State
and
Metropolitan Area
Data Book

2020

For Reference

State
and
Metropolitan Area
Data Book

2020

THIRD EDITION

Edited by Deirdre A. Gaquin
and Mary Meghan Ryan

ROWMAN & LITTLEFIELD
Lanham • Boulder • New York • London

Published by Rowman & Littlefield
A wholly owned subsidiary of The Rowman & Littlefield Publishing Group, Inc.
4501 Forbes Boulevard, Suite 200, Lanham, Maryland 20706
www.rowman.com

6 Tinworth Street, London SE11 5AL, United Kingdom

Library of Congress Control Number: 2020942091

ISBN: 978-1-64143-419-5
e-ISBN: 978-1-64143-420-1

∞™ The paper used in this publication meets the minimum requirements of American National Standard for Information Sciences—Permanence of Paper for Printed Library Materials, ANSI/NISO Z39.48-1992.

CONTENTS

PREFACE

This is the third edition of the *State and Metropolitan Area Data Book* (SMADB) produced by Bernan Press. The U.S. Census Bureau terminated its Statistical Compendia program in 2011. The Statistical Compendia program included the *Statistical Abstract of the United States* and its supplemental local area products—the *State and Metropolitan Area Data Book* and the *County and City Data Book* (CCDB). The Census Bureau published seven editions of SMADB, periodically since 1979, and 14 editions of CCDB, periodically since 1944. Since 1992, Bernan Press has produced 27 editions of *County and City Extra*, a comprehensive volume that combines some of the features of both SMADB and CCDB, and six editions of *Places, Towns, and Townships,* a companion volume with details about cities and towns not included in either CCDB or *County and City Extra*. Bernan continues to publish annual editions of *County and City Extra* that include most of the content of the former CCDB, plus many additional features. *County and City Extra* includes sections of state and metropolitan area data, but the *State and Metropolitan Area Data Book* includes a wider selection of state data, a table of data for micropolitan areas, and several tables that include the component counties of the metropolitan and micropolitan areas.

The SMADB is a convenient summary of statistics on the social and economic structure of the states, metropolitan areas, and micropolitan areas in the United States. It is designed to serve as a statistical reference and guide to other data publications and sources. The latter function is served by the source citations in Appendix A, "Source Notes and Explanations". This volume includes data from a variety of statistical publications and electronic sources, including nonprofit organizations, private businesses, as well as the majority of the federal statistical agencies. Publications and internet sites listed as sources usually contain additional detail and more comprehensive discussions of definitions and concepts than can be presented here. Data not available in printed publications issued by the contributing agency but obtained from websites are identified in the source notes. More information on the subjects covered in this publication is generally made available by its source, including additional methodological information about how the data are collected or produced.

Changes in this edition

All data have been updated to the most recent available year. All population and housing data have been updated based on the most recent population estimates from the Census Bureau. Detailed social and economic characteristics have been updated and expanded using the 1-year estimates from the American Community Survey, including information on health insurance, household type, migration, and commuting.

The results of the 2012 and 2016 presidential elections are included, as well as the 2018 congressional elections.

States. Data are presented for the United States, the 50 states, and the District of Columbia. There are 1,152 data items presented for these areas in Tables A-1 through A-81. The states and the District of Columbia are presented in alphabetical order under the U.S. total.

Metropolitan areas and metropolitan divisions. Data are presented for the 384 metropolitan areas and 31 metropolitan divisions defined as of September 2018. There are 164 data items presented for these areas in Tables B-1 through B-14.

Metropolitan areas and metropolitan divisions with their component counties. Data are presented for 49 data items in Tables C-1 through C-4. The 1180 counties and county equivalents are presented under their respective metropolitan area or metropolitan division.

Micropolitan areas with their component counties. Table D-1 includes 12 data items for 542 micropolitan areas and their 660 component counties. The metropolitan areas and their component counties are also included in Table D.

Appendixes. Appendix A provides information on source notes and explanations for the data items in

Tables A through D. Appendix B presents a brief introduction to central concepts of statistics and provides the methodological approach of principal sources. Appendix C presents a discussion of the geographic concepts relevant to this volume, as well as the current definitions for metropolitan areas. Appendix D offers a bibliography of the latest state specific abstracts published since 1999. For additional information on data presented, please consult the source publications available in local libraries, write to the agency indicated in the source notes, or visit the internet site listed.

Statistics for the nation. Extensive data at the national level can be found in the *ProQuest Statistical Abstract of the United States 2020,* co-published with Bernan Press.

Data for counties and cities may be found in Bernan's annual *County and City Extra*—the 28th edition is scheduled to publish in 2020—and Places, Towns, and Townships most recently published in 2016

GUIDE TO TABULAR PRESENTATION

Example of Table Structure:

Table A-20. Public Elementary and Secondary Schools—Finances and Teachers

| Geographic area | Total enrollment 2016–2017 (thousands)[1] | Revenues, 2016–2017 (millions of dollars) | | | |
| | | Total | Source | | |
			Local	State	Federal
United States..............................	50,513	705,267	316,635	331,322	57,311
Alabama.......................................	745	7,889	2,675	4,351	864
Alaska	133	2,508	554	1,601	354
Arizona..	1,113	10,259	4,155	4,778	1,326
Arkansas	493	5,619	2,042	2,951	626
California.....................................	6,309	88,109	29,813	50,841	7,455

[1]Enrollment represents the total count of pupils that are enrolled on or about October 1st of the survey year. These data are from the National Public Education Financial Survey.

Unit indicators show the specified quantities in which data items are presented. They are used for two primary reasons. Sometimes data are not available in absolute form. Other times, we round the numbers in order to save space to show more data, as in the case above.

If no unit indicator is shown, data presented are in absolute form (see Table B-1 for an example). When needed, unit indicators are found in the column or spanner headings for the data items as shown above.

Footnotes below the bottom rule of table pages give information relating to specific data items or figures within the table.

Further information on individual tables can be found in Appendix A, located in the back of the book.

Examples of Unit Indicator Interpretation table example:

Geographic area	Year	Item	Unit indicator	Number shown	Multiplier
United States..............................	2016–2017	Total enrollment	(thousands)	50,513	1,000
United States..............................	2016–2017	Revenues	(million dollars)	705,267	1,000,000

To determine the figure, it is necessary to multiply the number shown by the unit indicator.

Total enrollment, 2016–2017 = 50,513 * 1,000 or 50,513,000

Total revenues, 2016–2017 = 705,267 *1,000,000 or 705,267,000,000

In many tables, details will not add to the totals shown because of rounding.

EXPLANATION OF SYMBOLS AND TERMS

The following symbols, used in the tables throughout this book, are explained in condensed form in footnotes on the tables where they appear.

0   Represents zero or rounds to zero.

D   Figure withheld to avoid disclosure pertaining to a specific individual or organization; or does not meet statistical standards for reliability of derived figure.

NA Data not available.

X   Figure not applicable because column heading and stub line make entry impossible, absurd, or meaningless.

-   = Not available or withheld to avoid disclosure or does not meet statistical standards for reliability.

The following terms are also used throughout this publication:

Averages. An average is a single number or value that is often used to represent the "typical value" of a group of numbers. It is regarded as a measure of "location" or "central tendency" of a group of numbers.

The *arithmetic* mean is the type of average used most frequently. It is derived by summing the individual item values of a particular group and dividing the total by the number of items. The arithmetic mean is often referred to simply as the "mean" or "average."

The *median* of a group of numbers is the middle number or value when each item in the group is arranged according to size (lowest to highest or vice versa); it generally has the same number of items above it as well as below it. If there is an even number of items in the group, the median is taken to be the average of the two middle numbers.

Rates. A rate is a quantity or amount of an item measured in relation to a specified number of units of another item. For example, unemployment rate is the number of unemployed people per 100 people in the civilian labor force. Examples of other rates found in this publication include birth rate, which is the number of births per 1,000 population; infant death rate, the number of infant deaths per 1,000 live births; and crime rate, which is the number of serious offenses per 100,000 population.

A *per capita* figure represents a specific type of rate computed for every person in a specified group (or population).

It is derived by taking the total for a data item (such as income, taxes, or retail sales) and dividing it by the number of people in the specified population.

Ranks. Various data items in Tables A, States, and Tables B, Metropolitan Areas, of this publication are ranked from highest to lowest with a rank of 1 representing the highest rank. In both tables, when areas share the same rank, the next-lower rank is omitted.

In Table A, only the 50 states are ranked; the District of Columbia is not included in the state rankings. In Table B, only 384 metropolitan statistical areas (MSAs) are ranked. Not ranked are the 31 metropolitan divisions, which make up 11 metropolitan statistical areas. Areas not ranked are indicated by an "X" in the data cell.

Index numbers. An index number is a measure of difference or change, usually expressed as a percentage, relating one quantity (the variable) of a specified kind to another quantity of the same kind. Index numbers are widely used to express changes in prices over periods of time but may also be used to express differences between related subjects for a single point in time.

To compute a price index, a base year or period is selected. The base year price (of the commodity or service) is then designated as the base or reference price to which the prices for other years or periods are related. Many price indexes use the year 2000 as the base year; in tables, this is shown as "2000 = 100." A method of expressing the price relationship is: the price of a set of one or more items for a related year (e.g., 1990) divided by the price of the same set of items for the base year (e.g., 2000). The result multiplied by 100 provides the index number. When 100 is subtracted from the index number, the result equals the percentage change in price from the base year.

Current and constant dollars. Statistics in some tables are expressed in both current and constant dollars (for example, see Table A-40). Current dollar figures reflect actual prices or costs prevailing during the specified year(s). Constant dollar figures are estimates representing an effort to remove the effects of price changes from statistical series reported in dollar terms. In general, constant dollar series are derived by dividing current dollar estimates by the appropriate price index for the appropriate period (for example, the Consumer Price Index). The result is a series as it would presumably exist if prices were the same throughout, as in the base year; in other words, as if the dollar had constant purchasing power. Any changes in this constant dollar series would reflect only changes in real volume of output, income, expenditures, or other measure.

MAJOR FEDERAL DATA CONTACTS

To help *State and Metropolitan Area Data Book* users find more data and information about statistical publications, we are including this list of contacts for federal agencies with major statistical programs. The intent is to give a single, first-contact point-of-entry for users of statistics. These agencies will provide general information on their statistical programs and publications, as well as specific information on how to order their publications. We are also including the internet addresses for many of these agencies. These URLs were current in June 2020.

Executive Office of the President

Office of Management and Budget
Administrator
Office of Information and Regulatory Affairs
Office of Management and Budget
725 17th Street, NW
Washington, DC 20503
Information: 202-395-3080
https://www.whitehouse.gov/omb/

Department of Agriculture

Economic Research Service
U.S. Department of Agriculture
1400 Independence Ave., S.W.
Washington, DC 20250
Information: 202-720-2791
https://www.ers.usda.gov/

National Agriculture Statistics Service
USDA-NASS
1400 Independence Ave., SW
Washington, DC 20250
Information: 202-720-2791 or 800- 727-9540
https://www.nass.usda.gov/

Department of Commerce

U.S. Census Bureau
Customer Services Branch
U.S. Census Bureau
4600 Silver Hill Road
Washington, DC 20233
Information and publications: 1-800-923-8282
https://www.census.gov/

Department of Commerce—*Continued*

Bureau of Economic Analysis
1441 L Street, NW
Washington DC 20230
Information and publications: 202-606-9900
https://www.bea.gov/

International Trade Administration
1401 Constitution Ave., NW
Washington, DC 20230
Information: 1-800-872-8723
https://www.trade.gov/

National Oceanic and Atmospheric Administration
National Oceanic and Atmospheric Administration
Central Library
U.S. Department of Commerce
1315 East-West Highway
SSMC3, 2nd Floor
Silver Spring, MD 20910
Library: 301-713-2600 x.0157
https://library.noaa.gov/

Department of Defense

Department of Defense
Office of Public Communication
1400 Defense Pentagon
Washington, DC 20301-1400
Information: 703-571-3343
https://www.defense.gov/

Department of Education

National Library of Education
U.S. Department of Education
400 Maryland Avenue, SW
Washington, DC 20202
Education information and statistics: 1-800-872-5327
Education publications: 1-877-433-7827
https://www.ed.gov/

Department of Energy

Energy Information Administration
National Energy Information Center
1000 Independence Ave., SW

Department of Energy—*Continued*

Washington, DC 20585
Information and publications: 202-586-8800
https://www.eia.gov/

Department of Health and Human Services

Health Resources and Services Administration HRSA
Information Center
P.O. Box 2910
Merrifield, VA 22116
Information Center: 1-888-275-4772
https://www.hrsa.gov/ /

Substance Abuse and Mental Health Services Administration
1 Coke Cherry Road
Rockville, MD 20857
Information: 240-276-2130
Publications: 1-877-726-4727
https://www.samhsa.gov/

Centers for Disease Control and Prevention
Public Inquiries/MASO
1600 Clifton Road
Atlanta, GA 30333
Public inquires: 1-800-232-4636
https://www.cdc.gov/

Centers for Medicare and Medicaid Services (CMS)
U.S. Department of Health and Human Services 7500
Security Boulevard
Baltimore, MD 21244
Information: 1-877-267-2323
https://www.cms.gov/

National Center for Health Statistics
3311 Toledo Road
Hyattsville, MD 20782
Information: 1-800-232-4636
https://www.cdc.gov/nchs/

Department of Homeland Security

Office of Public Affairs
245 Murray Lane, SW
Washington, DC 20528
Information and publications: 202-282-8010
https://www.dhs.gov/

Department of Housing and Urban Development

Office of Community Planning and Development
451 7th St., SW
Washington, DC 20410
Information: 202-708-0006
Publications: 1-800-767-7468
https://www.hud.gov/program_offices/comm_planning

Departmentof the Interior

U.S. Geological Survey
Mineral resources program
USGS National Center
12201 Sunrise Valley Drive
Reston, VA 20192
Information and Publications: 1-888-275-8747
https://www.usgs.gov/energy-and-minerals/mineral-resources-program

Department of Justice

Bureau of Justice Statistics
Statistics Division
810 7th Street, NW
Washington, DC 20531
Information and publications: 202-307-0765
https://www.bjs.gov/

National Criminal Justice Reference Service
P.O. Box 6000
Rockville, MD 20849-6000
Publications: 1-800-851-3420
https://www.ncjrs.gov/

Federal Bureau of Investigation
J. Edgar Hoover Building
935 Pennsylvania Ave., NW
Washington, DC 20535-0001
Information: 202-324-3000
https://www.fbi.gov/

Department of Labor

Bureau of Labor Statistics
Office of Publications and Special Studies Services
Bureau of Labor Statistics
Postal Square Building
2 Massachusetts Ave., NE
Washington, DC 20212-0001
Information and publications: 202-691-5200
https://www.bls.gov/

Department of Labor—*Continued*

Employment and Training Administration
U.S. Department of Labor
Francis Perkins Building
200 Constitution Ave., NW
Washington, DC 20210
Information and publications: 1-877-872-5627
https://www.dol.gov/agencies/eta/

Department of Transportation

Federal Aviation Administration
800 Independence Ave., SW
Washington, DC 20591
Information and publications: 1-866-835-5322
https://www.faa.gov/

Bureau of Transportation Statistics
1200 New Jersey Avenue, SE
Washington, DC 20590
Products and statistical information: 1-800-853-1351
https://www.bts.gov/

Federal Highway Administration
Office of Public Affairs
U.S. Department of Transportation
1200 New Jersey Avenue, SE
Washington, DC 20590
Information: 202-366-0660
https://highways.dot.gov/

National Highway Traffic Safety Administration
Office of Public & Consumer Affairs
1200 New Jersey Avenue, SE,
West Building Washington, DC 20590
Information and publications: 1-888-327-4236
https://www.nhtsa.gov/

Department of the Treasury

Internal Revenue Service
Statistics of Income Division
Internal Revenue Service
P.O. Box 2608
Washington, DC 20013-2608
Information and publications: 202-874-0410
https://www.irs.gov/statistics

Department of Veterans Affairs

Department of Veterans Affairs
Office of Public Affairs
810 Vermont Ave., NW
Washington, DC 20420
Information: 202-461-7600
https://www.va.gov/

Independent Agencies

Administrative Office of the U.S. Courts
Office of Public Affairs
1 Columbus Circle, NE
Washington, DC 20544
Information: 202-502-2600
https://www.uscourts.gov/

Board of Governors of the Federal Reserve System
Division of Research and Statistics
Federal Reserve System
20th & Constitution Avenue, NW
Washington, DC 20551
Information: 202-452-3000
Publications: 202-452-3245
https://www.federalreserve.gov/

Environmental Protection Agency
Ariel Rios Building
1200 Pennsylvania Ave., NW
Washington, DC 20460
Publications: 1-800-490-9198
https://www.epa.gov/

National Science Foundation
Office of Legislation and Public Affairs
National Science Foundation
4201 Wilson Boulevard
Arlington, VA 22230
Information: 703-292-5111
https://www.nsf.gov/

Securities and Exchange Commission
Office of Public Affairs
Securities and Exchange Commission
100 F Street, NE
Washington, DC 20549
Information: 202-551-4120
Publications: 202-551-4040
https://www.sec.gov/

Social Security Administration
Office of Public Inquiries
6401 Security Boulevard
Baltimore, MD 21235
Information and Publications: 1-800-772-1213
https://www.ssa.gov/

PART A

STATES

Table A–1. Area and Population

Geographic area	Area, 2019 (sq. mi.) Total	Rank	Population 2019¹ (thousands)	2010¹ (thousands)	2000¹ (thousands)	Rank 2019	2010	2000	Per square mile of land area[2] 2019	2010	2000	Net change total[3]	Net international migration	Net domestic migration	Percent change 2010–2019	2000–2010
United States	3,533,044	X	328,240	308,758	281,425	X	X	X	92.9	87.4	79.7	19,481.4	7,859.9	0.0	6.3	9.7
Alabama	50,647	28	4,903	4,780	4,447	24	23	23	96.8	94.4	87.8	123.1	39.7	13.8	2.6	7.5
Alaska	571,017	1	732	710	627	48	47	48	1.3	1.2	1.1	21.3	16.5	-58.6	3.0	13.3
Arizona	113,653	6	7,279	6,392	5,131	14	16	20	64.0	56.3	45.2	886.4	142.1	453.7	13.9	24.6
Arkansas	52,038	27	3,018	2,916	2,673	33	32	33	58.0	56.0	51.4	101.8	23.2	11.4	3.5	9.1
California	155,854	3	39,512	37,255	33,872	1	1	1	253.5	239.1	217.4	2,257.7	1,021.5	-912.0	6.1	10.0
Colorado	103,637	8	5,759	5,029	4,302	21	22	24	55.6	48.5	41.5	729.4	95.7	351.9	14.5	16.9
Connecticut	4,843	48	3,565	3,574	3,406	29	29	29	736.2	738.1	703.3	-8.9	136.4	-200.3	-0.2	4.9
Delaware	1,949	49	974	898	784	45	45	45	499.6	460.8	402.1	75.8	13.2	39.5	8.4	14.6
District of Columbia	61	51	706	602	572	X	X	X	11,569.7	9,857.0	9,370.3	104.0	33.8	27.3	17.3	5.2
Florida	53,648	26	21,478	18,805	15,983	3	4	4	400.3	350.7	298.0	2,673.2	1,107.0	1289.6	14.2	17.6
Georgia	57,716	21	10,617	9,689	8,187	8	9	10	184.0	168.5	142.3	928.7	188.8	252.9	9.6	18.3
Hawaii	6,422	47	1,416	1,360	1,212	40	40	42	220.5	211.8	188.6	55.6	59.8	-70.2	4.1	12.3
Idaho	82,645	11	1,787	1,568	1,294	39	39	39	21.6	19.0	15.7	219.4	14.5	113.1	14.0	21.2
Illinois	55,514	24	12,672	12,832	12,420	6	5	5	228.3	231.1	223.7	-159.8	242.9	-865.9	-1.2	3.3
Indiana	35,826	38	6,732	6,484	6,081	17	15	14	187.9	181.0	169.7	248.2	99.1	-48.9	3.8	6.6
Iowa	55,854	23	3,155	3,047	2,926	31	30	30	56.5	54.5	52.4	108.2	47.8	-29.1	3.6	4.1
Kansas	81,758	13	2,913	2,853	2,689	35	33	32	35.6	34.9	32.9	60.2	51.1	-107.8	2.1	6.1
Kentucky	39,491	36	4,468	4,339	4,042	26	26	26	113.1	109.9	102.4	128.3	50.2	-13.3	3.0	7.3
Louisiana	43,204	33	4,649	4,533	4,469	25	25	22	107.6	104.9	103.4	115.3	45.0	-102.2	2.5	1.4
Maine	30,845	39	1,344	1,328	1,275	42	41	40	43.6	43.1	41.3	15.9	11.6	16.0	1.2	4.2
Maryland	9,711	42	6,046	5,774	5,297	19	19	19	622.6	594.8	545.6	271.9	199.0	-160.0	4.7	9.0
Massachusetts	7,801	45	6,893	6,548	6,349	15	14	13	883.5	839.5	814.0	344.7	361.8	-158.8	5.3	3.1
Michigan	56,606	22	9,987	9,884	9,938	10	8	8	176.4	174.8	175.8	102.7	193.0	-266.1	1.0	-0.6
Minnesota	79,626	14	5,640	5,304	4,919	22	21	21	70.8	66.6	61.8	335.7	114.4	-26.3	6.3	7.8
Mississippi	46,926	31	2,976	2,968	2,845	34	31	31	63.4	63.3	61.0	8.0	18.9	-80.2	0.3	4.3
Missouri	68,745	18	6,137	5,989	5,597	18	18	17	89.3	87.1	81.4	148.5	62.4	-60.5	2.5	7.0
Montana	145,548	4	1,069	989	902	43	44	44	7.3	6.8	6.2	79.4	6.4	49.4	8.0	9.7
Nebraska	76,817	15	1,934	1,826	1,711	37	38	38	25.2	23.8	22.3	108.1	35.1	-20.2	5.9	6.7
Nevada	109,860	7	3,080	2,701	1,998	32	35	35	28.0	24.6	18.2	379.5	22.4	234.6	14.1	35.1
New Hampshire	8,953	44	1,360	1,316	1,236	41	42	41	151.9	147.0	138.0	43.2	26.3	9.8	3.3	6.5
New Jersey	7,355	46	8,882	8,792	8,414	11	11	9	1,207.6	1,195.5	1,144.2	90.2	298.7	-491.2	1.0	4.5
New Mexico	121,312	5	2,097	2,059	1,819	36	36	36	17.3	17.0	15.0	37.6	26.6	-63.5	1.8	13.2
New York	47,124	30	19,454	19,378	18,977	4	3	3	412.8	411.2	402.7	75.4	698.0	-1379.2	0.4	2.1
North Carolina	48,620	29	10,488	9,536	8,046	9	10	11	215.7	196.1	165.6	952.3	163.7	475.5	10.0	18.5
North Dakota	68,995	17	762	673	642	47	48	47	11.0	9.7	9.3	89.5	12.7	34.7	13.3	4.7
Ohio	40,859	35	11,689	11,537	11,353	7	7	7	286.1	282.3	277.8	152.3	170.6	-217.5	1.3	1.6
Oklahoma	68,596	19	3,957	3,752	3,451	28	28	27	57.7	54.7	50.3	205.4	56.5	28.0	5.5	8.7
Oregon	95,988	10	4,218	3,831	3,421	27	27	28	43.9	39.9	35.6	386.7	58.2	233.5	10.1	12.0
Pennsylvania	44,742	32	12,802	12,703	12,281	5	6	6	286.1	283.9	274.5	99.1	274.1	-256.7	0.8	3.4
Rhode Island	1,034	50	1,059	1,053	1,048	44	43	43	1,024.5	1,018.5	1,014.0	6.4	36.9	-39.8	0.6	0.4
South Carolina	30,064	40	5,149	4,625	4,012	23	24	26	171.3	153.9	133.5	523.3	51.0	367.2	11.3	15.3
South Dakota	75,810	16	885	814	755	46	46	46	11.7	10.7	10.0	70.5	14.2	13.5	8.7	7.9
Tennessee	41,238	34	6,829	6,346	5,689	16	17	16	165.6	153.9	138.0	482.9	79.1	259.3	7.6	11.5
Texas	261,263	2	28,996	25,146	20,852	2	2	2	111.0	96.3	79.8	3,849.8	818.8	1145.6	15.3	20.6
Utah	82,377	12	3,206	2,764	2,233	30	34	34	38.9	33.6	27.2	442.1	48.1	82.1	16.0	23.8
Vermont	9,218	43	624	626	609	49	49	49	67.7	67.9	66.1	-1.7	7.5	-10.9	-0.3	2.8
Virginia	39,482	37	8,536	8,001	7,079	12	12	12	216.2	202.6	179.2	534.5	261.5	-71.1	6.7	13.0
Washington	66,455	20	7,615	6,725	5,894	13	13	15	114.6	101.2	88.7	890.4	234.8	336.3	13.2	14.1
West Virginia	24,041	41	1,792	1,853	1,808	38	37	37	74.5	77.1	75.2	-60.9	6.7	-43.0	-3.3	2.5
Wisconsin	54,167	25	5,822	5,687	5,364	20	20	18	107.5	105.0	99.0	135.1	59.3	-72.0	2.4	6.0
Wyoming	97,089	9	579	564	494	50	50	50	6.0	5.8	5.1	15.0	3.4	-13.5	2.7	14.1

Note: Survey, census, or data collection method is based on the "component of population change method" and the Census of Population and Housing. For information, see Appendix B, Limitations of the Data and Methodology, and Internet site https://www.census.gov/programs-surveys/popest/technical-documentation/methodology.html.

X. = Not applicable

[1]The 2019 population is estimated as of July 1, 2019. The April 1, 2010 and April 1, 2000 Population Estimates bases reflect modifications to the Census 2000 and 2010 population as documented in the Count Question Resolution program and geographic program revisions.

[2]People per square mile for 2010 and 2000 was calculated on the basis of land area data from the 2010 census. Land area in 2019 was used to calculate the people per square mile for 2019.

[3]The estimated components of population change will not sum to the numerical population change due to the process of controlling to national totals.

Sources: Area—U.S. Census Bureau, Gazetteer files, https://www.census.gov/geographies/reference-files/time-series/geo/gazetteer-files.html
Population and Population Change—U.S. Census Bureau, Population,Population Change, and Estimated Components of Population Change: April 1, 2010 to July 1, 2019
https://www.census.gov/data/tables/time-series/demo/popest/2010s-state-total.html
Table 1. Intercensal Estimates of the Resident Population for the United States, Regions, States, and Puerto Rico: April 1, 2000 to July 1, 2010
https://www.census.gov/data/tables/time-series/demo/popest/intercensal-2000-2010-state.html

Table A–2. Population by Age Group and Sex

Geographic area	Total	Under 5 years	5 to 17 years	18 to 24 years	25 to 34 years	35 to 44 years	45 to 54 years	55 to 64 years	65 to 74 years	75 to 84 years	85 years and over
United States	327,167	19,810	53,589	30,457	45,698	41,278	41,632	42,273	30,492	15,394	6,545
Alabama.....................	4,888	293	797	453	644	592	627	655	488	249	90
Alaska.......................	737	53	131	70	119	95	88	95	59	22	7
Arizona......................	7,172	436	1,207	687	986	880	851	866	726	390	142
Arkansas....................	3,014	190	513	281	397	369	369	384	296	157	59
California...................	39,557	2,441	6,549	3,745	6,044	5,256	5,072	4,781	3,285	1,640	744
Colorado	5,696	337	928	527	894	780	710	711	501	219	88
Connecticut.................	3,573	183	552	347	445	423	495	512	344	180	92
Delaware	967	55	149	84	129	111	122	136	108	53	20
District of Columbia	702	46	82	74	164	106	75	70	49	24	12
Florida........................	21,299	1,143	3,086	1,754	2,788	2,569	2,746	2,855	2,398	1,389	571
Georgia	10,519	657	1,848	1,010	1,473	1,373	1,411	1,286	895	418	147
Hawaii........................	1,420	88	216	121	203	181	171	181	149	71	41
Idaho.........................	1,754	116	331	163	231	220	200	215	168	81	29
Illinois.......................	12,741	761	2,097	1,176	1,770	1,640	1,640	1,665	1,142	584	267
Indiana.......................	6,692	419	1,150	656	877	822	840	873	616	309	131
Iowa..........................	3,156	198	533	319	398	380	371	418	301	160	79
Kansas.......................	2,912	189	517	295	383	356	336	373	263	134	66
Kentucky	4,468	275	733	418	585	552	577	597	435	215	81
Louisiana	4,660	307	789	425	667	584	563	606	428	209	81
Maine	1,338	64	186	107	160	152	180	212	163	79	33
Maryland.....................	6,043	365	976	531	835	774	819	813	545	267	118
Massachusetts.............	6,902	360	1,007	702	993	841	922	939	654	325	160
Michigan.....................	9,996	572	1,593	962	1,297	1,163	1,290	1,403	1,005	498	214
Minnesota	5,611	355	947	502	761	710	691	754	510	258	122
Mississippi..................	2,987	185	521	292	394	365	369	386	281	142	52
Missouri.....................	6,126	373	1,004	566	824	745	752	830	593	310	132
Montana......................	1,062	63	167	98	137	126	120	151	120	57	23
Nebraska	1,929	133	344	191	256	239	220	243	173	88	43
Nevada	3,034	186	503	249	445	403	395	377	293	140	43
New Hampshire.............	1,356	64	194	126	169	155	190	213	147	68	30
New Jersey	8,909	519	1,435	766	1,156	1,139	1,236	1,219	810	426	202
New Mexico	2,095	124	358	197	284	251	241	274	218	107	41
New York.....................	19,542	1,140	2,928	1,800	2,879	2,432	2,555	2,595	1,809	948	456
North Carolina..............	10,384	610	1,691	984	1,393	1,296	1,378	1,343	1,010	493	186
North Dakota................	760	55	124	85	115	90	80	95	64	34	19
Ohio..........................	11,689	695	1,899	1,068	1,545	1,391	1,485	1,612	1,150	588	256
Oklahoma	3,943	260	696	380	543	490	460	493	359	188	73
Oregon	4,191	234	639	365	596	560	513	544	448	206	84
Pennsylvania................	12,807	703	1,946	1,160	1,701	1,499	1,653	1,810	1,311	691	334
Rhode Island................	1,057	54	151	111	146	124	139	149	103	52	28
South Carolina	5,084	292	814	468	674	611	646	678	550	261	89
South Dakota	882	62	155	83	116	104	97	117	85	41	21
Tennessee	6,770	407	1,100	614	931	840	883	886	662	328	120
Texas.........................	28,702	2,024	5,374	2,796	4,236	3,882	3,553	3,234	2,167	1,035	400
Utah..........................	3,161	253	679	356	465	435	322	300	210	103	38
Vermont	626	30	86	67	74	71	81	96	73	34	14
Virginia	8,518	511	1,359	805	1,190	1,105	1,125	1,107	779	384	152
Washington..................	7,536	463	1,201	657	1,153	1,003	934	961	709	322	133
West Virginia...............	1,806	95	269	157	215	217	234	258	213	107	40
Wisconsin	5,814	334	942	552	737	705	738	821	572	285	129
Wyoming	578	36	99	52	78	73	65	80	58	27	11

Note: Survey, census, or data collection method is based on the Census of Population and Housing. For information, see Appendix B, Limitations of the Data and Methodology; https://www.census.gov/programs-surveys/popest/technical-documentation/methodology.html.

[1] As of July 1 for 2018. As of April 1 for decennial census years 2010 and 2000. All years include Armed Forces stationed in area.

Source: U.S. Census Bureau. Annual Estimates of the Resident Population for Selected Age Groups by Sex for the United States, States, Counties, and Puerto Rico Commonwealth and Municipios: April 1, 2010 to July 1, 2018 https://www.census.gov/programs-surveys/popest/data/tables.2018.html; Intercensal Estimates of the Resident Population by Sex and Age for States: April 1, 2000 to July 1, 2010 https://www.census.gov/data/tables/time-series/demo/popest/intercensal-2000-2010-state.html

Table A–2. Population by Age Group and Sex—*Continued*

Geographic area	Population under 18 years old (thousands)[1]			Population 65 years and over (thousands)[1]			Percentage of population, by age[1]						Males per 100 females 2018[1]
							Under 18 years			65 years and over			
	2018	2010	2000[2]	2018	2010	2000[2]	2018	2010	2000[2]	2018	2010	2000[2]	
United States	73,399	74,181	72,294	52,431	40268	34,992	22.4	24.0	25.7	16.0	13.0	12.4	97.0
Alabama......................	1,090	1,132	1,123	827	658	580	22.3	23.7	25.3	16.9	13.8	13.0	93.7
Alaska	184	187	191	87	55	36	24.9	26.4	30.4	11.8	7.7	5.7	109.0
Arizona.......................	1,643	1,629	1,367	1,258	882	668	22.9	25.5	26.6	17.5	13.8	13.0	98.9
Arkansas....................	703	711	680	512	420	374	22.7	25.0	27.3	14.3	11.4	10.6	96.5
California....................	8,990	9,295	9,250	5,669	4,247	3,596	22.7	25.0	27.3	14.3	11.4	10.6	98.8
Colorado....................	1,265	1,226	1,101	808	550	416	22.2	24.4	25.6	14.2	10.9	9.7	101.4
Connecticut................	735	817	842	615	507	470	20.6	22.9	24.7	17.2	14.2	13.8	95.3
Delaware....................	204	206	195	181	129	102	21.1	22.9	24.8	18.7	14.4	13.0	93.7
District of Columbia	127	101	115	85	69	70	18.1	16.8	20.1	12.1	11.4	12.2	90.3
Florida.......................	4,229	4,002	3,646	4,358	3,260	2,808	19.9	21.3	22.8	20.5	17.3	17.6	95.6
Georgia	2,506	2,492	2,169	1,460	1,032	785	23.8	25.7	26.5	13.9	10.7	9.6	94.7
Hawaii........................	303	304	296	261	195	161	21.4	22.3	24.4	18.4	14.3	13.3	100.2
Idaho..........................	447	429	369	278	195	146	25.5	27.4	28.5	15.9	12.4	11.3	100.5
Illinois........................	2,857	3,129	3,245	1,993	1,609	1,500	22.4	24.4	26.1	15.6	12.5	12.1	96.6
Indiana.......................	1,568	1,608	1,574	1,055	841	753	23.4	24.8	25.9	15.8	13.0	12.4	97.3
Iowa...........................	731	728	734	540	453	436	23.2	23.9	25.1	17.1	14.9	14.9	99.1
Kansas	706	727	713	462	376	356	24.2	25.5	26.5	15.9	13.2	13.3	99.3
Kentucky	1,009	1,023	995	731	578	505	22.6	23.6	24.6	16.4	13.3	12.5	97.1
Louisiana	1,096	1,118	1,220	718	558	517	23.5	24.7	27.3	15.4	12.3	11.6	95.4
Maine.........................	250	275	301	276	211	183	18.7	20.7	23.6	20.6	15.9	14.4	96.0
Maryland.....................	1,340	1,353	1,356	931	708	599	22.2	23.4	25.6	15.4	12.3	11.3	94.1
Massachusetts.............	1,367	1,419	1,500	1,139	903	860	19.8	21.7	23.6	16.5	13.8	13.5	94.3
Michigan.....................	2,165	2,344	2,596	1,717	1,362	1,219	21.7	23.7	26.1	17.2	13.8	12.3	97.0
Minnesota...................	1,303	1,284	1,287	890	683	594	23.2	24.2	26.2	15.9	12.9	12.1	99.2
Mississippi..................	706	756	775	474	380	344	23.6	25.5	27.3	15.9	12.8	12.1	94.1
Missouri	1,377	1,425	1,428	1,034	838	755	22.5	23.8	25.5	16.9	14.0	13.5	96.4
Montana......................	229	224	230	199	147	121	21.6	22.6	25.5	18.7	14.8	13.4	101.4
Nebraska....................	477	459	450	304	247	232	24.7	25.1	26.3	15.7	13.5	13.6	99.7
Nevada.......................	689	665	512	476	324	219	22.7	24.6	25.6	15.7	12.0	11.0	100.6
New Hampshire............	258	287	310	246	178	148	19	21.8	25.0	18.1	13.5	12.0	98.3
New Jersey	1,954	2,065	2,088	1,439	1,186	1,113	21.9	23.5	24.8	16.1	13.5	13.2	95.5
New Mexico	482	519	509	366	272	212	23	25.2	28.0	17.5	13.2	11.7	98.0
New York.....................	4,068	4,325	4,690	3,214	2,618	2,448	20.8	22.3	24.7	16.4	13.5	12.9	94.4
North Carolina.............	2,301	2,282	1,964	1,689	1,234	969	22.2	23.9	24.4	16.3	12.9	12.0	94.7
North Dakota...............	179	150	161	117	97	94	23.5	22.3	25.0	15.3	14.5	14.7	105.0
Ohio...........................	2,593	2,731	2,888	1,995	1,622	1,508	22.2	23.7	25.4	17.1	14.1	13.3	96.2
Oklahoma	956	930	892	620	507	456	24.3	24.8	25.9	15.7	13.5	13.2	98.1
Oregon	874	866	847	739	534	438	20.8	22.6	24.7	17.6	13.9	12.8	98.3
Pennsylvania..............	2,649	2,792	2,922	2,336	1,959	1,919	20.7	22.0	23.8	18.2	15.4	15.6	96.1
Rhode Island..............	205	224	248	182	152	152	19.4	21.3	23.6	17.2	14.4	14.5	94.7
South Carolina	1,106	1,080	1,010	900	632	485	21.8	23.4	25.2	17.7	13.7	12.1	94.0
South Dakota	218	203	203	147	117	108	24.7	24.9	26.8	16.6	14.3	14.3	102.0
Tennessee	1,506	1,496	1,399	1,110	853	703	22.2	23.6	24.6	16.4	13.4	12.4	95.3
Texas..........................	7,398	6,866	5,887	3,602	2,602	2,073	25.8	27.3	28.2	12.6	10.3	9.9	98.7
Utah...........................	932	871	719	350	249	190	29.5	31.5	32.2	11.1	9.0	8.5	101.5
Vermont	116	129	148	121	91	78	18.5	20.7	24.2	19.4	14.6	12.7	97.5
Virginia.......................	1,870	1,854	1,738	1,315	977	792	22	23.2	24.6	15.4	12.2	11.2	96.8
Washington.................	1,663	1,581	1,514	1,164	828	662	22.1	23.5	25.7	15.4	12.3	11.2	100.1
West Virginia...............	364	387	402	360	297	277	20.2	20.9	22.3	19.9	16.0	15.3	98.1
Wisconsin	1,276	1,339	1,369	985	777	703	22	23.6	25.5	17.0	13.7	13.1	99.0
Wyoming	135	135	129	95	70	58	23.3	24.0	26.1	16.5	12.4	11.7	104.0

Note: Survey, census, or data collection method is based on the Census of Population and Housing. For information, see Appendix B, Limitations of the Data and Methodology; https://www.census.gov/programs-surveys/popest/technical-documentation/methodology.html.
[1] As of July 1 for 2018. As of April 1 for decennial census years 2010 and 2000. All years include Armed Forces stationed in area.
[2] The April 1, 2000 population does not reflect modifications to the Census 2000 population as documented in the Count Question Resolution program and geographic program revisions.
Source: U.S. Census Bureau. Annual Estimates of the Resident Population for Selected Age Groups by Sex for the United States, States, Counties, and Puerto Rico Commonwealth and Municipios: April 1, 2010 to July 1, 2018 https://www.census.gov/programs-surveys/popest/data/tables.2018.html; Intercensal Estimates of the Resident Population by Sex and Age for States: April 1, 2000 to July 1, 2010 https://www.census.gov/data/tables/time-series/demo/popest/intercensal-2000-2010-state.html

Table A-3. Population, by Race and Hispanic Origin

Geographic area	All races[1] (thousands)		White alone[1] (thousands)		Black or African Amerian alone[1] (thousands)		American Indian and Alaska Native alone[1]		Asian alone[1]		Native Hawaiian and Other Pacific Islander alone[1]	
	2018[2]	2010[3]	2018[2]	2010[3]	2018[2]	2010[3]	2018[2]	2010[3]	2018[2]	2010[3]	2018[2]	2010[3]
United States	327,167	308,758	250,139	241,945	43,804	40,254	4,148	3,740	19,331	15,160	799	675
Alabama......................	4,888	4,780	3,380	3,363	1,311	1,259	34	33	73	55	5	5
Alaska........................	737	710	482	484	28	24	114	106	49	39	10	8
Arizona......................	7,172	6,392	5,938	5,419	364	281	380	335	264	188	20	16
Arkansas....................	3,014	2,916	2,385	2,342	472	454	30	26	50	38	11	7
California....................	39,557	37,255	28,532	27,637	2,556	2,487	651	622	6,064	5,038	200	181
Colorado	5,696	5,029	4,959	4,451	260	215	91	78	198	145	11	8
Connecticut.................	3,573	3,574	2,859	2,951	429	392	20	17	174	141	4	3
Delaware	967	898	672	646	222	196	6	6	40	29	1	1
District of Columbia	702	602	320	251	326	310	4	3	31	22	1	1
Florida........................	21,299	18,805	16,472	14,811	3,600	3,080	107	89	632	474	24	19
Georgia	10,519	9,689	6,361	6,146	3,411	2,994	55	49	453	323	12	10
Hawaii........................	1,420	1,360	364	349	31	22	6	5	535	532	145	138
Idaho..........................	1,754	1,568	1,632	1,476	16	11	30	26	28	20	4	3
Illinois........................	12,741	12,832	9,792	10,031	1,860	1,903	76	74	749	604	8	7
Indiana.......................	6,692	6,484	5,694	5,639	659	604	28	24	165	106	5	4
Iowa...........................	3,156	3,047	2,864	2,840	125	92	17	14	86	54	4	2
Kansas	2,912	2,853	2,515	2,501	179	173	35	33	91	70	4	3
Kentucky	4,468	4,339	3,914	3,864	376	343	13	12	73	50	4	3
Louisiana	4,660	4,533	2,930	2,903	1,526	1,463	37	33	84	72	3	3
Maine.........................	1,338	1,328	1,266	1,270	22	16	10	9	17	14	0	0
Maryland.....................	6,043	5,774	3,552	3,541	1,868	1,732	36	31	406	327	7	5
Massachusetts..............	6,902	6,548	5,577	5,525	617	504	34	30	493	360	7	6
Michigan.....................	9,996	9,884	7,924	7,950	1,408	1,416	73	68	337	243	4	3
Minnesota...................	5,611	5,304	4,718	4,623	380	281	77	67	289	218	4	3
Mississippi..................	2,987	2,968	1,766	1,790	1,129	1,104	18	17	32	26	2	2
Missouri......................	6,126	5,989	5,083	5,038	725	700	35	31	131	100	10	7
Montana......................	1,062	989	945	892	6	4	71	63	10	6	1	1
Nebraska.....................	1,929	1,826	1,703	1,649	99	86	29	23	52	33	1	1
Nevada.......................	3,034	2,701	2,254	2,107	306	231	51	43	264	203	24	19
New Hampshire.............	1,356	1,316	1,264	1,248	23	16	4	4	40	29	1	1
New Jersey	8,909	8,792	6,416	6,547	1,338	1,282	55	50	889	746	10	8
New Mexico	2,095	2,059	1,719	1,721	54	49	228	209	37	31	3	3
New York.....................	19,542	19,378	13,620	13,902	3,448	3,378	190	183	1,750	1,482	27	24
North Carolina..............	10,384	9,536	7,334	6,898	2,307	2,088	163	148	329	216	13	10
North Dakota...............	760	673	662	609	26	8	42	37	13	7	1	0
Ohio...........................	11,689	11,537	9,572	9,665	1,518	1,427	34	30	287	197	7	5
Oklahoma	3,943	3,752	2,924	2,852	307	284	367	336	92	67	8	5
Oregon.......................	4,191	3,831	3,636	3,403	93	74	76	67	202	145	19	15
Pennsylvania................	12,807	12,703	10,476	10,664	1,531	1,432	50	40	474	358	10	7
Rhode Island................	1,057	1,053	887	911	88	75	11	9	38	32	2	2
South Carolina	5,084	4,625	3,483	3,164	1,380	1,303	28	25	90	61	5	4
South Dakota	882	814	745	707	21	11	79	73	15	8	1	1
Tennessee	6,770	6,346	5,315	5,056	1,156	1,068	32	26	129	94	6	5
Texas..........................	28,702	25,146	22,625	20,390	3,674	3,071	291	251	1,486	1,000	42	31
Utah...........................	3,161	2,764	2,866	2,547	46	34	49	41	85	58	33	26
Vermont	626	626	590	599	9	6	2	2	13	8	0	0
Virginia	8,518	8,001	5,919	5,725	1,691	1,579	46	42	589	449	10	8
Washington..................	7,536	6,725	5,945	5,535	323	252	144	123	703	492	59	44
West Virginia................	1,806	1,853	1,688	1,747	65	64	5	4	15	13	1	0
Wisconsin	5,814	5,687	5,064	5,037	389	367	68	60	176	132	3	3
Wyoming	578	564	535	529	8	5	16	14	6	5	1	1

Note: Survey, census, or data collection method: based on the Census of Population and Housing. For information, see Appendix B, Limitations of the Data and Methodology, and www.census.gov/popest/methodology/index.html .

[1]Due to the complexities associated with the production of detailed characteristics' estimates at the state levels of geography may not necessarily sum to estimates at higher levels or geography.

[2]Population estimate as of July 1, 2018

[3]Population estimates for 2010 are for the base estimates and reflect changes to the Census 2010 population from the Count Question Resolution program and geographic program revisions.

Sources: U.S. Census Bureau, Annual Estimates of the Resident Population by Sex, Race, and Hispanic Origin for the United States and States: April 1, 2010 to July 1, 2018; https://www.census.gov/data/tables/time-series/demo/popest/2010s-state-detail.html

Table A-3. Population, by Race and Hispanic Origin—*Continued*

Geographic area	Two or more races[1] 2018[2]	Two or more races[1] 2010[3]	Hispanic or Latino origin[1,4] 2018[2]	Hispanic or Latino origin[1,4] 2010[3]	Non-Hispanic White alone[1] 2018[2]	Non-Hispanic White alone[1] 2010[3]	Percentage of total, 2018 White alone	Black or African American alone	American Indian and Alaska Native alone	Asian alone	Native Hawaiian and Other Pacific Islander alone	Two or more races	Hispanic or Latino origin	Non-Hispanic White alone
United States	8,946	6,984	59,872	50,479	197,546	197,326	76.5	13.4	1.3	5.9	0.2	2.7	18.3	60.4
Alabama......................	84	64	217	186	3,197	3,208	69.1	26.8	0.7	1.5	0.1	1.7	4.4	65.4
Alaska.........................	55	49	53	39	444	456	65.3	3.8	15.4	6.6	1.4	7.4	7.2	60.3
Arizona.......................	206	153	2,266	1,895	3,903	3,705	82.8	5.1	5.3	3.7	0.3	2.9	31.6	54.4
Arkansas....................	65	49	233	186	2,177	2,176	79.1	15.7	1.0	1.7	0.4	2.2	7.7	72.2
California....................	1,555	1,289	15,540	14,014	14,569	15,029	72.1	6.5	1.6	15.3	0.5	3.9	39.3	36.8
Colorado	177	132	1,235	1,039	3,868	3,529	87.1	4.6	1.6	3.5	0.2	3.1	21.7	67.9
Connecticut.................	87	70	590	479	2,376	2,557	80.0	12.0	0.6	4.9	0.1	2.4	16.5	66.5
Delaware	26	20	92	73	599	588	69.5	23.0	0.7	4.1	0.1	2.7	9.5	61.9
District of Columbia	20	14	79	55	260	210	45.6	46.4	0.6	4.4	0.1	2.8	11.3	37.1
Florida........................	464	332	5,562	4,224	11,399	10,927	77.3	16.9	0.5	3.0	0.1	2.2	26.1	53.5
Georgia......................	227	166	1,027	854	5,511	5,428	60.5	32.4	0.5	4.3	0.1	2.2	9.8	52.4
Hawaii........................	341	314	151	121	309	311	25.6	2.2	0.4	37.6	10.2	24.0	10.7	21.8
Idaho..........................	44	32	223	176	1,434	1,318	93.0	0.9	1.7	1.6	0.2	2.5	12.7	81.7
Illinois........................	256	211	2,214	2,028	7,773	8,183	76.9	14.6	0.6	5.9	0.1	2.0	17.4	61.0
Indiana.......................	141	108	475	390	5,277	5,295	85.1	9.8	0.4	2.5	0.1	2.1	7.1	78.9
Iowa...........................	61	45	194	152	2,691	2,704	90.7	4.0	0.5	2.7	0.1	1.9	6.2	85.3
Kansas.......................	88	73	351	300	2,203	2,234	86.4	6.1	1.2	3.1	0.1	3.0	12.1	75.7
Kentucky	88	67	172	133	3,766	3,750	87.6	8.4	0.3	1.6	0.1	2.0	3.8	84.3
Louisiana	80	60	244	193	2,729	2,741	62.9	32.7	0.8	1.8	0.1	1.7	5.2	58.6
Maine.........................	24	19	23	17	1,247	1,256	94.6	1.6	0.7	1.2	0.0	1.8	1.7	93.1
Maryland.....................	174	138	628	471	3,051	3,166	58.8	30.9	0.6	6.7	0.1	2.9	10.4	50.5
Massachusetts..............	174	123	847	628	4,928	5,037	80.8	8.9	0.5	7.1	0.1	2.5	12.3	71.4
Michigan.....................	249	203	519	436	7,485	7,580	79.3	14.1	0.7	3.4	0.0	2.5	5.2	74.9
Minnesota	143	111	309	250	4,459	4,411	84.1	6.8	1.4	5.1	0.1	2.5	5.5	79.5
Mississippi..................	39	30	100	81	1,686	1,724	59.1	37.8	0.6	1.1	0.1	1.3	3.4	56.5
Missouri	144	112	263	212	4,858	4,856	83.0	11.8	0.6	2.1	0.2	2.3	4.3	79.3
Montana......................	30	23	43	29	913	869	89.0	0.6	6.6	0.9	0.1	2.8	4.0	85.9
Nebraska....................	44	32	216	167	1,516	1,502	88.3	5.1	1.5	2.7	0.1	2.3	11.2	78.6
Nevada.......................	136	97	881	717	1,476	1,467	74.3	10.1	1.7	8.7	0.8	4.5	29.0	48.7
New Hampshire.............	24	19	53	37	1,220	1,217	93.2	1.7	0.3	3.0	0.0	1.8	3.9	90.0
New Jersey	200	160	1,839	1,555	4,893	5,238	72.0	15.0	0.6	10.0	0.1	2.3	20.6	54.9
New Mexico	54	46	1,029	953	778	838	82.0	2.6	10.9	1.8	0.2	2.6	49.1	37.1
New York.....................	507	410	3,754	3,417	10,831	11,345	69.7	17.6	1.0	9.0	0.1	2.6	19.2	55.4
North Carolina..............	237	175	997	800	6,526	6,236	70.6	22.2	1.6	3.2	0.1	2.3	9.6	62.8
North Dakota...............	17	11	30	13	638	598	87.0	3.4	5.5	1.8	0.1	2.2	3.9	84.0
Ohio	272	213	461	355	9,196	9,373	81.9	13.0	0.3	2.5	0.1	2.3	3.9	78.7
Oklahoma...................	245	207	429	332	2,576	2,579	74.2	7.8	9.3	2.3	0.2	6.2	10.9	65.3
Oregon.......................	164	127	556	450	3,155	3,012	86.8	2.2	1.8	4.8	0.5	3.9	13.3	75.3
Pennsylvania...............	266	202	976	720	9,742	10,109	81.8	12.0	0.4	3.7	0.1	2.1	7.6	76.1
Rhode Island................	30	25	168	131	761	811	83.9	8.4	1.1	3.6	0.2	2.8	15.9	72.0
South Carolina	98	68	296	236	3,239	2,968	68.5	27.1	0.5	1.8	0.1	1.9	5.8	63.7
South Dakota	21	16	36	22	718	690	84.4	2.4	9.0	1.7	0.1	2.4	4.1	81.4
Tennessee	132	96	381	290	4,990	4,807	78.5	17.1	0.5	1.9	0.1	2.0	5.6	73.7
Texas.........................	584	402	11,369	9,461	11,913	11,429	78.8	12.8	1.0	5.2	0.1	2.0	39.6	41.5
Utah...........................	82	58	450	358	2,466	2,226	90.7	1.4	1.5	2.7	1.1	2.6	14.2	78.0
Vermont	12	10	13	9	580	591	94.2	1.4	0.4	2.0	0.0	2.0	2.0	92.5
Virginia.......................	262	197	821	632	5,235	5,199	69.5	19.9	0.5	6.9	0.1	3.1	9.6	61.5
Washington..................	361	279	970	756	5,125	4,889	78.9	4.3	1.9	9.3	0.8	4.8	12.9	68.0
West Virginia................	32	25	30	22	1,662	1,728	93.5	3.6	0.3	0.8	0.0	1.8	1.7	92.1
Wisconsin...................	114	89	404	336	4,713	4,743	87.1	6.7	1.2	3.0	0.1	2.0	6.9	81.1
Wyoming	13	10	58	50	484	485	92.6	1.3	2.7	1.1	0.1	2.2	10.1	83.8

Note: Survey, census, or data collection method: based on the Census of Population and Housing. For information, see Appendix B, Limitations of the Data and Methodology, and www.census.gov/popest/methodology/index.html .

[1]Due to the complexities associated with the production of detailed characteristics' estimates at the state levels of geography may not necessarily sum to estimates at higher levels or geography.

[2]Population estimate as of July 1, 2018.

[3]Population estimates for 2010 are for the base estimates and reflect changes to the Census 2010 population from the Count Question Resolution program and geographic program revisions.

[4]Hispanic origin is considered an ethnicity and not a race; Hispanics may be any race.

Sources: U.S. Census Bureau, Annual Estimates of the Resident Population by Sex, Race, and Hispanic Origin for the United States and States: April 1, 2010 to July 1, 2018; https://www.census.gov/data/tables/time-series/demo/popest/2010s-state-detail.html

Table A-3. Population, by Race and Hispanic Origin—*Continued*

Geographic area	_ Percentage change, 2010–2018								
	All races	White alone	Black or African American alone	American Indian and Alaska Native alone	Asian alone	Native Hawaiian and Other Pacific Islander alone	Two or more races	Hispanic or Latino origin	Non-Hispanic White alone
United States	6.0	3.4	8.8	10.9	27.5	18.5	28.1	18.6	0.1
Alabama	2.3	0.5	4.1	4.5	32.5	0.0	31.2	17.0	-0.3
Alaska	3.8	-0.4	14.3	6.8	26.1	33.4	11.7	35.8	-2.6
Arizona	12.2	9.6	29.7	13.4	39.9	22.8	34.8	19.6	5.3
Arkansas	3.4	1.8	4.0	15.7	34.0	62.8	32.1	25.3	0.0
California	6.2	3.2	2.8	4.7	20.4	10.2	20.6	10.9	-3.1
Colorado	13.2	11.4	20.8	16.6	36.5	29.8	33.7	18.9	9.6
Connecticut	0.0	-3.1	9.5	19.2	23.7	10.0	22.9	23.1	-7.1
Delaware	7.7	4.1	13.1	8.9	34.9	52.0	30.5	25.6	1.9
District of Columbia	16.7	27.5	5.1	31.6	42.9	26.6	36.7	44.7	23.7
Florida	13.3	11.2	16.9	20.0	33.2	29.6	39.6	31.7	4.3
Georgia	8.6	3.5	13.9	12.9	40.2	18.9	36.5	20.3	1.5
Hawaii	4.4	4.2	38.6	13.5	0.6	4.7	8.5	25.3	-0.6
Idaho	11.9	10.6	44.1	18.1	38.9	39.4	38.1	26.7	8.8
Illinois	-0.7	-2.4	-2.3	2.3	23.9	13.6	21.5	9.2	-5.0
Indiana	3.2	1.0	9.1	13.3	56.7	28.6	31.0	21.9	-0.3
Iowa	3.6	0.9	35.9	22.9	58.0	74.9	35.1	28.3	-0.5
Kansas	2.0	0.6	3.1	5.4	31.0	26.4	20.0	17.0	-1.4
Kentucky	3.0	1.3	9.7	10.8	45.1	26.9	31.9	29.4	0.4
Louisiana	2.8	0.9	4.3	10.5	17.3	11.6	32.8	26.6	-0.4
Maine	0.8	-0.3	34.5	10.1	20.9	20.7	24.2	34.9	-0.7
Maryland	4.7	0.3	7.8	17.2	24.2	25.1	26.4	33.5	-3.6
Massachusetts	5.4	0.9	22.3	13.9	36.9	24.2	41.6	35.0	-2.2
Michigan	1.1	-0.3	-0.6	7.5	38.8	20.3	22.4	18.9	-1.2
Minnesota	5.8	2.0	35.4	13.8	32.7	40.1	28.2	23.6	1.1
Mississippi	0.6	-1.3	2.3	9.4	21.5	6.6	30.7	22.9	-2.2
Missouri	2.3	0.9	3.5	14.5	30.8	33.5	27.9	23.9	0.0
Montana	7.4	6.0	48.0	11.2	54.5	21.7	28.3	48.8	5.0
Nebraska	5.6	3.3	14.9	22.4	57.1	13.4	35.4	29.0	0.9
Nevada	12.4	7.0	32.3	18.4	29.9	24.1	39.7	23.0	0.7
New Hampshire	3.0	1.3	42.3	15.9	39.8	19.7	26.5	43.5	0.3
New Jersey	1.3	-2.0	4.3	9.6	19.2	29.1	25.7	18.3	-6.6
New Mexico	1.8	-0.1	9.3	9.4	19.2	8.7	17.2	8.0	-7.2
New York	0.8	-2.0	2.1	4.0	18.1	11.4	23.8	9.9	-4.5
North Carolina	8.9	6.3	10.5	10.5	52.5	26.0	35.5	24.6	4.6
North Dakota	13.0	8.6	210.7	13.6	90.9	71.6	55.6	119.3	6.6
Ohio	1.3	1.0	6.4	13.1	46.0	31.1	27.5	29.9	-1.9
Oklahoma	5.1	2.5	7.9	9.3	37.3	41.4	18.2	29.2	-0.1
Oregon	9.4	6.8	24.9	13.8	39.6	29.7	29.5	23.6	4.7
Pennsylvania	0.8	-1.8	6.9	24.7	32.3	41.3	31.8	35.6	-3.6
Rhode Island	0.4	-2.6	17.7	23.2	20.9	33.3	20.5	28.8	-6.1
South Carolina	9.9	10.1	5.9	12.3	46.9	30.2	42.7	25.6	9.1
South Dakota	8.4	5.4	99.4	9.1	94.1	44.5	33.8	64.6	4.1
Tennessee	6.7	5.1	8.2	21.2	36.9	19.7	37.5	31.3	3.8
Texas	14.1	11.0	19.6	15.8	48.6	35.5	45.0	20.2	4.2
Utah	14.4	12.5	35.0	19.4	47.7	28.6	41.5	25.6	10.8
Vermont	0.1	-1.4	35.6	6.5	55.9	41.1	21.0	36.1	-1.9
Virginia	6.5	3.4	7.1	11.8	31.1	21.9	32.9	29.9	0.7
Washington	12.1	7.4	27.9	17.8	43.1	35.6	29.3	28.4	4.8
West Virginia	-2.5	-3.4	2.1	13.9	21.4	8.9	26.3	35.7	-3.8
Wisconsin	2.2	0.5	6.0	12.4	33.6	29.5	28.7	20.2	-0.6
Wyoming	2.5	1.1	47.1	9.7	33.7	9.8	29.1	15.9	-0.1

Note: Survey, census, or data collection method: based on the Census of Population and Housing. For information, see Appendix B, Limitations of the Data and Methodology, and www.census.gov/popest/methodology/index.html .
Sources: U.S. Census Bureau, Annual Estimates of the Resident Population by Sex, Race, and Hispanic Origin for the United States and States: April 1, 2010 to July 1, 2018; https://www.census.gov/data/tables/time-series/demo/popest/2010s-state-detail.html

Table A–4. Population by Residence

Geographic area	Population by metropolitan residence, 2019				Population by metropolitan residence, 2019			Land area by metropolitan development, 2019			
	Total population	Population in metropolitan areas	Population in micropolitan areas	Population outside any core based statistical area	Population in metropolitan areas (percent)	Population in micropolitan areas (percent)	Population outside any core based statistical area (percent)	Total land area (square miles)	Land in metropolitan areas (percent)	Land in micropolitan areas (percent)	Land outside any core based statistical area (percent)
United States	328,239,523	282,828,515	27,252,936	18,158,072	86.2	8.3	5.5	3,533,043.725	28.0	20.3	51.7
Alabama	4,903,185	3,728,673	764,607	409,905	76.0	15.6	8.4	50,646.639	44.6	22.4	32.9
Alaska	731,545	493,166	45,875	192,504	67.4	6.3	26.3	571,016.948	5.9	1.3	92.8
Arizona......................	7,278,717	6,925,947	250,277	102,493	95.2	3.4	1.4	113,653.146	66.5	18.1	15.4
Arkansas...................	3,017,804	1,910,608	611,887	495,309	63.3	20.3	16.4	52,037.528	27.6	28.7	43.7
California...................	39,512,223	38,674,939	564,395	272,889	97.9	1.4	0.7	155,854.041	63.8	12.8	23.4
Colorado	5,758,736	5,043,251	406,134	309,351	87.6	7.1	5.4	103,637.497	23.2	21.7	55.1
Connecticut...............	3,565,287	3,384,954	180,333	0	94.9	5.1	0.0	4,842.684	81.0	19.0	0.0
Delaware	973,764	973,764	0	0	100.0	0.0	0.0	1,948.511	100.0	0.0	0.0
District of Columbia	705,749	705,749	0	0	100.0	0.0	0.0	61.136	100.0	0.0	0.0
Florida.......................	21,477,737	20,787,043	369,563	321,131	96.8	1.7	1.5	53,647.879	70.7	10.6	18.7
Georgia	10,617,423	8,811,718	1,023,365	782,340	83.0	9.6	7.4	57,716.331	43.5	21.8	34.8
Hawaii	1,415,872	1,141,980	273,806	86	80.7	19.3	0.0	6,422.425	27.4	72.4	0.2
Idaho.........................	1,787,065	1,327,492	318,464	141,109	74.3	17.8	7.9	82,645.130	29.9	22.0	48.0
Illinois.......................	12,671,821	11,246,743	819,853	605,225	88.8	6.5	4.8	55,513.723	40.8	25.5	33.8
Indiana......................	6,732,219	5,268,736	1,026,635	436,848	78.3	15.2	6.5	35,826.437	49.1	28.7	22.2
Iowa..........................	3,155,070	1,933,027	468,492	753,551	61.3	14.8	23.9	55,853.722	24.1	15.1	60.8
Kansas......................	2,913,314	2,025,859	502,785	384,670	69.5	17.3	13.2	81,758.475	15.1	18.3	66.7
Kentucky	4,467,673	2,659,326	910,128	898,219	59.5	20.4	20.1	39,491.383	27.3	24.8	47.9
Louisiana	4,648,794	3,914,867	436,459	297,468	84.2	9.4	6.4	43,204.489	53.8	19.2	27.0
Maine........................	1,344,212	798,925	122,302	422,985	59.4	9.1	31.5	30,844.799	19.3	2.8	77.9
Maryland	6,045,680	5,894,728	69,110	81,842	97.5	1.1	1.4	9,711.138	78.8	8.3	12.8
Massachusetts............	6,892,503	6,863,772	17,332	11,399	99.6	0.3	0.2	7,800.959	98.1	1.3	0.6
Michigan	9,986,857	8,184,614	1,003,256	798,987	82.0	10.0	8.0	56,605.933	28.3	29.4	42.3
Minnesota..................	5,639,632	4,392,182	731,920	515,530	77.9	13.0	9.1	79,625.878	30.1	24.3	45.6
Mississippi.................	2,976,149	1,439,512	963,883	572,754	48.4	32.4	19.2	46,925.533	24.9	33.3	41.8
Missouri.....................	6,137,428	4,602,874	696,145	838,409	75.0	11.3	13.7	68,745.459	28.3	19.5	52.2
Montana.....................	1,068,778	382,633	334,808	351,337	35.8	31.3	32.9	145,547.714	8.1	9.3	82.6
Nebraska....................	1,934,408	1,264,667	326,502	343,239	65.4	16.9	17.7	76,816.501	7.8	19.1	73.0
Nevada	3,080,156	2,798,273	249,485	32,398	90.8	8.1	1.1	109,860.373	13.3	51.7	35.0
New Hampshire...........	1,359,711	857,427	453,374	48,910	63.1	33.3	3.6	8,953.399	21.7	67.9	10.4
New Jersey	8,882,190	8,882,190			100.0	0.0	0.0	7,354.801	100.0	0.0	0.0
New Mexico	2,096,829	1,410,529	620,221	66,079	67.3	29.6	3.2	121,312.244	16.9	50.8	32.3
New York....................	19,453,561	18,094,588	973,657	385,316	93.0	5.0	2.0	47,123.773	48.4	29.0	22.7
North Carolina............	10,488,084	8,499,688	1,393,981	594,415	81.0	13.3	5.7	48,620.275	51.9	24.7	23.4
North Dakota..............	762,062	380,323	182,600	199,139	49.9	24.0	26.1	68,994.773	10.8	18.8	70.3
Ohio	11,689,100	9,382,254	1,860,387	446,459	80.3	15.9	3.8	40,858.759	42.8	38.7	18.5
Oklahoma...................	3,956,971	2,636,616	748,107	572,248	66.6	18.9	14.5	68,595.945	22.2	25.1	52.8
Oregon	4,217,737	3,536,983	578,243	102,511	83.9	13.7	2.4	95,988.003	22.2	40.7	37.1
Pennsylvania..............	12,801,989	11,355,102	1,075,044	371,843	88.7	8.4	2.9	44,741.693	51.5	29.0	19.5
Rhode Island..............	1,059,361	1,059,361	0	0	100.0	0.0	0.0	1,033.899	100.0	0.0	0.0
South Carolina	5,148,714	4,411,837	448,386	288,491	85.7	8.7	5.6	30,063.716	60.5	16.7	22.8
South Dakota	884,659	426,271	238,964	219,424	48.2	27.0	24.8	75,809.693	12.2	15.0	72.7
Tennessee	6,829,174	5,342,824	890,004	596,346	78.2	13.0	8.7	41,237.964	43.9	24.2	32.0
Texas........................	28,995,881	25,880,588	1,725,813	1,389,480	89.3	6.0	4.8	261,263.075	29.4	19.9	50.7
Utah..........................	3,205,958	2,870,657	187,272	148,029	89.5	5.8	4.6	82,376.887	29.0	14.9	56.0
Vermont.....................	623,989	220,411	236,024	167,554	35.3	37.8	26.9	9,217.879	13.6	42.8	43.6
Virginia......................	8,535,519	7,483,334	251,748	800,437	87.7	2.9	9.4	39,482.149	53.6	6.8	39.6
Washington................	7,614,893	6,834,200	600,763	179,930	89.7	7.9	2.4	66,455.115	48.7	24.5	26.8
West Virginia..............	1,792,147	1,155,956	294,459	341,732	64.5	16.4	19.1	24,041.128	37.3	14.8	47.9
Wisconsin	5,822,434	4,347,996	750,577	723,861	74.7	12.9	12.4	54,167.442	32.7	18.7	48.6
Wyoming	578,759	179,358	255,511	143,890	31.0	44.1	24.9	97,088.702	8.3	43.8	47.9

Table A–5. Households

Geographic area	Total households (thousands)		2018 percentage distribution											People per household	
			Family households						Nonfamily households			Households with one or more people—			
			Total¹		Married couple families		Female householder, no spouse present			Householder living alone					
	2018	2010	Family households, total	With own children under 18 years	Total	With own children under 18 years	Total	With own children under 18 years	Total	Total	65 years and over	under 18 years	65 years and over	2018	2010
United States	121,520	116,716	65.2	27.0	47.9	18.3	12.4	6.4	34.8	28.0	11.0	30.3	30.1	2.63	2.58
Alabama................	1,855	1,884	65.5	25.1	47.4	16.4	13.9	6.9	34.5	29.9	11.6	29.5	31.1	2.57	2.48
Alaska..................	255	258	65.8	30.1	50.2	21.8	9.5	5.4	34.2	26.0	8.1	34.2	24.7	2.79	2.65
Arizona.................	2,614	2,381	65.5	26.8	47.7	17.6	12.0	6.2	34.5	27.0	11.3	30.4	33.1	2.68	2.63
Arkansas	1,156	1,147	66.5	27.5	47.9	17.4	13.7	7.7	33.5	28.2	11.2	31.2	30.3	2.53	2.47
California..............	13,072	12,577	68.3	29.3	49.4	20.8	12.9	6.0	31.7	24.0	9.6	33.4	29.9	2.96	2.90
Colorado	2,177	1,973	63.1	27.4	49.1	20.1	9.5	5.1	36.9	28.1	9.7	30.0	26.3	2.56	2.49
Connecticut...........	1,378	1,371	64.7	26.9	47.2	18.0	12.7	6.6	35.3	29.1	12.2	29.2	31.0	2.51	2.52
Delaware..............	368	342	64.8	24.3	47.3	15.5	12.6	6.4	35.2	28.9	10.9	27.6	33.7	2.56	2.55
District of Columbia	287	267	42.3	17.6	25.4	9.2	13.3	6.8	57.7	45.6	11.5	19.6	22.5	2.31	2.11
Florida.................	7,809	7,421	64.4	22.9	46.6	14.7	12.8	6.2	35.6	29.0	13.1	26.2	37.2	2.67	2.48
Georgia	3,803	3,586	66.7	28.6	46.9	18.6	15.0	7.9	33.3	27.5	9.6	32.8	27.1	2.70	2.63
Hawaii..................	455	455	69.6	25.7	51.6	19.0	12.9	5.0	30.4	24.5	10.7	31.1	37.9	3.02	2.89
Idaho...................	640	579	68.4	29.0	54.5	21.4	9.4	5.3	31.6	25.4	10.4	31.9	29.9	2.69	2.66
Illinois.................	4,865	4,837	64.1	27.1	47.1	18.6	12.3	6.4	35.9	29.6	11.5	30.1	28.9	2.56	2.59
Indiana.................	2,599	2,502	64.8	27.3	48.0	18.0	11.7	6.6	35.2	28.9	11.1	30.6	28.4	2.50	2.52
Iowa....................	1,268	1,222	63.1	27.2	49.1	18.5	9.5	6.1	36.9	29.6	12.2	29.4	29.2	2.41	2.41
Kansas	1,133	1,112	64.1	28.5	50.4	20.5	9.6	5.8	35.9	29.2	11.3	31.2	28.3	2.50	2.49
Kentucky	1,733	1,720	65.7	26.9	48.4	17.9	12.5	6.6	34.3	28.1	11.0	31.1	29.5	2.50	2.45
Louisiana	1,737	1,728	63.6	26.4	43.1	15.8	15.4	8.3	36.4	30.6	11.0	30.5	29.1	2.61	2.55
Maine	570	557	60.1	21.7	46.8	14.6	9.0	5.1	39.9	30.8	13.8	24.3	34.4	2.28	2.32
Maryland...............	2,216	2,156	66.4	27.8	48.3	19.1	13.6	6.5	33.6	27.3	10.6	31.4	29.6	2.66	2.61
Massachusetts...........	2,624	2,547	62.7	25.9	46.7	18.4	11.8	6.0	37.3	29.0	12.0	28.5	30.8	2.54	2.48
Michigan...............	3,957	3,873	63.7	25.4	46.7	16.7	12.0	6.3	36.3	29.6	12.1	28.1	30.8	2.47	2.49
Minnesota..............	2,194	2,087	63.7	27.6	50.3	19.9	9.0	5.4	36.3	28.7	11.1	29.6	27.9	2.50	2.48
Mississippi.............	1,109	1,116	65.7	26.9	44.4	16.4	17.1	8.9	34.3	29.6	11.5	31.2	30.2	2.61	2.58
Missouri................	2,435	2,376	63.7	25.7	47.6	17.0	11.6	6.3	36.3	29.7	11.6	28.5	29.6	2.44	2.45
Montana................	431	410	61.6	24.2	49.4	17.0	8.0	4.7	38.4	30.0	12.1	26.9	32.2	2.40	2.35
Nebraska...............	765	721	63.4	28.8	49.6	20.3	9.3	6.0	36.6	29.6	11.8	31.0	27.9	2.45	2.46
Nevada.................	1,130	1,006	62.5	25.7	43.3	16.0	12.3	6.4	37.5	29.4	10.1	29.4	29.3	2.65	2.65
New Hampshire..........	531	519	64.3	23.4	51.6	16.6	8.5	4.6	35.7	27.6	11.4	25.8	31.9	2.47	2.46
New Jersey	3,250	3,214	68.7	28.7	51.2	21.0	12.6	5.7	31.3	26.0	11.1	31.6	31.5	2.69	2.68
New Mexico	794	791	62.4	24.1	43.4	14.5	13.3	6.8	37.6	31.1	12.3	28.2	32.6	2.58	2.55
New York................	7,367	7,318	62.9	25.4	44.0	17.1	14.0	6.4	37.1	29.9	12.1	28.6	31.4	2.57	2.57
North Carolina...........	4,011	3,745	65.4	26.6	47.9	17.6	13.0	6.9	34.6	28.5	10.9	30.1	29.5	2.52	2.48
North Dakota............	319	281	58.8	25.7	46.8	18.1	8.0	5.3	41.2	32.0	11.0	27.3	25.3	2.30	2.30
Ohio	4,685	4,603	62.4	25.6	45.1	16.1	12.5	7.0	37.6	31.1	12.0	28.6	29.9	2.43	2.44
Oklahoma	1,485	1,460	66.2	29.0	48.2	18.9	12.6	7.3	33.8	28.0	11.2	32.8	29.2	2.58	2.49
Oregon	1,640	1,519	62.7	25.1	48.4	17.6	9.6	5.3	37.3	27.3	11.9	27.7	31.9	2.50	2.47
Pennsylvania............	5,071	5,019	63.8	24.7	47.6	16.6	11.6	5.9	36.2	29.9	12.8	27.5	32.5	2.44	2.45
Rhode Island............	407	414	60.9	24.5	43.0	15.6	13.0	6.8	39.1	31.5	13.5	27.3	31.9	2.50	2.44
South Carolina	1,928	1,801	65.3	24.8	46.5	15.7	14.3	7.1	34.7	29.0	11.5	28.7	32.4	2.57	2.49
South Dakota	345	322	63.6	26.8	49.8	18.3	9.5	6.2	36.4	29.2	11.3	29.6	28.9	2.46	2.42
Tennessee	2,603	2,494	65.6	26.2	47.9	17.2	12.9	6.7	34.4	28.0	10.8	30.2	29.7	2.54	2.48
Texas...................	9,776	8,923	68.8	31.6	49.8	21.6	13.8	7.6	31.2	25.5	8.4	35.7	25.5	2.87	2.75
Utah....................	999	878	74.5	36.8	60.9	29.8	9.1	4.9	25.5	19.4	7.2	40.3	24.0	3.12	3.10
Vermont	261	256	59.6	21.6	47.0	14.9	8.0	4.5	40.4	31.3	13.0	24.3	33.2	2.30	2.34
Virginia.................	3,176	3,056	66.0	27.3	49.7	19.4	11.7	5.8	34.0	27.5	10.7	30.8	29.3	2.61	2.54
Washington.............	2,896	2,620	64.9	27.3	50.2	19.6	10.0	5.4	35.1	26.2	10.2	30.1	28.5	2.55	2.51
West Virginia............	735	764	62.9	22.4	47.3	14.8	11.0	5.6	37.1	31.1	13.6	26.5	35.0	2.39	2.36
Wisconsin...............	2,372	2,280	62.7	25.7	48.5	17.5	9.4	5.6	37.3	29.5	11.7	27.9	29.1	2.39	2.43
Wyoming	230	227	62.8	25.2	50.7	18.0	8.3	5.2	37.2	29.1	10.8	28.1	29.3	2.45	2.42

¹Total includes male householder with no spouse present (not shown separately).

Table A–6. Marital Status, 2018

Geographic area	Males 15 years and over						Females 15 years and over					
	Total (thousands)	Percentage					Total (thousands)	Percentage				
		Never married	Now married, except separated[1]	Separated[2]	Widowed	Divorced		Never married	Now married, except separated[1]	Separated[2]	Widowed	Divorced
United States	129,974	37.0	49.3	1.6	2.6	9.5	136,349	30.7	46.3	2.2	8.7	12.1
Alabama	1,903	34.1	49.3	1.9	3.1	11.6	2,084	28.1	45.7	2.7	10.3	13.2
Alaska	305	37.3	49.2	1.6	2.0	9.9	278	29.5	50.3	1.4	5.9	12.9
Arizona	2,868	36.7	48.0	1.5	2.7	11.1	2,940	30.0	46.2	2.0	8.5	13.3
Arkansas	1,179	32.3	50.8	2.0	3.0	11.9	1,251	26.5	46.7	2.4	10.2	14.3
California	15,847	40.9	47.8	1.6	2.2	7.5	16,237	33.9	45.3	2.4	7.7	10.8
Colorado	2,324	36.0	50.2	1.2	2.2	10.3	2,319	28.9	49.5	1.7	6.7	13.2
Connecticut	1,437	38.1	49.2	1.0	2.5	9.3	1,538	32.0	45.3	1.5	8.8	12.4
Delaware	383	37.4	49.4	1.4	3.0	8.8	416	31.1	45.4	1.9	8.5	13.0
District of Columbia	277	59.5	30.6	1.9	1.5	6.4	314	56.9	25.5	2.2	5.9	9.5
Florida	8,615	35.8	47.8	1.8	3.2	11.4	9,177	28.7	43.9	2.4	10.2	14.8
Georgia	4,057	37.8	48.4	1.7	2.4	9.7	4,395	32.4	44.2	2.5	8.2	12.7
Hawaii	580	38.4	50.0	1.1	2.5	8.0	584	29.4	49.2	1.5	10.0	10.0
Idaho	694	31.1	54.4	1.0	2.4	11.1	693	24.7	53.8	1.4	7.3	12.8
Illinois	5,059	38.4	49.2	1.3	2.7	8.4	5,322	32.5	46.0	1.7	8.7	11.0
Indiana	2,630	34.7	50.0	1.1	2.9	11.3	2,762	28.6	47.9	1.5	8.8	13.2
Iowa	1,253	34.0	52.0	0.9	3.0	10.1	1,293	26.9	50.5	1.2	9.4	11.9
Kansas	1,151	33.0	52.8	1.3	2.6	10.3	1,174	26.4	51.3	1.5	8.6	12.2
Kentucky	1,769	32.4	50.8	1.9	3.0	11.9	1,860	25.9	47.9	2.6	9.9	13.6
Louisiana	1,806	39.2	45.4	1.8	3.0	10.5	1,937	34.1	41.7	2.6	9.5	12.1
Maine	551	32.1	50.6	1.1	3.2	13.0	583	25.0	48.8	0.9	9.5	15.9
Maryland	2,362	37.5	49.9	1.5	2.4	8.7	2,570	32.8	45.4	2.3	8.0	11.5
Massachusetts	2,779	39.8	48.1	1.3	2.4	8.4	3,004	34.7	44.6	1.9	8.0	10.8
Michigan	4,017	36.6	49.0	1.0	2.8	10.6	4,203	30.4	46.7	1.3	9.0	12.6
Minnesota	2,239	35.6	51.8	0.9	2.3	9.4	2,286	29.1	51.0	1.2	7.4	11.3
Mississippi	1,147	36.6	46.8	2.4	3.4	10.8	1,254	31.9	42.0	3.0	10.7	12.4
Missouri	2,417	33.8	50.7	1.5	3.0	11.1	2,564	27.3	48.4	2.0	9.1	13.2
Montana	435	32.1	52.3	1.0	3.0	11.5	436	25.0	51.2	1.5	9.1	13.3
Nebraska	758	33.7	53.3	1.2	2.7	9.1	773	27.3	51.5	1.3	8.7	11.2
Nevada	1,228	37.2	45.7	1.5	2.7	12.9	1,231	29.8	44.9	2.0	7.7	15.6
New Hampshire	564	34.4	51.5	1.0	2.6	10.5	583	27.0	50.0	1.3	8.8	12.9
New Jersey	3,530	37.2	52.1	1.6	2.4	6.8	3,770	31.6	47.4	2.1	8.9	10.1
New Mexico	836	38.4	45.6	1.6	2.8	11.6	862	31.5	43.5	1.8	8.6	14.6
New York	7,765	40.5	47.8	1.8	2.5	7.3	8,403	35.5	42.7	2.7	8.9	10.2
North Carolina	4,078	34.9	50.7	2.3	2.8	9.4	4,408	29.4	46.2	2.9	9.4	12.1
North Dakota	312	37.4	50.3	0.6	2.8	8.9	297	27.3	53.3	0.9	8.5	10.0
Ohio	4,638	36.4	48.2	1.5	3.0	11.0	4,915	30.2	45.5	1.8	9.3	13.2
Oklahoma	1,543	33.0	50.2	1.8	3.2	12.0	1,602	25.9	47.9	2.2	9.7	14.2
Oregon	1,708	34.4	50.3	1.3	2.6	11.3	1,761	27.7	48.9	1.7	7.7	14.1
Pennsylvania	5,157	37.0	49.6	1.8	3.0	8.7	5,466	30.6	46.7	2.3	9.9	10.6
Rhode Island	429	42.9	43.7	1.2	2.8	9.4	461	35.9	40.9	1.6	9.5	12.1
South Carolina	1,998	35.7	48.5	2.5	3.2	10.1	2,168	30.4	44.4	2.8	10.1	12.3
South Dakota	351	34.4	52.3	0.7	2.3	10.3	351	28.0	50.0	1.5	8.5	11.6
Tennessee	2,661	34.0	50.3	1.8	2.8	11.1	2,857	28.0	47.0	2.5	9.3	13.3
Texas	11,100	37.1	49.7	1.9	2.3	9.1	11,435	30.9	46.7	2.8	7.8	11.8
Utah	1,193	33.4	55.9	1.3	1.6	7.9	1,190	27.7	55.0	1.6	5.5	10.2
Vermont	260	35.9	48.9	1.1	2.8	11.3	272	28.3	48.6	1.0	8.5	13.7
Virginia	3,393	35.7	50.8	2.0	2.8	8.7	3,573	29.7	47.7	2.5	8.6	11.6
Washington	3,055	35.2	51.7	1.3	2.2	9.6	3,088	27.5	50.5	1.6	7.2	13.3
West Virginia	742	31.9	50.0	1.5	3.6	12.9	766	24.9	48.0	1.3	11.2	14.6
Wisconsin	2,354	35.5	50.8	0.9	2.6	10.1	2,412	29.1	49.9	1.2	8.4	11.4
Wyoming	236	30.3	52.7	1.4	3.3	12.2	231	24.7	53.1	1.3	7.6	13.3

[1]Includes people whose current marriage has not ended through widowhood, divorce, or separation (regardless of previous marital history). The category may also include couples who live together or people in common-law marriages, if they consider this category the most appropriate.

[2]Includes people legally separated or otherwise absent from their spouse because of marital discord. Those without a final divorce decree are classified as "separated." This category also includes people who have been deserted or who have parted because they no longer want to live together but who have not obtained a divorce.

Table A–7. Residence One Year Ago, People Obtaining Legal Permanent Resident Status, and Language Spoken at Home, Selected Years

Geographic area	Residence 1 year ago, 2018 Population 1 year old and over (thousands)	Percentage of population who lived in same house 1 year ago	People obtaining lawful permanent resident status[1] Total 2018	2010	2005	Leading countries of birth, 2018 Mexico	Cuba	China	India	Dominican Republic	Phillippines	Vietnam	Language spoken at home, population 5 years old and over in the United States, 2018 All languages other than English Total (thousands)	Percentage of population	Percentage of population who speak Spanish
United States	323,532	86.0	1,090,482	1,035,265	1,116,252	161,779	76,413	65,089	59,801	54,621	45,907	33,813	67,269	21.9	13.5
Alabama......................	4,832	86.4	3,737	3,740	4,200	618	81	201	313	42	213	221	244	5.3	3.3
Alaska........................	727	83.7	1,375	1,703	1,524	86	8	42	10	57	511	31	111	16.3	3.8
Arizona......................	7,090	83.0	18,335	18,243	18,986	8,025	699	429	653	48	657	549	1,855	27.5	20.7
Arkansas....................	2,976	85.3	3,000	2,684	2,698	901	15	107	207	28	179	164	217	7.7	5.5
California....................	39,115	87.5	200,897	208,446	232,014	53,572	644	20,600	12,617	251	15,412	11,094	16,554	44.6	28.9
Colorado	5,633	82.1	13,913	12,489	11,975	4,053	286	509	399	39	350	520	897	16.7	11.6
Connecticut................	3,538	87.7	11,629	12,222	15,334	283	58	430	861	1,009	215	164	751	22.1	11.9
Delaware	959	89.0	1,831	2,198	2,991	214	16	99	206	65	69	32	119	13.1	7.2
District of Columbia	694	81.9	2,775	2,897	2,457	84	14	120	55	99	71	26	111	16.9	8.4
Florida........................	21,093	84.7	130,405	107,276	122,915	4,048	53,496	1,635	1,982	4,344	2,452	1,530	5,996	29.7	22.2
Georgia......................	10,410	85.6	26,725	24,833	31,527	3,451	571	996	2,450	450	610	1,405	1,385	14.0	8.0
Hawaii........................	1,404	86.3	5,430	7,037	6,480	69	D	417	29	D	3,229	191	367	27.5	2.5
Idaho..........................	1,735	82.9	2,728	2,556	2,768	837	5	93	32	D	101	35	179	10.9	8.2
Illinois........................	12,599	87.5	38,287	37,909	52,415	9,411	205	1,835	3,946	208	1,848	692	2,814	23.5	13.7
Indiana.......................	6,613	84.9	9,741	8,539	6,913	1,778	176	460	819	112	380	184	558	8.9	4.7
Iowa...........................	3,119	85.4	5,484	4,245	4,535	790	228	163	170	25	179	198	261	8.8	4.2
Kansas.......................	2,874	83.3	5,630	5,501	4,512	1,607	263	224	261	30	217	257	320	11.8	7.9
Kentucky....................	4,415	84.8	8,734	4,930	5,265	503	2,400	197	313	29	241	132	236	5.6	2.8
Louisiana	4,603	87.6	4,889	4,397	3,776	462	280	203	156	286	265	511	333	7.6	3.6
Maine.........................	1,324	86.4	1,749	1,349	1,907	10	D	58	41	16	82	49	78	6.1	0.8
Maryland....................	5,975	85.9	24,301	26,450	22,868	517	87	1,296	1,347	480	1,058	459	1,099	19.3	8.5
Massachusetts.............	6,834	87.4	33,174	31,069	34,232	292	91	2,212	1,606	5,234	284	1,086	1,591	24.3	9.4
Michigan....................	9,891	86.6	19,850	18,579	23,591	1,668	383	707	1,484	165	466	448	927	9.8	3.0
Minnesota..................	5,543	86.3	16,721	12,408	15,449	1,537	62	446	681	48	438	549	642	12.2	4.0
Mississippi.................	2,956	87.4	1,643	1,709	1,829	315	25	96	180	37	155	111	105	3.7	2.3
Missouri	6,053	85.3	7,638	7,151	8,742	774	294	373	437	67	331	375	364	6.3	2.5
Montana.....................	1,052	84.8	565	457	589	47	3	61	7	3	88	19	44	4.4	1.7
Nebraska....................	1,906	84.1	6,500	4,400	2,996	925	1,075	125	122	23	108	180	202	11.2	7.2
Nevada.......................	3,004	83.1	10,851	10,803	9,823	2,611	1,691	585	199	56	1,519	234	882	30.9	21.3
New Hampshire............	1,345	87.0	2,200	2,556	3,298	77	9	78	178	201	80	62	100	7.8	2.4
New Jersey	8,816	89.3	54,424	56,920	56,176	1,249	1,180	2,070	6,554	9,054	1,683	644	2,656	31.7	16.6
New Mexico	2,073	86.7	4,296	3,528	3,513	2,285	251	105	99	12	286	111	674	34.1	26.4
New York....................	19,330	89.6	134,839	147,999	136,815	2,786	780	16,381	4,267	24,871	2,275	585	5,645	30.7	14.9
North Carolina.............	10,275	84.9	20,838	16,112	16,710	3,566	580	770	1,440	590	609	717	1,178	12.0	7.8
North Dakota...............	750	83.1	1,674	1,058	864	54	13	22	42	5	162	19	52	7.4	1.9
Ohio...........................	11,555	85.6	18,809	13,585	16,892	814	98	801	1,356	328	1,095	306	807	7.3	2.4
Oklahoma	3,896	82.8	5,938	4,627	4,702	1,919	172	201	283	32	254	388	393	10.7	7.4
Oregon.......................	4,153	82.8	9,679	7,997	9,623	2,459	321	641	447	27	404	541	631	15.9	9.4
Pennsylvania..............	12,675	87.7	26,078	24,130	28,902	904	401	1,613	2,393	3,759	544	800	1,446	11.9	5.2
Rhode Island...............	1,048	88.6	4,336	4,027	3,852	55	25	99	80	1,476	49	37	218	21.7	12.3
South Carolina	5,029	85.7	5,078	4,401	5,028	721	120	236	417	94	271	219	353	7.4	4.6
South Dakota	871	85.0	1,132	987	881	76	40	38	34	3	64	8	56	6.8	2.1
Tennessee	6,693	85.3	9,590	8,156	8,960	1,293	391	346	636	96	573	231	466	7.3	4.2
Texas.........................	28,333	84.7	104,515	87,750	95,951	36,535	8,330	3,062	5,646	383	2,583	4,634	9,559	35.8	29.4
Utah...........................	3,115	83.0	5,723	6,085	5,082	1,564	51	201	135	40	192	140	461	15.8	10.8
Vermont	622	87.2	824	867	1,042	D	D	27	46	3	26	26	33	5.6	1.2
Virginia......................	8,424	84.8	27,426	28,607	27,095	840	314	1,007	1,756	235	1,109	1,121	1,312	16.4	7.5
Washington.................	7,453	81.9	26,029	22,283	26,480	3,413	96	2,269	1,859	40	1,553	1,609	1,418	20.0	8.6
West Virginia...............	1,788	88.7	675	729	847	31	11	66	31	9	89	25	42	2.5	1.1
Wisconsin	5,752	86.2	7,433	6,189	7,907	1,536	71	311	511	107	221	144	484	8.8	4.8
Wyoming	571	84.0	409	452	321	114	3	26	8	5	57	D	38	7.0	4.7

[1]People obtaining legal permanent resident status—Based on U.S. application Citizenship and Immigration Services (USCIS)-based case management systems that compile information supplied by aliens on the forms they are required to submit when applying for a legal status; for information, see Internet site www.dhs.gov/yearbook-immigration-statistics.
0 = zero.
D = Figure withheld to avoid disclosure pertaining to a specific organization or individual.
Sources: Residence 1 year ago—U.S. Census Bureau, 2018 American Community Survey; table DP02, "Selected Social Characteristics in the United States," using data.census.gov . People obtaining legal permanent resident status—U.S. Department of Homeland Security, Office of Immigration Statistics, 2018 Yearbook of Immigration Statistics, table 4 and Supplemental table 1 (www.dhs.gov/yearbook-immigration-statistics). Language—U.S. Census Bureau, 2018 American Community Survey, table DP02, "Selected Social Characteristics in the United States," using data.census.gov.

Table A–8. Place of Birth, 2018

Geographic area	Total population (thousands)	Percentage			Foreign born											
		Born in state of residence	Born in different state	Foreign born	Total (thousands)	Not a citizen	Entered the U.S. in 2010 or later	Europe	Born in							
									Asia					Latin America		
									Total	China	India	Philippines	Vietnam	Total	Mexico	El Salvador
United States	327,167	58.1	26.6	13.7	44,729	49.4	23.3	10.6	31.2	6.4	5.9	4.5	3.0	50.3	25.0	3.2
Alabama......................	4,888	69.3	26.4	3.3	163	58.7	28.4	12.8	32.3	5.8	6.4	2.7	4.0	47.5	26.7	0.7
Alaska........................	737	41.4	48.3	8.2	61	40.3	25.1	11.7	54.2	3.1	1.4	34.9	1.4	17.8	9.4	0.9
Arizona.......................	7,172	39.7	45.5	13.4	960	55.0	20.9	8.7	20.4	2.8	4.4	3.2	2.1	61.9	54.8	1.3
Arkansas.....................	3,014	61.6	32.9	4.8	144	65.0	24.1	6.3	23.2	2.1	4.6	2.2	4.1	62.0	40.8	10.6
California....................	39,557	55.8	15.9	26.9	10,626	47.5	17.2	6.4	39.7	9.2	5.0	8.0	4.8	49.9	38.1	4.3
Colorado....................	5,696	41.9	46.7	9.6	549	55.0	23.7	13.2	25.5	3.9	4.6	2.5	3.2	50.9	40.1	1.9
Connecticut................	3,573	54.7	26.9	14.6	520	47.0	25.0	21.6	24.2	5.0	8.9	1.3	1.2	46.0	4.6	1.5
Delaware....................	967	44.9	44.1	9.4	91	53.2	24.9	10.4	33.3	7.4	12.7	2.4	1.8	45.7	19.0	0.7
District of Columbia	702	37.1	46.6	13.9	98	54.7	32.8	18.7	20.7	4.5	2.2	1.8	1.5	39.8	3.0	11.0
Florida.......................	21,299	35.9	39.2	21.0	4,475	43.1	25.9	9.4	10.5	1.6	2.0	1.9	1.1	75.6	5.7	1.1
Georgia......................	10,519	54.8	33.7	10.1	1,064	54.9	25.5	7.9	30.9	4.2	8.6	1.6	3.7	48.2	22.5	2.6
Hawaii........................	1,420	53.0	25.3	18.7	266	41.5	23.4	3.8	77.8	10.0	0.7	46.7	3.4	5.6	1.9	0.1
Idaho.........................	1,754	46.5	46.3	6.0	105	56.8	18.4	10.3	20.4	3.9	2.5	4.3	2.2	62.1	52.3	1.4
Illinois.......................	12,741	67.0	17.8	14.1	1,791	48.3	18.6	20.2	32.1	4.9	9.8	5.1	1.5	42.8	35.3	0.5
Indiana.......................	6,692	67.9	26.1	5.3	354	59.1	31.2	11.7	35.5	7.3	8.9	3.0	1.8	42.1	30.5	1.7
Iowa..........................	3,156	69.9	23.9	5.5	175	61.0	37.9	11.1	39.0	6.2	5.4	2.5	4.7	32.8	24.0	1.4
Kansas.......................	2,912	59.5	32.3	7.2	209	59.9	28.7	5.6	33.3	4.7	7.4	2.5	5.6	53.4	41.6	2.4
Kentucky....................	4,468	68.8	26.6	3.8	169	59.4	38.3	14.1	34.0	5.7	6.5	3.9	2.8	39.9	17.5	1.1
Louisiana....................	4,660	78.1	17.0	4.2	195	60.1	34.2	7.2	32.2	3.9	2.6	4.8	9.6	54.6	15.3	2.5
Maine.........................	1,338	62.4	32.9	3.5	47	47.5	29.1	22.8	30.1	4.7	4.9	5.3	1.9	8.6	1.6	0.1
Maryland....................	6,043	47.4	35.9	15.1	915	46.5	25.2	8.3	31.0	6.6	6.2	3.8	2.0	39.3	3.7	11.1
Massachusetts.............	6,902	59.9	19.7	17.4	1,198	46.3	29.5	19.5	30.4	10.0	6.5	1.1	3.1	38.3	1.3	3.7
Michigan....................	9,996	76.2	16.0	7.0	695	46.4	30.7	17.9	52.3	6.5	11.0	3.1	2.0	18.9	12.1	0.4
Minnesota..................	5,611	67.4	23.1	8.6	484	47.3	30.0	10.0	37.3	4.7	6.2	2.2	3.7	23.0	12.4	1.5
Mississippi.................	2,987	71.7	25.2	2.4	71	62.5	38.5	13.4	31.8	4.6	7.3	4.5	4.8	47.9	24.8	0.3
Missouri	6,126	66.4	28.7	4.2	258	50.7	33.5	18.3	41.4	8.3	7.9	3.7	5.4	26.6	15.8	0.8
Montana.....................	1,062	52.8	44.1	2.2	23	41.9	25.3	27.6	29.9	5.0	1.7	8.0	3.7	23.2	10.5	0.0
Nebraska....................	1,929	64.3	27.6	7.2	139	60.0	32.2	8.0	27.8	2.4	4.6	3.0	3.4	52.6	32.0	4.5
Nevada......................	3,034	27.0	51.9	19.4	588	48.6	17.9	7.6	31.4	4.5	1.6	15.5	2.0	54.6	38.3	4.1
New Hampshire............	1,356	40.7	51.7	6.1	83	38.5	25.4	24.7	37.8	6.4	9.0	3.7	2.0	19.7	1.2	0.7
New Jersey	8,909	51.8	22.9	22.8	2,033	41.3	22.4	14.0	32.4	4.9	13.0	4.2	0.6	46.8	5.2	2.5
New Mexico	2,095	55.1	34.3	9.5	199	58.9	18.1	6.2	13.6	1.9	1.8	2.4	2.2	76.2	69.1	0.7
New York....................	19,542	62.7	12.0	22.8	4,447	41.6	22.2	15.7	29.4	10.9	3.6	1.9	0.6	48.1	5.0	2.3
North Carolina.............	10,384	55.8	34.9	7.9	824	60.9	26.0	10.3	28.5	4.1	9.1	2.0	2.1	51.4	28.1	3.4
North Dakota..............	760	63.1	31.2	4.7	36	55.5	44.2	9.4	40.0	1.4	4.7	6.2	1.9	13.0	3.9	0.6
Ohio..........................	11,689	74.9	19.5	4.8	556	47.2	33.2	18.0	43.2	7.6	11.8	2.9	2.1	19.6	8.6	1.3
Oklahoma	3,943	61.1	31.8	6.0	237	62.6	26.5	7.1	28.0	3.6	4.9	1.7	5.9	56.7	44.9	1.3
Oregon	4,191	45.4	43.1	10.3	432	54.7	23.8	14.2	32.9	6.5	4.7	3.9	5.1	43.2	35.2	1.7
Pennsylvania...............	12,807	71.7	19.1	7.2	923	46.2	30.3	18.4	38.8	8.7	10.2	2.2	3.5	31.4	5.9	0.9
Rhode Island..............	1,057	58.5	25.9	13.2	139	39.3	24.4	18.7	20.8	4.3	4.2	1.3	0.7	45.8	3.3	1.7
South Carolina	5,084	55.6	38.2	5.1	257	56.7	28.9	18.8	24.9	4.3	6.2	4.3	3.5	49.1	23.8	1.1
South Dakota	882	63.2	32.2	4.0	35	63.9	54.2	8.7	36.1	3.4	4.9	4.6	0.7	23.8	8.0	3.7
Tennessee	6,770	59.3	34.6	5.1	349	59.7	31.4	11.7	30.6	4.6	5.0	3.2	3.2	43.8	23.5	3.8
Texas.........................	28,702	59.4	21.8	17.2	4,928	62.3	24.1	4.0	22.9	3.2	5.9	2.2	3.6	66.5	50.8	4.6
Utah..........................	3,161	61.3	29.1	8.6	271	58.8	26.3	9.0	21.7	3.8	3.3	2.0	2.7	58.8	36.9	2.2
Vermont	626	49.2	44.9	4.9	31	39.3	23.6	28.9	31.9	9.5	2.5	2.9	1.5	12.1	1.7	0.4
Virginia	8,518	49.5	36.1	12.5	1,065	46.1	26.7	9.6	41.8	4.8	8.6	5.5	4.3	36.4	4.7	11.7
Washington................	7,536	46.3	37.2	14.7	1,105	51.3	26.8	14.2	43.8	9.3	8.2	6.1	5.9	29.6	22.9	1.3
West Virginia..............	1,806	68.7	29.2	1.5	28	48.2	30.2	18.7	44.8	8.7	5.7	5.5	2.4	25.6	9.5	2.4
Wisconsin	5,814	70.8	23.1	5.1	298	52.2	26.5	15.9	37.8	5.5	8.8	2.9	1.5	38.9	28.9	0.5
Wyoming	578	42.4	53.5	3.0	18	64.0	28.0	22.4	22.0	9.7	0.4	2.1	0.0	48.0	42.3	0.6

Table A–9. Live Births and Birth Rates

Geographic area	Total			Rate[1]			Percentage with low birth weight[2]			Rate[3] for teenage mothers[4]			Percentage to unmarried women		
	2018	2015	2010	2018	2015	2010	2018	2015	2010	2018	2015	2010	2018	2015	2010
United States	3,791,712	3,978,497	3,999,386	11.6	12.4	13.0	8.3	8.1	8.1	17.4	22.3	34.2	39.6	40.3	40.8
Alabama.....................	57,761	59,657	60,050	11.8	12.3	12.6	10.7	10.4	10.3	25.2	30.1	43.6	46.8	43.9	41.9
Alaska.......................	10,086	11,282	11,471	13.7	15.3	16.2	5.9	5.8	5.7	19.3	29.3	38.3	35.3	36.1	37.6
Arizona.....................	80,723	85,351	87,477	11.3	12.5	13.7	7.6	7.2	7.1	20.1	26.3	41.9	44.9	45.5	44.9
Arkansas..................	37,018	38,886	38,540	12.3	13.1	13.2	9.4	9.2	8.8	30.4	38.0	52.5	45.4	45.0	45.3
California..................	454,920	491,748	510,198	11.5	12.6	13.7	7.0	6.8	6.8	13.6	19.0	31.5	37.1	38.8	40.5
Colorado..................	62,885	66,581	66,355	11.0	12.2	13.2	9.4	9.0	8.8	14.3	19.3	33.4	23.2	22.7	23.9
Connecticut.............	34,725	35,746	37,708	9.7	10.0	10.6	7.6	7.9	8.0	8.3	10.1	18.7	37.1	37.5	37.4
Delaware.................	10,621	11,166	11,364	11.0	11.8	12.7	8.9	9.3	8.9	16.7	18.1	30.5	47.0	46.3	47.4
District of Columbia	9,212	9,578	9,165	13.1	14.2	15.2	10.0	10.0	10.2	19.3	25.6	45.4	46.5	49.3	54.8
Florida.....................	221,542	224,269	214,590	10.4	11.1	11.4	8.7	8.6	8.7	16.7	20.8	32.0	46.4	47.8	47.5
Georgia	126,172	131,404	133,947	12.0	12.9	13.8	10.1	9.5	9.7	20.6	25.6	41.4	45.1	45.2	45.8
Hawaii.....................	16,972	18,420	18,988	11.9	12.9	14.0	8.3	8.3	8.3	17.2	20.6	32.5	38.1	37.1	37.8
Idaho.......................	21,403	22,827	23,198	12.2	13.8	14.8	7.3	6.6	6.8	16.0	22.5	33.0	27.0	27.7	26.5
Illinois.....................	144,815	158,116	165,200	11.4	12.3	12.9	8.5	8.3	8.3	15.8	21.1	33.0	39.3	40.4	40.5
Indiana....................	81,646	84,040	83,940	12.2	12.7	12.9	8.1	8.0	8.0	21.8	26.0	37.3	43.2	43.3	43.0
Iowa........................	37,785	39,482	38,719	12.0	12.6	12.7	6.9	6.7	7.0	15.3	18.6	28.6	34.9	35.3	34.2
Kansas....................	36,261	39,154	40,649	12.5	13.4	14.2	7.4	6.8	7.1	20.0	25.5	39.3	36.4	36.0	37.8
Kentucky.................	53,922	55,971	55,784	12.1	12.6	12.9	8.9	8.7	9.0	27.3	32.4	46.2	41.9	41.6	41.2
Louisiana................	59,615	64,692	62,379	12.8	13.9	13.8	10.8	10.6	10.7	27.5	34.1	47.7	53.3	52.9	53.3
Maine......................	12,311	12,607	12,970	9.2	9.5	9.8	7.2	6.9	6.3	11.1	15.4	21.4	38.8	40.5	41.2
Maryland..................	71,080	73,616	73,801	11.8	12.3	12.8	8.8	8.6	8.8	14.1	17.0	27.3	39.2	40.1	41.9
Massachusetts..........	69,109	71,492	72,865	10.0	10.5	11.1	7.6	7.5	7.7	7.2	9.4	17.2	32.5	33.4	34.7
Michigan..................	110,032	113,312	114,531	11.0	11.4	11.6	8.5	8.5	8.4	15.8	19.4	30.1	40.8	41.9	41.8
Minnesota................	67,344	69,834	68,610	12.0	12.7	12.9	6.9	6.4	6.4	10.2	13.7	22.5	31.9	32.2	33.2
Mississippi...............	37,000	38,394	40,036	12.4	12.8	13.5	12.1	11.4	12.1	27.8	34.8	55.0	54.1	53.5	54.8
Missouri...................	73,269	75,061	76,759	12.0	12.3	12.8	8.7	8.3	8.2	21.6	25.0	37.1	40.3	40.4	40.2
Montana...................	11,513	12,583	12,060	10.8	12.2	12.2	7.4	7.1	7.5	17.2	25.3	35.0	34.9	36.3	36.4
Nebraska..................	25,488	26,679	25,918	13.2	14.1	14.2	7.6	7.1	7.1	16.7	22.0	31.1	32.5	32.9	33.6
Nevada....................	35,682	36,298	35,934	11.8	12.6	13.3	8.7	8.5	8.3	20.5	27.6	38.6	48.3	46.7	44.3
New Hampshire............	11,995	12,433	12,874	8.8	9.3	9.8	6.8	6.9	6.9	8.0	10.9	15.7	32.9	34.2	33.2
New Jersey	101,223	103,127	106,922	11.4	11.5	12.2	7.9	8.1	8.2	10.3	12.1	20.1	33.8	35.1	35.4
New Mexico	23,039	25,816	27,850	11.0	12.4	13.5	9.0	8.7	8.7	25.3	34.6	53.0	51.2	52.1	52.3
New York..................	226,238	237,274	244,375	11.6	12.0	12.6	8.1	7.8	8.2	11.7	14.6	22.7	37.5	39.5	41.7
North Carolina.............	118,954	120,843	122,350	11.5	12.0	12.8	9.2	9.1	9.1	18.7	23.6	38.3	40.9	41.0	42.0
North Dakota.............	10,636	11,314	9,104	14.0	14.9	13.5	6.6	6.2	6.7	16.4	22.2	28.8	31.9	31.6	32.7
Ohio........................	135,134	139,264	139,128	11.6	12.0	12.1	8.5	8.5	8.6	18.9	23.2	34.1	43.2	43.3	43.8
Oklahoma	49,800	53,122	53,238	12.6	13.6	14.2	8.3	7.9	8.4	27.2	34.8	50.4	42.2	41.8	41.8
Oregon	42,188	45,655	45,540	10.1	11.3	11.9	6.7	6.4	6.3	13.3	19.0	28.2	36.3	36.0	35.7
Pennsylvania.............	135,673	141,047	143,321	10.6	11.0	11.3	8.3	8.2	8.3	14.1	17.7	27.0	40.8	41.2	41.5
Rhode Island.............	10,506	10,993	11,177	9.9	10.4	10.6	7.6	7.6	7.7	11.5	14.3	22.3	43.6	45.1	45.0
South Carolina	56,669	58,139	58,342	11.1	11.9	12.6	9.6	9.5	9.9	22.0	26.2	42.6	46.2	46.5	47.6
South Dakota	11,893	12,336	11,811	13.5	14.4	14.5	6.6	6.1	6.8	20.4	26.4	34.9	36.1	37.2	37.6
Tennessee	80,751	81,685	79,495	11.9	12.4	12.5	9.3	9.2	9.0	25.3	30.5	43.2	43.5	43.9	44.1
Texas.......................	378,624	403,618	386,118	13.2	14.7	15.4	8.5	8.2	8.4	25.3	34.6	52.2	40.8	41.5	42.4
Utah........................	47,209	50,778	52,258	14.9	16.9	18.9	7.2	7.0	7.0	13.1	17.6	27.9	19.2	18.8	19.2
Vermont	5,432	5,903	6,223	8.7	9.4	9.9	7.0	6.6	6.1	8.8	11.6	17.9	38.5	40.2	39.2
Virginia....................	99,843	103,303	103,002	11.7	12.3	12.9	8.2	7.9	8.2	14.3	17.1	27.4	34.7	34.4	35.5
Washington...............	86,085	88,990	86,539	11.4	12.4	12.9	6.6	6.4	6.3	12.7	17.6	26.7	31.1	32.1	33.0
West Virginia.............	18,248	19,805	20,470	10.1	10.7	11.0	9.4	9.6	9.2	25.4	31.9	44.8	45.7	43.8	43.9
Wisconsin	64,098	67,041	68,487	11.0	11.6	12.0	7.7	7.3	7.0	13.0	16.2	26.2	37.4	37.5	36.7
Wyoming	6,562	7,765	7,556	11.4	13.2	13.4	9.4	8.6	9.0	20.8	29.2	39.0	33.3	33.9	34.0

[1]Birth rates are per 1,000 total population, estimated as of July 1.
[2]Less than 2,500 grams (5 pounds, 8 ounces).
[3]Per 1,000 estimated population in age group.
[4]Defined as mothers who are 15 to 19 years of age.

Table A–10. Births and Low Birth Weights by Race and Hispanic Origin, 2018

Geographic area	Births							Percentage wth low birth weights[3]			
	All Races[1]	White Non-Hispanic	Black Non-Hispanic	American Indian or Alaska Native	Asian	Native Hawaiian or Other Pacific Islander	Hispanic[2]	All races[1]	White non-Hispanic	Black non-Hispanic	Hispanic[2]
United States	3,791,712	1,956,413	552,029	29,092	240,798	9,476	886,210	8.3	6.9	14.1	7.5
Alabama.....................	57,761	33,776	17,597	148	903	46	4,403	10.7	8.1	16.4	7.6
Alaska........................	10,086	5,057	280	1,873	641	299	807	5.9	4.8	12.5	5.8
Arizona......................	80,723	32,805	4,305	4,155	2,908	248	34,084	7.6	7.0	12.4	7.3
Arkansas....................	37,018	23,609	6,966	220	775	498	4,099	9.4	7.7	16.0	7.4
California...................	454,920	123,139	22,380	1,411	68,444	1,732	211,271	7.0	5.8	12.1	6.7
Colorado....................	62,885	36,466	3,032	352	2,496	155	17,817	9.4	8.6	13.4	9.6
Connecticut................	34,725	18,488	4,423	38	2,232	5	8,762	7.6	6.0	12.6	8.1
Delaware	10,621	5,171	2,773	10	634	4	1,710	8.9	7.3	13.7	7.0
District of Columbia	9,212	3,040	4,252	15	444	2	1,296	10.0	5.2	14.6	6.8
Florida.......................	221,542	95,868	48,174	261	6,996	152	67,201	8.7	7.1	13.9	7.1
Georgia......................	126,172	55,676	43,746	102	5,768	104	17,432	10.1	7.3	14.8	7.3
Hawaii.......................	16,972	3,288	424	33	4,366	1,706	2,580	8.3	5.6	11.8	6.5
Idaho.........................	21,403	16,574	233	220	348	65	3,549	7.3	7.0	11.2	7.6
Illinois.......................	144,815	77,244	24,482	97	9,452	32	30,362	8.5	6.9	14.5	7.5
Indiana......................	81,646	59,520	10,242	73	2,382	59	7,867	8.1	7.1	13.8	7.1
Iowa..........................	37,785	29,327	2,615	152	1,176	149	3,694	6.9	6.3	11.3	7.6
Kansas	36,261	25,323	2,575	151	1,228	66	5,977	7.4	6.7	13.4	7.3
Kentucky	53,922	43,317	4,950	68	1,144	79	3,226	8.9	8.3	14.5	7.2
Louisiana	59,615	30,458	22,119	299	1,156	32	4,717	10.8	7.5	16.0	8.8
Maine........................	12,311	11,022	546	96	202	3	224	7.2	7.1	9.3	8.1
Maryland....................	71,080	29,585	21,893	83	4,928	31	12,470	8.8	6.7	12.6	6.9
Massachusetts.............	69,109	39,663	6,826	53	6,183	23	13,810	7.6	6.5	11.0	8.6
Michigan....................	110,032	74,777	20,558	412	4,395	34	7,139	8.5	6.8	14.9	7.3
Minnesota..................	67,344	46,014	8,207	983	5,298	57	4,991	6.9	5.9	10.2	7.6
Mississippi.................	37,000	18,597	15,797	221	411	17	1,666	12.1	8.6	17.0	7.1
Missouri.....................	73,269	53,697	10,589	140	1,698	199	4,409	8.7	7.3	15.9	7.3
Montana.....................	11,513	9,224	58	1,162	112	15	558	7.4	6.9	D	10.4
Nebraska....................	25,488	17,645	1,739	318	925	24	4,155	7.6	6.8	13.9	7.7
Nevada......................	35,682	13,021	4,564	280	2,613	340	13,307	8.7	7.7	12.7	7.7
New Hampshire.............	11,995	10,317	241	7	472	6	745	6.8	6.3	12.4	7.9
New Jersey	101,223	45,500	13,886	40	11,452	27	27,597	7.9	6.2	12.9	7.5
New Mexico	23,039	6,450	387	2,590	409	13	12,783	9.0	8.2	13.7	9.4
New York....................	226,238	110,840	33,145	395	24,383	50	51,755	8.1	6.3	12.9	8.2
North Carolina.............	118,954	63,514	27,670	1,448	4,834	151	18,360	9.2	7.4	14.4	7.5
North Dakota................	10,636	7,816	609	828	250	16	635	6.6	6.0	9.0	7.7
Ohio..........................	135,134	97,423	22,201	96	4,285	73	7,432	8.5	7.2	14.0	7.5
Oklahoma	49,800	28,444	4,136	4,557	1,306	214	7,545	8.3	7.8	15.3	7.0
Oregon	42,188	28,265	959	388	2,260	309	7,993	6.7	6.2	11.5	7.3
Pennsylvania...............	135,673	90,862	17,779	74	6,207	54	15,826	8.3	6.9	13.9	9.0
Rhode Island...............	10,506	6,008	783	36	519	5	2,756	7.6	6.6	11.7	7.9
South Carolina	56,669	31,890	16,681	106	1,172	50	5,255	9.6	7.0	15.2	7.3
South Dakota	11,893	8,481	416	1,645	224	7	661	6.6	6.1	8.4	7.4
Tennessee	80,751	53,256	15,921	79	1,877	69	7,824	9.3	7.8	15.1	7.2
Texas.........................	378,624	125,549	48,144	721	19,850	487	179,142	8.5	7.0	13.9	7.9
Utah..........................	47,209	34,303	521	418	1,131	468	8,133	7.2	6.6	10.6	8.6
Vermont	5,432	4,934	118	11	152	1	121	7.0	6.9	D	9.9
Virginia......................	99,843	54,798	20,860	157	7,625	103	14,397	8.2	6.6	13.3	6.9
Washington.................	86,085	49,019	3,922	1,166	8,729	1,159	16,073	6.6	5.7	9.8	6.7
West Virginia...............	18,248	16,621	626	14	176	2	378	9.4	9.2	13.6	7.9
Wisconsin	64,098	45,654	6,622	678	3,155	29	6,365	7.7	6.4	16.1	7.5
Wyoming	6,562	5,078	57	212	72	7	851	9.4	9.7	D	7.9

D = Figure does not meet standards of reliability or precision, based on fewer than 20 births.
[1] Includes other races not shown separately.
[2] People of Hispanic origin may be of any race. Births by Hispanic origin of mother.
[3] Less than 2,500 grams (5 pounds, 8 ounces).
[4] Number of births per 1,000 women age 15–44 years estimated.

Table A–11. Deaths and Death Rates, and Infant Deaths by Race and Hispanic Origin, 2017

Geographic area	Deaths Number (thousands)		Deaths Crude rate per 1,000 population[1]		Infant deaths[2] Number				Infant deaths[2] Mortality rate[2,3]			
	2015	2010	2015	2010	All races	Non-Hispanic White	Non-Hispanic Black	Hispanic or Latino	All races	Non-Hispanic White	Non-Hispanic Black	Hispanic or Latino
United States	2,814	2,468	8.6	8.0	22,335	9,359	6,730	4,808	5.79	4.61	11.46	5.35
Alabama	53	48	10.9	10.1	434	196	205	22	7.36	5.63	11.17	4.84
Alaska	4	4	6.0	5.2	59	25	-	-	5.65	4.35	-	-
Arizona	58	47	8.2	7.3	469	145	54	205	5.73	4.21	11.31	5.96
Arkansas	33	29	10.8	9.9	307	176	94	24	8.18	7.20	12.89	5.93
California	268	234	6.8	6.3	1,973	436	222	1,089	4.18	3.27	8.40	4.95
Colorado	38	31	6.8	6.3	291	149	31	96	4.52	3.90	8.71	5.30
Connecticut	31	29	8.7	8.0	160	63	47	41	4.54	3.28	10.29	4.64
Delaware	9	8	9.5	8.6	72	-	38	-	6.63	-	12.82	-
District of Columbia	5	5	7.2	7.8	77	-	57	-	8.05	-	12.19	-
Florida	204	174	9.7	9.2	1,358	453	515	353	6.07	4.64	10.22	5.26
Georgia	83	71	8.0	7.4	932	286	525	92	7.21	4.94	11.52	5.12
Hawaii	11	10	8.0	7.1	92	-	-	21	5.25	-	-	7.86
Idaho	14	11	8.2	7.3	102	77	-	-	4.60	4.42	-	-
Illinois	110	100	8.6	7.8	912	347	352	168	6.10	4.35	13.28	5.35
Indiana	66	57	9.8	8.8	600	361	163	58	7.30	5.91	15.34	7.56
Iowa	31	28	9.7	9.1	203	145	31	22	5.28	4.79	10.62	6.24
Kansas	27	25	9.3	8.6	221	130	34	43	6.05	5.00	11.79	7.21
Kentucky	48	42	10.8	9.7	355	275	54	20	6.48	6.15	10.07	6.33
Louisiana	46	41	9.8	9.0	431	146	252	28	7.06	4.59	11.05	5.86
Maine	15	13	11.0	9.6	70	64	-	-	5.69	5.75	-	-
Maryland	50	43	8.2	7.5	460	121	257	57	6.42	3.97	11.14	4.66
Massachusetts	59	53	8.6	8.0	262	121	50	71	3.71	2.91	6.82	5.22
Michigan	98	88	9.8	8.9	755	354	306	57	6.78	4.61	14.04	7.77
Minnesota	44	39	8.0	7.3	328	171	81	25	4.78	3.58	9.35	4.98
Mississippi	32	29	10.8	9.8	322	118	188	-	8.62	6.30	11.60	-
Missouri	62	55	10.1	9.2	456	284	146	-	6.24	5.18	12.95	-
Montana	10	9	9.7	8.9	64	42	-	-	5.42	4.39	-	-
Nebraska	17	15	8.8	8.3	144	94	20	20	5.58	5.18	10.36	4.56
Nevada	25	20	8.2	7.3	208	68	52	71	5.82	4.94	10.44	5.39
New Hampshire	13	10	9.3	7.7	51	41	-	-	4.21	3.87	-	-
New Jersey	75	69	8.3	7.9	453	139	155	124	4.47	3.00	10.98	4.53
New Mexico	19	16	8.9	7.7	140	33	-	81	5.89	4.96	-	6.06
New York	155	146	7.8	7.6	1,047	381	304	230	4.56	3.37	8.64	4.33
North Carolina	93	79	9.1	8.3	847	329	360	106	7.05	5.02	12.38	5.74
North Dakota	6	6	8.5	8.8	46	27	-	-	4.28	3.33	-	-
Ohio	124	109	10.6	9.4	983	527	383	54	7.18	5.26	15.89	7.23
Oklahoma	40	37	10.3	9.7	387	183	69	63	7.71	5.92	14.29	8.47
Oregon	37	32	8.8	8.3	236	138	-	58	5.41	4.57	-	7.01
Pennsylvania	136	125	10.6	9.8	841	435	268	100	6.11	4.63	13.53	6.31
Rhode Island	10	10	9.6	9.1	66	35	-	-	6.20	5.59	-	-
South Carolina	49	42	9.8	9.0	371	164	176	26	6.51	4.99	10.12	4.98
South Dakota	8	7	9.2	8.7	94	64	-	-	7.75	7.24	-	-
Tennessee	70	60	10.4	9.4	597	325	211	50	7.37	5.98	12.66	6.51
Texas	198	167	7.0	6.6	2,237	634	529	989	5.86	4.89	10.70	5.49
Utah	18	15	5.8	5.3	285	206	-	52	5.87	5.55	-	6.64
Vermont	6	5	9.6	8.6	27	22	-	-	4.77	4.25	-	-
Virginia	69	59	8.1	7.4	592	254	219	71	5.90	4.52	10.11	5.07
Washington	57	48	7.7	7.2	341	182	50	75	3.89	3.48	10.23	4.70
West Virginia	23	21	12.8	11.5	131	114	-	-	7.01	6.64	-	-
Wisconsin	53	47	9.1	8.3	414	205	128	49	6.37	4.37	17.28	7.69
Wyoming	5	4	8.2	7.9	32	26	-	-	4.64	4.72	-	-

Note: Survey, census, or data collection method is based on the National Vital Statistics System. For information, see Appendix B, Limitations of the Data and Methodology and www.cdc.gov/nchs/nvss.htm.
[1] Estimated resident population as of July 1.
[2] Infants are considered under 1 year of age.
[3] Per 1,000 live births. Infant deaths are based on decedent. Live births are based on races of mother.
- Not available; or data withheld to avoid disclosure; or does not meet statistical standards for reliability.

Table A–12. Age-Adjusted Death Rates, by Cause, 2017

Geographic area	All causes	Diseases of the heart	Malignant neoplasms	Chronic lower respiratory diseases	Accidents	Cerebro-vascular diseases	Alzheimer's disease	Diabetes mellitus	Influenza and pneumonia	Nephritis, nephrotic syndrome, and nephrosis	Intentional self-harm (suicide)
						Age-adjusted rates, 2017[1]					
United States	731.9	165.0	152.5	40.9	49.4	37.6	31.0	21.5	14.3	13.0	14.0
Alabama	917.7	223.2	170.0	57.8	53.8	50.0	45.2	19.8	20.2	16.5	16.6
Alaska	708.8	135.0	139.2	35.9	63.7	35.1	22.1	19.3	11.7	9.9	27.0
Arizona	678.5	141.9	135.8	42.7	56.2	30.8	35.1	23.7	10.1	6.2	18.2
Arkansas	900.1	223.8	173.6	66.7	51.8	43.8	39.4	32.4	19.8	19.7	20.8
California	618.7	142.9	136.7	32.2	33.1	37.6	37.1	22.1	14.6	8.9	10.5
Colorado	663.4	122.7	130.9	45.6	53.6	35.8	34.2	17.2	10.1	8.9	20.3
Connecticut	651.2	141.6	139.5	30.4	53.2	27.8	20.4	14.5	13.1	11.2	10.5
Delaware	749.6	158.4	160.4	40.7	61.9	46.2	30.5	19.1	14.9	16.1	11.6
District of Columbia	725.4	189.8	152.8	19.6	61.0	35.9	17.6	20.1	11.4	10.0	6.6
Florida	672.1	145.8	145.9	39.0	56.1	38.9	20.7	20.2	9.6	10.1	14.0
Georgia	793.7	175.8	154.9	46.2	45.2	43.5	46.0	21.5	13.8	18.6	13.6
Hawaii	584.9	129.8	128.6	19.0	35.7	37.5	19.7	15.9	29.6	10.7	15.2
Idaho	741.8	162.4	153.2	47.2	49.8	38.5	36.6	20.3	13.7	9.0	23.2
Illinois	724.2	163.3	157.9	37.6	44.4	38.9	25.6	19.2	15.6	16.8	11.2
Indiana	848.6	183.2	170.0	55.2	58.7	40.2	35.3	26.6	13.8	18.5	16.3
Iowa	737.0	167.4	158.0	46.5	42.7	32.8	35.3	22.8	13.2	8.8	15.0
Kansas	771.2	157.9	157.2	51.7	49.4	37.7	24.3	25.2	15.0	15.0	19.1
Kentucky	929.9	195.9	185.7	64.5	72.9	39.4	35.0	27.7	18.1	19.4	16.9
Louisiana	881.1	214.4	174.9	46.6	58.8	47.4	43.7	23.9	15.1	20.6	15.2
Maine	771.6	143.5	170.8	48.7	68.0	37.5	30.4	19.7	15.2	13.0	18.9
Maryland	718.1	164.5	151.5	29.9	36.9	40.2	17.1	20.3	14.0	11.9	9.8
Massachusetts	677.1	134.6	149.3	32.4	51.5	26.5	19.9	15.1	15.9	13.4	9.5
Michigan	783.5	196.1	161.3	44.3	53.0	39.3	34.5	22.1	14.2	14.7	14.1
Minnesota	656.4	119.1	146.8	36.3	44.6	32.6	34.9	19.3	9.9	7.7	13.8
Mississippi	951.3	231.6	183.1	58.3	56.3	51.1	49.5	33.3	23.0	21.7	15.0
Missouri	820.1	191.1	167.2	50.7	58.8	41.0	32.3	21.0	16.7	19.6	18.5
Montana	757.5	155.0	152.6	53.5	50.2	35.6	20.9	21.6	13.3	9.2	28.9
Nebraska	726.0	149.3	152.6	52.6	38.5	31.5	28.5	25.0	16.1	9.5	14.7
Nevada	765.5	199.3	155.3	50.0	47.8	35.9	27.3	18.3	19.6	9.0	20.3
New Hampshire	717.2	149.7	153.5	43.0	62.9	28.9	24.8	19.2	13.1	9.4	18.9
New Jersey	667.5	162.3	144.6	28.6	47.3	30.2	23.6	16.9	11.7	13.9	8.3
New Mexico	754.7	151.4	138.3	44.2	68.2	34.7	22.7	26.5	13.6	12.9	23.3
New York	623.6	171.2	141.2	28.9	35.5	24.6	13.2	16.8	17.7	9.1	8.1
North Carolina	785.6	156.5	157.1	45.3	56.3	43.0	37.3	23.6	17.5	17.0	14.3
North Dakota	692.7	137.8	142.6	38.3	41.3	35.4	36.5	21.8	15.3	12.9	20.1
Ohio	849.7	186.2	171.2	48.5	75.1	42.8	33.6	25.2	14.9	15.0	14.8
Oklahoma	902.4	237.2	177.3	65.8	62.5	43.3	39.3	30.6	13.9	10.2	19.1
Oregon	717.2	134.0	154.2	39.7	44.7	39.9	36.0	23.9	11.1	7.3	19.0
Pennsylvania	777.3	176.0	161.0	37.1	70.2	36.5	21.7	21.0	14.6	15.9	15.0
Rhode Island	713.4	155.7	154.2	36.2	60.0	29.4	27.3	18.8	13.9	11.6	11.8
South Carolina	828.0	172.0	162.7	47.9	60.2	44.9	44.9	24.5	12.3	15.5	16.3
South Dakota	736.6	150.1	156.9	45.3	56.1	36.7	36.9	24.9	19.0	6.8	22.5
Tennessee	897.1	202.2	173.4	57.4	63.0	45.0	46.7	21.2	21.3	14.4	16.8
Texas	735.7	169.2	146.5	40.5	38.8	41.3	38.5	22.9	11.2	16.0	13.4
Utah	700.1	150.2	120.3	32.1	44.2	36.2	42.1	22.9	13.3	9.7	22.7
Vermont	714.9	152.5	164.5	43.0	56.9	28.8	37.5	27.6	20.1	13.1	18.3
Virginia	719.4	154.5	152.6	34.9	44.0	37.5	36.9	21.6	12.6	5.2	13.4
Washington	688.6	138.8	148.4	38.0	44.0	36.9	46.0	21.6	18.2	17.1	16.9
West Virginia	957.1	192.0	179.4	64.3	100.3	41.8	30.6	34.0	19.4	12.5	21.1
Wisconsin	722.0	157.6	153.2	38.3	58.3	33.5	31.6	18.1	17.5	9.5	15.4
Wyoming	714.5	148.9	136.1	53.8	56.9	28.4	32.7	18.1	17.5	9.5	26.9

[1] Causes of death classified according to tenth revision of International Classification of Diseases. Rates per 100,000 population; age-adjusted rates per 100,000 U.S. standard population as of 2000. Rates for the United States and each state are based on populations estimated as of July 1, 2017.

Table A–13. Marriages and Divorces

Geographic area	Marriages[1] Rates per 1,000 population[3]			Divorces[2] Rates per 1,000 population[3]			Marital history, 2018 Median age at first marriage				Percent..		
	2018	2015	2010	2018	2015	2010	Men	Women	Total population age 15 and over	Ever married	Married within the past year	Divorced within the past year	Married two or more times
United States[4]	6.5	6.9	6.8	2.9	3.1	3.6	30.1	28.3	266,322,302	66.2	1.7	0.8	16.2
Alabama.........................	6.8	7.4	8.2	3.7	3.9	4.4	28.8	26.8	3,987,483	69.1	1.7	1.0	22.3
Alaska...........................	6.7	7.4	8.0	3.7	4.1	4.7	29.2	26.3	582,974	66.4	2.1	0.8	17.5
Arizona.........................	5.5	5.9	5.9	3.0	3.6	3.5	30.0	27.6	5,807,263	66.7	1.9	0.8	19.4
Arkansas.......................	8.9	10.0	10.8	4.1	4.8	5.7	27.4	26.6	2,429,708	70.7	1.9	1.2	25.3
California[5].....................	6.0	6.2	5.8	---	---	---	30.9	29.3	32,083,562	62.7	1.6	0.6	11.9
Colorado.......................	7.6	6.8	6.9	3.3	3.7	4.3	29.9	27.9	4,643,242	67.5	1.9	0.9	17.1
Connecticut...................	5.3	5.3	5.6	2.9	3.1	2.9	30.9	29.6	2,975,536	65.1	1.4	0.6	12.4
Delaware.......................	5.2	5.7	5.2	2.8	3.1	3.5	30.5	29.5	798,598	65.9	1.5	-	17.0
District of Columbia	7.8	8.2	7.6	2.5	2.8	2.8	31.8	31.0	590,722	41.9	2.4	0.5	7.0
Florida.........................	7.3	8.2	7.3	3.6	4.0	4.4	31.0	29.2	17,791,739	67.9	1.6	0.8	20.4
Georgia	6.4	6.2	7.3	2.5	---	---	30.0	28.0	8,451,927	65.0	1.7	0.8	17.7
Hawaii...........................	15.3	15.9	17.6	---	---	---	29.9	28.7	1,164,044	66.1	2.0	0.7	12.9
Idaho............................	7.8	8.2	8.8	3.8	4.1	5.2	26.9	26.7	1,386,609	72.1	2.4	0.8	21.5
Illinois..........................	5.5	5.9	5.7	1.5	2.2	2.6	30.6	29.1	10,381,247	64.6	1.7	0.6	13.4
Indiana..........................	6.6	6.9	6.3	---	---	---	28.8	27.1	5,392,554	68.4	1.7	0.9	19.5
Iowa.............................	5.7	6.3	6.9	2.2	1.2	2.4	28.3	26.4	2,545,586	69.6	1.8	0.6	16.3
Kansas..........................	5.4	5.9	6.4	2.3	2.8	3.7	28.1	26.1	2,325,350	70.4	1.9	0.8	19.0
Kentucky.......................	6.8	7.2	7.4	3.5	3.7	4.5	28.1	26.6	3,629,102	70.9	1.7	1.1	21.7
Louisiana	5.1	6.8	6.9	1.7	2.8	---	30.0	28.1	3,742,752	63.4	1.6	0.8	16.8
Maine...........................	7.4	7.6	7.1	3.2	3.4	4.2	29.6	28.8	1,134,585	71.6	1.3	0.8	19.8
Maryland........................	5.9	6.2	5.7	2.4	2.6	2.8	30.6	29.3	4,931,235	65.0	1.7	0.8	14.1
Massachusetts..............	6.3	5.5	5.6	2.1	2.6	2.5	31.0	29.9	5,783,050	62.8	1.6	0.6	10.6
Michigan........................	5.7	6.0	5.5	2.8	3.0	3.5	30.1	28.3	8,220,666	66.6	1.6	0.7	16.3
Minnesota......................	5.3	5.6	5.3	---	---	---	29.9	27.7	4,525,167	67.7	1.7	0.7	12.6
Mississippi.....................	6.3	7.0	4.9	2.7	3.4	4.3	27.6	27.3	2,401,006	65.9	1.8	0.8	20.1
Missouri........................	6.5	6.2	6.5	3.0	3.2	3.9	28.6	26.9	4,981,108	69.6	1.9	0.9	19.9
Montana........................	7.7	8.0	7.4	3.0	3.4	3.9	29.0	26.2	870,969	71.5	1.6	0.8	19.6
Nebraska.......................	6.0	6.4	6.6	2.9	3.2	3.6	28.0	26.4	1,531,482	69.5	1.7	0.7	15.9
Nevada..........................	26.7	31.0	38.3	4.4	4.6	5.9	30.2	28.3	2,459,348	66.5	1.8	1.0	20.6
New Hampshire.............	6.9	6.9	7.3	3.1	3.3	3.8	31.2	29.1	1,147,794	69.3	1.5	0.8	17.4
New Jersey	5.4	5.6	5.1	2.7	2.8	3.0	30.9	29.3	7,299,829	65.7	1.5	0.5	10.9
New Mexico	6.4	6.2	7.7	---	3.3	4.0	29.8	27.2	1,698,061	65.1	1.6	0.7	18.1
New York......................	7.1	7.1	6.5	2.8	2.7	2.9	31.0	29.8	16,168,651	62.1	1.6	0.6	10.3
North Carolina..............	6.4	7.0	6.6	3.1	3.1	3.8	29.5	28.1	8,485,855	67.9	1.7	0.8	18.4
North Dakota.................	5.7	6.2	6.5	2.6	2.8	3.1	28.9	26.7	609,824	67.5	2.0	0.6	13.7
Ohio............................	5.6	5.9	5.8	2.9	3.1	3.4	29.9	28.4	9,552,948	66.8	1.7	0.7	17.5
Oklahoma	6.4	7.4	7.2	3.8	4.4	5.2	27.8	26.4	3,144,933	70.7	2.1	1.1	23.3
Oregon..........................	6.3	6.9	6.5	3.4	3.4	4.0	29.9	27.8	3,469,423	69.0	1.9	0.9	19.8
Pennsylvania.................	5.5	5.7	5.3	2.6	2.6	2.7	30.6	28.9	10,622,654	66.3	1.5	0.7	13.8
Rhode Island.................	6.3	6.4	5.8	2.9	3.0	3.2	32.4	29.5	890,851	60.7	1.4	0.5	11.8
South Carolina	6.6	7.5	7.4	2.5	2.8	3.1	29.9	28.2	4,165,633	67.1	1.4	0.7	18.6
South Dakota	6.5	7.2	7.3	2.6	2.6	3.4	28.8	26.3	701,477	68.6	1.8	0.9	14.6
Tennessee	8.0	8.5	8.8	3.5	3.7	4.2	29.4	27.4	5,517,634	69.1	1.8	0.9	21.8
Texas...........................	6.1	7.2	7.1	2.6	2.6	3.3	29.2	27.3	22,535,123	66.1	1.9	0.8	17.1
Utah............................	8.4	8.1	8.5	3.8	3.6	3.7	26.8	24.8	2,382,849	69.4	2.3	0.8	15.7
Vermont	7.9	8.1	9.3	3.1	3.1	3.8	30.5	28.6	531,532	68.0	1.8	0.5	15.8
Virginia	6.4	7.0	6.8	3.1	3.3	3.8	29.9	27.9	6,966,390	67.4	1.9	0.8	16.4
Washington...................	6.0	6.2	6.0	3.3	3.4	4.2	29.7	27.9	6,142,755	68.7	1.9	0.8	17.9
West Virginia.................	6.1	6.6	6.7	3.3	4.0	5.1	29.2	26.9	1,507,317	71.6	1.6	0.9	22.0
Wisconsin	5.4	5.6	5.3	2.5	2.6	3.0	29.7	27.8	4,765,395	67.7	1.6	0.6	14.3
Wyoming.......................	7.1	7.3	7.6	3.8	4.1	5.1	29.3	26.0	466,760	72.5	2.0	0.9	22.2

[1]Data are accounts of marriages performed, except as noted.
[2]Includes annulments.
[3]Based on provisional counts of marriages by state occurrence; total population residing in area; population enumerated as of April 1 for 2000 and estimated as of July 1 for 2015 and 2018.
[4]U.S. total divorce rates are based solely on the combined counts and populations for reporting states and the District of Columbia.
[5]Marriage data include nonlicensed marriages registered.
--- = Not available

Table A–14. Health Care Services, Physicians, and Nurses

Geographic area	Establishments — Total (NAICS 62)	Establishments — Ambulatory Healthcare Services (NAICS 621)	Establishments — Hospitals (NAICS 622)	Establishments — Nursing and residential care facilities (NAICS 623)	Employees — Total (NAICS 62)	Employees — Ambulatory Healthcare Services (NAICS 621)	Employees — Hospitals (NAICS 622)	Employees — Nursing and residential care facilities (NAICS 623)	Annual payroll (NAICS 62) (millions of dollars)	Physicians[2] 2019 — Number	Physicians[2] 2019 — Rate per 100,000 population[3]	Nurses[2] 2019 — Number	Nurses[2] 2019 — Rate per 100,000 population[3]
United States[5]	897,635	625,395	7,020	89,876	20,241,438	7,406,773	6,001,339	3,514,416	995,684	685,830	208.9	3,233,380	985.1
Alabama	10,677	7,626	119	955	252,774	96,755	82,381	45,690	11,854	7,300	148.9	54,190	1,105.2
Alaska	2,702	1,755	28	397	52,228	19,308	16,250	5,737	3,022	1,200	164.0	6,750	922.7
Arizona	18,862	14,124	112	2,150	371,491	145,730	101,871	58,088	18,506	13,570	186.4	59,270	814.3
Arkansas	7,885	5,547	97	570	179,424	55,582	58,263	33,056	8,034	5,120	169.7	25,570	847.3
California	113,709	83,941	470	9,901	2,011,358	809,196	566,992	305,325	120,115	62,290	157.6	318,630	806.4
Colorado	16,745	12,569	108	1,038	315,864	126,124	89,754	48,403	16,148	9,310	161.7	55,980	972.1
Connecticut	11,085	7,475	52	1,279	290,886	98,605	68,729	64,128	14,210	9,550	267.9	37,490	1,051.5
Delaware	2,699	1,764	15	281	68,583	24,655	21,159	11,201	3,659	2,910	298.8	12,610	1,295.0
District of Columbia	2,212	1,221	14	182	72,997	23,127	26,950	7,033	4,365	4,370	619.2	11,830	1,676.2
Florida	61,562	48,717	337	3,987	1,134,627	480,710	327,918	195,913	56,858	45,540	212.0	194,310	904.7
Georgia	25,327	18,719	212	1,805	509,188	207,220	162,520	68,249	25,212	15,650	147.4	84,750	798.2
Hawaii	3,685	2,747	27	181	71,950	28,137	21,711	8,807	4,036	2,670	188.6	11,840	836.2
Idaho	5,322	3,740	53	440	96,205	32,889	32,583	15,273	4,203	1,220	68.3	14,930	835.4
Illinois	34,359	24,798	231	2,989	807,541	270,910	243,250	145,073	38,021	25,080	197.9	138,230	1,090.8
Indiana	16,965	11,173	178	2,227	432,565	166,278	125,172	81,622	20,187	11,740	174.4	72,920	1,083.1
Iowa	8,697	5,107	136	1,276	217,484	55,468	69,681	56,063	9,453	5,570	176.5	35,360	1,120.7
Kansas	8,136	5,102	157	1,058	193,428	61,779	58,096	44,203	8,385	4,110	141.1	33,160	1,138.2
Kentucky	11,823	7,861	149	1,071	260,461	89,650	90,602	47,036	12,108	6,070	135.9	47,530	1,063.9
Louisiana	12,702	9,034	231	1,051	298,483	102,057	101,682	45,636	12,926	6,450	138.7	44,850	964.8
Maine	4,790	2,492	42	932	112,277	33,452	36,021	24,680	5,247	3,830	284.9	16,280	1,211.1
Maryland	16,863	11,994	67	1,776	380,827	140,406	106,222	74,165	19,225	15,180	251.1	57,440	950.1
Massachusetts	19,495	11,770	129	2,849	641,269	201,695	195,835	116,689	33,050	27,560	399.9	88,540	1,284.6
Michigan	27,146	18,839	197	3,719	616,371	230,099	200,226	109,636	29,231	26,810	268.5	104,350	1,044.9
Minnesota	17,156	8,688	143	4,290	471,360	141,879	119,956	112,997	20,816	15,820	280.5	77,090	1,366.9
Mississippi	6,385	4,429	103	436	168,501	50,447	69,387	24,270	7,694	3,530	118.6	33,240	1,116.9
Missouri	20,978	11,643	183	1,848	413,376	131,790	131,791	80,262	18,505	10,770	175.5	74,980	1,221.7
Montana	3,731	2,198	67	427	72,425	22,089	24,734	13,214	3,310	2,100	196.5	10,990	1,028.3
Nebraska	5,818	3,755	106	485	133,276	37,475	45,107	28,607	6,271	4,230	218.7	25,370	1,311.5
Nevada	7,391	5,833	61	492	130,170	51,622	41,097	15,758	6,567	4,690	152.3	23,000	746.7
New Hampshire	3,754	2,419	35	314	94,601	32,810	29,368	16,362	4,942	3,200	235.3	15,650	1,151.0
New Jersey	28,096	21,252	121	2,150	598,540	244,095	158,066	99,789	29,981	24,210	272.6	87,470	984.8
New Mexico	5,146	3,524	60	402	126,231	41,219	36,345	14,983	5,408	3,300	157.4	18,720	892.8
New York	59,123	39,813	325	5,771	1,628,655	557,806	467,387	248,820	81,597	45,190	232.3	194,760	1,001.2
North Carolina	24,114	16,225	165	2,537	598,661	211,136	194,955	104,802	27,884	18,530	176.7	108,870	1,038.0
North Dakota	2,075	1,125	51	294	61,364	15,047	19,583	16,944	2,956	1,060	139.1	10,400	1,364.7
Ohio	29,739	19,718	256	3,559	845,432	287,865	266,371	166,355	38,896	27,950	239.1	137,200	1,173.7
Oklahoma	11,042	7,669	163	968	221,928	75,291	74,811	39,779	9,935	3,870	97.8	33,460	845.6
Oregon	14,082	8,527	67	2,678	261,317	97,871	72,436	53,171	13,339	8,600	203.9	39,300	931.8
Pennsylvania	37,840	24,780	336	4,181	1,032,307	348,204	289,124	218,721	48,545	28,630	223.6	158,270	1,236.3
Rhode Island	3,223	2,125	16	459	87,348	28,312	23,680	20,447	4,080	3,360	317.2	13,380	1,263.0
South Carolina	10,708	7,543	101	1,024	242,039	83,482	80,425	43,927	11,110	7,400	143.7	50,360	978.1
South Dakota	2,428	1,372	64	348	69,814	15,762	32,716	13,491	3,544	1,420	160.5	13,870	1,567.8
Tennessee	15,955	11,424	170	1,482	420,766	160,073	139,378	73,020	21,034	10,910	159.8	73,900	1,082.1
Texas	70,030	53,591	668	4,554	1,527,228	669,104	408,439	199,964	69,366	47,650	164.3	236,550	815.8
Utah	8,271	6,421	75	600	144,016	59,179	41,795	27,023	6,561	4,370	136.3	23,350	728.3
Vermont	2,134	1,230	16	225	48,633	16,633	15,007	8,353	2,256	1,660	266.0	7,510	1,203.5
Virginia	20,591	14,832	119	1,619	452,188	179,405	119,932	79,111	22,901	15,870	185.9	72,400	848.2
Washington	21,369	13,949	124	2,630	428,500	166,415	117,168	73,394	23,243	11,490	150.9	62,600	822.1
West Virginia	4,911	2,999	69	707	133,216	37,641	51,072	21,540	6,061	2,790	155.7	21,720	1,212.0
Wisconsin	16,084	8,909	161	3,147	408,348	134,782	115,013	82,170	19,234	12,180	209.2	62,790	1,078.4
Wyoming	2,013	1,287	34	135	32,917	9,507	12,328	5,436	1,595	1,060	183.2	5,480	946.9

[1] Data for 2017 are based on the 2017 North American Industry Classification System (NAICS).

[2] As of May. Physicians include the following Medical Doctors included in the Occupational Employment Statistics: Anesthesiologists; Family Medicine Physicians; General Internal Medicine Physicians; Obstetricians and Gynecologists; Pediatricians, General; Psychiatrists; Physicians, All Other, and Ophthalmologists, Except Pediatric; Surgeons, Except Ophthalmologists. Nurses include Registered Nurses, Nurse Anesthetists, Nurse Midwives, and Nurse Practitioners.

[3] Based on U.S. Census Bureau estimates as of July 1, 2019.

Table A–15. Employment in Health Care Occupations and Type of Health Insurance

Geographic area	Physicians and surgeons	Therapists	Registered nurses	Other nurses	Other diagnosing and treating practitioners	Health technologists and technicians	Nursing, psychiatric and home health aides	Occupational and physical therapist assistants and aides	Other healthcare supprt occupations
United States	959,512	887,315	3,312,948	228,275	1,067,195	3,141,970	3,476,199	151,536	1,496,496
Alabama	11,760	9,429	55,060	3,834	11,553	49,383	32,829	3,677	14,203
Alaska	2,015	1,969	6,163	582	3,758	5,605	8,059	324	4,068
Arizona	17,888	17,433	59,860	3,961	24,094	64,409	63,522	2,824	37,229
Arkansas	8,066	8,159	33,245	2,319	8,398	35,379	33,559	1,352	10,069
California	105,716	100,208	330,537	14,623	109,367	315,689	463,074	13,680	199,037
Colorado	15,879	17,537	55,974	3,550	25,014	49,013	45,502	1,675	32,240
Connecticut	14,413	13,136	38,289	2,759	13,585	35,388	49,312	1,362	15,664
Delaware	2,098	3,897	9,638	486	1,742	11,166	9,791	493	3,855
District of Columbia	4,199	956	3,294	438	2,352	2,769	6,019	194	1,810
Florida	61,409	55,212	211,021	15,086	60,537	208,765	172,428	9,393	107,439
Georgia	23,788	25,273	99,038	7,272	31,203	97,983	68,514	2,553	44,754
Hawaii	4,589	3,581	11,594	381	4,566	11,228	10,391	627	7,964
Idaho	3,463	3,869	16,782	1,334	4,845	15,502	15,921	447	7,249
Illinois	41,255	37,289	131,438	9,003	41,617	120,985	140,499	5,485	54,431
Indiana	14,340	23,365	74,571	5,420	20,990	68,860	58,858	2,815	29,313
Iowa	7,889	8,396	35,845	2,608	12,723	30,147	37,730	1,452	13,199
Kansas	8,516	8,873	34,614	2,603	10,667	28,312	28,549	1,868	13,174
Kentucky	10,132	14,143	51,163	4,071	13,664	48,269	40,668	2,483	16,591
Louisiana	7,419	11,186	51,537	3,740	11,265	48,999	48,746	2,897	18,438
Maine	4,722	4,673	15,152	1,672	4,862	14,861	19,182	493	6,092
Maryland	22,960	18,415	71,515	4,479	21,271	55,709	62,563	2,632	28,467
Massachusetts	35,216	21,853	92,782	8,073	27,246	75,580	83,955	3,244	39,109
Michigan	32,880	29,480	107,047	6,313	33,540	96,589	112,114	7,997	55,404
Minnesota	16,143	16,407	72,068	4,476	23,228	65,953	85,445	2,378	23,430
Mississippi	6,182	10,076	34,904	3,705	7,503	34,936	25,385	1,780	9,146
Missouri	18,155	16,105	66,859	5,635	17,656	70,052	64,944	3,430	23,912
Montana	2,226	2,985	13,260	859	4,354	9,263	11,014	279	5,129
Nebraska	4,261	7,231	22,613	1,168	7,455	16,428	23,692	840	7,632
Nevada	6,733	5,554	25,040	1,075	6,777	21,824	15,092	578	15,718
New Hampshire	4,237	3,689	15,553	1,237	6,265	15,205	13,274	238	7,452
New Jersey	34,270	26,740	98,817	5,663	30,154	82,748	83,023	3,861	42,366
New Mexico	5,334	6,000	14,620	1,561	6,645	14,717	25,317	636	10,043
New York	82,397	63,004	202,421	14,199	71,535	171,602	335,222	11,436	82,592
North Carolina	27,009	24,175	102,669	6,968	34,776	109,419	96,173	4,026	42,922
North Dakota	1,718	2,098	13,019	863	3,089	11,094	14,360	101	1,729
Ohio	38,729	31,688	141,536	11,017	37,584	134,435	134,234	9,562	51,757
Oklahoma	9,333	9,896	34,794	1,261	13,075	40,913	31,749	2,245	17,340
Oregon	12,570	12,574	39,849	2,777	15,578	38,231	52,215	1,965	25,215
Pennsylvania	44,666	46,201	150,319	12,057	49,315	147,948	177,678	7,450	50,920
Rhode Island	3,642	2,867	11,891	697	4,245	11,626	17,108	551	5,229
South Carolina	12,328	10,808	56,150	3,402	16,370	48,206	42,831	2,356	21,399
South Dakota	1,487	1,773	11,408	582	4,356	10,498	10,052	544	3,490
Tennessee	19,378	13,335	70,955	8,141	25,068	80,024	54,876	3,037	26,216
Texas	66,740	60,152	255,007	17,736	82,371	258,790	260,444	9,419	125,348
Utah	9,403	9,203	22,586	1,292	10,754	25,941	19,650	845	18,478
Vermont	2,812	2,548	6,839	422	1,803	9,027	7,515	30	2,942
Virginia	22,674	19,771	75,524	5,688	27,370	75,351	72,432	3,450	34,312
Washington	22,605	20,039	66,927	4,331	27,542	58,365	82,613	3,541	42,853
West Virginia	5,218	4,862	17,545	1,588	7,581	23,170	21,510	2,794	7,366
Wisconsin	17,211	17,399	67,841	4,430	23,647	60,101	82,135	3,669	29,372
Wyoming	1,439	1,803	5,775	838	2,240	5,513	4,431	528	2,389

Table A–15. Employment in Health Care Occupations and Type of Health Insurance—*Continued*

Geographic area	Total civilian noninstitutional population	Persons with no health insurance		Persons with private health insurance (percent)				Persons with public coverage (percent)				Percent with both private and public health insurance
		Number	Percent	Any type of private health insurance	Employer-based health insurance	Direct-purchase health insurance	TRICARE/military health coverage	Any type of public coverage	Medicare coverage	Medicaid/means tested coverage	VA health care	
United States	322,249,485	28,565,542	8.9	67.5	55.2	13.4	2.7	35.6	17.6	20.5	2.3	12.0
Alabama	4,810,094	481,259	10.0	66.6	53.6	13.4	4.6	37.2	20.5	19.7	2.9	13.8
Alaska	713,033	90,128	12.6	64.5	53.5	7.4	9.8	34.6	13.4	22.0	4.6	11.8
Arizona	7,064,799	749,977	10.6	62.6	50.4	12.8	3.3	39.3	19.2	22.4	3.0	12.5
Arkansas	2,960,503	243,585	8.2	60.4	47.2	13.5	3.3	44.2	20.5	27.1	3.1	12.8
California	39,062,465	2,825,620	7.2	63.7	52.3	12.6	1.8	38.4	15.2	26.4	1.6	9.4
Colorado	5,604,105	421,644	7.5	70.7	56.9	13.8	4.0	32.7	15.3	18.6	2.4	10.9
Connecticut	3,523,842	186,923	5.3	71.0	60.3	12.8	1.3	35.8	18.0	20.6	1.6	12.1
Delaware	952,211	53,962	5.7	70.6	59.7	13.2	2.8	39.8	20.8	21.4	2.0	16.1
District of Columbia	692,817	21,897	3.2	70.4	59.3	13.3	1.8	35.8	13.3	26.7	1.1	9.4
Florida	20,996,007	2,728,485	13.0	62.3	45.5	17.0	3.5	37.1	22.1	18.2	3.0	12.4
Georgia	10,334,958	1,411,183	13.7	65.8	53.9	11.9	3.9	31.2	15.9	17.4	2.5	10.6
Hawaii	1,368,549	55,799	4.1	76.3	62.9	12.2	9.2	35.2	19.3	17.7	2.8	15.7
Idaho	1,733,484	192,620	11.1	69.7	52.2	17.8	3.7	32.5	18.1	16.5	3.3	13.3
Illinois	12,563,908	874,608	7.0	70.2	59.3	12.8	1.1	33.9	16.6	19.2	1.7	11.0
Indiana	6,592,504	545,123	8.3	70.2	59.3	12.9	1.7	33.8	17.6	18.0	2.4	12.3
Iowa	3,113,029	147,039	4.7	74.8	60.3	16.8	1.8	35.4	18.2	19.2	2.7	14.9
Kansas	2,854,774	250,355	8.8	74.3	59.2	15.8	4.0	29.8	17.4	13.9	2.6	12.8
Kentucky	4,388,204	247,641	5.6	64.2	53.3	11.8	2.9	43.5	19.7	26.9	2.8	13.4
Louisiana	4,556,078	363,362	8.0	59.1	48.3	11.7	2.9	44.4	18.1	29.4	2.3	11.5
Maine	1,323,289	106,187	8.0	70.1	55.3	15.3	3.2	37.3	23.1	18.5	4.0	15.4
Maryland	5,943,064	356,708	6.0	74.0	63.0	12.4	3.8	33.3	16.6	18.8	2.0	13.3
Massachusetts	6,830,796	188,907	2.8	74.0	62.8	13.9	1.1	36.6	17.4	23.0	1.4	13.3
Michigan	9,888,529	534,551	5.4	71.1	60.5	13.0	1.3	39.1	19.6	22.5	2.1	15.6
Minnesota	5,553,564	244,379	4.4	76.1	62.3	15.8	1.4	33.2	16.7	18.0	2.5	13.7
Mississippi	2,919,673	354,151	12.1	60.5	47.9	12.7	3.7	38.9	19.5	23.4	2.4	11.5
Missouri	6,014,742	566,327	9.4	70.3	57.4	13.7	2.6	32.7	19.4	15.2	2.8	12.4
Montana	1,047,075	86,029	8.2	66.6	48.7	17.8	4.0	40.2	20.7	21.3	3.9	15.0
Nebraska	1,900,165	157,612	8.3	75.1	59.4	16.5	3.6	28.8	16.8	13.5	2.9	12.2
Nevada	2,998,585	336,191	11.2	64.9	53.5	11.3	3.5	34.9	17.1	19.2	3.4	11.0
New Hampshire	1,339,549	77,011	5.7	75.8	63.6	13.4	2.5	32.3	19.8	13.9	2.7	13.8
New Jersey	8,803,988	655,000	7.4	72.8	62.7	12.2	1.0	31.2	17.0	16.8	1.1	11.5
New Mexico	2,060,718	196,250	9.5	54.3	43.7	10.3	4.3	49.4	20.0	32.9	3.1	13.2
New York	19,302,636	1,041,233	5.4	67.2	56.4	13.3	0.9	39.9	17.8	26.2	1.4	12.5
North Carolina	10,183,721	1,092,046	10.7	67.3	52.7	14.7	4.5	34.7	18.6	18.2	3.0	12.8
North Dakota	743,793	53,935	7.3	79.7	61.9	19.0	3.6	26.5	16.3	11.3	2.9	13.5
Ohio	11,517,226	743,905	6.5	68.6	58.6	12.0	1.6	37.5	18.9	20.8	2.4	12.6
Oklahoma	3,861,581	548,316	14.2	64.1	50.8	13.5	3.9	34.6	18.2	17.7	3.4	12.9
Oregon	4,151,076	293,107	7.1	67.7	53.8	15.6	2.1	39.2	19.2	22.2	3.2	14.0
Pennsylvania	12,604,311	699,376	5.5	72.4	59.4	15.0	1.5	37.4	19.9	20.3	2.2	15.3
Rhode Island	1,041,309	42,481	4.1	70.0	57.5	14.2	2.3	38.7	19.1	23.6	2.3	12.8
South Carolina	4,990,240	522,459	10.5	65.9	51.8	14.2	4.8	37.8	20.4	19.7	3.3	14.2
South Dakota	864,598	84,707	9.8	72.0	54.8	17.5	4.1	30.4	17.9	13.8	3.6	12.2
Tennessee	6,667,784	674,865	10.1	65.8	52.5	13.6	3.6	37.1	18.9	20.6	2.7	13.0
Texas	28,243,191	5,002,893	17.7	61.8	51.0	11.2	3.0	29.0	13.7	17.0	2.2	8.6
Utah	3,135,573	295,364	9.4	78.5	64.6	14.8	2.5	21.3	11.9	10.4	1.7	9.2
Vermont	620,066	24,988	4.0	69.9	56.2	14.9	2.4	40.6	21.6	22.8	2.5	14.5
Virginia	8,301,038	731,469	8.8	75.4	59.7	14.1	7.8	28.6	17.2	12.1	2.9	12.8
Washington	7,427,599	477,284	6.4	70.6	57.6	12.8	4.3	35.9	17.0	20.8	2.6	12.9
West Virginia	1,776,965	114,106	6.4	62.8	53.4	10.6	2.5	47.1	23.9	26.4	3.8	16.3
Wisconsin	5,740,669	313,158	5.5	74.8	62.0	14.6	1.5	33.0	18.7	16.8	2.5	13.3
Wyoming	567,008	59,337	10.5	74.9	60.2	15.7	4.1	27.3	18.0	10.3	3.7	12.6

Table A–16. Health Indicators: Health Risks

Geographic area	Health risks										
	Adult Smoking (2016)	Youth Smoking (2015)	Adult Physical Activity (2013)	Youth Physical Activity (2015)	Adult Nutrition (2015)	Youth Nutrition (2015)	Adult Binge Drinking (2016)	Youth Binge Drinking (2015)	Observed Seat Belt Use (2014)	Youth Seat Belt Use (2015)	Youth Marijuana Use (2015)
United States[7]	17.0	10.8	50.5	48.6	22.3	14.8	16.9	17.7	87.0	93.9	21.7
Alabama	21.5	14.0	45.4	41.3	27.8	10.2	13.0	16.1	95.7	90.9	17.3
Alaska	19.0	11.1	55.3	44.2	18.9	14.2	18.2	12.5	88.4	90.6	19.0
Arizona	14.7	10.1	51.9	46.4	20.5	14.7	15.6	19.0	87.2	90.5	23.3
Arkansas	23.6	15.7	41.2	43.3	28.1	13.4	15.0	16.3	74.4	89.6	17.8
California	11.0	7.7	56.3	48.1	18.6	15.9	16.3	15.1	97.1	96.4	22.9
Colorado	15.6	--	60.4	--	17.8	--	19.0	--	82.4	--	--
Connecticut	13.4	10.3	50.9	45.3	19.5	12.8	16.7	14.0	85.1	91.7	20.4
Delaware	17.7	9.9	49.7	43.3	20.7	--	17.0	14.8	91.9	93.7	23.3
District of Columbia	14.7	--	57.7	30.5	19.1	12.1	25.5	8.3	93.2	--	28.7
Florida	15.5	9.9	50.2	41.9	21.3	15.5	15.5	15.3	88.8	91.5	21.5
Georgia	17.9	--	50.8	--	24.7	--	13.4	--	97.3	--	--
Hawaii	13.0	9.7	60.2	38.1	21.4	--	18.6	13.4	93.5	--	19.4
Idaho	14.5	9.7	53.9	53.1	18.7	11.3	16.1	15.6	80.2	94.3	17.0
Illinois	15.8	10.1	52.4	49.6	24.3	12.7	19.9	15.9	94.1	93.7	18.7
Indiana	21.1	11.2	44.1	46.5	26.7	9.8	17.5	17.4	90.2	94.1	16.4
Iowa	16.7	--	47.0	--	26.9	--	21.2	--	92.8	--	--
Kansas	17.2	--	49.1	--	22.3	--	16.0	--	85.7	--	--
Kentucky	24.5	16.9	46.0	37.0	24.6	11.1	14.6	17.7	86.1	90.9	17.2
Louisiana	22.8	--	45.2	--	31.0	--	16.9	--	84.1	--	--
Maine	19.8	11.2	53.6	41.2	18.3	--	18.3	11.7	85.0	93.7	19.9
Maryland	13.7	8.7	48.6	36.9	21.3	13.4	15.3	13.1	92.1	--	18.8
Massachusetts	13.6	7.7	54.5	45.2	18.3	12.0	17.8	17.7	76.6	--	24.5
Michigan	20.4	10.0	53.1	46.0	24.7	9.8	19.0	12.5	93.3	93.4	19.3
Minnesota	15.2	--	52.7	--	22.4	--	21.3	--	94.7	--	--
Mississippi	22.7	15.2	37.4	34.2	31.2	12.4	12.3	15.3	78.3	88.9	19.7
Missouri	22.1	11.0	48.7	45.7	23.3	10.5	18.3	19.5	78.8	91.9	16.3
Montana	18.5	13.1	57.8	54.0	19.3	13.3	18.9	20.7	74.0	90.5	19.5
Nebraska	17.0	13.3	50.1	52.8	24.8	13.2	20.0	14.3	79.0	88.7	13.7
Nevada	16.5	7.5	53.6	50.6	19.2	13.8	15.8	15.8	94.0	93.8	19.3
New Hampshire	18.0	9.3	55.4	46.9	17.3	--	18.0	16.8	70.4	91.8	22.2
New Jersey	14.0	--	50.5	--	22.1	--	16.0	--	87.6	--	--
New Mexico	16.6	11.4	55.0	52.2	21.5	16.4	15.0	14.6	92.1	94.0	25.3
New York	14.2	8.8	47.3	41.8	22.4	--	17.5	15.6	90.6	--	19.3
North Carolina	17.9	13.1	48.6	43.4	21.6	12.5	14.6	13.9	90.6	93.5	22.3
North Dakota	19.8	11.7	45.3	51.3	27.5	11.1	24.8	17.6	81.0	91.5	15.2
Ohio	22.5	--	49.5	--	24.8	--	17.9	--	85.0	--	--
Oklahoma	19.6	13.1	43.9	54.0	24.5	12.1	11.8	16.5	86.3	94.3	17.5
Oregon	16.2	--	64.1	--	16.5	--	16.3	--	97.8	--	--
Pennsylvania	18.0	12.9	47.8	45.6	24.2	10.7	19.4	15.4	83.6	89.1	18.2
Rhode Island	14.4	4.8	49.1	43.7	23.5	12.0	15.8	12.8	87.4	94.1	23.6
South Carolina	20.0	9.6	49.1	42.3	25.4	9.1	16.8	11.5	90.0	94.7	17.8
South Dakota	18.1	10.1	53.7	47.4	26.1	11.9	19.3	14.3	68.9	85.4	12.4
Tennessee	22.1	11.5	37.7	42.7	22.6	9.7	13.1	--	87.7	92.7	--
Texas	14.3	--	42.1	--	19.6	--	17.9	--	90.7	--	--
Utah	8.8	--	55.3	--	20.0	--	12.5	--	83.4	--	--
Vermont	17.0	10.8	58.8	45.8	17.6	18.1	18.4	16.0	84.1	--	22.4
Virginia	15.3	8.2	51.9	45.2	21.8	13.8	15.8	11.0	77.3	93.7	16.2
Washington	14.0	--	56.3	--	16.9	--	16.4	--	94.5	--	--
West Virginia	24.8	18.8	47.6	44.9	26.5	12.9	11.3	19.8	87.8	88.8	16.5
Wisconsin	17.1	--	53.4	--	24.0	--	24.6	--	84.7	--	--
Wyoming	19.0	15.7	54.2	50.7	21.5	13.9	18.4	19.7	79.2	89.3	18.3

Note: See Appendix A. Source Notes and Explanations for meanings of all indicators.
-- = Not available

Table A–17. Health Indicators: Health Conditions and Preventive Measures

Geographic area	Health Conditions							Preventive measures		
	HIV Diagnosis Rate (2014)	Adult Obesity (2016)	Youth Obesity (2015)	Diagnosed Diabetes (2014)	Diagnosed High Cholesterol (2013)	Diagnosed Hypertension (2013)	Medicated Hypertension (2013)	Colorectal Cancer Screening (2014)	Influenza Vaccination Coverage (2016)	Child Vaccination Coverage (2015)
United States[7]	16.5	30.1	13.9	9.1	38.4	31.4	78.1	68.8	46.8	72.2
Alabama	17.2	35.7	16.1	11.8	44.4	40.4	82.7	67.6	43.9	70.6
Alaska	6.8	31.4	14.0	7.6	38.6	29.8	61.3	64.3	39.1	66.3
Arizona	14.3	29.0	10.9	9.1	39.7	30.7	70.6	68.1	41.8	72.3
Arkansas	13.8	35.7	18.0	11.5	42.4	38.7	79.1	64.6	46.2	66.6
California	17.2	25.0	13.9	9.9	37.7	28.7	70.7	66.6	48.0	75.0
Colorado	9.0	22.3	--	6.9	34.8	26.3	69.2	69.3	49.9	75.4
Connecticut	10.0	26.0	12.3	8.0	37.8	31.3	76.0	76.1	52.7	80.6
Delaware	16.8	30.7	15.8	9.7	40.6	35.6	82.9	76.6	51.2	79.3
District of Columbia	66.9	22.6	15.1	9.1	34.0	28.4	73.6	70.3	48.3	76.3
Florida	31.3	27.4	12.3	9.4	40.3	34.6	79.4	69.9	43.3	66.6
Georgia	27.0	31.4	--	11.0	38.1	35.1	77.7	69.8	42.8	75.6
Hawaii	9.2	23.8	12.9	8.9	35.0	28.5	78.8	65.7	49.2	73.8
Idaho	2.0	27.4	11.1	7.0	38.4	29.4	71.9	66.4	39.5	71.6
Illinois	16.1	31.6	12.6	9.4	36.6	30.1	77.6	65.1	41.8	70.8
Indiana	9.0	32.5	13.6	9.7	39.8	33.5	79.7	65.0	43.6	74.7
Iowa	4.0	32.0	--	8.3	41.1	31.4	78.1	71.1	51.3	77.9
Kansas	5.8	31.2	--	9.5	38.1	31.3	78.5	67.8	43.9	75.2
Kentucky	9.9	34.2	18.5	11.3	43.2	39.1	81.3	69.6	45.0	73.0
Louisiana	36.6	35.5	--	10.4	40.7	39.9	80.8	66.4	41.6	70.8
Maine	5.2	29.9	13.3	7.8	39.7	33.3	79.6	78.1	49.9	71.8
Maryland	27.7	29.9	11.5	9.2	37.0	32.8	80.4	73.0	53.5	76.8
Massachusetts	12.8	23.6	11.0	8.8	36.5	29.4	75.8	77.9	50.3	78.5
Michigan	10.0	32.5	14.3	9.0	40.6	34.6	75.7	74.6	44.2	67.6
Minnesota	7.0	27.8	--	7.5	33.6	27.0	77.0	74.4	51.7	73.2
Mississippi	21.0	37.3	18.9	11.9	41.9	40.2	82.9	62.9	40.1	70.6
Missouri	9.9	31.7	13.1	10.0	38.8	32.1	82.9	66.7	46.4	71.0
Montana	1.9	25.5	10.3	7.6	35.7	29.3	73.5	66.8	42.2	68.1
Nebraska	6.1	32.0	13.0	8.4	37.4	30.3	78.5	67.6	52.3	73.8
Nevada	19.6	25.8	12.2	8.8	38.6	30.6	73.6	63.0	36.1	71.3
New Hampshire	3.6	26.6	12.2	7.8	36.7	30.1	76.8	77.8	50.4	74.1
New Jersey	20.4	27.4	--	8.6	39.2	31.1	78.0	67.7	49.1	76.5
New Mexico	8.2	28.3	15.6	10.4	36.8	29.5	74.0	63.0	49.2	70.1
New York	22.8	25.5	13.1	9.2	39.1	31.6	77.8	70.7	49.8	71.9
North Carolina	17.0	31.8	16.4	9.8	41.0	35.5	78.4	73.2	50.8	76.4
North Dakota	4.0	31.9	14.0	8.0	36.5	29.7	79.3	65.3	46.9	80.2
Ohio	10.3	31.5	--	10.3	37.5	33.5	79.4	67.6	46.6	68.3
Oklahoma	10.5	32.8	17.3	10.9	41.2	37.5	79.0	62.3	47.2	75.4
Oregon	7.3	28.7	--	8.0	37.0	31.8	71.2	70.6	40.0	67.4
Pennsylvania	12.2	30.3	14.0	9.6	38.5	33.7	80.5	69.6	53.3	72.8
Rhode Island	11.2	26.6	12.0	8.3	38.7	33.8	79.3	77.8	55.4	77.2
South Carolina	20.7	32.3	16.3	10.7	42.6	38.4	80.7	71.3	47.4	68.2
South Dakota	4.1	29.6	14.7	8.2	36.6	30.7	80.6	69.7	53.9	75.6
Tennessee	14.7	34.8	18.6	11.7	38.7	38.8	83.9	68.8	43.9	70.1
Texas	22.1	33.7	--	10.8	37.7	31.2	76.8	63.5	43.5	71.2
Utah	5.3	25.4	--	7.7	33.4	24.2	67.9	74.2	43.4	68.1
Vermont	3.5	27.1	12.4	6.9	35.2	31.1	72.6	75.3	47.3	75.6
Virginia	14.1	29.0	13.0	9.0	38.6	32.5	79.3	72.0	50.5	64.4
Washington	7.7	28.6	--	8.2	36.7	30.4	68.5	71.8	48.3	77.1
West Virginia	6.1	37.7	17.9	12.0	42.9	41.0	80.6	66.0	49.6	64.9
Wisconsin	4.8	30.7	--	8.0	36.3	32.3	77.2	75.9	43.7	68.8
Wyoming	2.4	27.7	11.0	7.8	35.0	28.7	74.5	61.8	38.9	73.3

Note: See Appendix A. Source Notes and Explanations for meanings of all indicators.
-- = Not available

Table A–18. People With and Without Health Insurance Coverage

Geographic area	All People									Children under 18 years old					
	Civilian noninstitutional population (thousands)			Number not covered (thousands)			Percentage of people not covered			Number not covered (thousands)			Percentage of children not covered		
	2018	2015	2010	2018	2015	2010	2018	2015	2010	2018	2015	2010	2018	2015	2010
United States	322,249	316,451	304,288	28,566	29,758	47,208	8.9	9.4	15.5	4,055	3,950	6,650	5.2	5.1	8.5
Alabama............................	4,810	4,781	4,703	481	484	687	10	10.1	14.6	41	37	76	3.5	3.2	6.3
Alaska..............................	713	713	689	90	106	137	12.6	14.9	19.9	18	21	25	9.4	10.8	12.8
Arizona............................	7,065	6,719	6,310	750	728	1,065	10.6	10.8	16.9	146	151	228	8.4	8.8	13.2
Arkansas..........................	2,961	2,924	2,868	244	278	501	8.2	9.5	17.5	34	39	56	4.5	5.3	7.5
California..........................	39,062	38,650	36,816	2,826	3,317	6,825	7.2	8.6	18.5	299	343	943	3.1	3.5	9.5
Colorado..........................	5,604	5,367	4,957	422	433	789	7.5	8.1	15.9	62	58	139	4.6	4.4	10.7
Connecticut......................	3,524	3,538	3,520	187	211	320	5.3	6.0	9.1	20	29	28	2.6	3.5	3.2
Delaware..........................	952	931	885	54	54	86	5.7	5.9	9.7	8	6	12	3.6	3.0	5.3
Distict of Columbia..........	693	661	594	22	25	45	3.2	3.8	7.6	2	2	3	1.8	1.5	2.4
Florida..............................	20,996	19,960	18,534	2,728	2,662	3,941	13	13.3	21.3	339	321	570	7.6	7.4	13.4
Georgia............................	10,335	10,024	9,520	1,411	1,388	1,876	13.7	13.9	19.7	217	190	272	8.1	7.2	10.3
Hawaii..............................	1,369	1,375	1,316	56	55	104	4.1	4.0	7.9	8	6	13	2.6	1.7	4.0
Idaho................................	1,733	1,632	1,552	193	180	275	11.1	11.0	17.7	29	26	50	6.1	5.8	11.0
Illinois..............................	12,564	12,680	12,673	875	900	1,746	7	7.1	13.8	102	87	162	3.4	2.8	4.9
Indiana.............................	6,593	6,520	6,391	545	628	948	8.3	9.6	14.8	109	117	157	6.6	7.0	9.2
Iowa.................................	3,113	3,080	3,005	147	155	280	4.7	5.0	9.3	21	29	34	2.7	3.8	4.4
Kansas.............................	2,855	2,850	2,804	250	261	389	8.8	9.1	13.9	38	40	66	5.1	5.2	8.5
Kentucky..........................	4,388	4,343	4,243	248	261	647	5.6	6.0	15.3	40	46	71	3.8	4.3	6.6
Louisiana	4,556	4,567	4,440	363	546	791	8	11.9	17.8	39	45	74	3.4	3.8	6.3
Maine...............................	1,323	1,315	1,313	106	111	133	8	8.4	10.1	15	16	12	5.5	5.7	4.2
Maryland..........................	5,943	5,909	5,688	357	389	641	6	6.6	11.3	47	57	75	3.3	4.0	5.2
Massachusetts.................	6,831	6,718	6,478	189	189	286	2.8	2.8	4.4	18	18	25	1.2	1.2	1.7
Michigan..........................	9,889	9,811	9,764	535	597	1,207	5.4	6.1	12.4	78	77	111	3.4	3.3	4.5
Minnesota........................	5,554	5,432	5,252	244	245	476	4.4	4.5	9.1	45	43	91	3.3	3.2	6.7
Mississippi.......................	2,920	2,928	2,903	354	372	528	12.1	12.7	18.2	35	36	74	4.7	4.6	9.1
Missouri...........................	6,015	5,969	5,880	566	583	774	9.4	9.8	13.2	83	89	99	5.7	6.0	6.6
Montana...........................	1,047	1,017	976	86	119	169	8.2	11.6	17.3	15	19	30	6.1	7.9	12.6
Nebraska..........................	1,900	1,866	1,802	158	154	208	8.3	8.2	11.5	26	27	29	5.2	5.5	5.9
Nevada.............................	2,999	2,856	2,669	336	351	604	11.2	12.3	22.6	58	56	126	8.0	7.9	18.0
New Hampshire.................	1,340	1,314	1,303	77	83	145	5.7	6.3	11.1	7	8	16	2.6	2.8	5.2
New Jersey	8,804	8,850	8,694	655	771	1,151	7.4	8.7	13.2	80	84	138	3.9	4.0	6.3
New Mexico......................	2,061	2,050	2,033	196	224	399	9.5	10.9	19.6	27	26	60	5.3	4.9	10.9
New York..........................	19,303	19,556	19,134	1,041	1,381	2,277	5.4	7.1	11.9	107	116	235	2.5	2.6	5.1
North Carolina..................	10,184	9,856	9,361	1,092	1,103	1,570	10.7	11.2	16.8	130	113	201	5.3	4.6	8.3
North Dakota....................	744	741	661	54	57	65	7.3	7.8	9.8	11	15	11	6.0	8.3	6.6
Ohio.................................	11,517	11,442	11,359	744	746	1,399	6.5	6.5	12.3	133	125	181	4.8	4.5	6.3
Oklahoma.........................	3,862	3,830	3,677	548	533	694	14.2	13.9	18.9	83	78	105	8.2	7.7	10.6
Oregon.............................	4,151	3,991	3,799	293	280	652	7.1	7.0	17.1	33	35	84	3.6	3.8	9.2
Pennsylvania....................	12,604	12,599	12,506	699	802	1,271	5.5	6.4	10.2	124	122	161	4.4	4.2	5.4
Rhode Island....................	1,041	1,041	1,037	42	59	126	4.1	5.7	12.2	5	8	15	2.2	3.6	6.1
South Carolina	4,990	4,801	4,537	522	523	795	10.5	10.9	17.5	56	48	113	4.7	4.2	9.8
South Dakota....................	865	841	798	85	86	99	9.8	10.2	12.4	13	15	18	5.9	7.0	8.6
Tennessee........................	6,668	6,496	6,260	675	667	899	10.1	10.3	14.4	83	69	90	5.2	4.4	5.7
Texas...............................	28,243	26,990	24,779	5,003	4,615	5,875	17.7	17.1	23.7	873	759	1,105	11.2	10.0	15.2
Utah.................................	3,136	2,971	2,750	295	311	422	9.4	10.5	15.3	72	70	102	7.4	7.3	11.1
Vermont...........................	620	620	620	25	24	50	4	3.8	8.0	2	2	3	2.0	1.4	2.0
Virginia............................	8,301	8,163	7,807	731	746	1,020	8.8	9.1	13.1	102	101	136	5.1	5.1	6.9
Washington......................	7,428	7,067	6,638	477	468	946	6.4	6.6	14.2	47	49	114	2.7	2.9	6.8
West Virginia....................	1,777	1,816	1,823	114	108	266	6.4	6.0	14.6	13	12	21	3.4	3.0	5.2
Wisconsin	5,741	5,699	5,613	313	323	529	5.5	5.7	9.4	51	50	76	3.8	3.7	5.4
Wyoming	567	577	555	59	66	83	10.5	11.5	14.9	10	12	13	7.1	8.1	8.8

Table A–19. Public and Private School Fall Enrollment

Geographic area	Total enrollment (thousands) 3-4	Percentage enrolled[1]	Percentage enrolled in public school[2]	Total enrollment (thousands) 5-17	Public (thousands)	Private (thousands)	Percentage enrolled in public school[2]	Total Fall 2006	Total Fall 2010	Total Fall 2016	PreK-8 Fall 2006	PreK-8 Fall 2010	PreK-8 Fall 2016	9-12 Fall 2006	9-12 Fall 2010	9-12 Fall 2016
United States	3,928	48.2	59.1	51,960	46,192	5,769	88.9	49,316	49,484	50,615	34,235	34,625	35,477	15,081	14,860	15,138
Alabama	53	44.1	60.2	771	682	89	88.5	744	756	745	529	534	522	215	222	223
Alaska	9	41.0	59.5	127	114	12	90.2	133	132	133	90	92	94	42	40	39
Arizona	66	37.4	62.2	1,164	1,059	105	91.0	1,068	1,072	1,123	760	752	784	309	320	339
Arkansas	37	48.7	69.4	492	445	47	90.4	476	482	493	337	346	350	140	136	143
California	500	48.9	58.3	6,379	5,802	577	91.0	6,407	6,290	6,309	4,410	4,294	4,368	1,997	1,996	1,942
Colorado	72	50.9	59.9	904	824	80	91.1	794	843	905	559	601	640	235	242	266
Connecticut	51	67.0	64.9	542	491	50	90.7	575	561	535	398	387	369	177	173	166
Delaware	12	47.5	67.2	143	128	16	89.0	122	129	136	85	90	96	37	39	41
District of Columbia	14	78.1	82.4	80	67	14	83.1	73	71	86	52	54	67	20	18	19
Florida	248	52.4	55.1	2,998	2,583	415	86.2	2,672	2,643	2,817	1,867	1,858	1,969	805	785	848
Georgia	139	49.2	63.5	1,805	1,618	187	89.6	1,629	1,677	1,764	1,167	1,202	1,246	463	475	519
Hawaii	18	48.9	39.2	208	173	35	83.2	181	180	182	126	128	131	55	52	50
Idaho	17	35.1	49.7	313	283	30	90.4	267	276	297	187	194	209	80	82	89
Illinois	172	55.5	63.1	2,032	1,806	225	88.9	2,118	2,092	2,027	1,478	1,455	1,409	641	637	618
Indiana	69	40.6	55.7	1,106	968	139	87.5	1,046	1,047	1,050	730	729	726	316	318	324
Iowa	37	44.8	72.9	521	475	46	91.2	483	496	510	326	348	363	157	148	147
Kansas	37	47.1	68.0	503	442	61	87.8	470	484	494	326	343	351	143	141	143
Kentucky	47	43.8	64.4	708	618	90	87.3	683	673	684	487	480	485	196	193	199
Louisiana	62	51.0	63.0	771	638	133	82.8	676	697	716	492	512	516	184	184	200
Maine	11	46.5	51.5	178	156	21	88.0	194	189	181	132	129	125	62	60	56
Maryland	71	47.6	49.1	948	805	143	85.0	852	852	886	579	588	630	273	264	256
Massachusetts	89	61.3	49.6	984	878	106	89.2	969	956	965	671	666	669	298	289	295
Michigan	109	45.8	67.4	1,548	1,387	161	89.6	1,723	1,587	1,529	1,171	1,076	1,047	552	511	481
Minnesota	71	50.6	61.9	918	823	95	89.6	841	838	875	558	570	607	282	268	268
Mississippi	38	49.1	66.7	508	451	58	88.7	495	491	483	356	351	345	139	140	138
Missouri	71	46.3	62.3	966	835	131	86.4	920	919	915	634	643	647	286	276	268
Montana	12	44.0	61.0	160	143	17	89.6	144	142	146	97	98	104	47	43	42
Nebraska	26	45.4	55.5	332	282	49	85.2	288	299	319	196	210	226	92	88	93
Nevada	29	37.4	65.3	484	448	36	92.6	425	437	474	303	307	334	122	130	140
New Hampshire	15	57.2	48.6	190	169	21	88.9	204	195	181	136	132	124	67	63	57
New Jersey	138	64.4	53.9	1,400	1,236	164	88.3	1,389	1,403	1,410	963	981	991	425	421	420
New Mexico	23	46.0	78.8	346	320	25	92.7	328	338	336	230	239	236	98	99	100
New York	281	60.1	58.0	2,844	2,432	412	85.5	2,810	2,735	2,730	1,887	1,869	1,887	922	866	843
North Carolina	112	45.5	53.6	1,635	1,445	190	88.4	1,444	1,491	1,550	1,027	1,058	1,080	417	432	470
North Dakota	8	37.2	68.1	117	107	10	91.1	97	96	110	64	66	79	32	30	30
Ohio	126	43.8	60.9	1,820	1,565	255	86.0	1,837	1,754	1,710	1,253	1,223	1,190	584	531	520
Oklahoma	46	42.1	73.7	675	612	63	90.6	639	660	694	460	483	504	179	176	190
Oregon	46	47.4	47.7	621	555	66	89.4	563	571	606	381	393	426	182	178	181
Pennsylvania	139	47.6	52.7	1,868	1,594	275	85.3	1,871	1,793	1,727	1,220	1,210	1,184	651	584	544
Rhode Island	10	39.2	59.1	144	124	20	86.2	152	144	142	102	98	99	50	46	43
South Carolina	52	44.6	58.3	793	713	79	90.0	708	726	771	501	516	548	207	210	223
South Dakota	11	44.7	71.6	150	135	14	90.3	121	126	136	83	88	99	38	38	38
Tennessee	65	38.5	58.2	1,062	921	142	86.7	978	987	1,002	692	702	708	286	286	294
Texas	350	42.3	63.6	5,211	4,832	379	92.7	4,600	4,936	5,361	3,320	3,587	3,836	1,280	1,349	1,525
Utah	44	43.7	58.2	660	614	46	93.0	523	586	660	371	425	471	152	161	189
Vermont	8	66.8	55.4	83	74	9	89.6	95	97	88	64	68	63	32	29	26
Virginia	101	48.9	45.1	1,328	1,178	150	88.7	1,220	1,251	1,287	842	871	898	379	380	389
Washington	89	46.9	46.9	1,161	1,036	125	89.2	1,027	1,044	1,102	695	714	762	332	330	339
West Virginia	14	36.0	81.8	255	235	20	92.1	282	283	274	198	201	194	84	81	79
Wisconsin	59	43.1	68.0	913	786	127	86.1	877	872	864	585	598	602	292	274	263
Wyoming	7	48.9	63.5	94	86	8	91.6	85	89	94	58	63	67	27	26	27

[1] As a percentage of all 3 and 4 year olds, including those not enrolled.
[2] As a percentage of those enrolled.

Table A–20. Public Elementary and Secondary Schools—Finances and Teachers

Geographic area	Total enrollment 2016-2017 (thousands)[1]	Revenues, 2016-2017 (millions of dollars)				Expenditures, 2016-2017		Current expenditures				Full-time equivalent teachers (thousands), 2018-2019[4]			Pupil-teacher ratio, 2018-2019[5]
		Total	Source			Total (millions of dollars)[2]	Per capita (dollars)[3]	Elementary and secondary schools (millions of dollars)	Average per pupil		Total	Elementary	Secondary	
			Local	State	Federal				Amount (dollars)	Rank				
United States	50,513	705,267	316,635	331,322	57,311	707,601	2,177.3	548,891	10,933		3,169.8	1,500.3	1,247.2	16.00
Alabama	745	7,889	2,675	4,351	864	8,030	1,647.4	7,085	9,528	41	42.1	16.9	19.7	17.56
Alaska	133	2,508	554	1,601	354	2,583	3,491.4	2,368	17,838	6	7.7	3.4	3.7	17.10
Arizona.....................	1,113	10,259	4,155	4,778	1,326	10,531	1,495.0	8,855	8,053	48	48.5	30.8	14.8	23.53
Arkansas..................	493	5,619	2,042	2,951	626	5,623	1,873.4	4,889	10,004	37	38.0	14.4	18.2	13.03
California..................	6,309	88,109	29,813	50,841	7,455	87,968	2,235.1	75,241	12,151	21	271.8	152.5	87.1	23.08
Colorado..................	905	10,601	5,292	4,602	706	10,633	1,894.7	8,815	9,849	39	53.1	24.8	23.3	17.15
Connecticut..............	535	11,584	6,586	4,494	504	11,574	3,238.9	9,736	19,929	3	42.8	24.3	15.4	12.30
Delaware..................	136	2,730	1,218	1,324	189	2,247	2,348.4	2,039	14,892	14	9.6	4.4	4.7	14.38
District of Columbia	86	2,526	2,288	(X)	238	2,626	3,778.7	1,860	22,561	2	7.3	3.3	2.7	12.82
Florida.....................	2,817	28,809	14,173	11,347	3,289	29,876	1,425.1	25,429	9,374	43	164.4	61.7	64.9	17.31
Georgia	1,764	20,444	9,079	9,440	1,925	20,344	1,954.3	17,999	10,274	34	117.2	43.6	45.9	15.08
Hawaii......................	182	2,844	58	2,534	252	2,779	1,950.8	2,600	14,322	16	12.1	5.6	5.5	14.94
Idaho.......................	297	2,575	616	1,707	253	2,560	1,490.6	2,202	7,554	50	16.7	8.4	7.6	18.54
Illinois.....................	2,027	35,480	19,457	13,711	2,312	34,588	2,706.7	31,046	15,517	12	132.4	85.5	39.8	14.97
Indiana.....................	1,050	11,953	3,891	7,087	974	11,867	1,782.3	10,424	9,823	40	61.2	27.2	29.4	17.26
Iowa........................	510	6,904	2,675	3,732	497	6,810	2,167.7	5,843	11,456	27	35.6	21.0	10.5	14.45
Kansas.....................	494	6,344	1,775	4,031	538	6,279	2,158.8	5,425	10,428	32	36.7	10.6	17.8	13.55
Kentucky..................	684	7,783	2,641	4,230	912	7,878	1,769.5	6,922	10,083	36	41.8	21.4	10.0	16.21
Louisiana..................	716	8,950	3,878	3,903	1,169	8,984	1,923.4	8,056	11,379	28	38.9	22.9	12.4	18.29
Maine.......................	181	2,820	1,532	1,093	195	2,838	2,126.7	2,527	14,633	15	15.0	9.1	4.5	12.00
Maryland...................	886	15,046	7,568	6,626	852	14,670	2,435.3	13,152	14,933	13	60.7	32.2	24.3	14.78
Massachusetts.............	965	18,424	10,494	7,000	930	17,910	2,610.8	15,574	17,718	7	73.9	41.9	26.1	13.03
Michigan...................	1,529	20,163	6,205	12,224	1,735	19,612	1,966.5	17,190	11,256	29	85.0	28.6	33.3	17.69
Minnesota.................	875	13,242	3,736	8,762	744	14,127	2,538.1	11,009	12,635	19	57.7	25.3	24.7	15.41
Mississippi................	483	4,753	1,665	2,416	673	4,674	1,563.8	4,233	8,755	47	32.0	12.7	13.3	14.75
Missouri	915	11,485	6,733	3,749	1,003	11,190	1,832.4	9,683	10,684	31	68.5	29.1	32.9	13.34
Montana....................	146	1,841	748	867	226	1,908	1,813.2	1,666	11,538	26	10.6	6.3	3.1	14.07
Nebraska...................	319	4,470	2,670	1,451	349	4,844	2,528.3	4,011	12,662	18	23.9	13.0	8.5	13.65
Nevada.....................	474	4,919	2,694	1,780	445	4,987	1,679.3	4,352	9,120	45	23.2	8.7	8.9	21.45
New Hampshire...........	181	3,132	1,951	1,007	174	3,083	2,285.7	2,804	15,958	10	14.6	8.9	4.8	12.19
New Jersey	1,410	30,368	16,178	12,921	1,270	29,839	3,358.2	26,533	19,585	4	116.2	55.0	37.6	12.05
New Mexico	336	4,024	708	2,726	589	3,901	1,865.0	3,308	9,949	38	21.1	7.6	8.0	15.78
New York...................	2,664	69,228	37,318	28,253	3,658	67,195	3,430.1	(X)	22,861	1	212.2	97.8	95.6	12.73
North Carolina............	1,550	14,481	3,782	9,058	1,641	15,390	1,498.8	13,939	8,995	46	100.2	61.2	29.1	15.49
North Dakota..............	110	1,757	579	1,015	163	1,825	2,417.0	1,509	13,767	17	9.5	5.5	3.2	12.02
Ohio	1,710	24,763	12,275	10,538	1,950	24,504	2,101.6	21,258	12,569	20	101.7	42.2	47.2	16.67
Oklahoma	694	6,361	2,627	3,008	726	6,229	1,584.4	5,474	7,921	49	42.4	20.0	18.3	16.46
Oregon	579	7,689	3,120	4,019	551	7,732	1,866.0	6,498	11,252	30	30.2	18.5	8.9	20.21
Pennsylvania..............	1,727	31,353	17,097	12,104	2,152	30,766	2,405.9	26,650	15,782	11	123.4	53.4	52.8	14.03
Rhode Island..............	142	2,561	1,281	1,087	193	2,592	2,455.2	2,288	16,620	8	10.7	6.2	3.8	13.34
South Carolina	771	9,993	4,212	4,868	913	9,722	1,936.1	8,106	10,419	33	52.7	33.5	15.6	14.81
South Dakota	136	1,580	834	540	205	1,572	1,800.6	1,353	10,117	35	9.9	5.5	2.5	14.09
Tennessee	1,002	10,077	4,286	4,629	1,162	10,418	1,552.9	9,190	9,246	44	64.1	40.3	18.4	15.72
Texas.......................	5,361	60,007	30,368	23,340	6,299	64,601	2,283.1	50,038	9,520	42	359.6	145.1	156.8	15.11
Utah........................	660	5,758	2,115	3,183	459	5,813	1,874.6	4,651	7,206	51	29.8	12.4	12.4	22.75
Vermont	88	1,742	68	1,561	114	1,797	2,879.0	1,635	19,480	5	8.3	2.5	2.7	10.50
Virginia....................	1,287	16,612	8,914	6,566	1,132	16,799	1,984.8	15,293	11,885	24	87.0	30.6	49.6	14.82
Washington................	1,102	15,655	4,737	9,846	1,071	16,008	2,156.4	13,191	11,971	22	61.8	28.5	25.5	18.17
West Virginia..............	274	3,526	1,205	1,917	404	3,488	1,919.5	3,144	11,745	25	18.9	8.3	9.1	14.17
Wisconsin..................	864	11,591	5,398	5,361	833	11,876	2,051.1	10,244	11,962	23	59.5	24.2	29.1	14.45
Wyoming	94	1,931	671	1,142	118	1,913	3,304.8	1,553	16,513	9	7.3	3.5	3.4	12.87

Note: Figures may not sum to totals because of rounding. Survey, census, or data collection method is based on U.S. Census Bureau, Public School Finance Data, see https://www.census.gov/programs-surveys/school-finances.html.
[1]Enrollment represents the total count of pupils that are enrolled on or about October 1st of the survey year. These data are from the National Public Education Financial Survey.
[2]Includes interest on school debt and other current expenditures not shown separately.
[3]Based on U.S. Census Bureau estimated resident population as of July 1, 2017.
[4]Schools classified by type of organization rather than by grade-group; elementary includes kindergarten; total includes ungraded teachers.
[5]Pupils that are enrolled on or about October 1st of the survey year.

Table A–21. Public High School Graduates and Educational Attainment

| Geographic area | Public high school graduates (thousands)[1] | | | | Educational attainment, 2018 | | | | | | |
| | | | | | | Percentage of people 25 years and over, by highest level completed | | | | | |
	2019–2020 Projected	2012–2013	2009–2010	1999–2000	Population 25 years and over (thousands)	Not a high school graduate	High school graduate	Some college, but no degree	Associate's degree	Bachelor's degree	Advanced degree[2]
United States	3,304	3,169	3,128	2,554	223,159	11.7	26.9	20.3	8.6	20.0	12.6
Alabama.......................	44	44	43	38	3,337	13.4	30.8	21.6	8.6	16.1	9.5
Alaska.........................	8	8	8	7	485	6.7	28.3	26.6	8.2	18.5	11.7
Arizona........................	70	62	61	38	4,840	12.5	24.0	25.0	8.9	18.6	11.2
Arkansas	31	29	28	27	2,022	12.8	34.0	22.3	7.6	14.7	8.6
California.....................	422	422	405	310	26,816	16.2	20.7	20.8	8.0	21.3	12.9
Colorado	58	51	49	39	3,900	8.1	20.8	20.9	8.4	26.0	15.7
Connecticut.................	36	39	34	32	2,493	9.1	26.9	16.6	7.9	21.8	17.8
Delaware	9	8	8	6	680	10.2	33.2	17.7	7.6	18.3	13.1
District of Columbia	4	4	4	3	500	7.9	16.6	12.3	2.8	25.9	34.5
Florida........................	175	158	156	107	15,302	11.5	28.7	19.7	9.7	19.1	11.3
Georgia	106	92	92	63	6,978	12.4	27.8	19.8	8.1	19.5	12.3
Hawaii.........................	11	11	11	10	996	8.0	26.8	20.6	11.1	22.0	11.5
Idaho...........................	19	17	18	16	1,144	9.1	27.8	25.5	9.9	18.7	9.0
Illinois	139	139	139	112	8,706	10.5	26.1	20.3	8.1	21.1	14.0
Indiana........................	70	67	65	57	4,468	11.0	33.1	19.9	8.9	17.3	9.8
Iowa............................	33	33	34	34	2,105	7.7	30.8	20.6	11.8	19.6	9.4
Kansas	33	32	32	29	1,911	9.0	25.4	22.8	8.9	21.1	12.8
Kentucky	44	43	43	37	3,039	13.2	32.6	20.8	8.6	14.5	10.3
Louisiana	40	38	37	38	3,126	14.2	34.3	20.8	6.5	15.9	8.4
Maine..........................	12	13	14	12	983	7.0	31.4	20.4	9.7	20.1	11.4
Maryland......................	60	59	59	48	4,167	9.5	24.2	18.7	6.8	21.9	18.9
Massachusetts..............	70	66	64	53	4,833	9.2	23.3	15.3	7.6	24.4	20.1
Michigan......................	98	104	111	98	6,870	8.9	28.7	23.2	9.6	18.0	11.5
Minnesota....................	59	58	60	57	3,809	6.6	24.2	20.8	11.7	24.2	12.5
Mississippi	27	27	25	24	1,977	14.6	29.8	22.3	10.1	14.4	8.8
Missouri	61	61	64	53	4,183	9.5	30.4	22.4	8.2	18.0	11.5
Montana.......................	10	9	10	11	736	6.1	27.9	24.5	9.7	20.7	11.0
Nebraska......................	23	20	19	20	1,266	8.6	25.8	22.4	10.9	21.3	11.1
Nevada........................	25	23	21	15	2,097	13.1	27.7	25.9	8.4	16.2	8.7
New Hampshire.............	13	14	15	12	971	6.9	27.7	18.4	10.2	22.4	14.5
New Jersey	96	96	96	74	6,189	9.8	26.3	16.4	6.6	24.8	16.0
New Mexico	21	19	19	18	1,416	14.6	26.1	23.6	8.0	15.7	12.0
New York......................	179	180	184	142	13,672	12.9	25.9	15.2	8.7	20.8	16.4
North Carolina..............	105	94	89	62	7,102	11.8	25.4	21.1	9.9	20.5	11.4
North Dakota................	7	7	7	9	501	7.7	25.9	21.9	14.9	22.1	7.6
Ohio............................	121	122	123	112	8,027	9.3	32.7	20.4	8.6	17.8	11.1
Oklahoma	42	37	39	38	2,608	11.6	31.3	23.5	8.0	16.7	9.0
Oregon	35	34	35	30	2,952	9.5	22.2	25.2	9.1	21.0	12.9
Pennsylvania................	118	130	131	114	8,995	9.0	34.6	15.9	8.6	19.2	12.7
Rhode Island................	10	10	10	8	741	10.9	28.4	18.0	8.3	19.9	14.5
South Carolina	47	42	40	32	3,492	11.6	29.9	20.1	10.2	18.0	10.4
South Dakota	8	8	8	9	583	7.7	31.0	19.9	12.2	20.2	9.0
Tennessee	64	61	62	42	4,641	12.2	31.8	21.0	7.5	17.3	10.2
Texas...........................	353	301	281	213	18,477	16.0	25.0	21.4	7.2	19.6	10.7
Utah............................	39	33	31	33	1,872	7.6	22.6	24.7	10.2	22.8	12.0
Vermont	6	6	7	7	446	6.5	28.6	17.7	8.6	23.1	15.6
Virginia	88	83	82	66	5,822	10.1	24.0	18.7	7.8	22.3	17.1
Washington..................	72	66	66	58	5,215	8.4	21.7	23.0	10.2	22.8	13.9
West Virginia................	17	18	18	19	1,281	12.2	39.7	19.2	7.5	12.8	8.5
Wisconsin	60	61	65	59	3,992	7.9	30.6	20.5	11.0	19.4	10.6
Wyoming	6	5	6	6	393	6.7	28.8	26.4	11.2	16.9	10.0

[1] For school year ending in year shown.
[2] Graduate or professional degree.

Table A–22. Institutions of Higher Education

| Geographic area | Fall enrollment in degree-granting institutions (thousands)[1] | | | | | | | | | Degrees conferred from degree-granting institutions, 2016–2017[2] | | | | | |
| | Total | | | Public | | | Private | | | Public | | Private nonprofit | | Private for-profit | |
	2017	2010	2000	2017	2010	2000	2017	2010	2000	Total	Percent Bachelor's	Total	Percent Bachelor's	Total	Percent Bachelor's
United States	19,766	21,019	15,312	14,560	15,142	11,753	5,205	5,877	3,560	2,603,534	49.0	1,064,839	53.2	279,344	40.8
Alabama..................	307	328	234	254	267	207	53	61	27	46,173	53.0	5,598	68.8	8,511	41.9
Alaska....................	27	35	28	26	32	27	1	2	1	3,868	50.2	134	47.8	49	0.0
Arizona..................	592	794	342	367	367	285	225	427	58	59,311	49.4	2,357	36.0	54,575	48.1
Arkansas................	164	176	115	147	156	102	17	20	13	28,102	47.8	3,634	72.1	142	28.9
California..............	2,714	2,715	2,257	2,247	2,223	1,928	467	492	329	330,842	46.1	89,963	45.1	41,104	45.8
Colorado	360	369	264	279	269	218	81	100	46	46,177	56.6	8,940	45.7	10,707	40.6
Connecticut............	198	199	161	116	127	101	81	72	60	21,645	54.8	20,752	50.7	1,501	65.6
Delaware...............	60	55	44	42	40	34	18	15	10	7,917	57.6	5,359	42.9	44	38.6
District of Columbia	96	92	73	5	6	5	91	86	67	807	48.0	23,410	37.0	1,531	30.0
Florida....................	1,071	1,125	708	798	790	557	273	335	151	171,190	42.3	52,268	44.0	17,225	48.3
Georgia	538	569	346	429	436	272	110	133	74	69,591	56.2	17,789	56.0	7,768	37.3
Hawaii	64	78	60	52	60	45	12	18	16	10,204	46.4	2,719	63.4	611	57.9
Idaho....................	132	85	66	76	64	54	56	21	12	12,165	54.2	6,982	73.5	210	12.9
Illinois..................	757	907	744	478	586	534	279	321	210	85,359	38.7	63,019	50.0	20,082	57.4
Indiana..................	399	459	314	302	338	240	97	122	74	57,126	57.6	22,829	64.3	1,998	19.5
Iowa.....................	261	382	189	170	178	135	91	204	54	29,431	45.8	14,202	68.2	10,424	43.5
Kansas..................	214	215	180	180	186	160	34	29	20	31,772	48.7	5,814	66.0	2,529	31.1
Kentucky...............	258	291	188	202	230	152	56	61	36	36,465	51.0	9,078	51.2	2,425	21.7
Louisiana	242	264	224	211	225	189	31	39	35	31,738	59.8	6,659	52.3	914	8.4
Maine...................	72	72	58	47	51	41	25	22	18	7,670	54.2	5,301	62.3	482	48.1
Maryland...............	364	378	274	304	310	224	61	68	50	57,086	48.5	15,239	39.7	1,047	39.5
Massachusetts..............	504	508	421	213	225	183	290	283	238	40,479	53.3	81,263	49.0	623	46.9
Michigan................	558	698	568	479	562	468	79	135	100	95,239	50.4	21,420	60.9	664	41.0
Minnesota..............	413	465	293	249	276	219	164	189	75	44,358	48.4	18,338	60.7	21,822	19.3
Mississippi..............	172	180	137	152	161	125	19	19	12	30,817	42.3	4,253	51.2	243	5.3
Missouri	383	445	321	236	256	202	148	189	120	45,706	49.1	38,127	47.7	2,380	24.1
Montana................	51	53	42	46	48	37	5	5	5	8,991	58.9	940	74.3	7	0.0
Nebraska...............	136	145	112	101	108	89	35	37	24	17,579	51.2	9,094	57.3	343	46.6
Nevada..................	118	129	88	108	113	83	10	16	5	16,027	50.9	1,403	29.8	961	39.0
New Hampshire............	149	76	62	40	44	36	109	31	26	8,450	60.2	18,184	53.8	0	
New Jersey	419	444	336	335	358	267	84	86	69	66,537	49.1	18,490	55.5	2,340	34.9
New Mexico	129	163	111	125	151	101	4	12	9	22,307	38.6	408	37.5	908	49.7
New York...............	1,260	1,305	1,043	697	724	583	563	582	460	139,156	47.0	141,918	49.6	11,611	34.1
North Carolina...........	564	586	405	455	475	329	109	111	75	85,757	46.1	24,372	60.5	2,505	27.2
North Dakota.............	54	57	40	48	49	36	6	8	4	9,688	59.2	1,147	57.5	177	16.9
Ohio.....................	650	745	550	497	548	411	152	198	138	95,592	51.6	34,238	63.1	4,110	17.3
Oklahoma	202	231	178	174	198	154	28	33	24	34,032	50.6	5,965	63.8	1,088	10.4
Oregon..................	230	252	183	192	208	155	38	44	28	36,228	50.1	10,806	46.3	722	35.3
Pennsylvania...........	717	805	610	401	433	339	316	372	270	81,127	59.9	78,523	54.6	6,008	21.6
Rhode Island.............	83	85	75	41	43	38	42	42	37	7,527	63.5	11,671	63.3	0	
South Carolina	246	257	186	201	205	156	46	52	30	35,369	54.1	7,283	79.0	2,456	38.6
South Dakota	54	58	43	45	45	35	9	14	8	8,364	55.7	1,550	74.9	431	57.5
Tennessee	323	352	264	223	242	203	100	109	61	41,238	54.1	21,322	60.0	2,940	23.0
Texas....................	1,631	1,536	1,034	1,448	1,334	897	182	202	137	242,991	44.3	35,749	58.0	7,838	32.2
Utah	332	256	164	180	179	123	152	77	41	32,621	49.8	31,211	64.7	1,364	31.2
Vermont	44	46	35	25	28	20	19	18	15	4,987	68.2	5,223	56.8	0	
Virginia	554	578	382	389	409	314	165	169	68	70,944	53.5	31,696	52.9	112	55.4
Washington.............	368	388	321	318	331	274	50	57	47	64,303	41.0	11,704	62.6	10,223	37.8
West Virginia.............	143	152	88	84	96	76	59	56	12	16,705	55.2	2,109	68.2	1,160	47.8
Wisconsin	341	384	307	280	301	250	61	83	57	46,768	58.8	14,310	65.8	11,549	49.2
Wyoming................	33	38	30	33	36	29	0	2	1	5,603	39.3	76	3.9	880	17.6

[1] Degree-granting institutions grant associate's or higher degrees and participate in Title IV federal financial aid programs.
[2] Totals include Associate's, Bachelor's, Master's, Ph.D., Ed.D., and comparable degrees at the doctoral level. Also includes most degrees formerly classified as first-professional, such as M.D., D.D.S., and law degrees conferred.

Table A-23. Violent Crimes and Crime Rates

Geographic area	Number[1] 2018	2015	2010	2005	Rate (per 100,000)[2] 2018 Total	Murder[3]	Rape[4]	Robbery	Aggravated assault	Total 2015	2010	2005
United States	1,245,065	1,197,704	1,251,248	1,390,745	380.6	5.0	42.6	86.2	246.8	372.6	404.5	469.0
Alabama......................	25,399	22,952	18,056	19,678	519.6	7.8	40.8	83.4	387.6	472.4	377.8	431.7
Alaska.........................	6,526	5,392	4,537	4,194	885.0	6.4	161.6	121.5	595.4	730.2	638.8	631.9
Arizona.......................	34,058	28,012	26,085	30,478	474.9	5.1	50.7	91.0	328.1	410.2	408.1	513.2
Arkansas....................	16,384	15,526	14,735	14,659	543.6	7.2	72.9	52.9	410.7	521.3	505.3	527.5
California....................	176,982	166,883	164,133	190,178	447.4	4.4	39.2	137.3	266.5	426.3	440.6	526.3
Colorado....................	22,624	17,515	16,133	18,498	397.2	3.7	71.5	66.7	255.4	321.0	320.8	396.5
Connecticut................	7,411	7,845	10,057	9,635	207.4	2.3	23.5	61.4	120.2	218.5	281.4	274.5
Delaware	4,097	4,720	5,575	5,332	423.6	5.0	34.9	89.5	294.2	499.0	620.9	632.1
District of Columbia[5]	6,996	8,531	8,004	8,032	995.9	22.8	64.1	343.8	565.3	1269.1	1330.2	1459.0
Florida........................	81,980	93,626	101,969	125,957	384.9	5.2	39.6	79.3	260.8	461.9	542.4	708.0
Georgia......................	34,355	38,643	39,072	40,725	326.6	6.1	25.2	78.7	216.6	378.3	403.3	448.9
Hawaii........................	3,532	4,201	3,574	3,253	248.6	2.5	44.0	66.6	135.5	293.4	262.7	255.1
Idaho..........................	3,983	3,568	3,465	3,670	227.1	2.0	45.1	11.4	168.6	215.6	221.0	256.8
Illinois........................	51,490	49,354	55,835	70,392	404.1	6.9	46.0	111.5	239.7	383.8	435.2	551.5
Indiana.......................	25,581	25,653	20,389	20,302	382.3	6.5	35.4	88.7	251.6	387.5	314.5	323.7
Iowa...........................	7,893	8,936	8,333	8,642	250.1	1.7	30.9	29.5	187.9	286.1	273.5	291.3
Kansas.......................	12,782	11,353	10,531	10,634	439.0	3.9	53.8	53.0	328.3	389.9	369.1	387.4
Kentucky	9,467	9,676	10,528	11,134	211.9	5.5	38.2	55.0	113.2	218.7	242.6	266.8
Louisiana	25,049	25,208	24,886	26,889	537.5	11.4	44.7	98.0	383.4	539.7	549.0	594.4
Maine	1,501	1,729	1,621	1,483	112.1	1.8	33.3	17.0	60.0	130.1	122.0	112.2
Maryland....................	28,320	27,462	31,620	39,369	468.7	8.1	32.8	160.8	267.0	457.2	547.7	703.0
Massachusetts...........	23,337	26,562	30,553	29,237	338.1	2.0	34.9	60.0	241.2	390.9	466.6	456.9
Michigan....................	44,918	41,231	48,460	55,877	449.4	5.5	76.9	56.6	310.3	415.5	490.3	552.1
Minnesota..................	12,369	13,319	12,515	15,243	220.4	1.9	43.9	52.5	122.2	242.6	236.0	297.0
Mississippi.................	6,999	8,254	8,003	8,131	234.4	5.7	18.0	53.4	157.2	275.8	269.7	278.4
Missouri.....................	30,758	30,261	27,252	30,477	502.1	9.9	47.5	84.8	359.8	497.4	455.0	525.4
Montana.....................	3,974	3,611	2,693	2,634	374.1	3.2	51.9	25.3	293.7	349.6	272.2	281.5
Nebraska....................	5,494	5,212	5,104	5,048	284.8	2.3	63.9	39.2	179.4	274.9	279.5	287.0
Nevada.......................	16,420	20,118	17,841	14,654	541.1	6.7	76.8	127.3	330.4	695.9	660.6	606.8
New Hampshire...........	2,349	2,652	2,198	1,729	173.2	1.5	39.4	26.5	105.8	199.3	167.0	132.0
New Jersey	18,537	22,879	27,055	30,919	208.1	3.2	16.0	71.4	117.4	255.4	307.7	354.7
New Mexico	17,949	13,681	12,126	13,541	856.6	8.0	64.6	135.1	648.9	656.1	588.9	702.2
New York.....................	68,495	75,165	75,977	85,839	350.5	2.9	33.6	93.1	220.9	379.7	392.1	445.8
North Carolina[6]............	39,210	34,852	34,653	40,650	377.6	6.0	25.4	81.1	265.1	347.0	363.4	468.1
North Dakota...............	2,133	1,812	1,513	625	280.6	2.4	52.2	20.8	205.2	239.4	225.0	98.2
Ohio...........................	32,723	33,898	36,366	40,273	279.9	4.8	45.3	78.6	151.2	291.9	315.2	351.3
Oklahoma...................	18,380	16,506	17,987	18,044	466.1	5.2	58.3	70.8	331.8	422.0	479.5	508.6
Oregon.......................	11,966	10,468	9,655	10,444	285.5	2.0	47.1	60.8	175.6	259.8	252.0	286.8
Pennsylvania..............	39,192	40,339	46,514	52,761	306.0	6.1	35.0	76.9	188.0	315.1	366.2	424.5
Rhode Island...............	2,317	2,562	2,701	2,703	219.1	1.5	45.5	42.9	129.2	242.5	256.6	251.2
South Carolina	24,825	24,700	27,648	32,384	488.3	7.7	47.9	69.9	362.8	504.5	597.7	761.1
South Dakota	3,570	3,289	2,186	1,363	404.7	1.4	69.6	29.7	304.0	383.1	268.5	175.7
Tennessee	42,226	40,400	38,921	44,891	623.7	7.4	41.7	106.2	468.5	612.1	613.3	752.8
Texas..........................	117,927	113,227	113,231	121,091	410.9	4.6	51.2	98.4	256.6	412.2	450.3	529.7
Utah...........................	7,368	7,071	5,879	5,612	233.1	1.9	55.5	39.1	136.6	236.0	212.7	227.2
Vermont......................	1,077	739	815	746	172.0	1.6	45.8	11.2	113.4	118.0	130.2	119.7
Virginia.......................	17,032	16,399	17,087	21,400	200.0	4.6	34.3	42.3	118.7	195.6	213.6	282.8
Washington.................	23,472	20,394	21,101	21,745	311.5	3.1	45.3	73.9	189.1	284.4	313.8	345.8
West Virginia...............	5,236	6,231	5,830	4,957	289.9	3.7	36.1	31.7	218.5	337.9	314.6	272.8
Wisconsin...................	17,176	17,647	14,142	13,371	295.4	3.0	38.7	60.0	193.7	305.8	248.7	241.5
Wyoming	1,226	1,302	1,104	1,172	212.2	2.3	42.1	17.3	150.6	222.1	195.9	230.1

[1]The violent crime figures include the offenses of murder, rape (revised definition for 2015, legacy definition for earlier years), robbery, and aggravated assault.
[2]Populations are U.S. Census Bureau estimates as of July 1 for each year except 2000 and 2010, which are decennial counts for April 1.
[3]Includes nonnegligent manslaughter.
[4]The figures shown in the rape (revised definition) column were estimated using the revised Uniform Crime Reporting (UCR) definition of rape.
[5]Includes offenses reported by the Metro Transit Police and the Arson Investigation Unit of the District of Columbia Fire and Emergency Medical Services.
[6]This state's agencies submitted rape data according to the legacy UCR definition of rape.

Table A–24. Property Crimes and Crime Rates

| Geographic area | Number[1] | | | | Rate (per 100,000)[2] | | | | | | |
| | 2018 | 2015 | 2010 | 2005 | 2018 | | | | Total | | |
					Total	Burglary	Larceny	Motor vehicle theft	2015	2010	2005
United States[3,4,5]	7,196,045	7,993,631	9,112,625	10,166,159	2,200	376.0	1,594.6	228.9	2,945.9	3,429.8	3,618.3
Alabama[5]	137,700	144,746	168,828	177,393	2,817	590.1	1,958.9	268.3	3,528.0	3,892.1	4,059.7
Alaska	24,339	20,806	20,259	23,975	3,301	539.6	2,219.0	541.9	2,836.8	3,612.5	3,682.5
Arizona	191,974	207,107	226,802	287,345	2,677	439.7	1,970.3	266.9	3,536.5	4,838.0	5,297.8
Arkansas	87,793	96,836	103,820	112,775	2,913	636.8	2,040.2	236.0	3,553.5	4,057.9	3,670.0
California	941,618	1,024,914	981,939	1,200,531	2,380	416.2	1,571.8	392.4	2,629.9	3,322.6	3,118.2
Colorado	152,163	144,136	135,001	188,449	2,672	375.2	1,915.9	380.5	2,674.5	4,039.5	3,648.6
Connecticut	60,055	65,066	78,259	89,794	1,681	222.5	1,251.8	206.7	2,188.8	2,558.0	2,908.0
Delaware	22,481	25,455	31,078	26,245	2,324	326.5	1,845.3	152.6	3,453.9	3,111.4	3,793.6
District of Columbia[4]	30,724	31,435	28,802	26,133	4,374	254.5	3,750.1	369.1	4,761.4	4,747.0	5,768.6
Florida	486,017	570,270	669,035	712,998	2,282	337.7	1,750.8	193.3	3,551.4	4,007.9	4,882.7
Georgia	270,738	308,723	353,449	378,534	2,574	431.3	1,907.0	235.4	3,639.2	4,172.3	4,246.4
Hawaii	40,772	54,346	45,667	61,115	2,870	396.4	2,076.2	397.7	3,349.6	4,792.6	4,955.1
Idaho	25,636	28,858	31,436	38,556	1,461	281.6	1,067.8	112.0	2,000.9	2,697.9	2,933.7
Illinois	246,264	255,729	349,064	393,148	1,933	306.7	1,472.3	153.8	2,718.1	3,080.3	3,629.4
Indiana	145,838	171,847	199,274	216,778	2,179	377.6	1,572.7	229.1	3,070.2	3,456.3	3,402.8
Iowa	53,385	63,957	68,740	84,056	1,692	352.6	1,190.4	148.5	2,253.6	2,833.7	2,967.3
Kansas	76,686	79,199	89,109	103,941	2,634	430.6	1,933.9	269.4	3,116.6	3,787.0	4,019.4
Kentucky	87,695	96,362	111,170	105,608	1,963	384.7	1,348.2	229.6	2,557.3	2,530.5	2,665.2
Louisiana	152,661	156,629	165,667	166,611	3,276	668.1	2,360.4	247.6	3,644.8	3,683.1	4,741.7
Maine	18,173	24,327	32,900	31,889	1,358	202.7	1,097.1	58.1	2,478.6	2,413.1	2,510.2
Maryland	122,864	139,048	173,309	198,483	2,033	312.6	1,519.8	200.9	2,995.5	3,544.1	4,029.5
Massachusetts	87,196	114,871	154,496	151,241	1,263	200.8	966.8	95.7	2,356.8	2,363.6	2,550.0
Michigan	165,280	187,101	271,501	312,843	1,654	316.6	1,162.3	174.6	2,748.8	3,091.1	3,554.9
Minnesota	111,874	121,984	136,431	158,301	1,994	288.4	1,524.8	180.5	2,569.0	3,084.1	3,207.6
Mississippi	71,766	84,790	88,596	95,231	2,403	697.8	1,561.2	144.0	2,983.0	3,260.1	3,643.5
Missouri	162,173	173,642	200,858	227,809	2,647	444.9	1,878.8	323.4	3,350.0	3,927.5	4,037.7
Montana	26,518	27,100	NA	29,407	2,496	306.6	1,926.5	263.2	NA	3,142.9	3,292.7
Nebraska	40,126	42,495	48,827	60,207	2,080	271.9	1,555.3	252.6	2,667.9	3,423.2	3,767.9
Nevada	73,985	77137	75,004	102,424	2,438	584.7	1,461.2	392.3	2,773.5	4,241.5	3,744.4
New Hampshire	16,935	23,229	29,230	23,532	1,249	136.2	1,048.2	64.1	2,219.8	1,796.4	2,257.8
New Jersey	125,156	145,701	183,042	203,391	1,405	215.9	1,065.1	123.9	2,080.1	2,333.0	2,776.6
New Mexico	71,657	77,094	70,776	79,995	3,420	767.8	2,166.1	485.8	3,425.9	4,148.3	4,761.0
New York	281,507	317,529	379,710	405,990	1,441	159.3	1,214.0	67.2	1,957.8	2,108.5	2,545.7
North Carolina	258,979	276,183	329,202	353,855	2,494	599.9	1,724.4	169.8	3,443.5	4,075.1	4,421.8
North Dakota	15,507	16,020	12,010	12,595	2,040	358.4	1,448.3	233.5	1,780.2	1,978.2	2,206.6
Ohio	254,496	300,525	376,836	419,899	2,177	412.2	1,594.6	170.3	3,266.1	3,662.7	3,707.7
Oklahoma	113,364	112,878	129,464	143,406	2,875	681.1	1,856.8	337.0	3,443.0	4,042.0	4,060.8
Oregon	121,278	118,719	116,657	160,199	2,894	389.1	2,109.9	395.1	3,039.3	4,399.8	4,494.7
Pennsylvania	190,816	232,085	276,366	300,444	1,490	211.6	1,175.9	102.4	2,173.1	2,417.2	2,575.3
Rhode Island	17,561	20,043	26,959	29,260	1,661	265.8	1,250.3	144.8	2,561.4	2,718.9	3,178.7
South Carolina	153,421	161,245	181,098	184,646	3,018	579.7	2,156.0	281.9	3,905.4	4,339.4	4,416.5
South Dakota	15,251	16,680	15,188	13,784	1,729	291.4	1,264.5	172.7	1,859.9	1,776.4	2,153.0
Tennessee	191,279	193,796	232,855	254,948	2,825	489.4	2,034.1	301.9	3,662.7	4,275.5	4,183.0
Texas	679,430	777,739	951,246	990,293	2,367	410.8	1,713.1	243.2	3,766.8	4,332.0	4,410.4
Utah	75,156	89,278	88,316	95,546	2,378	315.3	1,817.7	244.5	3,182.0	3,868.9	4,220.3
Vermont	8,036	8,806	14,160	14,210	1,283	234.2	1,008.5	40.4	2,262.3	2,280.7	2,873.4
Virginia	141,885	156,470	187,403	199,644	1,666	182.8	1,356.4	126.5	2,335.5	2,638.2	2,746.4
Washington	222,011	248,369	249,426	307,661	2,946	533.5	2,045.4	367.3	3,699.1	4,893.0	4,736.0
West Virginia	26,827	37,251	41,301	47,696	1,486	296.5	1,049.6	139.5	2,227.2	2,625.2	2,286.3
Wisconsin	90,686	113,924	142,781	147,275	1,560	242.5	1,168.9	148.5	2,508.6	2,660.2	2,972.3
Wyoming	10,313	11,151	13,869	16,070	1,785	264.0	1,375.9	145.2	2,456.6	3,155.3	3,031.5

[1]Property crimes include burglary, larceny-theft, and motor vehicle theft.
[2]Populations are U.S. Census Bureau estimates as of July 1 for each year except 2000 and 2010, which are decennial census counts.
[3]The crime figures have been adjusted
[4]Includes offenses reported by the police at the National Zoo and by Metro transit Police.
[5]Because of changes in the state's reporting practices, figures are not comparable to previous years' data.

Table A–25. Juvenile Arrests, Child Abuse Cases, and Correctional Population

Geographic area	Juvenile arrests, 2018			Child abuse and neglect cases reported and investigated, 2018				Estimated number and rate of persons supervised by U.S. adult correctional system by correctional status, 2016					
								Total correctional population[7]		Community supervision		Incarcerated	
	Total arrests[1]	Violent crime arrests[2]	Property crime arrests[3]	Number of reports[4]	Number of children who received an investigation or alternative response[5]	Number of victims[6]	First-time victims rate per 1,000 children	Total correctional population	Correctional supervision rate[9]	Number on probation or parole[8]	Community supervision rate[9]	Number in prison or local jail[10]	Incarceration rate[9]
United States	601,833	41,501	113,429	4,333,329	3,533,597	677,529	9.2	6,582,100	2,630	4,537,100	1,810	2,131,000	850
Alabama....................	3,578	296	959	42,379	38,634	12,158	11.2	99,800	2,640	60,700	1,610	40,900	1,080
Alaska.......................	1,687	206	439	16,818	12,749	2,615	14.2	12,900	2,320	8,400	1,520	4,400	800
Arizona.....................	20,478	1,127	3,298	109,432	87,862	15,504	9.4	137,500	2,570	84,800	1,590	55,000	1,030
Arkansas...................	7,697	427	1,423	70,372	58,823	8,538	12.1	72,100	3,150	51,500	2,250	24,000	1,050
California...................	42,958	7,210	7,484	439,435	360,040	63,795	7.1	536,100	1,770	333,300	1,100	202,700	670
Colorado...................	17,906	758	3,161	53,551	44,698	11,879	9.4	121,900	2,820	90,900	2,110	32,100	740
Connecticut...............	7,106	325	1,359	22,998	19,693	7,652	10.4	59,600	2,110	44,700	1,580	15,000	530
Delaware	2,851	302	547	13,745	12,180	1,251	6.1	22,400	2,980	15,800	2,100	6,600	880
District of Columbia	505	92	34	17,529	14,334	1,699	13.3	10,400	1,840	9,600	1,710	1,800	320
Florida......................	48,213	3,218	12,686	362,565	292,518	36,795	8.7	366,000	2,200	218,600	1,320	149,800	900
Georgia.....................	15,400	836	3,161	205,216	164,064	11,090	4.4	..	..	..	..	91,400	1,160
Hawaii.......................	1,762	104	309	3,938	3,817	1,265	4.2	27,500	2,450	21,900	1,950	5,600	500
Idaho........................	5,993	192	978	16,835	12,825	1,919	4.3	48,800	3,880	37,500	2,980	11,300	900
Illinois......................	7,366	786	1,876	186,008	146,141	31,515	11	204,200	2,070	143,400	1,450	60,800	620
Indiana.....................	8,831	615	1,784	223,929	161,340	25,731	16.4	159,900	3,150	116,700	2,300	43,200	850
Iowa.........................				57,422	38,631	11,764	16.1	46,700	1,940	35,100	1,460	13,400	560
Kansas......................	1,639	43	105	35,627	27,816	3,188	4.5	38,500	1,750	21,500	980	17,200	780
Kentucky	2,985	161	691	105,959	83,902	23,752	23.5	97,900	2,850	63,800	1,860	34,700	1,010
Louisiana	16,533	1,175	3,683	28,650	26,064	9,380	8.6	111,000	3,110	71,000	1,980	45,400	1,270
Maine.......................	2,845	51	673	13,123	11,031	3,481	13.9	10,300	960	6,800	630	4,100	380
Maryland...................	17,825	1,907	3,705	35,778	32,244	7,743	5.8	99,000	2,120	82,800	1,770	28,400	610
Massachusetts.............	4,508	464	615	92,554	76,244	25,812	18.9	82,900	1,520	63,600	1,170	19,400	360
Michigan	13,267	1,044	3,054	205,116	158,673	37,703	17.4	..	..	..	..	56,500	730
Minnesota	19,391	864	4,165	46,796	39,581	7,785	6	119,500	2,810	103,900	2,450	16,300	380
Mississippi.................	2,453	80	562	50,672	40,682	10,002	14.2	65,300	2,880	37,700	1,660	28,700	1,260
Missouri	15,560	893	2,886	109,779	81,059	5,662	4.1	105,900	2,240	61,600	1,300	44,300	940
Montana....................	3,722	81	666	19,453	15,300	3,763	16.4	15,200	1,860	10,200	1,250	5,700	700
Nebraska...................	6,985	207	1,426	29,909	24,329	2,635	5.5	23,300	1,620	14,600	1,010	8,800	610
Nevada......................	10,026	1,340	1,262	36,146	30,279	5,162	7.5	39,200	1,720	19,000	830	20,200	890
New Hampshire............	3,283	59	349	16,845	13,888	1,331	5.2	10,800	1,010	6,400	590	4,500	410
New Jersey	11,513	870	1,819	93,282	77,661	6,008	3.1	186,300	2,670	155,700	2,230	32,000	460
New Mexico	3,203	231	478	32,955	25,774	8,024	16.6	30,200	1,900	15,500	970	14,700	930
New York...................	14,434	1,207	3,468	275,323	218,684	68,785	16.9	212,100	1,360	142,400	910	74,400	480
North Carolina.............	11,088	757	2,673	130,554	112,261	6,502	2.8	149,300	1,890	95,200	1,210	54,100	680
North Dakota..............	4,009	91	435	8,102	7,295	2,097	11.7	10,300	1,770	7,100	1,230	3,100	540
Ohio	20,003	873	2,995	133,869	110,550	25,158	9.7	326,200	3,620	256,400	2,840	71,000	790
Oklahoma	7,701	392	1,641	68,665	58,958	15,355	16.1	74,500	2,510	35,500	1,190	39,000	1,310
Oregon	8,618	351	1,720	60,491	50,319	12,581	14.4	82,000	2,520	61,400	1,890	20,700	640
Pennsylvania...............	36,034	2,558	4,540	45,279	42,295	4,695	1.8	368,100	3,640	291,600	2,880	82,400	810
Rhode Island..............	2,373	121	406	13,060	10,841	3,644	17.8	24,300	2,850	23,200	2,730	3,100	370
South Carolina	10,803	616	2,328	104,611	82,617	19,130	17.3	68,800	1,770	36,700	940	32,100	820
South Dakota	4,886	92	657	4,111	3,761	1,426	6.6	15,000	2,290	9,300	1,420	5,800	880
Tennessee	19,692	1,421	3,843	104,250	87,384	9,186	6.1	119,400	2,310	74,700	1,440	48,400	930
Texas........................	55,458	3,946	10,127	315,263	281,562	63,271	8.6	681,900	3,290	482,900	2,330	218,500	1,050
Utah.........................	12,307	374	2,523	30,646	26,076	10,122	10.9	25,400	1,180	15,900	740	11,700	540
Vermont	702	40	100	5,393	4,485	958	8.3	7,400	1,450	5,800	1,150	1,700	340
Virginia	15,864	719	2,994	55,301	49,156	6,132	3.3	120,000	1,830	62,500	950	57,500	880
Washington................	10,996	866	2,274	59,952	46,131	4,498	2.7	127,000	2,230	100,600	1,760	30,400	530
West Virginia..............	496	38	55	58,860	52,276	6,946	19.1	20,100	1,380	10,100	690	10,100	690
Wisconsin	35,109	1,023	4,622	43,415	36,103	5,017	3.9	100,500	2,230	64,900	1,440	35,600	790
Wyoming	3,191	52	391	5,838	4,914	1,044	7.7	9,400	2,100	5,500	1,230	3,900	870

[1]Number of arrests. If an individual was arrested more than once, each arrest is counted. Does not include traffic arrests. The rape figures in this table are aggregate totals of the data submitted based on both the legacy and revised Uniform Crime Reporting definitions. Arrest figures may vary widely from state to state because some offenses are not considered crimes in some states.
[2]Violent crime includes murder or nonnegligent manslaughter, rape, robbery, and aggravated assault.
[3]Property crimes include burglary, larceny-theft, motor vehicle theft, and arson.
[4]The numbers of children are counted once for each investigation response or alternative response that reached a disposition (finding) for federal fiscal year 2017.
[5]The number of "Children subject of an investigation" is based on the "Unique count," counting a child once, regardless of the number of reports concerning that child, that received a CPS response in the year shown.
[6]Victims are defined as children for whom the State determined at least one maltreatment was substantiated or indicated; and a disposition of "substantiated," "indicated," or "alternative response victim" was assigned for a child in a specific report.
[7]Excludes, by jurisdiction, an estimated 83,700 prisoners held in jail, 24,000 probationers in prison, 24,400 probationers in jail, 24,500 parolees in jail, 13,000 parolees in prison, and 10,800 parolees on probation.
[8]Excludes an estimated 10,800 parolees on probation
[9]Rates were computed using estimates of the U.S. resident population of persons age 18 or older within jurisdiction.
[10]Excludes an estimated 83,700 prisoners held in local jails.
.. = Not available

Table A–26. State and Local Justice Employment and Expenditures, 2016

Geographic area	Number of employees				Total expenditures (in millions of dollars)			
	Total justice system	Police protection	Judicial and legal	Corrections	Total justice system	Police protection	Judicial and legal	Corrections
United States	2,129,988	977,613	438,273	714,102	233,484	109,210	46,257	78,017
Alabama.............................	28,180	14,821	5,076	8,283	2,336	1,251	362	722
Alaska................................	5,846	1,987	1,512	2,347	962	370	254	338
Arizona..............................	46,393	19,829	11,307	15,257	4,930	2,262	983	1,685
Arkansas...........................	21,452	9,289	3,864	8,299	1,507	691	220	596
California...........................	240,421	104,146	45,355	90,920	41,714	17,570	8,676	15,468
Colorado............................	35,674	15,992	8,151	11,531	3,941	1,873	754	1,313
Connecticut.......................	23,233	10,989	6,410	5,834	2,748	1,237	827	684
Delaware............................	7,584	2,692	1,948	2,944	864	348	208	308
District of Columbia	7,734	4,350	2,025	1,359	871	593	133	145
Florida................................	136,966	64,500	31,773	40,693	14,463	7,848	2,366	4,249
Georgia..............................	71,333	28,451	15,760	27,122	5,853	2,719	1,215	1,920
Hawaii...............................	9,957	4,182	3,414	2,361	971	459	294	217
Idaho.................................	10,845	4,238	2,339	4,268	1,000	457	200	343
Illinois...............................	82,305	45,273	14,165	22,867	8,618	5,216	1,549	1,852
Indiana..............................	37,503	16,961	8,118	12,424	2,986	1,255	572	1,159
Iowa..................................	15,681	7,832	3,277	4,572	1,581	779	358	444
Kansas..............................	20,470	9,712	4,270	6,488	1,645	799	330	516
Kentucky...........................	26,011	10,240	7,565	8,206	2,245	712	630	904
Louisiana...........................	38,860	18,710	7,703	12,447	3,471	1,614	718	1,138
Maine................................	6,169	3,164	1,081	1,924	672	295	112	264
Maryland............................	44,225	19,875	8,793	15,557	5,481	2,649	933	1,899
Massachusetts....................	44,046	22,070	9,758	12,218	4,709	2,502	1,088	1,119
Michigan............................	52,387	22,801	11,298	18,288	6,175	2,509	1,145	2,521
Minnesota..........................	30,201	13,299	6,681	10,221	3,667	1,922	731	1,013
Mississippi.........................	18,680	10,540	3,080	5,060	1,515	742	275	498
Missouri	43,182	19,430	8,420	15,332	3,266	1,744	561	960
Montana.............................	6,601	2,778	1,847	1,976	759	290	211	258
Nebraska...........................	12,038	5,251	2,229	4,558	1,144	459	186	500
Nevada..............................	18,190	7,990	4,480	5,720	2,372	1,184	476	712
New Hampshire..................	7,588	4,387	1,324	1,877	733	394	141	198
New Jersey	73,529	38,716	20,210	14,603	7,021	3,445	1,532	2,043
New Mexico	16,422	6,426	3,763	6,233	1,726	701	329	696
New York...........................	179,546	91,513	34,398	53,635	20,603	9,922	4,157	6,524
North Carolina....................	63,289	29,060	8,086	26,143	5,859	3,271	764	1,823
North Dakota......................	4,710	1,950	1,134	1,626	509	208	126	175
Ohio..................................	77,761	34,219	21,377	22,165	7,635	3,882	1,746	2,007
Oklahoma..........................	23,498	12,187	4,639	6,672	2,192	1,065	375	752
Oregon..............................	23,376	9,330	4,996	9,050	3,307	1,316	775	1,216
Pennsylvania......................	87,531	36,947	19,006	31,578	9,129	3,717	1,903	3,509
Rhode Island......................	5,934	3,157	1,324	1,453	804	436	147	222
South Carolina	30,816	14,672	5,151	10,993	2,308	1,194	359	755
South Dakota	4,924	2,272	1,073	1,579	472	201	91	180
Tennessee	42,721	21,942	8,020	12,759	3,796	1,855	765	1,176
Texas................................	177,323	78,259	29,378	69,686	16,544	7,615	3,008	5,921
Utah..................................	16,266	7,628	3,271	5,367	1,532	655	351	527
Vermont	3,586	1,732	763	1,091	406	188	81	137
Virginia	57,679	22,640	9,620	25,419	5,934	2,338	1,036	2,561
Washington........................	36,963	14,636	8,856	13,471	4,817	1,954	1,135	1,728
West Virginia......................	11,098	4,361	2,975	3,762	1,018	387	277	353
Wisconsin	38,114	18,085	6,137	13,892	4,091	1,873	663	1,554
Wyoming	5,147	2,102	1,073	1,972	583	242	126	215

Table A-27. Civilian Labor Force and Employment

Geographic area	Civilian noninstitutionalized population 16 years and over[1] (thousands)				Civilian labor force[1,2] (thousands)				Employed (thousands)			
	2019	2015	2010	2005	2019	2015	2010	2005	2019	2015	2010	2005
United States	259,175	250,801	237,830	226,082	163,539	157,130	153889	149,320	157538	148,834	139,064	141,730
Alabama.....................	3,862	3,797	3,690	3,477	2,242	2,161	2,196	2,146	2174	2,030	1,965	2,050
Alaska.......................	545	542	519	480	348	363	362	345	326	340	333	321
Arizona......................	5,713	5,274	4,897	4,465	3,551	3,164	3,090	2,883	3385	2,972	2,769	2,748
Arkansas....................	2,343	2,298	2,233	2,113	1,363	1,331	1,353	1,346	1314	1,264	1,242	1,275
California....................	31,107	30,301	28,543	26,762	19,412	18,829	18,336	17,530	18627	17,661	16,092	16,583
Colorado	4,545	4,231	3,871	3,548	3,149	2,825	2,724	2,564	3062	2,715	2,486	2,435
Connecticut.................	2,884	2,871	2,799	2,677	1,914	1,889	1,912	1,797	1842	1,781	1,737	1,709
Delaware	778	745	701	645	487	465	434	432	469	443	398	414
District of Columbia	577	556	503	467	410	389	346	316	387	362	314	295
Florida........................	17,410	16,258	14,946	13,895	10,337	9,594	9,212	8,721	10016	9,071	8,194	8,399
Georgia......................	8,196	7,759	7,324	6,748	5,110	4,769	4,697	4,586	4935	4,483	4,202	4,341
Hawaii........................	1,091	1,086	1,030	951	665	674	647	627	647	650	602	609
Idaho..........................	1,368	1,245	1,166	1,056	882	795	761	732	856	762	693	702
Illinois........................	10,001	10,053	9,905	9,611	6,447	6,506	6,625	6,398	6191	6,118	5,937	6,034
Indiana.......................	5,246	5,115	4,963	4,753	3,387	3,267	3,175	3,205	3275	3,109	2,846	3,030
Iowa...........................	2,468	2,430	2,358	2,275	1,739	1,698	1,678	1,630	1691	1,634	1,577	1,560
Kansas.......................	2,229	2,203	2,149	2,067	1,487	1,490	1,501	1,466	1440	1,427	1,395	1,392
Kentucky	3,494	3,441	3,350	3,207	2,073	1,981	2,054	2,000	1984	1,876	1,845	1,882
Louisiana	3,577	3,566	3,438	3,290	2,095	2,158	2,086	2,069	1994	2,022	1,920	1,921
Maine.........................	1,110	1,091	1,073	1,043	693	683	695	697	672	653	639	663
Maryland....................	4,761	4,695	4,489	4,254	3,261	3,142	3,074	2,925	3144	2,982	2,838	2,803
Massachusetts.............	5,635	5,502	5,252	5,064	3,817	3,589	3,480	3,384	3707	3,417	3,191	3,220
Michigan	7,993	7,882	7,739	7,737	4,937	4,759	4,799	5,083	4736	4,500	4,194	4,739
Minnesota..................	4,424	4,281	4,116	3,929	3,110	3,000	2,939	2,880	3009	2,889	2,721	2,763
Mississippi.................	2,287	2,278	2,228	2,143	1,276	1,265	1,307	1,317	1207	1,184	1,171	1,219
Missouri.....................	4,811	4,732	4,629	4,435	3,083	3,075	3,056	3,009	2982	2,921	2,764	2,847
Montana.....................	850	814	777	728	533	518	501	486	515	496	464	465
Nebraska....................	1,481	1,440	1,387	1,324	1,035	1,007	993	973	1004	977	947	936
Nevada......................	2,424	2,234	2,062	1,819	1,542	1,408	1,359	1,224	1482	1,313	1,175	1,174
New Hampshire............	1,121	1,089	1,056	1,019	774	746	738	726	754	721	695	700
New Jersey	7,071	7,012	6,864	6,631	4,493	4,487	4,555	4,392	4333	4,228	4,121	4,195
New Mexico	1,640	1,610	1,560	1,437	955	935	936	918	908	874	860	871
New York....................	15,656	15,717	15,386	15,008	9,514	9,559	9,595	9,461	9138	9,055	8,770	8,987
North Carolina.............	8,243	7,788	7,287	6,571	5,080	4,770	4,617	4,317	4884	4,498	4,116	4,091
North Dakota...............	582	579	521	492	404	413	378	356	394	401	364	344
Ohio...........................	9,239	9,124	8,971	8,820	5,802	5,699	5,847	5,890	5564	5,419	5,247	5,541
Oklahoma...................	3,029	2,971	2,832	2,658	1,841	1,832	1,768	1,703	1781	1,751	1,648	1,627
Oregon.......................	3,409	3,212	3,034	2,824	2,104	1,978	1,984	1,846	2025	1,867	1,773	1,732
Pennsylvania...............	10,277	10,214	10,049	9,702	6,492	6,413	6,381	6,251	6208	6,074	5,841	5,941
Rhode Island...............	864	855	842	837	556	554	567	566	536	521	503	537
South Carolina	4,063	3,819	3,565	3,234	2,376	2,273	2,156	2,069	2308	2,137	1,915	1,929
South Dakota	672	648	619	590	464	450	441	431	449	436	419	414
Tennessee..................	5,379	5,156	4,926	4,610	3,345	3,057	3,091	2,905	3232	2,885	2,792	2,743
Texas.........................	21,934	20,513	18,569	16,623	14,045	13,087	12,242	11,124	13552	12,506	11,245	10,523
Utah...........................	2,351	2,140	1,971	1,778	1,608	1,460	1,356	1,272	1566	1,407	1,250	1,221
Vermont......................	518	514	508	495	342	345	359	351	334	332	337	339
Virginia.......................	6,672	6,491	6,146	5,706	4,412	4,217	4,158	3,897	4289	4,029	3,860	3,758
Washington.................	6,020	5,617	5,246	4,817	3,914	3,551	3,511	3,264	3748	3,350	3,161	3,082
West Virginia...............	1,447	1,479	1,476	1,435	797	781	811	791	758	729	741	751
Wisconsin	4,633	4,544	4,436	4,285	3,105	3,092	3,082	3,021	3001	2,951	2,814	2,878
Wyoming	450	451	431	390	292	304	303	277	282	291	284	267

[1]Annual averages of monthly figures.

Table A-28. Civilian Labor Force and Unemployment

Geographic area	Civilian labor force participation, 2019[1,2,3]	Employment/ population ratio, 2019[3,4]	Unemployment[1] Total (thousands)				Rate[5]			
			2019	2015	2010	2005	2019	2015	2010	2005
United States[6]	63.1	60.8	6001	8,296	14,825	7,591	3.7	5.3	9.6	5.1
Alabama..................................	58.0	56.3	67	131	231	96	3.0	6.1	10.5	4.5
Alaska	63.8	59.9	21	24	28	24	6.1	6.5	7.9	6.9
Arizona...................................	62.2	59.2	167	192	320	135	4.7	6.1	10.4	4.7
Arkansas.................................	58.2	56.1	48	67	111	70	3.5	5.0	8.2	5.2
California................................	62.4	59.9	784	1,168	2,244	947	4.0	6.2	12.2	5.4
Colorado.................................	69.3	67.4	87	110	238	129	2.8	3.9	8.7	5.0
Connecticut.............................	66.4	63.9	71	108	174	88	3.7	5.7	9.1	4.9
Delaware.................................	62.6	60.2	18	23	37	18	3.8	4.9	8.4	4.1
District of Columbia	71.0	67.1	22	27	33	20	5.5	6.9	9.4	6.4
Florida....................................	59.4	57.5	321	523	1,018	322	3.1	5.5	11.1	3.7
Georgia	62.4	60.2	175	286	495	245	3.4	6.0	10.5	5.3
Hawaii	60.9	59.3	18	24	45	18	2.7	3.6	6.9	2.9
Idaho......................................	64.5	62.6	26	33	68	29	2.9	4.1	9.0	4.0
Illinois....................................	64.5	61.9	256	388	688	364	4.0	6.0	10.4	5.7
Indiana....................................	64.6	62.4	112	158	330	175	3.3	4.8	10.4	5.5
Iowa.......................................	70.5	68.5	48	64	101	70	2.7	3.8	6.0	4.3
Kansas....................................	66.7	64.6	47	62	106	74	3.2	4.2	7.1	5.0
Kentucky.................................	59.3	56.8	89	105	210	118	4.3	5.3	10.2	5.9
Louisiana................................	58.6	55.8	101	137	166	148	4.8	6.3	8.0	7.2
Maine......................................	62.4	60.5	21	30	57	34	3.0	4.4	8.1	4.9
Maryland.................................	68.5	66.0	117	160	235	121	3.6	5.1	7.7	4.1
Massachusetts.........................	67.7	65.8	111	172	289	164	2.9	4.8	8.3	4.8
Michigan.................................	61.8	59.2	201	258	605	344	4.1	5.4	12.6	6.8
Minnesota...............................	70.3	68.0	100	111	218	117	3.2	3.7	7.4	4.1
Mississippi..............................	55.8	52.8	69	81	136	99	5.4	6.4	10.4	7.5
Missouri..................................	64.1	62.0	102	155	293	162	3.3	5.0	9.6	5.4
Montana..................................	62.7	60.6	19	22	37	21	3.5	4.2	7.3	4.4
Nebraska.................................	69.9	67.8	32	30	46	37	3.0	3.0	4.6	3.8
Nevada....................................	63.6	61.1	60	95	184	50	3.9	6.7	13.5	4.1
New Hampshire.........................	69.0	67.3	20	25	43	26	2.5	3.4	5.8	3.6
New Jersey	63.5	61.3	160	260	434	197	3.6	5.8	9.5	4.5
New Mexico	58.2	55.4	46	61	76	47	4.9	6.5	8.1	5.1
New York.................................	60.8	58.4	377	504	826	474	4.0	5.3	8.6	5.0
North Carolina..........................	61.6	59.2	197	272	501	226	3.9	5.7	10.9	5.2
North Dakota............................	69.3	67.6	10	12	14	12	2.4	2.8	3.8	3.4
Ohio.......................................	62.8	60.2	239	280	600	349	4.1	4.9	10.3	5.9
Oklahoma................................	60.8	58.8	61	81	120	76	3.3	4.4	6.8	4.5
Oregon....................................	61.7	59.4	79	111	211	114	3.7	5.6	10.6	6.2
Pennsylvania............................	63.2	60.4	284	339	540	311	4.4	5.3	8.5	5.0
Rhode Island............................	64.3	62.0	20	33	63	29	3.6	6.0	11.2	5.0
South Carolina	58.5	56.8	68	136	241	139	2.8	6.0	11.2	6.7
South Dakota	69.0	66.7	15	14	22	16	3.3	3.1	5.0	3.8
Tennessee...............................	62.2	60.1	113	172	299	161	3.4	5.6	9.7	5.6
Texas......................................	64.0	61.8	494	582	997	601	3.5	4.4	8.1	5.4
Utah.......................................	68.4	66.6	42	53	106	52	2.6	3.6	7.8	4.1
Vermont..................................	66.0	64.5	8	12	22	12	2.4	3.6	6.1	3.5
Virginia...................................	66.1	64.3	123	188	297	139	2.8	4.5	7.1	3.6
Washington..............................	65.0	62.3	166	200	351	181	4.3	5.6	10.0	5.6
West Virginia............................	55.1	52.4	39	53	70	40	4.9	6.7	8.7	5.1
Wisconsin................................	67.0	64.8	104	141	267	143	3.3	4.5	8.7	4.7
Wyoming	65.0	62.6	11	13	20	10	3.6	4.3	6.4	3.6

[1] Annual averages of monthly figures.
[2] Percent of each specified group which is classified as either employed or unemployed.
[3] Preliminary data
[4] Percent of civilian noninstitutionalized population classified as employed.
[5] Percent unemployed of the civilian labor force.

Table A-29. Employed Civilians, by Occupation, May 2018 (thousands)

Geographic area	Total	Management occupations	Business and financial occupations	Computer and mathematical sciences	Architecture and engineering occupations	Life, physical, and social science occupations	Community and social service occupations	Legal occupations	Education, training, and library	Arts, design, entertainment, sports, and media	Health care practitioner and technical	Health care support
United States	146,875	8,054	8,184	4,553	2,593	1,289	2,244	1,151	8,887	2,018	8,673	6,522
Alabama............................	1,944	74	74	42	44	9	19	10	104	18	131	54
Alaska...............................	315	20	13	5	8	6	7	2	22	3	18	8
Arizona.............................	2,790	168	149	94	52	20	43	20	141	31	161	74
Arkansas...........................	1,210	63	50	23	13	6	14	6	74	9	81	36
California..........................	17,008	997	1,022	616	337	177	282	136	1,028	307	838	364
Colorado...........................	2,621	117	190	117	62	30	39	23	143	41	146	66
Connecticut.......................	1,660	117	90	48	35	12	34	13	121	22	103	51
Delaware...........................	449	19	28	17	7	5	7	5	25	4	32	12
District of Columbia	712	87	105	42	12	23	12	40	34	37	33	14
Florida..............................	8,609	400	460	207	106	40	102	88	432	105	532	253
Georgia	4,395	249	242	149	63	26	51	33	271	61	248	104
Hawaii...............................	642	34	28	10	9	6	11	4	43	9	32	20
Idaho................................	706	40	27	15	14	10	12	4	43	8	40	20
Illinois..............................	5,991	453	335	178	88	37	85	50	375	75	354	166
Indiana.............................	3,048	144	118	59	51	20	39	15	165	31	195	82
Iowa.................................	1,542	84	70	37	21	12	21	8	106	19	88	40
Kansas..............................	1,375	63	70	35	24	9	17	7	93	17	82	40
Kentucky	1,890	88	74	32	28	8	27	10	98	17	124	53
Louisiana	1,914	83	70	20	31	14	27	15	119	17	132	57
Maine................................	606	36	24	12	10	4	10	4	42	8	41	21
Maryland...........................	2,684	163	167	128	60	41	43	25	176	32	173	75
Massachusetts....................	3,571	294	206	141	75	54	84	30	245	52	243	106
Michigan............................	4,318	198	212	113	140	30	62	26	229	53	283	136
Minnesota..........................	2,868	171	165	96	56	26	58	20	166	40	191	83
Mississippi........................	1,124	56	32	12	14	6	14	6	75	8	80	31
Missouri............................	2,805	123	139	88	38	17	43	19	150	36	192	84
Montana............................	463	16	21	9	7	8	9	4	29	6	30	13
Nebraska...........................	978	51	50	31	12	7	14	5	59	11	63	28
Nevada..............................	1,347	64	49	20	14	8	13	9	55	19	63	26
New Hampshire...................	653	38	29	22	14	4	9	3	43	7	39	16
New Jersey	4,050	209	239	144	51	37	70	34	293	48	236	158
New Mexico	812	37	36	16	20	12	13	6	52	8	47	25
New York...........................	9,386	483	571	265	112	68	192	114	690	208	546	376
North Carolina....................	4,383	191	218	135	64	35	53	25	277	42	279	147
North Dakota......................	417	23	18	8	7	3	6	3	23	5	26	11
Ohio.................................	5,417	241	281	151	96	36	79	34	328	62	363	189
Oklahoma..........................	1,594	84	72	31	29	11	24	13	93	15	97	46
Oregon..............................	1,886	114	91	54	42	20	38	13	107	31	103	53
Pennsylvania......................	5,848	253	283	158	105	46	108	44	338	61	408	186
Rhode Island......................	482	21	28	14	9	3	9	4	33	7	33	18
South Carolina	2,062	89	76	40	40	9	25	14	114	19	126	55
South Dakota	422	12	20	8	5	4	7	2	25	5	31	11
Tennessee	2,957	170	127	56	45	17	32	15	156	32	195	73
Texas................................	12,114	551	595	364	235	81	117	81	764	138	679	314
Utah.................................	1,456	103	76	52	28	13	20	10	90	23	70	34
Vermont............................	305	16	15	7	6	3	10	2	26	6	19	7
Virginia.............................	3,833	174	275	207	77	32	59	36	245	49	211	95
Washington........................	3,259	166	218	165	75	36	49	22	188	49	165	87
West Virginia......................	697	31	23	11	9	6	11	5	45	5	59	22
Wisconsin..........................	2,849	126	142	78	52	20	39	14	165	32	171	71
Wyoming	269	12	9	3	4	4	4	2	20	3	15	7

[1]Due to separate processing and weighting procedures, totals for the United States differ from the results obtained by aggregating the totals for the States.
(D) = Data withheld to avoid disclosure or does not meet statistical standards.

Table A-29. Employed Civilians, by Occupation, May 2018 (thousands)—*Continued*

Geographic area	Protective services	Food preparation and serving related	Building and grounds cleaning and maintenance	Personal care and services	Sales and related	Office and administrative support	Farming, fishing, and forestry	Construction and extraction	Installation, maintenance, and repairs	Production	Transportation and material moving
United States	3,499	13,495	4,429	3,303	14,371	19,528	485	6,194	5,713	9,159	12,532
Alabama..................................	45	179	58	49	212	280	6	78	93	219	149
Alaska	8	27	10	13	26	52	1	18	17	10	23
Arizona...................................	78	265	85	112	289	472	12	124	113	112	172
Arkansas................................	27	109	35	36	125	170	6	45	57	119	105
California................................	386	1,595	482	954	1,634	2,439	227	658	530	836	1,161
Colorado................................	59	255	83	93	292	361	7	141	101	103	151
Connecticut............................	35	139	57	70	161	255	1	50	54	94	98
Delaware................................	10	43	16	16	48	71	1	16	17	20	30
District of Columbia	27	59	23	16	27	78	0	14	10	5	16
Florida....................................	235	934	329	250	1,059	1,452	18	393	359	309	544
Georgia..................................	106	419	112	108	472	643	11	147	182	312	385
Hawaii....................................	20	86	38	23	63	90	1	32	25	15	42
Idaho......................................	13	64	24	24	72	106	6	41	31	48	45
Illinois....................................	151	507	165	169	578	891	6	184	214	431	500
Indiana...................................	60	281	86	81	286	421	4	122	132	388	270
Iowa.......................................	23	132	47	53	155	218	6	67	67	149	120
Kansas...................................	29	123	40	50	128	219	4	58	60	115	94
Kentucky................................	38	178	50	57	178	288	4	71	87	197	180
Louisiana...............................	57	188	57	73	207	265	5	128	94	105	149
Maine.....................................	12	57	22	27	58	92	2	26	26	36	36
Maryland................................	73	225	86	92	262	389	3	119	104	81	165
Massachusetts.......................	77	308	105	162	317	497	2	129	103	152	190
Michigan................................	77	393	125	130	415	613	6	143	172	473	289
Minnesota..............................	44	242	86	144	277	406	4	101	100	214	178
Mississippi.............................	32	103	36	33	116	163	5	41	52	109	100
Missouri.................................	60	264	86	120	278	441	5	107	112	208	194
Montana.................................	8	51	20	16	49	68	2	28	22	18	29
Nebraska................................	16	83	29	30	95	150	3	44	41	77	78
Nevada...................................	43	188	71	81	140	204	1	74	52	52	102
New Hampshire......................	12	59	21	24	77	108	1	22	25	46	36
New Jersey	110	308	126	122	409	644	4	121	137	171	380
New Mexico	26	83	25	43	78	126	3	53	33	27	43
New York................................	313	773	311	454	923	1,481	5	346	312	328	515
North Carolina.......................	100	426	134	122	472	630	9	168	188	343	323
North Dakota..........................	7	35	14	18	39	57	1	33	23	24	34
Ohio..	120	505	157	145	515	816	5	188	207	497	402
Oklahoma...............................	36	159	44	43	163	254	3	86	77	108	107
Oregon...................................	33	183	55	85	180	276	13	83	66	119	128
Pennsylvania..........................	129	505	169	266	553	928	7	222	237	378	463
Rhode Island..........................	12	50	16	18	46	72	0	17	16	30	27
South Carolina	48	210	71	60	228	305	4	83	95	199	154
South Dakota	7	42	17	15	47	63	2	22	17	32	30
Tennessee..............................	71	278	81	80	288	469	5	96	128	266	277
Texas.....................................	292	1,161	335	416	1,276	1,995	24	629	521	680	866
Utah.......................................	23	111	45	45	140	239	1	88	55	94	95
Vermont..................................	5	27	11	14	28	41	1	13	12	20	17
Virginia...................................	103	335	126	127	398	542	6	158	159	181	238
Washington............................	66	294	89	121	307	442	20	161	129	178	233
West Virginia..........................	15	63	21	27	67	104	1	43	36	38	54
Wisconsin..............................	52	246	82	117	264	409	6	105	111	337	209
Wyoming	6	25	11	8	24	34	1	27	17	13	22

[1]Due to separate processing and weighting procedures, totals for the United States differ from the results obtained by aggregating the totals for the States.
(D) = Data withheld to avoid disclosure or does not meet statistical standards.

Table A-30. Private Industry Employment and Wages, 2018

Geographic area	Annual establishments	Average annual employment	Totral annual wages (in millions)	Annual average weekly wage	Annual wages per employee	Rank on annual wages
United States	9,711,681	124,551,838	7,124,159	1,100	57,198	(X)
Alabama................................	120,979	1,598,129	74,417	895	46,565	40
Alaska..................................	19,889	246,319	13,402	1,046	54,409	17
Arizona.................................	156,748	2,436,592	125,429	990	51,477	23
Arkansas...............................	86,265	1,014,114	44,339	841	43,722	47
California...............................	1,517,847	14,876,010	1,014,583	1,312	68,203	5
Colorado...............................	201,763	2,255,703	133,771	1,140	59,304	9
Connecticut............................	117,513	1,449,072	98,976	1,314	68,303	4
Delaware...............................	32,559	384,332	21,785	1,090	56,683	15
District of Columbia	39,325	534,661	47,149	1,696	88,184	1
Florida..................................	684,528	7,635,037	377,741	951	49,475	28
Georgia................................	270,541	3,777,824	204,738	1,042	54,195	18
Hawaii..................................	40,274	536,370	25,948	930	48,376	33
Idaho...................................	60,875	611,396	26,218	825	42,883	49
Illinois..................................	358,529	5,193,821	313,839	1,162	60,425	8
Indiana.................................	162,027	2,659,130	127,283	921	47,867	34
Iowa....................................	96,660	1,309,819	61,653	905	47,070	37
Kansas.................................	83,788	1,139,242	53,971	911	47,375	36
Kentucky	116,519	1,592,256	73,544	888	46,189	41
Louisiana	126,194	1,612,079	78,068	931	48,427	32
Maine...................................	49,812	518,990	23,322	864	44,938	44
Maryland...............................	169,835	2,188,298	128,523	1,129	58,732	10
Massachusetts........................	249,913	3,156,298	231,687	1,412	73,405	3
Michigan...............................	240,953	3,776,481	202,598	1,032	53,647	19
Minnesota..............................	168,785	2,498,328	146,023	1,124	58,448	12
Mississippi.............................	69,895	897,893	35,013	750	38,994	51
Missouri................................	191,036	2,381,261	118,086	954	49,590	27
Montana................................	47,900	381,664	16,149	814	42,312	50
Nebraska...............................	67,975	816,876	37,457	882	45,854	42
Nevada.................................	79,623	1,216,080	59,500	941	48,928	30
New Hampshire........................	50,054	574,083	33,029	1,106	57,533	14
New Jersey............................	263,159	3,472,611	226,946	1,257	65,353	7
New Mexico	56,219	645,435	28,264	842	43,790	46
New York...............................	622,828	8,017,398	589,087	1,413	73,476	2
North Carolina.........................	270,234	3,710,090	188,651	978	50,848	24
North Dakota...........................	29,879	346,756	18,432	1,022	53,157	20
Ohio....................................	283,135	4,687,246	234,290	961	49,985	26
Oklahoma..............................	104,889	1,285,704	60,137	899	46,774	38
Oregon.................................	149,168	1,648,323	85,839	1,001	52,077	21
Pennsylvania..........................	342,488	5,193,979	287,198	1,063	55,294	16
Rhode Island..........................	37,304	421,767	21,809	994	51,709	22
South Carolina	128,358	1,743,243	76,779	847	44,044	45
South Dakota	31,286	352,997	15,428	840	43,705	48
Tennessee.............................	157,381	2,560,978	129,795	975	50,682	25
Texas...................................	678,492	10,429,485	611,398	1,127	58,622	11
Utah....................................	99,566	1,247,220	60,580	934	48,572	31
Vermont................................	24,173	257,141	11,990	897	46,629	39
Virginia.................................	270,687	3,188,362	184,435	1,112	57,846	13
Washington............................	244,223	2,810,692	187,158	1,281	66,588	6
West Virginia...........................	47,091	559,118	25,593	880	45,774	43
Wisconsin..............................	167,652	2,497,801	122,275	941	48,953	29
Wyoming	24,873	207,335	9,831	912	47,418	35

(X) = Not applicable

Table A-31. Average Annual Employment by Industry and Wages

Geography area	Total, all industries	Goods-producing Total	Natural resources and mining	Construction	Manufacturing	Service-providing Total	Trade, transportation, and utilities	Information	Financial activities	Professional and business services	Education and health services	Leisure and hospitality	Other services
United States	124,551,838	21,810,990	1,937,219	7,225,870	12,647,900	102,740,848	27,406,633	2,815,363	8,187,308	20,872,036	22,632,823	16,196,857	4,501,913
Alabama	1,598,129	374,401	18,397	89,207	266,798	1,223,727	377,561	21,030	94,561	245,234	233,306	205,942	46,094
Alaska	246,319	42,311	13,863	15,820	12,628	204,007	64,423	5,617	11,425	27,327	49,563	35,577	9,960
Arizona	2,436,592	366,578	38,653	158,251	169,675	2,070,014	532,318	47,340	214,637	430,516	440,616	325,897	75,319
Arkansas	1,014,114	227,779	16,334	50,848	160,597	786,335	248,584	10,913	50,647	146,700	186,119	118,405	24,966
California	14,876,010	2,623,888	443,542	860,278	1,320,068	12,252,122	3,033,009	525,771	835,896	2,667,839	2,649,228	1,988,750	541,832
Colorado	2,255,703	366,739	46,357	173,096	147,285	1,888,964	466,602	75,076	164,801	423,946	335,274	339,407	82,040
Connecticut	1,449,072	224,541	5,272	58,769	160,500	1,224,532	296,173	31,734	123,655	221,029	326,866	157,709	66,913
Delaware	384,332	50,804	1,535	22,192	27,077	333,528	79,300	4,065	47,609	63,405	75,524	51,696	11,930
District of Columbia	534,661	16,956	32	15,588	1,336	517,706	33,021	19,174	27,284	167,694	116,911	79,571	73,442
Florida	7,635,037	985,180	72,507	541,083	371,590	6,649,857	1,772,605	138,995	570,645	1,365,136	1,287,814	1,226,786	279,269
Georgia	3,777,824	631,434	29,395	195,221	406,818	3,146,390	934,259	114,231	237,900	687,321	562,436	487,598	108,656
Hawaii	536,370	56,093	5,880	36,003	14,210	480,277	123,073	9,149	28,376	82,846	85,560	123,855	26,638
Idaho	611,396	141,255	26,636	46,827	67,792	470,141	139,473	8,798	32,493	91,631	100,212	78,912	18,622
Illinois	5,193,821	838,573	26,452	225,991	586,130	4,355,248	1,192,654	94,330	373,685	948,766	919,288	617,101	208,655
Indiana	2,659,130	704,101	21,236	141,028	541,836	1,955,030	591,234	29,375	133,603	342,835	459,398	310,335	87,997
Iowa	1,309,819	322,892	23,077	77,230	222,586	986,928	309,603	22,018	109,030	140,535	219,674	143,729	42,339
Kansas	1,139,242	245,546	19,284	61,206	165,056	893,696	263,858	18,664	73,500	179,413	195,132	129,372	33,757
Kentucky	1,592,256	347,958	18,569	77,934	251,454	1,244,298	399,946	21,989	92,881	217,081	267,486	197,894	46,476
Louisiana	1,612,079	331,102	43,598	151,993	135,510	1,280,977	377,555	22,869	85,071	213,171	300,015	236,357	45,904
Maine	518,990	88,264	7,143	29,285	51,836	430,727	118,191	7,397	29,811	69,285	118,009	68,406	18,021
Maryland	2,188,298	279,341	6,447	163,210	109,683	1,908,958	462,590	36,210	138,261	452,753	445,328	282,009	91,803
Massachusetts	3,156,298	413,372	9,626	158,656	245,091	2,742,926	577,061	91,783	217,151	587,518	773,683	375,767	119,963
Michigan	3,776,481	832,258	35,874	168,632	627,751	2,944,223	786,892	56,247	203,261	657,930	659,230	432,290	139,968
Minnesota	2,498,328	471,215	27,642	121,665	321,908	2,027,113	531,669	49,170	178,309	378,493	526,556	272,821	90,096
Mississippi	897,893	204,961	16,234	43,911	144,816	692,932	229,107	10,980	42,911	109,842	144,105	134,785	21,202
Missouri	2,381,261	412,466	16,642	122,662	273,163	1,968,794	537,150	47,666	162,755	385,727	454,728	305,418	75,350
Montana	381,664	62,140	12,503	29,077	20,560	319,525	91,355	6,350	21,204	42,410	73,530	66,044	18,301
Nebraska	816,876	167,950	15,823	52,320	99,807	648,926	189,793	17,653	66,245	119,167	138,155	92,581	25,333
Nevada	1,216,080	163,865	19,336	89,125	55,405	1,052,215	254,417	15,646	63,303	190,736	139,036	352,051	34,964
New Hampshire	574,083	100,091	2,619	26,890	70,582	473,992	139,183	12,351	33,486	82,831	112,567	71,975	20,991
New Jersey	3,472,611	414,904	12,165	157,147	245,593	3,057,707	876,344	69,519	242,994	671,419	656,716	385,616	135,824
New Mexico	645,435	110,225	35,856	47,224	27,145	535,210	135,970	12,015	32,955	106,930	128,590	97,785	20,964
New York	8,017,398	873,007	31,787	399,629	441,590	7,144,392	1,554,768	275,598	714,540	1,339,421	1,914,153	957,343	370,268
North Carolina	3,710,090	725,832	30,208	220,692	474,932	2,984,258	830,550	79,945	233,277	635,554	592,067	502,877	109,986
North Dakota	346,756	77,329	25,422	26,002	25,906	269,426	91,635	6,221	23,145	34,560	62,184	40,375	11,307
Ohio	4,687,246	948,179	28,520	220,709	698,950	3,739,067	1,017,249	70,930	293,549	729,430	904,140	566,681	156,685
Oklahoma	1,285,704	282,054	64,020	80,295	137,739	1,003,650	297,631	19,859	77,052	191,261	209,863	171,567	36,417
Oregon	1,648,323	352,784	53,530	104,561	194,693	1,295,539	349,656	34,277	84,865	248,627	288,939	210,781	77,296
Pennsylvania	5,193,979	878,244	52,523	255,910	569,811	4,315,734	1,117,054	85,970	325,130	806,555	1,209,344	571,799	199,883
Rhode Island	421,767	60,625	1,056	19,229	40,340	361,143	76,762	5,930	32,305	68,430	100,506	59,154	17,990
South Carolina	1,743,243	366,705	12,662	104,324	249,719	1,376,538	402,308	28,067	100,794	293,499	234,487	263,743	53,632
South Dakota	352,997	74,244	6,831	22,971	44,442	278,753	85,734	5,589	28,739	32,354	67,868	47,321	11,149
Tennessee	2,560,978	486,612	11,051	124,488	351,073	2,074,366	623,566	44,851	150,833	417,345	420,817	337,857	78,706
Texas	10,429,485	1,922,939	304,275	739,156	879,509	8,506,546	2,465,009	203,822	756,318	1,736,415	1,641,637	1,354,468	334,126
Utah	1,247,220	251,647	15,159	104,339	132,149	995,572	284,283	36,783	87,530	215,564	186,785	148,446	36,120
Vermont	257,141	49,019	3,930	15,262	29,827	208,122	54,476	4,280	11,814	28,976	62,630	37,198	8,748
Virginia	3,188,362	455,218	19,281	197,292	238,645	2,733,144	650,233	66,998	194,731	746,452	505,487	406,321	145,640
Washington	2,810,692	593,188	109,210	199,867	284,112	2,217,503	621,384	133,126	147,871	414,712	465,717	335,635	99,054
West Virginia	559,118	110,559	23,481	40,126	46,952	448,560	128,211	8,288	24,510	68,965	124,431	74,133	19,873
Wisconsin	2,497,801	630,163	32,257	122,396	475,510	1,867,638	541,333	47,152	148,837	327,719	434,143	282,313	84,183
Wyoming	207,335	53,462	23,488	20,253	9,721	153,873	49,819	3,554	11,124	18,733	26,972	36,403	7,261

[1]All estimates of labor and earnings provided by the Bureau of Labor Statistics (BLS) are based on the 2012 North American Industry Classification System (NAICS). National total may differ from sum of state total due to rounding. Annual employment data are the average employment by industry for the calendar year.

Table A-31. Average Annual Employment by Industry and Wages—*Continued*

| | Public administration employment | | | Annual wages per employee (dollars), 2018[1] | | | | |
| | | | | | Goods-producing | | | |
Geography area	Federal	State	Local	Total, all industries	Total	Natural resources and mining	Construction	Manufacturing
United States	2,795,195	69,945	170,478	57,198	65,814	59,628	62,727	68,525
Alabama........................	53,003	1,379	3,706	46,565	56,293	56,388	53,957	57,068
Alaska..........................	14,868	756	641	54,409	87,278	129,422	79,037	51,338
Arizona.........................	55,586	334	1,538	51,477	64,774	50,854	55,989	76,139
Arkansas.......................	20,103	1,059	1,973	43,722	47,958	47,616	47,988	47,984
California.......................	246,205	13,505	19,125	68,203	77,612	38,595	70,084	95,627
Colorado	52,841	702	1,536	59,304	69,028	88,489	62,414	70,677
Connecticut...................	18,097	627	2,188	68,303	78,210	40,054	69,727	82,569
Delaware	5,670	101	299	56,683	61,520	39,987	59,797	64,153
District of Columbia	196,240	12	25	88,184	73,445	37,833	71,845	92,958
Florida..........................	139,626	2,441	1,594	49,475	54,007	34,681	51,286	61,740
Georgia	101,387	2,684	3,919	54,195	58,941	42,010	61,018	59,168
Hawaii..........................	33,707	1,277	266	48,376	64,566	40,211	75,543	46,833
Idaho............................	13,086	493	1,674	42,883	52,906	39,998	44,285	63,932
Illinois..........................	79,162	143	6,363	60,425	71,224	50,101	71,957	71,895
Indiana.........................	38,031	1,417	2,988	47,867	61,399	48,605	58,404	62,680
Iowa.............................	17,590	1,567	3,354	47,070	58,348	42,989	57,435	60,257
Kansas	25,198	1,073	2,717	47,375	57,133	47,004	54,735	59,206
Kentucky.......................	35,365	2,596	1,978	46,189	57,872	56,223	53,957	59,208
Louisiana	31,138	1,352	3,443	48,427	71,483	84,277	63,892	75,881
Maine...........................	15,467	228	2,157	44,938	52,607	41,187	49,575	55,894
Maryland.......................	144,963	443	2,084	58,732	70,304	43,100	65,971	78,350
Massachusetts...............	45,397	2,266	4,302	73,405	84,188	61,244	78,802	88,576
Michigan.......................	52,243	1,112	4,875	53,647	65,327	40,516	62,378	67,537
Minnesota	32,049	1,485	4,021	58,448	66,163	50,521	67,248	67,096
Mississippi....................	25,150	1,112	1,800	38,994	49,308	47,028	50,325	49,254
Missouri........................	54,862	1,230	6,634	49,590	58,075	43,331	59,442	58,359
Montana........................	13,221	406	1,011	42,312	54,893	67,090	52,969	50,194
Nebraska.......................	16,807	851	1,913	45,854	50,607	41,084	51,657	51,566
Nevada.........................	19,081	617	320	48,928	62,817	82,872	61,123	58,543
New Hampshire..............	7,744	1,338	806	57,533	68,513	42,081	62,661	71,722
New Jersey	48,501	850	3,538	65,353	76,098	39,981	72,658	80,088
New Mexico	28,838	1,195	2,054	43,790	55,177	64,393	49,350	53,139
New York.......................	114,634	3,583	9,869	73,476	69,232	41,230	73,248	67,614
North Carolina................	72,753	1,447	4,939	50,848	57,369	39,062	54,587	59,827
North Dakota.................	9,337	377	985	53,157	71,022	95,073	64,586	53,882
Ohio.............................	78,638	1,149	11,401	49,985	61,108	51,145	61,194	61,487
Oklahoma......................	49,161	1,043	3,479	46,774	64,410	91,135	52,777	58,770
Oregon	28,097	908	3,588	52,077	62,613	37,495	60,523	70,641
Pennsylvania..................	96,947	1,451	9,153	55,294	63,835	62,951	66,852	62,561
Rhode Island..................	11,088	117	402	51,709	59,117	39,071	61,579	58,468
South Carolina	34,046	1,062	2,001	44,044	56,907	40,536	52,634	59,522
South Dakota	11,270	890	841	43,705	48,625	42,904	48,981	49,320
Tennessee	49,117	1,322	1,723	50,682	58,573	46,634	57,033	59,495
Texas............................	201,302	3,237	9,991	58,622	78,031	109,449	65,554	77,648
Utah	36,088	944	2,517	48,572	55,313	61,171	51,052	58,006
Vermont........................	7,000	251	798	46,629	55,119	38,605	51,025	59,390
Virginia.........................	179,578	2,287	3,440	57,846	58,592	47,043	58,050	59,974
Washington....................	74,798	1,073	2,355	66,588	65,840	33,346	64,432	79,321
West Virginia..................	23,497	1,066	1,972	45,774	68,893	80,012	72,255	60,459
Wisconsin	29,102	616	5,575	48,953	57,874	39,437	62,063	58,047
Wyoming	7,520	475	612	47,418	69,276	83,751	53,554	67,060

[1] All estimates of labor and earnings provided by the Bureau of Labor Statistics (BLS) are based on the 2012 North American Industry Classification System (NAICS). National total may differ from sum of state total due to rounding. Annual employment data are the average employment by industry for the calendar year.

Table A-31. Average Annual Employment by Industry and Wages—*Continued*

Geography area	Annual wages per employee (dollars), 2018[1]										
		Service-providing							Public administration		
	Total	Trade, transportation, and utlities	Information	Financial activities	Professional and business services	Education and health services	Leisure and hospitality	Other services	Federal	State	Local
United States	55,369	47,607	113,781	95,561	75,169	50,444	24,087	38,464	83,657	60,751	51,515
Alabama...............	43,589	41,970	60,025	69,240	55,653	46,432	16,798	37,839	83,424	53,853	41,931
Alaska...............	47,592	47,427	64,841	58,446	62,609	53,259	24,387	39,973	82,081	59,469	51,350
Arizona...............	49,122	46,734	75,499	70,877	56,745	51,125	24,580	37,697	78,120	58,960	48,138
Arkansas...............	42,495	41,450	53,828	58,119	60,316	42,468	16,536	34,843	70,535	47,846	38,748
California...............	66,188	52,020	188,173	107,228	91,070	52,187	30,527	40,668	85,563	80,316	65,286
Colorado...............	57,416	50,043	100,735	84,615	81,401	50,156	25,878	40,987	84,020	64,912	48,465
Connecticut...............	66,487	51,041	110,642	155,433	87,958	55,369	23,705	33,615	77,106	71,595	59,390
Delaware...............	55,947	40,843	65,782	95,574	80,066	53,795	20,414	34,259	74,175	58,222	53,483
District of Columbia	88,667	58,105	133,776	149,142	118,471	64,162	40,671	91,236	119,304	83,101	97,042
Florida...............	48,803	44,766	81,168	75,337	60,914	50,781	25,881	36,402	78,240	48,879	51,618
Georgia...............	53,242	49,352	96,613	84,587	66,989	52,062	20,604	36,377	78,756	49,102	42,255
Hawaii...............	46,486	44,653	69,442	67,068	54,157	53,215	34,017	36,930	79,519	51,838	70,708
Idaho...............	39,872	39,972	52,761	56,024	51,695	42,047	17,141	31,284	70,456	47,938	36,757
Illinois...............	58,346	51,570	91,164	109,598	76,586	50,959	23,765	42,392	79,997	68,266	51,317
Indiana...............	42,993	42,092	60,371	65,167	52,468	47,681	18,981	32,900	73,074	52,079	39,729
Iowa...............	43,380	40,539	58,519	73,894	54,071	43,022	16,799	34,313	66,332	68,905	42,759
Kansas...............	44,694	42,235	63,399	67,710	61,288	42,586	16,764	34,478	68,977	56,094	36,342
Kentucky...............	42,921	42,623	54,629	67,733	50,087	48,210	17,719	33,616	67,918	50,966	40,701
Louisiana...............	42,468	42,196	58,223	62,731	56,446	43,339	21,264	37,854	73,970	52,218	40,202
Maine...............	43,366	37,589	54,502	68,174	57,328	47,535	22,087	33,967	76,693	47,055	40,309
Maryland...............	57,039	46,648	92,844	94,201	79,500	54,310	24,012	43,222	105,797	58,256	57,540
Massachusetts...............	71,780	52,937	123,118	144,514	107,875	58,448	27,758	38,569	83,105	71,361	62,046
Michigan...............	50,346	47,200	73,556	71,568	69,377	49,739	20,566	33,275	78,351	63,464	47,535
Minnesota...............	56,655	49,570	78,903	95,604	82,535	51,469	22,507	34,221	74,709	64,997	49,870
Mississippi...............	35,944	36,497	49,173	53,281	42,132	41,620	17,523	34,491	70,772	48,236	36,062
Missouri...............	47,812	42,469	81,842	72,947	66,429	46,127	20,892	34,075	70,785	43,956	41,581
Montana...............	39,865	39,170	54,475	59,315	52,271	47,539	19,150	30,293	71,014	49,871	41,420
Nebraska...............	44,624	39,891	64,407	66,817	58,836	46,678	16,715	32,212	70,602	53,183	43,497
Nevada...............	46,765	44,190	70,292	66,612	61,821	54,167	33,688	37,484	74,160	56,443	56,680
New Hampshire...............	55,215	47,777	93,599	94,889	77,486	56,317	21,945	37,927	81,620	54,487	46,600
New Jersey...............	63,895	53,723	114,630	115,066	90,784	53,402	26,316	36,518	83,702	75,706	63,526
New Mexico...............	41,445	38,078	53,204	56,048	61,899	41,645	18,651	34,365	77,997	55,474	39,830
New York...............	73,995	51,832	129,853	186,871	95,057	53,467	33,850	41,910	81,432	70,645	68,166
North Carolina...............	49,262	43,092	83,920	87,311	65,609	48,381	19,767	35,102	71,559	51,955	46,118
North Dakota...............	48,029	49,819	70,208	63,251	61,774	51,404	17,889	37,216	67,173	55,430	41,459
Ohio...............	47,164	44,247	70,006	72,736	64,006	46,408	19,459	34,001	78,512	66,063	47,674
Oklahoma...............	41,817	41,554	58,997	58,044	52,227	45,570	18,204	35,221	71,246	49,492	39,598
Oregon...............	49,208	44,347	87,733	69,649	69,806	50,107	22,754	34,031	78,151	64,671	55,230
Pennsylvania...............	53,556	45,000	87,091	88,831	78,092	51,808	21,102	33,988	76,983	62,352	52,896
Rhode Island...............	50,465	43,902	74,327	88,061	68,957	48,716	22,818	33,322	83,388	71,685	61,031
South Carolina...............	40,617	39,429	61,977	61,713	50,391	45,993	17,991	32,985	70,584	49,010	44,357
South Dakota...............	42,394	39,650	49,334	60,160	56,384	50,399	16,954	32,874	66,785	49,934	36,196
Tennessee...............	48,831	46,137	73,821	76,718	59,851	52,099	23,524	35,137	81,746	52,167	42,382
Texas...............	54,234	52,337	87,085	83,356	74,443	48,036	21,861	39,429	80,130	59,947	46,768
Utah...............	46,868	44,163	78,404	67,933	59,543	43,696	20,121	35,627	71,940	55,859	37,271
Vermont...............	44,629	40,351	59,800	72,078	64,917	46,699	23,107	36,288	78,625	59,156	42,813
Virginia...............	57,722	43,886	100,731	85,723	87,511	49,627	20,678	42,804	95,979	52,154	46,018
Washington...............	66,788	63,994	194,631	80,466	82,245	51,354	25,357	40,310	81,787	65,065	59,477
West Virginia...............	40,076	38,698	52,508	53,206	51,745	46,182	17,916	31,425	78,420	44,192	39,112
Wisconsin...............	45,943	41,512	75,414	71,561	60,773	49,195	18,305	30,593	67,259	60,444	42,988
Wyoming...............	39,823	42,737	47,401	57,486	52,783	42,906	21,270	37,155	67,918	55,822	45,523

[1]All estimates of labor and earnings provided by the Bureau of Labor Statistics (BLS) are based on the 2012 North American Industry Classification System (NAICS). National total may differ from sum of state total due to rounding. Annual employment data are the average employment by industry for the calendar year.

Table A–32. Union Membership

Geographic area	2019 Total employed (thousands)	2019 Member of unions[1] Total (thousands)	2019 Member of unions[1] Percent of employed	2019 Represented by unions[2] Total (thousands)	2019 Represented by unions[2] Percent of employed	2018 Total employed (thousands)	2018 Members of unions[1] Total (thousands)	2018 Members of unions[1] Percent of employed	2018 Represented by unions[2] Total (thousands)	2018 Represented by unions[2] Percent of employed
United States	141,737	14,574	10.3	16,383	11.6	140,099	14,744	10.5	16,380	11.7
Alabama[3].....................	2,041	173	8.5	199	9.8	1,950	180	9.2	196	10.1
Alaska	282	48	17.1	53	18.7	299	55	18.5	60	20.0
Arizona[3].....................	3,028	174	5.7	214	7.1	2,943	156	5.3	191	6.5
Arkansas[3]..................	1,200	62	5.2	71	5.9	1,176	56	4.8	62	5.3
California......................	16,485	2,504	15.2	2,726	16.5	16,399	2,405	14.7	2,587	15.8
Colorado......................	2,631	237	9.0	259	9.8	2,564	281	11.0	307	12.0
Connecticut..................	1,680	244	14.5	269	16.0	1,677	268	16.0	280	16.7
Delaware	432	38	8.7	43	9.9	434	45	10.3	47	10.8
District of Columbia	361	34	9.3	37	10.2	354	35	9.9	41	11.6
Florida[3]......................	8,827	551	6.2	667	7.6	8,702	484	5.6	588	6.8
Georgia[3].....................	4,422	180	4.1	223	5.0	4,466	201	4.5	249	5.6
Hawaii	574	135	23.5	147	25.5	601	139	23.1	146	24.3
Idaho[3]........................	764	37	4.9	46	6.0	733	34	4.7	41	5.6
Illinois	5,658	771	13.6	832	14.7	5,694	786	13.8	839	14.7
Indiana[3]......................	3,007	249	8.3	296	9.8	3,049	269	8.8	283	9.3
Iowa[3].........................	1,543	97	6.3	122	7.9	1,461	113	7.7	129	8.8
Kansas[3]......................	1,280	112	8.7	130	10.1	1,283	90	7.0	129	10.1
Kentucky	1,786	144	8.0	169	9.5	1,812	161	8.9	207	11.4
Louisiana[3]	1,784	94	5.3	108	6.1	1,785	89	5.0	104	5.8
Maine	588	69	11.8	81	13.7	573	74	12.9	85	14.8
Maryland......................	2,912	330	11.3	371	12.8	2,784	307	11.0	336	12.1
Massachusetts...............	3,397	406	12.0	449	13.2	3,397	464	13.7	493	14.5
Michigan[3].....................	4,323	589	13.6	648	15.0	4,320	625	14.5	663	15.4
Minnesota	2,662	364	13.7	381	14.3	2,634	395	15.0	421	16.0
Mississippi[3]..................	1,105	70	6.3	93	8.4	1,121	58	5.1	80	7.1
Missouri	2,661	297	11.1	333	12.5	2,675	251	9.4	283	10.6
Montana.......................	437	46	10.5	52	12.0	427	50	11.8	60	14.0
Nebraska[3]....................	894	75	8.4	86	9.6	882	59	6.6	71	8.0
Nevada[3]......................	1,379	201	14.6	222	16.1	1,376	191	13.9	216	15.7
New Hampshire..............	677	69	10.3	79	11.6	664	68	10.2	77	11.6
New Jersey	4,094	642	15.7	712	17.4	3,935	587	14.9	639	16.2
New Mexico	813	58	7.1	72	8.8	812	56	6.8	67	8.2
New York......................	8,253	1,732	21.0	1,877	22.7	8,404	1,872	22.3	2,027	24.1
North Carolina[3].............	4,396	102	2.3	150	3.4	4,331	118	2.7	174	4.0
North Dakota[3]...............	356	21	6.0	27	7.5	343	18	5.2	23	6.7
Ohio	5,127	610	11.9	673	13.1	5,054	639	12.6	722	14.3
Oklahoma[3]...................	1,554	96	6.2	123	7.9	1,583	90	5.7	117	7.4
Oregon	1,772	255	14.4	277	15.7	1,738	242	13.9	256	14.7
Pennsylvania.................	5,642	676	12.0	740	13.1	5,575	701	12.6	748	13.4
Rhode Island.................	475	83	17.4	90	19.0	479	83	17.4	89	18.5
South Carolina[3].............	2,140	47	2.2	59	2.7	2,016	55	2.7	72	3.6
South Dakota[3]	395	22	5.6	26	6.7	387	22	5.6	28	7.1
Tennessee[3]...................	2,947	135	4.6	162	5.5	2,816	155	5.5	179	6.4
Texas[3]........................	12,334	497	4.0	642	5.2	11,989	512	4.3	653	5.4
Utah[3].........................	1,409	62	4.4	83	5.9	1,343	56	4.1	76	5.7
Vermont	290	33	11.2	35	12.0	291	31	10.5	34	11.6
Virginia[3]......................	3,881	156	4.0	201	5.2	3,875	168	4.3	213	5.5
Washington...................	3,393	638	18.8	684	20.2	3,270	649	19.8	671	20.5
West Virginia.................	704	72	10.2	78	11.1	684	68	10.0	74	10.8
Wisconsin	2,698	218	8.1	245	9.1	2,700	219	8.1	233	8.6
Wyoming[3]....................	243	18	7.3	21	8.7	235	15	6.5	18	7.7

[1]Members are employed workers who are union members.
[2]Covered members are workers covered by a collective bargaining agreement.
[3]Right-to-work state.

Table A-33. Median Income of Households in 2018 Inflation-Adjusted Dollars and Distribution by Income Level, 2018

Geographic area	Median household income (in 2018 inflation adjusted dollars)	Total number of households (thousands)	Percentage of households by income level (in 2018 inflation-adjusted dollars)									
			Under $10,000	$10,000–$14,999	$15,000–$24,999	$25,000–$34,999	$35,000–$49,999	$50,000–$74,999	$75,000–$99,999	$100,000–$149,999	$150,000–$199,999	$200,000 and over
United States	61,937	121,520	6.3	4.3	9.0	8.9	12.4	17.4	12.6	15.0	6.6	7.6
Alabama	49,861	1,855	9.1	6.0	11.9	10.1	13.0	17.4	12.0	12.1	4.4	4.0
Alaska	74,346	255	4.5	3.3	6.4	6.6	10.3	19.3	13.4	19.0	8.3	8.8
Arizona	59,246	2,614	6.0	3.6	9.5	9.3	13.5	19.1	13.1	14.2	5.7	5.8
Arkansas	47,062	1,156	8.2	6.1	12.3	11.3	15.2	17.8	10.6	11.3	3.8	3.6
California....................	75,277	13,072	5.1	3.9	7.5	7.2	10.4	15.6	12.3	16.6	8.9	12.4
Colorado.....................	71,953	2,177	4.9	3.3	7.2	7.4	11.7	17.5	13.6	17.5	8.2	8.7
Connecticut.................	76,348	1,378	5.3	3.9	7.2	7.2	10.1	15.5	12.2	16.9	9.3	12.4
Delaware.....................	64,805	368	6.0	4.0	8.3	9.3	11.5	18.2	13.7	15.7	6.6	6.6
District of Columbia	85,203	287	9.3	4.6	5.4	5.9	7.8	12.2	10.7	16.5	9.1	18.4
Florida........................	55,462	7,809	6.5	4.5	10.1	10.1	13.9	18.4	12.1	13.2	5.2	6.0
Georgia	58,756	3,803	7.1	4.1	9.5	9.5	12.8	17.8	12.3	14.2	5.9	6.7
Hawaii........................	80,212	455	5.3	2.2	6.1	7.2	10.5	15.5	13.3	20.1	9.6	10.2
Idaho..........................	55,583	640	5.5	4.3	10.2	9.4	15.3	21.1	12.4	13.1	4.5	4.2
Illinois........................	65,030	4,865	6.4	3.8	8.8	8.5	11.6	17.2	12.5	15.7	7.2	8.3
Indiana.......................	55,746	2,599	6.1	4.4	10.0	10.0	14.1	19.3	13.7	13.8	4.7	3.9
Iowa...........................	59,955	1,268	5.5	4.3	9.0	9.4	13.6	19.3	14.4	15.0	4.9	4.7
Kansas	58,218	1,133	5.7	4.4	9.5	10.1	13.6	18.7	13.2	13.9	5.7	5.2
Kentucky.....................	50,247	1,733	8.4	5.6	10.9	10.8	14.0	17.9	11.8	12.5	4.0	4.0
Louisiana	47,905	1,737	9.4	5.9	12.7	10.8	12.8	15.9	11.1	12.3	4.8	4.4
Maine.........................	55,602	570	6.2	5.5	9.9	9.4	13.9	18.1	13.5	14.1	4.9	4.3
Maryland.....................	83,242	2,216	4.8	2.9	5.9	6.0	9.9	15.7	13.2	18.8	10.2	12.5
Massachusetts	79,835	2,624	5.4	4.3	7.3	6.7	9.3	14.6	11.8	17.5	9.8	13.2
Michigan.....................	56,697	3,957	6.8	4.5	9.6	9.8	13.6	18.4	12.8	13.9	5.5	5.2
Minnesota...................	70,315	2,194	4.4	3.8	7.3	7.9	12.1	17.4	13.8	17.8	7.7	7.6
Mississippi..................	44,717	1,109	10.6	6.4	12.7	11.1	13.9	17.0	11.8	9.8	3.6	3.0
Missouri......................	54,478	2,435	6.3	4.9	10.1	10.4	14.4	18.6	12.4	13.2	4.8	5.0
Montana......................	55,328	431	6.3	5.1	9.8	10.3	13.8	19.9	13.2	12.8	4.7	4.0
Nebraska.....................	59,566	765	5.0	4.4	9.3	9.4	13.7	19.3	13.4	15.5	5.3	4.7
Nevada........................	58,646	1,130	6.6	3.7	8.7	9.4	14.3	18.4	13.3	14.5	5.9	5.4
New Hampshire.............	74,991	531	4.2	3.2	7.7	8.0	10.6	16.3	13.8	18.7	8.4	9.1
New Jersey	81,740	3,250	5.0	3.1	7.2	6.7	9.3	14.8	12.2	17.5	10.2	13.9
New Mexico	47,169	794	9.7	6.3	11.8	11.0	13.6	17.4	10.8	11.4	4.2	3.9
New York.....................	67,844	7,367	6.8	4.9	8.6	7.8	10.5	15.2	11.9	15.6	8.0	10.7
North Carolina..............	53,855	4,011	6.5	4.9	10.3	10.2	14.3	18.2	12.2	13.0	4.8	5.6
North Dakota................	63,837	319	5.8	4.0	8.1	8.2	13.2	18.3	13.7	17.5	6.3	5.1
Ohio...........................	56,111	4,685	7.0	4.7	9.8	9.8	13.5	18.3	12.9	14.1	5.1	4.8
Oklahoma....................	51,924	1,485	7.1	5.1	10.7	10.5	14.5	18.8	12.3	12.4	4.3	4.2
Oregon........................	63,426	1,640	5.3	4.0	8.5	8.9	12.8	18.1	13.6	15.5	6.5	6.7
Pennsylvania................	60,905	5,071	6.4	4.4	9.3	9.3	12.3	17.8	12.8	15.1	6.2	6.5
Rhode Island................	64,340	407	6.8	5.2	8.4	7.9	10.8	17.3	12.1	17.1	7.2	7.0
South Carolina	52,306	1,928	7.6	5.1	10.6	10.6	13.7	18.6	12.5	12.2	4.6	4.6
South Dakota	56,274	345	5.7	4.4	8.4	11.0	15.0	18.9	14.8	13.7	4.3	3.8
Tennessee	52,375	2,603	7.2	5.2	10.7	10.5	13.9	18.4	12.4	12.8	4.4	4.6
Texas..........................	60,629	9,776	6.5	4.3	9.0	9.1	12.7	17.7	12.3	14.8	6.5	7.2
Utah...........................	71,414	999	3.9	2.8	6.2	7.7	12.4	19.5	15.4	18.9	6.9	6.4
Vermont......................	60,782	261	5.9	4.8	8.4	8.9	12.5	18.6	14.7	16.0	5.4	4.8
Virginia.......................	72,577	3,176	5.2	3.6	7.4	7.5	11.3	16.3	12.8	16.7	8.4	10.7
Washington..................	74,073	2,896	4.6	3.0	6.9	7.1	11.5	17.5	13.5	17.7	8.6	9.7
West Virginia................	44,097	735	9.1	6.3	13.3	11.9	14.6	17.5	9.9	11.3	3.2	2.9
Wisconsin	60,773	2,372	5.0	4.4	8.8	9.5	13.5	19.3	13.8	15.6	5.4	4.7
Wyoming	61,584	230	5.3	3.4	9.4	9.9	13.0	18.2	13.9	16.2	5.9	4.9

Table A-34. Family Income and Families and Individuals Below Poverty: 2018

Geographic area	Median family income (in 2018 inflation-adjusted dollars)	Total number of families (thousands)	Percentage of families by income level						Families below poverty		Individuals below poverty		Children below poverty	
			Under $25,000	$25,000–$49,999	$50,000–$74,999	$75,000–$99,999	$100,000–$199,999	$200,000 and over	Number (thousands)	As a percentage of all families	Number (thousands)	As a percentage of all persons	Number (thousands)	As a percentage of all children
United States	76,401	79,242	12.3	19.0	17.8	14.3	26.8	9.9	7,369	9.3	41,852	13.1	12,998	18.0
Alabama	63,837	1,215	16.9	21.9	18.9	14.9	22.0	5.4	148	12.2	800	16.8	255	23.8
Alaska	89,847	168	8.8	14.5	18.4	14.1	33.2	11.0	13	7.5	79	10.9	25	14.1
Arizona	69,981	1,713	12.9	20.6	20.1	14.8	24.2	7.4	170	9.9	983	14.0	325	20.1
Arkansas	58,080	769	17.5	25.1	19.6	13.0	20.1	4.8	98	12.7	505	17.2	171	24.7
California	86,165	8,935	11.5	16.9	15.6	12.8	28.7	14.6	813	9.1	4,969	12.8	1,541	17.4
Colorado	88,955	1,373	8.4	15.8	16.8	15.3	31.8	11.9	85	6.2	537	9.6	149	11.9
Connecticut	98,100	892	9.1	14.4	14.6	12.7	32.4	16.8	63	7.1	361	10.4	102	14.1
Delaware	79,386	238	10.7	17.7	19.2	15.9	27.9	8.6	20	8.4	117	12.5	37	18.7
District of Columbia	117,713	122	14.5	11.4	11.3	8.3	24.1	30.3	14	11.3	108	16.2	29	23.1
Florida	66,995	5,027	13.5	22.3	19.6	14.1	22.7	7.7	488	9.7	2,841	13.6	819	19.7
Georgia	71,457	2,537	14.2	20.3	17.8	14.0	24.9	8.8	274	10.8	1,469	14.3	505	20.5
Hawaii	95,448	317	7.6	14.9	15.2	14.6	35.4	12.3	18	5.7	122	8.8	35	11.9
Idaho	65,987	438	11.8	22.6	23.0	14.8	22.5	5.3	36	8.2	203	11.8	63	14.3
Illinois	81,313	3,119	11.4	17.6	17.2	13.9	28.9	11.1	265	8.5	1,509	12.1	457	16.2
Indiana	70,150	1,683	12.5	20.7	20.8	16.6	24.1	5.3	157	9.3	853	13.1	275	18.0
Iowa	76,068	800	10.1	19.0	20.1	17.6	26.7	6.5	58	7.2	344	11.2	97	13.5
Kansas	74,042	727	10.9	20.1	19.7	16.2	26.2	7.0	58	8.0	338	12.0	103	14.9
Kentucky	62,228	1,139	16.7	23.1	19.2	14.2	21.6	5.2	144	12.6	730	16.9	226	23.0
Louisiana	61,847	1,105	18.8	22.3	17.3	13.0	22.7	6.0	150	13.6	844	18.6	283	26.2
Maine	72,390	343	10.7	21.4	19.5	16.8	25.6	6.0	25	7.3	152	11.6	35	14.5
Maryland	101,437	1,472	8.0	13.0	14.4	13.6	34.1	16.8	88	6.0	528	9.0	152	11.6
Massachusetts	101,548	1,644	8.9	13.6	14.0	12.5	33.1	17.9	107	6.5	664	10.0	164	12.2
Michigan	72,036	2,520	12.5	20.1	19.6	15.1	25.6	7.1	239	9.5	1,373	14.1	413	19.4
Minnesota	89,039	1,397	7.7	16.0	17.0	15.9	32.7	10.6	80	5.7	529	9.6	150	11.7
Mississippi	57,380	728	20.2	23.7	19.0	14.9	18.2	4.0	109	15.0	568	19.7	193	27.8
Missouri	69,188	1,551	12.5	22.1	19.7	15.1	23.8	6.9	140	9.0	786	13.2	247	18.3
Montana	68,940	266	11.1	22.2	21.4	16.2	23.5	5.6	20	7.7	135	13.0	36	16.0
Nebraska	75,990	486	10.1	19.3	19.7	16.5	27.5	6.8	34	7.1	206	11.0	60	12.9
Nevada	71,864	707	11.9	21.2	19.0	15.9	25.1	6.9	64	9.1	387	12.9	120	17.7
New Hampshire	93,930	342	6.8	14.9	16.4	15.5	34.2	12.2	16	4.7	100	7.6	27	10.6
New Jersey	101,404	2,232	9.2	13.5	13.6	12.8	32.7	18.1	154	6.9	832	9.5	264	13.7
New Mexico	58,760	495	19.5	23.0	19.3	12.8	19.9	5.3	75	15.1	399	19.5	124	26.3
New York	83,311	4,633	12.9	16.6	15.5	13.0	28.5	13.4	463	10.0	2,591	13.6	743	18.6
North Carolina	67,816	2,622	13.9	22.0	19.1	14.4	23.0	7.7	267	10.2	1,418	14.0	456	20.2
North Dakota	86,205	188	8.1	17.1	17.1	16.6	33.2	7.9	11	5.7	79	10.7	17	9.9
Ohio	72,028	2,924	12.7	20.2	19.2	15.4	25.8	6.8	284	9.7	1,579	13.9	496	19.5
Oklahoma	64,082	983	15.0	22.9	20.1	14.9	21.6	5.6	112	11.4	597	15.6	203	21.7
Oregon	77,655	1,028	10.7	18.8	18.6	15.1	27.7	9.0	82	8.0	517	12.6	134	15.7
Pennsylvania	77,491	3,235	11.1	18.7	18.4	15.1	27.8	8.9	262	8.1	1,518	12.2	435	16.8
Rhode Island	84,212	247	11.7	15.7	16.8	14.8	31.0	10.1	23	9.1	131	12.9	36	18.0
South Carolina	65,742	1,258	14.7	22.8	19.5	15.0	22.0	6.1	136	10.8	755	15.3	246	22.6
South Dakota	72,183	220	10.6	21.0	20.3	18.2	24.8	5.0	18	8.0	112	13.1	34	16.4
Tennessee	65,656	1,708	15.0	22.2	19.6	15.1	22.0	6.1	193	11.3	1,011	15.3	331	22.3
Texas	71,868	6,730	14.0	20.1	17.7	13.4	25.5	9.2	767	11.4	4,181	14.9	1,545	21.1
Utah	81,599	744	7.9	17.1	20.0	16.9	30.4	7.6	45	6.1	281	9.0	87	9.5
Vermont	80,452	156	9.4	17.6	18.6	18.8	28.8	6.9	10	6.2	66	11.0	14	12.1
Virginia	88,929	2,094	9.6	16.2	16.0	14.2	30.0	14.2	149	7.1	885	10.7	252	13.7
Washington	87,652	1,880	8.6	15.8	17.4	14.6	31.2	12.4	118	6.3	759	10.3	204	12.5
West Virginia	57,718	462	17.9	25.2	20.4	13.0	19.6	3.9	60	13.0	312	17.8	87	24.5
Wisconsin	76,814	1,487	9.7	18.9	20.0	16.6	28.1	6.7	104	7.0	626	11.0	175	14.0
Wyoming	78,352	145	9.8	19.2	18.3	16.7	29.4	6.6	10	7.1	62	11.1	18	13.8

Table A-35. Housing—Units and Characteristics: 2018

		Characteristics												
		Total units						Occupied units						
		Units in structure (percent)			Year built (percent)				Vehicles available (percent)				House heating fuel (percent)		
Geographic area	Total housing units	1-unit detached	1-unit attached	Mobile home	2010 or later	1990 to 2009	Before 1950	Total occupied housing units	None	1	2	3 or more	Utility gas	Electricity	Fuel oil, kerosene, etc.
United States	138,539,906	61.4	5.9	6.1	6.2	27.3	17.3	121,520,180	8.5	32.5	37.1	21.9	47.8	39.2	4.6
Alabama	2,274,711	68.3	1.5	13.2	7.4	33.7	8.9	1,855,184	6.3	31.7	36.2	25.8	27.1	65.7	0.1
Alaska	318,352	63.0	7.3	4.6	5.6	30.0	3.3	254,551	8.7	30.6	36.3	24.5	47.9	13.6	28.8
Arizona....................	3,035,902	64.2	4.6	10.3	7.0	43.3	2.9	2,614,298	6.0	35.0	37.7	21.3	32.9	60.4	0.1
Arkansas	1,380,521	69.9	1.7	11.4	8.3	32.9	8.4	1,156,347	6.5	32.0	38.3	23.2	37.0	51.7	0.1
California.................	14,277,867	57.3	7.1	3.7	4.1	21.8	14.8	13,072,122	6.9	30.2	36.9	26.0	63.8	26.7	0.3
Colorado.................	2,424,128	61.6	7.0	4.2	8.2	33.5	10.2	2,176,757	5.0	30.0	39.1	25.9	69.0	23.2	0.1
Connecticut.............	1,521,123	58.6	5.3	0.9	3.0	14.3	28.2	1,378,091	8.6	33.3	37.4	20.7	36.1	16.9	39.8
Delaware	438,659	57.5	17.0	9.0	8.9	31.6	12.7	367,671	6.4	31.6	42.4	19.6	42.9	33.4	11.5
District of Columbia	319,579	12.5	22.8	0.1	8.8	11.0	45.5	287,476	35.8	44.9	15.6	3.7	50.9	45.0	0.9
Florida....................	9,547,762	54.2	6.1	8.7	6.9	35.6	4.1	7,809,358	6.2	39.5	38.1	16.2	4.7	92.3	0.2
Georgia	4,326,266	66.3	3.8	8.7	7.2	40.9	6.8	3,803,012	6.2	32.2	37.9	23.6	38.8	55.3	0.2
Hawaii	546,261	52.8	9.2	0.2	5.2	26.7	7.1	455,309	8.6	33.0	35.4	23.0	2.4	29.6	0.0
Idaho......................	735,703	72.4	3.3	8.5	8.8	36.9	12.3	640,270	3.7	27.4	38.0	30.8	52.3	33.2	1.6
Illinois....................	5,376,176	58.4	5.8	2.4	3.0	22.0	27.3	4,864,864	10.8	34.5	36.4	18.3	76.9	17.3	0.1
Indiana	2,903,576	72.4	3.8	4.9	5.5	26.7	22.1	2,599,169	6.2	31.8	38.3	23.7	59.6	29.9	0.6
Iowa.......................	1,409,568	73.0	4.3	3.8	6.2	21.5	30.3	1,267,873	5.7	29.1	38.7	26.5	61.4	22.6	0.5
Kansas	1,280,553	72.7	4.4	4.3	5.7	24.1	21.8	1,133,408	5.3	29.6	38.0	27.0	64.7	25.0	0.2
Kentucky	1,995,187	67.5	2.6	11.8	6.1	31.5	14.3	1,732,713	6.9	32.0	38.2	23.0	36.8	52.6	0.8
Louisiana	2,076,136	65.6	2.7	12.9	7.8	26.3	10.4	1,737,220	8.3	37.2	37.0	17.5	33.0	64.4	0.1
Maine	746,592	69.0	2.1	8.3	4.7	24.1	27.9	570,307	7.4	32.9	40.5	19.2	7.8	7.3	62.4
Maryland.................	2,458,779	51.2	21.1	1.4	5.8	25.6	16.9	2,215,935	8.6	31.9	37.2	22.3	43.2	42.6	8.0
Massachusetts	2,915,043	51.4	5.5	0.8	4.1	14.4	37.2	2,624,294	12.5	35.0	36.2	16.4	52.4	16.6	25.1
Michigan	4,614,552	71.8	4.5	5.5	3.1	23.0	22.3	3,957,466	7.6	33.8	38.4	20.1	76.0	10.3	1.0
Minnesota	2,455,637	66.6	7.3	3.3	5.6	26.8	20.6	2,194,452	6.8	29.3	40.4	23.5	65.2	18.1	1.7
Mississippi	1,332,631	68.6	1.2	15.2	6.6	34.1	7.8	1,108,630	6.2	33.2	36.6	24.0	29.8	57.2	0.3
Missouri..................	2,806,296	69.8	3.6	6.3	5.2	26.7	18.9	2,434,806	6.9	32.4	37.7	23.0	50.1	37.1	0.2
Montana..................	515,161	69.4	3.9	9.9	7.2	28.8	17.7	431,421	5.1	26.5	37.5	30.9	52.2	24.3	0.9
Nebraska.................	845,011	72.0	4.2	3.7	6.3	22.9	24.8	765,490	5.1	29.3	39.1	26.5	60.1	29.6	0.4
Nevada...................	1,268,717	59.6	4.5	5.1	8.0	53.2	2.3	1,129,810	7.5	35.2	36.1	21.2	57.3	36.9	0.5
New Hampshire............	638,112	63.3	5.3	6.1	4.3	21.5	23.6	531,212	5.4	30.0	40.6	24.0	21.5	9.5	43.7
New Jersey	3,628,198	53.4	9.6	0.9	4.0	18.6	25.5	3,249,567	11.4	33.8	35.8	19.0	74.9	13.5	8.0
New Mexico	943,232	64.0	3.1	16.9	4.6	31.6	8.8	794,093	5.9	33.3	36.9	24.0	63.1	20.9	0.1
New York.................	8,363,847	41.8	5.0	2.2	3.2	12.2	39.9	7,367,015	29.3	32.5	25.8	12.4	59.7	12.1	19.8
North Carolina............	4,684,962	64.9	4.3	12.6	8.5	38.7	8.5	4,011,462	5.7	31.3	38.0	24.9	24.7	63.6	2.8
North Dakota.............	377,661	57.2	5.6	6.8	16.4	21.6	16.6	319,355	5.2	29.2	37.6	28.0	40.6	40.1	2.3
Ohio	5,217,617	68.4	4.6	3.7	3.7	21.2	26.0	4,685,447	8.0	33.2	37.4	21.4	65.5	24.3	2.0
Oklahoma................	1,743,073	73.0	1.9	9.1	8.2	23.7	12.6	1,485,310	5.6	31.8	38.6	24.0	51.1	39.4	0.2
Oregon....................	1,788,743	63.1	4.3	7.9	6.1	30.6	16.3	1,639,970	6.9	31.3	37.9	24.0	37.6	51.6	1.7
Pennsylvania.............	5,713,136	57.0	18.6	3.9	3.4	17.3	33.5	5,070,931	11.1	33.9	35.8	19.2	51.1	23.6	15.9
Rhode Island............	469,153	55.3	3.3	1.0	1.9	13.3	37.8	406,573	9.9	35.2	37.7	17.3	55.6	10.2	29.0
South Carolina	2,318,291	63.0	3.1	15.9	9.6	37.3	7.0	1,927,991	6.2	33.0	38.5	22.2	22.7	71.7	0.8
South Dakota	397,506	67.5	3.7	8.6	8.8	26.8	21.7	345,449	4.7	29.2	36.3	29.9	46.7	31.8	1.7
Tennessee	2,992,412	68.1	3.3	9.2	8.2	33.3	10.2	2,603,140	5.7	30.5	38.3	25.5	31.7	62.5	0.4
Texas	11,101,498	64.9	2.5	7.0	11.9	33.8	6.6	9,776,083	5.3	32.4	40.1	22.2	35.5	60.6	0.1
Utah	1,108,739	67.9	6.5	3.2	11.5	37.1	10.0	998,891	4.0	24.0	40.3	31.8	82.1	13.5	0.1
Vermont...................	337,133	67.0	4.4	6.4	4.3	20.7	29.0	261,373	6.3	34.1	41.8	17.8	18.1	5.4	41.7
Virginia...................	3,538,985	61.1	10.9	5.2	6.7	30.3	11.8	3,175,524	6.2	29.7	38.0	26.1	33.2	55.3	4.4
Washington	3,148,084	62.9	4.0	6.3	8.5	31.9	14.6	2,895,575	6.8	29.1	37.4	26.7	34.6	55.9	1.6
West Virginia..............	893,742	70.9	2.1	14.9	3.6	25.1	22.4	734,703	8.6	35.1	36.0	20.3	40.2	45.3	3.0
Wisconsin	2,710,718	66.6	4.1	3.4	4.5	26.1	24.8	2,371,960	6.3	31.8	40.2	21.8	66.0	15.6	1.9
Wyoming	278,615	65.7	4.4	12.9	7.9	26.3	16.1	230,252	4.4	24.8	37.1	33.7	61.6	22.3	0.2

Table A-36. Owner- and Renter-Occupied Units—Value and Gross Rent, 2018

Geographic Area	Owner-occupied units — Total units (thousands)	Median value (dollars)	Value—pct. Less than $100,000	Value—pct. $100,000–$199,999	Value—pct. $200,000–$499,000	Value—pct. $500,000 and over	Housing units with a mortgage — Total (thousands)	Median selected monthly owner costs (dollars)	Monthly owner costs 30 percent or more of household income (percent)	Renter-occupied units — Total units (thousands)	Median gross rent (dollars)	Gross rent—pct. Less than $500	Gross rent—pct. $500–$1,499	Gross rent—pct. $1,500 or more	Gross rent 30 percent or more of household income (percent of rental units paying rent)
United States	77,708,394	229,700	17.7	25.9	40.3	16.0	48,126,102	1,566	27.7	43,811,786	1,058	9.6	66.1	24.3	49.7
Alabama	1,262,257	147,900	33.0	33.8	28.8	4.3	694,367	1,164	23.6	592,927	788	18.1	76.9	5.0	47.9
Alaska	167,108	276,100	11.2	16.7	62.0	10.0	102,706	1,895	28.6	87,443	1,177	5.8	64.5	29.7	43.2
Arizona	1,694,367	241,100	13.9	23.6	51.7	10.9	1,072,502	1,417	26.9	919,931	1,036	5.9	76.5	17.7	47.1
Arkansas	760,401	133,100	36.6	36.2	23.5	3.7	410,135	1,071	22.8	395,946	731	18.5	78.1	3.5	45.8
California	7,165,664	546,800	4.7	5.4	35.4	54.5	4,988,711	2,345	38.2	5,906,458	1,520	4.9	44.1	50.9	54.6
Colorado	1,417,981	373,300	6.4	9.8	56.7	27.1	994,356	1,741	27.2	758,776	1,289	6.8	58.4	34.8	51.3
Connecticut	906,771	277,400	5.1	23.1	55.4	16.5	609,456	2,056	30.5	471,320	1,171	10.7	62.8	26.5	52.5
Delaware	261,145	255,300	9.9	22.0	59.3	9.0	165,425	1,566	30.9	106,526	1,108	9.1	73.3	17.6	52.6
District of Columbia	121,540	617,900	2.1	2.7	34.0	61.3	91,179	2,506	26.0	165,936	1,516	9.7	39.6	50.7	46.5
Florida	5,148,242	230,600	16.1	25.7	46.7	11.5	2,890,964	1,471	33.0	2,661,116	1,182	5.4	67.9	26.7	56.5
Georgia	2,426,435	189,900	20.8	32.2	38.3	8.6	1,568,112	1,395	25.1	1,376,577	1,008	9.9	75.7	14.5	49.7
Hawaii	265,364	631,700	2.1	3.5	29.3	65.0	170,872	2,354	38.8	189,945	1,613	6.9	38.3	54.7	52.9
Idaho	452,916	233,100	11.7	28.6	51.7	8.0	290,501	1,249	25.7	187,354	848	12.3	80.9	6.8	46.1
Illinois	3,210,113	203,400	19.2	30.0	41.2	9.6	2,002,424	1,665	27.2	1,654,751	995	10.4	69.7	19.9	47.4
Indiana	1,791,749	147,300	29.2	40.4	26.7	3.8	1,166,290	1,118	19.9	807,420	820	11.9	82.4	5.7	46.6
Iowa	903,751	152,000	28.6	37.5	30.8	3.1	543,108	1,234	19.9	364,122	777	15.3	79.0	5.8	42.4
Kansas	749,821	159,400	29.5	33.7	32.3	4.6	442,557	1,364	21.6	383,587	840	12.0	79.9	7.9	45.3
Kentucky	1,167,729	148,100	31.1	37.3	27.5	4.1	661,520	1,164	23.1	564,984	779	16.5	79.2	4.2	44.4
Louisiana	1,137,524	167,300	26.4	34.7	33.9	5.0	593,733	1,254	25.9	599,696	854	14.2	78.9	6.9	55.8
Maine	406,226	197,500	18.2	32.4	42.4	7.0	247,344	1,349	26.0	164,081	839	17.0	74.1	8.9	48.2
Maryland	1,482,669	324,800	6.2	14.7	58.2	20.8	1,073,634	1,955	27.1	733,266	1,371	8.1	51.1	40.8	49.8
Massachusetts	1,620,712	400,700	2.8	9.0	53.4	34.8	1,105,499	2,207	30.1	1,003,582	1,295	13.8	46.5	39.8	49.8
Michigan	2,817,484	162,500	27.3	34.7	32.9	5.1	1,671,899	1,270	22.7	1,139,982	861	12.7	78.9	8.4	48.3
Minnesota	1,567,939	235,400	11.1	27.5	52.6	8.8	1,024,974	1,559	21.4	626,513	969	13.1	70.2	16.8	46.2
Mississippi	756,195	123,300	41.1	33.5	22.8	2.6	365,204	1,132	25.1	352,435	777	17.0	79.7	3.2	50.0
Missouri	1,625,854	162,600	25.8	36.5	32.4	5.3	986,408	1,249	21.3	808,952	830	13.4	80.8	5.8	45.8
Montana	291,018	249,200	13.8	22.5	51.2	12.3	164,197	1,413	29.5	140,403	811	15.4	76.3	8.3	44.4
Nebraska	505,666	161,800	23.6	40.6	31.9	3.8	300,417	1,353	20.3	259,824	830	12.2	80.6	7.3	41.3
Nevada	641,551	292,200	7.2	15.2	64.2	13.3	435,070	1,528	30.2	488,259	1,108	3.8	77.0	19.2	51.1
New Hampshire	378,742	270,000	8.7	20.3	60.6	10.3	242,076	1,892	29.1	152,470	1,090	11.1	68.8	20.2	47.7
New Jersey	2,078,948	344,000	5.0	14.3	55.6	24.9	1,377,645	2,398	34.1	1,170,619	1,336	7.8	54.7	37.5	50.9
New Mexico	525,349	174,700	23.5	34.5	35.4	6.6	279,825	1,234	29.5	268,744	830	14.9	78.4	6.8	49.4
New York	3,953,785	325,500	13.6	20.0	35.5	30.9	2,366,391	2,098	32.8	3,413,230	1,274	10.9	50.8	38.4	52.0
North Carolina	2,612,904	180,600	22.3	33.4	36.7	7.7	1,623,735	1,284	24.9	1,398,558	900	10.6	79.3	10.1	47.8
North Dakota	199,467	198,700	21.9	28.6	43.8	5.6	106,417	1,425	17.4	119,888	808	12.3	79.6	8.0	38.5
Ohio	3,086,226	151,100	28.3	39.0	29.1	3.6	1,924,876	1,248	21.6	1,599,221	797	14.2	80.3	5.5	44.4
Oklahoma	971,990	140,000	33.9	37.3	24.8	4.1	522,069	1,214	22.6	513,320	808	12.6	81.7	5.6	43.6
Oregon	1,024,853	341,800	8.0	11.5	58.3	22.2	667,980	1,690	30.9	615,117	1,130	7.4	69.9	22.6	49.5
Pennsylvania	3,478,645	186,000	21.0	33.2	38.5	7.2	2,076,151	1,451	24.7	1,592,286	927	12.2	74.2	13.6	48.0
Rhode Island	251,354	273,800	4.5	18.5	65.1	12.0	171,436	1,830	32.8	155,219	998	16.5	69.4	14.0	47.1
South Carolina	1,335,486	170,800	26.5	31.8	34.1	7.6	780,604	1,225	25.6	592,505	892	11.6	78.3	10.2	48.7
South Dakota	234,487	171,500	24.4	34.5	36.0	5.1	129,323	1,301	22.1	110,962	734	19.0	76.5	4.5	41.0
Tennessee	1,723,984	177,500	22.9	33.9	36.2	7.1	1,010,900	1,228	24.3	879,156	861	13.5	77.4	9.0	48.7
Texas	6,034,082	186,000	23.2	30.6	37.8	8.4	3,408,366	1,603	27.4	3,742,001	1,046	6.8	74.6	18.6	48.7
Utah	703,983	303,300	5.6	14.2	65.5	14.8	491,897	1,531	23.2	294,908	1,043	7.1	75.1	17.8	44.3
Vermont	188,798	233,100	10.4	29.7	51.4	8.5	116,755	1,560	30.1	72,575	969	13.2	70.7	16.2	46.7
Virginia	2,093,205	281,700	10.9	21.6	46.7	20.7	1,419,521	1,752	25.5	1,082,319	1,215	7.6	58.5	33.9	48.5
Washington	1,818,988	373,100	6.1	11.0	51.8	31.1	1,233,756	1,883	29.1	1,076,587	1,316	6.2	55.1	38.7	47.7
West Virginia	532,674	121,300	41.2	34.2	22.3	2.3	244,953	1,001	22.9	202,029	735	21.2	74.7	4.1	49.3
Wisconsin	1,592,440	188,500	16.2	37.6	41.0	5.2	1,003,101	1,387	22.5	779,520	847	10.4	83.0	6.7	43.6
Wyoming	161,812	230,500	12.6	27.6	48.9	10.8	94,761	1,440	23.8	68,440	818	13.8	77.2	8.9	41.5

Table A-37. Home Ownership and Vacancy Rates

Geographic area	Homeownership rate[1]					Homeowner vacancy rates[2]					Rental vacancy rates[2]				
	2018	2017	2016	2015	2014	2018	2017	2016	2015	2014	2018	2017	2016	2015	2014
United States	64.4	63.9	63.4	63.7	64.5	1.5	1.6	1.7	1.8	1.9	6.9	7.2	6.9	7.1	7.6
Alabama...........................	70.3	70.0	69.7	70.0	72.1	1.9	2.2	2.5	2.7	2.5	13.2	14.0	14.6	14.9	14.0
Alaska..............................	63.7	65.5	65.2	62.3	64.9	1.8	1.4	1.3	1.9	2.2	11.1	7.4	8.1	6.8	6.8
Arizona............................	65.7	64.4	61.9	61.7	63.5	1.9	2.1	1.8	2.1	2.7	6.0	7.5	6.8	7.7	9.5
Arkansas..........................	64.7	65.0	67.6	67.1	65.4	2.1	2.3	3.4	2.7	3.3	9.9	11.6	11.1	11.3	14.7
California..........................	55.1	54.4	53.8	54.3	54.2	1.2	1.0	1.0	1.2	1.1	4.4	4.3	3.6	4.1	4.5
Colorado..........................	64.4	63.7	62.4	63.6	65.0	0.9	0.7	1.0	1.1	1.2	3.4	5.5	4.7	5.3	4.9
Connecticut......................	65.3	66.1	64.2	66.5	67.4	1.7	1.5	2.1	1.9	1.4	6.1	6.8	7.0	6.3	5.8
Delaware..........................	70.8	70.0	73.0	73.3	74.3	1.1	2.4	2.1	1.8	1.8	7.1	6.4	8.1	6.4	7.4
District of Columbia..........	39.9	40.3	40.8	40.4	41.5	1.2	2.1	1.6	1.6	1.6	7.9	7.1	5.8	5.4	6.5
Florida.............................	65.5	64.1	64.3	64.8	64.9	2.2	2.0	2.2	2.4	2.5	8.2	8.5	8.1	8.0	10.1
Georgia............................	63.8	62.8	62.3	62.9	62.9	1.6	1.4	1.7	2.6	2.8	7.1	7.6	7.2	8.0	9.7
Hawaii..............................	59.5	55.9	57.7	59.3	58.4	1.7	1.3	1.4	1.5	1.6	8.5	8.7	10.6	8.7	8.3
Idaho...............................	69.2	69.9	70.5	70.0	69.6	1.2	1.2	1.7	1.4	2.4	5.5	7.7	6.0	5.8	6.1
Illinois.............................	66.0	65.4	65.3	65.4	66.4	1.7	2.0	2.2	2.2	2.3	7.4	8.0	7.6	7.5	9.2
Indiana.............................	69.8	70.0	70.9	69.4	70.1	1.3	1.7	1.7	2.1	2.3	9.0	10.4	9.8	9.2	10.8
Iowa................................	68.9	70.0	70.0	68.8	69.4	1.5	2.0	1.1	0.8	2.0	7.4	7.0	5.4	5.7	5.7
Kansas.............................	67.3	66.0	67.1	64.9	64.7	1.6	1.7	1.6	1.6	2.2	10.5	11.5	11.1	12.0	8.8
Kentucky..........................	69.8	70.1	67.9	67.9	67.6	1.3	1.6	1.9	1.9	2.4	6.2	7.4	7.3	7.7	6.5
Louisiana.........................	65.7	66.1	64.2	63.3	65.3	1.9	1.9	2.1	2.2	2.1	10.1	10.7	11.4	10.0	8.4
Maine...............................	71.2	71.0	72.6	69.9	71.0	1.1	1.2	2.1	2.3	1.8	4.4	4.0	4.0	4.4	5.1
Maryland..........................	66.6	66.9	66.5	67.1	66.2	1.4	1.8	2.3	2.0	1.4	9.0	7.8	7.5	8.1	7.5
Massachusetts..................	61.5	60.0	59.7	60.5	63.0	1.0	1.0	1.2	1.4	1.3	4.2	4.9	4.1	4.2	5.6
Michigan..........................	73.0	72.9	72.8	74.6	73.8	1.2	0.9	1.3	1.5	1.5	7.4	7.6	7.5	7.4	8.2
Minnesota........................	69.8	72.7	72.4	70.1	71.4	0.4	1.1	0.9	1.0	1.4	5.0	5.8	4.2	4.9	5.6
Mississippi.......................	72.5	71.0	69.7	70.7	73.2	1.6	2.2	2.2	2.0	2.4	9.7	11.8	9.6	10.4	11.1
Missouri...........................	69.7	67.6	66.7	68.5	70.5	1.6	1.6	2.3	2.9	1.9	10.0	9.9	9.1	9.1	9.9
Montana...........................	67.4	67.6	67.1	66.4	66.9	1.4	2.0	2.1	1.7	1.6	5.9	6.9	6.0	3.9	4.0
Nebraska..........................	66.4	66.1	68.0	68.1	66.7	1.2	1.1	1.1	1.1	1.3	7.3	7.0	6.5	5.9	5.5
Nevada.............................	57.8	55.0	54.5	54.8	56.0	1.1	2.5	1.8	2.3	2.6	6.2	6.7	6.7	8.0	9.7
New Hampshire.................	73.4	71.6	71.8	71.6	72.2	0.9	1.2	1.6	1.8	1.8	3.7	3.7	4.6	5.7	5.6
New Jersey	65.0	64.1	62.2	64.0	65.2	1.5	1.9	2.2	1.6	1.6	5.0	4.9	5.5	5.5	6.2
New Mexico	68.0	66.6	67.4	66.5	66.3	2.0	2.6	2.0	2.8	2.1	9.1	10.5	9.5	10.3	10.8
New York..........................	51.0	51.1	51.5	51.5	52.9	1.7	2.1	2.0	2.0	1.7	5.2	5.2	5.2	5.1	4.9
North Carolina..................	65.2	66.3	65.7	65.2	66.4	1.4	1.9	2.1	2.6	2.2	7.1	7.8	8.3	9.8	8.1
North Dakota....................	61.9	62.6	61.4	61.8	64.5	2.4	1.7	1.8	1.7	0.9	14.3	16.7	15.4	9.6	8.6
Ohio................................	67.3	66.0	66.1	66.4	67.3	1.1	1.4	1.5	1.8	1.6	7.1	6.6	6.9	7.8	7.4
Oklahoma.........................	69.5	68.9	66.8	67.4	69.3	2.5	2.4	2.0	1.8	1.9	11.6	9.1	11.2	8.3	11.4
Oregon............................	62.0	61.8	62.6	61.1	62.8	1.3	1.1	1.4	1.5	1.8	4.6	5.6	4.4	4.6	4.1
Pennsylvania....................	69.9	68.6	68.5	69.6	69.7	1.6	1.8	1.7	2.2	2.2	6.7	7.2	6.3	7.2	8.7
Rhode Island....................	60.7	56.6	56.3	58.9	61.8	1.2	0.7	1.1	1.9	1.5	3.2	3.5	3.7	4.4	6.7
South Carolina	72.0	72.8	68.9	67.1	72.9	1.9	1.9	1.9	2.1	2.7	11.0	10.4	8.8	8.9	12.0
South Dakota	69.1	67.8	69.4	70.1	69.2	1.3	1.2	0.8	1.1	1.2	7.3	7.2	7.3	6.4	8.3
Tennessee	68.0	67.2	66.4	66.5	66.7	1.4	1.3	1.7	2.4	2.3	8.6	7.8	7.4	7.5	8.5
Texas...............................	62.7	61.7	61.5	61.9	62.2	1.4	1.6	1.8	1.5	1.5	8.9	9.8	9.4	9.6	9.5
Utah................................	72.2	71.0	71.3	69.9	70.9	1.0	1.1	0.9	1.1	1.5	5.4	6.2	5.7	5.1	8.6
Vermont...........................	71.4	71.1	71.3	71.8	73.5	1.1	1.3	1.6	2.0	1.9	4.2	3.6	4.5	4.5	5.0
Virginia............................	66.0	67.5	66.3	67.1	68.7	1.5	2.0	2.3	1.6	1.7	6.5	6.7	7.0	6.6	7.4
Washington......................	64.9	63.6	61.6	62.6	63.6	1.1	0.8	1.3	1.2	1.6	5.1	3.5	3.8	4.6	4.9
West Virginia....................	74.7	75.1	74.8	74.9	75.6	2.2	1.8	1.6	1.8	2.2	7.4	8.7	8.7	8.3	9.1
Wisconsin........................	67.9	68.0	67.7	66.6	67.8	1.4	1.1	1.5	1.2	1.7	4.6	4.8	5.3	5.3	4.6
Wyoming	71.1	70.4	70.2	69.9	70.8	2.6	2.7	2.2	1.3	1.6	13.0	14.7	12.2	9.8	8.0

[1]Proportion of owner households to occupied households.
[2]Proportion of the homeowner inventory that is vacant for sale.
[3]Proportion of the rental inventory that is vacant for rent.

Table A-38. Cost of Living Indicators—Housing, Public University, Energy Expenditures, and Motor Fuels Taxes

	Housing price indexes[1] (All-transactions index)				Average undergraduate tuition and fees and room and board rates charged for full-time students in degree-granting postsecondary institutions (dollars)						Public 2-year, tuition and required fees		
					Public 4-year institutions, in-state								
					2017–2018				2016–2017				
Geographic area	2018	2015	2010	2005	Total[2]	Tuition and required fees	Room	Board	Total	Tuition and required fees	In-state, 2017-2018	Out-of-state, 2017-2018	In-state, 2016-2017
United States	160.4	136.4	127.0	140.9	$20,050	$9,037	$6,227	$4,786	$19,488	$8,804	$3,243	$7,971	$3,156
Alabama	133.7	122.4	125.3	119.1	19,673	9,827	5,534	4,311	19,052	9,466	4,403	9,133	4,362
Alaska	179.1	170.4	156.2	140.5	18,373	7,221	6,209	4,943	17,370	7,210	-	-	3,820
Arizona	183.1	146.8	120.8	167.4	22,629	10,557	7,081	4,992	21,491	10,057	2,152	8,067	2,129
Arkansas	142.4	129.7	126.5	123.8	17,479	8,187	5,139	4,153	16,871	7,924	3,291	4,762	3,195
California	217.9	175.6	140.5	200.2	22,081	8,020	7,896	6,166	21,356	7,896	1,268	7,504	1,262
Colorado	188.9	145.3	118.3	122.3	21,514	9,540	5,858	6,116	20,943	9,352	3,638	10,354	3,565
Connecticut	134.0	130.5	139.3	153.8	25,182	12,355	7,032	5,795	24,174	11,726	4,312	12,879	4,189
Delaware	158.0	146.4	152.1	158.3	22,371	9,999	7,382	4,990	21,698	9,578	X	X	X
District of Columbia	326.0	267.2	208.1	202.1	X	5,756	X	X	X	5,612	X	X	X
Florida	199.2	155.0	131.0	184.7	14,896	4,455	5,856	4,585	14,806	4,435	2,506	9,111	2,552
Georgia	137.1	113.9	110.6	121.8	17,705	7,206	6,255	4,244	17,353	7,010	2,901	8,090	2,895
Hawaii	253.1	214.6	182.3	187.2	21,201	9,709	5,767	5,725	21,016	9,712	3,080	8,216	3,080
Idaho	182.9	141.3	131.0	132.9	15,455	7,247	3,911	4,297	14,457	7,005	3,282	7,732	3,227
Illinois	126.1	116.2	118.6	133.4	25,089	13,971	6,035	5,084	24,541	13,636	3,891	10,989	3,749
Indiana	130.7	113.7	109.9	113.3	19,297	9,038	5,476	4,783	19,001	8,876	4,255	8,211	4,175
Iowa	145.9	130.5	123.4	119.7	18,426	8,766	5,394	4,266	17,604	8,361	4,923	6,581	4,791
Kansas	145.6	127.4	122.4	119.4	17,963	8,737	4,813	4,414	17,560	8,489	3,382	4,611	3,221
Kentucky	143.8	126.0	122.3	119.3	20,745	10,365	5,889	4,490	19,673	10,014	4,106	13,825	3,962
Louisiana	160.9	148.9	140.1	124.4	18,835	9,165	5,664	4,007	18,319	8,813	4,093	7,057	4,031
Maine	164.9	144.5	144.6	154.2	19,500	9,664	5,028	4,808	19,073	9,219	3,698	6,498	3,673
Maryland	178.7	162.8	161.7	179.2	21,177	9,289	6,821	5,067	20,670	9,094	4,090	9,467	3,983
Massachusetts	170.0	144.8	135.7	159.0	25,229	12,778	7,771	4,680	24,473	12,331	4,991	10,006	4,785
Michigan	118.6	98.8	87.0	117.2	22,665	12,435	5,127	5,103	21,832	11,890	3,469	6,552	3,423
Minnesota	150.9	128.7	122.3	143.1	20,420	11,226	4,983	4,210	19,727	10,883	5,381	6,113	5,310
Mississippi	134.8	124.9	124.1	117.6	17,718	7,980	5,688	4,051	16,843	7,472	3,182	5,626	2,831
Missouri	141.6	123.8	122.3	126.8	18,106	8,387	6,016	3,703	17,639	8,176	3,273	6,157	3,028
Montana	193.1	168.3	154.4	139.8	15,800	6,783	4,184	4,834	15,241	6,503	3,631	8,482	3,381
Nebraska	151.7	130.3	118.3	117.6	18,449	8,188	5,517	4,744	17,379	7,732	3,212	4,101	2,991
Nevada	184.1	135.2	105.4	187.6	16,810	5,920	5,757	5,133	17,145	5,520	3,075	9,853	2,910
New Hampshire	163.2	140.5	138.0	160.9	27,570	15,949	7,047	4,574	26,968	15,491	7,337	15,907	7,002
New Jersey	164.2	151.2	155.5	171.0	26,542	13,633	7,966	4,943	26,070	13,297	4,536	8,049	4,366
New Mexico	148.2	135.4	140.6	131.6	15,803	6,718	4,567	4,518	15,528	6,825	1,666	5,318	1,590
New York	174.0	152.8	151.1	158.4	22,343	7,938	9,260	5,145	21,750	7,709	5,229	9,151	5,122
North Carolina	143.6	122.8	122.3	117.8	17,343	7,354	5,633	4,355	16,635	7,218	2,499	8,496	2,471
North Dakota	209.5	198.8	150.0	128.9	15,998	7,687	3,479	4,832	15,388	7,376	4,700	9,429	4,562
Ohio	121.0	105.3	104.3	115.2	21,674	10,026	6,632	5,017	20,961	9,827	3,672	7,456	3,654
Oklahoma	155.1	142.6	132.7	121.3	16,263	7,623	4,589	4,052	15,755	7,219	3,876	9,059	3,627
Oregon	201.9	158.2	138.1	140.5	22,710	10,363	7,262	5,085	21,324	9,739	4,487	8,503	4,262
Pennsylvania	161.1	145.6	145.2	141.5	25,795	14,534	6,743	4,518	25,331	14,068	5,173	13,679	5,048
Rhode Island	179.4	150.2	153.2	188.5	24,280	12,239	7,538	4,502	23,135	11,386	4,564	12,156	4,266
South Carolina	147.7	126.7	124.9	121.9	22,132	12,579	5,888	3,665	21,508	12,153	4,502	9,480	4,418
South Dakota	170.8	148.8	134.5	123.5	16,421	8,540	3,801	4,080	16,054	8,301	6,026	5,853	5,803
Tennessee	156.1	130.1	123.3	118.1	18,951	9,574	4,988	4,388	18,340	9,287	4,148	16,140	4,048
Texas	186.5	153.2	129.5	118.0	18,271	8,645	5,175	4,451	17,800	8,376	2,209	6,418	2,100
Utah	181.4	141.7	125.9	117.0	14,174	6,557	3,435	4,182	13,709	6,334	3,781	12,020	3,690
Vermont	167.7	157.6	158.2	151.4	27,782	16,103	7,381	4,297	26,786	15,537	6,414	12,678	6,222
Virginia	176.9	161.3	157.8	164.9	23,427	12,637	6,089	4,701	22,567	12,126	5,118	11,225	4,962
Washington	207.0	155.2	141.2	141.0	18,323	6,830	6,146	5,347	18,053	6,903	4,078	5,976	3,848
West Virginia	136.9	130.3	126.3	124.4	17,803	7,619	5,465	4,718	17,096	7,241	4,077	9,410	4,009
Wisconsin	141.3	122.4	124.0	130.5	16,544	8,475	4,864	3,205	16,246	8,419	4,337	6,257	4,292
Wyoming	192.4	179.2	165.7	141.4	14,486	4,443	4,493	5,550	14,354	4,311	3,142	7,678	2,987

[1] The housing price indexes reflect fluctuation from a base of 100. 100 represents the average price of a sample of local single-family homes in 2000. The indexes represent the change in value as of the end of the year shown.
[2] Costs include in-state tuition, required fees, and room and board.
(X) = Not applicable

Table A-38. Cost of Living Indicators—Housing, Public University, Energy Expenditures, and Motor Fuels Taxes—*Continued*

Geographic area	Energy expenditures[4], 2017			Tax rates[5] on motor fuel, 2018 (cents per gallon)			
	Expenditures (millions of dollars)	Energy expenditures per person (dollars)	Energy expenditures as percent of current-dollar GDP	Gasoline	Diesel	Liquefied Petroleum Gas	Gasohol
United States	1,136,496	3,495	5.83	18.4	24.4	13.6	18.4
Alabama	20,436	4,192	9.66	18.0	21.0	0.0	18.0
Alaska	5,112	6,910	9.89	8.0	8.0	0.0	8.0
Arizona	20,521	2,911	6.28	18.0	26.0	0.0	18.0
Arkansas	11,305	3,765	9.14	21.5	22.5	16.5	21.5
California	124,724	3,166	4.44	41.7	36.0	6.0	41.7
Colorado	16,391	2,919	4.72	22.0	20.5	9.0	22.0
Connecticut	12,536	3,508	4.72	25.0	41.7	0.0	25.0
Delaware	3,336	3,485	4.62	23.0	22.0	22.0	23.0
District of Columbia	1,970	2,832	1.46	23.5	23.5	0.0	23.5
Florida	57,074	2,721	5.83	27.5	27.5	0.0	27.5
Georgia	34,011	3,266	6.05	26.8	30.0	26.8	26.8
Hawaii	5,549	3,897	6.23	16.0	16.0	5.2	16.0
Idaho	6,311	3,672	8.71	33.0	33.0	23.2	33.0
Illinois	40,510	3,168	4.91	19.0	21.5	19.0	19.0
Indiana	27,101	4,069	7.72	30.0	49.0	0.0	30.0
Iowa	13,890	4,418	7.59	31.7	33.5	30.0	30.0
Kansas	11,180	3,841	6.98	24.0	26.0	23.0	24.0
Kentucky	17,338	3,893	8.63	24.6	21.6	24.6	24.6
Louisiana	32,041	6,860	13.45	20.0	20.0	14.6	20.0
Maine	5,624	4,213	9.11	30.0	31.2	0.0	23.0
Maryland	18,541	3,077	4.65	35.3	36.1	0.0	0.0
Massachusetts	23,206	3,381	4.29	24.0	24.0	24.9	24.0
Michigan	32,394	3,247	6.40	26.3	26.3	26.3	26.3
Minnesota	20,067	3,604	5.70	28.5	28.5	21.4	28.5
Mississippi	13,142	4,396	11.96	18.4	18.4	17.0	18.4
Missouri	21,162	3,464	6.96	17.0	17.0	17.0	17.0
Montana	4,578	4,347	9.73	32.3	30.0	5.2	32.3
Nebraska	8,244	4,299	6.95	28.9	28.9	28.0	28.9
Nevada	9,214	3,100	5.87	24.0	27.0	22.0	24.0
New Hampshire	5,193	3,847	6.40	23.8	23.8	22.2	23.8
New Jersey	29,541	3,323	4.93	37.1	40.1	5.3	37.1
New Mexico	7,368	3,520	7.82	17.0	21.0	12.0	17.0
New York	54,108	2,762	3.38	25.0	23.2	8.1	25.0
North Carolina	30,734	2,992	5.71	35.4	35.4	27.1	35.3
North Dakota	5,352	7,087	10.37	23.0	23.0	23.0	23.0
Ohio	40,371	3,461	6.25	28.0	28.0	28.0	28.0
Oklahoma	15,610	3,969	8.33	20.0	20.0	16.0	20.0
Oregon	13,019	3,140	5.76	34.0	34.0	26.2	34.0
Pennsylvania	43,927	3,434	5.84	57.6	74.1	42.5	57.6
Rhode Island	3,229	3,057	5.45	34.0	34.0	33.0	34.0
South Carolina	18,962	3,776	8.55	20.0	20.0	20.0	20.0
South Dakota	3,836	4,393	7.73	30.0	30.0	20.0	16.0
Tennessee	24,093	3,591	6.93	25.0	24.0	19.0	25.0
Texas	128,571	4,540	7.77	20.0	20.0	15.0	20.0
Utah	9,278	2,990	5.60	29.4	29.4	24.5	29.4
Vermont	2,589	4,145	7.94	30.5	31.0	0.0	0.0
Virginia	27,218	3,215	5.33	16.2	20.2	16.2	16.2
Washington	23,938	3,224	4.58	49.4	49.4	49.4	49.4
West Virginia	7,470	4,111	10.22	35.7	35.7	20.0	35.7
Wisconsin	20,408	3,523	6.35	30.9	30.9	22.6	30.9
Wyoming	4,442	7,672	11.81	24.0	24.0	24.0	24.0

[4]Expenditures are in nominal dollars and include taxes where data are available. Population estimated as of July 1.
[5]As of January 1 of the year shown. States vary in taxation of food and in local/state taxation practices. The United States entries are federal taxes. See the source for details.
(X) = Not applicable

Table A-39. Personal Income by State

Geographic area	Personal income, current dollars (billion dollars)										
	2018	2017	2016	2015	2014	2013	2012	2011	2010	2009	2008
United States	17,813	16,870	16,112	15,709	14,983	14,176	13,998	13,315	12,542	12,051	12,439
Alabama.....................	206	197	191	188	180	174	173	168	162	155	157
Alaska.......................	44	42	42	42	41	39	39	38	35	33	33
Arizona......................	318	300	282	271	257	243	237	226	216	212	223
Arkansas	130	125	120	117	114	107	107	100	93	90	92
California....................	2,514	2,370	2,264	2,172	2,021	1,886	1,852	1,738	1,628	1,554	1,607
Colorado	333	311	290	284	271	249	237	223	205	199	209
Connecticut.................	273	258	250	245	239	228	233	229	222	214	217
Delaware	51	48	46	45	43	41	40	40	37	36	36
District of Columbia	58	55	53	51	47	44	43	42	38	36	35
Florida........................	1,066	1,004	942	916	856	795	793	765	725	683	727
Georgia	489	464	440	424	401	374	369	359	335	328	334
Hawaii	79	76	73	70	67	63	62	60	57	56	56
Idaho.........................	77	72	68	66	62	58	56	53	50	48	50
Illinois	724	690	671	663	637	608	593	568	540	525	552
Indiana.......................	316	301	290	282	271	260	257	245	230	220	226
Iowa	158	149	145	144	139	134	132	126	116	113	116
Kansas	150	142	138	138	136	133	130	123	113	111	115
Kentucky	190	183	176	173	166	158	157	151	144	139	141
Louisiana	215	205	200	201	198	189	187	177	171	164	168
Maine.........................	65	62	60	58	56	53	53	52	50	49	49
Maryland.....................	383	365	354	342	326	314	315	306	289	279	281
Massachusetts	495	468	447	432	406	385	382	366	348	332	336
Michigan.....................	484	461	447	432	409	390	387	371	350	337	355
Minnesota	323	306	294	287	274	260	257	242	226	217	226
Mississippi	113	109	106	105	103	101	99	96	92	88	90
Missouri	293	279	270	262	253	244	242	230	221	216	220
Montana.....................	50	48	46	45	43	41	40	38	36	34	34
Nebraska....................	103	97	95	96	92	87	86	84	75	71	72
Nevada	149	139	131	126	117	109	109	105	101	97	103
New Hampshire.............	83	79	76	73	70	67	68	65	62	59	60
New Jersey	608	577	556	542	520	496	492	474	452	439	453
New Mexico	87	83	81	80	78	73	75	73	69	67	67
New York....................	1,342	1,286	1,203	1,163	1,115	1,070	1,057	1,004	950	913	929
North Carolina..............	479	454	433	420	398	376	380	355	342	338	351
North Dakota...............	42	40	40	41	42	39	39	33	29	26	27
Ohio..........................	570	544	524	515	496	476	469	451	422	410	421
Oklahoma...................	182	172	164	173	177	166	158	148	137	131	142
Oregon......................	213	201	190	181	168	157	154	146	139	135	140
Pennsylvania...............	720	680	660	644	619	593	588	563	534	512	524
Rhode Island...............	58	55	53	53	51	49	49	47	45	43	44
South Carolina	222	211	200	193	181	170	168	159	150	146	149
South Dakota	46	43	42	42	40	38	38	37	34	32	33
Tennessee	318	302	291	281	267	256	254	241	227	216	218
Texas........................	1,445	1,357	1,274	1,280	1,249	1,160	1,132	1,058	966	910	955
Utah..........................	146	137	129	122	113	106	103	96	89	87	90
Vermont.....................	34	32	32	31	30	29	28	27	26	25	26
Virginia......................	492	468	451	442	422	403	406	387	365	350	356
Washington.................	467	435	408	386	363	336	329	305	288	280	292
West Virginia...............	74	70	68	68	67	65	65	63	60	58	58
Wisconsin	300	285	275	269	258	248	246	235	222	216	219
Wyoming	35	33	32	33	33	31	31	28	26	24	27

Table A-39. Personal Income by State—*Continued*

Geographic area	Disposable personal income, current dollars (billion dollars)										
	2018	2017	2016	2015	2014	2013	2012	2011	2010	2009	2008
United States	15,737	14,826	14,157	13,773	13,200	12,501	12,491	11,864	11,306	10,900	10,933
Alabama	187	178	172	170	164	158	158	153	148	143	141
Alaska	40	38	38	39	38	35	36	35	33	30	30
Arizona	287	269	253	243	232	219	215	205	198	196	201
Arkansas	118	112	108	106	103	97	98	91	86	83	82
California	2,168	2,035	1,945	1,862	1,745	1,633	1,628	1,529	1,450	1,392	1,395
Colorado	293	271	252	248	238	219	210	197	184	179	182
Connecticut	232	218	211	205	201	192	201	197	194	188	183
Delaware	45	42	41	40	38	36	36	36	33	33	32
District of Columbia	49	47	45	43	40	38	37	36	34	31	30
Florida	964	903	846	813	766	713	720	695	667	629	653
Georgia	437	413	391	377	357	334	332	323	304	298	297
Hawaii	70	67	65	63	60	57	57	55	52	51	50
Idaho	69	65	61	59	56	53	51	48	46	45	45
Illinois	636	602	586	576	557	530	522	501	485	474	482
Indiana	284	269	260	252	244	234	233	221	210	201	202
Iowa	142	133	130	129	125	121	119	113	106	103	104
Kansas	134	127	124	124	122	119	118	110	103	101	102
Kentucky	170	163	157	155	149	142	142	137	131	127	125
Louisiana	196	186	181	182	180	171	170	162	158	151	151
Maine	59	56	53	52	50	48	48	47	46	45	44
Maryland	333	315	307	296	283	273	277	268	257	248	243
Massachusetts	422	397	379	364	343	327	331	315	306	293	286
Michigan	430	407	395	384	364	347	347	334	319	309	316
Minnesota	280	264	253	247	238	225	227	213	202	194	197
Mississippi	104	99	97	96	95	93	92	89	85	82	82
Missouri	261	248	240	232	226	218	218	208	201	197	195
Montana	45	43	41	40	38	36	37	34	33	31	31
Nebraska	92	87	85	86	82	78	78	76	68	65	65
Nevada	134	124	117	113	105	98	99	95	92	89	92
New Hampshire	75	70	68	65	63	61	62	59	57	54	54
New Jersey	527	497	480	467	450	429	432	414	401	390	388
New Mexico	80	75	74	73	71	67	69	67	64	61	61
New York	1,134	1,081	1,009	965	931	897	905	854	820	792	770
North Carolina	426	402	383	372	355	336	343	319	311	309	313
North Dakota	38	36	36	36	37	34	35	29	27	24	24
Ohio	509	484	466	458	442	423	420	403	381	371	373
Oklahoma	166	155	149	156	160	150	144	134	126	121	127
Oregon	186	174	165	158	148	138	137	130	124	122	122
Pennsylvania	639	599	582	567	548	525	525	502	481	462	461
Rhode Island	52	49	47	47	45	43	44	42	41	39	39
South Carolina	200	190	180	174	164	154	153	145	138	134	135
South Dakota	42	39	38	38	36	35	35	34	31	30	30
Tennessee	291	275	265	257	245	236	235	223	212	202	199
Texas	1,318	1,231	1,153	1,149	1,122	1,044	1,029	960	888	840	851
Utah	130	121	114	108	101	95	93	87	81	79	80
Vermont	30	29	28	28	27	26	26	25	24	23	23
Virginia	431	408	393	386	370	354	360	341	326	313	310
Washington	418	387	362	344	326	303	300	277	265	258	264
West Virginia	67	64	61	61	60	59	59	57	55	53	52
Wisconsin	266	252	242	238	230	220	220	210	200	195	194
Wyoming	32	29	29	30	29	27	27	26	23	22	23

Table A-40. Personal Income per Capita

Geographic area	Personal income per capita (current dollars)										
	2018	2017	2016	2015	2014	2013	2012	2011	2010	2009	2008
United States	54,446	51,885	49,870	48,978	47,058	44,851	44,599	42,735	40,546	39,284	40,904
Alabama......................	42,238	40,467	39,224	38,644	37,266	36,107	35,884	34,997	33,752	32,608	33,353
Alaska..........................	59,420	56,794	56,016	57,583	55,833	52,723	53,627	52,390	49,438	47,069	47,749
Arizona........................	44,329	42,505	40,671	39,676	38,226	36,602	36,123	34,968	33,635	33,418	35,563
Arkansas.....................	43,233	41,520	40,148	39,343	38,260	36,235	36,240	33,863	31,927	31,153	31,940
California.....................	63,557	60,156	57,739	55,758	52,324	49,277	48,798	46,170	43,634	42,044	43,890
Colorado	58,456	55,335	52,262	52,133	50,700	47,298	45,659	43,570	40,682	39,982	42,689
Connecticut.................	76,456	72,213	69,741	68,288	66,485	63,554	64,917	63,804	62,089	59,973	61,165
Delaware.....................	52,507	50,350	48,505	47,961	45,988	44,335	44,077	43,894	40,825	40,690	40,722
District of Columbia	82,005	78,969	77,475	75,439	71,334	67,939	68,418	67,441	63,597	60,448	61,117
Florida.........................	50,070	47,869	45,684	45,287	43,109	40,659	41,055	40,047	38,474	36,611	39,247
Georgia	46,482	44,536	42,693	41,681	39,795	37,549	37,254	36,580	34,522	34,042	35,175
Hawaii.........................	55,418	53,145	51,032	49,480	47,246	44,955	44,774	43,534	41,921	41,352	42,080
Idaho..........................	43,901	42,094	40,670	39,857	37,896	36,200	35,188	33,515	31,957	31,186	32,722
Illinois.........................	56,839	53,943	52,273	51,519	49,444	47,113	46,044	44,140	42,092	41,042	43,267
Indiana........................	47,149	45,225	43,741	42,627	41,099	39,648	39,334	37,653	35,454	34,102	35,228
Iowa...........................	50,124	47,458	46,431	46,224	44,799	43,472	42,906	40,952	38,104	37,136	38,537
Kansas	51,471	48,869	47,510	47,386	46,874	45,958	45,118	42,719	39,562	39,088	40,791
Kentucky.....................	42,458	40,999	39,638	39,093	37,584	35,919	35,753	34,626	33,141	32,157	32,757
Louisiana	46,242	43,938	42,726	43,034	42,684	40,911	40,556	38,710	37,649	36,457	37,891
Maine..........................	48,905	46,570	44,839	43,619	41,818	40,165	40,288	39,472	37,910	37,055	37,054
Maryland......................	63,354	60,512	59,029	57,139	54,687	53,052	53,546	52,437	50,007	48,755	49,428
Massachusetts.............	71,683	68,233	65,473	63,583	59,954	57,372	57,332	55,305	53,061	50,942	51,916
Michigan......................	48,423	46,258	44,868	43,533	41,147	39,361	39,059	37,512	35,391	34,030	35,700
Minnesota	57,515	54,919	53,209	52,315	50,254	47,941	47,860	45,353	42,606	41,015	43,104
Mississippi..................	37,834	36,375	35,613	35,022	34,545	33,852	33,309	32,163	30,902	29,855	30,479
Missouri......................	47,746	45,744	44,336	43,096	41,775	40,324	40,133	38,343	36,823	36,182	37,054
Montana......................	47,538	45,312	43,721	43,504	41,900	40,176	40,320	38,184	35,895	34,260	35,253
Nebraska.....................	53,263	50,663	49,703	50,588	48,948	46,592	46,562	45,429	40,920	39,264	40,225
Nevada........................	49,176	46,914	44,967	44,065	41,484	39,271	39,651	38,550	37,227	36,078	38,734
New Hampshire............	61,294	58,397	56,480	54,788	52,673	50,754	51,005	48,938	46,784	44,892	45,694
New Jersey	68,236	64,924	62,701	61,110	58,655	56,045	55,583	53,696	51,419	50,149	52,005
New Mexico	41,609	39,521	38,825	38,261	37,182	35,079	35,725	35,003	33,542	32,729	33,443
New York.....................	68,668	65,644	61,226	59,141	56,743	54,491	53,982	51,498	48,972	47,277	48,328
North Carolina.............	46,117	44,180	42,651	41,851	40,064	38,200	38,970	36,767	35,682	35,802	37,687
North Dakota...............	55,452	52,669	52,525	53,845	56,316	53,824	55,426	47,994	43,492	39,643	40,384
Ohio............................	48,739	46,651	45,040	44,340	42,754	41,098	40,634	39,071	36,575	35,532	36,596
Oklahoma....................	46,233	43,634	41,871	44,245	45,540	43,097	41,469	39,043	36,544	35,338	38,568
Oregon........................	50,843	48,372	46,498	45,182	42,483	40,015	39,601	37,821	36,122	35,481	37,067
Pennsylvania...............	56,225	53,144	51,614	50,378	48,431	46,411	46,019	44,210	42,047	40,390	41,512
Rhode Island...............	54,850	52,379	50,541	50,053	48,165	46,225	46,283	44,675	42,945	40,766	41,755
South Carolina	43,702	42,081	40,404	39,496	37,622	35,731	35,572	34,077	32,458	31,727	32,962
South Dakota	52,216	49,554	48,627	48,655	46,959	45,245	45,183	44,618	41,163	39,395	40,909
Tennessee	46,900	44,950	43,726	42,593	40,801	39,427	39,312	37,627	35,653	34,260	34,830
Texas..........................	50,355	47,929	45,616	46,577	46,289	43,781	43,397	41,244	38,274	36,711	39,271
Utah............................	46,320	44,002	42,375	40,867	38,517	36,725	36,139	34,200	32,156	31,833	33,857
Vermont......................	54,173	51,976	50,796	49,582	47,802	45,941	45,356	43,790	41,444	40,275	40,904
Virginia........................	57,799	55,306	53,605	52,892	50,754	48,855	49,585	47,775	45,496	44,122	45,437
Washington..................	62,026	58,550	55,884	53,840	51,518	48,304	47,768	44,709	42,676	41,958	44,558
West Virginia................	40,873	38,644	36,931	36,915	36,153	34,946	35,118	34,131	32,320	31,361	31,258
Wisconsin	51,592	49,290	47,550	46,681	44,939	43,184	43,034	41,178	38,997	38,070	38,910
Wyoming	60,361	56,377	54,610	57,101	56,708	52,892	53,527	49,992	45,714	43,738	48,593

Table A-40. Personal Income per Capita—*Continued*

Geographic area	Disposable personal income per capita (current dollars)										
	2018	2017	2016	2015	2014	2013	2012	2011	2010	2009	2008
United States	48,101	45,598	43,821	42,941	41,460	39,554	39,796	38,076	36,550	35,533	35,952
Alabama......................	38,215	36,474	35,382	34,945	33,855	32,770	32,805	31,861	30,992	29,994	29,972
Alaska	54,430	51,751	51,194	52,381	50,995	48,142	49,449	48,123	45,697	43,543	43,141
Arizona.......................	39,955	38,196	36,490	35,591	34,501	33,005	32,834	31,712	30,918	30,844	32,012
Arkansas.....................	39,171	37,443	36,185	35,516	34,621	32,750	33,039	30,788	29,278	28,545	28,699
California.....................	54,800	51,644	49,601	47,798	45,171	42,651	42,890	40,624	38,860	37,674	38,100
Colorado	51,405	48,341	45,492	45,521	44,493	41,578	40,420	38,484	36,377	35,961	37,308
Connecticut.................	65,063	60,909	59,090	57,281	55,911	53,357	55,794	54,909	54,307	52,725	51,566
Delaware	46,406	44,384	42,942	42,484	40,912	39,377	39,402	39,149	36,869	36,824	35,747
District of Columbia	70,167	67,127	65,928	63,871	60,782	57,908	58,843	58,434	55,855	52,744	51,884
Florida........................	45,273	43,058	40,989	40,216	38,546	36,465	37,244	36,391	35,368	33,714	35,269
Georgia	41,578	39,639	37,951	36,990	35,473	33,474	33,560	32,910	31,317	30,990	31,232
Hawaii........................	49,487	47,326	45,491	44,155	42,464	40,434	40,707	39,589	38,424	37,808	37,633
Idaho..........................	39,587	37,833	36,535	35,928	34,318	32,797	32,090	30,567	29,411	28,699	29,380
Illinois........................	49,890	47,091	45,717	44,807	43,180	41,102	40,551	38,930	37,800	37,021	37,837
Indiana.......................	42,383	40,457	39,149	38,195	37,014	35,671	35,648	33,963	32,291	31,143	31,436
Iowa...........................	44,965	42,304	41,461	41,309	40,183	38,967	38,661	36,963	34,724	33,926	34,559
Kansas	46,057	43,627	42,636	42,489	42,067	41,232	40,738	38,431	35,875	35,582	36,202
Kentucky	38,075	36,588	35,361	34,925	33,753	32,281	32,373	31,258	30,161	29,319	29,236
Louisiana	42,055	39,779	38,746	39,103	38,651	37,052	36,986	35,480	34,703	33,521	34,002
Maine.........................	43,909	41,603	40,020	39,063	37,649	36,086	36,500	35,710	34,626	33,864	33,166
Maryland.....................	55,128	52,275	51,091	49,431	47,452	46,059	47,013	45,951	44,321	43,202	42,795
Massachusetts.............	61,147	57,826	55,453	53,624	50,755	48,765	49,709	47,699	46,563	44,993	44,187
Michigan.....................	42,979	40,841	39,648	38,611	36,652	35,029	35,110	33,780	32,253	31,171	31,816
Minnesota...................	49,902	47,345	45,883	45,097	43,625	41,606	42,158	39,907	37,952	36,693	37,462
Mississippi..................	34,752	33,268	32,608	32,097	31,777	31,118	30,793	29,777	28,591	27,788	27,842
Missouri......................	42,647	40,653	39,422	38,286	37,341	36,090	36,249	34,579	33,558	33,003	32,892
Montana......................	42,627	40,439	38,989	38,728	37,341	35,975	36,388	34,583	32,841	31,256	31,495
Nebraska.....................	47,931	45,321	44,517	45,386	43,876	41,841	42,115	41,307	37,353	35,965	36,030
Nevada.......................	44,046	41,805	39,975	39,528	37,372	35,174	36,034	35,142	34,134	33,046	34,778
New Hampshire............	54,991	52,026	50,333	48,987	47,369	45,811	46,524	44,412	42,940	41,366	41,009
New Jersey	59,180	55,873	54,033	52,593	50,776	48,470	48,849	46,911	45,544	44,532	44,564
New Mexico	38,068	35,979	35,352	34,807	33,853	31,913	32,833	32,108	31,017	30,123	30,321
New York.....................	58,005	55,197	51,369	49,056	47,379	45,675	46,223	43,820	42,250	41,003	40,095
North Carolina..............	41,049	39,137	37,727	37,089	35,781	34,100	35,194	33,029	32,444	32,669	33,629
North Dakota...............	50,037	47,264	47,316	48,006	49,697	47,463	49,461	42,982	39,669	36,335	36,262
Ohio	43,579	41,472	40,039	39,411	38,104	36,573	36,387	34,941	33,036	32,221	32,372
Oklahoma...................	42,008	39,471	37,891	39,991	41,279	39,041	37,680	35,415	33,598	32,485	34,584
Oregon	44,397	41,992	40,330	39,303	37,221	35,057	35,196	33,535	32,433	31,978	32,497
Pennsylvania................	49,869	46,825	45,534	44,358	42,865	41,123	41,159	39,412	37,863	36,458	36,555
Rhode Island...............	48,742	46,238	44,637	44,316	42,726	41,055	41,629	39,969	38,961	37,035	36,979
South Carolina	39,401	37,755	36,216	35,529	34,058	32,272	32,448	31,037	29,842	29,214	29,730
South Dakota	47,755	45,027	44,227	44,268	42,787	41,378	41,557	41,274	38,423	36,845	37,513
Tennessee	42,922	40,956	39,853	38,927	37,460	36,285	36,452	34,860	33,300	32,075	31,898
Texas.........................	45,904	43,467	41,278	41,816	41,574	39,424	39,450	37,448	35,194	33,887	35,017
Utah	41,278	39,045	37,563	36,338	34,403	32,840	32,591	30,936	29,337	28,993	30,212
Vermont......................	48,620	46,444	45,485	44,448	42,944	41,346	41,216	39,648	37,993	36,957	36,564
Virginia.......................	50,627	48,162	46,738	46,154	44,504	42,848	43,985	42,145	40,612	39,498	39,621
Washington..................	55,452	52,165	49,670	48,030	46,268	43,494	43,471	40,567	39,235	38,737	40,163
West Virginia...............	37,061	34,985	33,433	33,300	32,656	31,617	31,984	30,861	29,568	28,701	28,069
Wisconsin	45,733	43,441	41,908	41,239	39,962	38,292	38,548	36,818	35,234	34,418	34,333
Wyoming	54,713	50,801	49,312	51,092	50,549	47,025	47,690	45,337	41,574	40,153	42,794

Table A-41. Earnings by Industry, 2018

Geographic area	Private earnings[1] (millions dollars)								
	Mining, quarrying, and oil and gas extraction (2017, NAICS 21)	Utilities (2017, NAICS 22)	Construction (2017, NAICS 23)	Manufacturing (2017, NAICS 31-33)	Wholesale trade (2017, NAICS 42)	Retail trade (2017, NAICS 44-45)	Transportation and warehousing (2017, NAICS 48-49)	Information (2017, NAICS 51)	Finance and insurance (2017, NAICS 52)
United States	158,353	100,500	771,088	1,155,693	586,568	705,796	492,416	438,069	894,866
Alabama	795	2,024	8,179	19,271	6,005	8,542	4,932	1,649	7,254
Alaska	2,426	309	2,198	959	529	1,694	2,105	539	686
Arizona	1,873	1,956	13,539	16,480	9,947	14,750	7,444	5,083	17,218
Arkansas	579	985	4,565	10,117	3,980	5,143	4,014	807	3,176
California	3,442	13,755	98,190	161,096	75,988	91,985	58,937	124,141	98,945
Colorado	14,127	1,270	18,773	13,669	11,294	12,091	9,603	6,360	14,302
Connecticut	167	945	9,487	19,790	7,424	9,279	5,137	4,279	27,167
Delaware	(D)	354	2,324	2,272	1,009	2,097	964	388	5,397
District of Columbia	55	454	1,493	157	722	1,094	573	3,033	3,790
Florida	519	4,386	44,261	30,884	33,722	47,123	23,552	16,682	46,478
Georgia	954	3,285	20,576	31,926	21,804	20,584	18,082	20,716	22,465
Hawaii	30	604	4,474	989	1,447	3,328	2,418	886	1,683
Idaho	252	386	3,988	6,066	2,275	4,050	1,673	645	2,206
Illinois	1,133	4,808	26,047	56,718	32,393	25,296	24,621	11,346	44,861
Indiana	631	1,960	13,677	45,236	10,638	12,807	10,120	2,617	10,215
Iowa	213	852	7,754	18,287	5,592	6,346	4,673	1,950	9,500
Kansas	1,597	917	5,878	13,022	5,316	5,572	5,633	3,439	6,400
Kentucky	791	851	7,668	19,236	6,048	7,712	8,072	1,783	7,301
Louisiana	6,739	1,173	14,037	13,903	6,059	9,084	6,747	1,761	5,844
Maine	25	215	3,069	3,914	1,621	3,235	1,112	534	2,456
Maryland	131	2,645	17,224	11,135	8,757	12,555	6,700	7,676	14,258
Massachusetts	142	2,711	22,604	27,938	15,278	16,444	7,490	13,478	37,389
Michigan	671	3,644	18,504	55,787	17,112	19,042	8,380	5,293	16,177
Minnesota	759	1,909	13,979	28,206	14,350	12,327	8,380	4,900	19,603
Mississippi	607	933	4,049	9,559	2,660	5,246	3,193	750	2,679
Missouri	337	1,698	12,538	22,730	11,057	11,993	7,511	4,765	15,861
Montana	1,179	344	2,826	1,402	1,271	2,576	1,280	494	1,447
Nebraska	145	1,563	4,379	7,175	3,731	4,183	7,403	1,520	5,752
Nevada	1,726	643	7,629	4,325	3,409	6,700	4,576	1,917	3,930
New Hampshire.............	73	341	4,151	6,494	3,228	4,308	871	1,488	3,714
New Jersey	863	3,051	21,457	31,134	25,583	23,244	16,870	11,013	32,863
New Mexico	2,833	499	3,579	1,776	1,483	3,613	1,671	899	1,941
New York	2,909	7,857	46,059	40,651	37,828	45,625	24,884	53,436	156,802
North Carolina.............	318	2,559	21,167	36,848	17,289	19,515	10,068	8,611	23,195
North Dakota...............	2,747	535	2,687	1,822	2,120	1,942	1,927	626	1,602
Ohio	2,243	2,906	24,072	58,528	21,587	22,781	18,084	6,703	25,095
Oklahoma	10,625	1,502	7,612	11,716	4,671	7,107	12,333	2,069	5,102
Oregon	164	793	10,647	17,632	6,956	9,571	4,863	3,982	6,431
Pennsylvania	4,540	3,906	30,161	48,479	21,907	25,229	26,474	24,272	30,130
Rhode Island................	(D)	198	2,244	3,170	1,722	2,285	761	574	3,217
South Carolina	176	1,592	9,533	20,106	6,250	9,621	4,548	2,952	7,881
South Dakota	97	240	2,132	3,101	1,665	2,170	977	509	3,133
Tennessee	329	398	15,619	27,307	11,119	15,551	13,125	4,289	12,861
Texas........................	80,828	9,986	85,047	91,855	58,338	59,740	60,103	22,098	71,941
Utah	831	793	8,872	10,410	4,920	8,194	4,537	3,802	6,921
Vermont	60	210	1,635	2,289	738	1,596	455	349	974
Virginia......................	649	2,099	18,715	18,915	11,220	16,232	9,958	5,759	18,700
Washington..................	504	730	22,691	29,423	13,244	28,296	11,086	29,554	12,539
West Virginia...............	2,471	706	4,102	3,800	1,542	2,964	1,635	606	1,446
Wisconsin	351	1,678	13,288	37,052	11,020	12,150	7,559	4,785	13,350
Wyoming	2,655	343	1,711	938	701	1,185	2,549	262	590

[1]All data estimates are in current dollars (not adjusted for inflation).
(D) = Data withheld to avoid disclosure or does not meet statistical standards, but the estimates for this item are included in the total.

Table A-41. Earnings by Industry, 2018—*Continued*

Geographic area	Private earnings[1] (million dollars)									Government and government enterprises		
	Real estate and rental and leasing (2017, NAICS 53)	Professional, scientific, and technical services (2017, NAICS 54)	Management of companies and enterprises (2017, NAICS 55)	Administrative and support and waste management and remediation services (2017, NAICS 56)	Educational services (2017, NAICS 61)	Health care and social assistance (2017, NAICS 62)	Arts, entertainment, and recreation (2017, NAICS 71)	Accommodation and food services (2017, NAICS 72)	Other services (except public administration) (2017, NAICS 81)	Federal, civilian	Military	State and local
United States	306,940	1,303,200	338,084	534,961	209,796	1,381,112	161,027	430,641	451,201	347,908	138,064	1,498,742
Alabama	1,955	11,809	1,882	5,129	1,139	14,845	638	4,191	5,581	6,441	1,832	19,179
Alaska	563	1,629	321	861	179	3,947	242	1,164	997	1,776	2,121	5,906
Arizona	5,903	17,083	3,215	13,601	3,274	26,847	2,963	8,816	7,685	6,334	2,252	25,194
Arkansas	1,403	4,075	4,755	2,932	705	10,192	342	2,413	3,106	2,074	708	10,598
California	58,031	221,379	40,653	74,488	26,665	167,510	31,725	62,509	62,184	30,659	15,984	240,179
Colorado	6,375	30,399	6,549	9,836	2,749	21,300	4,145	8,891	8,642	6,475	4,102	25,923
Connecticut	3,657	16,442	5,831	6,436	5,158	19,682	1,799	4,725	5,618	2,038	808	19,581
Delaware	850	3,911	1,335	1,586	381	5,075	312	1,224	1,128	614	475	4,527
District of Columbia	1,568	25,544	710	3,041	3,816	5,879	1,040	3,114	8,581	33,553	1,433	4,810
Florida	17,706	63,235	14,474	37,570	8,814	79,515	11,925	31,386	28,499	15,934	7,204	65,832
Georgia	8,890	34,409	10,455	17,842	5,354	34,514	2,526	11,252	11,355	11,630	6,818	38,036
Hawaii	1,864	3,122	1,006	2,619	820	5,616	735	5,309	2,269	3,901	4,890	7,106
Idaho	904	3,618	756	2,408	503	5,916	448	1,685	1,687	1,343	491	6,224
Illinois	12,765	62,037	14,454	25,128	10,701	54,664	6,853	16,849	19,881	9,237	2,720	59,219
Indiana	9,206	13,183	4,215	8,921	3,144	28,310	2,037	6,458	8,477	4,058	766	21,521
Iowa	1,424	5,459	1,995	3,194	1,501	11,371	618	2,909	3,891	1,701	399	15,497
Kansas	3,928	7,699	2,892	4,335	908	11,505	608	2,811	3,955	2,538	2,522	12,839
Kentucky	1,989	7,478	2,195	5,471	1,223	16,367	787	4,622	4,870	3,521	3,573	15,984
Louisiana	3,133	10,400	2,310	5,649	2,106	17,590	1,496	5,847	5,660	3,368	2,171	19,232
Maine	632	3,112	1,128	1,643	844	6,824	473	1,954	1,550	1,727	407	5,284
Maryland	12,184	34,422	4,083	10,690	5,530	27,771	3,240	7,623	9,310	26,746	4,208	29,309
Massachusetts	6,267	61,441	11,609	13,157	14,027	47,048	5,413	11,159	11,160	5,588	937	36,485
Michigan	7,696	35,538	10,273	14,756	3,665	40,514	2,623	10,017	12,002	5,966	738	39,037
Minnesota	3,629	21,484	12,000	7,594	3,252	31,257	2,632	6,015	7,957	3,501	706	26,344
Mississippi	897	3,185	1,208	2,604	739	8,314	313	3,038	2,791	2,602	1,541	11,491
Missouri	3,632	19,011	8,703	8,199	3,361	25,782	2,363	6,678	7,943	6,078	2,000	22,440
Montana	800	2,173	194	931	223	4,570	441	1,430	1,243	1,367	438	4,318
Nebraska	1,126	4,609	2,387	2,793	837	8,494	470	1,850	2,527	1,729	873	9,421
Nevada	2,037	6,954	4,182	4,833	679	9,247	2,532	14,591	3,367	2,064	1,336	11,905
New Hampshire.............	1,008	5,569	1,022	2,578	1,549	6,924	944	2,048	2,143	922	174	5,430
New Jersey	9,473	47,563	16,369	20,160	6,178	44,849	4,666	11,049	12,830	5,922	1,279	48,843
New Mexico	829	6,146	484	2,177	474	6,759	503	2,396	1,950	3,273	1,364	9,762
New York....................	27,932	119,460	25,071	36,991	28,524	111,503	20,249	30,140	31,629	13,631	3,224	139,166
North Carolina.............	6,700	30,508	10,883	15,059	6,031	33,542	3,878	11,769	11,928	7,598	10,797	42,250
North Dakota	955	1,546	546	767	164	3,991	143	826	1,055	914	779	3,980
Ohio	6,555	30,138	18,728	17,066	5,306	52,885	5,438	12,155	14,580	8,992	1,816	48,912
Oklahoma..................	1,898	7,044	1,981	5,167	977	12,954	793	3,996	4,433	5,104	2,320	16,182
Oregon	4,164	11,901	6,784	5,612	1,771	18,494	1,624	6,162	5,572	3,201	470	21,061
Pennsylvania...............	9,719	49,063	19,716	16,751	15,778	69,240	5,966	12,796	17,787	10,900	1,495	49,577
Rhode Island...............	651	3,139	1,934	1,594	1,482	5,209	523	1,473	1,397	1,347	481	4,488
South Carolina	3,090	11,373	2,247	8,096	1,497	13,516	1,089	6,333	5,746	3,515	3,683	21,260
South Dakota	500	1,326	621	621	289	4,722	200	1,064	1,141	1,098	455	3,461
Tennessee	5,503	17,174	6,215	11,806	3,144	35,010	4,985	9,063	9,677	5,852	815	23,525
Texas........................	25,899	106,515	20,727	48,930	10,678	99,705	8,901	35,564	36,813	23,543	13,041	115,049
Utah.........................	3,441	10,487	2,115	4,591	2,280	9,200	1,094	3,120	4,688	3,778	812	12,673
Vermont.....................	299	1,816	222	746	795	3,301	242	1,082	867	802	146	3,187
Virginia	5,983	60,283	11,273	16,875	4,363	30,867	2,675	10,050	13,172	27,735	13,117	37,627
Washington.................	7,119	30,363	6,219	11,892	2,752	32,526	3,048	10,721	10,171	8,902	6,051	41,552
West Virginia..............	649	3,151	686	1,742	349	7,374	254	1,669	1,632	2,713	300	6,302
Wisconsin	3,007	12,731	8,383	7,004	3,015	26,461	1,944	5,631	7,420	2,857	610	26,731
Wyoming....................	553	1,065	89	492	101	1,615	126	1,004	651	745	383	4,302

[1] All data estimates are in current dollars (not adjusted for inflation).
(D) = Data withheld to avoid disclosure or does not meet statistical standards, but the estimates for this item are included in the total.

Table A-42. Gross Domestic Product per State

Geographic area	Current dollars (millions)						Chained (millions of 2012 dollars)					
	2018	2017	2016	2015	2014	2013	2018	2017	2016	2015	2014	2013
United States	20,580,223	19,519,424	18,715,040	18,224,780	17,527,258	16,784,851	18,638,164	18,108,082	17,688,890	17,403,843	16,912,038	16,495,369
Alabama......................	221,736	210,364	203,830	200,403	194,211	191,481	198,436	193,024	190,703	189,339	186,849	188,165
Alaska........................	54,734	51,803	49,363	50,642	55,523	56,623	53,092	52,727	52,711	53,799	53,273	54,750
Arizona.......................	348,297	327,496	311,091	297,141	284,430	275,199	311,706	299,406	289,230	280,230	273,677	270,149
Arkansas.....................	128,419	123,383	120,375	118,761	117,337	114,252	117,294	115,347	114,541	113,861	112,932	111,779
California....................	2,997,733	2,819,111	2,657,798	2,553,772	2,395,162	2,262,771	2,721,651	2,610,682	2,500,950	2,428,598	2,312,540	2,220,868
Colorado	371,750	350,004	329,368	318,555	306,571	288,305	341,077	329,574	316,752	309,180	295,699	282,534
Connecticut.................	275,727	268,311	263,696	260,073	248,865	246,632	244,926	243,683	242,794	242,911	237,784	241,081
Delaware	73,481	70,775	69,550	70,969	66,891	60,666	62,765	62,740	63,109	65,876	63,500	59,157
District of Columbia	140,661	134,043	129,826	125,212	119,841	114,891	123,982	121,011	119,567	117,238	114,911	112,678
Florida........................	1,039,236	985,665	938,774	895,146	839,484	800,704	924,873	896,117	866,731	839,124	805,278	784,090
Georgia	592,153	566,474	539,525	513,566	485,817	460,585	528,999	516,594	498,267	481,576	465,646	450,772
Hawaii	93,798	89,429	85,844	82,710	77,854	75,788	82,652	80,716	78,905	77,185	74,529	74,278
Idaho..........................	77,052	72,723	69,029	66,004	63,522	61,018	70,500	67,818	65,535	63,098	61,395	59,831
Illinois........................	865,310	826,818	806,316	792,999	765,348	739,628	769,801	753,638	747,168	744,518	735,036	724,616
Indiana.......................	366,801	351,106	338,126	330,032	324,935	308,682	329,299	322,746	316,636	311,601	313,741	303,920
Iowa...........................	189,702	181,846	179,547	178,473	171,561	160,300	172,072	168,435	168,876	169,375	165,088	156,637
Kansas	168,318	161,220	156,857	152,374	148,226	143,221	154,583	151,466	149,928	146,173	143,425	140,506
Kentucky.....................	208,088	200,715	195,342	191,923	186,523	182,359	187,216	184,541	182,619	181,323	179,989	179,390
Louisiana	257,288	239,204	227,227	234,299	238,680	228,967	237,372	231,373	228,253	232,458	233,676	226,616
Maine.........................	64,856	62,040	59,754	57,526	55,795	53,719	57,450	56,189	54,971	53,781	53,418	52,505
Maryland.....................	412,584	394,259	384,889	367,097	352,047	341,255	368,860	360,030	356,818	345,230	338,734	334,939
Massachusetts.............	569,488	540,786	519,408	502,858	473,279	454,346	506,073	490,840	478,961	471,135	453,884	444,866
Michigan.....................	527,096	505,561	491,774	474,301	449,128	432,718	470,529	459,129	452,269	442,482	431,511	424,320
Minnesota	368,852	351,417	339,100	329,493	319,779	306,153	333,920	325,323	319,130	313,086	309,239	300,633
Mississippi..................	114,834	110,223	107,097	105,883	104,146	101,638	102,837	101,516	100,657	100,243	100,118	99,622
Missouri......................	318,921	304,946	297,583	294,795	284,713	277,851	284,924	278,192	275,501	276,700	273,171	271,902
Montana......................	50,327	47,559	45,458	46,153	44,496	43,141	46,220	45,029	44,265	44,871	43,174	42,434
Nebraska.....................	123,978	120,517	116,194	115,328	111,162	107,604	114,170	113,110	110,812	110,326	107,166	105,038
Nevada.......................	169,310	158,848	151,215	144,232	135,153	130,621	149,780	143,733	139,296	135,429	130,000	128,273
New Hampshire.............	84,464	80,900	78,478	76,033	72,340	70,182	75,833	74,119	72,816	71,511	69,545	68,800
New Jersey	622,003	595,325	582,428	569,680	546,687	533,687	555,755	543,530	539,943	535,299	525,729	523,334
New Mexico	100,297	94,267	91,044	90,969	92,481	88,411	93,605	91,344	91,268	91,201	89,275	86,506
New York.....................	1,668,866	1,604,134	1,539,555	1,487,754	1,427,495	1,355,581	1,435,636	1,418,942	1,389,681	1,372,163	1,349,268	1,319,299
North Carolina.............	563,691	538,402	519,122	503,629	475,995	455,522	497,331	485,499	475,339	469,479	455,046	445,361
North Dakota...............	56,082	52,472	50,833	55,012	58,650	53,882	52,873	51,015	51,036	54,902	56,523	52,531
Ohio...........................	675,905	645,326	622,835	610,772	593,355	561,046	196,525	191,544	190,110	195,902	187,739	550,800
Oklahoma....................	202,554	188,368	178,913	185,937	195,023	182,618	216,562	208,626	200,948	191,999	181,861	177,602
Oregon.......................	239,783	226,619	215,050	203,159	188,880	179,383	711,822	693,676	689,844	681,235	666,494	175,805
Pennsylvania...............	783,168	744,290	726,164	711,205	691,188	663,901	53,625	52,989	53,091	53,097	52,134	651,319
Rhode Island...............	60,588	58,506	57,694	56,759	54,427	53,210	201,873	195,460	189,900	183,562	178,940	52,085
South Carolina	233,930	223,111	212,987	203,921	191,938	183,015	207,203	201,873	195,460	189,900	183,562	178,940
South Dakota	52,015	49,739	48,606	47,752	46,047	44,815	46,491	45,619	45,686	45,443	44,153	43,602
Tennessee	364,105	345,950	335,026	322,664	303,809	292,804	323,675	313,837	308,032	301,587	291,688	286,801
Texas.........................	1,802,511	1,665,632	1,565,632	1,568,457	1,572,818	1,502,250	1,712,764	1,646,264	1,600,260	1,596,362	1,523,057	1,472,104
Utah	178,138	167,255	157,883	149,372	141,260	134,252	158,800	153,129	147,414	141,703	136,082	131,902
Vermont......................	33,256	32,210	31,659	30,730	29,701	29,099	29,750	29,407	29,363	28,907	28,522	28,499
Virginia.......................	532,893	509,373	493,878	484,217	463,478	455,070	477,006	464,793	456,676	454,953	445,869	446,560
Washington..................	565,831	524,815	491,358	470,329	442,201	419,345	511,672	483,773	459,754	444,319	425,763	411,141
West Virginia................	77,438	73,163	69,721	70,281	71,919	71,038	71,481	69,904	68,901	69,761	69,874	70,159
Wisconsin	336,294	321,988	313,532	305,817	293,885	282,385	301,623	294,657	290,750	287,164	282,079	276,190
Wyoming	39,119	37,454	35,740	37,722	39,436	38,923	38,040	37,997	38,053	39,723	38,718	38,504

Table A-43. Science and Engineering Indicators

Geographic area	Employment 2018			Field of Bachelor's degree for population 25 years and older, 2018		Masters Degrees Awarded, 2016-2017		
	Computer and Mathematical Occupations	Architecture and Engineering Occupations	Life, physical and social science occupations	Science and Engineering[1]	Science and Engineering Related Fields	Natural Sciences and Mathematics	Computer sciences	Engineering[3]
United States	5,037,751	2,952,377	1,489,027	25,618,830	7,043,367	32,513	46,555	60,244
Alabama................................	52,304	42,958	14,763	246,998	95,861	396	310	1,067
Alaska..................................	6,610	7,872	5,508	56,690	14,919	31	4	53
Arizona................................	101,946	67,562	23,543	478,973	141,290	450	798	1,169
Arkansas..............................	23,332	14,654	8,236	140,700	53,798	131	878	360
California..............................	698,428	427,283	207,131	3,816,380	749,708	2,827	4,008	8,338
Colorado	130,073	76,376	34,908	630,585	134,391	637	987	1,167
Connecticut..........................	58,487	45,508	18,514	363,319	87,052	802	621	990
Delaware..............................	13,331	7,261	7,123	72,769	19,920	103	234	127
District of Columbia	24,887	6,469	13,818	145,011	14,133	869	479	379
Florida.................................	251,438	134,774	56,106	1,460,500	515,257	1,602	1,542	2,503
Georgia	166,290	71,005	35,749	712,622	217,043	865	1,378	1,169
Hawaii.................................	13,197	10,749	6,409	128,217	30,325	73	24	50
Idaho...................................	19,333	15,256	8,823	113,662	35,126	79	26	136
Illinois.................................	204,291	96,064	52,767	1,014,507	289,736	1,669	3,848	3,152
Indiana................................	74,896	65,532	22,913	352,575	152,205	512	847	1,559
Iowa....................................	40,225	25,901	13,907	184,539	59,587	202	589	313
Kansas................................	40,313	26,266	10,948	188,489	73,429	250	120	534
Kentucky..............................	43,757	30,903	12,537	218,862	88,149	232	343	414
Louisiana.............................	32,056	37,627	18,447	211,264	96,877	657	170	275
Maine..................................	15,076	11,356	7,520	104,630	32,466	36	18	25
Maryland..............................	170,775	63,068	56,163	697,694	155,325	1,033	2,375	1,187
Massachusetts......................	162,152	84,922	71,796	891,926	184,094	1,805	1,869	2,890
Michigan..............................	131,453	137,887	37,571	674,089	226,621	1,026	957	3,211
Minnesota............................	107,379	63,572	33,611	476,235	136,798	473	694	582
Mississippi...........................	16,040	15,928	8,231	114,464	61,022	483	91	170
Missouri...............................	89,357	42,793	27,440	376,017	133,953	556	2,632	1,542
Montana...............................	10,713	6,806	6,375	78,742	27,763	95	17	61
Nebraska..............................	29,303	14,610	8,540	118,935	42,438	185	553	96
Nevada................................	28,583	17,987	8,075	164,652	53,270	76	61	86
New Hampshire......................	30,205	21,727	5,453	135,163	30,906	84	973	229
New Jersey	197,169	74,218	50,202	938,615	218,934	1,102	1,654	1,789
New Mexico	17,657	19,374	15,473	147,095	37,029	146	103	319
New York..............................	267,064	132,623	92,391	1,770,012	453,127	3,289	4,496	5,403
North Carolina.......................	158,525	79,814	47,323	772,203	207,107	1,007	1,021	1,407
North Dakota.........................	6,299	4,872	2,451	36,304	25,047	56	31	83
Ohio....................................	156,949	106,398	47,603	716,872	264,958	1,429	1,296	2,488
Oklahoma.............................	37,403	30,609	12,970	195,605	67,458	228	235	828
Oregon................................	70,693	47,319	22,687	394,665	91,243	284	152	483
Pennsylvania.........................	183,542	112,963	63,276	957,966	314,613	1,463	1,996	3,411
Rhode Island.........................	13,651	10,721	5,631	90,290	25,139	169	86	142
South Carolina	52,061	48,065	14,156	313,509	94,538	316	97	473
South Dakota	8,986	6,090	3,465	51,969	19,709	65	93	131
Tennessee............................	73,151	47,702	24,969	388,355	143,223	576	230	492
Texas..................................	401,110	255,119	101,127	1,970,427	519,136	2,214	3,839	5,910
Utah....................................	64,883	27,650	14,544	222,318	67,063	210	872	385
Vermont...............................	8,952	7,089	3,085	66,321	14,996	74	77	55
Virginia................................	241,196	83,013	43,939	923,915	176,031	596	1,735	1,083
Washington...........................	193,594	91,799	42,011	791,920	167,449	573	563	679
West Virginia.........................	14,289	11,783	6,207	78,147	38,852	89	225	228
Wisconsin.............................	80,389	59,130	29,905	383,221	133,704	336	300	575
Wyoming	3,958	5,350	2,687	39,892	10,549	52	8	41

Table A-44. Employment Establishment Changes by Number of Employees and State, 2014

State	Establishments in 2014			Establishment Entries			Establishment Exits			Net Change		
	Total	< 500	500+	Total	< 500	500+	Total	< 500	500+	Total	< 500	500+
United States	6,721,320	5,523,185	1,198,135	669,912	579,006	90,906	576,940	533,653	43,287	92,972	45,353	47,619
Alabama	90,262	70,728	19,534	7,362	6,082	1,280	6,673	6,081	592	689	1	688
Alaska	17,400	14,548	2,852	1,782	1,533	249	1,576	1,449	127	206	84	122
Arizona	117,069	91,396	25,673	12,907	10,763	2,144	10,889	9,796	1,093	2,018	967	1,051
Arkansas	58,857	47,759	11,098	4,918	4,290	628	4,717	4,385	332	201	-95	296
California	777,350	657,355	119,995	88,765	79,078	9,687	72,794	68,008	4,786	15,971	11,070	4,901
Colorado	135,227	112,607	22,620	15,835	13,921	1,914	12,729	11,887	842	3,106	2,034	1,072
Connecticut	79,574	65,711	13,863	6,748	5,715	1,033	6,410	5,849	561	338	-134	472
Delaware	21,558	16,895	4,663	2,134	1,788	346	1,866	1,601	265	268	187	81
District of Columbia	20,657	15,583	5,074	1,910	1,368	542	1,555	1,293	262	355	75	280
Florida	451,333	374,378	76,955	56,329	49,873	6,456	46,565	43,421	3,144	9,764	6,452	3,312
Georgia	195,566	154,470	41,096	20,904	17,484	3,420	17,455	16,086	1,369	3,449	1,398	2,051
Hawaii	28,929	23,948	4,981	2,415	2,037	378	2,167	2,017	150	248	20	228
Idaho	38,119	32,707	5,412	4,144	3,782	362	3,316	3,145	171	828	637	191
Illinois	277,513	229,422	48,091	26,184	22,461	3,723	23,847	22,027	1,820	2,337	434	1,903
Indiana	129,939	102,952	26,987	10,539	8,661	1,878	10,149	9,192	957	390	-531	921
Iowa	72,526	60,392	12,134	5,227	4,547	680	5,033	4,668	365	194	-121	315
Kansas	66,937	55,069	11,868	5,799	4,912	887	5,108	4,697	411	691	215	476
Kentucky	83,119	65,165	17,954	7,709	6,281	1,428	6,387	5,806	581	1,322	475	847
Louisiana	95,992	78,155	17,837	8,101	6,942	1,159	7,330	6,679	651	771	263	508
Maine	34,646	29,802	4,844	3,148	2,796	352	2,809	2,605	204	339	191	148
Maryland	122,252	99,347	22,905	11,641	9,609	2,032	10,087	9,195	892	1,554	414	1,140
Massachusetts	155,069	128,741	26,328	13,632	11,818	1,814	11,851	10,967	884	1,781	851	930
Michigan	193,589	160,279	33,310	16,527	14,153	2,374	15,311	14,167	1,144	1,216	-14	1,230
Minnesota	128,612	107,688	20,924	11,089	9,832	1,257	9,746	9,117	629	1,343	715	628
Mississippi	54,161	42,775	11,386	4,409	3,688	721	4,049	3,741	308	360	-53	413
Missouri	135,732	110,027	25,705	14,898	12,916	1,982	11,546	10,762	784	3,352	2,154	1,198
Montana	31,443	27,876	3,567	3,126	2,882	244	2,858	2,745	113	268	137	131
Nebraska	47,556	39,938	7,618	3,900	3,421	479	3,258	3,013	245	642	408	234
Nevada	53,710	42,753	10,957	7,010	6,205	805	5,428	4,963	465	1,582	1,242	340
New Hampshire	33,363	27,573	5,790	2,812	2,422	390	2,578	2,367	211	234	55	179
New Jersey	203,727	173,243	30,484	20,784	18,463	2,321	19,485	18,245	1,240	1,299	218	1,081
New Mexico	39,515	31,993	7,522	3,538	3,011	527	3,398	3,166	232	140	-155	295
New York	472,460	413,111	59,349	50,830	46,176	4,654	45,122	42,888	2,234	5,708	3,288	2,420
North Carolina	196,646	156,654	39,992	18,478	15,746	2,732	16,754	15,435	1,319	1,724	311	1,413
North Dakota	21,718	18,669	3,049	2,283	2,018	265	1,720	1,594	126	563	424	139
Ohio	228,034	179,108	48,926	17,773	14,224	3,549	16,525	14,990	1,535	1,248	-766	2,014
Oklahoma	83,796	69,092	14,704	7,639	6,732	907	6,800	6,371	429	839	361	478
Oregon	97,962	83,661	14,301	9,932	8,908	1,024	8,335	7,831	504	1,597	1,077	520
Pennsylvania	272,120	219,802	52,318	22,130	18,296	3,834	20,285	18,359	1,926	1,845	-63	1,908
Rhode Island	24,752	21,034	3,718	2,126	1,878	248	2,091	1,959	132	35	-81	116
South Carolina	92,292	72,832	19,460	8,435	7,201	1,234	7,492	6,936	556	943	265	678
South Dakota	23,189	20,317	2,872	1,881	1,727	154	1,782	1,726	56	99	1	98
Tennessee	121,014	92,747	28,267	10,849	8,568	2,281	9,572	8,630	942	1,277	-62	1,339
Texas	503,220	396,894	106,326	54,930	45,736	9,194	42,352	38,265	4,087	12,578	7,471	5,107
Utah	62,972	52,876	10,096	7,502	6,745	757	5,932	5,488	444	1,570	1,257	313
Vermont	18,658	16,491	2,167	1,544	1,414	130	1,474	1,402	72	70	12	58
Virginia	176,856	139,772	37,084	16,748	13,950	2,798	14,495	13,197	1,298	2,253	753	1,500
Washington	157,519	132,880	24,639	16,724	14,923	1,801	13,997	13,133	864	2,727	1,790	937
West Virginia	34,280	26,887	7,393	2,415	1,993	422	2,751	2,526	225	-336	-533	197
Wisconsin	124,208	103,167	21,041	9,666	8,433	1,233	8,894	8,298	596	772	135	637
Wyoming	18,322	15,916	2,406	1,801	1,604	197	1,597	1,485	112	204	119	85

Notes: Longitudinal data for establishments active (payroll) in the first quarter of the year. (Establishments with no employment in the first quarter were excluded.)

Table A-45. Employer Firms and Nonemployer Establishments

Geographic area	Firms, 2017 (thousands)				Employment, 2017 (thousands)			Annual payroll, 2017 (million dollars)			Nonemployer establishments[1]			
			By employment-size of enterprise			By employment-size of enterprise			By employment-size of enterprise		Number (thousands)		Receipts (millions)	
	2017	2010	Fewer than 20 employees	Fewer than 500 employees	Total	Fewer than 20 employees	Fewer than 500 employees	Total	Fewer than 20 employees	Fewer than 500 employees	2018	2010	2018	2010
United States	5,996.9	5,734.5	5,339.9	5,976.8	128,592	21,096	60,556	6,725,347	869,102	2,711,537	26,485.5	22,110.6	1,292,866.7	950,814
Alabama	74.3	75.5	61.9	71.7	1,690	273	803	71,746	9,614	30,986	336.4	320.6	14,797.0	12,111
Alaska	17.1	16.5	15.0	16.5	262	57	137	15,008	2,847	6,975	57.4	53.3	2,793.8	2,412
Arizona	109.8	102.2	93.4	106.5	2,449	356	1,066	113,491	14,229	43,182	502.6	396.0	23,719.1	16,864
Arkansas	50.9	51.1	43.0	49.1	1,031	177	491	42,306	5,972	17,132	209.2	192.0	9,171.9	7,499
California	763.8	690.5	676.9	757.5	14,897	2,605	7,225	955,044	125,502	375,608	3,453.8	2,814.4	189,304.5	138,315
Colorado	139.7	125.8	121.9	136.3	2,372	434	1,141	126,786	18,828	52,592	535.3	426.4	26,587.4	18,688
Connecticut	71.2	72.7	59.9	68.9	1,537	253	745	95,782	11,803	37,943	286.9	255.8	17,158.9	14,243
Delaware	20.4	19.7	16.4	19.0	401	64	187	21,976	2,833	8,524	68.6	53.9	4,504.8	2,792
District of Columbia	18.4	16.9	13.3	17.0	527	59	250	41,000	4,269	17,656	62.6	46.0	3,285.4	2,230
Florida	453.2	400.8	409.9	448.4	8,386	1,375	3,494	378,219	53,642	141,825	2,388.1	1,686.1	106,471.4	68,162
Georgia	180.7	170.2	155.5	176.4	3,889	584	1,678	191,941	22,914	69,961	955.6	771.2	39,863.1	28,043
Hawaii	25.6	25.4	21.3	24.6	544	90	276	24,366	3,650	11,307	112.6	92.1	5,556.1	4,066
Idaho	39.8	36.7	34.4	38.5	578	130	325	23,565	4,471	11,507	136.0	112.3	6,336.3	4,269
Illinois	256.5	253.6	221.9	251.7	5,498	827	2,477	301,444	36,060	120,256	996.7	903.0	44,899.3	35,305
Indiana	109.7	111.0	91.4	106.4	2,779	397	1,233	122,893	13,894	47,885	422.6	380.1	18,127.0	13,839
Iowa	63.2	63.4	53.6	61.2	1,354	218	650	58,926	7,544	25,143	212.3	201.4	9,723.7	7,607
Kansas	57.9	59.2	48.3	55.7	1,199	200	605	52,755	6,962	23,519	202.4	183.6	9,509.8	7,326
Kentucky	67.3	69.6	56.0	64.8	1,625	241	713	67,733	8,016	26,228	295.8	272.5	13,198.6	10,454
Louisiana	81.4	81.3	68.1	79.1	1,689	297	905	75,416	11,032	36,297	385.1	340.6	16,923.6	14,084
Maine	34.2	33.8	29.7	33.1	514	111	294	22,350	4,107	11,289	117.3	110.4	5,469.0	4,477
Maryland	110.0	108.2	92.7	107.0	2,336	380	1,156	126,633	17,076	56,807	510.7	424.2	23,049.1	17,833
Massachusetts	144.1	137.4	123.1	140.7	3,317	502	1,508	216,666	25,075	83,946	573.8	472.5	30,907.1	23,388
Michigan	174.1	174.3	149.1	170.7	3,860	629	1,892	186,679	25,162	81,627	730.7	679.8	32,700.7	25,659
Minnesota	119.4	117.7	101.5	116.5	2,685	391	1,259	142,130	16,071	54,885	416.5	381.8	19,994.8	15,550
Mississippi	44.5	45.8	37.3	42.7	940	162	437	35,367	5,149	14,929	222.2	196.2	9,164.2	7,299
Missouri	115.4	117.8	98.0	112.3	2,517	389	1,164	116,774	13,782	45,630	426.9	390.2	19,463.4	15,298
Montana	32.8	31.4	29.1	31.9	377	107	246	14,773	3,628	8,802	93.8	83.7	4,414.9	3,324
Nebraska	43.7	42.0	37.0	42.1	834	146	413	36,415	5,100	15,808	138.7	123.9	6,305.8	4,653
Nevada	52.6	47.4	43.6	50.3	1,192	170	503	50,961	7,405	20,473	245.4	177.2	12,646.4	8,796
New Hampshire	30.8	31.0	25.5	29.5	604	108	301	30,634	4,735	14,237	108.3	102.8	6,435.5	5,164
New Jersey	194.7	193.7	169.7	191.3	3,679	664	1,836	220,310	29,547	91,086	745.5	604.7	44,074.1	32,500
New Mexico	34.5	35.7	28.5	32.9	627	121	340	25,723	4,249	12,540	125.9	120.5	5,271.5	4,434
New York	465.6	444.9	416.6	460.8	8,261	1,515	4,110	547,344	69,384	219,739	1,804.2	1,575.8	98,252.1	71,776
North Carolina	177.8	168.9	152.9	174.0	3,774	608	1,711	175,696	22,127	65,858	787.9	640.7	34,400.9	24,682
North Dakota	19.8	18.2	16.4	18.9	341	68	195	16,337	2,722	8,360	56.5	47.8	2,948.3	2,021
Ohio	183.9	190.2	154.0	179.7	4,816	690	2,180	224,628	25,427	87,857	802.3	730.4	36,988.6	28,739
Oklahoma	72.9	72.0	62.2	70.7	1,361	247	710	59,670	8,891	27,601	291.5	263.0	13,907.1	11,313
Oregon	95.0	88.0	82.3	92.7	1,597	335	871	79,111	12,375	35,729	302.7	258.8	14,894.4	11,019
Pennsylvania	230.1	231.2	196.4	225.8	5,434	839	2,513	270,593	32,267	107,956	865.0	762.4	42,770.6	34,263
Rhode Island	24.2	24.6	20.2	23.1	436	82	229	20,945	3,392	9,935	83.1	71.9	3,887.0	3,113
South Carolina	83.0	78.9	70.2	80.4	1,867	290	817	76,707	10,300	29,652	364.0	295.6	16,174.0	11,400
South Dakota	22.4	21.6	18.9	21.5	360	76	209	14,719	2,575	7,552	68.4	60.2	3,339.0	2,376
Tennessee	99.4	98.0	81.9	96.0	2,650	364	1,117	120,114	13,785	46,189	540.0	465.5	26,244.1	19,008
Texas	442.6	394.4	381.1	436.5	10,580	1,578	4,769	544,773	66,485	212,326	2,514.3	1,934.5	125,732.8	85,935
Utah	66.6	57.7	57.2	64.5	1,283	206	590	58,192	7,736	24,034	246.8	192.0	11,761.1	8,005
Vermont	18.0	18.6	15.3	17.3	259	61	157	11,052	2,291	6,375	62.0	59.9	2,727.2	2,304
Virginia	153.4	149.3	130.7	149.8	3,311	534	1,558	177,106	21,872	73,409	633.0	510.3	28,429.4	21,157
Washington	155.6	144.4	135.9	152.5	2,769	533	1,404	169,766	22,547	67,341	491.9	405.3	25,002.7	18,134
West Virginia	26.7	29.6	22.1	25.4	549	98	270	22,287	3,091	9,415	88.2	90.1	3,467.4	3,153
Wisconsin	109.0	110.4	91.1	106.3	2,561	398	1,267	121,061	14,399	50,288	355.2	331.7	17,333.5	13,829
Wyoming	18.1	17.6	15.6	17.3	202	59	129	9,436	2,273	5,336	53.0	45.6	2,778.9	1,901

[1]Nonemployer business defined as a firm with no payroll or paid employees.

Table A-46. Private Nonfarm Establishments, Employment, and Payroll

Geographic area	Establishments 2017	2010	Net change, 2010–2017	Under 20	20 to 99	100 to 499	500 or more	Employment 2017	2010	Under 20	20 to 99	100 to 499	500 or more	Annual payroll 2017	2010
United States	7,860,674	7,396,628	464,046	6,712,629	956,298	170,788	20,959	128,592	111,970	30,196	38,019	32,294	28,082	6,725	4,941
Alabama	100,419	99,251	1,168	84,589	13,294	2,244	292	1,690	1,568	422	523	428	316	72	57
Alaska	21,279	19,985	1,294	18,917	1,981	343	38	262	255	82	77	68	36	15	13
Arizona	143,306	131,849	11,457	121,177	18,483	3,215	431	2,449	2,065	542	738	612	556	113	84
Arkansas	66,786	65,158	1,628	57,076	8,229	1,308	173	1,031	965	271	320	251	189	42	34
California	941,377	849,875	91,502	809,446	110,617	18,935	2,379	14,897	12,536	3,506	4,406	3,537	3,448	955	636
Colorado	169,842	151,973	17,869	148,077	18,385	3,034	346	2,372	1,955	605	719	571	477	127	89
Connecticut	89,574	89,234	340	75,782	11,385	2,179	228	1,537	1,437	358	450	400	329	96	80
Delaware	25,452	24,290	1,162	21,742	3,109	530	71	401	359	96	122	101	81	22	17
District of Columbia	23,585	21,502	2,083	19,065	3,633	796	91	527	463	92	150	156	129	41	31
Florida	557,308	491,150	66,158	490,704	55,256	10,129	1,219	8,386	6,627	1,906	2,199	1,872	2,408	378	253
Georgia	233,500	217,099	16,401	198,573	28,793	5,457	677	3,889	3,315	869	1,145	1,036	838	192	138
Hawaii	32,800	31,939	861	27,814	4,190	695	101	544	479	133	171	130	111	24	18
Idaho	47,574	43,450	4,124	42,048	4,801	647	78	578	488	181	185	120	93	24	16
Illinois	321,135	314,171	6,964	274,348	38,213	7,581	993	5,498	4,980	1,178	1,537	1,439	1,343	301	236
Indiana	148,377	145,019	3,358	123,343	20,586	3,950	498	2,779	2,400	608	827	748	597	123	90
Iowa	82,685	80,801	1,884	70,637	10,063	1,758	227	1,354	1,253	331	392	346	285	59	45
Kansas	74,947	74,301	646	63,619	9,487	1,653	188	1,199	1,127	298	376	315	210	53	43
Kentucky	91,241	90,771	470	76,533	12,147	2,270	291	1,625	1,457	379	477	439	331	68	52
Louisiana	106,599	103,365	3,234	89,921	14,191	2,247	240	1,689	1,600	440	565	405	278	75	62
Maine	41,622	40,571	1,051	36,702	4,194	672	54	514	481	159	163	125	67	22	17
Maryland	139,446	134,579	4,867	117,307	18,524	3,286	329	2,335	2,076	540	748	599	449	127	98
Massachusetts	179,828	169,790	10,038	151,844	22,804	4,604	576	3,317	2,929	701	920	871	825	217	158
Michigan	222,553	219,119	3,434	188,468	28,181	5,248	656	3,860	3,288	894	1,125	996	845	187	139
Minnesota	151,816	145,464	6,352	128,308	19,304	3,755	449	2,685	2,358	581	772	721	611	142	106
Mississippi	59,294	59,300	-6	50,667	7,352	1,123	152	939	882	250	290	216	183	35	29
Missouri	150,882	149,903	979	127,706	19,453	3,350	373	2,517	2,293	584	773	652	507	117	89
Montana	38,192	36,011	2,181	34,374	3,423	372	23	377	338	142	131	66	38	15	11
Nebraska	54,954	51,886	3,068	47,232	6,510	1,064	148	833	769	214	250	204	165	36	28
Nevada	66,430	59,207	7,223	56,475	8,223	1,499	233	1,192	1,003	256	323	278	334	51	38
New Hampshire	38,371	37,452	919	32,773	4,712	814	72	604	563	156	185	154	109	31	24
New Jersey	233,907	228,937	4,970	201,571	26,652	5,064	620	3,679	3,367	874	1,061	958	787	220	179
New Mexico	44,039	44,221	-182	37,684	5,478	814	63	626	600	183	212	149	83	26	21
New York	547,034	519,504	27,530	480,231	55,025	10,200	1,578	8,261	7,266	1,959	2,183	1,980	2,139	547	418
North Carolina	233,363	218,104	15,259	197,511	30,400	4,853	599	3,774	3,235	905	1,220	912	738	176	125
North Dakota	24,596	21,832	2,764	21,032	3,078	453	33	341	295	100	120	86	34	16	11
Ohio	253,001	253,491	-490	209,121	36,044	7,055	781	4,816	4,352	1,054	1,453	1,329	979	225	175
Oklahoma	93,674	90,050	3,624	80,290	11,464	1,736	184	1,361	1,241	367	451	329	215	60	46
Oregon	117,357	107,397	9,960	101,893	13,260	2,003	201	1,597	1,351	468	511	375	244	79	54
Pennsylvania	302,772	297,023	5,749	254,607	39,666	7,600	899	5,434	4,976	1,222	1,592	1,447	1,173	271	212
Rhode Island	28,783	28,521	262	24,715	3,408	594	66	436	399	111	134	106	86	21	17
South Carolina	109,238	102,045	7,193	92,628	14,013	2,292	305	1,866	1,503	439	553	422	452	77	53
South Dakota	27,099	25,622	1,477	23,664	2,965	427	43	360	329	107	114	83	55	15	11
Tennessee	137,918	131,582	6,336	113,907	19,823	3,720	468	2,650	2,264	578	783	710	579	120	88
Texas	592,677	522,146	70,531	496,331	79,947	14,612	1,787	10,580	8,785	2,345	3,195	2,798	2,242	545	387
Utah	80,140	68,820	11,320	69,112	9,223	1,571	234	1,282	1,021	289	364	303	326	58	38
Vermont	21,158	21,451	-293	18,699	2,129	298	32	259	264	83	82	56	38	11	9
Virginia	201,893	193,042	8,851	170,033	26,824	4,519	517	3,311	2,998	792	1,062	859	598	177	139
Washington	191,045	175,914	15,131	165,827	21,269	3,578	371	2,769	2,327	732	833	668	536	170	111
West Virginia	36,522	38,676	-2,154	31,200	4,548	695	79	549	560	160	178	128	83	22	19
Wisconsin	142,136	139,554	2,582	118,221	19,705	3,757	453	2,561	2,321	574	790	708	490	121	91
Wyoming	21,148	20,231	917	19,085	1,854	189	20	202	205	80	69	35	17	9	8

[1]Data provided by County Business Patterns is based on the North American Industry Classification System (NAICS). Data for 2017 is based on NAICS 2017. Data for 2010 is based on NAICS 2007.
[2]Employment is measured in March.

Table A-47. Foreign Direct Investment in the United States and U.S. Exports

| Geographic area | U.S. Foreign Majority-owned Affiliates[1] | | | | U.S. exports[2] (million dollars) | | | | U.S. agriculture exports[3] (million dollars) | | |
| | Number of affiliates with assets, sales, or net income greater than $20 million in 2017[4] | Employment of affiliates[5] (thousands) | | | 2019 | | | | | | |
		2015	2016	2017	Total exports	Rank	Percent change 2010–2019	2010	2018	2015	2010
United States	6,037	7,357.7	7,155.5	6,822.8	1,645,527		28.7	1,278,115	138,915.5	133,016.2	115,806.3
Alabama............................	669	113.9	111.1	104.6	20,748	23	33.8	15,505	1,348.8	1,216.8	1,134.8
Alaska...............................	168	18.1	18.6	16.3	4,969	40	19.7	4,152	16.6	14.5	11.5
Arizona..............................	846	113.6	108.4	104.4	24,691	19	57.8	15,652	1,466.7	1,283.3	1,070.1
Arkansas............................	487	46.4	45.6	46.1	6,226	36	20.8	5,156	3,013.5	3,135.4	3,190.1
California............................	2,365	802.8	772.1	734.2	173,326	2	21.0	143,269	23,304.9	22,843.9	15,355.4
Colorado............................	864	113.1	111.9	105.0	8,100	33	21.4	6,670	1,866.3	1,650.4	1,510.5
Connecticut........................	767	108.6	104.4	102.6	16,288	26	1.6	16,033	276.3	297.3	213.9
Delaware............................	400	25.5	27.1	25.2	4,428	42	-10.8	4,965	263.5	259.5	241.5
District of Columbia...............	346	23.1	22.8	23.5	3,681	43	145.3	1,501			
Florida...............................	1,355	368.1	366.4	331.2	56,038	7	1.5	55,227	3,146.3	3,493.8	2,963.2
Georgia..............................	1,212	259.3	246.3	228.9	41,225	12	43.6	28,704	2,865.0	2,846.2	2,587.9
Hawaii...............................	303	37.3	37.7	36.7	447	51	-34.8	685	307.9	367.4	308.3
Idaho................................	367	16.8	15.2	15.6	3,431	44	-33.4	5,150	2,076.1	1,860.4	1,488.4
Illinois...............................	1,478	353.0	348.6	321.7	59,924	6	20.4	49,767	8,488.3	8,033.9	7,463.9
Indiana..............................	869	203.0	196.0	189.7	39,393	13	37.4	28,670	4,649.5	4,705.6	4,298.9
Iowa.................................	466	58.2	59.3	59.9	13,187	28	21.0	10,895	10,646.9	9,987.1	9,367.5
Kansas..............................	582	60.8	58.2	56.1	11,615	31	17.0	9,927	4,881.7	4,163.5	4,666.6
Kentucky............................	697	138.8	133.5	120.2	33,095	16	71.3	19,320	2,221.5	2,099.7	1,515.1
Louisiana	556	70.0	69.1	67.5	63,674	4	54.0	41,348	1,443.2	1,566.0	1,509.5
Maine................................	355	34.8	34.3	34.3	2,711	46	-13.9	3,148	247.2	247.6	237.0
Maryland............................	776	120.1	120.0	116.9	13,072	29	28.6	10,168	668.8	669.9	565.2
Massachusetts.....................	1,013	216.6	215.5	203.0	26,118	18	-0.5	26,256	206.1	209.6	197.9
Michigan............................	1,119	270.3	251.5	243.3	55,315	8	24.3	44,504	2,827.0	2,855.3	2,355.2
Minnesota...........................	806	133.9	123.7	113.9	22,202	21	17.3	18,929	6,942.7	6,339.2	6,113.2
Mississippi..........................	438	39.9	37.3	37.4	11,898	30	43.9	8,267	1,935.6	1,840.0	1,784.3
Missouri.............................	730	128.6	116.7	109.8	13,400	27	3.7	12,920	3,938.5	3,610.9	3,484.7
Montana.............................	239	7.8	7.5	6.8	1,657	48	16.5	1,422	1,196.0	1,182.5	1,076.5
Nebraska............................	382	31.4	30.7	31.4	7,458	34	28.5	5,804	6,802.3	6,479.3	5,335.0
Nevada..............................	569	49.8	48.7	47.8	8,979	32	51.9	5,911	137.1	135.5	111.2
New Hampshire.....................	484	44.9	44.7	41.2	5,829	39	33.4	4,368	85.0	85.8	65.4
New Jersey	1,187	284.7	281.4	270.7	35,961	14	11.8	32,156	544.3	546.2	399.0
New Mexico	341	18.1	17.8	16.9	4,796	41	207.1	1,562	751.5	750.2	681.9
New York............................	1,733	493.9	495.2	477.9	73,275	3	8.3	67,686	1,459.1	1,452.8	1,224.7
North Carolina......................	1,104	279.2	264.6	252.6	34,357	15	38.4	24,817	3,470.4	3,573.0	3,391.0
North Dakota.......................	224	12.8	12.5	13.0	6,749	35	167.6	2,522	4,245.9	3,816.9	3,690.9
Ohio.................................	1,168	272.8	266.5	257.7	52,987	9	27.9	41,437	3,682.4	3,708.0	3,406.8
Oklahoma...........................	532	50.7	51.9	49.6	6,123	37	14.2	5,360	1,810.0	1,510.8	1,541.3
Oregon..............................	670	60.6	58.9	60.6	23,527	20	33.0	17,683	2,006.9	1,869.9	1,353.4
Pennsylvania.......................	1,128	309.2	303.5	291.4	42,535	10	22.1	34,826	2,056.5	2,038.0	1,615.3
Rhode Island.......................	368	26.4	25.9	25.5	2,679	47	37.7	1,946	34.5	32.6	31.7
South Carolina	795	145.5	139.6	134.6	41,456	11	104.1	20,316	864.2	808.2	808.8
South Dakota	237	12.6	12.5	11.9	1,354	50	7.2	1,263	3,560.4	3,702.2	2,964.3
Tennessee..........................	835	182.2	178.0	164.2	31,068	17	19.8	25,924	1,471.6	1,522.3	1,241.4
Texas................................	1,772	622.7	607.2	588.5	330,502	1	59.9	206,643	6,883.2	5,739.2	6,324.8
Utah.................................	519	48.2	47.0	42.6	17,344	25	27.8	13,572	430.0	432.0	329.9
Vermont.............................	216	10.1	10.5	11.0	3,022	45	-30.9	4,376	187.3	188.3	140.0
Virginia..............................	868	194.9	186.9	180.6	17,915	24	4.8	17,090	1,094.1	1,052.0	875.2
Washington.........................	979	127.7	120.0	113.3	60,122	5	12.9	53,244	3,614.5	3,476.9	2,800.6
West Virginia.......................	315	28.1	28.4	29.4	5,920	38	-7.9	6,427	160.3	143.8	115.2
Wisconsin...........................	737	107.6	104.6	97.3	21,669	22	9.5	19,783	2,979.5	2,868.5	2,411.6
Wyoming............................	184	7.7	8.0	7.2	1,366	49	38.9	983	339.4	304.2	235.5

[1]For calendar year. U.S. business enterprises that are more than 50 percent owned by foreign direct investors.
[2]For calendar year. National total includes Puerto Rico and US Virgin Islands. Foreign Trade Zone shipments are included in the U.S. total and distributed among individual states and territories. Unreported and estimated shipments are included in national totals.
[3]For calendar year. The U.S. totals include unallocated exports not included in states.
[4]National total includes data for territories as well as unspecified data (aircraft, railroad rolling stock, satellites, undersea cable, and trucks engaged in interstate transportation) and will differ from sum of state totals.
[5]National total includes data for territories and will differ from sum of state totals.
(D) = Withheld to avoid disclosure of individual companies.
(X) = Not applicable

Table A-48. Farms and Farm Earnings

Geographic Area	Farms (USDA)[1] (as of June 1)												Farm earnings (BEA)[2] (million dollars)			
	Number (thousands)				Land in farms (million acres)				Average acreage per farm							
	2018	2015	2012	2010	2018	2015	2012	2010	2018	2015	2012	2010	2018	2015	2012	2010
United States	2,029.2	2,068.0	2,170.0	2,200.9	899.5	912.0	914.0	920.0	443	441	421	418	67,932	87,500	93,338	67,945
Alabama	39.7	43.2	46.5	48.5	8.5	8.9	8.9	9.0	214	206	190	186	1,119	1,406	689	772
Alaska	1.0	0.8	0.7	0.7	0.9	0.8	0.9	0.9	850	1,092	1,294	1,294	11	12	11	6
Arizona	19.2	19.5	15.5	15.5	26.2	26.0	26.1	26.1	1,365	1,333	1,684	1,684	1,209	1,356	880	669
Arkansas	42.5	43.5	47.8	49.3	13.9	13.8	13.5	13.7	327	317	282	278	1,341	1,143	1,114	661
California	69.4	77.4	80.5	81.7	24.3	25.4	25.4	25.4	350	328	316	311	18,228	21,140	17,357	13,158
Colorado	38.9	34.2	36.3	36.1	31.8	31.7	31.3	31.2	817	927	862	864	863	1,596	1,248	1,014
Connecticut.................	5.5	6.0	4.9	4.9	0.4	0.4	0.4	0.4	69	73	82	82	172	188	251	207
Delaware	2.3	2.5	2.5	2.5	0.5	0.5	0.5	0.5	230	200	196	198	544	374	290	262
District of Columbia	(X)	(X)	(X)	(X)	(X)	(X)	(X)	(X)	(X)	(X)	(X)	(X)	(X)	(X)	(X)	(X)
Florida........................	47.5	47.3	47.5	47.5	9.7	9.5	9.3	9.3	204	200	195	195	2,396	3,565	2,783	2,482
Georgia	41.6	41.0	47.0	47.4	10.1	9.4	10.4	10.3	243	229	221	217	2,117	2,373	2,460	1,383
Hawaii	7.3	7.0	7.5	7.5	1.1	1.1	1.1	1.1	151	160	148	148	258	314	345	279
Idaho..........................	24.8	24.4	24.5	25.7	11.6	11.8	11.4	11.4	468	484	465	444	1,615	2,274	2,061	1,420
Illinois........................	72.0	73.4	74.3	76.0	27.0	26.8	26.6	26.7	375	365	358	351	2,973	293	3,061	2,558
Indiana	56.1	57.7	60.0	62.0	15.0	14.7	14.7	14.8	267	255	245	239	1,745	1,221	2,267	1,603
Iowa...........................	86.0	87.5	92.2	92.4	30.6	30.5	30.7	30.8	356	349	333	333	3,959	5,119	6,675	3,560
Kansas	58.9	60.4	65.5	65.5	45.8	46.0	46.0	46.2	778	762	702	705	1,385	1,727	3,033	2,516
Kentucky	75.1	76.4	85.5	85.7	12.9	13.0	14.0	14.0	172	170	164	163	1,153	1,374	921	340
Louisiana	27.4	26.9	29.0	30.0	8.0	7.8	8.0	8.1	292	288	274	268	602	541	1,182	798
Maine	7.6	8.2	8.1	8.1	1.3	1.5	1.4	1.4	171	177	167	167	157	234	268	264
Maryland.....................	12.4	12.2	12.8	12.8	2.0	2.0	2.1	2.1	161	166	160	160	388	446	627	385
Massachusetts	7.2	7.8	7.7	7.7	0.5	0.5	0.5	0.5	69	67	68	68	120	137	231	166
Michigan	47.0	51.5	54.7	54.9	9.8	10.0	9.9	10.0	209	193	181	182	1,075	1,089	1,644	1,405
Minnesota	68.5	73.6	79.4	81.0	25.5	25.9	26.8	26.9	372	352	338	332	1,852	3,180	5,977	3,140
Mississippi..................	34.7	36.7	42.3	42.4	10.4	10.8	11.2	11.2	300	294	264	263	1,232	687	808	879
Missouri......................	95.0	97.1	106.0	108.0	27.7	28.3	29.0	29.1	292	291	274	269	267	590	1,384	1,456
Montana......................	26.9	27.5	28.6	29.4	58.0	59.7	58.8	60.8	2,156	2,171	2,056	2,068	515	788	745	554
Nebraska.....................	45.9	48.7	46.7	47.2	45.0	45.2	45.5	45.6	980	928	974	966	2,182	5,177	4,562	3,115
Nevada	3.4	4.2	3.0	3.1	6.1	6.0	5.8	5.9	1,794	1,417	1,980	1,903	112	147	114	144
New Hampshire............	4.1	4.4	4.2	4.2	0.4	0.5	0.5	0.5	105	107	113	113	39	68	85	52
New Jersey	9.9	9.1	10.2	10.3	0.8	0.7	0.7	0.7	76	79	72	71	262	392	433	337
New Mexico	24.7	24.7	23.8	21.0	40.5	43.2	43.9	43.2	1,640	1,749	1,845	2,057	675	851	1,023	887
New York.....................	33.4	35.5	36.0	36.3	6.9	7.2	7.0	7.0	207	203	194	193	989	1,362	1,817	1,516
North Carolina.............	46.4	48.8	50.0	52.4	8.4	8.3	8.5	8.6	181	170	170	164	2,228	3,093	2,890	2,399
North Dakota...............	26.1	30.0	31.6	31.9	39.3	39.2	39.6	39.6	1,506	1,307	1,253	1,241	1,095	253	3,538	2,090
Ohio...........................	77.8	74.4	73.4	74.7	13.9	14.0	13.6	13.7	179	188	185	183	1,268	569	1,927	1,579
Oklahoma....................	77.3	78.0	85.5	86.5	34.2	34.2	34.8	35.2	442	438	407	407	672	1,870	1,756	809
Oregon	37.2	34.6	38.1	38.8	16.0	16.4	16.5	16.4	430	474	433	423	1,139	1,751	1,402	1,042
Pennsylvania................	53.0	57.9	62.1	63.2	7.3	7.7	7.7	7.8	138	133	124	123	991	1,639	2,055	1,342
Rhode Island................	1.1	1.2	1.2	1.2	0.1	0.1	0.1	0.1	55	56	57	57	37	30	26	27
South Carolina	24.6	24.4	26.7	27.0	4.8	5.0	4.8	4.9	195	205	180	181	118	144	476	485
South Dakota	29.6	31.3	31.0	31.8	43.2	43.3	43.7	43.7	1,459	1,383	1,408	1,374	1,472	1,604	2,505	1,703
Tennessee	70.0	67.3	76.0	78.3	10.9	10.9	10.8	10.9	156	162	142	139	-369	229	339	113
Texas.........................	247.0	242.0	244.7	247.5	127.0	130.0	128.0	130.4	514	537	523	527	2,021	6,133	2,602	3,251
Utah...........................	18.1	18.1	16.4	16.6	10.7	11.0	11.1	11.1	591	608	677	669	272	603	329	216
Vermont......................	6.8	7.3	7.0	7.0	1.2	1.3	1.2	1.2	176	171	174	174	154	213	255	193
Virginia.......................	42.5	45.0	46.2	47.3	7.8	8.1	8.1	8.1	184	180	174	170	205	437	658	353
Washington..................	35.7	36.0	39.3	39.5	14.7	14.7	14.8	14.8	412	408	377	375	3,854	4,817	3,345	2,507
West Virginia................	23.4	20.9	22.1	23.0	3.6	3.6	3.6	3.7	154	172	164	159	-63	-11	-5	-29
Wisconsin	64.8	68.9	76.8	78.0	14.3	14.4	15.0	15.2	221	209	195	195	1,119	2,669	2,758	1,754
Wyoming	11.9	11.6	10.8	11.0	29.0	30.4	30.2	30.2	2,437	2,621	2,796	2,745	167	293	136	120

[1]U.S. Department of Agriculture.
[2]Bureau of Economic Analysis. The estimates of earnings for 2000–2006 are based on the 2002 North American Industry Classification System (NAICS). The estimates for 2007 forward are based on the 2007 NAICS. All numbers provided are in current dollars (not adjusted for inflation).
(X) = Not applicable

Table A-49. Farm Finances and Income

Geographic Area	Value of agricultural sector productions[1] (million dollars)						Net farm income[2] (million dollars)					
	2018	2017	2016	2015	2014	2013	2018	2017	2016	2015	2014	2013
United States	413,920	413,879	399,273	429989	473521	473,063	83,777	75,060	62,263	81,586	92,238	123,694
Alabama..........................	6,565	6,400	50,811	52,171	58,986	54,680	1,413	1,492	976	16,713	1,756	1,896
Alaska............................	53	52	28,297	30,986	35,666	35,255	-6	-15	-6	6,026	-14	-12
Arizona...........................	4,669	4,972	23,650	28,274	29,169	28,178	928	1,005	1,092	5,126	578	1,121
Arkansas........................	10,034	9,845	22,513	25,045	26,396	26,540	1,807	1,732	845	4,826	2,110	2,602
California.......................	52,812	53,722	18,321	19,809	22,182	25,404	15,597	15,339	15,343	3,269	18,475	17,673
Colorado........................	8,066	7,997	17,772	18,146	21,098	23,287	1,259	1,038	1,263	3,118	1,222	1,394
Connecticut....................	726	739	16,658	17,397	18,262	18,744	165	161	67	2,981	105	230
Delaware........................	1,597	1,548	12,372	12,982	14,871	16,097	605	598	356	2,883	579	526
District of Columbia	X	X	X	X	X	X	X	X	X	X	X	X
Florida...........................	8,346	9,030	12,188	12,722	14,563	13,997	3,061	3,064	2,040	2,694	2,220	2,195
Georgia	10,230	10,143	11,605	11,582	13,733	13,932	2,306	2,700	1,945	2,538	2,359	2,716
Hawaii...........................	718	782	10,996	11,182	12,875	12,912	142	166	40	2,092	64	160
Idaho.............................	8,184	7,997	10,423	11,054	12,153	12,786	1,753	1,309	1,805	1,976	2,020	2,032
Illinois...........................	18,253	17,796	10,224	11,003	11,361	12,607	3,903	2,240	2,250	1,913	2,748	8,211
Indiana...........................	11,686	11,540	9,617	10,649	10,874	11,345	2,150	1,662	1,512	1,902	2,847	5,524
Iowa..............................	29,497	28,693	9,466	10,426	10,869	10,711	5,643	3,640	2,611	1,740	5,203	8,342
Kansas...........................	17,280	16,925	9,380	9,681	10,806	10,706	2,762	1,619	2,266	1,641	2,473	5,911
Kentucky........................	6,950	6,910	8,980	9,210	9,970	10,528	1,723	1,802	991	1,614	1,726	2,940
Louisiana........................	3,517	3,488	8,388	9,176	9,967	9,687	917	890	596	1,614	848	1,579
Maine............................	753	764	8,218	8,914	9,826	9,027	144	145	74	1,293	129	228
Maryland........................	2,683	2,797	7,803	8,746	9,413	8,929	539	711	404	1,257	637	898
Massachusetts................	577	589	7,389	8,706	9,357	8,629	72	69	-24	1,251	36	142
Michigan........................	8,434	8,151	7,378	8,375	9,312	8,372	1,089	831	72	1,238	657	1,830
Minnesota......................	18,165	18,088	7,286	8,334	8,890	8,256	2,860	2,269	1,119	1,222	3,280	5,628
Mississippi.....................	6,160	6,152	6,311	7,096	7,435	7,997	1,530	1,548	683	977	1,496	2,015
Missouri.........................	10,890	11,381	5,766	6,500	7,254	7,371	1,617	1,669	1,477	961	3,449	3,338
Montana.........................	4,377	4,027	5,708	6,122	7,043	6,932	1,093	517	698	938	665	1,220
Nebraska........................	22,510	21,911	5,567	5,916	6,918	6,687	2,590	2,183	3,861	826	5,744	7,429
Nevada...........................	748	745	5,546	5,616	5,889	5,640	85	83	9	783	154	51
New Hampshire...............	280	283	4,310	4,734	5,098	5,104	57	55	15	766	48	91
New Jersey	1,335	1,385	4,304	4,635	4,993	5,054	297	325	280	729	210	329
New Mexico....................	3,187	3,397	4,241	4,579	4,893	4,761	861	903	854	718	1,147	921
New York........................	5,685	5,932	4,010	4,296	4,461	4,640	1,073	1,311	705	611	1,685	1,857
North Carolina................	12,651	13,234	3,288	3,569	4,151	4,529	1,667	3,010	2,430	565	3,841	3,426
North Dakota..................	9,406	9,034	3,244	3,414	4,020	3,480	1,899	1,166	887	531	316	1,920
Ohio..............................	10,415	10,000	2,705	2,771	3,186	3,366	2,186	1,550	435	412	1,775	3,317
Oklahoma.......................	7,656	7,649	2,534	2,688	2,968	3,002	1,783	1,437	1,183	367	2,731	1,872
Oregon...........................	5,591	5,529	1,902	2,339	2,566	2,318	842	573	1,118	334	724	966
Pennsylvania..................	7,887	8,206	1,732	1,953	2,208	2,067	1,444	1,812	730	181	2,691	2,363
Rhode Island..................	92	90	1,358	1,442	1,668	1,517	30	27	3	172	7	19
South Carolina	2,851	2,871	1,311	1,372	1,349	1,350	275	359	153	170	250	748
South Dakota	10,687	10,041	905	980	1,107	1,000	2,574	1,344	1,353	162	2,138	3,691
Tennessee	4,213	4,310	859	926	1,024	970	325	460	210	154	689	1,412
Texas.............................	25,321	25,438	800	871	964	917	4,621	4,119	2,520	116	3,807	5,100
Utah..............................	1,964	2,017	758	851	883	906	474	391	331	115	558	541
Vermont.........................	828	889	699	838	877	854	148	193	135	77	305	281
Virginia..........................	4,404	4,499	692	786	797	774	656	795	356	67	757	1,007
Washington....................	10,238	10,566	578	652	697	740	2,271	2,556	2,389	61	1,739	2,359
West Virginia..................	900	922	275	326	329	338	87	128	22	22	55	115
Wisconsin......................	12,032	12,616	86	100	99	100	2,132	1,840	1,631	-9	2,889	3,279
Wyoming........................	1,816	1,785	47	45	48	42	327	238	159	-148	309	259

[1]The sum of the value of crop production, the value of livestock production, and revenues from services and forestry.
[2]Represents the value of agricultural sector production plus net government transactions (such as direct government payments) minus capital consumption, employee compensation, net rent received by nonoperator landlords, and interest payments.
(X) = Not applicable

Table A-50. Farm Income and Wealth Statistics

Geographic area	Direct government payments, 2018		Value of crop production, 2018		Value of animals and products production, 2018		Net farm income, 2018	
	Amount (in millions)	Share of U.S. direct government payments	Amount (in millions)	Share of U.S. value of crop production	Amount (in millions)	Share of U.S. value of animals and products production	Amount (in millions)	Share of U.S. net farm income
United States	13,669	(X)	188,575	(X)	177,519	(X)	83,777	(X)
Alabama	105	0.8	1,173	0.6	4,517	2.5	1,413	1.7
Alaska	12	0.1	31	0.0	10	0.0	-6	0.0
Arizona	59	0.4	2,357	1.2	1,739	1.0	1,807	2.2
Arkansas	629	4.6	3,230	1.7	5,601	3.2	15,597	18.6
California	275	2.0	37,807	20.0	11,691	6.6	1,259	1.5
Colorado	230	1.7	2,177	1.2	4,710	2.7	165	0.2
Connecticut	6	0.0	417	0.2	177	0.1	605	0.7
Delaware	17	0.1	245	0.1	1,134	0.6		
District of Columbia								
Florida	137	1.0	5,733	3.0	1,661	0.9	3,061	3.7
Georgia	326	2.4	2,817	1.5	6,053	3.4	2,306	2.8
Hawaii	14	0.1	428	0.2	165	0.1	142	0.2
Idaho	157	1.2	3,150	1.7	4,434	2.5	1,753	2.1
Illinois	1,051	7.7	14,465	7.7	2,392	1.3	3,903	4.7
Indiana	516	3.8	6,674	3.5	3,854	2.2	2,150	2.6
Iowa	1,184	8.7	12,205	6.5	14,320	8.1	5,643	6.7
Kansas	795	5.8	6,284	3.3	9,569	5.4	2,762	3.3
Kentucky	162	1.2	2,312	1.2	3,341	1.9	1,723	2.1
Louisiana	282	2.1	1,923	1.0	1,118	0.6	917	1.1
Maine	16	0.1	378	0.2	284	0.2	144	0.2
Maryland	39	0.3	823	0.4	1,364	0.8	539	0.6
Massachusetts	8	0.1	330	0.2	101	0.1	72	0.1
Michigan	232	1.7	4,160	2.2	3,299	1.9	1,089	1.3
Minnesota	827	6.0	8,436	4.5	7,513	4.2	2,860	3.4
Mississippi	366	2.7	1,923	1.0	3,314	1.9	1,530	1.8
Missouri	580	4.2	4,653	2.5	4,655	2.6	1,617	1.9
Montana	341	2.5	2,045	1.1	1,544	0.9	1,093	1.3
Nebraska	687	5.0	9,330	4.9	11,921	6.7	2,590	3.1
Nevada	15	0.1	169	0.1	487	0.3	85	0.1
New Hampshire	8	0.1	115	0.1	104	0.1	57	0.1
New Jersey	10	0.1	969	0.5	133	0.1	297	0.4
New Mexico	112	0.8	681	0.4	2,193	1.2	861	1.0
New York	81	0.6	1,967	1.0	3,057	1.7	1,073	1.3
North Carolina	106	0.8	3,149	1.7	7,641	4.3	1,667	2
North Dakota	739	5.4	6,776	3.6	1,224	0.7	1,899	2.3
Ohio	446	3.3	5,385	2.9	3,521	2.0	2,186	2.6
Oklahoma	334	2.4	1,221	0.6	5,519	3.1	1,783	2.1
Oregon	118	0.9	3,450	1.8	1,504	0.8	842	1.0
Pennsylvania	91	0.7	2,388	1.3	4,228	2.4	1,444	1.7
Rhode Island	2	0.0	44	0.0	29	0.0	30	0.0
South Carolina	57	0.4	992	0.5	1,397	0.8	275	0.3
South Dakota	803	5.9	5,044	2.7	4,167	2.3	2,574	3.1
Tennessee	139	1.0	1,910	1.0	1,387	0.8	325	0.4
Texas	850	6.2	5,993	3.2	14,974	8.4	4,621	5.5
Utah	63	0.5	460	0.2	1,246	0.7	474	0.6
Vermont	23	0.2	184	0.1	546	0.3	148	0.2
Virginia	76	0.6	1,247	0.7	2,218	1.2	656	0.8
Washington	197	1.4	6,970	3.7	2,508	1.4	2,271	2.7
West Virginia	12	0.1	153	0.1	519	0.3	87	0.1
Wisconsin	301	2.2	3,416	1.8	7,309	4.1	2,132	2.5
Wyoming	34	0.2	387	0.2	1,129	0.6	327	0.4

¹As determined by cash receipts; "Cattle" includes calves; "Greenhouse" includes nursery.
(X) = Not applicable

Table A-51. Natural Resource Industries and Minerals

Geographic Area	Natural resource industries (Includes Agriculture, forestry, fishing, and hunting [NAICS 11] and Mining quarrying, and oil and gas extraction NAICS 21)						Value of nonfuel mineral production (million dollars)			Mineral fuels, 2018		
	Establishments		Number of employees[2]		Annual payroll (million dollars)					Crude oil production (thousands of barrels)[3]	Natural gas production (millions of cubic feet)[4]	Coal production[5] (thousands of short tons)
	2017	2010	2014	2010	2014	2010	2020	2010	2005			
United States	49,092	48,783	742,141	737,637	57,609	51,428	86,300	64,000	55,400	4,011,521	32,823,295	756,167
Alabama	995	1,080	11,117	13,226	596	676	1,690	1,010	1,130	5,884	139,485	14,783
Alaska	633	541	10,370	11,984	1,215	1,260	3,130	3,240	1,500	174,800	341,315	902
Arizona.............................	433	431	12,928	11,699	780	697	6,970	6,700	4,350	11	46	6,550
Arkansas	984	1,076	9,274	13,345	484	707	901	630	597	5,018	589,973	-
California...........................	2,689	2,679	46,838	46,848	2,762	2,822	4,490	2,710	4,290	169,166	202,616	-
Colorado	1,489	1,572	22,861	25,203	2,334	2,239	1,790	1,930	1,750	177,817	1,831,325	14,026
Connecticut.......................	141	149	992	1,240	55	100	191	141	161	-	-	-
Delaware	53	54	251	224	16	8	30	13	20	-	-	-
District of Columbia	-	6	-	-	-	-	-	-	-	-	-	-
Florida...............................	1,321	1,248	11,957	17,382	508	633	3,370	2,080	2,910	1,839	788	
Georgia..............................	1,156	1,162	13,139	12,477	657	524	2,170	1,500	1,770	-	-	-
Hawaii...............................	48	50	344	494	18	16	134	112	125	-	-	-
Idaho.................................	596	580	6,307	5,748	340	268	185	1,200	896	88	1,861	-
Illinois...............................	864	887	9,728	9,883	621	609	1,470	910	1,210	8,420	2,418	49,563
Indiana..............................	575	561	7,748	7,794	433	447	695	837	894	1,684	5,054	34,598
Iowa..................................	582	462	4,874	3,558	272	180	836	542	659	-	-	-
Kansas..............................	1,114	1,201	7,748	9,860	414	509	1,070	1,040	873	34,714	201,505	-
Kentucky............................	625	882	11,100	23,048	647	1,434	591	742	782	2,265	83,973	39,567
Louisiana	2,018	2,195	43,056	53,794	3,219	3,735	614	492	397	48,841	2,810,636	1,483
Maine................................	957	807	3,211	3,575	166	138	102	114	141	-	-	-
Maryland............................	261	271	2,136	2,220	128	99	575	438	580	-	24	1,298
Massachusetts....................	418	442	2,043	2,100	120	115	289	194	250	-	-	-
Michigan............................	946	887	8,058	8,329	484	451	2,750	1,960	1,740	5,408	89,525	-
Minnesota..........................	725	615	7,741	7,568	562	528	5,300	3,860	2,190	-	-	-
Mississippi.........................	983	1,028	8,828	9,507	475	474	504	183	221	16,953	35,564	2,940
Missouri.............................	571	506	5,272	4,773	279	228	3,050	2,140	1,860	90	0	259
Montana.............................	675	712	6,506	7,085	533	485	1,280	1,120	847	21,540	43,524	38,610
Nebraska...........................	325	296	2,387	1,893	130	93	214	181	115	2,056	433	-
Nevada..............................	239	281	13,222	10,922	1,264	1,018	8,190	7,550	3,890	255	3	-
New Hampshire...................	195	184	862	764	50	35	156	100	88	-	-	-
New Jersey	296	307	2,222	2,976	124	121	377	232	356	-	-	-
New Mexico	821	773	17,555	15,064	1,286	1,087	1,090	1,010	1,150	248,958	1,485,142	10,792
New York...........................	898	909	6,569	7,146	342	358	1,870	1,290	1,290	221	11,798	-
North Carolina....................	1,024	967	8,073	7,218	379	277	1,420	908	862	-	-	-
North Dakota......................	640	399	15,820	8,825	1,530	746	58	88	35	461,531	705,789	29,643
Ohio..................................	984	1,001	11,842	10,376	735	543	1,400	1,080	1,210	23,224	2,409,153	8,993
Oklahoma..........................	2,933	2,972	42,083	41,956	3,548	3,343	1,070	646	616	200,685	2,946,117	610
Oregon..............................	1,497	1,396	14,027	13,173	680	457	499	292	439	-	499	-
Pennsylvania......................	1,540	1,553	26,843	25,714	2,063	1,757	2,100	1,530	1,560	6,478	6,210,673	49,883
Rhode Island......................	61	66	299	242	19	12	54	34	35	-	-	-
South Carolina	637	606	5,703	5,276	262	199	1,140	440	659	-	-	-
South Dakota	224	193	1,502	1,414	89	69	312	298	217	1,273	442	-
Tennessee.........................	444	453	4,507	4,641	237	205	1,420	814	771	210	3,538	232
Texas................................	8,940	8,591	210,426	169,074	20,864	15,352	6,470	2,560	2,710	1,609,075	7,847,102	24,823
Utah..................................	497	537	8,186	9,874	613	663	3,320	4,420	2,800	-	-	-
Vermont.............................	193	175	950	434	52	14	95	119	98	-	-	-
Virginia..............................	944	963	10,460	12,459	631	732	1,520	952	1,150	5	111,476	12,715
Washington........................	1,597	1,580	16,310	14,715	871	694	869	665	638	-	-	-
West Virginia......................	809	910	19,316	30,960	1,407	2,115	332	230	209	11,618	1,799,097	95,365
Wisconsin	734	652	10,577	5,176	852	273	1,950	651	570	-	-	-
Wyoming............................	768	935	17,973	23,790	1,463	1,848	2,630	1,860	1,300	87,955	1,640,264	304,188

[1]Includes Agriculture, forestry, fishing, and hunting (NAICS 11), and Mining, quarrying, and oil and gas extraction (NAICS 21). Data provided by County Business Patterns is based on the North American Industry Classification System (NAICS). Data for 2017 is based on NAICS 2017. Data for 2010 is based on NAICS 2007.
[2]Covers full- and part-time employees who are on the payroll in the pay period including March 12.
[3]U.S. totals include offshore production.
[4]Excludes nonhydrocarbon gases. U.S. total includes natural gas extracted from the Gulf of Mexico that is not distributed to states. The national total will therefore differ from the sum of state totals.
[5]Includes both surface and underground mines. U.S. total includes refuse recovery not distributed by state.
- = Not available

Table A-52. Agricultural Census

Geographic area	Number of farms (thousands)		Land in farms (millions of acres)		Average size of farm (acres)		Value of land and buildings[1] (million dollars)		Market value of agricultural products sold 2017	
	2017	2012	2017	2012	2017	2012	2017	2012	Products sold (million dollars)	Average per farm (dollars)
United States	2,042.2	2,109.3	900.2	914.5	441	434	2,679,001	2,268,537	388,523	190,245
Alabama......................	40.6	43.2	8.6	8.9	211	206	25,603	23,666	5,981	147,334
Alaska	1.0	0.8	0.9	0.8	858	1,094	610	519	71	71,171
Arizona......................	19.1	20.0	26.1	26.2	1369	1,312	21,191	16,886	3,852	201,824
Arkansas....................	42.6	45.1	13.9	13.8	326	306	43,935	36,416	9,651	226,420
California....................	70.5	77.9	24.5	25.6	348	328	229,363	160,525	45,154	640,297
Colorado	38.9	36.2	31.8	31.9	818	881	51,161	40,821	7,492	192,623
Connecticut.................	5.5	6.0	0.4	0.4	69	73	4,763	4,838	580	105,074
Delaware	2.3	2.5	0.5	0.5	228	208	4,420	4,153	1,466	636,826
District of Columbia	X	X	X	X	X	X	X	X	X	X
Florida........................	47.6	47.7	9.7	9.5	204	200	57,431	49,662	7,357	154,599
Georgia	42.4	42.3	10.0	9.6	235	228	34,926	29,676	9,573	225,577
Hawaii........................	7.3	7.0	1.1	1.1	155	161	10,590	10,229	564	76,938
Idaho.........................	25.0	24.8	11.7	11.8	468	474	33,513	26,130	7,567	302,746
Illinois	72.7	75.1	27.0	26.9	372	359	196,542	169,830	17,010	234,133
Indiana.......................	56.6	58.7	15.0	14.7	264	251	98,441	78,817	11,107	196,073
Iowa..........................	86.1	88.6	30.6	30.6	355	345	215,847	195,641	28,957	336,296
Kansas.......................	58.6	61.8	45.8	46.1	781	747	84,567	75,280	18,783	320,694
Kentucky.....................	76.0	77.1	13.0	13.0	171	169	48,848	39,459	5,738	75,533
Louisiana	27.4	28.1	8.0	7.9	292	281	24,350	20,176	3,173	115,861
Maine	7.6	8.2	1.3	1.5	172	178	3,394	3,356	667	87,758
Maryland.....................	12.4	12.3	2.0	2.0	160	166	15,644	14,073	2,473	198,955
Massachusetts.............	7.2	7.8	0.5	0.5	68	68	5,356	5,460	475	65,624
Michigan.....................	47.6	52.2	9.8	9.9	205	191	48,386	39,988	8,221	172,560
Minnesota	68.8	74.5	25.5	26.0	371	349	123,825	109,879	18,395	267,289
Mississippi..................	35.0	38.1	10.4	10.9	298	287	28,587	24,848	6,196	177,088
Missouri	95.3	99.2	27.8	28.3	291	285	94,031	78,885	10,526	110,427
Montana......................	27.0	28.0	58.1	59.8	2149	2,134	53,241	46,901	3,521	130,162
Nebraska	46.3	50.0	45.0	45.3	971	907	123,915	107,896	21,983	474,476
Nevada	3.4	4.1	6.1	5.9	1790	1,429	5,572	5,480	666	194,495
New Hampshire.............	4.1	4.4	0.4	0.5	103	108	2,225	1,975	188	45,548
New Jersey	9.9	9.1	0.7	0.7	74	79	9,888	9,147	1,098	111,095
New Mexico	25.0	24.7	40.7	43.2	1624	1,748	21,181	18,669	2,582	103,112
New York	33.4	35.5	6.9	7.2	205	202	22,172	18,678	5,369	160,572
North Carolina.............	46.4	50.2	8.4	8.4	182	168	39,138	36,506	12,901	277,924
North Dakota...............	26.4	31.0	39.3	39.3	1492	1,268	67,143	56,002	8,234	312,324
Ohio..........................	77.8	75.5	14.0	14.0	179	185	86,574	67,533	9,341	120,059
Oklahoma....................	78.5	80.2	34.2	34.4	435	428	59,220	46,049	7,466	95,065
Oregon.......................	37.6	35.4	16.0	16.3	424	460	38,840	30,676	5,007	133,103
Pennsylvania...............	53.2	59.3	7.3	7.7	137	130	47,688	41,796	7,759	145,962
Rhode Island...............	1.0	1.2	0.1	0.1	55	56	936	977	58	55,607
South Carolina	24.8	25.3	4.7	5.0	191	197	16,954	14,819	3,009	121,364
South Dakota	30.0	32.0	43.2	43.3	1443	1,352	89,437	72,968	9,722	324,397
Tennessee	70.0	68.1	10.9	10.9	155	160	42,601	38,749	3,799	54,284
Texas.........................	248.4	248.8	127.0	130.2	511	523	243,549	218,109	24,924	100,332
Utah	18.4	18.0	10.8	11.0	587	609	19,648	16,024	1,839	99,876
Vermont......................	6.8	7.3	1.2	1.3	175	171	4,226	4,011	781	114,713
Virginia.......................	43.2	46.0	7.8	8.3	180	180	36,061	35,752	3,961	91,625
Washington..................	35.8	37.2	14.7	14.7	410	396	40,943	33,906	9,635	269,172
West Virginia................	23.6	21.5	3.7	3.6	155	168	9,720	8,884	754	31,931
Wisconsin	64.8	69.8	14.3	14.6	221	209	70,212	57,167	11,427	176,368
Wyoming	11.9	11.7	29.0	30.4	2430	2,587	22,591	20,646	1,472	123,313

(X) = Not applicable

Table A-52. Agricultural Census—Continued

Geographic area	Total number of farm producers, 2017	Farms by value of sales, 2017						Cropland (thousand acres), 2017
		Less than $2,500	$2,500–$9,999	$10,000–$24,999	$25,000–$49,999	$50,000–$99,999	$100,000 or more	
United States	3,447,028	791,701	393,415	228,218	144,113	119,434	365,339	396,434
Alabama..............................	65,459	17,472	9,539	5,028	2,724	1,476	4,353	2,819
Alaska	1,847	312	270	191	68	59	90	84
Arizona...............................	33,847	12,802	2,886	1,228	512	390	1,268	1,287
Arkansas.............................	72,555	14,775	9,323	6,388	3,221	1,945	6,973	7,826
California............................	128,535	19,111	11,661	8,306	5,952	5,667	19,824	9,597
Colorado.............................	70,173	18,989	6,686	3,444	2,387	2,070	5,317	11,056
Connecticut.........................	9,771	2,464	1,407	608	338	241	463	149
Delaware.............................	3,963	611	254	235	113	120	969	452
District of Columbia	(X)	(X)	(X)	(X)	(X)	(X)	(X)	NA
Florida................................	79,933	23,558	9,676	4,842	2,592	2,010	4,912	2,826
Georgia	68,764	18,594	8,708	4,789	2,335	1,498	6,515	4,372
Hawaii	12,368	2,671	1854	1176	707	389	531	191
Idaho..................................	45,039	10,205	4,833	2,452	1,538	1,381	4,587	5,895
Illinois................................	118,141	23,276	9,174	5,848	4,919	5,724	23,710	24,003
Indiana...............................	95,845	18,583	10,056	6,092	4,117	4,069	13,732	12,910
Iowa...................................	145,432	25,204	7,955	6,065	5,651	7,600	33,629	26,546
Kansas................................	97,555	17,714	8,347	6,795	5,538	5,146	15,029	29,126
Kentucky.............................	125,155	31,921	18,021	10,120	5,949	3,470	6,485	6,630
Louisiana............................	44,272	12,802	5,865	2,869	1,705	1,036	3,109	4,346
Maine..................................	13,685	3,122	1,990	976	479	334	699	473
Maryland.............................	21,645	4,907	2,319	1,379	819	653	2,352	1,427
Massachusetts	13,371	3,258	1,519	774	526	405	759	172
Michigan	80,432	17,877	8813	5631	3519	3084	8717	7,925
Minnesota	113,415	21,107	8,218	5,822	4,737	6,467	22,471	21,787
Mississippi..........................	55,777	16,409	7,173	3,951	2,096	1,197	4,162	4,961
Missouri..............................	162,345	31,897	19,269	13,671	10,551	6,858	13,074	15,599
Montana..............................	48,161	9,962	3,678	2,235	2,138	2,119	6,916	16,406
Nebraska.............................	78,015	9,997	4,844	3,683	3,600	4,597	19,611	22,243
Nevada................................	6,055	1,164	741	362	222	199	735	795
New Hampshire.....................	7,346	1,856	1,052	502	287	160	266	108
New Jersey	16,873	4,472	2,111	1,014	629	537	1,120	463
New Mexico	41,670	14,486	5,132	1,811	1,055	876	1,684	1,826
New York.............................	58,870	10,313	6,518	4,861	2,854	2,304	6,588	4,291
North Carolina......................	74,958	18,113	10711	5645	2514	1716	7719	5,001
North Dakota........................	42,523	7,928	1,979	1,606	1,703	1,889	11,259	27,952
Ohio...................................	130,439	27,164	16,169	9,284	5,889	5,460	13,839	10,961
Oklahoma............................	130,434	29,701	17,271	11,574	6,888	4,947	8,150	11,716
Oregon	68,773	16,951	8,684	3,695	2,096	1,626	4,564	4,726
Pennsylvania........................	91,830	16,944	10,056	6,802	4,437	3,570	11,348	4,651
Rhode Island........................	1,868	396	255	116	94	73	109	18
South Carolina	39,332	13,163	5,181	2,489	1,132	738	2,088	2,035
South Dakota	49,547	7,468	2,673	2,228	2,128	2,733	12,738	19,814
Tennessee	114,285	30,890	18,085	9,568	4,874	2,284	4,282	5,286
Texas..................................	412,575	121,375	59,251	28,494	14,449	8,536	16,311	29,360
Utah	33,368	8,022	4119	2157	1205	988	1918	1,654
Vermont..............................	12,540	2,311	1,679	907	460	374	1,077	480
Virginia...............................	71,339	16,351	10,652	6,214	3,459	2,119	4,430	3,084
Washington..........................	64,290	16,663	7,297	3,051	1,877	1,341	5,564	7,489
West Virginia........................	38,409	11,052	7,185	2,871	1,217	474	823	948
Wisconsin............................	111,992	20,714	10,490	7,186	4,951	5,572	15,880	10,085
Wyoming	22,212	4,604	1,786	1,183	862	913	2,590	2,588

(X) = Not applicable

Table A-53. Utilities

Geographic area	Utilities[1] (NAICS 22)						Public water systems, 2012[3]			
	Establishments		Number of employees		Annual payroll[2] (million dollars)		Number of systems			
							Total	Community[4]	Non-transient, non-community[5]	Transient, non-community[6]
	2017	2010	2017	2010	2017	2010				
United States	18,965	17,600	644,703	638,058	67,433	55,396	152,143	50,452	17,594	84,097
Alabama	344	417	14,174	16,546	1,354	1,241	583	514	22	47
Alaska	106	91	2,070	1,988	196	155	1,446	413	237	796
Arizona	292	265	12,450	(D)	1,273	(D)	1,518	751	198	569
Arkansas	330	344	7,321	7,362	669	518	1,071	694	34	343
California	1,247	1,117	58,586	(D)	7,309	(D)	7,623	2,948	1,476	3,199
Colorado	405	385	10,668	8,837	987	713	1,979	874	168	937
Connecticut	134	169	7,779	(D)	897	1,163	2,491	502	540	1,449
Delaware	50	46	2,187	2,632	222	250	499	214	91	194
District of Columbia	55	45	1,857	(D)	303	(D)	7	5	2	0
Florida	866	585	26,834	26,859	2,807	2,113	5,370	1,646	805	2,919
Georgia	610	598	26,026	25,127	2,486	1,879	2,387	1,756	176	455
Hawaii	63	53	3,679	3,163	391	253	135	117	15	3
Idaho	214	192	3,961	2,887	364	206	1,971	736	232	1,003
Illinois	511	483	29,309	28,851	3,391	2,722	5,429	1,737	424	3,268
Indiana	636	626	15,611	16,176	1,471	1,234	4,073	787	587	2,699
Iowa	271	271	7,884	(D)	719	(D)	1,827	1,090	132	605
Kansas	246	197	7,119	6,502	705	513	997	876	41	80
Kentucky	356	341	8,629	8,310	765	663	439	387	17	35
Louisiana	483	537	11,147	(D)	1,041	(D)	1,342	992	142	208
Maine	117	96	2,440	2,311	202	153	1,895	376	370	1,149
Maryland	160	139	9,888	10,494	1,267	1,123	3,332	467	545	2,320
Massachusetts	287	281	12,617	12,861	1,473	1,319	8,529	2,319	718	5,492
Michigan	418	396	23,110	(D)	2,495	1,942	10,743	1,384	1,293	8,066
Minnesota	347	295	13,222	(D)	1,330	(D)	6,820	967	480	5,373
Mississippi	594	596	9,382	9,338	765	639	1,201	1,061	76	64
Missouri	373	357	15,561	16,665	1,548	1,355	2,746	1,424	217	1,105
Montana	211	200	3,058	2,972	262	231	2,170	727	284	1,159
Nebraska	120	105	1,141	(D)	107	(D)	1,337	600	143	594
Nevada	124	120	4,757	(D)	508	(D)	590	200	136	254
New Hampshire	123	113	3,256	3,492	320	298	2,479	699	455	1,325
New Jersey	364	375	20,117	18,018	2,487	1,823	3,709	582	738	2,389
New Mexico	227	231	4,506	5,017	402	379	1,083	572	134	377
New York	674	613	41,706	42,155	4,470	3,811	8,529	2,319	718	5,492
North Carolina	857	472	21,327	19,636	2,121	1,726	5,668	2,009	362	3,297
North Dakota	151	113	4,229	(D)	412	(D)	432	324	12	96
Ohio	704	696	23,380	(D)	2,348	(D)	4,561	1,209	669	2,683
Oklahoma	368	353	9,806	7,850	887	583	1,675	1,066	102	507
Oregon	282	291	8,034	7,395	789	614	2,494	882	321	1,291
Pennsylvania	854	783	29,868	31,133	3,194	2,956	8,460	1,954	1,177	5,329
Rhode Island	40	31	1,278	1,136	130	99	484	86	77	321
South Carolina	418	329	12,413	11,831	1,130	892	1,400	583	107	710
South Dakota	154	154	2,206	2,198	193	138	642	458	20	164
Tennessee	151	150	3,191	3,536	234	218	850	472	35	343
Texas	1,972	1,911	55,550	47,548	5,756	3,995	6,920	4,645	874	1,401
Utah	218	218	3,704	4,633	351	380	1,029	475	70	484
Vermont	70	59	1,282	2,067	134	182	1,403	418	252	733
Virginia	335	360	15,112	15,050	1,612	1,430	2,714	1,121	517	1,076
Washington	309	302	9,716	8,291	1,036	686	4,371	2,266	359	1,746
West Virginia	231	254	6,222	6,444	602	467	915	464	83	368
Wisconsin	347	317	12,699	13,484	1,284	1,168	11,470	1,055	891	9,524
Wyoming	146	128	2,634	2,492	232	196	789	315	97	377

[1]Data provided by County Business Patterns is based on the North American Industry Classification System (NAICS). Data for 2017 is based on NAICS 2017. Data for 2010 is based on NAICS 2007. Utilities data is for private use and excludes government employees, railroad employees, self-employed persons, and so on.
[2]National payroll figures include undisclosed data found at the State level and will therefore differ from the sum of the state totals.
[3]As of October. Covers public drinking water systems that provide water for human consumption through pipes and other constructed conveyances to at least 15 service connections or serve an average of at least 25 persons for at least 60 days a year. National totals differ from the sum of the state figures because national totals include water systems for Tribes and Territories.
[4]Includes any public water system that supplies water to the same population year-round.
[5]Includes any public water system that regularly supplies water to at least 25 of the same people at least six months per year but not year-round.
[6]Includes any public water system that provides water in a place, such as a gas station or a campground, where people do not remain for long periods of time and is open at least 60 days per year.
0 = Represents or rounds to zero
(D) = Data withheld to avoid disclosure or does not meet statistical standards.
NA = Not available

Table A-54. Energy Consumption

Geographic area	Total Primary Energy Consumption[1]		End-use sector, 2017[3] (trillion Btu)				Selected sources, 2017 (trillion Btu)				
	2017 (trillion Btu)	Per capita[2] (million Btu)	Residential	Commercial	Industrial[1]	Transportation	Petroleum[4]	Natural gas[5]	Coal	Nuclear	Renewable[6]
United States	97,622	300	19,864	17,864	31,873	28,020	36,262	28,042	13,840	8,419	10,896
Alabama.........................	1,901	390	324	254	822	501	537	682	379	446	276
Alaska..........................	608	822	53	59	333	163	224	344	16	0	24
Arizona.........................	1,475	209	401	355	230	489	532	336	335	338	170
Arkansas	1,058	352	202	173	397	286	327	318	268	133	116
California......................	7,881	200	1,416	1,473	1,818	3,175	3,534	2,189	34	187	1,230
Colorado	1,463	261	343	291	407	422	481	462	316	0	160
Connecticut..................	726	203	230	188	79	229	298	246	3	173	45
Delaware	270	282	60	57	84	70	103	103	5	0	8
District of Columbia	168	241	38	104	6	19	17	31	(Z)	0	2
Florida..........................	4,209	201	1,176	991	493	1,548	1,634	1,418	408	305	301
Georgia	2,802	269	666	533	759	844	917	709	344	353	286
Hawaii..........................	283	199	34	43	60	147	238	0	15	0	31
Idaho............................	554	322	135	92	168	159	177	116	3	0	173
Illinois..........................	3,872	303	892	796	1,176	1,008	1,242	1,035	685	1,017	266
Indiana.........................	2,701	406	498	357	1,232	614	736	748	929	0	176
Iowa.............................	1,559	496	221	190	848	300	411	376	300	55	455
Kansas	1,073	369	206	213	388	267	338	279	217	111	216
Kentucky	1,658	372	332	257	599	471	581	297	639	0	97
Louisiana	4,482	960	312	269	3,123	777	2,003	1,718	142	161	246
Maine	392	294	100	66	104	123	186	45	2	0	158
Maryland.......................	1,315	218	386	407	108	413	442	233	107	158	79
Massachusetts...............	1,424	208	410	402	155	458	553	463	12	53	96
Michigan.......................	2,775	278	725	599	716	735	847	909	499	339	238
Minnesota.....................	1,832	329	386	357	628	461	582	467	258	145	288
Mississippi....................	1,176	394	178	153	402	444	494	544	54	77	70
Missouri........................	1,726	283	471	403	301	551	604	265	710	87	95
Montana........................	421	399	96	81	127	117	173	83	156	0	141
Nebraska.......................	876	457	146	135	392	202	238	176	234	72	186
Nevada.........................	707	238	165	142	172	228	257	306	27	0	109
New Hampshire..............	318	235	100	70	46	102	153	54	4	105	65
New Jersey	2,135	240	536	560	257	783	907	734	17	356	83
New Mexico	683	327	112	122	229	220	252	250	199	0	76
New York.......................	3,684	188	1,055	1,117	388	1,125	1,291	1,280	20	441	484
North Carolina...............	2,503	244	649	567	562	725	818	520	350	443	239
North Dakota.................	631	836	69	88	343	131	186	112	398	0	161
Ohio.............................	3,644	312	839	682	1,197	926	1,111	1,015	811	185	148
Oklahoma......................	1,644	418	274	250	637	483	555	692	198	0	279
Oregon	1,032	249	264	202	261	305	335	263	19	0	505
Pennsylvania.................	3,808	298	871	631	1,355	951	1,201	1,404	670	870	233
Rhode Island.................	184	174	57	45	23	60	77	94.8	0	0	9
South Carolina	1,644	327	351	274	536	483	529	286	193	568	148
South Dakota	385	441	67	63	157	98	112	85	26	0	140
Tennessee	2,167	323	497	433	600	637	716	332	335	333	185
Texas............................	13,366	472	1,641	1,601	6,754	3,370	6,513	3,994	1,452	404	877
Utah.............................	829	267	175	171	222	261	298	231	275	0	64
Vermont........................	135	216	43	25	19	48	78	12	0	0	41
Virginia.........................	2,303	272	554	612	435	702	758	597	160	320	160
Washington	2,097	282	504	379	535	679	795	351	62	85	967
West Virginia.................	756	416	144	108	333	172	194	203	710	0	48
Wisconsin	1,806	312	414	366	600	426	520	505	389	101	191
Wyoming.......................	512	885	51	60	286	115	158	134	459	0	59

[1]U.S. total energy and U.S. industrial sector include 60.8 trillion Btu of net imports of coal coke that is not allocated to the states. U.S. total includes energy losses and co-products from the production of fuel ethanol which is not allocated to State figures.
[2]Based on estimated resident population as of July 1.
[3]End-use sector data include electricity sales and associated electrical system energy losses.
[4]Includes fuel ethanol blended into motor gasoline.
[5]Includes supplemental gaseous fuels.
[6]Includes conventional hydroelectric power, biomass (wood and biomass waste, fuel ethanol, and losses and co-products from fuel ethanol production), geothermal, solar thermal and photovoltaic, and wind energy.
0 = Represents zero or rounds to zero
(Z) = Less than .05 trillion Btu.

Table A-55. Energy Expenditures

Geographic area	Total expenditures, 2017[1,2,3]	Per capita[4] (dollars)	End-use sector, 2017[3] (million dollars)				Selected source, 2017 (million dollars)		
			Residential	Commercial	Industrial[2]	Transportation	Petroleum	Natural gas[6]	Coal
United States	1,136,496	3,489	246,110	184,761	190,934	514,692	631,717	142,245	30,326
Alabama................................	20,436	4,192	4,343	3,106	4,236	8,752	9,851	2,805	917
Alaska..................................	5,112	6,910	829	861	674	2,748	3,570	603	105
Arizona................................	20,521	2,925	4,909	3,712	2,015	9,885	11,284	1,778	750
Arkansas..............................	11,305	3,763	2,171	1,519	2,437	5,178	5,970	1,788	547
California..............................	124,724	3,155	22,640	22,426	14,242	65,416	71,487	14,480	127
Colorado..............................	16,391	2,923	3,513	2,690	2,438	7,750	9,082	2,151	563
Connecticut..........................	12,536	3,494	4,322	2,724	880	4,610	6,265	1,718	11
Delaware..............................	3,336	3,468	848	602	445	1,440	1,681	591	13
District of Columbia	1,970	2,839	461	1,122	57	330	350	332	(s)
Florida.................................	57,074	2,720	14,666	10,428	3,901	28,079	30,926	6,743	1,215
Georgia...............................	34,011	3,261	8,621.0	5,506.0	4,429.0	15,455.0	17,369.0	4,389.0	961
Hawaii.................................	5,549	3,887	826	1,005	947	2,772	3,757	91	46.0
Idaho..................................	6,311	3,676	1,272	738	1,131	3,171	3,711	584	6
Illinois.................................	40,510	3,164	9,345	6,629	6,129	18,408	21,138	6,744	1,359
Indiana................................	27,101	4,065	5,268	3,300	7,253	11,280	12,984	4,300	2,335
Iowa...................................	13,890	4,416	2,484	1,665	4,179	5,562	7,339	2,255	529
Kansas................................	11,180	3,838	2,445	2,107	1,927	4,700	5,641	1,436	373
Kentucky..............................	17,338	3,893	3,337	2,352	3,113	8,536	9,771	1,571	1,303
Louisiana.............................	32,041	6,840	3,306	2,591	15,968	10,177	20,841	5,085	427
Maine..................................	5,624	4,210	1,613	872	649	2,491	3,703	338	10
Maryland..............................	18,541	3,064	5,038	4,163	1,001	8,339	9,499	2,036	283
Massachusetts.......................	23,206	3,383	7,092.0	5,575.0	1,846.0	8,693.0	11,092.0	3,732.0	54
Michigan..............................	32,394	3,252	8,441	5,741	4,626	13,586	15,925	5,336	1,200.0
Minnesota............................	20,067	3,598	4,403	3,393	3,519	8,751	10,678	2,602	565
Mississippi...........................	13,142	4,404	2,288	1,735	2,048	7,071	7,824	1,999	143
Missouri...............................	21,162	3,462	5,124	3,599	2,314	10,124	11,469	2,077	1,332
Montana...............................	4,578	4,358	945	730	583	2,320	2,820	453	276
Nebraska..............................	8,244	4,294	1,442	1,075	1,935	3,792	4,549	926	327
Nevada................................	9,214	3,073	1,990	1,230	1,437	4,557	5,322	1,341	85
New Hampshire......................	5,193	3,867	1,713	943	503	2,034	3,105	415	16
New Jersey	29,541	3,280	6,894	6,397	2,138	14,113	16,178	4,475	52
New Mexico	7,368	3,529	1,254	1,127	946	4,041	4,675	736	392
New York..............................	54,108	2,726	16,448.0	14,348.0	3,005.0	20,307.0	24,594.0	9,314.0	69
North Carolina.......................	30,734	2,992	7,458	5,006	3,950	14,319	16,652	3,109	1,053.0
North Dakota.........................	5,352	7,085	677	749	1,704	2,221	3,239	291	600
Ohio....................................	40,371	3,463	9,481	6,132	7,559	17,198	20,381	5,849	1,775
Oklahoma.............................	15,610	3,971	3,040	2,169	2,656	7,745	9,183	2,230	374
Oregon................................	13,019	3,143	2,845	1,960	1,754	6,460	7,311	1,364	44
Pennsylvania.........................	43,927	3,430	11,858	5,863	7,919	18,287	23,221	6,898	1,576
Rhode Island.........................	3,229	3,047	1,053	736	298	1,143	1,557	654	—
South Carolina.......................	18,962	3,774	4,315	2,731	3,086	8,830	9,946	1,508	639
South Dakota	3,836	4,411	721	565	751	1,799	2,187	417	58
Tennessee............................	24,093	3,587	4,950	4,225	3,405	11,514	13,035	1,889	795
Texas..................................	128,571	4,542	18,561.0	13,397.0	41,408.0	55,205.0	87,311.0	12,441.0	2,557
Utah...................................	9,278	2,991	1,722	1,422	1,203	4,930	5,540	1,237	542.0
Vermont...............................	2,589	4,151	860	443	286	1,000	1,636	104	—
Virginia................................	27,218	3,213	6,537	5,046	2,682	12,953	14,695	3,060	477
Washington...........................	23,938	3,232	5,000	3,397	2,454	13,087	14,546	2,157	149
West Virginia.........................	7,470	4,114	1,555	979	1,829	3,107	3,981	536	1,621
Wisconsin.............................	20,408	3,521	4,655	3,414	3,865	8,474	10,248	2,867	893
Wyoming	4,442	7,668	532	512	1,446	1,952	2,598	412	783

[1]Total expenditures are the sum of purchases for each source (including retail electricity sales) less electric power sector purchases of fuel.
[2]Includes sources not shown separately, such as electricity imports and exports and coal coke net imports ($347 million in 2007), which are not included in the States.
[3]Excludes expenditures on energy sources such as hydroelectric, geothermal, wind, photovoltaic, or solar thermal. Also excluded are expenditures for reported amounts of energy consumed by the energy industry for production, transportation, and processing operations.
[4]Based on estimated resident population as of July 1.
[5]Includes fuel ethanol blended into motor gasoline.
[6]Includes supplemental gaseous fuels.
0 = Represents zero or amounts to zero

Table A-56. Construction

Geographic area	Construction (NAICS 23)									New Privately Owned Housing Units Authorized[3]			
	Nonfarm employment (thousands) (BLS)[1]			Earnings (BEA)[2] (million dollars)			Establishments			Total units		Valuation (thousands of dollars)	
	2019	2015	2010	2019	2015	2010	2017	2010	Net Change	2019	2015	2019	2015
United States	7,464.5	6,461	5,518	805,965	651,177	486,510	715,641	682,684	32,957	1,386,048	1,182,582	280,534,198	223,611,322
Alabama	93.5	81.6	87.2	8,752	7,198	6,760	7,535	8,235	-700	17,748	14,054	3,545,271	2,416,774
Alaska	16.4	17.6	16.6	2,265	2,424	2,285	2,461	2,461	0	1,680	1,298	412,921	324,596
Arizona.......................	170.7	127.9	111.5	15,023	9,871	8,017	12,380	12,091	289	46,580	28,910	10,850,556	6,985,714
Arkansas.....................	52.4	49.2	48.7	4,748	4,087	3,727	5,439	5,539	-100	12,723	8,500	2,171,607	1,380,106
California.....................	882.6	731.8	559.8	103,764	78,900	56,137	74,722	66,999	7,723	110,197	98,188	26,583,348	22,637,174
Colorado.....................	178.8	148.8	115.1	19,721	14,802	8,632	18,552	16,747	1,805	38,633	31,871	9,638,045	7,532,619
Connecticut.................	59.8	57.9	50.0	9,828	8,747	7,451	7,905	8,187	-282	5,854	6,077	1,354,391	1,282,308
Delaware	22.9	20.8	19.3	2,459	2,022	1,469	2,251	2,375	-124	6,539	5,221	849,102	641,676
District of Columbia	14.9	14.6	10.6	1,441	1,341	902	451	421	30	5,945	4,956	680,539	495,021
Florida........................	565.5	432.4	350.8	46,465	32,002	26,698	53,345	45,041	8,304	154,302	109,924	33,210,471	23,439,129
Georgia	203.4	166.5	149.7	21,712	15,927	11,862	18,192	17,482	710	53,823	45,549	10,681,578	7,955,101
Hawaii........................	37.2	35.0	28.9	4,590	3,953	3,074	2,881	2,738	143	4,093	5,422	1,283,822	1,582,395
Idaho..........................	52.8	38.2	31.3	4,351	3,032	2,022	6,949	6,358	591	17,716	9,954	3,401,488	1,934,066
Illinois........................	226.7	213.6	198.3	26,483	23,893	18,920	29,171	29,175	-4	20,524	19,571	3,726,457	4,136,596
Indiana.......................	146.2	127.1	115.7	14,329	11,699	9,208	13,456	13,756	-300	22,309	18,483	4,988,366	3,737,044
Iowa..........................	78.1	78.2	61.6	7,936	7,515	5,167	8,753	8,609	144	11,870	12,097	2,500,495	2,243,252
Kansas.......................	63.5	61.0	54.1	6,261	5,413	4,421	7,031	7,064	-33	7,961	8,644	1,682,921	1,646,377
Kentucky....................	80.3	75.8	67.9	7,999	6,977	5,200	7,335	7,770	-435	11,811	10,566	2,135,837	1,467,802
Louisiana	141.7	140.6	121.5	13,130	12,467	10,497	8,139	8,441	-302	15,793	13,830	3,136,086	2,777,014
Maine.........................	29.8	26.5	24.4	3,153	2,693	2,582	5,044	5,023	21	4,760	3,699	1,004,740	683,014
Maryland.....................	166.1	154.3	143.4	17,836	15,245	12,797	14,192	14,516	-324	18,491	17,057	3,754,023	3,080,620
Massachusetts.............	162.1	139.1	107.1	23,318	18,745	12,883	19,256	16,844	2,412	17,365	17,424	3,679,201	3,980,521
Michigan.....................	173.4	148.3	121.6	18,928	15,356	10,028	19,262	18,895	367	20,600	18,226	4,580,486	3,850,470
Minnesota...................	127.1	115.2	87.6	14,928	12,485	8,104	16,550	16,368	182	28,586	19,545	6,147,907	4,135,089
Mississippi..................	44.4	46.0	49.5	4,054	4,016	3,932	3,849	4,389	-540	6,952	6,845	1,240,886	1,078,138
Missouri......................	126.4	114.4	106.2	13,249	10,707	9,043	13,492	13,846	-354	17,460	18,344	3,388,568	3,146,410
Montana......................	30.1	26.5	22.6	2,945	2,495	1,854	5,476	5,111	365	4,776	4,826	855,745	827,389
Nebraska....................	53.5	49.0	41.7	4,588	4,421	4,311	6,481	5,810	671	8,025	8,096	1,325,156	1,317,315
Nevada.......................	96.2	70.2	59.3	8,548	5,642	6,852	4,979	5,003	-24	20,143	14,083	3,681,836	2,141,757
New Hampshire............	27.9	24.2	21.4	4,329	3,606	2,956	4,174	4,059	115	4,743	3,763	1,059,428	736,931
New Jersey	159.8	148.4	129.5	21,897	19,767	14,051	21,622	20,865	757	36,505	30,560	4,453,654	4,051,996
New Mexico	50.0	43.5	43.6	3,969	3,147	2,902	4,333	4,738	-405	5,020	4,599	1,121,875	872,141
New York....................	404.7	361.3	306.6	47,359	39,767	30,814	49,123	45,293	3,830	71,307	74,611	7,746,335	10,826,337
North Carolina.............	231.5	189.3	176.5	22,624	17,179	12,097	23,157	23,107	50	71,307	54,757	13,849,671	9,707,931
North Dakota...............	28.1	34.7	21.6	3,026	3,492	1,832	2,996	2,570	426	2,495	6,256	537,457	953,024
Ohio	226.0	200.5	168.8	24,480	20,320	14,129	19,907	20,620	-713	23,047	20,047	5,421,691	3,982,890
Oklahoma...................	82.6	77.4	67.0	7,973	7,541	6,079	8,359	8,086	273	12,152	11,545	2,482,605	2,216,234
Oregon.......................	108.9	83.3	67.6	11,254	7,764	5,320	12,871	11,797	1,074	22,037	17,510	4,447,105	3,591,958
Pennsylvania...............	260.6	235.4	214.9	30,938	26,086	20,663	26,689	26,835	-146	23,539	22,854	4,677,483	4,406,389
Rhode Island...............	19.9	17.0	15.9	2,333	1,951	1,742	3,161	3,091	70	1,400	998	280,414	211,614
South Carolina	107.3	87.0	79.4	10,114	7,436	5,213	9,853	9,688	165	36,034	31,030	8,006,648	6,242,696
South Dakota	23.6	22.2	20.1	2,209	1,961	1,500	3,394	3,158	236	4,415	4,482	836,315	740,741
Tennessee	129.8	112.7	100.7	16,514	12,793	9,269	10,048	10,025	23	41,361	32,219	7,876,497	5,596,464
Texas.........................	776.3	683.8	564.4	90,163	75,842	49,560	45,044	39,321	5,723	209,895	175,443	37,413,284	29,086,961
Utah	110.0	84.8	65.0	9,487	6,910	4,316	9,601	8,822	779	28,779	18,297	6,453,593	3,851,184
Vermont......................	15.3	15.1	13.5	1,654	1,554	1,463	2,698	2,784	-86	1,801	1,998	351,910	333,954
Virginia.......................	202.8	184.8	183.1	19,721	16,983	13,363	19,748	20,779	-1,031	32,418	28,469	5,793,753	4,724,305
Washington.................	220.2	173.2	140.7	24,119	16,934	11,650	23,660	21,027	2,633	48,424	40,374	10,223,055	8,518,859
West Virginia...............	36.0	32.5	32.8	3,447	2,900	2,610	3,085	3,659	-574	3,010	2,814	500,116	417,183
Wisconsin	124.0	109.4	94.6	13,500	11,219	8,369	13,867	14,325	-458	17,480	16,793	3,968,450	3,078,382
Wyoming.....................	22.7	23.3	22.3	2,049	1,950	1,775	2,722	2,741	-19	1,708	1,903	541,013	607,666

[1]All estimates of labor and earnings provided by BLS are based on the 2017 North American Industry Classification System (NAICS). Figure includes logging and mining with construction for Delaware, the District of Columbia, and Hawaii.
[2]Bureau of Economic Analysis. The estimates of earnings for 2010 are based on the 2007 North American Industry Classification System (NAICS). The estimates for 2015 are based on the 2012 NAICS. The estimates for 2019 are based in the 2017 NAICS. All dollars estimates are in current dollars and not adjusted for inflation.
[3]Data based on 20,100 places in the United States having building permits systems; see Source in Appendix A for details.

Table A-57. Manufactures (NAICS 31-33)

Geographic area	Nonfarm employment in manufacturing (BLS)[1] (thousands)			Earnings (BEA)[2] (million dollars)			Establishments[3]		Average hourly earnings of production workers[4] (dollars)		Value of shipments[5] (million dollars)	
	2019	2015	2010	2019	2015	2010	2017	2014	2016	2015	2016	2015
United States	12,793	12,336	11,528	1,191,275	1,060,471	877,372	290,936	292,543	23.28	22.61	5,354,694	5,519,018
Alabama	269	258	236	19,911	17,684	14,546	4,137	4,179	21.49	20.97	6,003	6,922
Alaska	13	14	13	1,017	1,010	723	534	529	21.40	20.65	55,065	53,520
Arizona	177	158	148	17,431	14,269	12,068	4,319	4,224	24.09	23.25	55,731	59,299
Arkansas	162	155	160	10,452	9,329	8,282	2,567	2,615	19.78	19.33	493,165	510,516
California	1,323	1,302	1,249	162,796	139,711	115,565	37,849	38,293	23.93	23.11	50,853	52,560
Colorado	150	141	124	14,610	12,394	9,660	5,108	4,958	23.25	22.89	56,376	58,212
Connecticut	162	157	163	20,636	18,869	23,703	3,979	4,198	26.62	25.55	16,558	18,664
Delaware	27	26	26	2,389	2,262	1,926	548	592	22.57	22.24	330	319
District of Columbia	1	1	1	148	171	136	116	98	20.06	19.72	104,865	104,382
Florida	385	343	309	32,797	26,373	21,817	13,390	12,912	22.09	21.37	166,678	167,614
Georgia	406	379	345	31,096	28,112	22,738	7,508	7,351	20.92	20.27	5,686	5,898
Hawaii	14	14	13	977	890	728	776	760	22.56	22.79	20,968	20,434
Idaho	69	62	53	6,096	4,913	3,464	1,873	1,753	23.43	22.84	252,503	259,556
Illinois	586	581	561	57,888	53,051	44,269	13,154	13,531	23.05	22.22	241,539	242,800
Indiana	542	518	446	45,601	40,991	31,872	8,045	8,036	23.24	22.61	105,663	115,490
Iowa	226	216	201	18,870	16,834	12,714	3,486	3,542	22.05	21.32	83,920	87,876
Kansas	167	161	158	13,207	14,329	11,166	2,760	2,831	24.11	23.49	128,159	132,081
Kentucky	252	241	209	20,089	17,591	13,598	3,691	3,755	23.16	22.99	156,874	173,426
Louisiana	138	144	138	14,445	13,425	11,596	3,173	3,255	29.20	28.05	15,169	15,928
Maine	53	51	51	4,104	3,600	3,340	1,683	1,645	24.09	23.56	41,214	39,898
Maryland	113	105	115	11,521	9,830	9,854	2,956	3,001	24.22	23.83	84,735	85,024
Massachusetts	244	249	252	28,299	27,111	24,808	6,418	6,654	25.05	24.92	261,293	263,936
Michigan	627	588	466	56,947	47,968	35,695	12,400	12,361	24.37	23.48	117,397	119,154
Minnesota	324	318	293	28,903	26,589	21,022	7,177	7,275	22.72	22.28	56,801	58,440
Mississippi	147	142	136	9,841	8,729	7,277	2,143	2,167	20.66	20.33	118,828	119,305
Missouri	277	261	246	23,838	20,927	16,914	5,770	5,946	24.94	24.40	9,396	9,708
Montana	21	19	17	1,469	1,225	953	1,330	1,251	23.75	23.34	53,112	56,112
Nebraska	100	97	92	7,323	6,920	5,155	1,758	1,795	20.96	20.00	16,682	16,139
Nevada	59	42	38	4,744	3,027	2,472	1,826	1,750	23.04	23.06	20,658	20,132
New Hampshire	72	67	66	6,769	5,741	5,159	1,787	1,806	23.24	22.76	90,605	94,141
New Jersey	252	239	252	32,517	25,879	25,597	7,328	7,537	23.83	23.36	12,674	13,539
New Mexico	29	28	29	1,964	1,942	1,902	1,325	1,350	23.79	23.25	148,469	150,457
New York	439	455	457	41,337	39,824	35,690	15,488	16,076	23.70	22.94	210,018	213,289
North Carolina	478	462	432	37,849	33,965	29,312	8,796	8,721	20.13	19.65	13,050	14,047
North Dakota	26	26	23	1,903	1,801	1,309	699	762	22.30	20.44	312,532	324,708
Ohio	701	687	621	60,651	54,540	43,823	13,902	14,208	23.33	22.82	56,775	63,105
Oklahoma	141	137	123	12,135	10,307	8,760	3,357	3,554	23.00	22.10	57,315	58,259
Oregon	198	186	164	17,983	15,463	12,289	5,547	5,314	24.11	23.25	217,753	222,391
Pennsylvania	575	568	560	50,398	45,343	39,802	13,502	13,684	23.58	22.98	11,344	11,966
Rhode Island	40	41	40	3,219	3,091	2,667	1,332	1,432	24.10	23.23	109,000	112,599
South Carolina	258	236	207	21,264	17,933	13,358	3,822	3,770	23.01	22.26	17,441	17,248
South Dakota	45	43	37	3,210	2,995	1,926	1,051	1,028	20.02	19.32	149,126	144,614
Tennessee	355	333	299	28,260	24,911	20,146	5,797	5,632	21.89	21.16	523,118	563,949
Texas	907	879	817	97,447	92,182	67,951	19,764	19,681	24.29	23.51	48,428	49,116
Utah	137	124	111	10,908	9,116	7,224	3,366	3,201	23.66	23.29	8,788	8,515
Vermont	30	31	31	2,377	2,213	2,130	1,030	989	23.20	22.09	99,131	101,551
Virginia	243	234	231	19,630	18,527	15,645	5,011	4,986	23.19	22.50	142,700	144,864
Washington	294	292	258	30,795	27,647	21,701	7,021	6,929	27.77	26.36	23,851	24,434
West Virginia	47	48	49	3,859	3,469	3,235	1,147	1,204	24.74	24.95	168,601	175,216
Wisconsin	484	467	431	38,362	34,562	29,082	8,817	8,858	22.20	21.47	6,742	7,649
Wyoming	10	10	9	993	888	601	573	564	32.17	30.35		

[1] All estimates of labor and earnings provided by the Bureau of Labor Statistics (BLS) are based on the 2017 North American Industry Classification System (NAICS). Earning estimates are in current dollars and not adjusted for inflation.
[2] Bureau of Economic Analysis. The estimates for 2010 are based on the 2007 North American Industry Classification System (NAICS); 2015 data are based on 2012 NAICS; 2019 data are based on 2017 NAICS. All dollars estimates are in current dollars and not adjusted for inflation.
[3] 2014 data for establishments are based on the 2012 North American Industry Classification System (NAICS); 2017 data are based on the 2017 NAICS. United States totals differ from the sum of the state figures because of differing benchmarks among states and differing industrial and geographic stratification.
[4] Data for average hourly earnings of production workers are provided in current dollars and not adjusted for inflation.
[5] Includes extensive and unmeasurable duplication from shipments between establishments in the same industry classification.
NA = Not available

Table A-58. Manufactures Summary and Export-Related Shipments and Employment

Geographic area	All employees Number	All employees Percentage change, 2010–2016	Payroll Total (million dollars)	Payroll Per employee (dollar)	Production workers Total	Production workers Hours (million)	Production workers Wages (million dollars)	Value added by manufactures[2] Total (million dollars)	Value added Per production worker (dollar)	Value of shipments[3] (million dollars)	Cost of materials (million dollars)	Capital expenditures (million dollars)
United States	11,112,764	5.2	643,406	57,898	7,733,162	15,681	364,985	2,408,996	311,515	5,354,694	2,942,556	168,318
Alabama	234,803	7.9	12,256	52,195	176,679	367	7,884	46,264	261,855	131,012	84,504	4,187
Alaska	12,178	14.7	590	48,431	10,176	21	442	2,212	217,420	6,003	3,933	204
Arizona	136,946	6.4	9,142	66,753	82,409	166	3,990	29,122	353,384	55,065	25,860	1,924
Arkansas	145,733	0.2	6,657	45,679	116,757	239	4,721	25,096	214,939	55,731	30,512	1,995
California	1,119,896	-0.7	73,011	65,194	706,390	1,422	34,022	255,636	361,891	493,165	238,271	13,063
Colorado	121,069	12.6	7,373	60,896	79,052	160	3,713	26,020	329,156	50,853	24,694	1,535
Connecticut	155,062	-0.4	10,968	70,731	87,968	178	4,730	32,663	371,311	56,376	23,599	1,452
Delaware	25,434	-11.1	1,455	57,216	17,901	36	816	5,870	327,905	16,558	10,640	500
District of Columbia ...	1259	-6.6	58	46,270	813	2	34	213	262,593	330	116	10
Florida	270,180	6.3	15,473	57,271	179,959	360	7,959	57,038	316,950	104,865	48,622	3,928
Georgia	351,951	11.8	18,119	51,482	265,733	539	11,282	71,133	267,687	166,678	95,931	4,451
Hawaii	11,513	7.3	568	49,359	7,149	14	312	2,093	292,744	5,686	3,543	130
Idaho	55,774	11.0	3,186	57,123	41,205	83	1,945	9,195	223,155	20,968	11,665	1,343
Illinois	538,183	-0.2	30,952	57,511	370,965	749	17,266	111,573	300,764	252,503	141,331	6,682
Indiana	476,417	14.7	26,341	55,290	357,501	737	17,133	102,353	286,302	241,539	139,185	7,047
Iowa	203,835	11.2	10,913	53,538	147,954	298	6,563	43,511	294,086	105,663	61,724	3,658
Kansas	154,684	4.5	8,626	55,762	110,902	221	5,318	33,892	305,605	83,920	49,927	2,212
Kentucky	230,763	17.1	12,487	54,110	178,593	369	8,550	45,084	252,440	128,159	82,825	3,904
Louisiana	113,914	-6.4	8,008	70,298	80,129	169	4,925	47,821	596,800	156,874	109,723	8,700
Maine	49,710	3.4	2,657	53,453	35,983	72	1,734	8,093	224,915	15,169	7,240	439
Maryland	91,791	-14.1	6,051	65,923	56,258	114	2,754	22,769	404,720	41,214	18,301	1,153
Massachusetts	223,996	-1.0	15,416	68,821	131,020	267	6,678	46,717	356,565	84,735	37,891	2,369
Michigan	555,005	26.6	32,361	58,307	398,946	815	19,868	103,771	260,112	261,293	157,767	7,410
Minnesota	297,770	3.4	16,961	56,961	197,099	396	8,984	56,929	288,836	117,397	60,798	3,420
Mississippi	130,537	1.2	6,329	48,483	103,082	209	4,324	21,760	211,095	56,801	34,820	1,590
Missouri	245,352	8.4	0	0	182,878	362	9,029	50,314	275,121	118,828	68,337	2,824
Montana	16,697	30.7	888	53,170	11,238	22	522	3,175	282,553	9,396	6,311	643
Nebraska	92,945	5.5	4,496	48,367	70,717	142	2,986	19,005	268,741	53,112	34,006	1,110
Nevada	41,356	5.3	2,311	55,887	27,759	57	1,312	8,702	313,493	16,682	7,958	457
New Hampshire	65,553	-6.4	4137	63,109	39,464	79	1845	11562	292986	20658	9,183	570
New Jersey	210,291	-12.6	13,237	62,946	139,870	286	6,818	45,823	327,608	90,605	44,907	2,738
New Mexico	21,747	-14.8	1,253	57,626	14,700	30	707	4,936	335,788	12,674	7,699	503
New York	395,129	-6.3	23,105	58,474	261,216	523	12,404	79,496	304,332	148,469	69,074	5,141
North Carolina	411,050	5.8	20,701	50,362	303,771	617	12,424	109,824	361,536	210,018	100,157	5,153
North Dakota	22,862	12.2	1,181	51,672	16,912	34	752	4,923	291,086	13,050	8,229	331
Ohio	642,945	9.6	36,033	56,044	460,781	945	22,047	129,554	281,162	312,532	182,566	10,755
Oklahoma	121,220	2.7	6,469	53,370	89,068	175	4,024	22,705	254,923	56,775	34,119	2,274
Oregon	160,128	27.8	9,543	59,598	108,945	217	5,222	27,846	255,597	57,315	29,664	2,623
Pennsylvania	522,221	-0.6	29,380	56,260	362,007	733	17,290	105,636	291,806	217,753	112,161	7,348
Rhode Island	36,081	-3.5	2,148	59,526	23,745	47	1,145	5,607	236,153	11,344	5,793	347
South Carolina	213,050	11.8	11,641	54,638	159,797	326	7,513	44,029	275,528	109,000	65,011	3,550
South Dakota	44,094	18.1	2,040	46,256	32,491	63	1,263	7,882	242,575	17,441	9,552	433
Tennessee	308,966	11.4	16,329	52,852	228,500	468	10,236	66,937	292,939	149,126	81,964	5,122
Texas	725,255	4.6	44,620	61,523	493,691	1,016	24,678	216,626	438,788	523,118	307,617	19,745
Utah	114,500	15.9	6,541	57,124	75,761	151	3,562	23,250	306,881	48,428	25,172	1,582
Vermont	27,420	-1.8	1,542	56,230	18,641	37	864	4,205	225,578	8,788	4,479	288
Virginia	222,824	-1.4	12,504	56,118	156,906	318	7,374	57,359	365,564	99,131	41,874	2,963
Washington	253,462	13.5	16,567	65,362	165,540	326	9,067	60,007	362,491	142,700	76,768	2,458
West Virginia	44,913	-8.6	2,594	57,750	31,981	66	1,623	11,341	354,612	23,851	12,377	680
Wisconsin	435,922	5.2	23,662	54,280	310,093	628	13,931	78,972	254,671	168,601	89,896	4,921
Wyoming	8,377	1.4	603	71,954	6,066	13	403	2,452	404,175	6,742	4,261	454

[1]Includes employment and payroll at administrative offices and auxiliary units. All employees represents the average of production workers plus all other employees for the payroll period ended nearest the 12th of March. Production workers represents the average of the employment for the payroll periods ended nearest the 12th of March, May, August, and November.
[2]Adjusted value added; takes into account (a) value added by merchandising operations (that is, difference between the sales value and cost of merchandise sold without further manufacture, processing, or assembly), plus (b) net change in finished goods and work-in-process inventories between beginning and end of year.
[3]Includes extensive and unmeasurable duplication from shipments between establishments in the same industry classification.
NA = Not available

Table A-59. Major Manufacturing Sectors, 2016

| Geographic area | Food manufacturing[1] (NAICS 311) | | | | Fabricated metal products[1] (NAICS 332) | | | |
| | Employment | | | Value of shipments (million dollars) | Employment | | | Value of shipments (million dollars) |
	Total	Percent of total manufacturing	Percent change, 2015–2016		Total	Percent of total manufacturing	Percent change, 2015–2016	
United States	1,417,046	12.8	1.9	764,787	1,327,632	11.9	-3.3	335,756
Alabama	30,333	12.9	1.3	11,079	22,231	9.5	-3.4	5,904
Alaska	8,833	72.5	-8.3	3,351	466	3.8	-6.0	108
Arizona	10,775	7.9	5.9	6,570	19,599	14	1	4,405
Arkansas	43,879	30.1	1.6	16,393	12,841	8.8	-4.4	4,244
California	156,164	13.9	2.9	76,519	120,229	10.7	-3.4	27,292
Colorado	18,343	15.2	3.0	10,422	13,229	10.9	-8.5	3,645
Connecticut	6,923	4.5	6.3	3,067	27,312	17.6	-2.6	7,063
Delaware	9,552	37.6	11.0	3,584	1,819	7.2	-4.2	365
District of Columbia	358	28	100	77	43	3.4	43.3	9
Florida	27,220	10.1	7.1	15,858	28,535	10.6	0.4	6,615
Georgia	59,872	17.0	0.8	28,941	27,108	7.7	2.4	8,090
Hawaii	4,926	42.8	0.9	1,449	414	3.6	-2.6	112
Idaho	14,975	26.8	-0.7	8,133	5,497	9.9	3.4	1,253
Illinois	75,849	14.1	4.0	45,172	84,075	16	-3	22,053
Indiana	34,649	7.3	-0.7	22,291	56,740	11.9	-2.3	16,098
Iowa	49,873	24.5	1.7	36,930	18,783	9.2	-4.9	4,691
Kansas	28,382	18.3	3.1	22,820	15,582	10.1	-3.9	3,531
Kentucky	27,850	12.1	6.4	13,764	20,032	8.7	-4.1	5,121
Louisiana	13,128	11.5	0.2	8,415	17,898	15.7	-8.4	3,968
Maine	4,481	9.0	-3.4	1,597	4,830	9.7	4.2	1,164
Maryland	12,907	14.1	-6.9	7,927	7,885	8.6	-1.0	1,898
Massachusetts	18,709	8.4	-1.6	7,524	29,532	13.2	1.3	8,975
Michigan	28,104	5.1	-2.9	16,310	75,198	13.5	-2.6	18,038
Minnesota	45,881	15.4	3.5	27,062	38,465	12.9	1.8	9,715
Mississippi	20,933	16.0	1.4	6,199	9,551	7.3	-9.4	2,662
Missouri	36,220	14.8	-4.7	22,612	28,699	11.7	-1.1	6,565
Montana	1,815	10.9	4.7	946	2,009	12.0	-1.9	431
Nebraska	35,163	37.8	3.6	28,825	8,051	8.7	-4.0	2,100
Nevada	5,062	12.2	8.1	2,284	5,533	13.4	9.3	1,232
New Hampshire	2,973	4.5	1.3	1,601	11,832	18.0	1.2	2,852
New Jersey	30,136	14.3	6.2	13,102	21,590	10.3	0.1	4,643
New Mexico	4,052	18.6	-6.9	2,898	1,943	8.9	-12.6	398
New York	41,681	10.5	0.4	19,669	48,493	12.3	-2.1	11,155
North Carolina	49,885	12.1	1.2	21,409	33,810	8.2	3.4	9,754
North Dakota	4,702	20.6	0.2	4,171	1,601	7.0	-16.6	370
Ohio	52,703	8.2	2.3	32,234	96,236	15.0	-4.4	27,902
Oklahoma	15,536	12.8	-1.2	7,804	21,511	17.7	-11.6	6,075
Oregon	24,055	15.0	7.1	9,227	15,221	9.5	0.7	3,188
Pennsylvania	66,158	12.7	2.7	34,295	73,423	14.1	-5.3	17,464
Rhode Island	2,574	7.1	2.0	658	8,843	24.5	-5.2	2,195
South Carolina	16,218	7.6	-5.8	7,154	22,265	10.5	-1.4	6,532
South Dakota	9,664	21.9	6.0	5,283	3,880	8.8	-3.4	821
Tennessee	36,062	11.7	1.7	20,642	36,303	11.7	1.1	9,412
Texas	82,409	11.4	2.9	43,331	106,213	14.6	-9.3	26,194
Utah	16,124	14.1	7.5	8,884	11,162	9.7	-1.7	2,869
Vermont	4,323	15.8	13.1	2,836	2,125	7.7	-3.0	405
Virginia	29,124	13.1	3.1	14,191	17,194	7.7	-1.7	5,059
Washington	33,223	13.1	-2.5	14,975	21,683	8.6	0.6	4,738
West Virginia					4,827	10.7	-10.1	1,591
Wisconsin	65,057	14.9	0.7	43,357	64,260	14.7	-5.9	14,468
Wyoming	438	5.2	-15.4	192	1,031	12.3	-10.0	319

[1] Data may not be available for all NAICS industries or geographies.

Table A-59. Major Manufacturing Sectors, 2016—*Continued*

Geographic area	Computer and electronic products[1] (NAICS 334)				Transportation equipment[1] (NAICS 336)			
	Employment			Value of shipments (million dollars)	Employment			Value of shipments (million dollars)
	Total	Percent of total manufacturing	Percent change, 2015–2016		Total	Percent of total manufacturing	Percent change, 2015–2016	
United States	768,650	6.9	-1.1	293,587	1,478,941	13.3	0.5	949,275
Alabama..........................	6,996	3.0	-11.0	2,476	57,030	24.3	5.1	52,178
Alaska	0	0.0	0.0	0	379	3.1	4.4	84
Arizona..........................	20,443	14.9	1.0	8,576	24,447	17.9	3.0	15,715
Arkansas	2,400	1.6	-2.0	638	13,017	8.9	-7.1	5,844
California........................	157,667	14.1	-1.3	61,636	113,528	10.1	0.6	48,071
Colorado	13,422	11.1	0.2	4,374	10,124	8.4	1.6	3,703
Connecticut....................	14,209	9.2	-2.2	4,978	47,236	30.5	-0.6	20,924
Delaware	1,710	6.7	5.9	642	489	1.9	10.1	116
District of Columbia	0	0.0	0.0	0	0	0.0	0.0	0
Florida............................	31,385	11.6	-3.7	10,975	28,221	10.4	1.2	8,791
Georgia	5,986	1.7	2.3	1,808	48,110	13.7	2.2	33,477
Hawaii	0	0.0	0.0	0	913	7.9	32.5	371
Idaho..............................	9,943	17.8	6.4	2,630	2,060	3.7	-6.4	553
Illinois............................	22,939	4.3	-6.6	8,976	51,056	9.5	-4.4	28,667
Indiana............................	13,421	2.8	0.3	5,469	121,265	25.5	1.7	81,049
Iowa................................	12,097	5.9	-1.1	3,813	14,004	6.9	-3.5	4,244
Kansas	6,868	4.4	-1.1	1,658	35,365	22.9	-11.1	21,399
Kentucky	3,106	1.3	5.0	880	63,956	27.7	5.5	50,260
Louisiana	952	0.8	-9.8	249	10,199	9.0	-14.6	2,702
Maine..............................	2,583	5.2	1.9	1,203	11,385	22.9	25.3	2,342
Maryland..........................	15,443	16.8	-0.9	6,988	5,293	5.8	4.4	1,951
Massachusetts..................	48,624	21.7	-0.1	22,513	6,986	3.1	-12.7	2,271
Michigan..........................	12,625	2.3	-0.6	3,520	161,397	29.1	3.6	124,070
Minnesota	35,107	11.8	0.3	11,523	11,972	4.0	-3.2	6,844
Mississippi......................	1,663	1.3	-10.3	298	24,703	18.9	2.6	11,679
Missouri..........................	6,355	2.6	4.8	2,564	43,424	17.7	2.3	34,478
Montana..........................	195	1.2	-	53	737	4.4	6.8	192
Nebraska..........................	4,131	4.4	-0.6	1,110	7,098	7.6	-5.0	2,467
Nevada............................	4,187	10.1	6.4	2,476	613	1.5	-18.0	254
New Hampshire..............	12,151	18.5	-0.6	4,065	3,310	5.0	2.8	772
New Jersey	21,356	10.2	2.7	7,049	3,730	1.8	2.9	1,016
New Mexico	3,427	15.8	-17.9	1,776	417	1.9	-15.4	149
New York........................	41,439	10.5	-0.5	13,377	19,176	4.9	-1.0	9,133
North Carolina................	13,710	3.3	-16.2	6,230	29,797	7.2	-4.9	23,639
North Dakota..................	1,373	6.0	-6.5	375	1,702	7.4	-12.7	501
Ohio................................	22,076	3.4	-0.8	6,479	115,400	17.9	-1.0	88,587
Oklahoma........................	3,647	3.0	-10.6	1,004	10,632	8.8	-7.1	5,068
Oregon............................	24,243	15.1	0.8	12,214	9,611	6.0	-3.7	3,128
Pennsylvania....................	28,594	5.5	1.4	10,734	35,478	6.8	0.7	19,307
Rhode Island....................	2,991	8.3	1.2	858	923	2.6	-4.8	253
South Carolina	4,379	2.1	2.9	2,768	35,418	16.6	3.5	28,784
South Dakota	1,965	4.5	-5.5	453	2,452	5.6	-15.7	772
Tennessee........................	6,519	2.1	-5.7	2,669	56,179	18.2	8.4	40,126
Texas..............................	55,580	7.7	-3.2	26,416	75,504	10.4	-2.4	62,081
Utah................................	13,814	12.1	0.9	4,640	10,355	9.0	6.8	4,147
Vermont..........................	4,529	16.5	-2.2	1,494	1,593	5.8	-7.5	405
Virginia............................	10,329	4.6	-2.5	3,415	38,343	17.2	-12.5	11,813
Washington......................	20,783	8.2	11.1	6,442	82,351	32.5	4.0	70,261
West Virginia..................	704	1.6	-15.0	169	5,552	12.4	-1.0	4,493
Wisconsin	20,285	4.7	1.1	8,864	25,928	5.9	7.4	10,099
Wyoming	217	2.6	-27.4	52	82	1.0	-31.1	46

[1]Data may not be available for all NAICS industries or geographies.

Table A-60. Information Industries

Geographic area	Nonfarm Employment (BLS)[1] (thousands)			Earnings (BEA)[2] (million dollars)			Establishments[3]								Net change, 2010–2017
							Total, 2017	Publishing, 2017	Motion Picture/ Sound Recording, 2017	Broadcasting, except Internet 2017	Tele-communications, 2017	Data Processing, hosting and related, 2017	Other Information services, 2017	Total, 2010	
	2019	2015	2010	2019	2015	2010									
United States	2,867.2	2,750.0	2,707.0	460,773	382,813	294,078	153,934	29,740	25,801	8,252	60,475	17,597	12,069	135,431	18,503
Alabama......................	21.2	21.4	24.0	1,745	1,589	1,603	1,735	308	124	160	957	126	60	1,587	148
Alaska........................	5.3	6.3	6.5	540	607	428	414	50	40	56	231	19	18	385	29
Arizona.......................	48.8	44.6	36.6	5,320	4,340	2,948	2,520	532	305	137	1,021	350	175	2,060	460
Arkansas.....................	11.3	13.5	15.3	889	1,005	1,203	1,150	185	105	114	593	109	44	1,052	98
California.....................	562.6	486.3	429.4	129,465	98,196	53,413	25,162	4,566	8,728	844	6,255	2,658	2,111	20,287	4,875
Colorado......................	76.0	70.7	72.0	7,406	6,824	7,398	3,615	843	447	161	1,298	572	294	2,940	675
Connecticut..................	31.5	32.4	31.7	4,598	4,197	3,411	1,804	400	237	101	673	198	195	1,649	155
Delaware.....................	3.9	4.7	6.0	399	452	570	584	118	54	17	238	90	67	402	182
District of Columbia	20.1	17.2	18.7	3,263	2,546	2,424	774	180	111	82	169	91	141	726	48
Florida........................	138.9	136.6	137.1	17,757	15,870	13,668	9,350	1,656	1,418	521	3,967	1,042	746	7,806	1,544
Georgia	117.0	111.5	98.0	21,721	17,161	14,877	4,697	847	724	288	1,988	556	294	4,064	633
Hawaii.........................	8.7	8.7	9.8	817	751	752	533	105	95	49	203	60	21	543	-10
Idaho..........................	9.0	9.3	9.6	682	628	593	799	169	75	60	350	90	55	702	97
Illinois........................	95.4	101.0	101.8	12,094	10,810	9,029	5,986	1,134	798	303	2,643	675	433	5,535	451
Indiana.......................	28.8	33.6	35.6	2,654	2,764	2,546	2,437	439	270	167	1,145	327	89	2,297	140
Iowa...........................	21.3	24.4	28.7	1,953	1,855	2,002	1,608	417	167	122	722	129	51	1,585	23
Kansas	18.1	21.1	26.8	3,550	2,433	1,428	1,439	277	128	124	701	121	88	1,437	2
Kentucky	21.6	22.7	24.7	1,844	1,772	2,362	1,794	298	159	161	820	286	70	1,487	307
Louisiana	22.2	26.4	24.7	1,804	1,875	1,647	1,528	243	154	114	836	126	55	1,393	135
Maine..........................	7.2	7.7	8.7	536	499	563	813	172	99	57	284	68	133	719	94
Maryland......................	35.3	38.6	44.0	8,018	7,120	8,019	2,546	478	331	118	1,065	374	180	2,417	129
Massachusetts..............	92.6	88.2	85.0	14,086	11,881	10,036	3,853	1,035	393	186	1,352	527	360	3,492	361
Michigan......................	55.2	56.6	54.8	5,446	5,297	4,477	4,084	692	430	213	1,811	431	507	3,451	633
Minnesota	46.8	51.3	54.1	4,941	4,982	4,455	2,787	694	384	178	1,051	299	181	2,568	219
Mississippi...................	10.7	12.7	12.3	739	828	691	1,020	158	47	107	609	67	32	918	102
Missouri......................	47.8	54.3	60.1	4,852	4,821	4,861	2,689	514	272	168	1,339	273	123	2,537	152
Montana......................	6.2	6.4	7.3	504	452	452	696	162	105	68	287	51	23	575	121
Nebraska.....................	17.2	18.3	17.5	1,533	1,364	1,125	977	238	96	75	424	99	45	934	43
Nevada........................	15.8	13.9	12.5	2,006	1,792	1,559	1,429	291	221	74	493	188	162	1,119	310
New Hampshire.............	12.4	12.5	11.4	1,556	1,454	1,168	771	206	74	40	296	98	57	723	48
New Jersey	67.4	74.4	79.2	10,922	11,050	9,274	3,888	717	477	98	1,712	602	282	3,841	47
New Mexico	11.2	12.7	14.4	923	918	932	822	144	94	80	385	71	48	791	31
New York.....................	278.3	264.9	253.1	55,427	46,464	34,409	11,741	2,111	3,248	489	3,383	1,000	1,510	11,014	727
North Carolina..............	76.2	76.2	68.3	8,381	7,795	5,633	3,918	786	475	245	1,720	460	232	3,576	342
North Dakota................	6.1	6.6	7.3	625	521	511	348	100	39	55	113	24	17	352	-4
Ohio...........................	69.5	71.6	77.6	6,761	6,573	8,692	4,298	784	408	224	2,114	576	192	4,055	243
Oklahoma....................	19.6	21.2	24.3	2,124	2,048	1,653	1,576	287	155	89	839	143	63	1,543	33
Oregon.......................	35.1	32.9	31.7	4,091	3,308	2,778	2,396	615	340	113	891	263	174	1,977	419
Pennsylvania................	86.9	84.9	93.3	25,858	23,626	19,557	5,574	919	533	266	2,356	806	694	5,010	564
Rhode Island................	5.9	8.6	10.0	581	813	832	453	96	52	27	167	55	56	415	38
South Carolina	27.1	26.9	25.9	3,025	2,248	2,003	1,639	303	149	117	822	162	86	1,393	246
South Dakota	5.5	5.9	6.5	523	492	433	474	133	54	61	169	38	19	419	55
Tennessee...................	45.5	44.4	45.0	4,417	3,772	3,471	2,789	473	533	235	1,186	250	112	2,421	368
Texas..........................	208.6	200.7	195.7	23,469	20,548	17,243	10,484	1,829	1,094	571	5,005	1,285	700	8,911	1,573
Utah...........................	39.9	34.6	29.3	4,198	3,032	2,138	1,746	410	305	56	544	264	167	1,375	371
Vermont......................	4.3	4.7	5.4	370	369	407	511	114	61	50	157	43	86	484	27
Virginia.......................	68.3	69.6	76.0	6,314	7,488	8,171	4,103	845	363	211	1,713	652	319	3,819	284
Washington..................	144.4	114.0	103.0	34,122	20,112	11,917	3,873	978	491	142	1,390	521	351	3,199	674
West Virginia................	8.1	9.7	10.3	598	746	667	675	100	42	58	418	37	20	747	-72
Wisconsin....................	47.0	48.9	46.7	5,059	4,472	3,420	2,632	523	253	161	1,382	217	96	2,399	233
Wyoming	3.4	3.8	3.9	263	250	231	400	66	44	39	188	28	35	300	100

[1]Employment estimates provided by the Bureau of Labor Statistics are based on the 2017 North American Industry Classification System (NAICS). The estimates for 2015 are based on the 2012 NAICS. The estimates for 2019 are based on
[2]The estimates of earnings provided by the Bureau of Economic Analysis for 2010 are based on the 2007 North American Industry Classification System (NAICS). the 2017 NAICS. All dollar estimates are in current dollars (not adjusted for inflation.)
[3]Data provided by County Business Patterns is based on the North American Industry Classification System (NAICS). Data for 2017 is based on NAICS 2017. Data for 2010 is based on NAICS 2007.

Table A-61. Wholesale and Retail Trade

Geographic area	Wholesale and retail nonfarm employment[1] (thousands)			Wholesale trade Earnings (BEA)[2] (million dollars)			Wholesale trade Establishments (NAICS 42)		Retail trade Earnings (BEA)[2] (million dollars)			Retail trade Establishments (NAICS 44 and 45)	
	2019	2015	2010	2019	2015	2010	2017	2014	2019	2015	2010	2017	2014
United States	21,496	21,460	19,893	607,508	553,067	440,078	409,656	416,593	725,996	651,772	540,618	1,064,449	1,065,368
Alabama	305	305	295	6,202	5,763	5,002	5,250	5,348	8,849	7,995	6,998	17,987	18,029
Alaska	42	44	42	560	507	433	753	745	1,739	1,704	1,546	2,489	2,496
Arizona	424	415	387	10,323	8,883	7,659	6,540	6,607	15,264	13,467	11,073	17,931	17,944
Arkansas	184	187	176	4,141	3,823	3,136	3,377	3,439	5,236	4,915	4,085	10,919	10,866
California	2,352	2,376	2,162	79,058	70,507	52,651	58,878	59,379	94,382	86,342	69,564	108,276	107,469
Colorado	382	366	328	12,008	10,230	7,775	7,225	7,206	12,577	10,753	8,758	18,892	18,643
Connecticut	235	247	241	7,446	7,271	6,278	4,097	4,324	9,387	9,074	7,958	12,462	12,542
Delaware	63	65	62	1,057	1,185	1,143	1,157	1,083	2,137	1,986	1,723	3,678	3,627
District of Columbia	28	27	23	836	700	556	405	452	1,113	950	750	1,783	1,740
Florida	1,462	1,416	1,247	35,190	30,759	23,681	31,283	31,443	47,938	42,654	33,396	74,530	73,200
Georgia	710	700	635	22,951	20,115	16,068	13,102	13,058	21,203	18,747	14,761	34,160	33,666
Hawaii	89	89	84	1,541	1,330	1,082	1,620	1,674	3,390	3,050	2,552	4,681	4,639
Idaho	119	112	100	2,463	2,053	1,537	2,169	2,050	4,168	3,728	3,004	6,131	5,818
Illinois	881	916	874	33,556	30,401	24,674	18,097	18,893	26,034	24,804	21,155	38,142	39,252
Indiana	439	444	418	10,917	9,918	7,947	7,609	7,684	13,139	11,878	10,048	21,343	21,431
Iowa	241	248	239	5,706	5,416	4,416	5,038	4,914	6,399	5,923	5,282	11,461	11,828
Kansas	200	209	198	5,387	5,064	4,385	4,436	4,497	5,622	5,425	4,830	10,074	10,391
Kentucky	285	284	272	6,302	5,591	4,583	4,279	4,315	7,893	7,063	6,309	15,035	15,223
Louisiana	292	306	288	6,251	5,933	5,008	5,337	5,482	9,219	8,927	7,788	16,614	16,596
Maine	100	102	100	1,651	1,533	1,267	1,540	1,575	3,363	2,940	2,748	6,238	6,304
Maryland	367	377	362	9,047	8,406	7,303	5,433	5,678	12,759	12,052	10,317	17,920	18,171
Massachusetts	475	477	461	15,829	14,144	12,495	7,567	7,875	17,335	14,897	13,264	24,129	24,136
Michigan	636	637	597	17,492	15,657	12,194	10,917	11,234	19,478	17,234	14,628	34,228	34,686
Minnesota	421	426	400	14,340	14,177	11,317	7,949	8,152	12,510	11,289	9,328	18,819	18,993
Mississippi	170	173	167	2,751	2,456	2,094	2,711	2,788	5,318	4,968	4,293	11,547	11,555
Missouri	428	432	415	11,183	10,597	8,495	7,625	7,789	12,189	11,571	10,217	20,730	21,228
Montana	76	76	70	1,323	1,237	898	1,600	1,580	2,658	2,327	2,255	4,742	4,757
Nebraska	145	152	145	3,886	3,711	2,976	3,201	3,162	4,280	3,896	3,265	7,132	7,240
Nevada	187	178	159	3,474	2,971	2,466	3,120	2,984	6,984	5,739	4,767	8,689	8,512
New Hampshire	122	123	118	3,335	3,083	2,289	1,830	1,847	4,451	4,007	5,183	6,023	6,044
New Jersey	665	676	645	26,135	24,718	20,450	13,859	14,236	24,059	21,363	18,150	31,354	31,685
New Mexico	111	115	111	1,597	1,456	1,371	1,747	1,855	3,618	3,529	3,197	6,333	6,557
New York	1,242	1,288	1,200	38,692	36,541	28,886	30,560	32,438	47,283	43,106	35,963	78,497	78,763
North Carolina	687	663	599	18,319	15,674	11,971	11,722	11,674	20,381	17,872	14,920	34,954	34,246
North Dakota	70	78	65	2,218	2,327	1,465	1,739	1,705	1,962	2,137	1,455	3,258	3,242
Ohio	790	806	767	22,327	20,311	16,159	13,678	14,217	23,295	21,336	18,641	35,550	36,260
Oklahoma	234	243	223	4,783	4,750	3,227	4,623	4,699	7,287	7,165	5,978	12,991	13,237
Oregon	286	276	250	7,292	6,300	6,047	5,336	5,345	9,824	8,352	6,816	14,336	13,994
Pennsylvania	825	856	844	22,580	21,542	18,023	14,299	14,832	25,859	24,291	22,657	42,608	43,598
Rhode Island	65	65	62	1,786	1,664	1,282	1,312	1,337	2,346	2,220	2,036	3,797	3,744
South Carolina	325	313	287	6,608	5,709	4,375	5,020	4,975	9,972	8,645	7,174	17,757	17,567
South Dakota	72	74	68	1,724	1,620	1,124	1,566	1,522	2,206	2,214	1,774	3,875	3,866
Tennessee	456	446	424	11,661	10,453	8,323	6,867	6,858	15,809	13,890	11,325	22,629	22,533
Texas	1,932	1,880	1,623	61,237	56,715	43,052	33,359	33,235	61,912	56,297	42,709	80,629	79,814
Utah	226	208	182	5,180	4,273	3,203	3,687	3,743	8,543	6,967	5,119	9,942	9,224
Vermont	46	47	47	745	688	619	790	813	1,624	1,501	1,315	3,232	3,400
Virginia	517	527	508	11,625	10,572	9,132	6,943	7,204	16,682	15,655	13,088	26,798	27,059
Washington	527	487	428	13,534	12,116	9,673	9,191	9,288	29,811	19,514	13,264	21,710	21,586
West Virginia	101	109	110	1,577	1,539	1,426	1,411	1,530	2,990	2,915	2,695	5,963	6,214
Wisconsin	422	427	406	10,946	9,827	7,853	6,973	6,985	12,307	11,272	9,427	18,880	19,143
Wyoming	37	40	38	735	849	607	829	845	1,212	1,226	1,073	2,571	2,610

[1]Estimates of labor provided by the Bureau of Labor Statistics (BLS) are based on the 2017 North American Industry Classification System (NAICS). Includes Wholesale trade (NAICS 42) and Retail trade (NAICS 44).
[2]Bureau of Economic Analysis. The estimates of earnings for 2010 are based on the 2007 North American Industry Classification System (NAICS). The estimates for 2015 are based on the 2012 NAICS. The estimates for 2019 are based on the 2017 NAICS. All dollars estimates are in current dollars and not adjusted for inflation.

Table A-62. Retail Trade Earnings, 2018

Geographic area	Total retail trade (million dollars)	Food services and drinking places (2017, NAICS 722) (million dollars)	Motor vehicle and parts dealers (2017, NAICS 441) Earnings (million dollars)	Percentage of all retail	Furniture and Home furnishings (2017, NAICS 442) Earnings (million dollars)	Percentage of all retail	Electronics and appliances (2017, NAICS 443) Earnings (million dollars)	Percentage of all retail	Building material and garden equipment and supplies dealers (2017, NAICS 444) Earnings (million dollars)	Percentage of all retail	Food and beverage stores (2017, NAICS 445) Earnings (million dollars)	Percentage of all retail	Health and personal care (2017, NAICS 446) Earnings (million dollars)	Percentage of all retail
United States	705,796	334,887	134,292	19.0	24,456	3.5	29,716	4.2	58,208	8.2	110,740	15.7	54,865	7.8
Alabama	8,542	3,625	1,875	21.9	283	3.3	320	3.8	854	10.0	971	11.4	789	9.2
Alaska	1,694	759	255	15.1	39	2.3	36	2.1	174	10.3	245	14.5	61	3.6
Arizona	14,750	6,818	2,823	19.1	753	5.1	672	4.6	1,146	7.8	2,247	15.2	997	6.8
Arkansas	5,143	2,121	1,136	22.1	150	2.9	161	3.1	447	8.7	622	12.1	433	8.4
California	91,985	49,989	14,937	16.2	3,246	3.5	3,762	4.1	6,366	6.9	17,333	18.8	6,992	7.6
Colorado	12,091	6,862	2,552	21.1	462	3.8	461	3.8	1,054	8.7	1,961	16.2	741	6.1
Connecticut	9,279	4,030	1,569	16.9	356	3.8	360	3.9	799	8.6	1,806	19.5	659	7.1
Delaware	2,097	1,018	451	21.5	101	4.8	101	4.8	203	9.7	345	16.5	170	8.1
District of Columbia	1,094	2,059	8	0.7	41	3.7	82	7.5	82	7.5	308	28.2	157	14.4
Florida	47,123	22,559	10,335	21.9	2,059	4.4	2,473	5.2	3,885	8.2	7,122	15.1	3,899	8.3
Georgia	20,584	9,560	4,229	20.5	968	4.7	1,219	5.9	1,765	8.6	2,858	13.9	1,555	7.6
Hawaii	3,328	2,551	479	14.4	81	2.4	80	2.4	200	6.0	664	19.9	246	7.4
Idaho	4,050	1,291	832	20.5	139	3.4	121	3.0	374	9.2	624	15.4	172	4.2
Illinois	25,296	13,501	4,481	17.7	924	3.7	1,763	7.0	1,891	7.5	3,962	15.7	2,538	10.0
Indiana	12,807	5,471	2,566	20.0	413	3.2	406	3.2	1,290	10.1	1,297	10.1	937	7.3
Iowa	6,346	2,199	1,338	21.1	187	3.0	241	3.8	645	10.2	1,097	17.3	394	6.2
Kansas	5,572	2,505	1,091	19.6	240	4.3	222	4.0	569	10.2	937	16.8	386	6.9
Kentucky	7,712	3,994	1,570	20.4	233	3.0	255	3.3	775	10.0	964	12.5	865	11.2
Louisiana	9,084	4,283	1,733	19.1	266	2.9	313	3.4	935	10.3	1,426	15.7	901	9.9
Maine	3,235	1,381	625	19.3	75	2.3	95	2.9	343	10.6	644	19.9	191	5.9
Maryland	12,555	6,146	2,511	20.0	454	3.6	486	3.9	1,136	9.0	2,810	22.4	920	7.3
Massachusetts	16,444	9,149	2,814	17.1	512	3.1	456	2.8	1,341	8.2	3,511	21.4	1,398	8.5
Michigan	19,042	8,014	4,217	22.1	632	3.3	867	4.6	1,926	10.1	2,560	13.4	1,752	9.2
Minnesota	12,327	4,991	2,222	18.0	418	3.4	459	3.7	1,108	9.0	1,865	15.1	966	7.8
Mississippi	5,246	1,981	1,075	20.5	124	2.4	151	2.9	514	9.8	604	11.5	503	9.6
Missouri	11,993	5,433	2,459	20.5	380	3.2	406	3.4	1,220	10.2	1,463	12.2	951	7.9
Montana	2,576	992	484	18.8	88	3.4	65	2.5	282	10.9	396	15.4	103	4.0
Nebraska	4,183	1,604	850	20.3	195	4.7	130	3.1	406	9.7	594	14.2	326	7.8
Nevada	6,700	3,787	1,353	20.2	212	3.2	245	3.7	386	5.8	927	13.8	437	6.5
New Hampshire	4,308	1,583	894	20.8	124	2.9	261	6.0	453	10.5	659	15.3	204	4.7
New Jersey	23,244	8,084	3,558	15.3	847	3.6	1,163	5.0	1,614	6.9	4,748	20.4	2,026	8.7
New Mexico	3,613	1,931	812	22.5	83	2.3	100	2.8	296	8.2	486	13.4	238	6.6
New York	45,625	23,807	5,781	12.7	1,382	3.0	2,265	5.0	3,090	6.8	8,081	17.7	5,138	11.3
North Carolina	19,515	9,976	4,516	23.1	677	3.5	763	3.9	1,868	9.6	2,592	13.3	1,551	7.9
North Dakota	1,942	641	417	21.5	68	3.5	79	4.1	226	11.7	201	10.3	125	6.4
Ohio	22,781	10,837	4,822	21.2	657	2.9	898	3.9	2,163	9.5	3,043	13.4	1,669	7.3
Oklahoma	7,107	3,556	1,525	21.5	282	4.0	240	3.4	760	10.7	927	13.0	576	8.1
Oregon	9,571	4,971	1,811	18.9	352	3.7	346	3.6	780	8.1	1,664	17.4	429	4.5
Pennsylvania	25,229	10,569	4,873	19.3	727	2.9	821	3.3	2,022	8.0	4,602	18.2	2,189	8.7
Rhode Island	2,285	1,267	371	16.3	65	2.8	70	3.1	181	7.9	438	19.2	291	12.7
South Carolina	9,621	4,824	1,964	20.4	282	2.9	334	3.5	1,001	10.4	1,439	15.0	755	7.8
South Dakota	2,170	676	485	22.4	63	2.9	72	3.3	231	10.6	250	11.5	88	4.1
Tennessee	15,551	7,112	3,404	21.9	580	3.7	691	4.4	1,344	8.6	1,953	12.6	1,256	8.1
Texas	59,740	30,278	14,382	24.1	2,183	3.7	2,777	4.6	4,742	7.9	8,807	14.7	3,967	6.6
Utah	8,194	2,360	1,595	19.5	332	4.0	320	3.9	609	7.4	833	10.2	694	8.5
Vermont	1,596	615	320	20.1	44	2.8	35	2.2	165	10.3	322	20.2	92	5.7
Virginia	16,232	8,203	3,595	22.1	628	3.9	754	4.6	1,359	8.4	2,646	16.3	1,114	6.9
Washington	28,296	8,516	3,099	11.0	597	2.1	788	2.8	1,665	5.9	2,598	9.2	914	3.2
West Virginia	2,964	1,228	619	20.9	65	2.2	99	3.3	308	10.4	351	11.8	313	10.6
Wisconsin	12,150	4,694	2,315	19.1	364	3.0	401	3.3	1,083	8.9	1,776	14.6	751	6.2
Wyoming	1,185	486	263	22.2	28	2.3	33	2.7	132	11.1	163	13.7	43	3.6

Table A-62. Retail Trade Earnings, 2018—*Continued*

Geographic area	Gasoline stations (2017, NAICS 447) (million dollars)		Clothing and clothing accessories (2017, NAICS 448) (million dollars)		Sporting goods, hobby, book, music stores (2017, NAICS 451)		General merchandise stores (2017, NAICS 452) (million dollars)		Miscellaneous stores (2017, NAICS 453)		Non-store retailers (2017, NAICS 454)	
	Earnings (million dollars)	Percentage of all retail	Earnings (million dollars)	Percentage of all retail	Earnings (million dollars)	Percentage of all retail	Earnings (million dollars)	Percentage of all retail	Earnings (million dollars)	Percentage of all retail	Earnings (million dollars)	Percentage of all retail
United States	38,592	5.5	43,391	6.1	18,612	2.6	96,456	13.7	39,302	5.6	57,166	8.1
Alabama	584	6.8	370	4.3	246	2.9	1,688	19.8	331	3.9	231	2.7
Alaska	89	5.2	71	4.2	61	3.6	412	24.3	142	8.4	109	6.4
Arizona	767	5.2	589	4.0	324	2.2	2,075	14.1	968	6.6	1,389	9.4
Arkansas	340	6.6	197	3.8	135	2.6	1,180	22.9	236	4.6	106	2.1
California	6,473	7.0	7,078	7.7	2,369	2.6	10,471	11.4	5,603	6.1	7,356	8.0
Colorado	545	4.5	581	4.8	561	4.6	1,697	14.0	884	7.3	592	4.9
Connecticut	420	4.5	738	8.0	246	2.7	826	8.9	533	5.7	967	10.4
Delaware	81	3.9	140	6.7	48	2.3	249	11.9	85	4.0	122	5.8
District of Columbia	22	2.0	105	9.6	36	3.3	128	11.7	72	6.5	52	4.7
Florida	1,467	3.1	3,125	6.6	1,070	2.3	6,506	13.8	2,163	4.6	3,019	6.4
Georgia	1,087	5.3	1,108	5.4	462	2.2	3,260	15.8	1,115	5.4	957	4.6
Hawaii	99	3.0	444	13.3	106	3.2	533	16.0	318	9.6	78	2.3
Idaho	275	6.8	117	2.9	131	3.2	548	13.5	222	5.5	496	12.3
Illinois	1,072	4.2	1,479	5.8	602	2.4	3,968	15.7	1,195	4.7	1,422	5.6
Indiana	777	6.1	1,196	9.3	265	2.1	2,132	16.6	636	5.0	893	7.0
Iowa	550	8.7	248	3.9	168	2.6	977	15.4	261	4.1	240	3.8
Kansas	342	6.1	224	4.0	185	3.3	889	16.0	261	4.7	226	4.1
Kentucky	457	5.9	290	3.8	169	2.2	1,455	18.9	355	4.6	323	4.2
Louisiana	750	8.3	425	4.7	195	2.1	1,575	17.3	431	4.7	134	1.5
Maine	223	6.9	128	4.0	88	2.7	367	11.3	181	5.6	277	8.6
Maryland	597	4.8	723	5.8	309	2.5	1,529	12.2	636	5.1	443	3.5
Massachusetts	470	2.9	1,125	6.8	492	3.0	1,492	9.1	911	5.5	1,923	11.7
Michigan	845	4.4	806	4.2	485	2.5	3,148	16.5	1,056	5.5	747	3.9
Minnesota	820	6.7	550	4.5	342	2.8	1,759	14.3	662	5.4	1,154	9.4
Mississippi	552	10.5	237	4.5	103	2.0	1,049	20.0	224	4.3	109	2.1
Missouri	951	7.9	575	4.8	319	2.7	2,047	17.1	538	4.5	684	5.7
Montana	278	10.8	73	2.9	97	3.7	345	13.4	275	10.7	91	3.5
Nebraska	407	9.7	158	3.8	111	2.6	612	14.6	141	3.4	254	6.1
Nevada	447	6.7	717	10.7	128	1.9	850	12.7	529	7.9	468	7.0
New Hampshire	182	4.2	193	4.5	163	3.8	426	9.9	256	5.9	494	11.5
New Jersey	840	3.6	1,893	8.1	1,210	5.2	2,269	9.8	1,245	5.4	1,832	7.9
New Mexico	290	8.0	184	5.1	80	2.2	680	18.8	267	7.4	98	2.7
New York	1,255	2.8	5,328	11.7	1,104	2.4	4,680	10.3	3,973	8.7	3,548	7.8
North Carolina	1,263	6.5	970	5.0	477	2.4	3,045	15.6	853	4.4	940	4.8
North Dakota	201	10.4	61	3.1	66	3.4	261	13.5	152	7.8	84	4.3
Ohio	1,399	6.1	1,316	5.8	602	2.6	3,227	14.2	1,149	5.0	1,837	8.1
Oklahoma	570	8.0	267	3.8	170	2.4	1,256	17.7	369	5.2	165	2.3
Oregon	533	5.6	568	5.9	324	3.4	1,413	14.8	722	7.5	630	6.6
Pennsylvania	1,094	4.3	1,356	5.4	655	2.6	3,123	12.4	1,266	5.0	2,502	9.9
Rhode Island	148	6.5	118	5.2	41	1.8	272	11.9	122	5.4	167	7.3
South Carolina	627	6.5	589	6.1	246	2.6	1,618	16.8	434	4.5	332	3.4
South Dakota	210	9.7	68	3.2	61	2.8	276	12.7	242	11.2	123	5.6
Tennessee	1,006	6.5	755	4.9	387	2.5	2,287	14.7	941	6.1	946	6.1
Texas	3,618	6.1	3,536	5.9	1,513	2.5	8,715	14.6	2,807	4.7	2,692	4.5
Utah	375	4.6	402	4.9	278	3.4	981	12.0	371	4.5	1,404	17.1
Vermont	126	7.9	74	4.6	54	3.4	100	6.3	103	6.4	159	10.0
Virginia	892	5.5	803	4.9	377	2.3	2,597	16.0	745	4.6	725	4.5
Washington	842	3.0	712	2.5	520	1.8	2,830	10.0	1,582	5.6	12,148	42.9
West Virginia	282	9.5	95	3.2	71	2.4	563	19.0	115	3.9	84	2.8
Wisconsin	902	7.4	442	3.6	328	2.7	1,883	15.5	562	4.6	1,343	11.1
Wyoming	146	12.3	43	3.6	35	2.9	187	15.8	62	5.2	52	4.4

Table A-63. Transportation and Commuting

| Geographic area | Transportation and warehousing (NAICS 48-49) | | | | | | | Workers 16 years and over, 2018 | | | | | | |
| | Nonfarm employment (BLS)[1] (thousands) | | Earnings (BEA)[2] (million dollars) | | Establishments[3] | | | Total workers (thousands) | Percentage of workers who | | | | Mean travel time to work (minutes) | Vehicle miles of travel, 2018 (billions) |
	2019	2015	2019	2015	2017	2010	Net change 2010–2017		Drove alone to work	Carpooled	Used public transportation[4]	Worked at home		
United States	5,618.1	4,858.6	523,010	423,869	237,308	208,474	28,834	154,609	76.3	9.0	4.9	5.3	27.1	3,240
Alabama	65.0	58.9	5,226	4,027	3,101	2,874	227	2,068	86.3	7.9	0.3	3.5	25.2	71
Alaska	20.3	19.6	2,218	1,970	1,179	1,113	66	355	68.0	12.3	1.2	5.3	19.1	5
Arizona	106.1	84.1	7,918	6,014	3,433	3,065	368	3,175	76.1	11.0	1.7	6.8	25.7	66
Arkansas	NA	NA	4,196	3,769	2,470	2,412	58	1,301	82.6	10.4	0.4	3.7	21.7	37
California	643.8	499.4	67,286	46,663	24,840	20,876	3,964	18,530	73.8	10.0	4.9	6.0	30.2	349
Colorado	86.9	72.2	10,395	10,054	3,776	3,340	436	2,963	74.9	8.6	2.8	8.6	25.9	54
Connecticut	51.8	44.4	5,422	4,990	1,672	1,641	31	1,793	77.9	8.1	4.4	5.7	26.8	32
Delaware	NA	NA	1,056	915	714	652	62	453	79.6	9.1	2.2	5.7	26.4	10
District of Columbia	NA	NA	560	567	158	182	-24	378	34.2	5.1	34.4	6.1	30.9	4
Florida	318.6	248.4	26,052	20,125	15,660	12,538	3,122	9,609	79.1	9.4	1.7	6.2	28.0	222
Georgia	214.4	174.1	17,170	15,370	6,962	5,831	1,131	4,891	79.4	9.4	2.0	5.9	29.0	131
Hawaii	30.5	27.3	2,537	2,044	926	856	70	707	67.3	14.7	5.7	5.4	27.6	11
Idaho	23.0	20.4	1,778	1,471	1,796	1,602	194	795	79.7	8.9	0.8	6.2	21.0	18
Illinois	299.3	261.2	25,649	23,446	16,203	12,151	4,052	6,192	72.7	8.3	9.4	5.1	29.4	108
Indiana	146.2	133.1	10,544	8,881	5,410	5,016	394	3,175	82.9	8.9	0.9	3.9	23.9	82
Iowa	63.2	60.1	4,811	4,324	3,679	3,620	59	1,589	81.6	8.1	1.0	5.1	19.5	33
Kansas	60.7	49.7	5,973	4,422	2,640	2,615	25	1,435	82.0	9.3	0.5	4.8	19.7	32
Kentucky	111.1	96.7	8,547	6,890	2,952	2,951	1	1,965	82.4	9.4	1.0	4.1	23.5	50
Louisiana	78.7	79.3	7,099	6,937	3,824	3,819	5	1,994	82.7	9.0	1.2	3.4	26.3	50
Maine	17.1	16	1,154	1,033	1,233	1,217	16	666	77.8	9.9	0.6	6.0	24.1	15
Maryland	92.4	77.2	6,884	6,054	3,525	3,307	218	3,066	74.3	8.8	7.9	5.2	33.3	60
Massachusetts	92.7	82.1	7,908	6,388	3,976	3,565	411	3,559	69.8	7.4	10.2	5.3	30.5	67
Michigan	139.2	115.6	10,904	8,622	6,624	5,482	1,142	4,616	82.0	8.9	1.4	4.1	24.7	102
Minnesota	97.2	86.2	8,796	7,224	4,832	4,549	283	2,923	77.7	8.4	3.5	6.1	23.8	60
Mississippi	52.8	45.1	3,407	2,637	2,113	2,077	36	1,217	85.5	8.9	0.3	2.6	25.0	41
Missouri	103.2	94.1	7,820	7,086	4,887	4,704	183	2,891	82.2	8.4	1.3	4.8	24.0	77
Montana	16.1	15.2	1,338	1,287	1,375	1,309	66	515	74.9	9.5	0.8	7.3	18.6	13
Nebraska	52.0	53.5	7,559	6,878	2,494	2,302	192	986	82.1	8.7	0.6	5.1	18.8	21
Nevada	70.4	56.6	4,918	3,981	1,643	1,392	251	1,427	78.3	10.5	2.9	4.2	24.9	28
New Hampshire	15.2	13.3	930	736	816	811	5	714	80.8	7.4	0.9	6.9	27.6	14
New Jersey	206.7	163.4	17,784	14,065	7,579	6,697	882	4,398	70.9	8.2	11.7	4.7	32.4	78
New Mexico	NA	NA	1,749	1,624	1,404	1,283	121	875	79.3	11.2	1.1	5.1	23.0	27
New York	272.4	246.9	26,159	23,343	13,107	11,985	1,122	9,311	53.1	6.3	28.0	4.5	34.0	124
North Carolina	145.0	120.7	10,740	8,665	6,135	5,342	793	4,859	80.6	9.3	1.0	6.0	24.8	121
North Dakota	20.5	22.8	2,061	2,347	1,471	1,175	296	399	82.2	8.7	0.7	3.7	17.7	10
Ohio	217.2	188.6	18,906	17,037	7,704	7,029	675	5,524	82.4	8.2	1.6	4.4	23.6	114
Oklahoma	56.2	47	12,898	13,548	2,751	2,596	155	1,777	82.5	9.5	0.5	4.1	22.1	45
Oregon	65.2	55.1	5,162	4,217	3,229	2,936	293	1,995	71.7	9.5	4.2	7.5	23.8	37
Pennsylvania	276.4	241.2	27,752	21,006	8,811	7,907	904	6,136	75.6	8.5	5.8	5.1	27.2	102
Rhode Island	11.4	10.3	795	683	699	640	59	520	81.3	8.1	2.2	3.7	25.0	8
South Carolina	71.7	60.3	4863	3877	2813	2,474	-2,474	2,303	81.4	9.4	0.6	5.0	25.1	57
South Dakota	NA	NA	1,010	953	1,259	1,134	125	448	81.1	8.8	0.2	6.2	17.3	10
Tennessee	178.8	153.7	13,915	11,473	4,327	4,161	166	3,093	83.1	9.0	0.6	4.7	25.4	81
Texas	529.7	458.1	63,337	42,844	19,964	15,745	4,219	13,337	80.7	9.8	1.3	5.2	26.7	282
Utah	61.5	50.6	4,847	3,909	2,344	2,051	293	1,514	75.7	11.1	2.2	6.9	22.0	32
Vermont	7.0	6.7	482	412	496	496	0	324	75.4	9.0	0.9	7.5	23.6	7
Virginia	131.1	116.3	10,477	9,312	5,086	4,779	307	4,221	76.7	9.1	4.5	5.6	28.7	85
Washington	111.1	97.9	11,852	9,079	5,463	4,847	616	3,660	71.0	9.8	7.0	6.5	28.4	62
West Virginia	NA	NA	1,674	1,601	1,184	1,249	-65	727	83.3	8.6	0.9	3.4	26.5	19
Wisconsin	103.6	94.2	7,833	6,884	5,630	5,189	441	2,957	81.7	7.5	1.5	4.8	22.0	66
Wyoming	12.3	13.1	2,659	2,185	939	890	49	285	75.8	10.2	1.2	6.2	16.2	10

[1] All estimates of labor provided by the Bureau of Labor Statistics (BLS) are based on the 2017 North American Industry. Classification System (NAICS). United States totals differ from the sum of the state figures because of differing benchmarks among states and differing industrial and geographic stratification.
[2] Bureau of Economic Analysis. The estimates of earnings for 2015 are based on the 2012 North American Industry Classification System (NAICS). The estimates for 2019 are based on the 2017 NAICS. All dollars estimates are in current dollars and not adjusted for inflation.
[3] Data for establishments in 2010 based on the 2007 North American Industry Classification System (NAICS); 2017 data are based on the 2017 NAICS.
[4] Excludes taxicab.
NA Not available
0 = Represents zero or rounds to zero

Table A-64. Motor Vehicle and Motorcycle Registrations, Bridges, and Drivers Licenses

Geographic area	Motor vehicle registrations Total[1] Number (thousands) 2018	2010	Automobile[2] (thousands) 2018	2010	Trucks[3] (thousands) 2018	2010	Motorcycle registrations[4] 2018	2010	Highway Vehicle-Miles Traveled[5] 2018	2008	Bridges, 2019 Total	Good condition	Fair condition	Poor condition	Drivers licenses[6] (thousands) 2018	2010
United States	273,602	242,061	111,242	130,892	152,702	110,322	8,666	8,010	3,240,327	2,973,509	617,084	279,582	291,339	46,163	227,558	210,115
Alabama......................	5,300	4,654	2,161	2,212	3,023	2,433	110	123	71,167	59,303	16,162	6,740	8,768	654	3,999	3,806
Alaska.......................	804	710	183	228	580	479	32	30	5,487	4,865	1,595	706	744	145	536	515
Arizona......................	5,806	4,320	2,392	2,201	3,236	2,114	170	137	66,145	61,628	8,320	5,098	3,085	137	5,285	4,444
Arkansas....................	2,817	2,073	921	945	1,793	1,120	91	76	36,675	33,163	12,902	6,598	5,678	626	2,145	2,078
California....................	31,022	31,014	15,066	17,978	15,034	12,981	823	760	348,796	327,286	25,771	13,707	10,267	1,797	27,039	23,753
Colorado	5,356	4,180	1,798	1,891	3,354	2,280	191	111	53,954	47,860	8,785	3,550	4,769	466	4,245	3,779
Connecticut................	2,880	3,082	1,307	1,986	1,474	1,085	88	66	31,596	31,737	4,336	1,256	2,805	275	2,606	2,935
Delaware	1,008	799	433	434	543	363	28	27	10,179	8,976	879	248	603	28	787	695
District of Columbia	352	212	210	160	133	49	4	2	3,691	3,611	244	60	174	10	528	385
Florida.......................	17,496	14,373	7,966	7,295	8,883	7,025	587	601	221,816	198,616	12,518	8,279	3,878	361	15,369	13,950
Georgia	8,513	7,702	3,557	3,739	4,715	3,939	204	197	131,456	109057	14,940	6,796	7,703	441	7,169	6,508
Hawaii	1,267	904	509	450	724	449	31	55	10,887	10,278	1,138	297	761	80	948	909
Idaho	1,880	1,325	599	541	1,211	780	67	53	17,709	15,251	4,493	1,282	2,916	295	1,253	1,070
Illinois.......................	10,589	10,079	4,478	5,773	5,757	4,287	320	350	107,954	106,079	26,825	13,084	11,334	2,407	8,715	8,374
Indiana......................	6,191	5,698	2,249	2,986	3,670	2,679	251	205	81,529	70,973	19,284	7,892	10,226	1,166	4,589	5,550
Iowa.........................	3,692	3,313	1,242	1,691	2,246	1,615	195	187	33,282	30,713	24,043	9,319	10,149	4,575	2,260	2,167
Kansas......................	2,684	2,436	975	880	1,607	1,552	95	87	32,190	29,727	24,934	13,468	10,186	1,280	2,149	2,033
Kentucky	4,368	3,589	1,722	1,890	2,534	1,684	101	72	49,544	47,534	14,394	4,908	8,444	1,042	3,033	2,950
Louisiana	3,885	4,086	1,389	1,917	2,353	2,146	114	69	50,045	45,091	12,884	6,244	4,939	1,701	3,425	3,134
Maine	1,126	1,054	391	519	679	531	51	56	14,784	14,559	2,461	748	1,399	314	1,041	1,020
Maryland....................	4,205	4,557	1,922	2,591	2,141	1,954	118	80	59,775	55,023	5,402	1,783	3,346	273	4,408	3,918
Massachusetts.............	5,061	5,334	2,183	3,145	2,696	2,177	169	159	66,772	54505	5,233	1,371	3,393	469	4,945	4,593
Michigan....................	8,387	9,286	3,024	5,136	5,096	4,122	258	281	102,398	101,825	11,244	4,304	5,723	1,217	7,154	7,083
Minnesota..................	5,404	4,848	1,977	2,459	3,166	2,370	242	255	60,438	57,995	13,346	8,085	4,630	631	3,391	3,281
Mississippi.................	2,067	2,016	825	1,144	1,206	863	28	28	40,730	43,711	17,019	10,682	4,853	1,484	2,058	1,928
Missouri.....................	5,499	5,153	2,102	2,579	3,215	2,564	154	109	76,595	68,273	24,494	10,228	12,119	2,147	4,273	4,246
Montana.....................	1,845	926	453	352	1,094	572	294	126	12,700	10,812	5,278	1,602	3,296	380	806	744
Nebraska....................	1,961	1,802	683	773	1,209	1,022	56	52	20,975	19,170	15,332	7,996	5,980	1,356	1,420	1,352
Nevada......................	2,514	1,362	1,074	690	1,362	669	75	67	28,319	20,780	2,029	1,009	994	26	1,983	1,691
New Hampshire............	1,346	1,203	507	619	757	582	79	80	13,776	13,040	2,502	1,323	966	213	1,162	1,037
New Jersey	6,055	6,628	2,754	3,972	3,125	2,632	151	328	77,539	73,629	6,786	1,825	4,432	529	6,343	5,953
New Mexico	1,824	1,612	656	703	1,103	906	60	53	27,288	26,279	4,014	1,517	2,277	220	1,458	1,406
New York	11,482	10,255	4,713	7,950	6,297	2,236	389	348	123,510	134085	17,540	6,348	9,447	1,745	12,194	11,286
North Carolina.............	8,210	5,743	3,394	3,282	4,596	2,427	188	134	121,127	101,712	18,407	7,087	9,606	1,714	7,509	6,537
North Dakota...............	900	736	240	341	618	392	39	34	9,856	7,820	4,329	2,352	1,515	462	561	483
Ohio.........................	10,914	9,801	4,604	5,615	5,859	4,139	410	384	114,474	108,302	27,167	16,101	9,609	1,457	8,033	7,963
Oklahoma...................	3,699	3,357	1,296	1,582	2,270	1,756	129	126	45,433	48,499	23,138	10,174	10,612	2,352	2,504	2,349
Oregon......................	3,943	3,050	1,489	1,489	2,303	1,546	134	108	36,848	33,468	8,211	2,850	4,935	426	2,931	2,770
Pennsylvania...............	10,728	9,991	4,424	5,682	5,875	4,275	373	412	102,109	107,848	22,911	7,330	12,080	3,501	8,991	8,737
Rhode Island...............	872	782	412	479	430	302	28	33	8,009	8,187	779	138	467	174	757	748
South Carolina	4,458	3,661	1,830	2,031	2,493	1,611	117	107	56,801	49,597	9,419	4,130	4,494	795	3,846	3,337
South Dakota	1,269	926	359	407	787	517	120	66	9,719	8,986	5,821	1,940	2,890	991	638	602
Tennessee	5,771	5,114	2,285	2,734	3,275	2,358	181	163	81,321	69,469	20,226	8,777	10,562	887	5,422	4,418
Texas........................	22,186	17,194	8,248	8,331	13,519	8,766	349	432	282,037	235382	54,432	27,958	25,749	725	17,370	15,158
Utah.........................	2,373	2,655	937	1,317	1,345	1,336	84	59	32,069	25,974	3,063	1,419	1,578	66	2,031	1,660
Vermont.....................	620	567	218	293	370	272	31	29	7,346	7,312	2,818	1,494	1,256	68	565	513
Virginia......................	7,605	6,149	3,268	3,510	4,106	2,623	196	74	85,336	82,278	13,933	4,670	8,656	607	5,929	5,402
Washington.................	7,152	4,683	2,965	2,600	3,928	2,071	236	218	62,367	55,558	8,300	4,307	3,609	384	5,910	5,106
West Virginia...............	1,694	1,436	560	703	1,070	730	61	49	19,447	20,774	7,291	1,861	3,899	1,531	1,137	1,206
Wisconsin	5,683	4,968	2,088	2,461	3,244	2,491	336	323	65,885	57,462	14,249	7,271	5,952	1,026	4,288	4,133
Wyoming	837	663	204	210	600	450	29	31	10,438	9,447	3,114	943	1,956	215	419	419

[1] Automobiles, trucks, and buses (excludes motorcycles). Excludes vehicles owned by military services.
[2] Includes private and commercially owned (including taxis). Excludes publicly owned.
[3] Includes private, commercial, and publicly owned trucks.
[4] Includes private and commercially owned. Excludes publicly owned.
[5] Travel for the rural minor collector and rural/urban local functional systems is estimated by the states based on a model or other means and provided to the FHWA on a summary basis. Travel for all other systems are estimated from State-provided data in the Highway Performance Monitoring System.
[6] Include restricted drivers and graduated driver license.

Table A-65. Traffic Fatalities and Seat Belt Use

| Geographic area | Traffic fatalities[1] | | | | | | Traffic fatalities in alcohol involved crashes, 2014 | | | | Rate of seat belt use[5] | | |
| | Number | | | Fatality rate[2] | | | | | By highest driver BAC in crash[4] | | | | |
	2014	2010	2005	2014	2010	2005	Total	Percent of all persons killed in crashes	Low alcohol: BAC 0.01 to 0.07	Alcohol impaired driving fatalities: BAC 0.08 or more	2014	2010	2007
United States	32,675	32,999	43,510	1.08	1.11	1.46	11,731	35.9	1,764	9,967	87.0	85.0	82.0
Alabama	820	862	1,148	1.25	1.34	1.92	312	38.0	48	264	95.7	91.4	82.3
Alaska	73	56	73	1.50	1.17	1.45	28	38.4	6	22	88.4	86.8	82.4
Arizona	770	759	1179	1.23	1.27	1.97	247	32.1	48	199	87.2	81.8	80.9
Arkansas	466	571	654	1.37	1.70	2.05	162	34.8	27	135	74.4	78.3	69.9
California	3074	2720	4333	0.92	0.84	1.32	1,053	34.3	171	882	97.1	96.2	94.6
Colorado	488	450	606	1.00	0.96	1.26	186	38.1	26	160	82.4	82.9	81.1
Connecticut	248	320	278	0.80	1.02	0.88	114	46.0	17	97	85.1	88.2	85.8
Delaware	121	101	133	1.26	1.13	1.40	52	43.0	3	49	91.9	90.7	86.6
District of Columbia	23	24	48	0.65	0.67	1.29	6	26.1	1	5	93.2	92.3	87.1
Florida	2,494	2444	3,518	1.24	1.25	1.75	807	32.4	122	685	88.8	87.4	79.1
Georgia	1,164	1247	1,729	1.04	1.12	1.52	325	27.9	47	278	97.3	89.6	89.0
Hawaii	95	113	140	0.93	1.13	1.39	35	36.8	3	32	93.5	97.6	97.6
Idaho	186	209	275	1.15	1.32	1.85	60	32.3	7	53	80.2	77.9	78.5
Illinois	924	927	1363	0.88	0.88	1.27	369	39.9	52	317	94.1	92.6	90.1
Indiana	746	754	938	0.94	1.00	1.31	239	32.0	34	205	90.2	92.4	87.9
Iowa	321	390	450	1.02	1.24	1.45	105	32.7	12	93	92.8	93.1	91.3
Kansas	385	431	428	1.25	1.44	1.44	121	31.4	18	103	85.7	81.8	75.0
Kentucky	672	760	985	1.40	1.58	2.08	197	29.3	26	171	86.1	80.3	71.8
Louisiana	737	721	963	1.53	1.59	2.14	301	40.8	48	253	84.1	75.9	75.2
Maine	131	161	169	0.92	1.11	1.13	50	38.2	6	44	85.0	82.0	79.8
Maryland	442	496	614	0.78	0.88	1.09	154	34.8	24	130	92.1	94.7	93.1
Massachusetts	328	347	441	0.57	0.64	0.80	154	47.0	21	133	76.6	73.7	68.7
Michigan	901	942	1,129	0.93	0.97	1.09	266	29.5	51	215	93.3	95.2	93.7
Minnesota	361	411	559	0.63	0.73	0.98	121	33.5	15	106	94.7	92.3	87.8
Mississippi	607	641	931	1.54	1.61	2.32	207	34.1	29	178	78.3	81.0	71.8
Missouri	766	821	1257	1.08	1.16	1.83	250	32.6	46	204	78.8	76.0	77.2
Montana	192	189	251	1.58	1.69	2.26	86	44.8	13	73	74.0	78.9	79.6
Nebraska	225	190	276	1.15	0.98	1.43	77	34.2	17	60	79.0	84.1	78.7
Nevada	290	257	427	1.15	1.16	2.06	113	39.0	20	93	94.0	93.2	92.2
New Hampshire	95	128	166	0.73	0.98	1.24	34	35.8	4	30	70.4	72.2	63.8
New Jersey	556	556	747	0.74	0.76	1.01	201	36.2	38	163	87.6	93.7	91.4
New Mexico	383	349	488	1.51	1.38	2.04	144	37.6	28	116	92.1	89.8	91.5
New York	1,039	1,201	1434	0.80	0.92	1.03	379	36.5	62	317	90.6	89.8	83.5
North Carolina	1,284	1320	1,547	1.19	1.29	1.53	427	33.3	49	378	90.6	89.7	88.8
North Dakota	135	105	123	1.28	1.27	1.62	66	48.9	11	55	81.0	74.8	82.2
Ohio	1,006	1080	1321	0.89	0.97	1.20	356	35.4	46	310	85.0	83.8	81.6
Oklahoma	669	668	803	1.40	1.40	1.71	181	27.1	27	154	86.3	85.9	83.1
Oregon	357	317	487	1.03	0.94	1.38	125	35.0	25	100	97.8	97.0	95.3
Pennsylvania	1195	1324	1,616	1.20	1.32	1.50	396	33.1	51	345	83.6	86.0	86.7
Rhode Island	52	67	87	0.68	0.81	1.05	19	36.5	1	18	87.4	78.0	79.1
South Carolina	824	809	1094	1.65	1.65	2.21	330	40.0	51	279	90.0	85.4	74.5
South Dakota	136	140	186	1.47	1.58	2.22	53	39.0	7	46	68.9	74.5	73.0
Tennessee	962	1,032	1270	1.33	1.47	1.79	312	32.4	45	267	87.7	87.1	80.2
Texas	3,538	3,023	3536	1.46	1.29	1.50	670	18.9	224	446	90.7	93.8	91.8
Utah	256	253	282	0.93	0.95	1.12	63	24.6	7	56	83.4	89.0	86.8
Vermont	44	71	73	0.62	0.98	0.95	14	31.8	5	9	84.1	85.2	87.1
Virginia	703	740	947	0.87	0.9	1.18	256	36.4	42	214	77.3	80.5	79.9
Washington	462	460	649	0.8	0.8	1.17	168	36.4	34	134	94.5	97.6	96.4
West Virginia	272	315	374	1.42	1.64	1.82	96	35.3	12	84	87.8	82.1	89.6
Wisconsin	507	572	815	0.84	0.96	1.36	203	40.0	37	166	84.7	79.2	75.3
Wyoming	150	155	170	1.59	1.66	1.88	53	35.3	5	48	79.2	78.9	72.2

[1]Traffic fatalities pertain to a police-reported crash involving a motor vehicle in transport on a trafficway in which at least one person dies within 30 days of the crash. Data include fatalities in crashes in which there was no driver or motorcycle rider present at the scene.
[2]Deaths per 100 million vehicle miles traveled.
[3]Data represents all fatalities (both operators and passengers) in which the operator of the crash had a BAC of .01 or above.
[4]BAC stands for blood alcohol concentration and is measured in grams per deciliter (g/dl).
[5]Seat belt use pertains to both drivers and passengers in front seat.
NA = Not available

Table A-66. Communications

Geographic area	Mobile wireless telephone subscribers[1] (thousands)			Total number of pay phones by state (as of March 31)		Internet use, 2018 (thousands)						
							Percent of households by type of internet plan			Percent of households without internet access by household income		
	2018	2013	2010	2014	2008	Total number of households	Cellular data plan	Cable, DSL, or satellite	Without an internet subscription	Less than $20,000	$20,000 to $74,999	$75,000 or more
United States	348,225	310,698	285,118	152,716	700,826	121,520,180	75.7	76.5	14.7	37.3	16.6	4.6
Alabama..........................	4,985	4,555	4,328	1,155	6,212	1,855,184	70.8	66.8	20.3	43.2	19.6	6.3
Alaska.............................	696	660	608	491	3,630	254,551	77.4	74.7	12.2	35.6	15.1	4.7
Arizona...........................	3,066	6,007	5,285	3,695	13,980	2,614,298	76.0	78.1	13.4	34.3	14.8	4.2
Arkansas.........................	7,001	2,852	2,673	734	3,128	1,156,347	68.0	61.8	22.8	44.9	22.6	7.9
California........................	43,336	36,446	33,839	25,846	96,328	13,072,122	80.7	83.0	11.1	31.8	13.9	3.8
Colorado.........................	5,936	5,062	4,687	2,235	8,224	2,176,757	80.5	83.8	10.4	30.4	13.1	3.3
Connecticut.....................	3,722	3,499	3,230	694	5,432	1,378,091	74.8	80.0	12.7	37.4	16.8	3.7
Delaware.........................	1,533	897	851	200	2,416	367,671	80.3	80.8	11.4	26.1	13.9	4.3
District of Columbia	959	1,381	1,249	344	3,956	287,476	79.2	79.6	13.8	39.3	17.2	4.3
Florida............................	21,884	18,985	17,251	6,871	34,412	7,809,358	75.3	77.5	14.5	33.3	15.2	5.5
Georgia...........................	11,054	9,959	9,063	2,056	14,817	3,803,012	75.2	75.8	16.1	38.5	17.8	5.1
Hawaii............................	1,576	1,389	1,252	4,203	5,703	455,309	78.6	78.5	14.1	38.9	19.5	5.5
Idaho..............................	1,695	1,402	1,277	712	2,299	640,270	76.4	78.7	13.4	34.5	14.1	3.5
Illinois............................	13,979	12,835	12,057	5,570	22,959	4,864,864	75.9	76.5	14.6	37.3	17.2	4.7
Indiana...........................	6,538	5,946	5,410	2,141	11,441	2,599,169	73.1	72.9	16.9	38.8	18.4	5.6
Iowa...............................	3,096	2,782	2,535	983	4,627	1,267,873	73.8	73.1	16.0	39.6	17.9	5.0
Kansas............................	3,202	2,840	2,560	705	3,675	1,133,408	75.2	74.9	15.4	37.5	16.9	4.9
Kentucky.........................	4,269	4,041	3,726	1,766	7,526	1,732,713	71.4	70.8	17.9	41.6	16.8	5.4
Louisiana........................	5,381	4,755	4,340	775	6,121	1,737,220	68.8	68.3	21.7	45.2	21.0	7.2
Maine..............................	1,296	1,202	1,124	318	3,410	570,307	69.8	76.8	15.4	38.0	15.9	4.3
Maryland.........................	6,700	5,857	5,560	1,724	17,808	2,215,935	80.4	80.7	11.6	35.6	16.7	3.8
Massachusetts..................	7,849	6,928	6,316	3,008	21,442	2,624,294	77.9	81.1	11.8	35.5	15.5	3.4
Michigan.........................	10,560	10,109	8,861	1,993	14,520	3,957,466	73.2	73.5	15.6	37.8	16.9	4.6
Minnesota........................	5,871	5,286	4,704	1,688	7,997	2,194,452	77.4	78.1	12.8	38.0	15.9	3.8
Mississippi.......................	2,780	2,685	2,440	326	4,093	1,108,630	69.0	59.9	23.5	45.5	22.1	7.9
Missouri..........................	6,305	5,748	5,309	1,345	8,160	2,434,806	74.5	71.4	16.8	39.7	17.5	5.3
Montana..........................	1,028	903	846	586	1,954	431,421	72.0	75.1	15.9	38.0	16.4	5.1
Nebraska.........................	1,983	1,738	1,523	1,744	4,646	765,490	76.7	76.6	13.8	36.2	14.7	4.7
Nevada............................	3,071	2,716	2,453	2,063	7,772	1,129,810	77.6	80.4	13.9	34.1	15.2	5.0
New Hampshire..................	1,330	1,211	1,170	350	3,648	531,212	75.6	82.8	10.5	33.3	12.6	3.7
New Jersey	10,076	8,732	8,601	4,516	36,832	3,249,567	80.1	81.4	11.8	35.6	16.3	3.8
New Mexico	2,044	1,804	1,689	654	4,614	794,093	66.1	66.2	22.7	44.4	22.4	7.8
New York.........................	23,875	21,444	19,504	28,025	94,876	7,367,015	74.6	76.5	14.5	37.0	17.2	4.6
North Carolina..................	10,214	9,021	8,526	3,289	17,905	4,011,462	73.0	75.9	16.3	39.0	17.1	4.9
North Dakota....................	773	702	623	205	705	319,355	71.4	74.6	19.5	47.0	20.5	9.5
Ohio...............................	12,501	12,198	10,511	4,194	19,335	4,685,447	73.8	76.2	15.2	36.8	15.9	4.6
Oklahoma........................	3,756	3,676	3,188	788	5,886	1,485,310	73.6	67.5	17.8	39.5	18.0	6.1
Oregon............................	4,262	3,601	3,340	1,859	8,251	1,639,970	79.0	79.4	11.7	30.8	13.0	4.3
Pennsylvania....................	13,558	12,318	11,424	7,424	35,204	5,070,931	73.6	76.0	15.5	38.2	17.9	4.3
Rhode Island....................	1,031	977	920	341	3,281	406,573	76.0	77.3	14.5	39.5	16.6	3.1
South Carolina..................	4,866	4,447	3,935	1,035	8,513	1,927,991	71.9	72.8	18.3	41.9	18.6	5.5
South Dakota	838	756	728	256	1,476	345,449	69.2	73.5	17.7	42.8	19.3	5.7
Tennessee.......................	7,262	6,596	6,193	1,369	9,706	2,603,140	72.9	70.4	17.7	42.1	17.9	4.7
Texas..............................	29,413	25,481	23,030	11,844	44,816	9,776,083	76.6	74.7	15.3	37.9	17.3	4.9
Utah...............................	2,945	2,489	2,251	901	3,897	998,891	81.1	84.8	9.8	30.8	11.5	4.0
Vermont...........................	587	521	485	213	1,664	261,373	62.8	76.6	16.9	39.2	18.5	7.1
Virginia...........................	8,572	7,966	7,595	2,090	22,463	3,175,524	77.5	76.1	14.1	40.9	18.0	4.2
Washington......................	7,620	6,547	6,022	3,182	14,999	2,895,575	81.4	83.1	9.8	29.6	12.4	3.3
West Virginia....................	1,590	1,536	1,500	2,355	5,736	734,703	62.8	70.6	20.7	41.9	18.9	6.9
Wisconsin........................	5,681	5,229	4,730	1,584	6,951	2,371,960	74.4	75.1	15.0	38.3	17.5	4.3
Wyoming	604	551	526	271	1,380	230,252	70.4	76.4	14.1	28.3	16.8	6.3

[1]As of December. All facilities-based wireless carriers are required to report, and to use the area codes of telephone numbers provided to subscribers to determine subscriber counts by state.

Table A-67. Financial Activities

| Geographic area | Nonfarm employment (BLS)[2] (thousands) | | | Financial activities[1] Earnings (BEA) (million dollars) | | | | | Establishments[3] | |
	2019	2015	2010	Financial Activities 2019 Total	Finance and Insurance	Real Estate and Rental and Leasing	2015	2010	2017	Net change 2010–2017
United States	8,619.0	8,197.0	7,695.0	1,256,344	933,386	322,958	1,005,631	813,261	884,792	63,971
Alabama.................................	96.3	98.3	92.0	9,532	7,446	2,086	8,301	6,240	11,694	519
Alaska....................................	11.7	12.5	12.2	1,306	710	596	1,244	1,296	1,748	142
Arizona..................................	229.9	176.3	167.6	25,197	18,902	6,295	18,361	11,216	19,626	2,221
Arkansas................................	62.5	51.4	48.8	4,857	3,393	1,465	4,202	3,120	7,531	261
California...............................	841.2	920.0	759.7	164,420	103,089	61,331	129,715	114,288	108,121	12,359
Colorado................................	173.9	158.5	144.3	21,858	15,111	6,747	16,865	8,573	22,459	3,333
Connecticut............................	123.8	142.3	135.2	30,971	27,183	3,788	25,744	32,852	9,340	-231
Delaware................................	47.7	45.2	42.7	6,435	5,544	891	6,002	5,027	3,250	148
District of Columbia	29.8	30.2	26.9	5,521	3,872	1,649	4,408	2,455	2,355	202
Florida...................................	590.9	539.8	478.0	67,490	48,822	18,668	49,982	31,903	69,705	10,188
Georgia..................................	250.2	237.3	218.5	32,722	23,368	9,354	24,847	15,853	27,411	2,119
Hawaii....................................	29.9	29.3	26.9	3,763	1,811	1,952	3,055	2,484	3,522	140
Idaho.....................................	36.8	29.7	29.2	3,323	2,358	966	2,595	1,869	5,553	598
Illinois...................................	411.1	409.6	371.6	60,605	47,233	13,372	52,033	33,673	34,843	13
Indiana..................................	141.5	138.8	130.9	20,441	10,804	9,636	17,665	14,918	16,096	569
Iowa......................................	109.7	98.3	101.3	11,362	9,884	1,478	9,798	8,402	9,467	658
Kansas...................................	77.3	70.6	72.2	10,729	6,627	4,102	8,526	6,881	9,415	493
Kentucky................................	93.4	85.7	85.7	9,588	7,461	2,128	8,200	6,261	10,220	223
Louisiana................................	92.2	98.4	91.4	9,076	5,795	3,281	8,263	6,694	12,617	643
Maine....................................	32.9	33.7	30.6	3,229	2,572	658	2,585	2,453	3,708	178
Maryland................................	143.8	158.8	144.4	27,054	14,484	12,570	21,820	16,919	14,181	467
Massachusetts........................	224.1	226.9	215.1	45,453	38,785	6,668	34,429	36,342	17,159	1,356
Michigan................................	224.5	216.1	188.1	25,188	17,151	8,036	21,366	15,989	21,268	46
Minnesota..............................	192.6	173.0	162.0	24,124	20,311	3,812	21,077	15,489	16,784	1,210
Mississippi.............................	44.5	45.8	44.5	3,667	2,731	936	3,392	2,500	7,101	-41
Missouri.................................	174.9	163.4	162.2	20,409	16,516	3,893	15,438	14,613	17,320	331
Montana................................	25.9	21.4	21.2	2,402	1,563	840	2,041	1,504	4,016	291
Nebraska...............................	75.2	64.5	68.9	7,206	6,021	1,185	5,792	4,580	6,746	569
Nevada..................................	69.0	64.3	52.9	6,397	4,256	2,141	4,686	3,173	8,868	1,015
New Hampshire........................	34.8	39.4	35.1	4,940	3,876	1,064	4,316	3,692	3,551	304
New Jersey.............................	252.3	279.7	251.6	43,187	33,346	9,841	36,444	34,937	21,228	157
New Mexico	35.6	34.9	33.0	2,943	2,059	885	2,649	2,147	5,087	45
New York................................	728.0	712.6	669.2	191,439	162,383	29,056	150,901	134,768	60,402	670
North Carolina.........................	252.6	198.4	199.9	32,153	25,107	7,046	23,753	23,409	26,001	2,635
North Dakota..........................	24.8	18.8	20.6	2,670	1,669	1,001	2,341	1,594	2,836	323
Ohio......................................	309.5	308.5	276.7	32,715	25,793	6,922	26,197	21,170	27,850	475
Oklahoma..............................	79.4	79.9	78.1	7,272	5,290	1,982	6,545	5,688	11,301	766
Oregon..................................	103.3	102.1	93.2	11,146	6,696	4,450	8,074	5,944	12,877	1,295
Pennsylvania..........................	329.7	335.7	310.9	41,425	31,370	10,055	36,458	23,896	28,165	1,056
Rhode Island..........................	35.3	34.3	30.7	3,983	3,295	688	3,510	2,861	2,553	81
South Carolina	104.6	92.5	91.9	11,406	8,145	3,260	9,720	6,782	13,306	1,251
South Dakota	29.0	28.5	28.9	3,748	3,215	533	3,011	3,045	3,124	297
Tennessee..............................	172.2	143.3	137.1	19,426	13,568	5,859	15,296	12,071	16,217	772
Texas....................................	801.0	609.5	625.4	104,086	76,573	27,513	79,665	55,172	72,782	8,813
Utah......................................	89.9	67.5	68.0	11,022	7,376	3,646	8,271	4,834	10,890	1,727
Vermont.................................	12.2	13.2	12.2	1,323	1,011	311	1,085	1,044	1,724	37
Virginia..................................	212.0	192.5	179.1	25,706	19,390	6,316	20,791	17,521	21,376	1,175
Washington............................	160.7	157.8	138.1	20,947	13,343	7,604	16,741	10,012	21,740	2,010
West Virginia..........................	29.2	30.0	28.6	2,151	1,482	669	1,880	1,793	3,510	-73
Wisconsin..............................	154.5	154.5	152.2	17,099	13,947	3,153	14,359	12,130	13,910	-11
Wyoming	11.2	10.8	10.8	1,233	651	582	1,193	1,187	2,238	146

[1] Includes Finance and Insurance (NAICS 52) and Real Estate and Rental and Leasing (NAICS 53).
[2] Based on the 2017 North American Industry Classification System (NAICS).
[3] 2017 data for establishments are based on the 2017 North American Industry Classification System (NAICS); 2010 data are based on the 2007 NAICS.

Table A-68. Professional and Business Services and Education and Health Services

| | Professional and business services[1] | | | | | | | | | Education and health services[2] | | | | | | | | |
| | Nonfarm employment (BLS)[3] (thousands) | | | Earnings (BEA)[4] (million dollars) | | | Establishments | | Net change, 2010–2017 | Nonfarm employment (BLS)[3] (thousands) | | | Earnings (BEA)[4] (million dollars) | | | Establishments | | Net change, 2010–2017 |
Geographic area	2019	2015	2010	2019	2015	2010	2017	2010		2019	2015	2010	2019	2015	2010	2017	2010	
United States	21,241	19,633	16,728	2,299,227	1,891,466	1,442,084	1,390,925	1,284,153	106,772	24,100	22,029	19,975	1,669,082	1,412,745	1,170,364	1,002,808	902,972	99,836
Alabama	251	229	210	19,888	16,176	13,913	14,628	14,067	561	250	227	214	16,770	14,757	12,646	11,557	11,073	484
Alaska	28	30	28	2,943	3,080	2,659	3,319	3,175	144	51	48	43	4,297	3,560	2,828	2,986	2,478	508
Arizona	445	398	341	36,253	29,265	22,872	27,898	25,374	2,524	462	397	345	32,007	25,749	21,487	21,048	18,307	2,741
Arkansas	145	139	119	12,383	10,214	7,704	9,901	9,423	478	194	175	166	11,376	9,585	8,010	8,511	8,006	505
California	2,721	2,481	2,073	357,654	287,722	209,137	178,099	159,144	18,955	2,803	2,455	2,127	205,993	167,297	129,804	128,263	112,953	15,310
Colorado	440	398	331	51,263	39,843	29,893	36,927	32,874	4,053	348	314	265	25,246	21,051	16,568	19,435	16,700	2,735
Connecticut	220	219	194	29,841	26,930	21,227	15,340	15,435	-95	339	327	307	25,829	23,044	20,586	12,556	11,553	1,003
Delaware	63	61	55	7,157	6,141	4,358	5,218	5,126	92	81	76	65	5,723	4,950	3,921	3,018	2,760	258
District of Columbia	171	162	148	30,620	26,314	21,217	7,195	6,292	903	130	131	108	9,982	8,897	7,161	2,830	2,671	159
Florida	1,392	1,223	1,006	122,411	95,530	73,097	119,328	103,692	15,636	1,340	1,200	1,071	92,529	78,150	64,365	68,665	60,038	8,627
Georgia	716	633	523	69,351	53,745	40,337	44,426	41,307	3,119	610	540	476	42,715	34,756	28,391	28,482	24,746	3,736
Hawaii	74	84	72	6,605	6,111	4,843	5,566	5,429	137	87	82	75	6,807	5,688	4,738	4,225	4,030	195
Idaho	97	82	75	7,339	5,414	4,644	7,443	6,614	829	111	98	84	6,927	5,650	4,381	5,829	5,143	686
Illinois	945	923	794	103,915	91,767	72,865	58,414	57,382	1,032	939	899	831	67,584	58,729	50,944	38,755	36,141	2,614
Indiana	344	331	276	27,404	22,814	17,369	21,597	20,926	671	482	451	420	32,943	27,522	22,872	18,593	16,671	1,922
Iowa	139	139	122	11,115	9,501	7,108	10,783	10,297	486	235	226	214	13,276	11,762	10,107	9,513	8,758	755
Kansas	179	179	152	15,609	14,239	9,556	11,640	11,233	407	202	194	180	12,953	11,529	9,693	8,856	8,451	405
Kentucky	217	218	181	15,782	13,704	10,867	12,975	12,782	193	283	264	254	18,270	15,554	13,281	12,728	11,834	894
Louisiana	216	214	193	19,038	17,830	14,540	17,603	16,704	899	320	305	271	21,188	18,190	15,182	13,973	12,975	998
Maine	69	65	57	6,211	4,930	3,908	6,003	5,676	327	129	123	119	8,088	6,879	6,101	5,303	5,261	42
Maryland	463	431	388	52,127	43,915	36,186	30,815	28,700	2,115	474	450	408	34,452	30,334	25,407	19,067	17,535	1,532
Massachusetts	602	536	464	92,402	71,210	52,439	34,348	32,205	2,143	812	762	688	63,755	55,986	45,748	22,682	20,771	1,911
Michigan	654	637	524	61,726	53,104	40,045	35,239	34,708	531	682	652	612	45,366	39,941	35,344	29,519	28,400	1,119
Minnesota	383	367	321	43,108	35,465	27,849	25,770	24,553	1,217	551	508	458	35,539	29,560	24,737	19,140	16,519	2,621
Mississippi	108	106	92	7,122	6,506	5,498	7,404	7,320	84	147	138	131	9,400	8,224	7,421	6,977	6,674	303
Missouri	382	369	318	36,989	31,569	25,110	23,248	21,844	1,404	485	448	416	30,510	26,117	22,242	22,639	17,642	4,997
Montana	43	40	39	3,485	2,913	2,309	5,836	5,347	489	79	72	64	5,038	4,162	3,371	4,115	3,723	392
Nebraska	120	116	101	10,174	8,960	6,722	7,861	7,384	477	157	150	141	9,788	8,055	6,824	6,381	5,713	668
Nevada	196	167	136	16,489	12,846	10,226	14,092	12,775	1,317	144	121	102	10,434	8,378	6,856	8,175	6,852	1,323
New Hampshire	84	77	64	9,616	7,649	5,810	6,300	6,320	-20	125	118	112	8,908	7,561	6,584	4,404	4,167	237
New Jersey	684	650	591	87,264	75,739	57,733	44,809	44,536	273	718	660	601	53,473	46,273	39,757	31,976	29,598	2,378
New Mexico	111	100	100	9,408	7,538	7,266	6,921	6,860	61	141	133	120	7,554	6,670	5,792	5,723	5,447	276
New York	1,375	1,267	1,099	193,936	161,299	123,471	92,463	86,697	5,766	2,140	1,891	1,680	147,687	120,889	101,872	67,448	63,220	4,228
North Carolina	649	589	485	59,606	47,692	34,750	39,999	35,726	4,273	626	574	537	41,711	35,001	29,602	27,064	25,309	1,755
North Dakota	33	36	28	2,823	2,829	1,660	3,096	2,579	517	67	60	55	4,503	3,695	2,750	2,251	1,980	271
Ohio	735	716	626	69,323	60,748	46,715	39,784	39,917	-133	940	906	841	60,422	52,979	45,216	32,815	31,030	1,785
Oklahoma	194	184	172	15,102	13,069	10,477	14,943	14,275	668	239	232	222	14,520	13,210	10,872	11,806	11,285	521
Oregon	254	229	189	25,542	20,618	13,487	19,373	17,523	1,850	301	258	229	21,305	17,668	13,940	15,690	13,591	2,099
Pennsylvania	815	780	690	90,004	76,740	60,668	48,582	46,684	1,898	1,296	1,191	1,128	88,976	76,159	65,006	41,713	39,477	2,236
Rhode Island	68	64	53	6,596	5,994	4,537	5,038	4,885	153	109	106	101	7,048	6,483	5,859	3,632	3,671	-39
South Carolina	298	263	216	22,832	17,819	13,338	17,759	15,732	2,027	258	235	210	15,624	13,313	10,842	11,910	10,781	1,129
South Dakota	33	31	28	2,726	2,351	1,769	3,287	3,031	256	74	69	65	5,286	4,466	3,481	2,667	2,529	138
Tennessee	427	393	304	37,844	28,248	21,955	20,237	18,858	1,379	442	415	376	39,711	36,935	28,594	17,348	16,059	1,289
Texas	1,792	1,598	1,281	187,918	151,635	108,563	104,401	89,234	15,167	1,741	1,579	1,381	116,329	98,148	78,126	77,365	64,826	12,539
Utah	224	195	152	18,664	13,690	9,453	16,024	13,082	2,942	210	183	155	12,158	9,495	7,510	9,471	7,718	1,753
Vermont	29	28	23	2,993	2,467	1,891	3,379	3,338	41	66	64	59	4,249	3,630	3,078	2,532	2,495	37
Virginia	767	702	650	93,039	77,674	65,957	43,939	40,413	3,526	555	514	463	36,706	31,762	26,623	23,738	20,663	3,075
Washington	435	389	326	51,108	39,487	30,795	33,512	29,891	3,621	502	449	425	37,420	29,642	23,737	24,283	21,596	2,687
West Virginia	69	67	61	5,673	4,568	3,671	4,567	4,671	-104	129	129	121	8,047	6,960	6,014	5,192	5,187	5
Wisconsin	326	315	274	29,037	24,324	18,384	20,020	19,045	975	464	436	408	30,877	26,128	22,639	17,752	15,995	1,757
Wyoming	19	19	17	1,764	1,528	1,237	3,576	3,068	508	29	27	26	1,784	1,620	1,456	2,207	1,970	237

[1]Professional, scientific and technical services; management of companies and enterprises; administrative and support and waste management and remediation services.
[2]Education services; health care and social assistance.
[3]Bureau of Labor Statistics.
[4]Bureau of Economic Analysis.

Table A-69. Leisure and Hospitality Services

| | Leisure and hospitality employees (BLS)¹ (includes Arts, Entertainment, and Recreation and Accommodations and Food Services) (thousands) | | | Arts, entertainment, and recreation services | | | | | | Accommodations and food services | | | | | |
| | | | | Earnings (BEA)² (million dollars) | | | Establishments³ | | Net change, 2010–2017 | Earnings (BEA)² (million dollars) | | | Establishments³ | | Net change, 2010–2017 |
	2019	2015	2010	2019	2015	2010	2017	2010		2019	2015	2010	2017	2010	
United States	16,466	15,160	13,049	169,106	139,202	107,317	143,396	123,151	20,245	454,928	368,965	265,015	726,167	643,960	82,207
Alabama	209	190	168	688	537	420	1,169	1,105	64	4,426	3,688	2,712	9,109	8,123	986
Alaska	36	35	32	249	220	155	577	548	29	1,224	1,130	904	2,218	1,993	225
Arizona	331	299	254	3,143	2,372	1,419	2,094	1,695	399	9,253	7,114	5,451	13,042	11,438	1,604
Arkansas	120	112	99	363	303	252	801	809	-8	2,569	2,108	1,620	5,969	5,290	679
California	2,033	1,830	1,501	33,583	28,379	22,716	26,451	20,205	6,246	67,530	51,021	33,446	89,612	75,463	14,149
Colorado	345	313	263	4,387	3,592	1,780	3,039	2,417	622	9,536	7,306	4,999	14,114	12,207	1,907
Connecticut	157	151	134	1,851	1,736	1,563	1,745	1,607	138	4,862	3,948	3,209	8,785	8,004	781
Delaware	53	49	44	337	339	394	446	410	36	1,307	1,033	753	2,211	1,910	301
District of Columbia	82	73	60	1,048	797	724	391	309	82	3,325	2,702	1,939	2,740	2,264	476
Florida	1,255	1,134	932	12,590	10,607	8,720	8896	7,462	1,434	32995	26812	20207	42,002	35,543	6,459
Georgia	502	448	374	2,777	2,178	1,846	3,476	2,696	780	11,904	9,788	7,138	21,236	18,567	2,669
Hawaii	127	115	100	786	632	480	510	494	16	5,648	4,454	3,221	3,866	3,483	383
Idaho	83	68	58	495	298	231	812	737	75	1,801	1,267	912	3,861	3,512	349
Illinois	621	578	515	7,092	6,256	4,032	5,232	4,450	782	17,765	15,048	11,140	28,967	26,879	2,088
Indiana	313	301	273	2,119	1,949	1,642	2,318	2,140	178	6,749	5,634	4,048	13,658	12,718	940
Iowa	144	141	130	647	593	574	1,456	1,457		2,993	2,611	1,826	7,281	6,918	363
Kansas	131	126	113	622	605	297	1,096	1,018	78	2,933	2,672	1,995	6,250	5,898	352
Kentucky	202	188	167	839	690	533	1,410	1,274	136	4,871	4,168	3,069	8,235	7,517	718
Louisiana	238	228	194	1,547	1,399	1,147	1,539	1,390	149	5,986	5,453	4,096	9,889	8,657	1,232
Maine	69	64	60	492	404	328	890	876	14	2,057	1,549	1,114	4,257	3,960	297
Maryland	282	268	230	3,134	3,145	1,407	2,166	2,037	129	8,065	6,494	5,067	12,151	10,986	1,165
Massachusetts	377	351	308	5,646	5,024	3,064	3,478	3,050	428	12,014	9,374	6,807	17,742	16,437	1,305
Michigan	434	414	378	2,661	2,329	2,252	3,494	3,520	-26	10,402	8,564	6,067	20,679	19,449	1,230
Minnesota	276	260	235	2,745	2,125	1,435	3,015	2,679	336	6,299	5,123	3,735	12,022	11,165	857
Mississippi	136	129	118	320	330	364	700	668	32	3,122	2,719	2,357	5,664	4,956	708
Missouri	309	293	272	2,428	2,595	1,994	2,300	2,111	189	6,995	5,816	4,539	12,918	12,313	605
Montana	67	63	56	450	385	298	1,236	1,150	86	1,507	1,270	869	3,577	3,391	186
Nebraska	94	89	81	500	398	294	928	855	73	1,929	1,631	1,201	4,631	4,243	388
Nevada	355	341	309	2,664	2,193	1,830	1,642	1,224	418	15,012	14,055	11,183	6,815	5,733	1,082
New Hampshire	73	69	62	987	789	638	819	721	98	2,143	1,702	1,258	3,794	3,538	256
New Jersey	394	360	334	4,966	3,605	2,715	3,846	3,418	428	11,196	9,514	7,619	21,551	19,543	2,008
New Mexico	99	93	84	543	467	454	719	654	65	2,525	2,143	1,714	4,410	4,089	321
New York	960	898	736	21,160	16,099	14,241	12,977	11,378	1,599	31,912	25,029	17,618	54,923	47,433	7,490
North Carolina	516	461	393	4,062	3,289	2,451	3,873	3,391	482	12,491	9,859	6,488	21,455	19,120	2,335
North Dakota	41	41	34	147	106	85	481	421	60	864	858	537	2,088	1,833	255
Ohio	569	539	475	5,585	4,590	3,623	4,019	3,860	159	12,687	10,815	7,538	24,371	23,143	1,228
Oklahoma	175	162	139	800	677	533	1,169	1,074	95	4,162	3,723	3,116	8,336	7,131	1,205
Oregon	214	192	162	1,694	1,320	693	2,000	1,639	361	6,495	4,824	3,087	11,700	10,319	1,381
Pennsylvania	577	545	501	6,348	5,059	4,104	4,889	4,508	381	13,344	11,356	8,779	28,862	27,683	1,179
Rhode Island	60	56	50	578	495	366	577	543	34	1,544	1,262	935	3,173	2,945	228
South Carolina	272	239	208	1,170	962	707	1,698	1,546	152	6,725	5,563	3,650	10,871	9,532	1,339
South Dakota	47	46	43	206	182	159	697	666	31	1,104	957	599	2,494	2,359	135
Tennessee	349	308	262	5,221	4,365	3,254	2,828	2,282	546	9,579	7,362	5,012	13,539	11,689	1,850
Texas	1,394	1,242	1,008	9,657	7,009	4,148	7,639	6,101	1,538	38,070	31,539	21,406	56,825	46,045	10,780
Utah	154	134	111	1,174	852	595	1,178	863	315	3,386	2,586	1,819	5,911	4,851	1,060
Vermont	37	36	32	244	227	197	468	436	32	1,128	932	674	1,985	1,896	89
Virginia	411	386	341	2,809	2,263	2,123	3,078	2,739	339	10,492	8,634	6,687	18,215	16,219	1,996
Washington	348	310	267	3,153	2,456	2,213	3,116	2,696	420	11,367	8,248	5,313	17,826	16,039	1,787
West Virginia	75	75	72	266	247	321	758	689	69	1,713	1,636	1,243	3,639	3,682	-43
Wisconsin	285	271	251	2,005	1,623	1,409	2,811	2,716	95	5,873	4,972	3,625	14,851	14,130	721
Wyoming	37	36	33	129	111	98	449	417	32	1,049	900	673	1,847	1,724	123

¹All estimates of labor and earnings provided by Bureau of Labor Statistics (BLS) are based on the 2017 North American Industry Classific System.
²Bureau of Economic Analysis. The estimates of earnings for 2010 are based on the 2007 North American Industry Classification System (NAICS). The estimates for 2017 are based on the 2017 NAICS. All dollars estimates are in current dollars and not adjusted for inflation.
³Data provided by County Business Patterns is based on the North American Industry Classification System (NAICS). Data for 2010 is based on NAICS 2007. Data for 2017 is based on NAICS 2017.

Table A–70. Travel and Tourism Indicators

Geographic area	International Tourists and Business Travelers, 2015		National parks[3] Recreational visits						
	Visa waiver[1]	Other[2]	2016	2015	2014	2013	2012	2011	2010
United States	22,419,941	46,605,955	330,971,688	307,247,252	292,800,082	273,630,895	282,765,682	276,626,130	279,337,864
Alabama	54,840	64,318	1,022,696	792,447	753,178	749,857	717,724	755,264	781,550
Alaska	66,080	53,831	2,783,011	2,664,293	2,684,693	2,585,980	2,412,524	2,333,919	2,274,843
Arizona	132,198	1,439,910	12,007,544	11,729,985	10,747,219	10,103,264	9,979,972	10,134,892	10,546,150
Arkansas	15,464	84,016	3,787,198	3,282,634	3,132,898	2,776,183	2,727,454	2,879,494	3,125,664
California	3,187,496	6,553,238	41,977,184	38,366,824	37,363,392	35,575,100	35,991,200	35,448,424	34,915,676
Colorado	182,823	341,195	7,457,420	7,077,287	6,031,874	5,393,745	5,811,546	5,819,069	5,635,307
Connecticut	80,168	106,905	39,079	47,220	34,082	22,862	21,465	22,415	19,313
Delaware	14,328	20,709	X	X	X	X	X	X	X
District of Columbia	187,677	209,320	42,700,159	41,801,278	37,701,216	34,202,516	34,286,073	30,579,692	33,140,005
Florida	3,106,583	6,713,838	10,855,364	10,639,976	10,667,459	10,282,814	10,366,613	10,580,858	9,222,981
Georgia	239,366	389,820	7,040,865	7,527,855	7,491,109	7,046,578	7,350,309	7,167,680	6,776,556
Hawaii	2,028,292	658,320	5,786,318	5,439,034	5,213,817	4,902,696	5,119,035	4,784,285	4,493,123
Idaho	16,539	18,549	629,191	601,777	553,739	614,412	553,554	601,668	530,977
Illinois	466,631	767,944	239,719	233,299	218,132	209,405	295,464	296,214	354,125
Indiana	56,298	95,435	1,949,880	1,887,762	1,778,385	1,935,295	2,148,903	2,094,529	2,395,485
Iowa	18,269	35,837	229,577	209,055	216,898	199,993	207,352	216,830	222,295
Kansas	16,385	58,842	121,249	115,903	98,591	91,930	101,752	90,383	100,361
Kentucky	28,322	43,403	1,882,702	1,760,944	1,828,192	1,604,722	1,717,853	1,666,505	1,797,894
Louisiana	101,918	189,638	500,797	494,688	510,522	624,047	625,913	577,755	496,329
Maine	32,644	30,473	3,317,250	2,823,741	2,574,717	2,265,631	2,431,052	2,374,645	2,504,208
Maryland	109,988	206,143	6,668,215	6,443,376	6,815,195	6,615,152	6,658,643	6,064,410	3,541,570
Massachusetts	499,014	513,779	10,127,182	9,399,919	9,850,586	9,678,050	10,487,447	10,231,394	9,913,501
Michigan	185,781	330,956	2,702,934	2,386,613	1,993,139	1,989,195	2,192,477	1,961,506	1,796,006
Minnesota	76,564	141,796	1,016,336	840,008	811,616	658,330	601,274	572,795	540,195
Mississippi	10,514	21,101	6,618,913	6,359,646	6,557,120	6,784,616	6,449,713	6,990,401	6,588,026
Missouri	39,731	87,152	2,824,117	3,247,219	3,385,772	3,888,912	4,171,826	3,913,220	4,140,544
Montana	25,480	19,452	5,655,262	4,967,752	4,590,398	4,281,517	4,451,755	4,061,967	4,584,011
Nebraska	190,311	266,704	307,208	291,235	254,198	257,903	304,046	276,058	290,323
Nevada	803,227	1,658,582	5,526,764	5,589,972	5,314,681	4,851,429	4,808,929	4,888,963	5,399,439
New Hampshire	29,485	22,838	42,377	39,242	37,785	37,837	33,663	32,695	30,941
New Jersey	383,663	606,510	4,829,258	4,205,734	4,389,637	5,028,646	4,885,202	5,357,781	5,858,443
New Mexico	17,000	280,377	1,872,044	1,714,677	1,602,114	1,512,529	1,502,808	1,491,144	1,657,550
New York	3,957,599	3,077,761	18,904,528	16,328,212	16,141,397	10,986,810	12,633,278	16,206,130	17,506,353
North Carolina	119,017	188,687	18,493,719	17,834,699	16,710,759	16,138,182	17,706,032	17,191,874	17,093,464
North Dakota	11,191	15,942	784,710	605,015	581,851	572,474	669,242	591,668	659,927
Ohio	97,809	161,867	2,818,683	2,624,146	2,470,177	2,404,918	2,611,158	2,417,080	2,738,275
Oklahoma	16,729	77,895	1,688,733	1,266,172	1,165,269	1,108,103	1,497,654	1,223,134	1,266,189
Oregon	92,913	121,884	1,328,643	1,154,108	1,033,254	969,051	875,271	839,614	888,358
Pennsylvania	191,286	240,571	11,070,572	9,935,361	9,005,244	9,137,524	8,768,869	8,526,173	8,970,475
Rhode Island	20,131	26,435	65,588	60,505	51,523	48,677	51,944	50,909	51,559
South Carolina	54,679	81,289	1,680,015	1,519,259	1,519,746	1,516,151	1,566,756	1,589,650	1,529,172
South Dakota	6,053	7,948	4,464,251	4,397,785	3,861,090	3,915,730	3,950,666	3,807,375	4,199,267
Tennessee	71,429	125,797	9,401,902	8,773,891	8,470,460	8,090,143	8,414,094	7,767,864	7,898,557
Texas	545,495	4,035,452	5,432,749	5,044,926	4,680,387	3,482,052	3,939,160	4,211,655	5,495,156
Utah	62,642	99,426	14,409,740	11,889,390	10,551,040	8,981,447	9,503,304	9,281,567	8,975,525
Vermont	29,127	15,668	55,716	35,003	39,086	34,112	32,403	29,049	31,209
Virginia	153,828	260,688	27,092,480	23,249,802	22,870,531	22,024,385	23,398,517	23,459,706	22,708,338
Washington	444,797	563,652	8,522,006	7,674,514	7,652,073	7,347,284	7,529,549	7,419,258	7,281,785
West Virginia	4,989	7,323	1,683,649	1,603,753	1,541,805	1,499,112	1,543,425	1,477,886	1,811,722
Wisconsin	53,108	82,476	537,925	544,223	625,850	320,027	273,933	312,905	251,145
Wyoming	11,286	10,393	7,461,666	7,250,657	6,387,455	6,079,578	6,194,752	5,955,778	6,307,997

[1] Includes GB, GMB, GT, GMT, WB, and WT admissions.
[2] Includes B1, B2 and a limited number of Border Crossing Card (BCC) admissions.
[3] For year ending June 30. Data are shown as reported by state park directors. In some states, park agency has under its control forests, fish and wildlife areas, and/or other areas. In other states agency is responsible for state parks only. Includes overnight visitors.
(X) = Not applicable

Table A-71. Government

Geographic area	Government employees (BLS)[1] (thousands)			Government earnings (BEA)[2] (million dollars)			Federal tax collections, 2018[3] (million dollars)	State tax collections[4] (million dollars)		
	2019	2015	2010	2019	2015	2010		2019	2015	2012
United States	22,923	22,029	22,490	2,051,421	1,823,646	1,668,220	3,465,467	1,090,242	916,488	796,918
Alabama	392	377	387	28,494	25,707	24,588	26,725	11,577	9,755	9,049
Alaska	80	82	85	9,972	9,462	8,450	5,287	1,781	864	7,049
Arizona	423	410	416	35,290	30,736	28,598	46,227	18,164	14,082	12,996
Arkansas	211	213	218	13,700	12,821	11,985	32,030	10,218	9,190	8,288
California	2,608	2,463	2,448	296,966	254,837	219,463	456,556	188,235	151,173	115,179
Colorado	455	417	394	38,466	32,614	28,462	58,708	15,870	12,811	10,263
Connecticut	236	239	247	22,673	21,894	19,653	53,729	17,994	16,232	15,481
Delaware	67	65	64	5,835	5,235	4,861	19,039	4,596	3,514	3,280
District of Columbia	239	238	247	40,862	35,468	33,082	28,444	8,679	7,087	X
Florida	1,123	1,082	1,112	91,717	81,731	80,167	205,694	44,800	37,218	32,997
Georgia	690	679	699	58,561	52,101	49,062	92,805	24,713	19,724	16,715
Hawaii	126	126	125	16,420	15,089	13,223	9,592	8,208	6,486	5,516
Idaho	127	119	119	8,387	7,155	6,499	10,858	4,884	3,975	3,374
Illinois	825	829	854	73,698	69,324	65,912	161,189	42,501	39,283	36,258
Indiana	429	427	437	27,184	24,513	23,458	58,699	20,171	17,400	16,289
Iowa	261	256	253	18,014	16,431	14,607	25,112	10,584	9,189	7,932
Kansas	260	257	262	18,610	17,002	15,717	25,814	10,030	7,884	7,418
Kentucky	311	319	317	23,438	22,590	22,680	34,755	12,896	11,598	10,619
Louisiana	331	327	366	25,364	23,327	23,839	41,982	11,749	9,719	8,994
Maine	101	100	104	7,725	6,798	6,364	7,925	4,674	4,064	3,777
Maryland	507	503	502	62,137	55,861	49,677	72,561	23,606	19,850	17,095
Massachusetts	457	451	439	44,665	40,115	33,197	117,998	31,805	27,012	22,821
Michigan	613	594	636	47,059	42,669	42,328	83,256	30,270	26,957	23,920
Minnesota	427	419	417	31,447	27,610	24,818	99,354	28,176	24,439	20,561
Mississippi	242	244	249	16,076	14,843	14,155	11,460	8,289	7,907	6,953
Missouri	436	434	448	31,442	29,248	27,990	63,139	13,181	11,956	10,802
Montana	91	90	92	6,279	5,667	5,157	6,229	3,169	2,843	2,459
Nebraska	174	171	170	12,308	11,153	9,982	25,312	5,755	5,087	4,367
Nevada	165	155	154	15,891	14,045	12,970	23,318	9,745	7,533	6,775
New Hampshire	90	90	96	6,711	6,225	5,912	12,291	2,969	2,488	2,205
New Jersey	606	614	642	57,725	53,803	51,665	138,977	38,844	31,568	27,456
New Mexico	189	191	200	15,097	13,752	13,176	9,002	7,428	6,009	5,471
New York	1,489	1,438	1,511	159,710	137,151	126,548	281,220	91,621	78,243	71,546
North Carolina	733	720	721	62,594	56,158	52,490	82,539	29,316	25,062	22,715
North Dakota	83	81	80	5,806	5,311	4,350	6,579	4,970	5,740	4,146
Ohio	786	771	786	61,212	55,444	51,932	140,891	30,147	28,297	25,928
Oklahoma	353	351	349	24,949	22,377	20,524	27,908	10,732	9,407	8,824
Oregon	299	301	300	25,879	21,754	19,401	33,802	13,960	10,575	8,728
Pennsylvania	707	705	771	63,631	59,192	57,335	136,269	43,132	36,110	32,950
Rhode Island	65	60	62	6,480	5,884	5,548	14,726	3,724	3,197	2,868
South Carolina	372	360	355	29,608	26,328	22,760	28,553	11,221	9,633	8,063
South Dakota	80	78	79	5,118	4,474	4,108	8,200	1,940	1,674	1,522
Tennessee	437	425	431	31,154	27,603	24,756	68,888	14,827	12,698	11,380
Texas	1,972	1,885	1,891	157,700	138,598	120,453	280,048	63,330	55,086	47,991
Utah	254	233	218	18,276	15,050	13,583	23,401	9,968	6,703	5,810
Vermont	57	56	55	4,263	3,855	3,368	4,418	3,429	3,043	2,731
Virginia	731	711	707	81,060	72,541	65,262	84,845	26,286	20,537	18,145
Washington	588	562	550	59,603	49,493	44,319	90,404	27,992	20,644	17,625
West Virginia	152	153	153	9,722	8,907	8,316	6,911	5,938	5,566	5,286
Wisconsin	406	409	420	30,861	28,452	27,014	51,993	20,039	17,019	15,995
Wyoming	69	71	71	5,580	5,247	4,452	4,931	2,111	2,356	2,305

[1] All estimates of labor and earnings provided by BLS are based on the 2007 North American Industry Classification System (NAICS). Government employment covers only civilian employees; military personnel are excluded. Employees of the Central Intelligence Agency, the National Security Agency, the National Imagery and Mapping Agency, and the Defense Intelligence Agency also are excluded.
[2] The estimates of earnings provided by the Bureau of Economic Analysis (BEA) for 2010–2015 are based on the 2007 North American Industry Classification System (NAICS). The estimates for 2019 are based on the 2017 NAICS. All dollar estimates are in current dollars (not adjusted for inflation). Includes Government enterprises.
[3] Excludes excise taxes collected by the Customs Service and the Alcohol and Tobacco Tax and Trade Bureau.
[4] Sum of State totals will differ from national total as the totals for the United States include revenue received from U.S. Armed Services overseas, Puerto Rico, and tax and excess withholding payments not classified by State, which contribute to the total amount of internal revenue collected by the federal government.

Table A-72. State Government Employment and Finances

Geographic area	Employment (full-time equivalent) Number (thousands) 2018	2012	Revenue (million dollars) Total 2018	2012	General, 2018 Total¹	Intergovernmental from federal government	Taxes	Expenditures (million dollars) Total 2018	2012	General, 2014 Total¹	Intergovernmental	Direct Education	Public welfare	Highway
United States	4,386	4,315	2,630,991	1,905,807	2,097,939	688,138	1,022,783	2,410,706	1,981,198	2,067,955	562,588	705,090	716,795	132,040
Alabama..................	92	89	34,407	28,970	28,251	10,303	11,056	33,899	27,687	29,952	7,007	12,052	8,613	2,017
Alaska.....................	24	27	9,919	14,983	8,152	3,457	1,642	11,979	11,729	10,446	649	1,373	2,830	1,325
Arizona....................	73	77	45,168	32,134	38,133	16,011	16,212	41,145	31,888	36,650	10,268	12,377	15,233	2,349
Arkansas..................	62	64	25,426	18,443	21,402	7,877	9,843	22,520	19,618	20,438	5,490	8,086	6,806	1,753
California.................	427	398	412,386	250,971	320,249	103,019	175,017	375,092	269,055	319,549	108,219	102,372	141,299	10,933
Colorado..................	89	74	42,390	25,688	30,879	9,403	14,802	37,449	28,238	31,696	7,519	12,636	9,804	2,058
Connecticut..............	59	61	35,139	27,328	30,490	7,440	19,082	28,071	28,370	22,583	5,908	7,355	4,883	1,611
Delaware..................	25	27	10,485	7,949	9,276	2,619	4,220	9,992	8,316	9,105	1,611	3,268	2,709	562
District of Columbia	(X)	(X)	(X)	(X)	(X)	(X)	(X)	(X)	(X)	(X)	(X)	(X)	(X)	(X)
Florida....................	181	181	110,235	83,670	91,783	28,299	45,961	96,822	79,482	86,783	18,959	28,660	27,813	8,435
Georgia	132	130	55,479	40,644	45,136	15,296	23,428	51,558	44,751	44,593	12,890	20,031	13,104	2,806
Hawaii....................	58	57	16,151	10,601	14,078	3,014	7,714	13,654	11,566	12,069	356	3,659	2,908	583
Idaho.....................	25	23	11,958	8,308	9,155	2,820	4,845	10,431	8,301	9,113	2,571	3,382	2,715	860
Illinois....................	122	130	92,718	68,902	72,948	22,430	39,857	92,468	72,622	76,875	21,110	19,255	25,366	5,151
Indiana...................	97	88	45,090	35,960	40,547	15,075	19,398	41,636	35,835	38,771	10,329	16,263	13,971	2,736
Iowa......................	51	48	28,868	21,080	24,072	6,076	10,088	23,877	20,408	20,953	5,373	7,371	6,261	2,376
Kansas...................	54	48	21,878	16,144	19,078	4,073	9,547	19,572	16,747	17,632	5,030	7,483	4,187	987
Kentucky	85	85	34,511	25,684	29,300	11,971	12,060	35,313	29,349	30,635	4,890	10,275	11,926	1,802
Louisiana	74	79	37,295	26,894	29,227	13,648	11,358	35,118	31,679	30,404	6,381	9,277	12,158	1,416
Maine.....................	20	21	10,658	8,418	8,815	3,013	4,411	9,237	9,128	8,155	1,347	2,177	3,325	766
Maryland..................	84	87	48,040	36,104	42,101	13,023	22,427	46,184	41,139	40,436	9,875	12,984	13,047	2,807
Massachusetts..............	104	95	68,542	49,237	58,095	17,101	29,655	67,366	56,685	56,701	9,435	13,318	23,881	2,602
Michigan..................	148	147	81,631	63,986	66,231	21,366	30,508	76,290	61,727	67,189	22,755	27,269	19,325	3,383
Minnesota.................	84	80	56,307	38,554	44,476	11,743	26,697	49,585	38,613	43,337	14,174	16,406	16,076	2,752
Mississippi................	55	58	23,421	18,765	19,137	8,272	7,891	21,833	20,051	18,660	4,861	5,752	6,579	1,157
Missouri..................	85	87	39,804	31,066	30,920	11,948	13,028	34,993	31,103	30,079	6,336	9,821	9,685	1,488
Montana..................	20	20	9,239	6,572	7,021	3,125	2,945	7,805	7,063	6,595	1,113	1,893	2,221	646
Nebraska..................	32	32	12,347	9,815	10,470	3,264	5,393	11,124	9,526	10,318	2,669	3,870	2,844	833
Nevada...................	30	27	21,772	14,318	16,088	5,454	9,157	17,415	13,477	14,611	5,180	5,653	3,956	1,044
New Hampshire.............	19	19	9,735	7,150	7,567	2,799	2,921	8,908	7,424	7,522	1,765	2,305	2,597	546
New Jersey	139	146	80,620	57,582	66,130	18,014	35,365	78,907	68,122	62,187	15,251	22,648	18,814	4,069
New Mexico	45	45	20,973	15,265	17,627	7,535	5,672	21,468	17,059	18,973	5,177	6,023	6,238	696
New York..................	248	237	223,526	179,605	175,700	64,588	88,541	213,163	181,226	173,767	63,492	46,901	71,581	7,382
North Carolina.............	140	150	67,303	56,469	56,344	18,705	27,855	60,929	53,624	54,506	14,706	21,895	15,124	5,297
North Dakota..............	18	19	8,880	7,773	7,747	1,742	4,205	7,216	6,315	6,539	1,995	2,336	1,556	752
Ohio......................	135	137	101,023	72,471	68,843	24,389	29,130	89,026	76,524	70,721	18,933	23,297	28,265	4,274
Oklahoma.................	63	65	26,986	23,248	22,075	7,101	9,564	25,315	22,599	21,148	4,471	8,068	6,810	2,215
Oregon...................	73	66	43,875	25,088	32,138	10,471	12,645	39,370	26,862	32,947	6,320	10,550	11,236	1,135
Pennsylvania..............	160	162	108,606	78,467	87,716	29,419	40,710	102,652	87,340	87,903	22,328	26,639	29,549	9,431
Rhode Island..............	18	19	9,905	7,987	8,406	2,869	3,483	9,472	8,326	8,070	1,308	2,165	3,261	412
South Carolina	80	79	35,446	26,132	28,178	9,917	10,550	35,003	27,668	28,985	6,768	10,412	8,053	1,895
South Dakota	14	14	5,615	4,352	4,410	1,499	1,918	5,243	4,424	4,646	872	1,609	1,173	641
Tennessee................	80	80	35,851	30,836	30,235	11,826	14,269	33,738	31,498	30,964	7,620	10,687	12,480	1,750
Texas.....................	308	301	171,756	130,720	137,623	47,202	60,329	150,890	125,953	132,368	31,521	56,461	39,408	9,485
Utah......................	62	53	24,322	15,601	18,688	4,724	8,039	21,888	17,109	19,664	4,167	9,030	3,898	1,375
Vermont..................	14	14	6,976	6,349	6,346	2,091	3,284	7,021	5,959	6,546	1,839	2,884	1,790	449
Virginia...................	126	126	62,587	43,138	50,882	10,958	23,489	56,367	46,760	50,396	12,258	17,422	11,684	5,422
Washington................	128	121	68,161	40,666	50,924	14,446	26,575	57,995	45,501	50,358	14,338	20,831	12,791	2,918
West Virginia..............	40	40	15,551	13,247	12,971	4,846	5,418	15,359	13,223	13,703	2,693	4,396	4,944	1,214
Wisconsin.................	71	71	54,526	35,881	36,278	9,494	18,743	42,178	37,753	36,484	11,109	12,317	11,162	2,938
Wyoming	12	14	7,505	6,599	5,602	2,364	1,837	6,169	5,774	5,230	1,354	1,898	854	505

¹Includes categories not shown separately.
(X) = Not applicable

Table A-73. State Government Tax Collections: 2016

Geographic area	Total[2] (million dollars)	Percent change, 2015-2016	Property taxes (million dollars)	State government tax collections, 2016[1]									
				Sales and gross receipts (million dollars)									
				Total	General sales and gross receipts	Selective sales taxes							
						Total	Alcoholic beverages	Amusements	Insurance premiums	Motor fuels	Public utilities	Tobacco products	Other selective sales
United States	929,891	1.3	18,291	441,289	292,411	148,878	6,612	7,589	20,449	43,855	13,291	18,010	38,951
Alabama	10,023	2.7	352	5,106	2,596	2,510	211	0	318	527	696	180	578
Alaska	897	-34.2	112	261	X	261	42	10	64	49	4	68	23
Arizona	13,680	-0.3	943	8,316	6,300	2,015	72	X	545	898	22	317	160
Arkansas	9,431	2.9	1,098	4,590	3,314	1,276	55	56	192	480	X	231	259
California	155,192	2.6	2,513	51,602	39,189	12,413	369	X	2,562	5,001	715	840	2,913
Colorado	13,021	2.1	X	5,123	2,840	2,283	43	116	278	667	X	201	977
Connecticut	15,290	-5.5	X	6,149	3,753	2,396	56	305	209	468	299	351	702
Delaware	3,522	0.2	X	539	X	539	20	X	96	125	55	112	130
District of Columbia	7,405	4.2	2,417	1,784	1,343	441	6	X	107	25	186	30	85
Florida	37,768	1.5	X	30,556	22,418	8,138	396	203	705	2,611	2,408	1,223	584
Georgia	21,455	8.7	962	8,408	5,480	2,928	191	X	429	1,655	X	220	434
Hawaii	6,919	6.7	X	4,316	3,206	1,110	51	X	158	93	153	125	531
Idaho	4,209	5.9	X	2,121	1,559	562	9	X	88	337	2	51	71
Illinois	38,907	-4.7	61	18,524	11,344	7,180	288	788	425	1,354	1,586	845	1,888
Indiana	17,632	1.1	11	10,662	7,306	3,356	48	579	235	845	215	443	988
Iowa	9,565	4.1	1	4,598	3,163	1,435	22	298	120	690	35	228	39
Kansas	8,059	2.2	664	4,325	3,240	1,085	134	0	306	451	0	147	47
Kentucky	11,646	0.4	563	5,495	3,267	2,228	132	0	146	850	64	242	790
Louisiana	9,498	-2.0	62	5,541	3,187	2,355	63	703	519	622	9	121	313
Maine	4,130	1.6	35	2,078	1,359	719	19	53	103	245	22	141	134
Maryland	20,894	4.5	748	8,939	4,504	4,435	32	650	553	1,018	138	395	1,649
Massachusetts	27,283	1.1	6	8,684	6,090	2,594	83	67	407	767	25	641	603
Michigan	27,609	2.4	2,061	13,331	9,264	4,068	156	113	330	1,017	29	946	1,472
Minnesota	25,189	3.7	850	10,121	5,584	4,537	88	56	458	901	0	650	2,382
Mississippi	7,660	-3.1	27	4,778	3,298	1,480	42	134	318	444	2	146	395
Missouri	12,297	2.4	31	5,302	3,536	1,766	37	368	401	717	X	102	141
Montana	2,628	-7.6	278	562	X	562	32	60	98	186	44	86	55
Nebraska	5,117	0.6	0	2,363	1,783	579	31	6	65	342	49	61	25
Nevada	8,026	6.5	280	6,348	4,266	2,082	45	930	310	316	23	175	282
New Hampshire	2,642	6.2	406	983	X	983	13	0	113	145	58	226	426
New Jersey	31,547	-0.1	5	13,173	9,268	3,906	139	209	605	554	965	677	756
New Mexico	5,275	-12.2	37	2,930	2,085	845	37	73	215	245	30	83	161
New York	81,350	4.0	X	24,790	13,534	11,256	300	1	1,539	1,612	914	1,247	5,622
North Carolina	26,213	4.5	X	11,150	7,188	3,962	379	0	503	1,936	0	286	857
North Dakota	3,709	-35.3	4	1,497	1,017	480	9	3	65	197	46	31	126
Ohio	28,695	1.4	X	18,231	12,227	6,005	101	269	579	1,856	1,157	1,009	1,029
Oklahoma	8,819	-9.0	X	3,778	2,471	1,307	120	21	323	464	46	316	16
Oregon	10,970	3.7	21	1,513	X	1,513	18	X	66	518	97	270	542
Pennsylvania	37,395	3.6	43	19,284	10,222	9,063	373	1,396	821	2,972	1,310	962	1,219
Rhode Island	3,246	2.5	3	1,665	974	692	20	X	114	90	104	144	218
South Carolina	9,457	-1.5	33	4,525	3,192	1,333	173	37	223	575	28	28	269
South Dakota	1,748	4.4	X	1,440	969	471	17	9	87	187	4	63	104
Tennessee	13,386	5.4	X	9,704	7,006	2,698	174	X	885	898	8	264	469
Texas	52,133	-5.4	X	46,371	32,131	14,239	1,192	30	2,171	3,500	605	1,480	5,254
Utah	7,083	5.7	X	3,032	2,084	948	52	X	133	420	24	120	200
Vermont	3,086	1.4	1,056	1,031	371	660	25	X	59	77	9	80	409
Virginia	21,213	3.3	30	6,880	3,932	2,948	269	0	485	896	122	179	998
Washington	22,280	7.9	2,062	17,636	13,560	4,076	348	X	535	1,458	489	451	794
West Virginia	5,128	-7.9	7	2,567	1,287	1,280	18	44	158	396	120	100	441
Wisconsin	17,649	3.7	171	7,763	5,059	2,705	59	0	197	1,043	369	650	387
Wyoming	1,914	-18.8	339	820	641	179	2	X	28	115	5	24	3

[1]The tax revenue data pertain to state fiscal years that end on June 30 in all but four states (NY, TX, AL, MI). Amounts shown for these four states reflect the different timing of their respective fiscal years, which were the 12-month periods ending on March 31 for New York, August 31 for Texas, and September 30 for Alabama and Michigan.
[2]Includes items not shown separately
0 = Represents zero or rounds to zero.
(D) = Data withheld to avoid disclosure or does not meet statistical standards.
(X) = Not applicable

Table A-74. Federal Government

| Geographic area | Total federal full time and part-time employment in thosands (BEA) | | | | | | Federal earnings (BEA) (million dollars) | | | | | |
| | Civilian | | | Military | | | Civilian | | | Military | | |
	2018	2015	2010	2018	2015	2010	2018	2015	2010	2018	2015	2010
United States	2,849.0	3,035.0	2,810.0	1,922.0	2,100.0	1,957.0	347.9	314.1	291.7	138.1	132.1	144.3
Alabama	53.1	58.5	53.1	28.6	32.8	29.8	6.4	6.0	5.7	1.8	1.7	2.0
Alaska	14.9	17.6	15.0	25.8	27.0	26.2	1.8	1.7	1.7	2.1	2.0	2.1
Arizona	55.7	60.0	54.7	34.0	34.9	31.8	6.3	5.7	5.2	2.3	2.0	2.3
Arkansas	20.2	22.9	20.3	14.8	18.1	17.2	2.1	1.9	1.9	0.7	0.8	0.9
California	246.7	269.1	245.1	205.8	223.8	204.3	30.7	27.6	25.7	16.0	14.9	16.3
Colorado	52.9	56.3	53.4	52.5	54.0	53.3	6.5	5.8	5.4	4.1	4.0	4.0
Connecticut	18.2	19.7	17.8	13.5	14.7	13.6	2.0	1.9	1.8	0.8	0.8	0.9
Delaware	5.7	6.2	5.7	8.5	8.7	8.7	0.6	0.6	0.5	0.5	0.4	0.5
District of Columbia	192.0	206.2	194.0	13.9	19.7	14.5	33.6	30.0	27.7	1.4	1.4	1.9
Florida	139.9	142.5	134.2	92.2	99.0	93.9	15.9	14.2	12.7	7.2	6.9	7.2
Georgia	101.5	107.8	99.0	90.2	103.5	94.6	11.6	10.4	9.9	6.8	6.8	7.5
Hawaii	33.7	34.9	33.1	55.2	56.2	58.2	3.9	3.5	3.2	4.9	5.0	4.7
Idaho	13.1	13.7	12.6	8.9	9.9	9.0	1.3	1.2	1.1	0.5	0.4	0.5
Illinois	79.3	92.0	80.0	43.9	47.8	42.0	9.2	8.6	8.6	2.7	2.3	2.9
Indiana	38.1	42.3	36.7	20.3	22.2	21.3	4.1	3.7	3.5	0.8	0.7	0.9
Iowa	17.6	19.2	17.5	11.3	13.0	12.0	1.7	1.6	1.5	0.4	0.4	0.5
Kansas	25.2	28.5	25.0	31.8	37.1	35.2	2.5	2.3	2.3	2.5	2.7	2.8
Kentucky	35.4	41.7	36.6	44.6	58.1	48.1	3.5	3.3	3.2	3.6	3.7	4.4
Louisiana	31.2	33.7	30.2	33.5	41.0	36.9	3.4	2.9	2.9	2.2	2.1	2.5
Maine	15.5	15.4	14.5	6.7	7.8	7.0	1.7	1.5	1.3	0.4	0.4	0.5
Maryland	174.1	172.0	173.1	49.9	46.4	49.9	26.7	24.0	21.1	4.2	4.0	3.6
Massachusetts	46.0	51.1	46.0	19.2	20.5	19.8	5.6	5.2	5.0	0.9	0.9	1.0
Michigan	52.4	57.5	51.5	17.6	20.7	18.4	6.0	5.5	5.1	0.7	0.7	0.9
Minnesota	32.1	34.7	31.6	19.7	20.9	19.9	3.5	3.2	3.0	0.7	0.6	0.8
Mississippi	25.2	27.3	25.3	27.0	31.2	27.3	2.6	2.4	2.3	1.5	1.4	1.8
Missouri	58.4	63.3	57.5	35.2	38.1	35.2	6.1	5.5	5.4	2.0	1.9	2.2
Montana	13.2	14.9	13.1	7.8	8.1	8.0	1.4	1.2	1.2	0.4	0.4	0.4
Nebraska	16.8	17.4	16.7	12.6	13.4	12.6	1.7	1.6	1.4	0.9	0.8	0.8
Nevada	19.3	18.7	18.6	18.4	17.0	17.8	2.1	1.8	1.6	1.3	1.2	1.1
New Hampshire	7.8	8.0	7.5	4.6	4.7	4.6	0.9	0.8	0.7	0.2	0.2	0.2
New Jersey	48.6	60.5	49.3	24.8	25.5	24.8	5.9	5.6	5.9	1.3	1.2	1.3
New Mexico	28.9	33.7	29.2	17.6	17.1	16.8	3.3	3.0	3.0	1.4	1.2	1.2
New York	115.0	132.8	115.1	55.2	60.2	57.1	13.6	12.6	12.1	3.2	3.1	3.6
North Carolina	72.9	72.1	70.4	127.7	144.9	129.0	7.6	6.8	5.9	10.8	10.4	11.3
North Dakota	9.4	10.2	9.2	11.8	11.7	11.6	0.9	0.8	0.8	0.8	0.7	0.7
Ohio	78.8	84.8	76.6	35.5	35.8	35.5	9.0	8.2	7.8	1.8	1.6	1.9
Oklahoma	49.2	50.5	47.0	33.7	39.6	33.4	5.1	4.6	4.3	2.3	2.2	2.6
Oregon	28.2	30.6	27.8	11.3	12.3	11.9	3.2	2.8	2.7	0.5	0.4	0.5
Pennsylvania	97.1	109.8	96.0	34.7	36.6	35.9	10.9	10.0	9.8	1.5	1.4	1.7
Rhode Island	11.1	10.7	10.5	6.7	7.3	7.2	1.3	1.2	1.1	0.5	0.5	0.5
South Carolina	34.1	34.4	32.9	52.9	54.5	53.5	3.5	3.1	2.8	3.7	3.6	3.6
South Dakota	11.3	12.0	11.1	8.1	8.8	8.0	1.1	1.0	0.9	0.5	0.4	0.5
Tennessee	49.6	53.6	49.6	20.4	23.6	21.8	5.9	5.4	4.9	0.8	0.8	1.1
Texas	202.0	210.4	195.0	172.6	183.6	171.6	23.5	20.9	19.2	13.0	12.5	13.2
Utah	36.1	38.0	35.0	16.3	16.9	16.1	3.8	3.3	3.1	0.8	0.7	0.9
Vermont	7.0	6.8	6.8	3.9	4.3	4.5	0.8	0.7	0.6	0.1	0.1	0.2
Virginia	199.3	191.2	196.4	136.5	152.4	140.2	27.7	24.9	21.9	13.1	12.8	13.7
Washington	74.9	75.7	73.3	73.9	81.7	75.6	8.9	7.8	7.1	6.1	5.9	6.2
West Virginia	23.6	24.5	23.3	8.5	10.0	9.0	2.7	2.4	2.2	0.3	0.3	0.4
Wisconsin	29.2	31.6	28.9	15.8	16.7	16.2	2.9	2.6	2.4	0.6	0.5	0.7
Wyoming	7.5	8.1	7.4	6.1	6.3	6.0	0.7	0.7	0.6	0.4	0.3	0.4

Table A-75. Federal Individual Income Tax Returns and Federal Real Estate

| Geographic area | Federal individual income tax returns | | | | | | | | | | Federal buildings, 2015 (million square feet) | | Federal Lands, 2015 |
| | Number of returns[1] (thousands) | | Adjusted gross income[2] (thousands of dollars) | | Adjusted gross income per return (dollars) | | Income tax[3] (thousands of dollars) | | Itemized Deductions, 2017 (thousands of dollars) | | | | |
	2017	2010	2017	2010	2017	2010	2017	2010	Total itemized deductions	Mortgage interest paid	Owned	Leased	Total, owned or leased (acres)
United States[5]	152,456	144,002	10,991,387	8,090,663	72,095	56,184	1,589,761	1,002,111	1,403,313	287,022	2,521	283.1	49,601,819
Alabama	2,060	2,102	118,876	98,932	57,707	47,060	14,449	10,778	13,039	2,758	51	4.0	282,211
Alaska	349	374	23,851	21,508	68,341	57,544	3,284	2,754	1,720	625	40	1.5	2,298,236
Arizona	3,023	2,719	193,797	135,801	64,108	49,952	25,595	15,144	22,963	6,018	51	4.3	4,628,488
Arkansas	1,233	1,224	73,645	55,981	59,728	45,723	8,911	5,720	8,288	1,272	22	1.4	780,210
California	18,099	16,684	1,521,053	1,026,911	84,041	61,551	234,500	133,458	252,954	54,755	269	20.0	4,813,512
Colorado	2,714	2,370	209,871	142,647	77,329	60,190	30,583	17,803	24,590	7,233	52	7.0	895,043
Connecticut	1,766	1,728	174,258	145,642	98,674	84,305	29,409	22,652	26,350	4,496	13	1.0	12,629
Delaware	464	428	31,276	23,888	67,405	55,844	4,072	2,699	3,769	1,030	6	0.4	12,479
District of Columbia	348	323	34,162	23,964	98,167	74,223	6,050	3,703	5,105	1,031	72	24.6	4,383
Florida	10,181	9,631	726,990	467,521	71,407	48,542	116,971	59,914	78,752	15,252	103	11.9	916,783
Georgia	4,543	4,590	298,099	216,008	65,617	47,065	40,049	24,703	43,384	8,414	112	10.3	1,011,373
Hawaii	693	653	45,428	33,362	65,553	51,062	5,688	3,502	5,800	1,863	47	1.7	429,370
Idaho	764	663	45,121	29,569	59,059	44,580	5,274	2,937	5,700	1,308	16	1.8	1,093,903
Illinois	6,129	6,044	455,607	362,262	74,336	59,939	67,180	46,803	54,969	10,939	61	5.8	236,325
Indiana	3,135	2,982	185,559	143,180	59,189	48,022	23,073	15,191	16,819	3,490	27	2.8	354,557
Iowa	1,458	1,400	92,282	72,095	63,294	51,499	11,251	7,572	10,520	1,821	15	1.9	254,665
Kansas	1,333	1,307	85,640	70,710	64,246	54,096	11,102	8,025	9,001	1,621	30	2.9	680,445
Kentucky	1,920	1,856	107,719	86,693	56,104	46,698	12,661	8,893	11,755	2,359	43	3.0	827,711
Louisiana	1,970	1,991	114,167	98,239	57,953	49,344	14,877	11,668	12,313	2,408	38	3.6	443,783
Maine	660	625	38,804	29,966	58,794	47,941	4,581	3,047	4,387	948	10	0.9	385,973
Maryland	2,986	2,787	235,433	189,301	78,846	67,914	32,942	23,632	40,983	9,426	113	20.4	216,905
Massachusetts	3,457	3,203	327,916	233,487	94,856	72,893	54,205	33,218	41,575	8,933	31	2.7	69,962
Michigan	4,763	4,607	299,669	227,557	62,916	49,396	39,851	25,396	30,754	6,287	24	5.0	165,791
Minnesota	2,772	2,561	205,975	152,396	74,306	59,505	28,235	18,219	27,051	5,735	19	2.3	101,830
Mississippi	1,235	1,283	60,763	53,325	49,201	41,547	6,575	5,592	7,174	1,193	40	2.3	564,739
Missouri	2,812	2,689	171,470	135,415	60,978	50,361	21,868	15,114	19,079	3,652	45	10.8	598,864
Montana	506	475	29,912	21,570	59,115	45,425	3,661	2,258	3,632	818	14	2.3	525,487
Nebraska	906	854	57,728	45,209	63,717	52,934	7,196	4,952	6,614	1,093	14	1.5	187,737
Nevada	1,418	1,264	94,289	66,772	66,494	52,829	13,802	8,423	10,906	2,598	26	2.1	5,418,573
New Hampshire	707	664	54,638	41,350	77,281	62,281	7,890	5,047	5,427	1,422	4	0.6	24,671
New Jersey	4,438	4,286	393,192	308,540	88,597	71,995	62,813	43,545	62,045	11,262	39	4.8	94,593
New Mexico	922	913	49,150	41,429	53,308	45,377	5,770	4,388	4,943	1,202	54	3.3	6,803,462
New York	9,695	9,272	836,755	628,370	86,308	67,770	140,510	91,175	132,916	17,181	82	8.6	201,814
North Carolina	4,578	4,203	286,383	207,775	62,556	49,438	36,903	22,165	33,993	7,654	88	4.8	661,173
North Dakota	363	330	24,152	18,586	66,534	56,241	3,372	2,266	1,773	391	15	1.1	628,688
Ohio	5,621	5,437	340,322	267,042	60,545	49,112	43,285	29,269	33,895	6,629	62	5.4	172,158
Oklahoma	1,630	1,590	97,446	79,531	59,783	50,007	12,018	8,856	10,842	1,793	50	5.3	1,113,278
Oregon	1,939	1,743	132,370	88,462	68,267	50,744	16,949	9,325	20,507	4,581	20	2.8	379,492
Pennsylvania	6,237	6,130	426,878	339,678	68,443	55,413	59,451	41,103	45,728	9,580	70	9.6	237,439
Rhode Island	537	509	35,968	28,279	66,980	55,548	4,850	3,344	4,503	1,033	11	0.6	3,135
South Carolina	2,241	2,052	132,262	94,103	59,019	45,863	16,233	9,463	15,790	3,551	50	2.2	512,685
South Dakota	419	394	26,394	19,818	62,993	50,327	3,477	2,278	2,065	387	15	0.9	553,501
Tennessee	3,036	2,847	183,899	136,096	60,573	47,810	24,585	15,292	15,186	3,640	48	3.2	483,932
Texas	12,521	10,996	886,241	620,581	70,780	56,439	133,417	80,302	95,704	17,438	167	22.8	2,276,885
Utah	1,326	1,135	89,567	58,858	67,547	51,875	10,946	5,769	13,283	3,161	28	2.9	3,376,514
Vermont	328	318	20,318	15,678	61,945	49,315	2,474	1,677	2,334	476	3	1.2	32,284
Virginia	3,961	3,729	309,804	245,073	78,214	65,713	44,246	31,185	42,810	11,457	151	28.4	739,443
Washington	3,568	3,169	298,356	190,783	83,620	60,201	45,091	23,868	29,934	9,247	78	5.4	1,701,670
West Virginia	767	783	40,036	35,604	52,198	45,457	4,467	3,639	3,064	660	22	2.6	158,665
Wisconsin	2,867	2,742	184,819	143,792	64,464	52,447	23,717	15,934	21,705	4,139	20	2.6	108,052
Wyoming	271	276	21,037	17,685	77,627	63,975	3,084	2,284	1,926	399	13	0.8	1,034,023

[1] Includes returns constructed by Internal Revenue Service for certain self-employment tax returns.

[2] Less deficit.

[3] Includes additional tax for tax preferences, self-employment tax, tax from investment credit recapture, and other income-related taxes. Total is before earned income credit.

[4] Federal real property is defined as any real property owned, leased, or otherwise managed by the federal government, within the United States, and improvements of federal lands. Federal real property shall exclude: interest in real property assets that have been disposed of for public benefit purposes pursuant to section 484 of title 40, United States Code, and are now held in private ownership; land easements or rights-of-way held by the federal government; public domain land (including lands withdrawn for military purposes) or land reserved or dedicated for national forest, national park, or national wildlife refuge purposes except for improvements on those lands; land held in trust or restricted fee status for individual Indians or Indian tribes; and land and interests in land that are withheld from the scope of this order by agency heads for reasons of national security, foreign policy, or public safety.

[5] For federal individual income tax returns, the states will not sum to U.S. totals. Totals include returns filed from Army Post Office and Fleet Post Office addresses by members of the armed forces stationed overseas; returns by other U.S. citizens abroad; and returns filed by residents of Puerto Rico with income from sources outside of Puerto Rico or with income earned as U.S. government employees.

Table A-76. Social Security, Food Stamps, and School Lunch Programs

	Social security benefits						Supplemental Nutrition Assistance Program (year ending September 30, 2016)					National school lunch program			
	Recipients Dec 31[1] (thousands)				Total monthly benefits, 2018 (million dollars)				Benefits issued			Participants (thousands)		Federal cost[4] (million dollars)	
	Total		Retired workers and dependents[1]		Total	Retired workers and dependents[1]	Number of households	Number of participants	Total (in thousands)	Per household	Per person				
Geographic area	2018	2011	2018	2011								2015	2019	2015	2019
United States	61,363	53,972	45,679	37,536	83,162	65,308	21,777,938	44,219,363	$66,539,351	$254.61	$125.40	30,496	29,552	13,003	14,199
Alabama...................	1,143	1,037	753	677	1,475	1,052	399,728	850,804	$1,254,835	$261.60	$122.91	531	500	230	250
Alaska.....................	101	82	77	64	131	105	34,648	82,326	$175,483	$422.07	$177.63	54	53	37	39
Arizona...................	1,349	1,105	1,057	906	1,874	1,530	427,061	960,105	$1,402,230	$273.62	$121.71	647	619	293	313
Arkansas.................	697	647	463	425	871	627	191,636	426,069	$577,775	$251.25	$113.01	321	313	144	155
California.................	5,963	5,130	4,690	4,151	7,935	6,443	2,093,562	4,340,042	$7,237,700	$288.09	$138.97	3,272	3,153	1,588	1,722
Colorado..................	875	721	683	591	1,202	977	225,334	475,690	$728,043	$269.25	$127.54	378	360	143	146
Connecticut..............	682	630	532	497	1,018	835	244,927	431,597	$685,510	$233.24	$132.36	288	284	105	130
Delaware..................	213	177	164	142	314	254	71,099	147,559	$220,683	$258.66	$124.63	98	98	38	42
District of Columbia	83	76	60	55	107	84	75,819	134,625	$210,436	$231.29	$130.26	53	53	28	29
Florida....................	4,626	3,894	3,595	3,170	6,265	5,074	1,870,739	3,454,530	$5,216,754	$232.38	$125.84	1,676	1,726	834	958
Georgia...................	1,830	1,524	1,312	1,145	2,411	1,839	800,670	1,733,473	$2,663,018	$277.17	$128.02	1,236	1,175	555	574
Hawaii....................	271	234	225	202	371	317	89,095	176,729	$484,225	$452.91	$228.33	110	104	48	48
Idaho.....................	346	279	263	223	458	366	79,531	185,303	$255,424	$267.63	$114.87	157	149	58	58
Illinois...................	2,243	2,065	1,699	1,570	3,097	2,457	996,092	1,914,393	$3,040,977	$254.41	$132.37	1,109	1,015	502	506
Indiana...................	1,350	1,220	975	891	1,877	1,446	328,688	741,610	$1,068,459	$270.89	$120.06	768	728	292	311
Iowa......................	647	592	498	458	882	712	178,874	380,705	$507,597	$236.48	$111.11	382	373	117	132
Kansas...................	553	499	415	376	768	612	114,392	253,833	$342,325	$249.38	$112.39	345	331	119	119
Kentucky.................	990	914	642	581	1,241	866	313,476	666,264	$980,977	$260.78	$122.70	525	515	225	267
Louisiana.................	908	809	593	525	1,109	775	422,090	927,168	$1,494,495	$295.06	$134.32	549	545	238	278
Maine.....................	344	307	249	223	435	333	98,549	189,245	$254,899	$215.54	$112.24	100	95	37	38
Maryland..................	1,001	873	763	687	1,436	1,153	388,957	744,343	$1,079,152	$231.21	$120.82	435	442	181	202
Massachusetts...........	1,273	1,161	936	860	1,759	1,374	450,364	779,192	$1,189,716	$220.14	$127.24	528	526	198	228
Michigan..................	2,209	2,017	1,597	1,463	3,124	2,405	777,906	1,473,614	$2,167,715	$232.22	$122.58	843	803	317	362
Minnesota................	1,033	905	808	722	1,457	1,197	231,228	478,783	$602,564	$217.16	$104.88	614	606	177	185
Mississippi...............	669	610	441	396	824	588	269,082	582,658	$814,421	$252.22	$116.48	385	354	188	192
Missouri..................	1,294	1,188	921	846	1,705	1,295	378,373	810,690	$1,182,958	$260.54	$121.60	604	559	234	241
Montana..................	234	198	182	158	303	246	54,612	116,626	$166,365	$253.86	$118.87	82	79	30	33
Nebraska.................	346	313	265	241	469	379	78,482	175,851	$240,677	$255.56	$114.05	241	244	81	88
Nevada...................	537	425	418	358	723	583	222,253	439,782	$629,520	$236.04	$119.29	216	230	109	119
New Hampshire............	306	263	225	201	438	345	48,037	98,464	$120,552	$209.13	$102.03	89	80	27	26
New Jersey	1,626	1,500	1,260	1,173	2,436	1,976	440,091	879,987	$1,223,052	$231.59	$115.82	696	667	278	301
New Mexico...............	437	371	319	279	549	425	216,877	471,247	$693,427	$266.44	$122.62	217	209	105	111
New York..................	3,627	3,337	2,739	2,523	5,045	4,004	1,635,764	2,968,227	$4,922,406	$250.77	$138.20	1,699	1,688	757	900
North Carolina.............	2,099	1,808	1,546	1,364	2,833	2,216	761,999	1,568,387	$2,248,947	$245.95	$119.49	904	835	416	433
North Dakota..............	134	121	103	92	175	140	25,262	54,252	$78,701	$259.62	$120.89	90	93	23	27
Ohio	2,356	2,166	1,691	1,564	3,105	2,361	793,923	1,608,633	$2,396,033	$251.50	$124.12	1,020	970	393	418
Oklahoma.................	789	717	555	506	1,024	770	276,268	612,869	$885,643	$267.15	$120.42	440	432	175	189
Oregon...................	872	735	680	598	1,194	971	419,778	734,864	$1,072,982	$213.01	$121.68	294	287	124	126
Pennsylvania.............	2,825	2,618	2,088	1,937	3,935	3,080	950,739	1,863,836	$2,729,025	$239.20	$122.02	1,035	1,012	403	461
Rhode Island..............	225	207	165	152	308	240	100,433	171,055	$271,960	$225.66	$132.49	76	78	32	35
South Carolina	1,143	956	835	720	1,554	1,206	378,328	805,012	$1,222,104	$269.19	$126.51	483	474	220	236
South Dakota	179	156	140	125	233	191	42,234	95,983	$144,590	$285.30	$125.53	107	105	31	33
Tennessee	1,453	1,288	1,020	916	1,913	1,442	547,850	1,113,231	$1,672,282	$254.37	$125.18	677	641	289	315
Texas.....................	4,224	3,552	3,084	2,660	5,496	4,238	1,588,116	3,768,472	$5,308,545	$278.56	$117.39	3,379	3,362	1,547	1,730
Utah......................	407	335	310	267	559	449	86,244	219,820	$301,870	$291.68	$114.44	334	332	113	119
Vermont..................	150	132	113	101	204	162	42,976	79,715	$116,470	$225.85	$121.76	49	46	17	17
Virginia...................	1,530	1,319	1,145	1,014	2,122	1,680	387,633	826,354	$1,169,413	$251.40	$117.93	703	704	246	288
Washington...............	1,347	1,127	1,038	907	1,914	1,547	546,931	1,011,412	$1,452,894	$221.37	$119.71	518	519	214	229
West Virginia..............	476	451	313	287	613	431	178,274	357,531	$499,059	$233.28	$116.32	194	187	80	94
Wisconsin.................	1,233	1,086	943	848	1,718	1,384	359,933	728,077	$922,851	$213.66	$105.63	542	504	192	198
Wyoming	112	94	87	75	156	126	14,367	33,853	$48,510	$281.37	$119.41	52	47	16	16

[1]Includes special benefits for persons age 72 and over not insured under regular or transitional provisions of Social Security Act.
[2]Unnegotiated checks not deducted.
[3]Includes benefits only and excludes administrative expenditures.
[4]Includes cash payments and commodity costs.

Table A-77. Social Insurance and Medical Programs

Geographic area	Supplemental security income Recipients (SSI) (thousands)[1]		Temporary assistance for Needy Families (TANF) Average number of recipients		Medicare enrollment (thousands)			Number of Children Ever Enrolled in Medicaid and CHIP during the year			
								CHIP		Medicaid	
	2018	2014	2018	2015	2019	2015	2010	2018	2015	2018	2015
United States	8,128	8,161	2,180,626	3,073,219	55,649	50,415	46,585	9,632,367	8,397,651	36,287,063	36,833,664
Alabama	162	175	18,422	31,774	968	900	845	222,072	133,043	538,567	658,242
Alaska	13	12	7,233	8,471	88	73	66	19,747	10,182	102,629	87,537
Arizona	119	119	14,938	24,869	1,212	1,041	930	127,063	38,811	887,183	942,546
Arkansas	105	111	6,214	10,855	591	555	531	98,127	112,071	413,369	364,822
California	1,238	1,146	767,126	1,114,580	5,582	5,038	4,757	1,976,284	1,912,128	4,671,066	4,888,674
Colorado	73	73	36,145	45,174	821	709	625	182,199	86,133	495,130	502,210
Connecticut	66	63	22,963	26,274	611	565	568	28,900	24,884	351,703	365,676
Delaware	17	17	10,349	12,789	192	167	149	13,958	16,379	108,522	100,258
District of Columbia	26	27	13,720	15,670	77	71	78	16,125	10,676	84,590	89,210
Florida	576	561	66,343	84,148	4,260	3,788	3,375	496,080	428,094	2,374,180	2,264,344
Georgia	259	256	20,664	25,853	1,581	1,401	1,236	262,135	230,815	1,315,810	1,341,668
Hawaii	23	24	12,174	21,735	236	215	206	29,375	27,239	145,454	143,075
Idaho	31	30	2,976	2,735	310	262	230	39,657	34,513	209,767	202,190
Illinois	267	276	22,225	41,886	2,017	1,870	1,839	296,186	330,571	1,422,984	1,540,694
Indiana	127	128	12,078	17,743	1,167	1,071	1,006	135,308	100,560	673,839	689,672
Iowa	51	51	19,984	28,565	581	534	517	99,314	82,657	335,207	334,419
Kansas	48	49	4,190	14,384	490	449	433	63,850	77,139	265,946	250,084
Kentucky	174	189	37,908	50,185	856	799	760	103,244	86,976	545,371	525,516
Louisiana	175	181	13,817	11,859	804	733	687	172,934	135,614	701,926	685,163
Maine	37	38	7,521	10,109	312	283	265	25,219	22,310	147,002	166,871
Maryland	121	118	43,136	46,480	895	812	785	151,179	142,327	506,314	532,090
Massachusetts	184	189	52,267	67,345	1,192	1,092	1,061	227,819	168,941	548,765	568,446
Michigan	272	275	30,442	52,225	1,933	1,785	1,651	81,391	119,699	1,165,320	1,139,982
Minnesota	94	94	40,821	43,155	942	848	786	4,043	3,835	654,776	599,730
Mississippi	117	126	8,295	13,972	564	527	497	88,491	87,105	422,523	447,883
Missouri	136	143	21,468	59,066	1,132	1,051	1,004	109,169	78,344	627,204	579,019
Montana	18	18	9,696	7,113	212	186	170	31,284	45,261	139,837	94,546
Nebraska	28	28	9,999	10,622	317	288	279	59,608	62,218	168,380	165,181
Nevada	57	50	23,564	28,802	473	406	357	71,994	61,908	476,068	352,510
New Hampshire	19	20	6,796	5,732	267	236	223	17,781	16,651	92,007	94,488
New Jersey	180	176	24,758	56,865	1,430	1,334	1,327	254,284	215,191	728,620	755,476
New Mexico	63	64	25,919	31,120	381	336	313	13,224	17,195	409,834	398,864
New York	629	654	203,008	256,741	3,252	3,007	2,988	768,259	630,732	2,167,369	2,293,708
North Carolina	229	235	25,503	23,920	1,857	1,669	1,490	296,759	234,654	1,144,978	1,145,975
North Dakota	8	8	2,517	2,917	120	109	109	8,689	4,955	53,988	61,525
Ohio	308	313	90,729	113,806	2,151	1,982	1,901	260,890	181,100	1,257,669	1,363,329
Oklahoma	96	97	13,904	15,802	673	624	603	206,350	190,858	516,560	519,694
Oregon	88	85	33,253	46,128	793	695	621	189,618	121,869	402,570	487,013
Pennsylvania	356	371	112,979	162,233	2,495	2,325	2,283	369,172	294,342	1,229,049	1,241,249
Rhode Island	33	33	9,976	29,733	194	179	183	35,920	31,324	112,369	99,712
South Carolina	115	118	17,608	23,572	1,004	882	774	111,051	98,336	655,634	619,859
South Dakota	15	15	6,011	5,935	161	144	137	20,129	16,216	74,208	80,764
Tennessee	176	184	47,253	87,101	1,259	1,153	1,058	107,140	106,215	904,130	819,456
Texas	650	666	55,346	70,524	3,783	3,328	3,001	1,136,587	1,049,623	3,456,176	3,535,755
Utah	32	31	8,338	9,018	360	311	283	60,423	55,285	235,144	254,776
Vermont	15	15	4,906	5,969	134	120	112	4,942	4,766	72,339	74,718
Virginia	156	155	33,917	51,341	1,356	1,217	1,141	207,725	189,366	658,138	675,868
Washington	149	151	55,117	75,739	1,235	1,085	972	87,732	46,037	822,258	787,486
West Virginia	72	78	12,916	16,139	409	390	382	39,419	48,278	236,174	297,450
Wisconsin	117	118	31,945	53,771	1,094	982	911	196,416	168,576	517,743	546,579
Wyoming	7	7	1,249	675	101	87	80	7,102	5,649	40,674	57,662

[1]Data cover federal SSI payments and/or federally administered state supplementation. National figures include data not distributed by state.

Table A-78. Government Transfer Payments to Individuals

Geographic area	Total government transfer payments (million dollars)					Program area 2018 (million dollars)						
	2018			2018	2010	Retirement and disability insurance benefits	Medical payments	Income maintenance benefits	Unemployment insurance benefits	Veterans benefits	Federal education and training assistance payments[2]	Other transfer receipts of individuals[3]
	Total	Percent change, 2010–2018	Per capita[1] (dollars)									
United States	2,971,451	27.8	9,082	2,971,451	2,325,117	1,007,322	1,355,734	259,860	27,569	109,886	69,053	65,430
Alabama...........................	47,222	24.3	9661	47,222	37978.34	17,881	18414.462	4,453	168	2,640	1,356	1,163
Alaska.............................	7,042	32.0	9,549	7,042	5,336	1,538	3,152	787	76	402	79	838
Arizona............................	63,501	32.6	8,854	63,501	47,886	21,954	27,905	4,610	290	2,511	3,479	1,070
Arkansas..........................	29,855	26.4	9,906	29,855	23,612	10,640	13,470	2,475	131	1,345	805	286
California.........................	346,145	29.7	8,751	346,145	266,907	101,523	170,722	32,340	4,924	10,201	9,773	7,366
Colorado..........................	42,931	45.1	7,538	42,931	29,593	14,583	19,631	2,875	378	2,373	1,006	747
Connecticut......................	35,452	22.0	9,923	35,452	29,066	11,973	17,548	2,481	607	672	634	708
Delaware..........................	10,464	46.2	10,819	10,464	7,158	3,705	4,946	663	68	315	383	158
District of Columbia	6,815	25.7	9,701	6,815	5,421	1,277	4,071	904	65	136	170	32
Florida.............................	204,099	34.6	9,582	204,099	151,686	73,749	86,729	16,458	443	8,494	3,934	9,280
Georgia............................	81,851	32.1	7,781	81,851	61,975	28,862	31,935	8,763	335	4,785	2,163	2,547
Hawaii.............................	12,090	30.2	8511	12,090	9,287	4,311	5078.479	1,219	146	684	202	118
Idaho...............................	13,883	35.5	7,914	13,883	10,249	5,586	5,434	986	90	616	292	465
Illinois.............................	106,651	14.4	8,371	106,651	93,254	37,391	46,996	10,601	1,640	2,464	2,634	1,937
Indiana............................	60,106	27.0	8,982	60,106	47,315	22,605	27,021	4,805	260	1,682	1,630	543
Iowa................................	27,579	27.0	8,738	27,579	21,721	10,529	12,010	1,913	370	786	761	475
Kansas............................	23,576	22.9	8,097	23,576	19,190	9,336	9,792	1,755	161	898	415	539
Kentucky..........................	45,160	27.4	10,106	45,160	35,454	15,493	21,134	3,763	326	1,595	1,394	412
Louisiana	46,017	33.4	9,875	46,017	34,490	13,661	23,053	4,670	186	1,637	1,087	634
Maine	14,265	25.9	10,658	14,265	11,331	5,156	6,383	920	93	680	238	481
Maryland..........................	52,649	34.3	8,713	52,649	39,194	17,192	25,425	4,200	513	2,020	953	929
Massachusetts..................	69,439	23.7	10,060	69,439	56,145	20,780	36,081	6,117	1,361	1,645	1,047	812
Michigan..........................	97,776	18.3	9782	97,776	82,685	37,247	43343.516	8,066	769	2,646	2,098	1,262
Minnesota........................	50,817	30.2	9,056	50,817	39,027	17,264	24,267	4,044	753	1,483	1,230	459
Mississippi.......................	29,276	21.5	9,803	29,276	24,090	9,995	13,127	2,958	88	1,088	740	586
Missouri...........................	56,443	23.9	9,213	56,443	45,572	20,706	25,284	4,039	299	2,159	1,147	1,381
Montana...........................	9,727	37.8	9,157	9,727	7,059	3,818	4,096	590	106	436	167	265
Nebraska..........................	15,508	30.7	8,038	15,508	11,868	5,882	6,177	1,134	77	716	333	737
Nevada............................	24,470	45.4	8,064	24,470	16,826	8,486	10,538	2,121	302	1,264	625	414
New Hampshire.................	12,376	35.5	9,124	12,376	9,136	5,119	5,315	578	66	458	297	228
New Jersey	83,808	18.5	9,408	83,808	70,718	29,615	37,911	7,224	1,876	1,520	1,696	1,872
New Mexico	20,683	30.3	9,870	20,683	15,879	6,579	9,573	2,134	133	1,011	435	325
New York..........................	222,370	21.9	11,379	222,370	182,471	61,179	122,661	21,485	2,021	3,453	4,254	2,763
North Carolina..................	92,688	31.2	8926	92,688	70,644	33,368	37345.581	8,227	206	5,201	2,250	3,663
North Dakota....................	6,076	33.7	7,994	6,076	4,543	2,256	2,622	489	91	230	104	107
Ohio................................	109,537	20.8	9,371	109,537	90,693	38,431	52,085	9,053	871	3,121	2,269	977
Oklahoma.........................	34,464	24.5	8,740	34,464	27,688	12,505	13,479	3,084	221	2,415	833	1,005
Oregon............................	40,005	36.6	9,546	40,005	29,282	14,393	18,288	2,938	487	1,728	583	604
Pennsylvania.....................	139,314	25.5	10,878	139,314	110,982	47,438	67,219	11,692	1,814	3,333	2,255	2,590
Rhode Island.....................	11,387	19.4	10,769	11,387	9,534	3,818	5,377	1,095	147	304	274	127
South Carolina	48,131	32.4	9,467	48,131	36,357	18,380	19,007	3,794	179	2,798	1,506	1,278
South Dakota	6,974	29.7	7,905	6,974	5,378	2,750	2,798	518	30	313	137	223
Tennessee........................	62,723	24.4	9,265	62,723	50,411	22,942	26,124	5,687	226	2,952	1,409	1,796
Texas...............................	214,052	35.0	7,458	214,052	158,614	66,200	95,713	22,069	2,057	11,529	4,348	5,390
Utah................................	18,462	34.1	5840	18,462	13,767	6,840	6718.369	1,674	150	687	749	897
Vermont...........................	6,823	27.6	10,894	6,823	5,348	2,383	3,187	573	62	184	189	101
Virginia............................	68,010	37.2	7,985	68,010	49,584	25,287	26,899	5,073	300	4,530	1,710	2,225
Washington......................	65,849	31.2	8,738	65,849	50,179	24,592	26,957	6,099	1,030	3,104	1,562	730
West Virginia....................	20,818	23.6	11,528	20,818	16,841	7,786	9,148	1,712	142	909	505	194
Wisconsin.........................	51,320	22.0	8,828	51,320	42,049	20,251	21,803	3,723	388	1,514	827	1,453
Wyoming..........................	4,776	31.1	8,268	4,776	3,642	2,086	1,742	225	47	219	85	237

[1]Based on estimated resident population as of July 1.
[2]Consists largely of federal fellowship payments (National Science Foundation fellowships and traineeships, subsistence payments to state maritime academy cadets, and other federal fellowships), interest subsidy on higher education loans, Pell grants, Job Corps payments, education exchange payments, and state education assistance.
[3]Consists largely of Bureau of Indian Affairs payments, Alaska Permanent Fund dividend payments, compensation of survivors of public safety officers, compensation of victims of crime, disaster relief payments, compensation for Japanese internment, the American Recovery and Reinvestment Act of 2009, funded Federal Additional Compensation for unemployment, COBRA premium reduction, and the Economic Recovery lump sum payment; and other special payments to individuals.

Table A-79. Department of Defense and Veterans

Geographic area	Department of Defense											Number of veterans[6] (thousands)	
	Personnel[1]						Defense spending, 2018[4]						
	Total			2019			State share of total U.S. defense spending (percent)	Defense spending as share of GDP (percent)	Defense spending per resident (dollars)	Payroll[5] ($ billions)	Contracts ($ billions)		
	2019	2016	2005	Active duty military[2]	Civilian[3]	Reserve and National Guard						2018	2010
United States	2,695,457	2,594,182	2,847,783	1,189,842	722,696	782,919	(X)	2.4	$1,528	141.2	$358.9	20,334	23,032
Alabama	51,958	51,316	61,943	8,858	24,211	18,889	3.1	6.9	3,150	3.2	12.2	373	424
Alaska	29,183	28,484	28,733	19,510	4,997	4,676	0.7	6.4	4,730	1.7	1.8	73	74
Arizona.............................	44,634	40,890	50,624	20,112	9,087	15,435	3.0	4.3	2,122	2.0	13.2	527	541
Arkansas	18,131	18,288	26,960	3,815	3,511	10,805	0.3	1.0	427	0.7	0.6	216	257
California...........................	286,560	243,053	295,517	164,770	64,465	57,325	11.5	1.9	1,459	15.2	42.5	1,752	1,943
Colorado............................	61,245	58,882	60,211	35,911	11,463	13,871	2.0	2.6	1,719	3.5	6.3	401	405
Connecticut.......................	15,715	13,543	17,617	6,294	2,577	6,844	3.2	5.7	4,439	0.7	15.2	188	231
Delaware...........................	9,987	9,747	10,595	3,585	1,351	5,051	0.1	0.7	553	0.4	0.1	73	33
District of Columbia	27,442	26,895	37,335	9,961	13,179	4,302	1.5	5.2	10,540	2.3	5.1	30	80
Florida..............................	136,071	120,425	134,621	66,229	32,491	37,351	4.8	2.3	1,132	7.2	16.9	1,570	1,588
Georgia	129,413	118,537	138,753	67,117	34,639	27,657	2.7	2.3	1,302	6.4	7.3	710	778
Hawaii	71,604	65,746	70,208	42,386	19,579	9,639	1.4	7.7	5,050	4.9	2.3	118	117
Idaho................................	10,608	9,532	12,630	3,579	1,501	5,528	0.1	0.8	355	0.4	0.2	128	139
Illinois..............................	57,022	53,295	73,180	20,601	12,117	24,304	2.0	1.1	790	2.2	7.9	637	804
Indiana.............................	30,652	30,615	32,896	1,065	11,600	17,987	0.9	1.2	691	1.3	3.3	429	517
Iowa.................................	12,822	12,361	16,837	278	1,440	11,104	0.5	1.2	730	0.3	2.0	209	248
Kansas	38,860	38,265	36,523	21,945	6,871	10,044	0.6	1.8	1,057	2.0	1.1	205	233
Kentucky	54,011	49,234	63,579	31,909	9,689	12,413	2.2	5.2	2,455	2.8	8.2	297	348
Louisiana	38,698	40,208	47,209	15,653	6,042	17,003	0.6	1.1	627	1.6	1.3	298	326
Maine...............................	12,995	12,586	14,270	844	8,601	3,550	0.4	2.9	1,422	0.7	1.2	115	135
Maryland...........................	94,618	90,861	84,264	29,335	46,347	18,936	5.0	6.0	4,169	7.4	17.8	399	464
Massachusetts...................	25,308	25,028	27,878	3,759	6,603	14,946	2.9	2.5	2,091	1.1	13.4	334	416
Michigan...........................	26,819	26,526	32,824	2,050	9,441	15,328	1.1	1.0	538	1.2	4.2	597	719
Minnesota.........................	21,802	21,407	28,686	658	2,255	18,889	0.7	1.0	641	0.5	3.1	331	387
Mississippi........................	37,624	34,293	39,252	12,401	9,284	15,939	1.7	7.2	2,774	1.7	6.6	191	231
Missouri............................	42,400	41,324	51,245	15,379	7,598	19,423	3.0	4.7	2,475	1.5	13.6	438	522
Montana............................	8,794	8,802	10,854	3,338	1,260	4,196	0.1	1.1	511	0.3	0.2	92	104
Nebraska...........................	16,251	16,244	19,515	6,235	4,033	5,983	0.3	1.2	790	0.9	0.6	133	145
Nevada.............................	21,978	20,041	18,221	11,517	2,624	7,837	0.6	1.8	1,023	1.1	2.0	229	233
New Hampshire.................	6,107	5,719	6,521	990	957	4,160	0.5	3.1	1,988	0.2	2.5	103	118
New Jersey	35,709	34,803	41,135	8,012	10,105	17,592	1.5	1.2	843	1.7	5.8	362	476
New Mexico	24,125	23,206	24,516	12,631	6,407	5,087	0.8	4.0	1,953	1.3	2.8	157	174
New York..........................	60,158	60,364	77,295	20,009	11,192	28,957	2.1	0.6	530	2.7	7.7	790	984
North Carolina...................	146,088	140,080	148,014	102,671	22,053	21,364	2.2	1.9	1,050	6.9	4.0	718	777
North Dakota.....................	13,482	12,973	14,516	7,393	1,683	4,406	0.2	1.4	1,028	0.6	0.2	56	57
Ohio.................................	61,562	59,635	64,979	6,986	26,596	27,980	1.9	1.4	819	3.2	6.4	775	943
Oklahoma..........................	59,344	56,040	62,850	21,307	24,918	13,119	1.3	3.2	1,658	3.0	3.5	306	347
Oregon..............................	13,904	14,197	17,605	1,565	2,891	9,448	0.3	0.7	401	0.5	1.2	306	340
Pennsylvania.....................	57,344	56,722	72,405	2,578	25,734	29,032	3.2	2.0	1,259	2.7	13.4	836	1,036
Rhode Island.....................	12,728	12,087	12,282	3,364	5,038	4,326	0.3	2.4	1,384	0.8	0.7	66	76
South Carolina	64,479	60,729	68,752	36,349	10,692	17,438	1.3	2.7	1,231	2.6	3.7	405	422
South Dakota	9,383	9,189	10,083	3,417	1,283	4,683	0.1	1.2	713	0.4	0.3	67	76
Tennessee.........................	26,571	26,718	31,751	2,454	6,157	17,960	0.6	0.8	439	1.0	2.0	470	534
Texas................................	226,043	211,680	225,990	122,891	47,728	55,424	10.2	2.8	1,770	10.9	39.9	1,596	1,690
Utah.................................	32,368	31,029	34,554	4,569	15,797	12,002	0.8	2.2	1,284	1.7	2.4	139	154
Vermont............................	4,171	4,219	4,919	167	551	3,453	0.1	1.9	1,026	0.1	0.5	44	52
Virginia.............................	253,531	208,262	243,871	130,547	96,726	26,258	11.2	10.3	6,603	18.0	38.2	739	828
Washington.......................	111,270	94,634	98,534	61,125	32,049	18,096	3.2	2.8	2,145	6.5	9.7	569	617
West Virginia.....................	9,886	9,969	12,756	189	1,775	7,922	0.2	1.0	438	0.3	0.5	144	180
Wisconsin.........................	17,852	17,677	23,571	1,083	2,449	14,320	0.8	1.1	671	0.5	3.4	371	437
Wyoming	7,210	6,762	7,904	3,166	1,059	2,985	0.1	1.2	818	0.3	0.2	49	56

[1]As of September 30.
[2]Military personnel include active duty personnel based ashore or afloat. Excluded are personnel temporarily shore-based in a transient status. Before 2005, active duty military strength data for U.S. Navy and Marine Corps service members were only enumerated for those who were shore-based; members who were not shore-based (afloat) did have their payroll included in the payroll outlay figures for their home port. Beginning with 2005 Service members in afloat status are included in the strength counts of their homeport locations. Reserve and National Guard personnel called to active duty under Title 10, United States Code 12304, are not included in the active duty military personnel counts.
[3]Civilian personnel includes United States citizens and foreign national direct hire civilians subject to Office of Management and Budget (OMB) ceiling controls and civilian personnel involved in civil functions in the United States. Excludes indirect-hire civilians and those direct-hire civilians not subject to OMB ceiling controls.
[4]For year ending September 30.
[5]Includes the gross earnings of civilian, active duty military personnel, reserve and national guard, and retired military for services rendered to the government and for cash allowances for benefits. Excludes employer's share of employee benefits, accrued military retirement benefits and most permanent change of stations costs.
[6]Includes only those veterans living as of September of the stated year. Veterans serving in more than one period of service are counted only once in the total. Veterans are considered any civilian honorably discharged from active duty, other than for training only without service-connected disability.

Table A-80. Elections

Geographic area	Voting-age population[1] (thousands)		Percent of voting-age population casting votes for President		Electoral votes cast for President[2]		Popular vote for President 2016		
								Percent of total	
	2016	2012	2016	2012	2016	2012	Total[3] (thousands)	Democratic	Republican
United States	249,485	240,186	54.8	53.8	R-306	D-232	136,787	48.0	45.8
Alabama.....................	3,766	3,698	56.4	56.1	R-9	R-9	2,123	34.4	62.1
Alaska........................	555	544	57.5	55.2	R-3	R-3	319	36.6	51.3
Arizona......................	5,300	4,932	48.6	46.6	R-11	R-11	2,573	45.1	48.7
Arkansas....................	2,283	2,238	49.5	47.8	R-6	R-6	1,131	33.7	60.6
California...................	30,157	28,801	47.0	45.3	D-55	D-55	14,182	61.7	31.6
Colorado	4,279	3,956	65.0	64.9	D-9	D-9	2,780	48.2	43.3
Connecticut................	2,823	2,797	58.3	55.7	D-7	D-7	1,645	54.6	40.9
Delaware....................	748	712	59.1	58.1	D-3	D-3	442	53.4	41.9
District of Columbia	560	523	55.8	56.2	D-3	D-3	313	90.5	4.1
Florida........................	16,466	15,315	57.2	55.3	R-29	D-29	9,420	47.8	49.0
Georgia......................	7,799	7,430	52.8	52.5	R-16	R-16	4,115	45.6	50.8
Hawaii........................	1,121	1,089	39.1	40.1	D-4	D-4	438	61.0	29.4
Idaho.........................	1,246	1,169	55.4	55.8	R-4	R-4	690	27.5	59.3
Illinois.......................	9,875	9,811	56.1	53.4	D-20	D-20	5,536	55.8	38.8
Indiana......................	5,058	4,946	54.1	53.1	R-11	R-11	2,735	37.8	56.9
Iowa..........................	2,404	2,351	65.1	67.3	R-6	D-6	1,566	41.8	51.2
Kansas.......................	2,192	2,162	54.0	53.7	R-6	R-6	1,184	36.1	56.7
Kentucky....................	3,426	3,362	56.2	53.5	R-8	R-8	1,924	32.7	62.5
Louisiana	3,568	3,484	56.9	57.2	R-8	R-8	2,029	38.4	58.1
Maine........................	1,077	1,063	71.7	68.2	D-3	D-4	772	46.3	43.5
Maryland....................	4,668	4,541	59.6	59.6	D-10	D-10	2,781	60.3	33.9
Massachusetts.............	5,434	5,245	62.2	60.7	D-11	D-11	3,379	59.1	32.3
Michigan....................	7,737	7,616	62.0	62.1	R-16	D-16	4,799	47.3	47.5
Minnesota..................	4,232	4,103	69.6	71.6	D-10	D-10	2,945	46.4	44.9
Mississippi..................	2,267	2,240	53.3	57.4	R-6	R-6	1,209	40.1	57.9
Missouri.....................	4,706	4,619	59.7	59.7	R-10	R-10	2,809	38.1	56.8
Montana.....................	815	783	60.7	61.8	R-3	R-3	495	35.9	56.5
Nebraska....................	1,434	1,392	58.9	57.1	R-5	R-5	844	33.7	58.7
Nevada......................	2,263	2,095	49.7	48.4	D-6	D-6	1,125	47.9	45.5
New Hampshire............	1,074	1,046	69.3	68.0	D-4	D-4	744	46.8	46.5
New Jersey	6,960	6,838	55.7	53.2	D-14	D-14	3,874	55.5	41.4
New Mexico	1,590	1,571	50.2	49.9	D-5	D-5	798	48.3	40.0
New York....................	15,565	15,307	50.1	46.5	D-29	D-29	7,802	56.1	32.4
North Carolina.............	7,848	7,466	60.4	60.3	R-15	R-15	4,742	46.2	49.8
North Dakota...............	582	545	59.2	59.3	R-3	R-3	344	27.2	63.0
Ohio..........................	9,002	8,881	61.1	62.8	R-18	D-18	5,496	43.6	51.7
Oklahoma...................	2,962	2,877	49.1	46.4	R-7	R-7	1,453	28.9	65.3
Oregon......................	3,225	3,039	62.1	58.9	D-7	D-7	2,001	50.1	39.1
Pennsylvania...............	10,109	10,024	60.5	57.3	R-20	D-20	6,115	47.9	48.6
Rhode Island...............	848	834	54.7	53.5	D-4	D-4	464	54.4	38.9
South Carolina	3,863	3,644	54.4	53.9	R-9	R-9	2,103	40.7	54.9
South Dakota	652	629	56.7	57.8	R-3	R-3	370	31.7	61.5
Tennessee	5,149	4,962	48.7	49.5	R-11	R-11	2,508	34.7	60.7
Texas.........................	20,568	19,074	43.6	41.9	R-38	R-38	8,969	43.2	52.2
Utah..........................	2,129	1,967	53.1	51.7	R-6	R-6	1,131	27.5	45.5
Vermont.....................	506	502	63.3	59.6	D-3	D-3	320	55.7	29.8
Virginia......................	6,542	6,329	60.9	60.9	D-13	D-13	3,983	49.8	44.4
Washington.................	5,659	5,312	58.6	58.8	D-12	D-12	3,317	52.5	36.8
West Virginia...............	1,456	1,471	49.0	45.6	R-5	R-5	713	26.5	68.6
Wisconsin	4,491	4,409	66.3	69.7	R-10	D-10	2,976	46.5	47.2
Wyoming	447	441	57.9	56.9	R-3	R-3	259	21.6	67.4

[1]Estimated population for those 18 years and over as of July 1 for the listed year. Includes armed forces stationed in each state, aliens, and institutionalized population.
[2]By major political party. D=Democratic, R=Republican.
[3]Includes other parties not shown separately.
(X) = Not applicable

Table A-80. Elections—*Continued*

Geographic area	Popular vote for President 2012 Total[3] (thousands)	2012 Percent of total Democratic	2012 Percent of total Republican	Votes cast for U.S. Senators 2018 Total[3] (thousands)	2018 Percent of total Democratic	2018 Percent of total Republican	2016 Total[3] (thousands)	2016 Percent of total Democratic	2016 Percent of total Republican	2014 Total[3] (thousands)	2014 Percent of total Democratic	2014 Percent of total Republican
United States	129,140	50.9	47.0	86,292	58.4	38.4	96,867	53.0	42.2	43,975	43.9	51.4
Alabama	2,074	38.4	60.5	(X)	(X)	(X)	2,087	35.9	64.0	818	0.0	97.3
Alaska	300	40.8	54.8	(X)	(X)	(X)	311	11.6	44.4	282	45.8	48.0
Arizona	2,299	44.6	53.7	2,384	50.0	47.6	2,531	40.7	53.7	(X)	(X)	(X)
Arkansas	1,069	36.9	60.6	(X)	(X)	(X)	1,108	36.2	59.8	848	39.4	56.5
California...................	13,039	60.2	37.1	11,113	100.0	0.0	12,244	100.0	0.0	(X)	(X)	(X)
Colorado	2,570	51.5	46.1	(X)	(X)	(X)	2,743	50.0	44.3	2,041	46.3	48.2
Connecticut................	1,558	58.1	40.7	1,387	56.8	39.3	1,596	57.7	34.6	(X)	(X)	(X)
Delaware	414	58.6	40.0	363	60.0	37.8	(X)	(X)	(X)	234	55.8	42.2
District of Columbia	294	90.9	7.3	(X)	(X)	(X)	(X)	(X)	(X)	(X)	(X)	(X)
Florida........................	8,474	50.0	49.1	8,190	49.9	50.1	9,302	44.3	52.0	(X)	(X)	(X)
Georgia	3,898	45.5	53.3	(X)	(X)	(X)	3,899	41.0	54.8	2,568	45.2	52.9
Hawaii	437	70.1	27.7	399	69.3	28.1	438	70.1	21.2	(X)	(X)	(X)
Idaho	652	32.6	64.5	(X)	(X)	(X)	679	27.7	66.1	437	34.7	65.3
Illinois	5,242	57.6	40.7	(X)	(X)	(X)	5,492	54.9	39.8	3,604	53.5	42.7
Indiana	2,625	43.9	54.1	2,283	44.8	50.7	2,733	42.4	52.1	(X)	(X)	(X)
Iowa	1,582	52.0	46.2	(X)	(X)	(X)	1,541	35.7	60.1	1,130	43.8	52.1
Kansas	1,160	38.0	59.7	(X)	(X)	(X)	1,178	32.2	62.2	866	0.0	53.1
Kentucky	1,797	37.8	60.5	(X)	(X)	(X)	1,903	42.7	57.3	1,436	40.7	56.2
Louisiana	1,994	40.6	57.8	(X)	(X)	(X)	1,997	35.3	62.1	1,523	38.1	61.0
Maine	725	55.4	40.3	646	10.3	34.6	(X)	(X)	(X)	617	30.8	67.0
Maryland....................	2,707	62.0	35.9	2,300	64.9	30.3	2,726	60.9	35.7	(X)	(X)	(X)
Massachusetts............	3,184	60.3	37.3	2,753	59.3	35.6	(X)	(X)	(X)	2,187	59.0	36.2
Michigan	4,731	54.2	44.7	4,237	52.3	45.8	(X)	(X)	(X)	3,122	54.6	41.3
Minnesota	2,937	52.7	45.0	2,597	60.3	36.2	(X)	(X)	(X)	1,982	53.2	42.9
Mississippi.................	1,286	43.8	55.3	936	39.5	58.5	(X)	(X)	(X)	632	37.9	59.9
Missouri.....................	2,757	44.4	53.8	2,442	45.6	51.4	2,803	46.4	49.2	(X)	(X)	(X)
Montana	484	41.7	55.4	504	50.3	46.8	(X)	(X)	(X)	370	40.1	57.8
Nebraska....................	794	38.0	59.8	699	38.6	57.7	(X)	(X)	(X)	540	31.5	64.3
Nevada.......................	1,015	52.4	45.7	972	50.4	45.4	1,108	47.1	44.7	(X)	(X)	(X)
New Hampshire.............	711	52.0	46.4	(X)	(X)	(X)	739	48.0	47.8	488	51.5	48.2
New Jersey	3,638	58.3	40.6	3,169	54.0	42.8	(X)	(X)	41.4	1,870	55.8	42.3
New Mexico	784	53.0	42.8	697	54.1	30.5	(X)	(X)	40.0	516	55.6	44.4
New York....................	7,117	60.8	31.2	6,251	60.1	27.7	7,801	61.3	32.4	(X)	(X)	(X)
North Carolina............	4,505	48.4	50.4	(X)	(X)	(X)	4,691	45.4	49.8	2,915	47.3	48.8
North Dakota...............	323	38.7	58.3	326	44.3	55.1	343	17.0	63.0	(X)	(X)	(X)
Ohio	5,581	50.7	47.7	4,411	53.4	46.6	5,374	37.2	51.7	821	28.5	68.0
Oklahoma...................	1,335	33.2	66.8	(X)	(X)	(X)	1,448	24.6	67.7	1,462	55.7	36.9
Oregon	1,789	54.2	42.1	(X)	(X)	(X)	1,952	56.6	33.3	(X)	(X)	(X)
Pennsylvania..............	5,742	52.1	46.7	5,009	55.7	42.6	6,052	47.3	48.8	317	70.6	29.2
Rhode Island..............	446	62.7	35.2	377	61.4	38.3	(X)	(X)	(X)	(X)	(X)	(X)
South Carolina	1,964	44.1	54.6	(X)	(X)	(X)	2,050	34.4	60.6	1,240	36.8	54.3
South Dakota	364	39.9	57.9	(X)	(X)	(X)	370	28.2	71.8	279	29.5	50.4
Tennessee	2,459	39.1	59.5	2,244	43.9	54.7	(X)	(X)	(X)	1,374	31.9	61.9
Texas.........................	7,994	41.4	57.2	8,372	48.3	50.9	1,116	27.1	68.1	4,648	34.4	61.6
Utah	1,017	24.7	72.8	1,063	30.9	62.6	320	60.0	32.3	(X)	(X)	(X)
Vermont.....................	299	66.6	31.0	278	0.0	26.9	(X)	(X)	(X)	2,184	49.1	48.3
Virginia......................	3,854	51.2	47.3	3,351	57.0	41.0	3,243	59.0	41.0	(X)	(X)	(X)
Washington................	3,126	56.2	41.3	3,086	58.4	41.6	(X)	(X)	(X)	454	34.5	62.1
West Virginia..............	670	35.5	62.3	586	49.6	46.3	2,949	46.8	50.2	(X)	(X)	(X)
Wisconsin	3,071	52.8	45.9	2,661	55.4	44.5	(X)	(X)	(X)	171	17.2	71.0
Wyoming	251	27.6	68.2	205,275	29.8	66.4	(X)	(X)	(X)			

[1]Estimated population for those 18 years and over as of July 1 for the listed year. Includes armed forces stationed in each state, aliens, and institutionalized population.
[2]By major political party. D=Democratic, R=Republican.
[3]Includes other parties not shown separately.
(X) = Not applicable

Table A–81. Composition of Congress and Public Officials

| Geographic area | Votes cast for U.S. Representatives[1] 2018 | | | Composition of 116th Congress, 2019[2] | | | | Composition of 115th Congress, 2017[3] | | | |
| | Total[5] | Percentage of total | | Senate[4] | | House of Representatives | | Senate | | House of Representatives | |
		Democratic	Republican	Democratic	Republican	Democratic	Republican	Democratic	Republican	Democratic	Republican
United States	114,016,831	52.9	44.3	45	53	232	197	46	52	193	237
Alabama	1,659,895	40.9	58.8	1	1	1	6	0	2	1	6
Alaska	282,166	46.5	53.1	0	2	0	1	0	2	0	1
Arizona	2,341,270	50.4	48.7	1	1	5	4	0	2	4	5
Arkansas	889,158	35.2	62.6	0	2	0	4	0	2	0	4
California	12,184,522	65.7	32.6	2	0	45	6	2	0	38	14
Colorado	2,513,907	53.4	43.0	1	1	4	3	1	1	3	4
Connecticut	1,379,808	58.6	37.1	2	0	5	0	2	0	5	0
Delaware	353,814	64.3	35.4	2	0	1	0	2	0	1	0
District of Columbia	X	X	X	X	X	X	X	X	X	X	X
Florida	7,021,476	47.1	52.3	0	2	13	14	1	1	11	16
Georgia	3,802,343	47.7	52.3	0	2	5	9	0	2	4	9
Hawaii	398,657	72.2	21.9	2	0	0	2	2	0	2	0
Idaho	595,724	34.8	61.8	0	2	2	0	0	2	0	2
Illinois	4,539,704	60.7	38.6	2	0	13	5	2	0	11	7
Indiana	2,256,149	44.3	55.3	0	2	2	7	1	1	2	7
Iowa	1,316,442	50.5	46.5	0	2	1	3	0	2	1	3
Kansas	1,050,322	44.2	53.6	0	2	1	3	0	2	0	3
Kentucky	1,569,798	39.0	59.6	0	2	1	5	0	2	1	5
Louisiana	1,460,593	37.9	57.2	0	2	1	5	0	2	1	5
Maine	631,334	54.4	39.6	0	1	2	0	0	1	1	1
Maryland	2,286,284	65.3	32.3	2	0	6	1	2	0	7	1
Massachusetts	2,752,665	70.6	18.1	2	0	9	0	2	0	9	0
Michigan	4,154,703	52.4	44.6	2	0	7	6	2	0	5	9
Minnesota	2,576,996	55.1	43.7	2	0	5	3	2	0	5	3
Mississippi	938,903	42.5	50.2	0	2	1	3	0	2	1	3
Missouri	2,418,413	42.5	55.0	0	2	2	6	1	1	2	6
Montana	504,421	46.2	50.9	1	1	0	1	1	1	0	0
Nebraska	696,570	38.0	62.0	0	2	0	3	0	2	0	3
Nevada	960,774	51.1	45.8	2	0	3	1	1	1	3	1
New Hampshire	570,744	54.5	43.6	2	0	2	0	2	0	2	0
New Jersey	3,098,743	59.9	38.7	2	0	10	2	2	0	7	5
New Mexico	693,311	58.3	38.2	2	0	3	0	2	0	2	1
New York	6,250,885	60.2	26.2	2	0	21	5	2	0	18	9
North Carolina	3,380,609	48.3	50.5	0	2	3	10	0	2	3	10
North Dakota	321,532	35.6	60.2	0	2	0	1	1	1	0	1
Ohio	4,406,358	47.3	52.0	1	1	4	12	1	1	4	12
Oklahoma	1,178,836	36.3	62.0	0	2	1	4	0	2	0	5
Oregon	1,847,646	57.4	38.0	2	0	4	1	2	0	4	1
Pennsylvania	4,929,875	55.0	44.8	1	1	9	9	1	1	5	13
Rhode Island	373,280	65.0	34.8	2	0	2	0	2	0	2	0
South Carolina	1,709,292	44.4	54.3	0	2	2	5	0	2	1	5
South Dakota	335,965	36.0	60.3	0	2	0	1	0	2	0	1
Tennessee	2,159,825	39.2	59.2	0	2	7	2	0	2	2	7
Texas	8,202,555	47.0	50.4	0	2	13	23	0	2	11	25
Utah	1,052,506	35.5	58.7	0	2	1	3	0	2	0	4
Vermont	278,230	67.8	25.4	1	0	1	0	1	0	1	0
Virginia	3,312,956	56.4	42.5	2	0	7	4	2	0	4	7
Washington	3,021,951	62.5	29.8	2	0	7	3	2	0	6	4
West Virginia	577,991	40.6	58.3	1	1	0	3	1	1	0	3
Wisconsin	2,571,655	53.2	45.6	1	1	3	4	1	1	3	5
Wyoming	205,275	29.2	62.3	0	2	0	1	0	2	0	1

[1]In each state, totals represent the sum of votes cast in each Congressional District or votes cast for Representative at Large in states where only one member is elected. In all years there are numerous districts within the state where either the Republican or Democratic party had no candidate. In some states the Republican and Democratic vote includes votes cast for the party candidate by endorsing parties.
[2]As of April 3, 2017.
[3]As of December 5, 2016.
[4]Vermont and Maine each had one had one Independent senator.
[5]Includes votes cast for minor parties not shown separately.
X = not applicable

PART B

METROPOLITAN AREAS

Table B-1. Area and Population

Metropolitan Statistical Area Metropolitan Division	Area 2019 (square miles)		Population			Rank			Persons per square mile of land Area		
	Total	Land	2019 Estimate (July 1)	2010 census estimates base (April 1)	2000 census estimates base (April 1)	2019	2010	2000	2019	2010	2000
Abilene, TX Metro Area	2,758	2,743	172,060	165,252	160,245	247	244	229	63	60	58
Akron, OH Metro Area	924	900	703,479	703,196	694,960	82	74	69	782	781	772
Albany, GA Metro Area	1,609	1,591	146,726	154,033	153,759	287	260	236	92	97	97
Albany-Lebanon, OR Metro Area	2,307	2,287	129,749	116,681	103,069	312	327	337	57	51	45
Albany-Schenectady-Troy, NY Metro Area	2,878	2,812	880,381	870,713	825,875	63	60	57	313	310	294
Albuquerque, NM Metro Area	9,296	9,283	918,018	887,063	729,649	61	59	65	99	96	79
Alexandria, LA Metro Area	2,026	1,963	152,037	153,918	145,035	275	263	250	77	78	74
Allentown-Bethlehem-Easton, PA-NJ Metro Area	1,475	1,453	844,052	821,273	740,395	70	67	64	581	565	510
Altoona, PA Metro Area	527	526	121,829	127,117	129,144	328	310	284	232	242	246
Amarillo, TX Metro Area	5,184	5,150	265,053	251,935	228,707	185	183	179	51	49	44
Ames, IA Metro Area	1,147	1,144	123,351	115,850	106,205	323	330	331	108	101	93
Anchorage, AK Metro Area	27,220	26,421	396,317	380,821	319,605	137	137	145	15	14	12
Ann Arbor, MI Metro Area	722	706	367,601	345,163	322,895	147	149	142	521	489	457
Anniston-Oxford, AL Metro Area	612	606	113,605	118,526	112,249	338	323	316	187	196	185
Appleton, WI Metro Area	1,042	956	237,974	225,667	201,602	195	196	193	249	236	211
Asheville, NC Metro Area	2,041	2,033	462,680	424,863	369,171	119	119	127	228	209	182
Athens-Clarke County, GA Metro Area	1,035	1,025	213,750	192,567	166,079	212	221	224	209	188	162
Atlanta-Sandy Springs-Alpharetta, GA Metro Area	8,835	8,685	6,020,364	5,286,718	4,263,438	9	9	11	693	609	491
Atlantic City-Hammonton, NJ Metro Area	672	556	263,670	274,525	252,552	187	169	169	474	494	455
Auburn-Opelika, AL Metro Area	616	608	164,542	140,287	115,092	261	287	308	271	231	189
Augusta-Richmond County, GA-SC Metro Area	3,582	3,481	608,980	564,893	508,032	95	95	93	175	162	146
Austin-Round Rock-Georgetown, TX Metro Area	4,280	4,222	2,227,083	1,716,323	1,249,763	29	35	40	527	407	296
Bakersfield, CA Metro Area	8,163	8,132	900,202	839,621	661,645	62	63	72	111	103	81
Baltimore-Columbia-Towson, MD Metro Area	3,105	2,602	2,800,053	2,710,598	2,552,994	21	20	19	1,076	1,042	981
Bangor, ME Metro Area	3,557	3,397	152,148	153,931	144,919	274	262	251	45	45	43
Barnstable Town, MA Metro Area	1,306	394	212,990	215,880	222,230	213	199	186	541	548	564
Baton Rouge, LA Metro Area	4,568	4,366	854,884	825,917	729,361	66	64	66	196	189	167
Battle Creek, MI Metro Area	718	706	134,159	136,150	137,985	306	297	268	190	193	195
Bay City, MI Metro Area	631	442	103,126	107,773	110,157	350	343	320	233	244	249
Beaumont-Port Arthur, TX Metro Area	2,390	2,101	392,563	388,749	385,090	140	134	118	187	185	183
Beckley, WV Metro Area	1,278	1,267	115,767	124,914	126,799	335	316	288	91	99	100
Bellingham, WA Metro Area	2,505	2,108	229,247	201,146	166,814	201	213	223	109	95	79
Bend, OR Metro Area	3,054	3,018	197,692	157,728	115,367	226	256	307	66	52	38
Billings, MT Metro Area	6,516	6,478	181,667	167,165	147,099	233	241	246	28	26	23
Binghamton, NY Metro Area	1,238	1,224	238,691	251,724	252,320	194	184	170	195	206	206
Birmingham-Hoover, AL Metro Area	4,565	4,489	1,090,435	1,061,039	981,525	50	51	49	243	236	219
Bismarck, ND Metro Area	4,345	4,281	128,949	110,625	96,784	314	341	348	30	26	23
Blacksburg-Christiansburg, VA Metro Area	1,090	1,074	167,531	162,960	151,272	257	245	241	156	152	141
Bloomington, IL Metro Area	1,186	1,183	171,517	169,577	150,433	249	236	242	145	143	127
Bloomington, IN Metro Area	799	780	169,230	159,535	142,349	253	253	259	217	205	183
Bloomsburg-Berwick, PA Metro Area	622	613	83,194	85,555	82,387	373	371	371	136	140	134
Boise City, ID Metro Area	11,833	11,767	749,202	616,566	464,840	78	87	102	64	52	40
Boston-Cambridge-Newton, MA-NH Metro Area	4,511	3,486	4,873,019	4,552,595	4,391,344	11	10	10	1,398	1,306	1,260
Boston, MA Div	1,658	1,113	2,031,884	1,888,025	1,812,937	-	-	-	1,826	1,696	1,629
Cambridge-Newton-Framingham, MA Div	1,675	1,310	2,400,733	2,246,215	2,188,815	-	-	-	1,833	1,715	1,670
Rockingham County-Strafford County, NH Div	1,178	1,063	440,402	418,355	389,592	-	-	-	414	394	367
Boulder, CO Metro Area	740	726	326,196	294,560	269,814	155	162	159	449	406	371
Bowling Green, KY Metro Area	1,639	1,615	179,240	158,613	134,976	239	255	271	111	98	84
Bremerton-Silverdale-Port Orchard, WA Metro Area	566	395	271,473	251,143	231,969	180	185	178	687	636	587
Bridgeport-Stamford-Norwalk, CT Metro Area	837	625	943,332	916,904	882,567	59	57	52	1,509	1,467	1,412
Brownsville-Harlingen, TX Metro Area	1,276	892	423,163	406,215	335,227	128	127	138	474	455	376
Brunswick, GA Metro Area	1,606	1,294	118,779	112,385	93,044	333	336	352	92	87	72
Buffalo-Cheektowaga, NY Metro Area	2,367	1,565	1,127,983	1,135,614	1,170,111	49	47	42	721	726	748
Burlington, NC Metro Area	434	423	169,509	151,155	130,800	251	270	280	401	357	309
Burlington-South Burlington, VT Metro Area	1,506	1,253	220,411	211,264	198,889	207	200	197	176	169	159
California-Lexington Park, MD Metro Area	764	359	113,510	105,144	86,211	339	346	363	316	293	240
Canton-Massillon, OH Metro Area	980	970	397,520	404,425	406,934	136	130	113	410	417	420
Cape Coral-Fort Myers, FL Metro Area	1,212	781	770,577	618,755	440,888	76	86	106	987	792	564
Cape Girardeau, MO-IL Metro Area	1,460	1,432	96,765	96,270	90,312	364	361	359	68	67	63
Carbondale-Marion, IL Metro Area	1,395	1,348	135,764	139,148	133,786	303	289	276	101	103	99
Carson City, NV Metro Area	157	145	55,916	55,269	52,457	384	384	384	386	381	363
Casper, WY Metro Area	5,376	5,341	79,858	75,448	66,533	378	379	379	15	14	12
Cedar Rapids, IA Metro Area	2,020	2,009	273,032	257,948	237,230	179	175	175	136	128	118
Chambersburg-Waynesboro, PA Metro Area	773	772	155,027	149,631	129,313	268	273	282	201	194	167
Champaign-Urbana, IL Metro Area	1,438	1,435	226,033	217,806	196,034	202	198	198	158	152	137
Charleston, WV Metro Area	2,668	2,647	257,074	277,985	286,046	189	168	156	97	105	108
Charleston-North Charleston, SC Metro Area	3,163	2,590	802,122	664,645	549,033	74	80	86	310	257	212
Charlotte-Concord-Gastonia, NC-SC Metro Area	5,714	5,597	2,636,883	2,243,963	1,742,647	22	23	28	471	401	311
Charlottesville, VA Metro Area	1,658	1,645	218,615	201,569	174,021	209	212	218	133	123	106
Chattanooga, TN-GA Metro Area	2,138	2,089	565,194	528,126	476,531	100	101	98	271	253	228
Cheyenne, WY Metro Area	2,688	2,686	99,500	91,885	81,607	358	367	372	37	34	30
Chicago-Naperville-Elgin, IL-IN-WI Metro Area	9,579	7,195	9,458,539	9,461,537	9,098,316	3	3	3	1,315	1,315	1,265
Chicago-Naperville-Evanston, IL Div	3,862	3,130	7,122,725	7,148,308	7,080,780	-	-	-	2,276	2,284	2,262
Elgin, IL Div	1,481	1,471	766,290	735,288	547,632	-	-	-	521	500	372

Table B-1. Area and Population—*Continued*

| Metropolitan Statistical Area Metropolitan Division | Area 2019 (square miles) | | Population | | | | | | | | |
| | | | 2019 Estimate (July 1) | 2010 census estimates base (April 1) | 2000 census estimates base (April 1) | Rank | | | Persons per square mile of land Area | | |
	Total	Land				2019	2010	2000	2019	2010	2000
Gary, IN Div....	2,113	1,878	703,428	708,117	675,971	-	-	-	375	377	360
Lake County-Kenosha County, IL-WI Div	2,122	716	866,096	869,824	793,933	-	-	-	1,210	1,215	1,109
Chico, CA Metro Area	1,677	1,636	219,186	220,005	203,171	208	197	192	134	134	124
Cincinnati, OH-KY-IN Metro Area	4,631	4,546	2,221,208	2,137,713	2,016,981	30	27	24	489	470	444
Clarksville, TN-KY Metro Area	2,242	2,158	307,820	273,942	232,000	164	171	177	143	127	108
Cleveland, TN Metro Area	774	763	124,942	115,747	104,015	320	331	333	164	152	136
Cleveland-Elyria, OH Metro Area	3,980	1,999	2,048,449	2,077,277	2,148,143	34	29	23	1,025	1,039	1,074
Coeur d'Alene, ID Metro Area	1,309	1,238	165,697	138,466	108,685	260	290	325	134	112	88
College Station-Bryan, TX Metro Area	2,133	2,100	264,728	228,668	184,885	186	194	208	126	109	88
Colorado Springs, CO Metro Area	2,689	2,684	745,791	645,612	537,484	79	83	88	278	241	200
Columbia, MO Metro Area	1,732	1,714	208,173	190,398	162,336	216	222	228	121	111	95
Columbia, SC Metro Area	3,834	3,703	838,433	767,469	647,158	71	72	75	226	207	175
Columbus, GA-AL Metro Area	2,818	2,786	321,048	308,478	293,518	160	156	152	115	111	105
Columbus, IN Metro Area	410	407	83,779	76,783	71,435	371	378	377	206	189	176
Columbus, OH Metro Area	4,850	4,797	2,122,271	1,900,008	1,675,013	32	32	31	442	396	349
Corpus Christi, TX Metro Area	1,873	1,532	429,024	405,025	380,783	127	129	121	280	264	249
Corvallis, OR Metro Area	678	675	93,053	85,581	78,153	366	370	374	138	127	116
Crestview-Fort Walton Beach-Destin, FL Metro Area	2,322	1,968	284,809	235,870	211,099	173	191	188	145	120	107
Cumberland, MD-WV Metro Area	757	750	97,284	103,272	102,008	362	348	342	130	138	136
Dallas-Fort Worth-Arlington, TX Metro Area	9,007	8,674	7,573,136	6,366,537	5,156,217	4	4	5	873	734	594
Dallas-Plano-Irving, TX Div	5,538	5,277	5,081,942	4,228,853	3,445,899	-	-	-	963	801	653
Fort Worth-Arlington-Grapevine, TX Div	3,469	3,397	2,491,194	2,137,684	1,710,318	-	-	-	733	629	504
Dalton, GA Metro Area	638	635	144,724	142,233	120,031	289	284	300	228	224	189
Danville, IL Metro Area	901	898	75,758	81,625	83,919	379	375	366	84	91	93
Daphne-Fairhope-Foley, AL Metro Area	2,027	1,590	223,234	182,265	140,415	203	227	263	140	115	88
Davenport-Moline-Rock Island, IA-IL Metro Area	2,314	2,270	379,172	379,681	376,019	144	138	124	167	167	166
Dayton-Kettering, OH Metro Area	1,290	1,282	807,611	799,280	805,816	73	70	59	630	623	629
Decatur, AL Metro Area	1,316	1,270	152,603	153,827	145,867	273	264	249	120	121	115
Decatur, IL Metro Area	586	581	104,009	110,777	114,706	348	340	310	179	191	198
Deltona-Daytona Beach-Ormond Beach, FL Metro Area	2,003	1,586	668,365	590,288	493,175	88	92	94	421	372	311
Denver-Aurora-Lakewood, CO Metro Area	8,403	8,345	2,967,239	2,543,608	2,179,240	19	21	22	356	305	261
Des Moines-West Des Moines, IA Metro Area	3,645	3,612	699,292	606,474	518,607	83	88	91	194	168	144
Detroit-Warren-Dearborn, MI Metro Area........	4,236	3,892	4,319,629	4,296,227	4,452,557	14	12	9	1,110	1,104	1,144
Detroit-Dearborn-Livonia, MI Div	673	612	1,749,343	1,820,473	2,061,162	-	-	-	2,858	2,975	3,369
Warren-Troy-Farmington Hills, MI Div	3,563	3,280	2,570,286	2,475,754	2,391,395	-	-	-	784	755	729
Dothan, AL Metro Area	1,729	1,716	149,358	145,640	130,861	283	279	279	87	85	76
Dover, DE Metro Area	798	586	180,786	162,350	126,697	235	248	289	309	277	216
Dubuque, IA Metro Area	616	608	97,311	93,643	89,143	361	364	360	160	154	147
Duluth, MN-WI Metro Area	12,205	10,522	288,732	290,636	286,544	170	164	155	27	28	27
Durham-Chapel Hill, NC Metro Area	2,350	2,290	644,367	564,193	474,991	92	96	100	281	246	207
East Stroudsburg, PA Metro Area	617	608	170,271	169,841	138,687	250	235	267	280	279	228
Eau Claire, WI Metro Area	1,686	1,646	169,304	161,383	148,337	252	249	244	103	98	90
El Centro, CA Metro Area	4,481	4,176	181,215	174,524	142,361	234	233	258	43	42	34
Elizabethtown-Fort Knox, KY Metro Area	1,218	1,190	153,928	148,331	133,896	270	275	274	129	125	112
Elkhart-Goshen, IN Metro Area	468	463	206,341	197,569	182,791	219	218	210	446	427	395
Elmira, NY Metro Area	411	407	83,456	88,847	91,070	372	369	355	205	218	224
El Paso, TX Metro Area	5,587	5,584	844,124	804,109	682,966	69	69	70	151	144	122
Enid, OK Metro Area	1,060	1,059	61,056	60,580	57,813	382	382	381	58	57	55
Erie, PA Metro Area	1,558	799	269,728	280,584	280,843	181	166	158	338	351	351
Eugene-Springfield, OR Metro Area	4,724	4,556	382,067	351,705	322,959	143	146	141	84	77	71
Evansville, IN-KY Metro Area	1,513	1,464	315,086	311,548	296,195	162	153	151	215	213	202
Fairbanks, AK Metro Area	7,435	7,330	96,849	97,585	82,840	363	357	369	13	13	11
Fargo, ND-MN Metro Area	2,820	2,810	246,145	208,777	174,367	193	206	217	88	74	62
Farmington, NM Metro Area	5,538	5,517	123,958	130,045	113,801	322	305	311	22	24	21
Fayetteville, NC Metro Area	1,651	1,638	526,719	481,011	427,634	108	108	108	322	294	261
Fayetteville-Springdale-Rogers, AR Metro Area	2,674	2,624	534,904	440,121	325,364	107	113	140	204	168	124
Flagstaff, AZ Metro Area	18,662	18,617	143,476	134,426	116,320	291	298	305	8	7	6
Flint, MI Metro Area	650	637	405,813	425,787	436,141	134	117	107	637	668	685
Florence, SC Metro Area	1,371	1,361	204,911	205,576	193,155	220	209	201	151	151	142
Florence-Muscle Shoals, AL Metro Area	1,343	1,261	147,970	147,137	142,950	285	277	257	117	117	113
Fond du Lac, WI Metro Area	766	720	103,403	101,623	97,296	349	350	347	144	141	135
Fort Collins, CO Metro Area	2,634	2,596	356,899	299,630	251,494	150	160	171	137	115	97
Fort Smith, AR-OK Metro Area	2,484	2,407	250,368	248,240	225,061	192	188	180	104	103	93
Fort Wayne, IN Metro Area	998	993	413,263	388,626	362,556	133	135	131	416	391	365
Fresno, CA Metro Area	6,011	5,958	999,101	930,507	799,407	54	56	60	168	156	134
Gadsden, AL Metro Area	549	535	102,268	104,429	103,459	353	347	336	191	195	193
Gainesville, FL Metro Area	2,737	2,343	329,128	305,076	266,842	154	158	161	140	130	114
Gainesville, GA Metro Area	429	393	204,441	179,724	139,277	221	228	265	520	457	354
Gettysburg, PA Metro Area	522	519	103,009	101,428	91,292	351	352	354	198	195	176
Glens Falls, NY Metro Area	1,777	1,698	125,148	128,946	124,345	318	307	290	74	76	73
Goldsboro, NC Metro Area	558	554	123,131	122,661	113,329	324	319	312	222	221	205
Grand Forks, ND-MN Metro Area	3,437	3,407	100,815	98,464	97,478	356	356	346	30	29	29
Grand Island, NE Metro Area	1,625	1,602	75,553	72,744	68,305	380	380	378	47	45	43
Grand Junction, CO Metro Area	3,341	3,329	154,210	146,733	116,255	269	278	306	46	44	35

Table B-1. Area and Population—*Continued*

Metropolitan Statistical Area Metropolitan Division	Area 2019 (square miles) Total	Land	Population 2019 Estimate (July 1)	2010 census estimates base (April 1)	2000 census estimates base (April 1)	Rank 2019	2010	2000	Persons per square mile of land Area 2019	2010	2000
Grand Rapids-Kentwood, MI Metro Area	3,804	2,689	1,077,370	993,663	935,433	51	52	51	401	370	348
Grants Pass, OR Metro Area	1,641	1,639	87,487	82,719	75,726	370	374	375	53	50	46
Great Falls, MT Metro Area	2,711	2,698	81,366	81,326	80,357	376	376	373	30	30	30
Greeley, CO Metro Area	4,017	3,985	324,492	252,827	180,926	156	179	213	81	63	45
Green Bay, WI Metro Area	2,849	1,870	322,906	306,241	282,599	158	157	157	173	164	151
Greensboro-High Point, NC Metro Area	2,020	1,994	771,851	723,923	643,430	75	73	76	277	258	205
Greenville, NC Metro Area	656	652	180,742	168,176	133,798	236	238	275	277	258	205
Greenville-Anderson, SC Metro Area	2,787	2,710	920,477	824,031	725,680	60	65	68	340	304	268
Gulfport-Biloxi, MS Metro Area	3,029	2,216	417,665	388,591	377,610	130	136	122	188	175	170
Hagerstown-Martinsburg, MD-WV Metro Area	1,019	1,008	288,104	269,146	222,771	171	173	182	286	267	221
Hammond, LA Metro Area	844	791	134,758	121,109	100,588	305	320	343	170	153	127
Hanford-Corcoran, CA Metro Area	1,392	1,390	152,940	152,974	129,461	272	265	281	110	110	93
Harrisburg-Carlisle, PA Metro Area	1,664	1,622	577,941	549,444	509,074	98	98	92	356	339	314
Harrisonburg, VA Metro Area	871	867	134,964	125,221	108,193	304	315	327	156	144	125
Hartford-East Hartford-Middletown, CT Metro Area	1,607	1,515	1,204,877	1,212,471	1,148,618	48	43	43	795	800	758
Hattiesburg, MS Metro Area	2,035	2,024	168,849	162,418	143,219	254	247	254	83	80	71
Hickory-Lenoir-Morganton, NC Metro Area	1,669	1,639	369,711	365,794	341,851	146	145	137	226	223	209
Hilton Head Island-Bluffton, SC Metro Area	1,625	1,231	222,195	187,010	141,615	204	225	261	180	152	115
Hinesville, GA Metro Area	1,006	917	80,994	77,929	71,914	377	377	376	88	85	78
Homosassa Springs, FL Metro Area	773	582	149,657	141,230	118,085	281	286	303	257	243	203
Hot Springs, AR Metro Area	735	678	99,386	95,999	88,068	359	362	361	147	142	130
Houma-Thibodaux, LA Metro Area	3,551	2,298	208,075	208,185	194,477	217	207	199	91	91	85
Houston-The Woodlands-Sugar Land, TX Metro Area	9,444	8,268	7,066,141	5,920,487	4,693,161	5	6	8	855	716	568
Huntington-Ashland, WV-KY-OH Metro Area	2,536	2,500	355,873	370,899	367,127	151	142	130	142	148	147
Huntsville, AL Metro Area	1,420	1,362	471,824	417,593	342,376	116	122	136	346	307	251
Idaho Falls, ID Metro Area	5,245	5,196	151,530	133,331	104,576	276	301	332	29	26	20
Indianapolis-Carmel-Anderson, IN Metro Area	4,341	4,307	2,074,537	1,888,075	1,658,462	33	33	32	482	438	385
Iowa City, IA Metro Area	1,194	1,182	173,105	152,586	131,676	246	266	278	146	129	111
Ithaca, NY Metro Area	492	475	102,180	101,592	96,501	354	351	349	215	214	203
Jackson, MI Metro Area	723	702	158,510	160,233	158,422	266	251	231	226	228	226
Jackson, MS Metro Area	5,494	5,405	594,806	587,115	546,955	97	93	87	110	109	101
Jackson, TN Metro Area	1,714	1,711	178,644	179,711	170,061	240	229	220	104	105	99
Jacksonville, FL Metro Area	3,698	3,202	1,559,514	1,345,594	1,122,750	40	40	44	487	420	351
Jacksonville, NC Metro Area	905	762	197,938	177,801	150,355	225	230	243	260	233	197
Janesville-Beloit, WI Metro Area	726	718	163,354	160,325	152,307	262	250	239	228	223	212
Jefferson City, MO Metro Area	2,279	2,248	151,235	149,820	140,052	278	272	264	67	67	62
Johnson City, TN Metro Area	864	854	203,649	198,757	181,607	222	217	211	238	233	213
Johnstown, PA Metro Area	694	688	130,192	143,695	152,598	311	281	238	189	209	222
Jonesboro, AR Metro Area	1,476	1,466	133,860	121,019	107,762	308	321	328	91	83	74
Joplin, MO Metro Area	1,268	1,263	179,564	175,509	157,322	238	232	232	142	139	125
Kahului-Wailuku-Lahaina, HI Metro Area	2,398	1,162	167,417	154,840	128,094	258	259	286	144	133	110
Kalamazoo-Portage, MI Metro Area	580	562	265,066	250,327	238,603	184	186	174	472	445	425
Kankakee, IL Metro Area	681	676	109,862	113,450	103,833	344	334	334	163	168	153
Kansas City, MO-KS Metro Area	7,373	7,256	2,157,990	2,009,355	1,811,254	31	30	26	297	277	250
Kennewick-Richland, WA Metro Area	3,025	2,942	299,612	253,328	191,822	166	178	203	102	86	65
Killeen-Temple, TX Metro Area	2,859	2,816	460,303	405,308	330,714	120	128	139	163	144	117
Kingsport-Bristol, TN-VA Metro Area	2,047	2,010	307,202	309,493	298,484	165	154	150	153	154	148
Kingston, NY Metro Area	1,161	1,124	177,573	182,519	177,749	241	226	214	158	162	158
Knoxville, TN Metro Area	3,347	3,220	869,046	815,025	727,600	64	68	67	270	253	226
Kokomo, IN Metro Area	294	293	82,544	82,748	84,964	375	373	365	282	282	290
La Crosse-Onalaska, WI-MN Metro Area	1,049	1,004	136,616	133,658	126,838	301	299	287	136	133	126
Lafayette, LA Metro Area	4,316	3,408	489,207	466,733	425,020	114	110	109	144	137	125
Lafayette-West Lafayette, IN Metro Area	1,651	1,642	233,002	210,310	186,960	197	202	207	142	128	114
Lake Charles, LA Metro Area	3,031	2,349	210,409	199,640	193,568	215	216	216	90	85	82
Lake Havasu City-Kingman, AZ Metro Area	13,461	13,332	212,181	200,182	155,032	214	214	235	16	15	12
Lakeland-Winter Haven, FL Metro Area	2,010	1,798	724,777	602,073	483,924	81	90	97	403	335	269
Lancaster, PA Metro Area	984	944	545,724	519,443	470,658	104	103	101	578	550	499
Lansing-East Lansing, MI Metro Area	2,256	2,229	550,391	534,684	519,415	103	100	90	247	240	233
Laredo, TX Metro Area	3,376	3,361	276,652	250,304	193,117	176	187	202	82	74	57
Las Cruces, NM Metro Area	3,815	3,808	218,195	209,217	174,682	210	205	216	57	55	46
Las Vegas-Henderson-Paradise, NV Metro Area	8,061	7,892	2,266,715	1,951,268	1,375,765	28	31	37	287	247	174
Lawrence, KS Metro Area	475	456	122,259	110,826	99,962	326	339	344	268	243	219
Lawton, OK Metro Area	1,726	1,702	126,415	130,288	121,610	315	304	295	74	77	71
Lebanon, PA Metro Area	363	362	141,793	133,597	120,327	295	300	298	392	369	333
Lewiston, ID-WA Metro Area	1,497	1,484	62,990	60,893	57,961	381	381	380	42	41	39
Lewiston-Auburn, ME Metro Area	497	468	108,277	107,709	103,793	346	344	335	231	230	222
Lexington-Fayette, KY Metro Area	1,484	1,470	517,056	472,103	408,326	109	109	112	352	321	278
Lima, OH Metro Area	407	403	102,351	106,313	108,473	352	345	326	254	264	269
Lincoln, NE Metro Area	1,422	1,409	336,374	302,157	266,787	152	159	162	239	214	189
Little Rock-North Little Rock-Conway, AR Metro Area	4,199	4,085	742,384	699,790	610,518	80	76	78	182	171	149
Logan, UT-ID Metro Area	1,841	1,828	142,165	125,442	102,720	293	314	340	78	69	56
Longview, TX Metro Area	2,723	2,680	286,657	280,007	256,152	172	167	166	107	104	96

Table B-1. Area and Population—*Continued*

Metropolitan Statistical Area Metropolitan Division	Area 2019 (square miles)		Population								
						Rank			Persons per square mile of land Area		
	Total	Land	2019 Estimate (July 1)	2010 census estimates base (April 1)	2000 census estimates base (April 1)	2019	2010	2000	2019	2010	2000
Longview, WA Metro Area	1,166	1,141	110,593	102,408	92,948	342	349	353	97	90	81
Los Angeles-Long Beach-Anaheim, CA Metro Area	5,699	4,851	13,214,799	12,828,957	12,365,627	2	2	2	2,724	2,645	2,549
Anaheim-Santa Ana-Irvine, CA Div	948	793	3,175,692	3,008,989	2,846,289	-	-	-	4,005	3,794	3,590
Los Angeles-Long Beach-Glendale, CA Div	4,751	4,059	10,039,107	9,819,968	9,519,338	-	-	-	2,473	2,419	2,345
Louisville/Jefferson County, KY-IN Metro Area	3,291	3,237	1,265,108	1,202,686	1,090,024	46	44	46	391	372	337
Lubbock, TX Metro Area	2,696	2,688	322,257	290,889	256,250	159	163	165	120	108	95
Lynchburg, VA Metro Area	2,147	2,120	263,566	252,654	222,317	188	181	185	124	119	105
Macon-Bibb County, GA Metro Area	1,738	1,724	229,996	232,245	222,368	200	193	184	133	135	129
Madera, CA Metro Area	2,153	2,137	157,327	150,834	123,109	267	271	292	74	71	58
Madison, WI Metro Area	3,386	3,309	664,865	605,466	535,421	89	89	89	201	183	162
Manchester-Nashua, NH Metro Area	892	877	417,025	400,706	380,841	131	131	120	476	457	434
Manhattan, KS Metro Area	1,888	1,835	130,285	127,094	108,999	310	311	323	71	69	59
Mankato, MN Metro Area	1,233	1,196	101,927	96,742	85,712	355	359	364	85	81	72
Mansfield, OH Metro Area	500	495	121,154	124,474	128,852	329	317	285	245	251	260
McAllen-Edinburg-Mission, TX Metro Area	1,583	1,571	868,707	774,764	569,463	65	71	82	553	493	363
Medford, OR Metro Area	2,801	2,783	220,944	203,204	181,269	206	211	212	79	73	65
Memphis, TN-MS-AR Metro Area	4,699	4,579	1,346,045	1,316,102	1,205,204	43	41	41	294	287	263
Merced, CA Metro Area	1,979	1,936	277,680	255,796	210,554	175	176	189	143	132	109
Miami-Fort Lauderdale-Pompano Beach, FL Metro Area	6,137	5,067	6,166,488	5,566,274	5,007,564	7	8	6	1,217	1,099	988
Fort Lauderdale-Pompano Beach-Sunrise, FL Div	1,323	1,203	1,952,778	1,748,146	1,623,018	-	-	-	1,623	1,453	1,349
Miami-Miami Beach-Kendall, FL Div	2,431	1,900	2,716,940	2,497,993	2,253,362	-	-	-	1,430	1,315	1,186
West Palm Beach-Boca Raton-Boynton Beach, FL Div	2,383	1,964	1,496,770	1,320,135	1,131,184	-	-	-	762	672	576
Michigan City-La Porte, IN Metro Area	613	598	109,888	111,466	110,106	343	337	321	184	186	184
Midland, MI Metro Area	528	516	83,156	83,621	82,874	374	372	368	161	162	161
Midland, TX Metro Area	1,818	1,815	182,603	141,671	120,755	232	285	297	101	78	67
Milwaukee-Waukesha, WI Metro Area	3,322	1,455	1,575,179	1,555,954	1,500,741	39	39	36	1,083	1,069	1,032
Minneapolis-St. Paul-Bloomington, MN Metro Area	7,520	7,048	3,640,043	3,333,628	3,016,562	16	16	16	516	473	428
Missoula, MT Metro Area	2,618	2,593	119,600	109,296	95,802	331	342	350	46	42	37
Mobile, AL Metro Area	2,733	2,310	429,536	430,719	417,940	126	116	110	186	186	181
Modesto, CA Metro Area	1,514	1,496	550,660	514,450	446,997	102	105	105	368	344	299
Monroe, LA Metro Area	2,343	2,282	200,261	204,487	201,074	224	210	196	88	90	88
Monroe, MI Metro Area	680	549	150,500	152,031	145,945	279	268	248	274	277	266
Montgomery, AL Metro Area	2,786	2,714	373,290	374,540	346,528	145	140	134	138	138	128
Morgantown, WV Metro Area	1,017	1,009	139,044	129,702	111,200	298	306	318	138	129	110
Morristown, TN Metro Area	793	717	142,749	136,858	123,081	292	295	293	199	191	172
Mount Vernon-Anacortes, WA Metro Area	1,917	1,730	129,205	116,892	102,979	313	326	339	75	68	60
Muncie, IN Metro Area	396	392	114,135	117,670	118,769	337	325	302	291	300	303
Muskegon, MI Metro Area	1,460	504	173,566	172,194	170,200	245	234	219	344	342	338
Myrtle Beach-Conway-North Myrtle Beach, SC-NC Metro Area	2,304	1,982	496,901	376,575	269,772	111	139	160	251	190	136
Napa, CA Metro Area	789	748	137,744	136,535	124,279	300	296	291	184	183	166
Naples-Marco Island, FL Metro Area	2,305	1,997	384,902	321,522	251,377	142	151	172	193	161	126
Nashville-Davidson--Murfreesboro--Franklin, TN Metro Area	5,766	5,689	1,934,317	1,646,183	1,358,992	36	37	38	340	289	239
New Bern, NC Metro Area	1,809	1,514	124,284	126,808	114,751	321	312	309	82	84	76
New Haven-Milford, CT Metro Area	862	605	854,757	862,442	824,008	67	62	58	1,413	1,426	1,363
New Orleans-Metairie, LA Metro Area	7,874	3,203	1,270,530	1,189,891	1,337,726	45	45	39	397	371	418
New York-Newark-Jersey City, NY-NJ-PA Metro Area	9,212	6,685	19,216,182	18,896,277	18,323,002	1	1	1	2,875	2,827	2,741
Nassau County-Suffolk County, NY Div	2,827	1,196	2,833,525	2,832,996	2,753,913	-	-	-	2,369	2,369	2,302
Newark, NJ-PA Div	2,256	2,181	2,167,829	2,146,271	2,098,843	-	-	-	994	984	962
New Brunswick-Lakewood, NJ Div	2,208	1,708	2,379,977	2,340,425	2,173,869	-	-	-	1,393	1,370	1,273
New York-Jersey City-White Plains, NY-NJ Div	1,921	1,600	11,834,851	11,576,585	11,296,377	-	-	-	7,397	7,235	7,061
Niles, MI Metro Area	1,581	568	153,401	156,808	162,453	271	257	227	270	276	286
North Port-Sarasota-Bradenton, FL Metro Area	1,618	1,300	836,995	702,312	589,959	72	75	80	644	540	454
Norwich-New London, CT Metro Area	772	665	265,206	274,070	259,088	183	170	163	399	412	390
Ocala, FL Metro Area	1,663	1,588	365,579	331,299	258,916	149	150	164	230	209	163
Ocean City, NJ Metro Area	620	251	92,039	97,257	102,326	367	358	341	367	387	407
Odessa, TX Metro Area	902	898	166,223	137,136	121,123	259	294	296	185	153	135
Ogden-Clearfield, UT Metro Area	8,635	7,230	683,864	597,162	485,401	85	91	96	95	83	67
Oklahoma City, OK Metro Area	5,582	5,512	1,408,950	1,253,002	1,095,421	41	42	45	256	227	199
Olympia-Lacey-Tumwater, WA Metro Area	774	722	290,536	252,260	207,355	168	182	191	402	349	287
Omaha-Council Bluffs, NE-IA Metro Area	4,407	4,346	949,442	865,347	767,041	57	61	62	218	199	176
Orlando-Kissimmee-Sanford, FL Metro Area	4,012	3,490	2,608,147	2,134,399	1,644,561	23	28	33	747	612	471
Oshkosh-Neenah, WI Metro Area	579	435	171,907	167,000	156,763	248	242	233	395	384	361
Owensboro, KY Metro Area	932	899	119,440	114,746	109,875	332	333	322	133	128	122
Oxnard-Thousand Oaks-Ventura, CA Metro Area	2,208	1,842	846,006	823,398	753,197	68	66	63	459	447	409
Palm Bay-Melbourne-Titusville, FL Metro Area	1,557	1,015	601,942	543,372	476,230	96	99	99	593	535	469
Panama City, FL Metro Area	1,033	759	174,705	168,850	148,217	244	237	245	230	222	195
Parkersburg-Vienna, WV Metro Area	612	599	89,339	92,667	93,859	368	366	351	149	155	157
Pensacola-Ferry Pass-Brent, FL Metro Area	2,048	1,669	502,629	448,991	412,153	110	111	111	301	269	247

Table B-1. Area and Population—*Continued*

Metropolitan Statistical Area Metropolitan Division	Area 2019 (square miles)		Population			Rank			Persons per square mile of land Area		
	Total	Land	2019 Estimate (July 1)	2010 census estimates base (April 1)	2000 census estimates base (April 1)	2019	2010	2000	2019	2010	2000
Peoria, IL Metro Area	3,401	3,334	400,561	416,253	405,149	135	123	114	120	125	122
Philadelphia-Camden-Wilmington, PA-NJ-DE-MD Metro Area	4,870	4,603	6,102,434	5,965,677	5,687,147	8	5	4	1,326	1,296	1,236
Camden, NJ Div	1,384	1,343	1,243,456	1,251,021	1,186,999	-	-	-	926	932	884
Montgomery County-Bucks County-Chester County, PA Div	1,868	1,838	1,984,174	1,924,229	1,781,233	-	-	-	1,080	1,047	969
Philadelphia, PA Div	333	318	2,150,811	2,084,769	2,068,414	-	-	-	6,764	6,556	6,503
Wilmington, DE-MD-NJ Div	1,284	1,104	723,993	705,658	650,501	-	-	-	656	639	589
Phoenix-Mesa-Chandler, AZ Metro Area	14,600	14,567	4,948,203	4,193,129	3,251,876	10	14	14	340	288	223
Pine Bluff, AR Metro Area	2,085	2,029	87,804	100,289	107,341	369	353	329	43	49	53
Pittsburgh, PA Metro Area	5,343	5,283	2,317,600	2,356,294	2,431,087	27	22	20	439	446	460
Pittsfield, MA Metro Area	946	927	124,944	131,274	134,953	319	303	272	135	142	146
Pocatello, ID Metro Area	2,590	2,516	95,489	90,661	83,103	365	368	367	38	36	33
Portland-South Portland, ME Metro Area	2,857	2,081	538,500	514,108	487,568	105	106	95	259	247	234
Portland-Vancouver-Hillsboro, OR-WA Metro Area	6,824	6,687	2,492,412	2,226,003	1,927,881	25	24	25	373	333	288
Port St. Lucie, FL Metro Area	1,441	1,115	489,297	424,107	319,426	113	120	146	439	380	286
Poughkeepsie-Newburgh-Middletown, NY Metro Area	1,664	1,608	679,158	670,280	621,517	86	79	77	422	417	387
Prescott Valley-Prescott, AZ Metro Area	8,128	8,123	235,099	211,017	167,517	196	201	221	29	26	21
Providence-Warwick, RI-MA Metro Area	2,236	1,587	1,624,578	1,601,206	1,582,997	38	38	35	1,024	1,009	997
Provo-Orem, UT Metro Area	5,550	5,396	648,252	526,885	376,774	91	102	123	120	98	70
Pueblo, CO Metro Area	2,398	2,386	168,424	159,063	141,472	256	254	262	71	67	59
Punta Gorda, FL Metro Area	858	681	188,910	159,967	141,627	229	252	260	277	235	208
Racine, WI Metro Area	792	333	196,311	195,428	188,831	227	220	204	590	587	568
Raleigh-Cary, NC Metro Area	2,148	2,118	1,390,785	1,130,493	797,071	42	48	61	657	534	376
Rapid City, SD Metro Area	6,267	6,248	142,107	126,400	112,818	294	313	314	23	20	18
Reading, PA Metro Area	866	856	421,164	411,570	373,638	129	126	126	492	481	436
Redding, CA Metro Area	3,847	3,775	180,080	177,221	163,256	237	231	226	48	47	43
Reno, NV Metro Area	6,806	6,580	475,642	425,442	342,885	115	118	135	72	65	52
Richmond, VA Metro Area	4,491	4,363	1,291,900	1,186,471	1,040,192	44	46	48	296	272	238
Riverside-San Bernardino-Ontario, CA Metro Area	27,408	27,277	4,650,631	4,224,948	3,254,821	13	13	13	170	155	119
Roanoke, VA Metro Area	1,895	1,868	313,222	308,666	288,309	163	155	154	168	165	154
Rochester, MN Metro Area	2,506	2,477	221,921	206,888	184,740	205	208	209	90	84	75
Rochester, NY Metro Area	5,246	3,266	1,069,644	1,079,704	1,062,452	52	50	47	328	331	325
Rockford, IL Metro Area	801	794	336,116	349,431	320,204	153	147	144	423	440	403
Rocky Mount, NC Metro Area	1,050	1,046	145,770	152,368	143,026	288	267	256	139	146	137
Rome, GA Metro Area	518	510	98,498	96,314	90,565	360	360	357	193	189	178
Sacramento-Roseville-Folsom, CA Metro Area	5,307	5,095	2,363,730	2,149,150	1,796,857	26	25	27	464	422	353
Saginaw, MI Metro Area	816	801	190,539	200,169	210,039	228	215	190	238	250	262
St. Cloud, MN Metro Area	1,803	1,751	201,964	189,093	167,392	223	224	222	115	108	96
St. George, UT Metro Area	2,430	2,427	177,556	138,115	90,354	242	292	358	73	57	37
St. Joseph, MO-KS Metro Area	1,676	1,656	125,223	127,319	122,336	317	309	294	76	77	74
St. Louis, MO-IL Metro Area	8,082	7,863	2,803,228	2,787,751	2,675,343	20	18	18	357	355	340
Salem, OR Metro Area	1,935	1,921	433,903	390,738	347,214	125	133	133	226	203	181
Salinas, CA Metro Area	3,771	3,282	434,061	415,059	401,762	124	124	115	132	126	122
Salisbury, MD-DE Metro Area	2,902	2,099	415,726	373,754	312,572	132	141	148	198	178	149
Salt Lake City, UT Metro Area	8,092	7,684	1,232,696	1,087,808	939,122	47	49	50	160	142	122
San Angelo, TX Metro Area	3,516	3,497	122,027	112,968	107,174	327	335	330	35	32	31
San Antonio-New Braunfels, TX Metro Area	7,371	7,313	2,550,960	2,142,520	1,711,703	24	26	30	349	293	234
San Diego-Chula Vista-Carlsbad, CA Metro Area	4,526	4,210	3,338,330	3,095,349	2,813,833	17	17	17	793	735	668
San Francisco-Oakland-Berkeley, CA Metro Area	3,426	2,470	4,731,803	4,335,593	4,123,740	12	11	12	1,916	1,755	1,669
Oakland-Berkeley-Livermore, CA Div	1,625	1,454	2,824,855	2,559,462	2,392,557	-	-	-	1,943	1,760	1,645
San Francisco-San Mateo-Redwood City, CA Div	973	496	1,648,122	1,523,701	1,483,894	-	-	-	3,323	3,072	2,995
San Rafael, CA Div	828	520	258,826	252,430	247,289	-	-	-	498	485	475
San Jose-Sunnyvale-Santa Clara, CA Metro Area	2,695	2,680	1,990,660	1,836,951	1,735,819	35	34	29	743	685	648
San Luis Obispo-Paso Robles, CA Metro Area	3,616	3,301	283,111	269,597	246,681	174	172	173	86	82	75
Santa Cruz-Watsonville, CA Metro Area	607	445	273,213	262,350	255,602	178	174	167	614	590	574
Santa Fe, NM Metro Area	1,911	1,910	150,358	144,232	129,292	280	280	283	79	76	68
Santa Maria-Santa Barbara, CA Metro Area	3,789	2,735	446,499	423,947	399,347	123	121	116	163	155	146
Santa Rosa-Petaluma, CA Metro Area	1,768	1,576	494,336	483,861	458,614	112	107	103	314	307	291
Savannah, GA Metro Area	1,567	1,349	393,353	347,597	293,000	139	148	153	292	258	217
Scranton--Wilkes-Barre, PA Metro Area	1,776	1,746	553,885	563,604	560,625	101	97	85	317	323	321
Seattle-Tacoma-Bellevue, WA Metro Area	6,309	5,870	3,979,845	3,439,808	3,043,878	15	15	15	678	586	519
Seattle-Bellevue-Kent, WA Div	4,503	4,202	3,074,865	2,644,586	2,343,058	-	-	-	732	629	558
Tacoma-Lakewood, WA Div	1,805	1,668	904,980	795,222	700,820	-	-	-	543	477	420
Sebastian-Vero Beach, FL Metro Area	617	503	159,923	138,028	112,947	265	293	313	318	274	225
Sebring-Avon Park, FL Metro Area	1,107	1,018	106,221	98,784	87,366	347	355	362	104	97	86
Sheboygan, WI Metro Area	1,271	512	115,340	115,512	112,646	336	332	315	225	226	220
Sherman-Denison, TX Metro Area	979	933	136,212	120,877	110,595	302	322	319	146	130	119
Shreveport-Bossier City, LA Metro Area	2,699	2,596	394,706	398,606	375,965	138	132	125	152	154	145
Sierra Vista-Douglas, AZ Metro Area	6,217	6,210	125,922	131,359	117,755	316	302	304	20	21	19
Sioux City, IA-NE-SD Metro Area	2,095	2,074	144,701	143,582	143,053	290	282	255	70	69	69

Table B-1. Area and Population—*Continued*

Metropolitan Statistical Area Metropolitan Division	Area 2019 (square miles)		Population								
	Total	Land	2019 Estimate (July 1)	2010 census estimates base (April 1)	2000 census estimates base (April 1)	Rank			Persons per square mile of land Area		
						2019	2010	2000	2019	2010	2000
Sioux Falls, SD Metro Area	2,586	2,575	268,232	228,264	187,093	182	195	206	104	89	73
South Bend-Mishawaka, IN-MI Metro Area	970	948	323,613	319,203	316,663	157	152	147	341	337	334
Spartanburg, SC Metro Area	819	808	319,785	284,304	253,791	161	165	168	396	352	314
Spokane-Spokane Valley, WA Metro Area	4,321	4,241	568,521	514,752	458,005	99	104	104	134	121	108
Springfield, IL Metro Area	1,192	1,183	206,868	210,170	201,437	218	203	194	175	178	170
Springfield, MA Metro Area	1,904	1,843	697,382	693,059	680,014	84	77	71	378	376	369
Springfield, MO Metro Area	3,021	3,007	470,300	436,756	368,374	117	114	128	156	145	123
Springfield, OH Metro Area	403	397	134,083	138,339	144,742	307	291	252	338	348	365
State College, PA Metro Area	1,113	1,109	162,385	154,005	135,758	264	261	270	146	139	122
Staunton, VA Metro Area	1,006	1,002	123,120	118,496	108,988	325	324	324	123	118	109
Stockton, CA Metro Area	1,427	1,392	762,148	685,306	563,598	77	78	84	548	492	405
Sumter, SC Metro Area	1,378	1,272	140,466	142,434	137,148	297	283	269	110	112	108
Syracuse, NY Metro Area	2,779	2,385	648,593	662,624	650,154	90	81	74	272	278	273
Tallahassee, FL Metro Area	2,603	2,388	387,227	368,771	320,304	141	143	143	162	154	134
Tampa-St. Petersburg-Clearwater, FL Metro Area	3,331	2,515	3,194,831	2,783,485	2,395,997	18	19	21	1,270	1,107	953
Terre Haute, IN Metro Area	1,935	1,910	186,367	189,774	188,184	230	223	205	98	99	99
Texarkana, TX-AR Metro Area	2,125	2,043	148,761	149,194	143,377	284	274	253	73	73	70
The Villages, FL Metro Area	580	557	132,420	93,420	53,345	309	365	383	238	168	96
Toledo, OH Metro Area	2,209	1,617	641,816	651,435	659,188	93	82	73	397	403	408
Topeka, KS Metro Area	3,290	3,233	231,969	233,860	224,551	199	192	181	72	72	69
Trenton-Princeton, NJ Metro Area	229	224	367,430	367,485	350,761	148	144	132	1,640	1,641	1,563
Tucson, AZ Metro Area	9,191	9,189	1,047,279	980,263	843,746	53	53	56	114	107	92
Tulsa, OK Metro Area	6,460	6,270	998,626	937,523	859,532	55	55	55	159	150	137
Tuscaloosa, AL Metro Area	3,558	3,493	252,047	239,214	212,983	190	190	187	72	68	61
Twin Falls, ID Metro Area	2,531	2,519	111,290	99,596	82,626	341	354	370	44	40	33
Tyler, TX Metro Area	950	921	232,751	209,725	174,706	198	204	215	253	228	190
Urban Honolulu, HI Metro Area	2,166	601	974,563	953,206	876,156	56	54	53	1,622	1,586	1,459
Utica-Rome, NY Metro Area	2,716	2,624	289,990	299,329	299,896	169	161	149	111	114	114
Valdosta, GA Metro Area	1,629	1,607	147,292	139,662	119,560	286	288	301	92	87	74
Vallejo, CA Metro Area	906	822	447,643	413,343	394,542	122	125	117	545	503	480
Victoria, TX Metro Area	1,748	1,734	99,742	94,003	91,016	357	363	356	58	54	52
Vineland-Bridgeton, NJ Metro Area	678	483	149,527	156,627	146,438	282	258	247	310	324	303
Virginia Beach-Norfolk-Newport News, VA-NC Metro Area	4,854	3,530	1,768,901	1,713,955	1,612,770	37	36	34	501	486	457
Visalia, CA Metro Area	4,839	4,824	466,195	442,182	368,021	118	112	129	97	92	76
Waco, TX Metro Area	1,834	1,803	273,920	252,766	232,093	177	180	176	152	140	129
Walla Walla, WA Metro Area	1,299	1,270	60,760	58,781	55,180	383	383	382	48	46	43
Warner Robins, GA Metro Area	531	526	185,409	167,626	134,433	231	240	273	352	319	255
Washington-Arlington-Alexandria, DC-VA-MD-WV Metro Area	7,003	6,568	6,280,487	5,649,688	4,849,948	6	7	7	956	860	738
Frederick-Gaithersburg-Rockville, MD Div	1,174	1,154	1,310,235	1,204,687	1,068,618	-	-	-	1,135	1,044	926
Washington-Arlington-Alexandria, DC-VA-MD-WV Div	5,829	5,414	4,970,252	4,445,001	3,781,330	-	-	-	918	821	698
Waterloo-Cedar Falls, IA Metro Area	1,514	1,503	168,522	167,819	163,706	255	239	225	112	112	109
Watertown-Fort Drum, NY Metro Area	1,857	1,269	109,834	116,232	111,738	345	328	317	87	92	88
Wausau-Weston, WI Metro Area	2,483	2,424	163,285	162,804	155,475	263	246	234	67	67	64
Weirton-Steubenville, WV-OH Metro Area	591	580	116,074	124,455	132,008	334	318	277	200	215	228
Wenatchee, WA Metro Area	4,843	4,740	120,629	110,887	99,219	330	338	345	25	23	21
Wheeling, WV-OH Metro Area	962	943	138,948	147,957	153,172	299	276	237	147	157	162
Wichita, KS Metro Area	4,181	4,148	640,218	623,061	571,166	94	85	81	154	150	138
Wichita Falls, TX Metro Area	2,675	2,620	151,254	151,474	151,524	277	269	240	58	58	58
Williamsport, PA Metro Area	1,244	1,229	113,299	116,102	120,044	340	329	299	92	94	98
Wilmington, NC Metro Area	1,263	1,064	297,533	254,879	201,389	167	177	195	280	240	189
Winchester, VA-WV Metro Area	1,069	1,063	140,566	128,452	102,997	296	308	338	132	121	97
Winston-Salem, NC Metro Area	2,040	2,009	676,008	640,503	569,207	87	84	83	336	319	283
Worcester, MA-CT Metro Area	2,100	2,024	947,404	916,763	860,054	58	58	54	468	453	425
Yakima, WA Metro Area	4,310	4,295	250,873	243,240	222,581	191	189	183	58	57	52
York-Hanover, PA Metro Area	911	904	449,058	435,015	381,751	121	115	119	497	481	422
Youngstown-Warren-Boardman, OH-PA Metro Area	1,744	1,702	536,081	565,782	602,964	106	94	79	315	332	354
Yuba City, CA Metro Area	1,252	1,235	175,639	166,898	139,149	243	243	266	142	135	113
Yuma, AZ Metro Area	5,519	5,514	213,787	195,750	160,026	211	219	230	39	36	29

Table B-2. Components of Population Change

Metropolitan Statistical Area Metropolitan Division	Components of population change, April 1 2010 (estimates base) to July 1, 2019 (estimate)								Population change, April 1, 2000 to April 1, 2010	
	Number									
	Total population change	Natural increase			Total migration	Net International migration	Net domestic migration	Percent change	Number	Percent change
		Total	Births	Deaths						
Abilene, TX Metro Area	6,808	6,432	21,881	15,449	431	3,167	-2,736	4.1	5,001	3.1
Akron, OH Metro Area	283	3,307	69,159	65,852	-2,597	13,086	-15,683	0.0	8,243	1.2
Albany, GA Metro Area	-7,307	5,423	18,764	13,341	-12,853	865	-13,718	-4.7	283	0.2
Albany-Lebanon, OR Metro Area	13,068	2,217	13,642	11,425	10,883	204	10,679	11.2	13,607	13.2
Albany-Schenectady-Troy, NY Metro Area	9,668	11,001	83,501	72,500	-858	16,398	-17,256	1.1	44,839	5.4
Albuquerque, NM Metro Area	30,955	28,587	95,682	67,095	2,884	11,273	-8,389	3.5	157,415	21.6
Alexandria, LA Metro Area	-1,881	3,625	18,768	15,143	-5,434	657	-6,091	-1.2	8,883	6.1
Allentown-Bethlehem-Easton, PA-NJ Metro Area	22,779	4,407	78,967	74,560	18,984	24,110	-5,126	2.8	80,872	10.9
Altoona, PA Metro Area	-5,288	-3,044	11,809	14,853	-2,137	266	-2,403	-4.2	-2,028	-1.6
Amarillo, TX Metro Area	13,118	12,500	33,935	21,435	497	6,326	-5,829	5.2	23,230	10.2
Ames, IA Metro Area	7,501	3,771	11,201	7,430	3,706	6,347	-2,641	6.5	9,645	9.1
Anchorage, AK Metro Area	15,496	33,779	54,430	20,651	-18,670	9,059	-27,729	4.1	61,216	19.2
Ann Arbor, MI Metro Area	22,438	13,531	33,966	20,435	9,093	18,202	-9,109	6.5	22,209	6.9
Anniston-Oxford, AL Metro Area	-4,921	-926	12,345	13,271	-3,943	554	-4,497	-4.2	6,345	5.7
Appleton, WI Metro Area	12,307	10,484	25,919	15,435	1,991	1,718	273	5.5	24,062	11.9
Asheville, NC Metro Area	37,817	-4,461	40,584	45,045	41,934	901	41,033	8.9	55,688	15.1
Athens-Clarke County, GA Metro Area	21,183	7,664	20,479	12,815	13,387	4,305	9,082	11.0	26,485	15.9
Atlanta-Sandy Springs-Alpharetta, GA Metro Area	733,646	343,765	673,437	329,672	389,077	144,048	245,029	13.9	1,023,312	24.0
Atlantic City-Hammonton, NJ Metro Area	-10,855	3,762	28,213	24,451	-14,717	7,275	-21,992	-4.0	21,969	8.7
Auburn-Opelika, AL Metro Area	24,255	7,301	16,800	9,499	16,776	4,442	12,334	17.3	25,208	21.9
Augusta-Richmond County, GA-SC Metro Area	44,087	19,584	68,807	49,223	24,442	5,614	18,828	7.8	56,841	11.2
Austin-Round Rock-Georgetown, TX Metro Area	510,760	149,806	239,673	89,867	355,902	62,740	293,162	29.8	466,558	37.3
Bakersfield, CA Metro Area	60,581	74,264	128,382	54,118	-13,469	7,091	-20,560	7.2	177,974	26.9
Baltimore-Columbia-Towson, MD Metro Area	89,455	85,415	309,615	224,200	5,900	63,529	-57,629	3.3	157,608	6.2
Bangor, ME Metro Area	-1,783	-1,025	13,391	14,416	-654	829	-1,483	-1.2	9,013	6.2
Barnstable Town, MA Metro Area	-2,890	-12,324	14,442	26,766	9,657	3,193	6,464	-1.3	-6,355	-2.9
Baton Rouge, LA Metro Area	28,967	39,336	104,150	64,814	-10,415	7,906	-18,321	3.5	96,559	13.2
Battle Creek, MI Metro Area	-1,991	1,283	15,001	13,718	-3,249	2,544	-5,793	-1.5	-1,837	-1.3
Bay City, MI Metro Area	-4,647	-1,418	9,713	11,131	-3,171	186	-3,357	-4.3	-2,384	-2.2
Beaumont-Port Arthur, TX Metro Area	3,814	12,241	49,027	36,786	-8,395	5,360	-13,755	1.0	3,659	1.0
Beckley, WV Metro Area	-9,147	-2,917	12,607	15,524	-6,186	457	-6,643	-7.3	-1,885	-1.5
Bellingham, WA Metro Area	28,101	6,275	20,961	14,686	21,826	3,788	18,038	14.0	34,332	20.6
Bend, OR Metro Area	39,964	3,342	16,324	12,982	36,236	-263	36,499	25.3	42,363	36.7
Billings, MT Metro Area	14,502	4,545	19,614	15,069	9,967	598	9,369	8.7	20,066	13.6
Binghamton, NY Metro Area	-13,033	-434	23,118	23,552	-12,668	3,636	-16,304	-5.2	-596	-0.2
Birmingham-Hoover, AL Metro Area	29,396	26,658	126,000	99,342	3,387	8,320	-4,933	2.8	79,510	8.1
Bismarck, ND Metro Area	18,324	6,700	15,869	9,169	11,386	1,131	10,255	16.6	13,841	14.3
Blacksburg-Christiansburg, VA Metro Area	4,571	962	13,760	12,798	3,636	5,090	-1,454	2.8	11,690	7.7
Bloomington, IL Metro Area	1,940	8,212	18,987	10,775	-6,357	6,019	-12,376	1.1	19,144	12.7
Bloomington, IN Metro Area	9,695	3,249	13,902	10,653	6,496	9,088	-2,592	6.1	17,187	12.1
Bloomsburg-Berwick, PA Metro Area	-2,361	-1,029	7,446	8,475	-1,264	514	-1,778	-2.8	3,174	3.9
Boise City, ID Metro Area	132,636	36,840	78,969	42,129	95,236	6,060	89,176	21.5	151,726	32.6
Boston-Cambridge-Newton, MA-NH Metro Area	320,424	141,612	475,777	334,165	182,147	285,199	-103,052	7.0	161,254	3.7
Boston, MA Div	143,859	63,607	201,427	137,820	81,556	132,497	-50,941	7.6	75,097	4.1
Cambridge-Newton-Framingham, MA Div	154,518	73,686	238,790	165,104	82,574	147,139	-64,565	6.9	28,768	7.4
Rockingham County-Strafford County, NH Div	22,047	4,319	35,560	31,241	18,017	5,563	12,454	5.3	57,389	2.6
Boulder, CO Metro Area	31,636	10,172	26,198	16,026	21,441	8,470	12,971	10.7	24,747	9.2
Bowling Green, KY Metro Area	20,627	5,949	19,566	13,617	14,662	4,654	10,008	13.0	23,632	17.5
Bremerton-Silverdale-Port Orchard, WA Metro Area	20,330	8,056	27,849	19,793	12,195	2,148	10,047	8.1	19,174	8.3
Bridgeport-Stamford-Norwalk, CT Metro Area	26,428	31,206	92,947	61,741	-4,739	44,863	-49,602	2.9	34,297	3.9
Brownsville-Harlingen, TX Metro Area	16,948	41,223	65,142	23,919	-24,410	4,200	-28,610	4.2	70,988	21.2
Brunswick, GA Metro Area	6,394	1,334	12,065	10,731	5,067	503	4,564	5.7	19,327	20.8
Buffalo-Cheektowaga, NY Metro Area	-7,631	-4	111,885	111,889	-6,892	24,110	-31,002	-0.7	-34,497	-2.9
Burlington, NC Metro Area	18,354	2,158	16,914	14,756	16,212	701	15,511	12.1	20,360	15.6
Burlington-South Burlington, VT Metro Area	9,147	5,838	20,120	14,282	3,497	5,694	-2,197	4.3	12,373	6.2
California-Lexington Park, MD Metro Area	8,366	5,788	12,990	7,202	2,616	1,323	1,293	8.0	18,932	22.0
Canton-Massillon, OH Metro Area	-6,905	-503	40,730	41,233	-6,051	1,073	-7,124	-1.7	-2,509	-0.6
Cape Coral-Fort Myers, FL Metro Area	151,822	-1,952	60,521	62,473	152,286	26,032	126,254	24.5	177,866	40.3
Cape Girardeau, MO-IL Metro Area	495	1,287	10,455	9,168	-771	1,220	-1,991	0.5	5,962	6.6
Carbondale-Marion, IL Metro Area	-3,384	1,846	14,376	12,530	-5,323	2,432	-7,755	-2.4	5,369	4.0
Carson City, NV Metro Area	647	-1,018	5,427	6,445	1,641	-181	1,822	1.2	2,817	5.4
Casper, WY Metro Area	4,410	3,455	9,996	6,541	826	506	320	5.8	8,915	13.4
Cedar Rapids, IA Metro Area	15,084	10,308	30,195	19,887	4,995	3,145	1,850	5.8	20,713	8.7
Chambersburg-Waynesboro, PA Metro Area	5,396	3,065	16,994	13,929	2,510	1,461	1,049	3.6	20,306	15.7
Champaign-Urbana, IL Metro Area	8,227	10,012	23,441	13,429	-1,912	17,285	-19,197	3.8	21,772	11.1
Charleston, WV Metro Area	-20,911	-5,096	27,559	32,655	-15,683	716	-16,399	-7.5	-8,063	-2.8
Charleston-North Charleston, SC Metro Area	137,477	34,811	86,195	51,384	101,288	8,231	93,057	20.7	115,606	21.1
Charlotte-Concord-Gastonia, NC-SC Metro Area	392,920	110,931	281,325	170,394	280,220	49,640	230,580	17.5	501,279	28.8
Charlottesville, VA Metro Area	17,046	5,913	20,988	15,075	11,220	6,113	5,107	8.5	27,540	15.8
Chattanooga, TN-GA Metro Area	37,068	7,014	58,213	51,199	30,065	3,828	26,237	7.0	51,619	10.8

Table B-2. Components of Population Change—Continued

Metropolitan Statistical Area Metropolitan Division	Components of population change, April 1 2010 (estimates base) to July 1, 2019 (estimate) — Number								Population change, April 1, 2000 to April 1, 2010	
	Total population change	Natural increase			Total migration	Net Inter-national migration	Net domestic migration	Percent change	Number	Percent change
		Total	Births	Deaths						
Cheyenne, WY Metro Area	7,615	4,474	11,829	7,355	3,119	429	2,690	8.3	10,278	12.6
Chicago-Naperville-Elgin, IL-IN-WI Metro Area	-2,998	438,246	1,085,985	647,739	-441,506	197,093	-638,599	0	363,223	4.0
Chicago-Naperville-Evanston, IL Div	-25,583	341,807	832,923	491,116	-367,592	175,553	-543,145	-0.4	67,481	1.0
Elgin, IL Div	31,002	47,553	87,955	40,402	-16,419	5,415	-21,834	4.2	187,709	34.3
Gary, IN Div	-4,689	12,957	75,224	62,267	-17,439	2,256	-19,695	-0.7	32,146	4.8
Lake County-Kenosha County, IL-WI Div	-3,728	35,929	89,883	53,954	-40,056	13,869	-53,925	-0.4	75,887	9.6
Chico, CA Metro Area	-819	782	22,527	21,745	-1,604	1,640	-3,244	-0.4	16,831	8.3
Cincinnati, OH-KY-IN Metro Area	83,495	73,617	253,180	179,563	11,213	31,157	-19,944	3.9	120,774	6.0
Clarksville, TN-KY Metro Area	33,878	27,663	47,474	19,811	5,746	6,228	-482	12.4	41,943	18.1
Cleveland, TN Metro Area	9,195	1,074	12,549	11,475	8,139	1,088	7,051	7.9	11,739	11.3
Cleveland-Elyria, OH Metro Area	-28,828	14,479	212,523	198,044	-42,445	36,318	-78,763	-1.4	-70,865	-3.3
Coeur d'Alene, ID Metro Area	27,231	4,026	16,346	12,320	23,102	-645	23,747	19.7	29,781	27.4
College Station-Bryan, TX Metro Area	36,060	16,008	28,760	12,752	19,989	12,665	7,324	15.8	43,783	23.7
Colorado Springs, CO Metro Area	100,179	47,495	87,988	40,493	52,570	11,220	41,350	15.5	108,125	20.1
Columbia, MO Metro Area	17,775	9,826	22,230	12,404	7,970	5,743	2,227	9.3	28,057	17.3
Columbia, SC Metro Area	70,964	25,002	86,594	61,592	46,188	13,450	32,738	9.2	120,318	18.6
Columbus, GA-AL Metro Area	12,570	15,057	42,452	27,395	-3,121	7,830	-10,951	4.1	14,937	5.1
Columbus, IN Metro Area	6,996	2,922	9,717	6,795	4,104	3,974	130	9.1	5,351	7.5
Columbus, OH Metro Area	220,263	108,626	251,291	142,665	112,154	58,853	53,301	11.6	226,994	13.6
Corpus Christi, TX Metro Area	23,999	21,115	53,060	31,945	2,943	5,884	-2,941	5.9	24,242	6.4
Corvallis, OR Metro Area	7,472	1,494	6,730	5,236	5,963	4,555	1,408	8.7	7,429	9.5
Crestview-Fort Walton Beach-Destin, FL Metro Area	48,939	10,408	31,828	21,420	38,062	3,974	34,088	20.7	24,769	11.7
Cumberland, MD-WV Metro Area	-5,988	-2,669	8,748	11,417	-3,284	583	-3,867	-5.8	1,237	1.2
Dallas-Fort Worth-Arlington, TX Metro Area	1,206,599	517,590	903,051	385,461	686,884	237,927	448,957	19	1,210,351	23.5
Dallas-Plano-Irving, TX Div	853,089	361,268	605,866	244,598	489,576	177,656	311,920	20.2	783,017	22.7
Fort Worth-Arlington-Grapevine, TX Div	353,510	156,322	297,185	140,863	197,308	60,271	137,037	16.5	427,334	25.0
Dalton, GA Metro Area	2,491	6,549	17,422	10,873	-4,009	625	-4,634	1.8	22,190	18.5
Danville, IL Metro Area	-5,867	484	9,452	8,968	-6,361	214	-6,575	-7.2	-2,294	-2.7
Daphne-Fairhope-Foley, AL Metro Area	40,969	1,650	20,641	18,991	38,880	1,343	37,537	22.5	41,849	29.8
Davenport-Moline-Rock Island, IA-IL Metro Area	-509	8,550	43,301	34,751	-8,953	5,209	-14,162	-0.1	3,669	1.0
Dayton-Kettering, OH Metro Area	8,331	10,890	88,783	77,893	-2,113	13,473	-15,586	1	-6,548	-0.8
Decatur, AL Metro Area	-1,224	915	16,512	15,597	-2,051	998	-3,049	-0.8	7,958	5.5
Decatur, IL Metro Area	-6,768	1,045	12,367	11,322	-7,840	463	-8,303	-6.1	-3,931	-3.4
Deltona-Daytona Beach-Ormond Beach, FL Metro Area	78,077	-21,838	52,064	73,902	99,352	11,264	88,088	13.2	97,124	19.7
Denver-Aurora-Lakewood, CO Metro Area	423,631	162,267	320,151	157,884	257,992	61,997	195,995	16.7	364,362	16.7
Des Moines-West Des Moines, IA Metro Area	92,818	40,673	85,530	44,857	51,899	11,716	40,183	15.3	87,867	16.9
Detroit-Warren-Dearborn, MI Metro Area	23,402	84,753	462,696	377,943	-61,318	110,907	-172,225	0.5	-156,267	-3.5
Detroit-Dearborn-Livonia, MI Div	-71,130	48,443	215,688	167,245	-121,285	38,142	-159,427	-3.9	-240,623	-11.7
Warren-Troy-Farmington Hills, MI Div	94,532	36,310	247,008	210,698	59,967	72,765	-12,798	3.8	84,356	3.5
Dothan, AL Metro Area	3,718	1,157	16,420	15,263	2,667	213	2,454	2.6	14,780	11.3
Dover, DE Metro Area	18,436	6,171	20,448	14,277	12,260	2,127	10,133	11.4	35,652	28.1
Dubuque, IA Metro Area	3,668	2,707	11,009	8,302	1,034	815	219	3.9	4,500	5.0
Duluth, MN-WI Metro Area	-1,904	-1,025	26,864	27,889	-609	1,537	-2,146	-0.7	4,094	1.4
Durham-Chapel Hill, NC Metro Area	80,174	25,573	65,747	40,174	54,198	19,005	35,193	14.2	89,200	18.8
East Stroudsburg, PA Metro Area	430	72	13,202	13,130	344	2,408	-2,064	0.3	31,145	22.5
Eau Claire, WI Metro Area	7,921	4,752	17,465	12,713	3,273	1,041	2,232	4.9	13,048	8.8
El Centro, CA Metro Area	6,691	18,410	27,894	9,484	-11,851	2,063	-13,914	3.8	32,163	22.6
Elizabethtown-Fort Knox, KY Metro Area	5,597	6,204	18,197	11,993	-784	2,157	-2,941	3.8	14,444	10.8
Elkhart-Goshen, IN Metro Area	8,772	13,069	28,381	15,312	-4,216	985	-5,201	4.4	14,768	8.1
Elmira, NY Metro Area	-5,391	94	8,887	8,793	-5,499	356	-5,855	-6.1	-2,221	-2.4
El Paso, TX Metro Area	40,015	74,054	121,572	47,518	-34,305	18,153	-52,458	5	121,163	17.7
Enid, OK Metro Area	476	2,377	8,684	6,307	-1,882	1,641	-3,523	0.8	2,767	4.8
Erie, PA Metro Area	-10,856	2,456	28,804	26,348	-13,316	5,680	-18,996	-3.9	-259	-0.1
Eugene-Springfield, OR Metro Area	30,362	588	32,589	32,001	29,917	5,052	24,865	8.6	28,745	8.9
Evansville, IN-KY Metro Area	3,538	4,334	34,097	29,763	-558	1,942	-2,500	1.1	15,353	5.2
Fairbanks, AK Metro Area	-736	11,008	15,436	4,428	-11,928	2,339	-14,267	-0.8	14,745	17.8
Fargo, ND-MN Metro Area	37,368	16,854	30,570	13,716	20,299	6,674	13,625	17.9	34,410	19.7
Farmington, NM Metro Area	-6,087	6,996	16,172	9,176	-13,162	109	-13,271	-4.7	16,244	14.3
Fayetteville, NC Metro Area	45,708	42,745	77,225	34,480	1,623	14,235	-12,612	9.5	53,370	12.5
Fayetteville-Springdale-Rogers, AR Metro Area	94,783	32,777	64,207	31,430	61,505	10,695	50,810	21.5	114,755	35.3
Flagstaff, AZ Metro Area	9,050	7,792	15,157	7,365	1,238	1,311	-73	6.7	18,111	15.6
Flint, MI Metro Area	-19,974	4,066	45,082	41,016	-24,248	1,840	-26,088	-4.7	-10,352	-2.4
Florence, SC Metro Area	-665	1,762	23,172	21,410	-2,246	819	-3,065	-0.3	12,416	6.4
Florence-Muscle Shoals, AL Metro Area	833	-2,523	14,204	16,727	3,481	767	2,714	0.6	4,187	2.9
Fond du Lac, WI Metro Area	1,780	1,399	10,048	8,649	432	1,265	-833	1.8	4,331	4.5
Fort Collins, CO Metro Area	57,269	11,605	31,320	19,715	45,121	4,487	40,634	19.1	48,121	19.1
Fort Smith, AR-OK Metro Area	2,128	5,187	29,653	24,466	-2,941	1,267	-4,208	0.9	23,216	10.3
Fort Wayne, IN Metro Area	24,637	20,290	51,797	31,507	4,659	5,989	-1,330	6.3	26,069	10.3
Fresno, CA Metro Area	68,594	80,755	142,608	61,853	-11,772	9,639	-21,411	7.4	131,089	7.2
Gadsden, AL Metro Area	-2,161	-1,921	10,979	12,900	-142	273	-415	-2.1	968	0.9
Gainesville, FL Metro Area	24,052	7,889	31,837	23,948	16,211	10,747	5,464	7.9	38,237	14.3
Gainesville, GA Metro Area	24,717	10,762	23,794	13,032	13,974	1,471	12,503	13.8	40,449	29.0

Table B-2. Components of Population Change—*Continued*

Metropolitan Statistical Area Metropolitan Division	Components of population change, April 1 2010 (estimates base) to July 1, 2019 (estimate)								Population change, April 1, 2000 to April 1, 2010	
	Number									
	Total population change	Natural increase			Total migration	Net International migration	Net domestic migration	Percent change	Number	Percent change
		Total	Births	Deaths						
Gettysburg, PA Metro Area	1,581	189	9,396	9,207	1,470	544	926	1.6	10,132	11.1
Glens Falls, NY Metro Area	-3,798	-1,334	10,739	12,073	-2,387	350	-2,737	-2.9	4,596	3.7
Goldsboro, NC Metro Area	470	4,411	15,461	11,050	-3,928	2,638	-6,566	0.4	9,344	8.2
Grand Forks, ND-MN Metro Area	2,351	5,350	13,041	7,691	-3,007	1,946	-4,953	2.4	986	1.0
Grand Island, NE Metro Area	2,809	4,006	10,352	6,346	-1,166	2,408	-3,574	3.9	4,431	6.5
Grand Junction, CO Metro Area	7,477	3,078	16,342	13,264	4,431	-173	4,604	5.1	30,462	26.2
Grand Rapids-Kentwood, MI Metro Area	83,707	55,687	125,556	69,869	28,532	17,629	10,903	8.4	58,231	6.2
Grants Pass, OR Metro Area	4,768	-3,219	7,810	11,029	7,981	-140	8,121	5.8	6,992	9.2
Great Falls, MT Metro Area	40	2,825	10,524	7,699	-2,753	759	-3,512	0	966	1.2
Greeley, CO Metro Area	71,665	22,092	37,587	15,495	49,035	2,484	46,551	28.3	71,921	39.8
Green Bay, WI Metro Area	16,665	13,646	36,179	22,533	3,288	3,355	-67	5.4	23,642	8.4
Greensboro-High Point, NC Metro Area	47,928	17,401	79,920	62,519	31,027	12,830	18,197	6.6	80,455	12.5
Greenville, NC Metro Area	12,566	7,944	19,462	11,518	4,658	1,371	3,287	7.5	34,369	25.7
Greenville-Anderson, SC Metro Area	96,446	21,138	96,861	75,723	75,133	13,917	61,216	11.7	98,355	13.6
Gulfport-Biloxi, MS Metro Area	29,074	10,483	46,703	36,220	18,654	5,595	13,059	7.5	10,965	2.9
Hagerstown-Martinsburg, MD-WV Metro Area	18,958	4,626	29,793	25,167	14,324	1,742	12,582	7	46,372	20.8
Hammond, LA Metro Area	13,649	6,635	17,863	11,228	7,015	508	6,507	11.3	20,519	20.4
Hanford-Corcoran, CA Metro Area	-34	14,271	21,880	7,609	-14,649	695	-15,344	0	23,521	18.2
Harrisburg-Carlisle, PA Metro Area	28,497	11,803	60,274	48,471	17,028	14,620	2,408	5.2	40,394	7.9
Harrisonburg, VA Metro Area	9,743	4,037	13,181	9,144	5,728	4,229	1,499	7.8	17,028	15.7
Hartford-East Hartford-Middletown, CT Metro Area	-7,594	13,025	110,209	97,184	-20,759	47,395	-68,154	-0.6	63,835	5.6
Hattiesburg, MS Metro Area	6,431	6,332	20,737	14,405	32	1,356	-1,324	4	19,199	13.4
Hickory-Lenoir-Morganton, NC Metro Area	3,917	-1,716	34,817	36,533	5,910	2,924	2,986	1.1	23,979	7.0
Hilton Head Island-Bluffton, SC Metro Area	35,185	5,746	21,847	16,101	29,093	3,536	25,557	18.8	45,395	32.1
Hinesville, GA Metro Area	3,065	11,489	15,546	4,057	-8,903	2,563	-11,466	3.9	6,005	8.4
Homosassa Springs, FL Metro Area	8,427	-13,385	9,689	23,074	21,756	331	21,425	6	23,144	19.6
Hot Springs, AR Metro Area	3,387	-2,502	10,186	12,688	5,924	-10	5,934	3.5	7,932	9.0
Houma-Thibodaux, LA Metro Area	-110	8,581	26,337	17,756	-8,622	1,553	-10,175	-0.1	13,707	7.0
Houston-The Woodlands-Sugar Land, TX Metro Area	1,145,654	540,027	889,610	349,583	602,610	333,553	269,057	19.4	1,227,326	26.2
Huntington-Ashland, WV-KY-OH Metro Area	-15,026	-3,285	37,621	40,906	-11,546	359	-11,905	-4.1	3,769	1.0
Huntsville, AL Metro Area	54,231	13,388	47,880	34,492	40,771	4,833	35,938	13	75,217	22.0
Idaho Falls, ID Metro Area	18,199	13,197	22,463	9,266	5,038	222	4,816	13.6	28,753	27.5
Indianapolis-Carmel-Anderson, IN Metro Area	186,462	97,491	246,099	148,608	89,578	43,502	46,076	9.9	229,623	13.8
Iowa City, IA Metro Area	20,519	10,606	19,234	8,628	9,929	7,862	2,067	13.4	20,910	15.9
Ithaca, NY Metro Area	588	1,506	7,735	6,229	-981	6,686	-7,667	0.6	5,079	5.3
Jackson, MI Metro Area	-1,723	1,215	16,506	15,291	-2,843	698	-3,541	-1.1	1,823	1.2
Jackson, MS Metro Area	7,691	21,259	70,872	49,613	-13,741	4,965	-18,706	1.3	40,160	7.3
Jackson, TN Metro Area	-1,067	1,711	20,312	18,601	-2,675	730	-3,405	-0.6	9,648	5.7
Jacksonville, FL Metro Area	213,920	52,866	167,526	114,660	160,572	34,089	126,483	15.9	222,841	19.8
Jacksonville, NC Metro Area	20,137	29,255	38,784	9,529	-10,285	7,624	-17,909	11.3	27,444	18.3
Janesville-Beloit, WI Metro Area	3,029	4,270	17,881	13,611	-1,131	397	-1,528	1.9	8,028	5.3
Jefferson City, MO Metro Area	1,415	4,291	16,332	12,041	-2,813	962	-3,775	0.9	9,745	7.0
Johnson City, TN Metro Area	4,892	-3,314	18,323	21,637	8,285	1,307	6,978	2.5	17,150	9.4
Johnstown, PA Metro Area	-13,503	-4,708	12,304	17,012	-8,837	384	-9,221	-9.4	-8,917	-5.8
Jonesboro, AR Metro Area	12,841	4,763	16,354	11,591	8,072	1,239	6,833	10.6	13,258	12.3
Joplin, MO Metro Area	4,055	5,310	22,013	16,703	-1,152	1,212	-2,364	2.3	18,187	11.6
Kahului-Wailuku-Lahaina, HI Metro Area	12,577	7,138	18,012	10,874	5,518	6,138	-620	8.1	26,746	20.9
Kalamazoo-Portage, MI Metro Area	14,739	9,446	28,774	19,328	5,485	4,483	1,002	5.9	11,724	4.9
Kankakee, IL Metro Area	-3,588	1,946	12,271	10,325	-5,547	530	-6,077	-3.2	9,617	9.3
Kansas City, MO-KS Metro Area	148,635	98,218	253,384	155,166	51,716	27,259	24,457	7.4	198,087	10.9
Kennewick-Richland, WA Metro Area	46,284	23,159	39,288	16,129	23,058	3,571	19,487	18.3	61,510	32.1
Killeen-Temple, TX Metro Area	54,995	43,397	68,686	25,289	11,142	13,598	-2,456	13.6	74,599	22.6
Kingsport-Bristol, TN-VA Metro Area	-2,291	-9,185	26,943	36,128	7,135	-122	7,257	-0.7	11,018	3.7
Kingston, NY Metro Area	-4,946	-1,139	14,405	15,544	-3,751	2,456	-6,207	-2.7	4,763	2.7
Knoxville, TN Metro Area	54,021	1,643	84,244	82,601	52,546	7,094	45,452	6.6	87,421	12.0
Kokomo, IN Metro Area	-204	153	9,085	8,932	-290	341	-631	-0.2	-2,212	-2.6
La Crosse-Onalaska, WI-MN Metro Area	2,958	2,447	13,220	10,773	572	341	231	2.2	6,822	5.4
Lafayette, LA Metro Area	22,474	23,870	62,244	38,374	-1,317	4,234	-5,551	4.8	41,716	9.8
Lafayette-West Lafayette, IN Metro Area	22,692	10,837	24,792	13,955	11,914	15,527	-3,613	10.8	23,345	12.5
Lake Charles, LA Metro Area	10,769	7,932	26,736	18,804	2,976	1,153	1,823	5.4	6,073	3.1
Lake Havasu City-Kingman, AZ Metro Area	11,999	-9,685	16,886	26,571	21,585	-1,496	23,081	6	45,150	29.1
Lakeland-Winter Haven, FL Metro Area	122,704	9,786	69,821	60,035	112,597	23,260	89,337	20.4	118,174	24.4
Lancaster, PA Metro Area	26,281	20,139	65,415	45,276	6,589	11,759	-5,170	5.1	48,788	10.4
Lansing-East Lansing, MI Metro Area	15,707	14,093	54,679	40,586	1,625	19,865	-18,240	2.9	15,269	2.9
Laredo, TX Metro Area	26,348	36,433	48,554	12,121	-10,078	7,043	-17,121	10.5	57,187	29.6
Las Cruces, NM Metro Area	8,978	12,954	27,022	14,068	-4,004	2,240	-6,244	4.3	34,520	19.8
Las Vegas-Henderson-Paradise, NV Metro Area	315,447	105,372	247,787	142,415	208,889	23,319	185,570	16.2	575,506	41.8
Lawrence, KS Metro Area	11,433	4,907	11,149	6,242	6,564	5,122	1,442	10.3	10,864	10.9
Lawton, OK Metro Area	-3,873	7,691	17,852	10,161	-11,769	2,831	-14,600	-3	8,678	7.1
Lebanon, PA Metro Area	8,196	1,613	15,092	13,479	6,716	4,877	1,839	6.1	13,250	11.0
Lewiston, ID-WA Metro Area	2,097	-293	6,567	6,860	2,421	-204	2,625	3.4	2,932	5.1
Lewiston-Auburn, ME Metro Area	568	1,802	11,771	9,969	-1,187	1,143	-2,330	0.5	3,917	3.8
Lexington-Fayette, KY Metro Area	44,953	21,545	57,894	36,349	23,522	11,848	11,674	9.5	63,777	15.6

Table B-2. Components of Population Change—*Continued*

Metropolitan Statistical Area Metropolitan Division	Components of population change, April 1 2010 (estimates base) to July 1, 2019 (estimate)								Population change, April 1, 2000 to April 1, 2010	
	Number									
	Total population change	Natural increase			Total migration	Net International migration	Net domestic migration	Percent change	Number	Percent change
		Total	Births	Deaths						
Lima, OH Metro Area	-3,962	1,560	11,697	10,137	-5,522	175	-5,697	-3.7	-2,158	-2.0
Lincoln, NE Metro Area	34,217	18,243	38,980	20,737	16,106	8,917	7,189	11.3	35,370	13.3
Little Rock-North Little Rock-Conway, AR Metro Area	42,594	28,130	88,569	60,439	14,662	7,696	6,966	6.1	89,278	14.6
Logan, UT-ID Metro Area	16,723	17,562	23,357	5,795	-854	2,240	-3,094	13.3	22,722	22.1
Longview, TX Metro Area	6,650	7,553	34,504	26,951	-805	1,888	-2,693	2.4	23,859	9.3
Longview, WA Metro Area	8,185	1,106	11,376	10,270	7,099	265	6,834	8	9,460	10.2
Los Angeles-Long Beach-Anaheim, CA Metro Area	385,842	753,642	1,500,780	747,138	-362,998	377,442	-740,440	3	463,319	3.7
Anaheim-Santa Ana-Irvine, CA Div	166,703	170,278	348,216	177,938	-1,103	84,009	-85,112	5.5	163,985	5.8
Los Angeles-Long Beach-Glendale, CA Div	219,139	583,364	1,152,564	569,200	-361,895	293,433	-655,328	2.2	299,334	3.1
Louisville/Jefferson County, KY-IN Metro Area	62,422	31,671	141,702	110,031	31,536	20,169	11,367	5.2	112,671	10.3
Lubbock, TX Metro Area	31,368	15,696	38,925	23,229	15,616	3,403	12,213	10.8	34,639	13.5
Lynchburg, VA Metro Area	10,912	1,841	26,279	24,438	9,174	3,531	5,643	4.3	30,342	13.6
Macon-Bibb County, GA Metro Area	-2,249	4,907	27,200	22,293	-7,136	1,769	-8,905		9,919	4.5
Madera, CA Metro Area	6,493	11,128	20,999	9,871	-4,704	-383	-4,321	4.3	27,732	22.5
Madison, WI Metro Area	59,399	28,060	67,559	39,499	31,480	15,600	15,880	9.8	70,028	13.1
Manchester-Nashua, NH Metro Area	16,319	9,873	39,447	29,574	6,672	13,569	-6,897	4.1	19,858	5.2
Manhattan, KS Metro Area	3,191	15,192	21,877	6,685	-12,490	7,782	-20,272	2.5	18,095	16.6
Mankato, MN Metro Area	5,185	3,828	10,317	6,489	1,386	1,510	-124	5.4	11,030	12.9
Mansfield, OH Metro Area	-3,320	-161	12,743	12,904	-3,119	238	-3,367	-2.7	-4,378	-3.4
McAllen-Edinburg-Mission, TX Metro Area	93,943	105,539	143,366	37,827	-11,366	11,748	-23,114	12.1	205,305	36.1
Medford, OR Metro Area	17,740	44	21,343	21,299	17,697	-141	17,838	8.7	21,936	12.1
Memphis, TN-MS-AR Metro Area	29,943	64,370	170,921	106,551	-34,521	13,637	-48,158	2.3	110,897	9.2
Merced, CA Metro Area	21,884	23,063	38,618	15,555	-1,110	463	-1,573	8.6	45,242	21.5
Miami-Fort Lauderdale-Pompano Beach, FL Metro Area	600,214	178,095	626,897	448,802	422,703	615,283	-192,580	10.8	558,730	11.2
Fort Lauderdale-Pompano Beach-Sunrise, FL Div	204,632	64,099	201,689	137,590	141,901	142,381	-480	11.7	125,128	7.7
Miami-Miami Beach-Kendall, FL Div	218,947	110,939	291,240	180,301	107,292	390,173	-282,881	8.8	244,651	10.9
West Palm Beach-Boca Raton-Boynton Beach, FL Div	176,635	3,057	133,968	130,911	173,510	82,729	90,781	13.4	188,951	16.7
Michigan City-La Porte, IN Metro Area	-1,578	1,109	12,075	10,966	-2,616	81	-2,697	-1.4	1,357	1.2
Midland, MI Metro Area	-465	1,232	7,933	6,701	-1,688	1,160	-2,848	-0.6	752	0.9
Midland, TX Metro Area	40,932	15,880	26,136	10,256	24,557	3,307	21,250	28.9	20,916	17.3
Milwaukee-Waukesha, WI Metro Area	19,225	59,009	182,815	123,806	-39,097	25,298	-64,395	1.2	55,213	3.7
Minneapolis-St. Paul-Bloomington, MN Metro Area	306,415	209,124	419,634	210,510	99,485	87,847	11,638	9.2	317,068	10.5
Missoula, MT Metro Area	10,304	3,212	11,126	7,914	7,109	1,271	5,838	9.4	13,494	14.1
Mobile, AL Metro Area	-1,183	11,538	53,087	41,549	-12,486	4,885	-17,371	-0.3	12,786	3.1
Modesto, CA Metro Area	36,210	32,649	70,420	37,771	3,879	4,607	-728	7	67,454	15.1
Monroe, LA Metro Area	-4,226	6,291	26,371	20,080	-10,438	779	-11,217	-2.1	3,410	1.7
Monroe, MI Metro Area	-1,531	841	14,053	13,212	-2,352	285	-2,637		6,079	4.2
Montgomery, AL Metro Area	-1,250	12,067	44,789	32,722	-13,366	4,233	-17,599	-0.3	28,013	8.1
Morgantown, WV Metro Area	9,342	3,498	13,166	9,668	5,765	3,321	2,444	7.2	18,510	16.6
Morristown, TN Metro Area	5,891	-1,020	13,994	15,014	6,971	839	6,132	4.3	13,774	11.2
Mount Vernon-Anacortes, WA Metro Area	12,313	2,574	13,426	10,852	9,769	1,610	8,159	10.5	13,914	13.5
Muncie, IN Metro Area	-3,535	-272	11,071	11,343	-3,241	1,422	-4,663	-3	-1,105	-0.9
Muskegon, MI Metro Area	1,372	3,782	19,514	15,732	-2,385	547	-2,932	0.8	1,994	1.2
Myrtle Beach-Conway-North Myrtle Beach, SC-NC Metro Area	120,326	-3,999	38,280	42,279	122,581	2,288	120,293	32	106,783	39.6
Napa, CA Metro Area	1,209	1,784	13,062	11,278	-469	1,157	-1,626	0.9	12,299	9.9
Naples-Marco Island, FL Metro Area	63,380	109	29,806	29,697	63,056	20,167	42,889	19.7	70,144	27.9
Nashville-Davidson--Murfreesboro--Franklin, TN Metro Area	288,134	88,741	216,969	128,228	197,758	39,422	158,336	17.5	287,194	21.1
New Bern, NC Metro Area	-2,524	3,352	15,570	12,218	-5,909	2,182	-8,091	-2	12,062	10.5
New Haven-Milford, CT Metro Area	-7,685	10,560	81,952	71,392	-18,293	32,843	-51,136	-0.9	38,448	4.7
New Orleans-Metairie, LA Metro Area	80,639	43,608	145,792	102,184	36,032	20,800	15,232	6.8	-147,837	-11.1
New York-Newark-Jersey City, NY-NJ-PA Metro Area	319,905	932,102	2,218,113	1,286,011	-611,662	837,005	-1,448,667	1.7	573,234	3.1
Nassau County-Suffolk County, NY Div	529	64,201	276,903	212,702	-63,021	50,245	-113,266	0	79,119	2.9
Newark, NJ-PA Div	21,558	75,389	225,372	149,983	-54,178	74,051	-128,229	1	47,535	2.5
New Brunswick-Lakewood, NJ Div	39,552	58,237	250,753	192,516	-18,365	60,896	-79,261	1.7	166,408	7.7
New York-Jersey City-White Plains, NY-NJ Div	258,266	734,275	1,465,085	730,810	-476,098	651,813	-1,127,911	2.2	280,172	2.5
Niles, MI Metro Area	-3,407	733	16,572	15,839	-4,107	3,175	-7,282	-2.2	-5,642	-3.5
North Port-Sarasota-Bradenton, FL Metro Area	134,683	-26,920	58,378	85,298	160,197	17,686	142,511	19.2	112,355	19.0
Norwich-New London, CT Metro Area	-8,864	2,357	24,643	22,286	-11,261	6,111	-17,372	-3.2	14,980	5.8
Ocala, FL Metro Area	34,280	-12,786	31,649	44,435	46,967	4,122	42,845	10.3	72,383	28.0
Ocean City, NJ Metro Area	-5,218	-4,081	7,966	12,047	-1,037	1,060	-2,097	-5.4	-5,065	-4.9
Odessa, TX Metro Area	29,087	15,113	26,048	10,935	13,561	2,296	11,265	21.2	16,013	13.2
Ogden-Clearfield, UT Metro Area	86,702	63,341	98,076	34,735	23,625	4,772	18,853	14.5	111,761	23.0
Oklahoma City, OK Metro Area	155,948	65,613	171,439	105,826	89,914	24,684	65,230	12.4	157,569	14.4
Olympia-Lacey-Tumwater, WA Metro Area	38,276	9,076	28,792	19,716	29,233	4,982	24,251	15.2	44,905	21.7
Omaha-Council Bluffs, NE-IA Metro Area	84,095	60,276	122,306	62,030	24,322	16,785	7,537	9.7	98,306	12.8
Orlando-Kissimmee-Sanford, FL Metro Area	473,748	103,875	259,676	155,801	368,588	181,996	186,592	22.2	489,841	29.8

Table B-2. Components of Population Change—Continued

Metropolitan Statistical Area Metropolitan Division	Components of population change, April 1 2010 (estimates base) to July 1, 2019 (estimate) Number								Population change, April 1, 2000 to April 1, 2010	
	Total population change	Natural increase			Total migration	Net International migration	Net domestic migration	Percent change	Number	Percent change
		Total	Births	Deaths						
Oshkosh-Neenah, WI Metro Area	4,907	3,727	17,264	13,537	1,311	1,101	210	2.9	10,233	6.5
Owensboro, KY Metro Area	4,694	2,968	14,338	11,370	1,824	1,091	733	4.1	4,873	4.4
Oxnard-Thousand Oaks-Ventura, CA Metro Area	22,608	41,771	93,266	51,495	-18,720	7,250	-25,970	2.7	70,196	9.3
Palm Bay-Melbourne-Titusville, FL Metro Area	58,570	-15,771	47,809	63,580	74,263	9,438	64,825	10.8	67,142	14.1
Panama City, FL Metro Area	5,855	3,934	20,996	17,062	1,770	3,938	-2,168	3.5	20,635	13.9
Parkersburg-Vienna, WV Metro Area	-3,328	-1,046	9,349	10,395	-2,196	-122	-2,074	-3.6	-1,191	-1.3
Pensacola-Ferry Pass-Brent, FL Metro Area	53,638	10,215	53,258	43,043	43,221	6,040	37,181	11.9	36,838	8.9
Peoria, IL Metro Area	-15,692	7,578	47,244	39,666	-23,246	3,815	-27,061	-3.8	11,102	2.7
Philadelphia-Camden-Wilmington, PA-NJ-DE-MD Metro Area	136,757	155,315	658,315	503,000	-14,959	156,632	-171,591	2.3	278,558	4.9
Camden, NJ Div	-7,565	23,704	126,951	103,247	-31,079	16,105	-47,184	-0.6	64,020	5.4
Montgomery County-Bucks County-Chester County, PA Div	59,945	28,001	186,504	158,503	33,544	37,079	-3,535	3.1	143,038	8.0
Philadelphia, PA Div	66,042	83,883	267,807	183,924	-16,558	92,611	-109,169	3.2	16,354	0.8
Wilmington, DE-MD-NJ Div	18,335	19,727	77,053	57,326	-866	10,837	-11,703	2.6	55,146	8.5
Phoenix-Mesa-Chandler, AZ Metro Area	755,074	247,209	540,924	293,715	505,500	106,785	398,715	18	941,251	28.9
Pine Bluff, AR Metro Area	-12,485	188	10,145	9,957	-12,826	182	-13,008	-12.4	-7,051	-6.6
Pittsburgh, PA Metro Area	-38,694	-35,527	218,159	253,686	-1,150	30,654	-31,804	-1.6	-74,785	-3.1
Pittsfield, MA Metro Area	-6,330	-3,812	9,885	13,697	-2,447	2,422	-4,869	-4.8	-3,678	-2.7
Pocatello, ID Metro Area	4,828	5,945	12,890	6,945	-1,126	1,771	-2,897	5.3	7,558	9.1
Portland-South Portland, ME Metro Area	24,392	762	45,771	45,009	23,980	6,493	17,487	4.7	26,536	5.4
Portland-Vancouver-Hillsboro, OR-WA Metro Area	266,409	96,518	253,110	156,592	169,456	47,983	121,473	12	298,115	15.5
Port St. Lucie, FL Metro Area	65,190	-6,266	39,334	45,600	71,121	8,993	62,128	15.4	104,681	32.8
Poughkeepsie-Newburgh-Middletown, NY Metro Area	8,878	22,759	69,991	47,232	-13,931	7,540	-21,471	1.3	48,774	7.8
Prescott Valley-Prescott, AZ Metro Area	24,082	-9,511	17,021	26,532	33,299	303	32,996	11.4	43,497	26.0
Providence-Warwick, RI-MA Metro Area	23,372	13,788	152,794	139,006	10,512	49,015	-38,503	1.5	18,214	1.2
Provo-Orem, UT Metro Area	121,367	90,108	112,018	21,910	31,402	7,531	23,871	23	150,111	39.8
Pueblo, CO Metro Area	9,361	1,417	17,214	15,797	8,038	458	7,580	5.9	17,591	12.4
Punta Gorda, FL Metro Area	28,943	-13,671	9,494	23,165	42,167	2,281	39,886	18.1	18,337	12.9
Racine, WI Metro Area	883	5,764	21,964	16,200	-4,815	747	-5,562	0.5	6,597	3.5
Raleigh-Cary, NC Metro Area	260,292	78,009	144,250	66,241	180,756	34,019	146,737	23	333,417	41.8
Rapid City, SD Metro Area	15,707	7,137	16,847	9,710	8,515	1,048	7,467	12.4	13,582	12.0
Reading, PA Metro Area	9,594	8,976	44,567	35,591	764	13,606	-12,842	2.3	37,918	10.1
Redding, CA Metro Area	2,859	-1,229	19,093	20,322	4,297	1,965	2,332	1.6	13,965	8.6
Reno, NV Metro Area	50,200	14,812	49,609	34,797	35,266	-307	35,573	11.8	82,554	24.1
Richmond, VA Metro Area	105,429	39,426	135,249	95,823	66,135	27,868	38,267	8.9	146,281	14.1
Riverside-San Bernardino-Ontario, CA Metro Area	425,683	289,072	560,691	271,619	138,230	26,965	111,265	10.1	970,145	29.8
Roanoke, VA Metro Area	4,556	-2,224	30,071	32,295	6,997	5,798	1,199	1.5	20,360	7.1
Rochester, MN Metro Area	15,033	12,126	26,680	14,554	3,014	5,386	-2,372	7.3	22,142	12.0
Rochester, NY Metro Area	-10,060	16,070	105,986	89,916	-25,978	20,870	-46,848	-0.9	17,245	1.6
Rockford, IL Metro Area	-13,315	8,421	38,636	30,215	-21,938	3,511	-25,449	-3.8	29,227	9.1
Rocky Mount, NC Metro Area	-6,598	580	15,786	15,206	-7,205	380	-7,585	-4.3	9,349	6.5
Rome, GA Metro Area	2,184	1,210	10,991	9,781	1,035	1,375	-340	2.3	5,749	6.3
Sacramento-Roseville-Folsom, CA Metro Area	214,580	94,910	252,144	157,234	120,948	51,225	69,723	10	352,294	19.6
Saginaw, MI Metro Area	-9,630	1,529	20,833	19,304	-11,236	1,809	-13,045	-4.8	-9,870	-4.7
St. Cloud, MN Metro Area	12,871	11,239	23,588	12,349	1,686	5,396	-3,710	6.8	21,701	13.0
St. George, UT Metro Area	39,441	9,223	20,632	11,409	29,998	100	29,898	28.6	47,761	52.9
St. Joseph, MO-KS Metro Area	-2,096	1,972	14,117	12,145	-4,042	1,720	-5,762	-1.6	4,991	4.1
St. Louis, MO-IL Metro Area	15,477	68,389	310,273	241,884	-52,131	32,872	-85,003	0.6	112,409	4.2
Salem, OR Metro Area	43,165	17,354	48,852	31,498	26,003	2,479	23,524	11	43,536	12.5
Salinas, CA Metro Area	19,002	35,696	58,879	23,183	-16,579	3,403	-19,982	4.6	13,299	3.3
Salisbury, MD-DE Metro Area	41,972	-505	38,714	39,219	42,177	4,614	37,563	11.2	61,188	19.6
Salt Lake City, UT Metro Area	144,888	109,213	171,087	61,874	36,389	31,265	5,124	13.3	148,686	15.8
San Angelo, TX Metro Area	9,059	4,943	14,767	9,824	4,081	492	3,589	8	5,794	5.4
San Antonio-New Braunfels, TX Metro Area	408,440	146,693	300,032	153,339	259,857	45,348	214,509	19.1	430,818	25.2
San Diego-Chula Vista-Carlsbad, CA Metro Area	242,981	204,933	398,611	193,678	40,821	107,098	-66,277	7.8	281,516	10.0
San Francisco-Oakland-Berkeley, CA Metro Area	396,210	202,172	477,380	275,208	194,735	231,599	-36,864	9.1	211,847	5.1
Oakland-Berkeley-Livermore, CA Div	265,393	131,117	291,168	160,051	134,876	130,281	4,595	10.4	166,905	7.0
San Francisco-San Mateo-Redwood City, CA Div	124,421	67,587	164,991	97,404	56,780	95,790	-39,010	8.2	39,808	2.7
San Rafael, CA Div	6,396	3,468	21,221	17,753	3,079	5,528	-2,449	2.5	5,134	2.1
San Jose-Sunnyvale-Santa Clara, CA Metro Area	153,709	126,304	220,891	94,587	28,415	152,520	-124,105	5	22,916	9.3
San Luis Obispo-Paso Robles, CA Metro Area	13,514	2,358	24,056	21,698	11,234	925	10,309	4.1	6,754	2.6
Santa Cruz-Watsonville, CA Metro Area	10,863	10,582	26,748	16,166	384	1,760	-1,376	4.2	14,935	11.6
Santa Fe, NM Metro Area	6,126	1,686	12,092	10,406	4,578	2,090	2,488	5.3	24,600	6.2
Santa Maria-Santa Barbara, CA Metro Area	22,552	23,723	52,100	28,377	-925	9,058	-9,983	2.2	25,254	5.5
Santa Rosa-Petaluma, CA Metro Area	10,475	8,237	45,881	37,644	2,497	3,206	-709	13.2	54,598	18.6
Savannah, GA Metro Area	45,756	19,377	47,201	27,824	26,251	6,261	19,990	-1.7	2,992	0.5
Scranton--Wilkes-Barre, PA Metro Area	-9,719	-12,308	52,222	64,530	3,012	14,117	-11,105	15.7	395,927	13.0
Seattle-Tacoma-Bellevue, WA Metro Area	540,037	201,727	426,466	224,739	338,123	198,637	139,486	16.3	301,530	12.9
Seattle-Bellevue-Kent, WA Div	430,279	155,468	321,252	165,784	274,525	183,553	90,972	13.8	94,397	13.5
Tacoma-Lakewood, WA Div	109,758	46,259	105,214	58,955	63,598	15,084	48,514	15.9	25,081	22.2
Sebastian-Vero Beach, FL Metro Area	21,895	-6,260	11,703	17,963	27,992	2,343	25,649	7.5	11,420	13.1
Sebring-Avon Park, FL Metro Area	7,437	-5,745	8,302	14,047	13,232	3,261	9,971			

Table B-2. Components of Population Change—*Continued*

Metropolitan Statistical Area Metropolitan Division	Components of population change, April 1 2010 (estimates base) to July 1, 2019 (estimate)								Population change, April 1, 2000 to April 1, 2010	
	Number									
	Total population change	Natural increase			Total migration	Net International migration	Net domestic migration	Percent change	Number	Percent change
		Total	Births	Deaths						
Sheboygan, WI Metro Area	-172	1,572	11,653	10,081	-1,697	754	-2,451	-0.1	2,864	2.5
Sherman-Denison, TX Metro Area	15,335	1,360	14,334	12,974	14,009	1,313	12,696	12.7	10,280	9.3
Shreveport-Bossier City, LA Metro Area	-3,900	14,744	52,173	37,429	-18,770	2,461	-21,231		22,639	6.0
Sierra Vista-Douglas, AZ Metro Area	-5,437	2,604	14,452	11,848	-8,272	2,499	-10,771	-4.1	13,602	11.6
Sioux City, IA-NE-SD Metro Area	1,119	7,700	19,546	11,846	-6,632	2,085	-8,717	0.8	526	0.4
Sioux Falls, SD Metro Area	39,968	19,508	35,744	16,236	20,333	6,431	13,902	17.5	41,169	22.0
South Bend-Mishawaka, IN-MI Metro Area	4,410	8,202	36,905	28,703	-3,668	5,192	-8,860	1.4	2,550	0.8
Spartanburg, SC Metro Area	35,481	6,361	33,877	27,516	29,139	1,679	27,460	12.5	30,526	12.0
Spokane-Spokane Valley, WA Metro Area	53,769	14,182	59,155	44,973	39,814	6,035	33,779	10.4	56,747	12.4
Springfield, IL Metro Area	-3,302	3,309	22,393	19,084	-6,530	2,178	-8,708	-1.6	8,733	4.3
Springfield, MA Metro Area	4,323	4,448	63,385	58,937	-85	30,334	-30,419	0.6	13,044	1.9
Springfield, MO Metro Area	33,544	13,234	52,176	38,942	20,399	2,408	17,991	7.7	68,335	18.6
Springfield, OH Metro Area	-4,256	-1,117	14,729	15,846	-3,061	459	-3,520	-3.1	-6,401	-4.4
State College, PA Metro Area	8,380	2,310	11,320	9,010	6,069	9,416	-3,347	5.4	18,243	13.4
Staunton, VA Metro Area	4,624	-682	11,545	12,227	5,343	1,059	4,284	3.9	9,508	8.7
Stockton, CA Metro Area	76,842	44,384	93,390	49,006	32,797	10,082	22,715	11.2	121,708	21.6
Sumter, SC Metro Area	-1,968	3,100	16,598	13,498	-5,029	1,120	-6,149	-1.4	5,293	3.9
Syracuse, NY Metro Area	-14,031	11,737	66,531	54,794	-25,820	13,114	-38,934	-2.1	12,466	1.9
Tallahassee, FL Metro Area	18,456	12,475	37,381	24,906	5,788	6,407	-619	5	48,466	15.1
Tampa-St. Petersburg-Clearwater, FL Metro Area	411,346	12,252	294,083	281,831	397,215	104,814	292,401	14.8	387,465	16.2
Terre Haute, IN Metro Area	-3,407	978	20,086	19,108	-4,333	1,587	-5,920	-1.8	1,587	0.8
Texarkana, TX-AR Metro Area	-433	2,625	17,822	15,197	-2,981	158	-3,139	-0.3	5,817	4.1
The Villages, FL Metro Area	39,000	-10,573	4,311	14,884	48,895	-134	49,029	41.7	40,075	75.1
Toledo, OH Metro Area	-9,619	12,412	71,848	59,436	-22,094	5,646	-27,740	-1.5	-7,753	-1.2
Topeka, KS Metro Area	-1,891	4,737	26,664	21,927	-6,550	1,618	-8,168	-0.8	9,316	4.1
Trenton-Princeton, NJ Metro Area	-55	11,634	38,444	26,810	-11,831	16,366	-28,197	0	16,750	4.8
Tucson, AZ Metro Area	67,016	21,542	107,047	85,505	46,336	22,079	24,257	6.8	136,517	16.2
Tulsa, OK Metro Area	61,103	35,371	121,193	85,822	26,210	14,415	11,795	6.5	78,000	9.1
Tuscaloosa, AL Metro Area	12,833	6,871	27,624	20,753	5,911	2,721	3,190	5.4	26,236	12.3
Twin Falls, ID Metro Area	11,694	6,569	14,844	8,275	5,159	2,539	2,620	11.7	16,970	20.5
Tyler, TX Metro Area	23,026	9,252	28,191	18,939	13,822	2,131	11,691	11	35,019	20.0
Urban Honolulu, HI Metro Area	21,357	50,711	121,272	70,561	-28,785	46,111	-74,896	2.2	77,050	8.8
Utica-Rome, NY Metro Area	-9,339	31	29,641	29,610	-9,340	5,250	-14,590	-3.1	-566	-0.2
Valdosta, GA Metro Area	7,630	7,791	18,666	10,875	-341	2,056	-2,397	5.5	20,100	16.8
Vallejo, CA Metro Area	34,300	18,081	47,682	29,601	16,528	6,691	9,837	8.3	18,756	4.8
Victoria, TX Metro Area	5,739	4,340	12,404	8,064	1,389	546	843	6.1	2,987	3.3
Vineland-Bridgeton, NJ Metro Area	-7,100	4,541	18,338	13,797	-11,725	3,190	-14,915	-4.5	10,195	7.0
Virginia Beach-Norfolk-Newport News, VA-NC Metro Area	54,946	78,552	209,617	131,065	-23,410	36,319	-59,729	3.2	101,184	6.3
Visalia, CA Metro Area	24,013	41,985	69,462	27,477	-17,932	-636	-17,296	5.4	74,160	20.2
Waco, TX Metro Area	21,154	12,895	33,987	21,092	8,384	2,630	5,754	8.4	20,673	8.9
Walla Walla, WA Metro Area	1,979	842	6,100	5,258	1,163	136	1,027	3.4	3,601	6.5
Warner Robins, GA Metro Area	17,783	8,835	21,567	12,732	8,970	2,828	6,142	10.6	33,169	24.7
Washington-Arlington-Alexandria, DC-VA-MD-WV Metro Area	630,799	428,108	743,898	315,790	200,650	326,958	-126,308	11.2	799,724	16.5
Frederick-Gaithersburg-Rockville, MD Div	105,548	75,081	145,718	70,637	30,709	78,342	-47,633	8.8	136,737	12.8
Washington-Arlington-Alexandria, DC-VA-MD-WV Div	525,251	353,027	598,180	245,153	169,941	248,616	-78,675	11.8	662,987	17.5
Waterloo-Cedar Falls, IA Metro Area	703	5,008	19,377	14,369	-4,194	2,815	-7,009	0.4	4,113	2.5
Watertown-Fort Drum, NY Metro Area	-6,398	10,875	19,170	8,295	-17,420	3,033	-20,453	-5.5	4,496	4.0
Wausau-Weston, WI Metro Area	481	3,423	17,162	13,739	-2,856	612	-3,468	0.3	7,329	4.7
Weirton-Steubenville, WV-OH Metro Area	-8,381	-5,260	10,356	15,616	-3,005	-176	-2,829	-6.7	-7,558	-5.7
Wenatchee, WA Metro Area	9,742	4,326	13,383	9,057	5,489	666	4,823	8.8	11,668	11.8
Wheeling, WV-OH Metro Area	-9,009	-4,101	13,249	17,350	-4,802	-57	-4,745	-6.1	-5,212	-3.4
Wichita, KS Metro Area	17,157	29,769	81,503	51,734	-12,358	9,096	-21,454	2.8	51,897	9.1
Wichita Falls, TX Metro Area	-220	2,932	17,382	14,450	-3,110	3,283	-6,393	-0.1	-50	0.0
Williamsport, PA Metro Area	-2,803	-325	11,394	11,719	-2,439	602	-3,041	-2.4	-3,930	-3.3
Wilmington, NC Metro Area	42,654	4,489	26,461	21,972	37,745	1,521	36,224	16.7	53,492	26.6
Winchester, VA-WV Metro Area	12,114	3,266	14,270	11,004	8,878	1,826	7,052	9.4	25,478	24.7
Winston-Salem, NC Metro Area	35,505	10,063	68,473	58,410	25,813	4,664	21,149	5.5	71,330	12.5
Worcester, MA-CT Metro Area	30,641	16,269	90,296	74,027	14,793	36,326	-21,533	3.3	56,710	6.6
Yakima, WA Metro Area	7,633	19,134	37,137	18,003	-11,510	-269	-11,241	3.1	20,659	9.3
York-Hanover, PA Metro Area	14,043	8,584	45,524	36,940	5,907	5,255	652	3.2	53,257	14.0
Youngstown-Warren-Boardman, OH-PA Metro Area	-29,701	-12,813	51,745	64,558	-16,642	2,675	-19,317	-5.2	-37,183	-6.2
Yuba City, CA Metro Area	8,741	10,299	23,119	12,820	-1,566	2,723	-4,289	5.2	27,753	19.9
Yuma, AZ Metro Area	18,037	14,964	28,472	13,508	2,839	7,552	-4,713	9.2	35,724	22.3

Table B-3. Population by Age, Race, and Hispanic Origin

	Population characteristics, 2018																
	Age (percent)										Race alone, not of Hispanic origin					Two or more races, not of Hispanic origin (percent)	Hispanic or Latino origin (percent)
Metropolitan Statistical Area Metropolitan Division	Under 5 years	5 to 14 years	15 to 24 years	25 to 34 years	35 to 44 years	45 to 54 years	55 to 64 years	65 to 74 years	75 to 84 years	85 years and over	White alone	Black or African-American alone	American Indian, Alaska native alone	Asian alone	Native Hawaiian, other Pacific Islander alone		
Abilene, TX Metro Area	6.9	13.1	16.8	14.7	11.8	10.3	11.4	8.2	4.8	2.0	64.3	7.4	0.4	1.9	0.1	1.9	23.9
Akron, OH Metro Area	5.4	11.3	14.0	12.9	11.4	13.0	14.4	10.3	5.1	2.3	79.5	12.4	0.2	3.4	0.0	2.3	2.2
Albany, GA Metro Area	6.2	13.4	15.6	13.0	11.7	11.9	12.5	9.4	4.4	1.7	40.2	54.3	0.2	1.2	0.1	1.2	2.8
Albany-Lebanon, OR Metro Area	6.1	12.5	11.7	13.5	11.9	11.8	13.8	11.1	5.5	2.0	84.7	0.6	1.2	1.1	0.2	2.9	9.3
Albany-Schenectady-Troy, NY Metro Area	5.2	10.9	14.5	13.1	11.9	13.2	14.0	10.1	4.9	2.4	79.5	8.1	0.2	4.5	0.1	2.3	5.4
Albuquerque, NM Metro Area	5.6	12.6	12.7	14.2	12.7	12.1	13.2	10.2	4.7	1.9	38.9	2.3	5.4	2.2	0.1	1.7	49.4
Alexandria, LA Metro Area	6.7	13.5	12.6	13.6	12.4	12.1	12.8	9.4	5.0	1.9	63.4	29.3	0.8	1.2	0.0	1.7	3.5
Allentown-Bethlehem-Easton, PA-NJ Metro Area	5.3	11.9	13.0	12.4	11.8	13.4	14.1	10.1	5.3	2.7	72.3	5.2	0.1	3.0	0.0	1.6	17.7
Altoona, PA Metro Area	5.3	11.6	11.2	12.3	11.4	12.8	14.6	11.5	6.3	3.0	94.6	1.9	0.1	0.7	0.0	1.4	1.3
Amarillo, TX Metro Area	7.0	14.4	13.5	14.7	13.1	11.5	11.7	8.2	4.2	1.6	59.0	6.1	0.5	3.5	0.0	1.6	29.2
Ames, IA Metro Area	4.7	9.7	29.1	12.9	10.4	9.2	10.5	7.6	3.9	1.9	85.6	2.4	0.2	6.8	0.0	1.5	3.4
Anchorage, AK Metro Area	7.2	13.9	13.4	16.5	13.2	12.1	12.4	7.5	2.8	1.0	63.1	4.3	7.6	7.7	2.0	7.1	8.2
Ann Arbor, MI Metro Area	4.9	10.4	22.1	14.5	11.4	11.6	11.3	8.4	3.8	1.6	70.0	12.0	0.3	9.6	0.0	3.2	4.8
Anniston-Oxford, AL Metro Area	5.8	12.0	12.9	13.2	11.9	12.5	14.0	10.6	5.3	1.8	72.0	20.9	0.4	0.9	0.1	1.8	3.9
Appleton, WI Metro Area	6.1	13.3	12.5	12.9	13.0	13.5	13.9	8.7	4.3	1.8	88.0	1.2	1.3	3.4	0.0	1.5	4.4
Asheville, NC Metro Area	4.9	10.3	10.5	12.6	12.3	12.8	14.3	12.9	6.6	2.7	85.1	4.4	0.4	1.2	0.1	1.7	7.1
Athens-Clarke County, GA Metro Area	5.4	11.4	22.0	14.3	11.9	11.1	10.8	8.0	3.8	1.4	65.6	20.1	0.2	3.6	0.0	1.7	8.7
Atlanta-Sandy Springs-Alpharetta, GA Metro Area	6.3	13.8	13.4	14.3	13.8	14.2	11.9	7.7	3.4	1.2	46.6	34.1	0.2	6.2	0.0	1.9	19.2
Atlantic City-Hammonton, NJ Metro Area	5.4	12.0	12.8	12.0	11.1	13.7	15.0	10.3	5.4	2.2	55.9	14.6	0.2	8.1	0.0	1.9	19.2
Auburn-Opelika, AL Metro Area	5.9	12.0	21.5	14.2	12.0	11.8	10.8	7.4	3.4	1.1	67.5	22.8	0.3	4.1	0.1	1.5	3.8
Augusta-Richmond County, GA-SC Metro Area	6.2	12.9	13.0	14.3	12.2	12.3	13.1	9.7	4.6	1.6	54.4	35.3	0.3	2.0	0.1	2.2	5.6
Austin-Round Rock-Georgetown, TX Metro Area	6.4	12.9	13.4	17.4	15.6	12.8	10.6	7.0	2.9	1.1	51.8	7.1	0.3	6.2	0.1	1.9	32.7
Bakersfield, CA Metro Area	7.8	16.5	14.7	15.6	12.8	11.2	10.5	6.6	3.2	1.2	33.5	5.2	0.6	4.7	0.1	1.9	54.0
Baltimore-Columbia-Towson, MD Metro Area	6.0	12.2	12.4	14.5	12.7	13.2	13.5	9.1	4.4	2.0	56.2	29.2	0.2	5.9	0.1	2.4	6.1
Bangor, ME Metro Area	4.7	10.1	13.5	13.2	11.4	13.2	15.2	10.9	5.4	2.4	93.7	0.9	1.2	1.1	0.0	1.7	1.4
Barnstable Town, MA Metro Area	3.7	8.4	9.9	8.9	8.7	12.1	17.6	17.4	9.2	4.0	89.8	3.1	0.6	1.5	0.0	1.8	3.2
Baton Rouge, LA Metro Area	6.5	13.0	14.8	14.3	12.8	12.1	12.3	8.7	4.0	1.5	56.7	35.6	0.3	2.1	0.0	1.2	4.1
Battle Creek, MI Metro Area	6.2	12.7	13.0	12.3	11.7	12.5	13.8	10.2	5.3	2.3	77.3	10.8	0.6	2.9	0.0	3.1	5.3
Bay City, MI Metro Area	5.0	11.5	11.4	12.3	11.4	12.7	15.3	11.6	6.1	2.7	89.9	1.7	0.5	0.6	0.0	1.9	5.4
Beaumont-Port Arthur, TX Metro Area	6.9	13.5	12.8	14.1	12.7	12.1	12.9	8.7	4.5	1.9	55.1	23.9	0.4	2.8	0.0	1.3	16.4
Beckley, WV Metro Area	5.3	12.0	10.7	11.8	12.6	12.5	14.3	12.4	6.0	2.4	89.2	6.6	0.2	0.7	0.0	1.7	1.5
Bellingham, WA Metro Area	5.3	10.9	17.0	13.8	11.9	11.3	12.4	10.7	4.7	1.9	78.7	1.1	2.6	4.5	0.3	3.4	9.5
Bend, OR Metro Area	5.1	11.5	10.4	13.0	13.2	12.7	14.1	12.7	5.4	1.9	87.1	0.5	0.7	1.2	0.1	2.3	8.1
Billings, MT Metro Area	6.0	13.2	11.6	13.3	12.4	11.8	14.0	10.4	5.1	2.3	86.9	0.6	3.7	0.7	0.1	2.5	5.5
Binghamton, NY Metro Area	5.2	10.9	16.3	11.2	10.5	11.8	14.7	10.4	6.0	3.0	85.4	4.5	0.2	3.6	0.0	2.3	3.9
Birmingham-Hoover, AL Metro Area	6.2	12.9	12.3	13.8	12.8	12.9	13.2	9.5	4.6	1.9	61.9	30.4	0.3	1.6	0.0	1.2	4.6
Bismarck, ND Metro Area	6.9	12.8	12.0	14.7	12.9	11.3	13.1	9.1	4.6	2.6	88.9	2.0	3.7	0.7	0.1	1.7	2.9
Blacksburg-Christiansburg, VA Metro Area	4.4	8.9	25.3	13.3	10.1	11.5	11.4	8.9	4.6	1.8	86.1	4.6	0.2	4.2	0.0	2.1	2.8
Bloomington, IL Metro Area	5.8	11.9	21.2	13.0	12.0	11.3	11.5	7.7	3.7	1.8	79.3	7.9	0.2	5.3	0.0	2.2	5.1
Bloomington, IN Metro Area	4.5	8.9	26.9	13.9	10.7	10.1	11.1	8.2	4.0	1.7	85.0	3.1	0.2	6.2	0.0	2.2	3.2
Bloomsburg-Berwick, PA Metro Area	4.8	10.3	16.6	11.4	10.6	12.2	14.3	11.0	6.0	2.9	92.6	1.7	0.1	1.6	0.0	1.0	2.9
Boise City, ID Metro Area	6.3	14.4	13.2	13.8	13.5	12.3	11.8	9.0	4.1	1.5	80.0	1.0	0.6	2.1	0.2	2.3	13.8
Boston-Cambridge-Newton, MA-NH Metro Area	5.3	10.9	13.7	15.2	12.5	13.4	13.3	9.0	4.5	2.2	70.1	7.9	0.1	8.4	0.0	1.8	11.5
Boston, MA Div	5.3	10.6	14.1	16.6	12.4	13.0	12.8	8.7	4.4	2.1	64.6	13.3	0.2	8.1	0.1	1.9	12.0
Cambridge-Newton-Framingham, MA Div	5.4	11.2	13.3	14.5	12.7	13.5	13.4	9.0	4.5	2.3	70.9	4.6	0.1	9.8	0.0	1.8	12.7
Rockingham County-Strafford County, NH Div	4.7	10.8	13.6	12.3	11.4	14.5	15.6	10.4	4.7	2.0	91.8	0.9	0.2	2.6	0.0	1.5	3.0
Boulder, CO Metro Area	4.4	11.0	18.4	14.0	12.5	12.7	12.6	8.8	3.8	1.6	77.6	1.0	0.4	4.8	0.1	2.3	13.9
Bowling Green, KY Metro Area	6.3	12.6	17.7	13.2	12.2	11.8	11.8	8.6	4.2	1.6	82.2	7.3	0.2	3.4	0.2	1.9	4.7
Bremerton-Silverdale-Port Orchard, WA Metro Area	5.8	11.3	13.0	14.7	11.9	11.7	13.8	11.1	4.9	1.9	76.3	2.8	1.4	5.2	0.9	5.4	8.0
Bridgeport-Stamford-Norwalk, CT Metro Area	5.5	12.8	13.3	11.4	12.4	14.4	14.0	8.7	4.7	2.5	61.5	11.0	0.1	5.7	0.0	1.5	20.2
Brownsville-Harlingen, TX Metro Area	8.1	16.8	16.0	12.4	12.2	11.2	9.7	7.6	4.2	1.7	8.8	0.4	0.1	0.7	0.0	0.2	89.8
Brunswick, GA Metro Area	5.5	12.0	11.8	11.9	11.2	12.9	14.3	12.3	6.1	2.0	67.8	23.5	0.3	1.2	0.1	1.6	5.5
Buffalo-Cheektowaga, NY Metro Area	5.4	11.1	12.7	14.0	11.2	12.8	14.7	10.2	5.3	2.6	77.1	12.0	0.6	3.2	0.0	1.9	5.2
Burlington, NC Metro Area	5.8	12.5	14.3	12.5	11.5	13.5	13.1	9.5	5.2	2.2	63.4	19.9	0.4	1.6	0.0	1.7	12.9
Burlington-South Burlington, VT Metro Area	4.9	10.4	17.5	13.7	11.8	12.5	13.8	9.2	4.3	2.0	89.5	2.0	0.4	3.7	0.0	2.1	2.2
California-Lexington Park, MD Metro Area	6.4	13.7	13.3	14.1	12.4	14.0	13.0	7.8	3.9	1.4	73.9	14.3	0.3	2.9	0.1	3.2	5.3
Canton-Massillon, OH Metro Area	5.6	11.9	12.3	11.8	11.3	12.9	14.6	11.1	5.9	2.6	87.0	7.3	0.2	0.9	0.0	2.4	2.1
Cape Coral-Fort Myers, FL Metro Area	4.6	9.9	10.0	11.0	10.3	11.7	14.1	15.5	9.6	3.5	66.8	8.1	0.2	1.7	0.0	1.3	21.9
Cape Girardeau, MO-IL Metro Area	5.7	12.1	16.2	12.4	11.2	11.6	13.2	9.9	5.4	2.3	85.7	8.2	0.3	1.5	0.0	2.0	2.2
Carbondale-Marion, IL Metro Area	5.6	11.0	16.6	13.2	11.6	11.4	12.7	10.2	5.4	2.2	82.8	9.0	0.3	2.2	0.0	2.1	3.5
Carson City, NV Metro Area	5.7	11.3	11.2	13.2	11.1	12.6	14.6	11.9	6.2	2.3	66.7	1.9	2.0	2.3	0.2	2.3	24.5
Casper, WY Metro Area	6.6	13.6	11.6	14.6	13.2	11.2	13.7	9.3	4.1	2.0	86.6	1.2	1.0	0.7	0.1	1.9	8.6
Cedar Rapids, IA Metro Area	6.2	12.9	12.7	13.2	12.8	12.6	13.1	9.3	4.9	2.2	87.1	5.0	0.2	2.2	0.1	2.2	3.1
Chambersburg-Waynesboro, PA Metro Area	6.0	12.3	11.4	12.0	11.6	13.3	13.6	10.8	6.1	2.7	87.7	3.4	0.2	1.1	0.1	1.7	5.9
Champaign-Urbana, IL Metro Area	5.5	10.3	25.1	14.1	10.9	10.9	7.7	3.7	1.8		69.0	12.2	0.2	10.2	0.1	2.6	5.8
Charleston, WV Metro Area	5.3	11.6	11.0	11.7	12.1	12.9	15.0	12.0	6.1	2.3	90.6	5.4	0.2	0.8	0.0	2.0	1.0
Charleston-North Charleston, SC Metro Area	6.1	12.2	12.2	15.7	13.2	12.6	12.8	9.6	4.2	1.5	64.4	25.5	0.4	2.0	0.1	2.0	5.7
Charlotte-Concord-Gastonia, NC-SC Metro Area	6.2	13.4	12.6	14.2	13.7	14.2	12.1	8.3	3.9	1.4	60.5	22.8	0.4	4.0	0.0	1.9	10.4
Charlottesville, VA Metro Area	5.3	10.6	15.4	14.1	11.9	11.9	13.0	10.5	5.2	2.1	75.3	11.9	0.2	4.7	0.1	2.4	5.5
Chattanooga, TN-GA Metro Area	5.7	11.8	12.0	13.6	12.3	13.0	13.6	10.4	5.3	2.2	78.1	13.5	0.3	1.7	0.1	1.6	4.7

Table B-3. Population by Age, Race, and Hispanic Origin—*Continued*

| | Population characteristics, 2018 | | | | | | | | | | | | | | | | |
| | Age (percent) | | | | | | | | | | Race alone, not of Hispanic origin | | | | | Two or more races, not of Hispanic origin (percent) | Hispanic or Latino origin (percent) |
Metropolitan Statistical Area / Metropolitan Division	Under 5 years	5 to 14 years	15 to 24 years	25 to 34 years	35 to 44 years	45 to 54 years	55 to 64 years	65 to 74 years	75 to 84 years	85 years and over	White alone	Black or African-American alone	American Indian, Alaska native alone	Asian alone	Native Hawaiian, other Pacific Islander alone		
Cheyenne, WY Metro Area	6.3	13.2	12.6	14.9	12.3	11.6	13.0	9.6	4.5	1.9	78.5	2.4	0.6	1.2	0.1	2.3	14.8
Chicago-Naperville-Elgin, IL-IN-WI Metro Area	6.0	12.7	13.0	14.4	13.3	13.1	12.8	8.5	4.2	1.9	52.6	16.3	0.1	7.0	0.0	1.5	22.4
Chicago-Naperville-Evanston, IL Div	6.0	12.4	12.6	15.2	13.4	13.0	12.7	8.4	4.2	1.9	49.2	18.5	0.1	7.9	0.0	1.5	22.7
Elgin, IL Div	6.3	14.5	14.9	12.2	13.6	13.6	12.0	7.8	3.7	1.5	61.4	6.0	0.1	3.8	0.0	1.5	27.3
Gary, IN Div	5.8	13.0	13.0	12.2	12.7	12.7	14.0	9.7	4.8	2.1	63.5	17.1	0.2	1.5	0.0	1.4	16.3
Lake County-Kenosha County, IL-WI Div	5.7	13.6	14.7	11.5	12.5	14.0	13.7	8.4	4.0	1.8	63.8	6.8	0.2	6.8	0.0	1.8	20.5
Chico, CA Metro Area	5.5	11.1	17.6	13.1	10.9	10.5	12.7	11.0	5.2	2.4	71.6	1.5	1.5	4.8	0.2	3.7	16.7
Cincinnati, OH-KY-IN Metro Area	6.2	13.2	13.3	13.5	12.3	12.9	13.5	9.0	4.4	1.8	79.3	12.4	0.2	2.8	0.1	2.0	3.3
Clarksville, TN-KY Metro Area	8.3	14.2	15.8	17.7	12.3	10.6	9.9	6.6	3.3	1.1	65.9	18.8	0.5	1.9	0.3	3.6	9.1
Cleveland, TN Metro Area	5.7	11.9	13.2	12.5	12.2	13.7	13.2	10.2	5.6		86.9	4.3	0.3	1.0	0.1	1.7	5.8
Cleveland-Elyria, OH Metro Area	5.6	11.7	12.3	13.0	11.6	12.9	14.5	10.4	5.5	2.6	69.6	19.8	0.2	2.5	0.0	1.9	6.0
Coeur d'Alene, ID Metro Area	6.0	12.9	11.4	12.9	12.0	12.1	13.7	11.5	5.5	1.9	90.4	0.4	1.1	0.9	0.1	2.2	4.8
College Station-Bryan, TX Metro Area	6.2	11.4	26.5	15.4	11.2	9.5	9.2	6.2	3.1	1.3	56.0	11.1	0.3	5.6	0.1	1.5	25.4
Colorado Springs, CO Metro Area	6.7	13.3	14.7	15.8	12.6	11.8	12.1	8.2	3.6	1.3	69.5	5.9	0.6	2.9	0.3	3.7	17.1
Columbia, MO Metro Area	5.8	11.4	21.3	14.9	11.8	10.5	11.2	7.8	3.6	1.7	79.7	9.1	0.4	4.6	0.1	2.8	3.3
Columbia, SC Metro Area	5.7	12.5	15.4	13.9	12.4	12.6	12.6	9.1	4.2	1.5	56.2	33.6	0.3	2.3	0.1	1.9	5.7
Columbus, GA-AL Metro Area	6.7	13.3	13.6	15.6	12.3	12.0	12.3	8.5	4.1	1.6	45.9	41.6	0.4	2.1	0.2	2.4	7.5
Columbus, IN Metro Area	6.6	13.3	12.0	14.5	12.4	12.6	12.4	9.4	5.0	2.0	81.4	2.1	0.2	7.8	0.0	1.5	6.9
Columbus, OH Metro Area	6.6	13.0	13.0	15.8	13.4	12.8	12.1	8.0	3.8	1.5	72.4	15.9	0.2	4.6	0.0	2.5	4.3
Corpus Christi, TX Metro Area	6.8	13.8	14.1	14.2	12.8	11.7	12.1	8.6	4.2	1.7	30.4	3.2	0.3	1.9	0.1	1.0	63.3
Corvallis, OR Metro Area	4.1	9.1	25.9	13.2	10.2	9.8	11.6	10.0	4.3	1.9	79.9	1.1	0.5	7.0	0.2	3.6	7.6
Crestview-Fort Walton Beach-Destin, FL Metro Area	6.4	12.0	11.4	15.0	12.2	11.8	14.0	10.3	5.1	1.8	76.0	8.4	0.6	2.6	0.1	3.4	8.8
Cumberland, MD-WV Metro Area	4.7	10.1	14.4	12.5	11.3	12.9	13.4	11.5	6.7	2.5	88.7	6.6	0.2	1.0	0.0	1.8	1.6
Dallas-Fort Worth-Arlington, TX Metro Area	6.9	14.6	13.5	14.9	14.1	13.3	11.3	6.9	3.1	1.2	45.4	15.9	0.4	7.2	0.1	1.8	29.2
Dallas-Plano-Irving, TX Div	6.9	14.6	13.5	15.1	14.4	13.4	11.1	6.8	3.0	1.1	42.9	16.6	0.3	8.4	0.1	1.7	30.0
Fort Worth-Arlington-Grapevine, TX Div	6.9	14.8	13.6	14.6	13.5	13.0	11.7	7.2	3.3	1.2	50.6	14.5	0.4	4.9	0.2	1.9	27.5
Dalton, GA Metro Area	6.5	14.5	13.5	13.2	12.5	13.7	11.8	8.4	4.4	1.5	64.4	2.8	0.2	1.1	0.0	1.1	30.3
Danville, IL Metro Area	6.4	13.2	11.7	12.0	11.5	11.9	14.0	10.8	6.1	2.5	77.9	13.5	0.2	0.9	0.0	2.2	5.2
Daphne-Fairhope-Foley, AL Metro Area	5.5	12.3	11.0	11.3	11.9	13.2	14.4	12.3	6.2	2.0	83.1	8.8	0.7	1.1	0.1	1.6	4.6
Davenport-Moline-Rock Island, IA-IL Metro Area	6.2	12.9	12.1	12.5	12.4	12.2	13.7	10.3	5.4	2.5	78.4	7.6	0.2	2.4	0.0	2.4	8.9
Dayton-Kettering, OH Metro Area	6.0	12.1	13.3	13.4	11.5	12.3	13.6	10.1	5.4	2.4	76.2	15.7	0.2	2.4	0.0	2.6	2.9
Decatur, AL Metro Area	5.9	12.7	11.8	12.2	11.9	13.9	13.9	10.4	5.6	1.8	75.6	12.3	1.8	0.6	0.1	2.6	7.1
Decatur, IL Metro Area	6.1	12.3	12.4	11.9	11.5	11.6	14.2	11.0	6.0	3.0	76.2	17.3	0.2	1.1	0.0	2.8	2.3
Deltona-Daytona Beach-Ormond Beach, FL Metro Area	4.6	9.8	10.9	11.3	10.3	12.2	15.4	14.4	8.0	3.1	71.8	10.3	0.3	2.0	0.0	1.7	13.9
Denver-Aurora-Lakewood, CO Metro Area	6.0	12.7	11.8	16.9	14.7	13.0	12.0	8.1	3.5	1.4	63.9	5.5	0.5	4.4	0.1	2.4	23.2
Des Moines-West Des Moines, IA Metro Area	7.0	14.1	12.5	14.6	13.8	12.5	11.9	8.0	3.8	1.8	81.0	5.3	0.2	4.3	0.1	1.9	7.2
Detroit-Warren-Dearborn, MI Metro Area	5.9	12.2	12.3	13.5	11.9	13.7	14.1	9.6	4.7	2.1	66.2	22.1	0.3	4.7	0.0	2.2	4.6
Detroit-Dearborn-Livonia, MI Div	6.5	13.0	12.7	14.2	11.7	13.0	13.3	9.0	4.3	2.1	49.5	38.3	0.3	3.5	0.0	2.3	6.1
Warren-Troy-Farmington Hills, MI Div	5.4	11.7	12.0	12.9	12.1	14.2	14.6	10.0	4.9	2.2	77.6	11.1	0.3	5.5	0.0	2.0	3.5
Dothan, AL Metro Area	5.9	12.6	11.6	12.5	12.1	13.0	13.5	11.0	5.7	2.0	69.7	23.7	0.5	0.8	0.1	1.8	3.5
Dover, DE Metro Area	6.3	12.8	13.8	13.6	11.6	12.1	12.8	10.0	5.3	1.8	60.9	25.5	0.6	2.3	0.1	3.3	7.4
Dubuque, IA Metro Area	6.3	12.6	14.0	12.7	11.1	11.8	13.6	9.7	5.6	2.7	90.6	3.4	0.2	1.3	0.4	1.5	2.5
Duluth, MN-WI Metro Area	5.1	11.1	14.4	11.7	11.5	11.7	15.2	11.1	5.5	2.6	90.8	1.1	2.5	1.0	0.0	2.4	1.7
Durham-Chapel Hill, NC Metro Area	5.6	11.4	14.4	14.8	12.8	12.9	12.7	9.4	4.2	1.7	55.0	26.5	0.3	4.8	0.0	2.0	11.3
East Stroudsburg, PA Metro Area	4.5	11.1	14.7	11.3	10.7	14.5	16.0	10.5	5.0	1.7	65.1	13.5	0.2	2.5	0.1	2.0	16.6
Eau Claire, WI Metro Area	5.7	11.8	16.2	13.2	11.9	11.7	13.0	9.8	4.7	2.1	91.1	1.4	0.5	3.2	0.0	1.5	2.3
El Centro, CA Metro Area	8.2	15.7	14.7	14.8	12.2	11.1	10.4	7.2	4.0	1.8	10.4	2.5	0.8	1.2	0.1	0.6	84.6
Elizabethtown-Fort Knox, KY Metro Area	6.3	13.6	13.0	13.4	13.0	13.1	13.3	8.5	4.2	1.6	79.6	9.7	0.4	1.8	0.2	3.0	5.3
Elkhart-Goshen, IN Metro Area	7.5	15.4	13.5	12.8	12.1	12.2	11.8	8.4	4.4	2.0	74.6	5.7	0.2	1.1	0.0	2.1	16.3
Elmira, NY Metro Area	5.6	12.0	12.0	12.4	11.7	12.7	14.7	10.6	5.6	2.7	86.2	6.0	0.3	1.5	0.0	2.9	3.2
El Paso, TX Metro Area	7.5	15.0	15.8	15.1	12.5	11.4	10.4	7.0	3.7	1.6	11.7	3.0	0.3	1.1	0.1	0.8	82.9
Enid, OK Metro Area	7.4	14.6	12.5	14.1	12.2	10.4	12.5	8.8	5.2	2.4	74.2	2.9	2.3	1.2	2.8	3.6	12.9
Erie, PA Metro Area	5.6	11.9	13.5	13.1	11.3	12.4	14.2	10.3	5.1	2.6	84.2	7.3	0.2	1.8	0.0	2.1	4.4
Eugene-Springfield, OR Metro Area	4.9	10.3	15.8	13.1	12.1	11.2	13.3	11.7	5.4	2.2	81.5	1.1	1.1	3.1	0.2	3.9	9.1
Evansville, IN-KY Metro Area	5.9	12.6	12.5	13.1	12.1	12.3	14.2	10.0	5.0	2.3	86.7	7.1	0.2	1.4	0.1	2.1	2.5
Fairbanks, AK Metro Area	7.6	13.1	16.6	18.7	12.5	10.2	11.0	7.2	2.4	0.7	69.3	4.9	7.4	3.4	0.5	6.2	8.4
Fargo, ND-MN Metro Area	7.2	12.6	17.6	16.5	13.0	10.3	10.5	7.0	3.4	1.9	84.9	5.6	1.3	3.0	0.0	1.9	3.2
Farmington, NM Metro Area	6.7	15.2	12.9	13.8	12.5	11.0	13.0	8.7	4.4	1.8	38.0	0.6	38.3	0.5	0.0	2.0	20.5
Fayetteville, NC Metro Area	7.6	13.9	15.2	16.8	12.6	11.3	10.8	7.1	3.5	1.2	47.0	32.6	2.0	2.2	0.3	3.6	12.3
Fayetteville-Springdale-Rogers, AR Metro Area	6.9	14.3	15.2	14.8	13.7	11.8	10.6	7.6	3.8	1.5	72.5	2.5	1.3	3.2	1.5	2.4	16.6
Flagstaff, AZ Metro Area	5.5	11.7	23.5	14.2	11.0	10.1	11.5	8.0	3.4	1.1	54.0	1.3	26.0	1.9	0.1	2.5	14.3
Flint, MI Metro Area	5.9	12.6	12.6	12.3	11.6	13.2	14.3	10.1	5.2	2.2	72.5	20.0	0.5	1.0	0.0	2.5	3.5
Florence, SC Metro Area	5.9	13.2	12.7	12.4	11.9	12.9	13.4	10.7	5.1	1.8	52.6	42.2	0.3	1.2	0.1	1.2	2.5
Florence-Muscle Shoals, AL Metro Area	5.3	11.2	13.5	12.2	11.0	12.8	13.9	11.4	6.4	2.3	82.3	12.2	0.4	0.7	0.0	1.6	2.8
Fond du Lac, WI Metro Area	5.3	12.3	12.2	11.9	12.1	13.0	14.7	10.5	5.4	2.6	89.3	1.9	0.4	1.9	0.0	1.2	5.3
Fort Collins, CO Metro Area	5.1	11.2	17.5	14.7	12.4	11.0	12.5	9.6	4.3	1.8	82.5	1.0	0.4	2.3	0.1	2.1	11.7
Fort Smith, AR-OK Metro Area	6.4	13.3	12.6	12.9	12.0	12.8	13.1	9.8	5.2	1.9	73.3	4.1	5.1	2.9	0.1	4.1	10.4
Fort Wayne, IN Metro Area	6.9	14.2	13.2	13.7	12.3	12.2	12.6	8.8	4.1	1.9	75.3	10.6	0.3	4.0	0.0	2.6	7.2
Fresno, CA Metro Area	7.8	16.1	14.3	15.3	12.6	11.1	10.4	7.2	3.5	1.6	29.0	4.6	0.6	10.2	0.1	1.9	53.5
Gadsden, AL Metro Area	5.8	11.8	12.1	12.1	12.0	13.5	13.7	11.3	5.7	1.9	77.7	15.5	0.4	0.8	0.0	1.6	4.0

Table B-3. Population by Age, Race, and Hispanic Origin—*Continued*

Metropolitan Statistical Area / Metropolitan Division	Under 5 years	5 to 14 years	15 to 24 years	25 to 34 years	35 to 44 years	45 to 54 years	55 to 64 years	65 to 74 years	75 to 84 years	85 years and over	White alone	Black or African-American alone	American Indian, Alaska native alone	Asian alone	Native Hawaiian, other Pacific Islander alone	Two or more races, not of Hispanic origin (percent)	Hispanic or Latino origin (percent)
Gainesville, FL Metro Area	5.2	10.2	21.4	14.8	10.8	10.2	11.7	9.4	4.5	1.8	64.5	17.8	0.3	5.2	0.1	2.4	9.8
Gainesville, GA Metro Area	6.6	14.2	13.6	13.0	12.5	13.5	11.8	8.8	4.5	1.6	60.3	7.3	0.2	2.0	0.0	1.3	29.0
Gettysburg, PA Metro Area	5.0	11.4	12.9	10.9	10.5	13.8	15.1	11.7	6.0	2.6	89.0	1.6	0.2	0.8	0.0	1.3	7.1
Glens Falls, NY Metro Area	4.6	10.5	10.9	12.1	11.2	14.0	15.8	12.1	6.2	2.6	92.9	2.1	0.2	0.7	0.0	1.3	2.8
Goldsboro, NC Metro Area	6.6	13.1	13.7	13.5	11.2	12.2	13.1	9.7	5.0	1.8	53.1	31.0	0.3	1.2	0.1	2.0	12.3
Grand Forks, ND-MN Metro Area	7.0	12.0	19.7	15.0	10.6	9.6	11.9	8.0	4.1	2.2	84.0	4.0	2.2	2.4	0.0	2.3	5.1
Grand Island, NE Metro Area	7.5	14.8	12.4	12.7	12.2	11.8	12.7	8.9	4.7	2.4	70.9	2.6	0.4	1.1	0.1	1.1	23.9
Grand Junction, CO Metro Area	5.7	12.3	12.8	13.1	12.1	11.0	14.0	11.1	5.6	2.4	81.1	0.7	0.7	0.9	0.1	1.7	14.8
Grand Rapids-Kentwood, MI Metro Area	6.5	13.4	14.4	14.5	12.4	12.1	12.5	8.4	4.1	1.8	78.2	6.7	0.3	2.8	0.0	2.1	9.7
Grants Pass, OR Metro Area	5.2	11.0	9.9	10.8	10.3	11.3	15.5	15.1	7.8	3.0	86.7	0.5	1.2	0.9	0.2	2.8	7.6
Great Falls, MT Metro Area	6.7	12.4	12.6	14.4	11.1	10.8	13.5	10.4	5.7	2.4	85.0	1.5	4.4	0.9	0.1	3.5	4.6
Greeley, CO Metro Area	7.3	14.8	13.2	15.3	13.7	12.1	11.5	7.7	3.3	1.2	65.4	1.2	0.5	1.6	0.1	1.6	29.6
Green Bay, WI Metro Area	6.2	13.1	12.7	12.9	12.4	13.0	13.9	9.4	4.6	1.9	83.2	2.3	2.3	2.8	0.0	1.8	7.6
Greensboro-High Point, NC Metro Area	5.8	12.4	13.8	13.1	11.9	13.6	13.1	9.6	4.8	1.9	57.9	27.1	0.4	4.0	0.1	1.9	8.6
Greenville, NC Metro Area	5.7	12.1	21.0	14.0	11.7	11.1	11.2	8.0	3.7	1.5	54.3	35.0	0.3	2.1	0.1	1.9	6.3
Greenville-Anderson, SC Metro Area	6.0	12.6	13.6	13.2	12.1	13.0	12.9	9.8	5.0	1.8	72.6	16.5	0.2	2.0	0.0	1.7	7.0
Gulfport-Biloxi, MS Metro Area	6.1	13.1	12.9	13.5	12.3	12.7	13.5	9.6	4.7	1.5	67.8	21.6	0.4	2.3	0.1	2.1	5.7
Hagerstown-Martinsburg, MD-WV Metro Area	5.8	12.5	11.7	13.3	12.5	14.1	13.5	9.8	4.8	1.9	81.6	9.2	0.2	1.4	0.0	2.7	4.8
Hammond, LA Metro Area	7.2	13.5	13.6	14.9	12.3	11.6	12.5	9.0	4.0	1.4	63.1	30.1	0.3	0.7	0.0	1.3	4.4
Hanford-Corcoran, CA Metro Area	7.5	15.4	15.1	17.0	13.8	11.5	9.5	5.9	3.1	1.2	31.8	6.1	0.9	3.9	0.2	2.2	55.0
Harrisburg-Carlisle, PA Metro Area	5.8	12.0	12.3	13.4	12.0	12.9	13.8	10.3	5.1	2.4	76.3	10.2	0.2	4.4	0.0	2.3	6.6
Harrisonburg, VA Metro Area	5.6	11.0	21.5	12.8	11.3	11.1	11.5	8.4	4.7	2.1	79.0	4.2	0.2	2.2	0.1	1.7	12.6
Hartford-East Hartford-Middletown, CT Metro Area	5.0	11.2	14.0	12.7	11.9	13.5	14.2	9.7	5.1	2.6	66.7	10.9	0.2	5.2	0.0	1.8	15.2
Hattiesburg, MS Metro Area	6.5	13.5	14.8	14.4	12.7	11.8	11.9	8.4	4.4	1.6	65.0	29.7	0.2	1.1	0.1	1.2	2.7
Hickory-Lenoir-Morganton, NC Metro Area	5.2	11.6	12.0	11.7	11.5	14.4	14.4	11.2	5.9	2.0	80.6	6.9	0.2	3.0	0.1	1.7	7.6
Hilton Head Island-Bluffton, SC Metro Area	5.2	10.5	12.0	11.4	10.1	10.7	13.8	15.8	8.0	2.4	64.8	20.7	0.2	1.2	0.1	1.6	11.4
Hinesville, GA Metro Area	9.7	14.4	16.4	18.7	11.7	9.9	9.8	6.0	2.6	0.7	42.8	38.3	0.5	1.8	0.5	3.8	12.4
Homosassa Springs, FL Metro Area	3.8	8.4	7.9	8.6	7.7	11.0	16.3	19.5	12.6	4.2	87.7	2.9	0.3	1.6	0.0	1.5	5.9
Hot Springs, AR Metro Area	5.4	11.2	10.7	11.4	11.0	12.0	14.5	13.4	7.6	2.8	81.8	8.5	0.6	0.9	0.1	2.3	5.9
Houma-Thibodaux, LA Metro Area	6.7	13.6	12.3	14.1	12.5	12.7	13.2	8.7	4.5	1.7	71.4	16.3	4.4	1.0	0.0	2.1	4.7
Houston-The Woodlands-Sugar Land, TX Metro Area	7.3	14.9	13.4	15.0	14.3	12.8	11.2	7.0	3.0	1.1	35.6	17.0	0.2	8.0	0.1	1.5	37.6
Huntington-Ashland, WV-KY-OH Metro Area	5.5	11.9	12.6	11.7	12.2	13.1	13.7	11.2	6.0	2.1	93.9	2.3	0.2	0.7	0.0	1.5	1.3
Huntsville, AL Metro Area	5.8	12.3	12.8	12.5	13.7	13.9	13.9	8.8	4.7	1.6	67.0	22.2	0.7	2.4	0.1	2.4	5.3
Idaho Falls, ID Metro Area	8.4	17.9	13.5	13.3	13.0	10.1	10.8	7.8	3.8	1.5	83.6	0.5	0.6	1.0	0.1	1.6	12.6
Indianapolis-Carmel-Anderson, IN Metro Area	6.6	13.9	12.8	14.4	13.3	12.9	12.4	8.2	3.9	1.6	72.0	15.4	0.2	3.4	0.0	2.1	6.9
Iowa City, IA Metro Area	6.0	11.3	22.7	14.9	11.9	10.3	10.3	7.6	3.4	1.7	79.6	6.3	0.2	6.0	0.0	2.9	5.9
Ithaca, NY Metro Area	3.8	8.1	29.2	12.8	10.4	10.1	11.2	8.9	3.8	1.8	77.0	4.0	0.3	10.5	0.0	2.6	5.3
Jackson, MI Metro Area	5.6	12.0	12.5	12.7	11.6	13.2	14.5	10.4	5.2	2.2	84.6	7.9	0.3	0.9	0.0	0.9	3.6
Jackson, MS Metro Area	6.2	13.6	13.8	14.0	12.9	12.3	12.7	8.8	4.1	1.7	45.2	50.0	0.1	1.2	0.0	1.6	2.6
Jackson, TN Metro Area	6.1	12.9	13.7	12.3	11.7	12.5	13.4	10.1	5.2	2.2	65.9	27.4	0.2	0.7	0.0		4.1
Jacksonville, FL Metro Area	6.2	12.6	11.9	14.6	12.7	13.0	13.3	9.7	4.4	1.7	62.7	21.3	0.3	4.1	0.1	2.4	9.2
Jacksonville, NC Metro Area	8.8	12.7	24.4	18.5	10.4	7.9	8.0	5.5	2.8	1.0	65.9	14.8	0.6	2.0	0.2	3.7	12.8
Janesville-Beloit, WI Metro Area	6.1	12.9	12.7	12.3	12.2	13.2	14.0	9.5	5.0	2.1	82.5	4.9	0.3	1.3	0.0	2.1	8.9
Jefferson City, MO Metro Area	5.9	12.5	12.9	13.3	12.7	12.9	13.4	9.7	4.8	2.0	86.2	7.9	0.4	0.9	0.1	1.8	2.7
Johnson City, TN Metro Area	4.8	10.6	13.4	12.3	11.4	13.5	13.9	11.4	6.2	2.2	90.5	3.2	0.3	1.1	0.0	1.6	3.3
Johnstown, PA Metro Area	5.0	10.7	12.6	10.4	10.7	12.6	15.4	12.5	6.6	3.4	92.7	3.4	0.1	0.5	0.1	1.5	1.7
Jonesboro, AR Metro Area	7.0	13.8	14.1	14.9	12.5	11.8	11.3	8.4	4.5	1.7	77.5	14.6	0.3	1.0	0.0	1.6	4.8
Joplin, MO Metro Area	6.6	13.7	13.0	13.3	12.1	12.0	12.7	9.4	5.1	2.0	84.4	1.7	1.7	1.3	0.0	3.0	7.4
Kahului-Wailuku-Lahaina, HI Metro Area	5.9	12.3	10.3	12.7	13.4	13.0	14.2	11.3	4.7	2.3	30.1	0.7	0.3	28.0	10.0	19.5	11.5
Kalamazoo-Portage, MI Metro Area	6.0	12.0	19.1	13.6	11.6	11.0	11.7	8.7	4.3	2.0	77.2	11.4	0.4	2.7	0.0	3.2	5.0
Kankakee, IL Metro Area	5.9	12.6	15.2	12.2	11.7	12.4	13.2	9.5	4.9	2.4	71.9	14.6	0.2	1.0	0.0	1.7	10.6
Kansas City, MO-KS Metro Area	6.5	13.6	12.1	14.3	13.2	12.6	12.9	8.7	4.2	1.9	72.4	12.3	0.4	3.0	0.2	2.5	9.2
Kennewick-Richland, WA Metro Area	7.7	16.2	13.3	14.2	13.0	11.2	11.2	8.0	3.7	1.4	60.3	1.7	0.6	2.8	0.2	2.3	32.2
Killeen-Temple, TX Metro Area	8.0	14.6	15.3	16.8	13.3	10.9	9.9	6.7	3.2	1.2	48.3	20.3	0.5	2.7	0.7	3.5	23.9
Kingsport-Bristol, TN-VA Metro Area	4.8	10.9	10.9	11.4	11.3	14.0	14.7	12.5	7.1	2.4	93.9	2.0	0.3	0.6	0.0	1.3	1.8
Kingston, NY Metro Area	4.4	10.0	12.4	12.6	11.6	13.8	15.5	11.6	5.6	2.6	78.9	6.1	0.2	2.0	0.0	2.2	10.5
Knoxville, TN Metro Area	5.4	11.5	13.5	12.7	11.9	13.1	13.6	10.7	5.5	2.1	86.4	5.9	0.3	1.6	0.1	1.8	4.0
Kokomo, IN Metro Area	6.0	12.7	11.9	12.0	11.3	12.6	14.0	11.0	6.1	2.4	85.0	7.5	0.3	1.2	0.0	2.5	3.5
La Crosse-Onalaska, WI-MN Metro Area	5.2	11.5	18.2	12.4	11.2	11.3	13.3	9.7	4.9	2.5	90.5	1.4	0.4	4.1	0.0	1.7	1.9
Lafayette, LA Metro Area	6.9	13.7	12.6	14.8	12.7	12.1	13.1	8.4	4.1	1.6	67.4	25.0	0.3	1.7	0.0	1.4	4.1
Lafayette-West Lafayette, IN Metro Area	5.9	11.7	24.5	13.7	10.7	10.3	10.4	7.5	3.8	1.7	78.4	4.6	0.2	7.1	0.0	1.8	7.8
Lake Charles, LA Metro Area	7.1	13.7	12.7	14.7	12.3	11.7	12.9	8.8	4.5	1.6	67.9	24.7	0.5	1.3	0.0	1.8	3.8
Lake Havasu City-Kingman, AZ Metro Area	4.4	9.7	9.2	10.2	9.0	10.9	16.3	17.2	10.2	2.9	76.9	1.1	2.1	1.1	0.2	1.8	16.8
Lakeland-Winter Haven, FL Metro Area	5.8	12.5	12.2	13.1	11.9	12.0	12.3	11.3	6.6	2.3	57.9	14.6	0.3	1.9	0.1	1.6	23.6
Lancaster, PA Metro Area	6.5	13.1	12.9	13.2	11.4	11.9	13.1	9.7	5.4	2.8	81.6	3.6	0.1	2.4	0.0	1.5	10.8
Lansing-East Lansing, MI Metro Area	5.6	11.4	17.8	13.4	11.5	11.9	12.9	9.4	4.4	1.8	78.0	7.8	0.4	4.6	0.0	2.8	6.3
Laredo, TX Metro Area	9.4	18.1	16.7	13.5	12.6	11.5	8.7	5.6	2.7	1.1	3.6	0.3	0.0	0.5	0.0	0.1	95.5
Las Cruces, NM Metro Area	6.4	13.9	18.6	13.0	11.0	10.2	11.1	9.1	4.9	1.9	26.9	1.6	0.8	1.1	0.1	1.0	68.6
Las Vegas-Henderson-Paradise, NV Metro Area	6.3	13.1	12.1	14.9	13.8	13.3	11.8	9.1	4.3	1.3	42.2	11.7	0.5	9.9	0.7	3.7	31.4
Lawrence, KS Metro Area	5.0	10.1	26.4	14.6	11.8	9.6	10.2	7.5	3.3	1.6	78.3	4.4	2.2	4.9	0.0	3.7	6.4

Table B-3. Population by Age, Race, and Hispanic Origin—*Continued*

Metropolitan Statistical Area Metropolitan Division	Under 5 years	5 to 14 years	15 to 24 years	25 to 34 years	35 to 44 years	45 to 54 years	55 to 64 years	65 to 74 years	75 to 84 years	85 years and over	White alone	Black or African-American alone	American Indian, Alaska native alone	Asian alone	Native Hawaiian, other Pacific Islander alone	Two or more races, not of Hispanic origin (percent)	Hispanic or Latino origin (percent)
Lawton, OK Metro Area	6.8	13.1	15.9	16.3	12.3	11.0	11.8	7.4	4.0	1.6	56.8	15.7	5.7	2.4	0.6	5.7	13.1
Lebanon, PA Metro Area	5.9	13.0	12.4	11.7	11.7	12.4	13.5	10.6	5.9	2.9	81.5	2.0	0.1	1.4	0.0	1.1	13.8
Lewiston, ID-WA Metro Area	5.6	11.7	11.4	12.7	11.3	11.7	14.3	11.6	6.7	2.9	88.0	0.5	4.0	0.9	0.1	2.4	4.1
Lewiston-Auburn, ME Metro Area	5.8	12.3	11.9	12.4	11.8	13.6	14.4	10.4	5.1	2.3	90.4	4.2	0.4	0.8	0.0	2.2	2.0
Lexington-Fayette, KY Metro Area	6.1	12.2	15.6	14.3	13.0	12.4	12.2	8.5	4.0	1.6	77.2	11.1	0.2	3.0	0.0	2.2	6.3
Lima, OH Metro Area	6.2	12.9	13.7	12.3	11.7	11.9	13.7	10.0	5.1	2.5	80.7	12.4	0.2	0.8	0.0	2.8	3.2
Lincoln, NE Metro Area	6.3	12.9	18.5	13.7	12.5	10.7	11.3	8.4	3.8	1.8	81.5	3.8	0.6	4.6	0.1	2.5	7.0
Little Rock-North Little Rock-Conway, AR Metro Area	6.4	13.1	13.3	14.2	12.9	12.3	12.5	9.2	4.4	1.7	66.8	23.7	0.4	1.7	0.0	1.9	5.4
Logan, UT-ID Metro Area	8.4	17.1	23.0	13.6	11.9	8.3	7.9	5.7	3.1	1.1	84.1	0.8	0.5	2.2	0.3	1.6	10.5
Longview, TX Metro Area	6.5	14.1	12.9	13.0	12.2	11.9	13.0	9.5	4.9	2.0	63.0	18.0	0.5	0.9	0.0	1.6	16.1
Longview, WA Metro Area	6.2	12.7	11.5	12.3	11.8	12.2	14.2	11.3	5.5	2.1	83.4	0.9	1.4	1.5	0.4	3.2	9.2
Los Angeles-Long Beach-Anaheim, CA Metro Area	6.0	12.1	13.1	15.8	13.5	13.5	12.2	7.9	4.1	1.9	29.5	6.4	0.2	16.2	0.2	2.3	45.2
Anaheim-Santa Ana-Irvine, CA Div.	5.9	12.2	13.0	14.5	12.9	14.0	12.7	8.4	4.4	2.0	40.1	1.6	0.2	20.9	0.2	2.7	34.2
Los Angeles-Long Beach-Glendale, CA Div.	6.0	12.0	13.2	16.2	13.7	13.3	12.0	7.8	4.0	1.9	26.1	8.0	0.2	14.7	0.2	2.1	48.6
Louisville/Jefferson County, KY-IN Metro Area	6.1	12.5	12.2	13.9	12.8	13.0	13.6	9.4	4.5	1.9	75.4	15.0	0.2	2.2	0.0	2.1	5.1
Lubbock, TX Metro Area	6.7	13.3	20.3	14.6	11.9	10.1	10.5	7.2	3.9	1.6	52.7	6.9	0.4	2.2	0.1	1.3	36.5
Lynchburg, VA Metro Area	5.3	10.9	16.5	12.3	10.1	12.3	13.8	10.7	5.8	2.3	75.9	17.2	0.4	1.6	0.0	1.9	3.0
Macon-Bibb County, GA Metro Area	6.2	13.2	13.4	13.0	11.6	12.6	13.4	9.9	4.9	1.8	48.7	44.9	0.2	1.7	0.0	1.4	3.1
Madera, CA Metro Area	7.6	15.5	13.9	14.0	12.6	11.5	11.0	8.4	4.0	1.5	33.7	3.3	1.1	2.0	0.1	1.5	58.3
Madison, WI Metro Area	5.6	11.6	15.8	15.0	13.1	12.1	12.4	8.8	3.9	1.8	81.9	4.5	0.3	5.3	0.0	2.1	5.8
Manchester-Nashua, NH Metro Area	5.2	11.4	12.4	13.7	12.2	14.4	14.9	9.3	4.4	2.0	84.1	2.5	0.2	4.4	0.0	1.8	7.0
Manhattan, KS Metro Area	7.6	11.9	26.4	17.5	11.0	7.4	8.0	5.9	2.8	1.5	73.9	8.0	0.6	3.7	0.4	3.5	9.9
Mankato, MN Metro Area	5.6	11.5	21.8	13.3	11.6	10.1	11.4	8.2	4.3	2.2	87.7	3.9	0.3	2.1	0.0	1.8	4.1
Mansfield, OH Metro Area	5.6	12.2	12.0	12.6	11.8	12.3	13.9	10.7	6.1	2.7	85.5	9.4	0.2	0.8	0.0	2.1	2.0
McAllen-Edinburg-Mission, TX Metro Area	8.9	18.2	16.4	13.5	12.6	11.0	8.3	6.2	3.5	1.4	6.0	0.4	0.1	0.9	0.0	0.2	92.4
Medford, OR Metro Area	5.6	11.7	10.9	12.7	11.8	11.5	14.0	13.0	6.3	2.6	80.4	0.8	0.9	1.4	0.3	2.9	13.2
Memphis, TN-MS-AR Metro Area	6.7	13.9	13.3	14.2	12.6	12.8	12.6	8.6	3.9	1.5	43.2	47.4	0.2	2.2	0.0	1.4	5.7
Merced, CA Metro Area	7.7	16.7	16.2	14.7	12.3	11.2	10.1	6.6	3.3	1.4	27.1	3.0	0.4	7.2	0.2	1.8	60.2
Miami-Fort Lauderdale-Pompano Beach, FL Metro Area	5.6	11.2	11.5	13.5	13.1	14.0	13.0	9.6	5.8	2.8	30.0	20.3	0.1	2.5	0.0	1.1	45.8
Fort Lauderdale-Pompano Beach-Sunrise, FL Div	5.8	11.8	11.5	13.5	13.4	14.1	13.4	9.3	5.0	2.4	35.6	28.3	0.2	3.7	0.1	1.6	30.4
Miami-Miami Beach-Kendall, FL Div	5.8	11.1	11.8	14.3	13.7	14.7	12.5	8.7	5.2	2.3	13.0	15.6	0.1	1.5	0.0	0.7	69.1
West Palm Beach-Boca Raton-Boynton Beach, FL Div.	5.1	10.6	10.9	12.0	11.5	12.8	13.3	11.6	8.1	4.3	54.1	18.6	0.2	2.8	0.0	1.4	22.9
Michigan City-La Porte, IN Metro Area	6.0	11.9	11.8	13.3	12.1	13.1	14.0	10.7	5.1	2.0	79.0	11.2	0.3	0.6	0.0	2.1	6.8
Midland, MI Metro Area	5.4	11.8	12.3	12.4	11.8	13.4	14.5	10.0	5.7	2.6	91.5	1.3	0.5	2.4	0.1	1.5	2.8
Midland, TX Metro Area	8.8	15.7	12.8	17.9	13.4	10.3	10.6	5.8	3.0	1.5	45.0	5.9	0.4	2.0	0.1	1.2	45.4
Milwaukee-Waukesha, WI Metro Area	6.2	12.9	12.8	14.0	12.6	12.5	13.4	9.0	4.4	2.2	66.3	16.4	0.4	4.0	0.0	1.9	10.9
Minneapolis-St. Paul-Bloomington, MN Metro Area	6.5	13.2	12.4	14.6	13.4	12.9	13.0	8.3	3.9	1.8	75.2	8.7	0.6	6.9	0.0	2.6	6.0
Missoula, MT Metro Area	5.1	10.6	17.1	15.6	12.9	10.9	12.2	9.8	4.3	1.6	89.2	0.4	2.4	1.8	0.1	2.8	3.3
Mobile, AL Metro Area	6.5	12.9	12.9	13.9	11.9	12.3	13.3	9.7	4.8	1.8	57.0	35.3	1.1	2.0	0.0	1.5	3.0
Modesto, CA Metro Area	7.2	15.3	13.9	14.5	12.7	11.9	11.3	7.7	3.8	1.6	41.1	2.7	0.5	5.4	0.7	2.6	47.0
Monroe, LA Metro Area	6.8	13.5	13.3	13.7	12.1	11.9	12.9	9.3	4.7	1.9	58.1	37.2	0.3	0.9	0.0	1.1	2.4
Monroe, MI Metro Area	5.3	12.0	12.0	11.7	11.6	13.8	15.5	10.6	5.3	2.2	91.2	2.5	0.3	0.7	0.0	1.7	3.7
Montgomery, AL Metro Area	6.4	12.8	13.1	14.1	12.7	12.8	12.8	9.0	4.6	1.7	47.9	44.9	0.3	2.2	0.1	1.4	3.3
Morgantown, WV Metro Area	5.0	9.4	20.2	16.2	12.2	11.2	11.4	8.8	4.0	1.6	89.9	3.2	0.2	2.8	0.0	1.9	2.0
Morristown, TN Metro Area	5.3	12.1	12.0	11.5	11.6	14.1	14.0	11.4	6.1	1.9	87.4	2.6	0.3	0.7	0.1	1.4	7.5
Mount Vernon-Anacortes, WA Metro Area	6.1	12.2	11.3	12.6	11.8	11.3	14.0	12.4	6.0	2.4	74.0	0.8	1.6	2.2	0.3	2.4	18.7
Muncie, IN Metro Area	4.9	10.1	22.9	11.5	10.0	11.4	12.0	9.5	5.3	2.3	86.7	7.0	0.2	1.3	0.1	2.1	2.6
Muskegon, MI Metro Area	6.1	13.0	12.3	13.1	12.0	12.3	14.3	10.2	4.8	2.0	76.3	13.8	0.7	0.6	0.0	2.6	5.8
Myrtle Beach-Conway-North Myrtle Beach, SC-NC Metro Area	4.4	9.8	9.7	10.9	10.6	12.1	16.4	17.3	6.9	1.9	78.8	12.0	0.5	1.1	0.1	1.8	5.7
Napa, CA Metro Area	5.1	11.7	12.3	12.3	12.6	13.2	13.6	10.8	5.7	2.6	52.0	2.1	0.4	8.4	0.3	2.4	34.5
Naples-Marco Island, FL Metro Area	4.4	9.6	9.6	9.5	9.7	11.5	13.4	15.8	11.8	4.6	62.5	6.7	0.2	1.4	0.0	0.9	28.2
Nashville-Davidson--Murfreesboro--Franklin, TN Metro Area	6.4	12.9	13.0	15.5	13.7	13.1	12.2	8.1	3.7	1.4	71.9	15.4	0.3	2.9	0.1	2.0	7.5
New Bern, NC Metro Area	5.9	11.4	14.4	13.0	10.6	10.6	13.6	11.9	6.2	2.4	66.3	21.3	0.5	2.6	0.1	2.3	6.9
New Haven-Milford, CT Metro Area	5.1	11.3	13.7	13.4	11.7	13.4	14.0	9.7	5.0	2.6	62.3	12.8	0.2	4.2	0.0	1.8	18.6
New Orleans-Metairie, LA Metro Area	6.3	12.3	11.6	14.8	12.9	12.5	13.7	9.6	4.4	1.8	51.4	34.9	0.4	2.8	0.0	1.5	9.0
New York-Newark-Jersey City, NY-NJ-PA Metro Area	6.1	11.8	12.2	14.8	13.1	13.4	13.0	8.8	4.7	2.3	45.6	16.0	0.2	11.7	0.0	1.6	24.9
Nassau County-Suffolk County, NY Div.	5.4	11.9	12.9	11.8	11.9	14.4	14.5	9.6	5.1	2.6	63.4	9.4	0.2	7.0	0.0	1.4	18.6
Newark, NJ-PA Div.	5.8	12.5	12.6	12.3	13.1	14.6	13.7	8.7	4.4	2.2	50.0	20.7	0.1	6.3	0.0	1.4	21.3
New Brunswick-Lakewood, NJ Div.	5.8	12.4	12.4	11.8	12.1	13.7	14.1	9.8	5.3	2.5	63.3	7.2	0.1	13.1	0.0	1.4	14.9
New York-Jersey City-White Plains, NY-NJ Div.	6.3	11.5	11.9	16.6	13.5	12.9	12.2	8.4	4.5	2.2	37.0	18.5	0.2	13.5	0.1	1.4	29.1
Niles, MI Metro Area	5.7	12.3	11.9	11.8	11.3	12.6	14.7	11.2	5.9	2.6	74.7	14.6	0.5	2.1	0.1	2.3	5.7
North Port-Sarasota-Bradenton, FL Metro Area	4.1	9.2	9.0	9.4	9.3	11.6	15.2	16.7	10.8	4.7	77.2	6.3	0.2	1.9	0.0	1.4	12.9
Norwich-New London, CT Metro Area	5.0	10.8	13.6	13.1	11.1	13.3	14.8	10.4	5.3	2.4	75.3	5.7	0.8	4.2	0.1	3.0	10.9
Ocala, FL Metro Area	4.9	10.5	9.8	10.9	9.8	11.4	13.7	15.6	10.1	3.2	70.1	12.5	0.3	1.7	0.1	1.6	13.6
Ocean City, NJ Metro Area	4.6	9.8	10.6	10.4	9.2	12.0	16.8	15.2	8.2	3.2	85.2	4.1	0.2	1.0	0.1	1.6	7.9

Table B-3. Population by Age, Race, and Hispanic Origin—*Continued*

| | Population characteristics, 2018 | | | | | | | | | | | | | | | | |
| Metropolitan Statistical Area Metropolitan Division | Age (percent | | | | | | | | | | Race alone, not of Hispanic origin | | | | | Two or more races, not of Hispanic origin (percent) | Hispanic or Latino origin (percent |
	Under 5 years	5 to 14 years	15 to 24 years	25 to 34 years	35 to 44 years	45 to 54 years	55 to 64 years	65 to 74 years	75 to 84 years	85 years and over	White alone	Black or African-American alone	American Indian, Alaska native alone	Asian alone	Native Hawaiian, other Pacific Islander alone		
Odessa, TX Metro Area	9.0	16.7	14.6	16.9	13.0	10.4	9.7	5.8	2.9	1.1	31.8	4.4	0.4	1.1	0.1	0.9	61.3
Ogden-Clearfield, UT Metro Area	8.1	17.5	14.3	14.3	14.3	10.4	10.0	6.5	3.2	1.2	81.0	1.2	0.5	1.6	0.5	2.1	13.1
Oklahoma City, OK Metro Area	6.8	13.9	13.9	14.8	13.1	11.6	12.0	8.3	4.0	1.6	63.9	10.4	3.8	3.3	0.1	4.7	13.7
Olympia-Lacey-Tumwater, WA Metro Area	5.8	12.0	11.7	14.5	13.5	12.2	13.0	10.7	4.7	1.9	74.6	3.2	1.3	6.0	0.9	4.9	9.2
Omaha-Council Bluffs, NE-IA Metro Area	7.2	14.2	12.9	14.4	13.3	12.0	12.2	8.2	3.8	1.7	75.8	7.6	0.4	3.1	0.1	2.3	10.7
Orlando-Kissimmee-Sanford, FL Metro Area	5.8	12.3	13.1	15.3	13.8	13.1	11.8	8.7	4.4	1.7	46.2	15.7	0.2	4.5	0.1	1.8	31.5
Oshkosh-Neenah, WI Metro Area	5.5	11.4	15.3	13.3	12.0	12.6	13.5	9.2	4.9	2.3	88.4	2.2	0.6	3.0	0.0	1.6	4.2
Owensboro, KY Metro Area	6.7	13.7	12.0	12.6	11.8	12.5	13.6	9.8	5.1	2.2	89.0	4.3	0.1	1.6	0.1	1.9	3.0
Oxnard-Thousand Oaks-Ventura, CA Metro Area	5.9	13.0	13.3	13.4	12.4	13.2	13.2	9.0	4.5	2.1	45.0	1.8	0.3	7.4	0.2	2.4	43.0
Palm Bay-Melbourne-Titusville, FL Metro Area	4.7	10.3	10.5	11.4	10.4	12.7	16.4	12.8	7.8	3.1	74.1	10.0	0.3	2.5	0.1	3.0	10.7
Panama City, FL Metro Area	6.1	12.0	11.3	14.4	12.1	12.8	14.2	9.9	5.1	2.1	76.1	11.2	0.6	2.2	0.1	3.0	6.7
Parkersburg-Vienna, WV Metro Area	5.6	11.7	10.9	11.4	11.9	13.3	14.8	11.7	6.5	2.2	95.2	1.2	0.2	0.6	0.0	1.6	1.1
Pensacola-Ferry Pass-Brent, FL Metro Area	5.9	11.9	13.6	14.4	11.7	12.3	13.7	9.9	4.9	1.7	70.7	16.7	0.7	2.9	0.1	3.0	5.8
Peoria, IL Metro Area	6.2	12.8	12.0	12.6	12.4	12.3	13.5	10.2	5.4	2.6	83.0	9.0	0.2	2.2	0.0	1.9	3.5
Philadelphia-Camden-Wilmington, PA-NJ-DE-MD Metro Area	5.8	12.1	12.7	14.4	12.3	13.1	13.6	9.1	4.6	2.2	61.4	20.5	0.2	6.2	0.0	1.9	9.7
Camden, NJ Div	5.5	12.4	12.3	13.1	12.5	13.9	14.1	9.3	4.7	2.1	65.2	16.0	0.2	5.0	0.0	2.1	11.5
Montgomery County-Bucks County-Chester County, PA Div	5.3	12.2	12.2	11.9	12.2	13.9	14.7	9.9	5.1	2.6	79.0	6.7	0.1	6.5	0.0	1.7	6.0
Philadelphia, PA Div	6.4	12.0	13.3	17.5	12.4	11.8	12.2	8.2	4.1	2.1	42.7	35.7	0.2	7.2	0.0	2.0	12.2
Wilmington, DE-MD-NJ Div	5.7	12.1	12.8	14.0	12.2	13.5	13.8	9.3	4.6	2.0	62.3	21.3	0.2	4.7	0.0	2.2	9.4
Phoenix-Mesa-Chandler, AZ Metro Area	6.3	13.4	13.2	14.5	13.0	12.4	11.6	9.1	4.8	1.8	55.1	5.4	1.9	4.1	0.2	2.2	31.2
Pine Bluff, AR Metro Area	5.7	11.8	13.7	13.4	12.0	12.5	13.6	10.2	5.1	2.0	46.5	48.7	0.3	0.7	0.1	1.2	2.4
Pittsburgh, PA Metro Area	5.1	10.5	11.6	13.4	11.5	12.8	15.1	11.1	5.9	3.0	85.3	8.4	0.1	2.6	0.0	1.8	1.8
Pittsfield, MA Metro Area	4.2	9.4	12.8	10.7	10.4	13.0	16.2	13.1	6.7	3.4	87.8	3.1	0.2	1.7	0.0	2.1	5.1
Pocatello, ID Metro Area	7.2	14.9	14.7	14.6	12.5	10.1	11.6	8.8	4.0	1.5	81.6	0.9	2.8	1.5	0.3	2.0	10.9
Portland-South Portland, ME Metro Area	4.8	10.5	11.4	12.9	11.9	13.6	15.4	11.5	5.5	2.4	92.1	2.1	0.3	1.8	0.0	1.8	2.0
Portland-Vancouver-Hillsboro, OR-WA Metro Area	5.7	12.1	11.7	15.4	14.7	13.1	12.3	9.2	4.0	1.7	72.8	3.0	0.7	7.1	0.5	3.6	12.2
Port St. Lucie, FL Metro Area	4.7	10.5	10.2	10.7	10.4	12.4	14.6	13.8	8.9	3.7	63.8	14.9	0.2	1.7	0.1	1.6	17.7
Poughkeepsie-Newburgh-Middletown, NY Metro Area	5.7	12.6	14.8	11.8	11.7	14.0	13.8	9.2	4.5	2.0	66.9	10.4	0.2	3.2	0.0	2.0	17.3
Prescott Valley-Prescott, AZ Metro Area	4.2	9.2	9.4	9.1	8.8	10.6	17.2	18.8	9.6	3.2	80.4	0.7	1.4	1.1	0.1	1.7	14.7
Providence-Warwick, RI-MA Metro Area	5.2	11.1	13.6	13.5	11.9	13.5	14.1	9.7	4.9	2.6	75.6	5.5	0.4	3.1	0.1	2.0	13.3
Provo-Orem, UT Metro Area	9.4	18.6	22.0	14.3	12.7	8.4	6.7	4.6	2.4	0.8	82.2	0.6	0.5	1.7	0.9	2.3	11.9
Pueblo, CO Metro Area	5.8	12.7	12.8	13.1	11.8	11.8	13.5	10.8	5.3	2.4	52.0	1.8	0.7	0.8	0.1	1.5	43.1
Punta Gorda, FL Metro Area	3.0	6.7	7.4	7.8	7.3	10.5	17.2	21.4	13.6	5.2	84.0	5.5	0.3	1.4	0.0	1.4	7.4
Racine, WI Metro Area	6.1	12.9	12.5	12.0	12.0	13.4	14.6	9.6	4.8	2.1	71.7	11.3	0.4	1.3	0.0	2.0	13.4
Raleigh-Cary, NC Metro Area	6.2	13.7	13.0	14.2	14.6	14.4	11.7	7.6	3.3	1.3	61.1	19.6	0.3	6.1	0.0	2.0	10.8
Rapid City, SD Metro Area	6.2	13.1	12.4	13.7	11.8	11.0	14.3	10.7	4.6	2.1	81.4	1.5	7.5	1.2	0.1	3.3	5.0
Reading, PA Metro Area	5.7	12.6	13.6	12.4	11.5	13.3	13.6	9.7	5.0	2.5	70.9	4.2	0.1	1.5	0.0	1.3	21.9
Redding, CA Metro Area	5.9	11.9	11.3	12.9	11.1	11.5	14.7	12.2	6.3	2.4	79.6	1.1	2.3	2.9	0.2	3.7	10.3
Reno, NV Metro Area	5.9	12.1	12.4	15.1	12.3	12.5	13.3	10.4	4.6	1.5	62.8	2.3	1.3	5.4	0.6	2.9	24.7
Richmond, VA Metro Area	5.8	12.0	12.6	14.6	12.7	13.3	13.5	9.4	4.3	1.8	57.1	29.7	0.4	4.1	0.1	2.2	6.5
Riverside-San Bernardino-Ontario, CA Metro Area	6.8	14.5	14.4	14.6	12.9	12.3	11.4	7.7	3.9	1.5	31.5	7.1	0.4	6.8	0.3	2.2	51.6
Roanoke, VA Metro Area	5.4	11.5	11.5	12.3	11.3	13.4	14.4	11.8	5.9	2.5	78.0	13.3	0.2	2.5	0.0	2.0	4.0
Rochester, MN Metro Area	6.7	13.8	11.4	13.5	12.8	11.8	13.4	9.1	5.0	2.5	84.0	4.6	0.2	4.7	0.0	1.9	4.5
Rochester, NY Metro Area	5.3	11.5	13.6	13.3	11.2	12.9	14.3	10.2	5.1	2.4	76.3	11.0	0.2	2.8	0.0	2.0	7.6
Rockford, IL Metro Area	6.3	13.2	12.6	12.3	11.8	13.1	13.6	9.9	5.2	2.2	69.1	11.3	0.2	2.6	0.0	2.2	14.6
Rocky Mount, NC Metro Area	5.6	12.6	12.5	11.8	11.2	12.9	14.6	11.4	5.4	2.1	44.7	46.4	0.5	0.6	0.1	1.4	6.3
Rome, GA Metro Area	6.1	13.0	14.0	12.9	12.0	12.6	12.6	9.5	5.2	2.0	70.9	14.4	0.2	1.5	0.1	1.6	11.3
Sacramento-Roseville-Folsom, CA Metro Area	6.0	12.9	13.2	14.3	13.0	12.5	12.6	9.1	4.4	1.9	51.8	7.0	0.5	13.7	0.8	4.3	21.8
Saginaw, MI Metro Area	5.7	11.8	13.3	12.5	10.9	12.5	14.1	10.9	5.7	2.6	69.2	18.5	0.3	1.4	0.0	1.9	8.5
St. Cloud, MN Metro Area	6.5	13.0	17.3	12.7	11.8	11.5	12.2	8.3	4.5	2.2	86.3	6.4	0.3	2.1	0.0	1.7	3.3
St. George, UT Metro Area	6.7	14.8	13.3	11.5	11.9	9.3	11.0	11.8	7.1	2.5	84.2	0.6	1.0	0.9	0.8	1.8	10.6
St. Joseph, MO-KS Metro Area	6.0	12.3	12.6	13.8	12.7	12.4	13.5	9.3	5.1	2.3	84.8	5.5	0.4	1.2	0.3	2.2	5.6
St. Louis, MO-IL Metro Area	6.0	12.4	12.1	13.7	12.5	12.7	14.2	9.5	4.8	2.2	73.7	18.3	0.2	2.7	0.0	1.9	3.1
Salem, OR Metro Area	6.5	13.7	13.8	13.7	12.6	11.5	12.0	9.5	4.7	1.9	67.4	1.1	1.2	2.2	0.8	2.8	24.5
Salinas, CA Metro Area	7.1	14.9	14.1	14.3	13.0	11.8	11.2	8.0	3.7	1.9	29.6	2.6	0.3	5.7	0.5	2.3	59.1
Salisbury, MD-DE Metro Area	5.2	10.8	12.3	10.9	9.9	11.7	15.2	14.6	7.1	2.4	71.1	17.5	0.4	1.7	0.0	2.0	7.2
Salt Lake City, UT Metro Area	7.5	15.4	14.0	16.3	14.7	11.2	10.0	6.6	3.0	1.2	71.4	1.7	0.7	4.3	1.6	2.3	18.2
San Angelo, TX Metro Area	6.8	13.4	15.3	15.4	11.6	10.3	11.6	8.7	4.8	2.0	53.0	3.6	0.4	1.2	0.1	1.5	40.3
San Antonio-New Braunfels, TX Metro Area	6.9	14.1	14.1	15.1	13.3	12.2	11.2	7.8	3.7	1.5	33.4	6.6	0.3	2.6	0.1	1.5	55.6
San Diego-Chula Vista-Carlsbad, CA Metro Area	6.2	11.9	13.7	16.5	13.4	12.4	11.8	8.1	4.0	1.9	45.2	4.7	0.4	12.0	0.4	3.3	34.0
San Francisco-Oakland-Berkeley, CA Metro Area	5.4	11.0	11.0	16.3	14.5	13.6	12.6	8.9	4.4	2.1	39.3	7.2	0.2	26.9	0.7	3.9	21.9
Oakland-Berkeley-Livermore, CA Div	5.7	12.0	11.8	15.1	14.4	13.6	12.6	8.6	4.1	1.9	36.0	9.7	0.3	25.5	0.7	4.1	23.8
San Francisco-San Mateo-Redwood City, CA Div	5.0	9.1	9.8	19.6	15.1	13.4	12.2	8.9	4.6	2.4	39.7	3.7	0.2	32.5	0.8	3.6	19.5
San Rafael, CA Div	4.6	11.6	10.4	8.7	11.7	15.5	15.2	12.9	6.4	3.0	71.5	2.5	0.2	6.3	0.2	3.3	16.1
San Jose-Sunnyvale-Santa Clara, CA Metro Area	6.0	12.4	12.2	16.2	14.4	13.7	11.8	7.5	4.0	1.9	31.1	2.3	0.2	36.6	0.3	3.0	26.4
San Luis Obispo-Paso Robles, CA Metro Area	4.6	10.0	18.2	11.5	11.1	10.9	13.7	11.9	5.6	2.5	68.6	1.7	0.5	3.6	0.1	2.6	22.8
Santa Cruz-Watsonville, CA Metro Area	5.1	10.9	18.2	12.1	11.7	12.2	13.4	10.5	4.1	1.9	56.9	1.0	0.4	4.6	0.1	3.0	34.1

Table B-3. Population by Age, Race, and Hispanic Origin—*Continued*

Metropolitan Statistical Area / Metropolitan Division	Age (percent)										Race alone, not of Hispanic origin					Two or more races, not of Hispanic origin (percent)	Hispanic or Latino origin (percent)
	Under 5 years	5 to 14 years	15 to 24 years	25 to 34 years	35 to 44 years	45 to 54 years	55 to 64 years	65 to 74 years	75 to 84 years	85 years and over	White alone	Black or African-American alone	American Indian, Alaska native alone	Asian alone	Native Hawaiian, other Pacific Islander alone		
Santa Fe, NM Metro Area	4.3	10.4	10.5	11.2	11.2	12.4	15.6	15.6	6.6	2.2	43.0	0.8	2.5	1.4	0.0	1.2	51.1
Santa Maria-Santa Barbara, CA Metro Area	6.2	12.4	19.3	13.3	11.3	10.7	11.3	8.4	4.5	2.4	44.1	1.8	0.4	5.4	0.2	2.3	45.8
Santa Rosa-Petaluma, CA Metro Area	5.0	11.2	11.6	12.9	12.5	12.7	14.4	12.1	5.2	2.4	63.1	1.6	0.7	4.2	0.3	2.8	27.2
Savannah, GA Metro Area	6.5	12.7	13.8	15.8	13.0	11.9	11.9	8.7	4.1	1.6	55.4	33.4	0.2	2.5	0.1	2.0	6.4
Scranton--Wilkes-Barre, PA Metro Area	5.2	11.2	12.3	12.6	11.3	13.2	14.2	11.0	6.0	3.0	82.6	3.5	0.1	1.9	0.0	1.3	10.5
Seattle-Tacoma-Bellevue, WA Metro Area	6.1	11.9	11.6	17.0	14.5	13.1	12.3	8.1	3.6	1.6	62.6	6.0	0.8	14.6	0.9	4.8	10.2
Seattle-Bellevue-Kent, WA Div	6.0	11.6	11.3	17.4	14.8	13.3	12.3	8.1	3.6	1.7	61.5	5.7	0.7	16.9	0.8	4.4	10.0
Tacoma-Lakewood, WA Div	6.7	13.1	12.6	15.7	13.3	12.4	12.5	8.4	3.9	1.5	66.3	7.0	1.2	6.6	1.6	6.2	11.1
Sebastian-Vero Beach, FL Metro Area	4.1	8.9	9.2	9.2	8.8	11.1	15.6	17.3	11.0	4.8	75.2	9.0	0.2	1.5	0.0	1.3	12.7
Sebring-Avon Park, FL Metro Area	4.6	9.7	8.9	9.7	8.7	9.8	13.4	16.6	13.4	5.2	66.4	9.6	0.4	1.4	0.0	1.3	20.8
Sheboygan, WI Metro Area	5.5	12.6	12.3	11.6	12.0	13.2	14.8	10.4	5.2	2.4	83.8	2.0	0.4	5.7	0.0	1.5	6.5
Sherman-Denison, TX Metro Area	6.4	13.4	12.4	12.4	11.6	12.3	13.9	10.3	5.0	5.3	75.0	5.9	1.3	1.5	0.1	2.4	13.8
Shreveport-Bossier City, LA Metro Area	6.7	13.5	12.4	14.2	12.5	11.6	12.9	9.4	4.8	2.0	52.5	39.8	0.4	1.4	0.1	1.7	4.1
Sierra Vista-Douglas, AZ Metro Area	5.8	12.1	12.5	12.5	11.0	10.6	13.2	12.7	7.3	2.3	54.9	3.9	0.8	2.0	0.3	2.4	35.6
Sioux City, IA-NE-SD Metro Area	7.3	14.6	13.7	12.8	12.0	11.8	12.4	9.0	4.5	1.9	71.4	3.5	1.5	2.7	0.2	2.1	18.5
Sioux Falls, SD Metro Area	7.6	14.6	12.2	15.3	13.5	11.5	12.0	8.2	3.4	1.8	84.6	5.1	1.9	2.1	0.0	2.0	4.3
South Bend-Mishawaka, IN-MI Metro Area	6.2	13.0	14.4	12.8	11.6	12.1	13.2	9.7	4.7	2.3	74.5	11.9	0.4	2.2	0.1	2.8	8.1
Spartanburg, SC Metro Area	6.1	13.0	13.1	13.8	11.9	13.3	12.7	9.6	4.9	1.6	68.0	20.5	0.2	2.4	0.0	1.7	7.1
Spokane-Spokane Valley, WA Metro Area	6.0	12.4	12.8	14.5	12.2	11.9	13.4	10.2	4.6	1.9	84.5	1.8	1.7	2.2	0.5	3.5	5.7
Springfield, IL Metro Area	5.6	12.6	12.0	12.5	12.3	12.8	14.3	10.5	5.1	2.3	81.1	12.1	0.2	2.0	0.0	2.3	2.3
Springfield, MA Metro Area	4.9	11.0	16.6	12.6	11.1	12.5	13.9	10.2	4.8	2.4	69.6	6.0	0.2	3.2	0.0	1.8	19.2
Springfield, MO Metro Area	6.3	12.5	15.3	13.4	12.0	11.7	12.3	9.3	5.0	2.1	89.6	2.4	0.6	1.6	0.1	2.3	3.4
Springfield, OH Metro Area	5.9	12.6	13.1	11.7	10.8	12.7	13.9	11.1	5.8	2.5	84.0	8.7	0.2	0.7	0.1	2.7	3.5
State College, PA Metro Area	3.9	8.5	26.4	13.9	10.7	11.1	11.4	8.1	4.3	1.9	85.2	3.6	0.1	6.5	0.1	1.5	3.0
Staunton, VA Metro Area	5.5	11.1	10.9	12.5	11.8	13.1	14.5	11.6	6.4	2.5	85.6	7.2	0.2	1.0	0.0	2.0	3.9
Stockton, CA Metro Area	7.1	15.5	14.2	14.1	13.0	12.2	11.2	7.5	3.6	1.6	31.0	7.1	0.4	15.5	0.6	3.4	41.9
Sumter, SC Metro Area	6.2	12.7	13.5	13.5	10.9	11.8	13.3	10.6	5.7	1.9	45.7	47.2	0.4	1.3	0.1	1.6	3.9
Syracuse, NY Metro Area	5.5	11.7	14.4	12.9	11.1	13.0	14.4	9.7	4.9	2.4	81.5	8.1	0.7	2.9	0.0	2.4	4.3
Tallahassee, FL Metro Area	5.3	10.7	21.3	14.1	11.4	11.0	11.7	9.0	3.9	1.5	55.6	32.5	0.3	3.0	0.0	1.9	6.7
Tampa-St. Petersburg-Clearwater, FL Metro Area	5.3	11.2	11.2	13.3	12.3	13.2	13.7	11.0	6.1	2.6	62.3	11.8	0.2	3.6	0.1	1.9	20.0
Terre Haute, IN Metro Area	5.7	11.6	15.4	12.9	11.7	12.3	13.0	10.0	5.1	2.2	89.4	5.0	0.3	1.3	0.0	1.8	2.2
Texarkana, TX-AR Metro Area	6.5	13.1	12.2	13.4	12.6	12.4	12.7	9.8	5.1	2.1	65.5	24.5	0.7	1.0	0.1	2.0	6.2
The Villages, FL Metro Area	2.0	4.0	4.2	5.8	5.9	6.7	13.9	33.1	20.2	4.3	85.1	7.0	0.3	0.9	0.1	0.9	5.7
Toledo, OH Metro Area	6.0	12.4	14.1	13.4	11.4	12.2	13.8	9.8	4.8	2.2	75.2	13.7	0.2	1.6	0.0	2.3	6.9
Topeka, KS Metro Area	6.1	13.3	12.3	11.9	11.7	12.0	14.2	10.6	5.4	2.4	77.7	6.1	1.2	1.2	0.1	3.1	10.5
Trenton-Princeton, NJ Metro Area	5.7	11.8	15.2	12.5	12.7	13.9	13.1	8.5	4.4	2.2	48.8	19.6	0.2	11.5	0.1	1.8	18.1
Tucson, AZ Metro Area	5.6	11.7	15.3	12.8	11.4	11.0	12.5	11.2	6.1	2.4	51.4	3.4	2.4	3.1	0.2	1.9	37.6
Tulsa, OK Metro Area	6.7	13.8	12.7	13.8	12.6	12.2	12.7	9.1	4.6	1.8	64.7	8.2	8.2	2.5	0.1	6.2	10.2
Tuscaloosa, AL Metro Area	6.0	11.5	18.5	14.4	11.8	11.4	12.0	8.6	4.1	1.7	58.0	35.6	0.2	1.4	0.0	1.1	3.7
Twin Falls, ID Metro Area	7.5	16.3	12.7	14.0	12.6	10.6	11.4	8.5	4.6	1.7	74.8	0.5	0.6	1.3	0.2	1.4	21.2
Tyler, TX Metro Area	6.9	13.6	13.7	13.7	11.8	11.7	12.2	9.2	5.2	2.1	59.3	17.2	0.3	1.7	0.1	1.5	19.9
Urban Honolulu, HI Metro Area	6.3	11.7	12.5	15.2	12.8	11.9	11.9	9.6	5.0	3.1	18.0	2.6	0.2	41.8	8.9	18.6	10.0
Utica-Rome, NY Metro Area	5.5	12.0	12.8	12.3	11.0	12.9	14.4	10.6	5.7	2.9	84.3	5.1	0.2	3.3	0.0	1.8	5.2
Valdosta, GA Metro Area	6.7	13.6	18.5	14.9	11.3	10.9	10.9	7.9	4.0	1.3	55.1	34.3	0.3	1.8	0.1	1.9	6.6
Vallejo, CA Metro Area	6.0	12.3	12.4	14.7	12.6	12.6	13.5	9.7	4.3	1.8	37.6	13.7	0.4	15.3	0.8	5.2	26.9
Victoria, TX Metro Area	6.8	14.0	13.3	13.7	12.0	11.1	12.6	9.4	5.0	2.2	45.3	5.6	0.3	1.2	0.0	1.0	46.6
Vineland-Bridgeton, NJ Metro Area	6.3	13.7	12.0	14.3	13.0	13.1	12.3	8.7	4.5	2.0	45.9	18.6	0.7	1.3	0.0	2.1	31.4
Virginia Beach-Norfolk-Newport News, VA-NC Metro Area	6.2	12.1	14.1	15.5	12.4	12.0	12.9	8.7	4.4	1.7	55.0	30.4	0.3	4.0	0.1	3.2	6.9
Visalia, CA Metro Area	7.9	17.7	15.1	14.2	12.7	11.0	9.9	6.7	3.3	1.4	28.1	1.2	0.7	3.3	0.1	1.4	65.2
Waco, TX Metro Area	6.9	13.4	18.1	13.3	11.5	10.8	11.4	8.3	4.4	2.0	55.3	14.6	0.3	1.6	0.1	1.6	26.5
Walla Walla, WA Metro Area	5.5	11.8	16.6	12.9	11.5	11.1	12.6	10.2	5.2	2.7	71.4	2.0	0.8	1.6	0.4	2.3	21.5
Warner Robins, GA Metro Area	6.4	14.2	13.8	14.4	12.8	12.6	12.6	8.0	4.0	1.3	54.0	33.5	0.3	2.8	0.1	2.4	6.9
Washington-Arlington-Alexandria, DC-VA-MD-WV Metro Area	6.5	12.7	12.4	15.0	14.4	13.8	12.2	7.8	3.6	1.6	45.2	25.0	0.2	10.6	0.1	2.8	16.1
Frederick-Gaithersburg-Rockville, MD Div	6.2	13.0	12.0	12.7	13.6	14.0	13.2	8.7	4.4	2.2	49.1	16.7	0.2	13.3	0.0	2.7	18.0
Washington-Arlington-Alexandria, DC-VA-MD-WV Div	6.5	12.7	12.5	15.5	14.6	13.7	12.0	7.6	3.4	1.4	44.1	27.2	0.2	9.9	0.1	2.9	15.6
Waterloo-Cedar Falls, IA Metro Area	6.2	12.2	17.3	12.5	11.5	10.7	12.4	9.6	5.1	2.5	84.0	7.6	0.2	2.1	0.3	2.0	3.8
Watertown-Fort Drum, NY Metro Area	7.8	12.8	15.6	17.1	11.6	10.4	10.9	8.0	4.0	1.7	81.2	6.2	0.5	1.6	0.2	2.5	7.8
Wausau-Weston, WI Metro Area	5.7	12.4	11.4	11.6	12.1	13.4	15.1	10.3	5.6	2.4	89.7	0.8	0.5	5.0	0.0	1.4	2.6
Weirton-Steubenville, WV-OH Metro Area	4.8	10.6	12.2	10.7	10.7	13.0	15.7	12.8	6.7	2.9	92.2	3.9	0.2	0.5	0.0	1.8	1.4
Wenatchee, WA Metro Area	6.4	13.8	12.2	12.5	11.8	11.2	13.5	10.9	5.4	2.3	66.2	0.5	0.8	1.0	0.2	1.7	29.7
Wheeling, WV-OH Metro Area	4.9	10.7	11.6	12.0	11.3	12.6	15.4	12.3	6.2	3.0	93.4	3.2	0.2	0.5	0.0	1.6	1.1
Wichita, KS Metro Area	6.7	14.5	13.4	13.7	12.3	11.5	12.9	8.7	4.3	2.0	71.6	7.4	0.8	3.8	0.1	3.0	13.4
Wichita Falls, TX Metro Area	6.2	12.5	16.0	14.5	11.5	11.0	12.8	8.6	4.9	2.1	67.9	9.3	0.8	1.9	0.1	2.2	17.9
Williamsport, PA Metro Area	5.3	11.6	12.3	13.1	11.1	12.6	14.6	10.8	5.7	2.8	90.6	4.5	0.2	0.6	0.0	2.0	2.1
Wilmington, NC Metro Area	5.1	10.8	14.9	12.9	12.4	12.8	13.3	10.9	5.0	1.9	76.9	13.5	0.4	1.3	0.1	1.8	6.0
Winchester, VA-WV Metro Area	6.0	12.3	12.1	12.2	12.1	13.7	13.7	10.5	5.3	2.1	81.3	5.0	0.2	1.6	0.0	2.1	9.7
Winston-Salem, NC Metro Area	5.6	12.5	12.7	12.3	11.7	13.9	13.8	10.2	5.2	2.1	67.9	17.8	0.3	1.9	0.0	1.6	10.5
Worcester, MA-CT Metro Area	5.3	11.7	13.6	13.0	12.1	14.2	14.4	9.2	4.4	2.1	76.8	4.4	0.2	4.8	0.0	1.8	12.0
Yakima, WA Metro Area	8.1	16.8	14.3	13.4	11.8	11.0	10.8	8.0	4.0	1.8	42.7	0.8	3.6	1.2	0.1	1.7	49.9
York-Hanover, PA Metro Area	5.7	12.5	12.0	12.4	12.0	13.7	14.2	10.1	5.2	2.2	82.9	5.7	0.2	1.5	0.0	1.8	7.9
Youngstown-Warren-Boardman, OH-PA Metro Area	5.2	11.1	12.2	11.5	10.9	12.7	15.1	11.9	6.4	3.1	82.8	10.6	0.2	0.7	0.0	1.8	3.7
Yuba City, CA Metro Area	7.4	15.0	13.3	14.9	12.3	11.3	11.7	8.2	4.3	1.7	49.3	2.8	1.2	12.1	0.3	3.9	30.3
Yuma, AZ Metro Area	7.2	14.0	15.3	13.9	11.0	10.1	9.8	9.2	7.1	2.5	30.4	1.9	1.0	1.2	0.1	1.1	64.3

Table B-4. Migration and Commuting, 2014–2018

Metropolitan Statistical Area Metropolitan Division	Migration 2014-2018			Commuting 2014-2018					
	Total population age 1 year and older	Percent who lived in the same house in prior year	Percent who lived outside this metro area in prior year	Total residents age 16 and older	Total who worked in this metro area	Lived and worked in this metro area	Employment/ residence ratio	Mean travel time to work	Percent who drove alone to work
Abilene, TX Metro Area	167,649	77.8	9.6	133,905	75,938	65,846	0.99	17.9	80.5
Akron, OH Metro Area	697,333	87.1	4.5	576,691	343,215	227,204	1.00	23.6	84.9
Albany, GA Metro Area	147,870	83.0	5.0	117,353	60,150	36,875	1.01	20.7	81.7
Albany-Lebanon, OR Metro Area	121,459	83.6	7.6	97,993	47,147	34,730	0.92	22.7	78.3
Albany-Schenectady-Troy, NY Metro Area	871,669	86.6	4.6	726,946	456,066	271,225	1.04	23.2	79.8
Albuquerque, NM Metro Area	899,901	86.0	4.2	727,544	405,033	338,304	0.99	23.6	80.3
Alexandria, LA Metro Area	151,968	88.1	4.1	120,780	61,101	49,279	1.02	23.6	82.5
Allentown-Bethlehem-Easton, PA-NJ Metro Area	826,357	87.6	4.4	678,717	368,203	235,808	0.91	27.9	81.6
Altoona, PA Metro Area	122,621	89.4	3.8	101,507	62,061	48,089	1.12	20.2	82.8
Amarillo, TX Metro Area	259,749	81.6	5.0	202,357	123,942	72,635	0.99	18.9	82.9
Ames, IA Metro Area	122,185	71.7	15.2	104,028	64,572	48,650	1.01	18.8	74.1
Anchorage, AK Metro Area	393,975	81.4	6.1	308,866	194,357	177,093	0.99	22.0	75.7
Ann Arbor, MI Metro Area	362,548	76.8	11.2	304,911	221,292	141,366	1.21	24.0	71.7
Anniston-Oxford, AL Metro Area	113,469	83.3	6.1	93,023	46,430	35,655	0.98	25.0	84.8
Appleton, WI Metro Area	231,727	90.1	4.4	184,749	121,220	74,374	0.97	19.9	85.6
Asheville, NC Metro Area	446,338	86.7	5.3	374,482	215,328	166,818	1.03	21.2	79.4
Athens-Clarke County, GA Metro Area	202,783	78.1	11.8	168,595	97,501	55,534	1.04	21.6	76.9
Atlanta-Sandy Springs-Alpharetta, GA Metro Area	5,710,378	84.9	4.2	4,504,186	2,793,291	1,476,240	1.01	31.9	77.6
Atlantic City-Hammonton, NJ Metro Area	265,749	87.0	4.7	217,525	125,833	99,696	1.01	24.3	77.2
Auburn-Opelika, AL Metro Area	157,620	80.0	10.8	128,804	62,013	49,399	0.86	22.2	84.4
Augusta-Richmond County, GA-SC Metro Area	586,368	85.8	5.3	471,087	255,636	150,363	1.01	24.0	84.0
Austin-Round Rock-Georgetown, TX Metro Area	2,033,267	81.4	6.7	1,622,868	1,087,164	803,044	1.01	27.1	76.5
Bakersfield, CA Metro Area	870,602	85.3	4.8	652,959	338,384	314,811	1.02	23.3	79.8
Baltimore-Columbia-Towson, MD Metro Area	2,762,167	86.6	3.9	2,245,696	1,373,002	743,609	0.99	31.0	76.6
Bangor, ME Metro Area	150,354	84.4	6.4	127,262	74,418	64,510	1.04	22.4	79.4
Barnstable Town, MA Metro Area	212,243	90.3	4.4	185,069	99,297	87,962	0.97	23.3	80.4
Baton Rouge, LA Metro Area	842,062	86.0	4.0	673,446	395,608	258,544	1.01	26.8	84.6
Battle Creek, MI Metro Area	132,832	84.5	5.4	106,909	63,624	45,967	1.11	20.2	82.5
Bay City, MI Metro Area	103,834	88.9	4.1	85,860	35,889	26,994	0.78	22.3	86.2
Beaumont-Port Arthur, TX Metro Area	390,494	85.5	4.8	310,364	169,128	120,808	1.03	21.9	88.3
Beckley, WV Metro Area	119,189	90.0	3.3	98,305	43,097	32,145	0.99	26.7	82.6
Bellingham, WA Metro Area	214,635	79.9	7.5	178,886	99,057	93,742	0.96	21.3	76.2
Bend, OR Metro Area	179,174	82.3	7.5	147,287	87,051	81,443	1.01	19.0	74.4
Billings, MT Metro Area	176,011	85.6	4.9	140,943	89,523	82,779	1.00	19.4	80.9
Binghamton, NY Metro Area	241,156	85.5	5.0	201,068	105,724	84,465	0.98	20.5	81.5
Birmingham-Hoover, AL Metro Area	1,069,198	85.6	3.9	860,385	493,788	346,670	1.02	26.2	84.6
Bismarck, ND Metro Area	124,274	85.0	5.6	100,157	66,881	51,726	0.98	18.3	84.8
Blacksburg-Christiansburg, VA Metro Area	165,165	78.7	10.0	143,157	79,428	51,626	1.06	20.4	79.4
Bloomington, IL Metro Area	171,228	83.6	7.1	139,889	93,976	79,765	1.05	18.0	80.6
Bloomington, IN Metro Area	164,746	70.4	13.4	141,854	84,418	66,324	1.06	20.6	73.3
Bloomsburg-Berwick, PA Metro Area	83,793	88.1	6.3	70,842	43,934	25,051	1.14	21.5	83.4
Boise City, ID Metro Area	686,649	82.9	5.7	535,507	319,953	263,983	0.99	22.0	79.8
Boston-Cambridge-Newton, MA-NH Metro Area …	4,761,559	86.6	4.1	3,958,927	2,711,143	1,555,847	1.07	31.4	66.7
Boston, MA Div	1,980,705	85.8	4.5	1,654,061	1,236,723	596,583	1.18	32.7	59.9
Cambridge-Newton-Framingham, MA Div	2,351,244	87.4	3.8	1,945,823	1,258,027	825,119	1.00	30.7	69.5
Rockingham County-Strafford County, NH Div	429,610	86.6	3.9	359,043	216,393	134,145	0.92	29.2	82.3
Boulder, CO Metro Area	318,101	77.4	11.9	265,772	203,314	135,818	1.20	22.8	65.4
Bowling Green, KY Metro Area	169,934	79.8	8.6	137,472	79,945	59,855	1.04	21.7	81.4
Bremerton-Silverdale-Port Orchard, WA Metro Area	259,484	82.0	8.8	214,355	112,820	100,683	0.91	30.4	69.3
Bridgeport-Stamford-Norwalk, CT Metro Area	934,145	88.2	4.7	754,186	470,317	357,071	1.01	30.7	72.3
Brownsville-Harlingen, TX Metro Area	415,868	91.4	2.3	305,790	150,129	140,115	0.96	20.2	84.9
Brunswick, GA Metro Area	115,238	84.7	6.7	93,548	49,941	39,073	1.00	21.9	82.1
Buffalo-Cheektowaga, NY Metro Area	1,118,893	88.3	2.9	929,003	545,470	471,714	1.01	21.7	82.5
Burlington, NC Metro Area	158,954	86.0	6.0	128,498	65,555	49,152	0.88	23.8	85.5
Burlington-South Burlington, VT Metro Area	215,872	82.5	6.5	181,573	124,390	98,996	1.05	22.3	75.2
California-Lexington Park, MD Metro Area	110,246	85.6	8.0	87,163	51,379	41,454	0.92	30.9	82.4
Canton-Massillon, OH Metro Area	396,879	87.1	3.6	324,886	176,128	136,820	0.94	22.3	84.6
Cape Coral-Fort Myers, FL Metro Area	711,922	85.2	6.5	603,414	278,036	256,435	0.95	27.3	79.9
Cape Girardeau, MO-IL Metro Area	95,883	82.0	6.9	78,257	45,671	34,617	1.05	21.1	80.9
Carbondale-Marion, IL Metro Area	136,972	82.2	8.2	113,675	59,333	39,308	1.05	21.2	81.9
Carson City, NV Metro Area	54,066	81.3	10.4	44,658	31,326	17,247	1.27	19.2	80.0
Casper, WY Metro Area	79,823	85.4	5.1	63,369	41,565	39,354	1.02	16.8	84.3
Cedar Rapids, IA Metro Area	265,454	86.4	4.9	212,714	142,496	116,099	1.02	19.5	84.4
Chambersburg-Waynesboro, PA Metro Area	152,008	89.2	4.0	123,224	63,323	49,228	0.88	24.8	82.2
Champaign-Urbana, IL Metro Area	223,408	78.2	11.9	187,640	115,447	98,511	1.05	18.2	71.3
Charleston, WV Metro Area	264,585	89.1	3.6	218,404	119,205	83,433	1.14	24.2	82.3
Charleston-North Charleston, SC Metro Area	749,471	84.0	6.0	609,639	375,054	246,439	1.01	26.1	81.0
Charlotte-Concord-Gastonia, NC-SC Metro Area	2,469,697	84.5	5.1	1,963,985	1,230,024	836,777	1.02	26.9	80.8
Charlottesville, VA Metro Area	211,744	81.1	8.9	176,721	114,522	53,848	1.10	23.4	72.9
Chattanooga, TN-GA Metro Area	545,968	86.9	4.4	448,217	260,107	184,277	1.04	23.5	83.0
Cheyenne, WY Metro Area	96,713	82.7	7.3	77,505	51,070	46,230	1.06	15.8	81.9
Chicago-Naperville-Elgin, IL-IN-WI Metro Area …	9,424,107	87.4	2.5	7,578,164	4,668,188	3,406,651	1.01	31.9	70.2
Chicago-Naperville-Evanston, IL Div	7,117,585	87.5	2.4	5,750,555	3,648,284	2,725,976	1.04	32.7	66.9
Elgin, IL Div	750,416	87.0	2.2	584,866	305,587	192,746	0.82	29.3	80.4

Table B-4. Migration and Commuting, 2014–2018—*Continued*

Metropolitan Statistical Area Metropolitan Division	Migration 2014-2018			Commuting 2014-2018					
	Total population age 1 year and older	Percent who lived in the same house in prior year	Percent who lived outside this metro area in prior year	Total residents age 16 and older	Total who worked in this metro area	Lived and worked in this metro area	Employment/ residence ratio	Mean travel time to work	Percent who drove alone to work
Gary, IN Div....................	694,115	87.3	2.3	558,037	276,521	198,163	0.89	28.4	84.1
Lake County-Kenosha County, IL-WI Div	861,991	86.8	3.6	684,706	437,796	289,766	1.00	29.5	78.4
Chico, CA Metro Area....................	225,108	81.7	6.5	186,682	91,774	83,716	1.00	21.0	75.3
Cincinnati, OH-KY-IN Metro Area........................	2,165,778	84.8	3.8	1,730,001	1,062,037	621,396	1.00	24.9	82.5
Clarksville, TN-KY Metro Area........................	291,591	78.2	10.2	225,143	126,586	87,470	0.95	23.7	84.6
Cleveland, TN Metro Area....................	119,995	84.6	5.5	97,908	49,571	37,377	0.93	22.0	82.6
Cleveland-Elyria, OH Metro Area........................	2,039,765	86.3	3.0	1,672,714	1,019,948	733,439	1.05	24.6	81.9
Coeur d'Alene, ID Metro Area........................	152,186	82.7	6.4	121,743	62,079	54,617	0.90	22.0	81.6
College Station-Bryan, TX Metro Area....................	250,877	72.4	12.8	206,419	119,584	101,731	1.02	18.4	79.4
Colorado Springs, CO Metro Area....................	703,228	77.6	10.3	557,771	342,021	322,761	0.98	23.7	77.4
Columbia, MO Metro Area....................	201,900	77.7	10.1	167,005	106,312	88,518	1.03	18.8	78.7
Columbia, SC Metro Area....................	807,198	82.8	7.3	655,793	398,125	259,936	1.02	24.0	80.6
Columbus, GA-AL Metro Area....................	315,909	79.0	9.1	252,141	147,666	87,414	1.07	22.4	80.2
Columbus, IN Metro Area....................	81,025	84.3	6.9	64,387	49,093	33,288	1.24	19.4	84.2
Columbus, OH Metro Area....................	2,028,092	82.9	4.6	1,618,783	1,050,862	748,706	1.03	23.8	82.5
Corpus Christi, TX Metro Area....................	421,434	82.1	5.7	331,876	197,918	165,114	1.03	20.1	83.7
Corvallis, OR Metro Area....................	89,132	74.2	14.0	76,953	44,792	33,211	1.06	18.9	65.5
Crestview-Fort Walton Beach-Destin, FL Metro Area.	262,713	80.2	9.4	214,636	134,556	105,099	1.08	24.7	82.2
Cumberland, MD-WV Metro Area....................	98,276	86.8	4.7	83,346	39,805	29,319	1.01	23.1	83.4
Dallas-Fort Worth-Arlington, TX Metro Area	7,092,122	83.9	4.2	5,499,329	3,568,376	2,479,115	1.01	28.2	80.8
Dallas-Plano-Irving, TX Div....................	4,747,609	83.8	4.2	3,680,032	2,482,331	1,640,297	1.04	28.4	79.9
Fort Worth-Arlington-Grapevine, TX Div	2,344,513	83.9	4.2	1,819,297	1,086,045	838,818	0.95	27.8	82.7
Dalton, GA Metro Area....................	141,442	91.1	3.2	110,629	68,166	43,891	1.07	22.6	86.4
Danville, IL Metro Area....................	77,449	88.0	3.5	61,864	30,476	26,007	0.98	19.7	84.4
Daphne-Fairhope-Foley, AL Metro Area....................	206,023	88.6	5.5	167,712	76,075	67,147	0.83	27.4	84.3
Davenport-Moline-Rock Island, IA-IL Metro Area	377,983	87.9	3.5	304,131	184,357	125,798	1.02	19.8	85.3
Dayton-Kettering, OH Metro Area....................	792,975	82.5	5.3	646,888	387,651	257,217	1.05	21.4	83.3
Decatur, AL Metro Area....................	150,636	88.2	3.9	121,728	56,821	38,770	0.90	24.5	88.7
Decatur, IL Metro Area....................	105,347	83.5	4.3	85,368	53,509	42,342	1.14	18.1	83.8
Deltona-Daytona Beach-Ormond Beach, FL Metro Area	628,560	86.5	6.7	535,659	220,885	195,649	0.86	25.9	81.2
Denver-Aurora-Lakewood, CO Metro Area	2,816,470	82.3	5.5	2,260,155	1,517,203	766,898	1.00	27.6	75.7
Des Moines-West Des Moines, IA Metro	661,902	82.4	5.4	519,516	358,130	262,672	1.02	20.5	83.5
Detroit-Warren-Dearborn, MI Metro Area...........	4,266,396	87.3	2.6	3,463,899	1,984,136	1,307,307	1.01	27.0	84.1
Detroit-Dearborn-Livonia, MI Div....................	1,738,297	86.9	2.5	1,389,038	781,063	530,982	1.09	25.3	80.6
Warren-Troy-Farmington Hills, MI Div	2,528,099	87.6	2.7	2,074,861	1,203,073	776,325	0.97	28.0	86.2
Dothan, AL Metro Area....................	146,305	88.1	4.0	118,189	61,125	43,650	1.01	22.7	87.5
Dover, DE Metro Area....................	172,647	85.4	6.6	138,560	71,444	57,182	0.90	25.8	82.3
Dubuque, IA Metro Area....................	95,670	84.6	6.5	77,130	58,041	46,340	1.17	16.2	82.9
Duluth, MN-WI Metro Area....................	286,741	84.6	5.3	239,145	140,836	111,725	1.02	20.6	79.5
Durham-Chapel Hill, NC Metro Area....................	610,513	81.8	8.5	502,755	338,072	178,987	1.12	24.6	76.1
East Stroudsburg, PA Metro Area	166,097	89.8	5.7	138,833	63,602	47,327	0.83	39.1	77.9
Eau Claire, WI Metro Area	164,709	82.7	6.2	135,137	88,110	63,277	1.02	19.9	81.2
El Centro, CA Metro Area....................	177,168	86.9	4.1	133,957	57,612	53,967	0.97	22.0	81.2
Elizabethtown-Fort Knox, KY Metro Area....................	148,779	80.4	10.1	118,392	63,690	45,851	0.92	24.3	82.9
Elkhart-Goshen, IN Metro Area....................	200,525	88.3	4.0	153,098	122,794	81,828	1.31	19.5	78.1
Elmira, NY Metro Area....................	84,926	88.4	4.1	69,181	37,576	27,631	1.03	19.6	82.9
El Paso, TX Metro Area	827,939	85.2	5.1	634,807	358,539	340,365	1.00	23.4	80.4
Enid, OK Metro Area....................	61,286	82.7	7.5	47,472	28,896	25,968	1.01	16.9	83.4
Erie, PA Metro Area....................	272,943	84.8	4.6	222,862	129,150	119,125	1.03	19.7	79.1
Eugene-Springfield, OR Metro Area	365,369	78.8	7.5	308,207	167,527	159,967	1.00	20.2	70.7
Evansville, IN-KY Metro Area....................	311,948	84.7	4.3	252,410	153,958	101,891	1.03	21.0	86.7
Fairbanks, AK Metro Area....................	97,893	78.4	10.0	77,606	51,102	50,249	0.99	18.6	75.2
Fargo, ND-MN Metro Area....................	233,470	78.2	8.1	188,228	139,020	103,896	1.04	16.9	82.5
Farmington, NM Metro Area....................	125,714	88.0	3.9	96,618	49,275	46,335	0.99	23.7	83.1
Fayetteville, NC Metro Area	507,336	80.3	10.5	396,885	216,724	161,891	0.96	23.7	81.9
Fayetteville-Springdale-Rogers, AR Metro Area	496,070	83.7	5.8	388,160	245,803	195,026	1.03	20.9	82.2
Flagstaff, AZ Metro Area....................	138,907	77.2	12.9	114,113	64,567	59,488	0.99	18.4	69.5
Flint, MI Metro Area....................	404,656	86.5	3.6	326,640	148,188	121,343	0.89	26.2	84.5
Florence, SC Metro Area	202,986	88.4	3.6	162,927	91,766	64,340	1.07	22.8	84.2
Florence-Muscle Shoals, AL Metro Area	145,647	85.5	5.1	120,435	59,237	43,052	0.96	23.5	88.8
Fond du Lac, WI Metro Area	101,390	87.8	5.2	82,623	48,697	37,288	0.92	20.1	83.1
Fort Collins, CO Metro Area....................	334,618	80.1	9.8	278,231	168,005	142,177	0.96	23.2	75.0
Fort Smith, AR-OK Metro Area....................	245,507	84.0	4.7	195,896	105,263	72,396	1.01	21.2	83.5
Fort Wayne, IN Metro Area....................	397,967	85.1	4.2	311,403	200,868	166,097	1.04	21.7	84.4
Fresno, CA Metro Area	964,182	85.0	3.6	727,089	387,148	351,800	1.00	22.6	78.5
Gadsden, AL Metro Area....................	101,901	85.3	4.6	83,391	36,800	30,032	0.89	24.0	85.5
Gainesville, FL Metro Area	317,894	79.0	10.0	268,268	149,910	121,289	1.05	23.4	75.6
Gainesville, GA Metro Area....................	193,658	87.2	6.0	151,110	94,150	62,485	1.04	26.7	80.9
Gettysburg, PA Metro Area	101,085	88.8	5.8	83,662	34,416	24,258	0.70	28.2	82.6
Glens Falls, NY Metro Area	125,317	86.8	4.8	105,604	54,909	33,963	0.93	24.5	81.6
Goldsboro, NC Metro Area	122,296	82.9	7.3	97,777	51,850	41,569	0.97	22.0	80.5
Grand Forks, ND-MN Metro Area....................	100,760	79.8	9.6	82,077	55,596	44,811	1.03	15.4	81.2
Grand Island, NE Metro Area....................	74,511	85.1	5.1	57,733	40,233	31,578	1.06	17.4	81.9

Table B-4. Migration and Commuting, 2014–2018—*Continued*

Metropolitan Statistical Area Metropolitan Division	Migration 2014-2018			Commuting 2014-2018					
	Total population age 1 year and older	Percent who lived in the same house in prior year	Percent who lived outside this metro area in prior year	Total residents age 16 and older	Total who worked in this metro area	Lived and worked in this metro area	Employment/ residence ratio	Mean travel time to work	Percent who drove alone to work
Grand Junction, CO Metro Area	148,308	80.9	7.5	120,743	66,163	64,041	0.97	20.2	78.4
Grand Rapids-Kentwood, MI Metro Area	1,041,322	84.1	4.9	826,836	548,639	406,386	1.05	21.7	81.9
Grants Pass, OR Metro Area	84,501	84.3	6.8	70,981	29,939	26,485	0.97	19.7	79.8
Great Falls, MT Metro Area	80,479	82.5	7.6	64,998	38,811	37,491	1.00	15.6	79.9
Greeley, CO Metro Area	291,199	82.8	9.2	224,773	119,335	86,809	0.83	27.3	80.1
Green Bay, WI Metro Area	313,884	86.1	4.6	251,646	171,672	133,903	1.05	20.0	83.7
Greensboro-High Point, NC Metro Area	749,512	86.2	5.2	608,791	371,211	262,031	1.07	22.5	83.4
Greenville, NC Metro Area	175,335	78.3	10.6	143,129	84,734	69,169	1.03	20.9	83.6
Greenville-Anderson, SC Metro Area	873,086	84.3	5.5	706,742	408,681	298,684	1.01	23.3	83.4
Gulfport-Biloxi, MS Metro Area	404,992	83.9	6.1	323,810	179,854	130,194	1.02	24.5	84.9
Hagerstown-Martinsburg, MD-WV Metro Area	277,667	87.0	5.7	224,745	107,367	73,794	0.85	30.4	81.7
Hammond, LA Metro Area	129,020	84.5	6.7	101,741	44,122	33,969	0.80	32.0	79.2
Hanford-Corcoran, CA Metro Area	148,252	80.2	9.3	113,475	56,576	42,927	1.02	22.9	76.4
Harrisburg-Carlisle, PA Metro Area	561,608	85.1	6.6	460,026	330,277	192,243	1.17	23.1	79.8
Harrisonburg, VA Metro Area	131,332	80.2	9.2	109,448	70,838	34,769	1.12	19.8	76.8
Hartford-East Hartford-Middletown, CT Metro Area	1,197,505	87.8	4.1	994,083	638,441	444,597	1.06	24.1	81.0
Hattiesburg, MS Metro Area	165,592	82.4	7.6	131,517	72,045	40,199	1.01	24.0	83.2
Hickory-Lenoir-Morganton, NC Metro Area	361,868	87.3	4.3	297,817	154,540	107,527	0.97	22.8	85.2
Hilton Head Island-Bluffton, SC Metro Area	208,568	82.6	9.2	173,752	91,485	76,060	1.00	23.8	76.8
Hinesville, GA Metro Area	78,626	71.2	15.6	59,587	34,803	22,630	1.01	23.2	81.6
Homosassa Springs, FL Metro Area	142,288	85.3	7.1	124,572	38,263	33,735	0.86	25.5	82.6
Hot Springs, AR Metro Area	97,315	84.4	6.2	80,534	40,527	34,043	1.03	21.7	79.0
Houma-Thibodaux, LA Metro Area	208,277	88.5	3.1	164,387	92,097	62,450	1.04	26.3	81.6
Houston-The Woodlands-Sugar Land, TX Metro Area	6,684,219	84.5	4.1	5,157,168	3,204,490	2,491,693	1.01	29.9	80.6
Huntington-Ashland, WV-KY-OH Metro Area	360,943	88.1	3.2	295,528	136,858	78,198	0.97	23.6	85.0
Huntsville, AL Metro Area	445,787	84.4	5.5	362,212	231,718	178,241	1.10	22.3	88.0
Idaho Falls, ID Metro Area	140,780	82.4	7.1	102,629	64,868	47,840	1.05	20.1	78.1
Indianapolis-Carmel-Anderson, IN Metro Area	1,983,612	85.0	3.8	1,561,137	993,155	618,397	1.01	25.0	83.9
Iowa City, IA Metro Area	166,682	76.9	9.9	137,561	97,260	75,342	1.06	19.3	71.0
Ithaca, NY Metro Area	102,133	75.0	13.8	89,418	60,191	43,778	1.24	18.9	61.3
Jackson, MI Metro Area	157,352	85.7	5.7	128,750	61,524	48,967	0.92	23.1	84.7
Jackson, MS Metro Area	591,859	85.6	4.4	468,515	268,141	153,186	1.03	24.5	86.1
Jackson, TN Metro Area	176,353	88.3	4.2	142,284	82,048	54,740	1.08	21.0	85.5
Jacksonville, FL Metro Area	1,457,321	81.3	6.3	1,179,239	697,552	537,572	1.01	26.7	80.8
Jacksonville, NC Metro Area	190,085	71.4	17.7	150,702	99,574	89,348	1.01	21.2	72.5
Janesville-Beloit, WI Metro Area	160,177	85.2	4.5	127,975	67,034	54,510	0.86	22.8	83.3
Jefferson City, MO Metro Area	149,427	85.8	6.2	120,983	74,635	47,519	1.06	21.1	84.1
Johnson City, TN Metro Area	199,498	84.3	5.6	167,256	83,565	53,956	0.97	21.4	85.5
Johnstown, PA Metro Area	133,371	88.2	4.4	111,584	52,003	41,411	0.93	24.6	82.3
Jonesboro, AR Metro Area	128,226	77.1	6.8	101,435	59,105	46,224	1.03	19.5	83.1
Joplin, MO Metro Area	175,307	86.3	4.6	138,375	86,120	58,421	1.05	18.8	82.7
Kahului-Wailuku-Lahaina, HI Metro Area	163,729	87.8	5.1	132,234	82,341	81,338	1.00	21.6	72.7
Kalamazoo-Portage, MI Metro Area	258,708	79.0	7.5	210,542	134,231	107,513	1.04	20.4	82.2
Kankakee, IL Metro Area	109,843	89.1	4.3	88,188	45,910	37,270	0.93	24.4	83.4
Kansas City, MO-KS Metro Area	2,080,919	84.6	4.0	1,646,607	1,068,913	651,988	1.02	23.1	83.5
Kennewick-Richland, WA Metro Area	280,902	83.5	4.9	211,683	120,704	86,377	0.97	21.8	80.9
Killeen-Temple, TX Metro Area	430,824	76.3	10.9	332,305	188,471	150,992	0.97	21.6	79.3
Kingsport-Bristol, TN-VA Metro Area	303,746	86.5	4.5	253,464	126,355	76,127	1.01	23.1	85.9
Kingston, NY Metro Area	177,690	88.8	5.1	150,935	68,778	56,157	0.81	28.4	77.2
Knoxville, TN Metro Area	837,452	85.1	4.9	690,279	397,873	277,440	1.03	23.7	84.3
Kokomo, IN Metro Area	81,663	84.3	5.6	66,064	39,912	28,760	1.10	19.5	83.9
La Crosse-Onalaska, WI-MN Metro Area	135,117	82.5	7.4	111,908	77,185	59,726	1.08	18.5	81.3
Lafayette, LA Metro Area	481,920	85.6	3.8	381,104	220,792	154,244	1.01	25.8	83.7
Lafayette-West Lafayette, IN Metro Area	223,394	75.0	10.8	183,896	112,567	87,960	1.04	19.4	75.8
Lake Charles, LA Metro Area	204,277	85.7	4.1	161,068	104,923	83,856	1.14	20.9	85.7
Lake Havasu City-Kingman, AZ Metro Area	204,536	80.5	8.9	173,770	58,533	56,381	0.84	20.8	80.0
Lakeland-Winter Haven, FL Metro Area	661,489	85.4	6.8	535,543	242,377	212,507	0.90	26.8	82.5
Lancaster, PA Metro Area	531,659	88.2	4.2	424,544	256,083	222,445	0.97	23.1	77.9
Lansing-East Lansing, MI Metro Area	539,155	80.8	7.6	445,431	260,715	157,850	1.01	22.1	79.8
Laredo, TX Metro Area	266,852	88.9	2.4	190,483	104,453	100,672	0.99	21.5	81.2
Las Cruces, NM Metro Area	213,004	84.8	6.8	167,514	80,231	71,458	0.91	20.9	81.2
Las Vegas-Henderson-Paradise, NV Metro Area	2,117,336	81.2	5.3	1,692,284	995,759	974,479	1.01	24.8	78.7
Lawrence, KS Metro Area	118,012	72.5	12.5	99,472	57,274	47,105	0.88	20.6	77.3
Lawton, OK Metro Area	126,647	71.8	14.2	101,033	60,016	54,142	1.03	17.2	72.6
Lebanon, PA Metro Area	137,117	86.5	5.8	110,484	55,453	41,483	0.84	22.6	81.0
Lewiston, ID-WA Metro Area	61,730	83.3	5.3	50,734	28,415	19,065	1.02	16.2	82.3
Lewiston-Auburn, ME Metro Area	106,172	84.6	5.9	86,464	49,753	36,695	0.95	23.9	79.3
Lexington-Fayette, KY Metro Area	500,668	77.9	7.3	406,426	278,022	183,618	1.10	21.5	79.6
Lima, OH Metro Area	102,536	84.0	6.1	82,330	52,588	37,369	1.11	19.1	85.8
Lincoln, NE Metro Area	322,921	79.0	7.8	259,535	183,890	162,375	1.04	19.3	81.3
Little Rock-North Little Rock-Conway, AR Metro Area	725,516	85.1	4.3	579,390	352,766	249,131	1.04	23.0	84.1
Logan, UT-ID Metro Area	133,279	80.3	8.3	98,026	61,501	56,100	0.96	17.9	75.3
Longview, TX Metro Area	280,734	84.2	7.0	221,449	121,459	77,770	1.01	22.5	84.8

Table B-4. Migration and Commuting, 2014–2018—*Continued*

Metropolitan Statistical Area / Metropolitan Division	Migration 2014-2018			Commuting 2014-2018					
	Total population age 1 year and older	Percent who lived in the same house in prior year	Percent who lived outside this metro area in prior year	Total residents age 16 and older	Total who worked in this metro area	Lived and worked in this metro area	Employment/ residence ratio	Mean travel time to work	Percent who drove alone to work
Longview, WA Metro Area	103,793	80.8	6.4	83,678	41,694	32,782	0.98	25.1	80.0
Los Angeles-Long Beach-Anaheim, CA Metro Area	13,111,211	88.7	2.7	10,653,248	6,522,483	5,699,633	1.04	30.4	75.1
Anaheim-Santa Ana-Irvine, CA Div	3,128,984	87.0	3.3	2,538,090	1,643,502	1,305,662	1.06	27.7	78.7
Los Angeles-Long Beach-Glendale, CA Div	9,982,227	89.2	2.6	8,115,158	4,878,981	4,393,971	1.03	31.3	73.9
Louisville/Jefferson County, KY-IN Metro Area	1,237,656	86.0	3.3	999,975	627,417	439,035	1.04	24.0	82.1
Lubbock, TX Metro Area	308,432	75.0	9.2	245,152	151,655	140,476	1.01	17.3	79.9
Lynchburg, VA Metro Area	257,529	85.5	5.9	215,207	112,937	57,781	0.95	23.8	81.7
Macon-Bibb County, GA Metro Area	226,565	84.9	5.5	181,922	98,131	58,660	1.08	23.4	83.3
Madera, CA Metro Area	152,969	88.4	5.2	117,191	49,361	34,953	0.91	27.1	76.8
Madison, WI Metro Area	639,882	81.9	6.4	526,164	389,130	315,284	1.08	21.7	74.7
Manchester-Nashua, NH Metro Area	406,742	84.5	6.7	335,710	200,517	145,770	0.91	28.2	81.4
Manhattan, KS Metro Area	131,647	73.3	13.6	106,214	73,729	48,026	1.05	16.4	77.7
Mankato, MN Metro Area	99,029	82.0	8.9	81,833	58,171	36,405	1.06	18.0	80.1
Mansfield, OH Metro Area	120,201	83.3	5.9	97,915	53,417	40,455	1.06	22.4	83.9
McAllen-Edinburg-Mission, TX Metro Area	836,243	90.6	2.5	597,554	301,967	288,486	0.96	22.1	80.3
Medford, OR Metro Area	212,170	80.7	6.0	174,754	91,392	86,785	1.00	18.9	76.1
Memphis, TN-MS-AR Metro Area	1,320,762	84.9	3.3	1,039,669	622,533	478,531	1.03	24.0	84.6
Merced, CA Metro Area	265,686	85.5	5.5	197,980	83,054	70,437	0.84	27.4	79.1
Miami-Fort Lauderdale-Pompano Beach, FL Metro	6,005,506	86.0	4.0	4,972,813	2,885,675	2,481,410	1.01	29.5	78.2
Fort Lauderdale-Pompano Beach-Sunrise, FL Div	1,888,071	84.3	4.2	1,548,232	848,903	713,669	0.91	28.4	79.9
Miami-Miami Beach-Kendall, FL Div	2,685,410	87.9	3.3	2,225,127	1,356,868	1,184,788	1.06	32.2	76.8
West Palm Beach-Boca Raton-Boynton Beach, FL Div	1,432,025	84.6	4.8	1,199,454	679,904	582,953	1.03	25.6	78.2
Michigan City-La Porte, IN Metro Area	109,321	83.4	7.7	89,337	41,377	31,697	0.90	22.9	83.7
Midland, MI Metro Area	82,586	87.3	5.7	67,652	40,115	26,615	1.06	21.6	85.4
Midland, TX Metro Area	166,792	82.3	8.8	125,973	104,909	72,165	1.24	18.9	85.6
Milwaukee-Waukesha, WI Metro Area	1,557,921	85.5	3.3	1,250,107	823,115	553,794	1.05	23.0	80.8
Minneapolis-St. Paul-Bloomington, MN Metro Area	3,498,186	85.3	3.4	2,789,737	1,919,075	1,094,206	1.01	25.4	77.6
Missoula, MT Metro Area	115,061	79.2	9.6	96,149	65,738	60,241	1.05	18.3	72.4
Mobile, AL Metro Area	425,865	87.7	3.1	341,515	186,141	157,547	1.05	25.3	86.2
Modesto, CA Metro Area	531,868	86.7	4.4	408,846	193,082	162,479	0.90	29.0	81.6
Monroe, LA Metro Area	202,011	89.2	3.8	159,789	81,206	66,967	1.01	21.8	85.6
Monroe, MI Metro Area	148,217	89.5	4.7	121,468	46,381	32,487	0.67	25.0	86.7
Montgomery, AL Metro Area	369,441	82.1	5.7	296,208	168,500	110,153	1.05	23.1	85.3
Morgantown, WV Metro Area	137,730	81.5	9.0	117,972	69,714	48,841	1.12	22.8	77.1
Morristown, TN Metro Area	138,452	88.4	5.8	113,323	51,025	31,825	0.89	25.2	80.9
Mount Vernon-Anacortes, WA Metro Area	122,859	83.5	7.5	99,600	55,878	43,110	1.02	26.2	77.5
Muncie, IN Metro Area	114,449	77.4	8.8	96,784	52,685	41,813	1.02	20.7	79.6
Muskegon, MI Metro Area	171,110	84.1	5.5	137,058	64,214	52,638	0.88	21.7	84.2
Myrtle Beach-Conway-North Myrtle Beach, SC-NC Metro Area	444,053	84.9	7.1	376,454	180,505	160,271	0.95	22.8	82.5
Napa, CA Metro Area	139,378	87.9	5.1	114,489	77,863	53,385	1.13	24.9	76.0
Naples-Marco Island, FL Metro Area	360,213	83.5	7.9	306,944	162,264	135,272	1.08	24.7	74.4
Nashville-Davidson--Murfreesboro--Franklin, TN Metro Area	1,817,409	83.5	5.4	1,454,612	967,102	618,179	1.04	27.5	81.4
New Bern, NC Metro Area	124,182	82.0	10.1	101,822	55,416	41,662	1.01	21.9	79.8
New Haven-Milford, CT Metro Area	851,227	88.0	4.5	705,188	392,142	306,523	0.93	25.3	78.1
New Orleans-Metairie, LA Metro Area	1,249,136	87.8	3.5	1,011,137	607,210	377,244	1.05	25.9	78.6
New York-Newark-Jersey City, NY-NJ-PA Metro Area	19,097,750	90.6	2.1	15,600,765	9,440,340	5,153,508	1.02	36.8	49.3
Nassau County-Suffolk County, NY Div	2,818,459	93.3	1.2	2,304,694	1,220,050	940,329	0.87	34.2	74.3
Newark, NJ-PA Div	2,140,862	90.6	1.9	1,732,126	1,021,016	532,598	0.96	33.4	70.6
New Brunswick-Lakewood, NJ Div	2,346,696	90.5	2.0	1,903,964	1,027,582	638,213	0.91	33.1	76.4
New York-Jersey City-White Plains, NY-NJ Div	11,791,733	90.0	2.3	9,659,981	6,171,692	3,042,368	1.09	38.8	33.7
Niles, MI Metro Area	153,133	85.0	5.9	124,462	69,181	56,830	0.98	19.7	81.4
North Port-Sarasota-Bradenton, FL Metro Area	779,987	84.3	6.9	671,415	317,166	248,126	1.00	24.9	81.0
Norwich-New London, CT Metro Area	266,544	85.4	6.6	221,822	136,203	109,292	0.99	23.5	79.8
Ocala, FL Metro Area	345,540	86.0	7.1	290,875	112,375	98,821	0.93	25.5	80.5
Ocean City, NJ Metro Area	93,056	88.4	5.9	79,298	41,715	31,574	1.00	22.7	80.4
Odessa, TX Metro Area	155,782	82.7	7.1	115,517	73,762	55,538	1.02	23.1	81.8
Ogden-Clearfield, UT Metro Area	642,335	85.0	5.2	470,483	252,146	181,762	0.83	22.7	80.1
Oklahoma City, OK Metro Area	1,351,759	82.1	5.0	1,064,983	661,517	468,656	1.01	22.7	82.9
Olympia-Lacey-Tumwater, WA Metro Area	272,020	80.5	9.4	222,075	114,559	92,059	0.90	26.3	79.1
Omaha-Council Bluffs, NE-IA Metro Area	910,234	84.0	4.4	710,666	478,728	330,949	1.01	20.3	84.2
Orlando-Kissimmee-Sanford, FL Metro Area	2,423,609	82.7	6.9	1,968,898	1,220,814	833,279	1.05	28.6	80.2
Oshkosh-Neenah, WI Metro Area	168,118	83.3	7.7	138,852	96,421	62,344	1.11	18.4	85.3
Owensboro, KY Metro Area	116,354	85.2	4.7	91,995	52,971	42,107	1.02	20.0	87.0
Oxnard-Thousand Oaks-Ventura, CA Metro Area	838,094	89.0	4.0	672,054	360,946	317,471	0.89	26.8	78.5
Palm Bay-Melbourne-Titusville, FL Metro Area	571,650	84.8	6.5	483,529	233,183	221,930	0.96	24.8	81.3
Panama City, FL Metro Area	180,081	80.1	8.0	147,639	84,715	77,299	1.03	23.3	81.4
Parkersburg-Vienna, WV Metro Area	90,298	89.2	4.0	74,324	40,264	29,356	1.06	21.2	81.6
Pensacola-Ferry Pass-Brent, FL Metro Area	476,584	81.6	8.6	390,549	202,179	161,979	0.94	24.8	78.4
Peoria, IL Metro Area	404,884	86.9	3.4	325,651	184,655	123,069	1.00	20.8	84.7

Table B-4. Migration and Commuting, 2014–2018—*Continued*

Metropolitan Statistical Area / Metropolitan Division	Migration 2014-2018			Commuting 2014-2018					
	Total population age 1 year and older	Percent who lived in the same house in prior year	Percent who lived outside this metro area in prior year	Total residents age 16 and older	Total who worked in this metro area	Lived and worked in this metro area	Employment/ residence ratio	Mean travel time to work	Percent who drove alone to work
Philadelphia-Camden-Wilmington, PA-NJ-DE-MD Metro Area	6,002,847	88.1	3.1	4,889,319	2,876,677	1,822,398	0.99	29.9	72.9
Camden, NJ Div	1,231,967	89.1	2.9	1,000,826	516,848	309,924	0.85	29.4	80.9
Montgomery County-Bucks County-Chester County,	1,945,090	89.2	2.9	1,587,941	1,029,473	621,365	1.02	29.2	79.8
Philadelphia, PA Div	2,111,395	86.6	3.3	1,718,832	985,807	638,292	1.05	32.3	57.3
Wilmington, DE-MD-NJ Div	714,395	87.8	3.5	581,720	344,549	252,817	0.99	26.4	80.7
Phoenix-Mesa-Chandler, AZ Metro Area	4,618,116	82.6	5.0	3,662,277	2,112,466	2,012,268	0.99	26.4	76.4
Pine Bluff, AR Metro Area	91,478	87.8	5.7	74,590	30,681	23,352	0.96	22.0	86.8
Pittsburgh, PA Metro Area	2,315,450	88.1	3.1	1,946,007	1,150,822	868,117	1.01	26.8	77.1
Pittsfield, MA Metro Area	126,371	87.4	4.6	108,363	64,335	57,731	1.02	19.9	77.5
Pocatello, ID Metro Area	91,319	81.3	7.8	70,633	37,945	33,438	0.96	17.6	76.8
Portland-South Portland, ME Metro Area	524,421	86.4	4.8	440,186	279,382	210,216	0.99	24.9	78.4
Portland-Vancouver-Hillsboro, OR-WA Metro Area	2,392,441	82.8	5.1	1,945,417	1,212,765	830,509	1.01	26.9	70.4
Port St. Lucie, FL Metro Area	459,264	86.0	7.4	385,633	163,273	123,396	0.87	26.8	78.5
Poughkeepsie-Newburgh-Middletown, NY Metro Area	665,433	90.2	2.5	537,051	268,277	209,557	0.85	33.0	75.0
Prescott Valley-Prescott, AZ Metro Area	223,104	83.6	8.7	191,513	78,358	75,280	0.95	23.4	76.2
Providence-Warwick, RI-MA Metro Area	1,599,747	87.7	3.7	1,329,819	719,618	488,811	0.91	26.0	80.5
Provo-Orem, UT Metro Area	589,994	79.0	8.4	416,561	250,037	223,722	0.93	21.8	73.4
Pueblo, CO Metro Area	162,989	83.8	6.1	131,204	65,284	59,277	0.98	22.0	82.8
Punta Gorda, FL Metro Area	175,798	84.4	9.6	157,559	51,461	40,862	0.87	24.9	79.1
Racine, WI Metro Area	192,915	87.6	4.9	154,976	79,939	57,790	0.86	24.3	84.0
Raleigh-Cary, NC Metro Area	1,287,680	83.4	6.5	1,017,630	653,537	502,366	0.99	26.2	79.8
Rapid City, SD Metro Area	135,070	82.5	7.9	107,593	69,984	57,602	1.01	18.2	81.9
Reading, PA Metro Area	412,417	86.9	4.5	333,733	177,067	146,950	0.89	24.9	79.8
Redding, CA Metro Area	177,154	85.2	5.7	144,873	71,306	65,717	1.01	20.4	81.8
Reno, NV Metro Area	448,983	81.2	6.2	365,834	223,395	205,368	1.00	21.6	77.8
Richmond, VA Metro Area	1,244,031	84.2	5.0	1,014,795	633,061	285,999	1.02	25.0	81.5
Riverside-San Bernardino-Ontario, CA Metro Area	4,461,967	86.3	4.7	3,471,149	1,624,255	1,313,436	0.87	32.4	78.5
Roanoke, VA Metro Area	310,064	85.2	4.9	256,380	158,617	69,720	1.08	23.6	82.4
Rochester, MN Metro Area	213,724	86.6	5.4	168,669	119,209	90,002	1.06	19.9	74.3
Rochester, NY Metro Area	1,064,603	85.6	4.2	876,224	518,296	423,022	1.01	21.4	81.4
Rockford, IL Metro Area	335,904	86.3	4.4	268,033	152,504	115,429	0.98	23.3	82.7
Rocky Mount, NC Metro Area	145,387	88.3	4.6	118,225	59,963	38,293	0.95	22.3	83.4
Rome, GA Metro Area	95,766	84.2	5.4	76,630	44,463	32,460	1.09	22.9	82.0
Sacramento-Roseville-Folsom, CA Metro Area	2,265,855	84.3	5.2	1,819,325	1,011,564	756,925	0.99	27.2	76.8
Saginaw, MI Metro Area	190,464	86.6	4.5	156,480	93,915	64,645	1.15	21.9	83.3
St. Cloud, MN Metro Area	194,177	81.6	8.2	155,357	111,737	75,408	1.07	21.2	80.5
St. George, UT Metro Area	158,573	83.2	8.3	121,955	64,755	60,737	1.01	17.5	77.5
St. Joseph, MO-KS Metro Area	124,870	84.0	6.3	102,062	59,813	41,995	1.04	18.8	83.7
St. Louis, MO-IL Metro Area	2,773,562	86.3	3.0	2,249,138	1,375,443	807,013	1.01	25.8	83.0
Salem, OR Metro Area	412,044	83.7	6.0	325,659	173,520	130,932	0.95	23.9	76.4
Salinas, CA Metro Area	427,668	87.9	6.1	331,250	184,127	166,857	0.98	22.7	71.2
Salisbury, MD-DE Metro Area	395,110	86.3	5.3	330,336	169,129	129,383	0.96	24.6	82.7
Salt Lake City, UT Metro Area	1,167,901	83.6	5.7	887,522	672,669	541,602	1.13	22.5	74.9
San Angelo, TX Metro Area	118,704	83.1	8.0	94,466	57,738	53,427	1.01	17.3	80.5
San Antonio-New Braunfels, TX Metro Area	2,393,841	83.8	5.0	1,874,643	1,100,656	942,594	0.99	26.3	79.8
San Diego-Chula Vista-Carlsbad, CA Metro Area	3,261,095	84.3	5.1	2,656,740	1,635,620	1,558,682	1.02	26.0	76.3
San Francisco-Oakland-Berkeley, CA Metro Area	4,624,391	86.9	4.9	3,837,904	2,410,577	1,485,220	1.03	33.6	58.1
Oakland-Berkeley-Livermore, CA Div	2,747,474	86.9	4.4	2,238,013	1,138,412	788,201	0.88	35.3	64.0
San Francisco-San Mateo-Redwood City, CA Div.	1,618,994	86.8	5.4	1,386,900	1,144,892	616,145	1.26	31.3	48.6
San Rafael, CA Div	257,923	86.6	6.0	212,991	127,273	80,874	0.99	32.5	65.3
San Jose-Sunnyvale-Santa Clara, CA Metro Area	1,959,326	85.6	6.0	1,582,829	1,109,551	839,835	1.13	28.9	75.1
San Luis Obispo-Paso Robles, CA Metro Area	279,210	82.1	7.8	236,821	127,166	114,769	0.99	22.2	74.0
Santa Cruz-Watsonville, CA Metro Area	270,904	85.5	7.0	226,263	119,655	101,581	0.91	27.0	69.0
Santa Fe, NM Metro Area	147,670	89.9	5.4	124,499	71,260	58,631	1.02	22.3	78.8
Santa Maria-Santa Barbara, CA Metro Area	438,786	80.5	7.2	355,380	219,845	193,820	1.06	19.8	67.9
Santa Rosa-Petaluma, CA Metro Area	496,731	86.2	5.3	412,126	231,728	210,600	0.94	25.4	74.7
Savannah, GA Metro Area	376,063	78.9	8.5	302,425	187,596	138,231	1.04	24.3	80.3
Scranton--Wilkes-Barre, PA Metro Area	551,705	87.8	3.9	459,294	260,357	205,517	1.01	22.1	80.8
Seattle-Tacoma-Bellevue, WA Metro Area	3,764,059	82.0	5.6	3,070,343	2,005,023	1,606,272	1.03	30.7	68.0
Seattle-Bellevue-Kent, WA Div	2,915,523	81.7	5.6	2,392,646	1,657,089	1,323,236	1.07	30.3	65.3
Tacoma-Lakewood, WA Div	848,536	82.7	5.3	677,697	347,934	283,036	0.86	32.0	78.3
Sebastian-Vero Beach, FL Metro Area	149,759	87.2	7.3	128,348	55,933	46,293	1.00	22.4	79.7
Sebring-Avon Park, FL Metro Area	101,453	83.9	7.5	86,414	31,179	28,516	0.97	19.9	77.9
Sheboygan, WI Metro Area	114,004	87.5	4.0	92,386	59,648	49,650	1.02	18.0	84.2
Sherman-Denison, TX Metro Area	126,925	82.4	7.8	101,316	52,241	42,003	0.91	25.1	78.4
Shreveport-Bossier City, LA Metro Area	396,646	87.6	3.3	314,330	178,549	123,835	1.03	21.7	86.2
Sierra Vista-Douglas, AZ Metro Area	124,759	82.6	10.1	101,377	45,338	42,920	0.98	20.6	78.8
Sioux City, IA-NE-SD Metro Area	141,614	87.0	4.9	109,994	73,291	49,323	1.02	17.9	82.9
Sioux Falls, SD Metro Area	251,854	83.1	5.5	195,439	142,368	103,362	1.02	18.4	84.4

Table B-4. Migration and Commuting, 2014–2018—*Continued*

Metropolitan Statistical Area Metropolitan Division	Migration 2014-2018			Commuting 2014-2018					
	Total population age 1 year and older	Percent who lived in the same house in prior year	Percent who lived outside this metro area in prior year	Total residents age 16 and older	Total who worked in this metro area	Lived and worked in this metro area	Employment/ residence ratio	Mean travel time to work	Percent who drove alone to work
South Bend-Mishawaka, IN-MI Metro Area	316,672	86.4	5.6	254,147	139,985	109,153	0.94	21.6	82.1
Spartanburg, SC Metro Area	298,887	85.1	5.6	239,693	146,966	106,192	1.08	22.7	84.4
Spokane-Spokane Valley, WA Metro Area	535,916	81.3	6.8	434,888	247,473	225,217	1.03	22.0	78.0
Springfield, IL Metro Area	207,807	84.1	4.4	168,295	110,434	89,821	1.10	20.2	83.5
Springfield, MA Metro Area	694,907	85.7	4.9	578,982	315,997	243,655	0.96	23.0	79.0
Springfield, MO Metro Area	453,311	81.6	6.1	366,504	216,493	154,507	1.03	21.9	82.5
Springfield, OH Metro Area	133,556	81.0	5.9	108,163	49,531	38,154	0.83	22.5	81.5
State College, PA Metro Area	160,061	75.6	13.3	139,946	83,077	67,625	1.10	20.3	68.5
Staunton, VA Metro Area	120,004	84.4	6.5	99,558	48,410	25,887	0.86	23.3	85.1
Stockton, CA Metro Area	722,181	85.4	5.5	553,741	260,066	208,986	0.88	33.2	78.2
Sumter, SC Metro Area	139,123	86.1	6.1	112,235	52,482	40,474	0.94	23.7	84.0
Syracuse, NY Metro Area	648,377	86.0	4.7	532,426	308,382	249,888	1.02	21.2	80.4
Tallahassee, FL Metro Area	376,105	77.8	9.4	315,130	182,646	149,115	1.03	23.2	81.5
Tampa-St. Petersburg-Clearwater, FL Metro Area	2,999,497	83.8	5.4	2,489,176	1,359,826	1,106,465	0.99	27.4	79.5
Terre Haute, IN Metro Area	185,403	81.9	6.7	152,345	78,680	57,099	0.97	22.2	83.1
Texarkana, TX-AR Metro Area	148,288	87.0	4.5	118,602	61,129	39,633	1.04	18.7	87.7
The Villages, FL Metro Area	120,514	87.3	8.2	113,104	32,616	16,358	1.34	24.8	74.8
Toledo, OH Metro Area	637,456	83.3	4.7	517,725	316,629	216,179	1.05	21.0	84.6
Topeka, KS Metro Area	230,590	85.9	4.5	183,958	110,146	86,502	1.01	20.3	82.8
Trenton-Princeton, NJ Metro Area	365,144	86.4	6.9	298,866	231,026	117,268	1.31	28.0	71.2
Tucson, AZ Metro Area	1,007,876	79.3	6.4	826,613	435,030	422,194	1.00	24.7	76.9
Tulsa, OK Metro Area	972,471	83.3	4.2	766,512	461,086	339,550	1.01	21.7	83.0
Tuscaloosa, AL Metro Area	246,912	84.4	7.4	202,966	108,787	88,533	1.02	24.0	85.4
Twin Falls, ID Metro Area	105,049	83.9	6.8	79,757	50,171	39,911	1.02	17.8	82.0
Tyler, TX Metro Area	222,459	85.9	6.3	175,423	104,811	84,340	1.07	23.8	84.1
Urban Honolulu, HI Metro Area	974,836	85.6	5.7	798,404	499,792	494,890	1.00	29.1	64.0
Utica-Rome, NY Metro Area	290,008	89.0	3.9	238,222	126,113	101,728	0.98	20.6	81.5
Valdosta, GA Metro Area	142,859	83.2	7.2	113,748	61,042	48,327	1.02	20.6	85.2
Vallejo, CA Metro Area	434,247	84.7	7.4	351,136	148,597	116,325	0.74	32.6	76.5
Victoria, TX Metro Area	98,184	84.2	4.7	77,205	45,691	37,497	1.02	20.7	80.1
Vineland-Bridgeton, NJ Metro Area	151,828	88.0	5.0	121,197	61,632	43,879	1.00	24.0	80.8
Virginia Beach-Norfolk-Newport News, VA-NC Metro Area	1,735,943	82.0	6.4	1,410,147	873,413	451,526	1.00	24.5	81.5
Visalia, CA Metro Area	453,749	88.2	2.9	332,597	163,753	146,551	0.95	22.7	78.1
Waco, TX Metro Area	262,175	80.8	7.2	207,716	122,501	106,495	1.04	19.9	82.1
Walla Walla, WA Metro Area	59,604	78.5	10.7	48,783	30,296	23,193	1.15	16.2	71.6
Warner Robins, GA Metro Area	176,305	84.4	7.4	138,575	79,374	56,377	0.99	21.9	84.7
Washington-Arlington-Alexandria, DC-VA-MD-WV Metro Area	6,074,957	84.8	4.9	4,882,612	3,411,898	1,640,648	1.05	34.7	66.0
Frederick-Gaithersburg-Rockville, MD Div.	1,273,573	85.9	4.5	1,020,127	629,814	411,108	0.93	34.7	67.9
Washington-Arlington-Alexandria, DC-VA-MD-WV Div.	4,801,384	84.6	5.0	3,862,485	2,782,084	1,229,540	1.08	34.7	65.5
Waterloo-Cedar Falls, IA Metro Area	168,041	81.6	6.7	137,078	92,135	73,575	1.06	17.0	81.3
Watertown-Fort Drum, NY Metro Area	112,346	79.2	11.7	89,445	56,364	50,437	1.06	17.8	77.4
Wausau-Weston, WI Metro Area	161,206	88.4	4.8	131,197	84,435	68,223	1.00	19.8	83.2
Weirton-Steubenville, WV-OH Metro Area	118,492	88.2	5.3	99,038	42,866	27,557	0.86	24.6	84.9
Wenatchee, WA Metro Area	115,926	87.5	4.6	91,322	50,748	36,362	0.96	18.7	78.7
Wheeling, WV-OH Metro Area	141,419	90.8	3.8	118,396	64,503	37,708	1.07	22.8	86.2
Wichita, KS Metro Area	627,837	84.0	4.1	489,423	305,164	263,224	1.00	19.6	83.8
Wichita Falls, TX Metro Area	149,041	80.6	9.3	120,907	68,433	59,696	1.00	16.5	77.4
Williamsport, PA Metro Area	113,652	86.3	4.8	94,029	54,663	44,739	1.03	20.4	82.1
Wilmington, NC Metro Area	280,243	83.1	7.7	234,096	140,360	106,532	1.06	21.7	81.6
Winchester, VA-WV Metro Area	134,485	87.9	5.3	109,576	63,603	28,160	0.98	30.9	79.2
Winston-Salem, NC Metro Area	654,702	86.4	5.1	530,161	273,103	186,758	0.93	23.5	84.1
Worcester, MA-CT Metro Area	930,014	88.7	4.3	763,816	403,156	325,283	0.86	28.9	80.8
Yakima, WA Metro Area	245,965	86.2	3.9	182,459	102,426	97,579	1.00	19.0	79.3
York-Hanover, PA Metro Area	439,146	87.6	4.1	356,928	183,199	149,267	0.84	27.1	84.4
Youngstown-Warren-Boardman, OH-PA Metro Area	539,467	88.8	3.3	448,625	228,507	166,129	0.96	22.1	85.6
Yuba City, CA Metro Area	168,886	84.3	5.9	130,208	56,528	34,642	0.83	28.3	78.8
Yuma, AZ Metro Area	204,595	81.8	7.4	160,374	74,825	73,494	0.96	20.0	81.6

Table B-5. Population and Household Characteristics, 2014–2018

Metropolitan Statistical Area Metropolitan Division Component Counties	Total households	Family households Total	With own children under 18 Total	Single parent headed (percent)	Householder living alone Total	Percent age 65 or older	Percent of households with one or more persons age 65 or older	Foreign-born population as a percent of total population	Non-citizens as a percent of total population	Speaking language other than English at home, persons 5 years and older (percent), 2014-2018
Abilene, TX Metro area	60,394	39,970	16,617	34.5	16,073	40.4	28.4	5.3	3.0	16.5
Akron, OH Metro area	286,378	177,612	70,517	34.8	89,725	38.0	29.1	4.8	2.5	6.1
Albany, GA Metro area	56,419	37,582	16,103	54.3	16,187	36.9	28.0	2.4	1.2	3.7
Albany-Lebanon, OR Metro area	47,030	31,814	12,552	33.9	11,926	46.4	33.1	4.6	2.8	7.7
Albany-Schenectady-Troy, NY Metro area	350,301	210,089	84,107	32.8	112,641	37.1	28.8	7.9	3.3	9.5
Albuquerque, NM Metro area	349,150	217,034	90,157	38.3	108,226	36.5	28.9	9.2	5.2	29.6
Alexandria, LA Metro area	54,989	37,059	15,711	43.1	15,781	41.1	30.3	2.9	1.8	5.7
Allentown-Bethlehem-Easton, PA-NJ Metro area	319,220	215,649	87,466	32.2	83,404	45.2	31.3	9.1	3.8	17.0
Altoona, PA Metro area	51,625	33,038	12,468	35.2	15,633	48.0	33.8	1.2	0.3	2.2
Amarillo, TX Metro area	96,613	64,719	29,664	30.4	27,226	35.5	25.4	10.1	6.9	21.3
Ames, IA Metro area	48,159	26,358	11,465	22.2	13,594	29.9	21.9	7.9	6.1	9.2
Anchorage, AK Metro area	137,403	91,871	43,992	29.3	34,151	27.1	20.3	8.9	3.4	14.9
Ann Arbor, MI Metro area	140,210	80,883	34,171	24.4	41,553	31.5	23.9	12.4	6.8	15.0
Anniston-Oxford, AL Metro area	45,033	30,833	11,798	39.8	12,067	40.5	30.7	2.7	1.4	4.2
Appleton, WI Metro area	92,514	63,076	28,253	24.7	23,953	37.7	24.6	3.7	1.7	6.6
Asheville, NC Metro area	190,162	115,649	40,884	29.3	61,710	42.8	34.7	5.5	3.1	7.6
Athens-Clarke County, GA Metro area	76,650	45,852	19,408	33.5	21,920	30.8	23.8	7.7	5.2	12.1
Atlanta-Sandy Springs-Alpharetta, GA Metro area	2,065,239	1,394,951	654,650	32.3	546,528	28.9	22.7	13.7	7.5	17.8
Atlantic City-Hammonton, NJ Metro area	99,874	66,553	27,418	39.9	27,528	46.2	32.6	16.2	6.9	26.9
Auburn-Opelika, AL Metro area	59,373	37,391	17,216	34.7	16,723	27.3	21.1	5.5	3.8	7.4
Augusta-Richmond County, GA-SC Metro area	214,489	144,313	58,647	39.1	60,423	37.9	28.8	4.8	2.5	6.8
Austin-Round Rock-Georgetown, TX Metro area	742,689	461,306	223,480	25.9	207,648	23.8	19.4	15.0	9.5	28.2
Bakersfield, CA Metro area	267,913	200,379	103,738	34.3	53,702	40.1	24.4	20.0	13.2	44.1
Baltimore-Columbia-Towson, MD Metro area	1,043,798	679,693	287,567	32.4	294,481	38.4	28.1	10.3	4.8	12.5
Bangor, ME Metro area	61,578	37,841	14,120	38.3	18,151	40.7	29.8	2.7	1.4	4.3
Barnstable Town, MA Metro area	94,292	58,164	16,019	29.8	30,369	55.6	45.6	7.8	3.4	8.6
Baton Rouge, LA Metro area	310,265	202,420	86,060	38.4	88,257	34.1	25.8	3.8	2.4	6.6
Battle Creek, MI Metro area	53,659	33,643	14,137	41.6	17,322	38.6	29.5	3.7	2.4	5.8
Bay City, MI Metro area	43,891	27,674	10,763	41.5	13,514	45.5	32.0	1.5	0.6	2.3
Beaumont-Port Arthur, TX Metro area	146,376	97,503	42,903	36.6	42,223	37.8	28.0	8.6	5.7	16.7
Beckley, WV Metro area	48,914	33,103	11,917	34.9	13,738	47.4	34.9	1.1	0.6	2.6
Bellingham, WA Metro area	85,008	51,611	20,510	27.2	23,264	41.0	29.4	10.2	5.0	11.5
Bend, OR Metro area	72,471	48,879	18,229	28.5	17,643	44.7	32.5	4.5	2.4	7.1
Billings, MT Metro area	73,272	45,733	19,413	30.1	22,183	38.5	28.6	2.0	0.9	4.0
Binghamton, NY Metro area	98,639	60,089	22,925	35.5	30,854	45.1	32.6	5.8	2.6	8.1
Birmingham-Hoover, AL Metro area	415,615	276,105	113,062	33.3	120,532	36.0	28.1	4.1	2.7	6.1
Bismarck, ND Metro area	53,781	33,668	15,011	28.4	15,558	36.0	24.7	1.9	1.0	4.4
Blacksburg-Christiansburg, VA Metro area	62,433	35,599	13,499	29.7	18,217	35.2	26.3	5.4	3.5	7.4
Bloomington, IL Metro area	66,159	40,460	18,268	25.4	18,922	31.1	22.4	7.0	4.4	8.4
Bloomington, IN Metro area	64,232	35,023	13,732	34.6	20,114	30.3	23.8	7.4	5.3	9.3
Bloomsburg-Berwick, PA Metro area	34,064	21,128	7,508	34.9	10,179	44.3	32.6	2.7	1.3	3.8
Boise City, ID Metro area	253,531	165,938	74,810	26.6	71,778	34.0	25.9	6.5	3.7	11.7
Boston-Cambridge-Newton, MA-NH Metro area	1,819,113	1,157,653	496,287	26.9	505,758	40.2	28.2	18.6	9.0	24.6
Boston, MA Div	757,727	459,484	196,163	30.0	226,091	38.4	27.7	20.3	9.7	26.8
Cambridge-Newton-Framingham, MA Div	892,691	583,344	255,113	24.7	239,246	41.6	28.6	19.6	9.7	26.3
Rockingham County-Strafford County, NH Div	168,695	114,825	45,011	25.8	40,421	41.8	28.6	5.0	2.2	6.2
Boulder, CO Metro area	125,894	73,589	33,113	25.2	35,388	33.9	23.8	10.8	6.2	16.0
Bowling Green, KY Metro area	64,721	42,777	18,934	33.8	16,925	36.6	25.9	7.1	4.8	9.8
Bremerton-Silverdale-Port Orchard, WA Metro area	101,662	68,471	27,322	29.4	25,792	41.6	30.4	6.4	2.3	7.1
Bridgeport-Stamford-Norwalk, CT Metro area	340,491	237,215	108,640	25.1	84,627	43.7	29.3	21.7	11.5	29.5
Brownsville-Harlingen, TX Metro area	123,185	97,344	48,550	37.2	22,945	49.1	30.6	23.5	16.1	73.1
Brunswick, GA Metro area	46,374	30,910	11,381	41.0	13,174	44.6	34.5	4.4	2.5	6.5
Buffalo-Cheektowaga, NY Metro area	476,058	283,954	114,680	37.6	159,804	40.9	30.0	6.5	3.1	9.3
Burlington, NC Metro area	64,059	41,309	17,763	38.3	19,046	42.4	29.7	7.9	5.5	12.6
Burlington-South Burlington, VT Metro area	86,949	52,366	21,861	28.2	24,236	39.9	25.9	7.4	3.5	8.6
California-Lexington Park, MD Metro area	40,332	28,405	13,016	26.5	9,741	32.8	23.5	4.8	2.2	7.3
Canton-Massillon, OH Metro area	163,775	107,103	42,184	37.6	47,520	42.5	31.8	2.0	0.8	3.6
Cape Coral-Fort Myers, FL Metro area	271,861	178,334	54,174	37.1	76,910	53.6	45.8	16.6	8.9	22.5
Cape Girardeau, MO-IL Metro area	36,358	23,432	9,040	31.8	9,964	41.9	29.7	2.4	1.8	3.1
Carbondale-Marion, IL Metro area	55,159	32,862	12,868	38.4	17,891	37.2	29.3	3.3	2.1	5.7
Carson City, NV Metro area	22,461	13,831	5,652	38.7	7,306	47.7	34.8	12.2	6.6	22.0
Casper, WY Metro area	32,851	20,315	8,967	36.6	10,243	37.9	24.8	2.6	1.5	6.5
Cedar Rapids, IA Metro area	108,235	69,044	30,950	29.3	31,397	38.7	26.9	3.6	2.1	4.8
Chambersburg-Waynesboro, PA Metro area	60,210	42,164	16,404	31.8	15,358	45.7	32.5	3.5	2.1	6.5
Champaign-Urbana, IL Metro area	89,199	47,310	20,285	31.2	31,587	26.0	21.8	11.2	7.8	16.3
Charleston, WV Metro area	110,903	71,150	25,233	36.6	34,060	41.9	33.6	1.4	0.6	1.8
Charleston-North Charleston, SC Metro area	285,962	183,029	74,840	33.1	82,904	32.1	26.1	4.9	2.8	6.8
Charlotte-Concord-Gastonia, NC-SC Metro area	934,829	628,544	284,500	31.2	250,403	32.1	24.4	9.8	6.1	13.8
Charlottesville, VA Metro area	82,869	51,293	20,770	26.7	23,265	37.0	29.6	9.2	5.5	11.0
Chattanooga, TN-GA Metro area	214,328	138,489	52,278	30.6	64,673	39.9	31.0	3.8	2.3	5.2

Table B-5. Population and Household Characteristics, 2014–2018—*Continued*

Metropolitan Statistical Area Metropolitan Division Component Counties	Total households	Family households Total	With own children under 18 Total	Single parent headed (percent)	Householder living alone Total	Percent age 65 or older	Percent of households with one or more persons age 65 or older	Foreign-born population as a percent of total population	Non-citizens as a percent of total population	Speaking language other than English at home, persons 5 years and older (percent), 2014-2018
Cheyenne, WY Metro area	39,179	26,007	11,399	29.8	11,024	37.2	27.3	3.2	1.7	6.4
Chicago-Naperville-Elgin, IL-IN-WI Metro Area	3,495,713	2,279,854	1,012,425	29.6	1,000,692	36.4	26.6	17.7	8.7	29.1
Chicago-Naperville-Evanston, IL Div	2,663,951	1,692,125	740,567	29.9	799,457	35.3	26.6	19.3	9.4	31.6
Elgin, IL Div	256,160	186,726	90,653	25.5	55,139	39.7	24.3	14.8	8.4	26.5
Gary, IN Div	267,507	179,558	76,301	37.4	74,707	39.7	29.4	5.9	2.5	11.9
Lake County-Kenosha County, IL-WI Div	308,095	221,445	104,904	25.1	71,389	41.8	26.1	16.2	8.1	25.1
Chico, CA Metro area	86,797	51,436	20,145	34.0	25,099	43.3	32.8	7.6	3.5	15.0
Cincinnati, OH-KY-IN Metro area	854,217	554,946	240,566	32.9	245,239	35.9	26.0	4.7	2.5	6.3
Clarksville, TN-KY Metro area	107,201	75,481	37,947	31.1	25,834	31.6	20.9	4.1	1.8	8.6
Cleveland, TN Metro area	46,936	32,232	12,489	31.7	12,424	40.5	30.6	5.2	3.5	7.2
Cleveland-Elyria, OH Metro area	857,453	519,251	211,297	38.7	289,391	38.8	30.3	5.8	2.3	10.1
Coeur d'Alene, ID Metro area	60,497	41,702	16,986	32.2	15,169	44.3	31.5	2.3	0.8	2.8
College Station-Bryan, TX Metro area	92,165	52,859	24,068	32.8	25,808	25.6	19.6	12.5	9.0	23.0
Colorado Springs, CO Metro area	263,562	180,269	82,692	27.9	66,480	33.8	23.6	6.8	3.2	11.7
Columbia, MO Metro area	79,944	46,873	20,391	29.1	24,062	29.2	21.8	5.8	3.7	7.3
Columbia, SC Metro area	308,718	198,294	83,795	38.2	91,245	33.0	26.3	5.0	2.9	7.6
Columbus, GA-AL Metro area	118,295	76,401	33,148	40.7	36,578	33.6	26.5	4.9	2.6	7.9
Columbus, IN Metro area	31,669	20,938	8,893	31.6	8,915	41.3	27.9	10.4	8.6	11.6
Columbus, OH Metro area	784,786	500,588	231,581	33.5	223,839	31.8	23.4	7.9	4.2	9.9
Corpus Christi, TX Metro area	152,047	104,465	45,529	36.7	38,005	36.9	27.5	8.1	5.1	36.4
Corvallis, OR Metro area	35,056	20,069	7,465	24.3	9,393	37.3	27.3	10.4	7.2	14.3
Crestview-Fort Walton Beach-Destin, FL Metro area	103,835	67,750	25,986	29.2	29,416	40.4	29.7	6.8	2.9	10.7
Cumberland, MD-WV Metro area	39,021	24,438	8,325	39.2	12,268	47.6	34.5	1.7	0.9	3.6
Dallas-Fort Worth-Arlington, TX Metro Area	2,510,847	1,744,338	861,103	29.6	624,714	28.8	21.4	18.5	11.8	31.6
Dallas-Plano-Irving, TX Div	1,689,084	1,162,836	579,484	28.8	427,718	27.6	20.7	20.4	13.3	34.2
Fort Worth-Arlington-Grapevine, TX Div	821,763	581,502	281,619	31.3	196,996	31.3	22.6	14.4	8.8	26.4
Dalton, GA Metro area	50,124	36,319	16,837	27.3	11,229	45.0	27.7	15.5	11.6	26.2
Danville, IL Metro area	31,180	19,598	8,037	44.2	9,859	45.4	33.3	2.2	1.2	4.6
Daphne-Fairhope-Foley, AL Metro area	78,622	51,359	18,035	25.0	23,893	42.2	35.0	3.4	1.9	5.4
Davenport-Moline-Rock Island, IA-IL Metro area	153,966	97,797	42,057	35.1	47,670	41.7	30.2	5.2	3.0	8.7
Dayton-Kettering, OH Metro area	330,381	204,592	86,031	39.1	105,409	38.2	29.6	4.5	2.2	5.6
Decatur, AL Metro area	58,457	40,527	15,722	32.5	15,953	44.1	30.6	3.5	2.6	6.2
Decatur, IL Metro area	44,113	26,739	10,476	42.4	15,267	40.1	31.7	2.0	1.0	3.5
Deltona-Daytona Beach-Ormond Beach, FL Metro area	253,614	158,577	48,016	37.4	76,629	50.9	41.9	8.4	3.2	14.1
Denver-Aurora-Lakewood, CO Metro area	1,094,028	689,095	317,442	26.8	309,219	30.6	22.8	12.3	7.2	20.1
Des Moines-West Des Moines, IA Metro area	260,852	169,174	82,114	28.1	72,313	35.9	23.8	7.6	4.4	10.9
Detroit-Warren-Dearborn, MI Metro area	1,690,744	1,082,379	451,055	34.1	516,343	38.1	28.7	9.8	4.3	13.3
Detroit-Dearborn-Livonia, MI Div	676,587	414,597	178,703	45.9	226,758	36.3	28.4	8.9	4.0	14.3
Warren-Troy-Farmington Hills, MI Div	1,014,157	667,782	272,352	26.4	289,585	39.6	28.9	10.4	4.5	12.7
Dothan, AL Metro area	56,401	37,430	14,306	38.7	16,504	42.1	32.4	2.0	1.1	3.5
Dover, DE Metro area	64,545	44,677	18,410	38.0	15,904	40.1	30.2	5.7	2.8	9.8
Dubuque, IA Metro area	38,330	25,272	10,809	30.2	10,795	37.7	27.7	2.7	1.5	4.1
Duluth, MN-WI Metro area	123,165	72,760	28,414	34.6	40,410	40.8	30.1	2.2	1.0	3.5
Durham-Chapel Hill, NC Metro area	241,274	149,205	62,953	36.0	72,854	31.5	25.6	11.5	7.5	15.9
East Stroudsburg, PA Metro area	56,770	40,250	15,054	28.9	13,378	42.2	32.2	10.2	3.1	15.8
Eau Claire, WI Metro area	66,238	40,794	17,390	29.4	19,520	39.8	27.5	2.8	1.3	5.2
El Centro, CA Metro area	44,057	33,880	15,296	35.4	8,817	44.5	32.0	31.1	15.6	76.0
Elizabethtown-Fort Knox, KY Metro area	57,403	39,661	16,978	31.4	15,005	34.5	25.1	3.4	1.4	5.6
Elkhart-Goshen, IN Metro area	72,329	52,027	24,366	33.8	16,422	39.4	26.6	7.8	5.4	18.8
Elmira, NY Metro area	34,373	21,610	8,773	41.5	10,459	43.6	31.0	3.0	1.3	4.2
El Paso, TX Metro area	266,624	195,651	92,023	36.2	62,094	35.0	25.8	24.9	13.5	71.3
Enid, OK Metro area	23,824	15,782	7,118	32.4	7,021	43.1	28.2	6.9	4.3	11.6
Erie, PA Metro area	110,050	69,095	29,112	40.4	33,234	41.0	29.7	4.8	2.7	7.1
Eugene-Springfield, OR Metro area	150,780	88,873	34,003	36.1	44,252	41.1	31.8	6.0	3.5	8.5
Evansville, IN-KY Metro area	128,119	81,449	33,581	35.6	38,591	37.3	27.8	2.6	1.4	3.4
Fairbanks, AK Metro area	36,513	24,057	11,871	27.7	9,053	24.0	18.2	5.2	2.3	10.1
Fargo, ND-MN Metro area	97,987	56,836	27,341	27.7	30,255	28.5	19.8	6.4	3.8	7.7
Farmington, NM Metro area	43,134	30,530	12,461	40.6	10,640	38.9	29.3	3.1	2.2	31.3
Fayetteville, NC Metro area	187,226	123,303	58,121	37.1	55,750	29.4	22.1	6.2	3.1	11.4
Fayetteville-Springdale-Rogers, AR Metro area	186,419	126,775	61,378	25.4	45,927	33.3	23.1	10.9	7.9	14.9
Flagstaff, AZ Metro area	47,276	29,278	10,709	33.0	11,830	31.0	24.7	4.8	2.9	24.6
Flint, MI Metro area	167,889	107,362	45,098	43.6	50,893	39.0	29.6	2.6	0.9	3.7
Florence, SC Metro area	78,643	52,211	20,916	42.5	22,802	41.2	30.7	2.5	1.1	3.2
Florence-Muscle Shoals, AL Metro area	60,313	39,636	14,749	32.0	17,682	45.6	32.9	1.9	1.2	3.0
Fond du Lac, WI Metro area	41,346	27,090	10,705	28.5	11,705	42.1	29.2	3.4	2.2	5.8
Fort Collins, CO Metro area	133,527	82,842	33,287	25.1	32,373	37.8	25.7	5.5	3.0	9.4
Fort Smith, AR-OK Metro area	96,547	65,833	27,037	33.8	26,560	41.4	29.5	6.0	3.4	10.4
Fort Wayne, IN Metro area	157,048	102,987	47,048	35.8	45,067	38.1	25.8	6.1	3.1	10.0
Fresno, CA Metro area	304,624	221,080	110,079	39.9	66,292	42.3	26.5	21.3	12.9	44.8
Gadsden, AL Metro area	38,777	26,139	9,686	35.5	11,275	48.8	33.8	2.9	1.8	3.9

Table B-5. Population and Household Characteristics, 2014–2018—*Continued*

Metropolitan Statistical Area Metropolitan Division Component Counties	Total households	Family households			Nonfamily households		Percent of households with one or more persons age 65 or older	Foreign-born population, 2014-2018		Speaking language other than English at home, persons 5 years and older (percent), 2014-2018
		Total	With own children under 18		Householder living alone			Foreign-born population as a percent of total population	Non-citizens as a percent of total population	
			Total	Single parent headed (percent)	Total	Percent age 65 or older				
Gainesville, FL Metro area............	119,992	65,187	24,201	34.6	42,065	30.1	27.3	9.1	4.6	12.5
Gainesville, GA Metro area............	63,931	47,761	21,029	27.8	13,066	42.8	28.9	16.7	12.4	28.8
Gettysburg, PA Metro area............	39,221	27,805	10,160	26.6	9,787	47.8	34.1	4.0	2.5	6.2
Glens Falls, NY Metro area............	51,562	32,648	11,486	35.4	15,287	44.0	33.7	2.9	1.1	5.0
Goldsboro, NC Metro area............	48,153	32,399	14,032	42.1	13,399	42.2	29.8	7.7	5.7	13.5
Grand Forks, ND-MN Metro area........	42,731	24,102	10,643	32.6	14,211	32.9	22.9	4.7	2.9	6.7
Grand Island, NE Metro area..........	28,878	19,506	9,245	37.1	7,574	44.4	27.8	11.6	8.4	18.5
Grand Junction, CO Metro area........	61,033	38,356	15,896	35.0	17,997	41.3	31.3	3.9	2.0	7.2
Grand Rapids-Kentwood, MI Metro area..	387,078	264,573	118,597	28.8	95,144	40.2	25.6	6.8	3.9	10.5
Grants Pass, OR Metro area...........	35,978	23,050	7,274	34.1	10,101	53.8	42.9	4.1	2.4	4.5
Great Falls, MT Metro area...........	34,444	21,358	8,683	33.5	10,982	42.6	30.2	2.1	0.8	3.0
Greeley, CO Metro area...............	102,101	74,632	35,708	22.3	20,859	37.6	23.6	8.7	5.7	19.3
Green Bay, WI Metro area.............	128,311	83,222	37,297	30.9	36,063	37.8	25.8	5.1	3.3	9.3
Greensboro-High Point, NC Metro area..	295,973	190,863	80,848	37.6	87,810	37.5	28.0	8.8	5.4	12.0
Greenville, NC Metro area............	69,169	41,214	18,435	39.4	20,427	28.9	22.9	4.7	3.0	7.0
Greenville-Anderson, SC Metro area ..	338,714	224,994	92,073	31.1	93,909	37.9	29.1	5.9	3.7	8.3
Gulfport-Biloxi, MS Metro area	155,946	102,708	42,362	42.0	44,756	37.4	28.5	3.8	1.9	6.2
Hagerstown-Martinsburg, MD-WV Metro area.......	106,267	71,969	29,897	33.6	28,024	41.5	29.4	4.2	1.9	6.1
Hammond, LA Metro area...............	47,527	31,606	12,801	41.7	13,234	36.7	26.9	2.2	1.3	4.5
Hanford-Corcoran, CA Metro area......	42,735	32,786	17,817	35.9	7,469	39.8	23.8	18.1	11.6	39.9
Harrisburg-Carlisle, PA Metro area...	228,652	146,356	58,978	32.3	67,852	40.3	29.7	6.5	3.2	10.2
Harrisonburg, VA Metro area..........	47,714	30,968	12,774	30.6	12,431	41.6	28.8	10.4	6.8	15.9
Hartford-East Hartford-Middletown, CT Metro Area	471,188	303,328	125,972	32.1	137,290	41.0	29.8	13.3	5.9	21.4
Hattiesburg, MS Metro area...........	61,603	40,759	18,201	38.0	16,832	36.7	25.5	2.3	1.4	3.2
Hickory-Lenoir-Morganton, NC Metro area.....	142,087	97,673	35,792	32.0	38,118	44.1	32.7	5.2	3.1	9.3
Hilton Head Island-Bluffton, SC Metro area	80,589	55,498	17,638	34.3	21,668	43.1	40.9	8.4	5.2	11.7
Hinesville, GA Metro area............	28,833	20,708	10,918	37.9	6,551	23.8	16.4	5.8	3.0	12.7
Homosassa Springs, FL Metro area	62,762	38,892	8,871	38.8	20,702	59.1	54.4	5.7	2.0	6.2
Hot Springs, AR Metro area	39,894	25,362	8,920	43.7	12,122	50.9	38.3	3.5	2.0	5.8
Houma-Thibodaux, LA Metro area	76,463	52,415	22,415	35.5	19,129	38.5	26.6	3.2	2.0	11.6
Houston-The Woodlands-Sugar Land, TX Metro area.........	2,310,213	1,634,300	806,362	29.9	558,256	28.6	21.7	23.4	14.4	39.0
Huntington-Ashland, WV-KY-OH Metro area.........	143,459	92,690	35,124	34.3	43,461	42.6	32.3	1.0	0.5	1.7
Huntsville, AL Metro area............	177,382	116,153	49,002	29.0	52,618	33.9	26.1	5.1	2.6	6.6
Idaho Falls, ID Metro area...........	48,697	35,981	17,750	22.0	10,752	41.0	25.7	5.2	2.9	10.9
Indianapolis-Carmel-Anderson, IN Metro area.......	767,335	491,176	227,223	33.6	226,705	32.9	24.0	6.8	4.3	9.5
Iowa City, IA Metro area.............	66,883	37,868	17,309	25.1	19,019	28.8	20.6	10.5	7.2	13.6
Ithaca, NY Metro area................	39,326	20,499	8,467	33.5	12,808	28.4	24.5	13.1	8.2	14.4
Jackson, MI Metro area...............	61,696	40,284	16,072	39.6	18,134	40.2	30.3	1.8	0.9	3.0
Jackson, MS Metro area...............	217,262	147,663	63,473	41.5	60,577	36.5	26.6	2.4	1.5	3.8
Jackson, TN Metro area...............	68,245	45,891	18,394	39.4	19,230	43.2	30.5	2.5	1.5	4.2
Jacksonville, FL Metro area..........	553,919	368,228	154,049	35.1	150,484	36.6	27.8	9.1	3.9	12.3
Jacksonville, NC Metro area..........	64,065	45,354	23,323	28.7	14,755	29.2	18.6	4.0	1.4	10.3
Janesville-Beloit, WI Metro area.....	64,538	41,895	17,888	39.3	18,272	41.9	28.2	4.5	2.6	8.2
Jefferson City, MO Metro area........	56,246	37,412	15,913	31.6	15,988	40.7	28.8	2.2	1.1	4.0
Johnson City, TN Metro area..........	84,305	53,403	19,712	35.3	25,436	39.1	31.4	3.1	2.0	3.9
Johnstown, PA Metro area.............	56,793	35,807	12,673	35.7	18,283	47.6	36.3	1.3	0.6	2.8
Jonesboro, AR Metro area.............	50,237	33,292	15,176	42.5	13,879	35.4	25.5	3.5	2.9	5.4
Joplin, MO Metro area................	67,529	45,095	19,756	29.5	18,367	43.3	28.6	3.8	2.5	6.7
Kahului-Wailuku-Lahaina, HI Metro area................	54,274	38,062	14,329	30.0	12,226	41.7	36.0	18.8	8.7	22.6
Kalamazoo-Portage, MI Metro area.....	102,809	60,903	26,699	34.0	31,074	36.4	25.6	5.0	2.8	7.1
Kankakee, IL Metro area..............	40,050	26,471	11,198	36.4	11,097	40.8	29.4	4.9	2.9	9.5
Kansas City, MO-KS Metro area	821,644	532,404	242,618	31.6	238,602	34.2	25.4	6.7	3.9	10.0
Kennewick-Richland, WA Metro area....	97,299	68,681	33,424	30.6	22,945	38.9	25.2	14.4	9.8	29.8
Killeen-Temple, TX Metro area........	150,293	105,502	52,547	33.4	37,767	29.1	21.2	7.8	3.8	18.2
Kingsport-Bristol, TN-VA Metro area..	128,069	84,109	29,344	34.9	39,038	45.5	35.7	1.5	0.7	2.3
Kingston, NY Metro area..............	69,539	42,806	15,985	34.5	21,405	44.9	34.0	7.8	3.3	11.4
Knoxville, TN Metro area.............	335,953	219,406	84,254	30.0	95,830	41.0	31.1	4.0	2.4	5.0
Kokomo, IN Metro area................	34,550	22,575	8,671	38.9	10,424	41.7	31.8	2.3	1.1	3.4
La Crosse-Onalaska, WI-MN Metro area..	55,500	33,153	13,988	27.0	16,298	38.0	27.3	2.7	0.8	6.4
Lafayette, LA Metro area.............	180,421	118,663	53,904	36.3	49,492	35.7	24.9	3.3	2.1	12.8
Lafayette-West Lafayette, IN Metro area..	83,779	48,905	21,857	31.6	24,493	30.0	22.6	9.9	7.5	13.6
Lake Charles, LA Metro area..........	80,013	52,452	22,882	38.9	23,093	35.8	26.6	2.9	1.6	6.7
Lake Havasu City-Kingman, AZ Metro area...........	85,485	54,107	15,142	43.2	24,932	53.4	47.3	6.7	3.5	11.1
Lakeland-Winter Haven, FL Metro area..	231,260	159,863	58,506	37.8	58,021	49.8	37.8	10.0	5.5	21.4
Lancaster, PA Metro area.............	199,889	139,910	56,015	25.0	47,998	44.8	30.9	5.0	2.3	17.1
Lansing-East Lansing, MI Metro area ..	213,752	129,704	53,138	33.7	63,983	35.9	26.6	6.3	3.8	8.7
Laredo, TX Metro area................	73,659	58,772	32,109	35.6	12,862	39.4	23.8	26.2	18.8	90.4
Las Cruces, NM Metro area............	77,453	52,524	23,638	37.0	19,725	37.8	29.0	17.6	11.1	51.6
Las Vegas-Henderson-Paradise, NV Metro area......	767,954	488,867	213,300	37.8	218,806	31.9	27.1	22.2	11.4	34.2
Lawrence, KS Metro area..............	46,294	25,119	11,000	26.2	14,055	27.6	20.7	7.3	4.8	10.1

Table B-5. Population and Household Characteristics, 2014–2018—*Continued*

Metropolitan Statistical Area Metropolitan Division Component Counties	Total households	Family households Total	With own children under 18 Total	Single parent headed (percent)	Householder living alone Total	Percent age 65 or older	Percent of households with one or more persons age 65 or older	Foreign-born population as a percent of total population	Non-citizens as a percent of total population	Speaking language other than English at home, persons 5 years and older (percent), 2014-2018
Lawton, OK Metro area	44,822	29,552	13,865	37.1	12,831	34.2	24.6	5.0	2.3	8.5
Lebanon, PA Metro area	53,281	36,955	14,319	33.0	13,546	47.1	33.1	4.1	1.9	13.0
Lewiston, ID-WA Metro area	25,473	16,464	6,203	37.6	7,277	43.8	34.2	2.0	0.8	4.3
Lewiston-Auburn, ME Metro area	45,491	27,667	11,774	38.7	13,553	41.9	28.8	3.3	1.5	10.5
Lexington-Fayette, KY Metro area	200,538	125,646	55,676	34.1	56,196	32.0	24.1	7.5	5.4	10.1
Lima, OH Metro area	40,537	26,653	11,385	40.4	11,729	39.0	30.0	1.4	0.7	2.9
Lincoln, NE Metro area	129,242	77,494	35,234	28.9	38,872	32.9	23.9	7.4	4.0	10.8
Little Rock-North Little Rock-Conway, AR Metro	282,138	183,179	78,798	37.0	83,593	34.3	26.1	4.2	2.6	6.5
Logan, UT-ID Metro area	41,939	31,651	16,050	15.9	6,784	41.8	20.4	6.5	4.3	10.6
Longview, TX Metro area	100,745	70,112	29,446	32.2	25,795	41.7	30.4	7.2	5.1	13.1
Longview, WA Metro area	41,397	27,113	10,766	37.2	11,487	46.7	33.2	4.1	2.0	6.9
Los Angeles-Long Beach-Anaheim, CA Metro area	4,338,482	2,948,986	1,277,324	30.2	1,064,363	35.5	27.8	33.3	15.9	54.0
Anaheim-Santa Ana-Irvine, CA Div	1,032,373	741,721	324,922	23.4	217,407	42.8	29.2	30.2	14.0	45.4
Los Angeles-Long Beach-Glendale, CA Div	3,306,109	2,207,265	952,402	32.5	846,956	33.7	27.3	34.2	16.6	56.6
Louisville/Jefferson County, KY-IN Metro area	488,638	311,337	129,729	35.0	147,821	36.1	27.4	5.6	3.1	7.2
Lubbock, TX Metro area	116,362	73,134	32,580	37.1	31,936	32.4	23.3	5.9	3.7	22.3
Lynchburg, VA Metro area	100,371	66,826	24,555	31.7	27,267	44.7	32.6	3.5	2.1	4.6
Macon-Bibb County, GA Metro area	85,991	54,277	21,503	45.1	27,971	36.5	29.5	2.7	1.2	4.2
Madera, CA Metro area	44,759	34,804	16,126	31.3	8,209	49.0	31.1	20.6	14.4	45.1
Madison, WI Metro area	268,213	158,241	70,576	27.2	79,244	31.1	23.1	7.5	4.4	10.3
Manchester-Nashua, NH Metro area	159,200	105,483	43,987	28.6	40,438	37.5	26.5	9.4	4.3	12.9
Manhattan, KS Metro area	48,097	29,471	15,239	25.9	13,429	25.8	17.8	7.3	4.5	11.5
Mankato, MN Metro area	38,521	23,526	10,456	33.1	9,991	36.3	23.9	4.4	2.8	6.0
Mansfield, OH Metro area	47,998	30,569	11,556	35.2	14,630	47.4	34.2	1.5	0.6	4.2
McAllen-Edinburg-Mission, TX Metro area	234,879	191,857	99,740	35.1	36,759	42.8	26.1	27.1	19.8	84.3
Medford, OR Metro area	87,417	55,629	21,940	36.9	24,815	51.0	36.5	6.1	3.5	9.9
Memphis, TN-MS-AR Metro area	495,110	323,100	139,477	43.3	145,541	32.5	25.5	5.3	3.4	7.8
Merced, CA Metro area	79,606	60,642	31,699	36.4	14,964	44.6	26.1	25.7	15.7	52.5
Miami-Fort Lauderdale-Pompano Beach, FL Metro Area	2,100,355	1,373,141	554,791	36.6	594,705	43.3	33.9	40.4	17.4	53.5
Fort Lauderdale-Pompano Beach-Sunrise, FL Div	682,088	436,468	182,756	36.5	198,194	40.9	30.9	33.7	13.7	40.7
Miami-Miami Beach-Kendall, FL Div	870,051	595,092	246,046	38.3	226,358	37.5	31.8	53.3	23.0	74.3
West Palm Beach-Boca Raton-Boynton Beach, FL Div	548,216	341,581	125,989	33.5	170,153	53.8	41.0	25.0	11.8	31.6
Michigan City-La Porte, IN Metro area	42,904	28,028	10,792	40.1	11,973	45.8	31.2	3.5	1.5	6.1
Midland, MI Metro area	34,017	23,191	9,235	26.9	8,888	40.7	28.6	3.9	2.5	4.2
Midland, TX Metro area	57,606	40,341	19,778	29.3	14,484	33.3	21.3	13.1	8.6	34.1
Milwaukee-Waukesha, WI Metro area	629,381	388,651	173,075	36.9	196,956	36.2	26.3	7.3	4.0	12.6
Minneapolis-St. Paul-Bloomington, MN Metro Area	1,360,921	878,612	408,762	27.0	378,380	34.9	23.9	10.6	5.0	14.4
Missoula, MT Metro area	48,608	27,292	11,687	28.7	15,020	32.4	25.1	2.9	1.5	4.7
Mobile, AL Metro area	161,838	105,996	42,348	40.9	48,703	36.4	29.4	3.2	1.5	4.7
Modesto, CA Metro area	172,682	127,767	62,209	32.2	35,424	43.5	27.9	20.6	11.5	42.5
Monroe, LA Metro area	74,168	47,834	20,206	43.3	23,122	38.8	29.1	1.6	0.9	2.5
Monroe, MI Metro area	59,279	40,823	15,656	30.2	15,918	43.0	30.0	2.2	0.9	3.1
Montgomery, AL Metro area	144,273	95,019	40,583	40.5	43,325	35.8	27.1	3.5	2.2	4.9
Morgantown, WV Metro area	51,239	29,122	11,060	26.9	16,258	29.0	24.8	4.6	3.3	6.5
Morristown, TN Metro area	53,269	37,118	12,973	28.8	13,583	44.8	33.6	4.1	3.3	6.5
Mount Vernon-Anacortes, WA Metro area	47,937	32,419	12,150	28.6	11,929	46.4	34.8	10.4	6.4	17.3
Muncie, IN Metro area	46,028	27,362	10,708	38.1	13,959	36.1	28.7	2.3	1.5	3.6
Muskegon, MI Metro area	65,619	44,389	18,145	40.3	17,454	43.5	30.0	1.8	0.9	3.4
Myrtle Beach-Conway-North Myrtle Beach, SC-NC.	182,812	120,322	36,262	37.7	51,164	44.2	39.4	5.5	3.1	6.8
Napa, CA Metro area	49,032	33,730	14,104	24.4	12,321	53.4	35.3	22.4	12.2	34.9
Naples-Marco Island, FL Metro area	140,942	95,659	27,608	34.8	37,773	59.6	50.1	25.0	14.3	33.3
Nashville-Davidson--Murfreesboro--Franklin, TN....	695,444	462,968	206,376	29.7	181,551	31.7	23.7	8.1	5.0	11.1
New Bern, NC Metro area	50,360	33,611	12,921	32.5	14,548	43.1	34.2	4.2	2.5	7.7
New Haven-Milford, CT Metro area	329,857	204,804	81,279	36.6	104,693	38.3	29.9	12.2	6.0	21.8
New Orleans-Metairie, LA Metro area	480,838	294,281	121,552	41.2	158,494	32.6	27.5	7.6	4.4	11.1
New York-Newark-Jersey City, NY-NJ-PA Metro Area	6,962,260	4,591,239	1,966,497	29.6	1,944,225	40.1	29.9	29.4	12.9	39.4
Nassau County-Suffolk County, NY Div	933,498	699,392	287,914	19.1	197,193	52.7	34.7	18.7	7.5	25.4
Newark, NJ-PA Div	774,797	535,661	243,438	29.6	204,384	40.0	28.7	23.0	10.2	31.0
New Brunswick-Lakewood, NJ Div	860,330	605,315	256,473	21.2	216,603	48.8	32.8	20.4	8.7	27.1
New York-Jersey City-White Plains, NY-NJ Div	4,393,635	2,750,871	1,178,672	33.9	1,326,045	36.9	28.5	35.0	15.4	46.8
Niles, MI Metro area	63,908	41,127	15,770	37.6	19,195	44.0	32.9	5.8	3.6	7.9
North Port-Sarasota-Bradenton, FL Metro area	324,203	205,134	56,282	34.3	98,649	59.1	49.4	12.5	6.2	14.9
Norwich-New London, CT Metro area	107,402	69,306	27,967	36.4	31,316	39.5	29.8	8.5	3.6	13.8
Ocala, FL Metro area	136,514	88,139	25,011	40.2	41,254	55.4	48.3	7.4	2.7	11.6
Ocean City, NJ Metro area	39,904	26,127	8,462	26.9	11,520	51.8	41.1	4.8	2.3	9.1
Odessa, TX Metro area	51,954	36,123	17,879	33.2	13,324	31.0	20.9	13.2	8.4	45.2

Table B-5. Population and Household Characteristics, 2014–2018—Continued

Metropolitan Statistical Area Metropolitan Division Component Counties	Total households	Family households Total	With own children under 18 Total	Single parent headed (percent)	Householder living alone Total	Percent age 65 or older	Percent of households with one or more persons age 65 or older	Foreign-born population as a percent of total population	Non-citizens as a percent of total population	Speaking language other than English at home, persons 5 years and older (percent), 2014-2018
Ogden-Clearfield, UT Metro area	205,890	160,623	82,486	19.4	37,096	37.1	22.5	5.4	2.9	10.9
Oklahoma City, OK Metro area	511,536	333,943	152,113	32.8	143,345	34.5	24.9	8.0	5.1	13.3
Olympia-Lacey-Tumwater, WA Metro area	108,070	71,946	30,554	30.6	28,017	40.4	29.1	7.8	3.1	11.4
Omaha-Council Bluffs, NE-IA Metro area	355,832	231,623	110,963	29.4	101,016	34.5	23.9	7.3	4.6	11.5
Orlando-Kissimmee-Sanford, FL Metro area	855,265	573,322	242,504	34.3	216,954	33.9	27.3	17.9	8.4	32.4
Oshkosh-Neenah, WI Metro area	70,173	42,219	17,952	31.2	21,331	38.0	26.5	3.5	1.7	6.1
Owensboro, KY Metro area	46,927	31,748	13,773	34.6	12,607	42.2	29.1	2.6	1.8	3.9
Oxnard-Thousand Oaks-Ventura, CA Metro area	271,226	197,226	84,465	24.9	58,566	44.7	31.2	22.0	11.3	38.4
Palm Bay-Melbourne-Titusville, FL Metro area	228,888	145,729	46,684	35.1	69,355	47.8	39.2	8.6	3.2	10.4
Panama City, FL Metro area	70,199	45,243	17,306	35.1	20,559	39.4	30.3	5.8	2.8	7.0
Parkersburg-Vienna, WV Metro area	38,517	24,905	9,358	36.0	11,671	45.4	33.6	1.0	0.3	1.7
Pensacola-Ferry Pass-Brent, FL Metro area	180,085	116,216	40,477	31.4	50,733	35.7	30.1	4.9	2.1	6.6
Peoria, IL Metro area	164,085	105,770	43,496	34.9	50,295	40.2	29.7	3.5	1.9	5.4
Philadelphia-Camden-Wilmington, PA-NJ-DE-MD Metro Area	2,264,041	1,467,360	616,210	32.9	659,350	39.1	29.0	10.8	4.9	15.9
Camden, NJ Div	457,241	315,182	132,416	30.5	118,967	43.0	29.9	9.2	3.6	15.1
Montgomery County-Bucks County-Chester County,	740,924	518,466	218,553	21.1	182,526	45.4	30.7	9.9	4.4	12.8
Philadelphia, PA Div	801,183	460,166	195,617	47.7	284,026	34.0	27.2	12.9	6.2	20.1
Wilmington, DE-MD-NJ Div	264,693	173,546	69,624	33.3	73,831	36.7	28.2	9.5	4.9	12.9
Phoenix-Mesa-Chandler, AZ Metro area	1,658,053	1,092,192	479,136	32.9	441,995	36.7	28.6	14.4	8.6	26.4
Pine Bluff, AR Metro area	34,064	21,416	8,010	45.1	11,331	37.4	31.2	1.6	1.1	3.5
Pittsburgh, PA Metro area	1,003,283	611,007	229,864	30.4	329,599	42.6	32.0	3.8	1.9	5.2
Pittsfield, MA Metro area	55,167	32,401	11,334	40.9	19,028	45.9	36.5	6.4	2.9	8.1
Pocatello, ID Metro area	33,422	22,083	10,224	25.2	8,935	37.8	26.5	5.0	3.0	9.6
Portland-South Portland, ME Metro area	220,198	137,347	52,629	28.8	62,893	42.0	30.8	4.9	2.1	7.1
Portland-Vancouver-Hillsboro, OR-WA Metro area	925,631	590,151	260,187	26.9	248,320	37.2	26.1	12.6	6.5	18.2
Port St. Lucie, FL Metro area	176,737	115,262	38,376	32.0	50,807	55.4	44.4	14.4	6.3	19.8
Poughkeepsie-Newburgh-Middletown, NY Metro Area	234,123	160,770	69,177	24.7	60,930	41.1	29.4	11.0	4.4	20.5
Prescott Valley-Prescott, AZ Metro area	96,007	60,712	16,306	31.1	28,697	57.0	47.8	6.3	3.0	10.7
Providence-Warwick, RI-MA Metro area	627,503	398,633	165,761	36.3	186,936	41.6	29.9	13.4	5.6	21.8
Provo-Orem, UT Metro area	164,039	133,892	74,148	12.5	19,673	37.5	18.5	7.1	4.6	14.3
Pueblo, CO Metro area	63,762	40,874	16,571	40.3	19,025	43.0	32.3	3.5	2.0	12.9
Punta Gorda, FL Metro area	76,150	48,430	9,278	35.5	23,137	64.8	58.1	10.3	4.2	10.0
Racine, WI Metro area	76,384	52,243	22,465	38.7	19,925	43.2	27.9	4.7	2.5	8.8
Raleigh-Cary, NC Metro area	482,401	328,591	163,719	26.2	121,376	29.4	21.3	12.0	7.1	15.8
Rapid City, SD Metro area	54,510	35,152	14,809	33.6	16,089	38.2	28.5	2.4	1.2	4.3
Reading, PA Metro area	154,467	106,646	44,401	34.3	38,954	46.1	30.9	7.5	3.8	19.0
Redding, CA Metro area	70,473	46,145	16,903	36.0	19,653	46.0	35.3	5.5	2.8	8.6
Reno, NV Metro area	179,230	110,685	47,727	32.3	52,154	37.7	28.6	13.9	7.3	23.2
Richmond, VA Metro area	476,706	306,819	128,159	33.4	139,240	36.9	27.7	7.8	4.0	10.2
Riverside-San Bernardino-Ontario, CA Metro Area	1,348,982	1,005,623	464,793	31.1	274,107	42.1	28.7	21.3	10.9	41.1
Roanoke, VA Metro area	128,792	82,624	30,968	35.7	39,151	41.8	32.8	4.8	2.9	5.9
Rochester, MN Metro area	85,917	58,091	26,650	25.8	22,531	38.8	26.6	8.3	4.4	10.8
Rochester, NY Metro area	431,331	266,609	109,703	37.7	133,198	41.3	29.8	7.0	3.1	11.5
Rockford, IL Metro area	133,339	87,653	37,875	40.9	38,487	41.7	29.3	8.7	4.5	15.3
Rocky Mount, NC Metro area	58,091	38,760	15,119	49.2	16,893	46.9	33.2	3.5	2.4	5.9
Rome, GA Metro area	35,633	24,857	9,694	36.6	9,245	45.9	31.0	6.9	4.7	10.0
Sacramento-Roseville-Folsom, CA Metro area	819,372	548,382	245,027	29.7	208,639	39.4	28.6	18.5	8.1	28.3
Saginaw, MI Metro area	78,648	49,725	20,104	41.8	24,068	41.4	31.5	2.5	1.3	4.8
St. Cloud, MN Metro area	75,108	48,378	21,951	30.7	20,113	33.6	24.0	6.2	4.0	8.8
St. George, UT Metro area	54,702	40,965	17,266	21.4	11,477	58.7	39.3	5.4	3.1	9.4
St. Joseph, MO-KS Metro area	47,075	29,590	12,151	35.6	14,399	43.4	30.2	3.0	2.0	4.7
St. Louis, MO-IL Metro area	1,118,263	719,254	303,162	33.1	333,278	38.3	27.9	4.7	2.3	6.4
Salem, OR Metro area	146,553	99,820	43,104	33.3	36,566	45.5	30.6	11.7	7.6	23.1
Salinas, CA Metro area	126,052	91,714	42,921	30.3	27,031	46.0	30.3	30.0	21.8	55.1
Salisbury, MD-DE Metro area	157,057	105,062	35,093	37.3	42,077	47.9	39.2	7.0	4.0	10.0
Salt Lake City, UT Metro area	389,330	274,967	136,698	22.9	87,585	33.4	21.7	12.3	7.6	20.3
San Angelo, TX Metro area	44,227	28,226	11,801	32.8	13,334	35.2	27.6	6.5	3.1	25.8
San Antonio-New Braunfels, TX Metro area	803,662	550,266	250,922	33.7	210,101	32.9	25.7	11.8	6.9	36.5
San Diego-Chula Vista-Carlsbad, CA Metro Area.	1,118,980	753,761	335,189	27.6	265,429	37.0	27.0	23.4	11.0	37.7
San Francisco-Oakland-Berkeley, CA Metro area.	1,692,047	1,086,572	471,387	22.9	445,496	38.1	28.5	30.6	13.5	41.1
Oakland-Berkeley-Livermore, CA Div	965,147	665,553	303,371	24.0	224,348	39.6	27.8	29.4	13.6	44.6
San Francisco-San Mateo-Redwood City, CA Div	621,642	355,334	138,980	20.6	188,956	34.1	28.1	34.6	13.8	22.7
San Rafael, CA Div	105,258	65,685	29,036	22.5	32,192	51.4	37.2	18.4	9.7	52.2
San Jose-Sunnyvale-Santa Clara, CA Metro area	653,265	470,615	219,701	18.9	133,473	37.5	26.3	38.2	18.0	17.9
San Luis Obispo-Paso Robles, CA Metro area	105,311	66,580	23,925	29.0	27,527	45.9	34.7	10.3	5.3	32.0
Santa Cruz-Watsonville, CA Metro area	95,756	61,058	24,883	27.3	24,586	43.9	31.4	17.9	11.2	34.5
Santa Fe, NM Metro area	61,972	36,678	12,964	40.9	21,094	42.8	37.0	12.5	8.6	39.7
Santa Maria-Santa Barbara, CA Metro area	144,962	95,270	42,395	30.1	34,270	48.0	31.2	22.9	15.1	39.7

Table B-5. Population and Household Characteristics, 2014–2018—*Continued*

Metropolitan Statistical Area / Metropolitan Division / Component Counties	Households, 2014-2018							Foreign-born population, 2014-2018		Speaking language other than English at home, persons 5 years and older (percent), 2014-2018
	Total households	Family households			Nonfamily households		Percent of households with one or more persons age 65 or older	Foreign-born population as a percent of total population	Non-citizens as a percent of total population	
		Total	With own children under 18		Householder living alone					
			Total	Single parent headed (percent)	Total	Percent age 65 or older				
Santa Rosa-Petaluma, CA Metro area	189,339	120,415	48,137	28.8	52,618	49.5	34.4	16.5	9.5	25.5
Savannah, GA Metro area	141,276	91,565	40,601	39.6	39,484	35.4	25.8	5.6	3.3	9.1
Scranton--Wilkes-Barre, PA Metro area	225,466	141,120	54,024	39.2	71,452	46.0	33.7	5.8	3.1	10.3
Seattle-Tacoma-Bellevue, WA Metro area	1,473,063	933,074	417,122	25.2	403,737	32.7	23.6	18.2	9.2	23.0
Seattle-Bellevue-Kent, WA Div	1,155,364	720,772	322,219	23.7	321,375	31.7	23.1	20.7	10.6	25.4
Tacoma-Lakewood, WA Div	317,699	212,302	94,903	30.3	82,362	36.4	25.3	9.8	4.3	14.6
Sebastian-Vero Beach, FL Metro area	57,403	35,755	8,468	26.4	18,801	61.2	52.6	10.0	4.8	13.4
Sebring-Avon Park, FL Metro area	41,026	26,755	7,202	34.3	12,388	61.3	55.3	10.9	6.6	19.0
Sheboygan, WI Metro area	47,303	30,933	12,979	28.3	13,891	41.1	29.1	5.7	2.3	9.7
Sherman-Denison, TX Metro area	47,957	32,759	13,383	32.6	13,016	42.5	32.0	6.3	4.6	11.2
Shreveport-Bossier City, LA Metro area	155,830	99,613	41,879	44.1	48,259	35.2	27.7	2.7	1.4	4.1
Sierra Vista-Douglas, AZ Metro area	49,250	32,319	12,129	34.5	14,586	49.6	39.2	11.0	5.0	29.0
Sioux City, IA-NE-SD Metro area	55,205	37,107	17,459	36.7	14,618	43.4	27.3	10.0	5.6	17.6
Sioux Falls, SD Metro area	100,022	64,442	31,233	29.7	28,783	33.9	22.7	5.9	3.6	7.9
South Bend-Mishawaka, IN-MI Metro area	122,096	78,997	33,503	35.3	36,347	39.8	29.0	5.6	3.3	8.6
Spartanburg, SC Metro area	114,640	78,311	32,023	34.9	30,864	40.0	29.5	6.4	3.5	10.1
Spokane-Spokane Valley, WA Metro area	215,922	137,900	58,659	32.5	62,103	39.3	28.6	5.2	2.3	6.9
Springfield, IL Metro area	88,859	54,291	22,942	40.0	28,753	37.5	28.1	2.9	1.5	4.6
Springfield, MA Metro area	268,036	167,272	68,369	41.8	80,967	42.1	30.8	8.3	3.6	20.6
Springfield, MO Metro area	184,429	116,440	49,528	29.3	52,943	39.1	27.8	2.4	1.3	4.7
Springfield, OH Metro area	54,905	35,710	14,318	43.9	15,916	45.5	32.6	2.2	1.3	3.9
State College, PA Metro area	57,908	32,728	12,638	18.8	17,345	30.9	25.0	8.7	6.3	11.6
Staunton, VA Metro area	48,961	31,931	11,634	30.9	14,405	46.4	34.8	3.0	1.7	4.0
Stockton, CA Metro area	226,727	168,502	83,489	31.9	45,993	42.4	27.3	23.3	12.1	41.0
Sumter, SC Metro area	54,464	36,691	13,585	45.4	15,604	40.1	31.9	2.9	1.8	5.5
Syracuse, NY Metro area	257,682	160,796	67,671	38.5	76,212	41.3	29.2	6.2	2.8	8.8
Tallahassee, FL Metro area	146,837	84,863	34,422	38.7	44,162	32.2	25.3	6.1	3.2	9.7
Tampa-St. Petersburg-Clearwater, FL Metro area	1,196,966	734,495	279,973	36.7	371,141	42.3	33.5	13.6	6.3	20.7
Terre Haute, IN Metro area	72,852	46,405	18,972	36.9	21,420	41.7	29.6	2.3	1.4	3.8
Texarkana, TX-AR Metro area	55,919	37,294	15,349	43.3	16,410	40.0	30.2	3.2	2.1	4.6
The Villages, FL Metro area	54,636	36,291	2,912	36.0	15,916	73.3	75.4	5.7	1.9	7.2
Toledo, OH Metro area	263,624	162,076	69,157	41.5	83,057	35.9	27.4	3.4	1.6	6.1
Topeka, KS Metro area	94,312	59,881	25,297	30.6	29,307	40.9	29.9	3.3	1.9	7.0
Trenton-Princeton, NJ Metro area	129,873	87,942	38,514	29.0	35,537	40.2	28.8	22.0	11.7	29.6
Tucson, AZ Metro area	400,907	246,861	97,019	38.7	121,700	39.7	33.1	13.0	6.7	28.5
Tulsa, OK Metro area	380,053	251,889	111,722	34.3	107,031	36.7	26.9	6.5	4.4	10.7
Tuscaloosa, AL Metro area	88,522	57,406	24,031	38.4	25,882	34.7	26.4	3.3	2.3	5.0
Twin Falls, ID Metro area	38,525	27,426	12,882	26.2	9,076	43.4	27.3	10.0	7.4	17.7
Tyler, TX Metro area	77,195	53,375	21,495	29.0	20,312	42.1	31.2	8.4	5.3	17.4
Urban Honolulu, HI Metro area	311,525	219,572	84,036	22.6	73,473	40.7	35.2	19.5	7.8	28.0
Utica-Rome, NY Metro area	114,597	72,529	29,559	38.7	35,169	44.5	32.5	6.6	2.7	10.6
Valdosta, GA Metro area	52,105	33,034	14,413	36.4	15,468	34.1	25.0	4.1	2.4	6.3
Vallejo, CA Metro area	149,067	107,267	44,814	34.0	32,847	41.9	30.1	20.0	8.1	29.8
Victoria, TX Metro area	35,225	24,404	10,019	32.2	8,978	42.6	31.2	6.4	4.1	23.5
Vineland-Bridgeton, NJ Metro area	50,608	34,788	15,255	47.4	13,015	44.6	30.2	10.4	6.8	27.9
Virginia Beach-Norfolk-Newport News, VA-NC Metro Area	658,516	440,513	188,926	36.4	177,512	36.4	26.5	6.5	2.7	9.0
Visalia, CA Metro area	136,106	104,650	54,508	35.2	24,996	42.6	25.5	22.2	15.0	51.0
Waco, TX Metro area	94,271	62,700	27,598	37.3	25,303	37.2	27.6	8.5	6.1	19.4
Walla Walla, WA Metro area	22,304	14,341	5,807	28.7	6,436	43.0	32.0	10.1	6.9	19.1
Warner Robins, GA Metro area	66,249	46,694	21,270	36.6	16,434	34.0	24.4	5.4	2.8	8.8
Washington-Arlington-Alexandria, DC-VA-MD-WV Metro Area	2,196,416	1,447,915	674,156	25.9	595,931	30.9	24.2	22.7	11.1	28.5
Frederick-Gaithersburg-Rockville, MD Div	461,632	324,098	151,465	23.3	112,263	39.4	27.8	28.1	13.0	35.4
Washington-Arlington-Alexandria, DC-VA-MD-WV Div	1,734,784	1,123,817	522,691	26.7	483,668	28.9	23.2	21.3	10.6	26.6
Waterloo-Cedar Falls, IA Metro area	67,698	41,797	17,769	33.0	20,498	40.8	28.6	4.8	2.8	7.3
Watertown-Fort Drum, NY Metro area	43,267	28,699	13,597	32.1	11,789	34.4	23.4	3.8	1.7	7.8
Wausau-Weston, WI Metro area	67,924	44,939	17,278	25.2	18,546	39.9	29.0	3.6	1.4	7.3
Weirton-Steubenville, WV-OH Metro area	50,017	31,554	10,646	39.0	15,853	48.3	36.3	1.3	0.4	2.0
Wenatchee, WA Metro area	43,102	29,391	11,938	31.4	11,239	44.4	33.0	13.0	8.5	26.8
Wheeling, WV-OH Metro area	55,783	35,023	12,247	34.1	18,154	47.9	35.8	1.2	0.4	1.7
Wichita, KS Metro area	242,956	157,689	72,705	32.6	72,399	36.8	26.3	7.3	4.0	12.3
Wichita Falls, TX Metro area	55,328	35,470	15,219	35.6	16,868	41.4	29.1	6.2	3.9	13.0
Williamsport, PA Metro area	45,897	29,880	11,743	33.6	13,285	41.2	31.5	1.9	0.9	3.7
Wilmington, NC Metro area	115,402	67,445	26,172	33.3	37,600	34.3	28.8	4.9	2.5	6.6
Winchester, VA-WV Metro area	51,190	35,168	13,876	30.4	13,245	45.4	31.8	6.5	4.2	9.7
Winston-Salem, NC Metro area	262,905	172,857	71,131	33.9	76,884	40.5	29.9	6.9	4.5	11.4
Worcester, MA-CT Metro area	351,743	231,427	98,640	30.8	96,285	40.6	27.9	11.1	5.2	18.2
Yakima, WA Metro area	82,300	59,595	29,344	38.6	18,560	41.7	27.9	18.1	13.1	40.3
York-Hanover, PA Metro area	171,244	118,697	48,430	31.7	41,968	44.9	30.1	3.9	1.8	7.5
Youngstown-Warren-Boardman, OH-PA Metro area	230,243	143,830	53,291	40.0	74,464	45.7	34.4	1.9	0.6	5.2
Yuba City, CA Metro area	58,539	42,280	20,469	32.9	12,755	43.7	28.3	17.9	8.9	32.1
Yuma, AZ Metro area	72,463	54,354	24,361	31.0	14,486	51.9	34.9	26.7	14.9	53.7

Table B-6. Enrollment, Teachers, and Educational Attainment

Metropolitan Statistical Area Metropolitan Division	Public school enrollment				Number of public school teachers		Pupil/teacher ratio		Educational attainment, 2014-2018		
	2017-2018			Percent change in total since 2007-2008	2017-2018	Percent change since 2007-2008	2017-2018	2007-2008	Population 25 years and over	High school graduate or less (percent)	Bachelor's degree or more (percent)
	Total	Pre-Kindergarten through Grade 8	Grades 9 through 12								
Abilene, TX Metro Area	29,599	21,667	7,932	6.9	2,094.4	-3.5	14.1	12.8	107,411	45.2	22.2
Akron, OH Metro Area	93,794	63,392	30,402	-12.1	5,600.9	-13.5	16.7	16.5	483,509	40.1	31.3
Albany, GA Metro Area	25,641	18,753	6,888	-8.4	1,460.3	-21.3	17.6	15.1	97,456	47.9	20.0
Albany-Lebanon, OR Metro Area	17,792	11,956	5,836	-8.5	928.4	2.1	19.2	21.4	85,098	40.1	19.5
Albany-Schenectady-Troy, NY Metro Area	117,306	80,335	36,971	-8.7	8,891.4	-11.7	13.2	12.8	606,254	34.2	36.8
Albuquerque, NM Metro Area	136,161	94,650	41,511	2.1	8,574.4	-5.3	15.9	14.7	620,953	36.1	31.6
Alexandria, LA Metro Area	26,467	18,834	7,633	-1.8	1,489.9	-21.5	17.8	14.2	102,758	53.7	18.6
Allentown-Bethlehem-Easton, PA-NJ Metro Area	121,386	82,119	39,267	-2.6	8,570.4	3.8	14.2	15.1	579,807	44.7	28.6
Altoona, PA Metro Area	17,414	11,981	5,433	-1.8	1,216.1	-6.8	14.3	13.6	88,518	54.5	20.8
Amarillo, TX Metro Area	50,148	36,133	14,015	11.3	3,465.6	6.3	14.5	13.8	169,856	41.2	24.1
Ames, IA Metro Area	15,361	10,721	4,640	4.0	1,035.7	-0.1	14.8	14.3	68,759	25.4	44.1
Anchorage, AK Metro Area	67,357	47,770	19,587	3.4	3,778.2	3.3	17.8	17.8	258,415	32.5	31.7
Ann Arbor, MI Metro Area	45,885	31,394	14,491	-1.1	2,822.5	4.7	16.3	17.2	227,170	19.7	55.2
Anniston-Oxford, AL Metro Area	17,567	12,323	5,244	-4.4	1,042.9	-11.9	16.8	15.5	79,135	48.4	18.0
Appleton, WI Metro Area	39,525	27,381	12,144	6.7	2,611.5	9.1	15.1	15.5	158,138	38.4	28.9
Asheville, NC Metro Area	54,735	37,881	16,854	2.0	3,742.6	0.9	14.6	14.5	330,742	34.4	34.8
Athens-Clarke County, GA Metro Area	29,681	20,589	9,092	23.6	2,130.7	15.1	13.9	13.0	124,111	37.6	38.2
Atlanta-Sandy Springs-Alpharetta, GA Metro area	1,019,091	709,430	309,661	12.2	65,116.9	1.6	15.7	14.2	3,805,068	34.9	37.8
Atlantic City-Hammonton, NJ Metro Area	42,486	29,437	13,049	-5.9	3,809.8	13.7	11.2	13.5	185,383	45.2	27.4
Auburn-Opelika, AL Metro Area	23,813	17,098	6,715	19.7	1,397.4	-0.3	17.0	14.2	94,988	33.6	34.1
Augusta-Richmond County, GA-SC Metro Area	97,028	68,925	28,103	3.3	6,037.6	-5.0	16.1	14.8	399,302	44.3	25.3
Austin-Round Rock-Georgetown, TX Metro Area	354,917	253,854	101,063	28.9	24,084.6	25.7	14.7	14.4	1,368,803	29.4	43.9
Bakersfield, CA Metro Area	188,436	132,740	55,696	10.5	7,910.9	-15.0	23.8	18.3	532,100	53.9	16.1
Baltimore-Columbia-Towson, MD Metro Area	404,712	289,417	115,295	5.4	26,591.3	-0.9	15.2	14.3	1,925,890	34.8	39.5
Bangor, ME Metro Area	19,843	13,787	6,056	-8.6	1,590.3	-15.6	12.5	11.5	107,392	42.0	27.1
Barnstable Town, MA Metro Area	24,628	16,450	8,178	-13.3	2,155.0	-5.7	11.4	12.4	165,336	28.8	42.8
Baton Rouge, LA Metro Area	130,784	93,718	37,066	8.5	7,491.3	-7.9	17.5	14.8	552,515	45.2	27.2
Battle Creek, MI Metro Area	20,366	13,799	6,567	-11.7	1,220.3	-19.2	16.7	15.3	91,073	45.3	21.2
Bay City, MI Metro Area	13,947	9,305	4,642	-11.0	743.6	-13.5	18.8	18.2	74,892	45.1	18.9
Beaumont-Port Arthur, TX Metro Area	68,412	49,633	18,779	0.2	4,560.7	-5.4	15.0	14.2	263,186	49.4	18.0
Beckley, WV Metro Area	18,539	13,408	5,131	-3.2	1,272.5	-5.9	14.6	14.2	86,340	56.6	17.1
Bellingham, WA Metro Area	27,537	18,905	8,632	4.2	1,498.8	8.7	18.4	19.2	142,652	31.0	33.9
Bend, OR Metro Area	26,449	18,138	8,311	7.8	1,251.7	6.0	21.1	20.8	130,615	28.8	34.2
Billings, MT Metro Area	26,321	18,896	7,425	7.9	1,750.4	1.9	15.0	14.2	122,434	36.7	30.7
Binghamton, NY Metro Area	33,017	22,670	10,347	-11.4	2,708.6	-14.6	12.2	11.8	163,689	41.6	27.7
Birmingham-Hoover, AL Metro Area	167,139	117,648	49,491	0.3	9,584.5	-15.0	17.4	14.8	738,052	38.9	30.7
Bismarck, ND Metro Area	18,224	13,127	5,097	18.8	1,298.8	18.8	14.0	14.0	85,918	32.0	32.6
Blacksburg-Christiansburg, VA Metro Area	18,156	12,533	5,623	-3.3	1,332.5	6.8	13.6	15.1	101,103	36.6	35.3
Bloomington, IL Metro Area	25,651	17,870	7,781	1.2	1,673.6	18.4	15.3	17.9	105,055	29.2	44.8
Bloomington, IN Metro Area	16,925	11,906	5,019	-3.6	1,033.9	0.0	16.4	17.0	98,190	33.9	40.6
Bloomsburg-Berwick, PA Metro Area	10,350	6,407	3,943	-11.2	827.3	-24.2	12.5	10.7	57,276	52.6	24.9
Boise City, ID Metro Area	124,890	86,695	38,195	15.3	6,600.2	14.8	18.9	18.9	452,892	34.6	31.0
Boston-Cambridge-Newton, MA-NH Metro Area	660,482	458,397	202,085	0.8	50,850.5	5.9	13.0	13.6	3,350,161	30.9	47.2
Boston, MA Div	266,310	185,106	81,204	2.1	19,981.5	6.2	13.3	13.9	1,390,797	32.4	45.6
Cambridge-Newton-Framingham, MA Div	334,993	233,122	101,871	1.8	26,131.7	8.0	12.8	13.6	1,655,423	29.5	50.0
Rockingham County-Strafford County, NH Div	59,179	40,169	19,010	-9.5	4,737.3	-5.3	12.5	13.1	303,941	31.7	39.3
Boulder, CO Metro Area	48,120	33,398	14,722	14.1	2,662.2	8.9	18.1	17.3	209,850	17.2	60.8
Bowling Green, KY Metro Area	27,257	19,264	7,993	14.1	1,645.9	13.4	16.6	16.5	108,494	46.6	25.4
Bremerton-Silverdale-Port Orchard, WA Metro Area	36,456	24,846	11,610	-5.7	1,963.5	-1.5	18.6	19.4	181,431	28.2	32.2
Bridgeport-Stamford-Norwalk, CT Metro Area	145,741	101,045	44,696	-1.8	11,470.3	5.4	12.7	13.6	641,790	31.8	47.4
Brownsville-Harlingen, TX Metro Area	105,578	74,295	31,283	5.4	6,835.7	3.9	15.4	15.2	245,532	58.8	17.3
Brunswick, GA Metro Area	18,087	13,032	5,055	-0.4	1,180.8	-7.7	15.3	14.2	81,517	45.0	24.5
Buffalo-Cheektowaga, NY Metro Area	152,786	105,470	47,316	-9.5	11,930.5	-9.6	12.8	12.8	794,320	37.6	31.8
Burlington, NC Metro Area	24,792	17,092	7,700	4.0	1,575.4	-0.1	15.7	15.1	108,031	42.0	24.0
Burlington-South Burlington, VT Metro Area	31,378	22,735	8,643	0.8	2,519.4	-4.4	12.5	11.8	145,567	30.6	44.0
California-Lexington Park, MD Metro Area	18,053	12,904	5,149	6.9	1,053.5	4.1	17.1	16.7	73,604	40.1	31.5
Canton-Massillon, OH Metro Area	59,036	40,025	19,011	-11.4	3,169.4	-11.9	18.6	18.5	279,261	47.4	22.1
Cape Coral-Fort Myers, FL Metro Area	93,221	64,796	28,425	16.1	5,858.0	16.6	15.9	16.0	537,841	42.8	27.8
Cape Girardeau, MO-IL Metro Area	13,245	9,589	3,656	-1.6	980.9	-2.8	13.5	13.3	63,519	46.0	26.3
Carbondale-Marion, IL Metro Area	19,211	13,633	5,578	-2.3	1,275.3	20.2	15.1	18.5	92,074	37.4	27.1
Carson City, NV Metro Area	8,200	5,680	2,520	2.0	459.1	-4.6	17.9	16.7	38,892	40.2	22.3
Casper, WY Metro Area	13,308	9,495	3,813	11.7	916.5	11.1	14.5	14.4	54,457	36.5	22.7
Cedar Rapids, IA Metro Area	44,244	30,996	13,248	6.6	2,895.3	-1.1	15.3	14.2	181,221	34.6	30.8
Chambersburg-Waynesboro, PA Metro Area	21,753	14,883	6,870	4.4	1,368.3	-5.8	15.9	14.4	107,004	55.3	21.0
Champaign-Urbana, IL Metro Area	28,250	20,148	8,102	5.4	2,091.2	24.1	13.5	15.9	132,829	27.8	43.0
Charleston, WV Metro Area	40,354	28,619	11,735	-7.8	2,703.2	-9.2	14.9	14.7	191,897	54.2	20.9
Charleston-North Charleston, SC Metro Area	115,584	83,875	31,709	22.7	7,562.9	17.8	15.3	14.7	521,770	35.0	34.8
Charlotte-Concord-Gastonia, NC-SC Metro Area	416,993	291,063	125,930	15.9	25,630.8	6.3	16.3	14.9	1,679,647	35.3	34.4
Charlottesville, VA Metro Area	27,037	18,804	8,233	5.7	1,555.6	-2.1	17.4	16.1	145,842	30.1	46.8
Chattanooga, TN-GA Metro Area	74,480	53,199	21,281	4.7	4,936.4	2.0	15.1	14.7	386,117	43.2	26.1

Table B-6. Enrollment, Teachers, and Educational Attainment—*Continued*

Metropolitan Statistical Area Metropolitan Division	Public school enrollment				Number of public school teachers		Pupil/teacher ratio		Educational attainment, 2014-2018		
		2017-2018									
	Total	Pre-Kindergarten through Grade 8	Grades 9 through 12	Percent change in total since 2007-2008	2017-2018	Percent change since 2007-2008	2017-2018	2007-2008	Population 25 years and over	High school graduate or less (percent)	Bachelor's degree or more (percent)
Cheyenne, WY Metro Area	15,280	10,991	4,289	11.2	1,109.7	4.0	13.8	12.9	65,774	32.6	28.7
Chicago-Naperville-Elgin, IL-IN-WI Metro Area	1,514,908	1,044,317	470,591	-4.9	93,362.7	11.7	16.2	19.1	6,436,872	35.8	37.4
Chicago-Naperville-Evanston, IL Div	1,104,420	766,528	337,892	-5.7	67,551.7	10.5	16.3	19.2	4,910,653	35.0	38.7
Elgin, IL Div	139,405	94,886	44,519	5.3	8,799.1	28.1	15.8	19.3	483,007	36.6	33.3
Gary, IN Div	115,379	78,923	36,456	-6.8	6,179.1	-2.7	18.7	19.5	474,068	46.2	23.0
Lake County-Kenosha County, IL-WI Div	155,704	103,980	51,724	-5.7	10,832.8	16.7	14.4	17.8	569,144	32.6	41.2
Chico, CA Metro Area	31,671	21,904	9,767	3.8	1,477.1	-17.3	21.4	17.1	147,890	33.4	26.5
Cincinnati, OH-KY-IN Metro Area	320,458	226,900	93,558	-2.6	17,195.8	-5.9	18.6	18.0	1,466,300	39.2	32.8
Clarksville, TN-KY Metro Area	47,797	34,383	13,414	13.4	2,824.1	8.6	16.9	16.2	181,897	40.2	23.8
Cleveland, TN Metro Area	18,374	12,644	5,730	3.4	1,137.0	1.6	16.2	15.9	83,140	49.6	20.3
Cleveland-Elyria, OH Metro Area	279,105	189,963	89,142	-11.1	16,079.0	-12.2	17.4	17.1	1,438,478	38.9	30.7
Coeur d'Alene, ID Metro Area	22,584	15,566	7,018	6.2	1,179.4	6.5	19.1	19.2	105,732	34.6	24.9
College Station-Bryan, TX Metro Area	36,596	26,400	10,196	19.7	2,602.8	17.4	14.1	13.8	139,084	36.7	36.7
Colorado Springs, CO Metro Area	123,769	87,407	36,362	12.9	7,300.7	6.8	17.0	16.0	460,298	26.6	37.8
Columbia, MO Metro Area	27,693	19,551	8,142	5.3	2,108.2	3.7	13.1	12.9	124,296	30.5	42.4
Columbia, SC Metro Area	139,221	96,980	42,241	15.5	9,649.1	11.2	14.4	13.9	537,058	37.6	31.9
Columbus, GA-AL Metro Area	49,885	35,259	14,626	-1.3	3,031.0	-12.7	16.5	14.6	210,140	42.5	23.9
Columbus, IN Metro Area	12,388	8,563	3,825	1.4	666.0	15.1	18.6	21.1	55,456	41.7	32.3
Columbus, OH Metro Area	335,619	232,547	103,072	9.3	17,068.0	2.5	19.7	18.4	1,373,112	36.6	36.1
Corpus Christi, TX Metro Area	77,791	54,866	22,925	1.5	5,065.3	-0.6	15.4	15.0	276,775	47.5	20.5
Corvallis, OR Metro Area	10,303	7,331	2,972	0.3	513.2	2.2	20.1	20.5	54,364	18.5	53.6
Crestview-Fort Walton Beach-Destin, FL Metro Area	41,163	29,731	11,432	13.1	2,408.0	-4.8	17.1	14.4	185,712	34.5	30.0
Cumberland, MD-WV Metro Area	12,779	9,088	3,691	-7.8	877.0	-12.8	14.6	13.8	69,438	53.4	17.3
Dallas-Fort Worth-Arlington, TX Metro Area	1,401,048	997,119	403,929	20.4	91,506.4	16.0	15.3	14.7	4,624,843	37.2	34.4
Dallas-Plano-Irving, TX Div	949,031	672,306	276,725	22.1	61,913.2	14.8	15.3	14.4	3,097,499	37.7	36.7
Fort Worth-Arlington-Grapevine, TX Div	452,017	324,813	127,204	16.9	29,593.2	18.5	15.3	15.5	1,527,344	39.5	29.9
Dalton, GA Metro Area	28,414	20,133	8,281	1.0	1,899.3	-1.8	15.0	14.6	92,955	62.1	13.9
Danville, IL Metro Area	12,647	9,033	3,614	-11.1	838.0	10.8	15.1	18.8	53,310	53.0	15.1
Daphne-Fairhope-Foley, AL Metro Area	31,782	22,359	9,423	21.0	1,766.5	-6.2	18.0	14.0	146,989	37.3	31.3
Davenport-Moline-Rock Island, IA-IL Metro Area	60,357	42,269	18,088	-1.3	4,055.5	10.4	14.9	16.7	262,111	39.9	26.7
Dayton-Kettering, OH Metro Area	112,438	79,619	32,819	-6.6	6,307.8	-4.6	17.8	18.2	547,728	37.7	29.1
Decatur, AL Metro Area	24,379	17,225	7,154	-3.1	1,432.9	-16.4	17.0	14.7	105,656	49.9	19.5
Decatur, IL Metro Area	15,970	11,480	4,490	-6.5	994.9	10.8	16.1	19.0	73,230	44.1	22.5
Deltona-Daytona Beach-Ormond Beach, FL Metro Area	75,989	52,366	23,623	-1.6	4,778.0	-11.2	15.9	14.4	470,654	42.1	23.7
Denver-Aurora-Lakewood, CO Metro Area	472,488	333,674	138,814	14.9	25,987.3	14.2	18.2	18.1	1,957,998	29.3	42.9
Des Moines-West Des Moines, IA Metro Area	118,165	84,277	33,888	19.1	7,565.4	9.9	15.6	14.4	444,801	33.4	35.8
Detroit-Warren-Dearborn, MI Metro Area	643,972	434,014	209,958	-12.8	34,995.2	-14.8	18.4	18.0	2,971,255	37.0	30.6
Detroit-Dearborn-Livonia, MI Div	273,943	188,499	85,444	-16.5	14,613.8	-20.5	18.7	17.8	1,178,363	44.1	23.3
Warren-Troy-Farmington Hills, MI Div	370,029	245,515	124,514	-9.9	20,381.4	-10.2	18.2	18.1	1,792,892	32.4	35.4
Dothan, AL Metro Area	22,026	15,569	6,457	4.4	1,211.9	-12.5	18.2	15.2	102,463	49.0	18.9
Dover, DE Metro Area	29,079	19,709	9,370	12.5	1,988.0	13.7	14.6	14.8	116,057	46.0	23.6
Dubuque, IA Metro Area	13,723	9,252	4,471	1.8	1,004.2	-6.3	13.7	12.6	64,565	40.6	30.5
Duluth, MN-WI Metro Area	39,459	27,741	11,718	-2.7	2,521.4	22.3	15.6	19.7	199,971	35.2	27.3
Durham-Chapel Hill, NC Metro Area	89,534	62,152	27,382	16.2	6,052.2	11.2	14.8	14.2	418,763	31.2	44.2
East Stroudsburg, PA Metro Area	23,313	15,504	7,809	-21.2	1,796.4	-23.7	13.0	12.6	115,370	46.1	24.4
Eau Claire, WI Metro Area	23,506	16,691	6,815	1.1	1,591.6	5.1	14.8	15.4	109,167	36.7	27.0
El Centro, CA Metro Area	38,706	26,294	12,412	5.3	1,700.8	-14.5	22.8	18.5	109,338	55.5	14.5
Elizabethtown-Fort Knox, KY Metro Area	24,670	17,020	7,650	3.6	1,465.9	0.3	16.8	16.3	100,054	42.8	20.8
Elkhart-Goshen, IN Metro Area	36,367	25,859	10,508	0.4	2,075.5	1.2	17.5	17.7	128,815	54.0	19.2
Elmira, NY Metro Area	11,883	8,539	3,344	-9.2	879.0	-24.7	13.5	11.2	59,921	45.7	23.9
El Paso, TX Metro Area	177,561	122,263	55,298	2.6	11,356.1	-1.3	15.6	15.0	511,137	46.5	22.7
Enid, OK Metro Area	11,551	8,600	2,951	20.6	666.5	4.0	17.3	14.9	40,501	48.6	22.4
Erie, PA Metro Area	38,018	26,235	11,783	-7.5	2,640.2	-1.2	14.4	15.4	187,964	47.7	27.7
Eugene-Springfield, OR Metro Area	45,324	31,452	13,872	-2.4	2,170.8	-4.7	20.9	20.4	251,966	32.1	29.6
Evansville, IN-KY Metro Area	44,652	31,214	13,438	2.3	3,064.0	15.1	14.6	16.4	216,047	43.0	25.2
Fairbanks, AK Metro Area	19,531	13,981	5,550	3.8	817.0	-4.2	23.9	22.1	61,838	27.8	32.6
Fargo, ND-MN Metro Area	35,394	25,656	9,738	26.5	2,542.6	33.1	13.9	14.6	147,524	26.6	37.9
Farmington, NM Metro Area	23,710	16,650	7,060	1.5	1,443.1	-9.3	16.4	14.7	81,510	46.5	15.2
Fayetteville, NC Metro Area	81,874	57,543	24,331	2.6	5,256.2	-3.5	15.6	14.6	322,672	37.8	23.2
Fayetteville-Springdale-Rogers, AR Metro Area	91,367	64,554	26,813	27.1	6,178.2	21.0	14.8	14.1	318,037	42.0	31.9
Flagstaff, AZ Metro Area	18,482	12,775	5,707	-5.6					82,119	31.8	35.6
Flint, MI Metro Area	64,045	43,632	20,413	-20.0	3,529.1	-20.3	18.1	18.1	278,730	41.5	20.9
Florence, SC Metro Area	33,357	23,637	9,720	-2.6	2,244.8	-2.4	14.9	14.9	139,171	50.1	21.1
Florence-Muscle Shoals, AL Metro Area	20,830	14,570	6,260	-3.3	1,268.7	-11.6	16.4	15.0	102,067	49.7	22.0
Fond du Lac, WI Metro Area	13,827	9,867	3,960	-3.3	923.6	0.2	15.0	15.5	71,153	44.9	22.7
Fort Collins, CO Metro Area	49,022	34,212	14,810	15.3	2,769.1	14.1	17.7	17.5	221,161	23.5	46.3
Fort Smith, AR-OK Metro Area	42,668	29,972	12,696	0.2	2,908.7	-5.4	14.7	13.9	166,806	51.9	16.9
Fort Wayne, IN Metro Area	60,483	42,019	18,464	-2.1	3,241.2	-6.1	18.7	17.9	263,078	40.1	27.5
Fresno, CA Metro Area	203,405	143,703	59,702	7.2	8,559.8	-20.0	23.8	17.7	596,505	47.7	20.7
Gadsden, AL Metro Area	15,260	10,561	4,699	-6.7	927.5	-11.2	16.5	15.7	71,995	48.4	17.7
Gainesville, FL Metro Area	39,166	28,161	11,005	1.3	-	-	-	67.3	200,322	35.0	36.5
Gainesville, GA Metro Area	35,414	24,732	10,682	7.1	2,241.6	-4.7	15.8	14.1	127,116	49.1	24.0

Table B-6. Enrollment, Teachers, and Educational Attainment—*Continued*

Metropolitan Statistical Area Metropolitan Division	Public school enrollment 2017-2018				Number of public school teachers		Pupil/teacher ratio		Educational attainment, 2014-2018		
	Total	Pre-Kindergarten through Grade 8	Grades 9 through 12	Percent change in total since 2007-2008	2017-2018	Percent change since 2007-2008	2017-2018	2007-2008	Population 25 years and over	High school graduate or less (percent)	Bachelor's degree or more (percent)
Gettysburg, PA Metro Area	13,969	9,532	4,437	-2.8	937.1	-3.6	14.9	14.8	71,478	51.9	22.4
Glens Falls, NY Metro Area	17,352	11,940	5,412	-13.7	1,487.6	-23.2	11.7	10.4	92,629	45.2	25.4
Goldsboro, NC Metro Area	19,521	13,839	5,682	-0.1	1,304.3	-3.7	15.0	14.4	82,105	46.4	19.5
Grand Forks, ND-MN Metro Area	14,519	10,399	4,120	3.8	1,146.1	2.4	12.7	12.5	62,366	32.5	31.0
Grand Island, NE Metro Area	14,939	10,650	4,289	11.6	1,078.4	9.6	13.9	13.6	49,298	45.3	20.5
Grand Junction, CO Metro Area	23,577	16,600	6,977	6.2	1,336.9	5.2	17.6	17.5	102,669	37.2	27.4
Grand Rapids-Kentwood, MI Metro Area	169,628	116,216	53,412	1.3	9,660.2	-3.0	17.6	16.8	684,898	36.7	32.1
Grants Pass, OR Metro Area	10,826	7,483	3,343	-3.3	516.7	1.4	21.0	22.0	63,006	40.7	17.2
Great Falls, MT Metro Area	11,653	8,460	3,193	-1.9	811.7	-4.7	14.4	13.9	55,249	39.9	26.0
Greeley, CO Metro Area	55,182	39,543	15,639	29.8	3,055.0	19.1	18.1	16.6	188,765	39.5	26.7
Green Bay, WI Metro Area	52,438	36,986	15,452	7.3	3,582.0	4.7	14.6	14.3	214,895	40.8	27.2
Greensboro-High Point, NC Metro Area	114,869	79,111	35,758	2.8	7,180.5	-5.1	16.0	14.8	512,752	40.3	28.9
Greenville, NC Metro Area	24,911	17,525	7,386	9.1	1,615.1	-1.9	15.4	13.9	106,889	34.2	31.8
Greenville-Anderson, SC Metro Area	139,533	99,647	39,886	9.7	8,637.0	5.3	16.2	15.5	594,838	41.6	28.6
Gulfport-Biloxi, MS Metro Area	64,822	46,210	18,612	8.4	4,176.9	1.0	15.5	14.5	274,769	42.7	21.5
Hagerstown-Martinsburg, MD-WV Metro Area	44,277	31,097	13,180	7.7	2,823.3	0.4	15.7	14.6	195,321	49.5	21.0
Hammond, LA Metro Area	19,698	14,345	5,353	1.1	1,122.0	-1.6	17.6	17.1	84,349	54.5	19.4
Hanford-Corcoran, CA Metro Area	28,794	20,283	8,511	6.1	1,265.4	-17.3	22.8	17.7	92,321	51.8	13.5
Harrisburg-Carlisle, PA Metro Area	85,464	58,276	27,188	7.6	5,743.3	-7.4	14.9	12.8	395,438	43.7	31.7
Harrisonburg, VA Metro Area	18,106	12,622	5,484	10.6	1,272.6	19.2	14.2	15.3	81,150	48.3	29.2
Hartford-East Hartford-Middletown, CT Metro area	175,691	121,368	54,323	-9.3	14,529.7	0.7	12.1	13.4	837,108	36.1	38.7
Hattiesburg, MS Metro Area	25,753	18,514	7,239	2.4	1,815.6	-0.9	14.2	13.7	107,682	40.2	28.0
Hickory-Lenoir-Morganton, NC Metro Area	53,170	36,322	16,848	-7.7	3,396.9	-13.6	15.7	14.7	257,924	49.3	18.3
Hilton Head Island-Bluffton, SC Metro Area	26,506	19,095	7,411	16.0	1,962.6	19.8	13.5	14.0	149,740	33.6	37.3
Hinesville, GA Metro Area	13,696	9,933	3,763	3.9	828.2	-0.1	16.5	15.9	46,944	42.4	17.6
Homosassa Springs, FL Metro Area	15,568	10,801	4,767	-3.7	981.0	-13.6	15.9	14.2	113,645	50.2	17.6
Hot Springs, AR Metro Area	15,346	10,948	4,398	10.0	1,045.5	-1.2	14.7	13.2	70,968	43.1	20.2
Houma-Thibodaux, LA Metro Area	32,383	23,507	8,876	-4.3	1,691.3	-31.5	19.1	13.7	140,118	61.4	16.1
Houston-The Woodlands-Sugar Land, TX Metro area	1,342,043	957,620	384,423	20.0	83,329.9	16.7	16.1	15.7	4,331,860	39.9	32.4
Huntington-Ashland, WV-KY-OH Metro Area	56,674	40,333	16,341	-3.6	3,757.5	-4.7	15.1	14.9	253,417	50.2	20.2
Huntsville, AL Metro Area	68,227	47,389	20,838	11.2	3,720.6	-9.9	18.3	14.8	308,079	33.1	38.3
Idaho Falls, ID Metro Area	32,099	22,968	9,131	20.8	1,596.9	18.4	20.1	19.7	85,756	35.4	28.4
Indianapolis-Carmel-Anderson, IN Metro Area	353,786	242,306	111,480	14.0	19,392.9	10.3	18.2	17.7	1,330,740	38.6	33.9
Iowa City, IA Metro Area	22,711	16,270	6,441	23.7	1,443.2	17.5	15.7	14.9	101,291	25.0	48.3
Ithaca, NY Metro Area	11,208	7,636	3,572	-7.5	1,064.4	-4.0	10.5	10.9	59,782	25.2	52.7
Jackson, MI Metro Area	23,286	15,918	7,368	-8.5	1,361.0	-11.7	17.1	16.5	109,811	42.4	21.4
Jackson, MS Metro Area	91,865	65,838	26,027	-3.5	5,915.3	-3.4	15.5	15.5	392,867	38.7	29.6
Jackson, TN Metro Area	28,023	20,027	7,996	1.8	1,811.2	1.1	15.5	15.4	118,969	50.3	21.7
Jacksonville, FL Metro Area	226,200	160,907	65,293	9.7	9,502.0	-15.6	23.8	18.3	1,013,985	37.3	30.5
Jacksonville, NC Metro Area	26,840	19,489	7,351	13.7	1,610.7	6.9	16.7	15.7	103,180	37.9	21.4
Janesville-Beloit, WI Metro Area	27,512	18,923	8,589	-2.9	1,899.5	-2.3	14.5	14.6	109,468	45.8	21.8
Jefferson City, MO Metro Area	20,622	14,360	6,262	2.9	1,568.4	2.0	13.1	13.0	103,086	45.9	27.0
Johnson City, TN Metro Area	26,665	18,540	8,125	-1.2	1,796.4	-0.4	14.8	15.0	141,513	46.4	26.1
Johnstown, PA Metro Area	17,311	11,868	5,443	-9.9	1,271.1	-7.6	13.6	14.0	96,069	53.6	21.4
Jonesboro, AR Metro Area	23,223	16,676	6,547	15.1	1,634.7	-6.3	14.2	11.6	84,033	48.6	23.1
Joplin, MO Metro Area	30,094	21,397	8,697	3.8	2,094.3	5.2	14.4	14.6	117,072	47.4	21.8
Kahului-Wailuku-Lahaina, HI Metro Area	22,071	15,873	6,198	4.9	1,425.5	7.6	15.5	15.9	117,206	39.8	26.6
Kalamazoo-Portage, MI Metro Area	35,339	24,588	10,751	0.3	2,007.5	-6.3	17.6	16.4	163,025	28.4	38.1
Kankakee, IL Metro Area	17,726	12,373	5,353	-10.4	1,146.8	12.4	15.5	19.4	72,819	45.7	21.0
Kansas City, MO-KS Metro Area	352,261	249,790	102,471	6.9	23,927.9	4.6	14.7	14.4	1,416,746	33.9	36.4
Kennewick-Richland, WA Metro Area	58,125	40,572	17,553	24.6	3,112.4	33.6	18.7	20.0	177,519	39.1	26.2
Killeen-Temple, TX Metro Area	87,433	63,973	23,460	15.3	5,746.8	7.2	15.2	14.2	268,518	36.2	22.7
Kingsport-Bristol, TN-VA Metro Area	41,949	29,006	12,943	-6.6	2,660.0	-13.4	15.8	14.6	222,976	50.7	20.6
Kingston, NY Metro Area	21,795	14,528	7,267	-15.9	1,706.3	-15.5	12.8	12.8	129,932	39.2	32.2
Knoxville, TN Metro Area	117,706	82,460	35,246	6.1	7,340.8	-0.3	16.0	15.1	584,297	42.6	29.0
Kokomo, IN Metro Area	13,707	9,340	4,367	-0.9	845.8	-2.5	16.2	16.0	57,038	47.6	21.2
La Crosse-Onalaska, WI-MN Metro Area	20,647	14,306	6,341	2.4	1,518.5	5.1	13.6	14.0	88,282	32.0	32.7
Lafayette, LA Metro Area	73,488	53,226	20,262	4.1	3,959.0	-18.5	18.6	14.5	323,023	53.0	22.8
Lafayette-West Lafayette, IN Metro Area	29,453	20,914	8,539	8.8	1,715.9	7.7	17.2	17.0	130,010	37.0	33.7
Lake Charles, LA Metro Area	35,793	25,850	9,943	5.1	2,202.5	-9.4	16.3	14.0	137,004	47.6	21.6
Lake Havasu City-Kingman, AZ Metro Area	23,647	17,009	6,638	-14.7	-	-	-	-	155,888	49.6	12.9
Lakeland-Winter Haven, FL Metro Area	104,026	72,988	31,038	11.2	6,508.0	-0.2	16.0	14.4	461,771	50.6	20.0
Lancaster, PA Metro Area	67,100	46,315	20,785	-3.9	4,717.7	-0.5	14.2	14.7	360,878	51.0	26.9
Lansing-East Lansing, MI Metro Area	80,044	52,862	27,182	-7.2	4,434.1	-11.8	18.1	17.2	351,688	32.7	32.0
Laredo, TX Metro Area	69,662	48,964	20,698	7.3	4,161.9	2.7	16.7	16.0	149,553	59.1	18.4
Las Cruces, NM Metro Area	39,972	27,878	12,094	2.4	2,470.2	-3.3	16.2	15.3	129,625	43.2	27.5
Las Vegas-Henderson-Paradise, NV Metro Area	361,599	256,501	105,098	17.0	17,411.9	9.9	20.8	19.5	1,454,973	42.9	23.9
Lawrence, KS Metro Area	15,225	10,453	4,772	8.7	1,053.6	10.3	14.5	14.7	68,491	22.5	50.4
Lawton, OK Metro Area	21,955	16,151	5,804	-4.3	1,364.2	-11.8	16.1	14.8	81,462	43.2	22.1
Lebanon, PA Metro Area	19,669	13,892	5,777	4.3	1,286.9	-0.7	15.3	14.6	95,065	57.1	20.3
Lewiston, ID-WA Metro Area	8,654	5,959	2,695	-3.8	518.9	0.7	16.7	17.5	43,929	39.7	21.4
Lewiston-Auburn, ME Metro Area	16,065	11,798	4,267	-1.2	1,279.1	-5.5	12.6	12.0	74,517	46.3	22.2

Table B-6. Enrollment, Teachers, and Educational Attainment—*Continued*

Metropolitan Statistical Area Metropolitan Division	Public school enrollment				Number of public school teachers		Pupil/teacher ratio		Educational attainment, 2014-2018		
		2017-2018									
	Total	Pre-Kindergarten through Grade 8	Grades 9 through 12	Percent change in total since 2007-2008	2017-2018	Percent change since 2007-2008	2017-2018	2007-2008	Population 25 years and over	High school graduate or less (percent)	Bachelor's degree or more (percent)
Lexington-Fayette, KY Metro Area	72,407	51,698	20,709	13.2	4,731.9	14.6	15.3	15.5	332,567	34.8	36.8
Lima, OH Metro Area	14,998	10,874	4,124	-11.8	914.9	-9.3	16.4	16.9	69,189	48.9	17.8
Lincoln, NE Metro Area	49,841	35,099	14,742	22.8	3,592.0	21.9	13.9	13.8	202,547	28.7	38.3
Little Rock-North Little Rock-Conway, AR Metro Area ...	118,208	84,941	33,267	9.7	7,931.0	-1.1	14.9	13.4	489,580	38.9	30.1
Logan, UT-ID Metro Area	30,112	21,520	8,592	16.6	-	-	-	22.6	69,341	29.2	35.5
Longview, TX Metro Area	53,274	38,306	14,968	5.8	3,834.6	1.0	13.9	13.3	187,509	47.9	18.6
Longview, WA Metro Area	17,477	11,962	5,515	-2.5	935.1	1.7	18.7	19.5	72,862	42.2	16.6
Los Angeles-Long Beach-Anaheim, CA Metro Area ...	1,966,228	1,336,522	629,706	-6.0	82,042.2	-25.8	24.0	18.9	8,997,001	39.6	33.7
Anaheim-Santa Ana-Irvine, CA Div.	485,622	324,634	160,988	0.3	18,969.6	-20.5	25.6	20.3	2,151,512	32.0	39.9
Los Angeles-Long Beach-Glendale, CA Div	1,480,606	1,011,888	468,718	-7.9	63,072.6	-27.3	23.5	18.5	6,845,489	42.0	31.8
Louisville/Jefferson County, KY-IN Metro Area	177,642	123,808	53,834	3.2	10,645.6	10.5	16.7	17.9	861,122	40.0	29.0
Lubbock, TX Metro Area	53,680	39,125	14,555	15.8	3,902.5	9.9	13.8	13.1	185,015	41.1	28.5
Lynchburg, VA Metro Area	32,312	22,414	9,898	-5.8	1,601.6	-25.0	20.2	16.1	174,249	42.9	27.1
Macon-Bibb County, GA Metro Area	36,661	26,706	9,955	-2.0	2,402.9	-3.7	15.3	15.0	153,202	48.1	23.5
Madera, CA Metro Area	31,694	22,292	9,402	10.7	1,368.9	-13.9	23.2	18.0	97,015	53.1	14.5
Madison, WI Metro Area	96,759	68,061	28,698	11.2	7,128.8	13.4	13.6	13.8	429,596	26.0	45.5
Manchester-Nashua, NH Metro Area	58,090	39,522	18,568	-11.0	4,437.1	-4.1	13.1	14.1	288,293	34.5	37.3
Manhattan, KS Metro Area	18,325	13,592	4,733	10.0	1,393.9	22.1	13.1	14.6	71,403	27.6	37.3
Mankato, MN Metro Area	13,996	9,911	4,085	14.9	890.6	16.7	15.7	16.0	60,545	32.5	33.2
Mansfield, OH Metro Area	17,688	12,570	5,118	-3.1	1,171.5	1.8	15.1	15.9	84,689	53.0	17.8
McAllen-Edinburg-Mission, TX Metro Area	225,402	159,107	66,295	16.2	14,681.3	15.9	15.4	15.3	473,253	58.7	18.4
Medford, OR Metro Area	29,626	20,813	8,813	4.1	1,405.3	4.3	21.1	21.1	152,902	36.7	27.4
Memphis, TN-MS-AR Metro Area	221,598	158,089	63,509	-2.9	13,491.8	-3.1	16.4	16.4	875,078	41.6	27.9
Merced, CA Metro Area	58,701	40,842	17,859	6.1	2,538.6	-17.7	23.1	17.9	158,034	56.5	14.0
Miami-Fort Lauderdale-Pompano Beach, FL Metro Area .	822,082	569,725	252,357	5.5	48,404.0	39.0	17.0	22.4	4,322,328	41.4	31.5
Fort Lauderdale-Pompano Beach-Sunrise, FL Div......	272,635	190,337	82,298	5.5	16,251.0	-	16.8	-	1,344,708	38.6	31.9
Miami-Miami Beach-Kendall, FL Div	354,840	245,203	109,637	1.6	19,340.0	-17.3	18.3	14.9	1,922,868	46.3	28.8
West Palm Beach-Boca Raton-Boynton Beach, FL Div	194,607	134,185	60,422	13.5	12,813.0	12.1	15.2	15.0	1,054,752	36.3	35.7
Michigan City-La Porte, IN Metro Area	16,613	11,329	5,284	-7.6	1,022.7	2.7	16.2	18.0	77,246	51.0	17.9
Midland, MI Metro Area	11,977	7,892	4,085	-14.9	660.1	-15.6	18.1	18.0	58,142	34.7	34.0
Midland, TX Metro Area	31,036	22,912	8,124	27.3	1,908.7	17.2	16.3	15.0	105,771	42.4	27.2
Milwaukee-Waukesha, WI Metro Area	229,208	159,151	70,057	-4.3	13,299.0	-7.1	17.2	16.7	1,064,700	35.5	35.1
Minneapolis-St. Paul-Bloomington, MN Metro Area	581,781	403,597	178,184	7.3	35,412.5	11.8	16.4	17.1	2,390,750	27.9	41.3
Missoula, MT Metro Area	13,887	9,838	4,049	5.3	896.7	3.3	15.5	15.2	77,154	25.8	42.5
Mobile, AL Metro Area	63,914	44,982	18,932	-4.3	3,511.7	-19.6	18.2	15.3	289,168	47.9	22.5
Modesto, CA Metro Area	109,808	76,263	33,545	7.0	4,746.5	-15.7	23.1	18.2	339,918	50.2	16.9
Monroe, LA Metro Area	35,055	25,173	9,882	-3.2	2,031.5	-19.9	17.3	14.3	133,698	51.4	21.7
Monroe, MI Metro Area	22,031	14,317	7,714	-17.0	1,137.4	-23.0	19.4	18.0	104,748	44.9	19.1
Montgomery, AL Metro Area	54,876	39,357	15,519	-2.2	3,057.8	-16.1	17.9	15.4	250,023	42.6	29.2
Morgantown, WV Metro Area	16,279	11,775	4,504	10.9	1,052.3	4.2	15.5	14.5	89,779	43.7	34.2
Morristown, TN Metro Area	21,348	15,069	6,279	2.2	1,328.1	2.7	16.1	16.1	97,651	58.3	15.3
Mount Vernon-Anacortes, WA Metro Area	19,419	13,557	5,862	-0.1	1,115.0	-	17.4	-	86,398	36.7	26.3
Muncie, IN Metro Area	15,538	10,700	4,838	-7.6	944.1	-10.9	16.5	15.9	71,116	45.3	24.3
Muskegon, MI Metro Area	27,455	18,552	8,903	-12.1	1,597.6	-11.1	17.2	17.4	117,584	43.7	19.1
Myrtle Beach-Conway-North Myrtle Beach, SC-NC	58,795	41,554	17,241	18.2	3,706.8	14.6	15.9	15.4	335,225	41.6	25.1
Napa, CA Metro Area	20,332	13,601	6,731	10.7	935.9	-19.2	21.7	15.9	98,220	32.9	34.9
Naples-Marco Island, FL Metro Area	46,832	32,272	14,560	9.6	3,006.0	4.3	15.6	14.8	274,710	39.0	36.2
Nashville-Davidson--Murfreesboro--Franklin, TN	283,782	202,579	81,203	19.2	17,945.2	16.4	15.8	15.4	1,234,861	37.2	35.1
New Bern, NC Metro Area	16,886	11,874	5,012	-5.0	1,113.8	-10.9	15.2	14.2	84,671	39.2	23.9
New Haven-Milford, CT Metro Area	120,820	83,324	37,496	-10.6	9,941.3	-0.4	12.2	13.5	595,852	40.8	34.9
New Orleans-Metairie, LA Metro Area	171,035	122,930	48,105	22.5	9,430.4	-8.1	18.1	13.6	874,498	41.8	29.8
New York-Newark-Jersey City, NY-NJ-PA Metro Area .	2,672,657	1,856,399	816,258	4.7	210,804.3	10.5	12.7	13.4	13,416,449	38.7	39.6
Nassau County-Suffolk County, NY Div	438,022	293,230	144,792	-5.7	33,581.5	-8.3	13.0	12.7	1,969,430	34.8	40.2
Newark, NJ-PA Div	343,959	240,234	103,725	1.4	29,212.9	21.4	11.8	14.1	1,482,481	37.2	40.1
New Brunswick-Lakewood, NJ Div	337,495	230,157	107,338	-3.3	29,545.0	26.2	11.4	14.9	1,638,106	34.6	41.6
New York-Jersey City-White Plains, NY-NJ Div.........	1,553,181	1,092,778	460,403	11.0	118,464.9	11.0	13.1	13.1	8,326,432	40.7	39.1
Niles, MI Metro Area	23,185	15,627	7,558	-10.1	1,294.8	-19.7	17.9	16.0	107,593	39.3	27.7
North Port-Sarasota-Bradenton, FL Metro Area	91,853	64,514	27,339	8.7	6,494.0	17.6	14.1	15.3	605,872	38.5	32.2
Norwich-New London, CT Metro Area	38,001	25,886	12,115	-11.2	3,185.8	-3.6	11.9	12.9	188,221	37.9	33.3
Ocala, FL Metro Area	43,119	30,274	12,845	1.3	2,571.0	-6.5	16.8	15.5	259,032	50.1	19.4
Ocean City, NJ Metro Area	12,110	8,452	3,658	-8.6	1,183.5	18.1	10.2	13.2	69,876	41.4	31.5
Odessa, TX Metro Area	34,880	25,871	9,009	29.9	2,121.0	23.1	16.4	15.6	93,728	54.1	15.6
Ogden-Clearfield, UT Metro Area	150,088	106,814	43,274	13.1	-	-	-	24.5	387,586	31.7	31.0
Oklahoma City, OK Metro Area	247,984	178,238	69,746	23.9	13,997.4	13.4	17.7	16.2	890,744	38.3	30.1
Olympia-Lacey-Tumwater, WA Metro Area	43,576	29,511	14,065	10.0	2,310.2	14.4	18.9	19.6	191,915	27.3	35.7
Omaha-Council Bluffs, NE-IA Metro Area	159,644	113,385	46,259	13.5	10,736.5	11.2	14.9	14.6	603,422	32.3	35.8
Orlando-Kissimmee-Sanford, FL Metro Area	387,697	268,442	119,255	11.4	25,170.0	14.9	15.4	15.9	1,668,607	36.7	31.3
Oshkosh-Neenah, WI Metro Area	23,062	16,189	6,873	-0.4	1,595.6	1.5	14.5	14.7	114,256	40.8	27.3
Owensboro, KY Metro Area	20,169	14,527	5,642	7.4	1,231.6	0.2	16.4	15.3	79,478	46.4	21.1
Oxnard-Thousand Oaks-Ventura, CA Metro Area	150,412	100,919	49,493	5.7	6,323.5	-14.5	23.8	19.2	566,685	34.5	33.1
Palm Bay-Melbourne-Titusville, FL Metro Area	73,524	51,084	22,440	-2.3	4,797.0	-2.2	15.3	15.3	426,776	36.6	29.3
Panama City, FL Metro Area	28,076	20,365	7,711	7.0	1,815.0	2.4	15.5	14.8	127,804	41.1	22.8

Table B-6. Enrollment, Teachers, and Educational Attainment—*Continued*

Metropolitan Statistical Area Metropolitan Division	Public school enrollment				Number of public school teachers		Pupil/teacher ratio		Educational attainment, 2014-2018		
	2017-2018			Percent change in total since 2007-2008	2017-2018	Percent change since 2007-2008	2017-2018	2007-2008	Population 25 years and over	High school graduate or less (percent)	Bachelor's degree or more (percent)
	Total	Pre-Kindergarten through Grade 8	Grades 9 through 12								
Parkersburg-Vienna, WV Metro Area	13,711	9,794	3,917	-6.0	954.5	-5.6	14.4	14.4	65,054	46.1	21.1
Pensacola-Ferry Pass-Brent, FL Metro Area	68,287	48,355	19,932	1.0	4,604.0	-6.7	14.8	13.7	327,072	36.2	27.0
Peoria, IL Metro Area	62,928	44,107	18,821	-3.4	4,316.3	19.4	14.6	18.0	281,053	39.0	27.4
Philadelphia-Camden-Wilmington, PA-NJ-DE-MD Metro Area	845,185	591,748	253,437	-0.7	60,026.0	0.5	14.1	14.2	4,172,132	39.1	37.0
Camden, NJ Div	189,664	132,695	56,969	-4.6	16,332.9	22.4	11.6	14.9	860,033	38.8	33.9
Montgomery County-Bucks County-Chester County,.	284,588	193,309	91,279	1.3	19,960.4	-3.4	14.3	13.6	1,371,616	31.0	46.8
Philadelphia, PA Div	267,327	192,835	74,492	-1.6	16,285.8	-14.9	16.4	14.2	1,445,255	46.1	31.1
Wilmington, DE-MD-NJ Div	103,606	72,909	30,697	4.2	7,446.9	13.6	13.9	15.2	495,228	41.5	32.7
Phoenix-Mesa-Chandler, AZ Metro Area	783,437	548,927	234,510	6.2	-	-	-	-	3,099,741	36.0	30.8
Pine Bluff, AR Metro Area	13,861	9,643	4,218	-17.1	1,051.6	-17.5	13.2	13.1	63,291	55.7	16.2
Pittsburgh, PA Metro Area	298,172	201,764	96,408	-9.0	21,212.3	-6.5	14.1	14.4	1,692,424	39.6	34.1
Pittsfield, MA Metro Area	15,784	10,875	4,909	-14.1	1,354.4	-11.8	11.7	12.0	92,946	38.8	33.4
Pocatello, ID Metro Area	16,532	11,658	4,874	7.7	856.4	4.0	19.3	18.6	58,269	36.1	26.3
Portland-South Portland, ME Metro Area	68,725	47,569	21,156	-7.6	5,704.5	-8.4	12.0	12.0	384,186	31.8	40.0
Portland-Vancouver-Hillsboro, OR-WA Metro Area	343,291	237,924	105,367	3.2	17,735.4	4.3	19.4	19.6	1,688,188	28.3	38.9
Port St. Lucie, FL Metro Area	61,227	41,630	19,597	4.0	2,465.0	-29.2	24.8	16.9	341,866	43.0	24.8
Poughkeepsie-Newburgh-Middletown, NY Metro Area	97,884	65,482	32,402	-13.2	7,482.7	-10.6	13.1	13.5	445,383	38.0	32.3
Prescott Valley-Prescott, AZ Metro Area	24,631	17,452	7,179	-12.6	-	-	-	-	171,813	35.4	25.2
Providence-Warwick, RI-MA Metro Area	222,681	154,444	68,237	-3.3	16,548.6	-1.8	13.5	13.7	1,123,418	41.9	31.4
Provo-Orem, UT Metro Area	150,018	107,716	42,302	28.0	-	-	-	24.8	295,568	22.6	39.6
Pueblo, CO Metro Area	31,810	19,737	12,073	17.4	1,583.4	3.6	20.1	17.7	111,894	39.2	22.0
Punta Gorda, FL Metro Area	15,901	10,337	5,564	-10.6	935.0	-14.3	17.0	16.3	145,220	43.5	23.2
Racine, WI Metro Area	28,109	19,129	8,980	-11.6	2,025.4	-0.1	13.9	15.7	133,019	41.6	24.7
Raleigh-Cary, NC Metro Area	220,288	153,883	66,405	23.1	13,774.5	15.7	16.0	15.0	866,151	26.8	45.9
Rapid City, SD Metro Area	20,596	14,906	5,690	7.5	1,296.9	0.5	15.9	14.8	92,322	35.1	30.0
Reading, PA Metro Area	65,331	44,190	21,141	-3.0	4,475.1	-8.7	14.6	13.7	281,665	50.8	24.5
Redding, CA Metro Area	26,965	18,359	8,606	0.6	1,229.7	-23.7	21.9	16.6	126,151	34.0	22.2
Reno, NV Metro Area	71,453	49,769	21,684	8.5	3,462.9	0.3	20.6	19.1	313,328	35.7	30.4
Richmond, VA Metro Area	195,240	136,573	58,667	2.2	11,338.8	6.6	17.2	18.0	866,483	35.7	36.6
Riverside-San Bernardino-Ontario, CA Metro Area	830,468	570,166	260,302	2.1	34,205.1	-17.9	24.3	19.5	2,861,981	46.0	21.1
Roanoke, VA Metro Area	44,428	31,036	13,392	-1.9	2,749.8	0.7	16.2	16.6	223,194	41.7	27.4
Rochester, MN Metro Area	34,964	24,471	10,493	6.9	2,287.7	14.7	15.3	16.4	146,683	30.2	37.6
Rochester, NY Metro Area	152,799	105,223	47,576	-9.7	12,639.4	-11.6	12.1	11.8	739,984	36.2	34.1
Rockford, IL Metro Area	54,479	38,082	16,397	-8.6	3,425.8	13.7	15.9	19.8	229,356	45.0	22.7
Rocky Mount, NC Metro Area	23,518	16,415	7,103	-11.5	1,428.1	-14.5	16.5	15.9	101,233	51.6	17.9
Rome, GA Metro Area	16,276	11,515	4,761	0.0	1,085.6	-10.5	15.0	13.4	64,087	52.1	20.4
Sacramento-Roseville-Folsom, CA Metro Area	373,673	259,615	114,058	9.5	16,282.2	-15.2	22.9	17.8	1,538,537	32.2	33.0
Saginaw, MI Metro Area	26,999	18,080	8,919	-19.2	1,509.0	-25.5	17.9	16.5	132,027	44.1	21.1
St. Cloud, MN Metro Area	31,122	21,179	9,943	11.4	1,537.0	-6.2	20.2	17.0	123,350	36.5	26.7
St. George, UT Metro Area	35,030	24,748	10,282	30.3	-	-	-	22.8	102,484	30.7	27.7
St. Joseph, MO-KS Metro Area	18,203	13,140	5,063	-1.7	1,412.0	-1.1	12.9	13.0	87,015	49.3	20.5
St. Louis, MO-IL Metro Area	403,204	282,705	120,499	-4.8	27,323.8	2.4	14.8	15.9	1,933,216	34.6	33.7
Salem, OR Metro Area	71,350	48,930	22,420	8.9	3,410.1	0.6	20.9	19.3	272,112	40.7	24.2
Salinas, CA Metro Area	79,663	57,483	22,180	13.6	3,516.6	-9.4	22.7	18.1	274,528	49.2	24.5
Salisbury, MD-DE Metro Area	53,630	38,187	15,443	9.1	3,964.0	10.6	13.5	13.7	283,818	45.2	26.4
Salt Lake City, UT Metro Area	236,779	166,981	69,798	11.4	-	-	-	24.2	739,492	32.7	33.9
San Angelo, TX Metro Area	20,309	14,678	5,631	10.3	-	-	-	-	76,915	44.9	24.0
San Antonio-New Braunfels, TX Metro Area	456,060	326,112	129,948	18.1	26,911.6	5.1	16.9	15.1	1,561,045	41.5	27.7
San Diego-Chula Vista-Carlsbad, CA Metro Area	502,778	344,665	158,113	4.9	21,167.4	-20.3	23.8	18.0	2,223,376	31.3	38.1
San Francisco-Oakland-Berkeley, CA Metro Area	592,806	407,322	185,484	12.5	26,344.6	-15.5	22.5	16.9	3,361,914	26.8	48.7
Oakland-Berkeley-Livermore, CA Div	404,617	279,174	125,443	12.2	17,577.0	-15.8	23.0	17.3	1,933,923	29.1	44.3
San Francisco-San Mateo-Redwood City, CA Div	154,630	104,971	49,659	11.5	7,143.8	-15.6	21.6	16.4	1,237,450	24.7	54.0
San Rafael, CA Div	33,559	23,177	10,382	21.8	1,623.8	-11.1	20.7	15.1	190,541	17.7	58.8
San Jose-Sunnyvale-Santa Clara, CA Metro Area	281,367	193,870	87,497	8.3	12,325.6	-14.1	22.8	18.1	1,361,877	26.9	50.4
San Luis Obispo-Paso Robles, CA Metro Area	34,663	23,566	11,097	2.0	1,575.7	-19.2	22.0	17.4	187,561	28.9	34.6
Santa Cruz-Watsonville, CA Metro Area	39,267	26,906	12,361	9.5	1,680.0	-15.3	23.4	18.1	178,865	29.4	40.0
Santa Fe, NM Metro Area	20,037	13,833	6,204	26.1	1,245.3	20.4	16.1	15.4	109,763	34.0	40.9
Santa Maria-Santa Barbara, CA Metro Area	69,625	48,929	20,696	8.2	3,070.7	-12.6	22.7	18.3	273,815	36.9	33.8
Santa Rosa-Petaluma, CA Metro Area	68,776	47,730	21,046	1.6	3,247.4	-18.9	21.2	16.9	357,968	30.7	34.9
Savannah, GA Metro Area	59,126	43,693	15,433	14.1	4,000.3	5.9	14.8	13.7	252,726	36.9	31.2
Scranton--Wilkes-Barre, PA Metro Area	73,900	51,904	21,996	-4.1	4,970.1	-15.6	14.9	13.1	395,765	48.4	24.7
Seattle-Tacoma-Bellevue, WA Metro Area	542,318	378,771	163,547	9.2	28,534.5	17.3	19.0	20.4	2,656,065	27.2	42.0
Seattle-Bellevue-Kent, WA Div	405,631	282,618	123,013	11.2	21,320.3	17.6	19.0	20.1	2,080,077	24.7	46.3
Tacoma-Lakewood, WA Div	136,687	96,153	40,534	3.6	7,214.2	16.4	18.9	21.3	575,988	36.2	26.4
Sebastian-Vero Beach, FL Metro Area	17,792	12,250	5,542	6.0	1,154.0	20.1	15.4	17.5	115,641	41.0	28.3
Sebring-Avon Park, FL Metro Area	12,414	8,828	3,586	-1.6	-	-	-	14.9	78,047	53.3	17.0
Sheboygan, WI Metro Area	18,833	12,966	5,867	-4.2	1,299.9	-4.8	14.5	14.4	80,103	43.6	23.9
Sherman-Denison, TX Metro Area	23,276	16,627	6,649	10.1	1,707.3	4.7	13.6	13.0	86,890	42.3	20.5
Shreveport-Bossier City, LA Metro Area	67,933	48,371	19,562	0.9	3,628.3	-18.4	18.7	15.1	268,096	45.7	23.5
Sierra Vista-Douglas, AZ Metro Area	19,262	13,400	5,862	-10.1	-	-	-	-	87,467	36.3	23.0
Sioux City, IA-NE-SD Metro Area	26,364	18,704	7,660	3.1	1,775.8	-5.3	14.8	13.6	92,117	46.7	22.3

Table B-6. Enrollment, Teachers, and Educational Attainment—*Continued*

Metropolitan Statistical Area Metropolitan Division	Public school enrollment				Number of public school teachers		Pupil/teacher ratio		Educational attainment, 2014-2018		
	2017-2018			Percent change in total since 2007-2008		Percent change since 2007-2008				High school graduate or less (percent)	Bachelor's degree or more (percent)
	Total	Pre-Kindergarten through Grade 8	Grades 9 through 12		2017-2018	2007-2008	2017-2018	2007-2008	Population 25 years and over		
Sioux Falls, SD Metro Area	44,014	32,234	11,780	28.8	2,887.9	26.0	15.2	14.9	167,016	33.7	33.0
South Bend-Mishawaka, IN-MI Metro Area	45,740	32,074	13,666	-7.2	2,554.7	-3.7	17.9	18.6	211,912	42.8	27.5
Spartanburg, SC Metro Area	50,393	35,841	14,552	9.7	3,542.5	12.8	14.2	14.6	203,339	44.1	23.8
Spokane-Spokane Valley, WA Metro Area	82,824	57,266	25,558	4.4	4,871.6	16.1	17.0	18.9	369,529	31.1	29.4
Springfield, IL Metro Area	31,709	22,456	9,253	-4.1	2,115.8	13.4	15.0	17.7	145,424	35.9	33.5
Springfield, MA Metro Area	99,971	69,677	30,294	-6.5	8,035.9	-6.7	12.4	12.4	468,899	40.0	32.4
Springfield, MO Metro Area	67,722	48,085	19,637	3.8	4,702.2	4.3	14.4	14.5	300,622	39.9	27.4
Springfield, OH Metro Area	20,716	14,601	6,115	-12.5	1,207.5	-7.5	17.2	18.1	92,344	49.3	18.6
State College, PA Metro Area	14,348	9,640	4,708	-7.5	1,129.8	-7.1	12.7	12.7	97,616	35.6	44.7
Staunton, VA Metro Area	16,235	11,375	4,860	-5.6	941.1	-11.8	17.3	16.1	87,111	47.9	25.9
Stockton, CA Metro Area	147,134	101,678	45,456	9.5	6,141.5	-17.1	24.0	18.1	458,237	49.3	18.4
Sumter, SC Metro Area	21,899	15,555	6,344	-5.6	1,342.0	-6.8	16.3	16.1	93,925	49.9	17.7
Syracuse, NY Metro Area	98,187	67,307	30,880	-9.9	7,510.8	-12.2	13.1	12.8	443,713	38.2	31.5
Tallahassee, FL Metro Area	47,813	34,288	13,525	1.1	2,594.0	-19.4	18.4	14.7	236,052	33.2	38.0
Tampa-St. Petersburg-Clearwater, FL Metro Area	414,624	291,714	122,910	6.3	27,169.0	3.9	15.3	14.9	2,174,962	39.8	29.6
Terre Haute, IN Metro Area	26,574	18,570	8,004	-9.9	1,627.9	-11.0	16.3	16.1	125,162	48.8	19.6
Texarkana, TX-AR Metro Area	26,609	19,297	7,312	2.0	2,030.6	-3.6	13.1	12.4	102,031	48.2	18.2
The Villages, FL Metro Area	8,648	6,317	2,331	15.0	-	-	-	15.6	108,330	38.7	31.1
Toledo, OH Metro Area	102,287	71,508	30,779	-5.2	5,579.6	-10.2	18.3	17.4	430,979	40.7	26.7
Topeka, KS Metro Area	37,761	26,392	11,369	-0.4	2,874.2	0.1	13.1	13.2	158,318	40.8	28.5
Trenton-Princeton, NJ Metro Area	52,521	36,059	16,462	0.8	4,605.9	32.4	11.4	15.0	247,693	36.5	42.0
Tucson, AZ Metro Area	142,863	99,636	43,227	-5.0	-	-	-	-	678,427	34.1	31.9
Tulsa, OK Metro Area	166,606	121,162	45,444	4.8	9,555.8	-2.3	17.4	16.2	652,789	40.1	27.2
Tuscaloosa, AL Metro Area	35,404	25,284	10,120	-0.2	2,001.8	-11.0	17.7	15.8	158,023	44.6	27.0
Twin Falls, ID Metro Area	20,918	15,114	5,804	24.6	1,122.7	17.5	18.6	17.6	67,338	43.2	19.4
Tyler, TX Metro Area	36,098	26,040	10,058	8.0	2,461.1	6.1	14.7	14.4	146,551	39.0	25.8
Urban Honolulu, HI Metro Area	121,109	87,385	33,724	-1.2	7,750.6	0.7	15.6	15.9	680,707	34.5	34.3
Utica-Rome, NY Metro Area	43,728	30,654	13,074	-5.0	3,357.3	-12.0	13.0	12.1	203,123	44.9	23.9
Valdosta, GA Metro Area	24,244	18,033	6,211	10.7	1,555.6	-0.2	15.6	14.0	88,012	47.8	23.0
Vallejo, CA Metro Area	64,253	44,301	19,952	-2.9	2,695.3	-29.4	23.8	17.3	299,653	35.3	26.2
Victoria, TX Metro Area	16,846	12,270	4,576	3.4	1,173.5	2.4	14.4	14.2	65,083	46.8	19.9
Vineland-Bridgeton, NJ Metro Area	26,240	19,348	6,892	4.8	2,297.2	18.0	11.4	12.9	103,911	60.6	14.7
Virginia Beach-Norfolk-Newport News, VA-NC Metro Area	267,569	187,812	79,757	-5.0	17,278.7	7.6	15.5	17.5	1,174,594	34.1	31.2
Visalia, CA Metro Area	103,835	73,596	30,239	11.1	4,430.7	-11.2	23.4	18.7	269,073	56.2	14.3
Waco, TX Metro Area	48,079	34,014	14,065	7.8	3,393.7	5.5	14.2	13.9	162,069	44.6	22.9
Walla Walla, WA Metro Area	8,763	5,896	2,867	-0.9	519.2	3.2	16.9	17.6	39,420	32.8	28.6
Warner Robins, GA Metro Area	33,136	23,742	9,394	9.9	2,100.8	-2.6	15.8	14.0	116,336	37.6	26.1
Washington-Arlington-Alexandria, DC-VA-MD-WV Metro Area	976,559	688,409	288,150	15.1	65,444.6	21.0	14.9	15.7	4,185,303	27.5	50.5
Frederick-Gaithersburg-Rockville, MD Div.	203,686	142,052	61,634	14.3	13,344.4	9.6	15.3	14.6	882,930	23.9	55.5
Washington-Arlington-Alexandria, DC-VA-MD-WV Div.	772,873	546,357	226,516	15.3	52,100.2	24.3	14.8	16.0	3,302,373	28.4	49.2
Waterloo-Cedar Falls, IA Metro Area	25,283	17,676	7,607	6.6	1,791.4	8.8	14.1	14.4	108,635	38.3	28.8
Watertown-Fort Drum, NY Metro Area	17,540	12,739	4,801	-4.9	1,323.5	-11.8	13.3	12.3	72,369	42.9	22.3
Wausau-Weston, WI Metro Area	23,997	16,852	7,145	-3.4	1,691.9	-0.3	14.2	14.6	113,775	43.6	24.3
Weirton-Steubenville, WV-OH Metro Area	15,785	11,381	4,404	-13.0	1,005.3	-17.4	15.7	14.9	85,899	52.2	16.9
Wenatchee, WA Metro Area	20,798	14,299	6,499	4.7	1,207.1	12.7	17.2	18.6	78,452	45.0	24.1
Wheeling, WV-OH Metro Area	18,964	13,595	5,369	-2.7	1,306.8	-0.4	14.5	14.8	103,629	49.2	20.9
Wichita, KS Metro Area	111,365	80,347	31,018	8.2	6,926.9	9.0	16.1	16.2	412,234	36.7	30.4
Wichita Falls, TX Metro Area	24,302	17,696	6,606	-4.3	1,838.7	-4.3	13.2	13.2	97,878	45.3	22.7
Williamsport, PA Metro Area	15,529	10,796	4,733	-8.1	1,061.0	-14.0	14.6	13.7	80,595	49.3	22.8
Wilmington, NC Metro Area	37,389	25,944	11,445	16.0	2,404.5	11.1	15.5	14.9	194,265	31.4	36.5
Winchester, VA-WV Metro Area	20,695	14,109	6,586	-1.7	1,267.1	-9.5	16.3	15.0	94,032	47.2	26.3
Winston-Salem, NC Metro Area	100,609	69,738	30,871	0.3	6,750.4	-2.7	14.9	14.5	453,838	43.1	26.4
Worcester, MA-CT Metro Area	142,435	98,502	43,933	-5.1	10,420.7	-0.4	13.7	14.4	645,393	38.6	34.5
Yakima, WA Metro Area	54,428	38,511	15,917	9.6	2,935.9	13.6	18.5	19.2	150,447	55.1	16.0
York-Hanover, PA Metro Area	64,142	44,308	19,834	0.8	4,250.2	-13.3	15.1	13.0	308,348	50.8	24.2
Youngstown-Warren-Boardman, OH-PA Metro Area	71,818	49,079	22,739	-17.3	4,536.8	-13.0	15.8	16.7	387,292	51.7	21.7
Yuba City, CA Metro Area	37,135	26,576	10,559	17.5	1,756.1	-5.0	21.1	17.1	109,422	43.8	17.3
Yuma, AZ Metro Area	37,712	25,760	11,952	-1.8	-	-	-	21.3	130,819	53.8	14.8

Table B-7. Median Income, Household Income Distribution, and Poverty Status, 2014–2018

Metropolitan Statistical Area Metropolitan Division	Total number of households, 2014-2018	Percent of households by income level, 2014-2018						Percent of households with earnings, 2014-2018	Percent of households receiving SNAP (food stamps), 2014-2018	Percent of group whose income in the past 12 months was below the poverty level, 2014-2018		
		Under $25,000	$25,000-$49,999	$50,000-$74,999	$75,000-$99,999	$100,000-$199,999	$200,000 and over			Individuals	Children under 18 years old	Families
Abilene, TX Metro Area	60,394	22.6	27.4	18.6	11.1	16.7	3.5	78.0	13.3	15.3	18.8	10.9
Akron, OH Metro Area	286,378	21.9	23.4	18.1	12.9	19.1	4.6	76.0	13.4	13.1	18.3	9.2
Albany, GA Metro Area	56,419	30.6	26.4	16.6	10.5	13.7	2.3	74.8	23.7	25.3	39.2	20.2
Albany-Lebanon, OR Metro Area	47,030	21.4	26.4	20.5	13.5	15.8	2.4	73.3	20.2	14.4	18.4	10.5
Albany-Schenectady-Troy, NY Metro Area	350,301	16.9	19.9	17.3	13.8	25.5	6.6	77.6	10.7	10.4	14.3	6.4
Albuquerque, NM Metro Area	349,150	24.3	24.0	17.8	12.0	17.5	4.3	74.8	15.1	17.2	23.8	12.9
Alexandria, LA Metro Area	54,989	29.3	25.9	16.1	11.1	14.9	2.8	71.4	17.4	19.5	25.0	15.3
Allentown-Bethlehem-Easton, PA-NJ Metro Area	319,220	17.1	21.4	18.5	13.7	23.1	6.3	76.8	11.3	10.7	16.5	7.7
Altoona, PA Metro Area	51,625	25.1	27.0	18.6	13.5	13.5	2.4	70.4	16.4	14.6	19.6	10.6
Amarillo, TX Metro Area	96,613	20.4	24.8	19.5	12.5	18.5	4.2	81.2	10.7	13.8	18.2	10.4
Ames, IA Metro Area	48,159	23.5	21.7	17.7	13.0	19.6	4.5	83.6	7.1	18.4	8.8	4.6
Anchorage, AK Metro Area	137,403	12.1	16.3	17.6	13.9	30.6	9.4	86.3	9.1	9.5	13.4	6.4
Ann Arbor, MI Metro Area	140,210	18.1	18.7	16.5	11.8	25.0	9.9	81.9	7.8	14.2	12.2	6.4
Anniston-Oxford, AL Metro Area	45,033	28.5	25.2	18.9	11.2	13.8	2.4	71.4	17.9	18.6	26.2	14.6
Appleton, WI Metro Area	92,514	15.1	22.4	19.3	15.6	23.8	3.9	80.7	7.2	8.0	11.1	5.9
Asheville, NC Metro Area	190,162	22.4	26.8	19.1	11.8	15.9	4.0	71.5	9.8	12.4	17.4	7.9
Athens-Clarke County, GA Metro Area	76,650	29.6	24.2	15.1	10.0	16.7	4.5	78.8	12.5	23.2	26.1	13.7
Atlanta-Sandy Springs-Alpharetta, GA Metro Area	2,065,239	17.3	21.4	18.0	13.0	22.3	8.0	83.3	11.4	13.1	18.8	9.8
Atlantic City-Hammonton, NJ Metro Area	99,874	20.8	21.8	16.8	12.1	22.3	6.2	76.7	14.0	14.3	22.6	10.9
Auburn-Opelika, AL Metro Area	59,373	29.8	21.8	15.7	11.2	17.4	4.1	77.6	11.7	21.4	22.3	12.8
Augusta-Richmond County, GA-SC Metro Area	214,489	24.9	24.2	17.7	12.5	17.4	3.4	74.7	15.2	17.4	26.3	13.5
Austin-Round Rock-Georgetown, TX Metro Area	742,689	14.3	19.1	17.8	13.2	25.8	9.8	86.3	7.3	11.6	14.5	7.6
Bakersfield, CA Metro Area	267,913	23.6	24.4	17.8	11.4	18.7	4.1	78.6	17.0	22.0	30.4	18.0
Baltimore-Columbia-Towson, MD Metro Area	1,043,798	15.2	16.9	15.9	12.9	28.4	10.7	80.1	11.7	10.4	13.6	6.9
Bangor, ME Metro Area	61,578	26.2	24.3	18.3	12.9	15.3	3.0	72.8	17.4	15.7	19.4	9.8
Barnstable Town, MA Metro Area	94,292	15.3	20.1	17.7	13.6	25.5	7.8	70.5	7.1	7.0	9.5	4.4
Baton Rouge, LA Metro Area	310,265	23.0	22.0	16.5	11.6	21.3	5.6	78.2	14.4	16.2	21.9	11.5
Battle Creek, MI Metro Area	53,659	25.0	27.2	19.7	11.0	14.4	2.6	71.8	15.0	16.9	25.8	13.0
Bay City, MI Metro Area	43,891	24.1	27.8	19.4	12.2	14.4	2.1	68.4	15.4	16.0	25.2	12.0
Beaumont-Port Arthur, TX Metro Area	146,376	25.0	23.7	17.1	11.2	19.1	3.9	74.8	15.3	16.5	24.0	12.8
Beckley, WV Metro Area	48,914	30.4	27.3	18.1	10.2	12.3	1.7	65.3	20.2	18.5	26.5	14.2
Bellingham, WA Metro Area	85,008	20.0	21.9	19.7	13.9	20.1	4.3	75.9	13.0	15.0	14.0	7.7
Bend, OR Metro Area	72,471	16.1	23.3	19.4	14.8	20.7	5.7	75.0	13.6	10.8	13.7	7.3
Billings, MT Metro Area	73,272	19.2	23.2	20.3	12.9	19.4	5.1	78.5	7.8	9.7	11.3	6.6
Binghamton, NY Metro Area	98,639	24.1	23.6	18.3	12.7	18.1	3.1	71.1	15.4	15.6	20.9	9.9
Birmingham-Hoover, AL Metro Area	415,615	23.1	22.4	17.7	12.3	19.2	5.3	75.7	12.5	14.9	20.7	11.2
Bismarck, ND Metro Area	53,781	15.3	20.4	17.8	14.7	26.2	5.6	82.3	5.3	8.3	8.3	4.8
Blacksburg-Christiansburg, VA Metro Area	62,433	25.9	21.6	19.8	12.2	16.3	4.2	75.4	8.4	21.6	16.2	8.8
Bloomington, IL Metro Area	66,159	19.8	18.9	17.0	13.3	24.9	6.2	80.4	9.8	14.6	11.9	7.6
Bloomington, IN Metro Area	64,232	27.7	24.7	17.3	10.5	16.1	3.6	80.5	8.8	23.2	21.3	11.4
Bloomsburg-Berwick, PA Metro Area	34,064	24.3	24.8	19.5	11.7	16.2	3.4	72.3	10.8	13.6	17.0	7.6
Boise City, ID Metro Area	253,531	20.0	23.6	20.0	12.8	19.0	4.7	78.5	10.1	12.6	14.9	8.2
Boston-Cambridge-Newton, MA-NH Metro Area	1,819,113	15.8	14.9	14.1	11.8	29.1	14.4	81.0	10.3	9.8	12.1	6.6
Boston, MA Div	757,727	17.9	15.0	13.9	11.4	28.2	13.7	80.4	12.3	11.8	14.7	8.0
Cambridge-Newton-Framingham, MA Div	892,691	14.7	14.5	13.7	11.7	29.5	15.9	81.3	9.5	8.8	10.7	6.1
Rockingham County-Strafford County, NH Div	168,695	11.8	16.2	17.0	13.7	30.9	10.4	82.0	5.1	6.2	7.7	3.7
Boulder, CO Metro Area	125,894	15.3	17.7	15.1	12.2	26.9	12.8	83.3	5.3	12.5	10.1	5.5
Bowling Green, KY Metro Area	64,721	25.1	25.7	19.0	12.3	14.6	3.3	76.4	13.2	17.9	23.2	12.8
Bremerton-Silverdale-Port Orchard, WA Metro Area	101,662	15.0	18.9	18.5	15.6	25.2	6.9	75.1	11.2	9.7	11.8	6.6
Bridgeport-Stamford-Norwalk, CT Metro Area	340,491	13.8	15.3	13.1	10.8	26.2	20.8	81.8	8.9	8.8	11.0	6.3
Brownsville-Harlingen, TX Metro Area	123,185	35.6	25.4	16.2	9.3	11.6	1.9	75.6	24.8	30.6	43.5	27.0
Brunswick, GA Metro Area	46,374	26.6	25.4	15.8	11.3	16.5	4.5	71.4	17.6	19.4	31.0	15.5
Buffalo-Cheektowaga, NY Metro Area	476,058	23.0	22.5	17.5	12.6	20.3	4.1	73.1	15.3	14.3	21.2	10.1
Burlington, NC Metro Area	64,059	25.5	28.4	16.5	10.9	16.2	2.4	76.0	15.4	16.8	25.3	12.7
Burlington-South Burlington, VT Metro Area	86,949	16.6	19.2	18.2	14.6	24.8	6.7	81.5	10.1	10.7	11.3	5.9
California-Lexington Park, MD Metro Area	40,332	11.5	14.9	14.4	13.8	35.6	9.8	82.7	9.7	8.3	11.5	6.0
Canton-Massillon, OH Metro Area	163,775	22.1	25.7	19.4	12.4	17.5	2.9	74.6	13.4	13.8	21.6	10.0
Cape Coral-Fort Myers, FL Metro Area	271,861	20.1	25.1	19.9	12.3	17.3	5.2	63.7	10.2	14.0	23.4	9.6
Cape Girardeau, MO-IL Metro Area	36,358	25.2	25.3	19.2	12.7	14.7	2.9	74.9	11.7	17.9	22.5	10.3
Carbondale-Marion, IL Metro Area	55,159	30.3	24.6	16.9	11.0	14.5	2.7	70.9	16.4	20.0	24.1	11.8
Carson City, NV Metro Area	22,461	21.0	26.9	19.3	12.4	16.7	3.8	72.4	12.4	13.7	21.1	9.8
Casper, WY Metro Area	32,851	17.0	24.3	19.4	13.8	21.5	4.0	81.3	6.7	9.6	11.2	5.8
Cedar Rapids, IA Metro Area	108,235	16.5	22.1	19.3	14.4	22.9	4.9	80.7	9.7	9.5	12.2	6.7
Chambersburg-Waynesboro, PA Metro Area	60,210	16.5	24.9	21.0	15.0	19.4	3.2	75.8	10.4	10.3	16.1	7.5
Champaign-Urbana, IL Metro Area	89,199	26.3	21.6	16.7	11.6	18.6	5.1	79.2	9.4	19.7	17.2	8.9
Charleston, WV Metro Area	110,903	28.8	26.5	17.9	10.3	13.3	3.2	66.9	17.4	18.5	27.3	14.1
Charleston-North Charleston, SC Metro Area	285,962	19.3	21.4	18.8	13.3	20.7	6.5	79.3	9.8	13.5	20.1	9.2
Charlotte-Concord-Gastonia, NC-SC Metro Area	934,829	18.6	22.8	18.2	12.8	20.6	7.0	81.2	10.6	12.8	18.2	9.5
Charlottesville, VA Metro Area	82,869	16.8	19.5	16.9	13.7	24.0	9.2	79.1	6.2	12.3	12.2	6.7
Chattanooga, TN-GA Metro Area	214,328	23.8	25.0	18.5	11.6	16.7	4.4	74.3	13.0	14.0	19.8	9.9
Cheyenne, WY Metro Area	39,179	17.3	20.9	19.5	14.7	23.9	3.8	79.0	7.0	10.0	12.2	7.2
Chicago-Naperville-Elgin, IL-IN-WI Metro Area	3,495,713	18.0	19.2	16.5	12.7	24.4	9.2	80.4	12.5	12.5	17.6	9.2
Chicago-Naperville-Evanston, IL Div	2,663,951	18.7	19.2	16.2	12.5	24.2	9.3	80.3	13.1	12.9	18.1	9.5
Elgin, IL Div	256,160	13.3	18.2	17.4	13.9	28.4	8.8	83.6	10.7	10.1	13.6	6.9

Table B-7. Median Income, Household Income Distribution, and Poverty Status, 2014–2018—*Continued*

Metropolitan Statistical Area / Metropolitan Division	Total number of households, 2,014-2,018	Percent of households by income level, 2014-2018						Percent of households with earnings, 2014-2018	Percent of households receiving SNAP (food stamps), 2014-2018	Percent of group whose income in the past 12 months was below the poverty level, 2014-2018		
		Under $25,000	$25,000-$49,999	$50,000-$74,999	$75,000-$99,999	$100,000-$199,999	$200,000 and over			Individuals	Children under 18 years old	Families
Gary, IN Div....................	267,507	20.7	23.2	18.4	13.9	20.3	3.7	76.1	12.1	14.6	23.0	11.3
Lake County-Kenosha County, IL-WI Div.............	308,095	14.0	17.3	16.2	12.5	26.5	13.6	82.2	9.8	9.3	12.7	6.9
Chico, CA Metro Area....................	86,797	27.3	24.1	16.5	10.8	16.9	4.4	70.1	11.9	20.1	20.8	11.5
Cincinnati, OH-KY-IN Metro Area....................	854,217	19.8	21.2	17.8	13.0	21.9	6.3	78.9	10.7	12.7	17.6	8.8
Clarksville, TN-KY Metro Area....................	107,201	21.8	27.0	20.8	12.8	15.1	2.5	79.4	13.5	15.1	19.3	12.0
Cleveland, TN Metro Area....................	46,936	24.2	28.6	18.1	11.9	14.5	2.7	75.3	14.9	16.5	23.9	12.2
Cleveland-Elyria, OH Metro Area....................	857,453	23.3	23.2	17.4	12.2	18.7	5.3	74.8	14.6	14.8	21.7	10.8
Coeur d'Alene, ID Metro Area....................	60,497	18.5	26.7	21.2	12.0	17.9	3.7	74.0	10.5	12.1	17.3	9.3
College Station-Bryan, TX Metro Area....................	92,165	27.9	23.5	15.7	11.6	16.6	4.7	83.2	8.6	23.2	20.5	12.3
Colorado Springs, CO Metro Area....................	263,562	16.2	21.0	19.5	13.8	23.7	5.9	81.8	9.6	10.8	14.4	7.7
Columbia, MO Metro Area....................	79,944	22.8	24.5	17.4	12.8	18.5	4.0	82.0	9.2	17.6	16.1	9.0
Columbia, SC Metro Area....................	308,718	21.7	24.1	19.3	13.1	17.6	4.2	78.4	12.9	15.2	20.5	10.9
Columbus, GA-AL Metro Area....................	118,295	28.5	24.6	18.0	11.5	14.1	3.2	74.0	17.6	19.5	28.0	14.7
Columbus, IN Metro Area....................	31,669	18.5	23.0	19.8	13.9	20.6	4.2	78.0	9.7	13.0	19.9	9.2
Columbus, OH Metro Area....................	784,786	18.4	21.8	18.1	13.4	22.2	6.2	81.2	12.0	13.7	19.2	9.6
Corpus Christi, TX Metro Area....................	152,047	22.5	23.0	18.3	12.6	19.2	4.3	79.9	16.6	16.4	23.5	12.7
Corvallis, OR Metro Area....................	35,056	24.2	19.9	15.3	13.1	21.1	6.4	76.0	11.6	19.4	12.9	7.5
Crestview-Fort Walton Beach-Destin, FL Metro Area	103,835	18.4	23.2	19.1	13.2	21.0	5.1	76.5	9.8	12.3	18.7	8.7
Cumberland, MD-WV Metro Area....................	39,021	27.2	27.7	19.9	11.2	12.3	1.7	67.5	16.8	15.9	21.3	11.2
Dallas-Fort Worth-Arlington, TX Metro Area	2,510,847	16.0	21.0	18.0	12.8	23.7	8.4	85.7	9.7	12.6	18.1	9.5
*Dallas-Plano-Irving, TX Div....................	1,689,084	15.9	20.8	17.6	12.5	24.1	9.1	86.4	9.2	12.6	18.2	9.5
Fort Worth-Arlington-Grapevine, TX Div*	821,763	16.1	21.5	18.9	13.4	23.0	7.1	84.1	10.6	12.5	18.0	9.3
Dalton, GA Metro Area....................	50,124	24.5	28.6	20.7	11.5	11.7	2.9	76.9	12.8	17.1	25.6	12.9
Danville, IL Metro Area....................	31,180	26.9	26.7	19.4	11.6	13.6	1.8	68.9	16.8	19.6	30.0	15.0
Daphne-Fairhope-Foley, AL Metro Area....................	78,622	19.7	24.4	19.3	12.3	19.1	5.1	71.8	7.5	10.6	13.4	7.3
Davenport-Moline-Rock Island, IA-IL Metro Area	153,966	20.5	23.9	19.5	13.4	19.1	3.6	75.1	11.8	13.1	19.3	9.6
Dayton-Kettering, OH Metro Area....................	330,381	23.1	23.9	18.3	12.2	18.6	4.0	74.9	13.1	15.3	22.6	11.5
Decatur, AL Metro Area....................	58,457	25.3	26.0	18.9	11.7	15.5	2.4	70.6	13.9	15.6	22.7	12.7
Decatur, IL Metro Area....................	44,113	25.3	24.3	18.0	12.8	16.1	3.5	71.9	17.5	16.2	25.7	11.8
Deltona-Daytona Beach-Ormond Beach, FL Metro Area.	253,614	23.8	28.0	19.1	11.8	14.3	3.0	64.7	13.0	14.6	21.2	9.3
Denver-Aurora-Lakewood, CO Metro Area.............	1,094,028	13.5	18.7	17.5	13.7	27.1	9.6	84.3	6.7	9.4	12.4	6.3
Des Moines-West Des Moines, IA Metro Area	260,852	15.5	20.5	18.9	14.6	24.0	6.4	83.2	11.5	10.0	13.0	6.5
Detroit-Warren-Dearborn, MI Metro Area...........	1,690,744	21.3	22.1	17.1	12.3	21.1	6.1	74.9	15.3	15.1	22.3	11.1
*Detroit-Dearborn-Livonia, MI Div....................	676,587	29.3	24.5	16.5	10.5	15.3	3.8	70.9	23.9	23.1	34.6	17.8
Warren-Troy-Farmington Hills, MI Div*	1,014,157	16.0	20.6	17.5	13.4	24.9	7.6	77.6	9.6	9.7	13.0	6.9
Dothan, AL Metro Area....................	56,401	29.1	25.9	17.8	10.7	13.7	2.8	70.2	15.8	18.8	28.8	14.3
Dover, DE Metro Area....................	64,545	18.9	24.0	19.4	14.6	19.6	3.6	76.3	16.2	13.6	20.5	10.4
Dubuque, IA Metro Area....................	38,330	18.9	21.7	20.0	16.0	19.3	4.1	79.2	9.7	11.7	14.8	7.2
Duluth, MN-WI Metro Area....................	123,165	21.8	24.7	19.1	13.2	18.0	3.2	72.3	10.5	14.1	15.9	7.8
Durham-Chapel Hill, NC Metro Area....................	241,274	20.0	22.3	17.2	12.3	20.3	7.9	80.7	10.8	14.8	20.6	10.0
East Stroudsburg, PA Metro Area....................	56,770	17.6	22.1	18.5	15.1	21.8	5.0	75.8	12.4	11.5	15.8	8.4
Eau Claire, WI Metro Area....................	66,238	20.6	24.3	19.2	14.1	18.7	3.1	78.4	10.7	13.1	13.7	6.9
El Centro, CA Metro Area....................	44,057	30.9	22.6	16.1	11.6	15.9	3.0	75.7	21.5	24.2	32.1	21.0
Elizabethtown-Fort Knox, KY Metro Area....................	57,403	21.3	25.8	19.6	12.8	18.0	2.5	76.5	13.0	13.6	19.3	10.4
Elkhart-Goshen, IN Metro Area....................	72,329	19.3	24.9	22.4	14.4	16.1	3.0	81.4	9.7	13.3	19.2	10.0
Elmira, NY Metro Area....................	34,373	23.1	24.0	19.3	12.8	17.6	3.2	71.6	15.1	14.8	20.8	10.8
El Paso, TX Metro Area....................	266,624	27.9	27.1	18.3	10.4	13.8	2.5	80.5	21.2	21.3	30.1	18.2
Enid, OK Metro Area....................	23,824	23.5	25.3	20.6	11.5	16.3	2.9	79.0	12.3	14.7	19.6	11.1
Erie, PA Metro Area....................	110,050	24.3	26.0	18.6	11.6	16.2	3.3	73.2	18.0	16.3	23.9	11.0
Eugene-Springfield, OR Metro Area....................	150,780	24.3	25.7	18.9	12.3	15.4	3.5	73.1	20.1	18.5	20.8	10.3
Evansville, IN-KY Metro Area....................	128,119	23.1	25.1	18.0	12.9	17.3	3.6	76.3	11.1	15.0	20.9	10.5
Fairbanks, AK Metro Area....................	36,513	10.9	19.8	17.9	15.9	28.5	7.1	88.4	6.9	8.1	10.4	5.0
Fargo, ND-MN Metro Area....................	97,987	18.3	21.5	18.4	15.1	20.6	6.0	85.3	7.3	10.9	11.0	5.9
Farmington, NM Metro Area....................	43,134	25.6	23.8	17.4	14.0	16.7	2.4	77.2	17.8	21.3	28.0	16.7
Fayetteville, NC Metro Area....................	187,226	25.2	27.5	19.0	12.2	14.1	2.1	77.9	16.5	18.2	25.6	14.5
Fayetteville-Springdale-Rogers, AR Metro Area	186,419	20.0	24.5	19.0	11.8	18.7	6.0	81.1	6.7	13.2	16.1	9.3
Flagstaff, AZ Metro Area....................	47,276	22.9	21.3	18.3	13.7	18.8	5.0	81.7	11.6	18.9	20.0	10.9
Flint, MI Metro Area....................	167,889	26.6	26.3	18.4	11.0	14.8	2.9	69.0	20.6	19.8	30.2	15.1
Florence, SC Metro Area....................	78,643	30.3	26.0	17.4	10.2	13.6	2.5	72.3	19.8	20.1	29.0	15.6
Florence-Muscle Shoals, AL Metro Area....................	60,313	27.3	25.7	19.3	11.6	13.6	2.6	68.2	12.5	15.6	21.0	11.3
Fond du Lac, WI Metro Area....................	41,346	17.6	23.9	21.2	14.6	20.0	2.7	77.7	9.6	9.0	12.3	6.1
Fort Collins, CO Metro Area....................	133,527	16.6	20.7	17.4	14.1	24.6	6.7	80.6	6.4	12.0	10.1	5.7
Fort Smith, AR-OK Metro Area....................	96,547	28.5	28.3	17.7	10.8	12.7	2.0	71.8	15.0	19.8	28.9	14.7
Fort Wayne, IN Metro Area....................	157,048	20.5	25.5	20.4	13.7	16.3	3.5	78.9	11.3	13.9	21.3	10.2
Fresno, CA Metro Area....................	304,624	25.2	23.7	17.4	11.6	17.6	4.4	79.3	20.1	24.1	34.3	19.7
Gadsden, AL Metro Area....................	38,777	29.1	25.9	17.6	12.3	12.9	2.3	67.7	14.1	17.3	30.0	13.4
Gainesville, FL Metro Area	119,992	29.4	23.3	17.6	10.7	14.5	4.5	74.6	12.0	21.4	22.7	11.7
Gainesville, GA Metro Area....................	63,931	17.3	24.7	19.2	13.9	19.8	5.2	80.0	10.5	14.6	22.6	10.8
Gettysburg, PA Metro Area....................	39,221	14.7	23.4	20.0	15.6	22.2	4.1	75.5	7.6	8.8	13.5	5.8
Glens Falls, NY Metro Area....................	51,562	19.7	24.0	19.4	13.9	19.6	3.4	73.7	13.5	11.2	15.4	7.5
Goldsboro, NC Metro Area....................	48,153	28.3	28.9	17.4	10.3	12.7	2.4	73.4	18.9	21.4	35.4	17.0
Grand Forks, ND-MN Metro Area....................	42,731	24.7	22.3	16.8	13.0	19.7	3.6	80.6	8.9	15.8	17.0	8.3

Table B-7. Median Income, Household Income Distribution, and Poverty Status, 2014–2018—*Continued*

Metropolitan Statistical Area Metropolitan Division	Total number of households, 2,014-2,018	Percent of households by income level, 2014-2018						Percent of households with earnings, 2014-2018	Percent of households receiving SNAP (food stamps), 2014-2018	Percent of group whose income in the past 12 months was below the poverty level, 2014-2018		
		Under $25,000	$25,000-$49,999	$50,000-$74,999	$75,000-$99,999	$100,000-$199,999	$200,000 and over			Individuals	Children under 18 years old	Families
Grand Island, NE Metro Area	28,878	20.9	24.5	20.2	14.3	17.3	2.9	81.8	11.1	12.5	18.2	9.8
Grand Junction, CO Metro Area	61,033	23.5	23.6	19.4	13.5	17.1	3.0	76.3	11.5	15.7	21.6	11.7
Grand Rapids-Kentwood, MI Metro Area	387,078	17.7	23.2	20.0	14.2	20.3	4.7	80.1	10.4	11.7	14.8	7.6
Grants Pass, OR Metro Area	35,978	28.1	28.1	19.4	11.9	9.7	2.8	62.2	22.4	18.6	26.8	13.0
Great Falls, MT Metro Area	34,444	24.0	27.9	19.0	10.2	15.2	3.7	73.8	10.6	12.8	14.8	8.9
Greeley, CO Metro Area	102,101	14.9	19.5	18.5	16.4	25.1	5.5	84.2	8.4	10.6	12.7	7.1
Green Bay, WI Metro Area	128,311	17.6	24.1	19.6	15.0	19.8	4.0	79.2	9.5	10.1	13.6	7.3
Greensboro-High Point, NC Metro Area	295,973	24.2	26.8	18.1	11.4	15.4	4.0	76.6	14.8	16.2	23.8	12.1
Greenville, NC Metro Area	69,169	29.5	24.6	17.3	10.1	15.3	3.1	79.5	15.1	23.9	27.8	15.0
Greenville-Anderson, SC Metro Area	338,714	23.3	24.9	18.3	12.4	17.0	4.1	76.2	11.1	14.3	18.9	10.1
Gulfport-Biloxi, MS Metro Area	155,946	26.2	25.9	18.6	12.6	14.1	2.5	73.4	15.9	18.3	27.1	14.7
Hagerstown-Martinsburg, MD-WV Metro Area	106,267	18.7	23.1	19.7	14.2	20.8	3.4	76.3	14.1	12.4	18.1	9.4
Hammond, LA Metro Area	47,527	30.7	22.4	16.9	11.3	16.2	2.4	75.4	20.9	22.0	31.6	16.8
Hanford-Corcoran, CA Metro Area	42,735	20.6	26.3	17.9	14.0	17.7	3.5	81.6	16.9	20.8	29.0	16.6
Harrisburg-Carlisle, PA Metro Area	228,652	16.2	22.7	19.4	14.7	21.7	5.2	77.8	10.0	10.1	15.5	6.7
Harrisonburg, VA Metro Area	47,714	20.7	25.7	19.7	13.3	17.1	3.3	80.1	8.8	16.5	12.7	8.7
Hartford-East Hartford-Middletown, CT Metro Area	471,188	16.3	18.1	15.2	13.2	27.2	10.1	78.3	13.0	10.1	13.4	6.8
Hattiesburg, MS Metro Area	61,603	30.2	23.9	17.4	11.3	14.7	2.5	75.5	16.6	21.3	26.7	15.5
Hickory-Lenoir-Morganton, NC Metro Area	142,087	26.1	27.2	19.0	12.2	12.8	2.7	72.9	14.1	15.3	21.6	11.6
Hilton Head Island-Bluffton, SC Metro Area	80,589	17.6	24.7	18.6	13.1	19.6	6.3	68.7	7.7	12.3	23.7	8.1
Hinesville, GA Metro Area	28,833	22.9	29.5	23.3	11.1	12.0	1.2	82.8	15.6	17.5	22.8	14.6
Homosassa Springs, FL Metro Area	62,762	28.7	31.4	18.6	8.9	10.4	2.0	50.5	12.9	16.7	29.0	11.1
Hot Springs, AR Metro Area	39,894	28.3	27.4	18.5	10.4	12.5	2.9	67.3	12.2	18.6	30.3	12.6
Houma-Thibodaux, LA Metro Area	76,463	25.9	23.3	17.0	11.8	18.4	3.6	75.1	14.6	18.8	25.6	14.2
Houston-The Woodlands-Sugar Land, TX Metro Area	2,310,213	17.8	20.8	17.1	12.1	22.8	9.5	85.7	11.5	14.2	20.7	11.4
Huntington-Ashland, WV-KY-OH Metro Area	143,459	30.2	25.0	17.5	11.0	13.7	2.7	65.0	17.3	18.9	24.7	13.9
Huntsville, AL Metro Area	177,382	20.6	20.8	16.5	12.5	22.8	6.7	78.2	10.7	13.3	19.2	9.7
Idaho Falls, ID Metro Area	48,697	18.1	25.1	20.8	13.2	18.7	4.1	80.7	11.6	11.3	14.2	8.3
Indianapolis-Carmel-Anderson, IN Metro Area	767,335	19.3	23.2	18.3	13.0	20.6	5.7	80.4	10.3	13.2	18.9	9.2
Iowa City, IA Metro Area	66,883	21.9	19.7	16.6	12.8	22.2	6.8	83.8	7.5	16.7	12.4	6.8
Ithaca, NY Metro Area	39,326	22.9	20.5	17.9	12.3	19.4	7.0	78.8	9.0	19.6	14.4	8.3
Jackson, MI Metro Area	61,696	22.9	25.9	19.5	12.7	16.2	2.9	72.6	14.0	14.1	22.6	10.3
Jackson, MS Metro Area	217,262	24.9	24.2	17.5	11.8	17.4	4.1	77.1	14.4	17.9	25.7	13.2
Jackson, TN Metro Area	68,245	27.7	27.1	18.0	11.1	13.4	2.7	71.2	17.4	18.7	28.6	14.2
Jacksonville, FL Metro Area	553,919	19.0	23.7	18.8	13.2	19.7	5.6	78.1	13.6	13.3	19.2	9.9
Jacksonville, NC Metro Area	64,065	20.0	30.6	21.5	12.9	13.5	1.5	82.5	12.3	13.8	19.0	10.9
Janesville-Beloit, WI Metro Area	64,538	20.0	24.5	20.4	14.7	17.8	2.5	76.7	16.3	13.6	21.4	10.6
Jefferson City, MO Metro Area	56,246	18.7	24.3	21.4	14.8	18.4	2.4	76.8	9.2	10.9	15.9	8.0
Johnson City, TN Metro Area	84,305	29.6	26.9	18.6	10.2	11.9	2.8	69.8	15.6	18.4	24.6	13.3
Johnstown, PA Metro Area	56,793	26.8	26.9	18.1	12.2	14.1	1.9	67.3	17.6	15.4	25.3	10.4
Jonesboro, AR Metro Area	50,237	28.5	27.0	17.7	11.2	12.4	3.1	76.9	14.9	19.0	26.2	13.9
Joplin, MO Metro Area	67,529	23.3	29.2	19.5	12.3	13.1	2.5	76.2	13.7	16.3	22.9	11.8
Kahului-Wailuku-Lahaina, HI Metro Area	54,274	14.3	16.9	17.4	15.2	27.3	8.8	80.9	9.9	9.7	11.7	6.6
Kalamazoo-Portage, MI Metro Area	102,809	20.7	25.4	18.1	11.7	19.0	5.0	78.0	12.4	16.1	18.0	9.5
Kankakee, IL Metro Area	40,050	22.3	20.7	20.1	13.9	19.6	3.5	75.3	16.9	14.8	20.6	10.5
Kansas City, MO-KS Metro Area	821,644	17.2	22.0	18.2	13.6	22.7	6.3	80.5	8.5	11.0	15.6	7.7
Kennewick-Richland, WA Metro Area	97,299	16.7	20.8	20.1	14.2	22.7	5.5	79.5	14.9	13.7	20.3	9.9
Killeen-Temple, TX Metro Area	150,293	19.8	26.0	21.0	13.6	16.6	3.0	80.7	13.5	13.7	19.5	10.8
Kingsport-Bristol, TN-VA Metro Area	128,069	28.7	28.0	18.1	10.5	12.3	2.4	66.6	16.6	17.3	27.2	12.9
Kingston, NY Metro Area	69,539	19.5	20.8	18.0	12.5	22.9	6.3	76.1	11.3	13.9	17.1	8.0
Knoxville, TN Metro Area	335,953	23.5	24.3	18.1	12.6	17.2	4.3	74.0	13.7	15.1	19.9	10.7
Kokomo, IN Metro Area	34,550	24.2	25.1	18.3	13.5	16.4	2.5	70.8	13.4	15.9	24.0	13.1
La Crosse-Onalaska, WI-MN Metro Area	55,500	17.9	26.4	19.4	13.2	19.0	4.0	79.2	8.3	12.4	8.3	5.0
Lafayette, LA Metro Area	180,421	25.9	23.7	16.7	11.5	17.8	4.4	77.1	15.1	18.5	25.3	13.7
Lafayette-West Lafayette, IN Metro Area	83,779	23.8	24.2	19.8	11.5	17.4	3.3	81.9	8.5	19.0	17.8	9.1
Lake Charles, LA Metro Area	80,013	26.1	24.3	16.4	11.2	18.0	4.0	76.0	13.5	16.6	24.5	13.0
Lake Havasu City-Kingman, AZ Metro Area	85,485	26.8	30.0	19.3	10.6	11.4	2.0	56.8	15.2	17.5	25.5	11.6
Lakeland-Winter Haven, FL Metro Area	231,260	23.2	28.3	19.7	11.9	14.0	2.8	69.1	15.4	16.6	26.0	12.5
Lancaster, PA Metro Area	199,889	15.8	22.5	20.1	15.0	22.0	4.6	79.7	8.9	10.0	14.1	6.4
Lansing-East Lansing, MI Metro Area	213,752	20.7	24.1	19.4	13.0	18.8	3.9	76.4	11.7	15.5	19.0	9.2
Laredo, TX Metro Area	73,659	31.5	25.2	16.0	10.0	14.3	3.0	82.8	28.0	30.1	40.5	26.2
Las Cruces, NM Metro Area	77,453	34.0	25.5	16.0	8.6	13.2	2.7	74.3	23.9	27.7	41.0	22.4
Las Vegas-Henderson-Paradise, NV Metro Area	767,954	19.7	24.6	19.0	13.2	18.9	4.7	78.9	13.0	14.1	20.2	10.5
Lawrence, KS Metro Area	46,294	23.6	22.1	17.7	11.1	21.0	4.5	84.4	6.1	18.7	12.3	7.6
Lawton, OK Metro Area	44,822	22.7	25.2	19.5	13.5	16.3	2.7	78.6	15.0	15.5	20.9	11.5
Lebanon, PA Metro Area	53,281	17.3	23.2	22.1	15.6	18.6	3.1	76.1	11.8	10.4	15.7	8.3
Lewiston, ID-WA Metro Area	25,473	21.4	26.3	19.7	13.8	16.5	2.3	70.6	14.0	14.0	19.5	8.4
Lewiston-Auburn, ME Metro Area	45,491	23.3	25.3	19.3	12.9	17.1	2.1	75.8	18.8	13.2	17.7	8.8
Lexington-Fayette, KY Metro Area	200,538	21.5	23.3	18.1	12.7	19.1	5.4	81.1	11.6	16.8	22.5	11.6
Lima, OH Metro Area	40,537	25.4	24.2	21.0	12.3	14.8	2.2	74.5	13.9	14.8	21.1	10.4
Lincoln, NE Metro Area	129,242	18.6	24.2	19.0	13.0	21.0	4.3	83.1	8.1	12.8	14.0	7.8
Little Rock-North Little Rock-Conway, AR Metro Area	282,138	22.5	25.1	18.0	12.0	18.1	4.4	77.2	10.2	15.1	20.7	10.5
Logan, UT-ID Metro Area	41,939	17.9	26.1	20.7	14.4	17.9	3.0	85.2	7.2	14.8	14.5	10.7
Longview, TX Metro Area	100,745	23.4	26.3	18.1	12.4	16.6	3.2	77.3	13.7	15.8	21.7	11.9

Table B-7. Median Income, Household Income Distribution, and Poverty Status, 2014–2018—*Continued*

Metropolitan Statistical Area Metropolitan Division	Total number of households, 2014-2018	Percent of households by income level, 2014-2018						Percent of households with earnings, 2014-2018	Percent of households receiving SNAP (food stamps), 2014-2018	Percent of group whose income in the past 12 months was below the poverty level, 2014-2018		
		Under $25,000	$25,000-$49,999	$50,000-$74,999	$75,000-$99,999	$100,000-$199,999	$200,000 and over			Individuals	Children under 18 years old	Families
Longview, WA Metro Area	41,397	23.0	25.1	18.8	12.9	17.4	2.9	68.9	22.2	16.0	20.7	11.6
Los Angeles-Long Beach-Anaheim, CA Metro Area	4,338,482	18.3	19.1	15.9	12.2	23.9	10.5	82.6	8.2	14.9	20.7	11.1
Anaheim-Santa Ana-Irvine, CA Div	1,032,373	13.3	15.7	15.2	12.8	28.7	14.3	82.7	6.4	11.5	15.2	7.9
Los Angeles-Long Beach-Glendale, CA Div	3,306,109	19.9	20.2	16.2	12.0	22.4	9.3	82.6	8.8	16.0	22.5	12.2
Louisville/Jefferson County, KY-IN Metro Area	488,638	20.5	23.6	18.6	12.9	19.3	5.1	77.8	11.1	13.0	18.8	9.3
Lubbock, TX Metro Area	116,362	25.0	25.0	17.4	12.0	16.2	4.4	82.3	12.7	19.0	21.0	12.0
Lynchburg, VA Metro Area	100,371	22.3	25.8	18.9	13.4	16.5	3.1	74.4	10.5	14.1	18.5	9.2
Macon-Bibb County, GA Metro Area	85,991	31.0	24.9	15.7	10.4	14.2	3.8	70.0	18.2	22.6	32.7	17.8
Madera, CA Metro Area	44,759	21.6	25.9	18.7	11.6	18.7	3.6	75.3	17.6	20.8	30.3	16.9
Madison, WI Metro Area	268,213	15.2	20.7	18.0	14.3	25.0	6.8	83.6	8.4	11.2	10.9	5.5
Manchester-Nashua, NH Metro Area	159,200	13.4	18.0	16.3	14.1	28.9	9.4	82.3	7.9	8.1	10.3	5.4
Manhattan, KS Metro Area	48,097	21.1	27.0	19.8	12.6	16.6	3.0	85.9	6.3	16.7	13.8	8.7
Mankato, MN Metro Area	38,521	18.9	24.2	17.9	14.9	20.0	4.1	82.4	7.9	15.2	10.4	6.9
Mansfield, OH Metro Area	47,998	25.1	27.1	20.0	12.4	13.3	2.1	70.9	15.2	14.3	19.4	10.1
McAllen-Edinburg-Mission, TX Metro Area	234,879	34.7	24.8	16.2	9.5	12.6	2.2	80.1	30.0	31.2	43.3	27.5
Medford, OR Metro Area	87,417	23.9	25.2	19.6	12.0	15.5	3.8	70.2	19.2	16.3	22.4	11.5
Memphis, TN-MS-AR Metro Area	495,110	25.1	23.7	17.3	11.5	17.7	4.7	78.9	16.8	18.6	29.3	14.2
Merced, CA Metro Area	79,606	23.8	26.1	18.8	11.8	15.6	3.9	78.7	19.7	22.7	32.3	19.0
Miami-Fort Lauderdale-Pompano Beach, FL Metro Area	2,100,355	23.0	23.4	17.3	11.3	18.1	6.9	77.3	17.6	15.4	21.3	11.9
Fort Lauderdale-Pompano Beach-Sunrise, FL Div	682,088	20.6	23.4	18.0	12.1	19.3	6.6	79.4	13.6	13.5	18.7	10.3
Miami-Miami Beach-Kendall, FL Div	870,051	27.0	23.9	16.7	10.6	16.0	5.9	79.9	25.4	18.0	24.2	14.7
West Palm Beach-Boca Raton-Boynton Beach, FL Div	548,216	19.6	22.7	17.4	11.5	20.1	8.7	70.6	10.3	12.8	19.1	9.0
Michigan City-La Porte, IN Metro Area	42,904	22.7	26.3	19.2	13.3	15.6	2.9	75.1	13.7	16.5	28.8	12.2
Midland, MI Metro Area	34,017	19.3	22.9	19.0	13.3	18.6	6.9	73.4	11.8	10.8	12.7	7.3
Midland, TX Metro Area	57,606	12.9	18.2	16.7	13.7	27.1	11.4	87.7	6.7	9.1	12.2	7.1
Milwaukee-Waukesha, WI Metro Area	629,381	20.6	21.9	17.4	12.8	21.4	6.0	77.8	14.2	14.0	20.3	9.8
Minneapolis-St. Paul-Bloomington, MN Metro Area	1,360,921	13.6	18.1	17.0	14.0	28.0	9.2	82.7	7.9	9.0	11.7	5.6
Missoula, MT Metro Area	48,608	24.2	24.7	18.3	11.8	16.7	4.2	80.6	12.2	14.9	13.1	7.6
Mobile, AL Metro Area	161,838	28.6	24.6	17.4	11.3	14.9	3.2	72.4	17.0	19.3	29.3	15.0
Modesto, CA Metro Area	172,682	19.9	23.7	18.7	13.0	20.2	4.5	78.2	14.7	16.1	21.7	12.7
Monroe, LA Metro Area	74,168	32.7	25.5	15.9	9.1	13.6	3.2	71.2	16.9	23.9	35.9	18.9
Monroe, MI Metro Area	59,279	17.6	22.5	19.6	14.4	22.7	3.2	73.5	12.3	10.6	14.3	7.2
Montgomery, AL Metro Area	144,273	26.1	22.9	17.2	12.3	17.7	3.8	75.2	17.3	18.3	27.9	14.4
Morgantown, WV Metro Area	51,239	26.4	24.1	17.4	10.2	16.8	5.1	76.3	11.1	19.9	18.1	9.7
Morristown, TN Metro Area	53,269	27.3	28.0	19.7	11.5	11.6	1.8	69.4	18.4	17.3	24.5	12.9
Mount Vernon-Anacortes, WA Metro Area	47,937	17.6	22.2	19.0	15.4	20.5	5.4	73.2	14.3	12.8	17.0	7.9
Muncie, IN Metro Area	46,028	29.9	26.7	17.8	10.8	12.0	2.8	73.4	14.1	21.5	24.8	13.0
Muskegon, MI Metro Area	65,619	24.1	27.6	20.1	11.2	14.5	2.5	73.1	18.8	17.1	24.5	12.5
Myrtle Beach-Conway-North Myrtle Beach, SC-NC	182,812	22.7	27.5	20.2	12.2	14.3	3.1	67.1	11.8	15.4	27.2	10.9
Napa, CA Metro Area	49,032	12.4	17.0	15.7	12.5	29.1	13.2	78.1	4.5	8.1	8.7	5.2
Naples-Marco Island, FL Metro Area	140,942	15.2	22.0	18.5	12.5	20.8	10.9	63.4	8.0	12.3	22.3	8.0
Nashville-Davidson--Murfreesboro--Franklin, TN	695,444	16.9	22.6	18.9	13.7	21.2	6.7	83.0	10.5	12.3	17.4	8.8
New Bern, NC Metro Area	50,360	23.7	26.9	19.8	11.9	14.5	3.1	71.0	14.4	16.0	26.4	11.0
New Haven-Milford, CT Metro Area	329,857	18.6	19.6	16.7	12.1	24.6	8.4	76.9	15.2	11.9	17.0	8.3
New Orleans-Metairie, LA Metro Area	480,838	26.1	22.7	16.4	11.3	18.1	5.4	76.9	13.9	17.5	25.8	12.9
New York-Newark-Jersey City, NY-NJ-PA Metro Area	6,962,260	18.8	16.9	14.3	11.4	25.3	13.3	79.4	13.3	13.5	18.7	10.3
Nassau County-Suffolk County, NY Div	933,498	10.7	12.9	12.7	12.1	33.4	18.1	80.4	5.6	6.4	8.2	4.4
Newark, NJ-PA Div	774,797	16.3	16.7	14.5	11.5	26.0	15.1	80.9	9.0	10.4	14.6	7.8
New Brunswick-Lakewood, NJ Div	860,330	13.4	16.1	14.9	12.4	29.3	13.9	78.2	5.9	8.2	11.8	5.7
New York-Jersey City-White Plains, NY-NJ Div	4,393,635	22.1	17.9	14.4	11.0	22.7	11.8	79.1	17.2	16.7	23.5	13.4
Niles, MI Metro Area	63,908	24.8	25.9	17.8	11.0	16.4	4.1	74.4	14.5	16.5	24.7	12.4
North Port-Sarasota-Bradenton, FL Metro Area	324,203	18.7	24.7	19.0	12.1	19.3	6.2	61.4	8.1	11.0	18.1	6.8
Norwich-New London, CT Metro Area	107,402	16.2	17.7	18.6	13.5	26.5	7.5	78.6	11.7	10.2	15.9	7.2
Ocala, FL Metro Area	136,514	25.8	30.4	19.8	10.3	11.3	2.4	57.8	15.7	16.6	28.4	12.0
Ocean City, NJ Metro Area	39,904	18.0	20.7	19.3	12.9	21.9	7.2	70.1	6.8	11.1	16.5	8.0
Odessa, TX Metro Area	51,954	17.8	23.1	18.9	13.4	21.6	5.1	86.2	11.9	11.8	15.2	9.2
Ogden-Clearfield, UT Metro Area	205,890	12.2	19.5	20.9	16.7	26.2	4.6	83.7	7.4	8.0	9.5	6.2
Oklahoma City, OK Metro Area	511,536	20.0	24.1	18.9	13.0	18.9	5.1	80.4	11.5	14.4	20.2	10.2
Olympia-Lacey-Tumwater, WA Metro Area	108,070	15.2	19.2	19.9	15.7	24.9	5.1	77.3	11.8	11.0	13.3	7.4
Omaha-Council Bluffs, NE-IA Metro Area	355,832	16.7	21.5	18.5	14.0	23.6	5.8	82.4	9.3	10.6	14.0	7.2
Orlando-Kissimmee-Sanford, FL Metro Area	855,265	20.4	25.0	19.1	12.4	17.9	5.2	79.8	14.5	14.7	21.0	11.0
Oshkosh-Neenah, WI Metro Area	70,173	18.9	24.6	20.4	13.6	18.5	4.0	77.9	9.7	11.9	14.9	6.2
Owensboro, KY Metro Area	46,927	23.1	26.8	18.7	12.6	15.7	3.1	73.6	11.6	15.9	22.7	11.9
Oxnard-Thousand Oaks-Ventura, CA Metro Area	271,226	12.2	16.5	15.8	14.1	29.0	12.4	81.3	7.2	9.6	12.9	6.6
Palm Bay-Melbourne-Titusville, FL Metro Area	228,888	20.8	24.9	19.5	12.3	18.0	4.5	67.4	10.7	12.7	18.5	8.8
Panama City, FL Metro Area	70,199	22.2	26.1	18.8	12.9	16.7	3.3	75.1	13.7	14.7	20.8	10.5
Parkersburg-Vienna, WV Metro Area	38,517	27.4	26.4	17.8	11.4	14.1	2.8	67.1	17.2	16.8	25.9	12.8
Pensacola-Ferry Pass-Brent, FL Metro Area	180,085	18.9	26.9	20.2	13.0	17.3	3.8	75.6	13.4	12.5	19.3	8.1
Peoria, IL Metro Area	164,085	19.9	22.8	19.8	13.5	19.5	4.6	74.5	12.7	12.7	17.1	8.9
Philadelphia-Camden-Wilmington, PA-NJ-DE-MD Metro Area	2,264,041	18.5	18.8	15.9	12.4	24.9	9.6	78.3	12.5	12.6	17.4	8.7
Camden, NJ Div	457,241	15.4	17.2	15.8	13.4	28.5	9.6	79.3	8.7	9.2	12.8	6.5

Table B-7. Median Income, Household Income Distribution, and Poverty Status, 2014–2018—*Continued*

Metropolitan Statistical Area Metropolitan Division	Total number of households, 2,014-2,018	Under $25,000	$25,000-$49,999	$50,000-$74,999	$75,000-$99,999	$100,000-$199,999	$200,000 and over	Percent of households with earnings, 2014-2018	Percent of households receiving SNAP (food stamps), 2014-2018	Individuals	Children under 18 years old	Families
Montgomery County-Bucks County-Chester County,..........	740,924	11.4	15.5	15.3	13.0	30.2	14.6	81.6	5.6	6.3	7.6	4.1
Philadelphia, PA Div..........	801,183	27.5	22.5	16.2	10.6	17.5	5.7	74.3	21.8	21.0	29.7	15.9
Wilmington, DE-MD-NJ Div..........	264,693	16.4	19.4	17.0	14.0	25.8	7.4	79.4	10.5	11.3	15.7	7.3
Phoenix-Mesa-Chandler, AZ Metro Area	1,658,053	18.3	22.6	18.8	13.0	21.0	6.4	77.8	10.3	14.7	21.0	10.6
Pine Bluff, AR Metro Area	34,064	33.1	26.8	17.5	9.9	10.9	1.8	67.3	18.7	22.3	35.2	16.8
Pittsburgh, PA Metro Area	1,003,283	21.3	22.2	17.7	12.8	20.5	5.6	74.2	12.6	11.5	15.6	7.7
Pittsfield, MA Metro Area..........	55,167	21.6	23.4	17.1	12.2	20.3	5.4	72.9	13.2	11.4	16.0	7.9
Pocatello, ID Metro Area	33,422	23.0	27.2	18.5	13.1	15.8	2.5	77.6	14.2	16.3	18.9	11.1
Portland-South Portland, ME Metro Area..........	220,198	16.5	20.2	18.6	14.4	23.9	6.3	78.5	9.5	9.2	11.0	5.5
Portland-Vancouver-Hillsboro, OR-WA Metro Area..	925,631	15.6	19.6	17.7	13.9	25.3	8.0	80.5	13.8	11.4	14.2	7.3
Port St. Lucie, FL Metro Area..........	176,737	22.1	25.8	19.3	12.4	15.3	5.1	64.7	10.7	13.5	19.9	9.5
Poughkeepsie-Newburgh-Middletown, NY Metro Area	234,123	15.5	17.6	15.3	13.1	29.2	9.1	79.3	9.4	10.7	16.1	7.4
Prescott Valley-Prescott, AZ Metro Area..........	96,007	23.2	26.6	21.3	11.4	14.6	2.9	60.9	9.3	14.0	18.8	8.8
Providence-Warwick, RI-MA Metro Area	627,503	20.9	19.4	16.4	12.7	24.0	6.6	76.1	15.9	12.5	17.6	9.0
Provo-Orem, UT Metro Area	164,039	13.1	20.3	20.2	15.5	25.3	5.5	88.8	6.3	11.2	9.9	7.8
Pueblo, CO Metro Area	63,762	27.4	27.0	17.4	12.1	13.9	2.3	52.3	18.5	19.0	25.9	14.5
Punta Gorda, FL Metro Area..........	76,150	22.6	28.3	20.3	11.7	13.7	3.4	52.3	8.7	11.1	18.3	7.5
Racine, WI Metro Area	76,384	19.0	21.9	19.6	14.0	21.2	4.2	77.5	15.6	12.1	17.7	8.7
Raleigh-Cary, NC Metro Area	482,401	14.0	20.2	17.6	13.6	25.9	8.8	84.7	7.9	10.5	14.4	7.2
Rapid City, SD Metro Area..........	54,510	19.2	25.3	20.7	13.8	17.1	3.9	79.2	10.4	12.2	17.3	8.2
Reading, PA Metro Area..........	154,467	18.7	21.7	18.9	14.1	22.2	4.4	77.4	13.5	12.8	20.0	9.1
Redding, CA Metro Area..........	70,473	24.2	25.1	18.5	11.5	16.9	3.9	68.0	10.9	17.1	23.3	10.8
Reno, NV Metro Area	179,230	17.7	23.0	19.3	13.2	20.9	5.9	78.6	9.9	12.1	15.4	7.7
Richmond, VA Metro Area..........	476,706	17.0	20.9	17.7	13.5	23.7	7.2	79.9	9.5	11.9	17.4	7.7
Riverside-San Bernardino-Ontario, CA Metro Area ..	1,348,982	19.2	21.5	17.9	13.2	22.6	5.6	79.0	12.4	15.9	22.3	12.4
Roanoke, VA Metro Area..........	128,792	21.6	24.2	19.5	13.1	17.8	4.0	74.1	10.9	13.4	20.2	9.6
Rochester, MN Metro Area..........	85,917	14.4	19.5	18.5	14.4	26.1	7.0	81.1	7.3	8.5	10.8	5.4
Rochester, NY Metro Area..........	431,331	20.8	23.3	18.1	12.7	20.5	4.7	74.8	14.0	13.8	20.0	9.7
Rockford, IL Metro Area..........	133,339	22.0	23.9	19.2	13.2	17.8	3.8	76.3	17.1	14.9	23.4	11.0
Rocky Mount, NC Metro Area	58,091	30.2	25.8	17.9	10.6	12.7	2.9	72.4	20.6	18.5	27.1	14.4
Rome, GA Metro Area	35,633	26.3	26.6	17.9	11.1	14.8	3.3	72.5	15.6	19.1	28.4	14.8
Sacramento-Roseville-Folsom, CA Metro Area	819,372	17.9	19.1	16.9	12.9	25.1	8.1	77.3	9.6	14.3	18.2	9.9
Saginaw, MI Metro Area..........	78,648	25.4	27.9	18.2	11.5	14.1	2.9	69.0	19.3	17.7	23.9	12.6
St. Cloud, MN Metro Area	75,108	18.4	23.8	19.3	14.8	20.1	3.7	81.3	9.7	13.0	16.2	7.2
St. George, UT Metro Area	54,702	17.7	25.3	22.0	13.1	17.6	4.3	69.4	8.4	12.4	16.3	8.7
St. Joseph, MO-KS Metro Area	47,075	23.5	25.4	20.7	12.9	15.1	2.5	75.2	12.1	15.6	23.5	11.3
St. Louis, MO-IL Metro Area..........	1,118,263	18.9	22.3	17.8	13.1	21.6	6.3	77.4	11.1	11.9	17.0	8.4
Salem, OR Metro Area	146,553	19.5	24.8	19.8	13.7	18.9	3.3	75.9	18.8	15.0	20.2	10.4
Salinas, CA Metro Area	126,052	14.7	21.3	19.2	13.7	22.8	8.2	81.6	7.1	14.1	21.2	10.5
Salisbury, MD-DE Metro Area	157,057	18.6	24.1	19.3	13.4	19.8	4.9	72.4	13.6	12.7	20.0	8.4
Salt Lake City, UT Metro Area	389,330	13.2	19.9	19.8	14.9	25.2	6.9	85.6	7.1	9.6	11.6	6.5
San Angelo, TX Metro Area	44,227	21.6	27.2	18.4	12.3	16.4	4.2	79.4	9.6	13.4	19.0	9.1
San Antonio-New Braunfels, TX Metro Area..........	803,662	20.3	22.7	18.7	12.9	20.0	5.6	80.5	11.9	14.9	21.1	11.3
San Diego-Chula Vista-Carlsbad, CA Metro Area	1,118,980	15.1	18.5	16.5	13.0	26.5	10.5	81.6	7.2	12.5	16.1	8.7
San Francisco-Oakland-Berkeley, CA Metro Area .	1,692,047	13.2	13.3	12.5	11.1	29.4	20.5	82.1	5.4	9.5	10.9	6.0
Oakland-Berkeley-Livermore, CA Div	965,147	13.1	14.4	13.6	11.9	29.9	17.1	82.4	6.5	10.0	11.8	6.7
San Francisco-San Mateo-Redwood City, CA Div.	621,642	13.7	11.8	11.0	10.1	28.8	24.7	82.2	4.2	9.1	9.2	5.0
San Rafael, CA Div	105,258	11.2	12.7	11.6	10.2	28.0	26.2	78.6	3.0	7.6	8.9	4.1
San Jose-Sunnyvale-Santa Clara, CA Metro Area.....	653,265	10.5	11.7	11.4	10.4	31.2	24.8	85.0	4.8	8.0	8.5	5.0
San Luis Obispo-Paso Robles, CA Metro Area	105,317	16.9	18.3	17.5	13.1	25.7	8.5	74.8	4.8	13.3	11.5	6.5
Santa Cruz-Watsonville, CA Metro Area	95,756	16.7	16.6	15.0	12.1	25.6	14.0	79.7	8.6	14.3	16.4	8.0
Santa Fe, NM Metro Area	61,972	18.8	23.6	18.5	12.1	20.0	7.0	73.5	9.9	12.8	18.9	8.6
Santa Maria-Santa Barbara, CA Metro Area	144,962	16.0	19.7	16.4	12.8	24.7	10.4	80.4	8.1	14.8	18.2	9.0
Santa Rosa-Petaluma, CA Metro Area..........	189,339	14.4	17.5	17.0	14.4	26.9	9.9	77.7	6.5	10.3	12.5	6.1
Savannah, GA Metro Area	141,276	20.8	23.0	17.9	13.5	19.9	4.8	80.3	12.4	14.5	19.9	10.7
Scranton--Wilkes-Barre, PA Metro Area..........	225,466	24.6	24.1	18.3	12.5	17.5	3.1	72.3	16.7	14.7	23.6	10.7
Seattle-Tacoma-Bellevue, WA Metro Area..........	1,473,063	13.0	16.5	16.3	13.5	28.9	11.9	82.8	10.2	9.6	11.8	6.1
Seattle-Beellevue-Kent, WA Div..........	1,155,364	12.4	15.5	15.4	13.1	30.1	13.6	83.7	9.3	9.2	10.9	5.7
Tacoma-Lakewood, WA Div..........	317,699	15.1	20.4	19.6	14.8	24.4	5.6	79.5	13.6	11.2	14.5	7.5
Sebastian-Vero Beach, FL Metro Area..........	57,403	21.5	26.0	18.6	11.7	15.8	6.4	57.6	9.9	12.2	19.4	6.5
Sebring-Avon Park, FL Metro Area..........	41,026	30.4	32.6	19.0	8.1	7.9	2.0	51.6	14.0	19.2	33.7	13.3
Sheboygan, WI Metro Area	47,303	17.6	24.3	21.3	14.5	19.3	3.0	78.1	9.5	7.6	9.4	4.9
Sherman-Denison, TX Metro Area	47,957	21.6	24.7	17.7	15.1	17.9	3.1	75.1	12.0	13.8	19.9	10.6
Shreveport-Bossier City, LA Metro Area..........	155,830	29.1	24.8	16.5	10.7	15.0	3.9	74.3	16.3	21.3	32.1	16.2
Sierra Vista-Douglas, AZ Metro Area..........	49,250	26.7	24.7	18.8	12.3	14.8	2.7	66.8	16.2	17.2	24.5	13.2
Sioux City, IA-NE-SD Metro Area..........	55,205	19.7	23.5	20.9	14.1	18.0	3.8	80.8	12.4	13.0	18.1	9.6
Sioux Falls, SD Metro Area	100,022	16.0	23.0	18.9	15.6	21.6	4.8	83.9	8.3	9.2	11.2	6.2
South Bend-Mishawaka, IN-MI Metro Area..........	122,096	22.8	25.8	18.7	12.7	16.1	3.9	77.0	11.5	15.1	22.2	10.9
Spartanburg, SC Metro Area	114,640	24.3	25.5	19.5	12.8	14.8	3.2	75.7	12.9	14.8	22.7	10.9
Spokane-Spokane Valley, WA Metro Area	215,922	21.3	25.1	18.5	13.3	17.8	4.0	75.1	17.0	14.5	17.9	9.3
Springfield, IL Metro Area	88,859	20.9	20.5	18.0	14.0	21.1	5.5	75.2	13.1	14.9	24.0	10.6
Springfield, MA Metro Area..........	268,036	22.9	21.9	16.4	12.5	21.1	5.2	74.3	18.2	15.6	22.5	11.1
Springfield, MO Metro Area	184,429	25.0	27.7	19.2	11.5	13.7	2.8	74.7	11.1	16.0	18.8	10.4

Table B-7. Median Income, Household Income Distribution, and Poverty Status, 2014–2018—Continued

Metropolitan Statistical Area Metropolitan Division	Total number of households, 2,014-2,018	Percent of households by income level, 2014-2018						Percent of households with earnings, 2014-2018	Percent of households receiving SNAP (food stamps), 2014-2018	Percent of group whose income in the past 12 months was below the poverty level, 2014-2018		
		Under $25,000	$25,000-$49,999	$50,000-$74,999	$75,000-$99,999	$100,000-$199,999	$200,000 and over			Individuals	Children under 18 years old	Families
Springfield, OH Metro Area	54,905	24.1	27.4	19.1	12.9	14.3	2.2	71.8	18.2	15.8	23.3	11.4
State College, PA Metro Area	57,908	22.2	22.0	16.3	12.4	21.6	5.5	78.6	6.8	18.4	11.8	5.5
Staunton, VA Metro Area	48,961	21.0	24.6	20.0	14.6	16.6	3.2	74.1	9.4	11.6	16.3	8.1
Stockton, CA Metro Area	226,727	19.9	21.6	17.6	12.7	22.3	5.8	79.6	14.5	15.9	21.8	12.7
Sumter, SC Metro Area	54,464	29.6	28.1	18.7	10.4	11.2	1.9	71.6	20.0	21.0	30.7	16.7
Syracuse, NY Metro Area	257,682	20.7	22.4	18.3	13.0	20.9	4.6	74.8	14.4	14.7	21.8	10.1
Tallahassee, FL Metro Area	146,837	24.1	25.5	16.7	12.3	17.1	4.3	78.5	13.8	20.0	21.5	10.8
Tampa-St. Petersburg-Clearwater, FL Metro Area	1,196,966	22.3	25.2	18.0	12.0	17.5	5.0	72.4	13.4	14.2	19.6	10.0
Terre Haute, IN Metro Area	72,852	25.8	27.7	19.3	11.6	13.6	1.9	74.3	14.1	16.8	21.2	11.8
Texarkana, TX-AR Metro Area	55,919	28.4	25.7	17.5	11.4	14.1	2.9	70.9	14.2	18.3	26.4	14.8
The Villages, FL Metro Area	54,636	18.1	26.4	21.3	14.9	16.4	2.9	34.1	4.8	8.8	22.6	5.0
Toledo, OH Metro Area	263,624	24.6	24.6	17.4	11.7	17.9	3.8	76.0	15.5	16.8	22.6	11.8
Topeka, KS Metro Area	94,312	19.8	25.0	19.4	14.5	18.2	3.1	75.2	8.4	12.0	15.0	7.7
Trenton-Princeton, NJ Metro Area	129,873	16.7	15.8	14.9	11.9	26.2	14.5	79.1	8.6	11.4	15.8	8.0
Tucson, AZ Metro Area	400,907	23.9	25.2	18.4	11.8	16.4	4.3	73.0	13.6	17.8	25.1	12.4
Tulsa, OK Metro Area	380,053	21.7	24.7	18.6	12.4	17.8	4.7	78.4	12.2	14.5	21.3	11.0
Tuscaloosa, AL Metro Area	88,522	27.8	22.9	17.7	12.0	16.2	3.4	74.3	12.7	19.2	24.8	12.9
Twin Falls, ID Metro Area	38,525	22.3	27.2	21.7	11.9	14.5	2.4	80.1	10.7	15.5	20.7	11.2
Tyler, TX Metro Area	77,195	22.5	24.4	18.3	12.2	17.9	4.8	75.8	11.7	16.4	22.7	11.8
Urban Honolulu, HI Metro Area	311,525	12.7	15.9	16.5	14.0	30.4	10.5	82.3	9.7	8.7	10.7	5.7
Utica-Rome, NY Metro Area	114,597	23.0	24.0	19.4	13.2	17.2	3.1	72.0	17.1	15.8	24.9	11.5
Valdosta, GA Metro Area	52,105	34.0	25.0	15.4	9.8	13.2	2.4	72.4	18.4	25.3	32.7	19.4
Vallejo, CA Metro Area	149,067	14.0	17.6	16.9	14.6	28.5	8.4	80.2	9.1	10.4	14.6	7.9
Victoria, TX Metro Area	35,225	21.7	23.3	16.7	12.6	21.2	4.6	78.0	12.1	15.3	21.6	11.4
Vineland-Bridgeton, NJ Metro Area	50,608	25.1	22.7	18.2	12.6	18.2	3.3	74.7	17.2	17.6	26.4	12.9
Virginia Beach-Norfolk-Newport News, VA-NC Metro Area	658,516	17.2	21.2	19.0	14.2	23.0	5.3	80.2	9.9	11.7	17.4	8.5
Visalia, CA Metro Area	136,106	26.5	25.7	17.7	11.1	15.2	3.8	79.7	22.4	25.5	34.0	21.4
Waco, TX Metro Area	94,271	26.9	25.1	17.1	11.1	16.3	3.5	77.6	13.3	19.6	26.6	13.5
Walla Walla, WA Metro Area	22,304	20.1	24.9	20.0	12.0	19.2	3.8	74.0	13.4	13.8	16.1	7.8
Warner Robins, GA Metro Area	66,249	21.8	23.1	19.0	12.6	20.0	3.6	77.7	14.6	16.5	23.0	13.3
Washington-Arlington-Alexandria, DC-VA-MD-WV Metro Area	2,196,416	10.4	12.9	13.9	12.6	32.6	17.7	85.7	7.1	8.0	10.3	5.4
Frederick-Gaithersburg-Rockville, MD Div	461,632	9.5	12.9	13.8	12.2	32.1	19.5	85.0	6.5	6.9	8.7	4.6
Washington-Arlington-Alexandria, DC-VA-MD-WV Metro Division	1,734,784	10.6	12.8	14.0	12.6	32.7	17.3	85.9	7.2	8.3	10.7	5.6
Waterloo-Cedar Falls, IA Metro Area	67,698	20.8	24.1	19.3	13.7	18.4	3.7	76.8	11.4	14.2	16.6	8.5
Watertown-Fort Drum, NY Metro Area	43,267	20.8	26.9	20.4	14.1	15.5	2.3	77.9	16.1	14.2	20.5	9.9
Wausau-Weston, WI Metro Area	67,924	18.0	25.2	18.9	15.2	19.2	3.6	78.6	9.6	9.3	12.5	5.8
Weirton-Steubenville, WV-OH Metro Area	50,017	27.2	26.8	19.0	11.9	13.3	1.7	67.9	16.0	16.0	24.8	10.9
Wenatchee, WA Metro Area	43,102	17.8	25.6	19.9	13.2	19.5	3.9	75.0	10.2	12.2	17.3	8.8
Wheeling, WV-OH Metro Area	55,783	26.4	25.1	17.3	12.5	15.9	2.8	68.9	12.7	13.9	19.1	9.1
Wichita, KS Metro Area	242,956	20.7	24.4	19.4	12.7	18.8	3.9	78.4	10.0	13.4	18.0	9.5
Wichita Falls, TX Metro Area	55,328	26.5	25.6	17.9	12.1	15.3	2.6	75.7	13.6	17.4	23.6	12.9
Williamsport, PA Metro Area	45,897	22.1	25.4	20.0	13.3	16.7	2.5	74.3	15.4	14.2	21.4	9.6
Wilmington, NC Metro Area	115,402	24.2	23.3	17.5	11.6	18.0	5.4	75.3	11.4	16.8	21.3	10.2
Winchester, VA-WV Metro Area	51,190	16.3	22.9	19.9	13.1	22.9	4.9	76.9	7.6	10.4	14.3	6.8
Winston-Salem, NC Metro Area	262,905	24.4	26.5	18.0	12.4	14.9	3.8	74.2	12.6	16.4	24.9	12.1
Worcester, MA-CT Metro Area	351,743	17.8	18.3	16.3	12.9	26.6	8.1	78.3	12.6	10.4	13.0	7.1
Yakima, WA Metro Area	82,300	21.8	28.3	20.6	12.3	14.1	2.9	78.3	22.5	18.2	26.4	14.2
York-Hanover, PA Metro Area	171,244	16.4	21.4	20.8	14.6	22.7	4.1	78.2	11.2	10.0	14.9	7.0
Youngstown-Warren-Boardman, OH-PA Metro Area	230,243	26.3	27.2	18.3	11.5	14.0	2.6	70.1	16.4	16.9	27.7	12.9
Yuba City, CA Metro Area	58,539	21.3	24.4	18.7	12.3	19.9	3.4	76.6	14.0	16.9	22.6	14.1
Yuma, AZ Metro Area	72,463	26.6	28.8	18.6	11.4	12.8	1.8	70.6	19.0	20.1	28.3	17.5

Table B-8. Health Insurance, Medicare, Social Security and Supplemental Security Income

Metropolitan Statistical Area / Metropolitan Division	Persons with no health insurance, 2014-2018		Persons who enrolled in Affordable Health Care Act plans, 2019		Persons with a disability, 2014-2018		Medicare program enrollment, 2018		Social Security program (OASDI) beneficiaries, December 2018			Supplemental Security Income program recipients, December 2018	
	Number	Percent	Number	Percent	Number	Percent	Number	Rate per 1000 persons	Number	Rate per 1000 persons	Retired workers, number	Number	Rate per 1000 persons
Abilene, TX Metro Area	21,930	13.9	4,242	2.5	25,556	16.2	30,593	178	32,580	190	21,910	4,441	26
Akron, OH Metro Area	40,916	5.9	13,588	1.9	90,804	13.0	141,444	201	143,430	204	98,305	17,540	25
Albany, GA Metro Area	23,357	15.9	4,506	3.0	21,748	14.8	28,253	189	31,375	209	20,755	6,694	45
Albany-Lebanon, OR Metro Area	8,627	7.1	2,989	2.3	21,389	17.5	28,702	225	31,215	245	21,605	3,576	28
Albany-Schenectady-Troy, NY Metro Area	35,305	4.1	-	-	105,213	12.1	176,792	200	187,730	213	133,880	20,023	23
Albuquerque, NM Metro Area	83,012	9.2	19,141	2.1	125,863	14.0	172,805	189	181,810	199	124,830	23,463	26
Alexandria, LA Metro Area	15,208	10.3	2,282	1.5	24,716	16.7	31,695	207	33,625	220	18,970	7,505	49
Allentown-Bethlehem-Easton, PA-NJ Metro Area	51,531	6.2	23,380	2.8	110,584	13.4	176,519	209	188,840	224	133,030	19,143	23
Altoona, PA Metro Area	6,490	5.3	2,587	2.1	21,325	17.4	30,751	251	30,915	252	20,525	4,451	36
Amarillo, TX Metro Area	39,762	15.6	6,500	2.4	29,369	11.5	42,547	160	43,775	165	30,095	4,385	17
Ames, IA Metro Area	5,221	4.3	1,396	1.1	10,836	8.9	18,901	152	19,225	155	14,500	985	8
Anchorage, AK Metro Area	50,226	13.0	9,875	2.5	44,929	11.6	50,482	127	52,565	132	36,990	7,571	19
Ann Arbor, MI Metro Area	13,963	3.9	10,392	2.8	32,757	9.1	57,651	155	59,320	160	42,645	5,446	15
Anniston-Oxford, AL Metro Area	10,686	9.4	3,472	3.0	23,598	20.8	27,138	238	30,220	264	17,925	4,532	40
Appleton, WI Metro Area	9,935	4.3	8,550	3.6	23,372	10.0	40,500	171	45,000	190	32,660	2,785	12
Asheville, NC Metro Area	47,096	10.6	31,852	6.9	65,090	14.6	114,510	249	119,995	261	88,250	9,456	21
Athens-Clarke County, GA Metro Area	25,525	12.5	6,476	3.1	24,903	12.2	32,719	155	35,510	168	24,430	4,748	23
Atlanta-Sandy Springs-Alpharetta, GA Metro Area	760,623	13.3	309,161	5.2	574,609	10.0	816,688	137	877,015	147	611,525	115,764	20
Atlantic City-Hammonton, NJ Metro Area	24,669	9.3	7,394	2.8	35,805	13.5	55,916	211	59,825	225	42,085	7,244	27
Auburn-Opelika, AL Metro Area	12,516	7.9	5,051	3.1	20,764	13.2	23,198	142	26,235	160	16,575	3,212	20
Augusta-Richmond County, GA-SC Metro Area	65,214	11.3	18,408	3.0	82,999	14.4	112,678	187	125,820	208	84,195	16,764	28
Austin-Round Rock-Georgetown, TX Metro Area	260,677	12.8	83,824	3.9	185,541	9.1	254,404	117	259,165	120	184,635	26,250	12
Bakersfield, CA Metro Area	77,216	9.0	-	-	95,441	11.2	115,517	129	124,855	139	81,405	33,789	38
Baltimore-Columbia-Towson, MD Metro Area	144,452	5.3	-	-	320,006	11.7	483,790	173	488,400	174	344,675	69,392	25
Bangor, ME Metro Area	14,300	9.5	6,251	4.1	27,898	18.6	36,197	240	38,030	252	23,560	5,452	36
Barnstable Town, MA Metro Area	6,858	3.2	-	-	27,848	13.2	74,517	349	72,365	339	57,185	3,139	15
Baton Rouge, LA Metro Area	78,718	9.4	18,749	2.2	120,520	14.4	139,962	164	147,580	173	89,675	25,064	29
Battle Creek, MI Metro Area	7,812	5.9	2,450	1.8	21,026	15.8	30,477	227	33,155	247	21,430	4,793	36
Bay City, MI Metro Area	5,758	5.5	2,484	2.4	16,395	15.8	26,082	251	29,265	282	18,940	3,234	31
Beaumont-Port Arthur, TX Metro Area	70,475	18.5	10,685	2.7	56,433	14.8	69,676	176	76,115	192	47,090	12,145	31
Beckley, WV Metro Area	8,825	7.5	1,155	1.0	28,372	24.3	30,785	263	34,590	295	18,620	5,681	48
Bellingham, WA Metro Area	13,971	6.5	-	-	28,370	13.2	44,820	199	45,540	202	33,410	4,303	19
Bend, OR Metro Area	15,426	8.6	11,405	5.9	22,836	12.7	42,618	222	45,135	235	35,180	2,312	12
Billings, MT Metro Area	15,119	8.6	5,517	3.1	22,133	12.6	35,386	196	37,150	206	27,280	2,664	15
Binghamton, NY Metro Area	10,134	4.2	-	-	36,983	15.4	55,371	231	60,175	251	41,175	8,199	34
Birmingham-Hoover, AL Metro Area	98,099	9.2	34,822	3.2	158,227	14.8	211,407	194	232,200	213	146,070	30,704	28
Bismarck, ND Metro Area	6,906	5.6	2,885	2.2	12,051	9.8	22,714	177	23,900	186	17,800	1,152	9
Blacksburg-Christiansburg, VA Metro Area	11,509	7.0	4,627	2.8	21,002	12.8	29,609	176	31,670	188	21,220	2,937	18
Bloomington, IL Metro Area	6,516	3.8	3,390	2.0	16,245	9.4	25,695	149	27,220	158	19,920	1,838	11
Bloomington, IN Metro Area	13,511	8.2	4,233	2.5	19,905	12.1	25,766	154	27,710	165	19,850	2,224	13
Bloomsburg-Berwick, PA Metro Area	3,997	4.8	2,035	2.4	11,243	13.5	18,783	224	20,355	243	14,705	1,764	21
Boise City, ID Metro Area	73,739	10.8	-	-	80,095	11.7	121,766	167	131,600	180	95,475	12,164	17
Boston-Cambridge-Newton, MA-NH Metro Area ...	145,277	3.0	83,824	0.3	506,275	10.6	853,812	175	822,065	169	577,810	104,098	21
Boston, MA Div	56,903	2.9	-	-	220,116	11.1	343,744	169	329,200	162	228,170	53,202	26
Cambridge-Newton-Framingham, MA Div	64,920	2.8	-	-	238,152	10.1	421,942	175	401,175	167	284,505	46,826	20
Rockingham County-Strafford County, NH Div	23,454	5.5	14,271	3.2	48,007	11.2	88,126	201	91,690	209	65,135	4,070	9
Boulder, CO Metro Area	16,064	5.0	-	-	25,747	8.1	50,147	154	46,360	142	35,615	2,243	7
Bowling Green, KY Metro Area	10,718	6.3	4,431	2.5	28,963	17.0	30,329	171	33,065	186	21,270	5,048	29
Bremerton-Silverdale-Port Orchard, WA Metro Area.	12,448	5.0	-	-	37,896	15.3	53,983	200	53,930	200	39,480	4,884	18
Bridgeport-Stamford-Norwalk, CT Metro Area	81,118	8.7	-	-	86,375	9.2	154,115	163	153,035	162	115,150	12,705	14
Brownsville-Harlingen, TX Metro Area	119,897	28.6	15,197	3.6	52,618	12.5	62,025	146	67,350	159	42,830	22,247	53
Brunswick, GA Metro Area	17,490	15.2	5,100	4.3	20,078	17.4	24,830	210	27,195	230	18,950	2,843	24
Buffalo-Cheektowaga, NY Metro Area	41,242	3.7	-	-	149,123	13.3	244,606	216	260,840	231	177,360	32,859	29
Burlington, NC Metro Area	18,968	11.9	6,215	3.7	22,761	14.3	32,440	195	35,480	213	25,740	3,548	21
Burlington-South Burlington, VT Metro Area	7,213	3.3	-	-	25,509	11.8	40,548	183	42,090	190	29,405	4,549	21
California-Lexington Park, MD Metro Area	6,292	5.8	-	-	13,583	12.5	16,117	143	16,715	148	11,500	1,692	15
Canton-Massillon, OH Metro Area	23,244	5.9	6,960	1.7	53,481	13.5	90,568	227	94,505	237	64,475	10,269	26
Cape Coral-Fort Myers, FL Metro Area	101,742	14.3	61,569	8.2	97,224	13.6	186,163	247	194,235	257	151,350	12,835	17
Cape Girardeau, MO-IL Metro Area	8,112	8.5	2,642	2.7	14,741	15.4	20,081	207	21,655	223	14,550	2,344	24
Carbondale-Marion, IL Metro Area	8,397	6.3	2,767	2.0	21,200	15.9	27,631	202	28,980	212	19,395	3,462	25
Carson City, NV Metro Area	5,547	10.6	1,442	2.6	11,509	21.9	13,449	243	13,525	244	10,350	1,044	19
Casper, WY Metro Area	10,684	13.5	2,716	3.4	11,612	14.6	13,950	176	15,045	190	10,465	1,276	16
Cedar Rapids, IA Metro Area	9,772	3.7	3,916	1.4	27,252	10.3	49,968	184	53,590	197	39,270	4,520	17
Chambersburg-Waynesboro, PA Metro Area	14,867	9.8	3,511	2.3	21,614	14.2	34,992	226	36,845	238	26,570	2,510	16
Champaign-Urbana, IL Metro Area	10,467	4.7	4,416	2.0	20,573	9.2	32,237	142	31,805	141	22,550	3,321	15
Charleston, WV Metro Area	16,652	6.3	2,699	1.0	52,809	19.9	66,602	256	73,600	283	42,985	11,589	45
Charleston-North Charleston, SC Metro Area	78,892	10.6	36,331	4.6	89,199	12.0	132,824	169	142,830	181	99,855	13,076	17
Charlotte-Concord-Gastonia, NC-SC Metro Area	262,985	10.6	128,178	4.9	268,687	10.8	402,788	155	437,635	169	311,645	43,092	17
Charlottesville, VA Metro Area	17,649	8.4	8,264	3.8	21,495	10.2	41,052	188	41,940	192	31,660	2,879	13
Chattanooga, TN-GA Metro Area	54,842	10.1	19,618	3.5	84,005	15.4	114,316	204	124,375	222	84,480	13,174	24
Cheyenne, WY Metro Area	7,859	8.3	2,951	3.0	12,614	13.4	18,498	187	19,040	192	13,640	1,485	15
Chicago-Naperville-Elgin, IL-IN-WI Metro Area ...	776,282	8.2	238,615	2.5	933,056	9.9	1,501,331	158	1,517,305	160	1,078,810	199,356	21
Chicago-Naperville-Evanston, IL Div	603,356	8.4	180,932	2.5	695,393	9.7	1,124,208	157	1,120,055	156	799,480	165,134	23

- = Data not available for states that have their own healthcare marketplaces.

Table B-8. Health Insurance, Medicare, Social Security and Supplemental Security Income—*Continued*

Metropolitan Statistical Area Metropolitan Division	Persons with no health insurance, 2014-2018		Persons who enrolled in Affordable Health Care Act plans, 2019		Persons with a disability, 2014-2018		Medicare program enrollment, 2018		Social Security program (OASDI) beneficiaries, December 2018			Supplemental Security Income program recipients, December 2018	
	Number	Percent	Number	Percent	Number	Percent	Number	Rate per 1000 persons	Number	Rate per 1000 persons	Retired workers, number	Number	Rate per 1000 persons
Elgin, IL Div	58,069	7.7	17,785	2.3	63,715	8.4	106,690	139	110,170	144	80,940	6,985	9
Gary, IN Div	55,734	8.0	14,767	2.1	92,453	13.3	133,746	191	147,225	210	97,495	15,270	22
Lake County-Kenosha County, IL-WI Div	59,123	6.9	25,131	2.9	81,495	9.5	136,687	157	139,855	161	100,895	11,967	14
Chico, CA Metro Area	16,561	7.4	-	-	38,146	17.0	49,813	215	52,010	225	35,745	10,748	47
Cincinnati, OH-KY-IN Metro Area	123,585	5.7	42,829	1.9	269,507	12.4	391,787	177	406,030	184	272,520	47,906	22
Clarksville, TN-KY Metro Area	23,275	8.5	5,282	1.7	42,481	15.6	43,188	141	50,195	164	29,805	6,636	22
Cleveland, TN Metro Area	14,097	11.7	4,186	3.4	21,579	18.0	26,708	216	29,685	240	19,545	3,153	26
Cleveland-Elyria, OH Metro Area	116,630	5.7	38,461	1.9	291,195	14.3	425,763	207	429,800	209	298,745	62,191	30
Coeur d'Alene, ID Metro Area	15,658	10.3	-	-	20,519	13.5	36,682	227	39,260	243	28,610	2,570	16
College Station-Bryan, TX Metro Area	33,586	13.5	5,062	1.9	23,007	9.2	30,422	116	31,505	120	21,605	4,480	17
Colorado Springs, CO Metro Area	50,703	7.5	-	-	84,911	12.5	110,678	150	115,050	156	79,280	9,374	13
Columbia, MO Metro Area	14,600	7.3	5,974	2.9	23,947	11.9	32,011	154	33,870	163	23,270	3,343	16
Columbia, SC Metro Area	78,024	9.9	31,813	3.8	109,390	13.9	144,117	173	160,075	192	111,055	16,285	20
Columbus, GA-AL Metro Area	37,465	12.5	8,777	2.8	53,439	17.8	57,224	180	64,660	203	39,810	11,072	35
Columbus, IN Metro Area	7,400	9.1	1,423	1.7	9,803	12.1	15,358	186	16,610	201	11,515	1,223	15
Columbus, OH Metro Area	143,034	7.1	40,078	1.9	241,210	11.9	318,444	151	321,010	152	215,540	45,791	22
Corpus Christi, TX Metro Area	72,124	17.1	12,663	3.0	58,030	13.7	70,603	165	75,395	176	47,810	13,890	32
Corvallis, OR Metro Area	5,045	5.6	2,576	2.8	9,842	11.0	16,060	174	16,080	175	12,370	1,046	11
Crestview-Fort Walton Beach-Destin, FL Metro Area	31,648	12.6	14,155	5.1	39,287	15.6	54,207	195	59,280	213	41,670	4,426	16
Cumberland, MD-WV Metro Area	5,032	5.4	331	0.3	18,062	19.3	23,470	240	24,530	251	16,240	3,054	31
Dallas-Fort Worth-Arlington, TX Metro Area	1,182,384	16.6	275,131	3.7	677,085	9.5	920,820	123	949,490	127	658,815	127,999	17
Dallas-Plano-Irving, TX Div	800,044	16.7	189,949	3.8	428,639	9.0	594,318	119	609,805	122	425,660	86,447	17
Fort Worth-Arlington-Grapevine, TX Div	382,340	16.2	85,182	3.5	248,446	10.5	326,502	133	339,685	138	233,155	41,552	17
Dalton, GA Metro Area	24,715	17.4	4,376	3.0	16,953	11.9	24,442	170	27,725	193	17,745	3,738	26
Danville, IL Metro Area	4,656	6.1	1,462	1.9	11,658	15.4	17,480	228	18,645	243	12,270	2,728	36
Daphne-Fairhope-Foley, AL Metro Area	20,864	10.2	10,989	5.0	28,863	14.0	51,023	234	56,005	257	39,725	3,505	16
Davenport-Moline-Rock Island, IA-IL Metro Area	19,315	5.1	7,887	2.1	45,301	12.0	77,681	204	82,215	216	60,390	7,530	20
Dayton-Kettering, OH Metro Area	49,689	6.3	12,954	1.6	115,097	14.6	163,669	203	165,895	206	113,115	20,077	25
Decatur, AL Metro Area	14,623	9.7	5,730	3.8	26,437	17.6	33,664	221	38,060	250	24,010	4,563	30
Decatur, IL Metro Area	5,067	4.9	2,010	1.9	15,950	15.3	23,987	229	25,200	241	17,395	3,282	31
Deltona-Daytona Beach-Ormond Beach, FL Metro Area	78,651	12.5	45,313	6.9	105,954	16.8	179,393	272	193,135	293	143,905	14,281	22
Denver-Aurora-Lakewood, CO Metro Area	225,972	8.0	-	-	264,392	9.4	407,731	139	397,570	136	294,005	35,929	12
Des Moines-West Des Moines, IA Metro Area	30,072	4.5	9,701	1.4	71,170	10.7	107,911	156	113,950	165	83,510	9,709	14
Detroit-Warren-Dearborn, MI Metro Area	258,669	6.0	123,069	2.8	604,330	14.1	827,842	191	890,375	206	592,050	133,599	31
Detroit-Dearborn-Livonia, MI Div	125,127	7.2	36,623	2.1	279,532	16.0	325,794	186	357,355	204	218,105	83,826	48
Warren-Troy-Farmington Hills, MI Div	133,542	5.3	86,446	3.4	324,798	12.8	502,048	195	533,020	207	373,945	49,773	19
Dothan, AL Metro Area	16,240	11.1	5,080	3.4	27,146	18.5	34,788	235	38,745	261	24,765	5,771	39
Dover, DE Metro Area	11,970	7.0	3,197	1.8	24,906	14.5	35,304	198	38,705	217	26,950	3,615	20
Dubuque, IA Metro Area	3,607	3.8	1,482	1.5	10,608	11.1	19,910	206	21,425	221	15,645	1,587	16
Duluth, MN-WI Metro Area	12,454	4.4	1,274	0.4	40,541	14.3	65,647	227	69,580	240	49,570	6,724	23
Durham-Chapel Hill, NC Metro Area	63,961	10.5	26,687	4.2	69,578	11.5	105,928	167	110,335	174	80,935	10,959	17
East Stroudsburg, PA Metro Area	11,760	7.1	5,369	3.2	25,498	15.3	32,825	194	36,780	217	24,465	3,081	18
Eau Claire, WI Metro Area	10,502	6.4	6,263	3.7	20,643	12.6	32,943	195	35,755	212	25,740	2,987	18
El Centro, CA Metro Area	15,883	9.3	-	-	24,557	14.4	30,496	168	33,480	184	21,385	10,405	57
Elizabethtown-Fort Knox, KY Metro Area	7,636	5.3	2,371	1.5	26,060	18.0	28,087	183	31,655	206	18,820	4,388	29
Elkhart-Goshen, IN Metro Area	30,489	15.2	3,191	1.6	26,390	13.1	33,899	165	36,290	177	25,950	2,997	15
Elmira, NY Metro Area	3,779	4.6	-	-	12,723	15.4	19,743	234	21,685	257	14,500	3,104	37
El Paso, TX Metro Area	169,064	20.7	44,441	5.3	113,687	13.9	126,667	150	134,570	159	82,460	29,452	35
Enid, OK Metro Area	7,850	13.1	2,177	3.6	8,793	14.6	11,718	192	12,585	207	8,430	1,322	22
Erie, PA Metro Area	14,798	5.5	5,493	2.0	41,391	15.3	58,480	215	64,055	235	42,915	10,419	38
Eugene-Springfield, OR Metro Area	27,921	7.6	13,318	3.5	61,964	16.9	85,276	225	88,925	234	64,320	9,592	25
Evansville, IN-KY Metro Area	21,388	6.9	7,486	2.4	47,797	15.4	64,499	205	70,505	224	47,340	7,119	23
Fairbanks, AK Metro Area	9,274	10.0	1,891	1.9	10,490	11.3	11,601	117	12,065	122	8,500	1,124	11
Fargo, ND-MN Metro Area	13,187	5.6	3,737	1.5	22,387	9.5	33,777	138	35,405	144	25,135	3,243	13
Farmington, NM Metro Area	18,305	14.5	1,112	0.9	18,712	14.8	20,509	164	23,220	186	14,485	3,970	32
Fayetteville, NC Metro Area	51,188	10.8	15,785	3.0	76,485	16.1	77,839	149	89,120	171	54,695	14,637	28
Fayetteville-Springdale-Rogers, AR Metro Area	52,005	10.4	13,748	2.6	50,913	10.2	78,774	150	86,985	165	59,015	8,208	16
Flagstaff, AZ Metro Area	17,200	12.3	4,103	2.9	16,525	11.9	19,476	136	20,985	147	15,155	2,473	17
Flint, MI Metro Area	22,905	5.6	7,507	1.8	67,799	16.7	88,584	218	100,420	247	63,085	16,524	41
Florence, SC Metro Area	21,814	10.7	8,542	4.2	34,150	16.8	44,075	215	49,190	240	31,920	8,467	41
Florence-Muscle Shoals, AL Metro Area	12,681	8.7	5,424	3.7	23,589	16.2	35,502	241	39,540	269	24,785	4,448	30
Fond du Lac, WI Metro Area	4,254	4.2	3,316	3.2	11,398	11.3	21,298	207	22,885	222	16,980	1,566	15
Fort Collins, CO Metro Area	21,078	6.3	-	-	33,021	9.8	59,736	170	58,480	167	44,650	2,590	7
Fort Smith, AR-OK Metro Area	27,924	11.3	6,119	2.4	49,381	20.0	53,075	212	59,970	240	36,050	8,640	35
Fort Wayne, IN Metro Area	36,591	9.2	9,463	2.3	50,895	12.7	71,746	175	79,125	193	55,120	8,516	21
Fresno, CA Metro Area	92,035	9.5	-	-	126,139	13.0	138,800	140	141,055	142	97,530	43,824	44
Gadsden, AL Metro Area	10,662	10.4	4,026	3.9	19,976	19.6	25,668	250	28,995	283	16,570	4,472	44
Gainesville, FL Metro Area	33,024	10.4	18,474	5.6	39,215	12.4	58,377	177	62,755	191	44,440	8,551	26
Gainesville, GA Metro Area	33,988	17.4	8,929	4.4	21,538	11.0	34,904	173	37,515	186	27,545	3,126	16
Gettysburg, PA Metro Area	5,804	5.8	2,850	2.8	13,565	13.5	23,888	232	24,985	243	18,930	1,114	11
Glens Falls, NY Metro Area	7,008	5.7	-	-	18,117	14.8	30,999	247	33,935	271	23,160	3,077	25
Goldsboro, NC Metro Area	15,791	13.2	3,966	3.2	19,818	16.5	23,482	191	26,225	213	16,985	4,145	34

- = Data not available for states that have their own healthcare marketplaces.

Table B-8. Health Insurance, Medicare, Social Security and Supplemental Security Income—*Continued*

Metropolitan Statistical Area Metropolitan Division	Persons with no health insurance, 2014-2018		Persons who enrolled in Affordable Health Care Act plans, 2019		Persons with a disability, 2014-2018		Medicare program enrollment, 2018		Social Security program (OASDI) beneficiaries, December 2018			Supplemental Security Income program recipients, December 2018	
	Number	Percent	Number	Percent	Number	Percent	Number	Rate per 1000 persons	Number	Rate per 1000 persons	Retired workers, number	Number	Rate per 1000 persons
Grand Forks, ND-MN Metro Area	5,957	6.0	1,854	1.8	11,156	11.2	16,811	164	17,790	174	12,715	1,346	13
Grand Island, NE Metro Area	8,862	11.9	3,527	4.7	9,569	12.8	13,517	178	14,230	188	10,450	1,123	15
Grand Junction, CO Metro Area	15,076	10.1	-	-	21,783	14.6	33,225	217	34,020	222	24,890	2,653	17
Grand Rapids-Kentwood, MI Metro Area	62,373	6.0	28,898	2.7	120,831	11.6	179,834	168	194,780	182	137,330	19,105	18
Grants Pass, OR Metro Area	6,898	8.1	2,937	3.4	16,638	19.6	26,108	299	27,795	318	20,410	2,886	33
Great Falls, MT Metro Area	6,897	8.8	2,186	2.7	11,634	14.9	17,509	215	18,625	228	13,315	1,817	22
Greeley, CO Metro Area	22,917	7.8	-	-	29,662	10.1	42,166	134	43,585	139	31,020	3,521	11
Green Bay, WI Metro Area	17,771	5.7	11,590	3.6	35,199	11.2	59,343	185	64,745	201	46,710	5,487	17
Greensboro-High Point, NC Metro Area	80,743	10.7	39,555	5.2	93,961	12.5	146,235	191	159,045	207	112,245	18,108	24
Greenville, NC Metro Area	19,292	10.9	8,454	4.7	22,494	12.8	29,002	161	31,560	175	20,510	5,687	32
Greenville-Anderson, SC Metro Area	96,871	11.1	39,914	4.4	124,311	14.2	179,943	199	196,870	217	135,970	17,989	20
Gulfport-Biloxi, MS Metro Area	58,948	14.8	10,727	2.6	67,056	16.8	79,059	190	89,535	215	57,090	11,794	28
Hagerstown-Martinsburg, MD-WV Metro Area	16,875	6.2	2,080	0.7	42,334	15.6	56,138	196	61,035	214	40,945	6,418	23
Hammond, LA Metro Area	14,494	11.2	2,495	1.9	25,980	20.0	22,489	168	24,405	182	14,100	5,069	38
Hanford-Corcoran, CA Metro Area	10,946	8.2	-	-	16,568	12.4	16,991	112	18,565	123	12,235	4,661	31
Harrisburg-Carlisle, PA Metro Area	34,005	6.1	12,980	2.3	69,204	12.4	116,344	203	122,060	212	88,260	11,408	20
Harrisonburg, VA Metro Area	16,466	12.5	4,756	3.5	14,835	11.3	22,746	168	24,270	179	17,650	1,890	14
Hartford-East Hartford-Middletown, CT Metro Area..	48,259	4.1	-	-	136,811	11.5	231,779	192	237,675	197	175,975	24,448	20
Hattiesburg, MS Metro Area	22,525	13.6	5,905	3.5	31,874	19.2	29,322	174	33,510	199	20,995	5,549	33
Hickory-Lenoir-Morganton, NC Metro Area	41,618	11.6	17,747	4.8	61,173	17.0	82,670	224	91,470	248	64,885	7,547	21
Hilton Head Island-Bluffton, SC Metro Area	24,821	12.3	9,821	4.5	27,608	13.6	55,195	254	57,000	262	45,640	2,568	12
Hinesville, GA Metro Area	9,555	13.0	1,645	2.0	10,631	14.5	8,660	108	10,515	131	6,025	1,543	19
Homosassa Springs, FL Metro Area	14,590	10.4	8,619	5.8	30,141	21.4	57,079	386	61,390	415	46,290	3,553	24
Hot Springs, AR Metro Area	10,831	11.2	3,001	3.0	19,870	20.5	28,340	286	30,635	309	20,870	3,846	39
Houma-Thibodaux, LA Metro Area	23,757	11.4	3,524	1.7	34,419	16.5	38,410	184	42,965	205	22,475	7,839	38
Houston-The Woodlands-Sugar Land, TX Metro Area	1,209,302	18.0	325,184	4.6	633,608	9.4	832,197	119	867,360	124	585,270	142,190	20
Huntington-Ashland, WV-KY-OH Metro Area	23,705	6.6	4,498	1.3	71,248	19.8	86,194	240	91,180	254	52,440	16,067	45
Huntsville, AL Metro Area	40,085	9.1	17,115	3.7	60,732	13.7	81,526	176	87,450	189	59,135	8,838	19
Idaho Falls, ID Metro Area	12,667	8.9	-	-	19,261	13.6	22,775	153	25,145	169	17,070	2,744	18
Indianapolis-Carmel-Anderson, IN Metro Area	175,036	8.8	51,460	2.5	246,371	12.4	329,069	161	357,685	175	244,780	37,048	18
Iowa City, IA Metro Area	9,860	5.9	2,569	1.5	12,819	7.7	24,507	141	25,155	145	18,705	2,082	12
Ithaca, NY Metro Area	3,740	3.7	-	-	9,285	9.1	16,442	160	16,625	162	12,340	1,456	14
Jackson, MI Metro Area	9,661	6.4	3,344	2.1	23,406	15.5	33,908	214	37,630	237	25,590	4,569	29
Jackson, MS Metro Area	63,879	10.9	18,045	3.0	74,966	12.8	107,078	179	119,100	199	77,515	21,515	36
Jackson, TN Metro Area	16,596	9.5	5,855	3.3	28,743	16.4	38,786	218	43,040	242	28,090	6,007	34
Jacksonville, FL Metro Area	160,962	11.1	79,912	5.2	193,831	13.4	278,360	181	297,885	194	208,075	33,690	22
Jacksonville, NC Metro Area	13,398	8.6	5,975	3.0	27,298	17.5	24,346	123	28,465	144	17,720	3,267	17
Janesville-Beloit, WI Metro Area	10,023	6.2	4,723	2.9	22,543	14.0	32,408	199	35,990	221	25,080	3,895	24
Jefferson City, MO Metro Area	13,271	9.3	3,375	2.2	18,301	12.8	28,979	191	32,875	217	22,180	2,530	17
Johnson City, TN Metro Area	19,684	9.9	6,180	3.0	39,095	19.7	48,956	242	53,495	264	34,675	5,732	28
Johnstown, PA Metro Area	6,094	4.6	3,103	2.4	24,029	18.3	36,068	274	38,905	295	25,395	4,772	36
Jonesboro, AR Metro Area	12,415	9.7	2,749	2.1	23,437	18.2	24,220	183	27,390	207	16,425	5,504	42
Joplin, MO Metro Area	22,877	13.0	5,539	3.1	25,318	14.4	35,079	196	38,650	216	25,045	4,526	25
Kahului-Wailuku-Lahaina, HI Metro Area	8,327	5.1	3,439	2.1	17,762	10.8	29,514	177	31,235	187	24,330	2,001	12
Kalamazoo-Portage, MI Metro Area	14,703	5.7	6,468	2.4	33,774	13.0	47,635	180	51,520	195	35,745	6,395	24
Kankakee, IL Metro Area	6,393	5.9	1,870	1.7	15,078	13.8	21,526	196	22,840	208	15,025	2,692	25
Kansas City, MO-KS Metro Area	190,346	9.1	70,976	3.3	254,802	12.2	360,063	168	377,470	176	267,005	33,713	16
Kennewick-Richland, WA Metro Area	27,888	9.9	-	-	37,042	13.2	44,579	151	47,205	159	32,825	5,735	19
Killeen-Temple, TX Metro Area	46,549	11.6	7,663	1.7	61,265	15.3	63,936	142	72,000	159	41,990	10,730	24
Kingsport-Bristol, TN-VA Metro Area	27,850	9.2	8,825	2.9	65,294	21.6	84,137	274	92,725	302	57,845	10,094	33
Kingston, NY Metro Area	10,239	5.9	-	-	24,210	13.8	39,991	224	42,145	236	29,810	4,075	23
Knoxville, TN Metro Area	74,514	8.9	28,817	3.4	125,108	15.0	185,833	216	200,290	233	135,020	21,008	24
Kokomo, IN Metro Area	6,273	7.7	1,315	1.6	14,301	17.6	19,419	236	21,530	261	14,870	2,249	27
La Crosse-Onalaska, WI-MN Metro Area	5,975	4.4	3,422	2.5	15,428	11.4	26,892	197	28,340	207	21,125	2,266	17
Lafayette, LA Metro Area	53,318	11.0	9,879	2.0	69,850	14.4	83,143	170	90,965	186	52,205	15,449	32
Lafayette-West Lafayette, IN Metro Area	20,118	9.0	4,277	1.9	26,243	11.7	32,441	141	35,240	153	24,630	2,775	12
Lake Charles, LA Metro Area	22,243	10.9	3,295	1.6	31,996	15.6	37,702	180	41,100	196	23,860	6,231	30
Lake Havasu City-Kingman, AZ Metro Area	21,042	10.4	6,227	3.0	45,731	22.5	64,270	307	69,740	333	52,520	4,602	22
Lakeland-Winter Haven, FL Metro Area	86,936	13.2	32,706	4.6	101,896	15.4	151,035	213	165,250	233	114,910	22,305	32
Lancaster, PA Metro Area	63,975	12.0	12,607	2.3	63,802	12.0	108,571	200	113,745	209	82,935	9,297	17
Lansing-East Lansing, MI Metro Area	29,723	5.5	11,938	2.2	75,340	13.9	100,469	183	110,965	202	76,995	12,085	22
Laredo, TX Metro Area	75,857	28.1	11,904	4.3	31,404	11.6	31,991	116	34,910	127	21,145	12,010	44
Las Cruces, NM Metro Area	23,944	11.3	5,591	2.6	29,042	13.7	39,585	182	42,740	197	28,835	8,267	38
Las Vegas-Henderson-Paradise, NV Metro Area	265,314	12.5	62,663	2.8	258,341	12.2	345,713	155	365,505	164	266,175	44,193	20
Lawrence, KS Metro Area	9,093	7.7	4,465	3.7	12,555	10.6	16,875	139	17,610	145	12,705	1,359	11
Lawton, OK Metro Area	15,267	13.2	3,343	2.6	22,101	19.1	19,739	156	22,400	178	13,525	3,362	27
Lebanon, PA Metro Area	12,919	9.4	2,655	1.9	18,058	13.2	31,323	222	33,255	235	24,585	2,586	18
Lewiston, ID-WA Metro Area	5,697	9.2	-	-	11,279	18.3	15,895	252	17,205	273	11,740	1,694	27
Lewiston-Auburn, ME Metro Area	8,840	8.3	3,529	3.3	17,430	16.4	24,387	227	26,250	244	16,965	4,177	39
Lexington-Fayette, KY Metro Area	34,939	7.0	10,586	2.0	65,927	13.2	83,248	161	88,070	170	59,955	11,300	22
Lima, OH Metro Area	6,807	6.7	1,075	1.0	15,701	15.5	21,762	212	22,930	223	15,185	2,977	29
Lincoln, NE Metro Area	23,335	7.2	12,717	3.8	34,415	10.7	51,852	155	52,605	157	38,550	5,125	15

- = Data not available for states that have their own healthcare marketplaces.

Table B-8. Health Insurance, Medicare, Social Security and Supplemental Security Income—*Continued*

Metropolitan Statistical Area Metropolitan Division	Persons with no health insurance, 2014-2018		Persons who enrolled in Affordable Health Care Act plans, 2019		Persons with a disability, 2014-2018		Medicare program enrollment, 2018		Social Security program (OASDI) beneficiaries, December 2018			Supplemental Security Income program recipients, December 2018	
	Number	Percent	Number	Percent	Number	Percent	Number	Rate per 1000 persons	Number	Rate per 1000 persons	Retired workers, number	Number	Rate per 1000 persons
Little Rock-North Little Rock-Conway, AR Metro Area	59,178	8.2	16,328	2.2	113,132	15.6	139,833	189	152,610	206	97,730	24,134	33
Logan, UT-ID Metro Area	10,368	7.7	8,778	6.2	12,305	9.1	15,708	112	16,835	120	12,070	1,012	7
Longview, TX Metro Area	49,013	17.7	11,112	3.9	40,291	14.6	55,071	193	59,960	210	38,470	8,760	31
Longview, WA Metro Area	6,074	5.8	-	-	21,713	20.9	25,755	236	28,005	257	18,700	3,914	36
Los Angeles-Long Beach-Anaheim, CA Metro Area	1,352,330	10.3	-	-	1,262,653	9.6	1,956,593	147	1,828,210	138	1,335,510	468,874	35
Anaheim-Santa Ana-Irvine, CA Div.	265,673	8.4	-	-	269,618	8.6	492,071	154	459,580	144	347,835	73,186	23
Los Angeles-Long Beach-Glendale, CA Div.	1,086,657	10.8	-	-	993,035	9.9	1,464,522	145	1,368,630	135	987,675	395,688	39
Louisville/Jefferson County, KY-IN Metro Area	72,328	5.9	25,475	2.0	175,116	14.2	237,905	188	253,440	200	169,090	32,933	26
Lubbock, TX Metro Area	42,412	13.7	8,091	2.5	43,818	14.2	47,319	148	49,685	156	32,920	6,715	21
Lynchburg, VA Metro Area	23,561	9.1	10,077	3.8	36,848	14.3	58,653	223	63,710	242	44,380	6,248	24
Macon-Bibb County, GA Metro Area	29,245	13.0	6,337	2.8	35,099	15.6	46,989	205	51,195	223	32,795	9,687	42
Madera, CA Metro Area	13,784	9.4	-	-	19,408	13.2	23,945	152	25,750	163	18,345	4,713	30
Madison, WI Metro Area	27,851	4.3	20,600	3.1	57,958	9.0	109,002	165	114,125	173	85,555	8,982	14
Manchester-Nashua, NH Metro Area	26,187	6.4	12,320	3.0	47,563	11.7	77,094	186	81,620	197	55,275	6,991	17
Manhattan, KS Metro Area	7,073	5.9	2,245	1.7	12,991	10.8	15,343	118	16,550	127	11,485	1,340	10
Mankato, MN Metro Area	3,533	3.6	-	-	10,339	10.4	16,853	166	17,570	173	12,865	1,325	13
Mansfield, OH Metro Area	9,058	7.9	2,019	1.7	18,516	16.1	27,833	230	29,515	244	20,000	3,515	29
McAllen-Edinburg-Mission, TX Metro Area	256,271	30.5	34,619	4.0	110,732	13.2	101,750	118	110,965	128	69,000	41,263	48
Medford, OR Metro Area	16,698	7.8	7,456	3.4	34,176	16.0	55,182	251	58,160	265	43,155	4,890	22
Memphis, TN-MS-AR Metro Area	150,546	11.4	39,063	2.9	170,905	12.9	221,334	165	241,820	180	157,085	45,330	34
Merced, CA Metro Area	23,145	8.7	-	-	36,206	13.6	35,367	129	38,490	140	25,395	10,949	40
Miami-Fort Lauderdale-Pompano Beach, FL Metro Area	960,517	16.0	801,102	12.9	656,645	10.9	1,089,022	176	1,078,480	174	804,260	231,366	37
Fort Lauderdale-Pompano Beach-Sunrise, FL Div.	277,323	14.6	242,609	12.4	208,108	11.0	315,183	162	325,960	167	240,200	45,513	23
Miami-Miami Beach-Kendall, FL Div.	487,884	18.1	422,183	15.3	272,374	10.1	457,926	166	430,415	156	313,510	162,011	59
West Palm Beach-Boca Raton-Boynton Beach, FL Div.	195,310	13.6	136,310	9.2	176,163	12.3	315,913	213	322,105	217	250,550	23,842	16
Michigan City-La Porte, IN Metro Area	8,901	8.7	2,552	2.3	14,194	13.8	22,688	206	25,220	229	17,200	2,199	20
Midland, MI Metro Area	3,954	4.8	2,121	2.5	11,275	13.6	17,687	213	19,715	237	13,600	1,504	18
Midland, TX Metro Area	29,154	17.3	3,827	2.1	15,856	9.4	19,341	109	19,895	112	13,225	2,042	12
Milwaukee-Waukesha, WI Metro Area	93,194	6.0	49,697	3.2	180,437	11.5	283,315	180	300,920	191	213,485	47,192	30
Minneapolis-St. Paul-Bloomington, MN Metro Area	158,856	4.5	4,520	0.1	346,041	9.8	561,436	155	573,200	159	423,455	60,674	17
Missoula, MT Metro Area	9,009	7.8	5,734	4.8	14,773	12.8	21,545	181	22,320	188	16,150	2,028	17
Mobile, AL Metro Area	49,044	11.6	17,411	4.0	61,310	14.4	86,822	202	97,125	226	59,025	15,592	36
Modesto, CA Metro Area	35,012	6.5	-	-	70,933	13.2	85,415	155	89,785	163	60,380	21,106	38
Monroe, LA Metro Area	22,414	11.3	4,021	2.0	26,617	13.4	39,405	195	42,530	210	25,885	9,675	48
Monroe, MI Metro Area	6,931	4.7	3,315	2.2	20,412	13.7	31,842	212	35,825	238	23,730	2,527	17
Montgomery, AL Metro Area	34,452	9.5	11,415	3.1	62,562	17.2	72,768	195	81,490	218	50,315	13,999	38
Morgantown, WV Metro Area	7,742	5.7	1,644	1.2	18,788	13.9	21,374	152	22,890	163	15,440	2,668	19
Morristown, TN Metro Area	14,617	10.6	4,514	3.2	27,739	20.1	34,014	240	38,005	268	23,970	4,515	32
Mount Vernon-Anacortes, WA Metro Area	9,415	7.7	-	-	18,353	15.0	30,272	236	31,270	244	23,335	2,369	19
Muncie, IN Metro Area	10,269	9.0	2,088	1.8	18,590	16.3	23,541	205	25,920	226	17,115	2,987	26
Muskegon, MI Metro Area	8,933	5.3	3,845	2.2	26,202	15.6	38,230	220	42,790	247	27,300	6,140	35
Myrtle Beach-Conway-North Myrtle Beach, SC-NC	59,090	13.3	30,220	6.3	75,273	16.9	137,640	286	150,455	313	115,310	8,156	17
Napa, CA Metro Area	9,015	6.5	-	-	16,313	11.8	28,982	208	27,500	197	20,710	2,116	15
Naples-Marco Island, FL Metro Area	59,734	16.5	33,814	8.9	41,329	11.4	96,286	254	96,650	255	78,075	4,182	11
Nashville-Davidson--Murfreesboro--Franklin, TN	178,465	9.8	65,940	3.5	217,617	11.9	290,766	153	313,505	165	218,605	30,290	16
New Bern, NC Metro Area	13,861	11.9	6,037	4.8	20,942	17.9	29,505	236	31,870	255	23,135	3,209	26
New Haven-Milford, CT Metro Area	44,329	5.2	-	-	97,095	11.4	162,961	190	166,945	195	120,335	20,825	24
New Orleans-Metairie, LA Metro Area	133,620	10.7	30,749	2.4	173,171	13.9	229,164	180	240,405	189	150,670	43,744	34
New York-Newark-Jersey City, NY-NJ-PA Metro Area	1,530,912	8.0	-	-	1,928,176	10.1	3,243,864	168	3,219,070	167	2,321,430	566,037	29
Nassau County-Suffolk County, NY Div.	144,309	5.1	-	-	253,889	9.0	548,935	193	559,390	197	403,645	36,190	13
Newark, NJ-PA Div.	199,910	9.3	58,237	2.7	217,521	10.2	358,678	165	364,260	168	265,320	46,482	21
New Brunswick-Lakewood, NJ Div.	157,515	6.7	74,513	3.1	241,205	10.3	461,160	194	471,550	198	352,010	31,705	13
New York-Jersey City-White Plains, NY-NJ Div.	1,029,178	8.7	67,496	0.6	1,215,561	10.3	1,875,091	158	1,823,870	153	1,300,455	451,660	38
Niles, MI Metro Area	12,004	7.8	4,441	2.9	22,803	14.8	35,252	229	37,950	246	26,840	4,550	30
North Port-Sarasota-Bradenton, FL Metro Area	93,640	12.0	47,923	5.8	115,657	14.8	236,218	288	243,950	297	193,375	10,576	13
Norwich-New London, CT Metro Area	10,953	4.3	-	-	33,086	12.9	54,551	205	56,960	214	40,905	4,506	17
Ocala, FL Metro Area	41,833	12.3	22,114	6.1	61,566	18.1	111,658	310	119,765	333	89,645	10,243	29
Ocean City, NJ Metro Area	5,510	6.0	3,817	4.1	12,960	14.1	27,134	293	28,810	311	22,035	1,697	18
Odessa, TX Metro Area	33,722	21.5	3,675	2.3	18,405	11.7	19,125	118	20,585	127	12,340	3,309	20
Ogden-Clearfield, UT Metro Area	48,698	7.5	31,657	4.7	66,797	10.3	83,658	124	86,600	128	59,920	6,675	10
Oklahoma City, OK Metro Area	172,118	12.8	56,384	4.0	186,234	13.8	222,512	159	239,780	172	163,555	27,379	20
Olympia-Lacey-Tumwater, WA Metro Area	14,937	5.6	-	-	34,776	13.0	58,057	203	61,460	215	43,630	5,381	19
Omaha-Council Bluffs, NE-IA Metro Area	73,104	8.0	29,136	3.1	98,896	10.9	148,714	158	153,240	163	108,035	15,034	16
Orlando-Kissimmee-Sanford, FL Metro Area	328,958	13.5	242,350	9.4	291,983	12.0	417,333	162	451,700	176	314,030	60,642	24
Oshkosh-Neenah, WI Metro Area	7,815	4.7	5,735	3.4	19,557	11.9	32,120	188	35,255	206	25,460	2,619	15
Owensboro, KY Metro Area	5,349	4.6	2,785	2.3	18,518	16.0	25,766	216	28,525	240	17,925	4,004	34
Oxnard-Thousand Oaks-Ventura, CA Metro Area	78,474	9.3	-	-	92,104	10.9	145,406	171	142,335	167	106,090	16,027	19
Palm Bay-Melbourne-Titusville, FL Metro Area	61,594	10.8	34,500	5.8	89,462	15.6	151,030	253	162,670	273	118,220	11,972	20

- = Data not available for states that have their own healthcare marketplaces.

Table B-8. Health Insurance, Medicare, Social Security and Supplemental Security Income—*Continued*

Metropolitan Statistical Area / Metropolitan Division	Persons with no health insurance, 2014-2018		Persons who enrolled in Affordable Health Care Act plans, 2019		Persons with a disability, 2014-2018		Medicare program enrollment, 2018		Social Security program (OASDI) beneficiaries, December 2018			Supplemental Security Income program recipients, December 2018	
	Number	Percent	Number	Percent	Number	Percent	Number	Rate per 1000 persons	Number	Rate per 1000 persons	Retired workers, number	Number	Rate per 1000 persons
Panama City, FL Metro Area	25,251	14.2	11,799	6.4	34,610	19.5	37,364	202	41,420	224	28,080	4,573	25
Parkersburg-Vienna, WV Metro Area	5,833	6.4	1,072	1.2	17,212	19.0	23,118	257	25,115	279	15,180	3,679	41
Pensacola-Ferry Pass-Brent, FL Metro Area	46,391	10.1	21,514	4.3	70,029	15.3	102,414	207	111,400	225	74,020	12,773	26
Peoria, IL Metro Area	19,572	4.9	7,880	2.0	48,171	12.0	83,260	207	89,475	222	64,070	8,116	20
Philadelphia-Camden-Wilmington, PA-NJ-DE-MD													
Me...	368,772	6.2	-	-	752,626	12.6	1,113,630	183	1,144,740	188	793,060	178,708	29
Camden, NJ Div	70,922	5.8	30,773	2.5	155,428	12.7	236,007	190	249,270	200	171,735	27,237	22
Montgomery County-Bucks County-Chester County,	87,789	4.5	75,461	3.8	193,210	10.0	384,742	194	388,310	196	289,575	19,723	10
Philadelphia, PA Div	172,304	8.1	73,468	3.4	320,902	15.2	361,814	168	368,030	171	235,095	118,030	55
Wilmington, DE-MD-NJ Div	37,757	5.3	-	-	83,086	11.7	131,067	181	139,130	192	96,655	13,718	19
Phoenix-Mesa-Chandler, AZ Metro Area	503,182	10.9	104,167	2.1	529,005	11.5	749,821	154	796,845	164	586,540	66,710	14
Pine Bluff, AR Metro Area	6,297	7.6	1,462	1.6	15,593	18.8	19,694	220	21,330	238	12,275	4,962	55
Pittsburgh, PA Metro Area	98,217	4.2	61,739	2.7	330,956	14.3	535,457	230	565,345	243	391,780	62,648	27
Pittsfield, MA Metro Area	3,696	3.0	-	-	19,657	15.7	34,062	270	34,670	274	23,855	3,916	31
Pocatello, ID Metro Area	8,686	9.5	-	-	14,956	16.3	16,073	169	16,910	178	11,090	2,094	22
Portland-South Portland, ME Metro Area	35,302	6.7	29,267	5.5	66,187	12.6	121,528	227	123,500	231	88,495	9,642	18
Portland-Vancouver-Hillsboro, OR-WA Metro Area...	157,533	6.6	75,152	3.0	289,207	12.0	411,295	166	418,265	169	308,410	44,901	18
Port St. Lucie, FL Metro Area	60,355	13.2	37,682	7.8	70,976	15.5	121,152	251	129,135	268	97,830	8,569	18
Poughkeepsie-Newburgh-Middletown, NY Metro Area	33,781	5.2	-	-	81,516	12.4	120,919	179	128,385	190	88,240	12,016	18
Prescott Valley-Prescott, AZ Metro Area	23,157	10.4	9,429	4.1	40,778	18.3	78,514	338	82,175	354	65,185	3,607	16
Providence-Warwick, RI-MA Metro Area	70,298	4.4	-	-	219,968	13.8	335,109	207	348,550	215	236,630	51,578	32
Provo-Orem, UT Metro Area	51,676	8.6	47,239	7.5	46,241	7.7	55,245	87	59,435	94	39,300	4,341	7
Pueblo, CO Metro Area	11,231	7.0	-	-	30,797	19.1	37,538	224	37,810	226	24,480	6,154	37
Punta Gorda, FL Metro Area	19,557	11.3	9,700	5.2	38,010	21.9	66,343	359	69,995	378	55,465	2,794	15
Racine, WI Metro Area	10,558	5.5	5,559	2.8	24,762	13.0	39,354	200	43,280	220	29,685	5,690	29
Raleigh-Cary, NC Metro Area	122,482	9.5	64,551	4.7	125,152	9.7	182,794	134	193,745	142	139,260	16,929	12
Rapid City, SD Metro Area	14,639	11.0	4,156	3.0	18,086	13.6	30,221	216	32,150	230	24,075	2,207	16
Reading, PA Metro Area	27,705	6.7	10,754	2.6	55,721	13.5	83,212	198	88,220	210	62,810	10,748	26
Redding, CA Metro Area	13,266	7.5	-	-	31,671	17.8	47,041	261	49,225	273	33,120	9,507	53
Reno, NV Metro Area	45,993	10.2	12,741	2.7	55,225	12.2	86,699	185	88,680	189	67,465	7,024	15
Richmond, VA Metro Area	108,655	8.8	50,523	3.9	151,817	12.3	225,959	176	240,905	188	172,675	27,144	21
Riverside-San Bernardino-Ontario, CA Metro Area ...	432,652	9.7	-	-	497,634	11.2	654,090	142	687,340	149	480,040	133,516	29
Roanoke, VA Metro Area	26,564	8.6	11,949	3.8	42,168	13.6	74,742	238	77,485	247	53,410	8,442	27
Rochester, MN Metro Area	9,738	4.6	-	-	22,062	10.3	39,522	180	41,075	187	31,405	2,777	13
Rochester, NY Metro Area	45,761	4.3	-	-	144,412	13.6	228,837	214	243,675	228	171,590	32,556	30
Rockford, IL Metro Area	21,907	6.5	8,374	2.5	45,590	13.6	67,311	199	72,225	214	49,820	8,046	24
Rocky Mount, NC Metro Area	15,305	10.5	5,202	3.6	23,996	16.5	32,746	224	36,045	247	24,110	6,267	43
Rome, GA Metro Area	13,028	13.8	3,313	3.4	14,534	15.3	20,266	207	22,595	231	14,820	3,305	34
Sacramento-Roseville-Folsom, CA Metro Area	134,416	5.9	-	-	266,412	11.7	407,955	174	403,655	172	286,915	79,481	34
Saginaw, MI Metro Area	9,964	5.3	4,119	2.2	31,394	16.6	44,841	235	49,690	260	32,065	8,456	44
St. Cloud, MN Metro Area	7,229	3.7	-	-	21,592	11.1	34,030	170	35,695	179	25,615	2,806	14
St. George, UT Metro Area	22,299	14.0	15,196	8.9	20,634	13.0	36,629	213	38,505	224	29,915	1,479	9
St. Joseph, MO-KS Metro Area	11,342	9.5	2,842	2.2	18,880	15.7	24,532	194	26,600	210	17,830	2,765	22
St. Louis, MO-IL Metro Area	193,018	7.0	102,066	3.6	351,991	12.7	534,222	190	564,635	201	388,070	57,409	21
Salem, OR Metro Area	33,086	8.1	10,875	2.5	60,767	14.8	80,805	187	85,860	199	62,590	9,169	21
Salinas, CA Metro Area	46,650	11.2	-	-	37,176	8.9	63,345	145	63,980	147	46,480	8,280	19
Salisbury, MD-DE Metro Area	26,790	6.9	6,588	1.6	52,948	13.6	106,508	260	113,465	277	87,630	7,877	19
Salt Lake City, UT Metro Area	130,303	11.1	68,466	5.6	111,131	9.4	145,587	119	151,295	124	105,730	14,202	12
San Angelo, TX Metro Area	17,440	15.1	3,707	3.1	16,067	13.9	21,875	181	23,290	192	16,210	2,885	24
San Antonio-New Braunfels, TX Metro Area	349,304	14.6	82,135	3.3	331,714	13.9	384,580	153	409,130	163	267,050	59,436	24
San Diego-Chula Vista-Carlsbad, CA Metro Area	279,602	8.7	-	-	314,897	9.8	517,013	155	506,500	152	371,270	82,195	25
San Francisco-Oakland-Berkeley, CA Metro Area .	232,541	5.0	-	-	457,048	9.8	759,895	161	696,970	147	525,730	128,782	27
Oakland-Berkeley-Livermore, CA Div	148,100	5.4	-	-	279,876	10.1	432,033	153	404,435	144	297,305	74,470	26
San Francisco-San Mateo-Redwood City, CA Div..	74,189	4.6	-	-	154,361	9.5	270,172	164	239,825	145	186,260	51,111	31
San Rafael, CA Div	10,252	4.0	-	-	22,811	8.9	57,690	222	52,710	203	42,165	3,201	12
San Jose-Sunnyvale-Santa Clara, CA Metro Area	96,092	4.9	-	-	157,341	8.0	272,118	136	244,710	122	184,015	44,905	23
San Luis Obispo-Paso Robles, CA Metro Area	20,715	7.5	-	-	31,615	11.5	61,978	218	60,800	214	47,035	4,416	16
Santa Cruz-Watsonville, CA Metro Area	17,004	6.2	-	-	30,314	11.1	48,749	178	47,750	174	35,985	5,517	20
Santa Fe, NM Metro Area	18,046	12.3	5,968	4.0	18,933	12.9	38,016	253	38,755	258	29,625	2,558	17
Santa Maria-Santa Barbara, CA Metro Area	46,478	10.6	-	-	43,333	9.9	74,689	167	73,785	165	54,775	8,553	19
Santa Rosa-Petaluma, CA Metro Area	34,386	6.9	-	-	60,313	12.1	103,045	206	100,180	200	76,445	8,815	18
Savannah, GA Metro Area	50,160	13.5	15,754	4.0	50,502	13.6	62,943	162	68,860	177	47,370	8,395	22
Scranton--Wilkes-Barre, PA Metro Area	28,669	5.3	15,289	2.8	84,520	15.5	131,593	237	140,655	253	95,625	17,544	32
Seattle-Tacoma-Bellevue, WA Metro Area..........	228,735	6.1	-	-	407,856	10.8	581,554	148	574,680	146	416,120	68,279	17
Seattle-Bellevue-Kent, WA Div	172,231	5.9	-	-	295,544	10.1	434,229	143	420,310	138	311,480	48,775	16
Tacoma-Lakewood, WA Div	56,504	6.7	-	-	112,312	13.4	147,325	165	154,370	173	104,640	19,504	22
Sebastian-Vero Beach, FL Metro Area	18,074	12.1	11,692	7.4	24,865	16.6	50,689	322	53,135	338	41,225	2,574	16
Sebring-Avon Park, FL Metro Area	12,786	12.7	5,521	5.2	20,634	20.4	32,509	308	34,855	331	26,490	2,873	27
Sheboygan, WI Metro Area	5,124	4.5	4,345	3.8	11,806	10.5	24,096	209	26,370	228	19,590	1,739	15
Sherman-Denison, TX Metro Area	21,458	16.9	4,348	3.2	21,177	16.7	27,388	204	28,785	215	19,905	2,997	22

- = Data not available for states that have their own healthcare marketplaces.

Table B-8. Health Insurance, Medicare, Social Security and Supplemental Security Income—*Continued*

Metropolitan Statistical Area Metropolitan Division	Persons with no health insurance, 2014-2018		Persons who enrolled in Affordable Health Care Act plans, 2019		Persons with a disability, 2014-2018		Medicare program enrollment, 2018		Social Security program (OASDI) beneficiaries, December 2018			Supplemental Security Income program recipients, December 2018	
	Number	Percent	Number	Percent	Number	Percent	Number	Rate per 1000 persons	Number	Rate per 1000 persons	Retired workers, number	Number	Rate per 1000 persons
Shreveport-Bossier City, LA Metro Area	38,680	9.9	6,794	1.7	56,249	14.4	75,510	190	79,980	201	50,440	18,374	46
Sierra Vista-Douglas, AZ Metro Area	9,568	8.2	2,615	2.1	19,874	17.1	31,364	247	33,555	265	24,225	3,144	25
Sioux City, IA-NE-SD Metro Area	11,086	7.8	2,843	2.0	17,048	12.0	25,787	179	27,715	193	19,620	2,369	17
Sioux Falls, SD Metro Area	17,044	6.8	7,156	2.7	24,720	9.8	45,187	170	47,335	178	35,245	3,376	13
South Bend-Mishawaka, IN-MI Metro Area	28,016	8.8	7,363	2.3	45,520	14.3	61,259	190	65,850	204	46,870	6,670	21
Spartanburg, SC Metro Area	32,538	10.9	11,772	3.8	44,894	15.1	63,581	203	69,760	222	46,085	7,170	23
Spokane-Spokane Valley, WA Metro Area	30,870	5.8	-	-	81,375	15.3	114,553	205	119,590	214	81,705	15,935	29
Springfield, IL Metro Area	8,593	4.1	3,914	1.9	28,822	13.9	42,688	206	45,915	221	32,845	4,696	23
Springfield, MA Metro Area	19,329	2.8	-	-	101,581	14.6	151,543	216	152,095	216	96,985	35,499	51
Springfield, MO Metro Area	49,723	11.0	20,412	4.4	67,596	14.9	92,272	198	98,320	211	66,005	9,797	21
Springfield, OH Metro Area	9,126	6.8	1,685	1.3	22,560	16.9	30,420	226	31,420	234	20,950	4,010	30
State College, PA Metro Area	8,550	5.5	2,955	1.8	15,018	9.6	23,921	147	25,100	154	18,890	1,407	9
Staunton, VA Metro Area	11,605	10.0	4,385	3.6	16,155	13.9	29,172	237	31,385	255	22,455	2,186	18
Stockton, CA Metro Area	53,972	7.5	-	-	89,397	12.4	109,424	145	113,525	151	77,155	28,104	37
Sumter, SC Metro Area	16,268	12.0	5,174	3.7	27,852	20.6	30,161	215	33,905	242	21,875	5,589	40
Syracuse, NY Metro Area	28,126	4.3	-	-	85,009	13.1	131,751	203	142,150	219	98,660	18,835	29
Tallahassee, FL Metro Area	33,170	9.0	18,739	4.9	47,560	12.9	62,955	164	68,220	177	49,725	10,056	26
Tampa-St. Petersburg-Clearwater, FL Metro Area	369,151	12.3	181,037	5.8	419,005	14.0	654,788	208	696,390	222	495,075	79,424	25
Terre Haute, IN Metro Area	15,779	8.8	3,415	1.8	32,926	18.4	39,117	210	43,050	231	28,550	4,842	26
Texarkana, TX-AR Metro Area	18,191	12.7	4,043	2.7	22,276	15.6	30,871	206	33,215	221	20,490	6,405	43
The Villages, FL Metro Area	6,881	6.2	4,588	3.6	21,913	19.6	71,185	553	71,555	556	62,540	1,632	13
Toledo, OH Metro Area	35,888	5.6	11,009	1.7	91,955	14.4	127,903	199	131,050	204	86,985	19,714	31
Topeka, KS Metro Area	17,623	7.7	5,741	2.5	33,005	14.4	50,261	216	52,475	226	36,280	5,558	24
Trenton-Princeton, NJ Metro Area	29,869	8.2	8,517	2.3	37,624	10.4	64,799	175	65,785	178	46,950	9,673	26
Tucson, AZ Metro Area	98,533	9.9	24,018	2.3	151,924	15.2	219,714	212	227,300	219	166,220	20,828	20
Tulsa, OK Metro Area	131,357	13.5	40,474	4.1	142,159	14.6	179,706	181	194,095	195	130,770	22,098	22
Tuscaloosa, AL Metro Area	19,261	7.8	6,566	2.6	34,412	14.0	46,907	186	52,700	209	30,815	8,846	35
Twin Falls, ID Metro Area	14,264	13.5	-	-	13,897	13.1	19,109	174	20,945	190	14,820	2,222	20
Tyler, TX Metro Area	38,284	17.2	9,368	4.1	29,973	13.5	44,090	192	46,250	201	31,925	5,467	24
Urban Honolulu, HI Metro Area	33,533	3.6	11,460	1.2	102,164	10.9	179,590	183	178,155	182	140,075	15,211	16
Utica-Rome, NY Metro Area	13,027	4.6	-	-	42,455	14.9	66,778	229	71,760	246	48,730	9,555	33
Valdosta, GA Metro Area	23,053	16.6	3,354	2.3	17,914	12.9	23,430	160	26,395	181	16,735	5,290	36
Vallejo, CA Metro Area	23,696	5.6	-	-	52,805	12.4	77,466	174	79,705	179	56,240	11,635	26
Victoria, TX Metro Area	15,199	15.4	2,813	2.8	14,928	15.2	18,765	188	19,975	201	13,090	2,646	27
Vineland-Bridgeton, NJ Metro Area	14,821	10.4	2,251	1.5	19,878	14.0	28,080	186	30,995	205	20,005	5,918	39
Virginia Beach-Norfolk-Newport News, VA-NC Metro Area	151,350	9.1	55,569	3.1	213,334	12.8	300,541	170	320,610	182	223,440	35,714	20
Visalia, CA Metro Area	44,779	9.8	-	-	55,228	12.1	61,354	132	66,085	142	44,575	18,732	40
Waco, TX Metro Area	39,465	15.2	5,340	2.0	36,096	13.9	46,354	171	49,415	182	32,515	7,982	29
Walla Walla, WA Metro Area	4,603	8.1	-	-	8,699	15.2	12,846	211	13,265	218	9,735	1,397	23
Warner Robins, GA Metro Area	21,088	12.0	4,905	2.7	24,335	13.9	29,839	163	32,300	177	21,075	4,849	27
Washington-Arlington-Alexandria, DC-VA-MD-WV Metro Area	486,015	8.0	-	-	524,830	8.6	837,971	134	785,149	125	584,128	88,102	14
Frederick-Gaithersburg-Rockville, MD Div.	88,261	6.9	-	-	109,731	8.6	200,886	154	182,320	139	139,160	16,385	13
Washington-Arlington-Alexandria, DC-VA-MD-WV Div.	397,754	8.3	-	-	415,099	8.6	637,085	129	602,829	122	444,968	71,717	15
Waterloo-Cedar Falls, IA Metro Area	8,481	5.0	2,046	1.2	18,783	11.2	33,632	198	36,085	213	25,720	3,518	21
Watertown-Fort Drum, NY Metro Area	6,105	6.0	-	-	14,598	14.2	19,859	178	22,240	199	14,765	2,652	24
Wausau-Weston, WI Metro Area	9,012	5.6	6,709	4.1	19,013	11.8	34,189	210	37,160	228	27,560	2,428	15
Weirton-Steubenville, WV-OH Metro Area	7,038	6.0	1,579	1.3	20,802	17.6	30,293	259	32,860	281	20,680	3,899	33
Wenatchee, WA Metro Area	10,951	9.4	-	-	18,414	15.8	24,787	207	25,960	216	19,800	1,929	16
Wheeling, WV-OH Metro Area	8,551	6.2	1,766	1.3	22,484	16.3	33,982	243	36,240	259	24,485	4,118	29
Wichita, KS Metro Area	65,501	10.4	18,180	2.9	80,770	12.9	110,595	174	120,290	189	83,615	12,679	20
Wichita Falls, TX Metro Area	18,574	13.7	4,304	2.8	22,796	16.8	28,309	187	30,560	202	19,700	4,351	29
Williamsport, PA Metro Area	6,612	5.9	2,592	2.3	17,383	15.6	26,306	231	28,645	252	20,255	3,222	28
Wilmington, NC Metro Area	29,142	10.4	18,442	6.3	37,629	13.5	57,027	194	61,085	208	44,475	5,214	18
Winchester, VA-WV Metro Area	14,613	10.9	4,126	3.0	19,597	14.6	27,279	195	29,275	209	21,215	2,337	17
Winston-Salem, NC Metro Area	74,014	11.3	31,783	4.7	83,707	12.8	135,805	202	147,600	220	104,890	14,201	21
Worcester, MA-CT Metro Area	24,891	2.7	-	-	112,789	12.2	176,353	186	179,225	189	120,090	24,837	26
Yakima, WA Metro Area	33,366	13.5	-	-	32,017	13.0	41,881	167	44,805	178	31,070	7,180	29
York-Hanover, PA Metro Area	24,793	5.6	11,131	2.5	59,799	13.6	90,732	202	97,620	218	70,125	8,302	19
Youngstown-Warren-Boardman, OH-PA Metro Area	33,485	6.3	9,248	1.7	82,471	15.5	134,944	250	142,795	265	94,130	18,821	35
Yuba City, CA Metro Area	14,964	8.9	-	-	24,604	14.6	29,408	168	31,340	179	19,930	7,825	45
Yuma, AZ Metro Area	26,772	13.3	3,517	1.7	24,108	12.0	34,532	163	38,745	183	27,365	4,683	22

- = Data not available for states that have their own healthcare marketplaces.

Table B-9. Housing Units and Building Permits

Metropolitan Statistical Area Metropolitan Division	Housing units 2018 (July 1 estimate)	2010 (July 1 estimate)	2000 (July 1 estimate)	Change 2010-2018 Number	Percent	Units per square mile of land area, 2018	New private housing units authorized by building permits, 2019 Number of units	Percent single family	Percent in structures with 5 or more units	Total value ($1000)
Abilene, TX Metro Area	71,930	69,748	65,395	2,182	3.1	26.2	350	95.4	0.0	70,888
Akron, OH Metro Area	315,499	312,633	291,804	2,866	0.9	350.6	521	99.6	0.0	268,779
Albany, GA Metro Area	65,547	64,509	62,170	1,038	1.6	41.2	363	39.4	60.6	49,396
Albany-Lebanon, OR Metro Area	50,883	48,870	42,661	2,013	4.1	22.2	634	60.6	39.4	112,408
Albany-Schenectady-Troy, NY Metro Area	410,490	393,605	364,471	16,885	4.3	146.0	1924	58.3	37.2	390,547
Albuquerque, NM Metro Area	392,050	375,161	307,455	16,889	4.5	42.2	2148	87.2	12.2	471,634
Alexandria, LA Metro Area	67,818	64,673	60,558	3,145	4.9	34.5	174	100.0	0.0	43,745
Allentown-Bethlehem-Easton, PA-NJ Metro Area	350,522	342,593	308,188	7,929	2.3	241.2	516	63.8	35.1	103,752
Altoona, PA Metro Area	56,945	56,304	55,077	641	1.1	108.3	13	100.0	0.0	1,547
Amarillo, TX Metro Area	109,989	103,513	92,624	6,476	6.3	21.4	472	94.5	0.0	111,563
Ames, IA Metro Area	52,800	48,567	41,681	4,233	8.7	46.2	341	19.4	79.8	41,906
Anchorage, AK Metro Area	160,226	154,498	104,318	5,728	3.7	6.1	1177	74.7	19.1	319,958
Ann Arbor, MI Metro Area	151,550	147,646	131,863	3,904	2.6	214.7	466	71.0	26.4	107,126
Anniston-Oxford, AL Metro Area	53,888	53,331	51,309	557	1.0	88.9	72	100.0	0.0	7,575
Appleton, WI Metro Area	98,527	92,938	78,841	5,589	6.0	103.1	405	83.5	8.1	110,065
Asheville, NC Metro Area	231,269	213,881	176,319	17,388	8.1	113.8	2678	73.8	26.2	641,158
Athens-Clarke County, GA Metro Area	86,439	81,776	67,872	4,663	5.7	84.3	1523	49.4	41.6	256,138
Atlanta-Sandy Springs-Alpharetta, GA	2,330,253	2,173,913	1,666,401	156,340	7.2	268.3	32729	79.9	19.6	6,774,312
Atlantic City-Hammonton, NJ Metro Area	128,409	126,776	114,431	1,633	1.3	231.0	956	38.0	61.2	147,622
Auburn-Opelika, AL Metro Area	70,369	62,722	50,508	7,647	12.2	115.7	2091	54.0	40.2	481,437
Augusta-Richmond County, GA-SC Metro	260,909	242,202	209,903	18,707	7.7	75.0	3145	82.6	12.8	564,490
Austin-Round Rock-Georgetown, TX Metro Area	853,701	708,577	502,748	145,124	20.5	202.2	32025	56.7	42.3	5,802,080
Bakersfield, CA Metro Area	300,377	284,767	232,436	15,610	5.5	36.9	1791	95.2	3.2	460,036
Baltimore-Columbia-Towson, MD Metro	1,164,130	1,132,766	1,050,614	31,364	2.8	447.4	6963	68.9	29.7	1,357,875
Bangor, ME Metro Area	76,136	73,937	66,999	2,199	3.0	22.4	163	69.3	0.0	30,768
Barnstable Town, MA Metro Area	164,321	160,372	147,569	3,949	2.5	417.1	59	94.9	0.0	27,292
Baton Rouge, LA Metro Area	368,882	340,862	293,107	28,020	8.2	84.5	3589	99.4	0.3	753,467
Battle Creek, MI Metro Area	60,864	61,023	58,824	-159	-0.3	86.2	3	100.0	0.0	629
Bay City, MI Metro Area	48,336	48,216	46,496	120	0.2	109.4	13	100.0	0.0	3,291
Beaumont-Port Arthur, TX Metro Area	171,510	162,803	156,951	8,707	5.3	81.6	607	99.0	0.0	128,191
Beckley, WV Metro Area	57,690	57,598	57,319	92	0.2	45.5	72	100.0	0.0	10,533
Bellingham, WA Metro Area	97,855	90,775	74,335	7,080	7.8	46.4	1752	44.5	50.9	332,552
Bend, OR Metro Area	91,041	80,233	55,131	10,808	13.5	30.2	2028	73.4	22.6	450,418
Billings, MT Metro Area	83,843	75,408	64,256	8,435	11.2	12.9	380	81.1	0.0	93,735
Binghamton, NY Metro Area	113,834	112,803	110,305	1,031	0.9	93.0	0	-	-	0
Birmingham-Hoover, AL Metro Area	488,586	469,503	423,274	19,083	4.1	108.8	3019	95.5	3.6	787,965
Bismarck, ND Metro Area	59,393	48,889	40,645	10,504	21.5	13.9	609	59.9	34.8	117,841
Blacksburg-Christiansburg, VA Metro	72,872	70,623	62,912	2,249	3.2	67.9	174	25.9	74.1	27,663
Bloomington, IL Metro Area	72,680	69,761	60,176	2,919	4.2	61.4	152	50.7	42.8	16,092
Bloomington, IN Metro Area	72,279	69,251	60,912	3,028	4.4	92.7	623	39.6	56.5	109,387
Bloomsburg-Berwick, PA Metro Area	38,557	37,507	35,405	1,050	2.8	62.9	123	76.4	7.3	27,689
Boise City, ID Metro Area	282,300	246,511	182,764	35,789	14.5	24.0	10659	71.2	25.9	2,073,996
Boston-Cambridge-Newton, MA-NH Metro	1,973,298	1,884,401	1,754,936	88,897	4.7	566.1	14777	29.3	64.9	2,832,416
Boston, MA Div	830,457	786,699	730,598	43,758	5.6	746.1	-	-	-	-
Cambridge-Newton-Framingham, MA Div	955,356	919,134	865,154	36,222	3.9	729.3	-	-	-	-
Rockingham County-Strafford County, Div	187,485	178,568	159,184	8,917	5.0	176.4	-	-	-	-
Boulder, CO Metro Area	137,435	127,149	112,068	10,286	8.1	189.3	1564	42.1	57.9	396,148
Bowling Green, KY Metro Area	76,043	68,964	58,620	7,079	10.3	47.1	745	77.4	12.6	151,708
Bremerton-Silverdale-Port Orchard, WA Metro Area	113,733	107,500	93,010	6,233	5.8	287.9	1117	83.3	15.4	303,274
Bridgeport-Stamford-Norwalk, CT Metro Area	374,481	361,481	340,078	13,000	3.6	599.2	2326	26.9	70.6	813,410
Brownsville-Harlingen, TX Metro Area	152,353	142,175	120,234	10,178	7.2	170.8	997	98.1	0.8	101,274
Brunswick, GA Metro Area	61,279	58,097	45,185	3,182	5.5	47.4	423	97.6	0.0	129,242
Buffalo-Cheektowaga, NY Metro Area	530,328	519,412	511,881	10,916	2.1	338.9	1721	54.6	42.8	411,721
Burlington, NC Metro Area	71,660	66,691	55,721	4,969	7.5	169.4	640	89.7	10.3	110,179
Burlington-South Burlington, VT Metro Area	98,398	92,508	82,989	5,890	6.4	78.5	509	49.3	42.2	99,043
California-Lexington Park, MD Metro	46,013	41,377	34,336	4,636	11.2	128.2	689	89.3	9.6	148,732
Canton-Massillon, OH Metro Area	180,617	178,924	170,237	1,693	0.9	186.2	558	73.8	19.7	115,821
Cape Coral-Fort Myers, FL Metro Area	399,729	371,257	247,782	28,472	7.7	511.8	9100	61.8	32.4	1,724,071
Cape Girardeau, MO-IL Metro Area	44,073	42,533	39,679	1,540	3.6	30.8	1	100.0	0.0	40
Carbondale-Marion, IL Metro Area	66,048	64,617	59,727	1,431	2.2	49.0	-	-	-	-
Carson City, NV Metro Area	24,026	23,537	21,369	489	2.1	165.7	248	69.4	29.4	53,457
Casper, WY Metro Area	37,181	33,905	29,952	3,276	9.7	7.0	180	82.8	0.0	36,184
Cedar Rapids, IA Metro Area	118,215	112,516	99,271	5,699	5.1	58.8	610	56.9	30.2	85,494
Chambersburg-Waynesboro, PA Metro Area	65,791	63,337	54,022	2,454	3.9	85.2	389	85.3	14.1	74,870
Champaign-Urbana, IL Metro Area	100,829	94,930	82,380	5,899	6.2	70.3	878	11.7	87.9	126,311
Charleston, WV Metro Area	131,510	131,446	132,388	64	0.0	49.7	168	88.7	6.0	15,574
Charleston-North Charleston, SC Metro Area	339,494	299,173	234,443	40,321	13.5	131.1	6754	70.6	29.0	1,413,327
Charlotte-Concord-Gastonia, NC-SC Metro Area	1,060,922	949,584	724,317	111,338	11.7	189.6	23293	64.4	35.0	4,761,217
Charlottesville, VA Metro Area	96,429	89,263	74,168	7,166	8.0	58.6	1028	68.5	30.9	247,358
Chattanooga, TN-GA Metro Area	246,062	234,608	206,170	11,454	4.9	117.8	2273	67.3	27.1	399,142
Cheyenne, WY Metro Area	43,894	40,558	34,317	3,336	8.2	16.3	429	89.3	5.1	80,200
Chicago-Naperville-Elgin, IL-IN-WI Metro Area	3,858,431	3,797,174	3,471,602	61,257	1.6	536.3	18021	42.1	51.6	3,349,614
Chicago-Naperville-Evanston, IL Div	2,946,802	2,909,629	2,720,412	37,173	1.3	941.5	-	-	-	-
Elgin, IL Div	272,919	263,647	193,493	9,272	3.5	185.5	-	-	-	-

Table B-9. Housing Units and Building Permits—*Continued*

Metropolitan Statistical Area Metropolitan Division	2018 (July 1 estimate)	2010 (July 1 estimate)	2000 (July 1 estimate)	Change 2010-2018 Number	Change 2010-2018 Percent	Units per square mile of land area, 2018	Number of units	Percent single family	Percent in structures with 5 or more units	Total value ($1000)
Gary, IN Div	302,903	294,266	270,298	8,637	2.9	161.3	-	-	-	-
Lake County-Kenosha County, IL-WI Div	335,807	329,632	287,399	6,175	1.9	469.0	-	-	-	-
Chico, CA Metro Area	100,033	95,923	85,759	4,110	4.3	61.1	894	39.5	52.7	135,499
Cincinnati, OH-KY-IN Metro Area	946,883	921,114	838,863	25,769	2.8	208.3	6050	73.6	25.1	1,350,044
Clarksville, TN-KY Metro Area	127,462	114,485	92,590	12,977	11.3	59.1	2273	80.8	13.2	311,478
Cleveland, TN Metro Area	53,208	49,445	44,347	3,763	7.6	69.7	498	71.1	15.7	72,686
Cleveland-Elyria, OH Metro Area	963,468	955,826	912,850	7,642	0.8	482.0	2980	84.6	10.0	762,553
Coeur d'Alene, ID Metro Area	72,499	63,376	46,939	9,123	14.4	58.6	2373	60.0	35.9	441,790
College Station-Bryan, TX Metro Area	110,833	95,224	75,583	15,609	16.4	52.8	1478	73.7	21.3	251,319
Colorado Springs, CO Metro Area	288,745	265,807	214,514	22,938	8.6	107.6	5508	73.5	23.9	1,709,856
Columbia, MO Metro Area	91,037	81,743	68,049	9,294	11.4	53.1	793	79.1	20.4	194,853
Columbia, SC Metro Area	359,526	332,208	270,721	27,318	8.2	97.1	4440	94.7	5.1	962,813
Columbus, GA-AL Metro Area	140,527	134,217	121,440	6,310	4.7	50.4	1070	63.6	35.5	190,074
Columbus, IN Metro Area	34,531	33,114	29,964	1,417	4.3	84.8	189	100.0	0.0	44,516
Columbus, OH Metro Area	869,366	821,697	710,597	47,669	5.8	181.2	8427	49.2	48.3	1,635,768
Corpus Christi, TX Metro Area	178,433	167,734	148,344	10,699	6.4	116.5	1068	99.1	0.0	183,511
Corvallis, OR Metro Area	38,451	36,321	32,074	2,130	5.9	57.0	416	22.1	72.1	76,927
Crestview-Fort Walton Beach-Destin,	151,330	137,659	108,371	13,671	9.9	76.9	3544	67.5	29.9	1,079,244
Cumberland, MD-WV Metro Area	45,977	46,335	45,158	-358	-0.8	61.3	40	100.0	0.0	8,905
Dallas-Fort Worth-Arlington, TX Metro Area	2,822,550	2,504,213	2,008,038	318,337	12.7	325.4	62563	56.2	42.7	12,705,862
Dallas-Plano-Irving, TX Div.	1,905,035	1,660,227	1,337,580	244,808	14.7	361.0	-	-	-	-
Fort Worth-Arlington-Grapevine, TX Div.	917,515	843,986	670,458	73,529	8.7	270.1	-	-	-	-
Dalton, GA Metro Area	56,311	55,890	45,456	421	0.8	88.7	-	-	-	-
Danville, IL Metro Area	36,129	36,310	36,375	-181	-0.5	40.2	0	-	-	0
Daphne-Fairhope-Foley, AL Metro Area	116,631	104,292	74,907	12,339	11.8	73.4	2687	80.3	17.4	515,101
Davenport-Moline-Rock Island, IA-IL	170,422	167,210	158,790	3,212	1.9	75.1	606	66.0	34.0	111,482
Dayton-Kettering, OH Metro Area	370,006	367,326	348,098	2,680	0.7	288.6	1114	88.3	11.0	357,566
Decatur, AL Metro Area	67,748	66,443	62,598	1,305	2.0	53.3	169	100.0	0.0	31,174
Decatur, IL Metro Area	50,393	50,481	50,260	-88	-0.2	86.7	16	100.0	0.0	4,112
Deltona-Daytona Beach-Ormond Beach,	314,618	302,940	237,753	11,678	3.9	198.4	3406	76.4	17.5	844,495
Denver-Aurora-Lakewood, CO Metro Area	1,195,422	1,079,739	897,927	115,683	10.7	143.3	19278	57.3	41.7	4,302,460
Des Moines-West Des Moines, IA Metro.	292,484	256,890	215,431	35,594	13.9	81.0	5189	74.0	25.3	1,220,230
Detroit-Warren-Dearborn, MI Metro area	1,912,679	1,886,206	1,800,731	26,473	1.4	491.4	7401	70.6	26.4	1,820,917
Detroit-Dearborn-Livonia, MI Div.	815,803	821,093	824,760	-5,290	-0.6	1333.0	-	-	-	-
Warren-Troy-Farmington Hills, MI Div	1,096,876	1,065,113	975,971	31,763	3.0	334.4	-	-	-	-
Dothan, AL Metro Area	69,817	66,975	60,008	2,842	4.2	40.7	271	80.8	17.7	58,749
Dover, DE Metro Area	73,093	65,533	50,778	7,560	11.5	124.7	1341	90.8	6.1	185,049
Dubuque, IA Metro Area	41,504	39,040	35,546	2,464	6.3	68.3	116	94.8	5.2	37,543
Duluth, MN-WI Metro Area	152,311	149,294	137,110	3,017	2.0	14.5	82	92.7	0.0	16,825
Durham-Chapel Hill, NC Metro Area	274,336	246,172	199,299	28,164	11.4	119.8	5795	61.4	38.0	1,144,958
East Stroudsburg, PA Metro Area	81,663	80,411	67,936	1,252	1.6	134.3	88	100.0	0.0	26,007
Eau Claire, WI Metro Area	73,014	69,415	60,549	3,599	5.2	44.4	707	61.4	22.2	134,261
El Centro, CA Metro Area	57,895	56,107	44,078	1,788	3.2	13.9	275	73.8	26.2	45,084
Elizabethtown-Fort Knox, KY Metro Area	66,008	61,321	54,010	4,687	7.6	55.5	2884	76.5	11.3	608,595
Elkhart-Goshen, IN Metro Area	79,492	77,785	70,116	1,707	2.2	171.7	491	86.6	4.9	92,168
Elmira, NY Metro Area	38,916	38,385	37,805	531	1.4	95.6	236	100.0	0.0	59,236
El Paso, TX Metro Area	301,219	272,544	226,965	28,675	10.5	53.9	2	100.0	0.0	400
Enid, OK Metro Area	26,798	26,824	26,057	-26	-0.1	25.3	26	100.0	0.0	6,412
Erie, PA Metro Area	121,617	119,243	114,508	2,374	2.0	152.2	57	71.9	24.6	13,346
Eugene-Springfield, OR Metro Area	163,472	156,254	139,383	7,218	4.6	35.9	956	65.3	31.8	191,003
Evansville, IN-KY Metro Area	143,102	138,831	127,819	4,271	3.1	97.7	894	69.0	24.3	187,709
Fairbanks, AK Metro Area	44,300	41,785	33,472	2,515	6.0	6.0	23	30.4	0.0	4,585
Fargo, ND-MN Metro Area	110,698	92,295	73,881	18,403	19.9	39.4	1408	65.5	33.9	286,100
Farmington, NM Metro Area	51,276	49,427	43,448	1,849	3.7	9.3	89	83.1	9.0	18,259
Fayetteville, NC Metro Area	220,824	201,216	170,293	19,608	9.7	134.8	1792	83.7	15.7	268,267
Fayetteville-Springdale-Rogers, AR Metro Area	211,085	188,799	136,102	22,286	11.8	80.4	6903	60.0	36.8	1,334,674
Flagstaff, AZ Metro Area	66,840	63,361	53,677	3,479	5.5	3.6	680	72.2	26.9	109,474
Flint, MI Metro Area	192,637	192,142	184,146	495	0.3	302.4	393	67.2	5.9	95,426
Florence, SC Metro Area	91,996	89,020	81,125	2,976	3.3	67.6	696	61.2	37.9	80,056
Florence-Muscle Shoals, AL Metro Area	72,194	69,582	65,562	2,612	3.8	57.3	235	88.9	8.5	26,928
Fond du Lac, WI Metro Area	45,361	43,940	39,365	1,421	3.2	63.0	177	36.7	58.8	26,616
Fort Collins, CO Metro Area	151,848	132,822	106,306	19,026	14.3	58.5	2541	62.8	34.5	557,835
Fort Smith, AR-OK Metro Area	111,636	107,638	95,567	3,998	3.7	46.4	512	61.1	1.6	88,662
Fort Wayne, IN Metro Area	174,162	166,611	151,894	7,551	4.5	175.4	1956	68.0	29.7	418,480
Fresno, CA Metro Area	333,769	316,068	271,364	17,701	5.6	56.0	3270	67.6	23.6	804,663
Gadsden, AL Metro Area	47,846	47,469	46,035	377	0.8	89.4	58	100.0	0.0	10,471
Gainesville, FL Metro Area	147,207	140,300	118,220	6,907	4.9	62.8	2126	27.2	72.6	259,651
Gainesville, GA Metro Area	74,423	68,887	51,793	5,536	8.0	189.4	1096	67.4	29.1	206,200
Gettysburg, PA Metro Area	42,563	40,866	35,977	1,697	4.2	82.0	220	100.0	0.0	67,925
Glens Falls, NY Metro Area	69,791	67,648	61,760	2,143	3.2	41.1	231	94.8	2.6	57,125
Goldsboro, NC Metro Area	54,474	53,013	47,559	1,461	2.8	98.3	-	-	-	-
Grand Forks, ND-MN Metro Area	48,429	44,028	41,397	4,401	10.0	14.2	145	62.1	31.0	33,988
Grand Island, NE Metro Area	32,026	30,231	28,072	1,795	5.9	20.0	105	67.6	24.8	19,156

Table B-9. Housing Units and Building Permits—*Continued*

Metropolitan Statistical Area Metropolitan Division	2018 (July 1 estimate)	2010 (July 1 estimate)	2000 (July 1 estimate)	Change 2010-2018 Number	Change 2010-2018 Percent	Units per square mile of land area, 2018	New private housing units authorized by building permits, 2019 Number of units	Percent single family	Percent in structures with 5 or more units	Total value ($1000)
Grand Junction, CO Metro Area	67,215	62,731	49,116	4,484	7.1	20.2	759	81.6	16.6	122,434
Grand Rapids-Kentwood, MI Metro Area	421,924	402,516	360,364	19,408	4.8	156.9	2874	54.3	42.1	538,751
Grants Pass, OR Metro Area	39,352	38,033	33,371	1,319	3.5	24.0	-	-	-	-
Great Falls, MT Metro Area	39,036	37,332	35,268	1,704	4.6	14.5	134	91.0	9.0	34,689
Greeley, CO Metro Area	112,465	96,455	67,151	16,010	16.6	28.2	3897	74.6	24.1	914,680
Green Bay, WI Metro Area	144,181	137,368	118,725	6,813	5.0	77.1	1011	62.5	36.5	223,421
Greensboro-High Point, NC Metro Area	337,407	323,151	276,354	14,256	4.4	169.2	2423	82.6	16.9	531,282
Greenville, NC Metro Area	80,265	75,114	58,528	5,151	6.9	123.1	706	42.6	44.9	107,616
Greenville-Anderson, SC Metro Area	389,705	362,468	313,676	27,237	7.5	143.8	6541	82.3	16.2	1,437,505
Gulfport-Biloxi, MS Metro Area	190,088	175,163	158,838	14,925	8.5	85.8	2188	93.0	4.8	387,096
Hagerstown-Martinsburg, MD-WV Metro	121,078	115,453	94,351	5,625	4.9	120.1	1523	88.0	2.1	290,920
Hammond, LA Metro Area	56,361	50,305	40,876	6,056	12.0	71.3	822	99.3	0.0	157,187
Hanford-Corcoran, CA Metro Area	46,645	43,910	36,687	2,735	6.2	33.6	-	-	-	-
Harrisburg-Carlisle, PA Metro Area	252,645	241,151	217,567	11,494	4.8	155.8	2009	57.3	36.4	357,379
Harrisonburg, VA Metro Area	54,165	51,229	41,199	2,936	5.7	62.5	361	100.0	0.0	106,897
Hartford-East Hartford-Middletown, CT Metro Area	517,040	507,344	472,786	9,696	1.9	341.3	1398	61.2	32.8	218,983
Hattiesburg, MS Metro Area	72,395	70,429	58,845	1,966	2.8	35.8	83	47.0	0.0	15,869
Hickory-Lenoir-Morganton, NC Metro Area	165,150	162,831	145,651	2,319	1.4	100.8	86	12.8	84.9	6,083
Hilton Head Island-Bluffton, SC Metro Area	113,319	103,417	69,299	9,902	9.6	92.1	882	97.3	2.7	297,004
Hinesville, GA Metro Area	35,570	32,896	26,370	2,674	8.1	38.8	754	37.9	61.5	112,500
Homosassa Springs, FL Metro Area	79,988	78,123	62,527	1,865	2.4	137.4	743	93.3	5.4	146,598
Hot Springs, AR Metro Area	51,026	50,554	45,085	472	0.9	75.3	117	40.2	51.3	20,378
Houma-Thibodaux, LA Metro Area	87,333	82,627	75,167	4,706	5.7	38.0	480	94.8	0.0	104,800
Houston-The Woodlands-Sugar Land, TX	2,637,765	2,301,060	1,798,493	336,705	14.6	319.0	61770	64.5	34.9	9,537,796
Huntington-Ashland, WV-KY-OH Metro Area	167,868	166,892	163,261	976	0.6	67.1	216	68.5	24.1	36,453
Huntsville, AL Metro Area	200,801	182,108	147,830	18,693	10.3	147.4	3517	95.3	2.4	515,414
Idaho Falls, ID Metro Area	54,717	49,884	38,252	4,833	9.7	10.5	1092	94.7	0.5	180,656
Indianapolis-Carmel-Anderson, IN Metro Area	867,936	817,626	705,444	50,310	6.2	201.5	9253	73.9	24.2	2,325,877
Iowa City, IA Metro Area	74,816	65,678	54,918	9,138	13.9	63.3	804	26.0	69.3	158,309
Ithaca, NY Metro Area	43,879	41,706	38,758	2,173	5.2	92.4	108	13.9	71.3	15,580
Jackson, MI Metro Area	69,685	69,456	63,169	229	0.3	99.3	6	100.0	0.0	952
Jackson, MS Metro Area	253,098	241,342	215,650	11,756	4.9	46.8	1181	81.4	18.6	272,297
Jackson, TN Metro Area	79,578	77,358	71,762	2,220	2.9	46.5	156	100.0	0.0	34,172
Jacksonville, FL Metro Area	655,272	599,393	477,477	55,879	9.3	204.6	14868	76.1	23.1	3,110,677
Jacksonville, NC Metro Area	80,259	68,742	56,207	11,517	16.8	105.3	1331	97.9	0.0	195,120
Janesville-Beloit, WI Metro Area	69,227	68,456	62,377	771	1.1	96.4	390	43.6	53.3	70,626
Jefferson City, MO Metro Area	65,369	63,625	57,024	1,744	2.7	29.1	-	-	-	-
Johnson City, TN Metro Area	98,048	93,939	82,219	4,109	4.4	114.8	231	58.4	38.1	37,160
Johnstown, PA Metro Area	66,022	65,666	65,793	356	0.5	96.0	4	100.0	0.0	950
Jonesboro, AR Metro Area	57,268	51,542	46,303	5,726	11.1	39.1	751	64.8	10.8	89,140
Joplin, MO Metro Area	76,587	75,025	67,733	1,562	2.1	60.6	254	79.5	3.9	37,112
Kahului-Wailuku-Lahaina, HI Metro Area	73,775	70,471	56,707	3,304	4.7	63.5	657	78.1	9.7	218,056
Kalamazoo-Portage, MI Metro Area	112,800	110,040	99,633	2,760	2.5	200.7	101	100.0	0.0	30,413
Kankakee, IL Metro Area	45,652	45,258	40,716	394	0.9	67.5	27	100.0	0.0	7,900
Kansas City, MO-KS Metro Area	918,595	872,502	760,905	46,093	5.3	126.6	9301	51.6	41.9	1,877,604
Kennewick-Richland, WA Metro Area	106,018	93,300	72,410	12,718	13.6	36.0	2464	67.7	28.7	565,449
Killeen-Temple, TX Metro Area	178,734	159,935	122,885	18,799	11.8	63.5	2537	89.8	0.0	418,681
Kingsport-Bristol, TN-VA Metro Area	149,725	147,058	136,645	2,667	1.8	74.5	26	76.9	0.0	4,903
Kingston, NY Metro Area	85,421	83,694	77,790	1,727	2.1	76.0	197	24.4	73.6	37,478
Knoxville, TN Metro Area	388,375	370,678	326,961	17,697	4.8	120.6	3575	73.1	26.7	706,013
Kokomo, IN Metro Area	39,567	38,681	37,685	886	2.3	135.0	221	31.2	68.8	26,613
La Crosse-Onalaska, WI-MN Metro Area	59,346	57,065	51,795	2,281	4.0	59.1	494	36.8	50.8	84,660
Lafayette, LA Metro Area	211,670	196,269	172,176	15,401	7.8	62.1	1643	98.5	1.5	351,248
Lafayette-West Lafayette, IN Metro Area	94,093	88,277	74,840	5,816	6.6	57.3	1297	34.6	64.5	199,055
Lake Charles, LA Metro Area	96,171	85,967	81,511	10,204	11.9	40.9	1127	74.4	19.5	176,430
Lake Havasu City-Kingman, AZ Metro Area	115,269	110,974	80,717	4,295	3.9	8.6	1106	94.4	0.0	229,785
Lakeland-Winter Haven, FL Metro Area	299,421	281,402	227,250	18,019	6.4	166.5	8032	75.7	23.4	1,599,226
Lancaster, PA Metro Area	212,205	203,230	180,611	8,975	4.4	224.8	89	62.9	7.9	17,867
Lansing-East Lansing, MI Metro Area	234,031	229,321	211,593	4,710	2.1	105.0	152	74.3	23.0	32,725
Laredo, TX Metro Area	84,455	73,684	55,740	10,771	14.6	25.1	1425	80.3	12.9	189,471
Las Cruces, NM Metro Area	89,049	81,795	65,878	7,254	8.9	23.4	975	89.5	9.8	230,221
Las Vegas-Henderson-Paradise, NV Metro Area	913,260	841,675	566,405	71,585	8.5	115.7	12714	73.6	24.5	2,486,264
Lawrence, KS Metro Area	51,073	46,803	40,436	4,270	9.1	112.0	373	46.6	49.6	67,792
Lawton, OK Metro Area	54,687	53,891	48,585	796	1.5	32.1	52	100.0	0.0	11,179
Lebanon, PA Metro Area	58,005	55,674	49,431	2,331	4.2	160.2	212	100.0	0.0	39,620
Lewiston, ID-WA Metro Area	27,990	27,331	25,382	659	2.4	18.9	54	5.6	90.7	4,700
Lewiston-Auburn, ME Metro Area	50,056	49,128	46,055	928	1.9	107.0	112	49.1	47.3	21,339
Lexington-Fayette, KY Metro Area	222,278	209,448	176,228	12,830	6.1	151.2	2887	45.5	52.1	459,009
Lima, OH Metro Area	45,186	44,989	44,276	197	0.4	112.1	6	66.7	0.0	1,193
Lincoln, NE Metro Area	140,692	127,883	111,111	12,809	10.0	99.9	1831	52.8	45.8	316,505
Little Rock-North Little Rock-Conway	328,596	307,604	262,950	20,992	6.8	80.4	2955	63.3	34.9	455,246
Logan, UT-ID Metro Area	47,144	41,677	33,015	5,467	13.1	25.8	569	32.0	60.8	90,552
Longview, TX Metro Area	119,545	115,106	107,679	4,439	3.9	44.6	166	91.6	7.2	30,869

Table B-9. Housing Units and Building Permits—*Continued*

Metropolitan Statistical Area Metropolitan Division	Housing units						New private housing units authorized by building permits, 2019			
	2018 (July 1 estimate)	2010 (July 1 estimate)	2000 (July 1 estimate)	Change 2010-2018 Number	Percent	Units per square mile of land area, 2018	Number of units	Percent single family	Percent in structures with 5 or more units	Total value ($1000)
Longview, WA Metro Area..................	44,968	43,481	38,767	1,487	3.4	39.4	230	100.0	0.0	52,254
Los Angeles-Long Beach-Anaheim, CA M	4,672,296	4,495,795	4,247,689	176,501	3.9	963.2	29927	30.9	62.3	6,825,816
Anaheim-Santa Ana-Irvine, CA Div...............	1,111,227	1,049,362	972,611	61,865	5.9	1401.3	-	-	-	-
Los Angeles-Long Beach-Glendale, CA.............	3,561,069	3,446,433	3,275,078	114,636	3.3	877.3	-	-	-	-
Louisville/Jefferson County, KY-IN M..............	547,551	526,286	465,528	21,265	4.0	169.2	5755	54.1	44.7	1,113,992
Lubbock, TX Metro Area.................	135,228	120,891	106,679	14,337	11.9	50.3	2253	66.9	26.1	399,992
Lynchburg, VA Metro Area.................	117,194	112,654	95,696	4,540	4.0	55.3	430	28.6	67.4	54,034
Macon-Bibb County, GA Metro Area	102,807	101,611	94,363	1,196	1.2	59.6	290	100.0	0.0	45,828
Madera, CA Metro Area.................	50,966	49,151	40,518	1,815	3.7	23.8	633	100.0	0.0	161,220
Madison, WI Metro Area.................	290,880	269,003	227,642	21,877	8.1	87.9	3736	41.4	54.5	837,262
Manchester-Nashua, NH Metro Area......................	172,031	166,147	150,436	5,884	3.5	196.2	517	61.1	30.4	99,394
Manhattan, KS Metro Area.................	56,560	51,592	42,765	4,968	9.6	30.8	304	76.6	22.0	75,945
Mankato, MN Metro Area.................	42,446	39,126	33,338	3,320	8.5	35.5	139	64.7	32.4	29,182
Mansfield, OH Metro Area.................	54,166	54,587	53,218	-421	-0.8	109.4	-	-	-	-
McAllen-Edinburg-Mission, TX Metro Area............	281,639	249,100	193,935	32,539	13.1	179.3	5362	63.1	17.3	762,047
Medford, OR Metro Area.................	96,241	91,018	76,129	5,223	5.7	34.6	660	75.8	20.0	147,163
Memphis, TN-MS-AR Metro Area.................	570,306	551,174	483,359	19,132	3.5	124.5	3664	90.3	9.4	775,285
Merced, CA Metro Area.................	85,756	83,715	68,875	2,041	2.4	44.3	175	100.0	0.0	39,908
Miami-Fort Lauderdale-Pompano Beach, FL Metro	2,548,762	2,464,332	2,158,776	84,430	3.4	503.0	20984	34.3	63.4	5,149,765
Fort Lauderdale-Pompano Beach-Sunrise, FL Div..	826,899	810,322	743,865	16,577	2.0	687.4	-	-	-	-
Miami-Miami Beach-Kendall, FL Div..............	1,031,955	989,277	855,553	42,678	4.3	543.1	-	-	-	-
West Palm Beach-Boca Raton-Boynton Beach, FL Div..	689,908	664,733	559,358	25,175	3.8	351.3	-	-	-	-
Michigan City-La Porte, IN Metro Area..............	49,225	48,458	45,724	767	1.6	82.3	111	100.0	0.0	26,864
Midland, MI Metro Area	37,114	35,962	33,906	1,152	3.2	71.9	45	86.7	0.0	6,338
Midland, TX Metro Area	63,756	56,270	50,118	7,486	13.3	35.1	1290	100.0	0.0	209,964
Milwaukee-Waukesha, WI Metro Area.................	681,189	669,927	619,802	11,262	1.7	468.2	2303	66.0	25.2	666,655
Minneapolis-St. Paul-Bloomington, MN...............	1,453,940	1,380,844	1,196,724	73,096	5.3	206.3	22466	42.3	56.7	4,942,301
Missoula, MT Metro Area.................	54,926	50,150	41,534	4,776	9.5	21.2	659	63.9	28.8	114,032
Mobile, AL Metro Area.................	193,261	187,174	173,660	6,087	3.3	83.7	715	99.6	0.0	160,970
Modesto, CA Metro Area.................	182,290	179,579	151,433	2,711	1.5	121.9	16	100.0	0.0	2,946
Monroe, LA Metro Area.................	93,564	88,343	83,808	5,221	5.9	41.0	465	67.7	23.7	89,844
Monroe, MI Metro Area.................	64,785	62,975	56,702	1,810	2.9	118.0	11	63.6	0.0	1,700
Montgomery, AL Metro Area.................	168,538	161,645	145,108	6,893	4.3	62.1	754	99.2	0.0	160,837
Morgantown, WV Metro Area.................	60,249	58,357	50,360	1,892	3.2	59.7	25	44.0	56.0	4,383
Morristown, TN Metro Area.................	62,682	61,436	54,010	1,246	2.0	87.4	-	-	-	-
Mount Vernon-Anacortes, WA Metro area.............	54,443	51,537	42,904	2,906	5.6	31.5	361	99.4	0.0	92,379
Muncie, IN Metro Area.................	52,727	52,342	51,122	385	0.7	134.5	23	100.0	0.0	2,287
Muskegon, MI Metro Area.................	74,305	73,553	68,781	752	1.0	147.4	43	100.0	0.0	8,565
Myrtle Beach-Conway-North Myrtle Bea..............	302,962	264,076	175,248	38,886	14.7	152.9	6440	94.4	4.5	1,198,440
Napa, CA Metro Area.................	55,460	54,798	48,719	662	1.2	74.1	-	-	-	-
Naples-Marco Island, FL Metro Area..............	218,281	197,494	146,520	20,787	10.5	109.3	3757	81.8	15.1	838,343
Nashville-Davidson--Murfreesboro--Franklin, TN....	789,006	693,656	566,084	95,350	13.7	138.7	21845	61.5	38.1	4,333,119
New Bern, NC Metro Area.................	60,236	57,495	49,745	2,741	4.8	39.8	-	-	-	-
New Haven-Milford, CT Metro Area..............	367,745	362,074	341,322	5,671	1.6	607.8	1092	20.2	72.6	127,500
New Orleans-Metairie, LA Metro Area..............	560,360	547,163	557,784	13,197	2.4	174.9	3957	80.3	13.2	823,267
New York-Newark-Jersey City, NY-NJ-P...........	7,756,101	7,534,655	7,104,331	221,446	2.9	1160.2	60746	18.8	76.0	8,530,349
Nassau County-Suffolk County, NY Div.............	1,050,369	1,038,590	982,427	11,779	1.1	878.2	-	-	-	-
Newark, NJ-PA Div.............	867,844	852,340	805,894	15,504	1.8	397.9	-	-	-	-
New Brunswick-Lakewood, NJ Div.............	976,318	955,508	878,952	20,810	2.2	571.6	-	-	-	-
New York-Jersey City-White Plains, N.............	4,861,570	4,688,217	4,437,058	173,353	3.7	3038.5	-	-	-	-
Niles, MI Metro Area.................	77,648	76,919	73,574	729	0.9	136.7	19	100.0	0.0	5,232
North Port-Sarasota-Bradenton, FL Me.............	438,533	401,416	322,435	37,117	9.2	337.3	9954	65.2	32.7	2,032,132
Norwich-New London, CT Metro Area..................	123,635	121,086	110,921	2,549	2.1	185.9	244	49.2	46.7	42,877
Ocala, FL Metro Area.................	170,504	164,110	123,249	6,394	3.9	107.4	2357	99.2	0.0	484,957
Ocean City, NJ Metro Area.................	99,436	98,416	91,226	1,020	1.0	396.2	870	63.2	11.3	267,136
Odessa, TX Metro Area.................	58,680	53,083	49,634	5,597	10.5	65.3	1782	41.7	58.1	297,179
Ogden-Clearfield, UT Metro Area..............	226,369	204,514	161,969	21,855	10.7	31.3	3555	71.8	22.8	781,542
Oklahoma City, OK Metro Area.................	579,374	539,740	473,659	39,634	7.3	105.1	6528	90.3	4.1	1,427,136
Olympia-Lacey-Tumwater, WA Metro area	117,872	108,496	87,059	9,376	8.6	163.3	1688	46.6	50.1	298,056
Omaha-Council Bluffs, NE-IA Metro area..............	390,430	362,976	313,007	27,454	7.6	89.8	4066	65.1	33.9	653,218
Orlando-Kissimmee-Sanford, FL Metro.............	1,050,625	943,156	690,045	107,469	11.4	301.0	24778	60.6	37.7	5,236,416
Oshkosh-Neenah, WI Metro Area..................	76,028	73,395	64,945	2,633	3.6	174.8	266	66.9	27.1	57,132
Owensboro, KY Metro Area.................	51,443	49,494	46,596	1,949	3.9	57.2	323	86.7	9.6	29,838
Oxnard-Thousand Oaks-Ventura, CA Met...............	291,019	281,774	252,796	9,245	3.3	158.0	657	19.2	71.8	107,655
Palm Bay-Melbourne-Titusville, FL Me.............	280,398	270,022	223,111	10,376	3.8	276.3	3864	55.5	44.4	892,207
Panama City, FL Metro Area.................	104,314	99,703	78,783	4,611	4.6	137.4	1186	64.7	34.8	218,024
Parkersburg-Vienna, WV Metro Area	43,618	43,451	43,068	167	0.4	72.8	117	43.6	0.0	15,910
Pensacola-Ferry Pass-Brent, FL Metro.............	215,538	201,643	174,356	13,895	6.9	129.1	3191	84.8	12.4	596,052
Peoria, IL Metro Area.................	183,251	180,551	169,873	2,700	1.5	55.0	54	63.0	37.0	14,952
Philadelphia-Camden-Wilmington, PA-N	2,497,485	2,434,697	2,286,358	62,788	2.6	542.6	15422	44.9	47.9	2,253,315
Camden, NJ Div.............	499,942	490,641	457,033	9,301	1.9	372.3	-	-	-	-
Montgomery County-Bucks County-Chest..........	789,061	764,615	689,131	24,446	3.2	429.3	-	-	-	-
Philadelphia, PA Div.............	913,704	893,300	879,239	20,404	2.3	2873.3	-	-	-	-
Wilmington, DE-MD-NJ Div.............	294,778	286,141	260,955	8,637	3.0	267.0	-	-	-	-

Table B-9. Housing Units and Building Permits—Continued

Metropolitan Statistical Area / Metropolitan Division	2018 (July 1 estimate)	2010 (July 1 estimate)	2000 (July 1 estimate)	Change 2010-2018 Number	Change 2010-2018 Percent	Units per square mile of land area, 2018	Number of units	Percent single family	Percent in structures with 5 or more units	Total value ($1000)
Phoenix-Mesa-Chandler, AZ Metro Area	1,939,993	1,802,038	1,342,946	137,955	7.7	133.2	35400	70.4	27.2	8,141,795
Pine Bluff, AR Metro Area	42,436	41,963	43,145	473	1.1	20.9	18	100.0	0.0	2,679
Pittsburgh, PA Metro Area	1,130,057	1,102,670	1,079,518	27,387	2.5	213.9	1555	58.1	38.2	350,075
Pittsfield, MA Metro Area	69,400	68,550	66,317	850	1.2	74.9	5	100.0	0.0	2,668
Pocatello, ID Metro Area	37,467	36,175	32,025	1,292	3.6	14.9	272	89.0	2.2	32,185
Portland-South Portland, ME Metro Area	275,711	262,973	234,119	12,738	4.8	132.5	3396	86.7	7.5	728,875
Portland-Vancouver-Hillsboro, OR-WA	1,008,433	926,044	794,512	82,389	8.9	150.8	2159	57.9	33.8	477,363
Port St. Lucie, FL Metro Area	223,169	215,201	157,691	7,968	3.7	200.2	1003	23.4	73.8	171,388
Poughkeepsie-Newburgh-Middletown, NY	265,390	255,847	229,638	9,543	3.7	165.0	1716	78.1	18.5	442,989
Prescott Valley-Prescott, AZ Metro Area	118,394	110,533	82,364	7,861	7.1	14.6	2048	77.9	8.5	418,595
Providence-Warwick, RI-MA Metro Area	705,431	694,167	657,795	11,264	1.6	444.5	6933	78.0	20.7	1,767,533
Provo-Orem, UT Metro Area	183,886	152,250	108,093	31,636	20.8	34.1	488	99.2	0.0	78,763
Pueblo, CO Metro Area	71,451	69,613	59,251	1,838	2.6	29.9	2244	88.9	5.1	604,878
Punta Gorda, FL Metro Area	105,172	100,685	80,155	4,487	4.5	154.4	245	61.6	34.3	62,846
Racine, WI Metro Area	82,907	82,211	74,909	696	0.8	249.0	14972	78.1	21.6	2,877,486
Raleigh-Cary, NC Metro Area	548,194	467,128	332,456	81,066	17.4	258.8	658	61.9	28.7	121,840
Rapid City, SD Metro Area	61,505	56,066	12,011	5,439	9.7	9.8	40	100.0	0.0	8,419
Reading, PA Metro Area	167,366	164,890	150,712	2,476	1.5	195.5	294	77.2	22.8	73,290
Redding, CA Metro Area	79,194	77,350	69,020	1,844	2.4	21.0	5189	40.1	57.9	975,703
Reno, NV Metro Area	203,135	187,007	146,669	16,128	8.6	30.9	8321	53.6	41.9	1,201,773
Richmond, VA Metro Area	525,984	499,436	429,539	26,548	5.3	120.6	14033	74.1	23.8	3,273,596
Riverside-San Bernardino-Ontario, CA	1,574,493	1,501,869	1,191,406	72,624	4.8	57.7	-	-	-	-
Roanoke, VA Metro Area	146,755	145,003	130,120	1,752	1.2	78.6	822	41.8	58.2	143,731
Rochester, MN Metro Area	95,296	88,292	74,524	7,004	7.9	38.5	1922	54.1	41.4	386,243
Rochester, NY Metro Area	482,293	469,716	440,207	12,577	2.7	147.7	250	71.6	0.0	33,598
Rockford, IL Metro Area	145,812	145,940	130,217	-128	-0.1	183.6	-	-	-	-
Rocky Mount, NC Metro Area	68,171	67,156	61,297	1,015	1.5	65.2	263	100.0	0.0	40,868
Rome, GA Metro Area	40,636	40,554	36,742	82	0.2	79.7	9373	76.5	21.3	2,487,621
Sacramento-Roseville-Folsom, CA Metro Area	911,208	872,424	718,998	38,784	4.4	178.8	64	48.4	0.0	9,100
Saginaw, MI Metro Area	87,817	86,834	85,696	983	1.1	109.6	5	100.0	0.0	1,385
St. Cloud, MN Metro Area	82,530	78,219	64,238	4,311	5.5	47.1	2766	64.4	29.3	457,877
St. George, UT Metro Area	71,363	57,883	36,848	13,480	23.3	29.4	0	-	-	0
St. Joseph, MO-KS Metro Area	54,067	53,659	50,694	408	0.8	32.6	6986	74.5	21.8	1,657,173
St. Louis, MO-IL Metro Area	1,262,828	1,226,066	1,126,418	36,762	3.0	160.6	1522	46.7	49.1	295,231
Salem, OR Metro Area	159,845	151,452	133,093	8,393	5.5	83.2	315	77.5	17.1	93,336
Salinas, CA Metro Area	142,399	139,088	132,051	3,311	2.4	43.4	3826	87.4	7.0	546,604
Salisbury, MD-DE Metro Area	251,593	231,517	185,724	20,076	8.7	119.9	10610	45.0	51.7	2,019,736
Salt Lake City, UT Metro Area	426,128	384,466	326,092	41,662	10.8	55.5	283	100.0	0.0	61,492
San Angelo, TX Metro Area	50,105	48,152	45,545	1,953	4.1	14.3	15919	57.3	41.1	2,859,241
San Antonio-New Braunfels, TX Metro Area	904,717	839,262	652,668	65,455	7.8	123.7	8082	37.4	56.2	1,706,587
San Diego-Chula Vista-Carlsbad, CA Metro Area	1,224,375	1,165,429	1,044,144	58,946	5.1	290.8	14132	28.7	69.3	3,839,132
San Francisco-Oakland-Berkeley, CA Metro Area	1,825,087	1,742,797	1,610,766	82,290	4.7	738.9	-	-	-	-
Oakland-Berkeley-Livermore, CA Div	1,030,996	983,391	897,252	47,605	4.8	709.1	-	-	-	-
San Francisco-San Mateo-Redwood City	680,909	648,138	608,358	32,771	5.1	1372.8	-	-	-	-
San Rafael, CA Div	113,182	111,268	105,156	1,914	1.7	217.7	6485	39.6	59.2	1,598,079
San Jose-Sunnyvale-Santa Clara, CA Metro Area	697,934	650,018	597,689	47,916	7.4	260.4	341	99.4	0.0	103,102
San Luis Obispo-Paso Robles, CA Metro Area	122,979	117,401	102,684	5,578	4.8	37.3	264	48.5	41.7	41,277
Santa Cruz-Watsonville, CA Metro Area	106,728	104,495	98,986	2,233	2.1	239.8	589	58.4	41.6	108,722
Santa Fe, NM Metro Area	73,456	71,359	57,920	2,097	2.9	38.5	258	93.4	6.6	128,089
Santa Maria-Santa Barbara, CA Metro	158,333	152,900	143,164	5,433	3.6	57.9	2244	88.8	11.2	718,585
Santa Rosa-Petaluma, CA Metro Area	205,225	204,661	183,846	564	0.3	130.2	2627	82.9	16.8	567,810
Savannah, GA Metro Area	163,944	151,365	123,434	12,579	8.3	121.5	59	96.6	0.0	13,826
Scranton--Wilkes-Barre, PA Metro Area	264,545	258,970	252,950	5,575	2.2	151.5	26584	32.9	61.7	5,552,819
Seattle-Tacoma-Bellevue, WA Metro Area	1,617,435	1,464,974	1,261,027	152,461	10.4	275.5	-	-	-	-
Seattle-Bellevue-Kent, WA Div	1,266,387	1,139,120	982,839	127,267	11.2	301.4	-	-	-	-
Tacoma-Lakewood, WA Div.	351,048	325,854	278,188	25,194	7.7	210.5	1240	92.2	0.0	462,631
Sebastian-Vero Beach, FL Metro Area	81,043	76,406	58,305	4,637	6.1	161.1	-	-	-	-
Sebring-Avon Park, FL Metro Area	55,759	55,395	48,964	364	0.7	54.8	14	100.0	0.0	4,617
Sheboygan, WI Metro Area	51,340	50,782	46,097	558	1.1	100.3	-	-	-	-
Sherman-Denison, TX Metro Area	56,731	53,747	48,441	2,984	5.6	60.8	-	-	-	-
Shreveport-Bossier City, LA Metro Area	184,376	173,982	160,060	10,394	6.0	71.0	1046	100.0	0.0	220,954
Sierra Vista-Douglas, AZ Metro Area	61,328	59,135	51,322	2,193	3.7	9.9	245	98.0	2.0	48,888
Sioux City, IA-NE-SD Metro Area	60,298	58,108	56,966	2,190	3.8	29.1	142	93.7	0.0	35,798
Sioux Falls, SD Metro Area	111,732	96,223	76,074	15,509	16.1	43.4	2023	63.7	34.8	343,247
South Bend-Mishawaka, IN-MI Metro Area	143,520	140,753	131,341	2,767	2.0	151.4	322	100.0	0.0	94,872
Spartanburg, SC Metro Area	131,451	122,741	107,505	8,710	7.1	162.7	2596	100.0	0.0	425,101
Spokane-Spokane Valley, WA Metro Area	241,728	223,028	193,291	18,700	8.4	57.0	3293	57.2	35.9	670,411
Springfield, IL Metro Area	97,681	95,622	90,921	2,059	2.2	82.6	179	37.4	46.9	29,016
Springfield, MA Metro Area	292,099	288,645	276,745	3,454	1.2	158.5	53	67.9	0.0	12,200
Springfield, MO Metro Area	205,482	192,605	157,347	12,877	6.7	68.3	834	86.3	5.5	180,213
Springfield, OH Metro Area	61,289	61,409	61,089	-120	-0.2	154.4	76	92.1	7.9	17,846
State College, PA Metro Area	67,144	63,383	53,367	3,761	5.9	60.5	311	82.6	16.1	84,767
Staunton, VA Metro Area	54,592	52,679	46,185	1,913	3.6	54.5	390	44.6	52.3	63,217

Table B-9. Housing Units and Building Permits—*Continued*

Metropolitan Statistical Area Metropolitan Division	2018 (July 1 estimate)	2010 (July 1 estimate)	2000 (July 1 estimate)	Change 2010-2018 Number	Change 2010-2018 Percent	Units per square mile of land area, 2018	Number of units	Percent single family	Percent in structures with 5 or more units	Total value ($1000)
Stockton, CA Metro Area	245,541	233,928	190,509	11,613	5.0	176.4	2203	84.8	15.2	637,810
Sumter, SC Metro Area	66,134	63,586	57,218	2,548	4.0	52.0	333	85.0	14.4	41,312
Syracuse, NY Metro Area	296,351	287,949	278,406	8,402	2.9	124.3	266	96.6	0.0	56,091
Tallahassee, FL Metro Area	172,340	163,239	137,424	9,101	5.6	72.2	2236	43.0	56.4	352,532
Tampa-St. Petersburg-Clearwater, FL	1,435,316	1,354,322	1,148,904	80,994	6.0	570.7	23558	62.3	36.6	5,077,562
Terre Haute, IN Metro Area	84,023	82,226	80,177	1,797	2.2	44.0	48	50.0	0.0	8,250
Texarkana, TX-AR Metro Area	66,152	64,307	60,796	1,845	2.9	32.4	31	100.0	0.0	6,451
The Villages, FL Metro Area	72,385	53,566	25,696	18,819	35.1	130.0	2928	90.7	9.3	740,077
Toledo, OH Metro Area	303,710	301,336	286,078	2,374	0.8	187.8	1264	60.8	35.8	223,192
Topeka, KS Metro Area	105,388	103,890	96,606	1,498	1.4	32.6	261	95.0	0.0	56,499
Trenton-Princeton, NJ Metro Area	145,121	143,219	133,584	1,902	1.3	647.9	538	33.6	56.1	52,640
Tucson, AZ Metro Area	462,749	441,605	369,335	21,144	4.8	50.4	4251	74.9	24.3	1,104,603
Tulsa, OK Metro Area	434,419	410,509	367,312	23,910	5.8	69.3	4300	78.4	20.4	860,210
Tuscaloosa, AL Metro Area	115,583	107,194	94,114	8,389	7.8	33.1	1329	36.5	51.8	252,915
Twin Falls, ID Metro Area	42,277	39,249	32,430	3,028	7.7	16.8	759	69.7	0.8	119,514
Tyler, TX Metro Area	91,101	87,371	72,139	3,730	4.3	98.9	416	94.2	0.0	111,255
Urban Honolulu, HI Metro Area	352,527	337,111	316,367	15,416	4.6	586.6	2608	37.2	61.9	708,995
Utica-Rome, NY Metro Area	139,327	137,620	134,947	1,707	1.2	53.1	23	34.8	52.2	2,052
Valdosta, GA Metro Area	62,357	57,629	48,366	4,728	8.2	38.8	1082	99.1	0.0	199,531
Vallejo, CA Metro Area	158,808	152,829	135,034	5,979	3.9	193.2	816	100.0	0.0	235,718
Victoria, TX Metro Area	40,870	39,135	36,473	1,735	4.4	23.6	-	-	-	-
Vineland-Bridgeton, NJ Metro Area	56,490	55,906	52,909	584	1.0	117.0	136	100.0	0.0	11,832
Virginia Beach-Norfolk-Newport News, Metro Area	739,946	704,515	639,332	35,431	5.0	209.6	5783	73.4	25.3	1,085,390
Visalia, CA Metro Area	150,210	141,946	120,048	8,264	5.8	31.1	1743	90.2	6.5	370,361
Waco, TX Metro Area	110,206	102,983	92,693	7,223	7.0	61.1	938	66.5	29.4	152,534
Walla Walla, WA Metro Area	24,902	23,477	21,202	1,425	6.1	19.6	117	94.9	0.0	33,596
Warner Robins, GA Metro Area	75,569	69,558	54,064	6,011	8.6	143.7	1176	84.7	15.3	213,694
Washington-Arlington-Alexandria, DC-VA-MD-WV Metro Area	2,381,919	2,243,007	1,921,499	138,912	6.2	362.7	26297	47.6	51.5	4,794,205
Frederick-Gaithersburg-Rockville, MD Div	489,705	466,254	409,906	23,451	5.0	424.4	-	-	-	-
Washington-Arlington-Alexandria, DC-VA-MD-WV Div.	1,892,214	1,776,753	1,511,593	115,461	6.5	349.5	-	-	-	-
Waterloo-Cedar Falls, IA Metro Area	74,423	71,388	66,483	3,035	4.3	49.5	109	88.1	4.6	27,447
Watertown-Fort Drum, NY Metro Area	60,049	58,002	54,136	2,047	3.5	47.3	129	100.0	0.0	17,189
Wausau-Weston, WI Metro Area	76,971	74,577	65,278	2,394	3.2	31.8	293	61.4	29.7	49,496
Weirton-Steubenville, WV-OH Metro Area	57,598	58,308	59,143	-710	-1.2	99.3	0	-	-	0
Wenatchee, WA Metro Area	55,247	51,553	43,484	3,694	7.2	11.7	658	81.9	13.5	130,198
Wheeling, WV-OH Metro Area	68,801	69,510	69,420	-709	-1.0	73.0	1	100.0	0.0	100
Wichita, KS Metro Area	273,884	263,417	239,216	10,467	4.0	66.0	1456	62.9	10.9	233,939
Wichita Falls, TX Metro Area	65,437	64,843	62,223	594	0.9	25.0	12	100.0	0.0	1,945
Williamsport, PA Metro Area	53,540	52,522	52,482	1,018	1.9	43.6	18	44.4	0.0	3,628
Wilmington, NC Metro Area	142,840	128,256	101,048	14,584	11.4	134.2	2924	45.2	54.7	615,960
Winchester, VA-WV Metro Area	60,900	56,977	45,320	3,923	6.9	57.3	859	79.4	11.2	157,305
Winston-Salem, NC Metro Area	301,120	287,238	246,938	13,882	4.8	149.9	2302	96.3	3.7	407,439
Worcester, MA-CT Metro Area	386,318	376,139	342,938	10,179	2.7	190.9	234	76.5	19.7	44,574
Yakima, WA Metro Area	89,130	85,595	79,292	3,535	4.1	20.8	879	46.9	42.1	143,317
York-Hanover, PA Metro Area	184,869	178,942	157,223	5,927	3.3	204.5	145	67.6	25.5	29,002
Youngstown-Warren-Boardman, OH-PA Metro Area	259,329	259,702	257,023	-373	-0.1	152.4	210	96.7	0.0	43,017
Yuba City, CA Metro Area	63,170	61,539	51,023	1,631	2.7	51.1	-	-	-	-
Yuma, AZ Metro Area	93,565	88,070	74,476	5,495	6.2	17.0	1158	99.5	0.0	178,370

Table B-10. Housing Units, 2014-2018

Metropolitan Statistical Area Metropolitan Division	Total housing units	Occupied housing units	1-unit detached	With 2 or more vehicles	Number	Owner-ship rate	With value under $200,000	With value of $500,000 or more	Number	Percent who pay 30% or more of income	Number	Percent who pay 30% or more of income
Abilene, TX Metro Area	71,259	60,394	72.2	60.2	37,520	62.1	79.1	2.1	18,002	24.8	22,874	47.8
Akron, OH Metro Area	314,626	286,378	69.2	58.0	190,669	66.6	69.3	2.8	123,032	22.1	95,709	47.7
Albany, GA Metro Area	65,197	56,419	63.5	53.8	30,470	54.0	79.8	1.8	17,454	25.3	25,949	50.5
Albany-Lebanon, OR Metro Area	50,011	47,030	67.6	64.9	29,910	63.6	49.7	5.3	19,079	31.0	17,120	51.5
Albany-Schenectady-Troy, NY Metro Area	405,385	350,301	56.7	54.9	224,214	64.0	47.2	4.5	144,607	24.1	126,087	46.5
Albuquerque, NM Metro Area	387,356	349,150	67.0	60.3	233,231	66.8	55.1	5.3	150,315	30.8	115,919	52.4
Alexandria, LA Metro Area	67,084	54,989	67.7	54.5	33,926	61.7	72.4	2.7	17,041	22.0	21,063	54.1
Allentown-Bethlehem-Easton, PA-NJ Metro Area	348,609	319,220	56.6	60.8	220,978	69.2	47.7	4.4	144,437	28.4	98,242	51.4
Altoona, PA Metro Area	56,767	51,625	71.7	55.6	36,221	70.2	78.5	1.9	19,758	21.0	15,404	49.1
Amarillo, TX Metro Area	108,469	96,613	70.7	61.6	61,727	63.9	74.0	2.9	35,171	22.8	34,886	45.3
Ames, IA Metro Area	51,305	48,159	58.0	62.6	28,045	58.2	61.7	2.4	17,345	18.1	20,114	53.6
Anchorage, AK Metro Area	158,249	137,403	57.4	65.5	88,571	64.5	23.1	10.5	62,555	28.0	48,832	48.0
Ann Arbor, MI Metro Area	150,400	140,210	57.5	56.7	85,122	60.7	37.8	11.5	56,948	22.8	55,088	50.2
Anniston-Oxford, AL Metro Area	53,682	45,033	71.5	63.7	31,286	69.5	79.4	2.3	16,475	23.4	13,747	48.2
Appleton, WI Metro Area	96,922	92,514	71.9	66.8	67,297	72.7	64.8	2.2	44,862	19.2	25,217	37.7
Asheville, NC Metro Area	224,820	190,162	65.6	60.9	128,345	67.5	47.5	8.7	72,528	27.5	61,817	51.0
Athens-Clarke County, GA Metro Area	85,107	76,650	58.3	61.7	41,807	54.5	58.6	6.1	25,215	24.8	34,843	55.7
Atlanta-Sandy Springs-Alpharetta, GA Metro Area	2,271,249	2,065,239	66.9	61.4	1,303,504	63.1	50.2	9.9	951,636	26.0	761,735	49.6
Atlantic City-Hammonton, NJ Metro Area	127,987	99,874	58.3	52.6	67,336	67.4	43.5	7.9	45,331	43.2	32,538	61.5
Auburn-Opelika, AL Metro Area	68,081	59,373	56.0	63.8	35,821	60.3	61.6	5.2	22,036	23.0	23,552	54.8
Augusta-Richmond County, GA-SC Metro Area	255,334	214,489	67.2	60.5	143,066	66.7	71.3	3.1	86,523	24.8	71,423	52.5
Austin-Round Rock-Georgetown, TX Metro Area	807,434	742,689	59.5	61.5	431,612	58.1	32.1	15.1	299,053	26.2	311,077	48.3
Bakersfield, CA Metro Area	295,756	267,913	71.7	62.3	155,395	58.0	48.3	4.9	108,795	34.1	112,518	54.2
Baltimore-Columbia-Towson, MD Metro Area	1,155,684	1,043,798	45.0	57.0	693,241	66.4	26.7	17.5	500,031	27.4	350,557	49.6
Bangor, ME Metro Area	75,490	61,578	64.4	57.1	42,921	69.7	74.4	1.5	25,783	25.5	18,657	50.4
Barnstable Town, MA Metro Area	163,181	94,292	81.8	59.0	74,991	79.5	7.1	28.9	46,555	40.8	19,301	55.0
Baton Rouge, LA Metro Area	361,235	310,265	66.1	58.2	211,654	68.2	59.6	4.9	123,375	23.2	98,611	51.4
Battle Creek, MI Metro Area	60,879	53,659	71.7	55.0	37,280	69.5	83.4	1.3	21,469	23.6	16,379	50.4
Bay City, MI Metro Area	48,260	43,891	77.5	57.6	34,103	77.7	85.5	1.3	18,127	25.5	9,788	46.9
Beaumont-Port Arthur, TX Metro Area	169,444	146,376	70.0	57.5	98,270	67.1	79.6	1.7	41,338	24.5	48,106	46.6
Beckley, WV Metro Area	57,751	48,914	75.6	55.4	37,118	75.9	85.7	1.8	16,709	23.6	11,796	45.6
Bellingham, WA Metro Area	95,567	85,008	64.5	64.9	52,715	62.0	17.9	17.9	34,851	32.4	32,293	56.0
Bend, OR Metro Area	86,875	72,471	74.2	69.0	47,606	65.7	18.1	23.3	32,356	33.9	24,865	52.5
Billings, MT Metro Area	81,361	73,272	66.8	67.8	50,909	69.5	42.2	6.3	32,496	27.5	22,363	44.4
Binghamton, NY Metro Area	113,316	98,639	62.7	53.2	66,754	67.7	83.3	1.6	36,482	23.6	31,885	52.9
Birmingham-Hoover, AL Metro Area	483,046	415,615	69.8	61.6	285,531	68.7	62.2	6.0	179,063	24.6	130,084	48.8
Bismarck, ND Metro Area	57,673	53,781	57.7	66.1	37,236	69.2	36.9	6.8	21,974	17.5	16,545	39.9
Blacksburg-Christiansburg, VA Metro Area	72,096	62,433	59.7	64.5	38,076	61.0	57.2	5.4	21,213	22.2	24,357	49.3
Bloomington, IL Metro Area	72,125	66,159	61.5	60.4	42,440	64.1	64.6	2.5	28,356	17.3	23,719	43.7
Bloomington, IN Metro Area	71,291	64,232	55.9	57.3	37,280	58.0	64.8	4.1	23,744	20.7	26,952	59.2
Bloomsburg-Berwick, PA Metro Area	38,259	34,064	68.1	59.3	23,606	69.3	67.8	2.8	12,508	23.5	10,458	44.9
Boise City, ID Metro Area	268,985	253,531	75.5	64.4	174,103	68.7	45.5	6.1	123,296	25.4	79,428	46.1
Boston-Cambridge-Newton, MA-NH Metro Area	1,945,646	1,819,113	47.8	52.0	1,121,715	61.7	9.1	35.6	793,136	30.6	697,398	49.5
Boston, MA Div	816,354	757,727	42.9	45.6	434,989	57.4	7.4	35.9	312,956	32.1	322,738	51.1
Cambridge-Newton-Framingham, MA Div	944,595	892,691	49.0	54.4	561,962	63.0	7.3	40.7	394,230	29.9	330,729	48.4
Rockingham County-Strafford County, NH Div	184,697	168,695	63.1	68.2	124,764	74.0	23.2	11.9	85,950	28.2	43,931	46.2
Boulder, CO Metro Area	134,326	125,894	58.9	63.1	78,093	62.0	10.3	44.2	54,539	25.9	47,801	56.6
Bowling Green, KY Metro Area	73,656	64,721	66.9	63.7	40,584	62.7	71.5	3.4	24,603	22.0	24,137	43.1
Bremerton-Silverdale-Port Orchard, WA Metro Area	111,801	101,662	69.2	66.6	67,694	66.6	23.0	18.3	47,199	29.8	33,968	48.0
Bridgeport-Stamford-Norwalk, CT Metro Area	370,999	340,491	57.5	61.8	229,169	67.3	13.4	40.5	161,030	35.8	111,322	55.2
Brownsville-Harlingen, TX Metro Area	149,556	123,185	64.0	54.1	82,110	66.7	88.6	1.4	34,401	33.2	41,075	54.6
Brunswick, GA Metro Area	60,319	46,374	59.9	58.9	30,967	66.8	65.4	8.2	17,005	30.1	15,407	48.6
Buffalo-Cheektowaga, NY Metro Area	527,448	476,058	60.7	48.8	314,110	66.0	72.3	2.7	190,664	21.4	161,948	49.5
Burlington, NC Metro Area	69,749	64,059	67.8	62.1	41,668	65.0	71.5	2.7	25,454	25.7	22,391	50.0
Burlington-South Burlington, VT Metro Area	96,722	86,949	57.8	60.2	57,474	66.1	26.7	10.2	39,501	29.4	29,475	52.4
California-Lexington Park, MD Metro Area	44,442	40,332	73.4	70.7	28,565	70.8	18.0	11.2	20,971	21.2	11,767	43.8
Canton-Massillon, OH Metro Area	180,148	163,775	75.4	60.9	112,838	68.9	79.5	1.9	70,971	21.2	50,937	42.6
Cape Coral-Fort Myers, FL Metro Area	388,044	271,861	55.3	52.0	191,954	70.6	48.1	10.8	98,530	34.9	79,907	52.1
Cape Girardeau, MO-IL Metro Area	43,436	36,358	71.0	63.0	24,671	67.9	74.9	3.2	14,286	23.7	11,687	43.0
Carbondale-Marion, IL Metro Area	65,828	55,159	63.9	55.7	34,906	63.3	81.5	1.5	18,049	21.8	20,253	52.8
Carson City, NV Metro Area	23,821	22,461	55.9	58.4	12,511	55.7	36.0	9.5	7,344	32.4	9,950	43.7
Casper, WY Metro Area	36,703	32,851	66.4	69.2	22,023	67.0	49.2	6.2	13,660	23.0	10,828	40.3
Cedar Rapids, IA Metro Area	116,571	108,235	70.5	64.9	81,436	75.2	68.2	3.1	53,304	19.4	26,799	41.0
Chambersburg-Waynesboro, PA Metro Area	65,192	60,210	65.7	66.4	42,159	70.0	60.8	3.1	25,674	24.7	18,051	40.2
Champaign-Urbana, IL Metro Area	99,071	89,199	56.7	51.0	49,725	55.7	68.4	2.9	31,725	21.0	39,474	54.0
Charleston, WV Metro Area	131,568	110,903	68.5	52.6	79,133	71.4	82.5	2.1	35,144	20.8	31,770	46.4
Charleston-North Charleston, SC Metro Area	326,417	285,962	61.2	60.0	188,371	65.9	44.4	14.1	126,703	29.9	97,591	50.9
Charlotte-Concord-Gastonia, NC-SC Metro Area	1,022,352	934,829	67.7	62.9	613,505	65.6	53.9	8.8	433,815	23.6	321,724	46.2
Charlottesville, VA Metro Area	94,528	82,869	63.4	62.9	52,377	63.2	26.4	18.8	34,087	25.1	30,492	47.7
Chattanooga, TN-GA Metro Area	242,075	214,328	70.5	61.3	144,223	67.3	66.7	4.6	84,297	23.6	70,105	47.3

Table B-10. Housing Units, 2014-2018—Continued

| | Housing units, 2014-2018 | | | | | | | | | | | |
Metropolitan Statistical Area Metropolitan Division	Total housing units	Occupied housing units	Percent of occupied units 1-unit detached	Percent of occupied units With 2 or more vehicles	Owner occupied units Number	Owner occupied units Ownership rate	Owner occupied units Percent With value under $200,000	Owner occupied units Percent With value of $500,000 or more	Housing units with a mortgage Number	Housing units with a mortgage Percent who pay 30% or more of income	Renter-occupied units Number	Renter-occupied units Percent who pay 30% or more of income
Cheyenne, WY Metro Area	42,922	39,179	65.0	66.4	27,332	69.8	44.9	4.4	17,674	23.4	11,847	46.0
Chicago-Naperville-Elgin, IL-IN-WI Metro Area	3,832,322	3,495,713	52.5	52.7	2,252,365	64.4	41.6	11.8	1,519,679	31.2	1,243,348	49.7
Chicago-Naperville-Evanston, IL Div	2,929,154	2,663,951	47.2	48.9	1,653,977	62.1	38.3	12.8	1,108,883	32.8	1,009,974	49.8
Elgin, IL Div	269,623	256,160	69.1	69.2	185,860	72.6	42.8	5.4	133,446	28.6	70,300	50.3
Gary, IN Div	299,965	267,507	72.9	59.2	191,248	71.5	68.4	2.9	125,563	23.1	76,259	49.3
Lake County-Kenosha County, IL-WI Div	333,580	308,095	67.3	66.6	221,280	71.8	41.8	17.3	151,787	28.5	86,815	48.4
Chico, CA Metro Area	98,743	86,797	62.2	61.5	51,358	59.2	36.2	10.9	30,553	34.9	35,439	62.0
Cincinnati, OH-KY-IN Metro Area	938,116	854,217	65.8	60.5	566,198	66.3	63.1	4.6	393,217	21.9	288,019	45.5
Clarksville, TN-KY Metro Area	124,402	107,201	69.9	63.9	62,464	58.3	72.2	2.1	41,652	25.1	44,737	47.2
Cleveland, TN Metro Area	52,104	46,936	69.8	64.5	31,440	67.0	70.5	2.9	18,012	25.8	15,496	44.2
Cleveland-Elyria, OH Metro Area	960,797	857,453	65.2	52.9	557,077	65.0	69.1	3.4	352,238	24.5	300,376	48.5
Coeur d'Alene, ID Metro Area	69,325	60,497	74.4	69.2	42,635	70.5	39.3	11.2	28,116	31.2	17,862	48.5
College Station-Bryan, TX Metro Area	105,574	92,165	52.9	59.9	46,687	50.7	59.5	5.4	24,331	26.1	45,478	57.1
Colorado Springs, CO Metro Area	281,748	263,562	68.0	66.3	169,806	64.4	31.1	10.1	125,296	27.9	93,756	51.6
Columbia, MO Metro Area	88,281	79,944	60.8	60.6	45,951	57.5	59.4	4.5	29,971	18.7	33,993	50.0
Columbia, SC Metro Area	351,181	308,718	66.0	60.7	208,031	67.4	68.4	4.7	132,236	25.0	100,687	50.6
Columbus, GA-AL Metro Area	139,159	118,295	66.5	55.9	65,660	55.5	70.4	3.1	40,808	31.0	52,635	50.8
Columbus, IN Metro Area	34,134	31,669	72.9	63.2	22,587	71.3	69.3	3.8	14,152	20.6	9,082	35.8
Columbus, OH Metro Area	855,015	784,786	62.2	60.2	481,952	61.4	58.7	5.1	344,117	21.8	302,834	44.5
Corpus Christi, TX Metro Area	176,002	152,047	67.7	57.9	90,175	59.3	76.8	2.8	47,170	26.8	61,872	48.1
Corvallis, OR Metro Area	38,037	35,056	58.8	61.3	19,922	56.8	19.2	14.1	11,911	24.6	15,134	59.3
Crestview-Fort Walton Beach-Destin, FL Metro Area	147,075	103,835	59.3	62.1	68,317	65.8	46.8	10.8	41,614	28.3	35,518	51.6
Cumberland, MD-WV Metro Area	46,106	39,021	72.1	56.9	27,151	69.6	78.3	1.6	14,298	21.7	11,870	49.7
Dallas-Fort Worth-Arlington, TX Metro Area	2,714,467	2,510,847	63.5	63.0	1,493,033	59.5	51.9	8.6	989,982	25.9	1,017,814	46.7
Dallas-Plano-Irving, TX Div	1,821,695	1,689,084	61.4	62.0	977,120	57.8	47.4	9.9	653,603	26.5	711,964	46.3
Fort Worth-Arlington-Grapevine, TX Div	892,772	821,763	67.8	65.0	515,913	62.8	60.4	6.0	336,379	24.8	305,850	47.4
Dalton, GA Metro Area	55,974	50,124	62.2	65.4	32,484	64.8	80.5	2.4	17,072	22.9	17,640	41.5
Danville, IL Metro Area	36,133	31,180	78.6	54.5	21,563	69.2	91.2	1.0	10,660	18.2	9,617	44.7
Daphne-Fairhope-Foley, AL Metro Area	111,945	78,622	62.6	63.8	57,881	73.6	53.8	7.7	34,276	27.8	20,741	48.3
Davenport-Moline-Rock Island, IA-IL Metro Area	169,585	153,966	72.9	60.2	108,682	70.6	74.3	2.2	67,638	20.6	45,284	45.5
Dayton-Kettering, OH Metro Area	369,022	330,381	70.1	57.5	208,694	63.2	76.4	2.0	134,480	21.4	121,687	45.6
Decatur, AL Metro Area	67,324	58,457	71.1	66.0	43,061	73.7	76.5	1.7	22,719	24.4	15,396	43.9
Decatur, IL Metro Area	50,464	44,113	78.1	53.7	30,676	69.5	85.0	1.3	16,581	20.3	13,437	48.1
Deltona-Daytona Beach-Ormond Beach, FL Metro Area	310,284	253,614	67.3	53.7	180,126	71.0	60.7	4.6	95,690	35.1	73,488	57.7
Denver-Aurora-Lakewood, CO Metro Area	1,154,952	1,094,028	59.2	63.5	695,394	63.6	15.5	22.4	526,052	26.1	398,634	50.1
Des Moines-West Des Moines, IA Metro Area	280,834	260,852	67.0	65.0	181,856	69.7	59.4	4.1	128,827	19.8	78,996	42.8
Detroit-Warren-Dearborn, MI Metro Area	1,900,988	1,690,744	70.3	55.9	1,163,420	68.8	61.9	4.9	716,405	24.3	527,324	50.4
Detroit-Dearborn-Livonia, MI Div	814,962	676,587	69.7	46.8	419,567	62.0	77.6	3.0	223,712	27.2	257,020	55.4
Warren-Troy-Farmington Hills, MI Div	1,086,026	1,014,157	70.7	62.0	743,853	73.3	53.0	6.0	492,693	23.1	270,304	45.9
Dothan, AL Metro Area	69,051	56,401	68.7	60.4	38,683	68.6	76.2	2.5	21,018	23.7	17,718	46.0
Dover, DE Metro Area	70,576	64,545	67.0	64.0	44,554	69.0	44.7	3.4	29,088	31.3	19,991	54.6
Dubuque, IA Metro Area	41,065	38,330	70.3	62.4	27,736	72.4	65.5	2.8	16,854	20.0	10,594	45.5
Duluth, MN-WI Metro Area	151,241	123,165	75.3	61.3	88,356	71.7	67.8	3.2	52,625	23.6	34,809	47.8
Durham-Chapel Hill, NC Metro Area	264,983	241,274	60.9	59.5	148,054	61.4	46.8	10.3	100,302	23.9	93,220	49.6
East Stroudsburg, PA Metro Area	81,328	56,770	82.4	64.5	44,118	77.7	63.9	2.4	29,188	38.0	12,652	51.9
Eau Claire, WI Metro Area	71,990	66,238	68.4	63.6	44,283	66.9	66.6	2.9	28,419	21.8	21,955	45.8
El Centro, CA Metro Area	57,468	44,057	64.1	62.5	25,717	58.4	57.8	2.4	16,986	36.2	18,340	55.5
Elizabethtown-Fort Knox, KY Metro Area	65,198	57,403	66.0	64.8	37,341	65.1	72.3	2.5	23,889	23.2	20,062	40.4
Elkhart-Goshen, IN Metro Area	78,804	72,329	72.3	62.2	49,784	68.8	76.1	2.4	32,936	17.3	22,545	42.2
Elmira, NY Metro Area	38,797	34,373	66.7	54.1	23,349	67.9	84.8	0.9	13,616	21.5	11,024	52.2
El Paso, TX Metro Area	294,927	266,624	67.0	60.2	163,901	61.5	84.1	1.3	94,441	32.6	102,723	49.3
Enid, OK Metro Area	26,792	23,824	80.6	62.0	15,355	64.5	80.3	1.7	7,015	22.0	8,469	39.9
Erie, PA Metro Area	121,124	110,050	65.9	51.6	72,413	65.8	76.4	2.3	41,842	22.1	37,637	47.3
Eugene-Springfield, OR Metro Area	161,531	150,780	62.1	57.9	88,435	58.7	34.1	8.5	56,365	33.9	62,345	56.5
Evansville, IN-KY Metro Area	141,753	128,119	73.0	59.9	87,163	68.0	75.3	2.6	56,029	21.0	40,956	50.0
Fairbanks, AK Metro Area	44,059	36,513	61.0	66.2	21,363	58.5	37.2	4.2	14,745	30.1	15,150	48.5
Fargo, ND-MN Metro Area	106,086	97,987	47.6	63.0	55,489	56.6	49.5	5.1	38,075	16.1	42,498	43.3
Farmington, NM Metro Area	50,931	43,134	57.2	65.1	30,986	71.8	69.8	3.4	14,417	25.5	12,148	42.7
Fayetteville, NC Metro Area	217,778	187,226	65.5	58.9	104,460	55.8	74.9	1.7	69,982	29.3	82,766	51.6
Fayetteville-Springdale-Rogers, AR Metro Area	202,807	186,419	69.0	64.8	113,242	60.7	60.9	5.7	73,978	18.7	73,177	39.7
Flagstaff, AZ Metro Area	65,438	47,276	62.8	63.7	28,637	60.6	38.6	15.1	15,656	27.8	18,639	53.2
Flint, MI Metro Area	192,073	167,889	74.6	53.8	116,693	69.5	84.3	1.8	67,407	26.4	51,196	53.0
Florence, SC Metro Area	90,780	78,643	62.4	56.6	52,599	66.9	77.5	1.9	27,874	25.2	26,044	48.8
Florence-Muscle Shoals, AL Metro Area	71,258	60,313	74.8	63.8	42,225	70.0	75.4	3.0	21,936	24.3	18,088	45.6
Fond du Lac, WI Metro Area	45,035	41,346	71.2	63.8	29,448	71.2	68.6	2.8	18,326	21.9	11,898	42.2
Fort Collins, CO Metro Area	145,672	133,527	66.4	69.6	86,247	64.6	14.9	17.8	60,146	26.4	47,280	56.5
Fort Smith, AR-OK Metro Area	110,572	96,547	71.1	59.7	64,306	66.6	80.9	2.1	34,602	22.8	32,241	46.2
Fort Wayne, IN Metro Area	171,627	157,048	74.7	60.1	109,215	69.5	78.4	2.3	71,977	18.1	47,833	45.1
Fresno, CA Metro Area	328,577	304,624	67.7	58.6	160,944	52.8	38.5	8.6	112,334	32.6	143,680	57.2
Gadsden, AL Metro Area	47,705	38,777	77.6	62.7	27,882	71.9	79.9	2.4	14,134	26.0	10,895	44.7

Table B-10. Housing Units, 2014-2018—*Continued*

Metropolitan Statistical Area / Metropolitan Division	Total housing units	Occupied housing units	Percent of occupied units 1-unit detached	With 2 or more vehicles	Owner occupied units Number	Owner-ship rate	Percent With value under $200,000	With value of $500,000 or more	Housing units with a mortgage Number	Percent who pay 30% or more of income	Renter-occupied units Number	Percent who pay 30% or more of income
Gainesville, FL Metro Area	144,199	119,992	49.6	51.7	71,320	59.4	62.9	4.7	38,002	27.6	48,672	57.3
Gainesville, GA Metro Area	71,903	63,931	71.6	68.1	43,871	68.6	54.7	7.7	27,920	28.0	20,060	46.4
Gettysburg, PA Metro Area	42,068	39,221	74.9	68.6	30,293	77.2	49.3	3.9	19,223	25.7	8,928	48.8
Glens Falls, NY Metro Area	69,221	51,562	72.4	57.9	37,054	71.9	61.5	5.7	21,706	28.8	14,508	52.1
Goldsboro, NC Metro Area	54,074	48,153	58.4	59.7	29,626	61.5	80.6	1.3	16,608	27.4	18,527	49.0
Grand Forks, ND-MN Metro Area	47,537	42,731	53.2	60.3	23,857	55.8	57.5	3.3	14,358	18.5	18,874	49.8
Grand Island, NE Metro Area	31,550	28,878	72.1	66.9	18,713	64.8	75.0	1.8	10,251	20.7	10,165	39.3
Grand Junction, CO Metro Area	65,878	61,033	69.1	62.2	41,030	67.2	45.4	8.0	27,676	29.6	20,003	53.6
Grand Rapids-Kentwood, MI Metro Area	413,926	387,078	67.9	63.6	280,715	72.5	64.7	3.8	180,835	19.9	106,363	46.8
Grants Pass, OR Metro Area	38,853	35,978	69.5	66.6	24,021	66.8	34.5	9.7	13,822	40.4	11,957	58.6
Great Falls, MT Metro Area	38,558	34,444	66.4	62.0	22,114	64.2	63.0	3.4	12,734	23.6	12,330	45.7
Greeley, CO Metro Area	106,198	102,101	73.2	73.1	74,144	72.6	28.9	10.8	55,224	27.3	27,957	48.1
Green Bay, WI Metro Area	142,410	128,311	67.9	64.7	87,661	68.3	64.4	3.0	56,530	21.0	40,650	41.0
Greensboro-High Point, NC Metro Area	332,867	295,973	64.7	59.9	185,404	62.6	69.4	3.9	120,655	25.8	110,569	49.2
Greenville, NC Metro Area	78,563	69,169	49.6	59.2	36,232	52.4	72.5	2.0	24,343	24.6	32,937	57.1
Greenville-Anderson, SC Metro Area	380,042	338,714	66.4	62.0	229,577	67.8	65.9	5.0	137,832	22.3	109,137	46.9
Gulfport-Biloxi, MS Metro Area	186,294	155,946	68.4	59.2	99,381	63.7	73.5	2.4	53,141	28.6	56,565	50.6
Hagerstown-Martinsburg, MD-WV Metro Area	119,230	106,267	64.9	63.2	74,467	70.1	53.6	3.3	49,920	26.4	31,800	44.7
Hammond, LA Metro Area	54,515	47,527	63.7	57.2	32,447	68.3	70.4	2.3	17,732	26.9	15,080	56.1
Hanford-Corcoran, CA Metro Area	45,792	42,735	70.6	63.6	22,114	51.7	48.9	4.9	15,331	29.7	20,621	49.0
Harrisburg-Carlisle, PA Metro Area	249,728	228,652	56.8	58.3	154,635	67.6	58.4	3.9	98,823	22.9	74,017	44.4
Harrisonburg, VA Metro Area	53,370	47,714	60.3	65.3	29,230	61.3	48.0	4.3	17,516	24.7	18,484	48.6
Hartford-East Hartford-Middletown, CT Metro Area	514,242	471,188	59.5	57.7	314,172	66.7	33.8	7.7	215,743	28.4	157,016	50.5
Hattiesburg, MS Metro Area	71,823	61,603	65.2	59.5	39,973	64.9	73.3	2.7	20,415	25.3	21,630	52.5
Hickory-Lenoir-Morganton, NC Metro Area	164,134	142,087	66.7	66.4	101,065	71.1	75.6	3.6	57,464	23.6	41,022	43.6
Hilton Head Island-Bluffton, SC Metro Area	109,393	80,589	61.4	57.8	57,394	71.2	34.4	22.2	33,429	38.7	23,195	54.5
Hinesville, GA Metro Area	34,674	28,833	56.1	57.9	14,230	49.4	84.1	1.2	9,209	29.2	14,603	52.1
Homosassa Springs, FL Metro Area	79,115	62,762	68.5	52.5	51,119	81.4	75.2	2.0	23,359	32.4	11,643	58.0
Hot Springs, AR Metro Area	50,862	39,894	66.1	57.7	26,955	67.6	70.5	5.0	13,996	27.0	12,939	52.0
Houma-Thibodaux, LA Metro Area	85,968	76,463	70.5	58.4	55,913	73.1	70.1	2.2	27,450	23.6	20,550	48.7
Houston-The Woodlands-Sugar Land, TX Metro Area	2,547,552	2,310,213	62.7	61.9	1,395,737	60.4	56.1	8.6	860,624	26.1	914,476	48.4
Huntington-Ashland, WV-KY-OH Metro Area	167,773	143,459	70.1	57.8	102,626	71.5	79.5	1.7	50,940	22.4	40,833	50.8
Huntsville, AL Metro Area	195,368	177,382	72.8	63.4	122,714	69.2	58.2	4.1	81,217	18.9	54,668	46.0
Idaho Falls, ID Metro Area	52,865	48,697	73.3	72.7	35,064	72.0	62.5	3.4	22,398	22.9	13,633	43.5
Indianapolis-Carmel-Anderson, IN Metro Area	852,999	767,335	69.0	60.4	499,406	65.1	66.2	4.7	359,192	20.2	267,929	48.6
Iowa City, IA Metro Area	71,966	66,883	52.8	59.7	40,890	61.1	48.2	6.3	26,926	20.5	25,993	56.0
Ithaca, NY Metro Area	43,048	39,326	50.8	47.3	21,749	55.3	50.2	4.7	13,155	26.5	17,577	60.3
Jackson, MI Metro Area	69,508	61,696	75.7	58.9	45,279	73.4	76.7	2.1	28,131	23.6	16,417	49.5
Jackson, MS Metro Area	249,857	217,262	70.6	61.3	146,607	67.5	70.2	3.8	86,318	25.3	70,655	49.2
Jackson, TN Metro Area	78,989	68,245	76.0	60.4	45,141	66.1	79.4	1.8	24,258	25.4	23,104	52.4
Jacksonville, FL Metro Area	634,729	553,919	63.6	58.2	353,750	63.9	53.3	7.6	237,161	28.3	200,169	51.0
Jacksonville, NC Metro Area	78,501	64,065	59.9	63.6	33,808	52.8	73.1	3.2	23,291	32.8	30,257	48.2
Janesville-Beloit, WI Metro Area	68,875	64,538	72.5	63.5	43,857	68.0	76.3	1.6	29,332	23.7	20,681	44.6
Jefferson City, MO Metro Area	64,872	56,246	72.4	64.3	40,133	71.4	67.7	2.1	23,423	19.2	16,113	38.3
Johnson City, TN Metro Area	97,040	84,305	65.9	62.0	56,276	66.8	71.3	3.6	29,696	26.4	28,029	47.5
Johnstown, PA Metro Area	65,878	56,793	74.1	54.4	42,013	74.0	84.6	1.2	19,299	20.6	14,780	44.4
Jonesboro, AR Metro Area	55,745	50,237	69.3	58.3	29,435	58.6	77.8	3.0	16,976	18.8	20,802	47.8
Joplin, MO Metro Area	75,559	67,529	76.8	61.3	45,097	66.8	81.1	2.3	25,896	21.0	22,432	44.9
Kahului-Wailuku-Lahaina, HI Metro Area	72,570	54,274	57.1	63.5	32,685	60.2	6.0	63.4	22,162	42.4	21,589	49.3
Kalamazoo-Portage, MI Metro Area	111,646	102,809	63.9	57.6	65,624	63.8	67.7	4.2	41,831	19.5	37,185	47.4
Kankakee, IL Metro Area	45,515	40,050	70.5	59.8	27,319	68.2	72.8	1.8	16,931	26.7	12,731	48.4
Kansas City, MO-KS Metro Area	901,895	821,644	70.0	61.6	535,338	65.2	58.8	5.3	359,523	21.7	286,306	44.1
Kennewick-Richland, WA Metro Area	102,679	97,299	65.2	70.4	66,594	68.4	47.4	5.3	43,615	22.6	30,705	45.7
Killeen-Temple, TX Metro Area	173,950	150,293	66.0	62.9	84,069	55.9	74.8	2.9	52,508	24.9	66,224	44.1
Kingsport-Bristol, TN-VA Metro Area	148,666	128,069	69.2	63.2	92,879	72.5	76.0	2.7	45,831	24.6	35,190	45.2
Kingston, NY Metro Area	84,874	69,539	69.6	58.9	47,815	68.8	41.2	7.3	27,977	35.8	21,724	59.7
Knoxville, TN Metro Area	382,020	335,953	68.8	64.1	230,941	68.7	62.2	5.9	132,768	23.8	105,012	46.6
Kokomo, IN Metro Area	39,188	34,550	75.5	58.0	23,617	68.4	85.7	1.5	14,867	18.3	10,933	44.4
La Crosse-Onalaska, WI-MN Metro Area	58,740	55,500	64.1	63.1	36,424	65.6	63.0	3.4	22,017	22.0	19,076	45.0
Lafayette, LA Metro Area	207,351	180,421	67.6	57.8	124,358	68.9	68.2	4.1	63,975	22.7	56,063	49.2
Lafayette-West Lafayette, IN Metro Area	92,657	83,779	65.3	58.8	49,233	58.8	71.9	2.3	33,292	17.2	34,546	53.4
Lake Charles, LA Metro Area	92,827	80,013	66.6	56.2	54,228	67.8	68.6	2.6	27,434	20.5	25,785	49.5
Lake Havasu City-Kingman, AZ Metro Area	113,876	85,485	60.4	57.8	58,675	68.6	64.8	3.2	31,417	34.1	26,810	45.5
Lakeland-Winter Haven, FL Metro Area	291,796	231,260	61.2	53.3	158,475	68.5	73.0	2.5	83,251	30.2	72,785	50.9
Lancaster, PA Metro Area	209,870	199,889	55.3	61.3	135,976	68.0	49.9	5.4	85,395	25.9	63,913	48.3
Lansing-East Lansing, MI Metro Area	232,362	213,752	68.5	58.7	141,315	66.1	74.4	2.0	91,426	21.2	72,437	48.8
Laredo, TX Metro Area	81,596	73,659	65.6	60.5	46,017	62.5	81.1	1.9	24,406	37.2	27,642	56.7
Las Cruces, NM Metro Area	87,096	77,453	57.9	62.7	47,873	61.8	72.4	3.1	25,556	32.5	29,580	52.6
Las Vegas-Henderson-Paradise, NV Metro Area	888,556	767,954	58.9	53.6	408,047	53.1	37.4	8.3	287,310	31.0	359,907	50.7
Lawrence, KS Metro Area	49,732	46,294	55.7	60.7	24,001	51.8	52.9	4.1	16,340	20.7	22,293	52.7

Table B-10. Housing Units, 2014-2018—*Continued*

			Housing units, 2014-2018									
			Percent of occupied units		Owner occupied units						Renter-occupied units	
							Percent		Housing units with a mortgage			
Metropolitan Statistical Area Metropolitan Division	Total housing units	Occupied housing units	1-unit detached	With 2 or more vehicles	Number	Owner-ship rate	With value under $200,000	With value of $500,000 or more	Number	Percent who pay 30% or more of income	Number	Percent who pay 30% or more of income
Lawton, OK Metro Area	54,690	44,822	72.5	59.5	24,949	55.7	75.9	2.3	15,150	22.8	19,873	42.3
Lebanon, PA Metro Area	57,336	53,281	60.1	61.6	37,201	69.8	63.6	2.6	22,600	24.3	16,080	44.0
Lewiston, ID-WA Metro Area	27,761	25,473	68.6	68.2	17,947	70.5	57.4	2.7	10,500	21.3	7,526	44.8
Lewiston-Auburn, ME Metro Area	49,735	45,491	58.7	56.5	29,272	64.3	71.9	1.5	19,531	26.6	16,219	45.7
Lexington-Fayette, KY Metro Area	218,435	200,538	65.1	58.7	117,905	58.8	58.8	6.5	80,534	21.1	82,633	46.5
Lima, OH Metro Area	45,063	40,537	74.8	60.1	26,952	66.5	83.5	1.2	15,869	19.3	13,585	47.2
Lincoln, NE Metro Area	136,297	129,242	61.9	61.6	78,366	60.6	63.1	3.5	52,310	19.6	50,876	45.5
Little Rock-North Little Rock-Conway, AR Metro Area	323,538	282,138	68.0	59.4	180,483	64.0	69.3	3.7	113,951	22.4	101,655	47.9
Logan, UT-ID Metro Area	45,408	41,939	66.1	73.0	27,041	64.5	43.9	5.7	18,070	24.5	14,898	48.2
Longview, TX Metro Area	118,776	100,745	68.1	62.7	68,830	68.3	75.8	2.9	32,649	24.0	31,915	46.8
Longview, WA Metro Area	44,419	41,397	69.0	63.7	27,338	66.0	51.4	4.1	17,608	28.3	14,059	53.3
Los Angeles-Long Beach-Anaheim, CA Metro Area	4,615,697	4,338,482	49.3	59.7	2,106,898	48.6	6.4	59.6	1,516,763	42.6	2,231,584	58.1
Anaheim-Santa Ana-Irvine, CA Div	1,091,376	1,032,373	50.7	68.3	592,269	57.4	6.2	71.6	422,707	39.5	440,104	57.2
Los Angeles-Long Beach-Glendale, CA Div	3,524,321	3,306,109	48.9	57.0	1,514,629	45.8	6.5	54.9	1,094,056	43.8	1,791,480	58.3
Louisville/Jefferson County, KY-IN Metro Area	539,867	488,638	69.4	58.6	326,705	66.9	62.8	4.9	215,702	21.8	161,933	44.9
Lubbock, TX Metro Area	130,854	116,362	66.8	59.3	64,869	55.7	74.9	2.9	35,541	24.6	51,493	54.7
Lynchburg, VA Metro Area	116,114	100,371	69.2	65.4	70,778	70.5	63.6	4.9	41,058	23.1	29,593	49.2
Macon-Bibb County, GA Metro Area	102,633	85,991	66.8	55.2	52,697	61.3	78.9	3.1	30,437	28.6	33,294	55.1
Madera, CA Metro Area	50,362	44,759	80.4	65.9	28,627	64.0	36.4	7.3	18,914	34.6	16,132	56.4
Madison, WI Metro Area	282,959	268,213	57.2	59.4	163,262	60.9	35.4	7.7	114,922	23.0	104,951	45.9
Manchester-Nashua, NH Metro Area	170,155	159,200	57.8	64.2	104,999	66.0	25.2	6.7	74,342	27.9	54,201	47.3
Manhattan, KS Metro Area	55,458	48,097	52.5	64.7	22,747	47.3	59.1	4.1	14,113	22.7	25,350	50.6
Mankato, MN Metro Area	41,451	38,521	62.0	66.2	25,321	65.7	59.6	2.9	15,997	21.5	13,200	49.0
Mansfield, OH Metro Area	54,280	47,998	74.0	58.0	32,616	68.0	86.0	1.8	18,734	23.1	15,382	43.8
McAllen-Edinburg-Mission, TX Metro Area	272,157	234,879	66.1	57.3	159,967	68.1	88.9	1.3	68,002	35.2	74,912	53.6
Medford, OR Metro Area	94,525	87,417	63.8	62.1	55,116	63.0	33.0	13.1	33,838	36.8	32,301	56.4
Memphis, TN-MS-AR Metro Area	564,505	495,110	69.3	56.5	297,000	60.0	68.3	4.1	193,914	26.9	198,110	52.9
Merced, CA Metro Area	84,795	79,606	76.0	64.4	41,378	52.0	41.2	8.7	27,707	35.2	38,228	52.4
Miami-Fort Lauderdale-Pompano Beach, FL Metro Area	2,520,412	2,100,355	41.8	51.6	1,248,511	59.4	36.5	15.4	743,896	41.4	851,844	62.9
Fort Lauderdale-Pompano Beach-Sunrise, FL Div	821,088	682,088	41.2	52.6	423,316	62.1	40.5	13.1	263,092	40.9	258,772	61.2
Miami-Miami Beach-Kendall, FL Div	1,016,653	870,051	39.8	50.7	449,056	51.6	32.6	16.3	278,079	44.1	420,995	65.3
West Palm Beach-Boca Raton-Boynton Beach, FL Div	682,671	548,216	45.7	52.0	376,139	68.6	36.5	17.0	202,725	38.2	172,077	60.0
Michigan City-La Porte, IN Metro Area	49,061	42,904	76.0	61.8	30,824	71.8	78.0	2.9	19,822	23.4	12,080	47.4
Midland, MI Metro Area	36,806	34,017	74.3	63.7	25,722	75.6	73.7	2.9	14,930	17.2	8,295	47.5
Midland, TX Metro Area	62,074	57,606	65.0	66.5	38,611	67.0	51.3	7.6	20,553	21.2	18,995	44.3
Milwaukee-Waukesha, WI Metro Area	676,538	629,381	54.8	54.6	378,275	60.1	48.6	6.3	255,723	25.7	251,106	49.3
Minneapolis-St. Paul-Bloomington, MN Metro Area	1,430,490	1,360,921	61.3	62.6	951,478	69.9	34.5	9.3	684,068	22.0	409,443	46.8
Missoula, MT Metro Area	53,259	48,608	60.3	62.8	28,553	58.7	24.8	9.6	17,610	31.2	20,055	49.8
Mobile, AL Metro Area	191,673	161,838	72.6	58.2	106,154	65.6	77.7	2.8	62,572	27.1	55,684	52.7
Modesto, CA Metro Area	181,213	172,682	75.9	65.0	99,079	57.4	27.5	9.0	69,104	34.5	73,603	54.5
Monroe, LA Metro Area	92,000	74,168	66.3	50.8	46,326	62.5	71.9	3.0	22,153	25.2	27,842	55.6
Monroe, MI Metro Area	64,005	59,279	77.4	65.7	47,473	80.1	69.3	1.7	30,920	22.3	11,806	50.7
Montgomery, AL Metro Area	166,861	144,273	70.7	58.3	92,999	64.5	69.7	3.4	59,602	23.8	51,274	51.5
Morgantown, WV Metro Area	60,065	51,239	57.4	57.4	32,155	62.8	61.6	5.7	16,341	17.1	19,084	52.1
Morristown, TN Metro Area	62,225	53,269	69.4	67.2	37,986	71.3	75.5	3.7	20,475	24.7	15,283	46.7
Mount Vernon-Anacortes, WA Metro Area	53,426	47,937	74.9	70.2	32,378	67.5	25.5	14.7	20,150	33.9	15,559	51.6
Muncie, IN Metro Area	52,710	46,028	73.1	57.4	29,688	64.5	87.8	1.7	18,102	19.8	16,340	54.8
Muskegon, MI Metro Area	73,962	65,619	77.2	57.9	48,916	74.5	82.9	1.7	29,008	22.4	16,703	53.2
Myrtle Beach-Conway-North Myrtle Beach, SC-NC	288,964	182,812	52.3	60.3	133,896	73.2	56.8	5.8	76,171	34.3	48,916	51.7
Napa, CA Metro Area	55,557	49,032	68.6	66.6	31,256	63.7	9.3	64.3	20,605	36.9	17,776	54.0
Naples-Marco Island, FL Metro Area	210,825	140,942	41.5	53.6	102,429	72.7	23.1	30.3	50,214	36.7	38,513	55.9
Nashville-Davidson--Murfreesboro--Franklin, TN	753,116	695,444	65.3	64.8	454,666	65.4	44.8	11.1	311,317	24.6	240,778	46.5
New Bern, NC Metro Area	59,590	50,360	66.5	59.7	32,576	64.7	67.8	4.4	19,575	29.2	17,784	46.3
New Haven-Milford, CT Metro Area	366,266	329,857	53.6	53.2	204,295	61.9	35.6	8.9	137,643	33.5	125,562	53.4
New Orleans-Metairie, LA Metro Area	556,563	480,838	61.4	50.6	298,208	62.0	53.4	7.2	171,332	30.9	182,630	57.1
New York-Newark-Jersey City, NY-NJ-PA Metro Area	7,683,042	6,962,260	35.9	37.1	3,568,464	51.3	10.6	39.5	2,297,914	40.3	3,393,796	53.3
Nassau County-Suffolk County, NY Div	1,046,997	933,498	78.1	66.5	750,198	80.4	6.3	35.2	493,401	41.5	183,300	58.1
Newark, NJ-PA Div	861,921	774,797	53.2	54.1	472,232	60.9	14.4	29.7	328,528	36.7	302,565	53.0
New Brunswick-Lakewood, NJ Div	969,964	860,330	63.7	60.5	620,975	72.2	15.8	23.3	407,568	36.0	239,355	52.1
New York-Jersey City-White Plains, NY-NJ Div	4,804,160	4,393,635	18.0	23.3	1,725,059	39.3	9.5	49.8	1,068,417	42.5	2,668,576	53.2
Niles, MI Metro Area	77,322	63,908	76.0	56.7	44,588	69.8	68.6	5.4	26,215	24.9	19,320	48.9
North Port-Sarasota-Bradenton, FL Metro Area	424,433	324,203	55.0	51.3	236,063	72.8	43.3	12.8	114,179	34.0	88,140	54.2
Norwich-New London, CT Metro Area	123,001	107,402	64.8	60.9	71,459	66.5	36.8	8.3	47,405	29.5	35,943	48.7
Ocala, FL Metro Area	167,450	136,514	66.8	48.8	103,534	75.8	74.2	2.7	50,734	32.3	32,980	49.1
Ocean City, NJ Metro Area	99,157	39,904	51.6	56.5	30,960	77.6	24.3	22.1	18,718	42.0	8,944	61.5
Odessa, TX Metro Area	57,669	51,954	62.2	61.6	34,099	65.6	74.9	2.6	16,292	24.6	17,855	40.8
Ogden-Clearfield, UT Metro Area	219,880	205,890	74.4	74.1	155,586	75.6	37.4	6.3	111,839	21.4	50,304	41.4

Table B-10. Housing Units, 2014-2018—*Continued*

Metropolitan Statistical Area Metropolitan Division	Total housing units	Occupied housing units	Percent of occupied units: 1-unit detached	Percent of occupied units: With 2 or more vehicles	Owner occupied: Number	Owner-ship rate	Percent With value under $200,000	Percent With value of $500,000 or more	Mortgage: Number	Mortgage: Percent who pay 30% or more of income	Renter: Number	Renter: Percent who pay 30% or more of income
Oklahoma City, OK Metro Area	568,965	511,536	72.1	62.4	325,889	63.7	68.4	4.2	202,183	23.2	185,647	45.4
Olympia-Lacey-Tumwater, WA Metro Area	115,193	108,070	67.8	65.6	68,791	63.7	25.4	9.7	46,590	29.4	39,279	50.5
Omaha-Council Bluffs, NE-IA Metro Area	382,538	355,832	71.3	62.2	232,750	65.4	63.7	3.7	161,999	21.3	123,082	44.6
Orlando-Kissimmee-Sanford, FL Metro Area	1,012,994	855,265	58.9	57.2	517,149	60.5	49.5	7.0	342,676	31.7	338,116	55.7
Oshkosh-Neenah, WI Metro Area	75,203	70,173	65.9	61.3	45,603	65.0	70.6	3.6	29,281	21.9	24,570	42.5
Owensboro, KY Metro Area	50,990	46,927	74.5	61.2	32,184	68.6	77.5	2.6	18,992	20.6	14,743	46.1
Oxnard-Thousand Oaks-Ventura, CA Metro Area	287,498	271,226	63.6	70.4	171,554	63.3	6.7	58.6	125,729	39.2	99,672	57.9
Palm Bay-Melbourne-Titusville, FL Metro Area	276,294	228,888	64.9	54.6	166,825	72.9	56.5	5.9	94,833	30.5	62,063	52.8
Panama City, FL Metro Area	102,266	70,199	49.5	57.5	44,545	63.5	59.5	4.2	25,533	30.5	25,654	52.5
Parkersburg-Vienna, WV Metro Area	43,556	38,517	75.5	56.7	27,733	72.0	79.5	1.7	14,517	21.8	10,784	50.9
Pensacola-Ferry Pass-Brent, FL Metro Area	210,912	180,085	70.9	60.1	118,863	66.0	66.5	4.6	73,383	27.0	61,222	48.6
Peoria, IL Metro Area	182,927	164,085	77.9	59.2	118,289	72.1	76.1	2.1	70,316	20.4	45,796	42.8
Philadelphia-Camden-Wilmington, PA-NJ-DE-MD Metro Area	2,478,671	2,264,041	44.3	52.2	1,523,999	67.3	37.3	11.0	1,019,819	30.0	740,042	51.9
Camden, NJ Div	497,809	457,241	63.0	60.4	334,040	73.1	43.5	5.4	232,285	32.7	123,201	53.9
Montgomery County-Bucks County-Chester County,	781,413	740,924	58.8	65.3	549,795	74.2	17.4	18.7	378,061	27.5	191,129	47.9
Philadelphia, PA Div	907,051	801,183	17.3	33.2	457,775	57.1	57.9	7.7	284,483	32.4	343,408	54.2
Wilmington, DE-MD-NJ Div	292,398	264,693	57.6	59.2	182,389	68.9	33.8	6.7	124,990	27.3	82,304	49.1
Phoenix-Mesa-Chandler, AZ Metro Area	1,890,525	1,658,053	65.4	57.7	1,035,227	62.4	40.0	10.9	708,729	27.2	622,826	48.1
Pine Bluff, AR Metro Area	42,380	34,064	68.8	55.8	22,160	65.1	88.8	1.3	10,628	27.9	11,904	47.2
Pittsburgh, PA Metro Area	1,122,290	1,003,283	67.5	54.0	700,468	69.8	68.4	4.0	407,321	21.4	302,815	44.6
Pittsfield, MA Metro Area	69,078	55,167	64.6	50.8	37,994	68.9	48.1	10.8	23,896	30.4	17,173	51.6
Pocatello, ID Metro Area	37,042	33,422	66.6	66.7	22,823	68.3	72.6	1.5	14,260	21.6	10,599	43.5
Portland-South Portland, ME Metro Area	271,466	220,198	67.2	60.8	157,131	71.4	31.4	10.5	107,343	28.4	63,067	48.1
Portland-Vancouver-Hillsboro, OR-WA Metro Area	979,612	925,631	61.8	60.3	573,334	61.9	15.2	21.1	413,966	29.4	352,297	50.5
Port St. Lucie, FL Metro Area	219,761	176,737	62.9	52.8	132,519	75.0	54.0	7.9	68,796	37.0	44,218	59.7
Poughkeepsie-Newburgh-Middletown, NY Metro Area	262,832	234,123	63.5	59.5	160,075	68.4	26.1	8.7	107,799	37.1	74,048	57.0
Prescott Valley-Prescott, AZ Metro Area	115,213	96,007	66.0	62.1	69,055	71.9	41.6	11.7	39,547	37.5	26,952	50.3
Providence-Warwick, RI-MA Metro Area	701,870	627,503	54.5	54.7	382,942	61.0	27.1	10.6	263,740	31.4	244,561	48.0
Provo-Orem, UT Metro Area	172,298	164,039	67.0	77.7	111,307	67.9	22.8	11.5	82,429	24.2	52,732	47.4
Pueblo, CO Metro Area	70,928	63,762	75.1	59.8	41,006	64.3	68.5	2.3	26,234	29.3	22,756	55.5
Punta Gorda, FL Metro Area	103,372	76,150	66.5	51.6	60,547	79.5	57.1	6.1	28,486	34.9	15,603	58.8
Racine, WI Metro Area	82,611	76,384	67.9	60.0	51,822	67.8	60.5	3.9	34,422	24.0	24,562	48.5
Raleigh-Cary, NC Metro Area	523,123	482,401	62.2	66.4	315,759	65.5	40.1	9.8	235,888	20.5	166,642	44.5
Rapid City, SD Metro Area	60,082	54,510	64.1	66.5	38,063	69.8	57.9	4.0	22,673	26.7	16,447	45.0
Reading, PA Metro Area	166,768	154,467	55.8	61.5	110,715	71.7	59.7	3.2	71,666	27.2	43,752	52.7
Redding, CA Metro Area	78,535	70,473	70.3	61.4	44,721	63.5	36.0	3.3	27,341	37.4	25,752	57.1
Reno, NV Metro Area	195,879	179,230	60.2	60.9	104,490	58.3	24.6	16.1	71,517	29.9	74,740	46.5
Richmond, VA Metro Area	517,109	476,706	69.5	62.5	311,526	65.3	40.3	8.6	223,476	26.0	165,180	50.0
Riverside-San Bernardino-Ontario, CA Metro Area	1,549,773	1,348,982	69.4	67.1	846,141	62.7	22.7	16.7	608,234	39.4	502,841	58.8
Roanoke, VA Metro Area	146,252	128,792	71.6	61.9	88,037	68.4	59.6	5.5	54,001	25.2	40,755	45.6
Rochester, MN Metro Area	92,468	85,917	70.8	65.1	64,875	75.5	53.7	5.8	42,505	19.6	21,042	44.0
Rochester, NY Metro Area	478,789	431,331	65.7	54.3	289,522	67.1	74.5	2.5	185,898	23.9	141,809	53.6
Rockford, IL Metro Area	145,837	133,339	71.5	58.3	90,295	67.7	82.6	1.3	58,297	25.3	43,044	47.7
Rocky Mount, NC Metro Area	67,821	58,091	62.8	59.5	36,801	63.4	81.9	1.6	21,609	28.5	21,290	48.8
Rome, GA Metro Area	40,505	35,633	71.5	59.8	21,469	60.3	74.3	3.3	12,424	25.7	14,164	49.7
Sacramento-Roseville-Folsom, CA Metro Area	896,341	819,372	68.4	62.3	491,785	60.0	14.3	25.1	353,469	33.6	327,587	54.5
Saginaw, MI Metro Area	87,377	78,648	76.0	56.5	56,288	71.6	84.9	1.5	30,164	24.5	22,360	53.2
St. Cloud, MN Metro Area	80,994	75,108	70.1	65.3	51,461	68.5	61.0	4.0	32,761	23.9	23,647	45.7
St. George, UT Metro Area	66,604	54,702	74.2	67.5	38,125	69.7	29.5	10.9	23,730	31.7	16,577	49.7
St. Joseph, MO-KS Metro Area	53,921	47,075	74.3	59.8	31,362	66.6	78.0	2.3	17,395	21.3	15,713	37.8
St. Louis, MO-IL Metro Area	1,251,497	1,118,263	70.1	59.1	769,933	68.9	60.7	5.4	507,538	22.8	348,330	47.8
Salem, OR Metro Area	156,952	146,553	63.7	63.0	88,910	60.7	39.4	7.3	58,819	29.3	57,643	50.8
Salinas, CA Metro Area	141,155	126,052	62.7	66.0	64,362	51.1	10.0	46.3	43,311	40.6	61,690	55.7
Salisbury, MD-DE Metro Area	245,421	157,057	59.3	62.3	115,189	73.3	42.9	9.9	68,908	31.9	41,868	52.3
Salt Lake City, UT Metro Area	411,725	389,330	64.1	67.1	262,327	67.4	26.1	12.6	192,134	24.5	127,003	45.0
San Angelo, TX Metro Area	49,740	44,227	70.0	58.3	27,858	63.0	74.8	2.8	14,190	24.8	16,369	48.1
San Antonio-New Braunfels, TX Metro Area	883,332	803,662	67.5	60.2	503,727	62.7	63.2	5.4	306,105	26.6	299,935	48.6
San Diego-Chula Vista-Carlsbad, CA Metro Area	1,204,884	1,118,980	51.2	64.0	593,890	53.1	8.1	53.1	429,792	39.7	525,090	57.0
San Francisco-Oakland-Berkeley, CA Metro Area	1,796,567	1,692,047	49.9	55.4	922,001	54.5	4.6	76.2	664,813	36.1	770,046	47.2
Oakland-Berkeley-Livermore, CA Div	1,013,280	965,147	58.3	62.0	562,662	58.3	5.6	67.3	415,480	35.0	402,485	51.0
San Francisco-San Mateo-Redwood City, CA Div.	670,419	621,642	35.0	44.0	292,139	47.0	3.0	90.9	201,220	37.4	329,503	41.9
San Rafael, CA Div	112,868	105,258	62.7	62.5	67,200	63.8	3.3	87.1	48,113	39.2	38,058	52.3
San Jose-Sunnyvale-Santa Clara, CA Metro Area	683,979	653,265	53.2	67.9	371,922	56.9	5.1	84.6	264,420	35.2	281,343	47.2
San Luis Obispo-Paso Robles, CA Metro Area	121,095	105,317	67.6	68.1	63,986	60.8	8.0	54.9	42,924	41.1	41,331	54.2
Santa Cruz-Watsonville, CA Metro Area	105,894	95,756	64.4	65.1	56,873	59.4	6.6	73.3	38,438	39.9	38,883	61.1
Santa Fe, NM Metro Area	72,928	61,972	63.8	61.8	43,572	70.3	30.7	21.4	25,379	35.5	18,400	47.9
Santa Maria-Santa Barbara, CA Metro Area	156,210	144,962	57.7	63.3	75,640	52.2	8.6	52.9	50,193	38.0	69,322	57.3

Table B-10. Housing Units, 2014-2018—Continued

	Housing units, 2014-2018											
			Percent of occupied units		Owner occupied units				Housing units with a mortgage		Renter-occupied units	
Metropolitan Statistical Area / Metropolitan Division	Total housing units	Occupied housing units	1-unit detached	With 2 or more vehicles	Number	Owner-ship rate	Percent With value under $200,000	Percent With value of $500,000 or more	Number	Percent who pay 30% or more of income	Number	Percent who pay 30% or more of income
Santa Rosa-Petaluma, CA Metro Area	207,631	189,339	67.8	65.1	115,093	60.8	9.2	59.0	77,494	38.9	74,246	55.3
Savannah, GA Metro Area	160,259	141,276	65.2	58.7	82,906	58.7	55.6	8.0	56,356	27.7	58,370	50.4
Scranton--Wilkes-Barre, PA Metro Area	263,059	225,466	64.7	53.1	152,502	67.6	73.5	2.2	82,800	26.0	72,964	44.9
Seattle-Tacoma-Bellevue, WA Metro Area	1,567,384	1,473,063	58.5	60.4	883,869	60.0	12.6	35.4	647,238	29.5	589,194	47.3
Seattle-Bellevue-Kent, WA Div	1,224,324	1,155,364	56.6	59.0	687,979	59.5	9.0	42.3	505,037	29.1	467,385	46.3
Tacoma-Lakewood, WA Div	343,060	317,699	65.3	65.6	195,890	61.7	24.9	11.2	142,201	30.9	121,809	51.3
Sebastian-Vero Beach, FL Metro Area	79,216	57,403	63.8	51.3	44,838	78.1	54.1	12.3	20,661	32.7	12,565	57.9
Sebring-Avon Park, FL Metro Area	55,578	41,026	58.6	42.3	30,913	75.3	83.5	1.6	12,205	30.3	10,113	54.2
Sheboygan, WI Metro Area	50,939	47,303	65.3	62.3	33,193	70.2	67.9	2.6	21,268	21.2	14,110	36.1
Sherman-Denison, TX Metro Area	55,441	47,957	73.4	63.1	32,331	67.4	73.2	2.9	16,275	23.8	15,626	43.8
Shreveport-Bossier City, LA Metro Area	182,087	155,830	66.8	54.6	95,464	61.3	68.4	3.7	54,136	27.8	60,366	56.0
Sierra Vista-Douglas, AZ Metro Area	60,883	49,250	63.8	62.0	34,066	69.2	70.2	2.1	19,149	28.8	15,184	46.4
Sioux City, IA-NE-SD Metro Area	59,601	55,205	72.8	64.6	36,874	66.8	78.2	1.7	20,823	17.1	18,331	39.2
Sioux Falls, SD Metro Area	106,557	100,022	64.5	65.4	67,050	67.0	57.7	4.4	45,412	18.3	32,972	41.3
South Bend-Mishawaka, IN-MI Metro Area	142,598	122,096	76.6	58.2	85,459	70.0	77.2	3.7	53,715	20.6	36,637	46.0
Spartanburg, SC Metro Area	127,850	114,640	69.6	63.3	79,791	69.6	74.7	3.3	47,962	23.0	34,849	46.2
Spokane-Spokane Valley, WA Metro Area	235,298	215,922	67.0	63.0	137,858	63.8	47.6	5.8	91,364	28.7	78,064	50.9
Springfield, IL Metro Area	97,138	88,859	72.4	55.5	61,663	69.4	72.7	2.4	37,857	19.1	27,196	48.0
Springfield, MA Metro Area	291,263	268,036	58.1	51.5	168,553	62.9	41.6	5.1	110,386	29.6	99,483	54.5
Springfield, MO Metro Area	201,850	184,429	72.6	60.9	115,834	62.8	72.0	2.9	72,780	21.8	68,595	48.9
Springfield, OH Metro Area	61,310	54,905	73.3	59.6	35,679	65.0	83.8	1.4	21,168	22.2	19,226	42.4
State College, PA Metro Area	66,312	57,908	58.8	55.5	35,807	61.8	43.5	8.6	21,309	21.9	22,101	57.0
Staunton, VA Metro Area	54,172	48,961	74.8	64.9	34,443	70.3	52.4	4.9	21,644	26.3	14,518	45.3
Stockton, CA Metro Area	241,055	226,727	73.4	65.9	126,097	55.6	23.8	15.9	90,636	34.2	100,630	55.5
Sumter, SC Metro Area	65,576	54,464	60.5	59.1	36,783	67.5	80.4	1.8	19,353	27.3	17,681	51.9
Syracuse, NY Metro Area	294,185	257,682	64.6	53.3	173,817	67.5	76.2	2.2	108,487	21.5	83,865	48.1
Tallahassee, FL Metro Area	168,755	146,837	54.7	56.6	85,457	58.2	59.0	4.7	52,082	26.6	61,380	57.6
Tampa-St. Petersburg-Clearwater, FL Metro Area	1,405,990	1,196,966	55.4	51.2	768,511	64.2	56.9	7.1	447,384	31.0	428,455	53.0
Terre Haute, IN Metro Area	83,504	72,852	74.7	60.0	48,975	67.2	86.3	1.2	29,954	17.4	23,877	51.0
Texarkana, TX-AR Metro Area	65,699	55,919	67.5	58.8	36,130	64.6	81.1	2.3	16,532	23.5	19,789	50.1
The Villages, FL Metro Area	69,130	54,636	80.4	33.3	49,041	89.8	32.3	8.5	19,464	36.6	5,595	57.5
Toledo, OH Metro Area	302,894	263,624	68.5	56.0	167,193	63.4	76.0	2.1	105,045	22.2	96,431	45.5
Topeka, KS Metro Area	104,953	94,312	74.5	62.2	64,197	68.1	76.8	1.7	38,996	21.6	30,115	44.9
Trenton-Princeton, NJ Metro Area	144,681	129,873	49.6	55.9	82,934	63.9	28.8	20.7	56,226	32.3	46,939	52.6
Tucson, AZ Metro Area	456,962	400,907	60.3	54.2	250,126	62.4	58.5	6.5	156,025	28.5	150,781	51.8
Tulsa, OK Metro Area	428,297	380,053	71.1	61.3	246,740	64.9	71.3	3.9	148,748	22.8	133,313	44.8
Tuscaloosa, AL Metro Area	112,985	88,522	60.1	59.5	57,352	64.8	67.6	3.9	33,779	26.5	31,170	51.6
Twin Falls, ID Metro Area	41,305	38,525	76.8	69.3	26,054	67.6	66.4	2.5	16,725	25.8	12,471	47.0
Tyler, TX Metro Area	89,766	77,195	68.6	61.8	50,844	65.9	68.0	4.4	26,657	25.6	26,351	48.5
Urban Honolulu, HI Metro Area	348,497	311,525	44.8	56.3	173,697	55.8	3.7	69.5	117,352	38.1	137,828	57.8
Utica-Rome, NY Metro Area	138,876	114,597	63.8	51.5	78,117	68.2	80.3	2.2	43,307	23.6	36,480	48.2
Valdosta, GA Metro Area	60,980	52,105	63.8	57.3	29,379	56.4	78.0	2.6	17,302	27.8	22,726	51.2
Vallejo, CA Metro Area	156,896	149,067	70.5	67.7	90,420	60.7	11.8	23.2	68,472	33.6	58,647	54.1
Victoria, TX Metro Area	40,579	35,225	68.1	61.3	23,690	67.3	73.4	2.3	11,400	24.0	11,535	49.1
Vineland-Bridgeton, NJ Metro Area	56,429	50,608	67.6	55.9	32,602	64.4	68.6	2.0	20,035	35.6	18,006	63.1
Virginia Beach-Norfolk-Newport News, VA-NC Metro Area	730,690	658,516	60.6	61.7	405,741	61.6	35.8	8.6	293,851	31.4	252,775	53.0
Visalia, CA Metro Area	147,791	136,106	75.1	62.9	77,314	56.8	53.3	6.4	54,356	38.0	58,792	55.6
Waco, TX Metro Area	107,681	94,271	68.7	59.1	56,074	59.5	74.4	2.8	30,096	28.8	38,197	52.8
Walla Walla, WA Metro Area	24,522	22,304	69.6	63.8	14,400	64.6	46.8	8.0	8,206	26.5	7,904	53.3
Warner Robins, GA Metro Area	73,762	66,249	71.3	62.2	42,543	64.2	76.9	1.4	28,441	21.7	23,706	46.6
Washington-Arlington-Alexandria, DC-VA-MD-WV Metro Area	2,341,735	2,196,416	46.4	57.3	1,395,212	63.5	10.7	36.3	1,089,629	27.1	801,204	48.1
Frederick-Gaithersburg-Rockville, MD Div	484,240	461,632	50.2	61.1	310,642	67.3	9.2	39.3	231,753	27.4	150,990	50.7
Washington-Arlington-Alexandria, DC-VA-MD-WV Div	1,857,495	1,734,784	45.4	56.3	1,084,570	62.5	11.2	35.4	857,876	27.1	650,214	47.4
Waterloo-Cedar Falls, IA Metro Area	73,491	67,698	72.8	62.9	46,746	69.1	71.9	2.0	28,619	19.9	20,952	46.6
Watertown-Fort Drum, NY Metro Area	59,801	43,267	57.4	54.8	24,108	55.7	71.3	3.2	13,909	24.2	19,159	46.5
Wausau-Weston, WI Metro Area	76,167	67,924	75.6	67.6	50,055	73.7	70.5	2.5	30,167	22.3	17,869	37.6
Weirton-Steubenville, WV-OH Metro Area	57,751	50,017	77.7	56.2	35,499	71.0	88.4	1.3	17,332	19.0	14,518	44.6
Wenatchee, WA Metro Area	54,118	43,102	68.2	68.3	28,959	67.2	28.6	12.1	17,593	28.4	14,143	38.1
Wheeling, WV-OH Metro Area	68,959	55,783	74.8	57.1	41,830	75.0	79.4	1.7	18,998	17.8	13,953	45.2
Wichita, KS Metro Area	270,145	242,956	73.1	63.1	159,062	65.5	76.1	2.2	99,458	20.7	83,894	45.4
Wichita Falls, TX Metro Area	65,333	55,328	73.5	58.6	35,524	64.2	83.9	1.5	17,776	25.9	19,804	49.5
Williamsport, PA Metro Area	53,340	45,897	69.0	59.5	31,852	69.4	70.5	2.7	18,634	25.5	14,045	48.6
Wilmington, NC Metro Area	137,845	115,402	62.1	60.7	71,092	61.6	43.6	9.9	48,066	32.8	44,310	53.7
Winchester, VA-WV Metro Area	59,469	51,190	71.8	67.6	35,774	69.9	42.4	5.4	23,457	24.6	15,416	45.3
Winston-Salem, NC Metro Area	295,862	262,905	68.4	61.9	175,467	66.7	70.9	3.9	109,705	23.9	87,438	48.5
Worcester, MA-CT Metro Area	383,474	351,743	57.7	58.0	230,641	65.6	29.5	6.8	162,609	27.4	121,102	49.0
Yakima, WA Metro Area	88,226	82,300	67.7	69.3	52,001	63.2	62.9	3.4	30,839	31.3	30,299	45.0
York-Hanover, PA Metro Area	183,379	171,244	63.7	65.4	127,920	74.7	61.3	2.5	83,625	26.2	43,324	50.6
Youngstown-Warren-Boardman, OH-PA Metro Area	259,354	230,243	76.1	56.1	161,867	70.3	83.1	1.4	87,173	22.7	68,376	48.1
Yuba City, CA Metro Area	62,685	58,539	70.2	64.8	33,947	58.0	35.2	8.3	22,486	34.3	24,592	51.5
Yuma, AZ Metro Area	91,685	72,463	52.4	57.6	48,612	67.1	79.2	1.3	28,065	32.4	23,851	45.3

Table B-11. Personal income and Earnings by Place of Work

Metropolitan Statistical Area Metropolitan Division	Personal Income										
	Total personal income			Percent change		Per capita personal income			Earnings (million dollars)		
	2018	2010	2005	2010-2018	2005-2010	2018	2010	2005	2018	2010	2005
Abilene, TX Metro Area	7,396,471	5,705,250	4,552,568	29.6	25.3	43,140	34,456	28,319	4,738	3,858	3,220
Akron, OH Metro Area	34,835,247	26,886,702	23,725,368	29.6	13.3	49,423	38,244	33,773	23,831	19,116	17,430
Albany, GA Metro Area	5,621,848	4,727,287	4,064,538	18.9	16.3	37,500	30,666	26,580	3,661	3,198	3,028
Albany-Lebanon, OR Metro Area	5,461,463	3,697,969	3,029,078	47.7	22.1	42,891	31,627	28,013	3,192	2,239	2,118
Albany-Schenectady-Troy, NY Metro Area	51,315,302	38,693,831	31,685,602	32.6	22.1	58,104	44,421	37,076	37,274	29,623	25,287
Albuquerque, NM Metro Area	38,960,264	30,634,965	25,413,256	27.2	20.5	42,536	34,438	31,392	26,042	21,663	19,244
Alexandria, LA Metro Area	6,733,129	5,361,291	4,527,139	25.6	18.4	43,995	34,793	30,603	4,202	3,537	2,950
Allentown-Bethlehem-Easton, PA-NJ Metro Area	45,618,354	34,563,981	29,310,311	32.0	17.9	54,120	42,053	37,208	28,712	22,106	20,034
Altoona, PA Metro Area	5,725,643	4,439,095	3,780,067	29.0	17.4	46,743	34,942	29,828	3,951	3,168	2,890
Amarillo, TX Metro Area	12,268,352	9,450,943	6,979,629	29.8	35.4	46,131	37,403	29,036	8,822	7,077	5,348
Ames, IA Metro Area	5,416,028	3,955,162	3,436,353	36.9	15.1	43,519	34,117	31,415	4,028	2,946	2,560
Anchorage, AK Metro Area	24,329,258	20,208,961	14,688,499	20.4	37.6	60,953	52,759	41,859	17,104	14,908	11,728
Ann Arbor, MI Metro Area	22,021,358	15,690,064	13,739,787	40.4	14.2	59,363	45,392	40,147	17,160	12,582	12,267
Anniston-Oxford, AL Metro Area	4,241,974	3,661,982	3,143,525	15.8	16.5	37,120	30,909	27,460	2,631	2,553	2,267
Appleton, WI Metro Area	12,145,541	8,669,917	7,443,643	40.1	16.5	51,134	38,372	34,473	8,697	6,385	5,906
Asheville, NC Metro Area	20,880,264	14,218,227	12,058,452	46.9	17.9	45,433	33,428	30,419	12,615	8,843	8,007
Athens-Clarke County, GA Metro Area	8,598,032	5,693,052	4,974,740	51.0	14.4	40,690	29,431	27,796	6,265	4,401	3,906
Atlanta-Sandy Springs-Alpharetta, GA Metro Area	312,213,493	203,513,558	183,620,829	53.4	10.8	52,473	38,379	38,488	241,551	159,712	153,538
Atlantic City-Hammonton, NJ Metro Area	12,917,979	10,708,168	9,127,596	20.6	17.3	48,668	38,989	33,764	9,311	8,182	7,953
Auburn-Opelika, AL Metro Area	6,235,716	4,131,431	3,244,253	50.9	27.3	38,036	29,341	25,721	3,507	2,336	2,065
Augusta-Richmond County, GA-SC Metro Area	25,407,239	18,732,472	15,493,330	35.6	20.9	42,053	33,067	29,162	17,386	13,103	11,347
Austin-Round Rock-Georgetown, TX Metro Area	127,439,164	70,355,303	52,344,576	81.1	34.4	58,773	40,726	36,016	100,077	54,518	43,145
Bakersfield, CA Metro Area	35,603,843	26,097,169	20,176,085	36.4	29.3	39,703	31,028	26,522	25,571	19,331	15,561
Baltimore-Columbia-Towson, MD Metro Area	174,900,870	132,299,439	112,150,514	32.2	18.0	62,402	48,716	42,413	127,665	96,235	82,275
Bangor, ME Metro Area	6,354,094	5,134,339	4,390,723	23.8	16.9	42,053	33,370	29,325	4,451	3,668	3,341
Barnstable Town, MA Metro Area	15,953,917	11,312,044	10,019,742	41.0	12.9	74,756	52,397	45,135	7,785	5,865	5,618
Baton Rouge, LA Metro Area	41,009,489	31,287,421	24,036,762	31.1	30.2	48,042	37,804	31,681	30,711	23,135	18,083
Battle Creek, MI Metro Area	5,416,654	4,337,337	3,958,299	24.9	9.6	40,276	31,903	28,488	4,137	3,405	3,230
Bay City, MI Metro Area	4,335,883	3,591,408	3,136,649	20.7	14.5	41,722	33,352	28,733	2,226	1,991	1,889
Beaumont-Port Arthur, TX Metro Area	17,622,789	13,655,532	10,809,511	29.1	26.3	44,527	35,081	28,041	12,843	10,128	8,150
Beckley, WV Metro Area	4,540,369	3,831,216	3,146,912	18.5	21.7	38,717	30,662	25,262	2,591	2,336	2,035
Bellingham, WA Metro Area	11,011,627	7,414,196	5,703,008	48.5	30.0	48,792	36,786	30,752	6,993	4,864	4,116
Bend, OR Metro Area	10,587,224	5,493,841	4,669,326	92.7	17.7	55,143	34,828	33,218	6,755	3,249	3,321
Billings, MT Metro Area	9,383,485	6,464,005	5,038,739	45.2	28.3	52,019	38,574	32,294	6,578	4,688	3,848
Binghamton, NY Metro Area	10,765,870	8,946,988	7,188,525	20.3	24.5	44,817	35,576	28,516	7,013	6,238	5,408
Birmingham-Hoover, AL Metro Area	55,469,335	41,703,186	36,624,610	33.0	13.9	50,979	39,279	35,983	39,693	30,296	28,068
Bismarck, ND Metro Area	7,258,313	4,776,622	3,375,405	52.0	41.5	56,564	42,990	33,138	5,124	3,556	2,629
Blacksburg-Christiansburg, VA Metro Area	6,483,480	4,707,296	4,035,455	37.7	16.6	38,538	28,855	25,802	4,527	3,322	3,175
Bloomington, IL Metro Area	8,499,762	6,822,087	5,497,638	24.6	24.1	49,180	40,175	34,296	6,984	6,101	5,139
Bloomington, IN Metro Area	7,037,172	4,913,993	4,121,467	43.2	19.2	41,947	30,688	27,459	4,800	3,525	3,119
Bloomsburg-Berwick, PA Metro Area	3,810,398	2,978,939	2,419,866	27.9	23.1	45,527	34,776	28,905	3,058	2,418	1,973
Boise City, ID Metro Area	33,580,111	20,737,699	17,633,546	61.9	17.6	45,973	33,563	32,238	23,472	14,893	13,540
Boston-Cambridge-Newton, MA-NH Metro Area	383,664,542	265,132,347	215,312,270	44.7	23.1	78,694	58,061	48,735	303,977	217,579	179,594
Boston, MA Div	165,583,381	114,957,000	90,225,112	44.0	27.4	81,537	60,670	49,454	146,965	105,472	86,069
Cambridge-Newton-Framingham, MA Div	188,678,903	130,151,426	107,792,059	45.0	20.7	78,441	57,764	49,361	139,130	99,221	81,833
Rockingham County-Strafford County, NH Div	29,402,258	20,023,921	17,295,099	46.8	15.8	66,935	47,848	42,196	17,882	12,885	11,693
Boulder, CO Metro Area	23,932,182	14,889,031	12,959,689	60.7	14.9	73,394	50,339	46,245	17,374	11,728	10,663
Bowling Green, KY Metro Area	6,518,937	4,732,922	3,923,750	37.7	20.6	36,740	29,704	26,890	4,577	3,294	2,987
Bremerton-Silverdale-Port Orchard, WA Metro Area	15,174,970	10,639,890	9,068,926	42.6	17.3	56,244	42,276	37,818	8,392	6,393	5,599
Bridgeport-Stamford-Norwalk, CT Metro Area	113,853,354	95,360,433	66,817,392	19.4	42.7	120,630	103,728	74,436	63,226	64,807	44,855
Brownsville-Harlingen, TX Metro Area	12,189,811	9,518,840	6,983,279	28.1	36.3	28,756	23,350	18,700	7,427	5,896	4,648
Brunswick, GA Metro Area	4,867,598	3,597,292	3,287,084	35.3	9.4	41,092	31,971	32,375	2,832	2,250	2,127
Buffalo-Cheektowaga, NY Metro Area	56,975,999	43,978,449	36,514,174	29.6	20.4	50,414	38,726	31,791	40,043	31,439	27,383
Burlington, NC Metro Area	6,548,003	4,846,334	4,003,936	35.1	21.0	39,342	32,002	28,741	3,724	2,849	2,711
Burlington-South Burlington, VT Metro Area	12,728,796	9,289,099	7,734,611	37.0	20.1	57,575	43,913	37,431	9,464	7,361	6,378
California-Lexington Park, MD Metro Area	6,401,617	4,961,849	3,661,019	29.0	35.5	56,820	46,915	37,793	4,702	3,721	2,690
Canton-Massillon, OH Metro Area	17,846,413	13,728,976	12,327,626	30.0	11.4	44,767	33,965	30,426	10,787	8,310	8,285
Cape Coral-Fort Myers, FL Metro Area	38,685,758	24,256,409	20,804,368	59.5	16.6	51,266	39,095	37,483	19,718	12,795	12,569
Cape Girardeau, MO-IL Metro Area	4,252,675	3,194,740	2,710,284	33.1	17.9	43,850	33,124	29,089	2,934	2,347	2,113
Carbondale-Marion, IL Metro Area	5,573,284	4,667,562	3,698,867	19.4	26.2	40,701	33,479	27,059	3,804	3,254	2,654
Carson City, NV Metro Area	2,812,458	2,431,986	1,374,248	15.6	77.0	50,754	44,229	24,548	2,390	2,302	1,159
Casper, WY Metro Area	5,488,907	3,727,816	2,746,085	47.2	35.8	69,379	49,395	39,274	4,202	2,867	1,990
Cedar Rapids, IA Metro Area	14,205,142	10,578,111	8,412,840	34.3	25.7	52,168	40,932	34,024	10,540	8,204	6,826
Chambersburg-Waynesboro, PA Metro Area	7,184,846	5,399,921	4,562,719	33.1	18.3	46,403	36,020	32,843	4,140	3,132	2,834
Champaign-Urbana, IL Metro Area	10,407,738	8,410,121	6,415,552	23.8	31.1	45,975	38,534	30,947	7,729	6,543	5,196
Charleston, WV Metro Area	11,468,907	9,958,597	8,361,125	15.2	19.1	44,053	35,848	29,880	8,941	7,862	6,923
Charleston-North Charleston, SC Metro Area	40,137,052	24,298,555	19,398,522	65.2	25.3	50,958	36,406	32,422	28,112	17,220	14,338
Charlotte-Concord-Gastonia, NC-SC Metro Area	135,350,409	87,057,935	70,783,635	55.5	23.0	52,176	38,691	36,100	105,406	67,933	58,741
Charlottesville, VA Metro Area	14,529,313	9,306,406	7,565,042	56.1	23.0	66,577	46,097	40,117	9,261	6,587	5,389
Chattanooga, TN-GA Metro Area	25,740,295	18,852,194	15,591,855	36.5	20.9	45,900	35,627	31,211	18,640	13,798	12,079
Cheyenne, WY Metro Area	5,150,637	3,936,992	3,137,052	30.8	25.5	52,039	42,684	36,591	3,801	2,872	2,258
Chicago-Naperville-Elgin, IL-IN-WI Metro Area	580,270,144	418,681,182	377,830,834	38.6	10.8	61,089	44,207	40,731	430,066	315,392	299,214
Chicago-Naperville-Evanston, IL Div	446,425,623	320,133,011	291,849,061	39.5	9.7	62,342	44,741	41,192	347,144	252,866	243,209
Elgin, IL Div	37,957,288	27,888,638	22,356,862	36.1	24.7	49,535	37,858	34,136	20,925	16,046	14,587
Gary, IN Div	32,894,999	24,898,486	21,827,467	32.1	14.1	46,900	35,159	31,552	18,862	15,270	13,920
Lake County-Kenosha County, IL-WI Div	62,992,234	45,761,047	41,797,444	37.7	9.5	72,395	52,550	49,493	43,135	31,209	27,498
Chico, CA Metro Area	10,255,376	7,309,787	6,164,088	40.3	18.6	44,346	33,235	28,703	5,984	4,378	4,016

Table B-11. Personal income and Earnings by Place of Work—*Continued*

Metropolitan Statistical Area Metropolitan Division	Total personal income 2018	Total personal income 2010	Total personal income 2005	Percent change 2010-2018	Percent change 2005-2010	Per capita personal income 2018	Per capita personal income 2010	Per capita personal income 2005	Earnings (million dollars) 2018	Earnings (million dollars) 2010	Earnings (million dollars) 2005
Cincinnati, OH-KY-IN Metro Area	119,887,654	86,411,968	75,654,735	38.7	14.2	54,176	40,366	36,409	86,578	64,868	58,287
Clarksville, TN-KY Metro Area	12,230,151	9,923,549	7,715,177	23.2	28.6	39,991	36,091	30,802	8,381	7,368	5,957
Cleveland, TN Metro Area	4,743,555	3,562,789	2,940,967	33.1	21.1	38,371	30,740	26,880	2,859	2,124	1,985
Cleveland-Elyria, OH Metro Area	110,538,721	82,196,381	75,099,017	34.5	9.5	53,738	39,604	35,563	82,220	62,191	59,679
Coeur d'Alene, ID Metro Area	7,265,573	4,461,860	3,682,987	62.8	21.1	44,987	32,134	29,237	3,940	2,600	2,377
College Station-Bryan, TX Metro Area	10,374,675	6,967,703	5,015,996	48.9	38.9	39,533	30,367	24,649	7,360	5,042	3,843
Colorado Springs, CO Metro Area	35,832,538	24,893,157	20,162,259	43.9	23.5	48,492	38,275	34,303	24,003	17,673	15,435
Columbia, MO Metro Area	9,662,239	6,958,980	5,560,147	38.8	25.2	46,510	36,446	31,546	6,832	5,097	4,295
Columbia, SC Metro Area	37,391,893	26,529,741	22,018,694	40.9	20.5	44,906	34,470	31,493	27,250	19,698	17,313
Columbus, GA-AL Metro Area	13,056,167	10,131,715	9,009,394	28.9	12.5	41,067	32,740	30,146	9,293	8,001	6,733
Columbus, IN Metro Area	4,131,157	2,893,676	2,453,889	42.8	17.9	49,922	37,668	33,314	4,029	2,559	2,286
Columbus, OH Metro Area	107,780,707	73,474,721	61,958,225	46.7	18.6	51,165	38,542	34,592	84,573	58,291	51,466
Corpus Christi, TX Metro Area	19,016,251	14,702,307	11,798,207	29.3	24.6	44,311	36,331	30,040	13,722	11,005	9,237
Corvallis, OR Metro Area	4,330,505	3,085,491	2,682,076	40.4	15.0	47,019	36,056	33,135	3,018	2,301	2,094
Crestview-Fort Walton Beach-Destin, FL Metro Area	14,393,306	9,559,627	8,547,685	50.6	11.8	51,655	40,520	36,617	9,469	6,462	6,359
Cumberland, MD-WV Metro Area	3,921,418	3,278,334	2,789,268	19.6	17.5	40,049	31,784	27,570	2,314	2,027	1,891
Dallas-Fort Worth-Arlington, TX Metro Area	417,480,554	262,043,276	212,703,311	59.3	23.2	55,886	40,994	37,170	334,735	210,167	181,366
Dallas-Plano-Irving, TX Div	293,143,908	177,669,534	146,032,505	65.0	21.7	58,545	41,833	38,307	250,379	151,784	131,924
Fort Worth-Arlington-Grapevine, TX Div	124,336,646	84,373,742	66,670,806	47.4	26.6	50,482	39,332	34,902	84,356	58,382	49,442
Dalton, GA Metro Area	5,228,926	3,651,564	3,558,793	43.2	2.6	36,316	25,666	26,581	4,387	3,216	3,558
Danville, IL Metro Area	3,032,359	2,647,762	2,200,608	14.5	20.3	39,481	32,433	26,601	1,893	1,715	1,542
Daphne-Fairhope-Foley, AL Metro Area	9,940,939	6,618,292	5,243,158	50.2	26.2	45,596	36,144	32,329	4,315	2,800	2,585
Davenport-Moline-Rock Island, IA-IL Metro Area	18,756,585	15,194,129	12,703,537	23.4	19.6	49,172	40,011	34,069	13,219	11,236	9,945
Dayton-Kettering, OH Metro Area	38,461,497	29,014,505	26,205,412	32.6	10.7	47,687	36,283	32,563	27,862	21,526	21,376
Decatur, AL Metro Area	5,887,132	4,818,572	4,183,243	22.2	15.2	38,719	31,300	28,189	3,452	2,867	2,717
Decatur, IL Metro Area	5,048,618	4,367,830	3,638,308	15.6	20.1	48,214	39,427	32,753	3,956	3,315	2,986
Deltona-Daytona Beach-Ormond Beach, FL Metro a	28,381,303	19,697,921	17,277,063	44.1	14.0	43,028	33,357	30,671	12,064	8,680	8,658
Denver-Aurora-Lakewood, CO Metro Area	188,515,221	111,542,391	97,009,527	69.0	15.0	64,287	43,660	41,586	145,819	87,401	80,152
Des Moines-West Des Moines, IA Metro Area	37,465,628	25,522,229	21,047,571	46.8	21.3	54,098	41,913	37,648	28,907	20,576	17,764
Detroit-Warren-Dearborn, MI Metro Area	229,674,196	163,054,960	163,362,941	40.9	-0.2	53,086	37,994	36,868	168,697	119,099	132,148
Detroit-Dearborn-Livonia, MI Div	75,316,539	58,973,262	58,850,370	27.7	0.2	42,942	32,489	30,022	62,999	47,810	52,947
Warren-Troy-Farmington Hills, MI Div	154,357,657	104,081,698	104,512,571	48.3	-0.4	60,002	42,029	42,299	105,698	71,289	79,201
Dothan, AL Metro Area	6,060,640	4,924,610	4,065,101	23.1	21.1	40,883	33,760	29,750	3,524	2,876	2,749
Dover, DE Metro Area	7,503,142	5,515,453	4,502,954	36.0	22.5	42,023	33,846	31,144	4,714	3,740	3,436
Dubuque, IA Metro Area	4,754,031	3,462,798	2,723,779	37.3	27.1	49,085	36,867	30,008	3,706	2,795	2,279
Duluth, MN-WI Metro Area	13,387,328	10,573,803	8,505,046	26.6	24.3	46,250	36,393	29,563	8,762	7,312	6,082
Durham-Chapel Hill, NC Metro Area	34,341,601	23,242,852	18,365,485	47.8	26.6	54,036	41,046	35,842	29,487	22,659	18,036
East Stroudsburg, PA Metro Area	7,241,661	5,419,411	4,779,892	33.6	13.4	42,722	31,908	29,497	3,978	3,367	2,915
Eau Claire, WI Metro Area	8,003,391	5,998,210	4,749,612	33.4	26.3	47,450	37,105	30,680	5,763	4,483	3,688
El Centro, CA Metro Area	6,722,874	5,146,671	3,843,753	30.6	33.9	36,974	29,455	24,622	4,609	3,645	2,910
Elizabethtown-Fort Knox, KY Metro Area	6,464,035	5,071,684	3,972,256	27.5	27.7	42,144	33,846	28,337	4,151	3,900	2,869
Elkhart-Goshen, IN Metro Area	9,623,587	6,003,170	5,892,501	60.3	1.9	46,816	30,404	30,651	10,030	5,487	6,433
Elmira, NY Metro Area	3,738,576	3,129,717	2,527,021	19.5	23.9	44,373	35,206	28,438	2,436	2,213	1,842
El Paso, TX Metro Area	30,301,514	22,892,407	16,751,349	32.4	36.7	35,836	28,363	22,900	21,022	16,180	12,558
Enid, OK Metro Area	2,708,506	2,373,651	1,797,543	14.1	32.0	44,465	39,081	31,339	1,794	1,609	1,256
Erie, PA Metro Area	12,216,339	9,717,399	8,138,952	25.7	19.4	44,903	34,606	29,360	7,972	6,685	6,217
Eugene-Springfield, OR Metro Area	17,431,415	11,916,860	10,326,208	46.3	15.4	45,919	33,862	30,748	10,932	7,749	7,472
Evansville, IN-KY Metro Area	14,888,076	11,818,127	9,959,401	26.0	18.7	47,313	37,903	32,778	10,400	8,947	7,940
Fairbanks, AK Metro Area	5,602,350	4,542,248	3,325,347	23.3	36.6	56,606	46,227	36,772	3,953	3,339	2,697
Fargo, ND-MN Metro Area	12,939,269	8,419,670	6,261,316	53.7	34.5	52,712	40,199	33,076	9,880	6,520	5,159
Farmington, NM Metro Area	4,433,145	3,961,771	3,104,292	11.9	27.6	35,453	30,428	24,872	3,065	2,924	2,398
Fayetteville, NC Metro Area	19,237,792	15,534,312	12,789,451	23.8	21.5	36,903	31,675	28,791	14,516	13,287	10,141
Fayetteville-Springdale-Rogers, AR Metro Area	34,354,146	17,091,019	13,264,268	101.0	28.9	65,306	38,642	34,429	17,713	10,760	9,537
Flagstaff, AZ Metro Area	6,875,489	4,631,674	3,744,647	48.4	23.7	48,129	34,406	29,480	4,353	3,138	2,613
Flint, MI Metro Area	16,710,172	12,926,987	12,563,100	29.3	2.9	41,068	30,420	28,391	9,311	7,435	8,216
Florence, SC Metro Area	8,283,087	6,446,200	5,536,629	28.5	16.4	40,413	31,344	27,799	5,729	4,417	4,066
Florence-Muscle Shoals, AL Metro Area	5,533,965	4,602,964	3,883,617	20.2	18.5	37,608	31,257	27,023	3,158	2,685	2,412
Fond du Lac, WI Metro Area	4,960,128	3,743,813	3,198,784	32.5	17.0	48,126	36,855	32,214	3,372	2,499	2,303
Fort Collins, CO Metro Area	18,993,920	11,252,959	9,383,173	68.8	19.9	54,188	37,454	34,106	12,316	7,604	6,836
Fort Smith, AR-OK Metro Area	9,455,644	7,397,525	6,193,319	27.8	19.4	37,800	29,789	26,253	6,138	5,202	4,905
Fort Wayne, IN Metro Area	18,891,419	13,413,626	11,885,735	40.8	12.9	46,141	34,456	31,660	14,126	10,308	9,752
Fresno, CA Metro Area	42,842,812	29,567,869	24,590,953	44.9	20.2	43,084	31,723	28,185	28,607	20,344	18,648
Gadsden, AL Metro Area	3,784,122	3,169,689	2,681,992	19.4	18.2	36,918	30,345	25,995	2,027	1,719	1,602
Gainesville, FL Metro Area	14,035,221	10,378,911	8,805,044	35.2	17.9	42,663	33,992	30,582	9,869	7,444	6,701
Gainesville, GA Metro Area	8,834,170	5,502,166	4,944,769	60.6	11.3	43,701	30,561	30,717	6,440	3,828	3,657
Gettysburg, PA Metro Area	5,055,502	3,788,328	3,184,784	33.4	19.0	49,173	37,333	32,298	2,362	1,778	1,705
Glens Falls, NY Metro Area	5,822,789	4,650,940	3,752,998	25.2	23.9	46,411	36,050	29,395	3,654	3,023	2,590
Goldsboro, NC Metro Area	4,741,631	3,884,495	3,223,114	22.1	20.5	38,472	31,607	27,546	2,840	2,501	2,171
Grand Forks, ND-MN Metro Area	5,183,480	3,718,077	2,910,438	39.4	27.7	50,670	37,697	29,766	3,748	2,812	2,305
Grand Island, NE Metro Area	3,321,648	2,510,001	2,051,601	32.3	22.3	43,817	34,418	29,789	2,480	1,897	1,590
Grand Junction, CO Metro Area	6,884,366	5,007,084	3,975,121	37.5	26.0	44,935	34,211	30,532	4,264	3,285	2,767
Grand Rapids-Kentwood, MI Metro Area	54,119,648	35,983,765	32,251,948	50.4	11.6	50,463	36,191	33,051	40,470	26,667	26,365
Grants Pass, OR Metro Area	3,581,121	2,493,113	2,193,668	43.6	13.7	40,977	30,083	27,196	1,780	1,215	1,258

Table B-11. Personal income and Earnings by Place of Work—Continued

Metropolitan Statistical Area Metropolitan Division	Personal Income								Earnings (million dollars)		
	Total personal income			Percent change		Per capita personal income					
	2018	2010	2005	2010-2018	2005-2010	2018	2010	2005	2018	2010	2005
Great Falls, MT Metro Area	3,879,504	3,125,339	2,463,626	24.1	26.9	47,518	38,347	30,780	2,518	2,147	1,744
Greeley, CO Metro Area	14,512,128	8,412,326	6,367,491	72.5	32.1	46,172	33,094	28,569	8,951	4,901	4,193
Green Bay, WI Metro Area	16,578,948	12,078,452	10,158,299	37.3	18.9	51,553	39,375	34,226	12,929	9,594	8,637
Greensboro-High Point, NC Metro Area	33,156,562	24,944,816	21,646,113	32.9	15.2	43,189	34,396	31,970	24,349	19,101	17,902
Greenville, NC Metro Area	7,410,874	5,499,331	4,275,890	34.8	28.6	41,191	32,569	28,905	5,231	3,959	3,220
Greenville-Anderson, SC Metro Area	40,084,909	27,098,891	22,383,450	47.9	21.1	44,213	32,822	29,334	28,184	18,922	16,895
Gulfport-Biloxi, MS Metro Area	15,340,477	13,254,712	11,288,717	15.7	17.4	36,878	34,047	28,321	10,783	9,846	8,237
Hagerstown-Martinsburg, MD-WV Metro Area	12,547,250	9,456,119	7,748,318	32.7	22.0	43,897	35,045	30,912	7,084	5,385	5,020
Hammond, LA Metro Area	5,213,875	3,995,727	2,810,109	30.5	42.2	38,974	32,892	26,266	2,607	2,397	1,633
Hanford-Corcoran, CA Metro Area	5,344,067	4,070,894	3,480,636	31.3	17.0	35,306	26,715	23,980	3,713	3,023	2,767
Harrisburg-Carlisle, PA Metro Area	30,085,436	22,331,977	19,239,195	34.7	16.1	52,354	40,596	36,592	26,357	19,941	18,145
Harrisonburg, VA Metro Area	5,373,366	3,842,746	3,224,329	39.8	19.2	39,721	30,644	27,652	4,202	3,190	2,803
Hartford-East Hartford-Middletown, CT Metro Area	77,610,163	61,473,373	51,515,061	26.3	19.3	64,337	50,634	43,365	61,216	49,541	44,434
Hattiesburg, MS Metro Area	6,503,256	4,967,645	3,910,385	30.9	27.0	38,648	30,503	26,018	4,259	3,294	2,768
Hickory-Lenoir-Morganton, NC Metro Area	14,681,083	11,080,715	9,966,803	32.5	11.2	39,849	30,309	28,142	9,443	7,211	7,270
Hilton Head Island-Bluffton, SC Metro Area	11,549,463	7,184,360	6,250,787	60.8	14.9	53,056	38,260	38,268	5,678	3,978	3,798
Hinesville, GA Metro Area	2,716,214	2,184,222	1,758,630	24.4	24.2	33,744	28,248	23,020	2,611	2,567	1,853
Homosassa Springs, FL Metro Area	5,609,441	4,322,621	3,618,459	29.8	19.5	37,920	30,620	27,046	2,007	1,740	1,591
Hot Springs, AR Metro Area	3,966,534	3,047,426	2,608,793	30.2	16.8	40,004	31,721	28,327	2,174	1,667	1,524
Houma-Thibodaux, LA Metro Area	9,228,613	8,197,584	5,816,313	12.6	40.9	44,127	39,365	29,014	6,620	6,385	4,205
Houston-The Woodlands-Sugar Land, TX Metro Area	392,394,285	267,613,203	201,134,921	46.6	33.1	56,077	44,997	38,431	312,329	217,779	169,703
Huntington-Ashland, WV-KY-OH Metro Area	14,476,675	11,948,084	9,551,087	21.2	25.1	40,299	32,200	25,991	8,798	7,553	6,363
Huntsville, AL Metro Area	22,947,407	16,818,957	12,676,948	36.4	32.7	49,595	40,115	34,007	18,622	14,212	11,313
Idaho Falls, ID Metro Area	6,771,676	4,390,404	3,534,984	54.2	24.2	45,477	32,811	30,419	4,848	3,484	2,825
Indianapolis-Carmel-Anderson, IN Metro Area	110,997,077	78,248,853	63,803,921	41.9	22.6	54,179	41,344	35,987	86,078	61,974	52,136
Iowa City, IA Metro Area	9,238,848	6,127,366	4,867,798	50.8	25.9	53,280	40,040	34,365	7,112	5,104	4,134
Ithaca, NY Metro Area	4,654,658	3,557,402	2,860,614	30.8	24.4	45,282	34,971	28,769	4,018	3,214	2,659
Jackson, MI Metro Area	6,326,183	4,859,884	4,477,594	30.2	8.5	39,832	30,351	27,462	4,105	3,061	3,069
Jackson, MS Metro Area	26,166,249	21,058,623	17,709,721	24.3	18.9	43,772	35,797	31,207	18,305	15,106	13,344
Jackson, TN Metro Area	7,170,532	5,783,868	4,813,319	24.0	20.2	40,226	32,175	27,644	5,066	4,068	3,751
Jacksonville, FL Metro Area	76,357,017	52,230,908	45,513,781	46.2	14.8	49,754	38,721	36,438	52,159	36,526	34,318
Jacksonville, NC Metro Area	9,121,475	7,826,773	5,067,689	16.5	54.4	46,142	41,879	32,236	6,747	6,284	3,943
Janesville-Beloit, WI Metro Area	7,210,874	5,419,969	4,804,600	33.0	12.8	44,204	33,817	30,649	4,592	3,304	3,427
Jefferson City, MO Metro Area	6,636,835	5,232,220	4,389,065	26.8	19.2	43,802	34,890	30,385	4,911	4,134	3,623
Johnson City, TN Metro Area	8,181,822	6,326,071	5,072,715	29.3	24.7	40,360	31,788	26,814	5,038	3,964	3,527
Johnstown, PA Metro Area	5,719,782	4,712,750	4,140,128	21.4	13.8	36,588	29,782	25,606	3,382	2,557	2,192
Jonesboro, AR Metro Area	4,849,042	3,611,286	2,882,475	34.3	25.3	36,588	30,700	26,864	4,921	3,918	3,453
Joplin, MO Metro Area	7,113,984	5,398,097	4,463,669	31.8	20.9	39,765	30,700	26,864	5,638	3,824	3,703
Kahului-Wailuku-Lahaina, HI Metro Area	8,204,107	5,536,704	4,704,262	48.2	17.7	49,040	35,699	32,794	9,333	6,758	6,316
Kalamazoo-Portage, MI Metro Area	12,905,261	9,129,445	7,876,080	41.4	15.9	48,723	36,409	32,377			
Kankakee, IL Metro Area	4,542,931	3,720,617	3,120,520	22.1	19.2	41,290	32,804	28,916	2,834	2,223	1,980
Kansas City, MO-KS Metro Area	115,303,009	82,754,866	66,337,271	39.3	24.7	53,788	41,103	34,742	87,372	64,297	53,991
Kennewick-Richland, WA Metro Area	13,109,607	9,661,802	6,616,507	35.7	46.0	44,256	37,808	30,201	9,545	7,499	5,368
Killeen-Temple, TX Metro Area	18,804,982	15,167,040	10,876,646	24.0	39.4	41,634	37,149	30,421	12,928	11,329	8,271
Kingsport-Bristol, TN-VA Metro Area	12,277,407	10,079,289	8,377,186	21.8	20.3	40,042	32,568	27,691	7,776	6,670	5,909
Kingston, NY Metro Area	9,012,508	6,976,549	5,826,954	29.2	19.7	50,462	38,247	31,939	4,480	3,694	3,085
Knoxville, TN Metro Area	39,343,358	28,329,224	23,670,534	38.9	19.7	45,739	34,718	30,789	28,589	20,933	18,620
Kokomo, IN Metro Area	3,446,353	2,578,070	2,568,666	33.7	0.4	41,842	31,153	30,441	2,680	2,033	2,633
La Crosse-Onalaska, WI-MN Metro Area	6,896,833	5,080,533	4,171,323	35.8	21.8	50,412	37,942	32,199	5,159	3,929	3,331
Lafayette, LA Metro Area	21,665,643	18,025,264	13,188,440	20.2	36.7	44,273	38,547	29,978	14,163	13,215	9,960
Lafayette-West Lafayette, IN Metro Area	9,196,588	6,556,542	5,430,670	40.3	20.7	39,969	31,121	27,616	7,036	4,983	4,437
Lake Charles, LA Metro Area	10,296,276	6,906,547	5,512,792	49.1	25.3	49,011	34,543	28,089	9,103	5,147	4,315
Lake Havasu City-Kingman, AZ Metro Area	6,946,164	5,124,399	4,508,683	35.6	13.7	33,148	25,582	23,884	2,997	2,288	2,293
Lakeland-Winter Haven, FL Metro Area	25,108,379	18,373,933	16,077,599	36.7	14.3	35,463	30,464	29,372	14,379	10,588	10,341
Lancaster, PA Metro Area	28,625,770	19,774,960	17,166,597	44.8	15.2	52,664	38,005	34,699	19,660	13,777	13,227
Lansing-East Lansing, MI Metro Area	23,000,426	17,633,905	15,709,754	30.4	12.2	41,812	32,967	29,337	16,122	12,909	12,206
Laredo, TX Metro Area	8,728,522	6,514,045	4,779,920	34.0	36.3	31,635	25,912	21,367	6,143	4,655	3,725
Las Cruces, NM Metro Area	7,954,729	6,343,985	4,711,013	25.4	34.7	36,570	30,196	24,900	4,678	4,135	3,270
Las Vegas-Henderson-Paradise, NV Metro Area	105,087,856	69,601,904	65,442,479	51.0	6.4	47,090	35,645	37,838	70,869	50,042	50,645
Lawrence, KS Metro Area	5,299,726	3,760,527	3,045,961	40.9	23.5	43,642	33,819	28,822	3,196	2,392	2,090
Lawton, OK Metro Area	5,238,405	4,686,111	3,445,744	11.8	36.0	41,509	35,617	28,366	3,606	3,515	2,584
Lebanon, PA Metro Area	6,832,788	4,936,259	4,172,784	38.4	18.3	48,352	36,936	33,066	3,619	2,734	2,390
Lewiston, ID-WA Metro Area	2,858,998	2,142,790	1,715,997	33.4	24.9	45,368	35,105	29,095	1,780	1,407	1,204
Lewiston-Auburn, ME Metro Area	4,471,723	3,662,513	3,190,503	22.1	14.8	41,528	34,004	29,720	3,105	2,494	2,211
Lexington-Fayette, KY Metro Area	24,736,885	17,583,206	14,942,038	40.7	17.7	47,875	37,141	34,200	18,921	14,079	12,904
Lima, OH Metro Area	4,395,648	3,484,154	3,009,436	26.2	15.8	42,816	32,758	28,162	3,483	2,844	2,668
Lincoln, NE Metro Area	16,691,498	11,691,240	9,830,342	42.8	18.9	49,886	38,590	34,436	12,583	9,110	7,946
Little Rock-North Little Rock-Conway, AR Metro Area	33,729,487	25,885,178	21,925,186	30.3	18.1	45,512	36,857	33,794	23,946	19,441	17,622
Logan, UT-ID Metro Area	5,447,370	3,564,862	2,605,752	52.8	36.8	38,690	28,255	23,146	3,733	2,513	1,903
Longview, TX Metro Area	11,912,035	10,223,575	7,705,594	16.5	32.7	41,630	36,448	28,982	8,233	7,410	5,550
Longview, WA Metro Area	4,903,274	3,611,372	2,750,569	35.8	31.3	44,990	35,282	28,493	2,978	2,304	1,887
Los Angeles-Long Beach-Anaheim, CA Metro Area	849,493,416	578,372,986	503,920,780	46.9	14.8	63,913	45,048	39,596	615,567	437,680	409,870
Anaheim-Santa Ana-Irvine, CA Div.	220,684,684	150,142,961	139,108,980	47.0	7.9	69,268	49,773	47,315	160,226	114,508	112,613

Table B-11. Personal income and Earnings by Place of Work—*Continued*

Metropolitan Statistical Area Metropolitan Division	Personal Income										
	Total personal income			Percent change		Per capita personal income			Earnings (million dollars)		
	2018	2010	2005	2010-2018	2005-2010	2018	2010	2005	2018	2010	2005
Los Angeles-Long Beach-Glendale, CA Div......	628,808,732	428,230,025	364,811,800	46.8	17.4	62,224	43,597	37,278	455,341	323,172	297,258
Louisville/Jefferson County, KY-IN Metro Area......	63,372,715	45,591,845	39,127,942	39.0	16.5	50,101	37,846	34,325	46,821	33,313	30,499
Lubbock, TX Metro Area	13,458,665	9,835,832	7,553,885	36.8	30.2	42,181	33,656	27,928	9,218	6,980	5,739
Lynchburg, VA Metro Area	10,632,655	8,338,197	6,905,113	27.5	20.8	40,374	32,960	28,950	6,385	5,329	4,718
Macon-Bibb County, GA Metro Area	9,434,368	7,590,079	6,770,495	24.3	12.1	41,066	32,684	29,679	6,550	5,129	4,849
Madera, CA Metro Area	6,290,616	4,295,560	3,457,218	46.4	24.2	39,897	28,446	24,639	4,142	2,816	2,426
Madison, WI Metro Area	39,209,592	26,341,322	22,762,076	48.9	15.7	59,371	43,424	39,722	30,975	21,143	19,221
Manchester-Nashua, NH Metro Area	25,390,957	19,093,904	16,752,532	33.0	14.0	61,147	47,610	42,264	18,972	14,197	12,921
Manhattan, KS Metro Area	6,007,400	5,071,745	3,256,735	18.4	55.7	46,008	39,462	29,262	4,711	4,345	2,725
Mankato, MN Metro Area	4,690,093	3,365,978	2,953,692	39.3	14.0	46,141	34,756	32,419	3,555	2,602	2,466
Mansfield, OH Metro Area	4,751,236	3,767,011	3,535,218	26.1	6.6	39,234	30,340	27,679	3,073	2,557	2,748
McAllen-Edinburg-Mission, TX Metro Area	22,869,174	17,084,134	12,072,246	33.9	41.5	26,410	21,925	17,885	14,786	10,778	8,255
Medford, OR Metro Area	10,232,320	6,760,361	5,972,219	51.4	13.2	46,603	33,246	30,674	6,137	4,139	4,086
Memphis, TN-MS-AR Metro Area	62,580,423	48,627,283	43,301,764	28.7	12.3	46,620	36,909	34,267	47,560	37,681	36,124
Merced, CA Metro Area	10,583,691	7,301,531	6,136,657	45.0	19.0	38,519	28,440	25,300	5,942	4,328	4,033
Miami-Fort Lauderdale-Pompano Beach, FL Metro	354,745,914	239,473,700	217,215,771	48.1	10.2	57,228	42,889	40,142	213,941	145,965	142,490
Fort Lauderdale-Pompano Beach-Sunrise, FL Div	98,087,689	71,456,951	66,369,584	37.3	7.7	50,269	40,767	37,993	63,266	46,306	43,461
Miami-Miami Beach-Kendall, FL Div	138,138,976	95,805,838	81,381,738	44.2	17.7	50,022	38,214	34,110	99,412	66,368	63,944
West Palm Beach-Boca Raton-Boynton Beach, FL Div.	118,519,249	72,210,911	69,464,449	64.1	4.0	79,760	54,554	54,338	51,263	33,291	35,085
Michigan City-La Porte, IN Metro Area	4,678,294	3,568,513	3,149,194	31.1	13.3	42,527	32,018	28,749	2,574	2,192	2,106
Midland, MI Metro Area	5,031,408	3,573,452	3,122,140	40.8	14.5	60,467	42,715	37,199	3,329	2,700	2,382
Midland, TX Metro Area	21,800,443	10,243,928	7,520,124	112.8	36.2	122,247	72,245	59,231	19,763	8,574	6,240
Milwaukee-Waukesha, WI Metro Area	89,846,100	67,895,636	59,294,589	32.3	14.5	57,005	43,616	38,948	67,043	52,444	48,155
Minneapolis-St. Paul-Bloomington, MN Metro Area..	227,292,301	154,354,201	136,156,811	47.3	13.4	62,889	46,214	42,764	171,629	120,727	111,802
Missoula, MT Metro Area	5,879,212	3,746,315	3,068,190	56.9	22.1	49,492	34,224	29,993	3,995	2,816	2,430
Mobile, AL Metro Area	16,418,051	13,708,434	11,280,821	19.8	21.5	38,170	31,810	27,076	12,353	10,192	8,675
Modesto, CA Metro Area	24,257,921	16,545,238	14,393,550	46.6	14.9	44,120	32,116	28,786	14,912	10,369	9,988
Monroe, LA Metro Area	8,185,652	6,629,892	5,415,661	23.5	22.4	40,482	32,393	26,864	5,143	4,341	3,756
Monroe, MI Metro Area	7,145,290	5,196,594	4,992,893	37.5	4.1	47,496	34,204	32,767	3,156	2,364	2,534
Montgomery, AL Metro Area	16,027,375	13,070,002	11,424,121	22.6	14.4	42,943	34,841	31,852	11,183	9,466	8,597
Morgantown, WV Metro Area	5,962,265	4,469,039	3,394,365	33.4	31.7	42,509	34,295	28,301	4,745	3,580	2,709
Morristown, TN Metro Area	5,077,850	3,848,707	3,229,568	31.9	19.2	35,829	28,105	24,925	3,088	2,299	2,276
Mount Vernon-Anacortes, WA Metro Area	6,802,660	4,466,693	3,610,887	52.3	23.7	53,060	38,192	32,624	4,101	2,704	2,435
Muncie, IN Metro Area	4,269,683	3,321,544	3,191,983	28.5	4.1	37,201	28,232	27,012	2,754	2,197	2,300
Muskegon, MI Metro Area	6,782,353	4,964,769	4,517,295	36.6	9.9	39,072	28,880	26,020	4,025	3,065	3,052
Myrtle Beach-Conway-North Myrtle Beach, SC-NC	18,610,259	11,316,565	9,059,535	64.5	24.9	38,700	29,913	28,512	9,582	6,242	6,082
Napa, CA Metro Area	10,454,107	6,388,392	5,759,965	63.6	10.9	74,984	46,696	44,178	7,607	4,711	4,326
Naples-Marco Island, FL Metro Area	35,080,466	20,182,883	18,077,850	73.8	11.6	92,686	62,564	58,799	11,636	7,516	7,938
Nashville-Davidson--Murfreesboro--Franklin, TN..	110,453,223	68,943,418	54,086,418	60.2	27.5	57,953	41,763	36,364	91,563	55,722	46,131
New Bern, NC Metro Area	5,416,600	4,573,112	3,749,986	18.4	22.0	43,257	35,888	31,837	3,461	3,204	2,746
New Haven-Milford, CT Metro Area	48,583,905	38,786,438	33,819,514	25.3	14.7	56,650	44,924	39,921	32,070	26,577	24,532
New Orleans-Metairie, LA Metro Area	66,608,812	50,931,119	43,647,642	30.8	16.7	52,431	42,609	31,482	46,738	38,470	32,367
New York-Newark-Jersey City, NY-NJ-PA Metro Area	1,480,232,981	1,033,820,797	862,421,257	43.2	19.9	76,681	54,631	46,445	1,088,320	784,300	673,641
Nassau County-Suffolk County, NY Div	223,660,292	163,568,660	138,598,578	36.7	18.0	78,769	57,674	49,323	123,440	98,368	80,414
Newark, NJ-PA Div	163,444,515	122,552,043	105,410,533	33.4	16.3	75,198	57,061	49,483	107,357	85,345	77,977
New Brunswick-Lakewood, NJ Div	166,817,620	120,146,077	104,417,801	38.8	15.1	69,978	51,283	45,721	106,341	77,090	69,674
New York-Jersey City-White Plains, NY-NJ Div.	926,310,554	627,554,017	513,994,345	47.6	22.1	77,795	54,113	45,307	751,183	523,496	445,576
Niles, MI Metro Area	7,310,968	5,661,580	4,894,114	29.1	15.7	47,430	36,120	30,876	4,532	3,697	3,468
North Port-Sarasota-Bradenton, FL Metro Area	46,387,945	29,331,427	28,603,450	58.2	2.5	56,462	41,702	42,391	21,130	13,571	15,559
Norwich-New London, CT Metro Area	15,810,805	12,716,139	11,014,231	24.3	15.5	59,264	46,410	40,844	11,004	9,569	8,844
Ocala, FL Metro Area	13,318,148	9,964,115	8,498,506	33.7	17.2	36,997	30,072	27,996	6,096	4,546	4,590
Ocean City, NJ Metro Area	5,634,744	4,344,431	4,082,240	29.7	6.4	60,877	44,686	41,123	2,947	2,265	2,361
Odessa, TX Metro Area	7,663,693	4,792,296	3,321,309	59.9	44.3	47,271	34,959	26,490	6,798	3,830	2,535
Ogden-Clearfield, UT Metro Area	29,695,058	19,319,224	15,377,014	53.7	25.6	43,988	32,213	28,881	17,737	11,764	10,121
Oklahoma City, OK Metro Area	67,827,244	48,691,611	39,469,521	39.3	23.4	48,571	38,712	33,987	50,042	36,140	30,729
Olympia-Lacey-Tumwater, WA Metro Area	14,803,331	10,255,275	8,113,695	44.3	26.4	51,684	40,535	35,740	9,076	6,318	5,289
Omaha-Council Bluffs, NE-IA Metro Area	54,682,155	38,968,526	31,147,406	40.3	25.1	58,037	44,912	38,250	41,158	29,846	24,226
Orlando-Kissimmee-Sanford, FL Metro Area	111,900,614	71,145,046	62,081,611	57.3	14.6	43,491	33,258	31,742	87,094	54,285	52,028
Oshkosh-Neenah, WI Metro Area	8,226,265	6,210,926	5,445,595	32.4	14.1	48,101	37,176	33,729	7,010	5,475	4,925
Owensboro, KY Metro Area	4,929,807	4,036,253	3,265,728	22.1	23.6	41,387	35,168	29,297	3,290	2,774	2,388
Oxnard-Thousand Oaks-Ventura, CA Metro Area ..	52,515,048	37,882,017	33,142,995	38.6	14.3	61,712	45,910	41,731	29,692	24,127	22,027
Palm Bay-Melbourne-Titusville, FL Metro Area	27,112,075	19,971,449	17,639,535	35.8	13.2	45,425	36,714	33,288	15,946	12,488	11,914
Panama City, FL Metro Area	8,010,201	6,221,309	5,316,165	28.8	17.0	43,231	36,768	32,631	5,156	4,105	3,834
Parkersburg-Vienna, WV Metro Area	3,780,296	3,001,028	2,509,990	26.0	19.6	41,988	32,375	27,090	2,308	2,034	1,901
Pensacola-Ferry Pass-Brent, FL Metro Area.........	21,407,914	15,799,407	13,358,921	35.5	18.3	43,259	35,036	30,398	12,530	9,512	8,714
Peoria, IL Metro Area	19,705,312	16,274,373	13,338,926	21.1	22.0	48,870	39,116	32,756	13,780	11,908	10,256
Philadelphia-Camden-Wilmington, PA-NJ-DE-MD Metro Area	392,847,384	287,527,441	244,711,399	36.6	17.5	64,440	48,154	41,981	275,920	207,890	185,442
Camden, NJ Div	71,055,003	55,443,269	47,173,264	28.2	17.5	57,124	44,300	38,217	43,422	34,388	31,533
Montgomery County-Bucks County-Chester County,	156,179,174	111,905,592	99,793,548	39.6	12.1	78,924	58,095	53,474	99,078	74,444	71,165

Table B-11. Personal income and Earnings by Place of Work—*Continued*

Metropolitan Statistical Area Metropolitan Division	Personal Income								Earnings (million dollars)		
	Total personal income			Percent change		Per capita personal income					
	2018	2010	2005	2010-2018	2005-2010	2018	2010	2005	2018	2010	2005
Philadelphia, PA Div	125,933,493	89,701,528	69,578,242	40.4	28.9	58,604	42,975	34,057	102,844	74,863	59,170
Wilmington, DE-MD-NJ Div	39,679,714	30,477,052	28,166,345	30.2	8.2	54,748	43,175	41,085	30,576	24,195	23,575
Phoenix-Mesa-Chandler, AZ Metro Area	224,072,103	146,975,844	131,180,038	52.5	12.0	46,125	34,955	34,752	159,709	105,013	101,366
Pine Bluff, AR Metro Area	3,093,074	2,787,368	2,511,182	11.0	11.0	34,554	27,844	24,165	2,011	1,961	1,871
Pittsburgh, PA Metro Area	135,002,633	101,016,521	85,247,831	33.6	18.5	58,072	42,857	35,902	98,029	73,299	64,144
Pittsfield, MA Metro Area	7,139,095	5,419,023	4,748,311	31.7	14.1	56,503	41,266	35,819	4,382	3,527	3,304
Pocatello, ID Metro Area	3,610,042	2,655,918	2,227,876	35.9	19.2	38,038	29,221	26,258	2,218	1,746	1,621
Portland-South Portland, ME Metro Area	30,921,024	22,245,639	19,238,097	39.0	15.6	57,751	43,288	37,701	21,336	15,968	14,135
Portland-Vancouver-Hillsboro, OR-WA Metro Area	141,269,916	89,153,740	74,811,330	58.5	19.2	56,991	39,940	36,188	103,525	66,040	59,659
Port St. Lucie, FL Metro Area	26,140,273	16,392,581	14,925,290	59.5	9.8	54,228	38,554	38,880	9,482	6,781	6,655
Poughkeepsie-Newburgh-Middletown, NY Metro Area	36,358,537	27,458,091	23,286,043	32.4	17.9	53,811	40,910	35,342	19,979	16,200	14,080
Prescott Valley-Prescott, AZ Metro Area	9,352,066	6,099,712	5,322,557	53.3	14.6	40,312	28,911	27,236	4,204	2,806	2,713
Providence-Warwick, RI-MA Metro Area	88,500,956	67,625,238	58,699,351	30.9	15.2	54,585	42,184	36,383	55,312	43,646	39,743
Provo-Orem, UT Metro Area	25,877,112	13,930,915	10,532,280	85.8	32.3	40,831	26,272	23,958	17,563	8,921	7,622
Pueblo, CO Metro Area	6,619,192	4,721,180	4,008,593	40.2	17.8	39,511	29,606	26,755	3,871	2,916	2,533
Punta Gorda, FL Metro Area	7,689,186	5,124,528	4,795,750	50.0	6.9	41,564	38,024	34,231	2,960	2,067	2,075
Racine, WI Metro Area	9,779,840	7,430,040	6,615,221	31.6	12.3	49,749	38,024	34,231	5,410	4,374	4,205
Raleigh-Cary, NC Metro Area	75,000,994	48,714,028	36,638,381	54.0	33.0	55,045	42,830	38,782	53,308	32,406	26,183
Rapid City, SD Metro Area	6,956,486	5,060,920	4,081,670	37.5	24.0	49,681	39,936	34,535	4,490	3,385	2,892
Reading, PA Metro Area	20,984,646	15,696,057	13,344,214	33.7	17.6	49,945	38,095	33,703	13,373	10,095	9,108
Redding, CA Metro Area	8,386,554	6,137,606	5,255,837	36.6	16.8	46,582	34,622	29,928	4,782	3,680	3,588
Reno, NV Metro Area	28,016,338	18,541,496	17,431,484	51.1	6.4	59,639	43,529	43,958	17,852	12,828	12,641
Richmond, VA Metro Area	73,485,301	51,016,738	44,166,287	44.0	15.5	57,301	42,935	39,562	54,229	38,913	35,242
Riverside-San Bernardino-Ontario, CA Metro Area	187,141,684	127,926,884	111,171,250	46.3	15.1	40,486	30,153	28,684	111,700	73,852	72,090
Roanoke, VA Metro Area	14,754,560	11,641,321	9,891,518	26.7	17.7	46,963	37,724	33,372	10,284	8,688	7,813
Rochester, MN Metro Area	12,160,015	8,847,715	7,081,858	37.4	24.9	55,323	42,698	35,914	9,539	7,245	6,123
Rochester, NY Metro Area	54,803,562	42,758,125	35,383,212	28.2	20.8	51,167	39,592	33,056	38,454	31,850	27,643
Rockford, IL Metro Area	14,967,703	11,831,811	10,187,088	26.5	16.1	44,328	33,883	30,327	10,440	8,060	7,814
Rocky Mount, NC Metro Area	5,767,561	4,874,454	4,126,589	18.3	18.1	39,498	31,981	28,067	3,303	3,103	2,955
Rome, GA Metro Area	3,772,493	2,917,603	2,634,666	29.3	10.7	38,524	30,258	27,930	2,637	2,095	1,942
Sacramento-Roseville-Folsom, CA Metro Area	131,984,004	88,581,303	76,702,441	49.0	15.5	56,278	41,131	37,694	92,719	64,066	61,258
Saginaw, MI Metro Area	7,394,256	6,099,417	5,612,153	21.2	8.7	38,754	30,518	27,064	5,559	4,499	4,641
St. Cloud, MN Metro Area	9,293,268	6,519,588	5,479,533	42.5	19.0	46,513	34,455	30,574	7,018	5,057	4,506
St. George, UT Metro Area	6,670,081	3,602,106	2,848,372	85.2	26.5	38,847	26,028	23,936	3,919	2,003	1,934
St. Joseph, MO-KS Metro Area	4,965,092	3,972,526	3,401,549	25.0	16.8	39,253	31,211	27,546	3,563	2,877	2,479
St. Louis, MO-IL Metro Area	156,778,821	118,383,785	101,878,567	32.4	16.2	55,883	42,432	37,314	109,871	85,994	77,020
Salem, OR Metro Area	18,456,831	12,317,582	10,188,406	49.8	20.9	42,714	31,463	27,682	12,386	8,400	7,377
Salinas, CA Metro Area	24,477,179	17,263,664	14,717,027	41.8	17.3	56,193	41,460	36,328	17,001	12,240	10,674
Salisbury, MD-DE Metro Area	19,800,550	13,636,949	11,560,726	45.2	18.0	48,296	36,382	33,441	11,009	7,836	7,578
Salt Lake City, UT Metro Area	63,249,028	39,344,828	32,338,111	60.8	21.7	51,736	36,047	32,428	56,956	35,920	29,815
San Angelo, TX Metro Area	5,616,169	4,173,139	3,273,183	34.6	27.5	46,406	36,793	30,368	3,594	2,810	2,308
San Antonio-New Braunfels, TX Metro Area	118,335,136	77,233,922	59,326,577	53.2	30.2	46,995	35,872	31,285	84,405	54,217	44,152
San Diego-Chula Vista-Carlsbad, CA Metro Area	205,236,393	136,969,778	122,936,302	49.8	11.4	61,386	44,137	41,838	148,502	101,819	97,098
San Francisco-Oakland-Berkeley, CA Metro Area	470,222,336	266,002,196	230,485,894	76.8	15.4	99,424	61,237	55,702	344,893	198,774	179,741
Oakland-Berkeley-Livermore, CA Div	222,646,436	129,745,614	115,232,657	71.6	12.6	79,038	50,571	47,216	132,025	86,809	83,663
San Francisco-San Mateo-Redwood City, CA Div	212,709,192	114,992,261	95,442,659	85.0	20.5	128,692	75,391	65,682	197,163	101,049	85,809
San Rafael, CA Div	34,866,708	21,264,321	19,810,578	64.0	7.3	134,275	84,080	81,122	15,704	10,917	10,268
San Jose-Sunnyvale-Santa Clara, CA Metro Area	212,331,990	111,534,137	91,261,494	90.4	22.2	106,213	60,564	52,754	194,331	103,477	86,178
San Luis Obispo-Paso Robles, CA Metro Area	16,612,046	10,855,099	9,229,260	53.0	17.6	58,491	40,233	35,687	10,031	6,799	6,211
Santa Cruz-Watsonville, CA Metro Area	19,021,010	12,794,043	10,529,273	48.7	21.5	69,355	48,616	41,886	9,606	7,838	6,321
Santa Fe, NM Metro Area	8,779,840	6,250,949	5,343,832	40.5	17.0	58,510	43,251	38,833	4,238	3,807	3,327
Santa Maria-Santa Barbara, CA Metro Area	27,992,849	19,354,013	17,055,537	44.6	13.5	62,690	45,621	41,795	18,535	13,562	12,139
Santa Rosa-Petaluma, CA Metro Area	32,246,609	20,830,579	18,884,982	54.8	10.3	64,501	42,969	40,531	19,537	13,294	12,676
Savannah, GA Metro Area	18,362,285	13,089,864	10,443,331	40.3	25.3	47,144	37,546	33,203	12,798	8,856	7,585
Scranton--Wilkes-Barre, PA Metro Area	25,649,394	20,574,826	17,450,039	24.7	17.9	46,175	36,496	31,348	16,621	13,399	12,261
Seattle-Tacoma-Bellevue, WA Metro Area	293,954,143	168,310,441	141,739,127	74.6	18.7	74,620	48,796	44,318	223,482	131,439	115,316
Seattle-Bellevue-Kent, WA Div	247,505,087	137,760,428	116,749,011	79.7	18.0	81,201	51,909	47,650	195,661	111,641	98,989
Tacoma-Lakewood, WA Div	46,449,056	30,550,013	24,990,116	52.0	22.2	52,114	38,409	33,403	27,822	19,799	16,327
Sebastian-Vero Beach, FL Metro Area	11,972,633	7,291,344	6,881,051	64.2	6.0	76,059	52,732	53,777	3,769	2,576	2,558
Sebring-Avon Park, FL Metro Area	3,526,778	2,839,216	2,369,188	24.2	19.8	33,453	28,785	24,779	1,516	1,271	1,180
Sheboygan, WI Metro Area	6,101,981	4,491,663	3,919,903	35.9	14.6	52,851	38,882	34,249	4,568	3,389	3,176
Sherman-Denison, TX Metro Area	5,653,755	3,904,991	3,158,882	44.8	23.6	42,195	32,265	27,310	3,008	2,265	2,008
Shreveport-Bossier City, LA Metro Area	18,489,212	15,702,599	12,164,595	17.7	29.1	46,509	39,263	31,753	12,133	11,274	9,029
Sierra Vista-Douglas, AZ Metro Area	5,109,813	4,556,212	3,530,461	12.2	29.1	40,308	34,563	28,067	2,829	2,855	2,242
Sioux City, IA-NE-SD Metro Area	7,281,785	5,872,816	4,769,135	24.0	23.1	50,586	40,812	34,099	5,174	4,503	3,808
Sioux Falls, SD Metro Area	15,811,766	10,620,149	7,805,480	48.9	36.1	59,520	46,356	37,780	12,090	8,287	6,249
South Bend-Mishawaka, IN-MI Metro Area	15,232,592	10,911,871	10,116,428	39.6	7.9	47,244	34,201	31,891	9,666	7,209	7,121
Spartanburg, SC Metro Area	13,543,549	9,117,819	7,738,833	48.5	17.8	43,148	32,021	29,260	10,023	6,699	6,083
Spokane-Spokane Valley, WA Metro Area	25,700,950	17,912,195	14,212,801	43.5	26.0	45,903	34,744	29,484	17,211	12,254	10,714
Springfield, IL Metro Area	10,131,128	8,255,598	6,839,175	22.7	20.7	48,793	39,226	33,364	7,428	6,396	5,640
Springfield, MA Metro Area	36,508,755	27,373,425	23,126,258	33.4	18.4	51,953	39,390	33,594	22,202	17,265	15,573
Springfield, MO Metro Area	19,510,460	13,975,534	12,090,217	39.6	15.6	41,780	31,959	30,009	13,388	9,908	9,406

Table B-11. Personal income and Earnings by Place of Work—*Continued*

Metropolitan Statistical Area Metropolitan Division	Personal Income										
	Total personal income			Percent change		Per capita personal income			Earnings (million dollars)		
	2018	2010	2005	2010-2018	2005-2010	2018	2010	2005	2018	2010	2005
Springfield, OH Metro Area	5,486,879	4,450,591	4,047,469	23.3	10.0	40,769	32,187	28,631	2,998	2,454	2,360
State College, PA Metro Area	7,520,504	5,506,441	4,513,504	36.6	22.0	46,193	35,706	31,011	6,292	4,769	4,063
Staunton, VA Metro Area	5,451,146	4,257,939	3,437,431	28.0	23.9	44,316	35,989	30,130	3,122	2,645	2,311
Stockton, CA Metro Area	33,866,043	22,508,045	19,744,981	50.5	14.0	44,995	32,755	30,054	19,207	13,724	13,310
Sumter, SC Metro Area	5,230,446	4,062,238	3,513,243	28.8	15.6	37,304	28,495	25,107	3,194	2,437	2,313
Syracuse, NY Metro Area	32,353,070	25,216,437	20,872,388	28.3	20.8	49,736	38,028	31,865	23,328	18,916	16,554
Tallahassee, FL Metro Area	16,407,638	12,804,173	10,972,926	28.1	16.7	42,601	34,668	31,874	11,564	9,327	8,591
Tampa-St. Petersburg-Clearwater, FL Metro Area	148,460,185	107,124,316	92,116,385	38.6	16.3	47,240	38,418	34,740	97,343	69,393	66,092
Terre Haute, IN Metro Area	7,148,511	5,801,484	4,952,866	23.2	17.1	38,299	30,611	26,341	4,280	3,832	3,453
Texarkana, TX-AR Metro Area	5,650,095	4,766,345	3,901,911	18.5	22.2	37,607	31,919	26,996	3,630	3,295	2,839
The Villages, FL Metro Area	5,935,589	2,805,571	1,683,009	111.6	66.7	46,100	29,758	24,300	1,929	1,124	778
Toledo, OH Metro Area	30,166,240	23,240,294	20,866,489	29.8	11.4	46,868	35,679	31,690	22,518	17,189	16,745
Topeka, KS Metro Area	10,703,205	8,555,962	7,112,845	25.1	20.3	46,017	36,521	31,168	7,618	6,070	5,276
Trenton-Princeton, NJ Metro Area	25,644,178	19,581,226	17,611,381	31.0	11.2	69,344	53,247	48,648	22,667	17,659	15,612
Tucson, AZ Metro Area	45,748,033	33,444,170	28,399,260	36.8	17.8	44,028	34,069	30,859	27,491	21,564	18,920
Tulsa, OK Metro Area	54,525,652	38,856,275	31,635,010	40.3	22.8	54,866	41,344	35,832	39,567	28,287	24,409
Tuscaloosa, AL Metro Area	9,564,524	7,554,904	6,325,105	26.6	19.4	37,983	31,546	28,463	6,696	5,231	4,594
Twin Falls, ID Metro Area	4,327,743	2,962,142	2,401,459	46.1	23.3	39,309	29,625	26,836	3,031	2,050	1,768
Tyler, TX Metro Area	12,714,831	8,856,467	6,481,476	43.6	36.6	55,229	42,092	33,870	9,684	6,808	5,210
Urban Honolulu, HI Metro Area	58,420,993	43,397,685	35,728,717	34.6	21.5	59,608	45,381	38,912	42,489	32,003	27,887
Utica-Rome, NY Metro Area	12,832,563	10,591,169	8,482,508	21.2	24.9	44,036	35,395	28,410	8,106	7,105	5,952
Valdosta, GA Metro Area	5,294,048	4,057,869	3,338,720	30.5	21.5	36,217	28,973	26,412	3,517	2,720	2,450
Vallejo, CA Metro Area	23,073,555	15,615,400	14,004,876	47.8	11.5	51,664	37,723	34,310	13,174	9,456	8,200
Victoria, TX Metro Area	4,579,306	3,420,315	2,889,484	33.9	18.4	45,968	36,350	31,571	2,765	2,346	2,017
Vineland-Bridgeton, NJ Metro Area	6,082,463	5,248,781	4,321,880	15.9	21.4	40,289	33,495	28,429	4,285	3,657	3,366
Virginia Beach-Norfolk-Newport News, VA-NC Metro Area	89,345,303	69,481,881	60,026,909	28.6	15.8	50,619	40,467	35,643	61,397	50,414	45,994
Visalia, CA Metro Area	18,830,069	13,499,399	10,660,604	39.5	26.6	40,420	30,473	26,131	11,660	8,506	7,411
Waco, TX Metro Area	11,103,692	7,925,194	6,472,890	40.1	22.4	40,831	31,225	26,883	7,983	5,753	4,964
Walla Walla, WA Metro Area	2,811,189	2,049,529	1,581,303	37.2	29.6	46,144	34,785	27,954	1,917	1,482	1,209
Warner Robins, GA Metro Area	7,665,919	5,819,814	4,625,417	31.7	25.8	41,944	34,542	30,641	5,181	4,272	3,561
Washington-Arlington-Alexandria, DC-VA-MD-WV Metro Area	453,978,195	331,670,527	272,956,715	36.9	21.5	72,483	58,410	51,631	369,185	283,470	236,773
Frederick-Gaithersburg-Rockville, MD Div	110,220,866	80,717,396	68,702,745	36.6	17.5	84,253	66,682	60,121	72,722	55,388	46,561
Washington-Arlington-Alexandria, DC-VA-MD-WV Div	343,757,329	250,953,131	204,253,970	37.0	22.9	69,375	56,168	49,290	296,463	228,082	190,212
Waterloo-Cedar Falls, IA Metro Area	7,815,019	6,037,465	4,990,164	29.4	21.0	46,063	35,953	30,566	5,805	4,690	3,990
Watertown-Fort Drum, NY Metro Area	5,243,969	4,824,770	3,507,876	8.7	37.5	46,924	41,381	30,910	3,960	3,967	2,818
Wausau-Weston, WI Metro Area	8,053,641	6,009,220	5,199,491	34.0	15.6	49,373	36,906	32,792	5,819	4,430	4,216
Weirton-Steubenville, WV-OH Metro Area	4,737,813	3,844,349	3,372,246	23.2	14.0	40,472	30,922	26,456	2,405	2,105	2,120
Wenatchee, WA Metro Area	5,999,700	3,799,818	2,946,346	57.9	29.0	50,021	34,149	28,503	3,629	2,397	2,065
Wheeling, WV-OH Metro Area	6,845,480	4,864,275	4,427,195	40.7	9.9	48,881	32,887	29,626	4,975	3,228	3,114
Wichita, KS Metro Area	33,060,860	24,196,893	19,392,269	36.6	24.8	51,854	38,784	32,979	23,178	17,909	14,612
Wichita Falls, TX Metro Area	6,585,897	5,697,899	4,577,043	15.6	24.5	43,527	37,573	30,281	4,068	3,950	3,299
Williamsport, PA Metro Area	4,981,132	3,971,445	3,338,203	25.4	19.0	43,823	34,168	28,403	3,407	2,767	2,510
Wilmington, NC Metro Area	12,752,177	8,743,765	7,555,558	45.8	15.7	43,311	34,195	32,723	8,414	5,941	5,353
Winchester, VA-WV Metro Area	6,735,251	4,708,233	3,910,273	43.1	20.4	48,174	36,590	33,181	4,297	3,028	2,822
Winston-Salem, NC Metro Area	30,115,104	22,866,797	19,821,371	31.7	15.4	44,850	35,657	32,882	18,710	14,950	13,501
Worcester, MA-CT Metro Area	52,891,807	39,446,298	33,004,787	34.1	19.5	55,801	42,926	36,799	31,780	23,854	21,386
Yakima, WA Metro Area	10,907,560	7,829,612	5,917,595	39.3	32.3	43,379	32,053	25,890	6,989	5,087	4,134
York-Hanover, PA Metro Area	22,464,381	17,537,523	14,765,850	28.1	18.8	50,113	40,279	36,096	13,238	10,777	10,109
Youngstown-Warren-Boardman, OH-PA Metro Area	22,874,791	18,590,681	17,194,841	23.0	8.1	42,443	32,914	29,432	13,641	11,580	11,923
Yuba City, CA Metro Area	7,505,397	5,588,084	4,406,327	34.3	26.8	42,925	33,441	28,419	4,114	3,174	2,617
Yuma, AZ Metro Area	7,569,100	5,368,937	4,281,382	41.0	25.4	35,682	27,234	23,943	5,173	3,585	3,129

Table B-12. Employees and Earnings by Selected Major Industries, 2018

Metropolitan Statistical Area Metropolitan Division	Employment 2018						Earnings 2018					
		Percent by selected major industries						Percent by selected major industries				
	Total	ManuD facturing	Finance and insurance	Professional scientific and technical services	Health care and social assistance	Government and government enterprises	Total (million dollars)	ManuD facturing	Finance and insurance	Professional scientific and technical services	Health care and social assistance	Government and government enterprises
Abilene, TX Metro Area	105,026	3.4	5.8	3.7	11.9	16.7	4,738	4.0	5.3	4.3	15.8	25.0
Akron, OH Metro Area	432,087	9.5	4.5	6.0	12.8	10.8	23,831	12.7	4.9	6.2	13.5	13.5
Albany, GA Metro Area	82,018	5.5	D	4.8	13.1	15.5	3,661	9.0	D	5.2	16.6	23.4
Albany-Lebanon, OR Metro Area	63,493	14.0	2.6	3.1	10.7	11.1	3,192	21.9	2.1	2.9	10.8	15.2
Albany-Schenectady-Troy, NY Metro Area	577,633	5.0	5.8	7.7	12.9	17.6	37,274	7.7	7.0	10.2	11.9	26.0
Albuquerque, NM Metro Area	510,248	3.7	4.1	8.8	D	17.2	26,042	4.5	4.6	13.6	D	25.1
Alexandria, LA Metro Area	81,408	5.6	D	3.7	16.8	17.4	4,202	7.6	D	4.0	19.4	23.7
Allentown-Bethlehem-Easton, PA-NJ Metro Area	482,097	8.4	4.0	4.9	14.7	8.9	28,712	13.1	3.8	5.2	16.5	11.2
Altoona, PA Metro Area	75,923	10.1	3.0	3.8	16.7	11.6	3,951	12.8	2.4	3.8	19.3	15.0
Amarillo, TX Metro Area	166,603	8.5	6.5	D	10.9	12.6	8,822	12.7	5.8	D	12.7	15.7
Ames, IA Metro Area	78,249	7.4	2.6	4.7	7.9	29.6	4,028	10.6	2.3	6.2	8.0	36.7
Anchorage, AK Metro Area	244,216	1.5	3.5	6.5	13.4	18.5	17,104	0.9	3.2	7.3	14.8	26.7
Ann Arbor, MI Metro Area	271,686	6.0	2.8	10.2	10.5	28.2	17,160	7.6	2.9	14.0	11.0	34.2
Anniston-Oxford, AL Metro Area	59,020	11.6	2.6	3.6	8.3	22.0	2,631	16.3	2.7	3.4	9.1	32.9
Appleton, WI Metro Area	156,716	15.6	5.9	D	D	8.8	8,697	21.2	7.0	D	D	11.3
Asheville, NC Metro Area	280,698	8.4	3.0	D	D	9.6	12,615	12.5	3.2	D	D	14.0
Athens-Clarke County, GA Metro Area	128,178	6.0	3.7	4.8	10.8	23.0	6,265	9.5	5.1	4.0	15.3	30.7
Atlanta-Sandy Springs-Alpharetta, GA Metro Area	3,875,139	4.8	5.2	8.7	8.9	9.0	241,551	6.4	7.3	12.3	8.8	11.0
Atlantic City-Hammonton, NJ Metro Area	169,240	1.6	3.2	4.4	12.9	13.6	9,311	1.8	2.6	6.2	15.8	23.1
Auburn-Opelika, AL Metro Area	84,897	8.1	2.8	4.9	5.5	21.9	3,507	11.7	2.8	4.6	5.9	33.9
Augusta-Richmond County, GA-SC Metro Area	323,779	7.0	2.6	D	9.9	20.0	17,386	10.2	2.6	D	10.3	28.0
Austin-Round Rock-Georgetown, TX Metro Area	1,506,528	4.5	5.7	D	8.0	11.8	100,077	7.4	5.9	D	7.6	13.6
Bakersfield, CA Metro Area	424,583	3.5	2.4	3.9	10.0	16.6	25,571	4.1	1.7	3.9	8.9	25.8
Baltimore-Columbia-Towson, MD Metro Area	1,868,945	3.4	4.9	9.3	13.1	14.7	127,665	4.6	6.7	13.2	12.1	22.0
Bangor, ME Metro Area	92,177	3.4	2.7	3.7	18.3	15.8	4,451	4.1	3.5	4.0	23.9	20.3
Barnstable Town, MA Metro Area	154,467	D	3.9	6.7	12.8	10.5	7,785	D	3.7	7.2	16.1	17.9
Baton Rouge, LA Metro Area	536,834	D	3.9	6.0	10.3	13.8	30,711	D	4.1	7.9	10.4	16.8
Battle Creek, MI Metro Area	70,390	17.2	2.4	5.4	15.0	16.0	4,137	22.1	1.6	9.1	14.5	21.2
Bay City, MI Metro Area	46,736	10.2	3.9	4.7	15.0	12.8	2,226	16.5	3.0	7.6	16.7	17.6
Beaumont-Port Arthur, TX Metro Area	213,977	D	D	4.5	10.7	11.5	12,843	D	D	6.0	10.1	12.9
Beckley, WV Metro Area	54,185	2.3	2.4	3.7	17.2	16.1	2,591	3.8	2.2	4.2	18.5	21.3
Bellingham, WA Metro Area	129,204	8.8	3.2	6.0	10.7	12.7	6,993	13.5	3.2	5.5	11.8	18.1
Bend, OR Metro Area	131,032	5.3	3.5	7.1	11.2	12.9	6,755	5.7	3.4	8.1	16.4	14.5
Billings, MT Metro Area	121,554	D	4.0	6.0	D	9.1	6,578	D	4.5	7.7	D	11.6
Binghamton, NY Metro Area	128,596	9.3	3.4	D	14.4	16.2	7,013	15.3	3.0	D	15.9	24.0
Birmingham-Hoover, AL Metro Area	669,420	5.8	7.2	D	10.8	12.4	39,693	7.1	10.3	D	14.1	14.3
Bismarck, ND Metro Area	93,626	2.1	4.8	5.5	14.9	15.5	5,124	3.3	5.0	7.9	17.8	19.2
Blacksburg-Christiansburg, VA Metro Area	89,158	13.6	2.2	5.9	8.2	25.0	4,527	20.6	1.5	7.0	8.3	15.1
Bloomington, IL Metro Area	112,062	2.9	20.9	D	9.6	14.1	6,984	3.0	37.7	D	9.5	15.1
Bloomington, IN Metro Area	99,028	9.5	2.5	4.6	D	24.9	4,800	14.1	2.5	6.5	D	31.0
Bloomsburg-Berwick, PA Metro Area	53,134	10.6	4.9	2.9	22.3	13.1	3,058	11.4	5.2	2.5	33.0	14.6
Boise City, ID Metro Area	446,444	7.1	4.8	D	11.3	11.3	23,472	14.4	5.3	D	12.7	13.7
Boston-Cambridge-Newton, MA-NH Metro Area ...	3,689,664	D	6.4	11.7	13.3	8.6	303,997	D	11.4	19.1	11.6	10.1
Boston, MA Div	1,652,749	D	9.0	10.3	15.2	9.2	146,965	D	19.1	17.5	13.4	10.8
Cambridge-Newton-Framingham, MA Div	1,751,274	6.8	4.3	13.5	12.2	8.0	139,130	11.0	3.9	21.7	9.9	9.3
Rockingham County-Strafford County, NH Div	285,641	D	4.9	8.8	9.7	9.7	17,882	D	6.0	12.4	10.2	10.5
Boulder, CO Metro Area	274,950	7.7	4.2	15.9	10.1	12.9	17,374	11.5	3.3	24.8	9.8	14.6
Bowling Green, KY Metro Area	102,531	D	D	3.6	11.1	12.0	4,577	D	D	4.1	14.5	14.6
Bremerton-Silverdale-Port Orchard, WA Metro Area	136,083	2.7	2.7	6.6	10.4	33.0	8,392	2.4	1.9	6.8	9.4	52.4
Bridgeport-Stamford-Norwalk, CT Metro Area	666,896	5.0	11.8	8.9	11.6	7.3	63,226	9.8	25.3	11.1	8.3	7.3
Brownsville-Harlingen, TX Metro Area	196,272	3.3	3.9	2.9	21.2	15.8	7,427	5.2	3.7	3.0	19.8	27.3
Brunswick, GA Metro Area	60,881	3.9	D	4.0	10.3	14.8	2,832	6.1	D	4.2	14.2	24.7
Buffalo-Cheektowaga, NY Metro Area	678,201	8.0	6.7	6.1	13.2	13.0	40,043	11.5	7.3	7.5	13.4	20.5
Burlington, NC Metro Area	84,379	11.5	3.4	3.5	13.4	9.0	3,724	15.7	3.8	3.8	20.5	11.1
Burlington-South Burlington, VT Metro Area	166,511	8.1	3.2	8.2	D	13.8	9,464	11.2	4.4	11.3	D	19.3
California-Lexington Park, MD Metro Area	62,531	1.2	1.5	17.2	8.0	27.3	4,702	0.8	0.7	22.7	6.4	47.4
Canton-Massillon, OH Metro Area	223,950	12.5	4.3	4.2	D	9.5	10,787	19.0	4.4	5.3	D	12.5
Cape Coral-Fort Myers, FL Metro Area	390,394	2.0	4.7	6.6	8.4	11.3	19,718	2.3	3.5	9.2	10.4	16.2
Cape Girardeau, MO-IL Metro Area	61,446	7.3	4.1	4.1	18.3	12.1	2,934	15.9	3.3	5.2	23.3	13.4
Carbondale-Marion, IL Metro Area	77,156	6.1	4.7	D	12.9	23.6	3,804	9.4	4.0	D	17.1	33.6
Carson City, NV Metro Area	39,764	7.1	6.0	4.2	11.9	24.3	2,390	8.6	3.6	4.2	14.0	35.9
Casper, WY Metro Area	54,703	3.4	4.6	4.5	12.3	10.9	4,202	3.3	2.3	3.8	10.7	10.6
Cedar Rapids, IA Metro Area	183,548	11.1	6.9	D	D	9.7	10,540	22.3	8.3	D	D	10.9
Chambersburg-Waynesboro, PA Metro Area	81,506	11.9	2.5	3.9	12.5	10.3	4,140	16.9	2.4	4.4	15.2	15.8
Champaign-Urbana, IL Metro Area	136,517	5.3	3.7	5.0	D	28.7	7,729	6.0	3.5	5.1	D	37.9
Charleston, WV Metro Area	153,289	D	D	D	D	17.3	8,941	D	D	D	D	17.3
Charleston-North Charleston, SC Metro Area	499,723	6.0	3.3	8.1	8.1	15.3	28,112	10.0	4.7	11.2	9.4	21.3
Charlotte-Concord-Gastonia, NC-SC Metro Area	1,638,822	7.2	6.9	D	7.4	9.9	105,406	8.5	12.3	D	6.8	11.0
Charlottesville, VA Metro Area	156,092	2.9	3.8	D	D	24.3	9,261	3.2	7.5	D	D	34.3
Chattanooga, TN-GA Metro Area	335,768	10.7	5.6	4.8	D	11.8	18,640	13.7	6.7	5.6	D	16.4
Cheyenne, WY Metro Area	69,933	2.3	6.9	4.8	7.6	25.2	3,801	3.9	3.7	5.8	8.1	38.9
Chicago-Naperville-Elgin, IL-IN-WI Metro Area ...	6,186,561	7.0	6.3	8.3	11.0	9.6	430,066	9.9	8.9	13.4	9.9	11.8
Chicago-Naperville-Evanston, IL Div	4,896,704	6.0	6.7	9.0	11.2	9.0	347,144	7.6	9.9	14.9	10.0	11.3
Elgin, IL Div	378,972	10.9	4.5	5.2	9.2	13.8	20,925	16.7	3.7	6.3	10.1	19.3

D = Not shown to avoid disclosure of confidential information

Table B-12. Employees and Earnings by Selected Major Industries, 2018—Continued

Metropolitan Statistical Area Metropolitan Division	Employment 2018						Earnings 2018					
		Percent by selected major industries						Percent by selected major industries				
	Total	Manufacturing	Finance and insurance	Professional scientific and technical services	Health care and social assistance	Government and government enterprises	Total (million dollars)	Manufacturing	Finance and insurance	Professional scientific and technical services	Health care and social assistance	Government and government enterprises
Gary, IN Div............................	352,845	10.4	3.1	4.0	13.8	10.5	18,862	20.2	2.8	3.9	15.2	10.3
Lake County-Kenosha County, IL-WI Div	558,040	11.3	6.2	6.8	8.4	12.2	43,135	20.8	5.6	9.1	7.1	13.3
Chico, CA Metro Area................	116,908	4.5	3.5	4.5	18.4	14.8	5,984	5.0	3.6	4.4	20.7	22.1
Cincinnati, OH-KY-IN Metro Area....................	1,398,413	8.9	D	6.7	11.8	9.7	86,578	13.4	D	8.3	11.9	11.0
Clarksville, TN-KY Metro Area....................	157,034	8.7	2.2	2.8	8.1	30.2	8,381	10.5	1.9	2.9	8.0	46.7
Cleveland, TN Metro Area................	62,680	15.2	3.1	D	D	9.6	2,859	22.9	2.5	D	D	12.0
Cleveland-Elyria, OH Metro Area....................	1,351,016	9.5	5.6	6.5	13.8	10.4	82,220	12.9	7.2	9.4	14.1	13.4
Coeur d'Alene, ID Metro Area....................	91,083	6.1	4.9	5.4	9.9	13.2	3,940	7.7	5.7	6.0	12.9	19.4
College Station-Bryan, TX Metro Area............	158,314	3.9	3.3	5.6	7.8	26.0	7,360	4.5	3.3	6.4	9.9	33.7
Colorado Springs, CO Metro Area....................	435,728	D	5.5	8.6	9.3	20.9	24,003	D	5.3	12.6	10.1	30.5
Columbia, MO Metro Area....................	143,236	3.7	5.3	5.0	9.4	24.1	6,832	5.2	8.0	5.5	10.9	34.7
Columbia, SC Metro Area....................	512,470	6.1	5.7	D	9.1	18.8	27,250	9.4	7.5	D	9.5	25.2
Columbus, GA-AL Metro Area................	182,468	6.4	8.0	D	9.8	24.3	9,293	8.4	12.4	D	10.5	35.4
Columbus, IN Metro Area................	61,915	32.5	2.4	4.4	7.5	11.0	4,029	48.8	2.6	4.3	6.9	8.7
Columbus, OH Metro Area....................	1,401,496	5.6	6.5	6.9	11.7	12.9	84,573	7.8	8.9	9.4	11.2	17.6
Corpus Christi, TX Metro Area....................	254,599	3.6	4.2	4.9	D	14.5	13,722	7.5	3.0	6.4	D	19.3
Corvallis, OR Metro Area................	52,126	6.7	2.6	8.2	13.7	18.8	3,018	11.1	2.2	7.7	16.5	30.1
Crestview-Fort Walton Beach-Destin, FL Metro Area	178,146	1.9	3.7	7.5	7.2	20.9	9,469	2.5	3.1	11.0	7.6	35.6
Cumberland, MD-WV Metro Area....................	47,612	10.0	2.9	3.4	17.7	16.5	2,314	14.6	3.1	2.7	20.0	23.6
Dallas-Fort Worth-Arlington, TX Metro Area	5,080,659	5.9	7.8	D	D	8.7	334,735	8.3	9.1	D	D	10.1
Dallas-Plano-Irving, TX Div	3,606,831	5.4	8.4	9.2	8.6	8.4	250,379	7.4	10.2	13.3	9.2	9.4
Fort Worth-Arlington-Grapevine, TX Div	1,473,828	7.1	6.3	5.2	9.1	9.4	84,356	11.1	5.7	5.9	9.9	12.2
Dalton, GA Metro Area................	81,001	31.4	2.2	D	D	9.0	4,387	36.6	1.8	D	D	10.3
Danville, IL Metro Area....................	35,863	14.0	4.5	2.1	9.0	16.9	1,893	21.2	3.8	1.4	9.3	23.2
Daphne-Fairhope-Foley, AL Metro Area............	115,166	4.3	4.0	4.6	9.5	9.4	4,315	6.9	3.9	5.3	12.8	13.8
Davenport-Moline-Rock Island, IA-IL Metro Area	231,770	10.6	4.4	D	D	12.0	13,219	14.3	4.0	D	D	15.7
Dayton-Kettering, OH Metro Area....................	487,119	9.2	4.3	6.9	14.2	14.0	27,862	12.2	4.9	9.2	15.6	21.8
Decatur, AL Metro Area....................	75,768	17.1	3.2	3.6	D	11.7	3,452	30.4	3.3	4.2	D	14.4
Decatur, IL Metro Area....................	62,811	18.4	4.2	3.5	14.3	9.6	3,956	31.2	3.5	3.6	12.9	10.7
Deltona-Daytona Beach-Ormond Beach, FL Metro Area.	294,806	4.4	4.3	5.4	13.0	8.4	12,064	7.1	4.0	5.8	17.4	13.7
Denver-Aurora-Lakewood, CO Metro Area............	2,094,120	D	D	D	D	10.5	145,819	D	D	D	D	11.9
Des Moines-West Des Moines, IA Metro Area	485,836	5.1	D	6.0	10.7	10.2	28,907	6.2	D	8.1	10.4	12.6
Detroit-Warren-Dearborn, MI Metro Area...........	2,628,870	10.3	4.9	10.1	12.6	7.8	168,697	14.9	5.5	15.3	11.6	9.7
Detroit-Dearborn-Livonia, MI Div.	968,969	10.2	4.1	7.7	14.5	9.5	62,999	14.8	4.7	12.1	13.3	12.1
Warren-Troy-Farmington Hills, MI Div	1,659,901	10.3	5.4	11.5	11.4	6.7	105,698	15.0	5.9	17.1	10.6	8.3
Dothan, AL Metro Area....................	79,403	7.1	3.2	3.5	D	14.4	3,524	8.0	3.3	4.9	D	19.4
Dover, DE Metro Area....................	93,124	D	4.5	D	12.0	24.8	4,714	D	2.8	D	12.4	36.8
Dubuque, IA Metro Area....................	73,999	13.4	7.7	3.9	12.9	7.0	3,706	20.9	10.0	4.8	14.1	8.1
Duluth, MN-WI Metro Area................	171,741	5.4	3.9	4.2	18.0	15.7	8,762	7.5	3.9	4.4	21.1	19.7
Durham-Chapel Hill, NC Metro Area....................	445,533	7.6	4.3	10.7	11.2	17.5	29,487	13.8	5.9	14.1	12.7	20.9
East Stroudsburg, PA Metro Area................	79,112	6.7	2.9	4.0	10.9	15.2	3,978	13.3	1.8	2.6	11.9	24.0
Eau Claire, WI Metro Area....................	112,157	10.3	4.8	3.9	14.8	11.2	5,763	13.5	5.1	4.1	19.6	14.6
El Centro, CA Metro Area....................	80,918	1.9	2.3	2.4	12.2	23.7	4,609	1.6	1.3	1.9	6.4	38.1
Elizabethtown-Fort Knox, KY Metro Area	78,130	10.6	3.1	3.2	7.1	25.8	4,151	14.5	2.8	2.9	6.4	40.6
Elkhart-Goshen, IN Metro Area....................	166,245	43.3	1.8	2.3	7.3	5.6	10,030	52.7	1.6	2.0	7.1	5.0
Elmira, NY Metro Area....................	43,868	11.9	3.3	3.1	16.0	14.2	2,436	16.6	4.0	3.0	16.9	22.9
El Paso, TX Metro Area....................	448,957	D	D	D	D	21.7	21,022	D	D	D	D	36.0
Enid, OK Metro Area....................	37,587	7.4	3.9	D	10.0	13.9	1,794	10.1	4.5	D	10.9	19.6
Erie, PA Metro Area....................	159,521	12.7	5.3	3.6	16.5	11.2	7,972	18.7	7.3	3.8	18.2	15.9
Eugene-Springfield, OR Metro Area....................	212,332	7.6	3.3	5.4	13.9	12.0	10,932	9.1	3.6	5.3	16.1	18.6
Evansville, IN-KY Metro Area....................	196,044	12.4	3.2	D	D	9.1	10,400	20.0	3.5	D	D	9.4
Fairbanks, AK Metro Area....................	59,454	1.5	1.7	4.3	10.2	33.8	3,953	1.1	1.3	3.5	10.7	47.3
Fargo, ND-MN Metro Area....................	180,612	6.0	6.8	5.3	13.4	11.5	9,880	7.4	8.1	6.3	15.0	13.9
Farmington, NM Metro Area....................	61,839	2.5	D	D	11.9	18.3	3,065	2.7	D	D	13.3	22.9
Fayetteville, NC Metro Area....................	257,954	4.3	2.1	D	7.6	36.1	14,516	4.9	1.6	D	5.8	57.9
Fayetteville-Springdale-Rogers, AR Metro Area	321,574	8.6	2.9	D	9.1	10.5	17,713	8.9	2.0	D	9.1	11.5
Flagstaff, AZ Metro Area....................	87,538	5.6	1.9	4.2	11.2	22.1	4,353	10.0	1.4	3.0	14.8	30.6
Flint, MI Metro Area....................	189,743	7.0	3.8	4.0	14.8	11.1	9,311	11.2	4.3	3.7	18.8	16.0
Florence, SC Metro Area....................	115,875	9.3	6.4	3.8	11.9	14.7	5,729	15.5	8.8	4.6	13.0	18.5
Florence-Muscle Shoals, AL Metro Area	76,121	12.8	3.8	3.0	9.3	13.7	3,158	19.5	3.8	2.9	12.4	20.0
Fond du Lac, WI Metro Area....................	61,500	18.9	4.0	2.8	11.2	9.3	3,372	25.7	3.9	2.8	12.9	11.8
Fort Collins, CO Metro Area....................	239,842	6.7	4.1	8.3	8.1	16.7	12,316	14.0	3.0	10.7	8.2	21.0
Fort Smith, AR-OK Metro Area....................	135,122	13.3	2.9	2.8	D	11.2	6,138	17.0	2.7	2.7	D	13.7
Fort Wayne, IN Metro Area....................	263,991	13.5	5.1	D	14.8	8.4	14,126	19.2	6.5	D	14.4	9.0
Fresno, CA Metro Area....................	510,394	5.4	3.9	3.9	14.3	14.9	28,607	6.0	3.6	4.1	19.0	22.7
Gadsden, AL Metro Area....................	50,804	11.4	3.5	2.8	D	11.4	2,027	15.7	3.7	2.7	D	15.0
Gainesville, FL Metro Area	198,261	3.1	3.8	D	14.2	22.9	9,869	4.3	4.7	D	17.2	35.5
Gainesville, GA Metro Area....................	119,901	17.8	4.2	3.4	12.0	9.5	6,440	19.7	4.5	3.7	16.1	10.8
Gettysburg, PA Metro Area....................	49,357	15.7	2.6	3.6	D	8.8	2,362	19.9	2.2	3.0	D	14.6
Glens Falls, NY Metro Area....................	71,640	9.0	3.7	4.2	12.8	13.8	3,654	14.0	3.6	4.1	14.1	20.9
Goldsboro, NC Metro Area....................	59,518	8.9	3.4	2.3	11.8	23.5	2,840	11.3	2.9	2.5	11.6	33.5
Grand Forks, ND-MN Metro Area....................	72,559	6.2	3.2	3.5	D	20.6	3,748	7.6	3.3	3.9	D	25.8
Grand Island, NE Metro Area....................	51,932	15.3	5.3	D	8.7	12.3	2,480	19.4	5.0	D	10.2	16.8

Table B-12. Employees and Earnings by Selected Major Industries, 2018—*Continued*

Metropolitan Statistical Area Metropolitan Division	Employment 2018						Earnings 2018					
	Total	Percent by selected major industries					Total (million dollars)	Percent by selected major industries				
		Manu-facturing	Finance and insurance	Professional scientific and technical services	Health care and social assistance	Government and government enterprises		Manu-facturing	Finance and insurance	Professional scientific and technical services	Health care and social assistance	Government and government enterprises
Grand Junction, CO Metro Area	91,009	3.9	4.3	4.7	13.3	11.6	4,264	4.4	4.4	4.7	16.7	16.0
Grand Rapids-Kentwood, MI Metro Area	734,356	16.8	4.4	D	D	7.1	40,470	24.4	5.0	D	D	9.4
Grants Pass, OR Metro Area	40,057	8.9	3.7	4.1	15.9	8.7	1,780	10.3	3.8	3.3	18.8	13.9
Great Falls, MT Metro Area	50,726	2.6	4.9	3.9	14.6	18.1	2,518	3.4	6.2	4.7	17.3	26.9
Greeley, CO Metro Area	162,136	9.1	4.2	4.3	7.0	11.1	8,951	11.2	3.3	3.8	7.0	11.3
Green Bay, WI Metro Area	222,303	14.3	D	D	D	10.4	12,929	17.1	D	D	D	12.2
Greensboro-High Point, NC Metro Area	478,400	11.9	4.9	4.9	10.4	9.5	24,349	16.6	6.4	6.6	11.6	11.6
Greenville, NC Metro Area	102,454	6.5	3.3	3.3	9.8	26.9	5,231	10.1	3.3	3.6	10.9	37.1
Greenville-Anderson, SC Metro Area	544,548	11.2	4.1	D	D	11.6	28,184	16.3	6.1	D	D	15.0
Gulfport-Biloxi, MS Metro Area	219,875	D	2.9	4.3	7.4	20.1	10,783	D	2.4	5.6	7.7	29.0
Hagerstown-Martinsburg, MD-WV Metro Area	141,104	6.8	5.1	4.1	12.1	13.5	7,084	10.0	6.3	4.2	13.7	19.9
Hammond, LA Metro Area	65,454	4.2	3.5	3.4	11.8	17.8	2,607	5.4	4.0	3.7	11.0	29.3
Hanford-Corcoran, CA Metro Area	63,771	8.1	1.7	1.9	11.7	31.4	3,713	8.8	1.2	1.5	9.9	47.1
Harrisburg-Carlisle, PA Metro Area	424,549	5.3	6.0	6.2	12.7	14.6	26,357	6.3	7.3	8.7	14.5	19.6
Harrisonburg, VA Metro Area	86,646	12.3	2.6	3.9	9.7	14.2	4,202	17.4	2.7	4.8	11.3	17.9
Hartford-East Hartford-Middletown, CT Metro Area	828,173	D	9.5	7.0	13.4	12.0	61,216	D	15.4	9.0	11.9	14.9
Hattiesburg, MS Metro Area	96,754	6.4	D	D	11.0	18.0	4,259	8.8	D	D	16.9	22.3
Hickory-Lenoir-Morganton, NC Metro Area	201,105	21.7	2.4	D	D	11.8	9,443	27.7	1.9	D	D	14.6
Hilton Head Island-Bluffton, SC Metro Area	127,088	1.2	3.5	D	7.9	17.4	5,678	1.2	4.1	D	8.9	29.1
Hinesville, GA Metro Area	42,175	D	D	D	D	54.6	2,611	D	D	D	D	73.4
Homosassa Springs, FL Metro Area	50,513	1.5	4.2	4.3	16.6	9.1	2,007	1.7	3.2	5.1	21.6	12.6
Hot Springs, AR Metro Area	53,599	5.1	3.9	3.9	16.7	9.1	2,174	7.4	3.8	3.8	22.3	13.1
Houma-Thibodaux, LA Metro Area	115,815	6.6	3.0	4.6	10.1	11.2	6,620	8.9	2.1	5.3	9.7	12.4
Houston-The Woodlands-Sugar Land, TX Metro Area	4,284,476	5.8	5.2	8.1	D	9.6	312,329	9.9	5.9	11.4	D	10.2
Huntington-Ashland, WV-KY-OH Metro Area	173,661	D	D	D	D	14.1	8,798	D	D	D	D	16.5
Huntsville, AL Metro Area	301,390	8.7	2.6	14.7	7.1	17.9	18,622	12.3	2.1	23.7	6.9	27.9
Idaho Falls, ID Metro Area	94,278	6.0	D	10.8	D	9.3	4,848	7.8	D	18.1	D	10.1
Indianapolis-Carmel-Anderson, IN Metro Area	1,355,155	7.1	5.3	D	D	10.5	86,078	10.8	6.8	D	D	10.9
Iowa City, IA Metro Area	131,571	4.7	3.5	3.8	8.1	31.0	7,112	6.8	2.9	3.6	7.3	43.9
Ithaca, NY Metro Area	70,894	4.9	2.6	7.1	D	8.8	4,018	6.9	2.5	7.2	D	12.4
Jackson, MI Metro Area	76,434	13.6	3.3	4.1	12.7	10.5	4,105	19.3	2.9	4.1	15.5	14.0
Jackson, MS Metro Area	384,815	5.8	5.3	5.0	12.1	16.4	18,305	8.2	6.4	6.9	13.6	21.6
Jackson, TN Metro Area	107,671	12.9	3.2	D	10.9	16.7	5,066	19.1	2.7	D	12.6	22.3
Jacksonville, FL Metro Area	935,281	3.7	8.1	7.0	11.6	9.8	52,159	5.4	11.3	8.8	13.1	13.6
Jacksonville, NC Metro Area	115,011	1.1	1.6	2.5	4.0	52.4	6,747	0.8	1.1	1.8	3.0	73.0
Janesville-Beloit, WI Metro Area	86,558	12.6	2.8	3.1	12.4	10.7	4,592	16.4	2.8	3.1	15.8	14.2
Jefferson City, MO Metro Area	101,578	6.9	D	3.9	8.3	25.2	4,911	9.7	D	4.9	8.9	31.2
Johnson City, TN Metro Area	106,890	7.6	5.0	D	D	15.9	5,038	11.0	4.8	D	D	21.8
Johnstown, PA Metro Area	66,287	6.6	4.9	4.6	18.7	12.1	3,122	9.6	5.2	5.2	21.9	17.3
Jonesboro, AR Metro Area	77,984	10.1	2.8	2.8	16.7	13.3	3,382	14.3	3.0	3.2	22.7	15.7
Joplin, MO Metro Area	103,562	13.4	2.7	3.1	13.3	9.8	4,921	22.7	2.8	3.4	15.6	10.6
Kahului-Wailuku-Lahaina, HI Metro Area	110,594	1.6	1.8	4.1	8.2	8.8	5,638	1.2	1.3	3.3	10.0	13.5
Kalamazoo-Portage, MI Metro Area	159,335	13.1	5.2	5.2	D	9.7	9,333	23.2	6.1	5.5	D	12.8
Kankakee, IL Metro Area	56,689	12.2	3.1	3.7	15.0	11.3	2,834	22.4	2.5	3.2	16.8	15.9
Kansas City, MO-KS Metro Area	1,408,379	5.8	6.4	9.3	10.8	11.5	87,372	7.5	8.4	13.2	10.9	13.7
Kennewick-Richland, WA Metro Area	156,436	5.7	2.7	7.8	11.0	13.3	9,545	6.3	2.2	12.3	10.9	17.8
Killeen-Temple, TX Metro Area	231,613	3.6	3.9	3.8	D	31.8	12,928	4.0	2.5	3.9	D	45.3
Kingsport-Bristol, TN-VA Metro Area	160,418	13.7	3.3	D	11.8	10.8	7,776	24.9	2.9	D	14.8	12.9
Kingston, NY Metro Area	92,469	4.3	3.5	5.6	13.1	14.6	4,480	6.7	3.1	4.9	13.8	28.0
Knoxville, TN Metro Area	515,988	7.9	D	7.2	D	11.6	28,589	11.1	D	10.4	D	14.1
Kokomo, IN Metro Area	49,415	24.1	2.9	2.8	12.6	10.8	2,680	45.5	2.9	2.1	13.1	9.5
La Crosse-Onalaska, WI-MN Metro Area	98,157	9.0	5.7	D	17.1	12.4	5,159	11.5	6.0	D	22.1	15.2
Lafayette, LA Metro Area	290,959	5.9	4.0	6.0	12.7	9.5	14,163	8.6	3.6	7.8	14.1	12.3
Lafayette-West Lafayette, IN Metro Area	130,007	D	2.7	4.3	D	20.5	7,036	D	2.7	5.7	D	24.3
Lake Charles, LA Metro Area	146,168	7.5	D	4.5	10.1	10.7	9,103	16.9	D	5.9	9.4	10.9
Lake Havasu City-Kingman, AZ Metro Area	71,666	5.2	3.3	3.7	12.7	11.2	2,997	6.5	2.7	3.2	19.9	16.9
Lakeland-Winter Haven, FL Metro Area	310,399	6.1	5.2	4.1	10.8	9.7	14,379	8.9	6.1	4.2	14.0	12.8
Lancaster, PA Metro Area	342,536	12.3	3.3	5.3	12.3	6.5	19,660	15.3	3.9	5.7	12.9	8.2
Lansing-East Lansing, MI Metro Area	302,536	7.6	5.9	D	11.2	18.0	16,122	11.3	7.7	D	12.5	26.1
Laredo, TX Metro Area	145,135	0.8	3.5	3.4	12.4	15.9	6,143	0.6	2.5	3.5	10.8	27.5
Las Cruces, NM Metro Area	102,594	2.8	3.0	5.6	16.2	19.9	4,678	3.4	2.7	6.4	16.0	29.7
Las Vegas-Henderson-Paradise, NV Metro Area	1,350,621	2.1	5.0	5.5	7.9	8.7	70,869	2.6	4.1	6.8	9.3	14.8
Lawrence, KS Metro Area	74,274	6.1	2.9	8.4	7.5	24.7	3,196	9.0	2.8	8.5	7.8	32.7
Lawton, OK Metro Area	68,946	D	3.2	3.9	6.1	38.5	3,606	D	2.7	3.8	5.8	53.2
Lebanon, PA Metro Area	68,829	14.3	2.4	3.5	11.7	12.2	3,619	17.6	2.1	3.1	11.8	18.8
Lewiston, ID-WA Metro Area	36,332	12.0	4.8	3.2	15.1	15.6	1,780	17.3	6.0	3.2	17.6	18.2
Lewiston-Auburn, ME Metro Area	63,344	8.5	3.8	5.2	17.0	9.3	3,105	10.7	4.7	6.1	20.6	11.7
Lexington-Fayette, KY Metro Area	356,470	8.9	3.2	D	9.7	15.2	18,921	13.8	3.4	D	11.5	20.9
Lima, OH Metro Area	64,205	14.6	3.0	3.1	17.3	9.7	3,483	24.9	2.3	3.0	20.4	12.3
Lincoln, NE Metro Area	235,742	5.9	6.2	6.1	D	15.3	12,583	8.2	7.3	7.8	D	21.2
Little Rock-North Little Rock-Conway, AR Metro Area	464,482	4.8	D	5.9	12.3	16.2	23,946	6.1	D	8.5	13.8	22.2
Logan, UT-ID Metro Area	85,452	14.5	3.9	D	D	15.2	3,733	20.1	3.6	D	D	19.3
Longview, TX Metro Area	173,710	9.6	4.5	4.0	D	9.0	8,233	15.4	3.9	5.1	D	10.6

Table B-12. Employees and Earnings by Selected Major Industries, 2018—*Continued*

Metropolitan Statistical Area Metropolitan Division	Employment 2018						Earnings 2018					
		Percent by selected major industries						Percent by selected major industries				
	Total	Manu-facturing	Finance and insurance	Professional scientific and technical services	Health care and social assistance	Government and government enterprises	Total (million dollars)	Manu-facturing	Finance and insurance	Professional scientific and technical services	Health care and social assistance	Government and government enterprises
Longview, WA Metro Area	50,753	13.4	2.8	3.2	13.2	13.3	2,978	21.5	2.1	2.8	12.7	15.6
Los Angeles-Long Beach-Anaheim, CA Metro Area	8,889,754	6.2	4.9	8.3	11.8	8.8	615,567	8.3	6.8	11.3	9.6	13.5
Anaheim-Santa Ana-Irvine, CA Div	2,308,542	7.5	6.5	9.3	9.7	7.2	160,226	10.8	9.4	11.7	8.9	10.3
Los Angeles-Long Beach-Glendale, CA Div	6,581,212	5.7	4.4	7.9	12.6	9.4	455,341	7.5	5.9	11.2	9.9	14.6
Louisville/Jefferson County, KY-IN Metro Area	829,070	9.9	6.3	5.7	11.3	9.2	46,821	14.0	9.4	7.5	12.6	11.1
Lubbock, TX Metro Area	200,848	2.7	6.0	4.5	D	16.0	9,218	3.3	6.5	5.1	D	25.0
Lynchburg, VA Metro Area	138,639	11.1	4.2	5.6	12.6	10.1	6,385	18.3	4.7	8.2	16.0	12.5
Macon-Bibb County, GA Metro Area	137,820	D	D	D	D	10.8	6,550	D	D	D	D	14.4
Madera, CA Metro Area	66,286	5.6	2.0	2.5	14.2	17.2	4,142	6.5	0.9	1.3	14.7	22.7
Madison, WI Metro Area	514,279	7.2	5.5	7.3	D	17.6	30,975	8.9	6.9	9.1	D	20.8
Manchester-Nashua, NH Metro Area	277,098	10.0	5.4	7.9	12.2	8.3	18,972	14.9	9.1	10.8	11.6	9.5
Manhattan, KS Metro Area	90,555	4.2	3.3	D	D	40.3	4,711	5.0	2.8	D	D	54.4
Mankato, MN Metro Area	72,337	11.2	3.5	D	D	12.4	3,555	15.7	3.5	D	D	17.3
Mansfield, OH Metro Area	65,434	16.0	2.9	2.5	13.1	12.1	3,073	23.3	2.6	2.4	14.9	17.4
McAllen-Edinburg-Mission, TX Metro Area	385,547	2.4	4.1	3.1	20.2	15.8	14,786	2.6	3.9	3.3	19.1	26.7
Medford, OR Metro Area	126,120	7.1	3.3	5.0	15.0	8.6	6,137	8.6	3.4	5.0	18.9	14.0
Memphis, TN-MS-AR Metro Area	863,932	5.4	3.8	4.7	11.5	10.3	47,560	9.4	5.8	4.2	12.9	13.3
Merced, CA Metro Area	106,327	9.5	2.4	2.3	10.5	18.2	5,942	10.5	2.1	1.7	9.7	26.3
Miami-Fort Lauderdale-Pompano Beach, FL Metro	4,069,251	2.6	6.2	7.6	10.3	8.1	213,941	3.3	8.0	10.9	11.2	12.3
Fort Lauderdale-Pompano Beach-Sunrise, FL Div	1,252,500	2.6	6.3	7.7	9.5	8.9	63,266	3.7	7.8	10.8	10.2	13.4
Miami-Miami Beach-Kendall, FL Div	1,858,895	2.7	5.5	7.2	10.2	8.1	99,412	2.8	7.8	10.4	11.0	12.6
West Palm Beach-Boca Raton-Boynton Beach, FL Div.	957,856	2.5	7.2	8.3	11.7	7.0	51,263	3.9	8.7	11.9	12.8	10.5
Michigan City-La Porte, IN Metro Area	53,496	15.0	2.5	3.2	11.1	12.9	2,574	21.7	2.7	2.9	13.4	14.4
Midland, MI Metro Area	48,061	13.7	2.8	4.4	13.4	7.0	3,329	24.7	2.3	3.3	11.0	6.8
Midland, TX Metro Area	161,109	2.9	D	5.0	4.5	6.3	19,763	2.1	D	3.1	2.4	3.6
Milwaukee-Waukesha, WI Metro Area	1,067,853	11.5	5.7	6.1	14.0	8.7	67,043	15.3	8.6	8.5	13.5	10.6
Minneapolis-St. Paul-Bloomington, MN Metro Area	2,546,419	8.2	6.7	D	12.2	10.4	171,629	11.1	10.1	D	10.8	11.9
Missoula, MT Metro Area	85,572	3.4	4.0	7.1	13.2	12.8	3,995	3.2	5.1	8.1	17.8	17.9
Mobile, AL Metro Area	245,447	8.4	4.2	5.5	11.5	11.7	12,353	15.8	5.4	8.3	12.2	14.8
Modesto, CA Metro Area	253,760	8.9	2.9	4.0	13.8	12.3	14,912	12.7	2.2	3.4	16.5	18.1
Monroe, LA Metro Area	117,114	6.3	5.3	D	D	11.3	5,143	9.6	5.9	D	16.9	16.0
Monroe, MI Metro Area	58,168	10.5	3.0	6.2	9.6	10.2	3,156	20.3	2.0	7.4	8.3	12.2
Montgomery, AL Metro Area	228,294	8.3	4.0	D	D	19.2	11,183	11.8	4.7	D	D	28.4
Morgantown, WV Metro Area	86,947	4.9	1.8	6.0	D	22.6	4,745	8.2	1.7	7.0	D	26.5
Morristown, TN Metro Area	67,771	19.3	2.2	D	D	11.7	3,088	27.2	1.6	D	D	14.1
Mount Vernon-Anacortes, WA Metro Area	71,106	9.3	3.8	4.8	8.5	16.9	4,101	14.2	4.6	4.7	7.1	22.8
Muncie, IN Metro Area	60,141	7.3	3.9	4.5	16.3	18.6	2,754	10.6	4.3	5.5	20.2	21.5
Muskegon, MI Metro Area	81,955	17.5	2.4	3.1	14.9	9.7	4,025	26.6	2.1	3.3	17.2	13.8
Myrtle Beach-Conway-North Myrtle Beach, SC-NC	238,527	2.3	3.9	4.3	7.9	10.2	9,582	3.3	5.1	4.7	11.3	16.0
Napa, CA Metro Area	107,800	14.0	2.8	5.4	9.2	10.4	7,607	22.8	3.1	5.2	9.1	14.7
Naples-Marco Island, FL Metro Area	230,183	2.2	6.3	6.1	10.2	6.2	11,636	3.4	7.3	10.9	12.9	8.9
Nashville-Davidson--Murfreesboro--Franklin, TN	1,366,725	6.5	D	7.5	10.2	8.5	91,563	7.3	D	10.2	18.6	8.7
New Bern, NC Metro Area	67,474	6.3	2.2	D	9.0	32.5	3,461	8.4	1.9	D	9.0	49.1
New Haven-Milford, CT Metro Area	512,713	6.3	4.7	6.0	15.8	10.0	32,070	8.6	4.0	8.3	15.4	14.6
New Orleans-Metairie, LA Metro Area	811,867	4.0	4.3	6.4	10.3	10.7	46,738	7.6	5.0	9.2	11.2	14.4
New York-Newark-Jersey City, NY-NJ-PA Metro Area.	12,917,191	D	7.8	9.0	13.4	10.1	1,088,320	D	15.9	13.1	10.5	13.1
Nassau County-Suffolk County, NY Div	1,815,390	D	7.3	7.5	14.5	10.6	123,440	D	7.3	9.1	16.1	17.9
Newark, NJ-PA Div	1,391,383	4.6	6.5	9.5	11.3	11.4	107,357	7.3	8.8	14.6	10.1	14.2
New Brunswick-Lakewood, NJ Div	1,500,279	4.4	5.7	9.4	11.9	9.6	106,341	10.8	5.6	13.4	10.9	12.3
New York-Jersey City-White Plains, NY-NJ Div	8,210,139	2.1	8.5	9.1	13.9	9.9	751,183	2.0	19.8	13.5	9.6	12.2
Niles, MI Metro Area	83,909	16.3	3.6	3.7	10.5	11.2	4,532	29.9	3.5	3.2	11.6	13.6
North Port-Sarasota-Bradenton, FL Metro Area	447,384	4.2	5.4	7.0	12.5	6.5	21,130	6.1	5.4	9.5	16.0	9.5
Norwich-New London, CT Metro Area	168,651	10.4	2.7	5.3	11.5	22.1	11,004	19.4	1.9	7.1	10.7	25.8
Ocala, FL Metro Area	154,258	6.0	4.1	4.7	13.4	10.2	6,096	8.9	3.4	5.1	19.0	14.9
Ocean City, NJ Metro Area	62,657	1.9	3.3	4.0	7.9	16.4	2,947	1.8	2.7	4.4	9.5	26.7
Odessa, TX Metro Area	103,385	5.6	2.8	3.2	5.5	10.0	6,798	6.9	2.0	3.2	4.7	10.5
Ogden-Clearfield, UT Metro Area	368,680	9.8	5.6	6.4	8.8	15.8	17,737	15.3	3.9	6.7	9.6	23.8
Oklahoma City, OK Metro Area	889,459	4.1	5.0	6.1	D	15.0	50,042	5.3	4.6	6.7	D	19.7
Olympia-Lacey-Tumwater, WA Metro Area	154,519	2.5	3.1	5.8	11.6	25.8	9,076	2.6	2.8	6.0	13.1	37.4
Omaha-Council Bluffs, NE-IA Metro Area	640,043	5.5	7.8	D	11.7	11.4	41,158	6.2	9.5	D	11.3	13.2
Orlando-Kissimmee-Sanford, FL Metro Area	1,712,125	3.0	4.7	7.2	9.1	7.6	87,094	4.6	5.9	10.5	11.0	10.4
Oshkosh-Neenah, WI Metro Area	117,122	20.1	4.5	4.8	10.0	10.6	7,010	27.7	5.0	5.9	9.2	11.6
Owensboro, KY Metro Area	68,030	13.6	D	D	D	10.0	3,290	22.6	D	D	D	11.3
Oxnard-Thousand Oaks-Ventura, CA Metro Area	475,749	6.1	5.5	7.6	10.3	10.7	29,692	8.7	5.5	7.8	9.7	17.2
Palm Bay-Melbourne-Titusville, FL Metro Area	303,181	9.0	4.0	7.5	12.4	10.5	15,946	18.9	3.4	9.7	13.3	14.9
Panama City, FL Metro Area	109,563	3.1	3.2	5.9	D	15.8	5,156	4.8	3.6	8.2	D	25.6
Parkersburg-Vienna, WV Metro Area	47,304	D	4.2	3.6	14.2	15.4	2,308	D	4.8	3.9	15.5	22.5
Pensacola-Ferry Pass-Brent, FL Metro Area	254,183	2.9	6.4	5.6	12.2	15.6	12,530	4.4	7.3	7.4	15.6	24.9
Peoria, IL Metro Area	225,817	10.8	D	4.9	14.7	10.8	13,780	23.1	D	6.4	15.0	12.1

Table B-12. Employees and Earnings by Selected Major Industries, 2018—*Continued*

Metropolitan Statistical Area Metropolitan Division	Employment 2018						Earnings 2018					
		Percent by selected major industries						Percent by selected major industries				
	Total	Manu-facturing	Finance and insurance	Professional scientific and technical services	Health care and social assistance	Government and government enterprises	Total (million dollars)	Manu-facturing	Finance and insurance	Professional scientific and technical services	Health care and social assistance	Government and government enterprises
Philadelphia-Camden-Wilmington, PA-NJ-DE-MD												
Metro Area	3,857,495	5.0	7.0	D	14.9	9.5	275,920	6.9	8.4	D	13.2	11.9
Camden, NJ Div	712,593	5.8	5.3	D	13.7	12.5	43,422	8.3	6.3	D	15.0	17.9
Montgomery County-Bucks County-Chester County,	1,433,189	6.6	7.8	10.8	13.1	6.2	99,078	9.3	8.2	16.8	11.6	7.7
Philadelphia, PA Div	1,254,359	2.9	5.3	7.5	18.4	11.0	102,844	4.0	7.0	12.1	13.9	12.9
Wilmington, DE-MD-NJ Div	457,354	4.2	11.6	7.3	13.2	11.3	30,576	6.8	16.9	11.7	13.2	13.7
Phoenix-Mesa-Chandler, AZ Metro Area	2,791,695	4.9	7.7	7.0	10.9	9.1	159,709	7.7	9.8	8.8	12.3	12.2
Pine Bluff, AR Metro Area	43,115	12.4	D	D	14.2	23.4	2,011	18.0	D	D	13.9	28.7
Pittsburgh, PA Metro Area	1,504,020	6.1	6.1	7.9	14.6	8.2	98,029	7.9	6.9	10.4	14.0	10.3
Pittsfield, MA Metro Area	86,070	5.1	3.6	6.5	16.6	10.1	4,382	9.0	4.5	8.6	19.3	14.3
Pocatello, ID Metro Area	52,633	6.8	4.9	4.2	12.3	18.0	2,218	11.1	5.5	3.9	14.0	23.1
Portland-South Portland, ME Metro Area	384,894	D	5.4	7.2	12.9	10.9	21,336	D	8.1	9.8	14.4	15.2
Portland-Vancouver-Hillsboro, OR-WA Metro Area..	1,613,028	8.6	4.5	D	D	9.4	103,525	12.8	5.1	D	D	13.4
Port St. Lucie, FL Metro Area	225,221	3.5	4.7	6.0	14.0	9.2	9,482	5.1	3.6	7.4	17.4	14.3
Poughkeepsie-Newburgh-Middletown, NY Metro Area	354,546	5.0	4.0	5.3	13.9	15.0	19,979	8.2	2.8	5.6	15.7	25.3
Prescott Valley-Prescott, AZ Metro Area	102,335	4.7	3.4	5.4	12.1	11.1	4,204	5.9	2.2	4.7	15.3	18.5
Providence-Warwick, RI-MA Metro Area	953,646	D	5.0	6.0	14.3	10.8	55,312	D	6.6	7.4	14.2	16.1
Provo-Orem, UT Metro Area	367,027	6.1	5.0	9.4	D	9.3	17,563	9.4	3.4	12.2	D	10.2
Pueblo, CO Metro Area	80,965	5.8	3.3	4.3	16.8	16.4	3,871	8.9	2.4	5.9	21.1	21.0
Punta Gorda, FL Metro Area	73,239	1.7	4.4	5.3	14.5	8.6	2,960	1.8	3.5	7.5	21.7	13.7
Racine, WI Metro Area	97,261	19.0	3.3	3.8	12.1	9.6	5,410	32.2	3.5	4.2	11.8	13.3
Raleigh-Cary, NC Metro Area	874,705	4.5	4.7	10.8	8.7	11.7	53,308	8.1	5.7	17.5	9.2	13.2
Rapid City, SD Metro Area	93,844	3.4	5.2	D	12.8	16.0	4,490	3.9	5.8	D	19.1	23.0
Reading, PA Metro Area	229,519	14.3	3.3	5.3	13.5	10.2	13,373	19.4	3.0	6.0	14.6	12.4
Redding, CA Metro Area	92,944	3.5	3.8	5.3	16.5	14.4	4,782	3.9	3.9	5.3	19.2	23.3
Reno, NV Metro Area	315,766	7.8	D	D	D	9.1	17,852	10.5	D	D	D	14.3
Richmond, VA Metro Area	864,428	4.0	D	7.1	11.0	14.7	54,229	5.3	D	10.4	11.3	17.7
Riverside-San Bernardino-Ontario, CA Metro Area ..	2,127,826	5.3	3.2	4.4	11.7	13.4	111,700	6.9	2.3	4.1	11.9	23.4
Roanoke, VA Metro Area	198,851	8.0	4.9	5.6	13.0	11.3	10,284	10.7	5.8	7.0	17.1	15.0
Rochester, MN Metro Area	153,399	7.4	2.8	3.2	32.6	8.6	9,539	10.4	2.0	2.2	49.0	9.4
Rochester, NY Metro Area	660,247	9.1	4.6	6.5	14.3	11.7	38,454	12.8	4.8	8.6	13.9	16.5
Rockford, IL Metro Area	188,290	17.8	4.0	3.5	13.7	9.2	10,440	26.6	4.9	3.2	15.9	12.4
Rocky Mount, NC Metro Area	74,042	13.6	2.9	3.5	D	14.7	3,303	22.0	2.9	3.3	D	19.0
Rome, GA Metro Area	53,711	12.3	3.3	D	17.1	11.1	2,637	17.7	2.7	D	25.3	13.9
Sacramento-Roseville-Folsom, CA Metro Area	1,384,512	3.0	4.9	7.1	11.8	18.3	92,719	3.6	5.4	8.7	12.2	31.0
Saginaw, MI Metro Area	108,324	12.1	4.3	3.5	15.9	10.2	5,559	19.9	4.8	4.0	18.9	14.0
St. Cloud, MN Metro Area	138,434	11.5	4.3	D	D	10.3	7,018	14.1	4.5	D	D	14.3
St. George, UT Metro Area	100,413	4.0	5.2	6.3	11.9	9.5	3,919	5.0	4.2	6.3	16.8	13.4
St. Joseph, MO-KS Metro Area	73,039	15.9	4.6	D	D	13.6	3,563	24.2	4.7	D	D	15.1
St. Louis, MO-IL Metro Area	1,797,783	D	6.0	6.6	13.1	10.0	109,871	D	9.1	9.4	12.8	11.9
Salem, OR Metro Area	228,186	6.4	3.3	4.0	12.7	18.2	12,386	6.3	3.0	4.1	14.8	29.3
Salinas, CA Metro Area	257,361	2.5	2.4	4.5	8.1	15.3	17,001	2.4	2.0	4.0	7.8	23.9
Salisbury, MD-DE Metro Area	224,502	D	3.5	D	11.4	11.3	11,009	D	3.1	D	15.0	15.6
Salt Lake City, UT Metro Area	946,278	6.5	8.2	D	8.0	12.1	56,956	8.3	9.0	D	7.6	14.8
San Angelo, TX Metro Area	74,744	D	D	D	11.2	17.0	3,594	D	D	D	14.1	23.0
San Antonio-New Braunfels, TX Metro Area	1,488,836	3.7	7.4	5.8	10.8	13.9	84,405	4.8	9.4	6.7	10.8	19.9
San Diego-Chula Vista-Carlsbad, CA Metro Area	2,176,967	5.6	4.4	10.2	9.5	16.0	148,502	8.6	4.6	14.7	8.5	23.3
San Francisco-Oakland-Berkeley, CA Metro Area .	3,436,995	4.6	5.6	13.5	10.4	9.6	344,893	6.1	8.4	19.3	7.7	11.6
Oakland-Berkeley-Livermore, CA Div	1,677,325	6.4	4.6	10.3	12.0	10.2	132,025	9.8	4.9	13.0	11.3	14.6
San Francisco-San Mateo-Redwood City, CA Div.	1,561,111	2.8	6.7	17.1	8.6	9.2	197,163	3.6	11.0	23.9	5.0	9.6
San Rafael, CA Div	198,559	3.2	5.7	12.6	11.1	8.2	15,704	6.1	6.2	15.3	10.4	11.8
San Jose-Sunnyvale-Santa Clara, CA Metro Area	1,473,886	12.1	3.6	D	9.6	6.9	194,331	22.3	2.7	D	6.1	6.0
San Luis Obispo-Paso Robles, CA Metro Area	176,059	5.3	3.2	7.4	10.1	13.3	10,031	6.0	3.2	7.9	10.4	20.8
Santa Cruz-Watsonville, CA Metro Area	157,613	5.6	3.0	8.0	12.1	13.0	9,606	7.4	3.1	8.0	13.2	19.2
Santa Fe, NM Metro Area	95,089	D	3.5	8.1	12.0	16.7	4,238	D	5.8	10.1	14.2	27.0
Santa Maria-Santa Barbara, CA Metro Area	281,958	5.2	3.0	7.7	10.1	13.9	18,535	7.1	2.9	10.0	10.8	20.1
Santa Rosa-Petaluma, CA Metro Area	311,917	8.5	3.5	7.5	12.5	9.6	19,537	12.3	3.7	7.4	13.2	13.5
Savannah, GA Metro Area	242,287	7.8	3.0	4.4	D	12.2	12,798	16.8	3.4	4.5	D	17.7
Scranton--Wilkes-Barre, PA Metro Area	326,594	9.0	4.8	D	10.1	9.4	16,621	11.8	5.4	D	D	14.2
Seattle-Tacoma-Bellevue, WA Metro Area	2,683,056	7.1	4.0	8.8	10.1	12.2	223,482	9.4	4.1	10.9	9.0	13.4
Seattle-Bellevue-Kent, WA Div	2,232,031	7.6	4.1	9.7	9.7	10.6	195,661	10.0	4.2	11.9	8.0	11.1
Tacoma-Lakewood, WA Div	451,025	4.3	3.7	4.4	12.2	20.2	27,822	5.3	3.3	4.0	16.2	29.6
Sebastian-Vero Beach, FL Metro Area	82,759	3.0	6.1	6.5	13.9	6.6	3,769	4.4	6.2	11.2	17.6	9.7
Sebring-Avon Park, FL Metro Area	40,885	2.0	3.2	3.5	15.8	10.5	1,516	2.6	2.7	3.1	23.2	16.3
Sheboygan, WI Metro Area	75,537	28.8	5.2	2.8	9.7	8.2	4,568	41.5	5.9	2.7	11.8	8.9
Sherman-Denison, TX Metro Area	70,943	8.6	5.6	3.8	15.2	10.3	3,008	14.4	5.3	3.7	19.7	14.2
Shreveport-Bossier City, LA Metro Area	242,082	4.1	3.8	D	13.4	14.4	12,133	6.5	3.3	D	16.5	22.3
Sierra Vista-Douglas, AZ Metro Area	51,617	1.7	3.0	5.8	8.9	29.3	2,829	1.2	2.8	7.1	9.1	47.7
Sioux City, IA-NE-SD Metro Area	96,357	D	4.9	2.8	D	10.3	5,174	D	5.3	3.6	D	12.0

Table B-12. Employees and Earnings by Selected Major Industries, 2018—*Continued*

Metropolitan Statistical Area Metropolitan Division	Employment 2018						Earnings 2018					
		Percent by selected major industries						Percent by selected major industries				
	Total	Manu-facturing	Finance and insurance	Professional scientific and technical services	Health care and social assistance	Government and government enterprises	Total (million dollars)	Manu-facturing	Finance and insurance	Professional scientific and technical services	Health care and social assistance	Government and government enterprises
Sioux Falls, SD Metro Area	204,698	D	D	4.7	D	7.7	12,090	D	D	5.4	D	8.4
South Bend-Mishawaka, IN-MI Metro Area	178,811	10.3	3.6	4.7	13.2	9.3	9,666	15.7	4.0	8.7	14.6	9.7
Spartanburg, SC Metro Area	186,651	17.8	2.8	4.2	D	11.8	10,023	27.0	4.3	4.2	D	15.1
Spokane-Spokane Valley, WA Metro Area	323,044	5.9	5.3	D	D	13.7	17,211	7.3	6.6	D	D	19.9
Springfield, IL Metro Area	129,873	2.8	6.4	5.2	D	16.2	7,428	3.1	7.0	6.1	D	23.9
Springfield, MA Metro Area	412,982	6.4	4.1	4.6	18.1	14.5	22,202	8.9	5.9	4.6	18.4	21.3
Springfield, MO Metro Area	287,746	6.2	4.6	5.1	13.5	10.6	13,388	9.8	5.0	8.0	17.4	13.5
Springfield, OH Metro Area	62,434	11.6	6.3	3.1	13.8	11.6	2,998	16.7	7.1	2.9	15.4	15.5
State College, PA Metro Area	118,052	4.0	2.4	5.5	8.8	40.5	6,292	5.1	2.2	6.0	10.3	47.9
Staunton, VA Metro Area	66,297	11.9	2.7	3.6	D	13.7	3,122	18.7	2.7	3.2	D	17.3
Stockton, CA Metro Area	340,035	6.2	3.4	3.1	11.1	13.1	19,207	7.8	2.8	2.8	11.9	21.6
Sumter, SC Metro Area	67,816	11.2	2.5	2.9	11.3	21.2	3,194	15.7	2.2	3.1	11.5	34.0
Syracuse, NY Metro Area	388,823	7.0	5.0	6.2	D	14.2	23,328	10.0	4.9	8.2	D	21.0
Tallahassee, FL Metro Area	233,838	1.7	4.0	7.4	D	25.8	11,564	2.1	4.5	11.3	D	34.6
Tampa-St. Petersburg-Clearwater, FL Metro Area	1,827,943	4.0	7.6	D	11.6	8.8	97,343	5.8	10.3	D	13.5	12.2
Terre Haute, IN Metro Area	92,047	12.4	3.1	2.6	12.8	15.4	4,280	18.1	3.3	2.6	14.9	18.2
Texarkana, TX-AR Metro Area	79,113	7.1	4.6	D	D	16.6	3,630	11.4	5.0	D	D	23.4
The Villages, FL Metro Area	44,814	3.0	5.7	5.1	12.5	11.0	1,929	4.9	4.1	5.5	14.9	20.1
Toledo, OH Metro Area	400,944	12.1	3.6	D	D	12.1	22,518	18.7	3.2	D	D	14.9
Topeka, KS Metro Area	145,718	5.7	6.9	D	13.6	19.1	7,618	7.2	9.9	D	14.6	22.4
Trenton-Princeton, NJ Metro Area	290,324	3.2	8.0	11.1	10.3	14.0	22,667	5.0	10.4	17.8	8.9	17.8
Tucson, AZ Metro Area	527,392	5.3	4.2	6.3	13.2	16.9	27,491	10.5	4.2	7.3	14.0	23.8
Tulsa, OK Metro Area	613,692	9.3	D	D	10.7	9.3	39,567	12.4	D	D	10.5	8.4
Tuscaloosa, AL Metro Area	142,408	12.8	D	D	D	20.4	6,696	21.0	D	D	D	27.9
Twin Falls, ID Metro Area	65,444	10.2	3.1	3.1	11.1	10.3	3,031	15.5	2.9	D	14.2	11.2
Tyler, TX Metro Area	151,640	3.9	5.2	5.2	16.4	9.7	9,684	4.3	3.8	5.4	16.2	9.7
Urban Honolulu, HI Metro Area	663,994	2.1	3.7	5.4	9.3	22.9	42,489	1.9	3.5	6.3	10.3	31.8
Utica-Rome, NY Metro Area	157,508	7.7	5.9	4.1	17.0	19.6	8,106	9.8	6.7	4.8	16.4	29.8
Valdosta, GA Metro Area	78,312	D	D	3.4	D	22.7	3,517	D	D	4.5	D	34.6
Vallejo, CA Metro Area	204,651	6.6	3.7	4.4	13.9	16.0	13,174	13.2	2.9	3.4	15.7	24.5
Victoria, TX Metro Area	58,455	D	4.2	3.5	D	12.1	2,765	D	3.5	3.5	D	15.9
Vineland-Bridgeton, NJ Metro Area	75,783	12.4	2.0	D	14.6	17.0	4,285	14.9	1.8	D	16.3	25.9
Virginia Beach-Norfolk-Newport News, VA-NC Metro Area	1,093,037	5.5	3.6	6.2	10.1	22.6	61,397	7.8	3.9	8.0	10.4	35.3
Visalia, CA Metro Area	210,856	6.6	2.8	2.6	8.6	16.0	11,660	8.2	2.2	2.3	7.2	24.7
Waco, TX Metro Area	162,771	10.7	D	3.9	9.9	12.0	7,983	17.4	D	4.7	10.6	15.8
Walla Walla, WA Metro Area	36,383	12.0	2.8	D	D	16.4	1,917	16.1	2.5	D	D	24.1
Warner Robins, GA Metro Area	98,347	D	D	5.6	D	31.5	5,181	D	D	6.3	D	52.9
Washington-Arlington-Alexandria, DC-VA-MD-WV Metro Area	4,445,776	D	D	D	D	17.6	369,185	D	D	D	D	26.9
Frederick-Gaithersburg-Rockville, MD Div	875,540	D	D	D	D	13.3	72,722	D	D	15.9	D	20.0
Washington-Arlington-Alexandria, DC-VA-MD-WV Metro Division	3,570,236	1.3	3.5	15.2	8.2	18.6	296,463	1.2	4.3	24.5	6.4	28.6
Waterloo-Cedar Falls, IA Metro Area	114,494	14.9	D	4.2	12.1	13.0	5,805	24.2	D	5.2	12.6	15.3
Watertown-Fort Drum, NY Metro Area	67,512	3.4	2.2	2.2	10.7	39.2	3,960	3.7	1.6	1.8	10.8	57.1
Wausau-Weston, WI Metro Area	107,758	18.7	7.9	3.2	10.6	9.5	5,819	23.0	9.8	4.3	14.5	11.7
Weirton-Steubenville, WV-OH Metro Area	49,923	11.1	3.0	D	15.8	12.2	2,405	19.0	2.7	D	17.4	13.4
Wenatchee, WA Metro Area	73,313	3.9	2.6	3.8	11.1	13.4	3,629	4.2	1.9	3.7	15.2	20.8
Wheeling, WV-OH Metro Area	83,476	3.7	3.8	4.0	D	11.6	4,975	5.0	3.5	11.9	D	11.1
Wichita, KS Metro Area	399,165	13.6	3.8	4.6	D	11.9	23,178	21.3	3.1	5.3	D	12.4
Wichita Falls, TX Metro Area	91,933	6.3	4.8	2.7	12.3	20.0	4,068	10.0	4.1	2.8	14.3	28.6
Williamsport, PA Metro Area	68,858	11.8	3.8	3.9	14.1	13.6	3,407	16.6	3.4	4.1	17.0	18.3
Wilmington, NC Metro Area	179,683	3.6	4.0	7.5	9.0	13.8	8,414	6.2	4.7	11.2	10.4	20.1
Winchester, VA-WV Metro Area	83,587	9.2	4.8	D	D	13.0	4,297	13.1	5.7	D	D	18.6
Winston-Salem, NC Metro Area	361,114	9.5	5.0	5.2	D	9.1	18,710	12.4	7.9	6.5	D	10.4
Worcester, MA-CT Metro Area	532,975	8.3	4.6	6.0	16.0	11.9	31,780	12.5	5.3	8.1	15.7	16.3
Yakima, WA Metro Area	135,686	6.9	2.3	2.5	13.3	14.0	6,989	8.7	2.0	2.5	14.5	18.8
York-Hanover, PA Metro Area	240,829	13.4	3.1	4.7	12.0	9.0	13,238	18.5	2.8	5.4	14.0	13.1
Youngstown-Warren-Boardman, OH-PA Metro Area	286,111	10.2	3.6	D	15.5	10.8	13,641	15.9	3.4	D	16.8	14.9
Yuba City, CA Metro Area	73,579	3.5	2.5	D	D	21.3	4,114	4.2	2.0	D	D	34.0
Yuma, AZ Metro Area	89,654	3.3	2.4	4.4	10.1	21.2	5,173	3.4	1.6	4.7	10.3	27.5

Table B-13. Civilian Labor Force

Metropolitan Statistical Area Metropolitan Division	Total labor force 2018	2015	2010	2005	Percent change 2005-2018	Number of unemployed 2018	2015	2010	2005	Unemployment rate 2018	2015	2010	2005
Abilene, TX Metro Area	77,053	74,814	76,448	80,081	-3.8	2,548	2,878	5,330	3,376	3.3	3.8	7.0	4.2
Akron, OH Metro Area	357,240	358,341	372,207	380,527	-6.1	16,597	17,753	39,167	22,421	4.6	5.0	10.5	5.9
Albany, GA Metro Area	66,101	64,306	69,533	72,558	-8.9	3,141	4,505	8,169	4,133	4.8	7.0	11.7	5.7
Albany-Lebanon, OR Metro Area	58,551	55,202	57,072	51,945	12.7	2,771	3,706	7,321	3,899	4.7	6.7	12.8	7.5
Albany-Schenectady-Troy, NY Metro Area	450,252	447,220	459,102	454,313	-0.9	16,972	19,937	33,405	18,042	3.8	4.5	7.3	4.0
Albuquerque, NM Metro Area	429,850	420,492	424,690	394,236	9.0	20,144	25,729	34,021	19,015	4.7	6.1	8.0	4.8
Alexandria, LA Metro Area	63,352	66,663	67,410	67,767	-6.5	3,411	4,381	5,197	4,185	5.4	6.6	7.7	6.2
Allentown-Bethlehem-Easton, PA-NJ Metro Area	435,921	430,138	419,462	407,310	7.0	19,528	23,063	38,745	19,882	4.5	5.4	9.2	4.9
Altoona, PA Metro Area	59,555	60,945	61,780	64,786	-8.1	2,505	3,139	4,948	3,351	4.2	5.2	8.0	5.2
Amarillo, TX Metro Area	132,065	130,406	129,609	127,588	3.5	3,637	4,022	7,355	5,068	2.8	3.1	5.7	4.0
Ames, IA Metro Area	72,572	72,781	68,178	62,296	16.5	1,233	1,914	3,088	1,953	1.7	2.6	4.5	3.1
Anchorage, AK Metro Area	199,604	203,007	200,237	185,756	7.5	11,988	11,457	14,379	10,988	6.0	5.6	7.2	5.9
Ann Arbor, MI Metro Area	194,621	188,340	182,801	189,926	2.5	5,928	7,019	14,832	8,467	3.0	3.7	8.1	4.5
Anniston-Oxford, AL Metro Area	45,972	45,928	51,559	53,955	-14.8	2,139	3,229	5,860	2,431	4.7	7.0	11.4	4.5
Appleton, WI Metro Area	131,547	129,417	127,900	119,949	9.7	3,613	5,017	10,026	5,304	2.7	3.9	7.8	4.4
Asheville, NC Metro Area	233,404	218,280	208,970	198,283	17.7	7,258	10,091	18,796	8,669	3.1	4.6	9.0	4.4
Athens-Clarke County, GA Metro Area	101,975	93,823	93,927	99,200	2.8	3,756	5,315	8,551	4,280	3.7	5.7	9.1	4.3
Atlanta-Sandy Springs-Alpharetta, GA Metro Area	3,071,572	2,839,005	2,720,049	2,584,602	18.8	115,989	161,855	280,009	138,928	3.8	5.7	10.3	5.4
Atlantic City-Hammonton, NJ Metro Area	118,969	126,383	140,598	136,314	-12.7	7,001	12,109	17,268	7,293	5.9	9.6	12.3	5.4
Auburn-Opelika, AL Metro Area	74,654	70,891	66,764	63,530	17.5	2,703	3,720	6,006	2,369	3.6	5.2	9.0	3.7
Augusta-Richmond County, GA-SC Metro Area	268,009	258,263	255,680	256,395	4.5	11,149	16,391	24,851	15,708	4.2	6.3	9.7	6.1
Austin-Round Rock-Georgetown, TX Metro Area	1,197,091	1,074,002	930,551	798,312	50.0	35,043	36,181	65,089	36,321	2.9	3.4	7.0	4.5
Bakersfield, CA Metro Area	386,997	390,337	371,515	326,748	18.4	30,865	39,860	58,154	27,342	8.0	10.2	15.7	8.4
Baltimore-Columbia-Towson, MD Metro Area	1,493,496	1,470,926	1,425,285	1,366,365	9.3	59,512	77,335	116,060	60,205	4.0	5.3	8.1	4.4
Bangor, ME Metro Area	77,127	76,846	79,017	77,286	-0.2	2,920	3,630	6,696	3,935	3.8	4.7	8.5	5.1
Barnstable Town, MA Metro Area	116,225	111,629	111,092	122,143	-4.8	4,974	6,815	11,030	6,022	4.3	6.1	9.9	4.9
Baton Rouge, LA Metro Area	427,887	430,728	400,736	372,571	14.8	18,886	23,798	31,482	26,240	4.4	5.5	7.9	7.0
Battle Creek, MI Metro Area	62,865	64,125	64,996	71,724	-12.4	2,646	3,276	7,607	4,799	4.2	5.1	11.7	6.7
Bay City, MI Metro Area	50,352	52,185	54,666	55,557	-9.4	2,410	3,020	6,319	3,949	4.8	5.8	11.6	7.1
Beaumont-Port Arthur, TX Metro Area	170,941	170,268	177,522	176,954	-3.4	10,320	11,352	19,886	13,557	6.0	6.7	11.2	7.7
Beckley, WV Metro Area	45,250	46,598	50,037	49,913	-9.3	2,572	3,635	4,396	2,552	5.7	7.8	8.8	5.1
Bellingham, WA Metro Area	111,670	104,151	104,359	102,524	8.9	5,295	6,239	9,892	5,399	4.7	6.0	9.5	5.3
Bend, OR Metro Area	95,367	84,779	81,238	74,532	28.0	4,020	4,985	11,243	4,282	4.2	5.9	13.8	5.7
Billings, MT Metro Area	91,688	91,118	86,507	88,352	3.8	3,076	3,062	5,115	3,137	3.4	3.4	5.9	3.6
Binghamton, NY Metro Area	107,364	110,126	124,412	122,597	-12.4	5,114	6,467	10,648	5,943	4.8	5.9	8.6	4.8
Birmingham-Hoover, AL Metro Area	519,731	510,052	512,474	500,789	3.8	18,186	27,462	49,502	20,484	3.5	5.4	9.7	4.1
Bismarck, ND Metro Area	66,293	65,955	63,257	59,910	10.7	1,861	1,719	2,458	1,824	2.8	2.6	3.9	3.0
Blacksburg-Christiansburg, VA Metro Area	81,916	82,249	80,561	76,695	6.8	2,577	3,852	6,763	3,130	3.1	4.7	8.4	4.1
Bloomington, IL Metro Area	87,889	90,917	96,138	87,165	0.8	3,680	4,340	6,787	3,554	4.2	4.8	7.1	4.1
Bloomington, IN Metro Area	79,040	76,649	78,052	78,446	0.8	2,917	3,901	6,551	3,969	3.7	5.1	8.4	5.1
Bloomsburg-Berwick, PA Metro Area	42,545	42,851	43,816	42,998	-1.1	1,912	2,299	3,850	2,386	4.5	5.4	8.8	5.5
Boise City, ID Metro Area	361,718	324,609	297,463	281,557	28.5	9,718	13,440	27,312	10,347	2.7	4.1	9.2	3.7
Boston-Cambridge-Newton, MA-NH Metro Area.	2,746,759	2,580,621	2,473,928	2,369,644	15.9	81,805	110,397	185,797	107,098	3.0	4.3	7.5	4.5
Boston, MA Div	1,134,416	1,058,743	1,014,209	946,385	19.9	35,344	47,522	80,235	45,077	3.1	4.5	7.9	4.8
Cambridge-Newton-Framingham, MA Div.	1,353,655	1,271,767	1,217,790	1,185,870	14.1	39,685	54,257	91,318	52,740	2.9	4.3	7.5	4.4
Rockingham County-Strafford County, NH Div.	258,688	250,111	241,929	237,389	9.0	6,776	8,618	14,244	9,281	2.6	3.4	5.9	3.9
Boulder, CO Metro Area	193,822	176,969	170,293	168,036	15.3	5,519	5,587	11,985	7,382	2.8	3.2	7.0	4.4
Bowling Green, KY Metro Area	83,443	77,899	77,926	74,979	11.3	3,219	3,711	7,767	4,071	3.9	4.8	10.0	5.4
Bremerton-Silverdale-Port Orchard, WA Metro Area	122,885	115,217	120,592	120,999	1.6	5,713	6,442	10,362	6,464	4.6	5.6	8.6	5.3
Bridgeport-Stamford-Norwalk, CT Metro Area	480,767	478,906	473,386	451,803	6.4	19,017	25,646	39,825	19,830	4.0	5.4	8.4	4.4
Brownsville-Harlingen, TX Metro Area	166,001	163,203	162,316	140,218	18.4	10,235	11,597	18,145	10,675	6.2	7.1	11.2	7.6
Brunswick, GA Metro Area	53,766	50,280	52,097	51,706	4.0	2,052	3,172	5,448	2,439	3.8	6.3	10.5	4.7
Buffalo-Cheektowaga, NY Metro Area	542,584	549,619	573,522	583,969	-7.1	24,771	30,124	49,093	30,659	4.6	5.5	8.6	5.3
Burlington, NC Metro Area	80,583	77,316	76,806	68,710	17.3	2,958	4,134	8,355	4,128	3.7	5.3	10.9	6.0
Burlington-South Burlington, VT Metro Area	128,380	126,065	126,401	117,420	9.3	2,810	3,697	6,406	3,886	2.2	2.9	5.1	3.3
California-Lexington Park, MD Metro Area	55,295	54,555	53,619	49,151	12.5	2,102	2,644	3,503	1,737	3.8	4.8	6.5	3.5
Canton-Massillon, OH Metro Area	199,318	199,765	206,242	204,520	-2.5	9,828	10,622	23,520	13,478	4.9	5.3	11.4	6.6
Cape Coral-Fort Myers, FL Metro Area	342,684	318,898	283,236	272,752	25.6	11,634	16,503	35,446	8,780	3.4	5.2	12.5	3.2
Cape Girardeau, MO-IL Metro Area	47,659	48,694	49,843	47,208	1.0	1,471	2,283	3,945	2,353	3.1	4.7	7.9	5.0
Carbondale-Marion, IL Metro Area	64,110	64,719	66,845	69,935	-8.3	3,247	3,901	6,172	3,522	5.1	6.0	9.2	5.0
Carson City, NV Metro Area	25,718	24,760	26,700	27,201	-5.5	1,216	1,784	3,600	1,234	4.7	7.2	13.5	4.5
Casper, WY Metro Area	39,059	42,882	39,894	39,124	-0.2	1,813	2,116	2,784	1,346	4.6	4.9	7.0	3.4
Cedar Rapids, IA Metro Area	143,364	144,834	145,538	138,103	3.8	3,986	5,587	8,775	6,023	2.8	3.9	6.0	4.4
Chambersburg-Waynesboro, PA Metro Area	77,064	77,794	75,712	76,938	0.2	2,846	3,857	6,455	2,642	3.7	5.0	8.5	3.4
Champaign-Urbana, IL Metro Area	114,099	113,059	118,153	110,243	3.5	5,016	5,817	9,661	4,512	4.4	5.1	8.2	4.1
Charleston, WV Metro Area	116,314	116,879	125,248	122,881	-5.3	6,127	7,899	10,458	6,297	5.3	6.8	8.3	5.1
Charleston-North Charleston, SC Metro Area	382,521	364,101	327,150	295,680	29.4	11,057	18,754	30,266	15,890	2.9	5.2	9.3	5.4
Charlotte-Concord-Gastonia, NC-SC Metro Area	1,343,488	1,251,898	1,152,331	1,010,941	32.9	49,044	68,629	135,364	54,693	3.7	5.5	11.7	5.4
Charlottesville, VA Metro Area	113,130	108,809	104,497	97,086	16.5	2,980	4,169	6,476	3,031	2.6	3.8	6.2	3.1
Chattanooga, TN-GA Metro Area	270,586	252,890	258,365	251,219	7.7	9,584	13,846	22,816	12,077	3.5	5.5	8.8	4.8
Cheyenne, WY Metro Area	47,682	48,668	46,182	41,359	15.3	1,847	1,942	3,090	1,701	3.9	4.0	6.7	4.1
Chicago-Naperville-Elgin, IL-IN-WI Metro Area.	4,876,393	4,892,095	4,872,958	4,698,563	3.8	197,067	289,857	514,472	275,641	4.0	5.9	10.6	5.9
Chicago-Naperville-Evanston, IL Div.	3,668,492	3,710,593	3,697,035	3,584,710	2.3	142,756	222,288	392,570	216,711	3.9	6.0	10.6	6.0
Elgin, IL Div.	397,049	388,695	386,048	347,149	14.4	18,272	21,847	41,722	18,758	4.6	5.6	10.8	5.4

Table B-13. Civilian Labor Force—*Continued*

Metropolitan Statistical Area / Metropolitan Division	Total labor force				Percent change 2005-2018	Number of unemployed				Unemployment rate			
	2018	2015	2010	2005		2018	2015	2010	2005	2018	2015	2010	2005
Gary, IN Div................	342,764	337,692	333,965	328,821	4.2	15,776	21,583	34,953	19,086	4.6	6.4	10.5	5.8
Lake County-Kenosha County, IL-WI Div	468,088	455,115	455,910	437,883	6.9	20,263	24,139	45,227	21,086	4.3	5.3	9.9	4.8
Chico, CA Metro Area...........	102,712	101,133	102,568	98,309	4.5	5,093	7,253	14,246	6,632	5.0	7.2	13.9	6.7
Cincinnati, OH-KY-IN Metro Area..........	1,127,192	1,088,283	1,107,357	1,100,966	2.4	44,607	49,086	109,770	60,101	4.0	4.5	9.9	5.5
Clarksville, TN-KY Metro Area.................	119,896	114,220	115,040	103,954	15.3	5,034	6,866	11,255	5,918	4.2	6.0	9.8	5.7
Cleveland, TN Metro Area..........	57,539	56,645	53,784	53,462	7.6	2,108	3,059	5,184	2,857	3.7	5.4	9.6	5.3
Cleveland-Elyria, OH Metro Area..........	1,035,340	1,030,083	1,052,045	1,078,484	-4.0	52,381	51,708	87,921	55,086	5.1	5.0	8.4	5.1
Coeur d'Alene, ID Metro Area..........	77,765	71,744	68,859	67,178	15.8	2,700	3,683	7,514	3,027	3.5	5.1	10.9	4.5
College Station-Bryan, TX Metro Area.................	132,760	123,710	115,448	102,867	29.1	3,931	4,279	7,609	4,380	3.0	3.5	6.6	4.3
Colorado Springs, CO Metro Area..........	349,735	319,422	318,662	301,904	15.8	13,737	14,579	29,786	15,860	3.9	4.6	9.3	5.3
Columbia, MO Metro Area..........	109,511	111,478	105,522	100,202	9.3	2,577	4,165	7,185	3,729	2.4	3.7	6.8	3.7
Columbia, SC Metro Area..........	398,497	398,461	372,407	355,320	12.2	13,181	21,796	34,814	20,316	3.3	5.5	9.3	5.7
Columbus, GA-AL Metro Area..........	130,453	128,789	133,165	132,476	-1.5	6,093	8,950	13,266	8,014	4.7	6.9	10.0	6.0
Columbus, IN Metro Area..........	45,295	43,575	38,387	37,388	21.1	1,185	1,576	3,660	1,812	2.6	3.6	9.5	4.8
Columbus, OH Metro Area..........	1,080,766	1,038,160	1,004,299	956,304	13.0	41,578	43,274	90,420	52,557	3.8	4.2	9.0	5.5
Corpus Christi, TX Metro Area..........	198,500	196,202	192,936	186,099	6.7	9,765	10,156	16,381	10,482	4.9	5.2	8.5	5.6
Corvallis, OR Metro Area..........	48,345	45,443	45,075	41,922	15.3	1,535	1,916	3,202	2,052	3.2	4.2	7.1	4.9
Crestview-Fort Walton Beach-Destin, FL Metro Area...	126,914	119,400	115,030	124,514	1.9	3,781	5,472	9,936	3,492	3.0	4.6	8.6	2.8
Cumberland, MD-WV Metro Area...........	44,246	43,884	46,781	48,703	-9.2	2,440	3,101	4,367	2,867	5.5	7.1	9.3	5.9
Dallas-Fort Worth-Arlington, TX Metro Area	3,869,662	3,556,612	3,273,368	2,998,404	29.1	135,325	144,171	264,282	156,327	3.5	4.1	8.1	5.2
Dallas-Plano-Irving, TX Div......................	2,631,424	2,401,661	2,192,401	2,004,189	31.3	92,386	95,891	175,976	105,630	3.5	4.0	8.0	5.3
Fort Worth-Arlington-Grapevine, TX Div	1,238,238	1,154,951	1,080,967	994,215	24.5	42,939	48,280	88,306	50,697	3.5	4.2	8.2	5.1
Dalton, GA Metro Area..........	61,199	61,498	64,820	66,501	-8.0	2,996	4,084	8,030	3,164	4.9	6.6	12.4	4.8
Danville, IL Metro Area..........	33,578	35,468	37,958	37,822	-11.2	2,074	2,498	4,341	2,378	6.2	7.0	11.4	6.3
Daphne-Fairhope-Foley, AL Metro Area.................	93,849	87,741	83,459	76,804	22.2	3,393	4,859	8,339	3,061	3.6	5.5	10.0	4.0
Davenport-Moline-Rock Island, IA-IL Metro Area ..	191,911	193,910	199,430	202,279	-5.1	8,011	10,793	16,387	9,189	4.2	5.6	8.2	4.5
Dayton-Kettering, OH Metro Area..........	386,050	381,610	401,835	404,463	-4.6	16,758	18,288	44,010	25,277	4.3	4.8	11.0	6.2
Decatur, AL Metro Area..........	70,258	68,614	72,718	71,679	-2.0	2,566	4,290	8,094	3,405	3.7	6.3	11.1	4.8
Decatur, IL Metro Area..........	49,961	50,566	55,193	52,836	-5.4	2,795	3,525	6,162	3,202	5.6	7.0	11.2	6.1
Deltona-Daytona Beach-Ormond Beach, FL Metro Area..........	300,516	281,928	279,521	274,669	9.4	11,376	16,727	34,326	10,374	3.8	5.9	12.3	3.8
Denver-Aurora-Lakewood, CO Metro Area	1,646,346	1,507,538	1,423,355	1,314,305	25.3	51,977	55,355	123,630	67,657	3.2	3.7	8.7	5.1
Des Moines-West Des Moines, IA Metro Area	372,879	359,227	341,880	314,920	18.4	9,069	12,962	20,097	12,730	2.4	3.6	5.9	4.0
Detroit-Warren-Dearborn, MI Metro Area.........	2,130,620	2,026,168	2,063,555	2,209,029	-3.5	91,155	119,158	285,929	153,998	4.3	5.9	13.9	7.0
Detroit-Dearborn-Livonia, MI Div.....................	794,466	760,432	802,754	910,762	-12.8	41,540	52,604	124,328	75,511	5.2	6.9	15.5	8.3
Warren-Troy-Farmington Hills, MI Div	1,336,154	1,265,736	1,255,801	1,298,267	2.9	49,615	66,554	161,601	78,487	3.7	5.3	12.9	6.0
Dothan, AL Metro Area...........	62,767	62,071	65,232	65,199	-3.7	2,551	3,871	6,231	2,545	4.1	6.2	9.6	3.9
Dover, DE Metro Area..........	78,124	76,292	72,711	72,015	8.5	3,239	4,108	6,461	2,621	4.1	5.4	8.9	3.6
Dubuque, IA Metro Area..........	55,213	55,752	54,215	50,793	8.7	1,333	2,058	3,136	2,196	2.4	3.7	5.8	4.3
Duluth, MN-WI Metro Area	148,405	148,438	150,703	147,148	0.9	5,584	7,328	12,334	7,525	3.8	4.9	8.2	5.1
Durham-Chapel Hill, NC Metro Area.................	328,244	309,917	290,122	268,243	22.4	11,289	15,457	24,044	11,941	3.4	5.0	8.3	4.5
East Stroudsburg, PA Metro Area	82,004	80,688	82,713	77,999	5.1	4,392	5,206	8,049	4,321	5.4	6.5	9.7	5.5
Eau Claire, WI Metro Area	92,860	91,311	90,289	86,404	7.5	2,648	3,779	6,767	3,943	2.9	4.1	7.5	4.6
El Centro, CA Metro Area	71,055	76,722	78,665	60,592	17.3	12,855	18,788	22,687	9,672	18.1	24.5	28.8	16.0
Elizabethtown-Fort Knox, KY Metro Area..........	67,543	64,236	65,301	65,279	3.5	2,830	3,263	6,682	3,982	4.2	5.1	10.2	6.1
Elkhart-Goshen, IN Metro Area..........	116,267	104,701	94,498	101,915	14.1	3,012	4,070	12,599	4,726	2.6	3.9	13.3	4.6
Elmira, NY Metro Area	35,373	37,455	41,594	40,595	-12.9	1,649	2,196	3,489	2,157	4.7	5.9	8.4	5.3
El Paso, TX Metro Area	360,802	343,150	342,254	291,338	23.8	15,300	17,720	31,324	20,532	4.2	5.2	9.2	7.0
Enid, OK Metro Area..........	27,330	30,120	28,519	28,304	-3.4	832	1,188	1,572	1,013	3.0	3.9	5.5	3.6
Erie, PA Metro Area..........	129,260	134,648	136,361	140,605	-8.1	6,087	7,397	12,687	7,562	4.7	5.5	9.3	5.4
Eugene-Springfield, OR Metro Area	181,761	172,577	178,303	173,600	4.7	8,165	10,028	19,648	10,664	4.5	5.8	11.0	6.1
Evansville, IN-KY Metro Area	164,282	158,689	159,288	159,088	3.3	5,249	6,789	14,106	8,159	3.2	4.3	8.9	5.1
Fairbanks, AK Metro Area..........	46,101	46,412	48,285	45,247	1.9	2,675	2,535	3,202	2,641	5.8	5.5	6.6	5.8
Fargo, ND-MN Metro Area..........	136,735	130,692	122,707	113,083	20.9	3,340	3,237	5,018	3,269	2.4	2.5	4.1	2.9
Farmington, NM Metro Area..........	52,537	55,754	54,860	54,461	-3.5	3,029	3,822	5,147	2,900	5.8	6.9	9.4	5.3
Fayetteville, NC Metro Area..........	200,668	196,424	198,447	190,865	5.1	10,030	14,168	20,674	10,330	5.0	7.2	10.4	5.4
Fayetteville-Springdale-Rogers, AR Metro Area	264,399	244,035	217,256	208,928	26.6	7,276	8,921	14,339	6,933	2.8	3.7	6.6	3.3
Flagstaff, AZ Metro Area..........	77,083	73,254	72,846	67,883	13.6	4,233	4,762	7,196	3,334	5.5	6.5	9.9	4.9
Flint, MI Metro Area..........	181,781	181,656	188,190	212,686	-14.5	8,894	11,088	26,272	16,784	4.9	6.1	14.0	7.9
Florence, SC Metro Area	96,082	95,508	94,763	92,386	4.0	3,639	6,509	11,303	8,149	3.8	6.8	11.9	8.8
Florence-Muscle Shoals, AL Metro Area..........	65,399	66,275	67,824	67,023	-2.4	2,840	4,827	7,178	3,508	4.3	7.3	10.6	5.2
Fond du Lac, WI Metro Area	57,658	57,033	56,516	55,868	3.2	1,519	2,325	4,801	2,567	2.6	4.1	8.5	4.6
Fort Collins, CO Metro Area..........	202,449	180,786	170,001	165,944	22.0	5,695	5,952	12,976	7,251	2.8	3.3	7.6	4.4
Fort Smith, AR-OK Metro Area	107,748	108,752	113,766	113,674	-5.2	3,978	5,597	9,450	5,092	3.7	5.1	8.3	4.5
Fort Wayne, IN Metro Area..........	202,508	195,019	193,545	196,585	3.0	6,335	8,899	20,853	10,347	3.1	4.6	10.8	5.3
Fresno, CA Metro Area..........	448,353	440,530	439,593	407,163	10.1	33,427	44,874	73,372	36,574	7.5	10.2	16.7	9.0
Gadsden, AL Metro Area..........	43,096	42,703	44,000	46,762	-7.8	1,768	2,639	4,807	2,220	4.1	6.2	10.9	4.7
Gainesville, FL Metro Area	161,134	152,226	152,571	147,618	9.2	5,400	7,304	13,105	4,495	3.4	4.8	8.6	3.0
Gainesville, GA Metro Area	102,169	92,527	86,546	82,801	23.4	3,235	4,493	8,341	3,702	3.2	4.9	9.6	4.5
Gettysburg, PA Metro Area	55,121	54,948	54,590	54,495	1.1	1,805	2,307	4,215	1,978	3.3	4.2	7.7	3.6
Glens Falls, NY Metro Area	59,873	60,892	64,387	67,615	-11.5	2,638	3,221	5,564	3,055	4.4	5.3	8.6	4.5
Goldsboro, NC Metro Area	52,731	53,753	54,808	51,135	3.1	2,271	3,257	5,021	2,675	4.3	6.1	9.2	5.2
Grand Forks, ND-MN Metro Area	54,699	54,585	55,022	54,988	-0.5	1,474	1,636	2,454	1,967	2.7	3.0	4.5	3.6

Table B-13. Civilian Labor Force—*Continued*

Metropolitan Statistical Area Metropolitan Division	Total labor force				Percent change 2005-2018	Number of unemployed				Unemployment rate			
	2018	2015	2010	2005		2018	2015	2010	2005	2018	2015	2010	2005
Grand Island, NE Metro Area	38,997	38,913	39,064	38,108	2.3	1,212	1,514	1,802	1,442	3.1	3.9	4.6	3.8
Grand Junction, CO Metro Area	76,060	71,875	76,113	70,811	7.4	3,111	3,959	8,337	3,461	4.1	5.5	11.0	4.9
Grand Rapids-Kentwood, MI Metro Area	577,594	551,669	514,558	518,278	11.4	17,403	21,405	54,027	30,775	3.0	3.9	10.5	5.9
Grants Pass, OR Metro Area	35,929	33,278	34,491	34,300	4.7	1,990	2,568	4,839	2,488	5.5	7.7	14.0	7.3
Great Falls, MT Metro Area	37,848	38,294	38,447	38,950	-2.8	1,362	1,547	2,451	1,671	3.6	4.0	6.4	4.3
Greeley, CO Metro Area	165,290	147,936	131,910	111,087	48.8	4,970	5,664	12,114	6,068	3.0	3.8	9.2	5.5
Green Bay, WI Metro Area	175,911	170,477	169,659	167,690	4.9	4,941	7,167	14,022	7,779	2.8	4.2	8.3	4.6
Greensboro-High Point, NC Metro Area	367,616	364,199	365,619	360,977	1.8	15,084	21,570	42,127	18,775	4.1	5.9	11.5	5.2
Greenville, NC Metro Area	89,961	87,726	85,917	73,488	22.4	3,811	5,311	8,743	4,253	4.2	6.1	10.2	5.8
Greenville-Anderson, SC Metro Area	424,424	417,458	390,067	384,213	10.5	13,176	22,029	40,692	23,672	3.1	5.3	10.4	6.2
Gulfport-Biloxi, MS Metro Area	170,934	169,894	179,666	182,838	-6.5	8,469	10,898	16,418	19,018	5.0	6.4	9.1	10.4
Hagerstown-Martinsburg, MD-WV Metro Area	139,261	137,998	134,502	118,393	17.6	5,902	7,348	12,354	5,027	4.2	5.3	9.2	4.2
Hammond, LA Metro Area	54,353	54,218	53,664	50,534	7.6	2,979	3,918	5,213	4,825	5.5	7.2	9.7	9.5
Hanford-Corcoran, CA Metro Area	57,865	57,756	59,440	53,840	7.5	4,481	6,065	9,583	5,083	7.7	10.5	16.1	9.4
Harrisburg-Carlisle, PA Metro Area	297,027	293,270	290,002	277,860	6.9	10,904	12,743	21,806	11,211	3.7	4.3	7.5	4.0
Harrisonburg, VA Metro Area	65,473	63,978	63,538	61,197	7.0	1,936	2,916	4,632	2,019	3.0	4.6	7.3	3.3
Hartford-East Hartford-Middletown, CT Metro Area	659,896	651,714	659,747	607,993	8.5	26,744	36,569	59,321	30,391	4.1	5.6	9.0	5.0
Hattiesburg, MS Metro Area	76,916	74,107	74,613	71,892	7.0	3,220	4,257	6,778	4,411	4.2	5.7	9.1	6.1
Hickory-Lenoir-Morganton, NC Metro Area	173,999	167,547	176,058	176,216	-1.3	6,179	9,432	23,608	11,597	3.6	5.6	13.4	6.6
Hilton Head Island-Bluffton, SC Metro Area	87,731	83,412	76,232	71,681	22.4	2,804	4,527	6,725	3,516	3.2	5.4	8.8	4.9
Hinesville, GA Metro Area	33,734	31,969	33,158	28,663	17.7	1,427	1,988	2,959	1,584	4.2	6.2	8.9	5.5
Homosassa Springs, FL Metro Area	47,799	47,745	52,847	51,324	-6.9	2,485	3,599	7,253	2,198	5.2	7.5	13.7	4.3
Hot Springs, AR Metro Area	40,797	39,930	41,563	41,936	-2.7	1,651	2,180	3,517	2,374	4.0	5.5	8.5	5.7
Houma-Thibodaux, LA Metro Area	88,248	99,639	95,980	96,374	-8.4	4,304	5,692	6,058	6,041	4.9	5.7	6.3	6.3
Houston-The Woodlands-Sugar Land, TX Metro Area	3,390,635	3,260,520	2,970,263	2,592,941	30.8	145,938	150,005	245,481	144,992	4.3	4.6	8.3	5.6
Huntington-Ashland, WV-KY-OH Metro Area	148,050	149,213	162,020	170,592	-13.2	8,388	9,546	14,955	9,475	5.7	6.4	9.2	5.6
Huntsville, AL Metro Area	222,145	210,925	208,154	193,890	14.6	7,723	11,559	17,873	7,254	3.5	5.5	8.6	3.7
Idaho Falls, ID Metro Area	70,273	64,865	63,062	61,167	14.9	1,675	2,289	4,404	1,887	2.4	3.5	7.0	3.1
Indianapolis-Carmel-Anderson, IN Metro Area	1,061,803	1,010,841	950,600	941,192	12.8	34,240	45,976	91,213	47,523	3.2	4.5	9.6	5.0
Iowa City, IA Metro Area	97,309	96,328	91,674	86,066	13.1	1,918	2,645	3,983	2,777	2.0	2.7	4.3	3.2
Ithaca, NY Metro Area	50,112	50,410	54,767	54,600	-8.2	1,829	2,216	3,370	1,947	3.6	4.4	6.2	3.6
Jackson, MI Metro Area	74,281	73,003	74,673	78,307	-5.1	2,930	3,872	9,109	5,363	3.9	5.3	12.2	6.8
Jackson, MS Metro Area	275,701	271,652	273,586	279,456	-1.3	11,698	14,881	24,632	16,858	4.2	5.5	9.0	6.0
Jackson, TN Metro Area	85,541	82,435	87,585	80,963	5.7	3,376	5,196	9,369	5,294	3.9	6.3	10.7	6.5
Jacksonville, FL Metro Area	773,494	719,099	697,120	635,531	21.7	26,270	38,724	74,912	23,855	3.4	5.4	10.7	3.8
Jacksonville, NC Metro Area	64,341	63,780	63,342	55,996	14.9	3,040	3,759	5,240	2,985	4.7	5.9	8.3	5.3
Janesville-Beloit, WI Metro Area	85,397	83,346	82,698	83,193	2.6	2,766	4,323	9,315	4,856	3.2	5.2	11.3	5.8
Jefferson City, MO Metro Area	73,535	75,582	77,926	77,810	-5.5	1,959	3,230	5,785	3,436	2.7	4.3	7.4	4.4
Johnson City, TN Metro Area	90,926	88,221	94,817	94,637	-3.9	3,450	5,277	9,092	5,000	3.8	6.0	9.6	5.3
Johnstown, PA Metro Area	58,344	62,286	66,751	67,122	-13.1	3,031	4,084	6,290	4,115	5.2	6.6	9.4	6.1
Jonesboro, AR Metro Area	64,389	61,036	58,533	56,567	13.8	2,053	2,818	4,548	2,910	3.2	4.6	7.8	5.1
Joplin, MO Metro Area	83,856	86,469	87,785	82,311	1.9	2,376	3,790	7,592	4,035	2.8	4.4	8.6	4.9
Kahului-Wailuku-Lahaina, HI Metro Area	86,137	83,739	78,966	74,992	14.9	2,109	3,107	6,743	2,026	2.4	3.7	8.5	2.7
Kalamazoo-Portage, MI Metro Area	132,886	129,090	129,632	132,576	0.2	4,537	5,632	12,975	6,954	3.4	4.4	10.0	5.2
Kankakee, IL Metro Area	55,920	54,856	57,060	52,672	6.2	3,032	3,704	7,069	3,348	5.4	6.8	12.4	6.4
Kansas City, MO-KS Metro Area	1,134,500	1,113,652	1,082,274	1,013,562	11.9	38,025	53,207	94,152	57,024	3.4	4.8	8.7	5.6
Kennewick-Richland, WA Metro Area	140,580	130,587	132,507	114,306	23.0	7,675	9,144	10,777	7,272	5.5	7.0	8.1	6.4
Killeen-Temple, TX Metro Area	175,915	169,972	166,193	149,377	17.8	7,213	7,905	12,704	7,716	4.1	4.7	7.6	5.2
Kingsport-Bristol, TN-VA Metro Area	137,055	136,480	144,661	140,267	-2.3	5,005	7,677	13,173	7,414	3.7	5.6	9.1	5.3
Kingston, NY Metro Area	88,712	88,315	93,606	91,816	-3.4	3,452	4,241	7,296	3,988	3.9	4.8	7.8	4.3
Knoxville, TN Metro Area	412,677	394,489	405,106	387,978	6.4	13,433	20,555	33,989	18,119	3.3	5.2	8.4	4.7
Kokomo, IN Metro Area	37,645	36,982	35,806	39,174	-3.9	1,529	1,846	4,506	2,567	4.1	5.0	12.6	6.6
La Crosse-Onalaska, WI-MN Metro Area	77,721	77,101	76,423	72,515	7.2	2,065	2,967	5,187	2,959	2.7	3.8	6.8	4.1
Lafayette, LA Metro Area	212,523	227,630	221,628	208,275	2.0	10,483	14,617	15,537	11,966	4.9	6.4	7.0	5.7
Lafayette-West Lafayette, IN Metro Area	116,750	111,801	105,647	99,273	17.6	3,700	4,796	9,555	4,862	3.2	4.3	9.0	4.9
Lake Charles, LA Metro Area	113,935	102,866	91,195	95,465	19.3	4,338	5,520	7,252	7,087	3.8	5.4	8.0	7.4
Lake Havasu City-Kingman, AZ Metro Area	85,442	79,550	82,726	89,079	-4.1	4,934	6,312	10,727	3,808	5.8	7.9	13.0	4.3
Lakeland-Winter Haven, FL Metro Area	298,759	279,553	278,479	258,158	15.7	12,156	17,728	33,811	10,479	4.1	6.3	12.1	4.1
Lancaster, PA Metro Area	281,433	275,782	268,014	267,575	5.2	9,542	11,335	20,089	9,773	3.4	4.1	7.5	3.7
Lansing-East Lansing, MI Metro Area	281,658	274,378	279,966	284,824	-1.1	10,195	12,740	28,549	17,918	3.6	4.6	10.2	6.3
Laredo, TX Metro Area	116,573	111,872	105,016	85,624	36.1	4,383	5,282	8,652	5,140	3.8	4.7	8.2	6.0
Las Cruces, NM Metro Area	96,769	94,548	93,597	85,089	13.7	5,470	6,881	7,260	4,792	5.7	7.3	7.8	5.6
Las Vegas-Henderson-Paradise, NV Metro Area	1,098,114	1,033,990	984,004	869,251	26.3	52,643	70,705	135,431	35,332	4.8	6.8	13.8	4.1
Lawrence, KS Metro Area	65,199	64,800	64,379	63,186	3.2	1,995	2,389	3,805	2,507	3.1	3.7	5.9	4.0
Lawton, OK Metro Area	51,314	52,569	54,506	48,573	5.6	1,984	2,285	3,164	2,164	3.9	4.3	5.8	4.5
Lebanon, PA Metro Area	71,222	70,011	70,062	70,117	1.6	2,677	3,167	5,236	2,519	3.8	4.5	7.5	3.6
Lewiston, ID-WA Metro Area	31,206	30,324	30,421	29,869	4.5	1,021	1,240	2,316	1,507	3.3	4.1	7.6	5.0
Lewiston-Auburn, ME Metro Area	55,449	54,794	55,909	57,033	-2.8	1,828	2,283	4,793	2,821	3.3	4.2	8.6	4.9
Lexington-Fayette, KY Metro Area	271,580	261,053	255,705	229,055	18.6	9,260	10,395	20,277	10,576	3.4	4.0	7.9	4.6
Lima, OH Metro Area	47,855	47,812	52,009	52,706	-9.2	2,147	2,321	5,567	3,291	4.5	4.9	10.7	6.2
Lincoln, NE Metro Area	182,114	176,131	171,332	165,264	10.2	4,633	4,668	7,202	5,800	2.5	2.7	4.2	3.5
Little Rock-North Little Rock-Conway, AR Metro Area	354,824	347,259	347,828	334,366	6.1	11,930	15,573	24,877	15,603	3.4	4.5	7.2	4.7

Table B-13. Civilian Labor Force—*Continued*

Metropolitan Statistical Area Metropolitan Division	Total labor force 2018	2015	2010	2005	Percent change 2005-2018	Number of unemployed 2018	2015	2010	2005	Unemployment rate 2018	2015	2010	2005
Logan, UT-ID Metro Area	70,182	66,495	63,444	63,440	10.6	1,847	2,046	3,808	2,048	2.6	3.1	6.0	3.2
Longview, TX Metro Area	127,980	131,409	133,429	133,117	-3.9	5,348	6,592	11,161	6,815	4.2	5.0	8.4	5.1
Longview, WA Metro Area	45,923	44,070	46,432	42,978	6.9	2,729	3,425	5,997	3,261	5.9	7.8	12.9	7.6
Los Angeles-Long Beach-Anaheim, CA Metro Area	6,761,767	6,575,553	6,454,562	6,367,520	6.2	287,370	400,998	764,850	315,711	4.2	6.1	11.8	5.0
Anaheim-Santa Ana-Irvine, CA Div	1,625,426	1,585,762	1,537,187	1,585,916	2.5	47,541	70,858	149,749	59,330	2.9	4.5	9.7	3.7
Los Angeles-Long Beach-Glendale, CA Div	5,136,341	4,989,791	4,917,375	4,781,604	7.4	239,829	330,140	615,101	256,381	4.7	6.6	12.5	5.4
Louisville/Jefferson County, KY-IN Metro Area	656,303	619,123	611,633	574,472	14.2	25,311	28,662	60,079	32,949	3.9	4.6	9.8	5.7
Lubbock, TX Metro Area	162,563	155,119	149,359	143,067	13.6	5,017	5,312	9,404	5,915	3.1	3.4	6.3	4.1
Lynchburg, VA Metro Area	122,127	122,371	126,345	116,542	4.8	4,217	6,001	9,890	4,736	3.5	4.9	7.8	4.1
Macon-Bibb County, GA Metro Area	104,769	102,334	105,508	110,115	-4.9	4,525	6,604	11,947	6,188	4.3	6.5	11.3	5.6
Madera, CA Metro Area	61,528	59,836	61,607	61,881	-0.6	4,316	6,290	10,241	4,866	7.0	10.5	16.6	7.9
Madison, WI Metro Area	387,610	376,890	360,360	351,442	10.3	8,900	12,654	22,972	11,816	2.3	3.4	6.4	3.4
Manchester-Nashua, NH Metro Area	236,915	229,847	226,152	226,188	4.7	6,223	8,177	13,911	8,202	2.6	3.6	6.2	3.6
Manhattan, KS Metro Area	59,199	59,731	61,340	55,950	5.8	1,916	2,402	3,647	2,369	3.2	4.0	5.9	4.2
Mankato, MN Metro Area	61,033	59,677	57,896	54,322	12.4	1,467	1,690	3,634	1,784	2.4	2.8	6.3	3.3
Mansfield, OH Metro Area	52,743	53,529	59,079	62,761	-16.0	2,583	2,990	7,171	4,227	4.9	5.6	12.1	6.7
McAllen-Edinburg-Mission, TX Metro Area	348,672	331,132	318,302	260,575	33.8	22,881	26,186	37,418	20,606	6.6	7.9	11.8	7.9
Medford, OR Metro Area	104,763	98,061	100,968	98,727	6.1	5,023	6,646	12,576	6,113	4.8	6.8	12.5	6.2
Memphis, TN-MS-AR Metro Area	631,817	611,593	632,306	597,083	5.8	26,126	38,257	61,189	36,464	4.1	6.3	9.7	6.1
Merced, CA Metro Area	115,408	114,106	113,579	98,738	16.9	9,574	12,953	20,388	9,858	8.3	11.4	18.0	10.0
Miami-Fort Lauderdale-Pompano Beach, FL Metro Area	3,150,518	2,985,017	2,807,697	2,710,277	16.2	114,247	162,024	302,108	97,777	3.6	5.4	10.8	3.6
Fort Lauderdale-Pompano Beach-Sunrise, FL Div	1,036,212	986,758	936,563	957,619	8.2	34,919	50,725	95,090	35,325	3.4	5.1	10.2	3.7
Miami-Miami Beach-Kendall, FL Div	1,383,302	1,308,410	1,225,397	1,147,797	20.5	53,279	75,983	136,171	36,360	3.9	5.8	11.1	3.2
West Palm Beach-Boca Raton-Boynton Beach, FL Div	731,004	689,849	645,737	604,861	20.9	26,049	35,316	70,847	26,092	3.6	5.1	11.0	4.3
Michigan City-La Porte, IN Metro Area	48,027	48,516	51,336	53,070	-9.5	2,102	3,045	6,178	3,221	4.4	6.3	12.0	6.1
Midland, MI Metro Area	40,611	41,412	41,219	41,907	-3.1	1,618	2,024	4,023	2,479	4.0	4.9	9.8	5.9
Midland, TX Metro Area	105,084	91,040	73,527	68,430	53.6	2,215	3,148	4,308	2,542	2.1	3.5	5.9	3.7
Milwaukee-Waukesha, WI Metro Area	824,848	822,755	817,477	782,820	5.4	26,358	40,446	73,100	38,774	3.2	4.9	8.9	5.0
Minneapolis-St. Paul-Bloomington, MN Metro Area	1,992,807	1,921,200	1,862,262	1,836,545	8.5	53,015	65,922	136,457	70,112	2.7	3.4	7.3	3.8
Missoula, MT Metro Area	63,069	60,506	58,536	57,899	8.9	2,100	2,376	4,292	2,282	3.3	3.9	7.3	3.9
Mobile, AL Metro Area	194,073	193,691	200,115	187,271	3.6	9,187	13,448	22,837	9,374	4.7	6.9	11.4	5.0
Modesto, CA Metro Area	243,538	241,118	243,274	226,627	7.5	15,598	22,882	41,092	19,042	6.4	9.5	16.9	8.4
Monroe, LA Metro Area	89,710	92,446	91,500	94,603	-5.2	5,013	6,666	8,560	6,172	5.6	7.2	9.4	6.5
Monroe, MI Metro Area	75,765	76,188	75,640	77,855	-2.7	3,169	3,480	8,869	4,826	4.2	4.6	11.7	6.2
Montgomery, AL Metro Area	172,376	171,292	175,499	168,497	2.3	6,709	10,018	17,267	7,413	3.9	5.8	9.8	4.4
Morgantown, WV Metro Area	68,646	65,065	63,289	58,509	17.3	2,980	3,286	3,949	2,308	4.3	5.1	6.2	3.9
Morristown, TN Metro Area	60,847	58,782	62,857	62,949	-3.3	2,339	3,731	7,365	3,706	3.8	6.3	11.7	5.9
Mount Vernon-Anacortes, WA Metro Area	60,278	56,640	59,114	56,282	7.1	3,126	3,863	6,456	3,498	5.2	6.8	10.9	6.2
Muncie, IN Metro Area	54,159	54,435	54,724	56,113	-3.5	2,173	3,103	6,322	3,851	4.0	5.7	11.6	6.9
Muskegon, MI Metro Area	78,196	77,270	77,712	90,054	-13.2	3,557	4,514	11,292	6,309	4.5	5.8	14.5	7.0
Myrtle Beach-Conway-North Myrtle Beach, SC-NC Metro Area	198,665	185,788	177,475	164,187	21.0	8,831	13,330	21,915	9,115	4.4	7.2	12.3	5.6
Napa, CA Metro Area	74,547	73,784	70,216	71,328	4.5	2,181	3,408	7,227	3,114	2.9	4.6	10.3	4.4
Naples-Marco Island, FL Metro Area	177,351	163,458	145,349	145,136	22.2	6,096	8,614	16,922	5,049	3.4	5.3	11.6	3.5
Nashville-Davidson--Murfreesboro--Franklin, TN...	1,031,834	926,750	867,293	769,804	34.0	28,089	41,820	74,643	35,013	2.7	4.5	8.6	4.5
New Bern, NC Metro Area	51,255	51,247	52,379	51,421	-0.3	2,147	3,083	5,612	2,412	4.2	6.0	10.7	4.7
New Haven-Milford, CT Metro Area	458,747	454,262	461,566	429,962	6.7	20,171	28,326	46,162	22,898	4.4	6.2	10.0	5.3
New Orleans-Metairie, LA Metro Area	594,960	604,753	570,730	9,021	6495.3	27,513	36,506	44,220	954	4.6	6.0	7.7	10.6
New York-Newark-Jersey City, NY-NJ-PA Metro area	9,608,604	9,618,446	9,480,794	9,181,112	4.7	384,043	516,048	847,752	451,051	4.0	5.4	8.9	4.9
Nassau County-Suffolk County, NY Div	1,485,659	1,473,327	1,469,298	1,467,327	1.2	54,979	65,932	109,582	60,389	3.7	4.5	7.5	4.1
Newark, NJ-PA Div	1,050,291	1,073,078	1,102,526	1,072,614	-2.1	45,136	62,367	103,038	48,671	4.3	5.8	9.3	4.5
New Brunswick-Lakewood, NJ Div	1,194,259	1,199,615	1,192,097	1,161,313	2.8	44,987	63,619	107,158	48,328	3.8	5.3	9.0	4.2
New York-Jersey City-White Plains, NY-NJ Div	5,878,395	5,872,416	5,716,873	5,479,858	7.3	238,941	324,130	527,974	293,663	4.1	5.5	9.2	5.4
Niles, MI Metro Area	73,328	73,366	76,628	79,071	-7.3	3,152	3,834	9,213	5,480	4.3	5.2	12.0	6.9
North Port-Sarasota-Bradenton, FL Metro Area	365,815	342,207	314,794	313,922	16.5	12,356	17,398	36,219	10,818	3.4	5.1	11.5	3.4
Norwich-New London, CT Metro Area	137,463	136,118	143,924	144,132	-4.6	5,431	8,087	12,851	6,473	4.0	5.9	8.9	4.5
Ocala, FL Metro Area	135,746	129,990	132,351	127,862	6.2	5,825	8,459	18,054	4,851	4.3	6.5	13.6	3.8
Ocean City, NJ Metro Area	45,785	48,038	50,213	57,700	-20.6	3,840	5,344	7,026	3,805	8.4	11.1	14.0	6.6
Odessa, TX Metro Area	85,132	79,838	68,186	62,285	36.7	2,289	3,702	5,661	2,827	2.7	4.6	8.3	4.5
Ogden-Clearfield, UT Metro Area	326,065	306,037	288,136	270,310	20.6	10,305	11,254	22,530	11,420	3.2	3.7	7.8	4.2
Oklahoma City, OK Metro Area	681,616	664,432	623,505	573,874	18.8	21,273	25,615	36,555	24,948	3.1	3.9	5.9	4.3
Olympia-Lacey-Tumwater, WA Metro Area	137,697	125,599	126,948	121,951	12.9	6,553	7,544	11,398	6,465	4.8	6.0	9.0	5.3
Omaha-Council Bluffs, NE-IA Metro Area	485,858	476,166	465,962	440,297	10.3	13,926	15,489	23,631	18,843	2.9	3.3	5.1	4.3
Orlando-Kissimmee-Sanford, FL Metro Area	1,337,790	1,218,997	1,137,389	1,015,778	31.7	43,843	63,039	126,244	36,571	3.3	5.2	11.1	3.6
Oshkosh-Neenah, WI Metro Area	92,956	91,455	92,450	91,185	1.9	2,524	3,876	7,224	4,025	2.7	4.2	7.8	4.4
Owensboro, KY Metro Area	56,392	53,738	55,465	55,137	2.3	2,278	2,496	5,237	3,291	4.0	4.6	9.4	6.0
Oxnard-Thousand Oaks-Ventura, CA Metro Area	425,728	427,597	430,010	415,958	2.3	16,066	24,125	46,586	19,733	3.8	5.6	10.8	4.7
Palm Bay-Melbourne-Titusville, FL Metro Area	276,558	256,081	265,643	260,435	6.2	9,746	15,388	29,886	9,466	3.5	6.0	11.3	3.6
Panama City, FL Metro Area	89,251	87,413	86,072	82,406	8.3	3,548	4,795	9,018	2,932	4.0	5.5	10.5	3.6

Table B-13. Civilian Labor Force—*Continued*

Metropolitan Statistical Area Metropolitan Division	Civilian Labor Force												
	Total labor force					Number of unemployed				Unemployment rate			
	2018	2015	2010	2005	Percent change 2005-2018	2018	2015	2010	2005	2018	2015	2010	2005
Parkersburg-Vienna, WV Metro Area	38,107	39,306	41,640	43,449	-12.3	2,127	2,566	3,785	2,423	5.6	6.5	9.1	5.6
Pensacola-Ferry Pass-Brent, FL Metro Area	225,952	211,775	211,246	203,128	11.2	7,825	11,302	20,778	7,689	3.5	5.3	9.8	3.8
Peoria, IL Metro Area	195,266	200,791	215,073	208,638	-6.4	10,218	13,064	21,763	9,946	5.2	6.5	10.1	4.8
Philadelphia-Camden-Wilmington, PA-NJ-DE-MD Metro Area	3,082,419	3,046,670	3,021,375	2,916,385	5.7	129,553	164,906	265,134	138,140	4.2	5.4	8.8	4.7
Camden, NJ Div	624,565	630,906	654,575	648,744	-3.7	26,391	37,614	65,915	28,272	4.2	6.0	10.1	4.4
Montgomery County-Bucks County-Chester County, PA Div	1,072,028	1,054,742	1,037,076	1,020,158	5.1	37,136	44,571	72,461	39,862	3.5	4.2	7.0	3.9
Philadelphia, PA Div	1,005,484	986,314	973,996	896,383	12.2	51,202	63,611	95,636	54,190	5.1	6.4	9.8	6.0
Wilmington, DE-MD-NJ Div	380,342	374,708	355,728	351,100	8.3	14,824	19,110	31,122	15,816	3.9	5.1	8.7	4.5
Phoenix-Mesa-Chandler, AZ Metro Area	2,407,742	2,179,351	2,073,297	1,943,498	23.9	101,259	113,536	199,291	80,003	4.2	5.2	9.6	4.1
Pine Bluff, AR Metro Area	35,409	36,238	42,560	46,561	-24.0	1,787	2,469	4,302	3,455	5.0	6.8	10.1	7.4
Pittsburgh, PA Metro Area	1,203,534	1,211,435	1,201,211	1,196,815	0.6	51,233	64,211	95,830	62,616	4.3	5.3	8.0	5.2
Pittsfield, MA Metro Area	66,109	65,305	68,182	72,664	-9.0	2,669	3,524	5,916	3,170	4.0	5.4	8.7	4.4
Pocatello, ID Metro Area	45,776	45,854	44,967	44,343	3.2	1,257	1,879	3,639	1,742	2.7	4.1	8.1	3.9
Portland-South Portland, ME Metro Area	298,848	285,272	283,871	285,935	4.5	8,418	10,326	20,111	11,150	2.8	3.6	7.1	3.9
Portland-Vancouver-Hillsboro, OR-WA Metro Area	1,313,057	1,229,252	1,207,836	1,093,793	20.0	51,060	64,214	123,712	64,508	3.9	5.2	10.2	5.9
Port St. Lucie, FL Metro Area	216,794	200,516	195,326	177,600	22.1	8,841	12,115	24,878	8,004	4.1	6.0	12.7	4.5
Poughkeepsie-Newburgh-Middletown, NY Metro Area	326,175	321,108	330,491	324,605	0.5	12,460	14,711	25,982	13,247	3.8	4.6	7.9	4.1
Prescott Valley-Prescott, AZ Metro Area	105,618	96,196	96,533	91,442	15.5	4,719	5,398	10,309	4,039	4.5	5.6	10.7	4.4
Providence-Warwick, RI-MA Metro Area	858,725	843,707	853,503	853,565	0.6	35,599	50,966	93,829	45,755	4.1	6.0	11.0	5.4
Provo-Orem, UT Metro Area	305,442	270,942	234,432	209,058	46.1	8,643	8,869	17,512	8,217	2.8	3.3	7.5	3.9
Pueblo, CO Metro Area	75,912	71,778	74,396	69,326	9.5	3,726	4,035	7,729	4,720	4.9	5.6	10.4	6.8
Punta Gorda, FL Metro Area	70,953	67,565	66,293	66,088	7.4	2,845	4,069	8,447	2,658	4.0	6.0	12.7	4.0
Racine, WI Metro Area	99,570	99,357	100,314	98,509	1.1	3,600	5,578	10,193	5,822	3.6	5.6	10.2	5.9
Raleigh-Cary, NC Metro Area	711,326	656,645	590,220	500,724	42.1	24,261	31,721	51,012	20,913	3.4	4.8	8.6	4.2
Rapid City, SD Metro Area	70,360	67,640	65,987	65,322	7.7	2,184	2,133	3,449	2,377	3.1	3.2	5.2	3.6
Reading, PA Metro Area	212,528	212,348	210,149	198,712	7.0	8,842	10,471	18,230	9,697	4.2	4.9	8.7	4.9
Redding, CA Metro Area	74,215	74,172	78,503	81,748	-9.2	3,669	5,764	13,169	5,922	4.9	7.8	16.8	7.2
Reno, NV Metro Area	252,010	226,753	222,838	210,769	19.6	9,153	14,167	28,873	8,320	3.6	6.2	13.0	3.9
Richmond, VA Metro Area	664,431	645,174	617,935	583,336	13.9	20,926	29,912	49,110	22,253	3.1	4.6	7.9	3.8
Riverside-San Bernardino-Ontario, CA Metro Area	2,053,401	1,954,227	1,866,722	1,704,048	20.5	86,587	128,453	255,547	90,008	4.2	6.6	13.7	5.3
Roanoke, VA Metro Area	156,379	156,920	159,127	149,437	4.6	4,639	6,975	12,036	5,268	3.0	4.4	7.6	3.5
Rochester, MN Metro Area	123,420	118,731	115,857	113,329	8.9	3,079	3,781	7,320	4,127	2.5	3.2	6.3	3.6
Rochester, NY Metro Area	522,110	525,497	546,181	547,998	-4.7	22,104	26,822	44,187	25,332	4.2	5.1	8.1	4.6
Rockford, IL Metro Area	167,669	168,604	177,519	165,009	1.6	9,618	11,627	24,853	10,543	5.7	6.9	14.0	6.4
Rocky Mount, NC Metro Area	65,029	66,712	72,954	68,411	-4.9	3,661	5,378	9,973	4,699	5.6	8.1	13.7	6.9
Rome, GA Metro Area	44,274	42,863	45,087	50,139	-11.7	1,906	2,861	5,337	2,598	4.3	6.7	11.8	5.2
Sacramento-Roseville-Folsom, CA Metro Area	1,095,762	1,053,823	1,049,782	1,011,984	8.3	40,617	61,730	129,718	49,365	3.7	5.9	12.4	4.9
Saginaw, MI Metro Area	86,849	88,365	90,722	98,365	-11.7	4,152	5,051	11,097	7,845	4.8	5.7	12.2	8.0
St. Cloud, MN Metro Area	111,550	109,703	106,774	102,805	8.5	3,400	4,128	8,017	4,511	3.0	3.8	7.5	4.4
St. George, UT Metro Area	73,929	63,647	56,776	56,944	29.8	2,517	2,597	5,955	2,305	3.4	4.1	10.5	4.0
St. Joseph, MO-KS Metro Area	63,265	65,762	66,123	64,845	-2.4	1,877	2,972	5,942	3,738	3.0	4.5	9.0	5.8
St. Louis, MO-IL Metro Area	1,459,246	1,466,763	1,478,087	1,426,498	2.3	49,950	74,051	141,696	78,966	3.4	5.0	9.6	5.5
Salem, OR Metro Area	201,371	189,258	191,735	183,380	9.8	8,696	11,225	20,861	11,592	4.3	5.9	10.9	6.3
Salinas, CA Metro Area	224,057	218,367	215,788	206,565	8.5	14,047	17,673	27,449	15,030	6.3	8.1	12.7	7.3
Salisbury, MD-DE Metro Area	191,345	182,963	176,882	181,096	5.7	9,321	11,672	17,292	8,031	4.9	6.4	9.8	4.4
Salt Lake City, UT Metro Area	653,521	614,874	575,832	542,619	20.4	19,912	21,036	44,360	21,872	3.0	3.4	7.7	4.0
San Angelo, TX Metro Area	56,312	56,139	54,143	53,733	4.8	1,781	2,290	3,524	2,299	3.2	4.1	6.5	4.3
San Antonio-New Braunfels, TX Metro Area	1,189,665	1,106,832	1,017,400	894,737	33.0	39,332	42,038	73,629	44,856	3.3	3.8	7.2	5.0
San Diego-Chula Vista-Carlsbad, CA Metro Area	1,592,193	1,550,059	1,515,198	1,489,799	6.9	52,663	80,584	162,932	64,093	3.3	5.2	10.8	4.3
San Francisco-Oakland-Berkeley, CA Metro Area	2,584,338	2,480,206	2,320,104	2,146,852	20.4	70,153	105,779	229,650	103,004	2.7	4.3	9.9	4.8
Oakland-Berkeley-Livermore, CA Div	1,412,785	1,364,794	1,308,069	1,244,122	13.6	43,238	66,270	143,043	62,132	3.1	4.9	10.9	5.0
San Francisco-San Mateo-Redwood City, CA Div	1,030,442	976,598	879,023	773,635	33.2	23,552	34,577	76,165	35,871	2.3	3.5	8.7	4.6
San Rafael, CA Div	141,111	138,814	133,012	129,095	9.3	3,363	4,932	10,442	5,001	2.4	3.6	7.9	3.9
San Jose-Sunnyvale-Santa Clara, CA Metro Area	1,079,673	1,042,939	954,431	839,860	28.6	28,843	44,279	100,626	45,288	2.7	4.2	10.5	5.4
San Luis Obispo-Paso Robles, CA Metro Area	140,920	139,039	133,651	131,479	7.2	4,151	6,574	13,442	5,600	2.9	4.7	10.1	4.3
Santa Cruz-Watsonville, CA Metro Area	142,618	143,323	141,717	142,992	-0.3	6,984	10,727	18,845	8,963	4.9	7.5	13.3	6.3
Santa Fe, NM Metro Area	73,974	73,358	74,289	76,704	-3.6	3,065	3,902	5,044	3,144	4.1	5.3	6.8	4.1
Santa Maria-Santa Barbara, CA Metro Area	216,698	217,344	212,267	213,206	1.6	8,437	11,501	20,587	9,244	3.9	5.3	9.7	4.3
Santa Rosa-Petaluma, CA Metro Area	262,348	257,893	244,634	253,410	3.5	7,187	11,565	26,534	11,205	2.7	4.5	10.8	4.4
Savannah, GA Metro Area	188,764	176,092	167,555	165,458	14.1	6,849	9,998	16,398	7,345	3.6	5.7	9.8	4.4
Scranton--Wilkes-Barre, PA Metro Area	276,860	279,077	281,094	277,022	-0.1	13,975	17,282	26,742	15,387	5.0	6.2	9.5	5.6
Seattle-Tacoma-Bellevue, WA Metro Area	2,113,294	1,978,480	1,888,261	1,727,043	22.4	81,595	94,675	182,292	83,495	3.9	4.8	9.7	4.8
Seattle-Bellevue-Kent, WA Div	1,689,157	1,586,608	1,492,417	1,357,888	24.4	59,648	69,336	141,024	60,809	3.5	4.4	9.4	4.5
Tacoma-Lakewood, WA Div	424,137	391,872	395,844	369,155	14.9	21,947	25,339	41,268	22,686	5.2	6.5	10.4	6.1
Sebastian-Vero Beach, FL Metro Area	65,104	61,131	61,384	59,484	9.4	2,786	4,200	8,536	2,846	4.3	6.9	13.9	4.8
Sebring-Avon Park, FL Metro Area	36,472	35,291	37,247	39,983	-8.8	1,756	2,653	4,660	1,690	4.8	7.5	12.5	4.2
Sheboygan, WI Metro Area	62,903	61,252	62,238	64,550	-2.6	1,571	2,310	5,782	2,557	2.5	3.8	9.3	4.0
Sherman-Denison, TX Metro Area	63,488	60,044	59,489	56,416	12.5	2,061	2,417	4,869	3,036	3.2	4.0	8.2	5.4

Table B-13. Civilian Labor Force—*Continued*

Metropolitan Statistical Area Metropolitan Division	Total labor force				Percent change 2005-2018	Number of unemployed				Unemployment rate			
	2018	2015	2010	2005		2018	2015	2010	2005	2018	2015	2010	2005
Shreveport-Bossier City, LA Metro Area	173,152	179,528	184,769	180,450	-4.0	8,833	12,048	13,940	10,785	5.1	6.7	7.5	6.0
Sierra Vista-Douglas, AZ Metro Area	49,774	50,302	57,023	55,774	-10.8	2,789	3,662	5,329	2,677	5.6	7.3	9.3	4.8
Sioux City, IA-NE-SD Metro Area	77,121	78,327	78,145	74,550	3.4	2,097	2,901	5,110	3,506	2.7	3.7	6.5	4.7
Sioux Falls, SD Metro Area	152,131	144,406	133,585	120,564	26.2	3,863	3,750	6,348	4,081	2.5	2.6	4.8	3.4
South Bend-Mishawaka, IN-MI Metro Area	161,106	154,398	155,045	161,819	-0.4	5,863	7,781	17,869	8,571	3.6	5.0	11.5	5.3
Spartanburg, SC Metro Area	147,900	139,770	131,818	131,691	12.3	4,604	8,003	15,613	9,830	3.1	5.7	11.8	7.5
Spokane-Spokane Valley, WA Metro Area	262,435	245,063	257,229	242,146	8.4	14,063	16,515	26,517	14,749	5.4	6.7	10.3	6.1
Springfield, IL Metro Area	111,638	112,216	115,866	112,103	-0.4	4,774	5,762	8,951	5,053	4.3	5.1	7.7	4.5
Springfield, MA Metro Area	364,152	349,615	346,424	351,559	3.6	14,677	19,925	31,750	18,321	4.0	5.7	9.2	5.2
Springfield, MO Metro Area	230,332	230,148	223,668	212,489	8.4	6,232	10,068	19,630	9,213	2.7	4.4	8.8	4.3
Springfield, OH Metro Area	62,963	64,039	68,266	70,529	-10.7	2,870	3,203	7,530	4,565	4.6	5.0	11.0	6.5
State College, PA Metro Area	79,859	77,749	77,338	72,388	10.3	2,585	3,087	4,599	2,896	3.2	4.0	5.9	4.0
Staunton, VA Metro Area	59,303	58,449	59,146	57,325	3.5	1,673	2,494	4,490	1,863	2.8	4.3	7.6	3.2
Stockton, CA Metro Area	326,387	314,590	311,437	283,588	15.1	19,571	27,961	51,442	22,299	6.0	8.9	16.5	7.9
Sumter, SC Metro Area	56,668	57,411	58,300	59,188	-4.3	2,365	4,046	7,476	5,175	4.2	7.0	12.8	8.7
Syracuse, NY Metro Area	306,225	309,294	331,466	330,039	-7.2	13,282	16,699	28,247	16,077	4.3	5.4	8.5	4.9
Tallahassee, FL Metro Area	193,504	184,837	190,683	179,409	7.9	6,692	9,715	16,084	5,754	3.5	5.3	8.4	3.2
Tampa-St. Petersburg-Clearwater, FL Metro Area	1,530,842	1,439,383	1,384,699	1,258,615	21.6	53,140	75,496	153,386	49,881	3.5	5.2	11.1	4.0
Terre Haute, IN Metro Area	84,428	84,286	88,535	88,748	-4.9	3,718	5,119	9,923	6,155	4.4	6.1	11.2	6.9
Texarkana, TX-AR Metro Area	64,702	64,678	68,991	68,421	-5.4	3,192	3,179	5,241	3,535	4.9	4.9	7.6	5.2
The Villages, FL Metro Area	31,241	28,592	25,310	25,555	22.3	1,592	2,205	3,355	870	5.1	7.7	13.3	3.4
Toledo, OH Metro Area	322,711	321,594	331,794	337,591	-4.4	16,139	16,537	37,425	22,742	5.0	5.1	11.3	6.7
Topeka, KS Metro Area	120,102	120,521	124,269	123,539	-2.8	4,150	5,105	8,766	6,765	3.5	4.2	7.1	5.5
Trenton-Princeton, NJ Metro Area	196,494	196,407	192,673	193,721	1.4	7,217	9,838	16,103	7,585	3.7	5.0	8.4	3.9
Tucson, AZ Metro Area	486,261	465,210	478,743	441,581	10.1	21,828	25,476	44,637	19,766	4.5	5.5	9.3	4.5
Tulsa, OK Metro Area	479,874	475,556	462,935	442,814	8.4	16,669	20,895	33,649	19,278	3.5	4.4	7.3	4.4
Tuscaloosa, AL Metro Area	118,203	115,845	111,365	103,279	14.5	4,566	6,710	11,197	4,220	3.9	5.8	10.1	4.1
Twin Falls, ID Metro Area	52,710	50,441	47,870	47,048	12.0	1,400	1,841	4,033	1,729	2.7	3.6	8.4	3.7
Tyler, TX Metro Area	107,543	103,817	101,151	95,360	12.8	3,909	4,636	8,041	4,800	3.6	4.5	7.9	5.0
Urban Honolulu, HI Metro Area	465,193	466,639	446,189	439,257	5.9	10,863	15,595	26,558	12,241	2.3	3.3	6.0	2.8
Utica-Rome, NY Metro Area	129,719	130,497	143,800	142,904	-9.2	5,872	7,214	11,275	6,957	4.5	5.5	7.8	4.9
Valdosta, GA Metro Area	64,535	62,724	64,076	64,829	-0.5	2,613	3,723	6,165	2,613	4.0	5.9	9.6	4.0
Vallejo, CA Metro Area	209,721	205,023	202,407	208,486	0.6	8,168	12,553	25,438	11,145	3.9	6.1	12.6	5.3
Victoria, TX Metro Area	46,675	48,819	46,435	47,296	-1.3	1,779	2,049	3,549	2,149	3.8	4.2	7.6	4.5
Vineland-Bridgeton, NJ Metro Area	64,289	67,457	72,664	69,082	-6.9	4,161	5,954	9,431	4,419	6.5	8.8	13.0	6.4
Virginia Beach-Norfolk-Newport News, VA-NC Metro Area	866,920	851,558	851,672	807,905	7.3	28,268	42,021	64,938	32,201	3.3	4.9	7.6	4.0
Visalia, CA Metro Area	204,589	202,210	203,021	183,305	11.6	19,649	23,500	34,911	17,286	9.6	11.6	17.2	9.4
Waco, TX Metro Area	125,454	119,119	120,142	119,278	5.2	4,499	4,851	8,923	6,079	3.6	4.1	7.4	5.1
Walla Walla, WA Metro Area	29,270	28,019	30,530	28,983	1.0	1,383	1,657	2,445	1,754	4.7	5.9	8.0	6.1
Warner Robins, GA Metro Area	82,108	76,762	80,017	73,947	11.0	3,410	4,709	7,236	3,770	4.2	6.1	9.0	5.1
Washington-Arlington-Alexandria, DC-VA-MD-WV Metro Area	3,400,352	3,280,584	3,157,966	2,911,638	16.8	112,310	144,949	200,520	100,722	3.3	4.4	6.3	3.5
Frederick-Gaithersburg-Rockville, MD Div	685,820	675,505	660,485	624,759	9.8	22,158	27,029	38,668	19,512	3.2	4.0	5.9	3.1
Washington-Arlington-Alexandria, DC-VA-MD-WV Metro Division	2,714,532	2,605,079	2,497,481	2,286,879	18.7	90,152	117,920	161,852	81,210	3.3	4.5	6.5	3.6
Waterloo-Cedar Falls, IA Metro Area	89,342	91,251	91,593	92,114	-3.0	2,352	4,006	5,451	3,867	2.6	4.4	6.0	4.2
Watertown-Fort Drum, NY Metro Area	44,691	46,507	50,310	47,105	-5.1	2,510	3,063	4,672	2,886	5.6	6.6	9.3	6.1
Wausau-Weston, WI Metro Area	89,436	88,716	89,181	90,188	-0.8	2,461	3,717	8,602	3,916	2.8	4.2	9.6	4.3
Weirton-Steubenville, WV-OH Metro Area	50,206	52,442	58,426	57,537	-12.7	3,106	3,933	7,781	4,349	6.2	7.5	13.3	7.6
Wenatchee, WA Metro Area	67,183	62,342	61,978	59,416	13.1	3,214	3,664	5,680	3,578	4.8	5.9	9.2	6.0
Wheeling, WV-OH Metro Area	66,156	65,824	69,968	68,509	-3.4	3,480	4,324	6,932	4,045	5.3	6.6	9.9	5.9
Wichita, KS Metro Area	306,191	307,285	315,454	307,282	-0.4	11,387	14,291	27,117	16,650	3.7	4.7	8.6	5.4
Wichita Falls, TX Metro Area	65,868	64,412	69,420	74,253	-11.3	2,223	2,766	5,320	3,376	3.4	4.3	7.7	4.5
Williamsport, PA Metro Area	57,134	60,858	59,485	59,297	-3.6	2,740	3,681	5,313	3,215	4.8	6.0	8.9	5.4
Wilmington, NC Metro Area	149,245	139,465	132,029	119,805	24.6	5,645	7,658	13,239	5,077	3.8	5.5	10.0	4.2
Winchester, VA-WV Metro Area	71,900	68,420	65,434	61,426	17.1	2,085	2,929	5,174	1,904	2.9	4.3	7.9	3.1
Winston-Salem, NC Metro Area	326,280	317,744	314,927	309,332	5.5	12,128	17,336	34,446	15,501	3.7	5.5	10.9	5.0
Worcester, MA-CT Metro Area	514,096	490,366	484,973	459,459	11.9	18,822	25,735	43,838	24,179	3.7	5.5	9.0	5.3
Yakima, WA Metro Area	129,176	121,673	122,140	117,560	9.9	8,190	9,901	12,972	9,133	6.3	8.1	10.6	7.8
York-Hanover, PA Metro Area	234,141	232,560	230,402	218,916	7.0	9,024	11,061	19,344	9,232	3.9	4.8	8.4	4.2
Youngstown-Warren-Boardman, OH-PA Metro Area	241,186	251,171	268,563	281,253	-14.2	13,973	15,295	31,809	19,330	5.8	6.1	11.8	6.9
Yuba City, CA Metro Area	74,555	72,495	75,029	65,683	13.5	5,255	7,357	13,599	6,170	7.0	10.1	18.1	9.4
Yuma, AZ Metro Area	97,636	93,659	92,816	76,067	28.4	16,639	20,318	23,316	12,063	17.0	21.7	25.1	15.9

Table B-14. Banking, Government Employment, and Private Business Establishments and Employment

Metropolitan Statistical Area Metropolitan Division	Banking 2019		Government Employment						Private nonfarm business				
			Federal civilian		Military		State and Local		Establishments		Employment		Annual payroll per employee 2017 (dollars)
	Number of offices	Deposits (million dollars)	2018	2010	2018	2010	2018	2010	2017	Change 2010-2017 (percent)	2017	Change 2010-2017 (percent)	
Abilene, TX Metro Area	49	3,199	1,276	1,474	4,666	5,128	11,553	12,035	3,969	1.8	58,400	4.6	36,851
Akron, OH Metro Area	195	14,741	2,231	2,517	1,761	1,821	42,692	46,488	16,425	-0.9	296,361	9.7	45,998
Albany, GA Metro Area	34	2,345	2,624	3,623	680	912	9,420	10,513	3,084	-6.8	46,015	3.5	38,081
Albany-Lebanon, OR Metro Area	24	1,154	309	346	301	331	6,439	6,613	2,612	6.9	36,602	15.4	41,268
Albany-Schenectady-Troy, NY Metro Area	282	30,263	6,685	7,241	3,344	3,108	91,832	96,554	21,565	2.4	353,006	9.2	49,480
Albuquerque, NM Metro Area	152	14,963	14,366	15,893	5,753	5,970	67,539	66,950	18,848	0.9	303,614	8.5	42,369
Alexandria, LA Metro Area	58	2,422	2,826	2,981	569	746	10,757	12,047	3,293	-4.5	47,260	-3.3	38,364
Allentown-Bethlehem-Easton, PA-NJ Metro Area	246	17,411	2,269	2,676	2,072	2,132	38,352	40,391	18,616	1.7	331,950	16.8	48,573
Altoona, PA Metro Area	56	2,653	1,114	1,083	303	334	7,418	8,240	3,185		52,981	5.0	37,979
Amarillo, TX Metro Area	69	7,342	2,247	2,330	610	601	18,201	18,077	6,369	5.6	95,807	8.1	41,364
Ames, IA Metro Area	49	2,946	1,030	1,443	436	493	21,672	20,759	2,680	2.9	38,790	12.6	40,981
Anchorage, AK Metro Area	43	6,459	8,555	10,078	12,615	14,807	24,055	24,620	11,056	6.1	162,723	1.6	58,657
Ann Arbor, MI Metro Area	88	9,775	4,036	3,738	626	687	71,897	68,948	8,212	3.9	152,087	14.7	54,635
Anniston-Oxford, AL Metro Area	32	1,976	3,747	5,518	522	636	8,699	8,030	2,319	-4.4	36,301	-1.8	34,374
Appleton, WI Metro Area	62	3,985	689	729	635	637	12,449	12,207	5,962	2.5	115,721	13.6	45,829
Asheville, NC Metro Area	109	8,128	3,512	3,973	1,056	1,074	22,279	23,954	13,001	13.0	172,341	21.5	39,052
Athens-Clarke County, GA Metro Area	53	4,869	1,069	1,708	611	827	27,779	25,987	4,755	8.3	65,041	21.1	38,076
Atlanta-Sandy Springs-Alpharetta, GA Metro Area	1,172	177,261	46,858	49,811	16,603	19,701	286,108	278,181	143,726	10.9	2,352,106	17.1	56,383
Atlantic City-Hammonton, NJ Metro Area	57	5,643	2,558	2,964	836	892	19,640	21,220	6,239	-3.7	103,653	-8.7	40,232
Auburn-Opelika, AL Metro Area	43	3,081	301	310	732	726	17,559	15,427	2,796	18.9	46,327	32.7	32,424
Augusta-Richmond County, GA-SC Metro Area	118	8,787	9,196	9,038	13,321	12,811	42,374	40,436	10,668	1.8	187,081	9.2	43,874
Austin-Round Rock-Georgetown, TX Metro Area	444	42,906	13,318	12,627	4,438	4,205	159,923	159,071	52,858	28.2	836,997	30.7	55,992
Bakersfield, CA Metro Area	90	9,320	10,690	10,947	3,939	3,817	55,700	47,586	12,924	8.4	189,762	8.5	45,048
Baltimore-Columbia-Towson, MD Metro Area	666	74,305	79,366	77,142	26,621	24,524	168,451	173,659	67,502	3.6	1,181,547	11.5	55,542
Bangor, ME Metro Area	46	3,098	1,152	1,416	454	489	12,997	13,322	4,084	-2.6	56,958	-1.1	40,788
Barnstable Town, MA Metro Area	100	8,277	1,610	1,918	1,189	1,274	13,409	12,521	8,681	5.7	78,050	13.4	46,242
Baton Rouge, LA Metro Area	229	20,634	2,921	3,422	3,318	4,351	67,730	75,043	18,669	3.7	346,458	11.1	48,685
Battle Creek, MI Metro Area	25	1,072	3,023	3,025	263	288	7,989	7,747	2,530	-5.6	53,335	12.8	48,972
Bay City, MI Metro Area	24	1,120	254	290	224	233	5,485	5,906	2,146	-6.3	29,870	1.8	40,263
Beaumont-Port Arthur, TX Metro Area	72	5,400	1,954	2,344	950	1,080	21,792	24,016	7,838	-1.1	132,171	4.6	48,836
Beckley, WV Metro Area	41	1,746	1,883	2,227	541	822	6,305	6,736	2,491	-8.5	33,038	-12.5	36,923
Bellingham, WA Metro Area	54	4,103	1,448	1,452	625	683	14,314	14,029	6,698	7.3	75,103	11.4	44,383
Bend, OR Metro Area	47	3,679	955	1,021	454	448	15,558	7,348	7,322	26.1	68,342	32.7	41,685
Billings, MT Metro Area	51	5,076	1,912	2,026	814	843	8,344	8,090	6,322	2.8	74,052	3.6	44,580
Binghamton, NY Metro Area	50	3,342	680	874	363	417	19,815	23,461	4,986	-2.5	79,415	-5.8	40,007
Birmingham-Hoover, AL Metro Area	302	41,431	8,833	9,552	4,828	5,284	69,223	68,353	24,719	1.4	436,077	4.1	49,197
Bismarck, ND Metro Area	59	4,280	1,235	1,294	762	811	12,505	11,484	3,926	13.3	56,813	10.1	45,394
Blacksburg-Christiansburg, VA Metro Area	56	3,149	386	548	571	558	21,372	19,424	3,158	-3.5	48,889	10.3	38,391
Bloomington, IL Metro Area	53	13,842	438	718	329	336	14,978	15,079	3,609	-2.5	71,642	-5.8	51,128
Bloomington, IN Metro Area	38	2,769	358	442	477	515	23,807	22,962	3,437	4.5	53,709	5.7	38,837
Bloomsburg-Berwick, PA Metro Area	32	1,425	189	230	202	217	6,555	6,658	1,883	1.7	36,923	8.0	48,745
Boise City, ID Metro Area	162	11,949	6,543	6,237	2,357	2,395	41,492	36,927	18,661	13.4	254,357	21.3	45,008
Boston-Cambridge-Newton, MA-NH Metro Area ...	1,508	357,415	35,722	40,092	14,183	14,994	268,722	260,539	130,876	7.1	2,534,539	13.9	70,913
Boston, MA Div	638	256,055	19,253	20,364	5,862	6,193	126,411	125,591	54,532	8.3	1,164,840	15.4	72,955
Cambridge-Newton-Framingham, MA Div	747	91,192	15,080	18,056	6,713	7,184	117,509	109,540	63,811	6.6	1,187,773	12.6	72,021
Rockingham County-Strafford County, NH Div	123	10,168	1,389	1,672	1,608	1,617	24,802	25,408	12,533	4.7	181,926	13.2	50,601
Boulder, CO Metro Area	100	10,513	2,023	2,325	829	900	32,716	28,565	12,551	9.7	153,690	15.3	60,564
Bowling Green, KY Metro Area	68	3,233	646	863	518	512	11,185	11,640	3,510	7.8	61,626	19.4	38,737
Bremerton-Silverdale-Port Orchard, WA Metro Area	56	3,396	19,786	16,071	11,527	10,856	13,581	13,263	5,928	4.8	59,021	4.9	39,958
Bridgeport-Stamford-Norwalk, CT Metro Area	354	48,906	2,848	3,469	1,874	1,799	43,905	44,109	27,207	0.7	429,679	9.1	82,149
Brownsville-Harlingen, TX Metro Area	70	4,234	3,452	3,050	928	1,051	26,696	27,858	6,377	0.8	107,239	8.6	27,372
Brunswick, GA Metro Area	37	2,182	1,994	1,976	389	426	6,644	8,298	2,904	1.5	35,077	8.8	34,208
Buffalo-Cheektowaga, NY Metro Area	255	46,080	9,464	10,548	1,962	2,102	76,634	82,542	27,534	2.4	482,984	6.0	43,949
Burlington, NC Metro Area	38	2,183	252	266	354	369	6,948	6,939	3,311	3.3	59,276	22.9	39,093
Burlington-South Burlington, VT Metro Area	69	5,258	4,051	3,508	1,441	1,461	17,535	16,580	6,919	3.0	102,620	4.8	47,118
California-Lexington Park, MD Metro Area	18	1,535	9,999	8,382	2,469	2,685	4,621	4,703	1,993	4.3	32,376	11.7	50,443
Canton-Massillon, OH Metro Area	116	7,402	1,031	1,300	1,012	1,025	19,188	19,444	8,635	-3.1	150,465	9.3	38,788
Cape Coral-Fort Myers, FL Metro Area	187	16,326	2,410	2,844	1,378	1,317	40,334	33,863	18,797	20.7	216,916	29.8	41,466
Cape Girardeau, MO-IL Metro Area	46	2,198	416	534	332	321	6,684	6,861	2,658	-15.0	39,925	-2.1	38,670
Carbondale-Marion, IL Metro Area	71	2,409	1,882	2,046	268	284	16,042	18,042	3,075	-2.6	43,560	6.7	34,842
Carson City, NV Metro Area	15	1,431	553	593	141	132	8,975	9,071	1,890	-11.7	20,905	-0.9	44,588
Casper, WY Metro Area	19	2,177	639	767	408	436	4,900	5,070	2,971	2.0	31,203	-4.4	48,104
Cedar Rapids, IA Metro Area	102	6,346	1,173	1,296	966	1,094	15,617	15,831	6,660	3.2	129,218	6.4	48,179
Chambersburg-Waynesboro, PA Metro Area	45	2,222	2,295	2,557	391	402	5,685	6,524	3,080	1.7	50,967	10.1	38,025
Champaign-Urbana, IL Metro Area	86	5,994	1,295	1,430	444	456	37,468	36,923	4,602	1.5	71,668	1.0	42,163
Charleston, WV Metro Area	76	6,662	2,351	2,349	1,227	1,538	22,947	24,513	5,799	-12.8	92,295	-13.9	43,813
Charleston-North Charleston, SC Metro Area	189	14,740	11,142	9,654	12,733	12,914	52,671	49,082	19,483	18.8	286,757	25.4	44,950
Charlotte-Concord-Gastonia, NC-SC Metro Area	507	206,223	10,784	10,469	6,378	6,271	144,423	135,968	62,039	13.7	1,058,398	23.3	53,265
Charlottesville, VA Metro Area	63	4,986	1,436	1,485	1,120	980	35,389	30,164	5,936	5.3	84,420	13.1	51,608
Chattanooga, TN-GA Metro Area	145	10,183	5,481	6,283	1,586	1,768	32,401	30,191	11,489	3.1	221,608	14.0	41,730

Table B-14. Banking, Government Employment, and Private Business Establishments and Employment—Continued

Metropolitan Statistical Area Metropolitan Division	Banking 2019		Government Employment						Private nonfarm business				
			Federal civilian		Military		State and Local		Establishments		Employment		
	Number of offices	Deposits (million dollars)	2018	2010	2018	2010	2018	2010	2017	Change 2010-2017 (percent)	2017	Change 2010-2017 (percent)	Annual payroll per employee 2017 (dollars)
Cheyenne, WY Metro Area	30	1,835	2,802	2,683	3,570	3,575	11,229	11,271	3,243	20.1	32,827	6.7	42,577
Chicago-Naperville-Elgin, IL-IN-WI Metro Area ...	2,636	415,680	54,115	61,516	33,406	36,816	509,052	516,234	247,182	4.4	4,165,528	9.7	59,356
Chicago-Naperville-Evanston, IL Div	1,979	360,448	44,584	50,580	14,614	14,960	379,755	385,434	192,272	4.6	3,317,834	10.4	60,346
Elgin, IL Div	214	15,098	1,959	2,257	1,512	1,504	48,900	47,299	17,135	6.5	237,763	10.2	44,736
Gary, IN Div	220	14,381	1,983	2,267	2,063	2,373	32,922	35,720	14,669	1.4	233,904	4.3	45,372
Lake County-Kenosha County, IL-WI Div	223	25,753	5,589	6,412	15,217	17,799	47,475	47,781	23,106	3.1	376,027	6.4	68,566
Chico, CA Metro Area	42	5,656	562	664	332	356	16,367	14,284	4,724	0.3	62,600	16.1	39,470
Cincinnati, OH-KY-IN Metro Area	699	138,987	15,066	17,879	5,886	5,940	114,491	115,390	46,963	1.5	946,308	8.1	50,970
Clarksville, TN-KY Metro Area	79	4,140	5,493	6,647	27,455	33,052	14,517	13,684	4,623	7.4	73,140	9.9	34,786
Cleveland, TN Metro Area	30	1,951	279	324	343	384	5,365	5,456	2,143	1.9	40,497	11.2	38,428
Cleveland-Elyria, OH Metro Area	621	72,791	18,664	20,079	5,591	5,887	115,799	119,547	51,086	-2.0	918,152	5.5	50,906
Coeur d'Alene, ID Metro Area	41	3,391	662	635	508	534	10,861	9,299	4,910	10.8	52,930	21.9	39,704
College Station-Bryan, TX Metro Area	70	5,987	832	1,194	562	593	39,843	34,451	4,980	14.6	75,731	28.2	37,126
Colorado Springs, CO Metro Area	134	8,635	12,120	12,909	37,466	39,199	41,605	36,228	18,262	10.4	248,023	13.8	46,388
Columbia, MO Metro Area	96	5,181	2,665	2,350	686	685	31,215	30,170	5,246	6.1	85,884	17.5	38,149
Columbia, SC Metro Area	171	19,730	10,413	10,863	12,408	13,603	73,363	68,968	17,554	2.7	295,371	9.1	42,714
Columbus, GA-AL Metro Area	57	9,367	6,712	6,563	19,323	22,185	18,240	18,319	5,863	0.2	99,653	4.3	41,778
Columbus, IN Metro Area	24	1,368	170	254	243	258	6,381	6,198	1,884	1.6	48,314	25.0	47,297
Columbus, OH Metro Area	538	62,066	14,667	15,660	5,744	5,483	160,381	151,225	42,559	5.9	874,951	15.3	49,560
Corpus Christi, TX Metro Area	96	6,165	5,705	6,826	4,730	4,583	26,360	26,808	9,086	3.4	155,845	12.9	41,935
Corvallis, OR Metro Area	15	1,301	480	592	255	287	9,071	9,883	2,148	4.3	28,322	15.5	49,755
Crestview-Fort Walton Beach-Destin, FL Metro Area	97	5,658	8,915	7,835	16,831	14,923	11,512	11,024	7,754	16.1	82,799	14.7	37,755
Cumberland, MD-WV Metro Area	24	927	564	659	337	344	6,954	7,555	1,999	-6.6	29,972	-0.5	36,638
Dallas-Fort Worth-Arlington, TX Metro Area	1,615	295,311	46,603	48,402	16,789	16,992	378,976	344,927	163,708	16.6	3,127,419	24.6	55,569
Dallas-Plano-Irving, TX Div	1,098	249,382	30,200	32,669	10,540	11,158	262,907	237,148	114,608	17.5	2,253,776	27.5	58,470
Fort Worth-Arlington-Grapevine, TX Div	517	45,929	16,403	15,733	6,249	5,834	116,069	107,779	49,100	14.4	873,643	17.8	48,082
Dalton, GA Metro Area	29	2,401	248	356	382	456	6,692	6,871	2,603	-3.4	55,284	-1.5	41,565
Danville, IL Metro Area	28	1,207	1,439	1,516	148	164	4,476	4,513	1,426	-7.3	24,093	-0.8	40,451
Daphne-Fairhope-Foley, AL Metro Area	92	4,554	357	370	980	883	9,468	8,259	5,384	15.4	61,792	20.8	33,783
Davenport-Moline-Rock Island, IA-IL Metro Area	134	8,153	5,709	7,814	1,384	1,440	20,737	20,742	8,878	-3.3	157,879	2.3	44,866
Dayton-Kettering, OH Metro Area	197	12,342	19,029	18,603	7,213	7,071	41,926	45,285	16,478	-1.6	326,374	9.1	45,336
Decatur, AL Metro Area	41	2,155	374	441	631	740	7,841	8,322	3,024	-2.7	46,522	1.2	42,219
Decatur, IL Metro Area	39	1,889	312	370	211	230	5,512	6,077	2,417	-3.7	44,389	-4.3	47,875
Deltona-Daytona Beach-Ormond Beach, FL Metro Area	141	12,244	1,477	1,710	1,247	1,231	21,986	24,220	15,027	11.1	168,368	18.3	35,491
Denver-Aurora-Lakewood, CO Metro Area	634	87,647	28,319	29,252	10,125	9,769	182,408	156,477	85,059	15.5	1,280,402	23.3	57,785
Des Moines-West Des Moines, IA Metro Area	225	20,533	6,353	6,348	2,576	2,718	40,509	38,836	17,416	11.2	329,004	15.3	51,360
Detroit-Warren-Dearborn, MI Metro Area	945	140,582	28,057	30,134	7,720	9,115	167,988	184,977	100,070	2.9	1,761,974	17.4	53,882
Detroit-Dearborn-Livonia, MI Div	306	57,108	13,864	15,948	3,190	3,922	74,728	87,636	32,444	-0.3	643,127	13.3	53,840
Warren-Troy-Farmington Hills, MI Div	639	83,474	14,193	14,186	4,530	5,193	93,260	97,341	67,626	4.6	1,118,847	19.9	53,907
Dothan, AL Metro Area	52	3,414	404	508	656	703	10,388	10,332	3,417	-2.0	50,838	2.4	39,204
Dover, DE Metro Area	32	2,111	1,672	1,971	4,314	4,422	17,122	17,009	3,583	12.0	52,481	13.1	39,381
Dubuque, IA Metro Area	38	2,945	266	274	355	407	4,529	4,366	2,797	2.2	54,767	8.3	42,826
Duluth, MN-WI Metro Area	92	4,545	1,600	2,098	1,061	1,164	24,245	24,527	7,394	-2.5	114,815	5.9	42,589
Durham-Chapel Hill, NC Metro Area	112	16,965	8,161	7,420	1,523	1,629	68,344	61,408	13,893	11.0	274,514	19.5	58,520
East Stroudsburg, PA Metro Area	48	2,736	3,211	4,702	448	458	8,357	9,338	3,385	-0.7	49,290	10.1	35,806
Eau Claire, WI Metro Area	54	2,967	546	648	423	442	11,557	11,372	4,242	1.8	72,741	7.6	48,803
El Centro, CA Metro Area	15	1,867	2,125	2,546	363	527	16,652	15,376	2,538	7.2	32,109	9.9	35,179
Elizabethtown-Fort Knox, KY Metro Area	45	2,270	5,373	6,405	5,101	12,012	9,667	8,244	2,616	-6.8	42,854	13.9	38,068
Elkhart-Goshen, IN Metro Area	57	3,384	272	307	601	659	8,405	8,267	4,949	1.2	132,095	40.1	47,387
Elmira, NY Metro Area	21	1,083	213	321	126	139	5,884	6,794	1,758	-5.3	30,377	-6.9	40,663
El Paso, TX Metro Area	91	8,756	13,064	12,910	27,349	23,721	56,879	54,946	14,599	9.0	237,730	14.7	32,155
Enid, OK Metro Area	25	1,514	497	556	1,431	1,536	3,287	3,784	1,645	0.0	21,514	-3.3	38,770
Erie, PA Metro Area	73	5,327	1,608	1,694	713	771	15,490	16,390	6,197	-1.4	115,178	3.1	39,422
Eugene-Springfield, OR Metro Area	74	5,533	1,818	1,917	987	1,044	22,691	24,224	9,959	3.7	125,153	12.1	40,501
Evansville, IN-KY Metro Area	97	6,364	1,310	1,349	942	1,032	15,570	15,096	7,741	1.9	144,467	1.1	43,123
Fairbanks, AK Metro Area	17	1,488	3,038	3,502	9,777	8,621	7,308	8,058	2,492	2.0	27,095	-0.2	50,510
Fargo, ND-MN Metro Area	94	8,778	2,588	2,455	1,313	1,328	16,842	15,291	6,917	9.8	122,574	13.1	45,867
Farmington, NM Metro Area	26	1,472	1,488	1,704	316	353	9,524	9,491	2,626	-7.0	34,753	-8.3	43,366
Fayetteville, NC Metro Area	83	4,672	15,592	13,503	46,799	54,989	30,790	30,768	7,833	0.9	120,741	3.0	33,997
Fayetteville-Springdale-Rogers, AR Metro Area	196	11,066	2,563	2,566	2,007	1,968	29,060	24,636	12,061	16.7	210,590	23.1	49,768
Flagstaff, AZ Metro Area	20	2,205	2,723	3,220	294	292	16,344	14,158	3,746	4.8	53,114	22.3	39,703
Flint, MI Metro Area	63	4,307	1,090	1,466	637	802	19,273	22,948	7,740	-2.1	121,169	9.8	40,743
Florence, SC Metro Area	53	2,989	690	985	775	898	15,626	15,529	4,225	-1.9	75,608	7.6	38,962
Florence-Muscle Shoals, AL Metro Area	48	2,840	866	1,415	612	710	8,930	9,902	3,213	-2.0	49,018	10.9	34,130
Fond du Lac, WI Metro Area	34	2,076	193	249	262	282	5,249	5,786	2,325	-4.7	43,479	12.3	43,045
Fort Collins, CO Metro Area	93	8,012	2,528	2,543	858	830	36,589	25,309	10,935	16.6	126,470	24.0	45,774
Fort Smith, AR-OK Metro Area	109	4,542	1,291	1,576	998	1,116	12,879	13,174	5,353	-2.4	91,556	-4.0	37,455
Fort Wayne, IN Metro Area	108	6,781	2,111	2,137	1,234	1,311	18,912	18,724	9,879	0.6	189,684	13.8	42,786
Fresno, CA Metro Area	126	14,298	10,081	10,754	1,572	1,802	64,161	56,293	16,881	7.0	261,800	16.3	43,232
Gadsden, AL Metro Area	24	1,138	308	437	421	500	5,086	5,137	1,978	-2.7	30,604	3.8	34,138
Gainesville, FL Metro Area	77	5,312	4,623	4,830	664	695	40,176	39,657	7,190	6.8	102,732	16.5	41,027
Gainesville, GA Metro Area	44	3,911	456	594	536	573	10,457	9,920	4,369	10.6	77,461	34.0	46,234

Table B-14. Banking, Government Employment, and Private Business Establishments and Employment—*Continued*

Metropolitan Statistical Area Metropolitan Division	Banking 2019 Number of offices	Banking 2019 Deposits (million dollars)	Federal civilian 2018	Federal civilian 2010	Military 2018	Military 2010	State and Local 2018	State and Local 2010	Establishments 2017	Establishments Change 2010-2017 (percent)	Employment 2017	Employment Change 2010-2017 (percent)	Annual payroll per employee 2017 (dollars)
Gettysburg, PA Metro Area	25	1,490	678	760	251	263	3,394	3,717	1,974	3.2	29,070	5.7	36,797
Glens Falls, NY Metro Area	48	2,757	316	431	192	208	9,394	10,013	3,345	-3.1	42,072	3.5	40,045
Goldsboro, NC Metro Area	25	1,549	1,225	1,309	4,708	4,885	8,073	8,486	2,175	-2.1	33,960	0.4	34,316
Grand Forks, ND-MN Metro Area	42	2,782	1,121	1,363	2,130	2,144	11,690	11,823	2,647	1.4	42,714	4.7	39,507
Grand Island, NE Metro Area	47	2,450	713	814	258	299	5,401	5,538	2,309	5.0	33,756	4.3	38,127
Grand Junction, CO Metro Area	38	2,774	1,583	1,606	379	395	8,590	8,113	4,446	-4.3	52,848	6.8	42,168
Grand Rapids-Kentwood, MI Metro Area	303	22,891	3,551	3,891	1,778	1,932	46,906	45,349	24,782	7.9	503,115	26.0	45,537
Grants Pass, OR Metro Area	20	1,520	261	324	204	232	3,019	3,015	2,030	0.8	23,460	22.3	34,366
Great Falls, MT Metro Area	23	1,450	1,702	1,858	3,499	3,583	3,962	4,209	2,458	0.2	30,445	0.5	38,271
Greeley, CO Metro Area	71	4,426	622	858	756	688	16,666	14,993	6,274	21.5	85,076	31.7	50,283
Green Bay, WI Metro Area	92	7,884	1,413	1,321	846	892	20,947	20,452	7,816	2.6	156,929	9.3	47,335
Greensboro-High Point, NC Metro Area	170	12,611	4,328	4,596	1,697	1,822	39,336	40,654	17,737	1.0	323,805	9.3	43,914
Greenville, NC Metro Area	40	2,319	722	578	424	419	26,419	23,319	3,584	0.4	60,749	7.8	39,964
Greenville-Anderson, SC Metro Area	236	17,460	2,771	2,781	3,364	3,641	57,277	51,048	20,111	7.4	340,562	14.5	42,759
Gulfport-Biloxi, MS Metro Area	124	6,022	8,858	9,083	9,833	12,743	25,474	25,370	7,473	-0.1	132,684	1.7	41,525
Hagerstown-Martinsburg, MD-WV Metro Area	80	3,980	3,952	4,606	1,150	1,114	13,946	14,215	5,315	-0.2	87,342	11.9	39,929
Hammond, LA Metro Area	35	2,004	366	455	491	587	10,774	11,273	2,426	8.1	36,408	14.2	37,251
Hanford-Corcoran, CA Metro Area	12	1,256	1,184	1,183	4,960	5,671	13,854	13,469	1,643	1.8	25,053	11.0	40,068
Harrisburg-Carlisle, PA Metro Area	181	16,329	7,338	7,964	2,163	2,127	52,598	56,582	13,767	2.7	277,210	6.9	47,973
Harrisonburg, VA Metro Area	49	2,366	357	396	408	398	11,558	9,938	3,094	3.5	51,926	2.7	37,670
Hartford-East Hartford-Middletown, CT Metro Area	345	46,307	6,255	6,791	2,433	2,346	90,881	91,528	29,521	-0.1	549,925	3.9	58,535
Hattiesburg, MS Metro Area	70	3,327	802	975	1,296	1,262	15,364	15,265	3,687	1.4	55,470	5.1	36,504
Hickory-Lenoir-Morganton, NC Metro Area	77	4,893	669	1,011	792	896	22,269	23,683	7,513	-1.6	135,351	12.3	38,351
Hilton Head Island-Bluffton, SC Metro Area	61	4,600	2,264	2,578	10,556	10,103	9,322	8,795	6,007	13.9	63,557	20.2	35,758
Hinesville, GA Metro Area	9	514	3,764	4,316	15,315	18,263	3,929	3,711	920	3.8	12,320	4.4	39,881
Homosassa Springs, FL Metro Area	37	2,283	244	274	254	284	4,109	4,740	2,774	4.0	30,047	20.1	34,922
Hot Springs, AR Metro Area	50	1,984	452	583	378	424	4,064	4,420	2,765	2.3	34,587	13.2	33,265
Houma-Thibodaux, LA Metro Area	67	4,343	411	588	869	1,080	11,683	13,537	4,581	-5.2	70,218	-8.0	46,841
Houston-The Woodlands-Sugar Land, TX Metro Area	1,416	249,551	29,205	30,568	15,035	15,244	369,011	340,505	142,141	16.2	2,599,675	19.5	60,616
Huntington-Ashland, WV-KY-OH Metro Area	117	6,013	3,300	3,608	1,427	1,565	19,677	20,800	7,012	-5.9	114,510	0.2	40,071
Huntsville, AL Metro Area	119	8,226	19,500	19,489	2,623	3,532	31,782	28,578	9,833	5.1	181,686	9.9	51,455
Idaho Falls, ID Metro Area	35	1,917	860	1,007	488	530	7,402	6,526	4,100	10.2	54,007	15.4	43,428
Indianapolis-Carmel-Anderson, IN Metro Area	522	54,169	17,067	17,493	6,555	6,819	118,561	114,753	47,389	6.1	911,388	17.3	48,930
Iowa City, IA Metro Area	53	4,478	2,176	1,819	636	647	37,913	32,558	3,984	6.4	70,971	10.4	43,031
Ithaca, NY Metro Area	26	2,106	257	314	161	167	5,840	6,442	2,377	2.5	48,258	6.2	39,906
Jackson, MI Metro Area	38	2,130	334	394	240	288	7,468	8,412	2,901	-3.9	50,191	12.3	48,039
Jackson, MS Metro Area	232	14,006	6,294	6,823	3,363	3,589	53,489	55,778	13,518	0.0	224,030	9.5	42,156
Jackson, TN Metro Area	72	3,171	613	785	487	592	16,860	16,414	3,920	-1.2	70,348	7.7	37,870
Jacksonville, FL Metro Area	277	65,384	18,315	18,071	13,275	18,634	60,163	60,141	38,202	12.1	577,874	19.8	46,031
Jacksonville, NC Metro Area	25	1,346	6,523	6,688	45,576	51,451	8,171	8,026	2,802	4.1	35,541	6.9	28,624
Janesville-Beloit, WI Metro Area	36	2,787	305	339	417	451	8,549	8,948	3,374	2.5	59,475	16.2	44,296
Jefferson City, MO Metro Area	60	4,747	819	904	498	536	24,239	26,730	3,549	-1.4	53,991	7.9	39,444
Johnson City, TN Metro Area	60	3,145	2,939	2,668	599	674	13,423	13,957	3,854	0.5	65,563	5.2	38,013
Johnstown, PA Metro Area	67	3,148	968	1,374	344	473	6,737	8,021	3,154	-8.2	46,317	-8.4	35,610
Jonesboro, AR Metro Area	56	3,105	394	526	501	532	9,463	8,718	2,879	4.1	46,190	16.8	37,698
Joplin, MO Metro Area	80	2,842	438	505	616	627	9,109	9,359	4,007	-5.6	70,980	-2.9	38,250
Kahului-Wailuku-Lahaina, HI Metro Area	37	3,689	856	978	1,192	1,161	7,658	8,853	4,705	8.6	64,947	13.2	41,234
Kalamazoo-Portage, MI Metro Area	54	3,474	683	1,033	416	469	14,400	14,732	5,641	0.2	109,826	6.9	47,285
Kankakee, IL Metro Area	36	1,870	253	281	212	226	5,949	6,153	2,347	-0.4	36,747	4.3	38,526
Kansas City, MO-KS Metro Area	694	61,307	27,887	28,991	11,012	11,674	122,680	126,545	52,650	6.2	954,263	12.1	50,947
Kennewick-Richland, WA Metro Area	52	3,245	1,224	1,446	752	802	18,767	16,669	6,120	16.5	87,957	17.5	49,729
Killeen-Temple, TX Metro Area	87	5,135	10,869	11,448	35,560	48,486	27,260	25,940	6,325	6.9	106,123	12.0	39,085
Kingsport-Bristol, TN-VA Metro Area	97	4,300	881	1,205	884	1,033	15,630	15,718	5,984	-1.8	104,278	1.4	43,064
Kingston, NY Metro Area	50	3,275	420	511	283	302	12,835	14,120	4,850	3.0	46,244	2.6	36,458
Knoxville, TN Metro Area	239	17,671	5,401	6,031	2,482	2,795	51,915	52,265	18,127	3.3	334,884	10.0	44,566
Kokomo, IN Metro Area	24	1,195	189	276	242	278	4,907	6,468	1,780	-1.8	31,996	12.6	42,988
La Crosse-Onalaska, WI-MN Metro Area	47	2,583	546	576	362	391	11,241	10,786	3,493	3.4	68,320	11.8	41,541
Lafayette, LA Metro Area	175	12,668	1,413	1,632	1,873	2,313	24,230	26,452	13,222	4.3	180,677	1.2	43,064
Lafayette-West Lafayette, IN Metro Area	68	3,398	535	768	703	729	25,465	24,196	4,347	6.6	77,501	18.2	42,093
Lake Charles, LA Metro Area	78	4,325	555	739	862	1,082	14,204	15,049	4,813	9.7	79,000	15.1	45,458
Lake Havasu City-Kingman, AZ Metro Area	39	3,050	444	677	447	440	7,140	7,541	3,784	1.9	41,986	5.7	34,802
Lakeland-Winter Haven, FL Metro Area	103	8,093	1,205	1,595	1,270	1,213	27,531	28,377	11,676	6.7	182,922	14.9	40,257
Lancaster, PA Metro Area	182	11,672	1,288	1,529	1,353	1,374	19,665	20,227	13,060	8.4	235,331	13.5	43,029
Lansing-East Lansing, MI Metro Area	119	7,660	2,109	2,541	1,042	1,389	51,160	52,372	10,735	-0.1	183,895	12.3	44,215
Laredo, TX Metro Area	57	6,540	3,486	3,418	536	575	19,044	18,682	5,434	15.4	78,875	24.2	29,149
Las Cruces, NM Metro Area	44	2,245	3,354	4,274	554	590	16,488	17,483	3,716	2.9	52,980	5.7	32,606
Las Vegas-Henderson-Paradise, NV Metro Area	335	264,275	13,307	12,390	15,777	14,203	88,088	83,755	45,830	15.7	857,591	17.2	41,766
Lawrence, KS Metro Area	51	2,324	430	526	451	481	17,497	14,612	2,727	3.8	40,467	8.2	31,222
Lawton, OK Metro Area	41	1,537	3,929	4,752	11,716	14,238	10,904	10,895	2,224	-3.3	32,718	-3.8	36,059
Lebanon, PA Metro Area	41	2,301	3,134	2,621	351	392	4,934	5,511	2,696	2.1	46,303	6.6	38,740
Lewiston, ID-WA Metro Area	19	732	250	280	184	217	5,232	5,016	1,581	0.4	22,882	9.5	39,203
Lewiston-Auburn, ME Metro Area	24	2,041	268	326	322	344	5,272	5,162	2,788	0.8	45,507	3.9	41,647

Table B-14. Banking, Government Employment, and Private Business Establishments and Employment—Continued

Metropolitan Statistical Area Metropolitan Division	Banking 2019 Number of offices	Banking 2019 Deposits (million dollars)	Federal civilian 2018	Federal civilian 2010	Military 2018	Military 2010	State and Local 2018	State and Local 2010	Establishments 2017	Establishments Change 2010-2017 (percent)	Employment 2017	Employment Change 2010-2017 (percent)	Annual payroll per employee 2017 (dollars)
Lexington-Fayette, KY Metro Area	183	10,747	4,561	4,783	1,561	1,555	48,233	45,317	12,488	5.7	228,183	14.1	44,062
Lima, OH Metro Area	30	1,837	328	406	248	264	5,670	6,287	2,383	-6.5	46,478	-0.1	40,612
Lincoln, NE Metro Area	137	9,083	3,434	3,051	1,123	1,228	31,612	31,094	9,041	10.0	144,760	11.1	42,055
Little Rock-North Little Rock-Conway, AR Metro Area...	303	23,910	9,662	9,854	6,188	8,350	59,338	62,213	18,201	3.4	283,598	2.8	44,410
Logan, UT-ID Metro Area	25	1,923	372	419	530	546	12,051	10,953	3,755	12.0	44,906	15.0	35,130
Longview, TX Metro Area	99	5,920	595	832	538	623	14,476	15,220	6,647	0.8	96,956	0.1	41,741
Longview, WA Metro Area	10	690	224	259	273	317	6,250	5,497	2,211	0.2	32,299	11.0	46,194
Los Angeles-Long Beach-Anaheim, CA Metro Area	2,354	568,516	59,045	65,195	22,106	23,985	703,644	667,241	372,217	12.5	5,324,257	9.7	58,676
Anaheim-Santa Ana-Irvine, CA Div	639	128,348	11,213	12,617	5,038	5,628	150,071	137,585	96,901	12.0	1,503,084	18.1	58,431
Los Angeles-Long Beach-Glendale, CA Div	1,715	440,168	47,832	52,578	17,068	18,357	553,573	529,656	275,316	12.6	3,821,173	6.7	58,773
Louisville/Jefferson County, KY-IN Metro Area	378	28,160	9,205	11,574	3,966	4,185	62,923	65,670	29,104	2.1	577,816	15.7	46,868
Lubbock, TX Metro Area	113	8,977	1,375	1,499	630	682	30,206	26,539	7,381	4.6	115,372	10.0	36,540
Lynchburg, VA Metro Area	86	4,981	567	833	831	827	12,628	13,794	5,998	5.3	99,184	9.9	39,729
Macon-Bibb County, GA Metro Area	49	3,739	1,125	1,499	602	829	13,213	14,152	5,168	-2.2	84,303	5.1	40,476
Madera, CA Metro Area	16	1,233	304	359	219	234	10,894	10,576	1,961	2.7	26,755	9.2	42,960
Madison, WI Metro Area	219	21,150	5,574	5,468	1,800	1,761	83,263	76,914	17,324	7.8	333,811	17.7	52,084
Manchester-Nashua, NH Metro Area	95	11,867	4,101	3,947	1,400	1,410	17,502	18,525	11,013	1.7	186,614	5.2	55,963
Manhattan, KS Metro Area	56	3,227	3,762	4,153	15,377	19,145	17,325	14,978	2,781	2.7	38,483	4.8	32,781
Mankato, MN Metro Area	42	2,447	297	395	352	355	8,346	7,995	2,679	5.2	50,288	11.0	38,244
Mansfield, OH Metro Area	45	1,898	664	721	287	304	6,990	7,542	2,662	-2.7	41,099	-3.4	34,991
McAllen-Edinburg-Mission, TX Metro Area	146	9,951	4,485	3,716	1,730	1,798	54,651	50,422	12,117	9.7	198,978	19.1	27,948
Medford, OR Metro Area	60	3,575	1,781	1,782	515	573	8,557	8,969	6,368	10.1	75,967	18.8	40,309
Memphis, TN-MS-AR Metro Area	359	31,871	14,077	15,306	5,361	6,683	69,714	74,093	25,596	-0.6	539,734	6.0	48,017
Merced, CA Metro Area	29	2,322	751	821	393	415	18,178	16,081	3,110	7.8	45,686	17.6	37,452
Miami-Fort Lauderdale-Pompano Beach, FL Metro	1,502	240,781	34,496	36,741	13,990	14,185	280,211	278,231	194,524	14.0	2,214,596	21.6	48,091
Fort Lauderdale-Pompano Beach-Sunrise, FL Div	442	55,525	7,081	8,964	3,912	3,941	99,880	92,658	61,032	9.9	705,667	18.9	47,519
Miami-Miami Beach-Kendall, FL Div	628	131,441	20,493	20,892	7,383	7,508	122,628	127,813	84,803	15.5	982,248	22.5	48,427
West Palm Beach-Boca Raton-Boynton Beach, FL Div	432	53,814	6,922	6,885	2,695	2,736	57,703	57,760	48,689	16.7	526,681	23.8	48,231
Michigan City-La Porte, IN Metro Area	23	1,708	177	220	328	376	6,421	7,080	2,314	-6.6	35,742	5.0	38,742
Midland, MI Metro Area	17	1,750	156	170	130	157	3,058	3,338	1,965	7.7	36,436	8.0	67,240
Midland, TX Metro Area	47	7,235	563	672	346	324	9,180	8,588	5,452	16.9	87,328	44.2	67,960
Milwaukee-Waukesha, WI Metro Area	484	63,063	10,620	11,224	4,356	4,841	77,446	80,297	38,690	0.7	783,764	6.3	52,206
Minneapolis-St. Paul-Bloomington, MN Metro Area	770	189,294	21,268	22,418	12,679	13,252	231,497	220,300	97,123	6.5	1,804,390	13.8	57,198
Missoula, MT Metro Area	36	2,449	1,426	1,604	531	539	9,008	8,732	4,458	6.9	50,107	8.4	37,140
Mobile, AL Metro Area	116	7,325	2,613	3,012	2,661	3,048	23,560	26,247	9,021	-0.3	156,341	2.8	45,322
Modesto, CA Metro Area	86	8,420	842	992	801	841	29,542	25,585	9,096	8.7	142,929	17.5	45,604
Monroe, LA Metro Area	61	3,536	586	779	737	989	11,917	14,330	5,067	0.6	72,184	2.1	37,599
Monroe, MI Metro Area	28	2,021	243	278	236	288	5,482	5,815	2,353	-1.3	37,086	6.9	43,565
Montgomery, AL Metro Area	103	8,476	6,498	7,131	4,252	4,790	33,020	34,227	7,741	0.0	130,956	3.1	40,712
Morgantown, WV Metro Area	48	3,052	2,017	2,020	633	634	16,959	17,125	2,951	7.6	53,463	20.4	45,080
Morristown, TN Metro Area	35	1,759	361	391	398	456	7,150	6,958	2,252	2.2	42,419	9.0	36,626
Mount Vernon-Anacortes, WA Metro Area	41	2,654	392	455	319	360	11,340	10,478	3,560	3.7	43,053	13.3	46,545
Muncie, IN Metro Area	29	2,797	305	357	322	374	10,571	10,448	2,455	0.6	42,508	18.4	36,262
Muskegon, MI Metro Area	35	1,606	365	433	281	343	7,329	8,311	3,165	-6.3	52,096	9.2	40,601
Myrtle Beach-Conway-North Myrtle Beach, SC-NC..	147	9,188	1,237	1,183	1,642	1,519	21,437	18,481	11,623	10.3	138,378	20.0	32,242
Napa, CA Metro Area	42	4,297	221	292	198	217	10,788	9,785	4,270	8.2	64,132	16.7	53,384
Naples-Marco Island, FL Metro Area	146	17,337	722	760	652	648	12,834	12,187	12,074	22.5	131,871	30.0	42,794
Nashville-Davidson--Murfreesboro--Franklin, TN.....	573	64,106	13,480	13,384	5,755	6,170	97,023	93,747	43,775	12.3	855,849	27.1	51,712
New Bern, NC Metro Area	23	1,602	5,905	5,767	7,494	9,853	8,546	8,637	2,542	-6.2	31,352	0.9	37,863
New Haven-Milford, CT Metro Area	245	32,723	5,520	5,975	1,907	1,855	44,087	45,157	19,562	-0.2	340,724	6.1	51,859
New Orleans-Metairie, LA Metro Area	317	35,906	12,972	13,068	7,665	9,111	66,436	78,855	31,166	6.0	494,676	9.2	47,490
New York-Newark-Jersey City, NY-NJ-PA Metro Area.	5,135	1,861,341	104,903	127,040	35,036	36,687	1,169,265	1,159,642	563,722	5.7	8,166,817	12.3	71,906
Nassau County-Suffolk County, NY Div	810	134,062	16,050	18,725	5,088	5,254	171,380	178,798	98,414	3.8	1,151,576	10.4	54,645
Newark, NJ-PA Div	717	86,720	16,494	18,564	4,457	4,547	137,771	145,611	57,626	-0.1	889,017	4.0	66,976
New Brunswick-Lakewood, NJ Div	767	90,396	9,523	15,397	5,177	5,965	129,286	131,147	64,530	4.8	967,636	10.8	60,427
New York-Jersey City-White Plains, NY-NJ Div....	2,841	1,550,163	62,836	74,354	20,314	20,921	730,828	704,086	343,152	7.5	5,158,588	14.6	78,763
Niles, MI Metro Area	51	2,208	334	396	259	316	8,830	9,135	3,543	-3.6	54,568	10.2	45,638
North Port-Sarasota-Bradenton, FL Metro Area	265	21,953	2,035	2,183	1,507	1,445	25,578	24,415	23,085	16.1	247,805	25.1	41,778
Norwich-New London, CT Metro Area	81	5,332	2,803	2,664	6,672	8,100	27,799	34,572	5,907	2.0	105,456	-1.5	50,532
Ocala, FL Metro Area	76	6,351	692	933	615	662	14,440	17,057	7,182	6.0	81,985	10.9	35,248
Ocean City, NJ Metro Area	46	3,133	452	527	1,162	1,067	8,633	8,924	3,850	-0.1	26,890	9.9	41,132
Odessa, TX Metro Area	37	3,412	195	217	313	313	9,782	9,619	3,639	12.5	59,190	20.8	54,374
Ogden-Clearfield, UT Metro Area	91	5,707	19,373	20,126	6,505	6,794	32,233	28,696	14,205	14.7	192,865	22.0	40,793
Oklahoma City, OK Metro Area	407	33,906	29,295	28,190	10,785	12,679	93,080	93,796	35,992	9.1	506,241	11.8	44,495
Olympia-Lacey-Tumwater, WA Metro Area	56	4,066	871	1,010	797	816	38,187	35,799	6,233	7.0	73,630	15.7	41,533
Omaha-Council Bluffs, NE-IA Metro Area	321	33,765	9,507	9,482	9,314	9,554	54,183	54,302	23,884	7.1	419,890	5.3	47,679
Orlando-Kissimmee-Sanford, FL Metro Area	522	52,936	14,609	12,778	4,642	4,573	111,032	101,234	64,912	17.9	1,072,635	25.3	43,274
Oshkosh-Neenah, WI Metro Area	35	2,321	416	531	435	463	11,556	11,873	3,627	0.7	85,726	2.7	50,909
Owensboro, KY Metro Area	46	3,077	314	367	370	390	6,104	9,809	2,629	2.5	47,181	5.9	39,313

Table B-14. Banking, Government Employment, and Private Business Establishments and Employment—*Continued*

Metropolitan Statistical Area / Metropolitan Division	Banking 2019: Number of offices	Banking 2019: Deposits (million dollars)	Government Employment: Federal civilian 2018	Federal civilian 2010	Military 2018	Military 2010	State and Local 2018	State and Local 2010	Private nonfarm business: Establishments 2017	Establishments Change 2010-2017 (percent)	Employment 2017	Employment Change 2010-2017 (percent)	Annual payroll per employee 2017 (dollars)
Oxnard-Thousand Oaks-Ventura, CA Metro Area	159	20,113	7,330	7,822	4,919	6,388	38,664	35,252	21,339	8.8	258,166	9.6	53,554
Palm Bay-Melbourne-Titusville, FL Metro Area	104	9,404	6,432	6,755	2,867	2,999	22,548	23,249	14,255	9.8	185,134	12.9	44,716
Panama City, FL Metro Area	49	3,637	3,917	3,796	4,127	4,255	9,273	10,727	4,700	5.0	63,126	16.0	35,582
Parkersburg-Vienna, WV Metro Area	30	1,695	2,428	2,266	421	477	4,451	4,787	2,038	-6.9	30,200	-8.7	34,505
Pensacola-Ferry Pass-Brent, FL Metro Area	85	7,419	6,673	7,247	11,672	13,797	21,351	21,344	9,604	5.7	133,544	15.2	40,278
Peoria, IL Metro Area	162	8,295	2,267	2,537	860	883	21,314	22,329	8,964	-5.3	163,411	-3.1	51,144
Philadelphia-Camden-Wilmington, PA-NJ-DE-MD Metro Area	1,631	459,935	51,275	57,922	22,732	22,714	293,612	298,843	148,311	2.5	2,628,893	8.6	57,685
Camden, NJ Div	308	29,387	7,627	9,193	7,690	7,363	73,520	77,174	28,054	0.2	458,427	7.7	49,370
Montgomery County-Bucks County-Chester County, PA Metro Division	677	63,925	6,011	7,918	5,125	5,657	77,996	80,098	60,276	3.2	1,011,898	9.2	60,977
Philadelphia, PA Div	448	63,840	32,136	35,577	6,499	6,181	99,260	98,846	41,085	3.5	848,150	9.8	57,027
Wilmington, DE-MD-NJ Div	198	302,782	5,501	5,234	3,418	3,513	42,836	42,725	18,896	1.4	310,418	4.5	61,034
Phoenix-Mesa-Chandler, AZ Metro Area	798	110,241	22,645	24,086	15,087	14,396	216,774	208,291	98,279	12.0	1,726,596	18.8	49,276
Pine Bluff, AR Metro Area	29	3,176	1,405	2,179	338	439	8,350	9,084	1,567	-7.9	21,677	-15.6	36,693
Pittsburgh, PA Metro Area	786	150,674	18,195	19,484	6,265	6,710	98,666	109,365	59,749	0.9	1,103,495	7.0	49,867
Pittsfield, MA Metro Area	59	4,597	384	501	290	336	8,060	8,104	3,872	-3.9	53,882	0.3	45,643
Pocatello, ID Metro Area	27	855	585	608	296	345	8,573	8,175	2,246	3.1	26,946	-0.3	34,919
Portland-South Portland, ME Metro Area	192	14,883	9,221	8,324	4,024	4,925	28,716	28,827	18,136	4.6	238,275	9.2	47,672
Portland-Vancouver-Hillsboro, OR-WA Metro Area	508	52,481	18,333	18,622	6,290	6,980	127,355	121,011	70,187	12.4	1,047,457	20.3	55,700
Port St. Lucie, FL Metro Area	100	9,373	1,027	1,302	909	932	18,818	18,329	11,313	14.7	117,217	18.4	37,735
Poughkeepsie-Newburgh-Middletown, NY Metro Area	184	15,378	5,772	6,777	7,245	7,114	40,242	43,728	17,203	3.3	215,318	7.9	43,360
Prescott Valley-Prescott, AZ Metro Area	49	4,091	1,503	1,551	508	473	9,344	9,529	5,985	6.1	61,048	20.1	34,754
Providence-Warwick, RI-MA Metro Area	400	42,660	12,265	12,052	7,999	8,736	82,871	81,025	41,395	0.4	637,255	7.9	47,290
Provo-Orem, UT Metro Area	84	8,840	1,079	1,218	2,431	2,332	30,699	26,814	13,738	27.1	215,315	38.8	43,212
Pueblo, CO Metro Area	41	1,754	1,093	1,038	414	443	11,780	11,821	3,117	-1.2	50,879	8.6	38,726
Punta Gorda, FL Metro Area	51	3,954	328	485	319	322	5,626	5,826	4,006	13.6	39,311	6.4	33,648
Racine, WI Metro Area	50	3,629	376	372	499	546	8,478	8,735	4,036	-0.3	66,364	3.4	46,954
Raleigh-Cary, NC Metro Area	297	28,588	6,026	5,835	3,649	3,514	92,843	86,870	33,877	17.1	520,170	26.7	52,969
Rapid City, SD Metro Area	33	2,790	2,991	2,989	4,047	4,340	7,993	7,576	4,565	8.0	54,904	13.1	40,082
Reading, PA Metro Area	115	16,614	933	1,227	1,044	1,096	21,325	22,965	8,435	1.8	153,071	7.3	46,071
Redding, CA Metro Area	36	3,336	1,300	1,512	305	288	11,813	11,692	4,195	-3.0	50,261	7.4	41,356
Reno, NV Metro Area	88	9,924	3,745	3,715	1,258	1,081	23,853	24,523	12,706	7.7	195,817	18.1	45,555
Richmond, VA Metro Area	302	117,658	16,960	15,781	13,962	12,357	95,720	95,281	31,770	6.1	541,040	16.0	50,098
Riverside-San Bernardino-Ontario, CA Metro Area	537	53,256	20,937	22,916	23,361	25,062	240,460	216,782	74,581	14.7	1,179,496	23.2	41,764
Roanoke, VA Metro Area	107	7,191	3,859	4,088	997	1,044	17,519	17,222	8,154	-0.4	140,143	6.0	42,599
Rochester, MN Metro Area	85	5,561	938	1,183	759	793	11,480	10,543	5,146	2.4	113,762	25.3	54,267
Rochester, NY Metro Area	231	19,211	5,013	5,017	1,722	1,793	70,688	73,089	24,870	3.2	453,814	8.0	45,204
Rockford, IL Metro Area	90	6,368	896	1,207	691	718	15,783	16,807	7,252	-3.4	134,942	6.9	44,519
Rocky Mount, NC Metro Area	34	2,343	372	527	315	373	10,229	10,974	2,745	-8.5	48,269	-2.6	36,681
Rome, GA Metro Area	20	1,628	203	262	256	303	5,505	6,791	2,018	1.9	36,648	7.9	38,873
Sacramento-Roseville-Folsom, CA Metro Area	381	55,169	14,244	14,773	4,200	4,340	235,311	235,575	49,002	10.1	743,106	19.6	53,582
Saginaw, MI Metro Area	46	2,157	1,483	1,608	308	387	9,283	10,203	4,212	-6.3	80,324	8.5	40,741
St. Cloud, MN Metro Area	62	5,479	2,472	2,100	672	704	11,132	11,834	5,384	2.8	100,928	12.9	43,909
St. George, UT Metro Area	31	2,507	591	615	660	614	8,314	6,517	5,076	33.0	50,267	39.6	35,409
St. Joseph, MO-KS Metro Area	49	2,230	643	671	414	456	8,862	9,428	2,806	-13.9	48,854	0.2	42,586
St. Louis, MO-IL Metro Area	895	89,456	28,396	31,214	13,358	14,347	137,317	144,086	70,881	1.3	1,249,653	7.1	51,038
Salem, OR Metro Area	80	6,137	1,419	1,823	1,014	1,091	39,150	39,046	9,717	8.0	121,784	13.7	39,361
Salinas, CA Metro Area	77	9,562	5,169	5,834	4,920	5,953	29,262	25,531	8,754	5.0	113,209	17.5	46,528
Salisbury, MD-DE Metro Area	151	79,846	1,161	1,362	1,895	1,739	22,230	21,512	10,627	2.2	128,997	14.4	38,077
Salt Lake City, UT Metro Area	211	551,719	12,572	13,050	4,981	5,248	97,414	83,957	33,247	12.6	608,961	21.0	50,546
San Angelo, TX Metro Area	31	2,747	1,217	1,419	3,455	3,449	8,040	8,054	2,879	8.1	40,571	10.9	39,287
San Antonio-New Braunfels, TX Metro Area	411	117,382	36,086	34,875	37,484	36,572	134,059	126,809	46,257	14.7	876,237	22.0	44,360
San Diego-Chula Vista-Carlsbad, CA Metro Area	583	91,328	47,693	47,256	100,840	110,957	199,539	180,293	85,077	12.2	1,266,620	15.0	57,617
San Francisco-Oakland-Berkeley, CA Metro Area	1,017	385,397	31,482	36,157	9,046	9,165	290,831	266,911	130,000	10.4	2,167,508	22.6	90,215
Oakland-Berkeley-Livermore, CA Div	495	104,492	13,647	15,819	5,609	5,532	152,395	138,604	64,046	10.5	1,026,993	20.0	70,760
San Francisco-San Mateo-Redwood City, CA Div.	434	268,346	17,123	19,422	2,942	3,004	123,372	114,376	55,884	11.2	1,039,154	26.9	111,757
San Rafael, CA Div	88	12,559	712	916	495	629	15,064	13,931	10,070	5.7	101,361	9.3	66,486
San Jose-Sunnyvale-Santa Clara, CA Metro Area	371	147,719	10,029	10,821	3,382	3,342	88,094	80,978	49,697	10.4	1,068,403	24.7	119,305
San Luis Obispo-Paso Robles, CA Metro Area	70	6,871	553	676	505	451	22,402	19,980	8,402	8.0	91,732	13.9	44,836
Santa Cruz-Watsonville, CA Metro Area	47	6,270	531	548	381	415	19,580	17,739	7,061	4.1	79,038	16.1	47,527
Santa Fe, NM Metro Area	33	3,112	940	1,182	387	387	14,545	17,436	4,759	-0.4	46,842	6.2	39,945
Santa Maria-Santa Barbara, CA Metro Area	96	12,670	3,521	4,138	3,059	3,399	32,525	30,841	11,761	4.9	149,750	11.3	52,892
Santa Rosa-Petaluma, CA Metro Area	119	14,563	1,354	1,796	1,445	1,445	27,264	25,005	14,174	7.5	173,035	21.0	52,031
Savannah, GA Metro Area	93	7,338	2,886	3,235	5,282	7,360	21,464	20,146	9,244	10.3	151,691	20.6	42,534
Scranton--Wilkes-Barre, PA Metro Area	203	12,393	4,261	4,734	1,389	1,508	25,198	27,328	13,149	-1.5	237,277	4.9	40,105
Seattle-Tacoma-Bellevue, WA Metro Area	866	112,179	33,909	37,691	44,415	51,907	248,048	230,168	106,194	9.7	1,726,886	20.3	71,091
Seattle-Bellevue-Kent, WA Div	699	99,820	21,944	24,488	13,411	14,286	200,128	184,114	88,106	9.9	1,469,804	21.3	75,252
Tacoma-Lakewood, WA Div	167	12,359	11,965	13,203	31,004	37,621	47,920	46,054	18,088	9.0	257,082	15.0	47,301
Sebastian-Vero Beach, FL Metro Area	44	4,699	362	388	272	278	4,787	5,242	4,326	11.8	45,434	21.8	38,359
Sebring-Avon Park, FL Metro Area	18	1,507	265	253	182	198	3,835	4,059	1,921	-3.0	20,766	10.4	32,758

Table B-14. Banking, Government Employment, and Private Business Establishments and Employment—*Continued*

Metropolitan Statistical Area Metropolitan Division	Banking 2019		Government Employment						Private nonfarm business				
			Federal civilian		Military		State and Local		Establishments		Employment		Annual payroll per employee 2017 (dollars)
	Number of offices	Deposits (million dollars)	2018	2010	2018	2010	2018	2010	2017	Change 2010-2017 (percent)	2017	Change 2010-2017 (percent)	
Sheboygan, WI Metro Area	37	2,159	203	235	322	341	5,654	5,759	2,659	-0.8	53,151	5.1	46,328
Sherman-Denison, TX Metro Area	41	2,584	337	435	259	276	6,718	6,123	2,561	1.6	39,443	1.5	37,840
Shreveport-Bossier City, LA Metro Area	115	7,474	4,806	4,847	6,634	7,505	23,379	29,990	9,215	0.6	140,406	-4.1	40,397
Sierra Vista-Douglas, AZ Metro Area	18	1,326	4,807	5,554	4,211	5,616	6,108	6,950	2,178	-8.1	24,819	-14.6	36,161
Sioux City, IA-NE-SD Metro Area	77	3,370	847	1,004	537	640	8,540	8,569	3,701	-2.0	67,718	2.8	39,970
Sioux Falls, SD Metro Area	141	673,331	2,714	2,643	1,511	1,516	11,453	10,127	7,827	11.4	143,288	16.7	45,170
South Bend-Mishawaka, IN-MI Metro Area	78	5,117	953	1,265	932	1,003	14,829	16,026	6,592	-1.9	129,862	10.7	41,101
Spartanburg, SC Metro Area	65	5,442	564	570	1,140	1,238	20,270	18,751	6,430	1.5	128,430	18.5	45,922
Spokane-Spokane Valley, WA Metro Area	110	9,132	5,130	5,072	4,410	4,357	34,620	33,747	14,121	6.5	199,588	10.8	45,037
Springfield, IL Metro Area	85	6,279	1,774	2,102	459	452	18,849	20,221	5,213	-2.8	85,368	2.6	41,294
Springfield, MA Metro Area	210	16,777	5,414	5,839	1,777	1,929	52,836	50,529	14,743	-0.7	242,907	1.9	43,461
Springfield, MO Metro Area	189	10,871	2,470	2,665	1,526	1,559	26,436	24,900	11,624	3.6	187,570	14.8	39,630
Springfield, OH Metro Area	35	1,621	561	714	332	355	6,367	6,440	2,238	-8.6	41,243	1.4	36,101
State College, PA Metro Area	55	3,501	480	547	446	449	46,859	45,224	3,361	5.4	46,119	7.1	39,277
Staunton, VA Metro Area	39	1,684	288	314	378	389	8,426	8,478	2,812	0.5	40,023	5.6	38,078
Stockton, CA Metro Area	101	10,861	3,081	4,361	1,146	1,143	40,339	32,388	11,512	6.3	190,958	18.9	44,060
Sumter, SC Metro Area	22	1,247	1,312	1,338	5,756	5,282	7,305	8,152	2,227	-4.6	36,794	10.3	35,116
Syracuse, NY Metro Area	153	12,909	5,039	4,924	1,127	1,347	48,923	51,688	15,252	-0.2	259,742	3.0	44,355
Tallahassee, FL Metro Area	81	8,620	2,076	2,113	691	813	57,569	59,342	9,067	4.4	110,687	6.8	40,254
Tampa-St. Petersburg-Clearwater, FL Metro Area	670	87,122	23,699	23,953	12,149	12,655	124,479	125,782	78,570	13.3	1,120,203	20.2	47,392
Terre Haute, IN Metro Area	63	2,874	1,300	1,472	535	625	12,295	12,760	3,811	-4.6	59,212	-2.3	37,585
Texarkana, TX-AR Metro Area	46	2,455	3,706	5,238	401	464	9,008	9,603	3,138	2.3	48,004	7.3	35,635
The Villages, FL Metro Area	28	2,974	1,638	1,510	210	174	3,102	2,993	1,575	38.5	22,470	57.6	37,753
Toledo, OH Metro Area	193	12,303	2,422	2,662	1,735	1,770	44,161	45,356	14,444	-1.5	275,095	6.1	44,904
Topeka, KS Metro Area	106	5,394	3,667	3,911	942	1,283	23,161	25,348	5,146	-4.7	85,514	-0.7	43,724
Trenton-Princeton, NJ Metro Area	139	17,429	2,253	2,502	720	766	37,656	42,321	9,732	-0.2	196,384	11.7	68,407
Tucson, AZ Metro Area	161	15,574	12,858	12,756	8,095	8,656	68,229	68,138	20,300	-0.1	320,502	6.4	41,905
Tulsa, OK Metro Area	280	26,636	4,739	5,121	3,628	4,031	48,912	49,929	24,510	1.8	401,196	9.1	47,411
Tuscaloosa, AL Metro Area	68	4,179	2,029	2,058	1,017	1,125	25,962	24,429	4,644	0.9	85,304	12.1	40,840
Twin Falls, ID Metro Area	35	1,694	440	501	347	384	5,967	5,341	3,223	5.6	37,498	16.4	33,963
Tyler, TX Metro Area	85	6,292	623	910	472	481	13,545	12,168	5,822	7.0	89,833	5.4	41,667
Urban Honolulu, HI Metro Area	181	36,270	31,078	31,825	52,011	53,162	68,777	67,001	21,628	0.2	366,570	9.1	46,945
Utica-Rome, NY Metro Area	71	4,474	2,418	3,012	496	542	27,978	29,910	6,029	-0.7	100,149	0.4	39,596
Valdosta, GA Metro Area	43	2,333	1,197	1,170	4,837	5,049	11,740	11,829	3,127	3.6	44,264	10.2	33,279
Vallejo, CA Metro Area	56	4,914	3,596	4,685	7,075	7,379	22,148	20,579	7,079	5.0	111,931	14.2	51,136
Victoria, TX Metro Area	25	2,194	198	435	201	222	6,692	6,852	2,434	2.9	33,922	8.1	43,066
Vineland-Bridgeton, NJ Metro Area	30	2,698	601	713	281	305	11,967	13,813	2,815	-5.2	47,231	4.9	39,809
Virginia Beach-Norfolk-Newport News, VA-NC Metro Area	307	26,275	58,287	50,346	81,626	95,421	107,630	113,211	38,430	0.4	621,229	3.4	42,640
Visalia, CA Metro Area	55	5,285	1,065	1,498	677	722	32,011	30,015	6,413	4.5	96,618	13.1	39,422
Waco, TX Metro Area	70	5,483	3,168	3,750	619	625	15,743	15,629	5,525	7.2	105,047	8.3	38,623
Walla Walla, WA Metro Area	19	1,273	1,375	1,262	147	174	4,452	4,509	1,385	0.2	20,322	3.2	39,598
Warner Robins, GA Metro Area	31	1,895	15,454	16,207	3,795	4,390	11,772	11,481	3,017	7.9	45,297	13.7	34,810
Washington-Arlington-Alexandria, DC-VA-MD-WV Metro Area	1,491	261,391	379,245	395,669	64,853	72,567	337,776	308,104	154,605	8.6	2,676,308	12.2	66,024
Frederick-Gaithersburg-Rockville, MD Div	349	47,646	51,343	52,179	9,732	8,270	55,599	51,093	33,674	4.5	529,923	10.1	61,143
Washington-Arlington-Alexandria, DC-VA-MD-WV Div	1,142	213,745	327,902	343,490	55,121	64,297	282,177	257,011	120,931	9.7	2,146,385	12.7	67,230
Waterloo-Cedar Falls, IA Metro Area	64	3,855	617	713	613	698	13,702	14,348	4,100	-0.8	75,798	0.8	41,548
Watertown-Fort Drum, NY Metro Area	34	1,624	3,216	3,762	14,961	18,927	8,314	8,313	2,444	-2.1	29,772	-0.7	36,967
Wausau-Weston, WI Metro Area	63	3,848	454	621	421	462	9,333	9,295	4,082	-0.8	73,859	9.9	42,541
Weirton-Steubenville, WV-OH Metro Area	39	1,860	252	392	396	452	5,460	5,773	2,190	-7.2	33,975	-8.5	37,464
Wenatchee, WA Metro Area	34	2,721	847	950	301	348	8,664	7,869	3,381	8.9	37,026	15.4	41,733
Wheeling, WV-OH Metro Area	59	3,800	595	745	490	570	8,618	9,617	3,304	-4.5	54,735	1.1	41,270
Wichita, KS Metro Area	232	15,907	5,035	6,362	5,162	5,391	37,483	36,079	14,811	0.7	261,264	2.2	44,430
Wichita Falls, TX Metro Area	44	2,687	1,888	2,304	6,146	7,104	10,327	10,837	3,424	-3.1	46,665	-1.4	35,663
Williamsport, PA Metro Area	47	2,506	370	544	278	301	8,719	9,402	2,731	-4.3	43,915		39,257
Wilmington, NC Metro Area	70	9,041	1,121	1,216	867	795	22,819	20,064	8,639	13.6	108,659	22.2	41,195
Winchester, VA-WV Metro Area	48	2,773	2,309	1,623	485	479	8,038	7,084	3,232	5.3	55,560	25.0	40,475
Winston-Salem, NC Metro Area	145	35,605	2,018	2,208	1,493	1,584	29,487	30,828	13,488	2.9	237,640	12.6	46,067
Worcester, MA-CT Metro Area	244	18,929	3,288	3,154	2,120	2,306	57,813	56,559	20,570	4.0	337,022	14.1	49,339
Yakima, WA Metro Area	50	3,388	1,243	1,383	736	844	17,068	16,096	4,765	1.7	70,083	12.3	40,427
York-Hanover, PA Metro Area	129	7,658	4,336	4,791	1,297	1,609	15,938	16,987	8,689	1.3	167,130	9.8	43,550
Youngstown-Warren-Boardman, OH-PA Metro Area	160	10,524	1,966	2,290	1,359	1,452	27,592	29,346	12,205	-5.0	192,993	-2.1	36,959
Yuba City, CA Metro Area	23	2,336	1,608	1,611	4,049	3,704	9,990	9,814	2,599	3.0	32,176	11.2	43,001
Yuma, AZ Metro Area	24	1,977	3,578	3,912	4,643	4,264	10,755	10,752	3,037	3.1	45,094	11.0	33,226

PART C

METROPOLITAN COUNTIES

185

Table C-1. Population and Population Characteristics

Metropolitan Statistical Area Metropolitan Division Component Counties	Population							Percent in each age group, 2018				Percent female
	2018 Estimate (July 1)	2010 census estimates base (April 1)	2000 census estimates base (April 1)	Net change		Percent change		Under 15 years	15 to 44 years	45 to 64 years	65 years and over	
				2010-2018	2000-2010	2010-2018	2000-2010					
Abilene, TX Metro Area	171,451	165,246	160,245	6,205	5,001	3.8	3.1	19.9	43.3	21.8	15.0	49.5
Callahan, TX	13,994	13,546	12,905	448	641	3.3	5.0	18.4	33.7	27.4	20.5	50.5
Jones, TX	19,817	20,192	20,785	-375	-593	-1.9	-2.9	14.1	44.9	25.4	15.6	37.3
Taylor, TX	137,640	131,508	126,555	6,132	4,953	4.7	3.9	21.0	44.0	20.7	14.4	51.2
Akron, OH Metro Area	704,845	703,203	694,960	1,642	8,243	0.2	1.2	16.7	38.3	27.4	17.6	51.4
Portage, OH	162,927	161,425	152,061	1,502	9,364	0.9	6.2	15.2	41.7	26.7	16.4	50.9
Summit, OH	541,918	541,778	542,899	140	-1,121	0.0	-0.2	17.1	37.3	27.6	17.9	51.5
Albany, GA Metro Area	149,917	154,042	153,759	-4,125	283	-2.7	0.2	19.7	40.3	24.4	15.6	52.9
Dougherty, GA	91,243	94,562	96,065	-3,319	-1,503	-3.5	-1.6	19.4	42.2	23.0	15.4	54.1
Lee, GA	29,764	28,298	24,757	1,466	3,541	5.2	14.3	21.3	40.1	25.9	12.6	49.9
Terrell, GA	8,611	9,507	10,970	-896	-1,463	-9.4	-13.3	19.2	34.9	26.1	19.8	52.1
Worth, GA	20,299	21,675	21,967	-1,376	-292	-6.3	-1.3	18.5	34.6	27.9	19.1	52.0
Albany-Lebanon, OR Metro Area	127,335	116,676	103,069	10,659	13,607	9.1	13.2	18.7	37.1	25.6	18.6	50.6
Linn, OR	127,335	116,676	103,069	10,659	13,607	9.1	13.2	18.7	37.1	25.6	18.6	50.6
Albany-Schenectady-Troy, NY Metro Area	883,169	870,714	825,875	12,455	44,839	1.4	5.4	16.0	39.4	27.1	17.5	51.0
Albany, NY	307,117	304,208	294,565	2,909	9,643	1.0	3.3	15.1	42.7	25.3	17.0	51.6
Rensselaer, NY	159,442	159,433	152,538	9	6,895	0.0	4.5	16.1	39.4	27.5	17.0	50.6
Saratoga, NY	230,163	219,593	200,635	10,570	18,958	4.8	9.4	16.3	36.4	29.2	18.1	50.5
Schenectady, NY	155,350	154,751	146,555	599	8,196	0.4	5.6	17.8	38.2	26.9	17.1	51.3
Schoharie, NY	31,097	32,729	31,582	-1,632	1,147	-5.0	3.6	14.1	34.8	29.2	21.9	49.8
Albuquerque, NM Metro Area	915,927	887,064	729,649	28,863	157,415	3.3	21.6	18.2	39.7	25.4	16.8	50.8
Bernalillo, NM	678,701	662,487	556,678	16,214	105,809	2.4	19.0	17.9	40.7	25.0	16.4	50.9
Sandoval, NM	145,179	131,620	89,908	13,559	41,712	10.3	46.4	19.0	37.0	26.3	17.7	51.0
Torrance, NM	15,591	16,375	16,911	-784	-536	-4.8	-3.2	16.8	35.2	27.3	20.7	47.0
Valencia, NM	76,456	76,582	66,152	-126	10,430	-0.2	15.8	19.3	37.0	26.1	17.7	49.8
Alexandria, LA Metro Area	153,044	153,918	145,035	-874	8,883	-0.6	6.1	20.1	38.7	25.0	16.2	50.5
Grant, LA	22,482	22,309	18,698	173	3,611	0.8	19.3	17.7	42.7	24.3	15.2	44.1
Rapides, LA	130,562	131,609	126,337	-1,047	5,272	-0.8	4.2	20.6	38.0	25.1	16.4	51.6
Allentown-Bethlehem-Easton, PA-NJ Metro Area	842,913	821,267	740,395	21,646	80,872	2.6	10.9	17.1	37.2	27.5	18.1	50.9
Warren, NJ	105,779	108,645	102,437	-2,866	6,208	-2.6	6.1	15.7	34.9	31.3	18.2	51.0
Carbon, PA	64,227	65,252	58,802	-1,025	6,450	-1.6	11.0	15.7	32.7	30.4	21.2	50.1
Lehigh, PA	368,100	349,676	312,090	18,424	37,586	5.3	12.0	18.6	38.8	25.9	16.7	51.0
Northampton, PA	304,807	297,694	267,066	7,113	30,628	2.4	11.5	16.2	37.2	27.6	19.0	50.8
Altoona, PA Metro Area	122,492	127,116	129,144	-4,624	-2,028	-3.6	-1.6	16.9	34.9	27.4	20.8	51.0
Blair, PA	122,492	127,116	129,144	-4,624	-2,028	-3.6	-1.6	16.9	34.9	27.4	20.8	51.0
Amarillo, TX Metro Area	265,947	251,937	228,707	14,010	23,230	5.6	10.2	21.4	41.4	23.2	14.1	49.7
Armstrong, TX	1,892	1,901	2,148	-9	-247	-0.5	-11.5	19.6	30.6	25.8	23.9	51.5
Carson, TX	6,005	6,186	6,516	-181	-330	-2.9	-5.1	19.4	35.1	25.9	19.5	49.9
Oldham, TX	2,131	2,052	2,185	79	-133	3.8	-6.1	16.9	40.3	27.8	15.0	48.0
Potter, TX	119,648	121,078	113,546	-1,430	7,532	-1.2	6.6	23.3	41.4	22.8	12.5	48.5
Randall, TX	136,271	120,720	104,312	15,551	16,408	12.9	15.7	19.9	41.7	23.3	15.1	50.8
Ames, IA Metro Area	124,451	115,850	106,205	8,601	9,645	7.4	9.1	14.4	52.5	19.7	13.4	48.1
Boone, IA	26,346	26,308	26,224	38	84	0.1	0.3	17.1	36.4	28.1	18.4	49.5
Story, IA	98,105	89,542	79,981	8,563	9,561	9.6	12.0	13.7	56.8	17.5	12.0	47.8
Anchorage, AK Metro Area	399,148	380,821	319,605	18,327	61,216	4.8	19.2	21.1	43.1	24.5	11.3	48.8
Anchorage, AK	291,538	291,829	260,283	-291	31,546	-0.1	12.1	20.6	44.2	24.2	11.1	49.1
Matanuska-Susitna, AK	107,610	88,992	59,322	18,618	29,670	20.9	50.0	22.4	40.2	25.5	11.9	48.1
Ann Arbor, MI Metro Area	370,963	345,104	322,895	25,859	22,209	7.5	6.9	15.3	48.0	22.9	13.8	50.4
Washtenaw, MI	370,963	345,104	322,895	25,859	22,209	7.5	6.9	15.3	48.0	22.9	13.8	50.4
Anniston-Oxford, AL Metro Area	114,277	118,594	112,249	-4,317	6,345	-3.6	5.7	17.8	38.0	26.5	17.7	51.9
Calhoun, AL	114,277	118,594	112,249	-4,317	6,345	-3.6	5.7	17.8	38.0	26.5	17.7	51.9
Appleton, WI Metro Area	237,524	225,664	201,602	11,860	24,062	5.3	11.9	19.4	38.4	27.4	14.8	49.9
Calumet, WI	50,159	48,973	40,631	1,186	8,342	2.4	20.5	19.4	36.3	29.2	15.1	49.6
Outagamie, WI	187,365	176,691	160,971	10,674	15,720	6.0	9.8	19.4	39.0	26.9	14.7	50.0
Asheville, NC Metro Area	459,585	424,859	369,171	34,726	55,688	8.2	15.1	15.2	35.4	27.1	22.2	51.9
Buncombe, NC	259,103	238,331	206,330	20,772	32,001	8.7	15.5	15.2	38.1	26.6	20.0	52.1
Haywood, NC	61,971	59,031	54,033	2,940	4,998	5.0	9.2	15.0	31.9	28.5	24.6	51.7
Henderson, NC	116,748	106,713	89,173	10,035	17,540	9.4	19.7	15.5	31.3	27.4	25.8	52.0
Madison, NC	21,763	20,784	19,635	979	1,149	4.7	5.9	14.5	35.8	27.4	22.3	50.7
Athens-Clarke County, GA Metro Area	211,306	192,564	166,079	18,742	26,485	9.7	15.9	16.8	48.1	22.0	13.1	51.9
Clarke, GA	127,330	116,697	101,489	10,633	15,208	9.1	15.0	14.8	56.2	18.1	11.0	52.6
Madison, GA	29,650	28,160	25,730	1,490	2,430	5.3	9.4	19.0	36.2	27.8	17.0	50.6
Oconee, GA	39,272	32,831	26,225	6,441	6,606	19.6	25.2	21.4	36.0	27.5	15.2	50.9
Oglethorpe, GA	15,054	14,876	12,635	178	2,241	1.2	17.7	17.1	35.2	28.8	18.9	50.6
Atlanta-Sandy Springs-Alpharetta, GA Metro Area	5,949,951	5,286,750	4,263,438	663,201	1,023,312	12.5	24.0	20.1	41.5	26.1	12.3	51.7
Barrow, GA	80,809	69,355	46,144	11,454	23,211	16.5	50.3	21.7	41.0	24.9	12.4	51.0
Bartow, GA	106,408	100,128	76,019	6,280	24,109	6.3	31.7	19.9	38.8	27.4	14.0	50.7
Butts, GA	24,193	23,667	19,522	526	4,145	2.2	21.2	17.4	40.4	26.7	15.5	47.2
Carroll, GA	118,121	110,580	87,268	7,541	23,312	6.8	26.7	19.5	42.6	24.3	13.6	51.2
Cherokee, GA	254,149	214,372	141,903	39,777	72,469	18.6	51.1	19.9	38.4	27.8	13.9	50.8
Clayton, GA	289,615	259,580	236,517	30,035	23,063	11.6	9.8	23.3	43.2	24.1	9.3	53.2
Cobb, GA	756,865	688,071	607,751	68,794	80,320	10.0	13.2	19.4	41.9	26.4	12.3	51.6
Coweta, GA	145,864	127,353	89,215	18,511	38,138	14.5	42.7	20.0	38.3	27.9	13.9	51.3
Dawson, GA	25,083	22,337	15,999	2,746	6,338	12.3	39.6	16.9	34.4	28.5	20.1	50.6
De Kalb, GA	756,558	691,971	665,865	64,587	26,106	9.3	3.9	19.6	43.1	24.9	12.4	52.7
Douglas, GA	145,331	132,305	92,174	13,026	40,131	9.8	43.5	21.0	40.6	26.9	11.5	52.5

Table C-1. Population and Population Characteristics—Continued

Metropolitan Statistical Area Metropolitan Division Component Counties	Population							Percent in each age group, 2018				Percent female
	2018 Estimate (July 1)	2010 census estimates base (April 1)	2000 census estimates base (April 1)	Net change		Percent change		Under 15 years	15 to 44 years	45 to 64 years	65 years and over	
				2010-2018	2000-2010	2010-2018	2000-2010					
Fayette, GA	113,459	106,564	91,263	6,895	15,301	6.5	16.8	17.9	34.1	29.8	18.2	51.5
Forsyth, GA	236,612	175,511	98,407	61,101	77,104	34.8	78.4	22.3	38.3	27.4	12.0	50.4
Fulton, GA	1,050,114	920,441	816,006	129,673	104,435	14.1	12.8	18.1	45.1	25.1	11.7	51.6
Gwinnett, GA	927,781	805,326	588,448	122,455	216,878	15.2	36.9	22.0	41.7	26.3	10.1	51.2
Haralson, GA	29,533	28,777	25,690	756	3,087	2.6	12.0	19.6	37.2	27.1	16.2	51.5
Heard, GA	11,879	11,825	11,012	54	813	0.5	7.4	18.6	36.0	28.0	17.5	50.2
Henry, GA	230,220	203,830	119,341	26,390	84,489	12.9	70.8	20.4	40.4	27.5	11.6	52.3
Jasper, GA	14,040	13,898	11,426	142	2,472	1.0	21.6	19.5	34.5	28.5	17.5	51.1
Lamar, GA	19,000	18,310	15,912	690	2,398	3.8	15.1	17.1	40.6	25.3	17.0	51.8
Meriwether, GA	21,068	21,983	22,534	-915	-551	-4.2	-2.4	17.8	34.3	27.5	20.4	52.1
Morgan, GA	18,853	17,863	15,457	990	2,406	5.5	15.6	18.6	33.3	28.0	20.0	51.9
Newton, GA	109,541	99,984	62,001	9,557	37,983	9.6	61.3	21.2	39.9	26.0	13.0	52.8
Paulding, GA	164,044	142,379	81,678	21,665	60,701	15.2	74.3	21.3	41.2	27.0	10.6	51.3
Pickens, GA	31,980	29,425	22,983	2,555	6,442	8.7	28.0	16.3	33.2	28.7	21.9	50.9
Pike, GA	18,634	17,874	13,688	760	4,186	4.3	30.6	18.5	37.4	28.2	15.9	50.8
Rockdale, GA	90,594	85,176	70,111	5,418	15,065	6.4	21.5	20.0	37.6	28.0	14.4	53.0
Spalding, GA	66,100	64,098	58,417	2,002	5,681	3.1	9.7	19.7	37.1	25.3	17.9	52.0
Walton, GA	93,503	83,767	60,687	9,736	23,080	11.6	38.0	20.1	37.7	26.7	15.5	51.3
Atlantic City-Hammonton, NJ Metro Area	265,429	274,521	252,552	-9,092	21,969	-3.3	8.7	17.4	35.9	28.7	17.9	51.6
Atlantic, NJ	265,429	274,521	252,552	-9,092	21,969	-3.3	8.7	17.4	35.9	28.7	17.9	51.6
Auburn-Opelika, AL Metro Area	163,941	140,300	115,092	23,641	25,208	16.9	21.9	17.8	47.7	22.6	11.9	50.8
Lee, AL	163,941	140,300	115,092	23,641	25,208	16.9	21.9	17.8	47.7	22.6	11.9	50.8
Augusta-Richmond County, GA-SC Metro Area	604,167	564,873	508,032	39,294	56,841	7.0	11.2	19.2	39.5	25.4	15.9	51.4
Burke, GA	22,423	23,311	22,243	-888	1,068	-3.8	4.8	21.4	36.3	26.6	15.6	52.4
Columbia, GA	154,291	124,041	89,288	30,250	34,753	24.4	38.9	20.9	40.4	25.2	13.5	51.2
Lincoln, GA	7,915	7,996	8,348	-81	-352	-1.0	-4.2	15.8	31.5	28.9	23.8	51.5
McDuffie, GA	21,531	21,867	21,231	-336	636	-1.5	3.0	21.0	35.1	26.4	17.5	53.2
Richmond, GA	201,554	200,569	199,775	985	794	0.5	0.4	19.2	43.2	23.6	14.1	51.6
Aiken, SC	169,401	160,114	142,552	9,287	17,562	5.8	12.3	18.0	35.8	26.9	19.4	51.7
Edgefield, SC	27,052	26,975	24,595	77	2,380	0.3	9.7	14.4	38.2	28.6	18.8	46.3
Austin-Round Rock-Georgetown, TX Metro Area	2,168,316	1,716,321	1,249,763	451,995	466,558	26.3	37.3	19.3	46.4	23.4	10.9	49.9
Bastrop, TX	86,976	74,202	57,733	12,774	16,469	17.2	28.5	21.0	37.1	26.8	15.2	49.1
Caldwell, TX	43,247	38,057	32,194	5,190	5,863	13.6	18.2	19.3	41.7	24.6	14.4	49.5
Hays, TX	222,631	157,099	97,589	65,532	59,510	41.7	61.0	19.2	48.3	21.5	11.0	50.3
Travis, TX	1,248,743	1,024,462	812,280	224,281	212,182	21.9	26.1	18.3	48.7	23.2	9.9	49.4
Williamson, TX	566,719	422,501	249,967	144,218	172,534	34.1	69.0	21.2	42.6	24.0	12.2	50.8
Bakersfield, CA Metro Area	896,764	839,619	661,645	57,145	177,974	6.8	26.9	24.3	43.1	21.7	11.0	48.7
Kern, CA	896,764	839,619	661,645	57,145	177,974	6.8	26.9	24.3	43.1	21.7	11.0	48.7
Baltimore-Columbia-Towson, MD Metro Area	2,802,789	2,710,602	2,552,994	92,187	157,608	3.4	6.2	18.2	39.6	26.7	15.5	51.8
Anne Arundel, MD	576,031	537,631	489,656	38,400	47,975	7.1	9.8	18.6	39.8	26.9	14.7	50.5
Baltimore, MD	828,431	805,229	754,292	23,202	50,937	2.9	6.8	18.0	38.4	26.5	17.2	52.6
Carroll, MD	168,429	167,142	150,897	1,287	16,245	0.8	10.8	17.5	35.6	30.1	16.8	50.5
Harford, MD	253,956	244,826	218,590	9,130	26,236	3.7	12.0	18.1	37.1	28.6	16.2	51.0
Howard, MD	323,196	287,123	247,842	36,073	39,281	12.6	15.8	19.9	38.8	27.5	13.8	51.1
Queen Anne's, MD	50,251	47,789	40,563	2,462	7,226	5.2	17.8	17.4	32.8	31.0	18.8	50.4
Baltimore city, MD	602,495	620,862	651,154	-18,367	-30,292	-3.0	-4.7	17.4	44.2	24.3	14.0	53.1
Bangor, ME Metro Area	151,096	153,932	144,919	-2,836	9,013	-1.8	6.2	14.9	38.1	28.4	18.7	50.5
Penobscot, ME	151,096	153,932	144,919	-2,836	9,013	-1.8	6.2	14.9	38.1	28.4	18.7	50.5
Barnstable Town, MA Metro Area	213,413	215,875	222,230	-2,462	-6,355	-1.1	-2.9	12.1	27.6	29.7	30.6	52.2
Barnstable, MA	213,413	215,875	222,230	-2,462	-6,355	-1.1	-2.9	12.1	27.6	29.7	30.6	52.2
Baton Rouge, LA Metro Area	853,610	825,920	729,361	27,690	96,559	3.4	13.2	19.5	41.9	24.4	14.2	51.1
Ascension, LA	124,672	107,215	76,627	17,457	30,588	16.3	39.9	22.3	40.6	25.3	11.8	50.6
Assumption, LA	22,300	23,416	23,388	-1,116	28	-4.8	0.1	17.6	36.3	28.0	18.0	51.5
East Baton Rouge, LA	440,956	440,169	412,852	787	27,317	0.2	6.6	19.0	44.0	22.8	14.2	52.2
East Feliciana, LA	19,305	20,276	21,360	-971	-1,084	-4.8	-5.1	15.1	37.1	30.1	17.7	45.7
Iberville, LA	32,721	33,404	33,320	-683	84	-2.0	0.3	17.0	40.2	27.0	15.8	49.4
Livingston, LA	139,567	128,015	91,814	11,552	36,201	9.0	39.4	21.3	40.5	25.0	13.2	50.7
Pointe Coupee, LA	21,940	22,805	22,763	-865	42	-3.8	0.2	18.0	33.9	27.5	20.6	51.9
St. Helena, LA	10,262	11,207	10,525	-945	682	-8.4	6.5	17.5	35.9	26.7	19.9	51.8
West Baton Rouge, LA	26,427	23,788	21,601	2,639	2,187	11.1	10.1	20.7	40.1	25.6	13.6	50.6
West Feliciana, LA	15,460	15,625	15,111	-165	514	-1.1	3.4	13.5	40.2	31.3	15.0	34.6
Battle Creek, MI Metro Area	134,487	136,148	137,985	-1,661	-1,837	-1.2	-1.3	18.9	36.9	26.3	17.8	51.1
Calhoun, MI	134,487	136,148	137,985	-1,661	-1,837	-1.2	-1.3	18.9	36.9	26.3	17.8	51.1
Bay City, MI Metro Area	103,923	107,773	110,157	-3,850	-2,384	-3.6	-2.2	16.5	35.1	28.0	20.4	50.9
Bay, MI	103,923	107,773	110,157	-3,850	-2,384	-3.6	-2.2	16.5	35.1	28.0	20.4	50.9
Beaumont-Port Arthur, TX Metro Area	395,780	388,749	385,090	7,031	3,659	1.8	1.0	20.3	39.5	25.0	15.1	49.4
Hardin, TX	57,207	54,635	48,073	2,572	6,562	4.7	13.7	20.4	36.7	26.2	16.7	50.7
Jefferson, TX	255,001	252,277	252,051	2,724	226	1.1	0.1	20.2	40.8	24.6	14.4	48.7
Orange, TX	83,572	81,837	84,966	1,735	-3,129	2.1	-3.7	20.7	37.5	25.7	16.1	50.4
Beckley, WV Metro Area	117,272	124,914	126,799	-7,642	-1,885	-6.1	-1.5	17.3	35.1	26.8	20.8	49.8
Fayette, WV	43,018	46,049	47,579	-3,031	-1,530	-6.6	-3.2	17.2	33.9	27.9	21.0	49.7
Raleigh, WV	74,254	78,865	79,220	-4,611	-355	-5.8	-0.4	17.4	35.8	26.2	20.6	49.9
Bellingham, WA Metro Area	225,685	201,146	166,814	24,539	34,332	12.2	20.6	16.2	42.7	23.7	17.4	50.5
Whatcom, WA	225,685	201,146	166,814	24,539	34,332	12.2	20.6	16.2	42.7	23.7	17.4	50.5
Bend, OR Metro Area	191,996	157,730	115,367	34,266	42,363	21.7	36.7	16.6	36.5	26.8	20.0	50.5
Deschutes, OR	191,996	157,730	115,367	34,266	42,363	21.7	36.7	16.6	36.5	26.8	20.0	50.5

Table C-1. Population and Population Characteristics—Continued

Metropolitan Statistical Area / Metropolitan Division / Component Counties	Population							Percent in each age group, 2018				Percent female
	2018 Estimate (July 1)	2010 census estimates base (April 1)	2000 census estimates base (April 1)	Net change		Percent change		Under 15 years	15 to 44 years	45 to 64 years	65 years and over	
				2010-2018	2000-2010	2010-2018	2000-2010					
Billings, MT Metro Area	180,385	167,165	147,099	13,220	20,066	7.9	13.6	19.2	37.3	25.7	17.8	50.6
Carbon, MT	10,714	10,078	9,552	636	526	6.3	5.5	14.0	29.5	30.8	25.8	49.4
Stillwater, MT	9,534	9,105	8,195	429	910	4.7	11.1	17.0	30.5	29.8	22.7	48.8
Yellowstone, MT	160,137	147,982	129,352	12,155	18,630	8.2	14.4	19.7	38.2	25.1	16.9	50.8
Binghamton, NY Metro Area	240,219	251,724	252,320	-11,505	-596	-4.6	-0.2	16.1	38.0	26.5	19.3	50.7
Broome, NY	191,659	200,675	200,536	-9,016	139	-4.5	0.1	15.9	39.2	25.9	19.1	50.8
Tioga, NY	48,560	51,049	51,784	-2,489	-735	-4.9	-1.4	17.0	33.4	29.3	20.3	50.3
Birmingham-Hoover, AL Metro Area	1,088,090	1,061,035	981,525	27,055	79,510	2.5	8.1	19.1	38.9	26.0	16.0	52.0
Bibb, AL	22,400	22,920	20,826	-520	2,094	-2.3	10.1	16.9	39.5	27.1	16.5	46.8
Blount, AL	57,840	57,321	51,024	519	6,297	0.9	12.3	19.0	36.0	26.7	18.2	50.7
Chilton, AL	44,153	43,630	39,593	523	4,037	1.2	10.2	19.5	37.2	26.5	16.8	50.9
Jefferson, AL	659,300	658,506	662,047	794	-3,541	0.1	-0.5	19.1	39.7	25.3	15.9	52.7
St. Clair, AL	88,690	83,345	64,742	5,345	18,603	6.4	28.7	18.9	36.9	27.5	16.6	50.4
Shelby, AL	215,707	195,313	143,293	20,394	52,020	10.4	36.3	19.2	38.3	27.2	15.3	51.7
Bismarck, ND Metro Area	128,320	110,625	96,784	17,695	13,841	16.0	14.3	19.8	39.5	24.4	16.3	49.7
Burleigh, ND	95,273	81,308	69,416	13,965	11,892	17.2	17.1	19.7	40.0	24.2	16.1	49.9
Morton, ND	31,095	27,469	25,303	3,626	2,166	13.2	8.6	19.8	38.7	24.7	16.7	49.4
Oliver, ND	1,952	1,848	2,065	104	-217	5.6	-10.5	21.3	29.2	27.4	22.2	47.7
Blacksburg-Christiansburg, VA Metro Area	168,234	162,962	151,272	5,272	11,690	3.2	7.7	13.3	48.6	22.9	15.2	49.2
Giles, VA	16,844	17,286	16,657	-442	629	-2.6	3.8	16.6	33.4	28.2	21.9	50.7
Montgomery, VA	98,985	94,422	83,629	4,563	10,793	4.8	12.9	12.9	54.2	20.4	12.6	48.0
Pulaski, VA	34,066	34,859	35,127	-793	-268	-2.3	-0.8	14.5	32.6	30.0	22.9	50.0
Radford City, VA	18,339	16,395	15,859	1,944	536	11.9	3.4	10.2	62.5	18.1	9.1	53.0
Bloomington, IL Metro Area	172,828	169,577	150,433	3,251	19,144	1.9	12.7	17.8	46.1	22.9	13.2	51.4
McLean, IL	172,828	169,577	150,433	3,251	19,144	1.9	12.7	17.8	46.1	22.9	13.2	51.4
Bloomington, IN Metro Area	167,762	159,536	142,349	8,226	17,187	5.2	12.1	13.4	51.4	21.2	13.9	50.3
Monroe, IN	146,917	137,959	120,563	8,958	17,396	6.5	14.4	12.9	54.0	19.9	13.1	50.3
Owen, IN	20,845	21,577	21,786	-732	-209	-3.4		17.0	33.3	30.4	19.3	50.0
Bloomsburg-Berwick, PA Metro Area	83,696	85,561	82,387	-1,865	3,174	-2.2	3.9	15.1	38.5	26.6	19.9	51.8
Columbia, PA	65,456	67,303	64,151	-1,847	3,152	-2.7	4.9	14.6	39.5	26.4	19.5	51.8
Montour, PA	18,240	18,258	18,236	-18	22	-0.1	0.1	16.9	34.9	27.2	21.0	51.7
Boise City, ID Metro Area	730,426	616,566	464,840	113,860	151,726	18.5	32.6	20.7	40.6	24.1	14.6	50.1
Ada, ID	469,966	392,371	300,904	77,595	91,467	19.8	30.4	19.5	41.3	24.8	14.4	49.9
Boise, ID	7,634	7,028	6,670	606	358	8.6	5.4	13.1	26.9	34.9	25.1	47.9
Canyon, ID	223,499	188,922	131,441	34,577	57,481	18.3	43.7	23.7	40.4	22.1	13.8	50.5
Gem, ID	17,634	16,719	15,181	915	1,538	5.5	10.1	18.7	32.3	27.2	21.9	50.0
Owyhee, ID	11,693	11,526	10,644	167	882	1.4	8.3	21.2	35.6	25.4	17.8	49.0
Boston-Cambridge-Newton, MA-NH Metro Area	4,875,390	4,552,598	4,391,344	322,792	161,254	7.1	3.7	16.2	41.4	26.7	15.7	51.4
Boston, MA Div	2,030,772	1,888,034	1,812,937	142,738	75,097	7.6	4.1	15.9	43.1	25.8	15.2	51.7
Norfolk, MA	705,388	670,907	650,308	34,481	20,599	5.1	3.2	17.0	38.1	28.0	16.9	51.9
Plymouth, MA	518,132	494,937	472,822	23,195	22,115	4.7	4.7	17.3	35.1	29.5	18.1	51.4
Suffolk, MA	807,252	722,190	689,807	85,062	32,383	11.8	4.7	13.9	52.7	21.4	12.0	51.7
Cambridge-Newton-Framingham, MA Div	2,405,352	2,246,204	2,188,815	159,148	57,389	7.1	2.6	16.6	40.6	26.9	15.8	51.3
Essex, MA	790,638	743,081	723,419	47,557	19,662	6.4	2.7	17.4	37.5	28.0	17.0	51.8
Middlesex, MA	1,614,714	1,503,123	1,465,396	111,591	37,727	7.4	2.6	16.3	42.1	26.4	15.3	51.0
Rockingham County-Strafford County, NH Div	439,266	418,360	389,592	20,906	28,768	5.0	7.4	15.5	37.3	30.2	17.1	50.6
Rockingham, NH	309,176	295,211	277,359	13,965	17,852	4.7	6.4	15.6	34.7	31.8	18.0	50.4
Strafford, NH	130,090	123,149	112,233	6,941	10,916	5.6	9.7	15.2	43.4	26.4	15.0	51.0
Boulder, CO Metro Area	326,078	294,561	269,814	31,517	24,747	10.7	9.2	15.5	44.9	25.3	14.3	49.7
Boulder, CO	326,078	294,561	269,814	31,517	24,747	10.7	9.2	15.5	44.9	25.3	14.3	49.7
Bowling Green, KY Metro Area	177,432	158,608	134,976	18,824	23,632	11.9	17.5	18.9	43.1	23.7	14.4	50.8
Allen, KY	21,122	19,968	17,800	1,154	2,168	5.8	12.2	19.0	35.8	27.6	17.6	50.5
Butler, KY	12,772	12,697	13,010	75	-313	0.6	-2.4	18.6	35.1	27.5	18.8	49.8
Edmonson, KY	12,274	12,177	11,644	97	533	0.8	4.6	14.9	36.2	28.2	20.7	49.8
Warren, KY	131,264	113,766	92,522	17,498	21,244	15.4	23.0	19.2	45.7	22.2	12.9	51.1
Bremerton-Silverdale-Port Orchard, WA Metro Area	269,805	251,143	231,969	18,662	19,174	7.4	8.3	17.1	39.6	25.5	17.8	48.9
Kitsap, WA	269,805	251,143	231,969	18,662	19,174	7.4	8.3	17.1	39.6	25.5	17.8	48.9
Bridgeport-Stamford-Norwalk, CT Metro Area	943,823	916,864	882,567	26,959	34,297	2.9	3.9	18.3	37.2	28.7	15.9	51.3
Fairfield, CT	943,823	916,864	882,567	26,959	34,297	2.9	3.9	18.3	37.2	28.7	15.9	51.3
Brownsville-Harlingen, TX Metro Area	423,908	406,215	335,227	17,693	70,988	4.4	21.2	25.0	40.6	20.9	13.5	51.3
Cameron, TX	423,908	406,215	335,227	17,693	70,988	4.4	21.2	25.0	40.6	20.9	13.5	51.3
Brunswick, GA Metro Area	118,456	112,371	93,044	6,085	19,327	5.4	20.8	17.5	34.8	27.2	20.4	52.3
Brantley, GA	18,897	18,414	14,629	483	3,785	2.6	25.9	19.3	36.2	27.9	16.6	50.7
Glynn, GA	85,219	79,625	67,568	5,594	12,057	7.0	17.8	17.7	35.4	26.5	20.2	52.9
McIntosh, GA	14,340	14,332	10,847	8	3,485	0.1	32.1	13.2	29.5	30.6	26.7	51.2
Buffalo-Cheektowaga, NY Metro Area	1,130,152	1,135,614	1,170,111	-5,462	-34,497	-0.5	-2.9	16.5	37.8	27.5	18.2	51.6
Erie, NY	919,719	919,129	950,265	590	-31,136	0.1	-3.3	16.6	38.4	27.1	17.9	51.6
Niagara, NY	210,433	216,485	219,846	-6,052	-3,361	-2.8	-1.5	16.3	35.5	29.1	19.1	51.3
Burlington, NC Metro Area	166,436	151,160	130,800	15,276	20,360	10.1	15.6	18.3	38.3	26.5	16.9	52.6
Alamance, NC	166,436	151,160	130,800	15,276	20,360	10.1	15.6	18.3	38.3	26.5	16.9	52.6
Burlington-South Burlington, VT Metro Area	221,083	211,262	198,889	9,821	12,373	4.6	6.2	15.4	43.0	26.2	15.4	50.8
Chittenden, VT	164,572	156,540	146,571	8,032	9,969	5.1	6.8	14.5	45.4	25.1	15.0	51.0
Franklin, VT	49,421	47,752	45,417	1,669	2,335	3.5	5.1	18.4	36.6	29.0	16.0	50.2
Grand Isle, VT	7,090	6,970	6,901	120	69	1.7	1.0	14.5	31.9	32.8	20.8	49.5
California-Lexington Park, MD Metro Area	112,664	105,143	86,211	7,521	18,932	7.2	22.0	20.0	39.9	27.0	13.1	50.2
St. Mary's, MD	112,664	105,143	86,211	7,521	18,932	7.2	22.0	20.0	39.9	27.0	13.1	50.2

Table C-1. Population and Population Characteristics—*Continued*

Metropolitan Statistical Area Metropolitan Division Component Counties	Population							Percent in each age group, 2018				Percent female
	2018 Estimate (July 1)	2010 census estimates base (April 1)	2000 census estimates base (April 1)	Net change		Percent change		Under 15 years	15 to 44 years	45 to 64 years	65 years and over	
				2010-2018	2000-2010	2010-2018	2000-2010					
Canton-Massillon, OH Metro Area	398,655	404,425	406,934	-5,770	-2,509	-1.4	-0.6	17.5	35.4	27.5	19.6	51.3
Carroll, OH	27,081	28,835	28,836	-1,754	-1	-6.1	0.0	16.9	32.4	29.6	21.1	49.9
Stark, OH	371,574	375,590	378,098	-4,016	-2,508	-1.1	-0.7	17.6	35.6	27.3	19.5	51.4
Cape Coral-Fort Myers, FL Metro Area	754,610	618,754	440,888	135,856	177,866	22.0	40.3	14.5	31.2	25.8	28.6	51.1
Lee, FL	754,610	618,754	440,888	135,856	177,866	22.0	40.3	14.5	31.2	25.8	28.6	51.1
Cape Girardeau, MO-IL Metro Area	96,982	96,274	90,312	708	5,962	0.7	6.6	17.8	39.7	24.8	17.6	51.3
Alexander, IL	6,060	8,238	9,590	-2,178	-1,352	-26.4	-14.1	19.3	30.0	28.8	21.9	51.6
Bollinger, MO	12,169	12,363	12,029	-194	334	-1.6	2.8	17.3	32.8	29.3	20.6	49.7
Cape Girardeau, MO	78,753	75,673	68,693	3,080	6,980	4.1	10.2	17.8	41.5	23.8	16.9	51.5
Carbondale-Marion, IL Metro Area	136,931	139,155	133,786	-2,224	5,369	-1.6	4.0	16.6	41.4	24.2	17.8	49.9
Jackson, IL	57,419	60,209	59,612	-2,790	597	-4.6	1.0	15.0	48.2	21.1	15.7	50.3
Johnson, IL	12,456	12,581	12,878	-125	-297	-1.0	-2.3	15.0	36.2	27.3	21.5	45.4
Williamson, IL	67,056	66,365	61,296	691	5,069	1.0	8.3	18.2	36.6	26.3	19.0	50.3
Carson City, NV Metro Area	55,414	55,274	52,457	140	2,817	0.3	5.4	16.9	35.5	27.2	20.3	48.7
Carson City city, NV	55,414	55,274	52,457	140	2,817	0.3	5.4	16.9	35.5	27.2	20.3	48.7
Casper, WY Metro Area	79,115	75,448	66,533	3,667	8,915	4.9	13.4	20.2	39.5	24.9	15.4	49.6
Natrona, WY	79,115	75,448	66,533	3,667	8,915	4.9	13.4	20.2	39.5	24.9	15.4	49.6
Cedar Rapids, IA Metro Area	272,295	257,943	237,230	14,352	20,713	5.6	8.7	19.1	38.7	25.7	16.4	50.5
Benton, IA	25,642	26,069	25,308	-427	761	-1.6	3.0	19.2	33.5	28.7	18.6	50.1
Jones, IA	20,744	20,636	20,221	108	415	0.5	2.1	17.5	34.4	27.5	20.6	48.3
Linn, IA	225,909	211,238	191,701	14,671	19,537	6.9	10.2	19.3	39.7	25.2	15.8	50.7
Chambersburg-Waynesboro, PA Metro Area	154,835	149,619	129,313	5,216	20,306	3.5	15.7	18.3	35.1	26.9	19.6	50.9
Franklin, PA	154,835	149,619	129,313	5,216	20,306	3.5	15.7	18.3	35.1	26.9	19.6	50.9
Champaign-Urbana, IL Metro Area	226,379	217,806	196,034	8,573	21,772	3.9	11.1	15.8	50.2	20.7	13.3	50.2
Champaign, IL	209,983	201,081	179,669	8,902	21,412	4.4	11.9	15.6	51.4	20.1	12.8	50.2
Piatt, IL	16,396	16,725	16,365	-329	360	-2.0	2.2	18.3	34.4	28.0	19.4	50.4
Charleston, WV Metro Area	260,342	277,983	286,046	-17,641	-8,063	-6.3	-2.8	16.9	34.8	27.9	20.5	51.3
Boone, WV	21,951	24,625	25,535	-2,674	-910	-10.9	-3.6	17.2	34.1	28.7	20.1	50.2
Clay, WV	8,632	9,384	10,330	-752	-946	-8.0	-9.2	18.2	32.6	28.6	20.6	49.5
Jackson, WV	28,706	29,214	28,000	-508	1,214	-1.7	4.3	17.4	33.4	28.8	20.4	50.3
Kanawha, WV	180,454	193,051	200,073	-12,597	-7,022	-6.5	-3.5	16.5	35.3	27.5	20.7	51.8
Lincoln, WV	20,599	21,709	22,108	-1,110	-399	-5.1	-1.8	18.3	33.4	28.8	19.5	50.5
Charleston-North Charleston, SC Metro Area	787,643	664,639	549,033	123,004	115,606	18.5	21.1	18.3	41.1	25.4	15.2	51.2
Berkeley, SC	221,091	178,316	142,651	42,775	35,665	24.0	25.0	20.0	41.1	25.1	13.8	50.3
Charleston, SC	405,905	350,150	309,969	55,755	40,181	15.9	13.0	16.7	41.7	25.2	16.4	51.6
Dorchester, SC	160,647	136,173	96,413	24,474	39,760	18.0	41.2	20.1	39.6	26.3	14.1	51.4
Charlotte-Concord-Gastonia, NC-SC Metro Area	2,594,090	2,243,926	1,742,647	350,164	501,279	15.6	28.8	19.6	40.5	26.3	13.6	51.5
Anson, NC	24,877	26,929	25,275	-2,052	1,654	-7.6	6.5	16.0	38.6	27.0	18.5	48.0
Cabarrus, NC	211,342	178,087	131,063	33,255	47,024	18.7	35.9	21.0	39.4	26.3	13.2	51.3
Gaston, NC	222,846	206,094	190,365	16,752	15,729	8.1	8.3	18.6	37.7	27.7	16.1	51.8
Iredell, NC	178,435	159,451	122,660	18,984	36,791	11.9	30.0	18.7	36.8	28.7	15.9	50.8
Lincoln, NC	83,770	77,985	63,780	5,785	14,205	7.4	22.3	17.1	34.5	30.7	17.7	50.3
Mecklenburg, NC	1,093,901	919,668	695,454	174,233	224,214	18.9	32.2	19.7	44.6	24.5	11.2	51.9
Rowan, NC	141,262	138,532	130,340	2,730	8,192	2.0	6.3	18.2	36.7	27.6	17.6	50.6
Union, NC	235,908	201,334	123,677	34,574	77,657	17.2	62.8	21.4	37.7	28.2	12.7	50.8
Chester, SC	32,251	33,147	34,068	-896	-921	-2.7	-2.7	18.6	34.5	28.2	18.8	51.8
Lancaster, SC	95,380	76,653	61,351	18,727	15,302	24.4	24.9	18.5	35.0	25.5	21.0	51.5
York, SC	274,118	226,046	164,614	48,072	61,432	21.3	37.3	20.1	38.8	26.9	14.3	51.8
Charlottesville, VA Metro Area	218,233	201,561	174,021	16,672	27,540	8.3	15.8	15.9	41.4	24.9	17.7	52.2
Albemarle, VA	108,718	98,988	79,236	9,730	19,752	9.8	24.9	16.3	40.0	25.0	18.6	52.2
Fluvanna, VA	26,783	25,744	20,047	1,039	5,697	4.0	28.4	16.1	35.3	28.3	20.2	54.3
Greene, VA	19,779	18,389	15,244	1,390	3,145	7.6	20.6	20.0	35.0	27.7	17.4	51.3
Nelson, VA	14,836	15,015	14,445	-179	570	-1.2	3.9	14.2	29.3	29.1	27.3	51.7
Charlottesville City, VA	48,117	43,425	45,049	4,692	-1,624	10.8	-3.6	13.8	54.3	20.3	11.6	51.5
Chattanooga, TN-GA Metro Area	560,793	528,150	476,531	32,643	51,619	6.2	10.8	17.5	37.9	26.6	18.0	51.5
Catoosa, GA	67,420	63,937	53,282	3,483	10,655	5.4	20.0	18.6	36.7	26.9	17.7	51.6
Dade, GA	16,226	16,635	15,154	-409	1,481	-2.5	9.8	15.9	37.8	27.0	19.3	50.9
Walker, GA	69,410	68,749	61,053	661	7,696	1.0	12.6	17.7	36.3	27.4	18.6	50.8
Hamilton, TN	364,286	336,486	307,896	27,800	28,590	8.3	9.3	17.4	38.9	26.1	17.6	51.7
Marion, TN	28,575	28,222	27,776	353	446	1.3	1.6	17.3	34.2	28.4	20.1	51.1
Sequatchie, TN	14,876	14,121	11,370	755	2,751	5.3	24.2	16.8	34.0	28.8	20.4	50.5
Cheyenne, WY Metro Area	98,976	91,885	81,607	7,091	10,278	7.7	12.6	19.5	39.8	24.7	16.0	49.3
Laramie, WY	98,976	91,885	81,607	7,091	10,278	7.7	12.6	19.5	39.8	24.7	16.0	49.3
Chicago-Naperville-Elgin, IL-IN-WI Metro Area .	9,498,716	9,461,539	9,098,316	37,177	363,223	0.4	4.0	18.8	40.7	25.9	14.6	51.0
Chicago-Naperville-Evanston, IL Div	7,160,934	7,148,261	7,080,780	12,673	67,481	0.2	1.0	18.5	41.2	25.7	14.6	51.2
Cook, IL	5,180,493	5,195,026	5,376,741	-14,533	-181,715	-0.3	-3.4	18.2	42.3	24.9	14.6	51.4
Du Page, IL	928,589	916,771	904,161	11,818	12,610	1.3	1.4	18.6	38.3	27.6	15.5	50.9
Grundy, IL	50,972	50,077	37,535	895	12,542	1.8	33.4	20.7	39.1	26.2	14.1	50.1
McHenry, IL	308,570	308,827	260,077	-257	48,750	-0.1	18.7	18.9	36.9	29.6	14.6	50.2
Will, IL	692,310	677,560	502,266	14,750	175,294	2.2	34.9	20.1	39.3	27.5	13.1	50.4
Elgin, IL Div	766,274	735,341	547,632	30,933	187,709	4.2	34.3	20.8	40.7	25.6	13.0	50.3
De Kalb, IL	104,143	105,160	88,969	-1,017	16,191	-1.0	18.2	17.6	47.7	22.0	12.6	50.5
Kane, IL	534,216	515,378	404,119	18,838	111,259	3.7	27.5	20.7	39.0	26.6	13.7	50.2
Kendall, IL	127,915	114,803	54,544	13,112	60,259	11.4	110.5	23.5	42.0	24.3	10.3	50.4
Gary, IN Div	701,386	708,117	675,971	-6,731	32,146	-1.0	4.8	18.8	37.9	26.7	16.6	51.2
Jasper, IN	33,370	33,481	30,043	-111	3,438	-0.3	11.4	18.9	36.9	26.6	17.6	50.3

Table C-1. Population and Population Characteristics—Continued

Metropolitan Statistical Area Metropolitan Division Component Counties	Population							Percent in each age group, 2018				Percent female
	2018 Estimate (July 1)	2010 census estimates base (April 1)	2000 census estimates base (April 1)	Net change		Percent change		Under 15 years	15 to 44 years	45 to 64 years	65 years and over	
				2010-2018	2000-2010	2010-2018	2000-2010					
Lake, IN	484,411	496,095	484,564	-11,684	11,531	-2.4	2.4	19.1	37.8	26.5	16.5	51.6
Newton, IN	14,011	14,239	14,566	-228	-327	-1.6	-2.2	17.3	34.4	28.9	19.5	49.5
Porter, IN	169,594	164,302	146,798	5,292	17,504	3.2	11.9	17.8	38.6	27.2	16.4	50.5
Lake County-Kenosha County, IL-WI Div	870,122	869,820	793,933	302	75,887	0.0	9.6	19.3	38.7	27.7	14.2	50.1
Lake, IL	700,832	703,396	644,356	-2,564	59,040	-0.4	9.2	19.5	38.6	27.7	14.2	50.0
Kenosha, WI	169,290	166,424	149,577	2,866	16,847	1.7	11.3	18.6	39.3	27.9	14.1	50.5
Chico, CA Metro Area	231,256	220,002	203,171	11,254	16,831	5.1	8.3	16.6	41.6	23.2	18.6	50.6
Butte, CA	231,256	220,002	203,171	11,254	16,831	5.1	8.3	16.6	41.6	23.2	18.6	50.6
Cincinnati, OH-KY-IN Metro Area	2,212,945	2,137,755	2,016,981	75,190	120,774	3.5	6.0	19.4	39.1	26.3	15.2	50.9
Dearborn, IN	49,568	50,033	46,109	-465	3,924	-0.9	8.5	18.0	35.1	29.2	17.7	50.3
Franklin, IN	22,736	23,096	22,151	-360	945	-1.6	4.3	18.6	34.4	28.5	18.4	50.0
Ohio, IN	5,844	6,107	5,623	-263	484	-4.3	8.6	15.3	31.3	31.2	22.1	50.5
Union, IN	7,037	7,516	7,349	-479	167	-6.4	2.3	16.5	34.5	29.6	19.4	50.4
Boone, KY	131,533	118,815	85,991	12,718	32,824	10.7	38.2	21.3	38.6	26.5	13.5	50.5
Bracken, KY	8,239	8,488	8,279	-249	209	-2.9	2.5	19.3	34.9	29.1	16.6	49.9
Campbell, KY	93,152	90,338	88,616	2,814	1,722	3.1	1.9	17.2	40.5	26.7	15.6	50.9
Gallatin, KY	8,832	8,586	7,870	246	716	2.9	9.1	20.0	37.5	28.6	14.0	49.4
Grant, KY	25,121	24,658	22,384	463	2,274	1.9	10.2	22.3	37.5	26.5	13.7	49.9
Kenton, KY	166,051	159,723	151,464	6,328	8,259	4.0	5.5	20.0	39.7	25.9	14.4	50.5
Pendleton, KY	14,529	14,875	14,390	-346	485	-2.3	3.4	18.4	35.2	30.3	16.1	49.0
Brown, OH	43,602	44,828	42,285	-1,226	2,543	-2.7	6.0	18.7	34.7	28.6	18.0	50.4
Butler, OH	382,378	368,135	332,807	14,243	35,328	3.9	10.6	19.3	40.3	25.7	14.7	50.9
Clermont, OH	205,466	197,365	177,977	8,101	19,388	4.1	10.9	18.9	36.8	28.0	16.3	50.7
Hamilton, OH	816,684	802,372	845,303	14,312	-42,931	1.8	-5.1	19.3	40.2	25.2	15.3	51.7
Warren, OH	232,173	212,820	158,383	19,353	54,437	9.1	34.4	20.0	37.4	28.1	14.5	49.7
Clarksville, TN-KY Metro Area	305,825	273,943	232,000	31,882	41,943	11.6	18.1	22.5	45.9	20.6	11.1	49.4
Christian, KY	71,671	73,938	72,265	-2,267	1,673	-3.1	2.3	23.4	46.8	17.6	12.3	46.5
Trigg, KY	14,643	14,329	12,597	314	1,732	2.2	13.7	17.9	31.0	28.9	22.3	50.4
Montgomery, TN	205,950	172,363	134,768	33,587	37,595	19.5	27.9	22.9	47.5	20.4	9.2	50.2
Stewart, TN	13,561	13,313	12,370	248	943	1.9	7.6	16.9	33.4	29.4	20.3	50.1
Cleveland, TN Metro Area	123,625	115,754	104,015	7,871	11,739	6.8	11.3	17.6	37.9	26.9	17.6	51.3
Bradley, TN	106,727	98,930	87,965	7,797	10,965	7.9	12.5	17.8	38.6	26.4	17.1	51.4
Polk, TN	16,898	16,824	16,050	74	774	0.4	4.8	15.8	33.4	29.9	21.0	50.7
Cleveland-Elyria, OH Metro Area	2,057,009	2,077,278	2,148,143	-20,269	-70,865	-1.0	-3.3	17.3	36.8	27.4	18.5	51.7
Cuyahoga, OH	1,243,857	1,280,115	1,393,978	-36,258	-113,863	-2.8	-8.2	17.1	38.0	26.7	18.2	52.3
Geauga, OH	94,031	93,409	90,895	622	2,514	0.7	2.8	18.1	32.2	29.3	20.4	50.4
Lake, OH	230,514	230,050	227,511	464	2,539	0.2	1.1	16.2	35.0	28.8	20.0	51.2
Lorain, OH	309,461	301,371	284,664	8,090	16,707	2.7	5.9	18.0	36.0	27.7	18.3	50.8
Medina, OH	179,146	172,333	151,095	6,813	21,238	4.0	14.1	18.0	35.0	29.1	17.9	50.5
Coeur d'Alene, ID Metro Area	161,505	138,466	108,685	23,039	29,781	16.6	27.4	18.9	36.4	25.8	19.0	50.6
Kootenai, ID	161,505	138,466	108,685	23,039	29,781	16.6	27.4	18.9	36.4	25.8	19.0	50.6
College Station-Bryan, TX Metro Area	262,431	228,668	184,885	33,763	43,783	14.8	23.7	17.6	53.1	18.7	10.6	49.6
Brazos, TX	226,758	194,861	152,415	31,897	42,446	16.4	27.8	17.4	56.1	17.4	9.2	49.5
Burleson, TX	18,389	17,187	16,470	1,202	717	7.0	4.4	18.4	32.9	28.3	20.4	50.8
Robertson, TX	17,284	16,620	16,000	664	620	4.0	3.9	20.2	35.0	25.5	19.3	50.9
Colorado Springs, CO Metro Area	738,939	645,609	537,484	93,330	108,125	14.5	20.1	19.9	43.2	23.8	13.1	49.5
El Paso, CO	713,856	622,250	516,929	91,606	105,321	14.7	20.4	20.1	43.7	23.4	12.8	49.5
Teller, CO	25,083	23,359	20,555	1,724	2,804	7.4	13.6	13.9	28.8	35.3	21.9	49.2
Columbia, MO Metro Area	207,745	190,393	162,336	17,352	28,057	9.1	17.3	17.2	48.0	21.7	13.1	51.1
Boone, MO	180,005	162,645	135,454	17,360	27,191	10.7	20.1	17.1	49.5	21.1	12.3	51.5
Cooper, MO	17,603	17,604	16,670	-1	934	0.0	5.6	17.4	39.2	25.4	17.9	47.8
Howard, MO	10,137	10,144	10,212	-7	-68	-0.1	-0.7	18.2	37.2	25.3	19.3	50.0
Columbia, SC Metro Area	832,666	767,476	647,158	65,190	120,318	8.5	18.6	18.2	41.7	25.2	14.9	51.5
Calhoun, SC	14,520	15,176	15,185	-656	-9	-4.3	-0.1	15.6	31.9	29.3	23.3	52.2
Fairfield, SC	22,402	23,960	23,454	-1,558	506	-6.5	2.2	15.7	32.3	30.3	21.7	52.2
Kershaw, SC	65,592	61,592	52,647	4,000	8,945	6.5	17.0	19.1	35.1	27.5	18.3	51.8
Lexington, SC	295,032	262,429	216,014	32,603	46,415	12.4	21.5	19.1	38.1	27.0	15.8	51.3
Richland, SC	414,576	384,450	320,677	30,126	63,773	7.8	19.9	17.7	46.5	23.0	12.7	51.7
Saluda, SC	20,544	19,869	19,181	675	688	3.4	3.6	18.2	34.6	27.4	19.8	49.3
Columbus, GA-AL Metro Area	317,922	308,455	293,518	9,467	14,937	3.1	5.1	19.9	41.5	24.3	14.3	50.5
Russell, AL	57,781	52,947	49,756	4,834	3,191	9.1	6.4	20.3	39.8	25.5	14.3	52.0
Chattahoochee, GA	10,684	11,267	14,882	-583	-3,615	-5.2	-24.3	19.7	65.1	10.3	4.8	36.0
Harris, GA	34,475	31,998	23,695	2,477	8,303	7.7	35.0	17.1	34.1	30.1	18.8	50.0
Marion, GA	8,351	8,738	7,144	-387	1,594	-4.4	22.3	17.0	32.6	30.4	20.0	50.8
Muscogee, GA	194,160	190,573	186,291	3,587	4,282	1.9	2.3	21.0	42.4	23.2	13.4	51.4
Stewart, GA	6,199	6,058	5,252	141	806	2.3	15.3	10.2	52.7	21.5	15.6	34.0
Talbot, GA	6,272	6,874	6,498	-602	376	-8.8	5.8	13.3	29.7	32.6	24.4	52.1
Columbus, IN Metro Area	82,753	76,786	71,435	5,967	5,351	7.8	7.5	19.9	38.9	24.9	16.3	49.7
Bartholomew, IN	82,753	76,786	71,435	5,967	5,351	7.8	7.5	19.9	38.9	24.9	16.3	49.7
Columbus, OH Metro Area	2,106,541	1,902,007	1,675,013	204,534	226,994	10.8	13.6	19.7	42.2	24.8	13.3	50.8
Delaware, OH	204,826	174,172	109,989	30,654	64,183	17.6	58.4	21.5	37.5	27.3	13.7	50.4
Fairfield, OH	155,782	146,182	122,759	9,600	23,423	6.6	19.1	19.6	37.5	27.1	15.8	50.2
Franklin, OH	1,310,300	1,163,532	1,068,978	146,768	94,554	12.6	8.8	19.7	45.0	23.2	12.0	51.1
Hocking, OH	28,385	29,373	28,241	-988	1,132	-3.4	4.0	17.8	34.5	28.6	19.1	50.4
Licking, OH	175,769	166,482	145,491	9,287	20,991	5.6	14.4	19.1	36.9	27.5	16.4	50.9
Madison, OH	44,413	43,438	40,213	975	3,225	2.2	8.0	16.8	39.5	28.2	15.5	45.8
Morrow, OH	35,112	34,829	31,628	283	3,201	0.8	10.1	18.3	34.9	29.5	17.2	50.2

Table C-1. Population and Population Characteristics—*Continued*

Metropolitan Statistical Area Metropolitan Division Component Counties	2018 Estimate (July 1)	2010 census estimates base (April 1)	2000 census estimates base (April 1)	Net change 2010-2018	Net change 2000-2010	Percent change 2010-2018	Percent change 2000-2010	Under 15 years	15 to 44 years	45 to 64 years	65 years and over	Percent female
Perry, OH	36,033	36,039	34,078	-6	1,961	0.0	5.8	19.3	35.7	28.5	16.5	49.9
Pickaway, OH	58,086	55,680	52,727	2,406	2,953	4.3	5.6	17.4	39.6	27.2	15.7	47.5
Union, OH	57,835	52,280	40,909	5,555	11,371	10.6	27.8	20.4	40.5	26.8	12.3	52.1
Corpus Christi, TX Metro Area	429,158	405,025	380,783	24,133	24,242	6.0	6.4	20.6	41.1	23.8	14.5	50.4
Nueces, TX	362,265	340,223	313,645	22,042	26,578	6.5	8.5	20.3	41.4	23.9	14.4	50.6
San Patricio, TX	66,893	64,802	67,138	2,091	-2,336	3.2	-3.5	22.2	39.4	23.5	15.0	49.7
Corvallis, OR Metro Area	92,101	85,582	78,153	6,519	7,429	7.6	9.5	13.2	49.2	21.3	16.2	49.8
Benton, OR	92,101	85,582	78,153	6,519	7,429	7.6	9.5	13.2	49.2	21.3	16.2	49.8
Crestview-Fort Walton Beach-Destin, FL Metro Area	278,644	235,868	211,099	42,776	24,769	18.1	11.7	18.4	38.6	25.8	17.2	49.4
Okaloosa, FL	207,269	180,825	170,498	26,444	10,327	14.6	6.1	18.8	40.4	24.7	16.0	49.3
Walton, FL	71,375	55,043	40,601	16,332	14,442	29.7	35.6	17.0	33.4	29.0	20.6	49.5
Cumberland, MD-WV Metro Area	97,915	103,245	102,008	-5,330	1,237	-5.2	1.2	14.8	38.2	26.3	20.7	48.5
Allegany, MD	70,975	75,047	74,930	-4,072	117	-5.4	0.2	14.2	39.7	25.8	20.3	47.9
Mineral, WV	26,940	28,198	27,078	-1,258	1,120	-4.5	4.1	16.3	34.4	27.7	21.7	50.2
Dallas-Fort Worth-Arlington, TX Metro Area	7,470,158	6,366,568	5,156,217	1,103,590	1,210,351	17.3	23.5	21.6	42.6	24.6	11.2	50.8
Dallas-Plano-Irving, TX Div	5,007,190	4,228,916	3,445,899	778,274	783,017	18.4	22.7	21.5	43.0	24.5	10.9	50.7
Collin, TX	1,005,146	782,220	491,675	222,926	290,545	28.5	59.1	21.2	41.6	26.2	11.0	50.8
Dallas, TX	2,637,772	2,366,683	2,218,899	271,089	147,784	11.5	6.7	21.9	44.0	23.3	10.7	50.6
Denton, TX	859,064	662,554	432,976	196,510	229,578	29.7	53.0	20.3	43.8	25.7	10.2	50.8
Ellis, TX	179,436	149,604	111,360	29,832	38,244	19.9	34.3	21.9	39.8	25.5	12.8	50.7
Hunt, TX	96,493	86,162	76,596	10,331	9,566	12.0	12.5	19.8	38.3	26.1	15.8	50.7
Kaufman, TX	128,622	103,363	71,313	25,259	32,050	24.4	44.9	23.0	40.5	24.6	11.9	50.7
Rockwall, TX	100,657	78,330	43,080	22,327	35,250	28.5	81.8	22.0	39.1	26.4	12.5	50.6
Fort Worth-Arlington-Grapevine, TX Div	2,462,968	2,137,652	1,710,318	325,316	427,334	15.2	25.0	21.7	41.7	24.7	11.8	50.9
Johnson, TX	171,361	150,940	126,811	20,421	24,129	13.5	19.0	21.5	39.0	25.4	14.1	50.1
Parker, TX	138,371	116,957	88,495	21,414	28,462	18.3	32.2	20.4	36.5	27.6	15.4	50.2
Tarrant, TX	2,084,931	1,810,655	1,446,219	274,276	364,436	15.1	25.2	21.9	42.4	24.4	11.3	51.1
Wise, TX	68,305	59,100	48,793	9,205	10,307	15.6	21.1	20.4	37.0	27.7	14.9	50.0
Dalton, GA Metro Area	143,983	142,221	120,031	1,762	22,190	1.2	18.5	21.0	39.2	25.5	14.3	50.4
Murray, GA	39,921	39,628	36,506	293	3,122	0.7	8.6	20.4	37.7	27.1	14.9	50.8
Whitfield, GA	104,062	102,593	83,525	1,469	19,068	1.4	22.8	21.3	39.8	24.9	14.0	50.2
Danville, IL Metro Area	76,806	81,625	83,919	-4,819	-2,294	-5.9	-2.7	19.7	35.1	25.9	19.3	50.2
Vermilion, IL	76,806	81,625	83,919	-4,819	-2,294	-5.9	-2.7	19.7	35.1	25.9	19.3	50.2
Daphne-Fairhope-Foley, AL Metro Area	218,022	182,264	140,415	35,758	41,849	19.6	29.8	17.8	34.2	27.6	20.4	51.5
Baldwin, AL	218,022	182,264	140,415	35,758	41,849	19.6	29.8	17.8	34.2	27.6	20.4	51.5
Davenport-Moline-Rock Island, IA-IL Metro Area	381,451	379,688	376,019	1,763	3,669	0.5	1.0	19.1	36.9	25.9	18.1	50.7
Henry, IL	49,090	50,485	51,020	-1,395	-535	-2.8		18.3	34.2	27.2	20.3	50.2
Mercer, IL	15,601	16,434	16,957	-833	-523	-5.1	-3.1	17.2	33.1	28.0	21.7	50.1
Rock Island, IL	143,477	147,546	149,374	-4,069	-1,828	-2.8	-1.2	18.7	36.6	25.5	19.3	50.7
Scott, IA	173,283	165,223	158,668	8,060	6,555	4.9	4.1	19.8	38.3	25.7	16.2	51.0
Dayton-Kettering, OH Metro Area	806,548	799,268	805,816	7,280	-6,548	0.9	-0.8	18.1	38.1	25.9	17.9	51.5
Greene, OH	167,995	161,576	147,886	6,419	13,690	4.0	9.3	17.1	40.2	25.6	17.2	50.7
Miami, OH	106,222	102,501	98,868	3,721	3,633	3.6	3.7	18.8	35.4	27.2	18.6	50.7
Montgomery, OH	532,331	535,191	559,062	-2,860	-23,871	-0.5	-4.3	18.3	38.0	25.7	18.0	51.8
Decatur, AL Metro Area	152,046	153,825	145,867	-1,779	7,958	-1.2	5.5	18.6	35.9	27.8	17.7	50.9
Lawrence, AL	32,957	34,339	34,803	-1,382	-464	-4.0	-1.3	17.8	34.5	29.1	18.7	51.3
Morgan, AL	119,089	119,486	111,064	-397	8,422	-0.3	7.6	18.8	36.3	27.4	17.5	50.7
Decatur, IL Metro Area	104,712	110,775	114,706	-6,063	-3,931	-5.5	-3.4	18.4	35.8	25.7	20.0	52.1
Macon, IL	104,712	110,775	114,706	-6,063	-3,931	-5.5	-3.4	18.4	35.8	25.7	20.0	52.1
Deltona-Daytona Beach-Ormond Beach, FL Metro Area	659,605	590,299	493,175	69,306	97,124	11.7	19.7	14.4	32.5	27.6	25.5	51.3
Flagler, FL	112,067	95,703	49,832	16,364	45,871	17.1	92.1	13.5	28.0	27.7	30.7	51.9
Volusia, FL	547,538	494,596	443,343	52,942	51,253	10.7	11.6	14.6	33.4	27.6	24.4	51.2
Denver-Aurora-Lakewood, CO Metro Area	2,932,415	2,543,602	2,179,240	388,813	364,362	15.3	16.7	18.7	43.4	25.0	13.0	50.0
Adams, CO	511,868	441,698	348,618	70,170	93,080	15.9	26.7	22.1	44.2	23.2	10.5	49.5
Arapahoe, CO	651,215	572,130	487,967	79,085	84,163	13.8	17.2	19.5	42.3	25.2	13.1	50.4
Broomfield, CO	69,267	55,856	38,272	13,411	17,584	24.0	45.9	18.8	41.9	25.5	13.8	50.3
Clear Creek, CO	9,605	9,064	9,322	541	-258	6.0	-2.8	12.5	32.7	34.5	20.3	47.2
Denver, CO	716,492	599,815	554,636	116,677	45,179	19.5	8.1	16.7	50.2	21.4	11.8	49.8
Douglas, CO	342,776	285,465	175,766	57,311	109,699	20.1	62.4	20.9	38.6	28.6	11.9	50.1
Elbert, CO	26,282	23,088	19,872	3,194	3,216	13.8	16.2	17.3	31.7	34.6	16.4	49.5
Gilpin, CO	6,121	5,453	4,757	668	696	12.3	14.6	12.5	32.8	37.7	16.9	47.5
Jefferson, CO	580,233	534,829	525,507	45,404	9,322	8.5	1.8	16.2	39.8	27.5	16.5	50.1
Park, CO	18,556	16,204	14,523	2,352	1,681	14.5	11.6	12.3	29.1	38.1	20.4	47.4
Des Moines-West Des Moines, IA Metro Area	692,556	606,474	518,607	86,082	87,867	14.2	16.9	21.1	40.9	24.4	13.7	50.6
Dallas, IA	90,180	66,138	40,750	24,042	25,388	36.4	62.3	23.5	41.9	22.6	12.0	50.7
Guthrie, IA	10,720	10,955	11,353	-235	-398	-2.1	-3.5	17.8	32.0	27.7	22.5	50.1
Jasper, IA	37,147	36,842	37,213	305	-371	0.8		18.4	35.6	26.9	19.1	48.9
Madison, IA	16,249	15,679	14,019	570	1,660	3.6	11.8	20.4	34.4	28.2	17.0	50.1
Polk, IA	487,204	430,632	374,601	56,572	56,031	13.1	15.0	21.0	41.8	24.2	13.1	50.7
Warren, IA	51,056	46,228	40,671	4,828	5,557	10.4	13.7	20.4	38.2	25.7	15.7	50.7
Detroit-Warren-Dearborn, MI Metro Area	4,326,442	4,296,290	4,452,557	30,152	-156,267	0.7	-3.5	18.1	37.7	27.8	16.4	51.3
Detroit-Dearborn-Livonia, MI Div	1,753,893	1,820,539	2,061,162	-66,646	-240,623	-3.7	-11.7	19.6	38.7	26.3	15.4	51.8
Wayne, MI	1,753,893	1,820,539	2,061,162	-66,646	-240,623	-3.7	-11.7	19.6	38.7	26.3	15.4	51.8
Warren-Troy-Farmington Hills, MI Div	2,572,549	2,475,751	2,391,395	96,798	84,356	3.9	3.5	17.1	37.1	28.8	17.1	50.9
Lapeer, MI	88,028	88,318	87,904	-290	414	-0.3	0.5	16.5	34.2	31.2	18.1	49.3

Table C-1. Population and Population Characteristics—*Continued*

Metropolitan Statistical Area Metropolitan Division Component Counties	Population 2018 Estimate (July 1)	2010 census estimates base (April 1)	2000 census estimates base (April 1)	Net change 2010-2018	Net change 2000-2010	Percent change 2010-2018	Percent change 2000-2010	Percent in each age group, 2018 Under 15 years	15 to 44 years	45 to 64 years	65 years and over	Percent female
Livingston, MI	191,224	180,961	156,951	10,263	24,010	5.7	15.3	16.9	34.7	31.1	17.2	49.9
Macomb, MI	874,759	841,039	788,149	33,720	52,890	4.0	6.7	17.2	37.5	28.4	17.0	51.3
Oakland, MI	1,259,201	1,202,384	1,194,156	56,817	8,228	4.7	0.7	17.1	37.8	28.3	16.8	51.0
St. Clair, MI	159,337	163,049	164,235	-3,712	-1,186	-2.3	-0.7	16.8	34.1	30.3	18.8	50.3
Dothan, AL Metro Area	148,245	145,641	130,861	2,604	14,780	1.8	11.3	18.4	36.2	26.5	18.8	51.8
Geneva, AL	26,314	26,787	25,764	-473	1,023	-1.8	4.0	17.8	34.0	27.9	20.3	51.2
Henry, AL	17,209	17,300	16,310	-91	990	-0.5	6.1	16.9	33.4	27.0	22.7	51.8
Houston, AL	104,722	101,554	88,787	3,168	12,767	3.1	14.4	18.9	37.2	26.1	17.8	52.0
Dover, DE Metro Area	178,550	162,349	126,697	16,201	35,652	10.0	28.1	19.0	39.0	24.9	17.1	51.8
Kent, DE	178,550	162,349	126,697	16,201	35,652	10.0	28.1	19.0	39.0	24.9	17.1	51.8
Dubuque, IA Metro Area	96,854	93,643	89,143	3,211	4,500	3.4	5.0	18.8	37.8	25.4	18.0	50.6
Dubuque, IA	96,854	93,643	89,143	3,211	4,500	3.4	5.0	18.8	37.8	25.4	18.0	50.6
Duluth, MN-WI Metro Area	289,457	290,638	286,544	-1,181	4,094	-0.4	1.4	16.2	37.7	26.9	19.2	49.5
Carlton, MN	35,837	35,386	31,671	451	3,715	1.3	11.7	18.4	36.4	28.1	17.1	47.8
Lake, MN	10,658	10,862	11,058	-204	-196	-1.9	-1.8	15.5	29.5	28.9	26.0	48.5
St. Louis, MN	199,754	200,231	200,528	-477	-297	-0.2	-0.1	15.8	38.6	26.2	19.4	49.8
Douglas, WI	43,208	44,159	43,287	-951	872	-2.2	2.0	16.3	36.7	28.4	18.6	49.9
Durham-Chapel Hill, NC Metro Area	635,527	564,191	474,991	71,336	89,200	12.6	18.8	17.0	42.0	25.6	15.4	51.9
Chatham, NC	73,139	63,481	49,329	9,658	14,152	15.2	28.7	16.6	30.3	28.7	24.4	52.2
Durham, NC	316,739	269,999	223,314	46,740	46,685	17.3	20.9	17.6	45.4	23.8	13.1	52.3
Granville, NC	60,115	57,531	48,498	2,584	9,033	4.5	18.6	16.7	36.1	30.1	17.1	49.0
Orange, NC	146,027	133,702	118,227	12,325	15,475	9.2	13.1	16.0	45.2	24.8	14.0	52.2
Person, NC	39,507	39,478	35,623	29	3,855	0.1	10.8	17.0	33.7	29.7	19.6	51.6
East Stroudsburg, PA Metro Area	169,507	169,832	138,687	-325	31,145	-0.2	22.5	15.6	36.8	30.4	17.2	50.5
Monroe, PA	169,507	169,832	138,687	-325	31,145	-0.2	22.5	15.6	36.8	30.4	17.2	50.5
Eau Claire, WI Metro Area	168,669	161,385	148,337	7,284	13,048	4.5	8.8	17.5	41.3	24.7	16.5	49.7
Chippewa, WI	64,135	62,506	55,195	1,629	7,311	2.6	13.2	18.2	35.8	28.0	18.0	48.2
Eau Claire, WI	104,534	98,879	93,142	5,655	5,737	5.7	6.2	17.1	44.6	22.6	15.7	50.6
El Centro, CA Metro Area	181,827	174,524	142,361	7,303	32,163	4.2	22.6	23.9	41.7	21.4	13.0	48.7
Imperial, CA	181,827	174,524	142,361	7,303	32,163	4.2	22.6	23.9	41.7	21.4	13.0	48.7
Elizabethtown-Fort Knox, KY Metro Area	153,378	148,340	133,896	5,038	14,444	3.4	10.8	19.9	39.4	26.4	14.3	50.1
Hardin, KY	110,356	105,538	94,174	4,818	11,364	4.6	12.1	20.5	39.8	25.8	14.0	50.2
Larue, KY	14,307	14,189	13,373	118	816	0.8	6.1	18.5	36.1	27.8	17.6	50.4
Meade, KY	28,715	28,613	26,349	102	2,264	0.4	8.6	18.4	39.4	28.2	14.0	49.6
Elkhart-Goshen, IN Metro Area	205,560	197,559	182,791	8,001	14,768	4.0	8.1	22.9	38.3	24.0	14.7	50.6
Elkhart, IN	205,560	197,559	182,791	8,001	14,768	4.0	8.1	22.9	38.3	24.0	14.7	50.6
Elmira, NY Metro Area	84,254	88,849	91,070	-4,595	-2,221	-5.2	-2.4	17.6	36.1	27.4	19.0	50.3
Chemung, NY	84,254	88,849	91,070	-4,595	-2,221	-5.2	-2.4	17.6	36.1	27.4	19.0	50.3
El Paso, TX Metro Area	845,553	804,129	682,966	41,424	121,163	5.2	17.7	22.5	43.3	21.9	12.3	50.7
El Paso, TX	840,758	800,653	679,622	40,105	121,031	5.0	17.8	22.5	43.3	21.9	12.3	50.7
Hudspeth, TX	4,795	3,476	3,344	1,319	132	37.9	3.9	17.9	47.8	18.9	15.4	47.0
Enid, OK Metro Area	60,913	60,580	57,813	333	2,767	0.5	4.8	21.9	38.8	22.9	16.4	50.2
Garfield, OK	60,913	60,580	57,813	333	2,767	0.5	4.8	21.9	38.8	22.9	16.4	50.2
Erie, PA Metro Area	272,061	280,584	280,843	-8,523	-259	-3.0	-0.1	17.6	37.9	26.6	18.0	50.6
Erie, PA	272,061	280,584	280,843	-8,523	-259	-3.0	-0.1	17.6	37.9	26.6	18.0	50.6
Eugene-Springfield, OR Metro Area	379,611	351,704	322,959	27,907	28,745	7.9	8.9	15.2	41.1	24.4	19.3	50.8
Lane, OR	379,611	351,704	322,959	27,907	28,745	7.9	8.9	15.2	41.1	24.4	19.3	50.8
Evansville, IN-KY Metro Area	314,672	311,548	296,195	3,124	15,353	1.0	5.2	18.5	37.7	26.5	17.3	51.3
Posey, IN	25,540	25,910	27,061	-370	-1,151	-1.4	-4.3	18.2	34.2	28.8	18.8	50.1
Vanderburgh, IN	180,974	179,703	171,922	1,271	7,781	0.7	4.5	18.1	39.3	25.7	16.9	51.5
Warrick, IN	62,567	59,689	52,383	2,878	7,306	4.8	13.9	19.4	35.7	27.4	17.5	51.0
Henderson, KY	45,591	46,246	44,829	-655	1,417	-1.4	3.2	19.3	35.8	27.3	17.6	51.7
Fairbanks, AK Metro Area	98,971	97,585	82,840	1,386	14,745	1.4	17.8	20.7	47.8	21.2	10.3	46.1
Fairbanks North Star, AK	98,971	97,585	82,840	1,386	14,745	1.4	17.8	20.7	47.8	21.2	10.3	46.1
Fargo, ND-MN Metro Area	245,471	208,777	174,367	36,694	34,410	17.6	19.7	19.8	47.1	20.8	12.3	49.7
Clay, MN	63,955	58,999	51,229	4,956	7,770	8.4	15.2	21.0	44.7	21.1	13.2	50.5
Cass, ND	181,516	149,778	123,138	31,738	26,640	21.2	21.6	19.3	47.9	20.7	12.0	49.4
Farmington, NM Metro Area	125,043	130,045	113,801	-5,002	16,244	-3.8	14.3	21.9	39.2	24.0	14.9	50.5
San Juan, NM	125,043	130,045	113,801	-5,002	16,244	-3.8	14.3	21.9	39.2	24.0	14.9	50.5
Fayetteville, NC Metro Area	521,308	481,004	427,634	40,304	53,370	8.4	12.5	21.5	44.6	22.0	11.9	50.5
Cumberland, NC	332,330	319,433	302,963	12,897	16,470	4.0	5.4	20.9	45.7	21.4	11.9	50.5
Harnett, NC	134,214	114,681	91,025	19,533	23,656	17.0	26.0	22.1	42.2	23.3	12.5	50.5
Hoke, NC	54,764	46,890	33,646	7,874	13,244	16.8	39.4	23.5	43.8	22.7	10.1	50.6
Fayetteville-Springdale-Rogers, AR Metro Area	526,050	440,119	325,364	85,931	114,755	19.5	35.3	21.2	43.7	22.3	12.8	50.2
Benton, AR	272,608	221,351	153,406	51,257	67,945	23.2	44.3	21.9	41.5	23.2	13.4	50.3
Madison, AR	16,481	15,722	14,243	759	1,479	4.8	10.4	19.5	34.4	27.1	19.1	50.1
Washington, AR	236,961	203,046	157,715	33,915	45,331	16.7	28.7	20.5	46.8	21.0	11.7	50.1
Flagstaff, AZ Metro Area	142,854	134,431	116,320	8,423	18,111	6.3	15.6	17.2	48.8	21.6	12.5	50.6
Coconino, AZ	142,854	134,431	116,320	8,423	18,111	6.3	15.6	17.2	48.8	21.6	12.5	50.6
Flint, MI Metro Area	406,892	425,789	436,141	-18,897	-10,352	-4.4	-2.4	18.5	36.5	27.6	17.5	51.8
Genesee, MI	406,892	425,789	436,141	-18,897	-10,352	-4.4	-2.4	18.5	36.5	27.6	17.5	51.8
Florence, SC Metro Area	204,961	205,571	193,155	-610	12,416	-0.3	6.4	19.1	37.0	26.3	17.6	53.2
Darlington, SC	66,802	68,609	67,394	-1,807	1,215	-2.6	1.8	18.2	35.7	27.2	19.0	52.8
Florence, SC	138,159	136,962	125,761	1,197	11,201	0.9	8.9	19.6	37.6	25.8	17.0	53.3
Florence-Muscle Shoals, AL Metro Area	147,149	147,137	142,950	12	4,187	0.0	2.9	16.5	36.8	26.7	20.0	52.0
Colbert, AL	54,762	54,428	54,984	334	-556	0.6		17.3	35.6	27.2	19.9	52.0
Lauderdale, AL	92,387	92,709	87,966	-322	4,743	-0.3	5.4	16.1	37.5	26.3	20.1	52.0

Table C-1. Population and Population Characteristics—*Continued*

Metropolitan Statistical Area Metropolitan Division Component Counties	Population							Percent in each age group, 2018				
	2018 Estimate (July 1)	2010 census estimates base (April 1)	2000 census estimates base (April 1)	Net change 2010-2018	Net change 2000-2010	Percent change 2010-2018	Percent change 2000-2010	Under 15 years	15 to 44 years	45 to 64 years	65 years and over	Percent female
Fond du Lac, WI Metro Area	103,066	101,627	97,296	1,439	4,331	1.4	4.5	17.6	36.2	27.7	18.5	50.8
Fond du Lac, WI	103,066	101,627	97,296	1,439	4,331	1.4	4.5	17.6	36.2	27.7	18.5	50.8
Fort Collins, CO Metro Area	350,518	299,615	251,494	50,903	48,121	17.0	19.1	16.2	44.6	23.5	15.7	50.1
Larimer, CO	350,518	299,615	251,494	50,903	48,121	17.0	19.1	16.2	44.6	23.5	15.7	50.1
Fort Smith, AR-OK Metro Area	250,148	248,277	225,061	1,871	23,216	0.8	10.3	19.6	37.5	25.9	16.9	50.9
Crawford, AR	63,406	61,948	53,247	1,458	8,701	2.4	16.3	20.1	37.0	26.2	16.6	50.7
Franklin, AR	17,810	18,129	17,771	-319	358	-1.8	2.0	18.6	35.6	26.5	19.3	50.0
Sebastian, AR	127,753	125,761	115,071	1,992	10,690	1.6	9.3	19.8	38.7	25.5	16.0	51.1
Sequoyah, OK	41,179	42,439	38,972	-1,260	3,467	-3.0	8.9	18.7	35.8	26.5	18.9	50.8
Fort Wayne, IN Metro Area	409,425	388,625	362,556	20,800	26,069	5.4	7.2	21.1	39.2	24.8	14.9	51.0
Allen, IN	375,351	355,335	331,849	20,016	23,486	5.6	7.1	21.3	39.6	24.5	14.6	51.1
Whitley, IN	34,074	33,290	30,707	784	2,583	2.4	8.4	19.0	35.3	27.7	18.0	50.2
Fresno, CA Metro Area	994,400	930,496	799,407	63,904	131,089	6.9	16.4	23.9	42.3	21.5	12.3	50.1
Fresno, CA	994,400	930,496	799,407	63,904	131,089	6.9	16.4	23.9	42.3	21.5	12.3	50.1
Gadsden, AL Metro Area	102,501	104,427	103,459	-1,926	968	-1.8	0.9	17.5	36.2	27.2	19.0	51.6
Etowah, AL	102,501	104,427	103,459	-1,926	968	-1.8	0.9	17.5	36.2	27.2	19.0	51.6
Gainesville, FL Metro Area	328,982	305,079	266,842	23,903	38,237	7.8	14.3	15.4	47.0	21.9	15.7	51.4
Alachua, FL	269,956	247,337	217,955	22,619	29,382	9.1	13.5	15.2	50.2	20.6	14.0	51.7
Gilchrist, FL	18,256	16,941	14,437	1,315	2,504	7.8	17.3	16.6	36.0	26.9	20.5	48.4
Levy, FL	40,770	40,801	34,450	-31	6,351	-0.1	18.4	16.2	30.8	28.3	24.8	51.2
Gainesville, GA Metro Area	202,148	179,726	139,277	22,422	40,449	12.5	29.0	20.8	39.0	25.2	14.9	50.3
Hall, GA	202,148	179,726	139,277	22,422	40,449	12.5	29.0	20.8	39.0	25.2	14.9	50.3
Gettysburg, PA Metro Area	102,811	101,424	91,292	1,387	10,132	1.4	11.1	16.3	34.4	28.9	20.4	50.8
Adams, PA	102,811	101,424	91,292	1,387	10,132	1.4	11.1	16.3	34.4	28.9	20.4	50.8
Glens Falls, NY Metro Area	125,462	128,941	124,345	-3,479	4,596	-2.7	3.7	15.1	34.2	29.8	20.9	49.6
Warren, NY	64,265	65,698	63,303	-1,433	2,395	-2.2	3.8	14.9	33.0	29.9	22.2	50.9
Washington, NY	61,197	63,243	61,042	-2,046	2,201	-3.2	3.6	15.3	35.5	29.8	19.5	48.2
Goldsboro, NC Metro Area	123,248	122,673	113,329	575	9,344	0.5	8.2	19.8	38.5	25.3	16.4	51.4
Wayne, NC	123,248	122,673	113,329	575	9,344	0.5	8.2	19.8	38.5	25.3	16.4	51.4
Grand Forks, ND-MN Metro Area	102,299	98,464	97,478	3,835	986	3.9	1.0	18.9	45.3	21.5	14.3	48.8
Polk, MN	31,529	31,600	31,369	-71	231	-0.2	0.7	20.3	36.0	25.7	18.0	49.8
Grand Forks, ND	70,770	66,864	66,109	3,906	755	5.8	1.1	18.3	49.4	19.5	12.7	48.4
Grand Island, NE Metro Area	75,808	72,736	68,305	3,072	4,431	4.2	6.5	22.3	37.3	24.5	16.0	49.6
Hall, NE	61,607	58,607	53,534	3,000	5,073	5.1	9.5	23.1	38.3	23.8	14.9	49.6
Howard, NE	6,468	6,274	6,567	194	-293	3.1	-4.5	20.3	31.9	26.7	21.1	49.3
Merrick, NE	7,733	7,855	8,204	-122	-349	-1.6	-4.3	18.2	33.8	27.5	20.6	49.9
Grand Junction, CO Metro Area	153,207	146,717	116,255	6,490	30,462	4.4	26.2	18.0	38.0	24.9	19.1	50.6
Mesa, CO	153,207	146,717	116,255	6,490	30,462	4.4	26.2	18.0	38.0	24.9	19.1	50.6
Grand Rapids-Kentwood, MI Metro Area	1,072,458	993,664	935,433	78,794	58,231	7.9	6.2	19.9	41.3	24.5	14.3	50.3
Ionia, MI	64,210	63,899	61,518	311	2,381	0.5	3.9	18.4	39.8	27.1	14.8	46.4
Kent, MI	653,786	602,628	574,335	51,158	28,293	8.5	4.9	20.1	41.9	24.3	13.7	50.7
Montcalm, MI	63,968	63,342	61,266	626	2,076	1.0	3.4	18.3	36.3	27.8	17.5	48.3
Ottawa, MI	290,494	263,795	238,314	26,699	25,481	10.1	10.7	19.9	41.5	23.7	15.0	50.6
Grants Pass, OR Metro Area	87,393	82,718	75,726	4,675	6,992	5.7	9.2	16.2	31.1	26.7	26.0	51.2
Josephine, OR	87,393	82,718	75,726	4,675	6,992	5.7	9.2	16.2	31.1	26.7	26.0	51.2
Great Falls, MT Metro Area	81,643	81,323	80,357	320	966	0.4	1.2	19.0	38.1	24.2	18.6	49.4
Cascade, MT	81,643	81,323	80,357	320	966	0.4	1.2	19.0	38.1	24.2	18.6	49.4
Greeley, CO Metro Area	314,305	252,847	180,926	61,458	71,921	24.3	39.8	22.1	42.2	23.6	12.2	49.6
Weld, CO	314,305	252,847	180,926	61,458	71,921	24.3	39.8	22.1	42.2	23.6	12.2	49.6
Green Bay, WI Metro Area	321,591	306,241	282,599	15,350	23,642	5.0	8.4	19.3	38.0	26.9	15.9	50.2
Brown, WI	263,378	248,007	226,778	15,371	21,229	6.2	9.4	19.8	39.4	26.0	14.9	50.4
Kewaunee, WI	20,383	20,574	20,187	-191	387	-0.9	1.9	17.3	34.4	28.8	20.4	49.3
Oconto, WI	37,830	37,660	35,634	170	2,026	0.5	5.7	16.7	31.2	31.8	20.4	48.8
Greensboro-High Point, NC Metro Area	767,711	723,885	643,430	43,826	80,455	6.1	12.5	18.2	38.9	26.7	16.3	52.2
Guilford, NC	533,670	488,421	421,048	45,249	67,373	9.3	16.0	18.4	40.8	25.7	15.2	52.7
Randolph, NC	143,351	141,823	130,454	1,528	11,369	1.1	8.7	18.3	35.5	28.5	17.7	50.7
Rockingham, NC	90,690	93,641	91,928	-2,951	1,713	-3.2	1.9	16.5	33.1	29.9	20.5	51.8
Greenville, NC Metro Area	179,914	168,167	133,798	11,747	34,369	7.0	25.7	17.8	46.7	22.3	13.2	53.0
Pitt, NC	179,914	168,167	133,798	11,747	34,369	7.0	25.7	17.8	46.7	22.3	13.2	53.0
Greenville-Anderson, SC Metro Area	906,626	824,035	725,680	82,591	98,355	10.0	13.6	18.6	39.0	25.9	16.6	51.4
Anderson, SC	200,482	186,943	165,740	13,539	21,203	7.2	12.8	18.9	36.3	26.8	18.0	51.9
Greenville, SC	514,213	451,184	379,616	63,029	71,568	14.0	18.9	19.2	39.3	25.7	15.8	51.5
Laurens, SC	66,994	66,535	69,567	459	-3,032	0.7	-4.4	18.1	35.9	27.5	18.5	51.7
Pickens, SC	124,937	119,373	110,757	5,564	8,616	4.7	7.8	15.7	43.5	24.3	16.5	50.2
Gulfport-Biloxi, MS Metro Area	415,978	388,575	377,610	27,403	10,965	7.1	2.9	19.2	38.7	26.2	15.9	50.9
Hancock, MS	47,334	44,014	42,967	3,320	1,047	7.5	2.4	16.6	34.3	29.3	19.8	51.1
Harrison, MS	206,650	187,105	189,601	19,545	-2,496	10.4	-1.3	20.1	39.9	25.1	15.0	51.0
Jackson, MS	143,277	139,668	131,420	3,609	8,248	2.6	6.3	19.1	38.2	26.9	15.9	50.8
Stone, MS	18,717	17,788	13,622	929	4,166	5.2	30.6	17.4	41.3	25.3	16.0	49.5
Hagerstown-Martinsburg, MD-WV Metro Area	285,836	269,143	222,771	16,693	46,372	6.2	20.8	18.3	37.6	27.6	16.5	49.7
Washington, MD	150,926	147,430	131,923	3,496	15,507	2.4	11.8	18.0	37.2	27.6	17.2	49.1
Berkeley, WV	117,123	104,172	75,905	12,951	28,267	12.4	37.2	19.3	38.9	27.2	14.7	50.4
Morgan, WV	17,787	17,541	14,943	246	2,598	1.4	17.4	14.3	31.6	31.0	23.1	49.9
Hammond, LA Metro Area	133,777	121,107	100,588	12,670	20,519	10.5	20.4	20.7	40.8	24.1	14.4	51.6
Tangipahoa, LA	133,777	121,107	100,588	12,670	20,519	10.5	20.4	20.7	40.8	24.1	14.4	51.6

Table C-1. Population and Population Characteristics—*Continued*

Metropolitan Statistical Area Metropolitan Division Component Counties	Population							Percent in each age group, 2018				Percent female
	2018 Estimate (July 1)	2010 census estimates base (April 1)	2000 census estimates base (April 1)	Net change		Percent change		Under 15 years	15 to 44 years	45 to 64 years	65 years and over	
				2010-2018	2000-2010	2010-2018	2000-2010					
Hanford-Corcoran, CA Metro Area	151,366	152,982	129,461	-1,616	23,521	-1.1	18.2	23.0	45.8	21.0	10.3	45.0
Kings, CA	151,366	152,982	129,461	-1,616	23,521	-1.1	18.2	23.0	45.8	21.0	10.3	45.0
Harrisburg-Carlisle, PA Metro Area	574,659	549,468	509,074	25,191	40,394	4.6	7.9	17.8	37.7	26.7	17.8	50.9
Cumberland, PA	251,423	235,405	213,674	16,018	21,731	6.8	10.2	16.8	38.4	26.3	18.5	50.5
Dauphin, PA	277,097	268,123	251,798	8,974	16,325	3.3	6.5	18.7	37.7	26.7	17.0	51.6
Perry, PA	46,139	45,940	43,602	199	2,338	0.4	5.4	17.6	34.4	29.5	18.5	49.4
Harrisonburg, VA Metro Area	135,277	125,221	108,193	10,056	17,028	8.0	15.7	16.6	45.6	22.6	15.2	51.2
Rockingham, VA	81,244	76,321	67,725	4,923	8,596	6.5	12.7	17.9	36.3	26.7	19.0	50.8
Harrisonburg City, VA	54,033	48,900	40,468	5,133	8,432	10.5	20.8	14.6	59.5	16.5	9.4	51.9
Hartford-East Hartford-Middletown, CT Metro Area	1,206,300	1,212,453	1,148,618	-6,153	63,835	-0.5	5.6	16.3	38.6	27.7	17.4	51.2
Hartford, CT	892,697	894,033	857,183	-1,336	36,850	-0.1	4.3	17.1	38.5	27.3	17.1	51.4
Middlesex, CT	162,682	165,676	155,071	-2,994	10,605	-1.8	6.8	14.0	34.8	30.9	20.3	51.3
Tolland, CT	150,921	152,744	136,364	-1,823	16,380	-1.2	12.0	13.8	43.6	26.8	15.8	49.9
Hattiesburg, MS Metro Area	168,267	162,418	143,219	5,849	19,199	3.6	13.4	20.0	42.0	23.7	14.4	52.1
Covington, MS	18,853	19,573	19,407	-720	166	-3.7	0.9	20.5	37.1	25.5	16.9	51.3
Forrest, MS	75,036	74,928	72,604	108	2,324	0.1	3.2	19.5	44.9	22.0	13.6	52.5
Lamar, MS	62,447	55,668	39,070	6,779	16,598	12.2	42.5	20.7	41.1	24.4	13.8	52.0
Perry, MS	11,931	12,249	12,138	-318	111	-2.6	0.9	18.7	35.9	27.1	18.3	51.1
Hickory-Lenoir-Morganton, NC Metro Area	368,416	365,830	341,851	2,586	23,979	0.7	7.0	16.8	35.2	28.8	19.1	50.5
Alexander, NC	37,353	37,185	33,603	168	3,582	0.5	10.7	16.5	34.8	28.7	20.0	49.1
Burke, NC	90,382	90,832	89,148	-450	1,684	-0.5	1.9	15.2	35.2	29.4	20.2	50.0
Caldwell, NC	82,029	83,060	77,415	-1,031	5,645	-1.2	7.3	16.4	34.0	29.8	19.9	50.5
Catawba, NC	158,652	154,753	141,685	3,899	13,068	2.5	9.2	18.1	36.0	28.1	17.9	51.2
Hilton Head Island-Bluffton, SC Metro Area	217,686	187,010	141,615	30,676	45,395	16.4	32.1	15.7	33.5	24.5	26.2	50.8
Beaufort, SC	188,715	162,231	120,937	26,484	41,294	16.3	34.1	15.5	33.1	24.1	27.3	51.0
Jasper, SC	28,971	24,779	20,678	4,192	4,101	16.9	19.8	17.1	36.3	27.3	19.4	49.5
Hinesville, GA Metro Area	80,495	77,919	71,914	2,576	6,005	3.3	8.4	24.1	46.8	19.7	9.3	49.4
Liberty, GA	61,497	63,588	61,610	-2,091	1,978	-3.3	3.2	24.6	47.7	18.5	9.3	49.3
Long, GA	18,998	14,331	10,304	4,667	4,027	32.6	39.1	22.5	44.1	23.7	9.6	49.6
Homosassa Springs, FL Metro Area	147,929	141,229	118,085	6,700	23,144	4.7	19.6	12.2	24.2	27.3	36.3	51.5
Citrus, FL	147,929	141,229	118,085	6,700	23,144	4.7	19.6	12.2	24.2	27.3	36.3	51.5
Hot Springs, AR Metro Area	99,154	96,000	88,068	3,154	7,932	3.3	9.0	16.6	33.1	26.5	23.8	51.9
Garland, AR	99,154	96,000	88,068	3,154	7,932	3.3	9.0	16.6	33.1	26.5	23.8	51.9
Houma-Thibodaux, LA Metro Area	209,136	208,184	194,477	952	13,707	0.5	7.0	20.3	38.9	25.9	14.9	50.9
Lafourche, LA	98,115	96,662	89,974	1,453	6,688	1.5	7.4	19.5	38.7	26.4	15.5	51.0
Terrebonne, LA	111,021	111,522	104,503	-501	7,019	-0.4	6.7	21.1	39.0	25.5	14.4	50.8
Houston-The Woodlands-Sugar Land, TX Metro Area	6,997,384	5,920,487	4,693,161	1,076,897	1,227,326	18.2	26.2	22.2	42.7	24.0	11.1	50.4
Austin, TX	29,989	28,412	23,590	1,577	4,822	5.6	20.4	19.6	34.6	26.8	19.0	50.1
Brazoria, TX	370,200	313,123	241,767	57,077	71,356	18.2	29.5	22.0	41.4	24.8	11.8	49.5
Chambers, TX	42,454	35,099	26,031	7,355	9,068	21.0	34.8	23.1	41.1	24.1	11.8	49.3
Fort Bend, TX	787,858	584,690	354,452	203,168	230,238	34.7	65.0	22.6	40.4	25.9	11.1	50.9
Galveston, TX	337,890	291,307	250,158	46,583	41,149	16.0	16.4	20.1	39.1	26.4	14.4	50.8
Harris, TX	4,698,619	4,093,188	3,400,578	605,431	692,610	14.8	20.4	22.3	44.0	23.2	10.5	50.3
Liberty, TX	86,323	75,641	70,154	10,682	5,487	14.1	7.8	22.1	40.2	24.9	12.8	50.4
Montgomery, TX	590,925	455,750	293,768	135,175	161,982	29.7	55.1	21.8	39.2	25.9	13.1	50.5
Waller, TX	53,126	43,277	32,663	9,849	10,614	22.8	32.5	20.4	45.9	21.9	11.8	50.2
Huntington-Ashland, WV-KY-OH Metro Area	359,228	370,896	367,127	-11,668	3,769	-3.1	1.0	17.4	36.5	26.8	19.3	51.0
Boyd, KY	47,240	49,538	49,752	-2,298	-214	-4.6	-0.4	17.5	35.2	27.8	19.5	50.2
Carter, KY	27,004	27,721	26,889	-717	832	-2.6	3.1	18.7	35.4	27.2	18.8	50.8
Greenup, KY	35,268	36,902	36,891	-1,634	11	-4.4	0.0	17.6	33.9	27.6	20.9	51.4
Lawrence, OH	59,866	62,448	62,319	-2,582	129	-4.1	0.2	17.9	35.5	27.8	18.9	51.3
Cabell, WV	93,224	96,297	96,784	-3,073	-487	-3.2	-0.5	16.4	40.7	24.1	18.8	51.1
Putnam, WV	56,682	55,495	51,589	1,187	3,906	2.1	7.6	18.1	35.6	28.0	18.3	50.8
Wayne, WV	39,944	42,495	42,903	-2,551	-408	-6.0		16.7	34.2	28.1	21.1	51.1
Huntsville, AL Metro Area	462,693	417,593	342,376	45,100	75,217	10.8	22.0	18.1	39.2	27.6	15.1	50.9
Limestone, AL	96,174	82,782	65,676	13,392	17,106	16.2	26.0	18.5	38.3	28.1	15.2	49.9
Madison, AL	366,519	334,811	276,700	31,708	58,111	9.5	21.0	18.0	39.4	27.5	15.0	51.1
Idaho Falls, ID Metro Area	148,904	133,329	104,576	15,575	28,753	11.7	27.5	26.2	39.8	20.9	13.1	49.9
Bonneville, ID	116,854	104,294	82,522	12,560	21,772	12.0	26.4	25.8	40.0	20.9	13.3	50.0
Butte, ID	2,611	2,893	2,899	-282	-6	-9.7	-0.2	19.6	30.5	26.4	23.4	49.5
Jefferson, ID	29,439	26,142	19,155	3,297	6,987	12.6	36.5	28.5	39.6	20.4	11.5	49.2
Indianapolis-Carmel-Anderson, IN Metro Area	2,048,703	1,888,085	1,658,462	160,618	229,623	8.5	13.8	20.5	40.5	25.3	13.7	51.1
Boone, IN	66,999	56,638	46,107	10,361	10,531	18.3	22.8	22.0	38.0	26.7	13.4	50.3
Brown, IN	15,234	15,245	14,957	-11	288	-0.1	1.9	14.1	29.9	31.9	24.1	50.7
Hamilton, IN	330,086	274,569	182,740	55,517	91,829	20.2	50.3	22.2	39.2	26.2	12.4	51.1
Hancock, IN	76,351	70,043	55,391	6,308	14,652	9.0	26.5	19.1	36.9	27.7	16.2	50.8
Hendricks, IN	167,009	145,414	104,093	21,595	41,321	14.9	39.7	20.5	39.5	26.2	13.9	50.0
Johnson, IN	156,225	139,857	115,209	16,368	24,648	11.7	21.4	20.5	39.7	25.2	14.6	50.6
Madison, IN	129,641	131,639	133,358	-1,998	-1,719	-1.5	-1.3	17.8	37.2	26.7	18.3	51.8
Marion, IN	954,670	903,389	860,454	51,281	42,935	5.7	5.0	20.8	42.8	23.7	12.6	50.3
Morgan, IN	70,116	68,943	66,689	1,173	2,254	1.7	3.4	18.3	35.1	29.7	16.9	50.3
Putnam, IN	37,779	37,952	36,019	-173	1,933	-0.5	5.4	16.0	41.4	26.0	16.6	47.5
Shelby, IN	44,593	44,396	43,445	197	951	0.4	2.2	18.6	35.8	28.4	17.1	50.3
Iowa City, IA Metro Area	173,401	152,586	131,676	20,815	20,910	13.6	15.9	17.3	49.5	20.6	12.7	50.4
Johnson, IA	151,260	130,882	111,006	20,378	19,876	15.6	17.9	16.8	51.6	19.8	11.7	50.4
Washington, IA	22,141	21,704	20,670	437	1,034	2.0	5.0	20.5	34.5	25.7	19.3	50.6

Table C-1. Population and Population Characteristics—Continued

Metropolitan Statistical Area Metropolitan Division Component Counties	Population							Percent in each age group, 2018				
	2018 Estimate (July 1)	2010 census estimates base (April 1)	2000 census estimates base (April 1)	Net change		Percent change		Under 15 years	15 to 44 years	45 to 64 years	65 years and over	Percent female
				2010-2018	2000-2010	2010-2018	2000-2010					
Ithaca, NY Metro Area	102,793	101,580	96,501	1,213	5,079	1.2	5.3	11.9	52.4	21.2	14.5	50.8
Tompkins, NY	102,793	101,580	96,501	1,213	5,079	1.2	5.3	11.9	52.4	21.2	14.5	50.8
Jackson, MI Metro Area	158,823	160,245	158,422	-1,422	1,823	-0.9	1.2	17.6	36.9	27.7	17.8	48.9
Jackson, MI	158,823	160,245	158,422	-1,422	1,823	-0.9	1.2	17.6	36.9	27.7	17.8	48.9
Jackson, MS Metro Area	597,788	587,115	546,955	10,673	40,160	1.8	7.3	19.7	40.7	25.0	14.6	52.0
Copiah, MS	28,543	29,447	28,757	-904	690	-3.1	2.4	19.1	37.6	25.7	17.6	51.9
Hinds, MS	237,085	245,365	250,800	-8,280	-5,435	-3.4	-2.2	20.0	41.8	24.1	14.1	53.3
Holmes, MS	17,622	19,483	21,609	-1,861	-2,126	-9.6	-9.8	21.2	39.8	23.9	15.0	52.2
Madison, MS	105,630	95,203	74,674	10,427	20,529	11.0	27.5	20.6	39.7	26.5	13.3	52.1
Rankin, MS	153,902	142,054	115,327	11,848	26,727	8.3	23.2	19.1	40.2	25.4	15.3	51.9
Simpson, MS	26,758	27,498	27,639	-740	-141	-2.7	-0.5	19.3	36.6	26.5	17.6	51.5
Yazoo, MS	28,248	28,065	28,149	183	-84	0.7	-0.3	18.4	45.6	22.7	13.3	42.4
Jackson, TN Metro Area	178,254	179,709	170,061	-1,455	9,648	-0.8	5.7	19.0	37.7	25.9	17.5	52.4
Chester, TN	17,276	17,145	15,540	131	1,605	0.8	10.3	17.9	40.5	24.5	17.2	51.9
Crockett, TN	14,328	14,576	14,532	-248	44	-1.7	0.3	19.4	35.3	26.5	18.8	52.2
Gibson, TN	49,045	49,687	48,152	-642	1,535	-1.3	3.2	20.1	36.0	25.8	18.1	52.1
Madison, TN	97,605	98,301	91,837	-696	6,464	-0.7	7.0	18.6	38.3	26.1	17.0	52.6
Jacksonville, FL Metro Area	1,534,701	1,345,591	1,122,750	189,110	222,841	14.1	19.8	18.7	39.2	26.3	15.8	51.2
Baker, FL	28,355	27,115	22,259	1,240	4,856	4.6	21.8	19.6	40.3	26.0	14.2	47.4
Clay, FL	216,072	190,865	140,814	25,207	50,051	13.2	35.5	18.9	37.7	27.6	15.8	50.7
Duval, FL	950,181	864,267	778,879	85,914	85,388	9.9	11.0	19.2	41.5	25.3	14.0	51.5
Nassau, FL	85,832	73,310	57,663	12,522	15,647	17.1	27.1	16.3	32.8	28.7	22.2	50.8
St. Johns, FL	254,261	190,034	123,135	64,227	66,899	33.8	54.3	17.7	33.7	28.4	20.2	51.2
Jacksonville, NC Metro Area	197,683	177,799	150,355	19,884	27,444	11.2	18.3	21.5	53.3	16.0	9.2	44.8
Onslow, NC	197,683	177,799	150,355	19,884	27,444	11.2	18.3	21.5	53.3	16.0	9.2	44.8
Janesville-Beloit, WI Metro Area	163,129	160,335	152,307	2,794	8,028	1.7	5.3	19.0	37.2	27.2	16.6	50.7
Rock, WI	163,129	160,335	152,307	2,794	8,028	1.7	5.3	19.0	37.2	27.2	16.6	50.7
Jefferson City, MO Metro Area	151,520	149,797	140,052	1,723	9,745	1.2	7.0	18.4	38.8	26.3	16.5	48.9
Callaway, MO	44,889	44,334	40,766	555	3,568	1.3	8.8	17.2	39.7	26.8	16.3	48.9
Cole, MO	76,796	75,975	71,397	821	4,578	1.1	6.4	18.6	38.8	26.1	16.6	49.5
Moniteau, MO	16,121	15,605	14,827	516	778	3.3	5.2	20.1	39.3	24.8	15.8	46.9
Osage, MO	13,714	13,883	13,062	-169	821	-1.2	6.3	19.1	35.6	27.8	17.4	48.5
Johnson City, TN Metro Area	202,719	198,757	181,607	3,962	17,150	2.0	9.4	15.4	37.4	27.4	19.8	51.1
Carter, TN	56,351	57,388	56,742	-1,037	646	-1.8	1.1	14.9	34.0	29.1	21.9	51.1
Unicoi, TN	17,761	18,311	17,667	-550	644	-3.0	3.6	15.0	32.8	29.0	23.2	50.9
Washington, TN	128,607	123,058	107,198	5,549	15,860	4.5	14.8	15.7	39.6	26.4	18.3	51.1
Johnstown, PA Metro Area	131,730	143,681	152,598	-11,951	-8,917	-8.3	-5.8	15.7	33.7	28.0	22.6	50.8
Cambria, PA	131,730	143,681	152,598	-11,951	-8,917	-8.3	-5.8	15.7	33.7	28.0	22.6	50.8
Jonesboro, AR Metro Area	132,532	121,020	107,762	11,512	13,258	9.5	12.3	20.7	41.6	23.1	14.6	51.4
Craighead, AR	108,558	96,443	82,148	12,115	14,295	12.6	17.4	20.9	42.8	22.4	13.8	51.4
Poinsett, AR	23,974	24,577	25,614	-603	-1,037	-2.5	-4.0	20.0	35.9	26.1	17.9	51.4
Joplin, MO Metro Area	178,902	175,509	157,322	3,393	18,187	1.9	11.6	20.4	38.4	24.8	16.4	50.8
Jasper, MO	120,636	117,391	104,686	3,245	12,705	2.8	12.1	20.8	39.8	23.8	15.6	51.2
Newton, MO	58,266	58,118	52,636	148	5,482	0.3	10.4	19.4	35.6	26.8	18.1	50.1
Kahului-Wailuku-Lahaina, HI Metro Area	167,207	154,840	128,094	12,367	26,746	8.0	20.9	18.2	36.4	27.2	18.3	50.3
Maui, HI	167,207	154,840	128,094	12,367	26,746	8.0	20.9	18.2	36.4	27.2	18.3	50.3
Kalamazoo-Portage, MI Metro Area	264,870	250,327	238,603	14,543	11,724	5.8	4.9	18.0	44.3	22.7	15.0	51.0
Kalamazoo, MI	264,870	250,327	238,603	14,543	11,724	5.8	4.9	18.0	44.3	22.7	15.0	51.0
Kankakee, IL Metro Area	110,024	113,450	103,833	-3,426	9,617	-3.0	9.3	18.5	39.1	25.5	16.9	50.8
Kankakee, IL	110,024	113,450	103,833	-3,426	9,617	-3.0	9.3	18.5	39.1	25.5	16.9	50.8
Kansas City, MO-KS Metro Area	2,143,651	2,009,341	1,811,254	134,310	198,087	6.7	10.9	20.1	39.6	25.4	14.8	50.9
Johnson, KS	597,555	544,181	451,086	53,374	93,095	9.8	20.6	20.1	39.9	25.5	14.5	50.9
Leavenworth, KS	81,352	76,211	68,691	5,141	7,520	6.7	10.9	19.9	40.1	25.6	14.5	46.8
Linn, KS	9,750	9,656	9,570	94	86	1.0	0.9	17.9	32.4	27.3	22.4	49.4
Miami, KS	33,680	32,781	28,351	899	4,430	2.7	15.6	19.9	34.9	28.4	16.7	50.3
Wyandotte, KS	165,324	157,525	157,882	7,799	-357	5.0	-0.2	23.7	40.8	23.2	12.3	50.4
Bates, MO	16,320	17,049	16,653	-729	396	-4.3	2.4	19.0	34.7	26.9	19.4	50.6
Caldwell, MO	9,108	9,424	8,969	-316	455	-3.4	5.1	19.3	33.9	27.1	19.8	49.3
Cass, MO	104,954	99,505	82,092	5,449	17,413	5.5	21.2	19.9	36.4	26.9	16.9	51.3
Clay, MO	246,365	221,943	184,006	24,422	37,937	11.0	20.6	20.0	40.5	25.4	14.1	50.9
Clinton, MO	20,470	20,743	18,979	-273	1,764	-1.3	9.3	19.2	34.6	28.1	18.1	49.7
Jackson, MO	700,307	674,134	654,880	26,173	19,254	3.9	2.9	19.7	40.2	25.1	14.9	51.6
Lafayette, MO	32,598	33,370	32,960	-772	410	-2.3	1.2	18.8	34.7	27.7	18.9	50.4
Platte, MO	102,985	89,325	73,781	13,660	15,544	15.3	21.1	19.7	39.6	26.2	14.5	50.7
Ray, MO	22,883	23,494	23,354	-611	140	-2.6	0.6	18.3	34.5	28.7	18.5	50.1
Kennewick-Richland, WA Metro Area	296,224	253,332	191,822	42,892	61,510	16.9	32.1	24.0	40.6	22.4	13.1	49.4
Benton, WA	201,877	175,169	142,475	26,708	32,694	15.2	22.9	22.4	39.0	23.7	14.9	49.9
Franklin, WA	94,347	78,163	49,347	16,184	28,816	20.7	58.4	27.4	43.9	19.6	9.2	48.3
Killeen-Temple, TX Metro Area	451,679	405,313	330,714	46,366	74,599	11.4	22.6	22.6	45.4	20.8	11.2	50.3
Bell, TX	355,642	310,159	237,974	45,483	72,185	14.7	30.3	23.6	45.1	20.5	10.8	50.3
Coryell, TX	74,808	75,474	74,978	-666	496	-0.9	0.7	19.4	50.2	20.1	10.3	50.3
Lampasas, TX	21,229	19,680	17,762	1,549	1,918	7.9	10.8	18.0	34.0	28.4	19.6	50.7
Kingsport-Bristol, TN-VA Metro Area	306,616	309,502	298,484	-2,886	11,018	-0.9	3.7	15.6	33.6	28.7	22.0	51.1
Hawkins, TN	56,530	56,829	53,563	-299	3,266	-0.5	6.1	16.1	33.2	29.5	21.1	50.9
Sullivan, TN	157,668	156,800	153,048	868	3,752	0.6	2.5	15.7	33.9	28.5	21.9	51.4
Scott, VA	21,534	23,170	23,403	-1,636	-233	-7.1	-1.0	14.5	32.1	29.2	24.2	49.7

Table C-1. Population and Population Characteristics—*Continued*

Metropolitan Statistical Area Metropolitan Division Component Counties	2018 Estimate (July 1)	2010 census estimates base (April 1)	2000 census estimates base (April 1)	Net change 2010-2018	Net change 2000-2010	Percent change 2010-2018	Percent change 2000-2010	Under 15 years	15 to 44 years	45 to 64 years	65 years and over	Percent female
Washington, VA	54,402	54,964	51,103	-562	3,861	-1.0	7.6	15.0	33.2	29.0	22.7	50.7
Bristol City, VA	16,482	17,739	17,367	-1,257	372	-7.1	2.1	16.6	35.7	26.7	21.1	52.6
Kingston, NY Metro Area	178,599	182,512	177,749	-3,913	4,763	-2.1	2.7	14.4	36.5	29.3	19.8	50.4
Ulster, NY	178,599	182,512	177,749	-3,913	4,763	-2.1	2.7	14.4	36.5	29.3	19.8	50.4
Knoxville, TN Metro Area	860,164	815,021	727,600	45,143	87,421	5.5	12.0	16.9	38.1	26.7	18.3	51.2
Anderson, TN	76,482	75,089	71,330	1,393	3,759	1.9	5.3	17.3	34.8	27.8	20.1	51.3
Blount, TN	131,349	123,098	105,823	8,251	17,275	6.7	16.3	16.4	34.9	28.4	20.2	51.5
Campbell, TN	39,583	40,723	39,854	-1,140	869	-2.8	2.2	16.9	34.2	28.2	20.7	50.9
Knox, TN	465,289	432,269	382,032	33,020	50,237	7.6	13.1	17.4	41.6	25.1	15.8	51.4
Loudon, TN	53,054	48,550	39,086	4,504	9,464	9.3	24.2	16.1	29.9	27.6	26.4	50.8
Morgan, TN	21,579	21,986	19,757	-407	2,229	-1.9	11.3	15.5	38.0	28.7	17.8	45.3
Roane, TN	53,140	54,199	51,910	-1,059	2,289	-2.0	4.4	15.0	31.9	30.2	22.8	51.2
Union, TN	19,688	19,107	17,808	581	1,299	3.0	7.3	17.9	34.5	29.3	18.3	50.7
Kokomo, IN Metro Area	82,366	82,752	84,964	-386	-2,212	-0.5	-2.6	18.7	35.3	26.6	19.5	51.5
Howard, IN	82,366	82,752	84,964	-386	-2,212	-0.5	-2.6	18.7	35.3	26.6	19.5	51.5
La Crosse-Onalaska, WI-MN Metro Area	136,808	133,660	126,838	3,148	6,822	2.4	5.4	16.6	41.7	24.6	17.1	51.0
Houston, MN	18,578	19,022	19,718	-444	-696	-2.3	-3.5	17.8	31.8	28.9	21.5	49.8
La Crosse, WI	118,230	114,638	107,120	3,592	7,518	3.1	7.0	16.4	43.3	23.9	16.4	51.2
Lafayette, LA Metro Area	489,364	466,736	425,020	22,628	41,716	4.8	9.8	20.5	40.1	25.2	14.2	51.3
Acadia, LA	62,190	61,787	58,861	403	2,926	0.7	5.0	21.6	37.8	25.4	15.3	51.2
Iberia, LA	70,941	73,094	73,266	-2,153	-172	-2.9	-0.2	21.6	37.4	26.0	15.0	51.1
Lafayette, LA	242,782	221,724	190,503	21,058	31,221	9.5	16.4	19.9	42.5	24.4	13.2	51.3
St. Martin, LA	53,621	52,160	48,583	1,461	3,577	2.8	7.4	20.2	38.2	26.6	15.0	50.8
Vermilion, LA	59,830	57,971	53,807	1,859	4,164	3.2	7.7	21.0	37.7	26.0	15.2	51.6
Lafayette-West Lafayette, IN Metro Area	230,091	210,305	186,960	19,786	23,345	9.4	12.5	17.6	48.9	20.7	12.9	49.1
Benton, IN	8,653	8,836	9,421	-183	-585	-2.1	-6.2	20.3	35.0	26.8	17.8	50.4
Carroll, IN	20,127	20,155	20,165	-28	-10	-0.1	0.0	18.1	34.1	28.2	19.6	49.7
Tippecanoe, IN	193,048	172,803	148,955	20,245	23,848	11.7	16.0	17.4	51.7	19.3	11.6	48.9
Warren, IN	8,263	8,511	8,419	-248	92	-2.9	1.1	18.4	32.7	28.8	20.2	50.6
Lake Charles, LA Metro Area	210,080	199,641	193,568	10,439	6,073	5.2	3.1	20.8	39.7	24.6	14.9	51.1
Calcasieu, LA	203,112	192,773	183,577	10,339	9,196	5.4	5.0	20.9	39.8	24.5	14.8	51.1
Cameron, LA	6,968	6,868	9,991	100	-3,123	1.5	-31.3	17.8	36.8	28.9	16.5	50.2
Lake Havasu City-Kingman, AZ Metro Area	209,550	200,182	155,032	9,368	45,150	4.7	29.1	14.1	28.4	27.2	30.3	49.4
Mohave, AZ	209,550	200,182	155,032	9,368	45,150	4.7	29.1	14.1	28.4	27.2	30.3	49.4
Lakeland-Winter Haven, FL Metro Area	708,009	602,098	483,924	105,911	118,174	17.6	24.4	18.3	37.2	24.3	20.2	51.0
Polk, FL	708,009	602,098	483,924	105,911	118,174	17.6	24.4	18.3	37.2	24.3	20.2	51.0
Lancaster, PA Metro Area	543,557	519,446	470,658	24,111	48,788	4.6	10.4	19.6	37.5	25.0	17.9	51.0
Lancaster, PA	543,557	519,446	470,658	24,111	48,788	4.6	10.4	19.6	37.5	25.0	17.9	51.0
Lansing-East Lansing, MI Metro Area	550,085	534,684	519,415	15,401	15,269	2.9	2.9	16.9	42.7	24.8	15.6	51.0
Clinton, MI	79,332	75,367	64,753	3,965	10,614	5.3	16.4	18.3	36.9	27.9	16.9	50.5
Eaton, MI	109,826	107,763	103,655	2,063	4,108	1.9	4.0	16.8	37.3	27.3	18.6	50.9
Ingham, MI	292,735	280,891	279,320	11,844	1,571	4.2	0.6	16.6	47.9	22.0	13.5	51.3
Shiawassee, MI	68,192	70,663	71,687	-2,471	-1,024	-3.5	-1.4	17.0	35.4	29.2	18.4	50.6
Laredo, TX Metro Area	275,910	250,304	193,117	25,606	57,187	10.2	29.6	27.5	42.9	20.1	9.5	50.9
Webb, TX	275,910	250,304	193,117	25,606	57,187	10.2	29.6	27.5	42.9	20.1	9.5	50.9
Las Cruces, NM Metro Area	217,522	209,202	174,682	8,320	34,520	4.0	19.8	20.3	42.6	21.3	15.8	50.9
Dona Ana, NM	217,522	209,202	174,682	8,320	34,520	4.0	19.8	20.3	42.6	21.3	15.8	50.9
Las Vegas-Henderson-Paradise, NV Metro Area	2,231,647	1,951,271	1,375,765	280,376	575,506	14.4	41.8	19.4	40.8	25.1	14.7	50.1
Clark, NV	2,231,647	1,951,271	1,375,765	280,376	575,506	14.4	41.8	19.4	40.8	25.1	14.7	50.1
Lawrence, KS Metro Area	121,436	110,826	99,962	10,610	10,864	9.6	10.9	15.1	52.8	19.8	12.3	50.2
Douglas, KS	121,436	110,826	99,962	10,610	10,864	9.6	10.9	15.1	52.8	19.8	12.3	50.2
Lawton, OK Metro Area	126,198	130,288	121,610	-4,090	8,678	-3.1	7.1	19.9	44.4	22.8	12.9	48.3
Comanche, OK	120,422	124,098	114,996	-3,676	9,102	-3.0	7.9	20.0	44.9	22.5	12.6	48.2
Cotton, OK	5,776	6,190	6,614	-414	-424	-6.7	-6.4	18.6	33.3	28.7	19.4	50.8
Lebanon, PA Metro Area	141,314	133,577	120,327	7,737	13,250	5.8	11.0	18.8	35.9	26.0	19.4	50.9
Lebanon, PA	141,314	133,577	120,327	7,737	13,250	5.8	11.0	18.8	35.9	26.0	19.4	50.9
Lewiston, ID-WA Metro Area	63,018	60,893	57,961	2,125	2,932	3.5	5.1	17.3	35.5	26.0	21.2	50.8
Nez Perce, ID	40,408	39,270	37,410	1,138	1,860	2.9	5.0	17.7	37.0	25.4	19.9	50.6
Asotin, WA	22,610	21,623	20,551	987	1,072	4.6	5.2	16.7	32.8	27.2	23.3	51.2
Lewiston-Auburn, ME Metro Area	107,679	107,710	103,793	-31	3,917	0.0	3.8	18.2	36.1	28.0	17.7	51.1
Androscoggin, ME	107,679	107,710	103,793	-31	3,917	0.0	3.8	18.2	36.1	28.0	17.7	51.1
Lexington-Fayette, KY Metro Area	516,697	472,103	408,326	44,594	63,777	9.4	15.6	18.4	42.9	24.5	14.2	51.0
Bourbon, KY	20,184	20,010	19,360	174	650	0.9	3.4	19.0	34.6	27.5	18.9	51.3
Clark, KY	36,249	35,603	33,144	646	2,459	1.8	7.4	18.6	35.6	27.9	17.9	51.2
Fayette, KY	323,780	295,867	260,512	27,913	35,355	9.4	13.6	17.6	45.9	23.2	13.3	50.9
Jessamine, KY	53,920	48,582	39,041	5,338	9,541	11.0	24.4	19.9	39.0	26.1	15.0	51.3
Scott, KY	56,031	47,102	33,061	8,929	14,041	19.0	42.5	21.0	41.4	25.6	12.0	50.7
Woodford, KY	26,533	24,939	23,208	1,594	1,731	6.4	7.5	18.1	34.5	28.6	18.8	51.9
Lima, OH Metro Area	102,663	106,315	108,473	-3,652	-2,158	-3.4	-2.0	19.0	37.7	25.6	17.6	49.6
Allen, OH	102,663	106,315	108,473	-3,652	-2,158	-3.4	-2.0	19.0	37.7	25.6	17.6	49.6
Lincoln, NE Metro Area	334,590	302,157	266,787	32,433	35,370	10.7	13.3	19.2	44.7	22.0	14.1	49.8
Lancaster, NE	317,272	285,407	250,291	31,865	35,116	11.2	14.0	19.2	45.0	21.9	13.9	49.8
Seward, NE	17,318	16,750	16,496	568	254	3.4	1.5	19.6	39.1	24.5	16.8	48.9
Little Rock-North Little Rock-Conway, AR Metro Area	741,104	699,796	610,518	41,308	89,278	5.9	14.6	19.5	40.4	24.8	15.3	51.6
Faulkner, AR	124,806	113,242	86,014	11,564	27,228	10.2	31.7	19.1	45.7	22.6	12.5	51.1

Table C-1. Population and Population Characteristics—*Continued*

Metropolitan Statistical Area Metropolitan Division Component Counties	Population							Percent in each age group, 2018				Percent female
	2018 Estimate (July 1)	2010 census estimates base (April 1)	2000 census estimates base (April 1)	Net change		Percent change		Under 15 years	15 to 44 years	45 to 64 years	65 years and over	
				2010-2018	2000-2010	2010-2018	2000-2010					
Grant, AR	18,188	17,842	16,464	346	1,378	1.9	8.4	18.2	36.5	27.3	18.0	50.6
Lonoke, AR	73,657	68,355	52,828	5,302	15,527	7.8	29.4	21.3	40.4	25.0	13.3	50.7
Perry, AR	10,352	10,441	10,209	-89	232	-0.9	2.3	18.4	33.3	28.1	20.2	50.6
Pulaski, AR	392,680	382,786	361,474	9,894	21,312	2.6	5.9	19.5	39.9	25.1	15.6	52.2
Saline, AR	121,421	107,130	83,529	14,291	23,601	13.3	28.3	19.1	37.7	25.5	17.8	51.0
Logan, UT-ID Metro Area	140,794	125,442	102,720	15,352	22,722	12.2	22.1	25.5	48.4	16.2	9.9	49.8
Franklin, ID	13,726	12,786	11,329	940	1,457	7.4	12.9	25.8	38.4	21.6	14.2	48.8
Cache, UT	127,068	112,656	91,391	14,412	21,265	12.8	23.3	25.4	49.5	15.6	9.5	49.9
Longview, TX Metro Area	286,143	280,011	256,152	6,132	23,859	2.2	9.3	20.6	38.1	24.9	16.4	50.2
Gregg, TX	123,707	121,745	111,379	1,962	10,366	1.6	9.3	21.7	39.2	23.7	15.4	51.4
Harrison, TX	66,726	65,644	62,110	1,082	3,534	1.6	5.7	20.9	36.8	25.4	16.9	51.1
Rusk, TX	54,450	53,307	47,372	1,143	5,935	2.1	12.5	18.4	39.6	25.4	16.6	46.1
Upshur, TX	41,260	39,315	35,291	1,945	4,024	4.9	11.4	19.7	34.8	27.2	18.4	50.6
Longview, WA Metro Area	108,987	102,408	92,948	6,579	9,460	6.4	10.2	18.9	35.7	26.4	18.9	50.5
Cowlitz, WA	108,987	102,408	92,948	6,579	9,460	6.4	10.2	18.9	35.7	26.4	18.9	50.5
Los Angeles-Long Beach-Anaheim, CA Metro Area.	13,291,486	12,828,946	12,365,627	462,540	463,319	3.6	3.7	18.0	42.4	25.7	13.9	50.7
Anaheim-Santa Ana-Irvine, CA Div.	3,185,968	3,010,274	2,846,289	175,694	163,985	5.8	5.8	18.1	40.4	26.7	14.8	50.6
Orange, CA.	3,185,968	3,010,274	2,846,289	175,694	163,985	5.8	5.8	18.1	40.4	26.7	14.8	50.6
Los Angeles-Long Beach-Glendale, CA Div.	10,105,518	9,818,672	9,519,338	286,846	299,334	2.9	3.1	18.0	43.1	25.3	13.6	50.7
Los Angeles, CA.	10,105,518	9,818,672	9,519,338	286,846	299,334	2.9	3.1	18.0	43.1	25.3	13.6	50.7
Louisville/Jefferson County, KY-IN Metro Area	1,264,908	1,202,695	1,090,024	62,213	112,671	5.2	10.3	18.6	38.8	26.6	16.0	51.2
Clark, IN	117,360	110,228	96,472	7,132	13,756	6.5	14.3	18.7	38.6	26.9	15.8	51.2
Floyd, IN	77,781	74,579	70,823	3,202	3,756	4.3	5.3	18.6	37.6	27.7	16.1	51.4
Harrison, IN	40,350	39,363	34,325	987	5,038	2.5	14.7	18.6	35.1	28.6	17.7	50.0
Washington, IN	27,943	28,262	27,223	-319	1,039	-1.1	3.8	18.6	35.8	28.5	17.1	50.2
Bullitt, KY	81,069	74,308	61,236	6,761	13,072	9.1	21.3	17.8	38.1	28.5	15.6	50.3
Henry, KY	16,106	15,415	15,060	691	355	4.5	2.4	19.1	35.1	28.2	17.6	50.5
Jefferson, KY	770,517	741,075	693,604	29,442	47,471	4.0	6.8	18.5	39.6	25.8	16.2	51.7
Oldham, KY	66,470	60,354	46,178	6,116	14,176	10.1	30.7	20.3	38.1	28.5	13.2	47.6
Shelby, KY	48,518	42,048	33,337	6,470	8,711	15.4	26.1	18.8	38.3	27.5	15.4	51.4
Spencer, KY	18,794	17,063	11,766	1,731	5,297	10.1	45.0	18.3	36.1	31.7	14.0	49.4
Lubbock, TX Metro Area	319,068	290,889	256,250	28,179	34,639	9.7	13.5	20.1	46.7	20.6	12.6	50.7
Crosby, TX	5,779	6,056	7,072	-277	-1,016	-4.6	-14.4	22.0	35.7	23.6	18.7	50.6
Lubbock, TX	307,412	278,918	242,628	28,494	36,290	10.2	15.0	20.0	47.2	20.4	12.4	50.7
Lynn, TX	5,877	5,915	6,550	-38	-635	-0.6	-9.7	22.7	36.2	24.3	16.8	49.0
Lynchburg, VA Metro Area	263,353	252,659	222,317	10,694	30,342	4.2	13.6	16.2	38.9	26.1	18.8	51.7
Amherst, VA	31,666	32,354	31,894	-688	460	-2.1	1.4	16.3	33.4	29.1	21.2	51.5
Appomattox, VA	15,841	15,029	13,705	812	1,324	5.4	9.7	17.6	34.3	27.4	20.7	51.4
Bedford, VA	78,747	74,936	60,371	3,811	14,565	5.1	24.1	16.0	31.8	30.9	21.3	50.7
Campbell, VA	54,973	54,807	51,078	166	3,729	0.3	7.3	15.7	36.1	28.3	19.9	51.4
Lynchburg City, VA	82,126	75,533	65,269	6,593	10,264	8.7	15.7	16.3	50.8	18.5	14.4	53.1
Macon-Bibb County, GA Metro Area	229,737	232,287	222,368	-2,550	9,919	-1.1	4.5	19.4	38.0	25.9	16.6	52.3
Bibb, GA	153,095	155,795	153,887	-2,700	1,908	-1.7	1.2	20.5	39.5	24.4	15.6	53.1
Crawford, GA	12,318	12,630	12,495	-312	135	-2.5	1.1	16.7	33.7	30.8	18.8	49.6
Jones, GA	28,616	28,667	23,639	-51	5,028	-0.2	21.3	18.6	36.0	27.7	17.6	51.6
Monroe, GA	27,520	26,173	21,757	1,347	4,416	5.1	20.3	16.6	35.7	29.2	18.5	50.1
Twiggs, GA	8,188	9,022	10,590	-834	-1,568	-9.2	-14.8	16.0	31.2	30.0	22.7	50.9
Madera, CA Metro Area	157,672	150,841	123,109	6,831	27,732	4.5	22.5	23.1	40.4	22.5	14.0	51.8
Madera, CA	157,672	150,841	123,109	6,831	27,732	4.5	22.5	23.1	40.4	22.5	14.0	51.8
Madison, WI Metro Area	660,422	605,449	535,421	54,973	70,028	9.1	13.1	17.2	43.8	24.4	14.5	50.1
Columbia, WI	57,358	56,849	52,468	509	4,381	0.9	8.3	17.3	35.6	29.2	17.9	48.9
Dane, WI	542,364	488,067	426,526	54,297	61,541	11.1	14.4	17.0	45.9	23.4	13.7	50.3
Green, WI	36,929	36,842	33,647	87	3,195	0.2	9.5	18.1	33.8	29.4	18.7	50.3
Iowa, WI	23,771	23,691	22,780	80	911	0.3	4.0	18.9	33.2	29.2	18.8	49.9
Manchester-Nashua, NH Metro Area	415,247	400,699	380,841	14,548	19,858	3.6	5.2	16.6	38.3	29.4	15.7	50.2
Hillsborough, NH	415,247	400,699	380,841	14,548	19,858	3.6	5.2	16.6	38.3	29.4	15.7	50.2
Manhattan, KS Metro Area	130,574	127,094	108,999	3,480	18,095	2.7	16.6	19.5	54.9	15.4	10.2	48.0
Geary, KS	32,594	34,354	27,947	-1,760	6,407	-5.1	22.9	27.7	51.5	12.2	8.6	47.2
Pottawatomie, KS	24,277	21,608	18,209	2,669	3,399	12.4	18.7	24.5	38.5	22.8	14.3	50.3
Riley, KS	73,703	71,132	62,843	2,571	8,289	3.6	13.2	14.3	61.8	14.4	9.5	47.5
Mankato, MN Metro Area	101,647	96,742	85,712	4,905	11,030	5.1	12.9	17.1	46.7	21.5	14.7	49.6
Blue Earth, MN	67,427	64,013	55,941	3,414	8,072	5.3	14.4	16.5	49.3	20.3	13.9	49.7
Nicollet, MN	34,220	32,729	29,771	1,491	2,958	4.6	9.9	18.5	41.6	23.7	16.2	49.5
Mansfield, OH Metro Area	121,099	124,474	128,852	-3,375	-4,378	-2.7	-3.4	17.9	36.4	26.2	19.5	49.2
Richland, OH	121,099	124,474	128,852	-3,375	-4,378	-2.7	-3.4	17.9	36.4	26.2	19.5	49.2
McAllen-Edinburg-Mission, TX Metro Area	865,939	774,768	569,463	91,171	205,305	11.8	36.1	27.1	42.5	19.3	11.1	51.0
Hidalgo, TX	865,939	774,768	569,463	91,171	205,305	11.8	36.1	27.1	42.5	19.3	11.1	51.0
Medford, OR Metro Area	219,564	203,205	181,269	16,359	21,936	8.1	12.1	17.2	35.4	25.4	22.0	51.2
Jackson, OR	219,564	203,205	181,269	16,359	21,936	8.1	12.1	17.2	35.4	25.4	22.0	51.2
Memphis, TN-MS-AR Metro Area	1,342,349	1,316,101	1,205,204	26,248	110,897	2.0	9.2	20.6	40.1	25.4	13.9	52.2
Crittenden, AR	48,342	50,906	50,866	-2,564	40	-5.0	0.1	22.4	38.6	24.8	14.1	52.4
De Soto, MS	182,001	161,267	107,199	20,734	54,068	12.9	50.4	20.8	40.5	25.7	12.9	51.8
Marshall, MS	35,451	37,145	34,993	-1,694	2,152	-4.6	6.1	17.3	37.2	28.0	17.5	50.4
Tate, MS	28,759	28,878	25,370	-119	3,508	-0.4	13.8	18.6	39.3	25.5	16.7	51.8
Tunica, MS	9,944	10,778	9,227	-834	1,551	-7.7	16.8	24.5	40.1	23.1	12.2	53.2
Fayette, TN	40,507	38,439	28,806	2,068	9,633	5.4	33.4	15.4	32.5	30.7	21.4	50.8

Table C-1. Population and Population Characteristics—*Continued*

Metropolitan Statistical Area Metropolitan Division Component Counties	Population							Percent in each age group, 2018				
	2018 Estimate (July 1)	2010 census estimates base (April 1)	2000 census estimates base (April 1)	Net change		Percent change		Under 15 years	15 to 44 years	45 to 64 years	65 years and over	Percent female
				2010-2018	2000-2010	2010-2018	2000-2010					
Shelby, TN	935,764	927,682	897,472	8,082	30,210	0.9	3.4	20.8	40.7	24.9	13.6	52.5
Tipton, TN	61,581	61,006	51,271	575	9,735	0.9	19.0	20.0	38.3	27.2	14.5	50.6
Merced, CA Metro Area	274,765	255,796	210,554	18,969	45,242	7.4	21.5	24.4	43.1	21.3	11.2	49.5
Merced, CA	274,765	255,796	210,554	18,969	45,242	7.4	21.5	24.4	43.1	21.3	11.2	49.5
Miami-Fort Lauderdale-Pompano Beach, FL Metro Area	6,198,782	5,566,294	5,007,564	632,488	558,730	11.4	11.2	16.8	38.0	27.0	18.2	51.4
Fort Lauderdale-Pompano Beach-Sunrise, FL Div...	1,951,260	1,748,146	1,623,018	203,114	125,128	11.6	7.7	17.6	38.3	27.5	16.6	51.3
Broward, FL Div	1,951,260	1,748,146	1,623,018	203,114	125,128	11.6	7.7	17.6	38.3	27.5	16.6	51.3
Miami-Miami Beach-Kendall, FL Div	2,761,581	2,498,013	2,253,362	263,568	244,651	10.6	10.9	16.8	39.8	27.1	16.2	51.5
Miami-Dade, FL	2,761,581	2,498,013	2,253,362	263,568	244,651	10.6	10.9	16.8	39.8	27.1	16.2	51.5
West Palm Beach-Boca Raton-Boynton Beach, FL Div	1,485,941	1,320,135	1,131,184	165,806	188,951	12.6	16.7	15.7	34.3	26.1	23.9	51.5
Palm Beach, FL	1,485,941	1,320,135	1,131,184	165,806	188,951	12.6	16.7	15.7	34.3	26.1	23.9	51.5
Michigan City-La Porte, IN Metro Area	110,007	111,463	110,106	-1,456	1,357	-1.3	1.2	17.8	37.2	27.1	17.9	48.5
La Porte, IN	110,007	111,463	110,106	-1,456	1,357	-1.3	1.2	17.8	37.2	27.1	17.9	48.5
Midland, MI Metro Area	83,209	83,626	82,874	-417	752	-0.5	0.9	17.2	36.5	27.9	18.4	50.7
Midland, MI	83,209	83,626	82,874	-417	752	-0.5	0.9	17.2	36.5	27.9	18.4	50.7
Midland, TX Metro Area	178,331	141,671	120,755	36,660	20,916	25.9	17.3	24.5	44.1	21.0	10.3	49.5
Martin, TX	5,753	4,799	4,746	954	53	19.9	1.1	26.4	38.7	23.7	11.3	49.4
Midland, TX	172,578	136,872	116,009	35,706	20,863	26.1	18.0	24.5	44.3	20.9	10.3	49.5
Milwaukee-Waukesha, WI Metro Area	1,576,113	1,555,954	1,500,741	20,159	55,213	1.3	3.7	19.1	39.3	26.0	15.6	51.2
Milwaukee, WI	948,201	947,736	940,164	465	7,572	0.0	0.8	20.2	42.5	23.7	13.6	51.6
Ozaukee, WI	89,147	86,395	82,317	2,752	4,078	3.2	5.0	17.2	34.0	29.0	19.7	50.8
Washington, WI	135,693	131,885	117,493	3,808	14,392	2.9	12.2	17.8	34.2	30.0	18.0	50.3
Waukesha, WI	403,072	389,938	360,767	13,134	29,171	3.4	8.1	17.3	34.8	29.2	18.7	50.8
Minneapolis-St. Paul-Bloomington, MN Metro Area	3,614,162	3,333,630	3,016,562	280,532	317,068	8.4	10.5	19.7	40.4	25.9	14.0	50.4
Anoka, MN	353,813	330,858	298,084	22,955	32,774	6.9	11.0	19.7	38.4	27.8	14.1	50.0
Carver, MN	103,551	91,086	70,205	12,465	20,881	13.7	29.7	21.9	37.9	28.2	12.0	50.4
Chisago, MN	55,922	53,890	41,101	2,032	12,789	3.8	31.1	18.6	36.4	29.5	15.4	48.4
Dakota, MN	425,423	398,583	355,904	26,840	42,679	6.7	12.0	20.2	38.5	27.1	14.2	50.7
Hennepin, MN	1,259,428	1,152,385	1,116,200	107,043	36,185	9.3	3.2	18.5	42.6	24.8	14.0	50.5
Isanti, MN	39,966	37,810	31,287	2,156	6,523	5.7	20.8	19.5	36.5	27.9	16.1	49.4
Le Sueur, MN	28,494	27,701	25,426	793	2,275	2.9	8.9	19.7	34.9	27.9	17.5	49.6
Mille Lacs, MN	26,139	26,097	22,330	42	3,767	0.2	16.9	20.0	34.5	27.2	18.3	49.7
Ramsey, MN	550,210	508,639	511,035	41,571	-2,396	8.2	-0.5	19.7	42.5	23.3	14.4	51.2
Scott, MN	147,381	129,912	89,498	17,469	40,414	13.4	45.2	22.7	39.4	27.1	10.9	50.2
Sherburne, MN	96,036	88,492	64,417	7,544	24,075	8.5	37.4	21.7	40.4	26.6	11.3	48.8
Washington, MN	259,201	238,114	201,130	21,087	36,984	8.9	18.4	20.1	37.1	27.8	15.0	50.6
Wright, MN	136,349	124,697	89,986	11,652	34,711	9.3	38.6	23.1	38.2	26.1	12.6	49.5
Pierce, WI	42,555	41,019	36,804	1,536	4,215	3.7	11.5	17.0	42.0	26.4	14.6	50.2
St. Croix, WI	89,694	84,347	63,155	5,347	21,192	6.3	33.6	20.4	37.3	28.2	14.1	50.1
Missoula, MT Metro Area	118,791	109,296	95,802	9,495	13,494	8.7	14.1	15.7	45.6	23.1	15.6	49.9
Missoula, MT	118,791	109,296	95,802	9,495	13,494	8.7	14.1	15.7	45.6	23.1	15.6	49.9
Mobile, AL Metro Area	430,135	430,726	417,940	-591	12,786	-0.1	3.1	19.3	38.7	25.6	16.3	52.3
Mobile, AL	413,757	413,145	399,843	612	13,302	0.1	3.3	19.4	38.9	25.5	16.2	52.4
Washington, AL	16,378	17,581	18,097	-1,203	-516	-6.8	-2.9	17.6	34.9	28.4	19.1	50.8
Modesto, CA Metro Area	549,815	514,451	446,997	35,364	67,454	6.9	15.1	22.5	41.1	23.2	13.2	50.5
Stanislaus, CA	549,815	514,451	446,997	35,364	67,454	6.9	15.1	22.5	41.1	23.2	13.2	50.5
Monroe, LA Metro Area	202,203	204,484	201,074	-2,281	3,410	-1.1	1.7	20.3	39.0	24.7	15.9	51.9
Morehouse, LA	25,398	27,979	31,021	-2,581	-3,042	-9.2	-9.8	20.2	35.5	25.6	18.8	51.9
Ouachita, LA	154,475	153,731	147,250	744	6,481	0.5	4.4	20.7	40.4	24.2	14.8	52.1
Union, LA	22,330	22,774	22,803	-444	-29	-1.9	-0.1	18.0	33.9	27.5	20.6	50.5
Monroe, MI Metro Area	150,439	152,024	145,945	-1,585	6,079	-1.0	4.2	17.3	35.3	29.3	18.1	50.6
Monroe, MI	150,439	152,024	145,945	-1,585	6,079	-1.0	4.2	17.3	35.3	29.3	18.1	50.6
Montgomery, AL Metro Area	373,225	374,541	346,528	-1,316	28,013	-0.4	8.1	19.2	39.9	25.6	15.3	52.4
Autauga, AL	55,601	54,574	43,671	1,027	10,903	1.9	25.0	19.2	38.4	26.9	15.6	51.4
Elmore, AL	81,887	79,293	65,874	2,594	13,419	3.3	20.4	18.2	39.7	26.9	15.1	51.7
Lowndes, AL	9,974	11,296	13,473	-1,322	-2,177	-11.7	-16.2	18.9	34.5	27.8	18.8	53.2
Montgomery, AL	225,763	229,378	223,510	-3,615	5,868	-1.6	2.6	19.6	40.6	24.7	15.1	52.8
Morgantown, WV Metro Area	140,259	129,710	111,200	10,549	18,510	8.1	16.6	14.4	48.6	22.6	14.4	48.4
Monongalia, WV	106,420	96,190	81,866	10,230	14,324	10.6	17.5	13.8	52.5	21.0	12.6	48.4
Preston, WV	33,839	33,520	29,334	319	4,186	1.0	14.3	16.0	36.3	27.7	20.0	48.7
Morristown, TN Metro Area	141,726	136,855	123,081	4,871	13,774	3.6	11.2	17.4	35.1	28.2	19.4	50.8
Grainger, TN	23,145	22,656	20,659	489	1,997	2.2	9.7	16.4	33.2	29.9	20.5	49.6
Hamblen, TN	64,569	62,531	58,128	2,038	4,403	3.3	7.6	19.0	35.9	26.6	18.5	51.2
Jefferson, TN	54,012	51,668	44,294	2,344	7,374	4.5	16.6	15.9	34.8	29.3	20.0	50.8
Mount Vernon-Anacortes, WA Metro Area	128,206	116,893	102,979	11,313	13,914	9.7	13.5	18.2	35.7	25.3	20.7	50.4
Skagit, WA	128,206	116,893	102,979	11,313	13,914	9.7	13.5	18.2	35.7	25.3	20.7	50.4
Muncie, IN Metro Area	114,772	117,664	118,769	-2,892	-1,105	-2.5	-0.9	15.0	44.4	23.4	17.1	51.7
Delaware, IN	114,772	117,664	118,769	-2,892	-1,105	-2.5	-0.9	15.0	44.4	23.4	17.1	51.7
Muskegon, MI Metro Area	173,588	172,194	170,200	1,394	1,994	0.8	1.2	19.1	37.4	26.6	17.0	50.3
Muskegon, MI	173,588	172,194	170,200	1,394	1,994	0.8	1.2	19.1	37.4	26.6	17.0	50.3
Myrtle Beach-Conway-North Myrtle Beach, SC-NC Metro Area	480,891	376,555	269,772	104,336	106,783	27.7	39.6	14.2	31.2	28.5	26.1	51.9
Brunswick, NC	136,744	107,429	73,143	29,315	34,286	27.3	46.9	12.6	26.5	29.4	31.5	52.2
Horry, SC	344,147	269,126	196,629	75,021	72,497	27.9	36.9	14.8	33.1	28.1	24.0	51.8

Table C-1. Population and Population Characteristics—*Continued*

Metropolitan Statistical Area Metropolitan Division Component Counties	Population							Percent in each age group, 2018				
	2018 Estimate (July 1)	2010 census estimates base (April 1)	2000 census estimates base (April 1)	Net change		Percent change		Under 15 years	15 to 44 years	45 to 64 years	65 years and over	Percent female
				2010-2018	2000-2010	2010-2018	2000-2010					
Napa, CA Metro Area	139,417	136,578	124,279	2,839	12,299	2.1	9.9	16.8	37.3	26.8	19.1	50.2
Napa, CA	139,417	136,578	124,279	2,839	12,299	2.1	9.9	16.8	37.3	26.8	19.1	50.2
Naples-Marco Island, FL Metro Area	378,488	321,521	251,377	56,967	70,144	17.7	27.9	14.0	28.8	24.9	32.2	50.7
Collier, FL	378,488	321,521	251,377	56,967	70,144	17.7	27.9	14.0	28.8	24.9	32.2	50.7
Nashville-Davidson--Murfreesboro--Franklin, TN	1,905,898	1,646,186	1,358,992	259,712	287,194	15.8	21.1	19.3	42.1	25.3	13.2	51.2
Cannon, TN	14,462	13,813	12,826	649	987	4.7	7.7	17.7	35.2	28.7	18.3	50.3
Cheatham, TN	40,439	39,106	35,912	1,333	3,194	3.4	8.9	18.1	36.9	30.1	15.0	50.3
Davidson, TN	692,587	626,560	569,891	66,027	56,669	10.5	9.9	17.8	46.8	23.1	12.2	51.7
Dickson, TN	53,446	49,650	43,156	3,796	6,494	7.6	15.0	19.0	37.2	27.7	16.2	50.9
Macon, TN	24,265	22,226	20,386	2,039	1,840	9.2	9.0	20.7	36.9	26.7	15.7	51.1
Maury, TN	94,340	80,932	69,498	13,408	11,434	16.6	16.5	19.7	38.0	26.4	15.9	51.8
Robertson, TN	71,012	66,332	54,433	4,680	11,899	7.1	21.9	19.7	37.6	27.9	14.8	50.6
Rutherford, TN	324,890	262,582	182,023	62,308	80,559	23.7	44.3	20.4	45.4	23.7	10.5	50.8
Smith, TN	19,942	19,149	17,712	793	1,437	4.1	8.1	18.6	36.1	28.4	17.0	50.3
Sumner, TN	187,149	160,634	130,449	26,515	30,185	16.5	23.1	19.4	37.4	27.3	15.9	51.2
Trousdale, TN	11,012	7,864	7,259	3,148	605	40.0	8.3	14.9	48.3	23.9	12.9	40.8
Williamson, TN	231,729	183,265	126,638	48,464	56,627	26.4	44.7	22.0	36.7	28.2	13.2	50.9
Wilson, TN	140,625	114,073	88,809	26,552	25,264	23.3	28.4	19.5	37.3	27.5	15.7	50.8
New Bern, NC Metro Area	125,219	126,813	114,751	-1,594	12,062	-1.3	10.5	17.3	38.1	24.2	20.4	49.6
Craven, NC	102,912	103,503	91,436	-591	12,067	-0.6	13.2	18.1	39.9	23.0	19.0	49.4
Jones, NC	9,637	10,167	10,381	-530	-214	-5.2	-2.1	15.2	31.7	30.5	22.6	51.0
Pamlico, NC	12,670	13,143	12,934	-473	209	-3.6	1.6	12.1	28.6	29.5	29.8	49.4
New Haven-Milford, CT Metro Area	857,620	862,456	824,008	-4,836	38,448	-0.6	4.7	16.4	38.9	27.3	17.4	51.8
New Haven, CT	857,620	862,456	824,008	-4,836	38,448	-0.6	4.7	16.4	38.9	27.3	17.4	51.8
New Orleans-Metairie, LA Metro Area	1,270,399	1,189,889	1,337,726	80,510	-147,837	6.8	-11.1	18.6	39.4	26.2	15.8	51.8
Jefferson, LA	434,051	432,573	455,466	1,478	-22,893	0.3	-5.0	18.5	38.0	26.4	17.1	51.6
Orleans, LA	391,006	343,828	484,674	47,178	-140,846	13.7	-29.1	16.9	43.2	25.1	14.8	52.7
Plaquemines, LA	23,410	23,039	26,757	371	-3,718	1.6	-13.9	21.5	39.2	25.9	13.4	49.6
St. Bernard, LA	46,721	35,897	67,229	10,824	-31,332	30.2	-46.6	22.6	41.7	24.3	11.4	51.0
St. Charles, LA	52,879	52,888	48,072	-9	4,816	0.0	10.0	20.3	38.4	27.8	13.6	50.9
St. James, LA	21,037	22,101	21,216	-1,064	885	-4.8	4.2	18.6	37.0	27.2	17.2	51.7
St. John the Baptist, LA	43,184	45,809	43,044	-2,625	2,765	-5.7	6.4	20.3	38.6	26.8	14.2	51.2
St. Tammany, LA	258,111	233,754	191,268	24,357	42,486	10.4	22.2	19.6	36.1	27.3	16.9	51.5
New York-Newark-Jersey City, NY-NJ-PA Metro Area	19,303,808	18,896,236	18,323,002	407,572	573,234	2.2	3.1	17.8	40.1	26.4	15.7	51.6
Nassau County-Suffolk County, NY Div	2,839,436	2,833,032	2,753,913	6,404	79,119	0.2	2.9	17.3	36.5	28.8	17.3	51.0
Nassau, NY	1,358,343	1,339,885	1,334,544	18,458	5,341	1.4	0.4	17.6	36.4	28.3	17.8	51.3
Suffolk, NY	1,481,093	1,493,147	1,419,369	-12,054	73,778	-0.8	5.2	17.1	36.7	29.3	16.9	50.8
Newark, NJ-PA Div	2,173,508	2,146,378	2,098,843	27,130	47,535	1.3	2.3	18.3	38.0	28.3	15.3	51.2
Essex, NJ	799,767	783,885	793,633	15,882	-9,748	2.0	-1.2	19.8	40.5	26.2	13.6	51.9
Hunterdon, NJ	124,714	127,357	121,989	-2,643	5,368	-2.1	4.4	15.0	32.8	33.6	18.5	50.5
Morris, NJ	494,228	492,314	470,212	1,914	22,102	0.4	4.7	16.9	36.0	30.0	17.1	50.9
Sussex, NJ	140,799	148,909	144,166	-8,110	4,743	-5.4	3.3	15.7	34.3	32.7	17.3	50.3
Union, NJ	558,067	536,567	522,541	21,500	14,026	4.0	2.7	19.4	39.0	27.2	14.4	51.2
Pike, PA	55,933	57,346	46,302	-1,413	11,044	-2.5	23.9	14.0	31.6	31.6	22.8	49.3
New Brunswick-Lakewood, NJ Div	2,383,854	2,340,277	2,173,869	43,577	166,408	1.9	7.7	18.2	36.3	27.8	17.6	51.2
Middlesex, NJ	829,685	809,924	750,162	19,761	59,762	2.4	8.0	17.9	40.4	26.7	15.0	50.7
Monmouth, NJ	621,354	630,374	615,301	-9,020	15,073	-1.4	2.4	17.1	34.8	30.6	17.6	51.4
Ocean, NJ	601,651	576,546	510,916	25,105	65,630	4.4	12.8	20.2	32.1	25.1	22.5	51.7
Somerset, NJ	331,164	323,433	297,490	7,731	25,943	2.4	8.7	17.6	36.5	30.3	15.6	51.1
New York-Jersey City-White Plains, NY-NJ Div	11,907,010	11,576,549	11,296,377	330,461	280,172	2.9	2.5	17.8	42.0	25.1	15.1	52.0
Bergen, NJ	936,692	905,143	884,118	31,549	21,025	3.5	2.4	17.3	36.8	28.7	17.2	51.5
Hudson, NJ	676,061	634,245	608,975	41,816	25,270	6.6	4.1	17.6	47.8	22.8	11.8	50.2
Passaic, NJ	503,310	501,609	489,049	1,701	12,560	0.3	2.6	19.9	39.8	25.8	14.5	51.2
Bronx, NY	1,432,132	1,384,603	1,332,650	47,529	51,953	3.4	3.9	20.8	42.7	23.8	12.8	52.9
Kings, NY	2,582,830	2,504,717	2,465,326	78,113	39,391	3.1	1.6	19.4	43.8	22.9	13.9	52.6
New York, NY	1,628,701	1,586,360	1,537,195	42,341	49,165	2.7	3.2	12.3	47.7	23.6	16.5	52.7
Putnam, NY	98,892	99,650	95,745	-758	3,905	-0.8	4.1	15.7	35.3	31.7	17.4	50.0
Queens, NY	2,278,906	2,230,578	2,229,379	48,328	1,199	2.2	0.1	17.0	40.6	26.8	15.7	51.5
Richmond, NY	476,179	468,730	443,728	7,449	25,002	1.6	5.6	18.0	38.2	27.6	16.2	51.5
Rockland, NY	325,695	311,694	286,753	14,001	24,941	4.5	8.7	23.5	36.5	24.3	15.7	50.9
Westchester, NY	967,612	949,220	923,459	18,392	25,761	1.9	2.8	17.9	37.1	28.0	17.1	51.6
Niles, MI Metro Area	154,141	156,811	162,453	-2,670	-5,642	-1.7	-3.5	18.0	35.0	27.3	19.7	51.1
Berrien, MI	154,141	156,811	162,453	-2,670	-5,642	-1.7	-3.5	18.0	35.0	27.3	19.7	51.1
North Port-Sarasota-Bradenton, FL Metro Area	821,573	702,314	589,959	119,259	112,355	17.0	19.0	13.2	27.7	26.8	32.2	52.0
Manatee, FL	394,855	322,879	264,002	71,976	58,877	22.3	22.3	15.0	30.6	26.9	27.4	51.7
Sarasota, FL	426,718	379,435	325,957	47,283	53,478	12.5	16.4	11.6	25.0	26.7	36.7	52.3
Norwich-New London, CT Metro Area	266,784	274,068	259,088	-7,284	14,980	-2.7	5.8	15.8	37.9	28.1	18.2	49.9
New London, CT	266,784	274,068	259,088	-7,284	14,980	-2.7	5.8	15.8	37.9	28.1	18.2	49.9
Ocala, FL Metro Area	359,977	331,299	258,916	28,678	72,383	8.7	28.0	15.4	30.6	25.1	28.9	52.0
Marion, FL	359,977	331,299	258,916	28,678	72,383	8.7	28.0	15.4	30.6	25.1	28.9	52.0
Ocean City, NJ Metro Area	92,560	97,261	102,326	-4,701	-5,065	-4.8	-4.9	14.4	30.2	28.8	26.6	51.1
Cape May, NJ	92,560	97,261	102,326	-4,701	-5,065	-4.8	-4.9	14.4	30.2	28.8	26.6	51.1
Odessa, TX Metro Area	162,124	137,136	121,123	24,988	16,013	18.2	13.2	25.7	44.5	20.1	9.7	49.1
Ector, TX	162,124	137,136	121,123	24,988	16,013	18.2	13.2	25.7	44.5	20.1	9.7	49.1

Table C-1. Population and Population Characteristics—*Continued*

Metropolitan Statistical Area / Metropolitan Division / Component Counties	Population							Percent in each age group, 2018				Percent female
	2018 Estimate (July 1)	2010 census estimates base (April 1)	2000 census estimates base (April 1)	Net change 2010-2018	Net change 2000-2010	Percent change 2010-2018	Percent change 2000-2010	Under 15 years	15 to 44 years	45 to 64 years	65 years and over	
Ogden-Clearfield, UT Metro Area	675,067	597,162	485,401	77,905	111,761	13.0	23.0	25.7	43.0	20.5	10.9	49.5
Box Elder, UT	54,950	49,978	42,745	4,972	7,233	9.9	16.9	26.5	39.9	20.7	12.9	49.3
Davis, UT	351,713	306,492	238,994	45,221	67,498	14.8	28.2	26.9	43.3	19.8	10.0	49.5
Morgan, UT	12,045	9,469	7,129	2,576	2,340	27.2	32.8	28.9	38.4	21.2	11.5	48.3
Weber, UT	256,359	231,223	196,533	25,136	34,690	10.9	17.7	23.6	43.4	21.3	11.7	49.7
Oklahoma City, OK Metro Area	1,396,445	1,252,990	1,095,421	143,455	157,569	11.4	14.4	20.7	41.8	23.6	13.9	50.7
Canadian, OK	144,447	115,540	87,697	28,907	27,843	25.0	31.7	21.9	41.2	24.0	13.0	50.4
Cleveland, OK	281,669	256,009	208,016	25,660	47,993	10.0	23.1	17.7	46.2	22.7	13.4	50.1
Grady, OK	55,551	52,428	45,516	3,123	6,912	6.0	15.2	19.7	37.1	27.0	16.2	50.0
Lincoln, OK	34,920	34,274	32,080	646	2,194	1.9	6.8	19.5	34.6	27.5	18.3	50.2
Logan, OK	47,291	41,854	33,924	5,437	7,930	13.0	23.4	18.8	38.7	26.7	15.8	50.4
McClain, OK	39,985	34,508	27,740	5,477	6,768	15.9	24.4	21.1	37.6	25.9	15.5	50.4
Oklahoma, OK	792,582	718,377	660,448	74,205	57,929	10.3	8.8	21.7	41.4	23.2	13.7	51.0
Olympia-Lacey-Tumwater, WA Metro Area	286,419	252,260	207,355	34,159	44,905	13.5	21.7	17.8	39.7	25.2	17.3	51.1
Thurston, WA	286,419	252,260	207,355	34,159	44,905	13.5	21.7	17.8	39.7	25.2	17.3	51.1
Omaha-Council Bluffs, NE-IA Metro Area	942,198	865,347	767,041	76,851	98,306	8.9	12.8	21.4	40.6	24.2	13.8	50.4
Harrison, IA	14,134	14,937	15,666	-803	-729	-5.4	-4.7	18.9	33.0	28.4	19.7	50.0
Mills, IA	15,063	15,059	14,547	4	512	0.0	3.5	19.2	33.6	28.8	18.4	49.7
Pottawattamie, IA	93,533	93,149	87,704	384	5,445	0.4	6.2	19.6	36.6	26.4	17.5	50.8
Cass, NE	26,159	25,241	24,334	918	907	3.6	3.7	19.7	34.2	28.5	17.5	49.6
Douglas, NE	566,880	517,114	463,585	49,766	53,529	9.6	11.5	21.6	42.1	23.3	13.0	50.6
Sarpy, NE	184,459	158,835	122,595	25,624	36,240	16.1	29.6	22.9	41.7	23.6	11.8	50.0
Saunders, NE	21,303	20,778	19,830	525	948	2.5	4.8	20.1	33.6	27.6	18.7	49.4
Washington, NE	20,667	20,234	18,780	433	1,454	2.1	7.7	19.7	34.3	28.2	17.8	49.9
Orlando-Kissimmee-Sanford, FL Metro Area	2,572,962	2,134,402	1,644,561	438,560	489,841	20.5	29.8	18.1	42.2	24.9	14.8	51.1
Lake, FL	356,495	297,052	210,528	59,443	86,524	20.0	41.1	15.8	31.7	25.8	26.7	51.6
Orange, FL	1,380,645	1,145,954	896,344	234,691	249,610	20.5	27.8	18.5	45.3	24.3	11.9	50.9
Osceola, FL	367,990	268,683	172,493	99,307	96,190	37.0	55.8	20.1	42.7	24.0	13.2	50.7
Seminole, FL	467,832	422,713	365,196	45,119	57,517	10.7	15.7	17.2	40.4	26.8	15.5	51.7
Oshkosh-Neenah, WI Metro Area	171,020	166,996	156,763	4,024	10,233	2.4	6.5	17.0	40.6	26.0	16.4	49.7
Winnebago, WI	171,020	166,996	156,763	4,024	10,233	2.4	6.5	17.0	40.6	26.0	16.4	49.7
Owensboro, KY Metro Area	119,114	114,748	109,875	4,366	4,873	3.8	4.4	20.4	36.4	26.0	17.1	50.9
Daviess, KY	101,104	96,643	91,545	4,461	5,098	4.6	5.6	20.4	36.8	25.8	16.9	51.1
Hancock, KY	8,758	8,565	8,392	193	173	2.3	2.1	20.9	35.0	27.1	17.0	48.7
McLean, KY	9,252	9,540	9,938	-288	-398	-3.0	-4.0	19.3	33.7	27.5	19.5	50.8
Oxnard-Thousand Oaks-Ventura, CA Metro Area	850,967	823,393	753,197	27,574	70,196	3.3	9.3	18.8	39.2	26.4	15.6	50.5
Ventura, CA	850,967	823,393	753,197	27,574	70,196	3.3	9.3	18.8	39.2	26.4	15.6	50.5
Palm Bay-Melbourne-Titusville, FL Metro Area	596,849	543,372	476,230	53,477	67,142	9.8	14.1	15.0	32.3	29.0	23.7	51.1
Brevard, FL	596,849	543,372	476,230	53,477	67,142	9.8	14.1	15.0	32.3	29.0	23.7	51.1
Panama City, FL Metro Area	185,287	168,852	148,217	16,435	20,635	9.7	13.9	18.1	37.7	27.1	17.1	50.4
Bay, FL	185,287	168,852	148,217	16,435	20,635	9.7	13.9	18.1	37.7	27.1	17.1	51.3
Parkersburg-Vienna, WV Metro Area	90,033	92,668	93,859	-2,635	-1,191	-2.8	-1.3	17.3	34.1	28.2	20.4	49.1
Wirt, WV	5,830	5,715	5,873	115	-158	2.0	-2.7	17.8	31.6	30.3	20.2	51.4
Wood, WV	84,203	86,953	87,986	-2,750	-1,033	-3.2	-1.2	17.3	34.3	28.0	20.4	50.0
Pensacola-Ferry Pass-Brent, FL Metro Area	494,883	448,991	412,153	45,892	36,838	10.2	8.9	17.8	39.7	26.0	16.5	50.5
Escambia, FL	315,534	297,620	294,410	17,914	3,210	6.0	1.1	17.6	40.4	25.2	16.8	49.0
Santa Rosa, FL	179,349	151,371	117,743	27,978	33,628	18.5	28.6	18.1	38.4	27.5	16.0	50.8
Peoria, IL Metro Area	403,217	416,251	405,149	-13,034	11,102	-3.1	2.7	19.0	36.9	25.8	18.3	48.0
Fulton, IL	34,844	37,069	38,250	-2,225	-1,181	-6.0	-3.1	16.1	36.2	27.1	20.6	50.4
Marshall, IL	11,534	12,638	13,180	-1,104	-542	-8.7	-4.1	16.3	31.9	28.3	23.5	51.5
Peoria, IL	180,621	186,496	183,433	-5,875	3,063	-3.2	1.7	19.8	38.5	24.7	17.1	50.5
Stark, IL	5,427	5,992	6,332	-565	-340	-9.4	-5.4	17.5	32.7	27.5	22.3	50.8
Tazewell, IL	132,328	135,392	128,485	-3,064	6,907	-2.3	5.4	18.8	36.0	26.5	18.8	50.1
Woodford, IL	38,463	38,664	35,469	-201	3,195	-0.5	9.0	19.6	35.7	26.6	18.1	51.6
Philadelphia-Camden-Wilmington, PA-NJ-DE-MD Metro Area	6,096,372	5,965,705	5,687,147	130,667	278,558	2.2	4.9	17.9	39.4	26.7	16.0	51.3
Camden, NJ Div	1,243,870	1,251,019	1,186,999	-7,149	64,020	-0.6	5.4	17.9	37.9	28.0	16.2	50.7
Burlington, NJ	445,384	448,730	423,394	-3,346	25,336	-0.7	6.0	17.0	37.1	29.0	16.9	51.8
Camden, NJ	507,078	513,719	508,932	-6,641	4,787	-1.3	0.9	18.8	38.7	26.8	15.7	51.3
Gloucester, NJ	291,408	288,570	254,673	2,838	33,897	1.0	13.3	17.7	37.7	28.7	15.8	51.0
Montgomery County-Bucks County-Chester County,	1,978,845	1,924,271	1,781,233	54,574	143,038	2.8	8.0	17.5	36.3	28.6	17.7	50.9
Bucks, PA	628,195	625,266	597,635	2,929	27,631	0.5	4.6	16.5	34.7	30.2	18.6	50.7
Chester, PA	522,046	499,133	433,501	22,913	65,632	4.6	15.1	18.5	37.1	28.0	16.3	51.3
Montgomery, PA	828,604	799,872	750,097	28,732	49,775	3.6	6.6	17.7	36.9	27.7	17.8	52.5
Philadelphia, PA Div	2,148,889	2,084,768	2,068,414	64,121	16,354	3.1	0.8	18.4	43.2	24.0	14.4	51.9
Delaware, PA	564,751	558,759	550,864	5,992	7,895	1.1	1.4	18.1	38.9	26.6	16.4	52.7
Philadelphia, PA	1,584,138	1,526,009	1,517,550	58,129	8,459	3.8	0.6	18.4	44.8	23.1	13.7	51.3
Wilmington, DE-MD-NJ Div	724,768	705,647	650,501	19,121	55,146	2.7	8.5	17.8	39.1	27.3	15.8	51.5
New Castle, DE	559,335	538,479	500,265	20,856	38,214	3.9	7.6	17.7	39.9	26.8	15.6	50.4
Cecil, MD	102,826	101,102	85,951	1,724	15,151	1.7	17.6	18.4	36.5	29.3	15.7	50.9
Salem, NJ	62,607	66,066	64,285	-3,459	1,781	-5.2	2.8	17.5	35.4	28.5	18.6	50.3
Phoenix-Mesa-Chandler, AZ Metro Area	4,857,962	4,193,127	3,251,876	664,835	941,251	15.9	28.9	19.7	40.6	24.0	15.7	50.5
Maricopa, AZ	4,410,824	3,817,359	3,072,149	593,465	745,210	15.5	24.3	19.8	40.9	24.1	15.2	47.9
Pinal, AZ	447,138	375,768	179,727	71,370	196,041	19.0	109.1	18.8	37.8	23.0	20.4	

Table C-1. Population and Population Characteristics—*Continued*

Metropolitan Statistical Area Metropolitan Division Component Counties	Population							Percent in each age group, 2018				
	2018 Estimate (July 1)	2010 census estimates base (April 1)	2000 census estimates base (April 1)	Net change 2010-2018	Net change 2000-2010	Percent change 2010-2018	Percent change 2000-2010	Under 15 years	15 to 44 years	45 to 64 years	65 years and over	Percent female
Pine Bluff, AR Metro Area	89,515	100,290	107,341	-10,775	-7,051	-10.7	-6.6	17.5	39.0	26.1	17.3	48.7
Cleveland, AR	8,018	8,692	8,571	-674	121	-7.8	1.4	17.8	33.6	27.6	21.0	50.4
Jefferson, AR	68,114	77,456	84,278	-9,342	-6,822	-12.1	-8.1	18.2	38.5	26.0	17.3	50.6
Lincoln, AR	13,383	14,142	14,492	-759	-350	-5.4	-2.4	13.6	45.1	26.0	15.3	38.2
Pittsburgh, PA Metro Area	2,324,743	2,356,302	2,431,087	-31,559	-74,785	-1.3	-3.1	15.6	36.5	27.9	20.0	51.3
Allegheny, PA	1,218,452	1,223,323	1,281,666	-4,871	-58,343	-0.4	-4.6	15.5	39.2	26.4	18.9	51.7
Armstrong, PA	65,263	68,944	72,392	-3,681	-3,448	-5.3	-4.8	15.9	32.0	30.1	22.0	50.2
Beaver, PA	164,742	170,549	181,412	-5,807	-10,863	-3.4	-6.0	16.0	33.7	28.8	21.5	51.4
Butler, PA	187,888	183,856	174,083	4,032	9,773	2.2	5.6	16.3	35.3	29.5	18.8	50.4
Fayette, PA	130,441	136,595	148,644	-6,154	-12,049	-4.5	-8.1	15.7	34.1	29.1	21.2	50.5
Washington, PA	207,346	207,841	202,897	-495	4,944	-0.2	2.4	16.0	34.5	28.9	20.6	50.9
Westmoreland, PA	350,611	365,194	369,993	-14,583	-4,799	-4.0	-1.3	14.9	32.3	30.1	22.7	51.1
Pittsfield, MA Metro Area	126,348	131,275	134,953	-4,927	-3,678	-3.8	-2.7	13.6	33.9	29.2	23.3	51.6
Berkshire, MA	126,348	131,275	134,953	-4,927	-3,678	-3.8	-2.7	13.6	33.9	29.2	23.3	51.6
Pocatello, ID Metro Area	94,906	90,661	83,103	4,245	7,558	4.7	9.1	22.1	41.8	21.7	14.3	50.2
Bannock, ID	87,138	82,842	75,565	4,296	7,277	5.2	9.6	21.7	42.4	21.7	14.2	50.3
Power, ID	7,768	7,819	7,538	-51	281	-0.7	3.7	26.3	36.0	22.2	15.4	49.1
Portland-South Portland, ME Metro Area	535,420	514,104	487,568	21,316	26,536	4.1	5.4	15.3	36.2	29.0	19.5	51.4
Cumberland, ME	293,557	281,676	265,612	11,881	16,064	4.2	6.0	15.3	38.0	28.3	18.4	51.5
Sagadahoc, ME	35,634	35,288	35,214	346	74	1.0	0.2	15.7	32.4	29.7	22.1	51.4
York, ME	206,229	197,140	186,742	9,089	10,398	4.6	5.6	15.2	34.4	29.9	20.5	51.2
Portland-Vancouver-Hillsboro, OR-WA Metro Area	2,478,810	2,225,996	1,927,881	252,814	298,115	11.4	15.5	17.8	41.8	25.5	14.9	50.5
Clackamas, OR	416,075	375,996	338,391	40,079	37,605	10.7	11.1	17.7	36.9	27.3	18.1	50.7
Columbia, OR	52,377	49,353	43,560	3,024	5,793	6.1	13.3	17.2	35.1	28.9	18.7	50.0
Multnomah, OR	811,880	735,148	660,486	76,732	74,662	10.4	11.3	15.8	46.1	24.6	13.4	50.5
Washington, OR	597,695	529,860	445,342	67,835	84,518	12.8	19.0	19.0	42.8	24.8	13.4	50.5
Yamhill, OR	107,002	99,209	84,992	7,793	14,217	7.9	16.7	18.2	39.7	24.9	17.1	49.9
Clark, WA	481,857	425,360	345,238	56,497	80,122	13.3	23.2	19.7	38.9	25.9	15.5	50.6
Skamania, WA	11,924	11,070	9,872	854	1,198	7.7	12.1	15.0	32.0	32.0	21.0	49.2
Port St. Lucie, FL Metro Area	482,040	424,107	319,426	57,933	104,681	13.7	32.8	15.3	31.4	27.0	26.4	50.9
Martin, FL	160,912	146,852	126,731	14,060	20,121	9.6	15.9	13.3	27.8	28.0	30.9	50.6
St. Lucie, FL	321,128	277,255	192,695	43,873	84,560	15.8	43.9	16.2	33.2	26.5	24.1	51.1
Poughkeepsie-Newburgh-Middletown, NY Metro Area	675,669	670,291	621,517	5,378	48,774	0.8	7.8	18.3	38.3	27.8	15.6	50.0
Dutchess, NY	293,718	297,462	280,150	-3,744	17,312	-1.3	6.2	15.0	37.9	29.5	17.6	50.2
Orange, NY	381,951	372,829	341,367	9,122	31,462	2.4	9.2	20.9	38.6	26.5	14.0	49.9
Prescott Valley-Prescott, AZ Metro Area	231,993	211,014	167,517	20,979	43,497	9.9	26.0	13.4	27.3	27.8	31.6	51.2
Yavapai, AZ	231,993	211,014	167,517	20,979	43,497	9.9	26.0	13.4	27.3	27.8	31.6	51.2
Providence-Warwick, RI-MA Metro Area	1,621,337	1,601,211	1,582,997	20,126	18,214	1.3	1.2	16.2	39.0	27.6	17.1	51.4
Bristol, MA	564,022	548,254	534,678	15,768	13,576	2.9	2.5	16.9	37.9	28.3	16.9	51.6
Bristol, RI	48,649	49,847	50,648	-1,198	-801	-2.4	-1.6	14.9	35.6	29.7	19.7	51.7
Kent, RI	163,861	166,113	167,090	-2,252	-977	-1.4	-0.6	15.3	36.0	29.9	18.9	51.7
Newport, RI	82,542	83,141	85,433	-599	-2,292	-0.7	-2.7	13.8	35.8	28.3	22.2	50.6
Providence, RI	636,084	626,762	621,602	9,322	5,160	1.5	0.8	17.0	41.8	25.9	15.3	51.3
Washington, RI	126,179	127,094	123,546	-915	3,548	-0.7	2.9	13.1	37.0	29.2	20.7	51.6
Provo-Orem, UT Metro Area	633,768	526,885	376,774	106,883	150,111	20.3	39.8	28.1	49.0	15.1	7.8	49.4
Juab, UT	11,555	10,246	8,238	1,309	2,008	12.8	24.4	28.4	40.7	18.8	12.1	48.7
Utah, UT	622,213	516,639	368,536	105,574	148,103	20.4	40.2	28.1	49.1	15.1	7.7	49.4
Pueblo, CO Metro Area	167,529	159,063	141,472	8,466	17,591	5.3	12.4	18.5	37.8	25.2	18.5	50.7
Pueblo, CO	167,529	159,063	141,472	8,466	17,591	5.3	12.4	18.5	37.8	25.2	18.5	50.7
Punta Gorda, FL Metro Area	184,998	159,964	141,627	25,034	18,337	15.6	12.9	9.6	22.4	27.7	40.2	51.2
Charlotte, FL	184,998	159,964	141,627	25,034	18,337	15.6	12.9	9.6	22.4	27.7	40.2	51.2
Racine, WI Metro Area	196,584	195,428	188,831	1,156	6,597	0.6	3.5	19.0	36.5	28.0	16.5	50.5
Racine, WI	196,584	195,428	188,831	1,156	6,597	0.6	3.5	19.0	36.5	28.0	16.5	50.5
Raleigh-Cary, NC Metro Area	1,362,540	1,130,488	797,071	232,052	333,417	20.5	41.8	19.9	41.9	26.1	12.1	51.3
Franklin, NC	67,560	60,553	47,260	7,007	13,293	11.6	28.1	17.9	36.0	29.3	16.8	50.6
Johnston, NC	202,675	168,877	121,965	33,798	46,912	20.0	38.5	21.0	38.4	27.2	13.3	51.0
Wake, NC	1,092,305	901,058	627,846	191,247	273,212	21.2	43.5	19.8	42.9	25.7	11.6	51.3
Rapid City, SD Metro Area	140,023	126,400	112,818	13,623	13,582	10.8	12.0	19.3	38.0	25.3	17.4	49.3
Meade, SD	28,294	25,443	24,253	2,851	1,190	11.2	4.9	19.3	41.5	24.0	15.3	48.0
Pennington, SD	111,729	100,957	88,565	10,772	12,392	10.7	14.0	19.3	37.1	25.6	18.0	49.6
Reading, PA Metro Area	420,152	411,556	373,638	8,596	37,918	2.1	10.1	18.3	37.5	26.9	17.2	50.8
Berks, PA	420,152	411,556	373,638	8,596	37,918	2.1	10.1	18.3	37.5	26.9	17.2	50.8
Redding, CA Metro Area	180,040	177,221	163,256	2,819	13,965	1.6	8.6	17.8	35.3	26.1	20.9	50.9
Shasta, CA	180,040	177,221	163,256	2,819	13,965	1.6	8.6	17.8	35.3	26.1	20.9	50.9
Reno, NV Metro Area	469,764	425,439	342,885	44,325	82,554	10.4	24.1	18.0	39.7	25.8	16.5	49.6
Storey, NV	4,029	4,014	3,399	15	615	0.4	18.1	9.7	24.1	34.7	31.5	48.8
Washoe, NV	465,735	421,425	339,486	44,310	81,939	10.5	24.1	18.1	39.9	25.7	16.4	49.6
Richmond, VA Metro Area	1,282,442	1,186,473	1,040,192	95,969	146,281	8.1	14.1	17.8	39.8	26.8	15.6	51.7
Amelia, VA	13,013	12,695	11,400	318	1,295	2.5	11.4	16.7	32.9	30.6	19.8	50.7
Charles City County, VA	6,941	7,256	6,926	-315	330	-4.3	4.8	12.1	29.5	33.8	24.6	51.8
Chesterfield, VA	348,556	316,239	259,903	32,317	56,336	10.2	21.7	19.4	38.5	27.1	14.9	51.8
Dinwiddie, VA	28,529	28,014	24,533	515	3,481	1.8	14.2	16.3	35.8	30.5	17.5	51.1
Goochland, VA	23,244	21,692	16,863	1,552	4,829	7.2	28.6	13.9	31.0	32.8	22.3	51.0
Hanover, VA	107,239	99,850	86,320	7,389	13,530	7.4	15.7	17.8	35.0	29.5	17.7	51.1
Henrico, VA	329,261	306,810	262,300	22,451	44,510	7.3	17.0	18.6	39.4	26.5	15.5	52.6

Table C-1. Population and Population Characteristics—*Continued*

Metropolitan Statistical Area Metropolitan Division Component Counties	Population							Percent in each age group, 2018				
	2018 Estimate (July 1)	2010 census estimates base (April 1)	2000 census estimates base (April 1)	Net change 2010-2018	Net change 2000-2010	Percent change 2010-2018	Percent change 2000-2010	Under 15 years	15 to 44 years	45 to 64 years	65 years and over	Percent female
King and Queen, VA	7,042	6,942	6,630	100	312	1.4	4.7	14.5	31.4	31.2	22.9	49.3
King William, VA	16,939	15,927	13,146	1,012	2,781	6.4	21.2	18.9	36.8	28.2	16.1	51.1
New Kent, VA	22,391	18,432	13,462	3,959	4,970	21.5	36.9	16.5	35.7	30.6	17.2	48.9
Powhatan, VA	29,189	28,064	22,377	1,125	5,687	4.0	25.4	14.8	34.1	32.8	18.2	48.2
Prince George, VA	38,082	35,719	33,047	2,363	2,672	6.6	8.1	17.9	43.2	24.9	14.0	45.9
Sussex, VA	11,237	12,070	12,504	-833	-434	-6.9	-3.5	12.8	42.1	27.3	17.8	40.7
Colonial Heights City, VA	17,833	17,410	16,897	423	513	2.4	3.0	20.0	35.8	24.6	19.6	54.2
Hopewell City, VA	22,596	22,591	22,354	5	237	0.0	1.1	22.1	37.9	24.3	15.7	53.4
Petersburg City, VA	31,567	32,435	33,740	-868	-1,305	-2.7	-3.9	19.6	37.4	26.1	17.0	54.0
Richmond City, VA	228,783	204,327	197,790	24,456	6,537	12.0	3.3	15.1	48.4	23.2	13.2	52.6
Riverside-San Bernardino-Ontario, CA Metro Area	4,622,361	4,224,966	3,254,821	397,395	970,145	9.4	29.8	21.3	41.9	23.7	13.1	50.2
Riverside, CA	2,450,758	2,189,765	1,545,387	260,993	644,378	11.9	41.7	20.7	40.9	23.9	14.4	50.2
San Bernardino, CA	2,171,603	2,035,201	1,709,434	136,402	325,767	6.7	19.1	21.9	43.0	23.5	11.6	50.2
Roanoke, VA Metro Area	314,172	308,669	288,309	5,503	20,360	1.8	7.1	16.9	35.1	27.8	20.2	51.6
Botetourt, VA	33,277	33,150	30,496	127	2,654	0.4	8.7	15.0	30.9	31.4	22.7	50.4
Craig, VA	5,064	5,175	5,091	-111	84	-2.1	1.6	13.9	30.9	31.8	23.4	50.5
Franklin, VA	56,195	56,135	47,286	60	8,849	0.1	18.7	15.6	30.9	29.9	23.5	50.8
Roanoke, VA	94,073	92,462	85,778	1,611	6,684	1.7	7.8	16.0	34.7	27.8	21.4	51.8
Roanoke City, VA	99,920	96,912	94,911	3,008	2,001	3.1	2.1	19.4	38.4	25.7	16.5	52.1
Salem City, VA	25,643	24,835	24,747	808	88	3.3	0.4	16.2	38.6	26.4	18.9	52.4
Rochester, MN Metro Area	219,802	206,882	184,740	12,920	22,142	6.2	12.0	20.4	37.7	25.3	16.6	50.8
Dodge, MN	20,822	20,087	17,731	735	2,356	3.7	13.3	21.1	37.7	26.5	14.7	50.1
Fillmore, MN	21,058	20,871	21,122	187	-251	0.9	-1.2	20.8	32.1	26.1	20.9	49.8
Olmsted, MN	156,277	144,260	124,277	12,017	19,983	8.3	16.1	20.6	39.3	24.6	15.5	51.2
Wabasha, MN	21,645	21,664	21,610	-19	54	-0.1	0.2	18.1	31.6	28.5	21.8	49.9
Rochester, NY Metro Area	1,071,082	1,079,697	1,062,452	-8,615	17,245	-0.8	1.6	16.9	38.1	27.2	17.8	51.4
Livingston, NY	63,227	65,207	64,328	-1,980	879	-3.0	1.4	14.4	39.6	28.2	17.9	49.8
Monroe, NY	742,474	744,399	735,343	-1,925	9,056	-0.3	1.2	17.1	39.1	26.5	17.2	51.7
Ontario, NY	109,864	108,090	100,224	1,774	7,866	1.6	7.8	16.4	35.0	28.7	19.9	51.0
Orleans, NY	40,612	42,883	44,171	-2,271	-1,288	-5.3	-2.9	15.7	36.6	29.8	17.9	50.1
Wayne, NY	90,064	93,754	93,765	-3,690	-11	-3.9	0.0	17.6	33.7	29.9	18.9	50.4
Yates, NY	24,841	25,364	24,621	-523	743	-2.1	3.0	18.1	34.9	26.2	20.8	51.4
Rockford, IL Metro Area	337,658	349,431	320,204	-11,773	29,227	-3.4	9.1	19.4	36.7	26.6	17.3	51.0
Boone, IL	53,577	54,167	41,786	-590	12,381	-1.1	29.6	19.8	37.0	27.4	15.8	50.0
Winnebago, IL	284,081	295,264	278,418	-11,183	16,846	-3.8	6.1	19.3	36.7	26.5	17.5	51.2
Rocky Mount, NC Metro Area	146,021	152,375	143,026	-6,354	9,349	-4.2	6.5	18.1	35.5	27.5	19.0	52.7
Edgecombe, NC	52,005	56,546	55,606	-4,541	940	-8.0	1.7	18.5	34.6	27.2	19.7	53.8
Nash, NC	94,016	95,829	87,420	-1,813	8,409	-1.9	9.6	17.9	35.9	27.6	18.5	52.1
Rome, GA Metro Area	97,927	96,314	90,565	1,613	5,749	1.7	6.3	19.1	38.9	25.2	16.7	51.7
Floyd, GA	97,927	96,314	90,565	1,613	5,749	1.7	6.3	19.1	38.9	25.2	16.7	51.7
Sacramento-Roseville-Folsom, CA Metro Area	2,345,210	2,149,151	1,796,857	196,059	352,294	9.1	19.6	18.9	40.4	25.2	15.5	51.1
El Dorado, CA	190,678	181,058	156,299	9,620	24,759	5.3	15.8	16.1	32.3	30.5	21.2	50.1
Placer, CA	393,149	348,503	248,399	44,646	100,104	12.8	40.3	18.2	35.4	26.8	19.6	51.1
Sacramento, CA	1,540,975	1,418,735	1,223,499	122,240	195,236	8.6	16.0	19.7	41.5	24.7	14.1	51.1
Yolo, CA	220,408	200,855	168,660	19,553	32,195	9.7	19.1	17.4	49.1	20.9	12.5	51.6
Saginaw, MI Metro Area	190,800	200,169	210,039	-9,369	-9,870	-4.7	-4.7	17.5	36.6	26.6	19.3	51.4
Saginaw, MI	190,800	200,169	210,039	-9,369	-9,870	-4.7	-4.7	17.5	36.6	26.6	19.3	51.4
St. Cloud, MN Metro Area	199,801	189,093	167,392	10,708	21,701	5.7	13.0	19.6	41.9	23.7	14.9	49.6
Benton, MN	40,545	38,451	34,226	2,094	4,225	5.4	12.3	21.4	40.5	24.1	14.1	50.1
Stearns, MN	159,256	150,642	133,166	8,614	17,476	5.7	13.1	19.1	42.2	23.5	15.1	49.5
St. George, UT Metro Area	171,700	138,115	90,354	33,585	47,761	24.3	52.9	21.6	36.7	20.3	21.5	50.5
Washington, UT	171,700	138,115	90,354	33,585	47,761	24.3	52.9	21.6	36.7	20.3	21.5	50.5
St. Joseph, MO-KS Metro Area	126,490	127,327	122,336	-837	4,991	-0.7	4.1	18.3	39.1	25.9	16.7	48.4
Doniphan, KS	7,682	7,948	8,249	-266	-301	-3.3	-3.6	17.5	37.2	25.7	19.6	49.7
Andrew, MO	17,607	17,297	16,492	310	805	1.8	4.9	18.9	35.0	27.6	18.5	50.3
Buchanan, MO	88,571	89,190	85,998	-619	3,192	-0.7	3.7	18.8	39.6	25.4	16.1	49.5
De Kalb, MO	12,630	12,892	11,597	-262	1,295	-2.0	11.2	14.3	42.0	27.1	16.6	37.4
St. Louis, MO-IL Metro Area	2,805,465	2,787,752	2,675,343	17,713	112,409	0.6	4.2	18.3	38.3	26.8	16.6	51.5
Bond, IL	16,630	17,768	17,633	-1,138	135	-6.4	0.8	15.8	38.4	27.3	18.6	48.0
Calhoun, IL	4,802	5,089	5,084	-287	5	-5.6	0.1	17.1	30.2	29.4	23.3	50.2
Clinton, IL	37,639	37,762	35,535	-123	2,227	-0.3	6.3	17.5	37.3	27.9	17.2	48.2
Jersey, IL	21,847	22,986	21,668	-1,139	1,318	-5.0	6.1	16.5	35.0	28.9	19.5	51.1
Macoupin, IL	45,313	47,765	49,019	-2,452	-1,254	-5.1	-2.6	17.3	34.6	28.2	19.9	50.5
Madison, IL	264,461	269,334	258,941	-4,873	10,393	-1.8	4.0	18.1	37.4	27.3	17.2	51.3
Monroe, IL	34,335	32,951	27,619	1,384	5,332	4.2	19.3	18.0	34.8	29.4	17.8	50.3
St. Clair, IL	261,059	270,062	256,082	-9,003	13,980	-3.3	5.5	19.4	38.0	26.7	15.8	51.8
Franklin, MO	103,670	101,495	93,807	2,175	7,688	2.1	8.2	19.0	35.2	28.4	17.4	50.3
Jefferson, MO	224,347	218,708	198,099	5,639	20,609	2.6	10.4	19.1	37.5	28.4	15.0	50.4
Lincoln, MO	57,686	52,565	38,944	5,121	13,621	9.7	35.0	21.1	38.5	27.1	13.4	50.0
St. Charles, MO	399,182	360,494	283,883	38,688	76,611	10.7	27.0	19.1	38.9	26.7	15.2	50.8
St. Louis, MO	996,945	998,986	1,016,315	-2,041	-17,329	-0.2	-1.7	18.1	37.2	26.6	18.1	52.6
Warren, MO	34,711	32,512	24,525	2,199	7,987	6.8	32.6	19.7	34.6	28.1	17.6	50.1
St. Louis city, MO	302,838	319,275	348,189	-16,437	-28,914	-5.1	-8.3	16.3	45.2	24.9	13.7	51.6
Salem, OR Metro Area	432,102	390,750	347,214	41,352	43,536	10.6	12.5	20.3	40.1	23.5	16.1	50.3
Marion, OR	346,868	315,343	284,834	31,525	30,509	10.0	10.7	20.6	40.0	23.7	15.7	50.2
Polk, OR	85,234	75,407	62,380	9,827	13,027	13.0	20.9	18.8	40.3	22.9	17.9	51.1

Table C-1. Population and Population Characteristics—Continued

Metropolitan Statistical Area / Metropolitan Division / Component Counties	2018 Estimate (July 1)	2010 census estimates base (April 1)	2000 census estimates base (April 1)	Net change 2010-2018	Net change 2000-2010	Percent change 2010-2018	Percent change 2000-2010	Under 15 years	15 to 44 years	45 to 64 years	65 years and over	Percent female
Salinas, CA Metro Area	435,594	415,061	401,762	20,533	13,299	4.9	3.3	22.0	41.4	23.0	13.6	49.1
Monterey, CA	435,594	415,061	401,762	20,533	13,299	4.9	3.3	22.0	41.4	23.0	13.6	49.1
Salisbury, MD-DE Metro Area	409,979	373,760	312,572	36,219	61,188	9.7	19.6	15.9	33.1	26.9	24.1	51.5
Sussex, DE	229,286	197,106	156,638	32,180	40,468	16.3	25.8	15.5	28.9	27.9	27.7	51.7
Somerset, MD	25,675	26,470	24,747	-795	1,723	-3.0	7.0	14.3	44.2	24.6	17.0	45.9
Wicomico, MD	103,195	98,733	84,644	4,462	14,089	4.5	16.6	18.2	41.6	24.3	15.9	52.6
Worcester, MD	51,823	51,451	46,543	372	4,908	0.7	10.5	14.0	29.5	28.7	27.8	51.5
Salt Lake City, UT Metro Area	1,222,540	1,087,808	939,122	134,732	148,686	12.4	15.8	22.9	45.1	21.2	10.8	49.8
Salt Lake, UT	1,152,633	1,029,590	898,387	123,043	131,203	12.0	14.6	22.7	45.2	21.3	10.9	49.8
Tooele, UT	69,907	58,218	40,735	11,689	17,483	20.1	42.9	27.1	43.2	20.5	9.2	49.4
San Angelo, TX Metro Area	121,022	112,968	107,174	8,054	5,794	7.1	5.4	20.2	42.3	21.9	15.5	50.2
Irion, TX	1,522	1,597	1,771	-75	-174	-4.7	-9.8	17.9	32.9	27.7	21.5	48.7
Sterling, TX	1,311	1,143	1,393	168	-250	14.7	-17.9	23.3	37.9	24.3	14.4	49.0
Tom Green, TX	118,189	110,228	104,010	7,961	6,218	7.2	6.0	20.2	42.5	21.8	15.5	50.3
San Antonio-New Braunfels, TX Metro Area	2,518,036	2,142,521	1,711,703	375,515	430,818	17.5	25.2	20.9	42.6	23.4	13.1	50.6
Atascosa, TX	50,310	44,911	38,628	5,399	6,283	12.0	16.3	22.7	39.0	23.6	14.7	50.1
Bandera, TX	22,824	20,489	17,645	2,335	2,844	11.4	16.1	13.7	27.2	32.1	27.0	50.4
Bexar, TX	1,986,049	1,714,772	1,392,931	271,277	321,841	15.8	23.1	21.3	44.0	22.5	12.1	50.6
Comal, TX	148,373	108,485	78,021	39,888	30,464	36.8	39.0	18.6	35.2	28.1	18.1	50.6
Guadalupe, TX	163,694	131,534	89,023	32,160	42,511	24.4	47.8	20.5	40.6	25.0	13.8	50.5
Kendall, TX	45,641	33,411	23,743	12,230	9,668	36.6	40.7	18.5	34.7	27.8	19.1	51.0
Medina, TX	50,921	46,006	39,304	4,915	6,702	10.7	17.1	18.8	37.9	26.6	16.7	48.4
Wilson, TX	50,224	42,913	32,408	7,311	10,505	17.0	32.4	19.4	36.5	28.2	16.0	49.9
San Diego-Chula Vista-Carlsbad, CA Metro Area	3,343,364	3,095,349	2,813,833	248,015	281,516	8.0	10.0	18.1	43.6	24.2	14.0	49.7
San Diego, CA	3,343,364	3,095,349	2,813,833	248,015	281,516	8.0	10.0	18.1	43.6	24.2	14.0	49.7
San Francisco-Oakland-Berkeley, CA Metro Area	4,729,484	4,335,587	4,123,740	393,897	211,847	9.1	5.1	16.4	41.9	26.2	15.5	50.5
Oakland-Berkeley-Livermore, CA Div	2,816,968	2,559,462	2,392,557	257,506	166,905	10.1	7.0	17.8	41.4	26.2	14.6	50.9
Alameda, CA	1,666,753	1,510,258	1,443,741	156,495	66,517	10.4	4.6	17.2	43.4	25.5	13.8	50.8
Contra Costa, CA	1,150,215	1,049,204	948,816	101,011	100,388	9.6	10.6	18.5	38.4	27.3	15.8	51.1
San Francisco-San Mateo-Redwood City, CA Div	1,652,850	1,523,702	1,483,894	129,148	39,808	8.5	2.7	14.1	44.4	25.6	15.9	49.7
San Francisco, CA	883,305	805,184	776,733	78,121	28,451	9.7	3.7	11.5	48.3	24.5	15.7	49.0
San Mateo, CA	769,545	718,518	707,161	51,027	11,357	7.1	1.6	17.1	40.0	26.8	16.1	50.6
San Rafael, CA Div	259,666	252,423	247,289	7,243	5,134	2.9	2.1	16.2	30.8	30.7	22.3	51.1
Marin, CA	259,666	252,423	247,289	7,243	5,134	2.9	2.1	16.2	30.8	30.7	22.3	51.1
San Jose-Sunnyvale-Santa Clara, CA Metro Area	1,999,107	1,836,937	1,735,819	162,170	101,118	8.8	5.8	18.3	42.7	25.5	13.5	49.4
San Benito, CA	61,537	55,265	53,234	6,272	2,031	11.3	3.8	21.3	40.7	25.1	12.9	49.9
Santa Clara, CA	1,937,570	1,781,672	1,682,585	155,898	99,087	8.8	5.9	18.3	42.8	25.5	13.5	49.4
San Luis Obispo-Paso Robles, CA Metro Area	284,010	269,597	246,681	14,413	22,916	5.3	9.3	14.6	40.7	24.6	20.1	49.3
San Luis Obispo, CA	284,010	269,597	246,681	14,413	22,916	5.3	9.3	14.6	40.7	24.6	20.1	49.3
Santa Cruz-Watsonville, CA Metro Area	274,255	262,356	255,602	11,899	6,754	4.5	2.6	16.0	42.0	25.6	16.5	50.5
Santa Cruz, CA	274,255	262,356	255,602	11,899	6,754	4.5	2.6	16.0	42.0	25.6	16.5	50.5
Santa Fe, NM Metro Area	150,056	144,227	129,292	5,829	14,935	4.0	11.6	14.7	33.0	28.0	24.3	51.5
Santa Fe, NM	150,056	144,227	129,292	5,829	14,935	4.0	11.6	14.7	33.0	28.0	24.3	51.5
Santa Maria-Santa Barbara, CA Metro Area	446,527	423,947	399,347	22,580	24,600	5.3	6.2	18.6	44.0	22.1	15.3	50.0
Santa Barbara, CA	446,527	423,947	399,347	22,580	24,600	5.3	6.2	18.6	44.0	22.1	15.3	50.0
Santa Rosa-Petaluma, CA Metro Area	499,942	483,868	458,614	16,074	25,254	3.3	5.5	16.1	37.0	27.2	19.7	51.2
Sonoma, CA	499,942	483,868	458,614	16,074	25,254	3.3	5.5	16.1	37.0	27.2	19.7	51.2
Savannah, GA Metro Area	389,494	347,598	293,000	41,896	54,598	12.1	18.6	19.2	42.6	23.9	14.3	51.5
Bryan, GA	38,109	30,215	23,417	7,894	6,798	26.1	29.0	24.3	42.3	22.8	10.6	50.7
Chatham, GA	289,195	265,126	232,048	24,069	33,078	9.1	14.3	17.9	43.1	23.6	15.4	51.9
Effingham, GA	62,190	52,257	37,535	9,933	14,722	19.0	39.2	22.0	40.7	25.6	11.6	50.2
Scranton--Wilkes-Barre, PA Metro Area	555,485	563,617	560,625	-8,132	2,992	-1.4	0.5	16.4	36.2	27.5	20.0	50.8
Lackawanna, PA	210,793	214,439	213,295	-3,646	1,144	-1.7	0.5	16.9	36.1	27.0	20.0	51.5
Luzerne, PA	317,646	320,895	319,250	-3,249	1,645	-1.0	0.5	16.1	36.4	27.6	19.9	50.5
Wyoming, PA	27,046	28,283	28,080	-1,237	203	-4.4	0.7	15.7	33.8	29.3	21.2	49.8
Seattle-Tacoma-Bellevue, WA Metro Area	3,939,363	3,439,805	3,043,878	499,558	395,927	14.5	13.0	18.1	43.1	25.4	13.4	49.9
Seattle-Bellevue-Kent, WA Div	3,048,064	2,644,588	2,343,058	403,476	301,530	15.3	12.9	17.6	43.6	25.6	13.3	49.8
King, WA	2,233,163	1,931,292	1,737,034	301,871	194,258	15.6	11.2	17.1	44.6	25.1	13.2	49.8
Snohomish, WA	814,901	713,296	606,024	101,605	107,272	14.2	17.7	19.0	40.6	27.0	13.5	49.8
Tacoma-Lakewood, WA Div	891,299	795,217	700,820	96,082	94,397	12.1	13.5	19.8	41.5	24.9	13.8	50.3
Pierce, WA	891,299	795,217	700,820	96,082	94,397	12.1	13.5	19.8	41.5	24.9	13.8	50.3
Sebastian-Vero Beach, FL Metro Area	157,413	138,028	112,947	19,385	25,081	14.0	22.2	13.0	27.2	26.7	33.0	52.1
Indian River, FL	157,413	138,028	112,947	19,385	25,081	14.0	22.2	13.0	27.2	26.7	33.0	52.1
Sebring-Avon Park, FL Metro Area	105,424	98,786	87,366	6,638	11,420	6.7	13.1	14.3	27.3	23.1	35.3	51.1
Highlands, FL	105,424	98,786	87,366	6,638	11,420	6.7	13.1	14.3	27.3	23.1	35.3	51.1
Sheboygan, WI Metro Area	115,456	115,510	112,646	-54	2,864	0.0	2.5	18.1	35.9	28.0	18.0	49.7
Sheboygan, WI	115,456	115,510	112,646	-54	2,864	0.0	2.5	18.1	35.9	28.0	18.0	49.7
Sherman-Denison, TX Metro Area	133,991	120,875	110,595	13,116	10,280	10.9	9.3	19.8	36.4	26.2	17.6	51.2
Grayson, TX	133,991	120,875	110,595	13,116	10,280	10.9	9.3	19.8	36.4	26.2	17.6	51.2
Shreveport-Bossier City, LA Metro Area	397,543	398,604	375,965	-1,061	22,639	-0.3	6.0	20.2	39.1	24.5	16.3	51.9
Bossier, LA	127,185	117,027	98,310	10,158	18,717	8.7	19.0	20.8	41.5	23.3	14.3	50.5
Caddo, LA	242,922	254,921	252,161	-11,999	2,760	-4.7	1.1	19.8	38.1	24.9	17.1	52.7
De Soto, LA	27,436	26,656	25,494	780	1,162	2.9	4.6	19.9	35.9	26.3	17.9	51.8
Sierra Vista-Douglas, AZ Metro Area	126,770	131,357	117,755	-4,587	13,602	-3.5	11.6	17.9	36.0	23.8	22.3	49.2
Cochise, AZ	126,770	131,357	117,755	-4,587	13,602	-3.5	11.6	17.9	36.0	23.8	22.3	49.2

Table C-1. Population and Population Characteristics—*Continued*

Metropolitan Statistical Area Metropolitan Division Component Counties	2018 Estimate (July 1)	2010 census estimates base (April 1)	2000 census estimates base (April 1)	Net change 2010-2018	Net change 2000-2010	Percent change 2010-2018	Percent change 2000-2010	Under 15 years	15 to 44 years	45 to 64 years	65 years and over	Percent female
Sioux City, IA-NE-SD Metro Area	143,950	143,579	143,053	371	526	0.3	0.4	21.9	38.5	24.2	15.4	50.1
Woodbury, IA	102,539	102,175	103,877	364	-1,702	0.4	-1.6	21.8	39.1	24.0	15.1	50.4
Dakota, NE	20,083	21,006	20,253	-923	753	-4.4	3.7	24.0	39.0	23.4	13.6	49.3
Dixon, NE	5,709	6,000	6,339	-291	-339	-4.9	-5.3	21.0	32.9	26.1	20.1	49.1
Union, SD	15,619	14,398	12,584	1,221	1,814	8.5	14.4	20.0	35.5	26.3	18.1	49.6
Sioux Falls, SD Metro Area	265,653	228,262	187,093	37,391	41,169	16.4	22.0	22.1	41.0	23.5	13.4	49.8
Lincoln, SD	58,807	44,823	24,131	13,984	20,692	31.2	85.7	23.8	40.8	22.5	12.9	50.5
McCook, SD	5,546	5,618	5,832	-72	-214	-1.3	-3.7	23.3	32.9	24.8	19.0	49.9
Minnehaha, SD	192,876	169,474	148,281	23,402	21,193	13.8	14.3	21.7	41.6	23.6	13.1	49.5
Turner, SD	8,424	8,347	8,849	77	-502	0.9	-5.7	20.1	33.1	26.0	20.7	49.7
South Bend-Mishawaka, IN-MI Metro Area	322,424	319,213	316,663	3,211	2,550	1.0	0.8	19.1	38.9	25.3	16.6	51.1
St. Joseph, IN	270,771	266,925	265,559	3,846	1,366	1.4	0.5	19.6	40.1	24.5	15.8	51.3
Cass, MI	51,653	52,288	51,104	-635	1,184	-1.2	2.3	16.7	32.9	29.4	21.0	49.8
Spartanburg, SC Metro Area	313,888	284,317	253,791	29,571	30,526	10.4	12.0	19.1	38.8	26.0	16.2	51.5
Spartanburg, SC	313,888	284,317	253,791	29,571	30,526	10.4	12.0	19.1	38.8	26.0	16.2	51.5
Spokane-Spokane Valley, WA Metro Area	559,891	514,752	458,005	45,139	56,747	8.8	12.4	18.4	39.5	25.3	16.8	50.4
Spokane, WA	514,631	471,229	417,939	43,402	53,290	9.2	12.8	18.5	40.4	25.0	16.2	50.4
Stevens, WA	45,260	43,523	40,066	1,737	3,457	4.0	8.6	17.7	30.0	29.0	23.3	50.1
Springfield, IL Metro Area	207,636	210,170	201,437	-2,534	8,733	-1.2	4.3	18.2	36.8	27.1	17.9	52.0
Menard, IL	12,288	12,705	12,486	-417	219	-3.3	1.8	17.9	34.5	28.2	19.4	51.3
Sangamon, IL	195,348	197,465	188,951	-2,117	8,514	-1.1	4.5	18.2	36.9	27.0	17.9	52.0
Springfield, MA Metro Area	702,724	693,058	680,014	9,666	13,044	1.4	1.9	15.9	40.3	26.4	17.4	52.0
Franklin, MA	70,963	71,377	71,535	-414	-158	-0.6	-0.2	14.2	33.8	29.9	22.0	51.5
Hampden, MA	470,406	463,625	456,228	6,781	7,397	1.5	1.6	17.6	39.2	26.4	16.8	51.7
Hampshire, MA	161,355	158,056	152,251	3,299	5,805	2.1	3.8	11.7	46.5	24.6	17.2	53.3
Springfield, MO Metro Area	466,978	436,709	368,374	30,269	68,335	6.9	18.6	18.8	40.8	24.0	16.5	51.0
Christian, MO	86,983	77,417	54,285	9,566	23,132	12.4	42.6	21.0	38.1	25.2	15.7	50.9
Dallas, MO	16,762	16,770	15,661	-8	1,109	0.0	7.1	19.6	32.4	27.8	20.3	50.1
Greene, MO	291,923	275,178	240,391	16,745	34,787	6.1	14.5	17.6	42.8	23.2	16.5	51.4
Polk, MO	32,201	31,137	26,992	1,064	4,145	3.4	15.4	18.7	38.8	24.5	18.0	50.9
Webster, MO	39,109	36,207	31,045	2,902	5,162	8.0	16.6	22.7	36.6	25.4	15.4	49.0
Springfield, OH Metro Area	134,585	138,341	144,742	-3,756	-6,401	-2.7	-4.4	18.4	35.6	26.6	19.4	51.6
Clark, OH	134,585	138,341	144,742	-3,756	-6,401	-2.7	-4.4	18.4	35.6	26.6	19.4	51.6
State College, PA Metro Area	162,805	154,001	135,758	8,804	18,243	5.7	13.4	12.3	51.0	22.4	14.2	47.4
Centre, PA	162,805	154,001	135,758	8,804	18,243	5.7	13.4	12.3	51.0	22.4	14.2	47.4
Staunton, VA Metro Area	123,007	118,496	108,988	4,511	9,508	3.8	8.7	16.6	35.3	27.6	20.5	50.8
Augusta, VA	75,457	73,753	65,615	1,704	8,138	2.3	12.4	15.4	34.2	29.3	21.0	49.3
Staunton City, VA	24,922	23,745	23,853	1,177	-108	5.0	-0.5	16.6	36.7	25.5	21.3	54.1
Waynesboro City, VA	22,628	20,998	19,520	1,630	1,478	7.8	7.6	20.3	37.3	24.4	18.0	52.3
Stockton, CA Metro Area	752,660	685,306	563,598	67,354	121,708	9.8	21.6	22.5	41.2	23.5	12.7	50.2
San Joaquin, CA	752,660	685,306	563,598	67,354	121,708	9.8	21.6	22.5	41.2	23.5	12.7	50.2
Sumter, SC Metro Area	140,212	142,441	137,148	-2,229	5,293	-1.6	3.9	18.9	37.9	25.1	18.1	51.7
Clarendon, SC	33,700	34,951	32,502	-1,251	2,449	-3.6	7.5	15.5	33.9	27.2	23.5	50.9
Sumter, SC	106,512	107,490	104,646	-978	2,844	-0.9	2.7	20.0	39.1	24.4	16.4	51.9
Syracuse, NY Metro Area	650,502	662,620	650,154	-12,118	12,466	-1.8	1.9	17.2	38.4	27.4	17.0	51.3
Madison, NY	70,795	73,451	69,441	-2,656	4,010	-3.6	5.8	15.4	37.5	28.8	18.3	50.7
Onondaga, NY	461,809	467,064	458,336	-5,255	8,728	-1.1	1.9	17.4	38.7	26.8	17.0	51.8
Oswego, NY	117,898	122,105	122,377	-4,207	-272	-3.4	-0.2	17.2	37.7	28.8	16.3	49.9
Tallahassee, FL Metro Area	385,145	368,770	320,304	16,375	48,466	4.4	15.1	16.0	46.8	22.7	14.5	51.9
Gadsden, FL	45,894	47,744	45,087	-1,850	2,657	-3.9	5.9	18.4	36.2	27.5	17.9	52.5
Jefferson, FL	14,288	14,759	12,902	-471	1,857	-3.2	14.4	14.3	32.2	29.9	23.5	47.6
Leon, FL	292,502	275,484	239,452	17,018	36,032	6.2	15.0	15.5	50.1	21.0	13.4	52.6
Wakulla, FL	32,461	30,783	22,863	1,678	7,920	5.5	34.6	17.6	38.2	28.6	15.7	46.6
Tampa-St. Petersburg-Clearwater, FL Metro Area	3,142,663	2,783,462	2,395,997	359,201	387,465	12.9	16.2	16.5	36.8	26.9	19.8	51.5
Hernando, FL	190,865	172,777	130,802	18,088	41,975	10.5	32.1	15.0	30.7	26.9	27.5	51.8
Hillsborough, FL	1,436,888	1,229,178	998,948	207,710	230,230	16.9	23.0	18.8	41.6	25.3	14.3	51.1
Pasco, FL	539,630	464,703	344,765	74,927	119,938	16.1	34.8	16.7	33.8	26.9	22.6	51.4
Pinellas, FL	975,280	916,804	921,482	58,476	-4,678	6.4	-0.5	13.3	32.5	29.4	24.8	52.0
Terre Haute, IN Metro Area	186,652	189,771	188,184	-3,119	1,587	-1.6	0.8	17.3	40.1	25.3	17.3	49.5
Clay, IN	26,170	26,884	26,556	-714	328	-2.7	1.2	18.9	35.8	27.5	17.9	50.6
Parke, IN	16,927	17,354	17,241	-427	113	-2.5	0.7	18.1	35.4	27.2	19.4	52.7
Sullivan, IN	20,690	21,475	21,751	-785	-276	-3.7	-1.3	15.6	39.4	27.0	18.0	45.7
Vermillion, IN	15,479	16,210	16,788	-731	-578	-4.5	-3.4	17.7	34.6	27.7	20.0	50.3
Vigo, IN	107,386	107,848	105,848	-462	2,000	-0.4	1.9	17.1	42.8	23.9	16.3	49.3
Texarkana, TX-AR Metro Area	150,242	149,194	143,377	1,048	5,817	0.7	4.1	19.6	38.3	25.1	17.0	50.2
Little River, AR	12,326	13,168	13,628	-842	-460	-6.4	-3.4	18.4	34.0	26.6	21.0	51.8
Miller, AR	43,592	43,462	40,443	130	3,019	0.3	7.5	19.7	37.8	25.6	16.9	50.9
Bowie, TX	94,324	92,564	89,306	1,760	3,258	1.9	3.6	19.8	39.0	24.7	16.5	49.7
The Villages, FL Metro Area	128,754	93,420	53,345	35,334	40,075	37.8	75.1	5.9	15.9	20.6	57.6	50.1
Sumter, FL	128,754	93,420	53,345	35,334	40,075	37.8	75.1	5.9	15.9	20.6	57.6	50.1
Toledo, OH Metro Area	643,640	651,435	659,188	-7,795	-7,753	-1.2	-1.2	18.4	38.9	26.0	16.7	51.2
Fulton, OH	42,276	42,698	42,084	-422	614	-1.0	1.5	19.3	35.4	27.6	17.8	50.3
Lucas, OH	429,899	441,815	455,054	-11,916	-13,239	-2.7	-2.9	19.2	38.4	26.1	16.3	51.5
Ottawa, OH	40,769	41,433	40,985	-664	448	-1.6	1.1	14.9	30.0	30.1	25.0	50.4
Wood, OH	130,696	125,489	121,065	5,207	4,424	4.1	3.7	16.9	44.1	23.7	15.3	50.7

Table C-1. Population and Population Characteristics—Continued

Metropolitan Statistical Area Metropolitan Division Component Counties	Population 2018 Estimate (July 1)	Population 2010 census estimates base (April 1)	Population 2000 census estimates base (April 1)	Net change 2010-2018	Net change 2000-2010	Percent change 2010-2018	Percent change 2000-2010	Under 15 years	15 to 44 years	45 to 64 years	65 years and over	Percent female
Topeka, KS Metro Area	232,594	233,867	224,551	-1,273	9,316	-0.5	4.1	19.4	35.9	26.2	18.4	51.1
Jackson, KS	13,280	13,460	12,657	-180	803	-1.3	6.3	20.4	33.5	27.0	19.1	50.0
Jefferson, KS	18,975	19,124	18,426	-149	698	-0.8	3.8	18.6	33.3	29.4	18.6	49.1
Osage, KS	15,941	16,294	16,712	-353	-418	-2.2	-2.5	18.9	33.0	28.3	19.8	49.9
Shawnee, KS	177,499	177,934	169,871	-435	8,063	-0.2	4.7	19.5	36.8	25.5	18.2	51.6
Wabaunsee, KS	6,899	7,055	6,885	-156	170	-2.2	2.5	18.9	32.3	28.8	20.0	48.9
Trenton-Princeton, NJ Metro Area	369,811	367,511	350,761	2,300	16,750	0.6	4.8	17.5	40.4	27.0	15.1	51.1
Mercer, NJ	369,811	367,511	350,761	2,300	16,750	0.6	4.8	17.5	40.4	27.0	15.1	51.1
Tucson, AZ Metro Area	1,039,073	980,263	843,746	58,810	136,517	6.0	16.2	17.3	39.5	23.4	19.8	50.8
Pima, AZ	1,039,073	980,263	843,746	58,810	136,517	6.0	16.2	17.3	39.5	23.4	19.8	50.8
Tulsa, OK Metro Area	993,797	937,532	859,532	56,265	78,000	6.0	9.1	20.5	39.1	24.8	15.5	50.9
Creek, OK	71,604	69,971	67,367	1,633	2,604	2.3	3.9	19.7	36.1	26.6	17.6	50.5
Okmulgee, OK	38,335	40,069	39,685	-1,734	384	-4.3	1.0	19.3	36.7	25.1	18.9	50.5
Osage, OK	47,014	47,476	44,437	-462	3,039		6.8	17.6	34.6	27.8	20.0	49.9
Pawnee, OK	16,390	16,579	16,612	-189	-33	-1.1	-0.2	19.5	34.2	27.0	19.3	50.4
Rogers, OK	91,984	86,918	70,641	5,066	16,277	5.8	23.0	19.0	37.7	26.9	16.4	50.1
Tulsa, OK	648,360	603,437	563,299	44,923	40,138	7.4	7.1	21.2	40.4	23.9	14.4	51.2
Wagoner, OK	80,110	73,082	57,491	7,028	15,591	9.6	27.1	20.0	37.8	25.9	16.3	50.5
Tuscaloosa, AL Metro Area	251,808	239,219	212,983	12,589	26,236	5.3	12.3	17.5	44.7	23.4	14.4	51.8
Greene, AL	8,233	9,043	9,974	-810	-931	-9.0	-9.3	18.3	33.1	26.2	22.3	52.8
Hale, AL	14,726	15,762	17,185	-1,036	-1,423	-6.6	-8.3	19.3	35.4	26.1	19.2	52.4
Pickens, AL	19,938	19,746	20,949	192	-1,203	1.0	-5.7	15.9	37.0	28.1	19.0	50.1
Tuscaloosa, AL	208,911	194,668	164,875	14,243	29,793	7.3	18.1	17.5	46.6	22.6	13.3	51.9
Twin Falls, ID Metro Area	110,096	99,596	82,626	10,500	16,970	10.5	20.5	23.9	39.3	22.0	14.9	50.3
Jerome, ID	24,015	22,366	18,342	1,649	4,024	7.4	21.9	26.2	38.6	22.2	13.0	49.0
Twin Falls, ID	86,081	77,230	64,284	8,851	12,946	11.5	20.1	23.2	39.5	21.9	15.4	50.6
Tyler, TX Metro Area	230,221	209,725	174,706	20,496	35,019	9.8	20.0	20.5	39.1	23.9	16.5	51.7
Smith, TX	230,221	209,725	174,706	20,496	35,019	9.8	20.0	20.5	39.1	23.9	16.5	51.7
Urban Honolulu, HI Metro Area	980,080	953,206	876,156	26,874	77,050	2.8	8.8	18.0	40.5	23.8	17.7	49.7
Honolulu, HI	980,080	953,206	876,156	26,874	77,050	2.8	8.8	18.0	40.5	23.8	17.7	49.7
Utica-Rome, NY Metro Area	291,410	299,330	299,896	-7,920	-566	-2.6	-0.2	17.4	36.1	27.3	19.2	50.3
Herkimer, NY	61,833	64,461	64,427	-2,628	34	-4.1	0.1	16.9	34.1	28.2	20.7	50.5
Oneida, NY	229,577	234,869	235,469	-5,292	-600	-2.3	-0.3	17.6	36.6	27.0	18.8	50.2
Valdosta, GA Metro Area	146,174	139,660	119,560	6,514	20,100	4.7	16.8	20.2	44.6	21.9	13.3	51.3
Brooks, GA	15,513	16,315	16,450	-802	-135	-4.9	-0.8	18.2	33.2	28.8	19.8	51.2
Echols, GA	4,000	4,027	3,754	-27	273	-0.7	7.3	22.2	40.6	24.3	13.0	48.3
Lanier, GA	10,340	10,070	7,241	270	2,829	2.7	39.1	20.5	39.8	25.6	14.1	49.5
Lowndes, GA	116,321	109,248	92,115	7,073	17,133	6.5	18.6	20.4	46.7	20.5	12.4	51.6
Vallejo, CA Metro Area	446,610	413,298	394,542	33,312	18,756	8.1	4.8	18.4	39.8	26.1	15.8	50.3
Solano, CA	446,610	413,298	394,542	33,312	18,756	8.1	4.8	18.4	39.8	26.1	15.8	50.3
Victoria, TX Metro Area	99,619	94,003	91,016	5,616	2,987	6.0	3.3	20.8	38.9	23.6	16.6	51.0
Goliad, TX	7,584	7,210	6,928	374	282	5.2	4.1	17.1	32.3	27.7	22.9	50.5
Victoria, TX	92,035	86,793	84,088	5,242	2,705	6.0	3.2	21.1	39.4	23.3	16.1	51.0
Vineland-Bridgeton, NJ Metro Area	150,972	156,633	146,438	-5,661	10,195	-3.6	7.0	20.0	39.3	25.4	15.3	49.0
Cumberland, NJ	150,972	156,633	146,438	-5,661	10,195	-3.6	7.0	20.0	39.3	25.4	15.3	49.0
Virginia Beach-Norfolk-Newport News, VA-NC Metro Area	1,765,042	1,713,954	1,612,770	51,088	101,184	3.0	6.3	18.4	42.0	24.9	14.8	50.8
Camden, NC	10,710	9,980	6,885	730	3,095	7.3	45.0	18.4	35.7	29.6	16.3	50.2
Currituck, NC	27,072	23,547	18,190	3,525	5,357	15.0	29.5	18.4	34.7	30.6	16.2	50.5
Gates, NC	11,573	12,184	10,516	-611	1,668	-5.0	15.9	16.2	31.8	31.7	20.2	50.5
Gloucester, VA	37,349	36,859	34,780	490	2,079	1.3	6.0	16.3	34.1	30.5	19.1	50.8
Isle of Wight, VA	36,953	35,274	29,728	1,679	5,546	4.8	18.7	17.0	33.4	30.4	19.1	51.0
James City County, VA	76,397	67,385	48,102	9,012	19,283	13.4	40.1	16.3	31.7	26.7	25.3	51.7
Mathews, VA	8,802	8,976	9,207	-174	-231	-1.9	-2.5	12.2	27.2	29.6	31.1	51.9
Southampton, VA	17,586	18,571	17,482	-985	1,089	-5.3	6.2	14.6	32.0	33.1	20.2	48.0
York, VA	67,846	65,239	56,297	2,607	8,942	4.0	15.9	19.3	37.9	26.7	16.1	51.0
Chesapeake City, VA	242,634	222,306	199,184	20,328	23,122	9.1	11.6	19.8	40.7	26.2	13.3	51.2
Franklin City, VA	8,013	8,580	8,346	-567	234	-6.6	2.8	19.7	33.9	26.7	19.7	54.9
Hampton City, VA	134,313	137,384	146,437	-3,071	-9,053	-2.2	-6.2	17.5	42.2	24.9	15.4	51.9
Newport News City, VA	178,626	180,994	180,150	-2,368	844	-1.3	0.5	19.7	44.3	23.0	13.1	51.7
Norfolk City, VA	244,076	242,827	234,403	1,249	8,424	0.5	3.6	16.9	51.2	20.7	11.2	47.9
Poquoson City, VA	12,190	12,157	11,566	33	591	0.3	5.1	17.9	34.7	28.1	19.4	50.0
Portsmouth City, VA	94,632	95,527	100,565	-895	-5,038	-0.9	-5.0	19.9	41.6	23.6	14.9	52.0
Suffolk City, VA	91,185	84,572	63,677	6,613	20,895	7.8	32.8	20.2	38.2	27.2	14.4	51.6
Virginia Beach City, VA	450,189	437,903	425,257	12,286	12,646	2.8	3.0	18.5	42.6	24.7	14.2	50.9
Williamsburg City, VA	14,896	13,689	11,998	1,207	1,691	8.8	14.1	9.4	56.7	17.6	16.3	54.0
Visalia, CA Metro Area	465,861	442,181	368,021	23,680	74,160	5.4	20.2	25.6	42.0	20.9	11.4	50.0
Tulare, CA	465,861	442,181	368,021	23,680	74,160	5.4	20.2	25.6	42.0	20.9	11.4	50.0
Waco, TX Metro Area	271,942	252,766	232,093	19,176	20,673	7.6	8.9	20.3	42.9	22.2	14.6	51.2
Falls, TX	17,335	17,867	18,576	-532	-709	-3.0	-3.8	17.5	38.4	25.9	18.2	52.5
McLennan, TX	254,607	234,899	213,517	19,708	21,382	8.4	10.0	20.5	43.2	21.9	14.4	51.1
Walla Walla, WA Metro Area	60,922	58,781	55,180	2,141	3,601	3.6	6.5	17.3	41.0	23.7	18.1	48.9
Walla Walla, WA	60,922	58,781	55,180	2,141	3,601	3.6	6.5	17.3	41.0	23.7	18.1	48.9
Warner Robins, GA Metro Area	182,766	167,602	134,433	15,164	33,169	9.0	24.7	20.6	40.9	25.2	13.2	51.6
Houston, GA	155,469	139,914	110,765	15,555	29,149	11.1	26.3	21.2	41.0	25.1	12.7	51.5
Peach, GA	27,297	27,688	23,668	-391	4,020	-1.4	17.0	17.3	40.8	25.9	16.0	51.8

Table C-1. Population and Population Characteristics—*Continued*

Metropolitan Statistical Area Metropolitan Division Component Counties	Population							Percent in each age group, 2018				Percent female
	2018 Estimate (July 1)	2010 census estimates base (April 1)	2000 census estimates base (April 1)	Net change 2010-2018	Net change 2000-2010	Percent change 2010-2018	Percent change 2000-2010	Under 15 years	15 to 44 years	45 to 64 years	65 years and over	
Washington-Arlington-Alexandria, DC-VA-MD-WV Metro Area	6,263,245	5,649,672	4,849,948	613,573	799,724	10.9	16.5	19.2	41.7	26.0	13.0	51.1
Frederick-Gaithersburg-Rockville, MD Div	1,308,215	1,205,355	1,068,618	102,860	136,737	8.5	12.8	19.2	38.3	27.2	15.3	51.5
Frederick, MD	255,648	233,391	195,277	22,257	38,114	9.5	19.5	19.0	38.5	28.1	14.5	50.7
Montgomery, MD	1,052,567	971,964	873,341	80,603	98,623	8.3	11.3	19.3	38.2	27.0	15.5	51.6
Washington-Arlington-Alexandria, DC-VA-MD-WV Division	4,955,030	4,444,317	3,781,330	510,713	662,987	11.5	17.5	19.2	42.7	25.7	12.4	51.0
District of Columbia	702,455	601,766	572,059	100,689	29,707	16.7	5.2	15.9	51.2	20.7	12.1	52.6
Calvert, MD	92,003	88,739	74,563	3,264	14,176	3.7	19.0	18.6	36.4	30.2	14.9	50.4
Charles, MD	161,503	146,565	120,546	14,938	26,019	10.2	21.6	19.6	38.8	29.1	12.5	51.8
Prince George's, MD	909,308	863,349	801,515	45,959	61,834	5.3	7.7	18.8	41.2	26.8	13.3	51.9
Arlington, VA	237,521	207,687	189,453	29,834	18,234	14.4	9.6	15.7	51.3	22.4	10.6	49.9
Clarke, VA	14,523	14,025	12,652	498	1,373	3.6	10.9	16.0	30.9	32.0	21.1	50.2
Culpeper, VA	51,859	46,691	34,262	5,168	12,429	11.1	36.3	20.6	36.7	27.0	15.7	50.0
Fairfax, VA	1,150,795	1,081,667	969,749	69,128	111,918	6.4	11.5	19.4	40.2	27.0	13.5	50.4
Fauquier, VA	70,675	65,236	55,139	5,439	10,097	8.3	18.3	18.9	35.0	29.6	16.4	50.5
Loudoun, VA	406,850	312,348	169,599	94,502	142,749	30.3	84.2	23.5	41.1	26.1	9.3	50.5
Madison, VA	13,295	13,309	12,520	-14	789	-0.1	6.3	16.4	31.7	29.6	22.3	51.7
Prince William, VA	468,011	401,997	280,813	66,014	121,184	16.4	43.2	22.7	41.8	25.6	9.9	50.0
Rappahannock, VA	7,252	7,503	6,983	-251	520	-3.3	7.4	13.1	28.8	30.8	27.3	50.9
Spotsylvania, VA	134,238	122,449	90,395	11,789	32,054	9.6	35.5	20.1	38.2	27.4	14.3	50.9
Stafford, VA	149,960	128,984	92,446	20,976	36,538	16.3	39.5	21.2	41.7	26.6	10.5	49.6
Warren, VA	40,003	37,435	31,584	2,568	5,851	6.9	18.5	18.2	36.4	29.3	16.0	50.2
Alexandria City, VA	160,530	140,008	128,283	20,522	11,725	14.7	9.1	16.0	48.2	24.3	11.5	51.9
Fairfax City, VA	24,574	22,554	21,498	2,020	1,056	9.0	4.9	21.7	38.3	25.7	14.3	50.3
Falls Church City, VA	14,772	12,279	10,377	2,493	1,902	20.3	18.3	22.1	37.3	27.4	13.2	50.9
Fredericksburg City, VA	29,144	24,178	19,279	4,966	4,899	20.5	25.4	18.0	50.0	20.8	11.2	53.8
Manassas City, VA	41,641	37,819	35,135	3,822	2,684	10.1	7.6	23.1	42.1	24.5	10.4	49.9
Manassas Park City, VA	17,307	14,241	10,290	3,066	3,951	21.5	38.4	18.3	47.8	25.9	8.0	48.5
Jefferson, WV	56,811	53,488	42,190	3,323	11,298	6.2	26.8	18.1	36.5	29.2	16.2	50.4
Waterloo-Cedar Falls, IA Metro Area	169,659	167,819	163,706	1,840	4,113	1.1	2.5	18.4	41.3	23.1	17.2	50.8
Black Hawk, IA	132,408	131,090	128,012	1,318	3,078	1.0	2.4	18.4	42.6	22.6	16.4	50.8
Bremer, IA	24,947	24,276	23,325	671	951	2.8	4.1	18.5	38.0	24.0	19.6	50.5
Grundy, IA	12,304	12,453	12,369	-149	84	-1.2	0.7	18.8	34.0	26.4	20.9	50.7
Watertown-Fort Drum, NY Metro Area	111,755	116,234	111,738	-4,479	4,496	-3.9	4.0	20.6	44.4	21.3	13.7	47.4
Jefferson, NY	111,755	116,234	111,738	-4,479	4,496	-3.9	4.0	20.6	44.4	21.3	13.7	47.4
Wausau-Weston, WI Metro Area	163,117	162,804	155,475	313	7,329	0.2	4.7	18.1	35.1	28.4	18.3	49.7
Lincoln, WI	27,689	28,743	29,641	-1,054	-898	-3.7	-3.0	14.6	31.4	32.6	21.5	49.3
Marathon, WI	135,428	134,061	125,834	1,367	8,227	1.0	6.5	18.8	35.9	27.6	17.7	49.7
Weirton-Steubenville, WV-OH Metro Area	117,064	124,450	132,008	-7,386	-7,558	-5.9	-5.7	15.4	33.6	28.7	22.4	51.3
Jefferson, OH	65,767	69,711	73,894	-3,944	-4,183	-5.7	-5.7	15.7	34.3	28.5	21.6	51.4
Brooke, WV	22,203	24,067	25,447	-1,864	-1,380	-7.7	-5.4	14.4	33.5	28.3	23.8	50.9
Hancock, WV	29,094	30,672	32,667	-1,578	-1,995	-5.1	-6.1	15.3	32.1	29.5	23.1	51.3
Wenatchee, WA Metro Area	119,943	110,887	99,219	9,056	11,668	8.2	11.8	20.2	36.5	24.8	18.5	49.8
Chelan, WA	77,036	72,460	66,616	4,576	5,844	6.3	8.8	19.5	36.2	25.3	19.1	50.0
Douglas, WA	42,907	38,427	32,603	4,480	5,824	11.7	17.9	21.4	37.1	23.9	17.6	49.3
Wheeling, WV-OH Metro Area	140,045	147,960	153,172	-7,915	-5,212	-5.3	-3.4	15.6	34.9	28.0	21.5	50.1
Belmont, OH	67,505	70,405	70,226	-2,900	179	-4.1	0.3	15.5	35.2	28.5	20.8	48.9
Marshall, WV	30,785	33,107	35,519	-2,322	-2,412	-7.0	-6.8	15.7	33.0	28.9	22.4	50.4
Ohio, WV	41,755	44,448	47,427	-2,693	-2,979	-6.1	-6.3	15.8	35.9	26.6	21.8	51.7
Wichita, KS Metro Area	637,578	623,063	571,166	14,515	51,897	2.3	9.1	21.2	39.4	24.3	15.0	50.4
Butler, KS	66,765	65,884	59,482	881	6,402	1.3	10.8	20.8	38.0	26.0	15.2	49.7
Harvey, KS	34,210	34,684	32,869	-474	1,815	-1.4	5.5	19.8	36.7	24.0	19.5	50.6
Sedgwick, KS	513,607	498,358	452,869	15,249	45,489	3.1	10.0	21.5	40.0	24.1	14.5	50.5
Sumner, KS	22,996	24,137	25,946	-1,141	-1,809	-4.7	-7.0	20.0	35.0	26.3	18.7	49.9
Wichita Falls, TX Metro Area	151,306	151,474	151,524	-168	-50	-0.1	0.0	18.7	42.0	23.8	15.6	48.5
Archer, TX	8,786	9,055	8,854	-269	201	-3.0	2.3	17.7	33.0	29.2	20.0	50.8
Clay, TX	10,456	10,754	11,006	-298	-252	-2.8	-2.3	16.2	31.3	29.8	22.7	50.2
Wichita, TX	132,064	131,665	131,664	399	1	0.3	0.0	18.9	43.4	22.9	14.7	48.3
Williamsport, PA Metro Area	113,664	116,114	120,044	-2,450	-3,930	-2.1	-3.3	17.0	36.5	27.2	19.3	51.0
Lycoming, PA	113,664	116,114	120,044	-2,450	-3,930	-2.1	-3.3	17.0	36.5	27.2	19.3	51.0
Wilmington, NC Metro Area	294,436	254,881	201,389	39,555	53,492	15.5	26.6	15.9	40.1	26.1	17.8	51.9
New Hanover, NC	232,274	202,683	160,307	29,591	42,376	14.6	26.4	15.3	41.6	25.3	17.7	52.3
Pender, NC	62,162	52,198	41,082	9,964	11,116	19.1	27.1	18.2	34.6	29.2	18.0	50.1
Winchester, VA-WV Metro Area	139,810	128,475	102,997	11,335	25,478	8.8	24.7	18.3	36.4	27.4	17.9	50.2
Frederick, VA	88,355	78,283	59,209	10,072	19,074	12.9	32.2	19.0	36.2	27.6	17.3	50.2
Winchester City, VA	28,108	26,223	23,585	1,885	2,638	7.2	11.2	19.1	40.5	24.4	15.9	51.3
Hampshire, WV	23,347	23,969	20,203	-622	3,766	-2.6	18.6	15.0	32.2	30.4	22.4	49.0
Winston-Salem, NC Metro Area	671,456	640,537	569,207	30,919	71,330	4.8	12.5	18.2	36.7	27.7	17.5	51.9
Davidson, NC	166,614	162,841	147,246	3,773	15,595	2.3	10.6	17.9	34.8	29.1	18.2	51.1
Davie, NC	42,733	41,221	34,835	1,512	6,386	3.7	18.3	17.0	32.3	29.6	21.2	51.2
Forsyth, NC	379,099	350,649	306,067	28,450	44,582	8.1	14.6	18.9	38.9	26.2	16.0	52.6
Stokes, NC	45,467	47,417	44,711	-1,950	2,706	-4.1	6.1	15.1	32.2	31.5	21.3	50.8
Yadkin, NC	37,543	38,409	36,348	-866	2,061	-2.3	5.7	17.0	33.3	29.6	20.2	50.8

Table C-1. Population and Population Characteristics—*Continued*

Metropolitan Statistical Area Metropolitan Division Component Counties	Population							Percent in each age group, 2018				Percent female
	2018 Estimate (July 1)	2010 census estimates base (April 1)	2000 census estimates base (April 1)	Net change		Percent change		Under 15 years	15 to 44 years	45 to 64 years	65 years and over	
				2010-2018	2000-2010	2010-2018	2000-2010					
Worcester, MA-CT Metro Area	947,866	916,764	860,054	31,102	56,710	3.4	6.6	17.0	38.7	28.6	15.8	50.7
Windham, CT	117,027	118,381	109,091	-1,354	9,290	-1.1	8.5	16.1	38.3	29.0	16.6	50.5
Worcester, MA	830,839	798,383	750,963	32,456	47,420	4.1	6.3	17.2	38.7	28.5	15.6	50.7
Yakima, WA Metro Area	251,446	243,240	222,581	8,206	20,659	3.4	9.3	24.9	39.6	21.8	13.7	50.0
Yakima, WA	251,446	243,240	222,581	8,206	20,659	3.4	9.3	24.9	39.6	21.8	13.7	50.0
York-Hanover, PA Metro Area	448,273	435,008	381,751	13,265	53,257	3.0	14.0	18.2	36.4	27.9	17.4	50.6
York, PA	448,273	435,008	381,751	13,265	53,257	3.0	14.0	18.2	36.4	27.9	17.4	50.6
Youngstown-Warren-Boardman, OH-PA Metro Area	538,952	565,781	602,964	-26,829	-37,183	-4.7	-6.2	16.3	34.5	27.8	21.4	51.0
Mahoning, OH	229,642	238,788	257,555	-9,146	-18,767	-3.8	-7.3	16.4	35.2	27.5	21.0	51.0
Trumbull, OH	198,627	210,325	225,116	-11,698	-14,791	-5.6	-6.6	16.7	33.7	28.0	21.6	51.3
Mercer, PA	110,683	116,668	120,293	-5,985	-3,625	-5.1	-3.0	15.6	34.6	28.2	21.7	50.6
Yuba City, CA Metro Area	174,848	166,902	139,149	7,946	27,753	4.8	19.9	22.4	40.4	23.0	14.2	49.8
Sutter, CA	96,807	94,756	78,930	2,051	15,826	2.2	20.1	21.5	39.3	23.9	15.4	50.2
Yuba, CA	78,041	72,146	60,219	5,895	11,927	8.2	19.8	23.5	41.9	21.9	12.8	49.4
Yuma, AZ Metro Area	212,128	195,750	160,026	16,378	35,724	8.4	22.3	21.1	40.2	19.9	18.8	48.5
Yuma, AZ	212,128	195,750	160,026	16,378	35,724	8.4	22.3	21.1	40.2	19.9	18.8	48.5

Table C-2. Population Characteristiics and Housing Units

Metropolitan Statistical Area Metropolitan Division Component counties	Population characteristics, 2018						Housing Units					
	Race alone or in combination, not of Hispanic origin (percent)										Percent change	
	White	Black or African-American	Asian	American Indian, Alaska Native	Native Hawaiian, Pacific Islander	Hispanic or Latino origin (percent)	2018 (July 1 estimate)	2015 (July 1 estimate)	2010 (July 1 estimate)	2000 (July 1 estimate)	2010-2018	2000-2010
Abilene, TX Metro Area	66.1	8.4	2.5	0.9	0.2	23.9	71,930	70,966	69,748	65,395	3.1	6.7
Callahan, TX	87.2	2.1	1.0	1.3	0.1	9.9	6,706	6,648	6,555	5,932	2.3	10.5
Jones, TX	59.2	12.5	0.7	0.8	0.1	27.8	7,437	7,422	7,415	7,253	0.3	2.2
Taylor, TX	64.9	8.5	3.0	0.9	0.2	24.8	57,787	56,896	55,778	52,210	3.6	6.8
Akron, OH Metro Area	81.7	13.8	4.0	0.7	0.1	2.2	315,499	314,190	312,633	291,804	0.9	7.1
Portage, OH	91.1	5.6	2.6	0.7	0.1	1.9	69,326	68,563	67,496	60,339	2.7	11.9
Summit, OH	78.8	16.3	4.4	0.8	0.1	2.2	246,173	245,627	245,137	231,465	0.4	5.9
Albany, GA Metro Area	41.1	55.1	1.5	0.6	0.1	2.8	65,547	65,103	64,509	62,170	1.6	3.8
Dougherty, GA	25.3	71.1	1.2	0.5	0.1	2.9	40,593	40,700	40,794	39,737	-0.5	2.7
Lee, GA	72.0	22.4	3.1	0.6	0.1	3.0	11,451	10,919	10,300	8,855	11.2	16.3
Terrell, GA	36.5	60.7	0.7	0.6	0.1	2.7	4,166	4,173	4,162	4,455	0.1	-6.6
Worth, GA	68.7	28.6	0.8	0.6	0.1	2.3	9,337	9,311	9,253	9,123	0.9	1.4
Albany-Lebanon, OR Metro Area	87.5	1.2	1.9	2.8	0.4	9.3	50,883	49,571	48,870	42,661	4.1	14.6
Linn, OR	87.5	1.2	1.9	2.8	0.4	9.3	50,883	49,571	48,870	42,661	4.1	14.6
Albany-Schenectady-Troy, NY Metro Area	81.6	9.4	5.3	0.6	0.1	5.4	410,490	402,290	393,605	364,471	4.3	8.0
Albany, NY	73.9	14.2	7.7	0.5	0.1	6.1	142,305	139,951	137,788	130,211	3.3	5.8
Rensselaer, NY	84.7	8.2	3.3	0.6	0.1	5.2	73,264	72,613	71,530	66,242	2.4	8.0
Saratoga, NY	91.7	2.4	3.7	0.5	0.1	3.4	107,374	103,387	98,811	87,017	8.7	13.6
Schenectady, NY	75.9	12.8	6.0	1.1	0.3	7.4	69,954	68,886	68,238	65,132	2.5	4.8
Schoharie, NY	94.2	1.9	1.1	0.7	0.1	3.3	17,593	17,453	17,238	15,869	2.1	8.6
Albuquerque, NM Metro Area	40.4	2.9	2.9	6.1	0.2	49.4	392,050	385,144	375,161	307,455	4.5	22.0
Bernalillo, NM	40.1	3.2	3.4	4.8	0.2	50.3	295,216	291,171	284,780	239,649	3.7	18.8
Sandoval, NM	44.7	2.6	2.0	13.0	0.2	39.4	57,328	55,087	52,422	35,726	9.4	46.7
Torrance, NM	51.9	1.9	0.8	3.1	0.2	43.8	8,098	7,999	7,811	7,276	3.7	7.4
Valencia, NM	33.3	1.3	0.8	4.5	0.1	61.0	31,408	30,887	30,148	24,804	4.2	21.5
Alexandria, LA Metro Area	64.9	30.2	1.6	1.5	0.1	3.5	67,818	66,671	64,673	60,558	4.9	6.8
Grant, LA	77.9	16.0	0.7	1.6	0.1	5.2	9,422	9,174	8,905	8,544	5.8	4.2
Rapides, LA	62.7	32.7	1.8	1.5	0.1	3.2	58,396	57,497	55,768	52,014	4.7	7.2
Allentown-Bethlehem-Easton, PA-NJ Metro Area	73.7	6.2	3.5	0.5	0.1	17.7	350,522	347,806	342,593	308,188	2.3	11.2
Warren, NJ	82.4	5.4	3.4	0.4	0.1	9.7	45,562	45,396	44,989	41,321	1.3	8.9
Carbon, PA	92.3	2.3	0.8	0.6	0.1	5.1	34,817	34,710	34,337	30,546	1.4	12.4
Lehigh, PA	64.9	6.8	4.0	0.4	0.1	25.4	146,707	145,079	142,814	129,237	2.7	10.5
Northampton, PA	77.5	6.5	3.4	0.5	0.1	13.8	123,436	122,621	120,453	107,084	2.5	12.5
Altoona, PA Metro Area	95.9	2.8	1.0	0.4	0.1	1.3	56,945	56,640	56,304	55,077	1.1	2.2
Blair, PA	95.9	2.8	1.0	0.4	0.1	1.3	56,945	56,640	56,304	55,077	1.1	2.2
Amarillo, TX Metro Area	60.4	6.9	3.9	1.0	0.1	29.2	109,989	107,924	103,513	92,624	6.3	11.8
Armstrong, TX	89.7	1.2	0.5	1.4	0.1	8.0	914	900	904	920	1.1	-1.7
Carson, TX	86.7	1.7	0.8	2.2	0.1	10.5	2,800	2,784	2,783	2,813	0.6	-1.1
Oldham, TX	78.5	3.6	1.5	1.3	0.0	16.3	859	850	842	815	2.0	3.3
Potter, TX	44.8	10.9	6.1	0.9	0.1	38.7	50,175	49,393	47,326	44,680	6.0	5.9
Randall, TX	72.3	3.8	2.1	1.0	0.1	22.3	55,241	53,997	51,658	43,396	6.9	19.0
Ames, IA Metro Area	87.1	3.1	7.5	0.5	0.1	3.4	52,800	50,600	48,567	41,681	8.7	16.5
Boone, IA	95.2	1.7	0.8	0.7	0.1	2.7	12,034	11,854	11,759	10,973	2.3	7.2
Story, IA	84.9	3.4	9.3	0.5	0.1	3.6	40,766	38,746	36,808	30,708	10.8	19.9
Anchorage, AK Metro Area	69.5	6.1	9.8	11.7	2.6	8.2	160,226	157,338	154,498	104,318	3.7	48.1
Anchorage, AK	63.8	7.6	12.3	12.0	3.3	9.3	118,236	115,645	113,147	100,661	4.5	12.4
Matanuska-Susitna, AK	85.0	2.1	3.2	10.9	0.8	5.1	41,990	41,693	41,351	3,657	1.5	1030.7
Ann Arbor, MI Metro Area	73.0	13.6	10.9	1.0	0.1	4.8	151,550	149,993	147,646	131,863	2.6	12.0
Washtenaw, MI	73.0	13.6	10.9	1.0	0.1	4.8	151,550	149,993	147,646	131,863	2.6	12.0
Anniston-Oxford, AL Metro Area	73.7	21.8	1.3	1.0	0.2	3.9	53,888	53,608	53,331	51,309	1.0	3.9
Calhoun, AL	73.7	21.8	1.3	1.0	0.2	3.9	53,888	53,608	53,331	51,309	1.0	3.9
Appleton, WI Metro Area	89.5	1.9	3.8	1.8	0.1	4.4	98,527	96,124	92,938	78,841	6.0	17.9
Calumet, WI	92.0	1.3	2.7	0.8	0.1	4.4	20,933	20,250	19,721	15,900	6.1	24.0
Outagamie, WI	88.8	2.1	4.1	2.1	0.1	4.4	77,594	75,874	73,217	62,941	6.0	16.3
Asheville, NC Metro Area	86.7	5.3	1.5	1.0	0.2	7.1	231,269	221,111	213,881	176,319	8.1	21.3
Buncombe, NC	85.3	7.1	1.8	1.0	0.2	6.7	126,567	118,930	113,540	94,451	11.5	20.2
Haywood, NC	93.6	1.6	0.7	1.1	0.1	4.1	35,567	35,289	34,976	28,812	1.7	21.4
Henderson, NC	84.6	4.0	1.5	1.0	0.2	10.4	58,097	56,083	54,753	43,299	6.1	26.5
Madison, NC	95.1	1.9	0.7	1.2	0.1	2.4	11,038	10,809	10,612	9,757	4.0	8.8
Athens-Clarke County, GA Metro Area	67.2	21.1	4.3	0.5	0.1	8.7	86,439	84,296	81,776	67,872	5.7	20.5
Clarke, GA	56.7	28.8	5.0	0.5	0.1	10.9	53,143	52,287	51,067	42,481	4.1	20.2
Madison, GA	82.9	9.9	2.1	0.8	0.1	5.8	12,022	11,949	11,807	10,565	1.8	11.8
Oconee, GA	85.5	5.7	4.7	0.4	0.1	5.1	14,593	13,481	12,410	9,450	17.6	31.3
Oglethorpe, GA	76.8	18.0	1.2	0.7	0.1	5.0	6,681	6,579	6,492	5,376	2.9	20.8
Atlanta-Sandy Springs-Alpharetta, GA Metro Area	48.3	35.3	6.8	0.7	0.1	10.9	2,330,253	2,240,371	2,173,913	1,666,401	7.2	30.5
Barrow, GA	72.4	13.1	4.2	0.7	0.1	11.5	28,951	27,464	26,414	17,532	9.6	50.7
Bartow, GA	78.9	11.8	1.3	0.8	0.1	8.8	41,532	40,250	39,835	29,150	4.3	36.7
Butts, GA	67.2	29.1	0.8	0.7	0.0	3.5	9,452	9,339	9,359	7,441	1.0	25.8
Carroll, GA	72.5	20.4	1.2	0.7	0.1	7.2	45,530	45,074	44,624	34,476	2.0	29.4
Cherokee, GA	80.1	7.7	2.6	0.7	0.1	10.8	94,218	87,760	82,460	52,924	14.3	55.8
Clayton, GA	11.0	71.4	5.4	0.7	0.2	13.3	105,859	104,930	104,825	87,260	1.0	20.1
Cobb, GA	53.4	28.8	6.2	0.7	0.1	13.2	302,646	295,323	286,536	239,141	5.6	19.8
Coweta, GA	72.4	18.8	2.7	0.7	0.1	7.1	55,398	52,805	50,247	33,555	10.3	49.7
Dawson, GA	93.1	1.3	1.1	0.9	0.1	4.8	11,771	10,830	10,437	7,228	12.8	44.4

Table C-2. Population Characteristiics and Housing Units—*Continued*

Metropolitan Statistical Area / Metropolitan Division / Component counties	Population characteristics, 2018						Housing Units					
	Race alone or in combination, not of Hispanic origin (percent)					Hispanic or Latino origin (percent)	2018 (July 1 estimate)	2015 (July 1 estimate)	2010 (July 1 estimate)	2000 (July 1 estimate)	Percent change	
	White	Black or African-American	Asian	American Indian, Alaska Native	Native Hawaiian, Pacific Islander						2010-2018	2000-2010
De Kalb, GA	30.6	54.9	7.1	0.7	0.1	8.6	314,302	307,163	304,962	262,573	3.1	16.1
Douglas, GA	40.7	48.5	2.1	0.8	0.2	10.0	53,033	52,150	51,662	35,166	2.7	46.9
Fayette, GA	63.1	24.7	6.0	0.7	0.2	7.4	43,033	41,626	40,801	33,003	5.5	23.6
Forsyth, GA	71.7	4.4	15.2	0.6	0.1	9.7	84,142	74,405	64,245	37,341	31.0	72.0
Fulton, GA	41.1	44.8	8.2	0.6	0.1	7.3	480,341	454,794	437,137	350,513	9.9	24.7
Gwinnett, GA	38.2	28.9	13.1	0.7	0.1	21.5	312,896	301,820	291,678	212,550	7.3	37.2
Haralson, GA	92.3	5.4	1.0	0.9	0.1	1.8	12,530	12,360	12,287	10,763	2.0	14.2
Heard, GA	86.6	10.8	0.8	0.9	0.1	2.8	5,229	5,172	5,145	4,528	1.6	13.6
Henry, GA	43.6	46.8	4.0	0.8	0.2	7.2	82,826	78,742	76,548	44,273	8.2	72.9
Jasper, GA	75.6	20.5	0.4	0.8	0.1	4.0	6,505	6,335	6,162	4,852	5.6	27.0
Lamar, GA	66.0	31.3	1.0	0.8	0.1	2.5	7,615	7,530	7,474	6,185	1.9	20.8
Meriwether, GA	58.0	39.8	0.7	0.8	0.1	2.2	10,015	9,954	9,953	9,245	0.6	7.7
Morgan, GA	73.6	22.9	0.9	0.7	0.1	3.3	7,845	7,587	7,475	6,191	4.9	20.7
Newton, GA	46.8	46.8	1.5	0.7	0.2	5.9	39,693	38,644	38,356	23,475	3.5	63.4
Paulding, GA	71.6	21.2	1.7	0.8	0.2	6.7	58,036	54,214	52,220	29,939	11.1	74.4
Pickens, GA	94.8	1.6	0.8	1.0	0.1	3.1	14,107	13,825	13,692	10,800	3.0	26.8
Pike, GA	88.4	10.0	0.8	0.7	0.1	1.6	7,055	6,876	6,836	5,031	3.2	35.9
Rockdale, GA	31.7	56.8	2.3	0.7	0.3	10.4	33,848	33,379	33,264	25,357	1.8	31.2
Spalding, GA	59.6	35.2	1.4	0.8	0.2	4.7	27,580	27,107	26,823	23,114	2.8	16.0
Walton, GA	75.3	18.9	1.9	0.6	0.1	4.7	34,265	32,913	32,456	22,795	5.6	42.4
Atlantic City-Hammonton, NJ Metro Area	57.5	15.6	9.0	0.6	0.1	19.2	128,409	127,856	126,776	114,431	1.3	10.8
Atlantic, NJ	57.5	15.6	9.0	0.6	0.1	19.2	128,409	127,856	126,776	114,431	1.3	10.8
Auburn-Opelika, AL Metro Area	68.9	23.5	4.7	0.7	0.1	3.8	70,369	67,039	62,722	50,508	12.2	24.2
Lee, AL	68.9	23.5	4.7	0.7	0.1	3.8	70,369	67,039	62,722	50,508	12.2	24.2
Augusta-Richmond County, GA-SC Metro Area	56.4	36.6	2.7	0.9	0.2	5.6	260,909	252,590	242,202	209,903	7.7	15.4
Burke, GA	48.7	47.8	0.7	0.8	0.2	3.3	10,072	9,956	9,869	8,879	2.1	11.1
Columbia, GA	70.7	19.0	5.4	0.8	0.3	6.9	58,736	54,830	48,883	33,713	20.2	45.0
Lincoln, GA	68.0	29.9	0.7	1.0	0.1	2.0	4,914	4,851	4,788	4,525	2.6	5.8
McDuffie, GA	54.6	42.4	0.7	0.7	0.1	3.2	9,361	9,322	9,316	8,946	0.5	4.1
Richmond, GA	36.3	57.6	2.5	0.9	0.3	5.0	89,092	87,698	86,412	82,336	3.1	5.0
Aiken, SC	67.6	25.8	1.5	1.1	0.1	5.9	77,687	75,159	72,367	62,250	7.4	16.3
Edgefield, SC	57.8	35.9	0.7	0.8	0.1	6.0	11,047	10,774	10,567	9,254	4.5	14.2
Austin-Round Rock-Georgetown, TX Metro Area	53.6	7.8	7.1	0.8	0.2	32.7	853,701	784,546	708,577	502,748	20.5	40.9
Bastrop, TX	53.3	7.3	1.0	1.0	0.1	38.7	30,168	29,319	29,349	22,429	2.8	30.9
Caldwell, TX	40.0	6.3	1.1	0.7	0.1	53.0	15,098	14,176	13,789	11,926	9.5	15.6
Hays, TX	54.7	4.3	2.1	0.8	0.1	39.6	82,002	73,370	59,753	36,310	37.2	64.6
Travis, TX	50.6	8.7	8.0	0.7	0.2	33.9	527,803	487,002	442,443	339,194	19.3	30.4
Williamson, TX	60.7	7.4	8.4	0.8	0.2	24.8	198,630	180,679	163,243	92,889	21.7	75.7
Bakersfield, CA Metro Area	35.2	5.9	5.5	1.2	0.3	54.0	300,377	293,523	284,767	232,436	5.5	22.5
Kern, CA	35.2	5.9	5.5	1.2	0.3	54.0	300,377	293,523	284,767	232,436	5.5	22.5
Baltimore-Columbia-Towson, MD Metro Area	58.2	30.6	6.8	0.8	0.2	6.1	1,164,130	1,150,687	1,132,766	1,050,614	2.8	7.8
Anne Arundel, MD	70.0	18.7	5.2	0.8	0.2	8.1	226,420	220,449	212,735	187,804	6.4	13.3
Baltimore, MD	58.5	30.4	7.0	0.8	0.1	5.7	337,210	336,095	335,705	314,305	0.4	6.8
Carroll, MD	90.3	4.5	2.6	0.5	0.1	3.7	63,726	63,234	62,416	54,589	2.1	14.3
Harford, MD	77.7	15.4	3.9	0.7	0.2	4.7	100,968	98,840	95,701	83,607	5.5	14.5
Howard, MD	54.0	21.0	20.5	0.8	0.2	7.1	120,838	116,457	109,617	93,391	10.2	17.4
Queen Anne's, MD	88.2	7.2	1.7	0.7	0.1	4.1	21,315	20,903	20,169	16,785	5.7	20.2
Baltimore city, MD	29.2	63.2	3.3	0.9	0.1	5.5	293,653	294,709	296,423	300,133	-0.9	-1.2
Bangor, ME Metro Area	95.3	1.4	1.5	2.1	0.1	1.4	76,136	75,089	73,937	66,999	3.0	10.4
Penobscot, ME	95.3	1.4	1.5	2.1	0.1	1.4	76,136	75,089	73,937	66,999	3.0	10.4
Barnstable Town, MA Metro Area	91.3	4.0	2.0	1.2	0.1	3.2	164,321	162,694	160,372	147,569	2.5	8.7
Barnstable, MA	91.3	4.0	2.0	1.2	0.1	3.2	164,321	162,694	160,372	147,569	2.5	8.7
Baton Rouge, LA Metro Area	57.7	36.3	2.4	0.7	0.1	4.1	368,882	357,315	340,862	293,107	8.2	16.3
Ascension, LA	69.2	23.9	1.6	0.7	0.1	5.7	48,680	45,505	41,007	29,398	18.7	39.5
Assumption, LA	66.4	30.0	0.5	0.9	0.1	3.1	10,867	10,640	10,368	9,654	4.8	7.4
East Baton Rouge, LA	45.5	47.3	3.7	0.6	0.1	4.2	195,190	192,115	187,509	169,395	4.1	10.7
East Feliciana, LA	54.9	43.3	0.5	1.0	0.1	1.7	8,552	8,305	8,033	7,920	6.5	1.4
Iberville, LA	48.3	48.8	0.5	0.5	0.1	2.7	13,583	13,181	12,719	11,935	6.8	6.6
Livingston, LA	88.5	7.0	0.9	0.8	0.1	3.8	58,274	55,190	50,444	36,552	15.5	38.0
Pointe Coupee, LA	61.2	35.9	0.5	0.5	0.0	2.9	11,613	11,409	11,148	10,318	4.2	8.0
St. Helena, LA	45.3	52.5	0.6	0.9	0.0	1.9	5,364	5,239	5,162	5,049	3.9	2.2
West Baton Rouge, LA	56.4	40.2	0.9	0.6	0.1	3.2	11,223	10,381	9,362	8,386	19.9	11.6
West Feliciana, LA	53.5	44.8	0.3	0.5	0.1	1.6	5,536	5,350	5,110	4,500	8.3	13.6
Battle Creek, MI Metro Area	80.2	12.9	3.4	1.4	0.1	5.3	60,864	60,885	61,023	58,824	-0.3	3.7
Calhoun, MI	80.2	12.9	3.4	1.4	0.1	5.3	60,864	60,885	61,023	58,824	-0.3	3.7
Bay City, MI Metro Area	91.7	2.8	0.8	1.1	0.1	5.4	48,336	48,213	48,216	46,496	0.2	3.7
Bay, MI	91.7	2.8	0.8	1.1	0.1	5.4	48,336	48,213	48,216	46,496	0.2	3.7
Beaumont-Port Arthur, TX Metro Area	56.3	24.6	3.1	0.8	0.1	16.4	171,510	168,625	162,803	156,951	5.3	3.7
Hardin, TX	87.5	6.0	0.9	0.9	0.1	5.9	25,004	24,055	22,661	19,936	10.3	13.7
Jefferson, TX	40.9	33.9	4.2	0.7	0.1	21.5	108,771	107,871	104,755	102,156	3.8	2.5
Orange, TX	81.7	9.1	1.5	1.1	0.1	8.0	37,735	36,699	35,387	34,859	6.6	1.5
Beckley, WV Metro Area	90.9	7.6	0.9	0.9	0.1	1.5	57,690	57,767	57,598	57,319	0.2	0.5
Fayette, WV	93.9	5.3	0.4	0.8	0.1	1.2	21,518	21,573	21,627	21,628	-0.5	0.0
Raleigh, WV	89.1	9.0	1.2	0.9	0.1	1.7	36,172	36,194	35,971	35,691	0.6	0.8

Table C-2. Population Characteristiics and Housing Units—*Continued*

Metropolitan Statistical Area / Metropolitan Division / Component counties	Population characteristics, 2018 — Race alone or in combination, not of Hispanic origin (percent)					Hispanic or Latino origin (percent)	Housing Units				Percent change	
	White	Black or African-American	Asian	American Indian, Alaska Native	Native Hawaiian, Pacific Islander		2018 (July 1 estimate)	2015 (July 1 estimate)	2010 (July 1 estimate)	2000 (July 1 estimate)	2010-2018	2000-2010
Bellingham, WA Metro Area	81.8	1.9	6.1	3.8	0.6	9.5	97,855	94,365	90,775	74,335	7.8	22.1
Whatcom, WA	81.8	1.9	6.1	3.8	0.6	9.5	97,855	94,365	90,775	74,335	7.8	22.1
Bend, OR Metro Area	89.3	0.9	2.0	1.7	0.4	8.1	91,041	84,483	80,233	55,131	13.5	45.5
Deschutes, OR	89.3	0.9	2.0	1.7	0.4	8.1	91,041	84,483	80,233	55,131	13.5	45.5
Billings, MT Metro Area	89.3	1.3	1.2	5.1	0.2	5.5	83,843	79,743	75,408	64,256	11.2	17.4
Carbon, MT	95.4	0.8	0.6	1.9	0.2	2.5	6,572	6,553	6,462	5,511	1.7	17.3
Stillwater, MT	93.7	0.6	0.9	2.0	0.2	4.4	4,879	4,876	4,807	3,985	1.5	20.6
Yellowstone, MT	88.6	1.4	1.3	5.5	0.2	5.8	72,392	68,314	64,139	54,760	12.9	17.1
Binghamton, NY Metro Area	87.5	5.9	4.4	0.7	0.1	3.9	113,834	113,027	112,803	110,305	0.9	2.3
Broome, NY	85.4	7.0	5.2	0.7	0.1	4.3	91,234	90,632	90,617	88,830	0.7	2.0
Tioga, NY	95.8	1.4	1.1	0.6	0.1	2.1	22,600	22,395	22,186	21,475	1.9	3.3
Birmingham-Hoover, AL Metro Area	63.0	31.0	1.9	0.7	0.1	4.6	488,586	480,077	469,503	423,274	4.1	10.9
Bibb, AL	75.5	21.7	0.4	0.8	0.1	2.6	9,239	9,114	8,990	8,362	2.8	7.5
Blount, AL	88.1	1.9	0.5	1.2	0.1	9.6	24,429	24,107	23,900	21,235	2.2	12.6
Chilton, AL	81.2	10.6	0.6	0.8	0.1	7.9	19,791	19,525	19,280	17,725	2.7	8.8
Jefferson, AL	50.7	43.8	2.1	0.6	0.1	4.0	309,560	306,046	300,648	288,547	3.0	4.2
St. Clair, AL	86.9	10.0	1.1	0.9	0.1	2.5	37,179	36,346	35,489	27,498	4.8	29.1
Shelby, AL	78.7	13.5	2.6	0.7	0.1	5.8	88,388	84,939	81,196	59,907	8.9	35.5
Bismarck, ND Metro Area	90.6	2.5	1.1	4.7	0.1	2.9	59,393	56,902	48,889	40,645	21.5	20.3
Burleigh, ND	90.2	2.9	1.2	4.8	0.1	2.6	43,152	41,454	35,874	29,137	20.3	23.1
Morton, ND	91.3	1.6	0.7	4.4	0.1	3.7	15,280	14,509	12,108	10,608	26.2	14.1
Oliver, ND	94.6	0.9	0.5	3.5	0.1	2.0	961	939	907	900	6.0	0.8
Blacksburg-Christiansburg, VA Metro Area	88.0	5.6	5.0	0.6	0.1	2.8	72,872	71,682	70,623	62,912	3.2	12.3
Giles, VA	95.7	2.2	0.8	0.6	0.1	1.9	8,359	8,356	8,322	7,763	0.4	7.2
Montgomery, VA	85.7	4.9	7.7	0.6	0.2	3.3	40,707	39,515	38,644	32,641	5.3	18.4
Pulaski, VA	92.3	6.0	0.7	0.6	0.1	1.8	17,286	17,284	17,237	16,362	0.3	5.3
Radford City, VA	85.0	11.1	2.6	0.7	0.1	3.0	6,520	6,527	6,420	6,146	1.6	4.5
Bloomington, IL Metro Area	81.4	9.3	6.0	0.5	0.1	5.1	72,680	71,844	69,761	60,176	4.2	15.9
McLean, IL	81.4	9.3	6.0	0.5	0.1	5.1	72,680	71,844	69,761	60,176	4.2	15.9
Bloomington, IN Metro Area	87.1	4.1	7.1	0.8	0.1	3.2	72,279	70,913	69,251	60,912	4.4	13.7
Monroe, IN	85.7	4.5	8.0	0.7	0.1	3.5	62,058	60,807	59,150	51,034	4.9	15.9
Owen, IN	97.1	0.9	0.8	0.9	0.1	1.5	10,221	10,106	10,101	9,878	1.2	2.3
Bloomsburg-Berwick, PA Metro Area	93.6	2.2	1.8	0.5	0.1	2.9	38,557	38,090	37,507	35,405	2.8	5.9
Columbia, PA	94.0	2.2	1.4	0.5	0.1	2.9	30,323	29,963	29,536	27,769	2.7	6.4
Montour, PA	91.9	2.2	3.5	0.4	0.1	2.9	8,234	8,127	7,971	7,636	3.3	4.4
Boise City, ID Metro Area	82.2	1.5	3.2	1.3	0.4	13.8	282,300	262,587	246,511	182,764	14.5	34.9
Ada, ID	86.9	1.9	4.1	1.1	0.5	8.3	186,481	171,977	159,814	119,537	16.7	33.7
Boise, ID	92.6	0.9	1.0	2.4	0.5	4.9	5,604	5,427	5,301	4,361	5.7	21.6
Canyon, ID	72.0	0.9	1.6	1.5	0.4	25.6	77,867	73,112	69,506	48,483	12.0	43.4
Gem, ID	89.5	0.5	1.4	1.9	0.2	8.4	7,407	7,214	7,104	5,919	4.3	20.0
Owyhee, ID	69.8	0.7	0.9	3.6	0.1	26.3	4,941	4,857	4,786	4,464	3.2	7.2
Boston-Cambridge-Newton, MA-NH Metro Area	71.8	8.7	9.2	0.5	0.1	11.5	1,973,298	1,931,147	1,884,401	1,754,936	4.7	7.4
Boston, MA Div	66.2	14.2	8.9	0.6	0.2	12.0	830,457	808,860	786,699	730,598	5.6	7.7
Norfolk, MA	76.1	7.8	12.7	0.4	0.1	4.8	280,291	275,842	270,625	255,470	3.6	5.9
Plymouth, MA	83.2	11.7	2.0	0.7	0.2	4.1	208,114	204,718	200,368	181,991	3.9	10.1
Suffolk, MA	46.6	21.5	9.8	0.7	0.2	23.4	342,052	328,300	315,706	293,137	8.3	7.7
Cambridge-Newton-Framingham, MA Div	72.6	5.4	10.7	0.4	0.1	12.7	955,356	938,894	919,134	865,154	3.9	6.2
Essex, MA	70.8	4.2	4.1	0.4	0.1	21.9	313,958	311,138	306,701	287,647	2.4	6.6
Middlesex, MA	73.5	6.0	13.9	0.4	0.1	8.3	641,398	627,756	612,433	577,507	4.7	6.0
Rockingham County-Strafford County, NH Div	93.2	1.4	3.2	0.7	0.1	3.0	187,485	183,393	178,568	159,184	5.0	12.2
Rockingham, NH	93.6	1.2	2.7	0.6	0.1	3.2	133,178	130,214	126,809	113,497	5.0	11.7
Strafford, NH	92.3	1.9	4.3	0.8	0.1	2.6	54,307	53,179	51,759	45,687	4.9	13.3
Boulder, CO Metro Area	79.8	1.5	6.1	0.9	0.2	13.9	137,435	132,710	127,149	112,068	8.1	13.5
Boulder, CO	79.8	1.5	6.1	0.9	0.2	13.9	137,435	132,710	127,149	112,068	8.1	13.5
Bowling Green, KY Metro Area	84.0	8.5	3.7	0.7	0.3	4.7	76,043	72,335	68,964	58,620	10.3	17.6
Allen, KY	96.0	1.9	0.4	0.8	0.0	2.2	9,507	9,422	9,316	8,098	2.1	15.0
Butler, KY	95.6	1.0	0.4	0.7	0.0	3.5	5,965	5,927	5,882	5,817	1.4	1.1
Edmonson, KY	95.8	2.4	0.6	1.0	0.0	1.3	6,607	6,547	6,478	6,120	2.0	5.8
Warren, KY	79.8	10.9	4.9	0.6	0.4	5.6	53,964	50,439	47,288	38,585	14.1	22.6
Bremerton-Silverdale-Port Orchard, WA Metro Area	81.2	4.3	8.0	2.9	1.7	8.0	113,733	110,752	107,500	93,010	5.8	15.6
Kitsap, WA	81.2	4.3	8.0	2.9	1.7	8.0	113,733	110,752	107,500	93,010	5.8	15.6
Bridgeport-Stamford-Norwalk, CT Metro Area	62.8	11.7	6.3	0.4	0.1	20.2	374,481	368,889	361,481	340,078	3.6	6.3
Fairfield, CT	62.8	11.7	6.3	0.4	0.1	20.2	374,481	368,889	361,481	340,078	3.6	6.3
Brownsville-Harlingen, TX Metro Area	9.0	0.5	0.8	0.2	0.0	89.8	152,353	148,192	142,175	120,234	7.2	18.2
Cameron, TX	9.0	0.5	0.8	0.2	0.0	89.8	152,353	148,192	142,175	120,234	7.2	18.2
Brunswick, GA Metro Area	69.3	24.4	1.5	0.8	0.2	5.5	61,279	59,811	58,097	45,185	5.5	28.6
Brantley, GA	93.7	4.3	0.5	1.3	0.0	2.0	8,155	8,104	8,086	6,540	0.9	23.6
Glynn, GA	64.9	27.2	1.9	0.7	0.2	6.8	43,512	42,234	40,774	32,836	6.7	24.2
McIntosh, GA	63.3	34.4	0.5	0.8	0.1	2.2	9,612	9,473	9,237	5,809	4.1	59.0
Buffalo-Cheektowaga, NY Metro Area	78.8	13.1	3.7	1.1	0.1	5.2	530,328	525,882	519,412	511,881	2.1	1.5
Erie, NY	76.8	14.1	4.3	0.9	0.1	5.7	429,714	425,782	420,202	416,085	2.3	1.0
Niagara, NY	87.5	8.6	1.5	1.6	0.1	3.1	100,614	100,100	99,210	95,796	1.4	3.6
Burlington, NC Metro Area	64.9	21.1	2.0	0.9	0.1	12.9	71,660	68,766	66,691	55,721	7.5	19.7
Alamance, NC	64.9	21.1	2.0	0.9	0.1	12.9	71,660	68,766	66,691	55,721	7.5	19.7

Table C-2. Population Characteristiics and Housing Units—*Continued*

Metropolitan Statistical Area Metropolitan Division Component counties	Population characteristics, 2018						Housing Units					
	Race alone or in combination, not of Hispanic origin (percent)					Hispanic or Latino origin (percent)	2018 (July 1 estimate)	2015 (July 1 estimate)	2010 (July 1 estimate)	2000 (July 1 estimate)	Percent change	
	White	Black or African-American	Asian	American Indian, Alaska Native	Native Hawaiian, Pacific Islander						2010-2018	2000-2010
Burlington-South Burlington, VT Metro Area	91.6	2.7	4.4	1.2	0.1	2.2	98,398	95,879	92,508	82,989	6.4	11.5
Chittenden, VT	90.2	3.2	5.5	0.8	0.1	2.4	70,352	68,371	65,822	59,077	6.9	11.4
Franklin, VT	95.7	1.2	1.2	2.4	0.1	1.7	22,714	22,299	21,627	19,242	5.0	12.4
Grand Isle, VT	95.0	1.4	0.8	3.3	0.1	2.1	5,332	5,209	5,059	4,670	5.4	8.3
California-Lexington Park, MD Metro Area	76.8	16.2	4.0	0.9	0.2	5.3	46,013	43,696	41,377	34,336	11.2	20.5
St. Mary's, MD	76.8	16.2	4.0	0.9	0.2	5.3	46,013	43,696	41,377	34,336	11.2	20.5
Canton-Massillon, OH Metro Area	89.3	9.0	1.2	0.8	0.1	2.1	180,617	179,855	178,924	170,237	0.9	5.1
Carroll, OH	97.2	1.2	0.6	0.9	0.1	1.4	13,626	13,641	13,693	13,036	-0.5	5.0
Stark, OH	88.7	9.6	1.3	0.8	0.1	2.2	166,991	166,214	165,231	157,201	1.1	5.1
Cape Coral-Fort Myers, FL Metro Area	67.9	8.8	2.1	0.5	0.1	21.9	399,729	381,640	371,257	247,782	7.7	49.8
Lee, FL	67.9	8.8	2.1	0.5	0.1	21.9	399,729	381,640	371,257	247,782	7.7	49.8
Cape Girardeau, MO-IL Metro Area	87.6	9.4	1.9	0.8	0.1	2.2	44,073	43,235	42,533	39,679	3.6	7.2
Alexander, IL	65.2	33.4	0.6	0.9	0.2	1.8	3,977	3,984	4,005	4,578	-0.7	-12.5
Bollinger, MO	97.0	0.9	0.4	1.4	0.1	1.4	5,883	5,888	5,879	5,537	0.1	6.2
Cape Girardeau, MO	87.8	8.9	2.2	0.8	0.1	2.4	34,213	33,363	32,649	29,564	4.8	10.4
Carbondale-Marion, IL Metro Area	84.7	10.2	2.8	0.8	0.1	3.5	66,048	65,715	64,617	59,727	2.2	8.2
Jackson, IL	76.3	16.3	4.5	1.0	0.2	4.5	29,026	28,975	28,619	26,888	1.4	6.4
Johnson, IL	89.5	7.2	0.5	0.7	0.1	3.1	5,642	5,629	5,601	5,066	0.7	10.6
Williamson, IL	91.0	5.5	1.7	0.8	0.1	2.8	31,380	31,111	30,397	27,773	3.2	9.4
Carson City, NV Metro Area	68.8	2.4	3.2	2.9	0.4	24.5	24,026	23,700	23,537	21,369	2.1	10.1
Carson City city, NV	68.8	2.4	3.2	2.9	0.4	24.5	24,026	23,700	23,537	21,369	2.1	10.1
Casper, WY Metro Area	88.4	1.9	1.2	1.7	0.2	8.6	37,181	36,504	33,905	29,952	9.7	13.2
Natrona, WY	88.4	1.9	1.2	1.7	0.2	8.6	37,181	36,504	33,905	29,952	9.7	13.2
Cedar Rapids, IA Metro Area	89.3	6.4	2.8	0.6	0.2	3.1	118,215	115,698	112,516	99,271	5.1	13.3
Benton, IA	97.2	1.2	0.5	0.5	0.1	1.5	11,180	11,134	11,094	10,393	0.8	6.7
Jones, IA	93.9	3.1	1.1	0.5	0.1	2.1	8,972	8,957	8,913	8,137	0.7	9.5
Linn, IA	88.0	7.3	3.2	0.6	0.2	3.4	98,063	95,607	92,509	80,741	6.0	14.6
Chambersburg-Waynesboro, PA Metro Area	89.3	4.5	1.4	0.6	0.1	5.9	65,791	64,930	63,337	54,022	3.9	17.2
Franklin, PA	89.3	4.5	1.4	0.6	0.1	5.9	65,791	64,930	63,337	54,022	3.9	17.2
Champaign-Urbana, IL Metro Area	71.3	13.6	11.3	0.5	0.2	5.8	100,829	98,169	94,930	82,380	6.2	15.2
Champaign, IL	69.3	14.5	12.2	0.5	0.2	6.1	93,396	90,793	87,662	75,562	6.5	16.0
Piatt, IL	97.2	1.2	0.8	0.5	0.1	1.4	7,433	7,376	7,268	6,818	2.3	6.6
Charleston, WV Metro Area	92.5	6.6	1.1	0.7	0.1	1.0	131,510	131,564	131,446	132,388	0.0	-0.7
Boone, WV	98.4	1.1	0.2	0.4	0.0	0.6	11,166	11,149	11,074	11,575	0.8	-4.3
Clay, WV	98.4	0.6	0.2	0.8	0.1	0.9	4,629	4,621	4,579	4,838	1.1	-5.4
Jackson, WV	97.8	1.1	0.4	0.8	0.0	1.0	13,433	13,364	13,310	12,283	0.9	8.4
Kanawha, WV	90.0	9.1	1.5	0.8	0.1	1.1	92,333	92,508	92,595	93,836	-0.3	-1.3
Lincoln, WV	98.6	0.7	0.3	0.6	0.0	0.7	9,949	9,922	9,888	9,856	0.6	0.3
Charleston-North Charleston, SC Metro Area	66.2	26.5	2.7	1.0	0.2	5.7	339,494	319,888	299,173	234,443	13.5	27.6
Berkeley, SC	65.8	25.2	3.5	1.2	0.2	6.9	85,956	80,065	73,844	55,081	16.4	34.1
Charleston, SC	66.3	27.2	2.2	0.7	0.1	5.1	191,891	180,890	170,157	141,817	12.8	20.0
Dorchester, SC	66.3	26.7	2.8	1.3	0.2	5.6	61,647	58,933	55,172	37,545	11.7	46.9
Charlotte-Concord-Gastonia, NC-SC Metro Area	62.2	24.0	4.5	0.9	0.1	10.4	1,060,922	1,003,886	949,584	724,317	11.7	31.1
Anson, NC	45.3	49.0	1.6	1.1	0.1	4.3	11,628	11,587	11,569	10,259	0.5	12.8
Cabarrus, NC	66.5	19.3	4.7	0.8	0.1	10.8	80,873	76,844	72,144	53,302	12.1	35.3
Gaston, NC	73.6	18.2	1.9	0.9	0.1	7.3	93,881	90,644	88,815	79,193	5.7	12.2
Iredell, NC	77.3	12.8	3.0	0.7	0.1	7.8	75,599	71,405	69,129	52,362	9.4	32.0
Lincoln, NC	86.3	6.2	0.9	0.8	0.1	7.2	36,767	34,476	33,549	26,006	9.6	29.0
Mecklenburg, NC	48.1	32.7	6.8	0.9	0.1	13.6	454,062	427,487	399,104	296,038	13.8	34.8
Rowan, NC	73.1	17.1	1.4	0.8	0.1	9.2	61,982	60,992	60,282	54,235	2.8	11.1
Union, NC	73.2	12.6	3.7	0.8	0.1	11.4	82,557	78,082	73,004	46,441	13.1	57.2
Chester, SC	60.1	37.8	0.6	1.0	0.1	2.1	14,795	14,737	14,706	14,416	0.6	2.0
Lancaster, SC	71.3	22.1	1.7	0.6	0.1	5.6	38,541	35,348	32,709	25,198	17.8	29.8
York, SC	72.0	20.1	2.9	1.3	0.1	5.7	110,237	102,284	94,573	66,867	16.6	41.4
Charlottesville, VA Metro Area	77.5	13.1	5.6	0.7	0.1	5.5	96,429	93,589	89,263	74,168	8.0	20.4
Albemarle, VA	78.7	10.6	6.5	0.6	0.1	5.9	46,076	44,290	42,175	33,867	9.2	24.5
Fluvanna, VA	80.1	16.4	1.3	0.8	0.2	3.6	11,047	10,763	10,427	8,081	5.9	29.0
Greene, VA	84.8	8.3	2.3	0.7	0.1	6.1	8,344	8,112	7,529	6,032	10.8	24.8
Nelson, VA	83.1	12.3	0.9	1.0	0.1	4.5	10,190	10,089	9,936	8,586	2.6	15.7
Charlottesville City, VA	68.4	19.2	8.6	0.6	0.2	5.7	20,772	20,335	19,196	17,602	8.2	9.1
Chattanooga, TN-GA Metro Area	79.7	14.4	2.0	0.8	0.1	4.7	246,062	240,246	234,608	206,170	4.9	13.8
Catoosa, GA	92.3	3.6	1.7	0.9	0.2	3.1	27,531	27,015	26,629	21,879	3.4	21.7
Dade, GA	95.0	1.6	1.3	1.2	0.1	2.3	7,302	7,271	7,309	6,253	-0.1	16.9
Walker, GA	92.2	5.3	0.9	0.8	0.1	2.3	30,458	30,223	30,104	25,750	1.2	16.9
Hamilton, TN	72.6	20.0	2.5	0.8	0.1	5.9	160,770	156,090	151,226	135,179	6.3	11.9
Marion, TN	93.1	4.8	0.8	1.0	0.1	1.8	13,497	13,185	12,962	12,200	4.1	6.2
Sequatchie, TN	94.9	1.2	0.6	1.2	0.1	3.5	6,504	6,462	6,378	4,907	2.0	30.0
Cheyenne, WY Metro Area	80.7	3.4	2.0	1.4	0.2	14.8	43,894	42,456	40,558	34,317	8.2	18.2
Laramie, WY	80.7	3.4	2.0	1.4	0.2	14.8	43,894	42,456	40,558	34,317	8.2	18.2
Chicago-Naperville-Elgin, IL-IN-WI Metro Area	54.0	17.0	7.7	0.5	0.1	22.4	3,858,431	3,819,770	3,797,174	3,471,602	1.6	9.4
Chicago-Naperville-Evanston, IL Div	50.6	19.2	8.6	0.4	0.1	22.7	2,946,802	2,920,517	2,909,629	2,720,412	1.3	7.0
Cook, IL	43.4	23.7	8.4	0.5	0.1	25.5	2,200,221	2,182,532	2,179,777	2,097,845	0.9	3.9
Du Page, IL	67.9	5.5	13.4	0.4	0.1	14.5	361,429	358,308	356,120	336,656	1.5	5.8
Grundy, IL	87.1	2.0	1.2	0.4	0.1	10.2	21,138	20,578	20,016	15,114	5.6	32.4

Table C-2. Population Characteristiics and Housing Units—*Continued*

Metropolitan Statistical Area / Metropolitan Division / Component counties	White	Black or African-American	Asian	American Indian, Alaska Native	Native Hawaiian, Pacific Islander	Hispanic or Latino origin (percent)	2018 (July 1 estimate)	2015 (July 1 estimate)	2010 (July 1 estimate)	2000 (July 1 estimate)	2010-2018	2000-2010
McHenry, IL	81.9	2.0	3.5	0.5	0.1	13.4	118,814	117,799	116,127	93,422	2.3	24.3
Will, IL	64.4	12.4	6.5	0.4	0.1	17.8	245,200	241,300	237,589	177,375	3.2	33.9
Elgin, IL Div.	62.7	6.7	4.4	0.4	0.1	27.3	272,919	267,925	263,647	193,493	3.5	36.3
De Kalb, IL	77.9	8.6	3.3	0.5	0.1	11.4	41,248	41,104	41,098	33,141	0.4	24.0
Kane, IL	58.0	6.0	4.7	0.4	0.1	32.2	189,472	185,344	182,158	140,480	4.0	29.7
Kendall, IL	70.0	8.0	3.8	0.3	0.1	19.5	42,199	41,477	40,391	19,872	4.5	103.3
Gary, IN Div.	64.8	17.9	1.8	0.6	0.1	16.3	302,903	298,497	294,266	270,298	2.9	8.9
Jasper, IN	92.4	1.2	0.6	0.6	0.1	6.1	13,641	13,446	13,187	11,287	3.4	16.8
Lake, IN	55.3	24.3	2.0	0.6	0.1	19.4	213,779	211,333	208,848	195,352	2.4	6.9
Newton, IN	91.9	1.1	0.6	0.8	0.1	6.4	6,095	6,065	6,029	5,765	1.1	4.6
Porter, IN	84.1	4.5	1.9	0.6	0.1	10.3	69,388	67,653	66,202	57,894	4.8	14.4
Lake County-Kenosha County, IL-WI Div	65.5	7.7	7.6	0.5	0.1	20.5	335,807	332,831	329,632	287,399	1.9	14.7
Lake, IL	62.6	7.6	9.0	0.5	0.1	22.2	265,150	262,868	260,330	227,135	1.9	14.6
Kenosha, WI	77.7	8.2	2.2	0.8	0.1	13.4	70,657	69,963	69,302	60,264	2.0	15.0
Chico, CA Metro Area	75.1	2.6	6.1	3.0	0.5	16.7	100,033	98,031	95,923	85,759	4.3	11.9
Butte, CA	75.1	2.6	6.1	3.0	0.5	16.7	100,033	98,031	95,923	85,759	4.3	11.9
Cincinnati, OH-KY-IN Metro Area	81.1	13.6	3.3	0.6	0.1	3.3	946,883	934,015	921,114	838,863	2.8	9.8
Dearborn, IN	97.3	1.2	0.7	0.6	0.1	1.3	20,615	20,348	20,182	17,901	2.1	12.7
Franklin, IN	97.2	0.7	1.2	0.6	0.0	1.2	9,814	9,677	9,551	8,648	2.8	10.4
Ohio, IN	97.4	1.0	0.5	0.6	0.1	1.5	2,860	2,824	2,779	2,410	2.9	15.3
Union, IN	96.5	1.4	1.0	0.8	0.1	1.8	3,259	3,244	3,239	3,086	0.6	5.0
Boone, KY	89.3	4.3	3.2	0.6	0.2	4.3	50,047	48,374	46,263	33,744	8.2	37.1
Bracken, KY	97.1	1.5	0.4	0.6	0.1	1.9	3,880	3,860	3,842	3,721	1.0	3.3
Campbell, KY	93.7	3.8	1.3	0.5	0.1	2.2	40,545	39,838	39,553	36,963	2.5	7.0
Gallatin, KY	92.6	2.5	0.4	0.7	0.1	5.5	3,944	3,894	3,793	3,368	4.0	12.6
Grant, KY	95.5	1.5	0.6	0.6	0.2	2.7	10,258	10,116	9,953	9,347	3.1	6.5
Kenton, KY	90.3	6.0	1.7	0.5	0.2	3.4	69,858	69,490	69,002	63,683	1.2	8.4
Pendleton, KY	97.2	1.3	0.5	0.7	0.1	1.4	6,396	6,366	6,338	5,781	0.9	9.6
Brown, OH	97.4	1.4	0.4	0.8	0.1	1.1	20,391	19,896	19,326	17,146	5.5	12.7
Butler, OH	82.6	9.9	4.2	0.6	0.1	4.9	152,718	150,330	148,367	130,273	2.9	13.9
Clermont, OH	94.8	2.3	1.7	0.7	0.1	2.0	83,793	82,415	80,735	69,284	3.8	16.5
Hamilton, OH	67.1	27.8	3.4	0.7	0.1	3.5	380,064	378,412	377,282	373,586	0.7	1.0
Warren, OH	87.3	4.2	6.7	0.5	0.1	2.8	88,441	84,931	80,909	59,922	9.3	35.0
Clarksville, TN-KY Metro Area	69.1	20.9	3.1	1.3	0.5	9.1	127,462	122,979	114,485	92,590	11.3	23.6
Christian, KY	68.0	23.2	2.2	1.1	0.5	8.1	30,007	29,824	29,466	27,325	1.8	7.8
Trigg, KY	90.0	8.2	0.7	0.9	0.2	2.3	7,965	7,904	7,813	6,734	1.9	16.0
Montgomery, TN	66.4	22.2	3.6	1.3	0.6	10.3	82,598	78,413	70,429	52,525	17.3	34.1
Stewart, TN	93.4	2.3	1.3	1.6	0.1	3.1	6,892	6,838	6,777	6,006	1.7	12.8
Cleveland, TN Metro Area	88.5	5.2	1.2	1.0	0.1	5.8	53,208	51,522	49,445	44,347	7.6	11.5
Bradley, TN	87.3	5.8	1.3	0.9	0.1	6.3	44,156	42,954	41,428	36,962	6.6	12.1
Polk, TN	96.3	1.1	0.5	1.4	0.1	2.2	9,052	8,568	8,017	7,385	12.9	8.6
Cleveland-Elyria, OH Metro Area	71.3	21.0	3.0	0.6	0.1	6.0	963,468	959,530	955,826	912,850	0.8	4.7
Cuyahoga, OH	60.5	30.9	3.8	0.6	0.1	6.2	617,889	619,310	621,554	617,165	-0.6	0.7
Geauga, OH	96.4	1.6	0.9	0.4	0.0	1.6	37,334	36,946	36,584	33,004	2.1	10.8
Lake, OH	89.2	5.3	1.9	0.5	0.1	4.7	103,281	102,339	101,230	93,679	2.0	8.1
Lorain, OH	80.3	9.6	1.7	0.8	0.1	10.2	131,916	129,672	127,135	111,814	3.8	13.7
Medina, OH	95.0	2.0	1.6	0.5	0.0	2.1	73,048	71,263	69,323	57,188	5.4	21.2
Coeur d'Alene, ID Metro Area	92.6	0.8	1.6	2.2	0.3	4.8	72,499	67,720	63,376	46,939	14.4	35.0
Kootenai, ID	92.6	0.8	1.6	2.2	0.3	4.8	72,499	67,720	63,376	46,939	14.4	35.0
College Station-Bryan, TX Metro Area	57.4	11.8	6.2	0.6	0.1	25.4	110,833	103,143	95,224	75,583	16.4	26.0
Brazos, TX	56.7	11.0	7.1	0.6	0.1	26.0	92,697	85,437	77,897	59,480	19.0	31.0
Burleson, TX	65.8	13.4	0.6	0.9	0.1	20.8	9,213	9,053	8,840	8,218	4.2	7.6
Robertson, TX	58.1	19.8	0.9	0.8	0.1	21.5	8,923	8,653	8,487	7,885	5.1	7.6
Colorado Springs, CO Metro Area	72.9	7.6	4.4	1.5	0.6	17.1	288,745	278,430	265,807	214,514	8.6	23.9
El Paso, CO	72.3	7.8	4.5	1.5	0.6	17.5	275,396	265,418	253,149	204,051	8.8	24.1
Teller, CO	90.4	1.3	1.6	1.8	0.2	6.8	13,349	13,012	12,658	10,463	5.5	21.0
Columbia, MO Metro Area	82.4	10.7	5.4	1.0	0.2	3.3	91,037	86,898	81,743	68,049	11.4	20.1
Boone, MO	81.1	11.2	6.1	1.0	0.2	3.5	78,940	74,812	69,695	56,980	13.3	22.3
Cooper, MO	89.7	8.2	0.9	1.1	0.1	2.1	7,505	7,501	7,466	6,713	0.5	11.2
Howard, MO	92.4	6.1	0.6	1.4	0.1	1.6	4,592	4,585	4,582	4,356	0.2	5.2
Columbia, SC Metro Area	57.8	34.8	2.8	0.8	0.2	5.7	359,526	346,856	332,208	270,721	8.2	22.7
Calhoun, SC	55.2	40.6	0.5	0.8	0.1	3.9	7,498	7,420	7,342	6,871	2.1	6.9
Fairfield, SC	39.6	58.0	0.9	0.8	0.1	2.2	11,946	11,814	11,686	10,406	2.2	12.3
Kershaw, SC	70.2	25.2	1.0	0.7	0.1	4.4	29,381	28,505	27,559	22,808	6.6	20.8
Lexington, SC	76.0	15.9	2.5	0.9	0.2	6.3	126,197	120,764	114,384	91,483	10.3	25.0
Richland, SC	43.9	48.7	3.6	0.8	0.2	5.2	175,070	168,998	161,943	130,581	8.1	24.0
Saluda, SC	58.9	24.9	0.5	0.7	0.1	16.2	9,434	9,355	9,294	8,572	1.5	8.4
Columbus, GA-AL Metro Area	47.9	43.1	2.8	1.0	0.3	7.5	140,527	138,418	134,217	121,440	4.7	10.5
Russell, AL	47.9	46.0	1.4	1.1	0.4	5.6	27,855	27,117	24,752	22,925	12.5	8.0
Chattahoochee, GA	60.3	21.0	4.1	1.6	0.9	16.1	3,338	3,353	3,375	3,324	-1.1	1.5
Harris, GA	78.1	17.2	1.6	0.8	0.2	3.8	14,344	13,862	13,410	10,417	7.0	28.7
Marion, GA	60.5	31.4	1.1	1.1	0.3	7.2	4,218	4,182	4,158	3,158	1.4	31.7
Muscogee, GA	42.3	48.2	3.6	0.9	0.3	7.7	85,008	84,141	82,737	76,363	2.7	8.3
Stewart, GA	24.6	40.8	2.8	1.1	0.1	31.5	2,338	2,350	2,381	2,357	-1.8	1.0
Talbot, GA	42.1	54.9	0.5	0.9	0.1	2.8	3,426	3,413	3,404	2,896	0.6	17.5

Table C-2. Population Characteristiics and Housing Units—*Continued*

Metropolitan Statistical Area Metropolitan Division Component counties	Population characteristics, 2018 Race alone or in combination, not of Hispanic origin (percent)					Hispanic or Latino origin (percent)	Housing Units				Percent change	
	White	Black or African-American	Asian	American Indian, Alaska Native	Native Hawaiian, Pacific Islander		2018 (July 1 estimate)	2015 (July 1 estimate)	2010 (July 1 estimate)	2000 (July 1 estimate)	2010-2018	2000-2010
Columbus, IN Metro Area	82.8	3.0	8.1	0.6	0.1	6.9	34,531	33,901	33,114	29,964	4.3	10.5
Bartholomew, IN	82.8	3.0	8.1	0.6	0.1	6.9	34,531	33,901	33,114	29,964	4.3	10.5
Columbus, OH Metro Area	74.7	17.5	5.3	0.8	0.1	4.3	869,366	847,735	821,697	710,597	5.8	15.6
Delaware, OH	86.3	4.5	7.9	0.5	0.1	2.7	74,520	70,659	66,488	43,212	12.1	53.9
Fairfield, OH	87.6	9.2	2.2	0.8	0.1	2.3	61,548	60,172	58,729	48,781	4.8	20.4
Franklin, OH	65.2	24.9	6.4	0.9	0.1	5.7	559,903	545,927	527,716	472,954	6.1	11.6
Hocking, OH	97.5	1.2	0.5	1.0	0.1	1.1	13,408	13,375	13,417	12,177	-0.1	10.2
Licking, OH	91.8	5.2	2.2	0.8	0.1	2.0	71,047	70,409	69,320	59,171	2.5	17.2
Madison, OH	89.8	7.2	1.7	0.8	0.1	2.1	16,118	16,041	15,941	14,407	1.1	10.6
Morrow, OH	97.2	1.2	0.6	0.8	0.1	1.5	14,338	14,230	14,160	12,182	1.3	16.2
Perry, OH	98.0	1.0	0.3	1.1	0.1	0.9	15,349	15,257	15,206	13,683	0.9	11.1
Pickaway, OH	94.0	4.6	0.8	0.8	0.1	1.4	21,566	21,282	21,268	18,689	1.4	13.8
Union, OH	90.6	3.3	5.1	0.6	0.1	1.8	21,569	20,383	19,452	15,341	10.9	26.8
Corpus Christi, TX Metro Area	31.3	3.5	2.3	0.6	0.1	63.3	178,433	174,860	167,734	148,344	6.4	13.1
Nueces, TX	29.9	3.9	2.4	0.6	0.1	64.2	149,950	147,606	141,184	123,317	6.2	14.5
San Patricio, TX	38.6	1.8	1.3	0.6	0.2	58.4	28,483	27,254	26,550	25,027	7.3	6.1
Corvallis, OR Metro Area	83.3	1.8	8.9	1.6	0.6	7.6	38,451	37,928	36,321	32,074	5.9	13.2
Benton, OR	83.3	1.8	8.9	1.6	0.6	7.6	38,451	37,928	36,321	32,074	5.9	13.2
Crestview-Fort Walton Beach-Destin, FL Metro Area	79.0	9.8	4.2	1.4	0.3	8.8	151,330	144,877	137,659	108,371	9.9	27.0
Okaloosa, FL	76.5	11.2	5.0	1.3	0.4	9.7	97,945	95,646	92,479	79,225	5.9	16.7
Walton, FL	86.4	5.8	2.0	1.7	0.2	6.4	53,385	49,231	45,180	29,146	18.2	55.0
Cumberland, MD-WV Metro Area	90.4	8.0	1.2	0.5	0.1	1.6	45,977	46,161	46,335	45,158	-0.8	2.6
Allegany, MD	88.6	9.5	1.4	0.5	0.1	1.9	32,826	33,036	33,294	32,984	-1.4	0.9
Mineral, WV	95.2	3.9	0.8	0.6	0.0	1.0	13,151	13,125	13,041	12,174	0.8	7.1
Dallas-Fort Worth-Arlington, TX Metro Area	47.0	16.7	7.9	0.9	0.2	29.2	2,822,550	2,657,652	2,504,213	2,008,038	12.7	24.7
Dallas-Plano-Irving, TX Div	44.4	17.4	9.1	0.8	0.1	30.0	1,905,035	1,776,921	1,660,227	1,337,580	14.7	24.1
Collin, TX	58.1	10.9	17.0	0.9	0.2	15.4	377,338	337,976	301,963	197,215	25.0	53.1
Dallas, TX	29.8	23.3	7.1	0.7	0.1	40.5	1,027,837	982,229	943,269	855,824	9.0	10.2
Denton, TX	60.3	11.0	10.3	1.0	0.2	19.5	319,948	289,364	257,163	170,445	24.4	50.9
Ellis, TX	61.2	11.4	1.1	1.0	0.2	26.6	63,512	58,376	54,484	39,443	16.6	38.1
Hunt, TX	72.6	8.7	1.8	1.5	0.2	17.0	38,084	37,331	36,770	32,600	3.6	12.8
Kaufman, TX	63.7	12.9	1.6	1.1	0.1	22.4	42,480	39,900	38,383	26,441	10.7	45.2
Rockwall, TX	71.8	7.2	3.7	0.9	0.2	18.0	35,836	31,745	28,195	15,612	27.1	80.6
Fort Worth-Arlington-Grapevine, TX Div	52.3	15.4	5.6	0.9	0.3	27.5	917,515	880,731	843,986	670,458	8.7	25.9
Johnson, TX	72.7	4.1	1.3	1.1	0.5	22.0	62,793	60,309	56,845	46,486	10.5	22.3
Parker, TX	84.3	1.9	1.0	1.4	0.1	12.8	50,820	48,829	46,777	34,361	8.6	36.1
Tarrant, TX	47.7	17.6	6.4	0.9	0.3	29.2	778,975	747,238	716,570	570,237	8.7	25.7
Wise, TX	77.6	1.7	0.9	1.4	0.1	19.7	24,927	24,355	23,794	19,374	4.8	22.8
Dalton, GA Metro Area	65.5	3.4	1.3	0.6	0.1	30.3	56,311	55,831	55,890	45,456	0.8	23.0
Murray, GA	82.8	1.3	0.6	0.7	0.1	15.6	16,168	16,010	15,983	14,391	1.2	11.1
Whitfield, GA	58.8	4.2	1.6	0.6	0.1	35.9	40,143	39,821	39,907	31,065	0.6	28.5
Danville, IL Metro Area	80.1	15.2	1.2	0.6	0.1	5.2	36,129	36,154	36,310	36,375	-0.5	-0.2
Vermilion, IL	80.1	15.2	1.2	0.6	0.1	5.2	36,129	36,154	36,310	36,375	-0.5	-0.2
Daphne-Fairhope-Foley, AL Metro Area	84.6	9.5	1.5	1.4	0.1	4.6	116,631	109,412	104,292	74,907	11.8	39.2
Baldwin, AL	84.6	9.5	1.5	1.4	0.1	4.6	116,631	109,412	104,292	74,907	11.8	39.2
Davenport-Moline-Rock Island, IA-IL Metro Area .	80.7	9.2	2.9	0.7	0.1	8.9	170,422	169,132	167,210	158,790	1.9	5.3
Henry, IL	91.5	2.6	0.7	0.5	0.1	6.0	22,168	22,178	22,158	21,304	0.0	4.0
Mercer, IL	96.0	1.3	0.7	0.5	0.0	2.5	7,424	7,391	7,359	7,111	0.9	3.5
Rock Island, IL	73.4	12.1	3.1	0.6	0.1	13.1	66,171	66,102	65,764	64,525	0.6	1.9
Scott, IA	82.3	9.4	3.5	0.8	0.1	6.9	74,659	73,461	71,929	65,850	3.8	9.2
Dayton-Kettering, OH Metro Area	78.5	17.3	3.1	0.9	0.1	2.9	370,006	368,529	367,326	348,098	0.7	5.5
Greene, OH	86.3	8.6	4.0	1.0	0.2	2.9	70,844	69,423	68,297	58,707	3.7	16.3
Miami, OH	93.9	3.6	2.1	0.6	0.1	1.7	44,351	44,304	44,263	40,621	0.2	9.0
Montgomery, OH	73.0	22.8	3.0	0.9	0.1	3.1	254,811	254,802	254,766	248,770	0.0	2.4
Decatur, AL Metro Area	78.0	13.2	0.8	3.4	0.1	7.1	67,748	67,086	66,443	62,598	2.0	6.1
Lawrence, AL	80.9	11.7	0.5	9.3	0.1	2.2	15,475	15,329	15,235	15,061	1.6	1.2
Morgan, AL	77.2	13.6	0.9	1.7	0.1	8.5	52,273	51,757	51,208	47,537	2.1	7.7
Decatur, IL Metro Area	78.8	19.5	1.6	0.6	0.1	2.3	50,393	50,492	50,481	50,260	-0.2	0.4
Macon, IL	78.8	19.5	1.6	0.6	0.1	2.3	50,393	50,492	50,481	50,260	-0.2	0.4
Deltona-Daytona Beach-Ormond Beach, FL Metro a	73.4	11.2	2.5	0.8	0.1	13.9	314,618	308,149	302,940	237,753	3.9	27.4
Flagler, FL	76.5	10.9	3.1	0.8	0.2	10.5	52,530	50,232	48,634	24,830	8.0	95.9
Volusia, FL	72.7	11.3	2.4	0.8	0.1	14.5	262,088	257,917	254,306	212,923	3.1	19.4
Denver-Aurora-Lakewood, CO Metro Area	66.1	6.5	5.4	1.1	0.3	23.2	1,195,422	1,134,731	1,079,739	897,927	10.7	20.2
Adams, CO	51.4	4.0	4.9	1.1	0.3	40.4	175,616	168,857	163,275	128,660	7.6	26.9
Arapahoe, CO	62.7	12.2	7.5	1.1	0.4	19.5	254,242	245,501	238,556	198,807	6.6	20.0
Broomfield, CO	78.9	1.9	8.0	1.0	0.2	12.6	28,937	27,053	22,674	14,786	27.6	53.3
Clear Creek, CO	89.9	1.5	1.4	1.5	0.1	7.4	5,810	5,753	5,676	5,119	2.4	10.9
Denver, CO	56.5	10.1	4.8	1.2	0.3	29.7	330,862	305,538	285,816	252,034	15.8	13.4
Douglas, CO	84.1	2.0	6.4	0.7	0.2	9.0	128,727	118,058	107,058	64,930	20.2	64.9
Elbert, CO	89.8	1.8	1.5	1.2	0.3	7.2	9,784	9,246	8,950	7,190	9.3	24.5
Gilpin, CO	89.1	1.5	1.9	1.8	0.3	7.3	3,724	3,625	3,571	2,952	4.3	21.0
Jefferson, CO	79.8	1.7	3.7	1.1	0.2	15.5	243,009	236,797	230,194	212,645	5.6	8.3
Park, CO	90.9	1.3	1.8	1.8	0.2	6.2	14,711	14,303	13,969	10,804	5.3	29.3

Table C-2. Population Characteristiics and Housing Units—*Continued*

Metropolitan Statistical Area Metropolitan Division Component counties	Population characteristics, 2018						Housing Units					
	Race alone or in combination, not of Hispanic origin (percent)										Percent change	
	White	Black or African-American	Asian	American Indian, Alaska Native	Native Hawaiian, Pacific Islander	Hispanic or Latino origin (percent)	2018 (July 1 estimate	2015 (July 1 estimate	2010 (July 1 estimate	2000 (July 1 estimate	2010-2018	2000-2010
Des Moines-West Des Moines, IA Metro Area	82.8	6.4	4.9	0.6	0.1	7.2	292,484	274,769	256,890	215,431	13.9	19.2
Dallas, IA	86.3	2.9	5.5	0.5	0.1	6.1	38,278	33,320	27,427	16,883	39.6	62.5
Guthrie, IA	95.6	1.0	0.6	0.8	0.1	3.0	5,815	5,770	5,757	5,482	1.0	5.0
Jasper, IA	94.3	2.7	1.0	0.6	0.1	2.5	16,333	16,225	16,184	15,657	0.9	3.4
Madison, IA	96.0	1.0	1.2	0.7	0.0	2.3	7,061	6,756	6,560	5,685	7.6	15.4
Polk, IA	79.2	8.2	5.7	0.6	0.1	8.5	204,633	193,327	182,540	156,480	12.1	16.7
Warren, IA	95.1	1.4	1.1	0.6	0.2	3.0	20,364	19,371	18,422	15,244	10.5	20.8
Detroit-Warren-Dearborn, MI Metro Area	68.1	23.2	5.4	0.9	0.1	4.6	1,912,679	1,895,282	1,886,206	1,800,731	1.4	4.7
Detroit-Dearborn-Livonia, MI Div	51.5	39.6	4.2	1.1	0.1	6.1	815,803	814,374	821,093	824,760	-0.6	-0.4
Wayne, MI	51.5	39.6	4.2	1.1	0.1	6.1	815,803	814,374	821,093	824,760	-0.6	-0.4
Warren-Troy-Farmington Hills, MI Div	79.5	12.0	6.2	0.9	0.1	3.5	1,096,876	1,080,908	1,065,113	975,971	3.0	9.1
Lapeer, MI	93.1	1.6	1.0	1.0	0.0	4.7	36,802	36,432	36,324	32,909	1.3	10.4
Livingston, MI	95.5	0.9	1.4	0.9	0.1	2.5	76,997	75,020	72,940	59,671	5.6	22.2
Macomb, MI	80.7	13.1	4.9	0.9	0.1	2.7	367,901	362,653	356,710	321,951	3.1	10.8
Oakland, MI	73.6	14.8	8.8	0.8	0.1	4.2	542,802	534,883	527,314	493,966	2.9	6.8
St. Clair, MI	93.0	3.5	1.0	1.1	0.1	3.4	72,374	71,920	71,825	67,474	0.8	6.4
Dothan, AL Metro Area	71.3	24.6	1.1	1.1	0.1	3.5	69,817	68,683	66,975	60,008	4.2	11.6
Geneva, AL	85.3	10.2	0.5	1.6	0.1	4.0	12,850	12,751	12,690	12,127	1.3	4.6
Henry, AL	70.6	26.6	0.5	0.9	0.1	2.7	9,183	9,063	8,902	8,064	3.2	10.4
Houston, AL	67.9	27.9	1.4	1.0	0.2	3.4	47,784	46,869	45,383	39,817	5.3	14.0
Dover, DE Metro Area	63.7	27.7	3.2	1.3	0.3	7.4	73,093	69,392	65,533	50,778	11.5	29.1
Kent, DE	63.7	27.7	3.2	1.3	0.3	7.4	73,093	69,392	65,533	50,778	11.5	29.1
Dubuque, IA Metro Area	92.1	4.3	1.7	0.5	0.5	2.5	41,504	40,826	39,040	35,546	6.3	9.8
Dubuque, IA	92.1	4.3	1.7	0.5	0.5	2.5	41,504	40,826	39,040	35,546	6.3	9.8
Duluth, MN-WI Metro Area	93.1	2.4	1.5	3.7	0.1	1.7	152,311	150,788	149,294	137,110	2.0	8.9
Carlton, MN	90.3	2.2	0.9	7.2	0.1	1.8	16,091	15,931	15,675	13,809	2.7	13.5
Lake, MN	96.3	1.2	0.8	1.5	0.1	1.7	7,995	7,881	7,687	6,863	4.0	12.0
St. Louis, MN	93.2	2.5	1.6	3.3	0.1	1.8	105,002	103,930	103,092	96,019	1.9	7.4
Douglas, WI	94.1	2.1	1.6	3.3	0.1	1.6	23,223	23,046	22,840	20,419	1.7	11.9
Durham-Chapel Hill, NC Metro Area	56.7	27.6	5.5	0.9	0.1	11.3	274,336	259,822	246,172	199,299	11.4	23.5
Chatham, NC	73.2	12.8	2.4	0.7	0.1	12.3	33,013	30,851	28,802	21,569	14.6	33.5
Durham, NC	44.2	37.2	6.0	1.0	0.1	13.7	138,954	130,073	120,597	96,123	15.2	25.5
Granville, NC	59.2	32.3	0.8	0.9	0.1	8.2	24,651	23,669	22,870	18,031	7.8	26.8
Orange, NC	71.3	12.3	9.1	1.0	0.1	8.6	59,184	56,849	55,684	47,999	6.3	16.0
Person, NC	67.6	28.0	0.6	1.1	0.1	4.4	18,534	18,380	18,219	15,577	1.7	17.0
East Stroudsburg, PA Metro Area	66.8	14.8	3.0	0.8	0.2	16.6	81,663	81,137	80,411	67,936	1.6	18.4
Monroe, PA	66.8	14.8	3.0	0.8	0.2	16.6	81,663	81,137	80,411	67,936	1.6	18.4
Eau Claire, WI Metro Area	92.5	2.0	3.7	0.9	0.1	2.3	73,014	71,328	69,415	60,549	5.2	14.6
Chippewa, WI	94.5	2.2	1.7	0.9	0.1	1.8	28,615	27,971	27,222	22,940	5.1	18.7
Eau Claire, WI	91.3	1.9	4.9	1.0	0.1	2.6	44,399	43,357	42,193	37,609	5.2	12.2
El Centro, CA Metro Area	10.8	2.6	1.5	0.9	0.1	84.6	57,895	57,206	56,107	44,078	3.2	27.3
Imperial, CA	10.8	2.6	1.5	0.9	0.1	84.6	57,895	57,206	56,107	44,078	3.2	27.3
Elizabethtown-Fort Knox, KY Metro Area	82.4	11.4	2.7	1.1	0.4	5.3	66,008	64,861	61,321	54,010	7.6	13.5
Hardin, KY	78.8	14.1	3.3	1.1	0.5	6.0	47,044	46,190	43,349	36,996	8.5	17.2
Larue, KY	93.0	4.0	0.5	0.9	0.1	3.2	6,402	6,335	6,182	5,881	3.6	5.1
Meade, KY	91.0	4.6	1.4	1.2	0.2	3.7	12,562	12,336	11,790	11,133	6.5	5.9
Elkhart-Goshen, IN Metro Area	76.6	7.0	1.5	0.7	0.1	16.3	79,492	78,492	77,785	70,116	2.2	10.9
Elkhart, IN	76.6	7.0	1.5	0.7	0.1	16.3	79,492	78,492	77,785	70,116	2.2	10.9
Elmira, NY Metro Area	88.9	8.0	2.0	0.7	0.1	3.2	38,916	38,760	38,385	37,805	1.4	1.5
Chemung, NY	88.9	8.0	2.0	0.7	0.1	3.2	38,916	38,760	38,385	37,805	1.4	1.5
El Paso, TX Metro Area	12.4	3.4	1.5	0.5	0.2	82.9	301,219	291,181	272,544	226,965	10.5	20.1
El Paso, TX	12.4	3.4	1.5	0.5	0.2	83.0	299,638	289,625	271,016	225,486	10.6	20.2
Hudspeth, TX	17.7	3.3	1.2	0.8	0.1	78.0	1,581	1,556	1,528	1,479	3.5	3.3
Enid, OK Metro Area	77.5	4.4	1.8	4.3	2.9	12.9	26,798	26,769	26,824	26,057	-0.1	2.9
Garfield, OK	77.5	4.4	1.8	4.3	2.9	12.9	26,798	26,769	26,824	26,057	-0.1	2.9
Erie, PA Metro Area	86.2	8.8	2.2	0.5	0.1	4.4	121,617	120,925	119,243	114,508	2.0	4.1
Erie, PA	86.2	8.8	2.2	0.5	0.1	4.4	121,617	120,925	119,243	114,508	2.0	4.1
Eugene-Springfield, OR Metro Area	85.2	2.0	4.5	2.8	0.6	9.1	163,472	160,646	156,254	139,383	4.6	12.1
Lane, OR	85.2	2.0	4.5	2.8	0.6	9.1	163,472	160,646	156,254	139,383	4.6	12.1
Evansville, IN-KY Metro Area	88.7	8.5	1.8	0.6	0.2	2.5	143,102	141,067	138,831	127,819	3.1	8.6
Posey, IN	96.8	1.7	0.7	0.6	0.1	1.3	11,544	11,428	11,211	11,098	3.0	1.0
Vanderburgh, IN	86.0	11.3	1.7	0.6	0.3	2.7	84,507	83,814	83,031	76,568	1.8	8.4
Warrick, IN	93.5	2.3	3.0	0.5	0.1	1.9	26,432	25,314	24,238	20,648	9.1	17.4
Henderson, KY	88.3	9.6	0.7	0.5	0.2	2.7	20,619	20,511	20,351	19,505	1.3	4.3
Fairbanks, AK Metro Area	75.0	6.4	5.2	10.9	0.9	8.4	44,300	43,896	41,785	33,472	6.0	24.8
Fairbanks North Star, AK	75.0	6.4	5.2	10.9	0.9	8.4	44,300	43,896	41,785	33,472	6.0	24.8
Fargo, ND-MN Metro Area	86.7	6.3	3.6	2.0	0.1	3.2	110,698	103,997	92,295	73,881	19.9	24.9
Clay, MN	88.7	4.7	2.0	2.2	0.1	4.6	26,804	25,555	24,031	19,798	11.5	21.4
Cass, ND	86.0	6.9	4.2	1.9	0.1	2.8	83,894	78,442	68,264	54,083	22.9	26.2
Farmington, NM Metro Area	39.8	1.1	0.9	39.8	0.1	20.5	51,276	50,736	49,427	43,448	3.7	13.8
San Juan, NM	39.8	1.1	0.9	39.8	0.1	20.5	51,276	50,736	49,427	43,448	3.7	13.8
Fayetteville, NC Metro Area	50.0	34.9	3.2	3.1	0.5	12.3	220,824	215,964	201,216	170,293	9.7	18.2
Cumberland, NC	45.9	39.6	3.9	2.6	0.6	11.9	147,109	145,080	136,013	118,799	8.2	14.5
Harnett, NC	63.5	22.6	1.9	1.8	0.3	13.0	52,548	50,432	46,898	38,844	12.0	20.7
Hoke, NC	42.2	35.9	2.2	9.6	0.4	13.6	21,167	20,452	18,305	12,650	15.6	44.7

Table C-2. Population Characteristiics and Housing Units—*Continued*

Metropolitan Statistical Area / Metropolitan Division / Component counties	White	Black or African-American	Asian	American Indian, Alaska Native	Native Hawaiian, Pacific Islander	Hispanic or Latino origin (percent)	2018 (July 1 estimate)	2015 (July 1 estimate)	2010 (July 1 estimate)	2000 (July 1 estimate)	2010-2018	2000-2010
Fayetteville-Springdale-Rogers, AR Metro Area	74.8	3.2	3.8	2.5	1.6	16.6	211,085	198,744	188,799	136,102	11.8	38.7
Benton, AR	75.2	2.3	4.6	2.7	0.7	16.9	108,486	100,183	93,366	64,682	16.2	44.3
Madison, AR	90.9	0.9	0.9	2.4	0.6	6.0	7,586	7,539	7,487	6,555	1.3	14.2
Washington, AR	73.2	4.3	3.2	2.3	2.6	17.1	95,013	91,022	87,946	64,865	8.0	35.6
Flagstaff, AZ Metro Area	56.2	2.0	2.8	27.1	0.4	14.3	66,840	64,722	63,361	53,677	5.5	18.0
Coconino, AZ	56.2	2.0	2.8	27.1	0.4	14.3	66,840	64,722	63,361	53,677	5.5	18.0
Flint, MI Metro Area	74.8	21.6	1.5	1.3	0.1	3.5	192,637	191,847	192,142	184,146	0.3	4.3
Genesee, MI	74.8	21.6	1.5	1.3	0.1	3.5	192,637	191,847	192,142	184,146	0.3	4.3
Florence, SC Metro Area	53.6	43.0	1.4	0.7	0.1	2.5	91,996	90,249	89,020	81,125	3.3	9.7
Darlington, SC	55.8	42.0	0.6	0.7	0.1	2.1	30,880	30,545	30,264	29,050	2.0	4.2
Florence, SC	52.5	43.5	1.7	0.7	0.2	2.7	61,116	59,704	58,756	52,075	4.0	12.8
Florence-Muscle Shoals, AL Metro Area	83.8	13.0	0.9	1.1	0.1	2.8	72,194	70,800	69,582	65,562	3.8	6.1
Colbert, AL	80.0	16.9	0.8	1.3	0.1	2.7	26,731	26,348	25,777	25,016	3.7	3.0
Lauderdale, AL	86.0	10.7	0.9	0.9	0.1	2.9	45,463	44,452	43,805	40,546	3.8	8.0
Fond du Lac, WI Metro Area	90.4	2.5	2.2	0.8	0.1	5.3	45,361	44,822	43,940	39,365	3.2	11.6
Fond du Lac, WI	90.4	2.5	2.2	0.8	0.1	5.3	45,361	44,822	43,940	39,365	3.2	11.6
Fort Collins, CO Metro Area	84.5	1.6	3.2	1.1	0.2	11.7	151,848	142,602	132,822	106,306	14.3	24.9
Larimer, CO	84.5	1.6	3.2	1.1	0.2	11.7	151,848	142,602	132,822	106,306	14.3	24.9
Fort Smith, AR-OK Metro Area	77.2	5.2	3.4	7.8	0.2	10.4	111,636	110,101	107,638	95,567	3.7	12.6
Crawford, AR	86.6	2.2	2.0	3.9	0.1	8.0	26,977	26,628	26,145	21,434	3.2	22.0
Franklin, AR	93.1	1.5	1.2	2.3	0.2	3.4	8,086	8,060	8,026	7,687	0.7	4.4
Sebastian, AR	72.1	8.0	5.2	3.4	0.2	14.6	57,218	56,344	54,785	49,453	4.4	10.8
Sequoyah, OK	71.8	2.6	1.0	29.9	0.1	4.3	19,355	19,069	18,682	16,993	3.6	9.9
Fort Wayne, IN Metro Area	77.8	12.5	4.5	0.8	0.1	7.2	174,162	170,397	166,611	151,894	4.5	9.7
Allen, IN	76.1	13.5	4.8	0.8	0.1	7.6	159,275	155,802	152,305	139,325	4.6	9.3
Whitley, IN	96.4	0.9	0.8	0.8	0.1	2.2	14,887	14,595	14,306	12,569	4.1	13.8
Fresno, CA Metro Area	30.7	5.3	11.2	1.1	0.3	53.5	333,769	325,963	316,068	271,364	5.6	16.5
Fresno, CA	30.7	5.3	11.2	1.1	0.3	53.5	333,769	325,963	316,068	271,364	5.6	16.5
Gadsden, AL Metro Area	79.2	16.3	0.9	1.1	0.1	4.0	47,846	47,628	47,469	46,035	0.8	3.1
Etowah, AL	79.2	16.3	0.9	1.1	0.1	4.0	47,846	47,628	47,469	46,035	0.8	3.1
Gainesville, FL Metro Area	66.7	19.0	6.1	0.7	0.2	9.8	147,207	142,779	140,300	118,220	4.9	18.7
Alachua, FL	63.1	21.3	7.3	0.6	0.2	10.3	118,968	115,055	112,854	95,637	5.4	18.0
Gilchrist, FL	87.4	6.1	0.8	1.1	0.1	6.1	7,578	7,425	7,309	5,939	3.7	23.1
Levy, FL	81.1	9.7	0.9	1.2	0.1	8.6	20,661	20,299	20,137	16,644	2.6	21.0
Gainesville, GA Metro Area	61.4	8.0	2.3	0.6	0.1	29.0	74,423	70,606	68,887	51,793	8.0	33.0
Hall, GA	61.4	8.0	2.3	0.6	0.1	29.0	74,423	70,606	68,887	51,793	8.0	33.0
Gettysburg, PA Metro Area	90.2	2.3	1.2	0.5	0.1	7.1	42,563	41,810	40,866	35,977	4.2	13.6
Adams, PA	90.2	2.3	1.2	0.5	0.1	7.1	42,563	41,810	40,866	35,977	4.2	13.6
Glens Falls, NY Metro Area	94.1	2.6	1.0	0.7	0.1	2.8	69,791	68,892	67,648	61,760	3.2	9.5
Warren, NY	94.8	1.9	1.2	0.7	0.1	2.7	40,199	39,514	38,763	34,940	3.7	10.9
Washington, NY	93.3	3.4	0.8	0.7	0.1	2.8	29,592	29,378	28,885	26,820	2.4	7.7
Goldsboro, NC Metro Area	54.8	32.2	1.9	0.9	0.2	12.3	54,474	53,867	53,013	47,559	2.8	11.5
Wayne, NC	54.8	32.2	1.9	0.9	0.2	12.3	54,474	53,867	53,013	47,559	2.8	11.5
Grand Forks, ND-MN Metro Area	86.2	4.7	3.1	3.2	0.2	5.1	48,429	47,209	44,028	41,397	10.0	6.4
Polk, MN	88.3	3.2	1.4	2.4	0.1	6.6	15,039	14,839	14,615	14,027	2.9	4.2
Grand Forks, ND	85.2	5.4	3.9	3.5	0.2	4.4	33,390	32,370	29,413	27,370	13.5	7.5
Grand Island, NE Metro Area	71.9	3.0	1.4	0.8	0.1	23.9	32,026	31,279	30,231	28,072	5.9	7.7
Hall, NE	66.7	3.5	1.6	0.7	0.1	28.5	25,076	24,436	23,574	21,637	6.4	9.0
Howard, NE	96.0	0.8	0.5	0.6	0.1	2.7	3,120	3,048	2,954	2,793	5.6	5.8
Merrick, NE	93.3	0.8	1.3	1.0	0.1	4.7	3,830	3,795	3,703	3,642	3.4	1.7
Grand Junction, CO Metro Area	82.7	1.3	1.4	1.4	0.2	14.8	67,215	65,297	62,731	49,116	7.1	27.7
Mesa, CO	82.7	1.3	1.4	1.4	0.2	14.8	67,215	65,297	62,731	49,116	7.1	27.7
Grand Rapids-Kentwood, MI Metro Area	80.2	8.0	3.4	0.9	0.1	9.7	421,924	410,066	402,516	360,364	4.8	11.7
Ionia, MI	89.7	5.1	0.7	1.0	0.1	4.8	25,028	24,798	24,773	22,140	1.0	11.9
Kent, MI	75.8	11.3	3.8	1.0	0.1	10.7	257,370	250,930	246,962	224,821	4.2	9.8
Montcalm, MI	93.0	3.0	0.6	1.2	0.1	3.6	28,681	28,350	28,222	26,002	1.6	8.5
Ottawa, MI	85.2	2.3	3.5	0.7	0.1	10.0	110,845	105,988	102,559	87,401	8.1	17.3
Grants Pass, OR Metro Area	89.3	1.0	1.7	2.9	0.4	7.6	39,352	38,565	38,033	33,371	3.5	14.0
Josephine, OR	89.3	1.0	1.7	2.9	0.4	7.6	39,352	38,565	38,033	33,371	3.5	14.0
Great Falls, MT Metro Area	88.3	2.4	1.8	6.4	0.3	4.6	39,036	38,392	37,332	35,268	4.6	5.9
Cascade, MT	88.3	2.4	1.8	6.4	0.3	4.6	39,036	38,392	37,332	35,268	4.6	5.9
Greeley, CO Metro Area	66.9	1.6	2.2	1.1	0.2	29.6	112,465	103,067	96,455	67,151	16.6	43.6
Weld, CO	66.9	1.6	2.2	1.1	0.2	29.6	112,465	103,067	96,455	67,151	16.6	43.6
Green Bay, WI Metro Area	84.9	3.2	3.2	3.0	0.1	7.6	144,181	141,565	137,368	118,725	5.0	15.7
Brown, WI	82.5	3.7	3.7	3.3	0.1	8.8	110,388	108,199	104,508	90,546	5.6	15.4
Kewaunee, WI	95.3	0.9	0.6	1.0	0.1	3.2	9,462	9,396	9,308	8,252	1.7	12.8
Oconto, WI	95.9	0.7	0.7	2.0	0.0	1.8	24,331	23,970	23,552	19,927	3.3	18.2
Greensboro-High Point, NC Metro Area	59.5	28.4	4.4	1.1	0.1	8.6	337,407	330,624	323,151	276,354	4.4	16.9
Guilford, NC	51.5	35.6	5.8	1.1	0.1	8.2	230,417	224,992	218,331	181,211	5.6	20.5
Randolph, NC	80.1	7.0	1.6	1.0	0.1	11.7	62,635	61,839	61,124	54,754	2.5	11.6
Rockingham, NC	74.0	19.8	0.9	0.9	0.1	6.2	44,301	43,793	43,696	40,389	1.4	8.2
Greenville, NC Metro Area	55.9	36.3	2.6	0.7	0.1	6.3	80,265	77,865	75,114	58,528	6.9	28.3
Pitt, NC	55.9	36.3	2.6	0.7	0.1	6.3	80,265	77,865	75,114	58,528	6.9	28.3

Table C-2. Population Characteristiics and Housing Units—*Continued*

Metropolitan Statistical Area / Metropolitan Division / Component counties	White	Black or African-American	Asian	American Indian, Alaska Native	Native Hawaiian, Pacific Islander	Hispanic or Latino origin (percent)	2018 (July 1 estimate)	2015 (July 1 estimate)	2010 (July 1 estimate)	2000 (July 1 estimate)	2010-2018	2000-2010
Greenville-Anderson, SC Metro Area	74.1	17.5	2.4	0.6	0.1	7.0	389,705	374,552	362,468	313,676	7.5	15.6
Anderson, SC	78.8	17.1	1.2	0.6	0.1	3.9	89,000	86,648	84,745	73,550	5.0	15.2
Greenville, SC	69.9	19.0	3.1	0.6	0.1	9.3	214,128	203,975	195,640	163,693	9.5	19.5
Laurens, SC	69.1	25.8	0.7	0.6	0.1	5.1	31,503	31,012	30,726	30,276	2.5	1.5
Pickens, SC	87.1	7.7	2.4	0.7	0.1	3.8	55,074	52,917	51,357	46,157	7.2	11.3
Gulfport-Biloxi, MS Metro Area	69.7	22.7	3.0	1.0	0.2	5.7	190,088	184,454	175,163	158,838	8.5	10.3
Hancock, MS	86.4	8.9	1.3	1.4	0.1	4.0	25,918	24,248	22,010	21,259	17.8	3.5
Harrison, MS	65.7	26.5	3.7	1.0	0.2	5.6	93,911	91,213	85,723	80,218	9.6	6.9
Jackson, MS	69.0	22.1	2.9	0.9	0.1	7.0	62,727	61,637	60,260	51,991	4.1	15.9
Stone, MS	77.0	20.3	0.8	0.9	0.1	2.2	7,532	7,356	7,170	5,370	5.0	33.5
Hagerstown-Martinsburg, MD-WV Metro Area	84.2	11.0	1.9	0.7	0.1	4.8	121,078	118,357	115,453	94,351	4.9	22.4
Washington, MD	80.7	13.5	2.4	0.6	0.2	5.4	61,638	61,264	60,812	53,123	1.4	14.5
Berkeley, WV	86.6	9.3	1.6	0.7	0.1	4.6	49,425	47,184	44,878	33,115	10.1	35.5
Morgan, WV	96.7	1.4	0.6	1.1	0.1	1.6	10,015	9,909	9,763	8,113	2.6	20.3
Hammond, LA Metro Area	64.3	30.8	1.0	0.8	0.1	4.4	56,361	53,622	50,305	40,876	12.0	23.1
Tangipahoa, LA	64.3	30.8	1.0	0.8	0.1	4.4	56,361	53,622	50,305	40,876	12.0	23.1
Hanford-Corcoran, CA Metro Area	33.7	6.9	4.9	1.4	0.4	55.0	46,645	45,247	43,910	36,687	6.2	19.7
Kings, CA	33.7	6.9	4.9	1.4	0.4	55.0	46,645	45,247	43,910	36,687	6.2	19.7
Harrisburg-Carlisle, PA Metro Area	78.4	11.7	4.9	0.6	0.1	6.6	252,645	248,276	241,151	217,567	4.8	10.8
Cumberland, PA	87.0	5.1	5.2	0.5	0.1	4.1	106,899	104,388	100,176	87,223	6.7	14.9
Dauphin, PA	67.7	19.5	5.4	0.7	0.1	9.6	124,805	123,182	120,544	111,348	3.5	8.3
Perry, PA	96.2	1.5	0.7	0.6	0.1	2.1	20,941	20,706	20,431	18,996	2.5	7.6
Harrisonburg, VA Metro Area	80.6	5.0	2.8	0.5	0.1	12.6	54,165	52,976	51,229	41,199	5.7	24.3
Rockingham, VA	89.5	2.7	1.1	0.5	0.1	7.3	35,852	34,827	33,724	27,448	6.3	22.9
Harrisonburg City, VA	67.2	8.5	5.2	0.5	0.2	20.6	18,313	18,149	17,505	13,751	4.6	27.3
Hartford-East Hartford-Middletown, CT Metro Area	68.3	11.9	5.8	0.6	0.1	15.2	517,040	512,673	507,344	472,786	1.9	7.3
Hartford, CT	62.2	14.3	6.2	0.6	0.1	18.5	380,471	377,747	374,407	353,505	1.6	5.9
Middlesex, CT	85.3	5.7	3.7	0.6	0.1	6.4	76,537	75,889	74,901	67,517	2.2	10.9
Tolland, CT	85.8	4.0	5.6	0.6	0.1	5.7	60,032	59,037	58,036	51,764	3.4	12.1
Hattiesburg, MS Metro Area	66.1	30.5	1.3	0.6	0.1	2.7	72,395	71,500	70,429	58,845	2.8	19.7
Covington, MS	61.2	36.2	0.6	0.5	0.1	2.4	8,739	8,628	8,507	8,104	2.7	5.0
Forrest, MS	58.1	38.4	1.3	0.6	0.1	2.9	33,215	32,793	32,304	29,610	2.8	9.1
Lamar, MS	74.8	21.3	1.8	0.6	0.1	2.7	24,770	24,481	24,094	16,013	2.8	50.5
Perry, MS	78.5	19.9	0.4	0.8	0.1	1.6	5,671	5,598	5,524	5,118	2.7	7.9
Hickory-Lenoir-Morganton, NC Metro Area	82.1	8.0	3.2	0.7	0.1	7.6	165,150	163,558	162,831	145,651	1.4	11.8
Alexander, NC	88.0	6.8	1.2	0.7	0.1	4.8	16,500	16,354	16,211	14,163	1.8	14.5
Burke, NC	82.9	7.6	3.9	0.8	0.2	6.2	41,314	40,944	40,859	37,600	1.1	8.7
Caldwell, NC	88.6	5.8	0.9	0.7	0.1	5.7	38,073	37,871	37,684	33,612	1.0	12.1
Catawba, NC	76.9	9.7	4.6	0.6	0.1	9.9	69,263	68,389	68,077	60,276	1.7	12.9
Hilton Head Island-Bluffton, SC Metro Area	66.2	21.6	1.7	0.6	0.2	11.4	113,319	107,304	103,417	69,299	9.6	49.2
Beaufort, SC	69.6	18.5	1.8	0.6	0.2	11.2	101,247	96,040	93,090	61,334	8.8	51.8
Jasper, SC	44.4	41.8	1.0	0.8	0.1	13.2	12,072	11,264	10,327	7,965	16.9	29.7
Hinesville, GA Metro Area	46.1	40.8	2.9	1.3	0.7	12.4	35,570	34,164	32,896	26,370	8.1	24.7
Liberty, GA	41.6	44.9	3.2	1.2	0.7	12.8	28,570	27,688	26,873	22,105	6.3	21.6
Long, GA	60.6	27.7	2.1	1.3	0.6	11.2	7,000	6,476	6,023	4,265	16.2	41.2
Homosassa Springs, FL Metro Area	89.1	3.5	2.0	0.9	0.1	5.9	79,988	78,682	78,123	62,527	2.4	24.9
Citrus, FL	89.1	3.5	2.0	0.9	0.1	5.9	79,988	78,682	78,123	62,527	2.4	24.9
Hot Springs, AR Metro Area	84.0	9.6	1.2	1.5	0.1	5.9	51,026	50,816	50,554	45,085	0.9	12.1
Garland, AR	84.0	9.6	1.2	1.5	0.1	5.9	51,026	50,816	50,554	45,085	0.9	12.1
Houma-Thibodaux, LA Metro Area	73.2	17.5	1.3	5.4	0.2	4.7	87,333	85,260	82,627	75,167	5.7	9.9
Lafourche, LA	78.4	14.3	1.1	3.6	0.1	4.4	41,622	40,216	38,786	35,045	7.3	10.7
Terrebonne, LA	68.7	20.3	1.4	6.9	0.3	5.1	45,711	45,044	43,841	40,122	4.3	9.3
Houston-The Woodlands-Sugar Land, TX Metro Area	36.9	17.7	8.6	0.6	0.1	37.6	2,637,765	2,502,850	2,301,060	1,798,493	14.6	27.9
Austin, TX	62.7	9.3	0.9	0.7	0.1	27.6	13,288	13,131	12,936	10,293	2.7	25.7
Brazoria, TX	47.6	14.7	7.4	0.7	0.1	31.1	139,490	130,221	118,855	91,210	17.4	30.3
Chambers, TX	67.4	8.6	1.5	0.8	0.1	22.8	16,151	14,930	13,395	10,418	20.6	28.6
Fort Bend, TX	34.1	21.0	21.5	0.6	0.1	24.7	260,754	233,475	198,045	117,523	31.7	68.5
Galveston, TX	58.5	13.3	3.9	0.8	0.1	25.0	148,274	142,314	132,783	112,369	11.7	18.2
Harris, TX	30.3	19.4	7.8	0.5	0.1	43.3	1,788,240	1,718,112	1,601,859	1,304,076	11.6	22.8
Liberty, TX	62.7	10.1	0.8	0.9	0.1	26.8	31,735	30,207	28,820	26,479	10.1	8.8
Montgomery, TX	66.6	5.7	3.6	0.8	0.2	24.8	222,592	204,022	178,487	114,095	24.7	56.4
Waller, TX	44.0	24.2	1.3	0.7	0.1	30.8	17,241	16,438	15,880	12,030	8.6	32.0
Huntington-Ashland, WV-KY-OH Metro Area	95.4	3.2	1.0	0.7	0.1	1.3	167,868	167,712	166,892	163,261	0.6	2.2
Boyd, KY	94.4	3.6	0.8	0.7	0.1	1.9	21,625	21,684	21,800	21,971	-0.8	-0.8
Carter, KY	97.5	1.0	0.4	0.7	0.0	1.3	12,535	12,432	12,317	11,576	1.8	6.4
Greenup, KY	97.2	1.3	0.7	0.9	0.0	1.1	16,342	16,349	16,326	16,016	0.1	1.9
Lawrence, OH	96.1	3.1	0.6	0.7	0.1	1.0	27,501	27,516	27,593	27,250	-0.3	1.3
Cabell, WV	92.3	6.2	1.7	0.7	0.1	1.4	46,327	46,421	46,162	45,645	0.4	1.1
Putnam, WV	96.5	1.8	1.1	0.7	0.1	1.2	24,249	24,001	23,458	21,674	3.4	8.2
Wayne, WV	98.0	1.0	0.5	0.8	0.0	0.7	19,289	19,309	19,236	19,129	0.3	0.6
Huntsville, AL Metro Area	69.1	23.3	3.1	1.5	0.2	5.3	200,801	192,724	182,108	147,830	10.3	23.2
Limestone, AL	78.0	14.4	2.0	1.4	0.1	6.1	36,529	35,835	35,024	27,082	4.3	29.3
Madison, AL	66.8	25.6	3.4	1.6	0.2	5.1	164,272	156,889	147,084	120,748	11.7	21.8

Table C-2. Population Characteristiics and Housing Units—*Continued*

Metropolitan Statistical Area Metropolitan Division Component counties	White	Black or African-American	Asian	American Indian, Alaska Native	Native Hawaiian, Pacific Islander	Hispanic or Latino origin (percent)	2018 (July 1 estimate)	2015 (July 1 estimate)	2010 (July 1 estimate)	2000 (July 1 estimate)	2010-2018	2000-2010
Idaho Falls, ID Metro Area	85.2	0.9	1.5	1.3	0.2	12.6	54,717	51,856	49,884	38,252	9.7	30.4
Bonneville, ID	84.4	1.0	1.6	1.3	0.3	13.3	43,775	41,419	39,784	30,656	10.0	29.8
Butte, ID	93.5	0.8	0.4	2.7	0.2	4.5	1,381	1,372	1,357	1,290	1.8	5.2
Jefferson, ID	87.7	0.5	1.1	1.1	0.2	10.6	9,561	9,065	8,743	6,306	9.4	38.6
Indianapolis-Carmel-Anderson, IN Metro Area	74.0	16.7	4.0	0.6	0.1	6.9	867,936	845,426	817,626	705,444	6.2	15.9
Boone, IN	91.6	2.6	3.6	0.6	0.1	3.2	27,553	26,064	22,812	18,115	20.8	25.9
Brown, IN	96.7	1.1	0.7	1.1	0.1	1.7	8,743	8,588	8,325	7,206	5.0	15.5
Hamilton, IN	85.2	5.1	7.1	0.4	0.1	4.1	129,523	120,219	107,290	70,555	20.7	52.1
Hancock, IN	93.6	3.4	1.3	0.7	0.1	2.4	30,589	29,321	28,199	21,927	8.5	28.6
Hendricks, IN	85.6	8.2	3.5	0.5	0.1	4.0	63,176	59,606	55,608	39,658	13.6	40.2
Johnson, IN	90.3	3.1	4.0	0.6	0.1	3.6	61,783	59,534	56,795	45,438	8.8	25.0
Madison, IN	86.6	9.6	0.9	0.7	0.1	4.1	59,132	59,016	59,061	57,003	0.1	3.6
Marion, IN	57.2	30.0	4.1	0.7	0.1	10.6	424,371	420,762	417,970	388,302	1.5	7.6
Morgan, IN	97.0	0.9	0.8	0.7	0.1	1.6	28,470	28,173	27,784	26,038	2.5	6.7
Putnam, IN	92.8	4.4	1.3	0.6	0.1	2.1	15,142	14,962	14,709	13,544	2.9	8.6
Shelby, IN	93.2	1.8	1.1	0.6	0.1	4.4	19,454	19,181	19,073	17,658	2.0	8.0
Iowa City, IA Metro Area	81.5	7.2	6.8	0.6	0.1	5.9	74,816	70,469	65,678	54,918	13.9	19.6
Johnson, IA	80.1	8.1	7.7	0.6	0.1	5.8	65,046	60,842	56,156	46,355	15.8	21.1
Washington, IA	91.6	1.6	0.9	0.5	0.1	6.5	9,770	9,627	9,522	8,563	2.6	11.2
Ithaca, NY Metro Area	79.6	5.2	12.0	0.8	0.2	5.3	43,879	42,651	41,706	38,758	5.2	7.6
Tompkins, NY	79.6	5.2	12.0	0.8	0.2	5.3	43,879	42,651	41,706	38,758	5.2	7.6
Jackson, MI Metro Area	87.1	9.7	1.2	1.0	0.1	3.6	69,685	69,418	69,456	63,169	0.3	10.0
Jackson, MI	87.1	9.7	1.2	1.0	0.1	3.6	69,685	69,418	69,456	63,169	0.3	10.0
Jackson, MS Metro Area	46.0	50.6	1.4	0.4	0.1	2.6	253,098	248,380	241,342	215,650	4.9	11.9
Copiah, MS	44.5	51.8	0.6	0.5	0.1	3.6	12,265	12,225	12,187	11,148	0.6	9.3
Hinds, MS	24.9	73.1	1.0	0.4	0.0	1.6	104,318	104,301	103,437	100,417	0.9	3.0
Holmes, MS	16.4	82.4	0.4	0.4	0.0	1.1	8,598	8,506	8,423	8,449	2.1	-0.3
Madison, MS	55.9	38.5	2.9	0.4	0.1	3.1	44,047	41,958	38,663	28,957	13.9	33.5
Rankin, MS	74.4	21.7	1.6	0.5	0.1	2.8	61,483	59,211	56,617	45,320	8.6	24.9
Simpson, MS	62.4	35.4	0.6	0.5	0.2	1.8	12,198	12,055	11,938	11,332	2.2	5.3
Yazoo, MS	34.9	57.2	0.7	0.6	0.1	7.5	10,189	10,124	10,077	10,027	1.1	0.5
Jackson, TN Metro Area	67.4	28.5	1.0	0.6	0.1	4.1	79,578	78,752	77,358	71,762	2.9	7.8
Chester, TN	86.7	10.5	0.9	1.0	0.1	2.8	7,158	7,083	6,994	6,210	2.3	12.6
Crockett, TN	74.8	14.8	0.4	0.6	0.1	10.9	6,420	6,398	6,422	6,148	0.0	4.5
Gibson, TN	78.7	18.9	0.4	0.6	0.1	2.8	22,622	22,471	22,030	21,056	2.7	4.6
Madison, TN	57.2	38.5	1.4	0.5	0.1	4.0	43,378	42,800	41,912	38,348	3.5	9.3
Jacksonville, FL Metro Area	64.8	22.4	5.1	0.8	0.2	9.2	655,272	624,193	599,393	477,477	9.3	25.5
Baker, FL	82.3	14.6	0.9	1.1	0.1	2.7	10,090	9,831	9,695	7,629	4.1	27.1
Clay, FL	74.6	12.5	4.2	1.0	0.3	10.3	81,785	78,737	75,589	54,138	8.2	39.6
Duval, FL	54.7	30.8	6.0	0.8	0.2	10.1	412,590	398,753	388,964	330,917	6.1	17.5
Nassau, FL	88.3	6.4	1.4	0.8	0.2	4.5	39,982	36,863	35,060	26,108	14.0	34.3
St. Johns, FL	84.0	5.9	3.9	0.6	0.2	7.2	110,825	100,009	90,085	58,685	23.0	53.5
Jacksonville, NC Metro Area	69.3	16.9	3.4	1.4	0.5	12.8	80,259	77,719	68,742	56,207	16.8	22.3
Onslow, NC	69.3	16.9	3.4	1.4	0.5	12.8	80,259	77,719	68,742	56,207	16.8	22.3
Janesville-Beloit, WI Metro Area	84.5	6.2	1.8	0.7	0.1	8.9	69,227	68,709	68,456	62,377	1.1	9.7
Rock, WI	84.5	6.2	1.8	0.7	0.1	8.9	69,227	68,709	68,456	62,377	1.1	9.7
Jefferson City, MO Metro Area	87.9	8.9	1.3	0.9	0.1	2.7	65,369	64,609	63,625	57,024	2.7	11.6
Callaway, MO	92.1	5.4	1.0	1.3	0.1	2.2	18,997	18,792	18,550	16,260	2.4	14.1
Cole, MO	83.1	13.3	1.7	0.8	0.2	2.9	33,508	33,041	32,306	29,099	3.7	11.0
Moniteau, MO	90.4	4.4	0.5	1.0	0.1	4.8	6,178	6,183	6,177	5,766	0.0	7.1
Osage, MO	98.0	0.7	0.4	0.7	0.1	1.0	6,686	6,593	6,592	5,899	1.4	11.7
Johnson City, TN Metro Area	92.0	4.0	1.4	0.8	0.1	3.3	98,048	96,512	93,939	82,219	4.4	14.3
Carter, TN	95.8	2.1	0.6	0.8	0.1	1.9	28,289	27,998	27,750	25,989	1.9	6.8
Unicoi, TN	93.8	0.8	0.4	0.9	0.1	5.1	8,910	8,890	8,832	8,242	0.9	7.2
Washington, TN	90.1	5.3	2.0	0.8	0.1	3.6	60,849	59,624	57,357	47,988	6.1	19.5
Johnstown, PA Metro Area	94.1	4.5	0.8	0.3	0.1	1.7	66,022	65,844	65,666	65,793	0.5	-0.2
Cambria, PA	94.1	4.5	0.8	0.3	0.1	1.7	66,022	65,844	65,666	65,793	0.5	-0.2
Jonesboro, AR Metro Area	79.1	15.6	1.3	0.8	0.1	4.8	57,268	55,038	51,542	46,303	11.1	11.3
Craighead, AR	77.1	17.0	1.5	0.8	0.1	5.2	46,255	44,077	40,613	35,241	13.9	15.2
Poinsett, AR	87.9	9.1	0.5	0.9	0.1	3.2	11,013	10,961	10,929	11,062	0.8	-1.2
Joplin, MO Metro Area	87.3	2.7	1.7	3.4	0.6	7.4	76,587	75,112	75,025	67,733	2.1	10.8
Jasper, MO	86.6	3.2	1.6	2.9	0.4	8.3	51,797	50,497	50,694	45,729	2.2	10.9
Newton, MO	88.7	1.7	1.8	4.3	1.1	5.6	24,790	24,615	24,331	22,004	1.9	10.6
Kahului-Wailuku-Lahaina, HI Metro Area	43.9	1.4	43.5	1.7	24.2	11.5	73,775	71,975	70,471	56,707	4.7	24.3
Maui, HI	43.9	1.4	43.5	1.7	24.2	11.5	73,775	71,975	70,471	56,707	4.7	24.3
Kalamazoo-Portage, MI Metro Area	80.2	13.5	3.4	1.2	0.1	5.0	112,800	111,174	110,040	99,633	2.5	10.4
Kalamazoo, MI	80.2	13.5	3.4	1.2	0.1	5.0	112,800	111,174	110,040	99,633	2.5	10.4
Kankakee, IL Metro Area	73.5	15.7	1.3	0.5	0.1	10.6	45,652	45,434	45,258	40,716	0.9	11.2
Kankakee, IL	73.5	15.7	1.3	0.5	0.1	10.6	45,652	45,434	45,258	40,716	0.9	11.2
Kansas City, MO-KS Metro Area	74.7	13.7	3.6	1.2	0.3	9.2	918,595	893,409	872,502	760,905	5.3	14.7
Johnson, KS	81.9	5.8	6.0	0.9	0.1	7.8	244,459	235,791	226,884	183,263	7.7	23.8
Leavenworth, KS	81.7	10.2	2.4	1.6	0.3	7.0	29,991	29,341	28,724	24,502	4.4	17.2
Linn, KS	95.1	1.3	0.6	2.0	0.1	2.9	5,660	5,552	5,450	4,724	3.9	15.4
Miami, KS	94.2	1.9	0.9	1.5	0.1	3.3	13,927	13,445	13,195	11,043	5.5	19.5

Table C-2. Population Characteristiics and Housing Units—*Continued*

Metropolitan Statistical Area / Metropolitan Division / Component counties	White	Black or African-American	Asian	American Indian, Alaska Native	Native Hawaiian, Pacific Islander	Hispanic or Latino origin (percent)	2018 (July 1 estimate)	2015 (July 1 estimate)	2010 (July 1 estimate)	2000 (July 1 estimate)	2010-2018	2000-2010
Wyandotte, KS	42.6	23.5	5.5	1.4	0.3	29.3	68,297	67,902	66,755	65,921	2.3	1.3
Bates, MO	95.7	1.8	0.4	1.6	0.1	2.2	7,842	7,854	7,842	7,268	0.0	7.9
Caldwell, MO	96.3	1.4	0.7	1.4	0.1	2.1	4,716	4,652	4,608	4,501	2.3	2.4
Cass, MO	89.8	5.1	1.4	1.4	0.2	4.6	42,427	40,942	40,069	31,905	5.9	25.6
Clay, MO	83.1	7.9	3.1	1.2	0.4	7.0	98,926	95,868	93,965	76,638	5.3	22.6
Clinton, MO	95.2	2.1	0.7	1.3	0.1	2.3	9,033	8,942	8,881	7,920	1.7	12.1
Jackson, MO	64.8	25.0	2.5	1.3	0.4	9.1	326,019	317,694	312,168	288,963	4.4	8.0
Lafayette, MO	93.8	3.0	0.8	1.3	0.2	2.9	14,826	14,778	14,720	13,727	0.7	7.2
Platte, MO	82.8	8.1	3.6	1.1	0.6	6.2	42,366	40,639	39,251	31,133	7.9	26.1
Ray, MO	95.2	2.1	0.5	1.1	0.2	2.5	10,106	10,009	9,990	9,397	1.2	6.3
Kennewick-Richland, WA Metro Area	62.4	2.4	3.6	1.4	0.3	32.2	106,018	100,936	93,300	72,410	13.6	28.8
Benton, WA	72.3	2.3	4.0	1.6	0.4	22.3	77,371	73,896	68,746	56,218	12.5	22.3
Franklin, WA	41.5	2.7	2.7	1.0	0.3	53.5	28,647	27,040	24,554	16,192	16.7	51.6
Killeen-Temple, TX Metro Area	51.3	22.4	4.0	1.2	1.0	23.9	178,734	171,619	159,935	122,885	11.8	30.2
Bell, TX	47.8	24.3	4.3	1.1	1.0	25.3	142,422	136,060	125,951	93,430	13.1	34.8
Coryell, TX	61.1	18.5	3.2	1.4	1.1	18.7	26,859	26,261	25,259	21,809	6.3	15.8
Lampasas, TX	74.2	4.3	1.8	1.7	0.5	19.8	9,453	9,298	8,725	7,646	8.3	14.1
Kingsport-Bristol, TN-VA Metro Area	95.1	2.7	0.8	0.7	0.1	1.8	149,725	148,009	147,058	136,645	1.8	7.6
Hawkins, TN	96.1	1.9	0.6	0.9	0.1	1.7	27,330	27,047	26,882	24,530	1.7	9.6
Sullivan, TN	94.7	3.0	1.0	0.8	0.1	1.9	75,729	74,379	73,809	69,225	2.6	6.6
Scott, VA	97.3	1.2	0.3	0.6	0.0	1.4	11,944	11,933	11,920	11,377	0.2	4.8
Washington, VA	96.1	1.9	0.7	0.5	0.0	1.6	25,992	25,908	25,659	23,050	1.3	11.3
Bristol City, VA	89.7	7.6	1.3	0.7	0.1	2.6	8,730	8,742	8,788	8,463	-0.7	3.8
Kingston, NY Metro Area	80.9	7.4	2.7	0.8	0.1	10.5	85,421	84,650	83,694	77,790	2.1	7.6
Ulster, NY	80.9	7.4	2.7	0.8	0.1	10.5	85,421	84,650	83,694	77,790	2.1	7.6
Knoxville, TN Metro Area	88.1	6.8	2.0	0.9	0.1	4.0	388,375	379,019	370,678	326,961	4.8	13.4
Anderson, TN	91.0	5.1	1.8	1.0	0.1	3.1	35,022	34,869	34,710	32,592	0.9	6.5
Blount, TN	92.4	3.7	1.2	0.9	0.1	3.5	58,673	56,646	55,340	47,243	6.0	17.1
Campbell, TN	97.5	0.8	0.5	1.0	0.1	1.3	21,172	20,590	20,012	18,571	5.8	7.8
Knox, TN	84.2	9.8	2.8	0.8	0.1	4.4	206,043	200,526	195,228	172,009	5.5	13.5
Loudon, TN	88.5	1.8	1.0	0.8	0.1	9.0	23,371	22,515	21,753	17,376	7.4	25.2
Morgan, TN	94.1	4.0	0.4	1.2	0.1	1.4	9,023	8,974	8,922	7,759	1.1	15.0
Roane, TN	94.3	3.4	0.9	1.2	0.1	2.0	25,600	25,667	25,739	23,447	-0.5	9.8
Union, TN	97.2	0.8	0.4	1.2	0.0	1.7	9,471	9,232	8,974	7,964	5.5	12.7
Kokomo, IN Metro Area	87.4	9.1	1.6	0.9	0.1	3.5	39,567	38,888	38,681	37,685	2.3	2.6
Howard, IN	87.4	9.1	1.6	0.9	0.1	3.5	39,567	38,888	38,681	37,685	2.3	2.6
La Crosse-Onalaska, WI-MN Metro Area	92.1	2.2	4.6	0.8	0.1	1.9	59,346	58,386	57,065	51,795	4.0	10.2
Houston, MN	97.2	1.3	0.9	0.6	0.1	1.2	8,777	8,705	8,603	8,186	2.0	5.1
La Crosse, WI	91.3	2.4	5.2	0.8	0.1	2.0	50,569	49,681	48,462	43,609	4.3	11.1
Lafayette, LA Metro Area	68.7	26.0	2.0	0.7	0.1	4.1	211,670	205,059	196,269	172,176	7.8	14.0
Acadia, LA	78.6	19.1	0.4	0.6	0.0	2.7	26,534	26,054	25,424	23,244	4.4	9.4
Iberia, LA	60.3	33.3	2.9	0.8	0.1	4.3	30,735	30,301	29,688	27,866	3.5	6.5
Lafayette, LA	66.6	27.2	2.2	0.7	0.1	4.6	104,039	99,572	93,883	78,232	10.8	20.0
St. Martin, LA	65.7	30.6	1.1	0.8	0.1	3.0	23,619	22,919	21,991	20,271	7.4	8.5
Vermilion, LA	79.7	15.1	2.3	0.7	0.1	3.7	26,743	26,213	25,283	22,563	5.8	12.1
Lafayette-West Lafayette, IN Metro Area	80.1	5.5	7.8	0.6	0.1	7.8	94,093	92,212	88,277	74,840	6.6	18.0
Benton, IN	93.4	1.4	0.4	0.6	0.1	5.2	3,928	3,914	3,929	3,828	0.0	2.6
Carroll, IN	94.9	1.1	0.3	0.5	0.0	4.1	9,674	9,505	9,476	8,700	2.1	8.9
Tippecanoe, IN	77.3	6.4	9.2	0.6	0.1	8.5	76,722	75,076	71,189	58,821	7.8	21.0
Warren, IN	96.7	0.8	0.7	0.7	0.1	2.0	3,769	3,717	3,683	3,491	2.3	5.5
Lake Charles, LA Metro Area	69.5	25.8	1.6	1.1	0.1	3.8	96,171	91,333	85,967	81,511	11.9	5.5
Calcasieu, LA	68.8	26.6	1.7	1.1	0.1	3.8	92,047	87,408	82,342	76,214	11.8	8.0
Cameron, LA	90.7	4.6	0.5	1.2	0.1	4.3	4,124	3,925	3,625	5,297	13.8	-31.6
Lake Havasu City-Kingman, AZ Metro Area	78.6	1.5	1.7	2.9	0.4	16.8	115,269	113,123	110,974	80,717	3.9	37.5
Mohave, AZ	78.6	1.5	1.7	2.9	0.4	16.8	115,269	113,123	110,974	80,717	3.9	37.5
Lakeland-Winter Haven, FL Metro Area	59.4	15.6	2.3	0.7	0.2	23.6	299,421	288,023	281,402	227,250	6.4	23.8
Polk, FL	59.4	15.6	2.3	0.7	0.2	23.6	299,421	288,023	281,402	227,250	6.4	23.8
Lancaster, PA Metro Area	83.0	4.6	2.7	0.4	0.1	10.8	212,205	208,700	203,230	180,611	4.4	12.5
Lancaster, PA	83.0	4.6	2.7	0.4	0.1	10.8	212,205	208,700	203,230	180,611	4.4	12.5
Lansing-East Lansing, MI Metro Area	80.6	9.5	5.3	1.2	0.1	6.3	234,031	231,407	229,321	211,593	2.1	8.4
Clinton, MI	91.4	2.7	2.1	1.0	0.1	4.5	31,952	31,347	30,695	24,796	4.1	23.8
Eaton, MI	84.9	7.8	2.9	1.1	0.1	5.5	47,668	47,299	47,052	42,294	1.3	11.2
Ingham, MI	72.7	13.9	8.1	1.3	0.1	7.9	124,140	122,537	121,258	115,321	2.4	5.1
Shiawassee, MI	95.3	1.2	0.8	1.1	0.1	3.0	30,271	30,224	30,316	29,182	-0.1	3.9
Laredo, TX Metro Area	3.7	0.3	0.6	0.1	0.0	95.5	84,455	80,071	73,684	55,740	14.6	32.2
Webb, TX	3.7	0.3	0.6	0.1	0.0	95.5	84,455	80,071	73,684	55,740	14.6	32.2
Las Cruces, NM Metro Area	27.8	1.9	1.4	1.2	0.1	68.6	89,049	86,130	81,795	65,878	8.9	24.2
Dona Ana, NM	27.8	1.9	1.4	1.2	0.1	68.6	89,049	86,130	81,795	65,878	8.9	24.2
Las Vegas-Henderson-Paradise, NV Metro Area	45.3	13.1	11.8	1.1	1.3	31.4	913,260	876,296	841,675	566,405	8.5	48.6
Clark, NV	45.3	13.1	11.8	1.1	1.3	31.4	913,260	876,296	841,675	566,405	8.5	48.6
Lawrence, KS Metro Area	81.8	6.0	6.0	3.6	0.2	6.4	51,073	48,730	46,803	40,436	9.1	15.7
Douglas, KS	81.8	6.0	6.0	3.6	0.2	6.4	51,073	48,730	46,803	40,436	9.1	15.7
Lawton, OK Metro Area	61.8	18.5	3.9	8.2	0.9	13.1	54,687	54,667	53,891	48,585	1.5	10.9
Comanche, OK	60.9	19.2	4.1	8.0	0.9	13.4	51,688	51,659	50,877	45,508	1.6	11.8

Table C-2. Population Characteristiics and Housing Units—*Continued*

Metropolitan Statistical Area / Metropolitan Division / Component counties	White	Black or African-American	Asian	American Indian, Alaska Native	Native Hawaiian, Pacific Islander	Hispanic or Latino origin (percent)	2018 (July 1 estimate)	2015 (July 1 estimate)	2010 (July 1 estimate)	2000 (July 1 estimate)	2010-2018	2000-2010
Cotton, OK	80.8	3.3	0.7	11.7	0.3	8.3	2,999	3,008	3,014	3,077	-0.5	-2.0
Lebanon, PA Metro Area	82.5	2.7	1.7	0.4	0.1	13.8	58,005	56,929	55,674	49,431	4.2	12.6
Lebanon, PA	82.5	2.7	1.7	0.4	0.1	13.8	58,005	56,929	55,674	49,431	4.2	12.6
Lewiston, ID-WA Metro Area	90.2	1.1	1.5	5.3	0.3	4.1	27,990	27,629	27,331	25,382	2.4	7.7
Nez Perce, ID	89.1	0.9	1.4	6.7	0.3	4.0	17,910	17,645	17,451	16,253	2.6	7.4
Asotin, WA	92.2	1.5	1.6	2.8	0.4	4.2	10,080	9,984	9,880	9,129	2.0	8.2
Lewiston-Auburn, ME Metro Area	92.5	5.3	1.4	1.1	0.1	2.0	50,056	49,622	49,128	46,055	1.9	6.7
Androscoggin, ME	92.5	5.3	1.4	1.1	0.1	2.0	50,056	49,622	49,128	46,055	1.9	6.7
Lexington-Fayette, KY Metro Area	79.2	12.5	3.5	0.6	0.1	6.3	222,278	216,276	209,448	176,228	6.1	18.9
Bourbon, KY	86.5	7.1	0.6	0.6	0.0	7.1	9,089	9,028	8,934	8,385	1.7	6.5
Clark, KY	91.3	5.5	0.8	0.6	0.1	3.1	15,952	15,781	15,709	13,835	1.5	13.5
Fayette, KY	73.3	16.3	4.9	0.7	0.1	7.4	142,680	139,541	135,386	116,750	5.4	16.0
Jessamine, KY	90.5	5.4	1.7	0.8	0.1	3.5	20,698	20,113	19,353	14,769	6.9	31.0
Scott, KY	88.8	6.4	1.6	0.6	0.1	4.4	22,631	20,812	19,342	13,065	17.0	48.0
Woodford, KY	87.3	5.7	0.9	0.5	0.1	7.0	11,228	11,001	10,724	9,424	4.7	13.8
Lima, OH Metro Area	83.4	14.5	1.1	0.7	0.1	3.2	45,186	45,011	44,989	44,276	0.4	1.6
Allen, OH	83.4	14.5	1.1	0.7	0.1	3.2	45,186	45,011	44,989	44,276	0.4	1.6
Lincoln, NE Metro Area	83.9	5.2	5.3	1.2	0.1	7.0	140,692	133,894	127,883	111,111	10.0	15.1
Lancaster, NE	83.3	5.4	5.5	1.2	0.2	7.2	133,479	126,817	121,003	104,669	10.3	15.6
Seward, NE	95.5	1.2	0.8	0.8	0.1	2.8	7,213	7,077	6,880	6,442	4.8	6.8
Little Rock-North Little Rock-Conway, AR Metro Area	68.5	24.7	2.2	1.1	0.1	5.4	328,596	320,953	307,604	262,950	6.8	17.0
Faulkner, AR	81.8	13.0	1.7	1.3	0.2	4.1	50,522	49,524	46,916	34,785	7.7	34.9
Grant, AR	93.5	3.1	0.6	1.2	0.0	2.9	8,046	7,945	7,765	6,978	3.6	11.3
Lonoke, AR	87.4	7.0	1.5	1.2	0.1	4.8	29,755	28,782	27,315	20,908	8.9	30.6
Perry, AR	93.6	2.7	0.6	2.0	0.1	3.1	4,990	4,951	4,910	4,709	1.6	4.3
Pulaski, AR	53.6	38.4	2.8	1.0	0.1	6.2	185,966	182,248	175,757	161,426	5.8	8.9
Saline, AR	85.3	8.5	1.6	1.1	0.1	5.0	49,317	47,503	44,941	34,144	9.7	31.6
Logan, UT-ID Metro Area	85.6	1.2	2.9	1.0	0.6	10.5	47,144	44,737	41,677	33,015	13.1	26.2
Franklin, ID	92.2	0.5	0.5	1.2	0.1	6.7	4,901	4,721	4,542	3,894	7.9	16.6
Cache, UT	84.8	1.2	3.2	1.0	0.6	10.9	42,243	40,016	37,135	29,121	13.8	27.5
Longview, TX Metro Area	64.5	18.9	1.2	1.0	0.1	16.1	119,545	118,398	115,106	107,679	3.9	6.9
Gregg, TX	58.6	21.2	1.7	0.9	0.1	19.2	52,103	51,667	49,554	46,426	5.1	6.7
Harrison, TX	64.4	21.4	0.9	1.0	0.1	13.6	28,726	28,337	27,737	26,333	3.6	5.3
Rusk, TX	64.4	18.0	0.8	0.9	0.1	17.3	21,604	21,469	21,190	19,930	2.0	6.3
Upshur, TX	82.0	8.7	0.6	1.4	0.1	9.0	17,112	16,925	16,625	14,990	2.9	10.9
Longview, WA Metro Area	86.4	1.6	2.4	3.1	0.6	9.2	44,968	44,178	43,481	38,767	3.4	12.2
Cowlitz, WA	86.4	1.6	2.4	3.1	0.6	9.2	44,968	44,178	43,481	38,767	3.4	12.2
Los Angeles-Long Beach-Anaheim, CA Metro Area	31.4	7.1	17.6	0.6	0.5	45.2	4,672,296	4,584,555	4,495,795	4,247,689	3.9	5.8
Anaheim-Santa Ana-Irvine, CA Div	42.6	2.1	22.8	0.6	0.6	34.2	1,111,227	1,080,780	1,049,362	972,611	5.9	7.9
Orange, CA	42.6	2.1	22.8	0.6	0.6	34.2	1,111,227	1,080,780	1,049,362	972,611	5.9	7.9
Los Angeles-Long Beach-Glendale, CA Div	27.9	8.7	16.0	0.6	0.4	48.6	3,561,069	3,503,775	3,446,433	3,275,078	3.3	5.2
Los Angeles, CA	27.9	8.7	16.0	0.6	0.4	48.6	3,561,069	3,503,775	3,446,433	3,275,078	3.3	5.2
Louisville/Jefferson County, KY-IN Metro Area	77.3	16.3	2.7	0.7	0.1	5.1	547,551	536,311	526,286	465,528	4.0	13.1
Clark, IN	85.1	9.5	1.5	0.7	0.2	5.5	51,086	49,673	47,846	41,354	6.8	15.7
Floyd, IN	89.8	6.8	1.5	0.7	0.1	3.4	33,014	32,478	31,989	29,199	3.2	9.6
Harrison, IN	96.6	1.2	0.7	0.7	0.1	2.0	17,187	16,859	16,548	13,798	3.9	19.9
Washington, IN	97.6	0.9	0.5	0.6	0.1	1.4	12,453	12,337	12,224	11,240	1.9	8.8
Bullitt, KY	95.7	1.8	0.9	0.9	0.1	2.1	31,940	30,771	29,388	23,322	8.7	26.0
Henry, KY	93.2	4.1	0.5	1.0	0.1	3.2	6,809	6,730	6,644	6,394	2.5	3.9
Jefferson, KY	69.1	23.3	3.6	0.7	0.1	5.7	347,117	341,839	337,589	306,844	2.8	10.0
Oldham, KY	89.7	4.9	2.1	0.7	0.1	4.1	22,293	21,430	20,723	15,793	7.6	31.2
Shelby, KY	81.6	8.1	1.5	0.7	0.2	10.0	18,257	17,152	16,617	12,975	9.9	28.1
Spencer, KY	95.4	2.3	0.6	0.6	0.1	2.2	7,395	7,042	6,718	4,609	10.1	45.8
Lubbock, TX Metro Area	53.8	7.4	2.6	0.7	0.2	36.5	135,228	128,767	120,891	106,679	11.9	13.3
Crosby, TX	40.5	3.4	0.4	0.8	0.1	55.8	2,902	2,902	2,900	3,196	0.1	-9.3
Lubbock, TX	54.2	7.6	2.7	0.7	0.2	35.9	129,655	123,191	115,315	100,814	12.4	14.4
Lynn, TX	49.9	2.7	0.3	0.6	0.0	47.2	2,671	2,674	2,676	2,669	-0.2	0.3
Lynchburg, VA Metro Area	77.6	18.5	2.0	0.8	0.1	3.0	117,194	115,623	112,654	95,696	4.0	17.7
Amherst, VA	76.8	20.4	0.9	1.5	0.1	2.6	14,227	14,138	13,990	12,989	1.7	7.7
Appomattox, VA	78.8	20.5	0.5	0.7	0.1	1.6	7,370	7,210	6,968	5,850	5.8	19.1
Bedford, VA	89.1	7.8	1.6	0.7	0.1	2.3	36,997	36,365	34,928	26,947	5.9	29.6
Campbell, VA	81.3	15.7	1.4	0.8	0.1	2.8	26,082	25,684	24,779	22,092	5.3	12.2
Lynchburg City, VA	64.3	29.4	3.3	0.7	0.2	4.4	32,518	32,226	31,989	27,818	1.7	15.0
Macon-Bibb County, GA Metro Area	49.8	45.8	2.0	0.6	0.1	3.1	102,807	102,521	101,611	94,363	1.2	7.7
Bibb, GA	39.0	55.9	2.5	0.6	0.2	3.4	70,044	70,259	69,795	67,328	0.4	3.7
Crawford, GA	74.3	21.2	1.3	1.0	0.0	3.5	5,391	5,341	5,294	4,890	1.8	8.3
Jones, GA	72.3	25.6	0.8	0.7	0.1	1.8	11,886	11,730	11,698	9,373	1.6	24.8
Monroe, GA	73.6	23.3	1.2	0.7	0.1	2.4	11,234	10,948	10,589	8,470	6.1	25.0
Twiggs, GA	56.8	40.6	0.5	0.8	0.1	2.5	4,252	4,243	4,235	4,302	0.4	-1.6
Madera, CA Metro Area	35.0	3.7	2.5	1.8	0.2	58.3	50,966	50,072	49,151	40,518	3.7	21.3
Madera, CA	35.0	3.7	2.5	1.8	0.2	58.3	50,966	50,072	49,151	40,518	3.7	21.3
Madison, WI Metro Area	83.9	5.7	6.1	0.7	0.1	5.8	290,880	279,114	269,003	227,642	8.1	18.2
Columbia, WI	93.5	2.1	1.1	0.9	0.1	3.4	26,912	26,411	26,150	22,790	2.9	14.7

Table C-2. Population Characteristiics and Housing Units—*Continued*

Metropolitan Statistical Area Metropolitan Division Component counties	White	Black or African-American	Asian	American Indian, Alaska Native	Native Hawaiian, Pacific Islander	Hispanic or Latino origin (percent)	2018 (July 1 estimate)	2015 (July 1 estimate)	2010 (July 1 estimate)	2000 (July 1 estimate)	2010-2018	2000-2010
Dane, WI	81.6	6.5	7.2	0.7	0.1	6.4	236,941	225,955	216,264	181,311	9.6	19.3
Green, WI	95.2	1.3	0.9	0.5	0.1	3.1	16,075	15,922	15,866	13,931	1.3	13.9
Iowa, WI	96.2	1.3	1.1	0.6	0.1	1.8	10,952	10,826	10,723	9,610	2.1	11.6
Manchester-Nashua, NH Metro Area	85.8	3.2	5.1	0.7	0.1	7.0	172,031	169,225	166,147	150,436	3.5	10.4
Hillsborough, NH	85.8	3.2	5.1	0.7	0.1	7.0	172,031	169,225	166,147	150,436	3.5	10.4
Manhattan, KS Metro Area	77.1	9.8	5.0	1.4	0.6	9.9	56,560	54,865	51,592	42,765	9.6	20.6
Geary, KS	60.8	20.2	5.0	2.0	1.4	16.6	15,385	15,363	14,613	11,925	5.3	22.5
Pottawatomie, KS	92.0	2.0	1.5	1.5	0.2	5.1	9,838	9,306	8,663	7,334	13.6	18.1
Riley, KS	79.4	7.8	6.1	1.2	0.4	8.5	31,337	30,196	28,316	23,506	10.7	20.5
Mankato, MN Metro Area	89.4	4.8	2.8	0.7	0.1	4.1	42,446	40,903	39,126	33,338	8.5	17.4
Blue Earth, MN	89.3	5.0	3.0	0.7	0.1	3.8	28,825	27,564	26,241	22,063	9.8	18.9
Nicollet, MN	89.6	4.3	2.2	0.7	0.1	4.7	13,621	13,339	12,885	11,275	5.7	14.3
Mansfield, OH Metro Area	87.5	10.8	1.1	0.7	0.1	2.0	54,166	54,313	54,587	53,218	-0.8	2.6
Richland, OH	87.5	10.8	1.1	0.7	0.1	2.0	54,166	54,313	54,587	53,218	-0.8	2.6
McAllen-Edinburg-Mission, TX Metro Area	6.2	0.5	1.0	0.1	0.0	92.4	281,639	267,197	249,100	193,935	13.1	28.4
Hidalgo, TX	6.2	0.5	1.0	0.1	0.0	92.4	281,639	267,197	249,100	193,935	13.1	28.4
Medford, OR Metro Area	83.2	1.4	2.3	2.4	0.6	13.2	96,241	93,692	91,018	76,129	5.7	19.6
Jackson, OR	83.2	1.4	2.3	2.4	0.6	13.2	96,241	93,692	91,018	76,129	5.7	19.6
Memphis, TN-MS-AR Metro Area	44.3	48.2	2.6	0.6	0.1	5.7	570,306	561,286	551,174	483,359	3.5	14.0
Crittenden, AR	42.6	54.4	0.9	0.6	0.1	2.6	21,822	21,729	21,499	20,571	1.5	4.5
De Soto, MS	64.4	29.5	1.9	0.5	0.1	5.1	68,518	65,033	61,759	41,441	10.9	49.0
Marshall, MS	48.4	47.7	0.4	0.6	0.1	3.9	15,820	15,311	14,909	13,275	6.1	12.3
Tate, MS	65.5	31.5	0.6	0.6	0.1	3.0	11,593	11,293	10,962	9,409	5.8	16.5
Tunica, MS	19.3	77.7	1.0	0.5	0.1	2.5	4,948	4,883	4,807	3,776	2.9	27.3
Fayette, TN	68.6	27.8	0.9	0.6	0.1	2.9	17,419	16,544	15,704	11,280	10.9	39.2
Shelby, TN	36.7	54.5	3.1	0.5	0.1	6.5	406,215	402,876	398,292	364,403	2.0	9.3
Tipton, TN	77.5	19.3	1.1	1.0	0.2	2.8	23,971	23,617	23,242	19,204	3.1	21.0
Merced, CA Metro Area	28.7	3.6	8.1	0.9	0.4	60.2	85,756	84,321	83,715	68,875	2.4	21.5
Merced, CA	28.7	3.6	8.1	0.9	0.4	60.2	85,756	84,321	83,715	68,875	2.4	21.5
Miami-Fort Lauderdale-Pompano Beach, FL Metro Area	30.8	21.1	3.0	0.3	0.2	45.8	2,548,762	2,503,145	2,464,332	2,158,776	3.4	14.2
Fort Lauderdale-Pompano Beach-Sunrise, FL Div.	36.8	29.4	4.4	0.4	0.3	30.4	826,899	817,247	810,322	743,865	2.0	8.9
Broward, FL	36.8	29.4	4.4	0.4	0.3	30.4	826,899	817,247	810,322	743,865	2.0	8.9
Miami-Miami Beach-Kendall, FL Div	13.5	16.0	1.8	0.2	0.1	69.1	1,031,955	1,007,301	989,277	855,553	4.3	15.6
Miami-Dade, FL	13.5	16.0	1.8	0.2	0.1	69.1	1,031,955	1,007,301	989,277	855,553	4.3	15.6
West Palm Beach-Boca Raton-Boynton Beach, FL Div	55.2	19.4	3.4	0.4	0.2	22.9	689,908	678,597	664,733	559,358	3.8	18.8
Palm Beach, FL	55.2	19.4	3.4	0.4	0.2	22.9	689,908	678,597	664,733	559,358	3.8	18.8
Michigan City-La Porte, IN Metro Area	80.9	12.6	0.9	0.7	0.1	6.8	49,225	49,003	48,458	45,724	1.6	6.0
La Porte, IN	80.9	12.6	0.9	0.7	0.1	6.8	49,225	49,003	48,458	45,724	1.6	6.0
Midland, MI Metro Area	92.9	1.9	2.8	1.0	0.1	2.8	37,114	36,681	35,962	33,906	3.2	6.1
Midland, MI	92.9	1.9	2.8	1.0	0.1	2.8	37,114	36,681	35,962	33,906	3.2	6.1
Midland, TX Metro Area	46.1	6.5	2.3	0.8	0.1	45.4	63,756	61,397	56,270	50,118	13.3	12.3
Martin, TX	49.8	2.1	0.6	0.6	0.1	47.4	1,897	1,876	1,852	1,898	2.4	-2.4
Midland, TX	46.0	6.7	2.3	0.8	0.1	45.3	61,859	59,521	54,418	48,220	13.7	12.9
Milwaukee-Waukesha, WI Metro Area	68.1	17.5	4.5	0.9	0.1	10.9	681,189	674,125	669,927	619,802	1.7	8.1
Milwaukee, WI	53.0	27.8	5.1	1.2	0.1	15.4	419,554	417,640	417,970	400,572	0.4	4.3
Ozaukee, WI	92.4	2.1	3.2	0.6	0.1	3.1	37,791	36,970	36,295	32,155	4.1	12.9
Washington, WI	93.7	1.8	1.8	0.6	0.1	3.2	57,201	55,892	54,741	46,072	4.5	18.8
Waukesha, WI	89.5	2.1	4.4	0.5	0.1	4.8	166,643	163,623	160,921	141,003	3.6	14.1
Minneapolis-St. Paul-Bloomington, MN Metro Area	77.6	10.1	7.8	1.3	0.1	6.0	1,453,940	1,419,178	1,380,844	1,196,724	5.3	15.4
Anoka, MN	83.1	7.9	5.6	1.4	0.1	4.7	133,192	130,124	126,790	108,640	5.0	16.7
Carver, MN	90.2	2.6	4.0	0.6	0.1	4.3	38,848	36,923	34,615	25,228	12.2	37.2
Chisago, MN	94.5	1.9	1.6	1.2	0.1	2.3	22,174	21,626	21,180	15,732	4.7	34.6
Dakota, MN	80.2	8.2	6.0	0.9	0.2	7.4	168,117	163,839	159,715	134,574	5.3	18.7
Hennepin, MN	71.3	15.0	8.4	1.4	0.1	7.0	537,756	525,440	509,558	469,998	5.5	8.4
Isanti, MN	95.3	1.3	1.6	1.3	0.1	2.1	16,212	15,621	15,330	12,129	5.8	26.4
Le Sueur, MN	92.1	1.0	0.9	0.8	0.1	6.2	12,809	12,575	12,420	10,896	3.1	14.0
Mille Lacs, MN	90.5	1.2	0.9	6.7	0.1	2.5	12,971	12,843	12,753	10,518	1.7	21.2
Ramsey, MN	64.2	14.0	16.1	1.4	0.2	7.6	220,680	218,447	217,163	206,701	1.6	5.1
Scott, MN	82.8	5.5	7.1	1.4	0.1	5.3	51,946	50,052	47,243	32,140	10.0	47.0
Sherburne, MN	92.7	3.6	1.9	1.0	0.1	2.7	34,312	33,174	32,395	23,146	5.9	40.0
Washington, MN	84.3	5.8	7.0	0.9	0.1	4.3	99,459	96,381	92,488	74,218	7.5	24.6
Wright, MN	93.7	2.3	1.9	0.7	0.1	3.1	52,458	50,637	49,047	34,773	7.0	41.0
Pierce, WI	95.3	1.3	1.6	0.9	0.1	2.1	16,693	16,405	16,141	13,521	3.4	19.4
St. Croix, WI	95.2	1.4	1.7	0.7	0.1	2.4	36,313	35,091	34,006	24,510	6.8	38.7
Missoula, MT Metro Area	91.9	1.0	2.7	3.9	0.2	3.3	54,926	52,496	50,150	41,534	9.5	20.7
Missoula, MT	91.9	1.0	2.7	3.9	0.2	3.3	54,926	52,496	50,150	41,534	9.5	20.7
Mobile, AL Metro Area	58.4	36.1	2.4	1.7	0.1	3.0	193,261	190,780	187,174	173,660	3.3	7.8
Mobile, AL	58.0	36.6	2.4	1.5	0.1	3.1	184,688	182,300	178,763	165,520	3.3	8.0
Washington, AL	66.3	23.9	1.1	8.4	0.2	1.6	8,573	8,480	8,411	8,140	1.9	3.3
Modesto, CA Metro Area	43.4	3.4	6.7	1.2	1.1	47.0	182,290	180,702	179,579	151,433	1.5	18.6
Stanislaus, CA	43.4	3.4	6.7	1.2	1.1	47.0	182,290	180,702	179,579	151,433	1.5	18.6

Table C-2. Population Characteristiics and Housing Units—*Continued*

Metropolitan Statistical Area Metropolitan Division Component counties	Population characteristiics, 2018						Housing Units					
	Race alone or in combination, not of Hispanic origin (percent)										Percent change	
	White	Black or African-American	Asian	American Indian, Alaska Native	Native Hawaiian, Pacific Islander	Hispanic or Latino origin (percent)	2018 (July 1 estimate)	2015 (July 1 estimate)	2010 (July 1 estimate)	2000 (July 1 estimate)	2010-2018	2000-2010
Monroe, LA Metro Area............................	59.0	37.9	1.1	0.6	0.1	2.4	93,564	91,296	88,343	83,808	5.9	5.4
Morehouse, LA........................	50.0	48.4	0.7	0.6	0.1	1.4	12,642	12,577	12,430	12,722	1.7	-2.3
Ouachita, LA..........................	59.0	38.0	1.3	0.6	0.1	2.2	69,018	67,141	64,556	60,217	6.9	7.2
Union, LA..............................	69.9	25.3	0.3	0.7	0.1	4.6	11,904	11,578	11,357	10,869	4.8	4.5
Monroe, MI Metro Area...........................	92.8	3.4	1.0	0.9	0.1	3.7	64,785	63,561	62,975	56,702	2.9	11.1
Monroe, MI............................	92.8	3.4	1.0	0.9	0.1	3.7	64,785	63,561	62,975	56,702	2.9	11.1
Montgomery, AL Metro Area.....................	49.0	45.7	2.6	0.7	0.1	3.3	168,538	166,028	161,645	145,108	4.3	11.4
Autauga, AL...........................	75.8	20.2	1.7	0.9	0.1	3.0	23,734	23,104	22,166	17,845	7.1	24.2
Elmore, AL............................	74.5	22.0	1.1	1.0	0.1	3.0	34,418	33,841	32,681	25,862	5.3	26.4
Lowndes, AL..........................	25.6	72.2	0.4	0.6	0.1	1.7	5,224	5,161	5,139	5,795	1.7	-11.3
Montgomery, AL......................	34.3	59.3	3.6	0.6	0.1	3.5	105,162	103,922	101,659	95,606	3.4	6.3
Morgantown, WV Metro Area....................	91.7	4.2	3.3	0.6	0.1	2.0	60,249	59,942	58,357	50,360	3.2	15.9
Monongalia, WV.......................	90.2	5.1	4.2	0.6	0.1	2.1	45,074	44,807	43,257	36,869	4.2	17.3
Preston, WV...........................	96.6	1.6	0.4	0.7	0.1	1.7	15,175	15,135	15,100	13,491	0.5	11.9
Morristown, TN Metro Area	88.8	3.4	0.9	0.8	0.2	7.5	62,682	62,033	61,436	54,010	2.0	13.7
Grainger, TN..........................	95.1	1.3	0.3	0.9	0.1	3.5	11,130	11,011	10,901	9,766	2.1	11.6
Hamblen, TN...........................	82.8	4.8	1.2	0.7	0.3	12.0	27,251	27,076	26,967	24,790	1.1	8.8
Jefferson, TN..........................	93.2	2.5	0.7	0.9	0.1	3.9	24,301	23,946	23,568	19,454	3.1	21.1
Mount Vernon-Anacortes, WA Metro Area...........	76.2	1.4	3.1	2.8	0.5	18.7	54,443	52,864	51,537	42,904	5.6	20.1
Skagit, WA............................	76.2	1.4	3.1	2.8	0.5	18.7	54,443	52,864	51,537	42,904	5.6	20.1
Muncie, IN Metro Area...........................	88.7	8.3	1.8	0.7	0.2	2.6	52,727	52,709	52,342	51,122	0.7	2.4
Delaware, IN...........................	88.7	8.3	1.8	0.7	0.2	2.6	52,727	52,709	52,342	51,122	0.7	2.4
Muskegon, MI Metro Area........................	78.8	15.4	1.0	1.6	0.1	5.8	74,305	73,761	73,553	68,781	1.0	6.9
Muskegon, MI..........................	78.8	15.4	1.0	1.6	0.1	5.8	74,305	73,761	73,553	68,781	1.0	6.9
Myrtle Beach-Conway-North Myrtle Beach, SC-NC	80.5	13.0	1.5	1.1	0.1	5.7	302,962	282,214	264,076	175,248	14.7	50.7
Brunswick, NC........................	83.5	10.9	1.0	1.3	0.1	4.9	92,264	84,443	77,772	51,833	18.6	50.0
Horry, SC	79.2	13.8	1.8	1.0	0.1	6.1	210,698	197,771	186,304	123,415	13.1	51.0
Napa, CA Metro Area............................	54.1	2.7	9.6	1.1	0.5	34.5	55,460	55,471	54,798	48,719	1.2	12.5
Napa, CA..............................	54.1	2.7	9.6	1.1	0.5	34.5	55,460	55,471	54,798	48,719	1.2	12.5
Naples-Marco Island, FL Metro Area..............	63.2	7.2	1.8	0.4	0.2	28.2	218,281	206,979	197,494	146,520	10.5	34.8
Collier, FL............................	63.2	7.2	1.8	0.4	0.2	28.2	218,281	206,979	197,494	146,520	10.5	34.8
Nashville-Davidson--Murfreesboro--Franklin, TN	73.7	16.5	3.5	0.8	0.1	7.5	789,006	734,328	693,656	566,084	13.7	22.5
Cannon, TN...........................	95.2	2.2	0.5	1.1	0.1	2.5	6,161	6,106	6,045	5,452	1.9	10.9
Cheatham, TN.........................	94.0	2.5	0.8	1.0	0.1	3.2	16,506	15,962	15,729	13,548	4.9	16.1
Davidson, TN..........................	58.1	28.3	4.6	0.8	0.1	10.4	319,529	297,862	284,192	253,627	12.4	12.1
Dickson, TN...........................	91.3	5.1	0.8	0.9	0.1	3.7	22,084	21,359	20,835	17,720	6.0	17.6
Macon, TN............................	92.6	1.4	0.8	0.9	0.1	5.4	10,422	10,092	9,862	8,940	5.7	10.3
Maury, TN............................	80.8	12.9	1.2	0.8	0.1	6.1	38,351	36,359	35,293	28,818	8.7	22.5
Robertson, TN.........................	84.4	8.1	0.8	0.8	0.1	7.3	27,756	26,746	26,139	21,155	6.2	23.6
Rutherford, TN........................	72.2	16.9	4.1	0.8	0.1	8.5	121,805	112,313	103,206	71,472	18.0	44.4
Smith, TN.............................	94.0	2.9	0.5	1.1	0.0	2.9	8,808	8,667	8,533	7,690	3.2	11.0
Sumner, TN...........................	85.4	8.6	1.8	0.8	0.1	5.1	73,725	68,951	66,089	51,969	11.6	27.2
Trousdale, TN.........................	85.3	12.6	0.7	0.7	0.0	2.4	3,667	3,467	3,371	3,100	8.8	8.7
Williamson, TN........................	85.8	4.9	5.4	0.6	0.1	4.9	85,029	76,041	68,656	47,442	23.8	44.7
Wilson, TN............................	86.3	8.0	2.1	0.9	0.1	4.5	55,163	50,403	45,706	35,151	20.7	30.0
New Bern, NC Metro Area........................	68.3	22.7	3.3	1.1	0.3	6.9	60,236	59,144	57,495	49,745	4.8	15.6
Craven, NC...........................	67.8	22.3	3.9	1.1	0.3	7.4	47,450	46,555	45,101	38,301	5.2	17.8
Jones, NC.............................	63.7	30.7	0.7	1.4	0.1	5.1	5,002	4,927	4,851	4,652	3.1	4.3
Pamlico, NC..........................	75.6	19.7	0.8	1.1	0.2	4.1	7,784	7,662	7,543	6,792	3.2	11.1
New Haven-Milford, CT Metro Area...............	63.9	14.0	4.7	0.6	0.1	18.6	367,745	365,480	362,074	341,322	1.6	6.1
New Haven, CT........................	63.9	14.0	4.7	0.6	0.1	18.6	367,745	365,480	362,074	341,322	1.6	6.1
New Orleans-Metairie, LA Metro Area.............	52.7	35.7	3.3	0.9	0.1	9.0	560,360	554,800	547,163	557,784	2.4	-1.9
Jefferson, LA..........................	53.6	27.5	4.6	0.8	0.1	14.9	188,657	188,472	189,142	188,204	-0.3	0.5
Orleans, LA...........................	31.8	60.0	3.3	0.7	0.1	5.6	191,627	191,885	190,086	215,500	0.8	-11.8
Plaquemines, LA......................	65.2	22.1	4.9	2.4	0.2	7.8	10,396	10,101	9,620	10,532	8.1	-8.7
St. Bernard, LA.......................	63.8	23.9	2.8	1.2	0.1	10.2	17,172	16,894	16,801	26,801	2.2	-37.3
St. Charles, LA........................	66.1	26.8	1.4	0.8	0.1	6.3	20,835	20,433	19,976	17,447	4.3	14.5
St. James, LA.........................	48.9	49.3	0.4	0.4	0.0	1.7	8,996	8,808	8,468	7,612	6.2	11.2
St. John the Baptist, LA	34.9	57.8	1.4	0.6	0.2	6.3	17,851	17,701	17,482	15,646	2.1	11.7
St. Tammany, LA......................	79.9	13.1	1.9	1.0	0.1	5.7	104,826	100,506	95,588	76,042	9.7	25.7
New York-Newark-Jersey City, NY-NJ-PA Metro Area	46.8	16.8	12.5	0.5	0.1	24.9	7,756,101	7,643,109	7,534,655	7,104,331	2.9	6.1
Nassau County-Suffolk County, NY Div..............	64.6	10.1	7.7	0.4	0.1	18.6	1,050,369	1,045,282	1,038,590	982,427	1.1	5.7
Nassau, NY...........................	60.4	12.2	11.1	0.4	0.1	17.2	473,496	470,992	468,473	458,537	1.1	2.2
Suffolk, NY...........................	68.3	8.1	4.6	0.5	0.1	19.8	576,873	574,290	570,117	523,890	1.2	8.8
Newark, NJ-PA Div...................	51.2	21.5	6.9	0.4	0.1	21.3	867,844	858,748	852,340	805,894	1.8	5.8
Essex, NJ.............................	31.6	39.6	6.2	0.5	0.1	23.5	318,813	314,725	313,100	301,201	1.9	3.9
Hunterdon, NJ........................	86.2	2.9	4.8	0.3	0.2	6.8	50,463	49,968	49,508	45,223	1.9	9.5
Morris, NJ............................	72.2	3.8	11.6	0.3	0.1	13.7	194,282	191,305	189,929	175,022	2.3	8.5
Sussex, NJ............................	87.0	2.6	2.6	0.4	0.1	8.6	62,464	62,338	61,942	56,760	0.8	9.1
Union, NJ.............................	40.9	21.7	6.0	0.4	0.1	32.3	202,688	201,508	199,570	193,056	1.6	3.4
Pike, PA..............................	81.1	6.3	1.8	0.8	0.1	11.4	39,134	38,904	38,385	34,632	2.0	10.8

Table C-2. Population Characteristiics and Housing Units—*Continued*

Metropolitan Statistical Area Metropolitan Division Component counties	White	Black or African-American	Asian	American Indian, Alaska Native	Native Hawaiian, Pacific Islander	Hispanic or Latino origin (percent)	2018 (July 1 estimate)	2015 (July 1 estimate)	2010 (July 1 estimate)	2000 (July 1 estimate)	2010-2018	2000-2010
New Brunswick-Lakewood, NJ Div	64.5	7.8	13.8	0.4	0.1	14.9	976,318	966,661	955,508	878,952	2.2	8.7
Middlesex, NJ	43.4	10.3	25.6	0.5	0.1	21.6	302,239	299,614	295,170	274,311	2.4	7.6
Monmouth, NJ	76.2	7.5	6.3	0.4	0.1	11.1	262,161	260,685	258,690	240,869	1.3	7.4
Ocean, NJ	85.4	3.6	2.3	0.3	0.1	9.5	284,906	280,489	278,422	250,088	2.3	11.3
Somerset, NJ	56.9	10.1	19.3	0.3	0.1	15.0	127,012	125,873	123,226	113,684	3.1	8.4
New York-Jersey City-White Plains, NY-NJ Div	38.3	19.4	14.4	0.6	0.2	29.1	4,861,570	4,772,418	4,688,217	4,437,058	3.7	5.7
Bergen, NJ	56.9	6.1	17.6	0.3	0.1	20.6	359,291	355,120	352,454	340,394	1.9	3.5
Hudson, NJ	29.9	11.5	16.6	0.4	0.1	42.9	284,142	277,802	270,970	241,063	4.9	12.4
Passaic, NJ	41.8	10.8	5.9	0.4	0.1	42.3	177,278	176,845	176,159	170,116	0.6	3.6
Bronx, NY	9.8	30.0	4.2	0.6	0.1	56.4	532,487	523,600	512,406	490,845	3.9	4.4
Kings, NY	37.8	31.0	13.4	0.6	0.2	19.1	1,053,767	1,025,756	1,002,175	932,114	5.1	7.5
New York, NY	48.7	13.5	13.6	0.5	0.1	25.9	886,249	866,516	848,011	799,670	4.5	6.0
Putnam, NY	79.0	3.3	2.7	0.4	0.1	15.8	38,680	38,575	38,216	35,134	1.2	8.8
Queens, NY	26.2	19.1	27.7	0.8	0.3	28.1	865,878	850,627	836,009	817,540	3.6	2.3
Richmond, NY	61.5	10.2	10.7	0.5	0.1	18.7	181,199	179,052	176,805	164,640	2.5	7.4
Rockland, NY	64.0	12.2	6.7	0.4	0.1	18.1	106,747	105,516	104,092	95,391	2.6	9.1
Westchester, NY	54.4	14.6	7.0	0.4	0.1	25.1	375,852	373,009	370,920	350,151	1.3	5.9
Niles, MI Metro Area	76.9	15.9	2.6	1.2	0.2	5.7	77,648	77,157	76,919	73,574	0.9	4.5
Berrien, MI	76.9	15.9	2.6	1.2	0.2	5.7	77,648	77,157	76,919	73,574	0.9	4.5
North Port-Sarasota-Bradenton, FL Metro Area	78.5	7.1	2.4	0.6	0.1	12.9	438,533	416,957	401,416	322,435	9.2	24.5
Manatee, FL	72.3	9.3	2.6	0.6	0.1	16.7	194,539	183,588	172,956	138,951	12.5	24.5
Sarasota, FL	84.2	5.0	2.2	0.6	0.1	9.3	243,994	233,369	228,460	183,484	6.8	24.5
Norwich-New London, CT Metro Area	77.9	7.4	5.2	1.8	0.2	10.9	123,635	122,642	121,086	110,921	2.1	9.2
New London, CT	77.9	7.4	5.2	1.8	0.2	10.9	123,635	122,642	121,086	110,921	2.1	9.2
Ocala, FL Metro Area	71.5	13.4	2.1	0.8	0.1	13.6	170,504	166,022	164,110	123,249	3.9	33.2
Marion, FL	71.5	13.4	2.1	0.8	0.1	13.6	170,504	166,022	164,110	123,249	3.9	33.2
Ocean City, NJ Metro Area	86.7	5.0	1.4	0.5	0.1	7.9	99,436	99,010	98,416	91,226	1.0	7.9
Cape May, NJ	86.7	5.0	1.4	0.5	0.1	7.9	99,436	99,010	98,416	91,226	1.0	7.9
Odessa, TX Metro Area	32.6	4.8	1.2	0.7	0.2	61.3	58,680	57,164	53,083	49,634	10.5	6.9
Ector, TX	32.6	4.8	1.2	0.7	0.2	61.3	58,680	57,164	53,083	49,634	10.5	6.9
Ogden-Clearfield, UT Metro Area	83.0	1.7	2.7	1.0	0.8	13.1	226,369	216,556	204,514	161,969	10.7	26.3
Box Elder, UT	88.4	0.7	1.5	1.2	0.3	9.5	19,085	18,386	17,370	14,279	9.9	21.6
Davis, UT	85.6	1.8	3.2	0.8	1.1	9.9	110,412	105,490	97,802	74,596	12.9	31.1
Morgan, UT	95.5	0.8	0.7	0.7	0.2	3.1	3,658	3,404	3,014	2,173	21.4	38.7
Weber, UT	77.6	1.9	2.3	1.1	0.6	18.7	93,214	89,276	86,328	70,921	8.0	21.7
Oklahoma City, OK Metro Area	68.2	12.1	4.1	6.8	0.2	13.7	579,373	564,228	539,740	473,659	7.3	14.0
Canadian, OK	79.6	4.3	3.8	7.2	0.2	9.3	48,961	47,699	45,867	34,213	6.7	34.1
Cleveland, OK	76.3	6.6	5.7	7.9	0.2	9.0	116,905	112,742	105,268	85,247	11.1	23.5
Grady, OK	85.6	3.2	0.8	9.1	0.2	5.9	23,018	22,695	22,232	19,497	3.5	14.0
Lincoln, OK	87.1	2.7	0.7	11.1	0.2	3.5	15,412	15,345	15,217	13,756	1.3	10.6
Logan, OK	81.2	9.3	1.0	6.1	0.2	6.5	17,609	17,430	17,216	13,989	2.3	23.1
McClain, OK	83.8	1.4	0.8	10.8	0.1	8.2	15,946	15,102	14,026	11,251	13.7	24.7
Oklahoma, OK	59.6	17.3	4.4	5.7	0.2	17.8	341,523	333,215	319,914	295,706	6.8	8.2
Olympia-Lacey-Tumwater, WA Metro Area	79.1	4.7	8.3	2.7	1.5	9.2	117,872	113,762	108,496	87,059	8.6	24.6
Thurston, WA	79.1	4.7	8.3	2.7	1.5	9.2	117,872	113,762	108,496	87,059	8.6	24.6
Omaha-Council Bluffs, NE-IA Metro Area	77.9	8.9	3.8	1.0	0.2	10.7	390,430	378,771	362,976	313,007	7.6	16.0
Harrison, IA	97.1	0.8	0.6	0.9	0.1	1.8	6,859	6,789	6,735	6,614	1.8	1.8
Mills, IA	94.9	1.1	0.7	1.0	0.2	3.3	6,142	6,133	6,111	5,684	0.5	7.5
Pottawattamie, IA	89.0	2.5	1.3	1.0	0.2	7.8	40,020	39,795	39,356	35,959	1.7	9.4
Cass, NE	95.0	1.2	0.8	1.1	0.1	3.4	11,659	11,352	11,125	10,212	4.8	8.9
Douglas, NE	71.2	12.5	4.8	1.1	0.2	12.8	237,306	229,554	219,959	193,366	7.9	13.8
Sarpy, NE	83.1	5.3	3.7	0.9	0.2	9.8	69,959	67,150	62,151	45,449	12.6	36.7
Saunders, NE	96.4	1.0	0.9	0.8	0.0	2.3	9,792	9,503	9,232	8,282	6.1	11.5
Washington, NE	95.3	1.2	0.8	0.8	0.1	3.1	8,693	8,501	8,307	7,441	4.6	11.6
Orlando-Kissimmee-Sanford, FL Metro Area	47.7	16.8	5.2	0.6	0.2	31.5	1,050,625	992,263	943,156	690,045	11.4	36.7
Lake, FL	70.8	11.2	2.6	0.8	0.2	16.0	160,467	150,682	145,164	103,959	10.5	39.6
Orange, FL	41.2	21.3	6.3	0.6	0.3	32.3	544,417	516,907	488,164	364,211	11.5	34.0
Osceola, FL	31.9	10.4	3.1	0.5	0.2	55.3	153,495	138,127	128,414	73,608	19.5	74.5
Seminole, FL	61.4	12.5	5.6	0.6	0.2	22.0	192,246	186,547	181,414	148,267	6.0	22.4
Oshkosh-Neenah, WI Metro Area	89.9	3.0	3.5	1.0	0.1	4.2	76,028	74,737	73,395	64,945	3.6	13.0
Winnebago, WI	89.9	3.0	3.5	1.0	0.1	4.2	76,028	74,737	73,395	64,945	3.6	13.0
Owensboro, KY Metro Area	90.8	5.7	1.8	0.5	0.1	3.0	51,443	50,803	49,494	46,596	3.9	6.2
Daviess, KY	89.8	6.5	2.0	0.4	0.1	3.2	43,374	42,764	41,491	38,591	4.5	7.5
Hancock, KY	96.4	2.0	0.4	0.8	0.0	1.6	3,753	3,746	3,735	3,610	0.5	3.5
McLean, KY	97.0	1.3	0.5	0.8	0.0	1.6	4,316	4,293	4,268	4,395	1.1	-2.9
Oxnard-Thousand Oaks-Ventura, CA Metro Area	47.2	2.3	8.8	0.8	0.4	43.0	291,019	285,863	281,774	252,796	3.3	11.5
Ventura, CA	47.2	2.3	8.8	0.8	0.4	43.0	291,019	285,863	281,774	252,796	3.3	11.5
Palm Bay-Melbourne-Titusville, FL Metro Area	76.2	11.1	3.5	0.8	0.2	10.7	280,398	274,026	270,022	223,111	3.8	21.0
Brevard, FL	76.2	11.1	3.5	0.8	0.2	10.7	280,398	274,026	270,022	223,111	3.8	21.0
Panama City, FL Metro Area	78.8	12.5	3.4	1.5	0.3	6.7	104,314	101,292	99,703	78,783	4.6	26.6
Bay, FL	78.8	12.5	3.4	1.5	0.3	6.7	104,314	101,292	99,703	78,783	4.6	26.6
Parkersburg-Vienna, WV Metro Area	96.7	2.1	0.9	0.7	0.1	1.1	43,618	43,502	43,451	43,068	0.4	0.9
Wirt, WV	98.1	1.0	0.5	0.8	0.1	0.8	3,332	3,273	3,236	3,263	3.0	-0.8
Wood, WV	96.6	2.2	0.9	0.7	0.1	1.2	40,286	40,229	40,215	39,805	0.2	1.0

Table C-2. Population Characteristiics and Housing Units—*Continued*

| | Population characteristics, 2018 | | | | | | Housing Units | | | | | |
| | Race alone or in combination, not of Hispanic origin (percent) | | | | | | | | | | Percent change | |
Metropolitan Statistical Area Metropolitan Division Component counties	White	Black or African-American	Asian	American Indian, Alaska Native	Native Hawaiian, Pacific Islander	Hispanic or Latino origin (percent)	2018 (July 1 estimate)	2015 (July 1 estimate)	2010 (July 1 estimate)	2000 (July 1 estimate)	2010-2018	2000-2010
Pensacola-Ferry Pass-Brent, FL Metro Area	73.4	18.0	4.2	1.6	0.3	5.8	215,538	208,420	201,643	174,356	6.9	15.7
Escambia, FL	66.9	24.1	4.6	1.6	0.4	5.8	142,471	139,343	136,790	124,889	4.2	9.5
Santa Rosa, FL	85.0	7.2	3.4	1.6	0.3	5.7	73,067	69,077	64,853	49,467	12.7	31.1
Peoria, IL Metro Area	84.8	10.3	2.7	0.6	0.1	3.5	183,251	182,851	180,551	169,873	1.5	6.3
Fulton, IL	92.5	4.2	0.5	0.6	0.0	3.1	16,372	16,286	16,195	16,240	1.1	-0.3
Marshall, IL	95.5	1.2	0.7	0.6	0.1	3.0	5,905	5,908	5,914	5,893	-0.2	0.4
Peoria, IL	72.3	20.3	4.6	0.6	0.1	4.9	83,638	83,784	83,055	78,421	0.7	5.9
Stark, IL	96.3	1.5	1.1	0.6	0.0	2.0	2,660	2,661	2,673	2,724	-0.5	-1.9
Tazewell, IL	95.2	1.9	1.3	0.6	0.1	2.3	59,036	58,729	57,552	53,057	2.6	8.5
Woodford, IL	96.4	1.2	1.0	0.5	0.1	1.9	15,640	15,483	15,162	13,538	3.2	12.0
Philadelphia-Camden-Wilmington, PA-NJ-DE-MD Metro Area	63.1	21.8	6.9	0.6	0.1	9.7	2,497,485	2,469,226	2,434,697	2,286,358	2.6	6.5
Camden, NJ Div	67.0	17.3	5.7	0.6	0.1	11.5	499,942	496,695	490,641	457,033	1.9	7.4
Burlington, NJ	69.0	18.2	6.2	0.7	0.1	8.3	179,893	178,090	175,683	161,925	2.4	8.5
Camden, NJ	57.8	19.8	6.5	0.6	0.1	17.2	206,146	206,135	204,923	199,227	0.6	2.9
Gloucester, NJ	79.8	11.5	3.7	0.5	0.1	6.4	113,903	112,470	110,035	95,881	3.5	14.8
Montgomery County-Bucks County-Chester County	80.6	7.6	7.1	0.5	0.1	6.0	789,061	777,652	764,615	689,131	3.2	11.0
Bucks, PA	85.2	4.7	5.7	0.5	0.1	5.5	251,515	248,752	246,048	226,193	2.2	8.8
Chester, PA	80.7	6.7	6.4	0.5	0.1	7.6	201,353	197,983	192,675	164,578	4.5	17.1
Montgomery, PA	77.1	10.5	8.7	0.4	0.1	5.3	336,193	330,917	325,892	298,360	3.2	9.2
Philadelphia, PA Div	44.3	37.0	7.8	0.7	0.1	12.2	913,704	903,721	893,300	879,239	2.3	1.6
Delaware, PA	68.0	22.9	6.7	0.6	0.1	3.9	224,871	223,857	222,998	217,129	0.8	2.7
Philadelphia, PA	35.9	42.1	8.2	0.8	0.1	15.2	688,833	679,864	670,302	662,110	2.8	1.2
Wilmington, DE-MD-NJ Div	64.1	22.7	5.3	0.7	0.1	9.4	294,778	291,158	286,141	260,955	3.0	9.7
New Castle, DE	58.7	26.3	6.3	0.7	0.1	10.3	224,499	220,945	217,571	200,131	3.2	8.7
Cecil, MD	86.9	7.9	1.9	0.8	0.1	4.6	42,676	42,587	41,136	34,658	3.7	18.7
Salem, NJ	75.6	14.7	1.4	0.7	0.2	9.5	27,603	27,626	27,434	26,166	0.6	4.8
Phoenix-Mesa-Chandler, AZ Metro Area	57.0	6.3	4.9	2.5	0.4	31.2	1,939,993	1,863,942	1,802,038	1,342,946	7.7	34.2
Maricopa, AZ	56.9	6.4	5.2	2.2	0.4	31.3	1,762,834	1,695,415	1,642,198	1,261,150	7.3	30.2
Pinal, AZ	58.3	5.4	2.3	5.2	0.5	30.4	177,159	168,527	159,840	81,796	10.8	95.4
Pine Bluff, AR Metro Area	47.6	49.5	0.9	0.8	0.1	2.4	42,436	42,345	41,963	43,145	1.1	-2.7
Cleveland, AR	85.6	12.2	0.3	0.9	0.0	2.4	4,105	4,087	4,067	3,842	0.9	5.9
Jefferson, AR	39.7	57.5	1.0	0.8	0.2	2.1	33,387	33,338	33,030	34,344	1.1	-3.8
Lincoln, AR	65.2	30.8	0.4	0.9	0.1	3.9	4,944	4,920	4,866	4,959	1.6	-1.9
Pittsburgh, PA Metro Area	86.9	9.6	3.0	0.5	0.1	1.8	1,130,057	1,118,113	1,102,670	1,079,518	2.5	2.1
Allegheny, PA	80.2	14.6	4.6	0.5	0.1	2.2	602,414	596,187	589,423	583,990	2.2	0.9
Armstrong, PA	97.9	1.4	0.5	0.4	0.0	0.8	32,782	32,752	32,545	32,382	0.7	0.5
Beaver, PA	91.3	7.7	0.8	0.5	0.1	1.6	79,659	79,111	78,242	77,827	1.8	0.5
Butler, PA	95.6	1.7	1.8	0.4	0.1	1.6	84,252	81,517	78,254	70,123	7.7	11.6
Fayette, PA	93.2	5.8	0.6	0.5	0.3	1.2	63,962	63,530	62,812	66,409	1.8	-5.4
Washington, PA	93.7	4.4	1.4	0.5	0.1	1.8	96,212	95,059	93,083	87,501	3.4	6.4
Westmoreland, PA	95.1	3.4	1.2	0.4	0.1	1.2	170,776	169,957	168,311	161,286	1.5	4.4
Pittsfield, MA Metro Area	89.8	4.3	2.2	0.6	0.1	5.1	69,400	68,910	68,550	66,317	1.2	3.4
Berkshire, MA	89.8	4.3	2.2	0.6	0.1	5.1	69,400	68,910	68,550	66,317	1.2	3.4
Pocatello, ID Metro Area	83.6	1.4	2.2	3.6	0.5	10.9	37,467	36,847	36,175	32,025	3.6	13.0
Bannock, ID	85.5	1.4	2.4	3.6	0.5	8.8	34,450	33,855	33,228	29,177	3.7	13.9
Power, ID	61.9	0.7	0.8	3.1	0.3	34.8	3,017	2,992	2,947	2,848	2.4	3.5
Portland-South Portland, ME Metro Area	93.8	2.7	2.4	1.0	0.1	2.0	275,711	269,292	262,973	234,119	4.8	12.3
Cumberland, ME	92.2	3.7	3.0	0.9	0.1	2.1	145,740	142,065	138,776	123,077	5.0	12.8
Sagadahoc, ME	96.0	1.4	1.3	1.1	0.1	1.8	18,935	18,637	18,306	16,524	3.4	10.8
York, ME	95.6	1.4	1.8	1.0	0.1	1.7	111,036	108,590	105,891	94,518	4.9	12.0
Portland-Vancouver-Hillsboro, OR-WA Metro Area	76.2	4.1	8.8	1.7	0.9	12.2	1,008,433	964,951	926,044	794,512	8.9	16.6
Clackamas, OR	84.5	1.7	6.1	1.6	0.6	8.9	169,240	163,355	157,166	137,556	7.7	14.3
Columbia, OR	91.3	1.2	2.2	3.0	0.5	5.4	21,413	21,010	20,721	17,650	3.3	17.4
Multnomah, OR	72.9	7.1	9.7	1.9	1.0	11.7	353,842	337,515	324,969	289,311	8.9	12.3
Washington, OR	68.5	3.0	13.3	1.3	0.9	17.0	232,451	223,165	212,797	179,873	9.2	18.3
Yamhill, OR	79.2	1.5	3.0	2.4	0.5	16.2	39,396	38,263	37,178	30,457	6.0	22.1
Clark, WA	81.4	3.2	6.3	1.8	1.3	10.0	186,167	175,867	167,574	135,069	11.1	24.1
Skamania, WA	90.2	1.2	1.7	3.0	0.4	6.3	5,924	5,776	5,639	4,596	5.1	22.7
Port St. Lucie, FL Metro Area	65.1	15.9	2.2	0.6	0.2	17.7	223,169	218,144	215,201	157,691	3.7	36.5
Martin, FL	79.1	5.8	1.8	0.5	0.1	13.9	80,410	79,511	78,367	65,864	2.6	19.0
St. Lucie, FL	58.1	21.0	2.4	0.6	0.2	19.5	142,759	138,633	136,834	91,827	4.3	49.0
Poughkeepsie-Newburgh-Middletown, NY Metro Area	68.6	11.6	3.9	0.7	0.1	17.3	265,390	261,501	255,847	229,638	3.7	11.4
Dutchess, NY	72.9	11.6	4.4	0.6	0.1	12.5	121,158	120,158	118,687	106,418	2.1	11.5
Orange, NY	65.3	11.6	3.4	0.7	0.1	21.0	144,232	141,343	137,160	123,220	5.2	11.3
Prescott Valley-Prescott, AZ Metro Area	81.9	1.1	1.6	2.3	0.3	14.7	118,394	113,704	110,533	82,364	7.1	34.2
Yavapai, AZ	81.9	1.1	1.6	2.3	0.3	14.7	118,394	113,704	110,533	82,364	7.1	34.2
Providence-Warwick, RI-MA Metro Area	77.4	6.7	3.7	0.9	0.2	13.3	705,431	699,962	694,167	657,795	1.6	5.5
Bristol, MA	84.1	5.7	2.9	0.7	0.2	8.4	236,274	233,446	230,606	217,298	2.5	6.1
Bristol, RI	93.0	1.9	2.9	0.6	0.2	3.2	21,056	20,957	20,840	19,907	1.0	4.7
Kent, RI	89.7	2.7	3.3	0.8	0.1	5.3	74,514	74,131	73,702	70,507	1.1	4.5
Newport, RI	87.8	5.0	2.7	1.0	0.2	6.0	42,666	42,315	41,830	39,639	2.0	5.5

Table C-2. Population Characteristiics and Housing Units—*Continued*

Metropolitan Statistical Area / Metropolitan Division / Component counties	White	Black or African-American	Asian	American Indian, Alaska Native	Native Hawaiian, Pacific Islander	Hispanic or Latino origin (percent)	2018 (July 1 estimate)	2015 (July 1 estimate)	2010 (July 1 estimate)	2000 (July 1 estimate)	2010-2018	2000-2010
Providence, RI	62.8	10.1	4.9	1.1	0.2	23.4	266,574	265,683	264,929	253,451	0.6	4.5
Washington, RI	92.5	2.1	2.6	1.4	0.1	3.3	64,347	63,430	62,260	56,993	3.4	9.2
Provo-Orem, UT Metro Area	84.4	1.0	2.8	0.9	1.6	11.9	183,886	167,201	152,250	108,093	20.8	40.9
Juab, UT	93.0	0.7	0.5	1.5	0.4	5.1	3,824	3,626	3,506	2,829	9.1	23.9
Utah, UT	84.2	1.0	2.8	0.9	1.6	12.0	180,062	163,575	148,744	105,264	21.1	41.3
Pueblo, CO Metro Area	53.4	2.3	1.2	1.4	0.2	43.1	71,451	70,652	69,613	59,251	2.6	17.5
Pueblo, CO	53.4	2.3	1.2	1.4	0.2	43.1	71,451	70,652	69,613	59,251	2.6	17.5
Punta Gorda, FL Metro Area	85.3	6.2	1.8	0.7	0.1	7.4	105,172	102,401	100,685	80,155	4.5	25.6
Charlotte, FL	85.3	6.2	1.8	0.7	0.1	7.4	105,172	102,401	100,685	80,155	4.5	25.6
Racine, WI Metro Area	73.6	12.7	1.6	0.8	0.1	13.4	82,907	82,481	82,211	74,909	0.8	9.7
Racine, WI	73.6	12.7	1.6	0.8	0.1	13.4	82,907	82,481	82,211	74,909	0.8	9.7
Raleigh-Cary, NC Metro Area	62.9	20.7	6.8	0.9	0.1	10.8	548,194	510,625	467,128	332,456	17.4	40.5
Franklin, NC	64.9	26.3	0.9	1.1	0.1	8.5	29,025	27,468	26,581	20,550	9.2	29.3
Johnston, NC	68.8	16.9	1.2	1.0	0.1	14.0	77,352	71,880	67,815	50,692	14.1	33.8
Wake, NC	61.7	21.1	8.3	0.8	0.1	10.3	441,817	411,277	372,732	261,214	18.5	42.7
Rapid City, SD Metro Area	84.4	2.3	1.9	9.7	0.2	5.0	61,505	59,340	56,066	12,011	9.7	366.8
Meade, SD	89.6	2.6	1.7	4.2	0.2	4.5	12,265	11,755	11,033	10,156	11.2	8.6
Pennington, SD	83.1	2.2	1.9	11.0	0.2	5.2	49,240	47,585	45,033	1,855	9.3	2327.7
Reading, PA Metro Area	72.2	5.1	1.8	0.4	0.1	21.9	167,366	166,382	164,890	150,712	1.5	9.4
Berks, PA	72.2	5.1	1.8	0.4	0.1	21.9	167,366	166,382	164,890	150,712	1.5	9.4
Redding, CA Metro Area	83.0	2.0	4.1	4.1	0.4	10.3	79,194	78,095	77,350	69,020	2.4	12.1
Shasta, CA	83.0	2.0	4.1	4.1	0.4	10.3	79,194	78,095	77,350	69,020	2.4	12.1
Reno, NV Metro Area	65.4	3.1	6.9	2.0	1.0	24.7	203,135	192,508	187,007	146,669	8.6	27.5
Storey, NV	86.3	2.3	2.9	2.7	0.7	7.6	2,054	2,024	1,994	1,610	3.0	23.9
Washoe, NV	65.3	3.1	6.9	2.0	1.0	24.8	201,081	190,484	185,013	145,059	8.7	27.5
Richmond, VA Metro Area	59.0	31.0	4.8	0.9	0.2	6.5	525,984	512,870	499,436	429,539	5.3	16.3
Amelia, VA	75.8	21.5	0.8	0.9	0.0	2.9	5,621	5,505	5,369	4,619	4.7	16.2
Charles City County, VA	45.5	46.9	1.3	7.8	0.2	1.8	3,378	3,336	3,234	2,912	4.5	11.1
Chesterfield, VA	63.3	24.8	4.5	0.8	0.1	9.2	132,356	127,804	122,722	98,229	7.9	24.9
Dinwiddie, VA	63.0	32.6	1.2	0.7	0.1	3.9	11,799	11,656	11,457	9,751	3.0	17.5
Goochland, VA	79.1	16.6	2.0	0.7	0.1	3.0	9,452	9,033	8,628	6,608	9.6	30.6
Hanover, VA	85.4	10.0	2.4	0.8	0.1	3.2	41,872	40,281	38,402	32,430	9.0	18.4
Henrico, VA	54.6	31.4	9.8	0.8	0.1	5.8	138,177	135,078	132,774	113,115	4.1	17.4
King and Queen, VA	68.0	28.1	0.8	2.3	0.1	3.3	3,512	3,472	3,415	3,015	2.8	13.3
King William, VA	79.1	16.7	1.7	2.2	0.1	2.7	7,155	6,740	6,534	5,219	9.5	25.2
New Kent, VA	80.3	14.4	1.8	2.0	0.2	3.7	8,728	8,064	7,326	5,239	19.1	39.8
Powhatan, VA	87.0	10.0	0.9	0.7	0.2	2.4	11,103	10,550	10,059	7,572	10.4	32.8
Prince George, VA	56.9	33.1	2.9	1.2	0.6	8.5	12,565	12,365	12,067	10,750	4.1	12.3
Sussex, VA	40.0	56.8	0.6	0.7	0.0	3.1	4,805	4,756	4,695	4,655	2.3	0.9
Colonial Heights City, VA	73.2	17.1	4.8	1.0	0.3	6.3	7,719	7,768	7,826	7,352	-1.4	6.4
Hopewell City, VA	48.1	43.4	2.0	1.1	0.4	8.3	10,328	10,282	10,155	9,755	1.7	4.1
Petersburg City, VA	16.6	77.8	1.5	1.0	0.2	5.2	16,349	16,346	16,382	15,973	-0.2	2.6
Richmond City, VA	43.2	48.0	3.0	0.8	0.1	7.1	101,065	99,834	98,391	92,345	2.7	6.5
Riverside-San Bernardino-Ontario, CA Metro Area	33.5	8.0	7.9	0.9	0.5	51.6	1,574,493	1,538,269	1,501,869	1,191,406	4.8	26.1
Riverside, CA	36.8	7.1	7.6	1.0	0.5	49.6	848,597	826,659	801,724	588,488	5.8	36.2
San Bernardino, CA	29.8	9.0	8.1	0.9	0.5	54.0	725,896	711,610	700,145	602,918	3.7	16.1
Roanoke, VA Metro Area	79.8	14.6	2.9	0.6	0.1	4.0	146,755	145,929	145,003	130,120	1.2	11.4
Botetourt, VA	93.9	3.8	1.1	0.7	0.0	1.8	14,927	14,778	14,573	12,645	2.4	15.2
Craig, VA	97.7	0.7	0.3	0.5	0.1	1.5	2,909	2,891	2,808	2,561	3.6	9.6
Franklin, VA	88.5	8.7	0.7	0.5	0.1	2.9	30,021	29,743	29,329	22,900	2.4	28.1
Roanoke, VA	87.0	6.9	4.0	0.5	0.1	3.1	41,023	40,640	40,087	36,224	2.3	10.7
Roanoke City, VA	60.7	30.9	3.9	0.8	0.1	6.5	47,008	47,035	47,360	45,379	-0.7	4.4
Salem City, VA	86.7	8.6	2.4	0.7	0.1	3.4	10,867	10,842	10,846	10,411	0.2	4.2
Rochester, MN Metro Area	85.7	5.5	5.6	0.6	0.1	4.5	95,296	90,740	88,292	74,524	7.9	18.5
Dodge, MN	93.2	1.1	1.2	0.8	0.1	5.1	8,339	8,129	7,955	6,691	4.8	18.9
Fillmore, MN	96.9	0.8	0.9	0.4	0.0	1.8	10,028	9,916	9,738	8,929	3.0	9.1
Olmsted, MN	81.9	7.3	7.4	0.6	0.1	5.0	66,672	62,528	60,600	49,818	10.0	21.6
Wabasha, MN	95.6	1.1	0.9	0.6	0.0	2.9	10,257	10,167	9,999	9,086	2.6	10.0
Rochester, NY Metro Area	78.1	12.2	3.5	0.7	0.1	7.6	482,293	476,661	469,716	440,207	2.7	6.7
Livingston, NY	92.1	3.1	1.8	0.7	0.1	3.7	27,616	27,390	27,088	24,257	1.9	11.7
Monroe, NY	72.2	16.0	4.4	0.6	0.1	9.0	329,190	325,394	320,971	304,908	2.6	5.3
Ontario, NY	91.1	3.1	1.7	0.5	0.1	5.0	51,204	49,984	48,561	42,697	5.4	13.7
Orleans, NY	87.8	7.0	0.8	1.0	0.1	4.9	18,598	18,550	18,440	17,385	0.9	6.1
Wayne, NY	91.7	4.0	1.1	0.7	0.1	4.5	41,798	41,569	41,113	38,861	1.7	5.8
Yates, NY	95.6	1.5	1.0	0.6	0.1	2.3	13,887	13,774	13,543	12,099	2.5	11.9
Rockford, IL Metro Area	71.2	12.7	3.1	0.7	0.1	14.6	145,812	145,835	145,940	130,217	-0.1	12.1
Boone, IL	73.5	3.1	1.8	0.7	0.1	22.4	20,097	20,068	19,981	15,524	0.6	28.7
Winnebago, IL	70.7	14.5	3.4	0.7	0.1	13.1	125,715	125,767	125,959	114,693	-0.2	9.8
Rocky Mount, NC Metro Area	45.8	47.4	0.9	1.0	0.1	6.3	68,171	67,575	67,156	61,297	1.5	9.6
Edgecombe, NC	37.1	57.8	0.4	0.7	0.2	4.8	25,028	24,843	24,838	24,059	0.8	3.2
Nash, NC	50.7	41.6	1.1	1.2	0.1	7.1	43,143	42,732	42,318	37,238	1.9	13.6
Rome, GA Metro Area	72.4	15.4	1.8	0.7	0.1	11.3	40,636	40,438	40,554	36,742	0.2	10.4
Floyd, GA	72.4	15.4	1.8	0.7	0.1	11.3	40,636	40,438	40,554	36,742	0.2	10.4

Table C-2. Population Characteristiics and Housing Units—*Continued*

Metropolitan Statistical Area / Metropolitan Division / Component counties	White	Black or African-American	Asian	American Indian, Alaska Native	Native Hawaiian, Pacific Islander	Hispanic or Latino origin (percent)	2018 (July 1 estimate)	2015 (July 1 estimate)	2010 (July 1 estimate)	2000 (July 1 estimate)	2010-2018	2000-2010
Sacramento-Roseville-Folsom, CA Metro Area	55.5	8.6	16.0	1.5	1.3	21.8	911,208	888,947	872,424	718,998	4.4	21.3
El Dorado, CA...............	80.5	1.4	6.1	1.8	0.5	12.9	91,105	89,009	88,191	71,727	3.3	23.0
Placer, CA...............	75.4	2.4	9.9	1.3	0.6	14.3	167,134	159,377	152,971	108,665	9.3	40.8
Sacramento, CA...............	48.1	11.8	18.7	1.5	1.7	23.4	574,438	563,620	556,128	476,695	3.3	16.7
Yolo, CA...............	49.8	3.4	17.1	1.3	0.9	31.9	78,531	76,941	75,134	61,911	4.5	21.4
Saginaw, MI Metro Area...............	71.0	19.8	1.7	0.9	0.1	8.5	87,817	87,150	86,834	85,696	1.1	1.3
Saginaw, MI...............	71.0	19.8	1.7	0.9	0.1	8.5	87,817	87,150	86,834	85,696	1.1	1.3
St. Cloud, MN Metro Area...............	87.9	7.2	2.6	0.7	0.1	3.3	82,530	80,115	78,219	64,238	5.5	21.8
Benton, MN...............	91.2	5.5	1.7	1.0	0.1	2.5	17,265	16,669	16,156	13,719	6.9	17.8
Stearns, MN...............	87.0	7.7	2.8	0.6	0.1	3.5	65,265	63,446	62,063	50,519	5.2	22.9
St. George, UT Metro Area...............	85.9	1.1	1.6	1.5	1.4	10.6	71,363	64,427	57,883	36,848	23.3	57.1
Washington, UT...............	85.9	1.1	1.6	1.5	1.4	10.6	71,363	64,427	57,883	36,848	23.3	57.1
St. Joseph, MO-KS Metro Area...............	86.9	6.8	1.5	1.1	0.3	5.6	54,067	53,873	53,659	50,694	0.8	5.8
Doniphan, KS...............	92.3	4.1	0.7	2.2	0.1	2.8	3,576	3,578	3,578	3,493	-0.1	2.4
Andrew, MO...............	95.4	1.7	0.8	0.8	0.1	2.6	7,337	7,334	7,312	6,690	0.3	9.3
Buchanan, MO...............	85.0	7.3	1.9	1.1	0.4	6.9	38,804	38,629	38,439	36,652	0.9	4.9
De Kalb, MO...............	84.6	12.0	0.6	0.8	0.2	2.8	4,350	4,332	4,330	3,859	0.5	12.2
St. Louis, MO-IL Metro Area...............	75.4	19.4	3.3	0.7	0.1	3.1	1,262,828	1,245,601	1,226,066	1,126,418	3.0	8.8
Bond, IL...............	88.9	6.8	1.1	0.9	0.1	3.6	7,286	7,166	7,096	6,713	2.7	5.7
Calhoun, IL...............	97.8	0.6	0.4	0.5	0.0	1.3	2,895	2,870	2,841	2,681	1.9	6.0
Clinton, IL...............	92.5	4.2	0.9	0.5	0.1	3.2	15,934	15,712	15,340	13,849	3.9	10.8
Jersey, IL...............	96.7	1.2	0.9	0.8	0.1	1.5	10,167	10,104	9,860	8,932	3.1	10.4
Macoupin, IL...............	97.0	1.5	0.6	0.7	0.0	1.3	21,787	21,663	21,588	21,132	0.9	2.2
Madison, IL...............	86.6	9.9	1.5	0.6	0.1	3.4	119,630	118,849	117,190	109,185	2.1	7.3
Monroe, IL...............	97.2	0.7	0.9	0.5	0.0	1.5	14,359	13,914	13,415	10,821	7.0	24.0
St. Clair, IL...............	63.5	31.6	2.3	0.7	0.2	4.2	120,596	119,442	116,436	104,692	3.6	11.2
Franklin, MO...............	96.3	1.5	0.8	0.9	0.1	1.8	45,533	44,413	43,469	38,456	4.7	13.0
Jefferson, MO...............	95.7	1.7	1.2	0.8	0.1	2.0	91,627	89,942	87,755	76,057	4.4	15.4
Lincoln, MO...............	94.6	2.7	0.8	0.9	0.1	2.6	21,847	21,399	21,036	15,642	3.9	34.5
St. Charles, MO...............	88.7	6.0	3.2	0.6	0.1	3.4	156,324	150,119	141,355	106,554	10.6	32.7
St. Louis, MO...............	67.5	25.8	5.3	0.6	0.1	3.0	441,973	438,873	438,037	424,238	0.9	3.3
Warren, MO...............	93.5	3.3	0.7	0.9	0.1	3.4	15,714	15,115	14,712	11,147	6.8	32.0
St. Louis city, MO...............	46.2	47.0	4.1	1.0	0.1	4.1	177,156	176,020	175,936	176,319	0.7	-0.2
Salem, OR Metro Area...............	70.1	1.8	3.2	2.3	1.1	24.5	159,845	155,480	151,452	133,093	5.5	13.8
Marion, OR...............	67.5	1.8	3.2	2.2	1.2	27.0	127,332	124,124	121,104	108,488	5.1	11.6
Polk, OR...............	80.5	1.7	3.1	3.1	0.7	14.3	32,513	31,356	30,348	24,605	7.1	23.3
Salinas, CA Metro Area...............	31.5	3.2	7.1	0.8	0.8	59.1	142,399	140,463	139,088	132,051	2.4	5.3
Monterey, CA...............	31.5	3.2	7.1	0.8	0.8	59.1	142,399	140,463	139,088	132,051	2.4	5.3
Salisbury, MD-DE Metro Area...............	73.0	18.8	2.1	0.9	0.1	7.2	251,593	242,332	231,517	185,724	8.7	24.7
Sussex, DE...............	76.9	13.1	1.6	1.0	0.1	9.3	141,101	132,803	123,392	93,535	14.4	31.9
Somerset, MD...............	53.4	43.0	1.3	0.9	0.2	3.6	11,490	11,317	11,153	10,099	3.0	10.4
Wicomico, MD...............	64.6	28.2	3.6	0.6	0.1	5.4	42,470	42,250	41,219	34,512	3.0	19.4
Worcester, MD...............	81.6	13.9	1.8	0.7	0.1	3.6	56,532	55,962	55,753	47,578	1.4	17.2
Salt Lake City, UT Metro Area...............	73.4	2.3	5.2	1.1	2.1	18.2	426,128	403,827	384,466	326,092	10.8	17.9
Salt Lake, UT...............	72.8	2.4	5.5	1.1	2.1	18.6	403,666	382,945	364,967	312,065	10.6	17.0
Tooele, UT...............	84.4	1.2	1.3	1.3	0.9	12.6	22,462	20,882	19,499	14,027	15.2	39.0
San Angelo, TX Metro Area...............	54.4	4.2	1.7	0.8	0.2	40.3	50,105	49,691	48,152	45,545	4.1	5.7
Irion, TX...............	71.6	1.5	0.3	1.6	0.1	26.3	862	859	855	909	0.8	-5.9
Sterling, TX...............	56.2	2.6	0.5	1.4	0.2	40.7	623	619	615	634	1.3	-3.0
Tom Green, TX...............	54.1	4.3	1.7	0.8	0.2	40.5	48,620	48,213	46,682	44,002	4.2	6.1
San Antonio-New Braunfels, TX Metro Area.........	34.7	7.2	3.2	0.6	0.2	55.6	904,717	873,964	839,262	652,668	7.8	28.6
Atascosa, TX...............	33.7	1.0	0.5	0.7	0.1	64.7	18,482	18,158	17,648	14,951	4.7	18.0
Bandera, TX...............	78.3	1.3	0.8	1.4	0.0	19.4	11,990	11,796	11,572	9,550	3.6	21.2
Bexar, TX...............	28.6	8.0	3.6	0.6	0.2	60.5	700,132	683,938	663,606	524,461	5.5	26.5
Comal, TX...............	68.3	2.6	1.7	0.9	0.1	27.8	60,948	53,551	47,300	33,022	28.9	43.2
Guadalupe, TX...............	51.6	8.5	2.6	0.8	0.3	38.3	60,135	55,469	50,245	33,817	19.7	48.6
Kendall, TX...............	72.8	1.4	1.6	1.0	0.1	24.4	16,563	15,359	14,091	9,709	17.5	45.1
Medina, TX...............	43.9	2.8	0.9	0.8	0.1	52.4	18,708	18,388	18,008	14,926	3.9	20.6
Wilson, TX...............	57.6	1.8	0.7	0.8	0.1	40.0	17,759	17,305	16,792	12,226	5.8	37.3
San Diego-Chula Vista-Carlsbad, CA Metro Area ..	48.1	5.7	14.1	0.9	0.8	34.0	1,224,375	1,194,262	1,165,429	1,044,144	5.1	11.6
San Diego, CA...............	48.1	5.7	14.1	0.9	0.8	34.0	1,224,375	1,194,262	1,165,429	1,044,144	5.1	11.6
San Francisco-Oakland-Berkeley, CA Metro Area ..	42.6	8.3	29.5	0.8	1.1	21.9	1,825,087	1,782,103	1,742,797	1,610,766	4.7	8.2
Oakland-Berkeley-Livermore, CA Div	39.5	11.0	28.2	0.9	1.2	23.8	1,030,996	1,004,470	983,391	897,252	4.8	9.6
Alameda, CA...............	34.5	11.6	33.8	0.8	1.3	22.4	615,077	595,742	582,866	541,385	5.5	7.7
Contra Costa, CA...............	46.8	10.0	20.0	1.0	0.9	25.8	415,919	408,728	400,525	355,867	3.8	12.5
San Francisco-San Mateo-Redwood City, CA Div..	42.7	4.6	35.1	0.7	1.3	19.5	680,909	664,940	648,138	608,358	5.1	6.5
San Francisco, CA...............	43.3	6.0	37.7	0.8	0.7	15.2	401,452	390,121	377,011	347,258	6.5	8.6
San Mateo, CA...............	42.1	3.0	32.1	0.6	1.9	24.3	279,457	274,819	271,127	261,100	3.1	3.8
San Rafael, CA Div...............	74.5	3.3	8.3	0.8	0.4	16.1	113,182	112,693	111,268	105,156	1.7	5.8
Marin, CA...............	74.5	3.3	8.3	0.8	0.4	16.1	113,182	112,693	111,268	105,156	1.7	5.8
San Jose-Sunnyvale-Santa Clara, CA Metro Area..	33.8	2.9	38.8	0.7	0.7	26.4	697,934	678,651	650,018	597,689	7.4	8.8
San Benito, CA...............	35.0	1.3	3.6	0.9	0.3	60.6	19,438	18,213	17,879	16,617	8.7	7.6
Santa Clara, CA...............	33.8	3.0	39.9	0.6	0.7	25.3	678,496	660,438	632,139	581,072	7.3	8.8

Table C-2. Population Characteristiics and Housing Units—*Continued*

Metropolitan Statistical Area Metropolitan Division Component counties	Population characteristics, 2018						Housing Units				Percent change	
	Race alone or in combination, not of Hispanic origin (percent)					Hispanic or Latino origin (percent)	2018 (July 1 estimate)	2015 (July 1 estimate)	2010 (July 1 estimate)	2000 (July 1 estimate)	2010-2018	2000-2010
	White	Black or African-American	Asian	American Indian, Alaska Native	Native Hawaiian, Pacific Islander							
San Luis Obispo-Paso Robles, CA Metro Area	71.0	2.3	5.0	1.3	0.4	22.8	122,979	120,247	117,401	102,684	4.8	14.3
San Luis Obispo, CA	71.0	2.3	5.0	1.3	0.4	22.8	122,979	120,247	117,401	102,684	4.8	14.3
Santa Cruz-Watsonville, CA Metro Area	59.6	1.7	6.3	1.2	0.4	34.1	106,728	105,527	104,495	98,986	2.1	5.6
Santa Cruz, CA	59.6	1.7	6.3	1.2	0.4	34.1	106,728	105,527	104,495	98,986	2.1	5.6
Santa Fe, NM Metro Area	44.1	1.1	1.7	3.1	0.1	51.1	73,456	72,782	71,359	57,920	2.9	23.2
Santa Fe, NM	44.1	1.1	1.7	3.1	0.1	51.1	73,456	72,782	71,359	57,920	2.9	23.2
Santa Maria-Santa Barbara, CA Metro Area	46.2	2.4	6.7	1.0	0.4	45.8	158,333	155,150	152,900	143,164	3.6	6.8
Santa Barbara, CA	46.2	2.4	6.7	1.0	0.4	45.8	158,333	155,150	152,900	143,164	3.6	6.8
Santa Rosa-Petaluma, CA Metro Area	65.8	2.4	5.6	1.6	0.6	27.2	205,225	207,870	204,661	183,846	0.3	11.3
Sonoma, CA	65.8	2.4	5.6	1.6	0.6	27.2	205,225	207,870	204,661	183,846	0.3	11.3
Savannah, GA Metro Area	57.2	34.6	3.1	0.8	0.2	6.4	163,944	158,340	151,365	123,434	8.3	22.6
Bryan, GA	75.7	15.7	2.8	1.0	0.3	7.3	14,795	13,406	11,888	8,759	24.5	35.7
Chatham, GA	49.9	41.3	3.5	0.7	0.2	6.6	125,680	123,676	119,533	100,374	5.1	19.1
Effingham, GA	79.8	14.8	1.5	0.9	0.1	4.8	23,469	21,258	19,944	14,301	17.7	39.5
Scranton--Wilkes-Barre, PA Metro Area	83.9	4.3	2.2	0.4	0.1	10.5	264,545	262,565	258,970	252,950	2.2	2.4
Lackawanna, PA	85.7	3.8	3.4	0.4	0.1	8.1	100,718	99,427	96,905	95,415	3.9	1.6
Luzerne, PA	81.6	4.9	1.6	0.4	0.1	12.9	150,302	149,670	148,798	144,811	1.0	2.8
Wyoming, PA	96.4	1.3	0.7	0.6	0.1	1.9	13,525	13,468	13,267	12,724	1.9	4.3
Seattle-Tacoma-Bellevue, WA Metro Area	66.9	7.6	17.1	2.0	1.5	10.2	1,617,435	1,541,678	1,464,974	1,261,027	10.4	16.2
Seattle-Bellevue-Kent, WA Div	65.5	7.1	19.4	1.8	1.2	10.0	1,266,387	1,202,179	1,139,120	982,839	11.2	15.9
King, WA	62.8	8.0	21.5	1.6	1.2	9.8	952,569	899,480	851,964	745,080	11.8	14.3
Snohomish, WA	72.7	4.6	13.6	2.2	1.1	10.4	313,818	302,699	287,156	237,759	9.3	20.8
Tacoma-Lakewood, WA Div	71.8	9.6	9.5	2.6	2.3	11.1	351,048	339,499	325,854	278,188	7.7	17.1
Pierce, WA	71.8	9.6	9.5	2.6	2.3	11.1	351,048	339,499	325,854	278,188	7.7	17.1
Sebastian-Vero Beach, FL Metro Area	76.4	9.7	1.9	0.6	0.1	12.7	81,043	78,300	76,406	58,305	6.1	31.0
Indian River, FL	76.4	9.7	1.9	0.6	0.1	12.7	81,043	78,300	76,406	58,305	6.1	31.0
Sebring-Avon Park, FL Metro Area	67.6	10.3	1.7	0.9	0.1	20.8	55,759	55,445	55,395	48,964	0.7	13.1
Highlands, FL	67.6	10.3	1.7	0.9	0.1	20.8	55,759	55,445	55,395	48,964	0.7	13.1
Sheboygan, WI Metro Area	85.2	2.8	6.1	0.8	0.1	6.5	51,340	50,786	50,782	46,097	1.1	10.2
Sheboygan, WI	85.2	2.8	6.1	0.8	0.1	6.5	51,340	50,786	50,782	46,097	1.1	10.2
Sherman-Denison, TX Metro Area	77.2	7.0	1.9	2.3	0.1	13.8	56,731	54,802	53,747	48,441	5.6	11.0
Grayson, TX	77.2	7.0	1.9	2.3	0.1	13.8	56,731	54,802	53,747	48,441	5.6	11.0
Shreveport-Bossier City, LA Metro Area	53.9	40.8	1.9	1.0	0.1	4.1	184,376	181,071	173,982	160,060	6.0	8.7
Bossier, LA	68.2	23.6	2.6	1.0	0.2	6.8	57,828	55,693	49,651	40,990	16.5	21.1
Caddo, LA	45.8	50.3	1.6	0.9	0.1	2.9	113,374	112,756	112,026	107,820	1.2	3.9
De Soto, LA	60.0	36.4	0.5	1.4	0.1	3.0	13,174	12,622	12,305	11,250	7.1	9.4
Sierra Vista-Douglas, AZ Metro Area	57.0	4.8	3.0	1.6	0.6	35.6	61,328	60,688	59,135	51,322	3.7	15.2
Cochise, AZ	57.0	4.8	3.0	1.6	0.6	35.6	61,328	60,688	59,135	51,322	3.7	15.2
Sioux City, IA-NE-SD Metro Area	73.4	4.6	3.2	2.2	0.3	18.5	60,298	59,278	58,108	56,966	3.8	2.0
Woodbury, IA	74.6	5.0	3.4	2.3	0.3	17.0	42,441	41,903	41,488	41,396	2.3	0.2
Dakota, NE	49.2	6.0	4.1	3.1	0.4	39.0	7,871	7,807	7,634	7,549	3.1	1.1
Dixon, NE	83.9	0.8	0.3	0.9	0.1	14.9	2,709	2,704	2,688	2,657	0.8	1.2
Union, SD	93.3	1.6	1.9	1.4	0.1	3.2	7,277	6,864	6,298	5,364	15.5	17.4
Sioux Falls, SD Metro Area	86.5	6.0	2.5	2.6	0.1	4.3	111,732	104,234	96,223	76,074	16.1	26.5
Lincoln, SD	94.3	2.2	1.7	1.1	0.1	2.2	21,099	19,574	17,950	9,343	17.5	92.1
McCook, SD	93.9	1.1	0.5	1.4	0.1	4.3	2,596	2,555	2,495	2,388	4.0	4.5
Minnehaha, SD	83.5	7.6	2.9	3.2	0.1	5.0	83,991	78,091	71,833	60,489	16.9	18.8
Turner, SD	95.7	0.8	0.4	1.3	0.1	2.8	4,046	4,014	3,945	3,854	2.6	2.4
South Bend-Mishawaka, IN-MI Metro Area	77.1	13.7	2.8	1.1	0.2	8.1	143,520	142,221	140,753	131,341	2.0	7.2
St. Joseph, IN	74.8	15.0	3.1	0.9	0.2	8.9	117,088	116,100	114,861	107,388	1.9	7.0
Cass, MI	89.0	6.7	1.2	2.1	0.1	4.0	26,432	26,121	25,892	23,953	2.1	8.1
Spartanburg, SC Metro Area	69.6	21.6	2.8	0.7	0.1	7.1	131,451	126,002	122,741	107,505	7.1	14.2
Spartanburg, SC	69.6	21.6	2.8	0.7	0.1	7.1	131,451	126,002	122,741	107,505	7.1	14.2
Spokane-Spokane Valley, WA Metro Area	87.8	3.0	3.5	3.0	0.8	5.7	241,728	231,892	223,028	193,291	8.4	15.4
Spokane, WA	87.7	3.2	3.7	2.7	0.9	5.9	219,880	210,380	201,853	175,610	8.9	14.9
Stevens, WA	89.3	1.0	1.5	7.3	0.4	3.8	21,848	21,512	21,175	17,681	3.2	19.8
Springfield, IL Metro Area	83.3	13.7	2.5	0.6	0.1	2.3	97,681	96,906	95,622	90,921	2.2	5.2
Menard, IL	96.8	1.5	0.7	0.8	0.1	1.6	5,749	5,701	5,658	5,299	1.6	6.8
Sangamon, IL	82.4	14.4	2.6	0.6	0.1	2.4	91,932	91,205	89,964	85,622	2.2	5.1
Springfield, MA Metro Area	71.2	7.0	3.7	0.7	0.1	19.2	292,099	290,780	288,645	276,745	1.2	4.3
Franklin, MA	92.1	2.0	2.3	1.0	0.2	4.2	34,172	33,986	33,767	31,970	1.2	5.6
Hampden, MA	63.2	8.8	2.9	0.6	0.1	26.1	193,870	193,359	192,243	186,025	0.8	3.3
Hampshire, MA	85.2	3.7	6.6	0.6	0.2	5.8	64,057	63,435	62,635	58,750	2.3	6.6
Springfield, MO Metro Area	91.8	3.4	2.1	1.5	0.2	3.4	205,482	199,980	192,605	157,347	6.7	22.4
Christian, MO	94.8	1.4	1.1	1.4	0.1	3.0	34,786	33,169	31,632	22,017	10.0	43.7
Dallas, MO	96.3	0.8	0.5	2.0	0.1	2.2	7,679	7,676	7,664	6,943	0.2	10.4
Greene, MO	89.8	4.6	2.8	1.6	0.2	3.9	134,568	130,954	125,573	105,011	7.2	19.6
Polk, MO	94.9	1.4	1.1	1.4	0.1	2.6	13,618	13,534	13,311	11,253	2.3	18.3
Webster, MO	95.8	1.5	0.6	1.6	0.1	2.1	14,831	14,647	14,425	12,123	2.8	19.0
Springfield, OH Metro Area	86.6	10.7	1.1	0.9	0.1	3.5	61,289	61,344	61,409	61,089	-0.2	0.5
Clark, OH	86.6	10.7	1.1	0.9	0.1	3.5	61,289	61,344	61,409	61,089	-0.2	0.5
State College, PA Metro Area	86.6	4.1	7.3	0.4	0.1	3.0	67,144	66,002	63,383	53,367	5.9	18.8
Centre, PA	86.6	4.1	7.3	0.4	0.1	3.0	67,144	66,002	63,383	53,367	5.9	18.8

Table C-2. Population Characteristiics and Housing Units—*Continued*

| Metropolitan Statistical Area Metropolitan Division Component counties | Population characteristics, 2018 | | | | | | Housing Units | | | | | |
| | Race alone or in combination, not of Hispanic origin (percent) | | | | | Hispanic or Latino origin (percent) | 2018 (July 1 estimate | 2015 (July 1 estimate | 2010 (July 1 estimate | 2000 (July 1 estimate | Percent change | |
	White	Black or African-American	Asian	American Indian, Alaska Native	Native Hawaiian, Pacific Islander						2010-2018	2000-2010
Staunton, VA Metro Area........	87.4	8.6	1.4	0.7	0.1	3.9	54,592	54,067	52,679	46,185	3.6	14.1
Augusta, VA........	91.8	5.1	0.9	0.6	0.1	2.9	32,732	32,241	31,221	26,773	4.8	16.6
Staunton City, VA........	83.4	13.5	2.0	0.9	0.1	3.2	11,840	11,815	11,739	10,472	0.9	12.1
Waynesboro City, VA........	77.2	14.7	2.1	1.0	0.2	8.3	10,020	10,011	9,719	8,940	3.1	8.7
Stockton, CA Metro Area........	33.9	8.2	17.6	1.2	1.0	41.9	245,541	238,545	233,928	190,509	5.0	22.8
San Joaquin, CA........	33.9	8.2	17.6	1.2	1.0	41.9	245,541	238,545	233,928	190,509	5.0	22.8
Sumter, SC Metro Area	47.0	48.1	1.8	0.8	0.2	3.9	66,134	65,351	63,586	57,218	4.0	11.1
Clarendon, SC........	48.8	47.4	0.9	0.6	0.1	3.2	17,850	17,700	17,475	15,354	2.1	13.8
Sumter, SC........	46.5	48.3	2.1	0.9	0.2	4.1	48,284	47,651	46,111	41,864	4.7	10.1
Syracuse, NY Metro Area........	83.7	9.5	3.6	1.2	0.1	4.3	296,351	293,098	287,949	278,406	2.9	3.4
Madison, NY........	94.4	2.4	1.3	1.0	0.1	2.3	32,394	32,117	31,781	28,706	1.9	10.7
Onondaga, NY........	79.1	12.7	4.6	1.4	0.1	5.1	209,347	206,678	202,522	196,811	3.4	2.9
Oswego, NY........	95.2	1.6	1.0	0.9	0.1	2.7	54,610	54,303	53,646	52,889	1.8	1.4
Tallahassee, FL Metro Area	57.3	33.5	3.6	0.8	0.1	6.7	172,340	167,452	163,239	137,424	5.6	18.8
Gadsden, FL........	33.3	55.6	0.8	0.5	0.1	10.5	20,658	19,663	19,523	17,725	5.8	10.1
Jefferson, FL........	61.4	34.4	0.8	0.8	0.1	3.9	6,769	6,681	6,634	5,277	2.0	25.7
Leon, FL........	58.1	32.2	4.4	0.7	0.1	6.6	131,211	127,956	124,257	104,525	5.6	18.9
Wakulla, FL........	81.8	13.8	1.1	1.3	0.2	3.8	13,702	13,152	12,825	9,897	6.8	29.6
Tampa-St. Petersburg-Clearwater, FL Metro Area	64.1	12.8	4.3	0.7	0.2	20.0	1,435,316	1,390,612	1,354,322	1,148,904	6.0	17.9
Hernando, FL........	78.8	6.0	1.8	0.8	0.2	14.2	87,526	85,608	84,535	63,113	3.5	33.9
Hillsborough, FL........	50.0	17.1	5.0	0.6	0.2	29.2	590,779	561,990	536,794	428,883	10.1	25.2
Pasco, FL........	75.6	6.5	3.3	0.7	0.1	15.8	246,921	237,055	229,309	174,667	7.7	31.3
Pinellas, FL........	75.5	11.4	4.2	0.7	0.2	10.0	510,090	505,959	503,684	482,241	1.3	4.4
Terre Haute, IN Metro Area........	91.1	6.1	1.6	0.8	0.1	2.2	84,023	83,267	82,226	80,177	2.2	2.6
Clay, IN........	97.2	1.3	0.5	0.7	0.1	1.4	11,784	11,793	11,700	11,145	0.7	5.0
Parke, IN........	95.1	3.0	0.3	0.7	0.0	1.6	8,260	8,153	8,091	7,543	2.1	7.3
Sullivan, IN........	92.9	5.2	0.5	0.9	0.1	1.8	8,958	8,937	8,939	8,826	0.2	1.3
Vermillion, IN........	97.6	1.0	0.5	0.7	0.1	1.3	7,489	7,514	7,487	7,419	0.0	0.9
Vigo, IN........	87.6	8.6	2.5	0.8	0.1	2.7	47,532	46,870	46,009	45,244	3.3	1.7
Texarkana, TX-AR Metro Area	67.3	25.6	1.3	1.5	0.1	6.2	66,152	65,417	64,307	60,796	2.9	5.8
Little River, AR........	74.6	20.6	0.7	2.4	0.1	3.7	6,527	6,490	6,461	6,443	1.0	0.3
Miller, AR........	70.3	25.9	0.7	1.4	0.1	3.6	19,597	19,512	19,305	17,784	1.5	8.6
Bowie, TX........	65.0	26.1	1.7	1.4	0.2	7.8	40,028	39,415	38,541	36,569	3.9	5.4
The Villages, FL Metro Area	85.8	7.4	1.1	0.7	0.1	5.7	72,385	67,906	53,566	25,696	35.1	108.5
Sumter, FL........	85.8	7.4	1.1	0.7	0.1	5.7	72,385	67,906	53,566	25,696	35.1	108.5
Toledo, OH Metro Area........	77.4	15.3	2.0	0.8	0.1	6.9	303,710	302,566	301,336	286,078	0.8	5.3
Fulton, OH........	89.8	1.1	0.7	0.6	0.1	8.9	17,574	17,475	17,426	16,269	0.8	7.1
Lucas, OH........	71.0	21.6	2.2	0.8	0.1	7.3	203,467	203,026	202,606	196,487	0.4	3.1
Ottawa, OH........	93.3	1.5	0.5	0.6	0.1	5.2	28,600	28,284	27,928	25,607	2.4	9.1
Wood, OH........	89.6	3.5	2.2	0.7	0.1	5.7	54,069	53,781	53,376	47,715	1.3	11.9
Topeka, KS Metro Area........	80.6	7.9	1.7	2.5	0.2	10.5	105,388	104,745	103,890	96,606	1.4	7.5
Jackson, KS........	86.9	1.5	0.8	9.3	0.1	4.6	5,882	5,808	5,781	5,113	1.7	13.1
Jefferson, KS........	95.1	1.2	0.5	2.0	0.2	2.9	8,424	8,290	8,166	7,530	3.2	8.4
Osage, KS........	94.8	1.4	0.7	1.5	0.1	3.4	7,599	7,549	7,507	7,038	1.2	6.7
Shawnee, KS........	76.8	9.9	2.0	2.1	0.2	12.6	80,167	79,818	79,209	73,887	1.2	7.2
Wabaunsee, KS........	93.9	1.6	0.8	1.8	0.1	4.3	3,316	3,280	3,227	3,038	2.8	6.2
Trenton-Princeton, NJ Metro Area........	50.3	20.5	12.4	0.5	0.2	18.1	145,121	144,486	143,219	133,584	1.3	7.2
Mercer, NJ........	50.3	20.5	12.4	0.5	0.2	18.1	145,121	144,486	143,219	133,584	1.3	7.2
Tucson, AZ Metro Area........	53.2	4.2	3.9	3.0	0.3	37.6	462,749	454,093	441,605	369,335	4.8	19.6
Pima, AZ........	53.2	4.2	3.9	3.0	0.3	37.6	462,749	454,093	441,605	369,335	4.8	19.6
Tulsa, OK Metro Area	70.3	9.7	3.1	13.0	0.2	10.2	434,419	425,302	410,509	367,312	5.8	11.8
Creek, OK........	82.1	3.4	1.0	16.1	0.2	4.3	30,786	30,349	29,809	28,038	3.3	6.3
Okmulgee, OK........	69.3	10.4	0.8	23.7	0.2	4.3	17,847	17,859	17,890	17,342	-0.2	3.2
Osage, OK........	69.9	12.5	0.6	20.6	0.1	3.7	21,944	21,648	21,170	18,867	3.7	12.2
Pawnee, OK........	81.9	1.7	0.7	18.1	0.2	3.2	7,841	7,799	7,749	7,478	1.2	3.6
Rogers, OK........	79.4	1.8	1.9	20.3	0.2	4.9	38,553	37,063	35,241	27,664	9.4	27.4
Tulsa, OK........	66.6	12.1	4.0	9.9	0.2	13.0	284,578	279,155	268,865	244,615	5.8	9.9
Wagoner, OK........	77.9	4.8	2.2	15.9	0.2	6.4	32,870	31,429	29,785	23,308	10.4	27.8
Tuscaloosa, AL Metro Area........	59.0	36.2	1.7	0.6	0.1	3.7	115,583	111,871	107,194	94,114	7.8	13.9
Greene, AL........	18.2	80.0	0.3	0.5	0.0	1.7	5,111	5,050	5,007	5,114	2.1	-2.1
Hale, AL........	40.3	58.1	0.4	0.5	0.0	1.4	7,845	7,750	7,663	7,763	2.4	-1.3
Pickens, AL........	54.8	40.5	0.4	0.5	0.0	4.8	9,623	9,533	9,486	9,525	1.4	-0.4
Tuscaloosa, AL........	62.3	32.5	1.9	0.6	0.1	3.9	93,004	89,538	85,038	71,712	9.4	18.6
Twin Falls, ID Metro Area........	76.1	0.8	1.7	1.3	0.3	21.2	42,277	40,801	39,249	32,430	7.7	21.0
Jerome, ID........	62.2	0.6	0.6	1.2	0.1	36.4	8,579	8,384	8,113	6,754	5.7	20.1
Twin Falls, ID........	80.0	0.9	2.1	1.3	0.4	16.9	33,698	32,417	31,136	25,676	8.2	21.3
Tyler, TX Metro Area........	60.7	18.1	2.0	0.8	0.2	19.9	91,101	89,181	87,371	72,139	4.3	21.1
Smith, TX........	60.7	18.1	2.0	0.8	0.2	19.9	91,101	89,181	87,371	72,139	4.3	21.1
Urban Honolulu, HI Metro Area........	31.8	3.7	57.1	1.5	21.5	10.0	352,527	345,698	337,111	316,367	4.6	6.6
Honolulu, HI........	31.8	3.7	57.1	1.5	21.5	10.0	352,527	345,698	337,111	316,367	4.6	6.6
Utica-Rome, NY Metro Area........	85.9	6.2	3.8	0.6	0.1	5.2	139,327	138,711	137,620	134,947	1.2	2.0
Herkimer, NY........	95.6	1.9	0.8	0.6	0.1	2.2	33,873	33,722	33,381	32,058	1.5	4.1
Oneida, NY........	83.3	7.3	4.6	0.6	0.1	6.1	105,454	104,989	104,239	102,889	1.2	1.3

Table C-2. Population Characteristiics and Housing Units—*Continued*

Metropolitan Statistical Area Metropolitan Division Component counties	White	Black or African-American	Asian	American Indian, Alaska Native	Native Hawaiian, Pacific Islander	Hispanic or Latino origin (percent)	2018 (July 1 estimate)	2015 (July 1 estimate)	2010 (July 1 estimate)	2000 (July 1 estimate)	2010-2018	2000-2010
Valdosta, GA Metro Area	56.7	35.3	2.4	0.8	0.2	6.6	62,357	59,869	57,629	48,366	8.2	19.2
Brooks, GA	58.1	35.2	1.3	1.0	0.1	5.9	7,808	7,753	7,716	7,139	1.2	8.1
Echols, GA	63.3	5.4	0.7	2.3	0.1	30.1	1,586	1,568	1,557	1,486	1.9	4.8
Lanier, GA	70.4	23.0	1.8	1.4	0.2	5.8	4,442	4,375	4,262	3,035	4.2	40.4
Lowndes, GA	55.1	37.5	2.7	0.7	0.2	5.9	48,521	46,173	44,094	36,706	10.0	20.1
Vallejo, CA Metro Area	41.9	15.9	18.3	1.3	1.6	26.9	158,808	155,605	152,829	135,034	3.9	13.2
Solano, CA	41.9	15.9	18.3	1.3	1.6	26.9	158,808	155,605	152,829	135,034	3.9	13.2
Victoria, TX Metro Area	46.2	6.2	1.4	0.6	0.1	46.6	40,870	40,631	39,135	36,473	4.4	7.3
Goliad, TX	58.6	4.7	0.5	0.8	0.0	36.4	3,798	3,756	3,712	3,439	2.3	7.9
Victoria, TX	45.2	6.3	1.5	0.5	0.1	47.4	37,072	36,875	35,423	33,034	4.7	7.2
Vineland-Bridgeton, NJ Metro Area	47.5	20.1	1.7	1.4	0.1	31.4	56,490	56,375	55,906	52,909	1.0	5.7
Cumberland, NJ	47.5	20.1	1.7	1.4	0.1	31.4	56,490	56,375	55,906	52,909	1.0	5.7
Virginia Beach-Norfolk-Newport News, VA-NC Metro Area	57.8	32.2	5.3	1.1	0.3	6.9	739,946	725,605	704,515	639,332	5.0	10.2
Camden, NC	82.6	13.1	2.7	1.2	0.2	3.0	4,303	4,189	4,107	2,992	4.8	37.3
Currituck, NC	89.0	6.4	1.2	1.1	0.2	4.0	16,051	15,349	14,478	10,783	10.9	34.3
Gates, NC	65.5	32.2	0.7	1.3	0.2	2.3	5,443	5,299	5,211	4,417	4.5	18.0
Gloucester, VA	86.7	9.1	1.5	1.2	0.2	3.8	16,755	16,330	15,875	14,525	5.5	9.3
Isle of Wight, VA	72.2	24.0	1.6	1.0	0.2	3.3	15,889	15,259	14,663	12,136	8.4	20.8
James City County, VA	77.7	14.4	3.6	0.9	0.2	5.9	33,763	32,459	30,136	21,046	12.0	43.2
Mathews, VA	87.2	9.4	1.4	1.2	0.2	2.8	5,757	5,734	5,673	5,318	1.5	6.7
Southampton, VA	62.5	35.5	0.8	0.9	0.2	1.8	7,657	7,586	7,484	7,071	2.3	5.8
York, VA	73.5	14.7	7.4	1.0	0.4	6.6	27,905	27,641	26,757	21,003	4.3	27.4
Chesapeake City, VA	59.6	31.2	4.8	1.0	0.2	6.5	91,765	88,793	83,404	72,906	10.0	14.4
Franklin City, VA	38.4	58.5	1.3	0.8	0.2	2.6	3,833	3,858	3,899	3,767	-1.7	3.5
Hampton City, VA	40.7	52.2	3.5	1.4	0.3	6.0	60,111	60,110	59,682	57,348	0.7	4.1
Newport News City, VA	45.6	43.3	4.6	1.2	0.3	9.2	78,010	77,388	76,416	74,312	2.1	2.8
Norfolk City, VA	46.0	42.8	4.9	1.3	0.4	8.4	98,218	96,597	95,091	94,375	3.3	0.8
Poquoson City, VA	92.9	1.8	3.4	0.8	0.1	3.1	4,835	4,759	4,730	4,304	2.2	9.9
Portsmouth City, VA	39.5	55.1	2.2	1.2	0.2	4.7	40,899	40,921	40,792	41,581	0.3	-1.9
Suffolk City, VA	51.2	43.1	2.7	0.9	0.2	4.7	37,338	35,485	33,113	24,891	12.8	33.0
Virginia Beach City, VA	64.5	21.0	8.9	1.0	0.3	8.3	186,117	182,629	178,076	162,628	4.5	9.5
Williamsburg City, VA	70.8	16.7	7.7	1.0	0.2	7.0	5,297	5,219	4,928	3,929	7.5	25.4
Visalia, CA Metro Area	29.4	1.6	3.9	1.2	0.2	65.2	150,210	146,500	141,946	120,048	5.8	18.2
Tulare, CA	29.4	1.6	3.9	1.2	0.2	65.2	150,210	146,500	141,946	120,048	5.8	18.2
Waco, TX Metro Area	56.8	15.5	2.0	0.7	0.1	26.5	110,206	106,309	102,983	92,693	7.0	11.1
Falls, TX	52.1	23.9	0.7	0.9	0.2	23.7	7,754	7,743	7,725	7,656	0.4	0.9
McLennan, TX	57.1	14.9	2.1	0.7	0.1	26.7	102,452	98,566	95,258	85,037	7.6	12.0
Walla Walla, WA Metro Area	73.4	2.6	2.6	1.7	0.6	21.5	24,902	24,352	23,477	21,202	6.1	10.7
Walla Walla, WA	73.4	2.6	2.6	1.7	0.6	21.5	24,902	24,352	23,477	21,202	6.1	10.7
Warner Robins, GA Metro Area	56.1	34.9	3.7	0.8	0.2	6.9	75,569	72,802	69,558	54,064	8.6	28.7
Houston, GA	57.8	33.1	4.1	0.9	0.2	6.7	63,958	61,316	58,484	44,914	9.4	30.2
Peach, GA	46.6	45.1	1.4	0.8	0.2	7.8	11,611	11,486	11,074	9,150	4.8	21.0
Washington-Arlington-Alexandria, DC-VA-MD-WV Metro Area	47.6	26.4	12.0	0.8	0.2	16.1	2,381,919	2,322,771	2,243,007	1,921,499	6.2	16.7
Frederick-Gaithersburg-Rockville, MD Div	51.5	18.0	14.6	0.6	0.2	18.0	489,705	482,111	466,254	409,906	5.0	13.7
Frederick, MD	75.1	11.1	5.7	0.7	0.1	10.2	99,041	94,538	90,298	73,727	9.7	22.5
Montgomery, MD	45.8	19.7	16.8	0.6	0.2	19.9	390,664	387,573	375,956	336,179	3.9	11.8
Washington-Arlington-Alexandria, DC-VA-MD-WV Division	46.6	28.6	11.3	0.8	0.2	15.6	1,892,214	1,840,660	1,776,753	1,511,593	6.5	17.5
District of Columbia	38.8	46.3	5.3	0.8	0.2	11.3	319,531	307,569	296,687	275,210	7.7	7.8
Calvert, MD	80.5	14.2	2.9	1.0	0.2	4.1	35,416	34,743	33,836	27,809	4.7	21.7
Charles, MD	41.3	50.4	4.4	1.6	0.2	6.0	61,248	58,791	55,123	44,193	11.1	24.7
Prince George's, MD	13.9	63.4	4.9	0.9	0.1	19.1	333,862	329,965	328,272	303,078	1.7	8.3
Arlington, VA	63.8	9.9	12.7	0.7	0.2	15.8	116,532	112,094	105,500	90,547	10.5	16.5
Clarke, VA	87.4	5.7	1.8	1.1	0.1	6.3	6,382	6,277	6,232	5,403	2.4	15.3
Culpeper, VA	72.6	15.8	2.2	0.8	0.1	11.3	18,946	18,297	17,666	12,919	7.2	36.7
Fairfax, VA	53.3	10.8	22.2	0.6	0.2	16.4	415,461	410,765	407,988	361,254	1.8	12.9
Fauquier, VA	81.6	8.8	2.2	0.8	0.1	8.9	27,140	26,408	25,634	21,167	5.9	21.1
Loudoun, VA	58.5	8.7	21.9	0.6	0.2	13.8	136,506	126,383	109,952	63,714	24.2	72.6
Madison, VA	86.9	10.6	0.9	1.0	0.1	3.1	6,104	6,016	5,939	5,256	2.8	13.0
Prince William, VA	45.4	22.6	10.8	0.9	0.3	24.2	150,444	145,778	137,580	99,170	9.4	38.7
Rappahannock, VA	90.5	5.4	1.2	1.0	0.2	3.8	3,984	3,951	3,897	3,319	2.2	17.4
Spotsylvania, VA	70.2	18.0	3.8	0.9	0.2	10.3	48,155	46,555	45,242	33,647	6.4	34.5
Stafford, VA	63.7	20.4	5.0	1.1	0.3	13.6	50,449	47,281	44,088	31,823	14.4	38.5
Warren, VA	88.7	5.9	1.8	0.9	0.1	4.9	16,501	16,168	15,980	13,340	3.3	19.8
Alexandria City, VA	54.1	23.2	8.0	0.7	0.2	16.7	76,529	76,178	72,410	64,533	5.7	12.2
Fairfax City, VA	57.5	6.6	20.5	0.8	0.2	17.4	9,095	8,808	8,675	8,244	4.8	5.2
Falls Church City, VA	74.2	5.4	11.9	0.8	0.1	11.1	6,019	5,995	5,471	4,764	10.0	14.8
Fredericksburg City, VA	62.2	25.5	4.0	0.9	0.3	11.0	11,730	11,510	10,490	8,935	11.8	17.4
Manassas City, VA	42.3	14.9	6.7	0.7	0.3	37.8	13,887	13,449	13,127	12,139	5.8	8.1
Manassas Park City, VA	34.2	14.8	12.3	0.9	0.2	40.1	4,875	4,894	4,893	3,404	-0.4	43.7
Jefferson, WV	86.1	7.6	2.1	1.0	0.1	5.8	23,418	22,785	22,071	17,725	6.1	24.5

Table C-2. Population Characteristiics and Housing Units—*Continued*

Metropolitan Statistical Area Metropolitan Division Component counties	Population characteristics, 2018						Housing Units					
	Race alone or in combination, not of Hispanic origin (percent)					Hispanic or Latino origin (percent)	2018 (July 1 estimate)	2015 (July 1 estimate)	2010 (July 1 estimate)	2000 (July 1 estimate)	Percent change	
	White	Black or African-American	Asian	American Indian, Alaska Native	Native Hawaiian, Pacific Islander						2010-2018	2000-2010
Waterloo-Cedar Falls, IA Metro Area	86.0	8.9	2.6	0.5	0.3	3.8	74,423	73,100	71,388	66,483	4.3	7.4
Black Hawk, IA	83.0	11.0	3.0	0.6	0.4	4.5	58,320	57,294	55,926	51,814	4.3	7.9
Bremer, IA	95.9	1.7	1.3	0.4	0.0	1.7	10,519	10,233	9,931	9,361	5.9	6.1
Grundy, IA	97.7	0.9	0.5	0.4	0.1	1.3	5,584	5,573	5,531	5,308	1.0	4.2
Watertown-Fort Drum, NY Metro Area	83.5	7.5	2.4	1.0	0.4	7.8	60,049	59,753	58,002	54,136	3.5	7.1
Jefferson, NY	83.5	7.5	2.4	1.0	0.4	7.8	60,049	59,753	58,002	54,136	3.5	7.1
Wausau-Weston, WI Metro Area	91.0	1.4	5.5	0.9	0.1	2.6	76,971	75,891	74,577	65,278	3.2	14.2
Lincoln, WI	96.4	1.3	0.7	1.0	0.1	1.7	17,237	17,017	16,791	14,736	2.7	13.9
Marathon, WI	89.9	1.4	6.5	0.9	0.1	2.8	59,734	58,874	57,786	50,542	3.4	14.3
Weirton-Steubenville, WV-OH Metro Area	93.9	5.1	0.7	0.6	0.1	1.4	57,598	57,855	58,308	59,143	-1.2	-1.4
Jefferson, OH	92.3	6.7	0.8	0.7	0.1	1.5	32,468	32,595	32,814	33,275	-1.1	-1.4
Brooke, WV	97.0	2.2	0.7	0.5	0.1	0.9	10,798	10,857	10,962	11,124	-1.5	-1.5
Hancock, WV	94.9	3.7	0.6	0.6	0.1	1.6	14,332	14,403	14,532	14,744	-1.4	-1.4
Wenatchee, WA Metro Area	67.8	0.9	1.5	1.6	0.3	29.7	55,247	53,476	51,553	43,484	7.2	18.6
Chelan, WA	69.1	0.9	1.5	1.7	0.3	28.3	38,074	36,892	35,525	30,497	7.2	16.5
Douglas, WA	65.4	0.9	1.4	1.6	0.3	32.1	17,173	16,584	16,028	12,987	7.1	23.4
Wheeling, WV-OH Metro Area	94.9	4.3	0.8	0.6	0.1	1.1	68,801	69,031	69,510	69,420	-0.9	0.1
Belmont, OH	94.1	5.2	0.6	0.6	0.1	1.0	32,155	32,226	32,441	31,446	-0.9	3.2
Marshall, WV	97.7	1.3	0.5	0.6	0.0	1.0	15,734	15,800	15,912	15,830	-1.1	0.5
Ohio, WV	94.2	5.0	1.1	0.7	0.1	1.2	20,912	21,005	21,157	22,144	-1.2	-4.5
Wichita, KS Metro Area	74.4	8.9	4.5	1.9	0.1	13.4	273,884	268,318	263,417	239,216	4.0	10.1
Butler, KS	90.7	2.8	1.7	2.0	0.1	5.0	27,084	26,656	26,088	23,296	3.8	12.0
Harvey, KS	84.5	2.7	1.3	1.5	0.1	12.1	14,878	14,711	14,538	13,419	2.3	8.3
Sedgwick, KS	70.8	10.5	5.2	1.9	0.2	14.9	220,933	216,001	211,921	191,611	4.3	10.6
Sumner, KS	91.7	1.9	0.7	2.6	0.1	5.4	10,989	10,950	10,870	10,890	1.1	-0.2
Wichita Falls, TX Metro Area	69.8	10.4	2.6	1.4	0.2	17.9	65,437	65,319	64,843	62,223	0.9	4.2
Archer, TX	89.5	1.5	0.7	1.4	0.1	8.2	4,173	4,149	4,109	3,847	1.6	6.8
Clay, TX	91.0	1.3	0.8	2.0	0.1	6.5	5,262	5,187	5,153	5,002	2.1	3.0
Wichita, TX	66.9	11.7	2.8	1.4	0.2	19.4	56,002	55,983	55,581	53,374	0.8	4.1
Williamsport, PA Metro Area	92.5	6.0	0.9	0.6	0.1	2.1	53,540	53,241	52,522	52,482	1.9	0.1
Lycoming, PA	92.5	6.0	0.9	0.6	0.1	2.1	53,540	53,241	52,522	52,482	1.9	0.1
Wilmington, NC Metro Area	78.5	14.5	1.8	1.0	0.1	6.0	142,840	135,158	128,256	101,048	11.4	26.9
New Hanover, NC	79.0	14.2	2.1	1.0	0.2	5.6	113,215	107,181	101,510	80,109	11.5	26.7
Pender, NC	76.7	15.6	0.9	1.1	0.1	7.4	29,625	27,977	26,746	20,939	10.8	27.7
Winchester, VA-WV Metro Area	83.3	6.3	2.1	0.7	0.1	9.7	60,900	58,662	56,977	45,320	6.9	25.7
Frederick, VA	84.5	5.5	2.2	0.7	0.1	9.1	34,843	32,878	31,399	23,481	11.0	33.7
Winchester City, VA	68.2	12.7	3.1	0.7	0.1	18.4	11,978	11,872	11,877	10,616	0.9	11.9
Hampshire, WV	96.7	1.7	0.4	0.7	0.1	1.6	14,079	13,912	13,701	11,223	2.8	22.1
Winston-Salem, NC Metro Area	69.4	18.8	2.2	0.8	0.1	10.5	301,120	293,206	287,238	246,938	4.8	16.3
Davidson, NC	81.1	10.3	1.8	0.9	0.1	7.3	75,582	73,543	72,681	62,800	4.0	15.7
Davie, NC	85.6	7.4	0.9	0.7	0.1	7.0	18,897	18,398	18,239	15,065	3.6	21.1
Forsyth, NC	58.1	27.0	2.9	0.8	0.1	13.0	166,917	161,764	157,022	133,852	6.3	17.3
Stokes, NC	92.3	4.4	0.5	0.8	0.1	3.1	22,313	22,105	21,947	19,332	1.7	13.5
Yadkin, NC	85.1	3.7	0.5	0.6	0.1	11.2	17,411	17,349	17,349	15,889	0.4	9.2
Worcester, MA-CT Metro Area	78.5	5.3	5.4	0.6	0.1	12.0	386,318	382,028	376,139	342,938	2.7	9.7
Windham, CT	83.9	2.7	1.8	1.1	0.1	12.3	49,833	49,549	49,082	44,066	1.5	11.4
Worcester, MA	77.7	5.6	5.9	0.6	0.1	11.9	336,485	332,479	327,057	298,872	2.9	9.4
Yakima, WA Metro Area	44.3	1.3	1.7	4.5	0.2	49.9	89,130	87,800	85,595	79,292	4.1	7.9
Yakima, WA	44.3	1.3	1.7	4.5	0.2	49.9	89,130	87,800	85,595	79,292	4.1	7.9
York-Hanover, PA Metro Area	84.6	6.9	1.9	0.5	0.1	7.9	184,869	182,663	178,942	157,223	3.3	13.8
York, PA	84.6	6.9	1.9	0.5	0.1	7.9	184,869	182,663	178,942	157,223	3.3	13.8
Youngstown-Warren-Boardman, OH-PA Metro Area	84.6	11.9	1.0	0.7	0.1	3.7	259,329	259,369	259,702	257,023	-0.1	1.0
Mahoning, OH	77.3	16.4	1.2	0.7	0.1	6.4	111,312	111,498	111,798	111,853	-0.4	0.0
Trumbull, OH	89.1	9.5	0.8	0.7	0.1	1.9	95,695	95,728	96,137	95,182	-0.5	1.0
Mercer, PA	91.7	6.9	1.1	0.5	0.1	1.6	52,322	52,143	51,767	49,988	1.1	3.6
Yuba City, CA Metro Area	52.9	4.0	13.8	2.6	0.7	30.3	63,170	62,394	61,539	51,023	2.7	20.6
Sutter, CA	48.3	3.1	18.1	2.0	0.7	31.5	34,477	34,182	33,880	28,383	1.8	19.4
Yuba, CA	58.5	5.1	8.6	3.4	0.8	28.7	28,693	28,212	27,659	22,640	3.7	22.2
Yuma, AZ Metro Area	31.4	2.3	1.7	1.3	0.2	64.3	93,565	90,882	88,070	74,476	6.2	18.3
Yuma, AZ	31.4	2.3	1.7	1.3	0.2	64.3	93,565	90,882	88,070	74,476	6.2	18.3

Table C-3. Personal Income and Earnings by Industry

Metropolitan Statistical Area / Metropolitan Division / Component counties	Personal Income — Total (million dollars) 2018	2010	Percent change 2010-2018	Per capita Personal Income 2018	2010	Percent change 2010-2018	Earnings 2018 — Total earnings (million dollars)	Manu-facturing	Retail Trade	Finance and Insurance	Professional, Scientic, and Technical Services	Health Care and Social Assistance	Government and Government Enterprises
Abilene, TX Metro Area	7,396	5,705	29.6	$43,140	$34,456	25.2	4,738	4.0	7.3	5.3	4.3	15.8	25.0
Callahan, TX	551	402	37.1	$39,392	$29,749	32.4	176	4.8	14.9	3.2	3.9	5.1	20.8
Jones, TX	606	517	17.1	$30,559	$25,551	19.6	262	3.6	5.2	3.6	1.8	3.8	47.8
Taylor, TX	6,240	4,786	30.4	$45,333	$36,305	24.9	4,299	4.0	7.1	5.5	4.5	17.0	23.7
Akron, OH Metro Area	34,835	26,887	29.6	$49,423	$38,244	29.2	23,831	12.7	7.5	4.9	6.2	13.5	13.5
Portage, OH	7,178	5,498	30.6	$44,055	$34,065	29.3	3,888	19.9	6.2	1.5	4.6	7.3	24.8
Summit, OH	27,657	21,389	29.3	$51,036	$39,489	29.2	19,942	11.2	7.8	5.6	6.6	14.7	11.3
Albany, GA Metro Area	5,622	4,727	18.9	$37,500	$30,666	22.3	3,661	9.0	6.9	D	5.2	16.6	23.4
Dougherty, GA	3,170	2,823	12.3	$34,744	$29,866	16.3	2,967	9.5	6.6	4.1	5.8	18.9	23.1
Lee, GA	1,407	1,022	37.7	$47,258	$35,959	31.4	377	5.6	7.6	2.7	D	D	22.4
Terrell, GA	347	293	18.7	$40,325	$30,719	31.3	132	8.3	10.4	5.0	1.8	D	23.9
Worth, GA	698	590	18.3	$34,380	$27,196	26.4	184	7.7	9.3	D	D	D	28.6
Albany-Lebanon, OR Metro Area	5,461	3,698	47.7	$42,891	$31,637	35.6	3,192	21.9	8.3	2.1	2.9	10.8	15.2
Linn, OR	5,461	3,698	47.7	$42,891	$31,637	35.6	3,192	21.9	8.3	2.1	2.9	10.8	15.2
Albany-Schenectady-Troy, NY Metro Area	51,315	38,694	32.6	$58,104	$44,421	30.8	37,274	7.7	5.3	7.0	10.2	11.9	26.0
Albany, NY	18,796	14,158	32.8	$61,201	$46,560	31.4	20,154	3.5	4.8	8.0	9.9	11.8	31.7
Rensselaer, NY	7,838	6,189	26.6	$49,156	$38,840	26.6	4,202	13.2	5.6	3.2	6.2	11.7	23.8
Saratoga, NY	15,563	10,768	44.5	$67,618	$48,921	38.2	7,169	13.5	6.2	8.9	9.5	10.7	16.4
Schenectady, NY	7,850	6,578	19.3	$50,533	$42,476	19.0	5,124	12.2	5.5	3.9	16.6	14.7	18.0
Schoharie, NY	1,268	1,001	26.7	$40,791	$30,632	33.2	625	3.1	6.6	4.2	2.5	8.9	34.5
Albuquerque, NM Metro Area	38,960	30,635	27.2	$42,536	$34,438	23.5	26,042	4.5	6.4	4.6	13.6	D	25.1
Bernalillo, NM	29,901	23,595	26.7	$44,057	$35,538	24.0	23,027	3.6	6.3	4.9	14.7	13.2	25.2
Sandoval, NM	6,032	4,495	34.2	$41,547	$33,943	22.4	1,959	14.4	6.3	2.2	5.5	10.0	23.3
Torrance, NM	472	409	15.3	$30,245	$24,948	21.2	176	2.7	10.7	1.8	2.9	D	29.4
Valencia, NM	2,555	2,135	19.7	$33,424	$27,805	20.2	880	6.0	8.9	2.0	2.9	8.2	26.4
Alexandria, LA Metro Area	6,733	5,361	25.6	$43,995	$34,793	26.4	4,202	7.6	10.1	D	4.0	19.4	23.7
Grant, LA	716	584	22.6	$31,828	$26,133	21.8	248	9.1	3.6	D	1.0	5.8	51.1
Rapides, LA	6,018	4,778	26.0	$46,090	$36,261	27.1	3,954	7.5	10.5	3.4	4.2	20.3	22.0
Allentown-Bethlehem-Easton, PA-NJ Metro Area	45,618	34,564	32.0	$54,120	$42,053	28.7	28,712	13.1	5.5	3.8	5.2	16.5	11.2
Warren, NJ	5,930	4,807	23.4	$56,058	$44,269	26.6	2,670	13.1	9.2	1.7	5.2	12.8	17.5
Carbon, PA	3,232	2,326	38.9	$50,322	$35,650	41.2	1,487	8.2	5.3	1.8	1.7	11.4	12.5
Lehigh, PA	19,735	15,339	28.7	$53,614	$43,806	22.4	15,706	12.6	4.6	3.6	5.4	21.5	8.9
Northampton, PA	16,721	12,092	38.3	$54,859	$40,588	35.2	8,850	14.8	5.9	5.2	5.4	9.7	13.2
Altoona, PA Metro Area	5,726	4,439	29.0	$46,743	$34,942	33.8	3,951	12.8	8.1	2.4	3.8	19.3	15.0
Blair, PA	5,726	4,439	29.0	$46,743	$34,942	33.8	3,951	12.8	8.1	2.4	3.8	19.3	15.0
Amarillo, TX Metro Area	12,268	9,451	29.8	$46,131	$37,403	23.3	8,822	12.7	7.1	5.8	D	12.7	15.7
Armstrong, TX	91	76	18.9	$47,995	$40,142	19.6	31	D	3.1	D	9.1	9.0	19.9
Carson, TX	278	237	17.6	$46,373	$38,435	20.7	509	D	1.2	D	1.3	D	4.7
Oldham, TX	105	87	20.0	$49,120	$42,550	15.4	79	D	1.5	0.9	D	D	23.3
Potter, TX	5,258	4,210	24.9	$43,945	$34,684	26.7	5,785	11.0	6.1	6.3	5.9	15.1	18.4
Randall, TX	6,536	4,841	35.0	$47,966	$39,944	20.1	2,417	4.2	10.9	5.9	4.6	9.5	11.1
Ames, IA Metro Area	5,416	3,955	36.9	$43,519	$34,117	27.6	4,028	10.6	5.1	2.3	6.2	8.0	36.7
Boone, IA	1,307	1,022	27.9	$49,606	$38,880	27.6	621	6.3	6.5	2.7	7.3	7.6	24.4
Story, IA	4,109	2,934	40.1	$41,885	$32,722	28.0	3,407	11.4	4.8	2.2	7.3	8.1	38.9
Anchorage, AK Metro Area	24,329	20,209	20.4	$60,953	$52,759	15.5	17,104	0.9	5.8	3.2	7.3	14.8	26.7
Anchorage, AK	19,390	16,606	16.8	$66,510	$56,616	17.5	15,181	0.9	5.4	3.3	7.6	14.7	26.9
Matanuska-Susitna, AK	4,939	3,603	37.1	$45,897	$40,152	14.3	1,923	1.0	9.0	2.2	4.3	15.2	25.2
Ann Arbor, MI Metro Area	22,021	15,690	40.4	$59,363	$45,392	30.8	17,160	7.6	3.8	2.9	14.0	11.0	34.2
Washtenaw, MI	22,021	15,690	40.4	$59,363	$45,392	30.8	17,160	7.6	3.8	2.9	14.0	11.0	34.2
Anniston-Oxford, AL Metro Area	4,242	3,662	15.8	$37,120	$30,909	20.1	2,631	16.3	7.6	2.7	3.4	9.1	32.9
Calhoun, AL	4,242	3,662	15.8	$37,120	$30,909	20.1	2,631	16.3	7.6	2.7	3.4	9.1	32.9
Appleton, WI Metro Area	12,146	8,670	40.1	$51,134	$38,372	33.3	8,697	21.2	6.1	7.0	D	D	11.3
Calumet, WI	2,547	1,829	39.2	$50,776	$37,308	36.1	907	31.4	6.8	3.8	D	D	11.1
Outagamie, WI	9,599	6,841	40.3	$51,230	$38,667	32.5	7,789	20.0	6.0	7.4	4.7	11.9	11.3
Asheville, NC Metro Area	20,880	14,218	46.9	$45,433	$33,428	35.9	12,615	12.5	8.1	3.2	D	D	14.0
Buncombe, NC	12,590	8,261	52.4	$48,592	$34,603	40.4	8,829	10.4	7.6	3.4	7.1	21.3	13.4
Haywood, NC	2,497	1,845	35.4	$40,290	$31,298	28.7	1,052	22.0	11.0	3.1	3.8	15.2	15.3
Henderson, NC	5,052	3,562	41.9	$43,276	$33,323	29.9	2,488	16.4	9.0	2.5	4.3	13.5	15.1
Madison, NC	741	551	34.4	$34,036	$26,519	28.3	245	8.7	6.0	1.5	D	D	20.4
Athens-Clarke County, GA Metro Area	8,598	5,693	51.0	$40,690	$29,431	38.3	6,265	9.5	6.3	5.1	4.0	15.3	30.7
Clarke, GA	4,325	3,019	43.3	$33,970	$25,709	32.1	4,880	10.9	6.7	5.6	3.2	16.8	35.2
Madison, GA	1,084	775	39.9	$36,557	$27,462	33.1	283	4.7	4.6	2.3	2.4	D	24.8
Oconee, GA	2,621	1,491	75.8	$66,740	$45,278	47.4	930	4.3	5.6	3.7	9.0	13.0	11.0
Oglethorpe, GA	568	409	38.7	$37,709	$27,471	37.3	171	5.8	2.1	2.3	1.7	D	17.7
Atlanta-Sandy Springs-Alpharetta, GA Metro Area	312,213	203,514	53.4	$52,473	$38,379	36.7	241,551	6.4	5.5	7.3	12.3	8.8	11.0
Barrow, GA	2,982	1,834	62.6	$36,898	$26,321	40.2	1,286	11.2	12.7	1.5	3.5	8.6	15.3
Bartow, GA	4,075	2,795	45.8	$38,298	$27,927	37.1	2,583	28.0	6.7	1.9	4.1	7.9	12.9
Butts, GA	830	600	38.2	$34,297	$25,275	35.7	391	14.2	8.0	1.6	D	D	24.8
Carroll, GA	4,556	3,176	43.4	$38,571	$28,702	34.4	2,730	20.5	6.3	2.0	D	16.2	17.1
Cherokee, GA	12,996	7,822	66.2	$51,137	$36,348	40.7	4,527	8.2	9.2	3.6	7.5	10.0	13.4
Clayton, GA	8,115	6,441	26.0	$28,020	$24,789	13.0	9,895	3.6	4.3	1.0	1.3	5.6	10.7
Cobb, GA	43,264	28,791	50.3	$57,162	$41,755	36.9	31,819	5.8	6.9	6.5	13.5	9.1	8.5
Coweta, GA	6,774	4,256	59.2	$46,438	$33,272	39.6	2,497	14.9	9.7	2.8	3.4	17.9	15.2
Dawson, GA	1,134	694	63.3	$45,201	$31,152	45.1	495	11.9	21.9	3.3	D	8.7	15.1

Table C-3. Personal Income and Earnings by Industry—*Continued*

| | Personal Income | | | | | | Earnings 2018 | | | | | | |
| | Total (million dollars) | | | Per capita Personal Income | | | | Earnings by Industry (percent) | | | | | |
Metropolitan Statistical Area Metropolitan Division Component counties	2018	2010	Percent change 2010-2018	2018	2010	Percent change 2010-2018	Total earnings (million dollars)	Manu-facturing	Retail Trade	Finance and Insurance	Professional, Scienfic, and Technical Services	Health Care and Social Assistance	Government and Government Enterprises
De Kalb, GA	38,487	26,055	47.7	$50,871	$37,626	35.2	26,206	3.9	5.7	6.4	9.2	11.8	14.2
Douglas, GA	5,120	3,785	35.3	$35,230	$28,546	23.4	2,613	10.6	10.5	2.0	3.0	10.2	15.7
Fayette, GA	7,206	4,797	50.2	$63,515	$44,859	41.6	3,065	13.1	6.9	3.6	8.0	15.5	13.6
Forsyth, GA	14,807	8,100	82.8	$62,580	$45,825	36.6	6,252	9.6	5.6	3.1	12.9	10.0	9.2
Fulton, GA	88,615	54,438	62.8	$84,386	$58,810	43.5	103,621	3.9	3.5	10.5	16.7	7.5	9.7
Gwinnett, GA	38,464	25,636	50.0	$41,458	$31,726	30.7	29,191	8.9	7.6	5.8	11.2	7.1	9.5
Haralson, GA	1,078	784	37.6	$36,508	$27,252	34.0	470	28.0	5.8	3.1	2.5	D	19.8
Heard, GA	370	285	29.9	$31,144	$24,066	29.4	163	21.9	2.0	0.7	1.0	D	23.0
Henry, GA	9,021	6,238	44.6	$39,184	$30,415	28.8	3,699	7.0	9.7	2.5	3.5	13.7	20.4
Jasper, GA	570	389	46.4	$40,606	$28,025	44.9	154	18.0	3.9	1.8	D	D	22.8
Lamar, GA	629	479	31.1	$33,079	$26,253	26.0	236	17.3	7.1	3.2	1.7	5.1	29.1
Meriwether, GA	734	597	22.9	$34,847	$27,376	27.3	327	23.2	4.0	1.6	0.6	D	21.5
Morgan, GA	953	601	58.6	$50,541	$33,571	50.5	434	18.7	7.5	3.9	D	D	15.0
Newton, GA	3,697	2,644	39.8	$33,750	$26,401	27.8	1,539	20.6	6.9	2.6	2.7	9.3	20.1
Paulding, GA	6,189	3,987	55.2	$37,727	$27,918	35.1	1,486	5.0	11.0	1.9	3.7	12.1	24.9
Pickens, GA	1,531	1,013	51.1	$47,887	$34,404	39.2	591	10.4	7.5	3.5	4.8	23.0	14.1
Pike, GA	743	512	45.0	$39,851	$28,564	39.5	191	13.0	4.9	2.3	D	D	22.6
Rockdale, GA	3,193	2,525	26.4	$35,244	$29,584	19.1	2,170	16.5	7.8	4.5	4.0	12.7	14.0
Spalding, GA	2,298	1,751	31.3	$34,772	$27,316	27.3	1,289	16.4	7.1	2.8	D	15.6	24.2
Walton, GA	3,783	2,486	52.1	$40,458	$29,621	36.6	1,629	15.6	6.2	2.4	3.2	8.2	16.1
Atlantic City-Hammonton, NJ Metro Area	12,918	10,708	20.6	$48,668	$38,989	24.8	9,311	1.8	7.0	2.6	6.2	15.8	23.1
Atlantic, NJ	12,918	10,708	20.6	$48,668	$38,989	24.8	9,311	1.8	7.0	2.6	6.2	15.8	23.1
Auburn-Opelika, AL Metro Area	6,236	4,131	50.9	$38,036	$29,341	29.6	3,507	11.7	6.8	2.8	4.6	5.9	33.9
Lee, AL	6,236	4,131	50.9	$38,036	$29,341	29.6	3,507	11.7	6.8	2.8	4.6	5.9	33.9
Augusta-Richmond County, GA-SC Metro Area	25,407	18,732	35.6	$42,053	$33,067	27.2	17,386	10.2	5.7	2.6	D	10.3	28.0
Burke, GA	797	652	22.2	$35,524	$27,960	27.1	1,337	2.5	2.2	0.6	4.7	D	7.3
Columbia, GA	7,633	5,011	52.3	$49,473	$40,098	23.4	2,295	10.4	11.6	2.3	7.5	12.0	18.1
Lincoln, GA	295	225	31.1	$37,333	$28,283	32.0	78	2.2	6.7	4.1	3.0	3.1	27.8
McDuffie, GA	796	610	30.5	$36,982	$27,984	32.2	395	25.2	7.9	2.8	2.0	D	21.6
Richmond, GA	7,699	6,129	25.6	$38,196	$30,506	25.2	8,528	7.8	4.4	2.1	5.3	12.7	42.5
Aiken, SC	7,201	5,376	34.0	$42,511	$33,490	26.9	4,396	15.4	6.0	4.5	9.1	7.9	11.7
Edgefield, SC	986	728	35.4	$36,436	$26,998	35.0	359	17.5	4.6	1.3	D	D	32.4
Austin-Round Rock-Georgetown, TX Metro Area	127,439	70,355	81.1	$58,773	$40,726	44.3	100,077	7.4	5.3	5.9	D	7.6	13.6
Bastrop, TX	3,180	2,129	49.3	$36,561	$28,633	27.7	1,304	6.1	9.5	2.7	3.9	7.2	21.4
Caldwell, TX	1,456	1,014	43.5	$33,668	$26,604	26.6	607	5.7	9.0	3.3	D	11.5	18.2
Hays, TX	9,733	5,239	85.8	$43,719	$33,116	32.0	4,737	8.5	8.8	2.5	6.0	8.1	19.8
Travis, TX	84,295	45,991	83.3	$67,504	$44,628	51.3	78,751	6.6	4.4	6.4	18.4	7.3	13.5
Williamson, TX	28,776	15,981	80.1	$50,776	$37,489	35.4	14,677	12.0	8.2	4.8	10.9	8.6	10.9
Bakersfield, CA Metro Area	35,604	26,097	36.4	$39,703	$31,028	28.0	25,571	4.1	6.2	1.7	3.9	8.9	25.8
Kern, CA	35,604	26,097	36.4	$39,703	$31,028	28.0	25,571	4.1	6.2	1.7	3.9	8.9	25.8
Baltimore-Columbia-Towson, MD Metro Area	174,901	132,299	32.2	$62,402	$48,716	28.1	127,665	4.6	4.5	6.7	13.2	12.1	22.0
Anne Arundel, MD	38,803	28,572	35.8	$67,363	$52,982	27.1	31,048	5.8	4.6	2.2	13.1	7.5	35.0
Baltimore, MD	50,995	39,768	28.2	$61,556	$49,306	24.8	32,319	4.6	6.3	10.2	10.6	13.7	17.5
Carroll, MD	10,618	8,065	31.6	$63,039	$48,233	30.7	4,145	7.8	8.0	3.5	10.4	13.8	14.8
Harford, MD	14,943	11,429	30.7	$58,841	$46,604	26.3	7,693	5.5	6.1	3.1	11.8	10.3	32.7
Howard, MD	25,344	18,499	37.0	$78,416	$64,092	22.3	17,528	4.8	4.6	6.2	26.2	7.3	9.1
Queen Anne's, MD	3,257	2,372	37.3	$64,810	$49,616	30.6	1,165	7.9	8.6	2.4	8.1	6.9	17.0
Baltimore city, MD	30,942	23,594	31.1	$51,357	$37,994	35.2	33,768	2.7	1.8	9.1	10.0	17.6	19.8
Bangor, ME Metro Area	6,354	5,134	23.8	$42,053	$33,370	26.0	4,451	4.1	8.7	3.5	4.0	23.9	20.3
Penobscot, ME	6,354	5,134	23.8	$42,053	$33,370	26.0	4,451	4.1	8.7	3.5	4.0	23.9	20.3
Barnstable Town, MA Metro Area	15,954	11,312	41.0	$74,756	$52,397	42.7	7,785	D	9.2	3.7	7.2	16.1	17.9
Barnstable, MA	15,954	11,312	41.0	$74,756	$52,397	42.7	7,785	D	9.2	3.7	7.2	16.1	17.9
Baton Rouge, LA Metro Area	41,009	31,287	31.1	$48,042	$37,804	27.1	30,711	D	5.6	4.1	7.9	10.4	16.8
Ascension, LA	6,212	4,285	45.0	$49,829	$39,719	25.5	3,735	27.2	6.1	1.8	3.2	5.2	9.6
Assumption, LA	1,043	785	32.9	$46,788	$33,641	39.1	296	13.2	5.5	3.4	D	D	18.7
East Baton Rouge, LA	22,659	17,668	28.3	$51,386	$40,103	28.1	20,971	6.9	5.4	5.1	10.2	12.8	17.3
East Feliciana, LA	826	679	21.6	$42,771	$33,649	27.1	355	8.0	3.8	2.9	D	10.9	52.8
Iberville, LA	1,355	1,088	24.5	$41,423	$32,592	27.1	1,689	38.3	2.1	1.0	D	D	12.6
Livingston, LA	5,674	4,241	33.8	$40,658	$32,957	23.4	1,760	10.7	9.7	3.4	4.0	7.4	19.6
Pointe Coupee, LA	973	804	21.1	$44,366	$35,231	25.9	363	7.6	9.0	5.6	D	D	18.0
St. Helena, LA	427	384	11.0	$41,592	$34,323	21.2	94	18.9	3.8	D	2.5	D	37.4
West Baton Rouge, LA	1,241	912	36.1	$46,976	$38,081	23.4	969	27.6	5.6	D	2.7	1.7	11.7
West Feliciana, LA	598	441	35.4	$38,655	$28,226	36.9	479	D	3.5	1.8	2.5	D	34.2
Battle Creek, MI Metro Area	5,417	4,337	24.9	$40,276	$31,903	26.2	4,137	22.1	4.8	1.6	9.1	14.5	21.2
Calhoun, MI	5,417	4,337	24.9	$40,276	$31,903	26.2	4,137	22.1	4.8	1.6	9.1	14.5	21.2
Bay City, MI Metro Area	4,336	3,591	20.7	$41,722	$33,352	25.1	2,226	16.5	7.8	3.0	7.6	16.7	17.6
Bay, MI	4,336	3,591	20.7	$41,722	$33,352	25.1	2,226	16.5	7.8	3.0	7.6	16.7	17.6
Beaumont-Port Arthur, TX Metro Area	17,623	13,656	29.1	$44,527	$35,081	26.9	12,843	D	6.3	D	6.0	10.1	12.9
Hardin, TX	2,630	1,919	37.1	$45,982	$35,020	31.3	842	D	10.3	D	5.4	15.5	15.1
Jefferson, TX	11,237	8,892	26.4	$44,065	$35,223	25.1	10,250	23.4	5.9	2.3	6.3	10.7	12.4
Orange, TX	3,756	2,845	32.0	$44,938	$34,684	29.6	1,750	33.0	6.5	3.2	4.2	4.2	14.3
Beckley, WV Metro Area	4,540	3,831	18.5	$38,717	$30,662	26.3	2,591	3.8	8.6	2.2	4.2	18.5	21.3
Fayette, WV	1,487	1,266	17.5	$34,577	$27,506	25.7	604	5.9	8.4	2.2	3.3	15.8	24.7
Raleigh, WV	3,053	2,565	19.0	$41,115	$32,503	26.5	1,987	3.1	8.6	2.1	4.5	19.3	20.2

Table C-3. Personal Income and Earnings by Industry—*Continued*

Metropolitan Statistical Area Metropolitan Division Component counties	Personal Income						Earnings 2018						
	Total (million dollars)			Per capita Personal Income			Total earnings (million dollars)	Earnings by Industry (percent)					
	2018	2010	Percent change 2010-2018	2018	2010	Percent change 2010-2018		Manufacturing	Retail Trade	Finance and Insurance	Professional, Scienfic, and Technical Services	Health Care and Social Assistance	Government and Government Enterprises
Bellingham, WA Metro Area	11,012	7,414	48.5	$48,792	$36,786	32.6	6,993	13.5	8.3	3.2	5.5	11.8	18.1
Whatcom, WA	11,012	7,414	48.5	$48,792	$36,786	32.6	6,993	13.5	8.3	3.2	5.5	11.8	18.1
Bend, OR Metro Area	10,587	5,494	92.7	$55,143	$34,828	58.3	6,755	5.7	7.9	3.4	8.1	16.4	14.5
Deschutes, OR	10,587	5,494	92.7	$55,143	$34,828	58.3	6,755	5.7	7.9	3.4	8.1	16.4	14.5
Billings, MT Metro Area	9,383	6,464	45.2	$52,019	$38,574	34.9	6,578	D	D	4.5	7.7	D	11.6
Carbon, MT	508	355	43.0	$47,442	$35,313	34.3	164	D	5.4	3.0	D	9.1	21.1
Stillwater, MT	494	329	50.0	$51,773	$36,064	43.6	290	4.9	D	0.6	2.2	D	9.3
Yellowstone, MT	8,382	5,780	45.0	$52,340	$38,949	34.4	6,123	6.4	7.1	4.8	8.2	17.3	11.5
Binghamton, NY Metro Area	10,766	8,947	20.3	$44,817	$35,576	26.0	7,013	15.3	6.4	3.0	D	15.9	24.0
Broome, NY	8,536	7,129	19.7	$44,540	$35,559	25.3	5,901	11.3	6.6	3.3	5.0	18.0	25.3
Tioga, NY	2,229	1,818	22.6	$45,910	$35,645	28.8	1,112	36.6	5.1	1.5	D	5.0	17.5
Birmingham-Hoover, AL Metro Area	55,469	41,703	33.0	$50,979	$39,279	29.8	39,693	7.1	5.4	10.3	D	14.1	14.3
Bibb, AL	678	573	18.3	$30,254	$25,055	20.8	262	8.8	6.5	1.6	1.9	8.8	26.2
Blount, AL	2,023	1,589	27.3	$34,976	$27,703	26.3	572	12.6	7.2	2.7	3.6	D	19.3
Chilton, AL	1,536	1,199	28.1	$34,798	$27,467	26.7	569	21.9	9.3	2.5	D	D	17.7
Jefferson, AL	36,084	27,718	30.2	$54,730	$42,115	30.0	30,084	6.5	4.7	9.7	9.6	16.1	15.5
St. Clair, AL	3,421	2,476	38.2	$38,569	$29,626	30.2	1,187	20.4	8.6	2.6	4.2	8.4	14.9
Shelby, AL	11,728	8,148	43.9	$54,369	$41,550	30.9	7,020	5.9	7.2	16.1	9.7	7.6	7.8
Bismarck, ND Metro Area	7,258	4,777	52.0	$56,564	$42,990	31.6	5,124	3.3	D	5.0	7.9	17.8	19.2
Burleigh, ND	5,542	3,623	53.0	$58,173	$44,348	31.2	4,184	1.8	7.4	5.1	8.0	19.9	20.8
Morton, ND	1,622	1,070	51.6	$52,153	$38,808	34.4	857	10.8	D	D	8.1	9.1	12.5
Oliver, ND	94	83	13.0	$48,290	$45,311	6.6	83	1.2	0.2	D	D	D	6.6
Blacksburg-Christiansburg, VA Metro Area	6,483	4,707	37.7	$38,538	$28,855	33.6	4,527	20.6	5.7	1.5	7.0	8.3	34.9
Giles, VA	676	542	24.6	$40,117	$31,309	28.1	291	25.7	7.7	2.1	10.6	D	16.6
Montgomery, VA	4,430	3,099	43.0	$37,759	$27,921	35.2	3,406	14.7	5.2	1.5	D	D	41.2
Pulaski, VA	1,378	1,066	29.2	$40,443	$30,613	32.1	830	43.2	6.8	1.3	D	7.8	15.3
Radford City, VA	NA	NA	NA	NA	NA	NA	NA	NA	NA	NA	NA	NA	NA
Bloomington, IL Metro Area	8,500	6,822	24.6	$49,180	$40,175	22.4	6,984	3.0	5.0	37.7	D	9.5	15.1
McLean, IL	8,500	6,822	24.6	$49,180	$40,175	22.4	6,984	3.0	5.0	37.7	D	9.5	15.1
Bloomington, IN Metro Area	7,037	4,914	43.2	$41,947	$30,688	36.7	4,800	14.1	5.2	2.5	6.5	D	31.0
Monroe, IN	6,202	4,272	45.2	$42,212	$30,833	36.9	4,463	11.4	5.3	2.5	6.9	13.5	32.5
Owen, IN	835	642	30.2	$40,081	$29,752	34.7	337	48.8	4.5	2.8	1.6	D	11.3
Bloomsburg-Berwick, PA Metro Area	3,810	2,979	27.9	$45,527	$34,776	30.9	3,058	11.4	4.6	5.2	2.5	33.0	14.6
Columbia, PA	2,763	2,207	25.2	$42,211	$32,771	28.8	1,631	19.0	7.2	2.7	2.7	10.8	20.8
Montour, PA	1,047	772	35.8	$57,426	$42,154	36.2	1,428	2.8	1.6	8.1	2.2	58.3	7.6
Boise City, ID Metro Area	33,580	20,738	61.9	$45,973	$33,563	37.0	23,472	14.4	7.6	5.3	D	12.7	13.7
Ada, ID	24,888	15,075	65.1	$52,958	$38,326	38.2	18,969	14.2	7.3	6.0	8.6	13.3	13.5
Boise, ID	331	216	53.4	$43,392	$30,818	40.8	88	3.6	3.1	D	D	D	33.5
Canyon, ID	7,304	4,696	55.5	$32,680	$24,803	31.8	4,011	16.3	9.3	2.6	3.6	10.7	13.7
Gem, ID	666	455	46.3	$37,796	$27,294	38.5	217	5.4	7.3	2.8	4.1	12.9	25.9
Owyhee, ID	390	294	32.5	$33,372	$25,663	30.0	187	5.4	4.9	D	2.5	D	17.5
Boston-Cambridge-Newton, MA-NH Metro Area	383,665	265,132	44.7	$78,694	$58,061	35.5	303,977	D	4.0	11.4	19.1	11.6	10.1
Boston, MA Div	165,583	114,957	44.0	$81,537	$60,670	34.4	146,965	D	3.8	19.1	17.5	13.4	10.8
Norfolk, MA	65,097	44,242	47.1	$92,285	$65,735	40.4	34,791	7.3	6.1	8.8	13.2	11.3	9.8
Plymouth, MA	34,977	23,865	46.6	$67,505	$48,122	40.3	16,442	5.7	7.7	5.5	7.3	13.5	17.8
Suffolk, MA	65,510	46,850	39.8	$81,152	$64,547	25.7	95,732	D	2.3	25.2	20.8	14.2	9.9
Cambridge-Newton-Framingham, MA Div	188,679	130,151	45.0	$78,441	$57,764	35.8	139,130	11.0	3.8	3.9	21.7	9.9	9.3
Essex, MA	53,374	38,579	38.4	$67,507	$51,750	30.4	29,732	16.0	5.8	4.0	10.6	15.4	12.6
Middlesex, MA	135,305	91,573	47.8	$83,795	$60,737	38.0	109,398	9.6	3.2	3.8	24.8	8.4	8.4
Rockingham County-Strafford County, NH Div	29,402	20,024	46.8	$66,935	$47,848	39.9	17,882	D	8.0	6.0	12.4	10.2	10.5
Rockingham, NH	22,823	15,334	48.8	$73,819	$51,927	42.2	13,873	10.5	8.0	5.6	12.5	9.1	7.8
Strafford, NH	6,579	4,690	40.3	$50,574	$38,071	32.8	4,009	D	7.9	7.2	11.8	14.0	20.0
Boulder, CO Metro Area	23,932	14,889	60.7	$73,394	$50,339	45.8	17,374	11.5	4.4	3.3	24.8	9.8	14.6
Boulder, CO	23,932	14,889	60.7	$73,394	$50,339	45.8	17,374	11.5	4.4	3.3	24.8	9.8	14.6
Bowling Green, KY Metro Area	6,519	4,733	37.7	$36,740	$29,704	23.7	4,577	D	6.6	D	4.1	14.5	15.2
Allen, KY	689	493	39.8	$32,643	$24,594	32.7	288	25.2	5.7	3.2	D	D	14.6
Butler, KY	440	344	27.7	$34,420	$27,030	27.3	178	29.7	3.3	2.3	1.4	D	18.3
Edmonson, KY	396	304	30.0	$32,253	$24,898	29.5	97	D	4.3	D	D	D	40.8
Warren, KY	4,994	3,591	39.1	$38,045	$31,412	21.1	4,014	18.7	6.8	3.7	4.5	15.4	13.7
Bremerton-Silverdale-Port Orchard, WA Metro Area	15,175	10,640	42.6	$56,244	$42,276	33.0	8,392	2.4	5.7	1.9	6.8	9.4	52.4
Kitsap, WA	15,175	10,640	42.6	$56,244	$42,276	33.0	8,392	2.4	5.7	1.9	6.8	9.4	52.4
Bridgeport-Stamford-Norwalk, CT Metro Area	113,853	95,360	19.4	$120,630	$103,728	16.3	63,226	9.8	4.9	25.3	11.1	8.3	7.3
Fairfield, CT	113,853	95,360	19.4	$120,630	$103,728	16.3	63,226	9.8	4.9	25.3	11.1	8.3	7.3
Brownsville-Harlingen, TX Metro Area	12,190	9,519	28.1	$28,756	$23,350	23.2	7,427	5.2	8.4	3.7	3.0	19.8	27.3
Cameron, TX	12,190	9,519	28.1	$28,756	$23,350	23.2	7,427	5.2	8.4	3.7	3.0	19.8	27.3
Brunswick, GA Metro Area	4,868	3,597	35.3	$41,092	$31,971	28.5	2,832	6.1	7.3	D	4.2	14.2	24.7
Brantley, GA	518	402	28.8	$27,413	$21,777	25.9	162	9.9	4.8	D	0.6	4.3	26.6
Glynn, GA	3,926	2,875	36.5	$46,073	$36,060	27.8	2,560	6.1	7.5	2.8	4.5	15.4	24.2
McIntosh, GA	423	320	32.4	$29,519	$22,345	32.1	109	0.5	7.9	0.6	3.1	2.2	34.4
Buffalo-Cheektowaga, NY Metro Area	56,976	43,978	29.6	$50,414	$38,726	30.2	40,043	11.5	6.1	7.3	7.5	13.4	20.5
Erie, NY	47,401	36,423	30.1	$51,539	$39,627	30.1	35,335	10.9	5.9	8.0	7.9	13.5	20.0
Niagara, NY	9,575	7,556	26.7	$45,501	$34,903	30.4	4,708	16.7	8.2	2.1	3.9	13.4	24.4
Burlington, NC Metro Area	6,548	4,846	35.1	$39,342	$32,002	22.9	3,724	15.7	8.6	3.8	3.8	20.5	11.1
Alamance, NC	6,548	4,846	35.1	$39,342	$32,002	22.9	3,724	15.7	8.6	3.8	3.8	20.5	11.1

Table C-3. Personal Income and Earnings by Industry—*Continued*

Metropolitan Statistical Area Metropolitan Division Component counties	Personal Income						Earnings 2018						
	Total (million dollars)			Per capita Personal Income			Total earnings (million dollars)	Earnings by Industry (percent)					
	2018	2010	Percent change 2010-2018	2018	2010	Percent change 2010-2018		Manu-facturing	Retail Trade	Finance and Insurance	Professional, Scienfic, and Technical Services	Health Care and Social Assistance	Government and Government Enterprises
Burlington-South Burlington, VT Metro Area	12,729	9,289	37.0	$57,575	$43,913	31.1	9,464	11.2	6.7	4.4	11.3	D	19.3
Chittenden, VT	10,025	7,269	37.9	$60,914	$46,369	31.4	8,092	10.6	6.7	4.8	12.6	15.3	17.5
Franklin, VT	2,284	1,695	34.7	$46,220	$35,461	30.3	1,273	15.9	7.4	1.7	3.4	13.1	31.0
Grand Isle, VT	420	324	29.5	$59,204	$46,659	26.9	99	2.9	D	2.7	7.0	D	18.9
California-Lexington Park, MD Metro Area	6,402	4,962	29.0	$56,820	$46,915	21.1	4,702	0.8	4.0	0.7	22.7	6.4	47.4
St. Mary's, MD	6,402	4,962	29.0	$56,820	$46,915	21.1	4,702	0.8	4.0	0.7	22.7	6.4	47.4
Canton-Massillon, OH Metro Area	17,846	13,729	30.0	$44,767	$33,965	31.8	10,787	19.0	7.0	4.4	5.3	D	12.5
Carroll, OH	1,075	850	26.4	$39,698	$29,473	34.7	423	17.8	6.6	1.4	3.2	D	13.9
Stark, OH	16,771	12,879	30.2	$45,136	$34,310	31.6	10,364	19.0	7.0	4.6	5.4	16.0	12.4
Cape Coral-Fort Myers, FL Metro Area	38,686	24,256	59.5	$51,266	$39,095	31.1	19,718	2.3	8.9	3.5	9.2	10.4	16.2
Lee, FL	38,686	24,256	59.5	$51,266	$39,095	31.1	19,718	2.3	8.9	3.5	9.2	10.4	16.2
Cape Girardeau, MO-IL Metro Area	4,253	3,195	33.1	$43,850	$33,124	32.4	2,934	15.9	7.9	3.3	5.2	23.3	13.4
Alexander, IL	210	219	-4.0	$34,713	$26,712	30.0	86	11.0	2.5	D	0.6	D	28.4
Bollinger, MO	395	321	23.0	$32,454	$26,008	24.8	104	6.4	6.9	D	2.4	D	22.1
Cape Girardeau, MO	3,647	2,654	37.4	$46,314	$34,974	32.4	2,744	16.4	8.1	3.4	5.4	24.0	12.6
Carbondale-Marion, IL Metro Area	5,573	4,668	19.4	$40,701	$33,479	21.6	3,804	9.4	6.4	4.0	D	17.1	33.6
Jackson, IL	2,141	1,891	13.2	$37,284	$31,316	19.1	1,857	7.2	5.5	2.1	D	17.6	39.7
Johnson, IL	448	336	33.3	$35,956	$26,638	35.0	133	1.9	3.5	D	2.7	D	49.9
Williamson, IL	2,985	2,441	22.3	$44,509	$36,744	21.1	1,814	12.2	7.6	6.2	D	17.8	26.2
Carson City, NV Metro Area	2,812	2,432	15.6	$50,754	$44,229	14.8	2,390	8.6	6.9	3.6	4.2	14.0	35.9
Carson City city, NV	2,812	2,432	15.6	$50,754	$44,229	14.8	2,390	8.6	6.9	3.6	4.2	14.0	35.9
Casper, WY Metro Area	5,489	3,728	47.2	$69,379	$49,395	40.5	4,202	3.3	4.8	2.3	3.8	10.7	10.6
Natrona, WY	5,489	3,728	47.2	$69,379	$49,395	40.5	4,202	3.3	4.8	2.3	3.8	10.7	10.6
Cedar Rapids, IA Metro Area	14,205	10,578	34.3	$52,168	$40,932	27.5	10,540	22.3	5.2	8.3	D	D	10.9
Benton, IA	1,385	1,051	31.7	$53,994	$40,359	33.8	526	27.1	7.4	3.2	D	D	17.2
Jones, IA	906	710	27.6	$43,652	$34,306	27.2	379	14.7	7.2	3.6	3.4	9.8	21.1
Linn, IA	11,915	8,817	35.1	$52,743	$41,650	26.6	9,635	22.3	5.0	8.7	6.0	11.0	10.1
Chambersburg-Waynesboro, PA Metro Area	7,185	5,400	33.1	$46,403	$36,020	28.8	4,140	16.9	6.6	2.4	4.4	15.2	15.8
Franklin, PA	7,185	5,400	33.1	$46,403	$36,020	28.8	4,140	16.9	6.6	2.4	4.4	15.2	15.8
Champaign-Urbana, IL Metro Area	10,408	8,410	23.8	$45,975	$38,534	19.3	7,729	6.0	6.2	3.5	5.1	D	37.9
Champaign, IL	9,518	7,687	23.8	$45,328	$38,141	18.8	7,462	6.0	6.2	3.5	5.1	14.3	38.4
Piatt, IL	890	723	23.0	$54,258	$43,284	25.4	267	6.5	5.9	5.9	3.4	D	24.4
Charleston, WV Metro Area	11,469	9,959	15.2	$44,053	$35,848	22.9	8,941	D	5.4	D	D	D	17.3
Boone, WV	737	741	-0.5	$33,592	$30,129	11.5	352	0.7	5.3	1.9	16.2	D	22.9
Clay, WV	267	237	12.5	$30,925	$25,310	22.2	68	D	6.3	D	D	16.3	35.5
Jackson, WV	1,095	791	38.5	$38,147	$27,053	41.0	1,169	12.0	3.6	1.1	3.4	D	6.4
Kanawha, WV	8,740	7,635	14.5	$48,435	$39,579	22.4	7,218	4.6	5.7	6.5	10.7	19.2	18.4
Lincoln, WV	629	554	13.6	$30,549	$25,555	19.5	134	0.5	7.2	D	3.7	14.9	33.6
Charleston-North Charleston, SC Metro Area	40,137	24,299	65.2	$50,958	$36,406	40.0	28,112	10.0	6.3	4.7	11.2	9.4	21.3
Berkeley, SC	8,935	5,323	67.8	$40,415	$29,670	36.2	4,414	14.7	6.4	2.4	19.6	3.4	15.0
Charleston, SC	24,954	14,606	70.8	$61,477	$41,616	47.7	21,426	8.1	6.1	5.4	10.0	10.9	23.0
Dorchester, SC	6,248	4,369	43.0	$38,892	$31,880	22.0	2,272	19.3	8.0	2.5	5.6	7.0	17.9
Charlotte-Concord-Gastonia, NC-SC Metro Area	135,350	87,058	55.5	$52,176	$38,691	34.9	105,406	8.5	5.3	12.3	D	6.8	11.0
Anson, NC	861	718	19.9	$34,616	$26,750	29.4	435	18.6	5.0	1.3	D	4.4	25.8
Cabarrus, NC	9,557	6,166	55.0	$45,220	$34,538	30.9	4,805	8.1	8.6	2.1	4.2	6.8	21.9
Gaston, NC	9,221	7,146	29.0	$41,379	$34,673	19.3	4,613	24.8	7.7	2.0	3.3	15.7	13.4
Iredell, NC	8,933	5,724	56.1	$50,065	$35,826	39.7	5,284	15.3	7.3	2.5	D	9.6	10.3
Lincoln, NC	3,836	2,459	56.0	$45,791	$31,488	45.4	1,469	22.3	7.4	2.7	5.4	5.0	16.1
Mecklenburg, NC	66,878	42,785	56.3	$61,137	$46,341	31.9	70,746	4.8	4.4	16.8	11.6	5.8	9.3
Rowan, NC	5,381	4,090	31.5	$38,089	$29,561	28.8	3,219	17.6	5.9	1.9	2.8	9.5	20.6
Union, NC	12,108	7,192	68.4	$51,326	$35,586	44.2	4,680	18.6	6.8	2.0	6.1	4.7	13.1
Chester, SC	1,097	848	29.4	$34,014	$25,574	33.0	624	40.2	4.2	1.6	2.7	5.1	16.0
Lancaster, SC	4,686	2,356	98.9	$49,127	$30,612	60.5	2,724	9.1	4.3	4.9	33.4	8.1	8.7
York, SC	12,792	7,572	68.9	$46,667	$33,379	39.8	6,807	13.3	6.9	5.8	7.4	8.3	12.3
Charlottesville, VA Metro Area	14,529	9,306	56.1	$66,577	$46,097	44.4	9,261	3.2	4.6	7.5	D	D	34.3
Albemarle, VA	11,702	7,240	61.6	$74,613	$50,753	47.0	8,450	3.0	4.5	8.0	9.9	10.4	35.3
Fluvanna, VA	1,197	888	34.8	$44,693	$34,437	29.8	308	3.6	3.5	1.3	D	6.0	28.7
Greene, VA	878	624	40.7	$44,383	$33,812	31.3	254	1.6	10.7	1.4	10.7	D	21.9
Nelson, VA	752	554	35.9	$50,717	$36,967	37.2	249	10.4	3.2	2.3	9.9	6.5	17.6
Charlottesville City, VA	NA	NA	NA	NA	NA	NA	NA	NA	NA	NA	NA	NA	NA
Chattanooga, TN-GA Metro Area	25,740	18,852	36.5	$45,900	$35,627	28.8	18,640	13.7	5.8	6.7	5.6	D	16.4
Catoosa, GA	2,370	1,795	32.0	$35,158	$28,017	25.5	900	10.4	14.0	4.2	2.3	10.1	18.1
Dade, GA	578	425	36.2	$35,640	$25,547	39.5	249	27.6	5.6	3.0	2.6	6.7	12.8
Walker, GA	2,278	1,791	27.2	$32,826	$26,007	26.2	847	31.0	5.2	4.7	D	4.7	21.7
Hamilton, TN	18,849	13,566	38.9	$51,743	$40,228	28.6	15,996	12.3	5.3	7.1	6.1	12.5	16.0
Marion, TN	1,099	871	26.2	$38,450	$30,863	24.6	475	28.6	8.2	2.2	D	6.8	16.4
Sequatchie, TN	565	404	39.9	$38,003	$28,611	32.8	173	12.8	10.1	6.5	D	D	24.5
Cheyenne, WY Metro Area	5,151	3,937	30.8	$52,039	$42,684	21.9	3,801	3.9	5.8	3.7	5.8	8.1	38.9
Laramie, WY	5,151	3,937	30.8	$52,039	$42,684	21.9	3,801	3.9	5.8	3.7	5.8	8.1	38.9
Chicago-Naperville-Elgin, IL-IN-WI Metro Area	580,270	418,681	38.6	$61,089	$44,207	38.2	430,066	9.9	4.6	8.9	13.4	9.9	11.8
Chicago-Naperville-Evanston, IL Div	446,426	320,133	39.5	$62,342	$44,741	39.3	347,144	7.6	4.2	9.9	14.9	10.0	11.3
Cook, IL	322,255	229,543	40.4	$62,205	$44,150	40.9	261,956	6.5	3.9	11.1	16.1	9.9	11.7
Du Page, IL	67,684	48,605	39.3	$72,889	$52,945	37.7	58,229	9.6	4.5	7.9	13.5	10.1	7.8
Grundy, IL	2,633	2,193	20.1	$51,657	$43,728	18.1	1,730	11.7	9.0	1.6	D	9.0	12.7

Table C-3. Personal Income and Earnings by Industry—*Continued*

Metropolitan Statistical Area / Metropolitan Division / Component counties	Personal Income — Total (million dollars) 2018	2010	Percent change 2010-2018	Per capita Personal Income 2018	2010	Percent change 2010-2018	Earnings 2018 — Total earnings (million dollars)	Manufacturing	Retail Trade	Finance and Insurance	Professional, Scienfic, and Technical Services	Health Care and Social Assistance	Government and Government Enterprises
McHenry, IL	17,194	12,868	33.6	$55,720	$41,635	33.8	7,023	17.5	7.6	2.9	5.6	10.4	16.3
Will, IL	36,660	26,924	36.2	$52,953	$39,664	33.5	18,206	12.3	6.5	2.5	5.9	10.2	14.7
Elgin, IL Div.	37,957	27,889	36.1	$49,535	$37,858	30.8	20,925	16.7	5.5	3.7	6.3	10.1	19.3
De Kalb, IL	4,262	3,295	29.4	$40,929	$31,335	30.6	2,638	12.6	7.5	2.7	D	11.5	29.9
Kane, IL	27,423	20,165	36.0	$51,333	$39,069	31.4	16,282	17.2	4.9	4.1	7.4	10.4	17.1
Kendall, IL	6,272	4,429	41.6	$49,033	$38,384	27.7	2,004	18.0	7.7	2.4	5.6	5.3	23.2
Gary, IN Div.	32,895	24,898	32.1	$46,900	$35,159	33.4	18,862	20.2	6.3	2.8	3.9	15.2	10.3
Jasper, IN	1,445	1,132	27.6	$43,293	$33,809	28.1	755	16.2	6.3	2.2	D	6.5	10.3
Lake, IN	21,882	16,958	29.0	$45,172	$34,194	32.1	13,595	19.9	6.2	2.8	3.8	16.5	10.6
Newton, IN	558	441	26.4	$39,818	$31,012	28.4	211	16.5	3.2	3.6	2.0	5.6	15.9
Porter, IN	9,010	6,366	41.5	$53,130	$38,701	37.3	4,301	22.1	6.8	2.7	5.0	13.3	9.3
Lake County-Kenosha County, IL-WI Div	62,992	45,761	37.7	$72,395	$52,550	37.8	43,135	20.8	6.7	5.6	9.1	7.1	13.3
Lake, IL	55,057	39,873	38.1	$78,559	$56,622	38.7	38,697	21.5	6.6	6.0	9.8	6.3	12.9
Kenosha, WI	7,935	5,888	34.8	$46,874	$35,337	32.6	4,438	15.0	7.0	1.7	2.9	13.8	16.4
Chico, CA Metro Area	10,255	7,310	40.3	$44,346	$33,235	33.4	5,984	5.0	9.0	3.6	4.4	20.7	22.1
Butte, CA	10,255	7,310	40.3	$44,346	$33,235	33.4	5,984	5.0	9.0	3.6	4.4	20.7	22.1
Cincinnati, OH-KY-IN Metro Area	119,888	86,412	38.7	$54,176	$40,366	34.2	86,578	13.4	5.3	D	8.3	11.9	11.0
Dearborn, IN	2,352	1,777	32.4	$47,454	$35,477	33.8	861	14.4	10.0	4.0	D	8.4	21.2
Franklin, IN	1,060	854	24.1	$46,629	$37,042	25.9	295	16.2	9.0	4.5	D	D	16.6
Ohio, IN	238	301	-20.9	$40,714	$49,333	-17.5	72	2.7	2.0	1.8	D	4.3	24.0
Union, IN	274	216	27.0	$38,998	$28,676	36.0	86	16.5	7.5	D	1.9	D	22.3
Boone, KY	6,314	4,429	42.6	$48,004	$37,103	29.4	5,968	17.2	6.3	4.6	4.5	5.6	7.8
Bracken, KY	303	247	22.4	$36,758	$29,053	26.5	82	D	2.8	D	2.5	8.5	25.3
Campbell, KY	4,566	3,268	39.7	$49,015	$36,060	35.9	2,016	9.6	7.4	2.3	8.1	12.2	20.2
Gallatin, KY	283	193	46.5	$32,065	$22,451	42.8	167	D	3.6	1.0	2.4	5.6	14.1
Grant, KY	907	697	30.1	$36,093	$28,245	27.8	313	13.2	10.7	1.6	6.7	D	20.7
Kenton, KY	9,628	6,823	41.1	$57,982	$42,654	35.9	5,655	8.6	4.9	9.8	6.8	16.0	13.1
Pendleton, KY	636	421	51.0	$43,757	$28,226	55.0	156	14.9	3.3	1.7	5.5	7.7	21.0
Brown, OH	1,625	1,279	27.0	$37,259	$28,503	30.7	538	9.7	7.4	2.2	D	10.1	24.6
Butler, OH	18,128	13,069	38.7	$47,408	$35,408	33.9	12,273	20.5	7.2	7.5	3.6	9.6	12.0
Clermont, OH	11,048	7,509	47.1	$53,770	$37,998	41.5	5,209	9.6	7.1	5.1	6.1	7.4	10.6
Hamilton, OH	48,643	36,123	34.7	$59,561	$45,026	32.3	45,529	11.9	3.9	8.8	10.9	14.1	10.1
Warren, OH	13,884	9,206	50.8	$59,799	$43,130	38.6	7,357	14.1	7.5	5.7	7.0	8.8	10.2
Clarksville, TN-KY Metro Area	12,230	9,924	23.2	$39,991	$36,091	10.8	8,381	10.5	5.9	1.9	2.9	8.0	46.7
Christian, KY	2,705	2,398	12.8	$37,742	$32,350	16.7	4,505	9.6	2.5	1.0	2.0	5.2	66.4
Trigg, KY	534	460	16.2	$36,495	$32,099	13.7	167	15.0	7.8	3.5	5.7	10.8	22.7
Montgomery, TN	8,450	6,574	28.5	$41,031	$37,968	8.1	3,500	11.2	10.3	3.1	4.3	11.7	22.5
Stewart, TN	540	491	10.0	$39,853	$36,806	8.3	209	15.7	4.3	1.4	D	3.9	48.1
Cleveland, TN Metro Area	4,744	3,563	33.1	$38,371	$30,740	24.8	2,859	22.9	7.4	2.5	D	D	12.0
Bradley, TN	4,173	3,112	34.1	$39,099	$31,405	24.5	2,715	23.7	7.4	2.5	D	D	11.2
Polk, TN	571	451	26.6	$33,772	$26,818	25.9	145	8.0	7.9	2.5	D	D	27.7
Cleveland-Elyria, OH Metro Area	110,539	82,196	34.5	$53,738	$39,604	35.7	82,220	12.9	4.8	7.2	9.4	14.1	13.4
Cuyahoga, OH	68,087	51,336	32.6	$54,739	$40,166	36.3	61,775	9.8	4.1	8.7	11.0	15.4	13.4
Geauga, OH	6,500	4,670	39.2	$69,129	$50,000	38.3	2,853	19.5	6.9	2.7	5.5	9.7	9.1
Lake, OH	11,694	8,748	33.7	$50,729	$38,034	33.4	6,565	28.0	7.0	2.2	4.9	10.1	12.4
Lorain, OH	14,281	10,437	36.8	$46,147	$34,621	33.3	6,659	22.3	6.9	2.4	3.9	11.7	17.6
Medina, OH	9,977	7,006	42.4	$55,691	$40,610	37.1	4,367	16.2	7.4	3.3	5.0	8.1	11.5
Coeur d'Alene, ID Metro Area	7,266	4,462	62.8	$44,987	$32,134	40.0	3,940	7.7	10.0	5.7	6.0	12.9	19.4
Kootenai, ID	7,266	4,462	62.8	$44,987	$32,134	40.0	3,940	7.7	10.0	5.7	6.0	12.9	19.4
College Station-Bryan, TX Metro Area	10,375	6,968	48.9	$39,533	$30,367	30.2	7,360	4.5	6.2	3.3	6.4	9.9	33.7
Brazos, TX	8,893	5,827	52.6	$39,216	$29,783	31.7	6,734	4.5	6.2	3.3	6.7	10.3	35.3
Burleson, TX	784	591	32.7	$42,629	$34,276	24.4	323	6.9	8.5	6.1	3.1	D	13.8
Robertson, TX	698	549	27.1	$40,394	$33,190	21.7	303	2.0	3.9	2.4	3.3	D	18.7
Colorado Springs, CO Metro Area	35,833	24,893	43.9	$48,492	$38,275	26.7	24,003	D	5.9	5.3	12.6	10.1	30.5
El Paso, CO	34,599	23,984	44.3	$48,467	$38,258	26.7	23,543	4.0	5.8	5.3	12.7	10.2	30.8
Teller, CO	1,234	909	35.7	$49,197	$38,742	27.0	460	D	7.8	2.8	7.2	5.0	16.7
Columbia, MO Metro Area	9,662	6,959	38.8	$46,510	$36,446	27.6	6,832	5.2	6.6	8.0	5.5	10.9	34.7
Boone, MO	8,584	6,115	40.4	$47,687	$37,468	27.3	6,405	4.9	6.4	8.2	5.7	11.3	35.6
Cooper, MO	685	530	29.2	$38,916	$30,111	29.2	291	6.1	9.2	5.5	2.6	8.5	23.1
Howard, MO	393	314	25.1	$38,796	$30,993	25.2	135	13.9	8.3	4.1	2.7	D	17.4
Columbia, SC Metro Area	37,392	26,530	40.9	$44,906	$34,470	30.3	27,250	9.4	6.1	7.5	D	9.5	25.2
Calhoun, SC	558	453	23.2	$38,451	$30,022	28.1	304	32.9	2.0	0.9	1.8	D	14.0
Fairfield, SC	823	685	20.2	$36,758	$28,727	28.0	454	9.7	7.1	0.8	D	5.0	18.1
Kershaw, SC	2,704	1,975	37.0	$41,227	$31,999	28.8	1,135	22.5	10.0	5.6	4.5	8.4	16.9
Lexington, SC	13,723	9,139	50.2	$46,513	$34,706	34.0	8,150	14.2	7.8	3.6	4.6	6.7	19.8
Richland, SC	18,875	13,700	37.8	$45,529	$35,515	28.2	16,955	5.4	5.1	9.9	9.6	11.2	28.9
Saluda, SC	708	578	22.6	$34,455	$29,003	18.8	251	36.4	4.2	1.5	1.0	D	22.7
Columbus, GA-AL Metro Area	13,056	10,132	28.9	$41,067	$32,740	25.4	9,293	8.4	4.6	12.4	D	10.5	35.4
Russell, AL	1,913	1,510	26.7	$33,104	$28,328	16.9	791	25.8	7.9	4.1	1.9	11.4	20.3
Chattahoochee, GA	332	343	-3.2	$31,115	$30,689	1.4	1,298	D	0.1	D	5.1	D	89.0
Harris, GA	1,636	1,165	40.5	$47,469	$36,224	31.0	298	17.6	2.4	2.6	D	D	24.4
Marion, GA	245	178	37.5	$29,333	$20,383	43.9	66	D	6.7	D	1.6	D	28.5
Muscogee, GA	8,572	6,640	29.1	$44,149	$34,745	27.1	6,705	7.6	5.2	16.5	5.8	12.4	27.5
Stewart, GA	141	120	17.4	$22,771	$19,716	15.5	89	D	2.1	D	D	D	29.7
Talbot, GA	216	175	23.5	$34,504	$25,520	35.2	46	0.2	1.6	6.8	D	D	27.3

Table C-3. Personal Income and Earnings by Industry—Continued

Metropolitan Statistical Area Metropolitan Division Component counties	Personal Income Total (million dollars) 2018	2010	Percent change 2010-2018	Per capita Personal Income 2018	2010	Percent change 2010-2018	Earnings 2018 Total earnings (million dollars)	Manu-facturing	Retail Trade	Finance and Insurance	Professional, Scienfic, and Technical Services	Health Care and Social Assistance	Government and Government Enterprises
Columbus, IN Metro Area	4,131	2,894	42.8	$49,922	$37,668	32.5	4,029	48.8	4.2	2.6	4.3	6.9	8.7
Bartholomew, IN	4,131	2,894	42.8	$49,922	$37,668	32.5	4,029	48.8	4.2	2.6	4.3	6.9	8.7
Columbus, OH Metro Area	107,781	73,475	46.7	$51,165	$38,542	32.8	84,573	7.8	5.0	8.9	9.4	11.2	17.6
Delaware, OH	15,176	9,423	61.1	$74,093	$53,815	37.7	7,736	7.1	6.5	10.7	10.9	8.1	8.4
Fairfield, OH	7,184	5,148	39.5	$46,113	$35,165	31.1	2,787	10.2	8.4	2.4	3.9	17.5	17.7
Franklin, OH	66,096	45,351	45.7	$50,443	$38,886	29.7	63,636	5.7	4.4	9.9	9.9	11.9	18.9
Hocking, OH	1,080	820	31.6	$38,047	$27,829	36.7	387	13.7	9.1	2.4	D	D	27.6
Licking, OH	8,096	5,772	40.3	$46,059	$34,626	33.0	3,997	14.2	8.8	5.9	5.7	10.7	15.1
Madison, OH	1,854	1,348	37.5	$41,751	$31,044	34.5	1,190	24.0	7.1	0.9	D	D	20.6
Morrow, OH	1,358	1,022	32.8	$38,666	$29,386	31.6	376	18.3	6.5	1.4	D	D	24.5
Perry, OH	1,340	996	34.6	$37,187	$27,627	34.6	492	12.7	5.0	2.0	1.9	D	19.1
Pickaway, OH	2,389	1,747	36.7	$41,131	$31,348	31.2	1,094	18.6	5.6	1.9	2.0	D	27.7
Union, OH	3,208	1,846	73.7	$55,470	$35,232	57.4	2,878	33.0	3.9	1.3	D	3.1	9.8
Corpus Christi, TX Metro Area	19,016	14,702	29.3	$44,311	$36,331	22.0	13,722	7.5	5.6	3.0	6.4	D	19.3
Nueces, TX	16,077	12,478	28.8	$44,378	$36,672	21.0	12,254	7.6	5.5	3.2	6.6	14.5	18.5
San Patricio, TX	2,940	2,225	32.1	$43,945	$34,527	27.3	1,468	7.3	6.4	1.6	4.2	D	25.4
Corvallis, OR Metro Area	4,331	3,085	40.4	$47,019	$36,056	30.4	3,018	11.1	4.9	2.2	7.7	16.5	30.1
Benton, OR	4,331	3,085	40.4	$47,019	$36,056	30.4	3,018	11.1	4.9	2.2	7.7	16.5	30.1
Crestview-Fort Walton Beach-Destin, FL Metro Area	14,393	9,560	50.6	$51,655	$40,520	27.5	9,469	2.5	7.5	3.1	11.0	7.6	35.6
Okaloosa, FL	10,130	7,376	37.3	$48,875	$40,818	19.7	7,691	2.7	6.7	3.2	11.9	7.4	41.0
Walton, FL	4,263	2,183	95.3	$59,728	$39,544	51.0	1,778	1.3	11.2	2.8	7.6	8.6	12.4
Cumberland, MD-WV Metro Area	3,921	3,278	19.6	$40,049	$31,784	26.0	2,314	14.6	7.3	3.1	2.7	20.0	23.6
Allegany, MD	2,876	2,399	19.9	$40,517	$32,000	26.6	1,825	9.5	7.6	3.5	2.8	22.4	25.2
Mineral, WV	1,046	879	18.9	$38,815	$31,209	24.4	488	34.1	6.4	1.6	2.6	11.1	17.7
Dallas-Fort Worth-Arlington, TX Metro Area	417,481	262,043	59.3	$55,886	$40,994	36.3	334,735	8.3	5.5	9.1	D	D	10.1
Dallas-Plano-Irving, TX Div	293,144	177,670	65.0	$58,545	$41,833	39.9	250,379	7.4	5.3	10.2	13.3	9.2	9.4
Collin, TX	66,213	38,782	70.7	$65,874	$49,188	33.9	42,604	7.9	6.9	13.0	13.9	9.8	8.8
Dallas, TX	155,610	96,799	60.8	$58,993	$40,804	44.6	177,483	6.5	4.6	10.6	13.9	9.1	8.6
Denton, TX	48,050	27,561	74.3	$55,933	$41,335	35.3	20,079	7.4	6.9	4.6	11.0	9.0	14.2
Ellis, TX	7,951	4,988	59.4	$44,313	$33,168	33.6	3,526	22.8	7.1	3.0	4.0	7.6	14.1
Hunt, TX	3,670	2,569	42.8	$38,029	$29,738	27.9	2,269	37.5	5.8	1.6	3.7	7.4	20.4
Kaufman, TX	5,510	3,382	62.9	$42,837	$32,556	31.6	2,091	14.5	7.5	3.3	D	7.4	20.6
Rockwall, TX	6,140	3,589	71.1	$61,003	$45,484	34.1	2,327	6.7	9.1	4.8	8.8	16.5	11.4
Fort Worth-Arlington-Grapevine, TX Div	124,337	84,374	47.4	$50,482	$39,332	28.3	84,356	11.1	6.2	5.7	5.9	9.9	12.2
Johnson, TX	7,145	4,935	44.8	$41,697	$32,628	27.8	3,285	14.6	9.0	2.4	3.1	7.2	14.9
Parker, TX	7,374	4,624	59.5	$53,289	$39,415	35.2	2,605	11.1	9.7	3.5	6.0	7.5	13.6
Tarrant, TX	106,829	72,761	46.8	$51,239	$40,033	28.0	76,946	10.9	5.9	6.0	6.1	10.3	12.0
Wise, TX	2,988	2,054	45.5	$43,752	$34,751	25.9	1,519	9.5	7.4	2.4	D	D	18.7
Dalton, GA Metro Area	5,229	3,652	43.2	$36,316	$25,666	41.5	4,387	36.6	5.5	1.8	D	D	10.3
Murray, GA	1,196	915	30.8	$29,968	$23,141	29.5	551	35.1	7.6	2.2	D	D	15.6
Whitfield, GA	4,033	2,737	47.4	$38,752	$26,637	45.5	3,836	36.9	5.2	1.7	8.0	10.0	9.5
Danville, IL Metro Area	3,032	2,648	14.5	$39,481	$32,433	21.7	1,893	21.2	5.8	3.8	1.4	9.3	23.2
Vermilion, IL	3,032	2,648	14.5	$39,481	$32,433	21.7	1,893	21.2	5.8	3.8	1.4	9.3	23.2
Daphne-Fairhope-Foley, AL Metro Area	9,941	6,618	50.2	$45,596	$36,144	26.2	4,315	6.9	11.6	3.9	5.3	12.8	13.8
Baldwin, AL	9,941	6,618	50.2	$45,596	$36,144	26.2	4,315	6.9	11.6	3.9	5.3	12.8	13.8
Davenport-Moline-Rock Island, IA-IL Metro Area	18,757	15,194	23.4	$49,172	$40,011	22.9	13,219	14.3	6.1	4.0	D	D	15.7
Henry, IL	2,213	1,856	19.2	$45,072	$36,778	22.6	876	10.4	7.2	5.8	D	11.8	24.4
Mercer, IL	703	608	15.6	$45,046	$37,051	21.6	199	16.5	6.5	4.3	1.7	D	22.5
Rock Island, IL	6,428	5,489	17.1	$44,802	$37,182	20.5	6,188	11.3	4.8	3.2	6.0	9.4	19.2
Scott, IA	9,413	7,242	30.0	$54,323	$43,817	24.0	5,956	18.0	7.2	4.5	5.2	14.1	10.6
Dayton-Kettering, OH Metro Area	38,461	29,015	32.6	$47,687	$36,283	31.4	27,862	12.2	5.3	4.9	9.2	15.6	21.8
Greene, OH	8,449	6,188	36.5	$50,291	$38,292	31.3	6,678	4.4	5.7	2.1	16.9	7.1	44.6
Miami, OH	5,051	3,669	37.7	$47,552	$35,797	32.8	2,674	29.4	6.8	2.4	3.6	9.3	12.7
Montgomery, OH	24,962	19,158	30.3	$46,891	$35,770	31.1	18,510	12.5	4.9	6.3	7.3	19.5	14.9
Decatur, AL Metro Area	5,887	4,819	22.2	$38,719	$31,300	23.7	3,452	30.4	6.4	3.3	4.2	D	14.4
Lawrence, AL	1,125	947	18.8	$34,125	$27,570	23.8	304	3.2	8.6	5.1	1.8	D	24.4
Morgan, AL	4,762	3,872	23.0	$39,991	$32,371	23.5	3,148	33.0	6.1	3.1	4.5	7.1	13.4
Decatur, IL Metro Area	5,049	4,368	15.6	$48,214	$39,427	22.3	3,956	31.2	4.9	3.5	3.6	12.9	10.7
Macon, IL	5,049	4,368	15.6	$48,214	$39,427	22.3	3,956	31.2	4.9	3.5	3.6	12.9	10.7
Deltona-Daytona Beach-Ormond Beach, FL Metro Area	28,381	19,698	44.1	$43,028	$33,357	29.0	12,064	7.1	9.7	4.0	5.8	17.4	13.7
Flagler, FL	5,180	3,161	63.8	$46,220	$32,905	40.5	1,444	3.8	10.5	3.8	6.3	12.5	16.2
Volusia, FL	23,202	16,537	40.3	$42,374	$33,445	26.7	10,620	7.5	9.6	4.1	5.8	18.1	13.3
Denver-Aurora-Lakewood, CO Metro Area	188,515	111,542	69.0	$64,287	$43,660	47.2	145,819	D	D	D	D	D	11.9
Adams, CO	22,171	13,645	62.5	$43,315	$30,754	40.8	17,352	6.4	5.2	1.7	4.3	8.0	22.1
Arapahoe, CO	39,190	23,553	66.4	$60,180	$40,979	46.9	30,926	1.9	5.3	12.2	15.1	10.7	9.4
Broomfield, CO	4,600	3,045	51.1	$66,410	$54,162	22.6	4,517	14.3	4.0	4.4	16.3	3.5	2.5
Clear Creek, CO	589	400	47.3	$61,300	$44,060	39.1	244	1.7	4.7	0.8	6.4	2.6	14.7
Denver, CO	57,211	29,589	93.4	$79,849	$49,041	62.8	59,581	2.8	2.5	7.4	14.4	6.5	11.0
Douglas, CO	25,250	15,418	63.8	$73,662	$53,727	37.1	11,349	1.4	6.8	12.3	18.1	8.8	7.6
Elbert, CO	1,507	911	65.4	$57,334	$39,368	45.6	304	2.6	6.4	2.1	11.0	D	15.9
Gilpin, CO	295	195	51.0	$48,128	$35,633	35.1	320	D	D	D	D	D	10.5
Jefferson, CO	36,865	24,262	52.0	$63,536	$45,278	40.3	21,029	12.0	6.6	3.6	14.3	10.7	14.1
Park, CO	837	524	59.8	$45,113	$32,175	40.2	197	2.6	7.6	1.6	9.8	2.3	21.7

Table C-3. Personal Income and Earnings by Industry—*Continued*

Metropolitan Statistical Area Metropolitan Division Component counties	Total (million dollars) 2018	2010	Percent change 2010-2018	Per capita Personal Income 2018	2010	Percent change 2010-2018	Total earnings (million dollars)	Manu-facturing	Retail Trade	Finance and Insurance	Professional, Scienfic, and Technical Services	Health Care and Social Assistance	Government and Government Enterprises
Des Moines-West Des Moines, IA Metro Area	37,466	25,522	46.8	$54,098	$41,913	29.1	28,907	6.2	5.6	D	8.1	10.4	12.6
Dallas, IA....................	5,963	3,270	82.4	$66,128	$48,989	35.0	3,415	4.8	6.7	40.0	5.7	8.0	7.8
Guthrie, IA..................	565	428	32.1	$52,694	$39,091	34.8	252	10.3	2.8	D	4.3	5.9	20.7
Jasper, IA...................	1,618	1,226	32.0	$43,551	$33,296	30.8	714	21.6	6.9	2.8	3.9	9.1	18.0
Madison, IA.................	804	587	36.9	$49,505	$37,330	32.6	258	4.5	7.4	5.0	4.1	5.7	23.5
Polk, IA.....................	25,927	18,259	42.0	$53,215	$42,230	26.0	23,505	5.9	5.3	18.8	8.8	10.9	12.7
Warren, IA..................	2,588	1,753	47.6	$50,698	$37,831	34.0	762	7.4	8.9	3.9	4.8	10.4	20.4
Detroit-Warren-Dearborn, MI Metro Area	229,674	163,055	40.9	$53,086	$37,994	39.7	168,697	14.9	5.4	5.5	15.3	11.6	9.7
Detroit-Dearborn-Livonia, MI Div.......	75,317	58,973	27.7	$42,942	$32,489	32.2	62,999	14.8	4.3	4.7	12.1	13.3	12.1
Wayne, MI...................	75,317	58,973	27.7	$42,942	$32,489	32.2	62,999	14.8	4.3	4.7	12.1	13.3	12.1
Warren-Troy-Farmington Hills, MI Div	154,358	104,082	48.3	$60,002	$42,029	42.8	105,698	15.0	6.1	5.9	17.1	10.6	8.3
Lapeer, MI...................	3,845	2,739	40.4	$43,679	$31,050	40.7	1,405	23.7	8.6	3.1	2.9	6.1	20.3
Livingston, MI..............	11,153	7,193	55.1	$58,326	$39,724	46.8	4,371	19.4	8.2	4.1	8.6	9.8	10.8
Macomb, MI.................	40,703	28,968	40.5	$46,530	$34,430	35.1	27,069	23.5	6.5	2.2	13.9	9.7	12.6
Oakland, MI.................	91,595	59,914	52.9	$72,741	$49,799	46.1	69,730	11.0	5.6	7.8	19.8	11.0	5.8
St. Clair, MI.................	7,061	5,268	34.0	$44,316	$32,380	36.9	3,123	19.8	7.4	2.2	3.9	14.6	17.4
Dothan, AL Metro Area..................	6,061	4,925	23.1	$40,883	$33,760	21.1	3,524	8.0	9.5	3.3	4.9	D	19.4
Geneva, AL..................	926	775	19.6	$35,192	$28,920	21.7	316	10.0	7.3	3.8	1.8	4.3	22.5
Henry, AL...................	695	534	30.1	$40,360	$30,867	30.8	240	10.6	4.5	2.8	14.1	D	16.0
Houston, AL.................	4,440	3,616	22.8	$42,398	$35,525	19.3	2,968	7.6	10.1	3.3	4.5	17.6	19.3
Dover, DE Metro Area..................	7,503	5,515	36.0	$42,023	$33,846	24.2	4,714	D	7.2	2.8	D	12.4	36.8
Kent, DE.....................	7,503	5,515	36.0	$42,023	$33,846	24.2	4,714	D	7.2	2.8	D	12.4	36.8
Dubuque, IA Metro Area..................	4,754	3,463	37.3	$49,085	$36,867	33.1	3,706	20.9	6.3	10.0	4.8	14.1	8.1
Dubuque, IA..................	4,754	3,463	37.3	$49,085	$36,867	33.1	3,706	20.9	6.3	10.0	4.8	14.1	8.1
Duluth, MN-WI Metro Area	13,387	10,574	26.6	$46,250	$36,393	27.1	8,762	7.5	6.7	3.9	4.4	21.1	19.7
Carlton, MN.................	1,545	1,165	32.5	$43,098	$32,906	31.0	841	13.9	5.1	4.5	2.7	11.2	37.4
Lake, MN....................	513	393	30.6	$48,132	$36,183	33.0	281	17.2	4.4	2.6	1.8	D	20.7
St. Louis, MN...............	9,472	7,551	25.4	$47,417	$37,730	25.7	6,521	5.3	7.1	4.1	5.2	25.5	17.2
Douglas, WI.................	1,858	1,464	26.9	$43,004	$33,180	29.6	1,119	12.7	6.4	2.2	1.8	8.1	20.4
Durham-Chapel Hill, NC Metro Area..................	34,342	23,243	47.8	$54,036	$41,046	31.6	29,487	13.8	3.4	5.9	14.1	12.7	20.9
Chatham, NC.................	4,611	2,852	61.7	$63,041	$44,678	41.1	978	9.7	7.6	2.7	11.1	12.8	16.3
Durham, NC.................	16,058	10,888	47.5	$50,698	$40,124	26.4	20,135	16.7	2.8	7.3	17.2	15.6	9.4
Granville, NC...............	2,324	1,733	34.1	$38,652	$30,050	28.6	1,436	26.1	4.0	1.1	1.5	D	41.4
Orange, NC..................	9,840	6,563	49.9	$67,385	$48,983	37.6	6,322	2.0	4.3	3.1	8.8	6.7	54.3
Person, NC..................	1,509	1,207	25.1	$38,202	$30,619	24.8	616	18.3	7.8	2.5	3.2	11.6	16.6
East Stroudsburg, PA Metro Area	7,242	5,419	33.6	$42,722	$31,908	33.9	3,978	13.3	7.8	1.8	2.6	11.9	24.0
Monroe, PA..................	7,242	5,419	33.6	$42,722	$31,908	33.9	3,978	13.3	7.8	1.8	2.6	11.9	24.0
Eau Claire, WI Metro Area	8,003	5,998	33.4	$47,450	$37,105	27.9	5,763	13.5	7.5	5.1	4.1	19.6	14.6
Chippewa, WI...............	2,961	2,206	34.2	$46,162	$35,219	31.1	1,667	24.1	9.7	1.8	3.2	9.7	14.3
Eau Claire, WI..............	5,043	3,792	33.0	$48,240	$38,299	26.0	4,097	9.2	6.6	6.4	4.4	23.7	14.7
El Centro, CA Metro Area	6,723	5,147	30.6	$36,974	$29,455	25.5	4,609	1.6	7.7	1.3	1.9	6.4	38.1
Imperial, CA.................	6,723	5,147	30.6	$36,974	$29,455	25.5	4,609	1.6	7.7	1.3	1.9	6.4	38.1
Elizabethtown-Fort Knox, KY Metro Area	6,464	5,072	27.5	$42,144	$33,846	24.5	4,151	14.5	6.2	2.8	2.9	6.4	40.6
Hardin, KY...................	4,792	3,803	26.0	$43,424	$35,554	22.1	3,731	14.4	6.0	2.6	3.0	6.3	42.8
Larue, KY...................	523	398	31.2	$36,525	$28,085	30.1	137	17.1	4.7	5.3	1.6	11.7	24.4
Meade, KY...................	1,149	871	32.0	$40,026	$30,327	32.0	282	13.5	8.9	3.0	3.0	6.2	20.0
Elkhart-Goshen, IN Metro Area	9,624	6,003	60.3	$46,816	$30,404	54.0	10,030	52.7	3.9	1.6	2.0	7.1	5.0
Elkhart, IN..................	9,624	6,003	60.3	$46,816	$30,404	54.0	10,030	52.7	3.9	1.6	2.0	7.1	5.0
Elmira, NY Metro Area	3,739	3,130	19.5	$44,373	$35,206	26.0	2,436	16.6	7.0	4.0	3.0	16.9	22.9
Chemung, NY................	3,739	3,130	19.5	$44,373	$35,206	26.0	2,436	16.6	7.0	4.0	3.0	16.9	22.9
El Paso, TX Metro Area	30,302	22,892	32.4	$35,836	$28,363	26.3	21,022	D	7.4	D	D	D	36.0
El Paso, TX..................	30,146	22,821	32.1	$35,856	$28,397	26.3	20,910	5.2	7.5	3.1	3.2	10.4	35.9
Hudspeth, TX................	156	71	118.5	$32,472	$20,528	58.2	112	D	0.7	D	D	D	56.5
Enid, OK Metro Area..................	2,709	2,374	14.1	$44,465	$39,081	13.8	1,794	10.1	6.7	4.5	D	10.9	19.6
Garfield, OK.................	2,709	2,374	14.1	$44,465	$39,081	13.8	1,794	10.1	6.7	4.5	D	10.9	19.6
Erie, PA Metro Area	12,216	9,717	25.7	$44,903	$34,606	29.8	7,972	18.7	6.5	7.3	3.8	18.2	15.9
Erie, PA.....................	12,216	9,717	25.7	$44,903	$34,606	29.8	7,972	18.7	6.5	7.3	3.8	18.2	15.9
Eugene-Springfield, OR Metro Area	17,431	11,917	46.3	$45,919	$33,862	35.6	10,932	9.1	7.8	3.6	5.3	16.1	18.6
Lane, OR....................	17,431	11,917	46.3	$45,919	$33,862	35.6	10,932	9.1	7.8	3.6	5.3	16.1	18.6
Evansville, IN-KY Metro Area	14,888	11,818	26.0	$47,313	$37,903	24.8	10,400	20.0	6.0	3.5	D	D	9.4
Posey, IN....................	1,231	979	25.7	$48,180	$37,869	27.2	753	47.6	4.5	2.2	D	2.7	8.2
Vanderburgh, IN.............	8,305	6,912	20.2	$45,893	$38,436	19.4	7,151	15.5	6.4	3.6	5.6	19.1	9.0
Warrick, IN..................	3,534	2,458	43.8	$56,476	$41,074	37.5	1,303	17.5	4.7	4.4	5.6	27.2	9.5
Henderson, KY...............	1,819	1,468	23.8	$39,891	$31,744	25.7	1,193	32.6	6.4	2.5	2.3	D	12.1
Fairbanks, AK Metro Area..................	5,602	4,542	23.3	$56,606	$46,227	22.5	3,953	1.1	5.5	1.3	3.5	10.7	47.3
Fairbanks North Star, AK.....	5,602	4,542	23.3	$56,606	$46,227	22.5	3,953	1.1	5.5	1.3	3.5	10.7	47.3
Fargo, ND-MN Metro Area..................	12,939	8,420	53.7	$52,712	$40,199	31.1	9,880	7.4	6.7	8.1	6.3	15.0	13.9
Clay, MN....................	2,762	2,007	37.6	$43,180	$33,931	27.3	1,320	7.9	7.1	2.4	4.4	10.9	23.1
Cass, ND....................	10,178	6,413	58.7	$56,070	$42,665	31.4	8,560	7.3	6.6	8.9	6.5	15.7	12.4
Farmington, NM Metro Area..................	4,433	3,962	11.9	$35,453	$30,428	16.5	3,065	2.7	8.7	D	D	13.3	22.9
San Juan, NM................	4,433	3,962	11.9	$35,453	$30,428	16.5	3,065	2.7	8.7	D	D	13.3	22.9
Fayetteville, NC Metro Area	19,238	15,534	23.8	$36,903	$31,675	16.5	14,516	4.9	5.1	1.6	D	5.8	57.9
Cumberland, NC.............	12,888	10,863	18.6	$38,780	$33,202	16.8	12,510	4.0	4.5	1.4	3.9	5.4	63.2
Harnett, NC..................	4,644	3,373	37.7	$34,604	$29,140	18.8	1,513	7.4	10.6	2.9	3.7	7.8	22.7
Hoke, NC....................	1,706	1,298	31.4	$31,148	$27,332	14.0	493	20.2	4.3	3.1	D	10.3	30.6

Table C-3. Personal Income and Earnings by Industry—*Continued*

Metropolitan Statistical Area Metropolitan Division Component counties	Personal Income						Earnings 2018						
	Total (million dollars)			Per capita Personal Income				Earnings by Industry (percent)					
	2018	2010	Percent change 2010-2018	2018	2010	Percent change 2010-2018	Total earnings (million dollars)	Manu-facturing	Retail Trade	Finance and Insurance	Professional, Scienfic, and Technical Services	Health Care and Social Assistance	Government and Government Enterprises
Fayetteville-Springdale-Rogers, AR Metro Area	34,354	17,091	101.0	$65,306	$38,642	69.0	17,713	8.9	5.3	2.0	D	9.1	11.5
Benton, AR	24,232	10,862	123.1	$88,890	$48,798	82.2	9,849	7.1	4.6	1.4	8.1	6.0	6.5
Madison, AR	585	377	55.3	$35,496	$24,015	47.8	248	22.8	6.9	1.9	D	4.6	13.6
Washington, AR	9,537	5,852	63.0	$40,247	$28,685	40.3	7,616	10.7	6.2	2.6	5.2	13.3	17.9
Flagstaff, AZ Metro Area	6,875	4,632	48.4	$48,129	$34,406	39.9	4,353	10.0	7.3	1.4	3.0	14.8	30.6
Coconino, AZ	6,875	4,632	48.4	$48,129	$34,406	39.9	4,353	10.0	7.3	1.4	3.0	14.8	30.6
Flint, MI Metro Area	16,710	12,927	29.3	$41,068	$30,420	35.0	9,311	11.2	8.5	4.3	3.7	18.8	16.0
Genesee, MI	16,710	12,927	29.3	$41,068	$30,420	35.0	9,311	11.2	8.5	4.3	3.7	18.8	16.0
Florence, SC Metro Area	8,283	6,446	28.5	$40,413	$31,344	28.9	5,729	15.5	6.9	8.8	4.6	13.0	18.5
Darlington, SC	2,503	1,984	26.2	$37,475	$28,953	29.4	1,467	25.8	5.3	2.1	1.6	10.3	13.2
Florence, SC	5,780	4,462	29.5	$41,833	$32,538	28.6	4,261	12.0	7.4	11.2	5.7	13.9	20.3
Florence-Muscle Shoals, AL Metro Area	5,534	4,603	20.2	$37,608	$31,257	20.3	3,158	19.5	9.2	3.8	2.9	12.4	20.0
Colbert, AL	2,102	1,725	21.8	$38,378	$31,646	21.3	1,555	29.3	7.9	3.3	1.6	7.5	20.6
Lauderdale, AL	3,432	2,877	19.3	$37,151	$31,029	19.7	1,603	10.0	10.6	4.4	4.2	17.1	19.4
Fond du Lac, WI Metro Area	4,960	3,744	32.5	$48,126	$36,855	30.6	3,372	25.7	6.2	3.9	2.8	12.9	11.8
Fond du Lac, WI	4,960	3,744	32.5	$48,126	$36,855	30.6	3,372	25.7	6.2	3.9	2.8	12.9	11.8
Fort Collins, CO Metro Area	18,994	11,253	68.8	$54,188	$37,454	44.7	12,316	14.0	6.3	3.0	10.7	8.2	21.0
Larimer, CO	18,994	11,253	68.8	$54,188	$37,454	44.7	12,316	14.0	6.3	3.0	10.7	8.2	21.0
Fort Smith, AR-OK Metro Area	9,456	7,398	27.8	$37,800	$29,789	26.9	6,138	17.0	6.8	2.7	2.7	14.4	13.7
Crawford, AR	2,089	1,679	24.4	$32,952	$27,097	21.6	1,076	22.3	6.5	2.1	D	6.8	11.9
Franklin, AR	610	467	30.7	$34,275	$25,762	33.0	286	18.0	6.8	1.4	D	7.3	21.2
Sebastian, AR	5,380	4,106	31.0	$42,110	$32,646	29.0	4,329	16.9	6.6	2.8	2.7	18.2	11.5
Sequoyah, OK	1,376	1,145	20.1	$33,420	$26,974	23.9	447	3.8	10.0	3.5	D	D	34.3
Fort Wayne, IN Metro Area	18,891	13,414	40.8	$46,141	$34,456	33.9	14,126	19.2	6.5	6.5	D	19.0	9.0
Allen, IN	17,374	12,307	41.2	$46,288	$34,576	33.9	13,304	17.4	6.6	6.8	4.9	19.9	8.9
Whitley, IN	1,517	1,107	37.1	$44,528	$33,176	34.2	821	47.2	5.7	2.0	D	5.8	9.5
Fresno, CA Metro Area	42,843	29,568	44.9	$43,084	$31,723	35.8	28,607	6.0	6.5	3.6	4.1	14.4	22.7
Fresno, CA	42,843	29,568	44.9	$43,084	$31,723	35.8	28,607	6.0	6.5	3.6	4.1	14.4	22.7
Gadsden, AL Metro Area	3,784	3,170	19.4	$36,918	$30,345	21.7	2,027	15.7	8.2	3.7	2.7	D	15.0
Etowah, AL	3,784	3,170	19.4	$36,918	$30,345	21.7	2,027	15.7	8.2	3.7	2.7	D	15.0
Gainesville, FL Metro Area	14,035	10,379	35.2	$42,663	$33,992	25.5	9,869	4.3	5.7	4.7	D	17.2	35.5
Alachua, FL	11,983	8,815	35.9	$44,390	$35,599	24.7	9,138	4.1	5.6	4.8	7.1	17.8	36.6
Gilchrist, FL	617	438	40.8	$33,774	$25,753	31.1	227	3.8	3.7	1.4	D	16.6	26.3
Levy, FL	1,435	1,126	27.4	$35,204	$27,661	27.3	504	8.9	10.0	3.1	3.7	6.6	20.5
Gainesville, GA Metro Area	8,834	5,502	60.6	$43,701	$30,561	43.0	6,440	19.7	5.8	4.5	3.7	16.1	10.8
Hall, GA	8,834	5,502	60.6	$43,701	$30,561	43.0	6,440	19.7	5.8	4.5	3.7	16.1	10.8
Gettysburg, PA Metro Area	5,056	3,788	33.4	$49,173	$37,333	31.7	2,362	19.9	6.1	2.2	3.0	D	14.6
Adams, PA	5,056	3,788	33.4	$49,173	$37,333	31.7	2,362	19.9	6.1	2.2	3.0	D	14.6
Glens Falls, NY Metro Area	5,823	4,651	25.2	$46,411	$36,050	28.7	3,654	14.0	8.5	3.6	4.1	14.1	20.9
Warren, NY	3,372	2,683	25.7	$52,475	$40,852	28.5	2,557	11.8	9.1	4.6	5.1	16.7	14.3
Washington, NY	2,451	1,968	24.5	$40,043	$31,072	28.9	1,097	19.2	7.3	1.3	1.6	8.0	36.5
Goldsboro, NC Metro Area	4,742	3,884	22.1	$38,472	$31,607	21.7	2,840	11.3	7.0	2.9	2.5	11.6	33.5
Wayne, NC	4,742	3,884	22.1	$38,472	$31,607	21.7	2,840	11.3	7.0	2.9	2.5	11.6	33.5
Grand Forks, ND-MN Metro Area	5,183	3,718	39.4	$50,670	$37,697	34.4	3,748	7.6	7.3	3.3	3.9	D	25.8
Polk, MN	1,539	1,166	32.1	$48,820	$36,838	32.5	816	14.5	6.0	2.5	1.9	D	20.2
Grand Forks, ND	3,644	2,553	42.8	$51,494	$38,103	35.1	2,932	5.7	7.7	3.5	4.5	16.8	27.3
Grand Island, NE Metro Area	3,322	2,510	32.3	$43,817	$34,418	27.3	2,480	19.4	8.1	5.0	D	10.2	16.8
Hall, NE	2,688	2,001	34.3	$43,625	$34,023	28.2	2,176	21.1	8.6	5.1	2.7	11.3	16.2
Howard, NE	268	220	21.9	$41,377	$34,958	18.4	98	2.9	7.0	5.1	D	7.0	38.1
Merrick, NE	366	290	26.4	$47,386	$36,948	28.3	205	8.7	3.7	3.9	1.3	D	12.8
Grand Junction, CO Metro Area	6,884	5,007	37.5	$44,935	$34,211	31.3	4,264	4.4	7.5	4.4	4.7	16.7	16.0
Mesa, CO	6,884	5,007	37.5	$44,935	$34,211	31.3	4,264	4.4	7.5	4.4	4.7	16.7	16.0
Grand Rapids-Kentwood, MI Metro Area	54,120	35,984	50.4	$50,463	$36,191	39.4	40,470	24.4	5.5	5.0	D	D	9.4
Ionia, MI	2,265	1,696	33.6	$35,273	$26,561	32.8	1,047	25.8	6.7	4.3	2.3	6.0	22.3
Kent, MI	35,262	23,498	50.1	$53,935	$38,970	38.4	29,206	20.6	5.5	5.9	7.0	15.5	7.4
Montcalm, MI	2,237	1,643	36.1	$34,972	$25,956	34.7	1,039	22.0	7.8	2.4	D	D	20.9
Ottawa, MI	14,356	9,146	57.0	$49,418	$34,629	42.7	9,178	36.5	5.0	2.7	4.5	5.2	13.0
Grants Pass, OR Metro Area	3,581	2,493	43.6	$40,977	$30,083	36.2	1,780	10.3	12.6	3.8	3.3	18.8	13.9
Josephine, OR	3,581	2,493	43.6	$40,977	$30,083	36.2	1,780	10.3	12.6	3.8	3.3	18.8	13.9
Great Falls, MT Metro Area	3,880	3,125	24.1	$47,518	$38,347	23.9	2,518	3.4	8.1	6.2	4.7	17.3	26.9
Cascade, MT	3,880	3,125	24.1	$47,518	$38,347	23.9	2,518	3.4	8.1	6.2	4.7	17.3	26.9
Greeley, CO Metro Area	14,512	8,412	72.5	$46,172	$33,094	39.5	8,951	11.2	5.6	3.3	3.8	7.0	11.3
Weld, CO	14,512	8,412	72.5	$46,172	$33,094	39.5	8,951	11.2	5.6	3.3	3.8	7.0	11.3
Green Bay, WI Metro Area	16,579	12,078	37.3	$51,553	$39,375	30.9	12,929	17.1	5.0	D	D	D	12.2
Brown, WI	13,912	10,022	38.8	$52,821	$40,333	31.0	11,901	16.5	5.0	8.5	6.2	14.1	11.6
Kewaunee, WI	942	748	25.9	$46,197	$36,395	26.9	444	25.1	4.1	D	3.5	D	17.0
Oconto, WI	1,725	1,308	31.9	$45,609	$34,683	31.5	584	23.3	6.0	1.8	D	11.2	20.2
Greensboro-High Point, NC Metro Area	33,157	24,945	32.9	$43,189	$34,396	25.6	24,349	16.6	6.0	6.4	6.6	11.6	11.6
Guilford, NC	24,482	17,911	36.7	$45,875	$36,584	25.4	20,250	14.2	5.9	7.2	7.4	12.0	11.2
Randolph, NC	5,306	4,197	26.4	$37,017	$29,562	25.2	2,688	31.3	5.7	2.3	2.5	8.6	12.9
Rockingham, NC	3,368	2,836	18.7	$37,137	$30,285	22.6	1,410	22.0	8.9	2.3	2.4	12.0	15.5
Greenville, NC Metro Area	7,411	5,499	34.8	$41,191	$32,569	26.5	5,231	10.1	6.4	3.3	3.6	10.9	37.1
Pitt, NC	7,411	5,499	34.8	$41,191	$32,569	26.5	5,231	10.1	6.4	3.3	3.6	10.9	37.1

Table C-3. Personal Income and Earnings by Industry—Continued

Metropolitan Statistical Area Metropolitan Division Component counties	Personal Income						Earnings 2018						
	Total (million dollars)			Per capita Personal Income			Total earnings (million dollars)	Earnings by Industry (percent)					
	2018	2010	Percent change 2010-2018	2018	2010	Percent change 2010-2018		Manu-facturing	Retail Trade	Finance and Insurance	Professional, Scienfic, and Technical Services	Health Care and Social Assistance	Government and Government Enterprises
Greenville-Anderson, SC Metro Area	40,085	27,099	47.9	$44,213	$32,822	34.7	28,184	16.3	6.3	6.1	D	D	15.0
Anderson, SC	7,961	5,728	39.0	$39,710	$30,611	29.7	4,149	26.1	8.2	2.1	4.3	8.1	20.6
Greenville, SC	25,014	16,128	55.1	$48,644	$35,629	36.5	20,314	12.5	5.8	7.6	9.9	10.2	11.5
Laurens, SC	2,319	1,828	26.9	$34,622	$27,478	26.0	1,351	41.3	4.1	1.4	D	D	16.6
Pickens, SC	4,791	3,415	40.3	$38,344	$28,618	34.0	2,369	16.9	7.9	2.2	3.4	8.7	34.1
Gulfport-Biloxi, MS Metro Area	15,340	13,255	15.7	$36,878	$34,047	8.3	10,783	D	6.0	2.4	5.6	7.7	29.0
Hancock, MS	1,669	1,472	13.4	$35,262	$33,386	5.6	1,057	7.8	4.4	1.5	11.8	5.7	38.5
Harrison, MS	7,709	6,526	18.1	$37,303	$34,740	7.4	5,756	D	7.1	2.7	4.6	8.7	34.1
Jackson, MS	5,373	4,766	12.7	$37,499	$34,176	9.7	3,732	37.2	4.6	2.1	5.7	7.2	18.6
Stone, MS	590	491	20.2	$31,516	$27,410	15.0	237	12.6	9.0	3.1	2.9	D	28.3
Hagerstown-Martinsburg, MD-WV Metro Area	12,547	9,456	32.7	$43,897	$35,045	25.3	7,084	10.0	8.2	6.3	4.2	13.7	19.9
Washington, MD	7,107	5,477	29.8	$47,092	$37,076	27.0	4,539	11.8	9.3	8.5	3.1	15.1	14.2
Berkeley, WV	4,826	3,485	38.5	$41,201	$33,317	23.7	2,376	7.0	6.1	2.2	6.3	11.9	30.6
Morgan, WV	614	494	24.4	$34,533	$28,219	22.4	170	6.4	7.4	3.5	3.6	D	21.2
Hammond, LA Metro Area	5,214	3,996	30.5	$38,974	$32,892	18.5	2,607	5.4	11.3	4.0	3.7	11.0	29.3
Tangipahoa, LA	5,214	3,996	30.5	$38,974	$32,892	18.5	2,607	5.4	11.3	4.0	3.7	11.0	29.3
Hanford-Corcoran, CA Metro Area	5,344	4,071	31.3	$35,306	$26,715	32.2	3,713	8.8	4.8	1.2	1.5	9.9	47.1
Kings, CA	5,344	4,071	31.3	$35,306	$26,715	32.2	3,713	8.8	4.8	1.2	1.5	9.9	47.1
Harrisburg-Carlisle, PA Metro Area	30,085	22,332	34.7	$52,354	$40,596	29.0	26,357	6.3	4.5	7.3	8.7	14.5	19.6
Cumberland, PA	13,864	9,980	38.9	$55,141	$42,304	30.3	10,618	5.8	5.5	7.7	11.2	12.2	15.3
Dauphin, PA	14,160	10,773	31.4	$51,100	$40,159	27.2	15,136	6.8	3.6	7.2	7.1	16.4	22.5
Perry, PA	2,062	1,579	30.6	$44,693	$34,381	30.0	603	5.1	7.6	3.5	3.6	6.5	21.2
Harrisonburg, VA Metro Area	5,373	3,843	39.8	$39,721	$30,644	29.6	4,202	17.4	6.1	2.7	4.8	11.3	17.9
Rockingham, VA	5,373	3,843	39.8	$39,721	$30,644	29.6	4,202	17.4	6.1	2.7	4.8	11.3	17.9
Harrisonburg City, VA	NA	NA	NA	NA	NA	NA	NA	NA	NA	NA	NA	NA	NA
Hartford-East Hartford-Middletown, CT Metro Area	77,610	61,473	26.3	$64,337	$50,634	27.1	61,216	D	4.7	15.4	9.0	11.9	14.9
Hartford, CT	57,894	45,736	26.6	$64,853	$51,089	26.9	51,534	11.7	4.4	17.7	9.5	11.7	13.2
Middlesex, CT	11,172	8,815	26.7	$68,673	$53,231	29.0	6,125	18.3	6.5	3.7	7.2	14.5	15.0
Tolland, CT	8,544	6,922	23.4	$56,614	$45,174	25.3	3,557	D	6.5	2.0	5.1	10.3	38.3
Hattiesburg, MS Metro Area	6,503	4,968	30.9	$38,648	$30,503	26.7	4,259	8.8	8.6	D	D	16.9	22.3
Covington, MS	674	540	24.9	$35,748	$27,559	29.7	347	18.4	5.9	1.8	D	5.6	18.3
Forrest, MS	2,917	2,353	24.0	$38,880	$31,372	23.9	2,624	9.3	6.7	2.9	2.9	16.6	27.9
Lamar, MS	2,531	1,762	43.6	$40,529	$31,443	28.9	1,133	1.4	14.2	5.4	7.0	22.2	11.5
Perry, MS	381	313	21.8	$31,934	$25,571	24.9	154	32.4	5.5	D	D	9.3	14.9
Hickory-Lenoir-Morganton, NC Metro Area	14,681	11,081	32.5	$39,849	$30,309	31.5	9,443	27.7	7.0	1.9	D	D	14.6
Alexander, NC	1,398	1,029	35.9	$37,438	$27,627	35.5	562	32.0	4.2	2.3	D	D	20.1
Burke, NC	3,187	2,481	28.5	$35,265	$27,394	28.7	1,666	25.9	5.4	1.9	2.6	17.5	24.3
Caldwell, NC	2,902	2,247	29.1	$35,374	$27,063	30.7	1,565	27.5	5.9	1.7	2.2	10.5	14.4
Catawba, NC	7,194	5,324	35.1	$45,342	$34,400	31.8	5,651	27.8	8.0	1.9	4.7	9.6	11.2
Hilton Head Island-Bluffton, SC Metro Area	11,549	7,184	60.8	$53,056	$38,260	38.7	5,678	1.2	8.6	4.1	D	8.9	29.1
Beaufort, SC	10,702	6,630	61.4	$56,711	$40,715	39.3	5,118	1.0	7.9	4.3	9.2	8.4	30.6
Jasper, SC	847	554	52.9	$29,242	$22,225	31.6	559	3.6	14.8	2.6	D	13.5	15.1
Hinesville, GA Metro Area	2,716	2,184	24.4	$33,744	$28,248	19.5	2,611	D	D	D	D	D	73.4
Liberty, GA	2,202	1,825	20.6	$35,805	$29,080	23.1	2,540	8.4	2.8	1.1	D	1.8	73.9
Long, GA	514	359	43.3	$27,071	$24,658	9.8	71	D	D	D	D	D	57.1
Homosassa Springs, FL Metro Area	5,609	4,323	29.8	$37,920	$30,620	23.8	2,007	1.7	11.3	3.2	5.1	21.6	12.6
Citrus, FL	5,609	4,323	29.8	$37,920	$30,620	23.8	2,007	1.7	11.3	3.2	5.1	21.6	12.6
Hot Springs, AR Metro Area	3,967	3,047	30.2	$40,004	$31,721	26.1	2,174	7.4	10.6	3.8	3.8	22.3	13.1
Garland, AR	3,967	3,047	30.2	$40,004	$31,721	26.1	2,174	7.4	10.6	3.8	3.8	22.3	13.1
Houma-Thibodaux, LA Metro Area	9,229	8,198	12.6	$44,127	$39,365	12.1	6,620	8.9	5.6	2.1	5.3	9.7	12.4
Lafourche, LA	4,621	3,914	18.1	$47,096	$40,447	16.4	2,998	7.3	4.4	1.5	3.0	6.3	15.6
Terrebonne, LA	4,608	4,284	7.6	$41,504	$38,426	8.0	3,622	10.1	6.6	2.6	7.1	12.5	9.7
Houston-The Woodlands-Sugar Land, TX Metro Area	392,394	267,613	46.6	$56,077	$44,997	24.6	312,329	9.9	4.5	5.9	11.4	D	10.2
Austin, TX	1,520	1,114	36.5	$50,702	$39,287	29.1	784	13.8	11.2	5.9	6.8	4.2	11.4
Brazoria, TX	17,488	11,609	50.6	$47,239	$36,917	28.0	9,426	21.2	5.8	2.0	5.0	8.3	13.9
Chambers, TX	2,279	1,388	64.1	$53,673	$39,167	37.0	1,375	28.6	3.3	1.0	4.7	D	11.2
Fort Bend, TX	45,333	27,609	64.2	$57,540	$46,775	23.0	16,916	13.6	8.0	4.3	9.1	9.6	11.1
Galveston, TX	17,498	11,900	47.0	$51,785	$40,689	27.3	8,304	13.4	6.6	5.8	5.8	6.3	28.9
Harris, TX	265,351	187,913	41.2	$56,474	$45,745	23.5	254,899	9.2	4.0	6.2	12.2	7.3	9.3
Liberty, TX	3,214	2,144	49.9	$37,237	$28,262	31.8	1,312	9.2	7.5	2.6	D	7.0	22.1
Montgomery, TX	37,586	22,559	66.6	$63,605	$49,125	29.5	18,093	5.9	5.8	5.9	10.2	8.5	10.2
Waller, TX	2,125	1,376	54.4	$39,995	$31,618	26.5	1,219	29.0	3.7	1.8	D	3.1	22.6
Huntington-Ashland, WV-KY-OH Metro Area	14,477	11,948	21.2	$40,299	$32,200	25.2	8,798	D	6.9	D	D	D	16.5
Boyd, KY	1,878	1,634	14.9	$39,746	$32,933	20.7	1,621	15.3	7.0	2.7	5.8	23.7	12.2
Carter, KY	833	715	16.5	$30,847	$25,759	19.8	287	12.3	10.3	4.1	3.0	7.7	23.1
Greenup, KY	1,444	1,214	19.0	$40,933	$32,905	24.4	544	10.9	5.9	2.6	D	25.1	15.0
Lawrence, OH	2,315	1,887	22.7	$38,673	$30,229	27.9	745	D	8.6	2.2	2.4	17.2	24.1
Cabell, WV	4,003	3,309	21.0	$42,939	$34,357	25.0	3,316	10.6	7.7	3.2	5.2	27.7	16.0
Putnam, WV	2,661	2,076	28.2	$46,941	$37,317	25.8	1,675	13.1	5.0	2.6	6.2	9.7	8.6
Wayne, WV	1,344	1,114	20.6	$33,637	$26,239	28.2	610	11.4	4.8	D	1.7	D	41.4
Huntsville, AL Metro Area	22,947	16,819	36.4	$49,595	$40,115	23.6	18,622	12.3	5.3	2.1	23.7	6.9	27.9
Limestone, AL	4,092	2,799	46.2	$42,546	$33,652	26.4	1,823	14.4	8.1	1.6	4.1	4.1	31.6
Madison, AL	18,856	14,020	34.5	$51,445	$41,715	23.3	16,799	12.1	5.0	2.2	25.8	7.2	27.5

Table C-3. Personal Income and Earnings by Industry—*Continued*

Metropolitan Statistical Area Metropolitan Division Component counties	Personal Income						Earnings 2018						
	Total (million dollars)			Per capita Personal Income			Total earnings (million dollars)	Earnings by Industry (percent)					
	2018	2010	Percent change 2010-2018	2018	2010	Percent change 2010-2018		Manu-facturing	Retail Trade	Finance and Insurance	Professional, Scienfic, and Technical Services	Health Care and Social Assistance	Government and Government Enterprises
Idaho Falls, ID Metro Area	6,772	4,390	54.2	$45,477	$32,811	38.6	4,848	7.8	13.4	D	18.1	D	10.1
Bonneville, ID	5,643	3,594	57.0	$48,287	$34,332	40.6	3,515	8.9	17.3	4.0	5.6	16.5	11.8
Butte, ID	102	83	22.2	$38,961	$28,567	36.4	896	0.4	0.2	D	74.4	D	1.8
Jefferson, ID	1,027	713	44.0	$34,900	$27,210	28.3	437	14.0	9.3	2.4	3.2	4.6	14.0
Indianapolis-Carmel-Anderson, IN Metro Area	110,997	78,249	41.9	$54,179	$41,344	31.0	86,078	10.8	5.6	6.8	D	D	10.9
Boone, IN	4,926	2,914	69.1	$73,531	$51,197	43.6	2,067	8.6	6.7	3.6	9.8	6.5	12.0
Brown, IN	713	521	36.7	$46,785	$34,286	36.5	172	6.5	8.6	2.1	7.3	9.6	20.7
Hamilton, IN	24,663	14,899	65.5	$74,717	$53,883	38.7	12,283	4.4	6.5	15.9	11.9	10.4	7.2
Hancock, IN	3,850	2,721	41.5	$50,422	$38,740	30.2	1,671	16.4	5.5	3.0	15.7	6.4	14.9
Hendricks, IN	8,291	5,516	50.3	$49,641	$37,807	31.3	4,327	6.8	11.5	2.3	D	7.1	13.8
Johnson, IN	7,551	5,204	45.1	$48,332	$37,100	30.3	3,475	12.0	9.4	4.4	5.2	12.9	13.3
Madison, IN	4,949	3,831	29.2	$38,172	$29,108	31.1	2,442	15.7	6.2	4.4	2.6	16.6	14.8
Marion, IN	49,586	37,742	31.4	$51,940	$41,723	24.5	56,638	11.4	4.6	5.8	9.6	14.2	10.9
Morgan, IN	3,098	2,361	31.2	$44,183	$34,141	29.4	1,018	17.3	7.2	4.0	D	9.2	13.6
Putnam, IN	1,416	1,068	32.5	$37,479	$28,178	33.0	777	23.0	5.2	3.0	1.8	D	16.4
Shelby, IN	1,956	1,470	33.0	$43,854	$33,180	32.2	1,207	33.1	4.8	1.7	2.6	6.3	13.6
Iowa City, IA Metro Area	9,239	6,127	50.8	$53,280	$40,040	33.1	7,112	6.8	5.3	2.9	3.6	7.3	43.9
Johnson, IA	7,967	5,278	50.9	$52,672	$40,188	31.1	6,402	6.2	5.3	2.9	3.6	7.4	47.3
Washington, IA	1,272	849	49.8	$57,438	$39,148	46.7	710	12.2	5.1	2.5	3.1	5.6	13.3
Ithaca, NY Metro Area	4,655	3,557	30.8	$45,282	$34,971	29.5	4,018	6.9	4.4	2.5	7.2	D	12.4
Tompkins, NY	4,655	3,557	30.8	$45,282	$34,971	29.5	4,018	6.9	4.4	2.5	7.2	D	12.4
Jackson, MI Metro Area	6,326	4,860	30.2	$39,832	$30,351	31.2	4,105	19.3	6.0	2.9	4.1	15.5	14.0
Jackson, MI	6,326	4,860	30.2	$39,832	$30,351	31.2	4,105	19.3	6.0	2.9	4.1	15.5	14.0
Jackson, MS Metro Area	26,166	21,059	24.3	$43,772	$35,797	22.3	18,305	8.2	7.1	6.4	6.9	13.6	21.6
Copiah, MS	948	809	17.1	$33,203	$27,497	20.8	411	30.7	6.9	1.5	2.1	D	19.5
Hinds, MS	9,320	8,417	10.7	$39,311	$34,254	14.8	8,705	3.6	4.8	6.0	6.5	16.3	31.7
Holmes, MS	500	473	5.7	$28,371	$24,379	16.4	166	16.8	8.1	5.0	6.0	D	39.6
Madison, MS	6,764	4,667	44.9	$64,033	$48,853	31.1	4,071	16.5	9.4	9.5	11.8	9.6	7.0
Rankin, MS	6,873	5,187	32.5	$44,661	$36,396	22.7	4,151	7.4	9.8	5.6	4.5	12.0	12.5
Simpson, MS	991	814	21.8	$37,036	$29,573	25.2	406	2.0	7.1	4.3	2.2	D	21.9
Yazoo, MS	770	691	11.5	$27,275	$24,553	11.1	395	13.4	5.7	2.1	1.3	D	41.6
Jackson, TN Metro Area	7,171	5,784	24.0	$40,226	$32,175	25.0	5,066	19.1	8.2	2.7	D	12.6	22.3
Chester, TN	581	454	28.0	$33,642	$26,416	27.4	237	14.3	8.7	2.0	2.7	D	25.2
Crockett, TN	524	464	12.9	$36,560	$31,802	15.0	245	33.4	18.3	1.9	2.9	D	19.3
Gibson, TN	1,896	1,542	22.9	$38,654	$31,017	24.6	863	20.7	10.5	3.5	D	D	19.5
Madison, TN	4,170	3,323	25.5	$42,720	$33,825	26.3	3,721	18.1	7.0	2.6	3.4	13.9	23.0
Jacksonville, FL Metro Area	76,357	52,231	46.2	$49,754	$38,721	28.5	52,159	5.4	6.9	11.3	8.8	13.1	13.6
Baker, FL	916	695	31.9	$32,313	$25,663	25.9	407	1.7	8.5	2.1	1.4	9.6	37.9
Clay, FL	9,271	6,490	42.9	$42,909	$33,903	26.6	3,211	3.2	9.7	3.1	9.9	18.9	14.7
Duval, FL	43,874	31,791	38.0	$46,174	$36,726	25.7	41,545	5.4	6.3	12.7	8.8	13.0	13.3
Nassau, FL	4,968	3,182	56.1	$57,877	$43,287	33.7	1,544	7.9	7.6	2.9	6.9	8.6	18.6
St. Johns, FL	17,328	10,073	72.0	$68,149	$52,671	29.4	5,453	6.9	8.9	7.9	9.6	11.3	12.2
Jacksonville, NC Metro Area	9,121	7,827	16.5	$46,142	$41,879	10.2	6,747	0.8	4.2	1.1	1.8	3.0	73.0
Onslow, NC	9,121	7,827	16.5	$46,142	$41,879	10.2	6,747	0.8	4.2	1.1	1.8	3.0	73.0
Janesville-Beloit, WI Metro Area	7,211	5,420	33.0	$44,204	$33,817	30.7	4,592	16.4	6.2	2.8	3.1	15.8	14.2
Rock, WI	7,211	5,420	33.0	$44,204	$33,817	30.7	4,592	16.4	6.2	2.8	3.1	15.8	14.2
Jefferson City, MO Metro Area	6,637	5,232	26.8	$43,802	$34,890	25.5	4,911	9.7	6.2	D	4.9	8.9	31.2
Callaway, MO	1,737	1,387	25.2	$38,686	$31,312	23.6	936	15.9	5.2	1.7	3.9	D	21.9
Cole, MO	3,670	2,904	26.4	$47,790	$38,134	25.3	3,423	4.8	6.5	5.2	5.8	11.1	36.0
Moniteau, MO	605	468	29.4	$37,533	$29,925	25.4	261	16.2	6.3	D	1.5	D	20.8
Osage, MO	625	473	32.1	$45,582	$34,106	33.6	291	42.4	5.3	2.4	0.9	3.9	13.5
Johnson City, TN Metro Area	8,182	6,326	29.3	$40,360	$31,788	27.0	5,038	11.0	7.9	4.8	D	D	21.8
Carter, TN	1,949	1,571	24.1	$34,579	$27,390	26.2	705	11.6	9.0	4.4	4.1	D	19.4
Unicoi, TN	665	556	19.6	$37,423	$30,401	23.1	346	38.9	4.7	1.5	D	7.9	15.1
Washington, TN	5,569	4,199	32.6	$43,299	$34,038	27.2	3,987	8.5	8.0	5.1	5.0	21.7	22.7
Johnstown, PA Metro Area	5,720	4,713	21.4	$43,420	$32,853	32.2	3,122	9.6	7.3	5.2	5.2	21.9	17.3
Cambria, PA	5,720	4,713	21.4	$43,420	$32,853	32.2	3,122	9.6	7.3	5.2	5.2	21.9	17.3
Jonesboro, AR Metro Area	4,849	3,611	34.3	$36,588	$29,782	22.9	3,382	14.3	7.5	3.0	3.2	22.7	15.7
Craighead, AR	4,074	2,932	39.0	$37,531	$30,307	23.8	3,044	14.4	7.7	3.1	3.4	24.0	15.4
Poinsett, AR	775	679	14.0	$32,315	$27,711	16.6	338	13.2	6.2	2.2	1.0	10.6	18.5
Joplin, MO Metro Area	7,114	5,398	31.8	$39,765	$30,700	29.5	4,921	22.7	7.6	2.8	3.4	15.6	10.6
Jasper, MO	4,822	3,575	34.9	$39,973	$30,384	31.6	3,650	25.6	7.7	2.9	3.9	10.7	10.3
Newton, MO	2,292	1,823	25.7	$39,334	$31,339	25.5	1,271	14.2	7.4	2.5	2.1	29.7	11.5
Kahului-Wailuku-Lahaina, HI Metro Area	8,204	5,537	48.2	$49,040	$35,699	37.4	5,638	1.2	8.0	1.3	3.3	10.0	13.5
Maui, HI	8,204	5,537	48.2	$49,040	$35,699	37.4	5,638	1.2	8.0	1.3	3.3	10.0	13.5
Kalamazoo-Portage, MI Metro Area	12,905	9,129	41.4	$48,723	$36,409	33.8	9,333	23.2	6.2	6.1	5.5	D	12.8
Kalamazoo, MI	12,905	9,129	41.4	$48,723	$36,409	33.8	9,333	23.2	6.2	6.1	5.5	D	12.8
Kankakee, IL Metro Area	4,543	3,721	22.1	$41,290	$32,804	25.9	2,834	22.4	6.5	2.5	3.2	16.8	15.9
Kankakee, IL	4,543	3,721	22.1	$41,290	$32,804	25.9	2,834	22.4	6.5	2.5	3.2	16.8	15.9
Kansas City, MO-KS Metro Area	115,303	82,755	39.3	$53,788	$41,103	30.9	87,372	7.5	D	8.4	13.2	10.9	13.7
Johnson, KS	44,225	29,474	50.0	$74,010	$54,015	37.0	31,634	4.8	5.1	11.3	13.3	11.2	6.9
Leavenworth, KS	3,486	2,656	31.2	$42,851	$34,720	23.4	2,084	4.2	3.5	3.2	5.5	4.6	59.9
Linn, KS	363	288	26.3	$37,267	$29,890	24.7	143	5.8	6.5	2.9	2.1	D	26.4
Miami, KS	1,642	1,192	37.7	$48,748	$36,248	34.5	596	7.0	6.6	3.6	4.1	10.9	20.8

Table C-3. Personal Income and Earnings by Industry—*Continued*

Metropolitan Statistical Area / Metropolitan Division / Component counties	Personal Income Total (million dollars) 2018	2010	Percent change 2010-2018	Per capita Personal Income 2018	2010	Percent change 2010-2018	Total earnings (million dollars)	Manufacturing	Retail Trade	Finance and Insurance	Professional, Scienfic, and Technical Services	Health Care and Social Assistance	Government and Government Enterprises
Wyandotte, KS	5,508	4,580	20.2	$33,315	$29,056	14.7	7,072	12.7	D	1.3	5.8	12.9	20.5
Bates, MO	634	517	22.7	$38,864	$30,343	28.1	240	3.8	9.3	D	5.5	D	26.8
Caldwell, MO	340	266	27.7	$37,301	$28,199	32.3	115	1.8	18.2	D	2.1	5.2	25.0
Cass, MO	4,949	3,547	39.5	$47,151	$35,557	32.6	1,657	7.6	9.6	3.2	4.3	9.3	18.2
Clay, MO	11,919	8,831	35.0	$48,381	$39,658	22.0	7,716	16.7	6.8	3.0	13.1	7.9	15.1
Clinton, MO	880	670	31.3	$42,988	$32,325	33.0	235	6.0	5.7	4.7	D	D	24.6
Jackson, MO	32,952	24,861	32.5	$47,054	$36,841	27.7	31,599	6.5	4.3	9.7	17.3	11.9	15.2
Lafayette, MO	1,373	1,077	27.5	$42,119	$32,261	30.6	504	10.7	7.4	3.8	D	D	22.5
Platte, MO	6,064	4,053	49.6	$58,878	$45,181	30.3	3,501	11.9	7.2	4.3	5.8	7.2	10.0
Ray, MO	968	742	30.4	$42,305	$31,587	33.9	276	15.4	9.2	2.5	3.8	D	27.3
Kennewick-Richland, WA Metro Area	13,110	9,662	35.7	$44,256	$37,808	17.1	9,545	6.3	6.3	2.2	12.3	10.9	17.8
Benton, WA	9,582	7,233	32.5	$47,465	$40,988	15.8	7,214	5.4	5.8	2.6	15.6	12.0	16.6
Franklin, WA	3,528	2,429	45.2	$37,390	$30,713	21.7	2,332	9.2	7.9	1.1	2.2	7.4	21.7
Killeen-Temple, TX Metro Area	18,805	15,167	24.0	$41,634	$37,149	12.1	12,928	4.0	5.8	2.5	3.9	D	45.3
Bell, TX	15,212	12,133	25.4	$42,773	$38,781	10.3	11,581	3.9	5.4	2.2	3.3	15.1	46.6
Coryell, TX	2,543	2,191	16.1	$33,996	$28,960	17.4	1,062	3.9	6.6	4.9	10.1	5.4	37.8
Lampasas, TX	1,050	843	24.5	$49,457	$42,661	15.9	284	8.9	18.3	4.8	4.8	D	20.5
Kingsport-Bristol, TN-VA Metro Area	12,277	10,079	21.8	$40,042	$32,568	22.9	7,776	24.9	7.5	2.9	D	14.8	12.9
Hawkins, TN	1,933	1,579	22.4	$34,188	$27,757	23.2	851	36.8	5.0	1.6	D	D	17.7
Sullivan, TN	6,718	5,351	25.5	$42,606	$34,137	24.8	5,003	25.2	7.2	3.0	4.0	17.0	9.5
Scott, VA	727	627	16.0	$33,769	$27,105	24.6	251	20.3	7.5	2.1	1.6	D	28.4
Washington, VA	2,900	2,523	15.0	$40,912	$34,686	17.9	1,672	18.5	9.8	3.6	3.9	11.9	18.1
Bristol City, VA	NA	NA	NA	NA	NA	NA	NA	NA	NA	NA	NA	NA	NA
Kingston, NY Metro Area	9,013	6,977	29.2	$50,462	$38,247	31.9	4,480	6.7	7.8	3.1	4.9	13.8	28.0
Ulster, NY	9,013	6,977	29.2	$50,462	$38,247	31.9	4,480	6.7	7.8	3.1	4.9	13.8	28.0
Knoxville, TN Metro Area	39,343	28,329	38.9	$45,739	$34,718	31.7	28,589	11.1	7.6	D	10.4	D	14.1
Anderson, TN	3,201	2,585	23.8	$41,853	$34,417	21.6	3,174	32.3	4.5	3.0	15.1	9.2	12.8
Blount, TN	5,647	3,929	43.7	$42,991	$31,891	34.8	3,491	20.2	8.5	4.7	6.4	9.0	14.1
Campbell, TN	1,345	1,106	21.6	$33,967	$27,140	25.2	553	14.8	8.8	2.9	D	D	20.6
Knox, TN	23,143	16,151	43.3	$49,738	$37,305	33.3	18,246	5.3	8.3	5.1	7.8	17.1	13.9
Loudon, TN	2,573	1,775	44.9	$48,491	$36,456	33.0	1,126	24.8	7.4	3.1	2.8	8.1	13.2
Morgan, TN	634	533	19.0	$29,380	$24,205	21.4	183	10.2	4.1	2.4	D	7.4	39.3
Roane, TN	2,178	1,779	22.4	$40,980	$32,839	24.8	1,628	4.4	3.8	0.7	49.5	6.1	13.7
Union, TN	624	472	32.2	$31,693	$24,695	28.3	188	17.1	6.4	D	3.8	4.3	23.7
Kokomo, IN Metro Area	3,446	2,578	33.7	$41,842	$31,153	34.3	2,680	45.5	6.1	2.9	2.1	13.1	9.5
Howard, IN	3,446	2,578	33.7	$41,842	$31,153	34.3	2,680	45.5	6.1	2.9	2.1	13.1	9.5
La Crosse-Onalaska, WI-MN Metro Area	6,897	5,081	35.8	$50,412	$37,942	32.9	5,159	11.5	5.9	6.0	D	22.1	15.2
Houston, MN	973	738	31.7	$52,354	$38,808	34.9	329	9.7	4.9	3.9	D	10.9	19.4
La Crosse, WI	5,924	4,342	36.4	$50,107	$37,799	32.6	4,831	11.6	5.9	6.2	4.2	22.8	14.9
Lafayette, LA Metro Area	21,666	18,025	20.2	$44,273	$38,547	14.9	14,163	8.6	7.1	3.6	7.8	14.1	12.3
Acadia, LA	2,320	1,959	18.4	$37,304	$31,660	17.8	946	7.6	7.1	3.2	4.7	11.9	16.8
Iberia, LA	2,786	2,596	7.3	$39,270	$35,509	10.6	1,844	14.3	6.9	3.3	3.2	7.6	14.5
Lafayette, LA	12,205	9,776	24.9	$50,273	$43,983	14.3	9,676	6.7	6.9	3.8	9.5	16.5	10.3
St. Martin, LA	2,019	1,703	18.5	$37,645	$32,590	15.5	794	23.3	9.0	2.5	5.0	8.7	14.4
Vermilion, LA	2,336	1,991	17.3	$39,042	$34,268	13.9	903	4.9	7.7	3.1	4.4	8.5	22.0
Lafayette-West Lafayette, IN Metro Area	9,197	6,557	40.3	$39,969	$31,121	28.4	7,036	D	4.9	2.7	5.7	D	24.3
Benton, IN	370	298	24.3	$42,775	$33,591	27.3	183	12.9	3.8	7.2	2.2	2.3	16.0
Carroll, IN	890	666	33.5	$44,201	$32,988	34.0	365	D	4.3	2.4	2.1	D	11.3
Tippecanoe, IN	7,562	5,296	42.8	$39,169	$30,596	28.0	6,339	23.4	5.0	2.7	6.1	13.3	25.6
Warren, IN	375	296	26.6	$45,419	$34,792	30.5	149	22.5	2.4	D	1.5	10.6	12.3
Lake Charles, LA Metro Area	10,296	6,907	49.1	$49,011	$34,543	41.9	9,103	16.9	5.9	D	5.9	10.9	10.9
Calcasieu, LA	9,946	6,672	49.1	$48,968	$34,568	41.7	7,763	18.6	6.9	2.3	6.4	10.9	12.2
Cameron, LA	350	234	49.7	$50,280	$33,846	48.6	1,340	6.7	0.3	D	2.8	0.4	3.5
Lake Havasu City-Kingman, AZ Metro Area	6,946	5,124	35.6	$33,148	$25,582	29.6	2,997	6.5	13.8	2.7	3.2	19.9	16.9
Mohave, AZ	6,946	5,124	35.6	$33,148	$25,582	29.6	2,997	6.5	13.8	2.7	3.2	19.9	16.9
Lakeland-Winter Haven, FL Metro Area	25,108	18,374	36.7	$35,463	$30,464	16.4	14,379	8.9	8.0	6.1	4.2	14.0	12.8
Polk, FL	25,108	18,374	36.7	$35,463	$30,464	16.4	14,379	8.9	8.0	6.1	4.2	14.0	12.8
Lancaster, PA Metro Area	28,626	19,775	44.8	$52,664	$38,005	38.6	19,660	15.3	7.5	3.9	5.7	12.9	8.2
Lancaster, PA	28,626	19,775	44.8	$52,664	$38,005	38.6	19,660	15.3	7.5	3.9	5.7	12.9	8.2
Lansing-East Lansing, MI Metro Area	23,000	17,634	30.4	$41,812	$32,967	26.8	16,122	11.3	5.6	7.7	D	12.5	26.1
Clinton, MI	3,690	2,634	40.1	$46,518	$34,936	33.2	1,172	11.8	8.4	3.9	D	6.9	14.5
Eaton, MI	4,689	3,562	31.6	$42,693	$33,053	29.2	2,933	18.1	6.9	16.1	3.1	5.4	14.4
Ingham, MI	11,932	9,346	27.7	$40,761	$33,247	22.6	10,950	9.2	4.7	6.3	7.3	14.9	31.1
Shiawassee, MI	2,689	2,092	28.6	$39,435	$29,617	33.1	1,068	13.8	8.8	2.7	4.7	13.5	19.9
Laredo, TX Metro Area	8,729	6,514	34.0	$31,635	$25,912	22.1	6,143	0.6	7.2	2.5	3.5	10.8	27.5
Webb, TX	8,729	6,514	34.0	$31,635	$25,912	22.1	6,143	0.6	7.2	2.5	3.5	10.8	27.5
Las Cruces, NM Metro Area	7,955	6,344	25.4	$36,570	$30,196	21.1	4,678	3.4	5.8	2.7	6.4	16.0	29.7
Dona Ana, NM	7,955	6,344	25.4	$36,570	$30,196	21.1	4,678	3.4	5.8	2.7	6.4	16.0	29.7
Las Vegas-Henderson-Paradise, NV Metro Area	105,088	69,602	51.0	$47,090	$35,645	32.1	70,869	2.6	7.2	4.1	6.8	9.3	14.8
Clark, NV	105,088	69,602	51.0	$47,090	$35,645	32.1	70,869	2.6	7.2	4.1	6.8	9.3	14.8
Lawrence, KS Metro Area	5,300	3,761	40.9	$43,642	$33,819	29.0	3,196	9.0	6.4	2.8	8.5	7.8	32.7
Douglas, KS	5,300	3,761	40.9	$43,642	$33,819	29.0	3,196	9.0	6.4	2.8	8.5	7.8	32.7
Lawton, OK Metro Area	5,238	4,686	11.8	$41,509	$35,617	16.5	3,606	D	5.1	2.7	3.8	5.8	53.2
Comanche, OK	4,997	4,464	11.9	$41,497	$35,600	16.6	3,509	8.5	5.1	2.7	3.8	5.9	53.4
Cotton, OK	241	222	8.7	$41,766	$35,956	16.2	97	D	4.8	2.7	1.9	3.2	46.5

Table C-3. Personal Income and Earnings by Industry—Continued

Metropolitan Statistical Area Metropolitan Division Component counties	Personal Income Total (million dollars) 2018	2010	Percent change 2010-2018	Per capita Personal Income 2018	2010	Percent change 2010-2018	Total earnings (million dollars)	Manu-facturing	Retail Trade	Finance and Insurance	Professional, Scienfic, and Technical Services	Health Care and Social Assistance	Government and Government Enterprises
Lebanon, PA Metro Area	6,833	4,936	38.4	$48,352	$36,936	30.9	3,619	17.6	7.7	2.1	3.1	11.8	18.8
Lebanon, PA	6,833	4,936	38.4	$48,352	$36,936	30.9	3,619	17.6	7.7	2.1	3.1	11.8	18.8
Lewiston, ID-WA Metro Area	2,859	2,143	33.4	$45,368	$35,105	29.2	1,780	17.3	9.0	6.0	3.2	17.6	18.2
Nez Perce, ID	1,794	1,363	31.6	$44,397	$34,669	28.1	1,342	20.8	7.7	7.1	2.9	16.1	18.5
Asotin, WA	1,065	780	36.6	$47,104	$35,893	31.2	438	6.6	13.0	2.7	4.1	22.0	17.3
Lewiston-Auburn, ME Metro Area	4,472	3,663	22.1	$41,528	$34,004	22.1	3,105	10.7	7.7	4.7	6.1	20.6	11.7
Androscoggin, ME	4,472	3,663	22.1	$41,528	$34,004	22.1	3,105	10.7	7.7	4.7	6.1	20.6	11.7
Lexington-Fayette, KY Metro Area	24,737	17,583	40.7	$47,875	$37,141	28.9	18,921	13.8	5.9	3.4	D	11.5	20.9
Bourbon, KY	896	628	42.6	$44,388	$31,459	41.1	492	13.1	8.2	3.6	2.4	7.9	10.8
Clark, KY	1,444	1,151	25.5	$39,848	$32,330	23.3	902	22.3	6.5	2.5	5.2	11.7	10.5
Fayette, KY	16,247	11,683	39.1	$50,180	$39,358	27.5	13,765	7.4	5.9	4.0	8.8	13.0	25.0
Jessamine, KY	2,344	1,582	48.2	$43,470	$32,486	33.8	1,098	16.8	11.6	1.8	D	6.8	12.5
Scott, KY	2,432	1,604	51.6	$43,409	$33,926	28.0	1,971	51.1	3.0	1.1	2.7	D	6.7
Woodford, KY	1,373	935	46.8	$51,753	$37,358	38.5	693	19.1	4.3	1.9	5.6	D	12.6
Lima, OH Metro Area	4,396	3,484	26.2	$42,816	$32,758	30.7	3,483	24.9	6.1	2.3	3.0	20.4	12.3
Allen, OH	4,396	3,484	26.2	$42,816	$32,758	30.7	3,483	24.9	6.1	2.3	3.0	20.4	12.3
Lincoln, NE Metro Area	16,691	11,691	42.8	$49,886	$38,590	29.3	12,583	8.2	5.7	7.3	7.8	D	21.2
Lancaster, NE	15,829	11,050	43.2	$49,889	$38,616	29.2	12,138	7.8	5.7	7.4	8.0	13.4	21.4
Seward, NE	863	641	34.7	$49,832	$38,153	30.6	445	19.5	4.9	4.4	2.8	D	16.2
Little Rock-North Little Rock-Conway, AR Metro Area	33,729	25,885	30.3	$45,512	$36,857	23.5	23,946	6.1	6.7	D	8.5	13.8	22.2
Faulkner, AR	4,692	3,536	32.7	$37,598	$31,007	21.3	2,502	8.6	8.4	3.0	13.3	14.3	17.8
Grant, AR	695	551	26.1	$38,201	$30,812	24.0	252	33.4	7.3	D	2.3	D	17.8
Lonoke, AR	2,855	2,207	29.4	$38,764	$32,109	20.7	801	12.5	8.5	5.5	3.8	9.5	19.6
Perry, AR	361	304	18.7	$34,877	$29,126	19.7	82	2.5	3.9	1.9	2.9	D	23.6
Pulaski, AR	20,100	15,708	28.0	$51,185	$40,952	25.0	18,845	5.2	6.0	8.2	8.5	13.8	23.5
Saline, AR	5,026	3,579	40.4	$41,397	$33,250	24.5	1,465	6.3	12.8	3.2	4.0	16.7	15.9
Logan, UT-ID Metro Area	5,447	3,565	52.8	$38,690	$28,255	36.9	3,733	20.1	6.9	3.6	D	D	19.3
Franklin, ID	495	335	47.6	$36,064	$26,233	37.5	216	8.4	8.6	2.2	D	D	22.2
Cache, UT	4,952	3,230	53.3	$38,974	$28,483	36.8	3,517	20.9	6.8	3.7	8.6	9.0	19.1
Longview, TX Metro Area	11,912	10,224	16.5	$41,630	$36,448	14.2	8,233	15.4	6.3	3.9	5.1	D	10.6
Gregg, TX	5,616	5,105	10.0	$45,401	$41,851	8.5	5,031	12.3	7.4	3.3	5.8	14.6	9.0
Harrison, TX	2,797	2,300	21.6	$41,917	$34,968	19.9	1,768	29.5	4.5	4.6	3.4	D	10.3
Rusk, TX	1,987	1,614	23.1	$36,485	$30,239	20.7	952	11.1	4.8	5.9	3.7	8.0	14.9
Upshur, TX	1,512	1,205	25.5	$36,645	$30,598	19.8	482	4.7	5.0	3.8	6.7	D	20.8
Longview, WA Metro Area	4,903	3,611	35.8	$44,990	$35,282	27.5	2,978	21.5	6.4	2.1	2.8	12.7	15.6
Cowlitz, WA	4,903	3,611	35.8	$44,990	$35,282	27.5	2,978	21.5	6.4	2.1	2.8	12.7	15.6
Los Angeles-Long Beach-Anaheim, CA Metro Area	849,493	578,373	46.9	$63,913	$45,048	41.9	615,567	8.3	5.2	6.8	11.3	9.6	13.5
Anaheim-Santa Ana-Irvine, CA Div	220,685	150,143	47.0	$69,268	$49,773	39.2	160,226	10.8	5.4	9.4	11.7	8.9	10.3
Orange, CA	220,685	150,143	47.0	$69,268	$49,773	39.2	160,226	10.8	5.4	9.4	11.7	8.9	10.3
Los Angeles-Long Beach-Glendale, CA Div	628,809	428,230	46.8	$62,224	$43,597	42.7	455,341	7.5	5.1	5.9	11.2	9.9	14.6
Los Angeles, CA	628,809	428,230	46.8	$62,224	$43,597	42.7	455,341	7.5	5.1	5.9	11.2	9.9	14.6
Louisville/Jefferson County, KY-IN Metro Area	63,373	45,592	39.0	$50,101	$37,846	32.4	46,821	14.0	5.2	9.4	7.5	12.6	11.1
Clark, IN	5,136	3,965	29.5	$43,763	$35,860	22.0	3,367	18.1	7.7	5.5	2.9	12.2	11.3
Floyd, IN	4,315	2,882	49.8	$55,480	$38,570	43.8	2,042	20.4	5.4	3.2	5.7	21.5	11.9
Harrison, IN	1,689	1,310	29.0	$41,862	$33,302	25.7	614	17.5	7.6	3.9	2.2	D	18.9
Washington, IN	1,065	792	34.5	$38,123	$27,986	36.2	393	25.2	9.5	2.7	1.7	D	15.3
Bullitt, KY	3,319	2,352	41.1	$40,935	$31,569	29.7	1,483	14.2	4.8	1.8	2.0	4.5	11.5
Henry, KY	612	465	31.5	$37,981	$30,245	25.6	179	18.7	4.0	2.8	D	D	25.0
Jefferson, KY	40,018	29,000	38.0	$51,937	$39,081	32.9	36,375	13.0	4.9	10.7	8.4	12.8	10.5
Oldham, KY	4,190	2,770	51.3	$63,039	$45,838	37.5	1,203	6.0	5.6	14.3	10.0	12.9	17.0
Shelby, KY	2,202	1,468	50.1	$45,392	$34,724	30.7	1,035	26.4	7.6	3.5	D	7.5	12.5
Spencer, KY	826	588	40.4	$43,960	$34,364	27.9	131	D	7.3	4.8	8.3	D	27.5
Lubbock, TX Metro Area	13,459	9,836	36.8	$42,181	$33,656	25.3	9,218	3.3	8.5	6.5	5.1	D	25.0
Crosby, TX	178	223	-20.3	$30,773	$37,012	-16.9	58	2.3	22.8	D	D	11.8	39.1
Lubbock, TX	13,086	9,395	39.3	$42,569	$33,516	27.0	9,082	3.3	8.5	6.4	5.1	15.1	24.8
Lynn, TX	195	218	-10.8	$33,119	$36,880	-10.2	79	2.6	3.4	D	D	D	41.6
Lynchburg, VA Metro Area	10,633	8,338	27.5	$40,374	$32,960	22.5	6,385	18.3	6.5	4.7	8.2	16.0	12.5
Amherst, VA	1,177	969	21.5	$37,160	$29,905	24.3	469	23.2	7.6	1.6	3.0	D	24.2
Appomattox, VA	607	464	30.7	$38,302	$30,754	24.5	173	2.6	13.1	1.9	4.0	D	26.6
Bedford, VA	3,678	2,721	35.2	$46,707	$36,261	28.8	1,180	13.6	6.8	3.6	7.4	11.4	15.4
Campbell, VA	5,171	4,184	23.6	$37,719	$32,074	17.6	4,563	19.6	6.1	5.3	9.1	18.0	10.0
Lynchburg City, VA	NA	NA	NA	NA	NA	NA	NA	NA	NA	NA	NA	NA	NA
Macon-Bibb County, GA Metro Area	9,434	7,590	24.3	$41,066	$32,684	25.6	6,550	D	D	D	D	D	14.4
Bibb, GA	6,385	5,264	21.3	$41,709	$33,784	23.5	5,500	7.8	7.1	12.8	5.5	22.1	11.9
Crawford, GA	416	356	17.0	$33,784	$28,184	19.9	86	1.1	2.9	D	7.2	8.3	27.0
Jones, GA	1,076	852	26.4	$37,618	$29,730	26.5	255	0.8	5.4	1.9	9.4	D	26.4
Monroe, GA	1,233	874	41.1	$44,790	$33,369	34.2	529	1.9	5.4	2.6	4.6	5.7	34.5
Twiggs, GA	324	245	32.0	$39,530	$27,335	44.6	180	D	D	D	D	4.7	9.6
Madera, CA Metro Area	6,291	4,296	46.4	$39,897	$28,446	40.3	4,142	6.5	4.7	0.9	1.3	14.7	22.7
Madera, CA	6,291	4,296	46.4	$39,897	$28,446	40.3	4,142	6.5	4.7	0.9	1.3	14.7	22.7
Madison, WI Metro Area	39,210	26,341	48.9	$59,371	$43,424	36.7	30,975	8.9	6.3	6.9	9.1	D	20.8
Columbia, WI	2,934	2,175	34.9	$51,147	$38,264	33.7	1,566	27.2	6.4	2.2	2.8	12.0	15.9
Dane, WI	33,249	21,893	51.9	$61,304	$44,752	37.0	27,660	7.2	5.5	7.5	9.8	9.8	21.6

Table C-3. Personal Income and Earnings by Industry—Continued

Metropolitan Statistical Area Metropolitan Division Component counties	Total (million dollars) 2018	2010	Percent change 2010-2018	Per capita Personal Income 2018	2010	Percent change 2010-2018	Total earnings (million dollars)	Manu-facturing	Retail Trade	Finance and Insurance	Professional, Scienfic, and Technical Services	Health Care and Social Assistance	Government and Government Enterprises
Green, WI	1,884	1,420	32.7	$51,026	$38,517	32.5	1,048	24.1	12.6	2.7	3.1	13.1	13.3
Iowa, WI	1,143	854	33.9	$48,073	$36,028	33.4	700	12.4	27.8	1.9	2.2	D	13.3
Manchester-Nashua, NH Metro Area	25,391	19,094	33.0	$61,147	$47,610	28.4	18,972	14.9	7.3	9.1	10.8	11.6	9.5
Hillsborough, NH	25,391	19,094	33.0	$61,147	$47,610	28.4	18,972	14.9	7.3	9.1	10.8	11.6	9.5
Manhattan, KS Metro Area	6,007	5,072	18.4	$46,008	$39,462	16.6	4,711	5.0	4.7	2.8	D	D	54.4
Geary, KS	1,594	1,434	11.2	$48,907	$40,679	20.2	2,200	1.9	1.9	0.7	D	1.2	80.5
Pottawatomie, KS	1,276	957	33.3	$52,564	$44,055	19.3	622	24.7	9.3	3.3	3.7	D	10.6
Riley, KS	3,137	2,681	17.0	$42,566	$37,469	13.6	1,888	2.0	6.4	5.1	6.4	11.6	38.3
Mankato, MN Metro Area	4,690	3,366	39.3	$46,141	$34,756	32.8	3,555	15.7	6.7	3.5	D	D	17.3
Blue Earth, MN	2,993	2,155	38.9	$44,383	$33,631	32.0	2,536	12.4	7.8	3.8	4.5	21.8	15.5
Nicollet, MN	1,697	1,211	40.2	$49,605	$36,958	34.2	1,019	23.9	4.1	2.7	D	D	21.9
Mansfield, OH Metro Area	4,751	3,767	26.1	$39,234	$30,340	29.3	3,073	23.3	7.9	2.6	2.4	14.9	17.4
Richland, OH	4,751	3,767	26.1	$39,234	$30,340	29.3	3,073	23.3	7.9	2.6	2.4	14.9	17.4
McAllen-Edinburg-Mission, TX Metro Area	22,869	17,084	33.9	$26,410	$21,925	20.5	14,786	2.6	9.7	3.9	3.3	19.1	26.7
Hidalgo, TX	22,869	17,084	33.9	$26,410	$21,925	20.5	14,786	2.6	9.7	3.9	3.3	19.1	26.7
Medford, OR Metro Area	10,232	6,760	51.4	$46,603	$33,246	40.2	6,137	8.6	10.0	3.4	5.0	18.9	14.0
Jackson, OR	10,232	6,760	51.4	$46,603	$33,246	40.2	6,137	8.6	10.0	3.4	5.0	18.9	14.0
Memphis, TN-MS-AR Metro Area	62,580	48,627	28.7	$46,620	$36,909	26.3	47,560	9.4	6.5	5.8	4.2	12.9	13.3
Crittenden, AR	1,788	1,480	20.8	$36,978	$29,038	27.3	986	15.6	7.0	1.8	2.0	10.3	15.1
De Soto, MS	7,408	5,148	43.9	$40,702	$31,821	27.9	3,560	8.4	10.9	2.5	2.4	11.2	11.7
Marshall, MS	1,147	930	23.3	$32,341	$25,096	28.9	454	15.2	7.4	3.6	1.0	D	14.6
Tate, MS	1,012	802	26.1	$35,182	$27,671	27.1	342	9.0	9.3	3.3	3.2	D	25.7
Tunica, MS	322	288	11.8	$32,425	$26,784	21.1	371	6.2	2.6	1.5	D	2.7	11.5
Fayette, TN	2,243	1,563	43.5	$55,364	$40,663	36.2	660	25.9	5.7	3.7	D	6.5	12.1
Shelby, TN	46,288	36,561	26.6	$49,465	$39,378	25.6	40,494	8.9	6.1	6.4	4.5	13.4	13.2
Tipton, TN	2,374	1,856	27.9	$38,547	$30,389	26.8	692	14.7	8.1	2.5	3.2	D	22.9
Merced, CA Metro Area	10,584	7,302	45.0	$38,519	$28,440	35.4	5,942	10.5	6.2	2.1	1.7	9.7	26.3
Merced, CA	10,584	7,302	45.0	$38,519	$28,440	35.4	5,942	10.5	6.2	2.1	1.7	9.7	26.3
Miami-Fort Lauderdale-Pompano Beach, FL Metro Area	354,746	239,474	48.1	$57,228	$42,889	33.4	213,941	3.3	7.1	8.0	10.9	11.2	12.3
Fort Lauderdale-Pompano Beach-Sunrise, FL Div.	98,088	71,457	37.3	$50,269	$40,767	23.3	63,266	3.7	8.1	7.8	10.8	10.2	13.4
Broward, FL	98,088	71,457	37.3	$50,269	$40,767	23.3	63,266	3.7	8.1	7.8	10.8	10.2	13.4
Miami-Miami Beach-Kendall, FL Div	138,139	95,806	44.2	$50,022	$38,214	30.9	99,412	2.8	6.6	7.8	10.4	11.0	12.6
Miami-Dade, FL	138,139	95,806	44.2	$50,022	$38,214	30.9	99,412	2.8	6.6	7.8	10.4	11.0	12.6
West Palm Beach-Boca Raton-Boynton Beach, FL Div	118,519	72,211	64.1	$79,760	$54,554	46.2	51,263	3.9	6.7	8.7	11.9	12.8	10.5
Palm Beach, FL	118,519	72,211	64.1	$79,760	$54,554	46.2	51,263	3.9	6.7	8.7	11.9	12.8	10.5
Michigan City-La Porte, IN Metro Area	4,678	3,569	31.1	$42,527	$32,018	32.8	2,574	21.7	6.7	2.7	2.9	13.4	14.4
La Porte, IN	4,678	3,569	31.1	$42,527	$32,018	32.8	2,574	21.7	6.7	2.7	2.9	13.4	14.4
Midland, MI Metro Area	5,031	3,573	40.8	$60,467	$42,715	41.6	3,329	24.7	3.9	2.3	3.3	11.0	6.8
Midland, MI	5,031	3,573	40.8	$60,467	$42,715	41.6	3,329	24.7	3.9	2.3	3.3	11.0	6.8
Midland, TX Metro Area	21,800	10,244	112.8	$122,247	$72,245	69.2	19,763	2.1	2.3	D	3.1	2.4	3.6
Martin, TX	322	207	56.0	$56,021	$42,949	30.4	205	3.5	5.9	D	1.0	2.1	18.3
Midland, TX	21,478	10,037	114.0	$124,455	$73,274	69.8	19,558	2.1	2.2	2.7	3.2	2.4	3.5
Milwaukee-Waukesha, WI Metro Area	89,846	67,896	32.3	$57,005	$43,616	30.7	67,043	15.3	5.1	8.6	8.5	13.5	10.6
Milwaukee, WI	45,124	35,777	26.1	$47,589	$37,727	26.1	39,320	11.3	4.3	9.3	8.8	15.5	12.9
Ozaukee, WI	7,488	5,397	38.7	$83,992	$62,485	34.4	3,214	24.4	5.5	7.0	9.5	13.7	9.1
Washington, WI	7,952	5,754	38.2	$58,601	$43,594	34.4	4,084	29.2	6.5	6.0	3.7	11.3	9.6
Waukesha, WI	29,283	20,968	39.7	$72,650	$53,760	35.1	20,425	18.9	6.3	8.1	8.6	10.0	6.8
Minneapolis-St. Paul-Bloomington, MN Metro Area	227,292	154,354	47.3	$62,889	$46,214	36.1	171,629	11.1	4.9	10.1	D	10.8	11.9
Anoka, MN	18,136	12,691	42.9	$51,258	$38,291	33.9	9,632	24.3	6.6	2.3	4.6	12.0	12.6
Carver, MN	7,388	4,704	57.1	$71,350	$51,468	38.6	3,446	25.4	4.1	2.8	6.1	11.5	10.6
Chisago, MN	2,726	1,892	44.1	$48,750	$35,102	38.9	1,054	14.7	7.9	1.7	9.5	20.2	15.8
Dakota, MN	25,802	17,842	44.6	$60,651	$44,694	35.7	15,644	12.2	7.1	10.4	6.9	8.1	11.8
Hennepin, MN	94,077	63,352	48.5	$74,698	$54,889	36.1	92,886	8.0	4.2	13.5	16.1	10.1	9.3
Isanti, MN	1,760	1,262	39.5	$44,049	$33,345	32.1	695	14.6	9.1	2.8	D	19.6	18.9
Le Sueur, MN	1,390	977	42.3	$48,799	$35,234	38.5	566	38.6	4.6	2.6	2.0	5.0	13.7
Mille Lacs, MN	1,087	817	33.1	$41,582	$31,317	32.8	530	7.9	6.5	3.2	3.2	D	36.0
Ramsey, MN	30,226	21,225	42.4	$54,934	$41,667	31.8	28,762	10.4	4.0	6.9	6.5	13.7	17.3
Scott, MN	8,797	5,782	52.1	$59,687	$44,304	34.7	4,183	16.9	5.7	2.7	6.2	7.7	16.1
Sherburne, MN	4,517	3,082	46.6	$47,031	$34,707	35.5	1,796	16.0	7.4	2.5	2.7	10.6	17.3
Washington, MN	17,607	11,384	54.7	$67,928	$47,643	42.6	6,478	13.8	7.9	6.5	6.9	13.5	12.6
Wright, MN	6,842	4,594	48.9	$50,181	$36,728	36.6	2,915	16.6	8.5	2.5	2.8	10.5	14.3
Pierce, WI	1,955	1,429	36.8	$45,936	$34,795	32.0	742	15.6	4.3	2.2	3.5	4.9	34.3
St. Croix, WI	4,982	3,320	50.0	$55,543	$39,337	41.2	2,299	21.8	7.4	3.7	5.2	12.6	14.1
Missoula, MT Metro Area	5,879	3,746	56.9	$49,492	$34,224	44.6	3,995	3.2	8.8	5.1	8.1	17.8	17.9
Missoula, MT	5,879	3,746	56.9	$49,492	$34,224	44.6	3,995	3.2	8.8	5.1	8.1	17.8	17.9
Mobile, AL Metro Area	16,418	13,708	19.8	$38,170	$31,810	20.0	12,353	15.8	6.3	5.4	8.3	12.2	14.8
Mobile, AL	15,823	13,183	20.0	$38,243	$31,896	19.9	12,014	15.1	6.4	5.6	8.5	12.5	14.9
Washington, AL	595	525	13.2	$36,323	$29,802	21.9	339	41.2	2.2	D	D	D	13.0
Modesto, CA Metro Area	24,258	16,545	46.6	$44,120	$32,116	37.4	14,912	12.7	7.1	2.2	3.4	16.5	18.1
Stanislaus, CA	24,258	16,545	46.6	$44,120	$32,116	37.4	14,912	12.7	7.1	2.2	3.4	16.5	18.1
Monroe, LA Metro Area	8,186	6,630	23.5	$40,482	$32,393	25.0	5,143	9.6	6.9	5.9	D	16.9	16.0
Morehouse, LA	978	846	15.6	$38,495	$30,352	26.8	384	10.1	7.9	3.1	2.1	D	16.8

Table C-3. Personal Income and Earnings by Industry—Continued

Metropolitan Statistical Area Metropolitan Division Component counties	Personal Income						Earnings 2018						
	Total (million dollars)			Per capita Personal Income			Total earnings (million dollars)	Earnings by Industry (percent)					
	2018	2010	Percent change 2010-2018	2018	2010	Percent change 2010-2018		Manu-facturing	Retail Trade	Finance and Insurance	Professional, Scienfic, and Technical Services	Health Care and Social Assistance	Government and Government Enterprises
Ouachita, LA	6,342	5,112	24.1	$41,053	$33,202	23.6	4,456	8.8	6.8	6.3	5.2	18.9	15.8
Union, LA	866	672	28.9	$38,794	$29,430	31.8	304	19.7	6.9	2.7	D	9.4	17.9
Monroe, MI Metro Area	7,145	5,197	37.5	$47,496	$34,204	38.9	3,156	20.3	6.0	2.0	7.4	8.3	12.2
Monroe, MI	7,145	5,197	37.5	$47,496	$34,204	38.9	3,156	20.3	6.0	2.0	7.4	8.3	12.2
Montgomery, AL Metro Area	16,027	13,070	22.6	$42,943	$34,841	23.3	11,183	11.8	6.1	4.7	D	D	28.4
Autauga, AL	2,314	1,827	26.7	$41,618	$33,360	24.8	694	17.4	8.1	3.1	3.4	9.6	18.7
Elmore, AL	3,461	2,702	28.1	$42,269	$33,950	24.5	1,121	15.6	10.9	2.9	4.3	8.8	22.6
Lowndes, AL	389	350	11.1	$38,991	$30,999	25.8	184	40.4	3.4	1.5	D	D	15.7
Montgomery, AL	9,863	8,192	20.4	$43,688	$35,693	22.4	9,185	10.3	5.4	5.1	7.9	11.5	30.1
Morgantown, WV Metro Area	5,962	4,469	33.4	$42,509	$34,295	24.0	4,745	8.2	5.2	1.7	7.0	D	26.5
Monongalia, WV	4,755	3,498	35.9	$44,679	$36,148	23.6	4,263	8.4	5.0	1.6	7.6	23.1	25.0
Preston, WV	1,208	971	24.3	$35,686	$28,950	23.3	482	5.9	6.5	2.1	2.1	D	40.2
Morristown, TN Metro Area	5,078	3,849	31.9	$35,829	$28,105	27.5	3,088	27.2	7.7	1.6	D	D	14.1
Grainger, TN	775	574	34.9	$33,490	$25,282	32.5	275	25.6	4.9	D	D	3.6	18.0
Hamblen, TN	2,366	1,845	28.2	$36,636	$29,509	24.2	1,925	32.5	8.4	1.6	2.0	11.8	12.8
Jefferson, TN	1,937	1,430	35.5	$35,866	$27,648	29.7	888	16.0	7.0	1.9	D	D	15.6
Mount Vernon-Anacortes, WA Metro Area	6,803	4,467	52.3	$53,060	$38,192	38.9	4,101	14.2	8.1	4.6	4.7	7.1	22.8
Skagit, WA	6,803	4,467	52.3	$53,060	$38,192	38.9	4,101	14.2	8.1	4.6	4.7	7.1	22.8
Muncie, IN Metro Area	4,270	3,322	28.5	$37,201	$28,232	31.8	2,754	10.6	8.6	4.3	5.5	20.2	21.5
Delaware, IN	4,270	3,322	28.5	$37,201	$28,232	31.8	2,754	10.6	8.6	4.3	5.5	20.2	21.5
Muskegon, MI Metro Area	6,782	4,965	36.6	$39,072	$28,880	35.3	4,025	26.6	9.9	2.1	3.3	17.2	13.8
Muskegon, MI	6,782	4,965	36.6	$39,072	$28,880	35.3	4,025	26.6	9.9	2.1	3.3	17.2	13.8
Myrtle Beach-Conway-North Myrtle Beach, SC-NC	18,610	11,317	64.5	$38,700	$29,913	29.4	9,582	3.3	11.0	5.1	4.7	11.3	16.0
Brunswick, NC	5,846	3,455	69.2	$42,749	$31,970	33.7	2,171	5.0	8.4	2.3	5.4	11.4	16.1
Horry, SC	12,765	7,862	62.4	$37,091	$29,090	27.5	7,412	2.8	11.8	5.9	4.5	11.3	16.0
Napa, CA Metro Area	10,454	6,388	63.6	$74,984	$46,696	60.6	7,607	22.8	4.6	3.1	5.2	9.1	14.7
Napa, CA	10,454	6,388	63.6	$74,984	$46,696	60.6	7,607	22.8	4.6	3.1	5.2	9.1	14.7
Naples-Marco Island, FL Metro Area	35,080	20,183	73.8	$92,686	$62,564	48.1	11,636	3.4	8.4	7.3	10.9	12.9	8.9
Collier, FL	35,080	20,183	73.8	$92,686	$62,564	48.1	11,636	3.4	8.4	7.3	10.9	12.9	8.9
Nashville-Davidson--Murfreesboro--Franklin, TN	110,453	68,943	60.2	$57,953	$41,763	38.8	91,563	7.3	6.0	D	10.2	18.6	8.7
Cannon, TN	522	386	35.5	$36,113	$27,940	29.3	148	10.1	5.8	D	2.5	10.9	23.2
Cheatham, TN	1,777	1,232	44.2	$43,932	$31,494	39.5	728	26.6	5.8	1.9	D	D	13.2
Davidson, TN	45,752	29,530	54.9	$66,060	$47,041	40.4	50,032	3.0	5.4	6.8	12.1	21.4	7.5
Dickson, TN	2,168	1,518	42.8	$40,556	$30,556	32.7	1,172	19.9	8.5	3.0	2.4	14.5	13.9
Macon, TN	808	577	40.1	$33,297	$25,931	28.4	334	12.5	11.3	5.4	D	D	19.1
Maury, TN	4,028	2,573	56.5	$42,696	$31,700	34.7	2,564	21.8	6.5	6.3	3.4	9.6	17.4
Robertson, TN	2,990	2,106	42.0	$42,104	$31,743	32.6	1,513	26.3	7.0	2.5	D	5.9	14.9
Rutherford, TN	13,331	8,245	61.7	$41,031	$31,265	31.2	9,789	24.1	6.8	3.6	3.5	8.7	14.3
Smith, TN	753	564	33.4	$37,742	$29,502	27.9	374	25.3	6.4	3.7	1.8	6.9	17.1
Sumner, TN	9,106	5,771	57.8	$48,656	$35,799	35.9	4,317	13.4	7.9	3.4	8.0	11.5	12.0
Trousdale, TN	331	231	43.5	$30,090	$29,334	2.6	138	13.0	7.7	2.6	2.8	D	20.3
Williamson, TN	21,985	12,033	82.7	$94,872	$65,353	45.2	17,095	2.0	5.4	10.1	12.9	23.6	4.9
Wilson, TN	6,904	4,178	65.2	$49,092	$36,428	34.8	3,360	9.8	11.3	3.9	5.4	7.7	10.1
New Bern, NC Metro Area	5,417	4,573	18.4	$43,257	$35,888	20.5	3,461	8.4	5.7	1.9	D	9.0	49.1
Craven, NC	4,494	3,797	18.4	$43,665	$36,444	19.8	3,188	8.8	5.5	2.0	D	8.6	50.8
Jones, NC	371	328	13.1	$38,536	$32,364	19.1	101	1.7	5.1	1.3	2.6	D	31.5
Pamlico, NC	552	448	23.0	$43,532	$34,191	27.3	171	4.8	10.9	1.8	3.8	D	29.0
New Haven-Milford, CT Metro Area	48,584	38,786	25.3	$56,650	$44,924	26.1	32,070	8.6	6.1	4.0	8.3	15.4	14.6
New Haven, CT	48,584	38,786	25.3	$56,650	$44,924	26.1	32,070	8.6	6.1	4.0	8.3	15.4	14.6
New Orleans-Metairie, LA Metro Area	66,609	50,931	30.8	$52,431	$42,609	23.1	46,738	7.6	5.4	5.0	9.2	11.2	14.4
Jefferson, LA	22,139	18,347	20.7	$51,005	$42,411	20.3	15,050	4.8	7.6	6.6	7.6	16.0	9.9
Orleans, LA	20,334	14,727	38.1	$52,004	$42,348	22.8	16,518	2.5	3.6	5.4	14.2	10.1	19.9
Plaquemines, LA	1,156	1,001	15.4	$49,376	$43,310	14.0	1,333	15.7	2.3	0.8	6.1	1.3	15.5
St. Bernard, LA	1,501	1,129	33.0	$32,130	$30,650	4.8	830	33.3	6.2	1.3	D	6.4	17.3
St. Charles, LA	2,610	2,111	23.6	$49,353	$39,966	23.5	2,425	34.0	2.8	1.0	D	3.1	10.2
St. James, LA	1,020	855	19.3	$48,484	$38,792	25.0	874	51.5	2.5	1.2	D	D	12.1
St. John the Baptist, LA	1,752	1,563	12.1	$40,573	$34,273	18.4	1,337	30.9	4.6	1.9	2.4	D	11.7
St. Tammany, LA	16,097	11,198	43.8	$62,366	$47,744	30.6	8,370	2.9	6.4	4.2	7.0	11.0	12.9
New York-Newark-Jersey City, NY-NJ-PA Metro area	1,480,233	1,033,821	43.2	$76,681	$54,631	40.4	1,088,320	D	4.5	15.9	13.1	10.5	13.1
Nassau County-Suffolk County, NY Div	223,660	163,569	36.7	$78,769	$57,674	36.6	123,440	D	6.8	7.3	9.1	16.1	17.9
Nassau, NY	122,032	87,966	38.7	$89,839	$65,564	37.0	62,939	D	7.4	7.3	9.9	19.9	15.3
Suffolk, NY	101,628	75,603	34.4	$68,617	$50,591	35.6	60,500	7.9	6.3	7.2	8.2	12.2	20.5
Newark, NJ-PA Div	163,445	122,552	33.4	$75,198	$57,061	31.8	107,357	7.3	4.6	8.8	14.6	10.1	14.2
Essex, NJ	53,951	40,729	32.5	$67,459	$51,947	29.9	35,882	4.2	3.5	11.4	10.1	11.1	20.1
Hunterdon, NJ	11,176	8,919	25.3	$89,610	$70,049	27.9	5,225	4.7	7.4	14.1	13.9	10.0	13.7
Morris, NJ	48,851	36,449	34.0	$98,842	$73,983	33.6	37,789	7.8	4.7	8.7	20.1	9.0	8.5
Sussex, NJ	8,695	7,059	23.2	$61,757	$47,429	30.2	3,192	7.0	7.9	2.8	7.6	13.0	20.5
Union, NJ	38,095	27,429	38.9	$68,262	$51,030	33.8	24,510	11.9	5.1	5.1	14.2	10.0	13.0
Pike, PA	2,677	1,968	36.0	$47,864	$34,306	39.5	759	1.6	8.0	2.0	4.4	8.4	26.5
New Brunswick-Lakewood, NJ Div	166,818	120,146	38.8	$69,978	$51,283	36.5	106,341	10.8	5.9	5.6	13.4	10.9	12.3
Middlesex, NJ	50,665	38,384	32.0	$61,065	$47,349	29.0	40,826	7.9	4.9	5.4	15.2	9.2	13.3

Table C-3. Personal Income and Earnings by Industry—*Continued*

| | Personal Income | | | | | | Earnings 2018 | | | | | | |
| | Total (million dollars) | | | Per capita Personal Income | | | Total earnings (million dollars) | Earnings by Industry (percent) | | | | | |
Metropolitan Statistical Area Metropolitan Division Component counties	2018	2010	Percent change 2010-2018	2018	2010	Percent change 2010-2018		Manu-facturing	Retail Trade	Finance and Insurance	Professional, Scienfic, and Technical Services	Health Care and Social Assistance	Government and Government Enterprises
Monmouth, NJ	49,695	36,269	37.0	$79,978	$57,526	39.0	24,090	3.4	7.2	6.3	12.3	16.1	13.5
Ocean, NJ	31,290	23,055	35.7	$52,008	$39,917	30.3	13,232	3.4	10.6	3.2	7.2	17.8	19.8
Somerset, NJ	35,168	22,438	56.7	$106,194	$69,235	53.4	28,192	24.7	4.2	6.6	14.4	5.8	6.2
New York-Jersey City-White Plains, NY-NJ Div	926,311	627,554	47.6	$77,795	$54,113	43.8	751,183	0.0	3.9	19.8	13.5	9.6	12.2
Bergen, NJ	80,509	59,877	34.5	$85,951	$66,064	30.1	47,888	6.8	7.0	5.3	11.0	14.5	9.6
Hudson, NJ	44,038	28,682	53.5	$65,139	$45,124	44.4	33,590	2.3	4.8	26.3	8.3	6.1	11.8
Passaic, NJ	25,452	20,377	24.9	$50,570	$40,587	24.6	14,344	11.4	8.3	3.4	7.0	13.7	19.6
Bronx, NY	53,528	41,481	29.0	$37,376	$29,899	25.0	27,553	1.3	5.5	1.4	1.7	24.9	31.0
Kings, NY	134,804	89,747	50.2	$52,192	$35,758	46.0	60,121	2.0	6.5	3.6	5.8	21.5	23.9
New York, NY	315,870	191,355	65.1	$193,940	$120,443	61.0	431,884	0.6	2.5	29.2	18.2	4.9	6.8
Putnam, NY	6,510	5,061	28.6	$65,833	$50,781	29.6	2,235	6.0	5.3	2.7	7.6	15.6	23.6
Queens, NY	113,437	83,138	36.4	$49,777	$37,202	33.8	62,936	2.2	5.0	3.6	3.1	14.2	24.1
Richmond, NY	27,023	20,364	32.7	$56,749	$43,363	30.9	10,466	D	7.0	2.0	4.2	21.3	26.1
Rockland, NY	19,693	15,179	29.7	$60,464	$48,572	24.5	10,310	8.0	7.0	3.3	9.4	16.1	19.1
Westchester, NY	105,446	72,294	45.9	$108,976	$76,048	43.3	49,855	5.3	4.6	10.4	11.9	13.9	15.8
Niles, MI Metro Area	7,311	5,662	29.1	$47,430	$36,120	31.3	4,532	29.9	5.4	3.5	3.2	11.6	13.6
Berrien, MI	7,311	5,662	29.1	$47,430	$36,120	31.3	4,532	29.9	5.4	3.5	3.2	11.6	13.6
North Port-Sarasota-Bradenton, FL Metro Area	46,388	29,331	58.2	$56,462	$41,702	35.4	21,130	6.1	8.8	5.4	9.5	16.0	9.5
Manatee, FL	18,707	12,156	53.9	$47,378	$37,586	26.1	8,430	7.7	9.0	3.8	7.3	14.1	10.7
Sarasota, FL	27,681	17,175	61.2	$64,868	$45,205	43.5	12,700	5.0	8.7	6.4	11.0	17.2	8.7
Norwich-New London, CT Metro Area	15,811	12,716	24.3	$59,264	$46,410	27.7	11,004	19.4	5.5	1.9	7.1	10.7	25.8
New London, CT	15,811	12,716	24.3	$59,264	$46,410	27.7	11,004	19.4	5.5	1.9	7.1	10.7	25.8
Ocala, FL Metro Area	13,318	9,964	33.7	$36,997	$30,072	23.0	6,096	8.9	10.8	3.4	5.1	19.0	14.9
Marion, FL	13,318	9,964	33.7	$36,997	$30,072	23.0	6,096	8.9	10.8	3.4	5.1	19.0	14.9
Ocean City, NJ Metro Area	5,635	4,344	29.7	$60,877	$44,686	36.2	2,947	1.8	9.6	2.7	4.4	9.5	26.7
Cape May, NJ	5,635	4,344	29.7	$60,877	$44,686	36.2	2,947	1.8	9.6	2.7	4.4	9.5	26.7
Odessa, TX Metro Area	7,664	4,792	59.9	$47,271	$34,959	35.2	6,798	6.9	5.9	2.0	3.2	4.7	10.5
Ector, TX	7,664	4,792	59.9	$47,271	$34,959	35.2	6,798	6.9	5.9	2.0	3.2	4.7	10.5
Ogden-Clearfield, UT Metro Area	29,695	19,319	53.7	$43,988	$32,213	36.6	17,737	15.3	6.7	3.9	6.7	9.6	23.8
Box Elder, UT	2,055	1,408	45.9	$37,390	$28,066	33.2	1,274	38.4	4.9	1.9	2.6	6.4	12.4
Davis, UT	16,280	10,236	59.0	$46,286	$33,244	39.2	9,473	11.8	6.7	2.8	8.1	7.8	28.3
Morgan, UT	631	360	75.2	$52,426	$37,854	38.5	187	9.2	6.6	9.0	8.7	4.4	14.5
Weber, UT	10,730	7,315	46.7	$41,853	$31,510	32.8	6,803	16.1	7.1	5.6	5.5	12.8	19.9
Oklahoma City, OK Metro Area	67,827	48,692	39.3	$48,571	$38,712	25.5	50,042	5.3	5.7	4.6	6.7	D	19.7
Canadian, OK	6,482	4,210	54.0	$44,878	$36,183	24.0	2,647	11.6	6.3	2.8	3.9	5.8	15.3
Cleveland, OK	12,702	9,360	35.7	$45,094	$36,410	23.9	5,472	4.7	8.4	3.9	7.0	9.4	30.6
Grady, OK	2,204	1,688	30.6	$39,675	$32,186	23.3	867	9.5	5.7	3.5	3.5	6.9	17.1
Lincoln, OK	1,245	952	30.7	$35,653	$27,721	28.6	442	7.5	6.8	9.8	3.2	D	20.1
Logan, OK	2,042	1,386	47.3	$43,169	$32,950	31.0	502	5.5	8.4	4.9	5.2	10.2	14.5
McClain, OK	1,805	1,230	46.7	$45,143	$35,411	27.5	649	5.7	8.5	4.1	4.3	6.1	16.2
Oklahoma, OK	41,348	29,866	38.4	$52,168	$41,435	25.9	39,462	4.8	5.1	4.8	7.0	12.5	18.7
Olympia-Lacey-Tumwater, WA Metro Area	14,803	10,255	44.3	$51,684	$40,535	27.5	9,076	2.6	6.3	2.8	6.0	13.1	37.4
Thurston, WA	14,803	10,255	44.3	$51,684	$40,535	27.5	9,076	2.6	6.3	2.8	6.0	13.1	37.4
Omaha-Council Bluffs, NE-IA Metro Area	54,682	38,969	40.3	$58,037	$44,912	29.2	41,158	6.2	5.1	9.5	D	11.3	13.2
Harrison, IA	635	534	18.9	$44,895	$35,785	25.5	239	10.5	7.8	5.6	4.1	D	20.7
Mills, IA	853	651	31.1	$56,647	$43,163	31.2	338	20.0	9.6	2.5	D	D	29.7
Pottawattamie, IA	4,265	3,176	34.3	$45,604	$34,013	34.1	2,542	15.5	7.7	2.4	3.3	12.7	15.2
Cass, NE	1,402	985	42.4	$53,602	$39,014	37.4	456	9.4	6.2	3.7	2.9	4.0	17.5
Douglas, NE	35,960	25,612	40.4	$63,435	$49,391	28.4	30,889	5.3	4.6	10.6	8.4	12.6	10.5
Sarpy, NE	9,284	6,382	45.5	$50,333	$39,958	26.0	5,650	4.2	5.7	9.0	7.0	5.4	24.6
Saunders, NE	1,112	775	43.5	$52,193	$37,117	40.6	398	6.6	6.3	4.7	4.9	4.9	22.9
Washington, NE	1,171	855	36.9	$56,640	$42,904	32.0	646	19.6	10.0	4.1	2.6	5.5	16.4
Orlando-Kissimmee-Sanford, FL Metro Area	111,901	71,145	57.3	$43,491	$33,258	30.8	87,094	4.6	6.9	5.9	10.5	11.0	10.4
Lake, FL	15,041	9,620	56.3	$42,190	$32,315	30.6	5,799	4.0	11.4	3.6	4.7	18.7	14.8
Orange, FL	61,642	38,834	58.7	$44,647	$33,810	32.1	61,710	5.0	5.9	5.4	11.3	10.2	10.0
Osceola, FL	12,271	7,148	71.7	$33,346	$26,489	25.9	5,587	1.8	10.2	1.7	3.8	15.6	15.7
Seminole, FL	22,947	15,543	47.6	$49,049	$36,739	33.5	13,998	4.0	8.3	10.6	11.9	9.9	8.1
Oshkosh-Neenah, WI Metro Area	8,226	6,211	32.4	$48,101	$37,176	29.4	7,010	27.7	4.6	5.0	5.9	9.2	11.6
Winnebago, WI	8,226	6,211	32.4	$48,101	$37,176	29.4	7,010	27.7	4.6	5.0	5.9	9.2	11.6
Owensboro, KY Metro Area	4,930	4,036	22.1	$41,387	$35,168	17.7	3,290	22.6	6.7	D	D	D	11.3
Daviess, KY	4,221	3,383	24.8	$41,754	$34,987	19.3	2,762	16.6	7.4	7.7	3.9	19.9	11.8
Hancock, KY	323	346	-6.5	$36,929	$40,442	-8.7	365	76.1	1.7	0.7	0.6	D	6.7
McLean, KY	385	307	25.4	$41,603	$32,266	28.9	163	5.6	6.0	D	D	3.8	14.8
Oxnard-Thousand Oaks-Ventura, CA Metro Area	52,515	37,882	38.6	$61,712	$45,910	34.4	29,692	8.7	7.2	5.5	7.8	9.7	17.2
Ventura, CA	52,515	37,882	38.6	$61,712	$45,910	34.4	29,692	8.7	7.2	5.5	7.8	9.7	17.2
Palm Bay-Melbourne-Titusville, FL Metro Area	27,112	19,971	35.8	$45,425	$36,714	23.7	15,946	18.9	6.9	3.4	9.7	13.3	14.9
Brevard, FL	27,112	19,971	35.8	$45,425	$36,714	23.7	15,946	18.9	6.9	3.4	9.7	13.3	14.9
Panama City, FL Metro Area	8,010	6,221	28.8	$43,231	$36,768	17.6	5,156	4.8	8.6	3.6	8.2	D	25.6
Bay, FL	8,010	6,221	28.8	$43,231	$36,768	17.6	5,156	4.8	8.6	3.6	8.2	D	25.6
Parkersburg-Vienna, WV Metro Area	3,780	3,001	26.0	$41,988	$32,375	29.7	2,308	D	8.8	4.8	3.9	15.5	22.5
Wirt, WV	187	140	33.8	$32,156	$24,463	31.4	34	D	6.3	2.6	2.1	11.0	39.6
Wood, WV	3,593	2,861	25.6	$42,669	$32,896	29.7	2,274	11.2	8.8	4.8	3.9	15.6	22.3
Pensacola-Ferry Pass-Brent, FL Metro Area	21,408	15,799	35.5	$43,259	$35,036	23.5	12,530	4.4	7.0	7.3	7.4	15.6	24.9
Escambia, FL	13,422	10,251	30.9	$42,537	$34,394	23.7	9,916	4.9	6.6	8.5	7.2	16.1	25.3

Table C-3. Personal Income and Earnings by Industry—*Continued*

Metropolitan Statistical Area Metropolitan Division Component counties	Personal Income Total (million dollars) 2018	2010	Percent change 2010-2018	Per capita Personal Income 2018	2010	Percent change 2010-2018	Earnings 2018 Total earnings (million dollars)	Manu-facturing	Retail Trade	Finance and Insurance	Professional, Scienfic, and Technical Services	Health Care and Social Assistance	Government and Government Enterprises
Santa Rosa, FL	7,986	5,549	43.9	$44,527	$36,288	22.7	2,614	2.6	8.5	2.8	8.3	13.5	23.0
Peoria, IL Metro Area	19,705	16,274	21.1	$48,870	$39,116	24.9	13,780	23.1	5.2	D	6.4	15.0	12.1
Fulton, IL	1,337	1,169	14.4	$38,361	$31,529	21.7	494	3.2	8.0	5.4	3.3	18.5	28.9
Marshall, IL	531	436	21.8	$46,015	$34,503	33.4	194	30.3	3.9	2.8	1.2	7.6	16.1
Peoria, IL	9,236	7,801	18.4	$51,135	$41,888	22.1	8,841	26.1	4.0	4.3	7.7	18.9	9.3
Stark, IL	233	195	19.3	$42,877	$32,670	31.2	90	23.2	8.1	D	D	4.7	18.9
Tazewell, IL	6,333	5,106	24.0	$47,862	$37,687	27.0	3,466	19.2	7.6	5.3	4.5	6.3	15.2
Woodford, IL	2,036	1,568	29.8	$52,928	$40,551	30.5	695	17.3	7.5	3.7	D	8.6	18.0
Philadelphia-Camden-Wilmington, PA-NJ-DE-MD Metro Area	392,847	287,527	36.6	$64,440	$48,154	33.8	275,920	6.9	4.9	8.4	D	13.2	11.9
Camden, NJ Div	71,055	55,443	28.2	$57,124	$44,300	28.9	43,422	8.3	8.0	6.3	D	15.0	17.9
Burlington, NJ	27,667	21,735	27.3	$62,120	$48,394	28.4	18,428	8.4	7.7	10.7	9.6	13.2	17.2
Camden, NJ	27,434	21,486	27.7	$54,103	$41,845	29.3	16,917	7.6	6.8	3.5	8.5	18.9	17.5
Gloucester, NJ	15,953	12,223	30.5	$54,745	$42,299	29.4	8,077	9.4	11.0	2.0	D	10.9	20.3
Montgomery County-Bucks County-Chester County	156,179	111,906	39.6	$78,924	$58,095	35.9	99,078	9.3	5.7	8.2	16.8	11.6	7.7
Bucks, PA	46,139	33,064	39.5	$73,447	$52,868	38.9	22,568	10.0	6.7	4.8	10.6	14.8	9.5
Chester, PA	43,249	30,768	40.6	$82,846	$61,545	34.6	27,680	7.1	6.0	12.9	17.3	7.7	7.8
Montgomery, PA	66,791	48,074	38.9	$80,606	$60,024	34.3	48,830	10.1	5.0	7.0	19.3	12.4	6.9
Philadelphia, PA Div	125,933	89,702	40.4	$58,604	$42,975	36.4	102,844	4.0	2.8	7.0	12.1	13.9	12.9
Delaware, PA	37,622	27,325	37.7	$66,617	$48,883	36.3	21,172	9.8	4.8	9.3	8.0	13.2	10.2
Philadelphia, PA	88,312	62,377	41.6	$55,747	$40,815	36.6	81,672	2.5	2.3	6.4	13.2	14.1	13.6
Wilmington, DE-MD-NJ Div	39,680	30,477	30.2	$54,748	$43,175	26.8	30,576	6.8	4.8	16.9	11.7	13.2	13.7
New Castle, DE	31,739	23,975	32.4	$56,745	$44,500	27.5	26,338	5.0	4.7	19.4	13.1	13.7	12.3
Cecil, MD	4,904	3,835	27.9	$47,695	$37,906	25.8	2,444	21.1	5.7	1.1	D	9.7	24.3
Salem, NJ	3,036	2,668	13.8	$48,496	$40,435	19.9	1,793	12.7	5.1	1.7	D	10.7	19.6
Phoenix-Mesa-Chandler, AZ Metro Area	224,072	146,976	52.5	$46,125	$34,955	32.0	159,709	7.7	6.6	9.8	8.8	12.3	12.2
Maricopa, AZ	210,370	138,119	52.3	$47,694	$36,108	32.1	155,445	7.7	6.5	10.0	9.0	12.4	11.6
Pinal, AZ	13,702	8,857	54.7	$30,644	$23,335	31.3	4,264	6.7	8.8	1.5	2.9	7.3	34.2
Pine Bluff, AR Metro Area	3,093	2,787	11.0	$34,554	$27,844	24.1	2,011	18.0	5.4	D	D	13.9	28.7
Cleveland, AR	323	249	29.7	$40,344	$28,745	40.4	89	7.2	1.7	D	D	5.7	19.3
Jefferson, AR	2,408	2,237	7.7	$35,356	$28,919	22.3	1,737	19.7	5.9	2.9	D	14.8	28.5
Lincoln, AR	361	301	19.9	$27,002	$21,390	26.2	185	7.1	2.8	2.0	0.7	8.7	35.8
Pittsburgh, PA Metro Area	135,003	101,017	33.6	$58,072	$42,857	35.5	98,029	7.9	5.1	6.9	10.4	14.0	10.3
Allegheny, PA	76,711	56,537	35.7	$62,958	$46,192	36.3	65,529	5.5	4.5	9.0	12.7	14.7	9.2
Armstrong, PA	2,970	2,460	20.8	$45,510	$35,716	27.4	1,245	10.2	6.2	2.6	2.4	14.0	14.9
Beaver, PA	8,033	6,311	27.3	$48,763	$36,981	31.9	4,097	13.0	5.7	2.0	4.3	14.5	13.4
Butler, PA	11,072	7,868	40.7	$58,927	$42,737	37.9	6,838	15.5	6.3	3.0	6.9	12.1	13.7
Fayette, PA	5,563	4,530	22.8	$42,649	$33,204	28.4	2,588	9.8	7.8	1.8	2.9	15.8	18.6
Washington, PA	12,351	8,832	39.8	$59,568	$42,478	40.2	8,256	9.2	4.6	2.8	6.3	10.4	8.5
Westmoreland, PA	18,302	14,479	26.4	$52,200	$39,652	31.6	9,475	14.5	7.6	3.2	6.1	12.6	12.3
Pittsfield, MA Metro Area	7,139	5,419	31.7	$56,503	$41,266	36.9	4,382	9.0	7.0	4.5	8.6	19.3	14.3
Berkshire, MA	7,139	5,419	31.7	$56,503	$41,266	36.9	4,382	9.0	7.0	4.5	8.6	19.3	14.3
Pocatello, ID Metro Area	3,610	2,656	35.9	$38,038	$29,221	30.2	2,218	11.1	7.1	5.5	3.9	14.0	23.1
Bannock, ID	3,325	2,424	37.2	$38,160	$29,198	30.7	1,981	8.4	8.0	6.0	4.3	15.7	24.2
Power, ID	285	232	22.8	$36,667	$29,462	24.5	237	33.6	D	1.3	1.1	D	13.4
Portland-South Portland, ME Metro Area	30,921	22,246	39.0	$57,751	$43,288	33.4	21,336	D	6.7	8.1	9.8	14.4	15.2
Cumberland, ME	18,354	12,978	41.4	$62,523	$46,109	35.6	14,601	6.5	6.3	10.6	11.6	16.4	10.9
Sagadahoc, ME	1,829	1,392	31.4	$51,325	$39,501	29.9	1,171	D	5.8	2.4	6.7	4.9	12.9
York, ME	10,738	7,876	36.3	$52,068	$39,937	30.4	5,563	11.8	7.8	2.7	5.6	11.0	26.9
Portland-Vancouver-Hillsboro, OR-WA Metro Area	141,270	89,154	58.5	$56,991	$39,940	42.7	103,525	12.8	5.6	5.1	D	D	13.4
Clackamas, OR	24,385	15,953	52.9	$58,608	$42,339	38.4	13,415	12.6	7.2	5.2	9.4	12.5	10.1
Columbia, OR	2,321	1,609	44.3	$44,312	$32,594	36.0	750	16.2	8.3	3.1	3.7	8.8	20.4
Multnomah, OR	46,967	29,792	57.6	$57,850	$40,407	43.2	44,589	6.3	4.8	6.2	12.8	11.3	17.2
Washington, OR	36,442	22,063	65.2	$60,971	$41,500	46.9	29,081	24.0	5.4	4.0	6.6	8.0	6.9
Yamhill, OR	4,866	3,243	50.0	$45,478	$32,661	39.2	2,450	20.3	6.5	2.7	4.4	12.1	13.8
Clark, WA	25,742	16,130	59.6	$53,423	$37,801	41.3	13,105	8.7	7.1	4.5	7.9	12.9	17.7
Skamania, WA	546	364	50.2	$45,802	$32,722	40.0	134	13.0	3.9	0.8	D	D	33.9
Port St. Lucie, FL Metro Area	26,140	16,393	59.5	$54,228	$38,554	40.7	9,482	5.1	8.4	3.6	7.4	17.4	14.3
Martin, FL	13,496	7,967	69.4	$83,873	$54,230	54.7	4,526	5.4	8.1	5.1	9.3	18.5	9.1
St. Lucie, FL	12,644	8,425	50.1	$39,374	$30,278	30.0	4,956	4.9	8.8	2.2	5.7	16.4	19.2
Poughkeepsie-Newburgh-Middletown, NY Metro Area	36,359	27,458	32.4	$53,811	$40,910	31.5	19,979	8.2	7.8	2.8	5.6	15.7	25.3
Dutchess, NY	16,555	12,529	32.1	$56,365	$42,081	33.9	9,027	11.0	6.9	3.1	5.6	16.6	21.8
Orange, NY	19,803	14,929	32.6	$51,848	$39,976	29.7	10,952	6.0	8.6	2.6	5.7	15.1	28.2
Prescott Valley-Prescott, AZ Metro Area	9,352	6,100	53.3	$40,312	$28,911	39.4	4,204	5.9	9.8	2.2	4.7	15.3	18.5
Yavapai, AZ	9,352	6,100	53.3	$40,312	$28,911	39.4	4,204	5.9	9.8	2.2	4.7	15.3	18.5
Providence-Warwick, RI-MA Metro Area	88,501	67,625	30.9	$54,585	$42,184	29.4	55,312	D	6.6	6.6	7.4	14.2	16.1
Bristol, MA	30,507	22,364	36.4	$54,089	$40,723	32.8	17,274	D	7.8	2.6	5.6	15.3	15.0
Bristol, RI	3,834	2,995	28.0	$78,805	$60,113	31.1	1,067	D	4.7	3.6	9.0	11.3	15.9
Kent, RI	9,777	7,507	30.2	$59,665	$45,214	32.0	5,600	9.8	8.7	6.2	8.3	14.6	12.8
Newport, RI	5,669	4,073	39.2	$68,679	$48,965	40.3	3,674	D	5.7	3.7	11.1	7.1	34.5
Providence, RI	30,619	24,417	25.4	$48,137	$38,892	23.8	23,257	6.4	4.9	11.1	8.2	15.3	14.3
Washington, RI	8,095	6,270	29.1	$64,158	$49,331	30.1	4,440	17.5	9.1	2.5	5.9	10.3	19.0

Table C-3. Personal Income and Earnings by Industry—*Continued*

Metropolitan Statistical Area Metropolitan Division Component counties	Personal Income Total (million dollars) 2018	2010	Percent change 2010-2018	Per capita Personal Income 2018	2010	Percent change 2010-2018	Total earnings (million dollars)	Earnings by Industry (percent) Manufacturing	Retail Trade	Finance and Insurance	Professional, Scienfic, and Technical Services	Health Care and Social Assistance	Government and Government Enterprises
Provo-Orem, UT Metro Area	25,877	13,931	85.8	$40,831	$26,272	55.4	17,563	9.4	9.3	3.4	12.2	D	10.2
Juab, UT	417	253	64.6	$36,087	$24,680	46.2	210	26.0	3.8	1.6	5.4	D	19.5
Utah, UT	25,460	13,678	86.1	$40,919	$26,303	55.6	17,354	9.2	9.4	3.4	12.3	8.9	10.1
Pueblo, CO Metro Area	6,619	4,721	40.2	$39,511	$29,606	33.5	3,871	8.9	8.3	2.4	5.9	21.1	21.0
Pueblo, CO	6,619	4,721	40.2	$39,511	$29,606	33.5	3,871	8.9	8.3	2.4	5.9	21.1	21.0
Punta Gorda, FL Metro Area	7,689	5,125	50.0	$41,564	$32,055	29.7	2,960	1.8	12.2	3.5	7.5	21.7	13.7
Charlotte, FL	7,689	5,125	50.0	$41,564	$32,055	29.7	2,960	1.8	12.2	3.5	7.5	21.7	13.7
Racine, WI Metro Area	9,780	7,430	31.6	$49,749	$38,024	30.8	5,410	32.2	6.1	3.5	4.2	11.8	13.3
Racine, WI	9,780	7,430	31.6	$49,749	$38,024	30.8	5,410	32.2	6.1	3.5	4.2	11.8	13.3
Raleigh-Cary, NC Metro Area	75,001	48,714	54.0	$55,045	$42,830	28.5	53,308	8.1	5.5	5.7	17.5	9.2	13.2
Franklin, NC	2,448	1,690	44.9	$36,238	$27,782	30.4	881	23.5	5.3	1.7	5.0	5.2	16.0
Johnston, NC	8,091	5,406	49.7	$39,922	$31,862	25.3	3,238	18.9	8.2	2.2	3.9	6.0	18.3
Wake, NC	64,462	41,618	54.9	$59,014	$45,891	28.6	49,189	7.1	5.3	6.0	18.7	9.4	12.8
Rapid City, SD Metro Area	6,956	5,061	37.5	$49,681	$39,936	24.4	4,490	3.9	7.6	5.8	D	19.1	23.0
Meade, SD	1,217	885	37.6	$43,015	$34,712	23.9	560	2.9	7.5	3.0	D	5.0	41.2
Pennington, SD	5,739	4,176	37.4	$51,369	$41,251	24.5	3,930	4.0	7.6	6.2	5.0	21.1	20.5
Reading, PA Metro Area	20,985	15,696	33.7	$49,945	$38,095	31.1	13,373	19.4	5.7	3.0	6.0	14.6	12.4
Berks, PA	20,985	15,696	33.7	$49,945	$38,095	31.1	13,373	19.4	5.7	3.0	6.0	14.6	12.4
Redding, CA Metro Area	8,387	6,138	36.6	$46,582	$34,622	34.5	4,782	3.9	9.2	3.9	5.3	19.2	23.3
Shasta, CA	8,387	6,138	36.6	$46,582	$34,622	34.5	4,782	3.9	9.2	3.9	5.3	19.2	23.3
Reno, NV Metro Area	28,016	18,541	51.1	$59,639	$43,529	37.0	17,852	10.5	D	D	D	D	14.3
Storey, NV	240	141	70.5	$59,651	$35,261	69.2	1,289	62.8	D	D	D	D	1.6
Washoe, NV	27,776	18,401	51.0	$59,639	$43,607	36.8	16,562	6.4	6.2	4.9	9.6	11.4	15.3
Richmond, VA Metro Area	73,485	51,017	44.0	$57,301	$42,935	33.5	54,229	5.3	D	D	10.4	11.3	17.7
Amelia, VA	583	428	36.2	$44,774	$33,554	33.4	184	7.3	3.9	1.3	2.8	8.6	16.3
Charles City County, VA	318	240	32.4	$45,824	$33,088	38.5	117	13.1	D	D	D	D	16.7
Chesterfield, VA	18,716	13,422	39.4	$53,695	$42,314	26.9	9,891	7.9	7.7	5.2	9.2	10.8	16.2
Dinwiddie, VA	3,145	2,665	18.0	$40,352	$34,217	17.9	1,833	8.0	8.5	3.8	2.1	D	22.1
Goochland, VA	2,337	1,490	56.8	$100,545	$68,536	46.7	2,093	2.0	1.2	54.2	3.0	1.6	4.3
Hanover, VA	6,462	4,435	45.7	$60,259	$44,392	35.7	3,573	7.1	8.9	2.0	5.7	11.9	9.5
Henrico, VA	22,006	14,412	52.7	$66,836	$46,896	42.5	18,139	3.5	5.0	12.6	11.3	12.8	7.9
King and Queen, VA	305	233	31.1	$43,361	$33,388	29.9	76	12.2	2.0	D	8.3	D	22.0
King William, VA	790	581	35.8	$46,612	$36,345	28.2	275	26.3	5.8	2.8	4.3	D	16.6
New Kent, VA	1,584	1,015	56.0	$70,743	$54,762	29.2	296	3.6	7.1	1.5	D	D	21.6
Powhatan, VA	1,652	1,108	49.1	$56,607	$39,414	43.6	486	3.6	6.8	2.7	10.2	5.2	23.1
Prince George, VA	2,353	1,884	24.9	$38,779	$32,320	20.0	2,687	13.2	2.1	0.5	D	D	61.4
Sussex, VA	353	319	10.4	$31,378	$26,598	18.0	209	1.9	7.2	0.8	D	D	38.1
Colonial Heights City, VA	NA	NA	NA	NA	NA	NA	NA	NA	NA	NA	NA	NA	NA
Hopewell City, VA	NA	NA	NA	NA	NA	NA	NA	NA	NA	NA	NA	NA	NA
Petersburg City, VA	NA	NA	NA	NA	NA	NA	NA	NA	NA	NA	NA	NA	NA
Richmond City, VA	12,882	8,784	46.7	$56,306	$43,004	30.9	14,369	3.6	2.1	8.8	15.5	11.9	26.0
Riverside-San Bernardino-Ontario, CA Metro Area	187,142	127,927	46.3	$40,486	$30,153	34.3	111,700	6.9	7.7	2.3	4.1	11.9	23.4
Riverside, CA	99,592	67,585	47.4	$40,637	$30,698	32.4	54,355	6.2	8.2	2.3	4.2	11.2	23.5
San Bernardino, CA	87,550	60,342	45.1	$40,316	$29,566	36.4	57,344	7.6	7.2	2.2	3.9	12.5	23.3
Roanoke, VA Metro Area	14,755	11,641	26.7	$46,963	$37,724	24.5	10,284	10.7	6.1	5.8	7.0	17.1	15.0
Botetourt, VA	1,673	1,306	28.1	$50,274	$39,332	27.8	677	18.8	4.8	1.7	3.0	D	13.7
Craig, VA	193	154	25.4	$38,185	$29,671	28.7	43	D	6.6	3.9	3.1	D	29.8
Franklin, VA	2,292	1,766	29.8	$40,781	$31,428	29.8	858	19.0	8.2	2.1	3.6	9.6	16.3
Roanoke, VA	6,255	4,916	27.2	$52,248	$41,910	24.7	4,057	13.3	5.9	5.8	8.1	D	16.9
Roanoke City, VA	4,342	3,500	24.0	$43,451	$36,185	20.1	4,649	D	6.0	7.0	7.2	21.7	13.2
Salem City, VA	NA	NA	NA	NA	NA	NA	NA	NA	NA	NA	NA	NA	NA
Rochester, MN Metro Area	12,160	8,848	37.4	$55,323	$42,698	29.6	9,539	10.4	4.7	2.0	2.2	49.0	9.4
Dodge, MN	999	752	32.9	$47,984	$37,313	28.6	458	27.6	3.2	2.0	2.4	D	16.2
Fillmore, MN	956	749	27.6	$45,378	$35,905	26.4	378	20.2	7.7	4.7	2.4	D	18.1
Olmsted, MN	9,151	6,553	39.6	$58,554	$45,342	29.1	8,281	8.4	4.6	1.8	2.2	55.3	8.3
Wabasha, MN	1,055	793	32.9	$48,724	$36,610	33.1	422	22.5	5.3	3.9	1.6	D	16.2
Rochester, NY Metro Area	54,804	42,758	28.2	$51,167	$39,592	29.2	38,454	12.8	5.5	4.8	8.6	13.9	16.5
Livingston, NY	2,903	2,177	33.3	$45,908	$33,374	37.6	1,659	8.1	5.0	1.0	D	7.5	30.8
Monroe, NY	39,315	30,935	27.1	$52,951	$41,546	27.5	29,631	11.7	5.1	5.5	10.4	15.1	13.9
Ontario, NY	5,878	4,258	38.0	$53,498	$39,365	35.9	3,765	15.1	7.8	3.3	3.7	12.5	19.2
Orleans, NY	1,582	1,303	21.5	$38,963	$30,410	28.1	878	18.8	5.5	2.1	1.8	D	37.6
Wayne, NY	4,147	3,290	26.0	$46,048	$35,095	31.2	2,046	26.1	6.4	1.7	2.3	7.2	26.4
Yates, NY	979	795	23.1	$39,402	$31,338	25.7	475	15.8	7.9	2.1	D	D	18.9
Rockford, IL Metro Area	14,968	11,832	26.5	$44,328	$33,883	30.8	10,440	26.6	6.1	4.9	3.2	15.9	12.4
Boone, IL	2,542	1,890	34.5	$47,437	$34,936	35.8	1,391	52.6	3.3	1.2	1.6	3.8	11.6
Winnebago, IL	12,426	9,942	25.0	$43,742	$33,691	29.8	9,050	22.7	6.6	5.5	3.5	17.8	12.5
Rocky Mount, NC Metro Area	5,768	4,874	18.3	$39,498	$31,981	23.5	3,303	22.0	8.0	2.9	3.3	D	19.0
Edgecombe, NC	1,817	1,605	13.2	$34,946	$28,345	23.3	860	19.1	11.4	1.4	1.5	D	29.2
Nash, NC	3,950	3,269	20.8	$42,016	$34,131	23.1	2,444	23.0	6.8	3.4	4.0	8.5	15.4
Rome, GA Metro Area	3,772	2,918	29.3	$38,524	$30,258	27.3	2,637	17.7	7.2	2.7	D	25.3	13.9
Floyd, GA	3,772	2,918	29.3	$38,524	$30,258	27.3	2,637	17.7	7.2	2.7	D	25.3	13.9
Sacramento-Roseville-Folsom, CA Metro Area	131,984	88,581	49.0	$56,278	$41,131	36.8	92,719	3.6	5.5	5.4	8.7	12.2	31.0
El Dorado, CA	12,864	8,721	47.5	$67,464	$48,147	40.1	5,108	4.0	6.3	9.8	8.0	11.2	18.7
Placer, CA	26,223	16,640	57.6	$66,700	$47,540	40.3	14,724	3.4	8.0	7.9	8.0	16.9	12.8

Table C-3. Personal Income and Earnings by Industry—Continued

Metropolitan Statistical Area / Metropolitan Division / Component counties	Personal Income Total (million dollars) 2018	2010	Percent change 2010-2018	Per capita Personal Income 2018	2010	Percent change 2010-2018	Total earnings (million dollars)	Manu-facturing	Retail Trade	Finance and Insurance	Professional, Scienfic, and Technical Services	Health Care and Social Assistance	Government and Government Enterprises
Sacramento, CA	80,969	55,137	46.9	$52,544	$38,790	35.5	62,693	3.2	5.1	5.0	9.6	12.1	34.0
Yolo, CA	11,928	8,083	47.6	$54,118	$40,200	34.6	10,195	5.6	4.1	1.4	5.0	6.5	44.6
Saginaw, MI Metro Area	7,394	6,099	21.2	$38,754	$30,518	27.0	5,559	19.9	7.2	4.8	4.0	18.9	14.0
Saginaw, MI	7,394	6,099	21.2	$38,754	$30,518	27.0	5,559	19.9	7.2	4.8	4.0	18.9	14.0
St. Cloud, MN Metro Area	9,293	6,520	42.5	$46,513	$34,455	35.0	7,018	14.1	7.4	4.5	D	D	14.3
Benton, MN	1,777	1,296	37.1	$43,830	$33,687	30.1	1,061	22.8	6.1	1.4	D	D	11.1
Stearns, MN	7,516	5,224	43.9	$47,196	$34,652	36.2	5,957	12.6	7.6	5.1	4.1	19.4	14.9
St. George, UT Metro Area	6,670	3,602	85.2	$38,847	$26,028	49.3	3,919	5.0	9.8	4.2	6.3	16.8	13.4
Washington, UT	6,670	3,602	85.2	$38,847	$26,028	49.3	3,919	5.0	9.8	4.2	6.3	16.8	13.4
St. Joseph, MO-KS Metro Area	4,965	3,973	25.0	$39,253	$31,211	25.8	3,563	24.2	6.4	4.7	D	D	15.1
Doniphan, KS	287	240	19.6	$37,405	$30,184	23.9	131	20.5	4.6	3.6	1.2	5.5	30.7
Andrew, MO	794	616	29.0	$45,118	$35,486	27.1	164	4.1	8.5	2.3	D	D	23.2
Buchanan, MO	3,526	2,818	25.1	$39,810	$31,641	25.8	3,091	26.8	6.2	4.7	4.2	15.9	12.7
De Kalb, MO	357	298	19.8	$28,294	$23,126	22.3	177	1.6	9.9	8.7	1.0	7.3	37.0
St. Louis, MO-IL Metro Area	156,779	118,384	32.4	$55,883	$42,432	31.7	109,871	D	5.2	9.1	9.4	12.8	11.9
Bond, IL	626	529	18.4	$37,653	$29,721	26.7	336	23.2	3.1	2.7	2.0	D	24.3
Calhoun, IL	204	173	17.8	$42,511	$34,016	25.0	50	D	8.5	6.3	2.2	D	30.0
Clinton, IL	1,816	1,385	31.1	$48,253	$36,609	31.8	742	9.4	9.0	3.0	2.6	11.0	21.5
Jersey, IL	907	780	16.3	$41,522	$33,944	22.3	298	3.6	9.2	4.0	6.7	D	28.5
Macoupin, IL	1,885	1,585	18.9	$41,607	$33,160	25.5	684	6.3	7.7	5.1	D	D	21.7
Madison, IL	12,401	9,926	24.9	$46,890	$36,852	27.2	7,106	16.0	6.2	3.1	6.2	11.3	16.2
Monroe, IL	2,015	1,468	37.2	$58,686	$44,500	31.9	583	6.4	8.4	5.8	7.9	6.3	17.5
St. Clair, IL	11,764	9,875	19.1	$45,061	$36,527	23.4	6,859	6.5	6.5	3.0	9.5	12.8	31.2
Franklin, MO	4,740	3,419	38.6	$45,719	$33,702	35.7	2,458	27.8	7.7	3.3	4.4	11.2	10.9
Jefferson, MO	9,598	7,183	33.6	$42,780	$32,782	30.5	3,058	10.5	8.8	3.2	3.8	12.3	17.6
Lincoln, MO	2,353	1,614	45.8	$40,788	$30,631	33.2	782	17.8	8.1	3.3	2.1	8.2	16.8
St. Charles, MO	21,454	14,457	48.4	$53,745	$39,960	34.5	10,334	13.9	7.5	6.6	5.5	10.2	11.2
St. Louis, MO	71,142	53,614	32.7	$71,360	$53,676	32.9	54,998	9.0	5.4	11.3	10.2	12.5	7.4
Warren, MO	1,447	1,020	41.8	$41,674	$31,323	33.0	481	26.9	5.8	3.2	D	D	16.1
St. Louis city, MO	14,428	11,355	27.1	$47,643	$35,560	34.0	21,102	8.4	1.4	10.8	13.1	16.3	14.0
Salem, OR Metro Area	18,457	12,318	49.8	$42,714	$31,463	35.8	12,386	6.3	6.4	3.0	4.1	14.8	29.3
Marion, OR	14,930	9,915	50.6	$43,042	$31,381	37.2	11,113	5.8	6.5	3.1	4.1	15.0	29.5
Polk, OR	3,527	2,403	46.8	$41,379	$31,804	30.1	1,273	10.0	5.4	1.8	3.5	12.8	28.1
Salinas, CA Metro Area	24,477	17,264	41.8	$56,193	$41,460	35.5	17,001	2.4	5.2	2.0	4.0	7.8	23.9
Monterey, CA	24,477	17,264	41.8	$56,193	$41,460	35.5	17,001	2.4	5.2	2.0	4.0	7.8	23.9
Salisbury, MD-DE Metro Area	19,801	13,637	45.2	$48,296	$36,382	32.7	11,009	D	8.7	3.1	D	15.0	15.6
Sussex, DE	11,541	7,236	59.5	$50,333	$36,564	37.7	5,761	D	9.0	2.6	D	15.2	11.3
Somerset, MD	810	680	19.1	$31,562	$25,701	22.8	505	3.7	3.0	D	2.2	D	44.0
Wicomico, MD	4,340	3,432	26.5	$42,054	$34,674	21.3	3,132	6.2	8.6	4.8	4.0	19.8	18.1
Worcester, MD	3,110	2,289	35.8	$60,007	$44,454	35.0	1,610	3.1	9.4	2.5	5.4	9.2	17.5
Salt Lake City, UT Metro Area	63,249	39,345	60.8	$51,736	$36,047	43.5	56,956	8.3	7.2	9.0	D	7.6	14.8
Salt Lake, UT	60,674	37,637	61.2	$52,639	$36,435	44.5	55,950	8.3	7.3	9.2	10.9	7.6	14.5
Tooele, UT	2,575	1,708	50.7	$36,836	$29,201	26.1	1,006	11.0	6.2	1.4	D	7.8	28.9
San Angelo, TX Metro Area	5,616	4,173	34.6	$46,406	$36,793	26.1	3,594	D	7.0	D	D	14.1	23.0
Irion, TX	104	70	48.3	$68,327	$43,635	56.6	83	D	1.8	D	D	0.1	7.8
Sterling, TX	76	41	85.0	$58,174	$36,248	60.5	43	0.4	2.6	D	D	D	19.7
Tom Green, TX	5,436	4,062	33.8	$45,993	$36,699	25.3	3,468	10.4	7.2	5.9	4.2	14.6	23.4
San Antonio-New Braunfels, TX Metro Area	118,335	77,234	53.2	$46,995	$35,872	31.0	84,405	4.8	6.0	9.4	6.7	10.8	19.9
Atascosa, TX	1,844	1,294	42.6	$36,660	$28,781	27.4	1,015	2.3	6.3	1.8	3.1	6.9	14.4
Bandera, TX	992	676	46.7	$43,459	$32,876	32.2	228	1.0	6.3	3.8	5.4	11.0	18.9
Bexar, TX	91,473	61,085	49.7	$46,058	$35,456	29.9	73,578	4.2	5.5	10.2	6.8	11.2	20.7
Comal, TX	8,616	4,821	78.7	$58,067	$44,118	31.6	3,980	5.2	10.3	3.5	6.7	10.0	11.1
Guadalupe, TX	7,335	4,508	62.7	$44,809	$33,996	31.8	2,877	23.8	7.3	2.1	3.2	6.1	15.0
Kendall, TX	3,846	2,035	89.0	$84,270	$60,526	39.2	1,502	4.6	13.2	8.2	15.4	8.6	9.2
Medina, TX	2,006	1,361	47.4	$39,403	$29,509	33.5	641	0.8	9.8	4.3	4.7	D	28.8
Wilson, TX	2,223	1,455	52.8	$44,255	$33,789	31.0	583	4.7	9.7	2.5	5.1	D	24.4
San Diego-Chula Vista-Carlsbad, CA Metro Area	205,236	136,970	49.8	$61,386	$44,137	39.1	148,502	8.6	4.8	4.6	14.7	8.5	23.3
San Diego, CA	205,236	136,970	49.8	$61,386	$44,137	39.1	148,502	8.6	4.8	4.6	14.7	8.5	23.3
San Francisco-Oakland-Berkeley, CA Metro Area	470,222	266,002	76.8	$99,424	$61,237	62.4	344,893	6.1	4.2	8.4	19.3	7.7	11.6
Oakland-Berkeley-Livermore, CA Div	222,646	129,746	71.6	$79,038	$50,571	56.3	132,025	9.8	5.1	4.9	13.0	11.3	14.6
Alameda, CA	127,746	72,841	75.4	$76,644	$48,142	59.2	90,616	11.7	5.0	3.4	13.9	10.0	15.5
Contra Costa, CA	94,900	56,904	66.8	$82,506	$54,063	52.6	41,410	5.7	5.3	8.3	11.2	14.1	12.6
San Francisco-San Mateo-Redwood City, CA Div	212,709	114,992	85.0	$128,692	$75,391	70.7	197,163	3.6	3.4	11.0	23.9	5.0	9.6
San Francisco, CA	115,445	61,873	86.6	$130,696	$76,808	70.2	126,048	1.6	3.3	12.7	26.8	4.5	11.8
San Mateo, CA	97,265	53,119	83.1	$126,392	$73,805	71.3	71,116	7.3	3.5	7.8	18.7	5.9	5.6
San Rafael, CA Div	34,867	21,264	64.0	$134,275	$84,080	59.7	15,704	6.1	7.1	6.2	15.3	10.4	11.8
Marin, CA	34,867	21,264	64.0	$134,275	$84,080	59.7	15,704	6.1	7.1	6.2	15.3	10.4	11.8
San Jose-Sunnyvale-Santa Clara, CA Metro Area	212,332	111,534	90.4	$106,213	$60,564	75.4	194,331	22.3	3.1	2.7	D	6.1	6.0
San Benito, CA	3,312	1,990	66.1	$53,822	$35,912	49.9	1,420	20.0	4.6	1.9	D	4.2	21.0
Santa Clara, CA	209,020	109,540	90.8	$107,877	$61,330	75.9	192,911	22.3	3.1	2.7	18.9	6.1	5.9
San Luis Obispo-Paso Robles, CA Metro Area	16,612	10,855	53.0	$58,491	$40,233	45.4	10,031	6.0	8.2	3.2	7.9	10.4	20.8
San Luis Obispo, CA	16,612	10,855	53.0	$58,491	$40,233	45.4	10,031	6.0	8.2	3.2	7.9	10.4	20.8
Santa Cruz-Watsonville, CA Metro Area	19,021	12,794	48.7	$69,355	$48,616	42.7	9,606	7.4	7.5	3.1	8.0	13.2	19.2
Santa Cruz, CA	19,021	12,794	48.7	$69,355	$48,616	42.7	9,606	7.4	7.5	3.1	8.0	13.2	19.2

Table C-3. Personal Income and Earnings by Industry—*Continued*

Metropolitan Statistical Area Metropolitan Division Component counties	Personal Income Total (million dollars) 2018	2010	Percent change 2010-2018	Per capita Personal Income 2018	2010	Percent change 2010-2018	Earnings 2018 Total earnings (million dollars)	Manu-facturing	Retail Trade	Finance and Insurance	Professional, Scienfic, and Technical Services	Health Care and Social Assistance	Government and Government Enterprises
Santa Fe, NM Metro Area	8,780	6,251	40.5	$58,510	$43,251	35.3	4,238	D	8.6	5.8	10.1	14.2	27.0
Santa Fe, NM	8,780	6,251	40.5	$58,510	$43,251	35.3	4,238	D	8.6	5.8	10.1	14.2	27.0
Santa Maria-Santa Barbara, CA Metro Area	27,993	19,354	44.6	$62,690	$45,621	37.4	18,535	7.1	5.5	2.9	10.0	10.8	20.1
Santa Barbara, CA	27,993	19,354	44.6	$62,690	$45,621	37.4	18,535	7.1	5.5	2.9	10.0	10.8	20.1
Santa Rosa-Petaluma, CA Metro Area	32,247	20,831	54.8	$64,501	$42,969	50.1	19,537	12.3	7.0	3.7	7.4	13.2	13.5
Sonoma, CA	32,247	20,831	54.8	$64,501	$42,969	50.1	19,537	12.3	7.0	3.7	7.4	13.2	13.5
Savannah, GA Metro Area	18,362	13,090	40.3	$47,144	$37,546	25.6	12,798	16.8	6.5	3.4	4.5	D	17.7
Bryan, GA	1,999	1,275	56.8	$52,456	$41,956	25.0	582	10.9	8.3	3.1	5.4	7.0	24.2
Chatham, GA	13,755	10,114	36.0	$47,563	$38,054	25.0	11,445	17.1	6.5	3.5	4.3	13.1	16.9
Effingham, GA	2,608	1,701	53.4	$41,942	$32,419	29.4	771	16.8	5.2	1.6	5.6	D	25.6
Scranton--Wilkes-Barre, PA Metro Area	25,649	20,575	24.7	$46,175	$36,496	26.5	16,621	11.8	6.8	5.4	D	D	14.2
Lackawanna, PA	10,061	8,172	23.1	$47,730	$38,092	25.3	6,363	10.3	6.8	6.2	5.9	18.8	13.0
Luzerne, PA	14,364	11,478	25.1	$45,219	$35,758	26.5	9,488	11.7	6.8	5.1	4.3	16.2	15.4
Wyoming, PA	1,225	925	32.4	$45,285	$32,756	38.2	770	25.1	6.0	1.9	D	D	10.0
Seattle-Tacoma-Bellevue, WA Metro Area	293,954	168,310	74.6	$74,620	$48,796	52.9	223,482	9.4	9.5	4.1	10.9	9.0	13.4
Seattle-Bellevue-Kent, WA Div	247,505	137,760	79.7	$81,201	$51,909	56.4	195,661	10.0	9.9	4.2	11.9	8.0	11.1
King, WA	201,962	109,194	85.0	$90,438	$56,333	60.5	169,033	7.1	10.4	4.2	12.8	7.9	10.6
Snohomish, WA	45,543	28,567	59.4	$55,888	$39,925	40.0	26,627	28.0	6.8	4.3	6.0	8.5	14.4
Tacoma-Lakewood, WA Div	46,449	30,550	52.0	$52,114	$38,409	35.7	27,822	5.3	6.3	3.3	4.0	16.2	29.6
Pierce, WA	46,449	30,550	52.0	$52,114	$38,409	35.7	27,822	5.3	6.3	3.3	4.0	16.2	29.6
Sebastian-Vero Beach, FL Metro Area	11,973	7,291	64.2	$76,059	$52,732	44.2	3,769	4.4	8.6	6.2	11.2	17.6	9.7
Indian River, FL	11,973	7,291	64.2	$76,059	$52,732	44.2	3,769	4.4	8.6	6.2	11.2	17.6	9.7
Sebring-Avon Park, FL Metro Area	3,527	2,839	24.2	$33,453	$28,785	16.2	1,516	2.6	10.9	2.7	3.1	23.2	16.3
Highlands, FL	3,527	2,839	24.2	$33,453	$28,785	16.2	1,516	2.6	10.9	2.7	3.1	23.2	16.3
Sheboygan, WI Metro Area	6,102	4,492	35.9	$52,851	$38,882	35.9	4,568	41.5	5.3	5.9	2.7	11.8	8.9
Sheboygan, WI	6,102	4,492	35.9	$52,851	$38,882	35.9	4,568	41.5	5.3	5.9	2.7	11.8	8.9
Sherman-Denison, TX Metro Area	5,654	3,905	44.8	$42,195	$32,265	30.8	3,008	14.4	7.9	5.3	3.7	19.7	14.2
Grayson, TX	5,654	3,905	44.8	$42,195	$32,265	30.8	3,008	14.4	7.9	5.3	3.7	19.7	14.2
Shreveport-Bossier City, LA Metro Area	18,489	15,703	17.7	$46,509	$39,263	18.5	12,133	6.5	7.4	3.3	D	16.5	22.3
Bossier, LA	5,615	4,376	28.3	$44,149	$37,185	18.7	3,376	5.0	9.1	2.6	5.5	8.7	33.4
Caddo, LA	11,761	10,427	12.8	$48,413	$40,795	18.7	8,232	6.5	6.9	3.7	5.2	20.8	17.9
De Soto, LA	1,113	900	23.7	$40,584	$33,747	20.3	526	17.4	6.0	2.0	D	D	20.9
Sierra Vista-Douglas, AZ Metro Area	5,110	4,556	12.2	$40,308	$34,563	16.6	2,829	1.2	6.7	2.8	7.1	9.1	47.7
Cochise, AZ	5,110	4,556	12.2	$40,308	$34,563	16.6	2,829	1.2	6.7	2.8	7.1	9.1	47.7
Sioux City, IA-NE-SD Metro Area	7,282	5,873	24.0	$50,586	$40,812	23.9	5,174	D	6.4	5.3	3.6	D	12.0
Woodbury, IA	4,510	3,715	21.4	$43,988	$36,282	21.2	3,172	14.0	8.4	2.9	3.7	15.9	15.0
Dakota, NE	840	613	37.0	$41,831	$29,159	43.5	899	42.6	3.9	7.7	D	3.0	8.7
Dixon, NE	252	208	21.0	$44,185	$34,819	26.9	127	D	1.4	1.8	D	D	16.4
Union, SD	1,679	1,336	25.7	$107,497	$92,203	16.6	976	12.5	3.1	11.1	6.3	21.4	4.4
Sioux Falls, SD Metro Area	15,812	10,620	48.9	$59,520	$46,356	28.4	12,090	D	6.9	D	5.4	D	8.4
Lincoln, SD	3,961	2,269	74.6	$67,364	$50,209	34.2	1,836	8.6	6.8	16.5	6.4	15.9	5.8
McCook, SD	291	226	29.0	$52,453	$40,218	30.4	130	D	5.1	3.2	2.6	9.5	10.9
Minnehaha, SD	11,037	7,781	41.8	$57,223	$45,785	25.0	9,825	8.0	7.1	18.1	5.5	20.0	9.0
Turner, SD	522	345	51.6	$62,019	$41,264	50.3	300	32.4	2.2	D	D	D	6.5
South Bend-Mishawaka, IN-MI Metro Area	15,233	10,912	39.6	$47,244	$34,201	38.1	9,666	15.7	6.1	4.0	8.7	14.6	9.7
St. Joseph, IN	12,909	9,263	39.4	$47,673	$34,716	37.3	8,993	15.3	6.2	4.0	9.1	15.2	8.9
Cass, MI	2,324	1,649	40.9	$44,994	$31,568	42.5	673	21.9	4.6	2.9	3.8	7.6	21.3
Spartanburg, SC Metro Area	13,544	9,118	48.5	$43,148	$32,021	34.7	10,023	27.0	6.1	4.3	4.2	D	15.1
Spartanburg, SC	13,544	9,118	48.5	$43,148	$32,021	34.7	10,023	27.0	6.1	4.3	4.2	D	15.1
Spokane-Spokane Valley, WA Metro Area	25,701	17,912	43.5	$45,903	$34,744	32.1	17,211	7.3	7.4	6.6	D	D	19.9
Spokane, WA	23,913	16,619	43.9	$46,466	$35,203	32.0	16,503	7.1	7.5	6.8	6.1	17.3	19.5
Stevens, WA	1,788	1,293	38.3	$39,505	$29,750	32.8	707	10.7	6.9	1.9	D	D	28.9
Springfield, IL Metro Area	10,131	8,256	22.7	$48,793	$39,226	24.4	7,428	3.1	5.6	7.0	6.1	D	23.9
Menard, IL	580	477	21.7	$47,233	$37,557	25.8	140	1.3	5.8	5.3	6.0	D	27.5
Sangamon, IL	9,551	7,779	22.8	$48,891	$39,333	24.3	7,289	3.1	5.6	7.1	6.1	20.7	23.8
Springfield, MA Metro Area	36,509	27,373	33.4	$51,953	$39,390	31.9	22,202	8.9	5.6	5.9	4.6	18.4	21.3
Franklin, MA	3,881	2,923	32.8	$54,689	$40,955	33.5	1,852	13.7	D	1.9	4.3	13.0	19.3
Hampden, MA	24,079	18,223	32.1	$51,187	$39,253	30.4	15,205	9.8	6.1	7.6	4.3	21.0	18.3
Hampshire, MA	8,549	6,227	37.3	$52,984	$39,087	35.6	5,144	4.6	6.2	2.5	5.5	12.6	30.9
Springfield, MO Metro Area	19,510	13,976	39.6	$41,780	$31,959	30.7	13,388	9.8	7.3	5.0	8.0	17.4	13.5
Christian, MO	3,506	2,355	48.9	$40,301	$30,247	33.2	1,073	7.7	9.2	4.6	5.3	6.6	17.4
Dallas, MO	556	420	32.4	$33,184	$25,120	32.1	164	6.1	10.5	4.1	1.6	D	20.8
Greene, MO	13,089	9,450	38.5	$44,837	$34,324	30.6	11,165	9.8	7.0	5.3	8.8	19.3	12.0
Polk, MO	1,085	787	37.8	$33,703	$25,266	33.4	514	4.2	7.9	3.1	D	11.2	32.6
Webster, MO	1,275	964	32.2	$32,589	$26,582	22.6	472	21.3	9.0	2.8	D	D	16.8
Springfield, OH Metro Area	5,487	4,451	23.3	$40,769	$32,187	26.7	2,998	16.7	6.4	7.1	2.9	15.4	15.5
Clark, OH	5,487	4,451	23.3	$40,769	$32,187	26.7	2,998	16.7	6.4	7.1	2.9	15.4	15.5
State College, PA Metro Area	7,521	5,506	36.6	$46,193	$35,706	29.4	6,292	5.1	4.3	2.2	6.0	10.3	47.9
Centre, PA	7,521	5,506	36.6	$46,193	$35,706	29.4	6,292	5.1	4.3	2.2	6.0	10.3	47.9
Staunton, VA Metro Area	5,451	4,258	28.0	$44,316	$35,989	23.1	3,122	18.7	6.4	2.7	3.2	D	17.3
Augusta, VA	5,451	4,258	28.0	$44,316	$35,989	23.1	3,122	18.7	6.4	2.7	3.2	D	17.3
Staunton City, VA	NA	NA	NA	NA	NA	NA	NA	NA	NA	NA	NA	NA	NA
Waynesboro City, VA	NA	NA	NA	NA	NA	NA	NA	NA	NA	NA	NA	NA	NA

Table C-3. Personal Income and Earnings by Industry—*Continued*

Metropolitan Statistical Area Metropolitan Division Component counties	Personal Income						Earnings 2018						
	Total (million dollars)			Per capita Personal Income				Earnings by Industry (percent)					
	2018	2010	Percent change 2010-2018	2018	2010	Percent change 2010-2018	Total earnings (million dollars)	Manu-facturing	Retail Trade	Finance and Insurance	Professional, Scienfic, and Technical Services	Health Care and Social Assistance	Government and Government Enterprises
Stockton, CA Metro Area	33,866	22,508	50.5	$44,995	$32,755	37.4	19,207	7.8	6.8	2.8	2.8	11.9	21.6
San Joaquin, CA	33,866	22,508	50.5	$44,995	$32,755	37.4	19,207	7.8	6.8	2.8	2.8	11.9	21.6
Sumter, SC Metro Area	5,230	4,062	28.8	$37,304	$28,495	30.9	3,194	15.7	6.5	2.2	3.1	11.5	34.0
Clarendon, SC	1,119	841	33.0	$33,197	$24,061	38.0	375	6.0	13.1	2.9	5.5	8.3	34.9
Sumter, SC	4,112	3,221	27.6	$38,603	$29,935	29.0	2,819	17.0	5.6	2.1	2.8	11.9	33.9
Syracuse, NY Metro Area	32,353	25,216	28.3	$49,736	$38,028	30.8	23,328	10.0	5.8	4.9	8.2	D	21.0
Madison, NY	3,151	2,467	27.7	$44,502	$33,599	32.5	1,441	13.9	8.7	2.1	4.5	D	23.0
Onondaga, NY	24,423	18,865	29.5	$52,886	$40,350	31.1	19,470	9.5	5.4	5.5	9.2	13.6	19.8
Oswego, NY	4,779	3,884	23.0	$40,538	$31,802	27.5	2,416	11.8	7.6	1.9	3.1	10.4	29.9
Tallahassee, FL Metro Area	16,408	12,804	28.1	$42,601	$34,668	22.9	11,564	2.1	5.6	4.5	11.3	D	34.6
Gadsden, FL	1,613	1,324	21.8	$35,139	$27,707	26.8	758	8.1	4.9	1.1	1.3	3.7	32.5
Jefferson, FL	582	465	25.3	$40,736	$31,495	29.3	156	0.3	5.9	2.0	5.3	D	20.2
Leon, FL	13,011	10,119	28.6	$44,482	$36,667	21.3	10,303	1.3	5.6	4.8	12.3	13.7	35.1
Wakulla, FL	1,202	896	34.1	$37,026	$29,076	27.3	347	14.4	7.2	4.2	6.9	5.4	31.0
Tampa-St. Petersburg-Clearwater, FL Metro Area	148,460	107,124	38.6	$47,240	$38,418	23.0	97,343	5.8	7.6	10.3	D	13.5	12.2
Hernando, FL	7,039	5,235	34.5	$36,878	$30,266	21.8	2,556	5.6	10.8	2.8	D	22.4	15.2
Hillsborough, FL	67,534	48,708	38.7	$47,000	$39,488	19.0	55,668	4.1	6.9	12.6	13.5	11.3	12.5
Pasco, FL	21,754	14,909	45.9	$40,313	$32,029	25.9	7,392	3.5	13.1	3.4	6.1	20.2	15.2
Pinellas, FL	52,133	38,272	36.2	$53,455	$41,763	28.0	31,728	9.5	7.4	8.4	10.4	15.1	10.8
Terre Haute, IN Metro Area	7,149	5,801	23.2	$38,299	$30,611	25.1	4,280	18.1	7.0	3.3	2.6	14.9	18.2
Clay, IN	1,011	807	25.2	$38,615	$30,073	28.4	440	40.5	6.8	2.4	1.5	6.6	14.2
Parke, IN	615	479	28.5	$36,345	$27,700	31.2	214	14.5	7.3	2.4	D	D	23.8
Sullivan, IN	728	612	19.0	$35,181	$28,591	23.0	354	11.2	5.4	2.2	1.8	D	27.3
Vermillion, IN	610	517	17.9	$39,411	$32,099	22.8	311	21.9	7.2	1.4	1.4	D	10.9
Vigo, IN	4,185	3,386	23.6	$38,970	$31,390	24.1	2,961	15.5	7.2	3.8	3.2	18.5	18.1
Texarkana, TX-AR Metro Area	5,650	4,766	18.5	$37,607	$31,919	17.8	3,630	11.4	7.3	5.0	D	D	23.4
Little River, AR	420	380	10.6	$34,086	$28,942	17.8	247	49.6	5.3	1.2	1.1	3.3	16.3
Miller, AR	1,456	1,240	17.4	$33,401	$28,474	17.3	781	22.8	5.1	2.3	D	D	15.3
Bowie, TX	3,774	3,146	20.0	$40,010	$33,961	17.8	2,601	4.4	8.1	6.2	3.2	19.2	26.5
The Villages, FL Metro Area	5,936	2,806	111.6	$46,100	$29,758	54.9	1,929	4.9	8.9	4.1	5.5	14.9	20.1
Sumter, FL	5,936	2,806	111.6	$46,100	$29,758	54.9	1,929	4.9	8.9	4.1	5.5	14.9	20.1
Toledo, OH Metro Area	30,166	23,240	29.8	$46,868	$35,679	31.4	22,518	18.7	6.1	3.2	D	D	14.9
Fulton, OH	1,928	1,447	33.2	$45,594	$33,947	34.3	1,222	38.5	5.3	2.0	D	D	12.6
Lucas, OH	19,900	15,427	29.0	$46,290	$34,948	32.5	15,691	15.7	6.6	3.6	6.5	17.0	14.6
Ottawa, OH	2,105	1,600	31.6	$51,637	$38,689	33.5	961	16.2	5.9	2.6	2.8	D	17.3
Wood, OH	6,233	4,766	30.8	$47,694	$37,839	26.0	4,644	24.1	4.7	2.2	3.9	7.1	16.0
Topeka, KS Metro Area	10,703	8,556	25.1	$46,017	$36,521	26.0	7,618	7.2	4.8	9.9	D	14.6	22.4
Jackson, KS	554	438	26.4	$41,686	$32,541	28.1	222	7.8	6.5	4.4	2.1	12.0	44.1
Jefferson, KS	844	658	28.2	$44,480	$34,392	29.3	252	7.5	3.7	2.4	D	D	21.1
Osage, KS	639	530	20.7	$40,102	$32,555	23.2	150	5.2	7.9	D	3.1	D	35.0
Shawnee, KS	8,318	6,653	25.0	$46,861	$37,301	25.6	6,909	7.2	4.7	10.5	7.1	15.3	21.4
Wabaunsee, KS	349	277	25.7	$50,534	$39,340	28.5	85	9.4	2.6	D	2.0	D	24.0
Trenton-Princeton, NJ Metro Area	25,644	19,581	31.0	$69,344	$53,247	30.2	22,667	5.0	3.7	10.4	17.8	8.9	17.8
Mercer, NJ	25,644	19,581	31.0	$69,344	$53,247	30.2	22,667	5.0	3.7	10.4	17.8	8.9	17.8
Tucson, AZ Metro Area	45,748	33,444	36.8	$44,028	$34,069	29.2	27,491	10.5	6.8	4.2	7.3	14.0	23.8
Pima, AZ	45,748	33,444	36.8	$44,028	$34,069	29.2	27,491	10.5	6.8	4.2	7.3	14.0	23.8
Tulsa, OK Metro Area	54,526	38,856	40.3	$54,866	$41,344	32.7	39,567	12.4	5.1	D	D	10.5	8.4
Creek, OK	2,921	2,309	26.5	$40,791	$32,885	24.0	1,310	23.2	5.2	3.1	2.9	9.3	14.5
Okmulgee, OK	1,302	1,104	17.9	$33,971	$27,550	23.3	565	16.2	8.6	4.9	3.8	D	33.6
Osage, OK	1,644	1,337	23.0	$34,971	$28,150	24.2	457	8.0	5.8	3.1	3.3	4.7	34.2
Pawnee, OK	587	488	20.3	$35,836	$29,411	21.8	220	1.8	7.8	D	15.7	10.9	27.8
Rogers, OK	4,214	2,977	41.6	$45,815	$34,217	33.9	1,914	21.9	6.4	2.5	D	6.8	21.7
Tulsa, OK	40,688	28,355	43.5	$62,756	$46,868	33.9	34,398	11.4	4.9	4.3	6.6	10.9	6.5
Wagoner, OK	3,168	2,286	38.6	$39,550	$31,129	27.1	703	17.3	7.3	2.6	3.5	D	14.7
Tuscaloosa, AL Metro Area	9,565	7,555	26.6	$37,983	$31,546	20.4	6,696	21.0	5.7	D	D	D	27.9
Greene, AL	266	240	11.0	$32,359	$26,675	21.3	100	29.0	5.1	D	D	D	29.8
Hale, AL	539	456	18.1	$36,585	$28,974	26.3	172	19.6	5.0	3.0	1.2	5.3	26.0
Pickens, AL	649	577	12.5	$32,551	$29,198	11.5	234	14.3	4.9	D	D	D	34.9
Tuscaloosa, AL	8,110	6,282	29.1	$38,822	$32,217	20.5	6,189	21.1	5.8	2.7	4.6	7.3	27.6
Twin Falls, ID Metro Area	4,328	2,962	46.1	$39,309	$29,625	32.7	3,031	15.5	7.9	2.9	D	14.2	11.2
Jerome, ID	917	647	41.7	$38,184	$28,815	32.5	685	14.2	6.0	1.0	D	4.0	8.0
Twin Falls, ID	3,411	2,315	47.3	$39,623	$29,859	32.7	2,346	16.0	8.5	3.4	3.9	17.3	12.1
Tyler, TX Metro Area	12,715	8,856	43.6	$55,229	$42,092	31.2	9,684	4.3	8.3	3.8	5.4	16.2	9.7
Smith, TX	12,715	8,856	43.6	$55,229	$42,092	31.2	9,684	4.3	8.3	3.8	5.4	16.2	9.7
Urban Honolulu, HI Metro Area	58,421	43,398	34.6	$59,608	$45,381	31.4	42,489	1.9	5.3	3.5	6.3	10.3	31.8
Honolulu, HI	58,421	43,398	34.6	$59,608	$45,381	31.4	42,489	1.9	5.3	3.5	6.3	10.3	31.8
Utica-Rome, NY Metro Area	12,833	10,591	21.2	$44,036	$35,395	24.4	8,106	9.8	6.0	6.7	4.8	16.4	29.8
Herkimer, NY	2,571	2,114	21.6	$41,581	$32,789	26.8	1,066	15.5	7.6	1.5	2.1	9.8	29.1
Oneida, NY	10,261	8,478	21.0	$44,697	$36,111	23.8	7,040	8.9	5.8	7.5	5.2	17.4	29.9
Valdosta, GA Metro Area	5,294	4,058	30.5	$36,217	$28,973	25.0	3,517	D	6.8	D	4.5	D	34.6
Brooks, GA	542	445	21.9	$34,944	$27,368	27.7	183	7.1	5.2	3.1	1.8	8.4	19.3
Echols, GA	112	80	39.7	$27,880	$19,859	40.4	27	D	D	D	0.0	D	37.9
Lanier, GA	285	215	32.3	$27,561	$21,336	29.2	84	9.8	D	D	1.4	2.4	43.8

Table C-3. Personal Income and Earnings by Industry—Continued

Metropolitan Statistical Area Metropolitan Division Component counties	Personal Income						Earnings 2018						
	Total (million dollars)			Per capita Personal Income			Total earnings (million dollars)	Earnings by Industry (percent)					
	2018	2010	Percent change 2010-2018	2018	2010	Percent change 2010-2018		Manu-facturing	Retail Trade	Finance and Insurance	Professional, Scienfic, and Technical Services	Health Care and Social Assistance	Government and Government Enterprises
Lowndes, GA	4,355	3,318	31.3	$37,443	$30,248	23.8	3,223	8.2	7.0	2.7	4.8	8.7	35.2
Vallejo, CA Metro Area	23,074	15,615	47.8	$51,664	$37,723	37.0	13,174	13.2	6.3	2.9	3.4	15.7	24.5
Solano, CA	23,074	15,615	47.8	$51,664	$37,723	37.0	13,174	13.2	6.3	2.9	3.4	15.7	24.5
Victoria, TX Metro Area	4,579	3,420	33.9	$45,968	$36,350	26.5	2,765	D	8.3	3.5	3.5	D	15.9
Goliad, TX	333	219	51.9	$43,858	$30,330	44.6	83	D	4.5	3.8	6.2	D	28.2
Victoria, TX	4,247	3,201	32.7	$46,142	$36,850	25.2	2,681	8.4	8.4	3.5	3.4	14.2	15.5
Vineland-Bridgeton, NJ Metro Area	6,082	5,249	15.9	$40,289	$33,495	20.3	4,285	14.9	7.5	1.8	D	16.3	25.9
Cumberland, NJ	6,082	5,249	15.9	$40,289	$33,495	20.3	4,285	14.9	7.5	1.8	D	16.3	25.9
Virginia Beach-Norfolk-Newport News, VA-NC Metro Area	89,345	69,482	28.6	$50,619	$40,467	25.1	61,397	7.8	5.0	3.9	8.0	10.4	35.3
Camden, NC	486	378	28.5	$45,335	$37,739	20.1	86	2.9	4.7	D	6.5	D	30.8
Currituck, NC	1,230	840	46.5	$45,435	$35,462	28.1	420	1.1	11.3	1.9	D	D	18.1
Gates, NC	417	369	13.1	$36,060	$30,342	18.8	76	D	6.3	3.7	3.8	D	35.2
Gloucester, VA	1,886	1,467	28.6	$50,502	$39,715	27.2	538	2.2	12.6	3.0	4.5	16.5	26.1
Isle of Wight, VA	2,044	1,599	27.8	$55,308	$45,286	22.1	798	28.0	3.2	2.3	5.4	D	12.2
James City County, VA	6,017	4,195	43.4	$65,906	$51,547	27.9	2,704	D	6.5	3.3	9.6	D	23.5
Mathews, VA	494	394	25.4	$56,088	$43,882	27.8	99	4.2	5.9	2.0	5.6	D	23.8
Southampton, VA	1,085	822	31.9	$42,381	$30,212	40.3	423	7.6	8.5	D	3.6	16.3	31.6
York, VA	4,731	3,744	26.4	$59,113	$48,361	22.2	1,591	1.7	8.5	1.7	D	D	32.1
Chesapeake City, VA	12,260	9,413	30.3	$50,529	$42,105	20.0	6,555	5.6	8.7	4.8	10.6	8.2	17.7
Franklin City, VA	NA	NA	NA	NA	NA	NA	NA	NA	NA	NA	NA	NA	NA
Hampton City, VA	5,849	4,940	18.4	$43,547	$35,969	21.1	4,427	3.9	4.6	1.5	10.0	9.3	48.4
Newport News City, VA	7,770	6,377	21.8	$43,501	$35,249	23.4	8,326	30.6	3.9	1.6	5.8	10.4	24.3
Norfolk City, VA	10,208	8,433	21.0	$41,822	$34,705	20.5	15,236	3.3	2.5	4.6	6.0	10.5	50.9
Poquoson City, VA	NA	NA	NA	NA	NA	NA	NA	NA	NA	NA	NA	NA	NA
Portsmouth City, VA	3,896	3,313	17.6	$41,169	$34,713	18.6	4,211	D	2.3	0.9	3.6	9.5	62.4
Suffolk City, VA	4,723	3,588	31.6	$51,798	$42,298	22.5	2,261	7.3	5.6	2.4	13.8	13.0	25.6
Virginia Beach City, VA	26,250	19,610	33.9	$58,308	$44,685	30.5	13,646	3.3	6.1	6.6	10.2	11.5	27.1
Williamsburg City, VA	NA	NA	NA	NA	NA	NA	NA	NA	NA	NA	NA	NA	NA
Visalia, CA Metro Area	18,830	13,499	39.5	$40,420	$30,473	32.6	11,660	8.2	6.2	2.2	2.3	7.2	24.7
Tulare, CA	18,830	13,499	39.5	$40,420	$30,473	32.6	11,660	8.2	6.2	2.2	2.3	7.2	24.7
Waco, TX Metro Area	11,104	7,925	40.1	$40,831	$31,225	30.8	7,983	17.4	6.6	D	4.7	10.6	15.8
Falls, TX	600	477	25.7	$34,619	$26,678	29.8	230	4.1	8.5	D	3.5	8.1	38.7
McLennan, TX	10,504	7,448	41.0	$41,254	$31,570	30.7	7,753	17.8	6.5	6.5	4.7	10.6	15.2
Walla Walla, WA Metro Area	2,811	2,050	37.2	$46,144	$34,785	32.7	1,917	16.1	4.7	2.5	D	D	24.1
Walla Walla, WA	2,811	2,050	37.2	$46,144	$34,785	32.7	1,917	16.1	4.7	2.5	D	D	24.1
Warner Robins, GA Metro Area	7,666	5,820	31.7	$41,944	$34,542	21.4	5,181	D	5.6	D	6.3	D	52.9
Houston, GA	6,627	5,024	31.9	$42,625	$35,693	19.4	4,608	7.9	5.5	1.7	6.8	5.9	56.7
Peach, GA	1,039	796	30.5	$38,066	$28,707	32.6	574	D	6.5	D	1.8	D	22.2
Washington-Arlington-Alexandria, DC-VA-MD-WV Metro Area	453,978	331,671	36.9	$72,483	$58,410	24.1	369,185	D	3.5	D	D	D	26.9
Frederick-Gaithersburg-Rockville, MD Div	110,221	80,717	36.6	$84,253	$66,682	26.4	72,722	D	4.1	D	15.9	D	20.0
Frederick, MD	15,817	11,549	37.0	$61,869	$49,312	25.5	8,250	D	7.1	D	D	D	19.5
Montgomery, MD	94,404	69,168	36.5	$89,690	$70,848	26.6	64,471	3.4	3.7	5.8	17.9	8.6	20.1
Washington-Arlington-Alexandria, DC-VA-MD-WV Division	343,757	250,953	37.0	$69,375	$56,168	23.5	296,463	1.2	3.3	4.3	24.5	6.4	28.6
District of Columbia	57,605	38,482	49.7	$82,005	$63,597	28.9	104,462	0.2	1.0	3.6	24.5	5.6	38.1
Calvert, MD	5,759	4,464	29.0	$62,591	$50,169	24.8	1,875	D	6.6	1.9	6.7	12.8	19.2
Charles, MD	9,214	7,033	31.0	$57,051	$47,795	19.4	3,073	1.4	12.1	2.0	6.0	10.5	32.2
Prince George's, MD	44,938	35,447	26.8	$49,420	$40,944	20.7	28,546	2.2	5.9	1.8	10.0	8.1	37.2
Arlington, VA	22,611	16,658	35.7	$95,198	$79,593	19.6	24,276	D	1.7	4.7	31.8	3.5	29.6
Clarke, VA	975	705	38.2	$67,111	$50,348	33.3	300	13.1	3.4	2.8	13.0	5.8	14.5
Culpeper, VA	2,412	1,720	40.2	$46,510	$36,724	26.6	1,113	8.6	7.9	2.3	6.7	12.7	20.4
Fairfax, VA	98,117	74,064	32.5	$82,441	$66,059	24.8	80,981	0.7	3.8	6.2	35.3	6.6	16.5
Fauquier, VA	5,003	3,625	38.0	$70,787	$55,384	27.8	1,860	3.1	6.8	3.5	15.7	9.2	20.3
Loudoun, VA	31,763	19,977	59.0	$78,070	$63,324	23.3	16,275	6.0	4.5	4.4	20.8	5.8	13.7
Madison, VA	649	450	44.3	$48,822	$33,815	44.4	210	7.9	21.2	1.2	2.1	D	17.5
Prince William, VA	28,846	21,494	34.2	$54,740	$46,843	16.9	13,439	D	6.8	2.0	D	D	27.9
Rappahannock, VA	475	367	29.6	$65,538	$48,903	34.0	120	3.8	4.7	D	17.0	3.8	17.5
Spotsylvania, VA	8,298	6,121	35.6	$50,790	$41,551	22.2	3,979	D	11.5	3.3	11.3	19.2	17.6
Stafford, VA	8,259	6,056	36.4	$55,076	$46,647	18.1	3,586	1.0	5.2	D	11.3	5.7	34.2
Warren, VA	1,870	1,385	35.0	$46,743	$36,924	26.6	783	10.3	6.9	2.7	4.9	11.4	17.9
Alexandria City, VA	14,128	10,784	31.0	$88,008	$76,627	14.9	10,477	D	3.8	3.6	26.5	4.9	31.1
Fairfax City, VA	NA	NA	NA	NA	NA	NA	NA	NA	NA	NA	NA	NA	NA
Falls Church City, VA	NA	NA	NA	NA	NA	NA	NA	NA	NA	NA	NA	NA	NA
Fredericksburg City, VA	NA	NA	NA	NA	NA	NA	NA	NA	NA	NA	NA	NA	NA
Manassas City, VA	NA	NA	NA	NA	NA	NA	NA	NA	NA	NA	NA	NA	NA
Manassas Park City, VA	NA	NA	NA	NA	NA	NA	NA	NA	NA	NA	NA	NA	NA
Jefferson, WV	2,836	2,120	33.8	$49,926	$39,541	26.3	1,107	4.7	5.1	2.2	7.7	8.4	31.7
Waterloo-Cedar Falls, IA Metro Area	7,815	6,037	29.4	$46,063	$35,953	28.1	5,805	24.2	6.4	D	5.2	12.6	15.3
Black Hawk, IA	5,927	4,580	29.4	$44,764	$34,917	28.2	4,885	26.2	6.5	4.5	5.6	13.2	14.9
Bremer, IA	1,233	932	32.2	$49,405	$38,377	28.7	619	17.2	7.2	14.7	2.8	D	19.5
Grundy, IA	655	525	24.8	$53,270	$42,130	26.4	301	6.8	3.6	D	3.1	D	13.0

Table C-3. Personal Income and Earnings by Industry—*Continued*

Metropolitan Statistical Area / Metropolitan Division / Component counties	Personal Income Total (million dollars)			Per capita Personal Income			Earnings 2018 Total earnings (million dollars)	Earnings by Industry (percent)					
	2018	2010	Percent change 2010-2018	2018	2010	Percent change 2010-2018		Manufacturing	Retail Trade	Finance and Insurance	Professional, Scienfic, and Technical Services	Health Care and Social Assistance	Government and Government Enterprises
Watertown-Fort Drum, NY Metro Area	5,244	4,825	8.7	$46,924	$41,381	13.4	3,960	3.7	6.1	1.6	1.8	10.8	57.1
Jefferson, NY	5,244	4,825	8.7	$46,924	$41,381	13.4	3,960	3.7	6.1	1.6	1.8	10.8	57.1
Wausau-Weston, WI Metro Area	8,054	6,009	34.0	$49,373	$36,906	33.8	5,819	23.0	5.9	9.8	4.3	14.5	11.7
Lincoln, WI	1,267	1,003	26.3	$45,766	$34,859	31.3	722	25.1	6.7	13.8	1.4	7.4	16.8
Marathon, WI	6,786	5,006	35.6	$50,111	$37,345	34.2	5,097	22.7	5.8	9.3	4.7	15.4	11.0
Weirton-Steubenville, WV-OH Metro Area	4,738	3,844	23.2	$40,472	$30,922	30.9	2,405	19.0	6.9	2.7	D	17.4	13.4
Jefferson, OH	2,585	2,098	23.2	$39,311	$30,120	30.5	1,320	9.6	7.8	2.0	D	D	15.4
Brooke, WV	927	743	24.7	$41,740	$30,972	34.8	482	23.4	7.3	1.7	D	D	9.9
Hancock, WV	1,226	1,003	22.2	$42,128	$32,705	28.8	602	36.1	4.5	4.8	5.0	8.2	11.7
Wenatchee, WA Metro Area	6,000	3,800	57.9	$50,021	$34,149	46.5	3,629	4.2	9.8	1.9	3.7	15.2	20.8
Chelan, WA	4,219	2,616	61.3	$54,763	$35,958	52.3	2,883	4.0	9.7	2.0	3.5	17.7	19.6
Douglas, WA	1,781	1,184	50.5	$41,508	$30,733	35.1	746	5.1	10.1	1.6	4.5	5.7	25.6
Wheeling, WV-OH Metro Area	6,845	4,864	40.7	$48,881	$32,887	48.6	4,975	5.0	5.9	3.5	11.9	D	11.1
Belmont, OH	2,864	2,145	33.5	$42,429	$30,493	39.1	1,441	3.4	9.4	2.3	2.7	13.3	16.5
Marshall, WV	1,263	930	35.7	$41,028	$28,135	45.8	1,344	9.2	3.1	0.9	1.8	D	7.7
Ohio, WV	2,718	1,789	51.9	$65,100	$40,205	61.9	2,190	3.5	5.4	6.0	24.2	19.6	9.6
Wichita, KS Metro Area	33,061	24,197	36.6	$51,854	$38,784	33.7	23,178	21.3	5.4	3.1	5.3	D	12.4
Butler, KS	3,082	2,417	27.5	$46,157	$36,669	25.9	1,330	17.7	5.6	3.2	4.1	12.0	21.2
Harvey, KS	1,439	1,181	21.9	$42,057	$33,984	23.8	895	27.0	5.4	3.0	3.6	D	11.4
Sedgwick, KS	27,620	19,776	39.7	$53,776	$39,621	35.7	20,522	21.5	5.4	3.0	5.6	11.0	11.7
Sumner, KS	920	824	11.8	$40,027	$34,153	17.2	431	13.8	5.5	4.4	2.6	6.4	21.8
Wichita Falls, TX Metro Area	6,586	5,698	15.6	$43,527	$37,573	15.8	4,068	10.0	7.3	4.1	2.8	14.3	28.6
Archer, TX	442	355	24.5	$50,310	$38,953	29.2	158	3.2	6.3	D	4.3	D	21.6
Clay, TX	443	381	16.3	$42,335	$35,456	19.4	102	4.5	8.8	D	4.1	D	28.1
Wichita, TX	5,701	4,962	14.9	$43,170	$37,650	14.7	3,808	10.5	7.3	4.1	2.7	15.0	28.9
Williamsport, PA Metro Area	4,981	3,971	25.4	$43,823	$34,168	28.3	3,407	16.6	6.4	3.4	4.1	17.0	18.3
Lycoming, PA	4,981	3,971	25.4	$43,823	$34,168	28.3	3,407	16.6	6.4	3.4	4.1	17.0	18.3
Wilmington, NC Metro Area	12,752	8,744	45.8	$43,311	$34,195	26.7	8,414	6.2	7.8	4.7	11.2	10.4	20.1
New Hanover, NC	10,520	7,166	46.8	$45,290	$35,250	28.5	7,658	6.2	7.9	5.0	11.7	10.6	19.9
Pender, NC	2,232	1,578	41.5	$35,914	$30,103	19.3	755	5.8	7.1	1.7	5.4	8.3	22.5
Winchester, VA-WV Metro Area	6,735	4,708	43.1	$48,174	$36,590	31.7	4,297	13.1	8.0	5.7	D	D	18.6
Frederick, VA	5,917	4,055	45.9	$50,802	$38,724	31.2	4,079	13.7	8.0	5.8	D	17.3	18.0
Winchester City, VA	NA	NA	NA	NA	NA	NA	NA	NA	NA	NA	NA	NA	NA
Hampshire, WV	819	653	25.3	$35,068	$27,264	28.6	218	2.8	9.4	4.4	2.9	D	29.3
Winston-Salem, NC Metro Area	30,115	22,867	31.7	$44,850	$35,657	25.8	18,710	12.4	6.7	7.9	6.5	D	10.4
Davidson, NC	6,512	5,005	30.1	$39,087	$30,732	27.2	2,822	22.0	6.3	1.8	2.8	9.0	13.3
Davie, NC	2,035	1,503	35.4	$47,630	$36,430	30.7	739	25.9	7.2	2.8	4.4	9.3	12.8
Forsyth, NC	18,502	13,862	33.5	$48,804	$39,449	23.7	14,152	9.3	6.7	9.8	7.7	19.8	9.1
Stokes, NC	1,675	1,351	24.0	$36,850	$28,531	29.2	425	10.7	9.5	2.8	2.9	10.7	23.1
Yadkin, NC	1,390	1,146	21.3	$37,027	$29,810	24.2	572	25.4	5.4	2.4	2.2	D	14.8
Worcester, MA-CT Metro Area	52,892	39,446	34.1	$55,801	$42,926	30.0	31,780	12.5	6.0	5.3	8.1	15.7	16.3
Windham, CT	5,531	4,470	23.7	$47,264	$37,708	25.3	2,732	18.5	8.0	1.7	3.6	14.9	19.4
Worcester, MA	47,361	34,976	35.4	$57,003	$43,698	30.4	29,048	12.0	5.8	5.8	8.5	15.8	16.0
Yakima, WA Metro Area	10,908	7,830	39.3	$43,379	$32,053	35.3	6,989	8.7	7.2	2.0	2.5	14.5	18.8
Yakima, WA	10,908	7,830	39.3	$43,379	$32,053	35.3	6,989	8.7	7.2	2.0	2.5	14.5	18.8
York-Hanover, PA Metro Area	22,464	17,538	28.1	$50,113	$40,279	24.4	13,238	18.5	5.6	2.8	5.4	14.0	13.1
York, PA	22,464	17,538	28.1	$50,113	$40,279	24.4	13,238	18.5	5.6	2.8	5.4	14.0	13.1
Youngstown-Warren-Boardman, OH-PA Metro Area	22,875	18,591	23.0	$42,443	$32,914	29.0	13,641	15.9	7.9	3.4	D	16.8	14.9
Mahoning, OH	9,897	8,275	19.6	$43,097	$34,714	24.1	6,037	10.3	7.8	3.1	4.4	19.3	16.6
Trumbull, OH	8,216	6,545	25.5	$41,363	$31,193	32.6	4,542	20.4	8.4	2.8	2.2	13.0	14.2
Mercer, PA	4,762	3,770	26.3	$43,024	$32,331	33.1	3,061	20.4	7.4	4.9	D	17.6	12.6
Yuba City, CA Metro Area	7,505	5,588	34.3	$42,925	$33,441	28.4	4,114	4.2	6.9	2.0	D	D	34.0
Sutter, CA	4,311	3,309	30.3	$44,535	$34,920	27.5	2,213	5.2	9.7	3.1	2.9	12.9	19.2
Yuba, CA	3,194	2,279	40.1	$40,929	$31,504	29.9	1,901	3.0	3.6	0.6	D	D	51.2
Yuma, AZ Metro Area	7,569	5,369	41.0	$35,682	$27,234	31.0	5,173	3.4	9.5	1.6	4.7	10.3	27.5
Yuma, AZ	7,569	5,369	41.0	$35,682	$27,234	31.0	5,173	3.4	9.5	1.6	4.7	10.3	27.5

Table C-4. Labor Force and Private Business Establishments and Employment

Metropolitan Statistical Area / Metropolitan Division / Component counties	Civilian Labor Force — Total 2018	2010	2005	Percent change 2010-2018	2005-2010	Unemployment rate 2018	2010	2005	Private nonfarm businesses — Establishments 2017	change 2010-2017	Employment 2017	Change 2010-2017	Annual payroll per employee 2017 (dollars)
Abilene, TX Metro Area	77,053	76,448	80,081	0.8	-4.5	3.3	7.0	4.2	3,969	1.8	58,400	4.6	$36,851
Callahan, TX	6,023	6,002	6,993	0.3	-14.2	3.4	7.3	4.1	216	-6.1	1,498	-1.3	$39,361
Jones, TX	5,721	6,161	7,869	-7.1	-21.7	4.8	8.8	5.4	276	-8.0	2,262	-11.2	$42,415
Taylor, TX	65,309	64,285	65,219	1.6	-1.4	3.2	6.8	4.1	3,477	3.2	54,640	5.5	$36,552
Akron, OH Metro Area	357,240	372,207	380,527	-4.0	-2.2	4.6	10.5	5.9	16,425	-0.9	296,361	9.7	$45,998
Portage, OH	86,523	90,710	89,469	-4.6	1.4	4.6	10.3	5.8	3,044	2.6	46,597	14.4	$39,370
Summit, OH	270,717	281,497	291,058	-3.8	-3.3	4.7	10.6	5.9	13,381	-1.6	249,764	8.8	$47,234
Albany, GA Metro Area	66,101	69,533	72,558	-4.9	-4.2	4.8	11.7	5.7	3,084	-6.8	46,015	3.5	$38,081
Dougherty, GA	38,361	41,490	41,217	-7.5	0.7	5.1	12.6	6.3	2,250	-8.4	37,251	0.2	$38,896
Lee, GA	14,885	14,345	16,403	3.8	-12.5	3.6	9.0	4.0	400	7.2	4,211	30.8	$36,075
Terrell, GA	3,673	3,917	4,586	-6.2	-14.6	6.6	12.2	6.9	172	-4.4	1,761	10.0	$33,857
Worth, GA	9,182	9,781	10,352	-6.1	-5.5	4.4	12.1	5.5	262	-12.7	2,792	14.3	$32,900
Albany-Lebanon, OR Metro Area	58,551	57,072	51,945	2.6	9.9	4.7	12.8	7.5	2,612	6.9	36,602	15.4	$41,268
Linn, OR	58,551	57,072	51,945	2.6	9.9	4.7	12.8	7.5	2,612	6.9	36,602	15.4	$41,268
Albany-Schenectady-Troy, NY Metro Area	450,252	459,102	454,313	-1.9	1.1	3.8	7.3	4.0	21,565	2.4	353,006	9.2	$49,480
Albany, NY	158,835	161,511	159,258	-1.7	1.4	3.7	7.0	3.9	9,533	0.7	178,772	6.4	$50,077
Rensselaer, NY	81,358	84,603	83,813	-3.8	0.9	3.9	7.8	4.2	2,983	0.1	43,481	5.0	$48,206
Saratoga, NY	118,982	118,048	119,981	0.8	-1.6	3.5	6.9	3.6	5,417	9.2	71,721	17.4	$49,342
Schenectady, NY	76,303	79,016	75,405	-3.4	4.8	4.0	7.6	4.2	3,045	-1.8	53,661	13.1	$49,860
Schoharie, NY	14,774	15,924	15,856	-7.2	0.4	4.8	8.9	5.0	587	5.6	5,371	-1.8	$37,980
Albuquerque, NM Metro Area	429,850	424,690	394,236	1.2	7.7	4.7	8.0	4.8	18,848	0.9	303,614	8.5	$42,369
Bernalillo, NM	329,380	326,594	305,757	0.9	6.8	4.5	7.7	4.7	15,964	0.1	268,114	10.3	$43,410
Sandoval, NM	64,633	60,901	50,173	6.1	21.4	5.0	8.4	5.2	1,766	9.6	24,047	-1.4	$36,891
Torrance, NM	5,603	6,028	7,606	-7.1	-20.7	7.6	11.6	5.5	207	-11.2	1,615	-10.1	$31,773
Valencia, NM	30,234	31,167	30,700	-3.0	1.5	5.5	9.6	5.3	911	1.2	9,838	-8.0	$29,135
Alexandria, LA Metro Area	63,352	67,410	67,767	-6.0	-0.5	5.4	7.7	6.2	3,293	-4.5	47,260	-3.3	$38,364
Grant, LA	8,071	8,590	8,558	-6.0	0.4	5.9	8.5	6.3	174	-7.4	1,876	12.8	$32,614
Rapides, LA	55,281	58,820	59,209	-6.0	-0.7	5.3	7.6	6.2	3,119	-4.4	45,384	-3.9	$38,602
Allentown-Bethlehem-Easton, PA-NJ Metro Area	435,921	419,462	407,310	3.9	3.0	4.5	9.2	4.9	18,616	1.7	331,950	16.8	$48,573
Warren, NJ	55,348	58,671	58,567	-5.7	0.2	3.8	9.8	4.0	2,450	-3.3	28,358	1.2	$44,058
Carbon, PA	31,526	31,786	30,223	-0.8	5.2	5.1	10.6	6.0	1,140	1.1	13,817	3.7	$31,763
Lehigh, PA	190,147	177,159	170,760	7.3	3.7	4.6	9.2	4.9	8,644	2.8	179,897	17.5	$52,860
Northampton, PA	158,900	151,846	147,760	4.6	2.8	4.4	8.8	5.0	6,382	2.5	109,878	22.5	$44,834
Altoona, PA Metro Area	59,555	61,780	64,786	-3.6	-4.6	4.2	8.0	5.2	3,185		52,981	5.0	$37,979
Blair, PA	59,555	61,780	64,786	-3.6	-4.6	4.2	8.0	5.2	3,185		52,981	5.0	$37,979
Amarillo, TX Metro Area	132,065	129,609	127,588	1.9	1.6	2.8	5.7	4.0	6,369	5.6	95,807	8.1	$41,364
Armstrong, TX	926	1,012	1,123	-8.5	-9.9	2.8	4.9	3.9	44	41.9	263	42.9	$34,403
Carson, TX	3,040	3,353	3,489	-9.3	-3.9	2.8	5.4	3.9	134	22.9	797	-80.4	$40,484
Oldham, TX	908	961	1,058	-5.5	-9.2	2.6	4.6	3.8	43	22.9	654	0.0	$36,300
Potter, TX	55,816	58,038	56,544	-3.8	2.6	2.9	6.3	4.6	3,509	-1.7	61,256	4.2	$41,125
Randall, TX	71,375	66,245	65,374	7.7	1.3	2.6	5.2	3.5	2,639	15.4	32,837	28.5	$41,988
Ames, IA Metro Area	72,572	68,178	62,296	6.4	9.4	1.7	4.5	3.1	2,680	2.9	38,790	12.6	$40,981
Boone, IA	14,816	14,843	15,374	-0.2	-3.5	2.1	5.7	3.5	573	0.0	7,063	11.6	$38,298
Story, IA	57,756	53,335	46,922	8.3	13.7	1.6	4.2	3.0	2,107	3.7	31,727	12.9	$41,578
Anchorage, AK Metro Area	199,604	200,237	185,756	-0.3	7.8	6.0	7.2	5.9	11,056	6.1	162,723	1.6	$58,657
Anchorage, AK	151,950	157,923	149,028	-3.8	6.0	5.5	6.6	5.5	8,759	3.4	144,029	-0.7	$60,551
Matanuska-Susitna, AK	47,654	42,314	36,728	12.6	15.2	7.6	9.4	7.6	2,297	17.5	18,694	24.2	$44,063
Ann Arbor, MI Metro Area	194,621	182,801	189,926	6.5	-3.8	3.0	8.1	4.5	8,212	3.9	152,087	14.7	$54,635
Washtenaw, MI	194,621	182,801	189,926	6.5	-3.8	3.0	8.1	4.5	8,212	3.9	152,087	14.7	$54,635
Anniston-Oxford, AL Metro Area	45,972	51,559	53,955	-10.8	-4.4	4.7	11.4	4.5	2,319	-4.4	36,301	-1.8	$34,374
Calhoun, AL	45,972	51,559	53,955	-10.8	-4.4	4.7	11.4	4.5	2,319	-4.4	36,301	-1.8	$34,374
Appleton, WI Metro Area	131,547	127,900	119,949	2.9	6.6	2.7	7.8	4.4	5,962	2.5	115,721	13.6	$45,829
Calumet, WI	27,919	27,304	25,092	2.3	8.8	2.6	6.9	4.1	878	2.1	12,053	4.0	$38,536
Outagamie, WI	103,628	100,596	94,857	3.0	6.1	2.8	8.1	4.5	5,084	2.5	103,668	14.9	$46,677
Asheville, NC Metro Area	233,404	208,970	198,283	11.7	5.4	3.1	9.0	4.4	13,001	13.0	172,341	21.5	$39,052
Buncombe, NC	139,319	123,680	115,125	12.6	7.4	3.0	8.6	4.4	8,544	18.7	121,073	26.5	$39,947
Haywood, NC	29,465	27,600	27,125	6.8	1.8	3.4	10.3	4.5	1,382	-2.2	15,084	7.9	$34,564
Henderson, NC	54,476	48,301	46,267	12.8	4.4	3.2	9.1	4.2	2,741	6.4	33,082	13.0	$38,885
Madison, NC	10,144	9,389	9,766	8.0	-3.9	3.6	10.4	5.1	334	6.4	3,102	9.1	$27,715
Athens-Clarke County, GA Metro Area	101,975	93,927	99,200	8.6	-5.3	3.7	9.1	4.3	4,755	8.3	65,041	21.1	$38,076
Clarke, GA	61,475	56,637	59,066	8.5	-4.1	4.0	9.3	4.5	3,040	4.9	47,747	12.1	$38,297
Madison, GA	13,689	13,374	15,469	2.4	-13.5	3.5	10.4	4.4	359	-1.6	2,054	-3.3	$31,216
Oconee, GA	19,687	16,837	17,109	16.9	-1.6	3.0	7.1	3.5	1,179	25.0	14,055	78.0	$38,909
Oglethorpe, GA	7,124	7,079	7,556	0.6	-6.3	3.7	9.6	4.6	177	-4.3	1,185	8.7	$31,165
Atlanta-Sandy Springs-Alpharetta, GA Metro Area	3,071,572	2,720,049	2,584,602	12.9	5.2	3.8	10.3	5.4	143,726	10.9	2,352,106	17.1	$56,383
Barrow, GA	39,665	34,670	30,504	14.4	13.7	3.3	10.8	4.8	1,234	21.0	16,931	32.7	$35,319
Bartow, GA	50,113	47,837	44,608	4.8	7.2	3.8	12.2	5.8	2,120	15.5	33,776	27.7	$41,449
Butts, GA	10,744	10,491	9,107	2.4	15.2	4.0	11.5	6.1	374	6.6	4,546	20.0	$35,893
Carroll, GA	55,383	51,817	50,679	6.9	2.2	4.0	11.7	5.5	2,090	5.5	35,576	20.9	$40,887
Cherokee, GA	132,799	112,578	99,737	18.0	12.9	3.1	8.8	4.2	5,419	19.7	53,665	43.7	$36,902
Clayton, GA	136,502	125,156	136,125	9.1	-8.1	4.9	13.5	6.9	3,782	-3.8	70,316	-0.6	$39,885
Cobb, GA	426,279	380,297	369,291	12.1	3.0	3.4	9.3	4.8	20,567	8.5	342,531	13.5	$56,083
Coweta, GA	73,505	64,319	55,824	14.3	15.2	3.4	9.7	4.9	2,475	21.5	34,066	31.2	$37,345
Dawson, GA	12,040	10,966	10,287	9.8	6.6	3.3	10.9	4.3	673	11.1	7,881	35.3	$25,606

Table C-4. Labor Force and Private Business Establishments and Employment—*Continued*

Metropolitan Statistical Area Metropolitan Division Component counties	Civilian Labor Force								Private nonfarm businesses				
	Total			Percent change		Unemployment rate			Establishments		Employment		Annual payroll per emplyee 2017 (dollars)
	2018	2010	2005	2010-2018	2005-2010	2018	2010	2005	2017	change 2010-2017	2017	Change 2010-2017	
De Kalb, GA	399,846	363,001	368,282	10.2	-1.4	4.0	10.8	6.1	17,036	6.0	271,992	7.7	$52,757
Douglas, GA	72,900	66,575	59,500	9.5	11.9	4.1	11.2	5.7	2,568	3.4	37,939	13.9	$36,568
Fayette, GA	57,768	52,927	53,172	9.1	-0.5	3.5	8.2	4.6	3,509	12.3	42,840	18.4	$38,993
Forsyth, GA	118,048	88,343	75,083	33.6	17.7	3.1	8.0	3.8	6,487	28.2	73,451	32.1	$46,954
Fulton, GA	555,127	485,002	457,326	14.5	6.1	4.0	10.5	5.8	36,792	11.5	813,418	19.4	$72,723
Gwinnett, GA	487,986	418,368	398,300	16.6	5.0	3.5	9.2	4.7	23,796	12.6	327,647	16.4	$50,161
Haralson, GA	12,508	12,385	12,834	1.0	-3.5	3.9	12.3	5.4	442	3.5	5,178	6.0	$49,922
Heard, GA	5,208	5,249	4,936	-0.8	6.3	3.9	12.1	5.8	126	5.0	1,138	9.8	$44,638
Henry, GA	113,843	101,141	88,594	12.6	14.2	4.1	10.3	5.3	3,764	15.7	52,020	28.1	$35,566
Jasper, GA	6,926	6,873	6,231	0.8	10.3	3.5	11.7	5.1	167	2.5	1,577	16.8	$30,821
Lamar, GA	8,118	8,160	7,764	-0.5	5.1	4.6	14.2	6.1	250	4.6	3,056	30.0	$30,861
Meriwether, GA	8,947	9,336	9,814	-4.2	-4.9	5.0	13.7	7.2	295	-4.8	3,179	-0.7	$36,538
Morgan, GA	9,067	8,630	8,932	5.1	-3.4	3.6	10.4	4.6	499	10.6	6,260	12.4	$33,962
Newton, GA	51,780	47,977	42,367	7.9	13.2	4.5	12.7	6.0	1,436	6.2	19,075	18.1	$43,959
Paulding, GA	83,868	73,735	58,563	13.7	25.9	3.4	10.0	4.7	1,985	24.1	19,407	34.4	$33,341
Pickens, GA	15,158	14,045	14,232	7.9	-1.3	3.5	11.0	4.2	717	10.0	6,634	22.4	$37,512
Pike, GA	8,756	8,505	7,706	3.0	10.4	3.6	10.7	5.7	270	11.6	1,903	30.1	$33,678
Rockdale, GA	44,875	41,960	39,089	6.9	7.3	4.4	11.3	5.8	2,035	-0.1	32,025	20.9	$43,996
Spalding, GA	28,551	28,669	28,138	-0.4	1.9	4.7	14.9	7.3	1,148	-1.5	16,739	2.6	$36,082
Walton, GA	45,262	41,037	37,577	10.3	9.2	3.6	10.6	4.8	1,670	10.2	17,340	17.4	$37,235
Atlantic City-Hammonton, NJ Metro Area	118,969	140,598	136,314	-15.4	3.1	5.9	12.3	5.4	6,239	-3.7	103,653	-8.7	$40,232
Atlantic, NJ	118,969	140,598	136,314	-15.4	3.1	5.9	12.3	5.4	6,239	-3.7	103,653	-8.7	$40,232
Auburn-Opelika, AL Metro Area	74,654	66,764	63,530	11.8	5.1	3.6	9.0	3.7	2,796	18.9	46,327	32.7	$32,424
Lee, AL	74,654	66,764	63,530	11.8	5.1	3.6	9.0	3.7	2,796	18.9	46,327	32.7	$32,424
Augusta-Richmond County, GA-SC Metro Area	268,009	255,680	256,395	4.8	-0.3	4.2	9.7	6.1	10,668	1.8	187,081	9.2	$43,874
Burke, GA	9,367	9,791	10,078	-4.3	-2.8	6.0	12.2	7.6	330	8.9	9,532	97.0	$78,105
Columbia, GA	74,950	61,522	56,828	21.8	8.3	3.5	7.3	4.6	2,404	12.8	31,817	21.1	$35,989
Lincoln, GA	3,611	3,679	3,615	-1.8	1.8	5.0	11.5	7.1	133	-10.1	838	-10.9	$30,057
McDuffie, GA	8,973	9,447	10,635	-5.0	-11.2	5.6	13.2	7.0	426	-4.1	6,613	7.1	$32,854
Richmond, GA	86,626	87,887	89,801	-1.4	-2.1	5.1	11.0	6.8	4,264	-2.2	85,058	5.6	$43,507
Aiken, SC	73,944	72,368	74,270	2.2	-2.6	3.3	9.3	5.9	2,797	1.4	48,486	0.6	$45,389
Edgefield, SC	10,538	10,986	11,168	-4.1	-1.6	3.5	9.9	7.2	314	-6.8	4,737	9.7	$36,844
Austin-Round Rock-Georgetown, TX Metro Area	1,197,091	930,551	798,312	28.6	16.6	2.9	7.0	4.5	52,858	28.2	836,997	30.7	$55,992
Bastrop, TX	41,491	35,289	33,653	17.6	4.9	3.4	8.2	5.1	1,355	34.2	14,332	31.1	$34,552
Caldwell, TX	19,092	16,661	15,967	14.6	4.3	3.6	8.6	5.3	616	15.6	5,980	11.5	$34,096
Hays, TX	114,386	80,387	67,038	42.3	19.9	3.0	7.0	4.5	4,259	33.6	59,314	58.2	$34,241
Travis, TX	721,786	575,630	502,123	25.4	14.6	2.8	6.8	4.5	35,717	25.6	599,954	27.5	$60,570
Williamson, TX	300,336	222,584	179,531	34.9	24.0	3.1	7.2	4.6	10,911	35.5	157,417	35.3	$49,525
Bakersfield, CA Metro Area	386,997	371,515	326,748	4.2	13.7	8.0	15.7	8.4	12,924	8.4	189,762	8.5	$45,048
Kern, CA	386,997	371,515	326,748	4.2	13.7	8.0	15.7	8.4	12,924	8.4	189,762	8.5	$45,048
Baltimore-Columbia-Towson, MD Metro Area	1,493,496	1,425,285	1,366,365	4.8	4.3	4.0	8.1	4.4	67,502	3.6	1,181,547	11.5	$55,542
Anne Arundel, MD	309,603	286,070	274,457	8.2	4.2	3.3	6.9	3.5	14,338	6.0	242,551	21.2	$55,895
Baltimore, MD	450,366	431,530	419,256	4.4	2.9	4.0	8.3	4.3	20,073	1.4	328,070	5.6	$50,917
Carroll, MD	94,339	92,598	91,900	1.9	0.8	3.2	6.8	3.3	4,209	-1.2	50,775	7.2	$40,134
Harford, MD	138,162	132,791	129,191	4.0	2.8	3.6	7.8	3.9	5,517	3.7	73,699	12.2	$44,500
Howard, MD	183,889	160,638	154,170	14.5	4.2	3.0	5.6	3.1	9,520	10.9	179,279	18.7	$63,217
Queen Anne's, MD	27,379	26,142	25,037	4.7	4.4	3.3	7.3	3.5	1,411	3.4	12,535	17.1	$38,466
Baltimore city, MD	289,758	295,516	272,354	-1.9	8.5	5.7	11.2	6.9	12,434	0.9	294,638	7.5	$61,874
Bangor, ME Metro Area	77,127	79,017	77,286	-2.4	2.2	3.8	8.5	5.1	4,084	-2.6	56,958	-1.1	$40,788
Penobscot, ME	77,127	79,017	77,286	-2.4	2.2	3.8	8.5	5.1	4,084	-2.6	56,958	-1.1	$40,788
Barnstable Town, MA Metro Area	116,225	111,092	122,143	4.6	-9.0	4.3	9.9	4.9	8,681	5.7	78,050	13.4	$46,242
Barnstable, MA	116,225	111,092	122,143	4.6	-9.0	4.3	9.9	4.9	8,681	5.7	78,050	13.4	$46,242
Baton Rouge, LA Metro Area	427,887	400,736	372,571	6.8	7.6	4.4	7.9	7.0	18,669	3.7	346,458	11.1	$48,685
Ascension, LA	62,979	53,392	45,815	18.0	16.5	4.1	7.5	6.5	2,290	16.1	39,313	29.5	$53,050
Assumption, LA	8,941	10,067	10,045	-11.2	0.2	6.7	11.6	9.9	249	-0.8	2,563	0.1	$42,482
East Baton Rouge, LA	232,663	221,984	212,877	4.8	4.3	4.3	7.6	6.9	12,347	1.3	247,884	7.7	$48,334
East Feliciana, LA	8,008	8,103	8,204	-1.2	-1.2	4.7	8.3	6.8	247	-6.8	3,197	-13.6	$40,384
Iberville, LA	14,190	14,031	12,609	1.1	11.3	6.2	10.0	9.0	542	2.1	11,323	22.1	$76,377
Livingston, LA	67,916	61,281	53,346	10.8	14.9	4.1	7.5	5.9	1,784	11.4	21,233	22.1	$34,518
Pointe Coupee, LA	9,999	10,001	9,917	0.0	0.8	5.4	8.7	8.9	342	-10.7	4,424	3.2	$41,070
St. Helena, LA	4,329	4,716	4,370	-8.2	7.9	6.6	13.1	14.1	115	-4.2	1,206	6.3	$34,461
West Baton Rouge, LA	13,528	11,924	10,456	13.5	14.0	4.4	7.9	7.0	567	13.4	12,277	16.0	$45,949
West Feliciana, LA	5,334	5,237	4,932	1.9	6.2	4.0	6.7	8.1	186	-4.1	3,038	22.1	$58,430
Battle Creek, MI Metro Area	62,865	64,996	71,724	-3.3	-9.4	4.2	11.7	6.7	2,530	-5.6	53,335	12.8	$48,972
Calhoun, MI	62,865	64,996	71,724	-3.3	-9.4	4.2	11.7	6.7	2,530	-5.6	53,335	12.8	$48,972
Bay City, MI Metro Area	50,352	54,666	55,557	-7.9	-1.6	4.8	11.6	7.1	2,146	-6.3	29,870	1.8	$40,263
Bay, MI	50,352	54,666	55,557	-7.9	-1.6	4.8	11.6	7.1	2,146	-6.3	29,870	1.8	$40,263
Beaumont-Port Arthur, TX Metro Area	170,941	177,522	176,954	-3.7	0.3	6.0	11.2	7.7	7,838	-1.1	132,171	4.6	$48,836
Hardin, TX	25,465	25,839	24,619	-1.4	5.0	5.2	9.9	6.6	810	4.0	9,496	14.2	$37,371
Jefferson, TX	108,181	113,217	111,553	-4.4	1.5	6.3	11.3	7.8	5,712	-0.9	103,722	5.0	$49,470
Orange, TX	37,295	38,466	40,782	-3.0	-5.7	5.7	11.7	8.0	1,316	-4.9	18,953	-1.8	$51,112
Beckley, WV Metro Area	45,250	50,037	49,913	-9.6	0.2	5.7	8.8	5.1	2,491	-8.5	33,038	-12.5	$36,923
Fayette, WV	15,785	17,567	17,747	-10.1	-1.0	6.4	10.0	5.8	721	-11.6	7,590	-12.8	$36,063
Raleigh, WV	29,465	32,470	32,166	-9.3	0.9	5.3	8.1	4.7	1,770	-7.2	25,448	-12.4	$37,180

Table C-4. Labor Force and Private Business Establishments and Employment—*Continued*

| | Civilian Labor Force | | | | | | | | Private nonfarm businesses | | | | |
| | Total | | | Percent change | | Unemployment rate | | | Establishments | | Employment | | Annual payroll per emplyee 2017 (dollars) |
Metropolitan Statistical Area Metropolitan Division Component counties	2018	2010	2005	2010-2018	2005-2010	2018	2010	2005	2017	change 2010-2017	2017	Change 2010-2017	
Bellingham, WA Metro Area	111,670	104,359	102,524	7.0	1.8	4.7	9.5	5.3	6,698	7.3	75,103	11.4	$44,383
Whatcom, WA	111,670	104,359	102,524	7.0	1.8	4.7	9.5	5.3	6,698	7.3	75,103	11.4	$44,383
Bend, OR Metro Area	95,367	81,238	74,532	17.4	9.0	4.2	13.8	5.7	7,322	26.1	68,342	32.7	$41,685
Deschutes, OR	95,367	81,238	74,532	17.4	9.0	4.2	13.8	5.7	7,322	26.1	68,342	32.7	$41,685
Billings, MT Metro Area	91,688	86,507	88,352	6.0	-2.1	3.4	5.9	3.6	6,322	2.8	74,052	3.6	$44,580
Carbon, MT	5,487	5,330	5,387	2.9	-1.1	3.5	6.4	3.8	405	3.6	2,169	1.9	$28,283
Stillwater, MT	4,932	4,762	4,386	3.6	8.6	3.4	5.8	3.5	258	2.4	2,426	10.5	$73,111
Yellowstone, MT	81,269	76,415	78,579	6.4	-2.8	3.3	5.9	3.5	5,659	2.8	69,457	3.4	$44,093
Binghamton, NY Metro Area	107,364	124,412	122,597	-13.7	1.5	4.8	8.6	4.8	4,986	-2.5	79,415	-5.8	$40,007
Broome, NY	84,592	97,844	96,287	-13.5	1.6	4.9	8.7	4.9	4,210	-2.3	71,176	-1.6	$40,475
Tioga, NY	22,772	26,568	26,310	-14.3	1.0	4.4	8.0	4.7	776	-3.8	8,239	-30.7	$35,962
Birmingham-Hoover, AL Metro Area	519,731	512,474	500,789	1.4	2.3	3.5	9.7	4.1	24,719	1.4	436,077	4.1	$49,197
Bibb, AL	8,661	8,934	8,861	-3.1	0.8	4.0	11.4	4.5	284	-3.1	3,484	19.1	$39,098
Blount, AL	25,006	24,906	26,446	0.4	-5.8	3.5	9.8	3.6	698	-0.4	6,645	3.3	$32,384
Chilton, AL	19,476	19,462	19,674	0.1	-1.1	3.6	10.3	3.9	756	2.9	7,892	16.8	$33,685
Jefferson, AL	314,014	318,520	317,359	-1.4	0.4	3.7	10.3	4.4	16,430	-1.1	315,802	0.0	$50,557
St. Clair, AL	39,683	38,280	33,750	3.7	13.4	3.5	10.1	4.0	1,313	8.4	18,226	41.6	$33,950
Shelby, AL	112,891	102,372	94,699	10.3	8.1	2.9	7.1	3.1	5,238	8.7	84,028	13.3	$50,600
Bismarck, ND Metro Area	66,293	63,257	59,910	4.8	5.6	2.8	3.9	3.0	3,926	13.3	56,813	10.1	$45,394
Burleigh, ND	49,251	46,337	44,286	6.3	4.6	2.6	3.6	2.8	3,013	12.0	45,596	6.1	$44,852
Morton, ND	16,169	15,993	14,527	1.1	10.1	3.3	4.6	3.6	869	18.2	10,664	23.6	$46,041
Oliver, ND	873	927	1,097	-5.8	-15.5	4.1	5.7	4.7	44	10.0	553	0.0	$77,640
Blacksburg-Christiansburg, VA Metro Area	81,916	80,561	76,695	1.7	5.0	3.1	8.4	4.1	3,158	-3.5	48,889	10.3	$38,391
Giles, VA	7,845	8,302	8,352	-5.5	-0.6	3.3	9.6	5.2	285	-6.6	3,716	-0.9	$37,997
Montgomery, VA	49,715	47,497	43,120	4.7	10.2	2.9	7.1	3.6	1,959	-1.5	30,027	15.3	$38,112
Pulaski, VA	16,055	16,975	17,995	-5.4	-5.7	3.5	11.1	4.5	602	-8.0	10,878	4.6	$40,061
Radford City, VA	8,301	7,787	7,228	6.6	7.7	3.7	9.3	4.6	312	-3.4	4,268	3.3	$36,447
Bloomington, IL Metro Area	87,889	96,138	87,165	-8.6	10.3	4.2	7.1	4.1	3,609	-2.5	71,642	-5.8	$51,128
McLean, IL	87,889	96,138	87,165	-8.6	10.3	4.2	7.1	4.1	3,609	-2.5	71,642	-5.8	$51,128
Bloomington, IN Metro Area	79,040	78,052	78,446	1.3	-0.5	3.7	8.4	5.1	3,437	4.5	53,709	5.7	$38,837
Monroe, IN	69,690	67,736	66,680	2.9	1.6	3.6	7.9	4.8	3,122	4.4	50,612	7.9	$39,245
Owen, IN	9,350	10,316	11,766	-9.4	-12.3	4.4	11.5	6.3	315	5.0	3,097	-20.7	$32,169
Bloomsburg-Berwick, PA Metro Area	42,545	43,816	42,998	-2.9	1.9	4.5	8.8	5.5	1,883	1.7	36,923	8.0	$48,745
Columbia, PA	33,495	34,737	34,035	-3.6	2.1	4.8	9.3	5.8	1,428	-0.5	22,024	2.2	$35,676
Montour, PA	9,050	9,079	8,963	-0.3	1.3	3.5	6.7	4.4	455	9.4	14,899	18.1	$68,063
Boise City, ID Metro Area	361,718	297,463	281,557	21.6	5.6	2.7	9.2	3.7	18,661	13.4	254,357	21.3	$45,008
Ada, ID	244,525	196,945	187,127	24.2	5.2	2.5	8.3	3.3	13,749	12.5	197,420	20.4	$48,194
Boise, ID	3,329	3,048	3,683	9.2	-17.2	4.2	10.6	4.5	160	11.1	666	26.4	$26,165
Canyon, ID	100,275	84,738	78,790	18.3	7.5	3.1	11.3	4.4	4,199	17.8	52,037	26.1	$34,519
Gem, ID	8,141	7,681	7,238	6.0	6.1	3.4	11.4	4.8	371	4.8	2,489	11.7	$26,802
Owyhee, ID	5,448	5,051	4,719	7.9	7.0	3.6	4.2	2.5	182	2.8	1,745	8.8	$30,512
Boston-Cambridge-Newton, MA-NH Metro Area	2,746,759	2,473,928	2,369,644	11.0	4.4	3.0	7.5	4.5	130,876	7.1	2,534,539	13.9	$70,913
Boston, MA Div	1,134,416	1,014,209	946,385	11.9	7.2	3.1	7.9	4.8	54,532	8.3	1,164,840	15.4	$72,955
Norfolk, MA	393,159	358,192	355,887	9.8	0.6	3.0	7.4	4.2	20,310	6.7	353,679	14.9	$56,556
Plymouth, MA	284,938	262,147	258,416	8.7	1.4	3.5	8.9	4.9	12,744	8.1	172,923	18.8	$47,547
Suffolk, MA	456,319	393,870	332,082	15.9	18.6	3.0	7.6	5.3	21,478	10.0	638,238	14.8	$88,926
Cambridge-Newton-Framingham, MA Div	1,353,655	1,217,790	1,185,870	11.2	2.7	2.9	7.5	4.4	63,811	6.6	1,187,773	12.6	$72,021
Essex, MA	429,887	392,103	375,771	9.6	4.3	3.4	8.7	5.3	19,100	6.8	294,751	12.1	$52,182
Middlesex, MA	923,768	825,687	810,099	11.9	1.9	2.7	6.9	4.1	44,711	6.5	893,022	12.8	$78,569
Rockingham County-Strafford County, NH Div	258,688	241,929	237,389	6.9	1.9	2.6	5.9	3.9	12,533	4.7	181,926	13.2	$50,601
Rockingham, NH	185,379	172,358	170,876	7.6	0.9	2.8	6.0	4.1	9,912	4.9	142,204	13.7	$51,540
Strafford, NH	73,309	69,571	66,513	5.4	4.6	2.3	5.7	3.4	2,621	4.2	39,722	11.3	$47,241
Boulder, CO Metro Area	193,822	170,293	168,036	13.8	1.3	2.8	7.0	4.4	12,551	9.7	153,690	15.3	$60,564
Boulder, CO	193,822	170,293	168,036	13.8	1.3	2.8	7.0	4.4	12,551	9.7	153,690	15.3	$60,564
Bowling Green, KY Metro Area	83,443	77,926	74,979	7.1	3.9	3.9	10.0	5.4	3,510	7.8	61,626	19.4	$38,737
Allen, KY	8,969	9,126	8,586	-1.7	6.3	3.7	11.7	6.5	234	-1.3	3,083	9.0	$33,812
Butler, KY	5,206	5,457	5,719	-4.6	-4.6	4.9	12.0	7.1	175	-7.4	1,876	12.2	$30,208
Edmonson, KY	4,868	5,122	5,408	-5.0	-5.3	5.3	13.3	7.1	114	-13.6	870	10.7	$27,897
Warren, KY	64,400	58,221	55,266	10.6	5.3	3.7	9.2	4.9	2,987	10.7	55,797	20.4	$39,465
Bremerton-Silverdale-Port Orchard, WA Metro Area	122,885	120,592	120,999	1.9	-0.3	4.6	8.6	5.3	5,928	4.8	59,021	4.9	$39,958
Kitsap, WA	122,885	120,592	120,999	1.9	-0.3	4.6	8.6	5.3	5,928	4.8	59,021	4.9	$39,958
Bridgeport-Stamford-Norwalk, CT Metro Area	480,767	473,386	451,803	1.6	4.8	4.0	8.4	4.4	27,207	0.7	429,679	9.1	$82,149
Fairfield, CT	480,767	473,386	451,803	1.6	4.8	4.0	8.4	4.4	27,207	0.7	429,679	9.1	$82,149
Brownsville-Harlingen, TX Metro Area	166,001	162,316	140,218	2.3	15.8	6.2	11.2	7.6	6,377	0.8	107,239	8.6	$27,372
Cameron, TX	166,001	162,316	140,218	2.3	15.8	6.2	11.2	7.6	6,377	0.8	107,239	8.6	$27,372
Brunswick, GA Metro Area	53,766	52,097	51,706	3.2	0.8	3.8	10.5	4.7	2,904	1.5	35,077	8.8	$34,208
Brantley, GA	7,351	7,468	7,559	-1.6	-1.2	4.5	12.7	5.4	191	7.9	1,244	-4.9	$32,959
Glynn, GA	40,225	38,340	38,916	4.9	-1.5	3.7	10.0	4.5	2,534	1.8	32,555	9.7	$34,583
McIntosh, GA	6,190	6,289	5,231	-1.6	20.2	4.0	10.6	5.4	179	-7.7	1,278	2.7	$25,879
Buffalo-Cheektowaga, NY Metro Area	542,584	573,522	583,969	-5.4	-1.8	4.6	8.6	5.3	27,534	2.4	482,984	6.0	$43,949
Erie, NY	443,446	465,675	472,255	-4.8	-1.4	4.4	8.3	5.2	22,940	2.4	421,508	6.1	$45,001
Niagara, NY	99,138	107,847	111,714	-8.1	-3.5	5.2	9.6	5.5	4,594	2.0	61,476	5.4	$36,739

Table C-4. Labor Force and Private Business Establishments and Employment—*Continued*

| | Civilian Labor Force | | | | | | | | Private nonfarm businesses | | | | |
| | Total | | | Percent change | | Unemployment rate | | | Establishments | | Employment | | Annual payroll per emplyee 2017 (dollars) |
Metropolitan Statistical Area Metropolitan Division Component counties	2018	2010	2005	2010-2018	2005-2010	2018	2010	2005	2017	change 2010-2017	2017	Change 2010-2017	
Burlington, NC Metro Area	80,583	76,806	68,710	4.9	11.8	3.7	10.9	6.0	3,311	3.3	59,276	22.9	$39,093
Alamance, NC	80,583	76,806	68,710	4.9	11.8	3.7	10.9	6.0	3,311	3.3	59,276	22.9	$39,093
Burlington-South Burlington, VT Metro Area	128,380	126,401	117,420	1.6	7.6	2.2	5.1	3.3	6,919	3.0	102,620	4.8	$47,118
Chittenden, VT	96,716	94,581	87,236	2.3	8.4	2.1	4.8	3.1	5,690	3.4	89,068	4.4	$47,986
Franklin, VT	27,610	27,686	25,936	-0.3	6.7	2.5	5.7	3.8	1,044	2.1	12,858	7.5	$41,623
Grand Isle, VT	4,054	4,134	4,248	-1.9	-2.7	3.2	6.9	5.0	185	-4.1	694	10.5	$37,625
California-Lexington Park, MD Metro Area	55,295	53,619	49,151	3.1	9.1	3.8	6.5	3.5	1,993	4.3	32,376	11.7	$50,443
St. Mary's, MD	55,295	53,619	49,151	3.1	9.1	3.8	6.5	3.5	1,993	4.3	32,376	11.7	$50,443
Canton-Massillon, OH Metro Area	199,318	206,242	204,520	-3.4	0.8	4.9	11.4	6.6	8,635	-3.1	150,465	9.3	$38,788
Carroll, OH	13,091	14,373	14,150	-8.9	1.6	5.3	13.0	6.9	473	0.6	6,285	29.6	$35,360
Stark, OH	186,227	191,869	190,370	-2.9	0.8	4.9	11.3	6.6	8,162	-3.3	144,180	8.6	$38,938
Cape Coral-Fort Myers, FL Metro Area	342,684	283,236	272,752	21.0	3.8	3.4	12.5	3.2	18,797	20.7	216,916	29.8	$41,466
Lee, FL	342,684	283,236	272,752	21.0	3.8	3.4	12.5	3.2	18,797	20.7	216,916	29.8	$41,466
Cape Girardeau, MO-IL Metro Area	47,659	49,843	47,208	-4.4	5.6	3.1	7.9	5.0	2,658	-15.0	39,925	-2.1	$38,670
Alexander, IL	2,153	2,971	3,319	-27.5	-10.5	7.9	11.7	8.6	92	-25.2	942	-25.2	$42,587
Bollinger, MO	5,498	5,842	5,856	-5.9	-0.2	3.6	10.1	6.2	201	-2.4	1,381	-0.7	$29,799
Cape Girardeau, MO	40,008	41,030	38,033	-2.5	7.9	2.8	7.3	4.5	2,365	-15.4	37,602	-1.4	$38,898
Carbondale-Marion, IL Metro Area	64,110	66,845	69,935	-4.1	-4.4	5.1	9.2	5.0	3,075	-2.6	43,560	6.7	$34,842
Jackson, IL	28,137	29,861	31,477	-5.8	-5.1	4.6	8.2	4.6	1,291	-5.3	17,273	0.3	$32,748
Johnson, IL	4,100	4,454	5,095	-7.9	-12.6	7.8	12.5	6.1	171	-6.0	1,281	-14.4	$23,191
Williamson, IL	31,873	32,530	33,363	-2.0	-2.5	5.1	9.7	5.3	1,613	0.1	25,006	13.2	$36,884
Carson City, NV Metro Area	25,718	26,700	27,201	-3.7	-1.8	4.7	13.5	4.5	1,890	-11.7	20,905	-0.9	$44,588
Carson City city, NV	25,718	26,700	27,201	-3.7	-1.8	4.7	13.5	4.5	1,890	-11.7	20,905	-0.9	$44,588
Casper, WY Metro Area	39,059	39,894	39,124	-2.1	2.0	4.6	7.0	3.4	2,971	2.0	31,203	-4.4	$48,104
Natrona, WY	39,059	39,894	39,124	-2.1	2.0	4.6	7.0	3.4	2,971	2.0	31,203	-4.4	$48,104
Cedar Rapids, IA Metro Area	143,364	145,538	138,103	-1.5	5.4	2.8	6.0	4.4	6,660	3.2	129,218	6.4	$48,179
Benton, IA	13,356	14,329	14,432	-6.8	-0.7	2.7	6.2	4.7	554	-3.1	4,341	0.2	$36,851
Jones, IA	10,484	11,106	10,423	-5.6	6.6	3.0	6.4	4.8	510	-0.2	4,508	-0.1	$34,679
Linn, IA	119,524	120,103	113,248	-0.5	6.1	2.8	6.0	4.3	5,596	4.2	120,369	6.9	$49,093
Chambersburg-Waynesboro, PA Metro Area	77,064	75,712	76,938	1.8	-1.6	3.7	8.5	3.4	3,080	1.7	50,967	10.1	$38,025
Franklin, PA	77,064	75,712	76,938	1.8	-1.6	3.7	8.5	3.4	3,080	1.7	50,967	10.1	$38,025
Champaign-Urbana, IL Metro Area	114,099	118,153	110,243	-3.4	7.2	4.4	8.2	4.1	4,602	1.5	71,668	1.0	$42,163
Champaign, IL	105,669	108,977	101,124	-3.0	7.8	4.4	8.2	4.1	4,273	2.2	69,309	1.4	$42,414
Piatt, IL	8,430	9,176	9,119	-8.1	0.6	4.3	7.8	4.0	329	-7.1	2,359	-8.7	$34,814
Charleston, WV Metro Area	116,314	125,248	122,881	-7.1	1.9	5.3	8.3	5.1	5,799	-12.8	92,295	-13.9	$43,813
Boone, WV	7,452	8,812	9,294	-15.4	-5.2	6.1	8.8	4.6	260	-17.7	3,617	-50.1	$37,841
Clay, WV	3,113	3,647	3,484	-14.6	4.7	8.4	14.1	7.8	85	-23.4	810	-43.9	$29,422
Jackson, WV	16,374	12,313	11,587	33.0	6.3	4.0	11.4	5.9	482	-9.1	6,908	4.4	$42,246
Kanawha, WV	82,263	92,603	90,679	-11.2	2.1	5.2	7.4	4.9	4,793	-12.6	79,121	-11.9	$44,794
Lincoln, WV	7,112	7,873	7,837	-9.7	0.5	6.9	11.7	6.4	179	-16.4	1,839	-11.6	$25,582
Charleston-North Charleston, SC Metro Area	382,521	327,150	295,680	16.9	10.6	2.9	9.3	5.4	19,483	18.8	286,757	25.4	$44,950
Berkeley, SC	101,127	82,740	71,630	22.2	15.5	3.0	10.0	5.3	3,214	22.5	49,941	33.6	$49,555
Charleston, SC	206,317	178,847	167,313	15.4	6.9	2.8	8.8	5.4	13,908	19.7	206,599	22.3	$45,023
Dorchester, SC	75,077	65,563	56,737	14.5	15.6	3.0	9.5	5.3	2,361	9.6	30,217	35.0	$36,840
Charlotte-Concord-Gastonia, NC-SC Metro Area	1,343,488	1,152,331	1,010,941	16.6	14.0	3.7	11.7	5.4	62,039	13.7	1,058,398	23.3	$53,265
Anson, NC	10,407	11,180	10,562	-6.9	5.9	4.5	14.1	7.4	400	-4.1	5,174	21.9	$29,541
Cabarrus, NC	106,601	89,049	77,153	19.7	15.4	3.6	11.5	4.6	4,404	12.7	66,651	19.3	$38,265
Gaston, NC	109,604	101,249	96,079	8.3	5.4	3.9	13.5	6.1	4,183	6.3	64,158	11.4	$38,029
Iredell, NC	87,984	78,671	72,392	11.8	8.7	3.6	12.9	5.0	4,781	12.5	67,463	19.7	$43,780
Lincoln, NC	42,654	39,984	36,213	6.7	10.4	3.4	12.7	5.6	1,716	12.7	19,275	17.8	$37,559
Mecklenburg, NC	611,673	502,428	426,529	21.7	17.8	3.7	10.7	5.0	32,102	15.1	623,205	23.9	$61,653
Rowan, NC	65,775	64,328	67,803	2.2	-5.1	3.9	14.1	5.4	2,630	2.5	44,192	13.6	$44,384
Union, NC	121,250	101,154	82,302	19.9	22.9	3.4	10.0	4.5	4,747	21.1	55,898	31.5	$39,388
Chester, SC	13,302	14,689	15,896	-9.4	-7.6	4.8	19.3	9.2	542	1.1	7,146	16.8	$42,570
Lancaster, SC	39,543	33,952	29,727	16.5	14.2	3.8	14.7	8.4	1,420	18.4	19,850	52.6	$46,096
York, SC	134,695	115,647	96,285	16.5	20.1	3.3	12.1	6.6	5,114	14.9	85,386	33.0	$43,918
Charlottesville, VA Metro Area	113,130	104,497	97,086	8.3	7.6	2.6	6.2	3.1	5,936	5.3	84,420	13.1	$51,608
Albemarle, VA	55,903	50,987	47,414	9.6	7.5	2.7	6.0	2.9	2,808	11.7	41,633	14.6	$48,231
Fluvanna, VA	13,553	13,078	12,793	3.6	2.2	2.5	6.3	3.1	395	-1.3	2,650	1.5	$37,945
Greene, VA	10,261	9,655	9,658	6.3	0.0	2.5	6.7	2.9	355	9.6	2,716	24.5	$32,556
Nelson, VA	7,399	7,574	7,424	-2.3	2.0	3.1	7.1	3.3	365	-5.4	3,289	8.6	$30,185
Charlottesville City, VA	26,014	23,203	19,797	12.1	17.2	2.5	6.1	3.8	2,013	0.0	34,132	11.9	$60,369
Chattanooga, TN-GA Metro Area	270,586	258,365	251,219	4.7	2.8	3.5	8.8	4.8	11,489	3.1	221,608	14.0	$41,730
Catoosa, GA	33,156	31,351	34,815	5.8	-9.9	3.4	8.6	4.4	945	2.2	11,974	-2.3	$32,007
Dade, GA	8,274	8,348	8,433	-0.9		3.6	8.7	4.8	215	-0.5	2,851	23.4	$30,600
Walker, GA	31,167	30,980	32,829	0.6	-5.6	3.9	10.3	5.0	682	-4.6	10,261	1.8	$32,662
Hamilton, TN	179,683	169,043	156,630	6.3	7.9	3.4	8.3	4.7	9,032	4.3	188,469	15.9	$43,347
Marion, TN	12,265	12,542	12,720	-2.2	-1.4	4.7	11.1	6.2	431	-2.5	6,121	16.2	$35,681
Sequatchie, TN	6,041	6,101	5,792		5.3	4.3	12.1	5.7	184	-0.5	1,932	5.2	$28,034
Cheyenne, WY Metro Area	47,682	46,182	41,359	3.2	11.7	3.9	6.7	4.1	3,243	20.1	32,827	6.7	$42,577
Laramie, WY	47,682	46,182	41,359	3.2	11.7	3.9	6.7	4.1	3,243	20.1	32,827	6.7	$42,577
Chicago-Naperville-Elgin, IL-IN-WI Metro Area	4,876,393	4,872,958	4,698,563	0.1	3.7	4.0	10.6	5.9	247,182	4.4	4,165,528	9.7	$59,356
Chicago-Naperville-Evanston, IL Div	3,668,492	3,697,035	3,584,710	-0.8	3.1	3.9	10.6	6.0	192,272	4.6	3,317,834	10.4	$60,346
Cook, IL	2,611,512	2,643,831	2,548,067	-1.2	3.8	4.0	10.9	6.4	133,666	4.5	2,405,790	10.9	$62,453

Table C-4. Labor Force and Private Business Establishments and Employment—*Continued*

Metropolitan Statistical Area / Metropolitan Division / Component counties	Civilian Labor Force Total 2018	Total 2010	Total 2005	Percent change 2010-2018	Percent change 2005-2010	Unemployment rate 2018	Unemployment rate 2010	Unemployment rate 2005	Establishments 2017	Establishments change 2010-2017	Employment 2017	Employment Change 2010-2017	Annual payroll per emplyee 2017 (dollars)
Du Page, IL	508,650	502,807	512,686	1.2	-1.9	3.1	8.9	4.7	34,041	2.8	581,197	4.8	$60,020
Grundy, IL	25,255	25,953	23,302	-2.7	11.4	4.7	13.3	7.1	1,187	10.5	16,898	12.8	$52,947
McHenry, IL	165,849	168,798	166,361	-1.7	1.5	3.5	10.5	5.1	7,961	1.8	85,331	5.1	$45,406
Will, IL	357,226	355,646	334,294	0.4	6.4	4.0	11.1	5.8	15,417	11.4	228,618	24.3	$45,124
Elgin, IL Div	397,049	386,048	347,149	2.8	11.2	4.6	10.8	5.4	17,135	6.5	237,763	10.2	$44,736
De Kalb, IL	55,487	56,390	53,459	-1.6	5.5	4.4	10.5	5.1	1,980	0.8	26,946	6.4	$39,892
Kane, IL	273,901	267,247	249,485	2.5	7.1	4.9	11.0	5.5	12,994	6.5	187,382	10.0	$46,708
Kendall, IL	67,661	62,411	44,205	8.4	41.2	3.5	10.1	5.0	2,161	12.2	23,435	16.4	$34,533
Gary, IN Div	342,764	333,965	328,821	2.6	1.6	4.6	10.5	5.8	14,669	1.4	233,904	4.3	$45,372
Jasper, IN	16,509	16,141	15,224	2.3	6.0	3.9	10.4	5.7	773	4.3	9,452	10.1	$37,708
Lake, IN	232,368	229,142	225,412	1.4	1.7	4.9	10.8	6.2	10,090	1.0	167,298	1.6	$45,855
Newton, IN	7,117	7,075	7,083	0.6	-0.1	4.3	11.3	5.4	242	-15.1	2,239	-11.0	$35,075
Porter, IN	86,770	81,607	81,102	6.3	0.6	3.8	9.5	4.8	3,564	3.3	54,915	13.1	$45,641
Lake County-Kenosha County, IL-WI Div	468,088	455,910	437,883	2.7	4.1	4.3	9.9	4.8	23,106	3.1	376,027	6.4	$68,566
Lake, IL	378,401	370,042	355,521	2.3	4.1	4.5	9.8	4.6	19,861	2.4	317,090	3.1	$73,841
Kenosha, WI	89,687	85,868	82,362	4.4	4.3	3.5	10.3	5.6	3,245	7.7	58,937	28.2	$40,183
Chico, CA Metro Area	102,712	102,568	98,309	0.1	4.3	5.0	13.9	6.7	4,724	0.3	62,600	16.1	$39,470
Butte, CA	102,712	102,568	98,309	0.1	4.3	5.0	13.9	6.7	4,724	0.3	62,600	16.1	$39,470
Cincinnati, OH-KY-IN Metro Area	1,127,192	1,107,357	1,100,966	1.8	0.6	4.0	9.9	5.5	46,963	1.5	946,308	8.1	$50,970
Dearborn, IN	26,132	25,524	26,428	2.4	-3.4	3.6	10.9	5.7	936	-3.3	12,647	-7.6	$36,497
Franklin, IN	11,395	11,395	12,052	0.0	-5.5	3.7	11.5	6.4	431	-1.8	5,075	10.8	$44,685
Ohio, IN	3,201	3,263	3,152	-1.9	3.5	3.5	11.1	5.3	75	-9.6	1,118	-11.9	$25,521
Union, IN	3,671	3,729	3,874	-1.6	-3.7	3.1	10.3	5.6	118	-4.8	880	2.6	$32,084
Boone, KY	70,741	63,271	59,889	11.8	5.6	3.4	8.9	4.8	3,110	10.3	81,027	31.3	$42,111
Bracken, KY	3,851	3,982	4,422	-3.3	-10.0	4.9	11.4	6.3	93	-5.1	978	14.7	$34,988
Campbell, KY	50,530	48,713	45,946	3.7	6.0	3.3	9.1	5.4	1,676	3.6	24,442	2.2	$36,859
Gallatin, KY	4,073	4,076	4,053	-0.1	0.6	4.1	12.3	5.9	87	-2.2	822	5.7	$31,861
Grant, KY	11,729	11,684	12,592	0.4	-7.2	4.3	11.8	5.5	374	-4.8	3,895	-2.8	$35,858
Kenton, KY	87,686	83,798	84,011	4.6	-0.3	3.4	9.8	5.0	3,157	1.3	56,608	-17.6	$50,441
Pendleton, KY	7,058	7,387	7,494	-4.5	-1.4	4.1	12.3	5.7	169	-8.6	1,753	9.7	$35,314
Brown, OH	19,478	21,125	22,047	-7.8	-4.2	5.4	13.3	7.0	535	-1.1	6,207	0.4	$29,102
Butler, OH	193,092	190,738	186,502	1.2	2.3	4.1	10.0	5.4	7,258	4.5	136,943	13.9	$43,956
Clermont, OH	105,585	104,819	104,576	0.7	0.2	4.1	10.4	5.5	3,574	0.6	50,416	12.9	$41,541
Hamilton, OH	412,156	413,738	419,952	-0.4	-1.5	4.1	9.9	5.6	21,018	-1.7	479,507	6.5	$57,441
Warren, OH	116,814	110,115	103,976	6.1	5.9	3.9	9.0	4.9	4,352	11.3	83,990	16.4	$50,242
Clarksville, TN-KY Metro Area	119,896	115,040	103,954	4.2	10.7	4.2	9.8	5.7	4,623	7.4	73,140	9.9	$34,786
Christian, KY	24,853	27,294	26,460	-8.9	3.2	5.2	11.7	7.0	1,336	-0.9	24,520	1.4	$36,940
Trigg, KY	6,001	6,440	6,469	-6.8	-0.4	4.7	14.1	6.6	233	-4.5	2,183	-7.1	$29,604
Montgomery, TN	83,866	75,637	65,160	10.9	16.1	3.8	8.5	4.9	2,892	13.4	45,042	16.5	$33,918
Stewart, TN	5,176	5,669	5,865	-8.7	-3.3	5.0	12.4	7.4	162	-0.6	1,395	2.6	$33,062
Cleveland, TN Metro Area	57,539	53,784	53,462	7.0	0.6	3.7	9.6	5.3	2,143	1.9	40,497	11.2	$38,428
Bradley, TN	50,258	46,448	46,242	8.2	0.4	3.6	9.4	5.3	1,920	2.1	39,049	11.8	$38,814
Polk, TN	7,281	7,336	7,220	-0.7	1.6	4.2	11.2	5.9	223	0.5	1,448	-3.5	$28,022
Cleveland-Elyria, OH Metro Area	1,035,340	1,052,045	1,078,484	-1.6	-2.5	5.1	8.4	5.1	51,086	-2.0	918,152	5.5	$50,906
Cuyahoga, OH	612,216	631,675	654,861	-3.1	-3.5	5.2	8.5	5.4	32,700	-2.9	662,119	5.1	$53,923
Geauga, OH	48,790	48,975	50,378	-0.4	-2.8	4.3	6.9	4.3	2,802	2.2	30,257	1.5	$41,387
Lake, OH	125,471	126,272	129,060	-0.6	-2.6	4.7	7.9	4.6	5,980	-2.6	85,528	3.2	$46,230
Lorain, OH	152,368	151,082	151,819	0.9	-0.5	5.4	9.1	5.2	5,623	-0.1	85,507	9.0	$41,849
Medina, OH	96,495	94,041	91,736	2.6	2.5	4.3	7.4	4.4	3,981	0.2	54,741	10.9	$41,130
Coeur d'Alene, ID Metro Area	77,765	68,859	67,178	12.9	2.5	3.5	10.9	4.5	4,910	10.8	52,930	21.9	$39,704
Kootenai, ID	77,765	68,859	67,178	12.9	2.5	3.5	10.9	4.5	4,910	10.8	52,930	21.9	$39,704
College Station-Bryan, TX Metro Area	132,760	115,448	102,867	15.0	12.2	3.0	6.6	4.3	4,980	14.6	75,731	28.2	$37,126
Brazos, TX	116,882	100,017	86,694	16.9	15.4	2.8	6.3	4.2	4,382	16.4	69,462	28.8	$36,804
Burleson, TX	8,223	7,870	8,615	4.5	-8.6	3.6	7.9	4.1	324	5.9	3,282	30.7	$41,391
Robertson, TX	7,655	7,561	7,558	1.2	0.0	4.1	9.2	5.0	274	-0.4	2,987	14.5	$39,927
Colorado Springs, CO Metro Area	349,735	318,662	301,904	9.8	5.6	3.9	9.3	5.3	18,262	10.4	248,023	13.8	$46,388
El Paso, CO	337,084	306,308	289,307	10.0	5.9	3.9	9.3	5.3	17,542	10.7	242,125	13.8	$46,643
Teller, CO	12,651	12,354	12,597	2.4	-1.9	3.7	9.4	4.9	720	3.4	5,898	13.4	$35,883
Columbia, MO Metro Area	109,511	105,522	100,202	3.8	5.3	2.4	6.8	3.7	5,246	6.1	85,884	17.5	$38,149
Boone, MO	97,114	92,559	85,727	4.9	8.0	2.3	6.5	3.6	4,652	7.3	79,836	19.3	$38,842
Cooper, MO	7,424	7,961	9,064	-6.7	-12.2	3.1	9.8	4.7	400	-4.1	3,881	-10.7	$29,007
Howard, MO	4,973	5,002	5,411	-0.6	-7.6	2.8	8.7	4.5	194	0.5	2,167	19.9	$28,984
Columbia, SC Metro Area	398,497	372,407	355,320	7.0	4.8	3.3	9.3	5.7	17,554	2.7	295,371	9.1	$42,714
Calhoun, SC	6,665	7,044	7,091	-5.4	-0.7	4.2	12.3	7.3	233	-4.1	3,332	9.9	$44,364
Fairfield, SC	9,786	10,672	11,316	-8.3	-5.7	6.2	14.6	7.8	320	0.6	7,746	70.1	$71,550
Kershaw, SC	28,930	28,136	28,995	2.8	-3.0	3.5	11.5	6.5	1,116	-2.2	15,297	16.1	$37,169
Lexington, SC	147,320	132,937	127,602	10.8	4.2	2.9	8.2	4.9	6,574	8.3	101,678	16.6	$38,314
Richland, SC	196,988	184,934	171,046	6.5	8.1	3.4	9.4	5.9	9,065	0.0	163,353	2.7	$44,850
Saluda, SC	8,808	8,684	9,270	1.4	-6.3	3.1	10.0	6.6	246	-5.7	3,965	10.2	$31,252
Columbus, GA-AL Metro Area	130,453	133,165	132,476	-2.0	0.5	4.7	10.0	6.0	5,863	0.2	99,653	4.3	$41,778
Russell, AL	23,753	23,814	21,501	-0.3	10.8	4.0	10.9	6.0	790	-5.7	11,100	4.5	$33,972
Chattahoochee, GA	1,988	2,218	2,657	-10.4	-16.5	5.6	10.9	10.6	111	65.7	1,967	213.7	$45,879
Harris, GA	16,736	16,415	15,281	2.0	7.4	3.4	7.7	4.2	435	9.3	4,204	25.1	$25,424
Marion, GA	3,435	3,723	3,410	-7.7	9.2	5.1	10.7	5.3	86	13.2	1,028	-13.0	$28,962

Table C-4. Labor Force and Private Business Establishments and Employment—*Continued*

Metropolitan Statistical Area / Metropolitan Division / Component counties	Civilian Labor Force								Private nonfarm businesses				
	Total			Percent change		Unemployment rate			Establishments		Employment		Annual payroll per emplyee 2017 (dollars)
	2018	2010	2005	2010-2018	2005-2010	2018	2010	2005	2017	change 2010-2017	2017	Change 2010-2017	
Muscogee, GA	79,354	81,718	84,703	-2.9	-3.5	5.1	10.1	6.2	4,315	-0.6	80,133	2.2	$43,881
Stewart, GA	2,352	2,402	1,951	-2.1	23.1	4.7	10.3	9.3	59	-20.3	717	-5.8	$31,820
Talbot, GA	2,835	2,875	2,973	-1.4	-3.3	5.0	10.1	7.1	67	9.8	504	-11.6	$40,107
Columbus, IN Metro Area	45,295	38,387	37,388	18.0	2.7	2.6	9.5	4.8	1,884	1.6	48,314	25.0	$47,297
Bartholomew, IN	45,295	38,387	37,388	18.0	2.7	2.6	9.5	4.8	1,884	1.6	48,314	25.0	$47,297
Columbus, OH Metro Area	1,080,766	1,004,299	956,304	7.6	5.0	3.8	9.0	5.5	42,559	5.9	874,951	15.3	$49,560
Delaware, OH	107,617	94,233	83,514	14.2	12.8	3.4	7.2	4.4	4,602	21.0	80,543	21.6	$52,418
Fairfield, OH	77,307	74,265	73,172	4.1	1.5	4.0	9.2	5.5	2,679	4.6	35,018	8.0	$35,271
Franklin, OH	685,914	626,837	601,304	9.4	4.2	3.8	8.9	5.4	28,412	4.8	641,881	14.5	$51,176
Hocking, OH	13,112	14,036	13,850	-6.6	1.3	5.1	11.7	7.7	488	1.5	5,279	6.2	$30,239
Licking, OH	89,021	87,551	81,708	1.7	7.2	4.0	9.6	5.9	3,031	3.7	53,281	15.2	$39,831
Madison, OH	20,584	20,665	19,828	-0.4	4.2	3.8	9.0	6.0	683	-2.3	13,993	37.7	$41,071
Morrow, OH	16,734	17,309	17,738	-3.3	-2.4	4.5	11.4	6.4	385	1.3	3,938	7.5	$32,997
Perry, OH	15,880	16,646	16,652	-4.6	0.0	5.6	13.4	8.4	430	1.4	4,329	13.0	$33,720
Pickaway, OH	26,268	26,100	24,055	0.6	8.5	4.3	10.6	7.2	795	-0.1	10,885	4.6	$38,019
Union, OH	28,329	26,657	24,483	6.3	8.9	3.5	8.4	5.1	1,054	5.2	25,804	23.9	$58,526
Corpus Christi, TX Metro Area	198,500	192,936	186,099	2.9	3.7	4.9	8.5	5.6	9,086	3.4	155,845	12.9	$41,935
Nueces, TX	168,149	162,502	156,542	3.5	3.8	4.7	8.1	5.4	8,025	3.4	140,760	12.3	$41,391
San Patricio, TX	30,351	30,434	29,557	-0.3	3.0	6.3	10.5	6.9	1,061	3.4	15,085	19.2	$47,007
Corvallis, OR Metro Area	48,345	45,075	41,922	7.3	7.5	3.2	7.1	4.9	2,148	4.3	28,322	15.5	$49,755
Benton, OR	48,345	45,075	41,922	7.3	7.5	3.2	7.1	4.9	2,148	4.3	28,322	15.5	$49,755
Crestview-Fort Walton Beach-Destin, FL Metro Area	126,914	115,030	124,514	10.3	-7.6	3.0	8.6	2.8	7,754	16.1	82,799	14.7	$37,755
Okaloosa, FL	96,270	89,046	96,570	8.1	-7.8	2.9	8.4	2.8	5,418	8.5	61,422	8.3	$39,057
Walton, FL	30,644	25,984	27,944	17.9	-7.0	3.1	9.4	2.8	2,336	38.9	21,377	38.6	$34,013
Cumberland, MD-WV Metro Area	44,246	46,781	48,703	-5.4	-3.9	5.5	9.3	5.9	1,999	-6.6	29,972	-0.5	$36,638
Allegany, MD	31,984	34,419	35,318	-7.1	-2.5	5.5	9.3	6.1	1,552	-7.1	23,844	0.4	$35,177
Mineral, WV	12,262	12,362	13,385	-0.8	-7.6	5.5	9.3	5.3	447	-4.7	6,128	-4.0	$42,322
Dallas-Fort Worth-Arlington, TX Metro Area	3,869,662	3,273,368	2,998,404	18.2	9.2	3.5	8.1	5.2	163,708	16.6	3,127,419	24.6	$55,569
Dallas-Plano-Irving, TX Div	2,631,424	2,192,401	2,004,189	20.0	9.4	3.5	8.0	5.3	114,608	17.5	2,253,776	27.5	$58,470
Collin, TX	545,243	425,252	367,439	28.2	15.7	3.3	7.2	4.7	24,118	36.1	419,266	45.2	$63,168
Dallas, TX	1,359,225	1,194,015	1,142,456	13.8	4.5	3.7	8.6	5.7	66,633	8.7	1,489,586	21.0	$60,564
Denton, TX	482,610	369,088	314,097	30.8	17.5	3.2	7.1	4.6	15,125	33.3	221,569	42.1	$44,730
Ellis, TX	89,935	75,674	66,297	18.8	14.1	3.3	8.0	5.3	3,002	22.8	45,132	43.3	$40,509
Hunt, TX	42,373	38,126	38,516	11.1		3.8	8.9	5.5	1,506	8.7	25,043	15.6	$53,380
Kaufman, TX	61,846	50,807	43,006	21.7	18.1	3.5	8.5	5.5	1,955	18.2	26,651	31.2	$37,439
Rockwall, TX	50,192	39,439	32,378	27.3	21.8	3.2	7.4	4.7	2,269	36.6	26,529	41.4	$37,952
Fort Worth-Arlington-Grapevine, TX Div	1,238,238	1,080,967	994,215	14.5	8.7	3.5	8.2	5.1	49,100	14.4	873,643	17.8	$48,082
Johnson, TX	79,949	71,940	72,108	11.1	-0.2	3.4	8.7	4.9	2,833	11.4	36,661	16.1	$40,982
Parker, TX	64,740	56,408	50,654	14.8	11.4	3.1	7.6	4.8	2,773	26.3	28,629	27.2	$39,794
Tarrant, TX	1,062,733	924,951	843,857	14.9	9.6	3.5	8.1	5.1	42,162	13.9	790,048	17.6	$48,784
Wise, TX	30,816	27,668	27,596	11.4	0.3	3.4	8.7	4.7	1,332	13.0	18,305	18.5	$44,976
Dalton, GA Metro Area	61,199	64,820	66,501	-5.6	-2.5	4.9	12.4	4.8	2,603	-3.4	55,284	-1.5	$41,565
Murray, GA	15,943	17,181	20,981	-7.2	-18.1	5.3	13.8	4.6	412	-1.2	7,619	-7.8	$34,466
Whitfield, GA	45,256	47,639	45,520	-5.0	4.7	4.7	11.9	4.8	2,191	-3.8	47,665	-0.4	$42,699
Danville, IL Metro Area	33,578	37,958	37,822	-11.5	0.4	6.2	11.4	6.3	1,426	-7.3	24,093	-0.8	$40,451
Vermilion, IL	33,578	37,958	37,822	-11.5	0.4	6.2	11.4	6.3	1,426	-7.3	24,093	-0.8	$40,451
Daphne-Fairhope-Foley, AL Metro Area	93,849	83,459	76,804	12.4	8.7	3.6	10.0	4.0	5,384	15.4	61,792	20.8	$33,783
Baldwin, AL	93,849	83,459	76,804	12.4	8.7	3.6	10.0	4.0	5,384	15.4	61,792	20.8	$33,783
Davenport-Moline-Rock Island, IA-IL Metro Area	191,911	199,430	202,279	-3.8	-1.4	4.2	8.2	4.5	8,878	-3.3	157,879	2.3	$44,866
Henry, IL	25,083	26,795	27,308	-6.4	-1.9	5.0	9.1	4.5	1,054	-6.7	13,304	1.8	$35,869
Mercer, IL	8,103	8,980	8,911	-9.8	0.8	5.3	9.9	5.5	272	-9.6	2,265	-3.1	$33,701
Rock Island, IL	71,847	76,522	77,924	-6.1	-1.8	5.2	9.5	4.6	3,077	-8.1	60,656		$51,224
Scott, IA	86,878	87,133	88,136	-0.3	-1.1	3.0	6.6	4.4	4,475	1.7	81,654	5.2	$41,919
Dayton-Kettering, OH Metro Area	386,050	401,835	404,463	-3.9	-0.6	4.3	11.0	6.2	16,478	-1.6	326,374	9.1	$45,336
Greene, OH	82,136	82,080	77,375	0.1	6.1	4.0	9.5	5.7	3,238	8.5	55,639	14.8	$42,268
Miami, OH	53,197	54,400	54,855	-2.2	-0.8	3.9	11.1	5.8	2,099	-1.4	36,143	9.5	$39,255
Montgomery, OH	250,717	265,355	272,233	-5.5	-2.5	4.5	11.4	6.5	11,141	-4.3	234,592	7.7	$47,000
Decatur, AL Metro Area	70,258	72,718	71,679	-3.4	1.4	3.7	11.1	4.8	3,024	-2.7	46,522	1.2	$42,219
Lawrence, AL	13,919	14,901	15,979	-6.6	-6.7	4.2	12.6	5.6	404	-2.4	3,256	-25.9	$29,728
Morgan, AL	56,339	57,817	55,700	-2.6	3.8	3.5	10.8	4.5	2,620	-2.7	43,266	4.1	$43,159
Decatur, IL Metro Area	49,961	55,193	52,836	-9.5	4.5	5.6	11.2	6.1	2,417	-3.7	44,389	-4.3	$47,875
Macon, IL	49,961	55,193	52,836	-9.5	4.5	5.6	11.2	6.1	2,417	-3.7	44,389	-4.3	$47,875
Deltona-Daytona Beach-Ormond Beach, FL Metro Area	300,516	279,521	274,669	7.5	1.8	3.8	12.3	3.8	15,027	11.1	168,368	18.3	$35,491
Flagler, FL	47,077	41,338	29,981	13.9	37.9	4.0	12.4	4.4	2,165	24.2	19,194	29.8	$32,544
Volusia, FL	253,439	238,183	244,688	6.4	-2.7	3.7	12.3	3.7	12,862	9.2	149,174	17.0	$35,870
Denver-Aurora-Lakewood, CO Metro Area	1,646,346	1,423,355	1,314,305	15.7	8.3	3.2	8.7	5.1	85,059	15.5	1,280,402	23.3	$57,785
Adams, CO	269,911	234,221	209,927	15.2	11.6	3.5	10.0	5.7	10,053	23.1	173,553	33.7	$49,059
Arapahoe, CO	362,692	316,886	298,738	14.5	6.1	3.2	8.6	5.1	19,014	13.4	293,379	24.3	$60,651
Broomfield, CO	39,816	31,538	24,506	26.2	28.7	2.9	7.4	4.8	2,158	25.7	46,084	43.0	$66,211
Clear Creek, CO	6,075	5,623	5,837	8.0	-3.7	3.0	8.1	4.7	353	2.9	2,961	16.8	$31,887
Denver, CO	412,817	347,590	302,009	18.8	15.1	3.2	9.1	5.7	25,694	16.5	444,646	20.7	$63,434
Douglas, CO	191,240	157,522	142,904	21.4	10.2	2.9	7.0	4.1	9,270	24.4	112,808	44.8	$59,252
Elbert, CO	14,963	12,755	12,895	17.3	-1.1	2.8	8.1	4.5	622	22.9	2,595	29.2	$40,066
Gilpin, CO	3,731	3,327	3,337	12.1	-0.3	2.5	8.0	4.8	125	14.7	4,885	10.6	$37,733

Table C-4. Labor Force and Private Business Establishments and Employment—*Continued*

Metropolitan Statistical Area Metropolitan Division Component counties	Civilian Labor Force								Private nonfarm businesses				
	Total			Percent change		Unemployment rate			Establishments		Employment		Annual payroll per emplyee 2017 (dollars)
	2018	2010	2005	2010-2018	2005-2010	2018	2010	2005	2017	change 2010-2017	2017	Change 2010-2017	
Jefferson, CO	334,242	304,252	304,514	9.9	-0.1	3.0	8.4	4.9	17,303	7.5	198,024	7.8	$46,995
Park, CO	10,859	9,641	9,638	12.6	0.0	2.9	8.1	4.7	467	4.0	1,467	20.6	$34,579
Des Moines-West Des Moines, IA Metro Area	372,879	341,880	314,920	9.1	8.6	2.4	5.9	4.0	17,416	11.2	329,004	15.3	$51,360
Dallas, IA	47,653	37,290	29,439	27.8	26.7	1.7	4.6	3.4	2,059	35.5	40,329	38.9	$51,886
Guthrie, IA	5,570	5,851	6,116	-4.8	-4.3	2.6	6.5	4.2	315	-2.5	2,336	-12.8	$32,673
Jasper, IA	19,266	19,022	18,644	1.3	2.0	2.6	7.3	5.9	756	-3.0	9,110	9.8	$34,403
Madison, IA	8,397	8,459	8,141	-0.7	3.9	3.2	6.4	4.5	405	11.3	2,736	4.0	$35,947
Polk, IA	264,356	244,906	227,980	7.9	7.4	2.5	6.0	4.0	12,995	9.2	265,640	13.2	$52,710
Warren, IA	27,637	26,352	24,600	4.9	7.1	2.3	5.6	3.7	886	14.3	8,853	11.1	$35,623
Detroit-Warren-Dearborn, MI Metro Area	2,130,620	2,058,555	2,209,029	3.5	-6.8	4.3	13.9	7.0	100,070	2.9	1,761,974	17.4	$53,882
Detroit-Dearborn-Livonia, MI Div	794,466	802,754	910,762	-1.0	-11.9	5.2	15.5	8.3	32,444	-0.3	643,127	13.3	$53,840
Wayne, MI	794,466	802,754	910,762	-1.0	-11.9	5.2	15.5	8.3	32,444	-0.3	643,127	13.3	$53,840
Warren-Troy-Farmington Hills, MI Div	1,336,154	1,255,801	1,298,267	6.4	-3.3	3.7	12.9	6.0	67,626	4.6	1,118,847	19.9	$53,907
Lapeer, MI	41,369	41,335	45,788	0.1	-9.7	5.2	16.3	7.5	1,702	7.9	18,583	26.7	$35,554
Livingston, MI	102,785	94,112	96,140	9.2	-2.1	3.3	11.2	5.2	4,384	8.8	52,688	21.1	$41,021
Macomb, MI	445,483	420,803	428,038	5.9	-1.7	4.0	13.9	6.6	19,195	8.1	309,802	22.7	$46,635
Oakland, MI	670,739	621,876	642,576	7.9	-3.2	3.3	11.8	5.5	39,250	2.9	696,367	19.2	$59,432
St. Clair, MI	75,778	77,675	85,725	-2.4	-9.4	4.7	16.4	7.7	3,095	-2.3	41,407	8.0	$40,030
Dothan, AL Metro Area	62,767	65,232	65,199	-3.8	0.1	4.1	9.6	3.9	3,417	-2.0	50,838	2.4	$39,204
Geneva, AL	10,851	11,559	11,628	-6.1	-0.6	3.9	10.4	3.9	400	-5.2	3,775	-4.7	$31,331
Henry, AL	6,766	7,259	7,469	-6.8	-2.8	4.4	10.9	4.3	297	-0.7	2,276	-17.6	$42,436
Houston, AL	45,150	46,414	46,102	-2.7	0.7	4.0	9.1	3.8	2,720	-1.6	44,787	4.3	$39,703
Dover, DE Metro Area	78,124	72,711	72,015	7.4	1.0	4.1	8.9	3.6	3,583	12.0	52,481	13.1	$39,381
Kent, DE	78,124	72,711	72,015	7.4	1.0	4.1	8.9	3.6	3,583	12.0	52,481	13.1	$39,381
Dubuque, IA Metro Area	55,213	54,215	50,793	1.8	6.7	2.4	5.8	4.3	2,797	2.2	54,767	8.3	$42,826
Dubuque, IA	55,213	54,215	50,793	1.8	6.7	2.4	5.8	4.3	2,797	2.2	54,767	8.3	$42,826
Duluth, MN-WI Metro Area	148,405	150,703	147,148	-1.5	2.4	3.8	8.2	5.1	7,394	-2.5	114,815	5.9	$42,589
Carlton, MN	17,655	17,794	17,021	-0.8	4.5	4.1	8.4	5.8	684	-4.3	8,000	-0.3	$41,754
Lake, MN	5,478	5,798	6,089	-5.5	-4.8	3.1	8.3	4.3	301	4.2	3,260	11.5	$37,705
St. Louis, MN	101,957	103,374	101,353	-1.4	2.0	3.7	8.1	5.0	5,374	-2.5	89,367	6.8	$43,375
Douglas, WI	23,315	23,737	22,685	-1.8	4.6	4.0	8.3	5.3	1,035	-3.5	14,188	3.3	$39,231
Durham-Chapel Hill, NC Metro Area	328,244	290,122	268,243	13.1	8.2	3.4	8.3	4.5	13,893	11.0	274,514	19.5	$58,520
Chatham, NC	34,637	30,661	30,758	13.0	-0.3	3.3	8.6	4.0	1,456	15.2	14,268	7.1	$34,112
Durham, NC	167,606	143,411	129,938	16.9	10.4	3.5	8.2	4.3	7,556	13.9	191,882	23.0	$65,902
Granville, NC	29,943	27,384	23,754	9.3	15.3	3.4	9.7	6.0	892	6.8	13,863	5.0	$38,324
Orange, NC	77,797	69,962	65,060	11.2	7.5	3.3	6.6	3.7	3,289	6.5	46,466	18.5	$45,342
Person, NC	18,261	18,704	18,733	-2.4	-0.2	4.1	12.4	6.4	700	-0.1	8,035	-0.9	$36,606
East Stroudsburg, PA Metro Area	82,004	82,713	77,999	-0.9	6.0	5.4	9.7	5.5	3,385	-0.7	49,290	10.1	$35,806
Monroe, PA	82,004	82,713	77,999	-0.9	6.0	5.4	9.7	5.5	3,385	-0.7	49,290	10.1	$35,806
Eau Claire, WI Metro Area	92,860	90,289	86,404	2.8	4.5	2.9	7.5	4.6	4,242	1.8	72,741	7.6	$48,803
Chippewa, WI	33,580	33,182	32,640	1.2	1.7	3.3	8.4	5.4	1,601	5.9	21,714	10.8	$38,814
Eau Claire, WI	59,280	57,107	53,764	3.8	6.2	2.6	7.0	4.1	2,641	-0.5	51,027	6.2	$53,054
El Centro, CA Metro Area	71,055	78,665	60,592	-9.7	29.8	18.1	28.8	16.0	2,538	7.2	32,109	9.9	$35,179
Imperial, CA	71,055	78,665	60,592	-9.7	29.8	18.1	28.8	16.0	2,538	7.2	32,109	9.9	$35,179
Elizabethtown-Fort Knox, KY Metro Area	67,543	65,301	65,279	3.4	0.0	4.2	10.2	6.1	2,616	-6.8	42,854	13.9	$38,068
Hardin, KY	49,149	46,901	46,216	4.8	1.5	4.1	9.7	5.8	2,089	-6.7	37,405	15.7	$38,474
Larue, KY	6,075	6,062	6,884	0.2	-11.9	4.4	11.3	6.3	202	-12.6	1,954	-9.2	$32,835
Meade, KY	12,319	12,338	12,179	-0.2	1.3	4.6	11.8	7.0	325	-3.8	3,495	10.6	$36,654
Elkhart-Goshen, IN Metro Area	116,267	94,498	101,915	23.0	-7.3	2.6	13.3	4.6	4,949	1.2	132,095	40.1	$47,387
Elkhart, IN	116,267	94,498	101,915	23.0	-7.3	2.6	13.3	4.6	4,949	1.2	132,095	40.1	$47,387
Elmira, NY Metro Area	35,373	41,594	40,595	-15.0	2.5	4.7	8.4	5.3	1,758	-5.3	30,377	-6.9	$40,663
Chemung, NY	35,373	41,594	40,595	-15.0	2.5	4.7	8.4	5.3	1,758	-5.3	30,377	-6.9	$40,663
El Paso, TX Metro Area	360,802	342,254	291,338	5.4	17.5	4.2	9.2	7.0	14,599	9.0	237,730	14.7	$32,155
El Paso, TX	359,136	340,841	290,010	5.4	17.5	4.2	9.2	7.0	14,569	9.1	237,385	14.7	$32,138
Hudspeth, TX	1,666	1,413	1,328	17.9	6.4	4.7	7.9	6.9	30	-11.8	345	7.1	$43,893
Enid, OK Metro Area	27,330	28,519	28,304	-4.2	0.8	3.0	5.5	3.6	1,645	0.0	21,514	-3.3	$38,770
Garfield, OK	27,330	28,519	28,304	-4.2	0.8	3.0	5.5	3.6	1,645	0.0	21,514	-3.3	$38,770
Erie, PA Metro Area	129,260	136,361	140,605	-5.2	-3.0	4.7	9.3	5.4	6,197	-1.4	115,178	3.1	$39,422
Erie, PA	129,260	136,361	140,605	-5.2	-3.0	4.7	9.3	5.4	6,197	-1.4	115,178	3.1	$39,422
Eugene-Springfield, OR Metro Area	181,761	178,303	173,600	1.9	2.7	4.5	11.0	6.1	9,959	3.7	125,153	12.1	$40,501
Lane, OR	181,761	178,303	173,600	1.9	2.7	4.5	11.0	6.1	9,959	3.7	125,153	12.1	$40,501
Evansville, IN-KY Metro Area	164,282	159,288	159,088	3.1	0.1	3.2	8.9	5.1	7,741	1.9	144,467	1.1	$43,123
Posey, IN	13,731	13,494	13,870	1.8	-2.7	2.8	7.8	4.9	512	0.4	9,126	8.9	$51,264
Vanderburgh, IN	95,249	92,127	91,447	3.4	0.7	3.2	8.9	5.2	5,066	1.9	104,527	-1.1	$42,690
Warrick, IN	33,148	30,817	30,602	7.6	0.7	2.9	8.0	4.7	1,166	8.0	14,644	16.3	$44,163
Henderson, KY	22,154	22,850	23,169	-3.0	-1.4	3.8	10.3	5.4	997	-3.9	16,170	-0.5	$40,389
Fairbanks, AK Metro Area	46,101	48,285	45,247	-4.5	6.7	5.8	6.6	5.8	2,492	2.0	27,095	-0.2	$50,510
Fairbanks North Star, AK	46,101	48,285	45,247	-4.5	6.7	5.8	6.6	5.8	2,492	2.0	27,095	-0.2	$50,510
Fargo, ND-MN Metro Area	136,735	122,707	113,083	11.4	8.5	2.4	4.1	2.9	6,917	9.8	122,574	13.1	$45,867
Clay, MN	35,791	33,883	30,853	5.6	9.8	2.9	5.5	3.4	1,342	5.3	17,905	6.7	$33,483
Cass, ND	100,944	88,824	82,230	13.6	8.0	2.3	3.5	2.7	5,575	11.0	104,669	14.2	$47,985
Farmington, NM Metro Area	52,537	54,860	54,461	-4.2	0.7	5.8	9.4	5.3	2,626	-7.0	34,753	-8.3	$43,366
San Juan, NM	52,537	54,860	54,461	-4.2	0.7	5.8	9.4	5.3	2,626	-7.0	34,753	-8.3	$43,366

Table C-4. Labor Force and Private Business Establishments and Employment—*Continued*

| | Civilian Labor Force | | | | | | | | Private nonfarm businesses | | | | |
| | Total | | | Percent change | | Unemployment rate | | | Establishments | | Employment | | Annual payroll per emplyee 2017 (dollars) |
Metropolitan Statistical Area / Metropolitan Division / Component counties	2018	2010	2005	2010-2018	2005-2010	2018	2010	2005	2017	change 2010-2017	2017	Change 2010-2017	
Fayetteville, NC Metro Area	200,668	198,447	190,865	1.1	4.0	5.0	10.4	5.4	7,833	0.9	120,741	3.0	$33,997
Cumberland, NC	127,957	131,096	127,153	-2.4	3.1	5.1	10.1	5.4	5,678	-0.5	93,171	0.2	$34,929
Harnett, NC	52,791	48,774	45,310	8.2	7.6	4.6	11.3	5.3	1,692	2.4	22,032	18.1	$31,084
Hoke, NC	19,920	18,577	18,402	7.2	1.0	5.0	10.1	5.8	463	14.0	5,538	-0.1	$29,912
Fayetteville-Springdale-Rogers, AR Metro Area	264,399	217,256	208,928	21.7	4.0	2.8	6.6	3.3	12,061	16.7	210,590	23.1	$49,768
Benton, AR	134,404	107,121	100,203	25.5	6.9	2.9	6.6	3.2	6,408	20.6	119,516	31.2	$56,486
Madison, AR	7,426	7,270	7,835	2.1	-7.2	2.9	7.1	3.7	211	14.7	2,496	9.3	$32,036
Washington, AR	122,569	102,865	100,890	19.2	2.0	2.6	6.5	3.4	5,442	12.6	88,578	14.0	$41,204
Flagstaff, AZ Metro Area	77,083	72,846	67,883	5.8	7.3	5.5	9.9	4.9	3,746	4.8	53,114	22.3	$39,703
Coconino, AZ	77,083	72,846	67,883	5.8	7.3	5.5	9.9	4.9	3,746	4.8	53,114	22.3	$39,703
Flint, MI Metro Area	181,781	188,190	212,686	-3.4	-11.5	4.9	14.0	7.9	7,740	-2.1	121,169	9.8	$40,743
Genesee, MI	181,781	188,190	212,686	-3.4	-11.5	4.9	14.0	7.9	7,740	-2.1	121,169	9.8	$40,743
Florence, SC Metro Area	96,082	94,763	92,386	1.4	2.6	3.8	11.9	8.8	4,225	-1.9	75,608	7.6	$38,962
Darlington, SC	30,086	30,590	30,588	-1.6	0.0	4.1	13.2	8.7	1,083	-4.2	17,652	-2.9	$42,764
Florence, SC	65,996	64,173	61,798	2.8	3.8	3.7	11.3	8.9	3,142	-1.1	57,956	11.3	$37,804
Florence-Muscle Shoals, AL Metro Area	65,399	67,824	67,023	-3.6	1.2	4.3	10.6	5.2	3,213	-2.0	49,018	10.9	$34,130
Colbert, AL	23,258	24,228	24,960	-4.0	-2.9	4.6	11.5	5.4	1,217	-5.2	23,258	24.4	$37,890
Lauderdale, AL	42,141	43,596	42,063	-3.3	3.6	4.2	10.1	5.1	1,996	0.2	25,760	1.1	$30,736
Fond du Lac, WI Metro Area	57,658	56,516	55,868	2.0	1.2	2.6	8.5	4.6	2,325	-4.7	43,479	12.3	$43,045
Fond du Lac, WI	57,658	56,516	55,868	2.0	1.2	2.6	8.5	4.6	2,325	-4.7	43,479	12.3	$43,045
Fort Collins, CO Metro Area	202,449	170,001	165,944	19.1	2.4	2.8	7.6	4.4	10,935	16.6	126,470	24.0	$45,774
Larimer, CO	202,449	170,001	165,944	19.1	2.4	2.8	7.6	4.4	10,935	16.6	126,470	24.0	$45,774
Fort Smith, AR-OK Metro Area	107,748	113,766	113,674	-5.3	0.1	3.7	8.3	4.5	5,353	-2.4	91,556	-4.0	$37,455
Crawford, AR	26,861	28,323	27,438	-5.2	3.2	3.6	8.2	4.4	1,072	-2.9	16,884	-22.0	$33,940
Franklin, AR	7,406	7,800	8,521	-5.1	-8.5	3.6	7.7	4.3	285	3.3	3,684	12.8	$34,819
Sebastian, AR	57,075	59,543	59,664	-4.1	-0.2	3.6	8.0	4.3	3,415	-2.9	63,892	-0.3	$40,028
Sequoyah, OK	16,406	18,100	18,051	-9.4	0.3	4.3	9.6	5.5	581	-1.2	7,096	11.0	$24,016
Fort Wayne, IN Metro Area	202,508	193,545	196,585	4.6	-1.5	3.1	10.8	5.3	9,879	0.6	189,684	13.8	$42,786
Allen, IN	184,863	175,942	178,905	5.1	-1.7	3.2	10.7	5.3	9,192	0.6	177,953	13.5	$43,014
Whitley, IN	17,645	17,603	17,680	0.2	-0.4	2.9	11.5	5.1	687	1.0	11,731	18.7	$39,337
Fresno, CA Metro Area	448,353	439,593	407,163	2.0	8.0	7.5	16.7	9.0	16,881	7.0	261,800	16.3	$43,232
Fresno, CA	448,353	439,593	407,163	2.0	8.0	7.5	16.7	9.0	16,881	7.0	261,800	16.3	$43,232
Gadsden, AL Metro Area	43,096	44,000	46,762	-2.1	-5.9	4.1	10.9	4.7	1,978	-2.7	30,604	3.8	$34,138
Etowah, AL	43,096	44,000	46,762	-2.1	-5.9	4.1	10.9	4.7	1,978	-2.7	30,604	3.8	$34,138
Gainesville, FL Metro Area	161,134	152,571	147,618	5.6	3.4	3.4	8.6	3.0	7,190	6.8	102,732	16.5	$41,027
Alachua, FL	137,339	128,370	123,550	7.0	3.9	3.3	8.0	2.9	6,195	7.1	94,515	16.0	$42,009
Gilchrist, FL	6,869	6,874	7,489	-0.1	-8.2	3.8	10.8	3.2	245	16.7	1,772	24.9	$33,537
Levy, FL	16,926	17,327	16,579	-2.3	4.5	3.8	11.9	3.8	750	1.8	6,445	22.0	$28,690
Gainesville, GA Metro Area	102,169	86,546	82,801	18.1	4.5	3.2	9.6	4.5	4,369	10.6	77,461	34.0	$46,234
Hall, GA	102,169	86,546	82,801	18.1	4.5	3.2	9.6	4.5	4,369	10.6	77,461	34.0	$46,234
Gettysburg, PA Metro Area	55,121	54,590	54,495	1.0	0.2	3.3	7.7	3.6	1,974	3.2	29,070	5.7	$36,797
Adams, PA	55,121	54,590	54,495	1.0	0.2	3.3	7.7	3.6	1,974	3.2	29,070	5.7	$36,797
Glens Falls, NY Metro Area	59,873	64,387	67,615	-7.0	-4.8	4.4	8.6	4.5	3,345	-3.1	42,072	3.5	$40,045
Warren, NY	31,709	34,154	35,471	-7.2	-3.7	4.6	9.0	4.6	2,276	-4.0	31,450	1.0	$39,937
Washington, NY	28,164	30,233	32,144	-6.8	-5.9	4.1	8.2	4.5	1,069		10,622	11.7	$40,363
Goldsboro, NC Metro Area	52,731	54,808	51,135	-3.8	7.2	4.3	9.2	5.2	2,175	-2.1	33,960	0.4	$34,316
Wayne, NC	52,731	54,808	51,135	-3.8	7.2	4.3	9.2	5.2	2,175	-2.1	33,960	0.4	$34,316
Grand Forks, ND-MN Metro Area	54,699	55,022	54,988	-0.6	0.1	2.7	4.5	3.6	2,647	1.4	42,714	4.7	$39,507
Polk, MN	16,786	17,156	16,899	-2.2	1.5	3.7	6.6	4.5	760	-1.4	9,346	-4.0	$36,712
Grand Forks, ND	37,913	37,866	38,089	0.1	-0.6	2.3	3.5	3.2	1,887	2.6	33,368	7.4	$40,290
Grand Island, NE Metro Area	38,997	39,064	38,108	-0.2	2.5	3.1	4.6	3.8	2,309	5.0	33,756	4.3	$38,127
Hall, NE	31,628	31,519	30,130	0.3	4.6	3.2	4.6	3.8	1,894	3.7	30,965	3.8	$38,469
Howard, NE	3,316	3,346	3,688	-0.9	-9.3	3.0	4.4	3.6	178	25.4	1,093	19.3	$33,104
Merrick, NE	4,053	4,199	4,290	-3.5	-2.1	2.8	4.5	3.7	237	3.0	1,698	3.9	$35,120
Grand Junction, CO Metro Area	76,060	76,113	70,811	-0.1	7.5	4.1	11.0	4.9	4,446	-4.3	52,848	6.8	$42,168
Mesa, CO	76,060	76,113	70,811	-0.1	7.5	4.1	11.0	4.9	4,446	-4.3	52,848	6.8	$42,168
Grand Rapids-Kentwood, MI Metro Area	577,594	514,558	518,278	12.3	-0.7	3.0	10.5	5.9	24,782	7.9	503,115	26.0	$45,537
Ionia, MI	30,119	29,931	30,924	0.6	-3.2	3.4	11.9	7.3	897	1.7	11,235	15.4	$37,268
Kent, MI	358,900	316,233	321,655	13.5	-1.7	3.0	10.1	5.8	16,750	9.1	365,651	25.7	$46,771
Montcalm, MI	28,474	27,809	29,471	2.4	-5.6	4.2	14.1	8.7	1,003	-3.5	13,080	12.3	$35,433
Ottawa, MI	160,101	140,585	136,228	13.9	3.2	2.8	10.3	5.2	6,132	7.8	113,149	30.1	$43,538
Grants Pass, OR Metro Area	35,929	34,491	34,300	4.2	0.6	5.5	14.0	7.3	2,030	0.8	23,460	22.3	$34,366
Josephine, OR	35,929	34,491	34,300	4.2	0.6	5.5	14.0	7.3	2,030	0.8	23,460	22.3	$34,366
Great Falls, MT Metro Area	37,848	38,447	38,950	-1.6	-1.3	3.6	6.4	4.3	2,458	0.2	30,445	0.5	$38,271
Cascade, MT	37,848	38,447	38,950	-1.6	-1.3	3.6	6.4	4.3	2,458	0.2	30,445	0.5	$38,271
Greeley, CO Metro Area	165,290	131,910	111,087	25.3	18.7	3.0	9.2	5.5	6,274	21.5	85,076	31.7	$50,283
Weld, CO	165,290	131,910	111,087	25.3	18.7	3.0	9.2	5.5	6,274	21.5	85,076	31.7	$50,283
Green Bay, WI Metro Area	175,911	169,659	167,690	3.7	1.2	2.8	8.3	4.6	7,816	2.6	156,929	9.3	$47,335
Brown, WI	143,673	137,150	135,667	4.8	1.1	2.7	7.9	4.5	6,580	3.2	144,871	10.2	$48,262
Kewaunee, WI	11,370	11,178	11,800	1.7	-5.3	2.9	8.2	4.5	461	-3.6	4,956	-9.6	$39,682
Oconto, WI	20,868	21,331	20,223	-2.2	5.5	3.3	10.7	5.7	775	0.9	7,102	5.4	$33,767
Greensboro-High Point, NC Metro Area	367,616	365,619	360,977	0.5	1.3	4.1	11.5	5.2	17,737	1.0	323,805	9.3	$43,914
Guilford, NC	260,591	252,010	240,605	3.4	4.7	4.1	11.1	5.1	13,562	2.2	262,080	10.7	$46,173

Table C-4. Labor Force and Private Business Establishments and Employment—*Continued*

Metropolitan Statistical Area / Metropolitan Division / Component counties	Civilian Labor Force								Private nonfarm businesses				Annual payroll per emplyee 2017 (dollars)
	Total			Percent change		Unemployment rate			Establishments		Employment		
	2018	2010	2005	2010-2018	2005-2010	2018	2010	2005	2017	change 2010-2017	2017	Change 2010-2017	
Randolph, NC	66,526	69,399	74,686	-4.1	-7.1	3.7	12.0	4.8	2,523	-2.5	39,187	6.3	$34,651
Rockingham, NC	40,499	44,210	45,686	-8.4	-3.2	4.5	13.2	6.6	1,652	-3.5	22,538	-0.4	$33,744
Greenville, NC Metro Area	89,961	85,917	73,488	4.7	16.9	4.2	10.2	5.8	3,584	0.4	60,749	7.8	$39,964
Pitt, NC	89,961	85,917	73,488	4.7	16.9	4.2	10.2	5.8	3,584	0.4	60,749	7.8	$39,964
Greenville-Anderson, SC Metro Area	424,424	390,067	384,213	8.8	1.5	3.1	10.4	6.2	20,111	7.4	340,562	14.5	$42,759
Anderson, SC	89,580	85,234	83,943	5.1	1.5	3.3	11.6	7.4	3,801	3.3	59,965	18.7	$38,827
Greenville, SC	248,725	220,209	209,830	12.9	4.9	2.9	9.6	5.5	13,369	10.7	237,218	14.7	$45,164
Laurens, SC	29,857	30,190	33,202	-1.1	-9.1	3.6	12.3	6.7	904	-4.2	16,753	6.2	$39,423
Pickens, SC	56,262	54,434	57,238	3.4	-4.9	3.4	10.9	6.5	2,037	0.5	26,626	9.7	$32,284
Gulfport-Biloxi, MS Metro Area	170,934	179,666	182,838	-4.9	-1.7	5.0	9.1	10.4	7,473	-0.1	132,684	1.7	$41,525
Hancock, MS	18,839	19,653	21,028	-4.1	-6.5	5.0	9.0	10.8	714	0.8	9,106	-9.7	$39,677
Harrison, MS	86,579	88,745	92,740	-2.4	-4.3	4.5	8.8	10.8	4,176	-0.7	74,790	8.1	$37,921
Jackson, MS	58,725	64,425	62,240	-8.8	3.5	5.5	9.5	9.9	2,309	1.1	45,794	-5.2	$48,411
Stone, MS	6,791	6,843	6,830	-0.8	0.2	5.4	10.6	7.7	274	-2.8	2,994	6.5	$31,853
Hagerstown-Martinsburg, MD-WV Metro Area	139,261	134,502	118,393	3.5	13.6	4.2	9.2	4.2	5,315	-0.2	87,342	11.9	$39,929
Washington, MD	74,742	75,805	67,796	-1.4	11.8	4.3	9.6	4.4	3,433	-1.6	60,244	9.1	$39,516
Berkeley, WV	56,576	51,020	43,568	10.9	17.1	4.1	8.6	4.0	1,654	4.2	25,095	21.5	$41,218
Morgan, WV	7,943	7,677	7,029	3.5	9.2	4.3	9.1	4.6	228	-8.4	2,003	-8.0	$36,212
Hammond, LA Metro Area	54,353	53,664	50,534	1.3	6.2	5.5	9.7	9.5	2,426	8.1	36,408	14.2	$37,251
Tangipahoa, LA	54,353	53,664	50,534	1.3	6.2	5.5	9.7	9.5	2,426	8.1	36,408	14.2	$37,251
Hanford-Corcoran, CA Metro Area	57,865	59,440	53,840	-2.6	10.4	7.7	16.1	9.4	1,643	1.8	25,053	11.0	$40,068
Kings, CA	57,865	59,440	53,840	-2.6	10.4	7.7	16.1	9.4	1,643	1.8	25,053	11.0	$40,068
Harrisburg-Carlisle, PA Metro Area	297,027	290,002	277,860	2.4	4.4	3.7	7.5	4.0	13,767	2.7	277,210	6.9	$47,973
Cumberland, PA	130,339	124,448	119,810	4.7	3.9	3.3	6.8	3.7	6,122	6.9	123,084	10.2	$45,189
Dauphin, PA	142,393	140,566	133,946	1.3	4.9	4.0	8.0	4.3	6,875	-0.2	147,918	4.5	$51,148
Perry, PA	24,295	24,988	24,104	-2.8	3.7	3.7	8.1	4.2	770	-3.3	6,208	1.1	$27,508
Harrisonburg, VA Metro Area	65,473	63,538	61,197	3.0	3.8	3.0	7.3	3.3	3,094	3.5	51,926	2.7	$37,670
Rockingham, VA	40,737	40,373	40,244	0.9	0.3	2.6	6.7	3.0	1,491	5.9	27,149	11.9	$41,555
Harrisonburg City, VA	24,736	23,165	20,953	6.8	10.6	3.5	8.3	3.9	1,603	1.3	24,777	-5.8	$33,413
Hartford-East Hartford-Middletown, CT Metro Area	659,896	659,747	607,993	0.0	8.5	4.1	9.0	5.0	29,521	-0.1	549,925	3.9	$58,535
Hartford, CT	480,319	479,963	437,887	0.1	9.6	4.2	9.4	5.3	22,880	0.2	459,840	3.9	$61,082
Middlesex, CT	93,078	93,292	89,289	-0.2	4.5	3.5	7.9	4.3	4,201	-0.5	62,799	8.7	$48,148
Tolland, CT	86,499	86,492	80,817	0.0	7.0	3.6	7.8	4.2	2,440	-1.9	27,286	-6.4	$39,515
Hattiesburg, MS Metro Area	76,916	74,613	71,892	3.1	3.8	4.2	9.1	6.1	3,687	1.4	55,470	5.1	$36,504
Covington, MS	8,288	8,235	8,793	0.6	-6.3	4.4	10.1	6.7	327	2.2	4,165	5.7	$33,692
Forrest, MS	33,763	34,083	35,646	-0.9	-4.4	4.4	9.8	6.2	1,779	-3.8	30,423	-2.2	$40,894
Lamar, MS	30,510	27,659	22,323	10.3	23.9	3.6	7.2	5.3	1,438	10.0	19,169	19.7	$29,165
Perry, MS	4,355	4,636	5,130	-6.1	-9.6	5.9	13.6	8.2	143	-10.1	1,713	2.0	$47,488
Hickory-Lenoir-Morganton, NC Metro Area	173,999	176,058	176,216	-1.2	-0.1	3.6	13.4	6.6	7,513	-1.6	135,351	12.3	$38,351
Alexander, NC	18,023	18,260	18,234	-1.3	0.1	3.2	13.1	5.4	566	-3.7	7,691	15.2	$32,853
Burke, NC	40,579	41,687	41,432	-2.7	0.6	3.6	12.9	6.3	1,438	-1.3	23,842	14.4	$34,257
Caldwell, NC	36,595	38,213	39,683	-4.2	-3.7	3.8	14.8	8.1	1,337	-5.2	21,119	13.9	$34,827
Catawba, NC	78,802	77,898	76,867	1.2	1.3	3.5	13.1	6.2	4,172	-0.2	82,699	11.0	$40,942
Hilton Head Island-Bluffton, SC Metro Area	87,731	76,232	71,681	15.1	6.3	3.2	8.8	4.9	6,007	13.9	63,557	20.2	$35,758
Beaufort, SC	75,517	65,336	61,574	15.6	6.1	3.2	8.7	4.9	5,347	13.3	54,957	16.5	$38,834
Jasper, SC	12,214	10,896	10,107	12.1	7.8	3.0	9.8	5.2	660	18.5	8,600	50.8	$39,881
Hinesville, GA Metro Area	33,734	33,158	28,663	1.7	15.7	4.2	8.9	5.5	920	3.8	12,320	4.4	$40,226
Liberty, GA	25,706	26,927	22,914	-4.5	17.5	4.3	9.0	5.9	847	4.1	12,003	4.7	$40,226
Long, GA	8,028	6,231	5,749	28.8	8.4	4.0	8.4	4.0	73	1.4	317	-4.5	$26,823
Homosassa Springs, FL Metro Area	47,799	52,847	51,324	-9.6	3.0	5.2	13.7	4.3	2,774	4.0	30,047	20.1	$34,922
Citrus, FL	47,799	52,847	51,324	-9.6	3.0	5.2	13.7	4.3	2,774	4.0	30,047	20.1	$34,922
Hot Springs, AR Metro Area	40,797	41,563	41,936	-1.8	-0.9	4.0	8.5	5.7	2,765	2.3	34,587	13.2	$33,265
Garland, AR	40,797	41,563	41,936	-1.8	-0.9	4.0	8.5	5.7	2,765	2.3	34,587	13.2	$33,265
Houma-Thibodaux, LA Metro Area	88,248	95,980	96,374	-8.1	-0.4	4.9	6.3	6.3	4,581	-5.2	70,218	-8.0	$46,841
Lafourche, LA	41,816	45,070	45,371	-7.2	-0.7	4.7	6.1	6.0	1,758	-8.6	25,894	-5.3	$47,055
Terrebonne, LA	46,432	50,910	51,003	-8.8	-0.2	5.0	6.5	6.5	2,823	-3.0	44,324	-9.5	$46,716
Houston-The Woodlands-Sugar Land, TX Metro Area	3,390,635	2,970,263	2,592,941	14.2	14.6	4.3	8.3	5.6	142,141	16.2	2,599,675	19.5	$60,616
Austin, TX	14,015	13,920	12,797	0.7	8.8	3.6	8.0	4.5	655	13.9	7,342	-22.2	$42,214
Brazoria, TX	175,989	155,227	133,540	13.4	16.2	4.5	8.5	5.7	5,667	17.6	90,444	28.7	$50,696
Chambers, TX	19,157	16,607	13,984	15.4	18.8	5.4	9.7	6.2	660	33.9	12,327	50.8	$66,468
Fort Bend, TX	382,102	298,162	235,000	28.2	26.9	4.0	7.6	5.2	13,459	45.9	169,355	47.4	$43,965
Galveston, TX	164,757	147,321	137,734	11.8	7.0	4.6	9.1	5.7	5,913	15.6	87,056	12.1	$39,672
Harris, TX	2,304,397	2,064,026	1,823,699	11.6	13.2	4.4	8.3	5.7	102,213	11.7	2,041,861	16.4	$64,017
Liberty, TX	32,303	30,614	31,272	5.5	-2.1	5.8	11.7	6.8	1,072	2.2	12,579	10.3	$41,196
Montgomery, TX	275,152	224,426	189,082	22.6	18.7	3.8	7.5	4.7	11,692	31.6	166,674	38.2	$55,314
Waller, TX	22,763	19,960	15,833	14.0	26.1	4.3	8.6	5.5	810	24.0	12,037	36.5	$43,067
Huntington-Ashland, WV-KY-OH Metro Area	148,050	162,020	170,592	-8.6	-5.0	5.7	9.2	5.6	7,012	-5.9	114,510	0.2	$40,071
Boyd, KY	18,099	20,421	22,989	-11.4	-11.2	5.9	10.2	5.9	1,242	-11.5	22,027	-9.1	$43,994
Carter, KY	9,894	11,925	13,629	-17.0	-12.5	9.2	14.1	8.3	406	0.0	4,892	-12.6	$26,079
Greenup, KY	13,459	15,351	17,203	-12.3	-10.8	6.6	11.5	6.4	456	-8.4	4,941	-0.1	$34,066
Lawrence, OH	23,690	27,703	28,685	-14.5	-3.4	5.6	10.3	6.2	806	-3.5	10,264	0.9	$30,790
Cabell, WV	41,287	43,292	44,041	-4.6	-1.7	4.7	7.2	4.5	2,397	-5.6	47,471	3.8	$39,740
Putnam, WV	26,118	26,390	26,468		-0.3	4.9	7.6	4.6	1,212	1.3	17,840	11.6	$46,465

Table C-4. Labor Force and Private Business Establishments and Employment—*Continued*

Metropolitan Statistical Area / Metropolitan Division / Component counties	Civilian Labor Force								Private nonfarm businesses				
	Total			Percent change		Unemployment rate			Establishments		Employment		Annual payroll per emplyee 2017 (dollars)
	2018	2010	2005	2010-2018	2005-2010	2018	2010	2005	2017	change 2010-2017	2017	Change 2010-2017	
Wayne, WV	15,503	16,938	17,577	-8.5	-3.6	6.0	8.5	5.2	493	-14.0	7,075	-6.8	$41,288
Huntsville, AL Metro Area	222,145	208,154	193,890	6.7	7.4	3.5	8.6	3.7	9,833	5.1	181,686	9.9	$51,455
Limestone, AL	42,393	38,321	35,123	10.6	9.1	3.5	9.6	4.4	1,379	9.3	17,747	28.1	$36,923
Madison, AL	179,752	169,833	158,767	5.8	7.0	3.5	8.3	3.6	8,454	4.5	163,939	8.2	$53,029
Idaho Falls, ID Metro Area	70,273	63,062	61,167	11.4	3.1	2.4	7.0	3.1	4,100	10.2	54,007	15.4	$43,428
Bonneville, ID	55,403	49,099	49,007	12.8	0.2	2.4	7.0	3.0	3,529	9.7	49,581	16.2	$44,359
Butte, ID	1,382	1,352	1,397	2.2	-3.2	3.2	7.2	4.3	58	-18.3	365	-50.5	$30,466
Jefferson, ID	13,488	12,611	10,763	7.0	17.2	2.3	7.1	3.3	513	18.5	4,061	19.7	$33,217
Indianapolis-Carmel-Anderson, IN Metro Area	1,061,803	950,600	941,192	11.7	1.0	3.2	9.6	5.0	47,389	6.1	911,388	17.3	$48,930
Boone, IN	35,904	29,394	27,178	22.1	8.2	2.7	7.6	4.1	1,525	14.1	24,773	46.8	$39,793
Brown, IN	7,659	7,566	8,002	1.2	-5.4	3.2	10.4	5.7	348	-4.1	2,402	9.3	$23,597
Hamilton, IN	181,103	144,861	130,720	25.0	10.8	2.7	6.7	3.5	9,057	22.5	145,220	45.8	$52,385
Hancock, IN	39,772	35,809	34,425	11.1	4.0	3.0	9.3	4.3	1,430	4.3	19,923	26.2	$44,575
Hendricks, IN	88,595	74,718	69,433	18.6	7.6	2.9	7.9	4.1	3,293	15.5	59,273	29.4	$39,557
Johnson, IN	82,164	71,598	70,047	14.8	2.2	2.9	8.8	4.4	3,168	7.9	49,398	32.2	$36,614
Madison, IN	59,431	59,406	63,209	0.0	-6.0	3.9	12.1	6.6	2,264	-3.3	35,756	4.8	$36,414
Marion, IN	490,706	452,835	459,492	8.4	-1.4	3.5	10.5	5.6	23,438	0.8	533,171	9.0	$52,602
Morgan, IN	36,392	35,025	37,206	3.9	-5.9	3.4	10.4	5.0	1,212	0.7	13,009	16.2	$35,848
Putnam, IN	16,882	16,674	17,804	1.2	-6.3	3.8	11.6	6.7	717	3.2	12,167	17.9	$33,241
Shelby, IN	23,195	22,714	23,676	2.1	-4.1	3.1	11.0	5.0	937	2.6	16,296	13.3	$41,969
Iowa City, IA Metro Area	97,309	91,674	86,066	6.1	6.5	2.0	4.3	3.2	3,984	6.4	70,971	10.4	$43,031
Johnson, IA	85,186	79,254	73,815	7.5	7.4	1.9	4.2	3.1	3,298	8.4	64,348	11.6	$43,872
Washington, IA	12,123	12,420	12,251	-2.4	1.4	2.3	5.1	3.7	686	-2.4	6,623	0.5	$34,855
Ithaca, NY Metro Area	50,112	54,767	54,600	-8.5	0.3	3.6	6.2	3.6	2,377	2.5	48,258	6.2	$39,906
Tompkins, NY	50,112	54,767	54,600	-8.5	0.3	3.6	6.2	3.6	2,377	2.5	48,258	6.2	$39,906
Jackson, MI Metro Area	74,281	74,673	78,307	-0.5	-4.6	3.9	12.2	6.8	2,901	-3.9	50,191	12.3	$48,039
Jackson, MI	74,281	74,673	78,307	-0.5	-4.6	3.9	12.2	6.8	2,901	-3.9	50,191	12.3	$48,039
Jackson, MS Metro Area	275,701	273,586	279,456	0.8	-2.1	4.2	9.0	6.0	13,518	0.0	224,030	9.5	$42,156
Copiah, MS	11,251	11,991	12,489	-6.2	-4.0	5.5	11.4	8.0	436	3.6	5,741	-2.0	$31,737
Hinds, MS	109,294	113,892	122,092	-4.0	-6.7	4.6	9.8	6.5	5,210	-9.7	98,943	4.0	$45,750
Holmes, MS	5,700	6,848	7,045	-16.8	-2.8	8.9	19.6	11.7	245	-6.1	2,122	3.9	$26,967
Madison, MS	53,303	48,712	44,044	9.4	10.6	3.7	7.4	5.1	3,126	10.8	51,993	22.2	$42,583
Rankin, MS	76,149	70,858	71,680	7.5	-1.1	3.4	6.9	4.5	3,686	7.7	55,248	11.3	$39,280
Simpson, MS	10,931	11,372	11,967	-3.9	-5.0	4.5	9.4	6.0	427	3.4	5,660	0.9	$27,039
Yazoo, MS	9,073	9,913	10,139	-8.5	-2.2	5.5	12.2	9.6	388	-4.7	4,323	13.1	$32,600
Jackson, TN Metro Area	85,541	87,585	80,963	-2.3	8.2	3.9	10.7	6.5	3,920	-1.2	70,348	7.7	$37,870
Chester, TN	8,422	8,363	7,533	0.7	11.0	3.8	10.0	6.0	242	0.0	3,083	9.8	$28,462
Crockett, TN	7,019	7,278	6,390	-3.6	13.9	3.9	11.6	7.8	224	0.4	2,003	1.5	$33,731
Gibson, TN	21,436	23,743	20,641	-9.7	15.0	4.5	12.0	8.5	928	-0.7	11,179	-3.9	$36,830
Madison, TN	48,664	48,201	46,399	1.0	3.9	3.8	10.0	5.6	2,526	-1.6	54,083	10.6	$38,775
Jacksonville, FL Metro Area	773,494	697,120	635,531	11.0	9.7	3.4	10.7	3.8	38,202	12.1	577,874	19.8	$46,031
Baker, FL	11,869	11,552	11,112	2.7	4.0	3.4	11.3	3.2	388	8.1	4,594	-12.7	$31,241
Clay, FL	106,276	95,867	86,643	10.9	10.6	3.3	9.9	3.4	3,891	10.6	43,306	19.1	$35,566
Duval, FL	487,844	454,798	421,549	7.3	7.9	3.6	11.4	4.0	25,750	8.7	450,794	17.8	$48,760
Nassau, FL	39,910	35,799	32,720	11.5	9.4	3.2	10.6	3.3	1,863	16.8	17,715	22.5	$35,774
St. Johns, FL	127,595	99,104	83,507	28.7	18.7	2.9	8.7	3.1	6,310	27.9	61,465	41.0	$37,455
Jacksonville, NC Metro Area	64,341	63,342	55,996	1.6	13.1	4.7	8.3	5.3	2,802	4.1	35,541	6.9	$28,624
Onslow, NC	64,341	63,342	55,996	1.6	13.1	4.7	8.3	5.3	2,802	4.1	35,541	6.9	$28,624
Janesville-Beloit, WI Metro Area	85,397	82,698	83,193	3.3	-0.6	3.2	11.3	5.8	3,374	2.5	59,475	16.2	$44,296
Rock, WI	85,397	82,698	83,193	3.3	-0.6	3.2	11.3	5.8	3,374	2.5	59,475	16.2	$44,296
Jefferson City, MO Metro Area	73,535	77,926	77,810	-5.6	0.1	2.7	7.4	4.4	3,549	-1.4	53,991	7.9	$39,444
Callaway, MO	21,087	22,377	22,596	-5.8		2.9	8.3	4.7	745	-2.1	11,725	4.7	$42,183
Cole, MO	38,229	40,685	40,148	-6.0	1.3	2.5	6.9	4.1	2,198	-1.7	35,600	6.9	$39,836
Moniteau, MO	7,223	7,397	7,564	-2.4	-2.2	3.0	8.4	5.1	330	-0.9	2,995	14.2	$31,358
Osage, MO	6,996	7,467	7,502	-6.3	-0.5	2.4	6.9	4.7	276	2.6	3,671	30.9	$33,488
Johnson City, TN Metro Area	90,926	94,817	94,637	-4.1	0.2	3.8	9.6	5.3	3,854	0.5	65,563	5.2	$38,013
Carter, TN	24,002	26,226	28,740	-8.5	-8.7	4.1	10.9	5.8	709	-3.0	9,143	1.2	$31,670
Unicoi, TN	7,065	7,919	8,144	-10.8	-2.8	4.9	11.9	6.2	242	-5.5	3,776	-7.0	$41,621
Washington, TN	59,859	60,672	57,753	-1.3	5.1	3.5	8.7	4.9	2,903	1.9	52,644	6.9	$38,855
Johnstown, PA Metro Area	58,344	66,751	67,122	-12.6	-0.6	5.2	9.4	6.1	3,154	-8.2	46,317	-8.4	$35,610
Cambria, PA	58,344	66,751	67,122	-12.6	-0.6	5.2	9.4	6.1	3,154	-8.2	46,317	-8.4	$35,610
Jonesboro, AR Metro Area	64,389	58,533	56,567	10.0	3.5	3.2	7.8	5.1	2,879	4.1	46,190	16.8	$37,698
Craighead, AR	54,120	47,796	45,084	13.2	6.0	3.1	7.4	4.8	2,528	5.2	42,356	17.6	$38,432
Poinsett, AR	10,269	10,737	11,483	-4.4	-6.5	3.8	9.3	6.6	351	-3.3	3,834	8.6	$29,592
Joplin, MO Metro Area	83,856	87,785	82,311	-4.5	6.7	2.8	8.6	4.9	4,007	-5.6	70,980	-2.9	$38,250
Jasper, MO	56,624	59,026	54,567	-4.1	8.2	2.7	8.5	4.8	2,795	-5.9	49,778	-8.6	$37,565
Newton, MO	27,232	28,759	27,744	-5.3	3.7	3.0	9.0	5.0	1,212	-4.9	21,202	13.6	$39,857
Kahului-Wailuku-Lahaina, HI Metro Area	86,137	78,966	74,992	9.1	5.3	2.4	8.5	2.7	4,705	8.6	64,947	13.2	$41,234
Maui, HI	86,137	78,966	74,992	9.1	5.3	2.4	8.5	2.7	4,705	8.6	64,947	13.2	$41,234
Kalamazoo-Portage, MI Metro Area	132,886	129,632	132,576	2.5	-2.2	3.4	10.0	5.2	5,641	0.2	109,826	6.9	$47,285
Kalamazoo, MI	132,886	129,632	132,576	2.5	-2.2	3.4	10.0	5.2	5,641	0.2	109,826	6.9	$47,285
Kankakee, IL Metro Area	55,920	57,060	52,672	-2.0	8.3	5.4	12.4	6.4	2,347	-0.4	36,747	4.3	$38,526
Kankakee, IL	55,920	57,060	52,672	-2.0	8.3	5.4	12.4	6.4	2,347	-0.4	36,747	4.3	$38,526

Table C-4. Labor Force and Private Business Establishments and Employment—*Continued*

	Civilian Labor Force								Private nonfarm businesses				
	Total			Percent change		Unemployment rate			Establishments		Employment		Annual payroll per emplyee 2017 (dollars)
Metropolitan Statistical Area Metropolitan Division Component counties	2018	2010	2005	2010-2018	2005-2010	2018	2010	2005	2017	change 2010-2017	2017	Change 2010-2017	
Kansas City, MO-KS Metro Area	1,134,500	1,082,274	1,013,562	4.8	6.8	3.4	8.7	5.6	52,650	6.2	954,263	12.1	$50,947
Johnson, KS	336,677	307,190	290,970	9.6	5.6	2.9	6.1	4.6	17,992	6.6	333,751	13.4	$54,384
Leavenworth, KS	36,546	34,342	33,105	6.4	3.7	3.6	7.6	6.1	1,263	6.5	14,737	10.7	$38,112
Linn, KS	4,448	4,534	4,897	-1.9	-7.4	5.9	11.2	7.2	199	11.2	1,268	10.1	$51,166
Miami, KS	17,469	17,111	16,335	2.1	4.8	3.6	7.6	5.1	733	2.1	6,751	3.4	$37,191
Wyandotte, KS	77,858	74,994	73,559	3.8	2.0	4.8	10.1	8.7	3,038	1.4	70,217	10.9	$47,667
Bates, MO	7,960	8,397	7,936	-5.2	5.8	3.8	11.0	6.4	351	0.0	2,891	2.0	$29,783
Caldwell, MO	4,404	4,560	4,406	-3.4	3.5	3.1	9.6	6.0	158	-4.2	1,364	73.5	$30,624
Cass, MO	54,386	53,355	48,720	1.9	9.5	3.1	9.6	5.1	1,983	6.8	21,781	22.4	$32,373
Clay, MO	134,903	125,001	111,211	7.9	12.4	2.9	8.4	4.6	5,142	8.2	104,822	26.8	$52,539
Clinton, MO	10,852	11,071	10,328	-2.0	7.2	3.2	9.7	5.4	368	-3.4	2,788	-9.7	$33,081
Jackson, MO	363,146	361,018	336,286	0.6	7.4	3.7	10.7	6.4	17,970	7.0	342,869	8.0	$51,568
Lafayette, MO	16,991	17,549	16,710	-3.2	5.0	3.2	9.8	5.5	706	-3.3	6,601	5.5	$31,260
Platte, MO	57,812	51,580	47,312	12.1	9.0	2.6	7.7	4.5	2,393	9.2	41,492	6.7	$43,823
Ray, MO	11,048	11,572	11,787	-4.5	-1.8	3.6	10.3	5.4	354	-8.5	2,931	0.6	$35,251
Kennewick-Richland, WA Metro Area	140,580	132,507	114,306	6.1	15.9	5.5	8.1	6.4	6,120	16.5	87,957	17.5	$49,729
Benton, WA	99,084	94,253	85,027	5.1	10.9	5.2	7.9	6.0	4,530	16.0	67,136	15.2	$51,874
Franklin, WA	41,496	38,254	29,279	8.5	30.7	6.1	8.8	7.4	1,590	18.2	20,821	25.5	$42,812
Killeen-Temple, TX Metro Area	175,915	166,193	149,377	5.8	11.3	4.1	7.6	5.2	6,325	6.9	106,123	12.0	$39,085
Bell, TX	142,270	131,835	114,094	7.9	15.5	4.1	7.7	5.0	5,186	8.7	92,327	13.6	$40,410
Coryell, TX	24,402	25,338	25,361	-3.7	-0.1	4.1	7.5	6.2	734	-2.8	9,653	-2.9	$29,456
Lampasas, TX	9,243	9,020	9,922	2.5	-9.1	3.7	7.1	4.3	405	3.8	4,143	16.8	$31,990
Kingsport-Bristol, TN-VA Metro Area	137,055	144,661	140,267	-5.3	3.1	3.7	9.1	5.3	5,984	-1.8	104,278	1.4	$43,064
Hawkins, TN	23,706	25,559	25,347	-7.2	0.8	4.0	10.9	6.2	615	0.0	10,639	23.8	$37,690
Sullivan, TN	70,100	73,637	71,480	-4.8	3.0	3.7	9.0	5.2	3,362	0.1	63,464	0.2	$47,439
Scott, VA	9,250	10,072	9,769	-8.2	3.1	3.2	8.5	5.3	271	-9.4	3,539	4.1	$30,689
Washington, VA	26,683	27,416	25,934	-2.7	5.7	3.4	7.9	4.5	1,149	-4.5	17,627	4.3	$37,664
Bristol City, VA	7,316	7,977	7,737	-8.3	3.1	3.7	8.8	5.5	587	-4.6	9,009	-15.6	$34,017
Kingston, NY Metro Area	88,712	93,606	91,816	-5.2	1.9	3.9	7.8	4.3	4,850	3.0	46,244	2.6	$36,458
Ulster, NY	88,712	93,606	91,816	-5.2	1.9	3.9	7.8	4.3	4,850	3.0	46,244	2.6	$36,458
Knoxville, TN Metro Area	412,677	405,106	387,978	1.9	4.4	3.3	8.4	4.7	18,127	3.3	334,884	10.0	$44,566
Anderson, TN	34,283	34,926	34,488	-1.8	1.3	3.8	9.3	5.1	1,575	-2.4	40,706	-2.2	$60,360
Blount, TN	62,275	61,408	59,009	1.4	4.1	3.2	9.1	4.7	2,357	3.6	42,917	12.9	$45,817
Campbell, TN	14,752	16,131	16,672	-8.5	-3.2	4.8	12.5	6.0	593	3.1	7,117	3.5	$31,599
Knox, TN	240,034	229,800	213,735	4.5	7.5	2.9	7.4	4.2	11,562	4.2	219,315	12.8	$42,843
Loudon, TN	22,857	22,352	21,651	2.3	3.2	3.4	9.3	4.7	949	7.8	13,186	11.9	$38,875
Morgan, TN	7,860	8,403	8,118	-6.5	3.5	4.5	11.4	7.5	159	-5.9	1,375	-14.0	$33,046
Roane, TN	23,153	24,323	25,587	-4.8	-4.9	4.1	9.2	5.8	733	-1.6	8,508	-0.1	$31,209
Union, TN	7,463	7,763	8,718	-3.9	-11.0	4.1	10.8	5.6	199	-2.0	1,760	3.8	$32,033
Kokomo, IN Metro Area	37,645	35,806	39,174	5.1	-8.6	4.1	12.6	6.6	1,780	-1.8	31,996	12.6	$42,988
Howard, IN	37,645	35,806	39,174	5.1	-8.6	4.1	12.6	6.6	1,780	-1.8	31,996	12.6	$42,988
La Crosse-Onalaska, WI-MN Metro Area	77,721	76,423	72,515	1.7	5.4	2.7	6.8	4.1	3,493	3.4	68,320	11.8	$41,541
Houston, MN	10,460	10,830	11,082	-3.4	-2.3	2.9	7.7	4.5	417	-7.5	4,509	12.0	$30,560
La Crosse, WI	67,261	65,593	61,433	2.5	6.8	2.6	6.6	4.0	3,076	5.1	63,811	11.8	$42,317
Lafayette, LA Metro Area	212,523	221,628	208,275	-4.1	6.4	4.9	7.0	5.7	13,222	4.3	180,677	1.2	$43,064
Acadia, LA	23,952	26,130	25,409	-8.3	2.8	5.4	7.3	6.1	1,122	1.2	12,554	-1.2	$31,730
Iberia, LA	28,639	32,240	32,671	-11.2	-1.3	5.8	8.6	6.7	1,602	-7.7	22,619	-20.7	$45,403
Lafayette, LA	113,337	113,571	104,121	-0.2	9.1	4.5	6.2	5.2	8,567	8.2	124,773	7.2	$44,733
St. Martin, LA	22,399	24,050	22,687	-6.9	6.0	5.2	8.0	6.0	931	5.3	11,219	2.3	$38,227
Vermilion, LA	24,196	25,637	23,387	-5.6	9.6	5.3	7.3	6.0	1,000	-2.3	9,512	-5.4	$36,264
Lafayette-West Lafayette, IN Metro Area	116,750	105,647	99,273	10.5	6.4	3.2	9.0	4.9	4,347	6.6	77,501	18.2	$42,093
Benton, IN	4,574	4,662	4,599	-1.9	1.4	3.2	9.2	5.3	173	-15.6	1,324	-14.2	$35,776
Carroll, IN	10,264	10,254	10,515	0.1	-2.5	3.3	9.9	5.2	396	-0.5	4,628	9.2	$36,820
Tippecanoe, IN	97,693	86,530	79,380	12.9	9.0	3.2	8.9	4.9	3,652	9.0	70,036	19.5	$42,664
Warren, IN	4,219	4,201	4,779	0.4	-12.1	3.2	10.5	4.5	126	2.4	1,513	29.2	$37,332
Lake Charles, LA Metro Area	113,935	91,195	95,465	24.9	-4.5	3.8	8.0	7.4	4,813	9.7	79,000	15.1	$45,458
Calcasieu, LA	109,878	87,896	91,004	25.0	-3.4	3.8	8.0	7.5	4,675	10.3	77,537	15.6	$44,610
Cameron, LA	4,057	3,299	4,461	23.0	-26.0	3.5	6.3	5.8	138	-7.4	1,463	-7.2	$90,436
Lake Havasu City-Kingman, AZ Metro Area	85,442	82,726	89,079	3.3	-7.1	5.8	13.0	4.3	3,784	1.9	41,986	5.7	$34,802
Mohave, AZ	85,442	82,726	89,079	3.3	-7.1	5.8	13.0	4.3	3,784	1.9	41,986	5.7	$34,802
Lakeland-Winter Haven, FL Metro Area	298,759	278,479	258,158	7.3	7.9	4.1	12.1	4.1	11,676	6.7	182,922	14.9	$40,257
Polk, FL	298,759	278,479	258,158	7.3	7.9	4.1	12.1	4.1	11,676	6.7	182,922	14.9	$40,257
Lancaster, PA Metro Area	281,433	268,014	267,575	5.0	0.2	3.4	7.5	3.7	13,060	8.4	235,331	13.5	$43,029
Lancaster, PA	281,433	268,014	267,575	5.0	0.2	3.4	7.5	3.7	13,060	8.4	235,331	13.5	$43,029
Lansing-East Lansing, MI Metro Area	281,658	279,966	284,824	0.6	-1.7	3.6	10.2	6.3	10,735	-0.1	183,895	12.3	$44,215
Clinton, MI	41,047	39,637	37,266	3.6	6.4	3.2	8.4	5.4	1,321	6.1	16,459	9.8	$38,934
Eaton, MI	56,986	57,180	58,653	-0.3	-2.5	3.5	9.6	5.5	2,130	3.3	41,483	10.7	$44,816
Ingham, MI	150,474	148,442	152,166	1.4	-2.4	3.6	10.3	6.4	6,143	-1.7	112,886	14.1	$45,716
Shiawassee, MI	33,151	34,707	36,739	-4.5	-5.5	4.3	12.9	8.0	1,141	-4.2	13,067	5.6	$35,990
Laredo, TX Metro Area	116,573	105,016	85,624	11.0	22.6	3.8	8.2	6.0	5,434	15.4	78,875	24.2	$29,149
Webb, TX	116,573	105,016	85,624	11.0	22.6	3.8	8.2	6.0	5,434	15.4	78,875	24.2	$29,149
Las Cruces, NM Metro Area	96,769	93,597	85,089	3.4	10.0	5.7	7.8	5.6	3,716	2.9	52,980	5.7	$32,606
Dona Ana, NM	96,769	93,597	85,089	3.4	10.0	5.7	7.8	5.6	3,716	2.9	52,980	5.7	$32,606
Las Vegas-Henderson-Paradise, NV Metro Area	1,098,114	984,004	869,251	11.6	13.2	4.8	13.8	4.1	45,830	15.7	857,591	17.2	$41,766
Clark, NV	1,098,114	984,004	869,251	11.6	13.2	4.8	13.8	4.1	45,830	15.7	857,591	17.2	$41,766

Table C-4. Labor Force and Private Business Establishments and Employment—*Continued*

Metropolitan Statistical Area Metropolitan Division Component counties	Civilian Labor Force								Private nonfarm businesses				
	Total			Percent change		Unemployment rate			Establishments		Employment		Annual payroll per employee 2017 (dollars)
	2018	2010	2005	2010-2018	2005-2010	2018	2010	2005	2017	change 2010-2017	2017	Change 2010-2017	
Lawrence, KS Metro Area	65,199	64,379	63,186	1.3	1.9	3.1	5.9	4.0	2,727	3.8	40,467	8.2	$31,222
Douglas, KS	65,199	64,379	63,186	1.3	1.9	3.1	5.9	4.0	2,727	3.8	40,467	8.2	$31,222
Lawton, OK Metro Area	51,314	54,506	48,573	-5.9	12.2	3.9	5.8	4.5	2,224	-3.3	32,718	-3.8	$36,059
Comanche, OK	48,566	51,497	45,272	-5.7	13.8	3.9	5.8	4.5	2,149	-3.2	31,539	-3.6	$36,144
Cotton, OK	2,748	3,009	3,301	-8.7	-8.8	3.1	6.7	3.7	75	-7.4	1,179	-10.7	$33,791
Lebanon, PA Metro Area	71,222	70,062	70,117	1.7	-0.1	3.8	7.5	3.6	2,696	2.1	46,303	6.6	$38,740
Lebanon, PA	71,222	70,062	70,117	1.7	-0.1	3.8	7.5	3.6	2,696	2.1	46,303	6.6	$38,740
Lewiston, ID-WA Metro Area	31,206	30,421	29,869	2.6	1.8	3.3	7.6	5.0	1,581	0.4	22,882	9.5	$39,203
Nez Perce, ID	21,053	20,088	19,352	4.8	3.8	2.8	6.7	4.4	1,132	-0.9	18,048	10.2	$39,493
Asotin, WA	10,153	10,333	10,517	-1.7	-1.7	4.4	9.4	6.3	449	3.9	4,834	6.8	$38,117
Lewiston-Auburn, ME Metro Area	55,449	55,909	57,033	-0.8	-2.0	3.3	8.6	4.9	2,788	0.8	45,507	3.9	$41,647
Androscoggin, ME	55,449	55,909	57,033	-0.8	-2.0	3.3	8.6	4.9	2,788	0.8	45,507	3.9	$41,647
Lexington-Fayette, KY Metro Area	271,580	255,705	229,055	6.2	11.6	3.4	7.9	4.6	12,488	5.7	228,183	14.1	$44,062
Bourbon, KY	9,704	10,064	9,810	-3.6	2.6	4.0	9.1	5.4	387	-0.8	5,403	-10.1	$39,789
Clark, KY	17,202	17,775	17,061	-3.2	4.2	4.1	10.8	5.5	749	-1.7	13,920	30.4	$37,593
Fayette, KY	174,849	163,286	146,365	7.1	11.6	3.3	7.4	4.5	8,730	5.9	161,160	12.5	$44,448
Jessamine, KY	26,425	24,710	21,888	6.9	12.9	3.6	8.5	4.7	1,134	10.0	16,487	18.4	$35,861
Scott, KY	28,607	25,429	20,631	12.5	23.3	3.3	8.7	4.9	930	10.6	23,472	23.2	$52,137
Woodford, KY	14,793	14,441	13,300	2.4	8.6	3.1	7.3	4.2	558	3.7	7,741	11.2	$43,624
Lima, OH Metro Area	47,855	52,009	52,706	-8.0	-1.3	4.5	10.7	6.2	2,383	-6.5	46,478	-0.1	$40,612
Allen, OH	47,855	52,009	52,706	-8.0	-1.3	4.5	10.7	6.2	2,383	-6.5	46,478	-0.1	$40,612
Lincoln, NE Metro Area	182,114	171,332	165,264	6.3	3.7	2.5	4.2	3.5	9,041	10.0	144,760	11.1	$42,055
Lancaster, NE	173,384	162,567	156,012	6.7	4.2	2.5	4.2	3.5	8,568	10.1	139,012	11.0	$42,426
Seward, NE	8,730	8,765	9,252	-0.4	-5.3	2.6	4.0	3.2	473	7.0	5,748	13.4	$33,078
Little Rock-North Little Rock-Conway, AR Metro Area	354,824	347,828	334,366	2.0	4.0	3.4	7.2	4.7	18,201	3.4	283,598	2.8	$44,410
Faulkner, AR	61,476	58,711	52,018	4.7	12.9	3.3	7.2	4.4	2,577	10.7	35,684	4.8	$38,865
Grant, AR	8,321	8,567	8,663	-2.9	-1.1	3.1	7.1	4.9	268	0.8	3,227	7.9	$33,333
Lonoke, AR	33,853	33,287	30,788	1.7	8.1	3.2	6.8	4.5	1,048	4.7	11,623	10.1	$33,292
Perry, AR	4,248	4,560	4,966	-6.8	-8.2	4.2	8.9	5.1	96	-15.0	734	-21.3	$29,896
Pulaski, AR	189,210	189,321	190,594	-0.1	-0.7	3.5	7.3	4.8	12,245	1.0	211,086	1.0	$47,420
Saline, AR	57,716	53,382	47,337	8.1	12.8	3.1	6.7	4.3	1,967	11.2	21,244	16.5	$32,091
Logan, UT-ID Metro Area	70,182	63,444	63,440	10.6	0.0	2.6	6.0	3.2	3,755	12.0	44,906	15.0	$35,130
Franklin, ID	6,920	6,195	6,218	11.7	-0.4	2.1	5.3	3.2	306	4.8	2,387	23.6	$30,526
Cache, UT	63,262	57,249	57,222	10.5	0.0	2.7	6.1	3.2	3,449	12.7	42,519	14.5	$35,389
Longview, TX Metro Area	127,980	133,429	133,117	-4.1	0.2	4.2	8.4	5.1	6,647	0.8	96,956	0.1	$41,741
Gregg, TX	57,815	60,363	60,526	-4.2	-0.3	4.1	7.9	4.9	4,054	1.1	63,827	0.8	$41,997
Harrison, TX	30,028	30,822	31,118	-2.6		4.4	9.4	5.6	1,281	-1.6	18,902	0.8	$40,979
Rusk, TX	22,296	23,961	22,712	-6.9	5.5	4.1	7.8	5.2	799	-1.5	9,603	-9.2	$44,442
Upshur, TX	17,841	18,283	18,761	-2.4	-2.5	4.2	8.8	5.0	513	9.1	4,624	9.7	$35,709
Longview, WA Metro Area	45,923	46,432	42,978	-1.1	8.0	5.9	12.9	7.6	2,211	0.2	32,299	11.0	$46,194
Cowlitz, WA	45,923	46,432	42,978	-1.1	8.0	5.9	12.9	7.6	2,211	0.2	32,299	11.0	$46,194
Los Angeles-Long Beach-Anaheim, CA Metro Area	6,761,767	6,454,562	6,367,520	4.8	1.4	4.2	11.8	5.0	372,217	12.5	5,324,257	9.7	$58,676
Anaheim-Santa Ana-Irvine, CA Div	1,625,426	1,537,187	1,585,916	5.7	-3.1	2.9	9.7	3.7	96,901	12.0	1,503,084	18.1	$58,431
Orange, CA	1,625,426	1,537,187	1,585,916	5.7	-3.1	2.9	9.7	3.7	96,901	12.0	1,503,084	18.1	$58,431
Los Angeles-Long Beach-Glendale, CA Div	5,136,341	4,917,375	4,781,604	4.5	2.8	4.7	12.5	5.4	275,316	12.6	3,821,173	6.7	$58,773
Los Angeles, CA	5,136,341	4,917,375	4,781,604	4.5	2.8	4.7	12.5	5.4	275,316	12.6	3,821,173	6.7	$58,773
Louisville/Jefferson County, KY-IN Metro Area	656,303	611,633	574,472	7.3	6.5	3.9	9.8	5.7	29,104	2.1	577,816	15.7	$46,868
Clark, IN	61,620	55,317	53,370	11.4	3.6	3.4	9.5	5.2	2,495	4.3	50,581	24.2	$38,010
Floyd, IN	41,401	37,858	37,486	9.4	1.0	3.3	8.9	5.2	1,873	6.8	27,360	6.3	$39,851
Harrison, IN	20,172	18,989	19,628	6.2	-3.3	3.5	9.9	6.3	694	3.6	9,089	-0.1	$33,592
Washington, IN	13,767	13,806	14,013	-0.3	-1.5	3.5	12.2	6.2	460	0.9	4,754	9.4	$31,920
Bullitt, KY	42,322	38,803	35,870	9.1	8.2	4.1	10.6	5.7	1,157	8.6	20,967	50.3	$34,971
Henry, KY	8,183	7,834	7,904	4.5	-0.9	3.9	9.9	5.7	208	-4.6	1,904	3.3	$32,597
Jefferson, KY	400,587	378,722	351,726	5.8	7.7	4.1	10.0	5.9	19,796	0.9	430,488	13.0	$50,292
Oldham, KY	33,270	29,248	26,226	13.8	11.5	3.3	7.5	4.8	1,210	-1.7	12,968	26.4	$40,479
Shelby, KY	24,920	21,851	20,059	14.0	8.9	3.5	8.9	5.2	992	10.8	18,496	63.2	$32,964
Spencer, KY	10,061	9,205	8,190	9.3	12.4	3.6	9.9	5.3	219	4.8	1,209	9.5	$25,585
Lubbock, TX Metro Area	162,563	149,359	143,067	8.8	4.4	3.1	6.3	4.1	7,381	4.6	115,372	10.0	$36,540
Crosby, TX	2,566	2,951	2,923	-13.0	1.0	4.5	8.0	5.4	95	-11.2	580	-30.0	$39,062
Lubbock, TX	157,225	143,339	137,313	9.7	4.4	3.1	6.3	4.1	7,202	5.1	114,071	10.4	$36,502
Lynn, TX	2,772	3,069	2,831	-9.7	8.4	3.2	6.6	5.8	84	-10.6	721	4.5	$40,538
Lynchburg, VA Metro Area	122,127	126,345	116,542	-3.3	8.4	3.5	7.8	4.1	5,998	5.3	99,184	9.9	$39,729
Amherst, VA	14,984	16,352	15,320	-8.4	6.7	3.3	8.1	4.1	574	-4.5	6,617	-1.2	$35,140
Appomattox, VA	7,083	7,343	6,824	-3.5	7.6	3.6	8.6	4.7	301	1.3	2,447	1.6	$25,927
Bedford, VA	38,097	39,053	36,472	-2.4	7.1	3.1	7.0	3.5	1,715	19.4	15,567	22.7	$38,263
Campbell, VA	26,036	27,756	26,677	-6.2	4.0	3.3	7.7	4.0	1,160	1.0	16,637	23.0	$45,607
Lynchburg City, VA	35,927	35,841	31,249	0.2	14.7	4.0	8.5	4.6	2,248	1.4	57,916	5.4	$39,542
Macon-Bibb County, GA Metro Area	104,769	105,508	110,115	-0.7	-4.2	4.3	11.3	5.6	5,168	-2.2	84,303	5.1	$40,476
Bibb, GA	69,212	70,225	72,845	-1.4	-3.6	4.5	11.6	5.8	4,149	-3.0	73,734	4.5	$41,065
Crawford, GA	5,703	5,769	6,269	-1.1	-8.0	4.2	11.4	5.9	105	7.1	507	-1.9	$32,980
Jones, GA	13,886	13,698	13,664	1.4	0.2	3.7	9.7	4.9	328	-3.0	2,614	5.0	$33,298
Monroe, GA	13,043	12,551	12,689	3.9	-1.1	3.7	10.2	5.1	514	3.6	5,902	-0.9	$37,564
Twiggs, GA	2,925	3,265	4,648	-10.4	-29.8	5.9	15.5	6.9	72	-6.5	1,546	118.7	$38,086

Table C-4. Labor Force and Private Business Establishments and Employment—*Continued*

Metropolitan Statistical Area Metropolitan Division Component counties	Civilian Labor Force								Private nonfarm businesses				
	Total			Percent change		Unemployment rate			Establishments		Employment		Annual payroll per emplyee 2017 (dollars)
	2018	2010	2005	2010-2018	2005-2010	2018	2010	2005	2017	change 2010-2017	2017	Change 2010-2017	
Madera, CA Metro Area	61,528	61,607	61,881	-0.1	-0.4	7.0	16.6	7.9	1,961	2.7	26,755	9.2	$42,960
Madera, CA	61,528	61,607	61,881	-0.1	-0.4	7.0	16.6	7.9	1,961	2.7	26,755	9.2	$42,960
Madison, WI Metro Area	387,610	360,360	351,442	7.6	2.5	2.3	6.4	3.4	17,324	7.8	333,811	17.7	$52,084
Columbia, WI	31,806	32,090	31,579	-0.9	1.6	2.7	8.5	4.4	1,439	3.2	20,900	10.0	$38,087
Dane, WI	320,589	293,224	285,593	9.3	2.7	2.2	5.9	3.1	14,313	8.6	289,898	18.8	$53,960
Green, WI	21,282	21,274	20,008	0.0	6.3	2.6	8.0	4.4	1,000	5.9	13,653	16.4	$41,734
Iowa, WI	13,933	13,772	14,262	1.2	-3.4	2.6	8.2	4.2	572	3.4	9,360	7.2	$40,342
Manchester-Nashua, NH Metro Area	236,915	226,152	226,188	4.8	0.0	2.6	6.2	3.6	11,013	1.7	186,614	5.2	$55,963
Hillsborough, NH	236,915	226,152	226,188	4.8	0.0	2.6	6.2	3.6	11,013	1.7	186,614	5.2	$55,963
Manhattan, KS Metro Area	59,199	61,340	55,950	-3.5	9.6	3.2	5.9	4.2	2,781	2.7	38,483	4.8	$32,781
Geary, KS	11,492	13,359	11,144	-14.0	19.9	4.8	9.2	5.9	557	-6.4	7,928	0.1	$31,303
Pottawatomie, KS	12,278	11,890	10,813	3.3	10.0	2.8	5.2	4.1	618	8.2	9,473	27.0	$39,184
Riley, KS	35,429	36,091	33,993	-1.8	6.2	2.9	5.0	3.7	1,606	4.1	21,082	-1.3	$30,460
Mankato, MN Metro Area	61,033	57,896	54,322	5.4	6.6	2.4	6.3	3.3	2,679	5.2	50,288	11.0	$38,244
Blue Earth, MN	40,277	38,114	35,479	5.7	7.4	2.5	6.4	3.3	1,992	4.7	37,124	9.1	$36,800
Nicollet, MN	20,756	19,782	18,843	4.9	5.0	2.2	6.1	3.2	687	6.7	13,164	16.8	$42,317
Mansfield, OH Metro Area	52,743	59,079	62,761	-10.7	-5.9	4.9	12.1	6.7	2,662	-2.7	41,099	-3.4	$34,991
Richland, OH	52,743	59,079	62,761	-10.7	-5.9	4.9	12.1	6.7	2,662	-2.7	41,099	-3.4	$34,991
McAllen-Edinburg-Mission, TX Metro Area	348,672	318,302	260,575	9.5	22.2	6.6	11.8	7.9	12,117	9.7	198,978	19.1	$27,948
Hidalgo, TX	348,672	318,302	260,575	9.5	22.2	6.6	11.8	7.9	12,117	9.7	198,978	19.1	$27,948
Medford, OR Metro Area	104,763	100,968	98,727	3.8	2.3	4.8	12.5	6.2	6,368	10.1	75,967	18.8	$40,309
Jackson, OR	104,763	100,968	98,727	3.8	2.3	4.8	12.5	6.2	6,368	10.1	75,967	18.8	$40,309
Memphis, TN-MS-AR Metro Area	631,817	632,306	597,083	-0.1	5.9	4.1	9.7	6.1	25,596	-0.6	539,734	6.0	$48,017
Crittenden, AR	21,467	22,819	22,513	-5.9	1.4	4.3	10.5	6.5	840	-3.7	13,288	-0.1	$33,202
De Soto, MS	89,980	79,619	71,502	13.0	11.4	3.8	7.5	4.1	2,910	15.4	53,045	30.3	$33,268
Marshall, MS	14,591	15,497	15,345	-5.8	1.0	5.0	12.1	8.5	431	0.9	6,573	5.8	$35,633
Tate, MS	12,259	12,631	11,896	-2.9	6.2	4.9	10.8	6.5	385	2.7	3,890	0.2	$30,374
Tunica, MS	4,477	5,027	4,505	-10.9	11.6	5.3	13.7	10.2	196	-10.1	6,927	-38.7	$31,554
Fayette, TN	18,769	18,830	15,955	-0.3	18.0	3.7	9.9	6.8	597	8.5	6,897	13.2	$42,072
Shelby, TN	442,379	448,829	428,931	-1.4	4.6	4.2	9.8	6.2	19,541	-2.5	440,133	4.9	$51,199
Tipton, TN	27,895	29,054	26,436	-4.0	9.9	4.2	11.3	6.4	696	-7.2	8,981	9.7	$35,048
Merced, CA Metro Area	115,408	113,579	98,738	1.6	15.0	8.3	18.0	10.0	3,110	7.8	45,686	17.6	$37,452
Merced, CA	115,408	113,579	98,738	1.6	15.0	8.3	18.0	10.0	3,110	7.8	45,686	17.6	$37,452
Miami-Fort Lauderdale-Pompano Beach, FL Metro Area	3,150,518	2,807,697	2,710,277	12.2	3.6	3.6	10.8	3.6	194,524	14.0	2,214,596	21.6	$48,091
Fort Lauderdale-Pompano Beach-Sunrise, FL Div.	1,036,212	936,563	957,619	10.6	-2.2	3.4	10.2	3.7	61,032	9.9	705,667	18.9	$47,519
Broward, FL	1,036,212	936,563	957,619	10.6	-2.2	3.4	10.2	3.7	61,032	9.9	705,667	18.9	$47,519
Miami-Miami Beach-Kendall, FL Div	1,383,302	1,225,397	1,147,797	12.9	6.8	3.9	11.1	3.2	84,803	15.5	982,248	22.5	$48,427
Miami-Dade, FL	1,383,302	1,225,397	1,147,797	12.9	6.8	3.9	11.1	3.2	84,803	15.5	982,248	22.5	$48,427
West Palm Beach-Boca Raton-Boynton Beach, FL Div	731,004	645,737	604,861	13.2	6.8	3.6	11.0	4.3	48,689	16.7	526,681	23.8	$48,231
Palm Beach, FL	731,004	645,737	604,861	13.2	6.8	3.6	11.0	4.3	48,689	16.7	526,681	23.8	$48,231
Michigan City-La Porte, IN Metro Area	48,027	51,336	53,070	-6.4	-3.3	4.4	12.0	6.1	2,314	-6.6	35,742	5.0	$38,742
La Porte, IN	48,027	51,336	53,070	-6.4	-3.3	4.4	12.0	6.1	2,314	-6.6	35,742	5.0	$38,742
Midland, MI Metro Area	40,611	41,219	41,907	-1.5	-1.6	4.0	9.8	5.9	1,965	7.7	36,436	8.0	$67,240
Midland, MI	40,611	41,219	41,907	-1.5	-1.6	4.0	9.8	5.9	1,965	7.7	36,436	8.0	$67,240
Midland, TX Metro Area	105,084	73,527	68,430	42.9	7.4	2.1	5.9	3.7	5,452	16.9	87,328	44.2	$67,960
Martin, TX	2,807	2,196	2,113	27.8	3.9	2.4	6.0	4.4	112	19.1	1,239	55.7	$54,370
Midland, TX	102,277	71,331	66,317	43.4	7.6	2.1	5.9	3.7	5,340	16.9	86,089	44.0	$68,156
Milwaukee-Waukesha, WI Metro Area	824,848	817,477	782,820	0.9	4.4	3.2	8.9	5.0	38,690	0.7	783,764	6.3	$52,206
Milwaukee, WI	472,701	476,449	451,298	-0.8	5.6	3.6	10.0	5.7	19,960	-0.3	452,210	1.8	$52,501
Ozaukee, WI	49,109	47,415	47,669	3.6	-0.5	2.5	7.1	3.7	2,820	2.7	40,528	17.0	$45,528
Washington, WI	77,606	75,604	71,985	2.6	5.0	2.5	8.1	4.2	3,259	3.7	51,260	13.0	$43,784
Waukesha, WI	225,432	218,009	211,868	3.4	2.9	2.7	7.3	3.8	12,651	1.0	239,766	12.5	$54,579
Minneapolis-St. Paul-Bloomington, MN Metro Area..	1,992,807	1,862,262	1,836,545	7.0	1.4	2.7	7.3	3.8	97,123	6.5	1,804,390	13.8	$57,198
Anoka, MN	196,586	187,355	189,702	4.9	-1.2	2.8	8.0	3.9	7,881	7.8	118,530	15.2	$46,618
Carver, MN	57,859	51,621	48,068	12.1	7.4	2.5	6.7	3.4	2,550	9.3	38,499	15.6	$52,778
Chisago, MN	29,662	29,314	27,047	1.2	8.4	3.4	8.9	4.8	1,276	2.7	13,765	6.5	$45,940
Dakota, MN	239,835	227,259	227,941	5.5	-0.3	2.5	7.0	3.6	10,707	8.3	183,119	14.1	$50,591
Hennepin, MN	703,310	650,891	652,568	8.1	-0.3	2.5	7.0	3.7	40,869	4.9	900,580	14.5	$64,051
Isanti, MN	21,134	20,561	21,044	2.8	-2.3	3.7	9.6	4.8	862	11.9	9,437	14.6	$38,608
Le Sueur, MN	15,962	15,715	14,186	1.6	10.8	4.1	8.9	5.4	717	3.8	7,862	29.0	$44,303
Mille Lacs, MN	12,788	13,152	11,974	-2.8	9.8	4.8	11.1	6.7	710	8.9	8,605	11.9	$32,997
Ramsey, MN	288,814	270,063	271,356	6.9	-0.5	2.7	7.5	3.9	13,579	2.7	298,031	4.8	$57,559
Scott, MN	82,820	74,150	69,821	11.7	6.2	2.5	6.9	3.5	3,398	10.5	48,790	29.8	$47,501
Sherburne, MN	51,700	48,989	46,529	5.5	5.3	3.2	8.4	4.3	2,106	11.0	22,422	15.9	$44,364
Washington, MN	141,974	132,046	125,591	7.5	5.1	2.5	6.7	3.5	5,946	11.9	79,574	21.1	$44,090
Wright, MN	74,674	70,095	62,757	6.5	11.7	3.0	8.0	4.3	3,391	13.2	37,596	21.4	$42,886
Pierce, WI	25,310	23,984	23,337	5.5	2.8	3.2	7.0	4.1	810	3.8	6,919	16.8	$34,025
St. Croix, WI	50,379	47,067	44,624	7.0	5.5	3.0	7.6	4.6	2,321	12.2	30,661	26.1	$40,795
Missoula, MT Metro Area	63,069	58,536	57,899	7.7	1.1	3.3	7.3	3.9	4,458	6.9	50,107	8.4	$37,140
Missoula, MT	63,069	58,536	57,899	7.7	1.1	3.3	7.3	3.9	4,458	6.9	50,107	8.4	$37,140
Mobile, AL Metro Area	194,073	200,115	187,271	-3.0	6.9	4.7	11.4	5.0	9,021	-0.3	156,341	2.8	$45,322
Mobile, AL	187,406	192,730	180,384	-2.8	6.8	4.7	11.3	5.0	8,813	-0.1	151,127	1.8	$44,265

Table C-4. Labor Force and Private Business Establishments and Employment—*Continued*

Metropolitan Statistical Area Metropolitan Division Component counties	Civilian Labor Force								Private nonfarm businesses				
	Total			Percent change		Unemployment rate			Establishments		Employment		Annual payroll per emplyee 2017 (dollars)
	2018	2010	2005	2010-2018	2005-2010	2018	2010	2005	2017	change 2010-2017	2017	Change 2010-2017	
Washington, AL	6,667	7,385	6,887	-9.7	7.2	5.8	14.2	6.2	208	-7.6	5,214	47.5	$75,984
Modesto, CA Metro Area	243,538	243,274	226,627	0.1	7.3	6.4	16.9	8.4	9,096	8.7	142,929	17.5	$45,604
Stanislaus, CA	243,538	243,274	226,627	0.1	7.3	6.4	16.9	8.4	9,096	8.7	142,929	17.5	$45,604
Monroe, LA Metro Area	89,710	91,500	94,603	-2.0	-3.3	5.6	9.4	6.5	5,067	0.6	72,184	2.1	$37,599
Morehouse, LA	10,193	11,097	11,717	-8.1	-5.3	8.2	15.4	9.2	458	-7.8	5,597	7.2	$28,903
Ouachita, LA	70,364	70,729	72,428	-0.5	-2.3	5.2	8.3	6.1	4,269	1.6	62,510	1.8	$38,721
Union, LA	9,153	9,674	10,458	-5.4	-7.5	5.7	10.4	6.2	340	0.6	4,077	1.2	$32,322
Monroe, MI Metro Area	75,765	75,640	77,855	0.2	-2.8	4.2	11.7	6.2	2,353	-1.3	37,086	6.9	$43,565
Monroe, MI	75,765	75,640	77,855	0.2	-2.8	4.2	11.7	6.2	2,353	-1.3	37,086	6.9	$43,565
Montgomery, AL Metro Area	172,376	175,499	168,497	-1.8	4.2	3.9	9.8	4.4	7,741	0.0	130,956	3.1	$40,712
Autauga, AL	25,957	25,713	23,949	0.9	7.4	3.6	8.9	3.8	869	-0.2	11,036	8.5	$32,705
Elmore, AL	37,215	36,683	34,448	1.5	6.5	3.4	9.1	3.7	1,179	6.1	14,743	7.1	$33,895
Lowndes, AL	3,625	4,350	4,952	-16.7	-12.2	7.3	18.5	8.0	108	-13.6	1,904	-9.8	$42,270
Montgomery, AL	105,579	108,753	105,148	-2.9	3.4	4.0	10.0	4.6	5,585	-0.9	103,273	2.3	$42,512
Morgantown, WV Metro Area	68,646	63,289	58,509	8.5	8.2	4.3	6.2	3.9	2,951	7.6	53,463	20.4	$45,080
Monongalia, WV	53,305	48,354	44,216	10.2	9.4	4.1	5.6	3.7	2,409	10.5	47,846	20.1	$46,268
Preston, WV	15,341	14,935	14,293	2.7	4.5	5.2	8.4	4.8	542	-3.7	5,617	23.2	$34,968
Morristown, TN Metro Area	60,847	62,857	62,949	-3.2	-0.1	3.8	11.7	5.9	2,252	2.2	42,419	9.0	$36,626
Grainger, TN	9,417	10,040	10,042	-6.2	0.0	4.0	12.7	6.0	234	5.9	2,443	21.2	$32,273
Hamblen, TN	27,421	28,403	29,400	-3.5	-3.4	3.8	11.6	5.8	1,314	0.0	28,825	7.2	$37,318
Jefferson, TN	24,009	24,414	23,507	-1.7	3.9	3.8	11.5	5.9	704	5.2	11,151	11.3	$35,791
Mount Vernon-Anacortes, WA Metro Area	60,278	59,114	56,282	2.0	5.0	5.2	10.9	6.2	3,560	3.7	43,053	13.3	$46,545
Skagit, WA	60,278	59,114	56,282	2.0	5.0	5.2	10.9	6.2	3,560	3.7	43,053	13.3	$46,545
Muncie, IN Metro Area	54,159	54,724	56,113		-2.5	4.0	11.6	6.9	2,455	0.6	42,508	18.4	$36,262
Delaware, IN	54,159	54,724	56,113		-2.5	4.0	11.6	6.9	2,455	0.6	42,508	18.4	$36,262
Muskegon, MI Metro Area	78,196	77,712	90,054	0.6	-13.7	4.5	14.5	7.0	3,165	-6.3	52,096	9.2	$40,601
Muskegon, MI	78,196	77,712	90,054	0.6	-13.7	4.5	14.5	7.0	3,165	-6.3	52,096	9.2	$40,601
Myrtle Beach-Conway-North Myrtle Beach, SC-NC	198,665	177,475	164,187	11.9	8.1	4.4	12.3	5.6	11,623	10.3	138,378	20.0	$32,242
Brunswick, NC	52,867	46,529	42,827	13.6	8.6	5.2	12.5	5.0	2,531	10.7	25,971	13.2	$36,148
Horry, SC	145,798	130,946	121,360	11.3	7.9	4.2	12.3	5.7	9,092	10.3	112,407	21.7	$31,339
Napa, CA Metro Area	74,547	70,216	71,328	6.2	-1.6	2.9	10.3	4.4	4,270	8.2	64,132	16.7	$53,384
Napa, CA	74,547	70,216	71,328	6.2	-1.6	2.9	10.3	4.4	4,270	8.2	64,132	16.7	$53,384
Naples-Marco Island, FL Metro Area	177,351	145,349	145,136	22.0	0.1	3.4	11.6	3.5	12,074	22.5	131,871	30.0	$42,794
Collier, FL	177,351	145,349	145,136	22.0	0.1	3.4	11.6	3.5	12,074	22.5	131,871	30.0	$42,794
Nashville-Davidson--Murfreesboro--Franklin, TN	1,031,834	867,293	769,804	19.0	12.7	2.7	8.6	4.5	43,775	12.3	855,849	27.1	$51,712
Cannon, TN	6,368	6,082	6,377	4.7	-4.6	3.2	11.1	5.3	211	28.7	1,637	18.8	$32,687
Cheatham, TN	21,459	20,210	20,229	6.2	-0.1	2.7	9.0	4.4	625	15.5	6,543	17.7	$42,918
Davidson, TN	396,574	342,404	301,917	15.8	13.4	2.6	8.2	4.5	19,881	9.7	448,759	21.1	$55,462
Dickson, TN	26,257	23,958	22,668	9.6	5.7	3.0	10.2	5.0	987	6.9	14,269	20.3	$34,163
Macon, TN	10,991	10,245	10,453	7.3	-2.0	3.2	11.2	5.7	313	-8.7	3,534	7.7	$32,071
Maury, TN	47,485	41,469	35,653	14.5	16.3	3.2	12.3	6.0	1,789	8.7	29,649	28.9	$44,189
Robertson, TN	36,975	33,768	31,473	9.5	7.3	3.1	9.2	4.9	1,178	11.1	19,852	26.9	$36,539
Rutherford, TN	176,691	140,219	117,742	26.0	19.1	2.7	8.9	4.2	5,319	18.3	112,802	36.7	$43,117
Smith, TN	9,145	8,934	9,047	2.4	-1.2	3.1	12.3	6.0	278	-1.8	3,881	14.1	$37,928
Sumner, TN	98,706	83,250	75,319	18.6	10.5	2.8	8.9	4.6	3,228	12.2	46,913	30.9	$41,717
Trousdale, TN	4,888	3,742	3,671	30.6	1.9	3.3	10.8	6.6	115	-8.7	1,432	32.7	$33,631
Williamson, TN	123,205	94,495	81,057	30.4	16.6	2.5	6.6	3.8	7,118	17.4	125,617	38.9	$61,882
Wilson, TN	73,090	58,517	54,198	24.9	8.0	2.8	8.4	4.6	2,733	16.3	40,961	40.5	$39,269
New Bern, NC Metro Area	51,255	52,379	51,421	-2.1	1.9	4.2	10.7	4.7	2,542	-6.2	31,352	0.9	$37,863
Craven, NC	41,528	42,279	40,795	-1.8	3.6	4.2	10.7	4.7	2,163	-6.2	28,282	0.3	$38,883
Jones, NC	4,379	4,598	4,935	-4.8	-6.8	4.2	11.2	4.9	138	-6.8	858	-13.8	$29,983
Pamlico, NC	5,348	5,502	5,691	-2.8	-3.3	4.1	10.2	4.5	241	-5.5	2,212	16.4	$27,877
New Haven-Milford, CT Metro Area	458,747	461,566	429,962	-0.6	7.4	4.4	10.0	5.3	19,562	-0.2	340,724	6.1	$51,859
New Haven, CT	458,747	461,566	429,962	-0.6	7.4	4.4	10.0	5.3	19,562	-0.2	340,724	6.1	$51,859
New Orleans-Metairie, LA Metro Area	594,960	570,730	NA	4.2	NA	4.6	7.7	NA	31,166	6.0	494,676	9.2	$47,490
Jefferson, LA	215,064	216,258	NA	-0.6	NA	4.4	7.4	NA	11,894	0.8	179,573	0.3	$46,220
Orleans, LA	178,845	162,592	NA	10.0	NA	5.0	8.7	NA	9,422	11.7	177,008	18.8	$46,324
Plaquemines, LA	9,992	10,028	NA	-0.4	NA	4.6	6.1	NA	660	-5.3	9,006	-10.6	$57,160
St. Bernard, LA	19,519	15,951	NA	22.4	NA	5.0	8.3	NA	678	6.3	8,087	20.1	$44,716
St. Charles, LA	24,916	25,481	NA	-2.2	NA	4.4	7.4	NA	993	4.2	20,472	2.3	$71,161
St. James, LA	9,327	10,130	NA	-7.9	NA	6.2	11.7	NA	318	0.3	6,760	-1.3	$71,055
St. John the Baptist, LA	19,641	21,535	NA	-8.8	NA	5.7	10.6	NA	732	-0.1	17,260	22.7	$52,474
St. Tammany, LA	117,656	108,755	NA	8.2	NA	4.2	6.3	NA	6,469	10.9	76,510	13.9	$42,781
New York-Newark-Jersey City, NY-NJ-PA Metro Area	9,608,604	9,480,794	9,181,112	1.3	3.3	4.0	8.9	4.9	563,722	5.7	8,166,817	12.3	$71,906
Nassau County-Suffolk County, NY Div	1,485,659	1,469,298	1,467,327	1.1	0.1	3.7	7.5	4.1	98,414	3.8	1,151,576	10.4	$54,645
Nassau, NY	707,875	691,435	689,655	2.4	0.3	3.5	7.1	4.0	48,608	3.2	566,051	10.7	$54,628
Suffolk, NY	777,784	777,863	777,672	0.0	0.0	3.9	7.7	4.2	49,806	4.3	585,525	10.1	$54,661
Newark, NJ-PA Div	1,050,291	1,102,526	1,072,614	-4.7	2.8	4.3	9.3	4.5	57,626	-0.1	889,017	4.0	$66,976
Essex, NJ	364,346	382,021	360,801	-4.6	5.9	5.2	10.8	5.6	18,874	-1.3	292,219	-0.8	$60,735
Hunterdon, NJ	63,020	68,281	71,103	-7.7	-4.0	3.3	7.4	3.1	3,813	-2.1	49,069	11.6	$64,471
Morris, NJ	252,984	264,785	267,019	-4.5	-0.8	3.3	7.4	3.3	16,962	1.1	305,297	11.0	$78,231
Sussex, NJ	72,560	82,239	82,976	-11.8	-0.9	4.0	9.4	3.9	3,224	-4.2	32,217	3.2	$41,976
Union, NJ	272,683	279,122	264,877	-2.3	5.4	4.3	9.5	4.8	13,821	1.4	201,537	-0.3	$65,182

NA = 2005 unemployment data are not available for this area because of Hurricane Katrina.

Table C-4. Labor Force and Private Business Establishments and Employment—*Continued*

Metropolitan Statistical Area Metropolitan Division Component counties	Civilian Labor Force								Private nonfarm businesses				
	Total			Percent change		Unemployment rate			Establishments		Employment		Annual payroll per emplyee 2017 (dollars)
	2018	2010	2005	2010-2018	2005-2010	2018	2010	2005	2017	change 2010-2017	2017	Change 2010-2017	
Pike, PA	24,698	26,078	25,838	-5.3	0.9	5.4	9.7	5.9	932	5.1	8,678	14.7	$29,847
New Brunswick-Lakewood, NJ Div	1,194,259	1,192,097	1,161,313	0.2	2.7	3.8	9.0	4.2	64,530	4.8	967,636	10.8	$60,427
Middlesex, NJ	435,053	424,100	414,728	2.6	2.3	3.6	9.0	4.2	21,850	3.3	393,849	9.6	$63,014
Monmouth, NJ	323,106	330,154	323,151	-2.1	2.2	3.7	8.7	4.1	19,294	2.4	242,695	12.0	$50,720
Ocean, NJ	266,971	264,400	248,890	1.0	6.2	4.3	10.3	4.7	13,380	13.1	144,569	16.2	$38,691
Somerset, NJ	169,129	173,443	174,544	-2.5	-0.6	3.4	7.6	3.4	10,006	2.8	186,523	7.9	$84,442
New York-Jersey City-White Plains, NY-NJ Div	5,878,395	5,716,873	5,479,858	2.8	4.3	4.1	9.2	5.4	343,152	7.5	5,158,588	14.6	$78,763
Bergen, NJ	472,001	478,945	465,823	-1.4	2.8	3.4	8.0	3.7	31,916	1.9	436,581	7.0	$61,377
Hudson, NJ	357,639	352,903	287,475	1.3	22.8	3.9	9.6	5.5	13,550	7.4	231,615	13.5	$72,567
Passaic, NJ	239,206	253,373	234,831	-5.6	7.9	5.1	11.4	5.5	12,158	4.4	144,817	0.9	$47,857
Bronx, NY	605,864	582,287	507,229	4.0	14.8	5.7	12.0	7.6	18,199	11.3	266,075	16.6	$45,577
Kings, NY	1,211,721	1,163,502	1,070,528	4.1	8.7	4.2	9.9	6.2	58,785	21.9	626,732	28.1	$41,059
New York, NY	919,101	881,204	902,717	4.3	-2.4	3.7	8.6	5.1	103,925	0.2	2,260,419	14.8	$112,042
Putnam, NY	51,085	52,594	56,067	-2.9	-6.2	3.7	7.2	3.7	2,898	-0.3	21,449	3.6	$45,003
Queens, NY	1,162,225	1,106,461	1,090,028	5.0	1.5	3.6	8.6	5.2	50,262	16.1	565,709	16.9	$49,922
Richmond, NY	220,621	216,950	231,455	1.7	-6.3	4.1	9.4	5.3	9,387	10.5	105,632	15.8	$41,839
Rockland, NY	154,676	149,978	151,221	3.1	-0.8	3.7	7.5	4.0	10,187	10.6	112,257	15.8	$46,650
Westchester, NY	484,256	478,676	482,484	1.2	-0.8	3.9	7.4	4.0	31,885	1.1	387,302	5.4	$66,571
Niles, MI Metro Area	73,328	76,628	79,071	-4.3	-3.1	4.3	12.0	6.9	3,543	-3.6	54,568	10.2	$45,638
Berrien, MI	73,328	76,628	79,071	-4.3	-3.1	4.3	12.0	6.9	3,543	-3.6	54,568	10.2	$45,638
North Port-Sarasota-Bradenton, FL Metro Area	365,815	314,794	313,922	16.2	0.3	3.4	11.5	3.4	23,085	16.1	247,805	25.1	$41,778
Manatee, FL	177,777	147,572	144,617	20.5	2.0	3.4	11.4	3.5	9,128	21.7	102,414	28.9	$38,626
Sarasota, FL	188,038	167,222	169,305	12.4	-1.2	3.4	11.6	3.4	13,957	12.8	145,391	22.6	$43,999
Norwich-New London, CT Metro Area	137,463	143,924	144,132	-4.5	-0.1	4.0	8.9	4.5	5,907	2.0	105,456	-1.5	$50,532
New London, CT	137,463	143,924	144,132	-4.5	-0.1	4.0	8.9	4.5	5,907	2.0	105,456	-1.5	$50,532
Ocala, FL Metro Area	135,746	132,351	127,862	2.6	3.5	4.3	13.6	3.8	7,182	6.0	81,985	10.9	$35,248
Marion, FL	135,746	132,351	127,862	2.6	3.5	4.3	13.6	3.8	7,182	6.0	81,985	10.9	$35,248
Ocean City, NJ Metro Area	45,785	50,213	57,700	-8.8	-13.0	8.4	14.0	6.6	3,850	-0.1	26,890	9.9	$41,132
Cape May, NJ	45,785	50,213	57,700	-8.8	-13.0	8.4	14.0	6.6	3,850	-0.1	26,890	9.9	$41,132
Odessa, TX Metro Area	85,132	68,186	62,285	24.9	9.5	2.7	8.3	4.5	3,639	12.5	59,190	20.8	$54,374
Ector, TX	85,132	68,186	62,285	24.9	9.5	2.7	8.3	4.5	3,639	12.5	59,190	20.8	$54,374
Ogden-Clearfield, UT Metro Area	326,065	288,136	270,310	13.2	6.6	3.2	7.8	4.2	14,205	14.7	192,865	22.0	$40,793
Box Elder, UT	25,435	23,644	22,413	7.6	5.5	3.0	8.5	4.3	1,164	12.9	17,663	9.9	$49,424
Davis, UT	170,592	146,959	135,870	16.1	8.2	2.9	7.0	3.9	7,332	18.4	91,392	27.9	$40,214
Morgan, UT	5,446	4,274	3,818	27.4	11.9	2.8	6.9	4.2	298	33.0	1,671	17.3	$44,227
Weber, UT	124,592	113,259	108,209	10.0	4.7	3.5	8.8	4.6	5,411	9.5	82,149	18.7	$39,513
Oklahoma City, OK Metro Area	681,616	623,505	573,874	9.3	8.6	3.1	5.9	4.3	35,992	9.1	506,241	11.8	$44,495
Canadian, OK	72,033	60,083	51,178	19.9	17.4	2.8	5.2	3.7	2,723	20.4	27,579	22.3	$39,007
Cleveland, OK	142,102	131,125	118,305	8.4	10.8	2.9	5.3	3.8	5,848	9.9	71,230	9.8	$35,456
Grady, OK	26,292	25,401	23,447	3.5	8.3	3.1	6.5	4.5	1,121	6.2	10,569	2.6	$35,359
Lincoln, OK	15,952	15,657	14,775	1.9	6.0	3.5	6.5	4.8	568	-0.5	5,403	1.9	$38,429
Logan, OK	21,953	19,805	18,151	10.8	9.1	3.0	5.7	3.9	850	18.5	6,440	11.4	$34,080
McClain, OK	19,424	17,180	14,736	13.1	16.6	2.8	5.6	4.2	879	16.3	7,983	15.5	$33,974
Oklahoma, OK	383,860	354,254	333,282	8.4	6.3	3.3	6.1	4.6	24,003	7.6	377,037	11.9	$47,347
Olympia-Lacey-Tumwater, WA Metro Area	137,697	126,948	121,951	8.5	4.1	4.8	9.0	5.3	6,233	7.0	73,630	15.7	$41,533
Thurston, WA	137,697	126,948	121,951	8.5	4.1	4.8	9.0	5.3	6,233	7.0	73,630	15.7	$41,533
Omaha-Council Bluffs, NE-IA Metro Area	485,858	465,962	440,297	4.3	5.8	2.9	5.1	4.3	23,884	7.1	419,890	5.3	$47,679
Harrison, IA	7,291	7,999	8,066	-8.9	-0.8	2.2	5.6	4.7	350	0.6	3,125	5.7	$36,151
Mills, IA	7,307	7,609	8,177	-4.0	-6.9	2.1	5.2	4.1	310	6.9	2,204	3.8	$35,608
Pottawattamie, IA	47,848	50,336	48,658	-4.9	3.4	2.3	5.8	4.9	1,980	-0.9	31,591	2.5	$36,488
Cass, NE	13,275	13,404	14,017	-1.0	-4.4	3.0	5.6	4.1	573	7.7	4,123	24.3	$36,005
Douglas, NE	293,923	279,280	266,086	5.2	5.0	3.1	5.1	4.5	15,795	5.6	311,361	0.3	$49,895
Sarpy, NE	94,057	84,923	72,972	10.8	16.4	2.7	4.4	3.4	3,714	18.8	56,945	43.8	$44,924
Saunders, NE	10,948	11,179	11,153	-2.1	0.2	2.7	4.8	3.9	558	11.8	3,873	11.2	$34,665
Washington, NE	11,209	11,232	11,168	-0.2	0.6	2.8	4.6	3.3	604	12.5	6,668	9.1	$44,920
Orlando-Kissimmee-Sanford, FL Metro Area	1,337,790	1,137,389	1,015,778	17.6	12.0	3.3	11.1	3.6	64,912	17.9	1,072,635	25.3	$43,274
Lake, FL	155,273	134,021	118,339	15.9	13.3	3.5	11.8	3.8	7,330	16.8	82,957	26.3	$34,833
Orange, FL	750,160	635,299	553,951	18.1	14.7	3.2	10.8	3.6	37,724	19.6	734,085	24.2	$45,189
Osceola, FL	177,919	137,372	116,456	29.5	18.0	3.6	12.5	3.8	6,279	30.2	80,578	35.4	$31,976
Seminole, FL	254,438	230,697	227,032	10.3	1.6	3.2	10.6	3.4	13,579	9.1	175,015	25.2	$44,446
Oshkosh-Neenah, WI Metro Area	92,956	92,450	91,185	0.5	1.4	2.7	7.8	4.4	3,627	0.7	85,726	2.7	$50,909
Winnebago, WI	92,956	92,450	91,185	0.5	1.4	2.7	7.8	4.4	3,627	0.7	85,726	2.7	$50,909
Owensboro, KY Metro Area	56,392	55,455	55,137	1.7	0.6	4.0	9.4	6.0	2,629	2.5	47,181	5.9	$39,313
Daviess, KY	48,018	46,881	46,341	2.4	1.2	4.0	9.3	5.8	2,327	2.6	42,622	6.0	$37,723
Hancock, KY	4,089	4,060	4,154	0.7	-2.3	4.2	10.3	6.2	134	1.5	3,288	2.0	$60,219
McLean, KY	4,285	4,524	4,642	-5.3	-2.5	4.9	10.2	7.2	168	1.8	1,271	15.2	$38,562
Oxnard-Thousand Oaks-Ventura, CA Metro Area	425,728	430,010	415,958	-1.0	3.4	3.8	10.8	4.7	21,339	8.8	258,166	9.6	$53,554
Ventura, CA	425,728	430,010	415,958	-1.0	3.4	3.8	10.8	4.7	21,339	8.8	258,166	9.6	$53,554
Palm Bay-Melbourne-Titusville, FL Metro Area	276,558	265,643	260,435	4.1	2.0	3.5	11.3	3.6	14,255	9.8	185,134	12.9	$44,716
Brevard, FL	276,558	265,643	260,435	4.1	2.0	3.5	11.3	3.6	14,255	9.8	185,134	12.9	$44,716
Panama City, FL Metro Area	89,251	86,072	82,406	3.7	4.4	4.0	10.5	3.6	4,700	5.0	63,126	16.0	$35,582
Bay, FL	89,251	86,072	82,406	3.7	4.4	4.0	10.5	3.6	4,700	5.0	63,126	16.0	$35,582
Parkersburg-Vienna, WV Metro Area	38,107	41,640	43,449	-8.5	-4.2	5.6	9.1	5.6	2,038	-6.9	30,200	-8.7	$34,505

Table C-4. Labor Force and Private Business Establishments and Employment—*Continued*

Metropolitan Statistical Area Metropolitan Division Component counties	Civilian Labor Force								Private nonfarm businesses				
	Total			Percent change		Unemployment rate			Establishments		Employment		Annual payroll per emplyee 2017 (dollars)
	2018	2010	2005	2010-2018	2005-2010	2018	2010	2005	2017	change 2010-2017	2017	Change 2010-2017	
Wirt, WV	2,171	2,292	2,505	-5.3	-8.5	7.0	12.5	7.4	49	-30.0	261	-32.4	$24,958
Wood, WV	35,936	39,348	40,944	-8.7	-3.9	5.5	8.9	5.5	1,989	-6.1	29,939	-8.4	$34,589
Pensacola-Ferry Pass-Brent, FL Metro Area	225,952	211,246	203,128	7.0	4.0	3.5	9.8	3.8	9,604	5.7	133,544	15.2	$40,278
Escambia, FL	145,298	139,913	135,677	3.8	3.1	3.5	10.1	3.9	6,859	3.6	106,907	12.2	$41,543
Santa Rosa, FL	80,654	71,333	67,451	13.1	5.8	3.3	9.3	3.6	2,745	11.4	26,637	29.3	$35,201
Peoria, IL Metro Area	195,266	215,073	208,638	-9.2	3.1	5.2	10.1	4.8	8,964	-5.3	163,411	-3.1	$51,144
Fulton, IL	15,224	17,592	17,566	-13.5	0.1	6.2	11.7	6.0	635	-9.2	6,219	-11.3	$30,398
Marshall, IL	5,510	6,427	7,115	-14.3	-9.7	5.2	10.3	4.4	259	-7.5	2,594	-12.5	$37,548
Peoria, IL	87,398	96,018	92,082	-9.0	4.3	5.5	10.5	4.9	4,373	-7.4	104,602	-1.4	$58,048
Stark, IL	2,587	3,029	2,833	-14.6	6.9	6.3	9.7	5.5	119	-1.7	997	10.0	$40,587
Tazewell, IL	65,386	71,668	69,006	-8.8	3.9	4.9	9.9	4.6	2,817	-1.1	40,721	-6.6	$40,303
Woodford, IL	19,161	20,339	20,036	-5.8	1.5	4.1	7.7	3.7	761	-3.9	8,278	2.5	$38,338
Philadelphia-Camden-Wilmington, PA-NJ-DE-MD Metro Area	3,082,419	3,021,375	2,916,385	2.0	3.6	4.2	8.8	4.7	148,311	2.5	2,628,893	8.6	$57,685
Camden, NJ Div	624,565	654,575	648,744	-4.6	0.9	4.2	10.1	4.4	28,054	0.2	458,427	7.7	$49,370
Burlington, NJ	227,445	237,144	237,927	-4.1	-0.3	3.8	9.0	3.9	10,444	0.5	180,194	3.8	$52,772
Camden, NJ	249,945	264,826	262,726	-5.6	0.8	4.6	10.9	4.8	11,518	-2.0	181,720	8.2	$49,570
Gloucester, NJ	147,175	152,605	148,091	-3.6	3.0	4.2	10.3	4.4	6,092	4.3	96,513	14.8	$42,641
Montgomery County-Bucks County-Chester County	1,072,028	1,037,076	1,020,158	3.4	1.7	3.5	7.0	3.9	60,276	3.2	1,011,898	9.2	$60,977
Bucks, PA	341,069	337,150	341,282	1.2	-1.2	3.7	7.6	4.1	19,355	2.8	252,929	4.7	$46,707
Chester, PA	281,572	269,540	256,305	4.5	5.2	3.2	6.2	3.6	14,593	5.8	250,337	11.4	$70,340
Montgomery, PA	449,387	430,386	422,571	4.4	1.8	3.4	6.9	3.9	26,328	2.1	508,632	10.4	$63,465
Philadelphia, PA Div	1,005,484	973,996	896,383	3.2	8.7	5.1	9.8	6.0	41,085	3.5	848,150	9.8	$57,027
Delaware, PA	295,898	286,187	279,252	3.4	2.5	4.0	8.0	4.6	12,921	1.2	211,442	4.9	$54,925
Philadelphia, PA	709,586	687,809	617,131	3.2	11.5	5.5	10.6	6.7	28,164	4.6	636,708	11.6	$57,725
Wilmington, DE-MD-NJ Div	380,342	355,728	351,100	6.9	1.3	3.9	8.7	4.5	18,896	1.4	310,418	4.5	$61,034
New Castle, DE	298,915	271,575	270,152	10.1	0.5	3.7	8.3	4.4	15,971	2.0	269,368	5.6	$62,774
Cecil, MD	52,632	51,981	49,714	1.3	4.6	4.4	9.5	4.6	1,770	-0.7	24,382	3.4	$47,760
Salem, NJ	28,795	32,172	31,234	-10.5	3.0	5.4	11.6	4.9	1,155	-3.2	16,668	-8.4	$52,321
Phoenix-Mesa-Chandler, AZ Metro Area	2,407,742	2,073,297	1,943,498	16.1	6.7	4.2	9.6	4.1	98,279	12.0	1,726,596	18.8	$49,276
Maricopa, AZ	2,229,526	1,919,590	1,856,076	16.1	3.4	4.1	9.5	4.0	94,566	11.9	1,675,392	18.7	$49,642
Pinal, AZ	178,216	153,707	87,422	15.9	75.8	5.0	10.7	5.6	3,713	15.9	51,204	23.3	$37,304
Pine Bluff, AR Metro Area	35,409	42,560	46,561	-16.8	-8.6	5.0	10.1	7.4	1,567	-7.9	21,677	-15.6	$36,693
Cleveland, AR	3,302	3,888	4,273	-15.1	-9.0	3.9	8.4	5.9	80	-1.2	530	15.0	$29,479
Jefferson, AR	28,066	33,973	37,037	-17.4	-8.3	5.3	10.4	7.6	1,316	-9.9	19,699	-16.8	$36,963
Lincoln, AR	4,041	4,699	5,251	-14.0	-10.5	4.3	9.4	7.6	171	6.9	1,448	-6.8	$35,662
Pittsburgh, PA Metro Area	1,203,534	1,201,211	1,196,815	0.2	0.4	4.3	8.0	5.2	59,749	0.9	1,103,495	7.0	$49,867
Allegheny, PA	645,169	636,093	628,051	1.4	1.3	4.0	7.6	5.0	33,762	1.2	711,354	7.4	$53,066
Armstrong, PA	32,148	33,637	32,901	-4.4	2.2	5.0	9.1	6.1	1,304	2.4	13,725	3.2	$36,674
Beaver, PA	84,057	85,611	89,335	-1.8	-4.2	4.5	8.6	5.6	3,407	-1.5	47,472		$40,331
Butler, PA	98,563	95,781	94,848	2.9	1.0	3.9	7.4	4.8	4,904	5.6	84,520	14.3	$46,158
Fayette, PA	57,081	59,533	65,225	-4.1	-8.7	5.8	10.7	7.0	2,574	-6.1	33,100	-8.6	$35,894
Washington, PA	106,001	105,280	102,273	0.7	2.9	4.3	8.1	5.5	5,205	3.5	86,267	9.4	$54,069
Westmoreland, PA	180,515	185,276	184,182	-2.6	0.6	4.4	8.2	5.3	8,593	-1.8	127,057	7.1	$40,196
Pittsfield, MA Metro Area	66,109	68,182	72,664	-3.0	-6.2	4.0	8.7	4.4	3,872	-3.9	53,882	0.3	$45,643
Berkshire, MA	66,109	68,182	72,664	-3.0	-6.2	4.0	8.7	4.4	3,872	-3.9	53,882	0.3	$45,643
Pocatello, ID Metro Area	45,776	44,967	44,343	1.8	1.4	2.7	8.1	3.9	2,246	3.1	26,946	-0.3	$34,919
Bannock, ID	41,686	41,095	40,549	1.4	1.3	2.7	8.0	3.9	2,071	2.6	24,760	-0.5	$34,555
Power, ID	4,090	3,872	3,794	5.6	2.1	2.9	9.2	4.7	175	8.7	2,186	1.8	$39,034
Portland-South Portland, ME Metro Area	298,848	283,871	285,935	5.3	-0.7	2.8	7.1	3.9	18,136	4.6	238,275	9.2	$47,672
Cumberland, ME	165,409	156,017	155,620	6.0	0.3	2.7	6.5	3.6	11,560	6.1	170,219	10.3	$50,134
Sagadahoc, ME	19,440	19,219	18,535	1.1	3.7	2.7	6.7	4.4	943	-0.6	13,477	0.9	$46,720
York, ME	113,999	108,635	111,780	4.9	-2.8	3.0	8.0	4.2	5,633	2.8	54,579	8.1	$40,230
Portland-Vancouver-Hillsboro, OR-WA Metro Area	1,313,057	1,207,836	1,093,793	8.7	10.4	3.9	10.2	5.9	70,187	12.4	1,047,457	20.3	$55,700
Clackamas, OR	218,998	202,654	190,177	8.1	6.6	3.8	10.1	5.5	12,103	12.6	146,934	6.8	$49,405
Columbia, OR	24,387	23,649	23,209	3.1	1.9	5.1	12.9	7.3	942	-1.1	8,492	22.8	$35,026
Multnomah, OR	456,886	418,838	360,354	9.1	16.2	3.7	9.6	6.1	27,628	12.1	440,774	19.1	$53,499
Washington, OR	322,574	289,670	268,325	11.4	8.0	3.5	9.0	5.2	15,651	10.6	280,275	27.7	$68,308
Yamhill, OR	54,524	51,226	44,039	6.4	16.3	3.8	10.4	6.1	2,547	11.4	30,776	11.0	$37,402
Clark, WA	230,353	216,620	202,656	6.3	6.9	4.8	12.9	6.7	11,114	17.0	138,535	28.6	$49,488
Skamania, WA	5,335	5,179	5,033	3.0	2.9	5.6	12.8	7.9	202	6.3	1,671	32.5	$32,022
Port St. Lucie, FL Metro Area	216,794	195,326	177,600	11.0	10.0	4.1	12.7	4.5	11,313	14.7	117,217	18.4	$37,735
Martin, FL	74,159	66,636	64,652	11.3	3.1	3.5	10.8	4.0	5,552	11.5	56,642	20.4	$39,463
St. Lucie, FL	142,635	128,690	112,948	10.8	13.9	4.4	13.8	4.8	5,761	18.0	60,575	16.7	$36,119
Poughkeepsie-Newburgh-Middletown, NY Metro area	326,175	330,491	324,605	-1.3	1.8	3.8	7.9	4.1	17,203	3.3	215,318	7.9	$43,360
Dutchess, NY	143,934	149,196	147,009	-3.5	1.5	3.7	7.7	3.9	7,607	2.2	96,703	0.3	$46,850
Orange, NY	182,241	181,295	177,596	0.5	2.1	3.9	8.0	4.2	9,596	4.2	118,615	15.1	$40,514
Prescott Valley-Prescott, AZ Metro Area	105,618	96,533	91,442	9.4	5.6	4.5	10.7	4.4	5,985	6.1	61,048	20.1	$34,754
Yavapai, AZ	105,618	96,533	91,442	9.4	5.6	4.5	10.7	4.4	5,985	6.1	61,048	20.1	$34,754
Providence-Warwick, RI-MA Metro Area	858,725	853,503	853,565	0.6	0.0	4.1	11.0	5.4	41,395	0.4	637,255	7.9	$47,290
Bristol, MA	302,918	286,799	287,829	5.6	-0.4	4.3	10.6	6.0	12,903	0.8	206,699	7.2	$45,852
Bristol, RI	26,082	26,957	28,254	-3.2	-4.6	3.5	9.7	4.3	1,269	3.2	14,570	10.8	$32,865

Table C-4. Labor Force and Private Business Establishments and Employment—*Continued*

Metropolitan Statistical Area Metropolitan Division Component counties	Civilian Labor Force								Private nonfarm businesses				Annual payroll per emplyee 2017 (dollars)
	Total			Percent change		Unemployment rate			Establishments		Employment		
	2018	2010	2005	2010-2018	2005-2010	2018	2010	2005	2017	change 2010-2017	2017	Change 2010-2017	
Kent, RI	90,476	94,263	96,472	-4.0	-2.3	3.7	11.1	4.8	4,698	-2.5	70,945	3.0	$45,474
Newport, RI	44,657	45,055	44,632	-0.9	0.9	3.5	10.0	4.6	2,760	0.1	31,763	10.6	$44,251
Providence, RI	325,587	328,921	323,279	-1.0	1.7	4.4	11.8	5.4	15,985	0.9	269,906	8.9	$50,253
Washington, RI	69,005	71,508	73,099	-3.5	-2.2	3.6	10.1	4.1	3,780	-0.3	43,372	10.4	$45,753
Provo-Orem, UT Metro Area	305,442	234,432	209,058	30.3	12.1	2.8	7.5	3.9	13,738	27.1	215,315	38.8	$43,212
Juab, UT	5,574	4,612	3,916	20.9	17.8	3.0	9.1	4.8	215	18.1	2,490	18.0	$34,037
Utah, UT	299,868	229,820	205,142	30.5	12.0	2.8	7.4	3.9	13,523	27.3	212,825	39.1	$43,320
Pueblo, CO Metro Area	75,912	74,396	69,326	2.0	7.3	4.9	10.4	6.8	3,117	-1.2	50,879	8.6	$38,726
Pueblo, CO	75,912	74,396	69,326	2.0	7.3	4.9	10.4	6.8	3,117	-1.2	50,879	8.6	$38,726
Punta Gorda, FL Metro Area	70,953	66,293	66,088	7.0	0.3	4.0	12.7	4.0	4,006	13.6	39,311	6.4	$33,648
Charlotte, FL	70,953	66,293	66,088	7.0	0.3	4.0	12.7	4.0	4,006	13.6	39,311	6.4	$33,648
Racine, WI Metro Area	99,570	100,314	98,509	-0.7	1.8	3.6	10.2	5.9	4,036	-0.3	66,364	3.4	$46,954
Racine, WI	99,570	100,314	98,509	-0.7	1.8	3.6	10.2	5.9	4,036	-0.3	66,364	3.4	$46,954
Raleigh-Cary, NC Metro Area	711,326	590,220	500,724	20.5	17.9	3.4	8.6	4.2	33,877	17.1	520,170	26.7	$52,969
Franklin, NC	30,642	27,954	25,987	9.6	7.6	4.0	10.9	4.8	1,061	15.2	10,437	12.4	$45,330
Johnston, NC	96,136	81,701	70,876	17.7	15.3	3.6	9.9	4.5	3,410	10.2	41,284	15.3	$36,036
Wake, NC	584,548	480,565	403,861	21.6	19.0	3.4	8.3	4.1	29,406	18.0	468,449	28.2	$54,631
Rapid City, SD Metro Area	70,360	65,987	65,322	6.6	1.0	3.1	5.2	3.6	4,565	8.0	54,904	13.1	$40,082
Meade, SD	14,107	13,148	12,738	7.3	3.2	3.3	5.3	3.8	707	5.4	5,399	7.7	$45,706
Pennington, SD	56,253	52,839	52,584	6.5	0.5	3.1	5.2	3.6	3,858	8.5	49,505	13.7	$39,468
Reading, PA Metro Area	212,528	210,149	198,712	1.1	5.8	4.2	8.7	4.9	8,435	1.8	153,071	7.3	$46,071
Berks, PA	212,528	210,149	198,712	1.1	5.8	4.2	8.7	4.9	8,435	1.8	153,071	7.3	$46,071
Redding, CA Metro Area	74,215	78,503	81,748	-5.5	-4.0	4.9	16.8	7.2	4,195	-3.0	50,261	7.4	$41,356
Shasta, CA	74,215	78,503	81,748	-5.5	-4.0	4.9	16.8	7.2	4,195	-3.0	50,261	7.4	$41,356
Reno, NV Metro Area	252,010	222,838	210,769	13.1	5.7	3.6	13.0	3.9	12,706	7.7	195,817	18.1	$31,521
Storey, NV	2,005	2,013	2,266	-0.4	-11.2	4.4	16.7	4.3	92	7.0	511	37.7	$45,592
Washoe, NV	250,005	220,825	208,503	13.2	5.9	3.6	12.9	3.9	12,614	7.7	195,306	18.1	$50,098
Richmond, VA Metro Area	664,431	617,935	583,336	7.5	5.9	3.1	7.9	3.8	31,770	6.1	541,040	16.0	$30,178
Amelia, VA	6,240	6,227	6,317	0.2	-1.4	3.2	8.5	3.5	275	-3.8	2,011	7.8	$43,671
Charles City County, VA	3,692	3,901	3,757	-5.4	3.8	3.9	9.6	4.4	150	7.9	1,625	37.2	$43,426
Chesterfield, VA	184,434	168,602	158,613	9.4	6.3	2.9	7.3	3.2	7,465	9.9	114,239	18.9	$40,763
Dinwiddie, VA	13,470	13,566	12,594	-0.7	7.7	3.5	8.8	4.1	356	-3.0	4,420	7.2	$94,027
Goochland, VA	10,913	10,483	10,343	4.1	1.4	3.0	7.2	3.0	677	8.5	14,793	34.5	$39,802
Hanover, VA	58,367	54,430	53,511	7.2	1.7	2.6	6.6	3.0	3,204	6.3	47,053	19.5	$52,165
Henrico, VA	180,933	167,701	156,494	7.9	7.2	3.0	7.3	3.4	9,444	8.6	175,591	13.1	
King and Queen, VA	3,849	3,592	3,263	7.2	10.1	3.0	8.1	4.0	120	12.1	644	-28.4	$38,540
King William, VA	9,004	8,656	7,911	4.0	9.4	2.9	7.5	3.5	337	0.9	3,455	21.1	$47,397
New Kent, VA	12,070	10,294	8,789	17.3	17.1	2.7	7.2	3.3	393	17.3	3,311	29.3	$34,965
Powhatan, VA	13,821	13,510	13,506	2.3	0.0	2.7	7.1	2.9	694	7.6	5,237	33.7	$37,979
Prince George, VA	14,955	13,962	15,026	7.1	-7.1	3.6	8.1	3.9	475	8.2	10,625	67.2	$33,751
Sussex, VA	3,822	4,281	4,408	-10.7	-2.9	4.9	11.4	5.9	185	-4.1	2,024	-8.3	$32,659
Colonial Heights City, VA	8,779	8,533	9,059	2.9	-5.8	3.3	8.3	4.1	665	-5.3	9,565	0.0	$26,605
Hopewell City, VA	9,703	9,864	10,276	-1.6	-4.0	4.8	11.6	5.8	413	-11.0	6,455	-1.6	$51,486
Petersburg City, VA	13,120	13,877	13,965	-5.5	-0.6	6.1	14.0	7.4	741	0.1	12,970	7.0	$38,470
Richmond City, VA	117,259	106,456	95,504	10.1	11.5	3.5	9.5	5.4	6,176	1.7	127,022	14.9	$58,219
Riverside-San Bernardino-Ontario, CA Metro Area	2,053,401	1,866,722	1,704,048	10.0	9.5	4.2	13.7	5.3	74,581	14.7	1,179,496	23.2	$41,764
Riverside, CA	1,092,371	976,444	852,578	11.9	14.5	4.4	13.8	5.4	38,946	16.1	575,169	26.0	$40,343
San Bernardino, CA	961,030	890,278	851,470	7.9	4.6	4.0	13.5	5.2	35,635	13.2	604,327	20.6	$43,116
Roanoke, VA Metro Area	156,379	159,127	149,437	-1.7	6.5	3.0	7.6	3.5	8,154	-0.4	140,143	6.0	$42,599
Botetourt, VA	17,222	17,700	17,017	-2.7	4.0	2.7	6.4	3.0	750	0.9	10,143	15.7	$43,281
Craig, VA	2,286	2,441	2,500	-6.3	-2.4	3.5	7.9	3.9	62	5.1	438	13.2	$25,628
Franklin, VA	26,271	27,622	25,337	-4.9	9.0	3.1	8.7	3.7	1,163	2.8	12,750	15.0	$29,070
Roanoke, VA	48,833	49,258	46,636	-0.9	5.6	2.7	6.3	3.0	2,029	-3.5	29,258	-3.7	$39,839
Roanoke City, VA	48,774	49,317	45,225	-1.1	9.0	3.2	8.7	4.2	3,132	-1.8	68,842	9.2	$44,743
Salem City, VA	12,993	12,789	12,722	1.6	0.5	2.9	6.9	3.2	1,018	5.6	18,712	0.5	$48,269
Rochester, MN Metro Area	123,420	115,857	113,329	6.5	2.2	2.5	6.3	3.6	5,146	2.4	113,762	25.3	$54,267
Dodge, MN	11,834	11,307	11,172	4.7	1.2	3.0	6.9	3.9	413	-1.9	4,684	15.4	$45,454
Fillmore, MN	11,534	11,246	11,274	2.6	-0.2	3.1	7.5	4.2	595	-4.6	4,757	-4.1	$34,709
Olmsted, MN	87,757	81,197	78,290	8.1	3.7	2.3	5.9	3.5	3,588	5.6	99,038	30.2	$56,561
Wabasha, MN	12,295	12,107	12,593	1.6	-3.9	2.9	7.1	4.1	550	-5.5	5,283	-7.9	$36,684
Rochester, NY Metro Area	522,110	546,181	547,998	-4.4	-0.3	4.2	8.1	4.6	24,870	3.2	453,814	8.0	$45,204
Livingston, NY	30,827	32,754	32,873	-5.9	-0.4	4.3	8.1	5.0	1,242		14,382	13.4	$34,572
Monroe, NY	362,858	378,251	376,359	-4.1	0.5	4.3	8.0	4.5	17,739	3.8	359,314	8.2	$45,822
Ontario, NY	55,149	56,368	56,825	-2.2	-0.8	3.9	7.4	4.5	2,977	6.6	47,030	10.6	$46,996
Orleans, NY	17,616	19,149	19,959	-8.0	-4.1	4.9	9.6	5.6	665	-0.9	8,315	1.4	$32,924
Wayne, NY	43,877	47,429	48,987	-7.5	-3.2	4.2	8.9	4.9	1,729	-0.2	19,772	0.4	$45,881
Yates, NY	11,783	12,230	12,995	-3.7	-5.9	3.8	7.4	4.3	518	-5.8	5,001		$32,212
Rockford, IL Metro Area	167,669	177,519	165,009	-5.5	7.6	5.7	14.0	6.4	7,252	-3.4	134,942	6.9	$44,519
Boone, IL	26,473	27,437	24,516	-3.5	11.9	5.8	13.8	6.6	850	-0.6	15,431	35.8	$54,851
Winnebago, IL	141,196	150,082	140,493	-5.9	6.8	5.7	14.0	6.3	6,402	-3.8	119,511	4.0	$43,185
Rocky Mount, NC Metro Area	65,029	72,954	68,411	-10.9	6.6	5.6	13.7	6.9	2,745	-8.5	48,269	-2.6	$36,681
Edgecombe, NC	21,741	25,501	24,224	-14.7	5.3	6.8	15.7	8.4	712	-11.6	11,899	-16.1	$31,161
Nash, NC	43,288	47,453	44,187	-8.8	7.4	5.1	12.6	6.0	2,033	-7.4	36,370	2.8	$38,487
Rome, GA Metro Area	44,274	45,087	50,139	-1.8	-10.1	4.3	11.8	5.2	2,018	1.9	36,648	7.9	$38,873

Table C-4. Labor Force and Private Business Establishments and Employment—*Continued*

Metropolitan Statistical Area Metropolitan Division Component counties	Civilian Labor Force								Private nonfarm businesses				
	Total			Percent change		Unemployment rate			Establishments		Employment		Annual payroll per emplyee 2017 (dollars)
	2018	2010	2005	2010-2018	2005-2010	2018	2010	2005	2017	change 2010-2017	2017	Change 2010-2017	
Floyd, GA	44,274	45,087	50,139	-1.8	-10.1	4.3	11.8	5.2	2,018	1.9	36,648	7.9	$38,873
Sacramento-Roseville-Folsom, CA Metro Area	1,095,762	1,049,782	1,011,984	4.4	3.7	3.7	12.4	4.9	49,002	10.1	743,106	19.6	$53,582
El Dorado, CA	91,589	91,129	91,050	0.5	0.1	3.6	12.2	4.8	4,516	6.0	46,146	12.5	$46,582
Placer, CA	185,213	173,338	164,249	6.9	5.5	3.2	11.6	4.3	10,816	16.2	149,730	26.5	$52,026
Sacramento, CA	710,442	683,127	664,327	4.0	2.8	3.8	12.6	4.9	29,515	8.8	481,229	19.1	$55,435
Yolo, CA	108,518	102,188	92,358	6.2	10.6	4.2	12.1	5.5	4,155	9.2	66,001	14.7	$48,494
Saginaw, MI Metro Area	86,849	90,722	98,365	-4.3	-7.8	4.8	12.2	8.0	4,212	-6.3	80,324	8.5	$40,741
Saginaw, MI	86,849	90,722	98,365	-4.3	-7.8	4.8	12.2	8.0	4,212	-6.3	80,324	8.5	$40,741
St. Cloud, MN Metro Area	111,550	106,774	102,805	4.5	3.9	3.0	7.5	4.4	5,384	2.8	100,928	12.9	$43,909
Benton, MN	21,666	21,100	22,165	2.7	-4.8	3.5	8.7	4.7	904	-0.1	15,878	13.6	$40,141
Stearns, MN	89,884	85,674	80,640	4.9	6.2	2.9	7.2	4.3	4,480	3.4	85,050	12.8	$44,612
St. George, UT Metro Area	73,929	56,776	56,944	30.2	-0.3	3.4	10.5	4.0	5,076	33.0	50,267	39.6	$35,409
Washington, UT	73,929	56,776	56,944	30.2	-0.3	3.4	10.5	4.0	5,076	33.0	50,267	39.6	$35,409
St. Joseph, MO-KS Metro Area	63,265	66,123	64,845	-4.3	2.0	3.0	9.0	5.8	2,806	-13.9	48,854	0.2	$42,586
Doniphan, KS	4,181	4,540	4,436	-7.9	2.3	3.5	8.8	6.3	164	0.6	1,587	36.6	$37,089
Andrew, MO	9,685	9,898	9,805	-2.2	0.9	2.7	8.3	5.2	288	-15.8	1,660	-5.6	$31,407
Buchanan, MO	44,570	46,660	45,542	-4.5	2.5	3.0	9.2	5.8	2,136	-15.4	43,439	-1.2	$43,584
De Kalb, MO	4,829	5,025	5,062	-3.9	-0.7	3.1	8.8	5.9	218	-5.2	2,168	15.3	$35,184
St. Louis, MO-IL Metro Area	1,459,246	1,478,087	1,426,498	-1.3	3.6	3.4	9.6	5.5	70,881	1.3	1,249,653	7.1	$51,038
Bond, IL	7,929	8,535	8,460	-7.1	0.9	4.4	10.0	5.4	323	-0.6	3,677	-4.6	$34,134
Calhoun, IL	2,340	2,499	2,552	-6.4	-2.1	5.3	10.0	6.1	78	-19.6	495	-18.0	$24,505
Clinton, IL	20,378	20,550	18,508	-0.8	11.0	3.6	7.3	4.7	874	0.5	8,974	1.4	$33,153
Jersey, IL	11,007	11,612	11,464	-5.2	1.3	4.9	9.2	5.3	422	-7.0	4,560	-3.8	$28,975
Macoupin, IL	23,066	24,782	24,383	-6.9	1.6	4.9	10.3	5.7	862	-9.5	8,162	-7.9	$32,786
Madison, IL	134,575	138,764	134,905	-3.0	2.9	4.5	9.8	5.5	5,757	-3.6	88,784	5.8	$41,745
Monroe, IL	18,595	18,008	17,252	3.3	4.4	3.5	7.3	4.2	807	2.8	8,487	15.5	$34,955
St. Clair, IL	127,192	133,097	121,152	-4.4	9.9	5.0	10.3	6.3	5,243	-3.9	76,350	-2.8	$38,778
Franklin, MO	52,287	53,456	52,490	-2.2	1.8	3.1	11.3	5.8	2,631	0.2	36,248	17.8	$37,923
Jefferson, MO	116,200	117,544	115,830	-1.1	1.5	3.1	10.4	5.4	3,973	-2.3	41,150	4.2	$35,276
Lincoln, MO	27,367	26,706	24,529	2.5	8.9	3.3	11.8	5.5	924	2.7	9,479	21.0	$38,431
St. Charles, MO	221,947	205,228	186,254	8.1	10.2	2.5	8.2	4.2	8,590	7.9	136,213	20.8	$42,933
St. Louis, MO	525,125	535,129	535,866	-1.9	-0.1	3.0	8.9	5.2	30,609	3.0	614,021	12.8	$57,105
Warren, MO	17,560	17,262	15,347	1.7	12.5	2.8	11.0	5.4	571	0.7	6,231	7.2	$37,322
St. Louis city, MO	153,678	164,915	157,506	-6.8	4.7	3.8	11.5	8.1	9,217	-0.2	206,822	-9.7	$56,314
Salem, OR Metro Area	201,371	191,735	183,380	5.0	4.6	4.3	10.9	6.3	9,717	8.0	121,784	13.7	$39,361
Marion, OR	161,676	155,350	147,824	4.1	5.1	4.3	11.2	6.5	8,267	7.8	107,121	11.4	$39,827
Polk, OR	39,695	36,385	35,556	9.1	2.3	4.4	9.7	5.6	1,450	9.4	14,663	33.2	$35,955
Salinas, CA Metro Area	224,057	215,788	206,565	3.8	4.5	6.3	12.7	7.3	8,754	5.0	113,209	17.5	$46,528
Monterey, CA	224,057	215,788	206,565	3.8	4.5	6.3	12.7	7.3	8,754	5.0	113,209	17.5	$46,528
Salisbury, MD-DE Metro Area	191,345	176,882	181,096	8.2	-2.3	4.9	9.8	4.4	10,627	2.2	128,997	14.4	$38,077
Sussex, DE	105,426	90,133	90,242	17.0	-0.1	3.7	8.5	3.7	5,606	4.5	69,318	22.0	$37,470
Somerset, MD	9,353	9,931	11,436	-5.8	-13.2	6.9	11.9	6.0	381	-0.5	3,905	3.9	$36,935
Wicomico, MD	51,041	50,381	51,702	1.3	-2.6	5.2	9.8	4.2	2,460	-2.7	37,158	4.7	$40,274
Worcester, MD	25,525	26,437	27,716	-3.4	-4.6	8.0	13.4	6.6	2,180	2.7	18,616	11.6	$36,195
Salt Lake City, UT Metro Area	653,521	575,832	542,619	13.5	6.1	3.0	7.7	4.0	33,247	12.6	608,961	21.0	$50,546
Salt Lake, UT	620,909	548,378	517,454	13.2	6.0	3.0	7.7	4.0	32,360	12.4	598,271	21.4	$50,775
Tooele, UT	32,612	27,454	25,165	18.8	9.1	3.5	8.3	4.4	887	19.2	10,690	2.6	$37,737
San Angelo, TX Metro Area	56,312	54,143	53,733	4.0	0.8	3.2	6.5	4.3	2,879	8.1	40,571	10.9	$39,287
Irion, TX	771	873	957	-11.7	-8.8	3.1	5.3	3.6	57	21.3	425	52.9	$54,574
Sterling, TX	582	675	937	-13.8	-28.0	3.3	4.7	2.8	51	88.9	306	39.7	$48,307
Tom Green, TX	54,959	52,595	51,839	4.5	1.5	3.2	6.6	4.3	2,771	7.0	39,840	10.4	$39,055
San Antonio-New Braunfels, TX Metro Area	1,189,665	1,017,400	894,737	16.9	13.7	3.3	7.2	5.0	46,257	14.7	876,237	22.0	$44,360
Atascosa, TX	21,247	19,631	19,011	8.2	3.3	3.8	8.2	5.2	811	28.9	10,887	68.1	$49,236
Bandera, TX	9,920	9,176	9,665	8.1	-5.1	3.4	7.8	4.5	399	10.8	3,198	59.1	$29,584
Bexar, TX	940,900	812,516	714,126	15.8	13.8	3.3	7.3	5.1	36,401	12.0	751,933	19.6	$45,020
Comal, TX	70,132	53,489	48,830	31.1	9.5	3.2	7.0	4.5	3,667	30.7	48,653	37.7	$39,817
Guadalupe, TX	79,824	64,924	51,700	22.9	25.6	3.1	6.7	4.6	2,120	19.1	33,654	33.5	$41,619
Kendall, TX	21,491	16,412	14,298	30.9	14.8	2.9	6.2	4.2	1,376	26.2	13,790	36.5	$42,010
Medina, TX	21,595	20,017	19,420	7.9	3.1	3.5	7.5	4.9	775	21.3	7,626	43.9	$33,157
Wilson, TX	24,556	21,235	17,687	15.6	20.1	3.1	6.8	4.8	708	34.3	6,496	36.0	$33,321
San Diego-Chula Vista-Carlsbad, CA Metro Area	1,592,193	1,515,198	1,489,799	5.1	1.7	3.3	10.8	4.3	85,077	12.2	1,266,620	15.0	$57,617
San Diego, CA	1,592,193	1,515,198	1,489,799	5.1	1.7	3.3	10.8	4.3	85,077	12.2	1,266,620	15.0	$57,617
San Francisco-Oakland-Berkeley, CA Metro Area	2,584,338	2,320,104	2,146,852	11.4	8.1	2.7	9.9	4.8	130,000	10.4	2,167,508	22.6	$90,215
Oakland-Berkeley-Livermore, CA Div	1,412,785	1,308,069	1,244,122	8.0	5.1	3.1	10.9	5.0	64,046	10.5	1,026,993	20.0	$70,760
Alameda, CA	848,215	782,522	734,258	8.4	6.6	3.0	10.9	5.1	40,095	11.3	690,339	22.7	$72,287
Contra Costa, CA	564,570	525,547	509,864	7.4	3.1	3.2	11.0	4.8	23,951	9.4	336,654	14.8	$67,630
San Francisco-San Mateo-Redwood City, CA Div	1,030,442	879,023	773,635	17.2	13.6	2.3	8.7	4.6	55,884	11.2	1,039,154	26.9	$111,757
San Francisco, CA	575,567	486,019	413,337	18.4	17.6	2.4	8.9	5.0	34,518	12.8	653,172	33.1	$104,009
San Mateo, CA	454,875	393,004	360,298	15.7	9.1	2.2	8.4	4.2	21,366	8.6	385,982	17.6	$124,869
San Rafael, CA Div	141,111	133,012	129,095	6.1	3.0	2.4	7.9	3.9	10,070	5.7	101,361	9.3	$66,486
Marin, CA	141,111	133,012	129,095	6.1	3.0	2.4	7.9	3.9	10,070	5.7	101,361	9.3	$66,486
San Jose-Sunnyvale-Santa Clara, CA Metro Area	1,079,673	954,431	839,860	13.1	13.6	2.7	10.5	5.4	49,697	10.4	1,068,403	24.7	$119,305
San Benito, CA	30,869	27,906	24,499	10.6	13.9	5.1	15.1	8.1	986	8.1	12,664	26.9	$45,477
Santa Clara, CA	1,048,804	926,525	815,361	13.2	13.6	2.6	10.4	5.3	48,711	10.4	1,055,739	24.6	$120,191

Table C-4. Labor Force and Private Business Establishments and Employment—*Continued*

Metropolitan Statistical Area Metropolitan Division Component counties	Civilian Labor Force								Private nonfarm businesses				
	Total			Percent change		Unemployment rate			Establishments		Employment		Annual payroll per emplyee 2017 (dollars)
	2018	2010	2005	2010-2018	2005-2010	2018	2010	2005	2017	change 2010-2017	2017	Change 2010-2017	
San Luis Obispo-Paso Robles, CA Metro Area	140,920	133,651	131,479	5.4	1.7	2.9	10.1	4.3	8,402	8.0	91,732	13.9	$44,836
San Luis Obispo, CA	140,920	133,651	131,479	5.4	1.7	2.9	10.1	4.3	8,402	8.0	91,732	13.9	$44,836
Santa Cruz-Watsonville, CA Metro Area	142,618	141,717	142,992	0.6	-0.9	4.9	13.3	6.3	7,061	4.1	79,038	16.1	$47,527
Santa Cruz, CA	142,618	141,717	142,992	0.6	-0.9	4.9	13.3	6.3	7,061	4.1	79,038	16.1	$47,527
Santa Fe, NM Metro Area	73,974	74,289	76,704	-0.4	-3.1	4.1	6.8	4.1	4,759	-0.4	46,842	6.2	$39,945
Santa Fe, NM	73,974	74,289	76,704	-0.4	-3.1	4.1	6.8	4.1	4,759	-0.4	46,842	6.2	$39,945
Santa Maria-Santa Barbara, CA Metro Area	216,698	212,267	213,206	2.1	-0.4	3.9	9.7	4.3	11,761	4.9	149,750	11.3	$52,892
Santa Barbara, CA	216,698	212,267	213,206	2.1	-0.4	3.9	9.7	4.3	11,761	4.9	149,750	11.3	$52,892
Santa Rosa-Petaluma, CA Metro Area	262,348	244,634	253,410	7.2	-3.5	2.7	10.8	4.4	14,174	7.5	173,035	21.0	$52,031
Sonoma, CA	262,348	244,634	253,410	7.2	-3.5	2.7	10.8	4.4	14,174	7.5	173,035	21.0	$52,031
Savannah, GA Metro Area	188,764	167,555	165,458	12.7	1.3	3.6	9.8	4.4	9,244	10.3	151,691	20.6	$42,534
Bryan, GA	17,868	14,455	15,280	23.6	-5.4	3.4	9.6	4.0	670	14.7	5,923	8.3	$30,235
Chatham, GA	140,971	127,323	124,569	10.7	2.2	3.7	9.9	4.6	7,834	10.4	137,942	21.4	$43,169
Effingham, GA	29,925	25,777	25,609	16.1	0.7	3.3	9.6	4.0	740	6.2	7,826	15.7	$40,652
Scranton--Wilkes-Barre, PA Metro Area	276,860	281,094	277,022	-1.5	1.5	5.0	9.5	5.6	13,149	-1.5	237,277	4.9	$40,105
Lackawanna, PA	105,330	106,992	105,324	-1.6	1.6	4.6	9.0	5.3	5,275	-1.8	90,517	-5.5	$39,381
Luzerne, PA	157,784	159,767	157,434	-1.2	1.5	5.4	10.0	5.8	7,210	-1.6	136,040	11.2	$39,801
Wyoming, PA	13,746	14,335	14,264	-4.1	0.5	4.5	8.8	5.2	664	2.6	10,720	31.1	$50,077
Seattle-Tacoma-Bellevue, WA Metro Area	2,113,294	1,888,261	1,727,043	11.9	9.3	3.9	9.7	4.8	106,194	9.7	1,726,886	20.3	$71,091
Seattle-Bellevue-Kent, WA Div	1,689,157	1,492,417	1,357,888	13.2	9.9	3.5	9.4	4.5	88,106	9.9	1,469,804	21.3	$75,252
King, WA	1,258,687	1,105,830	1,011,681	13.8	9.3	3.5	9.0	4.4	69,279	9.7	1,215,664	21.7	$79,392
Snohomish, WA	430,470	386,587	346,207	11.4	11.7	3.8	10.7	4.8	18,827	10.5	254,140	19.4	$55,449
Tacoma-Lakewood, WA Div	424,137	395,844	369,155	7.1	7.2	5.2	10.4	6.1	18,088	9.0	257,082	15.0	$47,301
Pierce, WA	424,137	395,844	369,155	7.1	7.2	5.2	10.4	6.1	18,088	9.0	257,082	15.0	$47,301
Sebastian-Vero Beach, FL Metro Area	65,104	61,384	59,484	6.1	3.2	4.3	13.9	4.8	4,326	11.8	45,434	21.8	$38,359
Indian River, FL	65,104	61,384	59,484	6.1	3.2	4.3	13.9	4.8	4,326	11.8	45,434	21.8	$38,359
Sebring-Avon Park, FL Metro Area	36,472	37,247	39,983	-2.1	-6.8	4.8	12.5	4.2	1,921	-3.0	20,766	10.4	$32,758
Highlands, FL	36,472	37,247	39,983	-2.1	-6.8	4.8	12.5	4.2	1,921	-3.0	20,766	10.4	$32,758
Sheboygan, WI Metro Area	62,903	62,238	64,550	1.1	-3.6	2.5	9.3	4.0	2,659	-0.8	53,151	5.1	$46,328
Sheboygan, WI	62,903	62,238	64,550	1.1	-3.6	2.5	9.3	4.0	2,659	-0.8	53,151	5.1	$46,328
Sherman-Denison, TX Metro Area	63,488	59,489	56,416	6.7	5.4	3.2	8.2	5.4	2,561	1.6	39,443	1.5	$37,840
Grayson, TX	63,488	59,489	56,416	6.7	5.4	3.2	8.2	5.4	2,561	1.6	39,443	1.5	$37,840
Shreveport-Bossier City, LA Metro Area	173,152	184,769	180,450	-6.3	2.4	5.1	7.5	6.0	9,215	0.6	140,406	-4.1	$40,397
Bossier, LA	57,620	56,576	51,496	1.8	9.9	4.3	6.1	5.4	2,495	3.7	37,205	5.6	$33,681
Caddo, LA	104,778	116,799	117,535	-10.3	-0.6	5.5	8.1	6.1	6,293		98,713	-7.5	$42,545
De Soto, LA	10,754	11,394	11,419	-5.6	-0.2	5.7	8.8	6.9	427	7.0	4,488	1.6	$48,844
Sierra Vista-Douglas, AZ Metro Area	49,774	57,023	55,774	-12.7	2.2	5.6	9.3	4.8	2,178	-8.1	24,819	-14.6	$36,161
Cochise, AZ	49,774	57,023	55,774	-12.7	2.2	5.6	9.3	4.8	2,178	-8.1	24,819	-14.6	$36,161
Sioux City, IA-NE-SD Metro Area	77,121	78,145	74,550	-1.3	4.8	2.7	6.5	4.7	3,701	-2.0	67,718	2.8	$39,970
Woodbury, IA	55,149	55,988	53,329	-1.5	5.0	2.5	6.6	4.8	2,639	-4.2	45,206	-2.8	$37,663
Dakota, NE	10,777	11,299	10,531	-4.6	7.3	3.5	7.3	4.7	449	4.2	11,935	18.4	$40,965
Dixon, NE	3,046	3,115	3,144	-2.2	-0.9	3.0	4.8	3.9	103	-8.8	1,035	-1.7	$34,853
Union, SD	8,149	7,743	7,546	5.2	2.6	3.2	5.8	4.0	510	7.1	9,542	15.8	$50,214
Sioux Falls, SD Metro Area	152,131	133,585	120,564	13.9	10.8	2.5	4.8	3.4	7,827	11.4	143,288	16.7	$45,170
Lincoln, SD	33,445	26,317	19,303	27.1	36.3	2.3	3.9	3.0	1,674	49.2	19,756	80.4	$46,289
McCook, SD	3,083	3,241	2,962	-4.9	9.4	2.5	4.9	3.4	192	9.7	979	9.9	$31,772
Minnehaha, SD	110,908	99,177	93,785	11.8	5.7	2.6	5.0	3.5	5,706	4.2	121,091	10.9	$45,205
Turner, SD	4,695	4,850	4,514	-3.2	7.4	2.7	4.6	3.7	255	1.2	1,462	-16.1	$36,111
South Bend-Mishawaka, IN-MI Metro Area	161,106	155,045	161,819	3.9	-4.2	3.6	11.5	5.3	6,592	-1.9	129,862	10.7	$41,101
St. Joseph, IN	136,728	130,462	134,160	4.8	-2.8	3.6	11.6	5.3	5,840	-2.0	122,005	10.5	$41,438
Cass, MI	24,378	24,583	27,659	-0.8	-11.1	4.1	11.4	5.1	752	-1.3	7,857	14.2	$35,859
Spartanburg, SC Metro Area	147,900	131,818	131,691	12.2	0.1	3.1	11.8	7.5	6,430	1.5	128,430	18.5	$45,922
Spartanburg, SC	147,900	131,818	131,691	12.2	0.1	3.1	11.8	7.5	6,430	1.5	128,430	18.5	$45,922
Spokane-Spokane Valley, WA Metro Area	262,435	257,229	242,146	2.0	6.2	5.4	10.3	6.1	14,121	6.5	199,588	10.8	$45,037
Spokane, WA	244,056	238,125	224,140	2.5	6.2	5.2	10.1	5.9	13,224	7.0	192,053	11.0	$45,315
Stevens, WA	18,379	19,104	18,006	-3.8	6.1	7.1	13.1	8.0	897	-0.4	7,535	5.5	$37,950
Springfield, IL Metro Area	111,638	115,866	112,103	-3.6	3.4	4.3	7.7	4.5	5,213	-2.8	85,368	2.6	$41,294
Menard, IL	6,689	7,150	6,982	-6.4	2.4	4.0	7.5	4.4	204	-9.3	1,351	-5.2	$32,549
Sangamon, IL	104,949	108,716	105,121	-3.5	3.4	4.3	7.7	4.5	5,009	-2.5	84,017	2.8	$41,434
Springfield, MA Metro Area	364,152	346,424	351,559	5.1	-1.5	4.0	9.2	5.2	14,743	-0.7	242,907	1.9	$43,461
Franklin, MA	41,365	39,971	39,577	3.5	1.0	3.0	7.6	4.3	1,574		20,307	4.7	$41,847
Hampden, MA	231,265	220,925	224,160	4.7	-1.4	4.6	10.3	5.8	9,584	-1.3	172,044	5.0	$45,113
Hampshire, MA	91,522	85,528	87,822	7.0	-2.6	3.0	7.0	4.0	3,585	1.2	50,556	-8.4	$38,485
Springfield, MO Metro Area	230,332	223,668	212,489	3.0	5.3	2.7	8.8	4.3	11,624	3.6	187,570	14.8	$39,630
Christian, MO	43,619	40,861	37,337	6.7	9.4	2.6	8.4	4.3	1,813	13.0	14,808	19.5	$30,683
Dallas, MO	6,966	7,285	7,448	-4.4	-2.2	3.9	12.6	5.4	286	13.0	2,199	-10.8	$18,544
Greene, MO	148,502	144,734	137,034	2.6	5.6	2.6	8.3	4.2	8,303	2.0	157,027	14.7	$40,911
Polk, MO	14,329	14,405	13,964	-0.5	3.2	3.6	10.3	4.9	563	-2.1	7,784	13.9	$42,646
Webster, MO	16,916	16,383	16,706	3.3	-1.9	3.1	10.5	4.7	659	2.2	5,752	18.0	$31,678
Springfield, OH Metro Area	62,963	68,266	70,529	-7.8	-3.2	4.6	11.0	6.5	2,238	-8.6	41,243	1.4	$36,101
Clark, OH	62,963	68,266	70,529	-7.8	-3.2	4.6	11.0	6.5	2,238	-8.6	41,243	1.4	$36,101
State College, PA Metro Area	79,859	77,338	72,388	3.3	6.8	3.2	5.9	4.0	3,361	5.4	46,119	7.1	$39,277
Centre, PA	79,859	77,338	72,388	3.3	6.8	3.2	5.9	4.0	3,361	5.4	46,119	7.1	$39,277
Staunton, VA Metro Area	59,303	59,146	57,325	0.3	3.2	2.8	7.6	3.2	2,812	0.5	40,023	5.6	$38,078

Table C-4. Labor Force and Private Business Establishments and Employment—*Continued*

Metropolitan Statistical Area Metropolitan Division Component counties	Civilian Labor Force								Private nonfarm businesses				
	Total			Percent change		Unemployment rate			Establishments		Employment		Annual payroll per emplyee 2017 (dollars)
	2018	2010	2005	2010-2018	2005-2010	2018	2010	2005	2017	change 2010-2017	2017	Change 2010-2017	
Augusta, VA	36,922	37,130	36,267	-0.6	2.4	2.7	7.1	3.1	1,423	2.4	20,507	10.7	$41,981
Staunton City, VA	11,920	11,846	11,231	0.6	5.5	2.9	7.8	3.3	767	-1.5	10,539	4.2	$31,802
Waynesboro City, VA	10,461	10,170	9,827	2.9	3.5	3.2	9.0	3.8	622		8,977	-2.8	$36,529
Stockton, CA Metro Area	326,387	311,437	283,588	4.8	9.8	6.0	16.5	7.9	11,512	6.3	190,958	18.9	$44,060
San Joaquin, CA	326,387	311,437	283,588	4.8	9.8	6.0	16.5	7.9	11,512	6.3	190,958	18.9	$44,060
Sumter, SC Metro Area	56,668	58,300	59,188	-2.8	-1.5	4.2	12.8	8.7	2,227	-4.6	36,794	10.3	$35,116
Clarendon, SC	12,548	13,881	12,742	-9.6	8.9	4.7	14.0	9.7	474	-7.6	5,396	-6.1	$27,052
Sumter, SC	44,120	44,419	46,446	-0.7	-4.4	4.0	12.5	8.5	1,753	-3.7	31,398	13.7	$36,502
Syracuse, NY Metro Area	306,225	331,466	330,039	-7.6	0.4	4.3	8.5	4.9	15,252	-0.2	259,742	3.0	$44,355
Madison, NY	32,630	35,586	36,109	-8.3	-1.4	4.8	8.3	5.1	1,402	-1.1	17,655	2.4	$36,535
Onondaga, NY	220,771	236,994	233,689	-6.8	1.4	4.0	8.0	4.5	11,714	-0.3	217,471	2.7	$45,186
Oswego, NY	52,824	58,886	60,241	-10.3	-2.2	5.5	10.6	6.2	2,136	1.2	24,616	5.3	$42,629
Tallahassee, FL Metro Area	193,504	190,683	179,409	1.5	6.3	3.5	8.4	3.2	9,067	4.4	110,687	6.8	$40,254
Gadsden, FL	18,500	20,080	20,488	-7.9	-2.0	4.6	11.8	3.9	653	1.1	7,936	-10.5	$43,668
Jefferson, FL	5,582	6,042	6,814	-7.6	-11.3	3.7	9.9	3.2	256	-1.2	1,628	-2.7	$33,127
Leon, FL	154,655	149,972	137,708	3.1	8.9	3.3	7.9	3.2	7,711	4.7	97,668	8.6	$40,414
Wakulla, FL	14,767	14,589	14,399	1.2	1.3	3.1	8.4	2.8	447	7.2	3,455	9.5	$31,265
Tampa-St. Petersburg-Clearwater, FL Metro Area	1,530,842	1,384,699	1,258,615	10.6	10.0	3.5	11.1	4.0	78,570	13.3	1,120,203	20.2	$47,392
Hernando, FL	70,465	66,470	57,093	6.0	16.4	4.5	13.5	4.9	3,311	13.0	35,165	23.4	$33,087
Hillsborough, FL	735,690	645,687	570,252	13.9	13.2	3.4	10.7	3.8	36,819	15.6	601,133	22.8	$50,558
Pasco, FL	231,983	207,364	177,737	11.9	16.7	3.8	11.9	4.4	9,686	16.3	98,898	31.3	$36,060
Pinellas, FL	492,704	465,178	453,533	5.9	2.6	3.3	10.8	3.9	28,754	9.5	385,007	13.6	$46,666
Terre Haute, IN Metro Area	84,428	88,535	88,748	-4.6	-0.2	4.4	11.2	6.9	3,811	-4.6	59,212	-2.3	$37,585
Clay, IN	12,332	13,180	13,314	-6.4		3.9	11.1	7.0	473	-5.4	5,948	18.7	$33,310
Parke, IN	7,169	7,332	8,111	-2.2	-9.6	4.0	10.9	6.5	266	4.7	2,118	-0.2	$33,521
Sullivan, IN	8,616	9,085	9,294	-5.2	-2.2	4.7	10.1	7.5	334	-5.4	4,066	16.3	$39,188
Vermillion, IN	7,169	7,810	8,131	-8.2	-3.9	5.5	12.9	7.4	268	-6.6	3,399	-14.2	$50,368
Vigo, IN	49,142	51,128	49,898	-3.9	2.5	4.4	11.2	6.8	2,470	-5.1	43,681	-5.0	$37,221
Texarkana, TX-AR Metro Area	64,702	68,991	68,421	-6.2	0.8	4.9	7.6	5.2	3,138	2.3	48,004	7.3	$35,635
Little River, AR	5,485	6,220	6,529	-11.8	-4.7	5.3	7.7	4.7	175	3.6	2,726	-6.0	$50,355
Miller, AR	19,722	20,560	19,724	-4.1	4.2	4.8	5.8	4.8	739	3.1	11,235	0.1	$35,550
Bowie, TX	39,495	42,211	42,168	-6.4	0.1	4.9	8.4	5.4	2,224	2.0	34,043	11.2	$34,484
The Villages, FL Metro Area	31,241	25,310	25,555	23.4	-1.0	5.1	13.3	3.4	1,575	38.5	22,470	57.6	$37,753
Sumter, FL	31,241	25,310	25,555	23.4	-1.0	5.1	13.3	3.4	1,575	38.5	22,470	57.6	$37,753
Toledo, OH Metro Area	322,711	331,794	337,591	-2.7	-1.7	5.0	11.3	6.7	14,444	-1.5	275,095	6.1	$44,904
Fulton, OH	22,228	23,144	23,151	-4.0	0.0	4.4	11.8	6.3	958	-1.4	16,206	9.3	$42,434
Lucas, OH	209,136	217,424	224,694	-3.8	-3.2	5.3	11.5	7.0	9,655	-2.9	192,945	2.4	$45,762
Ottawa, OH	20,986	22,678	21,855	-7.5	3.8	6.3	12.3	7.9	1,047	2.6	10,370	4.1	$42,998
Wood, OH	70,361	68,548	67,891	2.6	1.0	4.0	9.9	5.8	2,784	2.0	55,574	20.7	$43,004
Topeka, KS Metro Area	120,102	124,269	123,539	-3.4	0.6	3.5	7.1	5.5	5,146	-4.7	85,514	-0.7	$43,724
Jackson, KS	7,217	7,509	7,157	-3.9	4.9	3.0	6.2	5.8	255	-5.6	3,293	11.4	$27,980
Jefferson, KS	10,167	10,671	10,146	-4.7	5.2	3.3	7.5	5.2	323	0.6	2,313	-2.2	$37,738
Osage, KS	7,945	8,618	9,123	-7.8	-5.5	3.8	8.3	6.2	242	-10.4	1,586	-51.8	$32,294
Shawnee, KS	91,125	93,584	93,338	-2.6	0.3	3.5	7.0	5.5	4,193	-5.0	77,376	1.1	$44,979
Wabaunsee, KS	3,648	3,887	3,775	-6.1	3.0	3.2	6.5	4.5	133	6.4	946	-0.4	$29,707
Trenton-Princeton, NJ Metro Area	196,494	192,673	193,721	2.0	-0.5	3.7	8.4	3.9	9,732	-0.2	196,384	11.7	$68,407
Mercer, NJ	196,494	192,673	193,721	2.0	-0.5	3.7	8.4	3.9	9,732	-0.2	196,384	11.7	$68,407
Tucson, AZ Metro Area	486,261	478,743	441,581	1.6	8.4	4.5	9.3	4.5	20,300	-0.1	320,502	6.4	$41,905
Pima, AZ	486,261	478,743	441,581	1.6	8.4	4.5	9.3	4.5	20,300	-0.1	320,502	6.4	$41,905
Tulsa, OK Metro Area	479,874	462,935	442,814	3.7	4.5	3.5	7.3	4.4	24,510	1.8	401,196	9.1	$47,411
Creek, OK	31,623	31,807	32,063	-0.6	-0.8	3.8	8.6	5.7	1,348	-4.3	15,877	8.4	$41,271
Okmulgee, OK	15,918	16,887	16,816	-5.7	0.4	4.9	9.8	6.3	660	-5.7	6,538	-13.0	$32,492
Osage, OK	20,848	21,250	20,773	-1.9	2.3	4.3	7.8	4.8	599	-2.3	5,854	2.6	$33,983
Pawnee, OK	7,411	7,675	7,798	-3.4	-1.6	4.1	9.1	5.0	254	-12.1	2,693	9.3	$58,402
Rogers, OK	44,792	43,377	39,849	3.3	8.9	3.3	6.9	4.0	1,741	6.0	27,568	18.5	$49,086
Tulsa, OK	322,030	306,671	293,516	5.0	4.5	3.3	7.0	4.1	18,963	2.4	334,617	9.2	$48,256
Wagoner, OK	37,252	35,268	31,999	5.6	10.2	3.3	6.8	4.1	945	4.1	8,049	2.7	$36,846
Tuscaloosa, AL Metro Area	118,203	111,365	103,279	6.1	7.8	3.9	10.1	4.1	4,644	0.9	85,304	12.1	$40,840
Greene, AL	2,838	3,306	3,456	-14.2	-4.3	6.7	17.3	6.7	99	-7.5	1,256	-8.7	$34,708
Hale, AL	5,991	6,445	7,053	-7.0	-8.6	5.1	15.1	5.4	178	-7.3	1,921	-9.8	$36,179
Pickens, AL	7,805	7,699	7,960	1.4	-3.3	4.6	13.1	5.4	256	-11.4	2,654	-5.3	$32,523
Tuscaloosa, AL	101,569	93,915	84,810	8.1	10.7	3.7	9.2	3.7	4,111	2.4	79,473	13.9	$41,328
Twin Falls, ID Metro Area	52,710	47,870	47,048	10.1	1.7	2.7	8.4	3.7	3,223	5.6	37,498	16.4	$33,963
Jerome, ID	11,963	11,005	9,943	8.7	10.7	2.5	8.1	3.7	570	6.3	6,525	20.4	$38,256
Twin Falls, ID	40,747	36,865	37,105	10.5	-0.6	2.7	8.5	3.7	2,653	5.4	30,973	15.6	$33,058
Tyler, TX Metro Area	107,543	101,151	95,360	6.3	6.1	3.6	7.9	5.0	5,822	7.0	89,833	5.4	$41,667
Smith, TX	107,543	101,151	95,360	6.3	6.1	3.6	7.9	5.0	5,822	7.0	89,833	5.4	$41,667
Urban Honolulu, HI Metro Area	465,193	446,189	439,257	4.3	1.6	2.3	6.0	2.8	21,628	0.2	366,570	9.1	$46,945
Honolulu, HI	465,193	446,189	439,257	4.3	1.6	2.3	6.0	2.8	21,628	0.2	366,570	9.1	$46,945
Utica-Rome, NY Metro Area	129,719	143,800	142,904	-9.8	0.6	4.5	7.8	4.9	6,029	-0.7	100,149	0.4	$39,596
Herkimer, NY	27,990	31,552	31,671	-11.3	-0.4	4.9	8.6	5.3	1,130	-3.3	12,200	1.8	$37,177
Oneida, NY	101,729	112,248	111,233	-9.4	0.9	4.4	7.6	4.8	4,899	0.0	87,949	0.2	$39,931
Valdosta, GA Metro Area	64,535	64,076	64,829	0.7	-1.2	4.0	9.6	4.0	3,127	3.6	44,264	10.2	$33,279

Table C-4. Labor Force and Private Business Establishments and Employment—*Continued*

Metropolitan Statistical Area / Metropolitan Division / Component counties	Civilian Labor Force								Private nonfarm businesses				
	Total			Percent change		Unemployment rate			Establishments		Employment		Annual payroll per emplyee 2017 (dollars)
	2018	2010	2005	2010-2018	2005-2010	2018	2010	2005	2017	change 2010-2017	2017	Change 2010-2017	
Brooks, GA	7,044	7,309	8,289	-3.6	-11.8	3.9	9.6	4.3	211	6.0	2,189	9.7	$31,763
Echols, GA	1,900	1,876	2,314	1.3	-18.9	3.2	8.2	3.4	29	61.1	112	0.0	$35,384
Lanier, GA	3,845	3,872	3,810	-0.7	1.6	4.4	10.5	4.0	88	-20.7	848	-8.2	$28,940
Lowndes, GA	51,746	51,019	50,416	1.4	1.2	4.1	9.6	4.0	2,799	4.1	41,115	10.4	$33,443
Vallejo, CA Metro Area	209,721	202,407	208,486	3.6	-2.9	3.9	12.6	5.3	7,079	5.0	111,931	14.2	$51,136
Solano, CA	209,721	202,407	208,486	3.6	-2.9	3.9	12.6	5.3	7,079	5.0	111,931	14.2	$51,136
Victoria, TX Metro Area	46,675	46,435	47,296	0.5	-1.8	3.8	7.6	4.5	2,434	2.9	33,922	8.1	$43,066
Goliad, TX	3,305	3,356	3,397	-1.5	-1.2	3.8	7.4	4.8	124	12.7	841	6.3	$42,012
Victoria, TX	43,370	43,079	43,899	0.7	-1.9	3.8	7.7	4.5	2,310	2.4	33,081	8.1	$43,093
Vineland-Bridgeton, NJ Metro Area	64,289	72,664	69,082	-11.5	5.2	6.5	13.0	6.4	2,815	-5.2	47,231	4.9	$39,809
Cumberland, NJ	64,289	72,664	69,082	-11.5	5.2	6.5	13.0	6.4	2,815	-5.2	47,231	4.9	$39,809
Virginia Beach-Norfolk-Newport News, VA-NC Met	866,920	851,672	807,905	1.8	5.4	3.3	7.6	4.0	38,430	0.4	621,229	3.4	$42,640
Camden, NC	4,650	4,594	4,374	1.2	5.0	3.7	8.4	4.1	117	-1.7	533	-8.6	$29,953
Currituck, NC	13,633	12,189	12,065	11.8	1.0	3.6	8.9	3.0	665	13.9	4,577	18.3	$35,033
Gates, NC	5,309	5,460	4,918	-2.8	11.0	4.0	8.0	4.1	125	-3.8	880	-0.5	$27,189
Gloucester, VA	19,445	19,553	19,798	-0.6	-1.2	2.7	6.8	3.1	853	-4.7	7,418	1.5	$28,542
Isle of Wight, VA	19,135	18,800	17,369	1.8	8.2	3.0	7.1	3.7	670	4.5	9,690	-0.3	$47,868
James City County, VA	36,069	32,243	28,790	11.9	12.0	2.9	6.3	3.2	1,711	4.5	27,987	22.5	$37,717
Mathews, VA	4,111	4,224	4,396	-2.7	-3.9	3.0	6.3	3.0	188	5.0	1,095	12.8	$23,516
Southampton, VA	9,024	9,495	7,523	-5.0	26.2	2.8	8.6	4.2	217	-8.1	2,220	-29.2	$40,740
York, VA	32,590	31,289	30,554	4.2	2.4	2.8	6.1	3.1	1,462	0.8	19,156	10.4	$34,634
Chesapeake City, VA	121,125	113,319	111,678	6.9	1.5	3.0	7.2	3.6	5,461	1.4	91,514	10.5	$42,145
Franklin City, VA	3,587	3,708	3,725	-3.3	-0.5	4.4	12.6	5.2	271	-9.7	3,393	-4.6	$28,492
Hampton City, VA	64,378	66,666	66,763	-3.4	-0.1	4.0	9.0	4.5	2,347	-2.7	42,050	0.4	$42,003
Newport News City, VA	88,872	90,664	86,290	-2.0	5.1	3.6	8.3	4.5	3,794	0.9	89,422	4.4	$50,499
Norfolk City, VA	111,524	112,449	96,113	-0.8	17.0	3.6	8.8	5.1	5,377	-7.9	105,106	-8.5	$46,937
Poquoson City, VA	6,288	6,395	6,161	-1.7	3.8	2.7	6.1	2.9	212	-4.5	1,429	-1.7	$27,355
Portsmouth City, VA	44,095	45,461	44,821	-3.0	1.4	4.1	9.6	5.4	1,649	-6.7	25,286	-11.0	$41,092
Suffolk City, VA	44,014	41,753	37,792	5.4	10.5	3.2	7.6	4.0	1,649	10.1	22,489	8.7	$39,773
Virginia Beach City, VA	232,342	226,894	220,002	2.4	3.1	2.9	6.5	3.4	11,132	3.5	157,627	8.9	$40,358
Williamsburg City, VA	6,729	6,516	4,773	3.3	36.5	4.0	10.1	7.3	530	10.4	9,357	-4.5	$29,431
Visalia, CA Metro Area	204,589	203,021	183,305	0.8	10.8	9.6	17.2	9.4	6,413	4.5	96,618	13.1	$39,422
Tulare, CA	204,589	203,021	183,305	0.8	10.8	9.6	17.2	9.4	6,413	4.5	96,618	13.1	$39,422
Waco, TX Metro Area	125,454	120,142	119,278	4.4	0.7	3.6	7.4	5.1	5,525	7.2	105,047	8.3	$38,623
Falls, TX	6,668	7,242	7,276	-7.9	-0.5	3.9	8.5	6.2	223	-4.3	1,655	-9.6	$31,496
McLennan, TX	118,786	112,900	112,002	5.2	0.8	3.6	7.4	5.0	5,302	7.8	103,392	8.6	$38,737
Walla Walla, WA Metro Area	29,270	30,530	28,983	-4.1	5.3	4.7	8.0	6.1	1,385	0.2	20,322	3.2	$39,598
Walla Walla, WA	29,270	30,530	28,983	-4.1	5.3	4.7	8.0	6.1	1,385	0.2	20,322	3.2	$39,598
Warner Robins, GA Metro Area	82,108	80,017	73,947	2.6	8.2	4.2	9.0	5.1	3,017	7.9	45,297	13.7	$34,810
Houston, GA	70,197	67,099	62,594	4.6	7.2	4.0	8.5	4.8	2,548	10.7	38,741	15.1	$34,300
Peach, GA	11,911	12,918	11,353	-7.8	13.8	5.1	12.1	6.7	469	-5.4	6,556	6.0	$37,826
Washington-Arlington-Alexandria, DC-VA-MD-WV Metro Area	3,400,352	3,157,966	2,911,638	7.7	8.5	3.3	6.3	3.5	154,605	8.6	2,676,308	12.2	$66,024
Frederick-Gaithersburg-Rockville, MD Div	685,820	660,485	624,759	3.8	5.7	3.2	5.9	3.1	33,674	4.5	529,923	10.1	$61,143
Frederick, MD	130,831	127,913	120,349	2.3	6.3	3.5	6.9	3.1	6,214	7.2	89,981	11.1	$48,623
Montgomery, MD	554,989	532,572	504,410	4.2	5.6	3.2	5.6	3.1	27,460	3.9	439,942	9.9	$63,704
Washington-Arlington-Alexandria, DC-VA-MD-WV Division	2,714,532	2,497,481	2,286,879	8.7	9.2	3.3	6.5	3.6	120,931	9.7	2,146,385	12.7	$67,230
District of Columbia	404,610	346,065	315,616	16.9	9.6	5.6	9.4	6.4	23,585	9.7	527,004	13.8	$77,798
Calvert, MD	49,121	47,831	46,014	2.7	3.9	3.5	6.9	3.4	1,745	1.5	19,038	10.9	$46,175
Charles, MD	85,104	78,222	72,704	8.8	7.6	3.9	6.9	3.4	2,625	-1.6	32,830	4.4	$38,827
Prince George's, MD	504,423	479,626	442,341	5.2	8.4	4.1	7.5	4.5	15,300	7.4	266,260	11.9	$48,515
Arlington, VA	151,720	137,368	123,328	10.4	11.4	2.0	4.1	2.3	6,386	6.1	140,158	11.1	$81,204
Clarke, VA	7,545	7,695	7,738	-1.9	-0.6	2.9	6.7	2.6	353	-10.9	2,969	-8.3	$43,350
Culpeper, VA	24,178	23,263	19,022	3.9	22.3	2.8	7.2	3.3	1,019	7.6	12,752	13.6	$41,470
Fairfax, VA	630,229	610,521	568,187	3.2	7.5	2.4	5.1	2.6	31,388	9.1	613,931	9.8	$79,057
Fauquier, VA	36,319	35,763	35,413	1.6	1.0	2.6	6.2	2.7	1,899	6.4	18,900	17.0	$46,990
Loudoun, VA	216,433	175,439	147,280	23.4	19.1	2.5	5.1	2.4	10,605	31.4	160,171	36.5	$60,565
Madison, VA	7,261	7,169	7,172	1.3	0.0	2.4	6.3	3.1	269	-2.2	2,433	-5.9	$31,979
Prince William, VA	241,651	218,394	189,649	10.6	15.2	2.7	6.1	2.7	8,233	18.1	102,183	22.6	$45,395
Rappahannock, VA	3,701	4,025	4,112	-8.0	-2.1	2.7	6.3	2.6	211	14.7	1,078	16.9	$37,551
Spotsylvania, VA	66,032	63,357	61,880	4.2	2.4	3.0	7.0	2.7	2,522	9.9	30,960	20.5	$36,691
Stafford, VA	70,084	63,904	61,558	9.7	3.8	3.0	6.5	2.7	2,331	13.1	33,497	18.7	$42,678
Warren, VA	20,094	20,103	18,604	0.0	8.1	3.1	8.1	3.1	829	3.6	10,847	18.7	$35,914
Alexandria City, VA	100,409	90,361	84,746	11.1	6.6	2.2	4.9	2.6	4,670	4.0	82,656	4.9	$62,869
Fairfax City, VA	13,113	12,663	12,777	3.6	-0.9	2.3	5.4	2.7	1,982	-13.9	25,910	-6.7	$53,273
Falls Church City, VA	8,436	7,382	6,428	14.3	14.8	2.1	4.9	3.4	878	9.3	10,636	13.5	$51,109
Fredericksburg City, VA	13,690	12,423	11,225	10.2	10.7	3.5	9.0	4.5	1,401	5.5	20,124	-2.1	$41,895
Manassas City, VA	21,856	20,972	20,522	4.2	2.2	2.7	7.0	2.9	1,503	6.7	16,377	-26.4	$49,541
Manassas Park City, VA	8,944	8,066	6,519	10.9	23.7	2.7	6.2	2.5	327	16.0	3,177	6.6	$47,033
Jefferson, WV	29,579	26,869	24,044	10.1	11.7	3.3	6.7	3.3	870	1.0	12,494	27.5	$34,383
Waterloo-Cedar Falls, IA Metro Area	89,342	91,593	92,114	-2.5	-0.6	2.6	6.0	4.2	4,100	-0.8	75,798	0.8	$41,548
Black Hawk, IA	68,953	70,978	71,506	-2.9	-0.7	2.8	6.2	4.3	3,186	-1.3	63,375	-1.4	$41,165
Bremer, IA	13,845	13,861	13,732	-0.1	0.9	2.0	4.9	3.7	615	1.2	9,404	14.2	$42,037

Table C-4. Labor Force and Private Business Establishments and Employment—*Continued*

Metropolitan Statistical Area Metropolitan Division Component counties	Civilian Labor Force								Private nonfarm businesses				
	Total			Percent change		Unemployment rate			Establishments		Employment		Annual payroll per emplyee 2017 (dollars)
	2018	2010	2005	2010-2018	2005-2010	2018	2010	2005	2017	change 2010-2017	2017	Change 2010-2017	
Grundy, IA	6,544	6,754	6,876	-3.1	-1.8	2.5	5.7	3.8	299	1.0	3,019	10.7	$48,058
Watertown-Fort Drum, NY Metro Area	44,691	50,310	47,105	-11.2	6.8	5.6	9.3	6.1	2,444	-2.1	29,772	-0.7	$36,967
Jefferson, NY	44,691	50,310	47,105	-11.2	6.8	5.6	9.3	6.1	2,444	-2.1	29,772	-0.7	$36,967
Wausau-Weston, WI Metro Area	89,436	89,181	90,188	0.3	-1.1	2.8	9.6	4.3	4,082	-0.8	73,859	9.9	$42,541
Lincoln, WI	15,363	15,661	15,824	-1.9	-1.0	3.2	11.3	5.4	692	-3.6	8,706	4.6	$40,890
Marathon, WI	74,073	73,520	74,364	0.8	-1.1	2.7	9.3	4.1	3,390	-0.2	65,153	10.7	$42,761
Weirton-Steubenville, WV-OH Metro Area	50,206	58,426	57,537	-14.1	1.5	6.2	13.3	7.6	2,190	-7.2	33,975	-8.5	$37,464
Jefferson, OH	27,538	33,335	31,747	-17.4	5.0	6.3	14.5	7.7	1,252	-6.8	18,189	-5.9	$37,728
Brooke, WV	9,822	10,917	11,095	-10.0	-1.6	6.1	11.4	7.3	374	-6.7	7,262	-7.9	$38,390
Hancock, WV	12,846	14,174	14,695	-9.4	-3.5	5.9	12.1	7.4	564	-8.4	8,524	-14.2	$36,111
Wenatchee, WA Metro Area	67,183	61,978	59,416	8.4	4.3	4.8	9.2	6.0	3,381	8.9	37,026	15.4	$41,733
Chelan, WA	45,580	42,102	39,450	8.3	6.7	4.5	8.9	6.2	2,604	7.4	29,376	12.7	$43,222
Douglas, WA	21,603	19,876	19,966	8.7	-0.5	5.3	9.7	5.7	777	13.9	7,650	26.8	$36,014
Wheeling, WV-OH Metro Area	66,156	69,968	68,509	-5.4	2.1	5.3	9.9	5.9	3,304	-4.5	54,735	1.1	$41,270
Belmont, OH	30,588	33,462	32,494	-8.6	3.0	5.5	11.3	6.6	1,436	-3.8	19,443	4.7	$37,445
Marshall, WV	14,237	14,680	15,048	-3.0	-2.4	5.8	9.7	5.8	484	-1.8	8,707	6.7	$46,632
Ohio, WV	21,331	21,826	20,967	-2.3	4.1	4.6	7.9	4.9	1,384	-6.0	26,585	-3.0	$42,312
Wichita, KS Metro Area	306,191	315,454	307,282	-2.9	2.7	3.7	8.6	5.4	14,811	0.7	261,264	2.2	$44,430
Butler, KS	31,938	33,009	32,038	-3.2	3.0	3.5	7.8	5.5	1,348	4.8	13,659	2.9	$36,612
Harvey, KS	16,864	17,774	18,030	-5.1	-1.4	3.2	7.2	4.5	760	-6.7	13,087	4.6	$34,365
Sedgwick, KS	246,605	252,713	244,942	-2.4	3.2	3.8	8.8	5.5	12,225	0.9	230,156	2.2	$45,688
Sumner, KS	10,784	11,958	12,272	-9.8	-2.6	3.5	8.9	5.9	478	-2.8	4,362	-4.4	$32,705
Wichita Falls, TX Metro Area	65,868	69,420	74,253	-5.1	-6.5	3.4	7.7	4.5	3,424	-3.1	46,665	-1.4	$35,663
Archer, TX	4,184	4,601	5,289	-9.1	-13.0	3.1	6.7	3.5	213	15.8	1,109	-11.4	$36,459
Clay, TX	4,945	5,539	6,476	-10.7	-14.5	3.2	7.5	3.8	142	10.9	757	-22.0	$31,215
Wichita, TX	56,739	59,280	62,488	-4.3	-5.1	3.4	7.8	4.7	3,069	-4.7	44,799	-0.7	$35,718
Williamsport, PA Metro Area	57,134	59,485	59,297	-4.0	0.3	4.8	8.9	5.4	2,731	-4.3	43,915		$39,257
Lycoming, PA	57,134	59,485	59,297	-4.0	0.3	4.8	8.9	5.4	2,731	-4.3	43,915		$39,257
Wilmington, NC Metro Area	149,245	132,029	119,805	13.0	10.2	3.8	10.0	4.2	8,639	13.6	108,659	22.2	$41,195
New Hanover, NC	120,980	107,583	97,891	12.5	9.9	3.7	9.7	4.1	7,545	12.7	99,662	22.0	$42,127
Pender, NC	28,265	24,446	21,914	15.6	11.6	4.1	11.4	4.8	1,094	20.9	8,997	24.9	$30,864
Winchester, VA-WV Metro Area	71,900	65,434	61,426	9.9	6.5	2.9	7.9	3.1	3,232	5.3	55,560	25.0	$40,475
Frederick, VA	46,803	41,981	38,283	11.5	9.7	2.6	7.5	2.8	1,536	7.6	26,980	32.0	$41,858
Winchester City, VA	14,588	13,688	13,740	6.6	-0.4	2.9	8.3	3.1	1,372	5.1	25,971	21.7	$40,270
Hampshire, WV	10,509	9,765	9,403	7.6	3.8	4.2	9.1	4.1	324	-3.6	2,609	-1.6	$28,207
Winston-Salem, NC Metro Area	326,280	314,927	309,332	3.6	1.8	3.7	10.9	5.0	13,488	2.9	237,640	12.6	$46,067
Davidson, NC	80,112	80,622	78,306	-0.6	3.0	3.7	12.3	6.0	2,797	0.9	37,652	12.2	$37,940
Davie, NC	20,474	20,258	19,826	1.1	2.2	3.4	11.7	4.2	827	4.4	9,444	18.1	$33,472
Forsyth, NC	186,122	173,002	168,092	7.6	2.9	3.8	10.1	4.7	8,604	3.5	175,590	12.5	$49,673
Stokes, NC	21,781	22,847	23,944	-4.7	-4.6	3.6	11.4	5.0	647	6.2	6,305	14.8	$29,869
Yadkin, NC	17,791	18,198	19,164	-2.2	-5.0	3.4	11.0	4.6	613	-1.6	8,649	9.4	$33,794
Worcester, MA-CT Metro Area	514,096	484,973	459,459	6.0	5.6	3.7	9.0	5.3	20,570	4.0	337,022	14.1	$49,339
Windham, CT	63,426	64,653	60,903	-1.9	6.2	4.5	10.3	5.5	2,119	-1.4	31,180	10.3	$39,467
Worcester, MA	450,670	420,320	398,556	7.2	5.5	3.5	8.8	5.2	18,451	4.7	305,842	14.5	$50,345
Yakima, WA Metro Area	129,176	122,140	117,560	5.8	3.9	6.3	10.6	7.8	4,765	1.7	70,083	12.3	$40,427
Yakima, WA	129,176	122,140	117,560	5.8	3.9	6.3	10.6	7.8	4,765	1.7	70,083	12.3	$40,427
York-Hanover, PA Metro Area	234,141	230,402	218,916	1.6	5.2	3.9	8.4	4.2	8,689	1.3	167,130	9.8	$43,550
York, PA	234,141	230,402	218,916	1.6	5.2	3.9	8.4	4.2	8,689	1.3	167,130	9.8	$43,550
Youngstown-Warren-Boardman, OH-PA Metro Area	241,186	268,563	281,253	-10.2	-4.5	5.8	11.8	6.9	12,205	-5.0	192,993	-2.1	$36,959
Mahoning, OH	103,437	115,100	119,944	-10.1	-4.0	5.9	11.7	7.1	5,477	-5.5	86,091	3.3	$36,651
Trumbull, OH	87,662	99,834	105,645	-12.2	-5.5	6.2	13.2	7.0	3,963	-7.2	61,808	-12.4	$38,543
Mercer, PA	50,087	53,629	55,664	-6.6	-3.7	4.7	9.5	6.3	2,765	-0.7	45,094	4.1	$35,376
Yuba City, CA Metro Area	74,555	75,029	65,683	-0.6	14.2	7.0	18.1	9.4	2,599	3.0	32,176	11.2	$43,001
Sutter, CA	45,477	45,965	39,999	-1.1	14.9	7.5	18.4	9.6	1,780	4.4	21,864	10.8	$41,865
Yuba, CA	29,078	29,064	25,684	0.0	13.2	6.4	17.8	9.0	819	0.0	10,312	12.1	$45,410
Yuma, AZ Metro Area	97,636	92,816	76,067	5.2	22.0	17.0	25.1	15.9	3,037	3.1	45,094	11.0	$33,226
Yuma, AZ	97,636	92,816	76,067	5.2	22.0	17.0	25.1	15.9	3,037	3.1	45,094	11.0	$33,226

PART D

MICROPOLITAN AREAS

Table D-1. Population and Personal Income

Metropolitan or Micropolitan Statistical Area Metropolitan Division Component Counties	Population							Personal Income					
	2018 Estimate (July 1)	2010 census estimates base (April 1)	2000 census estimates base (April 1)	Net change		Percent change		Total (million dollars)		Percent change 2010-2018	Per capita	
				2010-2018	2000-2010	2010-2018	2000-2010	2018	2010		2018	2010
	1	2	3	4	5	6	7	8	9	10	11	12
Aberdeen, SD Micro area	43,191	40,603	39,827	2,588	776	6.4	1.9	2,271.7	1,674.3	35.7	$52,596	$41,120
Brown County, SD	39,316	36,532	35,460	2,784	1,072	7.6	3.0	2,070.1	1,521.9	36.0	$52,652	$41,524
Edmunds County, SD	3,875	4,071	4,367	-196	-296	-4.8	-6.8	201.6	152.3	32.4	$52,029	$37,474
Aberdeen, WA Micro area	73,901	72,798	67,194	1,103	5,604	1.5	8.3	2,987.8	2,227.6	34.1	$40,429	$30,581
Grays Harbor County, WA	73,901	72,798	67,194	1,103	5,604	1.5	8.3	2,987.8	2,227.6	34.1	$40,429	$30,581
Abilene, TX Metro area	171,451	165,246	160,245	6,205	5,001	3.8	3.1	7,396.5	5,705.3	29.6	$43,140	$34,456
Callahan County, TX	13,994	13,546	12,905	448	641	3.3	5.0	551.2	402.0	37.1	$39,392	$29,749
Jones County, TX	19,817	20,192	20,785	-375	-593	-1.9	-2.9	605.6	517.1	17.1	$30,559	$25,551
Taylor County, TX	137,640	131,508	126,555	6,132	4,953	4.7	3.9	6,239.6	4,786.2	30.4	$45,333	$36,305
Ada, OK Micro area	38,247	37,490	35,143	757	2,347	2.0	6.7	1,650.3	1,279.0	29.0	$43,148	$34,017
Pontotoc County, OK	38,247	37,490	35,143	757	2,347	2.0	6.7	1,650.3	1,279.0	29.0	$43,148	$34,017
Adrian, MI Micro area	98,266	99,892	98,890	-1,626	1,002	-1.6	1.0	3,891.3	3,017.6	29.0	$39,600	$30,287
Lenawee County, MI	98,266	99,892	98,890	-1,626	1,002	-1.6	1.0	3,891.3	3,017.6	29.0	$39,600	$30,287
Akron, OH Metro area	704,845	703,203	694,960	1,642	8,243	0.2	1.2	34,835.2	26,886.7	29.6	$49,423	$38,244
Portage County, OH	162,927	161,425	152,061	1,502	9,364	0.9	6.2	7,177.8	5,497.8	30.6	$44,055	$34,065
Summit County, OH	541,918	541,778	542,899	140	-1,121	0.0	-0.2	27,657.4	21,388.9	29.3	$51,036	$39,489
Alamogordo, NM Micro area	66,781	63,832	62,298	2,949	1,534	4.6	2.5	2,313.0	2,005.5	15.3	$34,636	$31,142
Otero County, NM	66,781	63,832	62,298	2,949	1,534	4.6	2.5	2,313.0	2,005.5	15.3	$34,636	$31,142
Albany, GA Metro area	149,917	154,042	153,759	-4,125	283	-2.7	0.2	5,621.8	4,727.3	18.9	$37,500	$30,666
Dougherty County, GA	91,243	94,562	96,065	-3,319	-1,503	-3.5	-1.6	3,170.1	2,822.7	12.3	$34,744	$29,866
Lee County, GA	29,764	28,298	24,757	1,466	3,541	5.2	14.3	1,406.6	1,021.8	37.7	$47,258	$35,959
Terrell County, GA	8,611	9,507	10,970	-896	-1,463	-9.4	-13.3	347.2	292.6	18.7	$40,325	$30,719
Worth County, GA	20,299	21,675	21,967	-1,376	-292	-6.3	-1.3	697.9	590.2	18.2	$34,380	$27,196
Albany-Lebanon, OR Metro area	127,335	116,676	103,069	10,659	13,607	9.1	13.2	5,461.5	3,698.0	47.7	$42,891	$31,637
Linn County, OR	127,335	116,676	103,069	10,659	13,607	9.1	13.2	5,461.5	3,698.0	47.7	$42,891	$31,637
Albany-Schenectady-Troy, NY Metro area	883,169	870,714	825,875	12,455	44,839	1.4	5.4	51,315.3	38,693.8	32.6	$58,104	$44,421
Albany County, NY	307,117	304,208	294,565	2,909	9,643	1.0	3.3	18,795.7	14,157.9	32.8	$61,201	$46,560
Rensselaer County, NY	159,442	159,433	152,538	9	6,895	0.0	4.5	7,837.5	6,188.7	26.6	$49,156	$38,840
Saratoga County, NY	230,163	219,593	200,635	10,570	18,958	4.8	9.4	15,563.2	10,767.8	44.5	$67,618	$48,921
Schenectady County, NY	155,350	154,751	146,555	599	8,196	0.4	5.6	7,850.3	6,578.0	19.3	$50,533	$42,476
Schoharie County, NY	31,097	32,729	31,582	-1,632	1,147	-5.0	3.6	1,268.5	1,001.4	26.7	$40,791	$30,632
Albemarle, NC Micro area	62,075	60,586	58,100	1,489	2,486	2.5	4.3	2,423.9	1,765.0	37.3	$39,047	$29,137
Stanly County, NC	62,075	60,586	58,100	1,489	2,486	2.5	4.3	2,423.9	1,765.0	37.3	$39,047	$29,137
Albert Lea, MN Micro area	30,444	31,254	32,584	-810	-1,330	-2.6	-4.1	1,394.6	1,096.5	27.2	$45,808	$35,141
Freeborn County, MN	30,444	31,254	32,584	-810	-1,330	-2.6	-4.1	1,394.6	1,096.5	27.2	$45,808	$35,141
Albertville, AL Micro area	96,109	93,019	82,231	3,090	10,788	3.3	13.1	3,464.2	2,767.5	25.2	$36,044	$29,719
Marshall County, AL	96,109	93,019	82,231	3,090	10,788	3.3	13.1	3,464.2	2,767.5	25.2	$36,044	$29,719
Albuquerque, NM Metro area	915,927	887,064	729,649	28,863	157,415	3.3	21.6	38,960.3	30,635.0	27.2	$42,536	$34,438
Bernalillo County, NM	678,701	662,487	556,678	16,214	105,809	2.4	19.0	29,901.5	23,595.4	26.7	$44,057	$35,538
Sandoval County, NM	145,179	131,620	89,908	13,559	41,712	10.3	46.4	6,031.8	4,495.1	34.2	$41,547	$33,943
Torrance County, NM	15,591	16,375	16,911	-784	-536	-4.8	-3.2	471.6	409.1	15.3	$30,245	$24,948
Valencia County, NM	76,456	76,582	66,152	-126	10,430	-0.2	15.8	2,555.4	2,135.4	19.7	$33,424	$27,805
Alexander City, AL Micro area	51,212	53,376	53,677	-2,164	-301	-4.1	-0.6	1,983.8	1,631.7	21.6	$38,736	$30,637
Coosa County, AL	10,715	11,758	12,202	-1,043	-444	-8.9	-3.6	335.7	279.3	20.2	$31,328	$23,706
Tallapoosa County, AL	40,497	41,618	41,475	-1,121	143	-2.7	0.3	1,648.1	1,352.4	21.9	$40,696	$32,606
Alexandria, LA Metro area	153,044	153,918	145,035	-874	8,883	-0.6	6.1	6,733.1	5,361.3	25.6	$43,995	$34,793
Grant Parish, LA	22,482	22,309	18,698	173	3,611	0.8	19.3	715.6	583.7	22.6	$31,828	$26,133
Rapides Parish, LA	130,562	131,609	126,337	-1,047	5,272	-0.8	4.2	6,017.6	4,777.6	26.0	$46,090	$36,261
Alexandria, MN Micro area	37,964	36,009	32,821	1,955	3,188	5.4	9.7	2,037.3	1,564.7	30.2	$53,665	$43,479
Douglas County, MN	37,964	36,009	32,821	1,955	3,188	5.4	9.7	2,037.3	1,564.7	30.2	$53,665	$43,479
Alice, TX Micro area	52,034	52,620	52,446	-586	174	-1.1	0.3	2,064.5	1,708.4	20.8	$39,676	$32,476
Duval County, TX	11,212	11,784	13,120	-572	-1,336	-4.9	-10.2	408.3	345.1	18.3	$36,418	$29,439
Jim Wells County, TX	40,822	40,836	39,326	-14	1,510	0.0	3.8	1,656.2	1,363.4	21.5	$40,570	$33,346
Allentown-Bethlehem-Easton, PA-NJ Metro area	842,913	821,267	740,395	21,646	80,872	2.6	10.9	45,618.4	34,564.0	32.0	$54,120	$42,053
Warren County, NJ	105,779	108,645	102,437	-2,866	6,208	-2.6	6.1	5,929.7	4,806.8	23.4	$56,058	$44,269
Carbon County, PA	64,227	65,252	58,802	-1,025	6,450	-1.6	11.0	3,232.0	2,326.3	38.9	$50,322	$35,650
Lehigh County, PA	368,100	349,676	312,090	18,424	37,586	5.3	12.0	19,735.3	15,339.3	28.7	$53,614	$43,806
Northampton County, PA	304,807	297,694	267,066	7,113	30,628	2.4	11.5	16,721.3	12,091.6	38.3	$54,859	$40,588
Alma, MI Micro area	40,599	42,476	42,285	-1,877	191	-4.4	0.5	1,536.0	1,219.7	25.9	$37,834	$28,745
Gratiot County, MI	40,599	42,476	42,285	-1,877	191	-4.4	0.5	1,536.0	1,219.7	25.9	$37,834	$28,745
Alpena, MI Micro area	28,360	29,601	31,314	-1,241	-1,713	-4.2	-5.5	1,162.3	943.0	23.3	$40,985	$31,947
Alpena County, MI	28,360	29,601	31,314	-1,241	-1,713	-4.2	-5.5	1,162.3	943.0	23.3	$40,985	$31,947
Altoona, PA Metro area	122,492	127,116	129,144	-4,624	-2,028	-3.6	-1.6	5,725.6	4,439.1	29.0	$46,743	$34,942
Blair County, PA	122,492	127,116	129,144	-4,624	-2,028	-3.6	-1.6	5,725.6	4,439.1	29.0	$46,743	$34,942
Altus, OK Micro area	24,949	26,446	28,439	-1,497	-1,993	-5.7	-7.0	961.2	896.7	7.2	$38,527	$33,860
Jackson County, OK	24,949	26,446	28,439	-1,497	-1,993	-5.7	-7.0	961.2	896.7	7.2	$38,527	$33,860
Amarillo, TX Metro area	265,947	251,937	228,707	14,010	23,230	5.6	10.2	12,268.4	9,450.9	29.8	$46,131	$37,403
Armstrong County, TX	1,892	1,901	2,148	-9	-247	-0.5	-11.5	90.8	76.4	18.8	$47,995	$40,142
Carson County, TX	6,005	6,186	6,516	-181	-330	-2.9	-5.1	278.5	236.9	17.6	$46,373	$38,435
Oldham County, TX	2,131	2,052	2,185	79	-133	3.8	-6.1	104.7	87.2	20.1	$49,120	$42,550
Potter County, TX	119,648	121,078	113,546	-1,430	7,532	-1.2	6.6	5,258.0	4,210.0	24.9	$43,945	$34,684
Randall County, TX	136,271	120,720	104,312	15,551	16,408	12.9	15.7	6,536.4	4,840.5	35.0	$47,966	$39,944
Americus, GA Micro area	34,969	37,827	36,966	-2,858	861	-7.6	2.3	1,227.8	1,029.4	19.3	$35,111	$27,305
Schley County, GA	5,236	5,010	3,766	226	1,244	4.5	33.0	162.0	127.0	27.6	$30,931	$25,316
Sumter County, GA	29,733	32,817	33,200	-3,084	-383	-9.4	-1.2	1,065.8	902.4	18.1	$35,847	$27,610
Ames, IA Metro area	124,451	115,850	106,205	8,601	9,645	7.4	9.1	5,416.0	3,955.2	36.9	$43,519	$34,117
Boone County, IA	26,346	26,308	26,224	38	84	0.1	0.3	1,306.9	1,021.5	27.9	$49,606	$38,880

Table D-1. Population and Personal Income—Continued

Metropolitan or Micropolitan Statistical Area Metropolitan Division Component Counties	Population							Personal Income				
	2018 Estimate (July 1)	2010 census estimates base (April 1)	2000 census estimates base (April 1)	Net change		Percent change		Total (million dollars)		Percent change 2010-2018	Per capita	
				2010-2018	2000-2010	2010-2018	2000-2010	2018	2010		2018	2010
Story County, IA	98,105	89,542	79,981	8,563	9,561	9.6	12.0	4,109.1	2,933.6	40.1	$41,885	$32,722
Amsterdam, NY Micro area	49,455	50,258	49,708	-803	550	-1.6	1.1	2,058.7	1,741.3	18.2	$41,628	$34,619
Montgomery County, NY	49,455	50,258	49,708	-803	550	-1.6	1.1	2,058.7	1,741.3	18.2	$41,628	$34,619
Anchorage, AK Metro area	399,148	380,821	319,605	18,327	61,216	4.8	19.2	24,329.3	20,209.0	20.4	$60,953	$52,759
Anchorage Municipality, AK	291,538	291,829	260,283	-291	31,546	-0.1	12.1	19,390.3	16,606.0	16.8	$66,510	$56,616
Matanuska-Susitna Borough, AK	107,610	88,992	59,322	18,618	29,670	20.9	50.0	4,938.9	3,603.0	37.1	$45,897	$40,152
Andrews, TX Micro area	18,128	14,786	13,004	3,342	1,782	22.6	13.7	906.6	540.1	67.9	$50,011	$36,375
Andrews County, TX	18,128	14,786	13,004	3,342	1,782	22.6	13.7	906.6	540.1	67.9	$50,011	$36,375
Angola, IN Micro area	34,586	34,173	33,214	413	959	1.2	2.9	1,495.2	1,047.5	42.7	$43,231	$30,687
Steuben County, IN	34,586	34,173	33,214	413	959	1.2	2.9	1,495.2	1,047.5	42.7	$43,231	$30,687
Ann Arbor, MI Metro area	370,963	345,104	322,895	25,859	22,209	7.5	6.9	22,021.4	15,690.1	40.4	$59,363	$45,392
Washtenaw County, MI	370,963	345,104	322,895	25,859	22,209	7.5	6.9	22,021.4	15,690.1	40.4	$59,363	$45,392
Anniston-Oxford, AL Metro area	114,277	118,594	112,249	-4,317	6,345	-3.6	5.7	4,242.0	3,662.0	15.8	$37,120	$30,909
Calhoun County, AL	114,277	118,594	112,249	-4,317	6,345	-3.6	5.7	4,242.0	3,662.0	15.8	$37,120	$30,909
Appleton, WI Metro area	237,524	225,664	201,602	11,860	24,062	5.3	11.9	12,145.5	8,669.9	40.1	$51,134	$38,372
Calumet County, WI	50,159	48,973	40,631	1,186	8,342	2.4	20.5	2,546.9	1,829.3	39.2	$50,776	$37,308
Outagamie County, WI	187,365	176,691	160,971	10,674	15,720	6.0	9.8	9,598.7	6,840.7	40.3	$51,230	$38,667
Arcadia, FL Micro area	37,489	34,862	32,209	2,627	2,653	7.5	8.2	885.1	767.0	15.4	$23,610	$21,957
De Soto County, FL	37,489	34,862	32,209	2,627	2,653	7.5	8.2	885.1	767.0	15.4	$23,610	$21,957
Ardmore, OK Micro area	58,311	57,149	54,452	1,162	2,697	2.0	5.0	2,455.9	1,937.5	26.8	$42,118	$33,860
Carter County, OK	48,177	47,733	45,621	444	2,112	0.9	4.6	2,075.4	1,660.7	25.0	$43,079	$34,737
Love County, OK	10,134	9,416	8,831	718	585	7.6	6.6	380.5	276.8	37.5	$37,547	$29,405
Arkadelphia, AR Micro area	22,061	22,993	23,546	-932	-553	-4.1	-2.3	801.1	636.5	25.9	$36,314	$27,760
Clark County, AR	22,061	22,993	23,546	-932	-553	-4.1	-2.3	801.1	636.5	25.9	$36,314	$27,760
Asheville, NC Metro area	459,585	424,859	369,171	34,726	55,688	8.2	15.1	20,880.3	14,218.2	46.9	$45,433	$33,428
Buncombe County, NC	259,103	238,331	206,330	20,772	32,001	8.7	15.5	12,590.4	8,260.9	52.4	$48,592	$34,603
Haywood County, NC	61,971	59,031	54,033	2,940	4,998	5.0	9.2	2,496.8	1,844.5	35.4	$40,290	$31,298
Henderson County, NC	116,748	106,713	89,173	10,035	17,540	9.4	19.7	5,052.4	3,561.8	41.8	$43,276	$33,323
Madison County, NC	21,763	20,784	19,635	979	1,149	4.7	5.9	740.7	551.0	34.4	$34,036	$26,519
Ashland, OH Micro area	53,745	53,140	52,523	605	617	1.1	1.2	2,066.0	1,564.6	32.0	$38,441	$29,343
Ashland County, OH	53,745	53,140	52,523	605	617	1.1	1.2	2,066.0	1,564.6	32.0	$38,441	$29,343
Ashtabula, OH Micro area	97,493	101,490	102,728	-3,997	-1,238	-3.9	-1.2	3,749.7	3,003.0	24.9	$38,461	$29,615
Ashtabula County, OH	97,493	101,490	102,728	-3,997	-1,238	-3.9	-1.2	3,749.7	3,003.0	24.9	$38,461	$29,615
Astoria, OR Micro area	39,764	37,026	35,630	2,738	1,396	7.4	3.9	1,792.1	1,247.7	43.6	$45,069	$33,642
Clatsop County, OR	39,764	37,026	35,630	2,738	1,396	7.4	3.9	1,792.1	1,247.7	43.6	$45,069	$33,642
Atchison, KS Micro area	16,193	16,921	16,774	-728	147	-4.3	0.9	606.2	499.4	21.4	$37,436	$29,627
Atchison County, KS	16,193	16,921	16,774	-728	147	-4.3	0.9	606.2	499.4	21.4	$37,436	$29,627
Athens, OH Micro area	65,818	64,764	62,223	1,054	2,541	1.6	4.1	2,190.0	1,782.0	22.9	$33,274	$27,342
Athens County, OH	65,818	64,764	62,223	1,054	2,541	1.6	4.1	2,190.0	1,782.0	22.9	$33,274	$27,342
Athens, TN Micro area	53,285	52,279	49,015	1,006	3,264	1.9	6.7	1,912.8	1,486.1	28.7	$35,897	$28,487
McMinn County, TN	53,285	52,279	49,015	1,006	3,264	1.9	6.7	1,912.8	1,486.1	28.7	$35,897	$28,487
Athens, TX Micro area	82,299	78,534	73,277	3,765	5,257	4.8	7.2	3,261.3	2,384.8	36.8	$39,627	$30,332
Henderson County, TX	82,299	78,534	73,277	3,765	5,257	4.8	7.2	3,261.3	2,384.8	36.8	$39,627	$30,332
Athens-Clarke County, GA Metro area	211,306	192,564	166,079	18,742	26,485	9.7	15.9	8,598.0	5,693.1	51.0	$40,690	$29,431
Clarke County, GA	127,330	116,697	101,489	10,633	15,208	9.1	15.0	4,325.4	3,018.5	43.3	$33,970	$25,709
Madison County, GA	29,650	28,160	25,730	1,490	2,430	5.3	9.4	1,083.9	774.6	39.9	$36,557	$27,462
Oconee County, GA	39,272	32,831	26,225	6,441	6,606	19.6	25.2	2,621.0	1,490.9	75.8	$66,740	$45,278
Oglethorpe County, GA	15,054	14,876	12,635	178	2,241	1.2	17.7	567.7	409.1	38.8	$37,709	$27,471
Atlanta-Sandy Springs-Alpharetta, GA Metro area	5,949,951	5,286,750	4,263,438	663,201	1,023,312	12.5	24.0	312,213.5	203,513.6	53.4	$52,473	$38,379
Barrow County, GA	80,809	69,355	46,144	11,454	23,211	16.5	50.3	2,981.7	1,833.9	62.6	$36,898	$26,321
Bartow County, GA	106,408	100,128	76,019	6,280	24,109	6.3	31.7	4,075.2	2,795.1	45.8	$38,298	$27,927
Butts County, GA	24,193	23,667	19,522	526	4,145	2.2	21.2	829.8	600.5	38.2	$34,297	$25,275
Carroll County, GA	118,121	110,580	87,268	7,541	23,312	6.8	26.7	4,556.0	3,176.3	43.4	$38,571	$28,702
Cherokee County, GA	254,149	214,372	141,903	39,777	72,469	18.6	51.1	12,996.3	7,821.7	66.2	$51,137	$36,348
Clayton County, GA	289,615	259,580	236,517	30,035	23,063	11.6	9.8	8,115.0	6,441.0	26.0	$28,020	$24,789
Cobb County, GA	756,865	688,071	607,751	68,794	80,320	10.0	13.2	43,263.7	28,791.4	50.3	$57,162	$41,755
Coweta County, GA	145,864	127,353	89,215	18,511	38,138	14.5	42.7	6,773.7	4,256.1	59.2	$46,438	$33,272
Dawson County, GA	25,083	22,337	15,999	2,746	6,338	12.3	39.6	1,133.8	694.3	63.3	$45,201	$31,152
De Kalb County, GA	756,558	691,971	665,865	64,587	26,106	9.3	3.9	38,486.8	26,055.1	47.7	$50,871	$37,626
Douglas County, GA	145,331	132,305	92,174	13,026	40,131	9.8	43.5	5,120.0	3,785.1	35.3	$35,230	$28,546
Fayette County, GA	113,459	106,564	91,263	6,895	15,301	6.5	16.8	7,206.3	4,797.1	50.2	$63,515	$44,859
Forsyth County, GA	236,612	175,511	98,407	61,101	77,104	34.8	78.4	14,807.1	8,099.6	82.8	$62,580	$45,825
Fulton County, GA	1,050,114	920,441	816,006	129,673	104,435	14.1	12.8	88,614.9	54,437.8	62.8	$84,386	$58,810
Gwinnett County, GA	927,781	805,326	588,448	122,455	216,878	15.2	36.9	38,464.2	25,636.0	50.0	$41,458	$31,726
Haralson County, GA	29,533	28,777	25,690	756	3,087	2.6	12.0	1,078.2	783.8	37.6	$36,508	$27,252
Heard County, GA	11,879	11,825	11,012	54	813	0.5	7.4	370.0	284.9	29.9	$31,144	$24,066
Henry County, GA	230,220	203,830	119,341	26,390	84,489	12.9	70.8	9,021.0	6,237.9	44.6	$39,184	$30,415
Jasper County, GA	14,040	13,898	11,426	142	2,472	1.0	21.6	570.1	389.4	46.4	$40,606	$28,025
Lamar County, GA	19,000	18,310	15,912	690	2,398	3.8	15.1	628.5	479.5	31.1	$33,079	$26,253
Meriwether County, GA	21,068	21,983	22,534	-915	-551	-4.2	-2.4	734.2	597.4	22.9	$34,847	$27,376
Morgan County, GA	18,853	17,863	15,457	990	2,406	5.5	15.6	952.8	600.7	58.6	$50,541	$33,571
Newton County, GA	109,541	99,984	62,001	9,557	37,983	9.6	61.3	3,697.0	2,644.2	39.8	$33,750	$26,401
Paulding County, GA	164,044	142,379	81,678	21,665	60,701	15.2	74.3	6,188.9	3,987.2	55.2	$37,727	$27,918
Pickens County, GA	31,980	29,425	22,983	2,555	6,442	8.7	28.0	1,531.4	1,013.4	51.1	$47,887	$34,404
Pike County, GA	18,634	17,874	13,688	760	4,186	4.3	30.6	742.6	512.0	45.0	$39,851	$28,564
Rockdale County, GA	90,594	85,176	70,111	5,418	15,065	6.4	21.5	3,192.9	2,525.4	26.4	$35,244	$29,584

Table D-1. Population and Personal Income—Continued

Metropolitan or Micropolitan Statistical Area / Metropolitan Division / Component Counties	2018 Estimate (July 1)	2010 census estimates base (April 1)	2000 census estimates base (April 1)	Net change 2010-2018	Net change 2000-2010	Percent change 2010-2018	Percent change 2000-2010	Total 2018	Total 2010	Percent change 2010-2018	Per capita 2018	Per capita 2010
Spalding County, GA	66,100	64,098	58,417	2,002	5,681	3.1	9.7	2,298.4	1,750.6	31.3	$34,772	$27,316
Walton County, GA	93,503	83,767	60,687	9,736	23,080	11.6	38.0	3,783.0	2,486.4	52.1	$40,458	$29,621
Atlantic City-Hammonton, NJ Metro area	265,429	274,521	252,552	-9,092	21,969	-3.3	8.7	12,918.0	10,708.2	20.6	$48,668	$38,989
Atlantic County, NJ	265,429	274,521	252,552	-9,092	21,969	-3.3	8.7	12,918.0	10,708.2	20.6	$48,668	$38,989
Atmore, AL Micro area	36,748	38,320	38,440	-1,572	-120	-4.1	-0.3	1,212.5	1,031.1	17.6	$32,996	$26,892
Escambia County, AL	36,748	38,320	38,440	-1,572	-120	-4.1	-0.3	1,212.5	1,031.1	17.6	$32,996	$26,892
Auburn, IN Micro area	43,226	42,229	40,285	997	1,944	2.4	4.8	1,904.9	1,330.0	43.2	$44,069	$31,434
De Kalb County, IN	43,226	42,229	40,285	997	1,944	2.4	4.8	1,904.9	1,330.0	43.2	$44,069	$31,434
Auburn, NY Micro area	77,145	80,017	81,963	-2,872	-1,946	-3.6	-2.4	3,257.9	2,605.6	25.0	$42,231	$32,611
Cayuga County, NY	77,145	80,017	81,963	-2,872	-1,946	-3.6	-2.4	3,257.9	2,605.6	25.0	$42,231	$32,611
Auburn-Opelika, AL Metro area	163,941	140,300	115,092	23,641	25,208	16.9	21.9	6,235.7	4,131.4	50.9	$38,036	$29,341
Lee County, AL	163,941	140,300	115,092	23,641	25,208	16.9	21.9	6,235.7	4,131.4	50.9	$38,036	$29,341
Augusta-Richmond County, GA-SC Metro area	604,167	564,873	508,032	39,294	56,841	7.0	11.2	25,407.2	18,732.5	35.6	$42,053	$33,067
Burke County, GA	22,423	23,311	22,243	-888	1,068	-3.8	4.8	796.6	652.1	22.2	$35,524	$27,960
Columbia County, GA	154,291	124,041	89,288	30,250	34,753	24.4	38.9	7,633.2	5,011.3	52.3	$49,473	$40,098
Lincoln County, GA	7,915	7,996	8,348	-81	-352	-1.0	-4.2	295.5	225.4	31.1	$37,333	$28,283
McDuffie County, GA	21,531	21,867	21,231	-336	636	-1.5	3.0	796.3	610.1	30.5	$36,982	$27,984
Richmond County, GA	201,554	200,569	199,775	985	794	0.5	0.4	7,698.6	6,129.2	25.6	$38,196	$30,506
Aiken County, SC	169,401	160,114	142,552	9,287	17,562	5.8	12.3	7,201.4	5,376.2	33.9	$42,511	$33,490
Edgefield County, SC	27,052	26,975	24,595	77	2,380	0.3	9.7	985.7	728.2	35.4	$36,436	$26,998
Augusta-Waterville, ME Micro area	122,083	122,154	117,114	-71	5,040	-0.1	4.3	5,486.4	4,567.1	20.1	$44,940	$37,412
Kennebec County, ME	122,083	122,154	117,114	-71	5,040	-0.1	4.3	5,486.4	4,567.1	20.1	$44,940	$37,412
Austin, MN Micro area	40,011	39,163	38,603	848	560	2.2	1.5	1,937.4	1,441.7	34.4	$48,423	$36,772
Mower County, MN	40,011	39,163	38,603	848	560	2.2	1.5	1,937.4	1,441.7	34.4	$48,423	$36,772
Austin-Round Rock-Georgetown, TX Metro area	2,168,316	1,716,321	1,249,763	451,995	466,558	26.3	37.3	127,439.2	70,355.3	81.1	$58,773	$40,726
Bastrop County, TX	86,976	74,202	57,733	12,774	16,469	17.2	28.5	3,180.0	2,129.2	49.4	$36,561	$28,633
Caldwell County, TX	43,247	38,057	32,194	5,190	5,863	13.6	18.2	1,456.0	1,014.4	43.5	$33,668	$26,604
Hays County, TX	222,631	157,099	97,589	65,532	59,510	41.7	61.0	9,733.1	5,239.4	85.8	$43,719	$33,116
Travis County, TX	1,248,743	1,024,462	812,280	224,281	212,182	21.9	26.1	84,294.6	45,991.2	83.3	$67,504	$44,628
Williamson County, TX	566,719	422,501	249,967	144,218	172,534	34.1	69.0	28,775.5	15,981.0	80.1	$50,776	$37,489
Bainbridge, GA Micro area	26,575	27,842	28,240	-1,267	-398	-4.6	-1.4	960.7	820.4	17.1	$36,150	$29,497
Decatur County, GA	26,575	27,842	28,240	-1,267	-398	-4.6	-1.4	960.7	820.4	17.1	$36,150	$29,497
Bakersfield, CA Metro area	896,764	839,619	661,645	57,145	177,974	6.8	26.9	35,603.8	26,097.2	36.4	$39,703	$31,028
Kern County, CA	896,764	839,619	661,645	57,145	177,974	6.8	26.9	35,603.8	26,097.2	36.4	$39,703	$31,028
Baltimore-Columbia-Towson, MD Metro area	2,802,789	2,710,602	2,552,994	92,187	157,608	3.4	6.2	174,900.9	132,299.4	32.2	$62,402	$48,716
Anne Arundel County, MD	576,031	537,631	489,656	38,400	47,975	7.1	9.8	38,803.4	28,572.1	35.8	$67,363	$52,982
Baltimore County, MD	828,431	805,229	754,292	23,202	50,937	2.9	6.8	50,994.5	39,768.2	28.2	$61,556	$49,306
Carroll County, MD	168,429	167,142	150,897	1,287	16,245	0.8	10.8	10,617.6	8,065.1	31.6	$63,039	$48,233
Harford County, MD	253,956	244,826	218,590	9,130	26,236	3.7	12.0	14,942.9	11,429.0	30.7	$58,841	$46,604
Howard County, MD	323,196	287,123	247,842	36,073	39,281	12.6	15.8	25,343.6	18,498.9	37.0	$78,416	$64,092
Queen Anne's County, MD	50,251	47,789	40,563	2,462	7,226	5.2	17.8	3,256.8	2,372.1	37.3	$64,810	$49,616
Baltimore city, MD	602,495	620,862	651,154	-18,367	-30,292	-3.0	-4.7	30,942.0	23,594.2	31.1	$51,357	$37,994
Bangor, ME Metro area	151,096	153,932	144,919	-2,836	9,013	-1.8	6.2	6,354.1	5,134.3	23.8	$42,053	$33,370
Penobscot County, ME	151,096	153,932	144,919	-2,836	9,013	-1.8	6.2	6,354.1	5,134.3	23.8	$42,053	$33,370
Baraboo, WI Micro area	64,249	61,965	55,225	2,284	6,740	3.7	12.2	3,107.4	2,247.9	38.2	$48,365	$36,222
Sauk County, WI	64,249	61,965	55,225	2,284	6,740	3.7	12.2	3,107.4	2,247.9	38.2	$48,365	$36,222
Bardstown, KY Micro area	45,851	43,443	37,477	2,408	5,966	5.5	15.9	1,946.0	1,384.5	40.6	$42,442	$31,733
Nelson County, KY	45,851	43,443	37,477	2,408	5,966	5.5	15.9	1,946.0	1,384.5	40.6	$42,442	$31,733
Barnstable Town, MA Metro area	213,413	215,875	222,230	-2,462	-6,355	-1.1	-2.9	15,953.9	11,312.0	41.0	$74,756	$52,397
Barnstable County, MA	213,413	215,875	222,230	-2,462	-6,355	-1.1	-2.9	15,953.9	11,312.0	41.0	$74,756	$52,397
Barre, VT Micro area	58,140	59,522	58,039	-1,382	1,483	-2.3	2.6	3,503.2	2,671.1	31.2	$60,255	$44,840
Washington County, VT	58,140	59,522	58,039	-1,382	1,483	-2.3	2.6	3,503.2	2,671.1	31.2	$60,255	$44,840
Bartlesville, OK Micro area	51,843	50,977	48,996	866	1,981	1.7	4.0	3,342.9	2,766.6	20.8	$64,481	$54,177
Washington County, OK	51,843	50,977	48,996	866	1,981	1.7	4.0	3,342.9	2,766.6	20.8	$64,481	$54,177
Batavia, NY Micro area	57,511	59,943	60,370	-2,432	-427	-4.1	-0.7	2,506.4	2,084.0	20.3	$43,582	$34,768
Genesee County, NY	57,511	59,943	60,370	-2,432	-427	-4.1	-0.7	2,506.4	2,084.0	20.3	$43,582	$34,768
Batesville, AR Micro area	55,044	53,905	51,352	1,139	2,553	2.1	5.0	1,877.9	1,517.8	23.7	$34,117	$28,075
Independence County, AR	37,678	36,641	34,233	1,037	2,408	2.8	7.0	1,322.0	1,060.1	24.7	$35,086	$28,800
Sharp County, AR	17,366	17,264	17,119	102	145	0.6	0.8	555.9	457.6	21.5	$32,012	$26,527
Baton Rouge, LA Metro area	853,610	825,920	729,361	27,690	96,559	3.4	13.2	41,009.5	31,287.4	31.1	$48,042	$37,804
Ascension Parish, LA	124,672	107,215	76,627	17,457	30,588	16.3	39.9	6,212.3	4,285.1	45.0	$49,829	$39,719
Assumption Parish, LA	22,300	23,416	23,388	-1,116	28	-4.8	0.1	1,043.4	784.9	32.9	$46,788	$33,641
East Baton Rouge Parish, LA	440,956	440,169	412,852	787	27,317	0.2	6.6	22,659.0	17,667.5	28.3	$51,386	$40,103
East Feliciana Parish, LA	19,305	20,276	21,360	-971	-1,084	-4.8	-5.1	825.7	678.8	21.6	$42,771	$33,649
Iberville Parish, LA	32,721	33,404	33,320	-683	84	-2.0	0.3	1,355.4	1,088.3	24.5	$41,423	$32,592
Livingston Parish, LA	139,567	128,015	91,814	11,552	36,201	9.0	39.4	5,674.5	4,240.8	33.8	$40,658	$32,957
Pointe Coupee Parish, LA	21,940	22,805	22,763	-865	42	-3.8	0.2	973.4	803.9	21.1	$44,366	$35,231
St. Helena Parish, LA	10,262	11,207	10,525	-945	682	-8.4	6.5	426.8	384.4	11.0	$41,592	$34,323
West Baton Rouge Parish, LA	26,427	23,788	21,601	2,639	2,187	11.1	10.1	1,241.4	912.2	36.1	$46,976	$38,081
West Feliciana Parish, LA	15,460	15,625	15,111	-165	514	-1.1	3.4	597.6	441.5	35.4	$38,655	$28,226
Battle Creek, MI Metro area	134,487	136,148	137,985	-1,661	-1,837	-1.2	-1.3	5,416.7	4,337.3	24.9	$40,276	$31,903
Calhoun County, MI	134,487	136,148	137,985	-1,661	-1,837	-1.2	-1.3	5,416.7	4,337.3	24.9	$40,276	$31,903
Bay City, MI Metro area	103,923	107,773	110,157	-3,850	-2,384	-3.6	-2.2	4,335.9	3,591.4	20.7	$41,722	$33,352
Bay County, MI	103,923	107,773	110,157	-3,850	-2,384	-3.6	-2.2	4,335.9	3,591.4	20.7	$41,722	$33,352
Bay City, TX Micro area	36,552	36,702	37,957	-150	-1,255	-0.4	-3.3	1,483.8	1,144.2	29.7	$40,596	$31,169

Table D-1. Population and Personal Income—Continued

Metropolitan or Micropolitan Statistical Area Metropolitan Division Component Counties	Population							Personal Income				
	2018 Estimate (July 1)	2010 census estimates base (April 1)	2000 census estimates base (April 1)	Net change		Percent change		Total (million dollars)		Percent change 2010-2018	Per capita	
				2010-2018	2000-2010	2010-2018	2000-2010	2018	2010		2018	2010
Matagorda County, TX	36,552	36,702	37,957	-150	-1,255	-0.4	-3.3	1,483.8	1,144.2	29.7	$40,596	$31,169
Beatrice, NE Micro area	21,493	22,311	22,993	-818	-682	-3.7	-3.0	1,071.7	864.6	24.0	$49,863	$38,824
Gage County, NE	21,493	22,311	22,993	-818	-682	-3.7	-3.0	1,071.7	864.6	24.0	$49,863	$38,824
Beaumont-Port Arthur, TX Metro area	395,780	388,749	385,090	7,031	3,659	1.8	1.0	17,622.8	13,655.5	29.1	$44,527	$35,081
Hardin County, TX	57,207	54,635	48,073	2,572	6,562	4.7	13.7	2,630.5	1,918.5	37.1	$45,982	$35,020
Jefferson County, TX	255,001	252,277	252,051	2,724	226	1.1	0.1	11,236.7	8,892.5	26.4	$44,065	$35,223
Orange County, TX	83,572	81,837	84,966	1,735	-3,129	2.1	-3.7	3,755.6	2,844.5	32.0	$44,938	$34,684
Beaver Dam, WI Micro area	87,847	88,759	85,897	-912	2,862	-1.0	3.3	3,935.4	3,124.1	26.0	$44,799	$35,205
Dodge County, WI	87,847	88,759	85,897	-912	2,862	-1.0	3.3	3,935.4	3,124.1	26.0	$44,799	$35,205
Beckley, WV Metro area	117,272	124,914	126,799	-7,642	-1,885	-6.1	-1.5	4,540.4	3,831.2	18.5	$38,717	$30,662
Fayette County, WV	43,018	46,049	47,579	-3,031	-1,530	-6.6	-3.2	1,487.4	1,266.2	17.5	$34,577	$27,506
Raleigh County, WV	74,254	78,865	79,220	-4,611	-355	-5.8	-0.4	3,052.9	2,565.0	19.0	$41,115	$32,503
Bedford, IN Micro area	45,668	46,129	45,922	-461	207	-1.0	0.5	1,854.8	1,421.9	30.4	$40,614	$30,842
Lawrence County, IN	45,668	46,129	45,922	-461	207	-1.0	0.5	1,854.8	1,421.9	30.4	$40,614	$30,842
Beeville, TX Micro area	32,587	31,861	32,359	726	-498	2.3	-1.5	927.3	807.4	14.9	$28,457	$25,340
Bee County, TX	32,587	31,861	32,359	726	-498	2.3	-1.5	927.3	807.4	14.9	$28,457	$25,340
Bellefontaine, OH Micro area	45,358	45,851	46,005	-493	-154	-1.1	-0.3	1,946.5	1,458.3	33.5	$42,914	$31,877
Logan County, OH	45,358	45,851	46,005	-493	-154	-1.1	-0.3	1,946.5	1,458.3	33.5	$42,914	$31,877
Bellingham, WA Metro area	225,685	201,146	166,814	24,539	34,332	12.2	20.6	11,011.6	7,414.2	48.5	$48,792	$36,786
Whatcom County, WA	225,685	201,146	166,814	24,539	34,332	12.2	20.6	11,011.6	7,414.2	48.5	$48,792	$36,786
Bemidji, MN Micro area	46,847	44,442	39,650	2,405	4,792	5.4	12.1	1,947.2	1,385.0	40.6	$41,565	$31,073
Beltrami County, MN	46,847	44,442	39,650	2,405	4,792	5.4	12.1	1,947.2	1,385.0	40.6	$41,565	$31,073
Bend, OR Metro area	191,996	157,730	115,367	34,266	42,363	21.7	36.7	10,587.2	5,493.8	92.7	$55,143	$34,828
Deschutes County, OR	191,996	157,730	115,367	34,266	42,363	21.7	36.7	10,587.2	5,493.8	92.7	$55,143	$34,828
Bennettsville, SC Micro area	26,398	28,935	28,818	-2,537	117	-8.8	0.4	833.2	641.7	29.8	$31,562	$22,190
Marlboro County, SC	26,398	28,935	28,818	-2,537	117	-8.8	0.4	833.2	641.7	29.8	$31,562	$22,190
Bennington, VT Micro area	35,631	37,125	36,994	-1,494	131	-4.0	0.4	1,940.4	1,493.9	29.9	$54,458	$40,286
Bennington County, VT	35,631	37,125	36,994	-1,494	131	-4.0	0.4	1,940.4	1,493.9	29.9	$54,458	$40,286
Berlin, NH Micro area	31,589	33,052	33,111	-1,463	-59	-4.4	-0.2	1,361.4	1,126.0	20.9	$43,098	$34,146
Coos County, NH	31,589	33,052	33,111	-1,463	-59	-4.4	-0.2	1,361.4	1,126.0	20.9	$43,098	$34,146
Big Rapids, MI Micro area	43,545	42,798	40,553	747	2,245	1.7	5.5	1,491.5	1,103.2	35.2	$34,252	$25,745
Mecosta County, MI	43,545	42,798	40,553	747	2,245	1.7	5.5	1,491.5	1,103.2	35.2	$34,252	$25,745
Big Spring, TX Micro area	36,459	35,012	33,627	1,447	1,385	4.1	4.1	1,467.7	1,030.2	42.5	$40,255	$29,441
Howard County, TX	36,459	35,012	33,627	1,447	1,385	4.1	4.1	1,467.7	1,030.2	42.5	$40,255	$29,441
Big Stone Gap, VA Micro area	41,980	45,443	44,027	-3,463	1,416	-7.6	3.2	1,384.9	1,391.1	-0.4	$32,988	$30,507
Wise County, VA	38,012	41,450	40,123	-3,438	1,327	-8.3	3.3	1,384.9	1,391.1	-0.4	$32,988	$30,507
Norton City, VA (included with Wise County)	3,968	3,993	3,904	-25	89	-0.6	2.3	-	-		-	-
Billings, MT Metro area	180,385	167,165	147,099	13,220	20,066	7.9	13.6	9,383.5	6,464.0	45.2	$52,019	$38,574
Carbon County, MT	10,714	10,078	9,552	636	526	6.3	5.5	508.3	355.4	43.0	$47,442	$35,313
Stillwater County, MT	9,534	9,105	8,195	429	910	4.7	11.1	493.6	329.0	50.0	$51,773	$36,064
Yellowstone County, MT	160,137	147,982	129,352	12,155	18,630	8.2	14.4	8,381.6	5,779.6	45.0	$52,340	$38,949
Binghamton, NY Metro area	240,219	251,724	252,320	-11,505	-596	-4.6	-0.2	10,765.9	8,947.0	20.3	$44,817	$35,576
Broome County, NY	191,659	200,675	200,536	-9,016	139	-4.5	0.1	8,536.5	7,128.7	19.7	$44,540	$35,559
Tioga County, NY	48,560	51,049	51,784	-2,489	-735	-4.9	-1.4	2,229.4	1,818.3	22.6	$45,910	$35,645
Birmingham-Hoover, AL Metro area	1,088,090	1,061,035	981,525	27,055	79,510	2.5	8.1	55,469.3	41,703.2	33.0	$50,979	$39,279
Bibb County, AL	22,400	22,920	20,826	-520	2,094	-2.3	10.1	677.7	573.1	18.3	$30,254	$25,055
Blount County, AL	57,840	57,321	51,024	519	6,297	0.9	12.3	2,023.0	1,589.4	27.3	$34,976	$27,703
Chilton County, AL	44,153	43,630	39,593	523	4,037	1.2	10.2	1,536.5	1,199.0	28.1	$34,798	$27,467
Jefferson County, AL	659,300	658,506	662,047	794	-3,541	0.1	-0.5	36,083.7	27,718.3	30.2	$54,730	$42,115
St. Clair County, AL	88,690	83,345	64,742	5,345	18,603	6.4	28.7	3,420.7	2,475.7	38.2	$38,569	$29,626
Shelby County, AL	215,707	195,313	143,293	20,394	52,020	10.4	36.3	11,727.9	8,147.7	43.9	$54,369	$41,550
Bismarck, ND Metro area	128,320	110,625	96,784	17,695	13,841	16.0	14.3	7,258.3	4,776.6	52.0	$56,564	$42,990
Burleigh County, ND	95,273	81,308	69,416	13,965	11,892	17.2	17.1	5,542.4	3,623.3	53.0	$58,173	$44,348
Morton County, ND	31,095	27,469	25,303	3,626	2,166	13.2	8.6	1,621.7	1,069.9	51.6	$52,153	$38,808
Oliver County, ND	1,952	1,848	2,065	104	-217	5.6	-10.5	94.3	83.4	13.1	$48,290	$45,311
Blackfoot, ID Micro area	46,236	45,605	41,735	631	3,870	1.4	9.3	1,680.0	1,291.7	30.1	$36,335	$28,224
Bingham County, ID	46,236	45,605	41,735	631	3,870	1.4	9.3	1,680.0	1,291.7	30.1	$36,335	$28,224
Blacksburg-Christiansburg, VA Metro area	168,234	162,962	151,272	5,272	11,690	3.2	7.7	6,483.5	4,707.3	37.7	$38,538	$28,855
Giles County, VA	16,844	17,286	16,657	-442	629	-2.6	3.8	675.7	542.1	24.6	$40,117	$31,309
Montgomery County, VA	98,985	94,422	83,629	4,563	10,793	4.8	12.9	4,430.0	3,098.9	43.0	$37,759	$27,921
Pulaski County, VA	34,066	34,859	35,127	-793	-268	-2.3	-0.8	1,377.7	1,066.3	29.2	$40,443	$30,613
Radford City, VA (included with Montgomery County personal income)	18,339	16,395	15,859	1,944	536	11.9	3.4	-	-		-	-
Bloomington, IL Metro area	172,828	169,577	150,433	3,251	19,144	1.9	12.7	8,499.8	6,822.1	24.6	$49,180	$40,175
McLean County, IL	172,828	169,577	150,433	3,251	19,144	1.9	12.7	8,499.8	6,822.1	24.6	$49,180	$40,175
Bloomington, IN Metro area	167,762	159,536	142,349	8,226	17,187	5.2	12.1	7,037.2	4,914.0	43.2	$41,947	$30,688
Monroe County, IN	146,917	137,959	120,563	8,958	17,396	6.5	14.4	6,201.7	4,272.2	45.2	$42,212	$30,833
Owen County, IN	20,845	21,577	21,786	-732	-209	-3.4		835.5	641.8	30.2	$40,081	$29,752
Bloomsburg-Berwick, PA Metro area	83,696	85,561	82,387	-1,865	3,174	-2.2	3.9	3,810.4	2,978.9	27.9	$45,527	$34,776
Columbia County, PA	65,456	67,303	64,151	-1,847	3,152	-2.7	4.9	2,763.0	2,207.4	25.2	$42,211	$32,771
Montour County, PA	18,240	18,258	18,236	-18	22	-0.1	0.1	1,047.4	771.5	35.8	$57,426	$42,154
Bluefield, WV-VA Micro area	106,279	114,157	114,449	-7,878	-292	-6.9	-0.3	4,038.2	3,604.9	12.0	$37,996	$31,549
Bland County, VA	6,293	6,824	6,871	-531	-47	-7.8	-0.7	234.9	190.2	23.5	$37,321	$27,976
Tazewell County, VA	40,855	45,068	44,598	-4,213	470	-9.3	1.1	1,588.8	1,421.3	11.8	$38,888	$31,495
Mercer County, WV	59,131	62,265	62,980	-3,134	-715	-5.0	-1.1	2,214.6	1,993.4	11.1	$37,452	$31,978

Table D-1. Population and Personal Income—*Continued*

Metropolitan or Micropolitan Statistical Area / Metropolitan Division / Component Counties	Population 2018 Estimate (July 1)	2010 census estimates base (April 1)	2000 census estimates base (April 1)	Net change 2010-2018	Net change 2000-2010	Percent change 2010-2018	Percent change 2000-2010	Personal Income Total (million dollars) 2018	2010	Percent change 2010-2018	Per capita 2018	Per capita 2010
Blytheville, AR Micro area	41,239	46,480	51,979	-5,241	-5,499	-11.3	-10.6	1,296.1	1,308.8		$31,428	$28,212
Mississippi County, AR	41,239	46,480	51,979	-5,241	-5,499	-11.3	-10.6	1,296.1	1,308.8		$31,428	$28,212
Bogalusa, LA Micro area	46,582	47,140	43,926	-558	3,214	-1.2	7.3	1,559.6	1,337.6	16.6	$33,480	$28,407
Washington Parish, LA	46,582	47,140	43,926	-558	3,214	-1.2	7.3	1,559.6	1,337.6	16.6	$33,480	$28,407
Boise City, ID Metro area	730,426	616,566	464,840	113,860	151,726	18.5	32.6	33,580.1	20,737.7	61.9	$45,973	$33,563
Ada County, ID	469,966	392,371	300,904	77,595	91,467	19.8	30.4	24,888.3	15,075.5	65.1	$52,958	$38,326
Boise County, ID	7,634	7,028	6,670	606	358	8.6	5.4	331.3	215.9	53.5	$43,392	$30,818
Canyon County, ID	223,499	188,922	131,441	34,577	57,481	18.3	43.7	7,303.9	4,696.4	55.5	$32,680	$24,803
Gem County, ID	17,634	16,719	15,181	915	1,538	5.5	10.1	666.5	455.5	46.3	$37,796	$27,294
Owyhee County, ID	11,693	11,526	10,644	167	882	1.4	8.3	390.2	294.4	32.5	$33,372	$25,663
Bonham, TX Micro area	35,286	33,910	31,242	1,376	2,668	4.1	8.5	1,326.9	943.1	40.7	$37,605	$27,805
Fannin County, TX	35,286	33,910	31,242	1,376	2,668	4.1	8.5	1,326.9	943.1	40.7	$37,605	$27,805
Boone, NC Micro area	55,945	51,057	42,695	4,888	8,362	9.6	19.6	2,052.3	1,493.1	37.5	$36,684	$29,295
Watauga County, NC	55,945	51,057	42,695	4,888	8,362	9.6	19.6	2,052.3	1,493.1	37.5	$36,684	$29,295
Borger, TX Micro area	21,198	22,249	23,857	-1,051	-1,608	-4.7	-6.7	880.8	766.7	14.9	$41,550	$34,518
Hutchinson County, TX	21,198	22,249	23,857	-1,051	-1,608	-4.7	-6.7	880.8	766.7	14.9	$41,550	$34,518
Boston-Cambridge-Newton, MA-NH Metro area	4,875,390	4,552,598	4,391,344	322,792	161,254	7.1	3.7	383,664.5	265,132.3	44.7	$78,694	$58,061
Boston, MA Div	2,030,772	1,888,034	1,812,937	142,738	75,097	7.6	4.1	165,583.4	114,957.0	44.0	$81,537	$60,670
Norfolk County, MA	705,388	670,907	650,308	34,481	20,599	5.1	3.2	65,096.8	44,242.3	47.1	$92,285	$65,735
Plymouth County, MA	518,132	494,937	472,822	23,195	22,115	4.7	4.7	34,976.5	23,865.0	46.6	$67,505	$48,122
Suffolk County, MA	807,252	722,190	689,807	85,062	32,383	11.8	4.7	65,510.1	46,849.7	39.8	$81,152	$64,547
Cambridge-Newton-Framingham, MA Div	2,405,352	2,246,204	2,188,815	159,148	57,389	7.1	2.6	188,678.9	130,151.4	45.0	$78,441	$57,764
Essex County, MA	790,638	743,081	723,419	47,557	19,662	6.4	2.7	53,373.8	38,578.8	38.4	$67,507	$51,750
Middlesex County, MA	1,614,714	1,503,123	1,465,396	111,591	37,727	7.4	2.6	135,305.1	91,572.6	47.8	$83,795	$60,737
Rockingham County-Strafford County, NH Div	439,266	418,360	389,592	20,906	28,768	5.0	7.4	29,402.3	20,023.9	46.8	$66,935	$47,848
Rockingham County, NH	309,176	295,211	277,359	13,965	17,852	4.7	6.4	22,823.1	15,333.7	48.8	$73,819	$51,927
Strafford County, NH	130,090	123,149	112,233	6,941	10,916	5.6	9.7	6,579.2	4,690.2	40.3	$50,574	$38,071
Boulder, CO Metro area	326,078	294,561	269,814	31,517	24,747	10.7	9.2	23,932.2	14,889.0	60.7	$73,394	$50,339
Boulder County, CO	326,078	294,561	269,814	31,517	24,747	10.7	9.2	23,932.2	14,889.0	60.7	$73,394	$50,339
Bowling Green, KY Metro area	177,432	158,608	134,976	18,824	23,632	11.9	17.5	6,518.9	4,732.9	37.7	$36,740	$29,704
Allen County, KY	21,122	19,968	17,800	1,154	2,168	5.8	12.2	689.5	493.1	39.8	$32,643	$24,594
Butler County, KY	12,772	12,697	13,010	75	-313	0.6	-2.4	439.6	344.2	27.7	$34,420	$27,030
Edmonson County, KY	12,274	12,177	11,644	97	533	0.8	4.6	395.9	304.5	30.0	$32,253	$24,898
Warren County, KY	131,264	113,766	92,522	17,498	21,244	15.4	23.0	4,994.0	3,591.2	39.1	$38,045	$31,412
Bozeman, MT Micro area	111,876	89,513	67,831	22,363	21,682	25.0	32.0	6,123.4	3,316.2	84.7	$54,734	$36,990
Gallatin County, MT	111,876	89,513	67,831	22,363	21,682	25.0	32.0	6,123.4	3,316.2	84.7	$54,734	$36,990
Bradford, PA Micro area	40,968	43,459	45,936	-2,491	-2,477	-5.7	-5.4	1,854.2	1,473.3	25.9	$45,261	$33,993
McKean County, PA	40,968	43,459	45,936	-2,491	-2,477	-5.7	-5.4	1,854.2	1,473.3	25.9	$45,261	$33,993
Brainerd, MN Micro area	94,408	91,077	82,249	3,331	8,828	3.7	10.7	4,360.0	3,106.2	40.4	$46,183	$34,036
Cass County, MN	29,519	28,567	27,150	952	1,417	3.3	5.2	1,400.5	992.1	41.2	$47,443	$34,622
Crow Wing County, MN	64,889	62,510	55,099	2,379	7,411	3.8	13.5	2,959.6	2,114.1	40.0	$45,610	$33,767
Branson, MO Micro area	55,852	51,675	39,703	4,177	11,972	8.1	30.2	2,008.2	1,516.2	32.4	$35,956	$29,208
Taney County, MO	55,852	51,675	39,703	4,177	11,972	8.1	30.2	2,008.2	1,516.2	32.4	$35,956	$29,208
Breckenridge, CO Micro area	31,007	27,994	23,548	3,013	4,446	10.8	18.9	2,101.1	1,210.1	73.6	$67,763	$43,100
Summit County, CO	31,007	27,994	23,548	3,013	4,446	10.8	18.9	2,101.1	1,210.1	73.6	$67,763	$43,100
Bremerton-Silverdale-Port Orchard, WA Metro area	269,805	251,143	231,969	18,662	19,174	7.4	8.3	15,175.0	10,639.9	42.6	$56,244	$42,276
Kitsap County, WA	269,805	251,143	231,969	18,662	19,174	7.4	8.3	15,175.0	10,639.9	42.6	$56,244	$42,276
Brenham, TX Micro area	35,108	33,695	30,373	1,413	3,322	4.2	10.9	1,834.9	1,433.8	28.0	$52,265	$42,542
Washington County, TX	35,108	33,695	30,373	1,413	3,322	4.2	10.9	1,834.9	1,433.8	28.0	$52,265	$42,542
Brevard, NC Micro area	34,215	33,091	29,334	1,124	3,757	3.4	12.8	1,439.4	988.1	45.7	$42,070	$29,864
Transylvania County, NC	34,215	33,091	29,334	1,124	3,757	3.4	12.8	1,439.4	988.1	45.7	$42,070	$29,864
Bridgeport-Stamford-Norwalk, CT Metro area	943,823	916,864	882,567	26,959	34,297	2.9	3.9	113,853.4	95,360.4	19.4	$120,630	$103,728
Fairfield County, CT	943,823	916,864	882,567	26,959	34,297	2.9	3.9	113,853.4	95,360.4	19.4	$120,630	$103,728
Brookhaven, MS Micro area	34,205	34,870	33,166	-665	1,704	-1.9	5.1	1,323.1	1,070.0	23.7	$38,682	$30,659
Lincoln County, MS	34,205	34,870	33,166	-665	1,704	-1.9	5.1	1,323.1	1,070.0	23.7	$38,682	$30,659
Brookings, OR Micro area	22,813	22,365	21,137	448	1,228	2.0	5.8	973.1	730.4	33.2	$42,657	$32,639
Curry County, OR	22,813	22,365	21,137	448	1,228	2.0	5.8	973.1	730.4	33.2	$42,657	$32,639
Brookings, SD Micro area	35,232	31,962	28,220	3,270	3,742	10.2	13.3	1,631.3	1,132.5	44.0	$46,302	$35,395
Brookings County, SD	35,232	31,962	28,220	3,270	3,742	10.2	13.3	1,631.3	1,132.5	44.0	$46,302	$35,395
Brownsville, TN Micro area	17,335	18,807	19,797	-1,472	-990	-7.8	-5.0	555.1	501.3	10.7	$32,023	$26,648
Haywood County, TN	17,335	18,807	19,797	-1,472	-990	-7.8	-5.0	555.1	501.3	10.7	$32,023	$26,648
Brownsville-Harlingen, TX Metro area	423,908	406,215	335,227	17,693	70,988	4.4	21.2	12,189.8	9,518.8	28.1	$28,756	$23,350
Cameron County, TX	423,908	406,215	335,227	17,693	70,988	4.4	21.2	12,189.8	9,518.8	28.1	$28,756	$23,350
Brownwood, TX Micro area	37,924	38,106	37,674	-182	432	-0.5	1.1	1,472.6	1,115.3	32.0	$38,830	$29,289
Brown County, TX	37,924	38,106	37,674	-182	432	-0.5	1.1	1,472.6	1,115.3	32.0	$38,830	$29,289
Brunswick, GA Metro area	118,456	112,371	93,044	6,085	19,327	5.4	20.8	4,867.6	3,597.3	35.3	$41,092	$31,971
Brantley County, GA	18,897	18,414	14,629	483	3,785	2.6	25.9	518.0	402.1	28.8	$27,413	$21,777
Glynn County, GA	85,219	79,625	67,568	5,594	12,057	7.0	17.8	3,926.3	2,875.4	36.5	$46,073	$36,060
McIntosh County, GA	14,340	14,332	10,847	8	3,485	0.1	32.1	423.3	319.8	32.4	$29,519	$22,345
Bucyrus-Galion, OH Micro area	41,550	43,783	46,966	-2,233	-3,183	-5.1	-6.8	1,608.2	1,318.5	22.0	$38,704	$30,135
Crawford County, OH	41,550	43,783	46,966	-2,233	-3,183	-5.1	-6.8	1,608.2	1,318.5	22.0	$38,704	$30,135
Buffalo-Cheektowaga, NY Metro area	1,130,152	1,135,614	1,170,111	-5,462	-34,497	-0.5	-2.9	56,976.0	43,978.4	29.6	$50,414	$38,726
Erie County, NY	919,719	919,129	950,265	590	-31,136	0.1	-3.3	47,401.1	36,422.8	30.1	$51,539	$39,627
Niagara County, NY	210,433	216,485	219,846	-6,052	-3,361	-2.8	-1.5	9,574.9	7,555.7	26.7	$45,501	$34,903
Burley, ID Micro area	44,689	43,019	41,590	1,670	1,429	3.9	3.4	1,873.8	1,321.1	41.8	$41,930	$30,609

Table D-1. Population and Personal Income—Continued

Metropolitan or Micropolitan Statistical Area Metropolitan Division Component Counties	Population							Personal Income				
	2018 Estimate (July 1)	2010 census estimates base (April 1)	2000 census estimates base (April 1)	Net change 2010-2018	Net change 2000-2010	Percent change 2010-2018	Percent change 2000-2010	Total (million dollars) 2018	Total (million dollars) 2010	Percent change 2010-2018	Per capita 2018	Per capita 2010
Cassia County, ID	23,864	22,964	21,416	900	1,548	3.9	7.2	1,079.1	748.3	44.2	$45,220	$32,421
Minidoka County, ID	20,825	20,055	20,174	770	-119	3.8	-0.6	794.7	572.9	38.7	$38,159	$28,526
Burlington, IA-IL Micro area	45,847	47,653	50,564	-1,806	-2,911	-3.8	-5.8	2,258.5	1,658.8	36.2	$49,261	$34,861
Henderson County, IL	6,709	7,328	8,213	-619	-885	-8.4	-10.8	281.4	233.6	20.5	$41,951	$31,806
Des Moines County, IA	39,138	40,325	42,351	-1,187	-2,026	-2.9	-4.8	1,977.0	1,425.3	38.7	$50,515	$35,419
Burlington, NC Metro area	166,436	151,160	130,800	15,276	20,360	10.1	15.6	6,548.0	4,846.3	35.1	$39,342	$32,002
Alamance County, NC	166,436	151,160	130,800	15,276	20,360	10.1	15.6	6,548.0	4,846.3	35.1	$39,342	$32,002
Burlington-South Burlington, VT Metro area	221,083	211,262	198,889	9,821	12,373	4.6	6.2	12,728.8	9,289.1	37.0	$57,575	$43,913
Chittenden County, VT	164,572	156,540	146,571	8,032	9,969	5.1	6.8	10,024.8	7,269.4	37.9	$60,914	$46,369
Franklin County, VT	49,421	47,752	45,417	1,669	2,335	3.5	5.1	2,284.3	1,695.5	34.7	$46,220	$35,461
Grand Isle County, VT	7,090	6,970	6,901	120	69	1.7	1.0	419.8	324.2	29.5	$59,204	$46,659
Butte-Silver Bow, MT Micro area	34,993	34,209	34,606	784	-397	2.3	-1.1	1,712.5	1,469.9	16.5	$48,939	$42,939
Silver Bow County, MT	34,993	34,209	34,606	784	-397	2.3	-1.1	1,712.5	1,469.9	16.5	$48,939	$42,939
Cadillac, MI Micro area	48,579	47,586	44,962	993	2,624	2.1	5.8	1,748.5	1,321.4	32.3	$35,993	$27,786
Missaukee County, MI	15,113	14,851	14,478	262	373	1.8	2.6	528.5	397.1	33.1	$34,972	$26,804
Wexford County, MI	33,466	32,735	30,484	731	2,251	2.2	7.4	1,220.0	924.3	32.0	$36,454	$28,231
Calhoun, GA Micro area	57,685	55,186	44,104	2,499	11,082	4.5	25.1	2,131.3	1,456.8	46.3	$36,947	$26,380
Gordon County, GA	57,685	55,186	44,104	2,499	11,082	4.5	25.1	2,131.3	1,456.8	46.3	$36,947	$26,380
California-Lexington Park, MD Metro area	112,664	105,143	86,211	7,521	18,932	7.2	22.0	6,401.6	4,961.8	29.0	$56,820	$46,915
St. Mary's County, MD	112,664	105,143	86,211	7,521	18,932	7.2	22.0	6,401.6	4,961.8	29.0	$56,820	$46,915
Cambridge, MD Micro area	31,998	32,623	30,674	-625	1,949	-1.9	6.4	1,489.9	1,166.3	27.7	$46,562	$35,680
Dorchester County, MD	31,998	32,623	30,674	-625	1,949	-1.9	6.4	1,489.9	1,166.3	27.7	$46,562	$35,680
Cambridge, OH Micro area	39,022	40,091	40,792	-1,069	-701	-2.7	-1.7	1,556.1	1,167.3	33.3	$39,878	$29,078
Guernsey County, OH	39,022	40,091	40,792	-1,069	-701	-2.7	-1.7	1,556.1	1,167.3	33.3	$39,878	$29,078
Camden, AR Micro area	28,883	31,496	34,534	-2,613	-3,038	-8.3	-8.8	1,052.9	928.8	13.4	$36,454	$29,572
Calhoun County, AR	5,277	5,368	5,744	-91	-376	-1.7	-6.5	181.7	138.3	31.4	$34,426	$25,797
Ouachita County, AR	23,606	26,128	28,790	-2,522	-2,662	-9.7	-9.2	871.2	790.5	10.2	$36,907	$30,349
Campbellsville, KY Micro area	36,598	35,773	34,445	825	1,328	2.3	3.9	1,276.7	996.5	28.1	$34,885	$27,749
Green County, KY	11,049	11,273	11,518	-224	-245	-2.0	-2.1	382.0	307.8	24.1	$34,570	$27,370
Taylor County, KY	25,549	24,500	22,927	1,049	1,573	4.3	6.9	894.7	688.7	29.9	$35,020	$27,922
Cañon City, CO Micro area	48,021	46,824	46,145	1,197	679	2.6	1.5	1,701.6	1,210.2	40.6	$35,435	$25,839
Fremont County, CO	48,021	46,824	46,145	1,197	679	2.6	1.5	1,701.6	1,210.2	40.6	$35,435	$25,839
Canton-Massillon, OH Metro area	398,655	404,425	406,934	-5,770	-2,509	-1.4	-0.6	17,846.4	13,729.0	30.0	$44,767	$33,965
Carroll County, OH	27,081	28,835	28,836	-1,754	-1.0	-6.1	0.0	1,075.1	850.2	26.5	$39,698	$29,473
Stark County, OH	371,574	375,590	378,098	-4,016	-2,508	-1.1	-0.7	16,771.4	12,878.8	30.2	$45,136	$34,310
Cape Coral-Fort Myers, FL Metro area	754,610	618,754	440,888	135,856	177,866	22.0	40.3	38,685.8	24,256.4	59.5	$51,266	$39,095
Lee County, FL	754,610	618,754	440,888	135,856	177,866	22.0	40.3	38,685.8	24,256.4	59.5	$51,266	$39,095
Cape Girardeau, MO-IL Metro area	96,982	96,274	90,312	708	5,962	0.7	6.6	4,252.7	3,194.7	33.1	$43,850	$33,124
Alexander County, IL	6,060	8,238	9,590	-2,178	-1,352	-26.4	-14.1	210.4	219.2	-4.0	$34,713	$26,712
Bollinger County, MO	12,169	12,363	12,029	-194	334	-1.6	2.8	394.9	321.1	23.0	$32,454	$26,008
Cape Girardeau County, MO	78,753	75,673	68,693	3,080	6,980	4.1	10.2	3,647.4	2,654.4	37.4	$46,314	$34,974
Carbondale-Marion, IL Metro area	136,931	139,155	133,786	-2,224	5,369	-1.6	4.0	5,573.3	4,667.6	19.4	$40,701	$33,479
Jackson County, IL	57,419	60,209	59,612	-2,790	597	-4.6	1.0	2,140.8	1,890.7	13.2	$37,284	$31,316
Johnson County, IL	12,456	12,581	12,878	-125	-297	-1.0	-2.3	447.9	335.9	33.3	$35,956	$26,638
Williamson County, IL	67,056	66,365	61,296	691	5,069	1.0	8.3	2,984.6	2,441.0	22.3	$44,509	$36,744
Carlsbad-Artesia, NM Micro area	57,900	53,823	51,658	4,077	2,165	7.6	4.2	3,133.7	2,352.3	33.2	$54,122	$43,642
Eddy County, NM	57,900	53,823	51,658	4,077	2,165	7.6	4.2	3,133.7	2,352.3	33.2	$54,122	$43,642
Carroll, IA Micro area	20,154	20,816	21,421	-662	-605	-3.2	-2.8	1,097.5	846.5	29.7	$54,456	$40,650
Carroll County, IA	20,154	20,816	21,421	-662	-605	-3.2	-2.8	1,097.5	846.5	29.7	$54,456	$40,650
Carson City, NV Metro area	55,414	55,274	52,457	140	2,817	0.3	5.4	2,812.5	2,432.0	15.6	$50,754	$44,229
Carson City city, NV	55,414	55,274	52,457	140	2,817	0.3	5.4	2,812.5	2,432.0	15.6	$50,754	$44,229
Casper, WY Metro area	79,115	75,448	66,533	3,667	8,915	4.9	13.4	5,488.9	3,727.8	47.2	$69,379	$49,395
Natrona County, WY	79,115	75,448	66,533	3,667	8,915	4.9	13.4	5,488.9	3,727.8	47.2	$69,379	$49,395
Cedar City, UT Micro area	52,775	46,163	33,779	6,612	12,384	14.3	36.7	1,699.2	1,052.7	61.4	$32,197	$22,755
Iron County, UT	52,775	46,163	33,779	6,612	12,384	14.3	36.7	1,699.2	1,052.7	61.4	$32,197	$22,755
Cedar Rapids, IA Metro area	272,295	257,943	237,230	14,352	20,713	5.6	8.7	14,205.1	10,578.1	34.3	$52,168	$40,932
Benton County, IA	25,642	26,069	25,308	-427	761	-1.6	3.0	1,384.5	1,051.2	31.7	$53,994	$40,359
Jones County, IA	20,744	20,636	20,221	108	415	0.5	2.1	905.5	709.8	27.6	$43,652	$34,306
Linn County, IA	225,909	211,238	191,701	14,671	19,537	6.9	10.2	11,915.1	8,817.2	35.1	$52,743	$41,650
Cedartown, GA Micro area	42,470	41,479	38,127	991	3,352	2.4	8.8	1,374.7	1,072.4	28.2	$32,368	$25,822
Polk County, GA	42,470	41,479	38,127	991	3,352	2.4	8.8	1,374.7	1,072.4	28.2	$32,368	$25,822
Celina, OH Micro area	40,959	40,814	40,924	145	-110	0.4	-0.3	2,111.9	1,501.7	40.6	$51,562	$36,820
Mercer County, OH	40,959	40,814	40,924	145	-110	0.4	-0.3	2,111.9	1,501.7	40.6	$51,562	$36,820
Central City, KY Micro area	30,774	31,499	31,839	-725	-340	-2.3	-1.1	1,043.0	867.6	20.2	$33,892	$27,407
Muhlenberg County, KY	30,774	31,499	31,839	-725	-340	-2.3	-1.1	1,043.0	867.6	20.2	$33,892	$27,407
Centralia, IL Micro area	37,620	39,437	41,691	-1,817	-2,254	-4.6	-5.4	1,619.9	1,352.5	19.8	$43,059	$34,311
Marion County, IL	37,620	39,437	41,691	-1,817	-2,254	-4.6	-5.4	1,619.9	1,352.5	19.8	$43,059	$34,311
Centralia, WA Micro area	79,604	75,457	68,600	4,147	6,857	5.5	10.0	3,459.0	2,464.2	40.4	$43,453	$32,636
Lewis County, WA	79,604	75,457	68,600	4,147	6,857	5.5	10.0	3,459.0	2,464.2	40.4	$43,453	$32,636
Chambersburg-Waynesboro, PA Metro area	154,835	149,619	129,313	5,216	20,306	3.5	15.7	7,184.8	5,399.9	33.1	$46,403	$36,020
Franklin County, PA	154,835	149,619	129,313	5,216	20,306	3.5	15.7	7,184.8	5,399.9	33.1	$46,403	$36,020
Champaign-Urbana, IL Metro area	226,379	217,806	196,034	8,573	21,772	3.9	11.1	10,407.7	8,410.1	23.8	$45,975	$38,534
Champaign County, IL	209,983	201,081	179,669	8,902	21,412	4.4	11.9	9,518.1	7,686.9	23.8	$45,328	$38,141
Piatt County, IL	16,396	16,725	16,365	-329	360	-2.0	2.2	889.6	723.2	23.0	$54,258	$43,284
Charleston, WV Metro area	260,342	277,983	286,046	-17,641	-8,063	-6.3	-2.8	11,468.9	9,958.6	15.2	$44,053	$35,848
Boone County, WV	21,951	24,625	25,535	-2,674	-910	-10.9	-3.6	737.4	741.3	-0.5	$33,592	$30,129
Clay County, WV	8,632	9,384	10,330	-752	-946	-8.0	-9.2	266.9	237.2	12.5	$30,925	$25,310

Table D-1. Population and Personal Income—Continued

Metropolitan or Micropolitan Statistical Area Metropolitan Division Component Counties	Population							Personal Income				
				Net change		Percent change		Total (million dollars)			Per capita	
	2018 Estimate (July 1)	2010 census estimates base (April 1)	2000 census estimates base (April 1)	2010-2018	2000-2010	2010-2018	2000-2010	2018	2010	Percent change 2010-2018	2018	2010
Jackson County, WV	28,706	29,214	28,000	-508	1,214	-1.7	4.3	1,095.1	790.9	38.5	$38,147	$27,053
Kanawha County, WV	180,454	193,051	200,073	-12,597	-7,022	-6.5	-3.5	8,740.3	7,635.3	14.5	$48,435	$39,579
Lincoln County, WV	20,599	21,709	22,108	-1,110	-399	-5.1	-1.8	629.3	553.8	13.6	$30,549	$25,555
Charleston-Mattoon, IL Micro area	61,693	64,921	64,449	-3,228	472	-5.0	0.7	2,559.2	2,116.1	20.9	$41,483	$32,595
Coles County, IL	50,885	53,876	53,196	-2,991	680	-5.6	1.3	2,086.0	1,737.7	20.0	$40,995	$32,259
Cumberland County, IL	10,808	11,045	11,253	-237	-208	-2.1	-1.8	473.1	378.3	25.1	$43,778	$34,230
Charleston-North Charleston, SC Metro area	787,643	664,639	549,033	123,004	115,606	18.5	21.1	40,137.1	24,298.6	65.2	$50,958	$36,406
Berkeley County, SC	221,091	178,316	142,651	42,775	35,665	24.0	25.0	8,935.4	5,323.4	67.9	$40,415	$29,670
Charleston County, SC	405,905	350,150	309,969	55,755	40,181	15.9	13.0	24,953.7	14,605.8	70.8	$61,477	$41,616
Dorchester County, SC	160,647	136,173	96,413	24,474	39,760	18.0	41.2	6,248.0	4,369.3	43.0	$38,892	$31,880
Charlotte-Concord-Gastonia, NC-SC Metro area	2,594,090	2,243,926	1,742,647	350,164	501,279	15.6	28.8	135,350.4	87,057.9	55.5	$52,176	$38,691
Anson County, NC	24,877	26,929	25,275	-2,052	1,654	-7.6	6.5	861.1	718.3	19.9	$34,616	$26,750
Cabarrus County, NC	211,342	178,087	131,063	33,255	47,024	18.7	35.9	9,556.9	6,166.2	55.0	$45,220	$34,538
Gaston County, NC	222,846	206,094	190,365	16,752	15,729	8.1	8.3	9,221.1	7,146.4	29.0	$41,379	$34,673
Iredell County, NC	178,435	159,451	122,660	18,984	36,791	11.9	30.0	8,933.3	5,723.8	56.1	$50,065	$35,826
Lincoln County, NC	83,770	77,985	63,780	5,785	14,205	7.4	22.3	3,835.9	2,459.3	56.0	$45,791	$31,488
Mecklenburg County, NC	1,093,901	919,668	695,454	174,233	224,214	18.9	32.2	66,878.2	42,784.8	56.3	$61,137	$46,341
Rowan County, NC	141,262	138,532	130,340	2,730	8,192	2.0	6.3	5,380.6	4,090.3	31.5	$38,089	$29,561
Union County, NC	235,908	201,334	123,677	34,574	77,657	17.2	62.8	12,108.1	7,192.2	68.4	$51,326	$35,586
Chester County, SC	32,251	33,147	34,068	-896	-921	-2.7	-2.7	1,097.0	847.9	29.4	$34,014	$25,574
Lancaster County, SC	95,380	76,653	61,351	18,727	15,302	24.4	24.9	4,685.7	2,356.3	98.9	$49,127	$30,612
York County, SC	274,118	226,046	164,614	48,072	61,432	21.3	37.3	12,792.4	7,572.5	68.9	$46,667	$33,379
Charlottesville, VA Metro area	218,233	201,561	174,021	16,672	27,540	8.3	15.8	14,529.3	9,306.4	56.1	$66,577	$46,097
Albemarle County, VA	108,718	98,988	79,236	9,730	19,752	9.8	24.9	11,702.0	7,240.4	61.6	$74,513	$50,753
Fluvanna County, VA	26,783	25,744	20,047	1,039	5,697	4.0	28.4	1,197.0	888.2	34.8	$44,693	$34,437
Greene County, VA	19,779	18,389	15,244	1,390	3,145	7.6	20.6	877.9	624.1	40.7	$44,383	$33,812
Nelson County, VA	14,836	15,015	14,445	-179	570	-1.2	3.9	752.4	553.7	35.9	$50,717	$36,967
Charlottesville City, VA (included with Albemarle County)	48,117	43,425	45,049	4,692	-1,624	10.8	-3.6	-	-	-	-	-
Chattanooga, TN-GA Metro area	560,793	528,150	476,531	32,643	51,619	6.2	10.8	25,740.3	18,852.2	36.5	$45,900	$35,627
Catoosa County, GA	67,420	63,937	53,282	3,483	10,655	5.4	20.0	2,370.3	1,795.3	32.0	$35,158	$28,017
Dade County, GA	16,226	16,635	15,154	-409	1,481	-2.5	9.8	578.3	424.6	36.2	$35,640	$25,547
Walker County, GA	69,410	68,749	61,053	661	7,696	1.0	12.6	2,278.4	1,791.4	27.2	$32,826	$26,007
Hamilton County, TN	364,286	336,486	307,896	27,800	28,590	8.3	9.3	18,849.2	13,565.6	38.9	$51,743	$40,228
Marion County, TN	28,575	28,222	27,776	353	446	1.3	1.6	1,098.7	870.9	26.2	$38,450	$30,863
Sequatchie County, TN	14,876	14,121	11,370	755	2,751	5.3	24.2	565.3	404.2	39.9	$38,003	$28,611
Cheyenne, WY Metro area	98,976	91,885	81,607	7,091	10,278	7.7	12.6	5,150.6	3,937.0	30.8	$52,039	$42,684
Laramie County, WY	98,976	91,885	81,607	7,091	10,278	7.7	12.6	5,150.6	3,937.0	30.8	$52,039	$42,684
Chicago-Naperville-Elgin, IL-IN-WI Metro area	9,498,716	9,461,539	9,098,316	37,177	363,223	0.4	4.0	580,270.1	418,681.2	38.6	$61,089	$44,207
Chicago-Naperville-Evanston, IL Div	7,160,934	7,148,261	7,080,780	12,673	67,481	0.2	1.0	446,425.6	320,133.0	39.5	$62,342	$44,741
Cook County, IL	5,180,493	5,195,026	5,376,741	-14,533	-181,715	-0.3	-3.4	322,255.0	229,542.8	40.4	$62,205	$44,150
Du Page County, IL	928,589	916,771	904,161	11,818	12,610	1.3	1.4	67,684.2	48,605.1	39.3	$72,889	$52,945
Grundy County, IL	50,972	50,077	37,535	895	12,542	1.8	33.4	2,633.0	2,193.0	20.1	$51,657	$43,728
McHenry County, IL	308,570	308,827	260,077	-257	48,750	-0.1	18.7	17,193.6	12,867.6	33.6	$55,720	$41,635
Will County, IL	692,310	677,560	502,266	14,750	175,294	2.2	34.9	36,659.8	26,924.5	36.2	$52,953	$39,664
Elgin, IL Div	766,274	735,341	547,632	30,933	187,709	4.2	34.3	37,957.3	27,888.6	36.1	$49,535	$37,858
De Kalb County, IL	104,143	105,160	88,969	-1,017	16,191	-1.0	18.2	4,262.4	3,294.8	29.4	$40,929	$31,335
Kane County, IL	534,216	515,378	404,119	18,838	111,259	3.7	27.5	27,422.8	20,165.2	36.0	$51,333	$39,069
Kendall County, IL	127,915	114,803	54,544	13,112	60,259	11.4	110.5	6,272.1	4,428.6	41.6	$49,033	$38,384
Gary, IN Div	701,386	708,117	675,971	-6,731	32,146	-1.0	4.8	32,895.0	24,898.5	32.1	$46,900	$35,159
Jasper County, IN	33,370	33,481	30,043	-111	3,438	-0.3	11.4	1,444.7	1,132.5	27.6	$43,293	$33,809
Lake County, IN	484,411	496,095	484,564	-11,684	11,531	-2.4	2.4	21,881.9	16,958.3	29.0	$45,172	$34,194
Newton County, IN	14,011	14,239	14,566	-228	-327	-1.6	-2.2	557.9	441.4	26.4	$39,818	$31,012
Porter County, IN	169,594	164,302	146,798	5,292	17,504	3.2	11.9	9,010.5	6,366.3	41.5	$53,130	$38,701
Lake County-Kenosha County, IL-WI Div	870,122	869,820	793,933	302	75,887	0.0	9.6	62,992.2	45,761.0	37.7	$72,395	$52,550
Lake County, IL	700,832	703,396	644,356	-2,564	59,040	-0.4	9.2	55,056.9	39,872.9	38.1	$78,559	$56,622
Kenosha County, WI	169,290	166,424	149,577	2,866	16,847	1.7	11.3	7,935.3	5,888.1	34.8	$46,874	$35,337
Chico, CA Metro area	231,256	220,002	203,171	11,254	16,831	5.1	8.3	10,255.4	7,309.8	40.3	$44,346	$33,235
Butte County, CA	231,256	220,002	203,171	11,254	16,831	5.1	8.3	10,255.4	7,309.8	40.3	$44,346	$33,235
Chillicothe, OH Micro area	76,931	78,078	73,345	-1,147	4,733	-1.5	6.5	2,841.9	2,252.9	26.1	$36,941	$28,845
Ross County, OH	76,931	78,078	73,345	-1,147	4,733	-1.5	6.5	2,841.9	2,252.9	26.1	$36,941	$28,845
Cincinnati, OH-KY-IN Metro area	2,212,945	2,137,755	2,016,981	75,190	120,774	3.5	6.0	119,887.7	86,412.0	38.7	$54,176	$40,366
Dearborn County, IN	49,568	50,033	46,109	-465	3,924	-0.9	8.5	2,352.2	1,777.0	32.4	$47,454	$35,477
Franklin County, IN	22,736	23,096	22,151	-360	945	-1.6	4.3	1,060.1	854.1	24.1	$46,629	$37,042
Ohio County, IN	5,844	6,107	5,623	-263	484	-4.3	8.6	237.9	300.7	-20.9	$40,714	$49,333
Union County, IN	7,037	7,516	7,349	-479	167	-6.4	2.3	274.4	216.1	27.0	$38,998	$28,676
Boone County, KY	131,533	118,815	85,991	12,718	32,824	10.7	38.2	6,314.1	4,429.3	42.6	$48,004	$37,103
Bracken County, KY	8,239	8,488	8,279	-249	209	-2.9	2.5	302.9	247.4	22.4	$36,758	$29,053
Campbell County, KY	93,152	90,338	88,616	2,814	1,722	3.1	1.9	4,565.8	3,267.5	39.7	$49,015	$36,060
Gallatin County, KY	8,832	8,586	7,870	246	716	2.9	9.1	283.2	193.4	46.4	$32,065	$22,451
Grant County, KY	25,121	24,658	22,384	463	2,274	1.9	10.2	906.7	697.1	30.1	$36,093	$28,245
Kenton County, KY	166,051	159,723	151,464	6,328	8,259	4.0	5.5	9,627.9	6,822.6	41.1	$57,982	$42,654
Pendleton County, KY	14,529	14,875	14,390	-346	485	-2.3	3.4	635.7	421.0	51.0	$43,757	$28,226
Brown County, OH	43,602	44,828	42,285	-1,226	2,543	-2.7	6.0	1,624.6	1,278.8	27.0	$37,259	$28,503
Butler County, OH	382,378	368,135	332,807	14,243	35,328	3.9	10.6	18,127.6	13,069.0	38.7	$47,408	$35,408
Clermont County, OH	205,466	197,365	177,977	8,101	19,388	4.1	10.9	11,047.9	7,508.7	47.1	$53,770	$37,998

Table D-1. Population and Personal Income—Continued

Metropolitan or Micropolitan Statistical Area Metropolitan Division Component Counties	2018 Estimate (July 1)	2010 census estimates base (April 1)	2000 census estimates base (April 1)	Net change 2010-2018	Net change 2000-2010	Percent change 2010-2018	Percent change 2000-2010	Total (million dollars) 2018	Total (million dollars) 2010	Percent change 2010-2018	Per capita 2018	Per capita 2010
Hamilton County, OH	816,684	802,372	845,303	14,312	-42,931	1.8	-5.1	48,642.7	36,123.1	34.7	$59,561	$45,026
Warren County, OH	232,173	212,820	158,383	19,353	54,437	9.1	34.4	13,883.7	9,206.2	50.8	$59,799	$43,130
Clarksburg, WV Micro area	92,822	94,197	92,144	-1,375	2,053	-1.5	2.2	4,186.4	3,204.9	30.6	$45,101	$33,970
Doddridge County, WV	8,406	8,201	7,403	205	798	2.5	10.8	242.6	139.7	73.7	$28,862	$17,036
Harrison County, WV	67,554	69,108	68,652	-1,554	456	-2.2	0.7	3,257.9	2,579.1	26.3	$48,226	$37,237
Taylor County, WV	16,862	16,888	16,089	-26	799	-0.2	5.0	685.9	486.2	41.1	$40,675	$28,792
Clarksdale, MS Micro area	22,628	26,145	30,622	-3,517	-4,477	-13.5	-14.6	767.4	750.1	2.3	$33,915	$28,734
Coahoma County, MS	22,628	26,145	30,622	-3,517	-4,477	-13.5	-14.6	767.4	750.1	2.3	$33,915	$28,734
Clarksville, TN-KY Metro area	305,825	273,943	232,000	31,882	41,943	11.6	18.1	12,230.2	9,923.5	23.2	$39,991	$36,091
Christian County, KY	71,671	73,938	72,265	-2,267	1,673	-3.1	2.3	2,705.0	2,398.0	12.8	$37,742	$32,350
Trigg County, KY	14,643	14,329	12,597	314	1,732	2.2	13.7	534.4	459.8	16.2	$36,495	$32,099
Montgomery County, TN	205,950	172,363	134,768	33,587	37,595	19.5	27.9	8,450.3	6,574.5	28.5	$41,031	$37,968
Stewart County, TN	13,561	13,313	12,370	248	943	1.9	7.6	540.4	491.3	10.0	$39,853	$36,806
Clearlake, CA Micro area	64,382	64,664	58,309	-282	6,355	-0.4	10.9	2,780.4	1,999.3	39.1	$43,185	$30,885
Lake County, CA	64,382	64,664	58,309	-282	6,355	-0.4	10.9	2,780.4	1,999.3	39.1	$43,185	$30,885
Cleveland, MS Micro area	31,333	34,153	40,633	-2,820	-6,480	-8.3	-15.9	1,197.3	1,014.0	18.1	$38,213	$29,733
Bolivar County, MS	31,333	34,153	40,633	-2,820	-6,480	-8.3	-15.9	1,197.3	1,014.0	18.1	$38,213	$29,733
Cleveland, TN Metro area	123,625	115,754	104,015	7,871	11,739	6.8	11.3	4,743.6	3,562.8	33.1	$38,371	$30,740
Bradley County, TN	106,727	98,930	87,965	7,797	10,965	7.9	12.5	4,172.9	3,111.8	34.1	$39,099	$31,405
Polk County, TN	16,898	16,824	16,050	74	774	0.4	4.8	570.7	451.0	26.5	$33,772	$26,818
Cleveland-Elyria, OH Metro area	2,057,009	2,077,278	2,148,143	-20,269	-70,865	-1.0	-3.3	110,538.7	82,196.4	34.5	$53,738	$39,604
Cuyahoga County, OH	1,243,857	1,280,115	1,393,978	-36,258	-113,863	-2.8	-8.2	68,087.1	51,335.6	32.6	$54,739	$40,166
Geauga County, OH	94,031	93,409	90,895	622	2,514	0.7	2.8	6,500.3	4,669.6	39.2	$69,129	$50,000
Lake County, OH	230,514	230,050	227,511	464	2,539	0.2	1.1	11,693.8	8,748.3	33.7	$50,729	$38,034
Lorain County, OH	309,461	301,371	284,664	8,090	16,707	2.7	5.9	14,280.8	10,437.3	36.8	$46,147	$34,621
Medina County, OH	179,146	172,333	151,095	6,813	21,238	4.0	14.1	9,976.8	7,005.5	42.4	$55,691	$40,610
Clewiston, FL Micro area	41,556	39,143	36,210	2,413	2,933	6.2	8.1	1,291.2	1,007.6	28.1	$31,071	$25,826
Hendry County, FL	41,556	39,143	36,210	2,413	2,933	6.2	8.1	1,291.2	1,007.6	28.1	$31,071	$25,826
Clinton, IA Micro area	46,518	49,117	50,149	-2,599	-1,032	-5.3	-2.1	2,058.1	1,723.8	19.4	$44,244	$35,109
Clinton County, IA	46,518	49,117	50,149	-2,599	-1,032	-5.3	-2.1	2,058.1	1,723.8	19.4	$44,244	$35,109
Clovis, NM Micro area	49,437	48,376	45,044	1,061	3,332	2.2	7.4	2,183.2	1,811.9	20.5	$44,161	$37,006
Curry County, NM	49,437	48,376	45,044	1,061	3,332	2.2	7.4	2,183.2	1,811.9	20.5	$44,161	$37,006
Coeur d'Alene, ID Metro area	161,505	138,466	108,685	23,039	29,781	16.6	27.4	7,265.6	4,461.9	62.8	$44,987	$32,134
Kootenai County, ID	161,505	138,466	108,685	23,039	29,781	16.6	27.4	7,265.6	4,461.9	62.8	$44,987	$32,134
Coffeyville, KS Micro area	32,120	35,468	36,252	-3,348	-784	-9.4	-2.2	1,206.9	1,121.6	7.6	$37,576	$31,727
Montgomery County, KS	32,120	35,468	36,252	-3,348	-784	-9.4	-2.2	1,206.9	1,121.6	7.6	$37,576	$31,727
Coldwater, MI Micro area	43,622	45,248	45,787	-1,626	-539	-3.6	-1.2	1,641.2	1,233.3	33.1	$37,622	$27,297
Branch County, MI	43,622	45,248	45,787	-1,626	-539	-3.6	-1.2	1,641.2	1,233.3	33.1	$37,622	$27,297
College Station-Bryan, TX Metro area	262,431	228,668	184,885	33,763	43,783	14.8	23.7	10,374.7	6,967.7	48.9	$39,533	$30,367
Brazos County, TX	226,758	194,861	152,415	31,897	42,446	16.4	27.8	8,892.6	5,827.5	52.6	$39,216	$29,783
Burleson County, TX	18,389	17,187	16,470	1,202	717	7.0	4.4	783.9	590.8	32.7	$42,629	$34,276
Robertson County, TX	17,284	16,620	16,000	664	620	4.0	3.9	698.2	549.4	27.1	$40,394	$33,190
Colorado Springs, CO Metro area	738,939	645,609	537,484	93,330	108,125	14.5	20.1	35,832.5	24,893.2	43.9	$48,492	$38,275
El Paso County, CO	713,856	622,250	516,929	91,606	105,321	14.7	20.4	34,598.5	23,983.9	44.3	$48,467	$38,258
Teller County, CO	25,083	23,359	20,555	1,724	2,804	7.4	13.6	1,234.0	909.2	35.7	$49,197	$38,742
Columbia, MO Metro area	207,745	190,393	162,336	17,352	28,057	9.1	17.3	9,662.2	6,959.0	38.8	$46,510	$36,446
Boone County, MO	180,005	162,645	135,454	17,360	27,191	10.7	20.1	8,583.9	6,114.5	40.4	$47,687	$37,468
Cooper County, MO	17,603	17,604	16,670	0	934	0.0	5.6	685.0	530.0	29.2	$38,916	$30,111
Howard County, MO	10,137	10,144	10,212	-7	-68	-0.1	-0.7	393.3	314.4	25.1	$38,796	$30,993
Columbia, SC Metro area	832,666	767,476	647,158	65,190	120,318	8.5	18.6	37,391.9	26,529.7	40.9	$44,906	$34,470
Calhoun County, SC	14,520	15,176	15,185	-656	-9	-4.3	-0.1	558.3	453.2	23.2	$38,451	$30,022
Fairfield County, SC	22,402	23,960	23,454	-1,558	506	-6.5	2.2	823.5	684.9	20.2	$36,758	$28,727
Kershaw County, SC	65,592	61,592	52,647	4,000	8,945	6.5	17.0	2,704.2	1,974.6	36.9	$41,227	$31,999
Lexington County, SC	295,032	262,429	216,014	32,603	46,415	12.4	21.5	13,722.9	9,139.4	50.2	$46,513	$34,706
Richland County, SC	414,576	384,450	320,677	30,126	63,773	7.8	19.9	18,875.2	13,700.2	37.8	$45,529	$35,515
Saluda County, SC	20,544	19,869	19,181	675	688	3.4	3.6	707.8	577.6	22.5	$34,455	$29,003
Columbus, GA-AL Metro area	317,922	308,455	293,518	9,467	14,937	3.1	5.1	13,056.2	10,131.7	28.9	$41,067	$32,740
Russell County, AL	57,781	52,947	49,756	4,834	3,191	9.1	6.4	1,912.8	1,510.1	26.7	$33,104	$28,328
Chattahoochee County, GA	10,684	11,267	14,882	-583	-3,615	-5.2	-24.3	332.4	343.4	-3.2	$31,115	$30,689
Harris County, GA	34,475	31,998	23,695	2,477	8,303	7.7	35.0	1,636.5	1,164.7	40.5	$47,469	$36,224
Marion County, GA	8,351	8,738	7,144	-387	1,594	-4.4	22.3	245.0	178.2	37.5	$29,333	$20,383
Muscogee County, GA	194,160	190,573	186,291	3,587	4,282	1.9	2.3	8,572.0	6,640.0	29.1	$44,149	$34,745
Stewart County, GA	6,199	6,058	5,252	141	806	2.3	15.3	141.2	120.2	17.5	$22,771	$19,716
Talbot County, GA	6,272	6,874	6,498	-602	376	-8.8	5.8	216.4	175.2	23.5	$34,504	$25,520
Columbus, IN Metro area	82,753	76,786	71,435	5,967	5,351	7.8	7.5	4,131.2	2,893.7	42.8	$49,922	$37,668
Bartholomew County, IN	82,753	76,786	71,435	5,967	5,351	7.8	7.5	4,131.2	2,893.7	42.8	$49,922	$37,668
Columbus, MS Micro area	58,930	59,779	61,586	-849	-1,807	-1.4	-2.9	2,268.7	1,875.7	21.0	$38,498	$31,368
Lowndes County, MS	58,930	59,779	61,586	-849	-1,807	-1.4	-2.9	2,268.7	1,875.7	21.0	$38,498	$31,368
Columbus, NE Micro area	33,363	32,237	31,662	1,126	575	3.5	1.8	1,647.7	1,201.7	37.1	$49,386	$37,197
Platte County, NE	33,363	32,237	31,662	1,126	575	3.5	1.8	1,647.7	1,201.7	37.1	$49,386	$37,197
Columbus, OH Metro area	2,106,541	1,902,007	1,675,013	204,534	226,994	10.8	13.6	107,780.7	73,474.7	46.7	$51,165	$38,542
Delaware County, OH	204,826	174,172	109,989	30,654	64,183	17.6	58.4	15,176.1	9,422.9	61.1	$74,093	$53,815
Fairfield County, OH	155,782	146,182	122,759	9,600	23,423	6.6	19.1	7,183.6	5,148.1	39.5	$46,113	$35,165
Franklin County, OH	1,310,300	1,163,532	1,068,978	146,768	94,554	12.6	8.8	66,096.1	45,350.8	45.7	$50,443	$38,886
Hocking County, OH	28,385	29,373	28,241	-988	1,132	-3.4	4.0	1,080.0	820.4	31.6	$38,047	$27,829
Licking County, OH	175,769	166,482	145,491	9,287	20,991	5.6	14.4	8,095.7	5,772.2	40.3	$46,059	$34,626

Table D-1. Population and Personal Income—*Continued*

Metropolitan or Micropolitan Statistical Area Metropolitan Division Component Counties	Population							Personal Income				
	2018 Estimate (July 1)	2010 census estimates base (April 1)	2000 census estimates base (April 1)	Net change		Percent change		Total (million dollars)		Percent change 2010-2018	Per capita	
				2010-2018	2000-2010	2010-2018	2000-2010	2018	2010		2018	2010
Madison County, OH	44,413	43,438	40,213	975	3,225	2.2	8.0	1,854.3	1,348.5	37.5	$41,751	$31,044
Morrow County, OH	35,112	34,829	31,628	283	3,201	0.8	10.1	1,357.7	1,022.4	32.8	$38,666	$29,386
Perry County, OH	36,033	36,039	34,078	-6	1,961	0.0	5.8	1,340.0	995.7	34.6	$37,187	$27,627
Pickaway County, OH	58,086	55,680	52,727	2,406	2,953	4.3	5.6	2,389.2	1,747.2	36.7	$41,131	$31,348
Union County, OH	57,835	52,280	40,909	5,555	11,371	10.6	27.8	3,208.1	1,846.5	73.7	$55,470	$35,232
Concord, NH Micro area	151,132	146,457	136,225	4,675	10,232	3.2	7.5	8,754.2	7,884.0	11.0	$57,924	$53,855
Merrimack County, NH	151,132	146,457	136,225	4,675	10,232	3.2	7.5	8,754.2	7,884.0	11.0	$57,924	$53,855
Connersville, IN Micro area	23,047	24,301	25,588	-1,254	-1,287	-5.2	-5.0	943.5	718.7	31.3	$40,939	$29,546
Fayette County, IN	23,047	24,301	25,588	-1,254	-1,287	-5.2	-5.0	943.5	718.7	31.3	$40,939	$29,546
Cookeville, TN Micro area	112,669	106,061	93,417	6,608	12,644	6.2	13.5	4,225.4	3,152.2	34.0	$37,503	$29,663
Jackson County, TN	11,758	11,632	10,984	126	648	1.1	5.9	366.7	291.5	25.8	$31,189	$25,080
Overton County, TN	22,068	22,080	20,118	-12	1,962	-0.1	9.8	743.7	568.1	30.9	$33,701	$25,720
Putnam County, TN	78,843	72,349	62,315	6,494	10,034	9.0	16.1	3,115.0	2,292.6	35.9	$39,509	$31,597
Coos Bay, OR Micro area	64,389	63,054	62,779	1,335	275	2.1	0.4	2,808.6	2,029.7	38.4	$43,620	$32,212
Coos County, OR	64,389	63,054	62,779	1,335	275	2.1	0.4	2,808.6	2,029.7	38.4	$43,620	$32,212
Cordele, GA Micro area	22,601	23,430	21,996	-829	1,434	-3.5	6.5	735.4	563.4	30.5	$32,540	$24,047
Crisp County, GA	22,601	23,430	21,996	-829	1,434	-3.5	6.5	735.4	563.4	30.5	$32,540	$24,047
Corinth, MS Micro area	36,925	37,060	34,558	-135	2,502	-0.4	7.2	1,329.4	1,017.1	30.7	$36,003	$27,411
Alcorn County, MS	36,925	37,060	34,558	-135	2,502	-0.4	7.2	1,329.4	1,017.1	30.7	$36,003	$27,411
Cornelia, GA Micro area	45,388	43,036	35,902	2,352	7,134	5.5	19.9	1,539.8	1,138.9	35.2	$33,925	$26,447
Habersham County, GA	45,388	43,036	35,902	2,352	7,134	5.5	19.9	1,539.8	1,138.9	35.2	$33,925	$26,447
Corning, NY Micro area	95,796	98,990	98,726	-3,194	264	-3.2	0.3	4,329.4	3,514.9	23.2	$45,194	$35,500
Steuben County, NY	95,796	98,990	98,726	-3,194	264	-3.2	0.3	4,329.4	3,514.9	23.2	$45,194	$35,500
Corpus Christi, TX Metro area	429,158	405,025	380,783	24,133	24,242	6.0	6.4	19,016.3	14,702.3	29.3	$44,311	$36,331
Nueces County, TX	362,265	340,223	313,645	22,042	26,578	6.5	8.5	16,076.7	12,477.8	28.8	$44,378	$36,672
San Patricio County, TX	66,893	64,802	67,138	2,091	-2,336	3.2	-3.5	2,939.6	2,224.5	32.1	$43,945	$34,527
Corsicana, TX Micro area	49,565	47,840	45,124	1,725	2,716	3.6	6.0	1,879.6	1,457.3	29.0	$37,922	$30,442
Navarro County, TX	49,565	47,840	45,124	1,725	2,716	3.6	6.0	1,879.6	1,457.3	29.0	$37,922	$30,442
Cortland, NY Micro area	47,823	49,294	48,599	-1,471	695	-3.0	1.4	1,946.0	1,555.2	25.1	$40,691	$31,556
Cortland County, NY	47,823	49,294	48,599	-1,471	695	-3.0	1.4	1,946.0	1,555.2	25.1	$40,691	$31,556
Corvallis, OR Metro area	92,101	85,582	78,153	6,519	7,429	7.6	9.5	4,330.5	3,085.5	40.4	$47,019	$36,056
Benton County, OR	92,101	85,582	78,153	6,519	7,429	7.6	9.5	4,330.5	3,085.5	40.4	$47,019	$36,056
Coshocton, OH Micro area	36,629	36,898	36,655	-269	243	-0.7	0.7	1,276.8	1,021.1	25.0	$34,856	$27,644
Coshocton County, OH	36,629	36,898	36,655	-269	243	-0.7	0.7	1,276.8	1,021.1	25.0	$34,856	$27,644
Craig, CO Micro area	13,188	13,791	13,184	-603	607	-4.4	4.6	555.6	447.7	24.1	$42,130	$32,455
Moffat County, CO	13,188	13,791	13,184	-603	607	-4.4	4.6	555.6	447.7	24.1	$42,130	$32,455
Crawfordsville, IN Micro area	38,346	38,121	37,629	225	492	0.6	1.3	1,536.0	1,274.5	20.5	$40,056	$33,455
Montgomery County, IN	38,346	38,121	37,629	225	492	0.6	1.3	1,536.0	1,274.5	20.5	$40,056	$33,455
Crescent City, CA Micro area	27,828	28,610	27,507	-782	1,103	-2.7	4.0	1,037.1	783.4	32.4	$37,268	$27,421
Del Norte County, CA	27,828	28,610	27,507	-782	1,103	-2.7	4.0	1,037.1	783.4	32.4	$37,268	$27,421
Crestview-Fort Walton Beach-Destin, FL Metro area	278,644	235,868	211,099	42,776	24,769	18.1	11.7	14,393.3	9,559.6	50.6	$51,655	$40,520
Okaloosa County, FL	207,269	180,825	170,498	26,444	10,327	14.6	6.1	10,130.3	7,376.4	37.3	$48,875	$40,818
Walton County, FL	71,375	55,043	40,601	16,332	14,442	29.7	35.6	4,263.1	2,183.2	95.3	$59,728	$39,544
Crossville, TN Micro area	59,673	56,062	46,802	3,611	9,260	6.4	19.8	2,184.8	1,636.7	33.5	$36,613	$29,125
Cumberland County, TN	59,673	56,062	46,802	3,611	9,260	6.4	19.8	2,184.8	1,636.7	33.5	$36,613	$29,125
Cullman, AL Micro area	83,442	80,406	77,483	3,036	2,923	3.8	3.8	3,304.9	2,457.4	34.5	$39,607	$30,544
Cullman County, AL	83,442	80,406	77,483	3,036	2,923	3.8	3.8	3,304.9	2,457.4	34.5	$39,607	$30,544
Cullowhee, NC Micro area	57,572	54,245	46,089	3,327	8,156	6.1	17.7	1,970.4	1,456.9	35.2	$34,226	$26,796
Jackson County, NC	43,327	40,261	33,121	3,066	7,140	7.6	21.6	1,423.0	1,051.2	35.4	$32,844	$26,048
Swain County, NC	14,245	13,984	12,968	261	1,016	1.9	7.8	547.4	405.6	35.0	$38,429	$28,951
Cumberland, MD-WV Metro area	97,915	103,245	102,008	-5,330	1,237	-5.2	1.2	3,921.4	3,278.3	19.6	$40,049	$31,784
Allegany County, MD	70,975	75,047	74,930	-4,072	117	-5.4	0.2	2,875.7	2,398.9	19.9	$40,517	$32,000
Mineral County, WV	26,940	28,198	27,078	-1,258	1,120	-4.5	4.1	1,045.7	879.4	18.9	$38,815	$31,209
Dallas-Fort Worth-Arlington, TX Metro area	7,470,158	6,366,568	5,156,217	1,103,590	1,210,351	17.3	23.5	417,480.6	262,043.3	59.3	$55,886	$40,994
Dallas-Plano-Irving, TX Div	5,007,190	4,228,916	3,445,899	778,274	783,017	18.4	22.7	293,143.9	177,669.5	65.0	$58,545	$41,833
Collin County, TX	1,005,146	782,220	491,675	222,926	290,545	28.5	59.1	66,212.7	38,781.7	70.7	$65,874	$49,188
Dallas County, TX	2,637,772	2,366,683	2,218,899	271,089	147,784	11.5	6.7	155,610.2	96,799.4	60.8	$58,993	$40,804
Denton County, TX	859,064	662,554	432,976	196,510	229,578	29.7	53.0	48,049.9	27,560.8	74.3	$55,933	$41,335
Ellis County, TX	179,436	149,604	111,360	29,832	38,244	19.9	34.3	7,951.4	4,987.6	59.4	$44,313	$33,168
Hunt County, TX	96,493	86,162	76,596	10,331	9,566	12.0	12.5	3,669.5	2,568.9	42.8	$38,029	$29,738
Kaufman County, TX	128,622	103,363	71,313	25,259	32,050	24.4	44.9	5,509.8	3,382.2	62.9	$42,837	$32,556
Rockwall County, TX	100,657	78,330	43,080	22,327	35,250	28.5	81.8	6,140.4	3,589.0	71.1	$61,003	$45,484
Fort Worth-Arlington-Grapevine, TX Div	2,462,968	2,137,652	1,710,318	325,316	427,334	15.2	25.0	124,336.6	84,373.7	47.4	$50,482	$39,332
Johnson County, TX	171,361	150,940	126,811	20,421	24,129	13.5	19.0	7,145.3	4,934.9	44.8	$41,697	$32,628
Parker County, TX	138,371	116,957	88,495	21,414	28,462	18.3	32.2	7,373.6	4,624.4	59.4	$53,289	$39,415
Tarrant County, TX	2,084,931	1,810,655	1,446,219	274,276	364,436	15.1	25.2	106,829.2	72,760.7	46.8	$51,239	$40,033
Wise County, TX	68,305	59,100	48,793	9,205	10,307	15.6	21.1	2,988.5	2,053.8	45.5	$43,752	$34,751
Dalton, GA Metro area	143,983	142,221	120,031	1,762	22,190	1.2	18.5	5,228.9	3,651.6	43.2	$36,316	$25,666
Murray County, GA	39,921	39,628	36,506	293	3,122	0.7	8.6	1,196.3	914.9	30.8	$29,968	$23,141
Whitfield County, GA	104,062	102,593	83,525	1,469	19,068	1.4	22.8	4,032.6	2,736.7	47.4	$38,752	$26,637
Danville, IL Metro area	76,806	81,625	83,919	-4,819	-2,294	-5.9	-2.7	3,032.4	2,647.8	14.5	$39,481	$32,433
Vermilion County, IL	76,806	81,625	83,919	-4,819	-2,294	-5.9	-2.7	3,032.4	2,647.8	14.5	$39,481	$32,433
Danville, KY Micro area	54,744	53,173	51,058	1,571	2,115	3.0	4.1	1,911.0	1,495.4	27.8	$34,907	$28,009
Boyle County, KY	30,100	28,437	27,697	1,663	740	5.8	2.7	1,137.2	877.3	29.6	$37,780	$30,603
Lincoln County, KY	24,644	24,736	23,361	-92	1,375	-0.4	5.9	773.8	618.1	25.2	$31,399	$25,001

Table D-1. Population and Personal Income—*Continued*

Metropolitan or Micropolitan Statistical Area Metropolitan Division Component Counties	Population							Personal Income				
	2018 Estimate (July 1)	2010 census estimates base (April 1)	2000 census estimates base (April 1)	Net change 2010-2018	Net change 2000-2010	Percent change 2010-2018	Percent change 2000-2010	Total (million dollars) 2018	Total (million dollars) 2010	Percent change 2010-2018	Per capita 2018	Per capita 2010
Danville, VA Micro area	101,642	106,550	110,156	-4,908	-3,606	-4.6	-3.3	3,912.9	3,092.8	26.5	$38,497	$29,037
Pittsylvania County, VA	60,949	63,473	61,745	-2,524	1,728	-4.0	2.8	3,912.9	3,092.8	26.5	$38,497	$29,037
Danville City, VA (included with Pittsylvania County personal Income)	40,693	43,077	48,411	-2,384	-5,334	-5.5	-11.0	-	-	-	-	-
Daphne-Fairhope-Foley, AL Metro area	218,022	182,264	140,415	35,758	41,849	19.6	29.8	9,940.9	6,618.3	50.2	$45,596	$36,144
Baldwin County, AL	218,022	182,264	140,415	35,758	41,849	19.6	29.8	9,940.9	6,618.3	50.2	$45,596	$36,144
Davenport-Moline-Rock Island, IA-IL Metro area..	381,451	379,688	376,019	1,763	3,669	0.5	1.0	18,756.6	15,194.1	23.4	$49,172	$40,011
Henry County, IL	49,090	50,485	51,020	-1,395	-535	-2.8		2,212.6	1,855.5	19.2	$45,072	$36,778
Mercer County, IL	15,601	16,434	16,957	-833	-523	-5.1	-3.1	702.8	608.0	15.6	$45,046	$37,051
Rock Island County, IL	143,477	147,546	149,374	-4,069	-1,828	-2.8	-1.2	6,428.0	5,488.7	17.1	$44,802	$37,182
Scott County, IA	173,283	165,223	158,668	8,060	6,555	4.9	4.1	9,413.2	7,241.9	30.0	$54,323	$43,817
Dayton, TN Micro area	33,044	31,800	28,400	1,244	3,400	3.9	12.0	1,128.4	880.7	28.1	$34,147	$27,648
Rhea County, TN	33,044	31,800	28,400	1,244	3,400	3.9	12.0	1,128.4	880.7	28.1	$34,147	$27,648
Dayton-Kettering, OH Metro area	806,548	799,268	805,816	7,280	-6,548	0.9	-0.8	38,461.5	29,014.5	32.6	$47,687	$36,283
Greene County, OH	167,995	161,576	147,886	6,419	13,690	4.0	9.3	8,448.7	6,187.7	36.5	$50,291	$38,292
Miami County, OH	106,222	102,501	98,868	3,721	3,633	3.6	3.7	5,051.1	3,668.6	37.7	$47,552	$35,797
Montgomery County, OH	532,331	535,191	559,062	-2,860	-23,871	-0.5	-4.3	24,961.7	19,158.2	30.3	$46,891	$35,770
Decatur, AL Metro area	152,046	153,825	145,867	-1,779	7,958	-1.2	5.5	5,887.1	4,818.6	22.2	$38,719	$31,300
Lawrence County, AL	32,957	34,339	34,803	-1,382	-464	-4.0	-1.3	1,124.7	946.9	18.8	$34,125	$27,570
Morgan County, AL	119,089	119,486	111,064	-397	8,422	-0.3	7.6	4,762.5	3,871.7	23.0	$39,991	$32,371
Decatur, IL Metro area	104,712	110,775	114,706	-6,063	-3,931	-5.5	-3.4	5,048.6	4,367.8	15.6	$48,214	$39,427
Macon County, IL	104,712	110,775	114,706	-6,063	-3,931	-5.5	-3.4	5,048.6	4,367.8	15.6	$48,214	$39,427
Decatur, IN Micro area	35,636	34,387	33,625	1,249	762	3.6	2.3	1,395.8	971.3	43.7	$39,167	$28,192
Adams County, IN	35,636	34,387	33,625	1,249	762	3.6	2.3	1,395.8	971.3	43.7	$39,167	$28,192
Defiance, OH Micro area	38,165	39,030	39,500	-865	-470	-2.2	-1.2	1,585.4	1,213.5	30.6	$41,540	$31,047
Defiance County, OH	38,165	39,030	39,500	-865	-470	-2.2	-1.2	1,585.4	1,213.5	30.6	$41,540	$31,047
Del Rio, TX Micro area	49,208	48,879	44,856	329	4,023	0.7	9.0	1,798.7	1,457.0	23.5	$36,554	$29,746
Val Verde County, TX	49,208	48,879	44,856	329	4,023	0.7	9.0	1,798.7	1,457.0	23.5	$36,554	$29,746
Deltona-Daytona Beach-Ormond Beach, FL Metro area	659,605	590,299	493,175	69,306	97,124	11.7	19.7	28,381.3	19,697.9	44.1	$43,028	$33,357
Flagler County, FL	112,067	95,703	49,832	16,364	45,871	17.1	92.1	5,179.7	3,161.4	63.8	$46,220	$32,905
Volusia County, FL	547,538	494,596	443,343	52,942	51,253	10.7	11.6	23,201.6	16,536.5	40.3	$42,374	$33,445
Deming, NM Micro area	23,963	25,095	25,016	-1,132	79	-4.5	0.3	746.2	675.9	10.4	$31,140	$26,949
Luna County, NM	23,963	25,095	25,016	-1,132	79	-4.5	0.3	746.2	675.9	10.4	$31,140	$26,949
Denver-Aurora-Lakewood, CO Metro area	2,932,415	2,543,602	2,179,240	388,813	364,362	15.3	16.7	188,515.2	111,542.4	69.0	$64,287	$43,660
Adams County, CO	511,868	441,698	348,618	70,170	93,080	15.9	26.7	22,171.3	13,645.4	62.5	$43,315	$30,754
Arapahoe County, CO	651,215	572,130	487,967	79,085	84,163	13.8	17.2	39,190.0	23,553.4	66.4	$60,180	$40,979
Broomfield County, CO	69,267	55,856	38,272	13,411	17,584	24.0	45.9	4,600.0	3,045.1	51.1	$66,410	$54,162
Clear Creek County, CO	9,605	9,064	9,322	541	-258	6.0	-2.8	588.8	399.8	47.3	$61,300	$44,060
Denver County, CO	716,492	599,815	554,636	116,677	45,179	19.5	8.1	57,211.4	29,588.9	93.4	$79,849	$49,041
Douglas County, CO	342,776	285,465	175,766	57,311	109,699	20.1	62.4	25,249.7	15,418.3	63.8	$73,662	$53,727
Elbert County, CO	26,282	23,088	19,872	3,194	3,216	13.8	16.2	1,506.9	911.1	65.4	$57,334	$39,368
Gilpin County, CO	6,121	5,453	4,757	668	696	12.3	14.6	294.6	195.1	51.0	$48,128	$35,633
Jefferson County, CO	580,233	534,829	525,507	45,404	9,322	8.5	1.8	36,865.4	24,261.5	52.0	$63,536	$45,278
Park County, CO	18,556	16,204	14,523	2,352	1,681	14.5	11.6	837.1	523.8	59.8	$45,113	$32,175
DeRidder, LA Micro area	37,253	35,654	32,986	1,599	2,668	4.5	8.1	1,593.8	1,259.3	26.6	$42,782	$35,141
Beauregard Parish, LA	37,253	35,654	32,986	1,599	2,668	4.5	8.1	1,593.8	1,259.3	26.6	$42,782	$35,141
Des Moines-West Des Moines, IA Metro area	692,556	606,474	518,607	86,082	87,867	14.2	16.9	37,465.6	25,522.2	46.8	$54,098	$41,913
Dallas County, IA	90,180	66,138	40,750	24,042	25,388	36.4	62.3	5,963.4	3,269.9	82.4	$66,128	$48,989
Guthrie County, IA	10,720	10,955	11,353	-235	-398	-2.1	-3.5	564.9	427.5	32.1	$52,694	$39,091
Jasper County, IA	37,147	36,842	37,213	305	-371	0.8		1,617.8	1,225.7	32.0	$43,551	$33,296
Madison County, IA	16,249	15,679	14,019	570	1,660	3.6	11.8	804.4	587.5	36.9	$49,505	$37,330
Polk County, IA	487,204	430,632	374,601	56,572	56,031	13.1	15.0	25,926.7	18,258.5	42.0	$53,215	$42,230
Warren County, IA	51,056	46,228	40,671	4,828	5,557	10.4	13.7	2,588.4	1,753.1	47.6	$50,698	$37,831
Detroit-Warren-Dearborn, MI Metro area	4,326,442	4,296,290	4,452,557	30,152	-156,267	0.7	-3.5	229,674.2	163,055.0	40.9	$53,086	$37,994
Detroit-Dearborn-Livonia, MI Div	1,753,893	1,820,539	2,061,162	-66,646	-240,623	-3.7	-11.7	75,316.5	58,973.3	27.7	$42,942	$32,489
Wayne County, MI	1,753,893	1,820,539	2,061,162	-66,646	-240,623	-3.7	-11.7	75,316.5	58,973.3	27.7	$42,942	$32,489
Warren-Troy-Farmington Hills, MI Div	2,572,549	2,475,751	2,391,395	96,798	84,356	3.9	3.5	154,357.7	104,081.7	48.3	$60,002	$42,029
Lapeer County, MI	88,028	88,318	87,904	-290	414	-0.3	0.5	3,845.0	2,738.8	40.4	$43,679	$31,050
Livingston County, MI	191,224	180,961	156,951	10,263	24,010	5.7	15.3	11,153.4	7,192.5	55.1	$58,326	$39,724
Macomb County, MI	874,759	841,039	788,149	33,720	52,890	4.0	6.7	40,702.9	28,968.1	40.5	$46,530	$34,430
Oakland County, MI	1,259,201	1,202,384	1,194,156	56,817	8,228	4.7	0.7	91,595.3	59,914.2	52.9	$72,741	$49,799
St. Clair County, MI	159,337	163,049	164,235	-3,712	-1,186	-2.3	-0.7	7,061.2	5,268.0	34.0	$44,316	$32,380
Dickinson, ND Micro area	31,916	24,983	23,524	6,933	1,459	27.8	6.2	1,960.4	1,279.8	53.2	$61,425	$50,902
Billings County, ND	919	784	888	135	-104	17.2	-11.7	68.6	41.5	65.3	$74,682	$53,008
Stark County, ND	30,997	24,199	22,636	6,798	1,563	28.1	6.9	1,891.8	1,238.3	52.8	$61,032	$50,834
Dixon, IL Micro area	34,223	36,031	36,062	-1,808	-31	-5.0	-0.1	1,430.1	1,187.0	20.5	$41,788	$32,995
Lee County, IL	34,223	36,031	36,062	-1,808	-31	-5.0	-0.1	1,430.1	1,187.0	20.5	$41,788	$32,995
Dodge City, KS Micro area	33,888	33,844	32,458	44	1,386	0.1	4.3	1,320.3	1,083.6	21.8	$38,962	$31,862
Ford County, KS	33,888	33,844	32,458	44	1,386	0.1	4.3	1,320.3	1,083.6	21.8	$38,962	$31,862
Dothan, AL Metro area	148,245	145,641	130,861	2,604	14,780	1.8	11.3	6,060.6	4,924.6	23.1	$40,883	$33,760
Geneva County, AL	26,314	26,787	25,764	-473	1,023	-1.8	4.0	926.0	774.5	19.6	$35,192	$28,920
Henry County, AL	17,209	17,300	16,310	-91	990	-0.5	6.1	694.6	533.9	30.1	$40,360	$30,867
Houston County, AL	104,722	101,554	88,787	3,168	12,767	3.1	14.4	4,440.0	3,616.1	22.8	$42,398	$35,525

Table D-1. Population and Personal Income—*Continued*

Metropolitan or Micropolitan Statistical Area Metropolitan Division Component Counties	Population							Personal Income				
	2018 Estimate (July 1)	2010 census estimates base (April 1)	2000 census estimates base (April 1)	Net change		Percent change		Total (million dollars)		Percent change 2010-2018	Per capita	
				2010-2018	2000-2010	2010-2018	2000-2010	2018	2010		2018	2010
Douglas, GA Micro area	51,390	50,736	45,022	654	5,714	1.3	12.7	1,659.9	1,242.8	33.6	$32,300	$24,321
Atkinson County, GA	8,297	8,382	7,609	-85	773	-1.0	10.2	253.2	182.6	38.7	$30,511	$21,828
Coffee County, GA	43,093	42,354	37,413	739	4,941	1.7	13.2	1,406.7	1,060.2	32.7	$32,644	$24,809
Dover, DE Metro area	178,550	162,349	126,697	16,201	35,652	10.0	28.1	7,503.1	5,515.5	36.0	$42,023	$33,846
Kent County, DE	178,550	162,349	126,697	16,201	35,652	10.0	28.1	7,503.1	5,515.5	36.0	$42,023	$33,846
Dublin, GA Micro area	63,842	65,298	60,288	-1,456	5,010	-2.2	8.3	2,228.0	1,808.3	23.2	$34,899	$27,704
Johnson County, GA	9,708	9,972	8,560	-264	1,412	-2.6	16.5	254.3	204.6	24.3	$26,195	$20,489
Laurens County, GA	47,325	48,445	44,874	-1,120	3,571	-2.3	8.0	1,768.6	1,432.9	23.4	$37,372	$29,605
Treutlen County, GA	6,809	6,881	6,854	-72	27		0.4	205.1	170.9	20.0	$30,119	$24,801
DuBois, PA Micro area	79,388	81,616	83,382	-2,228	-1,766	-2.7	-2.1	3,526.5	2,867.6	23.0	$44,421	$35,162
Clearfield County, PA	79,388	81,616	83,382	-2,228	-1,766	-2.7	-2.1	3,526.5	2,867.6	23.0	$44,421	$35,162
Dubuque, IA Metro area	96,854	93,643	89,143	3,211	4,500	3.4	5.0	4,754.0	3,462.8	37.3	$49,085	$36,867
Dubuque County, IA	96,854	93,643	89,143	3,211	4,500	3.4	5.0	4,754.0	3,462.8	37.3	$49,085	$36,867
Duluth, MN-WI Metro area	289,457	290,638	286,544	-1,181	4,094	-0.4	1.4	13,387.3	10,573.8	26.6	$46,250	$36,393
Carlton County, MN	35,837	35,386	31,671	451	3,715	1.3	11.7	1,544.5	1,165.4	32.5	$43,098	$32,906
Lake County, MN	10,658	10,862	11,058	-204	-196	-1.9	-1.8	513.0	392.7	30.6	$48,132	$36,183
St. Louis County, MN	199,754	200,231	200,528	-477	-297	-0.2	-0.1	9,471.7	7,551.3	25.4	$47,417	$37,730
Douglas County, WI	43,208	44,159	43,287	-951	872	-2.2	2.0	1,858.1	1,464.4	26.9	$43,004	$33,180
Dumas, TX Micro area	21,485	21,904	20,121	-419	1,783	-1.9	8.9	886.8	654.1	35.6	$41,275	$29,722
Moore County, TX	21,485	21,904	20,121	-419	1,783	-1.9	8.9	886.8	654.1	35.6	$41,275	$29,722
Duncan, OK Micro area	43,265	45,048	43,182	-1,783	1,866	-4.0	4.3	1,791.7	1,670.0	7.3	$41,413	$37,026
Stephens County, OK	43,265	45,048	43,182	-1,783	1,866	-4.0	4.3	1,791.7	1,670.0	7.3	$41,413	$37,026
Durango, CO Micro area	56,310	51,335	43,941	4,975	7,394	9.7	16.8	3,142.5	2,136.1	47.1	$55,807	$41,604
La Plata County, CO	56,310	51,335	43,941	4,975	7,394	9.7	16.8	3,142.5	2,136.1	47.1	$55,807	$41,604
Durant, OK Micro area	47,192	42,416	36,534	4,776	5,882	11.3	16.1	1,631.7	1,148.6	42.1	$34,575	$26,972
Bryan County, OK	47,192	42,416	36,534	4,776	5,882	11.3	16.1	1,631.7	1,148.6	42.1	$34,575	$26,972
Durham-Chapel Hill, NC Metro area	635,527	564,191	474,991	71,336	89,200	12.6	18.8	34,341.6	23,242.9	47.8	$54,036	$41,046
Chatham County, NC	73,139	63,481	49,329	9,658	14,152	15.2	28.7	4,610.7	2,852.3	61.6	$63,041	$44,678
Durham County, NC	316,739	269,999	223,314	46,740	46,685	17.3	20.9	16,058.0	10,887.9	47.5	$50,698	$40,124
Granville County, NC	60,115	57,531	48,498	2,584	9,033	4.5	18.6	2,323.6	1,732.8	34.1	$38,652	$30,050
Orange County, NC	146,027	133,702	118,227	12,325	15,475	9.2	13.1	9,840.0	6,563.1	49.9	$67,385	$48,983
Person County, NC	39,507	39,478	35,623	29	3,855	0.1	10.8	1,509.3	1,206.8	25.1	$38,202	$30,619
Dyersburg, TN Micro area	37,320	38,330	37,279	-1,010	1,051	-2.6	2.8	1,516.8	1,267.8	19.6	$40,642	$33,088
Dyer County, TN	37,320	38,330	37,279	-1,010	1,051	-2.6	2.8	1,516.8	1,267.8	19.6	$40,642	$33,088
Eagle Pass, TX Micro area	58,485	54,258	47,297	4,227	6,961	7.8	14.7	1,784.1	1,267.0	40.8	$30,505	$23,270
Maverick County, TX	58,485	54,258	47,297	4,227	6,961	7.8	14.7	1,784.1	1,267.0	40.8	$30,505	$23,270
Easton, MD Micro area	36,968	37,777	33,812	-809	3,965	-2.1	11.7	2,707.2	2,162.9	25.2	$73,232	$57,109
Talbot County, MD	36,968	37,777	33,812	-809	3,965	-2.1	11.7	2,707.2	2,162.9	25.2	$73,232	$57,109
East Stroudsburg, PA Metro area	169,507	169,832	138,687	-325	31,145	-0.2	22.5	7,241.7	5,419.4	33.6	$42,722	$31,908
Monroe County, PA	169,507	169,832	138,687	-325	31,145	-0.2	22.5	7,241.7	5,419.4	33.6	$42,722	$31,908
Eau Claire, WI Metro area	168,669	161,385	148,337	7,284	13,048	4.5	8.8	8,003.4	5,998.2	33.4	$47,450	$37,105
Chippewa County, WI	64,135	62,506	55,195	1,629	7,311	2.6	13.2	2,960.6	2,206.1	34.2	$46,162	$35,219
Eau Claire County, WI	104,534	98,879	93,142	5,655	5,737	5.7	6.2	5,042.8	3,792.1	33.0	$48,240	$38,299
Edwards, CO Micro area	54,993	52,196	41,659	2,797	10,537	5.4	25.3	4,297.8	2,319.4	85.3	$78,152	$44,515
Eagle County, CO	54,993	52,196	41,659	2,797	10,537	5.4	25.3	4,297.8	2,319.4	85.3	$78,152	$44,515
Effingham, IL Micro area	34,208	34,246	34,264	-38	-18	-0.1	-0.1	1,730.9	1,332.2	29.9	$50,599	$38,927
Effingham County, IL	34,208	34,246	34,264	-38	-18	-0.1	-0.1	1,730.9	1,332.2	29.9	$50,599	$38,927
El Campo, TX Micro area	41,619	41,280	41,188	339	92	0.8	0.2	1,726.1	1,401.6	23.2	$41,473	$33,952
Wharton County, TX	41,619	41,280	41,188	339	92	0.8	0.2	1,726.1	1,401.6	23.2	$41,473	$33,952
El Centro, CA Metro area	181,827	174,524	142,361	7,303	32,163	4.2	22.6	6,722.9	5,146.7	30.6	$36,974	$29,455
Imperial County, CA	181,827	174,524	142,361	7,303	32,163	4.2	22.6	6,722.9	5,146.7	30.6	$36,974	$29,455
El Dorado, AR Micro area	39,126	41,639	45,629	-2,513	-3,990	-6.0	-8.7	1,818.3	1,563.1	16.3	$46,474	$37,600
Union County, AR	39,126	41,639	45,629	-2,513	-3,990	-6.0	-8.7	1,818.3	1,563.1	16.3	$46,474	$37,600
Elizabeth City, NC Micro area	53,061	54,114	46,265	-1,053	7,849	-1.9	17.0	2,109.8	1,758.3	20.0	$39,762	$32,495
Pasquotank County, NC	39,639	40,661	34,897	-1,022	5,764	-2.5	16.5	1,562.4	1,306.2	19.6	$39,417	$32,150
Perquimans County, NC	13,422	13,453	11,368	-31	2,085	-0.2	18.3	547.4	452.1	21.1	$40,781	$33,534
Elizabethtown-Fort Knox, KY Metro area	153,378	148,340	133,896	5,038	14,444	3.4	10.8	6,464.0	5,071.7	27.5	$42,144	$33,846
Hardin County, KY	110,356	105,538	94,174	4,818	11,364	4.6	12.1	4,792.1	3,802.7	26.0	$43,424	$35,554
Larue County, KY	14,307	14,189	13,373	118	816	0.8	6.1	522.6	398.2	31.2	$36,525	$28,085
Meade County, KY	28,715	28,613	26,349	102	2,264	0.4	8.6	1,149.4	870.8	32.0	$40,026	$30,327
Elk City, OK Micro area	21,709	22,119	19,799	-410	2,320	-1.9	11.7	823.8	694.3	18.7	$37,948	$31,474
Beckham County, OK	21,709	22,119	19,799	-410	2,320	-1.9	11.7	823.8	694.3	18.7	$37,948	$31,474
Elkhart-Goshen, IN Metro area	205,560	197,559	182,791	8,001	14,768	4.0	8.1	9,623.6	6,003.2	60.3	$46,816	$30,404
Elkhart County, IN	205,560	197,559	182,791	8,001	14,768	4.0	8.1	9,623.6	6,003.2	60.3	$46,816	$30,404
Elkins, WV Micro area	28,823	29,405	28,262	-582	1,143	-2.0	4.0	1,053.0	852.0	23.6	$36,533	$29,015
Randolph County, WV	28,823	29,405	28,262	-582	1,143	-2.0	4.0	1,053.0	852.0	23.6	$36,533	$29,015
Elko, NV Micro area	54,463	50,929	46,942	3,534	3,987	6.9	8.5	2,535.5	2,071.7	22.4	$46,554	$40,562
Elko County, NV	52,460	48,942	45,291	3,518	3,651	7.2	8.1	2,455.6	2,006.7	22.4	$46,808	$40,882
Eureka County, NV	2,003	1,987	1,651	16	336	0.8	20.4	79.9	65.0	22.9	$39,903	$32,674
Ellensburg, WA Micro area	47,364	40,909	33,362	6,455	7,547	15.8	22.6	2,017.8	1,382.1	46.0	$42,603	$33,719
Kittitas County, WA	47,364	40,909	33,362	6,455	7,547	15.8	22.6	2,017.8	1,382.1	46.0	$42,603	$33,719
Elmira, NY Metro area	84,254	88,849	91,070	-4,595	-2,221	-5.2	-2.4	3,738.6	3,129.7	19.5	$44,373	$35,206
Chemung County, NY	84,254	88,849	91,070	-4,595	-2,221	-5.2	-2.4	3,738.6	3,129.7	19.5	$44,373	$35,206
El Paso, TX Metro area	845,553	804,129	682,966	41,424	121,163	5.2	17.7	30,301.5	22,892.4	32.4	$35,836	$28,363
El Paso County, TX	840,758	800,653	679,622	40,105	121,031	5.0	17.8	30,145.8	22,821.1	32.1	$35,856	$28,397
Hudspeth County, TX	4,795	3,476	3,344	1,319	132	37.9	3.9	155.7	71.3	118.4	$32,472	$20,528

Table D-1. Population and Personal Income—Continued

Metropolitan or Micropolitan Statistical Area Metropolitan Division Component Counties	Population							Personal Income				
	2018 Estimate (July 1)	2010 census estimates base (April 1)	2000 census estimates base (April 1)	Net change		Percent change		Total (million dollars)		Percent change 2010-2018	Per capita	
				2010-2018	2000-2010	2010-2018	2000-2010	2018	2010		2018	2010
Emporia, KS Micro area	36,035	36,482	38,965	-447	-2,483	-1.2	-6.4	1,401.3	1,093.1	28.2	$38,887	$30,003
Chase County, KS	2,629	2,790	3,030	-161	-240	-5.8	-7.9	121.9	88.8	37.3	$46,385	$31,892
Lyon County, KS	33,406	33,692	35,935	-286	-2,243	-0.8	-6.2	1,279.3	1,004.3	27.4	$38,297	$29,847
Enid, OK Metro area	60,913	60,580	57,813	333	2,767	0.5	4.8	2,708.5	2,373.7	14.1	$44,465	$39,081
Garfield County, OK	60,913	60,580	57,813	333	2,767	0.5	4.8	2,708.5	2,373.7	14.1	$44,465	$39,081
Enterprise, AL Micro area	51,909	49,952	43,615	1,957	6,337	3.9	14.5	2,237.0	1,778.8	25.8	$43,094	$35,431
Coffee County, AL	51,909	49,952	43,615	1,957	6,337	3.9	14.5	2,237.0	1,778.8	25.8	$43,094	$35,431
Erie, PA Metro area	272,061	280,584	280,843	-8,523	-259	-3.0	-0.1	12,216.3	9,717.4	25.7	$44,903	$34,606
Erie County, PA	272,061	280,584	280,843	-8,523	-259	-3.0	-0.1	12,216.3	9,717.4	25.7	$44,903	$34,606
Escanaba, MI Micro area	35,857	37,069	38,520	-1,212	-1,451	-3.3	-3.8	1,454.0	1,191.9	22.0	$40,551	$32,171
Delta County, MI	35,857	37,069	38,520	-1,212	-1,451	-3.3	-3.8	1,454.0	1,191.9	22.0	$40,551	$32,171
Espa±ola, NM Micro area	39,006	40,220	41,190	-1,214	-970	-3.0	-2.4	1,348.9	1,214.6	11.1	$34,582	$30,148
Rio Arriba County, NM	39,006	40,220	41,190	-1,214	-970	-3.0	-2.4	1,348.9	1,214.6	11.1	$34,582	$30,148
Eufaula, AL-GA Micro area	27,160	29,968	31,636	-2,808	-1,668	-9.4	-5.3	946.2	816.6	15.9	$34,839	$27,364
Barbour County, AL	24,881	27,457	29,038	-2,576	-1,581	-9.4	-5.4	875.8	758.9	15.4	$35,199	$27,767
Quitman County, GA	2,279	2,511	2,598	-232	-87	-9.2	-3.3	70.4	57.7	22.0	$30,902	$22,973
Eugene-Springfield, OR Metro area	379,611	351,704	322,959	27,907	28,745	7.9	8.9	17,431.4	11,916.9	46.3	$45,919	$33,862
Lane County, OR	379,611	351,704	322,959	27,907	28,745	7.9	8.9	17,431.4	11,916.9	46.3	$45,919	$33,862
Eureka-Arcata, CA Micro area	136,373	134,611	126,518	1,762	8,093	1.3	6.4	6,646.6	4,835.8	37.4	$48,739	$35,821
Humboldt County, CA	136,373	134,611	126,518	1,762	8,093	1.3	6.4	6,646.6	4,835.8	37.4	$48,739	$35,821
Evanston, WY Micro area	20,299	21,121	19,742	-822	1,379	-3.9	7.0	817.6	812.6	0.6	$40,280	$38,530
Uinta County, WY	20,299	21,121	19,742	-822	1,379	-3.9	7.0	817.6	812.6	0.6	$40,280	$38,530
Evansville, IN-KY Metro area	314,672	311,548	296,195	3,124	15,353	1.0	5.2	14,888.1	11,818.1	26.0	$47,313	$37,903
Posey County, IN	25,540	25,910	27,061	-370	-1,151	-1.4	-4.3	1,230.5	979.3	25.7	$48,180	$37,869
Vanderburgh County, IN	180,974	179,703	171,922	1,271	7,781	0.7	4.5	8,305.4	6,912.5	20.2	$45,893	$38,436
Warrick County, IN	62,567	59,689	52,383	2,878	7,306	4.8	13.9	3,533.5	2,457.9	43.8	$56,476	$41,074
Henderson County, KY	45,591	46,246	44,829	-655	1,417	-1.4	3.2	1,818.7	1,468.5	23.8	$39,891	$31,744
Fairbanks, AK Metro area	98,971	97,585	82,840	1,386	14,745	1.4	17.8	5,602.4	4,542.2	23.3	$56,606	$46,227
Fairbanks North Star Borough, AK	98,971	97,585	82,840	1,386	14,745	1.4	17.8	5,602.4	4,542.2	23.3	$56,606	$46,227
Fairfield, IA Micro area	18,381	16,840	16,181	1,541	659	9.2	4.1	777.9	543.2	43.2	$42,320	$32,265
Jefferson County, IA	18,381	16,840	16,181	1,541	659	9.2	4.1	777.9	543.2	43.2	$42,320	$32,265
Fairmont, MN Micro area	19,785	20,843	21,802	-1,058	-959	-5.1	-4.4	990.9	848.0	16.9	$50,083	$40,762
Martin County, MN	19,785	20,843	21,802	-1,058	-959	-5.1	-4.4	990.9	848.0	16.9	$50,083	$40,762
Fairmont, WV Micro area	56,097	56,418	56,598	-321	-180	-0.6	-0.3	2,355.0	1,962.5	20.0	$41,980	$34,715
Marion County, WV	56,097	56,418	56,598	-321	-180	-0.6	-0.3	2,355.0	1,962.5	20.0	$41,980	$34,715
Fallon, NV Micro area	24,440	24,877	23,982	-437	895	-1.8	3.7	1,067.1	828.7	28.8	$43,661	$33,390
Churchill County, NV	24,440	24,877	23,982	-437	895	-1.8	3.7	1,067.1	828.7	28.8	$43,661	$33,390
Fargo, ND-MN Metro area	245,471	208,777	174,367	36,694	34,410	17.6	19.7	12,939.3	8,419.7	53.7	$52,712	$40,199
Clay County, MN	63,955	58,999	51,229	4,956	7,770	8.4	15.2	2,761.6	2,006.8	37.6	$43,180	$33,931
Cass County, ND	181,516	149,778	123,138	31,738	26,640	21.2	21.6	10,177.7	6,412.8	58.7	$56,070	$42,665
Faribault-Northfield, MN Micro area	66,523	64,142	56,665	2,381	7,477	3.7	13.2	2,933.4	2,151.8	36.3	$44,096	$33,496
Rice County, MN	66,523	64,142	56,665	2,381	7,477	3.7	13.2	2,933.4	2,151.8	36.3	$44,096	$33,496
Farmington, MO Micro area	66,692	65,367	55,641	1,325	9,726	2.0	17.5	2,299.8	1,777.5	29.4	$34,485	$27,125
St. Francois County, MO	66,692	65,367	55,641	1,325	9,726	2.0	17.5	2,299.8	1,777.5	29.4	$34,485	$27,125
Farmington, NM Metro area	125,043	130,045	113,801	-5,002	16,244	-3.8	14.3	4,433.1	3,961.8	11.9	$35,453	$30,428
San Juan County, NM	125,043	130,045	113,801	-5,002	16,244	-3.8	14.3	4,433.1	3,961.8	11.9	$35,453	$30,428
Fayetteville, NC Metro area	521,308	481,004	427,634	40,304	53,370	8.4	12.5	19,237.8	15,534.3	23.8	$36,903	$31,675
Cumberland County, NC	332,330	319,433	302,963	12,897	16,470	4.0	5.4	12,887.6	10,863.4	18.6	$38,782	$33,202
Harnett County, NC	134,214	114,681	91,025	19,533	23,656	17.0	26.0	4,644.4	3,372.8	37.7	$34,604	$29,140
Hoke County, NC	54,764	46,890	33,646	7,874	13,244	16.8	39.4	1,705.8	1,298.2	31.4	$31,148	$27,332
Fayetteville-Springdale-Rogers, AR Metro area	526,050	440,119	325,364	85,931	114,755	19.5	35.3	34,354.1	17,091.0	101.0	$65,306	$38,642
Benton County, AR	272,608	221,351	153,406	51,257	67,945	23.2	44.3	24,232.1	10,862.0	123.1	$88,890	$48,798
Madison County, AR	16,481	15,722	14,243	759	1,479	4.8	10.4	585.0	376.7	55.3	$35,496	$24,015
Washington County, AR	236,961	203,046	157,715	33,915	45,331	16.7	28.7	9,537.1	5,852.4	63.0	$40,247	$28,685
Fergus Falls, MN Micro area	58,812	57,303	57,159	1,509	144	2.6	0.3	2,839.2	2,010.8	41.2	$48,275	$35,095
Otter Tail County, MN	58,812	57,303	57,159	1,509	144	2.6	0.3	2,839.2	2,010.8	41.2	$48,275	$35,095
Fernley, NV Micro area	55,808	51,980	34,501	3,828	17,479	7.4	50.7	2,160.5	1,458.5	48.1	$38,713	$28,025
Lyon County, NV	55,808	51,980	34,501	3,828	17,479	7.4	50.7	2,160.5	1,458.5	48.1	$38,713	$28,025
Findlay, OH Micro area	75,930	74,789	71,295	1,141	3,494	1.5	4.9	3,919.7	2,725.7	43.8	$51,623	$36,494
Hancock County, OH	75,930	74,789	71,295	1,141	3,494	1.5	4.9	3,919.7	2,725.7	43.8	$51,623	$36,494
Fitzgerald, GA Micro area	16,787	17,637	17,484	-850	153	-4.8	0.9	527.7	433.4	21.8	$31,436	$24,590
Ben Hill County, GA	16,787	17,637	17,484	-850	153	-4.8	0.9	527.7	433.4	21.8	$31,436	$24,590
Flagstaff, AZ Metro area	142,854	134,431	116,320	8,423	18,111	6.3	15.6	6,875.5	4,631.7	48.4	$48,129	$34,406
Coconino County, AZ	142,854	134,431	116,320	8,423	18,111	6.3	15.6	6,875.5	4,631.7	48.4	$48,129	$34,406
Flint, MI Metro area	406,892	425,789	436,141	-18,897	-10,352	-4.4	-2.4	16,710.2	12,927.0	29.3	$41,068	$30,420
Genesee County, MI	406,892	425,789	436,141	-18,897	-10,352	-4.4	-2.4	16,710.2	12,927.0	29.3	$41,068	$30,420
Florence, SC Metro area	204,961	205,571	193,155	-610	12,416	-0.3	6.4	8,283.1	6,446.2	28.5	$40,413	$31,344
Darlington County, SC	66,802	68,609	67,394	-1,807	1,215	-2.6	1.8	2,503.4	1,983.9	26.2	$37,475	$28,953
Florence County, SC	138,159	136,962	125,761	1,197	11,201	0.9	8.9	5,779.7	4,462.3	29.5	$41,833	$32,538
Florence-Muscle Shoals, AL Metro area	147,149	147,137	142,950	12	4,187	0.0	2.9	5,534.0	4,603.0	20.2	$37,608	$31,257
Colbert County, AL	54,762	54,428	54,984	334	-556	0.6		2,101.7	1,725.5	21.8	$38,378	$31,646
Lauderdale County, AL	92,387	92,709	87,966	-322	4,743	-0.3	5.4	3,432.3	2,877.5	19.3	$37,151	$31,029
Fond du Lac, WI Metro area	103,066	101,627	97,296	1,439	4,331	1.4	4.5	4,960.1	3,743.8	32.5	$48,126	$36,855
Fond du Lac County, WI	103,066	101,627	97,296	1,439	4,331	1.4	4.5	4,960.1	3,743.8	32.5	$48,126	$36,855
Forest City, NC Micro area	66,826	67,816	62,899	-990	4,917	-1.5	7.8	2,189.5	1,740.3	25.8	$32,764	$25,691
Rutherford County, NC	66,826	67,816	62,899	-990	4,917	-1.5	7.8	2,189.5	1,740.3	25.8	$32,764	$25,691

Table D-1. Population and Personal Income—*Continued*

Metropolitan or Micropolitan Statistical Area Metropolitan Division Component Counties	Population							Personal Income				
	2018 Estimate (July 1)	2010 census estimates base (April 1)	2000 census estimates base (April 1)	Net change		Percent change		Total (million dollars)		Percent change 2010-2018	Per capita	
				2010-2018	2000-2010	2010-2018	2000-2010	2018	2010		2018	2010
Forrest City, AR Micro area	25,439	28,254	29,329	-2,815	-1,075	-10.0	-3.7	711.0	647.6	9.8	$27,948	$22,968
St. Francis County, AR	25,439	28,254	29,329	-2,815	-1,075	-10.0	-3.7	711.0	647.6	9.8	$27,948	$22,968
Fort Collins, CO Metro area	350,518	299,615	251,494	50,903	48,121	17.0	19.1	18,993.9	11,253.0	68.8	$54,188	$37,454
Larimer County, CO	350,518	299,615	251,494	50,903	48,121	17.0	19.1	18,993.9	11,253.0	68.8	$54,188	$37,454
Fort Dodge, IA Micro area	36,277	38,013	40,235	-1,736	-2,222	-4.6	-5.5	1,650.4	1,308.4	26.1	$45,496	$34,538
Webster County, IA	36,277	38,013	40,235	-1,736	-2,222	-4.6	-5.5	1,650.4	1,308.4	26.1	$45,496	$34,538
Fort Leonard Wood, MO Micro area	52,014	52,274	41,165	-260	11,109	-0.5	27.0	2,107.2	2,036.1	3.5	$40,512	$38,526
Pulaski County, MO	52,014	52,274	41,165	-260	11,109	-0.5	27.0	2,107.2	2,036.1	3.5	$40,512	$38,526
Fort Madison-Keokuk, IA-IL-MO Micro area	58,741	62,095	65,589	-3,354	-3,494	-5.4	-5.3	2,494.7	2,003.4	24.5	$42,469	$32,274
Hancock County, IL	17,844	19,104	20,121	-1,260	-1,017	-6.6	-5.1	822.3	676.5	21.6	$46,081	$35,438
Lee County, IA	34,055	35,862	38,052	-1,807	-2,190	-5.0	-5.8	1,436.2	1,128.3	27.3	$42,174	$31,474
Clark County, MO	6,842	7,129	7,416	-287	-287	-4.0	-3.9	236.2	198.5	19.0	$34,516	$27,823
Fort Morgan, CO Micro area	28,558	28,159	27,171	399	988	1.4	3.6	1,304.7	873.0	49.5	$45,685	$30,912
Morgan County, CO	28,558	28,159	27,171	399	988	1.4	3.6	1,304.7	873.0	49.5	$45,685	$30,912
Fort Payne, AL Micro area	71,385	71,116	64,452	269	6,664	0.4	10.3	2,278.3	1,904.1	19.7	$31,916	$26,758
De Kalb County, AL	71,385	71,116	64,452	269	6,664	0.4	10.3	2,278.3	1,904.1	19.7	$31,916	$26,758
Fort Polk South, LA Micro area	48,860	52,334	52,531	-3,474	-197	-6.6	-0.4	1,990.0	1,864.7	6.7	$40,729	$35,373
Vernon Parish, LA	48,860	52,334	52,531	-3,474	-197	-6.6	-0.4	1,990.0	1,864.7	6.7	$40,729	$35,373
Fort Smith, AR-OK Metro area	250,148	248,277	225,061	1,871	23,216	0.8	10.3	9,455.6	7,397.5	27.8	$37,800	$29,789
Crawford County, AR	63,406	61,948	53,247	1,458	8,701	2.4	16.3	2,089.4	1,679.3	24.4	$32,952	$27,097
Franklin County, AR	17,810	18,129	17,771	-319	358	-1.8	2.0	610.4	467.2	30.7	$34,275	$25,762
Sebastian County, AR	127,753	125,761	115,071	1,992	10,690	1.6	9.3	5,379.6	4,105.6	31.0	$42,110	$32,646
Sequoyah County, OK	41,179	42,439	38,972	-1,260	3,467	-3.0	8.9	1,376.2	1,145.5	20.1	$33,420	$26,974
Fort Wayne, IN Metro area	409,425	388,625	362,556	20,800	26,069	5.4	7.2	18,891.4	13,413.6	40.8	$46,141	$34,456
Allen County, IN	375,351	355,335	331,849	20,016	23,486	5.6	7.1	17,374.2	12,307.0	41.2	$46,288	$34,576
Whitley County, IN	34,074	33,290	30,707	784	2,583	2.4	8.4	1,517.2	1,106.6	37.1	$44,528	$33,176
Frankfort, IN Micro area	32,250	33,219	33,866	-969	-647	-2.9	-1.9	1,263.3	992.8	27.2	$39,172	$29,885
Clinton County, IN	32,250	33,219	33,866	-969	-647	-2.9	-1.9	1,263.3	992.8	27.2	$39,172	$29,885
Frankfort, KY Micro area	73,478	70,730	66,798	2,748	3,932	3.9	5.9	3,013.2	2,390.2	26.1	$41,008	$33,797
Anderson County, KY	22,663	21,449	19,111	1,214	2,338	5.7	12.2	891.1	691.3	28.9	$39,321	$32,219
Franklin County, KY	50,815	49,281	47,687	1,534	1,594	3.1	3.3	2,122.0	1,698.9	24.9	$41,760	$34,484
Fredericksburg, TX Micro area	26,804	24,836	20,814	1,968	4,022	7.9	19.3	1,623.3	1,037.9	56.4	$60,561	$41,704
Gillespie County, TX	26,804	24,836	20,814	1,968	4,022	7.9	19.3	1,623.3	1,037.9	56.4	$60,561	$41,704
Freeport, IL Micro area	44,753	47,711	48,979	-2,958	-1,268	-6.2	-2.6	1,912.0	1,597.9	19.7	$42,722	$33,565
Stephenson County, IL	44,753	47,711	48,979	-2,958	-1,268	-6.2	-2.6	1,912.0	1,597.9	19.7	$42,722	$33,565
Fremont, NE Micro area	36,791	36,685	36,160	106	525	0.3	1.5	1,741.3	1,328.1	31.1	$47,330	$36,215
Dodge County, NE	36,791	36,685	36,160	106	525	0.3	1.5	1,741.3	1,328.1	31.1	$47,330	$36,215
Fremont, OH Micro area	58,799	60,946	61,792	-2,147	-846	-3.5	-1.4	2,447.4	1,968.3	24.3	$41,624	$32,327
Sandusky County, OH	58,799	60,946	61,792	-2,147	-846	-3.5	-1.4	2,447.4	1,968.3	24.3	$41,624	$32,327
Fresno, CA Metro area	994,400	930,496	799,407	63,904	131,089	6.9	16.4	42,842.8	29,567.9	44.9	$43,084	$31,723
Fresno County, CA	994,400	930,496	799,407	63,904	131,089	6.9	16.4	42,842.8	29,567.9	44.9	$43,084	$31,723
Gadsden, AL Metro area	102,501	104,427	103,459	-1,926	968	-1.8	0.9	3,784.1	3,169.7	19.4	$36,918	$30,345
Etowah County, AL	102,501	104,427	103,459	-1,926	968	-1.8	0.9	3,784.1	3,169.7	19.4	$36,918	$30,345
Gaffney, SC Micro area	57,078	55,488	52,537	1,590	2,951	2.9	5.6	1,894.8	1,502.0	26.2	$33,197	$27,047
Cherokee County, SC	57,078	55,488	52,537	1,590	2,951	2.9	5.6	1,894.8	1,502.0	26.2	$33,197	$27,047
Gainesville, FL Metro area	328,982	305,079	266,842	23,903	38,237	7.8	14.3	14,035.2	10,378.9	35.2	$42,663	$33,992
Alachua County, FL	269,956	247,337	217,955	22,619	29,382	9.1	13.5	11,983.4	8,814.7	35.9	$44,390	$35,599
Gilchrist County, FL	18,256	16,941	14,437	1,315	2,504	7.8	17.3	616.6	437.8	40.8	$33,774	$25,753
Levy County, FL	40,770	40,801	34,450	-31	6,351	-0.1	18.4	1,435.3	1,126.4	27.4	$35,204	$27,661
Gainesville, GA Metro area	202,148	179,726	139,277	22,422	40,449	12.5	29.0	8,834.2	5,502.2	60.6	$43,701	$30,561
Hall County, GA	202,148	179,726	139,277	22,422	40,449	12.5	29.0	8,834.2	5,502.2	60.6	$43,701	$30,561
Gainesville, TX Micro area	40,574	38,439	36,363	2,135	2,076	5.6	5.7	2,198.1	1,492.0	47.3	$54,174	$38,779
Cooke County, TX	40,574	38,439	36,363	2,135	2,076	5.6	5.7	2,198.1	1,492.0	47.3	$54,174	$38,779
Galesburg, IL Micro area	50,112	52,925	55,836	-2,813	-2,911	-5.3	-5.2	1,978.0	1,803.5	9.7	$39,471	$34,085
Knox County, IL	50,112	52,925	55,836	-2,813	-2,911	-5.3	-5.2	1,978.0	1,803.5	9.7	$39,471	$34,085
Gallup, NM Micro area	72,290	71,485	74,798	805	-3,313	1.1	-4.4	2,007.6	1,724.2	16.4	$27,771	$24,057
McKinley County, NM	72,290	71,485	74,798	805	-3,313	1.1	-4.4	2,007.6	1,724.2	16.4	$27,771	$24,057
Garden City, KS Micro area	40,554	40,767	45,054	-213	-4,287	-0.5	-9.5	1,803.2	1,473.1	22.4	$44,465	$35,969
Finney County, KS	36,611	36,785	40,523	-174	-3,738	-0.5	-9.2	1,580.6	1,290.4	22.5	$43,172	$34,919
Kearny County, KS	3,943	3,982	4,531	-39	-549		-12.1	222.6	182.7	21.8	$56,466	$45,662
Gardnerville Ranchos, NV Micro area	48,467	46,997	41,259	1,470	5,738	3.1	13.9	3,642.7	2,388.1	52.5	$75,159	$50,774
Douglas County, NV	48,467	46,997	41,259	1,470	5,738	3.1	13.9	3,642.7	2,388.1	52.5	$75,159	$50,774
Georgetown, SC Micro area	62,249	60,328	55,797	1,921	4,531	3.2	8.1	2,930.1	2,106.2	39.1	$47,071	$34,902
Georgetown County, SC	62,249	60,328	55,797	1,921	4,531	3.2	8.1	2,930.1	2,106.2	39.1	$47,071	$34,902
Gettysburg, PA Metro area	102,811	101,424	91,292	1,387	10,132	1.4	11.1	5,055.5	3,788.3	33.5	$49,173	$37,333
Adams County, PA	102,811	101,424	91,292	1,387	10,132	1.4	11.1	5,055.5	3,788.3	33.5	$49,173	$37,333
Gillette, WY Micro area	60,557	60,424	46,229	133	14,195	0.2	30.7	3,092.3	2,861.3	8.1	$51,064	$47,243
Campbell County, WY	46,140	46,133	33,698	7	12,435	0.0	36.9	2,437.3	2,327.6	4.7	$52,824	$50,333
Crook County, WY	7,450	7,083	5,887	367	1,196	5.2	20.3	343.3	260.7	31.7	$46,081	$36,612
Weston County, WY	6,967	7,208	6,644	-241	564	-3.3	8.5	311.7	272.9	14.2	$44,737	$37,914
Glasgow, KY Micro area	54,206	52,275	48,070	1,931	4,205	3.7	8.7	1,934.4	1,446.9	33.7	$35,685	$27,687
Barren County, KY	44,176	42,169	38,033	2,007	4,136	4.8	10.9	1,618.3	1,203.2	34.5	$36,633	$28,564
Metcalfe County, KY	10,030	10,106	10,037	-76	69	-0.8	0.7	316.1	243.7	29.7	$31,512	$24,044
Glens Falls, NY Metro area	125,462	128,941	124,345	-3,479	4,596	-2.7	3.7	5,822.8	4,650.9	25.2	$46,411	$36,050
Warren County, NY	64,265	65,698	63,303	-1,433	2,395	-2.2	3.8	3,372.3	2,682.7	25.7	$52,475	$40,852
Washington County, NY	61,197	63,243	61,042	-2,046	2,201	-3.2	3.6	2,450.5	1,968.2	24.5	$40,043	$31,072

Table D-1. Population and Personal Income—*Continued*

Metropolitan or Micropolitan Statistical Area Metropolitan Division Component Counties	Population							Personal Income				
	2018 Estimate (July 1)	2010 census estimates base (April 1)	2000 census estimates base (April 1)	Net change		Percent change		Total (million dollars)		Percent change 2010-2018	Per capita	
				2010-2018	2000-2010	2010-2018	2000-2010	2018	2010		2018	2010
Glenwood Springs, CO Micro area	77,720	73,538	58,663	4,182	14,875	5.7	25.4	6,243.7	3,684.3	69.5	$80,336	$50,296
Garfield County, CO	59,770	56,389	43,791	3,381	12,598	6.0	28.8	3,565.5	2,096.1	70.1	$59,653	$37,369
Pitkin County, CO	17,950	17,149	14,872	801	2,277	4.7	15.3	2,678.3	1,588.2	68.6	$149,207	$92,551
Gloversville, NY Micro area	53,591	55,520	55,073	-1,929	447	-3.5	0.8	2,310.4	1,861.3	24.1	$43,112	$33,560
Fulton County, NY	53,591	55,520	55,073	-1,929	447	-3.5	0.8	2,310.4	1,861.3	24.1	$43,112	$33,560
Goldsboro, NC Metro area	123,248	122,673	113,329	575	9,344	0.5	8.2	4,741.6	3,884.5	22.1	$38,472	$31,607
Wayne County, NC	123,248	122,673	113,329	575	9,344	0.5	8.2	4,741.6	3,884.5	22.1	$38,472	$31,607
Granbury, TX Micro area	60,537	51,163	41,100	9,374	10,063	18.3	24.5	3,071.7	1,967.3	56.1	$50,741	$38,373
Hood County, TX	60,537	51,163	41,100	9,374	10,063	18.3	24.5	3,071.7	1,967.3	56.1	$50,741	$38,373
Grand Forks, ND-MN Metro area	102,299	98,464	97,478	3,835	986	3.9	1.0	5,183.5	3,718.1	39.4	$50,670	$37,697
Polk County, MN	31,529	31,600	31,369	-71	231	-0.2	0.7	1,539.3	1,165.6	32.1	$48,820	$36,838
Grand Forks County, ND	70,770	66,864	66,109	3,906	755	5.8	1.1	3,644.2	2,552.5	42.8	$51,494	$38,103
Grand Island, NE Metro area	75,808	72,736	68,305	3,072	4,431	4.2	6.5	3,321.6	2,510.0	32.3	$43,817	$34,418
Hall County, NE	61,607	58,607	53,534	3,000	5,073	5.1	9.5	2,687.6	2,000.5	34.3	$43,625	$34,023
Howard County, NE	6,468	6,274	6,567	194	-293	3.1	-4.5	267.6	219.5	21.9	$41,377	$34,958
Merrick County, NE	7,733	7,855	8,204	-122	-349	-1.6	-4.3	366.4	290.0	26.3	$47,386	$36,948
Grand Junction, CO Metro area	153,207	146,717	116,255	6,490	30,462	4.4	26.2	6,884.4	5,007.1	37.5	$44,935	$34,211
Mesa County, CO	153,207	146,717	116,255	6,490	30,462	4.4	26.2	6,884.4	5,007.1	37.5	$44,935	$34,211
Grand Rapids, MN Micro area	45,108	45,051	43,992	57	1,059	0.1	2.4	1,970.5	1,459.3	35.0	$43,685	$32,407
Itasca County, MN	45,108	45,051	43,992	57	1,059	0.1	2.4	1,970.5	1,459.3	35.0	$43,685	$32,407
Grand Rapids-Kentwood, MI Metro area	1,072,458	993,664	935,433	78,794	58,231	7.9	6.2	54,119.6	35,983.8	50.4	$50,463	$36,191
Ionia County, MI	64,210	63,899	61,518	311	2,381	0.5	3.9	2,264.9	1,695.7	33.6	$35,273	$26,561
Kent County, MI	653,786	602,628	574,335	51,158	28,293	8.5	4.9	35,262.0	23,498.3	50.1	$53,935	$38,970
Montcalm County, MI	63,968	63,342	61,266	626	2,076	1.0	3.4	2,237.1	1,643.4	36.1	$34,972	$25,956
Ottawa County, MI	290,494	263,795	238,314	26,699	25,481	10.1	10.7	14,355.6	9,146.3	57.0	$49,418	$34,629
Grants, NM Micro area	26,746	27,215	25,595	-469	1,620	-1.7	6.3	752.4	641.5	17.3	$28,130	$23,481
Cibola County, NM	26,746	27,215	25,595	-469	1,620	-1.7	6.3	752.4	641.5	17.3	$28,130	$23,481
Grants Pass, OR Metro area	87,393	82,718	75,726	4,675	6,992	5.7	9.2	3,581.1	2,493.1	43.6	$40,977	$30,083
Josephine County, OR	87,393	82,718	75,726	4,675	6,992	5.7	9.2	3,581.1	2,493.1	43.6	$40,977	$30,083
Great Bend, KS Micro area	26,111	27,672	28,205	-1,561	-533	-5.6	-1.9	1,254.3	1,094.5	14.6	$48,036	$39,549
Barton County, KS	26,111	27,672	28,205	-1,561	-533	-5.6	-1.9	1,254.3	1,094.5	14.6	$48,036	$39,549
Great Falls, MT Metro area	81,643	81,323	80,357	320	966	0.4	1.2	3,879.5	3,125.3	24.1	$47,518	$38,347
Cascade County, MT	81,643	81,323	80,357	320	966	0.4	1.2	3,879.5	3,125.3	24.1	$47,518	$38,347
Greeley, CO Metro area	314,305	252,847	180,926	61,458	71,921	24.3	39.8	14,512.1	8,412.3	72.5	$46,172	$33,094
Weld County, CO	314,305	252,847	180,926	61,458	71,921	24.3	39.8	14,512.1	8,412.3	72.5	$46,172	$33,094
Green Bay, WI Metro area	321,591	306,241	282,599	15,350	23,642	5.0	8.4	16,578.9	12,078.5	37.3	$51,553	$39,375
Brown County, WI	263,378	248,007	226,778	15,371	21,229	6.2	9.4	13,911.9	10,022.1	38.8	$52,821	$40,333
Kewaunee County, WI	20,383	20,574	20,187	-191	387	-0.9	1.9	941.6	748.2	25.8	$46,197	$36,395
Oconto County, WI	37,830	37,660	35,634	170	2,026	0.5	5.7	1,725.4	1,308.1	31.9	$45,609	$34,683
Greeneville, TN Micro area	69,087	68,825	62,909	262	5,916	0.4	9.4	2,761.5	2,221.2	24.3	$39,971	$32,269
Greene County, TN	69,087	68,825	62,909	262	5,916	0.4	9.4	2,761.5	2,221.2	24.3	$39,971	$32,269
Greensboro-High Point, NC Metro area	767,711	723,885	643,430	43,826	80,455	6.1	12.5	33,156.6	24,944.8	32.9	$43,189	$34,396
Guilford County, NC	533,670	488,421	421,048	45,249	67,373	9.3	16.0	24,482.1	17,911.0	36.7	$45,875	$36,584
Randolph County, NC	143,351	141,823	130,454	1,528	11,369	1.1	8.7	5,306.5	4,197.4	26.4	$37,017	$29,562
Rockingham County, NC	90,690	93,641	91,928	-2,951	1,713	-3.2	1.9	3,367.9	2,836.5	18.7	$37,137	$30,285
Greensburg, IN Micro area	26,794	25,739	24,555	1,055	1,184	4.1	4.8	1,145.0	858.6	33.4	$42,733	$33,281
Decatur County, IN	26,794	25,739	24,555	1,055	1,184	4.1	4.8	1,145.0	858.6	33.4	$42,733	$33,281
Greenville, MS Micro area	45,063	51,135	62,977	-6,072	-11,842	-11.9	-18.8	1,692.9	1,543.8	9.7	$37,568	$30,213
Washington County, MS	45,063	51,135	62,977	-6,072	-11,842	-11.9	-18.8	1,692.9	1,543.8	9.7	$37,568	$30,213
Greenville, NC Metro area	179,914	168,167	133,798	11,747	34,369	7.0	25.7	7,410.9	5,499.3	34.8	$41,191	$32,569
Pitt County, NC	179,914	168,167	133,798	11,747	34,369	7.0	25.7	7,410.9	5,499.3	34.8	$41,191	$32,569
Greenville, OH Micro area	51,323	52,969	53,309	-1,646	-340	-3.1	-0.6	2,196.3	1,710.8	28.4	$42,793	$32,301
Darke County, OH	51,323	52,969	53,309	-1,646	-340	-3.1	-0.6	2,196.3	1,710.8	28.4	$42,793	$32,301
Greenville-Anderson, SC Metro area	906,626	824,035	725,680	82,591	98,355	10.0	13.6	40,084.9	27,098.9	47.9	$44,213	$32,822
Anderson County, SC	200,482	186,943	165,740	13,539	21,203	7.2	12.8	7,961.2	5,727.7	39.0	$39,710	$30,611
Greenville County, SC	514,213	451,184	379,616	63,029	71,568	14.0	18.9	25,013.6	16,128.4	55.1	$48,644	$35,629
Laurens County, SC	66,994	66,535	69,567	459	-3,032	0.7	-4.4	2,319.4	1,828.0	26.9	$34,622	$27,478
Pickens County, SC	124,937	119,373	110,757	5,564	8,616	4.7	7.8	4,790.6	3,414.8	40.3	$38,344	$28,618
Greenwood, MS Micro area	38,830	42,979	48,716	-4,149	-5,737	-9.7	-11.8	1,425.4	1,227.9	16.1	$36,709	$28,543
Carroll County, MS	9,911	10,597	10,769	-686	-172	-6.5	-1.6	372.8	296.1	25.9	$37,615	$27,926
Leflore County, MS	28,919	32,382	37,947	-3,463	-5,565	-10.7	-14.7	1,052.6	931.8	13.0	$36,399	$28,745
Greenwood, SC Micro area	70,741	69,711	66,271	1,030	3,440	1.5	5.2	2,647.4	2,101.3	26.0	$37,424	$30,110
Greenwood County, SC	70,741	69,711	66,271	1,030	3,440	1.5	5.2	2,647.4	2,101.3	26.0	$37,424	$30,110
Grenada, MS Micro area	21,055	21,905	23,263	-850	-1,358	-3.9	-5.8	750.2	651.4	15.2	$35,632	$29,825
Grenada County, MS	21,055	21,905	23,263	-850	-1,358	-3.9	-5.8	750.2	651.4	15.2	$35,632	$29,825
Gulfport-Biloxi, MS Metro area	415,978	388,575	377,610	27,403	10,965	7.1	2.9	15,340.5	13,254.7	15.7	$36,878	$34,047
Hancock County, MS	47,334	44,014	42,967	3,320	1,047	7.5	2.4	1,669.1	1,471.7	13.4	$35,262	$33,386
Harrison County, MS	206,650	187,105	189,601	19,545	-2,496	10.4	-1.3	7,708.7	6,525.9	18.1	$37,303	$34,740
Jackson County, MS	143,277	139,668	131,420	3,609	8,248	2.6	6.3	5,372.8	4,766.4	12.7	$37,499	$34,176
Stone County, MS	18,717	17,788	13,622	929	4,166	5.2	30.6	589.9	490.8	20.2	$31,516	$27,410
Guymon, OK Micro area	20,455	20,640	20,107	-185	533	-0.9	2.7	953.1	714.1	33.5	$46,597	$34,310
Texas County, OK	20,455	20,640	20,107	-185	533	-0.9	2.7	953.1	714.1	33.5	$46,597	$34,310
Hagerstown-Martinsburg, MD-WV Metro area	285,836	269,143	222,771	16,693	46,372	6.2	20.8	12,547.3	9,456.1	32.7	$43,897	$35,045
Washington County, MD	150,926	147,430	131,923	3,496	15,507	2.4	11.8	7,107.4	5,477.4	29.8	$47,092	$37,076
Berkeley County, WV	117,123	104,172	75,905	12,951	28,267	12.4	37.2	4,825.6	3,485.2	38.5	$41,201	$33,317

Table D-1. Population and Personal Income—*Continued*

Metropolitan or Micropolitan Statistical Area / Metropolitan Division / Component Counties	Population							Personal Income				
	2018 Estimate (July 1)	2010 census estimates base (April 1)	2000 census estimates base (April 1)	Net change		Percent change		Total (million dollars)		Percent change 2010-2018	Per capita	
				2010-2018	2000-2010	2010-2018	2000-2010	2018	2010		2018	2010
Morgan County, WV	17,787	17,541	14,943	246	2,598	1.4	17.4	614.2	493.6	24.4	$34,533	$28,219
Hailey, ID Micro area	23,728	22,494	19,982	1,234	2,512	5.5	12.6	2,615.1	1,347.2	94.1	$110,209	$60,109
Blaine County, ID	22,601	21,377	18,991	1,224	2,386	5.7	12.6	2,571.5	1,317.1	95.2	$113,780	$61,847
Camas County, ID	1,127	1,117	991	10	126	0.9	12.7	43.5	30.1	44.5	$38,600	$26,940
Hammond, LA Metro area	133,777	121,107	100,588	12,670	20,519	10.5	20.4	5,213.9	3,995.7	30.5	$38,974	$32,892
Tangipahoa Parish, LA	133,777	121,107	100,588	12,670	20,519	10.5	20.4	5,213.9	3,995.7	30.5	$38,974	$32,892
Hanford-Corcoran, CA Metro area	151,366	152,982	129,461	-1,616	23,521	-1.1	18.2	5,344.1	4,070.9	31.3	$35,306	$26,715
Kings County, CA	151,366	152,982	129,461	-1,616	23,521	-1.1	18.2	5,344.1	4,070.9	31.3	$35,306	$26,715
Hannibal, MO Micro area	38,804	38,948	37,915	-144	1,033	-0.4	2.7	1,589.8	1,300.2	22.3	$40,970	$33,365
Marion County, MO	28,592	28,781	28,289	-189	492	-0.7	1.7	1,174.2	953.8	23.1	$41,068	$33,137
Ralls County, MO	10,212	10,167	9,626	45	541	0.4	5.6	415.6	346.4	20.0	$40,698	$34,010
Harrisburg-Carlisle, PA Metro area	574,659	549,468	509,074	25,191	40,394	4.6	7.9	30,085.4	22,332.0	34.7	$52,354	$40,596
Cumberland County, PA	251,423	235,405	213,674	16,018	21,731	6.8	10.2	13,863.7	9,979.5	38.9	$55,141	$42,304
Dauphin County, PA	277,097	268,123	251,798	8,974	16,325	3.3	6.5	14,159.6	10,773.4	31.4	$51,100	$40,159
Perry County, PA	46,139	45,940	43,602	199	2,338	0.4	5.4	2,062.1	1,579.0	30.6	$44,693	$34,381
Harrison, AR Micro area	45,285	45,237	42,556	48	2,681	0.1	6.3	1,577.5	1,226.0	28.7	$34,834	$27,125
Boone County, AR	37,480	36,910	33,948	570	2,962	1.5	8.7	1,352.6	1,038.4	30.3	$36,089	$28,154
Newton County, AR	7,805	8,327	8,608	-522	-281	-6.3	-3.3	224.8	187.6	19.8	$28,808	$22,565
Harrisonburg, VA Metro area	135,277	125,221	108,193	10,056	17,028	8.0	15.7	5,373.4	3,842.7	39.8	$39,721	$30,644
Rockingham County, VA	81,244	76,321	67,725	4,923	8,596	6.5	12.7	5,373.4	3,842.7	39.8	$39,721	$30,644
Harrisonburg City, VA (included with Rockingham County personal income)	54,033	48,900	40,468	5,133	8,432	10.5	20.8	-	-	-	-	-
Hartford-East Hartford-Middletown, CT Metro area	1,206,300	1,212,453	1,148,618	-6,153	63,835	-0.5	5.6	77,610.2	61,473.4	26.3	$64,337	$50,634
Hartford County, CT	892,697	894,033	857,183	-1,336	36,850	-0.1	4.3	57,894.1	45,735.9	26.6	$64,853	$51,089
Middlesex County, CT	162,682	165,676	155,071	-2,994	10,605	-1.8	6.8	11,171.8	8,815.2	26.7	$68,673	$53,231
Tolland County, CT	150,921	152,744	136,364	-1,823	16,380	-1.2	12.0	8,544.3	6,922.2	23.4	$56,614	$45,174
Hastings, NE Micro area	31,511	31,367	31,151	144	216	0.5	0.7	1,548.4	1,152.9	34.3	$49,139	$36,801
Adams County, NE	31,511	31,367	31,151	144	216	0.5	0.7	1,548.4	1,152.9	34.3	$49,139	$36,801
Hattiesburg, MS Metro area	168,267	162,418	143,219	5,849	19,199	3.6	13.4	6,503.3	4,967.6	30.9	$38,648	$30,503
Covington County, MS	18,853	19,573	19,407	-720	166	-3.7	0.9	674.0	539.5	24.9	$35,748	$27,559
Forrest County, MS	75,036	74,928	72,604	108	2,324	0.1	3.2	2,917.4	2,353.2	24.0	$38,880	$31,372
Lamar County, MS	62,447	55,668	39,070	6,779	16,598	12.2	42.5	2,530.9	1,762.1	43.6	$40,529	$31,443
Perry County, MS	11,931	12,249	12,138	-318	111	-2.6	0.9	381.0	312.8	21.8	$31,934	$25,571
Hays, KS Micro area	28,710	28,452	27,507	258	945	0.9	3.4	1,334.0	1,115.3	19.6	$46,465	$39,238
Ellis County, KS	28,710	28,452	27,507	258	945	0.9	3.4	1,334.0	1,115.3	19.6	$46,465	$39,238
Heber, UT Micro area	75,173	59,849	44,951	15,324	14,898	25.6	33.1	7,289.8	3,349.1	117.7	$96,974	$55,684
Summit County, UT	41,933	36,324	29,736	5,609	6,588	15.4	22.2	5,518.6	2,587.2	113.3	$131,606	$70,882
Wasatch County, UT	33,240	23,525	15,215	9,715	8,310	41.3	54.6	1,771.2	761.9	132.5	$53,289	$32,223
Helena, MT Micro area	80,797	74,798	65,765	5,999	9,033	8.0	13.7	3,916.4	3,287.4	19.1	$48,472	$43,843
Jefferson County, MT	12,097	11,403	10,049	694	1,354	6.1	13.5	580.2	430.5	34.8	$47,960	$37,738
Lewis and Clark County, MT	68,700	63,395	55,716	5,305	7,679	8.4	13.8	3,336.2	2,856.9	16.8	$48,562	$44,938
Helena-West Helena, AR Micro area	18,029	21,755	26,445	-3,726	-4,690	-17.1	-17.7	561.2	574.1	-2.2	$31,128	$26,484
Phillips County, AR	18,029	21,755	26,445	-3,726	-4,690	-17.1	-17.7	561.2	574.1	-2.2	$31,128	$26,484
Henderson, NC Micro area	44,582	45,419	42,954	-837	2,465	-1.8	5.7	1,565.1	1,366.2	14.6	$35,105	$30,157
Vance County, NC	44,582	45,419	42,954	-837	2,465	-1.8	5.7	1,565.1	1,366.2	14.6	$35,105	$30,157
Hereford, TX Micro area	18,760	19,372	18,561	-612	811	-3.2	4.4	759.2	677.7	12.0	$40,470	$34,818
Deaf Smith County, TX	18,760	19,372	18,561	-612	811	-3.2	4.4	759.2	677.7	12.0	$40,470	$34,818
Hermiston-Pendleton, OR Micro area	88,888	87,062	81,543	1,826	5,519	2.1	6.8	3,520.7	2,660.8	32.3	$39,609	$30,476
Morrow County, OR	11,372	11,177	10,995	195	182	1.7	1.7	444.6	348.6	27.5	$39,095	$31,091
Umatilla County, OR	77,516	75,885	70,548	1,631	5,337	2.1	7.6	3,076.2	2,312.2	33.0	$39,684	$30,386
Hickory-Lenoir-Morganton, NC Metro area	368,416	365,830	341,851	2,586	23,979	0.7	7.0	14,681.1	11,080.7	32.5	$39,849	$30,309
Alexander County, NC	37,353	37,185	33,603	168	3,582	0.5	10.7	1,398.4	1,028.7	35.9	$37,438	$27,627
Burke County, NC	90,382	90,832	89,148	-450	1,684	-0.5	1.9	3,187.3	2,481.2	28.5	$35,265	$27,394
Caldwell County, NC	82,029	83,060	77,415	-1,031	5,645	-1.2	7.3	2,901.7	2,246.8	29.1	$35,374	$27,063
Catawba County, NC	158,652	154,753	141,685	3,899	13,068	2.5	9.2	7,193.6	5,324.0	35.1	$45,342	$34,400
Hillsdale, MI Micro area	45,749	46,686	46,527	-937	159	-2.0	0.3	1,674.3	1,306.9	28.1	$36,598	$28,019
Hillsdale County, MI	45,749	46,686	46,527	-937	159	-2.0	0.3	1,674.3	1,306.9	28.1	$36,598	$28,019
Hilo, HI Micro area	200,983	185,076	148,677	15,907	36,399	8.6	24.5	8,531.5	5,869.4	45.4	$42,449	$31,665
Hawaii County, HI	200,983	185,076	148,677	15,907	36,399	8.6	24.5	8,531.5	5,869.4	45.4	$42,449	$31,665
Hilton Head Island-Bluffton, SC Metro area	217,686	187,010	141,615	30,676	45,395	16.4	32.1	11,549.5	7,184.4	60.8	$53,056	$38,260
Beaufort County, SC	188,715	162,231	120,937	26,484	41,294	16.3	34.1	10,702.3	6,630.3	61.4	$56,711	$40,715
Jasper County, SC	28,971	24,779	20,678	4,192	4,101	16.9	19.8	847.2	554.1	52.9	$29,242	$22,225
Hinesville, GA Metro area	80,495	77,919	71,914	2,576	6,005	3.3	8.4	2,716.2	2,184.2	24.4	$33,744	$28,248
Liberty County, GA	61,497	63,588	61,610	-2,091	1,978	-3.3	3.2	2,201.9	1,825.2	20.6	$35,805	$29,080
Long County, GA	18,998	14,331	10,304	4,667	4,027	32.6	39.1	514.3	359.0	43.3	$27,071	$24,658
Hobbs, NM Micro area	69,611	64,727	55,511	4,884	9,216	7.5	16.6	3,093.3	2,144.7	44.2	$44,437	$33,200
Lea County, NM	69,611	64,727	55,511	4,884	9,216	7.5	16.6	3,093.3	2,144.7	44.2	$44,437	$33,200
Holland, MI Micro area	117,327	111,407	105,665	5,920	5,742	5.3	5.4	5,301.0	3,685.3	43.8	$45,182	$33,043
Allegan County, MI	117,327	111,407	105,665	5,920	5,742	5.3	5.4	5,301.0	3,685.3	43.8	$45,182	$33,043
Homosassa Springs, FL Metro area	147,929	141,229	118,085	6,700	23,144	4.7	19.6	5,609.4	4,322.6	29.8	$37,920	$30,620
Citrus County, FL	147,929	141,229	118,085	6,700	23,144	4.7	19.6	5,609.4	4,322.6	29.8	$37,920	$30,620
Hood River, OR Micro area	23,428	22,346	20,411	1,082	1,935	4.8	9.5	1,326.6	786.4	68.7	$56,624	$35,035
Hood River County, OR	23,428	22,346	20,411	1,082	1,935	4.8	9.5	1,326.6	786.4	68.7	$56,624	$35,035

Table D-1. Population and Personal Income—Continued

Metropolitan or Micropolitan Statistical Area Metropolitan Division Component Counties	Population							Personal Income				
	2018 Estimate (July 1)	2010 census estimates base (April 1)	2000 census estimates base (April 1)	Net change		Percent change		Total (million dollars)		Percent change 2010-2018	Per capita	
				2010-2018	2000-2010	2010-2018	2000-2010	2018	2010		2018	2010
Hope, AR Micro area	30,067	31,613	33,542	-1,546	-1,929	-4.9	-5.8	991.5	810.2	22.4	$32,976	$25,642
Hempstead County, AR	21,741	22,593	23,587	-852	-994	-3.8	-4.2	706.9	566.0	24.9	$32,515	$25,046
Nevada County, AR	8,326	9,020	9,955	-694	-935	-7.7	-9.4	284.6	244.2	16.5	$34,180	$27,140
Hot Springs, AR Metro area	99,154	96,000	88,068	3,154	7,932	3.3	9.0	3,966.5	3,047.4	30.2	$40,004	$31,721
Garland County, AR	99,154	96,000	88,068	3,154	7,932	3.3	9.0	3,966.5	3,047.4	30.2	$40,004	$31,721
Houghton, MI Micro area	38,332	38,781	38,317	-449	464	-1.2	1.2	1,465.1	1,132.3	29.4	$38,222	$29,108
Houghton County, MI	36,219	36,625	36,016	-406	609	-1.1	1.7	1,364.5	1,057.7	29.0	$37,674	$28,796
Keweenaw County, MI	2,113	2,156	2,301	-43	-145	-2.0	-6.3	100.6	74.6	34.9	$47,618	$34,385
Houma-Thibodaux, LA Metro area	209,136	208,184	194,477	952	13,707	0.5	7.0	9,228.6	8,197.6	12.6	$44,127	$39,365
Lafourche Parish, LA	98,115	96,662	89,974	1,453	6,688	1.5	7.4	4,620.8	3,913.8	18.1	$47,096	$40,447
Terrebonne Parish, LA	111,021	111,522	104,503	-501	7,019	-0.4	6.7	4,607.8	4,283.8	7.6	$41,504	$38,426
Houston-The Woodlands-Sugar Land, TX Metro area	6,997,384	5,920,487	4,693,161	1,076,897	1,227,326	18.2	26.2	392,394.3	267,613.2	46.6	$56,077	$44,997
Austin County, TX	29,989	28,412	23,590	1,577	4,822	5.6	20.4	1,520.5	1,114.2	36.5	$50,702	$39,287
Brazoria County, TX	370,200	313,123	241,767	57,077	71,356	18.2	29.5	17,487.9	11,608.5	50.6	$47,239	$36,917
Chambers County, TX	42,454	35,099	26,031	7,355	9,068	21.0	34.8	2,278.6	1,388.3	64.1	$53,673	$39,167
Fort Bend County, TX	787,858	584,690	354,452	203,168	230,238	34.7	65.0	45,333.5	27,609.5	64.2	$57,540	$46,775
Galveston County, TX	337,890	291,307	250,158	46,583	41,149	16.0	16.4	17,497.8	11,900.5	47.0	$51,785	$40,689
Harris County, TX	4,698,619	4,093,188	3,400,578	605,431	692,610	14.8	20.4	265,351.3	187,913.4	41.2	$56,474	$45,745
Liberty County, TX	86,323	75,641	70,154	10,682	5,487	14.1	7.8	3,214.4	2,143.9	49.9	$37,237	$28,262
Montgomery County, TX	590,925	455,750	293,768	135,175	161,982	29.7	55.1	37,585.5	22,558.8	66.6	$63,605	$49,125
Waller County, TX	53,126	43,277	32,663	9,849	10,614	22.8	32.5	2,124.8	1,376.1	54.4	$39,995	$31,618
Hudson, NY Micro area	59,916	63,057	63,094	-3,141	-37	-5.0	-0.1	3,343.9	2,640.2	26.7	$55,810	$41,891
Columbia County, NY	59,916	63,057	63,094	-3,141	-37	-5.0	-0.1	3,343.9	2,640.2	26.7	$55,810	$41,891
Huntingdon, PA Micro area	45,168	46,009	45,586	-841	423	-1.8	0.9	1,741.6	1,402.9	24.1	$38,558	$30,495
Huntingdon County, PA	45,168	46,009	45,586	-841	423	-1.8	0.9	1,741.6	1,402.9	24.1	$38,558	$30,495
Huntington, IN Micro area	36,240	37,123	38,075	-883	-952	-2.4	-2.5	1,532.7	1,180.7	29.8	$42,292	$31,811
Huntington County, IN	36,240	37,123	38,075	-883	-952	-2.4	-2.5	1,532.7	1,180.7	29.8	$42,292	$31,811
Huntington-Ashland, WV-KY-OH Metro area	359,228	370,896	367,127	-11,668	3,769	-3.1	1.0	14,476.7	11,948.1	21.2	$40,299	$32,200
Boyd County, KY	47,240	49,538	49,752	-2,298	-214	-4.6	-0.4	1,877.6	1,633.7	14.9	$39,746	$32,933
Carter County, KY	27,004	27,721	26,889	-717	832	-2.6	3.1	833.0	714.7	16.6	$30,847	$25,759
Greenup County, KY	35,268	36,902	36,891	-1,634	11	-4.4	0.0	1,443.6	1,213.5	19.0	$40,933	$32,905
Lawrence County, OH	59,866	62,448	62,319	-2,582	129	-4.1	0.2	2,315.2	1,887.0	22.7	$38,673	$30,229
Cabell County, WV	93,224	96,297	96,784	-3,073	-487	-3.2	-0.5	4,002.9	3,309.4	21.0	$42,939	$34,357
Putnam County, WV	56,682	55,495	51,589	1,187	3,906	2.1	7.6	2,660.7	2,075.8	28.2	$46,941	$37,317
Wayne County, WV	39,944	42,495	42,903	-2,551	-408	-6.0	-1.0	1,343.6	1,114.0	20.6	$33,637	$26,239
Huntsville, AL Metro area	462,693	417,593	342,376	45,100	75,217	10.8	22.0	22,947.4	16,819.0	36.4	$49,595	$40,115
Limestone County, AL	96,174	82,782	65,676	13,392	17,106	16.2	26.0	4,091.9	2,798.9	46.2	$42,546	$33,652
Madison County, AL	366,519	334,811	276,700	31,708	58,111	9.5	21.0	18,855.6	14,020.0	34.5	$51,445	$41,715
Huntsville, TX Micro area	72,480	67,861	61,758	4,619	6,103	6.8	9.9	2,030.6	1,510.1	34.5	$28,016	$22,128
Walker County, TX	72,480	67,861	61,758	4,619	6,103	6.8	9.9	2,030.6	1,510.1	34.5	$28,016	$22,128
Huron, SD Micro area	20,926	19,470	19,318	1,456	152	7.5	0.8	1,041.1	756.4	37.6	$49,751	$38,795
Beadle County, SD	18,883	17,399	17,023	1,484	376	8.5	2.2	929.9	675.9	37.6	$49,246	$38,830
Jerauld County, SD	2,043	2,071	2,295	-28	-224	-1.4	-9.8	111.2	80.5	38.1	$54,425	$38,498
Hutchinson, KS Micro area	62,342	64,511	64,790	-2,169	-279	-3.4	-0.4	2,563.0	2,174.4	17.9	$41,111	$33,686
Reno County, KS	62,342	64,511	64,790	-2,169	-279	-3.4	-0.4	2,563.0	2,174.4	17.9	$41,111	$33,686
Hutchinson, MN Micro area	35,873	36,645	34,898	-772	1,747	-2.1	5.0	1,762.6	1,304.9	35.1	$49,136	$35,661
McLeod County, MN	35,873	36,645	34,898	-772	1,747	-2.1	5.0	1,762.6	1,304.9	35.1	$49,136	$35,661
Idaho Falls, ID Metro area	148,904	133,329	104,576	15,575	28,753	11.7	27.5	6,771.7	4,390.4	54.2	$45,477	$32,811
Bonneville County, ID	116,854	104,294	82,522	12,560	21,772	12.0	26.4	5,642.5	3,593.6	57.0	$48,287	$34,332
Butte County, ID	2,611	2,893	2,899	-282	-6	-9.7	-0.2	101.7	83.3	22.1	$38,961	$28,567
Jefferson County, ID	29,439	26,142	19,155	3,297	6,987	12.6	36.5	1,027.4	713.5	44.0	$34,900	$27,210
Indiana, PA Micro area	84,501	88,889	89,605	-4,388	-716	-4.9	-0.8	3,373.6	2,805.1	20.3	$39,923	$31,566
Indiana County, PA	84,501	88,889	89,605	-4,388	-716	-4.9	-0.8	3,373.6	2,805.1	20.3	$39,923	$31,566
Indianapolis-Carmel-Anderson, IN Metro area	2,048,703	1,888,085	1,658,462	160,618	229,623	8.5	13.8	110,997.1	78,248.9	41.9	$54,179	$41,344
Boone County, IN	66,999	56,638	46,107	10,361	10,531	18.3	22.8	4,926.5	2,913.8	69.1	$73,531	$51,197
Brown County, IN	15,234	15,245	14,957	-11	288	-0.1	1.9	712.7	521.4	36.7	$46,785	$34,286
Hamilton County, IN	330,086	274,569	182,740	55,517	91,829	20.2	50.3	24,663.0	14,899.2	65.5	$74,717	$53,883
Hancock County, IN	76,351	70,043	55,391	6,308	14,652	9.0	26.5	3,849.8	2,720.7	41.5	$50,422	$38,740
Hendricks County, IN	167,009	145,414	104,093	21,595	41,321	14.9	39.7	8,290.5	5,516.4	50.3	$49,641	$37,807
Johnson County, IN	156,225	139,857	115,209	16,368	24,648	11.7	21.4	7,550.7	5,204.1	45.1	$48,332	$37,100
Madison County, IN	129,641	131,639	133,358	-1,998	-1,719	-1.5	-1.3	4,948.7	3,831.1	29.2	$38,172	$29,108
Marion County, IN	954,670	903,389	860,454	51,281	42,935	5.7	5.0	49,585.8	37,742.3	31.4	$51,940	$41,723
Morgan County, IN	70,116	68,943	66,689	1,173	2,254	1.7	3.4	3,097.9	2,361.0	31.2	$44,183	$34,141
Putnam County, IN	37,779	37,952	36,019	-173	1,933	-0.5	5.4	1,415.9	1,068.3	32.5	$37,479	$28,178
Shelby County, IN	44,593	44,396	43,445	197	951	0.4	2.2	1,955.6	1,470.4	33.0	$43,854	$33,180
Indianola, MS Micro area	25,735	29,383	34,369	-3,648	-4,986	-12.4	-14.5	794.2	713.1	11.4	$30,859	$24,605
Sunflower County, MS	25,735	29,383	34,369	-3,648	-4,986	-12.4	-14.5	794.2	713.1	11.4	$30,859	$24,605
Iowa City, IA Metro area	173,401	152,586	131,676	20,815	20,910	13.6	15.9	9,238.8	6,127.4	50.8	$53,280	$40,040
Johnson County, IA	151,260	130,882	111,006	20,378	19,876	15.6	17.9	7,967.1	5,278.2	50.9	$52,672	$40,188
Washington County, IA	22,141	21,704	20,670	437	1,034	2.0	5.0	1,271.7	849.2	49.8	$57,438	$39,148
Iron Mountain, MI-WI Micro area	29,704	30,591	32,560	-887	-1,969	-2.9	-6.0	1,488.7	1,112.5	33.8	$50,117	$36,408
Dickinson County, MI	25,383	26,168	27,472	-785	-1,304	-3.0	-4.7	1,253.8	942.3	33.1	$49,397	$36,023
Florence County, WI	4,321	4,423	5,088	-102	-665	-2.3	-13.1	234.8	170.2	38.0	$54,346	$38,697
Ithaca, NY Metro area	102,793	101,580	96,501	1,213	5,079	1.2	5.3	4,654.7	3,557.4	30.8	$45,282	$34,971
Tompkins County, NY	102,793	101,580	96,501	1,213	5,079	1.2	5.3	4,654.7	3,557.4	30.8	$45,282	$34,971

Table D-1. Population and Personal Income—*Continued*

Metropolitan or Micropolitan Statistical Area Metropolitan Division Component Counties	Population							Personal Income				
	2018 Estimate (July 1)	2010 census estimates base (April 1)	2000 census estimates base (April 1)	Net change		Percent change		Total (million dollars)		Percent change 2010-2018	Per capita	
				2010-2018	2000-2010	2010-2018	2000-2010	2018	2010		2018	2010
Jackson, MI Metro area	158,823	160,245	158,422	-1,422	1,823	-0.9	1.2	6,326.2	4,859.9	30.2	$39,832	$30,351
Jackson County, MI	158,823	160,245	158,422	-1,422	1,823	-0.9	1.2	6,326.2	4,859.9	30.2	$39,832	$30,351
Jackson, MS Metro area	597,788	587,115	546,955	10,673	40,160	1.8	7.3	26,166.2	21,058.6	24.3	$43,772	$35,797
Copiah County, MS	28,543	29,447	28,757	-904	690	-3.1	2.4	947.7	809.3	17.1	$33,203	$27,497
Hinds County, MS	237,085	245,365	250,800	-8,280	-5,435	-3.4	-2.2	9,319.9	8,417.1	10.7	$39,311	$34,254
Holmes County, MS	17,622	19,483	21,609	-1,861	-2,126	-9.6	-9.8	500.0	473.1	5.7	$28,371	$24,379
Madison County, MS	105,630	95,203	74,674	10,427	20,529	11.0	27.5	6,763.8	4,667.3	44.9	$64,033	$48,853
Rankin County, MS	153,902	142,054	115,327	11,848	26,727	8.3	23.2	6,873.4	5,187.1	32.5	$44,661	$36,396
Simpson County, MS	26,758	27,498	27,639	-740	-141	-2.7	-0.5	991.0	813.9	21.8	$37,036	$29,573
Yazoo County, MS	28,248	28,065	28,149	183	-84	0.7	-0.3	770.5	690.8	11.5	$27,275	$24,553
Jackson, OH Micro area	32,384	33,225	32,641	-841	584	-2.5	1.8	1,158.8	954.2	21.4	$35,783	$28,696
Jackson County, OH	32,384	33,225	32,641	-841	584	-2.5	1.8	1,158.8	954.2	21.4	$35,783	$28,696
Jackson, TN Metro area	178,254	179,709	170,061	-1,455	9,648	-0.8	5.7	7,170.5	5,783.9	24.0	$40,226	$32,175
Chester County, TN	17,276	17,145	15,540	131	1,605	0.8	10.3	581.2	454.2	28.0	$33,642	$26,416
Crockett County, TN	14,328	14,576	14,532	-248	44	-1.7	0.3	523.8	463.9	12.9	$36,560	$31,802
Gibson County, TN	49,045	49,687	48,152	-642	1,535	-1.3	3.2	1,895.8	1,542.5	22.9	$38,654	$31,017
Madison County, TN	97,605	98,301	91,837	-696	6,464	-0.7	7.0	4,169.7	3,323.3	25.5	$42,720	$33,825
Jackson, WY-ID Micro area	34,721	31,463	24,250	3,258	7,213	10.4	29.7	6,274.1	3,272.8	91.7	$180,700	$104,072
Teton County, ID	11,640	10,165	5,999	1,475	4,166	14.5	69.4	464.0	248.7	86.6	$39,858	$24,504
Teton County, WY	23,081	21,298	18,251	1,783	3,047	8.4	16.7	5,810.1	3,024.1	92.1	$251,728	$141,996
Jacksonville, FL Metro area	1,534,701	1,345,591	1,122,750	189,110	222,841	14.1	19.8	76,357.0	52,230.9	46.2	$49,754	$38,721
Baker County, FL	28,355	27,115	22,259	1,240	4,856	4.6	21.8	916.2	694.5	31.9	$32,313	$25,663
Clay County, FL	216,072	190,865	140,814	25,207	50,051	13.2	35.5	9,271.4	6,490.2	42.9	$42,909	$33,903
Duval County, FL	950,181	864,267	778,879	85,914	85,388	9.9	11.0	43,874.1	31,791.2	38.0	$46,174	$36,726
Nassau County, FL	85,832	73,310	57,663	12,522	15,647	17.1	27.1	4,967.7	3,182.1	56.1	$57,877	$43,287
St. Johns County, FL	254,261	190,034	123,135	64,227	66,899	33.8	54.3	17,327.7	10,072.9	72.0	$68,149	$52,671
Jacksonville, IL Micro area	38,902	40,900	42,153	-1,998	-1,253	-4.9	-3.0	1,615.6	1,389.5	16.3	$41,531	$34,029
Morgan County, IL	33,976	35,545	36,616	-1,569	-1,071	-4.4	-2.9	1,405.2	1,213.0	15.8	$41,359	$34,165
Scott County, IL	4,926	5,355	5,537	-429	-182	-8.0	-3.3	210.4	176.4	19.3	$42,720	$33,121
Jacksonville, NC Metro area	197,683	177,799	150,355	19,884	27,444	11.2	18.3	9,121.5	7,826.8	16.5	$46,142	$41,879
Onslow County, NC	197,683	177,799	150,355	19,884	27,444	11.2	18.3	9,121.5	7,826.8	16.5	$46,142	$41,879
Jacksonville, TX Micro area	52,592	50,834	46,659	1,758	4,175	3.5	8.9	1,812.7	1,427.4	27.0	$34,468	$28,019
Cherokee County, TX	52,592	50,834	46,659	1,758	4,175	3.5	8.9	1,812.7	1,427.4	27.0	$34,468	$28,019
Jamestown, ND Micro area	20,917	21,100	21,908	-183	-808	-0.9	-3.7	1,139.8	855.3	33.3	$54,491	$40,463
Stutsman County, ND	20,917	21,100	21,908	-183	-808	-0.9	-3.7	1,139.8	855.3	33.3	$54,491	$40,463
Jamestown-Dunkirk-Fredonia, NY Micro area	127,939	134,907	139,750	-6,968	-4,843	-5.2	-3.5	5,214.7	4,238.3	23.0	$40,759	$31,459
Chautauqua County, NY	127,939	134,907	139,750	-6,968	-4,843	-5.2	-3.5	5,214.7	4,238.3	23.0	$40,759	$31,459
Janesville-Beloit, WI Metro area	163,129	160,335	152,307	2,794	8,028	1.7	5.3	7,210.9	5,420.0	33.0	$44,204	$33,817
Rock County, WI	163,129	160,335	152,307	2,794	8,028	1.7	5.3	7,210.9	5,420.0	33.0	$44,204	$33,817
Jasper, AL Micro area	63,711	67,023	70,713	-3,312	-3,690	-4.9	-5.2	2,561.0	2,193.9	16.7	$40,197	$32,746
Walker County, AL	63,711	67,023	70,713	-3,312	-3,690	-4.9	-5.2	2,561.0	2,193.9	16.7	$40,197	$32,746
Jasper, IN Micro area	54,975	54,598	52,511	377	2,087	0.7	4.0	2,909.7	2,087.5	39.4	$52,928	$38,208
Dubois County, IN	42,565	41,888	39,674	677	2,214	1.6	5.6	2,404.4	1,689.9	42.3	$56,488	$40,326
Pike County, IN	12,410	12,710	12,837	-300	-127	-2.4	-1.0	505.3	397.6	27.1	$40,714	$31,236
Jefferson, GA Micro area	70,422	60,457	41,589	9,965	18,868	16.5	45.4	2,972.5	1,754.4	69.4	$42,211	$28,905
Jackson County, GA	70,422	60,457	41,589	9,965	18,868	16.5	45.4	2,972.5	1,754.4	69.4	$42,211	$28,905
Jefferson City, MO Metro area	151,520	149,797	140,052	1,723	9,745	1.2	7.0	6,636.8	5,232.2	26.8	$43,802	$34,890
Callaway County, MO	44,889	44,334	40,766	555	3,568	1.3	8.8	1,736.6	1,387.5	25.2	$38,686	$31,312
Cole County, MO	76,796	75,975	71,397	821	4,578	1.1	6.4	3,670.1	2,903.7	26.4	$47,790	$38,134
Moniteau County, MO	16,121	15,605	14,827	516	778	3.3	5.2	605.1	467.6	29.4	$37,533	$29,925
Osage County, MO	13,714	13,883	13,062	-169	821	-1.2	6.3	625.1	473.4	32.0	$45,582	$34,106
Jennings, LA Micro area	31,582	31,592	31,435	-10	157	0.0	0.5	1,337.0	1,004.8	33.1	$42,334	$31,764
Jefferson Davis Parish, LA	31,582	31,592	31,435	-10	157	0.0	0.5	1,337.0	1,004.8	33.1	$42,334	$31,764
Jesup, GA Micro area	29,808	30,099	26,565	-291	3,534	-1.0	13.3	952.5	831.5	14.6	$31,954	$27,647
Wayne County, GA	29,808	30,099	26,565	-291	3,534	-1.0	13.3	952.5	831.5	14.6	$31,954	$27,647
Johnson City, TN Metro area	202,719	198,757	181,607	3,962	17,150	2.0	9.4	8,181.8	6,326.1	29.3	$40,360	$31,788
Carter County, TN	56,351	57,388	56,742	-1,037	646	-1.8	1.1	1,948.6	1,570.8	24.1	$34,579	$27,390
Unicoi County, TN	17,761	18,311	17,667	-550	644	-3.0	3.6	664.7	555.9	19.6	$37,423	$30,401
Washington County, TN	128,607	123,058	107,198	5,549	15,860	4.5	14.8	5,568.6	4,199.4	32.6	$43,299	$34,038
Johnstown, PA Metro area	131,730	143,681	152,598	-11,951	-8,917	-8.3	-5.8	5,719.8	4,712.8	21.4	$43,420	$32,853
Cambria County, PA	131,730	143,681	152,598	-11,951	-8,917	-8.3	-5.8	5,719.8	4,712.8	21.4	$43,420	$32,853
Jonesboro, AR Metro area	132,532	121,020	107,762	11,512	13,258	9.5	12.3	4,849.0	3,611.3	34.3	$36,588	$29,782
Craighead County, AR	108,558	96,443	82,148	12,115	14,295	12.6	17.4	4,074.3	2,932.0	39.0	$37,531	$30,307
Poinsett County, AR	23,974	24,577	25,614	-603	-1,037	-2.5	-4.0	774.7	679.3	14.0	$32,315	$27,711
Joplin, MO Metro area	178,902	175,509	157,322	3,393	18,187	1.9	11.6	7,114.0	5,398.1	31.8	$39,765	$30,700
Jasper County, MO	120,636	117,391	104,686	3,245	12,705	2.8	12.1	4,822.1	3,574.9	34.9	$39,973	$30,384
Newton County, MO	58,266	58,118	52,636	148	5,482	0.3	10.4	2,291.9	1,823.2	25.7	$39,334	$31,339
Juneau, AK Micro area	32,113	31,275	30,711	838	564	2.7	1.8	2,188.3	1,727.6	26.7	$68,145	$55,045
Juneau City and Borough, AK	32,113	31,275	30,711	838	564	2.7	1.8	2,188.3	1,727.6	26.7	$68,145	$55,045
Kahului-Wailuku-Lahaina, HI Metro area	167,207	154,840	128,094	12,367	26,746	8.0	20.9	8,204.1	5,536.7	48.2	$49,040	$35,699
Maui County, HI (includes Kalawao County)	167,207	154,840	128,094	12,367	26,746	8.0	20.9	8,204.1	5,536.7	48.2	$49,040	$35,699
Kalamazoo-Portage, MI Metro area	264,870	250,327	238,603	14,543	11,724	5.8	4.9	12,905.3	9,129.4	41.4	$48,723	$36,409
Kalamazoo County, MI	264,870	250,327	238,603	14,543	11,724	5.8	4.9	12,905.3	9,129.4	41.4	$48,723	$36,409
Kalispell, MT Micro area	102,106	90,927	74,471	11,179	16,456	12.3	22.1	4,832.7	3,175.5	52.2	$47,331	$34,947
Flathead County, MT	102,106	90,927	74,471	11,179	16,456	12.3	22.1	4,832.7	3,175.5	52.2	$47,331	$34,947
Kankakee, IL Metro area	110,024	113,450	103,833	-3,426	9,617	-3.0	9.3	4,542.9	3,720.6	22.1	$41,290	$32,804

Table D-1. Population and Personal Income—Continued

Metropolitan or Micropolitan Statistical Area Metropolitan Division Component Counties	Population 2018 Estimate (July 1)	2010 census estimates base (April 1)	2000 census estimates base (April 1)	Net change 2010-2018	Net change 2000-2010	Percent change 2010-2018	Percent change 2000-2010	Personal Income Total (million dollars) 2018	2010	Percent change 2010-2018	Per capita 2018	Per capita 2010
Kankakee County, IL	110,024	113,450	103,833	-3,426	9,617	-3.0	9.3	4,542.9	3,720.6	22.1	$41,290	$32,804
Kansas City, MO-KS Metro area	2,143,651	2,009,341	1,811,254	134,310	198,087	6.7	10.9	115,303.0	82,754.9	39.3	$53,788	$41,103
Johnson County, KS	597,555	544,181	451,086	53,374	93,095	9.8	20.6	44,225.2	29,474.0	50.0	$74,010	$54,015
Leavenworth County, KS	81,352	76,211	68,691	5,141	7,520	6.7	10.9	3,486.0	2,656.4	31.2	$42,851	$34,720
Linn County, KS	9,750	9,656	9,570	94	86	1.0	0.9	363.4	287.7	26.3	$37,267	$29,890
Miami County, KS	33,680	32,781	28,351	899	4,430	2.7	15.6	1,641.8	1,191.9	37.7	$48,748	$36,248
Wyandotte County, KS	165,324	157,525	157,882	7,799	-357	5.0	-0.2	5,507.7	4,580.4	20.2	$33,315	$29,056
Bates County, MO	16,320	17,049	16,653	-729	396	-4.3	2.4	634.3	516.9	22.7	$38,864	$30,343
Caldwell County, MO	9,108	9,424	8,969	-316	455	-3.4	5.1	339.7	266.0	27.7	$37,301	$28,199
Cass County, MO	104,954	99,505	82,092	5,449	17,413	5.5	21.2	4,948.7	3,547.1	39.5	$47,151	$35,557
Clay County, MO	246,365	221,943	184,006	24,422	37,937	11.0	20.6	11,919.3	8,831.3	35.0	$48,381	$39,658
Clinton County, MO	20,470	20,743	18,979	-273	1,764	-1.3	9.3	880.0	670.4	31.3	$42,988	$32,325
Jackson County, MO	700,307	674,134	654,880	26,173	19,254	3.9	2.9	32,952.4	24,860.9	32.5	$47,054	$36,841
Lafayette County, MO	32,598	33,370	32,960	-772	410	-2.3	1.2	1,373.0	1,077.0	27.5	$42,119	$32,261
Platte County, MO	102,985	89,325	73,781	13,660	15,544	15.3	21.1	6,063.5	4,052.7	49.6	$58,878	$45,181
Ray County, MO	22,883	23,494	23,354	-611	140	-2.6	0.6	968.1	742.1	30.5	$42,305	$31,587
Kapaa, HI Micro area	72,133	67,095	58,463	5,038	8,632	7.5	14.8	3,564.5	2,375.4	50.1	$49,416	$35,341
Kauai County, HI	72,133	67,095	58,463	5,038	8,632	7.5	14.8	3,564.5	2,375.4	50.1	$49,416	$35,341
Kearney, NE Micro area	56,159	52,588	49,141	3,571	3,447	6.8	7.0	3,050.3	2,039.3	49.6	$54,315	$38,732
Buffalo County, NE	49,615	46,099	42,259	3,516	3,840	7.6	9.1	2,681.8	1,751.8	53.1	$54,052	$37,940
Kearney County, NE	6,544	6,489	6,882	55	-393	0.8	-5.7	368.5	287.5	28.2	$56,309	$44,381
Keene, NH Micro area	76,493	77,122	73,825	-629	3,297	-0.8	4.5	3,975.3	3,104.7	28.0	$51,969	$40,291
Cheshire County, NH	76,493	77,122	73,825	-629	3,297	-0.8	4.5	3,975.3	3,104.7	28.0	$51,969	$40,291
Kendallville, IN Micro area	47,532	47,540	46,275	-8	1,265	0.0	2.7	1,891.7	1,336.0	41.6	$39,798	$28,154
Noble County, IN	47,532	47,540	46,275	-8	1,265	0.0	2.7	1,891.7	1,336.0	41.6	$39,798	$28,154
Kennett, MO Micro area	29,423	31,953	33,155	-2,530	-1,202	-7.9	-3.6	1,004.2	967.9	3.8	$34,129	$30,300
Dunklin County, MO	29,423	31,953	33,155	-2,530	-1,202	-7.9	-3.6	1,004.2	967.9	3.8	$34,129	$30,300
Kennewick-Richland, WA Metro area	296,224	253,332	191,822	42,892	61,510	16.9	32.1	13,109.6	9,661.8	35.7	$44,256	$37,808
Benton County, WA	201,877	175,169	142,475	26,708	32,694	15.2	22.9	9,582.0	7,232.9	32.5	$47,465	$40,988
Franklin County, WA	94,347	78,163	49,347	16,184	28,816	20.7	58.4	3,527.6	2,428.9	45.2	$37,390	$30,713
Kerrville, TX Micro area	52,405	49,625	43,653	2,780	5,972	5.6	13.7	2,628.1	1,901.2	38.2	$50,150	$38,314
Kerr County, TX	52,405	49,625	43,653	2,780	5,972	5.6	13.7	2,628.1	1,901.2	38.2	$50,150	$38,314
Ketchikan, AK Micro area	13,918	13,519	14,070	399	-551	3.0	-3.9	940.9	740.7	27.0	$67,602	$54,602
Ketchikan Gateway Borough, AK	13,918	13,519	14,070	399	-551	3.0	-3.9	940.9	740.7	27.0	$67,602	$54,602
Key West, FL Micro area	75,027	73,090	79,589	1,937	-6,499	2.7	-8.2	6,911.4	4,464.5	54.8	$92,119	$60,973
Monroe County, FL	75,027	73,090	79,589	1,937	-6,499	2.7	-8.2	6,911.4	4,464.5	54.8	$92,119	$60,973
Kill Devil Hills, NC Micro area	36,501	33,920	29,967	2,581	3,953	7.6	13.2	2,055.5	1,381.6	48.8	$56,314	$40,657
Dare County, NC	36,501	33,920	29,967	2,581	3,953	7.6	13.2	2,055.5	1,381.6	48.8	$56,314	$40,657
Killeen-Temple, TX Metro area	451,679	405,313	330,714	46,366	74,599	11.4	22.6	18,805.0	15,167.0	24.0	$41,634	$37,149
Bell County, TX	355,642	310,159	237,974	45,483	72,185	14.7	30.3	15,211.9	12,132.7	25.4	$42,773	$38,781
Coryell County, TX	74,808	75,474	74,978	-666	496	-0.9	0.7	2,543.2	2,191.1	16.1	$33,996	$28,960
Lampasas County, TX	21,229	19,680	17,762	1,549	1,918	7.9	10.8	1,049.9	843.2	24.5	$49,457	$42,661
Kingsport-Bristol, TN-VA Metro area	306,616	309,502	298,484	-2,886	11,018	-0.9	3.7	12,277.4	10,079.3	21.8	$40,042	$32,568
Hawkins County, TN	56,530	56,829	53,563	-299	3,266	-0.5	6.1	1,932.7	1,578.6	22.4	$34,188	$27,757
Sullivan County, TN	157,668	156,800	153,048	868	3,752	0.6	2.5	6,717.6	5,351.0	25.5	$42,606	$34,137
Scott County, VA	21,534	23,170	23,403	-1,636	-233	-7.1		727.2	626.9	16.0	$33,769	$27,105
Washington County, VA	54,402	54,964	51,103	-562	3,861		7.6	2,900.0	2,522.8	15.0	$40,912	$34,686
Bristol City, VA (included with Washington County)	16,482	17,739	17,367	-1,257	372	-7.1	2.1	-	-	-	-	-
Kingston, NY Metro area	178,599	182,512	177,749	-3,913	4,763	-2.1	2.7	9,012.5	6,976.5	29.2	$50,462	$38,247
Ulster County, NY	178,599	182,512	177,749	-3,913	4,763	-2.1	2.7	9,012.5	6,976.5	29.2	$50,462	$38,247
Kingsville, TX Micro area	31,571	32,474	31,963	-903	511	-2.8	1.6	1,233.2	959.0	28.6	$39,060	$29,554
Kenedy County, TX	442	413	414	29		7.0	-0.2	19.3	12.5	54.4	$43,561	$30,014
Kleberg County, TX	31,129	32,061	31,549	-932	512	-2.9	1.6	1,213.9	946.5	28.3	$38,997	$29,548
Kinston, NC Micro area	55,976	59,511	59,648	-3,535	-137	-5.9	-0.2	2,290.6	1,911.9	19.8	$40,922	$32,137
Lenoir County, NC	55,976	59,511	59,648	-3,535	-137	-5.9	-0.2	2,290.6	1,911.9	19.8	$40,922	$32,137
Kirksville, MO Micro area	29,938	30,035	29,147	-97	888	-0.3	3.0	984.3	813.2	21.0	$32,877	$27,050
Adair County, MO	25,339	25,604	24,977	-265	627		2.5	850.8	696.6	22.1	$33,578	$27,187
Schuyler County, MO	4,599	4,431	4,170	168	261	3.8	6.3	133.4	116.6	14.4	$29,013	$26,256
Klamath Falls, OR Micro area	67,653	66,380	63,775	1,273	2,605	1.9	4.1	2,698.7	1,973.0	36.8	$39,891	$29,751
Klamath County, OR	67,653	66,380	63,775	1,273	2,605	1.9	4.1	2,698.7	1,973.0	36.8	$39,891	$29,751
Knoxville, TN Metro area	860,164	815,021	727,600	45,143	87,421	5.5	12.0	39,343.4	28,329.2	38.9	$45,739	$34,718
Anderson County, TN	76,482	75,089	71,330	1,393	3,759	1.9	5.3	3,201.0	2,584.9	23.8	$41,853	$34,417
Blount County, TN	131,349	123,098	105,823	8,251	17,275	6.7	16.3	5,646.9	3,928.9	43.7	$42,991	$31,891
Campbell County, TN	39,583	40,723	39,854	-1,140	869	-2.8	2.2	1,344.5	1,105.6	21.6	$33,967	$27,140
Knox County, TN	465,289	432,269	382,032	33,020	50,237	7.6	13.1	23,142.7	16,150.9	43.3	$49,738	$37,305
Loudon County, TN	53,054	48,550	39,086	4,504	9,464	9.3	24.2	2,572.6	1,775.4	44.9	$48,491	$36,456
Morgan County, TN	21,579	21,986	19,757	-407	2,229	-1.9	11.3	634.0	533.0	18.9	$29,380	$24,205
Roane County, TN	53,140	54,199	51,910	-1,059	2,289	-2.0	4.4	2,177.7	1,778.5	22.4	$40,980	$32,839
Union County, TN	19,688	19,107	17,808	581	1,299	3.0	7.3	624.0	472.1	32.2	$31,693	$24,695
Kokomo, IN Metro area	82,366	82,752	84,964	-386	-2,212	-0.5	-2.6	3,446.4	2,578.1	33.7	$41,842	$31,153
Howard County, IN	82,366	82,752	84,964	-386	-2,212	-0.5	-2.6	3,446.4	2,578.1	33.7	$41,842	$31,153
Laconia, NH Micro area	61,022	60,073	56,325	949	3,748	1.6	6.7	3,727.9	2,630.6	41.7	$61,091	$43,772
Belknap County, NH	61,022	60,073	56,325	949	3,748	1.6	6.7	3,727.9	2,630.6	41.7	$61,091	$43,772
La Crosse-Onalaska, WI-MN Metro area	136,808	133,660	126,838	3,148	6,822	2.4	5.4	6,896.8	5,080.5	35.8	$50,412	$37,942
Houston County, MN	18,578	19,022	19,718	-444	-696	-2.3	-3.5	972.6	738.4	31.7	$52,354	$38,808

Table D-1. Population and Personal Income—*Continued*

Metropolitan or Micropolitan Statistical Area Metropolitan Division Component Counties	Population							Personal Income				
	2018 Estimate (July 1)	2010 census estimates base (April 1)	2000 census estimates base (April 1)	Net change		Percent change		Total (million dollars)		Percent change 2010-2018	Per capita	
				2010-2018	2000-2010	2010-2018	2000-2010	2018	2010		2018	2010
La Crosse County, WI	118,230	114,638	107,120	3,592	7,518	3.1	7.0	5,924.2	4,342.1	36.4	$50,107	$37,799
Lafayette, LA Metro area	489,364	466,736	425,020	22,628	41,716	4.8	9.8	21,665.6	18,025.3	20.2	$44,273	$38,547
Acadia Parish, LA	62,190	61,787	58,861	403	2,926	0.7	5.0	2,319.9	1,959.0	18.4	$37,304	$31,660
Iberia Parish, LA	70,941	73,094	73,266	-2,153	-172	-2.9	-0.2	2,785.9	2,596.5	7.3	$39,270	$35,509
Lafayette Parish, LA	242,782	221,724	190,503	21,058	31,221	9.5	16.4	12,205.4	9,775.7	24.9	$50,273	$43,983
St. Martin Parish, LA	53,621	52,160	48,583	1,461	3,577	2.8	7.4	2,018.6	1,703.2	18.5	$37,645	$32,590
Vermilion Parish, LA	59,830	57,971	53,807	1,859	4,164	3.2	7.7	2,335.9	1,990.9	17.3	$39,042	$34,268
Lafayette-West Lafayette, IN Metro area	230,091	210,305	186,960	19,786	23,345	9.4	12.5	9,196.6	6,556.5	40.3	$39,969	$31,121
Benton County, IN	8,653	8,836	9,421	-183	-585	-2.1	-6.2	370.1	297.7	24.3	$42,775	$33,591
Carroll County, IN	20,127	20,155	20,165	-28	-10	-0.1	0.0	889.6	666.2	33.5	$44,201	$32,988
Tippecanoe County, IN	193,048	172,803	148,955	20,245	23,848	11.7	16.0	7,561.5	5,296.2	42.8	$39,169	$30,596
Warren County, IN	8,263	8,511	8,419	-248	92	-2.9	1.1	375.3	296.5	26.6	$45,419	$34,792
La Grande, OR Micro area	26,461	25,744	24,530	717	1,214	2.8	4.9	1,072.9	793.2	35.3	$40,547	$30,827
Union County, OR	26,461	25,744	24,530	717	1,214	2.8	4.9	1,072.9	793.2	35.3	$40,547	$30,827
LaGrange, GA-AL Micro area	103,649	101,210	95,362	2,439	5,848	2.4	6.1	3,692.7	2,926.9	26.2	$35,627	$28,930
Chambers County, AL	33,615	34,171	36,583	-556	-2,412	-1.6	-6.6	1,138.2	934.0	21.9	$33,859	$27,373
Troup County, GA	70,034	67,039	58,779	2,995	8,260	4.5	14.1	2,554.6	1,992.9	28.2	$36,476	$29,722
Lake Charles, LA Metro area	210,080	199,641	193,568	10,439	6,073	5.2	3.1	10,296.3	6,906.5	49.1	$49,011	$34,543
Calcasieu Parish, LA	203,112	192,773	183,577	10,339	9,196	5.4	5.0	9,945.9	6,672.5	49.1	$48,968	$34,568
Cameron Parish, LA	6,968	6,868	9,991	100	-3,123	1.5	-31.3	350.3	234.1	49.6	$50,280	$33,846
Lake City, FL Micro area	70,503	67,526	56,513	2,977	11,013	4.4	19.5	2,472.8	1,901.9	30.0	$35,074	$28,154
Columbia County, FL	70,503	67,526	56,513	2,977	11,013	4.4	19.5	2,472.8	1,901.9	30.0	$35,074	$28,154
Lake Havasu City-Kingman, AZ Metro area	209,550	200,182	155,032	9,368	45,150	4.7	29.1	6,946.2	5,124.4	35.6	$33,148	$25,582
Mohave County, AZ	209,550	200,182	155,032	9,368	45,150	4.7	29.1	6,946.2	5,124.4	35.6	$33,148	$25,582
Lakeland-Winter Haven, FL Metro area	708,009	602,098	483,924	105,911	118,174	17.6	24.4	25,108.4	18,373.9	36.7	$35,463	$30,464
Polk County, FL	708,009	602,098	483,924	105,911	118,174	17.6	24.4	25,108.4	18,373.9	36.7	$35,463	$30,464
Lamesa, TX Micro area	12,619	13,833	14,985	-1,214	-1,152	-8.8	-7.7	468.3	439.6	6.5	$37,111	$31,796
Dawson County, TX	12,619	13,833	14,985	-1,214	-1,152	-8.8	-7.7	468.3	439.6	6.5	$37,111	$31,796
Lancaster, PA Metro area	543,557	519,446	470,658	24,111	48,788	4.6	10.4	28,625.8	19,775.0	44.8	$52,664	$38,005
Lancaster County, PA	543,557	519,446	470,658	24,111	48,788	4.6	10.4	28,625.8	19,775.0	44.8	$52,664	$38,005
Lansing-East Lansing, MI Metro area	550,085	534,684	519,415	15,401	15,269	2.9	2.9	23,000.4	17,633.9	30.4	$41,812	$32,967
Clinton County, MI	79,332	75,367	64,753	3,965	10,614	5.3	16.4	3,690.4	2,634.4	40.1	$46,518	$34,936
Eaton County, MI	109,826	107,763	103,655	2,063	4,108	1.9	4.0	4,688.8	3,561.6	31.6	$42,693	$33,053
Ingham County, MI	292,735	280,891	279,320	11,844	1,571	4.2	0.6	11,932.1	9,346.1	27.7	$40,761	$33,247
Shiawassee County, MI	68,192	70,663	71,687	-2,471	-1,024	-3.5	-1.4	2,689.2	2,091.8	28.6	$39,435	$29,617
Laramie, WY Micro area	38,601	36,299	32,014	2,302	4,285	6.3	13.4	1,561.2	1,243.9	25.5	$40,444	$34,113
Albany County, WY	38,601	36,299	32,014	2,302	4,285	6.3	13.4	1,561.2	1,243.9	25.5	$40,444	$34,113
Laredo, TX Metro area	275,910	250,304	193,117	25,606	57,187	10.2	29.6	8,728.5	6,514.0	34.0	$31,635	$25,912
Webb County, TX	275,910	250,304	193,117	25,606	57,187	10.2	29.6	8,728.5	6,514.0	34.0	$31,635	$25,912
Las Cruces, NM Metro area	217,522	209,202	174,682	8,320	34,520	4.0	19.8	7,954.7	6,344.0	25.4	$36,570	$30,196
Dona Ana County, NM	217,522	209,202	174,682	8,320	34,520	4.0	19.8	7,954.7	6,344.0	25.4	$36,570	$30,196
Las Vegas, NM Micro area	32,097	34,260	35,306	-2,163	-1,046	-6.3	-3.0	1,114.2	1,052.9	5.8	$34,713	$30,704
Mora County, NM	4,506	4,881	5,180	-375	-299	-7.7	-5.8	160.1	211.4	-24.3	$35,534	$43,196
San Miguel County, NM	27,591	29,379	30,126	-1,788	-747	-6.1	-2.5	954.1	841.5	13.4	$34,579	$28,624
Las Vegas-Henderson-Paradise, NV Metro area	2,231,647	1,951,271	1,375,765	280,376	575,506	14.4	41.8	105,087.9	69,601.9	51.0	$47,090	$35,645
Clark County, NV	2,231,647	1,951,271	1,375,765	280,376	575,506	14.4	41.8	105,087.9	69,601.9	51.0	$47,090	$35,645
Laurel, MS Micro area	84,889	84,834	83,107	55	1,727	0.1	2.1	3,222.3	2,708.5	19.0	$37,959	$31,934
Jasper County, MS	16,428	17,065	18,149	-637	-1,084	-3.7	-6.0	612.5	496.8	23.3	$37,281	$29,204
Jones County, MS	68,461	67,769	64,958	692	2,811	1.0	4.3	2,609.9	2,211.7	18.0	$38,122	$32,619
Laurinburg, NC Micro area	34,810	36,160	35,998	-1,350	162	-3.7	0.5	1,156.7	1,054.8	9.7	$33,229	$29,248
Scotland County, NC	34,810	36,160	35,998	-1,350	162	-3.7	0.5	1,156.7	1,054.8	9.7	$33,229	$29,248
Lawrence, KS Metro area	121,436	110,826	99,962	10,610	10,864	9.6	10.9	5,299.7	3,760.5	40.9	$43,642	$33,819
Douglas County, KS	121,436	110,826	99,962	10,610	10,864	9.6	10.9	5,299.7	3,760.5	40.9	$43,642	$33,819
Lawrenceburg, TN Micro area	43,734	41,851	39,926	1,883	1,925	4.5	4.8	1,541.7	1,143.5	34.8	$35,252	$27,250
Lawrence County, TN	43,734	41,851	39,926	1,883	1,925	4.5	4.8	1,541.7	1,143.5	34.8	$35,252	$27,250
Lawton, OK Metro area	126,198	130,288	121,610	-4,090	8,678	-3.1	7.1	5,238.4	4,686.1	11.8	$41,509	$35,617
Comanche County, OK	120,422	124,098	114,996	-3,676	9,102	-3.0	7.9	4,997.2	4,464.2	11.9	$41,497	$35,600
Cotton County, OK	5,776	6,190	6,614	-414	-424	-6.7	-6.4	241.2	221.9	8.7	$41,766	$35,956
Lebanon, MO Micro area	35,713	35,571	32,513	142	3,058	0.4	9.4	1,305.6	963.6	35.5	$36,558	$27,008
Laclede County, MO	35,713	35,571	32,513	142	3,058	0.4	9.4	1,305.6	963.6	35.5	$36,558	$27,008
Lebanon, NH-VT Micro area	217,215	218,478	207,845	-1,263	10,633	-0.6	5.1	12,236.0	9,306.7	31.5	$56,332	$42,606
Grafton County, NH	89,786	89,137	81,743	649	7,394	0.7	9.0	5,425.4	4,039.8	34.3	$60,426	$45,326
Sullivan County, NH	43,144	43,739	40,458	-595	3,281	-1.4	8.1	2,229.8	1,689.2	32.0	$51,682	$38,601
Orange County, VT	28,999	28,941	28,226	58	715	0.2	2.5	1,367.9	1,075.1	27.2	$47,171	$37,139
Windsor County, VT	55,286	56,661	57,418	-1,375	-757	-2.4	-1.3	3,213.0	2,502.7	28.4	$58,116	$44,216
Lebanon, PA Metro area	141,314	133,577	120,327	7,737	13,250	5.8	11.0	6,832.8	4,936.3	38.4	$48,352	$36,936
Lebanon County, PA	141,314	133,577	120,327	7,737	13,250	5.8	11.0	6,832.8	4,936.3	38.4	$48,352	$36,936
Levelland, TX Micro area	22,980	22,927	22,716	53	211	0.2	0.9	895.6	833.8	7.4	$38,975	$36,487
Hockley County, TX	22,980	22,927	22,716	53	211	0.2	0.9	895.6	833.8	7.4	$38,975	$36,487
Lewisburg, PA Micro area	44,785	44,963	41,624	-178	3,339	-0.4	8.0	1,847.2	1,379.5	33.9	$41,246	$30,655
Union County, PA	44,785	44,963	41,624	-178	3,339	-0.4	8.0	1,847.2	1,379.5	33.9	$41,246	$30,655
Lewisburg, TN Micro area	33,683	30,608	26,767	3,075	3,841	10.0	14.3	1,264.8	836.3	51.2	$37,550	$27,257
Marshall County, TN	33,683	30,608	26,767	3,075	3,841	10.0	14.3	1,264.8	836.3	51.2	$37,550	$27,257
Lewiston, ID-WA Metro area	63,018	60,893	57,961	2,125	2,932	3.5	5.1	2,859.0	2,142.8	33.4	$45,368	$35,105
Nez Perce County, ID	40,408	39,270	37,410	1,138	1,860	2.9	5.0	1,794.0	1,363.0	31.6	$44,397	$34,669
Asotin County, WA	22,610	21,623	20,551	987	1,072	4.6	5.2	1,065.0	779.8	36.6	$47,104	$35,893

Table D-1. Population and Personal Income—*Continued*

Metropolitan or Micropolitan Statistical Area Metropolitan Division Component Counties	Population			Net change		Percent change		Personal Income			Per capita	
	2018 Estimate (July 1)	2010 census estimates base (April 1)	2000 census estimates base (April 1)	2010-2018	2000-2010	2010-2018	2000-2010	Total (million dollars) 2018	2010	Percent change 2010-2018	2018	2010
Lewiston-Auburn, ME Metro area	107,679	107,710	103,793	-31	3,917	0.0	3.8	4,471.7	3,662.5	22.1	$41,528	$34,004
Androscoggin County, ME	107,679	107,710	103,793	-31	3,917	0.0	3.8	4,471.7	3,662.5	22.1	$41,528	$34,004
Lewistown, PA Micro area	46,222	46,679	46,486	-457	193	-1.0	0.4	1,836.8	1,403.9	30.8	$39,738	$30,102
Mifflin County, PA	46,222	46,679	46,486	-457	193	-1.0	0.4	1,836.8	1,403.9	30.8	$39,738	$30,102
Lexington, NE Micro area	25,705	26,370	26,508	-665	-138	-2.5	-0.5	1,125.9	822.8	36.8	$43,802	$31,221
Dawson County, NE	23,709	24,326	24,365	-617	-39	-2.5	-0.2	1,020.8	738.1	38.3	$43,055	$30,356
Gosper County, NE	1,996	2,044	2,143	-48	-99	-2.3	-4.6	105.1	84.7	24.1	$52,671	$41,530
Lexington-Fayette, KY Metro area	516,697	472,103	408,326	44,594	63,777	9.4	15.6	24,736.9	17,583.2	40.7	$47,875	$37,141
Bourbon County, KY	20,184	20,010	19,360	174	650	0.9	3.4	895.9	628.2	42.6	$44,388	$31,459
Clark County, KY	36,249	35,603	33,144	646	2,459	1.8	7.4	1,444.4	1,151.0	25.5	$39,848	$32,330
Fayette County, KY	323,780	295,867	260,512	27,913	35,355	9.4	13.6	16,247.2	11,683.2	39.1	$50,180	$39,358
Jessamine County, KY	53,920	48,582	39,041	5,338	9,541	11.0	24.4	2,343.9	1,581.6	48.2	$43,470	$32,486
Scott County, KY	56,031	47,102	33,061	8,929	14,041	19.0	42.5	2,432.2	1,604.0	51.6	$43,409	$33,926
Woodford County, KY	26,533	24,939	23,208	1,594	1,731	6.4	7.5	1,373.2	935.2	46.8	$51,753	$37,358
Liberal, KS Micro area	21,780	22,950	22,510	-1,170	440	-5.1	2.0	841.2	682.6	23.2	$38,621	$29,714
Seward County, KS	21,780	22,950	22,510	-1,170	440	-5.1	2.0	841.2	682.6	23.2	$38,621	$29,714
Lima, OH Metro area	102,663	106,315	108,473	-3,652	-2,158	-3.4	-2.0	4,395.6	3,484.2	26.2	$42,816	$32,758
Allen County, OH	102,663	106,315	108,473	-3,652	-2,158	-3.4	-2.0	4,395.6	3,484.2	26.2	$42,816	$32,758
Lincoln, IL Micro area	28,925	30,305	31,183	-1,380	-878	-4.6	-2.8	1,109.0	919.9	20.6	$38,339	$30,375
Logan County, IL	28,925	30,305	31,183	-1,380	-878	-4.6	-2.8	1,109.0	919.9	20.6	$38,339	$30,375
Lincoln, NE Metro area	334,590	302,157	266,787	32,433	35,370	10.7	13.3	16,691.5	11,691.2	42.8	$49,886	$38,590
Lancaster County, NE	317,272	285,407	250,291	31,865	35,116	11.2	14.0	15,828.5	11,050.4	43.2	$49,889	$38,616
Seward County, NE	17,318	16,750	16,496	568	254	3.4	1.5	863.0	640.9	34.7	$49,832	$38,153
Little Rock-North Little Rock-Conway, AR Metro area	741,104	699,796	610,518	41,308	89,278	5.9	14.6	33,729.5	25,885.2	30.3	$45,512	$36,857
Faulkner County, AR	124,806	113,242	86,014	11,564	27,228	10.2	31.7	4,692.5	3,535.8	32.7	$37,598	$31,007
Grant County, AR	18,188	17,842	16,464	346	1,378	1.9	8.4	694.8	551.1	26.1	$38,201	$30,812
Lonoke County, AR	73,657	68,355	52,828	5,302	15,527	7.8	29.4	2,855.2	2,206.5	29.4	$38,764	$32,109
Perry County, AR	10,352	10,441	10,209	-89	232	-0.9	2.3	361.0	304.1	18.7	$34,877	$29,126
Pulaski County, AR	392,680	382,786	361,474	9,894	21,312	2.6	5.9	20,099.5	15,708.2	28.0	$51,185	$40,952
Saline County, AR	121,421	107,130	83,529	14,291	23,601	13.3	28.3	5,026.5	3,579.5	40.4	$41,397	$33,250
Lock Haven, PA Micro area	38,684	39,240	37,914	-556	1,326	-1.4	3.5	1,536.4	1,164.9	31.9	$39,716	$29,680
Clinton County, PA	38,684	39,240	37,914	-556	1,326	-1.4	3.5	1,536.4	1,164.9	31.9	$39,716	$29,680
Logan, UT-ID Metro area	140,794	125,442	102,720	15,352	22,722	12.2	22.1	5,447.4	3,564.9	52.8	$38,690	$28,255
Franklin County, ID	13,726	12,786	11,329	940	1,457	7.4	12.9	495.0	335.3	47.6	$36,064	$26,233
Cache County, UT	127,068	112,656	91,391	14,412	21,265	12.8	23.3	4,952.4	3,229.6	53.3	$38,974	$28,483
Logansport, IN Micro area	37,955	38,966	40,930	-1,011	-1,964	-2.6	-4.8	1,472.2	1,167.4	26.1	$38,788	$29,948
Cass County, IN	37,955	38,966	40,930	-1,011	-1,964	-2.6	-4.8	1,472.2	1,167.4	26.1	$38,788	$29,948
London, KY Micro area	148,320	148,099	144,931	221	3,168	0.1	2.2	4,806.0	3,975.3	20.9	$32,403	$26,819
Clay County, KY	20,105	21,729	24,556	-1,624	-2,827	-7.5	-11.5	614.5	513.7	19.6	$30,566	$23,718
Knox County, KY	31,304	31,888	31,795	-584	93	-1.8	0.3	921.3	774.2	19.0	$29,431	$24,306
Laurel County, KY	60,669	58,849	52,715	1,820	6,134	3.1	11.6	2,057.9	1,673.5	23.0	$33,921	$28,366
Whitley County, KY	36,242	35,633	35,865	609	-232	1.7	-0.6	1,212.2	1,013.9	19.6	$33,447	$28,386
Longview, TX Metro area	286,143	280,011	256,152	6,132	23,859	2.2	9.3	11,912.0	10,223.6	16.5	$41,630	$36,448
Gregg County, TX	123,707	121,745	111,379	1,962	10,366	1.6	9.3	5,616.5	5,105.3	10.0	$45,401	$41,851
Harrison County, TX	66,726	65,644	62,110	1,082	3,534	1.6	5.7	2,797.0	2,299.8	21.6	$41,917	$34,968
Rusk County, TX	54,450	53,307	47,372	1,143	5,935	2.1	12.5	1,986.6	1,613.6	23.1	$36,485	$30,239
Upshur County, TX	41,260	39,315	35,291	1,945	4,024	4.9	11.4	1,512.0	1,204.9	25.5	$36,645	$30,598
Longview, WA Metro area	108,987	102,408	92,948	6,579	9,460	6.4	10.2	4,903.3	3,611.4	35.8	$44,990	$35,282
Cowlitz County, WA	108,987	102,408	92,948	6,579	9,460	6.4	10.2	4,903.3	3,611.4	35.8	$44,990	$35,282
Los Alamos, NM Micro area	19,101	17,950	18,343	1,151	-393	6.4	-2.1	1,348.5	1,090.8	23.6	$70,600	$60,621
Los Alamos County, NM	19,101	17,950	18,343	1,151	-393	6.4	-2.1	1,348.5	1,090.8	23.6	$70,600	$60,621
Los Angeles-Long Beach-Anaheim, CA Metro area	13,291,486	12,828,946	12,365,627	462,540	463,319	3.6	3.7	849,493.4	578,373.0	46.9	$63,913	$45,048
Anaheim-Santa Ana-Irvine, CA Div	3,185,968	3,010,274	2,846,289	175,694	163,985	5.8	5.8	220,684.7	150,143.0	47.0	$69,268	$49,773
Orange County, CA	3,185,968	3,010,274	2,846,289	175,694	163,985	5.8	5.8	220,684.7	150,143.0	47.0	$69,268	$49,773
Los Angeles-Long Beach-Glendale, CA Div...	10,105,518	9,818,672	9,519,338	286,846	299,334	2.9	3.1	628,808.7	428,230.0	46.8	$62,224	$43,597
Los Angeles County, CA	10,105,518	9,818,672	9,519,338	286,846	299,334	2.9	3.1	628,808.7	428,230.0	46.8	$62,224	$43,597
Louisville/Jefferson County, KY-IN Metro area	1,264,908	1,202,695	1,090,024	62,213	112,671	5.2	10.3	63,372.7	45,591.8	39.0	$50,101	$37,846
Clark County, IN	117,360	110,228	96,472	7,132	13,756	6.5	14.3	5,136.1	3,965.1	29.5	$43,763	$35,860
Floyd County, IN	77,781	74,579	70,823	3,202	3,756	4.3	5.3	4,315.3	2,881.6	49.8	$55,480	$38,570
Harrison County, IN	40,350	39,363	34,325	987	5,038	2.5	14.7	1,689.1	1,309.7	29.0	$41,862	$33,302
Washington County, IN	27,943	28,262	27,223	-319	1,039	-1.1	3.8	1,065.3	792.0	34.5	$38,123	$27,986
Bullitt County, KY	81,069	74,308	61,236	6,761	13,072	9.1	21.3	3,318.5	2,351.8	41.1	$40,935	$31,569
Henry County, KY	16,106	15,415	15,060	691	355	4.5	2.4	611.7	465.1	31.5	$37,981	$30,245
Jefferson County, KY	770,517	741,075	693,604	29,442	47,471	4.0	6.8	40,018.0	29,000.3	38.0	$51,937	$39,081
Oldham County, KY	66,470	60,354	46,178	6,116	14,176	10.1	30.7	4,190.2	2,770.2	51.3	$63,039	$45,838
Shelby County, KY	48,518	42,048	33,337	6,470	8,711	15.4	26.1	2,202.3	1,467.7	50.1	$45,392	$34,724
Spencer County, KY	18,794	17,063	11,766	1,731	5,297	10.1	45.0	826.2	588.3	40.4	$43,960	$34,364
Lubbock, TX Metro area	319,068	290,889	256,250	28,179	34,639	9.7	13.5	13,458.7	9,835.8	36.8	$42,181	$33,656
Crosby County, TX	5,779	6,056	7,072	-277	-1,016	-4.6	-14.4	177.8	223.0	-20.3	$30,773	$37,012
Lubbock County, TX	307,412	278,918	242,628	28,494	36,290	10.2	15.0	13,086.2	9,394.7	39.3	$42,569	$33,516
Lynn County, TX	5,877	5,915	6,550	-38	-635	-0.6	-9.7	194.6	218.1	-10.8	$33,119	$36,880
Ludington, MI Micro area	29,100	28,691	28,274	409	417	1.4	1.5	1,212.5	910.7	33.1	$41,667	$31,709
Mason County, MI	29,100	28,691	28,274	409	417	1.4	1.5	1,212.5	910.7	33.1	$41,667	$31,709
Lufkin, TX Micro area	87,092	86,771	80,130	321	6,641	0.4	8.3	3,387.7	2,719.5	24.6	$38,897	$31,293

Table D-1. Population and Personal Income—*Continued*

Metropolitan or Micropolitan Statistical Area Metropolitan Division Component Counties	Population							Personal Income				
				Net change		Percent change		Total (million dollars)			Per capita	
	2018 Estimate (July 1)	2010 census estimates base (April 1)	2000 census estimates base (April 1)	2010-2018	2000-2010	2010-2018	2000-2010	2018	2010	Percent change 2010-2018	2018	2010
Angelina County, TX	87,092	86,771	80,130	321	6,641	0.4	8.3	3,387.7	2,719.5	24.6	$38,897	$31,293
Lumberton, NC Micro area	131,831	134,229	123,339	-2,398	10,890	-1.8	8.8	3,880.8	3,340.1	16.2	$29,438	$24,835
Robeson County, NC	131,831	134,229	123,339	-2,398	10,890	-1.8	8.8	3,880.8	3,340.1	16.2	$29,438	$24,835
Lynchburg, VA Metro area	263,353	252,659	222,317	10,694	30,342	4.2	13.6	10,632.7	8,338.2	27.5	$40,374	$32,960
Amherst County, VA	31,666	32,354	31,894	-688	460	-2.1	1.4	1,176.7	968.5	21.5	$37,160	$29,905
Appomattox County, VA	15,841	15,029	13,705	812	1,324	5.4	9.7	606.7	464.4	30.6	$38,302	$30,754
Bedford County, VA	78,747	74,936	60,371	3,811	14,565	5.1	24.1	3,678.0	2,721.2	35.2	$46,707	$36,261
Campbell County, VA	54,973	54,807	51,078	166	3,729	0.3	7.3	5,171.2	4,184.1	23.6	$37,719	$32,074
Lynchburg City, VA (included with Campbell County personal income)	82,126	75,533	65,269	6,593	10,264	8.7	15.7	-	-	-	-	-
Macomb, IL Micro area	29,955	32,610	32,913	-2,655	-303	-8.1	-0.9	1,159.0	1,053.5	10.0	$38,692	$32,289
McDonough County, IL	29,955	32,610	32,913	-2,655	-303	-8.1	-0.9	1,159.0	1,053.5	10.0	$38,692	$32,289
Macon-Bibb County, GA Metro area	229,737	232,287	222,368	-2,550	9,919	-1.1	4.5	9,434.4	7,590.1	24.3	$41,066	$32,684
Bibb County, GA	153,095	155,795	153,887	-2,700	1,908	-1.7	1.2	6,385.5	5,263.9	21.3	$41,709	$33,784
Crawford County, GA	12,318	12,630	12,495	-312	135	-2.5	1.1	416.2	355.6	17.0	$33,784	$28,184
Jones County, GA	28,616	28,667	23,639	-51	5,028	-0.2	21.3	1,076.5	851.6	26.4	$37,618	$29,730
Monroe County, GA	27,520	26,173	21,757	1,347	4,416	5.1	20.3	1,232.6	873.8	41.1	$44,790	$33,369
Twiggs County, GA	8,188	9,022	10,590	-834	-1,568	-9.2	-14.8	323.7	245.2	32.0	$39,530	$27,335
Madera, CA Metro area	157,672	150,841	123,109	6,831	27,732	4.5	22.5	6,290.6	4,295.6	46.4	$39,897	$28,446
Madera County, CA	157,672	150,841	123,109	6,831	27,732	4.5	22.5	6,290.6	4,295.6	46.4	$39,897	$28,446
Madison, IN Micro area	32,208	32,404	31,705	-196	699	-0.6	2.2	1,352.1	1,060.0	27.6	$41,981	$32,716
Jefferson County, IN	32,208	32,404	31,705	-196	699	-0.6	2.2	1,352.1	1,060.0	27.6	$41,981	$32,716
Madison, WI Metro area	660,422	605,449	535,421	54,973	70,028	9.1	13.1	39,209.6	26,341.3	48.9	$59,371	$43,424
Columbia County, WI	57,358	56,849	52,468	509	4,381	0.9	8.3	2,933.7	2,175.3	34.9	$51,147	$38,264
Dane County, WI	542,364	488,067	426,526	54,297	61,541	11.1	14.4	33,248.8	21,892.7	51.9	$61,304	$44,752
Green County, WI	36,929	36,842	33,647	87	3,195	0.2	9.5	1,884.4	1,419.8	32.7	$51,026	$38,517
Iowa County, WI	23,771	23,691	22,780	80	911	0.3	4.0	1,142.7	853.6	33.9	$48,073	$36,028
Madisonville, KY Micro area	45,068	46,918	46,519	-1,850	399	-3.9	0.9	1,768.3	1,471.4	20.2	$39,236	$31,414
Hopkins County, KY	45,068	46,918	46,519	-1,850	399	-3.9	0.9	1,768.3	1,471.4	20.2	$39,236	$31,414
Magnolia, AR Micro area	23,537	24,552	25,603	-1,015	-1,051	-4.1	-4.1	912.0	735.8	23.9	$38,749	$29,761
Columbia County, AR	23,537	24,552	25,603	-1,015	-1,051	-4.1	-4.1	912.0	735.8	23.9	$38,749	$29,761
Malone, NY Micro area	50,293	51,607	51,134	-1,314	473	-2.5	0.9	1,893.2	1,608.8	17.7	$37,644	$31,146
Franklin County, NY	50,293	51,607	51,134	-1,314	473	-2.5	0.9	1,893.2	1,608.8	17.7	$37,644	$31,146
Malvern, AR Micro area	33,701	33,011	30,353	690	2,658	2.1	8.8	1,030.6	834.5	23.5	$30,580	$25,114
Hot Spring County, AR	33,701	33,011	30,353	690	2,658	2.1	8.8	1,030.6	834.5	23.5	$30,580	$25,114
Manchester-Nashua, NH Metro area	415,247	400,699	380,841	14,548	19,858	3.6	5.2	25,391.0	19,093.9	33.0	$61,147	$47,610
Hillsborough County, NH	415,247	400,699	380,841	14,548	19,858	3.6	5.2	25,391.0	19,093.9	33.0	$61,147	$47,610
Manhattan, KS Metro area	130,574	127,094	108,999	3,480	18,095	2.7	16.6	6,007.4	5,071.7	18.4	$46,008	$39,462
Geary County, KS	32,594	34,354	27,947	-1,760	6,407	-5.1	22.9	1,594.1	1,433.5	11.2	$48,907	$40,679
Pottawatomie County, KS	24,277	21,608	18,209	2,669	3,399	12.4	18.7	1,276.1	957.2	33.3	$52,564	$44,055
Riley County, KS	73,703	71,132	62,843	2,571	8,289	3.6	13.2	3,137.2	2,681.0	17.0	$42,566	$37,469
Manitowoc, WI Micro area	79,074	81,442	82,887	-2,368	-1,445	-2.9	-1.7	3,769.9	3,112.2	21.1	$47,675	$38,266
Manitowoc County, WI	79,074	81,442	82,887	-2,368	-1,445	-2.9	-1.7	3,769.9	3,112.2	21.1	$47,675	$38,266
Mankato, MN Metro area	101,647	96,742	85,712	4,905	11,030	5.1	12.9	4,690.1	3,366.0	39.3	$46,141	$34,756
Blue Earth County, MN	67,427	64,013	55,941	3,414	8,072	5.3	14.4	2,992.6	2,155.2	38.9	$44,383	$33,631
Nicollet County, MN	34,220	32,729	29,771	1,491	2,958	4.6	9.9	1,697.5	1,210.7	40.2	$49,605	$36,958
Mansfield, OH Metro area	121,099	124,474	128,852	-3,375	-4,378	-2.7	-3.4	4,751.2	3,767.0	26.1	$39,234	$30,340
Richland County, OH	121,099	124,474	128,852	-3,375	-4,378	-2.7	-3.4	4,751.2	3,767.0	26.1	$39,234	$30,340
Marietta, OH Micro area	60,155	61,781	63,251	-1,626	-1,470	-2.6	-2.3	2,610.5	1,944.6	34.2	$43,396	$31,511
Washington County, OH	60,155	61,781	63,251	-1,626	-1,470	-2.6	-2.3	2,610.5	1,944.6	34.2	$43,396	$31,511
Marinette, WI-MI Micro area	63,417	65,778	68,710	-2,361	-2,932	-3.6	-4.3	2,781.6	2,185.7	27.3	$43,862	$33,303
Menominee County, MI	22,983	24,029	25,326	-1,046	-1,297	-4.4	-5.1	1,001.9	780.0	28.4	$43,594	$32,544
Marinette County, WI	40,434	41,749	43,384	-1,315	-1,635	-3.1	-3.8	1,779.7	1,405.6	26.6	$44,014	$33,739
Marion, IN Micro area	65,936	70,063	73,403	-4,127	-3,340	-5.9	-4.6	2,666.7	2,131.8	25.1	$40,444	$30,495
Grant County, IN	65,936	70,063	73,403	-4,127	-3,340	-5.9	-4.6	2,666.7	2,131.8	25.1	$40,444	$30,495
Marion, NC Micro area	45,507	44,996	42,151	511	2,845	1.1	6.7	1,550.7	1,180.6	31.3	$34,077	$26,178
McDowell County, NC	45,507	44,996	42,151	511	2,845	1.1	6.7	1,550.7	1,180.6	31.3	$34,077	$26,178
Marion, OH Micro area	65,256	66,501	66,217	-1,245	284	-1.9	0.4	2,496.2	1,940.5	28.6	$38,252	$29,201
Marion County, OH	65,256	66,501	66,217	-1,245	284	-1.9	0.4	2,496.2	1,940.5	28.6	$38,252	$29,201
Marquette, MI Micro area	66,516	67,071	64,634	-555	2,437	-0.8	3.8	2,663.0	2,171.0	22.7	$40,036	$32,365
Marquette County, MI	66,516	67,071	64,634	-555	2,437	-0.8	3.8	2,663.0	2,171.0	22.7	$40,036	$32,365
Marshall, MN Micro area	25,629	25,857	25,425	-228	432	-0.9	1.7	1,267.5	996.9	27.1	$49,455	$38,569
Lyon County, MN	25,629	25,857	25,425	-228	432	-0.9	1.7	1,267.5	996.9	27.1	$49,455	$38,569
Marshall, MO Micro area	22,895	23,370	23,756	-475	-386	-2.0	-1.6	883.3	769.0	14.9	$38,580	$32,833
Saline County, MO	22,895	23,370	23,756	-475	-386	-2.0	-1.6	883.3	769.0	14.9	$38,580	$32,833
Marshalltown, IA Micro area	39,981	40,648	39,311	-667	1,337	-1.6	3.4	1,745.3	1,373.8	27.0	$43,652	$33,736
Marshall County, IA	39,981	40,648	39,311	-667	1,337	-1.6	3.4	1,745.3	1,373.8	27.0	$43,652	$33,736
Martin, TN Micro area	33,415	35,015	34,895	-1,600	120	-4.6	0.3	1,246.9	1,016.4	22.7	$37,316	$29,004
Weakley County, TN	33,415	35,015	34,895	-1,600	120	-4.6	0.3	1,246.9	1,016.4	22.7	$37,316	$29,004
Martinsville, VA Micro area	63,855	67,996	73,346	-4,141	-5,350	-6.1	-7.3	2,513.8	2,071.0	21.4	$39,367	$30,504
Henry County, VA	50,953	54,182	57,930	-3,229	-3,748	-6.0	-6.5	2,513.8	2,071.0	21.4	$39,367	$30,504
Martinsville City, VA (included with Henry county personal income)	12,902	13,814	15,416	-912	-1,602	-6.6	-10.4	-	-	-	$31,013	$26,780
Maryville, MO Micro area	22,304	23,370	21,912	-1,066	1,458	-4.6	6.7	691.7	626.6	10.4	$31,013	$26,780
Nodaway County, MO	22,304	23,370	21,912	-1,066	1,458	-4.6	6.7	691.7	626.6	10.4	$31,013	$26,780

Table D-1. Population and Personal Income—Continued

Metropolitan or Micropolitan Statistical Area Metropolitan Division Component Counties	Population 2018 Estimate (July 1)	2010 census estimates base (April 1)	2000 census estimates base (April 1)	Net change 2010-2018	Net change 2000-2010	Percent change 2010-2018	Percent change 2000-2010	Personal Income Total (million dollars) 2018	Total 2010	Percent change 2010-2018	Per capita 2018	Per capita 2010
Mason City, IA Micro area	50,100	51,742	54,356	-1,642	-2,614	-3.2	-4.8	2,590.3	1,986.3	30.4	$51,702	$38,436
Cerro Gordo County, IA	42,647	44,151	46,447	-1,504	-2,296	-3.4	-4.9	2,274.9	1,714.5	32.7	$53,342	$38,881
Worth County, IA	7,453	7,591	7,909	-138	-318	-1.8	-4.0	315.4	271.8	16.0	$42,321	$35,848
Mayfield, KY Micro area	37,317	37,129	37,028	188	101	0.5	0.3	1,422.9	1,124.0	26.6	$38,130	$30,182
Graves County, KY	37,317	37,129	37,028	188	101	0.5	0.3	1,422.9	1,124.0	26.6	$38,130	$30,182
Maysville, KY Micro area	17,150	17,490	16,800	-340	690	-1.9	4.1	695.3	546.8	27.2	$40,541	$31,238
Mason County, KY	17,150	17,490	16,800	-340	690	-1.9	4.1	695.3	546.8	27.2	$40,541	$31,238
McAlester, OK Micro area	43,877	45,837	43,953	-1,960	1,884	-4.3	4.3	1,691.5	1,465.5	15.4	$38,551	$32,009
Pittsburg County, OK	43,877	45,837	43,953	-1,960	1,884	-4.3	4.3	1,691.5	1,465.5	15.4	$38,551	$32,009
McAllen-Edinburg-Mission, TX Metro area	865,939	774,768	569,463	91,171	205,305	11.8	36.1	22,869.2	17,084.1	33.9	$26,410	$21,925
Hidalgo County, TX	865,939	774,768	569,463	91,171	205,305	11.8	36.1	22,869.2	17,084.1	33.9	$26,410	$21,925
McComb, MS Micro area	39,563	40,407	38,940	-844	1,467	-2.1	3.8	1,228.4	1,090.5	12.6	$31,048	$26,961
Pike County, MS	39,563	40,407	38,940	-844	1,467	-2.1	3.8	1,228.4	1,090.5	12.6	$31,048	$26,961
McMinnville, TN Micro area	40,878	39,824	38,276	1,054	1,548	2.6	4.0	1,388.6	1,088.4	27.6	$33,970	$27,304
Warren County, TN	40,878	39,824	38,276	1,054	1,548	2.6	4.0	1,388.6	1,088.4	27.6	$33,970	$27,304
McPherson, KS Micro area	28,537	29,181	29,554	-644	-373	-2.2	-1.3	1,455.8	1,171.2	24.3	$51,016	$40,211
McPherson County, KS	28,537	29,181	29,554	-644	-373	-2.2	-1.3	1,455.8	1,171.2	24.3	$51,016	$40,211
Meadville, PA Micro area	85,063	88,750	90,366	-3,687	-1,616	-4.2	-1.8	3,485.0	2,792.9	24.8	$40,969	$31,518
Crawford County, PA	85,063	88,750	90,366	-3,687	-1,616	-4.2	-1.8	3,485.0	2,792.9	24.8	$40,969	$31,518
Medford, OR Metro area	219,564	203,205	181,269	16,359	21,936	8.1	12.1	10,232.3	6,760.4	51.4	$46,603	$33,246
Jackson County, OR	219,564	203,205	181,269	16,359	21,936	8.1	12.1	10,232.3	6,760.4	51.4	$46,603	$33,246
Memphis, TN-MS-AR Metro area	1,342,349	1,316,101	1,205,204	26,248	110,897	2.0	9.2	62,580.4	48,627.3	28.7	$46,620	$36,909
Crittenden County, AR	48,342	50,906	50,866	-2,564	40	-5.0	0.1	1,787.6	1,479.8	20.8	$36,978	$29,038
De Soto County, MS	182,001	161,267	107,199	20,734	54,068	12.9	50.4	7,407.9	5,148.0	43.9	$40,702	$31,821
Marshall County, MS	35,451	37,145	34,993	-1,694	2,152	-4.6	6.1	1,146.5	930.0	23.3	$32,341	$25,096
Tate County, MS	28,759	28,878	25,370	-119	3,508	-0.4	13.8	1,011.8	802.2	26.1	$35,182	$27,671
Tunica County, MS	9,944	10,778	9,227	-834	1,551	-7.7	16.8	322.4	288.3	11.8	$32,425	$26,784
Fayette County, TN	40,507	38,439	28,806	2,068	9,633	5.4	33.4	2,242.6	1,562.6	43.5	$55,364	$40,663
Shelby County, TN	935,764	927,682	897,472	8,082	30,210	0.9	3.4	46,287.8	36,560.7	26.6	$49,465	$39,378
Tipton County, TN	61,581	61,006	51,271	575	9,735	0.9	19.0	2,373.8	1,855.6	27.9	$38,547	$30,389
Menomonie, WI Micro area	45,131	43,865	39,858	1,266	4,007	2.9	10.1	1,802.9	1,374.0	31.2	$39,948	$31,307
Dunn County, WI	45,131	43,865	39,858	1,266	4,007	2.9	10.1	1,802.9	1,374.0	31.2	$39,948	$31,307
Merced, CA Metro area	274,765	255,796	210,554	18,969	45,242	7.4	21.5	10,583.7	7,301.5	45.0	$38,519	$28,440
Merced County, CA	274,765	255,796	210,554	18,969	45,242	7.4	21.5	10,583.7	7,301.5	45.0	$38,519	$28,440
Meridian, MS Micro area	100,948	107,445	106,569	-6,497	876	-6.0	0.8	3,721.1	3,194.2	16.5	$36,862	$29,693
Clarke County, MS	15,604	16,732	17,955	-1,128	-1,223	-6.7	-6.8	568.5	493.8	15.1	$36,431	$29,517
Kemper County, MS	10,027	10,446	10,453	-419	-7	-4.0	-0.1	293.7	237.8	23.5	$29,287	$22,735
Lauderdale County, MS	75,317	80,267	78,161	-4,950	2,106	-6.2	2.7	2,859.0	2,462.6	16.1	$37,959	$30,634
Mexico, MO Micro area	25,473	25,529	25,853	-56	-324	-0.2	-1.3	1,021.8	825.1	23.8	$40,111	$32,419
Audrain County, MO	25,473	25,529	25,853	-56	-324	-0.2	-1.3	1,021.8	825.1	23.8	$40,111	$32,419
Miami, OK Micro area	31,175	31,848	33,194	-673	-1,346	-2.1	-4.1	1,114.4	966.1	15.4	$35,746	$30,327
Ottawa County, OK	31,175	31,848	33,194	-673	-1,346	-2.1	-4.1	1,114.4	966.1	15.4	$35,746	$30,327
Miami-Fort Lauderdale-Pompano Beach, FL Metro area	6,198,782	5,566,294	5,007,564	632,488	558,730	11.4	11.2	354,745.9	239,473.7	48.1	$57,228	$42,889
Fort Lauderdale-Pompano Beach-Sunrise, FL Div.	1,951,260	1,748,146	1,623,018	203,114	125,128	11.6	7.7	98,087.7	71,457.0	37.3	$50,269	$40,767
Broward County, FL	1,951,260	1,748,146	1,623,018	203,114	125,128	11.6	7.7	98,087.7	71,457.0	37.3	$50,269	$40,767
Miami-Miami Beach-Kendall, FL Div	2,761,581	2,498,013	2,253,362	263,568	244,651	10.6	10.9	138,139.0	95,805.8	44.2	$50,022	$38,214
Miami-Dade County, FL	2,761,581	2,498,013	2,253,362	263,568	244,651	10.6	10.9	138,139.0	95,805.8	44.2	$50,022	$38,214
West Palm Beach-Boca Raton-Boynton Beach, FL Div	1,485,941	1,320,135	1,131,184	165,806	188,951	12.6	16.7	118,519.2	72,210.9	64.1	$79,760	$54,554
Palm Beach County, FL	1,485,941	1,320,135	1,131,184	165,806	188,951	12.6	16.7	118,519.2	72,210.9	64.1	$79,760	$54,554
Michigan City-La Porte, IN Metro area	110,007	111,463	110,106	-1,456	1,357	-1.3	1.2	4,678.3	3,568.5	31.1	$42,527	$32,018
La Porte County, IN	110,007	111,463	110,106	-1,456	1,357	-1.3	1.2	4,678.3	3,568.5	31.1	$42,527	$32,018
Middlesborough, KY Micro area	26,569	28,691	30,060	-2,122	-1,369	-7.4	-4.6	786.8	731.1	7.6	$29,612	$25,466
Bell County, KY	26,569	28,691	30,060	-2,122	-1,369	-7.4	-4.6	786.8	731.1	7.6	$29,612	$25,466
Midland, MI Metro area	83,209	83,626	82,874	-417	752	-0.5	0.9	5,031.4	3,573.5	40.8	$60,467	$42,715
Midland County, MI	83,209	83,626	82,874	-417	752	-0.5	0.9	5,031.4	3,573.5	40.8	$60,467	$42,715
Midland, TX Metro area	178,331	141,671	120,755	36,660	20,916	25.9	17.3	21,800.4	10,243.9	112.8	$122,247	$72,245
Martin County, TX	5,753	4,799	4,746	954	53	19.9	1.1	322.3	206.5	56.1	$56,021	$42,949
Midland County, TX	172,578	136,872	116,009	35,706	20,863	26.1	18.0	21,478.2	10,037.4	114.0	$124,455	$73,274
Milledgeville, GA Micro area	53,171	55,241	54,776	-2,070	465	-3.7	0.8	1,738.0	1,400.8	24.1	$32,687	$25,406
Baldwin County, GA	44,823	45,840	44,700	-1,017	1,140	-2.2	2.6	1,488.3	1,205.5	23.5	$33,203	$26,379
Hancock County, GA	8,348	9,401	10,076	-1,053	-675	-11.2	-6.7	249.8	195.2	28.0	$29,917	$20,696
Milwaukee-Waukesha, WI Metro area	1,576,113	1,555,954	1,500,741	20,159	55,213	1.3	3.7	89,846.1	67,895.6	32.3	$57,005	$43,616
Milwaukee County, WI	948,201	947,736	940,164	465	7,572	0.0	0.8	45,123.8	35,777.0	26.1	$47,589	$37,727
Ozaukee County, WI	89,147	86,395	82,317	2,752	4,078	3.2	5.0	7,487.6	5,397.2	38.7	$83,992	$62,485
Washington County, WI	135,693	131,885	117,493	3,808	14,392	2.9	12.2	7,951.8	5,753.8	38.2	$58,601	$43,594
Waukesha County, WI	403,072	389,938	360,767	13,134	29,171	3.4	8.1	29,283.0	20,967.7	39.7	$72,650	$53,760
Minden, LA Micro area	38,798	41,207	41,831	-2,409	-624	-5.8	-1.5	1,558.7	1,353.8	15.1	$40,175	$32,862
Webster Parish, LA	38,798	41,207	41,831	-2,409	-624	-5.8	-1.5	1,558.7	1,353.8	15.1	$40,175	$32,862
Mineral Wells, TX Micro area	28,875	28,122	27,026	753	1,096	2.7	4.1	1,129.7	882.6	28.0	$39,125	$31,427
Palo Pinto County, TX	28,875	28,122	27,026	753	1,096	2.7	4.1	1,129.7	882.6	28.0	$39,125	$31,427
Minneapolis-St. Paul-Bloomington, MN Metro area	3,614,162	3,333,630	3,016,562	280,532	317,068	8.4	10.5	227,292.3	154,354.2	47.3	$62,889	$46,214

Table D-1. Population and Personal Income—*Continued*

Metropolitan or Micropolitan Statistical Area Metropolitan Division Component Counties	Population							Personal Income				
	2018 Estimate (July 1)	2010 census estimates base (April 1)	2000 census estimates base (April 1)	Net change		Percent change		Total (million dollars)		Percent change 2010-2018	Per capita	
				2010-2018	2000-2010	2010-2018	2000-2010	2018	2010		2018	2010
Anoka County, MN	353,813	330,858	298,084	22,955	32,774	6.9	11.0	18,135.9	12,691.0	42.9	$51,258	$38,291
Carver County, MN	103,551	91,086	70,205	12,465	20,881	13.7	29.7	7,388.4	4,704.3	57.1	$71,350	$51,468
Chisago County, MN	55,922	53,890	41,101	2,032	12,789	3.8	31.1	2,726.2	1,892.2	44.1	$48,750	$35,102
Dakota County, MN	425,423	398,583	355,904	26,840	42,679	6.7	12.0	25,802.3	17,841.9	44.6	$60,651	$44,694
Hennepin County, MN	1,259,428	1,152,385	1,116,200	107,043	36,185	9.3	3.2	94,077.0	63,352.1	48.5	$74,698	$54,889
Isanti County, MN	39,966	37,810	31,287	2,156	6,523	5.7	20.8	1,760.5	1,262.3	39.5	$44,049	$33,345
Le Sueur County, MN	28,494	27,701	25,426	793	2,275	2.9	8.9	1,390.5	977.0	42.3	$48,799	$35,234
Mille Lacs County, MN	26,139	26,097	22,330	42	3,767	0.2	16.9	1,086.9	816.6	33.1	$41,582	$31,317
Ramsey County, MN	550,210	508,639	511,035	41,571	-2,396	8.2	-0.5	30,225.5	21,224.8	42.4	$54,934	$41,667
Scott County, MN	147,381	129,912	89,498	17,469	40,414	13.4	45.2	8,796.7	5,782.1	52.1	$59,687	$44,304
Sherburne County, MN	96,036	88,492	64,417	7,544	24,075	8.5	37.4	4,516.6	3,081.9	46.6	$47,031	$34,707
Washington County, MN	259,201	238,114	201,130	21,087	36,984	8.9	18.4	17,607.0	11,383.7	54.7	$67,928	$47,643
Wright County, MN	136,349	124,697	89,986	11,652	34,711	9.3	38.6	6,842.1	4,594.5	48.9	$50,181	$36,728
Pierce County, WI	42,555	41,019	36,804	1,536	4,215	3.7	11.5	1,954.8	1,429.4	36.8	$45,936	$34,795
St. Croix County, WI	89,694	84,347	63,155	5,347	21,192	6.3	33.6	4,981.8	3,320.3	50.0	$55,543	$39,337
Minot, ND Micro area	75,934	69,537	67,392	6,397	2,145	9.2	3.2	4,189.0	3,064.1	36.7	$55,166	$43,770
McHenry County, ND	5,816	5,392	5,987	424	-595	7.9	-9.9	303.8	236.1	28.7	$52,233	$43,700
Renville County, ND	2,374	2,470	2,610	-96	-140	-3.9	-5.4	144.8	119.8	20.9	$60,976	$48,209
Ward County, ND	67,744	61,675	58,795	6,069	2,880	9.8	4.9	3,740.4	2,708.3	38.1	$55,214	$43,599
Missoula, MT Metro area	118,791	109,296	95,802	9,495	13,494	8.7	14.1	5,879.2	3,746.3	56.9	$49,492	$34,224
Missoula County, MT	118,791	109,296	95,802	9,495	13,494	8.7	14.1	5,879.2	3,746.3	56.9	$49,492	$34,224
Mitchell, SD Micro area	23,166	22,836	21,880	330	956	1.4	4.4	1,230.1	948.3	29.7	$53,100	$41,569
Davison County, SD	19,790	19,504	18,741	286	763	1.5	4.1	1,005.2	770.2	30.5	$50,794	$39,533
Hanson County, SD	3,376	3,332	3,139	44	193	1.3	6.1	224.9	178.1	26.3	$66,614	$53,472
Moberly, MO Micro area	24,763	25,414	24,663	-651	751	-2.6	3.0	988.1	754.7	30.9	$39,903	$29,649
Randolph County, MO	24,763	25,414	24,663	-651	751	-2.6	3.0	988.1	754.7	30.9	$39,903	$29,649
Mobile, AL Metro area	430,135	430,726	417,940	-591	12,786	-0.1	3.1	16,418.1	13,708.4	19.8	$38,170	$31,810
Mobile County, AL	413,757	413,145	399,843	612	13,302	0.1	3.3	15,823.1	13,183.1	20.0	$38,243	$31,896
Washington County, AL	16,378	17,581	18,097	-1,203	-516	-6.8	-2.9	594.9	525.3	13.2	$36,323	$29,802
Modesto, CA Metro area	549,815	514,451	446,997	35,364	67,454	6.9	15.1	24,257.9	16,545.2	46.6	$44,120	$32,116
Stanislaus County, CA	549,815	514,451	446,997	35,364	67,454	6.9	15.1	24,257.9	16,545.2	46.6	$44,120	$32,116
Monroe, LA Metro area	202,203	204,484	201,074	-2,281	3,410	-1.1	1.7	8,185.7	6,629.9	23.5	$40,482	$32,393
Morehouse Parish, LA	25,398	27,979	31,021	-2,581	-3,042	-9.2	-9.8	977.7	846.0	15.6	$38,495	$30,352
Ouachita Parish, LA	154,475	153,731	147,250	744	6,481	0.5	4.4	6,341.7	5,112.0	24.1	$41,053	$33,202
Union Parish, LA	22,330	22,774	22,803	-444	-29	-1.9	-0.1	866.3	671.9	28.9	$38,794	$29,430
Monroe, MI Metro area	150,439	152,024	145,945	-1,585	6,079	-1.0	4.2	7,145.3	5,196.6	37.5	$47,496	$34,204
Monroe County, MI	150,439	152,024	145,945	-1,585	6,079	-1.0	4.2	7,145.3	5,196.6	37.5	$47,496	$34,204
Montgomery, AL Metro area	373,225	374,541	346,528	-1,316	28,013	-0.4	8.1	16,027.4	13,070.0	22.6	$42,943	$34,841
Autauga County, AL	55,601	54,574	43,671	1,027	10,903	1.9	25.0	2,314.0	1,826.6	26.7	$41,618	$33,360
Elmore County, AL	81,887	79,293	65,874	2,594	13,419	3.3	20.4	3,461.3	2,701.6	28.1	$42,269	$33,950
Lowndes County, AL	9,974	11,296	13,473	-1,322	-2,177	-11.7	-16.2	388.9	349.9	11.1	$38,991	$30,999
Montgomery County, AL	225,763	229,378	223,510	-3,615	5,868	-1.6	2.6	9,863.2	8,191.8	20.4	$43,688	$35,693
Montrose, CO Micro area	47,047	45,719	37,174	1,328	8,545	2.9	23.0	1,973.8	1,395.4	41.5	$41,955	$30,572
Montrose County, CO	42,214	41,277	33,432	937	7,845	2.3	23.5	1,685.6	1,223.1	37.8	$39,930	$29,697
Ouray County, CO	4,833	4,442	3,742	391	700	8.8	18.7	288.2	172.3	67.3	$59,639	$38,658
Morehead City, NC Micro area	69,524	66,463	59,383	3,061	7,080	4.6	11.9	3,431.7	2,648.0	29.6	$49,360	$39,702
Carteret County, NC	69,524	66,463	59,383	3,061	7,080	4.6	11.9	3,431.7	2,648.0	29.6	$49,360	$39,702
Morgan City, LA Micro area	49,774	54,650	53,500	-4,876	1,150	-8.9	2.1	1,955.1	1,961.9	-0.3	$39,280	$35,961
St. Mary Parish, LA	49,774	54,650	53,500	-4,876	1,150	-8.9	2.1	1,955.1	1,961.9	-0.3	$39,280	$35,961
Morgantown, WV Metro area	140,259	129,710	111,200	10,549	18,510	8.1	16.6	5,962.3	4,469.0	33.4	$42,509	$34,295
Monongalia County, WV	106,420	96,190	81,866	10,230	14,324	10.6	17.5	4,754.7	3,497.6	35.9	$44,679	$36,148
Preston County, WV	33,839	33,520	29,334	319	4,186	1.0	14.3	1,207.6	971.4	24.3	$35,686	$28,950
Morristown, TN Metro area	141,726	136,855	123,081	4,871	13,774	3.6	11.2	5,077.9	3,848.7	31.9	$35,829	$28,105
Grainger County, TN	23,145	22,656	20,659	489	1,997	2.2	9.7	775.1	574.4	34.9	$33,490	$25,282
Hamblen County, TN	64,569	62,531	58,128	2,038	4,403	3.3	7.6	2,365.5	1,844.5	28.2	$36,636	$29,509
Jefferson County, TN	54,012	51,668	44,294	2,344	7,374	4.5	16.6	1,937.2	1,429.7	35.5	$35,866	$27,648
Moscow, ID Micro area	40,134	37,243	34,935	2,891	2,308	7.8	6.6	1,659.2	1,220.6	35.9	$41,341	$32,765
Latah County, ID	40,134	37,243	34,935	2,891	2,308	7.8	6.6	1,659.2	1,220.6	35.9	$41,341	$32,765
Moses Lake, WA Micro area	97,331	89,124	74,698	8,207	14,426	9.2	19.3	3,872.7	2,708.9	43.0	$39,789	$30,243
Grant County, WA	97,331	89,124	74,698	8,207	14,426	9.2	19.3	3,872.7	2,708.9	43.0	$39,789	$30,243
Moultrie, GA Micro area	45,592	45,499	42,053	93	3,446	0.2	8.2	1,482.9	1,194.8	24.1	$32,526	$26,179
Colquitt County, GA	45,592	45,499	42,053	93	3,446	0.2	8.2	1,482.9	1,194.8	24.1	$32,526	$26,179
Mountain Home, AR Micro area	41,619	41,513	38,386	106	3,127	0.3	8.1	1,544.3	1,200.7	28.6	$37,106	$28,926
Baxter County, AR	41,619	41,513	38,386	106	3,127	0.3	8.1	1,544.3	1,200.7	28.6	$37,106	$28,926
Mountain Home, ID Micro area	27,259	27,040	29,130	219	-2,090	0.8	-7.2	1,004.6	762.1	31.8	$36,855	$28,100
Elmore County, ID	27,259	27,040	29,130	219	-2,090	0.8	-7.2	1,004.6	762.1	31.8	$36,855	$28,100
Mount Airy, NC Micro area	71,948	73,743	71,219	-1,795	2,524	-2.4	3.5	2,771.6	2,173.0	27.5	$38,522	$29,457
Surry County, NC	71,948	73,743	71,219	-1,795	2,524	-2.4	3.5	2,771.6	2,173.0	27.5	$38,522	$29,457
Mount Gay-Shamrock, WV Micro area	32,607	36,754	37,710	-4,147	-956	-11.3	-2.5	1,191.0	1,162.6	2.4	$36,525	$31,658
Logan County, WV	32,607	36,754	37,710	-4,147	-956	-11.3	-2.5	1,191.0	1,162.6	2.4	$36,525	$31,658
Mount Pleasant, MI Micro area	70,562	70,313	63,351	249	6,962	0.4	11.0	2,505.0	1,908.6	31.2	$35,501	$27,152
Isabella County, MI	70,562	70,313	63,351	249	6,962	0.4	11.0	2,505.0	1,908.6	31.2	$35,501	$27,152
Mount Pleasant, TX Micro area	46,066	44,735	39,667	1,331	5,068	3.0	12.8	1,650.7	1,297.4	27.2	$35,833	$28,947
Camp County, TX	13,033	12,401	11,549	632	852	5.1	7.4	503.9	396.4	27.1	$38,660	$31,977
Titus County, TX	33,033	32,334	28,118	699	4,216	2.2	15.0	1,146.8	900.9	27.3	$34,718	$27,788
Mount Sterling, KY Micro area	47,037	44,398	40,195	2,639	4,203	5.9	10.5	1,553.2	1,201.4	29.3	$33,021	$26,977

Table D-1. Population and Personal Income—Continued

Metropolitan or Micropolitan Statistical Area Metropolitan Division Component Counties	Population							Personal Income				
	2018 Estimate (July 1)	2010 census estimates base (April 1)	2000 census estimates base (April 1)	Net change		Percent change		Total (million dollars)		Percent change 2010-2018	Per capita	
				2010-2018	2000-2010	2010-2018	2000-2010	2018	2010		2018	2010
Bath County, KY	12,383	11,585	11,085	798	500	6.9	4.5	377.6	291.1	29.7	$30,496	$25,058
Menifee County, KY	6,451	6,304	6,556	147	-252	2.3	-3.8	195.5	155.5	25.7	$30,305	$24,424
Montgomery County, KY	28,203	26,509	22,554	1,694	3,955	6.4	17.5	980.1	754.8	29.8	$34,751	$28,428
Mount Vernon, IL Micro area	37,820	38,825	40,045	-1,005	-1,220	-2.6	-3.0	1,496.9	1,257.0	19.1	$39,581	$32,430
Jefferson County, IL	37,820	38,825	40,045	-1,005	-1,220	-2.6	-3.0	1,496.9	1,257.0	19.1	$39,581	$32,430
Mount Vernon, OH Micro area	61,893	60,932	54,500	961	6,432	1.6	11.8	2,609.5	1,905.3	37.0	$42,162	$31,186
Knox County, OH	61,893	60,932	54,500	961	6,432	1.6	11.8	2,609.5	1,905.3	37.0	$42,162	$31,186
Mount Vernon-Anacortes, WA Metro area	128,206	116,893	102,979	11,313	13,914	9.7	13.5	6,802.7	4,466.7	52.3	$53,060	$38,192
Skagit County, WA	128,206	116,893	102,979	11,313	13,914	9.7	13.5	6,802.7	4,466.7	52.3	$53,060	$38,192
Muncie, IN Metro area	114,772	117,664	118,769	-2,892	-1,105	-2.5	-0.9	4,269.7	3,321.5	28.5	$37,201	$28,232
Delaware County, IN	114,772	117,664	118,769	-2,892	-1,105	-2.5	-0.9	4,269.7	3,321.5	28.5	$37,201	$28,232
Murray, KY Micro area	39,135	37,190	34,177	1,945	3,013	5.2	8.8	1,398.0	1,146.3	22.0	$35,722	$30,692
Calloway County, KY	39,135	37,190	34,177	1,945	3,013	5.2	8.8	1,398.0	1,146.3	22.0	$35,722	$30,692
Muscatine, IA Micro area	42,929	42,749	41,722	180	1,027	0.4	2.5	2,041.4	1,547.0	32.0	$47,553	$36,188
Muscatine County, IA	42,929	42,749	41,722	180	1,027	0.4	2.5	2,041.4	1,547.0	32.0	$47,553	$36,188
Muskegon, MI Metro area	173,588	172,194	170,200	1,394	1,994	0.8	1.2	6,782.4	4,964.8	36.6	$39,072	$28,880
Muskegon County, MI	173,588	172,194	170,200	1,394	1,994	0.8	1.2	6,782.4	4,964.8	36.6	$39,072	$28,880
Muskogee, OK Micro area	68,362	70,988	69,451	-2,626	1,537	-3.7	2.2	2,512.9	2,141.4	17.3	$36,759	$30,111
Muskogee County, OK	68,362	70,988	69,451	-2,626	1,537	-3.7	2.2	2,512.9	2,141.4	17.3	$36,759	$30,111
Myrtle Beach-Conway-North Myrtle Beach, SC-NC Metro area	480,891	376,555	269,772	104,336	106,783	27.7	39.6	18,610.3	11,316.6	64.5	$38,700	$29,913
Brunswick County, NC	136,744	107,429	73,143	29,315	34,286	27.3	46.9	5,845.7	3,454.9	69.2	$42,749	$31,970
Horry County, SC	344,147	269,126	196,629	75,021	72,497	27.9	36.9	12,764.6	7,861.7	62.4	$37,091	$29,090
Nacogdoches, TX Micro area	65,711	64,524	59,203	1,187	5,321	1.8	9.0	2,480.9	2,001.5	24.0	$37,755	$30,941
Nacogdoches County, TX	65,711	64,524	59,203	1,187	5,321	1.8	9.0	2,480.9	2,001.5	24.0	$37,755	$30,941
Napa, CA Metro area	139,417	136,578	124,279	2,839	12,299	2.1	9.9	10,454.1	6,388.4	63.6	$74,984	$46,696
Napa County, CA	139,417	136,578	124,279	2,839	12,299	2.1	9.9	10,454.1	6,388.4	63.6	$74,984	$46,696
Naples-Marco Island, FL Metro area	378,488	321,521	251,377	56,967	70,144	17.7	27.9	35,080.5	20,182.9	73.8	$92,686	$62,564
Collier County, FL	378,488	321,521	251,377	56,967	70,144	17.7	27.9	35,080.5	20,182.9	73.8	$92,686	$62,564
Nashville-Davidson--Murfreesboro--Franklin, TN Metro area	1,905,898	1,646,186	1,358,992	259,712	287,194	15.8	21.1	110,453.2	68,943.4	60.2	$57,953	$41,763
Cannon County, TN	14,462	13,813	12,826	649	987	4.7	7.7	522.3	385.5	35.5	$36,113	$27,940
Cheatham County, TN	40,439	39,106	35,912	1,333	3,194	3.4	8.9	1,776.6	1,232.2	44.2	$43,932	$31,494
Davidson County, TN	692,587	626,560	569,891	66,027	56,669	10.5	9.9	45,752.1	29,529.9	54.9	$66,060	$47,041
Dickson County, TN	53,446	49,650	43,156	3,796	6,494	7.6	15.0	2,167.6	1,518.2	42.8	$40,556	$30,556
Macon County, TN	24,265	22,226	20,386	2,039	1,840	9.2	9.0	807.9	576.6	40.1	$33,297	$25,931
Maury County, TN	94,340	80,932	69,498	13,408	11,434	16.6	16.5	4,028.0	2,573.1	56.5	$42,696	$31,700
Robertson County, TN	71,012	66,332	54,433	4,680	11,899	7.1	21.9	2,989.9	2,105.6	42.0	$42,104	$31,743
Rutherford County, TN	324,890	262,582	182,023	62,308	80,559	23.7	44.3	13,330.6	8,244.7	61.7	$41,031	$31,265
Smith County, TN	19,942	19,149	17,712	793	1,437	4.1	8.1	752.6	564.2	33.4	$37,742	$29,502
Sumner County, TN	187,149	160,634	130,449	26,515	30,185	16.5	23.1	9,106.0	5,771.2	57.8	$48,656	$35,799
Trousdale County, TN	11,012	7,864	7,259	3,148	605	40.0	8.3	331.3	231.0	43.4	$30,090	$29,334
Williamson County, TN	231,729	183,265	126,638	48,464	56,627	26.4	44.7	21,984.7	12,033.3	82.7	$94,872	$65,353
Wilson County, TN	140,625	114,073	88,809	26,552	25,264	23.3	28.4	6,903.5	4,177.7	65.2	$49,092	$36,428
Natchez, MS-LA Micro area	50,764	53,121	54,587	-2,357	-1,466	-4.4	-2.7	1,701.5	1,619.1	5.1	$33,518	$30,310
Concordia Parish, LA	19,572	20,822	20,247	-1,250	575	-6.0	2.8	644.7	677.9	-4.9	$32,942	$32,531
Adams County, MS	31,192	32,299	34,340	-1,107	-2,041	-3.4	-5.9	1,056.8	941.1	12.3	$33,880	$28,890
Natchitoches, LA Micro area	38,659	39,569	39,080	-910	489	-2.3	1.3	1,540.9	1,248.1	23.5	$39,860	$31,576
Natchitoches Parish, LA	38,659	39,569	39,080	-910	489	-2.3	1.3	1,540.9	1,248.1	23.5	$39,860	$31,576
New Bern, NC Metro area	125,219	126,813	114,751	-1,594	12,062	-1.3	10.5	5,416.6	4,573.1	18.4	$43,257	$35,888
Craven County, NC	102,912	103,503	91,436	-591	12,067	-0.6	13.2	4,493.7	3,796.6	18.4	$43,665	$36,444
Jones County, NC	9,637	10,167	10,381	-530	-214	-5.2	-2.1	371.4	328.3	13.1	$38,536	$32,364
Pamlico County, NC	12,670	13,143	12,934	-473	209	-3.6	1.6	551.5	448.2	23.0	$43,532	$34,191
Newberry, SC Micro area	38,520	37,508	36,108	1,012	1,400	2.7	3.9	1,455.8	1,132.3	28.6	$37,793	$30,107
Newberry County, SC	38,520	37,508	36,108	1,012	1,400	2.7	3.9	1,455.8	1,132.3	28.6	$37,793	$30,107
New Castle, IN Micro area	48,271	49,466	48,508	-1,195	958	-2.4	2.0	1,850.5	1,435.4	28.9	$38,336	$28,981
Henry County, IN	48,271	49,466	48,508	-1,195	958	-2.4	2.0	1,850.5	1,435.4	28.9	$38,336	$28,981
New Castle, PA Micro area	86,184	91,140	94,643	-4,956	-3,503	-5.4	-3.7	3,786.0	3,116.7	21.5	$43,929	$34,248
Lawrence County, PA	86,184	91,140	94,643	-4,956	-3,503	-5.4	-3.7	3,786.0	3,116.7	21.5	$43,929	$34,248
New Haven-Milford, CT Metro area	857,620	862,456	824,008	-4,836	38,448	-0.6	4.7	48,583.9	38,786.4	25.3	$56,650	$44,924
New Haven County, CT	857,620	862,456	824,008	-4,836	38,448	-0.6	4.7	48,583.9	38,786.4	25.3	$56,650	$44,924
New Orleans-Metairie, LA Metro area	1,270,399	1,189,889	1,337,726	80,510	-147,837	6.8	-11.1	66,608.8	50,931.1	30.8	$52,431	$42,609
Jefferson Parish, LA	434,051	432,573	455,466	1,478	-22,893	0.3	-5.0	22,139.0	18,347.3	20.7	$51,005	$42,411
Orleans Parish, LA	391,006	343,828	484,674	47,178	-140,846	13.7	-29.1	20,333.7	14,727.2	38.1	$52,004	$42,348
Plaquemines Parish, LA	23,410	23,039	26,757	371	-3,718	1.6	-13.9	1,155.9	1,001.4	15.4	$49,376	$43,310
St. Bernard Parish, LA	46,721	35,897	67,229	10,824	-31,332	30.2	-46.6	1,501.1	1,128.7	33.0	$32,130	$30,650
St. Charles Parish, LA	52,879	52,888	48,072	-9	4,816	0.0	10.0	2,609.8	2,110.9	23.6	$49,353	$39,966
St. James Parish, LA	21,037	22,101	21,216	-1,064	885	-4.8	4.2	1,019.9	855.3	19.2	$48,484	$38,792
St. John the Baptist Parish, LA	43,184	45,809	43,044	-2,625	2,765	-5.7	6.4	1,752.1	1,562.6	12.1	$40,573	$34,273
St. Tammany Parish, LA	258,111	233,754	191,268	24,357	42,486	10.4	22.2	16,097.3	11,197.7	43.8	$62,366	$47,744
New Philadelphia-Dover, OH Micro area	92,176	92,587	90,914	-411	1,673	-0.4	1.8	3,996.5	2,970.5	34.5	$43,358	$32,096
Tuscarawas County, OH	92,176	92,587	90,914	-411	1,673	-0.4	1.8	3,996.5	2,970.5	34.5	$43,358	$32,096
Newport, OR Micro area	49,388	46,033	44,479	3,355	1,554	7.3	3.5	2,179.0	1,541.6	41.3	$44,119	$33,513
Lincoln County, OR	49,388	46,033	44,479	3,355	1,554	7.3	3.5	2,179.0	1,541.6	41.3	$44,119	$33,513
Newport, TN Micro area	35,774	35,642	33,565	132	2,077	0.4	6.2	1,142.7	904.0	26.4	$31,942	$25,364
Cocke County, TN	35,774	35,642	33,565	132	2,077	0.4	6.2	1,142.7	904.0	26.4	$31,942	$25,364

Table D-1. Population and Personal Income—Continued

Metropolitan or Micropolitan Statistical Area Metropolitan Division Component Counties	Population							Personal Income				
	2018 Estimate (July 1)	2010 census estimates base (April 1)	2000 census estimates base (April 1)	Net change		Percent change		Total (million dollars)		Percent change 2010-2018	Per capita	
				2010-2018	2000-2010	2010-2018	2000-2010	2018	2010		2018	2010
New Ulm, MN Micro area	25,111	25,893	26,911	-782	-1,018	-3.0	-3.8	1,330.7	1,005.6	32.3	$52,995	$38,913
Brown County, MN	25,111	25,893	26,911	-782	-1,018	-3.0	-3.8	1,330.7	1,005.6	32.3	$52,995	$38,913
New York-Newark-Jersey City, NY-NJ-PA Metro area	19,303,808	18,896,236	18,323,002	407,572	573,234	2.2	3.1	1,480,233.0	1,033,820.8	43.2	$76,681	$54,631
Nassau County-Suffolk County, NY Div	2,839,436	2,833,032	2,753,913	6,404	79,119	0.2	2.9	223,660.3	163,568.7	36.7	$78,769	$57,674
Nassau County, NY	1,358,343	1,339,885	1,334,544	18,458	5,341	1.4	0.4	122,032.0	87,966.0	38.7	$89,839	$65,564
Suffolk County, NY	1,481,093	1,493,147	1,419,369	-12,054	73,778	-0.8	5.2	101,628.3	75,602.7	34.4	$68,617	$50,591
Newark, NJ-PA Div	2,173,508	2,146,378	2,098,843	27,130	47,535	1.3	2.3	163,444.5	122,552.0	33.4	$75,198	$57,061
Essex County, NJ	799,767	783,885	793,633	15,882	-9,748	2.0	-1.2	53,951.1	40,729.4	32.5	$67,459	$51,947
Hunterdon County, NJ	124,714	127,357	121,989	-2,643	5,368	-2.1	4.4	11,175.7	8,918.6	25.3	$89,610	$70,049
Morris County, NJ	494,228	492,314	470,212	1,914	22,102	0.4	4.7	48,850.5	36,448.7	34.0	$98,842	$73,983
Sussex County, NJ	140,799	148,909	144,166	-8,110	4,743	-5.4	3.3	8,695.3	7,058.7	23.2	$61,757	$47,429
Union County, NJ	558,067	536,567	522,541	21,500	14,026	4.0	2.7	38,094.8	27,428.6	38.9	$68,262	$51,030
Pike County, PA	55,933	57,346	46,302	-1,413	11,044	-2.5	23.9	2,677.2	1,968.0	36.0	$47,864	$34,306
New Brunswick-Lakewood, NJ Div	2,383,854	2,340,277	2,173,869	43,577	166,408	1.9	7.7	166,817.6	120,146.1	38.8	$69,978	$51,283
Middlesex County, NJ	829,685	809,924	750,162	19,761	59,762	2.4	8.0	50,664.9	38,384.0	32.0	$61,065	$47,349
Monmouth County, NJ	621,354	630,374	615,301	-9,020	15,073	-1.4	2.4	49,694.8	36,269.2	37.0	$79,978	$57,526
Ocean County, NJ	601,651	576,546	510,916	25,105	65,630	4.4	12.8	31,290.5	23,054.9	35.7	$52,008	$39,917
Somerset County, NJ	331,164	323,433	297,490	7,731	25,943	2.4	8.7	35,167.6	22,437.9	56.7	$106,194	$69,235
New York-Jersey City-White Plains, NY-NJ Div	11,907,010	11,576,549	11,296,377	330,461	280,172	2.9	2.5	926,310.6	627,554.0	47.6	$77,795	$54,113
Bergen County, NJ	936,692	905,143	884,118	31,549	21,025	3.5	2.4	80,509.2	59,876.7	34.5	$85,951	$66,064
Hudson County, NJ	676,061	634,245	608,975	41,816	25,270	6.6	4.1	44,037.8	28,682.2	53.5	$65,139	$45,124
Passaic County, NJ	503,310	501,609	489,049	1,701	12,560	0.3	2.6	25,452.2	20,377.1	24.9	$50,570	$40,587
Bronx County, NY	1,432,132	1,384,603	1,332,650	47,529	51,953	3.4	3.9	53,527.8	41,480.9	29.0	$37,376	$29,899
Kings County, NY	2,582,830	2,504,717	2,465,326	78,113	39,391	3.1	1.6	134,804.0	89,747.2	50.2	$52,192	$35,758
New York County, NY	1,628,701	1,586,360	1,537,195	42,341	49,165	2.7	3.2	315,869.7	191,354.6	65.1	$193,940	$120,443
Putnam County, NY	98,892	99,650	95,745	-758	3,905	-0.8	4.1	6,510.4	5,060.9	28.6	$65,833	$50,781
Queens County, NY	2,278,906	2,230,578	2,229,379	48,328	1,199	2.2	0.1	113,437.4	83,137.7	36.4	$49,777	$37,202
Richmond County, NY	476,179	468,730	443,728	7,449	25,002	1.6	5.6	27,022.8	20,363.9	32.7	$56,749	$43,363
Rockland County, NY	325,695	311,694	286,753	14,001	24,941	4.5	8.7	19,692.8	15,178.9	29.7	$60,464	$48,572
Westchester County, NY	967,612	949,220	923,459	18,392	25,761	1.9	2.8	105,446.4	72,293.9	45.9	$108,976	$76,048
Niles, MI Metro area	154,141	156,811	162,453	-2,670	-5,642	-1.7	-3.5	7,311.0	5,661.6	29.1	$47,430	$36,120
Berrien County, MI	154,141	156,811	162,453	-2,670	-5,642	-1.7	-3.5	7,311.0	5,661.6	29.1	$47,430	$36,120
Nogales, AZ Micro area	46,511	47,420	38,381	-909	9,039	-1.9	23.6	1,816.6	1,395.2	30.2	$39,057	$29,421
Santa Cruz County, AZ	46,511	47,420	38,381	-909	9,039	-1.9	23.6	1,816.6	1,395.2	30.2	$39,057	$29,421
Norfolk, NE Micro area	48,504	48,270	49,538	234	-1,268	0.5	-2.6	2,487.6	1,782.7	39.5	$51,286	$36,859
Madison County, NE	35,392	34,876	35,226	516	-350	1.5		1,791.9	1,293.8	38.5	$50,630	$37,005
Pierce County, NE	7,142	7,266	7,857	-124	-591	-1.7	-7.5	408.1	273.5	49.2	$57,141	$37,665
Stanton County, NE	5,970	6,128	6,455	-158	-327	-2.6	-5.1	287.6	215.4	33.5	$48,167	$35,075
North Platte, NE Micro area	36,426	37,590	35,939	-1,164	1,651	-3.1	4.6	1,691.0	1,400.9	20.7	$46,423	$37,296
Lincoln County, NE	35,185	36,288	34,632	-1,103	1,656	-3.0	4.8	1,640.4	1,358.2	20.8	$46,623	$37,468
Logan County, NE	749	763	774	-14	-11	-1.8	-1.4	28.2	26.9	4.8	$37,603	$34,786
McPherson County, NE	492	539	533	-47	6	-8.7	1.1	22.4	15.8	41.8	$45,530	$29,308
North Port-Sarasota-Bradenton, FL Metro area	821,573	702,314	589,959	119,259	112,355	17.0	19.0	46,387.9	29,331.4	58.2	$56,462	$41,702
Manatee County, FL	394,855	322,879	264,002	71,976	58,877	22.3	22.3	18,707.4	12,156.5	53.9	$47,378	$37,586
Sarasota County, FL	426,718	379,435	325,957	47,283	53,478	12.5	16.4	27,680.5	17,175.0	61.2	$64,868	$45,205
North Vernon, IN Micro area	27,611	28,529	27,554	-918	975	-3.2	3.5	1,075.7	802.8	34.0	$38,959	$28,186
Jennings County, IN	27,611	28,529	27,554	-918	975	-3.2	3.5	1,075.7	802.8	34.0	$38,959	$28,186
North Wilkesboro, NC Micro area	68,557	69,310	65,632	-753	3,678	-1.1	5.6	2,507.5	1,957.4	28.1	$36,576	$28,258
Wilkes County, NC	68,557	69,310	65,632	-753	3,678	-1.1	5.6	2,507.5	1,957.4	28.1	$36,576	$28,258
Norwalk, OH Micro area	58,504	59,623	59,487	-1,119	136	-1.9	0.2	2,359.0	1,861.2	26.7	$40,323	$31,249
Huron County, OH	58,504	59,623	59,487	-1,119	136	-1.9	0.2	2,359.0	1,861.2	26.7	$40,323	$31,249
Norwich-New London, CT Metro area	266,784	274,068	259,088	-7,284	14,980	-2.7	5.8	15,810.8	12,716.1	24.3	$59,264	$46,410
New London County, CT	266,784	274,068	259,088	-7,284	14,980	-2.7	5.8	15,810.8	12,716.1	24.3	$59,264	$46,410
Oak Harbor, WA Micro area	84,460	78,508	71,558	5,952	6,950	7.6	9.7	4,706.5	3,171.4	48.4	$55,724	$40,303
Island County, WA	84,460	78,508	71,558	5,952	6,950	7.6	9.7	4,706.5	3,171.4	48.4	$55,724	$40,303
Ocala, FL Metro area	359,977	331,299	258,916	28,678	72,383	8.7	28.0	13,318.1	9,964.1	33.7	$36,997	$30,072
Marion County, FL	359,977	331,299	258,916	28,678	72,383	8.7	28.0	13,318.1	9,964.1	33.7	$36,997	$30,072
Ocean City, NJ Metro area	92,560	97,261	102,326	-4,701	-5,065	-4.8	-4.9	5,634.7	4,344.4	29.7	$60,877	$44,686
Cape May County, NJ	92,560	97,261	102,326	-4,701	-5,065	-4.8	-4.9	5,634.7	4,344.4	29.7	$60,877	$44,686
Odessa, TX Metro area	162,124	137,136	121,123	24,988	16,013	18.2	13.2	7,663.7	4,792.3	59.9	$47,271	$34,959
Ector County, TX	162,124	137,136	121,123	24,988	16,013	18.2	13.2	7,663.7	4,792.3	59.9	$47,271	$34,959
Ogden-Clearfield, UT Metro area	675,067	597,162	485,401	77,905	111,761	13.0	23.0	29,695.1	19,319.2	53.7	$43,988	$32,213
Box Elder County, UT	54,950	49,978	42,745	4,972	7,233	9.9	16.9	2,054.6	1,408.0	45.9	$37,390	$28,066
Davis County, UT	351,713	306,492	238,994	45,221	67,498	14.8	28.2	16,279.5	10,236.1	59.0	$46,286	$33,244
Morgan County, UT	12,045	9,469	7,129	2,576	2,340	27.2	32.8	631.5	360.4	75.2	$52,426	$37,854
Weber County, UT	256,359	231,223	196,533	25,136	34,690	10.9	17.7	10,729.5	7,314.6	46.7	$41,853	$31,510
Ogdensburg-Massena, NY Micro area	108,047	111,940	111,931	-3,893	9	-3.5	0.0	4,099.3	3,313.0	23.7	$37,940	$29,631
St. Lawrence County, NY	108,047	111,940	111,931	-3,893	9	-3.5	0.0	4,099.3	3,313.0	23.7	$37,940	$29,631
Oil City, PA Micro area	51,266	54,992	57,565	-3,726	-2,573	-6.8	-4.5	2,164.6	1,857.9	16.5	$42,223	$33,795
Venango County, PA	51,266	54,992	57,565	-3,726	-2,573	-6.8	-4.5	2,164.6	1,857.9	16.5	$42,223	$33,795
Okeechobee, FL Micro area	41,537	39,996	35,910	1,541	4,086	3.9	11.4	1,273.6	973.0	30.9	$30,661	$24,307
Okeechobee County, FL	41,537	39,996	35,910	1,541	4,086	3.9	11.4	1,273.6	973.0	30.9	$30,661	$24,307
Oklahoma City, OK Metro area	1,396,445	1,252,990	1,095,421	143,455	157,569	11.4	14.4	67,827.2	48,691.6	39.3	$48,571	$38,712
Canadian County, OK	144,447	115,540	87,697	28,907	27,843	25.0	31.7	6,482.5	4,209.6	54.0	$44,878	$36,183

Table D-1. Population and Personal Income—Continued

Metropolitan or Micropolitan Statistical Area Metropolitan Division Component Counties	Population							Personal Income				
	2018 Estimate (July 1)	2010 census estimates base (April 1)	2000 census estimates base (April 1)	Net change		Percent change		Total (million dollars)		Percent change 2010-2018	Per capita	
				2010-2018	2000-2010	2010-2018	2000-2010	2018	2010		2018	2010
Cleveland County, OK	281,669	256,009	208,016	25,660	47,993	10.0	23.1	12,701.6	9,360.2	35.7	$45,094	$36,410
Grady County, OK	55,551	52,428	45,516	3,123	6,912	6.0	15.2	2,204.0	1,687.9	30.6	$39,675	$32,186
Lincoln County, OK	34,920	34,274	32,080	646	2,194	1.9	6.8	1,245.0	952.4	30.7	$35,653	$27,721
Logan County, OK	47,291	41,854	33,924	5,437	7,930	13.0	23.4	2,041.5	1,385.8	47.3	$43,169	$32,950
McClain County, OK	39,985	34,508	27,740	5,477	6,768	15.9	24.4	1,805.0	1,230.1	46.7	$45,143	$35,411
Oklahoma County, OK	792,582	718,377	660,448	74,205	57,929	10.3	8.8	41,347.6	29,865.8	38.4	$52,168	$41,435
Olean, NY Micro area	76,840	80,343	83,955	-3,503	-3,612	-4.4	-4.3	3,073.2	2,665.1	15.3	$39,995	$33,219
Cattaraugus County, NY	76,840	80,343	83,955	-3,503	-3,612	-4.4	-4.3	3,073.2	2,665.1	15.3	$39,995	$33,219
Olympia-Lacey-Tumwater, WA Metro area	286,419	252,260	207,355	34,159	44,905	13.5	21.7	14,803.3	10,255.3	44.3	$51,684	$40,535
Thurston County, WA	286,419	252,260	207,355	34,159	44,905	13.5	21.7	14,803.3	10,255.3	44.3	$51,684	$40,535
Omaha-Council Bluffs, NE-IA Metro area	942,198	865,347	767,041	76,851	98,306	8.9	12.8	54,682.2	38,968.5	40.3	$58,037	$44,912
Harrison County, IA	14,134	14,937	15,666	-803	-729	-5.4	-4.7	634.5	533.5	18.9	$44,895	$35,785
Mills County, IA	15,063	15,059	14,547	4	512	0.0	3.5	853.3	650.7	31.1	$56,647	$43,163
Pottawattamie County, IA	93,533	93,149	87,704	384	5,445	0.4	6.2	4,265.4	3,175.6	34.3	$45,604	$34,013
Cass County, NE	26,159	25,241	24,334	918	907	3.6	3.7	1,402.2	984.7	42.4	$53,602	$39,014
Douglas County, NE	566,880	517,114	463,585	49,766	53,529	9.6	11.5	35,959.8	25,612.5	40.4	$63,435	$49,391
Sarpy County, NE	184,459	158,835	122,595	25,624	36,240	16.1	29.6	9,284.5	6,382.1	45.5	$50,333	$39,958
Saunders County, NE	21,303	20,778	19,830	525	948	2.5	4.8	1,111.9	774.6	43.5	$52,193	$37,117
Washington County, NE	20,667	20,234	18,780	433	1,454	2.1	7.7	1,170.6	854.8	36.9	$56,640	$42,904
Oneonta, NY Micro area	59,749	62,277	61,676	-2,528	601	-4.1	1.0	2,600.4	2,052.8	26.7	$43,522	$32,972
Otsego County, NY	59,749	62,277	61,676	-2,528	601	-4.1	1.0	2,600.4	2,052.8	26.7	$43,522	$32,972
Ontario, OR-ID Micro area	54,276	53,938	52,193	338	1,745	0.6	3.3	1,869.2	1,411.6	32.4	$34,438	$26,148
Payette County, ID	23,551	22,622	20,578	929	2,044	4.1	9.9	916.9	687.4	33.4	$38,933	$30,365
Malheur County, OR	30,725	31,316	31,615	-591	-299	-1.9	-0.9	952.2	724.3	31.5	$30,992	$23,103
Opelousas, LA Micro area	82,764	83,384	87,700	-620	-4,316	-0.7	-4.9	3,409.1	2,810.0	21.3	$41,191	$33,657
St. Landry Parish, LA	82,764	83,384	87,700	-620	-4,316	-0.7	-4.9	3,409.1	2,810.0	21.3	$41,191	$33,657
Orangeburg, SC Micro area	86,934	92,509	91,582	-5,575	927	-6.0	1.0	2,939.9	2,500.5	17.6	$33,818	$27,085
Orangeburg County, SC	86,934	92,509	91,582	-5,575	927	-6.0	1.0	2,939.9	2,500.5	17.6	$33,818	$27,085
Orlando-Kissimmee-Sanford, FL Metro area	2,572,962	2,134,402	1,644,561	438,560	489,841	20.5	29.8	111,900.6	71,145.0	57.3	$43,491	$33,258
Lake County, FL	356,495	297,052	210,528	59,443	86,524	20.0	41.1	15,040.6	9,620.3	56.3	$42,190	$32,315
Orange County, FL	1,380,645	1,145,954	896,344	234,691	249,610	20.5	27.8	61,642.2	38,834.1	58.7	$44,647	$33,810
Osceola County, FL	367,990	268,683	172,493	99,307	96,190	37.0	55.8	12,271.1	7,147.8	71.7	$33,346	$26,489
Seminole County, FL	467,832	422,713	365,196	45,119	57,517	10.7	15.7	22,946.7	15,542.7	47.6	$49,049	$36,739
Oshkosh-Neenah, WI Metro area	171,020	166,996	156,763	4,024	10,233	2.4	6.5	8,226.3	6,210.9	32.4	$48,101	$37,176
Winnebago County, WI	171,020	166,996	156,763	4,024	10,233	2.4	6.5	8,226.3	6,210.9	32.4	$48,101	$37,176
Oskaloosa, IA Micro area	22,000	22,382	22,335	-382	47	-1.7	0.2	966.1	723.7	33.5	$43,914	$32,294
Mahaska County, IA	22,000	22,382	22,335	-382	47	-1.7	0.2	966.1	723.7	33.5	$43,914	$32,294
Othello, WA Micro area	19,759	18,728	16,428	1,031	2,300	5.5	14.0	845.7	589.2	43.5	$42,800	$31,358
Adams County, WA	19,759	18,728	16,428	1,031	2,300	5.5	14.0	845.7	589.2	43.5	$42,800	$31,358
Ottawa, IL Micro area	148,163	154,901	153,098	-6,738	1,803	-4.3	1.2	6,671.4	5,403.9	23.5	$45,028	$34,912
Bureau County, IL	32,993	34,980	35,503	-1,987	-523	-5.7	-1.5	1,449.4	1,193.7	21.4	$43,931	$34,145
La Salle County, IL	109,430	113,915	111,509	-4,485	2,406	-3.9	2.2	4,884.1	3,976.2	22.8	$44,632	$34,935
Putnam County, IL	5,740	6,006	6,086	-266	-80	-4.4	-1.3	337.9	234.0	44.4	$58,869	$38,926
Ottawa, KS Micro area	25,631	25,996	24,784	-365	1,212	-1.4	4.9	1,086.3	836.6	29.8	$42,383	$32,195
Franklin County, KS	25,631	25,996	24,784	-365	1,212	-1.4	4.9	1,086.3	836.6	29.8	$42,383	$32,195
Ottumwa, IA Micro area	35,205	35,624	36,051	-419	-427	-1.2	-1.2	1,373.1	1,104.0	24.4	$39,002	$30,940
Wapello County, IA	35,205	35,624	36,051	-419	-427	-1.2	-1.2	1,373.1	1,104.0	24.4	$39,002	$30,940
Owatonna, MN Micro area	36,803	36,581	33,680	222	2,901	0.6	8.6	1,752.0	1,342.1	30.5	$47,604	$36,773
Steele County, MN	36,803	36,581	33,680	222	2,901	0.6	8.6	1,752.0	1,342.1	30.5	$47,604	$36,773
Owensboro, KY Metro area	119,114	114,748	109,875	4,366	4,873	3.8	4.4	4,929.8	4,036.3	22.1	$41,387	$35,168
Daviess County, KY	101,104	96,643	91,545	4,461	5,098	4.6	5.6	4,221.5	3,383.4	24.8	$41,754	$34,987
Hancock County, KY	8,758	8,565	8,392	193	173	2.3	2.1	323.4	345.8	-6.5	$36,929	$40,442
McLean County, KY	9,252	9,540	9,938	-288	-398	-3.0	-4.0	384.9	307.0	25.4	$41,603	$32,266
Oxford, MS Micro area	54,793	47,359	38,744	7,434	8,615	15.7	22.2	2,307.3	1,466.0	57.4	$42,110	$30,819
Lafayette County, MS	54,793	47,359	38,744	7,434	8,615	15.7	22.2	2,307.3	1,466.0	57.4	$42,110	$30,819
Oxnard-Thousand Oaks-Ventura, CA Metro area	850,967	823,393	753,197	27,574	70,196	3.3	9.3	52,515.0	37,882.0	38.6	$61,712	$45,910
Ventura County, CA	850,967	823,393	753,197	27,574	70,196	3.3	9.3	52,515.0	37,882.0	38.6	$61,712	$45,910
Ozark, AL Micro area	48,956	50,249	49,129	-1,293	1,120	-2.6	2.3	1,792.4	1,657.7	8.1	$36,613	$32,898
Dale County, AL	48,956	50,249	49,129	-1,293	1,120	-2.6	2.3	1,792.4	1,657.7	8.1	$36,613	$32,898
Paducah, KY-IL Micro area	96,647	98,757	98,765	-2,110	-8	-2.1	0.0	4,353.7	3,519.3	23.7	$45,048	$35,657
Massac County, IL	14,080	15,431	15,161	-1,351	270	-8.8	1.8	540.1	476.2	13.4	$38,360	$30,965
Ballard County, KY	7,979	8,246	8,286	-267	-40	-3.2	-0.5	302.7	253.6	19.4	$37,939	$30,702
Livingston County, KY	9,242	9,519	9,804	-277	-285	-2.9	-2.9	349.3	293.0	19.2	$37,792	$30,773
McCracken County, KY	65,346	65,561	65,514	-215	47	-0.3	0.1	3,161.6	2,496.5	26.6	$48,383	$38,092
Pahrump, NV Micro area	45,346	43,945	32,485	1,401	11,460	3.2	35.3	1,715.7	1,435.0	19.6	$37,835	$32,730
Nye County, NV	45,346	43,945	32,485	1,401	11,460	3.2	35.3	1,715.7	1,435.0	19.6	$37,835	$32,730
Palatka, FL Micro area	74,163	74,368	70,423	-205	3,945	-0.3	5.6	2,356.4	1,955.6	20.5	$31,773	$26,353
Putnam County, FL	74,163	74,368	70,423	-205	3,945	-0.3	5.6	2,356.4	1,955.6	20.5	$31,773	$26,353
Palestine, TX Micro area	58,057	58,459	55,109	-402	3,350	-0.7	6.1	1,988.0	1,562.5	27.2	$34,242	$26,710
Anderson County, TX	58,057	58,459	55,109	-402	3,350	-0.7	6.1	1,988.0	1,562.5	27.2	$34,242	$26,710
Palm Bay-Melbourne-Titusville, FL Metro area	596,849	543,372	476,230	53,477	67,142	9.8	14.1	27,112.1	19,971.5	35.8	$45,425	$36,714
Brevard County, FL	596,849	543,372	476,230	53,477	67,142	9.8	14.1	27,112.1	19,971.5	35.8	$45,425	$36,714
Pampa, TX Micro area	22,798	23,466	23,631	-668	-165	-2.8	-0.7	1,001.3	875.2	14.4	$43,921	$37,412
Gray County, TX	21,895	22,537	22,744	-642	-207	-2.8	-0.9	963.4	846.3	13.8	$44,002	$37,667
Roberts County, TX	903	929	887	-26	42	-2.8	4.7	37.9	28.8	31.6	$41,971	$31,197

Table D-1. Population and Personal Income—*Continued*

Metropolitan or Micropolitan Statistical Area Metropolitan Division Component Counties	Population							Personal Income				
	2018 Estimate (July 1)	2010 census estimates base (April 1)	2000 census estimates base (April 1)	Net change		Percent change		Total (million dollars)		Percent change 2010-2018	Per capita	
				2010-2018	2000-2010	2010-2018	2000-2010	2018	2010		2018	2010
Panama City, FL Metro area	185,287	168,852	148,217	16,435	20,635	9.7	13.9	8,010.2	6,221.3	28.8	$43,231	$36,768
Bay County, FL	185,287	168,852	148,217	16,435	20,635	9.7	13.9	8,010.2	6,221.3	28.8	$43,231	$36,768
Paragould, AR Micro area	45,325	42,090	37,331	3,235	4,759	7.7	12.7	1,581.6	1,172.2	34.9	$34,895	$27,777
Greene County, AR	45,325	42,090	37,331	3,235	4,759	7.7	12.7	1,581.6	1,172.2	34.9	$34,895	$27,777
Paris, TN Micro area	32,358	32,349	31,115	9	1,234	0.0	4.0	1,358.7	1,007.3	34.9	$41,989	$31,093
Henry County, TN	32,358	32,349	31,115	9	1,234	0.0	4.0	1,358.7	1,007.3	34.9	$41,989	$31,093
Paris, TX Micro area	49,728	49,789	48,499	-61	1,290	-0.1	2.7	2,027.0	1,630.2	24.3	$40,763	$32,723
Lamar County, TX	49,728	49,789	48,499	-61	1,290	-0.1	2.7	2,027.0	1,630.2	24.3	$40,763	$32,723
Parkersburg-Vienna, WV Metro area	90,033	92,668	93,859	-2,635	-1,191	-2.8	-1.3	3,780.3	3,001.0	26.0	$41,988	$32,375
Wirt County, WV	5,830	5,715	5,873	115	-158	2.0	-2.7	187.5	140.1	33.8	$32,156	$24,463
Wood County, WV	84,203	86,953	87,986	-2,750	-1,033	-3.2	-1.2	3,592.8	2,861.0	25.6	$42,669	$32,896
Parsons, KS Micro area	19,964	21,606	22,835	-1,642	-1,229	-7.6	-5.4	841.0	718.1	17.1	$42,127	$33,347
Labette County, KS	19,964	21,606	22,835	-1,642	-1,229	-7.6	-5.4	841.0	718.1	17.1	$42,127	$33,347
Payson, AZ Micro area	53,889	53,594	51,335	295	2,259	0.6	4.4	2,169.9	1,625.6	33.5	$40,267	$30,345
Gila County, AZ	53,889	53,594	51,335	295	2,259	0.6	4.4	2,169.9	1,625.6	33.5	$40,267	$30,345
Pearsall, TX Micro area	19,816	17,217	16,252	2,599	965	15.1	5.9	545.8	392.8	39.0	$27,545	$22,758
Frio County, TX	19,816	17,217	16,252	2,599	965	15.1	5.9	545.8	392.8	39.0	$27,545	$22,758
Pecos, TX Micro area	15,847	13,865	13,204	1,982	661	14.3	5.0	627.3	310.7	101.9	$39,584	$22,323
Loving County, TX	152	82	67	70	15	85.4	22.4	8.6	2.2	290.9	$56,730	$26,357
Reeves County, TX	15,695	13,783	13,137	1,912	646	13.9	4.9	618.7	308.5	100.6	$39,418	$22,298
Pella, IA Micro area	33,407	33,307	32,052	100	1,255	0.3	3.9	1,635.5	1,153.8	41.7	$48,956	$34,727
Marion County, IA	33,407	33,307	32,052	100	1,255	0.3	3.9	1,635.5	1,153.8	41.7	$48,956	$34,727
Pensacola-Ferry Pass-Brent, FL Metro area	494,883	448,991	412,153	45,892	36,838	10.2	8.9	21,407.9	15,799.4	35.5	$43,259	$35,036
Escambia County, FL	315,534	297,620	294,410	17,914	3,210	6.0	1.1	13,422.0	10,250.7	30.9	$42,537	$34,394
Santa Rosa County, FL	179,349	151,371	117,743	27,978	33,628	18.5	28.6	7,986.0	5,548.7	43.9	$44,527	$36,288
Peoria, IL Metro area	403,217	416,251	405,149	-13,034	11,102	-3.1	2.7	19,705.3	16,274.4	21.1	$48,870	$39,116
Fulton County, IL	34,844	37,069	38,250	-2,225	-1,181	-6.0	-3.1	1,336.7	1,168.9	14.4	$38,361	$31,529
Marshall County, IL	11,534	12,638	13,180	-1,104	-542	-8.7	-4.1	530.7	435.7	21.8	$46,015	$34,503
Peoria County, IL	180,621	186,496	183,433	-5,875	3,063	-3.2	1.7	9,236.0	7,800.5	18.4	$51,135	$41,888
Stark County, IL	5,427	5,992	6,332	-565	-340	-9.4	-5.4	232.7	195.0	19.3	$42,877	$32,670
Tazewell County, IL	132,328	135,392	128,485	-3,064	6,907	-2.3	5.4	6,333.4	5,106.1	24.0	$47,862	$37,687
Woodford County, IL	38,463	38,664	35,469	-201	3,195	-0.5	9.0	2,035.8	1,568.1	29.8	$52,928	$40,551
Peru, IN Micro area	35,567	36,905	36,082	-1,338	823	-3.6	2.3	1,246.2	947.5	31.5	$35,039	$25,740
Miami County, IN	35,567	36,905	36,082	-1,338	823	-3.6	2.3	1,246.2	947.5	31.5	$35,039	$25,740
Philadelphia-Camden-Wilmington, PA-NJ-DE-MD Metro area	6,096,372	5,965,705	5,687,147	130,667	278,558	2.2	4.9	392,847.4	287,527.4	36.6	$64,440	$48,154
Camden, NJ Div	1,243,870	1,251,019	1,186,999	-7,149	64,020	-0.6	5.4	71,055.0	55,443.3	28.2	$57,124	$44,300
Burlington County, NJ	445,384	448,730	423,394	-3,346	25,336	-0.7	6.0	27,667.4	21,734.7	27.3	$62,120	$48,394
Camden County, NJ	507,078	513,719	508,932	-6,641	4,787	-1.3	0.9	27,434.4	21,486.0	27.7	$54,103	$41,845
Gloucester County, NJ	291,408	288,570	254,673	2,838	33,897	1.0	13.3	15,953.1	12,222.6	30.5	$54,745	$42,229
Montgomery County-Bucks County-Chester County, PA Div	1,978,845	1,924,271	1,781,233	54,574	143,038	2.8	8.0	156,179.2	111,905.6	39.6	$78,924	$58,095
Bucks County, PA	628,195	625,266	597,635	2,929	27,631	0.5	4.6	46,139.3	33,064.2	39.5	$73,447	$52,868
Chester County, PA	522,046	499,133	433,501	22,913	65,632	4.6	15.1	43,249.2	30,767.7	40.6	$82,846	$61,545
Montgomery County, PA	828,604	799,872	750,097	28,732	49,775	3.6	6.6	66,790.7	48,073.8	38.9	$80,606	$60,024
Philadelphia, PA Div	2,148,889	2,084,768	2,068,414	64,121	16,354	3.1	0.8	125,933.5	89,701.5	40.4	$58,604	$42,975
Delaware County, PA	564,751	558,759	550,864	5,992	7,895	1.1	1.4	37,621.8	27,324.5	37.7	$66,617	$48,883
Philadelphia County, PA	1,584,138	1,526,009	1,517,550	58,129	8,459	3.8	0.6	88,311.7	62,377.0	41.6	$55,747	$40,815
Wilmington, DE-MD-NJ Div	724,768	705,647	650,501	19,121	55,146	2.7	8.5	39,679.7	30,477.1	30.2	$54,748	$43,175
New Castle County, DE	559,335	538,479	500,265	20,856	38,214	3.9	7.6	31,739.2	23,974.5	32.4	$56,745	$44,500
Cecil County, MD	102,826	101,102	85,951	1,724	15,151	1.7	17.6	4,904.3	3,834.8	27.9	$47,695	$37,906
Salem County, NJ	62,607	66,066	64,285	-3,459	1,781	-5.2	2.8	3,036.2	2,667.7	13.8	$48,496	$40,435
Phoenix-Mesa-Chandler, AZ Metro area	4,857,962	4,193,127	3,251,876	664,835	941,251	15.9	28.9	224,072.1	146,975.8	52.5	$46,125	$34,955
Maricopa County, AZ	4,410,824	3,817,359	3,072,149	593,465	745,210	15.5	24.3	210,370.2	138,119.2	52.3	$47,694	$36,108
Pinal County, AZ	447,138	375,768	179,727	71,370	196,041	19.0	109.1	13,701.9	8,856.6	54.7	$30,644	$23,335
Picayune, MS Micro area	55,387	55,752	48,621	-365	7,131	-0.7	14.7	2,006.7	1,750.2	14.7	$36,230	$31,419
Pearl River County, MS	55,387	55,752	48,621	-365	7,131	-0.7	14.7	2,006.7	1,750.2	14.7	$36,230	$31,419
Pierre, SD Micro area	20,672	19,988	19,253	684	735	3.4	3.8	1,158.1	906.5	27.8	$56,025	$45,226
Hughes County, SD	17,650	17,022	16,481	628	541	3.7	3.3	935.2	768.9	21.6	$52,986	$45,041
Stanley County, SD	3,022	2,966	2,772	56	194	1.9	7.0	223.0	137.5	62.2	$73,776	$46,289
Pine Bluff, AR Metro area	89,515	100,290	107,341	-10,775	-7,051	-10.7	-6.6	3,093.1	2,787.4	11.0	$34,554	$27,844
Cleveland County, AR	8,018	8,692	8,571	-674	121	-7.8	1.4	323.5	249.4	29.7	$40,344	$28,745
Jefferson County, AR	68,114	77,456	84,278	-9,342	-6,822	-12.1	-8.1	2,408.2	2,236.5	7.7	$35,356	$28,919
Lincoln County, AR	13,383	14,142	14,492	-759	-350	-5.4	-2.4	361.4	301.4	19.9	$27,002	$21,390
Pinehurst-Southern Pines, NC Micro area	98,682	88,242	74,769	10,440	13,473	11.8	18.0	5,063.1	3,545.2	42.8	$51,307	$40,019
Moore County, NC	98,682	88,242	74,769	10,440	13,473	11.8	18.0	5,063.1	3,545.2	42.8	$51,307	$40,019
Pittsburg, KS Micro area	39,019	39,135	38,242	-116	893	-0.3	2.3	1,479.6	1,220.4	21.2	$37,921	$31,156
Crawford County, KS	39,019	39,135	38,242	-116	893	-0.3	2.3	1,479.6	1,220.4	21.2	$37,921	$31,156
Pittsburgh, PA Metro area	2,324,743	2,356,302	2,431,087	-31,559	-74,785	-1.3	-3.1	135,002.6	101,016.5	33.6	$58,072	$42,857
Allegheny County, PA	1,218,452	1,223,323	1,281,666	-4,871	-58,343	-0.4	-4.6	76,711.2	56,537.2	35.7	$62,958	$46,192
Armstrong County, PA	65,263	68,944	72,392	-3,681	-3,448	-5.3	-4.8	2,970.1	2,459.6	20.8	$45,510	$35,716
Beaver County, PA	164,742	170,549	181,412	-5,807	-10,863	-3.4	-6.0	8,033.3	6,310.7	27.3	$48,763	$36,981
Butler County, PA	187,888	183,856	174,083	4,032	9,773	2.2	5.6	11,071.7	7,867.5	40.7	$58,927	$42,737
Fayette County, PA	130,441	136,595	148,644	-6,154	-12,049	-4.5	-8.1	5,563.2	4,530.3	22.8	$42,649	$33,204
Washington County, PA	207,346	207,841	202,897	-495	4,944	-0.2	2.4	12,351.2	8,832.4	39.8	$59,568	$42,478
Westmoreland County, PA	350,611	365,194	369,993	-14,583	-4,799	-4.0	-1.3	18,302.0	14,478.9	26.4	$52,200	$39,652

Table D-1. Population and Personal Income—*Continued*

Metropolitan or Micropolitan Statistical Area Metropolitan Division Component Counties	Population							Personal Income				
	2018 Estimate (July 1)	2010 census estimates base (April 1)	2000 census estimates base (April 1)	Net change		Percent change		Total (million dollars)		Percent change 2010-2018	Per capita	
				2010-2018	2000-2010	2010-2018	2000-2010	2018	2010		2018	2010
Pittsfield, MA Metro area	126,348	131,275	134,953	-4,927	-3,678	-3.8	-2.7	7,139.1	5,419.0	31.7	$56,503	$41,266
Berkshire County, MA	126,348	131,275	134,953	-4,927	-3,678	-3.8	-2.7	7,139.1	5,419.0	31.7	$56,503	$41,266
Plainview, TX Micro area	33,830	36,206	36,602	-2,376	-396	-6.6	-1.1	1,091.5	1,100.7	-0.8	$32,263	$30,348
Hale County, TX	33,830	36,206	36,602	-2,376	-396	-6.6	-1.1	1,091.5	1,100.7	-0.8	$32,263	$30,348
Platteville, WI Micro area	51,554	51,205	49,597	349	1,608	0.7	3.2	2,232.8	1,715.9	30.1	$43,310	$33,491
Grant County, WI	51,554	51,205	49,597	349	1,608	0.7	3.2	2,232.8	1,715.9	30.1	$43,310	$33,491
Plattsburgh, NY Micro area	80,695	82,131	79,894	-1,436	2,237	-1.7	2.8	3,557.1	2,895.9	22.8	$44,081	$35,275
Clinton County, NY	80,695	82,131	79,894	-1,436	2,237	-1.7	2.8	3,557.1	2,895.9	22.8	$44,081	$35,275
Plymouth, IN Micro area	46,248	47,050	45,128	-802	1,922	-1.7	4.3	1,911.4	1,467.0	30.3	$41,329	$31,213
Marshall County, IN	46,248	47,050	45,128	-802	1,922	-1.7	4.3	1,911.4	1,467.0	30.3	$41,329	$31,213
Pocatello, ID Metro area	94,906	90,661	83,103	4,245	7,558	4.7	9.1	3,610.0	2,655.9	35.9	$38,038	$29,221
Bannock County, ID	87,138	82,842	75,565	4,296	7,277	5.2	9.6	3,325.2	2,424.0	37.2	$38,160	$29,198
Power County, ID	7,768	7,819	7,538	-51	281	-0.7	3.7	284.8	231.9	22.8	$36,667	$29,462
Pleasant, WV-OH Micro area	56,697	58,290	57,026	-1,593	1,264	-2.7	2.2	2,085.3	1,713.6	21.7	$36,779	$29,321
Gallia County, OH	29,979	30,942	31,069	-963	-127	-3.1	-0.4	1,195.1	969.3	23.3	$39,864	$31,193
Mason County, WV	26,718	27,348	25,957	-630	1,391	-2.3	5.4	890.2	744.2	19.6	$33,318	$27,195
Ponca City, OK Micro area	44,161	46,562	48,080	-2,401	-1,518	-5.2	-3.2	1,805.3	1,568.4	15.1	$40,881	$33,779
Kay County, OK	44,161	46,562	48,080	-2,401	-1,518	-5.2	-3.2	1,805.3	1,568.4	15.1	$40,881	$33,779
Pontiac, IL Micro area	35,761	38,948	39,678	-3,187	-730	-8.2	-1.8	1,601.2	1,393.3	14.9	$44,775	$35,859
Livingston County, IL	35,761	38,948	39,678	-3,187	-730	-8.2	-1.8	1,601.2	1,393.3	14.9	$44,775	$35,859
Poplar Bluff, MO Micro area	56,040	56,900	54,376	-860	2,524	-1.5	4.6	1,913.1	1,709.5	11.9	$34,138	$30,050
Butler County, MO	42,639	42,794	40,867	-155	1,927	-0.4	4.7	1,505.2	1,334.7	12.8	$35,302	$31,193
Ripley County, MO	13,401	14,106	13,509	-705	597	-5.0	4.4	407.9	374.9	8.8	$30,437	$26,583
Portales, NM Micro area	18,743	19,840	18,018	-1,097	1,822	-5.5	10.1	739.3	634.5	16.5	$39,446	$31,690
Roosevelt County, NM	18,743	19,840	18,018	-1,097	1,822	-5.5	10.1	739.3	634.5	16.5	$39,446	$31,690
Port Angeles, WA Micro area	76,737	71,404	64,525	5,333	6,879	7.5	10.7	3,539.1	2,509.2	41.0	$46,120	$35,089
Clallam County, WA	76,737	71,404	64,525	5,333	6,879	7.5	10.7	3,539.1	2,509.2	41.0	$46,120	$35,089
Portland-South Portland, ME Metro area	535,420	514,104	487,568	21,316	26,536	4.1	5.4	30,921.0	22,245.6	39.0	$57,751	$43,288
Cumberland County, ME	293,557	281,676	265,612	11,881	16,064	4.2	6.0	18,354.2	12,977.7	41.4	$62,523	$46,109
Sagadahoc County, ME	35,634	35,288	35,214	346	74	1.0	0.2	1,828.9	1,391.6	31.4	$51,325	$39,501
York County, ME	206,229	197,140	186,742	9,089	10,398	4.6	5.6	10,737.9	7,876.3	36.3	$52,068	$39,937
Portland-Vancouver-Hillsboro, OR-WA Metro area	2,478,810	2,225,996	1,927,881	252,814	298,115	11.4	15.5	141,269.9	89,153.7	58.5	$56,991	$39,940
Clackamas County, OR	416,075	375,996	338,391	40,079	37,605	10.7	11.1	24,385.2	15,953.0	52.9	$58,608	$42,339
Columbia County, OR	52,377	49,353	43,560	3,024	5,793	6.1	13.3	2,320.9	1,608.7	44.3	$44,312	$32,594
Multnomah County, OR	811,880	735,148	660,486	76,732	74,662	10.4	11.3	46,966.9	29,792.1	57.6	$57,850	$40,407
Washington County, OR	597,695	529,860	445,342	67,835	84,518	12.8	19.0	36,442.2	22,063.0	65.2	$60,971	$41,500
Yamhill County, OR	107,002	99,209	84,992	7,793	14,217	7.9	16.7	4,866.3	3,243.2	50.0	$45,478	$32,661
Clark County, WA	481,857	425,360	345,238	56,497	80,122	13.3	23.2	25,742.3	16,130.0	59.6	$53,423	$37,801
Skamania County, WA	11,924	11,070	9,872	854	1,198	7.7	12.1	546.1	363.7	50.2	$45,802	$32,722
Port Lavaca, TX Micro area	21,561	21,382	20,647	179	735	0.8	3.6	833.7	637.3	30.8	$38,668	$29,901
Calhoun County, TX	21,561	21,382	20,647	179	735	0.8	3.6	833.7	637.3	30.8	$38,668	$29,901
Port St. Lucie, FL Metro area	482,040	424,107	319,426	57,933	104,681	13.7	32.8	26,140.3	16,392.6	59.5	$54,228	$38,554
Martin County, FL	160,912	146,852	126,731	14,060	20,121	9.6	15.9	13,496.1	7,967.3	69.4	$83,873	$54,230
St. Lucie County, FL	321,128	277,255	192,695	43,873	84,560	15.8	43.9	12,644.2	8,425.3	50.1	$39,374	$30,278
Portsmouth, OH Micro area	75,502	79,493	79,195	-3,991	298	-5.0	0.4	2,950.6	2,281.8	29.3	$39,080	$28,701
Scioto County, OH	75,502	79,493	79,195	-3,991	298	-5.0	0.4	2,950.6	2,281.8	29.3	$39,080	$28,701
Pottsville, PA Micro area	142,067	148,291	150,336	-6,224	-2,045	-4.2	-1.4	6,089.3	4,991.7	22.0	$42,862	$33,663
Schuylkill County, PA	142,067	148,291	150,336	-6,224	-2,045	-4.2	-1.4	6,089.3	4,991.7	22.0	$42,862	$33,663
Poughkeepsie-Newburgh-Middletown, NY Metro area	675,669	670,291	621,517	5,378	48,774	0.8	7.8	36,358.5	27,458.1	32.4	$53,811	$40,910
Dutchess County, NY	293,718	297,462	280,150	-3,744	17,312	-1.3	6.2	16,555.3	12,529.0	32.1	$56,365	$42,081
Orange County, NY	381,951	372,829	341,367	9,122	31,462	2.4	9.2	19,803.2	14,929.1	32.6	$51,848	$39,976
Prescott Valley-Prescott, AZ Metro area	231,993	211,014	167,517	20,979	43,497	9.9	26.0	9,352.1	6,099.7	53.3	$40,312	$28,911
Yavapai County, AZ	231,993	211,014	167,517	20,979	43,497	9.9	26.0	9,352.1	6,099.7	53.3	$40,312	$28,911
Price, UT Micro area	20,269	21,403	20,422	-1,134	981	-5.3	4.8	780.3	669.3	16.6	$38,499	$31,273
Carbon County, UT	20,269	21,403	20,422	-1,134	981	-5.3	4.8	780.3	669.3	16.6	$38,499	$31,273
Prineville, OR Micro area	23,867	20,978	19,182	2,889	1,796	13.8	9.4	977.2	597.1	63.7	$40,945	$28,589
Crook County, OR	23,867	20,978	19,182	2,889	1,796	13.8	9.4	977.2	597.1	63.7	$40,945	$28,589
Providence-Warwick, RI-MA Metro area	1,621,337	1,601,211	1,582,997	20,126	18,214	1.3	1.2	88,501.0	67,625.2	30.9	$54,585	$42,184
Bristol County, MA	564,022	548,254	534,678	15,768	13,576	2.9	2.5	30,507.1	22,364.2	36.4	$54,089	$40,723
Bristol County, RI	48,649	49,847	50,648	-1,198	-801	-2.4	-1.6	3,833.8	2,994.7	28.0	$78,805	$60,113
Kent County, RI	163,861	166,113	167,090	-2,252	-977	-1.4	-0.6	9,776.7	7,506.9	30.2	$59,665	$45,214
Newport County, RI	82,542	83,141	85,433	-599	-2,292	-0.7	-2.7	5,668.9	4,072.7	39.2	$68,679	$48,965
Providence County, RI	636,084	626,762	621,602	9,322	5,160	1.5	0.8	30,619.1	24,416.8	25.4	$48,137	$38,892
Washington County, RI	126,179	127,094	123,546	-915	3,548	-0.7	2.9	8,095.3	6,270.0	29.1	$64,158	$49,331
Provo-Orem, UT Metro area	633,768	526,885	376,774	106,883	150,111	20.3	39.8	25,877.1	13,930.9	85.8	$40,831	$26,272
Juab County, UT	11,555	10,246	8,238	1,309	2,008	12.8	24.4	417.0	253.3	64.6	$36,087	$24,680
Utah County, UT	622,213	516,639	368,536	105,574	148,103	20.4	40.2	25,460.1	13,677.6	86.1	$40,919	$26,303
Pueblo, CO Metro area	167,529	159,063	141,472	8,466	17,591	5.3	12.4	6,619.2	4,721.2	40.2	$39,511	$29,606
Pueblo County, CO	167,529	159,063	141,472	8,466	17,591	5.3	12.4	6,619.2	4,721.2	40.2	$39,511	$29,606
Pullman, WA Micro area	49,791	44,778	40,740	5,013	4,038	11.2	9.9	2,038.2	1,412.1	44.3	$40,935	$31,523
Whitman County, WA	49,791	44,778	40,740	5,013	4,038	11.2	9.9	2,038.2	1,412.1	44.3	$40,935	$31,523
Punta Gorda, FL Metro area	184,998	159,964	141,627	25,034	18,337	15.6	12.9	7,689.2	5,124.5	50.0	$41,564	$32,055
Charlotte County, FL	184,998	159,964	141,627	25,034	18,337	15.6	12.9	7,689.2	5,124.5	50.0	$41,564	$32,055

Table D-1. Population and Personal Income—*Continued*

Metropolitan or Micropolitan Statistical Area Metropolitan Division Component Counties	Population							Personal Income				
	2018 Estimate (July 1)	2010 census estimates base (April 1)	2000 census estimates base (April 1)	Net change		Percent change		Total (million dollars)		Percent change 2010-2018	Per capita	
				2010-2018	2000-2010	2010-2018	2000-2010	2018	2010		2018	2010
Quincy, IL-MO Micro area	75,546	77,306	78,771	-1,760	-1,465	-2.3	-1.9	3,427.4	2,745.7	24.8	$45,368	$35,488
Adams County, IL	65,691	67,097	68,277	-1,406	-1,180	-2.1	-1.7	3,080.0	2,460.3	25.2	$46,886	$36,633
Lewis County, MO	9,855	10,209	10,494	-354	-285	-3.5	-2.7	347.4	285.4	21.7	$35,249	$27,954
Racine, WI Metro area	196,584	195,428	188,831	1,156	6,597	0.6	3.5	9,779.8	7,430.0	31.6	$49,749	$38,024
Racine County, WI	196,584	195,428	188,831	1,156	6,597	0.6	3.5	9,779.8	7,430.0	31.6	$49,749	$38,024
Raleigh-Cary, NC Metro area	1,362,540	1,130,488	797,071	232,052	333,417	20.5	41.8	75,001.0	48,714.0	54.0	$55,045	$42,830
Franklin County, NC	67,560	60,553	47,260	7,007	13,293	11.6	28.1	2,448.2	1,689.6	44.9	$36,238	$27,782
Johnston County, NC	202,675	168,877	121,965	33,798	46,912	20.0	38.5	8,091.1	5,406.4	49.7	$39,922	$31,862
Wake County, NC	1,092,305	901,058	627,846	191,247	273,212	21.2	43.5	64,461.6	41,618.0	54.9	$59,014	$45,891
Rapid City, SD Metro area	140,023	126,400	112,818	13,623	13,582	10.8	12.0	6,956.5	5,060.9	37.5	$49,681	$39,936
Meade County, SD	28,294	25,443	24,253	2,851	1,190	11.2	4.9	1,217.1	884.7	37.6	$43,015	$34,712
Pennington County, SD	111,729	100,957	88,565	10,772	12,392	10.7	14.0	5,739.4	4,176.2	37.4	$51,369	$41,251
Raymondville, TX Micro area	21,515	22,136	20,082	-621	2,054	-2.8	10.2	615.2	509.0	20.9	$28,593	$22,899
Willacy County, TX	21,515	22,136	20,082	-621	2,054	-2.8	10.2	615.2	509.0	20.9	$28,593	$22,899
Reading, PA Metro area	420,152	411,556	373,638	8,596	37,918	2.1	10.1	20,984.6	15,696.1	33.7	$49,945	$38,095
Berks County, PA	420,152	411,556	373,638	8,596	37,918	2.1	10.1	20,984.6	15,696.1	33.7	$49,945	$38,095
Red Bluff, CA Micro area	63,916	63,440	56,039	476	7,401	0.8	13.2	2,715.4	1,829.4	48.4	$42,483	$28,780
Tehama County, CA	63,916	63,440	56,039	476	7,401	0.8	13.2	2,715.4	1,829.4	48.4	$42,483	$28,780
Redding, CA Metro area	180,040	177,221	163,256	2,819	13,965	1.6	8.6	8,386.6	6,137.6	36.6	$46,582	$34,622
Shasta County, CA	180,040	177,221	163,256	2,819	13,965	1.6	8.6	8,386.6	6,137.6	36.6	$46,582	$34,622
Red Wing, MN Micro area	46,403	46,185	44,127	218	2,058	0.5	4.7	2,484.9	1,834.8	35.4	$53,549	$39,703
Goodhue County, MN	46,403	46,185	44,127	218	2,058	0.5	4.7	2,484.9	1,834.8	35.4	$53,549	$39,703
Reno, NV Metro area	469,764	425,439	342,885	44,325	82,554	10.4	24.1	28,016.3	18,541.5	51.1	$59,639	$43,529
Storey County, NV	4,029	4,014	3,399	15	615	0.4	18.1	240.3	141.0	70.4	$59,651	$35,261
Washoe County, NV	465,735	421,425	339,486	44,310	81,939	10.5	24.1	27,776.0	18,400.5	51.0	$59,639	$43,607
Rexburg, ID Micro area	52,472	50,787	39,286	1,685	11,501	3.3	29.3	1,523.9	1,031.5	47.7	$29,042	$20,297
Fremont County, ID	13,168	13,236	11,819	-68	1,417	-0.5	12.0	486.0	336.4	44.5	$36,908	$25,441
Madison County, ID	39,304	37,551	27,467	1,753	10,084	4.7	36.7	1,037.9	695.0	49.3	$26,407	$18,488
Richmond, IN Micro area	65,936	68,996	71,097	-3,060	-2,101	-4.4	-3.0	2,736.7	2,130.6	28.4	$41,505	$30,928
Wayne County, IN	65,936	68,996	71,097	-3,060	-2,101	-4.4	-3.0	2,736.7	2,130.6	28.4	$41,505	$30,928
Richmond, VA Metro area	1,282,442	1,186,473	1,040,192	95,969	146,281	8.1	14.1	73,485.3	51,016.7	44.0	$57,301	$42,935
Amelia County, VA	13,013	12,695	11,400	318	1,295	2.5	11.4	582.6	427.7	36.2	$44,774	$33,554
Charles City County, VA	6,941	7,256	6,926	-315	330	-4.3	4.8	318.1	240.2	32.4	$45,824	$33,088
Chesterfield County, VA	348,556	316,239	259,903	32,317	56,336	10.2	21.7	18,715.7	13,421.9	39.4	$53,695	$42,314
Dinwiddie County, VA	28,529	28,014	24,533	515	3,481	1.8	14.2	3,144.6	2,665.1	18.0	$40,352	$34,217
Goochland County, VA	23,244	21,692	16,863	1,552	4,829	7.2	28.6	2,337.1	1,490.4	56.8	$100,545	$68,536
Hanover County, VA	107,239	99,850	86,320	7,389	13,530	7.4	15.7	6,462.1	4,434.7	45.7	$60,259	$44,392
Henrico County, VA	329,261	306,810	262,300	22,451	44,510	7.3	17.0	22,006.5	14,411.5	52.7	$66,836	$46,896
King and Queen County, VA	7,042	6,942	6,630	100	312	1.4	4.7	305.3	233.0	31.0	$43,361	$33,388
King William County, VA	16,939	15,927	13,146	1,012	2,781	6.4	21.2	789.6	581.5	35.8	$46,612	$36,345
New Kent County, VA	22,391	18,432	13,462	3,959	4,970	21.5	36.9	1,584.0	1,015.5	56.0	$70,743	$54,762
Powhatan County, VA	29,189	28,064	22,377	1,125	5,687	4.0	25.4	1,652.3	1,108.3	49.1	$56,607	$39,414
Prince George County, VA	38,082	35,719	33,047	2,363	2,672	6.6	8.1	2,353.1	1,883.8	24.9	$38,779	$32,320
Sussex County, VA	11,237	12,070	12,504	-833	-434	-6.9	-3.5	352.6	319.5	10.4	$31,378	$26,598
Colonial Heights City, VA (personal income included with Dinwiddie County)	17,833	17,410	16,897	423	513	2.4	3.0	-	-	-	-	-
Hopewell City, VA (personal income included with Prince George County)	22,596	22,591	22,354	5	237	0.0	1.1	-	-	-	-	-
Petersburg City, VA (personal income included with Dinwiddie County)	31,567	32,435	33,740	-868	-1,305	-2.7	-3.9	-	-	-	-	-
Richmond City, VA	228,783	204,327	197,790	24,456	6,537	12.0	3.3	12,881.8	8,783.8	46.7	$56,306	$43,004
Richmond-Berea, KY Micro area	106,566	97,592	86,179	8,974	11,413	9.2	13.2	3,717.6	2,816.0	32.0	$34,886	$28,682
Estill County, KY	14,198	14,679	15,307	-481	-628	-3.3	-4.1	448.0	378.2	18.5	$31,555	$25,704
Madison County, KY	92,368	82,913	70,872	9,455	12,041	11.4	17.0	3,269.6	2,437.8	34.1	$35,397	$29,207
Rio Grande City-Roma, TX Micro area	64,525	60,968	53,597	3,557	7,371	5.8	13.8	1,698.0	1,328.2	27.8	$26,316	$21,721
Starr County, TX	64,525	60,968	53,597	3,557	7,371	5.8	13.8	1,698.0	1,328.2	27.8	$26,316	$21,721
Riverside-San Bernardino-Ontario, CA Metro Area	4,622,361	4,224,966	3,254,821	397,395	970,145	9.4	29.8	187,141.7	127,926.9	46.3	$40,486	$30,153
Riverside County, CA	2,450,758	2,189,765	1,545,387	260,993	644,378	11.9	41.7	99,591.7	67,585.2	47.4	$40,637	$30,698
San Bernardino County, CA	2,171,603	2,035,201	1,709,434	136,402	325,767	6.7	19.1	87,550.0	60,341.6	45.1	$40,316	$29,566
Riverton, WY Micro area	39,531	40,123	35,804	-592	4,319	-1.5	12.1	1,724.8	1,439.7	19.8	$43,633	$35,813
Fremont County, WY	39,531	40,123	35,804	-592	4,319	-1.5	12.1	1,724.8	1,439.7	19.8	$43,633	$35,813
Roanoke, VA Metro area	314,172	308,669	288,309	5,503	20,360	1.8	7.1	14,754.6	11,641.3	26.7	$46,963	$37,724
Botetourt County, VA	33,277	33,150	30,496	127	2,654	0.4	8.7	1,673.0	1,305.7	28.1	$50,274	$39,332
Craig County, VA	5,064	5,175	5,091	-111	84	-2.1	1.6	193.4	154.2	25.4	$38,185	$29,671
Franklin County, VA	56,195	56,135	47,286	60	8,849	0.1	18.7	2,291.7	1,765.8	29.8	$40,781	$31,428
Roanoke County, VA	94,073	92,462	85,778	1,611	6,684	1.7	7.8	6,255.0	4,915.7	27.2	$52,248	$41,910
Roanoke City, VA	99,920	96,912	94,911	3,008	2,001	3.1	2.1	4,341.6	3,499.9	24.0	$43,451	$36,185
Salem City, VA (personal income included with Roanoke County)	25,643	24,835	24,747	808	88	3.3	0.4	-	-	-	-	-
Roanoke Rapids, NC Micro area	70,250	76,733	79,456	-6,483	-2,723	-8.4	-3.4	2,494.0	2,180.8	14.4	$35,501	$28,502
Halifax County, NC	50,574	54,627	57,370	-4,053	-2,743	-7.4	-4.8	1,821.3	1,595.8	14.1	$36,013	$29,295
Northampton County, NC	19,676	22,106	22,086	-2,430	20	-11.0	0.1	672.6	584.9	15.0	$34,185	$26,540
Rochelle, IL Micro area	50,923	53,497	51,032	-2,574	2,465	-4.8	4.8	2,380.9	1,889.9	26.0	$46,755	$35,376
Ogle County, IL	50,923	53,497	51,032	-2,574	2,465	-4.8	4.8	2,380.9	1,889.9	26.0	$46,755	$35,376

Table D-1. Population and Personal Income—*Continued*

Metropolitan or Micropolitan Statistical Area Metropolitan Division Component Counties	Population							Personal Income				
	2018 Estimate (July 1)	2010 census estimates base (April 1)	2000 census estimates base (April 1)	Net change		Percent change		Total (million dollars)		Percent change 2010-2018	Per capita	
				2010-2018	2000-2010	2010-2018	2000-2010	2018	2010		2018	2010
Rochester, MN Metro area	219,802	206,882	184,740	12,920	22,142	6.2	12.0	12,160.0	8,847.7	37.4	$55,323	$42,698
Dodge County, MN	20,822	20,087	17,731	735	2,356	3.7	13.3	999.1	752.0	32.9	$47,984	$37,313
Fillmore County, MN	21,058	20,871	21,122	187	-251	0.9	-1.2	955.6	749.2	27.5	$45,378	$35,905
Olmsted County, MN	156,277	144,260	124,277	12,017	19,983	8.3	16.1	9,150.7	6,553.1	39.6	$58,554	$45,342
Wabasha County, MN	21,645	21,664	21,610	-19	54	-0.1	0.2	1,054.6	793.4	32.9	$48,724	$36,610
Rochester, NY Metro area	1,071,082	1,079,697	1,062,452	-8,615	17,245	-0.8	1.6	54,803.6	42,758.1	28.2	$51,167	$39,592
Livingston County, NY	63,227	65,207	64,328	-1,980	879	-3.0	1.4	2,902.6	2,177.3	33.3	$45,908	$33,374
Monroe County, NY	742,474	744,399	735,343	-1,925	9,056	-0.3	1.2	39,315.0	30,934.8	27.1	$52,951	$41,546
Ontario County, NY	109,864	108,090	100,224	1,774	7,866	1.6	7.8	5,877.5	4,257.9	38.0	$53,498	$39,365
Orleans County, NY	40,612	42,883	44,171	-2,271	-1,288	-5.3	-2.9	1,582.4	1,302.8	21.5	$38,963	$30,410
Wayne County, NY	90,064	93,754	93,765	-3,690	-11	-3.9	0.0	4,147.3	3,290.2	26.1	$46,048	$35,095
Yates County, NY	24,841	25,364	24,621	-523	743	-2.1	3.0	978.8	795.2	23.1	$39,402	$31,338
Rockford, IL Metro area	337,658	349,431	320,204	-11,773	29,227	-3.4	9.1	14,967.7	11,831.8	26.5	$44,328	$33,883
Boone County, IL	53,577	54,167	41,786	-590	12,381	-1.1	29.6	2,541.5	1,890.1	34.5	$47,437	$34,936
Winnebago County, IL	284,081	295,264	278,418	-11,183	16,846	-3.8	6.1	12,426.2	9,941.7	25.0	$43,742	$33,691
Rockingham, NC Micro area	44,887	46,647	46,564	-1,760	83	-3.8	0.2	1,577.7	1,302.5	21.1	$35,148	$27,932
Richmond County, NC	44,887	46,647	46,564	-1,760	83	-3.8	0.2	1,577.7	1,302.5	21.1	$35,148	$27,932
Rockport, TX Micro area	23,792	23,158	22,497	634	661	2.7	2.9	1,151.3	868.3	32.6	$48,389	$37,455
Aransas County, TX	23,792	23,158	22,497	634	661	2.7	2.9	1,151.3	868.3	32.6	$48,389	$37,455
Rock Springs, WY Micro area	43,051	43,806	37,613	-755	6,193	-1.7	16.5	2,288.0	1,879.0	21.8	$53,145	$43,121
Sweetwater County, WY	43,051	43,806	37,613	-755	6,193	-1.7	16.5	2,288.0	1,879.0	21.8	$53,145	$43,121
Rocky Mount, NC Metro area	146,021	152,375	143,026	-6,354	9,349	-4.2	6.5	5,767.6	4,874.5	18.3	$39,498	$31,981
Edgecombe County, NC	52,005	56,546	55,606	-4,541	940	-8.0	1.7	1,817.4	1,605.1	13.2	$34,946	$28,345
Nash County, NC	94,016	95,829	87,420	-1,813	8,409	-1.9	9.6	3,950.2	3,269.4	20.8	$42,016	$34,131
Rolla, MO Micro area	44,732	45,156	39,825	-424	5,331	-0.9	13.4	1,750.4	1,338.0	30.8	$39,132	$29,518
Phelps County, MO	44,732	45,156	39,825	-424	5,331	-0.9	13.4	1,750.4	1,338.0	30.8	$39,132	$29,518
Rome, GA Metro area	97,927	96,314	90,565	1,613	5,749	1.7	6.3	3,772.5	2,917.6	29.3	$38,524	$30,258
Floyd County, GA	97,927	96,314	90,565	1,613	5,749	1.7	6.3	3,772.5	2,917.6	29.3	$38,524	$30,258
Roseburg, OR Micro area	110,283	107,684	100,399	2,599	7,285	2.4	7.3	4,456.3	3,331.8	33.8	$40,408	$30,955
Douglas County, OR	110,283	107,684	100,399	2,599	7,285	2.4	7.3	4,456.3	3,331.8	33.8	$40,408	$30,955
Roswell, NM Micro area	64,689	65,648	61,382	-959	4,266	-1.5	6.9	2,608.4	2,081.1	25.3	$40,322	$31,663
Chaves County, NM	64,689	65,648	61,382	-959	4,266	-1.5	6.9	2,608.4	2,081.1	25.3	$40,322	$31,663
Ruidoso, NM Micro area	19,556	20,495	19,411	-939	1,084	-4.6	5.6	817.3	644.0	26.9	$41,793	$31,488
Lincoln County, NM	19,556	20,495	19,411	-939	1,084	-4.6	5.6	817.3	644.0	26.9	$41,793	$31,488
Russellville, AR Micro area	85,535	83,939	75,608	1,596	8,331	1.9	11.0	2,974.3	2,314.0	28.5	$34,772	$27,463
Pope County, AR	64,000	61,754	54,469	2,246	7,285	3.6	13.4	2,256.7	1,769.1	27.6	$35,261	$28,484
Yell County, AR	21,535	22,185	21,139	-650	1,046	-2.9	4.9	717.5	544.9	31.7	$33,320	$24,601
Ruston, LA Micro area	47,196	46,740	42,509	456	4,231	1.0	10.0	1,907.2	1,447.9	31.7	$40,410	$30,905
Lincoln Parish, LA	47,196	46,740	42,509	456	4,231	1.0	10.0	1,907.2	1,447.9	31.7	$40,410	$30,905
Rutland, VT Micro area	58,672	61,653	63,400	-2,981	-1,747	-4.8	-2.8	3,071.0	2,490.3	23.3	$52,343	$40,441
Rutland County, VT	58,672	61,653	63,400	-2,981	-1,747	-4.8	-2.8	3,071.0	2,490.3	23.3	$52,343	$40,441
Sacramento-Roseville-Folsom, CA Metro area	2,345,210	2,149,151	1,796,857	196,059	352,294	9.1	19.6	131,984.0	88,581.3	49.0	$56,278	$41,131
El Dorado County, CA	190,678	181,058	156,299	9,620	24,759	5.3	15.8	12,863.9	8,721.0	47.5	$67,464	$48,147
Placer County, CA	393,149	348,503	248,399	44,646	100,104	12.8	40.3	26,223.1	16,640.2	57.6	$66,700	$47,540
Sacramento County, CA	1,540,975	1,418,735	1,223,499	122,240	195,236	8.6	16.0	80,969.1	55,136.7	46.9	$52,544	$38,790
Yolo County, CA	220,408	200,855	168,660	19,553	32,195	9.7	19.1	11,927.9	8,083.5	47.6	$54,118	$40,200
Safford, AZ Micro area	38,072	37,219	33,489	853	3,730	2.3	11.1	1,202.9	911.3	32.0	$31,597	$24,525
Graham County, AZ	38,072	37,219	33,489	853	3,730	2.3	11.1	1,202.9	911.3	32.0	$31,597	$24,525
Saginaw, MI Metro area	190,800	200,169	210,039	-9,369	-9,870	-4.7	-4.7	7,394.3	6,099.4	21.2	$38,754	$30,518
Saginaw County, MI	190,800	200,169	210,039	-9,369	-9,870	-4.7	-4.7	7,394.3	6,099.4	21.2	$38,754	$30,518
St. Cloud, MN Metro area	199,801	189,093	167,392	10,708	21,701	5.7	13.0	9,293.3	6,519.6	42.5	$46,513	$34,455
Benton County, MN	40,545	38,451	34,226	2,094	4,225	5.4	12.3	1,777.1	1,295.7	37.2	$43,830	$33,687
Stearns County, MN	159,256	150,642	133,166	8,614	17,476	5.7	13.1	7,516.2	5,223.9	43.9	$47,196	$34,652
St. George, UT Metro area	171,700	138,115	90,354	33,585	47,761	24.3	52.9	6,670.1	3,602.1	85.2	$38,847	$26,028
Washington County, UT	171,700	138,115	90,354	33,585	47,761	24.3	52.9	6,670.1	3,602.1	85.2	$38,847	$26,028
St. Joseph, MO-KS Metro area	126,490	127,327	122,336	-837	4,991	-0.7	4.1	4,965.1	3,972.5	25.0	$39,253	$31,211
Doniphan County, KS	7,682	7,948	8,249	-266	-301	-3.3	-3.6	287.3	240.3	19.6	$37,405	$30,184
Andrew County, MO	17,607	17,297	16,492	310	805	1.8	4.9	794.4	615.6	29.0	$45,118	$35,486
Buchanan County, MO	88,571	89,190	85,998	-619	3,192	-0.7	3.7	3,526.0	2,818.3	25.1	$39,810	$31,641
De Kalb County, MO	12,630	12,892	11,597	-262	1,295	-2.0	11.2	357.3	298.4	19.7	$28,294	$23,126
St. Louis, MO-IL Metro area	2,805,465	2,787,752	2,675,343	17,713	112,409	0.6	4.2	156,778.8	118,383.8	32.4	$55,883	$42,432
Bond County, IL	16,630	17,768	17,633	-1,138	135	-6.4	0.8	626.2	528.6	18.5	$37,653	$29,721
Calhoun County, IL	4,802	5,089	5,084	-287	5	-5.6	0.1	204.1	173.3	17.8	$42,511	$34,016
Clinton County, IL	37,639	37,762	35,535	-123	2,227	-0.3	6.3	1,816.2	1,385.3	31.1	$48,253	$36,609
Jersey County, IL	21,847	22,986	21,668	-1,139	1,318	-5.0	6.1	907.1	779.7	16.3	$41,522	$33,944
Macoupin County, IL	45,313	47,765	49,019	-2,452	-1,254	-5.1	-2.6	1,885.3	1,585.0	18.9	$41,607	$33,160
Madison County, IL	264,461	269,334	258,941	-4,873	10,393	-1.8	4.0	12,400.7	9,925.9	24.9	$46,890	$36,852
Monroe County, IL	34,335	32,951	27,619	1,384	5,332	4.2	19.3	2,015.0	1,468.4	37.2	$58,686	$44,500
St. Clair County, IL	261,059	270,062	256,082	-9,003	13,980	-3.3	5.5	11,763.6	9,874.7	19.1	$45,061	$36,527
Franklin County, MO	103,670	101,495	93,807	2,175	7,688	2.1	8.2	4,739.7	3,419.2	38.6	$45,719	$33,702
Jefferson County, MO	224,347	218,708	198,099	5,639	20,609	2.6	10.4	9,597.6	7,182.9	33.6	$42,780	$32,782
Lincoln County, MO	57,686	52,565	38,944	5,121	13,621	9.7	35.0	2,352.9	1,614.3	45.8	$40,788	$30,631
St. Charles County, MO	399,132	360,494	283,883	38,688	76,611	10.7	27.0	21,453.9	14,457.4	48.4	$53,745	$39,960
St. Louis County, MO	996,945	998,986	1,016,315	-2,041	-17,329	-0.2	-1.7	71,141.8	53,613.7	32.7	$71,360	$53,676
Warren County, MO	34,711	32,512	24,525	2,199	7,987	6.8	32.6	1,446.6	1,020.4	41.8	$41,674	$31,323
St. Louis city, MO	302,838	319,275	348,189	-16,437	-28,914	-5.1	-8.3	14,428.1	11,354.8	27.1	$47,643	$35,560

Table D-1. Population and Personal Income—*Continued*

Metropolitan or Micropolitan Statistical Area Metropolitan Division Component Counties	Population							Personal Income				
	2018 Estimate (July 1)	2010 census estimates base (April 1)	2000 census estimates base (April 1)	Net change		Percent change		Total (million dollars)		Percent change 2010-2018	Per capita	
				2010-2018	2000-2010	2010-2018	2000-2010	2018	2010		2018	2010
St. Marys, GA Micro area	53,677	50,512	43,664	3,165	6,848	6.3	15.7	1,938.4	1,468.2	32.0	$36,113	$28,981
Camden County, GA	53,677	50,512	43,664	3,165	6,848	6.3	15.7	1,938.4	1,468.2	32.0	$36,113	$28,981
St. Marys, PA Micro area	30,169	31,946	35,112	-1,777	-3,166	-5.6	-9.0	1,474.8	1,225.0	20.4	$48,886	$38,447
Elk County, PA	30,169	31,946	35,112	-1,777	-3,166	-5.6	-9.0	1,474.8	1,225.0	20.4	$48,886	$38,447
Salem, OH Micro area	102,665	107,852	112,075	-5,187	-4,223	-4.8	-3.8	3,902.6	3,191.3	22.3	$38,013	$29,579
Columbiana County, OH	102,665	107,852	112,075	-5,187	-4,223	-4.8	-3.8	3,902.6	3,191.3	22.3	$38,013	$29,579
Salem, OR Metro area	432,102	390,750	347,214	41,352	43,536	10.6	12.5	18,456.8	12,317.6	49.8	$42,714	$31,463
Marion County, OR	346,868	315,343	284,834	31,525	30,509	10.0	10.7	14,929.9	9,915.0	50.6	$43,042	$31,381
Polk County, OR	85,234	75,407	62,380	9,827	13,027	13.0	20.9	3,526.9	2,402.6	46.8	$41,379	$31,804
Salina, KS Micro area	60,203	61,700	59,760	-1,497	1,940	-2.4	3.2	2,958.1	2,295.0	28.9	$49,136	$37,089
Ottawa County, KS	5,802	6,091	6,163	-289	-72	-4.7	-1.2	239.0	211.4	13.1	$41,201	$34,678
Saline County, KS	54,401	55,609	53,597	-1,208	2,012	-2.2	3.8	2,719.1	2,083.6	30.5	$49,983	$37,352
Salinas, CA Metro area	435,594	415,061	401,762	20,533	13,299	4.9	3.3	24,477.2	17,263.7	41.8	$56,193	$41,460
Monterey County, CA	435,594	415,061	401,762	20,533	13,299	4.9	3.3	24,477.2	17,263.7	41.8	$56,193	$41,460
Salisbury, MD-DE Metro area	409,979	373,760	312,572	36,219	61,188	9.7	19.6	19,800.6	13,636.9	45.2	$48,296	$36,382
Sussex County, DE	229,286	197,106	156,638	32,180	40,468	16.3	25.8	11,540.7	7,235.7	59.5	$50,333	$36,564
Somerset County, MD	25,675	26,470	24,747	-795	1,723	-3.0	7.0	810.3	680.2	19.1	$31,562	$25,701
Wicomico County, MD	103,195	98,733	84,644	4,462	14,089	4.5	16.6	4,339.7	3,431.7	26.5	$42,054	$34,674
Worcester County, MD	51,823	51,451	46,543	372	4,908	0.7	10.5	3,109.8	2,289.4	35.8	$60,007	$44,454
Salt Lake City, UT Metro area	1,222,540	1,087,808	939,122	134,732	148,686	12.4	15.8	63,249.0	39,344.8	60.8	$51,736	$36,047
Salt Lake County, UT	1,152,633	1,029,590	898,387	123,043	131,203	12.0	14.6	60,673.9	37,636.5	61.2	$52,639	$36,435
Tooele County, UT	69,907	58,218	40,735	11,689	17,483	20.1	42.9	2,575.1	1,708.3	50.7	$36,836	$29,201
San Angelo, TX Metro area	121,022	112,968	107,174	8,054	5,794	7.1	5.4	5,616.2	4,173.1	34.6	$46,406	$36,793
Irion County, TX	1,522	1,597	1,771	-75	-174	-4.7	-9.8	104.0	70.1	48.4	$68,327	$43,635
Sterling County, TX	1,311	1,143	1,393	168	-250	14.7	-17.9	76.3	41.2	85.2	$58,174	$36,248
Tom Green County, TX	118,189	110,228	104,010	7,961	6,218	7.2	6.0	5,435.9	4,061.8	33.8	$45,993	$36,699
San Antonio-New Braunfels, TX Metro area	2,518,036	2,142,521	1,711,703	375,515	430,818	17.5	25.2	118,335.1	77,233.9	53.2	$46,995	$35,872
Atascosa County, TX	50,310	44,911	38,628	5,399	6,283	12.0	16.3	1,844.4	1,293.8	42.6	$36,660	$28,781
Bandera County, TX	22,824	20,489	17,645	2,335	2,844	11.4	16.1	991.9	676.0	46.7	$43,459	$32,876
Bexar County, TX	1,986,049	1,714,772	1,392,931	271,277	321,841	15.8	23.1	91,473.2	61,084.9	49.7	$46,058	$35,456
Comal County, TX	148,373	108,485	78,021	39,888	30,464	36.8	39.0	8,615.5	4,820.8	78.7	$58,067	$44,118
Guadalupe County, TX	163,694	131,534	89,023	32,160	42,511	24.4	47.8	7,334.9	4,507.8	62.7	$44,809	$33,996
Kendall County, TX	45,641	33,411	23,743	12,230	9,668	36.6	40.7	3,846.2	2,034.6	89.0	$84,270	$60,526
Medina County, TX	50,921	46,006	39,304	4,915	6,702	10.7	17.1	2,006.4	1,361.2	47.4	$39,403	$29,509
Wilson County, TX	50,224	42,913	32,408	7,311	10,505	17.0	32.4	2,222.7	1,454.9	52.8	$44,255	$33,789
San Diego-Chula Vista-Carlsbad, CA Metro area	3,343,364	3,095,349	2,813,833	248,015	281,516	8.0	10.0	205,236.4	136,969.8	49.8	$61,386	$44,137
San Diego County, CA	3,343,364	3,095,349	2,813,833	248,015	281,516	8.0	10.0	205,236.4	136,969.8	49.8	$61,386	$44,137
Sandpoint, ID Micro area	44,727	40,877	36,835	3,850	4,042	9.4	11.0	1,843.2	1,221.1	50.9	$41,209	$29,850
Bonner County, ID	44,727	40,877	36,835	3,850	4,042	9.4	11.0	1,843.2	1,221.1	50.9	$41,209	$29,850
Sandusky, OH Micro area	74,615	77,066	79,551	-2,451	-2,485	-3.2	-3.1	4,670.2	3,807.9	22.6	$62,591	$49,463
Erie County, OH	74,615	77,066	79,551	-2,451	-2,485	-3.2	-3.1	4,670.2	3,807.9	22.6	$62,591	$49,463
Sanford, NC Micro area	61,452	57,858	49,040	3,594	8,818	6.2	18.0	2,464.1	1,819.4	35.4	$40,098	$31,430
Lee County, NC	61,452	57,858	49,040	3,594	8,818	6.2	18.0	2,464.1	1,819.4	35.4	$40,098	$31,430
San Francisco-Oakland-Berkeley, CA Metro area	4,729,484	4,335,587	4,123,740	393,897	211,847	9.1	5.1	470,222.3	266,002.2	76.8	$99,424	$61,237
Oakland-Berkeley-Livermore, CA Div	2,816,968	2,559,462	2,392,557	257,506	166,905	10.1	7.0	222,646.4	129,745.6	71.6	$79,038	$50,571
Alameda County, CA	1,666,753	1,510,258	1,443,741	156,495	66,517	10.4	4.6	127,746.4	72,841.2	75.4	$76,644	$48,142
Contra Costa County, CA	1,150,215	1,049,204	948,816	101,011	100,388	9.6	10.6	94,900.0	56,904.4	66.8	$82,506	$54,063
San Francisco-San Mateo-Redwood City, CA Div..	1,652,850	1,523,702	1,483,894	129,148	39,808	8.5	2.7	212,709.2	114,992.3	85.0	$128,692	$75,391
San Francisco County, CA	883,305	805,184	776,733	78,121	28,451	9.7	3.7	115,444.6	61,873.0	86.6	$130,696	$76,808
San Mateo County, CA	769,545	718,518	707,161	51,027	11,357	7.1	1.6	97,264.6	53,119.2	83.1	$126,392	$73,805
San Rafael, CA Div	259,666	252,423	247,289	7,243	5,134	2.9	2.1	34,866.7	21,264.3	64.0	$134,275	$84,080
Marin County, CA	259,666	252,423	247,289	7,243	5,134	2.9	2.1	34,866.7	21,264.3	64.0	$134,275	$84,080
San Jose-Sunnyvale-Santa Clara, CA Metro area..	1,999,107	1,836,937	1,735,819	162,170	101,118	8.8	5.8	212,332.0	111,534.1	90.4	$106,213	$60,564
San Benito County, CA	61,537	55,265	53,234	6,272	2,031	11.3	3.8	3,312.0	1,993.7	66.1	$53,822	$35,912
Santa Clara County, CA	1,937,570	1,781,672	1,682,585	155,898	99,087	8.8	5.9	209,019.9	109,540.4	90.8	$107,877	$61,330
San Luis Obispo-Paso Robles, CA Metro area	284,010	269,597	246,681	14,413	22,916	5.3	9.3	16,612.0	10,855.1	53.0	$58,491	$40,233
San Luis Obispo County, CA	284,010	269,597	246,681	14,413	22,916	5.3	9.3	16,612.0	10,855.1	53.0	$58,491	$40,233
Santa Cruz-Watsonville, CA Metro area	274,255	262,356	255,602	11,899	6,754	4.5	2.6	19,021.0	12,794.0	48.7	$69,355	$48,616
Santa Cruz County, CA	274,255	262,356	255,602	11,899	6,754	4.5	2.6	19,021.0	12,794.0	48.7	$69,355	$48,616
Santa Fe, NM Metro area	150,056	144,227	129,292	5,829	14,935	4.0	11.6	8,779.8	6,250.9	40.5	$58,510	$43,251
Santa Fe County, NM	150,056	144,227	129,292	5,829	14,935	4.0	11.6	8,779.8	6,250.9	40.5	$58,510	$43,251
Santa Maria-Santa Barbara, CA Metro area	446,527	423,947	399,347	22,580	24,600	5.3	6.2	27,992.8	19,354.0	44.6	$62,690	$45,621
Santa Barbara County, CA	446,527	423,947	399,347	22,580	24,600	5.3	6.2	27,992.8	19,354.0	44.6	$62,690	$45,621
Santa Rosa-Petaluma, CA Metro area	499,942	483,868	458,614	16,074	25,254	3.3	5.5	32,246.6	20,830.6	54.8	$64,501	$42,969
Sonoma County, CA	499,942	483,868	458,614	16,074	25,254	3.3	5.5	32,246.6	20,830.6	54.8	$64,501	$42,969
Sault Ste. Marie, MI Micro area	37,517	38,669	38,543	-1,152	126	-3.0	0.3	1,285.7	1,080.8	19.0	$34,269	$27,991
Chippewa County, MI	37,517	38,669	38,543	-1,152	126	-3.0	0.3	1,285.7	1,080.8	19.0	$34,269	$27,991
Savannah, GA Metro area	389,494	347,598	293,000	41,896	54,598	12.1	18.6	18,362.3	13,089.9	40.3	$47,144	$37,546
Bryan County, GA	38,109	30,215	23,417	7,894	6,798	26.1	29.0	1,999.0	1,274.5	56.8	$52,456	$41,956
Chatham County, GA	289,195	265,126	232,048	24,069	33,078	9.1	14.3	13,754.9	10,114.5	36.0	$47,563	$38,054
Effingham County, GA	62,190	52,257	37,535	9,933	14,722	19.0	39.2	2,608.4	1,700.8	53.4	$41,942	$32,419
Sayre, PA Micro area	60,833	62,704	62,761	-1,871	-57	-3.0	-0.1	2,514.3	1,982.2	26.8	$41,331	$31,596
Bradford County, PA	60,833	62,704	62,761	-1,871	-57	-3.0	-0.1	2,514.3	1,982.2	26.8	$41,331	$31,596
Scottsbluff, NE Micro area	37,906	38,971	39,245	-1,065	-274	-2.7	-0.7	1,682.5	1,322.9	27.2	$44,387	$33,870
Banner County, NE	730	690	819	40	-129	5.8	-15.8	42.5	30.9	37.5	$58,252	$44,673
Scotts Bluff County, NE	35,989	36,970	36,951	-981	19	-2.7	0.1	1,589.7	1,247.7	27.4	$44,171	$33,670

Table D-1. Population and Personal Income—Continued

Metropolitan or Micropolitan Statistical Area Metropolitan Division Component Counties	Population							Personal Income				
	2018 Estimate (July 1)	2010 census estimates base (April 1)	2000 census estimates base (April 1)	Net change		Percent change		Total (million dollars)		Percent change 2010-2018	Per capita	
				2010-2018	2000-2010	2010-2018	2000-2010	2018	2010		2018	2010
Sioux County, NE	1,187	1,311	1,475	-124	-164	-9.5	-11.1	50.3	44.4	13.3	$42,404	$33,837
Scottsboro, AL Micro area	51,736	53,224	53,926	-1,488	-702	-2.8	-1.3	1,891.8	1,566.8	20.7	$36,567	$29,461
Jackson County, AL	51,736	53,224	53,926	-1,488	-702	-2.8	-1.3	1,891.8	1,566.8	20.7	$36,567	$29,461
Scottsburg, IN Micro area	23,878	24,187	22,960	-309	1,227	-1.3	5.3	894.8	667.1	34.1	$37,475	$27,607
Scott County, IN	23,878	24,187	22,960	-309	1,227	-1.3	5.3	894.8	667.1	34.1	$37,475	$27,607
Scranton--Wilkes-Barre, PA Metro area	555,485	563,617	560,625	-8,132	2,992	-1.4	0.5	25,649.4	20,574.8	24.7	$46,175	$36,496
Lackawanna County, PA	210,793	214,439	213,295	-3,646	1,144	-1.7	0.5	10,061.1	8,171.8	23.1	$47,730	$38,092
Luzerne County, PA	317,646	320,895	319,250	-3,249	1,645	-1.0	0.5	14,363.5	11,477.9	25.1	$45,219	$35,758
Wyoming County, PA	27,046	28,283	28,080	-1,237	203	-4.4	0.7	1,224.8	925.1	32.4	$45,285	$32,756
Searcy, AR Micro area	78,727	77,078	67,165	1,649	9,913	2.1	14.8	2,790.5	2,273.5	22.7	$35,445	$29,393
White County, AR	78,727	77,078	67,165	1,649	9,913	2.1	14.8	2,790.5	2,273.5	22.7	$35,445	$29,393
Seattle-Tacoma-Bellevue, WA Metro area	3,939,363	3,439,805	3,043,878	499,558	395,927	14.5	13.0	293,954.1	168,310.4	74.6	$74,620	$48,796
Seattle-Bellevue-Kent, WA Div	3,048,064	2,644,588	2,343,058	403,476	301,530	15.3	12.9	247,505.1	137,760.4	79.7	$81,201	$51,909
King County, WA	2,233,163	1,931,292	1,737,034	301,871	194,258	15.6	11.2	201,962.2	109,193.6	85.0	$90,438	$56,333
Snohomish County, WA	814,901	713,296	606,024	101,605	107,272	14.2	17.7	45,542.9	28,566.9	59.4	$55,888	$39,925
Tacoma-Lakewood, WA Div	891,299	795,217	700,820	96,082	94,397	12.1	13.5	46,449.1	30,550.0	52.0	$52,114	$38,409
Pierce County, WA	891,299	795,217	700,820	96,082	94,397	12.1	13.5	46,449.1	30,550.0	52.0	$52,114	$38,409
Sebastian-Vero Beach, FL Metro area	157,413	138,028	112,947	19,385	25,081	14.0	22.2	11,972.6	7,291.3	64.2	$76,059	$52,732
Indian River County, FL	157,413	138,028	112,947	19,385	25,081	14.0	22.2	11,972.6	7,291.3	64.2	$76,059	$52,732
Sebring-Avon Park, FL Metro area	105,424	98,786	87,366	6,638	11,420	6.7	13.1	3,526.8	2,839.2	24.2	$33,453	$28,785
Highlands County, FL	105,424	98,786	87,366	6,638	11,420	6.7	13.1	3,526.8	2,839.2	24.2	$33,453	$28,785
Sedalia, MO Micro area	42,542	42,201	39,403	341	2,798	0.8	7.1	1,606.5	1,317.0	22.0	$37,763	$31,162
Pettis County, MO	42,542	42,201	39,403	341	2,798	0.8	7.1	1,606.5	1,317.0	22.0	$37,763	$31,162
Selinsgrove, PA Micro area	40,540	39,719	37,546	821	2,173	2.1	5.8	1,720.9	1,313.9	31.0	$42,449	$33,090
Snyder County, PA	40,540	39,719	37,546	821	2,173	2.1	5.8	1,720.9	1,313.9	31.0	$42,449	$33,090
Selma, AL Micro area	38,310	43,818	46,365	-5,508	-2,547	-12.6	-5.5	1,380.1	1,232.2	12.0	$36,026	$28,093
Dallas County, AL	38,310	43,818	46,365	-5,508	-2,547	-12.6	-5.5	1,380.1	1,232.2	12.0	$36,026	$28,093
Seneca, SC Micro area	78,374	74,275	66,215	4,099	8,060	5.5	12.2	3,394.5	2,387.3	42.2	$43,312	$32,113
Oconee County, SC	78,374	74,275	66,215	4,099	8,060	5.5	12.2	3,394.5	2,387.3	42.2	$43,312	$32,113
Seneca Falls, NY Micro area	34,300	35,243	33,342	-943	1,901	-2.7	5.7	1,323.7	1,094.6	20.9	$38,593	$31,044
Seneca County, NY	34,300	35,243	33,342	-943	1,901	-2.7	5.7	1,323.7	1,094.6	20.9	$38,593	$31,044
Sevierville, TN Micro area	97,892	89,719	71,170	8,173	18,549	9.1	26.1	3,864.2	2,661.5	45.2	$39,474	$29,599
Sevier County, TN	97,892	89,719	71,170	8,173	18,549	9.1	26.1	3,864.2	2,661.5	45.2	$39,474	$29,599
Seymour, IN Micro area	44,111	42,376	41,335	1,735	1,041	4.1	2.5	1,884.5	1,456.7	29.4	$42,722	$34,207
Jackson County, IN	44,111	42,376	41,335	1,735	1,041	4.1	2.5	1,884.5	1,456.7	29.4	$42,722	$34,207
Shawano, WI Micro area	45,454	46,187	45,226	-733	961	-1.6	2.1	1,866.7	1,463.1	27.6	$41,068	$31,664
Menominee County, WI	4,658	4,232	4,562	426	-330	10.1	-7.2	141.5	108.2	30.8	$30,371	$25,338
Shawano County, WI	40,796	41,955	40,664	-1,159	1,291	-2.8	3.2	1,725.3	1,354.9	27.3	$42,290	$32,308
Shawnee, OK Micro area	72,679	69,443	65,521	3,236	3,922	4.7	6.0	2,722.3	2,378.9	14.4	$37,456	$34,164
Pottawatomie County, OK	72,679	69,443	65,521	3,236	3,922	4.7	6.0	2,722.3	2,378.9	14.4	$37,456	$34,164
Sheboygan, WI Metro area	115,456	115,510	112,646	-54	2,864	0.0	2.5	6,102.0	4,491.7	35.9	$52,851	$38,882
Sheboygan County, WI	115,456	115,510	112,646	-54	2,864	0.0	2.5	6,102.0	4,491.7	35.9	$52,851	$38,882
Shelby, NC Micro area	97,645	98,032	96,287	-387	1,745	-0.4	1.8	3,677.4	2,852.3	28.9	$37,661	$29,129
Cleveland County, NC	97,645	98,032	96,287	-387	1,745	-0.4	1.8	3,677.4	2,852.3	28.9	$37,661	$29,129
Shelbyville, TN Micro area	49,038	45,057	37,586	3,981	7,471	8.8	19.9	1,827.4	1,246.9	46.6	$37,266	$27,661
Bedford County, TN	49,038	45,057	37,586	3,981	7,471	8.8	19.9	1,827.4	1,246.9	46.6	$37,266	$27,661
Shelton, WA Micro area	65,507	60,692	49,405	4,815	11,287	7.9	22.8	2,801.5	1,991.4	40.7	$42,767	$32,788
Mason County, WA	65,507	60,692	49,405	4,815	11,287	7.9	22.8	2,801.5	1,991.4	40.7	$42,767	$32,788
Sheridan, WY Micro area	30,233	29,119	26,560	1,114	2,559	3.8	9.6	1,760.2	1,470.0	19.7	$58,223	$50,441
Sheridan County, WY	30,233	29,119	26,560	1,114	2,559	3.8	9.6	1,760.2	1,470.0	19.7	$58,223	$50,441
Sherman-Denison, TX Metro area	133,991	120,875	110,595	13,116	10,280	10.9	9.3	5,653.8	3,905.0	44.8	$42,195	$32,265
Grayson County, TX	133,991	120,875	110,595	13,116	10,280	10.9	9.3	5,653.8	3,905.0	44.8	$42,195	$32,265
Show Low, AZ Micro area	110,445	107,488	97,470	2,957	10,018	2.8	10.3	3,552.5	2,680.8	32.5	$32,165	$24,893
Navajo County, AZ	110,445	107,488	97,470	2,957	10,018	2.8	10.3	3,552.5	2,680.8	32.5	$32,165	$24,893
Shreveport-Bossier City, LA Metro area	397,543	398,604	375,965	-1,061	22,639	-0.3	6.0	18,489.2	15,702.6	17.7	$46,509	$39,263
Bossier Parish, LA	127,185	117,027	98,310	10,158	18,717	8.7	19.0	5,615.1	4,375.5	28.3	$44,149	$37,185
Caddo Parish, LA	242,922	254,921	252,161	-11,999	2,760	-4.7	1.1	11,760.6	10,427.1	12.8	$48,413	$40,795
De Soto Parish, LA	27,436	26,656	25,494	780	1,162	2.9	4.6	1,113.5	900.0	23.7	$40,584	$33,747
Sidney, OH Micro area	48,627	49,418	47,910	-791	1,508	-1.6	3.1	2,246.0	1,633.2	37.5	$46,188	$33,120
Shelby County, OH	48,627	49,418	47,910	-791	1,508	-1.6	3.1	2,246.0	1,633.2	37.5	$46,188	$33,120
Sierra Vista-Douglas, AZ Metro area	126,770	131,357	117,755	-4,587	13,602	-3.5	11.6	5,109.8	4,556.2	12.2	$40,308	$34,563
Cochise County, AZ	126,770	131,357	117,755	-4,587	13,602	-3.5	11.6	5,109.8	4,556.2	12.2	$40,308	$34,563
Sikeston, MO Micro area	38,458	39,188	40,422	-730	-1,234	-1.9	-3.1	1,546.8	1,301.9	18.8	$40,221	$33,169
Scott County, MO	38,458	39,188	40,422	-730	-1,234	-1.9	-3.1	1,546.8	1,301.9	18.8	$40,221	$33,169
Silver City, NM Micro area	27,346	29,510	31,002	-2,164	-1,492	-7.3	-4.8	1,121.9	892.6	25.7	$41,026	$30,379
Grant County, NM	27,346	29,510	31,002	-2,164	-1,492	-7.3	-4.8	1,121.9	892.6	25.7	$41,026	$30,379
Sioux City, IA-NE-SD Metro area	143,950	143,579	143,053	371	526	0.3	0.4	7,281.8	5,872.8	24.0	$50,586	$40,812
Woodbury County, IA	102,539	102,175	103,877	364	-1,702	0.4	-1.6	4,510.4	3,714.9	21.4	$43,988	$36,282
Dakota County, NE	20,083	21,006	20,253	-923	753	-4.4	3.7	840.1	613.3	37.0	$41,831	$29,159
Dixon County, NE	5,709	6,000	6,339	-291	-339	-4.9	-5.3	252.3	208.4	21.1	$44,185	$34,819
Union County, SD	15,619	14,398	12,584	1,221	1,814	8.5	14.4	1,679.0	1,336.2	25.7	$107,497	$92,203
Sioux Falls, SD Metro area	265,653	228,262	187,093	37,391	41,169	16.4	22.0	15,811.8	10,620.1	48.9	$59,520	$46,356
Lincoln County, SD	58,807	44,823	24,131	13,984	20,692	31.2	85.7	3,961.5	2,268.8	74.6	$67,364	$50,209
McCook County, SD	5,546	5,618	5,832	-72	-214	-1.3	-3.7	290.9	225.6	28.9	$52,453	$40,218
Minnehaha County, SD	192,876	169,474	148,281	23,402	21,193	13.8	14.3	11,037.0	7,781.2	41.8	$57,223	$45,785

Table D-1. Population and Personal Income—Continued

Metropolitan or Micropolitan Statistical Area Metropolitan Division Component Counties	2018 Estimate (July 1)	2010 census estimates base (April 1)	2000 census estimates base (April 1)	Net change 2010-2018	Net change 2000-2010	Percent change 2010-2018	Percent change 2000-2010	Total (million dollars) 2018	Total (million dollars) 2010	Percent change 2010-2018	Per capita 2018	Per capita 2010
Turner County, SD	8,424	8,347	8,849	77	-502	0.9	-5.7	522.4	344.6	51.6	$62,019	$41,264
Snyder, TX Micro area	16,866	16,919	16,361	-53	558	-0.3	3.4	710.0	621.4	14.3	$42,095	$36,708
Scurry County, TX	16,866	16,919	16,361	-53	558	-0.3	3.4	710.0	621.4	14.3	$42,095	$36,708
Somerset, KY Micro area	64,623	63,061	56,217	1,562	6,844	2.5	12.2	2,392.6	1,872.9	27.7	$37,024	$29,639
Pulaski County, KY	64,623	63,061	56,217	1,562	6,844	2.5	12.2	2,392.6	1,872.9	27.7	$37,024	$29,639
Somerset, PA Micro area	73,952	77,737	80,023	-3,785	-2,286	-4.9	-2.9	3,119.2	2,659.3	17.3	$42,179	$34,197
Somerset County, PA	73,952	77,737	80,023	-3,785	-2,286	-4.9	-2.9	3,119.2	2,659.3	17.3	$42,179	$34,197
Sonora, CA Micro area	54,539	55,368	54,501	-829	867	-1.5	1.6	2,609.0	1,909.2	36.7	$47,838	$34,592
Tuolumne County, CA	54,539	55,368	54,501	-829	867	-1.5	1.6	2,609.0	1,909.2	36.7	$47,838	$34,592
South Bend-Mishawaka, IN-MI Metro area	322,424	319,213	316,663	3,211	2,550	1.0	0.8	15,232.6	10,911.9	39.6	$47,244	$34,201
St. Joseph County, IN	270,771	266,925	265,559	3,846	1,366	1.4	0.5	12,908.5	9,262.6	39.4	$47,673	$34,716
Cass County, MI	51,653	52,288	51,104	-635	1,184	-1.2	2.3	2,324.1	1,649.2	40.9	$44,994	$31,568
Spartanburg, SC Metro area	313,888	284,317	253,791	29,571	30,526	10.4	12.0	13,543.5	9,117.8	48.5	$43,148	$32,021
Spartanburg County, SC	313,888	284,317	253,791	29,571	30,526	10.4	12.0	13,543.5	9,117.8	48.5	$43,148	$32,021
Spearfish, SD Micro area	25,741	24,090	21,802	1,651	2,288	6.9	10.5	1,293.0	906.7	42.6	$50,232	$37,460
Lawrence County, SD	25,741	24,090	21,802	1,651	2,288	6.9	10.5	1,293.0	906.7	42.6	$50,232	$37,460
Spencer, IA Micro area	16,134	16,667	17,372	-533	-705	-3.2	-4.1	837.0	655.0	27.8	$51,876	$39,374
Clay County, IA	16,134	16,667	17,372	-533	-705	-3.2	-4.1	837.0	655.0	27.8	$51,876	$39,374
Spirit Lake, IA Micro area	17,153	16,667	16,424	486	243	2.9	1.5	1,005.0	732.8	37.1	$58,592	$43,960
Dickinson County, IA	17,153	16,667	16,424	486	243	2.9	1.5	1,005.0	732.8	37.1	$58,592	$43,960
Spokane-Spokane Valley, WA Metro area	559,891	514,752	458,005	45,139	56,747	8.8	12.4	25,701.0	17,912.2	43.5	$45,903	$34,744
Spokane County, WA	514,631	471,229	417,939	43,402	53,290	9.2	12.8	23,912.9	16,619.1	43.9	$46,466	$35,203
Stevens County, WA	45,260	43,523	40,066	1,737	3,457	4.0	8.6	1,788.0	1,293.1	38.3	$39,505	$29,750
Springfield, IL Metro area	207,636	210,170	201,437	-2,534	8,733	-1.2	4.3	10,131.1	8,255.6	22.7	$48,793	$39,226
Menard County, IL	12,288	12,705	12,486	-417	219	-3.3	1.8	580.4	476.8	21.7	$47,233	$37,557
Sangamon County, IL	195,348	197,465	188,951	-2,117	8,514	-1.1	4.5	9,550.7	7,778.8	22.8	$48,891	$39,333
Springfield, MA Metro area	702,724	693,058	680,014	9,666	13,044	1.4	1.9	36,508.8	27,373.4	33.4	$51,953	$39,390
Franklin County, MA	70,963	71,377	71,535	-414	-158	-0.6	-0.2	3,880.9	2,922.8	32.8	$54,689	$40,955
Hampden County, MA	470,406	463,625	456,228	6,781	7,397	1.5	1.6	24,078.6	18,223.3	32.1	$51,187	$39,253
Hampshire County, MA	161,355	158,056	152,251	3,299	5,805	2.1	3.8	8,549.2	6,227.4	37.3	$52,984	$39,087
Springfield, MO Metro area	466,978	436,709	368,374	30,269	68,335	6.9	18.6	19,510.5	13,975.5	39.6	$41,780	$31,959
Christian County, MO	86,983	77,417	54,285	9,566	23,132	12.4	42.6	3,505.5	2,354.5	48.9	$40,301	$30,247
Dallas County, MO	16,762	16,770	15,661	-8	1,109	0.0	7.1	556.2	420.1	32.4	$33,184	$25,120
Greene County, MO	291,923	275,178	240,391	16,745	34,787	6.1	14.5	13,088.9	9,449.6	38.5	$44,837	$34,324
Polk County, MO	32,201	31,137	26,992	1,064	4,145	3.4	15.4	1,085.3	787.4	37.8	$33,703	$25,266
Webster County, MO	39,109	36,207	31,045	2,902	5,162	8.0	16.6	1,274.5	964.0	32.2	$32,589	$26,582
Springfield, OH Metro area	134,585	138,341	144,742	-3,756	-6,401	-2.7	-4.4	5,486.9	4,450.6	23.3	$40,769	$32,187
Clark County, OH	134,585	138,341	144,742	-3,756	-6,401	-2.7	-4.4	5,486.9	4,450.6	23.3	$40,769	$32,187
Starkville, MS Micro area	59,387	57,920	53,196	1,467	4,724	2.5	8.9	2,081.1	1,608.8	29.4	$35,043	$27,742
Oktibbeha County, MS	49,599	47,671	42,902	1,928	4,769	4.0	11.1	1,704.6	1,303.9	30.7	$34,367	$27,315
Webster County, MS	9,788	10,249	10,294	-461	-45	-4.5	-0.4	376.5	304.9	23.5	$38,464	$29,730
State College, PA Metro area	162,805	154,001	135,758	8,804	18,243	5.7	13.4	7,520.5	5,506.4	36.6	$46,193	$35,706
Centre County, PA	162,805	154,001	135,758	8,804	18,243	5.7	13.4	7,520.5	5,506.4	36.6	$46,193	$35,706
Statesboro, GA Micro area	77,296	70,246	55,983	7,050	14,263	10.0	25.5	2,503.0	1,849.5	35.3	$32,382	$26,211
Bulloch County, GA	77,296	70,246	55,983	7,050	14,263	10.0	25.5	2,503.0	1,849.5	35.3	$32,382	$26,211
Staunton, VA Metro area	123,007	118,496	108,988	4,511	9,508	3.8	8.7	5,451.1	4,257.9	28.0	$44,316	$35,989
Augusta County, VA	75,457	73,753	65,615	1,704	8,138	2.3	12.4	5,451.1	4,257.9	28.0	$44,316	$35,989
Staunton City, VA (personal income included with Augusta County)	24,922	23,745	23,853	1,177	-108	5.0	-0.5	-	-	-	-	-
Waynesboro City, VA (personal income included with Augusta County)	22,628	20,998	19,520	1,630	1,478	7.8	7.6	-	-	-	-	-
Steamboat Springs, CO Micro area	25,733	23,506	19,690	2,227	3,816	9.5	19.4	2,153.9	1,201.9	79.2	$83,702	$51,257
Routt County, CO	25,733	23,506	19,690	2,227	3,816	9.5	19.4	2,153.9	1,201.9	79.2	$83,702	$51,257
Stephenville, TX Micro area	42,446	37,900	33,001	4,546	4,899	12.0	14.8	1,679.7	1,078.1	55.8	$39,572	$28,434
Erath County, TX	42,446	37,900	33,001	4,546	4,899	12.0	14.8	1,679.7	1,078.1	55.8	$39,572	$28,434
Sterling, CO Micro area	21,528	22,709	20,504	-1,181	2,205	-5.2	10.8	1,036.8	786.4	31.8	$48,161	$35,693
Logan County, CO	21,528	22,709	20,504	-1,181	2,205	-5.2	10.8	1,036.8	786.4	31.8	$48,161	$35,693
Sterling, IL Micro area	55,626	58,494	60,653	-2,868	-2,159	-4.9	-3.6	2,448.4	2,053.9	19.2	$44,016	$35,123
Whiteside County, IL	55,626	58,494	60,653	-2,868	-2,159	-4.9	-3.6	2,448.4	2,053.9	19.2	$44,016	$35,123
Stevens Point, WI Micro area	70,942	70,021	67,182	921	2,839	1.3	4.2	3,255.2	2,412.3	34.9	$45,886	$34,448
Portage County, WI	70,942	70,021	67,182	921	2,839	1.3	4.2	3,255.2	2,412.3	34.9	$45,886	$34,448
Stillwater, OK Micro area	82,040	77,350	68,190	4,690	9,160	6.1	13.4	3,048.6	2,392.6	27.4	$37,159	$30,912
Payne County, OK	82,040	77,350	68,190	4,690	9,160	6.1	13.4	3,048.6	2,392.6	27.4	$37,159	$30,912
Stockton, CA Metro area	752,660	685,306	563,598	67,354	121,708	9.8	21.6	33,866.0	22,508.0	50.5	$44,995	$32,755
San Joaquin County, CA	752,660	685,306	563,598	67,354	121,708	9.8	21.6	33,866.0	22,508.0	50.5	$44,995	$32,755
Storm Lake, IA Micro area	19,874	20,265	20,411	-391	-146	-1.9	-0.7	993.7	759.0	30.9	$50,000	$37,288
Buena Vista County, IA	19,874	20,265	20,411	-391	-146	-1.9	-0.7	993.7	759.0	30.9	$50,000	$37,288
Sturgis, MI Micro area	61,043	61,295	62,422	-252	-1,127	-0.4	-1.8	2,372.5	1,784.3	33.0	$38,866	$29,115
St. Joseph County, MI	61,043	61,295	62,422	-252	-1,127	-0.4	-1.8	2,372.5	1,784.3	33.0	$38,866	$29,115
Sulphur Springs, TX Micro area	36,810	35,161	31,960	1,649	3,201	4.7	10.0	1,440.0	1,076.5	33.8	$39,120	$30,576
Hopkins County, TX	36,810	35,161	31,960	1,649	3,201	4.7	10.0	1,440.0	1,076.5	33.8	$39,120	$30,576
Summerville, GA Micro area	24,790	26,017	25,470	-1,227	547	-4.7	2.1	767.1	627.1	22.3	$30,946	$24,164
Chattooga County, GA	24,790	26,017	25,470	-1,227	547	-4.7	2.1	767.1	627.1	22.3	$30,946	$24,164
Sumter, SC Metro area	140,212	142,441	137,148	-2,229	5,293	-1.6	3.9	5,230.4	4,062.2	28.8	$37,304	$28,495
Clarendon County, SC	33,700	34,951	32,502	-1,251	2,449	-3.6	7.5	1,118.7	840.9	33.0	$33,197	$24,061

Table D-1. Population and Personal Income—Continued

Metropolitan or Micropolitan Statistical Area Metropolitan Division Component Counties	2018 Estimate (July 1)	2010 census estimates base (April 1)	2000 census estimates base (April 1)	Net change 2010-2018	Net change 2000-2010	Percent change 2010-2018	Percent change 2000-2010	Total (million dollars) 2018	Total (million dollars) 2010	Percent change 2010-2018	Per capita 2018	Per capita 2010
Sumter County, SC	106,512	107,490	104,646	-978	2,844	-0.9	2.7	4,111.7	3,221.3	27.6	$38,603	$29,935
Sunbury, PA Micro area	91,083	94,483	94,556	-3,400	-73	-3.6	-0.1	3,799.3	3,100.4	22.5	$41,712	$32,878
Northumberland County, PA	91,083	94,483	94,556	-3,400	-73	-3.6	-0.1	3,799.3	3,100.4	22.5	$41,712	$32,878
Susanville, CA Micro area	30,802	34,895	33,828	-4,093	1,067	-11.7	3.2	1,165.7	966.2	20.6	$37,844	$27,738
Lassen County, CA	30,802	34,895	33,828	-4,093	1,067	-11.7	3.2	1,165.7	966.2	20.6	$37,844	$27,738
Sweetwater, TX Micro area	14,751	15,215	15,802	-464	-587	-3.0	-3.7	635.6	473.7	34.2	$43,087	$31,066
Nolan County, TX	14,751	15,215	15,802	-464	-587	-3.0	-3.7	635.6	473.7	34.2	$43,087	$31,066
Syracuse, NY Metro area	650,502	662,620	650,154	-12,118	12,466	-1.8	1.9	32,353.1	25,216.4	28.3	$49,736	$38,028
Madison County, NY	70,795	73,451	69,441	-2,656	4,010	-3.6	5.8	3,150.5	2,467.5	27.7	$44,502	$33,599
Onondaga County, NY	461,809	467,064	458,336	-5,255	8,728	-1.1	1.9	24,423.2	18,864.6	29.5	$52,886	$40,350
Oswego County, NY	117,898	122,105	122,377	-4,207	-272	-3.4	-0.2	4,779.3	3,884.4	23.0	$40,538	$31,802
Tahlequah, OK Micro area	48,675	46,982	42,521	1,693	4,461	3.6	10.5	1,571.7	1,226.7	28.1	$32,290	$26,042
Cherokee County, OK	48,675	46,982	42,521	1,693	4,461	3.6	10.5	1,571.7	1,226.7	28.1	$32,290	$26,042
Talladega-Sylacauga, AL Micro area	79,828	82,283	80,321	-2,455	1,962	-3.0	2.4	2,771.5	2,278.1	21.7	$34,718	$27,748
Talladega County, AL	79,828	82,283	80,321	-2,455	1,962	-3.0	2.4	2,771.5	2,278.1	21.7	$34,718	$27,748
Tallahassee, FL Metro area	385,145	368,770	320,304	16,375	48,466	4.4	15.1	16,407.6	12,804.2	28.1	$42,601	$34,668
Gadsden County, FL	45,894	47,744	45,087	-1,850	2,657	-3.9	5.9	1,612.7	1,324.2	21.8	$35,139	$27,707
Jefferson County, FL	14,288	14,759	12,902	-471	1,857	-3.2	14.4	582.0	464.7	25.2	$40,736	$31,495
Leon County, FL	292,502	275,484	239,452	17,018	36,032	6.2	15.0	13,011.0	10,119.0	28.6	$44,482	$36,667
Wakulla County, FL	32,461	30,783	22,863	1,678	7,920	5.5	34.6	1,201.9	896.3	34.1	$37,026	$29,076
Tampa-St. Petersburg-Clearwater, FL Metro area..	3,142,663	2,783,462	2,395,997	359,201	387,465	12.9	16.2	148,460.2	107,124.3	38.6	$47,240	$38,418
Hernando County, FL	190,865	172,777	130,802	18,088	41,975	10.5	32.1	7,038.7	5,235.1	34.5	$36,878	$30,266
Hillsborough County, FL	1,436,888	1,229,178	998,948	207,710	230,230	16.9	23.0	67,533.9	48,707.7	38.7	$47,000	$39,488
Pasco County, FL	539,630	464,703	344,765	74,927	119,938	16.1	34.8	21,754.1	14,909.2	45.9	$40,313	$32,029
Pinellas County, FL	975,280	916,804	921,482	58,476	-4,678	6.4	-0.5	52,133.4	38,272.4	36.2	$53,455	$41,763
Taos, NM Micro area	32,835	32,935	29,979	-100	2,956	-0.3	9.9	1,262.7	954.9	32.2	$38,455	$29,029
Taos County, NM	32,835	32,935	29,979	-100	2,956	-0.3	9.9	1,262.7	954.9	32.2	$38,455	$29,029
Taylorville, IL Micro area	32,661	34,793	35,372	-2,132	-579	-6.1	-1.6	1,362.7	1,207.0	12.9	$41,724	$34,720
Christian County, IL	32,661	34,793	35,372	-2,132	-579	-6.1	-1.6	1,362.7	1,207.0	12.9	$41,724	$34,720
Terre Haute, IN Metro area	186,652	189,771	188,184	-3,119	1,587	-1.6	0.8	7,148.5	5,801.5	23.2	$38,299	$30,611
Clay County, IN	26,170	26,884	26,556	-714	328	-2.7	1.2	1,010.6	807.5	25.2	$38,615	$30,073
Parke County, IN	16,927	17,354	17,241	-427	113	-2.5	0.7	615.2	478.7	28.5	$36,345	$27,700
Sullivan County, IN	20,690	21,475	21,751	-785	-276	-3.7	-1.3	727.9	611.5	19.0	$35,181	$28,591
Vermillion County, IN	15,479	16,210	16,788	-731	-578	-4.5	-3.4	610.0	517.3	17.9	$39,411	$32,099
Vigo County, IN	107,386	107,848	105,848	-462	2,000	-0.4	1.9	4,184.8	3,386.5	23.6	$38,970	$31,390
Texarkana, TX-AR Metro area	150,242	149,194	143,377	1,048	5,817	0.7	4.1	5,650.1	4,766.3	18.5	$37,607	$31,919
Little River County, AR	12,326	13,168	13,628	-842	-460	-6.4	-3.4	420.2	380.0	10.6	$34,086	$28,942
Miller County, AR	43,592	43,462	40,443	130	3,019	0.3	7.5	1,456.0	1,240.4	17.4	$33,401	$28,474
Bowie County, TX	94,324	92,564	89,306	1,760	3,258	1.9	3.6	3,773.9	3,146.0	20.0	$40,010	$33,961
The Dalles, OR Micro area	26,505	25,211	23,791	1,294	1,420	5.1	6.0	1,157.2	845.1	36.9	$43,658	$33,422
Wasco County, OR	26,505	25,211	23,791	1,294	1,420	5.1	6.0	1,157.2	845.1	36.9	$43,658	$33,422
The Villages, FL Metro area	128,754	93,420	53,345	35,334	40,075	37.8	75.1	5,935.6	2,805.6	111.6	$46,100	$29,758
Sumter County, FL	128,754	93,420	53,345	35,334	40,075	37.8	75.1	5,935.6	2,805.6	111.6	$46,100	$29,758
Thomaston, GA Micro area	26,215	27,151	27,597	-936	-446	-3.4	-1.6	921.0	734.5	25.4	$35,133	$27,146
Upson County, GA	26,215	27,151	27,597	-936	-446	-3.4	-1.6	921.0	734.5	25.4	$35,133	$27,146
Thomasville, GA Micro area	44,448	44,724	42,737	-276	1,987	-0.6	4.6	1,971.5	1,491.4	32.2	$44,355	$33,326
Thomas County, GA	44,448	44,724	42,737	-276	1,987	-0.6	4.6	1,971.5	1,491.4	32.2	$44,355	$33,326
Tiffin, OH Micro area	55,207	56,742	58,683	-1,535	-1,941	-2.7	-3.3	2,190.7	1,703.5	28.6	$39,681	$30,088
Seneca County, OH	55,207	56,742	58,683	-1,535	-1,941	-2.7	-3.3	2,190.7	1,703.5	28.6	$39,681	$30,088
Tifton, GA Micro area	40,571	40,132	38,407	439	1,725	1.1	4.5	1,533.8	1,181.0	29.9	$37,805	$29,343
Tift County, GA	40,571	40,132	38,407	439	1,725	1.1	4.5	1,533.8	1,181.0	29.9	$37,805	$29,343
Toccoa, GA Micro area	26,035	26,173	25,435	-138	738	-0.5	2.9	1,013.2	744.6	36.1	$38,915	$28,490
Stephens County, GA	26,035	26,173	25,435	-138	738	-0.5	2.9	1,013.2	744.6	36.1	$38,915	$28,490
Toledo, OH Metro area	643,640	651,435	659,188	-7,795	-7,753	-1.2	-1.2	30,166.2	23,240.3	29.8	$46,868	$35,679
Fulton County, OH	42,276	42,698	42,084	-422	614		1.5	1,927.5	1,447.2	33.2	$45,594	$33,947
Lucas County, OH	429,899	441,815	455,054	-11,916	-13,239	-2.7	-2.9	19,900.1	15,427.1	29.0	$46,290	$34,948
Ottawa County, OH	40,769	41,433	40,985	-664	448	-1.6	1.1	2,105.2	1,600.1	31.6	$51,637	$38,689
Wood County, OH	130,696	125,489	121,065	5,207	4,424	4.1	3.7	6,233.4	4,765.9	30.8	$47,694	$37,839
Topeka, KS Metro area	232,594	233,867	224,551	-1,273	9,316	-0.5	4.1	10,703.2	8,556.0	25.1	$46,017	$36,521
Jackson County, KS	13,280	13,460	12,657	-180	803	-1.3	6.3	553.6	438.1	26.4	$41,686	$32,541
Jefferson County, KS	18,975	19,124	18,426	-149	698	-0.8	3.8	844.0	658.2	28.2	$44,480	$34,392
Osage County, KS	15,941	16,294	16,712	-353	-418	-2.2	-2.5	639.3	529.8	20.7	$40,102	$32,555
Shawnee County, KS	177,499	177,934	169,871	-435	8,063	-0.2	4.7	8,317.7	6,652.6	25.0	$46,861	$37,301
Wabaunsee County, KS	6,899	7,055	6,885	-156	170	-2.2	2.5	348.6	277.3	25.7	$50,534	$39,340
Torrington, CT Micro area	181,111	189,925	182,193	-8,814	7,732	-4.6	4.2	11,763.0	9,419.5	24.9	$64,949	$49,627
Litchfield County, CT	181,111	189,925	182,193	-8,814	7,732	-4.6	4.2	11,763.0	9,419.5	24.9	$64,949	$49,627
Traverse City, MI Micro area	149,914	143,365	131,342	6,549	12,023	4.6	9.2	7,543.4	4,995.9	51.0	$50,318	$34,853
Benzie County, MI	17,753	17,524	15,998	229	1,526	1.3	9.5	773.3	535.0	44.5	$43,557	$30,561
Grand Traverse County, MI	92,573	86,981	77,654	5,592	9,327	6.4	12.0	4,687.8	3,126.8	49.9	$50,639	$35,952
Kalkaska County, MI	17,824	17,147	16,571	677	576	3.9	3.5	617.1	447.1	38.0	$34,623	$26,081
Leelanau County, MI	21,764	21,713	21,119	51	594	0.2	2.8	1,465.1	887.0	65.2	$67,320	$40,833
Trenton-Princeton, NJ Metro area	369,811	367,511	350,761	2,300	16,750	0.6	4.8	25,644.2	19,581.2	31.0	$69,344	$53,247
Mercer County, NJ	369,811	367,511	350,761	2,300	16,750	0.6	4.8	25,644.2	19,581.2	31.0	$69,344	$53,247
Troy, AL Micro area	33,338	32,895	29,605	443	3,290	1.3	11.1	1,245.5	1,045.4	19.1	$37,359	$31,714
Pike County, AL	33,338	32,895	29,605	443	3,290	1.3	11.1	1,245.5	1,045.4	19.1	$37,359	$31,714

Table D-1. Population and Personal Income—*Continued*

Metropolitan or Micropolitan Statistical Area Metropolitan Division Component Counties	Population							Personal Income				
	2018 Estimate (July 1)	2010 census estimates base (April 1)	2000 census estimates base (April 1)	Net change		Percent change		Total (million dollars)		Percent change 2010-2018	Per capita	
				2010-2018	2000-2010	2010-2018	2000-2010	2018	2010		2018	2010
Truckee-Grass Valley, CA Micro area	99,696	98,745	92,033	951	6,712	1.0	7.3	6,161.1	4,502.9	36.8	$61,799	$45,583
Nevada County, CA	99,696	98,745	92,033	951	6,712	1.0	7.3	6,161.1	4,502.9	36.8	$61,799	$45,583
Tucson, AZ Metro area	1,039,073	980,263	843,746	58,810	136,517	6.0	16.2	45,748.0	33,444.2	36.8	$44,028	$34,069
Pima County, AZ	1,039,073	980,263	843,746	58,810	136,517	6.0	16.2	45,748.0	33,444.2	36.8	$44,028	$34,069
Tullahoma-Manchester, TN Micro area	104,001	100,209	93,024	3,792	7,185	3.8	7.7	4,046.5	3,064.4	32.0	$38,908	$30,625
Coffee County, TN	55,700	52,803	48,014	2,897	4,789	5.5	10.0	2,153.2	1,647.1	30.7	$38,656	$31,211
Franklin County, TN	41,890	41,064	39,270	826	1,794	2.0	4.6	1,628.7	1,225.7	32.9	$38,880	$29,925
Moore County, TN	6,411	6,342	5,740	69	602	1.1	10.5	264.6	191.6	38.1	$41,276	$30,274
Tulsa, OK Metro area	993,797	937,532	859,532	56,265	78,000	6.0	9.1	54,525.7	38,856.3	40.3	$54,866	$41,344
Creek County, OK	71,604	69,971	67,367	1,633	2,604	2.3	3.9	2,920.8	2,308.7	26.5	$40,791	$32,885
Okmulgee County, OK	38,335	40,069	39,685	-1,734	384	-4.3	1.0	1,302.3	1,104.3	17.9	$33,971	$27,550
Osage County, OK	47,014	47,476	44,437	-462	3,039	-1.0	6.8	1,644.1	1,337.2	23.0	$34,971	$28,150
Pawnee County, OK	16,390	16,579	16,612	-189	-33	-1.1	-0.2	587.3	488.2	20.3	$35,836	$29,411
Rogers County, OK	91,984	86,918	70,641	5,066	16,277	5.8	23.0	4,214.2	2,976.9	41.6	$45,815	$34,217
Tulsa County, OK	648,360	603,437	563,299	44,923	40,138	7.4	7.1	40,688.5	28,355.4	43.5	$62,756	$46,868
Wagoner County, OK	80,110	73,082	57,491	7,028	15,591	9.6	27.1	3,168.4	2,285.7	38.6	$39,550	$31,129
Tupelo, MS Micro area	165,867	161,544	150,807	4,323	10,737	2.7	7.1	6,218.4	4,729.1	31.5	$37,490	$29,268
Itawamba County, MS	23,517	23,401	22,770	116	631	0.5	2.8	816.8	643.8	26.9	$34,734	$27,491
Lee County, MS	85,202	82,910	75,755	2,292	7,155	2.8	9.4	3,572.9	2,662.9	34.2	$41,934	$32,130
Pontotoc County, MS	31,833	29,957	26,726	1,876	3,231	6.3	12.1	1,050.4	786.9	33.5	$32,996	$26,180
Prentiss County, MS	25,315	25,276	25,556	39	-280	0.2	-1.1	778.3	635.5	22.5	$30,743	$25,192
Tuscaloosa, AL Metro area	251,808	239,219	212,983	12,589	26,236	5.3	12.3	9,564.5	7,554.9	26.6	$37,983	$31,546
Greene County, AL	8,233	9,043	9,974	-810	-931	-9.0	-9.3	266.4	239.9	11.0	$32,359	$26,675
Hale County, AL	14,726	15,762	17,185	-1,036	-1,423	-6.6	-8.3	538.7	456.2	18.1	$36,585	$28,974
Pickens County, AL	19,938	19,746	20,949	192	-1,203	1.0	-5.7	649.0	576.6	12.6	$32,551	$29,198
Tuscaloosa County, AL	208,911	194,668	164,875	14,243	29,793	7.3	18.1	8,110.4	6,282.1	29.1	$38,822	$32,217
Twin Falls, ID Metro area	110,096	99,596	82,626	10,500	16,970	10.5	20.5	4,327.7	2,962.1	46.1	$39,309	$29,625
Jerome County, ID	24,015	22,366	18,342	1,649	4,024	7.4	21.9	917.0	647.0	41.7	$38,184	$28,815
Twin Falls County, ID	86,081	77,230	64,284	8,851	12,946	11.5	20.1	3,410.8	2,315.1	47.3	$39,623	$29,859
Tyler, TX Metro area	230,221	209,725	174,706	20,496	35,019	9.8	20.0	12,714.8	8,856.5	43.6	$55,229	$42,092
Smith County, TX	230,221	209,725	174,706	20,496	35,019	9.8	20.0	12,714.8	8,856.5	43.6	$55,229	$42,092
Ukiah, CA Micro area	87,606	87,850	86,265	-244	1,585	-0.3	1.8	4,393.4	3,312.6	32.6	$50,150	$37,729
Mendocino County, CA	87,606	87,850	86,265	-244	1,585	-0.3	1.8	4,393.4	3,312.6	32.6	$50,150	$37,729
Union, SC Micro area	27,410	28,972	29,881	-1,562	-909	-5.4	-3.0	897.5	757.7	18.5	$32,745	$26,193
Union County, SC	27,410	28,972	29,881	-1,562	-909	-5.4	-3.0	897.5	757.7	18.5	$32,745	$26,193
Union City, TN Micro area	30,267	31,807	32,450	-1,540	-643	-4.8	-2.0	1,230.8	1,017.8	20.9	$40,666	$31,986
Obion County, TN	30,267	31,807	32,450	-1,540	-643	-4.8	-2.0	1,230.8	1,017.8	20.9	$40,666	$31,986
Urbana, OH Micro area	38,754	40,099	38,890	-1,345	1,209	-3.4	3.1	1,591.0	1,235.2	28.8	$41,055	$30,821
Champaign County, OH	38,754	40,099	38,890	-1,345	1,209	-3.4	3.1	1,591.0	1,235.2	28.8	$41,055	$30,821
Urban Honolulu, HI Metro area	980,080	953,206	876,156	26,874	77,050	2.8	8.8	58,421.0	43,397.7	34.6	$59,608	$45,381
Honolulu County, HI	980,080	953,206	876,156	26,874	77,050	2.8	8.8	58,421.0	43,397.7	34.6	$59,608	$45,381
Utica-Rome, NY Metro area	291,410	299,330	299,896	-7,920	-566	-2.6	-0.2	12,832.6	10,591.2	21.2	$44,036	$35,395
Herkimer County, NY	61,833	64,461	64,427	-2,628	34	-4.1	0.1	2,571.1	2,113.6	21.6	$41,581	$32,789
Oneida County, NY	229,577	234,869	235,469	-5,292	-600	-2.3	-0.3	10,261.5	8,477.5	21.0	$44,697	$36,111
Uvalde, TX Micro area	26,846	26,405	25,926	441	479	1.7	1.8	1,059.3	793.5	33.5	$39,458	$30,009
Uvalde County, TX	26,846	26,405	25,926	441	479	1.7	1.8	1,059.3	793.5	33.5	$39,458	$30,009
Valdosta, GA Metro area	146,174	139,660	119,560	6,514	20,100	4.7	16.8	5,294.0	4,057.9	30.5	$36,217	$28,973
Brooks County, GA	15,513	16,315	16,450	-802	-135	-4.9	-0.8	542.1	444.7	21.9	$34,944	$27,368
Echols County, GA	4,000	4,027	3,754	-27	273	-0.7	7.3	111.5	79.8	39.7	$27,880	$19,859
Lanier County, GA	10,340	10,070	7,241	270	2,829	2.7	39.1	285.0	215.4	32.3	$27,561	$21,336
Lowndes County, GA	116,321	109,248	92,115	7,073	17,133	6.5	18.6	4,355.5	3,318.0	31.3	$37,443	$30,248
Vallejo, CA Metro area	446,610	413,298	394,542	33,312	18,756	8.1	4.8	23,073.6	15,615.4	47.8	$51,664	$37,723
Solano County, CA	446,610	413,298	394,542	33,312	18,756	8.1	4.8	23,073.6	15,615.4	47.8	$51,664	$37,723
Van Wert, OH Micro area	28,281	28,759	29,659	-478	-900	-1.7	-3.0	1,205.8	918.5	31.3	$42,638	$32,027
Van Wert County, OH	28,281	28,759	29,659	-478	-900	-1.7	-3.0	1,205.8	918.5	31.3	$42,638	$32,027
Vermillion, SD Micro area	14,041	13,868	13,537	173	331	1.2	2.4	554.4	444.3	24.8	$39,485	$32,131
Clay County, SD	14,041	13,868	13,537	173	331	1.2	2.4	554.4	444.3	24.8	$39,485	$32,131
Vernal, UT Micro area	35,438	32,588	25,224	2,850	7,364	8.7	29.2	1,118.5	997.7	12.1	$31,563	$30,728
Uintah County, UT	35,438	32,588	25,224	2,850	7,364	8.7	29.2	1,118.5	997.7	12.1	$31,563	$30,728
Vernon, TX Micro area	12,820	13,535	14,676	-715	-1,141	-5.3	-7.8	539.0	444.6	21.2	$42,041	$32,905
Wilbarger County, TX	12,820	13,535	14,676	-715	-1,141	-5.3	-7.8	539.0	444.6	21.2	$42,041	$32,905
Vicksburg, MS Micro area	46,176	48,771	49,644	-2,595	-873	-5.3	-1.8	1,827.6	1,623.4	12.6	$39,580	$33,243
Warren County, MS	46,176	48,771	49,644	-2,595	-873	-5.3	-1.8	1,827.6	1,623.4	12.6	$39,580	$33,243
Victoria, TX Metro area	99,619	94,003	91,016	5,616	2,987	6.0	3.3	4,579.3	3,420.3	33.9	$45,968	$36,350
Goliad County, TX	7,584	7,210	6,928	374	282	5.2	4.1	332.6	219.0	51.9	$43,858	$30,330
Victoria County, TX	92,035	86,793	84,088	5,242	2,705	6.0	3.2	4,246.7	3,201.4	32.7	$46,142	$36,850
Vidalia, GA Micro area	36,080	36,351	34,337	-271	2,014	-0.7	5.9	1,225.3	1,021.4	20.0	$33,961	$28,065
Montgomery County, GA	9,193	9,181	8,270	12	911	0.1	11.0	270.3	227.9	18.6	$29,408	$24,913
Toombs County, GA	26,887	27,170	26,067	-283	1,103	-1.0	4.2	954.9	793.6	20.3	$35,517	$29,123
Vincennes, IN Micro area	36,895	38,440	39,256	-1,545	-816	-4.0	-2.1	1,646.5	1,330.9	23.7	$44,626	$34,665
Knox County, IN	36,895	38,440	39,256	-1,545	-816	-4.0	-2.1	1,646.5	1,330.9	23.7	$44,626	$34,665
Vineland-Bridgeton, NJ Metro area	150,972	156,633	146,438	-5,661	10,195	-3.6	7.0	6,082.5	5,248.8	15.9	$40,289	$33,495
Cumberland County, NJ	150,972	156,633	146,438	-5,661	10,195	-3.6	7.0	6,082.5	5,248.8	15.9	$40,289	$33,495
Vineyard Haven, MA Micro area	17,352	16,535	14,987	817	1,548	4.9	10.3	1,626.3	1,060.0	53.4	$93,726	$63,965
Dukes County, MA	17,352	16,535	14,987	817	1,548	4.9	10.3	1,626.3	1,060.0	53.4	$93,726	$63,965

Table D-1. Population and Personal Income—*Continued*

Metropolitan or Micropolitan Statistical Area Metropolitan Division Component Counties	Population							Personal Income				
	2018 Estimate (July 1)	2010 census estimates base (April 1)	2000 census estimates base (April 1)	Net change		Percent change		Total (million dollars)		Percent change 2010-2018	Per capita	
				2010-2018	2000-2010	2010-2018	2000-2010	2018	2010		2018	2010
Virginia Beach-Norfolk-Newport News, VA-NC												
Metro area	1,765,042	1,713,954	1,612,770	51,088	101,184	3.0	6.3	89,345.3	69,481.9	28.6	$50,619	$40,467
Camden County, NC	10,710	9,980	6,885	730	3,095	7.3	45.0	485.5	377.7	28.5	$45,335	$37,739
Currituck County, NC	27,072	23,547	18,190	3,525	5,357	15.0	29.5	1,230.0	839.5	46.5	$45,435	$35,462
Gates County, NC	11,573	12,184	10,516	-611	1,668	-5.0	15.9	417.3	369.1	13.1	$36,060	$30,342
Gloucester County, VA	37,349	36,859	34,780	490	2,079	1.3	6.0	1,886.2	1,467.1	28.6	$50,502	$39,715
Isle of Wight County, VA	36,953	35,274	29,728	1,679	5,546	4.8	18.7	2,043.8	1,599.2	27.8	$55,308	$45,286
James City County, VA	76,397	67,385	48,102	9,012	19,283	13.4	40.1	6,016.7	4,195.1	43.4	$65,906	$51,547
Mathews County, VA	8,802	8,976	9,207	-174	-231	-1.9	-2.5	493.7	393.8	25.4	$56,088	$43,882
Southampton County, VA	17,586	18,571	17,482	-985	1,089	-5.3	6.2	1,084.9	822.3	31.9	$42,381	$30,212
York County, VA	67,846	65,239	56,297	2,607	8,942	4.0	15.9	4,731.1	3,743.8	26.4	$59,113	$48,361
Chesapeake City, VA	242,634	222,306	199,184	20,328	23,122	9.1	11.6	12,260.0	9,412.5	30.3	$50,529	$42,105
Franklin City, VA (personal income included with Southampton County)	8,013	8,580	8,346	-567	234	-6.6	2.8	-	-	-	-	-
Hampton City, VA	134,313	137,384	146,437	-3,071	-9,053	-2.2	-6.2	5,849.0	4,939.9	18.4	$43,547	$35,969
Newport News City, VA	178,626	180,994	180,150	-2,368	844	-1.3	0.5	7,770.4	6,377.5	21.8	$43,501	$35,249
Norfolk City, VA	244,076	242,827	234,403	1,249	8,424	0.5	3.6	10,207.9	8,433.4	21.0	$41,822	$34,705
Poquoson City, VA (personal income included with York County)	12,190	12,157	11,566	33	591	0.3	5.1	-	-	-	-	-
Portsmouth City, VA	94,632	95,527	100,565	-895	-5,038	-0.9	-5.0	3,895.9	3,313.2	17.6	$41,169	$34,713
Suffolk City, VA	91,185	84,572	63,677	6,613	20,895	7.8	32.8	4,723.2	3,587.9	31.6	$51,798	$42,298
Virginia Beach City, VA	450,189	437,903	425,257	12,286	12,646	2.8	3.0	26,249.7	19,610.1	33.9	$58,308	$44,685
Williamsburg City, VA (personal included with James City County)	14,896	13,689	11,998	1,207	1,691	8.8	14.1	-	-	-	-	-
Visalia, CA Metro area	465,861	442,181	368,021	23,680	74,160	5.4	20.2	18,830.1	13,499.4	39.5	$40,420	$30,473
Tulare County, CA	465,861	442,181	368,021	23,680	74,160	5.4	20.2	18,830.1	13,499.4	39.5	$40,420	$30,473
Wabash, IN Micro area	31,280	32,888	34,960	-1,608	-2,072	-4.9	-5.9	1,370.7	1,032.0	32.8	$43,820	$31,419
Wabash County, IN	31,280	32,888	34,960	-1,608	-2,072	-4.9	-5.9	1,370.7	1,032.0	32.8	$43,820	$31,419
Waco, TX Metro area	271,942	252,766	232,093	19,176	20,673	7.6	8.9	11,103.7	7,925.2	40.1	$40,831	$31,225
Falls County, TX	17,335	17,867	18,576	-532	-709	-3.0	-3.8	600.1	477.4	25.7	$34,619	$26,678
McLennan County, TX	254,607	234,899	213,517	19,708	21,382	8.4	10.0	10,503.6	7,447.8	41.0	$41,254	$31,570
Wahpeton, ND-MN Micro area	22,493	22,897	25,136	-404	-2,239	-1.8	-8.9	1,233.0	948.8	30.0	$54,817	$41,403
Wilkin County, MN	6,254	6,576	7,138	-322	-562	-4.9	-7.9	372.2	297.1	25.3	$59,516	$45,095
Richland County, ND	16,239	16,321	17,998	-82	-1,677	-0.5	-9.3	860.8	651.7	32.1	$53,007	$39,913
Walla Walla, WA Metro area	60,922	58,781	55,180	2,141	3,601	3.6	6.5	2,811.2	2,049.5	37.2	$46,144	$34,785
Walla Walla County, WA	60,922	58,781	55,180	2,141	3,601	3.6	6.5	2,811.2	2,049.5	37.2	$46,144	$34,785
Wapakoneta, OH Micro area	45,804	45,949	46,611	-145	-662	-0.3	-1.4	2,270.9	1,623.9	39.8	$49,578	$35,357
Auglaize County, OH	45,804	45,949	46,611	-145	-662	-0.3	-1.4	2,270.9	1,623.9	39.8	$49,578	$35,357
Warner Robins, GA Metro area	182,766	167,602	134,433	15,164	33,169	9.0	24.7	7,665.9	5,819.8	31.7	$41,944	$34,542
Houston County, GA	155,469	139,914	110,765	15,555	29,149	11.1	26.3	6,626.8	5,023.5	31.9	$42,625	$35,693
Peach County, GA	27,297	27,688	23,668	-391	4,020	-1.4	17.0	1,039.1	796.3	30.5	$38,066	$28,707
Warren, PA Micro area	39,498	41,811	43,863	-2,313	-2,052	-5.5	-4.7	1,693.5	1,415.8	19.6	$42,875	$33,894
Warren County, PA	39,498	41,811	43,863	-2,313	-2,052	-5.5	-4.7	1,693.5	1,415.8	19.6	$42,875	$33,894
Warrensburg, MO Micro area	53,652	52,595	48,258	1,057	4,337	2.0	9.0	1,973.2	1,522.5	29.6	$36,777	$28,881
Johnson County, MO	53,652	52,595	48,258	1,057	4,337	2.0	9.0	1,973.2	1,522.5	29.6	$36,777	$28,881
Warsaw, IN Micro area	79,344	77,354	74,057	1,990	3,297	2.6	4.5	3,792.6	2,653.0	43.0	$47,799	$34,303
Kosciusko County, IN	79,344	77,354	74,057	1,990	3,297	2.6	4.5	3,792.6	2,653.0	43.0	$47,799	$34,303
Washington, IN Micro area	33,147	31,654	29,820	1,493	1,834	4.7	6.2	1,394.3	1,006.5	38.5	$42,064	$31,730
Daviess County, IN	33,147	31,654	29,820	1,493	1,834	4.7	6.2	1,394.3	1,006.5	38.5	$42,064	$31,730
Washington, NC Micro area	47,079	47,768	44,958	-689	2,810	-1.4	6.3	1,960.5	1,593.9	23.0	$41,643	$33,340
Beaufort County, NC	47,079	47,768	44,958	-689	2,810	-1.4	6.3	1,960.5	1,593.9	23.0	$41,643	$33,340
Washington-Arlington-Alexandria, DC-VA-MD-WV Metro area	6,263,245	5,649,672	4,849,948	613,573	799,724	10.9	16.5	453,978.2	331,670.5	36.9	$72,483	$58,410
Frederick-Gaithersburg-Rockville, MD Div	1,308,215	1,205,355	1,068,618	102,860	136,737	8.5	12.8	110,220.9	80,717.4	36.6	$84,253	$66,682
Frederick County, MD	255,648	233,391	195,277	22,257	38,114	9.5	19.5	15,816.6	11,549.1	37.0	$61,869	$49,312
Montgomery County, MD	1,052,567	971,964	873,341	80,603	98,623	8.3	11.3	94,404.3	69,168.3	36.5	$89,690	$70,848
Washington-Arlington-Alexandria, DC-VA-MD-WV Div	4,955,030	4,444,317	3,781,330	510,713	662,987	11.5	17.5	343,757.3	250,953.1	37.0	$69,375	$56,168
District of Columbia County,	702,455	601,766	572,059	100,689	29,707	16.7	5.2	57,604.8	38,481.5	49.7	$82,005	$63,597
Calvert County, MD	92,003	88,739	74,563	3,264	14,176	3.7	19.0	5,758.5	4,464.4	29.0	$62,591	$50,169
Charles County, MD	161,503	146,565	120,546	14,938	26,019	10.2	21.6	9,213.9	7,033.4	31.0	$57,051	$47,795
Prince George's County, MD	909,308	863,349	801,515	45,959	61,834	5.3	7.7	44,938.2	35,447.5	26.8	$49,420	$40,944
Arlington County, VA	237,521	207,687	189,453	29,834	18,234	14.4	9.6	22,611.4	16,657.9	35.7	$95,198	$79,593
Clarke County, VA	14,523	14,025	12,652	498	1,373	3.6	10.9	974.7	705.4	38.2	$67,111	$50,348
Culpeper County, VA	51,859	46,691	34,262	5,168	12,429	11.1	36.3	2,412.0	1,720.1	40.2	$46,510	$36,724
Fairfax County, VA	1,150,795	1,081,667	969,749	69,128	111,918	6.4	11.5	98,116.8	74,063.9	32.5	$82,441	$66,059
Fauquier County, VA	70,675	65,236	55,139	5,439	10,097	8.3	18.3	5,002.9	3,624.7	38.0	$70,787	$55,384
Loudoun County, VA	406,850	312,348	169,599	94,502	142,749	30.3	84.2	31,762.7	19,977.3	59.0	$78,070	$63,324
Madison County, VA	13,295	13,309	12,520	-14	789	-0.1	6.3	649.1	449.8	44.3	$48,822	$33,815
Prince William County, VA	468,011	401,997	280,813	66,014	121,184	16.4	43.2	28,845.5	21,493.8	34.2	$54,740	$46,843
Rappahannock County, VA	7,252	7,503	6,983	-251	520	-3.3	7.4	475.3	366.6	29.7	$65,538	$48,903
Spotsylvania County, VA	134,238	122,449	90,395	11,789	32,054	9.6	35.5	8,298.2	6,121.4	35.6	$50,790	$41,551
Stafford County, VA	149,960	128,984	92,446	20,976	36,538	16.3	39.5	8,259.2	6,056.4	36.4	$55,076	$46,647
Warren County, VA	40,003	37,435	31,584	2,568	5,851	6.9	18.5	1,869.9	1,384.7	35.0	$46,743	$36,924
Alexandria City, VA	160,530	140,008	128,283	20,522	11,725	14.7	9.1	14,127.9	10,784.5	31.0	$88,008	$76,627
Fairfax City, VA (personal income included with Fairfax County)	24,574	22,554	21,498	2,020	1,056	9.0	4.9	-	-	-	-	-
Falls Church City, VA (personal income included with Fairfax County)	14,772	12,279	10,377	2,493	1,902	20.3	18.3	-	-	-	-	-

Table D-1. Population and Personal Income—*Continued*

Metropolitan or Micropolitan Statistical Area Metropolitan Division Component Counties	Population							Personal Income				
	2018 Estimate (July 1)	2010 census estimates base (April 1)	2000 census estimates base (April 1)	Net change		Percent change		Total (million dollars)		Percent change 2010-2018	Per capita	
				2010-2018	2000-2010	2010-2018	2000-2010	2018	2010		2018	2010
Fredericksburg City, VA (personal income included with Spotsylvania county)..........	29,144	24,178	19,279	4,966	4,899	20.5	25.4	-	-	-	-	-
Manassas City, VA (personal income included with Prince William County)	41,641	37,819	35,135	3,822	2,684	10.1	7.6	-	-	-	-	-
Manassas Park City, VA (personal income included with Prince William County)	17,307	14,241	10,290	3,066	3,951	21.5	38.4	-	-	-	-	-
Jefferson County, WV	56,811	53,488	42,190	3,323	11,298	6.2	26.8	2,836.3	2,119.6	33.8	$49,926	$39,541
Washington Court House, OH Micro area	28,666	29,035	28,433	-369	602	-1.3	2.1	1,102.2	852.0	29.4	$38,449	$29,362
Fayette County, OH.......................	28,666	29,035	28,433	-369	602	-1.3	2.1	1,102.2	852.0	29.4	$38,449	$29,362
Waterloo-Cedar Falls, IA Metro area.....................	169,659	167,819	163,706	1,840	4,113	1.1	2.5	7,815.0	6,037.5	29.4	$46,063	$35,953
Black Hawk County, IA	132,408	131,090	128,012	1,318	3,078	1.0	2.4	5,927.1	4,580.0	29.4	$44,764	$34,917
Bremer County, IA.......................	24,947	24,276	23,325	671	951	2.8	4.1	1,232.5	932.4	32.2	$49,405	$38,377
Grundy County, IA.......................	12,304	12,453	12,369	-149	84	-1.2	0.7	655.4	525.1	24.8	$53,270	$42,130
Watertown, SD Micro area..............	34,126	33,128	31,437	998	1,691	3.0	5.4	1,657.4	1,211.5	36.8	$48,567	$36,561
Codington County, SD...................	28,015	27,225	25,897	790	1,328	2.9	5.1	1,387.2	1,023.8	35.5	$49,518	$37,624
Hamlin County, SD.......................	6,111	5,903	5,540	208	363	3.5	6.6	270.2	187.7	44.0	$44,209	$31,683
Watertown-Fort Atkinson, WI Micro area..............	85,129	83,683	74,021	1,446	9,662	1.7	13.1	3,936.4	2,983.6	31.9	$46,241	$35,638
Jefferson County, WI...................	85,129	83,683	74,021	1,446	9,662	1.7	13.1	3,936.4	2,983.6	31.9	$46,241	$35,638
Watertown-Fort Drum, NY Metro area	111,755	116,234	111,738	-4,479	4,496	-3.9	4.0	5,244.0	4,824.8	8.7	$46,924	$41,381
Jefferson County, NY....................	111,755	116,234	111,738	-4,479	4,496	-3.9	4.0	5,244.0	4,824.8	8.7	$46,924	$41,381
Wauchula, FL Micro area...............	27,245	27,731	26,938	-486	793	-1.8	2.9	770.6	639.4	20.5	$28,285	$23,062
Hardee County, FL.......................	27,245	27,731	26,938	-486	793	-1.8	2.9	770.6	639.4	20.5	$28,285	$23,062
Wausau-Weston, WI Metro area	163,117	162,804	155,475	313	7,329	0.2	4.7	8,053.6	6,009.2	34.0	$49,373	$36,906
Lincoln County, WI.......................	27,689	28,743	29,641	-1,054	-898	-3.7	-3.0	1,267.2	1,003.1	26.3	$45,766	$34,859
Marathon County, WI....................	135,428	134,061	125,834	1,367	8,227	1.0	6.5	6,786.4	5,006.1	35.6	$50,111	$37,345
Waycross, GA Micro area...............	55,069	55,067	51,119	2	3,948	0.0	7.7	1,909.0	1,536.6	24.2	$34,666	$27,872
Pierce County, GA.......................	19,389	18,762	15,636	627	3,126	3.3	20.0	699.3	541.2	29.2	$36,065	$28,768
Ware County, GA.........................	35,680	36,305	35,483	-625	822	-1.7	2.3	1,209.8	995.4	21.5	$33,906	$27,408
Weatherford, OK Micro area...............	29,036	27,469	26,142	1,567	1,327	5.7	5.1	1,209.4	928.3	30.3	$41,652	$33,783
Custer County, OK.......................	29,036	27,469	26,142	1,567	1,327	5.7	5.1	1,209.4	928.3	30.3	$41,652	$33,783
Weirton-Steubenville, WV-OH Metro area............	117,064	124,450	132,008	-7,386	-7,558	-5.9	-5.7	4,737.8	3,844.3	23.2	$40,472	$30,922
Jefferson County, OH....................	65,767	69,711	73,894	-3,944	-4,183	-5.7	-5.7	2,585.4	2,098.3	23.2	$39,311	$30,120
Brooke County, WV......................	22,203	24,067	25,447	-1,864	-1,380	-7.7	-5.4	926.8	743.2	24.7	$41,740	$30,972
Hancock County, WV....................	29,094	30,672	32,667	-1,578	-1,995	-5.1	-6.1	1,225.7	1,002.8	22.2	$42,128	$32,705
Wenatchee, WA Metro area...............	119,943	110,887	99,219	9,056	11,668	8.2	11.8	5,999.7	3,799.6	57.9	$50,021	$34,149
Chelan County, WA......................	77,036	72,460	66,616	4,576	5,844	6.3	8.8	4,218.7	2,616.1	61.3	$54,763	$35,958
Douglas County, WA.....................	42,907	38,427	32,603	4,480	5,824	11.7	17.9	1,781.0	1,183.7	50.5	$41,508	$30,733
West Plains, MO Micro area...............	40,076	40,398	37,238	-322	3,160	-0.8	8.5	1,364.8	1,095.3	24.6	$34,055	$27,001
Howell County, MO......................	40,076	40,398	37,238	-322	3,160	-0.8	8.5	1,364.8	1,095.3	24.6	$34,055	$27,001
West Point, MS Micro area...............	19,386	20,634	21,979	-1,248	-1,345	-6.0	-6.1	759.8	605.6	25.5	$39,191	$29,476
Clay County, MS.........................	19,386	20,634	21,979	-1,248	-1,345	-6.0	-6.1	759.8	605.6	25.5	$39,191	$29,476
Wheeling, WV-OH Metro area...............	140,045	147,960	153,172	-7,915	-5,212	-5.3	-3.4	6,845.5	4,864.3	40.7	$48,881	$32,887
Belmont County, OH.....................	67,505	70,405	70,226	-2,900	179	-4.1	0.3	2,864.2	2,144.9	33.5	$42,429	$30,493
Marshall County, WV....................	30,785	33,107	35,519	-2,322	-2,412	-7.0	-6.8	1,263.0	930.4	35.7	$41,028	$28,135
Ohio County, WV........................	41,755	44,448	47,427	-2,693	-2,979	-6.1	-6.3	2,718.3	1,788.9	52.0	$65,100	$40,205
Whitewater, WI Micro area...............	103,718	102,228	93,759	1,490	8,469	1.5	9.0	5,188.2	3,617.6	43.4	$50,023	$35,398
Walworth County, WI....................	103,718	102,228	93,759	1,490	8,469	1.5	9.0	5,188.2	3,617.6	43.4	$50,023	$35,398
Wichita, KS Metro area...............	637,578	623,063	571,166	14,515	51,897	2.3	9.1	33,060.9	24,196.9	36.6	$51,854	$38,784
Butler County, KS.......................	66,765	65,884	59,482	881	6,402	1.3	10.8	3,081.7	2,416.6	27.5	$46,157	$36,669
Harvey County, KS......................	34,210	34,684	32,869	-474	1,815	-1.4	5.5	1,438.8	1,180.6	21.9	$42,057	$33,984
Sedgwick County, KS...................	513,607	498,358	452,869	15,249	45,489	3.1	10.0	27,620.0	19,776.0	39.7	$53,776	$39,621
Sumner County, KS.....................	22,996	24,137	25,946	-1,141	-1,809	-4.7	-7.0	920.5	823.7	11.8	$40,027	$34,153
Wichita Falls, TX Metro area...............	151,306	151,474	151,524	-168	-50	-0.1	0.0	6,585.9	5,697.9	15.6	$43,527	$37,573
Archer County, TX.......................	8,786	9,055	8,854	-269	201	-3.0	2.3	442.0	354.9	24.5	$50,310	$38,953
Clay County, TX.........................	10,456	10,754	11,006	-298	-252	-2.8	-2.3	442.7	380.7	16.3	$42,335	$35,456
Wichita County, TX......................	132,064	131,665	131,664	399	1	0.3	0.0	5,701.2	4,962.3	14.9	$43,170	$37,650
Williamsport, PA Metro area...............	113,664	116,114	120,044	-2,450	-3,930	-2.1	-3.3	4,981.1	3,971.4	25.4	$43,823	$34,168
Lycoming County, PA....................	113,664	116,114	120,044	-2,450	-3,930	-2.1	-3.3	4,981.1	3,971.4	25.4	$43,823	$34,168
Williston, ND Micro area...............	35,350	22,399	19,761	12,951	2,638	57.8	13.3	2,434.7	1,325.6	83.7	$68,874	$58,687
Williams County, ND....................	35,350	22,399	19,761	12,951	2,638	57.8	13.3	2,434.7	1,325.6	83.7	$68,874	$58,687
Willmar, MN Micro area...............	42,855	42,239	41,203	616	1,036	1.5	2.5	2,342.8	1,691.0	38.5	$54,667	$40,036
Kandiyohi County, MN...................	42,855	42,239	41,203	616	1,036	1.5	2.5	2,342.8	1,691.0	38.5	$54,667	$40,036
Wilmington, NC Metro area...............	294,436	254,881	201,389	39,555	53,492	15.5	26.6	12,752.2	8,743.8	45.8	$43,311	$34,195
New Hanover County, NC...............	232,274	202,683	160,307	29,591	42,376	14.6	26.4	10,519.7	7,165.9	46.8	$45,290	$35,250
Pender County, NC......................	62,162	52,198	41,082	9,964	11,116	19.1	27.1	2,232.5	1,577.9	41.5	$35,914	$30,103
Wilmington, OH Micro area...............	42,057	42,035	40,543	22	1,492	0.1	3.7	1,923.2	1,520.7	26.5	$45,728	$36,284
Clinton County, OH......................	42,057	42,035	40,543	22	1,492	0.1	3.7	1,923.2	1,520.7	26.5	$45,728	$36,284
Wilson, NC Micro area...............	81,455	81,218	73,814	237	7,404	0.3	10.0	3,299.0	2,730.2	20.8	$40,501	$33,588
Wilson County, NC......................	81,455	81,218	73,814	237	7,404	0.3	10.0	3,299.0	2,730.2	20.8	$40,501	$33,588
Winchester, VA-WV Metro area............	139,810	128,475	102,997	11,335	25,478	8.8	24.7	6,735.3	4,708.2	43.1	$48,174	$36,590
Frederick County, VA...................	88,355	78,283	59,209	10,072	19,074	12.9	32.2	5,916.5	4,055.0	45.9	$50,802	$38,724
Winchester City, VA (included with Frederick County).......................	28,108	26,223	23,585	1,885	2,638	7.2	11.2	-	-	-	-	-
Hampshire County, WV.................	23,347	23,969	20,203	-622	3,766	-2.6	18.6	818.7	653.3	25.3	$35,068	$27,264

Table D-1. Population and Personal Income—*Continued*

Metropolitan or Micropolitan Statistical Area / Metropolitan Division / Component Counties	Population							Personal Income				
	2018 Estimate (July 1)	2010 census estimates base (April 1)	2000 census estimates base (April 1)	Net change 2010-2018	Net change 2000-2010	Percent change 2010-2018	Percent change 2000-2010	Total (million dollars) 2018	Total (million dollars) 2010	Percent change 2010-2018	Per capita 2018	Per capita 2010
Winfield, KS Micro area	35,218	36,309	36,291	-1,091	18	-3.0	0.0	1,363.2	1,146.9	18.9	$38,707	$31,585
Cowley County, KS	35,218	36,309	36,291	-1,091	18	-3.0	0.0	1,363.2	1,146.9	18.9	$38,707	$31,585
Winnemucca, NV Micro area	16,786	16,521	16,106	265	415	1.6	2.6	787.7	675.3	16.6	$46,927	$40,724
Humboldt County, NV	16,786	16,521	16,106	265	415	1.6	2.6	787.7	675.3	16.6	$46,927	$40,724
Winona, MN Micro area	50,825	51,461	49,985	-636	1,476	-1.2	3.0	2,543.1	1,803.1	41.0	$50,036	$35,056
Winona County, MN	50,825	51,461	49,985	-636	1,476	-1.2	3.0	2,543.1	1,803.1	41.0	$50,036	$35,056
Winston-Salem, NC Metro area	671,456	640,537	569,207	30,919	71,330	4.8	12.5	30,115.1	22,866.8	31.7	$44,850	$35,657
Davidson County, NC	166,614	162,841	147,246	3,773	15,595	2.3	10.6	6,512.5	5,005.1	30.1	$39,087	$30,732
Davie County, NC	42,733	41,221	34,835	1,512	6,386	3.7	18.3	2,035.4	1,502.9	35.4	$47,630	$36,430
Forsyth County, NC	379,099	350,649	306,067	28,450	44,582	8.1	14.6	18,501.7	13,862.1	33.5	$48,804	$39,449
Stokes County, NC	45,467	47,417	44,711	-1,950	2,706	-4.1	6.1	1,675.4	1,350.9	24.0	$36,850	$28,531
Yadkin County, NC	37,543	38,409	36,348	-866	2,061	-2.3	5.7	1,390.1	1,145.7	21.3	$37,027	$29,810
Wisconsin Rapids-Marshfield, WI Micro area	73,055	74,749	75,555	-1,694	-806	-2.3	-1.1	3,414.8	2,725.4	25.3	$46,743	$36,429
Wood County, WI	73,055	74,749	75,555	-1,694	-806	-2.3	-1.1	3,414.8	2,725.4	25.3	$46,743	$36,429
Woodward, OK Micro area	24,174	24,232	22,561	-58	1,671	-0.2	7.4	1,091.7	852.3	28.1	$45,159	$35,288
Ellis County, OK	3,952	4,151	4,075	-199	76	-4.8	1.9	203.8	166.7	22.3	$51,570	$40,089
Woodward County, OK	20,222	20,081	18,486	141	1,595	0.7	8.6	887.9	685.6	29.5	$43,906	$34,290
Wooster, OH Micro area	115,967	114,516	111,564	1,451	2,952	1.3	2.6	5,107.1	3,689.6	38.4	$44,039	$32,254
Wayne County, OH	115,967	114,516	111,564	1,451	2,952	1.3	2.6	5,107.1	3,689.6	38.4	$44,039	$32,254
Worcester, MA-CT Metro area	947,866	916,764	860,054	31,102	56,710	3.4	6.6	52,891.8	39,446.3	34.1	$55,801	$42,926
Windham County, CT	117,027	118,381	109,091	-1,354	9,290	-1.1	8.5	5,531.1	4,470.1	23.7	$47,264	$37,708
Worcester County, MA	830,839	798,383	750,963	32,456	47,420	4.1	6.3	47,360.7	34,976.2	35.4	$57,003	$43,698
Worthington, MN Micro area	21,924	21,378	20,832	546	546	2.6	2.6	988.8	786.3	25.8	$45,100	$36,697
Nobles County, MN	21,924	21,378	20,832	546	546	2.6	2.6	988.8	786.3	25.8	$45,100	$36,697
Yakima, WA Metro area	251,446	243,240	222,581	8,206	20,659	3.4	9.3	10,907.6	7,829.6	39.3	$43,379	$32,053
Yakima County, WA	251,446	243,240	222,581	8,206	20,659	3.4	9.3	10,907.6	7,829.6	39.3	$43,379	$32,053
Yankton, SD Micro area	22,869	22,438	21,652	431	786	1.9	3.6	1,149.7	889.9	29.2	$50,275	$39,664
Yankton County, SD	22,869	22,438	21,652	431	786	1.9	3.6	1,149.7	889.9	29.2	$50,275	$39,664
York-Hanover, PA Metro area	448,273	435,008	381,751	13,265	53,257	3.0	14.0	22,464.4	17,537.5	28.1	$50,113	$40,279
York County, PA	448,273	435,008	381,751	13,265	53,257	3.0	14.0	22,464.4	17,537.5	28.1	$50,113	$40,279
Youngstown-Warren-Boardman, OH-PA Metro area	538,952	565,781	602,964	-26,829	-37,183	-4.7	-6.2	22,874.8	18,590.7	23.0	$42,443	$32,914
Mahoning County, OH	229,642	238,788	257,555	-9,146	-18,767	-3.8	-7.3	9,897.0	8,275.0	19.6	$43,097	$34,714
Trumbull County, OH	198,627	210,325	225,116	-11,698	-14,791	-5.6	-6.6	8,215.8	6,545.5	25.5	$41,363	$31,193
Mercer County, PA	110,683	116,668	120,293	-5,985	-3,625	-5.1	-3.0	4,762.0	3,770.2	26.3	$43,024	$32,331
Yuba City, CA Metro area	174,848	166,902	139,149	7,946	27,753	4.8	19.9	7,505.4	5,588.1	34.3	$42,925	$33,441
Sutter County, CA	96,807	94,756	78,930	2,051	15,826	2.2	20.1	4,311.3	3,308.8	30.3	$44,535	$34,920
Yuba County, CA	78,041	72,146	60,219	5,895	11,927	8.2	19.8	3,194.1	2,279.3	40.1	$40,929	$31,504
Yuma, AZ Metro area	212,128	195,750	160,026	16,378	35,724	8.4	22.3	7,569.1	5,368.9	41.0	$35,682	$27,234
Yuma County, AZ	212,128	195,750	160,026	16,378	35,724	8.4	22.3	7,569.1	5,368.9	41.0	$35,682	$27,234
Zanesville, OH Micro area	86,183	86,086	84,585	97	1,501	0.1	1.8	3,500.2	2,650.4	32.1	$40,614	$30,743
Muskingum County, OH	86,183	86,086	84,585	97	1,501	0.1	1.8	3,500.2	2,650.4	32.1	$40,614	$30,743
Zapata, TX Micro area	14,190	14,018	12,182	172	1,836	1.2	15.1	401.5	334.9	19.9	$28,294	$23,775
Zapata County, TX	14,190	14,018	12,182	172	1,836	1.2	15.1	401.5	334.9	19.9	$28,294	$23,775

APPENDIXES

APPENDIX A.
SOURCE NOTES AND EXPLANATIONS

This appendix presents General Notes on population and economic and government censuses followed by source notes and explanations of the data items presented in table sets A through D of this publication. These table sets vary in both geographic and data coverage.

Each table set begins with the table number and title, followed by the source citation for these items, and related definitions and other explanatory text on the source.

GENERAL NOTES

Population

Decennial censuses. The population statistics for 2010 and earlier are based on results from the censuses of population and housing, conducted by the U.S. Census Bureau as of April 1 in each of those years. As provided by Article 1, Section 2, of the U.S. Constitution, adopted in 1787, a census has been taken every 10 years since 1790. The original purposes of the census were to apportion the seats in the U.S. House of Representatives based on the population of each state and to derive an equitable tax on each state for the payment of the Revolutionary War debt. Through the years, the nation's needs and interests have become more complex, and the content of the decennial census has changed accordingly. At present, census data not only are used to apportion seats in the House and to aid legislators in the realignment of legislative district boundaries but are also used in the distribution of billions of federal dollars each year and are vital to state and local governments and to private firms for such functions as market analysis, site selection, and environmental impact studies.

The decennial censuses prior to 2010 used both short- and long-form questionnaires to gather information. The short form asked a limited number of basic questions. These questions were asked of all people and housing units and are often referred to as 100 percent questions because they were asked of the entire population. In 2010, these became the only questions because the long-form questionnaire has been replaced by the American Community Survey. The population items include sex, age, race, Hispanic or Latino, household relationship, and group quarters. Housing items include occupancy status, vacancy status, tenure (owner occupied or renter occupied), and mortgage status. The long form of the earlier censuses asked more detailed information on a sample basis and included the 100 percent questions as well as questions on education, employment, income, ancestry, homeowner costs, units in a structure, number of rooms, etc. For information about the 2010 census, see www.census.gov/2010census/. For information about the 2000 census, see www.census.gov/main/www/cen2000.html.

Persons enumerated in the census were counted as inhabitants of their usual place of residence, which generally means the place where a person lives and sleeps most of the time. This place is not necessarily the same as the legal residence, voting residence, or domicile. In the vast majority of cases, however, the use of these different bases of classification would produce substantially the same statistics, although appreciable differences may exist for a few areas.

The implementation of this usual-residence practice has resulted in the establishment of residence rules for certain categories of persons whose usual place of residence is not immediately apparent (e.g., college students were counted at their college residence). As in the above example, persons were not always counted as residents of the place where they happened to be staying on census day. However, persons without a usual place of residence were counted where they were enumerated.

For links to information on procedures and concepts used for the 2010 Census of Population and Housing, as well as a facsimile of the questionnaires and descriptions of the data products resulting from the census, see U.S. Census Bureau, see www.census.gov/programs-surveys/decennial-census/data/datasets.2010.html.

Population estimates. The U.S. Census Bureau annually produces estimates of resident population for each state and county using a component of population change method at the county level. To produce the state population estimates, all county populations within each state are summed.

The Census Bureau develops county population estimates with a component of population change method in which they use administrative records and other data to estimate the household and group quarters population.

For the household population, the components of population change are births, deaths, net domestic migration, and net international migration. The Census Bureau measures change in the nonhousehold, or group quarters, population by the net change in the population living in group quarters facilities.

A major assumption underlying this approach is that changes in selected administrative and other data sources closely approximate the components of population change. Therefore, Census Bureau demographers separately estimate each component of population change based on administrative records, including registered births and deaths, federal income tax returns, medicare enrollees, and military movement. The Census Bureau also separately estimates net international migration using information from the American Community Survey (ACS), the decennial census, and other data sources.

Most administrative record data sources lag the current estimate year by as much as 2 years. As a result, the Census Bureau projects the data for the current year based on past years' data. As updated data become available, the Census Bureau revises the projected input data so that each vintage's estimates are always based on the most recent data available.

The Census Bureau produces the estimate of each county's population, starting with the base population from either the 2010 census (for the July 1, 2010, estimates) or the revised population estimate for the prior year (for the July 1, 2011, and later estimates). The Census Bureau then adds or subtracts the demographic components of population change calculated for that time period. The Census Bureau will then add the estimates of net domestic migration, net international migration and the net change in the group quarters population.

State and county estimates may also incorporate other changes due to corrections made since the 2010 census. The corrections occur outside the component estimation framework and are the result of successful local challenges or special censuses.

The results of the 2010 census are used as the base population for subsequent annual population estimates. The enumerated resident population in the 2010 census is the starting point for the post-2010 population estimates. The Census Bureau will modify this enumerated population in two ways to produce the April 1, 2010, population estimates base. First, they reconcile the Census 2010 race categories with the race categories that appear in their administrative records data by recoding the "Some other race" 2010 census responses to one or more of the five 1997 Office of Management and Budget (OMB) race categories: White, Black or African American, American

Indian and Alaska Native, Asian, and Native Hawaiian and Other Pacific Islander. Second, they update the population estimates base to reflect changes to the 2010 census population due to the Count Question Resolution program, legal boundary updates and other geographic program revisions.

The birth and death components are estimated using data from two sources. Where possible, members of the Federal State Cooperative Program for Population Estimates (FSCPE) provide summary data on all registered births and deaths to residents of their respective states and counties from 2010 to the most recent calendar year. The National Center for Health Statistics (NCHS) also provides birth and death data, but these data are not as current as those available from members of the FSCPE. However, the NCHS data include individual record data on each registered birth and death by state, county, month, sex, race, Hispanic origin, and age (for deaths). Where FSCPE vital data are not available, only NCHS data is used.

County birth totals from FSCPE and NCHS sources are controlled to the national NCHS birth total for the corresponding year. Then the county-level sex, race, and Hispanic origin distribution of NCHS births for that year is applied to these totals to derive births for each demographic group for all U.S. counties. Estimates of annual deaths for demographic groups are calculated in similar fashion. The Census Bureau reconciles county death totals from the two data sources to the NCHS national death total for the corresponding year and assigns the county-level age, sex, race, and Hispanic origin distribution of NCHS deaths for that year. Since they produce estimates for July 1 of each year, the Census Bureau uses the NCHS month-of-occurrence information to derive births and deaths for the July 1 to June 30 period for each year.

The Census Bureau produces separate population estimates for the populations under 18, age 18 to 64 and age 65 and over, mainly because different data are used to measure the domestic migration of these three populations. To determine the net domestic migration for the population under the age of 65, the Census Bureau uses data derived from federal income tax returns supplied by the Internal Revenue Service (IRS). The data used is limited to filers and their dependents under 65.

To calculate net domestic migration rates the Census Bureau will subtract the out-migrants from the in-migrants for each county to produce the number of net migrants. Then, they will divide the number of IRS-based net migrants in each county by the number of individuals represented on the tax returns in the first year in each county.

To determine the net migration for the age of 65 and over, the Census Bureau uses medicare enrollment data from the Centers for Medicare and Medicaid (CMS.)

International migration is considered any change of residence across the borders of the United States (50 states and District of Columbia). The net international migration component of the population estimates combines four parts: (a) net international migration of the foreign born, (b) net migration between the United States and Puerto Rico, (c) net migration of natives to and from the United States, and (d) net movement of the Armed Forces population between the United States and overseas.

Net international migration of the foreign-born population is estimated in two parts, immigration and emigration. The estimate of immigration utilizes information from the American Community Survey (ACS) on the reported residence of the foreign-born population in the prior year. The foreign born who reported being abroad in the year prior to the survey are considered immigrants.

Group quarters population data are used from two sources to estimate the change in the group quarters (GQ) populations: (1) Census 2010 group quarters population by single year of age and facility type (i.e., correctional institutions, juvenile facilities, nursing homes, other institutional facilities, university dormitories, military barracks, other non-institutional facilities) for each sub-county area (e.g., cities and towns) and (2) a time series of individual GQ records from the Group Quarters Report (GQR) prepared by the FSCPE members.

For further elaboration and explanation regarding Census Bureau methodology for population estimates, including information on net international migration, group quarters population, and estimations of the county populations, see https://www.census.gov/programs-surveys/popest/technical-documentation/methodology.html

American Community Survey

The American Community Survey (ACS) is a nationwide survey designed to provide communities with a fresh look at how they are changing. It was designed to eliminate the need for the long form in the 2010 and subsequent censuses. The ACS collects information from U.S. households similar to what was collected on the 2000 census long form, such as income, commute time to work, home value, veteran status, and other important data. As with the official U.S. census, information about individuals will remain confidential.

The ACS collects and produces population and housing information every year instead of every 10 years. About three million households are surveyed each year.

Collecting data every year reduces the cost of the official decennial census and provides more up-to-date information throughout the decade about trends in the U.S. population at the local community level. The ACS began in 1996 and has expanded each subsequent year.

Each year, 1-year estimates are available for geographic areas with a population of 65,000 or more. This includes the nation, all states and the District of Columbia, all congressional districts, approximately 800 counties, and 500 metropolitan and micropolitan statistical areas, among others. Between 2008 and 2012, the ACS released 3-year estimates for geographic areas with a population of 20,000 or more, including the nation, all states and the District of Columbia, all congressional districts, approximately 1,800 counties, and 900 metropolitan and micropolitan statistical areas, among others. When these 3-year estimates were discontinued, they were replaced by 1-year Supplemental Estimates with less detail than the regular 1-year estimates, but providing data for geographic areas with 20,000 to 65,000 residents. For areas with a population less than 20,000, 5-year estimates are available. The first 5-year estimates, based on the ACS data collected from 2005 through 2009, were released in 2010. Since then, 5-year estimates are released every year.

More information on the American Community Survey can be found at www.census.gov/acs/www.

Economic Censuses

The economic census is the major source of facts about the structure and functioning of the nation's economy. It provides essential information for government, business, industry, and the general public. It furnishes an important part of the framework for such composite measures as the gross domestic product estimates, input/output measures, production and price indexes, and other statistical series that measure short-term changes in economic conditions. Title 13 of the U.S. Code (Sections 131, 191, and 224) directs the Census Bureau to take the economic census every 5 years, covering years ending in "2" and "7." The economic censuses form an integrated program at 5-year intervals since 1967 and before that for 1963, 1958, and 1954. Prior to that time, the individual censuses were taken separately at varying intervals. Beginning with the 1997 Economic Census data, the census presents data based on the North American Industry Classification System.

The economic censuses are collected on an establishment basis. An establishment is generally a single physical location where business is conducted or where services or industrial operations are performed (e.g., factory, mill, store, hotel, movie theater, mine, farm, airline terminal, sales office, warehouse, or central administrative office). A company operating at more than one location is required to file a separate report for each store, factory, shop, or other location. Each establishment is assigned a separate industry classification based on its primary activity and not that of its parent company. Establishments responding to the establishment survey are classified into industries on the basis of their principal product or activity (determined by annual sales volume) in accordance with the *North American Industry Classification System—United States, 2017* manual available at https:// www.census.gov/cgi-bin/sssd/naics/naicsrch?chart=2017.

More detailed information about the scope, coverage, classification system, data items, and publications for each of the economic censuses and related surveys can be found at https://www.census.gov/programs-surveys/ economic-census.html.

Data from the 2017 Economic Census are currently being released through the Census Bureau's data.census.gov, the Census Bureau's online system for access and dissemination of data. The 2017 data were not available in time for this book.

North American Industry Classification System (NAICS) Sector

The North American Industry Classification System (NAICS) was developed under the direction and guidance of the Office of Management and Budget (OMB) as the standard for use by federal statistical agencies in classifying business establishments for the collection, tabulation, presentation, and analysis of statistical data describing the U.S. economy. Use of the standard provides uniformity and comparability in the presentation of these statistical data. NAICS is based on a production-oriented concept, meaning that it groups establishments into industries according to similarity in the processes used to produce goods or services. Previous census data were presented based on the Standard Industrial Classification (SIC) system developed in 1937. Due to this change, comparability between census years and data found in previous books will be limited.

There are 20 NAICS sectors, which are further subdivided into subsectors (three-digit codes), industry groups (four-digit codes), and, as implemented in the United States, industries (five- and six-digit codes). For more information regarding the classifications see https://www.census. gov/cgi-bin/sssd/naics/naicsrch?chart=2017

The **Agriculture, Forestry, Fishing, and Hunting** (NAICS 11) sector comprises establishments primarily engaged in growing crops, raising animals, harvesting timber, and harvesting fish and other animals from a farm, ranch, or their natural habitats.

The establishments in this sector are often described as farms, ranches, dairies, greenhouses, nurseries, orchards, or hatcheries. A farm may consist of a single tract of land or a number of separate tracts, which may be held under different tenures. For example, one tract may be owned by the farm operator and another rented. It may be operated by the operator alone or with the assistance of members of the household or hired employees, or it may be operated by a partnership, corporation, or other type of organization. When a landowner has one or more tenants, renters, croppers, or managers, the land operated by each is considered a farm. The sector distinguishes two basic activities: agricultural production and agricultural support activities. Agricultural production includes establishments performing the complete farm or ranch operation, such as farm owner-operators, tenant farm operators, and sharecroppers. Agricultural support activities include establishments that perform one or more activities associated with farm operation, such as soil preparation, planting, harvesting, and management, on a contract or fee basis.

Excluded from the Agriculture, Forestry, Fishing, and Hunting sector are establishments primarily engaged in agricultural research and establishments primarily engaged in administering programs for regulating and conserving land, mineral, wildlife, and forest use. These establishments are classified in Industry 54171, Research and Development in the Physical, Engineering, and Life Sciences; and Industry 92412, Administration of Conservation Programs, respectively.

For information on the subsectors of Agriculture, Forestry, Fishing, and Hunting (NAICS 11), see <www.census.gov/eos/www/naics/>.

The **Mining, Quarrying, and Oil and Gas Extraction** sector (NAICS 21) comprises establishments that extract naturally occurring mineral solids, such as coal and ores; liquid minerals, such as crude petroleum; and gases, such as natural gas. The term mining is used in the broad sense to include quarrying, well operations, beneficiating (e.g., crushing, screening, washing, and flotation), and other preparation customarily performed at the mine site or as a part of mining activity.

The Mining, Quarrying, and Oil and Gas Extraction sector distinguishes two basic activities: mine operation and mining support activities. Mine operation includes establishments operating mines, quarries, or oil and gas wells on their own account or for others on a contract or fee basis. Mining support activities include establishments that perform exploration (except geophysical surveying) and/ or other mining services on a contract or fee basis (except mine site preparation and construction of oil/gas pipelines).

Establishments in the Mining, Quarrying, and Oil and Gas Extraction sector are grouped and classified according to the natural resource mined or to be mined. Industries include establishments that develop the mine site, extract the natural resources, and/or those that beneficiate (i.e., prepare) the mineral mined. Beneficiation is the process whereby the extracted material is reduced to particles that can be separated into mineral and waste, the former suitable for further processing or direct use. The operations that take place in beneficiation are primarily mechanical, such as grinding, washing, magnetic separation, and centrifugal separation. In contrast, manufacturing operations primarily use chemical and electrochemical processes, such as electrolysis and distillation. However, some treatments, such as heat treatments, take place in both the beneficiation and the manufacturing (i.e., smelting/refining) stages. The range of preparation activities varies by mineral and the purity of any given ore deposit. While some minerals, such as petroleum and natural gas, require little or no preparation, others are washed and screened, while yet others, such as gold and silver, can be transformed into bullion before leaving the mine site.

Mining, beneficiating, and manufacturing activities often occur in a single location. Separate receipts will be collected for these activities whenever possible. When receipts cannot be broken out between mining and manufacturing, establishments that mine or quarry nonmetallic minerals, and then beneficiate the nonmetallic minerals into more finished manufactured products are classified based on the primary activity of the establishment. A mine that manufactures a small amount of finished products will be classified in Sector 21, Mining, Quarrying, and Oil and Gas Extraction. An establishment that mines whose primary output is a more finished manufactured product will be classified in Sector 31–33, Manufacturing.

For information on the subsectors of Mining, Quarrying, and Oil and Gas Extraction (NAICS 21), see <www.census.gov/eos/www/naics/>.

The **Utilities** sector (NAICS 22) comprises establishments engaged in the provision of the following utility services: electric power, natural gas, steam supply, water supply, and sewage removal. Within this sector, the specific activities associated with the utility services provided vary by utility: electric power includes generation, transmission, and distribution; natural gas includes distribution; steam supply includes provision and/or distribution; water supply includes treatment and distribution; and sewage removal includes collection, treatment, and disposal of waste through sewer systems and sewage treatment facilities.

Excluded from this sector are establishments primarily engaged in waste management services classified in Subsector 562, Waste Management and Remediation

Services. These establishments also collect, treat, and dispose of waste materials; however, they do not use sewer systems or sewage treatment facilities.

For information on the subsectors of Utilities (NAICS 22), see <www.census.gov/eos/www/naics/>.

The **Construction** sector (NAICS 23) comprises establishments primarily engaged in the construction of buildings or engineering projects (e.g., highways and utility systems). Establishments primarily engaged in the preparation of sites for new construction and establishments primarily engaged in subdividing land for sale as building sites also are included in this sector.

Construction work done may include new work, additions, alterations, or maintenance and repairs. Activities of these establishments generally are managed at a fixed place of business, but they usually perform construction activities at multiple project sites. Production responsibilities for establishments in this sector are usually specified in (1) contracts with the owners of construction projects (prime contracts) or (2) contracts with other construction establishments (subcontracts).

Establishments primarily engaged in contracts that include responsibility for all aspects of individual construction projects are commonly known as general contractors, but also may be known as design-builders, construction managers, turnkey contractors, or (in cases where two or more establishments jointly secure a general contract) joint-venture contractors. Construction managers that provide oversight and scheduling only (i.e., agency) as well as construction managers that are responsible for the entire project (i.e., at risk) are included as general contractor type establishments. Establishments of the "general contractor type" frequently arrange construction of separate parts of their projects through subcontracts with other construction establishments.

Establishments primarily engaged in activities to produce a specific component (e.g., masonry, painting, and electrical work) of a construction project are commonly known as specialty trade contractors. Activities of specialty trade contractors are usually subcontracted from other construction establishments, but especially in remodeling and repair construction, the work may be done directly for the owner of the property.

Establishments primarily engaged in activities to construct buildings to be sold on sites that they own are known as operative builders, but also may be known as speculative builders or merchant builders. Operative builders produce buildings in a manner similar to general contractors, but their production processes also include site acquisition and securing of financial backing.

Operative builders are most often associated with the construction of residential buildings. Like general contractors, they may subcontract all or part of the actual construction work on their buildings.

There are substantial differences in the types of equipment, work force skills, and other inputs required by establishments in this sector. To highlight these differences and variations in the underlying production functions, this sector is divided into three subsectors.

Subsector 236, Construction of Buildings, comprises establishments of the general contractor type and operative builders involved in the construction of buildings. Subsector 237, Heavy and Civil Engineering Construction, comprises establishments involved in the construction of engineering projects. Subsector 238, Specialty Trade Contractors, comprises establishments engaged in specialty trade activities generally needed in the construction of all types of buildings. Force account construction is construction work performed by an enterprise primarily engaged in some business other than construction for its own account and use, using employees of the enterprise. This activity is not included in the construction sector unless the construction work performed is the primary activity of a separate establishment of the enterprise. The installation and the ongoing repair and maintenance of telecommunications and utility networks are excluded from construction when the establishments performing the work are not independent contractors. Although a growing proportion of this work is subcontracted to independent contractors in the Construction Sector, the operating units of telecommunications and utility companies performing this work are included with the telecommunications or utility activities.

For information on the subsectors of Construction (NAICS 23), see <www.census.gov/eos/www/naics/>.

The **Manufacturing** sector (NAICS 31–33) comprises establishments engaged in the mechanical, physical, or chemical transformation of materials, substances, or components into new products. The assembling of component parts of manufactured products is considered manufacturing, except in cases where the activity is appropriately classified in Sector 23, Construction.

Establishments in the Manufacturing sector are often described as plants, factories, or mills and characteristically use power-driven machines and materials-handling equipment. However, establishments that transform materials or substances into new products by hand or in the workers home and those engaged in selling to the general public products made on the same premises from which they are sold, such as bakeries, candy stores, and custom tailors, may also be included in this sector.

Manufacturing establishments may process materials or may contract with other establishments to process their materials for them. Both types of establishments are included in manufacturing.

The materials, substances, or components transformed by manufacturing establishments are raw materials that are products of agriculture, forestry, fishing, mining, or quarrying as well as products of other manufacturing establishments. The materials used may be purchased directly from producers, obtained through customary trade channels, or secured without recourse to the market by transferring the product from one establishment to another, under the same ownership.

The new product of a manufacturing establishment may be finished in the sense that it is ready for utilization or consumption, or it may be semifinished to become an input for an establishment engaged in further manufacturing. For example, the product of the alumina refinery is the input used in the primary production of aluminum; primary aluminum is the input to an aluminum wire drawing plant; and aluminum wire is the input for a fabricated wire product manufacturing establishment.

The subsectors in the Manufacturing sector generally reflect distinct production processes related to material inputs, production equipment, and employee skills. In the machinery area, where assembling is a key activity, parts and accessories for manufactured products are classified in the industry of the finished manufactured item when they are made for separate sale. For example, a replacement refrigerator door would be classified with refrigerators and an attachment for a piece of metal working machinery would be classified with metal working machinery. However, components, input from other manufacturing establishments, are classified based on the production function of the component manufacturer. For example, electronic components are classified in Subsector 334, Computer and Electronic Product Manufacturing and stampings are classified in Subsector 332, Fabricated Metal Product Manufacturing.

Manufacturing establishments often perform one or more activities that are classified outside the Manufacturing sector of NAICS. For instance, almost all manufacturing has some captive research and development or administrative operations, such as accounting, payroll, or management. These captive services are treated the same as captive manufacturing activities. When the services are provided by separate establishments, they are classified to the NAICS sector where such services are primary, not in manufacturing.

The boundaries of manufacturing and the other sectors of the classification system can be somewhat blurry. The establishments in the manufacturing sector are engaged in the transformation of materials into new products. Their output is a new product. However, the definition of what constitutes a new product can be somewhat subjective. As clarification, the following activities are considered manufacturing in NAICS: Milk bottling and pasteurizing; Grinding of lenses to prescription; Water bottling and processing; Wood preserving; Fresh fish packaging (oyster shucking, electroplating, plating, metal heat fish filleting); Treating and polishing for the trade; Apparel jobbing (assigning of materials lapidary work for the trade, to contract factories or shops for fabricating signs and advertising displays, fabrication or other contract operations); Rebuilding or remanufacturing as well as contracting on materials owned by others; Machinery (i.e., automotive parts); Printing and related activities; Ship repair and renovation; Ready-mixed concrete production; Machine shops; Leather converting; and Tire retreading.

Conversely, there are activities that are sometimes considered manufacturing, but which for NAICS are classified in another sector (i.e., not classified as manufacturing). They include: (1) Logging, classified in Sector 11, Agriculture, Forestry, Fishing, and Hunting, is considered a harvesting operation; (2) The beneficiating of ores and other minerals, classified in Sector 21, Mining, Quarrying, and Oil and Gas Extraction, is considered part of the activity of mining; (3) The construction of structures and fabricating operations performed at the site of construction by contractors, is classified in Sector 23, Construction; (4) Establishments engaged in breaking of bulk and redistribution in smaller lots, including packaging, repackaging, or bottling products, such as liquors or chemicals; the customized assembly of computers; sorting of scrap; mixing paints to customer order; and cutting metals to customer order, classified in Sector 42, Wholesale Trade or Sector 44–45, Retail Trade, produce a modified version of the same product, not a new product; and (5) Publishing and the combined activity of publishing and printing, classified in Sector 51, Information, perform the transformation of information into a product whereas the value of the product to the consumer lies in the information content, not in the format in which it is distributed (i.e., the book or CD-ROM).

For information on the subsectors of Manufacturing (NAICS 31–33), see https://www.census.gov/eos/www/naics/.

The **Wholesale Trade** sector (NAICS 42) comprises establishments engaged in wholesaling merchandise, generally without transformation, and rendering services incidental to the sale of merchandise. The merchandise described in this sector includes the outputs of agriculture, mining, manufacturing, and certain information industries, such as publishing.

The wholesaling process is an intermediate step in the distribution of merchandise. Wholesalers are organized to sell or arrange the purchase or sale of (a) goods for resale (i.e., goods sold to other wholesalers or retailers), (b) capital or durable nonconsumer goods, and (c) raw and intermediate materials and supplies used in production.

Wholesalers sell merchandise to other businesses and normally operate from a warehouse or office. These warehouses and offices are characterized by having little or no display of merchandise. In addition, neither the design nor the location of the premises is intended to solicit walk-in traffic. Wholesalers do not normally use advertising directed to the general public. Customers are generally reached initially via telephone, in-person marketing, or by specialized advertising that may include internet and other electronic means. Follow-up orders are either vendor-initiated or client-initiated, generally based on previous sales, and typically exhibit strong ties between sellers and buyers. In fact, transactions are often conducted between wholesalers and clients that have long-standing business relationships.

This sector comprises two main types of wholesalers: merchant wholesalers that sell goods on their own account and business-to-business electronic markets, agents, and brokers that arrange sales and purchases for others generally for a commission or fee.

1. Establishments that sell goods on their own account are known as wholesale merchants, distributors, jobbers, drop shippers, and import/export merchants. Also included as wholesale merchants are sales offices and sales branches (but not retail stores) maintained by manufacturing, refining, or mining enterprises apart from their plants or mines for the purpose of marketing their products. Merchant wholesale establishments typically maintain their own warehouse where they receive and handle goods for their customers. Goods are generally sold without transformation, but may include integral functions, such as sorting, packaging, labeling, and other marketing services.

2. Establishments arranging for the purchase or sale of goods owned by others or purchasing goods, generally on a commission basis are known as business-to-business electronic markets, agents and brokers, commission merchants, import/export agents and brokers, auction companies, and manufacturers representatives. These establishments operate from offices and generally do not own or handle the goods they sell.

Some wholesale establishments may be connected with a single manufacturer and promote and sell the particular manufacturers' products to a wide range of other wholesalers or retailers. Other wholesalers may be connected to a retail chain, or limited number of retail chains, and only provide a variety of products needed by that particular retail operation(s). These wholesalers may obtain the products from a wide range of manufacturers. Still other wholesalers may not take title to the goods, but act as agents and brokers for a commission.

Although, in general, wholesaling normally denotes sales in large volumes, durable nonconsumer goods may be sold in single units. Sales of capital or durable nonconsumer goods used in the production of goods and services, such as farm machinery, medium and heavy-duty trucks, and industrial machinery, are always included in Wholesale trade. For information on the subsectors of Wholesale Trade sector (NAICS 42), see <www.census.gov/eos/www/naics/>.

The **Retail Trade** sector (NAICS 44–45) comprises establishments engaged in retailing merchandise, generally without transformation, and rendering services incidental to the sale of merchandise.

The retailing process is the final step in the distribution of merchandise; retailers are, therefore, organized to sell merchandise in small quantities to the general public. This sector comprises two main types of retailers: store and nonstore retailers.

Store retailers operate fixed point-of-sale locations, located and designed to attract a high volume of walk-in customers. In general, retail stores have extensive displays of merchandise and use mass-media advertising to attract customers. They typically sell merchandise to the general public for personal or household consumption, but some also serve business and institutional clients. These include establishments, such as office supply stores, computer and software stores, building materials dealers, plumbing supply stores, and electrical supply stores. Catalog showrooms, gasoline stations, automotive dealers, and mobile home dealers are treated as store retailers.

In addition to retailing merchandise, some types of store retailers are also engaged in the provision of after-sales services, such as repair and installation. For example, new automobile dealers, electronics and appliance stores, and musical instrument and supplies stores often provide repair services. As a general rule, establishments engaged in retailing merchandise and providing after-sales services are classified in this sector.

The first 11 subsectors of retail trade are store retailers. The establishments are grouped into industries and industry groups typically based on one or more of the following criteria:

1. The merchandise line or lines carried by the store; for example, specialty stores are distinguished from general-line stores.

2. The usual trade designation of the establishments. This criterion applies in cases where a store type is well recognized by the industry and the public, but difficult to define strictly in terms of merchandise lines carried; for example, pharmacies, hardware stores, and department stores.

3. Capital requirements in terms of display equipment; for example, food stores have equipment requirements not found in other retail industries.

4. Human resource requirements in terms of expertise; for example, the staff of an automobile dealer requires knowledge in financing, registering, and licensing issues that are not necessary in other retail industries.

Nonstore retailers, like store retailers, are organized to serve the general public, but their retailing methods differ. The establishments of this subsector reach customers and market merchandise with methods, such as the broadcasting of "infomercials," the broadcasting and publishing of direct-response advertising, the publishing of paper and electronic catalogs, door-to-door solicitation, in-home demonstration, selling from portable stalls (street vendors, except food), and distribution through vending machines. Establishments engaged in the direct sale (nonstore) of products, such as home heating oil dealers and home delivery newspaper routes are included here.

The buying of goods for resale is a characteristic of retail trade establishments that particularly distinguishes them from establishments in the agriculture, manufacturing, and construction industries. For example, farms that sell their products at or from the point of production are not classified in retail, but rather in agriculture. Similarly, establishments that both manufacture and sell their products to the general public are not classified in retail, but rather in manufacturing. However, establishments that engage in processing activities incidental to retailing are classified in retail. This includes establishments, such as optical goods stores that do in-store grinding of lenses, and meat and seafood markets.

Wholesalers also engage in the buying of goods for resale, but they are not usually organized to serve the general public. They typically operate from a warehouse or office and neither the design nor the location of these premises is intended to solicit a high volume of walk-in traffic. Wholesalers supply institutional, industrial, wholesale, and retail clients; their operations are, therefore, generally organized to purchase, sell, and deliver merchandise in larger quantities. However, dealers of durable nonconsumer goods, such as farm machinery and heavy-duty trucks, are included in wholesale trade even if they often sell these products in single units.

For information on the subsectors of Retail Trade (NAICS 44–45), see <www.census.gov/eos/www /naics/>.

The **Transportation and Warehousing** sector (NAICS 48–49) includes industries providing transportation of passengers and cargo, warehousing and storage for goods, scenic and sightseeing transportation, and support activities related to modes of transportation. Establishments in these industries use transportation equipment or transportation related facilities as a productive asset. The type of equipment depends on the mode of transportation. The modes of transportation are air, rail, water, road, and pipeline.

The Transportation and Warehousing sector distinguishes three basic types of activities: subsectors for each mode of transportation, a subsector for warehousing and storage, and a subsector for establishments providing support activities for transportation. In addition, there are subsectors for establishments that provide passenger transportation for scenic and sightseeing purposes, postal services, and courier services.

A separate subsector for support activities is established in the sector because, first, support activities for transportation are inherently multimodal, such as freight transportation arrangement, or have multimodal aspects. Secondly, there are production process similarities among the support activity industries.

One of the support activities identified in the support activity subsector is the routine repair and maintenance of transportation equipment (e.g., aircraft at an airport, railroad rolling stock at a railroad terminal, or ships at a harbor or port facility). Such establishments do not perform complete overhauling or rebuilding of transportation equipment (i.e., periodic restoration of transportation equipment to original design specifications) or transportation equipment conversion (i.e., major modification to systems). An establishment that primarily performs factory (or shipyard) overhauls, rebuilding, or conversions of aircraft, railroad rolling stock, or a ship is classified in Subsector 336, Transportation Equipment Manufacturing, according to the type of equipment.

Many of the establishments in this sector often operate on networks, with physical facilities, labor forces, and equipment spread over an extensive geographic area.

Warehousing establishments in this sector are distinguished from merchant wholesaling in that the warehouse establishments do not sell the goods.

Excluded from this sector are establishments primarily engaged in providing travel agent services that support transportation and other establishments, such as hotels, businesses, and government agencies. These establishments are classified in Sector 56, Administrative and Support and Waste Management and Remediation Services. Also, establishments primarily engaged in providing rental and leasing of transportation equipment without operator are classified in Subsector 532, Rental and Leasing Services.

For information on the subsectors of Transportation and Warehousing sector (NAICS 48–49) see <www.census.gov/eos/www/naics/>.

The **Information** sector (NAICS 51) comprises establishments engaged in the following processes: (a) producing and distributing information and cultural products, (b) providing the means to transmit or distribute these products as well as data or communications, and (c) processing data.

The main components of this sector are the publishing industries, including software publishing, and both traditional publishing and publishing exclusively on the internet; the motion picture and sound recording industries; the broadcasting industries, including traditional broadcasting and those broadcasting exclusively over the internet; the telecommunications industries; web search portals, data processing industries, and the information services industries.

The expressions "information age" and "global information economy" are used with considerable frequency today. The general idea of an "information economy" includes both the notion of industries primarily producing, processing, and distributing information, as well as the idea that every industry is using available information and information technology to reorganize and make themselves more productive.

For the purposes of NAICS, it is the transformation of information into a commodity that is produced and distributed by a number of growing industries that is at issue. The Information sector groups three types of establishments: (1) those engaged in producing and distributing information and cultural products; (2) those that provide the means to transmit or distribute these products as well as data or communications; and (3) those that process data. Cultural products are those that directly express attitudes, opinions, ideas, values, and artistic creativity; provide entertainment; or offer information and analysis concerning the past and present. Included in this definition are popular, mass-produced products as well as cultural products that normally have a more limited audience, such as poetry books, literary magazines, or classical records.

The unique characteristics of information and cultural products, and of the processes involved in their production and distribution, distinguish the Information sector from the goods-producing and service-producing sectors. Some of these characteristics are:

1. Unlike traditional goods, an "information or cultural product," such as a newspaper online or television program, does not necessarily have tangible qualities, nor is it necessarily associated with a particular form. A movie can be shown at a movie theater, on a television broadcast, through video-on-demand, or rented at a local video store. A sound recording can be aired on radio, embedded in multimedia products, or sold at a record store.

2. Unlike traditional services, the delivery of these products does not require direct contact between the supplier and the consumer.

3. The value of these products to the consumer lies in their informational, educational, cultural, or entertainment content, not in the format in which they are distributed. Most of these products are protected from unlawful reproduction by copyright laws.

4. The intangible property aspect of information and cultural products makes the processes involved in their production and distribution very different from goods and services. Only those possessing the rights to these works are authorized to reproduce, alter, improve, and distribute them. Acquiring and using these rights often involves significant costs. In addition, technology is revolutionizing the distribution of these products. It is possible to distribute them in a physical form, via broadcast, or online.

5. Distributors of information and cultural products can easily add value to the products they distribute. For instance, broadcasters add advertising not contained in the original product. This capacity means that unlike traditional distributors, they derive revenue not from sale of the distributed product to the final consumer, but from those who pay for the privilege of adding information to the original product. Similarly, a directory and mailing list publisher can acquire the rights to thousands of previously published newspaper and periodical articles and add new value by providing search and software and organizing the information in a way that facilitates research and retrieval. These products often command a much higher price than the original information.

The distribution modes for information commodities may either eliminate the necessity for traditional manufacture, or reverse the conventional order of manufacture-distribute. A newspaper distributed online, for example, can be printed locally or by the final consumer. Similarly, packaged software, is now available mainly online. The NAICS Information sector is designed to make such economic changes transparent as they occur, or to facilitate designing surveys that will monitor the new phenomena and provide data to analyze the changes.

Many of the industries in the NAICS Information sector are engaged in producing products protected by copyright law or in distributing them (other than distribution by traditional wholesale and retail methods). Examples are traditional publishing industries, software and directory and mailing list publishing industries, and film and sound industries. Broadcasting and telecommunications industries and information providers and processors are also included in the Information sector because their technologies are so closely linked to other industries in the Information sector.

For information on the subsectors of Information sector (NAICS 51), see <www.census.gov/eos /www/naics/>.

The **Finance and Insurance** sector (NAICS 52) comprises establishments primarily engaged in financial transactions (transactions involving the creation, liquidation, or change in ownership of financial assets) and/or in facilitating financial transactions. Three principal types of activities are identified:

1. Raising funds by taking deposits and/or issuing securities and, in the process, incurring liabilities. Establishments engaged in this activity use raised funds to acquire financial assets by making loans and/ or purchasing securities. Putting themselves at risk, they channel funds from lenders to borrowers and transform or repackage the funds with respect to maturity, scale, and risk. This activity is known as financial intermediation.

2. Pooling of risk by underwriting insurance and annuities. Establishments engaged in this activity collect fees, insurance premiums, or annuity considerations; build up reserves; invest those reserves; and make contractual payments. Fees are based on the expected incidence of the insured risk and the expected return on investment.

3. Providing specialized services facilitating or supporting financial intermediation, insurance, and employee benefit programs.

In addition, monetary authorities charged with monetary control are included in this sector.

The subsectors, industry groups, and industries within the NAICS Finance and Insurance sector are defined on the basis of their unique production processes. As with all industries, the production processes are distinguished by their use of specialized human resources and specialized physical capital. In addition, the way in which these establishments acquire and allocate financial capital, their source of funds, and the use of those funds provides a third basis for distinguishing characteristics of the production process. For instance, the production process in raising funds through deposit taking is different from the process of raising funds in bond or money markets. The process of making loans to individuals also requires different production processes than does the creation of investment pools or the underwriting of securities.

Most of the Finance and Insurance subsectors contain one or more industry groups of (1) intermediaries with similar patterns of raising and using funds and (2) establishments engaged in activities that facilitate, or are otherwise related to, that type of financial or insurance intermediation. Industries within this sector are defined in terms of activities for which a production process can be specified, and many of these activities are not exclusive to a particular type of financial institution. To deal with the varied activities taking place within existing financial institutions, the approach is to split these institutions into components performing specialized services. This requires defining the units engaged in providing those services and developing procedures that allow for their delineation. These units are the equivalents for finance and insurance of the establishments defined for other industries.

The output of many financial services, as well as the inputs and the processes by which they are combined, cannot be observed at a single location and can only be defined at a higher level of the organizational structure of the enterprise. Additionally, a number of independent activities that represent separate and distinct production processes may take place at a single location belonging to a multilocation financial firm. Activities are more likely to be homogeneous with respect to production characteristics than are locations, at least in financial services. The classification defines activities broadly enough that it can be used both by those classifying by location and by those employing a more top-down approach to the delineation of the establishment.

Establishments engaged in activities that facilitate, or are otherwise related to, the various types of intermediation have been included in individual subsectors, rather than in a separate subsector dedicated to services alone because these services are performed by intermediaries, as well as by specialist establishments, the extent to which the activity of the intermediaries can be separately identified is not clear.

The Finance and Insurance sector has been defined to encompass establishments primarily engaged in financial transactions; that is, transactions involving the creation, liquidation, change in ownership of financial assets; or in facilitating financial transactions. Financial industries are extensive users of electronic means for facilitating the verification of financial balances, authorizing transactions, transferring funds to and from transactors accounts, notifying banks (or credit card issuers) of the individual transactions, and providing daily summaries. Since these transaction-processing activities are integral to the production of finance and insurance services, establishments that principally provide a financial transaction processing service are classified to this sector, rather than to the data processing industry in the Information sector.

Legal entities that hold portfolios of assets on behalf of others are significant and data on them are required for a variety of purposes. Thus for NAICS, these funds, trusts, and other financial vehicles are the fifth subsector of the Finance and Insurance sector. These entities earn interest, dividends, and other property income, but have little or no employment and no revenue from the sale of services. Separate establishments and employees devoted to the management of funds are classified in Industry Group 5239, Other Financial Investment Activities.

For information on the subsectors of **Finance and Insurance** sector (NAICS 52), see <wwwcensus.gov/eos/www/naics/>.

The **Real Estate and Rental and Leasing** sector (NAICS 53) comprises establishments primarily engaged in renting, leasing, or otherwise allowing the use of tangible or intangible assets, and establishments providing related services. The major portion of this sector comprises establishments that rent, lease, or otherwise allow the use of their own assets by others. The assets may be tangible, as is the case of real estate and equipment, or intangible, as is the case with patents and trademarks.

This sector also includes establishments primarily engaged in managing real estate for others, selling, renting and/or buying real estate for others, and appraising real estate. These activities are closely related to this sector's main activity, and it was felt that from a production basis they would best be included here. In addition, a substantial proportion of property management is self-performed by lessors.

The main components of this sector are the real estate lessors industries (including equity real estate investment trusts (REITs)); equipment lessors industries (including motor vehicles, computers, and consumer goods); and lessors of nonfinancial intangible assets (except copyrighted works).

Excluded from this sector are establishments primarily engaged in renting or leasing equipment with operators. Establishments renting or leasing equipment with operators are classified in various subsectors of NAICS depending on the nature of the services provided (e.g., transportation, construction, agriculture). These activities are excluded from this sector because the client is paying for the expertise and knowledge of the equipment operator, in addition to the rental of the equipment. In many cases, such as the rental of heavy construction equipment, the operator is essential to operate the equipment.

For information on the subsectors of Real Estate and Rental and Leasing sector (NAICS 53), see <www.census.gov/eos/www/naics/>.

The **Professional, Scientific, and Technical Services** sector (NAICS 54) comprises establishments that specialize in performing professional, scientific, and technical activities for others. These activities require a high degree of expertise and training. The establishments in this sector specialize according to expertise and provide these services to clients in a variety of industries and, in some cases, to households. Activities performed include: legal advice and representation; accounting, bookkeeping, and payroll services; architectural, engineering, and specialized design services; computer services; consulting services; research services; advertising services; photographic services; translation and interpretation services; veterinary services; and other professional, scientific, and technical services.

This sector excludes establishments primarily engaged in providing a range of day-to-day office administrative services, such as financial planning, billing and recordkeeping, personnel, and physical distribution and logistics. These establishments are classified in Sector 56, Administrative and Support and Waste Management and Remediation Services.

For information on the subsectors of Professional, Scientific, and Technical Services sector (NAICS 54) see <www.census.gov/eos/www/naics/>.

The **Management of Companies and Enterprises** sector (NAICS 55) comprises (1) establishments that hold the securities of (or other equity interests in) companies and enterprises for the purpose of owning a controlling interest or influencing management decisions or (2) establishments (except government establishments) that administer, oversee, and manage establishments of the company or enterprise and that normally undertake the

strategic or organizational planning and decision-making role of the company or enterprise. Establishments that administer, oversee, and manage may hold the securities of the company or enterprise.

Establishments in this sector perform essential activities that are often undertaken, in-house, by establishments in many sectors of the economy. By consolidating the performance of these activities of the enterprise at one establishment, economies of scale are achieved.

Government establishments primarily engaged in administering, overseeing, and managing governmental programs are classified in Sector 92, Public Administration. Establishments primarily engaged in providing a range of day-to-day office administrative services, such as financial planning, billing and recordkeeping, personnel, and physical distribution and logistics are classified in Industry 56111, Office Administrative Services.

For information on the subsectors of Management of Companies and Enterprises sector (NAICS 55), see <www.census.gov/eos/www/naics/>.

The **Administrative and Support and Waste Management and Remediation Services** sector (NAICS 56) comprises establishments performing routine support activities for the day-to-day operations of other organizations. These essential activities are often undertaken in-house by establishments in many sectors of the economy. The establishments in this sector specialize in one or more of these support activities and provide these services to clients in a variety of industries and, in some cases, to households. Activities performed include: office administration, hiring and placing of personnel, document preparation and similar clerical services, solicitation, collection, security and surveillance services, cleaning, and waste disposal services.

The administrative and management activities performed by establishments in this sector are typically on a contract or fee basis. These activities may also be performed by establishments that are part of the company or enterprise. However, establishments involved in administering, overseeing, and managing other establishments of the company or enterprise, are classified in Sector 55, Management of Companies and Enterprises. Establishments in Sector 55 normally undertake the strategic and organizational planning and decision-making role of the company or enterprise. Government establishments engaged in administering, overseeing, and managing governmental programs are classified in Sector 92, Public Administration.

For information on the subsectors of Administrative and Support and Waste Management and Remediation

Services sector (NAICS 56), see <www.census.gov/eos/www/naics/>.

The **Educational Services** sector (NAICS 61) comprises establishments that provide instruction and training in a wide variety of subjects. This instruction and training is provided by specialized establishments, such as schools, colleges, universities, and training centers. These establishments may be privately owned and operated for profit or not for profit, or they may be publicly owned and operated. They may also offer food and/or accommodation services to their students.

Educational services are usually delivered by teachers or instructors that explain, tell, demonstrate, supervise, and direct learning. Instruction is imparted in diverse settings, such as educational institutions, the workplace, or the home, and through diverse means, such as correspondence, television, the internet, or other electronic and distance-learning methods. The training provided by these establishments may include the use of simulators and simulation methods. It can be adapted to the particular needs of the students, for example, sign language can replace verbal language for teaching students with hearing impairments. All industries in the sector share this commonality of process, namely, labor inputs of instructors with the requisite subject matter expertise and teaching ability.

For information on the subsectors of Educational Services sector (NAICS 61), see <www.census.gov/eos/www/naics/>.

The **Health Care and Social Assistance** sector (NAICS 62) comprises establishments providing health care and social assistance for individuals. The sector includes both health care and social assistance because it is sometimes difficult to distinguish between the boundaries of these two activities. The industries in this sector are arranged on a continuum starting with those establishments providing medical care exclusively, continuing with those providing health care and social assistance, and finally finishing with those providing only social assistance. The services provided by establishments in this sector are delivered by trained professionals. All industries in the sector share this commonality of process, namely, labor inputs of health practitioners or social workers with the requisite expertise. Many of the industries in the sector are defined based on the educational degree held by the practitioners included in the industry.

Excluded from this sector are aerobic classes in Subsector 713, Amusement, Gambling, and Recreation Industries and nonmedical diet and weight reducing centers in Subsector 812, Personal and Laundry Services. Although these can be viewed as health services, these services are not typically delivered by health practitioners.

For information on the subsectors of Health Care and Social Assistance sector (NAICS 62), see <http://www.census.gov/eos/www/naics/>.

The **Arts, Entertainment, and Recreation** sector (NAICS 71) includes a wide range of establishments that operate facilities or provide services to meet varied cultural, entertainment, and recreational interests of their patrons. This sector comprises (1) establishments that are involved in producing, promoting, or participating in live performances, events, or exhibits intended for public viewing; (2) establishments that preserve and exhibit objects and sites of historical, cultural, or educational interest; and (3) establishments that operate facilities or provide services that enable patrons to participate in recreational activities or pursue amusement, hobby, and leisure-time interests.

Some establishments that provide cultural, entertainment, or recreational facilities and services are classified in other sectors. Excluded from this sector are: (1) establishments that provide both accommodations and recreational facilities, such as hunting and fishing camps and resort and casino hotels are classified in Subsector 721, Accommodation; (2) restaurants and night clubs that provide live entertainment in addition to the sale of food and beverages are classified in Subsector 722, Food Services and Drinking Places; (3) motion picture theaters, libraries and archives, and publishers of newspapers, magazines, books, periodicals, and computer software are classified in Sector 51, Information; and (4) establishments using transportation equipment to provide recreational and entertainment services, such as those operating sightseeing buses, dinner cruises, or helicopter rides, are classified in Subsector 487, Scenic and Sightseeing Transportation.

For information on the subsectors of **Arts, Entertainment, and Recreation** sector (NAICS 71) see <www.census.gov/eos/www/naics/>.

The **Accommodation and Food Services** sector (NAICS 72) comprises establishments providing customers with lodging and/or preparing meals, snacks, and beverages for immediate consumption. The sector includes both accommodation and food services establishments because the two activities are often combined at the same establishment.

Excluded from this sector are civic and social organizations, amusement and recreation parks, theaters, and other recreation or entertainment facilities providing food and beverage services.

For information on the subsectors of Accommodation and Food Services sector (NAICS 72), see <www.census.gov/eos/www/naics/>.

The **Other Services** (except Public Administration) sector (NAICS 81) comprises establishments engaged in providing services not specifically provided for elsewhere in the classification system. Establishments in this sector are primarily engaged in activities, such as equipment and machinery repairing, promoting or administering religious activities, grantmaking, advocacy, and providing dry cleaning and laundry services, personal care services, death care services, pet care services, photofinishing services, temporary parking services, and dating services.

Private households that engage in employing workers on or about the premises in activities primarily concerned with the operation of the household are included in this sector.

Excluded from this sector are establishments primarily engaged in retailing new equipment and also performing repairs and general maintenance on equipment. These establishments are classified in Sector 44–45, Retail Trade.

For information on the subsectors of **Other Services** (except Public Administration) sector (NAICS 81) see <www.census.gov/eos/www/naics/>.

The **Public Administration** sector (NAICS 92) consists of establishments of federal, state, and local government agencies that administer, oversee, and manage public programs and have executive, legislative, or judicial authority over other institutions within a given area. These agencies also set policy, create laws, adjudicate civil and criminal legal cases, provide for public safety and for national defense. In general, government establishments in the Public Administration sector oversee governmental programs and activities that are not performed by private establishments. Establishments in this sector typically are engaged in the organization and financing of the production of public goods and services, most of which are provided for free or at prices that are not economically significant.

Government establishments also engage in a wide range of productive activities covering not only public goods and services but also individual goods and services similar to those produced in sectors typically identified with private-sector establishments. In general, ownership is not a criterion for classification in NAICS. Therefore, government establishments engaged in the production of private-sector-like goods and services should be classified in the same industry as private-sector establishments engaged in similar activities.

As a practical matter, it is difficult to identify separate establishment detail for many government agencies. To the extent that separate establishment records are available, the administration of governmental programs is classified in Sector 92, Public Administration, while the operation of that same governmental program is classified elsewhere in NAICS based on the activities performed. For example, the governmental administrative authority for an airport is classified in Industry 92612, Regulation and Administration of Transportation Programs, while operating the airport is classified in Industry 48811, Airport Operations. When separate records for multiestablishment companies are not available to distinguish between the administration of a governmental program and the operation of it, the establishment is classified in Sector 92, Public Administration.

Examples of government-provided goods and services that are classified in sectors other than Public Administration include: schools, classified in Sector 61, Educational Services; hospitals, classified in Subsector 622, Hospitals; establishments operating transportation facilities, classified in Sector 48–49, Transportation and Warehousing; the operation of utilities, classified in Sector 22, Utilities; and the Government Printing Office, classified in Subsector 323, Printing and Related Support Activities.

For information on the subsectors of Public Administration sector (NAICS 92), see <http://www.census.gov/eos/www/naics/>.

Census of Governments

A Census of Governments is taken at 5-year intervals as required by law under Title 13, U.S. Code, Section 161. The purpose of the Census of Governments is to provide periodic and comprehensive statistics about governments and governmental activities for all state and local governments in the U.S. Local governments include counties, cities, townships, special districts, and school districts. Data are obtained on government organizations, finances, and employment. Organization data include location, type, and characteristics of local governments and officials. Finances and employment data are the same as in comparable annual surveys and include revenue, expenditure, debt, assets, employees, payroll, and benefits. The U.S. Code, Title 13, requires this census and provides for voluntary responses. The 2012 census, similar to those taken since 1957, covers three major subject fields—government organization, public employment, and government finances.

The concept of local governments as defined by the Census Bureau covers three general-purpose governments (county, municipal, and township) and two limited-purpose governments (school district and special district). For information on the history, methodology, and concepts for the Census of Governments, see the *Governments Finance and Employment Classification Manual* at www.census.gov/govs/classification/.

The term "full-time equivalent employment" refers to a computed statistic representing the number of full-time employees that could have been employed if the reported number of hours worked by part-time employees had been worked by full-time employees. This statistic is calculated separately for each function of a government by dividing the "part-time hours paid" by the standard number of hours for full-time employees in the particular government and then adding the resulting quotient to the number of full-time employees.

Revenue includes all amounts of money received by a government from external sources during its fiscal year (i.e., those originating "outside the government"), net of refunds and other correcting transactions, other than issuance of debt, sale of investments, and agency or private trust transactions. Under this definition, revenue excludes amounts transferred from other funds or agencies of the same government. General revenue covers all government revenue except liquor stores revenue, insurance trust revenue, and utility revenue. Taxes are compulsory contributions exacted by a government for public purposes except employee and employer assessments for retirement and social insurance purposes, which are classified as insurance trust revenue. All tax revenue is classified as general revenue and comprises amounts received (including interest and penalties but excluding protested amounts and refunds) from all taxes imposed by a government. Local government tax revenue excludes any amounts from shares of state imposed and collected taxes, which are classified as intergovernmental revenue. Property taxes are taxes conditioned on ownership of property and measured by its value. This category includes general property taxes related to property as a whole, real and personal, tangible or intangible, whether taxed at a single rate or at classified rates, and taxes on selected types of property, such as motor vehicles or on certain or all intangibles. Direct expenditure includes payments to employees, suppliers, contractors, beneficiaries, and other final recipients of government payment; i.e., all expenditure other than intergovernmental expenditure, while general expenditure covers all government expenditure other than the specifically enumerated kinds of expenditure classified as utility expenditure, liquor stores expenditure, and employee retirement or other insurance trust expenditure.

Census of Agriculture

The Census Bureau took a census of agriculture every 10 years from 1840 to 1920; since 1925, this census has been taken roughly once every 5 years. The 1997 Census of Agriculture was the first one conducted by the National Agricultural Statistics Service of the U.S. Department of Agriculture. Over time, the definition of a farm has varied. For recent censuses (including the 2017 census), a farm has been defined as any place from which $1,000 or more of agricultural products were produced and sold or normally would have been sold during the census year. The census of agriculture is the leading source of facts and statistics about the Nation's agricultural production. It provides a detailed picture of U.S. farms and ranches every five years and is the only source of uniform, comprehensive agricultural data for every state and county or county equivalent in the U.S.

TABLE A—STATES

Table A, States, presents 81 tables with 1,152 items of data for each state, the United States as a whole, and the District of Columbia. These tables are numbered A-1 through A-81.

A number of the statistics in Tables A-1 through A-81 are also presented for metropolitan areas in Tables B-1 through B-14, for metropolitan area component counties in Tables C-1 through C-4, and for metropolitan and micropolitan areas in Table D-1.

Table A-1. Area and Population

Sources: Area—U.S. Census Bureau, National Counties Gazetteer file, 2019; https://www.census.gov/geographies/reference-files/time-series/geo/gazetteer-files.html; Population—U.S. Census Bureau, Population, Population Change, and Estimated Components of Population Change: April 1, 2010 to July 1, 2019, https://www.census.gov/data/tables/time-series/demo/popest/2010s-state-total.html; Intercensal Estimates of the Resident Population for the United States, Regions, States, and Puerto Rico: April 1, 2000 to July 1, 2010, https://www.census.gov/data/tables/time-/demo/popest/intercensal-2000-2010-state.html.

Land area. The Census Bureau provides land area for the decennial censuses and updates it in annual Gazetteer files. Area was calculated from the specific set of boundaries recorded for the entity (in this case, states and counties) in the Census Bureau's geographic database.

Land area measurements may disagree with the information displayed on census maps and in the TIGER® file because, for area measurement purposes, features identified as "intermittent water" and "glacier" are reported as land area. TIGER® is an acronym for the digital (computer-readable) geographic database that automates the mapping and related geographic activities required to support the Census Bureau's census and survey programs; TIGER® stands for Topologically Integrated Geographic Encoding and Referencing system.

The accuracy of any area measurement figure is limited by the inaccuracy inherent in (1) the location and shape of the various boundary features in the database and (2) rounding affecting the last digit in all operations that compute and/ or sum the area measurement. Identification of land and inland, coastal, and territorial is for statistical purposes and does not necessarily reflect legal definitions thereof.

Population estimates for 2019 and other intercensal years and population estimates base data for 2010 and 2000 were used to calculate rates or describe various population characteristics in Tables A-2 through A-81.

The 2000 and 2010 decennial census counts are the estimates base numbers, reflecting modifications to the Census 2000 and 2010 population as documented in the Count Question Resolution program and geographic program revisions. The 2000 decennial population counts are from the short-form questionnaires that were asked of all people and housing units and are often referred to as 100 percent questions because they are asked of the entire population. In 2010, all people and households answered on a short form. For more information on the decennial census and population estimates, see General Notes.

Persons enumerated in the census were counted as inhabitants of their usual place of residence, which generally means the place where a person lives and sleeps the majority of the time. This place is not necessarily the same as the legal residence, voting residence, or domicile. In the vast majority of cases, however, the use of these different bases of classification would produce substantially the same statistics, although appreciable differences may exist for a few areas.

The implementation of this usual-residence practice has resulted in the establishment of residence rules for certain categories of persons whose usual place of residence is not immediately apparent (e.g., college students were counted at their college residence). As in the above example, persons were not always counted as residents of the place where they happened to be staying on census day. However, persons without a usual place of residence were counted where they were enumerated.

Rank numbers are assigned on the basis of area size for the rank of area and by population size for rank of population, with each state placed in descending order, largest to smallest. Where ties—two or more states with identical area or populations occur—the same rank is assigned to each of the tied states. In such cases, the following rank number(s) is omitted so that the lowest rank is usually equal to the number of states ranked.

Persons per square mile, also known as population density, is the average number of inhabitants per square mile

of land area. These figures are derived by dividing the total number of residents by the number of square miles of land area in the specified geographic area. To determine population per square kilometer, multiply the population per square mile by .386103.

Net change represents the increase or decrease between the 2 years shown. **Percent change** represents the increase or decrease between the 2 years shown as a percentage of the beginning population.

Refer to the General Notes on population estimates for explanations of **international migration** and **domestic migration**.

Table A-2. Population by Age Group and Sex

Sources: U.S. Census Bureau. Annual Estimates of the Resident Population for Selected Age Groups by Sex for the United States, States, Counties, and Puerto Rico Commonwealth and Municipios: April 1, 2010 to July 1, 2018 https://www.census.gov/programs-surveys/popest/data/tables.2018.html; U.S Census Bureau. Intercensal Estimates of the Resident Population by Sex and Age for States: April 1, 2000 to July 1, 2010 https://www.census.gov/data/tables/time-series/demo/popest/intercensal-2000-2010-state.html

Refer to the General Notes on population estimates for explanations of **population by age and sex**.

Table A-3. Population by Race and Hispanic Origin

Sources: U.S. Census Bureau, Annual Estimates of the Resident Population by Sex, Race, and Hispanic Origin for the United States and States: April 1, 2010 to July 1, 2018; https://www.census.gov/data/tables/time-series/demo/popest/2010s-state-detail.html

Race. The racial classifications used by the Census Bureau adhere to the October 30, 1997, *Federal Register Notice* entitled "Revisions to the Standards for the Classification of Federal Data on Race and Ethnicity" issued by the Office of Management and Budget (OMB); https://www.census.gov/topics/population/race/about.html.

These standards govern the categories used to collect and present federal data on race and ethnicity. The OMB requires federal agencies to use a minimum of five race categories: White, Black or African American, American Indian and Alaska Native, Asian, and Native Hawaiian and Other Pacific Islander. For respondents unable to identify with any of these five race categories, the OMB approved including a sixth category, "Some other race," beginning with the Census 2000 questionnaire.

The question on race for Census 2000 was different from past census in several ways. Most significant was that respondents were given the option of selecting one or more race categories to indicate their racial identities. Because of these changes, the Census 2000 and 2010 data on race are not directly comparable with data from the 1990 census or earlier censuses. Caution is recommended when interpreting changes in the racial composition of the U.S. population over time.

Population estimates by race and Hispanic origin are calculated using a distributive cohort component method. Previously developed resident state population estimates by age and sex and residential national population estimates by age, sex, race, and Hispanic origin are used as a base. Estimated post-censal changes in the corresponding populations are applied with a cohort component model. These distributions are applied to the original state age-sex and national characteristics estimates.

White refers to people having origins in any of the original peoples of Europe, the Middle East, or North Africa. It includes people who indicated their race or races as White or wrote in entries such as Irish, German, Italian, Lebanese, Near Easterner, Arab, or Polish.

Black or African American refers to people having origins in any of the Black racial groups of Africa. It includes people who indicated their race or races as Black, African American, or Negro or wrote in entries such as African American, Afro American, Nigerian, or Haitian.

American Indian and Alaska Native refers to people having origins in any of the original peoples of North and South America (including Central America) and who maintain tribal affiliation or community attachment. It includes people who indicated their race or races by marking this category or writing in their principal or enrolled tribe, such as Rosebud Sioux, Chippewa, or Navajo.

Asian refers to people having origins in any of the original peoples of the Far East, Southeast Asia, or the Indian subcontinent. It includes people who indicated their race or races as Asian Indian, Chinese, Filipino, Korean, Japanese, Vietnamese, or Other Asian or wrote in entries such as Burmese, Hmong, Pakistani, or Thai.

Native Hawaiian and Other Pacific Islander refers to people having origins in any of the original peoples of Hawaii, Guam, Samoa, or other Pacific Islands. It includes people who indicated their race or races as Native Hawaiian, Guamanian or Chamorro, Samoan, or Other Pacific Islander or wrote in entries such as Tahitian, Mariana Islander, or Chuukese.

Two or more races. People may have chosen to provide two or more races either by checking two or more race response check boxes, by providing multiple write-in responses, or by some combination of check boxes and write-in responses. The race response categories shown on the questionnaire were collapsed into the five minimum race groups by the OMB.

Hispanic or Latino. People who identify with the terms "Hispanic" or "Latino" are those who classify themselves in one of the specific Hispanic or Latino categories listed on the questionnaire, such as Mexican, Puerto Rican, or Cuban, as well as those who indicate that they are other Spanish, Hispanic, or Latino. Origin can be viewed as the heritage, nationality group, lineage, or country of birth of the person or the person's parents or ancestors before their arrival in the United States. People who identify their origin as Spanish, Hispanic, or Latino may be any race.

The concept of race, as used by the Census Bureau, reflects self-identification by people according to the race or races with which they most closely identify. These categories are sociopolitical constructs and should not be interpreted as being scientific or anthropological in nature. Furthermore, the race categories include both racial and national-origin groups.

Traditional and current data collection and classification treat race and Hispanic origin as two separate and distinct concepts in accordance with guidelines from the OMB. Race and Hispanic origin are two separate concepts in the federal statistical system. People who are Hispanic may be any race, and people in each race group may be either Hispanic or non-Hispanic. Also, each person has two attributes, their race (or races) and whether or not they are Hispanic. The overlap of race and Hispanic origin is the main comparability issue. For example, Black Hispanics (Hispanic Blacks) are included in both the number of Blacks and in the number of Hispanics. For further information, see www.census.gov/population/www/socdemo/compraceho.html.

Table A-4. Population by Residence

Sources: U.S. Census Bureau. Population—Population and Housing Units Estimates Data; https://www.census.gov/programs-surveys/popest/data/tables.html; Land—2019 Gazetteer files https://www.census.gov/geographies/reference-files/time-series/geo/gazetteer-files.html;

The U.S. Office of Management and Budget (OMB) defines Metropolitan and Micropolitan Statistical Areas according to published standards that are applied to the Census Bureau data. The general concept of a Metropolitan or Micropolitan Statistical Area (collectively referred to as Core Based Statistical Areas, or CBSAs) is that of an area containing a recognized population nucleus and adjacent communities that have a high degree of integration with that nucleus.

A **Metropolitan Statistical Area** is defined by OMB as a CBSA associated with at least one urbanized area that has a population of at least 50,000. The Metropolitan Statistical Area comprises the central county or counties containing the core, plus adjacent outlying counties having a high degree of social and economic integration with the central county as measured through commuting. A **core** is a densely settled concentration of population, comprising either an urbanized area or urban cluster.

A **Micropolitan Statistical Area** is defined as a CBSA associated with at least one urban cluster that has a population of at least 10,000, but less than 50,000. The micropolitan area comprises the central county or counties containing the core, plus adjacent outlying counties having a high degree of social and economic integration with the central county as a measure through commuting. For more information on metropolitan and micropolitan statistical areas, see OMB Bulletin No. 18.04 at https://www.census.gov/programs-surveys/metro-micro.html.

The metropolitan and micropolitan statistical area population estimates are based upon the county estimates. The county estimates methodology is available at: https://www.census.gov/programs-surveys/popest/technical-documentation/methodology.html.

Table A-5. Households

Sources: For 2018 data, U.S. Census Bureau, American Community Survey, 2018 1-year file, Table DP02. Selected Social Characteristics in the United States . For 2010 data, U.S. Census Bureau, Profile of General Population and Housing Characteristics: 2010; 2010 Census Summary File 1 (SF1) 100 percent data, Table H13. data.census.gov.

A **household** consists of all the people who occupy a housing unit. A house, an apartment or other group of rooms, or a single room, is regarded as a housing unit when it is occupied or intended for occupancy as separate living quarters; that is, when the occupants do not live and eat with any other persons in the structure and there is direct access from the outside or through a common hall. A household includes the related family members and all the unrelated people, if any, such as lodgers, foster children, wards, or employees who share the housing unit. A person living alone in a housing unit, or a group of unrelated people sharing a housing unit such as partners or roomers, is also counted as a household. The count of households excludes group quarters. **People per household** (or average household size) is a measure obtained by dividing the number of people in households by the total number of households (or householder).

A **family household** is a household maintained by a householder who is in a family (persons related by birth, marriage, or adoption) and includes any unrelated people (unrelated subfamily members and/or secondary individuals) who may be residing there. The number of family households is equal to the number of families. The count of family household members differs from the count of family members, however, in that the family household members include all people living in the household, whereas family members include only the householder and his/her relatives. The expression "**married-couple**" before the term "household," "family," or "subfamily" indicates that the household, family, or subfamily is maintained by a married couple. **Female householder, no spouse present** includes a family with a female who maintains a household with no spouse.

A **nonfamily household** consists of the householder who lives alone or with nonrelatives only.

Own child category is a never-married child under 18 years old who is a son or daughter of the householder by birth, marriage, or adoption.

For more information regarding household data, see https://www.census.gov/topics/families.html.

Table A-6. Marital Status, 2018

Source: U.S. Census Bureau--American Community Survey 2018 1-year estimates, Table DP02. Selected Social Characteristics in the United States; data.census.gov.

Marital status refers to how people responded when asked if they were now married, widowed, divorced, separated, or never married. Couples who live together (unmarried people, people in common-law marriages) were allowed to report the marital status they considered the most appropriate.

Never married includes all people who have never been married, including people whose only marriage(s) was annulled.

Now married, except separated includes people whose current marriage has not ended through widowhood, divorce, or separation (regardless of previous marital history). The category also includes couples who live together or people in common-law marriages if they consider this category the most appropriate.

Separated includes people legally separated or otherwise absent from their spouse because of marital discord. This category also includes people who have been deserted or who have parted because they no longer want to live together but who have not obtained a divorce.

Widowed includes widows and widowers who have not remarried.

Divorced includes people who are legally divorced and who have not remarried. Those without a final divorce decree are classified as "separated."

Table A-7. Residence 1 Year Ago, People Obtaining Legal Permanent Resident Status, and Language Spoken at Home

Sources: Residence 1 year ago and Language—U.S. Census Bureau, 2018 American Community Survey; table DP02. Selected Social Characteristics in the United States. www.census.gov/acs/www/; data.census.gov.

People obtaining legal permanent resident status—U.S. Department of Homeland Security, Office of Immigration Statistics, 2018 Yearbook of Immigration Statistics, table 4 and Supplemental table 1. www.dhs.gov/yearbook-immigration-statistics.

Language—U.S. Census Bureau, 2015 American Community Survey, table B06007, "Place of Birth by Language Spoken at Home and Ability to Speak English in the United States," data.census.gov.

Residence 1 year ago. The American Community Survey asked those participants who had moved from another residence in the United States 1 year earlier to report the city, town, or post office, the name of the U.S. county, state, and ZIP Code where they lived 1 year ago. People living outside of the United States were asked to report the name of the foreign country or U.S. Island Area where they were living 1 year ago. "Residence 1 year ago" is used in conjunction with location of current residence to determine the extent of residential mobility of the population and the resulting redistribution of the population across the various states, metropolitan areas, and regions of the country. When no information on previous residence was reported for a person, information for other family members, if available, was used to assign a location of residence 1 year ago. All cases of nonresponse or incomplete response that were not assigned a previous residence based on information from other family members were allocated to the previous residence of another person with similar characteristics who provided complete information.

ACS participants were also asked if they sometimes or always spoke a language other than English at home. **Language other than English** includes anyone responding yes to this question but does not include the speaking of a language only at school or if speaking is limited to a few expressions or slang. People reporting they did speak another language at home were asked to identify the language spoken.

People obtaining lawful permanent resident status refers to an alien admitted to the United States as a lawful permanent resident. Permanent residents are also commonly referred to as immigrants; however, the Immigration and Nationality Act (INA) broadly defines an immigrant as any alien in the United States, except one legally admitted under specific nonimmigrant categories (INA section 101(a) (15)). An illegal alien who entered the United States without inspection, for example, would be strictly defined as an immigrant under the INA but is not a permanent resident alien. Lawful permanent residents are legally accorded the privilege of residing permanently in the United States. They may be issued immigrant visas by the Department of State overseas or adjusted to permanent resident status by the Department of Homeland Security in the United States.

Table A-8. Place of Birth, 2018

Sources: U.S. Census Bureau, American Community Survey 2018; 1-year estimates; DP02: Selected Social Characteristics in the United States, and table C05006, Place of Birth for the Foreign-Born Population; data.census.gov.

Place of birth. Participants of the American Community Survey were asked where they were born and were asked to select from two categories: (1) in the United States or (2) outside the United States. Respondents selecting category 1 were then asked to report the name of the state while respondents selecting category 2 were then asked to report the name of the foreign country, or Puerto Rico, Guam, etc. People not reporting a place of birth were assigned the state or country of birth of another family member, or were allocated the response of another individual with similar characteristics. People born outside the United States were asked to report their place of birth according to current international boundaries. Since numerous changes in boundaries of foreign countries have occurred in the last century, some people may have reported their place of birth in terms of boundaries that existed at the time of their birth or emigration, or in accordance with their own national preference.

The **foreign-born** population includes anyone who was not a U.S. citizen at birth. This includes respondents who indicated they were a U.S. citizen by naturalization or not a U.S. citizen. This excludes people born in the United States, Puerto Rico or a U.S. Island Area such as Guam or the U.S. Virgin Islands, or people born in a foreign country to a U.S. citizen parent(s).

Table A-9. Live Births and Birth Rates

Source: U.S. National Center for Health Statistics, National Vital Statistics Reports (NVSR), Births: Final Data for 2018, Vol. 68, No. 13, November 27, 2019; Final Data for 2015, Vol. 66, No. 1, January 5, 2017; Final Data for 2010, Vol. 61, No. 1, August 28, 2012 https://www.cdc.gov/nchs/products/nvsr.htm.

The National Vital Statistics System (NVSR) is an intergovernmental data system with the purpose of collecting and disseminating the nation's official vital statistics. These data are provided through contracts between NCHS and vital registration systems operated in the various jurisdictions legally responsible for the registration of vital events—births, deaths, marriages, divorces, and fetal deaths. In the United States, legal authority for the registration of these events resides individually with the 50 States, 2 cities (Washington, DC, and New York City), and 5 territories (Puerto Rico, the Virgin Islands, Guam, American Samoa, and the Commonwealth of the Northern Mariana Islands). These jurisdictions are responsible for maintaining registries of vital events and for issuing copies of birth, marriage, divorce, and death certificates.

Birth statistics are limited to events occurring during the year. The data are by place of residence and exclude events occurring to nonresidents of the United States. Births that occur outside the United States are excluded.

Birth rates represent the number of births per 1,000 resident population estimated as of July 1 for 2018 and 2015 and enumerated as of April 1 for 2010 (decennial census year).

Births to **unmarried women.** The mother's marital status is based on a question on the birth certificate. In most states, the question is: "Mother married? (At birth, conception, or any time between) (Yes or No)." If the question is answered "no," then the birth is considered nonmarital.

Teenage mothers are considered anyone under the age of 20.

Low birth weight is defined as less than 2,500 grams or 5 pounds, 8 ounces.

Table A-10. Births and Low Birth Weights by Race and Hispanic Origin: 2015

Source: U.S. National Center for Health Statistics, National Vital Statistics Reports (NVSR). Final Data 2018, Vol. 68, No. 13, November 27, 2019, https://www.cdc.gov/nchs/products/nvsr.htm

Births by race. For information on how the National Vital Statistics System, the National Center for Health Statistics (NCHS) collects and publishes data, see appendix entry for Table A-9.

Race and Hispanic origin are reported separately on the birth certificate. Beginning with the 1989 data year, NCHS started tabulating its birth data primarily by race of the mother. In 1988 and prior years, births were tabulated by the race of the child, which was determined from the race of the parents as entered on the birth certificate. Race categories are consistent with the 1997 Office of Management and Budget standards.

Infants born at less than 2,500 grams or 5 pounds, 8 ounces are considered to have a **low birth weight.**

Table A-11. Deaths and Death Rates

Sources: U.S. National Center for Health Statistics, National Vital Statistics Reports (NVSR). Final Data 2017, Vol. 68, No. 9, June 24, 2019, https://www.cdc.gov/nchs/products/nvsr.htm

Deaths. Mortality data for 2017 and 2010 are based on the continuous receipt and processing of statistical records by the National Center for Health Statistics (NCHS). NCHS received the data from states' vital registration systems through the Vital Statistics Cooperative Program.

Death statistics are limited to events occurring during the year. The data are by place of residence and exclude events occurring to nonresidents of the United States. Deaths that occur outside the United States are excluded. **Death rates** represent the number of deaths per 1,000 resident population estimated as of April 1 for 2010 (decennial census year) and July 1 for 2017.

Infant mortality rates are calculated by dividing the preliminary number of infant deaths that occurred during the year by the number of live births for the same period and are presented as rates per 1,000 live births.

Table A-12. Age-Adjusted Death Rates by Cause: 2017

Source: U. S. National Center for Health Statistics, National Vital Statistics Reports (NVSR): Deaths: Final Data for 2017, Vol. 68, No. 9, Supplemental table I-16; www.cdc.gov/nchs/data/nvsr/nvsr68/nvsr68_09-508.pdf.

Death rates by cause. Mortality statistics by cause of death are compiled in accordance with World Health Organization (WHO) regulations, which specify that member nations classify causes of death according to the current revision of the *International Statistical Classification of Diseases and Related Health Problems* (ICD). Effective with deaths occurring in 1999, the United States began using the Tenth Revision of this classification. Tabulations of cause-of-death statistics are based solely on the underlying cause of death. The underlying cause is defined by the WHO as "the disease or injury which initiated the train of events leading directly to death, or the circumstances of the accident or violence which produced the fatal injury." The underlying cause is selected from the conditions entered by the physician in the cause of death section of the death certificate. When more than one cause or condition is entered by the physician, the underlying cause is determined by the sequence of conditions on the certificate, provisions, of the ICD, and associated selection rules and modifications.

Age-adjusted rates are mortality rates adjusted for the different age distributions of separate populations. Certain causes of death can be more probable with a certain age group and will distort an area's risk of suffering from certain injuries or diseases. An age-adjusted rate will control the impact a particular age group will have on the death rate of an area and will allow the user to compare mortality risks between areas with different age groups or in a time series. Age-adjusted rates should be viewed as relative indexes rather than actual measures of mortality risk. The age-adjusted rates provided by the National Vital Statistics Reports (NVSR) were computed by the direct method of applying age-specific death rates to the U.S. standard population age distribution.

The rates of almost all causes of death vary by age. Age adjustment is a technique for "removing" the effects of age from crude rates, so as to allow meaningful comparisons across populations with different underlying age structures. For example, comparing the crude rate of heart disease in Florida to that of California is misleading, because the relatively older population in Florida will lead to a higher crude death rate, even if the age-specific rates of heart disease in Florida and California are the same. For such a comparison, age-adjusted rates are preferable. Age-adjusted rates should be viewed as relative indexes rather than as direct or actual measures of mortality risk.

Table A-13. Marriages and Divorces

Sources: Marriage and divorce rates--U.S. National Center for Health Statistics, National Vital Statistics System; https://www.cdc.gov/nchs/nvss/marriage-divorce.htm.

Marital history-- U.S. Census Bureau, 2018 American Community Survey, Table B12007, Median age at first marriage; Table B12501, Marriages in the last year by sex by marital status for the population 15 years and over; Table B12503, Divorces in the last year by sex by marital status for the population 15 years and over; Table B12505. Number of times married by sex by marital status for the population 15 years and over. data.census.gov.

Marriage and divorce. Information on the total rates of marriages and divorces at the national and state levels are published in the NCHS National Vital Statistics System. The collection of detailed data was suspended beginning in January 1996 (see Federal Register Notice, December 15, 1995). Beginning with the June 2003 data, detailed state tables of marriage and divorce levels have been included in the monthly reports of provisional data published in the NCHS National Vital Statistics Reports. Prior to this, these data were available in the "Detailed Statistical Tables" section of NCHS's Data Warehouse website.

Marriage and divorce rates (per 1000 people) provided by NVSS are based on all events occurring in the state that were received in the registration offices during a 1-month period. The yearly figures are derived from summing all 12 months. Divorce figures include reported annulments. There is considerable variability among the states in the procedures that are used to submit the counts of marriages and divorces to NCHS and in the extent to which the states update their counts of marriages and divorces as new information is received. Therefore, counts vary in their completeness.

Information on marital history is from the 2018 American Community Survey. Persons age 15 and older were asked about their marital status. Those who were "ever married" (including those now married, separated, widowed, or divorced) were asked if they had been married, widowed, or divorced in the past 12 months. They were asked how many times (once, two times, or three or more times) they have been married, and the year of their last marriage.

The median age at first marriage is calculated indirectly by estimating the proportion of young people who will marry during their lifetime, calculating one-half of this proportion, and determining the age (at the time of the survey) of people at this half-way mark by osculatory interpolation. It does not represent the actual median age of the population who married during the calendar year. It is shown to the nearest tenth of a year. Henry S. Shryock and Jacob S. Siegel outline the osculatory procedure in *Methods and Materials of Demography*, First Edition (May 1973), Volume 1, pages 291-296.

Table A-14. Health Care Services, Physicians, and Nurses.

Sources: Health care services—U.S. Census Bureau, County Business Patterns, annual https://www.census.gov/programs-surveys/cbp.html

Physicians and Nurses—Bureau of Labor Statistics, Occupational Employment Statistics, Occupational

Employment and Wages; May 2019 Wage and Employment Statistics; <https://www.bls.gov/oes/home.htm>.

County Business Patterns (CBP) is an annual series that provides subnational economic data by industry. The series is useful for studying the economic activity of small areas, analyzing economic changes over time, and as a benchmark for statistical series, surveys, and databases between economic censuses. CBP covers most of the country's economic activity. The series excludes data on self-employed individuals, employees of private households, railroad employees, agricultural production employees, and most government employees.

CBP data are extracted from the Business Register, the Census Bureau's file of all known single- and multiestablishment companies. The Annual Company Organization Survey and quinquennial economic censuses provide individual establishment data for multilocation firms. Data for single-location firms are obtained from various programs conducted by the Census Bureau, such as the economic censuses, the Annual Survey of Manufactures, and Current Business Surveys, as well as from administrative records of the Internal Revenue Service (IRS), the Social Security Administration (SSA), and the Bureau of Labor Statistics (BLS).

An **establishment** is a single physical location at which business is conducted or services or industrial operations are performed. It is not necessarily identical with a company or enterprise, which may consist of one or more establishments. When two or more activities are carried on at a single location under a single ownership, all activities generally are grouped together as a single establishment. The entire establishment is classified on the basis of its major activity and all data are included in that classification. Establishment counts represent the number of locations with paid employees any time during the year.

Paid **employment** consists of full- and part-time employees, including salaried officers and executives of corporations, who are on the payroll in the pay period including March 12. Included are employees on paid sick leave, holidays, and vacations; not included are proprietors and partners of unincorporated businesses.

Total **payroll** includes all forms of compensation, such as salaries, wages, reported tips, commissions, bonuses, vacation allowances, sick-leave pay, employee contributions to qualified pension plans, and the value of taxable fringe benefits. For corporations, it includes amounts paid to officers and executives; for unincorporated businesses, it does not include profit or other compensation of proprietors or partners. Payroll is reported before deductions for social security, income tax, insurance, union dues, etc.

Health Care and Social Assistance (NAICS 62) combines Ambulatory Health Care Services (NAICS 621), Hospitals (NAICS 622), Nursing and Residential Care Facilities (NAICS 623), and Social Assistance (NAICS 624.) Social Assistance is not presented separately in this table. For more information on health care services (2017, NAICS 62), see General Notes or internet site <https://www.census.gov/eos/www/naics/>.

The numbers of **physicians** and **nurses** are from the Occupational Employment Statistics (OES) program, which produces employment and wage estimates annually for over 800 occupations. The OES survey is a semi-annual mail survey of non-farm establishments. The BLS produces the survey materials and selects the establishments to be surveyed. The sampling frame (the list from which establishments to be surveyed are selected) is derived from the list of establishments maintained by State Workforce Agencies (SWAs) for unemployment insurance purposes. Establishments to be surveyed are selected in order to obtain data from every metropolitan and non-metropolitan area in every State, across all surveyed industries, and from establishments of varying sizes. The SWAs mail the survey materials to the selected establishments and make follow-up calls to request data from nonrespondents or to clarify data. The collected data are used to produce occupational estimates at the National, State, and sub-State levels.

Table A-15. Health Care Employment and Type of Health Insurance

Source: U.S. Census Bureau, American Community Survey 2018.

Employment in Health Care Occupations Table B24010. Sex by occupation for the civilian employed population 16 years and over.

Health Insurance: C27002. Private health insurance status by sex by age; C27003. Public health insurance status by sex by age; C27004. Employer based health insurance by sex by age; C27005. Direct-purchase health insurance by sex by age; C27006. Medicare coverage by sex by age; C27007. Medicaid/means-tested public coverage by sex by age; C27008. TRICARE/military health coverage by sex by age; C27009. VA health care by sex by age; C27010. Types of Healath Insurance Coverage by Age. data.census.gov

Health care employment is from the occupation data in the American Community Survey. Occupation describes the kind of work a person does on the job. Occupation data were derived from answers to two questions: "What kind of work was this person doing?" and "What were this person's most important activities or duties?" These questions were asked of all people 15 years old and over who had worked in the past 5 years. For employed people, the data refer to the person's job during the previous week. For those who worked two or more jobs, the data refer to the job where the person worked the greatest number of hours. For unemployed people and people who are not currently employed but report having a job within the last five years, the data refer to their last job. Table A-15 includes only employed persons aged 16 or older.

Occupation statistics are compiled from data that are coded based on the Standard Occupational Classification (SOC) Manual: 2018 (http://www.bls.gov/soc), published by the Executive Office of the President, Office of Management and Budget.

Census occupation codes, based on the 2018 SOC, provide 569 specific occupational categories, for employed people, including military, arranged into 23 major occupational groups. Respondents provided the data for the tabulations by writing on the questionnaires descriptions of the kind of work and activities they are doing. These write-ins are converted to a code category through automated coding. Cases not autocoded on both industry and occupation are sent to the clerical staff in the National Processing Center (NPC) in Jeffersonville, Indiana, who assign codes by comparing these descriptions to entries in the Alphabetical Index of Industries and Occupations (https://www.census.gov/topics/employment/industry-occupation/guidance/indexes.html)

The ACS combines some occupations.

- "Therapists" include occupational, physical, radiation, recreational, and respiratory therapists; speech-language pathologists; exercise physiologists; and all other therapists.

- "Physicians and Surgeons" include Emergency Medicine Physicians, Radiologists, Anesthesiologists, Cardiologists, Dermatologists, Family Medicine Physicians, General Internal Medicine Physicians, Neurologists, Obstetricians and Gynecologists, Pediatricians, Physician Pathologists, Psychiatrists, Surgeons, and Physicians, all other.

- "Other nurses" include nurse anesthetists, nurse midwives, and nurse practitioners.

- "Other health diagnosing and treating practitioners" include chiropractors, dentists, dietitians and nutritionists, optometrists, pharmacists, physician assistants, podiatrists, audiologists, veterinarians, acupuncturists, and all other health diagnosing and treating practitioners.

- "Health technologists and technicians" include clinical laboratory technologists and technicians, dental hygienists, cardiovascular technologists and technicians, diagnostic medical sonographers, radiologic technologists and technicians, Magnetic resonance imaging technologists, nuclear medicine technologists, medical dosimetrists, emergency medical technicians, paramedics, pharmacy technicians, psychiatric technicians, surgical technologists, veterinary technologists and technicians, dietetic technicians, ophthalmic medical technicians, licensed practical and licensed vocational nurses, medical records specialists, dispensing opticians, miscellaneous health technologists and technicians, and all other healthcare practitioners and technical occupations.

- "Other healthcare support occupations" include massage therapists, dental assistants, medical assistants, medical transcriptionists, pharmacy aides, veterinary assistants and laboratory animal caretakers, phlebotomists, and all other healthcare support workers, including medical equipment preparers.

Health Insurance Coverage. In the 2018 American Community Survey, respondents were instructed to report their current coverage and to mark "yes" or "no" for each of the eight types listed:

a. Insurance through a current or former employer or union (of this person or another family member)

b. Insurance purchased directly from an insurance company (by this person or another family member)

c. Medicare, for people 65 and older, or people with certain disabilities

d. Medicaid, Medical Assistance, or any kind of government-assistance plan for those with low incomes or a disability

e. TRICARE or other military health care

f. VA (including those who have ever used or enrolled for VA health care)

g. Indian Health Service

h. Any other type of health insurance or health coverage plan (Respondents who answered "yes" to question h were asked to provide their other type of coverage in a write-in field.)

Health insurance coverage in the ACS and other Census Bureau surveys define coverage to include plans and programs that provide comprehensive health coverage. Plans that provide insurance for specific conditions or situations such as cancer and long-term care policies are not considered coverage. Likewise, other types of insurance like dental, vision, life, and disability insurance are not considered health insurance coverage.

In defining types of coverage, write-in responses were reclassified into one of the first seven types of coverage or determined not to be a coverage type. Write-in responses that referenced the coverage of a family member were edited to assign coverage based on responses from other family members. As a result, only the first seven types of health coverage are included in the data. An eligibility edit was applied to give Medicaid, Medicare, and TRICARE coverage to individuals based on program eligibility rules. TRICARE or other military health care was given to active-duty military personnel and their spouses and children. Medicaid or other means-tested public coverage was given to foster children, certain individuals receiving Supplemental Security Income or Public Assistance, and the spouses and children of certain Medicaid beneficiaries. Medicare coverage was given to people 65 and older who received Social Security or Medicaid benefits. People were considered insured if they reported at least one "yes" to Questions a to f.

People who had no reported health coverage, or those whose only health coverage was Indian Health Service, were considered uninsured. For reporting purposes, the Census Bureau broadly classifies health insurance coverage as private health insurance or public coverage.

Private health insurance is a plan provided through an employer or union, a plan purchased by an individual from a private company, or TRICARE or other military health care. Respondents reporting a "yes" to the types listed in parts a, b, or e were considered to have private health insurance. Public health coverage includes the federal programs Medicare, Medicaid, and VA Health Care (provided through the Department of Veterans Affairs); the Children's Health Insurance Program (CHIP); and individual state health plans. Respondents reporting a "yes" to the types listed in c, d, or f were considered to have public coverage. The types of health insurance are not mutually exclusive; people may be covered by more than one at the same time.

Table A-16. Health Indicators: Health Risks

Source: U.S. Centers for Disease Control and Prevention, Atlanta, GA. Sortable Risk Factors and Health Indicators. https://sortablestats.cdc.gov/#/.

Health Indicators. The CDC's Sortable Risk Factors and Health Indicators website compiles data from various published CDC and federal sources into a format that allows users to view, sort, and analyze data at state/territory, regional, and national levels.

Table A-16 includes the following indicators for the United States and each state:

Adult Smoking (2016). The percent of adults (age 18+) who currently smoke cigarettes (**Source:** *Behavioral Risk Factor Surveillance System*) Includes all 50 states, DC and territories (Guam, Puerto Rico, and the U.S. Virgin Islands).

Youth Smoking (2015). The percent of High school students who smoked cigarettes on one or more days in the last 30 days. (**Source:** *Youth Risk Behavior Surveillance System (YRBSS), 2015*) National percentage is based on a separate, nationally representative survey. It is not based on results from individual state and territorial surveys. Data not available in MN, OR, and WA. 2015 Data not available in CO, GA, IA, KS, LA, NJ, OH, TX, UT, WI.

Adult Physical Activity (2013). The percent of adults that participated in 150 minutes or more of Aerobic Physical Activity per week. (**Source:** *Behavioral Risk Factors Surveillance System (BRFSS)*) Includes all 50 states, DC and territories (Guam, Puerto Rico, and the U.S. Virgin Islands). National data based on median state prevalence of these 54 areas.

Youth Physical Activity (2015). The percent of high school students that are physically active at least 60 minutes per day on five or more days. (**Source:** *Youth Risk Behavior Surveillance System (YRBSS), 2015*) Physically active is defined as doing any kind of physical activity that increased the heart rate and made them breathe hard some of the time during the 7 days before the survey. National percentage is based on a separate, nationally representative survey. It is not based on results from individual state and territorial surveys. Data not available in MN, OR, and WA. 2015 Data not available in CO, GA, IA, KS, LA, NJ, OH, TX, UT, WI.

Adult Nutrition (2015). The percent of adults that consume vegetables less than one time per day. (**Source:** *Behavioral Risk Factors Surveillance System*) Includes all 50 states, DC and territories (Guam, Puerto Rico, and the U.S. Virgin Islands). National data based on median state prevalence of these 54 areas.

Youth Nutrition (2015). The percent of high school students that ate vegetables three or more times per day (**Source:** *Youth Risk Behavior Surveillance System (YRBSS), 2015*) National percentage is based on a separate, nationally representative survey. It is not based on results from individual state and territorial surveys. Data not available in MN, OR, and WA. 2015 Data not available in CO, GA, IA, KS, LA, NJ, OH, TX, UT, WI

Adult Binge Drinking (2016). The percent of adults (age over 18) who are binge drinkers: males having five or more drinks on one occasion, females having four or more drinks on one occasion. (**Source:** *Behavioral Risk Factor Surveillance System*) Includes all 50 states, DC and territories (Guam, Puerto Rico, and the U.S. Virgin Islands). National data based on median state prevalence of these 54 areas.

Youth Binge Drinking (2015). The percent of high school students reporting having five or more drinks of alcohol in a row within a couple of hours on at least 1 day in the last 30 days (**Source:** *Youth Risk Behavior Surveillance System (YRBSS), 2015*) National percentage is based on a separate, nationally representative survey. It is not based on results from individual state and territorial surveys. Data not available in MN, OR, and WA. 2015 Data not available in CO, GA, IA, KS, LA, NJ, OH, TX, UT, WI

Observed Seat Belt Use (2014). The percent of observed seat belt use among front seat occupants based on probability samples in all 50 states (**Source:** *National Highway Traffic Safety Administration (NHTSA)*). NHTSA's National Occupant Protection Use Survey (NOPUS) is a national probability-based survey. National average of 85% includes 50 states, DC, and territories.

Youth Seat Belt Use (2015). Percent of high school students who wore a seat belt sometimes, most of the time, or always (**Source:** *Youth Risk Behavior Surveillance System (YRBSS), 2015*) National percentage is based on a separate, nationally representative survey. It is not based on results from individual state and territorial surveys. Data not available in MN, OR, and WA. 2015 Data not available in CO, GA, IA, KS, LA, NJ, OH, TX, UT, WI

Youth Marijuana Use (2015). The percent of high school students who used marijuana on at least 1 or more days in the last 30 days (**Source:** *Youth Risk Behavior Surveillance System (YRBSS), 2015*). National percentage is based on a separate, nationally representative survey. It is not based on results from individual state and territorial surveys. Data not available in MN, OR, and WA. 2015 Data not available in CO, GA, IA, KS, LA, NJ, OH, TX, UT, WI.

Table A-17. Health Indicators: Health Conditions and Preventive Measures

Source: U.S. Centers for Disease Control and Prevention, Atlanta, GA. Sortable Risk Factors and Health Indicators. https://sortablestats.cdc.gov/#/.

Health Indicators. The CDC's Sortable Risk Factors and Health Indicators website compiles data from various published CDC and federal sources into a format that allows users to view, sort, and analyze data at state/territory, regional, and national levels.

Table A-17 includes the following indicators:

HIV Diagnosis Rate (2014). The rate of persons diagnosed with HIV infection per 100,000 population (**Source:** *CDC HIV Surveillance Report*). Diagnoses of HIV infection refers to laboratory-confirmatory evidence of HIV infection cases reported to CDC annually. The estimated rates of diagnoses of HIV infection are based on data from 46 states and 5 territories (American Samoa, Guam, the Northern Mariana Islands, Puerto Rico, and the U.S. Virgin Islands) that have had confidential name-based HIV infection reporting for a sufficient length of time (i.e., since at least January 2007, and reporting to CDC since at least June 2007). This figure does not include persons living with HIV who have NOT been diagnosed (20% of all persons living with HIV). Rates are per 100,000 population based on 2009 population estimates, and are statistical adjusted to account for reporting delays, but not for incomplete reporting.

Adult Obesity (2016). The percent of adults (age 18 and older) who are obese (Body Mass Index>30) (**Source:** *Behavioral Risk Factor Surveillance System 2012*). Includes all 50 states, DC and territories (Guam, Puerto Rico, and the U.S. Virgin Islands). National data based on median state prevalence of these 54 areas.

Youth Obesity (2015). Indicator: The percent of high school students who are obese (Body Mass Index= the 95th percentile for age/sex) (**Source:** *Youth Risk Behavior Surveillance System (YRBSS), 2015*). National percentage is based on a separate, nationally representative survey. It is not based on results from individual state and territorial surveys. Data not available in MN, OR, and WA. 2015 Data not available in CO, GA, IA, KS, LA, NJ, OH, TX, UT, WI.

Diagnosed Diabetes (2014). The percent of adults (age 18+) ever told by health professional that they have diabetes (**Source:** *Behavioral Risk Factor Surveillance System (BRFSS), 2014*). Women diagnosed only during pregnancy (gestational diabetes) and persons who reported they are pre-or borderline diabetic are excluded. Includes all 50 states, DC and territories (Guam, Puerto Rico, and the U.S. Virgin Islands). National data based on median state prevalence of these 54 areas (median %=9.5).

Diagnosed High Cholesterol (2013). The percent of adults who have had their blood cholesterol checked and have been told it was high (**Source:** *Behavioral Risk Factor Surveillance System (BRFSS))*. Includes all 50 states, DC and territories (Guam, Puerto Rico, and the U.S. Virgin Islands). National data based on median state prevalence of these 54 areas (median %=38.4).

Diagnosed Hypertension (2013). The percent of adults (age 18+) ever told by a health professional that they have high blood pressure. (**Source:** *Behavioral Risk Factor Surveillance System)*. Includes all 50 states, DC and territories (Guam, Puerto Rico, and the U.S. Virgin Islands). National data based on median state prevalence of these 54 areas (median %=30.9).

Medicated Hypertension (2013). The percent of adults (age 18+) currently taking medicine for high blood pressure (hypertension) (**Source:** *Behavioral Risk Factor Surveillance System)*. Percent is based on a subset of persons having been told by health professionals that they have high blood pressure. Data includes all 50 states, DC and territories (Guam, Puerto Rico, and the U.S. Virgin Islands). National data based on median state prevalence of these 54 areas.

Colorectal Cancer Screening (2014). The percent of persons age 50+ who have ever had a sigmoidoscopy or colonoscopy (**Source:** *Behavioral Risk Factor Surveillance System)*. Includes all 50 states, DC and territories (Guam, Puerto Rico, and the U.S. Virgin Islands). National data based on median state prevalence of these 54 areas (median %=64.2).

Influenza Vaccination Coverage (2016). The percent of persons aged 6 months and older who received a seasonal influenza vaccination with the past year (**Source:** *Fluvaxview)* Combines estimates from the National Immunization Survey (NIS) and the Behavioral Risk Factor Surveillance System (BRFSS), from all 50 states and DC to estimate national and state level influenza vaccination coverage. National and regional rates exclude U.S. territories.

Child Vaccination Coverage (2015). The percent of children aged 19 to 35 months receiving the recommended doses of DTaP, polio, MMR, Hib, hepatitis B, Varicella and PCV. (**Source:** *National Immunization Survey (NIS))*. The Advisory Committee on Immunization Practices recommended series of vaccinations for children aged 19 to 35

months include at least four doses of diphtheria-tetanus-acellular pertussis (DTaP), at least three doses of polio, at least one dose of measles-mumps-rubella (MMR), at least three or four doses of Haemophilus influenzae B (Hib) depending on product type received, at least three doses of hepatitis B antigens, at least one dose of varicella, and at least four doses of PCV. In 2009, the full series was modified to include 3 or 4 doses of Hib vaccine (depending on product type received); which differs from the 2007 and 2008 full series included 3 doses of Hib vaccine.

Table A-18. People with and without Health Insurance Coverage

Source: U.S. Census Bureau, American Community Survey, Health Insurance Coverage in the United States, 2018, historical tables. https://www.census.gov/data/tables/time-series/demo/health-insurance/historical-series/hic.html

Each year the Census Bureau issues a report on health insurance in the United States. This report presents statistics on health insurance coverage based on information collected in the Current Population Survey Annual Social and Economic Supplements (CPS ASEC) and the American Community Survey (ACS). Table A-18 is from the ACS data.

People who had no reported health coverage, or those whose only health coverage was Indian Health Service, were considered uninsured. For reporting purposes, the Census Bureau broadly classifies health insurance coverage as private health insurance or public coverage.

Private health insurance is a plan provided through an employer or union, a plan purchased by an individual from a private company, or TRICARE or other military health care. Public health coverage includes the federal programs Medicare, Medicaid, and VA Health Care (provided through the Department of Veterans Affairs); the Children's Health Insurance Program (CHIP); and individual state health plans. The types of health insurance are not mutually exclusive; people may be covered by more than one at the same time.

Table A-19. Public and Private School Fall Enrollment

Sources: Total enrollment—U.S. Census Bureau, *2018 American Community Survey*; table C14003, "School enrollment by type of school by age for the population 3 years and over"; data.census.gov; Public enrollment—U.S. National Center for Education Statistics, Digest of Education Statistics, annual. https://nces.ed.gov/programs/digest/d18/index.asp

Total (public and private) enrollment data are provided by the American Community Survey. For information on the American Community Survey, see General Notes.

Total enrollment rate is the average percent of people aged 3–4 or 5–17 years who are enrolled in public or private school based on enumerated resident population for the ages of 3–4 or 5–17 as of July 1.

Public enrollment data are from the Common Core of Data (CCD), which is the National Center for Education Statistics' (NCES) primary database on elementary and secondary public education in the United States. The CCD, collected annually, is a comprehensive, national statistical database of all public elementary and secondary schools and school districts and contains data that are comparable across all states.

Data are collected for a particular school year via an online reporting system open to state education agencies during the school year. Beginning with the 2006–07 school year, nonfiscal CCD data are collected through the Department of Education's Education Data Exchange Network (EDEN). Since the CCD is a universe collection, CCD data are not subject to sampling errors. However, nonsampling errors could come from two sources: nonresponse and inaccurate reporting.

Table A-20. Public Elementary and Secondary Schools—Finances and Teachers

Source: U.S. Department of Education, National Center for Education Statistics, Common Core of Data (CCD), "National Public Education Financial Survey (State Fiscal)", 2016-17 v.1a; "School District Finance Survey (F-33)", 2016-17 (FY 2017) v.1a; "State Nonfiscal Public Elementary/Secondary Education Survey", 2018-19 v.1a.

Enrollment is the "Fall Membership", the total count of pupils that are enrolled on or about October 1st of the survey year.

Total Revenues is the sum of subtotals for Local Government, State Government, Intermediate Government Agencies, and Federal Government. Does not include other sources of revenue.

Local Revenues is the sum of Local Revenues and Revenues from Intermediate Agencies.

State Revenues are revenues received by the Local Education Agencies (LEAs) from the state and includes unrestricted and restricted grants-in-aid, revenue in lieu of taxes, and payments for, or on behalf of, LEAs.

Total Expenditures is the sum of Total Expenditures for Education, Direct State Support Expenditures for Private School Students, and Interest on long term debt.

Current expenditures are for public elementary and secondary education, grades prekindergarten through grade 12, including ungraded students. Expenditures for equipment, non-public education, school construction, debt financing and community services are excluded from this data item. Expenditures by state governments for and on behalf of LEAs are included in these expenditures, and all other expenditures here. This is the sum of expenditures for Instruction, Support Services, and Non-instructional Services (excluding Community Services) and Direct Program Support (excluding Support for Private school Students), and excludes Property expenditures.

Total Current Expenditures per pupil is the total current expenditures for public elementary and secondary education divided by the fall membership as reported in the state finance file. The Expenditures for equipment, non-public education, school construction, debt financing and community services are excluded from this data item.

A **teacher** is a professional school staff member who instructs students in prekindergarten, kindergarten, grades 1 through 12, or ungraded classes, and who maintains daily student attendance records. The number of teachers represents full- time equivalent (FTE), computed by dividing the amount of time employed by the time normally required for a full-time position.

A kindergarten teacher is a teacher of a group or class that is part of a public school program and is taught during the year preceding first grade.

An elementary teacher is a teacher of a group or class that is within a general level of instruction classified by state and local practice as elementary, generally including grades 1 through 8.

A secondary school teacher is a teacher of a group or class that is within a general level of instruction classified by state and local practice as high school, generally including grades 9 through 12.

The **pupil/teacher ratio** includes teachers for students with disabilities and other special teachers, while these teachers are generally excluded from class size calculations. The student count for the pupil/teacher ratio includes all students enrolled in the fall of the school year.

Table A-21. Public High School Graduates and Educational Attainment

Sources: Public high school graduates—U.S. National Center for Education Statistics, Digest of Education Statistics, annual. https://nces.ed.gov/programs/digest/d18/index.asp);

Attainment—U.S. Census Bureau, 2018 American Community Survey, Table B15003, "Educational Attainment for the Population 25 Years and Over" (data.census.gov)

A **high school graduate** is defined as an individual who has received formal recognition from school authorities, by the granting of a diploma, for completing a prescribed course of study. This definition does not include other high school completers or high school equivalency recipients. Projections of graduates could be affected by changes in policies influencing graduation requirements.

Data on **educational attainment** are derived from questions asked of all respondents to the American Community Survey, and data presented here are tabulated for people 25 years old and over. Respondents are classified according to the highest degree or the highest level of school completed. Persons currently enrolled in school are asked to report the level of the previous grade attended or the highest degree received. **High school graduate** refers to respondents who received a high school diploma or the equivalent, such as passing the test of General Educational Development (G.E.D.), and did not attend college. **Some college, but no degree** refers to respondents who have attended college for some amount of time but have no degree. The category **associate's degree** includes people whose highest degree is an associate's degree, which generally requires 2 years of college-level work and is either in an occupational program that prepares them for a specific occupation, or an academic program primarily in the arts and sciences. The course work may or may not be transferable to a **bachelor's degree**. **Advanced degree** refers to a graduate or professional degree.

Table A-22. Institutions of Higher Education

Source: Fall enrollment and degrees conferred—U.S. National Center for Education Statistics, Digest of Education Statistics, annual. https://nces.ed.gov/programs/digest/d18/index.asp

Higher education is identified by the National Center for Education Statistics (NCES) as the study beyond secondary school at an institution that offers programs terminating in an associate, baccalaureate, or higher degrees. The data shown are based upon the Integrated Postsecondary Education Data System (IPEDS), established as the core postsecondary education data collection program for NCES. IPEDS is a system of surveys designed to collect data from all primary providers of postsecondary education in such areas as enrollment, program completions, faculty, staff, and finances. See the sources for methodological details.

Degrees conferred refer to awards conferred by a college, university, or other postsecondary educational institution as official recognition for the successful completion of a program of studies.

Table A-23. Violent Crimes and Crime Rates

Source: U.S. Federal Bureau of Investigation, *Crime in the United States*, annual. https://ucr.fbi.gov/crime-in-the-u.s/2018/crime-in-the-u.s.-2018

Data presented on crime are through the voluntary contribution of crime statistics by law enforcement agencies across the United States. The Uniform Crime Reporting (UCR) program provides periodic assessments of crime in the nation as measured by offenses coming to the attention of the law enforcement community. UCR program contributors compile and submit their crime data in one of two means: either directly to the FBI or through the state UCR programs.

Caution is advised when comparing data between areas based on these respective Crime Index figures. Assessing criminality and law enforcement's responses from area to area should encompass many elements (i.e., population density and urbanization, population composition, stability of population, modes of transportation, commuting patterns and highway systems, economic conditions, cultural conditions, family conditions, climate, effective strength and emphasis of law enforcement agencies, attitudes of citizenry toward crime, and crime reporting practices). These elements may have a significant impact on crime reporting. Also, not all law enforcement agencies provide data for all 12 months of the year and some agencies fail to report at all. Data in this publication are presented as reported to the FBI.

Data presented reflect the Hierarchy Rule, which requires that only the most serious offense in a multiple-offense criminal incident be counted. In descending order of severity, the violent crimes are murder and nonnegligent manslaughter, forcible rape, robbery, and aggravated assault, followed by the property crimes of burglary, larceny-theft, and motor vehicle theft. The Hierarchy Rule does not apply to the offense of arson.

Violent crimes include four crime categories: (1) Murder and nonnegligent manslaughter, as defined in the UCR program, is the willful (nonnegligent) killing of one human being by another. This offense excludes deaths caused by negligence, suicide, or accident; justifiable homicides; and attempts to murder or assaults to murder. (2) In 2013, the FBI UCR Program began collecting rape data under a revised definition, used in this book for the 2015 data. Previously, offense data for forcible rape were collected under the legacy UCR definition: the carnal knowledge of a female forcibly and against her will. Beginning with the 2013 data year, the term "forcible" was removed from the offense title, and the definition was changed. The revised UCR definition of rape is: penetration, no matter how slight, of the vagina or anus with any body part or object, or oral penetration by a sex organ of another person, without the consent of the victim. Attempts or assaults to commit rape are also included in the statistics presented here; however, statutory rape and incest are excluded. (3) Robbery is the taking or attempting to take anything of value from the care, custody, or control of a person or persons by force or threat of force or violence and/or by putting the victim in fear. (4) Aggravated assault is an unlawful attack by one person upon another for the purpose of inflicting severe or aggravated bodily injury. This type of assault is usually accompanied by the use of a weapon or by means likely to produce death or great bodily harm. Attempts are included since an injury does not necessarily have to result when a gun, knife, or other weapon is used, which could and probably would result in a serious personal injury if the crime were successfully completed.

Rates are based on Census Bureau resident population enumerated as of April 1 for decennial census years and estimated as of July 1 for other years.

Table A-24. Property Crimes and Crime Rates

Source: U.S. Federal Bureau of Investigation, *Crime in the United States*, annual. https://ucr.fbi.gov/crime-in-the-u.s/2018/crime-in-the-u.s.-2018

For information on the Uniform Crime Reporting (UCR) program and comparability of data, see appendix entry for Table A-23.

In general, property crimes include four crime categories: (1) Burglary is the unlawful entry of a structure to commit a felony or theft. (2) Larceny-theft is the unlawful taking, carrying, leading, or riding away of property from the possession or constructive possession of another. It includes crimes such as shoplifting, pocket picking, purse snatching, thefts from motor vehicles, thefts of motor vehicle parts and accessories, bicycle thefts, etc., in which no use of force, violence, or fraud occurs. This crime category does not include embezzlement, "con" games, forgery, worthless checks, and motor vehicle theft. (3) Motor vehicle theft is the theft or attempted theft of a motor vehicle. This definition excludes the taking of a motor vehicle for temporary use by those persons having lawful access. (4) Arson is any willful or malicious burning or attempt to burn, with or without intent to defraud, a dwelling house, public building, motor vehicle or aircraft, personal property of another, etc. Only fires determined through investigation to have been willfully or maliciously set are classified as arson. Fires of suspicious or unknown origins are excluded.

Table A-25. Juvenile Arrests, Child Abuse Cases, and Prisoners

Sources: Juvenile arrests—*Crime in the United States*, annual. https://ucr.fbi.gov/crime-in-the-u.s/2018/crime-in-the-u.s.-2018 ; Child abuse and neglect—U.S. Department of Health and Human Services, Administration on Children, Youth and Families, *Child Maltreatment 2015* https://www.acf.hhs.gov/cb/resource/child-maltreatment-2018; Estimated number and rate of persons supervised by adult correctional system—Bureau of Justice Statistics, *Correctional Populations in the United States, 2016* https://www.bjs.gov/index.cfm?ty=pbdetail&iid=6226

Juvenile arrests. The FBI's Uniform Crime Reporting (UCR) Program counts one arrest for each separate instance in which a person is arrested, cited, or summoned for an offense. The UCR Program collects arrest data on 28 offenses, (https://ucr.fbi.gov/crime-in-the-u.s/2018/crime-in-the-u.s.-2018/topic-pages/offenses-known-to-law-enforcement) Because a person may be arrested multiple times during a year, the UCR arrest figures do not reflect the number of individuals who have been arrested; rather, the arrest data show the number of times that persons are arrested, as reported by law enforcement agencies to the UCR Program. Juveniles include all persons under 18. Traffic arrests are not included. The rape figures in this table are aggregate totals of the data submitted based on both the legacy and revised Uniform Crime Reporting definitions. Drunkenness is considered a crime in some states; therefore, the figures vary from state to state.

Data on **child abuse and neglect cases** are collected and analyzed through the National Child Abuse and Neglect Data System (NCANDS) by the Children's Bureau, Administration on Children, Youth, and Families in the Administration for Children and Families, U.S. Department of Health and Human Services. The number of investigations includes assessments and is based on the total number of investigations that received a disposition. The number of children subject of an investigation of assessment is based on the total number of children for whom an alleged maltreatment was substantiated, indicated, or assessed to have occurred or the child was at risk of occurrence. A victim is defined as a child for whom the state determined at least one maltreatment was substantiated or indicated.

Each state has its own definitions of child abuse and neglect based on minimum standards set by federal law. Federal legislation provides a foundation for states by identifying a minimum set of acts or behaviors that define child abuse and neglect. The *Federal Child Abuse Prevention and Treatment Act* (CAPTA), (42 U.S.C.A. §5106g), as amended by the *Keeping Children and Families Safe Act of 2003*, defines child abuse and neglect as: Any recent act or failure to act on the part of a parent or caretaker which results in death, serious physical or emotional harm, sexual abuse or exploitation; or an act or failure to act which presents an imminent risk of serious harm.

Within the minimum standards set by CAPTA, each state is responsible for providing its own definitions of child abuse and neglect. Most states recognize four major types of maltreatment: neglect, physical abuse, sexual abuse, and psychological maltreatment.

Data for persons supervised by the U.S. adult correctional system were published in *Correctional Populations in the United States*, compiled from the Annual Probation Survey, Annual Parole Survey, Census of Jail Inmates, Deaths in Custody Reporting Program—Annual Summary on Inmates under Jail Jurisdiction, and National Prisoner Statistics program.

Table A-26. State and Local Justice Employment and Expenditures

Source: U.S. Bureau of Justice Statistics, Justice Expenditure and Employment Extracts, Preliminary 2016; https://www.bjs.gov/index.cfm?ty=pbdetail&iid=6728

Justice expenditure and employment data are extracted from the Census Bureau's Annual Government Finance Survey and Annual Survey of Public Employment. **Employees** include both full-time and part-time employees. **Expenditure** refers to all amounts of money paid out other than for retirement of debt, investment in securities, extensions of loans, or agency transactions. It includes only external cash payments and excludes any intragovernmental transfers and noncash transactions. It also includes any payments financed from borrowing, fund balances, intergovernmental revenue, and other current revenue.

Police protection is the function of enforcing the law, and preserving order and traffic safety and apprehending those who violate the law, whether these activities are performed by a police department, a sheriff's department, or a special police force maintained by an agency whose primary responsibility is outside the justice system but that has a police force to perform these activities in its specialized area (geographic or functional). Data for police protection cover all activities concerned with the enforcement of law and order, including coroners' offices, police-training academies, investigation bureaus, and local jails, "lockup," or other detention facilities not intended to serve as correctional facilities. **Judicial and legal** services covers all civil and criminal activities associated with courts, including prosecution and public defense. Data for **corrections** cover all activities pertaining to the confinement and correction of adults and minors accused or convicted of criminal offenses. Any pardon, probation, and parole activities also are included here.

Table A-27. Civilian Labor Force and Employment

Source: U.S. Bureau of Labor Statistics, Local Area Unemployment Statistics program. https://www.bls.gov/lau/rdscnp16.htm

The **civilian noninstitutionalized population** includes persons 16 years of age and older residing in the 50 states and the District of Columbia who are not inmates of institutions (for example, penal and mental facilities, homes for the aged), and who are not on active duty in the armed forces. The **civilian labor force** comprises all civilians 16 years old and over classified as employed or unemployed. Employed persons are all civilians who, during the survey week, did any work at all as paid employees, in their own business, profession, or on their own farm or who worked 15 hours or more as unpaid workers in an enterprise operated by a member of the family. It also includes all those who were not working but who had jobs or businesses from which they were temporarily absent because of illness, bad weather, vacation, labor-management disputes, job training, or personal reasons, whether they were paid for the time off or were seeking other jobs. Each employed person is counted only once regardless of how many jobs he or she may have.

Table A-28. Civilian Labor Force and Unemployment

Source: U.S. Bureau of Labor Statistics, Local Area Unemployment Statistics program. https://www.bls.gov/lau/rdscnp16.htm

Unemployed persons are all civilians 16 years old and over who had no employment during the survey week, were available for work, except for temporary illness, and had actively pursued employment some time during the prior 4 weeks. Active efforts include sending out resumes, placing or answering advertisements, and contacting potential employers regarding employment opportunities. Those engaged in passive methods of job seeking are not classified as unemployed. Persons who were laid off or were waiting to report to a new job within 30 days did not need to be looking for work to be classified as unemployed. The **unemployment rate** for all civilian workers represents the number of unemployed as a percent of the civilian labor force.

Table A-29. Employed Civilians by Occupation

Source: U.S. Bureau of Labor Statistics, Occupational Employment Statistics program. https://www.bls.gov/oes/home.htm

An **occupation** is a set of activities or tasks that employees are paid to perform. Employees who perform essentially the same tasks are in the same occupation, whether or not they work in the same industry. Some occupations are concentrated in a few particular industries; other occupations are found in many industries.

Table A-30. Private Industry Employment and Wages

Sources: U.S. Bureau of Labor Statistics, Quarterly Census of Employment and Wages https://data.bls.gov/cew/apps/table_maker/v4/table_maker.htm#type=0&year=2018&qtr=A&own=0&ind=10&supp=1

Data from the Quarterly Census of Employment and Wages (QCEW) program (ES-202 program for employment and average annual pay) are the product of a federal-state cooperative program. The QCEW program derives its data from quarterly tax reports submitted to State Employment Security Agencies by over eight million employers subject to state unemployment insurance (UI) laws and from federal agencies subject to the Unemployment Compensation for Federal Employees (UCFE) program. This includes 99.7 percent of all wage and salary civilian employment. The summaries are a result of the administration of state unemployment insurance programs that require most employers to pay quarterly taxes based on the employment and wages of workers covered.

The QCEW program is an employer reported measure and therefore associated with filled jobs, whether full or part-time, and place of work. If a person holds two jobs, the person would be counted twice in QCEW data. Programs which measure full-time equivalent positions or vacant positions target a different concept, as do household reported measures, which more typically show number of people with jobs, regardless of how many, and keep track of them by place or residence. The QCEW program, by definition, measures employment covered by unemployment insurance laws. In excluding self-employed jobs, and others, it differs significantly from those programs that include that employment.

Average annual wages per employee for any given industry are computed by dividing total annual wages by annual average employment. A further division by 52 yields average weekly wages per employee. Annual pay data only approximate annual earnings, because an individual may not be employed by the same employer all year or may work for more than one employer at a time. Average weekly or annual pay is affected by the ratio of full-time to part-time workers, as well as by the numbers of individuals in high- and low-paying occupations. When comparing average pay levels among states and industries, data users should take these factors into consideration. For example, industries characterized by high proportions of part-time workers will show average weekly wage levels appreciably less than the weekly pay levels of regular full-time employees in these industries. The opposite is true of industries with low proportions of part-time workers and of industries that typically schedule heavy weekend and overtime work. Average wage data also may be influenced by work stoppages, labor turnover, retroactive payments, seasonal factors, and bonus payments.

Table A-31. Average Annual Employment By industry and Wages

Sources: U.S. Bureau of Labor Statistics, Quarterly Census of Employment and Wages : https://data.bls.gov/cew/apps/data_views/data_views.htm#tab=Tables

See the text for Table A-30 for explanations of employment and annual pay data for the Quarterly Census of Employment and Wages program. Refer to General Notes to see information on different industries defined using the North American Industry Classification System (NAICS).

Table A-32. Union Membership

Sources: U.S. Bureau of Labor Statistics. BLS news release 20-0108 "Union Members—2019". https://www.bls.gov/news.release/pdf/union2.pdf

The Bureau of Labor Statistics (BLS) provides information on union membership. The estimates from BLS are obtained from the Current Population Survey (CPS), which provides basic information on the labor force, employment, and unemployment. The survey is conducted monthly for the Bureau of Labor Statistics by the U.S. Census Bureau from a scientifically selected national sample of about 60,000 eligible households.

Table A-33. Median Income of Households in 2018 Inflation-Adjusted Dollars and Distribution by Income Level

Source: U.S. Census Bureau, American Community Survey, 2018. Table S1901. Income in the Past 12 Months (In 2018 Inflation-Adjusted Dollars). data.census.gov

Median income divides the income distribution into two equal parts: one-half of the cases falling below the median income and one-half above the median. For households and families, the median income is based on the distribution of the total number of households and families including those with no income. The median income for individuals is based on individuals 15 years old and over with income. Median income for households, families, and individuals is computed on the basis of a standard distribution. Median income is rounded to the nearest whole dollar. Median income figures are calculated using linear interpolation if the width of the interval containing the estimate is $2,500 or less. If the width of the interval containing the estimate is greater than $2,500, Pareto interpolation is used.

Income of households includes the income of the householder and all other individuals 15 years old and over in the household, whether they are related to the householder or not. Because many households consist of only one person, average household income is usually less than average family income. Although the household income statistics cover the past 12 months, the characteristics of individuals and the composition of households refer to the time of interview. Thus, the income of the household does not include amounts received by individuals who were members of the household during all or part of the past 12 months if these individuals no longer resided in the household at the time of interview. Similarly, income amounts reported by individuals who did not reside in the household during the past 12 months but who were members of the household at the time of interview are included. However, the composition of most households was the same during the past 12 months as at the time of interview.

For the definition of a **household**, see appendix entry for Table A-5.

Table A-34. Family Income and Families and Individuals Below Poverty: 2015

Source: U.S. Census Bureau, American Community Survey, 2018. Table S1901. Income in the Past 12 Months (In 2018 Inflation-Adjusted Dollars). Table S1701. Poverty Status in the Past 12 Months; Table S1702. Poverty Status in the Past 12 Months of Families. data.census.gov

In compiling statistics on family income, the incomes of all members 15 years old and over related to the householder are summed and treated as a single amount. Although the family income statistics cover the past 12 months, the characteristics of individuals and the composition of families refer to the time of enumeration. Thus, the income of the family does not include amounts received by individuals who were members of the family during all or part of the

past 12 months if these individuals no longer resided with the family at the time of enumeration. Similarly, income amounts reported by individuals who did not reside with the family during the past 12 months but who were members of the family at the time of enumeration are included. However, the composition of most families was the same during the past 12 months as at the time of enumeration. See appendix entry for Table A-33 for information on **Median income**.

Poverty status is determined using thresholds arranged in a two-dimensional matrix. The matrix consists of family size cross-classified by presence and number of family members under age 18 years old. Unrelated individuals and two-person families are further differentiated by age of reference person. To determine a person's poverty status, one compares the person's total family income in the last 12 months with the poverty threshold appropriate for that person's family size and composition. If the total income of that person's family is less than the threshold appropriate for that family, then the person is considered poor or "below the poverty level," together with every member of his or her family. If a person is not living with anyone related by birth, marriage, or adoption, then the person's own income is compared with his or her poverty threshold. The total number of people below the poverty level was the sum of people in families and the number of unrelated individuals with incomes in the last 12 months below the poverty level.

Poverty thresholds can be found at https://www.census.gov/data/tables/time-series/demo/income-poverty/historical-poverty-thresholds.html

Table A-35. Housing—Units and Characteristics

Source: U.S. Census Bureau, American Community Survey, 2018. Table DP04. Selected Housing Characteristics. data.census.gov.

A **housing unit** is a house, apartment, mobile home or trailer, group of rooms, or single room occupied or, if vacant, intended for occupancy as separate living quarters. Separate living quarters are those in which the occupants do not live and eat with any other persons in the structure and that have direct access from the outside of the building through a common hall. For vacant units, the criteria of separateness and direct access are applied to the intended occupants whenever possible.

Units in structure. A structure is a separate building that either has open spaces on all sides or is separated from other structures by dividing walls that extend from ground to roof. In determining the number of units in a structure, all housing units, both occupied and vacant, are counted. Stores and office space are excluded. The statistics are presented for the number of housing units in structures of specified type and size, not for the number of residential buildings. **Mobile Homes** include both occupied and vacant mobile homes to which no permanent rooms have been added are counted in this category. Mobile homes used only for business purposes or for extra sleeping space and mobile homes for sale on a dealer's lot, at the factory, or in storage are not counted in the housing inventory. **1-Unit, Detached** are any 1-unit structure detached from any other house, that is, with open space on all four sides. Such structures are considered detached even if they have an adjoining shed or garage. A one-family house that contains a business is considered detached as long as the building has open space on all four sides. Mobile homes to which one or more permanent rooms have been added or built also are included. **1-Unit, Attached** include any 1-unit structure that has one or more walls extending from ground to roof separating it from adjoining structures. In row houses (sometimes called townhouses), double houses, or houses attached to nonresidential structures, each house is a separate, attached structure if the dividing or common wall goes from ground to roof.

Year structure built refers to when the building was first constructed, not when it was remodeled, added to, or converted. Housing units under construction are included as vacant housing if they meet the housing unit definition— that is, all exterior windows, doors, and final usable floors are in place. For mobile homes, houseboats, RVs, etc., the manufacturer's model year was assumed to be the year built. The data relate to the number of units built during the specified periods that were still in existence at the time of enumeration.

A housing unit is classified as **occupied** if it is the current place of residence of the person or group of people living in it at the time of enumeration, or if the occupants are only temporarily absent from the residence for 2 months or less; that is, away on vacation or a business trip. If all the people staying in the unit at the time of the interview are staying there for 2 months or less, the unit is considered to be temporarily occupied, and classified as "vacant." The occupants may be a single family, one person living alone, two or more families living together, or any other group of related or unrelated people who share living quarters. Occupied rooms or suites of rooms in hotel, motels, and similar places are classified as housing units only when occupied by permanent residents, that is, people who consider the hotel as their current place of residence or have no current place of residence elsewhere. If any of the occupants in rooming or boarding houses, congregate housing, or continuing care facilities live separately from others in the building and have direct access, their quarters are classified as separate housing units.

Data on **vehicles available** show the number of passenger cars, vans, and pickup or panel trucks of one-ton capacity or less kept at home and available for the use of household members. Vehicles rented or leased for 1 month or more, company vehicles, and police and government vehicles are included if kept at home and used for nonbusiness purposes. Dismantled or immobile vehicles are excluded. Vehicles kept at home but used only for business purposes also are excluded.

House heating fuel data refer to occupied housing units. The data show the type of fuel used most to heat the house, apartment, or mobile home. Utility gas includes gas piped through underground pipes from a central system to serve the neighborhood. Electricity is generally supplied by means of above or underground electric power lines.

Table A-36. Owner- and Renter-Occupied Units—Value and Gross Rent

Source: U.S. Census Bureau, American Community Survey, 2018. Table DP04. Selected Housing Characteristics. data.census.gov

A housing unit is **owner-occupied** if the owner or co-owner lives in the unit even if it is mortgaged or not fully paid for. The owner or co-owner must live in the unit. The unit is owner-occupied if someone who lives in the household is purchasing the house with a mortgage or some other debt arrangement such as a deed of trust, trust deed, contract to purchase, land contract, or purchase agreement. The unit also is considered owned with a mortgage if it is built on leased land and there is a mortgage on the unit. Mobile homes occupied by owners with installment loan balances also are included in this category.

Value is the respondent's estimate of how much the property (house and lot, mobile home and lot, or condominium unit) would sell for if it were for sale. If the house or mobile home was owned or being bought, but the land on which it sits was not, the respondent was asked to estimate the combined value of the house or mobile home and the land. **Median value** divides the value distribution into two equal parts: one-half of the cases falling below the median value of the property and one-half above the median.

Renter Occupied includes all occupied housing units that are not owner occupied, whether they are rented for cash rent or occupied without payment of cash rent. "No cash rent" units are generally provided free by friends or relatives or in exchange for services such as resident manager, caretaker, minister, or tenant farmer. Housing units on military bases also are classified as "No cash rent." "Rented for cash rent" includes units in continuing care, sometimes called life care arrangements. These arrangements usually involve a contract between one or more individuals and a health services provider guaranteeing the individual shelter, usually a house or apartment, and services, such as meals or transportation to shopping or recreation.

Gross rent is the contract rent plus the estimated average monthly cost of utilities (electricity, gas, and water and sewer) and fuels (oil, coal, kerosene, wood, etc.) if these are being paid for by the renter (or paid for the renter by someone else). The **median rent** divides the rent distribution into two equal parts: one-half of the cases falling below the median contract rent and one-half above the median.

Table A-37. Home Ownership and Vacancy Rates

Sources: U.S. Census Bureau, Current Population Survey/Housing Vacancy Survey https://www.census.gov/housing/hvs/index.html

Vacancy rates and **homeownership rates** are based on data obtained from the Current Population Survey/Housing Vacancy Survey (CPS/HVS). Beginning in 2003, new weighting procedures based on the 2000 decennial census were implemented. The CPS/HVS includes the civilian noninstitutionalized population. This universe includes civilians in households, people in noninstitutional group quarters (other than military barracks), and military in households living off post or with their families on post (as long as at least one household member is a civilian adult). The universe excludes other military in households and in group quarters (barracks) and people living in institutions. The weighting is controlled to independent counts of housing units for the month of the estimate. The sample size consists of approximately 71,000 addresses per month. A unit is in sample for 4 consecutive months, out for 8 months, back in sample for 4 months, and then retired from the sample. A housing unit is vacant if no one is living in it at the time of the interview, unless its occupants are only temporarily absent. In addition, a vacant unit may be one that is owned entirely by persons who have a usual residence elsewhere. **Rental vacancy rate** is the proportion of the rental inventory that is vacant for rent. The **homeowner vacancy rate** is the proportion of the homeowner inventory that is vacant for sale. The proportion of owner households to occupied households is termed the homeownership rate. It is computed by dividing the number of owner households by the number of occupied households.

Table A-38. Cost of Living Indicators— Housing, Public University, Hospital Stays, Energy Expenditures, and Utilities

Sources: Housing price index—Federal Housing Finance Agency, Annual House Price Indexes, https://www.fhfa.

gov/DataTools/Downloads/Pages/House-Price-Index.aspx ; Average undergraduate tuition and fees—U.S. National Center for Education Statistics, Digest of Education Statistics 2018, http://nces.ed.gov/programs/digest/; Energy expenditures, U.S. Department of Energy, Energy Price and Expenditure Estimates, https://www.eia.gov/state/seds/sep_prices/notes/pr_print.pdf; Gasoline state tax rates—U.S. Department of Transportation, Federal Highway Administration, https://www.fhwa.dot.gov/policyinformation/statistics/2018/mf121t.cfm.

Data on **housing prices** are collected through the Federal Housing Finance Board's Monthly Interest Rate Survey (MIRS). This survey provides monthly information on interest rates, loan terms, and house prices by property type, by loan type, and by lender type, as well as information on 15- and 30-year fixed-rate loans. The sample consists of mortgage lenders who were asked to report the terms and conditions on all single-family, fully amortized, purchase-money, nonfarm loans that they close during the last 5 business days of the month. The survey excludes FHA-insured and VA-guaranteed loans, multifamily loans, mobile home loans, and loans created by refinancing another mortgage.

The indexes in this table are developmental annual state indexes. Indexes are calibrated using appraisal values and sales prices for mortgages bought or guaranteed by Fannie Mae and Freddie Mac. This table shows the index value with a base of 100 to represent the value in 2000. Other bases are available from when they were first recorded (1975) and 1990.

Data on **undergraduate tuition, fees, room, and board** are for the entire academic year and are average charges for full-time students. In-state tuition and fees were weighted by the number of full-time-equivalent undergraduates, but were not adjusted to reflect the number of students who were state residents. Out-of-state tuition and fees were weighted by the number of first-time freshmen attending the institution in fall 2016 from out of state. Institutional room and board rates are weighted by the number of full-time students. Degree-granting institutions grant associate's or higher degrees and participate in Title IV federal financial aid programs. Detail may not sum to totals because of rounding.

Energy expenditure data refers to money directly spent by consumers to purchase energy. Expenditures equal the amount of energy used by the consumer times the price per unit paid by the consumer. In the calculation of the amount of energy used, process fuel and intermediate products are not included. Population estimates used to calculate per capita data are provided by the Census Bureau's population estimates.

This table shows **motor-fuel tax rates** that are levied as a dollar amount per volume of motor fuel. Taxes that apply to all petroleum products with distinguishing motor fuel are omitted. The gasohol rates shown are for gasoline blended with 10 percent ethanol. NOTE: The States which have exemptions are Hawaii (1 cent), Iowa (2 cents) Maine (6.5 cents), and Montana (4 cents). Tax rates include other miscellanous tax (enviromental, etc.).

Table A-39. Personal Income by State

Source: U.S. Bureau of Economic Analysis, Regional Economic Accounts https://www.bea.gov/regional/index.htm

Personal income data are based on the Regional Economic Information System; see Appendix B for additional information. Personal Income is the income that is received by all persons from all sources. It is calculated as the sum of wage and salary disbursements, supplements to wages and salaries, proprietors' income with inventory valuation and capital consumption adjustments, rental income of persons with capital consumption adjustment, personal dividend income, personal interest income, and personal current transfer receipts, less contributions for government social insurance. The personal income of an area is the income that is received by, or on behalf of, all the individuals who live in the area; therefore, the estimates of personal income are presented by the place of residence of the income recipients.

Disposable income is total personal income minus personal current taxes. It is personal income that is available for spending or saving.

Estimates are in current dollars (not adjusted for inflation.) For explanations of current versus constant dollars, see appendix entry for Table A-42.

Table A-40. Personal Income per Capita

Source: U.S. Bureau of Economic Analysis, Regional Economic Accounts https://www.bea.gov/regional/index.htm

Personal income data are based on the Regional Economic Information System; see Appendix B for additional information. Personal Income is the income that is received by all persons from all sources. It is calculated as the sum of wage and salary disbursements, supplements to wages and salaries, proprietors' income with inventory valuation and capital consumption adjustments, rental income of persons with capital consumption adjustment, personal dividend income, personal interest income, and personal current transfer receipts, less contributions for government social insurance. The personal income of an

area is the income that is received by, or on behalf of, all the individuals who live in the area; therefore, the estimates of personal income are presented by the place of residence of the income recipients.

Disposable income is total personal income minus personal current taxes. It is personal income that is available for spending or saving.

Estimates are in current dollars (not adjusted for inflation.) For explanations of current versus constant dollars, see appendix entry for Table A-42.

Table A-41. Earnings by Industry

Source: U.S. Bureau of Economic Analysis, Regional Economic Accounts, https://www.bea.gov/regional/index.htm

The components of **earnings** are wage and salary disbursements, other labor income, and proprietors' income. Wage and salary disbursements are defined as monetary remuneration of employees, including corporate officers; commissions, tips, and bonuses; and "pay-in-kind" that represents income to the recipient. They are measured before such deductions as social security contributions and union dues. All disbursements in the current period are covered. "Pay-in-kind" represents allowances for food, clothing, and lodging paid in kind to employees, which represent income to them, valued at the cost to the employer. Other labor income consists of employer contributions to privately administered pension and welfare funds and a few small items such as directors' fees, compensation of prison inmates, and miscellaneous judicial fees. Proprietors' income is the monetary income and income in-kind of proprietorships and partnerships, including the independent professions and of tax-exempt cooperatives. Refer to General Notes for information on specific industries.

Table A-42. Gross Domestic Product by State

Source: Bureau of Economic Analysis, Regional Economic Accounts https://www.bea.gov/regional/index.htm

Total **Gross Domestic Product** (GDP) by state is the value added in production by the labor and capital located in a state. GDP for a state is derived as the sum of the gross state product originating in all industries in a state. In concept, an industry's GDP by state, referred to as its "value added," is equivalent to its gross output (sales or receipts and other operating income, commodity taxes, and inventory change) minus its intermediate inputs (consumption of goods and services purchased from other U.S. industries or imported). GDP by state is therefore the state counterpart of the nation's gross domestic product (GDP), BEA's featured measure of U.S. output.

GDP by state for the nation differs from GDP for the following reasons: GDP by state excludes and GDP includes the compensation of federal civilian and military personnel stationed abroad and government consumption of fixed capital for military structures located abroad and for military equipment, except office equipment and GDP by state and GDP have different revision schedules.

Current-dollar estimates are the market value of an item and reflect the prices of the period being measured. **Chained dollars** are a measure used to express real prices, or prices that have been adjusted to account for inflation in order to represent a dollar's purchasing power. A chain-dollar estimate is a measure used to approximate the chained-typed index level and is calculated by taking the current-dollar level of a series in the base period and multiplying it by the change in the chained-type quantity index number for the series since the base period.

A chained-type index is an index based on the linking (chaining) of indexes to create a time series. Annual chained-type Fisher indices are used in BEA's national income and product accounts (NIPAs) whereby Fisher ideal price indices are calculated using the weights of adjacent years. Those annual changes are then multiplied (chained) together, forming the chained-type index time series. Chained-dollar estimates correctly show growth rates for a series, but are not additive in periods other than the base period.

Table A-43. Science and Engineering Indicators

Sources: Employment and Field of Bachelor's Degree—U.S. Census Bureau, American Community Survey, 2018 1-year file, Table S2401 Occupation by Sex for the Employed Population 25 Years and Over and Table S1501 Field of Bachelor's Degree for First Major; Master's Degrees—U.S. National Center for Education Statistics, Digest of Education Statistics, annual. https://nces.ed.gov/programs/digest/d18/index.asp.

Science and Engineering employment is from the occupation data in the American Community Survey. Occupation describes the kind of work a person does on the job. Occupation data were derived from answers to two questions: "What kind of work was this person doing?" and "What were this person's most important activities or duties?" These questions were asked of all people 15 years old and over who had worked in the past 5 years. For employed people, the data refer to the person's job during the previous week. For those who worked two or more jobs, the data refer to the job where the person

worked the greatest number of hours. For unemployed people and people who are not currently employed but report having a job within the last five years, the data refer to their last job. Table A-43 includes only employed persons aged 16 or older.

Occupation statistics are compiled from data that are coded based on the Standard Occupational Classification (SOC) Manual: 2018 (http://www.bls.gov/soc), published by the Executive Office of the President, Office of Management and Budget.

Census occupation codes, based on the 2018 SOC, provide 569 specific occupational categories, for employed people, including military, arranged into 23 major occupational groups. Respondents provided the data for the tabulations by writing on the questionnaires descriptions of the kind of work and activities they are doing. These write-ins are converted to a code category through automated coding. Cases not autocoded on both industry and occupation are sent to the clerical staff in the National Processing Center (NPC) in Jeffersonville, Indiana, who assign codes by comparing these descriptions to entries in the Alphabetical Index of Industries and Occupations (https://www.census.gov/topics/employment/industry-occupation/guidance/indexes.html).

For the detailed list of occupations, see

https://www2.census.gov/programs-Surveys/acs/tech_docs/code_lists/2018_ACS_Code_Lists.pdf?#

Data on field of bachelor's degree were derived from answers to a question that was asked only of persons with a bachelor's degree or higher. Eligible respondents were asked to list the specific major(s) of any bachelor's degree received. This question does not ask for the field of any other type of degree earned (such as master's or doctorate).

For the detailed list of fields of degree, see

https://www2.census.gov/programs-surveys/acs/tech_docs/subject_definitions/2018_ACSSubjectDefinitions.pdf?#

The Master's Degrees awarded are from the Integrated Postsecondary Education Data System (IPEDS), Fall 2017, Completions component, Natural sciences and mathematics includes biological and biomedical sciences; physical sciences; science technologies/technicians; and mathematics and statistics. Engineering includes engineering; engineering technologies/technicians; mechanic and repair technologies/technicians; and construction trades.

Table A-44. Employment Establishment Changes by Firm Size and State, 2014

Source: U.S. Census Bureau, Business Dynamic Statistics, https://www.census.gov/programs-surveys/bds.html

BDS provides annual measures of business dynamics (such as job creation and destruction, establishment births and deaths, and firm startups and shutdowns) for the economy and aggregated by establishment and firm characteristics. Firms are an aggregation of all establishments owned by a parent company with some annual payroll. Establishment entries represent all establishments initially counted in a given state during the calendar year, while establishment exits measure those that have left the state during the year.

For information regarding establishments, employment, and annual payroll, see appendix entry for Table A-14.

Table A-45. Employer Firms and Nonemployer Establishments

Sources: Employer firms—U.S. Small Business Administration, Office of Advocacy, Research and Statistics, https://www.sba.gov/advocacy/firm-size-data ; U.S. Census Bureau, Statistics of U.S. Businesses, https://www.census.gov/programs-surveys/susb.html Nonemployer establishments—U.S. Census Bureau, Nonemployer Statistics, https://www.census.gov/programs-surveys/nonemployer-statistics/data/tables.html

The Census Bureau provides the Office of Advocacy of the U.S. Small Business Administration with data on employer firm size in the Statistics of U.S. Businesses (SUSB). A **firm** is defined as the aggregation of all establishments owned by a parent company (within a geographic location and/ or industry) that have some annual payroll. A firm may be located in one or more places. SUSBs employer data contain the number of firms, number of establishments, employment, and annual payroll for employment size of firm categories by location and industry. The employer data consist of static and dynamic data. Data are static or a "snapshot" of firms at a point in time. Industries are defined according to the North American Industry Classification System (NAICS) thereafter.

A **nonemployer** business is one that has no paid employees, has annual business receipts of $1,000 or more ($1 or more in the construction industries), and is subject to federal income taxes. Nonemployer businesses are generally small, such as real estate agents and independent contractors. Nonemployers constitute nearly three-quarters of all businesses, but they contribute only about 3 percent of overall sales and receipts data.

For information regarding establishments, employment, and annual payroll, see appendix entry for Table A-14.

Table A-46. Private Nonfarm Establishments, Employment, and Payroll

Source: U.S. Census Bureau, County Business Patterns, annual. https://www.census.gov/programs-surveys/cbp.html.

Data excludes governmental establishments except for wholesale liquor establishments, retail liquor stores, federally chartered savings institutions, federally chartered credit unions, and hospitals. Establishments without a fixed location or having an unknown county location within a state are included under a "state-wide" geography classification. For state data, a firm is defined as an aggregation of all establishments owned by a parent company within a state. Establishments are nonfarm locations with active payroll in any quarter.

For information regarding establishments, employment, and annual payroll, see appendix entry for Table A-14.

Table A-47. Foreign Direct Investment in the United States and U.S. Exports

Sources: U.S. affiliates—Bureau of Economic Analysis, International Economic Accounts, Foreign direct investment in the United States. https://www.bea.gov/international// and https://www.bea.gov/international/di1fdiop.htm. U.S. exports—U.S. Census Bureau, Foreign Trade Statistics, http://www.census.gov/foreign-trade/statistics/state/origin_movement/index.html. U.S. agricultural exports—U.S. Department of Agriculture, Economic Research Service, U.S. Agricultural Trade database, https://www.ers.usda.gov/data-products/state-export-data/.

Foreign direct investment data in the United States are based on a survey of operations of nonbank U.S. affiliates that are majority-owned by foreign direct investors.

A **U.S. affiliate** is a U.S. business enterprise in which there is foreign direct investment; that is, in which a single foreign person owns or controls, directly or indirectly, 10 percent or more of the voting securities of an incorporated U.S. business enterprise. "Person" is broadly defined to include any individual, corporation, branch, partnership, associated group, association, estate trust, or other organization and any government. A "foreign person" is any person that resides outside the United States; that is, outside the 50 states, the District of Columbia, the Commonwealth of Puerto Rico, and all U.S. territories and possessions.

Export statistics consist of goods valued at more than $2,500 per commodity shipped by individuals and organizations (including exporters, freight forwarders, and carriers) from the United States to other countries. Exports are valued at the F.A.S. (free alongside ship) value of merchandise at the U.S. port of export, based on the transaction price including inland freight, insurance, and other charges incurred in placing the merchandise alongside the carrier at the U.S. port of exportation. Data on the value of U.S. agricultural exports by state of production are estimated by the Economic Research Service (ERS) using the customs district-level export data compiled by the Census Bureau and the state-level agricultural production data supplied by the National Agricultural Statistics Service (NASS). From these approximations a state that is the largest producer of an agricultural commodity will also account for the largest share of U.S. exports of that commodity.

U.S. agricultural commodity exports are often produced in inland states. From the farm, a commodity is sold to a local elevator, which in turn may sell it to a larger elevator located at a major transportation hub, which then moves the commodity to a port. As the commodity passes through several states before being exported, the state-of-origin often is lost or the product commingled with similar product from other states. Frequently, the state from which the commodity began its export journey, not necessarily the state in which the commodity was produced, is reported by the exporter. To more accurately reflect the situation for inland agricultural producing States, ERS calculates U.S. state agricultural exports based on a state's share of production of the exported commodity.

Table A-48. Farms and Farm Earnings

Sources: Farms—U.S. Department of Agriculture, National Agricultural Statistics Service, Farms and Land in Farms, 2016 Summary http://usda.mannlib.cornell.edu/usda/current/FarmLandIn/FarmLandIn-02-17-2017.pdf Earnings—U.S. Bureau of Economic Analysis, Regional Economic Accounts https://www.bea.gov/regional/index.htm.

A **farm** is any place from which $1,000 or more of agricultural products were produced and sold, or normally would have been sold, during the year. Government payments are included in sales. Ranches, institutional farms, experimental and research farms, and Indian Reservations are included as farms. Places with the entire acreage enrolled in the Conservation Reserve Program (CRP), Wetlands Reserve Program (WRP), or other government programs are counted as farms.

The acreage designated as "**land in farms**" consists primarily of agricultural land used for crops, pasture, or grazing. It also includes woodland and wasteland not actually under cultivation or used for pasture or grazing, provided it was part of the farm operator's total operation. Large acreages of woodland or wasteland held for nonagricultural purposes are not included. Land in farms includes

Conservation Reserve, Wetlands Reserve Programs, or other government programs.

Average acreage per farm was calculated by dividing the total land in farms for an area by the number of farms in that area.

Farm earnings comprises the net income of sole proprietors, partners, and hired laborers arising directly from the current production of agricultural commodities, either livestock or crops. It includes net farm proprietors' income and the wages and salaries, pay-in-kind, and supplements to wages and salaries of hired farm laborers; but specifically excludes the income of nonfamily farm corporations.

Table A-49. Farm Finances and Income

Source: U.S. Department of Agriculture, Economic Research Service, Farm Income and Wealth Statistics, https://www.ers.usda.gov/data-products/farm-income-and-wealth-statistics/data-files-us-and-state-level-farm-income-and-wealth-statistics/

The value of agricultural sector production is the sum of the value of crop production, the value of livestock production, and revenues from services and forestry in the value added table. The value of crop production and livestock production encompass cash receipts, home consumption, and inventory change. Revenues from services and forestry include machine hire and custom work income, sales of forestry products from farms, farm-related income, and gross imputed rental value of farm dwellings. The income and expenses associated with operators' dwellings are included in this account.

Net farm income is that portion of the net value added by agriculture to the national economy earned by farm operators. Farm operators typically benefit most from the increases and assimilate most of the declines arising from short-term, unanticipated weather and market conditions. Net farm income is a value of production measure indicating the farm operators' share of the net value added to the national economy within a calendar year, independent of whether it is received in cash or a non-cash form such as increases/decreases in inventories and imputed rental for the farm operator's dwelling.

Table A-50. Farm Income and Wealth Statistics

Sources: Government Payments—U.S. Department of Agriculture, Economic Research Service, Farm Income and Wealth Statistics, https://www.ers.usda.gov/data-products/farm-income-and-wealth-statistics.aspx;

Government payments consist of direct cash payments received by the farm operators. This includes disaster payments, loan deficiency payments from prior participation, payments from Conservation Reserve Programs (CRP), the Wetlands Reserve Programs (WRP), other conservation programs, and all other federal farm programs under which payments were made directly to farm operators. Commodity Credit Corporation (CCC) proceeds and federal crop insurance payments were not tabulated in this category.

Farm marketings represent quantities of agricultural products sold by farmers multiplied by prices received per unit of production at the local market. Information on prices received for farm products is generally obtained from surveys of firms (such as grain elevators, packers, and processors) purchasing agricultural commodities directly from producers. In some cases, the price information is obtained directly from the producers.

Table A-51. Natural Resource Industries and Minerals

Sources: Natural resource industries—U.S. Census Bureau, County Business Patterns, https://www.census.gov/programs-surveys/cbp.html; Nonfuel Mineral Production—United States Geological Survey "Mineral Commodities Summaries—2020 Tables https://minerals.usgs.gov/minerals/pubs/mcs/; Mineral fuels--U.S. Energy Information Administration. www.eia.gov/petroleum/supply/annual/volume1/, https://www.eia.gov/naturalgas/ https://www.eia.gov/coal/

Natural Resource Industries as presented here includes Agriculture, Forestry, Fishing, and Hunting (NAICS 11), Mining (NAICS 21), Wood Product Manufacturing (NAICS 321), and Paper Manufacturing (NAICS 322). For information on establishments, employment, and payroll, see the appendix entry for Table A-15. For detailed information on industry sectors and subsectors, see the General Notes of this appendix for the North American Industry Classification System (NAICS). Both Wood Product Manufacturing and Paper Manufacturing are subsectors of Manufacturing.

Nonfuel mineral production. The U.S. Geological Survey (USGS) collects information about the quantity and quality of all mineral resources. See the source listed for more detailed information on nonfuel mineral production.

The Energy Information Administration (EIA) collects production data on an ongoing basis for crude oil, natural gas, and coal.

Table A-52. Agriculture Census

Source: U.S. Department of Agriculture, National Agricultural Statistics Service, 2017 Census of Agriculture and 2012 Census of Agriculture https://www.nass.usda.gov/Publications/AgCensus/2017/index.php

A **farm** is any place from which $1,000 or more of agricultural products were produced and sold, or normally would have been sold, during the year. Government payments are included in sales. Ranches, institutional farms, experimental and research farms, and Indian Reservations are included as farms. Places with the entire acreage enrolled in the Conservation Reserve Program (CRP), Wetlands Reserve Program (WRP), or other government programs are counted as farms.

The acreage designated as "**land in farms**" consists primarily of agricultural land used for crops, pasture, or grazing. It also includes woodland and wasteland not actually under cultivation or used for pasture or grazing, provided it was part of the farm operator's total operation. Large acreages of woodland or wasteland held for nonagricultural purposes are not included. Land in farms includes Conservation Reserve, Wetlands Reserve Programs, or other government programs.

Market value of agricultural products sold represents the gross market value before taxes and production expenses of all agricultural products sold or removed from the place in 2007 regardless of who received the payment. It is equivalent to total sales and it includes sales by the operators as well as the value of any shares received by partners, landlords, contractors, or others associated with the operation. It includes value of direct sales and the value of commodities placed in the Commodity Credit Corporation (CCC) loan program. Market value of agricultural products sold does not include payments received for participation in other federal farm programs. Also, it does not include income from farm-related sources such as custom work and other agricultural services or income from nonfarm sources. The value of crops sold in 2007 or 2002 does not necessarily represent the sales from crops harvested in 2007 or 2002. Data may include sales from crops produced in earlier years and may exclude some crops produced in the stated years but held in storage and not sold. Sales figures are expressed in current dollars.

Farms by combined government payments and market value of agricultural products sold represent the value of products sold plus government payments. Total value of products sold combines total sales not under production contract and total sales under production contract. Government payments consist of government payments received from the Conservation Reserve Program (CRP), Wetlands Reserve Program (WRP), Farmable Wetlands Program (FWP), or Conservation Reserve Enhancement Program (CREP) plus government payments received from federal, state, and local programs other than the CRP, WRP, FWP, and CREP, and Commodity Credit Corporation loans.

The term **producer** designates a person who who is involved in making decisions for the farm operation.

Decisions may include decisions about such things as planting, harvesting, livestock management, and marketing. The producer may be the owner, a member of the owner's household, a hired manager, a tenant, a renter, or a sharecropper. If a person rents land to others or has land worked on shares by others, he/she is considered the producer only of the land which is retained for his/her own operation.

Table A-53. Utilities

Sources: Private utilities—U.S. Census Bureau, County Business Patterns, https://www.census.gov/programs-surveys/cbp.html. Water systems— Environmental Protection Agency https://www.epa.gov/ground-water-and-drinking-water/safe-drinking-water-information-system-sdwis-federal-reporting

Private utilities. Refer to General Notes to see information on the private utilities industry defined using the North American Industry Classification System (NAICS). See the appendix entry for Table A-15 for information on establishments, employees, and annual payroll. For information on what constitutes residential, see appendix entry for Table A-54.

Data on **water systems** are obtained by the Environmental Protection Agency through the Safe Drinking Water Information System/Federal Version (SDWIS/FED), a database designed and implemented to meet the EPAs needs in the oversight and management of the Safe Drinking Water Act (SDWA). The database contains data submitted by states and EPA regions in conformance with reporting requirements established by statute, regulation, and guidance. Community systems include any public water system that supplies water to the same population year-round. Nontransient noncommunity systems include any public water system that regularly supplies water to at least 25 of the same people at least 6 months per year, but not year-round. Transient noncommunity systems include any public water system that provides water in a place such as a gas station or a campground where people do not remain for long periods of time.

Table A-54. Energy Consumption

Source: U.S. Energy Information Administration, State Energy Data System (SEDS), <https://www.eia.gov/state/seds/

Energy consumption is the use of energy as a source of heat or power or as an input in the manufacturing process. Data on energy consumption are from the State Energy Data System (SEDS), which is maintained and operated by the Energy Information Administration (EIA). SEDS has two principal objectives: (1) to provide state

energy consumption, price, and expenditure estimates to members of Congress, federal and state agencies, and the general public and (2) to provide the historical series necessary for EIAs energy models.

An **end-use sector** is a firm or individual that purchases products for its own consumption and not for resale (i.e., an ultimate consumer).

The **residential sector** is the energy-consuming sector that consists of living quarters for private households. Common uses of energy associated with this sector include space heating, water heating, air conditioning, lighting, refrigeration, cooking, and running a variety of other appliances. The residential sector excludes institutional living quarters.

The **commercial sector** is the energy-consuming sector that consists of service-providing facilities and equipment of: businesses; federal, state, and local governments; and other private and public organizations, such as religious, social, or fraternal groups. The commercial sector includes institutional living quarters. It also includes sewage treatment facilities. Common uses of energy associated with this sector include space heating, water heating, air conditioning, lighting, refrigeration, cooking, and running a wide variety of other equipment. This sector includes generators that produce electricity and/or useful thermal output primarily to support the activities of the above-mentioned commercial establishments.

Industrial sector: An energy-consuming sector that consists of all facilities and equipment used for producing, processing, or assembling goods. The industrial sector encompasses the following types of activity: Manufacturing (NAICS codes 31–33); Agriculture, Forestry, Fishing, and Hunting (NAICS code 11); Mining, including oil and gas extraction (NAICS code 21); and Construction (NAICS code 23). Overall energy use in this sector is largely for process heat and cooling and powering machinery, with lesser amounts used for facility heating, air conditioning, and lighting. Fossil fuels are also used as raw material inputs to manufactured products. This sector includes generators that produce electricity and/or useful thermal output primarily to support the above-mentioned industrial activities.

Transportation sector: An energy-consuming sector that consists of all vehicles whose primary purpose is transporting people and/or goods from one physical location to another. Included are automobiles; trucks; buses; motorcycles; trains, subways, and other rail vehicles; aircraft; and ships, barges, and other waterborne vehicles. Vehicles whose primary purpose is not transportation (e.g., construction cranes and bulldozers, farming vehicles, and warehouse tractors and forklifts) are classified in the sector of their primary use. In this report, natural gas used in the operation of natural gas pipelines is included in the transportation sector.

Petroleum is a broadly defined class of liquid hydrocarbon mixtures. Included are crude oil, lease condensate, unfinished oils, refined products obtained from the processing of crude oil, and natural gas plant liquids. Volumes of finished petroleum products include nonhydrocarbon compounds, such as additives and detergents, after they have been blended into the products.

Hydroelectric Power is the production of electricity from the kinetic energy of falling water.

Nuclear electric power (nuclear power) is the electricity generated by the use of the thermal energy released from the fission of nuclear fuel in a reactor.

Table A-55. Energy Expenditures

Source: U.S. Energy Information Administration, https://www.eia.gov/state/seds/.

Energy expenditures refer to the money directly spent by consumers to purchase energy. Expenditures equal the amount of energy used by the consumer times the price per unit paid by the consumer. In the calculation of the amount of energy used, process fuel and intermediate products are not included.

Data on energy expenditures are from the State Energy Data System (SEDS), which is maintained and operated by the Energy Information Administration (EIA). For more information about the SEDS, end-use sector, or the various types of energy, see the appendix entry for Table A-54.

Table A-56. Construction

Sources: Employment—U.S. Bureau of Labor Statistics, Current Employment Statistics Program, <https://www.bls.gov/sae/home.htm>; Earnings—U.S. Bureau of Economic Analysis, Survey of Current Business https://www.bea.gov/regional/index.htm/; Establishments--U.S. Census Bureau, County Business Patterns, https://www.census.gov/programs-surveys/cbp.html; New housing units—U.S. Census Bureau, New Residential Construction, https://www.census.gov/construction/nrc/index.html.

Construction. Refer to General Notes of this appendix to see information on the Construction industry defined using the North American Industry Classification System (NAICS).

Data for nonfarm **employment** are based on the Current Employment Statistics (CES) survey of payroll records

covering over 390,000 businesses on a monthly basis. Employment is defined as the total number of persons on establishment payrolls employed full- or part-time who received pay for any part of the pay period, which includes the 12th day of the month. Temporary and intermittent employees are included, as are any workers who are on paid sick leave, on paid holiday, or who work during only part of the specified pay period. A striking worker who only works a small portion of the survey period, and is paid, would be included as employed under the CES definitions. Persons on the payroll of more than one establishment are counted in each establishment. Data exclude proprietors, self-employed, unpaid family or volunteer workers, farm workers, and domestic workers. Persons on layoff the entire pay period, on leave without pay, on strike for the entire period, or who have not yet reported for work are not counted as employed.

For information on **earnings**, see appendix entry for Table A-41.

Statistics on **housing units authorized by building permits** include housing units issued in local permit-issuing jurisdictions by a building or zoning permit. Not all areas of the country require a building or zoning permit. The statistics only represent those areas that do require a permit. Current surveys indicate that construction is undertaken for all but a very small percentage of housing units authorized by building permits. A major portion typically gets under way during the month of permit issuance and most of the remainder begin within the three following months. Because of this lag, the housing unit authorization statistics do not represent the number of units actually put into construction for the period shown, and should therefore not be directly interpreted as "housing starts."

Table A-57. Manufactures

Sources: Employment and average hourly earnings—U.S. Bureau of Labor Statistics, Current Employment Statistics Program, https://www.bls.gov/sae/home.htm; Earnings—U.S. Bureau of Economic Analysis, Survey of Current Business, https://www.bea.gov/regional/index.htm; Establishments—U.S. Census Bureau, County Business Patterns, https://www.census.gov/programs-surveys/cbp.html; Value of shipments—U.S. Census Bureau, https://www.census.gov/manufacturing/m3/index.html.

Manufactures. Refer to General Notes of this appendix to see information on the Manufacturing industry defined using the North American Industry Classification System (NAICS). See the notes and explanations for Table A-56 for information on employment. For information regarding earnings, see appendix entry for Table A-41. For information on establishments, see appendix entry for Table A-14.

Average hourly earnings are on a "gross" basis. They reflect not only changes in basic hourly and incentive wage rates, but also such variable factors as premium pay for overtime and late-shift work and changes in output of workers paid on an incentive plan. They also reflect shifts in the number of employees between relatively high-paid and low-paid work and changes in workers' earnings in individual establishments. Averages for groups and divisions further reflect changes in average hourly earnings for individual industries. Averages of hourly earnings differ from wage rates. Earnings are the actual return to the worker for a stated period; rates are the amount stipulated for a given unit of work or time. The earnings series do not measure the level of total labor costs on the part of the employer because the following are excluded: benefits, irregular bonuses, retroactive items, payroll taxes paid by employers, and earnings for those employees not covered under production worker, construction worker, or non-supervisory employee definitions.

Value of shipments includes the received or receivable net selling values, free on board plant (exclusive of freight and taxes), of all products shipped, both primary and secondary, as well as all miscellaneous receipts, such as receipts for contract work performed for others, installation and repair, sales of scrap, and sales of products bought and sold without further processing. Included are all items made by or for the establishments from material owned by it, whether sold, transferred to other plants of the same company, or shipped on consignment. The net selling value of products made in one plant on a contract basis from materials owned by another was reported by the plant providing the materials. In the case of multiunit companies, the manufacturer was requested to report the value of products transferred to other establishments of the same company at full economic or commercial value, including not only the direct cost of production but also a reasonable proportion of "all other costs" (including company overhead) and profit.

Table A-58. Manufactures Summary and Export-Related Shipments and Employment

Sources: Manufactures summary—U.S. Census Bureau, Annual Survey of Manufactures, Geographic Area Statistics< https://www.census.gov/programs-surveys/asm.html

Employees includes all full-time and part-time employees on the payrolls of operating manufacturing establishments during any part of the pay period that included the 12th of the months specified on the report form. Included are employees on paid sick leave, paid holidays, and paid vacations; not included are proprietors and partners of unincorporated businesses. These individuals consist of all full-time and part-time employees who are on the payrolls of establishments who worked or received pay for

any part of the pay period including the 12th of March, May, August, and November.

Payroll includes the gross earnings of all employees on the payrolls of operating manufacturing establishments paid in the calendar year. Payroll includes all forms of compensation, such as salaries, wages, commissions, dismissal pay, bonuses, vacation and sick leave pay, and compensation in kind, prior to such deductions as employees' social security contributions, withholding taxes, group insurance, union dues, and savings bonds. The total includes salaries of officers of corporations. It excludes payments to proprietors or partners of unincorporated concerns. Also excluded are payments to members of Armed Forces and pensioners carried on the active payrolls of manufacturing establishments, and employers' social security contributions or other nonpayroll labor costs, such as employees' pension plans, group insurance premiums, and workers' compensation.

Production workers are the number of workers (up through the line-supervisor level) engaged in fabricating, processing, assembling, inspecting, receiving, storing, handling, packing, warehousing, shipping (but not delivering), maintenance, repair, janitorial and guard services, product development, auxiliary production for plant's own use (e.g., power plant), recordkeeping, and other services closely associated with these production operations at the establishment. Employees above the working-supervisor level are excluded from this item.

Production worker hours include all hours worked or paid for at the manufacturing plant, including actual overtime hours (not straight-time equivalent hours). It excludes hours paid for vacations, holidays, or sick leave when the employee is not at the establishment.

Value added by manufactures measures manufacturing activity derived by subtracting the cost of materials, supplies, containers, fuel, purchased electricity, and contract work from the value of shipments (products manufactured plus receipts for services rendered). The result of this calculation is adjusted by the addition of value added by merchandising operations (i.e., the difference between the sales value and the cost of merchandise sold without further manufacture, processing, or assembly) plus the net change in finished goods and work-in-process between the beginning- and end-of-year inventories. For those industries where value of production is collected instead of value of shipments, value added is adjusted only for the change in work-in-process inventories between the beginning and end of year. For those industries where value of work done is collected, the value added does not include an adjustment for the change in finished goods or work-in-process inventories. This item avoids the duplication in the figure for value of shipments that results from the use of products of some establishments as materials by others.

Value of Shipments includes the received or receivable net selling values, "Free on Board" (FOB) plant (exclusive of freight and taxes), of all products shipped, both primary and secondary, as well as all miscellaneous receipts, such as receipts for contract work performed for others, installation and repair, sales of scrap, and sales of products bought and sold without further processing. Included are all items made by or for the establishments from material owned by it, whether sold, transferred to other plants of the same company, or shipped on consignment.

Cost of materials refers to direct charges actually paid or payable for items consumed or put into production during the year, including freight charges and other direct charges incurred by the establishment in acquiring these materials. It includes the cost of materials or fuel consumed, whether purchased by the individual establishment from other companies, transferred to it from other establishments of the same company, or withdrawn from inventory during the year.

Capital Expenditures includes all expenditures during the year for both new and used structures and equipment chargeable to asset accounts for which depreciation or amortization accounts are ordinarily maintained. Also includes capitalized leasehold improvements and capitalized interest charges on loans used to finance capital projects.

Table A-59. Major Manufacturing Sectors:

Sources: U.S. Census Bureau, Annual Survey of Manufactures, Geographic Area Statistics https://www.census.gov/programs-surveys/asm.html;

Refer to General Notes of this appendix to see information on the Manufacturing industry and major sectors defined using the North American Industry Classification System (NAICS). See appendix entry for Table A-14 for information on the County Business Patterns. See the notes and explanations for Table A-57 and A-58 for information on employment and value of shipments.

Table A-60. Information Industries

Sources: Employment—U.S. Bureau of Labor Statistics; State and Metro Area Employment, Hours, & Earnings; SAE Databases: Employment, Hours, and Earnings-State and Metro Area; www.bls.gov/sae/home.htm\ Earnings—U.S. Bureau of Economic Analysis, Regional Economic Accounts, State Annual Personal Income and Employment; https://www.bea.gov/regional/index.htm. Establishments—U.S. Census Bureau, County Business

Patterns, annual; https://www.census.gov/programs-surveys/cbp.html.

Refer to General Notes to see an explanation of the Information industry defined using the North American Industry Classification System (NAICS). See notes and explanations for Table A-56 for information on employment. For information on earnings, see appendix entry for Table A-41. For information on establishments, see appendix entry for Table A-14.

Table A-61. Wholesale and Retail Trade

Sources: Employment—U.S. Bureau of Labor Statistics; State and Metro Area Employment, Hours, & Earnings; SAE Databases: Employment, Hours, and Earnings-State and Metro Area; www.bls.gov/sae/home.htm\ Earnings—U.S. Bureau of Economic Analysis, Regional Economic Accounts, State Annual Personal Income and Employment; https://www.bea.gov/regional/index.htm. Establishments—U.S. Census Bureau, County Business Patterns, annual; https://www.census.gov/programs-surveys/cbp.html.

Refer to General Notes to see information on the Wholesale Trade and Retail Trade industries defined using the North American Industry Classification System (NAICS). See notes and explanations for Table A-56 for information on employment. For information on earnings, see appendix entry for Table A-41. For information on establishments, see appendix entry for Table A-14.

Table A-62. Retail Trade Earnings

Source: Earnings—U.S. Bureau of Economic Analysis, Regional Economic Accounts, State Annual Personal Income and Employment; https://www.bea.gov/regional/index.htm

Refer to General Notes to see information on the Retail Trade industry defined using the North American Industry Classification System (NAICS). For information on earnings, see appendix entry for Table A-41.

Table A-63. Transportation and Commuting

Sources: Employment—U.S. Bureau of Labor Statistics, Current Employment Statistics Program, see https://www.bls.gov/sae/home.htm; Earnings—U.S. Bureau of Economic Analysis, Survey of Current Business, https://www.bea.gov/regional/index.htm; Establishments—U.S. Census Bureau, County Business Patterns, https://www.census.gov/programs-surveys/cbp.html; Workers 16 and over— U.S. Census Bureau, American Community Survey 2018, Table DP03. Selected Economic Characteristics, data.census.gov; Vehicle miles of travel—U.S. Federal

Highway Administration, Highway Statistics, annual, < https://www.fhwa.dot.gov/policyinformation/statistics. cfm >;

Refer to General Notes to see information on the Transportation and Warehousing industry defined using the North American Industry Classification System (NAICS). See the notes and explanations for Table A-56 for information on employment and Table A-41 for information on earnings. For information on establishments, see appendix entry for Table A-14.

Means of transportation to work refers to the principal mode of travel or type of conveyance that the worker usually used to get from home to work during the week. People who used different means of transportation on different days of the week were asked to specify the one they used most often, that is, the greatest number of days. People who used more than one means of transportation to get to work each day were asked to report the one used for the longest distance during the work trip. The category, "Public transportation," includes workers who used a bus or trolley bus, streetcar or trolley car, subway or elevated, railroad, or ferryboat, even if each mode is not shown separately in the tabulation. The category, "Drove alone," includes people who usually drove alone to work as well as people who were driven to work by someone who then drove back home or to a non-work destination. The category, "Carpooled," includes workers who reported that two or more people usually rode to work in the vehicle during the reference week.

Vehicle miles of travel data are collected by the Federal Highway Administration (FHWA). Vehicle miles of travel are miles of travel by all types of motor vehicles as determined by the states on the basis of actual traffic counts and established estimating procedures.

Table A-64. Motor Vehicle and Motorcycle Registrations, Highway Mileage, Bridges, and Driver's Licenses

Sources: Registrations, highway mileage, and driver's licenses—U.S. Federal Highway Administration, Highway Statistics, annual, http://www.fhwa.dot.gov/policy/ohpi/hss/hsspubs.cfm;

Vehicle registration data are collected by the Federal Highway Administration (FHWA) from state motor vehicle registration agencies. Accordingly, registration practices and dates do vary. For uniformity, data have been adjusted to a calendar-year basis as registration years in states differ. Registration data include publicly, privately, and commercially owned vehicles.

Total **highway mileage** includes roads and streets in the functional systems, which are assigned to groups according

to the character service they are intended to provide. The functional systems are (1) **arterial highways** that generally handle the long trips, (2) **collector facilities** that collect and disperse traffic between the arterials and the lower systems, and (3) **local roads and streets** that primarily serve direct access to residential areas. The **interstate system** connects, as directly as practicable, the nation's principal metropolitan areas, cities, and industrial centers.

Data on **bridges** are based on the National Bridge Inventory (NBI). The NBI is a compilation of data supplied by states as required by the National Bridge Inspection Standards for bridges located on public roads. The database is maintained in a format prescribed by the Recording and Coding Guide for the Structure Inventory and Appraisal of the Nation's Bridges. Bridges are structurally deficient if they have been restricted to light vehicles, require immediate rehabilitation to remain open, or are closed. Bridges are functionally obsolete if they have deck geometry, load-carrying capacity, clearance or approach roadway alignment that no longer meet the criteria for the system of which the bridge is carrying a part.

Driver's licenses. Each state and the District of Columbia administers its own driver licensing system. Since 1954, all states have required drivers to be licensed, and since 1959, all states have required examination prior to licensing. Tests of knowledge of state driving laws and practices, vision, and driving proficiency are now required for new licensees.

Table A-65. Traffic Fatalities and Seat Belt Use

Sources: Traffic fatalities— U.S. National Highway Traffic Safety Administration, Fatality Analysis Reporting System, https://www.nhtsa.gov/research-data/fatality-analysis-reporting-system-fars . Seat belts— U.S. Department of Transportation, National Highway Traffic Safety Administration, Seat Belt Use in 2014: Use Rates in the States and Territories.

Traffic fatalities. The National Highway Traffic Safety Administration (NHTSA) has a cooperative agreement with an agency in each state's government to provide information on all qualifying fatal crashes in the state. These agreements are managed by regional contracting Officer's Technical Representatives located in the 10 NHTSA regional offices.

A fatal crash involves a motor vehicle in transport on a traffic way in which at least one person dies within 30 days of the crash. **Traffic fatality rate** is per 100 million vehicle miles traveled.

Traffic fatalities in alcohol-involved crashes include both drivers and occupants. Only the BAC of the operator is considered when classifying data as alcohol-involved.

Blood alcohol content (BAC) is measured as a percentage by weight of alcohol in the blood (grams/deciliter). A positive BAC level (0.01 g/dl and higher) indicates that alcohol was consumed by the person tested.

Seat belt use. Data for states are based on observational surveys conducted in accordance with Section 157, Title 23, U.S. Code. For national figures, data are based on the National Occupant Protection Use Survey (NOPUS). Motorists observed in the survey were counted as "belted" if they appeared to have a shoulder belt across the front of their body.

Table A-66. Communications

Sources: Mobile wireless subscribers—Federal Communications Commission, https://www.fcc.gov/general/iatd-data-statistical-reports and: https://apps.fcc.gov/edocs_public/attachmatch/DOC-329975A1.pdf; Number of payphones by state-Federal Communications Commission internet Use—U.S. Census Bureau American Community Survey 2018 1-year estimates; data.census.gov.

The FCC's local competition and broadband data gathering program collects data on **mobile wireless** telephone subscribership and high-speed connections from telecommunications carriers twice a year using FCC Form 477.

The American Community Survey asked respondents about computer use in their household and if any member of the household has access to the internet. Households with access includes housing units where someone pays to access the internet through a service such as a data plan for a smartphone; a broadband internet service such as cable, fiber optic or DSL; satellite; dial-up; or other type of service. This will normally refer to a service that someone is billed for directly for internet alone or sometimes as part of a bundle.

Table A-67. Financial Activities

Sources: Employment—U.S. Bureau of Labor Statistics, Current Employment and Statistics Program, <https://www.bls.gov/sae/home.htm>; Earnings—U.S Bureau of Economic Analysis, Survey of Current Business, < https://www.bea.gov/regional/index.htm/>; Establishments—U.S. Census Bureau, County Business Patterns, https://www.census.gov/programs-surveys/cbp.html >;

Refer to General Notes to see information on Financial Activities defined using the North American Industry Classification System (NAICS). Financial Activities includes NAICS codes 52 (Finance and Insurance) and 53 (Real Estate and Rental and Leasing.) See notes and explanations for Table A-56 for information on employment. For information on earnings, see appendix entry

for Table A-41. For information on establishments, see appendix entry for Table A-14.

Table A-68. Professional and Business Services and Education and Health Services

Sources: Employment—U.S. Bureau of Labor Statistics, Current Employment Statistics Program, <https://www.bls.gov/sae/home.htm>; Earnings—U.S. Bureau of Economic Analysis, Survey of Current Business, https://www.bea.gov/regional/index.htm; Establishments—U.S. Census Bureau, County Business Patterns, https://www.census.gov/programs-surveys/cbp.html

Professional and Business Services includes Professional, Scientific, and Technical Services; Management of Companies and Enterprises; and Administrative and Support and Waste Management and Remediation Services.

Education and Health Services includes Educational Services and Health Care and Social Assistance. Refer to General Notes to see information on the above industries defined using the North American Industry Classification System (NAICS).

For information on employment, see appendix entry for Table A-56. For information on earnings, see appendix entry for Table A-41. For information on establishments, see appendix entry for Table A-14.

Table A-69. Leisure and HospitalityServices

Sources: Employment—U.S. Bureau of Labor Statistics, Current Employment Statistics Program, https://www.bls.gov/sae/home.htm; Earnings—U.S. Bureau of Economic Analysis, Survey of Current Business, https://www.bea.gov/regional/index.htm; Establishments—U.S. Census Bureau, County Business Patterns, https://www.census.gov/programs-surveys/cbp.html

Refer to General Notes to see information on **Arts, Entertainment, and Recreation Services** and **Accommodation and Food Services** industries defined using the North American Industry Classification System (NAICS). For information on employment, see appendix entry for Table A-56. For information on earnings, see appendix entry for Table A-41. For information on establishments, see appendix entry for Table A-14.

Table A-70. Travel and Tourism Indicators

Sources:;Travel and Tourism Indicators—U.S. Department of Homeland Security, Office of Immigration Statistics, 2015 Year Book of Immigration Statistics, see https://www.dhs.gov/immigration-statistics/yearbook/2015; National parks— U.S. National Park Service, https://irma.nps.gov/STATS/Reports/National

International visitors for pleasure: *The Yearbook of Immigration Statistics* is a compendium of tables that provides data on foreign nationals who, during a fiscal year, were granted lawful permanent residence (i.e., admitted as immigrants or became legal permanent residents), were admitted into the United States on a temporary basis (e.g., tourists, students, or workers), applied for asylum or refugee status, or were naturalized. A nonimmigrant is defined by Section 101(a)(15) of the Immigration and Nationality Act (INA) as an alien who is not an immigrant and is admitted in one of the nonimmigrant alien classes of admission. Nonimmigrant admissions refer to number of events (i.e., entries into the United States) rather than persons. As such, one nonimmigrant may enter the United States more than once, and each entry would count as a separate admission record.

Visitors to national parks. A visit is defined as the entry of any person, except National Park Service (NPS) personnel, onto lands or waters administered by the NPS. A visit may occur as a recreation visit or a nonrecreation visit. A same-day reentry, negligible transit, and an entry to a detached portion of the same park on the same day are considered to be a single visit. Visits are reported separately for two contiguous parks.

Table A-71. Government

Sources: Employment—U.S. Bureau of Labor Statistics, Current Employment Statistics Program, (CES), https://www.bls.gov/sae/data.htm; Earnings—U.S. Bureau of Economic Analysis, https://www.bea.gov/regional/index.htm/; Federal tax collections—Internal Revenue Service, Data Book 2018, https://www.irs.gov/uac/tax-stats ; State tax collections—U.S. Census Bureau, Federal, state and local governments, Tax collections, State government tax collections, annual, see also, https://www.census.gov/govs/

For information on **earnings**, refer to appendix entry for Table A-41. Government employment covers only civilian workers. Government enterprises are government agencies that cover a substantial portion of their operating costs by selling goods and services to the public and that maintain separate accounts. For addition information regarding employment, refer to the notes and explanations for Table A-56.

Data on **federal tax collections** are provided by the Internal Revenue Service (IRS) through the Statistics of Income (SOI) program. This program pulls data electronically from the master file and augments the data with items captured from the hard copies of taxpayers' returns. The IRS processes about 200 million tax returns each year, and SOI uses approximately half a million of these for statistics. Classification by state is based on the individual's address (or, in the case of businesses,

the location of the principal office or place of business). However, some individuals may use the address of a tax attorney or accountant. Sole proprietors, partners in a partnership, or shareholders in an "S" corporation may use their business addresses. Such addresses could have been located in a state other than the state in which the individual resided. Similarly, taxes withheld reported by employers located near a state boundary might include substantial amounts withheld from salaries of employees who reside in a neighboring state. Also, while taxes of corporations may be paid from the principal office, the operations of these corporations may be located in one or more other state(s).

State tax collections data are collected by the Census Bureau through an Annual Survey of State Government Tax Collection. These statistics are of all 50 state governments in the United States and are for state governments only. They should not be interpreted as state area data (state plus local government tax collections combined). The state government tax data presented by the Census Bureau may differ from data published by state governments because the Census Bureau may be using a different definition of which organizations are covered under the term, "state government." For the purpose of State Government Tax Collections statistics, the term "state government" refers not only to the executive, legislative, and judicial branches of a given state, but it also includes agencies, institutions, commissions, and public authorities that operate separately or somewhat autonomously from the central state government but where the state government maintains administrative or fiscal control over their activities as defined by the Census Bureau. The tax revenue data pertain to state fiscal years that end on June 30, in all but four states (NY, TX, AL, MI). Amounts shown for these four states reflect the different timing of their respective fiscal years, which were the 12-month periods ending on March 31, for New York, August 31 for Texas, and September 30, for Alabama and Michigan.

Table A-72. State Government Employment and Finances

Sources: Employment—U.S. Census Bureau, State Government Employment and Payroll Data and Annual Survey of State Government Finances; https://www.census.gov/govs/

The Census Bureau collects data on **state government employment** by conducting an Annual Survey of Government Employment. Alternatively, every 5 years, in years ending in a "2" or "7," a Census of Governments, including an employment portion, is conducted. For both the census and the annual surveys, the employment detail is equivalent.

Employment refers to all persons gainfully employed by and performing services for a government. **Employees** include all persons paid for personal services performed, including persons paid from federally funded programs, paid elected or appointed officials, persons in a paid leave status, and persons paid on a per-meeting, annual, semiannual, or quarterly basis. Unpaid officials, pensioners, persons whose work is performed on a fee basis, and contractors and their employees are excluded from the count of employees. **Full-time equivalent** employment refers to a computed statistic representing the number of full-time employees who could have been employed if the reported number of hours worked by part-time employees had been worked by full-time employees. This statistic is calculated separately for each function of a government by dividing the "part-time hours paid" by the standard number of hours for full-time employees in the particular government and then adding the resulting quotient to the number of full-time employees.

Finance data are collected by the Census Bureau through the Annual Survey of Government Finances, which covers all state and local governments in the United States. The survey content includes the entire range of government finance activities: revenue, expenditure, debt, and assets.

Revenue includes all amounts of money received by a government from external sources during its fiscal year net of refunds and other correcting transactions, other than issuance of debt, sale of investments, and agency or private trust transactions. Revenue excludes amounts transferred from other funds or agencies of the same government. Revenue comprises amounts received by all agencies, boards, commissions, or other organizations categorized as dependent on the government concerned. Stated in terms of the accounting procedures from which these data originate, revenue covers receipts from all accounting funds of a government, other than intragovernmental service (revolving), agency, and private trust funds.

General revenue comprises all revenue except that classified as liquor store, utility, or insurance trust revenue. Generally, the basis for this distinction is not the fund or administrative unit established to account for and control a particular activity, but rather the nature of the revenue source involved. Within general revenue are four main categories: taxes, intergovernmental revenue, current charges, and miscellaneous general revenue.

Intergovernmental revenue comprises monies from other governments, including grants, shared taxes, and contingent loans and advances for support of particular functions or for general financial support; any significant and identifiable amounts received as reimbursement for performance of governmental services for other governments; and any other form of revenue representing the sharing by other governments in the financing of activities administered by the receiving government. All intergovernmental revenue is reported in the general government sector, even if it is used to support activities in other sectors (such as utilities). Intergovernmental revenue excludes amounts received from the sale of property, commodities, and utility services to other governments (which are reported in different revenue categories). It also excludes amounts received from other governments as the employer share or for support of public employee retirement or other insurance trust funds of the recipient government, which are treated as insurance trust revenue.

Taxes are compulsory contributions exacted by a government for public purposes, other than for employee and employer assessments and contributions to finance retirement and social insurance trust systems and for special assessments to pay capital improvements. Tax revenue comprises gross amounts collected (including interest and penalties) minus amounts paid under protest and amounts refunded during the same period. It consists of all taxes imposed by a government whether the government collects the taxes itself or relies on another government to act as its collection agent.

Expenditure includes all amounts of money paid out by a government during its fiscal year—net of recoveries and other correcting transactions—other than for retirement of debt, purchase of investment securities, extension of loans, and agency or private trust transactions. Under this definition, expenditure relates to external payments of a government and excludes amounts Transferred to funds or agencies of the same government (other than payments to intragovernmental service funds).

Expenditure includes payments from all sources of funds, including not only current revenues but also proceeds from borrowing and prior year fund balances. Note, however, that the Census Bureau's finance statistics do not relate expenditure to their source of funding. Expenditure includes amounts spent by all agencies, boards, commissions, or other organizations categorized as dependent on the government concerned.

General expenditure comprises all expenditure except that classified as liquor store, utility, or insurance trust expenditure. As noted above, it includes all such payments regardless of the source of revenue from which they were financed. General government expenditures are classified by function and character and object.

Intergovernmental expenditure is defined as amounts paid to other governments for performance of specific functions or for general financial support. Includes grants, shared taxes, contingent loans and advances, and any significant and identifiable amounts or reimbursement paid to other governments for performance of general government services or activities. By definition, it excludes amounts paid to other governments for purchase of commodities, property, or utility services and for any tax levied as such on facilities of the government.

Direct expenditure comprises all final expenditures paid to current employees, former employees (retirees) and to private sector entities outside of the government itself (e.g., all expenditure other than intergovernmental expenditure).

Education expenditures cover the operation, maintenance, and construction of public schools and facilities for elementary and secondary education (kindergarten through high school), vocational-technical education, and other educational institutions except those for higher education. Covers operations by independent governments (school districts) as well as those operated as integral agencies of state, county, municipal, or township governments. Also covers financial support of public elementary and secondary schools.

Public welfare expenditures are those cash payments made directly to individuals contingent upon their need, other than those under federal categorical assistance programs.

Highway expenditures include maintenance, operation, repair, and construction of highways, streets, roads, alleys, sidewalks, bridges, tunnels, ferry boats, viaducts, and related nontoll structures.

Table A-73. State Government Tax Collections

Source: U.S. Census Bureau, Annual Survey of State Government Tax Collection, https://www.census.gov/programs-surveys/stc.html

Data on **state government tax collections** are collected by the Census Bureau by conducting an Annual Survey of State Government Tax Collection. The data are on the fiscal year tax collections of all 50 state governments in the United States and are for state governments only. They should not be interpreted as state area data (state plus local government tax collections combined). See appendix entry for Table A-71 for more information.

Property taxes include three types, all having in common the use of value as a basis for the tax. General property taxes, relating to property as a whole, taxed at a single rate or at classified rates according to the class of property. Property refers to real property (e.g., land and structures)

as well as personal property; personal property can be either tangible (e.g., automobiles and boats) or intangible (e.g., bank accounts and stocks and bonds). Special property taxes, levied on selected types of property (e.g., oil and gas properties, house trailers, motor vehicles, and intangibles) and subject to rates not directly related to general property tax rates. Taxes based on income produced by property as a measure of its value on the assessment date. For more information on **Taxes**, see appendix entry for Table A-71 and A-72.

Sales and gross receipts taxes are taxes on goods and services, measured on the basis of the volume or value of their transfer, upon gross receipts or gross income there from, or as an amount per unit sold; and related taxes based upon use, storage, production, importation, or consumption of goods and service.

General sales and gross receipts taxes are applicable with only specified exceptions to sales of all types of goods and services or to all gross receipts, whether at a single rate or at classified rates, and sales use taxes.

Table A-74. Federal Government

Sources: U.S. Bureau of Economic Analysis, https://www.bea.gov/regional/index.htm;

Federal employment. Employment is a count of jobs, both full-time and part-time. It includes wage and salary jobs, sole proprietorships, and individual general partners, but not unpaid family workers nor volunteers. Federal civilian employment includes civilian employees of the federal government, including congressional staff and the U.S. Postal Service. The federal military category includes government establishments primarily engaged in national security and national affairs.

Earnings is the sum of three components of personal income--wages and salaries, supplements to wages and salaries, and proprietors' income. It can be used in the analyses of regional economies as a proxy for the income that is generated from participation in current production. Earnings estimates for 1929-47 are assumed to be on a place-of-residence basis; explicit adjustments were made for the principal interstate commuting flows.

Table A-75. Federal Individual Income Tax Returns

Sources: Tax returns—U.S. Internal Revenue Service, Internal Revenue Service Data Book; https://www.irs.gov/statistics/soi-tax-stats-individual-income-tax-state-data. Property and land—U.S. General Services Administration, Federal Real Property Profile, annual, see internet site https://www.gsa.gov.

For information on **federal individual income tax returns**, see appendix entry for Table A-71 or consult the source.

Data on **federally owned property** and **federal lands** are collected through the General Services Administration's (GSA's) Federal Real Property Profile (FRPP) reporting system. Contributing agencies provide data annually based on their real property holdings as of September 30. Land acreage is divided into urban and rural categories. Leased land is usually not reported if it is included with a building lease. Buildings are roofed and walled structures built for permanent use. Buildings owned by the government, whether or not located on government-owned land, are included in the data. Buildings under construction are included only if they were available for use as of September 30 of the year shown.

Table A-76. Social Security, Supplemental Nutrition Assistance Programs, and School Lunch Programs

Sources: Social Security—U.S. Social Security Administration, Annual Statistical Supplement, https://www.ssa.gov/policy/docs/statcomps/supplement/; Federal food stamp and national school lunch programs—U.S. Department of Agriculture, Food and Nutrition Service, Supplemental Nutrition Assistance Program, Annual State Level Data, https://www.fns.usda.gov/pd/supplemental-nutrition-assistance-program-snap.

Social security. The Old-Age, Survivors, and Disability Insurance Program (OASDI) provides monthly benefits for retired and disabled insured workers and their dependents and to survivors of insured workers. To be eligible for benefits, a worker must have had a specified period of employment in which OASDI taxes were paid. The data were derived from the Master Beneficiary Record (MBR), the principal administrative file of social security beneficiaries. Data for total recipients and retired workers include persons with special age-72 benefits. Special age-72 benefit represents the monthly benefit payable to men who attained age 72 before 1972 and for women who attained age 72 before 1970 and who do not have sufficient quarters to qualify for a retired-worker benefit under either the fully or the transitionally insured status provision.

As of October 1, 2008, **Supplemental Nutrition Assistance Program** (SNAP) was the new name for the federal Food Stamp Program. SNAP is the federal name for the program. State programs may have different names. SNAP provides low-income households with electronic benefits that can be used at most grocery stores. The U.S. Department of Agriculture administers SNAP at the federal level through its Food and Nutrition Service (FNS). State agencies administer the program at state and local levels, including determination of eligibility and allotments, and distribution of benefits. Consult source for more information on program.

The **National School Lunch Program** covers public and private elementary and secondary schools and residential child care institutions. Costs include federal cash reimbursements at rates set by law for each meal served and commodity costs. The Food and Nutrition Service administers the program at the federal level. At the state level, the National School Lunch Program is usually administered by state education agencies, which operate the program through agreements with school food authorities. Consult source for more information on program.

Table A-77. Social Insurance and Medical Programs

Sources: U.S. Social Security Administration, Annual Statistical Supplement to the Social Security Bulletin; https://www.ssa.gov/policy/docs/statcomps/ssi_sc/; TANF—U.S. Administration for Children and Families, Temporary Assistance for Needy Families (TANF) Program, Administration for Children and families

https://www.acf.hhs.gov/sites/default/files/ofa/2018tanf_totalrecipients_03252019_508.pdf

Medicare enrollment—U.S. Centers for Medicare and Medicaid Services, Medicare State Enrollment, https://www.cms.hhs.gov/medicareEnrpts/; Number of Children Ever Enrolled in Medicaid and CHIP, https://www.medicaid.gov/sites/default/files/2019-12/fy-2018-childrens-enrollment-report.pdf

The **Supplemental Security Income** (SSI) program provides cash payments in accordance with nationwide eligibility requirements to people with limited income and resources who are aged, blind, or disabled. An aged person is defined as an individual who is 65 years old or over. A blind person is anyone with vision of 20/200 or less with the use of correcting lens in the better eye or with tunnel vision of 20 degrees or less. The disabled classification refers to any person unable to engage in any substantial gainful activity by reason of any medically determinable physical or mental impairment expected to result in death or that has lasted or can be expected to last for a continuous period of at least 12 months. For a child under 18 years, eligibility is based on disability or severity comparable with that of an adult, since the criterion of "substantial gainful activity" is inapplicable for children.

The **Temporary Assistance for Needy Families** (TANF) program is a time-limited program that assists families with children when the parents or other responsible relatives cannot provide for the family's basic needs. The federal government provides grants to states to run the TANF program so that the states decide on the design of the program, the type and amount of assistance payments, the range of other services to be provided, and the rules for determining who is eligible for benefits. Prior to TANF, the cash assistance program to families was called Aid to Families with Dependent Children (1980–1996). Under the new welfare law (Personal Responsibility Reconciliation Act of 1996), the program became TANF.

Medicare. Since July 1966, the federal medicare program has provided two coordinated plans for nearly all people age 65 and over: (1) a hospital insurance plan, which covers hospital and related services and (2) a voluntary supplementary medical insurance plan, financed partially by monthly premiums paid by participants, which partly covers physicians' and related medical services. Such insurance also applies, since July 1973, to disabled beneficiaries of any age after 24 months of entitlement to cash benefits under the social security or railroad retirement programs and to persons with end-state renal disease.

Medicaid is a health insurance program for certain low-income people. These include: certain low-income families with children; aged, blind, or disabled people on supplemental security income; certain low-income pregnant women and children; and people who have very high medical bills. Medicaid is funded and administered through a state-federal partnership. Although there are broad federal requirements for medicaid, states have a wide degree of flexibility to design their program. States have authority to establish eligibility standards, determine what benefits and services to cover, and set payment rates. All states, however, must cover these basic services: inpatient and outpatient hospital services; doctors' services, family planning, and periodic health checkups; and diagnosis and treatment for children.

Center for Medicare and Medicaid Service (CMS) administers the Children's Health Insurance Program (CHIP). Children began receiving insurance through CHIP in 1997 and the program helped states expand health care coverage to more than 5 million of the nation's uninsured children. The program was reauthorized on February 4, 2009, when the President signed into law the Children's Health Insurance Program Reauthorization Act of 2009 (CHIPRA or Public Law 111-3). CHIPRA finances the Children's Health Insurance Program (CHIP) through Fiscal Year (FY) 2013.

The Children's Health Insurance Program is jointly financed by the federal and state governments and is administered by the states. Within broad federal guidelines, each state determines the design of its program, eligibility groups, benefit packages, payment levels for coverage, and administrative and operating procedures.

CHIP provides a capped amount of funds to states on a matching basis. Federal payments under title XXI to states are based on state expenditures under approved plans effective on or after October 1, 1997.

Table A-78. Government Transfer Payments to Individuals

Source: U.S. Bureau of Economic Analysis, "Regional Accounts Data, Annual State Personal Income," <https://www.bea.gov/regional/index.htm>,

Personal current transfer receipts are personal income that are payments to persons for which no current services are performed. It consists of payments to individuals and to nonprofit institutions by federal, state, and local governments and by businesses. Government transfer payments to individuals consist of: retirement and disability insurance benefits, medical benefits, income maintenance benefits, unemployment insurance compensation, veteran's benefits, federal education and training assistance, and other transfer receipts of individuals from governments.

Retirement and disability insurance benefits consist of Old-Age, Survivors, and Disability (OASDI) benefits; railroad retirement and disability benefits; federal and state workers' compensation; temporary disability benefits; black lung benefits; and Pension Benefit Guaranty benefits.

Medical payments include medical benefits, public assistance medical care, and military medical insurance benefits. Medicare benefits are federal government payments made through intermediaries to beneficiaries for the care provided to individuals under the medicare program. Public assistance medical care benefits are received by low-income individuals. These payments consist mainly of the payments made through intermediaries to the vendors for care provided to individuals under the federally assisted, state-administered medicaid program and State Children's Health Insurance Program (SCHIP) and under the general assistance medical programs of state and local governments. Military medical insurance benefits are vendor payments made under the TriCare Management Program, formerly called the Civilian Health and Medical Plan of the Uniformed Services program, for the medical care of dependents of active duty military personnel and of retired military personnel and their dependents at nonmilitary medical facilities.

Income maintenance benefits consist largely of supplemental security income payments, family assistance, food stamp payments, and other assistance payments, including general assistance.

Unemployment insurance benefits are made up of state unemployment compensation; unemployment compensation of federal civilian employees, railroad employees, and veterans; and trade adjustment allowances. State unemployment compensation are benefits consisting mainly of the payments received by individuals under state-administered unemployment insurance (UI) programs, but they include the special benefits authorized by federal legislation for periods of high unemployment. The provisions that govern the eligibility, timing, and amount of benefit payments vary among the states, but the provisions that govern the coverage and financing are uniform nationally. Unemployment compensation of federal civilian employees are benefits received by former federal employees under a federal program administered by the state employment security agencies. Unemployment compensation of railroad employees are benefits received by railroad workers who are unemployed because of sickness or because work is unavailable in the railroad industry and in related industries, such as carrier affiliates. This UI program is administered by the Railroad Retirement Board (RRB) under a federal program that is applicable throughout the nation. Unemployment compensation of veterans are benefits that are received by unemployed veterans who have recently separated from military service and who are not eligible for military retirement benefits. The compensation is paid under a federal program that is administered by the state employment security agencies. Trade adjustment allowances are the payments received by workers who are unemployed because of the adverse economic effects of international trade arrangements.

Veterans' benefits include veterans' pension and disability benefits, veterans' readjustment benefits, veterans' life insurance benefits, and other assistance to veterans (federal government payments received by paraplegics and by certain other disabled veterans to purchase automobiles and other conveyances, state and local government payments of assistance to indigent veterans, and the state and local government payments of bonuses to veterans).

Federal education and training assistance consists of federal fellowships, higher education student assistance, Job Corps payments, and interest payments on guaranteed student loans. Federal fellowships consist of the payments to outstanding science students who receive National Science Foundation (NSF) grants, the subsistence payments to the cadets at the six state maritime academies, and the payments for all other federal fellowships. Higher education student assistance consists of the federal payments, called Pell Grants, for an undergraduate education for students with low incomes. Job Corps payments are primarily the allowances for living expenses received by economically disadvantaged individuals who are between the ages of 16 and 21 and who are enrolled in the designated vocational and educational training programs. These benefits also include the adjustment allowances received by trainees upon the successful completion of their training. Interest payments on guaranteed student loans are made by the Department of Education to commercial lending institutions on behalf of the individuals who receive low-interest, deferred-payment loans from these institutions in order to pay the expenses of higher education.

Other transfer receipts of individuals from governments consist largely of Bureau of Indian Affairs payments, education exchange payments, Alaska Permanent Fund dividend payments, compensation of survivors of public safety officers, compensation of victims of crime, disaster relief payments, compensation for Japanese internment, and other special payments to individuals.

Table A-79. Department of Defense and Veterans

Sources: Department of Defense—U.S. Department of Defense, Military and Civilian Personnel by Service/Agency by State/Country https://www.dmdc.osd.mil/appj/dwp/searchResults.jsp?search=by+state and https://www.oea.gov/dsbs-fy2018. Veterans—U.S. Department of Veterans Affairs, Office of Policy, Planning, and Preparedness, see https://www.va.gov/vetdata/

The **Department of Defense** (DoD) is responsible for providing the military forces of the United States. It includes the Office of the Secretary of Defense, the Joint Chiefs of Staff, the Army, the Navy, the Air Force, and the defense agencies. The President serves as Commander in Chief of the armed forces; from him, the authority flows to the Secretary of Defense and through the Joint Chiefs of Staff to the commanders of unified and specified commands (e.g., U.S. Strategic Command).

DoD personnel data include active duty military, civilian, and Reserve and National Guard. Expenditures include payroll outlays, contracts, and grants. Payroll outlays consist of active duty military pay, civilian pay, Reserve and National Guard pay, and retired military pay. Contracts include supply and equipment contracts, RDT&E contracts, service contracts, construction contracts, and civil function contracts. Consult the source for more information.

Veterans. The Office of Policy in the Department of Veterans Affairs (VA) is responsible for administering a range of programs and analyses concerning veteran surveys, demographics, and population estimates. Within the Office of Policy, the Office of the actuary (OACT) develops estimates and projections of the veteran population and their characteristics.

The Department of Veterans Affairs (VA) provides official estimates and projections of the veteran population using the Veteran Population Model (VetPop). The model is updated periodically for improved methodology, more recent data, and changing needs. For each year, VetPop generates the number of veterans by selected characteristics: at the state and/or national levels—by age, gender, period of service, race/ethnicity, rank (Officer/Enlisted), and branch of service; at the county level—by age and gender. Veteran's data is derived from a combination of decennial census data, Defense Manpower Data Center (DMDC) losses, and GORGO, the projection model used by Department of Defense's Office of the Actuary.

A veteran is someone 18 years and older (there are a few 17-year-old veterans) who is not currently on active duty, but who once served on active duty in the U.S. Army, Navy, Air Force, Marine Corps, or Coast Guard, or who served in the Merchant Marine during World War II. There are many groups whose active service makes them veterans including: those who incurred a service-connected disability during active duty for training in the Reserves or National Guard, even though that service would not otherwise have counted for veteran status; members of a national guard or reserve component who have been ordered to active duty by order of the President or who have a full-time military job. The latter are called AGRs (Active Guard and Reserve). No one who has received a dishonorable discharge is a veteran.

Table A-80. Elections

Sources: Voting-age population, 2016—U.S. Census Bureau, Population estimates, https://www.census.gov/data/tables/2016/demo/popest/state-detail.html; Electoral votes, 2012 percent of voting-age population voting for President, votes for President and votes for Senators—U.S. Congress, Clerk of the House, Statistics of the Presidential and Congressional Election, biennial, see history.house.gov/Institution/Election-Statistics/2018election/ history.house.gov/Institution/Election-Statistics/2016election/ and history.house.gov/Institution/Election-Statistics/2014election/.

The **voting-age population** relates to people 18 years old and over in all states and the District of Columbia. Data include armed forces stationed in each state, aliens, and the institutionalized population.

Votes cast for President. The Constitution specifies how the President and Vice President are selected. Each state elects, by popular vote, a group of electors equal in number to its total of members of Congress. The 23rd Amendment, adopted in 1961, grants the District of Columbia three presidential electors, a number equal to that of the least populous state. A majority vote of all electors is necessary to elect the President and Vice President. If no candidate receives a majority, the House of Representatives, with each state having one vote, is empowered to elect the President and Vice President, again, with a majority of votes required.

Votes cast for U.S. Senators. The U.S. Senate is composed of 100 members, two from each state, who are elected to serve for a term of 6 years. One-third of the Senate is elected every 2 years. Senators were originally chosen by the state legislatures. The 17th Amendment to the Constitution, adopted in 1913, prescribed that Senators be elected by popular vote.

Table A-81. Composition of Congress and Public Officials

Sources: U.S. Congress, Clerk of the House, Statistics of the Presidential and Congressional Election, biennial, see history.house.gov/Institution/Election-Statistics/2018election/ and history.house.gov/Institution/Election-Statistics/2016election/; Composition of Congress—Office of the Clerk, Official List of Members by State, annual, see also http://clerk.house.gov/

In each state, totals for votes cast for Representatives represent the sum of votes cast in each Congressional District or votes cast for Representatives at Large in states where only one member is elected. In all years, there are numerous districts within the state where either the Republican or Democratic party had no candidate. In some states, the Republican and Democratic vote includes votes cast for the party candidate by endorsing parties. Refer to the notes and explanations for Table A-82 for information on Senators.

TABLE B. METROPOLITAN AREAS

Table B consists of 14 tables (B-1 through B-14) with 164 data items for 384 metropolitan statistical areas (MSAs), and 31 metropolitan divisions within 11 large metropolitan statistical areas. They are presented alphabetically in each of the 14 tables.

All summaries, including historical data, are presented for the areas as currently defined. Where possible, the original figures have been retabulated to reflect the status of metropolitan area boundaries as of September 14, 2018. For more information on these areas, see Appendix C, Geographic Concepts and Codes.

Table B-1. Area and Population

Sources: Area—U.S. Census Bureau, 2019 U.S. Gazetteer Files, https://www.census.gov/geographies/reference-files/time-series/geo/gazetteer-files.html;

Population—Population and Housing Units Estimates Data; https://www.census.gov/programs-surveys/popest/data/tables.html.

Total area. Area measurement data provide the size, in square miles, of geographic entities for which the Census Bureau tabulates and disseminates data. Area is calculated from the specific boundary recorded for each entity (in this case, metropolitan areas) in the Census Bureau's geographic database.

Area measurements may disagree with the information displayed on the Census Bureau maps and in the MAF. TIGER database because, for area measurement purposes, features identified as "intermittent water" and "glacier" are reported as land area. The accuracy of any area measurement data is limited by the accuracy inherent in (1) the location and shape of the various boundary information in the database, (2) the location and shapes of the shorelines of water bodies in that database, and (3) rounding affecting the last digit in all operations that compute and/or sum the area measurements. Identification of land and inland, coastal, and territorial is for statistical purposes and does not necessarily reflect legal definitions thereof.

Population numbers for 2010 and 2000 are counts of the resident population on April 1 of those decennial census years. The April 1 estimates base populations for 2010 and 2000 may differ from the April 1 census count due to legal boundary updates, other geographic program changes, and Count Question Resolution actions.

Population estimates for 2019 measure the estimated population from the calculated number of people living in an area as of July 1. The Census Bureau develops county population estimates with a component of population change method in which they use administrative records and other data to estimate the household and group quarters population. For the household population, the components of population change are births, deaths, net domestic migration, and net international migration. They measure change in the nonhousehold, or group quarters, population by the net change in the population living in group quarters facilities.

A major assumption underlying this approach is that changes in selected administrative and other data sources closely approximate the components of population change. Therefore, Census Bureau demographers separately estimate each component of population change based on administrative records, including registered births and deaths, federal income tax returns, medicare enrollees, and military movement. They also separately estimate net international migration using information

from the American Community Survey (ACS), the decennial census, and other data sources.

Most administrative record data sources lag the current estimate year by as much as 2 years, therefore, the Census Bureau projects the data for the current year based on past years' data. As updated data become available, they revise the projected input data so that each vintage's estimates are always based on the most recent data available.

For more information on the method used for these estimates, see Appendix B, Limitations and Methodology, and the website at https://www.census.gov/programs-surveys/popest/technical-documentation/methodology.html.

Rank numbers are assigned on the basis of population size, with each metropolitan area placed in descending order, largest to smallest. Where ties occur (two or more areas with identical populations) the same rank is assigned to each of the tied metropolitan areas. In such cases, the following rank number(s) is omitted so that the lowest rank is usually equal to the number of metropolitan areas ranked.

People per square mile of land area, also known as population density, is the average number of inhabitants per square mile of land area. These figures are derived by dividing the total number of residents by the number of square miles of land area in the specified geographic area.

Table B-2. Components of Population Change

Sources: U.S. Census Bureau, Population Estimates, Cumulative Estimates of the Components of Resident Population Change for Metropolitan Statistical Areas: April 1, 2010 to July 1, 2019; https://www.census.gov/programs-surveys/popest/data/data-sets.html.

The Census Bureau develops county population estimates with a component of population change method in which they use administrative records and other data to estimate the household and group quarters population. For the household population, the components of population change are births, deaths, net domestic migration, and net international migration. They measure change in the nonhousehold, or group quarters, population by the net change in the population living in group quarters facilities.

A major assumption underlying this approach is that changes in selected administrative and other data sources closely approximate the components of population change. Therefore, Census Bureau demographers separately estimate each component of population change based on administrative records, including registered births and deaths, federal income tax returns, medicare enrollees, and military movement. They also separately estimate net international migration using information from the American Community Survey (ACS), the decennial census, and other data sources.

Most administrative record data sources lag the current estimate year by as much as 2 years, therefore, the Census Bureau projects the data for the current year based on past years' data. As updated data become available, they revise the projected input data so that each vintage's estimates are always based on the most recent data available.

The Census Bureau produces the estimate of each county's population, starting with the base population from either the 2010 census (for the July 1, 2010, estimates) or the revised population estimate for the prior year (for the July 1, 2011, and later estimates). They then add or subtract the demographic components of population change calculated for that time period. Basically, they add the estimated number of births and subtract the estimated number of deaths for the time period. Next, they add the estimates of net domestic migration, net international migration, and the net change in the group quarters population. The definitions of these concepts follow.

The Census Bureau produces separate population estimates for the populations under age 65 and age 65 and over, mainly because different data are used to measure the domestic migration of these two populations. For the population under age 65, they use person-level data from individual federal tax returns to estimate net domestic migration. They use medicare enrollment data to calculate measures of migration for the population age 65 and over because this population is not always well represented on tax returns. County total population estimates are the sum of the estimates of the population under age 65 and age 65 years and over.

State and county estimates may also incorporate other changes due to corrections made since the 2010 census. The corrections occur outside the component estimation framework and are the result of successful local challenges or special censuses.

Natural increase. Births minus deaths. The rate of natural increase expresses natural increase during a time period as a percentage of an area's population at the midpoint of the time period.

Net international migration. Any change of residence across the borders of the United States (50 states and District of Columbia). The Census Bureau makes estimates of net international migration for the nation, states, and counties. They estimate net international migration in four parts: (1) net international migration of the foreign

born, (2) net migration between the United States and Puerto Rico, (3) net migration of natives to and from the United States, and (4) net movement of the Armed Forces population between the United States and overseas. The largest component, net international migration of the foreign born, includes lawful permanent residents (immigrants), temporary migrants (such as students), humanitarian migrants (such as refugees), and people illegally present in the United States. Currently, they do not estimate these components individually.

Net Domestic Migration. The difference between domestic in-migration to an area and domestic out-migration from the same area during a time period. Domestic in- and out-migration consist of moves where both the origin and the destination are within the United States (excluding Puerto Rico).

Percentage population change is the difference between the population of an area at the beginning and end of a time period, expressed as a percentage of the beginning population.

Table B-3. Population by Age, Race, and Hispanic origin

Sources: U.S. Census Bureau, County Population Estimates by age, sex, race, and Hispanic origin, https://www.census.gov/programs-surveys/popest/data/tables.2018.html

Age, sex, and race estimates are based on the distributed cohort component method. For an overview, see https://www.census.gov/programs-surveys/popest/technical-documentation/methodology.html.

Age. The age classification is based on the age of the person in complete years as of July 1. The age of the person usually was derived from their date of birth information.

Race. The concept of race, as used by the Census Bureau, reflects self-identification by people according to the race or races with which they most closely identify. People may choose to report more than one race to indicate their racial mixture. These categories are sociopolitical constructs and should not be interpreted as being scientific or anthropological in nature. Furthermore, the race categories include both racial and national-origin groups. Caution must be used when interpreting changes in the racial composition of the U.S. population over time. The racial classifications used by the Census Bureau adhere to the December 15, 2000 (revised from October 30, 1997), *Federal Register Notice* entitled, "Revisions to the Standards for the Classification of Federal Data on Race and Ethnicity" issued by the OMB, https://www.census.gov/topics/population/race/about.html. These standards govern the categories used to collect and present federal data on race and ethnicity. The OMB required federal agencies to use a minimum of five race categories: White, Black or African American, American Indian and Alaska Native, Asian, and Native Hawaiian and Other Pacific Islander. For respondents unable to identify with any of these five race categories, the OMB approved including a sixth category "Some other race."

The Census 2010 question on race included three areas where respondents could write in a more specific race group. The response categories and write-in answers can be combined to create the five minimum OMB race categories plus "Some other race." People who responded to the question on race by indicating only one race are referred to as the race alone population or the group that reported only one race category.

White. A person having origins in any of the original peoples of Europe, the Middle East, or North Africa. It includes people who indicate their race as "White" or report entries such as Irish, German, Italian, Lebanese, Near Easterner, Arab, or Polish.

Black or African American. A person having origins in any of the Black racial groups of Africa. It includes people who indicate their race as "Black, African American, or Negro," or who provide written entries such as African American, Afro American, Kenyan, Nigerian, or Haitian.

American Indian and Alaska Native. A person having origins in any of the original peoples of North and South America including Central America, and who maintain tribal affiliation or community attachment. It includes people who classify themselves as described below.

American Indian. Includes people who indicate their race as "American Indian," entered the name of an Indian tribe, or report such entries as Canadian Indian, French-American Indian, or Spanish-American Indian.

Alaska Native. Includes written responses of Eskimos, Aleuts, and Alaska Indians as well as entries such as Arctic Slope, Inupiat, Yupik, Alutiiq, Egeik, and Pribilovian. The Alaska tribes are the Alaskan Athabascan, Tlingit, and Haida.

Asian. A person having origins in any of the original peoples of the Far East, Southeast Asia, or the Indian subcontinent including Cambodia, China, India, Japan, Korea, Malaysia, Pakistan, the Philippine Islands, Thailand, and Vietnam. It includes "Asian Indian," "Chinese," "Filipino," "Korean," "Japanese," "Vietnamese," and "Other Asian."

Asian Indian includes people who indicate their race as "Asian Indian" or identify themselves as Bengalese, Bharat, Dravidian, East Indian, or Goanese. *Chinese*

includes people who indicate their race as "Chinese" or who identify themselves as Cantonese or Chinese American. In some census tabulations, written entries of Taiwanese are included with Chinese while in others they are shown separately. *Filipino* includes people who indicate their race as "Filipino" or who report entries such as Philipano, Philipine, or Filipino American. *Japanese* includes people who indicate their race as "Japanese" or who report entries such as Nipponese or Japanese American. *Korean* includes people who indicate their race as "Korean" or who provide a response of Korean American. *Vietnamese* includes people who indicate their race as "Vietnamese" or who provide a response of Vietnamese American.

Native Hawaiian and Other Pacific Islander. A person having origins in any of the original peoples of Hawaii, Guam, Samoa, or other Pacific Islands. It includes people who indicate their race as "Native Hawaiian," "Guamanian or Chamorro," "Samoan," and "Other Pacific Islander."

Native Hawaiian includes people who indicate their race as "Native Hawaiian" or who identify themselves as "Part Hawaiian" or "Hawaiian." *Guamanian or Chamorro* includes people who indicate their race as such, including written entries of Chamorro or Guam. *Samoan* includes people who indicate their race as "Samoan" or who identified themselves as American Samoan or Western Samoan. *Other Pacific Islander* includes people who provided a write-in response of a Pacific Islander group such as Tahitian, Northern Mariana Islander, Palauan, Fijian, or a cultural group, such as Melanesian, Micronesian, or Polynesian.

Hispanic or Latino origin. People who identify with the terms "Hispanic" or "Latino" are those who classify themselves in one of the specific Hispanic or Latino categories listed on the questionnaire—"Mexican," "Puerto Rican," or "Cuban"—as well as those who indicate that they are "other Spanish, Hispanic, or Latino." Origin can be viewed as the heritage, nationality group, lineage, or country of birth of the person or the person's parents or ancestors before their arrival in the United States. People who identify their origin as Spanish, Hispanic, or Latino may be of any race.

Table B-4. Migration and Commuting, 2014-2018

Source: U.S. Census Bureau, American Community Survey, "B07001: Geographical Mobility in the Past Year for Current Residence in the United States, 2014-2018"; "B08604: Worker Population for Workplace Geography, 2014-2018"; "B08007: Place of Work for Workers 16 years Old and Over—State and County level, 2014-2018"; "B08134 and B08135: B08006: Sex of Workers by Means of Transportation to Work, 2014-2018; Aggregate Travel Time to Work and Means of Transportation to Work by Travel Time to Work, 2014-2018" data.census.gov.

Residence one year ago. For the American Community Survey, people who had moved from another residence in the United States or Puerto Rico 1 year earlier were asked to report the exact address (number and street name); the name of the city, town, or post office; the name of the U.S. county or municipio in Puerto Rico; state or Puerto Rico; and the ZIP Code where they lived 1 year ago. People living outside the United States and Puerto Rico were asked to report the name of the foreign country or U.S. Island Area where they were living 1 year ago.

The tabulation category, "Same house," includes all people 1 year and over who did not move during the 1 year as well as those who had moved and returned to their residence 1 year ago. The category, "Different house in the United States" includes people who lived in the United States 1 year earlier but in a different house or apartment from the one they occupied at the time of interview. These movers are then further subdivided according to the type of move. In most tabulations, movers within the U.S. are divided into three groups according to their previous residence: "Different house, same county," "Different county, same state," and "Different state." The last group may be further subdivided into region of residence 1 year ago. An additional category, "Abroad," includes those whose previous residence was in a foreign country, Puerto Rico, American Samoa, Guam, the Northern Marianas, or the U.S. Virgin Islands, including members of the Armed Forces and their dependents. Residence 1 year ago is used in conjunction with location of current residence to determine the extent of residential mobility of the population and the resulting redistribution of the population across the various states, metropolitan areas, and regions of the country. In Table B-4, the migration refers to the metropolitan areas.

Place of Work. Data were tabulated for workers 16 years old and over, that is, members of the Armed Forces and civilians who were at work during the reference week. Data on place of work refer to the geographic location at which workers carried out their occupational activities during the reference week.

In the American Community Survey, the exact address (number and street name) of the place of work was asked, as well as the place (city, town, or post office); whether the place of work was inside or outside the limits of that city or town; and the county, state or foreign country, and ZIP Code. If the respondent's employer operated in more than one location, the exact address of the location

or branch where he or she worked was requested. When the number and street name were unknown, a description of the location, such as the building name or nearest street or intersection, was to be entered. People who worked at more than one location during the reference week were asked to report the location at which they worked the greatest number of hours. People who regularly worked in several locations each day during the reference week were requested to give the address at which they began work each day. For cases in which daily work did not begin at a central place each day, the respondent was asked to provide as much information as possible to describe the area in which he or she worked most during the reference week.

Employment/residence ratio. The employment/residence ratio is a measure of the total number of workers working in an area or place, relative to the total number of workers living in the area or place. It is often used as a rough indication of the jobs-workers balance in an area/place, although it does not take into account whether the resident workers possess the skills needed for the jobs available in their particular area/place. The employment/residence ratio is calculated by dividing the number of total workers working in an area/place by the number of total workers residing in the area/place. When the ratio is greater than 1.00, there are more workers coming into the metropolitan area. When the ratio is less than 1.00, more of the metropolitan area residents commute to jobs outside of the area.

Means of Transportation to Work. Means of transportation to work refers to the principal mode of travel or type of conveyance that the worker usually used to get from home to work during the reference week.

People who used different means of transportation on different days of the week were asked to specify the one they used most often, that is, the greatest number of days. People who used more than one means of transportation to get to work each day were asked to report the one used for the longest distance during the work trip. The category, "Car, truck, or van," includes workers using a car (including company cars but excluding taxicabs), a truck of one-ton capacity or less, or a van.

Private Vehicle Occupancy. Private vehicle occupancy refers to the number of people who usually rode to work in the vehicle during the reference week. The category, "Drove alone," includes people who usually drove alone to work as well as people who were driven to work by someone who then drove back home or to a non-work destination.

Mean Travel Time to Work (in Minutes). Mean travel time to work (in minutes) is the average travel time that workers usually took to get from home to work (one way) during the reference week. This measure is obtained by dividing the total number of minutes taken to get from home to work (the aggregate travel time) by the number of workers 16 years old and over who did not work at home. The travel time includes time spent waiting for public transportation, picking up passengers and carpools, and time spent in other activities related to getting to work. The aggregate travel time to work used to calculate mean travel time to work is rounded to the nearest tenth of a minute.

Table B-5. Population and Household Characteristics 2014-2018

Source: U.S. Census Bureau, American Community Survey, "DP02. Selected Social Characteristics in the United States: 2014-2018; data.census.gov.

Household. A household includes all the people who occupy a housing unit as their usual place of residence.

Family household. A family includes a householder and one or more people living in the same household who are related to the householder by birth, marriage, or adoption. All people in a household who are related to the householder are regarded as members of his or her family. A family household may contain people not related to the householder, but those people are not included as part of the householder's family in census tabulations. Thus, the number of family households is equal to the number of families, but family households may include more members than do families. A household can contain only one family for purposes of census tabulations. Not all households contain families since a household may comprise a group of unrelated people or one person living alone.

With own children under 18. Households that include never-married children under 18 years who are sons or daughters by birth, stepchildren, or adopted children of the householder.

Single-parent household. A family household with own children of the householder, with a male or female householder with no spouse present.

Nonfamily Household. A householder living alone or with nonrelatives only. Unmarried couples households, whether opposite-sex or same-sex, with no relatives of the householder present are tabulated in nonfamily households.

Foreign-born population. The Census Bureau separates the U.S. resident population into two groups based on whether or not a person was a U.S. citizen at the time of birth. Anyone born in the United States or U.S. Island Area (such as Puerto Rico) or born abroad to a U.S. citizen parent is a U.S. citizen at the time of birth and consequently included in the *native population*. The term *foreign-born population* refers to anyone who is not a U.S. citizen at birth. This includes naturalized U.S. citizens, legal permanent resident aliens (immigrants), temporary migrants (such as students), humanitarian migrants (such as refugees), and people illegally present in the United States. Non-citizens are foreign-born individuals who have not become naturalized U.S. citizens.

Language Spoken at Home by the Respondent. The American community Survey asked about languages spoken at home in an effort to measure the current use of languages other than English. This category included persons 5 years old and over and excluded respondents who spoke a language other than English exclusively outside of the home.

Table B-6. Enrollment, Teachers, and Educational Attainment

Sources: Enrollment, number of teachers, and pupil/teacher ratio—National Center for Education Statistics, Common Core of Data, <https://nces.ed.gov/ccd/elsi/>; Educational attainment— U.S. Census Bureau, American Community Survey, DP02. Selected Social Characteristics in the United States: 2014-2018; data.census.gov.

Enrollment, teachers, and pupil/teacher ratio. The Common Core of Data (CCD) is the Department of Education's primary database on public elementary and secondary education in the United States. CCD is a comprehensive, annual, national statistical database of all public elementary and secondary schools and school districts, which contains data that are designed to be comparable across all states.

The objectives of the CCD are twofold: first, to provide an official listing of public elementary and secondary schools and school districts in the nation, which can be used to select samples for other NCES surveys. And second, to provide basic information and descriptive statistics on public elementary and secondary schools and schooling in general.

The CCD survey annually collects data about all public elementary and secondary schools, all local education agencies, and all state education agencies throughout the United States. CCD contains three categories of information: general descriptive information on schools and school districts; data on students and staff; and fiscal data. Much of the data are obtained from administrative records maintained by the state education agencies (SEAs) (the State survey), but there are also surveys of the School Districts and the individual schools.

The numbers of students enrolled in public schools and full-time equivalent teachers are provided by the schools in the school survey.

Educational Attainment. Educational attainment data in this table include persons who are 25 years old and over. In the American Community Survey, respondents are classified according to the highest degree or the highest level of school completed. The question included instructions for persons currently enrolled in school to report the level of the previous grade attended or the highest degree received. The category "High School Graduate or Less" includes people whose highest degree was a high school diploma or its equivalent, and people who had not graduated from high school. The category "Bachelor's degree or higher" includes those who received a bachelor's, master's, or professional or doctorate degree.

Table B-7. Household Income and Poverty Status: 2014-2018

Source: U.S. Census Bureau, American Community Survey, DP03. Selected Economic Characteristics in the United States: 2014-2918; data.census.gov.

Income. Total income is the sum of the amounts reported separately for wage or salary income; net self-employment income; interest, dividends, or net rental or royalty income or income from estates and trusts; Social Security or Railroad Retirement income; Supplemental Security Income (SSI); public assistance or welfare payments; retirement, survivor, or disability pensions; and all other income. Receipts from the following sources are not included as income: capital gains, money received from the sale of property (unless the recipient was engaged in the business of selling such property); the value of income "in kind" from food stamps, public housing subsidies, medical care, employer contributions for individuals, etc.; withdrawal of bank deposits; money borrowed; tax refunds; exchange of money between relatives living in the same household; gifts and lump-sum inheritances, insurance payments, and other types of lump-sum receipts.

Income of households includes the income of the householder and all other individuals 15 years old and over. In compiling statistics on family and household income, the incomes of all persons 15 years old and over in the household (or family) are summed and treated as a single amount. Although the income statistics cover the past 12 months, the characteristics of individuals and the composition of families refer to the time of enumeration. Thus, the income of the family or household does not include amounts received by individuals who were members of the family or household during all or part of the past 12 months if these individuals no longer resided with the family at the time of enumeration. Similarly, income amounts reported by individuals who did not reside with the family or in the household during the past 12 months but who were members of the family or household at the time of enumeration are included. However, the composition of most families and most households was the same during the past 12 months as at the time of interview.

Earnings are defined as the sum of wage or salary income and net income from self-employment. "Earnings" represent the amount of income received regularly for people 16 years old and over before deductions for personal income taxes, Social Security, bond purchases, union dues, Medicare deductions, etc. An individual with earnings is one who has either wage/salary income or self-employment income, or both. Respondents who "break even" in self-employment income and therefore have zero self-employment earnings also are considered "individuals with earnings."

SNAP. Respondents were asked if one or more of the current household members received Supplemental Nutrition Assistance Program (SNAP) benefits during the past 12 months. SNAP benefits were referred to as Food Stamps until 2008.

Poverty status is determined using thresholds arranged in a two-dimensional matrix. The matrix consists of family size cross-classified by presence and number of family members under age 18 years old. Unrelated individuals and two-person families are further differentiated by age of reference person. To determine a person's poverty status, one compares the person's total family income in the last 12 months with the poverty threshold appropriate for that person's family size and composition. If the total income of that person's family is less than the threshold appropriate for that family, then the person is considered poor or "below the poverty level," together with every member of his or her family. If a person is not living with anyone related by birth, marriage, or adoption, then the person's own income is compared with his or her poverty threshold. The total number of people below the poverty level was the sum of people in families and the number of unrelated individuals with incomes in the last 12 months below the poverty level. The average poverty threshold for a family of four in 2018 was $25,701. See https://www.census.gov/topics/income-poverty/poverty.html for more information and detailed poverty thresholds.

Table B-8. Health Insurance, Disability, Medicare, Social Security, and Supplemental Security Income

Sources: Persons with no health insurance--U.S. Census Bureau, American Community Survey, DP03. Selected Economic Characteristics in the United States: 2014-2018. Persons with a disability--U.S. Census Bureau, American Community Survey, S1810. Persons with a Disability, 2014-2018: data.census.gov. Affordable Care Act Enrollment—2019 Marketplace Open Enrollment Period Public Use Files; www.cms.gov/Research-Statistics-Data-and-Systems/Statistics-Trends-and-Reports/Marketplace-Products/2019_Open_Enrollment . Medicare program enrollment--Centers for Medicare and Medicaid Services, CMS Statistics: Medicare Enrollment, www.cms.hhs.gov/MedicareEnrpts/. Social security--U.S. Social Security Administration, OASDI Beneficiaries by State and County, www.ssa.gov/policy/docs/statcomps/oasdi_sc/2018/index.html. Supplemental security income--U.S. Social Security Administration, SSI Recipients by State and County, www.ssa.gov/policy/docs/statcomps/ssi_sc/2018/index.html.

Health Insurance. In the American Community Survey, respondents were instructed to report their current coverage for each of eight types of health insurance: Insurance through a current or former employer or union (of this person or another family member); Insurance purchased directly from an insurance company (by this person or another family member); Medicare, for people 65 and older, or people with certain disabilities; Medicaid, Medical Assistance, or any kind of government-assistance plan for those with low incomes or a disability; TRICARE or other military health care; VA (including those who have ever used or enrolled for VA health care); Indian Health Service; or any other type of health insurance or health coverage plan.

Disability status. Disability is defined as the product of interactions among individuals' bodies; their physical, emotional, and mental health; and the physical and social environment in which they live, work, or play. Disability exists where this interaction results in limitations of activities and restrictions to full participation at school, at work, at home, or in the community. For example, disability may exist where a person is limited in their ability to work due to job discrimination against persons with specific health conditions; or, disability may exist where a child has difficulty learning because the school cannot accommodate the child's deafness. In an attempt to capture a variety of characteristics that encompass the definition of disability, the ACS identifies serious difficulty with four basic areas of functioning–hearing, vision, cognition, and ambulation.

Affordable Care Act enrollment. The number of persons enrolled through the Affordable Care Act includes the total number of submitted applications as of December 22, 2018 for the 39 states that used the HealthCare.gov platform, including the Federally-facilitated Marketplace, State Partnership Marketplaces and supported State-based Marketplaces. This includes applications that were created through the automatic re-enrollment process

The county numbers have been aggregated to metropolitan areas. Data are not available for metropolitan areas that are completely or primarily in states that have their own Healthcare marketplaces: California, Colorado, Connecticut, the District of Columbia, Idaho, Maryland, Massachusetts, Minnesota. New York, Rhode Island, Vermont, and Washington.

Medicare enrollment. When first implemented in 1966, Medicare covered only most persons age 65 and over. By the end of 1966, 3.7 million persons had received at least some health care services covered by Medicare. In 1973, other groups became eligible for Medicare benefits: persons who are entitled to social security or Railroad Retirement disability benefits for at least 24 months; persons with end stage renal disease (ESRD) requiring continuing dialysis or kidney transplant; and certain otherwise non-covered aged persons who elect to buy into Medicare.

Medicare consists of two primary parts: Hospital Insurance (HI), also known as Part A, and Supplementary Medical Insurance (SMI), also known as Part B. Health care services covered under Medicare's Hospital Insurance include inpatient hospital care, skilled nursing facility care, home health agency care, and hospice care. SMI coverage is optional and requires payment of a monthly premium.

The enrollment counts are determined using a person-year methodology, calculated by summing the total number of months that each person is enrolled and dividing by 12.

Social Security

The Old-Age, Survivors, and Disability Insurance Program (OASDI) provides monthly benefits for retired and disabled insured workers and their dependents and to survivors of insured workers. To be eligible for benefits, a worker must have had a specified period of employment in which OASDI taxes were paid. A worker becomes eligible for full retirement benefits at age 65 through 67 (depending on the year of birth), although reduced benefits may be obtained at age 62; the worker's spouse is under the same limitations. Survivor benefits are payable to dependents of deceased insured workers. Disability benefits are payable to an insured worker under age 65 with a prolonged disability and to that person's dependents on the same basis as dependents of a retired worker. Also, disability benefits are payable at age 50 to the disabled widow or widower of a deceased worker who was fully insured at the time of death. A lump-sum benefit is generally payable on the death of an insured worker to a spouse or minor children.

The data were derived from the Master Beneficiary Record (MBR), the principal administrative file of social security beneficiaries. Data for total recipients and retired workers include persons with special age-72 benefits. Special age-72 benefit represents the monthly benefit payable to men who attained age-72 before 1972 and for women who attained age 72 before 1970 and who do not have sufficient quarters to qualify for a retired-worker benefit under either the fully or the transitionally insured status provision.

Supplemental security income. The Supplemental Security Income (SSI) program provides cash payments in accordance with nationwide eligibility requirements to people with limited income and resources who are aged, blind, or disabled. Under the SSI program, each person living in his or her own household is provided a cash payment from the federal government that is sufficient, when added to the person's countable income (the total gross money income of an individual less certain exclusions), to bring the total monthly income up to a specified level (the federal benefit rate). If the individual or couple is living in another household, the guaranteed level is reduced by one-third.

An aged person is defined as an individual who is 65 years old or over. A blind person is anyone with vision of 20/200 or less with the use of correcting lens in the better eye or with tunnel vision of 20 degrees or less. The disabled classification refers to any person unable to engage in any substantial gainful activity by reason of any medically determinable physical or mental impairment expected to result in death or that has lasted or can be expected to last for a continuous period of at least 12 months. For a child under 18 years, eligibility is based on disability or severity comparable with that of an adult, since the criterion of "substantial gainful activity" is inapplicable for children.

Table B-9. Housing Units and Building Permits

Sources: Housing units—U.S. Census Bureau, "Housing Unit Estimates for Counties: April 1, 2010 to July 1,

2018," https://www.census.gov/programs-surveys/popest/data/data-sets.2018.html. Building permits—U.S. Census Bureau, Building Permits Survey, Permits by metropolitan area 2019; https://www.census.gov/construction/bps/msaannual.html.

Housing unit estimates are developed by using building permits, mobile home shipments, and estimates of housing unit loss to measure housing unit change since the last census. For more information see https://www.census.gov/programs-surveys/popest/technical-documentation/methodology.html.

Building permits data are based on reports submitted by local building permit officials in response to a Census Bureau mail survey. They are obtained using Form C-404, "Report of New Privately Owned Residential Building or Zoning Permits Issued." Data are collected from individual permit offices, most of which are municipalities; the remainder are counties, townships, or New England and Middle Atlantic-type towns. Currently, there are 20,000 permit-issuing places. When a report is not received, missing data are either (1) obtained from the Survey of Use of Permits, which is used to collect information on housing starts, or (2) imputed.

The data relate to new private housing units intended for occupancy on a housekeeping basis. They exclude mobile homes (trailers), hotels, motels, and group residential structures, such as nursing homes and college dormitories. They also exclude conversions of and alterations to existing buildings. A housing unit consists of a room or group of rooms intended for occupancy as separate living quarters by a family, by a group of unrelated persons living together, or by a person living alone.

Table B-10. Housing Units: 2014-2018

Source: U.S. Census Bureau, American Community Survey, DP04. Selected Housing Characteristics: 2014-2018. data.census.gov.

A **housing unit** is a house, apartment, mobile home or trailer, group of rooms, or single room occupied or, if vacant, intended for occupancy as separate living quarters. Separate living quarters are those in which the occupants do not live and eat with any other persons in the structure and which have direct access from the outside of the building or through a common hall. A housing unit is classified as occupied if it is the usual place of residence of the person or group of people living in it at the time of census enumeration or if the occupants are only temporarily absent; that is, away on vacation or business. All occupied housing units are classified as either owner occupied or renter occupied. A housing unit is owner occupied if the owner or co-owner lives in the unit even if it is mortgaged or not fully paid for. All occupied housing units that are not owner occupied, whether they are rented for cash rent or occupied without payment of cash rent, are classified as renter occupied.

One-unit detached is a one-unit structure detached from any other house, that is, with open space on all four sides. Such structures are considered detached even if they have an adjoining shed or garage. A one-family house that contains a business is considered detached as long as the building has open space on all four sides. Mobile homes to which one or more permanent rooms have been added or built also are included.

Ownership rate is computed by dividing the number of owner-occupied housing units by the number of occupied housing units. A housing unit is **owner-occupied** if the owner or co-owner lives in the unit even if it is mortgaged or not fully paid for. The owner or co-owner must live in the unit. The unit is owner-occupied if someone who lives in the household is purchasing the house with a mortgage or some other debt arrangement such as a deed of trust, trust deed, contract to purchase, land contract, or purchase agreement. The unit also is considered owned with a mortgage if it is built on leased land and there is a mortgage on the unit. Mobile homes occupied by owners with installment loan balances also are included in this category.

Selected monthly owner costs were obtained for owner-occupied units. Selected monthly owner costs are the sum of payments for mortgages, deeds of trust, contracts to purchase, or similar debts on the property (including payments for the first mortgage, second mortgages, home equity loans, and other junior mortgages); real estate taxes; fire, hazard, and flood insurance on the property; utilities (electricity, gas, and water and sewer); and fuels (oil, coal, kerosene, wood, etc.). It also includes, where appropriate, the monthly condominium fee for condominiums and mobile home costs (installment loan payments, personal property taxes, site rent, registration fees, and license fees). Selected monthly owner costs were tabulated for all owner-occupied units, and usually are shown separately for units "with a mortgage" and for units "not mortgaged." Table B-10 includes only those units with a mortgage.

To inflate selected monthly owner costs from previous years, the dollar values are inflated to the latest year's dollar values by multiplying by a factor equal to the average annual Consumer Price Index (CPI-U-RS) factor for the current year, divided by the average annual CPI-U-RS factor for the earliest year.

Monthly rent refers to the **gross rent** which is the contract rent plus the estimated average monthly cost of utilities (electricity, gas, and water and sewer) and fuels (oil, coal, kerosene, wood, etc.) if these are paid by the renter (or paid for the renter by someone else). Gross rent is intended to eliminate differentials that result from varying practices with respect to the inclusion of utilities and fuels as part of the rental payment. The estimated costs of water and sewer, and fuels are reported on a 12-month basis but are converted to monthly figures for the tabulations.

Vehicles available. The question on vehicles available was asked at occupied housing units. These data show the number of passenger cars, vans, and pickup or panel trucks of one-ton capacity or less kept at home and available for the use of household members. Vehicles rented or leased for one month or more, company vehicles, and police and government vehicles are included if kept at home and used for non-business purposes. Dismantled or immobile vehicles are excluded. Vehicles kept at home but used only for business purposes also are excluded.

Table B-11. Personal Income and Earnings by Place of Work

Sources: U.S. Bureau of Economic Analysis, Regional Economic Accounts, Local Area Personal Income and Employment, https://www.bea.gov/data/by-place-county-metro-local.

Personal income is the income that is received by all persons from all sources. It is calculated as the sum of wage and salary disbursements, supplements to wages and salaries, proprietors' income with inventory valuation and capital consumption adjustments, rental income of people with capital consumption adjustment, personal dividend income, personal interest income, and personal current transfer receipts, less contributions for government social insurance.

The personal income of an area is the income that is received by, or on behalf of, all the individuals who live in the area; therefore, the estimates of personal income are presented by the place of residence of the income recipients.

Personal income differs by definition from money income, which is prepared by the Census Bureau, in that money income is measured before deduction of personal contributions for social insurance and does not include imputed income, lump-sum payments, and income received by quasi-individuals. Money income does include income from private pensions and annuities and from interpersonal transfer, such as child support; therefore it is not comparable to personal income. Total personal income is adjusted to place of residence.

About 90 percent of the state and county estimates of personal income are based on census data and on administrative-records data that are collected by other federal agencies. The data from censuses are mainly collected from the recipient of the income. The most important sources of census data for the state and county estimates are the census of agriculture and the census of population and housing that are conducted by the Census Bureau. The data from administrative records may originate either from the recipients of the income or from the source of the income. These data are a byproduct of the administration of various federal and state government programs. The most important sources of these data are as follows: the state unemployment insurance programs of the Employment and Training Administration, Department of Labor; the social insurance programs of the Social Security Administration and the Health Care Financing Administration, Department of Health and Human Services; the federal income tax program of the Internal Revenue Service, Department of the Treasury; the veterans benefit programs of the Department of Veterans Affairs; and the military payroll systems of the Department of Defense. The remaining 10 percent of the estimates are based on data from other sources. For example, the estimates of the components of farm proprietors' income, a component of personal income, are partly based on the state estimates of farm income and the county estimates of case receipts, crop production, and livestock inventory that are prepared by the Department of Agriculture, which uses sample surveys, along with census data and administrative-records data, to derive its estimates.

Total **earnings** cover wage and salary disbursements, supplements to wages and salaries, and proprietor's income. Wage and salary disbursements consists of the monetary remuneration of employees, including corporate officers salaries and bonuses, commissions, pay-in-kind, incentive payments, and tips. It reflects the amount of payments disbursed, but not necessarily earned during the year. It is measured before deductions, such as social security contributions and union dues. Wage and salary disbursements includes stock options of nonqualified plans at the time that they have been exercised by the individual. Stock options are reported in wage and salary disbursements. The value that is included in wages is the difference between the exercise price and the price that the stock options were granted. Supplements to wages and salaries consists of employer contributions for employee pension and insurance funds and of employer contributions for government social insurance. Proprietor's income is the current-production income (including income in kind) of sole proprietorships and partnerships and of tax-exempt cooperatives. Corporate directors' fees are included in proprietors' income, but the imputed net rental income of owner-occupants of all dwellings is included in rental

income of persons. Proprietors' income excludes dividends and monetary interest received by nonfinancial business and rental incomes received by persons not primarily engaged in the real estate business; these incomes are included in dividends, net interest, and rental income of persons, respectively.

Table B-12. Employees and Earnings by Selected Major Industries: 2018

Sources: U.S. Bureau of Economic Analysis, Regional Economic Accounts, Local Area Personal Income and Employment, https://www.bea.gov/data/by-place-county-metro-local.

The estimates of employment and earnings from 2015 are based on the 2012 North American Industry Classification System (NAICS). For more information on NAICS please visit http://www.census.gov/eos/www/naics/index.html.

The BEA employment series for states and local areas comprises estimates of the number of jobs, full-time plus part-time, by place of work. Full-time and part-time jobs are counted at equal weight. Employees, sole proprietors, and active partners are included, but unpaid family workers and volunteers are not included.

Earnings by place of work is the sum of Wage and Salary Disbursements, supplements to wages and salaries and proprietors' income.

Table B-13. Civilian Labor Force and Banking

Sources: Civilian labor force, U.S. Bureau of Labor Statistics (BLS), *Local Area Unemployment Statistics, Annual Averages*, www.bls.gov/lau/.

Civilian Labor Force

Civilian labor force data are the product of a federal-state cooperative program in which state employment security agencies prepare labor force and unemployment estimates under concepts, definitions, and technical procedures established by the BLS. These data for substate areas are produced by the BLS primarily for use in allocating funds under various federal legislative programs. Users of these data are cautioned that, because of the small size of many of the areas, as well as limitations of the data inputs, the estimates are subject to considerable, but nonquantifiable, error. An explanation of the technical procedures used to develop monthly and annual local area labor force estimates appears monthly in the Explanatory Note for state and area unemployment data in the BLS periodical, *Employment and Earnings*. Additional information may also be found at the BLS Web site at <www.bls.gov/opub/hom/>.

The civilian labor force comprises all persons in the civilian noninstitutional population classified as either employed or unemployed. Employed persons are persons 16 years and over in the civilian noninstitutional population who, during the reference week, (a) did any work at all (at least 1 hour) as paid employees; worked in their own business, profession, or on their own farm, or worked 15 hours or more as unpaid workers in an enterprise operated by a member of the family; and (b) all those who were not working but who had jobs or businesses from which they were temporarily absent because of vacation, illness, bad weather, childcare problems, maternity or paternity leave, labor-management dispute, job training, or other family or personal reasons, whether or not they were paid for the time off or were seeking other jobs. Each employed person is counted only once, even if he or she holds more than one job. Excluded are persons whose only activity consisted of work around their own house (painting, repairing, or own home housework) or volunteer work for religious, charitable, and other organizations.

Unemployed people are all civilians aged 16 years and older who had no employment during the reference week, were available for work, except for temporary illness, and had made specific efforts to find employment sometime during the 4-week period ending with the reference week. Persons who were waiting to be recalled to a job from which they had been laid off need not have been looking for work to be classified as unemployed. The unemployment rate for all civilian workers represents the number of unemployed as a percent of the civilian labor force.

Table B-14. Banking, Government Employment, and Private Business Establishments and Employment

Sources: Banking—U. S. Federal Deposit Insurance Corporation (FDIC) https://www7.fdic.gov/sod/; Government Employment--U.S. Bureau of Economic Analysis—Regional Economic Accounts Local Area Personal Income and Employment; https://www.bea.gov/data/by-place-county-metro-local; Private nonfarm business—County Business Patterns https://www.census.gov/programs-surveys/cbp.html.

Banking. The FDIC (Federal Deposit Insurance Corporation) and OTS (Office of Thrift Supervision) collect deposit data on each office of every FDIC-insured bank and saving association as of June 30 of each year in the Summary of Deposits (SOD) survey. The FDIC surveys all FDIC-insured commercial banks, savings banks, and U.S. branches of foreign banks, and the OTS surveys all savings associations. Data presented here exclude U.S. branch offices of foreign banks. For all counties, individual banking offices—not the combined totals of the bank—are the source of the data.

Insured **savings institutions** include all FDIC-insured (OTS-Regulated and FDIC-Regulated) financial institutions that operate under federal or state banking charters. The number of **banking offices** in any given area includes every location at which deposit business is transacted. Banking office is defined to include all offices and facilities that actually hold deposits, but to exclude loan production offices, computer centers, and other non-deposit installations, such as automated teller machines (ATMs). The term "offices" includes both main offices and branches. An institution with four branches operates a total of five offices.

Government Employment. Employment is measured as the average annual sum of full-time and part-time jobs. The estimates are on a place-of-work basis. State and local government employment includes person employed in all state and local government agencies and enterprises. Data for federal civilian employment include civilian employees of the federal government, including civilian employees of the Department of Defense. Military employment includes all persons on active duty status.

County Business Patterns (CBP) is an annual series that provides subnational economic data by industry. The series is useful for studying the economic activity of small areas; analyzing economic changes over time; and as a benchmark for statistical series, surveys, and databases between economic censuses. CBP covers most of the country's economic activity. The series excludes data on self-employed individuals, employees of private households, railroad employees, agricultural production employees, and most government employees. The County Business Patterns program has tabulated on a North American Industry Classification System (NAICS) basis since 1998. Data for 1997 and earlier years are based on the Standard Industrial Classification (SIC) system. For more information on the relationship between the two systems, see Concordances <www.census.gov/eos/www/naics/concordances/concordances.html>.

CBP data are extracted from the Business Register, the Census Bureau's file of all known single and multiestablishment companies. The Annual Company Organization Survey and quinquennial economic censuses provide individual establishment data for multilocation firms. Data for single-location firms are obtained from various programs censuses, the Annual Survey of Manufactures, and Current Business Surveys, as well as from administrative records of the Internal Revenue Service (IRS), the Social Security Administration (SSA), and the Bureau of Labor Statistics (BLS).

An **establishment** is a single physical location at which business is conducted or services or industrial operations are performed. It is not necessarily identical with a company or enterprise, which may consist of one or more establishments. When two or more activities are carried on at a single location under a single ownership, all activities generally are grouped together as a single establishment. The entire establishment is classified on the basis of its major activity and all data are included in that classification. Establishment-size designations are determined by paid employment in the mid-March pay period. The size group "1 to 4" includes establishments that did not report any paid employees in the mid-March pay period but paid wages to at least one employee at some time during the year.

Establishment counts represent the number of locations with paid employees any time during the year. This series excludes governmental establishments except for wholesale liquor establishments (NAICS 4248), retail liquor stores (NAICS 44531), federally-chartered savings institutions (NAICS 522120), federally-chartered credit unions (NAICS 522130), and hospitals (NAICS 622).

Total payroll includes all forms of compensation, such as salaries, wages, reported tips, commissions, bonuses, vacation allowances, sick-leave pay, employee contributions to qualified pension plans, and the value of taxable fringe benefits. For corporations, it includes amounts paid to officers and executives; for unincorporated businesses, it does not include profit or other compensation of proprietors or partners. Payroll is reported before deductions for social security, income tax, insurance, union dues, etc. First-quarter payroll consists of payroll during the January-to-March quarter.

Paid employment consists of full- and part-time employees, including salaried officers and executives of corporations, who are on the payroll in the pay period including March 12. Included are employees on paid sick leave, holidays, and vacations; not included are proprietors and partners of unincorporated businesses.

TABLE C. METROPOLITAN AREAS WITH COMPONENT COUNTIES

Table C consists of 4 tables (C-1 through C-4) with 50 data items for 384 metropolitan statistical areas (MSAs), 31 metropolitan divisions (in 11 large metropolitan statistical areas), and 1,180 counties within the metropolitan areas. They are presented alphabetically in each of the 4 tables, with counties listed alphabetically within each metropolitan area.

All summaries, including historical data, are presented for the areas as currently defined. Where possible, the original figures have been retabulated to reflect the status of

metropolitan area boundaries as of September 14, 2018. For more information on these areas, see Appendix C, Geographic Concepts and Codes.

Table C-1. Population and Population Characteristics

Sources: Population and change—U.S. Census Bureau, Population Estimates Program, Population and Housing Unit Estimates Datasets. www.census.gov/programs-surveys/popest/data/data-sets.html

Population numbers for 2010 and 2000 are counts of the resident population on April 1 of those decennial census years. The April 1 estimates base population may differ from the April 1 census count due to legal boundary updates, other geographic program changes, and Count Question Resolution actions.

Population estimates for 2019 and 2018 measure the estimated population from the calculated number of people living in an area as of July 1. The Census Bureau develops county population estimates with a component of population change method in which they use administrative records and other data to estimate the household and group quarters population. For the household population, the components of population change are births, deaths, net domestic migration, and net international migration. They measure change in the nonhousehold, or group quarters, population by the net change in the population living in group quarters facilities.

A major assumption underlying this approach is that changes in selected administrative and other data sources closely approximate the components of population change. Therefore, Census Bureau demographers separately estimate each component of population change based on administrative records, including registered births and deaths, federal income tax returns, medicare enrollees, and military movement. They also separately estimate net international migration using information from the American Community Survey (ACS), the decennial census, and other data sources.

Most administrative record data sources lag the current estimate year by as much as 2 years. Therefore, the Census Bureau projects the data for the current year based on past years' data. As updated data become available, they revise the projected input data so that each vintage's estimates are always based on the most recent data available.

For more information on the method used for these estimates, see Appendix B, Limitations and Methodology, and the website at <http://www.census.gov/programs-surveys/popest/technical-documentation.html.

Age. The age classification is based on the age of the person in complete years as of July 1, 2018. The age of the person usually was derived from their date of birth information.

Table C-2. Population Characteristics and Housing Units

Sources: Population estimates by race and housing unit estimates—U.S. Census Bureau, Population Estimates Program, Population and Housing Unit Estimates Datasets www.census.gov/programs-surveys/popest/data/datasets.html

Race. The concept of race, as used by the Census Bureau, reflects self-identification by people according to the race or races with which they most closely identify. These categories are sociopolitical constructs and should not be interpreted as being scientific or anthropological in nature. Furthermore, the race categories include both racial and national-origin groups. Caution must be used when interpreting changes in the racial composition of the U.S. population over time. The racial classifications used by the Census Bureau adhere to the December 15, 2000 (revised from October 30, 1997), *Federal Register Notice* entitled, "Revisions to the Standards for the Classification of Federal Data on Race and Ethnicity" issued by the OMB. These standards govern the categories used to collect and present federal data on race and ethnicity. The OMB required federal agencies to use a minimum of five race categories: White, Black or African American, American Indian and Alaska Native, Asian, and Native Hawaiian and Other Pacific Islander. For respondents unable to identify with any of these five race categories, the OMB approved including a sixth category "Some other race." See http://www.census.gov/topics/population/race.html.

The Census 2010 question on race included three areas where respondents could write in a more specific race group. The response categories and write-in answers can be combined to create the five minimum OMB race categories plus "Some other race."

People who responded to the question on race by indicating only one race are referred to as the "race alone" population or the group that reported only one race category. Table C-2 uses the "race alone or in combination" categories, which include all people who indicated a particular race, whether or not they indicated other races. Thus, the percentages of the individual groups may add up to more than 100 percent, because individuals can be in more than one group.

White. A person having origins in any of the original peoples of Europe, the Middle East, or North Africa. It includes people who indicate their race as "White" or report entries such as Irish, German, Italian, Lebanese, Near Easterner, Arab, or Polish.

Black or African American. A person having origins in any of the Black racial groups of Africa. It includes people who indicate their race as "Black, African American, or Negro," or who provide written entries such as African American, Afro American, Kenyan, Nigerian, or Haitian.

American Indian and Alaska Native. A person having origins in any of the original peoples of North and South America including Central America, and who maintain tribal affiliation or community attachment. It includes people who classify themselves as described below.

American Indian. Includes people who indicate their race as "American Indian," entered the name of an Indian tribe, or report such entries as Canadian Indian, French-American Indian, or Spanish-American Indian.

Alaska Native. Includes written responses of Eskimos, Aleuts, and Alaska Indians as well as entries such as Arctic Slope, Inupait, Yupik, Alutiiq, Egeik, and Pribilovian. The Alaska tribes are the Alaskan Athabascan, Tlingit, and Haida.

Asian. A person having origins in any of the original peoples of the Far East, Southeast Asia, or the Indian subcontinent including Cambodia, China, India, Japan, Korea, Malaysia, Pakistan, the Philippine Islands, Thailand, and Vietnam. It includes "Asian Indian," "Chinese," "Filipino," "Korean," "Japanese," "Vietnamese," and "Other Asian."

Asian Indian includes people who indicate their race as "Asian Indian" or identify themselves as Bengalese, Bharat, Dravidian, East Indian, or Goanese. *Chinese* includes people who indicate their race as "Chinese" or who identify themselves as Cantonese or Chinese American. In some census tabulations, written entries of Taiwanese are included with Chinese while in others they are shown separately. *Filipino* includes people who indicate their race as "Filipino" or who report entries such as Philipano, Philipine, or Filipino American. *Japanese* includes people who indicate their race as "Japanese" or who report entries such as Nipponese or Japanese American. *Korean* includes people who indicate their race as "Korean" or who provide a response of Korean American. *Vietnamese* includes people who indicate their race as "Vietnamese" or who provide a response of Vietnamese American.

Native Hawaiian and Other Pacific Islander. A person having origins in any of the original peoples of Hawaii,

Guam, Samoa, or other Pacific Islands. It includes people who indicate their race as "Native Hawaiian," "Guamanian or Chamorro," "Samoan," and "Other Pacific Islander."

Native Hawaiian includes people who indicate their race as "Native Hawaiian" or who identify themselves as "Part Hawaiian" or "Hawaiian." *Guamanian or Chamorro* includes people who indicate their race as such, including written entries of Chamorro or Guam. *Samoan* includes people who indicate their race as "Samoan" or who identified themselves as American Samoan or Western Samoan. *Other Pacific Islander* includes people who provided a write-in response of a Pacific Islander group such as Tahitian, Northern Mariana Islander, Palauan, Fijian, or a cultural group, such as Melanesian, Micronesian, or Polynesian.

Hispanic or Latino origin. People who identify with the terms "Hispanic" or "Latino" are those who classify themselves in one of the specific Hispanic or Latino categories listed on the questionnaire—"Mexican," "Puerto Rican," or "Cuban"—as well as those who indicate that they are "other Spanish, Hispanic, or Latino." Origin can be viewed as the heritage, nationality group, lineage, or country of birth of the person or the person's parents or ancestors before their arrival in the United States. People who identify their origin as Spanish, Hispanic, or Latino may be of any race.

Housing unit estimates are developed by using building permits, mobile home shipments, and estimates of housing unit loss to measure housing unit change since the last census. For more information see http://www.census.gov/programs-surveys/popest/technical-documentation.html.

Table C-3. Personal Income and Earnings by Industry

Source: Personal income and earnings, U.S. Bureau of Economic Analysis, Regional Economic Accounts, State and Local Area Personal Income and Employment: https://www.bea.gov/data/by-place-county-metro-local. Population for per capita income—U.S. Census Bureau, compiled from Population and Housing Unit Estimates Tables, https://www.census.gov/programs-surveys/popest/data/tables.2018.html.

Personal income is the income that is received by all persons from all sources. It is calculated as the sum of wage and salary disbursements, supplements to wages and salaries, proprietors' income with inventory valuation and capital consumption adjustments, rental income of people with capital consumption adjustment, personal dividend income, personal interest income, and personal current transfer receipts, less contributions for government social insurance.

The personal income of an area is the income that is received by, or on behalf of, all the individuals who live in the area; therefore, the estimates of personal income are presented by the place of residence of the income recipients.

Personal income differs by definition from money income, which is prepared by the Census Bureau, in that money income is measured before deduction of personal contributions for social insurance and does not include imputed income, lump-sum payments, and income received by quasi-individuals. Money income does include income from private pensions and annuities and from interpersonal transfer, such as child support; therefore it is not comparable to personal income. Total personal income is adjusted to place of residence.

Per Capita personal income is the personal income of a given area divided by the resident population of the area, using the July 1 population estimate of the year shown.

About 90 percent of the state and county estimates of personal income are based on census data and on administrative-records data that are collected by other federal agencies. The data from censuses are mainly collected from the recipient of the income. The most important sources of census data for the state and county estimates are the census of agriculture and the census of population and housing that are conducted by the Census Bureau. The data from administrative records may originate either from the recipients of the income or from the source of the income. These data are a byproduct of the administration of various federal and state government programs. The most important sources of these data are as follows: the state unemployment insurance programs of the Employment and Training Administration, Department of Labor; the social insurance programs of the Social Security Administration and the Health Care Financing Administration, Department of Health and Human Services; the federal income tax program of the Internal Revenue Service, Department of the Treasury; the veterans benefit programs of the Department of Veterans Affairs; and the military payroll systems of the Department of Defense. The remaining 10 percent of the estimates are based on data from other sources. For example, the estimates of the components of farm proprietors' income, a component of personal income, are partly based on the state estimates of farm income and the county estimates of case receipts, crop production, and livestock inventory that are prepared by the Department of Agriculture, which uses sample surveys, along with census data and administrative-records data, to derive its estimates.

Total **earnings** cover wage and salary disbursements, supplements to wages and salaries, and proprietor's income.

Wage and salary disbursements consists of the monetary remuneration of employees, including corporate officers salaries and bonuses, commissions, pay-in-kind, incentive payments, and tips. It reflects the amount of payments disbursed, but not necessarily earned during the year. It is measured before deductions, such as social security contributions and union dues. Wage and salary disbursements includes stock options of nonqualified plans at the time that they have been exercised by the individual. Stock options are reported in wage and salary disbursements. The value that is included in wages is the difference between the exercise price and the price that the stock options were granted. Supplements to wages and salaries consists of employer contributions for employee pension and insurance funds and of employer contributions for government social insurance. Proprietor's income is the current-production income (including income in kind) of sole proprietorships and partnerships and of tax-exempt cooperatives. Corporate directors' fees are included in proprietors' income, but the imputed net rental income of owner-occupants of all dwellings is included in rental income of persons. Proprietors' income excludes dividends and monetary interest received by nonfinancial business and rental incomes received by persons not primarily engaged in the real estate business; these incomes are included in dividends, net interest, and rental income of persons, respectively.

The estimates of earnings from 2018 are based on the 2017 North American Industry Classification System (NAICS). For more information on NAICS please visit <http://www.census.gov/eos/www/naics/>.

Earnings by place of work is the sum of Wage and Salary Disbursements, supplements to wages and salaries and proprietors' income.

Table C-4. Labor Force and Private Business Establishments and Employment

Sources: Civilian labor force--U.S. Bureau of Labor Statistics, Local Area Unemployment, Annual Averages <www.bls.gov/lau/>. Private nonfarm businesses--U.S. Census Bureau, County Business Patterns http://www.census.gov/programs-surveys/cbp.html.

Civilian Labor Force

Civilian labor force data are the product of a federal-state cooperative program in which state employment security agencies prepare labor force and unemployment estimates under concepts, definitions, and technical procedures established by the BLS. These data for substate areas are produced by the BLS primarily for use in allocating funds under various federal legislative programs. Users of these data are cautioned that, because of the small size of many of the areas, as well as limitations of the data inputs, the estimates are subject to considerable, but nonquantifiable, error. An explanation of the technical procedures used to develop monthly and annual local area labor force estimates appears monthly in the Explanatory Note for state and area unemployment data in the BLS periodical, *Employment and Earnings*. Additional information may also be found at the BLS Web site at <www.bls.gov/opub/hom/>.

The civilian labor force comprises all persons in the civilian noninstitutional population classified as either employed or unemployed. Employed persons are persons 16 years and over in the civilian noninstitutional population who, during the reference week, (a) did any work at all (at least 1 hour) as paid employees; worked in their own business, profession, or on their own farm, or worked 15 hours or more as unpaid workers in an enterprise operated by a member of the family; and (b) all those who were not working but who had jobs or businesses from which they were temporarily absent because of vacation, illness, bad weather, childcare problems, maternity or paternity leave, labor-management dispute, job training, or other family or personal reasons, whether or not they were paid for the time off or were seeking other jobs. Each employed person is counted only once, even if he or she holds more than one job. Excluded are persons whose only activity consisted of work around their own house (painting, repairing, or own home housework) or volunteer work for religious, charitable, and other organizations.

Unemployed people are all civilians aged 16 years and older who had no employment during the reference week, were available for work, except for temporary illness, and had made specific efforts to find employment sometime during the 4-week period ending with the reference week. Persons who were waiting to be recalled to a job from which they had been laid off need not have been looking for work to be classified as unemployed. The unemployment rate for all civilian workers represents the number of unemployed as a percent of the civilian labor force.

County Business Patterns (CBP) is an annual series that provides subnational economic data by industry. The series is useful for studying the economic activity of small areas; analyzing economic changes over time; and as a benchmark for statistical series, surveys, and databases between economic censuses. CBP covers most of the country's economic activity. The series excludes data on self-employed individuals, employees of private households, railroad employees, agricultural production employees, and most government employees. The County Business Patterns program has tabulated on a North American Industry Classification System (NAICS) basis since 1998. Data for 1997 and earlier years are based on the Standard Industrial Classification (SIC) system. For more information on the relationship between the two systems, see Concordances <www.census.gov/eos/www/naics/concordances/concordances.html>.

CBP data are extracted from the Business Register, the Census Bureau's file of all known single and multiestablishment companies. The Annual Company Organization Survey and quinquennial economic censuses provide individual establishment data for multilocation firms. Data for single-location firms are obtained from various programs censuses, the Annual Survey of Manufactures, and Current Business Surveys, as well as from administrative records of the Internal Revenue Service (IRS), the Social Security Administration (SSA), and the Bureau of Labor Statistics (BLS).

An **establishment** is a single physical location at which business is conducted or services or industrial operations are performed. It is not necessarily identical with a company or enterprise, which may consist of one or more establishments. When two or more activities are carried on at a single location under a single ownership, all activities generally are grouped together as a single establishment. The entire establishment is classified on the basis of its major activity and all data are included in that classification. Establishment-size designations are determined by paid employment in the mid-March pay period. The size group "1 to 4" includes establishments that did not report any paid employees in the mid-March pay period but paid wages to at least one employee at some time during the year.

Establishment counts represent the number of locations with paid employees any time during the year. This series excludes governmental establishments except for wholesale liquor establishments (NAICS 4248), retail liquor stores (NAICS 44531), federally-chartered savings institutions (NAICS 522120), federally-chartered credit unions (NAICS 522130), and hospitals (NAICS 622).

Total payroll includes all forms of compensation, such as salaries, wages, reported tips, commissions, bonuses, vacation allowances, sick-leave pay, employee contributions to qualified pension plans, and the value of taxable fringe benefits. For corporations, it includes amounts paid to officers and executives; for unincorporated businesses, it does not include profit or other compensation of proprietors or partners. Payroll is reported before deductions for social security, income tax, insurance, union dues, etc. First-quarter payroll consists of payroll during the January-to-March quarter.

Paid employment consists of full- and part-time employees, including salaried officers and executives of corporations, who are on the payroll in the pay period including

March 12. Included are employees on paid sick leave, holidays, and vacations; not included are proprietors and partners of unincorporated businesses.

TABLE D. METROPOLITAN AND MICROPOLITAN AREAS WITH COMPONENT COUNTIES

Table D consists of 1 table (D-1) with 12 data items for 926 Core Based Statistical Areas (384 metropolitan statistical areas and 542 micropolitan statistical areas), 31 metropolitan divisions within the largest metropolitan areas, and 1,840 counties within the metropolitan and micropolitan areas. They are presented alphabetically, with counties listed alphabetically within each micropolitan area.

All summaries, including historical data, are presented for the areas as currently defined. Where possible, the original figures have been retabulated to reflect the status of metropolitan and micropolitan area boundaries as of September 14, 2018. For more information on these areas, see Appendix C, Geographic Concepts and Codes.

Table D-1. Population and Personal Income

Sources: Population—U.S. Censu3s Bureau, Population Estimates Program, Population and Housing Unit Estimates Datasets www.census.gov/programs-surveys/popest/data/data-sets.html; Personal income—U.S. Bureau of Economic Analysis, Regional Economic Accounts, State and Local Area Personal Income https://bea.gov/regional/index.htm.

Population numbers for 2010 and 2000 are counts of the resident population on April 1 of those decennial census years. The April 1 estimates base population may differ from the April 1 census count due to legal boundary updates, other geographic program changes, and Count Question Resolution actions.

Population estimates for 2019 measure the estimated population from the calculated number of people living in an area as of July 1. The Census Bureau develops county population estimates with a component of population change method in which they use administrative records and other data to estimate the household and group quarters population. For the household population, the components of population change are births, deaths, net domestic migration, and net international migration. They measure change in the nonhousehold, or group quarters, population by the net change in the population living in group quarters facilities.

A major assumption underlying this approach is that changes in selected administrative and other data sources closely approximate the components of population change. Therefore, Census Bureau demographers separately estimate each component of population change based on administrative records, including registered births and deaths, federal income tax returns, medicare enrollees, and military movement. They also separately estimate net international migration using information from the American Community Survey (ACS), the decennial census, and other data sources.

Most administrative record data sources lag the current estimate year by as much as 2 years. Therefore, the Census Bureau projects the data for the current year based on past years' data. As updated data become available, they revise the projected input data so that each vintage's estimates are always based on the most recent data available.

For more information on the method used for these estimates, see Appendix B, Limitations and Methodology, and the website at <http://www.census.gov/programs-surveys/popest/technical-documentation.html >.

Personal income is the income that is received by all persons from all sources. It is calculated as the sum of wage and salary disbursements, supplements to wages and salaries, proprietors' income with inventory valuation and capital consumption adjustments, rental income of people with capital consumption adjustment, personal dividend income, personal interest income, and personal current transfer receipts, less contributions for government social insurance.

The personal income of an area is the income that is received by, or on behalf of, all the individuals who live in the area; therefore, the estimates of personal income are presented by the place of residence of the income recipients.

Per Capita personal income is the personal income of a given area divided by the resident population of the area, using the July 1 population estimate of the year shown. Personal income differs by definition from money income, which is prepared by the Census Bureau, in that money income is measured before deduction of personal contributions for social insurance and does not include imputed income, lump-sum payments, and income received by quasi-individuals. Money income does include income from private pensions and annuities and from interpersonal transfer, such as child support; therefore it is not comparable to personal income. Total personal income is adjusted to place of residence.

About 90 percent of the state and county estimates of personal income are based on census data and on administrative-records data that are collected by other federal agencies. The data from censuses are mainly collected from the recipient of the income. The most important sources of census data for the state and county estimates are the census of agriculture and the census of population and housing that are conducted by the Census Bureau. The data from administrative records may originate either from the recipients of the income or from the source of the income. These data are a byproduct of the administration of various federal and state government programs. The most important sources of these data are as follows: the state unemployment insurance programs of the Employment and Training Administration, Department of Labor; the social insurance programs of the Social Security Administration and the Health Care Financing Administration, Department of Health and Human Services; the federal income tax program of the Internal Revenue Service, Department of the Treasury; the veterans benefit programs of the Department of Veterans Affairs; and the military payroll systems of the Department of Defense. The remaining 10 percent of the estimates are based on data from other sources. For example, the estimates of the components of farm proprietors' income, a component of personal income, are partly based on the state estimates of farm income and the county estimates of case receipts, crop production, and livestock inventory that are prepared by the Department of Agriculture, which uses sample surveys, along with census data and administrative-records data, to derive its estimates.

APPENDIX B.
LIMITATIONS OF THE DATA AND METHODOLOGY

INTRODUCTION

The data presented in this *State and Metropolitan Area Data Book* came from many sources. The sources include not only federal statistical bureaus and other organizations that collect and issue statistics as their principal activity, but also governmental administrative and regulatory agencies, private research bodies, trade associations, insurance companies, health associations, and private organizations such as the National Education Association and philanthropic foundations. Consequently, the data vary considerably as to reference periods, definitions of terms and, for ongoing series, the number and frequency of time periods for which data are available.

The statistics presented were obtained and tabulated by various means. Some statistics are based on complete enumerations or censuses while others are based on samples. Some information is extracted from records kept for administrative or regulatory purposes (school enrollment, hospital records, securities registration, financial accounts, social security records, income tax returns, and so on), while other information is obtained explicitly for statistical purposes through interviews or by mail. The estimation procedures used vary from highly sophisticated scientific techniques to crude "informed guesses."

Each set of data relates to a group of individuals or units of interest referred to as the *target universe* or *target population*, or simply as the *universe* or *population*. Prior to data collection the target universe should be clearly defined. For example, if data are to be collected for the universe of households in the United States, it is necessary to define a "household." The target universe may not be completely traceable. Cost and other considerations may restrict data collection to a survey universe based on some available list and that list may be inaccurate or out of date. This list is called a *survey frame* or *sampling frame*.

The data in many tables are based on data obtained for all population units, a census, or on data obtained for only a portion, or sample, of the population units. When the data presented are based on a sample, the sample is usually a scientifically selected probability sample. This is a sample selected from a list or sampling frame in such a way that every possible sample has a known chance of

selection and usually each unit selected can be assigned a number, greater than zero and less than or equal to one, representing its likelihood or probability of selection.

For large-scale sample surveys, the probability sample of units is often selected as a multistage sample. The first stage of a multistage sample is the selection of a probability sample of large groups of population members, referred to as primary sampling units (PSUs). For example, in a national multistage household sample, PSUs are often counties or groups of counties. The second stage of a multistage sample is the selection, within each PSU selected at the first stage, of smaller groups of population units, referred to as secondary sampling units. In subsequent stages of selection, smaller and smaller nested groups are chosen until the ultimate sample of population units is obtained. To qualify a multistage sample as a probability sample, all stages of sampling must be carried out using probability-sampling methods.

Prior to selection at each stage of a multistage (or a singlestage) sample, a list of the sampling units or sampling frame for that stage must be obtained. For example, for the first stage of selection of a national household sample, a list of the counties and county groups that form the PSUs must be obtained. For the final stage of selection, lists of households, and sometimes persons within the households, have to be compiled in the field. For surveys of economic entities and for the economic censuses the Census Bureau generally uses a frame constructed from the Census Bureau's Business Register. The Business Register contains all establishments with payroll in the United States including small single establishment firms as well as large multiestablishment firms.

Wherever the quantities in a table refer to an entire universe, but are constructed from data collected in a sample survey, the table quantities are referred to as *sample estimates*. In constructing a sample estimate, an attempt is made to come as close as is feasible to the corresponding universe quantity that would be obtained from a complete census of the universe. Estimates based on a sample will, however, generally differ from the hypothetical census figures. Two classifications of errors are associated with estimates based on sample surveys: (1) *sampling error*—the error arising from the use of a sample, rather than a census, to estimate population quantities and (2) *nonsampling error*—those errors arising from nonsampling sources. As discussed below, the magnitude of the sampling error for an estimate can usually be estimated from the sample data. However, the magnitude of the nonsampling error for an estimate can rarely be estimated. Consequently, actual error in an estimate exceeds the error that can be estimated.

The particular sample used in a survey is only one of a large number of possible samples of the same size, which could have been selected using the same sampling procedure. Estimates derived from the different samples would, in general, differ from each other. The *standard error* (SE) is a measure of the variation among the estimates derived from all possible samples. The standard error is the most commonly used measure of the sampling error of an estimate. Valid estimates of the standard errors of survey estimates can usually be calculated from the data collected in a probability sample. For convenience, the standard error is sometimes expressed as a percent of the estimate and is called the relative standard error or *coefficient of variation* (CV). For example, an estimate of 200 units with an estimated standard error of 10 units has an estimated CV of 5 percent.

A sample estimate and an estimate of its standard error or CV can be used to construct interval estimates that have a prescribed confidence that the interval includes the average of the estimates derived from all possible samples with a known probability. To illustrate, if all possible samples were selected under essentially the same general conditions, and using the same sample design, and if an estimate and its estimated standard error were calculated from each sample, then: 1) approximately 68 percent of the intervals from one standard error below the estimate to one standard error above the estimate would include the average estimate derived from all possible samples; 2) approximately 90 percent of the intervals from 1.6 standard errors below the estimate to 1.6 standard errors above the estimate would include the average estimate derived from all possible samples; and 3) approximately 95 percent of the intervals from two standard errors below the estimate to two standard errors above the estimate would include the average estimate derived from all possible samples.

Thus, for a particular sample, one can say with the appropriate level of confidence (e.g., 90 percent or 95 percent) that the average of all possible samples is included in the constructed interval. Example of a confidence interval: an estimate is 200 units with a standard error of 10 units. An approximately 90 percent confidence interval (plus or minus 1.6 standard errors) is from 184 to 216.

All surveys and censuses are subject to nonsampling errors. Nonsampling errors are of two kinds *random and nonrandom*. Random nonsampling errors arise because of the varying interpretation of questions (by respondents or interviewers) and varying actions of coders, keyers, and other processors. Some randomness is also introduced when respondents must estimate. Nonrandom nonsampling errors result from total nonresponse (no usable data obtained for a sampled unit), partial or item nonresponse (only a portion of a response may be usable), inability or unwillingness on the part of respondents to provide correct information, difficulty interpreting questions, mistakes in recording or keying data, errors of collection or processing, and coverage problems (overcoverage and undercoverage of the target universe). Random nonresponse errors usually, but not always, result in an understatement of sampling errors and thus an overstatement of the precision of survey estimates. Estimating the magnitude of nonsampling errors would require special experiments or access to independent data and, consequently, the magnitudes are seldom available.

Nearly all types of nonsampling errors that affect surveys also occur in complete censuses. Since surveys can be conducted on a smaller scale than censuses, nonsampling errors can presumably be controlled more tightly. Relatively more funds and effort can perhaps be expended toward eliciting responses, detecting and correcting response error, and reducing processing errors. As a result, survey results can sometimes be more accurate than census results.

To compensate for suspected nonrandom errors, adjustments of the sample estimates are often made. For example, adjustments are frequently made for nonresponse, both total and partial. Adjustments made for either type of nonresponse are often referred to as *imputations*. Imputation for total nonresponse is usually made by substituting for the questionnaire responses of the nonrespondents the "average" questionnaire responses of the respondents. These imputations usually are made separately within various groups of sample members, formed by attempting to place respondents and nonrespondents together that have "similar" design or ancillary characteristics. Imputation for item nonresponse is usually made by substituting for a missing item the response to that item of a respondent having characteristics that are "similar" to those of the nonrespondent.

For an estimate calculated from a sample survey, the *total error* in the estimate is composed of the sampling error, which can usually be estimated from the sample, and the nonsampling error, which usually cannot be estimated from the sample. The total error present in a population quantity obtained from a complete census is composed of only nonsampling errors. Ideally, estimates of the total error associated with data given in these tables should be given. However, due to the unavailability of estimates of nonsampling errors, only estimates of the levels of sampling errors, in terms of estimated standard errors or coefficients of variation, are available. To obtain estimates of the estimated standard errors from the sample of interest, obtain a copy of the referenced report, which appears at the end of each table.

Source of Additional Material: The Federal Committee on Statistical Methodology (FCSM) is an interagency committee dedicated to improving the quality of federal statistics <http://www.fcsm.gov/>.

Principal databases: Beginning below are brief descriptions of 18 of the sample surveys, censuses, and administrative collections that provide a substantial portion of the data contained in this publication.

U.S. DEPARTMENT OF AGRICULTURE

National Agriculture Statistics Service (NASS)

Census of Agriculture

Universe, Frequency, and Types of Data: Complete count of U.S. farms and ranches conducted once every 5 years with data at the national, state, and county level. Data published on farm numbers and related items/characteristics.

Type of Data Collection Operation: Complete census for number of farms; land in farms; farm income; agriculture products sold; farms by type of organization; total cropland; irrigated land; farm operator characteristics; livestock and poultry inventory and sales; and selected crops harvested. Market value of land, buildings, and products sold, total farm production expenses, machinery and equipment, and fertilizer and chemicals.

Data Collection and Imputation Procedures: Data collection is by mailing questionnaires to all farmers and ranchers. Producers can return their forms by mail or online. Nonrespondents are contacted by telephone and correspondence follow-ups. Imputations were made for all nonresponse item/characteristics and coverage adjustments were made to account for missed farms and ranches. The response rate for the 2007 census was 85.2 percent.

Estimates of Sampling Error: Weight adjustments were made to account for the undercoverage and whole-unit nonresponse of farms on the Census Mail List (CML). These were treated as sampling errors.

Other (Nonsampling) Errors: Nonsampling errors are due to incompleteness of the census mailing list, duplications on the list, respondent reporting errors, errors in editing reported data, and in imputation for missing data. Evaluation studies are conducted to measure certain nonsampling errors such as list coverage and classification error. It is a reasonable assumption that the net effect of nonmeasurable errors is zero (the positive errors cancel the negative errors).

Sources of Additional Material: U.S. Department of Agriculture, National Agricultural Statistics Service (NASS), 2007 Census of Agriculture, Appendix A-1 Census of Agriculture Methodology, Appendix B-1 General Explanation and Census of Agriculture Report Form.

Multiple Frame Surveys

Universe, Frequency, and Types of Data: Surveys of U.S. farm operators to obtain data on major livestock inventories, selected crop acreage and production, grain stocks, and farm labor characteristics, farm economic data, and chemical use data. Estimates are made quarterly, semiannually, or annually depending on the data series.

Type of Data Collection Operation: Primary frame is obtained from general or special purpose lists, supplemented by a probability sample of land areas used to estimate for list incompleteness.

Data Collection and Imputation Procedures: Mail, telephone, or personal interviews used for initial data collection. Mail nonrespondent follow-up by phone and personal interviews. Imputation based on average of respondents.

Estimates of Sampling Error: Estimated CVs range from 1 percent to 2 percent at the U.S. level for crop and livestock data series and 3 to 5 percent for economic data. Regional CVs range from 3 to 6 percent, while state estimate CVs run 5 to 10 percent.

Other (Nonsampling) Errors: In addition to above, replicated sampling procedures used to monitor effects of changes in survey procedures.

Sources of Additional Material: U.S. Department of Agriculture, National Agricultural Statistics Service (NASS), USDA's National Agricultural Statistics Service: The Fact Finders of Agriculture, March 2007.

U.S. BUREAU OF LABOR STATISTICS

Current Employment Statistics (CES) Program

Universe, Frequency, and Types of Data: Monthly survey drawn from a sampling frame of over 8 million unemployment insurance tax accounts in order to obtain data by industry on employment, hours, and earnings.

Type of Data Collection Operation: The CES sample included about 145,000 businesses and government agencies, which represent approximately 557,000 individual worksites.

Data Collection and Imputation Procedures: Each month, the state agencies cooperating with Bureau of Labor Statistics (BLS), as well as BLS Data Collection Centers, collect data through various automated collection modes and mail. BLS Washington staff prepares national estimates of employment, hours, and earnings while states use the data to develop state and area estimates.

Estimates of Sampling Errors: The relative standard error for total nonfarm employment is 0.1 percent. A birth/death model adjusts for the impact of business openings and closings. From April through December 2012, the cumulative birth/death model added 755,000 employees.

Other (nonsampling) Errors: Estimates of employment adjusted annually to reflect complete universe. Average adjustment is 0.2 percent over the last decade, with an absolute range from less than 0.1 percent to 0.6 percent.

Sources of Additional Material: U.S. Bureau of Labor Statistics, Employment & Earnings Online. See <www.bls.gov/opub/ee/home.htm>.

U.S. DEPARTMENT OF COMMERCE

U.S. BUREAU OF ECONOMIC ANALYSIS (BEA)

Regional Economic Accounts

Universe, Frequency, and Types of Data: The Regional Economic Accounts website contains estimates of personal income and its components and employment for local areas such as states, counties, metropolitan areas, and micropolitan areas.

Type of Data Collection Operation: The estimates of personal income are primarily based on administrative records data, census data, and survey data.

Data Collection and Imputation Procedures: The data are collected from administrative records, which may come from the recipients of the income or from the sources of the income. These data are a byproduct of the administration of various federal and state government programs. The most important sources of these data are—the state unemployment insurance programs of the Bureau of Labor Statistics (BLS), the social insurance programs of the Centers for Medicare and Medicaid Services, federal income tax program of the Internal

Revenue Service, veterans benefit programs of the U.S. Department of Veterans Affairs, and military payroll systems of the U.S. Department of Defense.

The data from censuses are mainly collected from the recipients of income. The most important sources for these data are the Census of Agriculture at the U.S. Department of Agriculture (USDA) and the Census of Population and Housing conducted by the U.S. Census Bureau. Other sources may include estimates of farm proprietors' income by the USDA, wages and salaries from County Business Patterns from the Census Bureau, and the Quarterly Census of Employment and Wages by the Department of Labor.

Estimates of Sampling Error: Not applicable, except component variables may be subject to error.

Other (Nonsampling) Errors: Nonsampling errors in the administrative data sets may affect personal income estimates.

Sources of Additional Material: Methodological information on other Bureau of Economic Analysis (BEA) datasets such as "State Personal Income" and "Gross State Product" may be found at <www.bea.gov/regional/methods.cfm>.

U.S. CENSUS BUREAU

American Community Survey (ACS)

Universe, Frequency, and Types of Data: Nationwide survey to obtain annual data about demographic, social, economic, and housing characteristics of housing units and the people residing in them. It covers the household population and, beginning in 2006, also includes the group quarters population living in prisons, nursing homes and college dormitories, and other group quarters.

Type of Data Collection Operation: Housing unit address sampling is performed twice a year in both August and January. First-phase of sampling defines the universe for the second stage of sampling through two steps. First, all addresses that were eligible for the second phase sampling within the past 4 years are excluded from eligibility. This ensures that no address is in sample more than once in any 5-year period. The second step is to select a 20 percent systematic sample of "new" units, i.e., those units that have never appeared on a previous Master Address File (MAF) extract. All new addresses are systematically assigned to either the current year or to one of four back-samples. This procedure maintains five equal partitions of the universe. The second-phase sampling is done on the current year's partition and results in approximately 3,000,000 housing unit addresses in the United States and

36,000 in Puerto Rico. Group quarter sampling is performed separately from the housing unit sampling. The sampling begins with separating the small (15 persons or fewer) and the large (more than 15 persons) group quarters. The target sampling rate for both groups is a 2.5 percent sample of the group quarters population. It results in approximately 200,000 group quarters residents being selected in the United States, and an additional 1,000 in Puerto Rico.

Data Collection and Imputation Procedures: The American Community Survey is conducted every month on independent samples. Each housing unit in the independent monthly samples is mailed a prenotice letter announcing the selection of the address to participate, a survey questionnaire package, and a reminder postcard. These sample units addresses receive a second (replacement) questionnaire package if the initial questionnaire has not been returned by mid-month. Sample addresses for which a questionnaire is not returned in the mail and a telephone number is not available are forwarded to telephone centers for follow-up. Interviewers attempt to contact and interview these mail nonresponse cases by telephone. Sample addresses that are still unresponsive after 2 months of attempts are forwarded for a possible personal visit. Unresponsive addresses are subsampled at rates between 1 in 3 and 2 in 3. Those addresses selected through this process are assigned to Field Representatives (FRs), who visit the addresses, verify their existence, determine their occupancy status, and conduct interviews. Collection of group quarters data is conducted by FRs only. Their methods include completing the questionnaire while speaking to the resident in person or over the telephone, or leaving paper questionnaires for residents to complete for themselves and then pick them up later. This last option is used for data collection in federal prisons. If needed, a personal interview can be conducted with a proxy, such as a relative or guardian. After data collection is completed, any remaining incomplete or inconsistent information on the questionnaire is imputed during the final automated edit of the collected data.

Estimates of Sampling Error: The data in the ACS products are estimates and can vary from the actual values that would have been obtained by conducting a census of the entire population. The estimates from the chosen sample addresses can also vary from those that would have been obtained from a different set of addresses. This variation causes uncertainty, which can be measured using statistics such as standard error, margin of error, and confidence interval. All ACS estimates are accompanied by margins of error to assist users.

Other (Nonsampling) Errors: Nonsampling Error—In addition to sampling error, data users should realize that other types of errors may be introduced during any of the various complex operations used to select, collect, and process survey data. An important goal of the ACS is to minimize the amount of nonsampling error introduced through coverage issues in the sample list, nonresponse from sample housing units, and transcribing or editing data. One way of accomplishing this is by finding additional sources of addresses, following up on nonrespondents, and maintaining quality control systems.

Sources of Additional Material: U.S. Census Bureau, American Community Survey Web site at www.census.gov/acs; U.S. Census Bureau, American Community Survey Accuracy of the Data documents at <http://www.census.gov/acs/www/UseData/Accuracy/Accuracy1.htm>.

Annual Survey of Manufactures (ASM)

Universe, Frequency, and Types of Data: The Annual Survey of Manufactures is conducted annually, except for years ending in "2" and "7", for all manufacturing establishments having one or more paid employees. The purpose of the ASM is to provide key intercensal measures of manufacturing activity, products, and location for the public and private sectors. The ASM provides statistics on employment, payroll, worker hours, payroll supplements, cost of materials, value added by manufacturing, capital expenditures, inventories, and energy consumption. It also provides estimates of value of shipments for 1,800 classes of manufactured products.

Type of Data Collection Operation: The ASM includes approximately 50,000 establishments selected from the census universe of 328,500 manufacturing establishments. Approximately 15,400 large establishments are selected with certainty, and the remaining establishments are selected with probability proportional to a composite measure of establishment size. The survey is updated from two sources: Internal Revenue Service (IRS) administrative records are used to include new single-unit manufacturers and the Company Organization Survey identifies new establishments of multiunit forms.

Data Collection and Imputation Procedures: Survey is conducted by mail with phone and mail follow-ups of nonrespondents. Imputation (for all nonresponse items) is based on previous year reports, or for new establishments in survey, on industry averages.

Estimates of Sampling Error: Estimated relative standard errors for number of employees, new expenditures, and for value added totals are given in annual publications. For U.S.-level industry statistics, most estimated relative standard errors are 2 percent or less, but vary considerably for detailed characteristics.

Other (Nonsampling) Errors: The unit response rate is about 85 percent. Nonsampling errors include those due to collection, reporting, and transcription errors, many of which are corrected through computer and clerical checks.

Sources of Additional Material: U.S. Census Bureau, *Annual Survey of Manufactures,* <www.census.gov/manufacturing/asm/index.html>.

State Government Tax Collections (STC)

Universe, Frequency, and Types of Data: The universe for the State Tax Collections Survey covers the 50 state governments only. No local governments are included in the universe for each state. The data have been collected annually since 1939. Statistics on the State Government Tax Collections Survey include measurement of tax by category: Property Tax, Sales and Gross Receipts Taxes, License Taxes, Income Taxes, and Other Taxes. Each tax category is broken down into subcategories (e.g., motor fuel sales, alcoholic beverage sales, motor vehicle licenses, alcoholic beverage licenses). There are currently 25 different tax codes that state tax revenue may fall into.

Type of Data Collection Operation: Most of the data in this report were gathered by a mail canvass of appropriate state government offices that are directly involved with state-administered taxes. There are approximately one hundred offices that are canvassed to collect data from all fifty states. Follow-up procedures include the use of mail, telephone, and email until data are received.

Data Editing and Imputation Procedures: Data are processed from several collection methods including direct response to survey forms from state government officials, as well as from the compilation of administrative records and supplemental sources. Regardless of the collection method, these data are edited using ratio edits of the current year's value to the prior year's value. The fifty state governments provide the Census Bureau with administrative records from their central accounting systems. These administrative records are unique to each state as each state is legally organized differently from every other state and, as such, each state has a unique organizational and accounting structure. It is the responsibility of the Census Bureau to classify the different accounting and organizational structures into uniform tax categories so that entities with different methods of government accounting can be presented on a comparable basis. The records represent the core, or central, state government and are limited to tax revenue. Data on state government tax revenues are compiled from state administrative records by Census Bureau employees, according to the Census Bureau's classification methodology. When state records do not include full tax revenue detail or reporting

units do not respond, supplemental data sources from external financial reports or the Census Bureau's *Annual Survey of State Government Finances and Quarterly Summary of State and Local Government Tax Revenue* are required to complete the datasets. This procedure is called imputation. Supplemental records are merged with data from the state governments. Although every effort is made to obtain financial information from all state government entities, financial statements may not be available at the time the Census Bureau closes the processing, or governmental entities may not respond to the Census Bureau's requests. Every year the data are subject to revisions as new data become available.

Estimates of Sampling Error: These data are not subject to sampling error because this is a complete enumeration of all 50 state governments.

Other (Nonsampling) Errors: Despite efforts made in all phases of collection, processing, and tabulation to minimize errors, the survey is subject to nonsampling errors such as the inability to obtain data for every variable for all units, inaccuracies in classification, mistakes in keying and coding, and coverage errors.

Sources of Additional Material: For further information, see the *Government Finance and Employment Classification Manual* <www.census.gov/govs/classification/> and the *2007 Census of Governments* <www.census.gov/govs/cog/>.

Annual Survey of Public Employment and Payroll (ASPEP)

Universe, Frequency, and Types of Data: The population of interest for this survey includes the civilian employees of all federal government agencies (except the Central Intelligence Agency, the National Security Agency, and the Defense Intelligence Agency), all agencies of the 50 state governments, and 89,476 local governments (i.e., counties, municipalities, townships, special districts, and school districts) including the District of Columbia. Data have been collected annually since 1957. A census is conducted every 5 years (years ending in "2" and "7"). A sample of state and local governments is used to collect data in the intervening years. A new sample is selected every 5 years (in years ending in "4" and "9"). The survey provides data on full-time and part-time employment, part-time hours worked, full-time equivalent employment, and payroll statistics by governmental function (i.e., elementary and secondary education, higher education).

Type of Data Collection Operation: Data collected for the Annual Survey of Government Employment are public record and are not confidential, as authorized by Title 13, U.S. Code, Section 9. Census Bureau staff compiled federal government data from records of the U.S. Office of Personnel Management (OPM). These data are based on the Monthly Report of Federal Civilian Employment. Census Bureau staff collected some state government data through special arrangements, referred to as central collection agreements, wherein data for multiple state agencies or school districts are reported by a central respondent generally in an electronic file. Forty-five of the state governments provided data from central payroll records for all or most of their agencies/institutions. Data for agencies and institutions for the remaining state governments were obtained by mail canvass questionnaires. Local governments were also canvassed using a mail questionnaire. All respondents receiving the mail questionnaire had the option of responding electronically using the Web site developed for reporting data.

Data Editing and Imputation Procedures: Editing is a process that ensures survey data are accurate, complete, and consistent. Efforts are made at all phases of collection, processing, and tabulation to minimize errors. Although some edits are built into the internet data collection instrument and the data entry programs, the majority of the edits are performed post collection. Edits consist primarily of two types: (1) *consistency edits* and (2) *historical ratio edits* of the current year's reported value to the prior year's value. The *consistency edits* check the logical relationships of data items reported on the form. For each function where employees are reported, the *historical ratio edits* compare data from two different time periods.

Not all respondents answer every item on the questionnaire. There are also questionnaires that are not returned despite efforts to gain a response. Imputation is the process of filling in missing or invalid data with reasonable values in order to have a complete data set for analytical purposes. For nonresponding governments, the imputations were based on recently reported historical data from either a prior year annual survey or the most recent Census of Governments. These data were adjusted by a growth rate that was determined by the growth of responding units that were similar (in size, geography, and type of government) to the nonrespondent. If there was no recent historical data available, the imputations were based on the data from a randomly selected responding donor that was similar to the nonrespondent. In cases where good secondary data sources exist, the data from those sources were used.

Estimates of Sampling Error: The intercensal data come from a sample rather than a census of all possible units. The particular sample that was selected is one of a larger number of possible samples of the same size and sample design that could have been selected. Each sample would have yielded different estimates. The estimated coefficients of variation, which are provided for each estimate on www.census.gov/govs , are an estimate of this sampling variability.

Other (Nonsampling) Errors: Although every effort is made in all phases of collection, processing, and tabulation to minimize errors, the data are subject to nonsampling errors such as inability to obtain data for every variable from all units in the population of interest, inaccuracies in classification, response errors, misinterpretation of questions, mistakes in keying and coding, and coverage errors. The data processing section describes our efforts to mitigate errors due to nonresponse, keying, reporting errors, etc.

Sources of Additional Material: For further information, see the *Government Finance and Employment Classification Manual* <www.census.gov/govs/classification/> and the *2007 Census of Governments* <www.census.gov/govs/cog/>.

Annual Finance Survey (AFS)

Universe, Frequency, and Types of Data: The population of interest for this survey contains the 50 state governments and 89,476 local governments (counties, municipalities, townships, special districts, and school districts) including the District of Columbia. In years ending in "2" and "7" the entire universe is canvassed. In intervening years, a sample of the population of interest is surveyed. The survey coverage includes all state and local governments in the United States.

The survey collects financial data. Revenue data include taxes (i.e., property, sales, tobacco, motor vehicle, licensing and permit), charges, interest, and other earnings. Expenditure data include total by function (i.e., education, highways, airports, water and sewerage, health, hospitals, corrections, fire and police protection), and by accounting category (i.e., current operations and capital outlays). Debt data include issuance, retirement, and amounts outstanding. Financial assets data include securities and other holdings, by type.

Type of Data Collection Operation: The data collection for the state and local finance survey (both census and sample survey) is made up of three modes to obtain data: mail canvass, internet collection, and central collection from state sources. Collection methods vary by state and type of government. Administrative data are compiled for most state government agencies and the 48 largest and most complex county and municipal governments. The survey melds several government finance surveys, including the Survey of Local Government Finances, Survey of Public-Employee Retirement Systems, Integrated Post-secondary Educational Data System (IPEDS) from the National Center for Education Statistics (NCES), State Government Finances Survey, and the Survey of Public Elementary-Secondary Education Finances.

Data Editing and Imputation Procedures: Not all respondents answer every item on the questionnaire. There are also questionnaires that are not returned despite efforts to gain a response. Imputation is the process of filling in missing or invalid data with reasonable values in order to have a complete data set for analytical purposes. For nonresponding governments, imputations for missing units are based on recently reported historical data from either a prior year annual survey or the most recent census, adjusted by a growth rate. If no historical data are available, data from a randomly selected similar unit are used for the imputation.

Editing is a process that ensures data are accurate, complete, and consistent. Efforts are made at all phases of collection, processing, and tabulation to minimize errors. Although some edits are built into the internet data collection instrument and the data entry programs, the majority of the edits are performed post collection. Data are checked for internal consistency within the questionnaire and for historical accuracy.

Estimates of Sampling Error: In census years, all of the units in the population are surveyed, and there is no sampling error. In the intercensal years, the population is sampled, and the estimates are subject to sampling error. The coefficient of variation is a measure of sampling variability expressed as a percentage of the estimated total. Generally, the estimated coefficients of variation for state and local government revenues, expenditures, debt, or assets are under 3 percent in each state. Coefficients of variation for the estimates are given in the tables on the website www.census.gov/govs/estimate/index.html.

Other (Nonsampling) Errors: Although every effort is made in all phases of collection, processing, and tabulation to minimize errors, the data are subject to nonsampling errors such as inability to obtain data for every variable from all units in the population of interest, inaccuracies in classification, response errors, misinterpretation of questions, mistakes in keying and coding, and coverage errors.

Sources of Additional Material: For more information on the survey, see www.census.gov/govs/estimate/index.html. On that site, see the *Survey Methodology* and *Government Finance and Employment Classification Manual*.

Economic Census

(Industry Series, Geographic Area Series, and Subject Series Reports) (for NAICS sectors 21 to 81).

Universe, Frequency, and Types of Data.

Conducted every 5 years to obtain data on number of establishments, number of employees, payroll, total sales/receipts/revenue, and other industry- specific statistics.

The universe is all establishments with paid employees excluding agriculture, forestry, fishing and hunting, and government. (Nonemployer Statistics, discussed separately, covers those establishments without paid employees.)

Type of Data Collection Operation: All large employer firms were surveyed (i.e., all employer firms above payroll-size cutoff s established to separate large from small employers) plus, in most sectors, a sample of the small employer firms.

Data Collection and Imputation Procedures: Mail questionnaires were used with both mail and telephone follow-ups for nonrespondents. Businesses also had the option to respond electronically. Data for nonrespondents and for small employer firms not mailed a questionnaire were obtained from administrative records of other federal agencies or imputed.

Estimates of Sampling Error: Not applicable for basic data such as sales, revenue, receipts, payroll, etc., for sectors other than Construction (NAICS 23). Estimates of sampling error for construction industries are included with the data as published on the Census Bureau Web site.

Other (Nonsampling) Errors: Establishment response rates by NAICS sector in 2002 ranged from 80 percent to 89 percent. Nonsampling errors may occur during the collection, reporting, keying, and classification of the data.

Sources of Additional Material U.S. Census Bureau, see www.census.gov/econ/census07/www/methodology/.

Census of Population

Universe, Frequency, and Types of Data: Complete count of U.S. population conducted every 10 years since 1790. Data obtained on number and characteristics of people in the United States.

Type of Data Collection Operation: The 2010 census consisted of one form for 100 percent of the population. On this 2010 questionnaire and on the 100 percent questionnaire of the 1990 and 2000 censuses, the 100 percent items included: age, date of birth, sex, race, Hispanic origin, relationship to householder, homeownership and mortgage status. In 1980, approximately 19 percent of the housing units were included in the sample that received a longer questionnaire; in 1990 and 2000, approximately 17 percent were included in the sample. By 2010, the sample had been eliminated and replaced the ongoing American Community Survey.

Data Collection and Imputation Procedures: In 1980, 1990, 2000, and 2010 mail questionnaires were used extensively with personal interviews in the remainder. Extensive telephone and personal follow-up for nonrespondents was done in the censuses. Imputations were made for missing characteristics.

Estimates of Sampling Error: The 2010 census included no sampling. In prior censuses, sampling errors for data were estimated for all items collected by sample and varied by characteristic and geographic area. The coefficients of variation (CVs) for national and state estimates were generally very small.

Other (Nonsampling) Errors: Since 1950, evaluation programs have been conducted to provide information on the magnitude of some sources of nonsampling errors such as response bias and undercoverage in each census. Results from the evaluation program for the 1990 census indicated that the estimated net undercoverage amounted to about 1.5 percent of the total resident population. For the 2000 census, the evaluation program indicated a net overcount of 0.5 percent of the resident population.

Sources of Additional Material: U.S. Census Bureau, The Coverage of Population in the 1980 Census, PHC80-E4; *Content Reinterview Study: Accuracy of Data for Selected Population and Housing Characteristics as Measured by Reinterview*, PHC80-E2; *1980 Census of Population*, Vol. 1, (PC80-1), Appendixes B, C, and D. *Content Reinterview Survey: Accuracy of Data for Selected Population and Housing Characteristics as Measured by Reinterview*, 1990, CPH-E-1; Effectiveness of Quality Assurance, CPH-E-2; Programs to Improve Coverage in the 1990 Census, 1990, CPH-E-3. For 2000 census evaluations, see www.census.gov/pred/www . For 2010 census evaluations, see www.census.gov/2010census/about/cpex.php.

County Business Patterns

Universe, Frequency, and Types of Data: County Business Patterns is an annual tabulation of basic data items extracted from the Business Register, a file of all known single- and multi-location employer companies maintained and updated by the U.S. Census Bureau. Data include number of establishments, number of employees, first quarter and annual payrolls, and number of establishments by employment size class. Data are excluded for self-employed individuals, private households, railroad employees, agricultural production workers, and most government employees.

Type of Data Collection Operation: The annual Company Organization Survey provides individual establishment data for multi-location companies. Data for single establishment companies are obtained from various Census Bureau programs, such as the Annual Survey of Manufactures and Current Business Surveys, as well as from administrative records of the Internal Revenue Service, the Social Security Administration, and the Bureau of Labor Statistics.

Estimates of Sampling Error: Not applicable.

Other (Nonsampling) Error: The data are subject to nonsampling errors, such as inability to identify all cases in the universe; definition and classification difficulties; differences in interpretation of questions; errors in recording or coding the data obtained; and estimation of employers who reported too late to be included in the tabulations and for records with missing or misreported data.

Sources of Additional Materials: U.S. Census Bureau, County Business Patterns, <www.census.gov/econ/cbp/index.html>.

Current Population Survey (CPS)

Universe, Frequency, and Types of Data: Nationwide monthly sample designed primarily to produce national and state estimates of labor force characteristics of the civilian noninstitutionalized population 16 years of age and older.

Type of Data Collection Operation: Multistage probability sample that currently includes 72,000 households from 824 sample areas. Sample size increased in some states to improve data reliability for those areas on an annual average basis. A continual sample rotation system is used. Households are in sample 4 months, out for 8 months, and in for 4 more. Month-to-month overlap is 75 percent; year-to-year overlap is 50 percent.

Data Collection and Imputation Procedures: For first and fifth months that a household is in sample, personal interviews; other months, approximately 85 percent of the data collected by phone. Imputation is done for item nonresponse. Adjustment for total nonresponse is done by a predefined cluster of units, by state, metropolitan status and CBSA size; for item nonresponse imputation varies by subject matter.

Estimates of Sampling Error: The national total estimates of the civilian labor force and of employment have monthly CVs of about .2 percent and annual average CVs of about .1 percent. Unemployment is a much smaller characteristic and consequently has substantially larger CVs than the civilian labor force or employment. The national unemployment rate, the most important

CPS statistic, has a monthly CV of about 2 percent and an annual average CV of about 1 percent. Assuming a 6 percent unemployment rate, states have annual average CVs of about 8 percent. The estimated CVs for family income and poverty rate for all persons in 2005 are .4 percent and 1.2 percent, respectively. CVs for subnational areas, such as states, tend to be larger and vary by area.

Other (Nonsampling) Errors: Estimates of response bias on unemployment are available. Estimates of the unemployment rate from reinterviews range from –2.4 percent to 1.0 percent of the basic CPS unemployment rate (over a 30-month span from January 2004 through June 2006). Eligible CPS households are approximately 82 percent of the assigned households, with a corresponding response rate of 92 percent.

Sources of Additional Material: U.S. Census Bureau and Bureau of Labor Statistics, Current Population Survey: Design and Methodology, (Technical Paper 66), available on the internet www.census.gov/prod/2006pubs/tp-66.pdf and the Bureau of Labor Statistics, <www.bls.gov/cps/> and the *BLS Handbook of Methods*, Chapter 1, available at <www.bls.gov/opub/hom/homch1_a.htm> .

Monthly Survey of Construction

Universe, Frequency, and Types of Data: Survey conducted monthly of newly constructed housing units (excluding mobile homes). Data are collected on the start, completion, and sale of housing. (Annual figures are aggregates of monthly estimates.)

Type of Data Collection Operation: A multistage probability sample of approximately 900 of the 20,000 permit-issuing jurisdictions in the United States was selected. Each month in each of these permit offices, field representatives list and select a sample of permits for which to collect data. to obtain data in areas where building permits are not required, a multistage probability sample of 80 land areas (census tracts or subsections of census tracts) was selected. All roads in these areas are canvassed and data are collected on all new residential construction found. Sampled buildings are followed up until they are completed (and sold, if for sale).

Data Collection and Imputation Procedures: Data are obtained by telephone inquiry and/or field visit. Nonresponse/ undercoverage adjustment factors are used to account for late reported data.

Estimates of Sampling Error: Estimated CV of 5 percent to 6 percent for estimates of national totals of units started, but may be higher than 20 percent for estimated

totals of more detailed characteristics, such as housing units in multiunit structures.

Other (Nonsampling) Errors: Response rate is over 90 percent for most items. Nonsampling errors are attributed to definitional problems, differences in interpretation of questions, incorrect reporting, inability to obtain information about all cases in the sample, and processing errors.

Sources of Additional Material All data are available at www.census.gov/const/www/newresconstindex.html. Further documentation of the survey is also available at that site.

Nonemployer Statistics

Universe, Frequency, and Types of Data: Nonemployer statistics are an annual tabulation of economic data by industry for active businesses without paid employees that are subject to federal income tax. Data showing the number of firms and receipts by industry are available for the United States, states, counties, and metropolitan areas. Most types of businesses covered by the Census Bureau's economic statistics programs are included in the nonemployer statistics. Tax-exempt and agricultural-production businesses are excluded from nonemployer statistics.

Type of Data Collection Operation: The universe of nonemployer firms is created annually as a byproduct of the Census Bureau's Business Register processing for employer establishments. If a business is active but without paid employees, then it becomes part of the potential nonemployer universe. Industry classification and receipts are available for each potential nonemployer business. These data are obtained primarily from the annual business income tax returns of the Internal Revenue Service (IRS). The potential nonemployer universe undergoes a series of complex processing, editing, and analytical review procedures at the Census Bureau to distinguish nonemployers from employers and to correct and complete data items used in creating the data tables.

Estimates of Sampling Error: Not applicable.

Other (Nonsampling) Errors: The data are subject to nonsampling errors, such as industry misclassification as well as errors of response, keying, nonreporting, and coverage.

Sources of Additional Material: U.S. Census Bureau, Nonemployer Statistics <www.census.gov/econ/nonemployer/index.html> .

Population Estimates

Universe, Frequency, and Types of Data: The U.S. Census Bureau annually produces estimates of total resident population for each state and county. County population estimates are produced with a component of population change method, while the state population estimates are solely the sum of the county populations.

Type of Data Collection Operation: The Census Bureau develops county population estimates with a demographic procedure called an "administrative records component of population change" method. A major assumption underlying this approach is that the components of population change are closely approximated by administrative data in a demographic change model. In order to apply the model, Census Bureau demographers estimate each component of population change separately. For the population residing in households the components of population change are births, deaths, and net migration, including net international migration. For the nonhousehold population, change is represented by the net change in the population living in group quarters facilities.

Estimates of Sampling Error: Not applicable.

Other (Nonsampling) Errors: Not available.

Sources of Additional Material: U.S. Census Bureau, "Methodology for the United States Resident Population Estimates by Age, Sex, Race, and Hispanic Origin and the State and County Total Resident Population Estimates" at <www.census.gov/popest/methodology/index.html >.

U.S. DEPARTMENT OF EDUCATION

National Center for Education Statistics Integrated Postsecondary Education Data Survey (IPEDS), Completions

Universe, Frequency, and Types of Data: Annual survey of all Title IV (federal financial aid) eligible postsecondary institutions to obtain data on earned degrees and other formal awards, conferred by field of study, level of degree, sex, and by racial/ethnic characteristics (every other year prior to 1989, then annually).

Type of Data Collection Operation: Complete census.

Data Collection and Imputation Procedures: Data are collected through a web-based survey in the fall of every year. Missing data are imputed by using data of similar institutions.

Estimates of Sampling Error: Not applicable.

Other (Nonsampling) Errors: For 2010-2011, the response rate for degree-granting institutions was 100.0 percent.

Sources of Additional Material: U.S. Department of Education, National Center for Education Statistics (NCES), *Postsecondary Institutions and Price of Attendance in 2011-12; Degrees and Other Awards Conferred: 2010-11; and 12-Month Enrollment: 2010-11: First Look (Provisional Data)*. See <www.nces.ed.gov/ipeds/> .

U.S. FEDERAL BUREAU OF INVESTIGATION

Uniform Crime Reporting (UCR) Program

Universe, Frequency, and Types of Data: Monthly reports on the number of criminal offenses that become known to law enforcement agencies. Data are also collected on crimes cleared by arrest or exceptional means; age, sex, and race of arrestees and for victims and offenders for homicides, number of law enforcement employees, on fatal and nonfatal assaults against law enforcement officers, and on hate crimes reported.

Type of Data Collection Operation: Crime statistics are based on reports of crime data submitted either directly to the FBI by contributing law enforcement agencies or through cooperating state UCR Programs.

Data Collection and Imputation Procedures: States with UCR programs collect data directly from individual law enforcement agencies and forward reports, prepared in accordance with UCR standards, to the FBI. Accuracy and consistency edits are performed by the FBI.

Estimates of Sampling Error: Not applicable.

Other (Nonsampling) Errors: During 2011, law enforcement agencies active in the UCR Program represented 97.8 percent of the total population. The coverage amounted to 98.8 percent of the U.S. population in metropolitan statistical areas, 92.3 percent of the population in cities outside metropolitan areas, and 93.1 percent in nonmetropolitan counties.

Sources of Additional Material: U.S. Department of Justice, Federal Bureau of Investigation, *Crime in the United States*, annual, *Hate Crime Statistics*, annual, *Law Enforcement Officers Killed and Assaulted*, annual, <www.fbi.gov/about-us/cjis/ucr >.

U.S. INTERNAL REVENUE SERVICE

Individual Income Tax Returns

Universe, Frequency, and Types of Data: Annual study of unaudited individual income tax returns, Forms 1040, 1040A, and 1040EZ, filed by U.S. citizens and residents. Data provided on various financial characteristics by size of adjusted gross income, marital status, and by taxable and nontaxable returns. Data by state, based on the population of returns filed, also include returns from 1040NR, filed by nonresident aliens plus certain self-employment tax returns.

Type of Data Collection Operation: Stratified probability sample of 308,946 returns for tax year 2010. The sample is classified into sample strata based on the larger of total income or total loss amounts, the size of business plus farm receipts, and other criteria such as the potential usefulness of the return for tax policy modeling. Sampling rates for sample strata varied from 0.01 percent to 100 percent.

Data Collection and Imputation Procedures: Computer selection of sample of tax return records. Data adjusted during editing for incorrect, missing, or inconsistent entries to ensure consistency with other entries on return.

Estimates of Sampling Error: Estimated CVs for tax year 2010: adjusted gross income less deficit 0.09 percent; salaries and wages 0.17 percent; and tax-exempt interest received 1.25 percent. (State data not subject to sampling error.)

Other (Nonsampling) Errors: Processing errors and errors arising from the use of tolerance checks for the data.

Sources of Additional Material: U.S. Internal Revenue Service, *Statistics of Income, Individual Income Tax Returns,* annual, (Publication 1304). www.irs.gov/uac/ SOI-Tax-Stats-Individual-Income-Tax-Returns-Publication-1304-%28Complete-Report%29

NATIONAL CENTER FOR HEALTH STATISTICS (NCHS)

National Vital Statistics System

Universe, Frequency, and Types of Data: Annual data on births and deaths in the United States.

Type of Data Collection Operation: Mortality data based on complete file of death records, except 1972, based on 50 percent sample. Natality statistics 1951–1971, based on 50 percent sample of birth certificates, except a 20 percent to 50 percent sample in 1967, received by NCHS.

Data Collection and Imputation Procedures: Reports based on records from registration offices of all states, District of Columbia, New York City, Puerto Rico, Virgin Islands, Guam, American Samoa, and Northern Marianas.

Estimates of Sampling Error: For recent years, there is no sampling for these files; the files are based on 100 percent of events registered.

Other (Nonsampling) Errors: It is believed that more than 99 percent of the births and deaths occurring in this country are registered.

Sources of Additional Material U.S. National Center for Health Statistics, *Vital Statistics of the United States,* Vol. I and Vol. II annual, and the *National Vital Statistics Reports.* See the NCHS Web site at < www.cdc.gov/nchs/ nvss.htm> .

NATIONAL HIGHWAY TRAFFIC SAFETY ADMINISTRATION (NHTSA)

Fatality Analysis Reporting System (FARS)

Universe, Frequency, and Types of Data: FARS is a census of all fatal motor vehicle traffic crashes that occur throughout the United States including the District of Columbia and Puerto Rico on roadways customarily open to the public. The crash must be reported to the state/jurisdiction and at least one directly related fatality must occur within 30 days of the crash.

Type of Data Collection Operation: One or more analysts, in each state, extract data from the official documents and enter the data into a standardized electronic database.

Data Collection and Imputation Procedures: Detailed data describing the characteristics of the fatal crash, the vehicles and persons involved are obtained from police crash reports, driver and vehicle registration records, autopsy reports, highway department, etc. Computerized edit checks monitor the accuracy and completeness of the data. The FARS incorporates a sophisticated mathematical multiple imputation procedure to develop a probability distribution of missing blood alcohol concentration (BAC) levels in the database for drivers, pedestrians, and cyclists.

Estimates of Sampling Error: Since this is census data, there are no sampling errors.

Other (Nonsampling) Errors: FARS represents a census of all police-reported crashes and captures all data reported at the state level. FARS data undergo a rigorous quality control process to prevent inaccurate reporting. However, these data are highly dependent on the accuracy of the police accident reports. Errors or omissions within police accident reports may not be detected.

Sources of Additional Material: The FARS Coding and Validation Manual, ANSI D16.1 Manual on Classification of Motor Vehicle Traffic Accidents (Sixth Edition). <www.nhtsa.gov/FARS>

APPENDIX C.
GEOGRAPHIC CONCEPTS

Geographic Concepts

STATES

States are the major political units of the United States. The District of Columbia is treated as a state equivalent in this publication. Tables A-1 through A-81 present data for the United States, the 50 states, and the District of Columbia. For census purposes, states are often grouped into geographic regions and divisions. However, Table A only uses an alphabetical state presentation.

METROPOLITAN AND MICROPOLITAN STATISTICAL AREAS

The U.S. Office of Management and Budget (OMB) defines metropolitan and micropolitan statistical areas according to published standards that are applied to U.S. Census Bureau data. The general concept of a metropolitan or micropolitan statistical area is that of a core area containing a substantial population nucleus, together with adjacent communities having a high degree of economic and social integration with that core. The term "core based statistical area" (CBSA) refers collectively to metropolitan and micropolitan statistical areas.

The major purpose of CBSAs is to enable all federal agencies to use the same geographic definitions in tabulating and publishing data for metropolitan and micropolitan areas. The definitions are designed to serve a wide variety of statistical and analytical purposes; adoption of the area for any specific purpose should be judged in terms of appropriateness for that purpose. While the definitions have been developed for statistical use by federal agencies, state and local governments as well as private business firms have often found the definitions helpful in presenting data for metropolitan and micropolitan areas.

The official 2010 Standards for Defining Metropolitan and Micropolitan Statistical Areas may be found on the OMB website at https://www.govinfo.gov/content/pkg/FR-2010-06-28/pdf/2010-15605.pdf. OMB Bulletin 18-04, which was issued on September 14, 2018, provides the listing of metropolitan and micropolitan statistical areas found in this publication; this document and related documents may be found at https://www.census.gov/programs-surveys/metro-micro/about/omb-bulletins.html. Metropolitan areas presented in tables B-1 through B-14 and C-1 through C-4 and micropolitan areas presented in table D-1 of this publication are those county-based areas defined in that bulletin.

Historical development. In 1910, the Census Bureau introduced "metropolitan districts" as an area classification. This marked the first use by the Census Bureau of a unit for reporting population data for large cities, together with their suburbs. Originally, only cities of at least 200,000 population were designated as the core of a metropolitan district. By 1940, the concept had been expanded to apply to a city of 50,000 or more inhabitants. The metropolitan district was generally defined to include contiguous minor civil divisions (MCDs) and incorporated places having a population density of at least 150 persons per square mile; therefore, the boundaries did not necessarily follow county lines.

A major limitation of the metropolitan district concept, from the standpoint of statistical presentation, was that not many data items beyond those available from the census of population and housing were available for MCDs and smaller places. The applicability of the metropolitan district concept also was limited because other generally similar area classifications were in use (e.g., the industrial areas of the census of manufactures and the labor market areas of the Labor Department's Employment and Training Administration), which were defined in different ways.

The standard metropolitan area (SMA) concept was developed in 1949 by the Bureau of the Budget (now OMB), with the advice of the newly established Federal Committee on Standard Metropolitan Areas, to overcome the above difficulties. It was designed so that a wide variety of statistical data on metropolitan areas might be presented for a uniform set of geographic areas. The SMAs consisted of one or more contiguous counties containing at least one city of 50,000 or more inhabitants. Additional counties had to meet certain criteria of metropolitan character and of social and economic integration with the central county in order to be included in an SMA.

Changes in the official criteria have been made at the time of each census since 1950. None of these changes have involved significant deviations from the basic metropolitan concept. Several modifications have been made in the rules for determining how large a city must be to have a metropolitan division defined. Criteria changes also have been made to reflect changing national conditions. For example, the 1949 rule specified that a county must have less than 25 percent of its workers engaged in agriculture. However, with a rapidly decreasing proportion of the population engaged in farming, this requirement has been eliminated because practically no counties are still affected by it. In 1959, the designation "standard metropolitan area" was changed to "standard metropolitan statistical area" (SMSA) to emphasize the nature and purpose of the areas. The SMSA designation was changed to the MSA/CMSA/PMSA designations in June 1983. The term "core based statistical area" (CBSA) was adopted in 2000 and refers collectively to metropolitan and micropolitan statistical areas.

The metropolitan and micropolitan statistical areas used in this book are based on application of 2010 standards that appeared in the Federal Register on June 28, 2010, to 2010 decennial census data and subsequent population estimates. Metropolitan and micropolitan statistical area definitions were announced by OMB effective June 6, 2003, and subsequently updated. The lists of metropolitan and micropolitan statistical areas definitions may be found at https://www.census.gov/programs-surveys/metro-micro.html.

Defining metropolitan and micropolitan statistical areas. The 2000 standards provide that each CBSA must contain at least one urban area of 10,000 or more population. Each metropolitan statistical area must have at least one urbanized area of 50,000 or more inhabitants. Each micropolitan statistical area must have at least one urban cluster of at least 10,000 but less than 50,000 population.

Under the standards, the county (or counties) in which at least 50 percent of the population resides within urban areas of 10,000 or more population, or that contain at least 5,000 people residing within a single urban area of 10,000 or more population, is identified as a "central county" (counties). Additional outlying counties" are included in the CBSA if they meet specified requirements of commuting to or from the central counties. Counties or equivalent entities form the geographic "building blocks" for metropolitan and micropolitan statistical areas throughout the United States and Puerto Rico.

If specified criteria are met, a metropolitan statistical area containing a single core with a population of 2.5 million or more may be subdivided to form smaller groupings of counties referred to as "metropolitan divisions."

Principal cities and metropolitan and micropolitan statistical area titles. The largest city in each metropolitan or micropolitan statistical area is designated a "principal city." Additional cities qualify if specified requirements are met concerning population size and employment. The title of each metropolitan or micropolitan statistical area consists of the names of up to three of its principal cities and the name of each state into which the metropolitan or micropolitan statistical area extends. Titles of metropolitan divisions also typically are based on principal city names but in certain cases consist of county names.

Defining New England city and town areas. In view of the importance of cities and towns in New England, the 2010 standards also provide for a set of geographic areas that are defined using cities and towns in the six New England states. The New England city and town areas (NECTAs) are defined using the same criteria as metropolitan and micropolitan statistical areas and are identified as either metropolitan or micropolitan, based, respectively, on the presence of either an urbanized area of 50,000 or more population or an urban cluster of at least 10,000 but less than 50,000 population. If the specified criteria are met, a NECTA containing a single core with a population of at least 2.5 million may be subdivided to form smaller groupings of cities and towns referred to as New England city and town area divisions. NECTAs are not included in this book.

Changes in definitions over time. Changes in the definitions of these statistical areas since the 1950 census have consisted chiefly of:

- The recognition of new areas as they reached the minimum required city or urbanized area population

- The addition of counties (or cities and towns in New England) to existing areas as new decennial census data showed them to qualify.

- In some instances, formerly separate areas have been merged, components of an area have been transferred from one area to another, or components have been dropped from an area. The large majority of changes have taken place on the basis of decennial census data. However, Census Bureau data serve as the basis for intercensal updates in specified circumstances.

Because of these historical changes in geographic definitions, users must be cautious in comparing data for these statistical areas from different dates. For some purposes, comparisons of data for areas as defined at given dates may be appropriate; for other purposes, it may be preferable to maintain consistent area definitions. OMB bulletins since 2003 can be found at https://www.census.gov/programs-surveys/metro-micro/about/omb-bulletins.

html. Historical metropolitan area definitions are available for 1999, 1993, 1990, 1983, 1981, 1973, 1970, 1963, 1960, and 1950.

A map of metropolitan and micropolitan areas can be found at https://www.census.gov/geographies/reference-maps/2018/geo/cbsa.html.

COUNTIES

The primary political divisions of most states are termed "counties," which are the basic building blocks for metropolitan areas. In Louisiana, these divisions are known as "parishes." In Alaska, which has no counties, the county equivalents are the organized "boroughs" and the "census areas" that are delineated for statistical purposes by the State of Alaska and the Census Bureau. In four states (Maryland, Missouri, Nevada, and Virginia), there are one or more cities that are independent of any county organization and thus constitute primary divisions of their states. These cities are known as "independent cities" and are treated as equivalent to counties for statistical purposes. The District of Columbia has no primary divisions, and the entire area is considered equivalent to a county for statistical purposes.

Tables C-1 through C-4 present data for the 384 metropolitan statistical areas, 31 metropolitan divisions, and their 1,180 component counties defined as of September 2018. Table D-1 presents data for the 926 Core Based Statistical Areas—384 metropolitan statistical areas and 542 micropolitan statistical areas--and the 1,840 counties within those areas.

APPENDIX D.
GUIDE TO STATE STATISTICAL ABSTRACTS AND STATE INFORMATION

The bibliography below includes the most recent statistical abstracts for states. For some states, a near equivalent has been listed in substitution for, or in addition to, a statistical abstract. All sources contain statistical tables on a variety of subjects for the state as a whole, its component parts, or both. Internet sites also contain statistical data.

Alabama
University of Alabama, Center for Business and
    Economic Research
P.O. Box 870221
Tuscaloosa, AL 35487-0221
Phone: 205-348-6191. Fax: 205-348-2951
Internet site https://cber.culverhouse.ua.edu/

Alabama Economic Outlook, 2020. Revised annually

Alaska
State of Alaska, Department of Commerce,
    Community and Economic Development
550 West 7th Avenue, Suite 1535
Anchorage, AK 99501-3587
Phone: 907-269-8100. Fax 907-269-8125
Internet site http://commerce.alaska.gov/

The Alaska Economic Performance Report, 2013. Online.
https://www.commerce.alaska.gov/web/Portals/6/
    pub/2013_Alaska_Economic_Performance

Arizona
Arizona Commerce Authority
100 North 7th Avenue
Suite 400
Phoenix, AZ 85007
Phone: 602-845-1200
Internet site: www.azcommerce.com/data/
    az-at-a-glance/

University of Arizona, Economic and Business Research
    Center
1130 East Helen Street, McClelland Hall, Room 103
P.O. Box 210108
Tucson, AZ 85721-0108
Phone: 520-621-2155. Fax: 520-621-2150
Internet site http://ebr.eller.arizona.edu/

Arizona— *Continued*
Arizona's Economy. Quarterly Online
https://www.azeconomy.org/archive/

Arizona Economic Outlook; Online
https://www.azeconomy.org/data/forecast-data/

Arkansas
University of Arkansas at Little Rock, Arkansas
    Economic Development Institute
College of Business
2801 South University Avenue
Little Rock, AR 72204-1099
Phone: 501-569-8519. Fax: 501-569-8538.
Internet site https://ualr.edu/aedi/

Arkansas State and County Economic Data, 2017.
    Annual
https://youraedi.com/pubs/2017/17_04_StateNCounty.
    pdf

Arkansas Personal Income Handbook, 2017
ps://youraedi.com/pubs/2017/17_03_PIH.pdf

California
California Department of Finance
915 L Street
Sacramento, CA 95814
Phone: 916-445-3878
Internet site http://www.dof.ca.gov/Reports/

Colorado
University of Colorado at Boulder, University
    Libraries
184 UCB
1720 Pleasant Street
Boulder, CO 80309-0184
Phone: 303-492-8705
Internet site https://www.colorado.edu/libraries/
https://libguides.colorado.edu/strategies/government

Colorado Office of Economic Development and
    International Trade
1600 Broadway, Suite 2500
Denver, CO 80202

Colorado—*Continued*
Phone: 303-892-3840. Fax: 303-892-3848
Internet site https://choosecolorado.com/

Connecticut
Connecticut Department of Economic and Community
    Development
450 Columbus Boulevard
Hartford, CT 06103
Phone: 860-500-2300
Internet site www.ct.gov/ecd/site/default.asp

The Connecticut Economic Digest
www.ct.gov/ecd/cwp/view.
    asp?a=1106&q=303286&ecdNav=|

Connecticut Town Profiles, 2019
www.cerc.com/TownProfiles/default.asp

Delaware
Delaware Division of Small Business
99 Kings Highway, Dover, DE 19901
Phone: 302-739-4271. Fax: 302-739-5749
Internet site http://dedo.delaware.gov

2017 Delaware Data Book. Online
https://business.delaware.gov/wp-content/uploads/
    sites/118/2017/09/DE_DataBook.pdf

District of Columbia
Small Business Resource Center
64 New York Avenue NW, Suite 3149
Washington, DC 20002
Phone: 202-671-1552
Internet site https://business.dc.gov/sbrc.

Florida
University of Florida, Bureau of Economic and
    Business Research,
Ayers Technology Plaza
720 SW 2nd Ave Ste 150
    PO Box 117148
Gainesville, FL 32611
Phone: 352-392-0171 Fax: 888-534-2404
Internet site www.bebr.ufl.edu/

Print versions of the *Florida Statistical Abstract*, the *Florida County Perspective*, and *the Florida County Rankings* were discontinued in 2011. However, most data from these publications are available online at: http://www.bebr.ufl.edu/data

Georgia
University of Georgia, Terry College of Business
Selig Center for Economic Growth

Georgia—*Continued*
Athens, GA 30602-6269
Phone: 706-542-8100. Fax: 706-542-3835
Internet site http://terry.uga.edu/selig/

Georgia Statistical Abstract, ceased after 2015
Georgia Economic Outlook, 2020
The Multicultural Economy 2019
www.terry.uga.edu/about/centers-institutes/selig/
    publications

Hawaii
State of Hawaii, Department of Business, Economic
    Development and Tourism
P.O. Box 2359, Honolulu, HI 96804
Phone: 808-586-2355
Internet site www.hawaii.gov/dbedt/

The State of Hawaii Data Book 2018. Annual.
http://dbedt.hawaii.gov/economic/

Idaho
Idaho Department of Commerce
P.O. Box 83720
Boise, ID 83720-0093
Phone: 208-287-0772
Internet site http://commerce.idaho.gov/

Illinois
Illinois Department of Commerce and Economic
    Opportunity
100 W. Randolph
Chicago, IL 60601
Phone: 312-814-7179
http://www.ildceo.net/dceo/

2019 Illnois Economic Report
https://www2.illinois.gov/ides/lmi/Annual%20Report/
    EconomicReport_2019.pdf

Indiana
Indiana University, Kelley School of Business
Indiana Business Research Center
100 South College Avenue, Suite 240
Bloomington, IN 47404
Phone: 812-855-5507
Internet site www.stats.indiana.edu/

STATS Indiana. Online only

Iowa
Iowa State University, University Extension
Iowa Community Indicators Program
2159 Beardshear Hall
Ames, IA 50011-2046

Iowa—*Continued*
Phone: 800-262-3804
https://www.icip.iastate.edu

State Library of Iowa, State Data Center of Iowa
Capital Building, Second Floor
1007 E. Grand Ave
Des Moines, IA 50319
Phone: 800-248-4483. Fax: 515-242-6543
Internet site https://www.iowadatacenter.org/

Kansas
University of Kansas, Institute for Policy and Social
    Research
1541 Lilac Lane, 607 Blake Hall
Lawrence, KS 66045-3129
Phone: 785-864-3701. Fax: 785-864-3683
Internet site www.ipsr.ku.edu/

Kansas Statistical Abstract, 2018. 53rd ed. Online only
https://ipsr.ku.edu/ksdata/ksah/

Kentucky
Kentucky Cabinet for Economic Development
Old Capitol Annex, 300 West Broadway
Frankfort, KY 40601-1975
Phone: 800-626-2930. Fax: 502-564-3256
Internet site www.thinkkentucky.com/

Kentucky Deskbook of Economic Statistics, 2009. Online
    only
http://dspace.kdla.ky.gov:8080/jspui/
    bitstream/10602/2500/3/2009_Deskbook_Part1.pdf

Kentucky Economic Development Guide
https://siteselection.com/cc/kentucky/2019/index.cfm

Louisiana
Louisiana State Census Data Center
Division of Administration, Office of Technology
    Services
1201 N. Third St, Suite 7-210
Baton Rouge, LA 70802
Phone: 225-342-7000
Internet site https://www.louisiana.gov/
    demographics-and-geography/

Maine
Maine Department of Administration and Financial
    Services
State Economist
78 State House Station
Augusta, ME 04333
Phone: 207-624-7800
Internet site https://www.maine.gov/dafs/economist/

Maryland
Maryland Department of Panning
301 West Preston Street, Suite 1101
Baltimore, MD 21201
Phone: 410-767-4500

Maryland State Data Center
http://www.mdp.state.md.us/msdc/

2018 Maryland Statistical Handbook
https://planning.maryland.gov/MSDC/Documents/
    md-statistical-handbook.pdfpdf

Massachusetts
Economic and Public Policy Research
UMass Donahue Institute
100 Venture Way, Suite 9
Hadley, MA 01035
Phone: 413-545-0001
Internet site: http://www.donahue.umassp.edu/
    business-groups/economic-public-policy-research

MassBenchmarks, monthly journal
http://www.donahue.umassp.edu/our-publications/
    massbenchmarks2

Michigan
Michigan Economic Development Corporation
300 North Washington Square
Lansing, MI 48913
Phone: 1-888-522-0103
Internet site https://www.michiganbusiness.org/

Minnesota
Minnesota Department of Employment and Economic
    Development (DEED)
1st National Bank Building
332 Minnesota Street, Suite E200
Saint Paul, MN 55101-1351
Phone: 651-259-7114
Internet site: https://mn.gov/deed/

Minnesota State Demographic Center
658 Cedar Street, Room 300
Saint Paul, MN 55155
Internet Site www.demography.state.mn.us/.

Mississippi
Mississippi State University Libraries
P.O. Box 5408
Mississippi State, MS 39762-5408
Phone: 662-325-7668
Mississippi Statistical Resources
Internet site http://guides.library.msstate.edu/content.
    php?pid=15893&sid=106686

Missouri
University of Missouri-Columbia
Economic and Policy Analysis Research Center
10 Professional Building, Columbia, MO 65211
Phone: 573-882-4805. Fax: 573-882-5563
Internet site: https://eparc.missouri.edu/

Missouri Statistical Data Archive. Online only
Internet site https://eparc.missouri.edu/publications/
archive/archive.html

Montana
Montana Department of Commerce
Census and Economic Information Center
301 South Park Avenue, P.O. Box 200533
Helena, MT 59620-0533
Phone: 406-841-2742
Internet site http://ceic.mt.gov/

Nebraska
Nebraska Department of Economic Development
301 Centennial Mall South, 4th Floor
Lincoln, NE 68508
Phone: 800-426-6505.
Internet site http://info.neded.org/

Nevada
Nevada Department of Administration
Division of Budget and Planning
209 East Musser Street, Room 200
Carson City, NV 89701-4298
Phone: 775-684-0222. Fax: 775-684-0260

New Hampshire
New Hampshire Office of Strategic Initiatives
Governor Hugh J. Gallen State Office Park
Johnson Hall, 3rd Floor
107 Pleasant Street
Concord, NH 03301
Phone: 603-271-2155. Fax 603-271-2615
Internet site https://www.nh.gov/osi/index.htm

New Jersey
State of New Jersey Department of Labor and
    Workforce Development
1 John Fitch Plaza, P.O. Box 110
Trenton, NJ 08611
Phone: 609-984-2595. Fax: 609-984-6833
Internet site https://www.nj.gov/labor/

Labor Market Information. Online only
Internet site https://nj.gov/labor/lpa/LMI_index.html

New Mexico
University of New Mexico
Bureau of Business and Economic Research, MSC06
    3510
1 University of New Mexico
Albuquerque, NM 87131-0001
Phone: 505-277-2216.
Internet site https://bber.unm.edu/data-bank

New York
Nelson A. Rockefeller Institute of Government,
411 State Street,
Albany, NY 12203-1003.
Phone: 518-445-4150
Internet site www.rockinst.org/

New York State Statistical Yearbook
https://rockinst.org/data-hub/new-york-data-sets/

North Carolina
North Carolina Office of State Budget and
    Management
MSC 20320
Raleigh, NC 27699-0320
Phone: 984-236-0600
Internet site www.osbm.state.nc.us/

How North Carolina Ranks, 2018
https://files.nc.gov/ncosbm/documents/files/state_
    rankings18.pdf

North Dakota
North Dakota Department of Commerce
Economic Development & Finance Division
P.O. Box 2057
Bismarck, North Dakota 58502-2057
Phone: 701-328-5300.
http://www.business.nd.gov/

Ohio
Ohio Development Services Agency
77 South High Street, 29th Floor
Columbus, OH 43215
Phone: 800-848-1300
Internet site https://development.ohio.gov/reports/
    reports_research.htm#

Oklahoma
University of Oklahoma,
Michael F. Price College of Business
Center for Economic and Management Research
307 West Brooks, Suite 4

Oklahoma—*Continued*
Norman OK 73019
Phone: 405-325-2931, Fax: 405-325-7688
Internet site http://www.ou.edu/price/centersresearch/
cemr

Statistical Abstract of Oklahoma
http://www.ou.edu/price/centersresearch/cemr/
cemr_publications

Oregon
Oregon State Archives
800 Summer Street, NE
Salem, OR 97310
Phone: 503-373-0701. Fax: 503-378-4118.

Oregon Blue Book, 2019-2020. Biennial
Internet site https://sos.oregon.gov/blue-book/Pages/
default.aspx

Pennsylvania
Penn State Harrisburg
Pennsylvania State Data Center
Institute of State and Regional Affairs
777 West Harrisburg Pike,
Middletown, PA 17057-4898
Phone: 717-948-6336. Fax: 717-948-6754
Internet site http://pasdc.hbg.psu.edu

Pennsylvania Statistical Abstract, 2015. Also Available on
CD-ROM.
https://pasdc.hbg.psu.edu/Publications/
Pennsylvania-Abstract
Pennsylvania Facts, 2020
https://pasdc.hbg.psu.edu/sdc/pasdc_files/pastats/
PAFacts2020.pdf

Rhode Island
Rhode Island Economic Development Corporation
315 Iron Horse Way, Suite 101
Providence, RI 02908
Phone: 401-278-9100. Fax 401-273-8270
Internet site www.riedc.com/r/index.html
Rhode Island Economic Development Corporation
http://www.riedc.com/data-and-publications/
economy-and-workforce

South Carolina
South Carolina Revenue and Fiscal Affairs Office
1000 Assembly Street
Rembert Dennis Building, Suite 421
Columbia, SC 29201
Phone: 803-734-3793

South Carolina—*Continued*
South Carolina Statistical Abstract, 2012. Also available
on CD-ROM.
https://guides.statelibrary.sc.gov/
sc-government-statistics/statistics

South Dakota
South Dakota Governor's Office on Economic
Development
711 E. Wells Ave.
Pierre, South Dakota 57501
Phone: 605-773-4633
https://sdgoed.com/

Tennessee
University of Tennessee
Boyd Center for Business and Economic Research
College of Business Administration
916 Volunteer Boulevard
Knoxville, TN 37996-0500
Phone: 865-974-5441
Internet site http://cber.bus.utk.edu/Default.htm

Tennessee State Data Center
http://tndata.utk.edu/

Texas
Texas Almanac, University of North Texas
History Department
1155 Union Circle #310650, Denton, TX 76203-5017
Phone: 940-369-5200
https://texashistory.unt.edu/explore/collections/
TXALC/

Texas Almanac
Internet site www.texasalmanac.com/

Texas Demographic Center
University of Texas at San Antonio
501 W Cesar E Chavez Blvd
San Antonio, TX 78207-4415
Phone: 210-458-6543. Fax: 210-458-6541
Internet site http://txsdc.utsa.edu/

Utah
Governor's Office of Planning and Budget
Demographic and Economic Analysis, 150
P.O. Box 132210
Salt Lake City, UT 84114-2210
Phone 801-538-1027. Fax: 801-538-1547
https://www.utah.gov/about/demographics.html

Utah—*Continued*
Spring 2013 Data Guide
2013 Economic Outlook
Internet site http://www.governor.utah.gov/dea/

Vermont
Department of Labor
Economic and Labor Market Information
P.O. Box 488
Montpelier, VT 05601-0488
Phone: 802-828-4157. Fax: 802-828-4050

Economic and Labor Market Information
Internet site www.vtlmi.info/

Virginia
Weldon Cooper Center for Public Service
2400 Old Ivy Road
Charlottesville, VA 22903
434-982-5522. Fax: 434-982-5524
Internet site www.coopercenter.org/

Washington
Washington State Office of Financial Management
P.O. Box 43113
Olympia, WA 98504-3113
Phone: 360-902-0599
Internet site www.ofm.wa.gov/

Washington State Data Book, 2019
http://www.ofm.wa.gov/databook/default.asp

West Virginia
West Virginia University
College of Business and Economics
Bureau of Business and Economic Research
P.O. Box 6025, Morgantown, WV 26506
Phone: 304-293-7831
Internet site www.be.wvu.edu/bber/index.htm

2019 West Virginia County Data Profiles.
https://business.wvu.edu/research-outreach/
   bureau-of-business-and-economic-research/
   wv-county-profiles
West Virginia Economic Outlook, 2020. Annual
https://researchrepository.wvu.edu/bureau_be/311/

Wisconsin
Wisconsin Legislative Reference Bureau
One East Main Street, Suite 200
Madison, WI 53703
608-5045802

2019-2020 Wisconsin Blue Book. Biennial
Internet site https://legis.wisconsin.gov/lrb/blue-book/

Wyoming
Department of Administration and Information
Economic Analysis Division
2800 Central Avenue
Cheyenne, WY 82002-0060
Phone: 307-777-7504.
Internet site http://eadiv.state.wy.us/

Wyoming 2019 – Just the Facts
http://eadiv.state.wy.us/Wy_facts/facts2019.pdf

KEY FEDERAL WEBSITES WITH STATE-LEVEL INFORMATION
Many federal government agencies publish state-level information. The sites listed below have large concentrations of state-level information on easy-to-locate websites.

U.S. BUREAU OF ECONOMIC ANALYSIS
Gross State Product and Personal income at
www.bea.gov/regional/index.htm

U.S. BUREAU OF LABOR STATISTICS
Current Employment Statistics at
www.bls.gov/sae/home.htm
Geographic Profile of Employment and
   Unemployment at
www.bls.gov/gps/home.htm
State occupational injuries, illnesses, and fatalities at
www.bls.gov/iif/oshstate.htm

U.S. CENSUS BUREAU
American Community Survey data at
www.census.gov/acs/www/
Annual Survey of Manufactures at
https://www.census.gov/programs-surveys/asm.html
Building permits at
http://www.census.gov/construction/bps/
County Business Patterns at
https://www.census.gov/programs-surveys/cbp.html
Economic Census at
www.census.gov/programs-surveys/economic-census.
   html
Foreign trade at
www.census.gov/foreign-trade/statistics/state/
Population and Housing unit estimates at
www.census.gov/popest/

State and County QuickFacts profiles at
https://www.census.gov/quickfacts
State government finances at
https://www.census.gov/programs-surveys/state.html
State government employment and payroll at
https://www.census.gov/programs-surveys/apes.html

U.S. DEPARTMENT OF AGRICULTURE
Economic Research Service
Agricultural Exports at
https://www.ers.usda.gov/data-products/foreign-
    agricultural-trade-of-the-united-states-fatus/
    us-agricultural-trade-data-update/
Farm Income Wealth and Statistics at
https://www.ers.usda.gov/data-products/
    farm-income-and-wealth-statistics/
State Fact Sheets at
www.ers.usda.gov/StateFacts/
National Agricultural Statistics Service
Census of Agriculture at
www.agcensus.usda.gov/

U.S. DEPARTMENT OF HEALTH AND HUMAN
    SERVICES
Centers for Disease Control and Prevention
Behavioral Risk Factor Surveillance System at
www.cdc.gov/brfss/
Fast Stats A to Z at
https://www.cdc.gov/nchs/fastats/default.htm
Substance Abuse and Mental Health Services
    Administration
State-level data at
http://www.samhsa.gov/

ENERGY INFORMATION ADMINISTRATION
Energy consumption at
www.eia.doe.gov/emeu/states/_seds.html
General state information at
https://www.eia.gov/state/

NATIONAL CENTER OF EDUCATION
    STATISTICS
State Education Data Profiles at
https://nces.ed.gov/nationsreportcard/**states**/

NATIONAL SCIENCE FOUNDATION
Science and Engineering State Profiles at
http://www.nsf.gov/statistics/states/

U.S. DEPARTMENT OF TRANSPORTATION
Federal Highway Administration
Highway statistics at
www.fhwa.dot.gov/policy/ohpi/hss/index.cfm

Federal Highway Administration
State traffic safety information at
http://www.fhwa.dot.gov/publications/research/
    safety/06099/appendb.cfm

INDEX